THE COMPLETE POETRY AND ESSENTIAL PROSE OF JOHN MILTON

John Milton

The Complete Poetry and Essential Prose of John Milton

Edited by William Kerrigan,
John Rumrich,
and Stephen M. Fallon

THE MODERN LIBRARY
NEW YORK

2007 Modern Library Edition

Published in the United States by Modern Library,
an imprint of The Random House Publishing Group,
a division of Random House, Inc., New York.

Grateful acknowledgment is made to Yale University Press
for permission to reprint material from three volumes from
The Complete Prose Works of John Milton, edited by Maurice Kelley
and John Carey: vol. 1 (copyright © 1953 by Yale University), vol. 4
(copyright © 1966 by Yale University), and volume 6 (copyright © 1973
by Yale University). Reprinted by permission.

Illustration credits can be found on page ix.

LIBRARY OF CONGRESS CATALOGING-IN-PUBLICATION DATA
Milton, John, 1608–1674.
[Selections. 2007]
The complete poetry and essential prose of John Milton/edited by
William Kerrigan, John Rumrich, and Stephen M. Fallon.
p. cm.
"This edition contains all of Milton's poetry and a generous portion
of his most vital prose. The texts of both have been almost
entirely modernized"—General preface.
ISBN 978-0-679-64253-4
I. Kerrigan, William II. Rumrich, John Peter
III. Fallon, Stephen M. IV. Title.
PR3553.K47 2007
821'.4—dc22 2007003087

Printed in the United States of America on acid-free paper

www.modernlibrary.com

2 4 6 8 9 7 5 3

Contents

List of Illustrations *ix*
General Preface *xi*
References and Abbreviations *xvii*
A Chronology of Milton's Life *xxi*
Minutes of the Life of Mr. John Milton, by John Aubrey *xxiii*
A Chronology of Milton's Poetry *xxxi*

ENGLISH POEMS

Psalm 114 3
Psalm 136 4
On the Death of a Fair Infant Dying of a Cough 6
At a Vacation Exercise 11
Song: On May Morning 15
The Fifth Ode of Horace, Lib. I 16
On the Morning of Christ's Nativity 18
The Passion 30
On Shakespeare 34
On the University Carrier 35
Another on the Same 36
An Epitaph on the Marchioness of Winchester 37
L'Allegro 41
Il Penseroso 46
Arcades 52
At a Solemn Music 57
On Time 58
Upon the Circumcision 60

A Masque Presented at Ludlow Castle, 1634 [Comus] 61
Lycidas 99
Psalms 80–88 110
Psalms 1–8 123
Translations from the Prose Works 132

ENGLISH AND ITALIAN SONNETS

Sonnets 1–23 139
On the New Forcers of Conscience Under the Long Parliament 163

LATIN AND GREEK POEMS

Elegiac Verses

"Get up, go, get up, it's time now" 169
Kings should not oversleep 170
The Fable of the Peasant and the Lord 170
A Philosopher to a King 171

Book of Elegies

Elegy 1. To Charles Diodati 172
Elegy 2. On the Death of the Beadle of Cambridge University 175
Elegy 3. On the Death of the Bishop of Winchester 177
Elegy 4. To Thomas Young, his tutor, at present performing the office of chaplain among the English merchants living in Hamburg 180
Elegy 5. On the Arrival of Spring 185
Elegy 6. To Charles Diodati, staying in the country 190
Elegy 7 194
A postscript to his elegies 198
On the Gunpowder Plot 198
On the same 199
On the same 199
On the same 200
On the Inventor of Gunpowder 200
To Leonora singing in Rome 200
To the same 201
To the same 202

Book of Miscellaneous Poems

On the Death of the Vice-Chancellor, a Physician 203
On the Fifth of November 205
On the Death of the Bishop of Ely 213
That Nature does not suffer from old age 215
Of the Platonic Idea as understood by Aristotle 218
To His Father 220
Psalm 114 225
To Salzilli, the Roman poet, being ill. Scazons 226
Manso 227
Epitaph for Damon 232
On the Engraver of His Portrait 242
To John Rouse, Librarian of Oxford University 243
Epigram from *A Defense of the English People* 247
Epigrams from *A Second Defense* 248

LATE MASTERPIECES

Introduction to *Paradise Lost* 251
Paradise Lost 283
Book I 293; *Book II* 323; *Book III* 359; *Book IV* 384; *Book V* 418; *Book VI* 445; *Book VII* 476; *Book VIII* 497; *Book IX* 517; *Book X* 552; *Book XI* 585; *Book XII* 611
Introduction to *Paradise Regained* 631
Paradise Regained 635
Book I 635; *Book II* 650; *Book III* 664; *Book IV* 678
Introduction to *Samson Agonistes* 699
Samson Agonistes 707

PROSE WORKS

Familiar Letters

Diodati Greets Milton Cheerfully 767
Diodati Greets Milton 767
To Alexander Gill 768
Letter to a Friend 769

To Charles Diodati 772
To the Same 773
Sir Henry Wotton to Milton 775
To Lukas Holste in the Vatican at Rome 777
To Leonard Philaras 779
To the Most Distinguished Mr. Henry de Brass 781

Prolusions

Prolusion 1 785
Prolusion 7 793

Controversial Prose

Selections from *Of Reformation* 805
A Selection from *The Reason of Church Government Urged Against Prelaty, The Second Book* 835
A Selection from *An Apology for Smectymnuus* 845
Selections from *The Doctrine and Discipline of Divorce* 853
Areopagitica 923
Of Education 967
Selections from *Tetrachordon* 983
Selections from *The Tenure of Kings and Magistrates* 1021
Selections from *Eikonoklastes* 1057
Selections from *Second Defense of the English People* 1069
The Ready and Easy Way to Establish a Free Commonwealth 1111
Selections from *Christian Doctrine* 1137

Works Cited 1335
Index 1349

List of Illustrations

All Illustrations are used with permission.

The "Onslow" portrait of Milton at age twenty-one, artist unknown. National Portrait Gallery, London. *frontispiece,* 2

Paradise Lost 4.257–90. *Paradise Lost. A Poem in Twelve Books,* 1674. Harry Ransom Humanities Research Center. x

Portrait of Milton at age ten, by Cornelius Janssen. The Pierpont Morgan Library/Art Resource, N.Y. xxx

Lycidas 123–65. *Facsimile of the Manuscript of Milton's Minor Poems, Preserved in the Library of Trinity College, Cambridge.* Cambridge University Press, 1899. Harry Ransom Humanities Research Center. 107

Frontispiece portrait of John Milton, by William Marshall. *Poems of Mr. John Milton, both English and Latin, Compos'd at Several Times,* 1645. Harry Ransom Humanities Research Center. 243

Frontispiece portrait of John Milton, by William Faithorne. *The History of Britain,* 1670. Harry Ransom Humanities Research Center. 250

Paradise Lost, title page. *Paradise Lost. A Poem in Twelve Books,* 1674. Harry Ransom Humanities Research Center. 283

Fall of the Angels. The Caedmon Poems . . . and Facsimiles of the Illustrations in the Junius Manuscript. E. P. Dutton & Co., 1916. 322

Satan on His Throne, by John Martin. *The Paradise Lost of John Milton.* C. Whittingham, 1846. Harry Ransom Humanities Research Center. 358

Raphael Visits Adam and Eve, by Gustave Doré. *Milton's Paradise Lost.* Illustrated by Gustave Doré. Cassell, Petter, Galpin & Co., 1882. Harry Ransom Humanities Research Center. 417

Expulsion of the Rebel Angels, by Francis Hayman. *Paradise Lost. A Poem in Twelve Books.* J. and R. Tonson and S. Draper, 1749. Harry Ransom Humanities Research Center. 475

The Serpent Stands Before Eve, by Edward Burney. *Milton's Paradise Lost.* C. Whittingham, 1800. Harry Ransom Humanities Research Center. 551

Aeropagitica, title page. *Areopagitica: A Speech of John Milton for the Liberty of Unlicenc'd Printing, to the Parlament of England,* 1644. Harry Ransom Humanities Research Center. 922

Frontispiece portrait of Charles I, by William Marshall. *Eikon Basilike: The Pourtraicture of his Sacred Majestie in his Solitudes and Sufferings,* 1649. Harry Ransom Humanities Research Center. 1056

Another ſide, umbrageous Grots and Caves
Of coole receſs, o're which the mantling vine
Layes forth her purple Grape, and gently creeps
Luxuriant; mean while murmuring waters fall
Down the ſlope hills, diſperſt, or in a Lake,
That to the fringed Bank with Myrtle crownd,
Her chryſtal mirror holds, unite thir ſtreams.
The Birds thir quire apply; aires, vernal aires,
Breathing the ſmell of field and grove, attune
The trembling leaves, while Univerſal *Pan*
Knit with the *Graces* and the *Hours* in dance
Led on th' Eternal Spring. Not that faire field
Of *Enna*, where *Proſerpin* gathering flours
Her ſelf a fairer Floure by gloomie *Dis*
Was gatherd, which coſt *Ceres* all that pain
To ſeek her through the world; nor that ſweet Grove
Of *Daphne* by *Orontes*, and th' inſpir'd
Caſtalian Spring, might with this Paradiſe
Of *Eden* ſtrive; nor that *Nyſeian* Ile
Girt with the River *Triton*, where old *Cham*,
Whom Gentiles *Ammon* call and *Lybian Jove*,
Hid *Amalthea* and her Florid Son
Young *Bacchus* from his Stepdame *Rhea's* eye;
Nor where *Abaſſin* Kings thir iſſue Guard,
Mount *Amara*, though this by ſom ſuppos'd
True Paradiſe under the *Ethiop* Line
By *Nilus* head, encloſd with ſhining Rock,
A whole days journy high, but wide remote
From this *Aſſyrian* Garden, where the Fiend
Saw undelighted all delight, all kind
Of living Creatures new to ſight and ſtrange:
Two of far nobler ſhape erect and tall,
Godlike erect, with native Honour clad
In naked Majeſtie ſeemd Lords of all,

And

Book IV, lines 257 to 290, from the second edition of *Paradise Lost* (1674).

General Preface

This edition contains all of Milton's poetry and a generous portion of his most vital prose. Milton is among the greatest of authors. In preparing this edition, we have tried our level best to present and elucidate his writings in all their glorious detail. The texts of both poetry and prose have been almost entirely modernized. We have removed his italics, updated his spelling, dropped most of his capitalizations, revised his punctuation, and added quotation marks to the spoken and quoted passages. While there are obvious virtues in retaining the original presentation of these works, especially since Milton appears to have exerted at least some influence on many of the texts published in his lifetime, these benefits are outweighed, in our opinion, by the supreme benefit of making this difficult author as readable as possible for modern students. Old spelling texts are available online and in college and university libraries, indeed in many municipal libraries, and should a reader become particularly fascinated with a specific passage or work, we strongly recommend that these versions be consulted.

An important check on full-throttle modernization is a series of textual effects radiating from the fact that Milton was writing metrical verse in the seventeenth century. Take the example of elision. Milton freely indulged in this poetic convention. At will he was able to elide a syllable, making an entire iambic beat vanish. All he had to do was leave out a vowel, or replace a vowel with an apostrophe, in order to make a trisyllable such as *opening* into the bisyllabic *op'ning*. Our text retains significant elisions. We have been able to dispense with some few elisions because of changes in pronunciation. In the seventeenth century one could or could not pronounce the *-ed* suffix of past tense verbs. Milton, like other poets of the period, regularly indicated by orthography whether or not a particular *-ed* was to be voiced. In both the 1667 and 1674 editions of *Paradise Lost,* a fallen Eve returns to Adam in Book 9 with the following words: "Hast thou not wonderd, Adam, at my stay?" (l. 856). As the spelling indicates, Milton intended the third syllable of *wondered* to remain silent. In modern English, however, there is no third syllable in *wondered.* It is only and always bisyllabic. A modernized edition can therefore safely print the line without indicating elision: "Hast thou not wondered, Adam, at my stay?" On the other hand, when an *–ed* is to be pronounced, adding an extra syllable unvoiced in today's English, a modern edition must indicate this fact with an accent mark (*wonderèd*).

Another type of elision cancels a familiar sound in order to create a brand-new sound. In Book 9 of *Paradise Lost,* as Adam and Eve awaken after the evening of their fall, shame seems to gather in their genitals, which they hasten to cover with leaves. Milton compares this practice, the advent of clothing in Eden, to observations made by Christopher Columbus: "Columbus found th' American so girt" (9.1116). Here the absence of the *e* in *the* indicates that the *th*-sound must be merged with the first syllable of *American.* The new sound (*tha*) is counted as one syllable only, one iambic beat, so the line scans: "Cŏ lúm/bŭs foúnd/thă mér/ĭ cán/sŏ gírt." With this example we have almost crossed the mysterious gap from verse technique to poetic beauty. As Milton writes about the disappearance of genitals behind leafy coverings, he himself makes a letter disappear behind a leaflike apostrophe. What Columbus saw in "th' American" is what we see in just those words on the page. Milton does not really, at least in this particular example, design an elaborate effect around the connection between covering and eliding. He rather seems to beckon toward the pure possibility of such effects, inviting us to behold the worlds of potential meaning opened by a single implicit metaphor linking a technique of the poem (elision) to its story (clothing).

In that direction lies the opulence of Milton's verse. Another example will make the point. For here the author is not just showing us how he might weave his technique into the meaning of his story but really doing it, and with a skill no other English poet has excelled. Just before Eve returns to him, fallen in his absence, Adam has a premonition: "Yet oft his heart, divine of something ill,/Misgave him; he the falt'ring measure felt" (9.845–46). The lines are perfectly regular iambic pentameter, the norm of the poem. But this regularity is achieved only by virtue of the elision of the middle syllable of *faltering.* (In the 1667 and 1674 editions, the word printed here was *faultring.*) Dire consequences lurk like a premonition, like the onset of punishment, behind this innocent word. Its first syllable puns on *fall* and *fault.* Its missing second syllable, hidden behind the elision, threatens the iambic norm with an anapestic foot. That imaginary foot would produce the metrical equivalent of cardiac arrhythmia, a faltering of the human heartbeat. Like Adam, we feel "the falt'ring measure" pressing against the surface of iambic regularity. The primal fault of Adam and Eve, Milton told us in the opening lines of his epic, "Brought Death into the world, and all our woe" (1.3). Many books later, as the climax foretold at the opening looms near, a meaning-laden *falt'ring* traces at the level of meter the forthcoming fruit of the Fall.

Milton's poetry is replete with such beauties. Our main concern has been to preserve these energies in the new format of modern English. Modernized texts are regarded with suspicion in some quarters of the academic world. No one should imagine, however, that this particular modernizing was carried out in slapdash fashion. Far from it. Errors creep into every edition, as they creep into every book. Yet we have tried to produce texts that meet the highest standards of accuracy. Our modernized *Paradise Lost* derives from the second edition of 1674, our *Paradise Regained* and *Samson Agonistes* from the first edition of 1671, and shorter compositions from the 1645 *Poems,* supplemented with those first printed in the second edition of 1673. Key textual variants, cruxes, and puzzles are discussed individually in the notes.

If our texts aim toward the present, our headnotes and annotations pull readers back into Milton's world. The notes are copious, and they are extensively cross-referenced. We certainly have not tried to supply our readers with everything they might need to understand and assess this author, for that would be neither possible nor desirable. Like all editions, this one is just a beginning. But it is meant to be a serious beginning. Milton is the most learned of the major English writers. Our notes contain such things as old meanings of English words, Greek and Latin roots still signifying in Milton's English, classical and biblical allusions, literary analogues both similar and contrasting, important differences between printed texts or printed and manuscript texts. We take note of extraordinary prosodic effects in Milton's poetry, echoes within and among his works, new developments in his thought and attitudes, puns and putdowns. We have tried as concisely as possible to convey information about historical events, literary conventions, outmoded scientific ideas, theological disputes, and in general all ideas and assumptions unfamiliar to modern readers. For disputed passages, of which there are many, we have usually summarized the interpretive options and, when we felt pretty sure of our grounds, assessed their probability.

Milton's so-called minor poems have been organized in a manner unique to this edition. By "minor poems" is meant, in effect, everything besides *Paradise Lost, Paradise Regained,* and *Samson Agonistes,* which are conventionally termed his "major works." Some editions try to retain the order in which these shorter poems appeared in Milton's 1645 *Poems,* finding a way to tip in works that first appeared in his 1673 *Poems,* translations found in his prose works, or pieces never published during his lifetime but discovered subsequently by scholars. Other editions try to present all the minor poems in their probable order of composition. The results in both cases are chaotic to the modern eye. Poems in different languages jostle against one another. Some works, particularly the shortest of the minor poems, seem to get lost in the mix and, even if all the poems in an edition have been numbered sequentially, remain quite difficult to locate without consulting a table of contents that is itself difficult to locate.

No doubt this teeming profusion is revealing. It shows that the young Milton did in fact move from language to language, genre to genre, turning the different aspects of his education into different expressions of his developing literary ambitions. But we think that little will be lost in the way of revelation by reconfiguring the minor poems, while a little more will be gained in the way of clarity and ease of use. We have therefore divided them into three groups. "English Poems," much the largest one, contains all the poems Milton wrote in

English, including classical and biblical translations, with the exception of his sonnets. A second group, "English and Italian Sonnets," includes the poems entitled "Sonnets" and numbered in both the 1645 and 1673 editions; the sonnets group has the further justification that its poems should for some purposes be studied together, given their power and originality in the history of this poetic form. A final category, "Latin and Greek Poems," contains all the poems written in those languages. Within each section, the works have been placed in their probable order of composition. "A Chronology of Milton's Poetry," prepared by Stephen B. Dobranski, allows readers to determine at a glance the likely time frame for the composition of any poem printed in this edition.

We have printed the major poems in their traditional order: *Paradise Lost, Paradise Regained, Samson Agonistes.* During the last half century, a small number of scholars have urged an earlier date for the composition of *Samson Agonistes.* We continue to believe that the verse drama was probably Milton's final poem.

By his contemporaries Milton was better known for his prose than his poetry. From 1641 to his death, in 1674, he published (not counting a handful of extremely short works) twenty books of prose, five in Latin and fifteen in English. The majority of these were meant to influence immediate political circumstances during the Civil War and its aftermath. He opposed episcopacy and monarchy, attacked censorship, advocated representative government, and defended the execution of Charles I. Stepping back from the turbulence of political events, he also produced treatises on theology, logic, and grammar, and histories of Great Britain and Muscovy (Russia). These books fill eight fat volumes in the Yale University Press edition of Milton's *Complete Prose Works.*

We have selected prose works first of all for their intrinsic excellence. Few would question the merit of Milton's abiding classics *Areopagitica,* the first book devoted to freedom of the press, and *Of Education,* his remarkable outline for the reform of contemporary pedagogy. There is also a great deal of fascinating self-reflection scattered like the dismembered body of an autobiography throughout his polemical tracts. We have reprinted selections of this sort from *The Reason of Church Government, An Apology for Smectymnuus,* and the *Second Defense of the English People,* as well as a group of his familiar letters and two of his early "prolusions" or academic exercises. Our selections from the polemical *Of Reformation* and *Eikonoklastes* display the high-minded fervor of Milton's political commitments.

Early on, though confident in his powers as a poet, Milton seems somewhat uneasy in the medium of prose, which he calls the work of his "left hand." The result is a vivid, image-laden style that at times becomes undisciplined. Such prose presents serious difficulties for modernizers. Milton's language does not have the tight structure of end-stops found in modern sentences and paragraphs. The second unit of *Of Reformation,* for example, runs to 375 words. Modernizing, we break this unit up into three sentences of 191, 88, and 96 words. Dividing Miltonic prose into shorter sentences and paragraphs certainly makes it easier to read, and as with the poetry, readability has been our goal. But we are painfully aware that Milton's relentless rhythms have been muted and his twisty syntax reduced.

A quieter, more assured style marks the two divorce tracts, *The Doctrine and Discipline of Divorce* and *Tetrachordon.* We reprint substantial portions of these books. Increasingly viewed as pivotal in Milton's career, they reflect the chastening experience of his initially unhappy first marriage as he faces the challenge of interpreting Scripture against the grain of its apparent sense. In two other works, *The Tenure of Kings and Magistrates* and *The Ready and Easy Way,* the reader will be able to follow the full development of arguments that establish Milton as a major political thinker and simultaneously show him reacting in personal ways to the pressure of great events, as one king is beheaded and another, his son, is crowned eleven years later. The final set of selections, from Milton's theological treatise *Christian Doctrine,* is our most controversial choice, since a few scholars have recently tried to cast doubt on his authorship of the work. We remain convinced not only of his authorship (see our introduction to the work) but also of its signal importance for understanding the beliefs embedded in his major poems. For the *Christian Doctrine,* as for all other Latin prose, we print with permission translations originally made for the *Complete Prose Works.*

We are mindful of our profound debts to previous editors and annotators, so much so that a catalog of some of their names has for us an epic ring: John Leonard, John Carey, Alastair Fowler, Merritt Y. Hughes, Douglas Bush, B. A. Wright, A.W. Verity, Rev. Henry J. Todd, Thomas Warton, Thomas Newton, Jonathan Richardson, Patrick Hume. An edition of this scope and thoroughness represents a departure for our publisher. At Random House, MJ Devaney was the first editor to champion our book. After her retirement, Judy Sternlight expertly guided the edition through to publication. We were ably assisted in our editorial work by Phillip Albonetti, Yaser Amad, Sara Berry, Gina Marie Cora, Marlene Daut, Jonathan Lamb, Mary Maddox, Heidi Meurer, Jennifer Nichols, Nunzio N. D'Alessio, Sarah Dawson, Joel Dodson, Claire Fallon, Joseph Rumrich, Rania Salah, Dan Shore, Shea Suski, Natalie Tenner, and Amelia Kerrigan. For this edition, Milton's foreign-language poetry (a few pieces in Italian and Greek but mostly Latin verse) has been newly translated into English prose by Gordon Braden.

References and Abbreviations

Most of the many editions, books, and articles cited in the notes and headnotes can be found, alphabetized by author, in Works Cited at the end of this volume. Where an author's surname is given without a date, it means that only one of this author's works has been cited in the edition. Where a name is coupled with a date, it means that at least two works by this author have been cited. Multiple entries in Works Cited are arranged chronologically. Books that Milton refers to in passing in his prose works receive a full citation in our notes and do not reappear in Works Cited.

We use these abbreviations for works by John Milton:

1637	*A Masque Presented at Ludlow Castle* (1637).
1645	*Poems of Mr. John Milton* (1645).
1667	*Paradise Lost. A Poem Written in Ten Books* (1667).
1671	*Paradise Regained. A Poem in IV Books. To which is added Samson Agonistes* (1671).
1674	*Paradise Lost. A Poem in Twelve Books. The Second Edition ...* (1674).
BMS	Bridgewater manuscript of *Masque.*
CMS	Manuscript of poems by Milton at Trinity College, Cambridge.
Yale	*Complete Prose Works of John Milton,* ed. Don M. Wolfe et al. (8 vols., Yale Univ. Press, 1953–80).
Animad	*Animadversions on the Remonstrant's Defense*
Apology	*An Apology for Smectymnuus*
Areop	*Areopagitica*
CD	*Christian Doctrine*
Damon	*Epitaph for Damon*
DDD	*The Doctrine and Discipline of Divorce*
Eikon	*Eikonoklastes*
Il Pens	*Il Penseroso*
L'All	*L'Allegro*
Lyc	*Lycidas*
Masque	*A Masque Presented at Ludlow Castle*
Nat Ode	*On the Morning of Christ's Nativity*

Of Ed	*Of Education*
Of Ref	*Of Reformation*
PL	*Paradise Lost*
PR	*Paradise Regained*
RCG	*The Reason of Church Government Urged Against Prelaty*
REW	*The Ready and Easy Way to Establish a Free Commonwealth*
SA	*Samson Agonistes*
TKM	*The Tenure of Kings and Magistrates*
1Def	*Pro Populo Anglicano Defensio* (*A Defense of the English People*)
2Def	*Defensio Secunda* (*Second Defense of the English People*)

We use the following abbreviations for works by Shakespeare:

ADO	*Much Ado About Nothing*
ANT	*Antony and Cleopatra*
AWW	*All's Well That Ends Well*
AYL	*As You Like It*
COR	*Coriolanus*
HAM	*Hamlet*
1H4	*The First Part of King Henry the Fourth*
2H4	*The Second Part of King Henry the Fourth*
H5	*King Henry the Fifth*
JC	*Julius Caesar*
LLL	*Love's Labor's Lost*
LR	*King Lear*
MAC	*Macbeth*
MM	*Measure for Measure*
MND	*A Midsummer Night's Dream*
MV	*The Merchant of Venice*
OTH	*Othello*
ROM	*Romeo and Juliet*
R2	*King Richard the Second*
R3	*King Richard the Third*
TMP	*The Tempest*
TN	*Twelfth Night*
TRO	*Troilus and Cressida*
VEN	*Venus and Adonis*
WIV	*The Merry Wives of Windsor*
WT	*The Winter's Tale*

Unless otherwise indicated, we quote the Bible from the *AV* (King James Version), and use standard abbreviations when referring to its books; we sometimes cite *Geneva* (*The Geneva Bible,* 1588). Poetry in English, except where otherwise indicated, we cite from the Oxford authors series. Classical works are cited from the Loeb Classical Library unless otherwise noted, with standard abbreviations, such as, prominently, *Il.* and *Od.* for Homer's *Iliad* and *Odyssey, Ec.* and *Aen.* for Vergil's *Eclogues* and *Aeneid,* and *Her.* and *Met.* for Ovid's *Heroides* and *Metamorphoses.*

We also use these abbreviations:

Torquato Tasso, *GL*	*Gerusalemme Liberata*
Ludovico Ariosto, *OF*	*Orlando Furioso*
Edmund Spenser, *SC, FQ*	*The Shepheardes Calender, The Faerie Queene*

A Chronology of Milton's Life

1608 (December 9) John Milton born on Bread Street in London.

1615 (November 24?) Brother Christopher born.

1620 (?) Enters St. Paul's School under the headmastership of Alexander Gill, Sr. Begins his friendship with Charles Diodati. Thomas Young tutors Milton at home.

1625 (February 12) Admitted to Christ's College, Cambridge.

1629 (March 26) Receives his B.A. degree. In December writes *On the Morning of Christ's Nativity.*

1632 (July 3) Receives his M.A. degree. Retires to his father's country house at Hammersmith for continued study.

1634 (September 29) *A Masque* performed at Ludlow Castle in Wales.

1635 or 36 Moves with his parents to Horton.

1637 *A Masque* published (dated 1637 but possibly published in 1638). Mother, Sara, dies in Horton on April 3. *Lycidas* written in November and published the next year.

1638–9 Milton tours the Continent from April or May 1638 to July or August 1639. Charles Diodati dies in August 1638.

1639 Settles in London, where he makes his living as a tutor.

1641 Earliest antiprelatical tracts—*Of Reformation* (May), *Of Prelatical Episcopacy* (June or July), *Animadversions on the Remonstrant's Defense* (July)—published.

1642 Publishes *The Reason of Church Government* (January or February) and *An Apology for Smectymnuus* (April). Marries Mary Powell in June or July. In August she leaves him and the Civil War begins.

1643 *The Doctrine and Discipline of Divorce* published in August.

1644 The second edition of *The Doctrine and Discipline of Divorce* published in February; *Of Education* in June; *The Judgment of Martin Bucer* in August; *Areopagitica* in November.

1645 Two more divorce pamphlets, *Tetrachordon* and *Colasterion,* published in March. Reconciles with Mary in July or August and moves to a larger house in Barbican in September.

1646 *Poems of Mr. John Milton* published in January, dated 1645. Daughter Anne born July 29.

1647 (March 13) On or about this date his father dies, leaving Milton the Bread Street house and a moderate estate. (September–October) Moves to a smaller house in High Holborn.

1648 (October 25) Daughter Mary born.

1649 (January 30) Charles I executed. *Eikon Basilike* published a week later. (February 13) *The Tenure of Kings and Magistrates* published, with a second edition in September. (March 15) Appointed Secretary for Foreign Tongues and ordered to answer *Eikon Basilike.* (May 11) Salmasius's *Defensio Regia* arrives in England. (October 6) *Eikonoklastes* published, answering *Eikon Basilike.*

1651 (February 24) The *Pro Populo Anglicano Defensio* (*A Defense of the English People*) published, answering Salmasius. (March 16) Son John born.

1652 (February or March) Total blindness descends. Daughter Deborah born May 2. Wife Mary dies on May 5. Son John dies in June.

1653 Duties as Secretary for Foreign Tongues are reduced by the addition of an assistant. Cromwell installed as Protector in December.

1654 *Defensio Secunda* (*Second Defense of the English People*) published in May.

1655 Milton is pensioned in April and though he continues to work for the Protectorate, devotes more time to private studies. *Pro Se Defensio* (*Defense of Himself*) published in August.

1656 (November 12) Marries Katharine Woodcock.

1657 (October 19) Daughter Katharine born.

1658 Probably begins work on *Paradise Lost.* Wife Katharine dies on February 3. Daughter Katharine dies on March 17. Cromwell dies in September, succeeded by his son Richard.

1659 *A Treatise of Civil Power* published in February. Richard Cromwell resigns in May. *Considerations Touching the Likeliest Means to Remove Hirelings out of the Church* published in August.

1660 *The Ready and Easy Way to Establish a Free Commonwealth* published in February, with a second edition in April. Charles II proclaimed king in May. Milton arrested and imprisoned between September and November and released in December.

1663 (February 24) Marries Elizabeth Minshull. Moves to a house in Artillery Walk, near Bunhill Fields.

1665 Around June, moves to Chalfont St. Giles to avoid the London plague.

1667 (October or November) *Paradise Lost* published as a poem in ten books.

1670 (around November 1) *History of Britain* published.

1671 *Paradise Regained* and *Samson Agonistes* published.

1672 *Artis Logicae* (*The Art of Logic*) published.

1673 *Of True Religion* published. An enlarged edition of *Poems* published, also including *Of Education.*

1674 *Epistolae Familiarum* (*Familiar Letters*) published, including his *Prolusions. Paradise Lost. A Poem in Twelve Books* published around July 1. Milton dies November 9 or 10 and is buried in St. Giles, Cripplegate.

Minutes of the Life of Mr. John Milton

John Aubrey

There are several seventeenth-century Milton biographers, including the anonymous biographer (most likely Milton's friend Cyriack Skinner), the Oxford historian Anthony à Wood, Milton's nephew and former student Edward Phillips, and the deist John Toland. One can find their works in Helen Darbishire's *The Early Lives of Milton* (1932), which attributes the anonymous biography to Edward Phillips's brother, John. We choose to print the biographical notes gathered by the antiquarian John Aubrey, which are notable for their author's extraordinary attention to personal details and efforts to verify his information by consulting those who knew Milton well, including the poet's widow, his brother, and some of his friends.

Aubrey's manuscript notes are loosely organized, partly chronologically and partly by the person interviewed. Our text follows the chronologically arranged version established by Andrew Clark (2:62–72). Those wanting to identify the sources of individual comments may consult Clark's edition or Darbishire's. We have reproduced Clark's interpolated headings, but we have in some places made different choices in our inclusions and exclusions. We have also modernized the text, changing punctuation and spelling. Aubrey's notes are peppered with ellipses, where he leaves blanks to be filled in should further information appear. Bracketed ellipses in our text indicate places where we omit material found in Clark's edition; otherwise the ellipses are Aubrey's.

[His parentage]

His mother was a Bradshaw.

Mr. John Milton was of an Oxfordshire family.

His grandfather, . . . , (a Roman Catholic), of Holton, in Oxfordshire, near Shotover.

His father was brought up in the University of Oxon, at Christ Church, and his grandfather disinherited him because he kept not to the Catholic religion (he found a Bible in English in his chamber). So thereupon he came to London, and became a scrivener (brought up by a friend of his; was not an apprentice) and got a plentiful estate by it, and left it off many years before he died. He was an ingenious man; delighted in music; composed many songs now in print, especially that of *Oriana*.[1]

I have been told that the father composed a song of fourscore parts for the Landgrave of Hesse, for which [his] highness sent a medal of gold, or a noble present. He died about 1647; buried in Cripplegate church, from his house in the Barbican.

[His birth]

His son John was born in Bread Street, in London, at the Spread Eagle, which was his house (he had also in that street another house, the Rose, and other houses in other places).

He was born Anno Domini . . . the . . . day of . . . , about . . . o'clock in the . . .

(John Milton was born the 9th of December, 1608, *die Veneris*;[2] half an hour after 6 in the morning.)

[His precocity]

Anno Domini 1619, he was ten years old, as by his picture; and was then a poet.

[School, college, and travel]

His schoolmaster then was a Puritan, in Essex, who cut his hair short.

He went to school to old Mr. Gill, at Paul's School. Went at his own charge only to Christ's College in Cambridge at fifteen, where he stayed eight years at least. Then he traveled into France and Italy (had Sir H. Wotton's commendatory letters). At Geneva he contracted a great friendship with the learned Dr. Diodati of Geneva (*vide* his poems). He was acquainted with Sir Henry Wotton, ambassador at Venice, who delighted in his company. He was several years <*Quaere*, how many? *Resp.*, two years> beyond sea, and returned to England just upon the breaking out of the civil wars.

From his brother, Christopher Milton: When he went to school, when he was very young, he studied very hard and sat up very late, commonly till twelve or

1. ***Oriana:*** Milton's father contributed a song, "Fair Orian," to *The Triumphs of Oriana* (1601), a volume of songs dedicated to Queen Elizabeth I.
2. ***die Veneris:*** Venus's Day, i.e., Friday.

one o'clock at night, and his father ordered the maid to sit up for him; and in those years (10) composed many copies of verses which might well become a riper age. And was a very hard student in the university, and performed all his exercises there with very good applause. His first tutor there was Mr. Chapell; from whom receiving some unkindness <whipped him>; he was afterwards (though it seemed contrary to the rules of the college) transferred to the tuition of one Mr. Tovell,[3] who died parson of Lutterworth.

He went to travel about the year 1638 and was abroad about a year's space, chiefly in Italy.

[Return to England]

Immediately after his return he took a lodging at Mr. Russell's, a tailor, in St. Bride's churchyard, and took into his tuition his [Milton's] sister's two sons, Edward and John Phillips, the first 10, the other 9 years of age; and in a year's time made them capable of interpreting a Latin author at sight, etc., and within three years they went through the best of Latin and Greek poets: Lucretius and Manilius <and with him the use of the globes and some rudiments of arithmetic and geometry> of the Latins; Hesiod, Aratus, Dionysius Afer, Oppian, Apollonii *Argonautica,* and Quintus Calaber. Cato, Varro, and Columella *De re rustica* were the very first authors they learned. As he was severe on the one hand, so he was most familiar and free in his conversation to those to whom most sour in his way of education. N.B. he made his nephews songsters, and sing, from the time they were with him.

[First wife and children]

He married his first wife, Mary Powell of Fosthill,[4] at Shotover, in Oxonshire, Anno Domini . . . ; by whom he had four children. [He] hath two daughters living: Deborah was his amanuensis (he taught her Latin, and to read Greeke to him when he had lost his eyesight, which was anno Domini . . .).

[Separation from his first wife]

She went from him to her mother's at . . . in the king's quarters, near Oxford, anno Domini . . . ; and wrote the *Triplechord* about divorce.[5]

Two opinions do not well on the same bolster. She was a . . . Royalist, and went to her mother to the King's quarters, near Oxford. I have perhaps so much charity to her that she might not wrong his bed: but what man, especially con-

3. I.e., Nathaniel Tovey.

4. I.e., Forest Hill.

5. **Triplechord** ***about divorce:*** most likely *Tetrachordon* (four strings).

templative, would like to have a young wife environed and stormed by the sons of Mars, and those of the enemy party?

His first wife (Mrs. Powell, a Royalist) was brought up and lived where there was a great deal of company and merriment <dancing, etc.>. And when she came to live with her husband, at Mr. Russell's in St. Bride's churchyard, she found it very solitary; no company came to her; oftentimes heard his nephews beaten and cry. This life was irksome to her, and so she went to her parents at Fosthill. He sent for her, after some time; and I think his servant was evilly entreated: but as for manner of wronging his bed, I never heard the least suspicions; nor had he, of that, any jealousy.

[Second wife]

He had a middle wife, whose name was Katharine Woodcock. No child living by her.

[Third wife]

He married his second [sic] wife, Elizabeth Minshull, anno . . . (the year before the sickness): a gentle person, a peaceful and agreeable humor.

[His public employment]

He was Latin secretary to the Parliament.

[His blindness]

His sight began to fail him at first upon his writing against Salmasius, and before 'twas full completed one eye absolutely failed. Upon the writing of other books after that, his other eye decayed.

His eyesight was decaying about 20 years before his death. His father read without spectacles at 84. His mother had very weak eyes, and used spectacles presently after she was thirty years old.

[Writings after his blindness]

After he was blind he wrote these following books, viz.: *Paradise Lost, Paradise Regained, Grammar, Dictionary* (imperfect).

I heard that after he was blind that he was writing a Latin dictionary (in the hands of Moses Pitt). *Vidua affirmat*[6] she gave all his papers (among which this

6. **Vidua affirmat:** His widow maintains.

dictionary, imperfect) to his nephew, a sister's son, that he brought up . . . Phillips, who lives near the Maypole in the Strand. She has a great many letters by her from learned men, his acquaintance, both of England and beyond the sea.

[His later residences]

He lived in several places, e.g., Holborn near Kingsgate. He died in Bunhill, opposite the Artillery-garden wall.

[His death and burial]

He died of the gout, struck in the 9th or 10th of November, 1674, as appears by his apothecary's book.

He lies buried in St. Giles Cripplegate, upper end of the chancel at the right hand, *vide* his gravestone. Memorandum: his stone is now removed, for about two years since (now 1681) the two steps to the communion table were raised. I guess John Speed[7] and he lie together.

[Personal characteristics]

His harmonical and ingenious soul did lodge in a beautiful and well-proportioned body—*"In toto nusquam corpore menda fuit,"* Ovid.[8]

He was a spare man. He was scarce so tall as I am, [. . .] of middle stature.

He had auburn hair. His complexion exceeding fair—he was so fair that they called him *the Lady of Christ's College.* Oval face. His eye a dark gray.

He had a delicate tuneable voice, and had good skill. His father instructed him. He had an organ in his house; he played on that most.

Of a very cheerful humor. He would be cheerful even in his gout-fits, and sing.

He was very healthy and free from all diseases: seldom took any physic (only sometimes he took manna):[9] only towards his latter end he was visited with the gout, spring and fall.

He had a very good memory; but I believe that his excellent method of thinking and disposing did much to help his memory.

7. ***John Speed:*** author of *The History of Great Britain,* he is buried in St. Giles, as is John Foxe, author of *The Book of Martyrs* and *Acts and Monuments.*

8. 1 *Amores* 5.18: "There was not a blemish on her body."

9. ***manna:*** a mild laxative.

He pronounced the letter R <*littera canina*[10]> very hard (a certain sign of a satirical wit—from John Dryden.).

[Portraits of him]

Write his name in red letters on his pictures, with his widow, to preserve.[11]

His widow has his picture, drawn very well and like, when a Cambridge-scholar, which ought to be engraven; for the pictures before his books are not *at all* like him.

[His habits]

His exercise was chiefly walking.

He was an early riser <*scil.* at 4 a clock *manè*[12]>; yea, after he lost his sight. He had a man read to him. The first thing he read was the Hebrew bible, and that was at 4 h. *manè*, 1/2 h. plus. Then he contemplated.

At 7 his man came to him again, and then read to him again and wrote till dinner; the writing was as much as the reading. His (2nd) daughter, Deborah, could read to him in Latin, Italian and French, and Greek. [She] married in Dublin to one Mr. Clarke <sells silk, etc.>; very like her father. The other sister is Mary, more like her mother.

After dinner he used to walk 3 or 4 hours at a time (he always had a garden where he lived); went to bed about 9.

Temperate man, rarely drank between meals.

Extreme pleasant in his conversation and at dinner, supper, etc; but satirical.

[Notes about some of his works]

From Mr. E. Phillips:—All the time of writing his *Paradise Lost,* his vein began at the autumnal equinoctial, and ceased at the vernal or thereabouts (I believe about May); and this was 4 or 5 years of his doing it. He began about 2 years before the king came in, and finished about three years after the king's restoration.[13]

In the 4th book of *Paradise Lost* there are about six verses of Satan's exclamation to the sun, which Mr. E. Phillips remembers about 15 or 16 years before ever

10. **littera canina:** dog letter, so called because making a continuous *r* sound resembles a dog's growl when threatening attack.
11. A note to himself.
12. **Scil. . . . manè:** It is well known (*scilicet*) . . . in the morning.
13. I.e., Milton composed his epic between 1658 and 1663.

his poem was thought of, which verses were intended for the beginning of a tragedy which he had designed, but was diverted from it by other business.

Whatever he wrote against monarchy was out of no animosity to the king's person, or out of any faction or interest, but out of a pure zeal to the liberty of mankind, which he thought would be greater under a free state than under a monarchial government. His being so conversant in Livy and the Roman authors, and the greatness he saw done by the Roman commonwealth, and the virtue of their great commanders induced him to.

From Mr. Abraham Hill:—Memorandum: his sharp writing against Alexander More, of Holland, upon a mistake, notwithstanding he had given him by the ambassador all satisfaction to the contrary: viz. that the book called *Clamor* was writ by Peter du Moulin. Well, that was all one; he having writ it,[14] it should go into the world; one of them was as bad as the other.

Memorandum:—Mr. Theodore Haak. Regiae Societatis Socius, hath translated half his *Paradise Lost* into High Dutch in such blank verse, which is very well liked of by Germanus Fabricius, Professor at Heidelberg, who sent to Mr. Haak a letter upon this translation: *"incredibile est quantum nos omnes affecerit gravitas styli, et copia lectissimorum verborum,"*[15] etc.—*vide* the letter.

Mr. John Milton made two admirable panegyrics, as to sublimity of wit, one on Oliver Cromwell, and the other on Thomas, Lord Fairfax, both which his nephew Mr. Phillips hath. But he hath hung back these two years, as to imparting copies to me for the collection of mine [. . .]. Were they made in commendation of the devil, 'twere all one to me: 'tis the ὕψος[16] that I look after. I have been told that 'tis beyond Waller's or anything in that kind.[17] [. . .]

[His acquaintance]

He was visited much by learned [men]; more than he did desire.

He was mightily importuned to go into France and Italy. Foreigners came much to see him, and much admired him, and offered to him great preferments to come over to them; and the only inducement of several foreigners that came over into England was chiefly to see Oliver Protector and Mr. John Milton; and would see the house and chamber where he was born. He was much more admired abroad than at home.

14. Milton published his *Second Defense of the English People* (1654), with its attack on More as the author of the *Cry of the King's Blood* (*Regii Sanguinis Clamor*), even after learning that another had written the book.

15. "It is incredible how much the dignity of his style and his most excellent diction have affected all of us."

16. ὕψος: loftiness, altitude.

17. We omit here a catalog of Milton's works.

His familiar learned acquaintance were Mr. Andrew Marvell, Mr. Skinner, Dr. Pagett, M.D.

Mr. . . . [Cyriack] Skinner, who was his disciple.

John Dryden, Esq., Poet Laureate, who very much admires him, and went to him to have leave to put his *Paradise Lost* into a drama in rhyme. Mr. Milton received him civilly, and told him *he would give him leave to tag his verses.*[18]

His widow assures me that Mr. T. Hobbes was not one of his acquaintance, that her husband did not like him at all, but he would acknowledge him to be a man of great parts, and a learned man. Their interests and tenets did run counter to each other, *vide* Mr. Hobbes' *Behemoth.*

18. John Dryden's *The State of Innocence, and Fall of Man: An Opera Written in Heroique Verse,* based on *Paradise Lost,* was published in 1677. A *tag* was an ornamental, metal-tipped lace or string that dangled from a garment.

"Anno Domini 1619, he was ten years old, as by his picture; and was then a poet."

A Chronology of Milton's Poetry

Title of Poem	Composition	Earliest Print Publication
A Paraphrase on Psalm 114	1624	1645, 1673
Psalm 136	1624	1645, 1673
Apologus de Rustico et Hero	1624?*	1673
Carmina Elegiaca	1624?*	1876
Ignavus satrapam	1624?*	1876
Philosophus ad regem	1624?*	1645, 1673
Elegia prima	1626 (early April?)	1645, 1673
Elegia tertia, In Obitum Praesulis Wintoniensis	1626 ("Autumn 1626")	1645, 1673
Elegia secunda, In Obitum Praeconis Adademici	1626 ("Autumn 1626")	1645, 1673
In Obitum Praesulis Eliensis	1626 ("Autumn 1626")	1645, 1673
In Obitum Procancellarii Medici	1626 ("Autumn 1626")	1645, 1673
In Proditionem Bombardicam	1626?**	1645, 1673
In eandem	1626?** (post Mar. 1625 b/c ref to KJ I's death)	1645, 1673
In eandem	1626?**	1645, 1673
In eandem	1626?**	1645, 1673
In inventorem Bombardae	1626?**	1645, 1673
In quintum Novembris	1626 (Nov.)	1645, 1673
Elegia quarta	1627 (btwn Mar. 11 & Apr. 28)	1645, 1673
Elegia septima	1627 (May?)	1645, 1673 [1628—poem to Alexander Gill, Jr.?]
On the Death of a Fair Infant Dying of a Cough	1628 (Jan.–April)	1673
De Idea Platonica	1628 (June)? 1631?	1645, 1673
At a Vacation Exercise in the College	1628 (near July 4 or as late as Oct.)	1673
Elegia quinta	1629 (spring)	1645, 1673
Song. On May Morning	1629 (or 1630 or early 1631) (spring)	1645, 1673

Title of Poem	Composition	Earliest Print Publication
Sonnet I ("O Nightingale")	1629 (or 1630) (spring)	1645, 1673
Sonnet 2 ("Enchanting lady")	1629 (Michaelmas term)?	1645, 1673
Sonnet 3 ("As on a rugged hill")	1629 (Michaelmas term)?	1645, 1673
Canzone ("Ladies and young men in love")	1629 (Michaelmas term)?	1645, 1673
Sonnet 4 ("Diodati—and I will tell you")	1629 (Michaelmas term)?	1645, 1673
Sonnet 5 ("Surely, my lady, your beautiful eyes")	1629 (Michaelmas term)?	1645, 1673
Sonnet 6 ("A young, quiet, naïve lover")	1629 (Michaelmas term)?	1645, 1673
The Fifth Ode of Horace. Book I.	1629 (late)? (Campbell: "wholly undatable")	1673
On the Morning of Christ's Nativity	1629 (Dec. 25)	1645, 1673
Elegia sexta	1629 (late Dec.)	1645, 1673
The Passion	1630? (Mar. 26, Good Friday)	1645, 1673
On Shakespeare	1630	1632, 1645, 1664, 1673
On the University Carrier	1631 (soon after Jan. 1)	1645, 1658, 1673
Another on the Same	1631 (soon after Jan. 1)	1640, 1657, 1645, 1658, 1673
Epitaph on the Marchioness of Winchester	1631 (Easter term)	1645, 1673
Naturam non pati senium	1631? (June 1631, per Shawcross; also 1628–32)	1645, 1673
L'Allegro	1631? (summer 1631, per Oras)	1645, 1673
Il Penseroso	1631? (summer 1631, per Oras)	1645, 1673
Ad Patrem	1631? (per Bush; Shawcross: 1638; also 1632–45)	1645, 1673
Sonnet 7 ("How soon hath time")	1631 (Dec.)	1645, 1673
Elegiac couplet on Ariosto	1632?	1931-38 ?
Arcades	1632 (late summer)	1645, 1673
At a Solemn Musick	1632?	1645, 1673
On Time	1632–33? (Shawcross: 1637)	1645, 1673
Upon the Circumcision	1633?	1645, 1673
A Masque Presented at Ludlow Castle	1634 (Sept.)	1637, 1645, 1673
Psalm 114	1634 (Nov.)	1645, 1673
Haec ego mente (appended to *Elegia septima*)	1635? (Carey: "must . . . be post-1628")	1645, 1673
Lycidas	1637 (Nov.)	1638, 1645, 1673
Fix here ye	1638 (Apr.?)	1876
Ad Salsillum poetam Romanum	1638 (Oct.–Nov.?)	1645, 1673

TITLE OF POEM	COMPOSITION	EARLIEST PRINT PUBLICATION
Mansus	1638 (Dec.) or 1639 (Jan.–Feb.)	1645, 1673
Ad Leonoram Romae canentem	1639 (Feb.) or 1638 (Oct.–Nov.)	1645, 1673
Ad eandem ("The poet Torquato")	1639 (Feb.) or 1638 (Oct.–Nov.)	1645, 1673
Ad eandem ("Why, credulous Naples")	1639 (Feb.) or 1638 (Oct.–Nov.)	1645, 1673
Epitaphium Damonis	1639 (autumn)	1640, 1645, 1673
Translations from *Of Reformation*	1641 (Jan.–May)	1641 (May)
Translation from *Reason of Church-Government*	1641–42 (Aug. 4–Jan. 1)	1642 (late Jan. or Feb.)
Translations from *Apology against a Pamphlet*	1642 (Apr.)	1642 (Apr.)
Sonnet 8 ("Captain, or Colonel")	1642 (Nov.?)	1645, 1673
Sonnet 10 ("Daughter to that good Earle")	1642–45	1645, 1673
Sonnet 9 ("Lady, that in the prime")	1643–45	1645, 1673
Translation from *Areopagitica*'s title page	1644 (Nov.)	1644 (Nov. 23)
Translation from *Tetrachordon*	1645 (Feb.)	1645 (Mar. 4)
In Effigiei ejus Sculptorem	1645	1645, 1673
Sonnet 13 ("Harry, whose tuneful")	1646 (Feb. 9)	1648, 1673
Sonnet 12 ("I did but prompt the age")	1646	1673
On the New Forcers of Conscience	1646 (Shawcross: early 1647)	1673
Sonnet 14 ("When Faith and Love")	1646 (Dec.)	1673
Ad Joannem Rousium	1647 (Jan. 23)	1673
Sonnet 11 ("A book was writ of late")	1647?	1673
Psalms 80-88	1648 (Apr.)	1673
Sonnet 15 ("Fairfax, whose name in arms")	1648 (btwn July 8 & Aug. 17)	1694
Translation from *Tenure of Kings & Magistrates*	1649 (Feb.)	1649 (Feb. 13)
Translations from *History of Britain*	1649 (Feb.–Mar.)	1670
Verse from *Pro Populo Anglicano Defensio*	1650	1651 (Feb. 24)
Sonnet 16 ("Cromwell, our chief of men")	1652 (May)	1694
Sonnet 17 ("Vane, young in years")	1652 (June–July)	1662, 1694
Psalms 1-8	1653 (Aug. 8–14)	1673
Verses from *Defensio Secunda*	1653–54	1654 (May 30)
Sonnet 18 ("Avenge O Lord")	1655 (shortly after June 20)	1673
Sonnet 19 ("When I consider")	1655 (btwn July & Oct.)°	1673
Sonnet 20 ("Lawrence of virtuous")	1655 (Oct.–Nov.?)	1673
Sonnet 21 ("Cyriack, whose grandsire")	1655 (Oct.–Dec.?)	1673
Sonnet 22 ("Cyriack, this three years' day")	1655 (Oct.–Dec.?)	1694
Sonnet 23 ("Methought I saw")	1652? 1658?	1673

Title of Poem	Composition	Earliest Print Publication
Paradise Lost	1640s?, 1658–63? (per Aubrey)	1667 (Aug.?), 1674 (July 6?)
Paradise Regained	1665 (Aug.)–1670?	1671
Samson Agonistes	1660s?	1671

* = composed during Milton's school days ** = evidently composed for academic celebrations of Guy Fawkes Day ° = also dated as early as 1651 or 1652

English Poems

"He had auburn hair. His complexion exceeding fair—he was so fair that they called him *the Lady of Christ's College*" (see Aubrey, p. xxvii).

PSALM 114

The 1645 *Poems* informed its readers that "this and the following Psalm were done by the author at fifteen years old." They could well have been school exercises, as is usually assumed, but Milton's father's combination of faith and musical skill expressed itself in a keen appreciation for the Psalter. Milton Sr. in fact contributed six settings to Thomas Ravenscroft's *The Whole Book of Psalms* (1621). These translations are his son's earliest surviving English compositions.

When the blest seed of Terah's faithful son,
After long toil their liberty had won,
And passed from Pharian fields to Canaan land,
Led by the strength of the Almighty's hand,
Jehovah's wonders were in Israel shown,
His praise and glory was in Israel known.
That saw the troubled sea, and shivering fled,
And sought to hide his froth-becurlèd head
Low in the earth; Jordan's clear streams recoil,
As a faint host that hath received the foil.
The high, huge-bellied mountains skip like rams
Amongst their ewes, the little hills like lambs.
Why fled the ocean? And why skipped the mountains?
Why turnèd Jordan toward his crystal fountains?
Shake earth, and at the presence be aghast
Of him that ever was, and ay shall last,
That glassy floods from rugged rocks can crush,
And make soft rills from fiery flint-stones gush.

1. **faithful son:** Abraham.
3. **Pharian:** Egyptian.
10. **foil:** defeat.

PSALM 136

Let us with a gladsome mind
Praise the Lord, for he is kind,
  For his mercies ay endure,
  Ever faithful, ever sure.

Let us blaze his name abroad,
For of gods he is the God;
  For, &c.

O let us his praises tell,
Who doth the wrathful tyrants quell.
  For, &c.

Who with his miracles doth make
Amazèd heav'n and earth to shake.
  For, &c.

Who by his wisdom did create
The painted heav'ns so full of state.
  For, &c.

Who did the solid earth ordain
To rise above the wat'ry plain.
  For, &c.

Who by his all-commanding might,
Did fill the new-made world with light.
  For, &c.

And caused the golden-tressèd sun,
All the day long his course to run.
  For, &c.

The hornèd moon to shine by night,
Amongst her spangled sisters bright.
  For, &c.

10. **Who:** 1673. 1645 has *that* here and in lines 13, 17, 21, and 25. In each case we follow 1673.

He with his thunder-clasping hand,
Smote the first-born of Egypt land.
For, &c.

And in despite of Pharaoh fell,
He brought from thence his Israel.
For, &c.

The ruddy waves he cleft in twain,
Of the Erythraean main.
For, &c.

The floods stood still like walls of glass,
While the Hebrew bands did pass.
For, &c.

But full soon they did devour
The tawny king with all his power.
For, &c.

His chosen people he did bless
In the wasteful wilderness.
For, &c.

In bloody battle he brought down
Kings of prowess and renown.
For, &c.

He foiled bold Seon and his host,
That ruled the Amorean coast.
For, &c.

And large-limbed Og he did subdue,
With all his over-hardy crew.
For, &c.

And to his servant Israel
He gave their land therein to dwell.
For, &c.

46. **Erythraean:** adjective from the Greek for "red," applied by Herodotus 1.180; 2.8, 158 to the Red Sea.

65. **Seon:** Sihon, King of the Amorites (Num. 21.21–32).

66. **Amorean:** Amorite.

69. **Og:** giant King of Bashan, slain by Moses (Num. 21.33–35).

73. **his servant Israel:** Jacob.

He hath with a piteous eye
Beheld us in our misery.
For, &c.

And freed us from the slavery
Of the invading enemy.
For, &c.

All living creatures he doth feed,
And with full hand supplies their need.
For, &c.

Let us therefore warble forth
His mighty majesty and worth.
For, &c.

That his mansion hath on high
Above the reach of mortal eye.
For his mercies ay endure,
Ever faithful, ever sure.

ON THE DEATH OF A FAIR INFANT DYING OF A COUGH

This work belongs to a group of English lyrics that first appeared in the 1673 *Poems.* Based on the testimony of Milton's nephew Edward Phillips (Darbishire 1932, 62), the subject of the poem has generally been thought to have been Anne Phillips (b. January 1626 and d. January 1628), Milton's niece, and the mother addressed in the last stanza his sister Anne Phillips. Carey argues against these identifications, primarily on the grounds that Milton was nineteen and could not have written the elegy, as he claims to have, *Anno aetatis 17* (at the age of seventeen). The alternative is that Milton, whether unconsciously or not, backdated the poem (LeComte 7–8). Others of Carey's arguments seem tendentious. He takes "Summer's chief honor if thou hadst outlasted/Bleak Winter's force that made thy blossom dry" to assert that the child did not outlive a single winter (and therefore could not have been little Anne Phillips, who lived two years), whereas in fact the lines declare that the child did not outlive the winter in which she contracted the cough "that made thy blossom dry," and are therefore consistent with the Anne Phillips hypothesis.

In Stanza 5 the poem erupts with questions that always haunt tragic deaths.

Why did God permit this infant to die? "Could Heav'n for pity thee so strictly doom?" These painful questions open up the large subject of theodicy, the justification of God's ways to men, that will occupy the argumentative center of *Paradise Lost.* In this early lyric, perhaps his first original poem in English, Milton tries to lay doubts to rest by finding a providential scheme within which the infant's death can be seen as a divine attempt to bring Earth and Heaven closer together or improve the lot of mankind.

The poem ends with a prophecy that we take literally: "This if thou do he will an offspring give,/That till the world's last end shall make thy name to live." Hoping to make "offspring" metaphorical, modern editors often cite God's promise to the eunuchs in Isaiah 56.5: "Even unto them will I give . . . a name better than of sons and daughters: I will give them an everlasting name, that shall not be cut off." So Milton's "offspring" becomes salvation and eternal bliss, matters that render trivial all parental concern with earthly offspring. But Milton does not say that the fame of the offspring is eternal. Quite the opposite, he says that it will last until the end of the world. Recourse to Isaiah in interpreting "Fair Infant" probably does not occur before 1921 (Hughes et al. 2:135). Proponents clearly hope that the biblical passage can fend off the apparent sense of Milton's lines, which in turn is thought to suppose a Milton so fame-crazed that he would console a patient sister with the promise of another child with a glorious future. But that is precisely what he has done. Milton's sister was indeed pregnant at the time of the fair infant's death, and she gave birth to Elizabeth Phillips in April 1628.

ANNO AETATIS 17

I

O fairest flower no sooner blown but blasted,
Soft silken primrose fading timelessly,
Summer's chief honor if thou hadst outlasted
Bleak Winter's force that made thy blossom dry;
For he being amorous on that lovely dye
    That did thy cheek envermeil, thought to kiss
But killed alas, and then bewailed his fatal bliss.

1–2. **O fairest . . . fading:** The opening echoes *The Passionate Pilgrim* 10.1–2: "Sweet rose, fair flower, untimely plucked, soon faded,/Plucked in the bud and faded in the spring!" This work was ascribed to Shakespeare in 1599 and 1640, but we now believe that Shakespeare wrote only five of its twenty sonnets. The author of the one echoed by Milton is unknown.

1. **blown:** bloomed.

2. **timelessly:** unseasonably, not in due time.

3. **chief honor:** that for which Summer would be honored.

5. **amorous on:** in love with.

6. **envermeil:** tinge with vermilion.

6–7. **thought to kiss/But killed:** Shakespeare also conjoins *kiss* and *kill* in *VEN* 1110 and *OTH* 5.2.356–57.

II

For since grim Aquilo his charioteer
By boist'rous rape th' Athenian damsel got,
He thought it touched his deity full near,
If likewise he some fair one wedded not,
Thereby to wipe away th' infamous blot
Of long-uncoupled bed, and childless eld,
Which 'mongst the wanton gods a foul reproach was held.

III

So mounting up in icy-pearlèd car,
Through middle empire of the freezing air
He wandered long, till thee he spied from far;
There ended was his quest, there ceased his care.
Down he descended from his snow-soft chair,
But all unwares with his cold-kind embrace
Unhoused thy virgin soul from her fair biding place.

IV

Yet art thou not inglorious in thy fate;
For so Apollo, with unweeting hand
Whilom did slay his dearly-lovèd mate,
Young Hyacinth born on Eurotas' strand,
Young Hyacinth the pride of Spartan land;
But then transformed him to a purple flower:
Alack that so to change thee Winter had no power.

8–9. In Ovid, Boreas, the north wind, also called Aquilo, snatches away Orithyia, daughter of the king of Athens (*Met.* 6.682–710). Milton makes Aquilo into Winter's charioteer, and his *boist'rous rape* into the incitement of Winter's lust.

13. **eld:** old age.

15. **icy-pearlèd car:** chariot decorated with hailstones.

16. **middle empire:** the middle of the three traditional regions of air.

19. **snow-soft chair:** another description of the chariot of line 15, now seemingly cushioned with snow.

20. **cold-kind embrace:** an embrace kind in its intention but chilling in its consequences.

23–27. Apollo accidentally killed his beloved Hyacinthus with a discus and made a brightly colored (*purpureus*) flower spring from his blood (Ovid, *Met.* 10.162–216). At least one commentator (Servius; see Allen 49) blamed Boreas (Aquilo) for the accident.

23. **unweeting:** a variant of *unwitting.*

25. **born . . . strand:** Hyacinthus was born in Sparta, which is situtated on the river Eurotas.

V

Yet can I not persuade me thou art dead
Or that thy corse corrupts in earth's dark womb,
Or that thy beauties lie in wormy bed,
Hid from the world in a low delvèd tomb;
Could Heav'n for pity thee so strictly doom?
  O no! For something in thy face did shine
Above mortality that showed thou wast divine.

VI

Resolve me then O soul most surely blest
(If so it be that thou these plaints dost hear),
Tell me bright spirit where'er thou hoverest,
Whether above that high first-moving sphere
Or in the Elysian fields (if such there were).
  O say me true if thou wert mortal wight,
And why from us so quickly thou didst take thy flight.

VII

Wert thou some star which from the ruined roof
Of shaked Olympus by mischance didst fall;
Which careful Jove in nature's true behoof
Took up, and in fit place did reinstall?
Or did of late Earth's sons besiege the wall
  Of sheeny Heav'n, and thou some goddess fled
Amongst us here below to hide thy nectared head?

36. **Resolve me:** Answer my questions, solve my problems (*OED* 3.11b).

39. **first-moving sphere:** the *primum mobile,* the outermost sphere of the Ptolemaic universe.

40. **Elysian fields:** home of the blessed dead in Homer (*Od.* 4.561–69) and Plato (*Phaedo* 112E).

45. **behoof:** benefit.

47. **Earth's sons:** the Giants, who warred against the gods (Hesiod, *Theog.* 183–85).

VIII

Or wert thou that just maid who once before
Forsook the hated earth, O tell me sooth,
And cam'st again to visit us once more?
Or wert thou that sweet smiling youth?
Or that crowned matron, sage white-robèd Truth?
    Or any other of that Heav'nly brood
Let down in cloudy throne to do the world some good?

IX

Or wert thou of the golden-wingèd host,
Who having clad thyself in human weed,
To earth from thy prefixèd seat didst post,
And after short abode fly back with speed,
As if to show what creatures Heav'n doth breed,
    Thereby to set the hearts of men on fire
To scorn the sordid world, and unto Heav'n aspire?

X

But O why didst thou not stay here below
To bless us with thy Heav'n-loved innocence,
To slake his wrath whom sin hath made our foe,
To turn swift-rushing black perdition hence,
Or drive away the slaughtering pestilence,
    To stand 'twixt us and our deservèd smart?
But thou canst best perform that office where thou art.

50. **that just maid:** Astraea, goddess of Justice, who fled the earth when corruption followed the golden age. See *Nat Ode* 141–46.

53. Something apparently dropped out of this line when the poem was first printed, in 1673. It is missing a metrical foot, and the *youth* lacks his allegorical identity. Words such as *Mercy* and *Virtue* have been inserted between *thou* and *that,* which saves the meter; but these allegorical figures are never male, and *youth* in Milton always refers to a male.

54. **white-robèd Truth:** See Cesare Ripa, *Iconologia* 530.

57. **golden-wingèd host:** the angels.

59. **prefixèd:** preordained.

66. **his:** God's.

68. **pestilence:** There was a major outbreak of plague in 1625–26. Milton could be assuming that the birth of Anne Phillips *did* drive away that plague. She will be an even more effective advocate in Heaven.

XI

Then thou the mother of so sweet a child
Her false imagined loss cease to lament,
And wisely learn to curb thy sorrows wild;
Think what a present thou to God hast sent,
And render him with patience what he lent;
This if thou do he will an offspring give,
That till the world's last end shall make thy name to live.

71. **Then thou:** The address has shifted from the dead child to its mother.

75. **render:** give back; **lent:** The idea that life is lent to us by God and in the end must be paid back was commonplace (see Jonson, "On My First Son" 3–5, "On My First Daughter" 2–4).

76–77. See headnote.

AT A VACATION EXERCISE

At some point during the summer vacation months (July through October) of 1628, Milton presided over festive exercises at Christ's College. In keeping with the traditions behind such saturnalian occasions, he first of all delivered the two raucous Latin orations that constitute Prolusion 6. The speeches were peppered with boisterous jokes about gender, sex, farts, and the like. Then the master of ceremonies broke into these pentameter English couplets. Milton's opening address to the English language, including his dismissal of the stylistic tastes of "late fantastics" (l. 20), is playful. With "Yet I had rather, if I were to choose" (l. 29), the tone shifts from schoolboy fun to personal yearnings serious enough to be already drafting at age nineteen a life plan dedicated to their realization: for a noble epic subject, an answerable style, a unique access to the divine secrets of the universe, and an enraptured audience. After exhibiting his literary dreams, Milton returns via a beautiful imitation of Horace (see 53–58n) to the business at hand, which is to play out the role of mocking the "Ens," or Father of the concepts of Aristotelian logic first adopted in the earlier Latin segment of the college entertainment. In graver minds, however, the hall must have kept on shimmering with the revelation of what this amusing student, if he were to choose, would rather be doing.

The work was first printed in 1673.

ANNO AETATIS 19

The Latin speeches ended, the English thus began.

Hail native language, that by sinews weak
Didst move my first endeavoring tongue to speak,
And mad'st imperfect words with childish trips,
Half unpronounced, slide through my infant lips,
Driving dumb silence from the portal door,
Where he had mutely sat two years before:
Here I salute thee and thy pardon ask,
That now I use thee in my latter task:
Small loss it is that thence can come unto thee,
I know my tongue but little grace can do thee:
Thou need'st not be ambitious to be first,
Believe me I have thither packed the worst:
And, if it happen as I did forecast,
The daintiest dishes shall be served up last.
I pray thee then, deny me not thy aid
For this same small neglect that I have made:
But haste thee straight to do me once a pleasure,
And from thy wardrobe bring thy chiefest treasure;
Not those new-fangled toys, and trimming slight
Which takes our late fantastics with delight,
But cull those richest robes, and gay'st attire
Which deepest spirits, and choicest wits desire:
I have some naked thoughts that rove about
And loudly knock to have their passage out;
And weary of their place do only stay
Till thou hast decked them in thy best array;
That so they may without suspect or fears
Fly swiftly to this fair assembly's ears;
Yet I had rather, if I were to choose,
Thy service in some graver subject use,

12. **thither:** in the Latin oration that preceded these English couplets.

19. **new-fangled toys:** idle fancies, appealing in their novelty.

20. **takes:** captivates, puts a spell upon; **late fantastics:** in the immediate context, showy dressers; but since dressing throughout lines 18–26 refers metaphorically to adopting a poetic style or manner, the *late* (recent) *fantastics* apparently names a modish school of writers given to fanciful notions. Some have taken Milton to be criticizing the metaphysical manner, but he might just as well be tweaking a form of expression cultivated by some of his fellow students.

27. **suspect:** suspicion.

29–52. Here Milton digresses from the academic conviviality of the immediate occasion to reveal his literary ambitions.

Such as may make thee search thy coffers round,
Before thou clothe my fancy in fit sound:
Such where the deep transported mind may soar
Above the wheeling poles, and at Heav'n's door
Look in, and see each blissful deity
How he before the thunderous throne doth lie,
Listening to what unshorn Apollo sings
To th' touch of golden wires, while Hebe brings
Immortal nectar to her kingly sire:
Then passing through the spheres of watchful fire,
And misty regions of wide air next under,
And hills of snow and lofts of pilèd thunder,
May tell at length how green-eyed Neptune raves,
In Heav'n's defiance mustering all his waves;
Then sing of secret things that came to pass
When beldam Nature in her cradle was;
And last of kings and queens and heroes old,
Such as the wise Demodocus once told
In solemn songs at King Alcinous' feast,
While sad Ulysses' soul and all the rest
Are held with his melodious harmony
In willing chains and sweet captivity.
But fie my wand'ring Muse, how thou dost stray!
Expectance calls thee now another way;
Thou know'st it must be now thy only bent
To keep in compass of thy predicament:
Then quick about thy purposed business come,
That to the next I may resign my room.

Then ENS is represented as Father of the Predicaments, his ten sons, whereof the eldest stood for SUBSTANCE with his Canons, which ENS thus speaking, explains.

32. **fancy:** invention.
33. **deep:** high (Lat. *altus* means both "high" and "deep").
34. **the wheeling poles:** the spheres of the Ptolemaic universe.
37. **unshorn:** stock epithet for Apollo.
38. **Hebe:** goddess of youth, daughter of Zeus.
40. **spheres of watchful fire:** The celestial spheres were manned by watchful angels.
42. **lofts:** layers or stages of air; **pilèd:** stockpiled.
48. **Demodocus:** minstrel who sang of the fall of Troy at the court of Alcinous (*Od.* 8.487–543) and brought tears to the eyes of Odysseus.
53. Milton's abrupt return to the occasion echoes Horace's rejection of epic Trojan tales (*Quo, Musa, tendis?*) in *Odes* 3.3.70.
53–58. Milton in the role of Ens or Father on this occasion must now introduce by name his ten Sons, the "categories" Aristotle defined in his *Categories.* The Muse's *bent* (aim) must be to keep within the *compass* (limits) of her *predicament,* or present situation. In scholastic logic based on Aristotle, the grammatical "accidents" that befell a "substance" or particular entity were called "predicaments."

Good luck befriend thee son; for at thy birth
The fairy ladies danced upon the hearth;
Thy drowsy nurse hath sworn she did them spy
Come tripping to the room where thou didst lie;
And sweetly singing round about thy bed
Strew all their blessings on thy sleeping head.
She heard them give thee this, that thou shouldst still
From eyes of mortals walk invisible;
Yet there is something that doth force my fear,
For once it was my dismal hap to hear
A sibyl old, bow-bent with crookèd age,
That far events full wisely could presage,
And in time's long and dark prospective glass
Foresaw what future days should bring to pass.
"Your Son," said she, "(nor can you it prevent)
Shall subject be to many an accident.
O'er all his brethren he shall reign as king,
Yet every one shall make him underling,
And those that cannot live from him asunder
Ungratefully shall strive to keep him under;
In worth and excellence he shall outgo them,
Yet being above them, he shall be below them;
From others he shall stand in need of nothing,
Yet on his brothers shall depend for clothing.
To find a foe it shall not be his hap,
And Peace shall lull him in her flow'ry lap;
Yet shall he live in strife, and at his door
Devouring War shall never cease to roar:
Yea, it shall be his natural property
To harbor those that are at enmity."
What power, what force, what mighty spell, if not
Your learned hands, can loose this Gordian knot?

The next, QUANTITY and QUALITY, spoke in prose, then RELATION was called by his name.

66. **walk invisible:** Because substance is an abstraction known only through particular accidents, Milton jokingly suggests that his personified Substance received at birth the gift of invisibility.

71. **time's . . . glass:** a crystal in which future events can be seen.

87–88. Cp. Aristotle, *Categories* 5.4a: "But what is most characteristic of substance appears to be this: that, although it remains, notwithstanding, numerically one and the same, it is capable of being the recipient of contrary qualifications."

90. **loose this Gordian knot:** overcome the paradoxes of Aristotle's logic. The knot to which the proverb alludes was originally tied by Gordius. The oracle declared that whoever untied it would rule Asia. Alexander cut it.

Rivers arise; whether thou be the son
Of utmost Tweed, or Ouse, or gulfy Dun,
Or Trent, who like some Earth-born giant spreads
His thirty arms along th' indented meads,
Or sullen Mole that runneth underneath,
Or Severn swift, guilty of maiden's death,
Or rocky Avon, or of sedgy Lea,
Or coaly Tyne, or ancient hallowed Dee,
Or Humber loud that keeps the Scythian's name,
Or Medway smooth, or royal-towered Thame.

The rest was prose.

91. **Rivers arise:** Two brothers named Rivers (George and Nizel) had been admitted to Christ's College in 1628. One of them played Relation, and is here *called by his name.* Milton proceeds to burlesque the catalogs of rivers found in Spenser (*FQ* 4.11.24–47) and often in Drayton's *Polyolbion.*

92. **gulfy:** full of eddies.

95. **sullen:** flowing sluggishly.

99. The name of the river *Humber* supposedly came from a Scythian invader who drowned in it after being defeated by Locrine.

SONG: ON MAY MORNING

Dates from 1629 to 1631 have been proposed for this poem in the absence of any evidence. Whenever Milton wrote this aubade or dawn song, it is a small gem. It hearkens back to Elizabethan songs such as Thomas Nashe's "Spring, the sweet spring" (the opening poem in Francis Turner Palgrave's famous anthology *The Golden Treasury*) and Shakespeare's "It was a lover and his lass" (from *AYL* 5.3). Like his predecessors, and it must be said, without a hint of what is popularly known as Puritanism, Milton joins in the ritual dance of the year's renewal, the return of flowers, the reaffirmation of "Mirth and youth, and warm desire." The lyric is an "early song," sung on the dawn of a May morning with the early charm of the English Renaissance song still blossoming in its shifting meters and exuberant enjambments.

As he often does, Milton saves the most remarkable effect for the end. We "wish thee long" when of course May is never long enough, and our annual wishes are doomed to disappointment. The message of the final words rolls back retrospectively through the entire poem, and we behold a second time, under the sign of "gone too soon," the dawn of a May morning. The effect anticipates what the mature poet will achieve with the endless spring of Paradise: represent it responsively and thoroughly while all the while making us ever more hopelessly aware of its having been lost too soon.

Now the bright morning Star, day's harbinger,
Comes dancing from the East, and leads with her
The flow'ry May, who from her green lap throws
The yellow cowslip, and the pale primrose.
    Hail bounteous May that dost inspire
    Mirth and youth, and warm desire;
    Woods and groves are of thy dressing,
    Hill and dale doth boast thy blessing.
Thus we salute thee with our early song,
And welcome thee, and wish thee long.

1. **morning Star:** Venus.
3. Milton's flower-throwing *May* recalls Spenser's "faire May . . . throwing flowers out of her lap around" (*FQ* 7.7.34).

THE FIFTH ODE OF HORACE, LIB. I

This famous translation appeared for the first time in the 1673 *Poems.* Proponents of a late date, noting likenesses between the translation and Milton's mature style, suppose that he was deliberately studying Horace in an attempt to perfect his own literary gifts. But the fact that we have no other examples of such studious translations (unless we imagine that Milton was primarily tinkering with his style in the Psalm paraphrases) argues for an earlier date, perhaps 1629, on the assumption that the poem grew out of an academic exercise. It was not unusual for teachers to have their students compete in translating or adapting a classical work. By the eighteenth century, the practice extended to Milton's works. Thomas Warton in his 1785 edition notes that "Mr. Benson [presumably William Benson (1682–1754), who erected the Milton monument in Westminster Abbey] gave medals as prizes for the best verses that were produced on Milton at all our great schools."

The Horace translation was in fact immensely popular in the eighteenth century. "From 1700 to 1837," Raymond Havens reports, "no fewer than eighty-three poems, and probably many more, were written in Milton's Horatian stanza, which thus had a vogue almost as great, in proportion to the length and importance of the poem, as any of his own verse-forms enjoyed" (560). The best-known of the imitations is Collins's *Ode to Evening,* and the influence of Milton's unrhymed lines of shifting length can still be heard in such Victorian pieces as Tennyson's "Tears, idle tears" and Arnold's *Philomela.*

It is doubtful that Milton himself would have considered this vogue a sign of artistic health. The words of the headnote, "as near as the language will permit," indicate his awareness that this version of a Horatian ode is not a manifesto or an exemplar but a tour de force, a fantastic one-off. For the language does not permit. English word order cannot approach the free arrangements possible in an inflected language. Nor can Latin quantitative measures be imposed but for an enchanted moment on the accentual-syllabic system native to English. The poem affords us a brief look at an ideal English classicism that never happened. "Milton's youthful version of the Pyrrha Ode . . . is the only English translation in which it is really possible to perceive something of what makes the original what it is: the inimitable combination of difficulty and ease, artifice and grace, gravity and lightness" (Leishman, 52–53).

Quis multa gracilis te puer in rosa

Rendered almost word for word without rhyme according to the Latin measure, as near as the language will permit.

What slender youth bedewed with liquid odors
   Courts thee on roses in some pleasant cave,
   Pyrrha? For whom bind'st thou
   In wreaths thy golden hair,
Plain in thy neatness? O how oft shall he
On faith and changèd gods complain: and seas
   Rough with black winds and storms
   Unwonted shall admire:
Who now enjoys thee credulous, all gold,
Who always vacant, always amiable
   Hopes thee, of flattering gales
   Unmindful? Hapless they
To whom thou untried seem'st fair. Me in my vowed
Picture the sacred wall declares t' have hung
   My dank and dropping weeds
   To the stern god of sea.

5. **Plain in thy neatness:** Milton's restrained rendition of Horace's famously rich *simplex munditie* (or *simplex munditiis,* as modern editions read). The phrase has been taken as a comment on Horace's own poetic art but in context asserts that *Pyrrha* is ordinarily plain in adorning herself, which makes the wreaths of her current hairdo all the more suggestive of a new love interest.

8. **shall admire:** shall wonder at (in surprise).

9. **all gold:** entirely pure, gold through and through (not just in the tresses).

10. **vacant:** without other lovers; **amiable:** lovable.

11. **flattering:** treacherous, deceitful.

13–16. **Me . . . sea:** *Vota* or "vows" were prayers to the gods to avert some danger, accompanied by the promise of a thanksgiving offering should the danger pass. They were often commemorated by placing a votive tablet containing an inscription or a picture summarizing the vow on the wall of the temple. Horace's thankful speaker, having escaped metaphorical shipwreck (ill-fated love) through the favor of Neptune, has pictured himself hanging clothes still wet from the sea on the walls of Neptune's temple.

ON THE MORNING OF CHRIST'S NATIVITY

Though by no means the earliest of Milton's poems, the *Nativity Ode,* as it is commonly called, was printed first in both the 1645 and 1673 *Poems,* as if its author (or its publisher, or both) were entirely confident of the work's power. Here the mature poet presents his calling card. For the first time we see him shift from a personal voice seeking inspiration in the opening four stanzas to a communal voice performing our human part in the celestial harmonies that accompany the Incarnation, and defining with authoritative ease the proportions of joy and sorrow, wonder and apprehension, pride and shame, appropriate to this watershed moment. Other Nativity odes of the period dwelled on the paradox of an eternal God become a mortal child; Milton does that briefly in Stanza 2 of his induction. Other Nativity odes dwelled as modern Christmas cards do on the tender love passing back and forth between Mary and the infant Jesus; Milton touches on this theme in his final stanza. What Milton's poem has, in place of the conventional themes that consumed other lyrics on this topic, is a sense of the meaning of the Nativity within the full scope of Christian history, and an interest in the relationship between Christianity and the various cultures, religions, and artistic traditions found in the world at its advent.

Two of the most influential treatments of the ode are Arthur Barker's account of its structure (1940–41) and Rosemond Tuve's study of its imagery (37–72). See also the important recent studies by C.W.R.D. Moseley (99–114), David Quint, and Mary Oates O'Reilly.

Composed 1629

I

This is the month, and this the happy morn
Wherein the Son of Heav'n's eternal King,
Of wedded maid, and virgin mother born,
Our great redemption from above did bring;
For so the holy sages once did sing,
    That he our deadly forfeit should release,
And with his Father work us a perpetual peace.

1. **this the happy morn:** Milton told Diodati that he began the poem on Christmas morning 1629. See *Elegy 6* 88.

5. **holy sages:** Hebrew prophets.

6. **deadly forfeit:** sin and its penalty, death.

II

That glorious form, that light unsufferable,
And that far-beaming blaze of majesty,
Wherewith he wont at Heav'n's high council table,
To sit the midst of trinal unity,
He laid aside; and here with us to be,
   Forsook the courts of everlasting day,
And chose with us a darksome house of mortal clay.

III

Say Heav'nly Muse, shall not thy sacred vein
Afford a present to the infant God?
Hast thou no verse, no hymn, or solemn strain,
To welcome him to this his new abode,
Now while the heav'n by the sun's team untrod,
   Hath took no print of the approaching light,
And all the spangled host keep watch in squadrons bright?

IV

See how from far upon the eastern road
The star-led wizards haste with odors sweet:
O run, prevent them with thy humble ode,
And lay it lowly at his blessèd feet;
Have thou the honor first, thy Lord to greet,
   And join thy voice unto the angel choir,
From out his secret altar touched with hallowed fire.

8. **unsufferable:** unbearable.

10. **wont:** was accustomed.

14. **house of mortal clay:** the human body. Cp. *Passion* 15–17.

15. **Heav'nly Muse:** Milton's first reference in a poem to the source of inspiration he would later invoke in *PL* 1.6. One of her names (*PL* 7.1–2) is Urania, the classical Muse of astronomy, but elevated to the Christian or Heavenly Muse in du Bartas's *La Muse Chrestiene* (1574). **sacred vein:** aptitude for religious verse.

19. **Now:** referring to the first Christmas morning, to which the poet has been imaginatively transported. On the complex time schemes and shifting verb tenses of the poem, see Nelson 32–33, 41–52, and Tayler 1979, 34–40.

22. **eastern road:** leading from the East (i.e., Asia) to Bethlehem.

23. **star-led wizards:** the Magi (Matt. 2); **odors:** spices (the frankincense and myrrh of Matt. 2.11).

24. **prevent:** come before. Milton implores the Muse to complete his poem-present, begun on Christmas morning (see 1n), before January 6, when the Epiphany (the manifestation of Jesus to the Gentiles, represented by the Magi) is traditionally celebrated. Given the poem's time play, Milton may be asking that his verses arrive in Bethlehem before the Magi.

28. An inverted line: the voice (27) is touched with hallowed fire from out the secret (*retired, set apart*) altar. In Isa. 6.6–7 an angel touches the prophet's lips with a burning coal from God's altar. Cp. *RCG* (p. 843).

The Hymn

I

It was the winter wild,
While the Heav'n-born-child,
    All meanly wrapped in the rude manger lies;
Nature in awe to him
Had doffed her gaudy trim
    With her great master so to sympathize:
It was no season then for her
To wanton with the sun her lusty paramour.

II

Only with speeches fair
She woos the gentle air
    To hide her guilty front with innocent snow,
And on her naked shame,
Pollute with sinful blame,
    The saintly veil of maiden white to throw,
Confounded, that her maker's eyes
Should look so near upon her foul deformities.

34. **so to sympathize:** be in accord with (by divesting herself of her glory).

35. **season:** both "time of year" and "proper occasion."

39. **front:** face.

41. **Pollute:** tainted by the Fall and its consequences; **blame:** culpability, not reproof.

43. **Confounded:** ashamed.

III

But he her fears to cease,
Sent down the meek-eyed Peace;
She crowned with olive green, came softly sliding
Down through the turning sphere
His ready harbinger,
With turtle wing the amorous clouds dividing,
And waving wide her myrtle wand,
She strikes a universal peace through sea and land.

IV

No war, or battle's sound
Was heard the world around:
The idle spear and shield were high up hung,
The hookèd chariot stood
Unstained with hostile blood,
The trumpet spake not to the armèd throng,
And kings sat still with awful eye,
As if they surely knew their sov'reign Lord was by.

V

But peaceful was the night
Wherein the Prince of Light
His reign of peace upon the earth began:
The Winds with wonder whist,
Smoothly the waters kissed,
Whispering new joys to the mild Ocean,
Who now hath quite forgot to rave,
While birds of calm sit brooding on the charmèd wave.

45. **cease:** end.

46. **meek-eyed:** gently, mercifully gazing (as opposed to the judgmental look Nature feared); **Peace:** Descending as in a court masque, with her emblematic olive crown and myrtle wand, Peace personifies the *pax romana,* during which Jesus was born, and prefigures the *perpetual peace* (7) to come at the end of time.

48. **turning sphere:** In the Ptolemaic universe, the outermost sphere imparts motion to the others while our planet rests at the stationary center (cp. Plato, *Phaedrus* 247b; Vergil, *Aen.* 6.797).

49. **harbinger:** forerunner.

50. **turtle:** turtledove; **amorous clouds:** surrounding and clinging to *Peace* as if in love with her.

51. **myrtle:** plant sacred to Venus.

56. **hookèd:** Chariots are "armed with hooks" (scythes) in 2 Macc. 13.2.

59. **awful:** filled with awe.

64. **whist:** hushed, silent.

68. **birds of calm:** halcyons (kingfishers). The ancients (Aristotle, *History of the Animals* 5.8) believed that calm seas always prevailed during the two midwinter weeks when the halcyons were brooding on their floating nests, laying eggs. **charmèd:** under a spell.

VI

The Stars with deep amaze
Stand fixed in steadfast gaze,
    Bending one way their precious influence,
And will not take their flight,
For all the morning light,
    Or Lucifer that often warned them thence;
But in their glimmering orbs did glow,
Until their Lord himself bespake, and bid them go.

VII

And though the shady gloom
Had given day her room,
    The Sun himself withheld his wonted speed,
And hid his head for shame,
As his inferior flame,
    The new-enlightened world no more should need;
He saw a greater sun appear
Than his bright throne, or burning axletree could bear.

VIII

The shepherds on the lawn,
Or ere the point of dawn,
    Sat simply chatting in a rustic row;
Full little thought they then,
That the mighty Pan
    Was kindly come to live with them below;
Perhaps their loves, or else their sheep,
Was all that did their silly thoughts so busy keep.

71. *Influence* is the astrological term for an ethereal liquid sent from the stars to the earth for good or ill (La Primaudaye 135–39). Here all the stars direct their influence (benign, presumably) toward Bethlehem. Cp. *PL* 9.105–7.

73. **For all:** in spite of.

74. **Lucifer:** the morning star. Venus is "otherwise called Hesperus and Vesper and Lucifer, both because he seemeth to be one of the brightest stars, and also first riseth and setteth last" (E.K.'s gloss on "December," in Spenser, *SC*).

75. **orbs:** the concentric hollow spheres that in the Ptolemaic scheme carry the stars and planets around the earth.

81. **As:** as if, or because.

83. **greater sun:** Christ. See Mal. 4.2; *PL* 5.171–72.

84. **throne:** described by Ovid in *Met.* 2.24; **axletree:** the axle of the sun's chariot.

86. **Or ere:** before; **point of dawn:** daybreak.

89. **mighty Pan:** Spenser also called Christ "mighty Pan" in *SC*, "May" 54, and E.K.'s gloss on the passage retells from Plutarch the story of how, at the time of the Crucifixion, a voice in the Mediterranean cried out that great Pan was dead (*The Obsolescence of Oracles* 418).

92. **silly:** simple, harmless.

IX

When such music sweet
Their hearts and ears did greet,
As never was by mortal finger strook,
Divinely-warbled voice
Answering the stringèd noise,
As all their souls in blissful rapture took:
The Air such pleasure loath to lose,
With thousand echoes still prolongs each Heav'nly close.

X

Nature that heard such sound
Beneath the hollow round
Of Cynthia's seat, the airy region thrilling,
Now was almost won
To think her part was done,
And that her reign had here its last fulfilling;
She knew such harmony alone
Could hold all Heav'n and Earth in happier union.

XI

At last surrounds their sight
A globe of circular light,
That with long beams the shame-faced Night arrayed;
The helmèd Cherubim
And sworded Seraphim,
Are seen in glittering ranks with wings displayed,
Harping in loud and solemn choir,
With unexpressive notes to Heav'n's new-born heir.

98. **took:** captivated, put under a spell.

100. **close:** conclusion of a musical phrase, theme, or movement.

102–3. **hollow . . . seat:** the sphere of the moon; **airy region thrilling:** piercing the air between the moon and the earth.

104. **won:** persuaded.

110. **globe:** The Latin *globus* can mean both "troop" and "sphere." Both meanings are appropriate here as the globe of light gradually reveals *glittering ranks* (114) of angels.

114. **displayed:** unfolded.

116. **unexpressive:** indescribable.

XII

Such music (as 'tis said)
Before was never made,
But when of old the sons of morning sung,
While the Creator great
His constellations set,
And the well-balanced world on hinges hung,
And cast the dark foundations deep,
And bid the welt'ring waves their oozy channel keep.

XIII

Ring out ye crystal spheres,
Once bless our human ears,
(If ye have power to touch our senses so)
And let your silver chime
Move in melodious time,
And let the base of heav'n's deep organ blow,
And with your ninefold harmony
Make up full consort to th' angelic symphony.

119. **when of old:** See Job 38.4–7.

122. **well-balanced world:** Cp. *PL* 7.242: "And Earth self-balanced on her center hung"; **hinges:** supports; in this case probably the two poles of the axis about which the earth revolves. This line comes at the poem's midpoint.

124. **welt'ring:** tumbling; **oozy:** slimy, muddy.

125. **ye crystal spheres:** Each of the planetary spheres was believed to produce a unique note of the overall "music of the spheres," normally inaudible on the fallen Earth. Here Milton imagines that vast music joining in the higher harmony of the *angelic symphony* (132).

126. **Once:** only.

130. **the base:** The lowest note of the celestial music is that of the Earth (with the likely implication that this base note has been silent or out of tune since the Fall).

131. **ninefold:** Cp. the "nine enfolded spheres" of *Arcades* 64, while in *PL* 3.481–83 there are ten spheres. It is likely that Milton prefers nine spheres in this instance because they correlate with the nine orders of angels.

132. **full consort to:** full harmony with (there being a sphere answerable to every order of angel); **symphony:** harmony (not the modern sense of a particular form of musical composition).

XIV

For if such holy song
Enwrap our fancy long,
Time will run back, and fetch the age of gold,
And speckled Vanity
Will sicken soon and die,
And lep'rous Sin will melt from earthly mold,
And Hell itself will pass away,
And leave her dolorous mansions to the peering day.

XV

Yea Truth and Justice then
Will down return to men,
Orbed in a rainbow; and, like glories wearing,
Mercy will sit between,
Throned in celestial sheen,
With radiant feet the tissued clouds down steering,
And Heav'n as at some festival,
Will open wide the gates of her high palace hall.

XVI

But wisest Fate says no,
This must not yet be so,
The babe lies yet in smiling infancy,
That on the bitter cross
Must redeem our loss;
So both himself and us to glorify:
Yet first to those ychained in sleep,
The wakeful trump of doom must thunder through the deep.

135. **age of gold:** Christian interpretation of Vergil's *Ec.* 4 led to an association between the Nativity and the restoration of Saturn's age of gold.

136. **speckled:** spotted.

138. **mold:** the material (earth and clay) from which man was made.

140. **peering:** Opinion is divided between "just now appearing" and "overlooking, prying."

141–48. In classical terms, the return of Justice (Astraea) will reinaugurate the golden age (135n). Peace (45–52), Truth, Justice, and Mercy are the four daughters of God. They often debate the fate of fallen man, then achieve reconciliation through their unanimous approval of Christ's sacrifice. See also *Eikon* in Yale 3:583–84.

143–44. The 1645 version is "Th' enamelled arras of the rainbow wearing,/And Mercy set between." Mercy set between recalls Christ's position in *the midst of trinal unity* (11).

146. **tissued:** woven with gold or silver threads. Mercy's descent on a cloud again suggests (see 46n) the machinery of court masques.

148. **gates:** See Ps. 24.7.

155. **ychained:** a Spenserian archaism; **sleep:** death.

156. **wakeful:** arousing.

XVII

With such a horrid clang
As on Mount Sinai rang
While the red fire, and smold'ring clouds out brake:
The agèd earth aghast
With terror of that blast,
Shall from the surface to the center shake;
When at the world's last session,
The dreadful judge in middle air shall spread his throne.

XVIII

And then at last our bliss
Full and perfect is,
But now begins; for from this happy day
Th' old Dragon under ground
In straiter limits bound,
Not half so far casts his usurpèd sway,
And wroth to see his kingdom fail,
Swinges the scaly horror of his folded tail.

157. **clang:** the sound of a trumpet.

158. **As on Mount Sinai:** God appears on Sinai "in thunders and lightnings . . . and the voice of the trumpet exceeding loud" (Exod. 19.16). The *As* joining these two events has providential force, since the fearful appearance on Sinai typologically foreshadows the Last Judgment.

161. **that blast:** the thundering *trump of doom* (156).

163. **session:** the sitting of a court of justice.

164. **middle air:** the clouds in which Christ will return (Dan. 7.13; Matt. 24.30). Clouds inhabit the middle of the three traditional regions of air (Svendsen 1969, 88).

168. **old Dragon:** Rev. 20.2: "The dragon, that old serpent, which is the devil."

171. **wroth:** stirred to wrath.

172. **Swinges:** lashes.

XIX

The Oracles are dumb,
No voice or hideous hum
Runs through the archèd roof in words deceiving.
Apollo from his shrine
Can no more divine,
With hollow shriek the steep of Delphos leaving.
No nightly trance, or breathèd spell,
Inspires the pale-eyed priest from the prophetic cell.

XX

The lonely mountains o'er,
And the resounding shore,
A voice of weeping heard, and loud lament;
From haunted spring, and dale
Edged with poplar pale,
The parting Genius is with sighing sent;
With flow'r-inwoven tresses torn,
The Nymphs in twilight shade of tangled thickets mourn.

XXI

In consecrated earth,
And on the holy hearth,
The Lars and Lemures moan with midnight plaint;
In urns, and altars round,
A dear and dying sound
Affrights the flamens at their service quaint;
And the chill marble seems to sweat,
While each peculiar power forgoes his wonted seat.

173–236. Christ's expulsion of the pagan gods was a familiar topos—see Tuve 66n for theological versions. In *PL* 1.373–521, the pagan gods are identified with fallen angels.

173. **Oracles are dumb:** The chief source for the belief that pagan oracles ceased to speak at Christ's birth is Plutarch's *The Obsolescence of Oracles.* See also Sir Thomas Browne, *Pseudodoxia Epidemica* 7.12.

175. **words deceiving:** See *PR* 1.430–31.

178. **Delphos:** Delphi.

179. **nightly:** by night, nocturnal (not "occurring every night"); **breathèd spell:** Lucan reports that a vapor in the cave at Delphi produced the ability to prophesy (*Pharsalia* 5.82–85).

186. **Genius:** classical god of a locale.

187. **flow'r-inwoven tresses torn:** The garlands are signs of joy and celebration, now turned to devastation by the birth of Christ. Tearing of the hair is a gesture of lamentation (Ezra 9.3).

191. **Lars:** *lares,* Roman household gods whose worship took place in a separate apartment called *lararia* or hearth; **Lemures:** Roman spirits of dead bad men, supposed to wander at night and trouble the living.

194. **flamens:** priests; **quaint:** elaborate.

195. **seems to sweat:** a dire sign.

XXII

Peor and Baälim
Forsake their temples dim,
With that twice-battered god of Palestine,
And moonèd Ashtaroth,
Heav'n's queen and mother both,
Now sits not girt with tapers' holy shine;
The Libyc Hammon shrinks his horn;
In vain the Tyrian maids their wounded Thammuz mourn.

XXIII

And sullen Moloch fled,
Hath left in shadows dread,
His burning idol all of blackest hue;
In vain with cymbals' ring,
They call the grisly king,
In dismal dance about the furnace blue;
The brutish gods of Nile as fast,
Isis and Orus, and the dog Anubis haste.

197. **Peor and Baälim:** Peor was a local (Moabite) manifestation of Baäl (pl. Baälim), originally a Phoenician sun god whose worship became widespread and diverse in the ancient Middle East. Cp. Num. 25.3, 5.18; Deut. 3.29; *PL* 1.406–17n.

199. **twice-battered god:** Dagon. The Philistines twice set his image beside the Ark. The first morning he had fallen on his face, and the second his head and the palms of his hands were cut off (1 Sam. 5.2–4). Cp. *PL* 1.457–66.

200. **moonèd Ashtaroth:** Ashtareth is the Hebrew name for the Syrian Astarte, a fertility goddess associated with the moon. As with Baälim, Milton uses the plural Ashtaroth to indicate her various local manifestations.

203. **Libyc Hammon:** the Egyptian god Ammon, represented as a ram with massive horns; **shrinks his horn:** draws in his horn; hence, withdraws from a position of prominence (*OED* 13).

204. **Tyrian:** Phoenician; **Thammuz:** The Phoenician original of the Greek Adonis was annually slain by a wild boar and then resurrected: but not this year. See Ezek. 8.14.

205. **sullen:** baleful; **Moloch:** an Ammonite brass idol in whose flames the Hebrews sacrificed their children while priests drowned out the screams with trumpets and timbrels.

211. **brutish:** worshiped as animal forms.

212. **Isis . . . Orus . . . Anubis:** *Isis,* sister and wife of Osiris, was the Egyptian moon goddess. Horus (*Orus*), sometimes identified with the sun, was her child. The jackal-headed *Anubis* was the offspring of Osiris and Nephthys, another of his sisters.

XXIV

Nor is Osiris seen
In Memphian grove, or green,
    Trampling the unshow'red grass with lowings loud:
Nor can he be at rest
Within his sacred chest,
    Naught but profoundest Hell can be his shroud;
In vain with timbrelled anthems dark
The sable-stolèd sorcerers bear his worshipped ark.

XXV

He feels from Judah's land
The dreaded infant's hand,
    The rays of Bethlehem blind his dusky eyn;
Nor all the gods beside,
Longer dare abide,
    Not Typhon huge ending in snaky twine:
Our babe to show his Godhead true,
Can in his swaddling bands control the damnèd crew.

213. **Osiris:** the chief Egyptian god, worshiped in the form of a black bull (hence his *lowings loud,* 215).

215. **unshow'red:** not rained on.

217. **sacred chest:** Set, the Egyptian god of darkness, imprisoned Osiris in a chest, and threw it into the Nile.

218. **shroud:** place of retreat.

219. **timbrelled:** accompanied by tambourines.

220. **sable-stolèd:** black robed; **worshipped ark:** Herodotus 2.63: "The image of the god [Osiris], in a little wooden gilt casket, is carried . . . from the temple by the priests."

221. **Judah's land:** where Bethlehem lies—Isa. 19.17: "The land of Judah shall be a terror unto Egypt."

226. **Typhon:** The last-mentioned of the Egyptian gods has a *snaky twine* because the Egyptian Set, brother and enemy to Osiris, was confused with the Greek Typhon, a monster human above the waist but with great coils of twisted serpents below it.

227–28. Just as the break between Christian and pagan seems absolute, Milton compares the victorious Christ child to the infant Hercules, who strangled two serpents sent by Juno to kill him. On Hercules as a pagan type of Christ, see Hughes 1953, 106, and Allen 129–30.

XXVI

So when the Sun in bed,
Curtained with cloudy red,
Pillows his chin upon an orient wave,
The flocking shadows pale,
Troop to th' infernal jail,
Each fettered ghost slips to his several grave,
And the yellow-skirted fays
Fly after the Night-steeds, leaving their moon-loved maze.

XXVII

But see the virgin blest,
Hath laid her babe to rest.
Time is our tedious song should here have ending:
Heav'n's youngest teemèd star,
Hath fixed her polished car,
Her sleeping Lord with handmaid lamp attending:
And all about the courtly stable,
Bright-harnessed angels sit in order serviceable.

231. **orient:** eastern, bright.

232–34. It was a popular belief that ghosts and other spirits fled the dawn. See Shakespeare, *HAM* 1.1.152, 1.5.89–91, and *MND* 3.2.379–84.

234. **fettered ghost:** dead soul whose earthly interests tie it to this world. Cp. *Masque* 470–75.

235. **fays:** fairies. Milton seems to be the first to make them *yellow-skirted.*

236. **Night-steeds:** horses that draw the chariot of Night; **moon-loved maze:** "fairy rings," the markings left by their circle dance; the dance is *moon-loved* because loved by the moon, or loved by fairies when the moon shines, or both.

239. **our tedious song:** It was conventional modesty for a poet to refer to his work (usually toward the end of it) as *tedious.* See Gascoigne, "Gascoigne's woodmanship" 150; Browne, *Britannia's Pastorals* 2.3.482.

240. **youngest teemèd:** latest born.

241. **fixed:** "The star, which they saw in the east, went before them, till it came and stood over where the young child was" (Matt. 2.9).

244. **Bright-harnessed:** clad in bright armor; **serviceable:** ready to serve.

THE PASSION

The opening of this poem clearly alludes to *On the Morning of Christ's Nativity,* which was begun at Christmas 1629. So *The Passion* was probably written in 1630, perhaps at Easter time. The poems on the birth and death of Christ also seem related to *Upon the Circumcision,* in that all three take as their subjects a liturgical moment from the life of Christ and both *The Passion* and *Upon the Circumcision* refer to the *Nativity Ode.*

The most interesting thing about this lyric is the fact that Milton could not finish it, and marked the impasse with a prose postscript in which the subject of Christ's Passion is declared to be "above the years he had when he wrote it." Milton might at the time have been singling out the Passion for another treatment in the future, but as it happened his major work on the life of Christ, *Paradise Regained,* focused on the temptation in the wilderness.

The eight emphatic lines on the Crucifixion in *Paradise Lost* (12.412–19) were the best he had to offer on that topic. Unlike Richard Crashaw or even George Herbert, Milton never warmed to the subject of Christ's blood. His religious poetry (with the partial exception of *Upon the Circumcision*) is notably distant from the Eucharist. Unlike the *Nativity Ode, The Passion* does not find typological energy in its segment of Christ's life. The lyric moves in space, from landscape to landscape, but not in melodious time.

I

Erewhile of music, and ethereal mirth,
Wherewith the stage of air and earth did ring,
And joyous news of Heav'nly infant's birth,
My muse with angels did divide to sing;
But headlong joy is ever on the wing,
   In wintry solstice like the shortened light
Soon swallowed up in dark and long out-living night.

II

For now to sorrow must I tune my song,
And set my harp to notes of saddest woe,
Which on our dearest Lord did seize ere long,
Dangers, and snares, and wrongs, and worse than so,
Which he for us did freely undergo.
   Most perfect hero, tried in heaviest plight
Of labors huge and hard, too hard for human wight.

4. **divide:** meaning both "share" (with the angels) and "perform divisions" (musical variations on a theme).

6. Like the shortened daylight at the winter solstice.

13. **Most perfect hero:** Hercules is a type or prefiguration of Christ. See *Nat Ode* 227–28n.

III

He sov'reign priest, stooping his regal head
That dropped with odorous oil down his fair eyes,
Poor fleshly tabernacle enterèd,
His starry front low-roofed beneath the skies;
O what a mask was there, what a disguise!
Yet more; the stroke of death he must abide,
Then lies him meekly down fast by his brethren's side.

IV

These latter scenes confine my roving verse,
To this horizon is my Phoebus bound,
His Godlike acts, and his temptations fierce,
And former sufferings other where are found;
Loud o'er the rest Cremona's trump doth sound;
Me softer airs befit, and softer strings
Of lute, or viol still, more apt for mournful things.

V

Befriend me Night, best patroness of Grief,
Over the pole thy thickest mantle throw,
And work my flattered fancy to belief,
That heav'n and earth are colored with my woe;
My sorrows are too dark for day to know:
The leaves should all be black whereon I write,
And letters where my tears have washed a wannish white.

15. **sov'reign priest:** Two of Christ's three offices are King and Priest (*CD* 1.15).

16. **dropped with odorous oil:** The name Christ means "anointed" in Greek.

17. **fleshly tabernacle:** For the body as tabernacle, see 2 Cor. 5.1, 2 Pet. 1.13–14.

26. **Cremona's trump:** Milton expresses admiration for the Neo-Latin *Christiad* (1535) of Marco Girolamo Vida, a native of Cremona.

28. **still:** quiet.

30. **pole:** sky.

34–35. Though editors often maintain otherwise, we have no seventeenth-century elegies printed on black pages with white letters. But elegies were often printed with a band of black on the edge of the page. Milton, Carey suggests, wishes that his pages were *all* (entirely) black.

VI

See see the chariot, and those rushing wheels
That whirled the prophet up at Chebar flood;
My spirit some transporting cherub feels,
To bear me where the towers of Salem stood,
Once glorious towers, now sunk in guiltless blood;
There doth my soul in holy vision sit
In pensive trance, and anguish, and ecstatic fit.

VII

Mine eye hath found that sad sepulchral rock
That was the casket of Heav'n's richest store,
And here though grief my feeble hands uplock,
Yet on the softened quarry would I score
My plaining verse as lively as before;
For sure so well instructed are my tears,
That they would fitly fall in ordered characters.

VIII

Or should I thence, hurried on viewless wing,
Take up a weeping on the mountains wild,
The gentle neighborhood of grove and spring
Would soon unbosom all their echoes mild,
And I (for grief is easily beguiled)
Might think th' infection of my sorrows loud,
Had got a race of mourners on some pregnant cloud.

This subject the author finding to be above the years he had when he wrote it, and nothing satisfied with what was begun, left it unfinished.

37. **the prophet:** Ezekiel. He saw the chariot of God borne by cherubim near the river Chebar (Ezek. 1 and 10).

39. **Salem:** Jerusalem.

42. **ecstatic:** outside the body.

43. **that sad sepulchral rock:** the Holy Sepulchre in Jerusalem (Mark 15.46).

44. **casket:** treasure chest.

47. **plaining:** mourning; **lively:** vividly, feelingly.

49. **in ordered characters:** in letters (*characters*) so ordered as to spell the words of my poem.

50. **viewless:** invisible.

56. **got:** begot. Milton glances at the myth of Ixion. He tried to rape Hera, but she substituted a cloud for herself, and on that cloud Ixion begot a race of centaurs (Pindar, *Pyth.* 2.21–24).

ON SHAKESPEARE

This poem is dated 1630 in the 1645 *Poems,* but if actually written that early, was not published until the Second Folio of 1632, where it appeared anonymously under the title "An Epitaph on the Admirable Dramatic Poet W. Shakespeare." We know nothing of the circumstances linking Milton to the makers of the Second Folio.

It is satisfying in several ways that this should be the first printed of Milton's English poems. The great poet of the age to come begins his career by honoring the great poet of the age just past. He does so by calling attention early on to the extraordinary fame, the amazing hold on living memory, that is to this day such a remarkable aspect of the Shakespeare phenomenon.

What needs my Shakespeare for his honored bones,
The labor of an age in pilèd stones,
Or that his hallowed relics should be hid
Under a star-ypointing pyramid?
Dear son of Memory, great heir of Fame,
What need'st thou such weak witness of thy name?
Thou in our wonder and astonishment
Hast built thyself a livelong monument.
For whilst to th' shame of slow-endeavoring art,
Thy easy numbers flow, and that each heart
Hath from the leaves of thy unvalued book
Those Delphic lines with deep impression took,
Then thou our fancy of itself bereaving,
Dost make us marble with too much conceiving;
And so sepulchered in such pomp dost lie,
That kings for such a tomb would wish to die.

1–2. It seems likely that the idea of the Folio as a monument (though hardly original) derives in this case from poems affixed to the First Folio, especially Ben Jonson's *To the Memory of . . . Shakespeare* 22–24.

3. **hallowed relics:** Shakespeare's (metaphorical) sainthood is implied.

4. **star-ypointing:** pointing to the stars. An archaism popularized by Spenser, the *y*-prefix is a metrically handy vestige of Middle English. Usually joined to past participles (cp. *Nat Ode* 155, *L'All* 12), here it is used with the present. The bibliographical record suggests that this ungrammatical combination of past and present tenses was intended.

8. **livelong:** durable. The 1632 Folio reads "lasting." The usage is unique and seems designed to stress Shakespeare's *living* presence.

10. **numbers:** rhythmic verses. As Heming and Condell remarked in their preface to the First Folio, "His mind and hand went together. And what he thought, he uttered with that easiness, that we have scarce received from him a blot in his papers." Cp. "inspires/Easy my unpremeditated verse" (*PL* 9.23–24). *That* substitutes for *whilst* (9).

11. **unvalued:** The primary sense is "invaluable," but "not regarded as valuable" lurks in the background (it was so used by Shakespeare).

12. **Delphic:** Apollo, the god of poetry, had his oracle at Delphi.

14. **make us marble:** Cp. *Il Pens* 42n. It is not the book that entombs Shakespeare but its en-

ON THE UNIVERSITY CARRIER

Who sickened in the time of his vacancy,
being forbid to go to London, by reason
of the plague.

Thomas Hobson drove a weekly coach from Cambridge to the Bull Inn, Bishopgate Street, in London, and also rented horses. He must have been a notable figure in the university, since his death on New Year's Day of 1631 inspired a number of poems, including two by Milton himself. The carrier's insistence that customers take the mount standing nearest the stable door or go without is said to have originated the proverbial phrase "Hobson's choice" (the title of a memorable 1954 David Lean film).

The plague of 1630 closed the university, resulting in a suspension of Hobson's routine. Though he escaped the plague, his vacation led to a decline and eventually, so it was thought, to his death.

Here lies old Hobson, Death hath broke his girt,
And here alas, hath laid him in the dirt;
Or else the ways being foul, twenty to one,
He's here stuck in a slough, and overthrown.
'Twas such a shifter, that if truth were known,
Death was half glad when he had got him down;
For he had any time this ten years full,
Dodged with him, betwixt Cambridge and the Bull.
And surely, Death could never have prevailed,
Had not his weekly course of carriage failed;
But lately finding him so long at home,
And thinking now his journey's end was come,
And that he had ta'en up his latest inn,
In the kind office of a chamberlain
Showed him his room where he must lodge that night,
Pulled off his boots, and took away the light:
If any ask for him, it shall be said,
"Hobson has supped, and 's newly gone to bed."

---

tranced readers; **conceiving:** both "taking into the mind, becoming possessed" and "imagining, forming mental representations."

1. **girt:** girth or saddle belt.

5. **'Twas:** he was; **shifter:** trickster.

7. **he:** probably Hobson, but possibly Death.

8. **Dodged with him:** shifted position so as to baffle him; **the Bull:** Bull Inn (see headnote).

14. **chamberlain:** the attendant at an inn in charge of the bedchambers.

ANOTHER ON THE SAME

Strenuous, repetitive wit is familiar enough in Donne, Jonson, Herrick, Lovelace, and other seventeenth-century writers. But the second Hobson epigram is the only example of this period style in Milton's work. The quick spurt of higher wit at the end of the poem, where the account of Hobson's work suddenly merges with Milton's own artistic work and the poem itself passes away, anticipates the far more sublime passage merging poet and poem in the epilogue to *Lycidas.*

Here lieth one who did most truly prove,
That he could never die while he could move,
So hung his destiny never to rot
While he might still jog on, and keep his trot,
Made of sphere-metal, never to decay
Until his revolution was at stay.
Time numbers motion, yet (without a crime
'Gainst old truth) motion numbered out his time;
And like an engine moved with wheel and weight,
His principles being ceased, he ended straight;
Rest that gives all men life, gave him his death,
And too much breathing put him out of breath;
Nor were it contradiction to affirm
Too long vacation hastened on his term.
Merely to drive the time away he sickened,
Fainted, and died, nor would with ale be quickened;
"Nay," quoth he, on his swooning bed outstretched,
"If I may not carry, sure I'll ne'er be fetched,
But vow though the cross doctors all stood hearers,
For one carrier put down to make six bearers."
Ease was his chief disease, and to judge right,

5. **sphere-metal:** The celestial spheres were thought to have been made of an indestructible material (Aristotle, *On the Heavens* 1.3).

6. **at stay:** at a standstill.

7. **Time numbers motion:** Aristotle defines time as the measure of motion (*Physics* 4.11–12).

8. **motion . . . time:** But in the case of Hobson, motion measured time (since his time was up when he stopped moving).

9. **engine:** machine (specifically, a clock).

10. **principles:** forces that achieve a regular result; **straight:** immediately.

14. **term:** end, but punning on "university term."

15. **drive the time away:** banish the time; but the idle carrier also desires employment, and in this sense would *drive the time away.*

18. A play on the phrase "fetch and carry," with *fetched* meaning "restored to consciousness."

19. **cross doctors:** the university professors who oppose Hobson's crossings to London.

20. **put down:** both "removed from office" and "killed"; **bearers:** both "carriers" and "pallbearers."

He died for heaviness that his cart went light,
His leisure told him that his time was come,
And lack of load made his life burdensome,
That even to his last breath (there be that say't)
As he were pressed to death, he cried, "More weight."
But had his doings lasted as they were,
He had been an immortal carrier.
Obedient to the moon he spent his date
In course reciprocal, and had his fate
Linked to the mutual flowing of the seas,
Yet (strange to think) his wain was his increase:
His letters are delivered all and gone,
Only remains this superscription.

22. **heaviness:** sadness.
26. **pressed to death:** a mode of execution used on prisoners who would not plead. They were put beneath boards on which rocks were placed and might cry out for more weight (a quicker death).
29–30. **Obedient . . . reciprocal:** Like the tides, he went back and forth each month (between Cambridge and London) in obedience to the moon.
32. **wain:** wagon, with a pun on *wane,* meaning "decrease, waste."
34. **this superscription:** the address on a letter and the inscription on a gravestone. Milton alludes to the poem itself, which is just now, in its final line, *delivered all and gone.*

AN EPITAPH ON THE MARCHIONESS OF WINCHESTER

Jane Savage married Lord John Paulet, the Marquis of Winchester, in 1622. She died at the age of twenty-three, soon after giving birth to a stillborn son on April 15, 1631; the cause of death was apparently an infection spread from a lanced abscess in her cheek. Other poems for the Marchioness survive, and lines 53–60 suggest that a volume by Cambridge elegists was at least planned. We know of nothing to connect Milton to this Roman Catholic family, though there is some evidence that Jane at the end of her life was inclining toward Protestantism (R. F. Williams 2:106).

In its tetrameter couplets, mixing regular with "headless" or trochaic lines, and in its confident classicism, the poem recalls Ben Jonson. But the climactic allusion to the biblical figure of Rachel has the same easy inventiveness with which the Jonsonian tradition approaches classical materials, and is therefore pure Milton.

This rich marble doth inter
The honored wife of Winchester,
A viscount's daughter, an earl's heir,
Besides what her virtues fair
Added to her noble birth,
More than she could own from earth.
Summers three times eight save one
She had told, alas too soon,
After so short time of breath,
To house with darkness, and with death.
Yet had the number of her days
Been as complete as was her praise,
Nature and fate had had no strife
In giving limit to her life.
Her high birth, and her graces sweet,
Quickly found a lover meet;
The virgin choir for her request
The god that sits at marriage feast;
He at their invoking came
But with a scarce-well-lighted flame;
And in his garland as he stood,
Ye might discern a cypress bud.
Once had the early matrons run
To greet her of a lovely son,
And now with second hope she goes,
And calls Lucina to her throes;
But whether by mischance or blame
Atropos for Lucina came;
And with remorseless cruelty,
Spoiled at once both fruit and tree:
The hapless babe before his birth
Had burial, yet not laid in earth,
And the languished mother's womb
Was not long a living tomb.

11–14. If her life had been as long as her praise were full, then the natures of those who mourn her would not feel cheated by fate.

16. In 1622, at the age of fourteen, she married John Paulet.

17. **request:** invoke.

18. **god:** Hymen.

20. Hymen's torch also sputtered at the ill-fated wedding of Orpheus and Eurydice (Ovid, *Met.* 10.6–7).

22. **cypress:** a tree long associated with mourning.

23. **early matrons:** timely midwives.

24. **greet her of:** congratulate her on; **son:** Charles, born 1629.

25. **second hope:** hope of a second child.

26. **Lucina:** Roman goddess of childbirth.

28. **Atropos:** The last of the three Fates; she cuts the thread of life.

31–32. **before his birth/Had burial:** Before she died, Jane delivered a stillborn boy.

So have I seen some tender slip
Saved with care from winter's nip,
The pride of her carnation train,
Plucked up by some unheedy swain,
Who only thought to crop the flow'r
New shot up from vernal show'r;
But the fair blossom hangs the head
Sideways as on a dying bed,
And those pearls of dew she wears,
Prove to be presaging tears
Which the sad morn had let fall
On her hast'ning funeral.
Gentle lady, may thy grave
Peace and quiet ever have;
After this thy travail sore
Sweet rest seize thee evermore,
That to give the world increase,
Shortened hast thy own life's lease;
Here, besides the sorrowing
That thy noble house doth bring,
Here be tears of perfect moan
Wept for thee in Helicon,
And some flowers, and some bays,
For thy hearse to strew the ways,
Sent thee from the banks of Came,
Devoted to thy virtuous name;
Whilst thou bright saint high sit'st in glory,
Next her much like to thee in story,
That fair Syrian shepherdess,
Who after years of barrenness,
The highly favored Joseph bore
To him that served for her before,
And at her next birth much like thee,
Through pangs fled to felicity,
Far within the bosom bright

35. **slip:** a shoot or sprig of a plant. In the forthcoming simile, the *slip* is Jane, the *unheedy swain* is death, and the *flow'r* is her stillborn son.

44. **presaging tears:** tears wept in advance of the fact of death, as if in premonition.

49. **travail:** labor, including the pain of childbirth.

50. **seize thee:** establish you in a place of dignity. *Sweet rest* is personified.

54. **bring:** bring forth.

56. **Helicon:** a mountain sacred to the Muses; some take it as a reference to Cambridge.

59. **Came:** the river Cam, which flows through Cambridge.

63. **Syrian shepherdess:** Rachel, Jacob's wife, who bore Joseph, then died giving birth to a second son, Benjamin.

66. **him:** Jacob; Gen. 29.20: "And Jacob served seven years for Rachel."

Of blazing majesty and light;
There with thee, new welcome saint,
Like fortunes may her soul acquaint,
With thee there clad in radiant sheen,
No marchioness, but now a queen.

73. **With thee there:** The reversal of *There with thee* (71) is an early appearance of one of Milton's trademark effects.

L'ALLEGRO and IL PENSEROSO

The companion poems, as *L'Allegro* (Ital. for "the joyful man") and *Il Penseroso* (Ital. for "the pensive man") are termed, do not appear in the Trinity College manuscript and are therefore difficult to date. Their rustic settings suggest the years following Cambridge, when Milton lived in his father's country homes at Hammersmith (1632–35) and Horton (1635–38), but they could just as well have been written earlier, during a normal college vacation.

The poems were widely and almost studiously imitated during the eighteenth century (Havens 236–75) and, at least in the academic study of Milton, retain their prestige today, despite the fact that the artful echoing between and within the poems, combined with their prosodic exuberance, apparently places them at some distance from theoretical concerns prominent in contemporary literary criticism. But absence can itself become a topic. Annabel Patterson (1988), with Raymond Williams in mind, observes that the ideal landscapes of the poems have been censored of any indications of real work. Marshall Grossman helps to fill in the picture by noting an anxiety over living off the labor of others.

Are the poems complementary or disjunctive? It belongs to their art that they are both. On the one hand, the goddess scornfully dismissed at the beginning of each poem is not the goddess celebrated in the other poem but her pathological antitype. The poems do not expressly reject each other. On the other hand, both speakers are trying to seal pacts with their respective goddesses. If Mirth can provide the bounties sought by the happy man, he declares, "Mirth with thee, I mean to live," and the pensive man adopts the same formula in his closing address to Melancholy. Each, should his terms be met, has a commitment to devote his life to his respective goddess. There is no hint that they are simply shopping around for the best deal and after their evocations of an ideal day will find out what's on offer from rival goddesses.

It seems clear that the pensive man wants more than the companion speaker, though this observation should not be taken to suggest that the happy man does not want a very great deal. Specifically, he wants a sure antidote to eating cares, a place in a literary tradition that includes Jonson and Shakespeare, and access to a music more powerful than that of Orpheus. But the pensive man wants liberty of contemplation, the high magic of the Platonic and Hermetic traditions, the genres of tragedy and epic, the narrative enchantment of Chaucer, mysterious dreams, a religious music able to bring all Heaven before his eyes, time to acquire universal knowledge, and in the end "something like prophetic strain." Mirth's gifts would make any wise man happy. The gifts of Melancholy are those of a life of planned accomplishment similar to Milton's.

L'ALLEGRO

Hence loathèd Melancholy,
    Of Cerberus, and blackest Midnight born,
In Stygian cave forlorn
    'Mongst horrid shapes, and shrieks, and sights unholy,
Find out some uncouth cell,
    Where brooding Darkness spreads his jealous wings,
And the night-raven sings;
    There under ebon shades, and low-browed rocks,
As ragged as thy locks,
    In dark Cimmerian desert ever dwell.
But come thou goddess fair and free,
In Heav'n yclept Euphrosyne,
And by men, heart-easing Mirth,
Whom lovely Venus at a birth
With two sister Graces more
To ivy-crownèd Bacchus bore;
Or whether (as some sager sing)
The frolic wind that breathes the spring,

1. **loathèd Melancholy:** Melancholy entered the Renaissance in two main traditions. In Galenic medicine it was a pathological condition caused by excessive black bile. But Aristotle remarked briefly that all extraordinary men in the arts and sciences were melancholic, thus associating melancholy with genius (see Wittkower and Wittkower 102). The *loathèd Melancholy* dismissed here is the Galenic kind, not the *divinest* variety of the companion poem.

2. An invented genealogy. Erebus is the traditional husband of Night; Milton mates her with *Cerberus,* the hound of Hades, whose name means "heart-devouring."

3. According to Vergil, *Aen.* 6.418, Cerberus lived in a cave near the river Styx.

5. **uncouth:** desolate.

7. **night-raven:** a bird, perhaps an owl or night heron, associated with evil omens.

8. **shades:** trees.

9. **ragged:** rugged.

10. **Cimmerian:** Cimmerians live in perpetual darkness (Homer, *Od.* 11.13–19).

11. **fair and free:** a common romance formula, also found in Jonson's *Epigram 76;* **free:** of gentle birth and breeding.

12. **yclept:** called; **Euphrosyne:** Mirth, one of the three sister Graces. The other two were Aglais (Brilliance) and Thalia (Bloom).

14. **at a birth:** at one birth.

17. **some sager sing:** Milton invents this genealogy.

Zephyr with Aurora playing,
As he met her once a-Maying,
There on beds of violets blue,
And fresh-blown roses washed in dew,
Filled her with thee a daughter fair,
So buxom, blithe, and debonair.
Haste thee nymph, and bring with thee
Jest and youthful Jollity,
Quips and Cranks, and wanton Wiles,
Nods, and Becks, and wreathèd Smiles,
Such as hang on Hebe's cheek,
And love to live in dimple sleek;
Sport that wrinkled Care derides,
And Laughter holding both his sides.
Come, and trip it as ye go
On the light fantastic toe,
And in thy right hand lead with thee,
The mountain nymph, sweet Liberty;
And if I give thee honor due,
Mirth, admit me of thy crew
To live with her, and live with thee,
In unreprovèd pleasures free;
To hear the lark begin his flight,
And singing startle the dull night,
From his watch-tower in the skies,
Till the dappled dawn doth rise;
Then to come in spite of sorrow,
And at my window bid good morrow,
Through the sweet-briar, or the vine,
Or the twisted eglantine.

20. **a-Maying:** a reference to the May Day observances condemned by some Puritans.

24. **buxom, blithe, and debonair:** The three adjectives were often connected, as in Thomas Randolph's "A bowl of wine is wondrous boon cheer/To make one blithe, buxom, and debonair" (*Aristippus* 18); **buxom:** unresisting, yielding; **blithe:** happy; **debonair:** good-looking, affable, and in this case literally *de bon air,* given that the father is a wind.

27. **Quips:** sharp remarks; **Cranks:** jokes where a word (*heart-easing,* say) is twisted to resemble another of diverse meaning (*heart-eating*).

28. **Nods:** gestures of salutation; **Becks:** A beck is probably an upward movement of the head ("come on") corresponding to a beckoning by hand.

29. **Hebe:** goddess of youth.

33. **trip it:** dance.

34. **fantastic:** whimsical, fancifully conceived (transferred from the dance to the foot or *toe* of the dancer). In the form of "trip the light fantastic," this has become one of Milton's gifts to the proverb hoard of our language, but while *trip* may continue to suggest dancing to some users, *light fantastic* has become vaguely attached to neon lights or dramatically lit nightclubs, and *toe,* initially left out in tribute to the familiarity of the line, has been forgotten.

40. **unreprovèd:** blameless.

45. **Then to come:** Some think that the lark comes to the speaker's window, but most modern editions favor L'Allegro; **in spite of:** in defiance of.

48. **eglantine:** another name for sweetbriar.

While the cock with lively din,
Scatters the rear of darkness thin,
And to the stack, or the barn door,
Stoutly struts his dames before,
Oft list'ning how the hounds and horn,
Cheerly rouse the slumb'ring morn,
From the side of some hoar hill,
Through the high wood echoing shrill.
Some time walking not unseen
By hedge-row elms, on hillocks green,
Right against the eastern gate,
Where the great sun begins his state,
Robed in flames, and amber light,
The clouds in thousand liveries dight.
While the plowman near at hand,
Whistles o'er the furrowed land,
And the milkmaid singeth blithe,
And the mower whets his scythe,
And every shepherd tells his tale
Under the hawthorn in the dale.
Straight mine eye hath caught new pleasures
Whilst the landscape round it measures,
Russet lawns, and fallows gray,
Where the nibbling flocks do stray,
Mountains on whose barren breast
The laboring clouds do often rest:
Meadows trim with daisies pied,
Shallow brooks, and rivers wide.
Towers, and battlements it sees
Bosomed high in tufted trees,
Where perhaps some beauty lies,

50. **Scatters the rear:** The image is of an army in retreat, its back part being scattered by pursuing forces.

55. **hoar:** probably just a color word, denoting the frost-colored mists covering the hills in summertime.

57. **Some time walking:** "In those vernal seasons of the year, when the air is calm and pleasant, it were an injury and sullenness against nature not to go out, and see her riches, and partake in her rejoicing with heaven and earth" (*Of Ed,* p. 980).

60. **state:** royal progress (as when the monarch goes on a journey of state).

62. **dight:** clothed.

67. **tells his tale:** Editors have long argued about whether this means "counts his sheep" or "tells his story (of love)." Given the time of day, the first seems likelier.

71. **Russet lawns:** unplowed lands whose grasses have been turned reddish brown by the sun; **fallows:** plowed but unseeded lands.

75. **pied:** variegated.

78. **tufted:** growing in clusters.

79. **lies:** dwells.

The cynosure of neighboring eyes.
Hard by, a cottage chimney smokes,
From betwixt two agèd oaks,
Where Corydon and Thyrsis met,
Are at their savory dinner set
Of herbs, and other country messes,
Which the neat-handed Phyllis dresses;
And then in haste her bower she leaves,
With Thestylis to bind the sheaves;
Or if the earlier season lead
To the tanned haycock in the mead,
Sometimes with secure delight
The upland hamlets will invite,
When the merry bells ring round,
And the jocund rebecks sound
To many a youth, and many a maid,
Dancing in the checkered shade;
And young and old come forth to play
On a sunshine holiday,
Till the livelong daylight fail,
Then to the spicy nut-brown ale,
With stories told of many a feat,
How fairy Mab the junkets ate;
She was pinched, and pulled she said,
And he by friar's lantern led,
Tells how the drudging goblin sweat,
To earn his cream-bowl duly set,
When in one night, ere glimpse of morn,
His shadowy flail hath threshed the corn
That ten day-laborers could not end,

80. **cynosure:** that which serves to direct. Mariners steered by the polestar (Cynosure). So the beautiful lady is the constant referent by means of which men plot their courses.

83. **Corydon and Thyrsis:** common names in Renaissance pastoral.

91. **secure:** carefree.

94. **rebecks:** fiddles.

102. **Mab:** queen of the fairies, famously described by Shakespeare's Mercutio (*ROM* 1.4.54–95); **junkets:** cream cheeses or other dishes made with cream.

103. **She:** woman relating her tale of the supernatural to the group, just as, in the next line, *he* is a man telling his; **pinched:** Mab "pinches country wenches,/If they rub not clean their benches" (Jonson, *The Satyr* 58–59).

104. **friar's lantern:** unexplained. Milton seems to have in mind misleading lights such as the jack-o'-lantern or will-o'-the-wisp, but editors have yet to find one connected to a friar.

105. **drudging goblin:** Hobgoblin, a.k.a. Robin Goodfellow or Puck, takes up the drudgery of country maids in Jonson's *Love Restored* 59.

106. **cream-bowl:** conventional reward for a *drudging goblin.*

109. **end:** put in a barn. In one night the hobgoblin threshes more corn than ten men could *end* in a day.

Then lies him down the lubber fiend,
And stretched out all the chimney's length,
Basks at the fire his hairy strength;
And crop-full out of doors he flings,
Ere the first cock his matin rings.
Thus done the tales, to bed they creep,
By whispering winds soon lulled asleep.
Towered cities please us then,
And the busy hum of men,
Where throngs of knights and barons bold,
In weeds of peace high triumphs hold,
With store of ladies, whose bright eyes
Rain influence, and judge the prize
Of wit, or arms, while both contend
To win her grace, whom all commend.
There let Hymen oft appear
In saffron robe, with taper clear,
And pomp, and feast, and revelry,
With mask, and antique pageantry,
Such sights as youthful poets dream
On summer eves by haunted stream.
Then to the well-trod stage anon,
If Jonson's learned sock be on,
Or sweetest Shakespeare, Fancy's child,
Warble his native wood-notes wild.
And ever against eating cares,
Lap me in soft Lydian airs,
Married to immortal verse
Such as the meeting soul may pierce

110. **lubber:** an inferior household servant, a drudge.

111. **chimney's:** fireplace's.

113. **crop-full:** completely full.

120. **weeds of peace:** courtly garments.

121. **store of:** plenty of.

122. **Rain influence:** Astrologically, *influence* is a tenuous but efficacious liquid supposed to flow from the stars. In love poetry, the lady's eyes were often compared to stars; hence the eyes of these ladies are said to *rain influence* on those whom they favor with a glance.

125. **Hymen:** marriage god, as usual wearing a *saffron robe* and carrying a torch (*taper*).

131. **anon:** instantly.

132. **learned sock:** The *sock* or low-heeled slipper of the Greek comic actor here stands for comedy itself. Jonson was (and wanted to be thought) a particularly learned playwright, the opposite of the warbling Shakespeare.

135. **eating cares:** translates Horace's *curas edacis* (*Odes* 2.11.18).

136. **Lap me:** enfold me, as in a garment; **soft Lydian airs:** Plato condemns effeminate Lydian music in favor of the martial Phrygian and solemn Dorian modes (*Rep.* 3.398–99). On Milton's unusual endorsement of it, see Hughes 1925.

137. **Married:** The marriage of music and verse was a poetic commonplace, as Warton demonstrated. Cp. *Solemn Music* 2–3.

138. **meeting:** coming forward in response or welcome (in this particular case, *meeting* in the sense of "anticipating harmony").

In notes, with many a winding bout
Of linkèd sweetness long drawn out,
With wanton heed, and giddy cunning,
The melting voice through mazes running;
Untwisting all the chains that tie
The hidden soul of harmony;
That Orpheus' self may heave his head
From golden slumber on a bed
Of heaped Elysian flow'rs, and hear
Such strains as would have won the ear
Of Pluto, to have quite set free
His half-regained Eurydice.
These delights, if thou canst give,
Mirth with thee, I mean to live.

139. **bout:** a movement turning or circling back on itself.

141. **wanton heed, and giddy cunning:** "The adjectives describe the appearance, the nouns the reality" (R. C. Browne).

145. **Orpheus' self:** Orpheus himself. To regain his dead wife, Eurydice, he sang for Proserpine and Pluto; **heave:** lift with effort.

147. **Elysian:** According to Ovid (*Met.* 11.61–66), Orpheus was reunited with Eurydice in the Elysian fields after his death at the hands of the Maenads, but there is no reference to her presence here.

147–50. **and hear . . . Eurydice:** The strains that Orpheus now hears would have convinced Pluto *to have quite set free* his captive—that is, released Eurydice without the condition (a fatal one in the event) that Orpheus could not look back at her as they walked out of Hades. Had Orpheus commanded this music, Eurydice would have been *entirely* regained.

151–52. Milton evokes the close of Marlowe's much-imitated "The Passionate Shepherd to His Love": "If these delights thy mind may move,/Then live with me, and be my love."

IL PENSEROSO

Hence vain deluding joys,
    The brood of Folly without father bred,
How little you bestead,
    Or fill the fixèd mind with all your toys;
Dwell in some idle brain,
    And fancies fond with gaudy shapes possess,
As thick and numberless
    As the gay motes that people the sunbeams,

1. **joys:** The poem begins, like *L'Allegro,* with a judgmental dismissal of a parody of the opposite goddess.

2. **without father bred:** either raised without a father, hence by implication bastards, or conceived without a father, hence unnatural.

3. **bestead:** help.

6. **fancies fond:** foolish fancies.

Or likest hovering dreams,
The fickle pensioners of Morpheus' train.
But hail thou goddess, sage and holy,
Hail divinest Melancholy,
Whose saintly visage is too bright
To hit the sense of human sight;
And therefore to our weaker view,
O'erlaid with black, staid Wisdom's hue.
Black, but such as in esteem,
Prince Memnon's sister might beseem,
Or that starred Ethiop queen that strove
To set her beauty's praise above
The sea nymphs, and their powers offended.
Yet thou art higher far descended,
Thee bright-haired Vesta long of yore,
To solitary Saturn bore;
His daughter she (in Saturn's reign,
Such mixture was not held a stain);
Oft in glimmering bow'rs, and glades
He met her, and in secret shades
Of woody Ida's inmost grove,
While yet there was no fear of Jove.
Come pensive nun, devout and pure,
Sober, steadfast, and demure,
All in a robe of darkest grain,
Flowing with majestic train,
And sable stole of cypress lawn,
Over thy decent shoulders drawn.
Come, but keep thy wonted state,

10. **pensioners:** attendants or dependents; *Morpheus:* son of Sleep and god of dreams.

11–55. The welcome to Melancholy, with her genealogy and her companions, parallels *L'Allegro* 11-36. For the identity of this Melancholy, see *L'Allegro* 1n.

14. **hit:** suit, agree with.

18. **Memnon's sister:** Memnon, the handsome dark-hued King of Ethiopia, fought for the Trojans and was slain by Achilles. Eventually tradition gave him a beautiful sister, as in Lydgate's *Troy Book* 5.2887–906.

19. **starred Ethiop queen:** A second ideal of black beauty is Cassiopea, who boasted that she was more beautiful than the Nereids. She is *starred* because after her death Neptune transformed her into a constellation.

23. **Vesta:** daughter of Saturn, goddess of flocks and herbs and households, and devoted to virginity. Milton invented the idea of Vesta as Melancholy's mother.

24. **Saturn:** This god had long been associated with the melancholic or saturnine temperament. See Klibansky et al.

27. **glimmering bow'rs:** retreats overarched with trees, through which light glimmers.

28–30. Eventually, knowing that one of his sons was destined to usurp his throne, a fearful Saturn ate his children; the siring of Melancholy took place before that fear.

33. **grain:** hue.

35. **sable stole:** long black robe; **cypress lawn:** fine linen.

36. **decent:** comely, handsome.

With even step, and musing gait,
And looks commercing with the skies,
Thy rapt soul sitting in thine eyes:
There held in holy passion still,
Forget thyself to marble, till
With a sad leaden downward cast,
Thou fix them on the earth as fast.
And join with thee calm Peace, and Quiet,
Spare Fast, that oft with gods doth diet,
And hears the Muses in a ring,
Ay round about Jove's altar sing.
And add to these retired Leisure,
That in trim gardens takes his pleasure;
But first, and chiefest, with thee bring,
Him that yon soars on golden wing,
Guiding the fiery-wheelèd throne,
The Cherub Contemplation,
And the mute Silence hist along,
'Less Philomel will deign a song,
In her sweetest, saddest plight,
Smoothing the rugged brow of Night,
While Cynthia checks her dragon yoke,
Gently o'er th' accustomed oak;
Sweet bird that shunn'st the noise of folly,
Most musical, most melancholy!
Thee chantress oft the woods among,
I woo to hear thy evensong;
And missing thee, I walk unseen
On the dry smooth-shaven green,
To behold the wand'ring moon,
Riding near her highest noon,
Like one that had been led astray
Through the heav'n's wide pathless way;
And oft, as if her head she bowed,

39. **commercing:** communicating.

42. **Forget thyself to marble:** become so entranced that your body is like a statue. Cp. *On Shakespeare* 14.

43. **sad:** serious (not "sorrowful"); **leaden:** Astrology associated lead with saturnine influences; **cast:** expression.

44. **fast:** fixedly.

48. **Ay:** continually. Muses dance around Jove's altar in Hesiod, *Theog.* 1–10.

53. **fiery-wheelèd throne:** Cp. God's chariot (Ezek. 1 and 10), which also appears in *The Passion* 36–40.

54. **Cherub Contemplation:** According to traditional angelology, the cherubim contemplate God. *Cherub* is the singular of cherubim.

55. **hist along:** summoned without noise.

56. **Philomel:** the nightingale. See *Masque* 234n; **deign:** grant.

59. **Cynthia:** goddess of the moon, associated with Hecate and her dragon-drawn chariot.

Stooping through a fleecy cloud.
Oft on a plat of rising ground,
I hear the far-off curfew sound,
Over some wide-watered shore,
Swinging slow with sullen roar;
Or if the air will not permit,
Some still removèd place will fit,
Where glowing embers through the room
Teach light to counterfeit a gloom,
Far from all resort of mirth,
Save the cricket on the hearth,
Or the bellman's drowsy charm,
To bless the doors from nightly harm:
Or let my lamp at midnight hour,
Be seen in some high lonely tow'r,
Where I may oft outwatch the Bear,
With thrice-great Hermes, or unsphere
The spirit of Plato to unfold
What worlds, or what vast regions hold
The immortal mind that hath forsook
Her mansion in this fleshly nook:
And of those daemons that are found
In fire, air, flood, or under ground,
Whose power hath a true consent
With planet, or with element.
Sometime let gorgeous Tragedy
In sceptered pall come sweeping by,
Presenting Thebes, or Pelops' line,
Or the tale of Troy divine.

73. **plat:** plot, a small piece of land.

74. **curfew:** bell rung (usually at 9:00 P.M.) as a sign to put out fires.

83. **bellman:** night watchman calling the hours; Herrick's "The Bell-man" provides examples of his charms.

87. **outwatch the Bear:** Since Ursa Major (*the Bear*) never sets but simply disappears in the morning sky, the phrase means "stay awake all night."

88. **thrice-great Hermes:** Hermes Trismegistus, alleged author of the *Corpus Hermeticum,* for centuries wrongly supposed to be the earliest work of Western philosophy. In Hermes one could read of spells for summoning the dead. See Milton's *Of the Platonic Idea* 33; **unsphere:** call down from the planetary sphere (where it now resides).

93. **daemons:** In Hermeticism, spiritual beings corresponding to the four elements inhabit the entire cosmos. For the Christian Platonist Marsilio Ficino, the Greek-Platonic notion of daemons or attendant spirits was equivalent to angels (*Commentary on Plato's Symposium,* 110–13).

95. **consent:** accord.

98. **pall:** robe (Lat. *palla*) symbolic of tragedy.

99. **Thebes:** Aeschylus, Sophocles, and Euripides all set tragedies in Thebes; **Pelops' line:** The descendants of Pelops included tragic characters such as Atreus, Thyestes, Agamemnon, Orestes, Electra, and Iphigenia.

100. **tale of Troy divine:** Sophocles and Euripides set tragedies in Troy. Homer calls the city "divine" in *Od.* 11.86, 17.293.

Or what (though rare) of later age,
Ennobled hath the buskined stage.
But, O sad virgin, that thy power
Might raise Musaeus from his bower,
Or bid the soul of Orpheus sing
Such notes as warbled to the string,
Drew iron tears down Pluto's cheek,
And made Hell grant what love did seek.
Or call up him that left half-told
The story of Cambuscan bold,
Of Camball, and of Algarsife,
And who had Canace to wife,
That owned the virtuous ring and glass,
And of the wondrous horse of brass,
On which the Tartar king did ride;
And if aught else, great bards beside,
In sage and solemn tunes have sung,
Of tourneys and of trophies hung;
Of forests, and enchantments drear,
Where more is meant than meets the ear.
Thus, Night, oft see me in thy pale career,
Till civil-suited Morn appear,
Not tricked and frounced as she was wont,
With the Attic boy to hunt,
But kerchiefed in a comely cloud,
While rocking winds are piping loud,
Or ushered with a shower still,
When the gust hath blown his fill,
Ending on the rustling leaves,

102. **buskined:** dressed for the performance of tragedies in the "buskin," a high boot worn by Greek tragic actors, as opposed to the "sock" of comic actors (see *L'All* 132n).

104. **Musaeus:** a mythical early poet sometimes said to be the son of Orpheus.

105–8. Whereas the Orphic music requested at the end of *L'Allegro* (see 147–50n) is higher than that sung by Orpheus himself, the magus of *Il Penseroso* would hear the exact song Orpheus performed.

109. **him:** Chaucer, who left his *Squire's Tale* unfinished. The tale mixes Arabic settings with Western chivalry.

112. The line echoes Spenser's continuation of the *Squire's Tale* in *FQ* 4.3.52; **to wife:** as wife.

113. **virtuous:** endowed with magical power.

114. **wondrous horse of brass:** The brass horse was *wondrous* in being able to bear its rider any distance within twenty-four hours.

120. **more . . . than meets the ear:** allegorical writing, such as Spenser practiced. *Meets* is likely intended to remind us of "the meeting soul" of *L'Allegro* 138, where the harmonies of the music are fully realized through the ear.

121. **pale career:** moonlit course.

122. **civil-suited:** soberly dressed. Cp. Shakespeare, *ROM* 3.2.10–11: "civil Night,/Thou sober-suited matron."

123. **tricked and frounced:** adorned and with curled hair.

124. **Attic boy:** Aurora or Morning loved the young Cephalus, an ardent hunter (Ovid, *Met.* 7.690–865).

127. **still:** quiet.

With minute drops from off the eaves.
And when the Sun begins to fling
His flaring beams, me goddess bring
To archèd walks of twilight groves,
And shadows brown that Sylvan loves
Of pine, or monumental oak,
Where the rude axe with heavèd stroke,
Was never heard the nymphs to daunt,
Or fright them from their hallowed haunt.
There in close covert by some brook,
Where no profaner eye may look,
Hide me from Day's garish eye,
While the bee with honeyed thigh,
That at her flow'ry work doth sing,
And the waters murmuring
With such consort as they keep,
Entice the dewy-feathered Sleep;
And let some strange mysterious dream
Wave at his wings in airy stream,
Of lively portraiture displayed,
Softly on my eyelids laid.
And as I wake, sweet music breathe
Above, about, or underneath,
Sent by some spirit to mortals good,
Or th' unseen Genius of the wood.
But let my due feet never fail,
To walk the studious cloister's pale,
And love the high embowèd roof,
With antique pillars' massy proof,
And storied windows richly dight,
Casting a dim religious light.
There let the pealing organ blow,
To the full-voiced choir below,

130. **minute:** small.
134. **Sylvan:** Roman god of the woods, subsequently identified with Pan.
139. **close covert:** a secret retreat inside dense growth.
141. **garish:** excessively bright.
145. **consort:** musical harmony.
148. **Wave at his wings:** Milton is describing a dream that begins, in the waking state, as a stream of moving images (*lively portraiture*) borne on the wings of Sleep.
154. **Genius of the wood:** See *Arcades* 62–78.
156. **pale:** enclosure.
157. **embowèd:** vaulted.
158. **massy proof:** proven strong in their massiveness (i.e., able to uphold the heavy roof).
159. **storied:** ornamented with biblical stories; **dight:** decorated.
160. **dim religious light:** Cp. Donne, *A Hymn to Christ:* "Churches are best for prayer that have least light"; also the dim churches of More's *Utopia,* built that way because "overmuch light doth disperse men's cogitations" (230).

In service high, and anthems clear,
As may with sweetness, through mine ear,
Dissolve me into ecstasies,
And bring all Heav'n before mine eyes.
And may at last my weary age
Find out the peaceful hermitage,
The hairy gown and mossy cell,
Where I may sit and rightly spell,
Of every star that heav'n doth show,
And every herb that sips the dew;
Till old experience do attain
To something like prophetic strain.
These pleasures Melancholy give,
And I with thee will choose to live.

164. **As:** such as.
165. **Dissolve me into ecstasies:** "separate my soul from my body."
169. **hairy gown:** traditional garb of the ascetic.
170. **spell:** learn.
171–72. The shift from *star* to *herb* recalls the downward course of Melancholy's stare in 39–44.
173. **old experience:** long study.
174. **strain:** melody, whether of song or poetry (*OED* 3.12, 12b). Cp. *Lyc* 87: "That strain I heard was of a higher mood."
175–76. See *L'All* 151–52n.

ARCADES

Arcades, probably the opening of a larger entertainment, was performed in honor of Alice, Dowager Countess of Derby, at some point in the early 1630s. Then in her seventies, she was a veteran of early Stuart masquing, having performed in Jonson's *Masque of Blackness* (1605) and *Masque of Beauty* (1607), and having been the main presence in John Marston's *The . . . Lord and Lady of Huntingdon's Entertainment of their right Noble Mother Alice* (1607, but not published until 1801). Milton would have been particularly aware that his beloved Spenser had dedicated *Tears of the Muses* (1591) to her, represented her under the name "Amaryllis" in *Colin Clouts Come Home Again* (1595), and in both works boasted of being her kin (she was born Alice Spenser). So Milton was not just augmenting a literary fame first spread by Spenser, although that aspect of the piece was no doubt gratifying. He was also honoring Spenser's blood.

Alice married Sir Thomas Egerton, Lord Keeper, in 1600, and his son Sir John subsequently wed her daughter. In 1617 Sir John Egerton was created the first Earl of Bridgewater, and was appointed Lord Lieutenant of Wales in 1631. Milton's *A Masque* (*Comus*) celebrates Egerton's assumption of his duties in Wales.

Henry Lawes, a family friend to the musically minded Miltons, was music tutor to the earl's children. It seems a reasonable conjecture that he was responsible on this occasion for steering the Bridgewater family toward a young and unknown poet, just as he was responsible for the more important commission to write *A Masque.*

Milton compliments Alice more extravagantly than Spenser. He does not praise her more outrageously than Marston; no one could. But Milton, while submitting to the conventions of the masque, is far more loyal than Marston to a much older literary genre: pastoral. He can imagine no higher praise for a great figure like Countess Alice than to enshrine her as the supreme rural queen in Arcadia, held in awe by the genius of the woods and sought by a pilgrim band of nymphs and shepherds.

Part of an entertainment presented to the Countess Dowager of Darby at Harefield, by some noble persons of her family, who appear on the scene in pastoral habit, moving toward the seat of state, with this song.

1. *Song*

Look nymphs, and shepherds look,
What sudden blaze of majesty
Is that which we from hence descry
Too divine to be mistook:
    This, this is she
To whom our vows and wishes bend,
Here our solemn search hath end.

Fame that her high worth to raise,
Seemed erst so lavish and profuse,
We may justly now accuse
Of detraction from her praise;
    Less than half we find expressed,
    Envy bid conceal the rest.

Title. **Arcades:** Arcadians. Arcadia is a Greek valley long associated with the pastoral genre. In the Renaissance, both Sannazaro and Sidney set pastoral fictions there.

6. **vows:** prayers, promises made to gods.

8–13. The passage alludes to poetic praises of the countess once written by Spenser and others but today reduced to a trickle.

8. **raise:** extol, exalt.

9. **erst:** formerly.

12. **Less than half:** Cp. the Queen of Sheba to Solomon: "Behold, the half was not told me" (1 Kings 10.7).

Mark what radiant state she spreads,
In circle round her shining throne,
Shooting her beams like silver threads:
This, this is she alone,
    Sitting like a goddess bright,
    In the center of her light.

Might she the wise Latona be,
Or the towered Cybele,
Mother of a hundred gods;
Juno dares not give her odds;
    Who had thought this clime had held
    A deity so unparalleled?

As they come forward, the Genius of the Wood appears, and turning toward them, speaks.

Genius. Stay gentle swains, for though in this disguise,
I see bright honor sparkle through your eyes;
Of famous Arcady ye are, and sprung
Of that renownèd flood, so often sung,
Divine Alpheus, who by secret sluice,
Stole under seas to meet his Arethuse;
And ye the breathing roses of the wood,
Fair silver-buskined Nymphs as great and good,
I know this quest of yours, and free intent
Was all in honor and devotion meant
To the great mistress of yon princely shrine,
Whom with low reverence I adore as mine,
And with all helpful service will comply
To further this night's glad solemnity;
And lead ye where ye may more near behold
What shallow-searching Fame hath left untold;

14. **radiant state:** The word *state* could refer to splendor befitting the great, or a raised chair beneath a canopy, or the canopy alone. The third meaning best suits the context.
20. **Latona:** mother of Apollo and Diana.
21. **Cybele:** Phrygian goddess identified with Rhea and Ops, the wife of Saturn and mother of Jove, Juno, and other deities. Vergil describes her wearing a towered crown and clutching a hundred of her grandchildren (*Aen.* 6.784–87).
23. **give her odds:** offer to compete with her on terms that favor the countess.
30. **secret sluice:** hidden channel.
31. **Arethuse:** nymph devoted to Diana, who turned *Arethuse* into a stream to help her flee the river god *Alpheus.* Arethuse flowed under the sea to the island of Ortygia in Syracuse, Sicily. Alpheus pursued her there, and their waters mingled in a fountain.
32. **breathing:** fragrant.
33. **silver-buskined:** clad in high silver boots.
34. **free:** noble, generous.
37. **low reverence:** deep bow.
39. **solemnity:** festive ceremony.
41. **shallow-searching:** looking superficially. Cp. the attack on fame in 8–13.

Which I full oft amidst these shades alone
Have sat to wonder at, and gaze upon:
For know by lot from Jove I am the pow'r
Of this fair wood, and live in oaken bow'r,
To nurse the saplings tall, and curl the grove
With ringlets quaint, and wanton windings wove.
And all my plants I save from nightly ill,
Of noisome winds, and blasting vapors chill.
And from the boughs brush off the evil dew,
And heal the harms of thwarting thunder blue,
Or what the cross dire-looking planet smites,
Or hurtful worm with cankered venom bites.
When evening gray doth rise, I fetch my round
Over the mount, and all this hallowed ground,
And early ere the odorous breath of morn
Awakes the slumb'ring leaves, or tasseled horn
Shakes the high thicket, haste I all about,
Number my ranks, and visit every sprout
With puissant words, and murmurs made to bless;
But else in deep of night when drowsiness
Hath locked up mortal sense, then listen I
To the celestial sirens' harmony,
That sit upon the nine enfolded spheres,
And sing to those that hold the vital shears,
And turn the adamantine spindle round,
On which the fate of gods and men is wound.
Such sweet compulsion doth in music lie,
To lull the daughters of Necessity,
And keep unsteady Nature to her law,
And the low world in measured motion draw

49. **blasting:** withering.
50. **evil dew:** mildew.
51. **thwarting thunder blue:** *Thunder* here stands for *lightning*. Its blue light is *thwarting*, cutting across the sky.
52. **cross dire-looking planet:** Saturn, *cross* (adverse) because *dire-looking* (of evil aspect in an astrological sense).
53. **worm with cankered venom:** The term *cankerworm* was applied to caterpillars and insect larvae that eat leaves and buds. Cp. *Lyc* 45.
54. **fetch my round:** make my customary circuit.
57. **tasseled horn:** ornamented hunting horn.
59. **Number my ranks:** count my trees in their rows (like soldiers in a formation).
60. **puissant . . . bless:** potent magic charms and blessings.
63. **celestial sirens' harmony:** In Plato's *Rep.* 10.616–17, each of the celestial spheres has a siren who sings one note; together these notes make up the music of the spheres.
65. **those that hold the vital shears:** In Plato (see 63n) the celestial spheres are threaded on the spindle of Necessity. Her daughters, the three Fates, sit around her and turn the spindle. In this line Milton imagines that all three of the Fates wield the *shears* that cut life's thread (technically, that is the job of Atropos). *Vital* here means "fatal to life."
71. **measured:** rhythmical.

After the heavenly tune, which none can hear
Of human mold with gross unpurgèd ear;
And yet such music worthiest were to blaze
The peerless height of her immortal praise,
Whose luster leads us, and for her most fit,
If my inferior hand or voice could hit
Inimitable sounds; yet as we go,
Whate'er the skill of lesser gods can show,
I will assay, her worth to celebrate,
And so attend ye toward her glittering state;
Where ye may all that are of noble stem
Approach, and kiss her sacred vesture's hem.

2. *Song*

O'er the smooth enameled green
Where no print of step hath been,
    Follow me as I sing,
    And touch the warbled string.
Under the shady roof
Of branching elm star-proof,
    Follow me,
I will bring you where she sits,
Clad in splendor as befits
    Her deity.
Such a rural queen
All Arcadia hath not seen.

3. *Song*

Nymphs and shepherds dance no more
    By sandy Ladon's lilied banks.
On old Lycaeus or Cyllene hoar,
    Trip no more in twilight ranks;
Though Erymanth your loss deplore,

72. **none can hear:** Cp. *Nat Ode* 125n, and *Prolusion* 2 (Yale 1:238).
73. **mold:** the earth from which our bodies are formed.
74. **blaze:** proclaim.
77. **hit:** imitate perfectly.
80. **assay:** attempt.
81. **state:** chair of state.
84. **enameled:** adorned with many colors (referring here to flowers of many colors).
89. **star-proof:** admitting no starlight, with perhaps the astrological sense of "admitting no malign celestial influences."
97. **Ladon:** a river in Arcadia that empties into the Alpheus (see 31n).
98–102. *Lycaeus, Cyllene, Erymanth,* and *Maenalus* are all mountains in Arcadia.

A better soil shall give ye thanks.
From the stony Maenalus,
Bring your flocks, and live with us;
Here ye shall have greater grace,
To serve the Lady of this place.
Though Syrinx your Pan's mistress were,
Yet Syrinx well might wait on her.
Such a rural queen
All Arcadia hath not seen.

106. **Syrinx:** A nymph pursued by Pan. She ran into the river Ladon and became a reed.

AT A SOLEMN MUSIC

Some poems in the Trinity College manuscript appear as fair copies. Others seem to have been composed in the manuscript itself. *At a Solemn Music* belongs to this second category, as there are four distinct drafts, the first one written on the reverse of the leaf containing the end of *Arcades* and the last a fair copy. It seems a safe bet that the poem was begun soon after *Arcades*. The pastoral entertainment cannot be securely dated, though 1632 seems likely (Campbell 47).

The title means "At a Sacred Concert." Listening appreciatively to a piece of vocal music inspires a lofty meditation on the place of music in the universe and its history. Leo Spitzer's *Classical and Christian Ideas of World Harmony*, a classic of intellectual history, explores the traditions behind the poem and also contains a discussion of it (see as well Heninger).

Blest pair of sirens, pledges of Heav'n's joy,
Sphere-borne harmonious sisters, Voice and Verse,
Wed your divine sounds, and mixed power employ
Dead things with inbreathed sense able to pierce,
And to our high-raised fantasy present
That undisturbèd song of pure concent,
Ay sung before the sapphire-colored throne
To him that sits thereon

1. **sirens:** Plato identified celestial music with the songs of eight sirens (*Rep.* 10.616–17). Cp. *Arcades* 63–64; **pledges:** both "offspring" and "assurances."

4. The songs of Orpheus had this power, as in *PL* 7.34–36. Cp. *Masque* 561–62.

6. **concent:** concord.

7. **Ay:** forever; **sapphire-colored throne:** God's throne; see Ezek. 1.26.

With saintly shout, and solemn jubilee,
Where the bright Seraphim in burning row
Their loud uplifted angel trumpets blow,
And the Cherubic host in thousand choirs
Touch their immortal harps of golden wires,
With those just spirits that wear victorious palms,
Hymns devout and holy psalms
Singing everlastingly;
That we on earth with undiscording voice
May rightly answer that melodious noise;
As once we did, till disproportioned sin
Jarred against nature's chime, and with harsh din
Broke the fair music that all creatures made
To their great Lord, whose love their motion swayed
In perfect diapason, whilst they stood
In first obedience, and their state of good.
O may we soon again renew that song,
And keep in tune with Heav'n, till God ere long
To his celestial consort us unite,
To live with him, and sing in endless morn of light.

9. **jubilee:** joyful shouting. The Hebrew Jubilee was a ritual emancipation of slaves celebrated every fifty years. Christians considered it a type of the Atonement.

14. **those just spirits:** justified spirits, the saints. Cp. Rev. 7.9: "a great multitude . . . clothed in white robes, and palms in their hands."

17. **undiscording:** Milton's coinage suggests not mere concord, but a concord won from a constant victory over discord.

19. **disproportioned:** disharmonious.

23. **diapason:** complete concord.

27. **consort:** harmony of voices, company of musicians.

ON TIME

Editors generally date this poem in the early 1630s. In the Trinity College manuscript, a phrase is written beneath the title "On Time." All that is legible today is the words "set on a clock case," which have been scored out. The manuscript was ill-handled for many years, and by the time it was photographed for facsimile reproduction in 1899, a strip of paper had been pasted over the top left side of this page (fol. 8). On the basis of eighteenth- and nineteenth-century transcriptions, we know that originally something was written before "set"—probably "to be." But we do not know whether the author considered "to be set on a clock case," before he struck it out, as a subtitle or an alternative title. Presumably the word *set* indicates that the poem is to be glued onto the clock case, perhaps to the back of the case's door.

The clock Milton has in mind is the one modern horologists call a "lantern clock." It was the earliest household clock manufactured in England. Made of brass, it sat on a wall shelf. The two ends of a line threaded in the mechanism of the clock hung through a hole in the shelf. A lead weight was affixed to the short end of the line, and its subsequent graduated descent drove the mechanism. After about thirty hours, the weight had to be transferred to the other side (now the short side) of the line. A lantern clock had one dial for marking hours and a twelve-hour face. In the 1630s, when Milton wrote this poem, England stood on the brink of an industrial boom in clockmaking that would last through the next century and well into the nineteenth. English makers would capture much of the European market from their main competitors in Germany, and the excellent design and accuracy of the English clock would become a matter of considerable national pride. The long good time of this British industry could be said to have begun when, in 1631, a royal patent was granted to the London Guild of Clockmakers. Milton's lyric enters the history of British clocks on the threshold of a major economic triumph.

Fly envious Time, till thou run out thy race,
Call on the lazy leaden-stepping hours,
Whose speed is but the heavy plummet's pace;
And glut thyself with what thy womb devours,
Which is no more than what is false and vain,
And merely mortal dross;
So little is our loss,
So little is thy gain.
For when as each thing bad thou hast entombed,
And last of all, thy greedy self consumed,
Then long eternity shall greet our bliss
With an individual kiss;
And joy shall overtake us as a flood,
When everything that is sincerely good

1. **envious:** The adjective was conventionally attached to personified *Time,* but in this poem the malice is specific: Time envies man because Time has no stake in Eternity, no share in the Christian promise of salvation.
2. **leaden-stepping:** The mechanisms of early lantern clocks were driven by the graduated falling of lead-weighted cords.
3. **plummet:** the lead weight referred to in 2n.
4. **womb:** stomach.
7–8. Milton returned to the end-words of these lines for the titles of *Paradise Lost* and *Paradise Regained.*
9. **when as:** when. The *whens* of lines 9, 14, and 19 refer, as it were, to the first moment after time, to eternity in its sudden newness.
12. **individual kiss:** an indivisible and therefore unending kiss; but the word *individual* was just acquiring its modern sense of "peculiar to a particular person," and Milton might be suggesting that the joy of salvation will be felt by the individual soul not (as in Averroism) by a collective world-soul. A professor at Milton's college, Henry More, was for a time an Averroist (Nicolson 1960, 299–300).
14. **sincerely:** wholly.

And perfectly divine,
With Truth, and Peace, and Love shall ever shine
About the supreme throne
Of him, t' whose happy-making sight alone,
When once our Heav'nly-guided soul shall climb,
Then all this earthy grossness quit,
Attired with stars, we shall forever sit,
Triumphing over Death, and Chance, and thee, O Time.

18. **happy-making sight:** anglicizes the theological term "beatific vision."
20. **quit:** left behind.
21. **Attired with stars:** Cp. Rev. 12.1: "upon her head a crown of twelve stars."
22. **Chance:** The defeat of chance is a common motive in Christian thought. See Boethius, *The Consolation of Philosophy*, 5.1 and *passim*.

UPON THE CIRCUMCISION

Though often dated in 1633, this poem's evident connection with both the *Nativity Ode* and *The Passion* may argue for an earlier composition. If it were the last written of the three, *Upon the Circumcision* could be viewed as literary redemption for the failure of *The Passion*. Here Milton *is* able to deal with the death of Christ, but at a temporal distance made possible by traditional typology. The first blood of the circumcision prefigures the sacrifice of the Crucifixion; Milton's climactic association of the wound of the circumcision knife with the spear wound after Christ's death on the Cross belongs to the design of Christian history. The struggle between love and law announced in the center of the poem suggests Paul, and the "circumcision" of the "heart" (the poem's final word) was indeed a favorite theme of the Apostle (see 28n).

Ye flaming Powers, and wingèd warriors bright,
That erst with music, and triumphant song
First heard by happy watchful shepherds' ear,
So sweetly sung your joy the clouds along
Through the soft silence of the list'ning night;
Now mourn, and if sad share with us to bear
Your fiery essence can distill no tear,
Burn in your sighs, and borrow

1. **Powers:** one of the nine orders of angels in Pseudo-Dionysius, but here naming all angels.
2. **erst:** formerly, alluding like the opening of *The Passion* to the *Nativity Ode*.
6–9. Milton suggests that the angels, if they cannot ordinarily cry, could burn, and with this sunlike heat draw up to Heaven the seas of tears wept on Earth.

Seas wept from our deep sorrow;
He who with all Heav'n's heraldry whilere
Entered the world, now bleeds to give us ease;
Alas, how soon our sin
  Sore doth begin
    His infancy to seize!
O more exceeding love or law more just?
Just law indeed, but more exceeding love!
For we by rightful doom remédiless
Were lost in death, till he that dwelt above
High throned in secret bliss, for us frail dust
Emptied his glory, ev'n to nakedness;
And that great cov'nant which we still transgress
Entirely satisfied,
And the full wrath beside
Of vengeful Justice bore for our excess,
And seals obedience first with wounding smart
This day: but O ere long
  Huge pangs and strong
    Will pierce more near his heart.

10. **Heav'n's heraldry:** heraldic pomp (of the Nativity); **whilere:** a while back.
11. **now bleeds:** at the circumcision.
12–14. The shrinking lines imitate the seizing.
12. **our sin:** the Fall, which makes Christ's sacrifice necessary.
15–16. Christ's sacrifice is the defeat of law (the law demanding our death), symbolized by the circumcision knife, by love (forgiveness), symbolized by his blood.
21. **that great cov'nant:** the Mosaic Law.
22. Cp. *PL* 3.212: "The rigid satisfaction, death for death."
24. **excess:** violation of the law.
28. **Will pierce:** alluding to the spear thrust into Christ's side (John 19.34). The first blood of the circumcision is a type or prefiguration of the Crucifixion. Herbert connected that final wound with the birth of Eve from the side of Adam and the origin of the Eucharist: "They will pierce my side . . . /That as sin came, so sacraments might flow" ("The Sacrifice" 246–47); **heart:** See Paul's discussion of the circumcision of the heart in Rom. 2.28–29, 3.30, 4.9–17; Col. 2.11–14; et cetera.

A MASQUE PRESENTED AT LUDLOW CASTLE, 1634 [COMUS]

This work is commonly known under the title *Comus,* which it was given when revised for the stage in the eighteenth century. In its three printings during Milton's lifetime, it was uniformly entitled *A Masque Presented at Ludlow Castle.*

The masque was performed on Michaelmas night (September 29) 1634 in the great hall at Ludlow Castle in Shropshire to celebrate the first visit of the Earl of Bridgewater, recently appointed Lord President of the Council of Wales and

Lord Lieutenant of the Welsh and border counties, to the territory he was now to administer. It is misleading to speak of roles and parts with regard to the court masque of the seventeenth century, since these were not off-the-rack characters open to any actor or actress but tailor-made for specific people. The Lady was Bridgewater's daughter, Alice Egerton, age fifteen; the Elder and Younger Brothers were Bridgewater's sons John, Viscount Brackley, age eleven, and Lord Thomas Egerton, age nine. It may help to explain how *A Masque* could be at once a public performance and a personal statement to note that the masquing family (older sister and two younger brothers) mirrors, with Milton in the role of the Older Brother, the poet's own family (an older sister, Ann, a younger brother, Christopher).

The Attendant Spirit was the music tutor of the Egerton children, Henry Lawes, a man with a great deal of experience in this dramatic genre (see the headnotes to *Arcades* and *Sonnet 13*). He wrote the songs for *Masque,* and supervised its anonymous publication in 1637. The Earl of Bridgewater was the stepson and son-in-law of the Countess Dowager of Derby, for whom Milton had devised *Arcades,* which had also been staged by Lawes. It seems likely that the success of *Arcades* encouraged Lawes to commission a second, more ambitious work from the young Milton.

Besides the versions printed in 1637, 1645, and 1673, there are two significant manuscripts. Milton seems to have made his initial entries in the Trinity College manuscript (*CMS*) in 1632 and continued to revise the work throughout his lifetime. Several fair copies are believed to have been made at various stages of the *CMS* text, and there is now good reason to think (Sprott, Gaskell, Brown) that the other significant manuscript, the so-called Bridgewater manuscript (*BMS*) kept among the papers of the Egerton family, is one of those copies, a rather poor one done by a scribe perhaps as early as 1634. But the *BMS* was once considered the acting text used in 1634, and quite possibly in the hand of Henry Lawes. This mistaken conception of the *BMS* figures in a good bit of now dubious theorizing about the political, psychological, or philosophical meaning of supposed revisions to the performance version of *A Masque.*

The anonymous 1637 edition is prefaced by a letter from Henry Lawes to the work's Elder Brother, John Egerton. Lawes reveals that, although he has had many requests for copies of the masque, a burden this publication intends to shed, the entertainment is "not openly acknowledged by the author." It would seem that only a reluctant author, and not Lawes, could have chosen the odd Vergilian epigraph (*Ec.* 2.58–59) for the 1637 *Masque: Eheu quid volui misero mihi: floribus austrum Perditus* ("Did I mean my own destruction when I let the south wind blow upon my flowers?"). Whatever was meant by this strangely apprehensive epigraph, Milton seems entirely proud of the work by 1645, where *A Masque* is placed last among the English poems, prefaced by the Lawes letter from 1637 and a second letter from the poet and diplomat Sir Henry Wotton, thanking Milton for sending him "a dainty piece of entertainment." The letters are absent in 1673, no doubt because Milton had outgrown this simplistic technique for courting prestige.

The history of the court masque has been studied by Enid Welsford, John Demaray, and Cedric Brown. A new slant on the genre, aimed at linking aesthetic and political analysis, emerged in Stephen Orgel's *The Illusion of Power* (1975), one of the founding studies of the so-called New Historicism, whose influence can be felt in the treatment of masques in Graham Parry's *The Golden Age Restor'd: The Culture of the Stuart Court, 1603–42* (1981) and Jonathan Goldberg's *James I and the Politics of Literature* (1983). But histories of masquing of any kind tend to illuminate Milton's sharp differences with standard procedures. Ben Jonson introduced the character of Comus to the English masque tradition in *Pleasure Reconciled with Virtue* (performed in 1618 but not printed until 1640). Jonson's Comus was a god of gluttony, patron of meat and drink, and was whisked away by Hercules in the first antimasque; he bears little if any relation to Milton's wily sorcerer. The Circe episode of the *Odyssey* was a popular source of plot devices ("hinges," as Jonson called them) in the masque tradition. William Browne's *Inner Temple Masque* and Aurelian Townshend's *Tempe Restored* are the two examples most frequently mentioned by critics and editors, though again, it is immediately clear that neither work has, or even aspires to, the philosophical concentration of *Masque*. Among stage plays, George Peele's *An Old Wives' Tale* is credited with the plot of two brothers having to rescue a sister from an evil enchanter. There are also intriguing connections with John Fletcher's *The Faithful Shepherdess*, which contains an ardent defense of chastity against its enemies, and a villain who defends unchastity by reference to nature's foison. Finally, the Shakespearean vigor of phrase and figure in *A Masque* has often been noted (Leavis).

Explanations for the peculiarities of the work, especially its interest in chastity, have been sought in topical events. Barbara Breasted and Rosemary Mundhenk pointed to the sexual outrages committed by the Second Earl of Castlehaven, who was the brother-in-law of Bridgewater's wife. He was tried and executed in 1631 for a number of sexual crimes involving his wife and his servants. Leah Marcus pled for the importance of the illiterate serving maid Margery Evans, who had perhaps been raped and wrongfully jailed in 1631, and whose appeal came under the jurisdiction of the Earl of Bridgewater. These attempts to situate *Masque* in its historical milieu suggest that its elevated conception of chastity was meant to dissociate the Egerton family from scandal and can be thought of as emanating, not from anything unusual or interesting in the soul of Milton, but rather from the immediate concerns of his patrons. Such arguments can never be what they most want to be—a bulwark against the possibility of psychological explanation. For even if we suppose that "base the entertainment on chastity" was part of Milton's commission, there is no reason why something in his soul might not have responded, "That's no problem, believe me."

The Persons

The Attendant Spirit, afterwards in the habit of Thyrsis
Comus, with his crew
The Lady
1. Brother
2. Brother
Sabrina the Nymph.

The chief persons which presented were
The Lord Brackley,
Mr. Thomas Egerton his brother,
The Lady Alice Egerton.

The first scene discovers a wild wood.

The Attendant Spirit descends or enters.

Before the starry threshold of Jove's court
My mansion is, where those immortal shapes
Of bright aërial spirits live ensphered
In regions mild of calm and serene air,
Above the smoke and stir of this dim spot,
Which men call earth, and with low-thoughted care
Confined and pestered in this pinfold here,
Strive to keep up a frail and feverish being
Unmindful of the crown that Virtue gives
After this mortal change, to her true servants
Amongst the enthroned gods on sainted seats.
Yet some there be that by due steps aspire

[**Stage direction**]: The printed versions of 1637, 1645, and 1673 have "Attendant Spirit," while *CMS* and *BMS* have "a guardian spirit, or daemon."

3. **ensphered:** in their allotted sphere, like the spirit of Plato in *Il Pens* 88–89.

5. **smoke and stir:** the corrupt atmosphere (*rank vapors* in 17) of this place and the pointless strife of most of its inhabitants (*Strive* in 8); the quasi-hendiadys evokes Shakespeare (see Wright 1981).

6. **men call earth:** Socrates says that the earth we take for granted is a misty hollow, whereas the true earth's surface lies among the stars (Plato, *Phaedo* 109–11).

7. **pestered:** crowded; restrained, by shackles or a tether; **pinfold:** holding pen for animals.

10. **mortal change:** death, the change from mortal existence. Cp. *immortal change* (841).

To lay their just hands on that golden key
That opes the palace of eternity:
To such my errand is, and but for such,
I would not soil these pure ambrosial weeds
With the rank vapors of this sin-worn mold.
But to my task. Neptune, besides the sway
Of every salt flood, and each ebbing stream,
Took in by lot 'twixt high and nether Jove
Imperial rule of all the sea-girt isles
That like to rich and various gems inlay
The unadornèd bosom of the deep,
Which he to grace his tributary gods
By course commits to several government,
And gives them leave to wear their sapphire crowns,
And wield their little tridents; but this isle,
The greatest and the best of all the main,
He quarters to his blue-haired deities,
And all this tract that fronts the falling sun
A noble peer of mickle trust and power
Has in his charge, with tempered awe to guide
An old and haughty nation proud in arms:
Where his fair offspring nursed in princely lore
Are coming to attend their father's state,
And new-entrusted scepter, but their way
Lies through the perplexed paths of this drear wood,
The nodding horror of whose shady brows
Threats the forlorn and wand'ring passenger.
And here their tender age might suffer peril,
But that by quick command from sov'reign Jove
I was dispatched for their defense and guard;
And listen why, for I will tell ye now
What never yet was heard in tale or song
From old or modern bard in hall or bow'r.

13. **golden key:** Cp. the "golden key" of *Lyc* 111, which also opens the gates of Heaven.

16. **weeds:** clothes, specifically the *sky robes* of l. 83.

17. **sin-worn mold:** could be either the pestilent earth or the pestilent body. From which side of his garments is the soiling expected?

18. **sway:** rule.

20. **Took . . . Jove:** After Saturn's overthrow, Neptune and his brothers, Jove and Pluto (*nether Jove*), divided the universe by casting lots (*Il.* 15.187–93).

27. **this isle:** Britain.

29. **quarters:** assigns.

30. **this tract:** Wales and the Welsh Marches.

31. **noble peer:** the Earl of Bridgewater; **mickle:** great.

33. **nation:** Wales.

35. **state:** throne (cp. "seat of state" in the headnote of *Arcades*).

37. **perplexed:** entangled; **wood:** Cp. Dante, *Inf.* 1–3, and Spenser, *FQ* 1.1.7–10.

38. **nodding:** The *shady brows* of the forest bend over or droop.

45. **hall or bow'r:** rooms in a castle: the common *hall* where feasts were hosted, and the *bower* or bedroom.

Bacchus that first from out the purple grape
Crushed the sweet poison of misusèd wine,
After the Tuscan mariners transformed,
Coasting the Tyrrhene shore, as the winds listed,
On Circe's island fell (who knows not Circe
The daughter of the Sun? Whose charmèd cup
Whoever tasted, lost his upright shape,
And downward fell into a groveling swine).
This nymph that gazed upon his clust'ring locks,
With ivy berries wreathed, and his blithe youth,
Had by him, ere he parted thence, a son
Much like his father, but his mother more,
Whom therefore she brought up and Comus named,
Who ripe and frolic of his full-grown age,
Roving the Celtic and Iberian fields,
At last betakes him to this ominous wood,
And in thick shelter of black shades embowered,
Excels his mother at her mighty art,
Off'ring to every weary traveler,
His orient liquor in a crystal glass,
To quench the drought of Phoebus, which as they taste
(For most do taste through fond intemperate thirst)
Soon as the potion works, their human count'nance,
Th' express resemblance of the gods, is changed
Into some brutish form of wolf, or bear,
Or ounce, or tiger, hog, or bearded goat,
All other parts remaining as they were;
And they, so perfect is their misery,

48. **the Tuscan mariners transformed:** Bacchus transformed his abductors into dolphins (Ovid, *Met.* 3.582–691).

49. **Tyrrhene shore:** coast of Italy facing Sardinia and Corsica.

51. **daughter of the Sun:** as Circe is said to be in Homer (*Od.* 10.135–38); **charmèd cup:** The Circe of Homer and Ovid does offer men a cup, but her wand effects their metamorphosis into animals (*Od.* 10.233–39; *Met.* 14.277–80); the expanded role of the cup in Milton suggests temptation and moral choice.

55. **ivy berries:** Bacchus is often represented with a crown woven of grapevine and ivy.

56. **a son:** Comus, from the Greek *komos* or "revelry," was a minor deity in classical culture, associated with the marriage ceremony and drunkenness; he appears as a belly god in Jonson's mask *Pleasure Reconciled to Virtue* (1618). Milton here invents his parentage.

59. **frolic of his full-grown age:** sportive with his mature powers.

60. **Celtic, and Iberian:** French and Spanish.

65. **orient:** bright.

66. **drought of Phoebus:** thirst brought on by the sun.

66–77. Milton's account differs from Homer's in the following particulars: the potion, not the wand, effects the change; only the head is changed; the victims are not transformed into swine only but into various beasts; they do not realize their change (in Homer they yearn to be men again); they forget their friends and their birthplace.

67. **fond:** foolish.

71. **ounce:** lynx.

73. **perfect:** complete.

Not once perceive their foul disfigurement,
But boast themselves more comely than before,
And all their friends and native home forget
To roll with pleasure in a sensual sty.
Therefore when any favored of high Jove
Chances to pass through this advent'rous glade,
Swift as the sparkle of a glancing star,
I shoot from Heav'n to give him safe convoy,
As now I do: but first I must put off
These my sky robes spun out of Iris' woof,
And take the weeds and likeness of a swain
That to the service of this house belongs,
Who with his soft pipe and smooth-dittied song,
Well knows to still the wild winds when they roar,
And hush the waving woods, nor of less faith,
And in this office of his mountain watch,
Likeliest, and nearest to the present aid
Of this occasion. But I hear the tread
Of hateful steps, I must be viewless now.

Comus enters with a charming-rod in one hand, his glass in the other, with him a rout of monsters headed like sundry sorts of wild beasts, but otherwise like men and women. Their apparel glistering, they come in making a riotous and unruly noise, with torches in their hands.

Comus.
The star that bids the shepherd fold,
Now the top of heav'n doth hold,
And the gilded car of day,
His glowing axle doth allay
In the steep Atlantic stream,
And the slope sun his upward beam
Shoots against the dusky pole,
Pacing toward the other goal

79. **advent'rous:** dangerous.
83. **Iris' woof:** rainbow-colored thread.
84. **weeds:** clothes; **swain:** shepherd.
84–88. A compliment to Henry Lawes, put somewhat awkwardly into his own mouth (he played the Attendant Spirit).
87. **knows to:** knows how to.
88. **nor of less faith:** "nor is his loyalty less than his musical skill."
90. **Likeliest:** fittest (to aid).
90–91. **nearest . . . occasion:** help closest to the situation.
92. **viewless:** invisible.
93. **star:** Hesperus, the evening star; **fold:** pen their sheep.
95. **gilded car of day:** the chariot of the sun.
96. **allay:** cool.
97. **steep:** swift-flowing.
98. **slope sun:** descending, so that only its *upward beam* is still visible.
99. **dusky pole:** northern sky.

Of his chamber in the east.
Meanwhile welcome joy, and feast,
Midnight shout, and revelry,
Tipsy dance, and jollity.
Braid your locks with rosy twine,
Dropping odors, dropping wine.
Rigor now is gone to bed,
And Advice with scrupulous head,
Strict Age, and sour Severity,
With their grave saws in slumber lie.
We that are of purer fire
Imitate the starry choir,
Who in their nightly watchful spheres,
Lead in swift round the months and years.
The sounds and seas with all their finny drove
Now to the moon in wavering morris move,
And on the tawny sands and shelves,
Trip the pert fairies and the dapper elves;
By dimpled brook and fountain brim,
The wood-nymphs decked with daisies trim
Their merry wakes and pastimes keep:
What hath night to do with sleep?
Night hath better sweets to prove,
Venus now wakes, and wakens Love.
Come let us our rites begin,
'Tis only daylight that makes sin,
Which these dun shades will ne'er report.
Hail goddess of nocturnal sport,
Dark-veiled Cotytto, t' whom the secret flame
Of midnight torches burns; mysterious dame
That ne'er art called, but when the dragon womb

105. **rosy twine:** roses twisted together.

110. **saws:** maxims; dictates.

111. **purer fire:** It was a commonplace that men were composed of the four elements. Comus asserts that the fire in their makeup is of the *purer* kind found in the stars, and that this affinity makes their dance like the stars' movements.

113. **watchful spheres:** Angelic intelligences were thought to guide or watch over the planetary spheres.

115. **sounds and seas:** straits and open seas.

116. **morris:** folk dance associated with May Day ceremonies. It used pantomine to tell elaborate stories, and its performers wore bells on their costumes. Will Kemp, Shakespeare's clown, once morrised for nine days in journeying from London to Norwich (Lee and Onions 2:238–40).

117. **shelves:** sandbanks.

118. **Trip:** dance; **pert:** brisk.

121. **wakes:** nocturnal revels.

129. **Cotytto:** Roman authors associated this Thracian goddess with licentious rites performed at night (Juvenal 2.91–92; Horace, *Epod.* 17.56–57).

131. **dragon womb:** Renaissance commentators assumed that the dragon-drawn chariot of *Met.* 7.218–19 belonged to Hecate, daughter of Night (Harding 50), patroness of witchcraft, and companion to Milton's Cotytto.

Of Stygian darkness spits her thickest gloom,
And makes one blot of all the air,
Stay thy cloudy ebon chair,
Wherein thou rid'st with Hecat', and befriend
Us thy vowed priests, till utmost end
Of all thy dues be done, and none left out,
Ere the blabbing eastern scout,
The nice Morn on th' Indian steep
From her cabined loophole peep,
And to the tell-tale Sun descry
Our concealed solemnity.
Come, knit hands, and beat the ground,
In a light fantastic round.

The Measure

Break off, break off, I feel the different pace
Of some chaste footing near about this ground.
Run to your shrouds, within these brakes and trees;
Our number may affright: some virgin sure
(For so I can distinguish by mine art)
Benighted in these woods. Now to my charms,
And to my wily trains; I shall ere long
Be well stocked with as fair a herd as grazed
About my mother Circe. Thus I hurl
My dazzling spells into the spongy air,
Of power to cheat the eye with blear illusion,
And give it false presentments, lest the place
And my quaint habits breed astonishment,
And put the damsel to suspicious flight,
Which must not be, for that's against my course;
I under fair pretence of friendly ends,
And well-placed words of glozing courtesy

138. **blabbing eastern scout:** the sun, a *blabbing* tattletale because it makes ill deeds visible to others.

139. **nice:** modest, fastidious; but as Carey points out, the classical Aurora was hardly that, and Comus may be mocking her hypocrisy; **Indian steep:** mountains (Leonard thinks the Himalayas) in the eastern land of India.

140. **cabined loophole:** a small window, such as a porthole.

142. **concealed solemnity:** secret rites.

144. **light fantastic round:** a nimble ring dance that will seem to bring grotesque fancies to life. Cp. *L'All* 34.

[**Stage direction**] **Measure:** song and dance.

147. **shrouds:** hiding places.

151. **trains:** allurements.

153–54. **hurl . . . air:** At this point Comus throws some sort of sparkle dust into the air, which is *spongy* because it takes in and retains the effect.

155. **blear:** dim, misty.

156. **false presentments:** illusions.

157. **quaint habits:** curious clothes.

161. **glozing:** flattering.

Baited with reasons not unplausible
Wind me into the easy-hearted man,
And hug him into snares. When once her eye
Hath met the virtue of this magic dust,
I shall appear some harmless villager
Whom thrift keeps up about his country gear;
But here she comes, I fairly step aside
And hearken, if I may her business hear.

The Lady enters.

Lady. This way the noise was, if mine ear be true,
My best guide now; methought it was the sound
Of riot and ill-managed merriment,
Such as the jocund flute or gamesome pipe
Stirs up among the loose unlettered hinds,
When for their teeming flocks and granges full
In wanton dance they praise the bounteous Pan,
And thank the gods amiss. I should be loath
To meet the rudeness and swilled insolence
Of such late wassailers; yet O where else
Shall I inform my unacquainted feet
In the blind mazes of this tangled wood?
My brothers when they saw me wearied out
With this long way, resolving here to lodge
Under the spreading favor of these pines,
Stepped as they said to the next thicket side
To bring me berries, or such cooling fruit
As the kind hospitable woods provide.
They left me then, when the gray-hooded Ev'n
Like a sad votarist in palmer's weed
Rose from the hindmost wheels of Phoebus' wain.
But where they are, and why they came not back,

163. **Wind me:** insinuate myself; **easy-hearted:** gullible, trusting.
165. **virtue:** efficacy.
166–69. Here we compromise between 1673 and the two earlier versions of 1637 and 1645. Our l. 167, present in the early texts, dropped out in 1673, which also printed our ll. 168–69 in the reverse order. We keep the earlier line and the earlier order of 168–69, but emend l. 169 from its initial form ("And hearken, if I may, her business here") to the version established in the 1673 Errata.
168. **fairly:** quietly.
174. **loose unlettered hinds:** lewd, illiterate farmhands.
175. **teeming:** multiplying; **granges:** barns.
176. **Pan:** Greek god of woods and shepherds.
177. **amiss:** in the wrong way.
178. **swilled:** drunken.
179. **wassailers:** revelers.
180. **inform:** find guidance for.
189. **votarist:** one bound by a vow (here a vow of pilgrimage); **palmer's weed:** pilgrim's clothes.
190. **wain:** chariot.

Is now the labor of my thoughts; 'tis likeliest
They had engaged their wand'ring steps too far,
And envious darkness, ere they could return,
Had stole them from me, else O thievish Night
Why shouldst thou, but for some felonious end,
In thy dark lantern thus close up the stars,
That Nature hung in heav'n, and filled their lamps
With everlasting oil, to give due light
To the misled and lonely traveler?
This is the place, as well as I may guess,
Whence even now the tumult of loud mirth
Was rife, and perfect in my listening ear,
Yet naught but single darkness do I find.
What might this be? A thousand fantasies
Begin to throng into my memory
Of calling shapes, and beck'ning shadows dire,
And airy tongues, that syllable men's names
On sands, and shores, and desert wildernesses.
These thoughts may startle well, but not astound
The virtuous mind, that ever walks attended
By a strong siding champion Conscience.——
O welcome pure-eyed Faith, white-handed Hope,
Thou hovering angel girt with golden wings,
And thou unblemished form of Chastity,
I see ye visibly, and now believe
That he, the Supreme Good, t' whom all things ill
Are but as slavish officers of vengeance,
Would send a glist'ring guardian if need were
To keep my life and honor unassailed.
Was I deceived, or did a sable cloud
Turn forth her silver lining on the night?
I did not err, there does a sable cloud
Turn forth her silver lining on the night,
And casts a gleam over this tufted grove.

193. **engaged:** pledged.
194. **envious:** malicious.
197. **dark lantern:** a lantern with a gate to shut up its light. What in this production will count as starlight (221–25) may at this point be shuttered in a dark lantern. See 331n.
203. **rife:** loud; **perfect in:** perfectly clear to.
204. **single:** total.
207–9. **calling shapes . . . wildernesses:** Sources have been adduced, but Milton was drawing on motifs common in travel literature and folklore.
212. **siding champion:** a champion that takes one's side.
215. **unblemished form of Chastity:** The Lady places Chastity of some sort after Faith and Hope, where St. Paul leads one to expect Charity (1 Cor. 13.13). Does *unblemished* modify *form,* suggesting that the Lady sees the essence or idea of Chastity? Or does it modify *form of Chastity,* suggesting that another form of it is blemished?
221–25. The repetition of the interrogative as a declarative is an effect borrowed from Ovid, *Fasti* 5.549.

I cannot hallo to my brothers, but
Such noise as I can make to be heard farthest
I'll venture, for my new enlivened spirits
Prompt me; and they perhaps are not far off.

Song

Sweet Echo, sweetest Nymph that liv'st unseen
Within thy airy shell
By slow Meander's margent green,
And in the violet-embroidered vale
Where the love-lorn nightingale
Nightly to thee her sad song mourneth well.
Canst thou not tell me of a gentle pair
That likest thy Narcissus are?
O if thou have
Hid them in some flow'ry cave,
Tell me but where,
Sweet queen of parley, daughter of the sphere.
So may'st thou be translated to the skies,
And give resounding grace to all heav'n's harmonies.

Comus. Can any mortal mixture of earth's mold
Breathe such divine enchanting ravishment?
Sure something holy lodges in that breast,
And with these raptures moves the vocal air
To testify his hidden residence;
How sweetly did they float upon the wings
Of silence, through the empty-vaulted night
At every fall smoothing the raven down
Of darkness till it smiled: I have oft heard

230. **Echo:** Because Echo chattered while Zeus dallied with other women, Hera condemned her never to say anything except what had just been said to her. She became one of the lovers of Narcissus.

231. **airy shell:** the arched sky.

232. **Meander:** winding river in Asia Minor, perhaps as classical code for the Severn; **margent:** bank.

234. **love-lorn:** The term, which Milton was among the first to use, originally meant not "abandoned by one's love" but "ruined by one's love," as Philomela was ruined by Tereus.

236–37. Are the brothers like *Narcissus* in being youthful and attractive or because, like *Narcissus* and his image, they resemble each other and are inseparable?

241. **parley:** conversation; **daughter of the sphere:** born in the mortal, sublunary sphere.

242. **translated:** taken to Heaven.

243. **resounding grace:** a perfect term for what Echo might add to heavenly harmonies; the phrase occurs in "the only Alexandrine in *Comus,* mimicking the lengthening of heaven's song by Echo" (Carey).

248. **his:** its, referring to *something holy* in line 246.

249. **they:** referring to *these raptures* in line 247.

251. **fall:** cadence.

My mother Circe with the Sirens three,
Amidst the flow'ry-kirtled Naiades
Culling their potent herbs and baleful drugs,
Who as they sung, would take the prisoned soul,
And lap it in Elysium; Scylla wept,
And chid her barking waves into attention,
And fell Charybdis murmured soft applause:
Yet they in pleasing slumber lulled the sense,
And in sweet madness robbed it of itself,
But such a sacred and home-felt delight,
Such sober certainty of waking bliss
I never heard till now. I'll speak to her
And she shall be my queen.——Hail, foreign wonder!
Whom certain these rough shades did never breed,
Unless the goddess that in rural shrine
Dwell'st here with Pan or Sylvan, by blest song
Forbidding every bleak unkindly fog
To touch the prosperous growth of this tall wood.
Lady. Nay gentle shepherd, ill is lost that praise
That is addressed to unattending ears;
Not any boast of skill, but extreme shift
How to regain my severed company
Compelled me to awake the courteous Echo
To give me answer from her mossy couch.
Comus. What chance good Lady hath bereft you thus?
Lady. Dim darkness and this leafy labyrinth.
Comus. Could that divide you from near-ushering guides?
Lady. They left me weary on a grassy turf.
Comus. By falsehood, or discourtesy, or why?
Lady. To seek i' the valley some cool friendly spring.
Comus. And left your fair side all unguarded, Lady?
Lady. They were but twain, and purposed quick return.

253. **Sirens three:** the sea nymphs whose song led sailors to their doom (*Od.* 12.166–200). There is no classical precedent for associating them with Circe, but they appear as Circe's attendants in William Browne's *Inner Temple Mask,* 1–96.

254. **flow'ry-kirtled:** wearing skirts of flowers; **Naiades:** nymphs of rivers and springs, four of whom serve Circe in *Od.* 10.348–51.

255. **potent herbs:** In Vergil, *Aen.* 7.19, Circe uses *potentibus herbis* to transform men into beasts.

256–59. In Ovid, *Met.* 14.8–74, *Circe* transforms the nymph *Scylla* into first a monster, then the treacherous rock facing *Charybdis.* Here both become the enchanted audience of Circe's song.

257. **lap it in Elysium:** wrap the soul in bliss.

261. **robbed it of itself:** rendered it unconscious.

262. **home-felt:** heartfelt.

267. **Unless the goddess:** i.e., unless you are the goddess.

268. **Sylvan:** Sylvanus, god of the woods, sometimes identified with *Pan.*

272. **unattending:** inattentive.

273. **extreme shift:** "my last chance, given the circumstances."

277–90. The passage is an example of stichomythia, or dialogue in single lines, a common device in Greek and Renaissance drama.

Comus. Perhaps forestalling night prevented them.
Lady. How easy my misfortune is to hit!
Comus. Imports their loss, beside the present need?
Lady. No less than if I should my brothers lose.
Comus. Were they of manly prime or youthful bloom?
Lady. As smooth as Hebe's their unrazored lips.
Comus. Two such I saw, what time the labored ox
In his loose traces from the furrow came,
And the swinked hedger at his supper sat;
I saw them under a green mantling vine
That crawls along the side of yon small hill,
Plucking ripe clusters from the tender shoots;
Their port was more than human, as they stood;
I took it for a fairy visïon
Of some gay creatures of the element
That in the colors of the rainbow live
And play i' th' plighted clouds. I was awestruck,
And as I passed, I worshipped; if those you seek,
It were a journey like the path to Heav'n
To help you find them.
Lady.   Gentle villager
What readiest way would bring me to that place?
Comus. Due west it rises from this shrubby point.
Lady. To find out that, good shepherd, I suppose,
In such a scant allowance of starlight,
Would overtask the best land-pilot's art,
Without the sure guess of well-practiced feet.
Comus. I know each lane, and every alley green,
Dingle, or bushy dell of this wild wood,
And every bosky bourn from side to side
My daily walks and ancient neighborhood,
And if your stray attendance be yet lodged,
Or shroud within these limits, I shall know
Ere morrow wake, or the low-roosted lark
From her thatched pallet rouse; if otherwise
I can conduct you, Lady, to a low

285. **prevented:** anticipated.
286. **hit:** guess.
290. **Hebe:** the goddess of youth.
291. **what time:** at the time when.
292. **traces:** straps.
293. **swinked hedger:** workman tired (*swinked*) from cutting hedges.
294. **mantling:** spreading.
297. **port:** deportment, bearing.
299. **element:** sky.
301. **plighted:** folded.
311. **alley:** path.
312. **Dingle:** wooded hollow.
313. **bosky bourn:** bushy stream.
315. **stray attendance:** missing attendants.
316. **shroud:** seek shelter.
318. **if otherwise:** if you prefer.

But loyal cottage, where you may be safe
Till further quest.
Lady. Shepherd I take thy word,
And trust thy honest offered courtesy,
Which oft is sooner found in lowly sheds
With smoky rafters, than in tap'stry halls
And courts of princes, where it first was named
And yet is most pretended: in a place
Less warranted than this, or less secure
I cannot be, that I should fear to change it.
Eye me blest Providence, and square my trial
To my proportioned strength. Shepherd lead on.—

The two brothers

Elder brother. Unmuffle ye faint stars, and thou fair moon
That wont'st to love the traveler's benison,
Stoop thy pale visage through an amber cloud,
And disinherit Chaos, that reigns here
In double night of darkness and of shades;
Or if your influence be quite dammed up
With black usurping mists, some gentle taper,
Though a rush candle from the wicker hole
Of some clay habitation, visit us
With thy long leveled rule of streaming light,
And thou shalt be our star of Arcady,
Or Tyrian Cynosure.
Second brother. Or if our eyes
Be barred that happiness, might we but hear
The folded flocks penned in their wattled cotes,

322–26. **And trust . . . pretended:** The sentiment appears in Ariosto, *OF* 14.62, but near replicas abound. "Full of courtesy, full of craft" was a proverb of the day (Tilley C732).

327. **warranted:** protected against danger.

329. **square:** bring into alignment with (my allotted strength).

331. **Unmuffle:** remove the covering of darkness; perhaps the line triggers a stage effect, such as the uncovering of lit tapers or the opening of dark lanterns (see 197n).

332. **wont'st:** is accustomed to; **benison:** blessing.

334. **disinherit:** dispossess; **Chaos:** Night and Chaos are paired also in *PL* 2.894–97.

335. **shades:** trees.

336. **influence:** Astrologers taught that an ethereal liquid or *influence* flowed from the stars to affect human destiny.

338. **rush candle:** pith of a rush plant dipped in tallow; its light was feeble; **wicker hole:** window made of plaited twigs.

341. **star of Arcady:** The Elder Brother alludes to Ovid's myth (*Met.* 2.409–531) of Callisto, princess of Arcadia, who was raped by Jove and bore a child, Arcas, whom Juno changed into the constellation Ursa Major (*star of Arcady*). Greek sailors steered by it.

342. **Tyrian Cynosure:** Ursa Minor, by which Phoenician (*Tyrian*) sailors steered.

344. **wattled cotes:** animal pens made of stakes interlaced with branches and twigs.

Or sound of pastoral reed with oaten stops,
Or whistle from the lodge, or village cock
Count the night watches to his feathery dames,
'Twould be some solace yet, some little cheering
In this close dungeon of innumerous boughs.
But O that hapless virgin our lost sister,
Where may she wander now, whither betake her
From the chill dew, amongst rude burs and thistles?
Perhaps some cold bank is her bolster now
Or 'gainst the rugged bark of some broad elm
Leans her unpillowed head fraught with sad fears.
What if in wild amazement and affright,
Or while we speak within the direful grasp
Of savage hunger, or of savage heat?
Elder brother. Peace brother, be not over-exquisite
To cast the fashion of uncertain evils;
For grant they be so, while they rest unknown,
What need a man forestall his date of grief,
And run to meet what he would most avoid?
Or if they be but false alarms of fear,
How bitter is such self-delusïon?
I do not think my sister so to seek,
Or so unprincipled in virtue's book,
And the sweet peace that goodness bosoms ever,
As that the single want of light and noise
(Not being in danger, as I trust she is not)
Could stir the constant mood of her calm thoughts,
And put them into misbecoming plight.
Virtue could see to do what Virtue would
By her own radiant light, though sun and moon
Were in the flat sea sunk. And Wisdom's self

345. **pastoral reed:** the shepherd's pipe, made of oat straw; **stops:** finger holes.
349. **close:** confined.
356. **amazement:** frenzy.
357–65. This passage from the printed texts appears in neither of the manuscripts, which have in its place the following lines: "So fares as did forsaken Proserpine/When the big rolling flakes of pitchy clouds/And darkness wound her in."
358. of the hunger of savage beasts or the lust of savage men.
359. **over-exquisite:** excessively precise.
360. **cast:** forecast (as in "casting a horoscope"); **fashion:** form.
361. **be so:** be evils.
362. **forestall:** introduce before the proper time. A proverb of the day was "He that seeks trouble never misses it" (Tilley T532).
366. **so to seek:** so without resources, so much at a loss.
367. **unprincipled:** uninstructed.
368. **bosoms:** encloses in its bosom.
369. **single:** mere.
372. **misbecoming:** unbecoming.
373–74. **Virtue . . . light:** Editors cite Jonson (*Pleasure Reconciled to Virtue* 339–42) and Spenser (*FQ* 1.1.12), but the phrasing (albeit not the sense) is closer to Shakespeare's "Lovers can see to do their amorous rights/By their own beauties" (*ROM* 3.2.8–9).
375. **Wisdom's self:** Wisdom herself.

Oft seeks to sweet retired solitude,
Where with her best nurse Contemplatïon
She plumes her feathers, and lets grow her wings
That in the various bustle of resort
Were all to-ruffled, and sometimes impaired.
He that has light within his own clear breast
May sit i' th' center, and enjoy bright day,
But he that hides a dark soul and foul thoughts
Benighted walks under the midday sun;
Himself is his own dungeon.
Second brother. 'Tis most true
That musing Meditation most affects
The pensive secrecy of desert cell,
Far from the cheerful haunt of men and herds,
And sits as safe as in a senate-house;
For who would rob a hermit of his weeds,
His few books, or his beads, or maple dish,
Or do his gray hairs any violence?
But beauty like the fair Hesperian tree
Laden with blooming gold, had need the guard
Of dragon watch with unenchanted eye,
To save her blossoms, and defend her fruit
From the rash hand of bold incontinence.
You may as well spread out the unsunned heaps
Of miser's treasure by an outlaw's den,
And tell me it is safe, as bid me hope
Danger will wink on opportunity,
And let a single helpless maiden pass
Uninjured in this wild surrounding waste.
Of night or loneliness it recks me not,
I fear the dread events that dog them both,
Lest some ill-greeting touch attempt the person
Of our unownèd sister.
Elder brother. I do not, brother,
Infer, as if I thought my sister's state

376. **seeks to:** repairs to.
380. **all to-ruffled:** very much ruffled.
382. **center:** center of the earth.
386. **affects:** is drawn to, has affection for.
387. **secrecy:** seclusion.
389. **senate-house:** the safest of places, being both public and the center of law and order.
390. **weeds:** clothes.
391. **beads:** rosary.
393. **Hesperian tree:** The tree bearing golden apples was guarded by the Hesperides (three daughters of Hesperus) and by a dragon.
401. **wink on:** overlook.
404. **it recks me not:** I don't care (whether we are talking about the effects of night or loneliness).
406. **ill-greeting:** greeting with evil intent; **touch:** sexual touch; **attempt:** try to ravish.
407. **unownèd:** lost.
408. **Infer, as if I thought:** argue as one who thought.

Secure without all doubt, or controversy:
Yet where an equal poise of hope and fear
Does arbitrate th' event, my nature is
That I incline to hope, rather than fear,
And gladly banish squint suspicïon.
My sister is not so defenseless left
As you imagine; she has a hidden strength
Which you remember not.
Second brother. What hidden strength,
Unless the strength of Heav'n, if you mean that?
Elder brother. I mean that too, but yet a hidden strength
Which if Heav'n gave it, may be termed her own:
'Tis chastity, my brother, chastity:
She that has that, is clad in complete steel,
And like a quivered nymph with arrows keen
May trace huge forests, and unharbored heaths,
Infamous hills, and sandy perilous wilds,
Where through the sacred rays of chastity,
No savage fierce, bandit, or mountaineer
Will dare to soil her virgin purity:
Yea there, where very desolation dwells
By grots and caverns shagged with horrid shades,
She may pass on with unblenched majesty,
Be it not done in pride, or in presumption.
Some say no evil thing that walks by night
In fog, or fire, by lake, or moorish fen,
Blue meager hag, or stubborn unlaid ghost,
That breaks his magic chains at curfew time,
No goblin, or swart fairy of the mine,
Hath hurtful power o'er true virginity.
Do ye believe me yet, or shall I call
Antiquity from the old schools of Greece
To testify the arms of chastity?

409. **without:** beyond.
413. **squint:** looking obliquely: a behavior thought to characterize suspicious people.
419. **if:** even if.
422. **quivered nymph:** a nymph devoted to Diana, and therefore to both archery and chastity.
423. **trace:** walk through.
426. **bandit:** from the Italian *bandito,* meaning originally "someone placed under the ban of excommunication"; **mountaineer:** mountain savage.
429. **shagged:** covered with shrubs; **horrid:** bristling.
430. **unblenched:** unfaltering.
432. Evoking *HAM* I.I.120–23: "Some say . . . no spirit dare stir abroad."
434. **Blue:** livid; **meager:** emaciated.
435. **curfew time:** when the evening bell was rung (usually 9:00 P.M.).
436. **swart:** black.
439. **old schools:** the various schools of ancient philosophy.

Hence had the huntress Dian her dread bow,
Fair silver-shafted queen forever chaste,
Wherewith she tamed the brinded lioness
And spotted mountain pard, but set at naught
The frivolous bolt of Cupid; gods and men
Feared her stern frown, and she was queen o' th' woods.
What was that snaky-headed Gorgon shield
That wise Minerva wore, unconquered virgin,
Wherewith she freezed her foes to congealed stone,
But rigid looks of chaste austerity,
And noble grace that dashed brute violence
With sudden adoration and blank awe?
So dear to Heav'n is saintly chastity,
That when a soul is found sincerely so,
A thousand liveried angels lacky her,
Driving far off each thing of sin and guilt,
And in clear dream and solemn vision
Tell her of things that no gross ear can hear,
Till oft converse with Heav'nly habitants
Begin to cast a beam on th' outward shape,
The unpolluted temple of the mind,
And turns it by degrees to the soul's essence,
Till all be made immortal: but when lust
By unchaste looks, loose gestures, and foul talk,
But most by lewd and lavish act of sin,
Lets in defilement to the inward parts,
The soul grows clotted by contagion,
Embodies and imbrutes, till she quite lose

443. **brinded:** tawny.

444. **pard:** panther or leopard.

445. **bolt:** arrow.

447–48. **that snaky-headed . . . wore:** *Minerva,* who changed Medusa's hair to snakes because Neptune violated her in Minerva's temple, wore the image of that snaky head on her shield. Like Medusa herself, the image turned opponents to stone. Ironically, the Lady, rather than an opponent of chastity, will become paralyzed in Milton's mask.

452. **blank:** rendering powerless.

455. Cp. the *thousand fantasies* of line 205.

458. **no gross ear can hear:** Cp. *Arcades* 72–73.

459–63. **Till . . . immortal:** The rather uncommon idea of body being gradually transformed into spirit or soul also appears in *PL* 5.497–500. This notion is mostly found among occultists influenced by Neoplatonism and Hermeticism; see, for example, George Rust, *A Letter of Resolution Concerning Origen.*

459. **oft converse:** frequent spiritual intercourse, possibly including conversation. Cp. *PL* 7.9.

460–61. **outward shape . . . mind:** The temple of the mind is a virgin (*unpolluted*) body.

462. **it:** the outward shape, the body.

463. **all:** the entirety of the person, body and soul. Despite the body-soul dualism implicit in its emphasis on chastity, *A Masque* also yearns for a Hebraic sense of their indivisibility. These contrary impulses will settle into the mature monism or animate materialism of *PL* 5.469–503 (S. Fallon 1991, 83).

465–75. Milton follows Plato's *Phaedo* 81 in this account of lewd souls becoming embodied (the opposite of chastity's transformation of body into soul).

465. **lavish:** lascivious.

The divine property of her first being.
Such are those thick and gloomy shadows damp
Oft seen in charnel vaults, and sepulchers
Lingering, and sitting by a new-made grave,
As loath to leave the body that it loved,
And linked itself by carnal sensualty
To a degenerate and degraded state.
Second brother. How charming is divine philosophy!
Not harsh and crabbèd as dull fools suppose,
But musical as is Apollo's lute,
And a perpetual feast of nectared sweets,
Where no crude surfeit reigns.
Elder brother. List, list, I hear
Some far-off hallo break the silent air.
Second brother. Methought so too; what should it be?
Elder brother. For certain
Either someone like us night-foundered here,
Or else some neighbor woodman, or at worst,
Some roving robber calling to his fellows.
Second brother. Heav'n keep my sister. Again, again, and near.
Best draw, and stand upon our guard.
Elder brother. I'll hallo;
If he be friendly he comes well, if not,
Defense is a good cause, and Heav'n be for us.

The Attendant Spirit habited like a shepherd

That hallo I should know, what are you? Speak;
Come not too near, you fall on iron stakes else.
Spirit. What voice is that, my young lord? Speak again.
Second brother. O brother, 'tis my father's shepherd sure.
Elder brother. Thyrsis? Whose artful strains have oft delayed
The huddling brook to hear his madrigal,
And sweetened every muskrose of the dale,

469. **property:** essential character.

470–75. Milton adapts Plato's *Phaedo* 81.

474. **sensualty:** Though our text is modernized, we prefer *sensualty,* found in the *CMS* and 1645, to the unmetrical *sensuality,* found in the *BMS,* 1637, and 1673.

478. **musical as is Apollo's lute:** Cp. Shakespeare, *LLL* 4.3.339–40: "Sweet and musical/As bright Apollo's lute."

480. **crude:** indigestible.

483. **night-foundered:** engulfed in night.

[**Stage direction**] **habited:** dressed.

491. **iron stakes:** swords.

494. **Thyrsis:** The name of the singer of Theocritus's first eclogue and one of the competing singers in Vergil, *Ec.* 7, hence an embodiment of pastoral tradition. Milton speaks of himself as Thyrsis in *Damon.* There follows a second compliment to the musical talents of Henry Lawes (see 84–88).

495. **huddling:** crowding together, presumably to hear Thyrsis's song.

How cam'st thou here good swain? Hath any ram
Slipped from the fold, or young kid lost his dam,
Or straggling wether the pent flock forsook?
How couldst thou find this dark sequestered nook?
Spirit. O my loved master's heir, and his next joy,
I came not here on such a trivial toy
As a strayed ewe, or to pursue the stealth
Of pilfering wolf; not all the fleecy wealth
That doth enrich these downs, is worth a thought
To this my errand, and the care it brought.
But O my virgin Lady, where is she?
How chance she is not in your company?
Elder brother. To tell thee sadly shepherd, without blame,
Or our neglect, we lost her as we came.
Spirit. Ay me unhappy! Then my fears are true.
Elder brother. What fears good Thyrsis? Prithee briefly show.
Spirit. I'll tell ye. 'Tis not vain or fabulous
(Though so esteemed by shallow ignorance)
What the sage poets taught by th' Heav'nly Muse,
Storied of old in high immortal verse
Of dire Chimeras and enchanted isles,
And rifted rocks whose entrance leads to Hell,
For such there be, but unbelief is blind.
    Within the navel of this hideous wood,
Immured in cypress shades a sorcerer dwells
Of Bacchus and of Circe born, great Comus,
Deep skilled in all his mother's witcheries,
And here to every thirsty wanderer,
By sly enticement gives his baneful cup,
With many murmurs mixed, whose pleasing poison
The visage quite transforms of him that drinks,
And the inglorious likeness of a beast
Fixes instead, unmolding reason's mintage
Charactered in the face; this have I learnt
Tending my flocks hard by i' th' hilly crofts

499. **wether:** castrated ram.
501. **next:** nearest.
502. **toy:** trifle.
506. **To this:** compared to this.
508. **How chance:** how does it chance that.
515. **sage poets . . . Muse:** The sage poets are not necessarily Christian, for Milton believed that poetic "abilities, wheresoever they be found, are the inspired gift of God" (p. 841). He probably had in mind Homer, Vergil, Tasso, Ariosto, and Spenser.
516. **Storied:** narrated.
517. **Chimeras:** monsters composed of lion, goat, and dragon parts.
518. **rifted:** split.
520. **navel:** center.
530. **Charactered:** engraved, like a face on a coin.
531. **crofts:** pieces of enclosed ground used for pasture or tillage.

That brow this bottom glade, whence night by night
He and his monstrous rout are heard to howl
Like stabled wolves, or tigers at their prey,
Doing abhorrèd rites to Hecate
In their obscurèd haunts of inmost bow'rs.
Yet have they many baits, and guileful spells
T' inveigle and invite th' unwary sense
Of them that pass unweeting by the way.
This evening late, by then the chewing flocks
Had ta'en their supper on the savory herb
Of knot-grass dew-besprent, and were in fold,
I sat me down to watch upon a bank
With ivy canopied, and interwove
With flaunting honeysuckle, and began
Wrapped in a pleasing fit of melancholy
To meditate my rural minstrelsy
Till fancy had her fill; but ere a close
The wonted roar was up amidst the woods,
And filled the air with barbarous dissonance,
At which I ceased, and listened them a while,
Till an unusual stop of sudden silence
Gave respite to the drowsy-frighted steeds
That draw the litter of close-curtained Sleep;
At last a soft and solemn breathing sound
Rose like a steam of rich distilled perfumes,
And stole upon the air, that even Silence
Was took ere she was ware, and wished she might
Deny her nature, and be never more
Still to be so displaced. I was all ear,
And took in strains that might create a soul
Under the ribs of Death. But O ere long
Too well I did perceive it was the voice

532. **brow:** make a brow in relation to, overlook.

534. **stabled wolves:** a crux: "wolves put in a stable" seems a surreal picture, though it has Vergilian precedent (*Aen.* 7.15–20); "wolves having broken into the fold" is of a piece with "tigers at their prey," but *stabled* must be wrenched to produce this sense; appealing to "stabled" in *PL* 11.752, some have suggested "wolves in their lairs." Like Hughes et al. 2:921–22, we prefer the first suggestion.

539. **unweeting:** unaware.

542. **knot-grass:** applied to various plants with knotty stems; **dew-besprent:** sprinkled with dew.

545. **flaunting:** waving gaily.

547. **meditate:** practice.

548. **ere a close:** before the conclusion of a single musical phrase or cadence.

550. **barbarous dissonance:** Cp. *PL* 7.32.

552. **stop of sudden silence:** referring to the sudden breaking off of the dance (145).

553. **drowsy-frighted:** drowsy but frightened; some editors, on the sole authority of *CMS*, print "drowsy-flighted."

554. **litter:** chariot.

555. **sound:** the Lady's song.

558. **took:** charmed.

Of my most honored Lady, your dear sister.
Amazed I stood, harrowed with grief and fear,
And "O poor hapless nightingale," thought I,
"How sweet thou sing'st, how near the deadly snare!"
Then down the lawns I ran with headlong haste
Through paths and turnings often trod by day,
Till guided by mine ear I found the place
Where that damned wizard hid in sly disguise
(For so by certain signs I knew) had met
Already, ere my best speed could prevent,
The aidless innocent Lady his wished prey,
Who gently asked if he had seen such two,
Supposing him some neighbor villager;
Longer I durst not stay, but soon I guessed
Ye were the two she meant; with that I sprung
Into swift flight, till I had found you here,
But further know I not.
Second brother. O night and shades,
How are ye joined with Hell in triple knot
Against th' unarmèd weakness of one virgin
Alone and helpless! Is this the confidence
You gave me brother?
Elder brother. Yes, and keep it still,
Lean on it safely; not a period
Shall be unsaid for me: against the threats
Of malice or of sorcery, or that power
Which erring men call chance, this I hold firm,
Virtue may be assailed, but never hurt,
Surprised by unjust force, but not enthralled,
Yea even that which mischief meant most harm,
Shall in the happy trial prove most glory.
But evil on itself shall back recoil,
And mix no more with goodness, when at last
Gathered like scum, and settled to itself,
It shall be in eternal restless change

566. **hapless nightingale:** The Lady's song alluded to Philomela (234n). She sang, the Attendant Spirit implies, better than she knew.

585. **period:** sentence.

586. **for me:** for my part.

587. **that power:** Since the Elder Brother is swearing against this power, perhaps against the threats of this power, it seems unlikely that he alludes to providence, as Hughes et al. maintain. Perhaps he means "whatever gods there may be (behind the illusion of chance) that have been thought to say something contrary to what I am about to profess."

589–90. The Elder Brother has seemed to be saying, unrealistically, that virtue could repel or prevent physical assault. He now declares more convincingly that virtue cannot be destroyed by physical assault.

594. **when:** till.

Self-fed and self-consumed; if this fail,
The pillared firmament is rottenness,
And earth's base built on stubble. But come let's on.
Against th' opposing will and arm of Heav'n
May never this just sword be lifted up.
But, for that damned magician, let him be girt
With all the grisly legions that troop
Under the sooty flag of Acheron,
Harpies and Hydras, or all the monstrous forms
'Twixt Africa and Ind, I'll find him out,
And force him to restore his purchase back,
Or drag him by the curls to a foul death,
Cursed as his life.
Spirit. Alas good vent'rous youth,
I love thy courage yet, and bold emprise,
But here thy sword can do thee little stead;
Far other arms and other weapons must
Be those that quell the might of Hellish charms;
He with his bare wand can unthread thy joints,
And crumble all thy sinews.
Elder brother. Why prithee shepherd
How durst thou then thyself approach so near
As to make this relation?
Spirit. Care and utmost shifts
How to secure the Lady from surprisal
Brought to my mind a certain shepherd lad
Of small regard to see to, yet well skilled
In every virtuous plant and healing herb

597. **Self-fed and self-consumed:** as indeed evil is in *PL* 2.798–800; 10.629–37; **if this fail:** if what I have said prove false.

598–99. **The pillared firmament . . . stubble:** The created universe is imagined as a building with a foundation (*earth's base*) on which pillars (see Job 26.11) support the dome of the sky. If evil should prove to belong to the design of creation, then the pillars would be rotten, the foundation resting on flimsy *stubble* (short stalks left after harvest).

604. **Acheron:** one of the four rivers of Hades (cp. *PL* 2.578).

605. **Harpies and Hydras:** *Harpies* were rapacious birds with women's faces; the *Hydra,* eventually slain by Hercules, was a water serpent with heads that multiplied when cut off.

606. **Ind:** India.

607. **purchase:** ill-gotten prizes.

610. **emprise:** either "undertaking" (what he has just vowed to do) or "enterprise" (general spiritedness).

611. **stead:** service.

614. **bare:** mere; **unthread:** dislocate, take out of their sockets.

615. **crumble:** shrivel up.

617. **relation:** report; **shifts:** plans in exigent circumstances.

619. **shepherd lad:** almost certainly Milton himself, as the poet memorializes his friendship with Lawes.

620. **Of small regard to see to:** is "characteristic in its proud modesty, corresponding to the 'uncouth swain' of *Lycidas*" (Wright 1981). The knowledge of plants and herbs (see *Il Pens* 172) has poetic utility here, in the flower catalog of *Lycidas,* and in Milton's epic account of the Garden of Eden.

That spreads her verdant leaf to the morning ray.
He loved me well, and oft would beg me sing,
Which when I did, he on the tender grass
Would sit, and hearken even to ecstasy,
And in requital ope his leathern scrip,
And show me simples of a thousand names
Telling their strange and vigorous faculties;
Amongst the rest a small unsightly root,
But of divine effect, he culled me out;
The leaf was darkish, and had prickles on it,
But in another country, as he said,
Bore a bright golden flower, but not in this soil:
Unknown, and like esteemed, and the dull swain
Treads on it daily with his clouted shoon,
And yet more med'cinal is it than that Moly
That Hermes once to wise Ulysses gave;
He called it Haemony, and gave it me,
And bade me keep it as of sov'reign use
'Gainst all enchantments, mildew blast, or damp
Or ghastly Furies' apparition;
I pursed it up, but little reck'ning made,
Till now that this extremity compelled;
But now I find it true, for by this means
I knew the foul enchanter though disguised,
Entered the very lime-twigs of his spells,
And yet came off: if you have this about you
(As I will give you when we go) you may
Boldly assault the necromancer's hall;
Where if he be, with dauntless hardihood,
And brandished blade rush on him, break his glass,
And shed the luscious liquor on the ground,
But seize his wand; though he and his cursed crew
Fierce sign of battle make, and menace high,

626. **scrip:** small bag carried by shepherds.

627. **simples:** medicinal herbs; **thousand names:** Cp. lines 205, 455.

635. **clouted:** patched, mended.

636. **Moly:** Hermes gave this plant, which has a white flower and black root, to Odysseus to protect him against Circe's spells. Commentators often supposed it to represent temperance or education.

638. **Haemony:** Milton invented this herb, and no one is sure what, beyond competing with Homer, he had in mind. The term might derive from Haemonia (Thessaly, associated with magic), or *haimonios* (Gk. for "bloodred"), which sometimes leads interpreters to the blood of Christ. Hanford and B. A. Wright (1938) saw it as a symbol of Milton's youthful Christian-Platonic philosophy. Others take it as a symbol of Christian grace.

640. **blast:** infection; mildew was thought to be seriously malignant; **damp:** noxious vapor.

642. **little reck'ning made:** took little heed.

646. **lime-twigs:** traps, alluding to the practice of catching birds by spreading lime on branches.

Vulcan vomit smoke,
retire, if he but shrink.
sis, lead on apace, I'll follow thee,
gel bear a shield before us.

a stately palace, set out with all manner of deliciousness: soft music, tables spread with all dainties. Comus appears with his rabble, and the Lady set in an enchanted chair, to whom he offers his glass, which she puts by, and goes about to rise.

Comus. Nay, Lady, sit; if I but wave this wand,
Your nerves are all chained up in alabaster,
And you a statue; or as Daphne was
Root-bound, that fled Apollo.
Lady. Fool, do not boast;
Thou canst not touch the freedom of my mind
With all thy charms, although this corporal rind
Thou hast immanacled, while Heav'n sees good.
Comus. Why are you vexed Lady? Why do you frown?
Here dwell no frowns, nor anger, from these gates
Sorrow flies far: see, here be all the pleasures
That fancy can beget on youthful thoughts
When the fresh blood grows lively, and returns
Brisk as the April buds in primrose season.
And first behold this cordial julep here
That flames and dances in his crystal bounds
With spirits of balm and fragrant syrups mixed.
Not that Nepenthes which the wife of Thone
In Egypt gave to Jove-born Helena
Is of such power to stir up joy as this,
To life so friendly, or so cool to thirst.
Why should you be so cruel to yourself,
And to those dainty limbs which Nature lent

[Stage direction] **puts by:** refuses; **goes about:** attempts.

660. **nerves:** sinews.

661. *Daphne* was turned into a laurel as she ran away from a lustful Apollo (Ovid, *Met.* 1.545–52). But this metamorphosis saved her from a sexual predator, and it is therefore somewhat odd that Comus would threaten the Lady with Daphne's fate. The Apollo-Daphne myth was central to the tradition of Petrarchan love poetry.

663. "Though his body be thrown into fetters, no bondage can enchain his soul," as Cicero (*On the Chief Good and Evil* 3.22) and others have observed. The issue is not rape. As the Lady realizes, Comus wants her to consent, in a free mental act, to his seduction. Cp. line 1019.

672. **julep:** sweet drink.

674. **balm:** aromatic fragrance.

675–76. Helen slips *Nepenthes,* a potion for dispelling grief given her by the Egyptian wife of Thone, into Menelaus's drink (Homer, *Od.* 4.219–32).

679. Cp. *SA* 784.

For gentle usage and soft delicacy?
But you invert the cov'nants of her trust,
And harshly deal like an ill borrower
With that which you received on other terms,
Scorning the unexempt condition
By which all mortal frailty must subsist,
Refreshment after toil, ease after pain,
That have been tired all day without repast,
And timely rest have wanted; but fair virgin
This will restore all soon.
Lady. 'Twill not false traitor,
'Twill not restore the truth and honesty
That thou hast banished from thy tongue with lies.
Was this the cottage and the safe abode
Thou told'st me of? What grim aspects are these,
These ugly-headed monsters? Mercy guard me!
Hence with thy brewed enchantments, foul deceiver.
Hast thou betrayed my credulous innocence
With vizored falsehood and base forgery,
And wouldst thou seek again to trap me here
With lickerish baits fit to ensnare a brute?
Were it a draft for Juno when she banquets,
I would not taste thy treasonous offer; none
But such as are good men can give good things,
And that which is not good, is not delicious
To a well-governed and wise appetite.
Comus. O foolishness of men! that lend their ears
To those budge doctors of the Stoic fur,
And fetch their precepts from the Cynic tub,
Praising the lean and sallow Abstinence.
Wherefore did Nature pour her bounties forth,

681. **usage:** active use, as opposed to mere hoarding.

682. **the cov'nants of her trust:** the particular clauses of the agreement governing Nature's loan. The financial metaphors throughout this passage suggest a libertine parody of the parable of the talents in Matt. 25.

685. **unexempt condition:** condition from which no one is exempt.

694. **aspects:** countenances.

698. **vizored:** hidden, as the face is hidden by a visor.

700. **lickerish:** pleasant to the taste; the word also means "lustful."

703. "A bad man's gifts convey no benefit" (Euripides, *Medea* 618).

707. **budge doctors:** pompous academics, with *budge* referring to a fur worn on academic gowns; **Stoic:** The school of Stoic philosophers opposed luxury and hedonism.

708. **Cynic tub:** The school of Cynicism opposed not only riches but the ordinary pleasures of life. Diogenes the Cynic for a time resided in a tub.

710–36. Most of the sources adduced by scholars pertain to the idea that beauty must be seen, not the argument about Nature's abundance. The nurse in Seneca's *Hippolytus* 469–81, maintaining that without copulation Nature would

With such a full and unwithdrawing hand,
Covering the earth with odors, fruits, and flocks,
Thronging the seas with spawn innumerable,
But all to please and sate the curious taste?
And set to work millions of spinning worms,
That in their green shops weave the smooth-haired silk
To deck her sons, and that no corner might
Be vacant of her plenty, in her own loins
She hutched th' all-worshipped ore and precious gems
To store her children with; if all the world
Should in a pet of temperance feed on pulse,
Drink the clear stream, and nothing wear but frieze,
Th' All-giver would be unthanked, would be unpraised,
Not half his riches known, and yet despised,
And we should serve him as a grudging master,
As a penurious niggard of his wealth,
And live like Nature's bastards, not her sons,
Who would be quite surcharged with her own weight,
And strangled with her waste fertility;
Th' earth cumbered, and the winged air darked with plumes,
The herds would over-multitude their lords,
The sea o'erfraught would swell, and th' unsought diamonds
Would so emblaze the forehead of the deep,
And so bestud with stars, that they below
Would grow inured to light, and come at last
To gaze upon the sun with shameless brows.
List, Lady, be not coy, and be not cozened
With that same vaunted name Virginity:

---

be empty, anticipates the argument in reverse. The closest analogue is Colax's penultimate speech in Thomas Randolph's *The Muses' Looking-Glass* 2.3 (see Smith 1922).

714. **sate:** satisfy entirely; **curious:** fastidious, but with a suggestion of searching out all possibilities, however rare or perverse.

716. **green shops:** green workshops (in mulberry trees).

719. **hutched:** stored in a coffer.

721. **a pet of:** a foolish craze for; **pulse:** food consisting of vegetables that are also seeds (beans, lentils, et cetera); Daniel and his companions favored this diet at the court of Nebuchadnezzar (Dan. 1.8–16).

722. **frieze:** coarse woolen cloth.

727. **like Nature's bastards:** like illegitimate children who make no claim to their parent's property.

728. **surcharged:** overloaded.

729. **strangled:** suffocated.

732–36. The *deep* is the central portion of the earth, and its *forehead* is the part of the deep closest to the surface. To inhabitants of the deep, gems shining in the forehead appear like stars, and if left unmined would eventually lure them to the surface.

737–54. On the idea that beauty should be public and mutual, not solitary, see Sidney, *Arcadia* 3.10; Daniel, *Complaint of Rosamond* 512–32; Drayton, *England's Heroical Epistles,* "King John to Matilda," 119–56; and Carew, "To A.L. Persuasions to Love": "That rich treasure/Of rare beauty . . ./Was Bestowed on you by Nature/To be enjoyed, and 'twere a sin/There to be scarce, where she hath been/So prodigal of her best graces" (8–13).

738. **vaunted:** boasted or bragged of, highly prized.

Beauty is Nature's coin, must not be hoarded,
But must be current, and the good thereof
Consists in mutual and partaken bliss,
Unsavory in th' enjoyment of itself.
If you let slip time, like a neglected rose
It withers on the stalk with languished head.
Beauty is Nature's brag and must be shown
In courts, at feasts, and high solemnities
Where most may wonder at the workmanship;
It is for homely features to keep home,
They had their name thence; coarse complexïons
And cheeks of sorry grain will serve to ply
The sampler, and to tease the housewife's wool.
What need a vermeil-tinctured lip for that,
Love-darting eyes, or tresses like the morn?
There was another meaning in these gifts,
Think what, and be advised, you are but young yet.
Lady. I had not thought to have unlocked my lips
In this unhallowed air, but that this juggler
Would think to charm my judgment, as mine eyes,
Obtruding false rules pranked in reason's garb.
I hate when Vice can bolt her arguments
And Virtue has no tongue to check her pride:
Impostor, do not charge most innocent Nature,
As if she would her children should be riotous
With her abundance; she good cateress
Means her provision only to the good
That live according to her sober laws,
And holy dictate of spare Temperance:
If every just man that now pines with want
Had but a moderate and beseeming share
Of that which lewdly-pampered Luxury
Now heaps upon some few with vast excess,
Nature's full blessings would be well dispensed

Marlowe, *Hero and Leander,* 1.209: "This idol which you term virginity."

740. **current:** in circulation (referring to *Nature's coin*).

745. **brag:** show, display.

750. **grain:** color; **ply:** work at.

751. **tease:** comb out in preparation for spinning.

752. **vermeil:** vermilion.

757. **juggler:** sorcerer, trickster.

759. **pranked:** dressed up.

760. **bolt:** sift, pick (from the bolting or sifting of the meal from the bran in milling).

768–74. Cp. *LR* 3.4.28–35, 4.1.68–72: "Let the superfluous and lust-dieted man/That slaves your ordinance, that will not see/Because he does not feel, feel now your power quickly;/So distribution should undo excess,/And each man have enough."

…rfluous even proportion,
…o whit encumbered with her store;
…the Giver would be better thanked,
… due paid, for swinish gluttony
Ne'er looks to Heav'n amidst his gorgeous feast,
But with besotted base ingratitude
Crams, and blasphemes his feeder. Shall I go on?
Or have I said enough? To him that dares
Arm his profane tongue with contemptuous words
Against the sun-clad power of Chastity,
Fain would I something say, yet to what end?
Thou has nor ear nor soul to apprehend
The sublime notion and high mystery
That must be uttered to unfold the sage
And serious doctrine of Virginity,
And thou art worthy that thou shouldst not know
More happiness than this thy present lot.
Enjoy your dear wit and gay rhetoric
That hath so well been taught her dazzling fence,
Thou art not fit to hear thyself convinced;
Yet should I try, the uncontrollèd worth
Of this pure cause would kindle my rapt spirits
To such a flame of sacred vehemence
That dumb things would be moved to sympathize,
And the brute earth would lend her nerves and shake,
Till all thy magic structures reared so high
Were shattered into heaps o'er thy false head.
Comus. She fables not, I feel that I do fear
Her words set off by some superior power;
And though not mortal, yet a cold shudd'ring dew
Dips me all o'er, as when the wrath of Jove

778. **besotted:** morally stupefied.

779–806. **Shall I . . . more strongly:** Though missing from the two manuscripts, this passage appears in all three of the texts (1637, 1645, 1673) published in Milton's lifetime.

785. **high mystery:** religious truth known only through divine revelation.

786–87. **sage/And serious:** Milton refers to "our sage and serious poet Spenser" in *Areop* (p. 939).

787. **Virginity:** As Leonard notes, "virginity" in Protestant thought could include chaste marriage; see Calvin, *Institutes* 4.12.28: "The second kind of virginity is the chaste love of marriage." But the Lady gives no indication that she is using the word as a synonym for "chastity in general," and Comus has accused her of being deceived by that "vaunted name Virginity."

790. **gay:** showy, specious.

791. **fence:** skill in verbal fencing.

793. **uncontrollèd:** unchecked; indisputable.

796. **dumb things:** creatures without the power of speech.

797. Horace, *Odes* 1.34.9, feels a thunderbolt strike so magnificently that it shakes his skepticism about the gods.

803. **Dips me:** suffuses me with moisture; **Jove:** He defeated Saturn and the Titans with thunderbolts, then imprisoned the Titans in *Erebus* (the dark underworld).

Speaks thunder and the chains of Erebus
To some of Saturn's crew. I must dissemble,
And try her yet more strongly. Come, no more,
This is mere moral babble, and direct
Against the canon laws of our foundation;
I must not suffer this, yet 'tis but the lees
And settlings of a melancholy blood;
But this will cure all straight, one sip of this
Will bathe the drooping spirits in delight
Beyond the bliss of dreams. Be wise, and taste.—

The brothers rush in with swords drawn, wrest his glass out of his hand, and break it against the ground; his rout make sign of resistance, but are all driven in; the Attendant Spirit comes in.

Spirit. What, have you let the false enchanter scape?
O ye mistook, ye should have snatched his wand
And bound him fast; without his rod reversed,
And backward mutters of dissevering power,
We cannot free the Lady that sits here
In stony fetters fixed, and motionless;
Yet stay, be not disturbed, now I bethink me,
Some other means I have which may be used,
Which once of Meliboeus old I learnt,
The soothest shepherd that e'er piped on plains.
    There is a gentle nymph not far from hence,
That with moist curb sways the smooth Severn stream,
Sabrina is her name, a virgin pure;

804. **thunder and the chains of Erebus:** an example of zeugma, the double use of a verb: Jove "speaks" in the thunder, and "speaks the sentence of" Erebus on the defeated Titans.

808. **canon laws:** rules, but also glancing at the church's Canon Law; **foundation:** institution such as a church or college.

810. **melancholy blood:** The heaviest, darkest human blood is saturated with the melancholic humor, which is the cause of madness.

816. **rod reversed:** Circe reverses her wand to free Odysseus's men (Ovid, *Met.* 14.300). Sandys 1632 identified the wand with "sinister persuasions to pleasure" and the reversed wand with "discipline, and a view of their own deformity" (481).

817. **backward mutters:** spells muttered backward to free the Lady. Spenser's Britomart forces an enchanter to reverse his incantation and so release Amoret (*FQ* 3.12.36).

822. **Meliboeus:** He is a character in Vergil's first eclogue. Most editors suppose him to represent Spenser, the author to whom Milton is first of all indebted for his knowledge of Sabrina's story (*FQ* 2.10.14–19).

823. **soothest:** most truthful.

824–41. In the oldest source, Geoffrey of Monmouth's *History of Britain* 2.4–5, which Milton follows closely when retelling the story in his own *History of Britain* (Yale 5:18), *Sabrina* is the adulterous child of *Locrine* and Estrildis. *Guendolen,* his previous wife and queen, defeats and kills Locrine in battle, and for revenge throws Estrildis and Sabrina into the stream, which she names Sabrina (in time altered to *Severn*). Like Drayton, Milton has Sabrina transformed into a goddess by *Nereus*'s daughters (*Polyoblion* 5.1–30).

825. **sways:** rules.

Whilom she was the daughter of Locrine,
That had the scepter from his father Brute.
She guiltless damsel, flying the mad pursuit
Of her enragèd stepdame Guendolen,
Commended her fair innocence to the flood
That stayed her flight with his cross-flowing course;
The water nymphs that in the bottom played
Held up their pearlèd wrists and took her in,
Bearing her straight to agèd Nereus' hall,
Who piteous of her woes, reared her lank head,
And gave her to his daughters to imbathe
In nectared lavers strewed with asphodel,
And through the porch and inlet of each sense
Dropped in ambrosial oils till she revived,
And underwent a quick immortal change,
Made goddess of the river; still she retains
Her maiden gentleness, and oft at eve
Visits the herds along the twilight meadows,
Helping all urchin blasts and ill-luck signs
That the shrewd meddling elf delights to make,
Which she with precious vialed liquors heals.
For which the shepherds at their festivals
Carol her goodness loud in rustic lays,
And throw sweet garland wreaths into her stream
Of pansies, pinks, and gaudy daffodils.
And, as the old swain said, she can unlock
The clasping charm, and thaw the numbing spell,
If she be right invoked in warbled song,
For maidenhood she loves, and will be swift
To aid a virgin, such as was herself
In hard-besetting need; this will I try,
And add the power of some adjuring verse.

831. **Commended her fair innocence:** There is no suggestion of Sabrina's suicide in Geoffrey of Monmouth (824–41n). Milton also stresses her virginity.

834. **pearlèd wrists:** Water nymphs favor pearl adornments, as is clear from a stage direction in Ben Jonson's *Mask of Blackness:* his water nymphs wear on "the front, ear, necks and wrists, ornament of the most choice and orient pearl."

835. **Nereus:** a sea god who fathered fifty Nereids.

838. **lavers:** basins; **asphodel:** the immortal flower that grows in Homer's Elysian fields (*Od.* 11.539).

845. **Helping all urchin blasts:** remedying infections caused by ill spirits.

846. **shrewd:** mischievous.

852. **old swain:** Meliboeus.

853. **clasping charm . . . spell:** Leonard suggests that a distinction is intended between the *clasping charm,* which simply holds the Lady to the chair, and the more serious *numbing spell,* which renders her speechless and unconscious.

858. **adjuring:** entreating.

Song

Sabrina fair,
    Listen where thou art sitting
Under the glassy, cool, translucent wave,
    In twisted braids of lilies knitting
The loose train of thy amber-dropping hair;
    Listen for dear honor's sake,
    Goddess of the silver lake,
        Listen and save.

Listen and appear to us
In name of great Oceanus,
By th' earth-shaking Neptune's mace,
And Tethys' grave majestic pace,
By hoary Nereus' wrinkled look,
And the Carpathian wizard's hook,
By scaly Triton's winding shell,
And old sooth-saying Glaucus' spell,
By Leucothea's lovely hands,
And her son that rules the strands,
By Thetis' tinsel-slippered feet,
And the songs of Sirens sweet,
By dead Parthenope's dear tomb,

863. **amber-dropping:** *Amber* in this context could be either a color word or an odor word (a shortened form of *ambergris*—the morbid intestinal secretion of a whale, but nonetheless a valued source of perfumes).

864. **honor's sake:** Female honor in this period almost always centers on chastity. In the seventeenth century, this concept gradually came under attack by male poets (Donne, Carew, Rochester) and even by a female poet (Aphra Behn).

865. **lake:** Vergil terms the Tiber a *lacus* in *Aen.* 8.66, 74.

867–89. These lines contain the *adjuring verse* mentioned in line 858.

868. **Oceanus:** father of all rivers.

869. **earth-shaking:** Homeric epithet for Poseidon/*Neptune,* god of the sea and earthquakes; **mace:** trident.

870. **Tethys:** wife of Oceanus and mother of rivers.

871. **Nereus:** See 835n.

872. **Carpathian wizard:** Proteus, who lived in the Carpathian Sea, was the shepherd of Neptune's seals.

873. **Triton:** Neptune's herald, bearing a conch shell; **winding:** sounding, trumpeting.

874. **Glaucus:** a fisherman who became a sea god when he ate a magical herb (Ovid, *Met.* 13.904–68).

875. **Leucothea:** After leaping from a cliff to avoid the wrathful Juno, Ino was made the sea god *Leucothea* by Neptune (Ovid, *Met.* 4.512–42).

876. **her son:** Melicertes, whom Ino (see previous note) was holding when she jumped into the sea. Nepture turned him into Palaemon, god of harbors.

877. **Thetis:** a Nereid described by Homer as "silver-footed" (*Il.* 18.127), the mother of Achilles.

878. Even though the sweetness of their song is emphasized, it is odd that this catalog of benign sea deities should arrive at the *Sirens,* companions of Circe who lured sailors to their deaths (see 252–57).

879. **Parthenope:** a Siren who drowned herself when Odysseus escaped; she is supposed to be buried in Naples (Ovid, *Met.* 14.101).

And fair Ligea's golden comb,
Wherewith she sits on diamond rocks
Sleeking her soft alluring locks,
By all the nymphs that nightly dance
Upon thy streams with wily glance,
Rise, rise, and heave thy rosy head
From thy coral-paven bed,
And bridle in thy headlong wave,
Till thou our summons answered have.
          Listen and save.

Sabrina rises, attended by water-nymphs, and sings.

   By the rushy-fringèd bank,
Where grows the willow and the osier dank,
   My sliding chariot stays,
Thick set with agate, and the azurn sheen
Of turkis blue, and emerald green
   That in the channel strays,
Whilst from off the waters fleet
Thus I set my printless feet
O'er the cowslip's velvet head,
   That bends not as I tread,
Gentle swain, at thy request
   I am here.

Spirit. Goddess dear
We implore thy powerful hand
To undo the charmèd band
Of true virgin here distressed,
Through the force, and through the wile
Of unblest enchanter vile.
Sabrina. Shepherd 'tis my office best
To help ensnarèd chastity;
Brightest Lady look on me,
Thus I sprinkle on thy breast
Drops that from my fountain pure,
I have kept of precious cure;

880. **Ligea:** another of the Sirens: Vergil described her shining tresses (*Georg.* 4.336).
893. **azurn:** azure.
894. **turkis:** turquoise.
897. **printless feet:** feet that leave no footprints; cp. Shakespeare, *TMP* 5.1.34.
904. **charmèd band:** bonds secured by a magical charm.
906. **force . . . wile:** On force and fraud as the two great instruments of achievement, see Machiavelli, *Discourses* 2.13.

Thrice upon thy finger's tip,
Thrice upon thy rubied lip,
Next this marble venomed seat
Smeared with gums of glutinous heat
I touch with chaste palms moist and cold,
Now the spell hath lost his hold;
And I must haste ere morning hour
To wait in Amphitrite's bower.

Sabrina descends, and the Lady rises out of her seat.

Spirit. Virgin, daughter of Locrine
Sprung of old Anchises' line,
May thy brimmèd waves for this
Their full tribute never miss
From a thousand petty rills,
That tumble down the snowy hills:
Summer drought, or singèd air
Never scorch thy tresses fair,
Nor wet October's torrent flood
Thy molten crystal fill with mud;
May thy billows roll ashore
The beryl and the golden ore;
May thy lofty head be crowned
With many a tower and terrace round,
And here and there thy banks upon
With groves of myrrh and cinnamon.
Come Lady while Heaven lends us grace,
Let us fly this cursèd place,
Lest the sorcerer us entice
With some other new device.
Not a waste or needless sound
Till we come to holier ground.
I shall be your faithful guide
Through this gloomy covert wide,
And not many furlongs thence
Is your father's residence,
Where this night are met in state

917. **glutinous:** sticky, gluey; critics often hear sexual undertones (Flosdorf 4–5; Kerrigan 1983, 45–48; Marcus 1983, 317).

918. **cold:** in antithesis to the heat of the previous line, and implying "chaste."

921. **Amphitrite:** wife of Neptune.

923. **Anchises' line:** the line of Trojan kings of Britain descended from Anchises, father of Aeneas; see Geoffrey of Monmouth, *History of Britain.*

924. **brimmèd:** full to the river's brim.

928. **singèd:** scorching.

Many a friend to gratulate
His wishèd presence, and beside
All the swains that there abide,
With jigs and rural dance resort;
We shall catch them at their sport,
And our sudden coming there
Will double all their mirth and cheer;
Come let us haste, the stars grow high,
But Night sits monarch yet in the mid sky.

The scene changes, presenting Ludlow Town and the President's castle. Then come in country dancers, after them the Attendant Spirit with the two brothers and the Lady.

Song

Spirit. Back, shepherds, back, enough your play,
Till next sunshine holiday,
Here be without duck or nod
Other trippings to be trod
Of lighter toes, and such court guise
As Mercury did first devise
With the mincing Dryades
On the lawns and on the leas.

This second song presents them to their father and mother.

Noble Lord, and Lady bright,
I have brought ye new delight,
Here behold so goodly grown
Three fair branches of your own;
Heav'n hath timely tried their youth,
Their faith, their patience, and their truth.

949. **gratulate:** welcome.

959. **sunshine holiday:** Cp. *L'All* 98.

960. **duck or nod:** awkward curtsy or bow.

961. **trippings:** dances.

962. **guise:** manner; the Attendant Spirit is contrasting the country dancers who have just performed with the court dancers about to perform.

963. **Mercury:** Though not the inventor of dance, he figured prominently in court masques, and his appearance here is doubly appropriate owing to his gift of Moly to Odysseus.

964. **mincing:** Quoted by the *OED* as an instance of "mincing" 1.b, "behaving in an affectedly dainty manner," but Demaray explains that "mince" is also "a dancing term that meant doubling the time to make twice as many steps to a musical measure" (118). While this meaning is not recorded in the *OED,* see Shakespeare, *MV* 3.4.67: "I'll . . . turn two mincing steps into a manly stride"; **Dryades:** forest nymphs.

970. **timely:** early.

970–71. The meter, the phrasing, the rhyme are all suggestive of Jonson (see *His Excuse for Loving*).

And sent them here through hard assays
With a crown of deathless praise,
To triumph in victorious dance
O'er sensual folly and intemperance.

The dances ended, the Spirit epilogizes.

Spirit. To the ocean now I fly,
And those happy climes that lie
Where day never shuts his eye,
Up in the broad fields of the sky:
There I suck the liquid air
All amidst the gardens fair
Of Hesperus, and his daughters three
That sing about the golden tree:
Along the crispèd shades and bow'rs
Revels the spruce and jocund Spring;
The Graces and the rosy-bosomed Hours,
Thither all their bounties bring,
There eternal Summer dwells,
And west winds with musky wing
About the cedarn alleys fling
Nard and Cassia's balmy smells.
Iris there with humid bow
Waters the odorous banks that blow
Flowers of more mingled hue
Than her purfled scarf can show,
And drenches with Elysian dew
(List mortals, if your ears be true)
Beds of hyacinth and roses

972. **assays:** trials.

976. **ocean:** In Plato (*Phaedo* 112e) the river Ocean lies on the genuine surface of the earth, which is among the stars.

980. **liquid:** clear, bright.

982–83. Hesiod, *Theog.* 215, says that the Hesperides "tend the fair apples beyond glorious Okeanos."

984. **crispèd shades:** leafy boughs *crisped* or curled by both leaves and shadows.

985. **spruce:** lively.

986. **Graces:** three goddesses who attended Venus and were in the Renaissance associated with a wide range of bounties; **Hours:** three goddesses who preside over the seasons. Graces and Hours dance together in *PL* 4.267.

988. In 1637, 1645, and *CMS,* this line began with "That," meaning "so that." But the word is canceled by the errata of 1673 (the last text Milton corrected).

990. **cedarn:** composed of cedars.

991. **Nard and Cassia:** fragrant plants.

992. **Iris:** goddess of the rainbow.

993. **blow:** bring into bloom.

995. **purfled:** variegated.

997. Cp. *PL* 7.30–31, where Milton also expresses his literary aspiration while dividing his audience into high and low, worthy and unworthy.

Where young Adonis oft reposes,
Waxing well of his deep wound
In slumber soft, and on the ground
Sadly sits th' Assyrian queen;
But far above in spangled sheen
Celestial Cupid, her famed son, advanced,
Holds his dear Psyche sweet entranced
After her wand'ring labors long,
Till free consent the gods among
Make her his eternal bride,
And from her fair unspotted side
Two blissful twins are to be born,
Youth and Joy; so Jove hath sworn.
    But now my task is smoothly done,
I can fly, or I can run
Quickly to the green earth's end,
Where the bowed welkin slow doth bend,
And from thence can soar as soon
To the corners of the moon.
    Mortals that would follow me,
Love Virtue, she alone is free;
She can teach ye how to climb
Higher than the sphery chime;
Or if Virtue feeble were,
Heav'n itself would stoop to her.

999. **Adonis:** Loved by Venus, he was killed by a boar, then brought back to life in the Garden of Adonis. Spenser's famous version of the Garden of Adonis (*FQ* 3.6.46–48) is set on this earth. Milton translates the locale to the heavens and fuses it with the garden of the Hesperides.

1000. **Waxing:** growing.

1002. Venus and Adonis make love in Spenser's garden but not in Milton's. Although recovery appears imminent, Venus is sad.

1004–8. Apuleius, *The Golden Ass* 4.28–6.24, tells the story of Cupid's love for the mortal Psyche (Gk. for "soul"). She underwent many trials before Venus allowed her to marry her son. See Milton's allusion to her in *Areop* (p. 938).

1004. **Celestial Cupid:** His double nature (son of Venus, yet residing on a celestial plane higher than hers) reminds some readers of Christ; **advanced:** raised, elevated.

1011. **Youth and Joy:** In Apuleius Psyche gives birth to Voluptas, in Spenser to Pleasure. Milton invents the twins and one of their identities (Joy was obviously suggested by Voluptas and Pleasure). Cp. Milton's *Apology* (p. 851): "The first and chiefest office of love begins and ends in the soul, producing those happy twins of her divine generation, knowledge and virtue."

1015. **bowed welkin:** either "arched vault of the sky" or "the vault of the sky arched by a rainbow"; **slow doth bend:** Beheld from the western boundary of the earth, the sky seems in its vastness to bend slowly.

1017. **corners of the moon:** horns of the moon.

1021. Above the spheres of the Ptolemaic universe and the music they make, which is to say, in Heaven.

1023. **stoop:** bow down, descend, with the paradoxical connotations of humbling oneself (*OED* 2a) and being condescending (*OED* 2c). In 1639 Milton, traveling abroad, copied the final two lines in the album of the Cerdogni family of Geneva.

LYCIDAS

The year 1637 must have seemed more than usually marked by death to the twenty-eight-year-old Milton. His mother, Sara, died on April 3. Soon thereafter the plague came to Horton, where Milton was living with his father, and lasted through August. Ben Jonson, intestate and apparently senile, died on August 6, and three days later was buried, amid a large party of mourners, under the pavement in the north aisle of Westminister Abbey. There were plans for a monument, but life moves on, and they came to nothing. On August 10, Edward King, a Fellow of Christ's College, Cambridge, preparing himself to become an Anglican clergyman, set sail from Chester Bay to visit his family in Ireland. While the vessel was coasting along the shores of northern Wales, it struck a rock. The only surviving account tells us that King was thrown onto his knees by the force of the collision and stayed there, praying, as the ship went down.

A volume of memorial elegies was planned by King's Cambridge friends. We have no evidence that Milton was a close acquaintance, but at such times the entire university community conventionally shared the grief. Milton was asked to contribute late in the death-packed year of 1637. In the Trinity College manuscript, *Lycidas* is dated "Novemb: 1637," the same month in which Milton was planning to take rooms in London. *Justa Eduardo King* (Obsequies for Edward King) was published in Cambridge at the University Press early in 1638. It was a twinned or double book, not unlike Milton's 1645 and 1673 *Poems,* in that it contained two title pages followed by separately paginated sections in different languages. The first, in Latin, introduced twenty-three elegies in Latin and Greek. The second and English title page, headed "Obsequies to the memory of Mr. Edward King," announced thirteen English poems. The last of these, and the final poem in the volume, was Milton's *Lycidas,* printed without a headnote and signed with his initials.

It is one of the most famous, most powerful, and most studied poems in English literature. Two anthologies provide good starting places for beginners. Scott Elledge's *Milton's "Lycidas": Edited to Serve as an Introduction to Criticism* is particularly focused on the tradition behind the poem and the precise sense of its words. C. A. Patrides's *Milton's Lycidas: The Tradition and the Poem* is more expansive and contains some of the best essays on the work written in the twentieth century, as well as a valuable review of the history of *Lycidas* criticism by M. H. Abrams (216–35).

In the end, Lycidas is appointed "genius of the shore," in which office he shall be good "to all that wander in that perilous flood." As an enduring presence in the minds of its readers, the poem *Lycidas* has often served as spiritual companion and guardian. On Ralph Waldo Emerson's first voyage to Europe, his ship encountered a fierce Atlantic storm, and for three days passengers lived in fear of drowning at sea. Emerson calmed himself by retrieving *Lycidas* from memory, "clause by clause, here a verse and there a word, as Isis in the fable the broken body of Osiris" (R. D. Richardson 131). The meaning of the poem, and the meaning of teaching the poem, are the twinned subjects of a remarkable short story, "Wash Far Away," by the poet and scholar John Berryman (1976).

The headnote was added in 1645. At that time, as Milton looked back on his pastoral elegy, he felt that the words of denunciation he had penned in 1637 for St. Peter (130–31) had prophesied the overthrow of the Anglican establishment.

In this monody the author bewails a learned friend, unfortunately drowned in his passage from Chester on the Irish Seas, 1637. And by occasion foretells the ruin of our corrupted clergy, then in their height.

Yet once more, O ye laurels, and once more
Ye myrtles brown, with ivy never sere,
I come to pluck your berries harsh and crude,
And with forced fingers rude,
Shatter your leaves before the mellowing year.
Bitter constraint, and sad occasion dear,
Compels me to disturb your season due:
For Lycidas is dead, dead ere his prime,
Young Lycidas, and hath not left his peer:
Who would not sing for Lycidas? He knew
Himself to sing, and build the lofty rhyme.
He must not float upon his wat'ry bier

Headnote: The headnote was added in 1645. The *CMS* has only the first sentence; **monody:** in Greek literature, a dirge performed by a single voice; **by occasion:** A main difference between Protestant and Catholic meditation in Milton's day is that the latter concentrated on preset subjects, while the former was prompted by events and was therefore "by occasion" (see the full title of Donne's *The Anatomy of the World* and Huntley 123).

1. **Yet once more:** Heb. 12.26–27, alluding to Hag. 2.6–7: "Yet once more I shake not the earth only, but also heaven. And this word, Yet once more, signifieth the removing of those things that are shaken, as of things that are made, that those things which cannot be shaken may remain." On the biographical and generic senses of the apocalyptic opening, see Tayler 1979, 48–50. **laurels:** the crown of the poet was traditionally woven of laurels, sacred to Apollo.

2. **myrtles:** sacred to Venus and symbolic of love or love poetry; **ivy:** sacred to Bacchus and sometimes symbolic of learning or immortality; **never sere:** evergreen.

3. **crude:** unripe.

4. **rude:** ungentle (*forced*) or unskilled.

5. **Shatter:** scatter, destroy.

6. **occasion:** see note to headnote; **dear:** heartfelt.

8. **Lycidas:** a reasonably common name in classical pastoral. See Theocritus 7 and 27.42; Bion 2, 6; Vergil, *Ec.* 7.67, 9, and also Milton's *Damon* 132. Herrick's *Hesperides* contains "An Eclogue or Pastoral between Endimion Porter and Lycidas Herrick." There appears to be no particular significance to Milton's choice of this name.

8–9. Cp. the repeated name in Spenser's *Astrophel:* "Young Astrophel, the pride of shepherds praise,/Young Astrophel, the rustic lasses love."

10. Cp. Vergil, *Ec.* 10.3: "Who would not sing for Gallus?"; **He knew:** he knew how.

11. **build:** a classical idiom, as in Horace, *Epod.* 1.3.24: "You build charming poetry"; **rhyme:** verse (not necessarily rhymed).

Unwept, and welter to the parching wind,
Without the meed of some melodious tear.
 Begin then, sisters of the sacred well,
That from beneath the seat of Jove doth spring;
Begin, and somewhat loudly sweep the string.
Hence with denial vain, and coy excuse;
So may some gentle muse
With lucky words favor my destined urn,
And as he passes turn,
And bid fair peace be to my sable shroud.
For we were nursed upon the self-same hill,
Fed the same flock, by fountain, shade, and rill.
 Together both, ere the high lawns appeared
Under the opening eyelids of the morn,
We drove afield, and both together heard
What time the grayfly winds her sultry horn,
Batt'ning our flocks with the fresh dews of night,
Oft till the star that rose, at evening, bright
Toward heav'n's descent had sloped his westering wheel.
Meanwhile the rural ditties were not mute,
Tempered to th' oaten flute,
Rough satyrs danced, and fauns with cloven heel
From the glad sound would not be absent long,

13. **welter:** roll to and fro.

14. **meed:** merited honor; **melodious tear:** poetic elegy. Collections of elegies issued by the universities were often entitled *Lacrymae* (Lat.: "tears").

15. **Begin then:** a formula for prompting the Muses found in Theocritus 1.64, the refrain of Moschus's *Lament for Bion,* and Vergil, *Ec.* 10.6; **well:** a spring, probably Aganippe on Mount Helicon, near the altar to Zeus, though sometimes explained as the Pierian spring, birthplace of the Muses, on Mount Olympus. Either could be referred to as the *seat of Jove.*

18. **coy:** shyly reserved or retiring.

19. **So:** on condition that I sing for Lycidas; **muse:** poet.

20. **lucky:** presaging good luck (by wishing me well); **urn:** grave.

22. **sable:** black.

23. **self-same hill:** probably Christ's College, Cambridge, which both Milton and King attended.

25. **lawns:** glades, the open spaces between woods.

26. **opening:** The 1638 edition read "glimmering"; **eyelids of the morn:** See Job 41.18.

28. **What time:** at the time when; **grayfly:** used of various insects; **winds:** blows; **sultry horn:** the metaphorical instrument by means of which grayflies hum in the midday heat. Browne discusses the question in *Pseudodoxia Epidemica* 3.27.10.

29. **Batt'ning:** fattening.

30. **star:** Hesperus, the evening star, whose appearance signals the shepherd to fold his flocks, as in *Masque* 93.

31. **westering:** Hesperus appears to set in the west.

32. **ditties:** In Milton's day the word *ditty* could refer to any kind of song and lacked the modern connotation of triviality.

33. **Tempered to:** attuned to; **oaten flute:** Pipes made from oat straw were traditional instruments of pastoral music.

34. **satyrs . . . fauns:** Greek *satyrs* had a human form, save for pointed ears and a tail. They were later identified with *fauns,* half human and half goat (*with cloven heel*).

And old Damaetas loved to hear our song.
But O the heavy change, now thou art gone,
Now thou art gone, and never must return!
Thee shepherd, thee the woods, and desert caves,
With wild thyme and the gadding vine o'ergrown,
And all their echoes mourn.
The willows, and the hazel copses green,
Shall now no more be seen,
Fanning their joyous leaves to thy soft lays.
As killing as the canker to the rose,
Or taint-worm to the weanling herds that graze,
Or frost to flowers, that their gay wardrobe wear,
When first the whitethorn blows;
Such, Lycidas, thy loss to shepherd's ear.
Where were ye nymphs when the remorseless deep
Closed o'er the head of your loved Lycidas?
For neither were ye playing on the steep,
Where your old bards, the famous Druids lie,
Nor on the shaggy top of Mona high,
Nor yet where Deva spreads her wizard stream:
Ay me, I fondly dream!
Had ye been there—for what could that have done?
What could the Muse herself that Orpheus bore,
The Muse herself, for her enchanting son
Whom universal Nature did lament,

36. **Damaetas:** a traditional pastoral name. Milton may have had a specific tutor in mind; William Chappell and Joseph Mede are the two most popular candidates.

39–44. In Moschus's *Lament for Bion,* the orchards and groves bewail his loss; see also Ovid on the death of Orpheus (*Met.* 11.44–46).

40. **gadding:** wandering.

45. **canker:** a name given to caterpillars and insect larvae that harmed the leaves and buds of plants.

46. **taint-worm:** possibly "husk," a parasite fatal to newly weaned sheep.

48. **whitethorn:** hawthorn.

50. **Where were ye nymphs:** Speakers in Theocritus (1.66–69) and Vergil (*Ec.* 10.9–12) also interrogate nymphs.

52. **steep:** This might refer to a mountain in Wales but probably alludes to an island, though which one the author had in mind remains unclear. Bardsey, whose name proclaims an association with bards, seems the best candidate, though it is not near the island of *Mona.* Milton may have been misled on Mona's proximity to Bardsey by an ambiguous Latin sentence in Camden's *Britannia.* See Hughes et al. 2:655 for details.

53. For a similar reference to the Druids as poets, see *Manso* 43.

54. **Mona:** Anglesey; Drayton, *Polyolbion* 9.425–29, remembering Tacitus, said that this island was once covered with sacred oaks (*shaggy*).

55. **Deva:** the river Dee, *wizard* because associated with magicians and divination.

56. **fondly:** foolishly; **dream:** give voice to the foolish thought "If only the Muses had been here."

58–63. The Muse is Calliope, inspirer of epic poetry. Her son Orpheus, still in love with Eurydice, was torn to pieces by the resentful Maenads, females devoted to Bacchus. All *Nature did lament* as his head, still singing, floated down the river Hebrus into the Aegean Sea, arriving finally at the island of Lesbos (Ovid, *Met.* 9.1–66; Vergil, *Georg.* 4.485–527). Cp. *PL* 7.32–38.

When by the rout that made the hideous roar,
His gory visage down the stream was sent,
Down the swift Hebrus to the Lesbian shore.
Alas! What boots it with uncessant care
To tend the homely slighted shepherd's trade,
And strictly meditate the thankless muse?
Were it not better done as others use,
To sport with Amaryllis in the shade,
Or with the tangles of Neaera's hair?
Fame is the spur that the clear spirit doth raise
(That last infirmity of noble mind)
To scorn delights, and live laborious days;
But the fair guerdon when we hope to find,
And think to burst out into sudden blaze,
Comes the blind Fury with th' abhorrèd shears,
And slits the thin-spun life. "But not the praise,"
Phoebus replied, and touched my trembling ears.
"Fame is no plant that grows on mortal soil,

61. **rout:** band (with negative connotation, as here).

64. **What boots it:** Of what advantage or profit is it?

65. **homely:** humble; **slighted:** treated with indifference or disdain; **shepherd's trade:** writing poetry.

66. **strictly:** rigorously (note *with uncessant care* in l. 64); **meditate the thankless muse:** compose poetry at the bidding of a muse who cannot protect me from death; the idiom "meditate the Muse" is found in Vergil, *Ec.* 1.2. Some editors take *thankless* to refer to an ungrateful public.

67. **use:** are accustomed to doing.

68. **Amaryllis:** Amaryllis, though she appears in Theocritus, is particularly associated with Vergil; see especially *Ec.* 2.14–16, since Milton evokes its phrasing.

69. **Neaera:** She appears in classical literature, and her hair was ever worthy of comment, but Milton almost certainly has in mind the Neaera of the sixteenth-century Dutch Neo-Latin lyricist Johannes Secundus (*Basia* 7, 8).

70. **Fame is the spur:** This declaration has become proverbial and is the title of a 1947 British film of a novel by the same name; **clear:** noble, pure (from Lat. *clarus*).

71. **That last infirmity of noble mind:** Milton is here imitating a classical maxim found in numerous writers, including Tacitus 4.6: "Even in the case of wise men the desire for glory is last cut off." Milton's contemporary Owen Felltham put it this way in *Of Fame:* "Desire of glory is the last garment that even wise men lay aside. For this we may trust Tacitus" (*Resolves* 47).

73. **guerdon:** reward (fame, in this case).

74. **sudden blaze:** flash of glory; *blaze* could mean "to make public." Cp. *PL* 10.453; *PR* 3.47.

75. **blind Fury with th' abhorrèd shears:** Atropos, the third of the Fates, is here represented as a *Fury,* normally thought of as an agent of vengeance, and as *blind,* not a usual attribute of either Fates or Furies. Death is fierce and purposeless.

76. **slits:** cuts (not lengthwise).

77. **touched my trembling ears:** echoing Vergil, *Ec.* 6.3–4, where the poet is probably alluding to Callimachus, *Aetia,* Fragment 1. The gesture both warns the poet to stop and reminds him of something he has forgotten. Also, in ancient Rome, witnesses were summoned by a touch on the ear. Masson's suggestion that a person's ears were thought to tingle when someone else was talking about him is probably irrelevant, since *trembling* is most likely a transferred epithet and refers to the trembling of the poet's ears *after* they have been touched by *Phoebus* Apollo. Apollo as the god of poetry appropriately concludes the first and classical section of the poem, in which shepherding represents writing poetry.

Nor in the glistering foil
Set off to th' world, nor in broad rumor lies,
But lives and spreads aloft by those pure eyes,
And perfect witness of all-judging Jove;
As he pronounces lastly on each deed,
Of so much fame in Heav'n expect thy meed."
O fountain Arethuse, and thou honored flood,
Smooth-sliding Mincius, crowned with vocal reeds,
That strain I heard was of a higher mood:
But now my oat proceeds,
And listens to the herald of the sea
That came in Neptune's plea.
He asked the waves, and asked the felon winds,
"What hard mishap hath doomed this gentle swain?"
And questioned every gust of rugged wings
That blows from off each beakèd promontory:
They knew not of his story,
And sage Hippotades their answer brings,
That not a blast was from his dungeon strayed;
The air was calm, and on the level brine,
Sleek Panope with all her sisters played.
It was that fatal and perfidious bark
Built in th' eclipse, and rigged with curses dark,
That sunk so low that sacred head of thine.
Next Camus, reverend sire, went footing slow,

79. **glistering foil:** thin leaf of gold or silver placed under a precious stone to enhance its brilliance.

80. **nor in broad rumor lies:** Cp. Pope, *Essay on Man:* "What's fame, a fancied life in other's breath?"

84. **meed:** reward (lifting the idea of fame as *guerdon* from earth to Heaven). See 14n.

85–87. The poem returns to pastoral after the "higher mood" of Phoebus's speech. *Arethuse,* invoked by Theocritus (1.117), represents Greek pastoral, while the river *Mincius,* celebrated by Vergil, represents Roman pastoral. The river god Alpheus pursued the nymph Arethusa, who turned into a river herself; they ran untainted through the sea and emerged, mingling, in the Sicilian spring named Arethusa.

87. **mood:** musical mode.

88. **oat:** pipe made from oat straw, whose song is symbolic of pastoral verse.

89–131. A procession of mourners is conventional in pastoral elegy. See Milton's *Damon* 69–90.

89. **herald:** Triton, Neptune's son.

90. **in Neptune's plea:** to plead Neptune's innocence of the charge of responsibility for Lycidas's (King's) death by calling a number of witnesses.

91. **felon:** wild, with also the sense of "criminal," in that the winds are at this point presumed to be guilty of Lycidas's death.

93–94. **beakèd promontory** and **rugged wings** is a classic example of transferred epithet: *beakèd* belongs with *wings* and *promontory* with *rugged.*

96. **Hippotades:** Aeolus, son of Hippotes and god of winds, who kept them imprisoned in a cavern (Vergil, *Aen.* 1.52–63).

99. **Panope:** one of the fifty Nereids (sea nymphs).

103. **Camus:** the god of the river Cam, representing Cambridge University; **footing slow:** The Cam does move slowly, but a fanciful pun on the derivation of *pedant* from the Italian *pedare* ("to foot it") has been suggested. A personification of Camus appears prominently in Phineas Fletcher's *Piscatory Eclogues.*

His mantle hairy, and his bonnet sedge,
Inwrought with figures dim, and on the edge
Like to that sanguine flower inscribed with woe.
"Ah! Who hath reft," quoth he, "my dearest pledge?"
Last came, and last did go,
The pilot of the Galilean lake;
Two massy keys he bore of metals twain
(The golden opes, the iron shuts amain).
He shook his mitred locks, and stern bespake,
"How well could I have spared for thee, young swain,
Enow of such as for their bellies' sake,
Creep and intrude, and climb into the fold?
Of other care they little reck'ning make,
Than how to scramble at the shearers' feast,
And shove away the worthy bidden guest.
Blind mouths! that scarce themselves know how to hold
A sheep-hook, or have learned aught else the least
That to the faithful herdman's art belongs!
What recks it them? What need they? They are sped;
And when they list, their lean and flashy songs
Grate on their scrannel pipes of wretched straw;

104. **hairy:** Academic gowns were fur-trimmed; **sedge:** a name applied to various plants growing near water. Crowns of sedge were conventional for river gods in masques.

105. **Inwrought:** worked in, sewn in.

106. **sanguine flower:** the hyacinth, on whose leaves Apollo inscribed AIAI ("Alas, alas"), because the plant sprang from the blood of his beloved Hyacinthus. See *Fair Infant* 23–27.

107. **reft:** taken; **pledge:** child. Cp. *PL* 2.818.

109. **pilot:** St. Peter, the fisherman of Galilee and founder of the Christian Church, to whom Jesus said he would give "the keys of the kingdom of Heaven" (Matt. 16), to bind and to loose. King had intended to take holy orders. For the two keys, see also *PL* 3.484–85 and *Areop* (p. 934).

111. **amain:** vehemently.

112. **mitred:** As the first bishop of the Christian Church, St. Peter wears a miter.

113. **for:** instead of; **swain:** shepherd.

113–29. This attack on ecclesiastical corruption resembles numerous passages from the Bible (Ezek. 34, John 10, 1 Peter 4) and Christian literature (Dante, *Par.* 27.55–57; Petrarch, *Ec.* 6 and 7; Spenser, *SC*, "May" and "September").

114. **Enow:** the plural of *enough.*

115. **climb:** John 10.1: "He that entereth not by the door into the sheepfold, but climbeth up some other way."

117. **scramble:** contend with a crowd for a share of food, coin, wealth (*OED* 2); **shearers' feast:** festive supper given to the workers after sheep shearing (thus metaphorical here for the temporal rewards of the priesthood).

119. **Blind mouths:** Ruskin's famous comment still seems definitive: "A 'bishop' means 'a person who sees.' A 'pastor' means 'a person who feeds.' The most unbishoply character a man can have is therefore to be blind. The most unpastoral is, instead of feeding, to want to be fed—to be a mouth. Take the two reverses together, and you have 'blind mouths'" (*Sesame and Lilies* 1.22).

120. **or have learned aught else:** In his prose works, Milton often railed against the ignorance of the Anglican clergy. See *Apology* (Yale 1:933–35) and *Eikon* (Yale 3:437–38).

121. **faithful herdman's art:** the offices of the priesthood.

122. **What recks it them?:** What do they care?; **sped:** satisfied, well off.

123. **list:** please; **lean:** because yielding no sustenance; **flashy:** insipid, watery (not the modern "showy").

124. **scrannel:** thin, harsh-sounding.

The hungry sheep look up, and are not fed,
But swoll'n with wind, and the rank mist they draw,
Rot inwardly, and foul contagion spread:
Besides what the grim wolf with privy paw
Daily devours apace, and nothing said.
But that two-handed engine at the door,
Stands ready to smite once, and smite no more."
  Return Alpheus, the dread voice is past
That shrunk thy streams; return Sicilian muse,
And call the vales, and bid them hither cast
Their bells, and flow'rets of a thousand hues.
Ye valleys low, where the mild whispers use
Of shades and wanton winds, and gushing brooks,
On whose fresh lap the swart star sparely looks,
Throw hither all your quaint enameled eyes,
That on the green turf suck the honeyed showers,
And purple all the ground with vernal flowers.
Bring the rathe primrose that forsaken dies,
The tufted crow-toe, and pale jessamine,
The white pink, and the pansy freaked with jet,
The glowing violet,
The musk-rose, and the well-attired woodbine,
With cowslips wan that hang the pensive head,

125. "They [the prelates] have fed themselves, and not their flocks" (*Animad* in Yale 1:726).

126. **swoll'n with wind:** suffering from the disease of sheep rot. Cp. the similar metaphor for the effects on the laity of ecclesiastical corruption in Petrarch, *Ec.* 6.21–31, 7.19–27, 9, and Dante, *Par.* 29.106–7; **draw:** inhale.

128. **grim wolf:** the Roman Catholic Church, especially the Jesuits, since the coat of arms of their founder, St. Ignatius, featured two gray wolves. Milton seems to be deploring the secret conversion of high-placed Anglicans to the old faith; **privy:** secret.

130. **two-handed engine:** The most famous crux in Milton. The phrasing (*smite once, and . . . no more*) recalls the opening lines (*Yet once more . . . and once more*) but with the shift from repetition to apocalyptic finality that St. Paul found in the very meaning of "Yet once more" (see 1n). Perhaps the most convincing of the many attempts to solve the crux is Tayler's identification of the two-handed engine with St. Peter's keys (1979, 234–36). **at the door:** ready to hand, soon to strike. Cp. Matt. 24.33.

132. **Alpheus:** See 85–87n.

135. **bells:** bell-shaped flowers.

136. **use:** haunt, habitually resort.

137. **shades:** tree-shaded places (B. A. Wright); **wanton:** unrestrained (blowing where they list).

138. **whose:** referring back to the *valleys low;* **swart star:** Sirius, the Dog Star, which rises during the hot "dog days" of summer. The star is *swart,* darkened by heat.

139. **quaint:** attractively adorned; **enameled:** many-colored.

141. **purple:** make bright.

142. **rathe:** early.

142–50. There are two versions of this passage in *CMS,* one of which is nearly identical to the printed text. The other, which has psychological interest, begins: "Bring the rathe primrose that unwedded dies/Colouring the pale cheek of unenjoyed love." Cp. Shakespeare, *WT* 4.4.122–24.

143. **tufted:** growing in clusters; **crow-toe:** wild hyacinth; **jessamine:** jasmine.

144. **freaked:** flecked or streaked.

146. **woodbine:** honeysuckle.

147. **wan:** pale.

Recalls Il Penseroso

Lycidas 33

and when they list thire leane and flashie songs
grate on thire scrannel pipes of wretched straw
the hungrie sheepe looke up and are not fed
but swolne wth wind, and the rank mist they draw
rot inwardly, and foule contagion spred
besides what the grim wolfe wth privie paw
dayly devours apace, and ~~nothing~~ sed little
but that two-handed engine at the dore
stands readie to smite once and smite no more
Returne Alpheus the dred voice is past
that shrunk thy streams, returne Sicilian Muse
and call the vales and bid them hither cast
thire bells and flowrets of a thousand hues
yee vallies low where the mild whispers use
of shades, and wanton winds, and gushing brooks
on whose fresh lap the swart starre ~~sparely~~ looks *sparely ~~faintly~~
*~~bring~~ hither all yor quaint enameld eyes *throw
that on the greene terfe suck the honied showrs
and purple all the ground wth ~~vernal flowrs~~ bring the rathe ...
to strew the laureat herse where Lycid lies
for so to interpose a little ease
let our ~~sad~~ *fraile thoughts dally wth false surmise
Ay mee whilst thee ~~floods~~ and sounding seas shores
wash farre away, where ere thy bones are hurld
whether beyond the stormie Hebrides
where thou perhapps under the humming tide
visitst the bottome of the monstrous world
or whether thou to our moist vows denied
sleepst by the fable of ~~Corineus~~ old Bellerus
where the great vision of the guarded mount
looks toward Namancos and Bayona's hold
looke homeward Angel now and melt wth ruth
and O yee Dolphins waft the haplesse youth
Weepe no more wofull shepheards weepe no more
for Lycidas yr ...

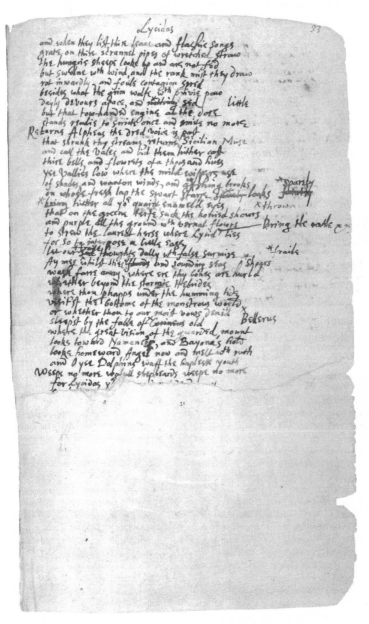

Lines 123–66 of *Lycidas,* from the Cambridge Manuscript.

And every flower that sad embroidery wears:
Bid amaranthus all his beauty shed,
And daffadillies fill their cups with tears,
To strew the laureate hearse where Lycid lies.
For so to interpose a little ease,
Let our frail thoughts dally with false surmise.
Ay me! Whilst thee the shores, and sounding seas
Wash far away, where'er thy bones are hurled,
Whether beyond the stormy Hebrides,
Where thou perhaps under the whelming tide
Visit'st the bottom of the monstrous world;
Or whether thou to our moist vows denied,
Sleep'st by the fable of Bellerus old,
Where the great vision of the guarded mount
Looks toward Namancos and Bayona's hold;
Look homeward angel now, and melt with ruth.
And, O ye dolphins, waft the hapless youth.
Weep no more, woeful shepherds, weep no more,
For Lycidas your sorrow is not dead,
Sunk though he be beneath the wat'ry floor,
So sinks the day-star in the ocean bed,
And yet anon repairs his drooping head,

148. **sad:** sober-colored; **embroidery:** markings on the flowers.

149. **amaranthus:** the name (from Gk. for "unfading") of both a genus of ornamental plants and an imaginary immortal flower (cp. *PL* 3.353–57).

151. **laureate:** decked with the laurels (both wreaths and poems) invoked in the poem's opening line. Memorial stanzas were sometimes attached to a hearse.

152–62. T. S. Eliot wrote of this passage that "for the single grandeur of sound, there is nothing finer in poetry" (*On Poetry and Poets,* 164).

153. **false surmise:** That the body of Lycidas lies on a laureate hearse is one false surmise; according to Brooks and Hardy (183), the ritual of strewing apparently sympathetic (but actually indifferent) flowers is another.

157. **whelming:** *CMS* and 1638 have "humming."

158. **bottom . . . world:** the bottom of the sea, a realm of monsters.

159. **moist vows:** tearful funeral rites.

160. **fable of Bellerus:** The hero or giant Bellerus seems to have been invented by Milton in order to make *Bellerium,* as Land's End is known in Latin, eponymous.

161. **great vision . . . mount:** According to Camden's *Britannia,* the archangel Michael appeared to monks on St. Michael's Mount. A section of the rock is called "St. Michael's Chair."

162. **Namancos and Bayona's hold:** the district of Namancos and the stronghold of Bayona in Spain, one of England's traditional enemies. Camden remarked that "there is no other place in this island [save Land's End] that looks towards Spain" (B. A. Wright).

163. **Look homeward angel:** Michael is asked to turn his gaze away from Spain to the Irish Sea, which somewhere contains the body of Lycidas.

164. **ye dolphins:** Dolphins are invoked to minister to the body primarily because they had performed this service for the poet Arion (Herodotus 1.24) and the infant Melicertes (Ovid, *Met.* 4.481–54). They have also served as symbols of the resurrection; **waft:** convey from sea to land.

165. The repeated *no more . . . no more* continues the pattern established in the opening lines and line 131, and shifts from apocalyptic finality (see 130n) to the certitude of faith, which ends mourning.

166. **your sorrow:** the object of your sorrow.

168. **day-star:** the sun.

And tricks his beams, and with new-spangled ore,
Flames in the forehead of the morning sky:
So Lycidas sunk low, but mounted high,
Through the dear might of him that walked the waves,
Where other groves, and other streams along,
With nectar pure his oozy locks he laves,
And hears the unexpressive nuptial song,
In the blest kingdoms meek of joy and love.
There entertain him all the saints above,
In solemn troops, and sweet societies
That sing, and singing in their glory move,
And wipe the tears for ever from his eyes.
Now, Lycidas, the shepherds weep no more;
Henceforth thou art the genius of the shore,
In thy large recompense, and shalt be good
To all that wander in that perilous flood.
Thus sang the uncouth swain to th' oaks and rills,
While the still Morn went out with sandals gray;
He touched the tender stops of various quills,
With eager thought warbling his Doric lay:
And now the sun had stretched out all the hills,
And now was dropped into the western bay;

170. **tricks:** dresses anew; **ore:** gold.

171. **forehead:** forefront. Shakespeare has "the forehead of the morning" in *COR* 2.1.57.

173. **him that walked the waves:** "A designation of our Saviour, by a miracle [Matt. 14.25–31] which bears an immediate reference to the subject of the poem" (Warton).

174. **groves, and other streams:** Cp. Rev. 22.1-2.

175. **nectar:** the drink of the gods; **oozy:** still wet from the sea; **laves:** washes.

176. **unexpressive:** inexpressible; **nuptial song:** the song sung at the nuptials of the lamb in Rev. 19.5.

178. **the saints above:** The word *saints* can mean "all of the redeemed in Heaven," but Milton also used it to refer to angels.

181. Cp. Rev. 21.4: "And God shall wipe away all tears from their eyes" (also Isa. 25.8). Milton transfers the action from God to the saints.

183. **genius:** the guardian spirit of a locality. A sudden shift from Christian to classical, as Milton again refuses to sever the two cultural traditions.

184. **thy large recompense:** God's generous recompense to Lycidas for his early and terrifying death.

185. The poet himself has been among the first to benefit from the offices of Lycidas.

186–93. The epilogue has the form of an *ottava rima* stanza (eight iambic pentameter lines rhyming abababcc).

186. **uncouth:** unknown, unskilled; **oaks and rills:** The pastoral community of shepherds, the processions of gods and goddesses, the divine speakers—all suddenly disappear. The poem was sung to an empty landscape.

188. **tender:** either frail or responsive; **stops:** finger holes; **various quills:** the hollow reeds of the shepherd's pipes, *various* because of the mixture of styles in the poem.

189. **With eager thought:** eager, that is, after the hesitant beginning; **Doric:** The earliest pastoral poets (Theocritus, Moschus, and Bion) wrote in the Doric dialect.

190. "The setting sun had stretched out the shadows of the hills."

At last he rose, and twitched his mantle blue:
Tomorrow to fresh woods, and pastures new.

192. **he:** For a moment *he* is ambiguously both the poet and the sun. The ambiguity is not dispelled by *twitched his mantle blue,* which could refer in some fashion to the morning sky. **twitched:** pulled up around his shoulders (in preparing to depart); **blue:** Literary shepherds mostly wore gray mantles, but blue ones were not unknown (William Browne, *Shepherd's Pipe* 2.37–38).

193. **fresh woods, and pastures new:** These could refer in general to changes in the future (editors often mention Milton's forthcoming journey to the continent), or to the landscape of Heaven that awaits the faithful. Poetically and autobiographically, they could also refer to the epic poem customarily undertaken after the completion of the young poet's pastoral songs.

PSALMS 80–88

Milton's headnote expresses a pronounced concern with the literalness of these efforts. Deviations from that standard must wear italics. As first printed in 1673, the translations also had marginal notes giving sometimes the Hebrew, sometimes a full English version of the Hebrew, at a few of the places where Milton expanded or paraphrased the original. This fussiness over what is and what is not in the Bible relates these Psalm translations to seventeenth-century controversies over the metrical Psalter. In 1647 the Westminster Assembly appointed a committee to revise the Francis Rous Psalter of 1641. For practical purposes they divided the Psalms into four groups, the third of which began, suggestively, with Psalm 80, just like Milton's group (Hunter 1961). Other political contexts have been explored (Boddy; Hill, 381–82).

The translations were given a date of April 1648 in the second edition of the *Poems.* Our notes make some use of Milton's original marginalia.

Nine of the Psalms done into meter, wherein all but what is in a different character, are the very words of the text, translated from the original.

Psalm 80

1) Thou shepherd that dost Israel *keep*
Give ear *in time of need,*
Who leadest like a flock of sheep
Thy lovèd Joseph's seed,
That sitt'st between the Cherubs *bright*
Between their wings outspread
Shine forth, *and from thy cloud give light,*
And on our foes thy dread.

2) In Ephraim's view and Benjamin's,
And in Manasseh's sight
Awake thy strength, come, and *be seen*
To save us *by thy might.*
3) Turn us again, *thy grace divine*
To us O God *vouchsafe;*
Cause thou thy face on us to shine
And then we shall be safe.
4) Lord God of Hosts, how long wilt thou,
How long wilt thou declare
Thy smoking wrath *and angry brow*
Against thy people's prayer?
5) Thou feed'st them with the bread of tears,
Their bread with tears they eat,
And mak'st them largely drink the tears
Wherewith their cheeks are wet.
6) A strife thou mak'st us *and a prey*
To every neighbor foe;
Among themselves they laugh, they play,
And flouts at us they throw.
7) Return us, *and thy grace divine,*
O God of Hosts *vouchsafe;*
Cause thou thy face on us to shine,
And then we shall be safe.
8) A vine from Egypt thou hast brought,
Thy free love made it thine,
And drov'st out nations *proud and haught*
To plant this *lovely* vine.
9) Thou didst prepare for it a place
And root it deep and fast
That it *began to grow apace,*
And filled the land *at last.*
10) With her *green* shade *that* covered *all,*
The hills were *overspread;*
Her boughs *as high as* cedars tall
Advanced their lofty head.
11) Her branches *on the western side*
Down to the sea she sent,
And *upward* to that river *wide*
Her other branches *went.*

11. **Awake:** *Gnorera* means "arouse."
19. **smoking wrath:** *Gnashanta* means "you are smoking."
23. **largely:** *Shalish* means "third of a measure."
27–28. **laugh . . . throw:** *Jilgnagu* means "mock."

12) Why hast thou laid her hedges low
And broken down her fence,
That all may pluck her, as they go,
With rudest violence?
13) The *tuskèd* boar out of the wood
Upturns it by the roots,
Wild beasts there browse, and make their food
Her grapes and tender shoots.
14) Return now, God of Hosts, look down
From Heav'n, thy seat divine,
Behold *us, but without a frown,*
And visit this *thy* vine.
15) Visit this vine, which thy right hand
Hath set, and planted *long,*
And the young branch, that for thyself
Thou hast made firm and strong.
16) But now it is consumed with fire,
And cut *with axes* down;
They perish at thy dreadful ire,
At thy rebuke and frown.
17) Upon the man of thy right hand
Let thy *good* hand be *laid,*
Upon the Son of Man, whom thou
Strong for thyself hast made.
18) So shall we not go back from thee
To ways of sin and shame,
Quicken us thou, then *gladly* we
Shall call upon thy name.
Return us, *and thy grace divine*
Lord God of Hosts *vouchsafe,*
Cause thou thy face on us to shine,
And then we shall be safe.

Psalm 81

1) To God our strength sing loud, *and clear*
Sing loud to God *our King,*
To Jacob's God, *that all may hear*
Loud acclamations ring.
2) Prepare a hymn, prepare a song,
The timbrel hither bring;
The *cheerful* psalt'ry bring along
And harp *with* pleasant *string;*
3) Blow, *as is wont,* in the new moon

With trumpets' *lofty sound,*
Th' appointed time, the day whereon
Our solemn feast *comes round.*
4) This was a statute *giv'n of old*
For Israel *to observe,*
A law of Jacob's God, *to hold*
From whence they might not swerve.
5) This he a testimony ordained
In Joseph, *not to change,*
When as he passed through Egypt land;
The tongue I heard, was strange.
6) From burden, *and from slavish toil*
I set his shoulder free;
His hands from pots, *and miry soil*
Delivered were *by me.*
7) When trouble did thee sore assail,
On me then didst thou call,
And I to free thee *did not fail,*
And led thee out of thrall.
I answered thee in thunder deep
With clouds encompassed round;
I tried thee at the water *steep*
Of Meriba *renowned.*
8) Hear O my people, *hearken well,*
I testify to thee
Thou ancient stock of Israel,
If thou wilt list to me,
9) Throughout the land of thy abode
No alien god shall be,
Nor shalt thou to a foreign god
In honor bend thy knee.
10) I am the Lord thy God which brought
Thee out of Egypt land;
Ask large enough, and I, *besought,*
Will grant thy full demand.
11) And yet my people would not *hear,*
Nor hearken to my voice;
And Israel *whom I loved so dear*
Misliked me for his choice.
12) Then did I leave them to their will
And to their wand'ring mind;

29. **in thunder deep:** *Besether ragnam* means "in the secret place of thunder."

Their own conceits they followed still,
Their own devices blind.
13) O that my people would *be wise*
To serve me *all their days,*
And O that Israel would *advise*
To walk my *righteous* ways.
14) Then would I soon bring down their foes
That now so proudly rise,
And turn my hand against *all those*
That are their enemies.
15) Who hate the Lord should *then be fain*
To bow to him and bend,
But *they, his people, should remain,*
Their time should have no end.
16) And we would feed them *from the shock*
With flour of finest wheat,
And satisfy them from the rock
With honey *for their meat.*

Psalm 82

1) God in the great assembly stands
Of kings and lordly states,
Among the gods on both his hands
He judges and debates.
2) How long will ye pervert the right
With judgment false and wrong,
Favoring the wicked *by your might,*
Who thence grow bold and strong?
3) Regard the weak and fatherless,
Despatch the poor man's cause,
And raise the man in deep distress
By just and equal laws.
4) Defend the poor and desolate,
And rescue from the hands
Of wicked men the low estate
Of him *that help demands.*
5) They know not nor will understand,
In darkness they walk on;

1. **great assembly:** *Bagnadath-el* means "assembly of God."

3. **Among . . . hands:** *Bekerev* means "in the midst of."

5–6. **pervert . . . wrong:** *Tishphetu gnavel* means "judge falsely."

9–10. **Regard . . . cause:** *Shiphtu-dal* means "judge the poor."

The earth's foundations are all moved
    And out of order gone.
6) I said that ye were gods, yea all
    The sons of God most high,
7) But ye shall die like men, and fall
    As other princes *die.*
8) Rise God, judge thou the earth *in might,*
    This *wicked* earth redress,
For thou art he who shalt by right
    The nations all possess.

19–20. **moved . . . gone:** *Jimmotu* means "moved."

25–26. **judge . . . redress:** *Shophta* means "judge."

Psalm 83

1) Be not thou silent *now at length,*
    O God hold not thy peace,
Sit not thou still O God of *strength,*
    We cry and do not cease.
2) For lo thy *furious* foes *now* swell
    And storm outrageously,
And they that hate thee *proud and fell*
    Exalt their heads full high.
3) Against thy people they contrive
    Their plots and counsels deep;
Them to ensnare they chiefly strive
    Whom thou dost hide and keep.
4) "Come let us cut them off," say they,
    "Till they no nation be,
That Israel's name forever may
    Be lost in memory."
5) For they consult with all their might,
    And all as one in mind
Themselves against thee they unite
    And in firm union bind.
6) The tents of Edom, and the brood
    Of *scornful* Ishmael,
Moab, with them of Hagar's blood

5–6. **swell . . . outrageously:** *Jehemajun* means "are in tumult."

9–10. **contrive . . . counsels:** *Jagnarimu Sod* means "deliberate cunningly."

11. **Them to ensnare:** *Jithjagnatsu gnal* means "conspire against."

12. **Whom . . . keep:** *Tsephuneca* means "your hidden things."

17. **with all their might:** *Lev jachdau* means "together with one heart."

That in the desert dwell,
7) Gebal and Ammon *there conspire,*
And *hateful* Amalek,
The Philistines, and they of Tyre
Whose bounds the sea doth check.
8) With them *great* Ashur also bands
And doth confirm the knot;
All these have lent their armèd hands
To aid the sons of Lot.
9) Do to them as to Midian *bold*
That wasted all the coast,
To Sisera, and as *is told*
Thou didst to Jabin's *host,*
When at the brook of Kishon *old*
They were repulsed and slain,
10) At Endor quite cut off, and rolled
As dung upon the plain.
11) As Zeb and Oreb evil sped
So let their princes speed,
As Zeba, and Zalmunna *bled*
So let their princes *bleed.*
12) *For they amidst their pride* have said,
"By right now shall we seize
God's houses, and *will now invade*
Their stately palaces."
13) My God, O make them as a wheel,
No quiet let them find,
Giddy and *restless* let *them reel*
Like stubble from the wind.
14) As *when* an *aged* wood takes fire
Which on a sudden strays,
The *greedy* flame runs higher and higher
Till all the mountains blaze;
15) So with thy whirlwind them pursue,
And with thy tempest chase;
16) And till they yield thee honor due,
Lord fill with shame their face.
17) Ashamed and troubled let them be,
Troubled and shamed forever,
Ever confounded, and so die

47–48. **God's houses . . . stately palaces:** Milton's note asserts that the Hebrew *Neoth Elihim* can mean both English phrases.

With shame, *and 'scape it never.*
18) Then shall they know that thou whose name
Jehovah is alone,
Art the Most High, *and thou the same*
O'er all the earth *art one.*

Psalm 84

1) How lovely are thy dwellings fair!
O Lord of Hosts, how dear
The *pleasant* tabernacles are!
Where thou dost dwell so near.
2) My soul doth long and almost die
Thy courts O Lord to see;
My heart and flesh aloud do cry,
O living God, for thee.
3) There ev'n the sparrow *freed from wrong*
Hath found a house of *rest;*
The swallow there, to lay her young
Hath built her *brooding* nest;
Ev'n *by* thy altars Lord of Hosts
They find their safe abode,
And home they fly from round the coasts
Toward thee, my King, my God.
4) Happy, who in thy house reside
Where thee they ever praise;
5) Happy, whose strength in thee doth bide,
And in their hearts thy ways.
6) They pass through Baca's *thirsty* vale,
That dry and barren ground,
As through a fruitful wat'ry dale
Where springs and show'rs abound.
7) They journey on from strength to strength
With joy and gladsome cheer
Till all before *our* God at *length*
In Sion do appear.
8) Lord God of Hosts hear *now* my prayer,
O Jacob's God give ear;
9) Thou God our shield look on the face
Of thy anointed *dear.*
10) For one day in thy courts *to be*
Is better, *and more blest*
Than *in the joys of vanity,*
A thousand days *at best.*

I in the temple of my God
Had rather keep a door,
Than dwell in tents, *and rich abode*
With sin *for evermore.*
11) For God the Lord both sun and shield
Gives grace and glory *bright;*
No good from them shall be withheld
Whose ways are just and right.
12) Lord *God* of Hosts *that reign'st on high,*
That man is *truly* blest,
Who *only* on thee doth rely,
And in thee only rest.

Psalm 85

1) Thy land to favor graciously
Thou hast not Lord been slack;
Thou hast from *hard* captivity
Returnèd Jacob back.
2) Th' iniquity thou didst forgive
That wrought thy people woe,
And all their sin, *that did thee grieve*
Hast hid *where none shall know.*
3) Thine anger all thou hadst removed,
And *calmly* didst return
From thy fierce wrath which we had proved
Far worse than fire to burn.
4) God of our saving health and peace,
Turn us, and us restore;
Thine indignation cause to cease
Toward us, *and chide no more.*
5) Wilt thou be angry without end,
For ever angry thus?
Wilt thou thy frowning ire extend
From age to age on us?
6) Wilt thou not turn, and *hear our voice*
And us again revive,
That so thy people may rejoice
By thee preserved alive?
7) Cause us to see thy goodness Lord,
To us thy mercy show;
Thy saving health to us afford
And life in us renew.
8) *And now* what God the Lord will speak

I will *go straight and* hear,
For to his people he speaks peace
And to his saints *full dear;*
To his dear saints he will speak peace,
But let them never more
Return to folly, *but surcease*
To trespass as before.
9) Surely to such as do him fear
Salvation is at hand
And Glory shall *ere long appear*
To dwell within our land.
10) Mercy and Truth *that long were missed*
Now *joyfully* are met;
Sweet Peace and Righteousness have kissed
And hand in hand are set.
11) Truth from the earth *like to a flow'r*
Shall bud and blossom *then,*
And Justice from her Heav'nly bower
Look down *on mortal men.*
12) The Lord will also then bestow
Whatever thing is good;
Our land shall forth in plenty throw
Her fruits *to be our food.*
13) Before him Righteousness shall go
His royal harbinger,
Then will he come, and not be slow;
His footsteps cannot err.

Psalm 86

1) Thy *gracious* ear, O Lord, incline,
O hear me *I thee pray,*
For I am poor, and almost pine
With need, *and sad decay.*
2) Preserve my soul, for I have trod
Thy ways, and love the just;
Save thou thy servant O my God
Who *still* in thee doth trust.
3) Pity me Lord for daily thee
I call; 4) O make rejoice
Thy servant's soul; for Lord to thee
I lift my soul *and voice;*
5) For thou art good, thou Lord art prone
To pardon, thou to all

Art full of mercy, thou *alone*
   To them that on thee call.
6) Unto my supplication Lord
   Give ear, and to the cry
Of my *incessant* prayers afford
   Thy hearing graciously.
7) I in the day of my distress
   Will call on thee *for aid;*
For thou wilt *grant* me *free access*
   And answer, *what I prayed.*
8) Like thee among the gods is none
   O Lord, nor any works
Of all that other gods have done
   Like to thy *glorious* works.
9) The nations all whom thou hast made
   Shall come, *and all shall frame*
To bow them low before thee Lord,
   And glorify thy name.
10) For great thou art, and wonders great
   By thy strong hand are done;
Thou *in thy everlasting seat*
   Remainest God alone.
11) Teach me O Lord thy way *most right;*
   I in thy truth will bide;
To fear thy name my heart unite,
   So shall it never slide.
12) Thee will I praise O Lord my God
   Thee honor, and adore
With my whole heart, and blaze abroad
   Thy name for evermore.
13) For great thy mercy is toward me,
   And thou hast freed my soul,
Ev'n from the lowest Hell set free,
   From deepest darkness foul.
14) O God the proud against me rise
   And violent men are met
To seek my life, and in their eyes
   No fear of thee have set.
15) But thou Lord art the God most mild,
   Readiest thy grace to show,
Slow to be angry, and *art styled*
   Most merciful, most true.
16) O turn to me *thy face at length,*
   And me have mercy on;

Unto thy servant give thy strength,
And save thy handmaid's son.
17) Some sign of good to me afford,
And let my foes *then* see
And be ashamed, because thou Lord
Dost help and comfort me.

Psalm 87

1) Among the holy mountains *high*
Is his foundation fast,
There seated in his sanctuary,
His temple there is placed.
2) Sion's *fair* gates the Lord loves more
Than all the dwellings *fair*
Of Jacob's *land, though there be store,*
And all within his care.
3) City of God, most glorious things
Of thee *abroad* are spoke;
4) I mention Egypt, *where proud kings*
Did our forefathers yoke;
I mention Babel to my friends,
Philistia *full of scorn,*
And Tyre with Ethiop's *utmost ends:*
Lo this man there was born.
5) But *twice that praise shall in our ear*
Be said of Sion *last:*
This and this man was born in her,
High God shall fix her fast.
6) The Lord shall write it in a scroll
That ne'er shall be outworn,
When he the nations doth enroll,
That this man there was born.
7) Both they who sing, and they who dance
With sacred songs are there,
In thee *fresh brooks, and soft streams glance*
And all my fountains *clear.*

Psalm 88

1) Lord God that dost me save and keep,
All day to thee I cry;
And all night long, before thee *weep*
Before thee *prostrate lie.*

2) Into thy presence let my prayer
With sighs devout ascend;
And to my cries, that *ceaseless are,*
Thine ear with favor bend.
3) For cloyed with woes and trouble store
Surcharged my soul doth lie;
My life *at death's uncheerful door*
Unto the grave draws nigh.
4) Reckoned I am with them that pass
Down to the *dismal* pit;
I am a man, but weak alas
And for that name unfit.
5) From life discharged and parted quite
Among the dead *to sleep,*
And like the slain *in bloody fight*
That in the grave lie *deep,*
Whom thou rememberest no more,
Dost never more regard:
Them from thy hand delivered o'er
Death's hideous house hath barred.
6) Thou in the lowest pit *profound*
Hast set me *all forlorn,*
Where thickest darkness *hovers round,*
In horrid deeps *to mourn.*
7) Thy wrath *from which no shelter saves*
Full sore doth press on me;
Thou break'st upon me all thy waves,
And all thy waves break me.
8) Thou dost my friends from me estrange,
And mak'st me odious,
Me to them odious, *for they change,*
And I here pent up thus.
9) Through sorrow, and affliction great
Mine eye grows dim and dead;
Lord all the day I thee entreat,
My hands to thee I spread.
10) Wilt thou do wonders on the dead,
Shall the deceased arise
And praise thee *from their loathsome bed*
With pale and hollow eyes?
11) Shall they thy loving kindness tell

31–32. **Thou break'st . . . break me:** Although Milton's note claims that either line 31 or line 32 would correctly translate the original, only the first would.

On whom the grave *hath hold,*
Or they *who* in perdition *dwell*
Thy faithfulness *unfold?*
12) In darkness can thy mighty *hand*
Or wondrous acts be known,
Thy justice in the *gloomy* land
Of *dark* oblivion?
13) But I to thee O Lord do cry
Ere yet my life be spent,
And *up to thee* my prayer *doth hie*
Each morn, and thee prevent.
14) Why wilt thou Lord my soul forsake,
And hide thy face from me,
15) That am already bruised, and shake
With terror sent from thee;
Bruised, and afflicted and *so low*
As ready to expire,
While I thy terrors undergo
Astonished with thine ire.
16) Thy fierce wrath over me doth flow,
Thy threat'nings cut me through.
17) All day they round about me go,
Like waves they me pursue.
18) Lover and friend thou hast removed
And severed from me far.
They *fly me now* whom I have loved,
And as in darkness are.

59. **shake:** Milton seems not to have considered that the Hebrew word can also be taken to mean "youth."

PSALMS 1–8

Milton's headnotes give the precise date of each of these translations except for the first.

There is more metrical variety here than in the group from 1648. These translations also have a strikingly high percentage of run-on lines. Their relationship to political circumstances has been variously assessed (Fixler 182; Hill 383). Others (Studley, Rohr-Sauer) stress the fact that Milton had been blind for only a year and a half in August 1653, and call attention in particular to the rendering of blindness in Psalm 6.

Psalm 1

Done into verse, 1653

Blest is the man who hath not walked astray
In counsel of the wicked, and i' th' way
Of sinners hath not stood, and in the seat
Of scorners hath not sat. But in the great
Jehovah's law is ever his delight,
And in his law he studies day and night.
He shall be as a tree which planted grows
By wat'ry streams, and in his season knows
To yield his fruit, and his leaf shall not fall,
And what he takes in hand shall prosper all.
Not so the wicked, but as chaff which fanned
The wind drives, so the wicked shall not stand
In judgment, or abide their trial then,
Nor sinners in th' assembly of just men.
For the Lord knows th' upright way of the just,
And the way of bad men to ruin must.

Psalm 2

Here Milton uses *terza rima,* Dante's measure, where propulsive force is customarily provided by rhyme, not syntax, because the second and unrhymed line of each tercet supplies the rhyme-sound for the next tercet. Lawrence Binyon, poet and translator of Dante, clearly felt a kind of formal violence in Milton's lawless, overflowing syntax: "In the *Divina Commedia* each tercet is a stanza complete in itself, and almost always closed by a full stop. . . . Milton, with his instinct for moving on in a continuous motion and making his pauses without reference to the stanza, largely annuls the value of the rhymes" (185).

Done August 8, 1653. Terzetti

Why do the Gentiles tumult, and the nations
  Muse a vain thing, the kings of th' earth upstand
  With power, and princes in their congregations
Lay deep their plots together through each land,
  Against the Lord and his Messiah dear?
  Let us break off, say they, by strength of hand

Their bonds, and cast from us, no more to wear,
    Their twisted cords: he who in Heaven doth dwell
    Shall laugh, the Lord shall scoff them, then severe
Speak to them in his wrath, and in his fell
    And fierce ire trouble them; but I saith he
    Anointed have my king (though ye rebel)
On Sion my holy hill. A firm decree
    I will declare; the Lord to me hath said,
    Thou art my Son, I have begotten thee
This day; ask of me, and the grant is made;
    As thy possession I on thee bestow
    Th' heathen, and as thy conquest to be swayed
Earth's utmost bounds: them shalt thou bring full low
    With iron scepter bruised, and them disperse
    Like to a potter's vessel shivered so.
And now be wise at length ye kings averse,
    Be taught ye judges of the earth; with fear
    Jehovah serve, and let your joy converse
With trembling; kiss the Son lest he appear
    In anger and ye perish in the way,
    If once his wrath take fire like fuel sere.
Happy all those who have in him their stay.

Psalm 3

August 9, 1653
When he fled from Absalom

Lord how many are my foes,
        How many those
    That in arms against me rise.
        Many are they
    That of my life distrustfully thus say,
"No help for him in God there lies."
But thou Lord art my shield, my glory;
        Thee through my story
    Th' exalter of my head I count;
        Aloud I cried
    Unto Jehovah; he full soon replied
And heard me from his holy mount.
I lay and slept, I waked again,
        For my sustain
    Was the Lord. Of many millions
        The populous rout

I fear not though encamping round about
They pitch against me their pavilions.
Rise Lord, save me my God for thou
Hast smote ere now
On the cheek-bone all my foes,
Of men abhorred
Hast broke the teeth. This help was from the Lord;
Thy blessing on thy people flows.

Psalm 4

August 10, 1653

Answer me when I call,
God of my righteousness;
In straits and in distress
Thou didst me disenthrall
And set at large; now spare,
Now pity me, and hear my earnest prayer.
Great ones how long will ye
My glory have in scorn,
How long be thus forborne
Still to love vanity,
To love, to seek, to prize
Things false and vain and nothing else but lies?
Yet know the Lord hath chose,
Chose to himself apart
The good and meek of heart
(For whom to choose he knows);
Jehovah from on high
Will hear my voice what time to him I cry.
Be awed, and do not sin,
Speak to your hearts alone,
Upon your beds, each one,
And be at peace within.
Offer the offerings just
Of righteousness and in Jehovah trust.
Many there be that say
Who yet will show us good?
Talking like this world's brood;
But Lord, thus let me pray,
On us lift up the light,
Lift up the favor of thy count'nance bright.
Into my heart more joy

And gladness thou hast put
Than when a year of glut
Their stores doth over-cloy
And from their plenteous grounds
With vast increase their corn and wine abounds.
In peace at once will I
Both lay me down and sleep,
For thou alone dost keep
Me safe where'er I lie;
As in a rocky cell
Thou Lord alone in safety mak'st me dwell.

Psalm 5

August 12, 1653

Jehovah to my words give ear,
My meditation weigh,
The voice of my complaining hear,
My King and God, for unto thee I pray.
Jehovah thou my early voice
Shalt in the morning hear;
I' th' morning I to thee with choice
Will rank my prayers, and watch till thou appear.
For thou art not a God that takes
In wickedness delight;
Evil with thee no biding makes;
Fools or mad men stand not within thy sight.
All workers of iniquity
Thou hat'st; and them unblest
Thou wilt destroy that speak a lie;
The bloody and guileful man God doth detest.
But I will in thy mercies dear,
Thy numerous mercies, go
Into thy house; I in thy fear
Will towards thy holy temple worship low.
Lord lead me in thy righteousness,
Lead me because of those
That do observe if I transgress;
Set thy ways right before, where my step goes.
For in his falt'ring mouth unstable
No word is firm or sooth;
Their inside, troubles miserable;
An open grave their throat, their tongue they smooth.

God, find them guilty, let them fall
By their own counsels quelled;
Push them in their rebellions all
Still on; for against thee they have rebelled;
Then all who trust in thee shall bring
Their joy, while thou from blame
Defend'st them; they shall ever sing
And shall triumph in thee, who love thy name.
For thou Jehovah wilt be found
To bless the just man still,
As with a shield thou wilt surround
Him with thy lasting favor and good will.

Psalm 6

August 13, 1653

Lord in thine anger do not reprehend me,
Nor in thy hot displeasure me correct;
Pity me Lord for I am much deject,
Am very weak and faint; heal and amend me,
For all my bones, that even with anguish ache,
Are troubled, yea my soul is troubled sore;
And thou O Lord how long? Turn Lord, restore
My soul, O save me for thy goodness' sake,
For in death no remembrance is of thee;
Who in the grave can celebrate thy praise?
Wearied I am with sighing out my days,
Nightly my couch I make a kind of sea;
My bed I water with my tears; mine eye
Through grief consumes, is waxen old and dark
I' th' midst of all mine enemies that mark.
Depart all ye that work iniquity.
Depart from me, for the voice of my weeping
The Lord hath heard, the Lord hath heard my prayer;
My supplication with acceptance fair
The Lord will own, and have me in his keeping.
Mine enemies shall all be blank and dashed
With much confusion; then grow red with shame;
They shall return in haste the way they came
And in a moment shall be quite abashed.

Psalm 7

August 14, 1653
Upon the words of Chush the Benjamite against him

Lord my God to thee I fly;
Save me and secure me under
Thy protection while I cry,
Lest as a lion (and no wonder)
He haste to tear my soul asunder,
Tearing and no rescue nigh.

Lord my God if I have thought
Or done this, if wickedness
Be in my hands, if I have wrought
Ill to him that meant me peace,
Or to him have rendered less,
And not freed my foe for naught;

Let th' enemy pursue my soul
And overtake it, let him tread
My life down to the earth and roll
In the dust my glory dead,
In the dust and there outspread
Lodge it with dishonor foul.

Rise Jehovah in thine ire,
Rouse thyself amidst the rage
Of my foes that urge like fire;
And wake for me, their fury assuage;
Judgment here thou didst engage
And command which I desire.

So th' assemblies of each nation
Will surround thee, seeking right,
Thence to thy glorious habitation
Return on high and in their sight.
Jehovah judgeth most upright
All people from the world's foundation.

Judge me Lord, be judge in this
According to my righteousness
And the innocence which is
Upon me: cause at length to cease

Of evil men the wickedness
And their power that do amiss.

But the just establish fast,
Since thou art the just God that tries
Hearts and reins. On God is cast
My defense, and in him lies,
In him who both just and wise
Saves th' upright of heart at last.

God is a just judge and severe,
And God is every day offended;
If th' unjust will not forbear,
His sword he whets, his bow hath bended
Already, and for him intended
The tools of death, that waits him near.

(His arrows purposely made he
For them that persecute.) Behold
He travails big with vanity,
Trouble he hath conceived of old
As in a womb, and from that mold
Hath at length brought forth a lie.

He digged a pit, and delved it deep,
And fell into the pit he made;
His mischief that due course doth keep,
Turns on his head, and his ill trade
Of violence will undelayed
Fall on his crown with ruin steep.

Then will I Jehovah's praise
According to his justice raise,
And sing the name and deity
Of Jehovah the Most High.

Psalm 8

August 14, 1653

O Jehovah our Lord how wondrous great
    And glorious is thy name through all the earth!
So as above the heavens thy praise to set
    Out of the tender mouths of latest birth,

Out of the mouths of babes and sucklings thou
Hast founded strength because of all thy foes
To stint th' enemy, and slack th' avenger's brow
That bends his rage thy providence to oppose.

When I behold thy heavens, thy fingers' art,
The moon and stars which thou so bright hast set
In the pure firmament, then saith my heart,
O what is man that thou rememb'rest yet,

And think'st upon him; or of man begot
That him thou visit'st and of him art found?
Scarce to be less than gods, thou mad'st his lot,
With honor and with state thou hast him crowned.

O'er the works of thy hand thou mad'st him Lord,
Thou hast put all under his lordly feet,
All flocks, and herds, by thy commanding word,
All beasts that in the field or forest meet,

Fowl of the heavens, and fish that through the wet
Sea-paths in shoals do slide, and know no dearth.
O Jehovah our Lord how wondrous great
And glorious is thy name through all the earth.

"Fix here"

When Alfred Norwood found Milton's *Commonplace Book* in 1874, he also discovered this couplet written on the back of a letter from Henry Lawes.

Fix here ye overdated spheres
That wing the restless foot of time.

1. **overdated:** outdated, worn out.

TRANSLATIONS FROM THE PROSE WORKS

FROM *Of Reformation* (1641)

1)

Ah Constantine, of how much ill was cause
Not thy conversion, but those rich domains
That the first wealthy Pope received of thee.

Dante, *Inferno* 19.115–17

2)

Founded in chaste and humble poverty,
'Gainst them that raised thee dost thou lift thy horn?
Impudent whore, where hast thou placed thy hope?
In thy adulterers, or thy ill-got wealth?
Another Constantine comes not in haste.

Petrarch, *Rime* 138.9–13

3)

And to be short, at last his guide him brings
Into a goodly valley, where he sees
A mighty mass of things strangely confused,
Things that on earth were lost, or were abused.

Ariosto, *Orlando Furioso* 34.73

4)

Then passed he to a flow'ry mountain green,
Which onced smelt sweet, now stinks as odiously;
This was that gift (if you the truth will have)
That Constantine to good Sylvestro gave.

Ariosto, *Orlando Furioso* 34.80

FROM *The Reason of Church Government* (1641)

5)

When I die, let the earth be rolled in flames.

Dio, *Roman History* 58.23

FROM *An Apology for Smectymnuus* (1642)

6)

Laughing to teach the truth
What hinders? As some teachers give to boys
Junkets and knacks, that they may learn apace.

Horace, *Satires* 1.1.24–26

7)

Jesting decides great things
Stronglier, and better oft than earnest can.

Horace, *Satires* 1.10.14-15

8)

'Tis you that say it, not I; you do the deeds,
And your ungodly deeds find me the words.

Sophocles, *Electra* 624-25

FROM THE TITLE PAGE OF *Areopagitica* (1644)

9)

This is true liberty, when freeborn men
Having to advise the public may speak free,
Which he who can, and will, deserves high praise;
Who neither can nor will, may hold his peace;
What can be juster in a state than this?

Euripides, *Supplices* 438–41

FROM *Tetrachordon* (1645)

10)

Whom do we count a good man, whom but he
Who keeps the laws and statues of the Senate,
Who judges in great suits and controversies,
Whose witness and opinion wins the cause;
But his own house, and the whole neighborhood
Sees his foul inside through his whited skin.

Horace, *Epistles* 1.16.40–45

FROM *The Tenure of Kings and Magistrates* (1649)

11)

There can be slain
No sacrifice to God more acceptable
Than an unjust and wicked king.

Seneca, *Hercules Furens* 922–24

FROM *The History of Britain* (1670)

12)

Goddess of shades, and huntress, who at will
Walk'st on the rolling sphere, and through the deep,
On thy third reign the earth look now, and tell
What land, what seat of rest thou bidd'st me seek,
What certain seat, where I may worship thee
For ay, with temples vowed, and virgin choirs.

Geoffrey of Monmouth, *History* I.II

13)

Brutus far to the west, in th' ocean wide
Beyond the realm of Gaul, a land there lies,
Sea-girt it lies, where giants dwelt of old;
Now void, it fits thy people; thither bend
Thy course, there shalt thou find a lasting seat,
There to thy sons another Troy shall rise,
And kings be born of thee, whose dreaded might
Shall awe the world, and conquer nations bold.

Geoffrey of Monmouth, *History* I.II

14)

Low in a mead of kine under a thorn,
Of head bereft li'th poor Kenelm king-born.

Flores Historiarum for 821 C.E.

English and Italian Sonnets

Introduction to English and Italian Sonnets

Milton wrote twenty-four sonnets. The impulse to isolate this group from his other minor poems can be traced back to the various numbering schemes found in both the manuscript and printed versions during Milton's lifetime. In the 1645 *Poems*, ten sonnets were numbered from 1 to 10. The 1673 edition added nine more, ending with number 19. In the Trinity College manuscript (*CMS*), three sonnets (18–20 in the present edition) and four lines of another (our 21) are missing, but the sonnets present in the manuscript are numbered through to 23, and there is even a marginal note after *Sonnet 12* indicating that *On the New Forcers of Conscience* was "to come in here." Milton's editors have chosen to use the *CMS* numbering so persistently that generations of readers have known individual poems by these numbers. Here we print the standard twenty-three, followed by the one maverick sonnet (*On the New Forcers*) that, despite the marginal note, never got to be one of that number.

It was of course conventional to number sonnets, since they often formed an aggregate unit, a "sequence," held together by a narrative and by persistent thematic concerns. Milton's sonnet group clearly does not aspire to this conventional sort of unity. Why, then, did he number them? He must in some measure have been calling attention to his career-long interest in the form, and even to the possibility that, should the poems be read as a group, he might be seen to have done something interesting or original with that form.

The interest came in two phases. A youthful period from 1629 to 1632 produced a fragmentary group of Italian poems. Milton wrote no other poems in this language; his main ambition in Italian was to explore, in the correct Tuscan dialect, the origins of the love sonnet: *Questa è lingua di cui si vanta Amore* ("This is the tongue in which Love glories" [*Canzone* 15]). For this edition, the Italian poems have been newly translated into English prose by Gordon Braden.

Milton followed these experiments with one strikingly powerful religious meditation, *Sonnet 7*. There had been other religious sonnets written in England, notably Donne's *La Corona* and several sets of *Holy Sonnets*, but nothing in Donne's Jesuit-influenced meditations on death and apocalypse anticipated Milton's effort to gather religious strength in contemplating the end of an apparently unpromising youth. At the time of *Sonnet 7*'s composition, in 1632, there was only one other English sonnet of comparable power on a comparable subject, George Herbert's "The Answer."

Milton's most distinctive contributions to the history of the English sonnet came in the second phase of his sonnet writing, which began in 1642 and perhaps continued (depending on the date of *Sonnet 23*) to 1658. These sonnets have real people in them, whereas love sonnets tend notoriously to drift away from actual human beings with genuine names into cloudy realms of myth and metaphor. In the manner of Tasso's *Heroic Sonnets,* Milton addressed poems to great men such as Fairfax and Cromwell, but more often he used the form to celebrate his male and female friendships. His adaptations of Horatian conventions of address leave the impression that the sonnets are commentaries on proper names, enumerating virtues that these names are widely held to possess. Although Ben Jonson did not write sonnets, his habit of beginning poems with names ("Camden, most reverend head," "Donne, the delight of Phoebus," "Roe, and my joy to name") must have been an influence. Thirteen of the sonnets, opening with the name or title of the addressee, might with an eye toward *Paradise Lost* be termed personal invocations.

Milton's mature sonnets are all in some fashion occasional. Though few in number, they capture a broad range of human experiences. They register quiet moments of unpretentious conversation (21) as well as moments of sublime political outrage (18). They contain the evolution of his political beliefs and his lofty disappointment with the public he was trying to sway as a pamphleteer. They represent the initial emotional turmoil of blindness (19), then return to the subject for a glimpse, rare in literature, of spiritual serenity (22), only to close with clear evidence that the loss of sight blended into his other grievings (23).

It was in fact the writing of sonnets that kept Milton's poetic talents well-honed during the years of political commitment and public service, when he was unable to begin something on the scale of *Paradise Lost.* They do not sound like anyone else's sonnets. Shakespeare is closer to Petrarch than Milton's mature sonnets are to either predecessor. Wordsworth made this point in his polemical sonnet "Scorn not the Sonnet." His history of the form associates it with a number of objects: it was a key to Shakespeare, a lute to Petrarch, a pipe to Tasso, a crown to Dante, a lamp to Spenser. We come at the end to Milton, who can be listed among the authors who made the form into a musical instrument, but one able to emit a louder and more soulful music than was previously known:

and, when a damp
Fell round the path of Milton, in his hand
The Thing became a trumpet; whence he blew
Soul-animating strains—alas, too few!

SONNET 1

The first six sonnets, dealing with love, are thought to be early and to have been composed in less than a year, probably in 1629. The vogue of the English love sonnet had ended over thirty years before. But Milton's initial approach to the form is in important ways Italianate. He never writes in the so-called Shakespearean pattern of three quatrains and a couplet, but always in the Italian or Petrarchan pattern of two quatrains (the octave) and two tercets (the sestet), with the quatrains always rhyming abba (not interlaced abab, as in Shakespeare) and with shifting rhyme schemes in the sestet.

"O Nightingale," though often compared with *Song: On May Morning,* lacks the communal voice of that finer lyric. Generically the poem is a complaint in which the speaker, having suffered failures in love, seeks to enlist curative forces to end his misery.

O Nightingale, that on yon bloomy spray
Warblest at eve, when all the woods are still,
Thou with fresh hope the lover's heart dost fill,
While the jolly Hours lead on propitious May;
Thy liquid notes that close the eye of day,
First heard before the shallow cuckoo's bill
Portend success in love; O if Jove's will
Have linked that amorous power to thy soft lay,
Now timely sing, ere the rude bird of hate
Foretell my hopeless doom in some grove nigh:
As thou from year to year hast sung too late
For my relief, yet hadst no reason why:
Whether the Muse or Love call thee his mate,
Both them I serve, and of their train am I.

4. **Hours:** the goddesses of the seasons, usually three in number (spring, summer, winter).

5–7. To hear a cuckoo (later the *bird of hate*) was a bad omen; to hear a nightingale was a good omen. "The nightingale and the cuckoo sing both in one month," warned a Renaissance proverb (Tilley N181).

6. **shallow:** shrill.

13. **mate:** This word "has the primary meaning 'companion' but in its context also carries an allusion to the vulgar idea of 'mating' " (Honigmann 87).

SONNET 2

The end of *Elegy 6* probably alludes to this little group of Italian pieces. Eschewing the latest styles in Italian love poetry, Milton returned to the literary mannerisms of Petrarch, Bembo, and Tasso. Whatever the motives behind these poems might have been, among them was the desire to achieve an authentic feel for the origins of the love sonnet.

The prose translation of *Sonnet 2,* as of all Milton's non-English poems, was done for this edition by Gordon Braden.

Donna leggiadra il cui bel nome onora
L'erbosa val di Reno, e il nobil varco,
Ben è colui d'ogni valore scarco
Qual tuo spirto gentil non innamora,
Che dolcemente mostrasi di fuora
De' suoi atti soavi giammai parco,
E i don', che son d'amor saette ed arco,
Là onde l'alta tua virtù s'infiora.
Quando tu vaga parli, o lieta canti
Che mover possa duro alpestre legno,
Guardi ciascun agli occhi, ed agli orecchi
L'entrata, chi di te si trova indegno.
Grazia sola di sù gli vaglia, innanzi
Che'l disio amoroso al cuor s'invecchi.

Enchanting lady whose fair name[1] honors the grassy valley of the Reno and the noble crossing, he is indeed empty of all worth whom your gentle spirit does not enamor, which sweetly expresses itself, never grudging in its graceful actions nor in the favors which are Love's arrow and bow, there[8] where your lofty virtue is decked with flowers. When in beauty you speak or in happiness you sing with the power to move hard alpine timber,[10] let every man guard the entrance to his eyes and to his ears who finds himself unworthy of you. May grace alone from above help him before amorous desire ages itself in his heart.

1. Milton divulges the lady's name by referring to the region of Italy named Emilia, where the Reno river flows (Smart 137–44).
8. **Là:** in her eyes.
10. First the lady's song has the power of Orpheus, then it becomes Siren-like in testing the self-discipline of the unworthy.

SONNET 3

Qual in colle aspro, a l'imbrunir di sera,
L'avvezza giovinetta pastorella
Va bagnando l'erbetta strana e bella
Che mal si spande a disusata spera
Fuor di sua natia alma primavera,
Così Amor meco insù la lingua snella
Desta il fior novo di strania favella,

As on a rugged hill, at the darkening of evening, the experienced young shepherdess goes watering the strange and beautiful little plant which can scarcely spread its leaves in an unfamiliar place, far from its lifegiving native springtime, so on my agile

Mentre io di te, vezzosamente altera,
Canto, dal mio buon popol non inteso,
E'l bel Tamigi cangio col bel Arno.
Amor lo volse, ed io a l'altrui peso
Seppi ch'Amor cosa mai volse indarno.
Deh! Foss'il mio cuor lento e'l duro seno
A chi pianta dal ciel sì buon terreno.

10. Milton has exchanged the Thames for the Arno, which is to say, given up English for Tuscan Italian. On the preeminence of the Tuscan dialect, see Prince 4–13.

tongue Love awakens the new flower of a strange language while of you, charmingly proud, I sing, unintelligible to my own good people, and change the beautiful Thames for the beautiful Arno.[10] Love willed it, and I knew from the distress of others that Love never willed anything in vain. Ah, would that my slow heart and hard breast might be as good soil for Him who plants from Heaven!

CANZONE

Since the *canzone* normally had several stanzas, this single-stanza lyric is, strictly speaking, not a *canzone* but a *canzone* stanza. It is not a sonnet either, but we print it here in order not to separate it from the other Italian lyrics.

Ridonsi donne e giovani amorosi
M'accostandosi attorno, e perché scrivi,
Perché tu scrivi in lingua ignota e strana
Verseggiando d'amor, e come t'osi?
Dinne, se la tua speme sia mai vana,
E de' pensieri lo miglior t'arrivi;
Così mi van burlando, altri rivi,
Altri lidi t'aspettan, ed altre onde
Nelle cui verdi sponde
Spuntati ad or, ad or a la tua chioma
L'immortal guiderdon d'eterne frondi:
Perché alle spalle tue soverchia soma?
Canzon dirotti, e tu per me rispondi:
Dice mia donna, e'l suo dir è il mio cuore,
Questa è lingua di cui si vanta Amore.

7. **altri rivi:** other languages.

Ladies and young men in love laugh, crowding around me. "And why do you write, and why do you write in an unknown and strange tongue, versifying about love, and how do you dare to? Tell us, so that your hope not be vain and the best of your wishes succeed." So they tease me: "Other streams,[7] other shores wait for you, and other waters by whose green side now and again there grows for your hair the immortal guerdon of eternal leaves. Why add a great load to your shoulders?" Canzone, I will tell you, and you answer for me. My Lady says—and her speaking is my heart—"This is the tongue in which Love glories."

SONNET 4

Diodati, e te'l dirò con maraviglia,
  Quel ritroso io ch'amor spreggiar solea
  E de' suoi lacci spesso mi ridea,
  Già caddi, ov' uom dabben talor s'impiglia.
Nè treccie d'oro, nè guancia vermiglia
  M'abbaglian sì, ma sotto nova idea
  Pellegrina bellezza che'l cuor bea,
  Portamenti alti onesti, e nelle ciglia
Quel sereno fulgor d'amabil nero,
  Parole adorne di lingua più d'una,
  E'l cantar che di mezzo l'emispero
Traviar ben può la faticosa luna;
  E degli occhi suoi avventa sì gran fuoco
  Che l'incerar gli orecchi mi fia poco.

Diodati[1]—and I will tell you with amazement—such a coy one as I who used to scorn Love and often laughed at his snares, have now fallen where an honest man sometimes entangles himself. Neither golden tresses nor rosy cheeks dazzle me so, but a foreign beauty based on a new idea cheers my heart: a noble, modest bearing, and under her eyebrows such serene radiance of lovely blackness, speech adorned with more than one tongue, and singing which could well lead the weary moon astray from the middle of the sky, and from her eyes shoots such a great fire that it would do me little good to seal up my ears.[14]

1. **Diodati:** Charles Diodati, the friend whom Milton addressed in his first and sixth elegies, and whose death he commemorated in *Epitaph for Damon.*

14. Odysseus puts wax in the ears of his crew to prevent them from hearing of the song of the Sirens (*Od.* 12). In this case, wax would be useless because of the lady's visual power.

SONNET 5

Per certo i bei vostr' occhi, donna mia,
  Esser non può che non sian lo mio sole;
  Sì mi percuoton forte, come ei suole
  Per l'arene di Libia chi s'invia,
Mentre un caldo vapor (nè senti' pria)
  Da quel lato si spinge ove mi duole,
  Che forse amanti nelle lor parole
  Chiaman sospir; io non so che si sia:
Parte rinchiusa e turbida si cela
  Scossomi il petto, e poi n'uscendo poco
  Quivi d'attorno o s'agghiaccia, o s'ingiela;
Ma quanto agli occhi giunge a trovar loco
  Tutte le notti a me suol far piovose
  Finché mia Alba rivien colma di rose.

Surely, my lady, your beautiful eyes cannot help but be my sun; they strike me as powerfully as he does someone who travels across the sands of Libya. At the same time a hot vapor[5] (I have not felt it before) bursts from that side where I hurt—perhaps what lovers in their language call a sigh; I do not know what it is. Part of it, pent up and stormy, hides itself, shaking my breast, and then a little of it escaping either chills or freezes round about. But as much of it as finds its way to my eyes makes all nights tearful until my Dawn returns, crowned with roses.

5. **caldo vapor:** hot vapors in the heart are especially prominent in troubadour love poetry (Klein 73–85).

SONNET 6

Giovane piano, e semplicetto amante
  Poiché fuggir me stesso in dubbio sono,
  Madonna a voi del mio cuor l'umil dono
  Farò divoto; io certo a prove tante
L'ebbi fedele, intrepido, costante,
  Di pensieri leggiadro, accorto, e buono;
  Quando rugge il gran mondo, e scocca il tuono,
  S'arma di sé, e d'intero diamante,
Tanto del forse, e d'invidia sicuro,
  Di timori, e speranze al popol use
  Quanto d'ingegno e d'alto valor vago,
E di cetra sonora, e delle Muse:
  Sol troverete in tal parte men duro
  Ove amor mise l'insanabil ago.

A young, quiet, naïve lover, since I am in doubt how to escape from myself, I will, my lady, make you the devout humble gift of my heart. With certainty in many tests I have found it faithful, fearless, constant, graceful in its thoughts, shrewd, and good; when the whole world roars and the thunder shakes, it arms itself with itself and with solid adamant, as safe from doubt and envy, from the fears and hopes of ordinary people, as it is avid for intelligence and true worth, and for the sounding lyre and for the Muses. You will find it less hard only where Love has set an incurable sting.

SONNET 7

The *CMS* contains two drafts, likely dating from 1633, of a letter to an unknown friend. The friend (possibly Milton's former tutor Thomas Young) had apparently chided Milton for wasting time with his studies and admonished him to seek ordination immediately. In the first draft of his reply, Milton denied that he was wasting time and, in his defense, alluded to the parables of the talents (Matt. 25.14–30) and the vineyard (Matt. 20.1–16). "Yet that you may see that I am something suspicious of myself, and do take notice of a certain belatedness in me, I am the bolder to send you some of my nightward thoughts some while since (because they come in not altogether unfitly) made up in a Petrarchan stanza" (p. 771). Milton then quoted *Sonnet 7,* in which he does indeed "take notice of a certain belatedness in me." The poem was probably composed on or about Milton's twenty-third birthday (December 9, 1631).

The octave, with its realization that youth is gone and there's nothing to show for it, tacitly creates a desire to act. But the sestet, turning in a new direction announced by the opening word *Yet,* replaces this desire with patience and confidence. Apparent delay becomes appropriate preparation. Time the thief becomes Time the guide. If Milton has the grace to harmonize his actions with the will of Heaven, he is as timely-happy as a mortal can be. The temptation to act now, followed by the resolve not to act just yet, is central to both *Sonnet 19* and the portrayal of Christ in *Paradise Regained.*

The syntax evokes three quatrains and a couplet, superimposing the ghost of the English Shakespearean sonnet on Milton's "Petrarchan stanza."

How soon hath Time the subtle thief of youth,
Stol'n on his wing my three and twentieth year!
My hasting days fly on with full career,
But my late spring no bud or blossom shew'th.
Perhaps my semblance might deceive the truth,
That I to manhood am arrived so near,
And inward ripeness doth much less appear,
That some more timely-happy spirits endu'th.
Yet be it less or more, or soon or slow,
It shall be still in strictest measure even
To that same lot, however mean or high,
Toward which Time leads me, and the will of Heaven;
All is, if I have grace to use it so,
As ever in my great Taskmaster's eye.

1. **subtle:** cunning, with the emphasis on how the theft is scarcely noticed until it is fully accomplished.
2. **on his wing:** by his act of flight. Wings were among Time's conventional attributes.
3. **full career:** full speed.
4. **bud or blossom:** A despairing phrase, since the speaker not only has no complete accomplishment (*blossom*) but also no nascent work-in-progress (*bud*). Buds, blossoms, and flowers were common metaphors for poems.
5. **semblance:** appearance. "Although I am past forty, there is scarcely anyone to whom I do not seem younger by about ten years" (*2Def* p. 1080).
8. **timely-happy spirits:** men whose accomplishments are in harmony with their years; **endu'th:** endows.
9. **it:** inward ripeness.
10. **still:** always.
10–11. **even/To:** level with.
13–14. "All that I do in time is as though done in eternity, provided that I have the grace to act in accord with God's will."
14. **Taskmaster:** See the parable of the laborers in the vineyard (Matt. 20.1–16).

SONNET 8

In the *CMS* this sonnet has two titles, "On his door when the city expected an assault" (in the hand of a copyist, and struck out) and "When the assault was intended to the city" (in the poet's hand). While it was probably never actually tacked to Milton's door, the poem does have the form of an inscription addressed to the soldier of a conquering army who comes upon the door to Milton's home. That a poet can indeed create enduring fame and "spread thy name o'er lands and seas" is proven by the two examples of literary clemency in the sestet, both of which crossed from Greece to England centuries before and were obviously still remembered.

The assault in question was expected in 1642, when the retreat of the Parliamentary army left the road to London open to Royalist troops. In October 1642, Londoners worked feverishly digging trenches and barricading the streets in order to prevent invasion. On November 12, Charles I and his army advanced as far as Brentford but retreated in the face of the Parliamentary army of the Earl of Essex. Milton wrote the sonnet at some time during this period of anticipated attack.

Captain or colonel, or knight in arms,
  Whose chance on these defenseless doors may seize,
  If deed of honor did thee ever please,
  Guard them, and him within protect from harms;
He can requite thee, for he knows the charms
  That call fame on such gentle acts as these,
  And he can spread thy name o'er lands and seas,
  Whatever clime the sun's bright circle warms.
Lift not thy spear against the muses' bower:
  The great Emathian conqueror bid spare
  The house of Pindarus, when temple and tower
Went to the ground: and the repeated air
  Of sad Electra's poet had the power
  To save th' Athenian walls from ruin bare.

1. **colonel:** a trisyllable, pronounced "coronel."

2. **defenseless doors:** Milton's lodging was outside the gates of the city.

3. I.e., if ever deed of honor did thee please.

10. **Emathian conqueror:** Alexander the Great. When his army sacked Thebes, he spared a house once occupied by Pindar (Plutarch, *Alexander* 11).

12–14. When an army of Spartans, Thebans, and Corinthians had defeated Athens and were about to raze it to the ground, a man from Phocis sang the first Chorus from Euripides' *Electra.* All were moved to compassion and refused to destroy a city that had produced such a poet (Plutarch, *Lysander* 15).

12. **repeated air:** recited chorus (see previous note).

SONNET 9

Presumably, since this poem follows *Sonnet 8* in the *CMS,* it was written after 1642, but the lady has not been satisfactorily identified. Some (Honigmann, Miller) have supposed that she was Mary Powell herself, despite the fact that what little we know of her youthful character hardly suggests a woman who had turned her back on marriage and earthly pleasure.

Lady that in the prime of earliest youth,
  Wisely hast shunned the broad way and the green,
  And with those few art eminently seen,
  That labor up the hill of heav'nly truth,
The better part with Mary, and with Ruth,
  Chosen thou hast, and they that overween,
  And at thy growing virtues fret their spleen,
  No anger find in thee, but pity and ruth.
Thy care is fixed, and zealously attends
  To fill thy odorous lamp with deeds of light,
  And hope that reaps not shame. Therefore be sure
Thou, when the bridegroom with his feastful friends
  Passes to bliss at the midhour of night,
  Hast gained thy entrance, virgin wise and pure.

1. **prime:** the "springtime" of human life.
2. **broad way:** "Broad is the way that leadeth to destruction" (Matt. 7.13); **and the green:** See Job 8.12–13 on the greenness of the paths of those who forget God.
4. **hill of heav'nly truth:** Cp. Donne, *Sat.* 3.79–81; and for the history of the trope, see Milgate 290–92.
5. **The better part:** While Martha bustled, Mary sat at the feet of Christ. After Martha complained, Christ said, "One thing is needful: and Mary hath chosen that good part" (Luke 10.39–42); **Ruth:** The widowed Ruth lived with her mother-in-law rather than seek a new husband (Ruth 1.14).
6. **overween:** presume (to criticize you).
11. **hope that reaps not shame:** Cp. Rom. 5.5 ("And hope maketh none ashamed") and 10.11 ("Whosoever believeth in him shall not be ashamed").
11–14. Cp. the parable of the wise and foolish virgins in Matt. 25.1–13.
12. **feastful:** festive.
14. **entrance:** Besides the parable of the virgins (see 11–14n), Milton glances at John 10.9: "I am the door: by me if any man enter in, he shall be saved."

SONNET 10

Edward Phillips relates that "Our Author, now as it were a single man again, made it his chief diversion now and then in an evening to visit the Lady Margaret Lee. . . . This lady being a woman of great wit and ingenuity, had a particular honor for him, and took much delight in his company, as likewise her husband Captain Hobson . . . and what esteem he at the same time had for her, appears by a sonnet he made in praise of her" (Darbishire 64). The allusion to Milton being "as it were a single man" dates his acquaintance with Lady Margaret and his composition of this sonnet somewhere between July 1642, when Mary Powell Milton left him to return to her family, and early summer 1645, when the couple reconciled.

The poem, a notable feat of technical virtuosity, places one coherent syntactical structure between the two appositives at its ends ("Daughter to that good

Earl . . . , honored Margaret"), meditating on a woman and her names in such a way that she is indeed related truly (as daughter to that good Earl) and then shown to possess his virtues (as honored Margaret).

Daughter to that good Earl, once President
  Of England's Council, and her Treasury,
  Who lived in both, unstained with gold or fee,
  And left them both, more in himself content,
Till the sad breaking of that Parliament
  Broke him, as that dishonest victory
  At Chaeronea, fatal to liberty,
  Killed with report that old man eloquent,
Though later born, than to have known the days
  Wherein your father flourished, yet by you
  Madam, methinks I see him living yet;
So well your words his noble virtues praise,
  That all both judge you to relate them true,
  And to possess them, honored Margaret.

1. **good Earl:** Having studied law, James Ley held several high positions in the reign of James I and was named Lord High Treasurer in 1624. Charles I created him Earl of Marlborough. Resigning as Treasurer in 1628, he was appointed President of the Council.

5–6. Ley died on March 14, 1629, twelve days after Charles had unsuccessfully tried to adjourn an unruly Parliament.

6. **dishonest:** shameful.

7. **Chaeronea:** Milton remembers the story that the rhetorician Isocrates died of voluntary starvation after Philip of Macedon's defeat of Athenian and Theban forces at Chaeronea (Dionysius of Halicarnassus, *Commentaries on the Ancient Orators,* "Isocrates").

13. **all:** all that hear you.

SONNET 11

This poem was numbered 12 in the *CMS* but became *Sonnet 11* in the 1673 *Poems.* Some editions revert to the manuscript numbering. *Tetrachordon,* along with *Colasterion,* was published in March 1645. The phrase *of late* means "recently." Yet the publication must have been far enough in the past for the minor vogue of the book, "now seldom pored on," to have been exhausted.

A book was writ of late called *Tetrachordon;*
  And woven close, both matter, form and style;
  The subject new: it walked the town a while,
  Numb'ring good intellects; now seldom pored on.

Cries the stall-reader, "Bless us! What a word on
A title page is this!" and some in file
Stand spelling false, while one might walk to Mile-
End Green. Why is it harder, sirs, than Gordon,
Colkitto, or Macdonnel, or Galasp?
Those rugged names to our like mouths grow sleek
That would have made Quintilian stare and gasp.
Thy age, like ours, O soul of Sir John Cheke,
Hated not learning worse than toad or asp,
When thou taught'st Cambridge and King Edward Greek.

1. **Tetrachordon:** The title of Milton's divorce pamphlet, *Tetrachordon,* is an elaborate conceit summarizing the entire work. The Greek term alludes to a four-note scale, the notes in this case being the four main treatments of marriage in the Bible (Gen. 1.27–28, 2.18, 23–24; Deut. 24.1–5; Matt. 5.31–32, 19.3–11; 1 Cor. 7.10–16). The argument of the pamphlet tries to bring these disparate passages into harmony.

3. **walked the town:** Cp. Horace, *Epist.* 1.20, where the poet consigns his book to a doomed life of prostitution.

4. **Numb'ring good intellects:** both "attracting good intellects among its readers" and "determining the number of good intellects."

5. **stall-reader:** one who browses in the stall outside a bookshop.

6. **in file:** in a row (along the stall).

7. **spelling false:** misinterpreting.

7–8. **Mile-/End Green:** Mile-End, the first mile stone outside Aldgate, marked the eastern boundary of London.

8–9. *Gordon* perhaps refers to George, Lord Gordon; *Macdonnel* (MacDonald) and *Colkitto* (Coll Keitache, a nickname given one of the MacDonalds) were Scottish officers serving in the Royalist army of the Earl of Montrose. *Galasp* is George Gillespie, a member of the Westminster Assembly.

10. **rugged:** hard to pronounce, ill-tuned; **like:** similarly ill-tuned; **sleek:** easy.

11. **Quintilian:** first-century Roman rhetorician whose *Institutes* 1.5.8 condemned barbarous (foreign) words.

12. **Sir John Cheke:** This English educator, the first Professor of Greek at Cambridge, tutored King Edward VI, whose name appears on the title page of *Tetrachordon* because Milton wanted to call attention to a congenial marriage law passed during "those best and purest times" of his reign (p. 987).

12–14. Here Milton puts *like ours* where it may appear to mean "like our age hates learning." But he almost certainly meant to say that Cheke's age, unlike the current one, honored learning. A modern author with this sense in mind would have written "Thy age . . . hated not learning, like ours [like ours does], worse than toad or asp."

SONNET 12

Milton's second sonnet on his divorce tracts, probably written in 1646, makes it clear that his arguments fared no better with his contemporaries than the Greek title of *Tetrachordon.* For a year after its publication, *The Doctrine and Discipline of Divorce,* the first and most often printed of the divorce pamphlets, seems to have occasioned conversation rather than written responses. When the printed notices began to appear, in late 1644, they were mostly by Presbyterians, overwhelmingly negative, and virtually without exception exercises in ridicule rather than reasoned argument (Parker 1971, 17–24). Milton felt that he had become infamous without being given a fair hearing. In the grand ironic reversal of this sonnet, he turns his readers' hostile judgment of his book into an appallingly accurate judgment of themselves.

On the Same

I did but prompt the age to quit their clogs
  By the known rules of ancient liberty,
  When straight a barbarous noise environs me
  Of owls and cuckoos, asses, apes and dogs.
As when those hinds that were transformed to frogs
  Railed at Latona's twin-born progeny
  Which after held the sun and moon in fee.
  But this is got by casting pearl to hogs;
That bawl for freedom in their senseless mood,
  And still revolt when truth would set them free.
  License they mean when they cry liberty;
For who loves that, must first be wise and good;
  But from that mark how far they rove we see
  For all this waste of wealth, and loss of blood.

1. **clogs:** weights or encumbrances put upon beasts to keep them from straying.
2. **known rules:** Mosaic divorce law.
3. **barbarous noise environs me:** Cp. *Lyc* 61; *PL* 7.36–37.
5–7. *Latona* with her twin children, Apollo and Diana, subsequently the deities of the sun and the moon, tried to drink from a pond. When peasants muddied the water, she transformed them into frogs (Ovid, *Met.* 6.317–81).
7. **in fee:** in absolute possession.
8. **this is got by:** this is what you get from; **casting pearl to hogs:** "Neither cast ye your pearls before swine, lest they trample them under their feet, and turn again and rend you" (Matt. 7.6).
10. The line has two senses: "And always revolt against the truth that would set them free" and "And always backslide into mental clogs rather than accept the truth that would set them free" (Leonard).
11. **License:** licentiousness, with a possible pun on license to print.
12. "None can love freedom heartily but good men; the rest love not freedom but license" (*TKM* p. 1024).
13. **mark:** target (of first being wise and good? of loving true liberty?); **rove:** shoot arrows away from the mark.
14. **For all:** in spite of; **this waste . . . blood:** this expenditure of wealth and loss of life (in the Civil War). Milton rails against the Presbyterians for rendering the sacrifices of the Civil War pointless because they have not, as promised, produced liberty but instead renewed ancient habits of spiritual bondage.

SONNET 13

Milton's admiration for the person and art of Henry Lawes was not affected in the slightest by the musician's ardent royalism. Nor was Lawes himself affected in the slightest by the young poet's equally ardent Puritanism. From 1630 Lawes was a member of the King's Private Music, which involved composing, planning, directing, and performing in court entertainments. During these years he continued his role as music tutor to the children of the Egerton family, and it was in this capacity that he was responsible for commissioning the young and unknown Milton to write the words for *Arcades* and *A Masque.*

As a musician, Lawes did not actually create a new style in songs. His work belonged to a period style in the middle seventeenth century that reversed an older manner by allowing poetry some role in determining the music.

To Mr. H. Lawes, on his Airs

Harry, whose tuneful and well-measured song
  First taught our English music how to span
  Words with just note and accent, not to scan
  With Midas' ears, committing short and long,
Thy worth and skill exempts thee from the throng,
  With praise enough for Envy to look wan;
  To after-age thou shalt be writ the man
  That with smooth air couldst humor best our tongue.
Thou honor'st verse, and verse must lend her wing
  To honor thee, the priest of Phoebus' choir
  That tun'st their happiest lines in hymn or story.
Dante shall give Fame leave to set thee higher
  Than his Casella, whom he wooed to sing
  Met in the milder shades of Purgatory.

2. **to span:** to measure, as with the hand; here referring to the words matched with notes of proper length and stress.

3. **to scan:** to determine the number and nature of poetic feet.

4. **With Midas' ears:** to scan improperly or tastelessly; Midas was given ass's ears as a punishment for preferring the music of Pan to that of Apollo (Ovid, *Met.* 11.146–79); **committing short and long:** placing a long syllable in a short note, or vice versa.

5. **exempts thee:** singles thee out.

12–14. On the threshold of Purgatory, Dante greets the shade of his friend Casella, a Florentine musician, and asks for a song; Casella proceeds to sing Dante's *Amor che me la mente mi ragiona* (*Purg.* 2.76–117).

14. **milder shades:** The threshold was less dark than the rest of Purgatory.

SONNET 14

The first of the three drafts of this poem in the *CMS* bears the title "On the religious memory of Mrs. Catharine Thomason my Christian friend." Mrs. Thomason, who died in December 1646, was the wife of George Thomason, a bookseller whose extensive collection of Civil War pamphlets is now housed in the British Museum and contains over 22,000 items printed between 1640 and 1660. He was a Presbyterian whose sympathies, in the later 1640s, swung toward the king. His wife, Catharine, was the ward and niece of the bookseller to whom George was originally apprenticed. Her love for books and learning is evident from her husband's will, which disperses her library to her children (she left eight of them) in the hope that they "will remember to whom they [the books] did once belong" and "will make the better use of them for their precious and dear mother's sake" (Hughes et al. 2:407).

When Faith and Love which parted from thee never,
  Had ripened thy just soul to dwell with God,
  Meekly thou didst resign this earthy load
  Of death, called life, which us from life doth sever.
Thy works and alms and all thy good endeavor
  Stayed not behind, nor in the grave were trod;
  But as Faith pointed with her golden rod,
  Followed thee up to joy and bliss forever.
Love led them on, and Faith who knew them best
  Thy handmaids, clad them o'er with purple beams
  And azure wings, that up they flew so dressed,
And spake the truth of thee on glorious themes
  Before the Judge, who thenceforth bid thee rest
  And drink thy fill of pure immortal streams.

1. **Faith and Love:** "The parts of Christian doctrine are two: Faith, or knowledge of God, and Love, or the worship of God" (*CD* 1.1, p. 1145).

8. **Followed thee up:** Rev. 14.13: "Blessed are the dead which die in the Lord . . . their works do follow them."

9. **Faith who knew them best:** Faith who best knew them (works, alms, all good endeavor) to be.

13. **the Judge:** Christ.

14. Cp. Ps. 36.8–9; Rev. 22.1, 17.

SONNET 15

Though present in the *CMS,* the Fairfax sonnet did not appear in the 1645 or 1673 *Poems.* It was first printed in Edward Phillips's edition of the *Letters of State* in 1694.

General Thomas Fairfax of the Parliamentary army had won victory after victory over Royalist forces since 1643, and his siege on Colchester in June through August 1948 was no exception. But while Fairfax was occupied with Colchester, the Scottish army invaded England in July, inspiring the many local rebellions Milton refers to as "Hydra heads." It would seem that Milton has not yet heard of Cromwell's victories over the invaders (see *Sonnet 16*). His wish that Fairfax could turn his talents from defeating the enemy to reforming Parliament's own scandalous practices was in vain. Unable to support the beheading of Charles I backed by Cromwell and his army, Fairfax in 1650 retired from public life to his country estate, where the young Andrew Marvell would tutor his daughter Maria and write in his honor "Upon Appleton House, to my Lord Fairfax," one of the greatest poems of the century.

On the Lord General Fairfax, at the Siege of Colchester

Fairfax, whose name in arms through Europe rings
  Filling each mouth with envy, or with praise,
  And all her jealous monarchs with amaze,
  And rumors loud, that daunt remotest kings,
Thy firm unshaken virtue ever brings
  Victory home, though new rebellions raise
  Their Hydra heads, and the false North displays
  Her broken league, to imp their serpent wings,
O yet a nobler task awaits thy hand;
  For what can war, but endless war still breed,
  Till truth and right from violence be freed,
And public faith cleared from the shameful brand

5. **virtue:** the sum of manly powers, including courage and moral worth.

7. **Hydra heads:** Whenever Hercules cut off one of Hydra's many heads, two grew in its place; **false North:** The Scots, having signed a treaty with Charles I, invaded England in July 1648.

8. **broken league:** The Scottish invasion was thought by its opponents (which included Milton) to be a violation of the Solemn League and Covenant; **imp:** engraft feathers to improve the wings' flight.

12. **public faith:** Honigmann shows that Parliament referred to the public funding of the Civil War as the "public faith." Loans were solicited, then not repaid (for a time Milton himself lost much of his fortune in this manner) and the funds subsequently mismanaged, such that the Parliamentary army was always being promised "public faith" compensation that never arrived in full. See the digression on the Long Parliament in the manuscript of *The History of Britain,* where Milton denounces the scheme (Yale 5:444).

Of public fraud. In vain doth valor bleed
While avarice and rapine share the land.

SONNET 16

Like *Sonnet 15*, this poem appears in the *CMS* but was first printed by Edward Phillips in his 1694 *Letters of State.* Cromwell was a member of the Parliamentary committee to which the title alludes. In May 1652, when Milton apparently wrote the poem, the committee was considering a proposal that Parliament establish a national church and pay its clergy; dissent would be tolerated so long as it respected fifteen fundamental doctrines. The chief proponent of the scheme was John Owen, who had served as Cromwell's chaplain. Milton, like Cromwell, favored a wider scope of toleration. In the sonnet Milton urges the Puritan leader to embrace the separation of church and state, refusing "to bind our souls with secular chains," and repudiate the "hireling wolves" of a state-funded clergy.

To the Lord General Cromwell, May 1652, On the proposals of certain ministers at the Committee for Propagation of the Gospel

Cromwell, our chief of men, who through a cloud
  Not of war only, but detractions rude,
  Guided by faith and matchless fortitude
  To peace and truth thy glorious way hast ploughed,
And on the neck of crownèd Fortune proud
  Hast reared God's trophies and his work pursued,
  While Darwen stream with blood of Scots imbrued,
  And Dunbar field resounds thy praises loud,
And Worcester's laureate wreath; yet much remains
  To conquer still; peace hath her victories
  No less renowned than war, new foes arise
Threat'ning to bind our souls with secular chains:

1. **through a cloud:** Cp. Marvell's *Horatian Ode,* 13–16.

2. **detractions rude:** Milton catalogs some of them in *A Second Defense* (Yale 4:662–66).

5. **neck of crownèd Fortune:** alluding to the beheading of Charles I in January 1649.

6. **reared God's trophies:** A *trophy* was originally a structure erected on the battlefield or in a public place.

7. **Darwen stream:** This stream is near the place where Cromwell routed the invading Scottish army in August 1648.

8. **Dunbar field:** Cromwell defeated the Scottish army here in September 1650.

9. **Worcester's laureate wreath:** Cromwell scored a decisive victory over Charles II at Worcester in September 1651 (on the anniversary of his victory at Dunbar).

11. **new foes:** proponents of government-enforced conformity to a national church.

Help us to save free conscience from the paw
Of hireling wolves whose Gospel is their maw.

14. **hireling wolves:** Milton's contemptuous phrase for mercenary clergymen paid by the government; cp. John 10.13. In the Bible, enemies of Christ and Christianity are often represented as wolves (Matt. 7.15; Acts 20.29). Cp. *Lyc* 113–22.

SONNET 17

Although it appears in the *CMS,* this poem was first published in George Sikes's *Life and Death of Sir Henry Vane* (1662).

The elder Vane, also named Henry (1589-1655), served Charles I as Privy Councillor (1630), Treasurer of the Household (1639), and Secretary of State (1640). But his son Vane the Younger (1613–62) was deeply sympathetic toward the Puritans. For a time he lived in New England, where he became Governor of the Massachusetts Bay Colony (1636–37). Returning to England, he was appointed Secretary of the Navy and opposed the court party in Parliament. When Milton addressed him in this sonnet, in 1652, he was a member of the Council of State considering the same proposals that Cromwell had been implored to reject in *Sonnet 16.* Milton praised him for understanding the separation of "spiritual power and civil," which is the basis of religious freedom.

The ideal alliance between Cromwell and Vane forged in *Sonnets 16* and *17* did not survive long in the realm of history. Vane deplored Cromwell's dissolution of the Long Parliament in 1653 and retired from public life during the Protectorate. Upon Cromwell's death, he tried unsuccessfully to prevent the return of Charles II. After a two-year imprisonment, Vane was tried for treason, convicted, and executed in 1662.

To Sir Henry Vane the Younger

Vane, young in years, but in sage counsel old,
Than whom a better senator ne'er held
The helm of Rome, when gowns not arms repelled
The fierce Epirot and the African bold;
Whether to settle peace or to unfold
The drift of hollow states, hard to be spelled,

3. **gowns not arms:** The *gowns* or togas of the senators represent civil as opposed to military power.
4. **fierce Epirot and the African bold:** Both Pyrrhus, King of Epirus, and Hannibal invaded Italy in the third century B.C.E. and inspired noble resistance in the Roman senate.
6. **drift:** scheme, plot; **hollow:** false, insincere; **spelled:** discovered.

Then to advise how war may best, upheld,
Move by her two main nerves, iron and gold,
In all her equipage; besides to know
Both spiritual power and civil, what each means,
What severs each, thou hast learnt, which few have done.
The bounds of either sword to thee we owe;
Therefore on thy firm hand religion leans
In peace, and reckons thee her eldest son.

8. **iron and gold:** In his *Commonplace Book,* Milton quoted Machiavelli's *Discourses* 2.10 on the sinews of war being steel rather than gold (Yale 1:498).

9. **equipage:** apparatus of war.

12. **bounds of either sword:** limits of the jurisdiction of the two swords, spiritual and civil (church and state).

14. **eldest son:** despite Vane being, as we are told in the opening words of the sonnet, *young in years.*

SONNET 18

This poem was occasioned by events that took place in the Italian Alps in April through May 1655.

The Vaudois or Waldensians, who traced their origins to the twelfth century and according to some retained an Apostolic purity in matters of worship, lived in Alpine villages in France and Italy. In Italy the sect had been granted the right to settle in the Piedmont Valley by the Duke of Savoy, but the Vaudois had infiltrated villages forbidden by the treaty. The duke dispatched an army. In April 1655 around 1,712 Vaudois were massacred with great ferocity—burned alive, impaled, mutilated, hurled from precipices. Some fled for France and died of exposure in the mountains. When their leaders called for support from Protestant states, England responded fervently. Cromwell commanded a general fast, raised thousands of pounds for the victims, formed an alliance, wrote to various European leaders, including the Duke of Savoy, sent an envoy (Sir Michael Morland) to the duke, and seriously considered sending an army. Milton wrote this sonnet.

On the Late Massacre in Piedmont

Avenge O Lord thy slaughtered saints, whose bones
Lie scattered on the Alpine mountains cold,
Ev'n them who kept thy truth so pure of old

1. **Avenge:** The word is being used with biblical force; see Rev. 6.9–10 and Luke 18.7–8.

When all our fathers worshipped stocks and stones,
Forget not: in thy book record their groans
Who were thy sheep and in their ancient fold
Slain by the bloody Piemontese that rolled
Mother with infant down the rocks. Their moans
The vales redoubled to the hills, and they
To Heav'n. Their martyred blood and ashes sow
O'er all th' Italian fields where still doth sway
The triple tyrant: that from these may grow
A hundredfold, who having learnt thy way
Early may fly the Babylonian woe.

4. **stocks and stones:** a standard phrase (*OED* "stock," 1d); see Jer. 2.27, 3.9.
5. **thy book:** the book of human actions to be consulted on Judgment Day; see Rev. 5.1.
10–13. Editors often cite the old saying that "the blood of martyrs is the seed of faith."
12. **triple tyrant:** The pope wore a three-tiered miter.
13. **thy way:** the true faith.
14. Puritans identified the Church of Rome with the Babylon whose doom was prophesied in Rev. 17–18. There are also Old Testament prophecies of the destruction of Babylon, with warnings to flee before the calamity occurs (Jer. 50–51, Isa. 48).

SONNET 19

This poem presents several points of controversy.

What is its date? What is its mood? Some experts, thinking the poem to have been written soon after Milton's total loss of sight in 1652, stress the author's uncertainty over whether God will ever ask him to work again. The main spiritual task of the poem is Milton's need to resign himself to this uncertainty. Others would date the poem later, in 1655–56, on the assumption that the sonnets were numbered chronologically in the 1673 *Poems,* and *Sonnet 18* was pretty clearly written in 1655. But the sonnets are *not* placed in perfectly sequential order (Morse). It is moreover hard to believe that someone who had just published *A Second Defense* (1654) and the *Defense of Himself* (1655) would speak of himself as uselessly hoarding his one talent. The year 1652 is the more probable date of composition.

Why would Milton say, whether in 1652 or 1655–56, that blindness had come to him "Ere half my days"? The poet was, after all, forty-three in 1652. It has been suggested that his father, who died at eighty-four, encouraged a sanguine calculation of the time allotted him on this earth; but if Milton believed that he had not yet reached the halfway point in 1652, he must have been confident in outliving his father. We have no solution to this difficulty and would simply remark that Milton wanted to do a very great deal in this life.

What does the analogy at the end of the poem mean? In the sonnet as a whole, Milton defeats beforehand a threatened impatience. He imagines God come to assess his labors, finding that he has done nothing since his blindness, and chiding him for that inactivity. Milton imagines that he would in turn chide God Himself by asking, "Doth God exact day labor, light denied?" Milton calls this a "murmur," a complaint, and we therefore know its tone to be sarcastic. "God, are you really being Godlike in chiding me for my lack of labor? How can you expect me to work in the dark night of my blindness?" But patience overcomes this fantasized complaint, and in the process lays to rest the terrifying implications of the parable of the talents (see Haskin 29–53). God will not chide. God, unlike an earthly taskmaster, does not need our work or our talents. Acceptance of the will of God is itself service enough. Then Milton alludes to angels that "post," doing the bidding of God, as opposed to angels "who only stand and wait." Both serve God. *Wait* may mean "attend as a servant" but surely also has the common sense of "stay in expectation," waiting to be given a bidding to do, a job to complete. For the time being, waiting is God's bidding. But Milton, it once again seems appropriate to remark, wanted to do a very great deal in this life.

When I consider how my light is spent,
 Ere half my days, in this dark world and wide,
 And that one talent which is death to hide,
 Lodged with me useless, though my soul more bent
To serve therewith my Maker, and present
 My true account, lest he returning chide,
 "Doth God exact day labor, light denied?"
 I fondly ask; but patience to prevent
That murmur soon replies, "God doth not need
 Either man's work or his own gifts; who best
 Bear his mild yoke, they serve him best; his state

1. **When I consider:** The opening is formulaic; cp. Shakespeare, *Sonnet 15*: "When I consider everything that grows."

3. **that one talent:** See the parable of the talents in Matt. 25.14–30. The man with one talent hid it and was punished by being cast into the outer darkness.

4. **useless:** not in use, with a glance at usury (see Matt. 25.27); **bent:** determined.

5. **therewith:** with my spent light and useless talent as the cause or occasion of this greater determination to serve (*OED* 3b).

6. **true account:** Cp. "my certain account" in *Apology* (Yale 1:869).

7. Cp. "I must work the works of him that sent me, while it is day: the night cometh when no man can work" (John 9.4). Cp. also the parable of the vineyard, where all the day laborers, no matter how long they work, receive the same wages (Matt. 20.1–16).

8. **fondly:** foolishly.

9. **murmur:** complaint.

11. **mild yoke:** "My yoke is easy" (Matt. 11.30).

Is kingly. Thousands at his bidding speed
And post o'er land and ocean without rest:
They also serve who only stand and wait."

12–14. In the traditional angelology of Pseudo-Dionysius and Aquinas, the five lower orders are sent out to execute God's will, while the four higher orders stand ever in God's presence and transmit his commands to the lower orders. But Milton seems not to have accepted this distinction. Leonard rightly notes that in *Paradise Lost* all the angels, however exalted their rank, carry messages and perform tasks. The word *only* in line 14 implies that standing and waiting is not as dignified as posting *o'er land and ocean;* and *wait* may well imply that in the future a command will be given (see headnote).

SONNET 20

Phillips says that "young Lawrence (the son of him that was President of Oliver's Council), to whom there is a sonnet among the rest, in his printed poems," frequently visited Milton after his move to Petty France, Westminster, in 1651 (Darbishire 74).

The "virtuous father," Henry Lawrence (1600–64), entered public life in 1648, attaching himself to Cromwell. He sat in successive Parliaments, became Lord President of the Council of State, and served as Keeper of the Library at St. James House. He wrote several theological treatises. In *A Second Defense,* Milton calls him a man "of supreme genius, cultivated in the liberal arts" (p. 1105).

His son and Milton's friend, Edward Lawrence (1633–57), became a member of Parliament in 1656 and died the next year at the age of twenty-four. Milton may have tutored him. The idea of retiring inside during a long and dark winter to enjoy the classical pleasures of wine, music, poetry, and free conversation is a major motif in Royalist poets of the so-called Cavalier school, such as Lovelace ("The Grasshopper"), Cowley ("The Grasshopper," the essay "Of Liberty"), and Herrick ("To Live Merrily, and to Trust to Good Verses"). All of them were inspired by the work of Ben Jonson, as was the young Milton. Here the mature sonneteer appropriates this Jonsonian and ultimately Horatian genre in the service of a Puritan conviviality.

Lawrence of virtuous father virtuous son,
Now that the fields are dank, and ways are mire,

1. **father:** Henry Lawrence, whom Cromwell appointed permanent chairman of the Council of State in January 1654. Carey notes the Horatian character of the first line's syntax. Cp. *Odes* 1.16.1: *O matre pulchra filia pulchrior* ("O maiden fairer than thy mother fair").

Where shall we sometimes meet, and by the fire
Help waste a sullen day, what may be won
From the hard season gaining? Time will run
On smoother, till Favonius re-inspire
The frozen earth, and clothe in fresh attire
The lily and rose, that neither sowed nor spun.
What neat repast shall feast us, light and choice,
Of Attic taste, with wine, whence we may rise
To hear the lute well touched, or artful voice
Warble immortal notes and Tuscan air?
He who of those delights can judge, and spare
To interpose them oft, is not unwise.

4. **waste:** spend, pass.
5. **hard season:** winter.
6. **Favonius:** the west wind, Zephyrus.
8. **neither sowed nor spun:** See Matt. 6.28–29.
9. **neat:** simple and elegant.
10. **Of Attic taste:** such as would have been preferred or appreciated in Athens.
12. **Tuscan air:** Italian song; according to Phillips, Milton shipped home from Italy "a chest or two of choice music books of the best masters flourishing about that time in Italy" (Darbishire 59).
13. **spare:** A crux: Some take *spare* to mean "forbear," in which case Milton is telling Lawrence to have a restricted number of good times, while others think *spare* means "spare the time," in which case Milton is telling Lawrence to have all the good times he can manage. It seems ominous for the "spare the time" camp that no one has yet found an example of the use of *spare* in which the direct object (time) is understood and the verb is followed by an infinitive. But Bush defends "spare the time" nonetheless (Hughes et al., 2:475–76).

SONNET 21

This second sonnet on conviviality is addressed to Cyriack Skinner (1627–1700). Milton may have tutored him in the 1640s. According to Phillips, he was in the 1650s a frequent visitor to Milton's home (Darbishire 74). Skinner is now widely believed to be the so-called "anonymous biographer," author of a short life of Milton that is our main source for certain biographical details.

Cyriack, whose grandsire on the Royal Bench
Of British Themis, with no mean applause
Pronounced and in his volumes taught our laws,

1. **grandsire:** Skinner's maternal grandfather was Sir Edward Coke (1552–1634), a famous lawyer, scholar, and defender of Parliamentary rights who became Chief Justice of the King's Bench in 1613.
2. **Themis:** Roman goddess of Justice.

Which others at their bar so often wrench;
Today deep thoughts resolve with me to drench
In mirth, that after no repenting draws;
Let Euclid rest and Archimedes pause,
And what the Swede intend, and what the French.
To measure life learn thou betimes, and know
Toward solid good what leads the nearest way;
For other things mild Heav'n a time ordains,
And disapproves that care, though wise in show,
That with superfluous burden loads the day,
And when God sends a cheerful hour, refrains.

4. **others at their bar:** other judges in their courts.
5–6. "Resolve with me today to drench deep thoughts in mirth."
6. **no repenting draws:** Cp. Jonson, "Inviting a Friend to Supper," 39–41.
7. "Drop for now your study of geometry and physics."
8. **Swede:** may be Charles X, who invaded Poland in 1655; the French were at war with Spain in 1655.
9. **betimes:** while time remains.
11. **a time ordains:** See Eccles. 3.1: "To every thing there is a time, and a time to every purpose under heaven."

SONNET 22

In another sonnet addressed to Cyriack Skinner (see headnote to *Sonnet 21*), Milton revisits the subject of his blindness. The poem was perhaps written in 1655–56. His confidence in God's guidance is far more settled and serene here than in the turbulent *Sonnet 19*.

Cyriack, this three years' day these eyes, though clear
To outward view, of blemish or of spot,
Bereft of light their seeing have forgot,
Nor to their idle orbs doth sight appear
Of sun or moon or star throughout the year,
Or man or woman. Yet I argue not
Against Heaven's hand or will, nor bate a jot
Of heart or hope, but still bear up and steer

1. **this three years' day:** for the last three years.
1–2. **clear . . . spot:** When a political opponent charged him with being hideously ugly, Milton replied that in fact his blind eyes looked just like ordinary eyes (p. 1079), and Skinner confirms the point (Darbishire 32).
4. **orbs:** eyeballs.
7. **hand or will:** executive powers or commands; **bate a jot:** endure the slightest reduction.
8. **bear up:** The primary sense (linking with *steer*) is nautical: put the helm "up" so as to bring the vessel into the direction of the wind. But "keep up my courage" is in the background.

Right onward. What supports me dost thou ask?
The conscience, friend, to have lost them overplied
In liberty's defense, my noble task,
Of which all Europe talks from side to side.
This thought might lead me through the world's vain masque
Content though blind, had I no better guide.

10. **conscience:** consciousness.

11. **In liberty's defense:** In January 1650, the Council of State ordered Milton to reply to Salmasius's *Defensio Regia.* He later said that his physicians had advised him that the task would result in blindness. Milton persisted, sacrificing his eyesight "for the greatest possible benefit to the state" (p. 1082).

12. **all Europe talks:** Not quite, but the *First Defense* did achieve some European notoriety (see Parker 1971, 32–38).

13. **vain masque:** The idea of life as a staged drama was commonplace; Bacon's *Of Truth* takes note of "the masques and mummeries and triumphs of the world."

SONNET 23

It is regrettable that one of Milton's most moving lyrics, possibly the most moving, should be enveloped in an unpoetic atmosphere of puzzle solving and scholarly debate. But that is the situation. For two centuries editors had assumed that the "late espousèd saint" of this sonnet was Katharine Woodcock, Milton's second wife. Then in 1945, William R. Parker wrote the first of a number of pieces urging the claims of Mary Powell, Milton's first wife.

Many of the facts cut in two directions. For example, Mary died in May 1652, three days after giving birth to Deborah, her third daughter. Katharine died in February 1658. Although she had given birth to a daughter in October 1657 (who would outlive her by only six weeks), Katharine's death was due not to childbirth but to consumption. With regard to which dead wife is Milton most likely to have thought of the Old Testament ritual of purification after childbirth? Katharine died long after the time prescribed for this purification (eighty days if the child was a daughter) had expired, whereas Mary did not survive the purification period. Milton might have thought: "Katharine lived beyond the time of uncleanness yet was not returned to me, save in a dream." But he might equally well have thought: "Mary did not live through the time of uncleanness. Would that she had, and would that she had been returned to me, as she is in this dream." It is well to bear in mind, whatever one decides, that the poem's "purification in the Old Law" is metaphorical for the wife's return to her husband, again to be "mine," and in the larger design of the poem prepares for the higher purity of her mind in line 9.

Milton, entirely blind in 1652, never saw Katharine but enjoyed "full sight" of Mary for many years. Which wife is more likely to be veiled? Katharine, the wife he never saw? So many interpreters have decided. It may be significant that Admetus does not recognize Alcestis while she is veiled, whereas Milton, surely, is in no doubt over the identity of the veiled shade in his dream. Perhaps the veiled face symbolizes his blindness, the fact that in this life he could form no image of her face even if she were to return to him. In Heaven he will behold her without the "restraint" of blindness. Thus far the evidence favors Katharine. But what is implied and not implied by "such, as yet once more I trust to have/Full sight of her in Heaven without restraint"? The phrase "yet once more," which seems to allude in a personal and mysterious way to *Lycidas,* implies that the event in question will occur three times (once, once more, yet once more). Now the lines favor Mary Powell by suggesting that Milton has had "full sight" of her on this earth, in this dream (the veil not counting against "full sight"), and trusts to see her again in Heaven. But Katharine Woodcock is not entirely ruled out. The "yet" in "yet once more" could conceivably be an intensive, indicating that the event will happen twice (once, yet once more). Milton could be saying that he has full sight of Katharine in the dream (the subsequent detail of the veil again being regarded in the context of the dream's "day" as no compromise in "full sight") and will see her face-to-face in Heaven.

The poem achieves inner coherence no matter which woman a reader has in mind. It may point us toward the sonnet's emotional force to glance briefly at the way in which possession is drawn out in the course of the poem. "Methought": the dream vision was mine, entirely private, more so than I knew at the time. It was a vision of "my" late saint, and this blossoms into a still more emphatic "Mine" at the opening of line 5. He trusts "to have" full sight of her in Heaven. To "my fancied sight," the goodness in her face could not be plainer. Then at last she (in answer to the poet's desire?) inclines "to embrace me." But Milton awakes, she disappears, and in the end all of the poem's yearning mineness has only the empty, sightless "my night." How fragile, how pregnant with despair, was that opening "Methought"!

But Gerald Hammond has recently suggested that the cruel twist of fate at the end of the poem can also be viewed as a display of mental strength. The dreamer appears to remain entirely passive. He confesses to no coaxing, no response; the veiled woman bends to embrace him. The speaker's one positive act is to awaken at just that moment. Could it be an escape? The embraces of a woman come back from the grave might restore to a man everything he has lost and most desires to have again, but they might also draw him into the dead world of the past. Perhaps Milton, in losing the image he thought was "mine," regains his life. Perhaps his awakening "is not passive, but an act of heroic resistance" (Hammond 216).

Methought I saw my late espousèd saint
Brought to me like Alcestis from the grave,
Whom Jove's great son to her glad husband gave,
Rescued from death by force though pale and faint.
Mine as whom washed from spot of child-bed taint
Purification in the Old Law did save,
And such, as yet once more I trust to have
Full sight of her in Heaven without restraint,
Came vested all in white, pure as her mind:
Her face was veiled, yet to my fancied sight,
Love, sweetness, goodness in her person shined
So clear, as in no face with more delight.
But O as to embrace me she inclined,
I waked, she fled, and day brought back my night.

1. **Methought I saw:** As in *Sonnet 19,* the opening is formulaic; see Ralegh's "Methought I saw the grave where Laura lay." **late espousèd saint:** Critics make a great deal of whether *late* modifies *espousèd,* which would make the phrase mean "recently married saint" and cast doubt on Mary Powell as the woman in question, or instead modifies *espousèd saint,* which would make the phrase mean "recently deceased wife." The first reading is strained.

2. **Alcestis:** In Euripides' *Alcestis,* Admetus can escape death by persuading someone to die in his place, and his wife, Alcestis, volunteers. Hercules rescues her from Death and returns her, pale, trembling, and veiled, to her husband.

5. **as whom:** as one whom.

5–6. God lays down the ritual prescriptions for purifying women immediately after childbirth in Lev. 12. During this time, women would not be seen by their husbands.

7. **yet once more:** The opening phrase of *Lycidas.* See headnote.

8. **without restraint:** Hammond (217, 221–23) notes the erotic force of "restraint" in *PL* 8.628. The end of the purification ritual signaled a resumption of sexual relations.

9. **all in white:** Cp. Rev. 7.13–14, 19.8.

10. **Her face was veiled:** as was the face of Alcestis (see 2n), though Milton, unlike Admetus, immediately recognizes his wife.

13–14. Among the numerous classical precedents for this failed embrace are Aeneas's three attempts to clasp the shade of his wife (*Aen.* 2.789–95) and Achilles' attempt to embrace the dream image of Patroclus (*Il.* 23.99–107).

ON THE NEW FORCERS OF CONSCIENCE UNDER THE LONG PARLIAMENT

Milton entered the pamphlet wars of the 1640s as a supporter of the Presbyterians in their struggle against Anglican Prelacy. *An Apology for Smectymnuus* (1642) took up the cause of five Presbyterian ministers who, under the joint pseudonym SMECTYMNUUS, were engaged in disputes with Bishop Joseph Hall. But by the time *On the New Forcers of Conscience* was written, probably late in 1646, Milton was firmly allied with Independents in opposition to the Presbyterians, who in his mind had come to resemble the Anglican prelates they had originally sought to oust.

In 1643 the Long Parliament appointed the Westminster Assembly to reorganize the Anglican Church. Presbyterians enjoyed an overwhelming majority in the Assembly, and they are the "New Forcers of Conscience" to whom Milton's poem is addressed. They used their power to thwart the aims of the Independents in the Assembly, who preferred toleration and liberty of conscience to the advantages of compulsory conformity. Although Parliament in August 1646 accepted the Assembly's plan to ordain ministers by Presbyterian synods or classes (Milton's "classic hierarchy"), the poem supposes that the rampant abuses of the Presbyterians will soon lead to their comeuppance in Parliament.

The poem has the form of a *sonetto caudato* or "tailed sonnet." Rather than come to closure at line 14, it produces a half-line (tailed line) and a couplet, then a second half-line or tail, before delivering the pentameter couplet at the end. Italian poets had used the tailed sonnet for humorous and satirical subjects.

Because you have thrown off your prelate lord,
And with stiff vows renounced his liturgy
To seize the widowed whore Plurality
From them whose sin ye envied, not abhorred,
Dare ye for this adjure the civil sword
To force our consciences that Christ set free,
And ride us with a classic hierarchy
Taught ye by mere A.S. and Rutherford?
Men whose life, learning, faith and pure intent
Would have been held in high esteem with Paul
Must now be named and printed heretics
By shallow Edwards and Scotch What-d'ye-call:

1. **you:** The poem is addressed to Presbyterians in the Westminster Assembly; **thrown off your prelate lord:** Parliament had resolved to abolish episcopacy in 1643, though it was not formally outlawed until the decree of 1646.

2. **his liturgy:** Archbishop Laud's version of the *The Book of Common Prayer*, abolished in 1645.

3. **Plurality:** the practice of holding more than one ministerial living. Presbyterians criticized Anglicans for this abuse but were now guilty of it themselves.

4. **abhorred:** a play on *whore* found in *OTH* (4.2.161–62) and *MM* (3.1.101).

5. **for this:** for the widowed whore Plurality; **adjure:** charge, entreat.

6. **force . . . free:** Milton believed that compelled conformity to the national church was a violation of Christian liberty.

7. **ride us:** tyrannize over us; **classic hierarchy:** Parliament decreed that English congregations were to be grouped in Presbyteries or "Classes" in the Scottish manner.

8. **A.S.:** Adam Stewart, a Scottish divine who wrote pamphlets (signed with his initials) attacking the Independents; **Rutherford:** Samuel Rutherford, another and more substantial opponent of independency who resided in London from 1643 to 1647 as a commissioner of the Church of Scotland to the Westminster Assembly.

12. **shallow Edwards:** Thomas Edwards, an English Presbyterian, was the University Preacher at Cambridge and author of *Gangraena* (1646), which listed among numerous heresies Milton's doctrine of divorce. **Scotch What-d'ye-call:** often assumed without real evidence to be Robert Baillie, a Scottish Commissioner on the Assembly whose *Dissausive from the Errors of the Time* (1645) also attacked Milton's views on divorce.

But we do hope to find out all your tricks,
Your plots and packings worse than those of Trent,
That so the Parliament
May with their wholesome and preventive shears
Clip your phylacteries, though balk your ears,
And succor our just fears
When they shall read this clearly in your charge:
"New *Presbyter* is but old *Priest* writ large."

14. **packings:** corrupt manipulations of a deliberative body. **Trent:** The Council of Trent was intended to reform the doctrines of the Roman Catholic Church in response to the Reformation. But it was manipulated by the papacy and became a standard Protestant example of Catholic hypocrisy and treachery.

17. **phylacteries:** ostentatious and hypocritical signs of piety; **balk your ears:** intentionally omit (to clip) your ears. Parliament will not punish the hypocritical Presbyterians by cutting off their ears, which is how William Prynne (1600–69) was twice punished. He lost most of his ears for supposedly slandering the king and queen in *Histrio-Mastix* (1633), and then the remnants of them for Presbyterian attacks on the Anglican Church in 1637.

19. **they:** Parliament; **your charge:** the indictment that will be brought against the Presbyterians.

20. Etymologically, *priest* is an abbreviated form of *presbyter* (from Gk. for "elder" and "priest"). Hence "Priest" *writ large* (written out in full) would be *presbyter.*

Latin and Greek Poems

Carmina Elegiaca [*Elegiac Verses*]

When A. I. Horwood discovered Milton's *Commonplace Book* in 1874, he also found a holograph page containing the poem *Ignavus satrapam* and a fragment of a Latin prose composition on early rising. The two poems are almost certainly early school exercises, possibly from 1624.

Surge, age, surge, leves, iam convenit, excute somnos,
  Lux oritus, tepidi fulcra relinque tori.
Iam canit excubitor gallus, praenuntius ales
  Solis, et invigilans ad sua quemque vocat.
Flammiger Eois Titan caput exerit undis
  Et spargit nitidum laeta per arva iubar.
Daulias argutum modulatur ab ilice carmen
  Edit et excultos mitis alauda modos.
Iam rosa fragrantes spirat silvestris odores,
  Iam redolent violae luxuriatque seges.
Ecce novo campos Zephyritis gramine vestit
  Fertilis, et vitreo rore madescit humus.
Segnes invenias molli vix talia lecto
  Cum premat imbellis lumina fessa sopor.
Illic languentes abrumpunt somnia somnos
  Et turbant animum tristia multa tuum;
Illic tabifici generantur semina morbi.
  Qui pote torpentem posse valere virum?
Surge, age, surge, leves, iam convenit, excute somnos,
  Lux oritur, tepidi fulcra relinque tori.

Get up, go, get up, it's time now, throw off worthless sleep, the light is rising, leave the frame of your warm bed! The watchman rooster is already singing, the winged harbinger of the sun, and, wide awake, calls each to his own business. The flame-bearing Titan[5] lifts his head out of Dawn's waves and scatters gleaming light over the happy fields. The Daulian[7] sings a sharp song from the oak tree, and the gentle lark puts forth exquisite notes. Now the wild rose breathes out sweet odors, now the violets are fragrant and the wheat fields run riot. Look, fruitful Zephyritis[11] dresses the fields with new grass, and the earth is moist with glassy dew. Sluggard, you will hardly find such things in your soft bed while unwarlike sleep presses your tired eyes. There dreams interrupt your languid slumber, and many troubling things disturb your spirit; there the seeds of wasting diseases are born. How can a lazy man be healthy? Get up, go, get up, it's time now, throw off worthless sleep, the light is rising, leave the frame of your warm bed!

5. **Titan:** the sun.
7. **Daulias:** the swallow.
11. **Zephyritis:** Zephyr's consort is Flora, goddess of spring.

IGNAVUS SATRAPAM

[*Kings should not oversleep*]

Ignavus satrapam dedecet inclytum
Somnus qui populo multifido praeest.
Dum Dauni veteris filius armiger
Stratus purpureo procubuit [toro]
Audax Euryalus, Nisus et impiger
Invasere cati nocte sub horrida
Torpentes Rutilos castraque Volscia:
Hinc caedes oritur clamor et absonus.

Ignoble sleep is unfitting for a famous satrap who rules a nation of many parts. While the arms-bearing son of old Daunus[3] lay stretched on a bed[4] of purple, bold Euryalus and unsluggish Nisus, a shrewd pair, on a harsh night invaded the drowsy Rutilians and the Volscian camp. Whence arose slaughter and confused outcry.

3. The camp of Turnus is attacked in *Aen.* 9.176-449.
4. The word *toro* is a conjecture; the last word of the line is missing from the manuscript.

APOLOGUS DE RUSTICO ET HERO

[*The Fable of the Peasant and the Lord*]

This work first appeared at the end of the *Elegiarum Liber* in the *Poems* of 1673. It is almost universally considered an early school exercise. The fable appears in Aesop, but Milton's model is Mantuan, *Opera* (Paris, 1513), 194.

Rusticus ex malo sapidissima poma quotannis
  Legit, et urbano lecta dedit domino:
Hic incredibili fructus dulcedine captus
  Malum ipsam in proprias transtulit areolas.
Hactenus illa ferax, sed longo debilis aevo,
  Mota solo assueto, protinus aret iners.
Quod tandem ut patuit domino, spe lusus inani,
  Damnavit celeres in sua damna manus.
Atque ait, Heu quanto satius fuit illa coloni
  (Parva licet) grato dona tulisse animo!
Possem ego avaritiam frenare, gulamque voracem:
  Nunc periere mihi et fetus et ipsa parens.

A peasant picked very tasty fruit every year from an apple tree, and gave the choicest to his lord in the city; captivated by the fruit's incredible sweetness, he transplanted the tree itself into his own garden. Fruitful up to then, but weak from old age, when moved from its accustomed soil, it immediately withers and becomes barren. Then, when this became clear to the lord, fooled by vain hope, he cursed the quickness of his hands in his own undoing. And he said, "Alas, how much better it was to receive my tenant's gifts, small as they were, with a grateful spirit! Would that I could have restrained my greed and voracious gluttony; now I have lost both the offspring and the parent itself."

PHILOSOPHUS AD REGEM

[*A Philosopher to a King*]

These Greek verses were printed in the 1645 and 1673 *Poems*. Though we cannot supply a certain date, the work was probably a school exercise.

Philosophus ad regem quendam qui eum ignotum et insontem inter reos forte captum inscius damnaverat τὴν ἐπὶ θανάτῳ πορευόμενος, haec subito misit

Ὦ ἄνα εἰ ὀλέσῃς με τὸν ἔννομον, οὐδέ τιν' ἀνδρῶν
Δεινὸν ὅλως δράσαντα, σοφώτατον ἴσθι κάρηνον
Ῥηϊδίως ἀφέλοιο, τὸ δ' ὕστερον αὖθι νοήσεις,
Μαψιδίως δ' ἄρ' ἔπειτα τεὸν πρὸς θυμὸν ὀδύρῃ,
Τοιόν δ' ἐκ πόλιος περιώνυμον ἄλκαρ ὀλέσσας.

A philosopher being conveyed to his death suddenly sent this to a certain king who unknowingly had condemned him after he had been accidentally taken, unrecognized and innocent, in the company of criminals.

O master, if you destroy me, a law-abiding man who has done no harm at all to anyone, know that you blithely take off a head of great wisdom, but afterward you will quickly understand, and then you will vainly lament in your heart that you deprived the city of such a widely renowned guardian.

Elegiarum Liber [*Book of Elegies*]

ELEGIA PRIMA AD CAROLUM DIODATUM
[*Elegy 1. To Charles Diodati*]

This poem, probably written in 1626, is addressed to Charles Diodati (1609–1638), the great friend of Milton's youth. They attended St. Paul's together. Diodati went up to Oxford in 1623, while Milton, for reasons that remain unclear, did not enter Cambridge until February 1625. It has often been supposed that in the passage in which Milton refers to himself as an "exile" (ll. 17–20) he is discussing an altercation with his tutor William Chappell that resulted in a suspension. But, as Carey rightly points out, the evidence is weak, and Milton's "exile" was probably a normal college vacation.

Tandem, care, tuae mihi pervenire tabellae,
  Pertulit et voces nuntia charta tuas,
Pertulit occidua Devae Cestrensis ab ora
  Vergivium prono qua petit amne salum.
Multum, crede, iuvat terras aluisse remotas
  Pectus amans nostri, tamque fidele caput,
Quodque mihi lepidum tellus longinqua sodalem
  Debet, at unde brevi reddere iussa velit.
Me tenet urbs reflua quam Thamesis alluit unda,
  Meque nec invitum patria dulcis habet.
Iam nec arundiferum mihi cura revisere Camum,
  Nec dudum vetiti me laris angit amor.
Nuda nec arva placent, umbrasque negantia molles;

At last, dear friend, your tablets have reached me, and the paper messenger has brought your voice, brought it from the western bank of Chester's Dee, where it seeks the Irish Sea with a downward flow. Believe me, it is a great joy that faraway lands have nurtured a heart which loves us, and so faithful a head, and that a distant country owes me a charming companion but is willing to pay the debt quickly when ordered. The city which the Thames washes with retreating waves holds me, and my sweet homeland does not keep me against my will. Nor do I now have any interest in returning to the reedy Cam; nor does love of

Quam male Phoebicolis convenit ille locus!
Nec duri libet usque minas perferre magistri
Caeteraque ingenio non subeunda meo.
Si sit hoc exilium, patrios adiisses penates,
Et vacuum curis otia grata sequi,
Non ego vel profugi nomen sortemve recuso,
Laetus et exilii conditione fruor.
O utinam vates nunquam graviora tulisset
Ille Tomitano flebilis exul agro;
Non tunc Ionio quicquam cessisset Homero
Neve foret victo laus tibi prima Maro.
Tempora nam licet hic placidis dare libera Musis,
Et totum rapiunt me mea vita libri.
Excipit hinc fessum sinuosi pompa theatri,
Et vocat ad plausus garrula scena suos.
Seu catus auditur senior, seu prodigus haeres,
Seu procus, aut posita casside miles adest,
Sive decennali foecundus lite patronus
Detonat inculto barbara verba foro,
Saepe vafer gnato succurrit servus amanti,
Et nasum rigidi fallit ubique patris;
Saepe novos illic virgo mirata calores
Quid sit amor nescit, dum quoque nescit, amat.
Sive cruentatum furiosa Tragoedia sceptrum
Quassat, et effusis crinibus ora rotat;
Et dolet, et specto, iuvat et spectasse dolendo;
Interdum et lacrimis dulcis amaror inest:
Seu puer infelix indelibata reliquit
Gaudia, et abrupto flendus amore cadit;
Seu ferus e tenebris iterat Styga criminis ultor,
Conscia funereo pectora torre movens;

my recently forbidden hearth god torment me; nor are bare fields attractive, denying soft shade. How badly that place suits Phoebus's followers.[14] It is not pleasing to keep bearing the threats of a harsh master[15] and other things intolerable to my talent. If this is exile—to have returned to my homeland gods and pursue a welcome leisure free from worries—I have not shunned the name, nor do I refuse the fate, and I am happy to rejoice in the condition of exile. Oh, would that bard[21] had never borne anything worse, that tearful exile in the fields of Tomis; then he would not have yielded to Ionic Homer,[23] nor would the highest praise have been yours, defeated Vergil. For here it is possible to give free time to the peaceful Muses, and my books (my life) take me over completely. The spectacle of the curved theater attracts one when tired, and the chatty stage summons its applause. Sometimes a crafty old man is being heard, or a prodigal heir, or a wooer, or a soldier with his helmet off is there, or a lawyer rich from a ten-year-old case declaims barbarous words to an ignorant forum. Often a clever slave helps out a son in love, and fools the nose of his stern father at every turn; often then a virgin, surprised by new passion, does not know what love is, and loves even as she does not know. Sometimes furious Tragedy shakes a bloody scepter and twists her face, her hair streaming; and it is painful, and I watch, and it is a joy to have watched in pain. And sometimes there is a sweet bitterness in tears, as when an unhappy boy abandoned unconsummated joys, and falls to be wept over, his love extinguished; or when from the shadows a fierce avenger of crime

14. **Phoebicolis:** poets.
15. The stern tutor is usually identified as William Chappell. Aubrey (p. xxv) is responsible for the familiar but dubious notion that Chappell whipped Milton.
21. **vates:** Ovid, whom Augustus exiled to Tomis on the Black Sea.
23. **Ionio:** Smyrna in Ionia was one of the cities that claimed to be the birthplace of Homer.

Seu maeret Pelopeia domus, seu nobilis Ili,
Aut luit incestos aula Creontis avos.
Sed neque sub tecto semper nec in urbe latemus,
Irrita nec nobis tempora veris eunt.
Nos quoque lucus habet vicina consitus ulmo
Atque suburbani nobilis umbra loci.
Saepius hic blandas spirantia sidera flammas
Virgineos videas praeteriisse choros.
Ah quoties dignae stupui miracula formae
Quae posset senium vel reparare Iovis;
Ah quoties vidi superantia lumina gemmas,
Atque faces quotquot volvit uterque polus;
Collaque bis vivi Pelopis quae brachia vincant,
Quaeque fluit puro nectare tincta via,
Et decus eximium frontis, tremulosque capillos,
Aurea quae fallax retia tendit Amor;
Pellacesque genas, ad quas hyacinthia sordet
Purpura, et ipse tui floris, Adoni, rubor.
Cedite laudatae toties Heroides olim,
Et quaecunque vagum cepit amica Iovem.
Cedite Achaemeniae turrita fronte puellae,
Et quot Susa colunt, Memnoniamque Ninon.
Vos etiam Danae fasces submittite Nymphae,
Et vos Iliacae, Romuleaeque nurus;
Nec Pompeianas Tarpeia Musa columnas
Iactet, et Ausoniis plena theatra stolis.
Gloria Virginibus debetur prima Britannis;

recrosses the Styx, moving guilty hearts with his funereal torch; or when the house of Pelops[45] grieves, or that of noble Ilus, or Creon's palace atones for incestuous ancestors. But we do not always hide indoors or in the city, nor is springtime wasted on us. A grove nearby, thickly planted with elm, holds us, and the noble shade of a site just outside the city. Often here you can see groups of young girls pass by: stars breathing forth seductive flames. Ah, how many times I have been amazed at the miracles of a worthy figure which could reverse the old age of Jove! Ah, how many times I have seen eyes outshining jewels and all the torches which revolve around either pole! And necks which would outdo the shoulders of twice-living Pelops[57] and the path[58] that runs dyed with pure nectar; and an exceptionally beautiful forehead, and dancing hair which treacherous Love casts as a golden net; and enticing cheeks beside which the purple hyacinth seems dull, and even the blush of your flower,[62] Adonis! Surrender, you heroines praised so many times in the past,[63] and whatever mistress trapped fickle Jove! Surrender, you women of Persia with the towering headdresses, and all of you who inhabit Susa[66] and Memnon's Nineveh! And you Greek nymphs, put down your fasces, and you young women of Troy and of Rome. And let the Tarpeian Muse[69] not boast of Pompey's colonnade, and the theaters crowded with Italian gowns. The prime glory is owed to the virgins of Britain; foreign woman, let it be enough for you to come next. And you, city of

45. **Pelopeia domus:** The descendants of Pelops (Atreus, Thyestes, Agamemnon, Orestes, Electra, Iphigenia) were destined for tragedy. Cp. *Il Pens* 99–100.

57. Pelops was killed by his father, Tantalus, and served to the gods. Demeter ate a part of his shoulder. When Pelops was restored to life, the gods gave him an ivory shoulder (Ovid, *Met.* 6.403–11).

58. **via:** the Milky Way.

62. **tui floris, Adoni:** Venus caused the anemone to grow from Adonis's blood.

63. Milton alludes to the heroines of Ovid's *Heroides.*

66. **Susa:** a major city in Persia.

69. **Tarpeia Musa:** Ovid, who lived near the Tarpeian rock. He thought Pompey's colonnade and the Roman theater were the best places to meet women (*Ars Amatoria* 1.67, 3.387).

Extera sat tibi sit foemina posse sequi.
Tuque urbs Dardaniis Londinum structa colonis
Turrigerum late conspicienda caput,
Tu nimium felix intra tua moenia claudis
Quicquid formosi pendulus orbis habet.
Non tibi tot caelo scintillant astra sereno
Endymioneae turba ministra deae,
Quot tibi conspicuae formaque auroque puellae
Per media radiant turba videnda vias.
Creditur huc gemenis venisse invecta columbis
Alma pharetrigero milite cincta Venus,
Huic Cnidon, et riguas Simoentis flumine valles,
Huic Paphon, et roseam posthabitura Cypron.
Ast ego, dum pueri sinit indulgentia caeci,
Moenia quam subito linquere fausta paro;
Et vitare procul malefidae infamia Circes
Atria, divini Molyos usus ope.
Stat quoque iuncosas Cami remeare paludes,
Atque iterum raucae murmur adire Scholae.
Interea fidi parvum cape munus amici,
Paucaque in alternos verba coacta modos.

London, built by Trojan settlers,[73] whose tower-bearing head can be seen from far around, you are too happy for enclosing within your walls whatever beauty the pendulous earth holds. There are not as many stars shining for you in the calm heavens—the crowd attending on Endymion's goddess—as there are girls brilliant with beauty and gold, a crowd to be seen shining throughout your streets. It is believed that nurturing Venus, surrounded by her quiver-bearing soldiery, came here, carried by her twin doves, thinking Cnidos and the valleys watered by the river Sinois inferior to this, and Paphos and rosy Cyprus. But I, while the indulgence of the blind boy permits, am preparing to leave these happy walls as soon as possible, and to leave far behind the infamous halls of faithless Circe, using the aid of divine moly.[88] I am set to return to the reedy marshes of the Cam, and again to join the tumult of the noisy university. In the meantime, take this small gift from a loyal friend, a few words forced into alternating meter.[92]

73. According to ancient legends popularized by Geoffrey of Monmouth, Britain was founded by a Trojan named Brutus, the great-grandson of Aeneas.

88. **Molyos:** The herb moly protects Homer's Odysseus against the charms of Circe (*Od.* 10.305).

92. **alternos . . . modos:** The alternating pentameter and hexameter lines of the elegiac couplet.

ELEGIA SECUNDA. IN OBITUM PRAECONIS ACADEMICI CANTABRIGIENSIS

[*Elegy 2. On the Death of the Beadle of Cambridge University*]

The subject of this elegy is Richard Ridding, for thirty years the Senior Esquire Bedell (hence Beadle) of the university. He resigned his post in September 1626 and died soon thereafter.

Milton dated the poem in his standard manner. The Latin tag means "At the age of seventeen."

ANNO AETATIS 17

Te, qui conspicuus baculo fulgente solebas
  Palladium toties ore ciere gregem,
Ultima praeconum praeconem te quoque saeva
  Mors rapit, officio nec favet ipsa suo.
Candidiora licet fuerint tibi tempora plumis
  Sub quibus accipimus delituisse Iovem,
O dignus tamen Haemonio iuvenescere succo,
  Dignus in Aesonios vivere posse dies,
Dignus quem Stygiis medica revocaret ab undis
  Arte Coronides, saepe rogante dea.
Tu si iussus eras acies accire togatas,
  Et celer a Phoebo nuntius ire tuo,
Talis in Iliaca stabat Cyllenius aula
  Alipes, aetherea missus ab arce Patris.
Talis et Eurybates ante ora furentis Achillei
  Rettulit Atridae iussa severa ducis.
Magna sepulchrorum regina, satelles Averni
  Saeva nimis Musis, Palladi saeva nimis,
Quin illos rapias qui pondus inutile terrae?
  Turba quidem est telis ista petenda tuis.
Vestibus hunc igitur pullis Academia luge,
  Et madeant lachrymis nigra feretra tuis.
Fundat et ipsa modos querebunda Elegeia
    tristes,
  Personet et totis naenia moesta scholis.

AT AGE 17

You who, illustrious with your shining staff,[1] used to rouse the Palladian flock[2] so many times with your voice—cruel death, the ultimate herald, takes you, also a herald, and shows no favor to his own profession. Though your temples may have been whiter than the feathers under which we are told Jove hid himself,[6] O! worthy nevertheless to be made young again with Haemonian juice,[7] worthy to be able to live to Aeson's age, worthy for the son of Coronis to have recalled from the waters of Styx with his medical art, at the goddess's repeated request.[9] If you were ordered to assemble a betogaed line, and to go as a swift messenger from your Phoebus,[12] so stood winged Hermes[13] in the Trojan court, sent from the aerial citadel of his father, and so Eurybates[15] delivered to the face of enraged Achilles the stern orders of lord Atrides. Great queen of tombs, servant of Avernus,[17] too cruel to the Muses, too cruel to Pallas, why do you not take those who are a useless burden on the earth? There is a crowd of such at which to aim your weapons. Therefore, Academy, in dark clothing mourn this man, and let the black bier be wet with your tears; and let plaintive Elegy herself pour out sorrowful harmonies, and sad dirges resound in all the schools.

1. **baculo:** the beadle's mace, carried in academic ceremonies.
2. The university is filled with devotees of Pallas, goddess of wisdom and learning.
6. Jove raped Leda in the shape of a swan.
7. Medea revives Jason's father, Aeson, with drugs from Thessaly (Ovid, *Met.* 7.251–93).
9. Asclepius, who restored Hippolytus to life in Ovid's *Fasti* 6.743–56.
12. **Phoebo:** the vice-chancellor.
13. Mercury (called *Cyllenius* because born on Mount Cyllene) is sent by his father, Jupiter, to guide Priam to Achilles (*Il.* 23.336–467).
15. **Eurybates:** One of the heralds Agamemnon sends to seize the captive Briseis from Achilles (*Il.* 1.318–44).
17. Avernus is a lake near Venice close to the cave where Aeneas descended to the underworld (*Aen.* 6.106–7); it is used poetically as a name for the underworld.

ELEGIA TERTIA, IN OBITUM PRAESULIS WINTONIENSIS

[*Elegy 3. On the Death of the Bishop of Winchester*]

This poem was occasioned by the death of the famous Anglican divine Lancelot Andrewes on September 25, 1626. Andrewes was greatly admired by T. S. Eliot, the most important literary tastemaker of the twentieth century. According to Eliot, his sermons "rank with the finest English prose of their time, of any time," and the spiritual wisdom of Andrewes makes Donne the preacher seem "a little of the religious spellbinder" or "the sorcerer of emotional orgy" (1964, 299, 302). But Eliot was admittedly conservative in religious (and other) matters. In his third political pamphlet, *The Reason of Church Government* (1641), Milton devoted some irritable pages to Andrewes's "shallow reasonings" about prelacy (Yale 1:768–79).

ANNO AETATIS 17

Moestus eram, et tacitus nullo comitante sedebam,
  Haerebantque animo tristia plura meo,
Protinus en subiit funestae cladis imago
  Fecit in Angliaco quam Libitina solo;
Dum procerum ingressa est splendentes marmore turres
  Dira sepulchrali mors metuenda face;
Pulsavitque auro gravidos et iaspide muros,
  Nec metuit satrapum sternere falce greges.
Tunc memini clarique ducis, fratrisque verendi
  Intempestivis ossa cremata rogis.
Et memini Heroum quos vidit ad aethera raptos,
  Flevit et amissos Belgia tota duces.
At te praecipue luxi, dignissime praesul,
  Wintoniaeque olim gloria magna tuae;
Delicui fletu, et tristi sic ore querebar,

3. During 1625 over 35,000, about a sixth of the city's population, died of the plague in London and its environs (Wilson 1963, 174–75).

4. **Libitina:** goddess of corpses.

5. Horace's *Odes* 1.4.13–14 is the best-known version of this commonplace.

11. **Heroum:** Among the prominent Englishmen to die in the Low Countries were the earls of Oxford and Southampton, and Sir Horace Vere. Breda fell to the Spaniards in May 1625.

AT AGE 17

I was sad, and sat silent, with no companion, and many sorrows clung to my soul—then suddenly came a vision of the grim killing[3] which Libitina[4] had done on English soil, while dreadful death, fearsome with her sepulchral torch, entered the splendidly marble palaces of the great,[5] and beat down walls heavy with gold and jasper, and did not fear to cut down a flock of satraps with her scythe. Then I remembered the bones of a famous lord and his respected brother, burned on untimely pyres. And I remembered the heroes[11] whom all Belgia saw snatched up into the skies and mourned as lost leaders. But especially I mourned you, most worthy bishop, once the great glory of your Winchester; I melted with weeping, and thus complained in a sad voice: "Sav-

Mors fera, Tartareo diva secunda Iovi,
Nonne satis quod silva tuas persentiat iras,
Et quod in herbosos ius tibi detur agros,
Quodque afflata tuo marcescant lilia tabo,
Et crocus, et pulchrae Cypridi sacra rosa?
Nec sinis ut semper fluvio contermina quercus
Miretur lapsus praetereuntis aquae.
Et tibi succumbit liquido quae plurima caelo
Evehitur pennis quamlibet augur avis,
Et quae mille nigris errant animalia silvis,
Et quod alunt mutum Proteos antra pecus.
Invida, tanta tibi cum sit concessa potestas,
Quid iuvat humana tingere caede manus?
Nobileque in pectus certas acuisse sagittas,
Semideamque animam sede fugasse sua?
Talia dum lacrimans alto sub pectore volvo,
Roscidus occiduis Hesperus exit aquis,
Et Tartessiaco submerserat aequore currum
Phoebus ab eoo littore mensus iter.
Nec mora, membra cavo posui refovenda cubili;
Condiderant oculos noxque soporque meos,
Cum mihi visus eram lato spatiarier agro;
Heu nequit ingenium visa referre meum.
Illic punicea radiabant omnia luce,
Ut matutino cum iuga sole rubent.
Ac veluti cum pandit opes Thaumantia proles,
Vestitu nituit multicolore solum.
Non dea tam variis ornavit floribus hortos
Alcinoi, Zephyro Chloris amata levi.

16. **Tartareo . . . Iovi:** Pluto, the Jove of the underworld.
20. **Cypridi:** Venus, to whom Cyprus was sacred.
26. **Proteos:** Proteus herded Neptune's seals.
32. **Hesperus:** the evening star.
33. **Tartessiaco . . . aequore:** the Atlantic Ocean.
41. **Thaumantia proles:** Iris, goddess of the rainbow.
44. **Chloris:** the Roman goddess of flowers, whose name changed to Flora after Zephyrus wooed her (Ovid, *Fasti* 5.195–378).

age Death, goddess second only to Tartarean Jove,[16] is it not enough that the woods feel your anger, and that you are given power over grassy fields, and that lilies wither when breathed upon by your poison, and also the crocus and the rose, sacred to beautiful Cypris;[20] or that you do not allow the oak next to the river to watch forever the flow of the passing water? And whatever bird, although an augur, that is carried on its wings through the liquid heavens succumbs to you, and however many thousands of animals wander in the dark forests, and whatever silent herd the caves of Proteus nurture.[26] Invidious one, since so much power is granted you, why does it please you to stain your hands with human slaughter, and to have sharpened sure arrows against a noble breast, and to have driven a half-divine soul from its home?" While, weeping, I turn such things over in my heart, dewy Hesperus[32] leaves the western waters, and Phoebus, having marked his journey from the eastern shore, had submerged his chariot in the Tartessian sea.[33] Without delay, I laid my body that needed restoring on my hollow bed, and night and sleep had closed my eyes, when I seemed to be wandering in a large field—alas, my skill cannot relate what I saw. There everything shone with a red light, as when mountaintops blush with the morning sun; and as when Thaumas's daughter[41] opens up her riches, the earth gleamed in multicolored clothing. The goddess Chloris,[44] loved by gentle Zephyrus, did not ornament the gardens of Alcinous with such varied flowers. Silver rivers wash

Flumina vernantes lambunt argentea campos,
Ditior Hesperio flavet arena Tago.
Serpit odoriferas per opes levis aura Favoni,
Aura sub innumeris humida nata rosis.
Talis in extremis terrae Gangetidis oris
Luciferi regis fingitur esse domus.
Ipse racemiferis dum densas vitibus umbras
Et pellucentes miror ubique locos,
Ecce mihi subito praesul Wintonius astat,
Sidereum nitido fulsit in ore iubar;
Vestis ad auratos defluxit candida talos,
Infula divinum cinxerat alba caput.
Dumque senex tali incedit venerandus amictu,
Intremuit laeto florea terra sono.
Agmina gemmatis plaudunt caelestia pennis,
Pura triumphali personat aethra tuba.
Quisque novum amplexu comitem cantuque salutat,
Hosque aliquis placido misit ab ore sonos:
Nate veni, et patrii felix cape gaudia regni,
Semper ab hinc duro, nate, labore vaca.
Dixit, et aligerae tetigerunt nablia turmae,
At mihi cum tenebris aurea pulsa quies.
Flebam turbatos Cephaleia pellice somnos;
Talia contingant somnia saepe mihi.

the springtime fields; the sand is more golden than Hesperian Tagus.[46] The gentle breeze of Favonius[47] steals through odor-bearing riches—a moist breeze born from innumerable roses. Such is imagined to be the home of King Lucifer on the far shores of the land of Ganges. While I gaze on the shadows dense with grape-bearing vines and shining spaces in all directions, lo! suddenly the Bishop of Winchester stands next to me. A starry brightness shone from his radiant face; his white clothing flowed down to his golden ankles, a white fillet girded his divine head. And as the reverend old man moved in such clothing, the flowery earth trembled with a happy sound. Heaven's host applauds with jeweled wings, the pure ether resounds with a triumphal trumpet. Each salutes the new comrade with embrace and song, and one with peaceful mouth uttered these sounds: "Come, son, and in happiness take the joys of the paternal kingdom; from now on, son, be forever free of hard labor."[64] He spoke, and the winged troop touched their harps; but my golden repose was dispersed with the shadows. I wept for the dreams disturbed by Cephalus's mistress;[67] may such dreams come to me often.[68]

46. **Tago:** the Tagus, a river in Spain known for its golden sand.

47. **Favoni:** Zephyrus, the west wind.

64. Cp. Rev. 14.13: "They may rest from their labors."

67. **Cephaleia pellice:** Aurora, goddess of the dawn.

68. **Talia . . . mihi:** Milton adapts the famous last line of Ovid's *Amores* 1.5, which commemorates a delightfully unexpected afternoon of lovemaking with Corinna.

ELEGIA QUARTA. AD THOMAM IUNIUM PRAECEPTOREM SUUM, APUD MERCATORES ANGLICOS HAMBURGAE AGENTES PASTORIS MUNERE FUNGENTEM

[*Elegy 4. To Thomas Young, his tutor, at present performing the office of chaplain among the English merchants living in Hamburg*]

The Scotsman Thomas Young (1587?–1655) tutored the young Milton for some period between his arrival in London around 1618 and 1620, when he departed for Hamburg and the eleven-year-old Milton moved on to St. Paul's grammar school. Young returned to England in 1628 and received the vicarage of Stowmarket in Suffolk. His sympathies were deeply Presbyterian. In the early 1640s, Young was one of the five authors comprehended in the joint pseudonym Smectymnuus (his initials supplied the *ty* in the middle). He was appointed to the Westminster Assembly in 1643 and to the Mastership of Jesus College, Cambridge, in 1644. Young was ousted from the Cambridge post in 1650 for refusing to accept the terms of the Engagement (a secret treaty between Charles I and the Scottish Commissioners trading three years of Presbyterian government in the English Church for a Scottish invasion of England) and returned to Stowmarket. It is hard to believe that Milton did not have his old friend and teacher somewhere in mind when, in the digression on the Long Parliament in *The History of Britain,* he complained of avaricious divines who "accept besides one, sometimes two or more of the best livings, collegiate masterships in the universities, rich lectures in the city, setting sail to all winds that might blow gain into their covetous bosoms" (Yale 5:446).

ANNO AETATIS 18

Curre per immensum subito mea littera pontum;
I, pete Teutonicos laeve per aequor agros;
Segnes rumpe moras, et nil, precor, obstet eunti,
Et festinantis nil remoretur iter.
Ipse ego Sicanio fraenantem carcere ventos
Aeolon, et virides sollicitabo deos,
Caeruleamque suis comitatam Dorida nymphis,
Ut tibi dent placidam per sua regna viam.
At tu, si poteris, celeres tibi sume iugales,

AT AGE 18

Run quickly, my letter, across the huge ocean;[1] go, seek the Teutonic fields across the smooth sea. Break off lazy delays, and let nothing, I pray, get in your way, and let nothing slow your journey as you hurry. I myself will solicit Aeolus, who holds back the winds in their Sicilian cave, and the green gods, and cerulean Doris[7] in company with her nymphs, to give you a peaceful path through their kingdom. And you, if you can, take up that swift

1. An imitation of Ovid's *Tristia* 3.7.1–2.
7. **Dorida:** wife of Nereus and mother of the fifty Nereids.

Vecta quibus Colchis fugit ab ore viri;
Aut queis Triptolemus Scythicas devenit in oras,
Gratus Eleusina missus ab urbe puer.
Atque ubi Germanas flavere videbis arenas,
Ditis ad Hamburgae moenia flecte gradum,
Dicitur occiso quae ducere nomen ab Hama,
Cimbrica quem fertur clava dedisse neci.
Vivit ibi antiquae clarus pietatis honore
Praesul Christicolas pascere doctus oves;
Ille quidem est animae plusquam pars altera nostrae,
Dimidio vitae vivere cogor ego.
Hei mihi quot pelagi, quot montes interiecti
Me faciunt alia parte carere mei!
Charior ille mihi quam tu doctissime Graium
Cliniadi, pronepos qui Telamonis erat;
Quamque Stagirites generoso magnus alumno,
Quem peperit Libyco Chaonis alma Iovi.
Qualis Amyntorides, qualis Philyreius heros
Myrmidonum regi, talis et ille mihi.
Primus ego Aonios illo praeeunte recessus
Lustrabam, et bifidi sacra vireta iugi;
Pieriosque hausi latices, Clioque favente,
Castalio sparsi laeta ter ora mero.
Flammeus at signum ter viderat arietis Aethon,

team with which the Colchian[10] fled the presence of her husband, or the one in which the gracious boy Triptolemus,[11] sent from the Eleusinian city, came to the Scythian shores. And when you see the golden sands of Germany, bend your course to the walls of wealthy Hamburg, which is said to have gotten its name from the death of Hama,[15] whom a Danish club is reported to have sent to death. There lives a pastor famous for honoring the ancient faith, learned in the tending of Christian sheep. He indeed is more than the other part of my soul;[19] I am forced to live half a life. Alas, how many seas, how many mountains in between make me lack my other part! He is dearer to me than you, most learned of the Greeks,[23] were to the son of Clinias, who was the descendant of Telamon; than the great Stagirite[25] to his noble alumnus, whom the kindly woman of Chaonia bore to Libyan Jove. As the son of Amyntor, as the Philyrean hero to the king of the Myrmidons, so also he to me. With him leading me, I first traveled the Aonian retreats and the sacred green precincts of the forked mountain[30] and drank the Pierian waters, and with Clio's[31] favor sprinkled my happy mouth three times with Castalian wine. But three times fiery Aethon[33]

10. **Colchis:** Medea, who fled in a dragon-drawn chariot after killing her children.

11. Triptolemus also drove a chariot drawn by dragons (Ovid, *Met.* 5.642–61).

15. **Hama:** There was a story that Hamburg took its name from the Saxon champion Hama, who was killed by a Danish giant on the spot where the city now stands.

19. Evoking Horace's farewell to Vergil, *animae dimidium meae* ("half of my own soul"), in *Odes* 1.3.8.

23. **doctissime Graium:** Socrates, whose friendship with Alcibiades is represented in Plato's *Symposium.*

25. **Stagirites:** Aristotle, a native of Stageira, tutored Alexander the Great, who according to Plutarch (*Alexander* 2–3) was sired by Jupiter Ammon in the form of a snake.

30. **bifidi . . . iugi:** Parnassus, sacred to Apollo and the Muses.

31. **Clio:** the Muse of history.

33. **Aethon:** one of the horses of the sun's chariot. The arithmetic of the passage has been much debated.

Induxitque auro lanea terga novo,
Bisque novo terram sparsisti Chlori senilem
Gramine, bisque tuas abstulit Auster opes:
Necdum eius licuit mihi lumina pascere vultu,
Aut linguae dulces aure bibisse sonos.
Vade igitur, cursuque Eurum praeverte sonorum;
Quam sit opus monitis res docet, ipsa vides.
Invenies dulci cum coniuge forte sedentem,
Mulcentem gremio pignora chara suo,
Forsitan aut veterum praelarga volumina patrum
Versantem, aut veri biblia sacra Dei;
Caelestive animas saturantem rore tenellas,
Grande salutiferae religionis opus.
Utque solet, multam sit dicere cura salutem,
Dicere quam decuit, si modo adesset, herum.
Haec quoque paulum oculos in humum defixa modestos,
Verba verecundo sis memor ore loqui:
Haec tibi, si teneris vacat inter praelia Musis
Mittit ab Angliaco littore fida manus.
Accipe sinceram, quamvis sit sera, salutem;
Fiat et hoc ipso gratior illa tibi.
Sera quidem, sed vera fuit, quam casta recepit
Icaris a lento Penelopeia viro.
Ast ego quid volui manifestum tollere crimen,
Ipse quod ex omni parte levare nequit?
Arguitur tardus merito, noxamque fatetur,
Et pudet officium deseruisse suum.
Tu modo da veniam fasso, veniamque roganti;
Crimina diminui, quae patuere, solent.
Non ferus in pavidos rictus diducit hiantes,
Vulnifico pronos nec rapit ungue leo.
Saepe sarissiferi crudelia pectora Thracis
Supplicis ad moestas delicuere preces.
Extensaeque manus avertunt fulminis ictus,
Placat et iratos hostia parva deos.
Iamque diu scripsisse tibi fuit impetus illi,
Neve moras ultra ducere passus Amor.
Nam vaga Fama refert, heu nuntia vera malorum!
In tibi finitimis bella tumere locis,

looked upon the sign of the Ram and covered its woolly back with new gold, and twice, Chloris, you sprinkled the aged earth with new grass, and twice Auster[36] took your riches away; and I have not yet been allowed to feast my eyes on his face, or to drink with my ear the sweet sounds of his tongue. Go, therefore, and outstrip loud Eurus[39] in your course; the situation shows, you yourself see how urgent my orders are. You will perhaps find him sitting with his sweet wife, caressing in his lap their dear love tokens; or perhaps going through the great volumes of the ancient fathers, or the Holy Bible of the true God; or watering tender souls with heavenly dew, the great task of the religion of salvation. As is the custom, take care to speak a hearty greeting, such as would have befitted your master, if only he were there. Briefly fixing your modest eyes on the ground, remember also to speak these words in a respectful voice: "A faithful hand sends you these from the English shore, if there is time for the soft Muses amid the battles.[51] Accept a sincere greeting, though it is late; and may it be for this very reason the more welcome to you. Late indeed, but true, was that which chaste Penelope, daughter of Icarius, received from her tardy husband.[56] But why did I want to excuse this manifest guilt, when he himself cannot in any way minimize it? He is rightly accused of delay, and confesses his guilt, and is ashamed to have failed his office. Forgive him now that he has confessed and begs for pardon; crimes tend to diminish when they are laid open. The wild beast does not spread its gaping jaws for those that tremble, and the lion does not seize with its wounding claw those that lie

36. **Auster:** the south wind.

39. **Eurum:** the east wind.

51. **praelia:** Hamburg was not attacked in the Thirty Years' War, though armies passed near it.

56. **lento Penelopeia viro:** Odysseus.

Teque tuamque urbem truculento milite cingi,
  Et iam Saxonicos arma parasse duces.
Te circum late campos populatur Enyo,
  Et sata carne virum iam cruor arva rigat.
Germanisque suum concessit Thracia Martem;
  Illuc Odrysios Mars pater egit equos.
Perpetuoque comans iam deflorescit oliva,
  Fugit et aerisonam Diva perosa tubam,
Fugit io terris, et iam non ultima virgo
  Creditur ad superas iusta volasse domos.
Te tamen interea belli circumsonat horror,
  Vivis et ignoto solus inopsque solo;
Et, tibi quam patrii non exhibuere penates,
  Sede peregrina quaeris egenus opem.
Patria, dura parens, et saxis saevior albis
  Spumea quae pulsat littoris unda tui,
Siccine te decet innocuos exponere foetus,
  Siccine in externam ferrea cogis humum,
Et sinis ut terris quaerant alimenta remotis
  Quos tibi prospiciens miserat ipse Deus,
Et qui laeta ferunt de caelo nuntia, quique
  Quae via post cineres ducat ad astra, docent?
Digna quidem Stygiis quae vivas clausa tenebris,
  Aeternaque animae digna perire fame!

prone. The cruel hearts of the spear-bearing Thracians have often melted at the mournful prayers of a suppliant. Outstretched hands ward off the lightning bolt, and a small offering placates the angry gods. For a long time now he has had the urge to write you, nor did Love tolerate any further delay. For now busy Rumor reports—alas, true messenger of evils!—that wars arise in the areas near you, and you and your city are encircled by a fierce army, and the Saxon lords[74] have already prepared for war. Enyo[75] devastates the countryside widely about you, and even now blood waters fields sown with men's flesh. Thrace has surrendered its own Mars to the Germans, and Father Mars has driven Odrysian horses there. The ever leafy olive is withering now, and the goddess[80] who hates the brazen-sounding trumpet has fled—look, she has fled from the earth!—and now the just virgin[81] is not believed the last to have flown to heavenly homes. Meanwhile the horror of war sounds about you, and you live alone and impoverished in an unknown land, and in your need seek in a foreign home the sustenance which the Penates of your homeland did not provide you. Harsh parent homeland, and more cruel than the white rocks which the foaming waves of your shore batter, is it right for you to expose your innocent offspring this way? Is this how you, with a heart of iron, force them onto foreign soil, and allow them to seek sustenance in distant lands—those whom God Himself, out of care for you, had sent, and who carry the happy message from Heaven, and who teach the way that after ashes leads to the stars? You are worthy indeed to live shut up in Stygian shad-

74. **Saxonicos . . . duces:** probably Dukes Frederick, William, and Bernard, sons of Duke John of Saxe-Weimar.

75. **Enyo:** goddess of war.

80. **Diva:** Eirene, goddess of peace.

81. **virgo:** Astraea, goddess of justice, the last of the gods to leave earth (Ovid, *Met.* 1.149–50).

Haud aliter vates terrae Thesbitidis olim
Pressit inassueto devia tesqua pede,
Desertasque Arabum salebras, dum regis Achabi
Effugit atque tuas, Sidoni dira, manus.
Talis et horrisono laceratus membra flagello,
Paulus ab Aemathia pellitur urbe Cilix;
Piscosaeque ipsum Gergessae civis Iesum
Finibus ingratus iussit abire suis.
At tu sume animos, nec spes cadat anxia curis
Nec tua concutiat decolor ossa metus.
Sis etenim quamvis fulgentibus obsitus armis,
Intententque tibi millia tela necem,
At nullis vel inerme latus violabitur armis,
Deque tuo cuspis nulla cruore bibet.
Namque eris ipse Dei radiante sub aegide tutus;
Ille tibi custos, et pugil ille tibi;
Ille Sionaeae qui tot sub moenibus arcis
Assyrios fudit nocte silente viros;
Inque fugam vertit quos in Samaritidas oras,
Misit ab antiquis prisca Damascus agris,
Terruit et densas pavido cum rege cohortes,
Aere dum vacuo buccina clara sonat,
Cornea pulvereum dum verberat ungula campum,
Currus arenosam dum quatit actus humum,
Auditurque hinnitus equorum ad bella ruentum,
Et strepitus ferri, murmuraque alta virum.
Et tu (quod superest miseris) sperare memento,
Et tua magnanimo pectore vince mala.
Nec dubites quandoque frui melioribus annis,
Atque iterum patrios posse videre lares.

97. **vates terrae Thesbitidis:** Elijah, who fled from Ahab.

102. Paul, born in Tarsus in Cilicia, was scourged and imprisoned at Philippi in Macedonia.

103. See Matt. 8.28–34.

113. In 2 Kings 19.35–36, God destroys Sennacherib's army before the walls of Jerusalem.

115. In 2 Kings 7.6–7, God scatters the army of King Ben-hadad by causing them to hear the sounds of a great enemy force.

119. A variation on a familiar Vergilian tag (*Aen.* 8.596).

ows, and worthy to die from the soul's eternal hunger! Not otherwise the Tishbite prophet[97] once walked with unaccustomed foot the desolate pathways and rough deserts of Arabia as he fled the hands of King Ahab and of you, dire woman of Sidon. And in the same way Paul of Cilicia, his limbs torn by the horrid-sounding lash, was driven from the Emathian city;[102] and the ungrateful citizenry of the fishing village of Gergessa ordered Jesus himself[103] to leave their territory. But summon your spirit, and do not let anxious hope yield to worries or discoloring fear shake your bones. For though you are surrounded by glittering weapons and a thousand spears threaten you with death, still your unarmed side will not be pierced by any weapon, and no spearhead drink your blood. For you yourself will be safe beneath God's radiant shield, He your guardian and He your fighter—He who in the silent night beneath the walls of Zion[113] routed so many men of Assyria, and turned to flight those whom age-old Damascus sent from her ancient fields against the land of the Samaritans,[115] and terrified the dense cohorts along with their trembling king, while the clear trumpet sounds in the empty air, while the horny hoof pounds the dusty plane,[119] while the driven chariot beats the sandy soil, and the neighing of horses is heard as they run to battle, and the clangor of iron, and the deep roaring of men. And you, remember what is left for the wretched—to hope; and conquer your misfortunes with your great heart. And do not let yourself doubt that someday you will enjoy better times, and you will again be able to see the Lares of your homeland."

ELEGIA QUINTA. IN ADVENTUM VERIS

[*Elegy 5. On the Arrival of Spring*]

Milton's version of this popular topos in Renaissance Latin verse is now considered one of the best of the period. The poem links the renewal of the year with the renewal of literature, and to enact that connection Milton produced what A. S. P. Woodhouse termed a "distillation of the whole body of classic myth relatable to love and the coming of spring" (1943, 72). In other words, the elegy is a pastiche, but a glorious one, packed with artifice of the highest order.

ANNO AETATIS 20

In se perpetuo Tempus revolubile gyro
  Iam revocat Zephyros vere tepente, novos.
Induiturque brevem Tellus reparata iuventam,
  Iamque soluta gelu dulce virescit humus.
Fallor? an et nobis redeunt in carmina vires,
  Ingeniumque mihi munere veris adest?
Munere veris adest, iterumque vigescit ab illo
  (Quis putet?) atque aliquod iam sibi poscit opus.
Castalis ante oculos, bifidumque cacumen
    oberrat,
  Et mihi Pyrenen somnia nocte ferunt.
Concitaque arcano fervent mihi pectora motu,
  Et furor, et sonitus me sacer intus agit.
Delius ipse venit, video Peneide lauro
  Implicitos crines, Delius ipse venit.
Iam mihi mens liquidi raptatur in ardua coeli,
  Perque vagas nubes corpore liber eo.
Perque umbras, perque antra feror, penetralia
    vatum,
  Et mihi fana patent interiora deum.
Intuiturque animus toto quid agatur Olympo,
  Nec fugiunt oculos Tartara caeca meos.
Quid tam grande sonat distento spiritus ore?
  Quid parit haec rabies, quid sacer iste furor?
Ver mihi, quod dedit ingenium, cantabitur illo;

AT AGE 20

Time, turning upon itself in an endless circle, now as the spring warms itself calls back fresh zephyrs, and restored Earth puts on brief youth, and now, freed from the cold, the soil grows pleasantly green. Am I wrong, or does power also return to our songs, and is inspiration at hand for me as the spring's gift? It is the spring's gift, and flourishes again because of it (who would have thought?) and now demands some task for itself. Castalia comes before my eyes, and the forked peak;[9] and at night dreams bring Pirene[10] to me. And my heart is struck and burns with a mysterious impulse, and fury and sacred sound rouse me inwardly. The Delian[13] himself comes, I see hair bound with Penean laurel, the Delian himself comes. Now my mind is rapt into the heights of the liquid heavens, and free of the body I go through the wandering clouds. Through the shadows I am carried, through the inmost caves of the poets, and the inmost shrines of the gods are open to me. The soul comprehends what is happening anywhere on Olympus, nor does blind Tartarus escape my eyes. What grand thing does the spirit

9. **Castalis . . . cacumen:** See *Elegy 4* 30n.

10. **Pyrenen:** Pirene, a Corinthian fountain sprung from the hoof mark of Pegasus and sacred to the Muses.

13. **Delius:** Apollo (born on the island of Delos); **Peneide lauro:** Daphne, daughter of the river god Peneus, was changed into a laurel as she fled Apollo.

Profuerint isto reddita dona modo.
Iam, Philomela, tuos foliis adoperta novellis
Instituis modulos, dum silet omne nemus.
Urbe ego, tu silva, simul incipiamus utrique,
Et simul adventum veris uterque canat.
Veris io rediere vices; celebremus honores
Veris, et hoc subeat Musa perennis opus.
Iam sol Aethiopas fugiens Tithoniaque arva,
Flectit ad Arctoas aurea lora plagas.
Est breve noctis iter, brevis est mora noctis opacae,
Horrida cum tenebris exulat illa suis.
Iamque Lycaonius plaustrum caeleste Bootes
Non longa sequitur fessus ut ante via;
Nunc etiam solitas circum Iovis atria toto
Excubias agitant sidera rara polo.
Nam dolus, et caedes, et vis cum nocte recessit,
Neve giganteum dii timuere scelus.
Forte aliquis scopuli recubans in vertice pastor,
Roscida cum primo sole rubescit humus,
Hac, ait, hac certe caruisti nocte puella
Phoebe tua, celeres quae retineret equos.
Laeta suas repetit silvas, pharetramque resumit
Cynthia, Luciferas ut videt alta rotas,
Et tenues ponens radios gaudere videtur
Officium fieri tam breve fratris ope.

sing with a wide-open mouth? What does this madness, this sacred fury give birth to? The spring, which gave me this inspiration, will be sung by it; in this way the repaid gifts will show a profit. Now Philomela,[25] hidden in new foliage, you begin your music while the entire grove is silent. I in the city, you in the woods, let us both begin, and let each simultaneously sing the arrival of spring. The spring—hail!—has returned again, let us celebrate in honor of the spring, and let the perennial[30] Muse take on this task. Now the sun, fleeing from the Ethiopians and the Tithonian fields,[31] turns his golden reins toward the Arctic regions. Night's journey is brief, dark night's stay is brief; shuddering, she goes into exile with her shadows, and now Lycaonian[35] Bootes does not, as before, wearily follow the heavenly wagon in a long journey; now only a few stars in the whole sky keep their regular patrol around Jove's halls. For deceit and murder and violence have left with the night, nor have the gods feared the wickedness of the Giants.[40] Perhaps some shepherd, leaning against a rock's peak when the dewy earth reddens at the first sunlight, says, "This, certainly this night, Phoebus, you were missing the girl who would hold back your swift horses." Cynthia[46] happily returns to her forests and takes up her quiver when from on high she sees the light-bringing wheels, and as she puts down her own soft beams seems to rejoice that her task has become so short with the help of

25. **Philomela:** the nightingale.
30. **perennis:** So 1673; 1645 reads *"quotannis."* Milton changed the word after his political opponent Salmasius, a famous classicist, noted the long last syllable in *"quotannis."*
31. The sun has left the Ethiopians (i.e., the equator) and the East (associated with Tithonus, husband of the dawn goddess) to move northward.
35. **Lycaonius:** northern.
40. **giganteum:** Giants attacked the gods during the Iron Age, after Justice had fled the earth (Ovid, *Met.* 1.151f).
46. **Cynthia:** Diana, the moon goddess.

Desere, Phoebus ait, thalamos Aurora seniles;
  Quid iuvat effoeto procubuisse toro?
Te manet Aeolides viridi venator in herba,
  Surge, tuos ignes altus Hymettus habet.
Flava verecundo dea crimen in ore fatetur,
  Et matutinos ocyus urget equos.
Exuit invisam Tellus rediviva senectam,
  Et cupit amplexus Phoebe subire tuos;
Et cupit, et digna est, quid enim formosius illa,
  Pandit ut omniferos luxuriosa sinus,
Atque Arabum spirat messes, et ab ore venusto
  Mitia cum Paphiis fundit amoma rosis.
Ecce coronatur sacro frons ardua luco,
  Cingit ut Idaeam pinea turris Opim;
Et vario madidos intexit flore capillos,
  Floribus et visa est posse placere suis.
Floribus effusos ut erat redimita capillos,
  Taenario placuit diva Sicana deo.
Aspice Phoebe tibi faciles hortantur amores,
  Mellitasque movent flamina verna preces.
Cinnamea Zephyrus leve plaudit odorifer ala,
  Blanditiasque tibi ferre videntur aves.
Nec sine dote tuos temeraria quaerit amores
  Terra, nec optatos poscit egena toros;
Alma salutiferum medicos tibi gramen in usus
  Praebet, et hinc titulos adiuvat ipsa tuos.
Quod si te pretium, si te fulgentia tangunt
  Munera (muneribus saepe coemptus Amor)
Illa tibi ostentat quascunque sub aequore vasto,
  Et superiniectis montibus abdit opes.
Ah quoties cum tu clivoso fessus Olympo
  In vespertinas praecipitaris aquas,

her brother. "Aurora," says Phoebus, "leave the chamber of old age;[49] what is the point of lying in an exhausted bed? The hunter Aeolides waits for you in the green grass; rise, lofty Hymettus holds your passion." The golden-haired goddess professes her guilt with a shamefaced look, and drives the horses of the morning faster. Reborn Earth sheds her hated old age and yearns, Phoebus, for your embraces—and yearns and is worthy, for what is more beautiful than she, as, luxuriant, she bares her all-nurturing breasts and breathes the harvests of Arabia, and from her lovely mouth pour forth sweet spices together with Paphian roses? Look! her high forehead is crowned with a sacred grove, just as a tower of pines girds Idaean Ops;[62] and she weaves varied flowers into her wet hair, and seems to have the power of charming with her own flowers. When she had knit her flowing hair with flowers, the Sicilian goddess[66] charmed the Taenarian god. Look, Phoebus: easy loves call to you, and the vernal winds carry honeyed prayers. Fragrant Zephyrus lightly beats his cinnamon wings, and birds seem to bring entreaties to you. Nor does inconsiderate Earth seek your love without a dowry, nor does she sue in poverty for the union for which she hopes. Bountiful, she offers you health-bringing herbs for medical use, and in so doing she herself enhances your titles. If this reward, if these dazzling gifts move you (love is often purchased with gifts), she displays before you whatever riches she hides under the vast ocean and the piled up mountains. Ah, how many times, when, tired from the steeps of Olympus you plunge into the evening waters, she says, "Why, Phoebus, does

49. Aurora's husband, Tithonus, was given immortality by the gods but not eternal youth. He therefore suffered the afflictions of old age, including impotence.

62. **Idaeam pinea turris Opim:** Cybele, a Phrygian fertility goddess, was worshiped in Rome as Ops, goddess of plenty. Ida was covered with pines, her sacred tree. She wore a turreted headdress.

66. **diva Sicana:** Proserpina. Pluto ravishes her in Ovid, *Met.* 5.385–408.

Cur te, inquit, cursu languentem Phoebe diurno
Hesperiis recipit caerula mater aquis?
Quid tibi cum Tethy? Quid cum Tartesside lympha?
Dia quid immundo perluis ora salo?
Frigora Phoebe mea melius captabis in umbra;
Huc ades, ardentes imbue rore comas.
Mollior egelida veniet tibi somnus in herba;
Huc ades, et gremio lumina pone meo.
Quaque iaces circum mulcebit lene susurrans
Aura per humentes corpora fusa rosas.
Nec me (crede mihi) terrent Semeleia fata,
Nec Phaetonteo fumidus axis equo;
Cum tu Phoebe tuo sapientius uteris igni,
Huc ades et gremio lumina pone meo.
Sic Tellus lasciva suos suspirat amores;
Matris in exemplum caetera turba ruunt.
Nunc etenim toto currit vagus orbe Cupido,
Languentesque fovet solis ab ignes faces.
Insonuere novis lethalia cornua nervis,
Triste micant ferro tela corusca novo.
Iamque vel invictam tentat superasse Dianam,
Quaeque sedet sacro Vesta pudica foco.
Ipsa senescentem reparat Venus annua formam,
Atque iterum tepido creditur orta mari.
Marmoreas iuvenes clamant *Hymenaee* per urbes,
Littus *io Hymen,* et cava saxa sonant.
Cultior ille venit tunicaque decentior apta;
Puniceum redolet vestis odora crocum.
Egrediturque frequens ad amoeni gaudia veris
Virgineos auro cincta puella sinus.
Votum est cuique suum, votum est tamen omnibus unum,
Ut sibi quem cupiat det Cytherea virum.

83. **Tethy:** Tethys, mother of rivers.

91. **Semeleia fata:** Semele, loved by Zeus, was persuaded by the jealous Hera to ask her lover to appear to her in his divine splendor. He did so, and Semele was consumed by fire (Ovid, *Met.* 3.253–315).

101. Diana, goddess of the moon, was patroness of virginity. Vesta was goddess of the household; her priestesses were Vestal virgins.

105. Hymen, god of marriage, appears in the refrains (*io Hymen Hymenaee* and *Hymen o Hymenaee, Hymen ades o Hymenaee!*) of two of Catullus's epithalamia.

112. **Cytherea:** Venus.

the blue mother receive you in the Hesperian waters when you are exhausted from your daily round? What is Tethys[83] to you? What is the water of Tartessus, that you should wash your divine face in the unclean sea? You will do better, Phoebus, seeking coolness in my shade; come here, soak your flaming hair in the dew. Softer sleep will come to you on the cold grass; come here, and place your eyes upon my breast. And where you lie, the air, whispering softly, will stroke the bodies stretched out on dewy roses. Trust me, the fate of Semele[91] does not frighten me, nor the chariot smoking from Phaethon's horses. Since you, Phoebus, use your fire more wisely, come here, and place your eyes upon my breast." Thus lascivious Earth breathes out her love; the rest of her company rush to their mother's example. For now fickle Cupid runs everywhere in the world, and rekindles his languishing torches with the fire of the sun. His lethal bow sounds with new strings, and his glittering darts shine grimly with new iron. And now he attempts to defeat unconquered Diana,[101] and chaste Vesta, who tends the holy fire. Each year Venus herself renews her aging beauty, and is believed to rise again from the warm sea. Through marble cities young men cry out, "Hymenaeus!"[105] and the shore and the hollow rocks sound, "Io Hymen!" Well-dressed he comes, and handsome in his well-fitting tunic; his perfumed clothing smells like red crocus. Many a girl, her virgin breasts bound with gold, comes out into the joys of the pleasant spring. Each has her own prayer, but it is the same prayer for all: that Cytherea[112] give each the man she desires. Now the shepherd also plays on

Nunc quoque septena modulatur arundine pastor,
Et sua quae iungat carmina Phyllis habet.
Navita nocturno placat sua sidera cantu,
Delphinasque leves ad vada summa vocat.
Iupiter ipse alto cum coniuge ludit Olympo,
Convocat et famulos ad sua festa deos.
Nunc etiam Satyri cum sera crepuscula surgunt,
Pervolitant celeri florea rura choro,
Silvanusque sua Cyparissi fronde revinctus,
Semicaperque deus, semideusque caper.
Quaeque sub arboribus Dryades latuere vetustis
Per iuga, per solos expatiantur agros.
Per sata luxuriat fruticetaque Maenalius Pan,
Vix Cybele mater, vix sibi tuta Ceres;
Atque aliquam cupidus praedatur Oreada Faunus,
Consulit in trepidos dum sibi nympha pedes,
Iamque latet, latitansque cupit male tecta videri,
Et fugit, et fugiens pervelit ipsa capi.
Dii quoque non dubitant caelo praeponere silvas,
Et sua quisque sibi numina lucus habet.
Et sua quisque diu sibi numina lucus habeto,
Nec vos arborea dii precor ite domo.
Te referant miseris te Iupiter aurea terris
Saecla! Quid ad nimbos aspera tela redis?
Tu saltem lente rapidos age Phoebe iugales
Qua potes, et sensim tempora veris eant.
Brumaque productas tarde ferat hispida noctes,
Ingruat et nostro serior umbra polo.

his sevenfold pipe, and Phyllis[114] has her own songs to join to his. The sailor calms his stars with a nighttime song and calls the agile dolphins to the surface of the waves.[116] Jupiter himself sports with his wife on high Olympus and summons the attendant gods to his feast. And now satyrs, when the late dusk rises, fly over the flowery countryside in swift chorus, and Silvanus bound with his cypress leaves[121]—the half-goat god and the half-god goat. And the Dryads who hid in the ancient trees range through the peaks, through the lonely fields. Maenalian Pan[125] frolics through the crops and through the bushes; Mother Cybele, Ceres[126] herself are scarcely safe from him. And lusty Faunus[127] catches some Oread while the nymph trusts in her trembling feet, and now is hidden, and hiding, badly concealed, wishes to be seen, and flees, and, fleeing, herself wishes to be captured. The gods also do not hesitate to prefer the woods to the heavens, and each grove has its own deities. And long may each grove have its own deities; do not leave your arboreal home, gods, I pray. Let ages of gold bring you back, Jupiter, to the unhappy earth! Why return to the clouds, your harsh weapons? At least drive your swift team as slowly as you can, Phoebus, and let spring's time go gradually. And let rough winter slowly bring its drawn-out nights, and let a later shadow threaten our sky.

114. **Phyllis:** generic name in pastoral for a shepherdess.

116. Pliny (9.8.24–8) held that dolphins were susceptible to music.

121.. Silvanus, the wood god, loved the boy Cyparissus, who was transformed into a cypress after dying of grief for a pet deer that Silvanus killed.

125. **Maenalius Pan:** Maenalus was an Arcadian mountain sacred to Pan.

126. **Cybele:** See 62n. Ceres was her daughter.

127. **Oreada:** An Oread was a mountain nymph; **Faunus:** a Roman wood god.

ELEGIA SEXTA. AD CAROLUM DIODATUM RURI COMMORANTEM

[*Elegy 6. To Charles Diodati, staying in the country*]

This poem, concluding with a reference to the recent composition of the *Nativity Ode,* seems to have been written soon after Christmas 1629. Diodati had apparently sent Milton a letter in a classical language in which he apologized for his uninspired verses and playfully asked Milton for a sign of his affection. Critics often disagree over the tone of Milton's poetic reply. Some recognize a serious personal dedication in his account of the Pythagorean sacrifices required of the heroic poet. Others discern a jocularity running throughout the work, its opening hyperboles about elegiac verse yielding with no shift in tone to its concluding hyperboles about heroic verse.

Qui cum idibus Decemb. scripsisset, et sua carmina excusari postulasset si solito minus essent bona, quod inter lautitias quibus erat ab amicis exceptus, haud satis felicem operam Musis dare se posse affirmabat, hunc habuit responsum.

Mitto tibi sanam non pleno ventre salutem,
Qua tu distento forte carere potes.
At tua quid nostram prolectat Musa Camenam,
Nec sinit optatas posse sequi tenebras?
Carmine scire velis quam te redamemque colamque,
Crede mihi vix hoc carmine scire queas,
Nam neque noster amor modulis includitur arctis,
Nec venit ad claudos integer ipse pedes.
Quam bene solennes epulas, hilaremque Decembrim,
Festaque coelifugam quae coluere Deum,
Deliciasque refers, hyberni gaudia ruris,
Haustaque per lepidos Gallica musta focos.

8. **claudos integer ipse pedes:** The "limping feet" of the alternating hexameters and pentameters in elegy was Ovid's joke (*Tristia* 3.1.11–12).

Who, when he had written on the Ides of December and asked for his own poems to be excused if they were less good than usual, because, he claimed, with the entertainment in which he had been caught up by his friends, he was not able to give sufficiently fruitful attention to the Muses, received this reply.

I send you, on an empty stomach, a wish for health which you, with a full one, perhaps need. But why does your muse coax forth ours, and not allow her to pursue the shadows she hopes for? Should you want to learn in poetry how much I return your love and am devoted to you, believe me, you can scarcely learn it from this poem. For neither is our love encompassed by tight-fitting metrics nor, being healthy, does it come on limping feet.[8] How well you describe the solemn banquets, and the December cheer, and the feasts which honor the heaven-fleeing god, and the delights, the joys of the country in winter, and the Gallic must

Quid quereris refugam vino dapibusque poesin?
  Carmen amat Bacchum, carmina Bacchus amat.
Nec puduit Phoebum virides gestasse corymbos,
  Atque hederam lauro praeposuisse suae.
Saepius Aoniis clamavit collibus *Euoe*
  Mista Thyoneo turba novena choro.
Naso Corallaeis mala carmina misit ab agris;
  Non illic epulae non sata vitis erat.
Quid nisi vina, rosasque racemiferumque Lyaeum
  Cantavit brevibus Teia Musa modis?
Pindaricosque inflat numeros Teumesius Euan,
  Et redolet sumptum pagina quaeque merum;
Dum gravis everso currus crepat axe supinus,
  Et volat Eleo pulvere fuscus eques.
Quadrimoque madens Lyricen Romanus Iaccho
  Dulce canit Glyceran, flavicomamque Chloen.
Iam quoque lauta tibi generoso mensa paratu,
  Mentis alit vires, ingeniumque fovet.
Massica foecundam despumant pocula venam,
  Fundis et ex ipso condita metra cado.
Addimus his artes, fusumque per intima Phoebum
  Corda; favent uni Bacchus, Apollo, Ceres.
Scilicet haud mirum tam dulcia carmina per te
  Numine composito tres peperisse deos.
Nunc quoque Thressa tibi caelato barbitos auro

drunk in front of charming fireplaces. Why do you complain that poetry is a fugitive from wine and feasting?[13] Song loves Bacchus, Bacchus loves songs. Phoebus was not ashamed to have worn green clusters of ivy berries, or to prefer ivy to his own laurel. The crowd of nine, mixed with the Bacchic chorus, often cried out "Euoe!"[17] in the Aonian hills. Naso sent bad poems from the fields of the Coralli; there were no banquets there, the vine was not cultivated.[20] What besides wine and roses and cluster-bearing Lyaeus did the muse of Teos[22] sing in his brief measures? Boeotian Bacchus[23] filled the verses of Pindar, and every page smells of the wine he drank, while the heavy chariot clatters upside down with its axle in the air, and the horseman flies by, dark with the dust of Elis. Drunk with four-year-old wine, the Roman lyricist[27] sings sweetly of Glycera and golden-haired Chloe, and now a sumptuous table with choice appointments nourishes your mind's strength, warms your wit. Cups of Massic wine[31] foam out a fertile vein, and you pour out verses stored in the bottle itself. We add artistic skill to these, and Phoebus poured through the innermost heart; Bacchus, Apollo, Ceres show their favor in unison. Surely it is no wonder that three gods, with their combined divinity, have given birth to such sweet songs through you. Now too the Thracian lyre[37] with its golden decoration, softly plucked with a

13. A distinction between poetic inspiration by God (or a god) and poetic inspiration by wine (*must* is new wine) was not uncommon in Renaissance literature.

17. **Euoe:** the cry of Bacchic revelers; **turba novena:** the nine Muses.

20. In exile on the Black Sea, Ovid wrote *Tristia*, *Ex Ponto*, and *Ibis*. The Coralli were a local tribe of Geats who had little interest in his poetry. (They didn't drink wine either.)

22. **Teia Musa:** the legendery poet Anacreon.

23. **Teumesius Euan:** Bacchus. Milton is referring to Pindar's celebration of chariot races in the Olympic games (*Olymp.* 2–4).

27. **Lyricen Romanus:** Horace. Glycera and Chloe both appear as love interests in his *Odes*.

31. **Massica:** Mount Massicus was famous for its wine (Horace, *Odes* 1.1.19).

37. **Thressa tibi caelato barbitos:** The lyre is Thracian because Orpheus was a "Thracian bard" (*PL* 7.34).

Insonat arguta molliter icta manu;
Auditurque chelys suspensa tapetia circum,
Virgineos tremula quae regat arte pedes.
Illa tuas saltem teneant spectacula Musas,
Et revocent, quantum crapula pellit iners.
Crede mihi dum psallit ebur, comitataque plectrum
Implet odoratos festa chorea tholos,
Percipies tacitum per pectora serpere Phoebum,
Quale repentinus permeat ossa calor;
Perque puellares oculos digitumque sonantem
Irruet in totos lapsa Thalia sinus.
Namque elegia levis multorum cura deorum est,
Et vocat ad numeros quemlibet illa suos;
Liber adest elegis, Eratoque, Ceresque, Venusque,
Et cum purpurea matre tenellus Amor.
Talibus inde licent convivia larga poetis,
Saepius et veteri commaduisse mero.
At qui bella refert, et adulto sub Iove caelum,
Heroasque pios, semideosque duces,
Et nunc sancta canit superum consulta deorum,
Nunc latrata fero regna profunda cane,
Ille quidem parce Samii pro more magistri
Vivat, et innocuos praebeat herba cibos;
Stet prope fagineo pellucida lympha catillo,
Sobriaque e puro pocula fonte bibat.
Additur huic scelerisque vacans et casta iuventus,
Et rigidi mores, et sine labe manus.
Qualis veste nitens sacra, et lustralibus undis
Surgis ad infensos augur iture deos.
Hoc ritu vixisse ferunt post rapta sagacem
Lumina Tiresian, Ogygiumque Linon,
Et lare devoto profugum Calchanta, senemque

skillful hand, plays for you; and amid hung tapestries the harp is heard, which guides virginal feet with its quivering art. Let those sights, in any case, occupy your muse, and recall whatever sluggish drunkenness drives away. Believe me, when the ivory plucks the strings and the festive crowd, in time with the lyre, fills the perfumed halls, you will feel Phoebus creep quietly through your heart, as a sudden warmth spreads through your bones; and by way of girlish eyes and the sounding finger, gliding Thalia[48] will overrun your entire breast. For light Elegy is cared for by many of the gods, and she calls whomever she pleases to her numbers; Liber is there in elegiacs, and Erato[51] and Ceres and Venus, and tender little Love with his rosy mother. So great banquets are right for such poets, and frequently getting drunk on old wine; but he who tells of wars, and of heaven under the rule of Jove in his maturity, and reverent heroes and semidivine leaders, and sings now of the sacred deliberations of the supreme gods, now of the deep realm where the fierce dog barks[58]—let him live sparingly, like the master of Samos,[59] and let plants provide him with harmless food; let the clearest water stand nearby in a beechwood vessel, and let him drink sober drafts from a pure spring. Add to this a youth free of crime and chaste, and strict morals, and a hand free from stain. In such a manner do you, prophet, splendid in sacred clothing, with purifying waters, rise to go before the hostile gods. In this way they say wise Tiresias lived after the loss of his eyes, and Ogygian Linus,[68] and Calchas in flight from his accursed home, and Orpheus in old age, when the wild beasts

48. **Thalia:** Muse of lyric poetry, according to Horace (*Odes* 4.6.25).

51. **Erato:** Muse of love poetry, according to Ovid (*Ars Am.* 2.16).

58. **cane:** Cerberus, watchdog of Hades.

59. **Samii pro more magistri:** Pythagoras, who lived by ascetic rules.

68. Milton invents the self-denials of these shadowy figures.

Orpheon edomitis sola per antra feris;
Sic dapis exiguus, sic rivi potor Homerus
Dulichium vexit per freta longa virum,
Et per monstrificam Perseiae Phoebados aulam,
Et vada femineis insidiosa sonis,
Perque tuas rex ime domos, ubi sanguine nigro
Dicitur umbrarum detinuisse greges.
Diis etenim sacer est vates, divumque sacerdos,
Spirat et occultum pectus, et ora Iovem.
At tu siquid agam scitabere (si modo saltem
Esse putas tanti noscere siquid agam)
Paciferum canimus caelesti semine regem,
Faustaque sacratis saecula pacta libris,
Vagitumque Dei, et stabulantem paupere tecto
Qui suprema suo cum patre regna colit.
Stelliparumque polum, modulantesque aethere turmas,
Et subito elisos ad sua fana deos.
Dona quidem dedimus Christi natalibus illa;
Illa sub auroram lux mihi prima tulit.
Te quoque pressa manent patriis meditata cicutis;
Tu mihi, cui recitem, iudicis instar eris.

had been tamed in the solitary caves. Like them, spare in his diet and drinking from the stream,[71] Homer brought the man of Dulichium through the wide seas, and through the monster-making halls of the daughter of Perse and Phoebus,[73] and the shallows treacherous with female sounds,[74] and through your house, infernal king, where he is said to have detained crowds of shadows with black blood. For a bard is sacred to the gods, and a priest to the gods, and both his hidden heart and his mouth breathe forth Jove. But if you would know what I am doing (if indeed you think it worthwhile to know what I am doing), we are singing the peace-bringing king of heavenly seed, and the happy ages promised in the sacred books, and the baby cries of God, and the stabling under a poor roof of him who inhabits the highest kingdom with his father, and the star-spawning sky, and the hosts making music in the air, and the gods suddenly shattered in their own shrines. These gifts indeed we have given for Christ's birthday; these the first light brought me at dawn. For you also[89] are waiting modest things composed on paternal pipes; you to whom I recite them will be as it were my judge.

71. Here Milton deliberately contradicts Horace, who said that no good poet was a water drinker (*Epist.* 1.19.1–6).

73. **Perseiae Phoebados:** Circe.

74. **femineis insidiosa sonis:** the song of the Sirens. Odysseus descends to Hades in *Od.* 11.

89. It is debated whether these lines continue to allude to the ode *On the Morning of Christ's Nativity* or might instead refer to other poems (Carey 1964; Hughes et al. 1:26).

ELEGIA SEPTIMA
[*Elegy 7*]

Whereas the other dated elegies make use of arabic numerals, this one is dated with an ordinal. *Anno aetatis undevigesimo* would usually mean "in the nineteenth year of his age," when he was eighteen, throughout most of 1627. But considering that *anno aetatis* in conjunction with an arabic numeral always means "at the age of . . ." in Milton, some scholars suppose that the author of *Elegy 7* was nineteen.

Assuming that the poem was written around May Day 1627, and is earlier than *Elegy 5* and *Elegy 6*, Milton might have removed it from its chronological position and placed it at the end of his little book of elegies because the poem makes the best fit with his retraction, *Haec ego mente.*

ANNO AETATIS UNDEVIGESIMO

Nondum blanda tuas leges Amathusia noram,
Et Paphio vacuum pectus ab igne fuit.
Saepe cupidineas, puerilia tela, sagittas,
Atque tuum sprevi maxime, numen, Amor.
Tu puer imbelles dixi transfige columbas;
Conveniunt tenero mollia bella duci:
Aut de passeribus tumidos age, parve, triumphos;
Haec sunt militiae digna trophaea tuae.
In genus humanum quid inania dirigis arma?
Non valet in fortes ista pharetra viros.
Non tulit hoc Cyprius (neque enim Deus ullus ad iras
Promptior), et duplici iam ferus igne calet.
Ver erat, et summae radians per culmina villae
Attulerat primam lux tibi Maie diem:
At mihi adhuc refugam quaerebant lumina noctem,
Nec matutinum sustinuere iubar.
Astat Amor lecto, pictis Amor impiger alis;
Prodidit astantem mota pharetra Deum;
Prodidit et facies, et dulce minantis ocelli,

1. **Amathusia:** Venus, here named after her shrine at Amathus on Cyprus.
2. **Paphio:** Venus had a temple at Paphos on Cyprus.
11. **Cyprius:** Cupid, whose mother, Venus, was called "Cypris" from her associations with Cyprus (see 1n, 2n).

IN HIS NINETEENTH YEAR

I did not yet know your laws, enticing Amathusia,[1] and my heart was empty of Paphian[2] fire. Often I have scorned Cupid's arrows—childish weapons—and your divinity, Love. "Boy," I said, "shoot down harmless doves; soft wars are right for a tender general. Or stage pompous triumphs over sparrows, little one; these are trophies worthy of your campaign. Why attack the human race with useless armaments? That quiver has no power against real men." The Cyprian boy[11] did not tolerate this (for no god is quicker to anger) and now burns in his rage with redoubled fire. It was spring, and the light shining on the top of the farmhouse brought your first day, May. But my eyes still sought fleeing night and did not bear the morning light. Love stood next to the bed, restless Love with colored wings. The moving quiver gave him away as he stood there; and his face gave him away, and his sweetly menacing eyes, and all those things

Et quicquid puero dignum et Amore fuit.
Talis in aeterno iuvenis Sigeius Olympo
Miscet amatori pocula plena Iovi;
Aut qui formosas pellexit ad oscula nymphas
Thiodamantaeus naiade raptus Hylas;
Addideratque iras, sed et has decuisse putares,
Addideratque truces, nec sine felle minas.
Et miser exemplo sapuisses tutius, inquit;
Nunc mea quid possit dextera testis eris.
Inter et expertos vires numerabere nostras,
Et faciam vero per tua damna fidem.
Ipse ego si nescis strato Pythone superbum
Edomui Phoebum, cessit et ille mihi;
Et quoties meminit Peneidos, ipse fatetur
Certius et gravius tela nocere mea.
Me nequit adductum curvare peritius arcum,
Qui post terga solet vincere Parthus eques.
Cydoniusque mihi cedit venator, et ille
Inscius uxori qui necis author erat.
Est etiam nobis ingens quoque victus Orion,
Herculeaeque manus, Herculeusque comes.
Iupiter ipse licet sua fulmina torqueat in me,
Haerebunt lateri spicula nostra Iovis.
Caetera quae dubitas melius mea tela docebunt,
Et tua non leviter corda petenda mihi.
Nec te stulte tuae poterunt defendere Musae,
Nec tibi Phoebaeus porriget anguis opem.
Dixit, et aurato quatiens mucrone sagittam,
Evolat in tepidos Cypridos ille sinus.
At mihi risuro tonuit ferus ore minaci,

that were worthy of a boy and of Love. He was like the Sigean youth[21] who mixes full cups for his lover Jove on eternal Olympus; or like Theodamas's son Hylas,[24] abducted by a Naiad, he who lured the beautiful nymphs to his kisses—and he added anger (but you would think it became him), and he added bitter threats, not without rancor. And he said, "Unhappy man, it would have been safer to have learned from example; now you will be witness to what my right hand can do. You will be numbered among those who have known my power, and indeed I will gain credibility through your punishment. I myself, in case you do not know, tamed proud Phoebus after he had struck down Python,[31] and he yielded to me; and whenever he remembers the daughter of Peneus, he himself admits that my arrows hurt more surely and more deeply. The Parthian horseman, who is used to winning behind his back, cannot bend a taut bow more skillfully than I. And the Cydonian hunter[37] yields to me, and he who unknowingly was the author of his wife's death. And even huge Orion[39] was also outdone by me, and the hands of Hercules, and the companion of Hercules.[40] Let Jupiter himself spin his thunderbolts at me, our arrows will stick in Jove's side. On other things which you doubt, my weapons will better convince you, and your own heart, at which I will aim with no lack of seriousness. Fool, your muses will not be able to defend you, nor will Phoebus's serpent extend you any aid." He spoke, and shaking a gold-tipped arrow,[47] he flew away into the warm bosom of Cypris. And when he thundered fierce at me with his menacing speech, I laughed, and

21. **iuvenis Sigeius:** Ganymede, the Trojan boy who served as Zeus's cupbearer.

24. **Hylas:** a youth loved by Hercules. Trying to fetch water from a pool, he was pulled down by amorous nymphs.

31. Apollo taunted Cupid for presuming to use the bow. Cupid promptly shot him with a golden arrow (love) and Daphne with a leaden one (antipathy). See Ovid, *Met.* 1.452–567.

37. Crete was famous for its archers. **ille/Inscius:** Cephalus, who heard a sound in the bushes, threw his spear and killed his wife, Procris (Ovid, *Met.* 7.835–62).

39. Orion pursued the seven daughters of Altas (Pleiades).

40. Deianira, wife of Hercules, scolds him for his submission to Omphale, who dressed him as a maid and forced him to spin for her (Ovid, *Her.* 9.47).

47. See 31n.

Et mihi de puero non metus ullus erat.
Et modo qua nostri spatiantur in urbe Quirites,
Et modo villarum proxima rura placent.
Turba frequens, facieque simillima turba dearum,
Splendida per medias itque reditque vias.
Auctaque luce dies gemino fulgore coruscat,
Fallor? an et radios hinc quoque Phoebus habet.
Haec ego non fugi spectacula grata severus,
Impetus et quo me fert iuvenilis agor.
Lumina luminibus male providus obvia misi,
Neve oculos potui continuisse meos.
Unam forte aliis supereminuisse notabam;
Principium nostri lux erat illa mali.
Sic Venus optaret mortalibus ipsa videri,
Sic regina Deum conspicienda fuit.
Hanc memor obiecit nobis malus ille Cupido,
Solus et hos nobis texuit ante dolos.
Nec procul ipse vafer latuit, multaeque sagittae,
Et facis a tergo grande pependit onus.
Nec mora; nunc ciliis haesit, nunc virginis ori,
Insilit hinc labiis, insidet inde genis;
Et quascunque agilis partes iaculator oberrat,
Hei mihi, mille locis pectus inerme ferit.
Protinus insoliti subierunt corda furores;
Uror amans intus, flammaque totus eram.
Interea misero quae iam mihi sola placebat
Ablata est, oculis non reditura meis.
Ast ego progredior tacite querebundus, et excors,
Et dubius volui saepe referre pedem.
Findor; et haec remanet, sequitur pars altera votum;
Raptaque tam subito gaudia flere iuvat.

there was no fear of the boy in me. And sometimes the places where our citizens stroll in the city[51] are pleasant, and sometimes the nearby countryside of the farmhouses. A dense crowd, much like a crowd of goddesses in their faces, goes to and fro, shining in the middle of the road. With its light enhanced, the day gleams with double splendor; am I wrong, or does Phoebus take his beams from them? I did not in sternness flee this welcome spectacle, and I was driven where youthful impulse carried me. With bad foresight I sent my eyes to meet theirs, nor could I hold back my sight. By chance I noticed one standing out above the others; that light was the beginning of my trouble. Such would Venus herself have hoped to appear to mortals; such the queen of the gods must have looked. That mindful, evil Cupid thrust her in our way, and he alone wove these plots for us ahead of time. The trickster himself hid not far away, and many arrows and a heavy load of torches hung on his back. No delay, now he clung to the eyelids, now to the virgin's mouth, from here he jumps to the lips, then he resides in the cheeks; and to whatever part the agile archer flits, alas for me, he strikes my unarmed heart in a thousand places. Unfamiliar furies immediately overran my heart, I burn inwardly in love, and I was all aflame. Meanwhile, she who was now the only one to please me in my misery was taken away, never to return to my sight. But I go about, silently complaining and out of my mind, and confused, I often wanted to retrace my steps. I am torn, and this part stays and the other part follows my hope, and it is sweet to weep for pleasure so suddenly taken back. In such a way did

51. The favorite places to walk in London in the seventeenth century were Gray's Inn Fields, Lincoln's Inn Fields, Moorfields, and the Temple Garden.

Sic dolet amissum proles Iunonia coelum,
Inter Lemniacos praecipitata focos.
Talis et abreptum solem respexit, ad Orcum
Vectus ab attonitis Amphiaraus equis.
Quid faciam infelix, et luctu victus? Amores
Nec licet inceptos ponere, neve sequi.
O utinam spectare semel mihi detur amatos
Vultus, et coram tristia verba loqui!
Forsitan et duro non est adamante creata,
Forte nec ad nostras surdeat illa preces.
Crede mihi nullus sic infeliciter arsit;
Ponar in exemplo primus et unus ego.
Parce precor teneri cum sis Deus ales amoris;
Pugnent officio nec tua facta tuo.
Iam tuus O certe est mihi formidabilis arcus,
Nate dea, iaculis nec minus igne potens:
Et tua fumabunt nostris altaria donis,
Solus et in superis tu mihi summus eris.
Deme meos tandem, verum nec deme furores;
Nescio cur, miser est suaviter omnis amans:
Tu modo da facilis, posthaec mea siqua futura est,
Cuspis amaturos figat ut una duos.

Jove's offspring[81] grieve for lost heaven after being hurled down among the Lemnian households; and so did Amphiaraus,[84] being carried off to Orcus by his crazed horses, look back at the sun that was being snatched away. What am I to do, unhappy, overcome with grief? It is not allowed either to put down the love that has begun or to follow it. Oh, would it be given to me to see that beloved face once, and to give my sad speech in private. And possibly she was not created out of hard adamant, and perhaps she would not be deaf to our prayers. Believe me, no one burned so unhappily; I may be put down as the first and only example. Spare me, I pray, since you are the winged god of tender love; do not let your deeds war against your office. Now your bow is surely terrifying to me, son of a goddess, powerful with your arrows and no less so with your fire; and your altars will smoke with my offerings, and you alone will be supreme to me among the gods. Please take away my ravings— But no, do not take them away. I do not know why, every lover is agreeably miserable. Just be kind enough to grant, if after this any female is to be mine, that one arrowhead transfix two loving hearts.

81. Vulcan (Hephaestus), the son of Juno (Hera), was hurled from heaven by Jove (Zeus) and fell for an entire day, landing on the island of Lemnos (*Il.* 1.590–93).

84. **Amphiaraus:** one of the seven against Thebes; he knew the cause was unjust and fled in shame when the attack failed. To save him from disgrace, Zeus opened the earth so that he and his chariot were dropped into Hades (Statius, *Thebaid* 7.690–823).

HAEC EGO MENTE

[*A postscript to his elegies*]

Haec ego mente olim laeva, studioque supino
  Nequitiae posui vana trophaea meae.
Scilicet abreptum sic me malus impulit error,
  Indocilisque aetas prava magistra fuit.
Donec Socraticos umbrosa Academia rivos
  Praebuit, admissum dedocuitque iugum.
Protinus extinctis ex illo tempore flammis,
  Cincta rigent multo pectora nostra gelu.
Unde suis frigus metuit puer ipse sagittis,
  Et Diomedeam vim timet ipsa Venus.

These empty trophies to my wantonness I once made with a frivolous mind and perverse enthusiasm. Clearly malign error drove me when I was abducted this way, and untaught youth was my depraved teacher—until shady Academia offered its Socratic streams,[5] and made me unlearn the burden which I had taken up. With my flames quenched immediately from that time on, our heart stiffens, encased in thick ice. Whence the boy himself fears the cold on his arrows, and Venus herself dreads the strength of Diomedes.

5. Cp. *An Apology* (p. 851): "Thus from the laureate fraternity of poets, riper years, and the ceaseless round of study and reading led me to the shady spaces of philosophy, but chiefly to the divine volumes of Plato."

IN PRODITIONEM BOMBARDICAM

[*On the Gunpowder Plot*]

The four epigrams on the Gunpowder Plot, and the one on the inventor of gunpowder, were probably composed for the academic observance of Guy Fawkes Day. They were placed in the *Elegiarum Liber* in 1645 and 1673, as were the Leonora poems that follow them, because they were written in the elegiac meter.

Cum simul in regem nuper satrapasque Britannos
  Ausus es infandum perfide Fauxe nefas,
Fallor? an et mitis voluisti ex parte videri,
  Et pensare mala cum pietate scelus?
Scilicet hos alti missurus ad atria caeli,
  Sulphureo curru flammivolisque rotis.
Qualiter ille feris caput inviolabile Parcis
  Liquit Iordanios turbine raptus agros.

When, treacherous Fawkes, you once lately dared unspeakable evil against the king and satraps of Britain, am I wrong or did you wish to seem kind in part and to mitigate your crime with malign piety—planning, it would seem, to send them to the halls of highest heaven in a sulfureous chariot with wheels of spinning fire? Just so did that man[7] whose head could not be touched by the Fates leave the Jordanian fields, carried off in a whirlwind.

7. **ille:** Elijah, who was taken into Heaven without dying (2 Kings 2.7).

IN EANDEM

[*On the same*]

Siccine tentasti caelo donasse Iacobum
Quae septemgemino Belua monte lates?
Ni meliora tuum poterit dare munera numen,
Parce precor donis insidiosa tuis.
Ille quidem sine te consortia serus adivit
Astra, nec inferni pulveris usus ope.
Sic potius foedos in caelum pelle cucullos,
Et quot habet brutos Roma profana deos,
Namque hac aut alia nisi quemque adiuveris arte,
Crede mihi caeli vix bene scandet iter.

So you tried to give James to heaven, you beast[2] that hides in the seven hills? Unless your divinity can give better offerings, I pray spare us your gifts, traitor. He has indeed without you gone late to his kindred stars,[6] not using the aid of your infernal powder. Instead, blow foul monks to heaven that way,[7] and all the brutish gods that profane Rome holds! For believe me, unless you help them with this or another craft, scarcely any will climb the path to heaven.

2. **Belua:** Protestants identified the beast of Rev. 13.1 with the Catholic Church.
6. James I died on March 27, 1625.
7. Cp. *PL* 3.473–94.

IN EANDEM

[*On the same*]

Purgatorem animae derisit Iacobus ignem,
Et sine quo superum non adeunda domus.
Frenduit hoc trina monstrum Latiale corona
Movit et horrificum cornua dena minax.
Et nec inultus ait temnes mea sacra Britanne,
Supplicium spreta relligione dabis.
Et si stelligeras unquam penetraveris arces,
Non nisi per flammas triste patebit iter.
O quam funesto cecinisti proxima vero,
Verbaque ponderibus vix caritura suis!
Nam prope Tartareo sublime rotatus ab igni
Ibat ad aethereas umbra perusta plagas.

James derided the soul's purgatorial fire,[1] without which the house of the gods cannot be approached. The triple-crowned monster of Latium[3] gnashed his teeth at this and, horrific and menacing, shook his ten horns.[4] And he said, "Briton, you will not scorn my sacred things unavenged; you will suffer punishment for spurning religion. And if you ever enter into the starry citadels, it will only be if a bitter path through flames opens up." Oh, how close you sang to the deadly truth, words barely failing to have weight! For he almost went on high, whirled by Tartarean fire, to the airy precincts as a charred ghost.

1. James I condemned the idea of Purgatory (McIlwain 125).
3. **Latiale:** Roman. The triple-crowned monster is the pope.
4. **cornua dena:** See Rev. 13.1.
11. **Tartareo:** infernal, horrible.

IN EANDEM

[*On the same*]

Quem modo Roma suis devoverat impia diris,
  Et Styge damnarat Taenarioque sinu,
Hunc vice mutata iam tollere gestit ad astra,
  Et cupit ad superos evehere usque deos.

Him whom impious Rome once denounced with curses and damned to Styx and the Taenarian gulf,[2] now with a different approach she works to lift up to the stars and wants to convey to the highest gods.

2. **Taenarioque sinu:** See *Elegy* 5.66n. Baptized a Catholic, James was raised a Protestant. Catholics considered him excommunicate.

IN INVENTOREM BOMBARDAE

[*On the Inventor of Gunpowder*]

Iapetionidem laudavit caeca vetustas,
  Qui tulit aethereain solis ab axe facem;
At mihi maior erit, qui lurida creditur arma,
  Et trifidum fulmen surripuisse Iovi.

Blind antiquity praised the son of Iapetus,[1] who brought the heavenly torch from the sun's chariot; but to me he will be a greater man who is believed to have taken the lurid armaments and triple thunder of Jove.

1. **Iapetionidem:** Prometheus, who stole fire from heaven. In *PL* 6.470–506, Satan is the inventor of gunpowder.

AD LEONORAM ROMAE CANENTEM

[*To Leonora singing in Rome*]

Leonora Baroni was a well-known Italian singer. During his travels through Europe, Milton made two visits to Rome, in October–November 1638 and January–February 1639.

These three poems bring the *Elegiarum Liber* to a close.

Angelus unicuique suus (sic credite gentes)
  Obtigit aethereis ales ab ordinibus.
Quid mirum, Leonora tibi si gloria maior?
  Nam tua praesentem vox sonat ipsa Deum.
Aut Deus, aut vacui certe mens tertia coeli

A special winged angel—believe it so, peoples—has been allotted to each one from the heavenly orders. Why would it be surprising if your glory, Leonora, would be greater, for the sound of your voice makes God present. Either God or certainly a third mind[5]

5. **mens tertia:** perhaps the third person of the Trinity, perhaps the Neoplatonic World-Soul.

Per tua secreto guttura serpit agens;
Serpit agens, facilisque docet mortalia corda
Sensim immortali assuescere posse sono.
Quod si cuncta quidem Deus est, per cunctaque fusus,
In te una loquitur, caetera mutus habet.

from the empty sky glides affectingly in secret through your throat—glides affectingly, and with ease teaches mortal hearts to become accustomed bit by bit to immortal sound. For if God is indeed all things, and is suffused through all things, in you alone He speaks, and possesses other things in silence.

AD EANDEM

[*To the same*]

Altera Torquatum cepit Leonora poetam,
Cuius ab insano cessit amore furens.
Ah miser ille tuo quanto felicius aevo
Perditus, et propter te Leonora foret!
Et te Pieria sensisset voce canentem
Aurea maternae fila movere lyrae,
Quamvis Dircaeo torsisset lumina Pentheo
Saevior, aut totus desipuisset iners,
Tu tamen errantes caeca vertigine sensus
Voce eadem poteras composuisse tua;
Et poteras aegro spirans sub corde quietem
Flexanimo cantu restituisse sibi.

Another Leonora captured the poet Torquato;[1] in his rage he surrendered to insane love for her. Ah, unhappy man, how much more blessedly he would have perished in your time, and because of you, Leonora! And he would have heard you, singing with your Pierian[5] voice, stroke the golden strings of your mother's[6] lyre. Even if he rolled his eyes more savagely than Dircaean Pentheus,[7] or became totally mindless and inert, you could still have calmed his senses with your voice as they wandered blindly whirling; and breathing peace into his sick heart, you could have restored him with a mind-bending song.

1. **Torquatum:** The poet Torquato Tasso (1544–95) suffered from insanity due, it was said, to his love for Leonora d'Este, the sister of his patron, the Duke of Ferrara.
5. **Pieria:** birthplace of the Muses.
6. Leonora's mother was a musician.
7. **Dircaeo:** Theban; **Pentheo:** Pentheus, an opponent of the Dionysian rites. The Bacchantes tore him to pieces.

AD EANDEM

[*To the same*]

Credula quid liquidam Sirena Neapoli iactas,
  Claraque Parthenopes fana Acheloiados,
Littoreamque tua defunctam naiada ripa
  Corpora Chalcidico sacra dedisse rogo?
Illa quidem vivitque, et amoena Tibridis unda
  Mutavit rauci murmura Pausilipi.
Illic Romulidum studiis ornata secundis,
  Atque homines cantu detinet atque deos.

Credulous Naples, why do you boast of the melodious siren and the famous shrine of Achelous's daughter Parthenope[2]—that when the Naiad of the coast died on your shore, you placed her sacred body on a Chalcidian[4] pyre? She is in fact alive, and changed the rumble of noisy Posilipo[6] for the pleasant waters of the Tiber. There, honored with the enthusiastic favor of the sons of Romulus, she entrances both men and gods with her song.

2. **Parthenopes:** one of the Sirens. See *Masque* 879n.
4. **Chalcidico:** Neapolitan.
6. **Pausilipi:** Naples, which Leonora has left for Rome. There was a tunnel through Mount Posilipo famous for its noisy traffic.

Sylvarum Liber
[*Book of Miscellaneous Poems*]

IN OBITUM PROCANCELLARII MEDICI
[*On the Death of the Vice-Chancellor, a Physician*]

John Gostlin, Master of Caius and Regius Professor of Physic, served as Vice-Chancellor in 1626 and died on October 21. Milton having been seventeen, not sixteen, at the time of his death, the Latin heading is in error.

ANNO AETATIS 16

Parere fati discite legibus,
Manusque Parcae iam date supplices,
  Qui pendulum telluris orbem
    Iapeti colitis nepotes.
Vos si relicto mors vaga Taenaro
Semel vocarit flebilis, heu morae
  Tentantur incassum dolique;
    Per tenebras Stygis ire certum est.
Si destinatam pellere dextera
Mortem valeret, non ferus Hercules
  Nessi venenatus cruore
    Aemathia iacuisset Oeta.

2. **Parcae:** Milton alludes to one of the three Fates, but which one is unclear.
4. **Iapeti:** Iapetus was the father of Prometheus, who created man, and therefore a common ancestor of mankind.
5. **Taenaro:** There was supposed to be an entrance to Hades near this mountain.
10. The poison in Nessus's bloody shirt drove Hercules to suicide on *Oeta,* the mountain range between Aetolia and Thessaly.

AT AGE 16

Learn to obey the laws of fate, and now lift suppliant hands to Parca,[2] you sons of Iapetus[4] who inhabit earth's pendant globe. If wandering, mournful death, leaving Taenarus,[5] once calls you, alas delays and tricks are tried in vain; travel to the shades of Styx is certain. If a strong arm could repel destined death, fierce Hercules[10] would not have lain on Emathian Oeta, poisoned with the blood of Nessus; Ilium would not have seen Hector cut down by the shameful fraud of envious

Nec fraude turpi Palladis invidae
Vidisset occisum Ilion Hectora, aut
Quem larva Pelidis peremit
Ense Locro, Iove lacrimante.
Si triste fatum verba Hecateia
Fugare possint, Telegoni parens
Vixisset infamis, potentique
Aegiali soror usa virga.
Numenque trinum fallere si queant
Artes medentum, ignotaque gramina,
Non gnarus herbarum Machaon
Eurypyli cecidisset hasta.
Laesisset et nec te Philyreie
Sagitta echidnae perlita sanguine,
Nec tela te fulmenque avitum
Caese puer genitricis alvo.
Tuque O alumno maior Apolline,
Gentis togatae cui regimen datum,
Frondosa quem nunc Cirrha luget,
Et mediis Helicon in undis,
Iam praefuisses Palladio gregi
Laetus, superstes, nec sine gloria,
Nec puppe lustrasses Charontis
Horribiles barathri recessus.
At fila rupit Persephone tua
Irata, cum te viderit artibus
Succoque pollenti tot atris

Pallas,[13] nor he whom the phantom of Peleus's son killed[15] with a Locrian sword while Jove wept. If Hecate's words could drive away sad fate, the infamous parent of Telegonus[18] would have lived, and Aegialus's sister,[20] using her powerful wand. If doctors' arts and unknown plants could cheat the triune divinity, Machaon,[23] an expert with herbs, would not have fallen to Euripylus's spear. Nor would an arrow smeared with the hydra's blood have wounded you, son of Philyra;[25] nor the weapons and thunder of your grandfather have wounded you, boy cut from the womb of your mother.[28] And you, O greater than your pupil Apollo, to whom was given the government of the betogaed society, whom leafy Cirrha[31] now mourns, and also Helicon amid its waters, you would still be leading Pallas's flock:[33] happy, a survivor, and not without glory—nor would you be traveling the horrid recesses of the underworld in Charon's[35] boat. But angry Persephone[37] cut your thread when she saw you had snatched so many from the dark

13. Disguised as Hector's brother Deiphobus, Pallas Athena persuaded Hector to fight Achilles. After Achilles missed him with his first cast, she retrieved his spear (*Il.* 22.226–404).

15. Sarpedon was killed by Patroclus, who wore the armor of Achilles. Zeus wept because Sarpedon was his son (*Il.* 16.458–505).

18. **Telegoni parens:** Circe. Telegonus was her child by Odysseus.

20. **Aegiali soror:** Medea, who murdered her brother Absyrtus or Aegialeus.

23. **Machaon:** Son of Asclepius, he tended the Greek army at Troy (*Il.* 2.732).

25. **Philyreie:** the centaur Chiron, who died when accidentally wounded by a poisoned arrow.

28. **puer:** Asclepius, whose skill as a physician was so great that he could revive the dead. To prevent that, Zeus killed him with a thunderbolt.

31. **Cirrha:** a town near Delphi sacred to Apollo.

33. **Palladio gregi:** the students of Cambridge University.

35. **Charontis:** Charon was the ferryman of the Styx.

37. **Persephone:** queen of Hades; her Latin name is Proserpina (see l. 46).

Faucibus eripuisse mortis.
Colende praeses, membra precor tua
Molli quiescant cespite, et ex tuo
Crescant rosae, calthaeque busto,
Purpureoque hyacinthus ore.
Sit mite de te iudicium Aeaci,
Subrideatque Aetnaea Proserpina,
Interque felices perennis
Elysio spatiere campo.

45. **Aeaci:** Aeacus, one of the three judges of the dead in Hades.

46. **Aetnaea:** Sicilian (from Mount Etna).

jaws of death with your arts and powerful medicine. Reverend Governor, I pray that your limbs rest on soft turf, and that on your tomb roses flourish, and marigolds, and the hyacinth with its purple face. May Aeacus's[45] judgment on you be gentle, and may Etnaean[46] Proserpina smile, and may you walk forever among the blessed in the Elysian field.

IN QUINTUM NOVEMBRIS

[*On the Fifth of November*]

Like the four Latin epigrams on the Gunpowder Plot, *On the Fifth of November* was probably written for an academic celebration of the nation's deliverance from Catholic treachery on Guy Fawkes Day. As the young Milton's only epic work and only characterization of Satan, it has been scrutinized for anticipations of *Paradise Lost.*

ANNO AETATIS 17

Iam pius extrema veniens Iacobus ab arcto
Teucrigenas populos, lateque patentia regna
Albionum tenuit, iamque inviolabile foedus
Sceptra Caledoniis coniunxerat Anglica Scotis:
Pacificusque novo felix divesque sedebat
In solio, occultique doli securus et hostis:
Cum ferus ignifluo regnans Acheronte tyrannus,
Eumenidum pater, aethereo vagus exul Olympo,
Forte per immensum terrarum erraverat orbem,

1. James came from Scotland to rule England in 1603. The plotters finally decided to blow up Parliament on November 5, 1605.

7. Acheron, one of the rivers of Hades (not the burning one, which is Phlegethon), could stand for the region as a whole.

AT AGE 17

Now, coming from the farthest north,[1] devout James took over the Troy-born people and the widely spread realms of Albion, and now an inviolable treaty brought the English scepter to the Caledonian Scots. The peacemaker sat happy and wealthy on his new throne, secure from hidden plot or enemy, while the fierce tyrant ruling over fiery Acheron,[7] the father of the Eumenides, a wandering exile from heavenly Olympus, happened to roam across the great globe of the earth, counting his allies in

Dinumerans sceleris socios, vernasque fideles,
Participes regni post funera moesta futuros;
Hic tempestates medio ciet aere diras,
Illic unanimes odium struit inter amicos,
Armat et invictas in mutua viscera gentes;
Regnaque olivifera vertit florentia pace,
Et quoscunque videt purae virtutis amantes,
Hos cupit adiicere imperio, fraudumque magister
Tentat inaccessum sceleri corrumpere pectus,
Insidiasque locat tacitas, cassesque latentes
Tendit, ut incautos rapiat, ceu Caspia tigris
Insequitur trepidam deserta per avia praedam
Nocte sub illuni, et somno nictantibus astris.
Talibus infestat populos Summanus et urbes
Cinctus caeruleae fumanti turbine flammae.
Iamque fluentisonis albentia rupibus arva
Apparent, et terra Deo dilecta marino,
Cui nomen dederat quondam Neptunia proles
Amphitryoniaden qui non dubitavit atrocem
Aequore tranato furiali poscere bello,
Ante expugnatae crudelia saecula Troiae.
At simul hanc opibusque et festa pace beatam
Aspicit, et pingues donis Cerealibus agros,
Quodque magis doluit, venerantem numina veri
Sancta Dei populum, tandem suspiria rupit
Tartareos ignes et luridum olentia sulphur.
Qualia Trinacria trux ab Iove clausus in Aetna
Efflat tabifico monstrosus ab ore Tiphoeus.
Ignescunt oculi, stridetque adamantinus ordo
Dentis, ut armorum fragor, ictaque cuspide cuspis.
Atque pererrato solum hoc lacrimabile mundo
Inveni, dixit, gens haec mihi sola rebellis,
Contemtrixque iugi, nostraque potentior arte.

crime and his faithful slaves,[10] who would be sharers in his kingdom after their miserable funerals. Here he stirs up fearsome storms in the middle air,[12] there he creates hate between friends of a single mind, and arms unconquered peoples against one another's vitals, and overturns kingdoms that were flourishing in olive-bearing peace; and whatever lovers of pure virtue he sees, these he longs to add to his empire, and, a master of deceit, he tries to corrupt the heart closed off to sin and sets silent traps and spreads hidden nets to catch the unwary, just as the Caspian tigress tracks her trembling prey through the pathless deserts, on a moonless night while the stars wink with sleepiness. In such a way does Summanus,[23] wrapped in a smoking cloud of blue flame, assault nations and cities. And now white land with resounding cliffs appears, and territory dear to the god of the sea, to which long ago Neptune's offspring[27] gave his name—he who after crossing the sea did not hesitate to challenge the fierce son of Amphitryon to furious war before the cruel time of Troy's destruction.

But as soon as he sees this place blessed with wealth and festive peace, and the fields rich with the gifts of Ceres, and—what grieved him more—a people worshiping the sacred power of the true God, at length he broke into sighs smelling of Tartarean fire and yellow sulfur: such as savage, monstrous Typhoeus,[37] imprisoned by Jove in Trinacrian Etna, breathes forth from his corrosive mouth. His eyes flare, the adamantine array of his teeth grinds with a noise like that of arms and of spear struck by spear. "And after wandering over the entire world," he

10. **vernas:** slaves by birth. The phrase *vernasque fideles* smacks of a predestination that the mature Milton would repudiate.

12. **medio . . . aere:** the middle region of the air, where devils reside throughout Milton's work.

23. **Summanus:** god of midnight storms.

27. **Neptunia proles:** Albion, the legendary king of Britain who named the island after himself. Hercules (*Amphitryoniaden*) killed him in Gaul.

37. For Typhoeus, see *PL* 1.198–99.

Illa tamen, mea si quicquam tentamina possunt,
Non feret hoc impune diu, non ibit inulta.
Hactenus, et piceis liquido natat aere pennis;
Qua volat, adversi praecursant agmine venti,
Densantur nubes, et crebra tonitrua fulgent.
Iamque pruinosas velox superaverat Alpes,
Et tenet Ausoniae fines, a parte sinistra
Nimbifer Appenninus erat, priscique Sabini,
Dextra veneficiis infamis Hetruria, nec non
Te furtiva Tibris Thetidi videt oscula dantem;
Hinc Mavortigenae consistit in arce Quirini.
Reddiderant dubiam iam sera crepuscula lucem,
Cum circumgreditur totam Tricoronifer urbem,
Panificosque deos portat, scapulisque virorum
Evehitur, praeeunt summisso poplite reges,
Et mendicantum series longissima fratrum;
Cereaque in manibus gestant funalia caeci,
Cimmeriis nati in tenebris, vitamque trahentes.
Templa dein multis subeunt lucentia taedis
(Vesper erat sacer iste Petro) fremitusque canentum
Saepe tholos implet vacuos, et inane locorum.
Qualiter exululat Bromius, Bromiique caterva,
Orgia cantantes in Echionio Aracyntho,
Dum tremit attonitus vitreis Asopus in undis,
Et procul ipse cava responsat rupe Cithaeron.
His igitur tandem solenni more peractis,
Nox senis amplexus Erebi taciturna reliquit,
Praecipitesque impellit equos stimulante flagello,

52. **Thetidi:** Thetis (by synecdoche the sea itself).

60. The Cimmerians live on the edge of the world in utter darkness (Homer, *Od.* 11.13–22).

64. **Bromius:** Bacchus, whose celebrations were noisy.

said, "this is the only thing I have found to make me weep; this nation is the only one rebellious to me, and scornful of my yoke, and more powerful than our art. Still, if my attempts have any effect, it will not go unpunished long, it will not go without retribution." So much, and he swims through the liquid air on wings of pitch; where he flies, contrary winds run before in a mass, clouds thicken, and dense thunder flashes.

And now he speedily crossed the frosty Alps and reaches Italian territory; on the left were the cloud-bearing Apennines and the ancient Sabines, on the right Tuscany notorious for poisons, nor does he fail to see you, running Tiber, giving kisses to Thetis;[52] here he alights at the citadel of Mars-born Quirinus. Now late dusk had brought back uncertain light, when the wearer of the triple crown tours the entire city and carries gods made of bread, and is borne on men's shoulders. Kings precede him on bended knee, and a very long line of begging friars, and blindly they carry wax tapers in their hands—born and dragging out their life in Cimmerian darkness.[60] Then they enter into temples lit with many torches (this was the eve sacred to Peter), and the roar often fills the empty domes and the vacant spaces. In such a way Bromius[64] wails, and Bromius's company, singing orgiastic songs on Echionian Aracynthus, while stunned Asopus trembles in his glassy waters, and from far away Cithaeron itself echoes from its hollow cliff.

So when these things had finally been done according to solemn rite, silent Night left the embrace of aged Erebus and drove her horses headlong with her stinging whip: sightless

Captum oculis Typhlonta, Melanchaetemque ferocem,
Atque Acherontaeo prognatam patre Siopen
Torpidam, et hirsutis horrentem Phrica capillis.
Interea regum domitor, Phlegetontius haeres
Ingreditur thalamos (neque enim secretus adulter
Producit steriles molli sine pellice noctes);
At vix compositos somnus claudebat ocellos,
Cum niger umbrarum dominus, rectorque silentum,
Praedatorque hominum falsa sub imagine tectus
Astitit. Assumptis micuerunt tempora canis,
Barba sinus promissa tegit, cineracea longo
Syrmate verrit humum vestis, pendetque cucullus
Vertice de raso, et ne quicquam desit ad artes,
Cannabeo lumbos constrinxit fune salaces,
Tarda fenestratis figens vestigia calceis.
Talis uti fama est, vasta Franciscus eremo
Tetra vagabatur solus per lustra ferarum,
Silvestrique tulit genti pia verba salutis
Impius, atque lupos domuit, Libicosque leones.
  Subdolus at tali Serpens velatus amictu
Solvit in has fallax ora execrantia voces;
Dormis nate? Etiamne tuos sopor opprimit artus?
Immemor O fidei, pecorumque oblite tuorum,
Dum cathedram venerande tuam, diademaque triplex
Ridet Hyperboreo gens barbara nata sub axe,
Dumque pharetrati spernunt tua iura Britanni:
Surge, age, surge piger, Latius quem Caesar adorat,
Cui reserata patet convexi ianua caeli,
Turgentes animos, et fastus frange procaces,
Sacrilegique sciant, tua quid maledictio possit,

Typhlon and ferocious Melanchaetes and stolid Siope, sired by an Acherontean father, and bristling Phrix with his shaggy hair. Meanwhile, the breaker of kings, the heir of Phlegethon, enters his bridal chamber (for the secret adulterer does not spend fruitless nights without a soft whore), but sleep had scarcely closed his composed eyes when the black lord of the shadows, the ruler of the silent, the predator of men, stood there, dressed in a false image: his temples gleam with applied whiteness,[80] a streaming beard covers his chest, his ashen clothing sweeps the ground with a long train, and his cowl hangs from his shaved head, and lest anything be lacking in his artfulness, he bound his salacious loins with a rope of hemp, fitting his slow feet into latticed shoes. So, the story goes, did Francis in the vast desert travel alone through the vile haunts of animals and, unholy himself, brought the holy words of salvation to the people of the forest, and tamed the wolves and the Libyan lions.

Treacherous and veiled in such clothing, the deceitful serpent opened his accursed mouth with these words: "Are you sleeping, son? Does sleep still oppress your limbs? O forgetful of your faith, and oblivious of your flock, while a barbarous nation born under the Hyperborean sky mocks your throne and triple diadem—you who should be worshiped—and while British archers spurn your laws: arise, act, arise, sluggard, whom Latin Caesar adores, for whom the locked gates of arched Heaven stand open, break their swollen spirits and their stubborn pride, and let the sacrilegious know what your curse can do, and what the guardianship of the apostolic

80. Cp. Satan's disguise in *PR* 1.314–20, 497–98.

Et quid Apostolicae possit custodia clavis;
Et memor Hesperiae disiectam ulciscere classem,
Mersaque Iberorum lato vexilla profundo,
Sanctorumque cruci tot corpora fixa probrosae,
Thermodoontea nuper regnante puella.
At tu si tenero mavis torpescere lecto
Crescentesque negas hosti contundere vires,
Tyrrhenum implebit numeroso milite Pontum,
Signaque Aventino ponet fulgentia colle:
Relliquias veterum franget, flammisque cremabit,
Sacraque calcabit pedibus tua colla profanis,
Cuius gaudebant soleïs dare basia reges.
Nec tamen hunc bellis et aperto Marte lacesses,
Irritus ille labor; tu callidus utere fraude,
Quaelibet haereticis disponere retia fas est;
Iamque ad consilium extremis rex magnus ab oris
Patricios vocat, et procerum de stirpe creatos,
Grandaevosque patres trabea, canisque verendos;
Hos tu membratim poteris conspergere in auras,
Atque dare in cineres, nitrati pulveris igne
Aedibus iniecto, qua convenere, sub imis.
Protinus ipse igitur quoscumque habet Anglia fidos
Propositi, factique mone, quisquamne tuorum
Audebit summi non iussa facessere Papae?
Perculsosque metu subito, casumque stupentes
Invadat vel Gallus atrox, vel saevus Iberus
Saecula sic illic tandem Mariana redibunt,
Tuque in belligeros iterum dominaberis Anglos.
Et nequid timeas, divos divasque secundas

key[101] can do; remember, and avenge Hesperia's[102] shattered fleet and the banners of the Iberians sunk in the wide ocean, and the bodies of so many saints fixed to the shameful cross[104] while the Thermodontean girl reigned of late. But if you prefer to languish in a soft bed and refuse to quell the enemy's growing strength, he will fill the Tyrrhenian Sea with a great army and plant his gleaming standards on the Aventine hill; he will smash your ancient relics and burn them in the flames, and tread with profane feet on your holy neck—you whose sandals kings rejoiced to kiss. Still, you shouldn't challenge him in battle and open war—that would be useless labor—but be clever and use trickery: it's lawful to spread any sort of net for heretics. And now the great king is summoning patricians from the farthest territories for counsel, and those born in the lineage of the great, and aged fathers venerated for their gown and white hair; these you could spatter piecemeal into the air and turn into ashes with the fire of nitrate powder injected into the depths of the buildings where they convene. Therefore you should yourself immediately alert whatever faithful England still has concerning this plan and action; who of your people would dare not carry out the orders of the supreme pope? Either the ferocious Gaul or the savage Iberian will invade them when they are overwhelmed with sudden fear, stunned at the event; so at last the Marian ages will return there, and you will again rule over the warlike English. And to keep you from being afraid, know that the gods and goddesses are favorable, all the divinities that are celebrated in your holidays." He spoke, and dropping his as-

101. **Apostolicae . . . clavis:** the Catholic doctrine by which each successive pope inherits the keys of the kingdom given originally to Peter (Matt. 16.19).

102. *Hesperiae* here refers to Spain. The passage alludes to the defeat of the Armada in 1588.

104. Omitting the Protestants burned by Mary, Satan remembers only the Catholics put to death under Elizabeth.

Accipe, quotque tuis celebrantur numina fastis.
Dixit et adscitos ponens malefidus amictus
Fugit ad infandam, regnum illaetabile, Lethen.
Iam rosea Eoas pandens Tithonia portas
Vestit inauratas redeunti lumine terras;
Maestaque adhuc nigri deplorans funera nati
Irrigat ambrosiis montana cacumina guttis;
Cum somnos pepulit stellatae ianitor aulae
Nocturnos visus, et somnia grata revolvens.
Est locus aeterna septus caligine noctis
Vasta ruinosi quondam fundamina tecti,
Nunc torvi spelunca Phoni, Prodotaeque bilinguis
Effera quos uno peperit Discordia partu.
Hic inter caementa iacent praeruptaque saxa,
Ossa inhumata virum, et traiecta cadavera ferro;
Hic Dolus intortis semper sedet ater ocellis,
Iurgiaque, et stimulis armata Calumnia fauces,
Et furor, atque viae moriendi mille videntur
Et timor, exanguisque locum circumvolat Horror,
Perpetuoque leves per muta silentia Manes,
Exululat tellus et sanguine conscia stagnat.
Ipsi etiam pavidi latitant penetralibus antri
Et Phonos, et Prodotes, nulloque sequente per antrum,
Antrum horrens, scopulosum, atrum feralibus umbris,
Diffugiunt sontes, et retro lumina vortunt;
Hos pugiles Romae per saecula longa fideles
Evocat antistes Babylonius, atque ita fatur.
Finibus occiduis circumfusum incolit aequor
Gens exosa mihi, prudens Natura negavit
Indignam penitus nostro coniungere mundo;

sumed attire, the deceiver fled to unspeakable Lethe, his joyless kingdom.

Now rosy Tithonia,[133] opening the gates of dawn, clothes the gilded earth with returning light and, still mournfully weeping for the death of her black son, sprinkles the mountain peaks with ambrosial drops, when the gatekeeper of the starry palace has driven off sleep, rolling away nocturnal visions and welcome dreams.

There is a place enclosed within the eternal cloud of night, once the vast foundations of a ruined building, now the cave of grim Murder and double-tongued Treason, whom fierce Discord spawned in one birth. Here amid rubble and sharp rocks[143] lie the unburied bones of men and corpses pierced with iron; here dark Guile sits forever with his twisted eyes, and Quarrel, and Calumny, armed with a mouth of spikes, and Fury, and a thousand ways to die are seen, and Fear. Bloodless Horror and insubstantial ghosts fly perpetually around the place in the mute silence, and the conscience-stricken Earth wails[150] and is pooled with blood. Even Murder and Treason themselves hide in fear within the depths of the cavern, and though no one pursues them through that cavern—a horrid cavern, rocky, dark with deathly shadows—they flee guiltily, and turn to look behind. The Babylonian[156] priest summons these pugilists who have been faithful to Rome for long ages, and speaks so: "In the sea that flows around the western lands lives a nation hateful to me; prudent Nature refused to join it to our world for being utterly unworthy. This I order: hurry there with speedy step, and let the king and his satraps together, that

133. **Tithonia:** Aurora, wife of Tithonus.

143. **praeruptaque:** So 1673; 1645 had "semifractaque." Another change prompted by the metrical criticisms of Salmasius (see *Elegy* 5.30n).

150. **Exululat:** So 1673; 1645 had "Exululant." The translation of 148–50 follows the errata sheet for 1673, discovered in 1695. See Hughes et al., 1:191–92.

156. **Babylonius:** In Protestant literature of this period, the Babylon of Rev. 14.8 and 17.5 is commonly identified with Rome.

Illuc, sic iubeo, celeri contendite gressu,
Tartareoque leves difflentur pulvere in auras
Et rex et pariter satrapae, scelerata propago;
Et quotquot fidei caluere cupidine verae
Consilii socios adhibete, operisque ministros.
Finierat, rigidi cupide paruere gemelli.
  Interea longo flectens curvamine caelos
Despicit aetherea dominus qui fulgurat arce,
Vanaque perversae ridet conamina turbae,
Atque sui causam populi volet ipse tueri.
  Esse ferunt spatium, qua distat ab Aside terra
Fertilis Europe, et spectat Mareotidas undas;
Hic turris posita est Titanidos ardua Famae
Aerea, lata, sonans, rutilis vicinior astris
Quam superimpositum vel Athos vel Pelion Ossae.
Mille fores aditusque patent, totidemque fenestrae,
Amplaque per tenues translucent atria muros;
Excitat hic varios plebs agglomerata susurros;
Qualiter instrepitant circum mulctralia bombis
Agmina muscarum, aut texto per ovilia iunco,
Dum Canis aestivum coeli petit ardua culmen.
Ipsa quidem summa sedet ultrix matris in arce,
Auribus innumeris cinctum caput eminet olli,
Queis sonitum exiguum trahit, atque levissima captat
Murmura, ab extremis patuli confinibus orbis.
Nec tot Aristoride servator inique iuvencae
Isidos, immiti volvebas lumina vultu,
Lumina non unquam tacito nutantia somno,
Lumina subiectas late spectantia terras.
Istis illa solet loca luce carentia saepe

criminal brood, be scattered by Tartarean powder to the soft breezes. And call upon however many have been hot with desire for the true faith to be fellow conspirators and accomplices in the deed." He had finished, and the stern twins eagerly obeyed.

Meanwhile, the Lord who, bending the heavens in a wide arc, shoots lightning from his airy citadel, looks down and laughs at the vain efforts of that perverse mob, and he decides to defend his people's cause himself. There is said to be an area where fertile Europe is separated from the Asian land and looks toward the waters of Mareotis; here the steep tower of Fame,[172] child of Titans, is located: brazen, wide, resounding, reaching nearer to the ruddy stars than Athos or Pelion piled upon Ossa. A thousand doors and entrances stand open, and as many windows, and its large rooms gleam through the thin walls; the people crowded together here stir up variable murmurs, as when an army of flies makes a rumbling sound around the milk pails[178] or the sheepfolds of woven rushes, while the lofty Dog Star seeks the summertime peak of heaven. She herself sits, her mother's avenger, at the summit of the citadel; she holds her head high, covered with innumerable ears, with which she catches the slightest sound and gathers the lightest murmurs from the farthest confines of the wide world. Son of Arestor,[185] unjust guardian of the heifer Isis, you did not roll as many eyes in your unkind face, eyes never nodding in quiet sleep, eyes watching over the lands stretching widely below. With these she is accustomed to often scanning places empty of light, untouched even by the radiant sun. And talking with a

172. The main classical sources for the description of Fame and her tower are Ovid, *Met.* 12.39–63, and Vergil, *Aen.* 4.173–88.

178. The simile of the flies buzzing about the milk pail comes from Homer (*Il.* 2.469–73, 16.641–43). Cp. *PR* 4.15–17.

185. Argus, sometimes said to be the son of Arestor, was set to watch Io by the jealous Juno.

Perlustrare, etiam radianti impervia soli.
Millenisque loquax auditaque visaque linguis
Cuilibet effundit temeraria; veraque mendax
Nunc minuit, modo confictis sermonibus auget.
Sed tamen a nostro meruisti carmine laudes
Fama, bonum quo non aliud veracius ullum,
Nobis digna cani, nec te memorasse pigebit
Carmine tam longo; servati scilicet Angli
Officiis vaga diva tuis, tibi reddimus aequa.
Te Deus aeternos motu qui temperat ignes,
Fulmine praemisso alloquitur, terraque tremente:
Fama siles? an te latet impia Papistarum
Coniurata cohors in meque meosque Britannos,
Et nova sceptrigero caedes meditata Iacobo?
Nec plura, illa statim sensit mandata Tonantis,
Et satis ante fugax stridentes induit alas,
Induit et variis exilia corpora plumis;
Dextra tubam gestat Temesaeo ex aere sonoram.
Nec mora iam pennis cedentes remigat auras,
Atque parum est cursu celeres praevertere nubes,
Iam ventos, iam solis equos post terga reliquit:
Et primo Angliacas solito de more per urbes
Ambiguas voces, incertaque murmura spargit,
Mox arguta dolos, et detestabile vulgat
Proditionis opus, nec non facta horrida dictu,
Authoresque addit sceleris, nec garrula caecis
Insidiis loca structa silet; stupuere relatis,
Et pariter iuvenes, pariter tremuere puellae,
Effaetique senes pariter, tantaeque ruinae
Sensus ad aetatem subito penetraverat omnem.

thousand tongues, she recklessly pours out to anyone what she has heard and seen; and being a liar, sometimes she shrinks the truth, and then augments it with fictitious reports. But still you have earned praise in our song,[194] Fame, a good thing than which none is more true—you are worthy to be sung by us, and there will never be cause to regret having remembered you in such a lengthy song; we English, surely saved through your offices, wandering goddess, give you your due. God, who guides the eternal fires in their motion, having sent down a thunderbolt, addressed you while the earth trembled: "Fame, are you silent? Is this unholy cohort of papists conspiring against me and my Britons, this innovative murder planned against scepter-bearing James hidden from you?" No more; she immediately sensed the commands of the Thunderer and, swift enough before this, put on whirring wings, and put varied feathers on her slender body; in her right hand she brings a loud trumpet of Temesaean brass. No delay, but she now rows with her wings through the yielding air; and it is not enough to outstrip the swift clouds in her course, she left now the winds, now the horses of the sun behind her back. And first, in her usual way, she scatters conflicting stories and uncertain murmurs throughout the cities of England; soon she clearly publicizes the plots and the detestable work of treason and actions horrible to speak of, and adds the crime's authors; nor as she talks away is she silent about the sites prepared for the blind ambush. People were stunned at these reports, young men and girls and weak old men trembled in equal measure, and the sense of great disaster suddenly struck all ages

194. The Gunpowder Plot was discovered when Lord Monteagle in October 1605 received an anonymous letter warning him to stay away from the opening of Parliament. Alerted, the government searched the cellar of the House of Lords, found the gunpowder, and arrested the custodian Guy Fawkes.

Attamen interea populi miserescit ab alto
Aethereus pater, et crudelibus obstitit ausis
Papicolum; capti poenas raptantur ad acres;
At pia thura Deo, et grati solvuntur honores;
Compita laeta focis genialibus omnia fumant,
Turba choros iuvenilis agit: Quintoque Novembris
Nulla dies toto occurrit celebratior anno.

221. **Aethereus pater:** a pagan phrase given a Christian sense (Martial 9.35.10, 9.36.7; Claudian 22.26).

to the heart. But in the meantime the heavenly father[221] pities his people from on high, and stopped the papists' cruel venture. Captured, they are hurried off to harsh punishment; but holy incense is offered to God, and grateful honors. The happy crossroads all smoke with festive bonfires; a crowd of young people leads the dance: no day in the entire year comes with more celebration than the fifth of November.

IN OBITUM PRAESULIS ELIENSIS

[*On the Death of the Bishop of Ely*]

Nicholas Felton died in October 1626, less than a month after Lancelot Andrewes (see *Elegy 3* headnote), whom he had succeeded as Bishop of Ely. Felton and Andrewes were in fact close friends. Both men were scholars, fellows, and masters of Pembroke College, Cambridge, and both served as translators of the Authorized Version.

ANNO AETATIS 17

Adhuc madentes rore squalebant genae,
Et sicca nondum lumina;
Adhuc liquentis imbre turgebant salis,
Quem nuper effudi pius,
Dum maesta charo iusta persolvi rogo
Wintoniensis praesulis,
Cum centilinguis Fama (proh semper mali
Cladisque vera nuntia)
Spargit per urbes divitis Britanniae,
Populosque Neptuno satos,
Cessisse morti, et ferreis sororibus
Te generis humani decus,
Qui rex sacrorum illa fuisti in insula
Quae nomen Anguillae tenet.

1. Milton is alluding to his grief for, and elegy for, Lancelot Andrewes (*Elegy 3*).
11. **sororibus:** the three Fates.
14. **Anguillae:** Ely means "eel-island."

AT AGE 17

My cheeks, still wet,[1] were caked with dew, and my eyes not yet dry; they were still swollen with the rain of salt water which in my reverence I had lately poured out while I performed my sad rites at the dear grave of the Bishop of Winchester, when hundred-tongued Fame (always, alas, a true messenger of evil and disaster) scattered it through the cities of wealthy Britain and the people descended from Neptune that you, the glory of the human race, who were king of the holy men in that island which has the name of Ely,[14] had succumbed to death and to the iron sisters.[11] Then straightway my troubled heart

Tunc inquietum pectus ira protinus
  Ebulliebat fervida,
Tumulis potentem saepe devovens deam:
  Nec vota Naso in Ibida
Concepit alto diriora pectore,
  Graiusque vates parcius
Turpem Lycambis execratus est dolum,
  Sponsamque Neobolen suam.
At ecce diras ipse dum fundo graves,
  Et imprecor neci necem,
Audisse tales videor attonitus sonos
  Leni, sub aura, flamine:
Caecos furores pone, pone vitream
  Bilemque et irritas minas.
Quid temere violas non nocenda numina,
  Subitoque ad iras percita?
Non est, ut arbitraris elusus miser,
  Mors atra Noctis filia,
Erebove patre creta, sive Erinnye,
  Vastove nata sub Chao:
Ast illa caelo missa stellato, Dei
  Messes ubique colligit;
Animasque mole carnea reconditas
  In lucem et auras evocat:
Ut cum fugaces excitant Horae diem
  Themidos Iovisque filiae;
Et sempiterni ducit ad vultus patris;
  At iusta raptat impios
Sub regna furvi luctuosa Tartari,
  Sedesque subterraneas.
Hanc ut vocantem laetus audivi, cito
  Foedum reliqui carcerem,
Volatilesque faustus inter milites
  Ad astra sublimis feror:
Vates ut olim raptus ad coelum senex

seethed with fervent anger, cursing many times the goddess with power over tombs. Naso did not conceive with his deep heart more frightful curses against Ibis,[18] and the Greek bard[20] more sparingly execrated Lycambis's shameful deceit and his bride Neobole. But behold, while I pour out heavy imprecations and call down death upon Death, I seem, astonished, to hear, in a light breath under the breeze, sounds such as these: "Put away blind rage, put away glassy bile and useless threats. Why do you recklessly affront divinities that cannot be harmed and are quickly roused to anger? Death is not, as you think in your delusion and misery, the dark daughter of Night,[32] or sprung from her father Erebus, or from a Fury, or born under vast Chaos: but sent from the starry heaven, she everywhere gathers God's harvest; she summons souls buried in a mass of flesh up into the light and air—as when the fleeing Hours,[39] daughters of Themis and Jove, rouse the day—and she leads them before the face of the eternal Father; but being just, she hurries the impious down to the sorrowful kingdom of swarthy Tartarus and his subterranean habitations. Glad when I heard her call, I quickly left the foul prison, and was carried in happiness among flying soldiers to the stars on high, like the ancient prophet[49] hurried up to Heaven

18. Ovid in his exile wrote *Ibis,* an invective against an unidentified enemy.

20. **Graiusque vates:** Archilochus, a Greek poet of the seventh or eighth century B.C.E., avenged himself after an unsuccessful courtship with such scathing poems that both the father and the daughter hanged themselves (Horace, *Epist.* 1.19.23–31).

32. Death is the daughter of Night in Hesiod, *Theog.* 758–59.

39. **Horae:** the Hours, goddesses of the seasons.

49. **Vates:** Elijah; see 2 Kings 2.11.

Auriga currus ignei.
Non me Bootis terruere lucidi
Sarraca tarda frigore, aut
Formidolosi Scorpionis brachia,
Non ensis Orion tuus.
Praetervolavi fulgidi solis globum,
Longeque sub pedibus deam
Vidi triformem, dum coercebat suos
Fraenis dracones aureis.
Erraticorum siderum per ordines,
Per lacteas vehor plagas,
Velocitatem saepe miratus novam,
Donec nitentes ad fores
Ventum est Olympi, et regiam Chrystallinam, et
Stratum smaragdis Atrium.
Sed hic tacebo, nam quis effari queat
Oriundus humano patre
Amœnitates illius loci? mihi
Sat est in aeternum frui.

driving a chariot of fire. Bright Boötes's Wagon, slow from the cold, did not terrify me, nor did the arms of the formidable Scorpion, nor did your sword, Orion. I flew past the globe of the blazing sun, and far beneath my feet I saw the triform[57] goddess as she controlled her dragons with reins of gold. I am carried through the ranks of the wandering stars, through the Milky Way, often marveling at my new speed, until I have come to the shining gates of Olympus and the crystalline palace and the forecourt paved with emerald. But here I fall silent, for who born of a human father could speak the pleasures of that place? It is enough for me to enjoy them for eternity."

57. **triformem:** The moon has a triune divinity as Luna (in the heavens), Diana (on earth), and Hecate (in Hades).

NATURAM NON PATI SENIUM

[*That Nature does not suffer from old age*]

This work contributes to an important seventeenth-century debate. The idea that Nature is in a state of decay or corruption was proposed in England as early as 1580 but received a full exposition in Geoffrey Goodman's *The Fall of Man* (1616). Goodman was answered by George Hakewill's *Apology of the Power and Providence of God in the Government of the World. Or an Examination and Censure of the Common Error Touching Nature's Perpetual and Universal Decay* (1627). The issue did not bear exclusively on the natural world. When debaters came to consider whether or not human genius was in decline, they inevitably spawned another major controversy over the relative merits of the ancients and the moderns, and that debate, several times ignited in the Restoration and eighteenth century, eventually mutated into nineteenth- and twentieth-century disputes about the idea of progress (Jones 22–40).

The second edition of Hakewill's *Apology* in 1630 contained an account of a notable phlebotomy performed by Theodore Diodati, Charles's father. But Milton might have read the 1627 edition. Or the ideas might have been in the Cambridge air. Though it seems an academic exercise, this poem cannot be reliably dated.

Heu quam perpetuis erroribus acta fatiscit
Avia mens hominum, tenebrisque immersa profundis
Oedipodioniam volvit sub pectore noctem!
Quae vesana suis metiri facta deorum
Audet, et incisas leges adamante perenni
Assimilare suis, nulloque solubile saeclo
Consilium fati perituris alligat horis.
Ergone marcescet sulcantibus obsita rugis
Naturae facies, et rerum publica mater
Omniparum contracta uterum sterilescet ab aevo?
Et se fassa senem male certis passibus ibit
Sidereum tremebunda caput? num tetra vetustas
Annorumque aeterna fames, squalorque situsque
Sidera vexabunt? An et insatiabile Tempus
Esuriet Caelum, rapietque in viscera patrem?
Heu, potuitne suas imprudens Iupiter arces
Hoc contra munisse nefas, et temporis isto
Exemisse malo, gyrosque dedisse perennes?
Ergo erit ut quandoque sono dilapsa tremendo
Convexi tabulata ruant, atque obvius ictu
Stridat uterque polus, superaque ut Olympius aula
Decidat, horribilisque retecta Gorgone Pallas.
Qualis in Aegaeam proles Iunonia Lemnon
Deturbata sacro cecidit de limine caeli.
Tu quoque Phoebe tui casus imitabere nati
Praecipiti curru, subitaque ferere ruina
Pronus, et extincta fumabit lampade Nereus,

Alas, driven by such enduring errors, the wayward mind of men grows weary and, immersed in deep shadows, revolves an Oedipodean night in the heart! Insanely it dares to measure the deeds of gods by its own, and to assimilate laws cut in eternal adamant to its own, and to bind fate's plan, unrevokable by any era, to the hours about to perish. Will therefore the face of Nature wither, covered with furrowing wrinkles, and the general mother[9] of things grow stale, shrunken from age in her all-parenting womb? And will she, showing that she is old, move badly with uncertain steps, shaking her starry head? Will foul old age and the years' eternal hunger and filth and rot trouble the stars? And will insatiable Time[14] devour Heaven, and thrust his father into his bowels? Alas, could improvident Jupiter not have fortified his own citadels against this outrage and exempted them from this evil of Time and given them eternal circuits? Therefore it will happen that the collapsed floor of the arched sky will fall with a great sound, and each pole, feeling the blow, will screech, and the Olympian will fall from his house above, and also Pallas,[22] horrifying with her Gorgon uncovered. In such a way did Juno's offspring,[23] hurled from the sacred threshold of heaven, fall to Aegean Lemnos. You too, Phoebus, will imitate the downfall of your son[25] in your headlong chariot, and you will be carried downward to sudden ruin, and Nereus will smoke from your quenched lamp and give out funereal hisses from the astonished sea. Then even the peak of lofty Haemus will shatter when its foundations are torn apart; and

9. **mater:** Ge, Earth, was the common ancestor of gods and men according to Hesiod, *Theog.* 117–63.

14. For centuries Chronos (Time) had been mistakenly identified with Cronos/Saturn, who devoured the children Rhea bore him (Panofsky 69–94).

22. Pallas Athena wears the Gorgon Medusa's head on her shield.

23. **proles Iunonia:** Vulcan, Juno's son; see *Elegy 7* 81–82n.

25. **tui . . . nati:** Phaethon. He lost control of his father's horses when driving the chariot of the sun; Zeus had to stop him with a thunderbolt.

Et dabit attonito feralia sibila ponto.
Tunc etiam aerei divulsis sedibus Haemi
Dissultabit apex, imoque allisa barathro
Terrebunt Stygium deiecta Ceraunia Ditem
In superos quibus usus erat, fraternaque bella.
At Pater omnipotens fundatis fortius astris
Consuluit rerum summae, certoque peregit
Pondere fatorum lances, atque ordine summo
Singula perpetuum iussit servare tenorem.
Volvitur hinc lapsu mundi rota prima diurno,
Raptat et ambitos socia vertigine caelos.
Tardior haud solito Saturnus, et acer ut olim
Fulmineum rutilat cristata casside Mavors.
Floridus aeternum Phoebus iuvenile coruscat,
Nec fovet effoetas loca per declivia terras
Devexo temone Deus; sed semper amica
Luce potens eadem currit per signa rotarum,
Surgit odoratis pariter formosus ab Indis
Aethereum pecus albenti qui cogit Olympo
Mane vocans, et serus agens in pascua coeli;
Temporis et gemino dispertit regna colore.
Fulget, obitque vices alterno Delia cornu,
Caeruleumque ignem paribus complectitur ulnis.
Nec variant elementa fidem, solitoque fragore
Lurida perculsas iaculantur fulmina rupes.
Nec per inane furit leviori murmure Corus,
Stringit et armiferos aequali horrore Gelonos
Trux Aquilo, spiratque hiemem, nimbosque volutat.
Utque solet, Siculi diverberat ima Pelori
Rex maris, et rauca circumstrepit aequora concha
Oceani tubicen, nec vasta mole minorem

the uprooted Ceraunian mountains, which had been used against the gods, and fraternal war, cast into the depths of the underworld, will terrify Stygian Dis. But the omnipotent father, having set the stars more strongly in their place,[33] took care concerning the sum of things, and poised fate's scales with a sure weight, and commanded each thing to keep a perpetual movement within a supreme order. Hence the first wheel of the universe turns on a daily cycle,[37] and it speeds the heavenly sphere with an allied rotation. Saturn is no slower than his custom, and, as fiercely as ever, Mars flashes red lightning from his crested helmet. Phoebus gleams in the flower of eternal youth; the god does not warm the exhausted earth from a chariot steered downward through the sloping regions but, always powerful with a friendly light, drives through the same wheel tracks. He rises just as beautiful from the perfumed Indies who, summoning the dawn, gathers the eternal herd into whitening Olympus and, driving them out later into the pastures of heaven, divides Time's kingdom into two colors; and Delia[49] shines and dies by turns with alternating horns, and embraces the blue fire in the same arms. Nor do the elements break faith; lurid lightning smashes the stricken rocks with its usual crash. Nor does Corus[53] rage through the empty air with a lighter roar, and fierce Aquilo[55] confines the armed Gelonians with the same shuddering, and breathes forth winter, and tumbles the clouds. As he's used to, the king of the sea batters the base of Sicilian Pelorus, and Ocean's trumpeter[58] surrounds the sea with the sound of a raucous conch shell, nor do the

33. The passage echoes Ovid, Met. 2.300, where Earth begs Jove to kill Phaethon in order to prevent the world from being destroyed.

37. Milton turns from myths of a violent end to the enduring order of the cosmos as imaged by the Ptolemaic spheres.

49. **Delia:** Diana, moon goddess, born on the island of Delos.

53. **Corus:** the northwest wind.

55. **Aquilo:** the northeast wind.

58. **tubicen:** Triton, Neptune's herald.

Aegaeona ferunt dorso Balearica cete.
Sed neque Terra tibi saecli vigor ille vetusti
Priscus abest; servatque suum Narcissus odorem,
Et puer ille suum tenet et puer ille decorem
Phoebe tuusque et Cypri tuus, nec ditior olim
Terra datum sceleri celavit montibus aurum
Conscia, vel sub aquis gemmas. Sic denique in aevum
Ibit cunctarum series iustissima rerum,
Donec flamma orbem populabitur ultima, late
Circumplexa polos, et vasti culmina caeli,
Ingentique rogo flagrabit machina mundi.

Balearic whales carry on their backs an Aegaeon[59] any less vast in bulk. And you, Earth, are not lacking in that ancient vigor of the old days, and Narcissus keeps his odor; and that boy of yours,[62] Phoebus, and that boy of yours, Cypris, keep their attractiveness, nor was it a wealthier Earth that once, for conscience, hid gold dedicated to crime in the mountains, or jewels under the waters. So, then, the very just course of all things will continue forever, until the last fire[67] devastates the world, broadly enveloping the poles and the summits of vast heaven, and the fabric of the universe blazes on a huge pyre.

59. **Aegaeona:** a giant monster known to gods as Briareos (*Il.* 1.403–4). See *PL* 1.199–201.

62. On Apollo and Hyacinthus, see *Fair Infant* 23–27n; Ovid relates that Venus turned Adonis into an anemone after he was killed by a boar (*Met.* 10.728–39).

67. 2 Pet. 3.10 provides biblical sanction for the idea of a final conflagration.

DE IDEA PLATONICA QUEMADMODEM ARISTOTELES INTELLEXIT

[*Of the Platonic Idea as understood by Aristotle*]

In a letter to his friend Alexander Gill dated July 2, 1628, Milton discusses some verses he has been writing for another student to recite in the philosophical disputation at the Cambridge Commencement (held the day before the letter is dated). Milton describes the *leviculas . . . nugas* (trivial jokes) in these lines, and Carey plausibly suggests that *De Idea* fits this characterization better than *Naturam non pati senium.*

The poem adopts the role of literal-minded Aristotelian so uncompromisingly that it becomes a satire of Aristotle as much as of Plato. Aristotle's main criticisms of the doctrine of ideas are found in *Metaphysics* 1.9, 7.8.

Dicite sacrorum praesides nemorum deae,
Tuque O noveni perbeata numinis
Memoria mater, quaeque in immenso procul
Antro recumbis otiosa Aeternitas,
Monumenta servans, et ratas leges Iovis,
Caelique fastos atque ephemeridas deum,
Quis ille primus cuius ex imagine
Natura sollers finxit humanum genus,
Aeternus, incorruptus, aequaevus polo,
Unusque et universus, exemplar Dei?
Haud ille Palladis gemellus innubae
Interna proles insidet menti Iovis;
Sed quamlibet natura sit communior,
Tamen seorsus extat ad morem unius,
Et, mira, certo stringitur spatio loci;
Seu sempiternus ille siderum comes
Caeli pererrat ordines decemplicis,
Citimumve terris incolit lunae globum:
Sive inter animas corpus adituras sedens
Obliviosas torpet ad Lethes aquas:
Sive in remota forte terraum plaga
Incedit ingens hominis archetypus gigas,
Et diis tremendus erigit celsum caput
Atlante maior portitore siderum.
Non cui profundum caecitas lumen dedit
Dircaeus augur vidit hunc alto sinu;
Non hunc silenti nocte Pleiones nepos
Vatum sagaci praepes ostendit choro;
Non hunc sacerdos novit Assyrius, licet
Longos vetusti commemoret atavos Nini,

Speak, goddesses[1] who preside over the sacred groves, and you, Memory,[3] most blessed mother of the nine divinities, and Eternity,[4] you who recline unbusied far away in a great cavern, guarding the records and the established laws of Jove, the calendar of heaven and the logbook of the gods: Who was that first being from whose image skillful Nature fashioned the human race—eternal, uncorrupted, as old as the sky, unique and universal, the pattern for God? He does not reside as a child inside the mind of Jove, as twin brother to unmarried Pallas; but although his nature is more general, still he exists separately, in the manner of an individual, and, amazingly, is confined within definite boundaries of space. Perhaps, eternal companion of the stars, he wanders through the ranks of the tenfold heavens, or he inhabits the globe of the moon, the one nearest to Earth; or, sitting among the souls waiting for a body,[19] he dozes beside the forgetful waters of Lethe; or maybe in a remote tract of the world, man's archetype walks as an immense giant, and, bigger than Atlas, lifter of the stars, he raises his lofty head to frighten the gods. The Dircaean augur,[26] to whom blindness gave profound illumination, did not see him in his deep heart; Pleione's swift grandson[27] did not display him to the wise chorus of bards in the silent night; the Assyrian priest[29] did not know him, though he remembered the lengthy ancestry of Ninus,[30] and primordial

1. The goddesses might be Diana and her nymphs, who attend at births and are associated with groves, or more probably the nine Muses.
3. **Memoria:** Mnemosyne, mother of the Muses.
4. The idea of a mysterious old man controlling events from a remote cave can be found in Claudian 22.424–40 and Boccaccio (who calls him Eternity) in *De Genealogiis Deorum* 1.2.
19. The doctrine of metempsychosis is found in *Phaedo* 70–72 and Vergil, *Aen.* 6.713–51.
26. **Dircaeus augur:** Tiresias, the blind Theban prophet.
27. **Pleiones nepos:** Mercury, grandson of Atlas and Pleione.
29. It is uncertain which Assyrian sage Milton has in mind.
30. **Nini:** Ninus, founder of the Assyrian monarchy.

Priscumque Belon, inclitumque Osiridem.
Non ille trino gloriosus nomine
Ter magnus Hermes (ut sit arcani sciens)
Talem reliquit Isidis cultoribus.
At tu perenne ruris Academi decus
(Haec monstra si tu primus induxti scholis)
Iam iam poetas urbis exules tuae
Revocabis, ipse fabulator maximus,
Aut institutor ipse migrabis foras.

31. **Belon:** The Assyrian god Bel was called Baal by the Hebrews.

33. **Ter magnus Hermes:** On the tradition of "Hermes Trismegistus" see Yates 1–156.

35. **Academi decus:** Plato, who excluded poets from his ideal state (*Rep.* 10.595–607).

Belus,[31] and famous Osiris. Nor did that glorious one with the triple name, Thrice Great Hermes[33] (even if he was knowledgeable about secret things), bequeath such a one to the worshipers of Isis. But you, enduring glory of the rustic Academy[35] (if you were the first to bring such monsters into the schools), now, now you, the greatest storyteller, will call back the poets banished from your city, or else you, its founder, will depart.

AD PATREM

[*To His Father*]

This poem cannot be securely dated but probably belongs to the decade of the 1630s, and likely to the first half of it.

Only two of Milton's poems, *To His Father* and *Fair Infant,* deal directly with his birth family, and the English elegy does not expressly acknowledge that the dead child was Milton's niece or its mother his sister.

In his prose works, Milton left two grateful accounts of the "ceaseless diligence and care of my father" (p. 839; also p. 1090) in providing him with a first-rate education. Sincere gratitude is surely among the emotions in *To His Father.* But here, uniquely, we have evidence of a rift between Milton and his father on the key matter of his poetic vocation. For however long a time, whether a month or years, in whatever manner, whether jokingly or solemnly or with some of each, John Milton, Sr., expressed a desire that his son abandon poetry as a central ambition and turn to something more worldly and practical. The poem is one of the earliest of many self-defenses in Milton's work.

Nunc mea Pierios cupiam per pectora fontes
Irriguas torquere vias, totumque per ora
Volvere laxatum gemino de vertice rivum;
Ut tenues oblita sonos audacibus alis
Surgat in officium venerandi Musa parentis.
Hoc utcunque tibi gratum pater optime carmen

1. **Pierios . . . fontes:** Pieria was the birthplace of the Muses.

Now I would wish the Pierian fountains[1] to divert their watery channels into my heart, and the entire stream loosed from the twin peaks to pour through my mouth, so that the Muse, forgetting trivial songs, may rise on bold wings to the duty of reverencing my parent. However wel-

Exiguum meditatur opus, nec novimus ipsi
Aptius a nobis quae possint munera donis
Respondere tuis, quamvis nec maxima possint
Respondere tuis, nedum ut par gratia donis
Esse queat, vacuis quae redditur arida verbis.
Sed tamen haec nostros ostendit pagina census,
Et quod habemus opum charta numeravimus ista,
Quae mihi sunt nullae, nisi quas dedit aurea Clio
Quas mihi semoto somni peperere sub antro,
Et nemoris laureta sacri Parnassides umbrae.
Nec tu vatis opus divinum despice carmen,
Quo nihil aethereos ortus, et semina caeli,
Nil magis humanam commendat origine mentem,
Sancta Prometheae retinens vestigia flammae.
Carmen amant superi, tremebundaque Tartara carmen
Ima ciere valet, divosque ligare profundos,
Et triplici duros Manes adamante coercet.
Carmine sepositi retegunt arcana futuri
Phoebades, et tremulae pallentes ora Sibyllae;
Carmina sacrificus sollennes pangit ad aras,
Aurea seu sternit motantem cornua taurum;
Seu cum fata sagax fumantibus abdita fibris
Consulit, et tepidis Parcam scrutatur in extis.
Nos etiam patrium tunc cum repetemus Olympum,
Aeternaeque morae stabunt immobilis aevi,
Ibimus auratis per caeli templa coronis,
Dulcia suaviloquo sociantes carmina plectro,
Astra quibus, geminique poli convexa sonabunt.

come to you, best father, she is devising this song, a slight work, and we ourselves do not know a more suitable offering in payment for your gifts, although the greatest offering could not repay your gifts, still less could arid thanks which is given in vain words be equal to your gifts. But still, this page shows our account, and we have numbered on this paper what wealth we have: of which I have none except what golden Clio[14] has given, which my sleep has spawned in a remote cavern, and the laurel groves in the sacred wood, the shades of Parnassus. But do not look down on the poet's work, divine song; nothing more commends our celestial origins and heavenly seeds, nothing, because of its origin, more commends the human mind, keeping the sacred traces of Promethean fire.[20] The gods love song, song has power to stir the shuddering depths of Tartarus and bind the gods of the deep, and constricts the harsh shades with threefold adamant. With song the priestesses of Phoebus and the trembling, pale-mouthed Sibyls[25] uncover the secrets of the distant future; the sacrificing priest crafts songs at the solemn altar, whether he slays a bull tossing its golden horns, or when he skillfully reads the fates hidden in the smoking organs and seeks out Parca in the warm entrails. And when we return to our fatherland Olympus, and the eternal intervals of unmoving time stand still, we will go with golden crowns through the temples of heaven,[32] wedding sweet songs to the smooth-voiced lyre, with which the stars and the vaults of both poles will sound.

14. **Clio:** in Roman times the Muse of history.

20. Prometheus, who stole fire from heaven and gave it to man. "Prometheus clearly and expressly signifies Providence" (Bacon, *Wisdom of the Ancients,* "Prometheus").

25. **Phoebades:** priestesses of Apollo; **Sibyllae:** prophetesses, such as the Cumaean sibyl, who guides Aeneas through the underworld in *Aen.* 6.

32. The gold crowns come from Rev. 4.4, the harps from 5.8.

Spiritus et rapidos qui circinat igneus orbes
Nunc quoque sidereis intercinit ipse choreis
Immortale melos, et inenarrabile carmen;
Torrida dum rutilus compescit sibila Serpens,
Demissoque ferox gladio mansuescit Orion;
Stellarum nec sentit onus Maurusius Atlas.
Carmina regales epulas ornare solebant,
Cum nondum luxus, vastaeque immensa vorago
Nota gulae, et modico spumabat coena Lyaeo.
Tum de more sedens festa ad convivia vates,
Aesculea intonsos redimitus ab arbore crines,
Heroumque actus, imitandaque gesta canebat,
Et Chaos, et positi late fundamina mundi,
Reptantesque deos, et alentes numina glandes,
Et nondum Aetnaeo quaesitum fulmen ab antro.
Denique quid vocis modulamen inane iuvabit,
Verborum sensusque vacans, numerique loquacis?
Silvestres decet iste choros, non Orphea, cantus,
Qui tenuit fluvios et quercubus addidit aures
Carmine, non cithara, simulachraque functa canendo
Compulit in lacrimas: habet has a carmine laudes.
  Nec tu perge precor sacras contemnere Musas,
Nec vanas inopesque puta, quarum ipse peritus
Munere, mille sonos numeros componis ad aptos,
Millibus et vocem modulis variare canoram
Doctus, Arionii merito sis nominis haeres.
Nunc tibi quid mirum, si me genuisse poetam
Contigerit, charo si tam prope sanguine iuncti
Cognatas artes, studiumque affine sequamur:
Ipse volens Phoebus se dispertire duobus,
Altera dona mihi, dedit altera dona parenti,

The fiery spirit[35] which circles the rapid spheres is itself now singing immortal music and indescribable song among the starry choirs, while the ruddy serpent[38] suppresses his scorching hisses, and fierce Orion, dropping his sword, grows calm, and Mauretanian Atlas does not feel the weight of the stars. Songs used to adorn regal banquets, when luxury and the huge maw of endless gluttony were not yet known and dinner foamed with Lyaeus in moderation. Then, by custom, the bard, sitting at the festive banquet, his uncut hair crowned with oak leaves, sang of the actions of heroes, deeds to be imitated, and of chaos and the broad foundations on which the universe is set, and of deities crawling and of acorns[48] feeding gods, and of the thunderbolt not yet sought from the cave of Etna. In the end, what good is an empty modulation of the voice, lacking words and sense and expressive meter? That is fitting for woodland choruses, not for Orpheus's music, which entranced streams and gave ears to oak trees with his song, not with his lyre, and brought dead phantoms to tears with his singing; he earned his praises from song. Do not, I pray, keep scorning the sacred Muses, and do not think them vain and useless, you who skilled in their gift set a thousand songs to fit rhythm, having learned to vary the melodious voice in a thousand tunes, so as to be a worthy heir of Arion's[60] name. Why should it surprise you if it happened I was begotten a poet—if, so closely joined to you by dear blood, we pursued related arts and kindred study? Phoebus,[64] wishing to distribute himself between two, gave one gift to me, the other to my parent, and we

35. Milton appears to be saying that his own *spiritus* leaves his body to join the high songs sung at the topmost rung of the universe. Carey 1964 cites Cicero's *Somnium Scipionis* and Macrobius's commentary on it.

38. **Serpens:** the constellation of the Serpent.

48. **glandes:** Ovid says that men in the Golden Age, before there was agriculture, ate acorns from Jove's tree (*Met.* 1.106).

60. **Arionii:** Arion charmed a dolphin with his lyre (Herodotus 1.23–24).

64. Apollo is the god of both music and poetry.

Dividuumque deum genitorque puerque
tenemus.
Tu tamen ut simules teneras odisse Camenas,
Non odisse reor, neque enim, pater, ire iubebas
Qua via lata patet, qua pronior area lucri,
Certaque condendi fulget spes aurea nummi;
Nec rapis ad leges, male custoditaque gentis
Iura, nec insulsis damnas clamoribus aures.
Sed magis excultam cupiens ditescere mentem,
Me procul urbano strepitu, secessibus altis
Abductum Aoniae iucunda per otia ripae,
Phoebaeo lateri comitem sinis ire beatum.
Officium chari taceo commune parentis,
Me poscunt maiora; tuo pater optime sumptu
Cum mihi Romuleae patuit facundia linguae,
Et Latii veneres, et quae Iovis ora decebant
Grandia magniloquis elata vocabula Graiis,
Addere suasisti quos iactat Gallia flores,
Et quam degeneri novus Italus ore loquelam
Fundit, Barbaricos testatus voce tumultus,
Quaeque Palaestinus loquitur mysteria vates.
Denique quicquid habet caelum, subiectaque
coelo
Terra parens, terraeque et coelo interfluus aer,
Quicquid et unda tegit, pontique agitabile
marmor,
Per te nosse licet, per te, si nosse libebit.
Dimotaque venit spectanda scientia nube,
Nudaque conspicuos inclinat ad oscula vultus,
Ni fugisse velim, ni sit libasse molestum.
I nunc, confer opes quisquis malesanus avitas
Austriaci gazas, Peruanaque regna praeoptas.

possess the divided god as father and son. Though you pretend to have hated the soft Muses, I do not think you did, for you did not, father, order me to go where the broad way lies open, where the field of wealth is more inviting, and confident, golden hope of making money shines out; nor do you hurry me off to law and the nation's badly kept statutes, nor do you condemn my ears to that ridiculous clamor. But, wishing to enrich my cultivated mind, you allow me, far removed from the city's noise, in deep seclusion, to pass through the joyful leisure of the Aonian banks,[75] a happy comrade by the side of Phoebus. I say nothing about the common office of a loving parent; greater things summon me. When, best father, at your expense the eloquence of the tongue of Romulus was laid open to me, the beauties of Latin and the grand, exalted words of the magniloquent Greeks, which suited the mouth of Jove, you persuaded me to add those flowers of which France boasts, and the speech that the new Italian pours forth from a degenerate mouth, attesting with his voice the barbarian incursions, and the mysteries that the Palestinian prophet speaks. Finally, whatever heaven holds, and parental earth that lies under heaven, and the air flowing between earth and heaven, and whatever the waves and the moving marble of the sea cover, because of you I can learn, because of you, if I want to learn it. With the cloud moved away, Science comes to be viewed, and naked bends her illustrious face to be kissed, unless I wish to flee, unless it be unappealing to taste. Go now, accumulate wealth, whoever insanely prefers the ancestral jewels of Austria and the kingdoms of Peru.[94] What

75. **Aoniae . . . ripae:** The fountains of Aganippe and Hippocrene near Mount Helicon in Aonia (the Muses were termed Aonides) inspired those who drank from them.

94. **Peruanaque regna:** Spain conquered gold-rich Peru in the 1530s.

Quae potuit maiora pater tribuisse, vel ipse
Iupiter, excepto, donasset ut omnia, coelo?
Non potiora dedit, quamvis et tuta fuissent,
Publica qui iuveni commisit lumina nato
Atque Hyperionios currus, et fraena diei,
Et circum undantem radiata luce tiaram.
Ergo ego iam doctae pars quamlibet ima catervae
Victrices hederas inter, laurosque sedebo;
Iamque nec obscurus populo miscebor inerti,
Vitabuntque oculos vestigia nostra profanos.
Este procul vigiles curae, procul este querelae,
Invidiaeque acies transverso tortilis hirquo;
Saeva nec anguiferos extende Calumnia rictus;
In me triste nihil foedissima turba potestis,
Nec vestri sum iuris ego; securaque tutus
Pectora, vipereo gradiar sublimis ab ictu.
  At tibi, care pater, postquam non aequa merenti
Posse referre datur, nec dona rependere factis,
Sit memorasse satis, repetitaque munera grato
Percensere animo, fidaeque reponere menti.
  Et vos, O nostri, iuvenilia carmina, lusus,
Si modo perpetuos sperare audebitis annos,
Et domini superesse rogo, lucemque tueri,
Nec spisso rapient oblivia nigra sub Orco,
Forsitan has laudes, decantatumque parentis
Nomen, ad exemplum, sero servabitis aevo.

99. **Hyperionios currus:** Hyperion, father of Helios, often stands for the sun itself.

118. **Orco:** Hades.

greater things could a father have bestowed, even if Jove himself had given all (with the exception of heaven)? He did not give more precious gifts, even if they had been given safely, who entrusted to his young son the common light and Hyperion's chariot[99] and the reins of day and the tiara billowing with radiant light. Therefore I, already part, though at the lowest rank, of the learned company, will sit among the triumphant ivies and laurels, and now I will no longer mingle in obscurity with the witless mob, and our footsteps will shun profane eyes. Be far away, wide-eyed worries, be far away, complaints and invidious looks twisted askance like a goat; do not reach your snake-bearing jaws toward me, savage Calumny. The foul gang of you can do nothing painful to me, nor am I under your law; safe in an untroubled heart, I shall walk above the viperous stroke. But for you, dear father, since I cannot repay you equally to your deserving or match gifts with deeds, let it be enough to have memorialized them, to count up your repeated favors with a grateful spirit, and to secure them in a faithful mind. And you, O our playthings, poems of our youth, if only you dare hope for endless years and to outlive your master's pyre and see the light, and black oblivion does not hurry you beneath crowded Orcus,[118] perhaps these praises and this singing of my father's name you will preserve as an example for a later age.

PSALM 114

In a 1634 letter to his friend Alexander Gill, who had himself published Latin and Greek poetry, Milton mentions his recent translation of a psalm into Greek heroic verse and notes that this was his first attempt to write Greek poetry since leaving school (Yale 1:321–22). This is almost certainly the work in question.

'Ισραὴλ ὅτε παῖδες, ὅτ' ἀγλαὰ φῦλ' 'Ιακώβου
Αἰγύπτιον λίπε δῆμον, ἀπεχθέα βαρβαρόφωνον,
Δὴ τότε μοῦνον ἔην ὅσιον γένος υἷες 'Ιοῦδα.
'Εν δὲ θεὸς λαοῖσι μέγα κρείων βασίλευεν.
Εἶδε καὶ ἐντροπάδην φύγαδ' ἐρρώησε θάλασσα
Κύματι εἰλυμένη ῥοθίῳ, ὁ δ' ἄρ' ἐστυφελίχθη
'Ιρὸς 'Ιορδάνης ποτὶ ἀργυροειδέα πηγήν.
'Εκ δ' ὄρεα σκαρθμοῖσιν ἀπειρέσια κλονέοντο,
'Ως κριοὶ σφριγόωντες ἐϋτραφερῷ ἐν ἀλωῇ.
Βαιότεραι δ' ἅμα πᾶσαι ἀνασκίρτησαν ἐρίπναι,
Οἷα παραὶ σύριγγι φίλῃ ὑπὸ μητέρι ἄρνες.
Τίπτε σύ γ' αἰνὰ θάλασσα πέλωρ φυγάδ' ἐρρώησας
Κύματι εἰλυμένη ῥοθίῳ; τί δ' ἄρ' ἐστυφελίχθης
'Ιρὸς 'Ιορδάνη ποτὶ ἀργυροειδέα πηγήν;
Τίπτ' ὄρεα σκαρθμοῖσιν ἀπειρέσια κλονέεσθε
'Ως κριοὶ σφριγόωντες ἐϋτραφερῷ ἐν ἀλωῇ;
Βαιότεραι τί δ' ἄρ' ὕμμες ἀνασκιρτήσατ' ἐρίπναι,
Οἷα παραὶ σύριγγι φίλῃ ὑπὸ μητέρι ἄρνες;
Σείεο γαῖα τρέουσα θεὸν μεγάλ' ἐκτυπέοντα
Γαῖα θεὸν τρείουσ' ὕπατον σέβας 'Ισσακίδαο
"Ος τε καὶ ἐκ σπιλάδων ποταμοὺς χέε μορμύροντας,
Κρήνην τ' ἀέναον πέτρης ἀπὸ δακρυοέσσης.

When the children of Israel, when the glorious tribes of Jacob left the hateful, barbarian-tongued country of Egypt, then indeed the sons of Judah were the only holy nation; God ruled the people with great power. The sea knew it and rushed headlong in flight, wrapped in a roaring wave, and sacred Jordan was thrust back to its silvery source. Limitless mountains ran bounding out, like lusty rams in a luxurious garden. At the same time, all the lower peaks skipped like lambs to the sound of a panpipe around their dear mother. Why, you dread monster sea, did you rush in flight, wrapped in a roaring wave? Why, you sacred Jordan, were you thrust back to your silvery source? Why, you limitless mountains, did you run bounding out like lusty rams in a luxurious garden? Why, you lower peaks, did you skip like lambs to the sound of a panpipe around their dear mother? Quake, earth, in fear of the great-thundering God—in fear, earth, of God, the highest majesty of the children of Isaac, who pours the raging rivers forth from the rocks and the everflowing spring from the weeping stone.

AD SALSILLUM POETAM ROMANUM AEGROTANTEM. SCAZONTES

[*To Salzilli, the Roman poet, being ill. Scazons*]

Little is known of Giovanni Salzilli. Milton met him in Rome, probably during his first visit, in October–November 1638. Salzilli wrote a brief Latin poem in which he prefers Milton to Homer, Vergil, and Tasso. Milton printed the work, along with other commendatory pieces, as a preface to his Latin poems in 1645 and alludes to its flattery at the beginning of *To Salzilli.*

The poem is written in scazons, or "limping" iambic lines that end in a spondee or trochee.

O Musa gressum quae volens trahis claudum,
Vulcanioque tarda gaudes incessu,
Nec sentis illud in loco minus gratum,
Quam cum decentes flava Deiope suras
Alternat aureum ante Iunonis lectum,
Adesdum et haec s'is verba pauca Salsillo
Refer, camena nostra cui tantum est cordi,
Quamque ille magnis praetulit immerito divis.
Haec ergo alumnus ille Londini Milto,
Diebus hisce qui suum linquens nidum
Polique tractum (pessimus ubi ventorum,
Insanientis impotensque pulmonis
Pernix anhela sub Iove exercet flabra),
Venit feraces Itali soli ad glebas,
Visum superba cognitas urbes fama
Virosque doctaeque indolem iuventutis,
Tibi optat idem hic fausta multa Salsille,
Habitumque fesso corpori penitus sanum;
Cui nunc profunda bilis infestat renes,
Praecordiisque fixa damnosum spirat.
Nec id pepercit impia quod tu Romano
Tam cultus ore Lesbium condis melos.
O dulce divum munus, O Salus Hebes
Germana! Tuque Phoebe morborum terror

2. Vulcan's fall from heaven left him lame. See *Elegy* 7.81n.
4. Juno promised Aeolus the nymph Dëiope as a reward for sending a storm upon the Trojan fleet.
22. Alcaeus and Sappho were natives of Lesbos.
23. Hebe is the goddess of youth.

O Muse who willingly drags a limping gait and enjoys moving slow with Vulcan's walk,[2] nor thinks this any less welcome in its place than when blond Dëiope[4] dances on her well-formed legs in front of Juno's golden bed: come and, if you are willing, take these few words to Salzilli, to whom our poetry is so dear that he undeservedly prefers it to the divine greats. This, therefore, from Milton, child of London, who lately leaving his nest and portion of the sky (where the worst of winds, unable to control its crazed lungs, blows breathless gusts around rapidly under Jove), comes to the fertile earth of Italy's soil, to see its renowned cities of proud fame, its men and the excellence of its learned youth: this same man wishes you much happiness, Salzilli, and good health throughout your wearied body—in which excessive bile now plagues the kidneys and, fixed in the chest, breathes forth poison; nor in its impiety has it spared you for composing with such cultivation Lesbian lyrics[22] for a Roman mouth. O sweet gift of the gods, O health, sister of Hebe![23] and you, Phoebus, the terror of diseases since

Pythone caeso, sive tu magis Paean
Libenter audis, hic tuus sacerdos est.
Querceta Fauni, vosque rore vinoso
Colles benigni, mitis Evandri sedes,
Siquid salubre vallibus frondet vestris,
Levamen aegro ferte certatim vati.
Sic ille charis redditus rursum Musis
Vicina dulci prata mulcebit cantu.
Ipse inter atros emirabitur lucos
Numa, ubi beatum degit otium aeternum,
Suam reclivis semper Aegeriam spectans.
Tumidusque et ipse Tibris hinc delinitus
Spei favebit annuae colonorum:
Nec in sepulchris ibit obsessum reges
Nimium sinistro laxus irruens loro;
Sed frena melius temperabit undarum,
Adusque curvi salsa regna Portumni.

the slaying of Python,[25] or if you prefer to be called Paean: this man is your priest. Oak forests of Faunus,[27] and hills rich with dew that smells of wine, gentle seat of Evander,[28] if anything medicinal flourishes in your valleys, bear that comfort quickly to the sick bard. Restored again thus to his dear muses, he will soothe the neighboring meadows with his sweet song. Numa[34] himself will wonder among the dark groves, where he spends his blessed eternal leisure, reclining and gazing forever on his Egeria. And charmed this way, even swollen Tiber[36] will be kind to the farmers' yearly hope; nor, running with the left rein too loose, will he go to besiege kings in their tombs, but will manage the waves' harness better, as far as the salty kingdom of curved Portumnus.

25. **Pythone caeso:** Python was a monstrous serpent slain by Apollo, who is the god of healing as well as of poetry and music.
27. **Fauni:** Faunus, Roman god of woods, identified with Pan.
28. **Evandri sedes:** Evander founded the city of Pallanteum on the banks of the Tiber where Rome was to stand.
34. **Numa:** Numa, the second of Rome's legendary kings, learned wisdom from the water nymph Egeria.
36. Horace describes how the Tiber flooded *monumenta regis* (*Odes* 1.2.15).

MANSO

Giovanni Battista Manso (c. 1560–1645) was a patron of the arts who had befriended two notable Italian poets, Torquato Tasso and Giambattista Marino. His services to literature overshadowed his own work, which included poetry, philosophical dialogues, and a *Life of Tasso.* Milton met Manso in Naples in 1638 and later remembered him as "a man of high rank and influence, to whom the famous Italian poet, Torquato Tasso, dedicated his work on friendship. As long as I was there I found him a very true friend. He personally conducted me through the various quarters of the city and the Viceregal Court, and more than once came to my lodgings to call. When I was leaving he gravely apologized because even though he had especially wished to show me many more attentions, he could not do so in that city, since I was unwilling to be circumspect in regard to religion" (p. 1092). Milton certainly means to establish in this passage that the future public opponent of Catholicism and apologist of the English Revolution was already on display in his reckless outspokenness in Italy, and one might expect a certain degree of exaggeration. But the Latin couplet by Manso that Milton printed in 1645 among the poems prefacing his Latin verse also calls attention to his Protestantism: "If your religious persuasions were equal to your mind, your handsome figure, your fame, your face, and your manners, then—good heavens!—you would be an angel, not an Englishman." When he invented the character of Abdiel in *Paradise Lost,* one might reply, Milton found a way to be both.

Manso has often been judged one of the best of Milton's Latin pieces.

Ioannes Baptista Mansus Marchio Villensis vir ingenii laude, tum literarum studio, nec non et bellica virtute apud Italos clarus in primis est. Ad quem Torquati Tassi dialogus extat de Amicitia scriptus; erat enim Tassi amicissimus; ab quo etiam inter Campaniae principes celebratur, in illo poemate cui titulus *Gerusalemme conquistata, lib. 20.*

Fra cavalier magnanimi, è cortesi
Risplende il Manso . . .

Is authorem Neapoli commorantem summa benevolentia prosecutus est, multaque ei detulit humanitatis officia. Ad hunc itaque hospes ille antequam ab ea urbe discederet, ut ne ingratum se ostenderet, hoc carmen misit.

Haec quoque Manse tuae meditantur carmina laudi
Pierides, tibi Manse choro notissime Phoebi,
Quandoquidem ille alium haud aequo est dignatus honore
Post Galli cineres, et Maecenatis Hetrusci.
Tu quoque si nostrae tantum valet aura Camenae,

1. **quoque:** Many other poems had been addressed to Manso.

2. **Pierides:** the Muses.

4. **Galli:** Cornelius Gallus, an elegiac poet and friend to Vergil; **Maecenatis:** Maecenas, patron of Vergil, Horace, and other poets.

Giovanni Battista Manso, Marquis of Villa, is among the most famous men in Italy because of his reputation for intelligence, as well as his devotion to literature and his courage in war. There is a dialogue of Torquato Tasso's, "On Friendship," written to him; for he was a very close friend of Tasso's, who celebrated him among the princes of Campania in his poem entitled "Jerusalem Conquered," Book 20: "Among the great-hearted and courtly knights Manso shines out . . ." He attended the author with great benevolence while he was staying in Naples, and did him many kind services. So, before he left that city, in order not to seem ungrateful as a guest, he sent him this poem.

Manso, the Pierians[2] also[1] rehearse this poem in your praise—for you, Manso, well known to Phoebus's choir, inasmuch as no one else is worthy of equal honor since the funerals of Gallus and Etruscan Maecenas.[4] You too, if the breath of our Muse has such power, will sit

Victrices hederas inter, laurosque sedebis.
Te pridem magno felix concordia Tasso
Iunxit, et aeternis inscripsit nomina chartis.
Mox tibi dulciloquum non inscia Musa Marinum
Tradidit; ille tuum dici se gaudet alumnum,
Dum canit Assyrios divum prolixus amores;
Mollis et Ausonias stupefecit carmine nymphas.
Ille itidem moriens tibi soli debita vates
Ossa, tibi soli supremaque vota reliquit.
Nec manes pietas tua chara fefellit amici;
Vidimus arridentem operoso ex aere poetam.
Nec satis hoc visum est in utrumque, et nec pia cessant
Officia in tumulo; cupis integros rapere Orco,
Qua potes, atque avidas Parcarum eludere leges:
Amborum genus, et varia sub sorte peractam
Describis vitam, moresque, et dona Minervae;
Aemulus illius Mycalen qui natus ad altam
Rettulit Aeolii vitam facundus Homeri.
Ergo ego te Clius et magni nomine Phoebi
Manse pater, iubeo longum salvere per aevum
Missus Hyperboreo iuvenis peregrinus ab axe.
Nec tu longinquam bonus aspernabere Musam,
Quae nuper gelida vix enutrita sub Arcto
Imprudens Italas ausa est volitare per urbes.
Nos etiam in nostro modulantes flumine cygnos
Credimus obscuras noctis sensisse per umbras,
Qua Thamesis late puris argenteus urnis
Oceani glaucos perfundit gurgite crines.
Quin et in has quondam pervenit Tityrus oras.

among the victorious ivy and laurels.[6] Happy concord once bound you to the great Tasso and wrote your names on eternal pages. Soon the knowing Muse entrusted sweet-voiced Marino[9] to you, and he rejoices to be called your student while he sings at length the Assyrian love story of the gods; and smoothly he struck the Italian nymphs dumb with his song. Accordingly, when he died he left his bones, as was fated, to you alone,[13] left his final wishes to you alone. Nor did your loving piety disappoint your friend's shade; we have seen the smiling poet in well-worked bronze. Nor did this seem enough for either, and your pious offices do not end at the grave; you long to snatch them intact away from Orcus, where you can, and escape the hungry laws of the Parcae; you are writing about their lineage, and life lived with mixed luck, and their habits, and the gifts of Minerva: emulating him who, born near lofty Mycale,[22] eloquently wrote the life of Aeolian Homer. Therefore, Father Manso, in the name of Clio and great Phoebus, I, a young man sent as a pilgrim from the Hyperborean[26] sky, order you to be healthy throughout a long life. Nor in your goodness will you spurn a distant Muse who, barely nourished of late under the frigid Bear, imprudently dares to fly through the cities of Italy. We also believe that we have heard swans[30] singing in our river in the dark shadows of night, where silver Thames pours forth her blue-gray hair broadly from pure urns in Ocean's stream. Why, Tityrus[34] once visited these

6. See *To His Father* 102. The ivy and laurel are emblematic of poetry or poetic distinction.

9. **Marinum:** The Italian poet Giambattista Marino (1569–1625), whose *L'Adone* (1623) tells of Venus and Adonis.

13. Milton suggests that Manso took charge of burying Marino and erecting his monument, but we have no corroborating evidence. Nor do we have Manso's biography of Marino.

22. The *Life of Homer* is no longer attributed to Herodotus.

26. **Hyperboreo:** Diodorus Siculus 2.47.1 placed the island of the Hyperboreans in the ocean beyond Gaul.

30. **cygnos:** swans (i.e., poets), as in Jonson calling Shakespeare the "Sweet Swan of Avon."

34. **Tityrus:** Spenser's name for Chaucer (*SC*, "February" 92).

Sed neque nos genus incultum, nec inutile Phoebo,
Qua plaga septeno mundi sulcata Trione
Brumalem patitur longa sub nocte Booten.
Nos etiam colimus Phoebum, nos munera Phoebo
Flaventes spicas, et lutea mala canistris,
Halantemque crocum (perhibet nisi vana vetustas)
Misimus, et lectas Druidum de gente choreas.
(Gens Druides antiqua sacris operata deorum
Heroum laudes imitandaque gesta canebant.)
Hinc quoties festo cingunt altaria cantu
Delo in herbosa Graiae de more puellae
Carminibus laetis memorant Corineida Loxo,
Fatidicamque Upin, cum flavicoma Hecaerge,
Nuda Caledonio variatas pectora fuco.
Fortunate senex, ergo quacunque per orbem
Torquati decus, et nomen celebrabitur ingens,
Claraque perpetui succrescet fama Marini,
Tu quoque in ora frequens venies plausumque virorum,
Et parili carpes iter immortale volatu.
Dicetur tum sponte tuos habitasse penates
Cynthius, et famulas venisse ad limina Musas:
At non sponte domum tamen idem, et regis adivit
Rura Pheretiadae caelo fugitivus Apollo;
Ille licet magnum Alciden susceperat hospes;
Tantum ubi clamosos placuit vitare bubulcos,
Nobile mansueti cessit Chironis in antrum,
Irriguos inter saltus frondosaque tecta

shores. But we are not an uncultured nation, or useless to Phoebus, who endure wintry Boötes in the long night in that part of the world furrowed by the sevenfold Triones.[36] We also cultivate Phoebus, we have sent Phoebus offerings:[38] golden grain, and red apples in baskets, and the fragrant crocus (unless tradition has it wrong), and choice choirs from the race of Druids. (The Druids, an ancient race engaged in the rituals of the gods,[42] sang the praises and exemplary deeds of heroes.) Hence whenever, according to custom, Greek girls surround the altars on grassy Delos with festive singing, they commemorate with happy songs Corineus's daughter Loxo[46] and prophetic Upis, along with golden-haired Hecaerge, who adorn their naked breasts with Caledonian dye. Lucky old man, since wherever throughout the world the glory of Torquato and his great name are celebrated, and the bright fame of undying Marino grows, you too will come often to the lips and the applause of men, and will take an immortal journey with equal flight. It will be said that Cynthius[55] of his own free will dwelt with your hearth gods, and the Muses came as servants to your doors; but not of his own free will did that same Apollo, a fugitive from heaven, visit the farm of the king who was Pheres's son, even though that man had as a host taken in great Alcides.[58] Whenever it pleased him to get away from the noisy plowmen, he retired to the noble cave of gentle Chiron,[60] amid the moist glades and leafy shelters by

36. Ursa Major has seven prominent stars and was often compared to oxen yoked to a wagon.

38. Callimachus relates that the Hyperborean maidens Loxo, Upis, and Hecaerge brought offerings of corn to Apollo and Artemis at Delos (*Hymn* 4.283–99).

42. See *Lyc* 53n on Druids and Bards.

46. **Corineida:** daughter of Corineus, who accompanied the Trojan Brutus to Britain and came to govern Cornwall. See Geoffrey of Monmouth, *History of Britain* 1.12.

55. **Cynthius:** Apollo, born on Mount Cynthus.

58. See *Sonnet 23* 2n.

60. **Chironis:** Chiron the centaur, tutor of many heroes.

Peneium prope rivum: ibi saepe sub ilice nigra
Ad citharae strepitum blanda prece victus amici
Exilii duros lenibat voce labores.
Tum neque ripa suo, barathro nec fixa sub imo
Saxa stetere loco; nutat Trachinia rupes,
Nec sentit solitas, immania pondera, silvas;
Emotaeque suis properant de collibus orni,
Mulcenturque novo maculosi carmine lynces.
Diis dilecte senex, te Iupiter aequus oportet
Nascentem, et miti lustrarit lumine Phoebus,
Atlantisque nepos; neque enim nisi charus ab ortu
Diis superis poterit magno favisse poetae.
Hinc longaeva tibi lento sub flore senectus
Vernat, et Aesonios lucratur vivida fusos,
Nondum deciduos servans tibi frontis honores,
Ingeniumque vigens, et adultum mentis acumen.
O mihi si mea sors talem concedat amicum,
Phoebaeos decorasse viros qui tam bene norit,
Si quando indigenas revocabo in carmina reges,
Arturumque etiam sub terris bella moventem;
Aut dicam invictae sociali foedere mensae,
Magnanimos Heroas, et (O modo spiritus adsit)
Frangam Saxonicas Britonum sub Marte phalanges.
Tandem ubi non tacitae permensus tempora vitae,
Annorumque satur cineri sua iura relinquam,
Ille mihi lecto madidis astaret ocellis,
Astanti sat erit si dicam sim tibi curae;
Ille meos artus liventi morte solutos,

the banks of Peneus; there often, under a black oak, yielding to his friend's gentle prayer, he eased the harsh labors of exile with his voice to the sound of his lute. Then neither the riverbanks nor the boulders lodged in the bottom of the abyss stayed in their place; the Trachinian cliff nodded and did not feel the immense weight of its accustomed forest, and the ash trees were moved and hurried down from their hills, and the spotted lynxes were soothed by the novel song. Old man dear to the gods, Jupiter must have been favorable at your birth, and Phoebus looked at you with kind eyes, and also Atlas's grandson;[72] for unless dear to the heavenly gods from the start, one could not have befriended a great poet. That is why your long old age is a springtime of late-blooming flowers, and in its vigor gains Aesonian[75] spindles, still preserving the not yet decaying honors of your face,[76] lively in intellect and mature sharpness of mind. O, may my luck provide me with such a friend who knows well how to honor Phoebus's men, if ever I recall our native kings into song,[80] and Arthur, waging war even under the earth, or tell of the great-hearted heroes of the table made unconquerable by their joint oath, and (O may the spirit only be there) smash the Saxon phalanxes with British warfare. When at last I have measured out the time of a

72. **nepos:** Mercury, god of eloquence.

75. **Aesonios:** See *Elegy 2* 7–8n.

76. There is evidence that Manso delighted his friends by removing his wig and displaying his baldness (Masson 1965, 1:813).

80. These lines are the earliest statement of Milton's interest in writing an Arthurian epic. See also *Damon* 162–71. Arthur does not appear in the list of twenty-eight subjects from British history that Milton set down in the *CMS* as possible material for an epic poem.

Curaret parva componi molliter urna.
Forsitan et nostros ducat de marmore vultus,
Nectens aut Paphia myrti aut Parnasside lauri
Fronde comas, at ego secura pace quiescam.
Tum quoque, si qua fides, si praemia certa bonorum,
Ipse ego caelicolum semotus in aethera divum,
Quo labor et mens pura vehunt, atque ignea virtus
Secreti haec aliqua mundi de parte videbo
(Quantum fata sinunt), et tota mente serenum
Ridens purpureo suffundar lumine vultus,
Et simul aethereo plaudam mihi laetus Olympo.

life that has not been silent, and full of years I leave to the ashes their due, he would stand by my bed with moist eyes, and it will be enough if I say to him standing there, "Let me be in your care." My limbs, unstrung by livid death, he would take care to compose in a small urn; and perhaps he might transpose my features into marble, binding the hair with a Paphian wreath[92] of myrtle or a Parnassian one of laurel, and I will rest in secure peace. Then also, if any faith, if any reward for good men is certain, I, far away in the ether of the divine gods, where work and a pure mind and fiery virtue lead, will watch these things from some part of the secret world (as much as the Fates permit), and laughing serenely with my whole mind, I will be suffused in my face with ruddy light and at the same time applaud myself in happiness on ethereal Olympus.

92. **Paphia:** Paphos, where there was a temple of Venus, to whom the myrtle was sacred. After Daphne was transformed into a laurel, Apollo entwined laurel in his hair, bow, quiver, and lyre.

EPITAPH FOR DAMON

Milton's closest friend, Charles Diodati, died in England in August 1638 while Milton was traveling in Italy. The poem itself (ll. 13–17) tells us that it was written soon after his return to England in the summer of 1639. One copy survives of a small private printing in 1640.

Epitaphium Damonis is in obvious ways a Latin *Lycidas.* Both are pastoral elegies profoundly knowledgeable about the history of the form, both were occasioned by the deaths of young men, and both rise to consoling visions of the dead shepherds being welcomed into Heaven. But all the similarities point to differences. Latin brings the *Epitaphium* closer to the pastoral tradition, as does the refrain based on the final line of Vergil's final eclogue. Milton genuinely loved Diodati, whereas he seems to have been at best a distant acquaintance of Edward King. Finally, the vision of Heaven at the climax of *Lycidas* seems rather sedate in comparison with the Christian bacchanalian at the end of *Epitaphium Damonis,* all the more striking because of the absence of an epilogue.

Argumentum

Thyrsis et Damon eiusdem viciniae pastores, eadem studia sequuti a pueritia amici erant, ut qui plurimum. Thyrsis animi causa profectus peregre de obitu Damonis nuntium accepit. Domum postea reversus et rem ita esse comperto, se, suamque solitudinem hoc carmine deplorat. Damonis autem sub persona hic intelligitur Carolus Deodatus ex urbe Hetruriae Luca paterno genere oriundus, caetera Anglus; ingenio, doctrina, clarissimisque caeteris virtutibus, dum viveret, iuvenis egregius.

Thyrsis and Damon, shepherds of the same district, pursuing the same studies, were friends from boyhood, the closest possible. Thyrsis, traveling abroad for pleasure, received news of Damon's death. After returning home and on verifying that the report was true, he wept for himself and his loneliness in this song. By the name "Damon" here is meant Charles Diodati, descended from the Tuscan city of Lucca on his father's side, and otherwise an Englishman: while he lived, an extraordinary young man for talent, learning, and other most distinguished virtues.

Himerides nymphae (nam vos et Daphnin et Hylan,
Et plorata diu meministis fata Bionis)
Dicite Sicelicum Thamesina per oppida carmen:
Quas miser effudit voces, quae murmura Thyrsis,
Et quibus assiduis exercuit antra querelis
Fluminaque, fontesque vagos, nemorumque recessus,
Dum sibi praereptum queritur Damona, neque altam
Luctibus exemit noctem loca sola pererrans.
Et iam bis viridi surgebat culmus arista,
Et totidem flavas numerabant horrea messes,
Ex quo summa dies tulerat Damona sub umbras,
Nec dum aderat Thyrsis; pastorem scilicet illum
Dulcis amor Musae Thusca retinebat in urbe.
Ast ubi mens expleta domum pecorisque relicti
Cura vocat, simul assueta seditque sub ulmo,
Tum vero amissum tum denique sentit amicum,
Coepit et immensum sic exonerare dolorem.

Himeran nymphs[1] (for you memorialized Daphnis and Hylas and the long-lamented fate of Bion[2]), speak a Sicilian song through the villages of the Thames: the cries, the moans which Thyrsis[4] poured out in his misery, the unremitting complaints with which he troubled the caves and the rivers and the wandering fountains and the depths of the groves while he lamented that Damon was snatched from him, nor did he exempt dark night from his grieving as he wandered the lonely sites. And already the stalk twice thrust upward with a green beard, and as many times the granaries counted the golden harvest since the last day took Damon into the shadows, and yet Thyrsis was not there; for sweet love of the Muse detained that shepherd in a Tuscan city. But when his full mind and care for the flock left behind called him home, and he sat down under his familiar elm, then truly, then at last he felt the loss of his friend,

1. **Himerides:** pastoral Muses, after the two rivers named Himera in Sicily, home to Theocritus, Bion, and Moschus. The young shepherd Daphnis is mourned in Theocritus's first eclogue, which is the earliest pastoral elegy. On Hylas, see *Elegy 7* 24n.

2. Bion is mourned in *Lament for Bion* (Moschus 3), the first pastoral elegy on the death of a poet.

4. **Thyrsis:** Milton adopts the name of the shepherd who mourns for Daphnis in Theocritus 1.

Ite domum impasti, domino iam non vacat, agni.
Hei mihi! quae terris, quae dicam numina coelo,
Postquam te immiti rapuerunt funere, Damon;
Siccine nos linquis, tua sic sine nomine virtus
Ibit, et obscuris numero sociabitur umbris?
At non ille animas virga qui dividit aurea,
Ista velit, dignumque tui te ducat in agmen,
Ignavumque procul pecus arceat omne silentum.
Ite domum impasti, domino iam non vacat, agni.
Quicquid erit, certe, nisi me lupus ante videbit,
Indeplorato non comminuere sepulcro,
Constabitque tuus tibi honos, longumque vigebit
Inter pastores: illi tibi vota secundo
Solvere post Daphnin, post Daphnin dicere laudes
Gaudebunt, dum rura Pales, dum Faunus amabit:
Si quid id est, priscamque fidem coluisse, piumque,
Palladiasque artes, sociumque habuisse canorum.
Ite domum impasti, domino iam non vacat, agni.
Haec tibi certa manent, tibi erunt haec praemia Damon.
At mihi quid tandem fiet modo? quis mihi fidus
Haerebit lateri comes, ut tu saepe solebas
Frigoribus duris, et per loca foeta pruinis,
Aut rapido sub sole, siti morientibus herbis?
Sive opus in magnos fuit eminus ire leones,
Aut avidos terrere lupos praesepibus altis?

and began to unburden himself of his immense grief:

"Go home unfed, lambs; your master has no time for you now.[18] Alas for me! what gods on earth, what gods in the sky will I call, now that they have taken you away from me, Damon, with a pitiless funeral? Is this how you leave us, will your virtue go this way without a name and join the number of the obscure shades? But may he[23] who divides the souls with his golden wand not want this, and may he lead you to a company worthy of you, and keep back all the ignoble herd of the silent.

"Go home unfed, lambs; your master has no time for you now. Whatever happens, surely, unless a wolf sees me first,[27] you will not wither in an unlamented tomb, and your honor will survive for you, and will long flourish among the shepherds. They will take pleasure in swearing oaths to you, second after Daphnis, and in speaking your praises, after Daphnis, as long as Pales, as long as Faunus[32] loves the country: if it counts for anything to have cultivated the ancient faith and piety and the arts of Pallas,[34] and to have had a singer for a companion.

"Go home unfed, lambs; your master has no time for you now. These things remain certain for you, these will be your rewards, Damon; but what then will become of me? What faithful companion will cling to my side, as you often used to do in the harsh cold, and in places teeming with frost, or under the scorching sun when the plants were dying of thirst? Whether our task was to track great lions from a distance or to frighten hungry wolves from the tall sheepfolds, who will

18. Milton's refrain reworks the last line of Vergil's last eclogue, *Ite domum saturae, venit Hesperus, ite capellae* (Go home, my full-fed goats, the evening star comes, go home).

23. **ille:** Mercury. According to Vergil, *Aen.* 4.242–44, Mercury uses his wand (*virga*) to summon ghosts.

27. An old superstition held that a man seen by a wolf before he saw it would be struck dumb.

32. **Pales:** Roman goddess of shepherds. For Faunus, see *To Salzilli* 27n.

34. Pallas Athena was goddess of wisdom; Diodati studied at Oxford and Geneva. The poetic friend is Milton.

Quis fando sopire diem cantuque solebit?
Ite domum impasti, domino iam non vacat, agni.
Pectora cui credam? quis me lenire docebit
Mordaces curas, quis longam fallere noctem
Dulcibus alloquiis, grato cum sibilat igni
Molle pyrum, et nucibus strepitat focus, at malus Auster
Miscet cuncta foris, et desuper intonat ulmo?
Ite domum impasti, domino iam non vacat, agni.
Aut aestate, dies medio dum vertitur axe,
Cum Pan aesculea somnum capit abditus umbra,
Et repetunt sub aquis sibi nota sedilia nymphae,
Pastoresque latent, stertit sub sepe colonus,
Quis mihi blanditiasque tuas, quis tum mihi risus,
Cecropiosque sales referet, cultosque lepores?
Ite domum impasti, domino iam non vacat, agni.
At iam solus agros, iam pascua solus oberro,
Sicubi ramosae densantur vallibus umbrae,
Hic serum expecto; supra caput imber et Eurus
Triste sonant, fractaeque agitata crepuscula silvae.
Ite domum impasti, domino iam non vacat, agni.
Heu quam culta mihi prius arva procacibus herbis
Involvuntur, et ipsa situ seges alta fatiscit!
Innuba neglecto marcescit et uva racemo,
Nec myrteta iuvant; ovium quoque taedet, at illae
Moerent, inque suum convertunt ora magistrum.
Ite domum impasti, domino iam non vacat, agni.
Tityrus ad corylos vocat, Alphesiboeus ad ornos,
Ad salices Aegon, ad flumina pulcher Amyntas,

65. **Innuba:** The idea of the vine being "wedded" to the elm or poplar was a commonplace of Latin poetry; Horace calls trees without vines "celibate" or "widowed" (*Odes* 2.15.4, 4.5.30).

be easing the day with talk and song?

"Go home unfed, lambs; your master has no time for you now. To whom will I entrust my heart? Who will teach me to soften biting cares, who to cheat the long night with sweet conversation while a soft pear hisses before the welcome fire, and the hearth crackles with nuts, but outside evil Auster roils everything and thunders in the elm up above?

"Go home unfed, lambs; your master has no time for you now. Or in the summer, while the day turns to noontime, when Pan catches his sleep, concealed in the shade of oaks, and nymphs go back to their well-known stations beneath the water, and the shepherds are hidden, and the farmer snores under the hedge, who will bring back to me your flatteries, who will bring back to me your laughter and Athenian wit and cultivated charms?

"Go home unfed, lambs; your master has no time for you now. But now I wander alone through the fields, alone through the pastures; anywhere that the branched shadows are made thick by the valleys, there I wait for evening. Above my head the rain and Eurus make a sad sound, and the troubled twilight of the shattered frost.

"Go home unfed, lambs; your master has no time for you now. Alas, how my once cultivated fields are overrun with unrestrained weeds, and the tall grain itself droops from neglect! The unwed grapes[65] rot, their clusters untended, nor does the myrtle give pleasure; even the sheep are wearisome, and they grieve and turn their faces to their master.

"Go home unfed, lambs; your master has no time for you now. Tityrus calls to the hazels, Alphesiboeus to the ash trees, Aegon

Hic gelidi fontes, hic illita gramina musco,
Hic Zephyri, hic placidas interstrepit arbutus undas;
Ista canunt surdo, frutices ego nactus abibam.
  Ite domum impasti, domino iam non vacat, agni.
Mopsus ad haec, nam me redeuntem forte notarat
(Et callebat avium linguas, et sidera Mopsus)
Thyrsi, quid hoc? dixit, quae te coquit improba bilis?
Aut te perdit amor, aut te male fascinat astrum,
Saturni grave saepe fuit pastoribus astrum,
Intimaque obliquo figit praecordia plumbo.
  Ite domum impasti, domino iam non vacat, agni.
Mirantur nymphae, et quid te Thyrsi futurum est?
Quid tibi vis? aiunt, non haec solet esse iuventae
Nubila frons, oculique truces, vultusque severi;
Illa choros, lususque leves, et semper amorem
Iure petit; bis ille miser qui serus amavit.
  Ite domum impasti, domino iam non vacat, agni.
Venit Hyas, Dryopeque, et filia Baucidis Aegle,
Docta modos, citharaeque sciens, sed perdita fastu,
Venit Idumanii Chloris vicina fluenti;
Nil me blanditiae, nil me solantia verba,
Nil me, si quid adest, movet, aut spes ulla futuri.
  Ite domum impasti, domino iam non vacat, agni.
Hei mihi quam similes ludunt per prata iuvenci,
Omnes unanimi secum sibi lege sodales,
Nec magis hunc alio quisquam secernit amicum

88. **Hyas:** Hyas is killed by a lioness in Ovid, *Fasti* 5.169–82, though Milton may have a nymph in mind. **Dryope:** appears in Ovid, *Met.* 9.331–93.

90. The river Chelmer in Essex flows into Blackwater Bay. Camden in his *Britannia* identified the river with with Ptolemy's *Idumanius fluvius.*

to the willows, handsome Amyntas to the streams: 'Here are cold fountains, here grass spread with moss, here zephyrs, here the arbutus mixes its noise with the placid waves.' They sing to a deaf person; reaching the bushes, I escaped.

"Go home unfed, lambs; your master has no time for you now. At this Mopsus, for he happened to see me leaving (and Mopsus knows the languages of the birds and the stars), said, 'Thyrsis, what is this? What unhealthy bile troubles you? Either love slays you, or an evil star bewitches you; Saturn's star has often been grim for shepherds, it pierces the innermost heart with its slanting lead.'

"Go home unfed, lambs; your master has no time for you now. The nymphs wonder, and say, 'What will become of you, Thyrsis? What do you want? The forehead of youth is not usually cloudy like this, or the eyes angry, or the looks severe; by rights it seeks out dances and easygoing games and, always, love; he is twice as wretched who loves too late.'

"Go home unfed, lambs; your master has no time for you now. Hyas[88] came, and Dryope, and Aegle, the daughter of Baucis, learned in music, knowledgeable about the lyre, but undone by her fastidiousness; Chloris, from near the Idumanian river,[90] came. Blandishments do not, comforting words do not move me, or anything that is at hand, or any hope of the future.

"Go home unfed, lambs; your master has no time for you now. Alas for me, how alike are the young bulls playing in the meadow, all comrades agreed with each other in their law; none singles out one friend more than another from the herd. In the

De grege; sic densi veniunt ad pabula thoes,
Inque vicem hirsuti paribus iunguntur onagri;
Lex eadem pelagi, deserto in littore Proteus
Agmina phocarum numerat, vilisque volucrum
Passer habet semper quicum sit, et omnia circum
Farra libens volitet, sero sua tecta revisens;
Quem si fors letho obiecit, seu milvus adunco
Fata tulit rostro, seu stravit arundine fossor,
Protinus ille alium socio petit inde volatu.
Nos durum genus, et diris exercita fatis
Gens homines aliena animis, et pectore discors;
Vix sibi quisque parem de millibus invenit unum,
Aut si sors dederit tandem non aspera votis,
Illum inopina dies qua non speraveris hora
Surripit, aeternum linquens in saecula damnum.
  Ite domum impasti, domino iam non vacat, agni.
Heu quis me ignotas traxit vagus error in oras
Ire per aereas rupes, Alpemque nivosam!
Ecquid erat tanti Romam vidisse sepultam,
Quamvis illa foret, qualem dum viseret olim,
Tityrus ipse suas et oves et rura reliquit;
Ut te tam dulci possem caruisse sodale,
Possem tot maria alta, tot interponere montes,
Tot silvas, tot saxa tibi, fluviosque sonantes?
Ah certe extremum licuisset tangere dextram,
Et bene compositos placide morientis ocellos,
Et dixisse vale, nostri memor ibis ad astra.
  Ite domum impasti, domino iam non vacat, agni.

same way wolves[97] go in packs for food, and shaggy asses are joined with their mates in turn. The law of the sea is the same: on the deserted shore Proteus[99] counts his company of seals. And the sparrow, the most insignificant of birds, always has someone to be with, to fly freely about all the grain, returning in the evening to his own home: whom if chance hurled to death, whether the kite bore its fate in a curved beak or a farmworker brought it down with his shaft, he then straightway seeks another as a companion in flight. We men are a hard race, a tribe drawn by a dire fate, unfriendly in spirit and troubled at heart; each finds scarcely one partner in a thousand, or if a fortune not hostile to our prayers finally gives us one, the unexpected day, the hour for which you had not hoped, snatches him away, leaving eternal loss for all time.

"Go home unfed, lambs; your master has no time for you now. Alas, what inconstant error dragged me to unknown shores, to go through the airy cliffs, the snowy Alps! Was it so important to have seen Rome in its tomb—even if it had been as it was when Tityrus[117] once left his sheep and fields to see it—that I should leave you, such a sweet companion, that I should interpose so many deep seas, so many mountains, so many forests, so many rocks, so many sounding rivers between us? Ah, surely it would have been permitted to touch his hand at the end, and the gently closed eyes of the peacefully dying man, and to have said, 'Farewell, you will go to the stars remembering us.'

"Go home unfed, lambs; your

97. **thoes:** probably refers to a kind of weasel, though Milton seems to have thought that it means "wolves."

99. Proteus, the sea god, knew all things and could change his shape to avoid answering questions (see *Areop*, p. 962).

117. *Tityrus* here means Vergil's Tityrus, who saw Rome in its early days of splendor (*Ec.* 1.26), not Chaucer, as in *Manso* 34.

Quamquam etiam vestri nunquam meminisse pigebit,
Pastores Thusci, Musis operata iuventus,
Hic charis, atque lepos; et Thuscus tu quoque Damon,
Antiqua genus unde petis Lucumonis ab urbe.
O ego quantus eram, gelidi cum stratus ad Arni
Murmura, populeumque nemus, qua mollior herba,
Carpere nunc violas, nunc summas carpere myrtos,
Et potui Lycidae certantem audire Menalcam.
Ipse etiam tentare ausus sum, nec puto multum
Displicui, nam sunt et apud me munera vestra
Fiscellae, calathique et cerea vincla cicutae;
Quin et nostra suas docuerunt nomina fagos
Et Datis, et Francinus, erant et vocibus ambo
Et studiis noti, Lydorum sanguinis ambo.
  Ite domum impasti, domino iam non vacat, agni.
Haec mihi tum laeto dictabat roscida luna,
Dum solus teneros claudebam cratibus hoedos.
Ah quoties dixi, cum te cinis ater habebat,
Nunc canit, aut lepori nunc tendit retia Damon,
Vimina nunc texit, varios sibi quod sit in usus;
Et quae tum facile sperabam mente futura
Arripui voto levis, et praesentia finxi,
Heus bone numquid agis? nisi te quid forte retardat,
Imus? et arguta paulum recubamus in umbra,
Aut ad aquas Colni, aut ubi iugera Cassibelauni?

master has no time for you now. Yet still it will never trouble me to remember you, shepherds of Tuscany, young men devoted to the Muses: Grace is here, and Charm; and you also were a Tuscan, Damon,[127] whence you take your ancestry from the ancient city of Lucca. O, how grand I felt, stretched out by the murmurs of the cold Arno and the poplar grove, where the grass was softer, to pluck now violets, now myrtle sprays, and I could hear Menalcas in a contest[132] with Lycidas. I even dared to compete, and I don't think I greatly displeased, for your gifts[134] are still with me: baskets of twigs and baskets of wicker and the wax fastenings of a panpipe. And indeed Dati and Francini[137] taught their beech trees our name, and they were both of them famous for voice and learning, and both of Lydian blood.

"Go home unfed, lambs; your master has no time for you now. These things the dewy moon used to say to me then when I was happy, while in solitude I shut the tender kids up in their pens. Ah, how many times I said, when dark ashes held you, 'Now Damon is singing, or puts out nets for the hare, now he weaves wickerwork, for which he has various uses.' And I lightly seized with a wish future things which I then readily hoped for in my mind and pretended they were present: 'Hello, good fellow, what are you up to? Unless something happens to hold you back, shall we go and rest awhile in the rustling shade, either by the waters of the Colne[149] or where the acres of Cassivellaunus are? You

127. Diodati's forebears came from Lucca; see Dorian 5. *Lucumonis lucumo* (inspired person) was a name given to Etruscan princes and priests.
132. Via the pastoral convention of the singing match between shepherds, Milton alludes to the poetry contests in the Florentine academies (p. 840).
134. **munera:** perhaps an allusion to the poetic encomia that Milton placed before his Latin verse in the 1645 *Poems.*
137. Milton refers to two friends he made in Italy, Carlo Dati and Antonio Francini, both of whom wrote commendatory poems included in the 1645 *Poems* (see previous note).
149. **Colni:** The river Colne flows near Horton.

Tu mihi percurres medicos, tua gramina, succos,
Helleborumque, humilesque crocos, foliumque hyacinthi,
Quasque habet ista palus herbas, artesque medentum.
Ah pereant herbae, pereant artesque medentum
Gramina, postquam ipsi nil profecere magistro.
Ipse etiam, nam nescio quid mihi grande sonabat
Fistula, ab undecima iam lux est altera nocte,
Et tum forte novis admoram labra cicutis,
Dissiluere tamen rupta compage, nec ultra
Ferre graves potuere sonos; dubito quoque ne sim
Turgidulus, tamen et referam, vos cedite silvae.
Ite domum impasti, domino iam non vacat, agni.
Ipse ego Dardanias Rutupina per aequora puppes
Dicam, et Pandrasidos regnum vetus Inogeniae,
Brennumque Arviragumque duces, priscumque Belinum,
Et tandem Armoricos Britonum sub lege colonos;

will run through your medicines[150] for me, your plants and juices: hellebore and the humble crocus and the leaf of the hyacinth, whatever herbs and medical arts this marsh holds.' Ah, curse the herbs, curse the medical arts, the plants, now that they did no good for their own master. And myself—for my pipe played someting grand, I know not what, it is now the next day after the eleventh night, and then by chance I had placed my lips on new reeds, but they fell apart, their fastening broken, and they could no longer carry serious tunes, and I am unsure if I am being grandiose, but still I will recite; yield, you forests.[160]

"Go home unfed, lambs; your master has no time for you now. I myself will tell[162] of the Trojan keels through the Rutupian sea, and the ancient kingdom of Inogene,[163] daughter of Pandrasus, and the leaders Brennus and Arviragus, and old Belinus,[164] and Armorican settlers[165] at last

150. This passage is sometimes taken to suggest that the "certain shepherd lad" of *Masque* 618–28 is Diodati.

160. **vos cedite silvae:** Vergil's Gallus turns away from pastoral with the words *concedite silvae* (*Ec.* 10.63).

162. On Milton's plans for a British epic, see the less detailed account in *Manso* 80–84.

163. Pandrasus gave his daughter Inogene in marriage to the Trojan Brutus after Brutus defeated him. See Milton's *History of Britain* (Yale 5:11–13).

164. Brennus and Belinus were legendary British kings who conquered Rome (Geoffrey of Monmouth, *History of Britain* 3.1–10). Arviragus was King Cymbeline's son; Shakespeare rendered these characters in his *Cymbeline.*

165. British historians liked to believe that Constantine had founded a colony of veteran British soldiers in Gaul.

Tum gravidam Arturo fatali fraude Iogernen,
Mendaces vultus, assumptaque Gorlois arma,
Merlini dolus. O mihi tum si vita supersit,
Tu procul annosa pendebis fistula pinu
Multum oblita mihi, aut patriis mutata Camenis
Brittonicum strides, quid enim? omnia non licet uni
Non sperasse uni licet omnia; mi satis ampla
Merces, et mihi grande decus (sim ignotus in aevum
Tum licet, externo penitusque inglorius orbi)
Si me flava comas legat Usa, et potor Alauni,
Vorticibusque frequens Abra, et nemus omne Treantae,
Et Thamesis meus ante omnes, et fusca metallis
Tamara, et extremis me discant Orcades undis.
Ite domum impasti, domino iam non vacat, agni.
Haec tibi servabam lenta sub cortice lauri,
Haec, et plura simul, tum quae mihi pocula Mansus,
Mansus Chalcidicae non ultima gloria ripae,
Bina dedit, mirum artis opus, mirandus et ipse,
Et circum gemino caelaverat argumento:

under British law; then Igraine,[166] heavy with Arthur through a fateful deception, the lying appearance, the putting on of Gorlois's armor—Merlin's trick. O, if life then is left to me, you, pipe,[169] will hang far off on an aged pine tree, all forgotten by me; or, changed to homeland muses, you will whistle a British theme. What then? All things are not allowed for one man, to hope for all things is not allowed for one man; it will be large enough reward for me, and great glory for me (let me be forever unknown and utterly without fame in the outside world) if yellow-haired Ouse[175] reads me, and the drinker of the Alne, and Humber, thick with eddies, and every grove of the Trent, and my Thames above all, and the Tamar,[178] dark with minerals, and the Orkneys in their distant waves study me.

"Go home unfed, lambs; your master has no time for you now. These things I was keeping for you under the rubbery bark of the laurel,[180] these and more as well, the twin cups which Manso[181]—Manso, not the least glory of the Chalcidian[182] shore—gave me, a wonderful work of art, and he himself a wonder, and he had engraved it about with a double theme: in the middle the water of the Red Sea and the perfumed spring, the long shores of Arabia and the forests exuding balsam; among

166. Uther Pendragon appeared to Igraine in the form of her dead husband, Gorlois, King of Cornwall, and fathered Arthur (Geoffrey of Monmouth, *History of Britain* 8.19).

169. **fistula:** the pastoral pipe. Commentators debate whether Milton is abandoning pastoral poetry or Latin poetry.

175. **Usa:** the river Ouse, initiating a catalog of English rivers; **potor Alauni:** Camden says that both the Alne in Northumberland and the united Stour and Avon in Hampshire bore the Latin name *Alaunus.*

178. **Tamara:** The Tamar flows between Cornwall and Devonshire; **Orcades:** the Orkney Islands.

180. Milton probably got the idea of verses carved or written on laurel bark from Vergil, *Ec.* 5.13-14.

181. **Mansus:** See the headnote to *Manso.* Some have taken the cups to be symbolic of other gifts from Manso—copies of his books, perhaps.

182. **Chalcidicae:** Neapolitan. Naples was settled by colonists from Chalcis.

In medio rubri maris unda, et odoriferum ver,
Littora longa Arabum, et sudantes balsama silvae;
Has inter Phoenix divina avis, unica terris,
Caeruleum fulgens diversicoloribus alis,
Auroram vitreis surgentem respicit undis.
Parte alia polus omnipatens, et magnus Olympus,
Quis putet? hic quoque Amor, pictaeque in nube pharetrae,
Arma corusca, faces, et spicula tincta pyropo;
Nec tenues animas, pectusque ignobile vulgi
Hinc ferit, at circum flammantia lumina torquens,
Semper in erectum spargit sua tela per orbes
Impiger, et pronos nunquam collimat ad ictus;
Hinc mentes ardere sacrae, formaeque deorum.
Tu quoque in his, nec me fallit spes lubrica Damon,
Tu quoque in his certe es, nam quo tua dulcis abiret
Sanctaque simplicitas, nam quo tua candida virtus?
Nec te Lethaeo fas quaesivisse sub Orco,
Nec tibi conveniunt lacrimae, nec flebimus ultra;
Ite procul lacrimae, purum colit aethera Damon,
Aethera purus habet, pluvium pede reppulit arcum;
Heroumque animas inter, divosque perennes,
Aethereos haurit latices et gaudia potat
Ore sacro. Quin tu coeli post iura recepta
Dexter ades, placidusque fave quicunque vocaris,
Seu tu noster eris Damon, sive aequior audis

these the phoenix,[187] the divine bird, unique in the world, gleaming blue with its multicolored wings, watches Aurora rising from the glassy waves. In another part, the unbounded sky and great Olympus—who would have thought?—here also Love,[191] and in a cloud his colorful quivers, his gleaming arms, his torches, and his arrows coated with golden bronze. From here he does not strike at frivolous souls or the ignoble heart of the mob, but turning his flaming eye about, he always, tirelessly, casts his weapons upward into the spheres, and never aims a downward blow. From this source sacred minds catch fire, and the forms of the gods.

"You too are among these—and slippery hope does not deceive me, Damon—you too are surely among these, for where would your sweet and holy simplicity go, or your pure white virtue? Nor is it lawful to have looked for you down in Lethaean Orcus,[201] nor are tears fitting for you, and we will weep no longer. Be gone far away, tears. Damon inhabits the pure heavens;[203] in his purity he possesses the heavens, he spurns the rainbow with his foot. Among the souls of heroes and the eternal gods he drinks heavenly liquid and downs its joys with his holy mouth. So now, after receiving your due in heaven, you are at my right hand; favor me also in your kindness, however you are called: whether you will be our Damon, or whether you prefer Diodati, by which divine

187. It has been suggested that Milton borrowed details from *De Ave Phoenice*, attributed to Lactantius, one of his favorite theologians, or from Tasso's *Le Fenice*.

191. Plato distinguished between the vulgar and the heavenly Aphrodite (*Symposium* 180–85). Ficino adapted the distinction to his Christian Neoplatonism in *Commentary on Plato's Symposium* 2.6.

201. See *Elegy 7* 83n.

203. Daphnis is deified in Vergil, *Ec.* 5.56–59.

Diodatus, quo te divino nomine cuncti
Coelicolae norint, silvisque vocabere Damon.
Quod tibi purpureus pudor, et sine labe iuventus
Grata fuit, quod nulla tori libata voluptas,
En etiam tibi virginei servantur honores;
Ipse caput nitidum cinctus rutilante corona,
Laetaque frondentis gestans umbracula palmae
Aeternum perages immortales hymenaeos;
Cantus ubi, choreisque furit lyra mista beatis,
Festa Sionaeo bacchantur et Orgia thyrso.

name[210] all the gods know you, and you will be called Damon in the woodlands. Because blushing modesty and a youth without stain pleased you, because the joy of the marriage bed[213] was never tasted, lo, virginal honors are reserved for you. Girt about your shining head with a glowing crown,[215] and bearing the happy shade of a leafy palm,[216] you will partake forever in an immortal wedding,[217] where there is singing and the lyre rages in the midst of blessed dances, and orgiastic feasts have their bacchic celebration under the thyrsus[219] of Zion."

210. **divino nomine:** probably an allusion to Diodati's name, which means "God-given."

213. **tori:** Leonard, opposing the idea that Milton was interested in chastity to the point of disparaging marriage, translates *torus* as "bed" rather than "marriage bed." Cp. Rev. 14.4: "These are they which were not defiled with women."

215. **corona:** Cp. the "crown of glory" in 1 Pet. 5.4.

216. **palmae:** Cp. Rev. 7.9: "A great multitude, which no man could number . . . stood before the throne, and before the Lamb, clothed with white robes, and palms in their hands."

217. **hymenaeos:** Cp. Rev. 19.7: "Let us be glad and rejoice . . . for the marriage of the Lamb is come."

219. The thyrsus was a vine-leaved staff carried by Bacchic celebrants.

IN EFFIGIEI EIUS SCULPTOR

[*On the Engraver of His Portrait*]

Milton clearly felt that the frontispiece portrait to the 1645 *Poems,* engraved by the well-known artist William Marshall, did not do justice to his looks. He took his revenge by having the artist engrave these verses beneath the imperfect likeness. Marshall, having no Greek and expecting no attack, dutifully complied, thereby serving notice of his poor skill as an artist, his ignorance as a linguist, and his gullibility as a judge of men. The verses suggest that the engraving might better be regarded as Marshall's self-portrait.

Ἀμαθεῖ γεγράφθαι χειρὶ τήνδε μὲν εἰκόνα
Φαίης τάχ' ἂν πρὸς εἶδος αὐτοφυὲς βλέπων.
Τὸν δ' ἐκτυπωτὸν οὐκ ἐπιγνόντες φίλοι
Γελᾶτε φαύλου δυσμίμημα ζωγράφου.

You might readily say that this picture was drawn with an ignorant hand if you saw the real image; if you don't recognize the man being pictured, friends, laugh at this bad imitation of a worthless artist.

AD IOANNEM ROUSIUM, OXONIENSIS ACADEMIAE BIBLIOTHECARIUM

[*To John Rouse, Librarian of Oxford University*]

Soon after the 1645 *Poems* appeared, Milton sent a copy to Rouse, along with the eleven prose pamphlets he had so far published, for deposit in the Bodleian Library. Somehow the *Poems* was lost in transit, and Rouse requested a second copy. Milton sent one, enclosing a manuscript of this poem. Both the manuscript and, apparently, the book are in the Bodleian to this day.

De libro Poematum amisso, quem ille sibi denuo mitti postulabat, ut cum aliis nostris in Bibliotheca publica reponeret, Ode

Ode on a lost book of poems, which he asked to have sent to him again, so that he could put it in the public library with our others

"... if you don't recognize the man being pictured, friends, laugh at this bad imitation of a worthless artist."

Strophe 1

Gemelle cultu simplici gaudens liber,
Fronde licet gemina,
Munditieque nitens non operosa,
Quam manus attulit
Iuvenilis olim,
Sedula tamen haud nimii poetae;
Dum vagus Ausonias nunc per umbras
Nunc Britannica per vireta lusit
Insons populi, barbitoque devius
Indulsit patrio, mox itidem pectine Daunio
Longinquum intonuit melos
Vicinis, et humum vix tetigit pede;

Antistrophe

Quis te, parve liber, quis te fratribus
Subduxit reliquis dolo,
Cum tu missus ab urbe,
Docto iugiter obsecrante amico,
Illustre tendebas iter
Thamesis ad incunabula
Caerulei patris,
Fontes ubi limpidi
Aonidum, thyasusque sacer
Orbi notus per immensos
Temporum lapsus redeunte coelo,
Celeberque futurus in aevum?

1. The English and Latin works in the 1645 *Poems* had separate title pages and pagination.
10. **Daunio:** Italian.
18. **Thamesis:** the upper reaches of the Thames. Oxford lies at the confluence of the Thames and the Cherwell.
21. **Aonidum:** the Muses.

STROPHE 1

Twin-born book,[1] rejoicing in a single cover, though with a double leaf, and shining with unfussy neatness, which a youthful hand, earnest but not too much the poet, once bestowed while he amused himself wandering now through Italian shade and now through British greenery, unspoiled by people, and off by himself indulged his native lyre: soon in the same way with his Daunian[10] plectrum he sounded a far-off song for his neighbors, and scarcely touched the ground with his foot:

ANTISTROPHE

Who, little book, who stole you away by trickery from your brothers, when, sent from the city at the steady imploring of my learned friend, you were making the illustrious journey to the cradle of the Thames,[18] the blue father, where the clear fountains of the Aonides[21] are, and the sacred Bacchic dance known to the world across an immense lapse of time with the turning heavens, and to be renowned forever?

Strophe 2

Modo quis deus, aut editus deo
Pristinam gentis miseratus indolem
(Si satis noxas luimus priores
Mollique luxu degener otium)
Tollat nefandos civium tumultus,
Almaque revocet studia sanctus
Et relegatas sine sede Musas
Iam pene totis finibus Angligenum;
Immundasque volucres
Unguibus imminentes
Figat Apollinea pharetra,
Phineamque abigat pestem procul amne
Pegaseo?

STROPHE 2

But what god or offspring of a god,[25] having pity for the ancient character of our nation (if we have sufficiently atoned for our earlier crimes and our laziness corrupted with womanish luxury), might take away the accursed upheaval of our citizens, and in holiness recall the nourishing studies[30] and the banished Muses now almost totally without a home within all the territory of England, and with Apollo's quiver transfix the loathsome birds[33] hovering with their claws and drive the Phinean plague beyond the river of Pegasus?

Antistrophe

Quin tu, libelle, nuntii licet mala
Fide, vel oscitantia
Semel erraveris agmine fratrum,
Seu quis te teneat specus,
Seu qua te latebra, forsan unde vili
Callo tereris institoris insulsi,
Laetare felix; en iterum tibi
Spes nova fulget posse profundam
Fugere Lethen, vehique superam
In Iovis aulam remige penna;

ANTISTROPHE

But you, little book, though by the bad faith or weariness of the messenger you have wandered this once from the company of your brothers, whether a ditch keeps you, or some hiding place whence you will be rubbed by the vile skin of a stupid shopkeeper: cheer up, lucky one; behold, new hope shines again for you to be able to avoid deep Lethe,[45] and be borne to the high hall of Jove with your wing as oarsman.

25. Cp. Horace's appeal to an unnamed hero in *Odes* 1.2.25–52.
30. From 1642 to 1646, when it surrendered to Fairfax, Oxford was the Royalists' headquarters, and the usual activities of the university were suspended.
33. The prophet Phineas was punished by Zeus with blindness and visits from the Harpies until delivered by the Argonauts (Apollonius of Rhodes 2.178–310).
45. **Lethen:** the river of oblivion in Hades.

Strophe 3

Nam te Rousius sui
Optat peculi, numeroque iusto
Sibi pollicitum queritur abesse,
Rogatque venias ille cuius inclyta
Sunt data virum monumenta curae:
Teque adytis etiam sacris
Voluit reponi quibus et ipse praesidet
Aeternorum operum custos fidelis,
Quaestorque gazae nobilioris
Quam cui praefuit Ion,
Clarus Erechtheides,
Opulenta dei per templa parentis
Fulvosque tripodas, donaque Delphica
Ion Actaea genitus Creusa.

STROPHE 3

For Rouse wants you for his property and complains that, though you were promised to him, you are missing from the rightful list, and asks that you come—he into whose care have been given the famous monuments of men—and wished that you be placed in the sacred precincts over which he presides himself as the faithful guardian of eternal works, custodian of a nobler treasure[55] than that of which Ion, the famous descendant of Erechtheus, had charge in the opulent temples of his father the god, the yellow tripods and the Delphic gifts—Ion, born of Actaean[60] Creusa.

Antistrophe

Ergo tu visere lucos
Musarum ibis amoenos,
Diamque Phoebi rursus ibis in domum
Oxonia quam valle colit
Delo posthabita,
Bifidoque Parnassi iugo:
Ibis honestus,
Postquam egregiam tu quoque sortem
Nactus abis, dextri prece sollicitatus amici.
Illic legeris inter alta nomina
Authorum, Graiae simul et Latinae
Antiqua gentis lumina, et verum decus.

ANTISTROPHE

Therefore you will go to see the pleasant groves of the Muses, and you will go again to the divine house of Phoebus which he inhabits in the valley of Oxford, preferring it to Delos[65] and twin-peaked Parnassus; you will go in honor, since you also depart in possession of extraordinary luck, summoned by prayer of a beneficent friend. There you will be read among the greatest authorial names, the ancient lights and true glory of both the Greek race and the Latin.

Epodos

Vos tandem haud vacui mei labores,
Quicquid hoc sterile fudit ingenium;
Iam sero placidam sperare iubeo
Perfunctam invidia requiem, sedesque beatas

EPODE

Then you are not in vain, my labors, whatever that sterile talent has poured forth; now at last I order you to look forward to a calm rest, done with envy, and the happy home which good

55. Milton is thinking of Euripides' *Ion.* The hero, son of Apollo, becomes guardian of his shrine and its treasures at Delphi.

60. **Actaea:** Attic (from Acte, an early name for Attica).

65. **Delo:** Delos, birthplace of Apollo.

Quas bonus Hermes
Et tutela dabit solers Rousi,
Quo neque lingua procax vulgi penetrabit,
atque longe
Turba legentum prava facesset;
At ultimi nepotes,
Et cordatior aetas
Iudicia rebus aequiora forsitan
Adhibebit integro sinu.
Tum livore sepulto,
Si quid meremur sana posteritas sciet
Rousio favente.

Ode tribus constat Strophis totidemque Antistrophis una demum epodo clausis, quas, tametsi omnes nec versuum numero, nec certis ubique colis exacte respondeant, ita tamen secuimus, commode legendi potius, quam ad antiquos concinendi modos rationem spectantes. Alioquin hoc genus rectius fortasse dici monostrophicum debuerat. Metra partim sunt κατὰ σχέσιν, partim ἀπολελυμένα. Phaleucia quae sunt, spondaeum tertio loco bis admittunt, quod idem in secundo loco Catullus ad libitum fecit.

Hermes[77] and the wise protection of Rouse will provide, where the unruly tongue of the mob will not penetrate, and the degenerate crowd of readers stays far away. But future descendants and a more sensible age will perhaps make fairer judgments with an unprejudiced heart. Then, with spite buried, a sane posterity will, thanks to Rouse, know if we have deserved anything.

The ode consists of three strophes and as many antistrophes, closed at the end with one epode: which, although they do not all correspond exactly in the number of verses or everywhere in precise metrical units, still we have divided up this way, more for the sake of convenience in reading than observing the rule of the ancient forms of prosody. In other regards this form should perhaps more accurately be called "monostrophic." The metrics are partly "responsive" and partly "irregular." The lines that are Phaleucian twice allow a spondee in the third foot, which Catullus did freely in the second foot.

77. Hermes is the god of eloquence, roads, the lyre, and wisdom, and the conductor of shades.

EPIGRAM FROM *A DEFENSE OF THE ENGLISH PEOPLE*

Milton's *Defensio* was published in 1651, in answer to the *Defensio Regia Pro Carolo I* (1649) by the renowned classical scholar Claude de Saumaise, or Salmasius (1588–1653). Milton ridicules Salmasius' ignorance of English words and offers this epigram, an adaptation of Persius, *Prologue* 8–14, in which the imitated words are italicized.

Quis expedivit Salmasio suam Hundredam,
Picamque *docuit nostra verba conari*?
Magister artis venter, et Iacobei
Centum, exulantis viscera marsupii regis.
Quod si dolosi spes refulserit nummi,
Ipse Antichristi qui modo primatum Papae
Minatus uno est dissipare sufflatu,
Cantabit ultro Cardinalitium *melos.*

Who set Salmasius *loose* with his "hundreda,"[1] and *taught the magpie to try our vocabulary? His stomach is his schoolteacher,* and a hundred Jacobuses,[3] the innards of the exiled king's purse. *If hope of a dishonest penny glitters,* that man, who once threatened to blow away the supremacy of the papal antichrist[6] with one puff, will willingly *sing* the Cardinals' *tune.*

1. Saumaise mistakenly gave the plural of *hundred* as *hundreda* (*Defensio Regia* 204).
3. It was widely rumored that Charles I promised to reward Saumaise with a hundred Jacobuses (a gold coin valued at twenty-two shillings).
6. **primatum Papae:** Salmasius was also the author of *De Primatu Papae* (1645), which challenged papal authority.

EPIGRAMS FROM *A SECOND DEFENSE*

1. Salmasius died the year before Milton published his *Defensio Secunda* (1654). Milton explains that he wrote this epigram, centered on the old joke (Martial, *Epigrams* 3.2.1–5) that worthless books are good for wrapping fish, in the expectation that Salmasius would reply to his initial *Defensio* of 1652 (Yale 4:581).

Gaudete scombri, et quicquid est piscium salo,
Qui frigida hieme incolitis algentes freta;
Vestrum misertus ille Salmasius eques
Bonus amicire nuditatem cogitat;
Chartaeque largus apparat papyrinos
Vobis cucullos praeferentes Claudii
Insignia nomenque et decus Salmasii,
Gestetis ut per omne cetarium forum
Equitis clientes, scriniis mungentium
Cubito virorum, et capsulis gratissimos.

Rejoice, mackerels, and whatever fish there are in the sea[1] who, freezing, inhabit the frigid ocean in winter: out of pity for you, that good Sir Salmon[3] plans to clothe your nakedness and, generous with paper, is preparing papyrus hoods[6] for you, bearing the insignia, name, and honor of Claude Saumaise, so that as the knight's retainers you may bear them through the entire fish market, most welcome in the boxes and cartons of the men who wipe their noses on their elbows.[10]

1. This line parodies Catullus 31.13–14.
3. Milton puns on "Salmasius" and the Latin *salmo* (salmon).
6. **cucullos:** both "cowls" and "conical wrappers for merchandise," as also in Martial, *Epigrams* 3.2.5.
10. It was an ancient commonplace that fishmongers wiped their noses on their sleeves.

2. This adaptation of Juvenal 2.20–21 was directed against Alexander More, an opponent of the regicide whom Milton accused of having seduced Salmasius' maid.

de virtute loquutus
Clunem agitas: ego te ceventem, More, verebor?

having talked of virtue, you hunt for ass; shall I be in awe of you, More, when you grind your hips?

Late Masterpieces

Gul. Faithorne ad Vivum
Delin. et sculpsit.
Ioannis Miltoni Effigies Ætat: 62.
1670.

Milton at sixty-two, engraving by William Faithorne
from the frontispiece to Milton's *History of Britain* (1670).

Introduction to *Paradise Lost*

Milton became entirely blind in 1652, just a short while before the death of his first wife, Mary Powell Milton, followed six weeks later by the death of their infant son, John. He married again in 1656. In 1658 Katharine Woodcock Milton died of complications arising from childbirth, again followed about six weeks later by the death of their infant daughter, Katharine. The political cause to which Milton had devoted two decades of his life suffered a resounding defeat with Charles II's ascent to the throne in 1660. Through this time of loss and reversal, Milton kept busy on various prose projects, including his theological treatise *Christian Doctrine,* a Latin thesaurus, and his *History of Britain.* He translated a group of Psalms in 1653. He wrote the occasional sonnet. Then, probably before the Restoration, he shook off potential depression, concentrated his powers, and began composing the greatest long poem in the English language. "His great works," Samuel Johnson declared, "were performed under discountenance, and in blindness, but difficulties vanished at his touch; he was born for whatever is arduous" (Thorpe 88).

Though Edward Phillips did not mention these dates in his life of Milton, he told John Aubrey that the poem was begun "about 2 years before the king came in, and finished about three years after the king's restoration" (xxviii). Although Milton associated literary creativity with the temperate Mediterranean climate that had nurtured Homer and Vergil, he himself composed *Paradise Lost* only during the winter, from the autumnal to the vernal equinox. Various secretaries copied it down. Milton's habit was to rise early in the morning with "ten, twenty, or thirty verses" (Darbishire 73) ready for dictation. If his amanuensis happened to be late, he had a little joke ready, and "would complain, saying *he wanted to be milked*" (Darbishire 33).

A major poem had long been his chief ambition. As early as *At a Vacation Exercise* in 1628, the nineteen-year-old undergraduate had magically suspended the expectations of a humorous ritual occasion to evoke the highest raptures of epic, "where the deep transported mind may soar/Above the wheeling poles, and at Heav'n's door/Look in," and "sing of secret things that came to pass/When beldam Nature in her cradle was." For a time, as references in *Manso* and *Epitaph for Damon* reveal, he considered a specifically British poem shaped from

Arthurian materials. Such a work would be "doctrinal and exemplary to a nation" (*RCG*, p. 841). We do not know precisely why Milton abandoned this plan. He might have come to feel that a patriotic epic was simply too provincial, or that the choice of an early British king for a hero would commit the work to some degree of monarchism; then, too, he might have realized as maturity settled on him that he could admire Spenser without trying to duplicate his achievement.

The first plans for a work on the Fall of man in the Garden of Eden appear in four outlines for a tragic drama in the Trinity College manuscript (*CMS*), probably drafted in the early 1640s. The third of these is called "Paradise Lost." Adam and Eve do not take the stage until after the Fall, presumably because their "first naked glory" (*PL* 9.1115) could not be accommodated in a fallen theater. In the fourth and final version, which shifts from the outline format to narrative prose, Milton roughs in some features of *Paradise Lost.* Satan has a new prominence. The work will end with the expelling angel showing Adam a pageant about the fallen world he is soon to enter.

The Book

Paradise Lost was published in 1667 by the bookseller Samuel Simmons, whose London shop was near Aldersgate. The Pierpont Morgan Library in New York possesses a manuscript of Book 1 of the poem in the hand of a copyist, and corrected by as many as five other hands, that was used to set the type for this edition (see Darbishire 1931 for a photographic facsimile). The contract stipulated that Milton was to be paid five pounds for the manuscript, another five pounds upon the sale of a first edition of thirteen hundred copies, and yet another five pounds upon the sale of a second edition of the same size. The earliest title page of the 1667 quarto identifies Paradise Lost as "A POEM Written in TEN BOOKS By *JOHN MILTON.*" Sales were apparently sluggish. Through 1668 and 1669, the edition was issued with four more title pages, as Simmons added Milton's note on unrhyming verse and his prose arguments summarizing the action of the poem book by book. When the first printing finally sold out in April 1669, Milton was paid a second five pounds.

It was perhaps Dryden's announcement in April 1674 that he would transform *Paradise Lost* into a heroic opera (this "never acted" opera was published as *The State of Innocence* in 1677) that led Simmons to print a second and octavo edition of the epic in July 1674. This book contained prefatory poems by Samuel Barrow (in Latin) and Andrew Marvell (in English). The epic was "amended, enlarged, and differently disposed as to the number of books, by his own hand, that is by his own appointment [by someone acting as his agent]" (Edward Phillips in Darbishire, 1932, 75). The shift from ten to twelve books meant dividing the original Book 7 into the new Books 7 and 8, with the addition of four new lines at the beginning of Book 8; the long Book 10 of the first edition was divided into Books 11 and 12, with five new lines at the beginning of Book 12. There were four other major revisions (the reworking of 1.5104–5, the expansion at 5.636–41, the addition of 11.485–87, the alteration of 11.551). The authority of the second edition cannot be doubted in these matters. An unwell Milton made an oral will on or about July 20, 1674, two weeks after the second publication of *Paradise Lost,* and died on November 9, 1674. The second edition of *Paradise Lost* was the last printing over which he exerted control.

There are thirty-seven substantive differences between the two editions. In thirteen of these, the quarto text supplies the superior reading; in only eight is the octavo text superior; editors differ over the remaining sixteen (Moyles 22–26). It would seem from this evidence that editors should not, as many have claimed to do, adopt the 1674 octavo as a copy text and automatically follow it with regard to the accidentals of spelling and punctuation (Moyles 28). There are over eight hundred variants of this kind between the two editions. We have treated each as a separate case rather than defer to the rule of the copy text.

Simmons published a third edition in 1678. A printer named Brabazon Aylmer purchased the poem from Simmons in 1680, then sold half of it to a young entrepreneur named Jacob Tonson. He was Dryden's chief publisher and would become known for his beautiful editions of Shakespeare and Spenser. But Milton was his great love and, happily enough for a businessman, his great moneymaker too. He and Aylmer printed a folio-size fourth edition of the epic in 1688, adding illustrations, a frontispiece portrait of Milton, and an epigram by Dryden in which Milton is said to be the union of Homer and Vergil. Tonson purchased Aylmer's half of the poem in 1691. He also obtained from Aylmer the manuscript of Book 1 now owned by the Pierpont Morgan Library. For the sixth edition, of 1695, Tonson added 321 pages of explanatory notes by Patrick Hume; no other English poem had ever been so lavishly annotated. Tonson and his family would print *Paradise Lost,* and other works by Milton, in various configurations again and again throughout the eighteenth century. When asked which poet had brought him the greatest financial profit, Tonson without hesitation replied "Milton" (Lynch 126). He had his portrait painted holding a copy of *Paradise Lost.*

In 1732 a cantankerous, seventy-year-old academic named Richard Bentley, then England's foremost classicist and a specialist in textual emendation, published a notorious edition of *Paradise Lost.* Believing that he had purified textual corruption in classical authors such as Manilius, Bentley brought the same methods to Milton's modern epic. Blind, Milton was unable to correct wayward copyists. But Bentley, suspecting a more deliberate and insidious errancy, posited the existence of a "phantom" editor. Befuddled by Milton's learning and linguistic precision, this unknown person rewrote the text to suit his own imbecility. Today the Bentley edition seems a work of glaring subjectivity. Truths about the epic, such as the immense thoughtfulness manifest in its details, do not break into the editor's awareness because his attention is devoted wholly to his own theory and method. It was hardly a compliment to Milton to suppose that *Paradise Lost* as readers knew it was a work of genius systematically effaced by the work of a moron. But modern critics such as William Empson, Christopher Ricks, and John Leonard have been inspired by Bentley's scrutiny of the minutiae of Milton's style. Textual emendation became the rage in Shakespeare studies in the eighteenth century and is still widely practiced today. The aberration of Bentley's *Paradise Lost* aside, it never caught on among Milton's editors.

The next notable edition was Thomas Newton's beautiful two-volume variorum of 1749. Its copious and often unequaled annotations were mostly reprinted, with the addition of many new ones, in the 1826 variorum of Milton's entire poetic works assembled by Reverend Henry Todd. Anyone who becomes seriously curious about the meaning of a particular word or passage in Milton will want to go back to Todd and Newton, and behind them to the first of Milton's annotators, Patrick Hume. They will also want to explore works such as Jonathan Richardson's *Explanatory Notes and Remarks on Milton's Paradise Lost* (1734) and James Paterson's *A Complete Commentary with Etymological, Explanatory, Critical and Classical Notes on Milton's "Paradise Lost"* (1744). There are many subtleties, exactitudes, and points of information in these notes for which we, like other modern editors, have simply found no room.

Among the editions of the last century or so, we were most surprised to discover the sustained elucidation of A. W. Verity, who is largely forgotten today; besides the excellence of their commentary, his notes teem with examples of Romantic and Victorian imitation of Milton and will prove useful in future studies of that subject. In working on this edition, we came to think of Verity as the unknown god of Milton annotation. We also paid especially close attention to the thoughtful notes of Alastair Fowler and John Leonard, and consulted Merritt Hughes, Douglas Bush, Scott Elledge, and Roy Flannagan, among others.

Cosmos

Heaven sits atop Milton's cosmos. Beneath it lies Chaos. We sense that both of these realms have, so to speak, been around forever. It would be a nice point in Milton's theology to ask whether Chaos precedes Heaven or vice versa, since the very existence of God seems to require an abode, and therefore a Heaven of some sort, while on the other hand Chaos appears to be the precondition of all creations, including those of the Son, the angels, and Heaven. As the poem begins, these two established cosmic areas have been joined by two new spaces. At the bottom of Chaos stands Hell, the elder of the new realms. Between Heaven and Chaos, suspended on a golden chain affixed to Heaven (2.1004–6), lies the most recent of God's creations: our Earth, including the planets and stars surrounding it.

Readers of the poem are usually familiar with dualistic visions of Heaven, in which the realm of the divine is carefully separated from such imperfect earthly things as body and alteration. But Milton's universe is monistic. Everything stems from "one first matter" (5.472). Instead of excluding materiality, pleasure, pain, appetite, sexuality, and time from Heaven, Milton welcomes them in. As on Earth, day and night alternate in Heaven; Heaven's night is not the darkness of Earth's but rather comparable to earthly twilight (5.627–29, 645–46, 685–86). Beneath the very Mount of God is a cave "Where light and darkness in perpetual round/Lodge and dislodge by turns, which makes through Heav'n/Grateful vicissitude, like day and night" (6.6–8). Milton's God, satisfying an appetite for vicissitude, resides on time.

Angels live large in a Heaven that is vast but not infinite. When Satan leaves the military camp near the deity, he and his followers retreat to the "palace of great Lucifer" in north Heaven (5.760). Apparently, on the model of the court and the country, angels live in estates various distances from the mountainous throne of God. Buildings designed by angelic architects, radiant with gems and precious metals, grace the realm. The orders of angels (Seraphim, Cherubim, Thrones, Dominations, Virtues, Powers, Principalities, Archangels, Angels) were strictly hierarchical in traditional Christian thought. At times in Milton, the terms carry their old hierarchical force, but often they are used interchangeably, as a pool of synonyms for the generic angel. Milton is rather insistent on the point that while likenesses between Heaven and Earth may be necessary fictions, they could also be ontologically sound (5.571–76). "O Earth, how like to Heav'n!" Satan exclaims (9.99). Heaven has vales, streams, breezes, trees, flowers, and vines. The vegetation produces ambrosial food, "the growth of Heaven" (5.635). Heaven and Earth, like spirit and matter or men and angels, differ "but in degree, of kind the same" (5.490).

Although Chaos can be studied in terms of antecedents in classical literature and philosophy (Chambers 1963), its appearance in the epic owes its problematic character to Milton's theology. Chaos is infinite, and filled by a ubiquitous God who has nonetheless withdrawn his creative will from chaotic matter (7.168–73). None of the categorical binaries established during the creation of Genesis inhere in Chaos. It is neither this nor that, "neither sea, nor shore, nor air, nor fire,/But all these in their pregnant causes mixed/Confus'dly" (2.912–14); therefore Satan, as he traverses this indeterminate space, confusedly mixes locomotions, "And swims or sinks, or wades, or creeps, or flies" (2.950). The "embryon atoms" (2.900) of Chaos are "the womb of Nature" (2.911), the pure potential that the Son first circumscribes with golden compasses when creating our universe (7.225–31) and will doubtless use again in creating new worlds (2.915–16). Chaos cannot be good until God has infused it with creative order. It is at least morally neutral, at best thoroughly praiseworthy, as a part of the process by which God makes and sustains all things.

But alongside the language of atomism, Milton gives us a mythic Chaos, personified as the ruler of his realm, or rather its "Anarch" (2.988), since Chaos is by definition without rule. This Chaos, speaking for his consort, Night, and for a shadowy pack of Hesiodic creatures and personifications (2.963–67), expresses his resentment over recent losses (the creations of Hell and our universe) and supports Satan's mission on the assumption that "Havoc and spoil and ruin are my gain" (2.1009). We thus arrive at paradox. Theologically, Chaos is neutral or better. Mythically, in terms of the epic narrative, Chaos is the ally of Satan.

Jewish and Christian theologians have sometimes distinguished the Bible from other Mesopotamian creation myths in which the god-hero defeats a chaos monster, out of whose slain body the world is made; in Genesis, by contrast, the world is initially good, and God affirms its goodness on every day of the creation. Evil appears with the fall of man (Ricoeur 172, 175–210), though of course the enigmatic presence of the snake promises a backstory of some kind. For Ricoeur the matter at stake here is whether religious symbols are recessive, and must always point backward to the defeat of Chaos, or whether they can look toward novel futures, as is apparently the case with the messianic and eschatological strands of Judaism and Christianity. Regina Schwartz, defending Milton's mythic Chaos, argues that the separation of evil from the Creation is not really true of the Bible, and is patently untrue of *Paradise Lost,* where Chaos gives Satan his nod of approval. All of God's revelations, all of Satan's subsequent defeats, echo the initial triumph over Chaos, and redemption itself is but a repetition of that original victory (Schwartz 8–39; see also Leonard 2000, xx–xxi).

John Rumrich, defending the theological Chaos, notes that the irony of Chaos's expression of solidarity with Satan lies in the old Anarch's failure to understand that Satanic evil is rigid, not anarchic, a fixed posture of defiance and disobedience (1995, 1035–44). We see this in Book 10, where Sin and Death are building a bridge through Chaos to link Earth and Hell, and a double-crossed Chaos seethes at this new incursion into his realm:

> On either side
> Disparted Chaos overbuilt exclaimed,
> And with rebounding surge the bars assailed,
> That scorned his indignation. (10.415-18)

Chaos, Rumrich maintains, is "a part of the deity, arguably feminine, over which the eternal father does not exercise control, from which, in other words, the father is absent as an active, governing agent" (1995, 1043; see also Danielson 32–57).

Expelled from Heaven, the rebel angels fall for nine days and nights through Chaos to Hell (6.871), which "Yawning received them whole, and on them closed" (6.875). They land on a burning sulfurous lake. After spending another nine days and nights stretched out dazed or unconscious on this lake (1.50–53), they awaken to the baleful prospect of Hell. Milton famously describes it as "darkness visible" (1.63), a place where fire burns without giving off light. Its purpose is not clear to the fallen angels. Among the first topics addressed in Hell is whether the Hell is for punishment or confinement (1.146–52).

In Milton's day the idea of Hell and its eternal torments was just entering a period of declining popularity among educated Europeans (Walker). Americans in particular, remembering such figures as Jonathan Edwards, tend to associate Puritanism with resistance to this trend. Milton exposes the simplicity of this view. His narrator introduces Hell as a "dungeon" for "torture without end" (1.61–69). But beyond the nine days in burning sulfur, we do not observe much in the way of punishment. To be sure, there are the more or less classical touches of the devils' periodic exposure to the extremes of ice and fire (2.596–603); the frustrating waters of Lethe, which shrink from seekers of oblivion (2.604–14); the terrifying monsters bred in Hell (2.622–28); the annual metamorphosis of the demons into serpents (10.572–77). But nothing here approaches the individualized tortures inflicted over and over on the inmates of Dante's Hell. Perhaps the difference lies in the fact that Milton's Hell is inhabited by fallen angels only, whereas Dante's is peopled. But there is no direct allusion in *Paradise Lost* to tortures awaiting the damned in the future. William Empson, a critic acutely attuned to the idea of God as torturer, found no evidence of this despicable notion in *Paradise Lost*: "Milton's God is not interested in torture, and never suggests that he uses it to improve people's characters" (1965, 273). For Milton, one has the impression, exile from God is the primal punishment, and all others merely the flash points of low imaginations.

As for confinement, the only exit from Hell is through a locked gate. But the key has been entrusted to Sin (2.774–77, 850–53, 871–89). She alone can unlock the gate, and does, and is incapable of closing it. At the end of time, Hell may indeed become a dungeon of torment (10.629–37), the universe's vacuum-cleaner bag, but in the meantime devils will possess the fallen earth, especially its air. Milton's Hell is more importantly a spiritual condition. "The mind is its own place," Satan declares, "and in itself/Can make a Heav'n of Hell, a Hell of Heav'n" (1.254–55). It can certainly do the second, as we see in the birth of Sin from the mind of Satan. Out of the "darkness" of a painful headache, "flames thick and fast" appear (2.754): a precise echo of Hell's "darkness visible." Even in Heaven, Satan has Hell within him, "nor from Hell/One step no more than from himself can fly/By change of place" (4.21–23).

The first half of *Paradise Lost* begins with Milton's search for a Heavenly Muse who was present at the Creation, "and with mighty wings outspread/Dove-like sat'st brooding on the vast abyss" (1.20–21). Only with this Muse illuminating what is dark in him, raising and supporting what is low in him, can Milton create the poem. The second half of *Paradise Lost* begins in Book 7 with a direct and expanded account of this miracle. It is the perfect fit between inspiration and subject matter: the metaphorical creation of the poem now recounts the actual Creation. This world, the handiwork of God, was the single greatest stimulus to Milton's imagination.

We find many examples of this literary excitement in Milton's treatment of astronomy. He met the blind Galileo in 1638 or 1639, when the Inquisition had confined him to his villa outside of Florence. The "Tuscan artist" is the only contemporary mentioned in the epic. There are three explicit references (1.287–91, 3.588–90, 5.261–63). To these must be added passages that allude to one or another of Galileo's discoveries, such as newly sighted stars (7.382–84), the nature of the Milky Way (7.577–81), the phases of Venus (7.366), the moons of Jupiter (8.148–52), and the freshly detailed description of the moon (7.375–78, 8.145–48). This fascination extends to other matters concerning the new astronomy of the seventeenth century. Milton returns four times to the question of whether there has been from the beginning, or may be in the future, a plurality of inhabited worlds (2.912, 7.191, 7.621–22, 8.148–52). He leaves open debated matters such as whether the earth rotates on its axis (4.591–95). When he writes of the "three different motions" of the earth (8.130), we can infer a somewhat detailed knowledge of Copernicus (Babb 81–82), the champion of the heliocentric universe, who wrote at length about the three motions (daily rotation, annual revolution about the sun, and the slow movement about the ecliptic, or "trepidation," causing the precession of the equinoxes).

On the large question of whether to prefer the modern "Copernican" heliocentric model or the ancient "Ptolemaic" geocentric model of the universe, Milton has Raphael, Adam's first angelic educator, insist on the undecidability of such matters (8.66–178). But it would have been impossible to represent cosmic space with any precision without making a choice, and in point of fact the design of the poem's universe is Ptolemaic. Earth is the still point of the turning world. The spheres of the moon, sun, Mercury, Venus, Mars, Jupiter, and Saturn turn about a central Earth. Beyond them is the eighth sphere of the fixed stars, so called because they do not appear to change their positions with regard to one another. The ninth is the so-called crystalline sphere, whose vibrations cause the "trepidation" (3.483). Finally, the primum mobile, the outer circle moved directly by God, encases this entire mesh of spheres within spheres.

Did Milton see the heavens through a telescope? Might he, to broach the most exciting thought of all, have looked through Galileo's telescope? Such speculations, common in the discipline of Milton studies, are inspired by his epic's unprecedented aesthetics of space. If Milton ultimately sided with the ancients in universe design, his rendering of the great vistas both seen and traversed by space-traveling angels opens a whole new area in modern literary sublimity. "Milton's canvas in *Paradise Lost* is the vastest used by an English artist" (Nicolson 1960, 187). Dante's universe is finished. Milton's is a work in progress. The novelties of Earth and Hell have reorganized space itself; more novelties can be anticipated. Novelty in the representation of space is a conscious literary feature of the epic, and stands for its modernity. When Satan throws his shield over his back, Milton interposes, between our mental sight and its object, the "optic glass" of Galileo:

> the broad circumference
> Hung on his shoulders like the moon, whose orb
> Through optic glass the Tuscan artist views

At evening from the top of Fesole,
Or in Valdarno, to descry new lands,
Rivers or mountains in her spotty globe. (1.286–91)

Homer had compared the brightness of Achilles' shield to the moon. Milton switches the focus from brightness, so crucial in Greek poetics, to size, so crucial in his poetics, and relocates the old simile inside the circle of Galileo's telescope. This invention, he implies, is the only modern device to expand the imaginative range of poetry, to provide a worldly conceptualization of what it means to describe immortals and inquire into the ways of God. Notice how, once Galileo is introduced, the passage forgets Satan and the narrative line of the poem to celebrate the wandering curiosity of Galileo's viewing and descrying eye. For Milton, the Tuscan artist represents curiosity rewarded: despite Catholic dogmatism, Galileo wanted to see, and he did see, which is what the blind narrator of *Paradise Lost* seeks in his invocation to light at the opening of Book 3.

Many of the poem's best sidereal effects derive from what Alastair Fowler calls "an entire fictive astronomy," whose implications Milton works out "with ingenuity reminiscent of science fiction" (1998, 35). Before the Fall, Milton postulates, the path of the sun never deviates from the equator. The axis of the earth is perfectly parallel to the axis of the sun. The sun is always in Aries. There is no precession of equinoxes. Day and night are always of equal duration. There are no seasons. Within the beautiful simplicity of this system, Milton arranges the various journeys and arrivals of his poem. An extraordinary number of important things happen at the four cardinal points of the day, dawn and dusk, noon and midnight (Cirillo 1962).

Allusions to the zodiac and the constellations are often both realistic and symbolic. Milton rarely underlines, rarely sticks an elbow in our ribs. When Satan leaves our world in Book 10, "Betwixt the Centaur and the Scorpion steering / His zenith, while the Sun in Aries rose" (328–29), the author expects a very great deal of his reader. She must know that the constellation Anguis, the body of the serpent held by Ophiuchus, lies between the Centaur and the Scorpion. She must recall that, some 5,833 lines ago, Satan entered our world (3.555–61), and Milton described his view in such a way that he must have been gazing out from the head of Anguis. A reader able to put all this together realizes that Satan enters through the head and exits from the tail of the serpent. She appreciates a scatological joke. She is reminded of eating and digestion, which is rather a serious matter in *Paradise Lost.* She recalls with a dawning sense of complexity that Satan in Eden possesses the serpent through its mouth. And so on. As one of the finest of Milton's eighteenth-century commentators put it, "A reader of Milton must be always upon duty; he is surrounded with sense, it rises in every line, every word is to the purpose. . . . All has been considered, and demands and merits observation" (Richardson in Darbishire 1932, 315).

It will not surprise close students of Milton to learn that there is a passage in the poem that apparently calls into question everything we have said about the energy, originality, and sublimity of his cosmos. For what are we to make of Raphael's dismissive rebuke to the ambitions of astronomers (8.66–178)? God will laugh at their attempts to divulge his secrets. Adam is advised to leave the heavens to their own workings: "be lowly wise" (173). The speech is not, as it has sometimes been taken to be, an all-out attack on the new learning that elsewhere seems to intrigue and inspire the poet. God is in fact pictured laughing at the old Ptolemaic astronomers, adding orbits within orbits and strange counterpressures ("build, unbuild") in order to make the model fit the appearances (Babb 88):

> perhaps to move
> His laughter at their quaint opinions wide
> Hereafter, when they come to model heav'n
> And calculate the stars, how they will wield
> The mighty frame, how build, unbuild, contrive
> To save appearances, how gird the sphere
> With centric and eccentric scribbled o'er,
> Cycle and epicycle, orb in orb. (8.77–84)

The angel also insists that man is not the only being who must discipline his curiosity; the workings of the universe have been kept secret from "man or angel" (see also 7.122–24). And no doubt Raphael has a point in maintaining that the correctness of this or that celestial picture makes no difference to life on Earth, which must be the focus of our wisdom.

Still, censuring a desire to understand the heavens seems directly contrary in spirit to the passage on Satan's shield, with its excited shift of focus to the knowledge-hungry eyes of Galileo surveying the moon. Perhaps Nicolson was right in supposing that there were "two persistent aspects of Milton's personality, one satisfied with proportion and limitation, the other revelling in the luxuriant and the unrestrained" (1960, 186). Then again, it is possible that the dismissal of astronomy belongs not to a conflict between contentment and aspiration but to the structure of aspiration. This divine disapproval could be viewed as a scientific expression of the general sense of trespass Milton encounters when approaching God. "May I express thee unblamed" (3.3)? He cannot reach the heights without taking liberties.

Theology

Milton's theology is systematic, Christian, Protestant, and for the most part quite standard. That much is evident from his epic argument, which incorporates the familiar locales, actors, and events of Christian orthodoxy: Heaven, Hell, an almighty and all-knowing deity, hateful rebel angels, benevolent unfallen angels, Adam and Eve, a garden Paradise on Earth, the Fall, Original Sin, the penalty of mortality, and, in prospect, satisfaction of that penalty through sacrifice of God's only begotten Son. Indeed, this large conformity has permitted generations of Milton scholars to downplay or ignore his unorthodoxy. Yet, despite the substantially ordinary Christianity of *Paradise Lost,* Milton did endorse various theological opinions deemed heretical, some criminally so in the view of seventeenth-century civil and ecclesiastical authorities.

A few of these unorthodox beliefs figure crucially in *Paradise Lost.* Most do not. On the one hand, Milton's advocacy of adult baptism by immersion, for example, and his rejection of obligatory Sabbath observation, though significant enough in the religious politics of the seventeenth century, do not bear on his epic. Vitalist monism and insistence on creation *ex deo,* on the other hand, are grand generative heresies foundational to the fictional world imagined by Milton—its spiritual-natural ground rules, as detailed in the preceding section. The three great religious debates of seventeenth-century England, and the heresies that correspond to them, are even more overtly pertinent, especially to the declared intention of the epic narrative to "justify the ways of God to men." The first of these controversies concerns the means of salvation (soteriology); the second, church government (ecclesiology); and the third, the status of the Son of God (Christology).

Most Christians in a relatively tolerant age would deem Milton's theological opinions as they relate to the first two of these controversies unremarkable and, in any case, his own business. But his opinions concerning the Son of God still register as heretical according to most Christian sects. They have also been a focus of sometimes heated scholarly controversy for nearly two centuries, since the manuscript of his theological treatise, *Christian Doctrine,* was discovered in 1823. The longest chapter of the treatise criticizes the orthodox doctrine of the Trinity as a logical impossibility devoid of scriptural authority and depicts the Son as a distinctly lesser God: the first of all creatures, begotten in time, and variously inferior to his father. That Milton's arguments should therefore be classified as Arian and contrary to Nicene formulations ("true God from true God . . . of one essence with the Father") was the seemingly inescapable conclusion endorsed by theologically informed Milton scholars from the time of Bishop Sumner, the original translator of the treatise, through the era of C. S. Lewis and Maurice Kelley in the mid–twentieth century. Orthodox believers who saw Milton as a bulwark of traditional Christianity were discomfited, the unorthodox heartened. Thus in 1826 the American Unitarian clergyman William Ellery Channing, a forerunner of Transcendentalism, enthusiastically grouped Milton with other celebrated seventeenth-century antitrinitarians: "our Trinitarian adversaries are perpetually ringing in our ears the names of Fathers and Reformers. We take MILTON, LOCKE, and NEW-

TON, and place them in our front, and want no others to oppose to the whole army of great names on the opposite side. Before these intellectual suns, the stars of self-named orthodoxy 'hide their diminished heads' " (35–36).

Readers who found *Paradise Lost* nonetheless orthodox comforted themselves with the often repeated observation that before the discovery of the treatise readers better informed theologically than their twentieth-century counterparts failed to suspect Milton's epic of heresy. C. S. Lewis reasoned that Milton when he composed his epic must have deliberately set aside his theological eccentricities in order to appeal to the majority of Christian readers (90–91). This surmise segued into the still current argument that because the theological treatise is inconsistent with the epic, the former should not be relied on as a guide to understanding the latter (Patrides 1976; Campbell et al. 110).

Such claims simply do not hold water. John Toland, writing Milton's life in 1698, declined to defend *Paradise Lost* "against those people who brand [it] with heresy" (128), indicating that such complaints were fairly common even before the discovery of the treatise. Unlike Toland, Jonathan Richardson, writing in 1734, says he cannot in good conscience "pass over in silence another conjecture which some have made, . . . that Milton was an Arian; and this is built on certain passages in *Paradise Lost*" (xlix). Theologically acute readers like Daniel Defoe (1660–1731) objected to Milton's account of the Son's exaltation (5.600–615) for laying, in Defoe's words, a "foundation for the corrupt doctrine of Arius" (75). A century later, shortly after *Christian Doctrine* was published, Thomas Macaulay remarked that "we can scarcely conceive that any person could have read *Paradise Lost* without suspecting him of [Arianism]" (3). Suspicion falls short of conviction, however, and unsupported by the evidence of the theological treatise, the Arianism of the epic is "no other than a conjecture" (Richardson, xlix). The mutedness of the epic's heretical account of the Son has been persuasively attributed to Milton's discretion in an intolerant age and the narrative disposition of epic (Rajan 23–31). Milton's main goal in *Paradise Lost* is to tell a story, not to argue doctrine.

The challenge to this commonsense observation mounted by W. B. Hunter, C. A. Patrides, and J. H. Adamson was complicated, recondite, and to the embarrassment of Milton scholarship, highly successful. Hunter originally argued that Milton's version of the godhead exemplified a not always unorthodox strain of early church opinion, called "subordinationism," which conceived of the Christian Trinity in terms of Platonic hypostases. Ralph Cudworth does in 1678 use the key term *subordination* in explaining the beliefs of the "Platonic Christian" and in asserting that such beliefs were consistent with those of "the generality of Christian doctors for the first three hundred years after the apostles' times" (2:417). This claim is not controversial, but it has no bearing on Milton's alleged orthodoxy. Like Arius before him, Milton was not a Platonic theologian, not when it came to his insistence on the absolute singularity of infinite God or on the finite existence of the Son. And even if Milton had been one of Cudworth's Platonic Christians, by the seventeenth century the Platonist version of the Christian Trinity did qualify as heretical. The subordinationism attributed to Milton is in short, per Michael Bauman's definitive formulation, "not orthodox, and Milton does not teach it" (1987, 133). Despite these flaws, Hunter's argument prevailed for an entire generation, so that in scholarship from the 1970s and '80s one generally finds the evasive and misleading label "subordinationist" in discussions of Milton's depiction of the Son.

Less controversial by far are Milton's opinions on how salvation occurs, perhaps because these opinions are now predominant among orthodox Christians and because Milton's God himself details them in a plain theological exposition difficult to misconstrue (3.173–202). During Milton's lifetime the Calvinist theory of salvation, and predestination as its distinctive tenet, reigned in England and especially in the Puritan culture that nurtured the young poet. Opposed to Calvinist orthodoxy was Arminianism, so called after the Dutch clergyman Jacobus Arminius (1560–1609), whose deviations from determinist doctrine were condemned at the grand Calvinist council of the early seventeenth century, the Synod of Dort (1618–19). According to articles endorsed at Dort, neither the blessed nor the damned can influence their respective fates. For the sake of his glory, God extends saving grace to a few utterly depraved sinners, thereby expressing his mercy. Also for his glory's sake, but additionally to exemplify divine justice, God consigns the rest of humanity (a large majority) to eternal torment. As for human liberty, even unfallen Adam and Eve were never free to obey, as Calvin insists: "God foreknew what end man was to have before he created him, and consequently foreknew because he so ordained by his decree" (3.23.7).

Arminians, by contrast, held that human beings are created free and, once fallen, receive sufficient grace to effect salvation, provided that they embrace the opportunity rather than reject it. The dependence of such a moral framework on human choice seems to have struck Calvin as a self-evident slight to divine omnipotence, as if "God ordained nothing except to treat man according to his own deserts" (3.23.7). The notion that the deity would leave individual human beings to determine their own fates roused Calvin's indignation. Four main claims distinguish the Arminians' "barren invention," as he called it (3.23.7). First, God's grace is universal, extended to all humanity. Second, this grace is not irresistible, which is to say, as an anti-Calvinistic Thomas Jefferson insists in his summary of Arminian beliefs, "man is always *free* and at liberty to receive or reject grace." Third, as Jefferson continues, divine justice "would not permit [God] to punish men for crimes they are predestinated to commit" (1:554). And last, foreknowledge and causation are distinct, even in a time line created, governed, and immutably foreseen by an omnipotent and omniscient God.

In England before the 1640s, clergy who held Arminius's heterodox opinions regarding salvation tended to be high-ranking and conservative, adhering to and even embellishing sacramental ritual and set liturgical forms that to Puritan sensibilities smacked of Roman Catholicism. This religiously and politically conservative English clergy presided over a top-down episcopal hierarchy whose regime complemented and reinforced the Stuart monarchy's civil sway—hence the so-called "thorough" government of church and state during the 1630s, when king and bishop sought to rule without Parliamentary interference. Continental followers of Arminius, by contrast, remained largely Calvinist in devotional culture and practice. Their deviations from Calvinist orthodoxy, moreover, were republican not authoritarian in their political implications, as Jefferson's enthusiastic assessment suggests. Yet Arminian English bishops were oblivious to any such implications and, though in the minority, used their power to institute and enforce their cultural and governmental preferences, even when doing so meant outraging consciences or ruthlessly punishing dissent. Such impositions grated on the Puritans, who, regardless of their views on salvation, deplored episcopal pomp, debunked most sacraments, and endorsed plain spontaneity in worship.

During the 1640s, the defeat of the high-church, anti-Calvinist elite and the ready resort of the now predominant Presbyterian faction to its own coercive policies seem to have freed Milton to argue explicitly in behalf of rational choosing and free will. For all his support of the Presbyterian faction against the prelates, Milton had never endorsed predestination. His Arminian tendencies become unmistakable in the divorce tracts and in *Areopagitica*'s exaltation of rational choice, toleration, and individual accountability. Milton insists that God created man free, and if Adam had not been free, he might as well have been a puppet: "a mere artificial Adam, such an Adam as he is in the motions" (p. 944). By the end of the 1640s, Milton's contention that the English have every right to try and execute King Charles rests on an anti-Presbyterian first premise, all the more provocative for being presented as a self-evident truth: "No man who knows aught can be so stupid [as] to deny that all men naturally were born free, being the image and resemblance of God himself" (*TKM*, p. 1028). At this distance, it seems clear that Milton's breach with the Presbyterians rests on differing conceptions of the dignity of the human subject. By the time he comes to write his epic, choice and responsibility are for Milton the very stuff of human morality and of human desert (Danielson; S. Fallon 1998). Most Presbyterians, by contrast, deemed the ethical categories of choice and responsibility meaningless or wickedly delusional.

In *Paradise Lost,* it is only to the characterization of Satan and his followers that the language of predestination applies. Hell is thus described as a "prison ordained" to which they have been eternally "decreed, / Reserved and destined" (1.71, 2.160–61). Like stereotypical Calvinists, certain devils spend vast stretches of time debating "of providence, foreknowledge, will and fate / Fixed fate, free will, foreknowledge absolute"—i.e., "in wand'ring mazes lost" (2.559–61). Fate is their preferred ideological fiction as they persistently elide their responsibility for rebelling against the only divine right monarch whose legitimacy Milton ever acknowledged. When they debate policy and strategy, they do so in "synods," a term historically associated with the determinist doctrinal pronouncements of Calvinist and Presbyterian assemblies (2.391).

Even the narrative and dramatic stress placed on Satan's role and character, which some have deemed disproportionate, is an indicator of Milton's distance from the determinist tenets of the Presbyterians. The serpent's temptation is beside the point in Calvinist theology, as indeed is any agency outside God. The Fall is divinely ordained. Calvin's deity was a volitional black hole, obviating the need for a malevolent opponent who sparks evil. For Milton, by contrast, temptation is an ethical state crucial to theodicy, permitting merit to the creature, as in the case of Abdiel, while at the same time justifying the redemption of humanity: unlike the irreversibly damned rebel angels, "man falls deceived/By the other first" (3.130–31). Most important, the freedom and accountability presumed by temptation prevent humanity's recriminations against God "as if predestination overruled/Their will" (3.114–15). The justification of God's ways to men turns out to be largely an Arminian response to the Calvinist insistence on the bondage of the will. Foreknowledge does not predetermine; the choices of unfallen humanity are free: "authors to themselves in all/Both what they judge and what they choose; for so/I formed them free" (3.122–24). As Perez Zagorin observes, Milton's "loyalty to the principle of liberty as he understood it was absolute" (114). It was a matter of doing justice to man and God.

To God more than to man, however. Liberty is a state that we ordinarily associate with human beings, but from Milton's highly theocentric and theodical perspective, freedom is primarily and definitively a quality essential to the nature of God. Only because the human race is created in the image of God is it self-evident that humanity is born free. The only necessity that applies to God is that he not involve himself in contradiction. Any action he takes must therefore conform to the good, goodness being definitive of divine identity rather than a limitation on his freedom. Though raised in the highly Calvinist culture of seventeenth-century London, Milton insists on the freedom allowed humanity in Arminian theology because his God must not be held liable for the sins of humanity, as Calvin's was. The necessity that God's deeds be good ones does not wed God to any particular action, however; his "goodness" remains "free/To act or not" (7.171–72). Such freedom holds true even concerning the generation of the Son. God is under no necessity to beget a second divinity; he freely chooses to do so. The Son, in his turn, freely offers himself as a sacrifice on behalf of humanity (3.236–65). Adam and Eve echo and also mediate the praiseworthy choices of the Father and Son when they decide to procreate and so begin the line that will produce their redeemer (10.867–1096). So the theodicy comes full circle, with goodness remaining free at every juncture to act or not.

Genre

"The greatest writer who has ever existed of a limited genre"—that is how T. S. Eliot in 1926 described Milton. The initial superlative hints at a magnanimous finish, but Eliot instead concludes by demeaning genre and diminishing his praise: "Instead of poetry, you get *genres* of poetry" (1993, 201). Centuries earlier, Thomas Rymer had also denied the authenticity of Milton's poetry, snidely describing *Paradise Lost* as a work that "some are pleased to call a poem" (1678, 143). He even omits it from a summary of English heroic poetry that culminates instead with Davenant's *Gondibert* (1651) and Cowley's *Davideis* (1656) (1694, preface). Rymer condemns Milton for not being sufficiently generic, whereas Eliot criticizes him for being excessively generic. Their shared disdain may owe less to Milton's artistic fraudulence than to the not uncommon tendency of lesser artists to mitigate the achievements of greater ones. Rymer is more easily cleared from that suspicion. True to his name, he scorned unrhymed narrative verse as prose, an arbitrary genre distinction but one general at the time as the note on verse affixed to the first edition attests. By contrast, Eliot's dedication to the proposition that genre is an ersatz proxy for true poetry remains a head-scratcher, even in its historical context.

According to the *OED,* the term *genre* did not enter English usage until the nineteenth century. The concept of literary kind had by then already been debated for millennia, however, energetically so during the European Renaissance, when genre was held in very high esteem, not least by Milton himself. His ideal curriculum includes prosody as a necessary technical study, but far above it in real dignity he places the "sublime art" that teaches "the laws" governing "true" poems, whether epic, dramatic, or lyric (*Of Ed;* see pp. 977–78). The reverential diction is telling. Taken together with the related claim that Scripture offers the most perfect instances of the major genres (*RCG;* see p. 841), it suggests that for Milton, as for Sir Philip Sidney before him, literary genres were divinely authorized modes of mimesis, corresponding to the Creator's arrangement of reality. Compared with any individual poem, genre was the more real thing, and indeed "the first thing the reader needs to know about *Paradise Lost,*" according to C. S. Lewis (1).

Eliot's low regard for genre may have stemmed from discomfort with prescriptive rules for poetry. Milton does insist on "laws" for poems, after all. But his neoclassicism is distinct from the neoclassicism that prevailed in England after the Restoration, Rymer being one of its chief proponents. Through the sixteenth and well into the seventeenth century, Italy was the center of cultural authority in Europe. Its cities "swarmed with critics," according to Rymer, but as "swarmed" suggests, the Italian critical hegemony lacked uniformity or a common national focus. During the first half of the seventeenth century, the individualism of the Italian swarm gradually gave way to the regimentation of the French. "From Italy, France took the cudgels," the pugnacious Rymer put it, tracing French ascendancy to Cardinal Richelieu's amalgamation of cultural with political authority at the increasingly absolutist French court (1694, A2r–v). Milton, however, never acknowledged the cultural turn away from his beloved Italy. His ambitions as an epic poet crystallized during his visit to Italy (1638–39), and his disdain for France was quite general and persistent. His masterworks of the Restoration display a sublime if studied indifference to Gallic dictates, and his conception of literary genre, epic specifically, owes a great deal to the formative influence of sixteenth-century Italians, Torquato Tasso most prominently.

Milton refers to Tasso repeatedly in poems composed during his visit to Italy (see, e.g., *Manso*), and when in *The Reason of Church Government* he discusses epic, Tasso alone is named in the company of Homer and Vergil (see pp. 840–41). It was Tasso who originally argued that the "laws of poetry" are divinely established realities, "essential and fixed by the very nature and law of things" (Kates 36). A poet did not need to conform to fixed rules derived from authoritative precedent but could instead embody the objectively based laws of poetry according to the judgment of natural reason, judgment informed not only by subjective experience and the efforts of precursors but also by, most crucially for a Christian poet, scriptural revelation. Milton may have adored Homer above all other poets, but to fulfill his own poetic vocation in the genre that Homer epitomized, Milton characteristically believed himself morally obliged to manifest the epic genre on his own terms, taking full advantage of his access to Christian doctrine. In short, the heroic poem as Milton conceived it was more adaptable to the individual poet's conception of truth than a rote critic like Rymer could stomach.

English critics nursed on Gallic canons early on censured *Paradise Lost* for its wantonness. John Dennis in 1704 described it as "the most lofty but most irregular poem that has been produced by the mind of man" (bv), and unlike Dennis, who ultimately judges *Paradise Lost* above the critical law, subsequent neoclassical critics typically laud Milton's loftiness and rue his irregularities. Milton's idiosyncratic version of epic defies standard definitions because it is unusually inclusive, almost all-encompassing. Northrop Frye calls it "the story of all things," yet even that broad rubric seems inadequate (1965, 3). The reach of *Paradise Lost* extends far beyond creation, affording local habitation and a name even to the uncreated realm of the Anarch Chaos and comprising the infinite and eternal together with the finite and fleeting. In its "diffuse" form, epic is the only genre that Milton discusses in *The Reason for Church Government* for which he cites no scriptural precedent. This tantalizing omission may in part suggest that Milton did not consider any book in the Bible, not even Genesis, both unified and ample enough to qualify.

In her magisterial study of Milton and genre, Barbara Lewalski tracks Milton's use of virtually every subgenre recognized by Renaissance rhetoricians and deems *Paradise Lost* "an encyclopedia of literary forms" (1985, 125). Jonathan Richardson makes much the same point in defending Milton's masterwork as "a composition . . . not reducible under any known denomination," "the quintessence of all that is excellent in writing" (cxlv, clii). If in its encompassing formal plenitude *Paradise Lost* violates the "limited genre" defined by neoclassical critics, its promiscuity is nonetheless profoundly classical in spirit. Aristotle himself distinguishes epic from other genres by its capacity to assimilate within a single narrative other modes, such as the dramatic or lyric, and their various subgenres (26). Book 4 illustrates Milton's singular gift for subduing such multiplicity under a unified narrative arc. The basic story line—Satan's intrusion into Paradise leading ultimately to his apprehension and expulsion—occasions, among other genre variations, authorial apostrophe, Satanic soliloquy, landscape poetry with features of the country house tradition, various love lyrics, metamorphic tales of origin, evening prayer, and confrontational martial dialogue. Nor was epic originally confined to what Voltaire in his *Essai sur la poésie épique* defined as "narratives in verse of warlike adventures" (331), which Milton scorned as "tedious havoc" (*PL* 9.30).

Deriving from the Greek word for "story" or "story-related," *epic* seems to have been a broader category for the early Greeks, virtually indistinguishable from what is now meant by narrative in general. Aristocratic martial and amorous encounters are undeniably the stuff of Homeric epic, and of mock epic (Homer is supposed to have composed one of those, too), but Hesiod's overtly didactic narratives also qualified, as did Orphic poems celebrating religious mysteries. In each case, the bard tells a story meant to epitomize and even justify the supernaturally shaped course of human events. Milton observes the familiar trappings and formal insignia of epic: invocations, extended similes, catalogs, epithets, and the rest. But he does so idiosyncratically, in line with his highly individual Christian faith. The invocations exemplify this characteristic willingness to interpret the "laws" of epic according to his own situation. Embracing and expanding on a liberty asserted previously by Tasso, he uses the invocations as occasions to speak not simply in his own voice but to an unprecedented extent of himself and his anxious situation, "in darkness, and with dangers compassed round" (7.27).

When Aristotle described epic as an inclusive, composite form, he was distinguishing it from drama, the genre that shows rather than tells and brooks no authorial narration. By contrast, the authorial voice in epic sometimes withdraws in favor of storytelling characters involved in dramatic dialogue or lyrical self-expression. Aristotle thought drama the nobler genre, not only purer in mode but also more disciplined in plot than sprawling epic (26). Early modern theorists, however, focused on the magnitude of solitary authorial effort rather than on the purity of the form or concentrated efficiency of the action. The actors in a drama, furthermore, "share the poet's praise," as Dryden says (1800, 1:436). Such critics were nearly unanimous in accounting epic, precisely because it is vast, complicated, and solitary in execution, as "the greatest work which the soul of man is capable to perform" (Dryden 1800, 1:425). Milton, of course, as if to satisfy classical as well as modern standards of preeminence, composed both a capacious epic and a stringent classical tragedy (one never designed for staging or actors' shares). Still, the most momentous and defining artistic decision he ever made came down to a choice between these two great genres.

When he originally conceived the story of the Fall as the subject of a tragedy, Milton honored the long-standing critical consensus that unhappy events are best reserved for dramatic presentation—an affinity of form and subject acknowledged in the epic's most genre-conscious moment, the invocation to Book 9. As if to signal this anomaly formally, the same invocation fails to do what invocations by their very name promise they will do: invoke. Acknowledging his dependence on the Muse only in the last line, Milton devotes this "invocation" instead to justifying his deviation from mainline epic into tragedy. For, despite his concessions, Milton clearly thought that in choosing to tell this sad story in the grandest narrative genre, he had made a good trade-off. The story of the Fall allows him, as he indicates in the invocation, to redefine heroism in accordance with his Christian faith (9.13–41). More important, if "an epic poem must either be national or mundane," as Coleridge claimed, once an author has chosen the mundane, the goal must be to tell a story "common to all mankind" (1886, 240). This is a tall order, but in a Christian culture, the story of Adam and Eve, though tragic, more than fills the bill. Not simply the greatest story ever told, it is every story ever told: Milton's "Adam and Eve are all men and women inclusively," as Coleridge observed (240). If he could not claim to invent the epic mode, as Homer had, Milton could reinvent it in light of Christian revelation and aspire to include all other epics, all other narratives of any kind.

The other main advantage of arranging the story of man's first disobedience as a narrative and not a tragic drama was the chance to exploit the single most definitive formal requirement of an epic narrative—that it begin in the midst of things. Milton made much of this opportunity: a titanic Satan and his followers, first rolling in hellfire and then debating revenge, followed by the farsighted judgment of a Zeus-like God and his obsequious adherents in Heaven. Indeed, the opening books are so striking that they have largely determined the poem's reception in modern times. These books address received traditions of heroic poetry overtly and extensively, and they also contain, according to many readers, the most poetic energy and the thematic designs crucial to the work as a whole.

To revive a thesis that originated in the early eighteenth century and fell out of fashion in the twentieth, we think it likely that Milton's inspiration for making Satan weltering in Hell his "midst of things" was the pre-Norman, English tradition of biblical poetry, especially the Old English *Genesis B,* long attributed to Caedmon. No one denies that Milton had opportunity to become acquainted with this and other works in the Caedmon manuscripts, discovered in 1651 by the philologist Franciscus Junius, then residing in London. If Milton was given access to the manuscripts while he was still sighted, he probably took note of the illustrations, including one of the rebel angels plunging headlong into the jaws of Leviathan (see p. 322). Scholars have argued, not without evidence, that Milton's competency in Old English was at best slight and that any acquaintance he might have had with the Caedmon poems, whether in manuscript or in print, would therefore have been superficial and inconsequential. Yet even a superficial acquaintance would have left him aware that *Genesis B* begins, as *Paradise Lost* does, with Satan and his thanes rallying in Hell. Furthermore, as French Fogle's introduction to Milton's *History of Britain* observes, Milton's access to freshly published Old English texts and translations was extensive (Yale 5: xxxvi–xxxvii). The conception of Christ prevalent in England until the Conquest, "which views the cross from the perspective of world history and emphasizes its victorious aspect, the conquest of Satan," was far more amenable to him than the later emphasis on the sufferings of Christ (Huttar 242).

While Milton dismissed the monks who wrote the early history of Britain as "ill gifted with utterance" (Yale, 5:288), it does not follow that he would have disdained the Anglo-Saxon language. His schoolmaster at St. Paul's, Alexander Gill, was an advocate of the English vernacular and demonstrably knowledgeable about Old English (Fletcher 1:185). The common complaint that *Paradise Lost* is replete with Latinisms, an English estranged from its vernacular roots, is unjustified, as Fowler's edition repeatedly observes. On the contrary, Milton's English is generally idiomatic. When in 1807 James Ingram translated the first fifteen lines of *Paradise Lost* into Old English, he left the syntax virtually untouched and required substitutes for ten loan words only (47–48). We think it not only fitting but probable that the catalyst for Milton's choice of epic subject once he had abandoned the British theme was the coincidental discovery in the 1650s of a native tradition of biblical poetry written before the Conquest.

Prosody and Style

Paradise Lost is written in unrhymed pentameter lines, or blank verse. Early in the sixteenth century, the Earl of Surrey adopted this form for his partial translation of Vergil's *Aeneid,* and toward the end of that century it became the conventional medium of Elizabethan drama. Shakespeare's plays are primarily written in blank verse. But Spenser had not used it. Milton's choice of blank verse was a daring one, for at that time there was no long blank-verse poem of much distinction in English or any other language. It was largely because of Milton's precedent that blank verse established itself as early as James Thomson's *Seasons* (1726–30) as the preferred metrical form for long and ambitious English poems. Wordworth's *The Prelude;* Keats's *Hyperion;* Tennyson's *The Princess, Enoch Arden,* and *The Idylls of the King;* Browning's *The Ring and the Book;* Arnold's *Empedocles on Etna;* the long narratives of Edwin Arlington Robinson; sections of Crane's *The Bridge;* Stevens's *Sunday Morning* and *Notes toward a*

Supreme Fiction; Frost's *Home Burial;* and Betjeman's *Summoned by Bells* are all written in blank verse.

Milton organized his narrative into verse paragraphs, within which he devised syntactical patterns famous for their length and lucidity. Having freed himself from the ancient bondage of rhyme, he created musical effects with consonance, dissonance, alliteration, repetition, and even the occasional internal rhyme. He particularly excelled in the "turn of words," as it was called in the seventeenth and eighteenth centuries—repeating the same words in a reversed or modified order. Dryden tells us that he once looked for these turns in Milton but failed to find them (*Essays* 2:108–9). In fact the effect is everywhere, as in "though fall'n on evil days,/On evil days though fall'n" (7.25–26), which reminded Emerson of "the reflection of the shore and trees in water" (R. Richardson 318). When the Father announces the forthcoming creation in Book 7, "Glory they sung to the most high" (182), then "Glory to him" (184), the Son who has just defeated the rebel angels, and finally, with a turn of words, "to him/Glory and praise" (186–87). Through creation the Son will "diffuse" the glory of the Father "to worlds and ages infinite" (190–91), and in this very passage we feel that glory has been squeezed from the word *glory* and diffused from clause to clause. Some of the best-known turns include Eve's initial infatuation with her image in the pool ("Pleased I soon returned,/... Pleased it returned as soon") at 4.460–65, and Eve's great love lyric enclosed by the brackets of "Sweet is" and "is sweet" (4.641–56); inside them she lists the same natural beauties twice, once as sweet, once again as not sweet. Addison thought this last "one of the finest turns of words that I have ever seen" (Shawcross 1:142).

Distinguished achievement in sound effects is an excellence that no one has ever seriously denied to Milton. His verse has few rivals in what Hazlitt termed "the adaptation of the sound and movement of the verse to the meaning of the passage" (Thorpe 104). Sometimes the adaptations are relatively simple, like certain film scores. As Satan struggles through Chaos, the verse also seems to have trouble making headway: "So he with difficulty and labor hard/Moved on, with difficulty and labor he" (2.1021–22). When he hears "a universal hubbub wild/Of stunning sounds" (2.951–52), it is clear that *universal* and *wild* are ways of defining what the word *hubbub,* all meaning aside, delivers to us purely through its sound. *Stunning sounds* echoes the chaotic crack of *hubbub,* as if sounds had indeed been stunned. Sometimes the adaptation of sound to meaning is wittier, more conceptual. When Satan departs from Pandaemonium, the philosophical devils "reasoned high/of providence, foreknowledge, will and fate,/fixed fate, free will, foreknowledge absolute,/And found no end, in wand'ring mazes lost" (2.558–61). Milton makes the catalog of philosophical concepts into a little semantic labyrinth in which "foreknowledge, will and fate" enough resemble "fixed fate, free will, foreknowledge absolute" to make us wonder how they are alike, how not alike. Have we really gone anywhere in moving from one line to the next?

When the poem introduces a distinction, the difference is likely to be taken up, explored, and often complicated by the verse. In Book 4, for example, the narrator reads gender differences from the naked bodies of Adam and Eve, and the result is the greatest politically incorrect passage in English poetry. "For contemplation he and valor formed,/For softness she and sweet attractive grace" (297–98). We can see immediately that alliteration serves Eve. The poetry is already indicating its willingness to interfere with the passage's legalism, but for now there is no time to explore the bond between Eve and poetic beauty. The law must be pronounced. Adam is formed for God, she for God in him. His forehead and eye "declared/Absolute rule" (300–301).

At this point Milton begins to describe their differing hair treatments, Adam's first:

> Hyacinthine locks
> Round from his parted forelock manly hung
> Clust'ring, but not beneath his shoulders broad. (301–3)

The two run-on lines imitate the fall of his hair (*Hyacinthine* implies that it is black), while the strong end-stop of line 303 puts a limit to its hanging down. *But not* has an almost corrective force, as if things might have been getting out of hand. They immediately do. Eve's blond tresses introduce four straight run-on lines, followed by four more end-stopped lines:

> She as a veil down to the slender waist
> Her unadornèd golden tresses wore
> Disheveled, but in wanton ringlets waved
> As the vine curls her tendrils, which implied
> Subjection, but required with gentle sway,
> And by her yielded, by him best received,
> Yielded with coy submission, modest pride,
> And sweet reluctant amorous delay. (304–11)

He the cluster, she the vine. He words in their stable sense, words as law, words that set limits; she words as their sense is in transit, disheveled, drawn out variously from line to line, creeping and curling with wanton implication. Syntax flows across the unit of the line. Milton's verse becomes femalelike in describing femaleness, then arrives at the key word *Subjection* in line 308, which mates with all the verbs to come. Enjambment stops. We have returned to the matter of the law, but in, so to speak, another semantic universe. Subjection is what is *required,* what is *yielded,* what is *best received,* and again what is *yielded.* It is their bond, and also their sexual spark. He requires and receives it; she yields and yields it. Lacking compulsion, it is no longer "subjection" in the usual sense but rather her free consent.

This passage begins with the law of gender difference, yet by its end we find that law realized in amorous love and artistic excitement. Eve yields her subjection with "coy submission, modest pride," both phrases being oxymorons, and the first of them of particular richness in Renaissance love poetry (Kerrigan and Braden 204–18). An oxymoron naturally requires two words, a plus and a minus, a point and a counterpoint. The last line, with Eve-like luxuriance, doubles the oxymoron quotient with four perfect words, oxymoronic in various ways: *reluctant* crosses *amorous, amorous* crosses *delay, delay* crosses *reluctant.* But all of them and their nest of contradictory combinations are *sweet,* the very word that Eve will turn so memorably a few hundred lines later, enclosing the couple's love and their lapsing days of Paradise in its embrace. They will not make love until the end of the day. Eve's *sweet . . . delay* is an oxymoronic union of desire and control, consent and refusal, passion and rule, profusion and limit, fusing the various contraries of the passage. Adam also participates in this knot of contraries. *Gentle sway* is the first oxymoron of the passage, and links to *delay* through a delayed rhyme. Of "Yielded with coy submission, modest pride,/ And sweet reluctant amorous delay," Walter Savage Landor remarked, "I would rather have written these two lines than all the poetry that has been written since Milton's time in all the regions of the earth" (Thorpe 368–69).

Milton's style marries male and female, "which two great sexes animate the world" (8.151). There is male law. There are requirements, fixed meanings, ripe clusters of sense. But there is energy as well, and the energy in this poetry is female, vinelike, curling here and then back, various in its repetition, paradoxical, nurturing underbrushes of implication that modify and even revise the abstract fixities of law.

Diction

Johnson proclaimed that Milton "wrote no language, but has formed what Butler calls a Babylonish Dialect" (Thorpe 86). Yet his strictures on Milton are almost always wrong or exaggerated. A recent study such as John Hale's *Milton's Languages* is from the outset friendlier toward the multilingual characteristics of Milton's style than would have been possible in the confines of Johnson's linguistic patriotism. Modern statistical studies have demonstrated that the style of *Paradise Lost* is neither as archaic nor as Latinate as some of its critics have imagined (Boone). Milton is a learned author, to be sure, but a student determined to appreciate at least some of the learning in his language will be not be led away from the genius of ordinary English. T. S. Eliot, writing in the Johnson tradition, emphasized "the remoteness of Milton's verse from ordinary speech" (Thorpe 321). But in fact Milton's poetry enriches ordinary speech in new and surprising ways.

Now and then Milton will use a word in its classical or etymological sense, waving aside its derived meaning in English. In "There went a fame in Heav'n" (1.651), *fame* has its Roman sense of "word spoken." An imperial Milton banishes the English sense. Similarly, *succinct* in "His habit fit for speed succinct" (3.643) has the Latin meaning of "tucked under, tight-fitted." Christopher Ricks has shown that Milton will sometimes insist on the etymological sense when naming an unfallen world in which words with definitions involving immorality are not yet appropriate (109–17). At their creation the rivers of the earth run "with serpent error wand'ring" (7.302), but *error* in the Latin sense of "wandering" contains no taint of crime or mistake. Words too have their original innocence. In order to grasp this last example, a reader must see that the Latin definition is in meaningful dialogue with the derived sense, and that the rejection of the ordinary English meaning, far from being arbitrary, belongs to the larger significance of the passage.

Milton "was not content," Walter Raleigh observed, "to revive the exact classical meaning in place of the vague or weak English acceptation; he often kept both senses, and loaded the word with two meanings at once" (1900, 209). When the hair of the angel Uriel falls "Illustrious on his shoulders" (3.627), Milton refers at once to the luster or brightness of the hair and the august reputation of the angel. As it approaches Eve in Book 9, the snake is "voluble" (436). In its classical sense, the word denotes the coiling motion of the snake, but in its newer English sense, it announces the serpent's forthcoming talkativeness (Ricks 108). Beelzebub refers to Chaos as "the vast abrupt" (2.409), where *abrupt* seems first of all to retain its Latin sense of "broken off, precipitous." The rebel angels have fallen through Chaos and have some idea of what it means to traverse this abyss of indefiniteness. Whoever enters Chaos breaks off from the stabilities of Heaven and Hell. But the English meanings seem also in play when we note that Milton has transformed an adjective into a noun. Chaos itself will be a constant sequence of abrupt changes, a place where interruption is not a surprise but the norm.

There is a fund of linguistic peculiarities in *Paradise Lost.* Milton, for example, likes the sequence adjective + noun + adjective, as in *universal hubbub wild* or *vast profundity obscure.* He was not the first to try this sequence, but it is a good bet that, wherever we encounter it in subsequent English verse, Milton is probably on the author's mind; Arnold's "vast edges drear" in "Dover Beach" hopes to remind us of the seething Chaos of *Paradise Lost.* F. T. Prince (112–29) discussed Milton's interest in a related sequence found in Italian verse as early as Dante: adjective + noun + and + adjective, as in "Sad task and hard" (5.564) or "Sad resolution and secure" (6.541). Does the second adjective come in as an afterthought? The *task,* let us say, is primarily *sad,* so much so that one forgets for a moment that it is *hard* as well. Or does the second adjective bear the main emotion? A *sad* task would be burden enough, but this one is, more important, *hard.* Milton enjoyed playing with this scheme. He experimented, for example, with distancing the adjectives: "pleasing was his shape, / And lovely" (9.503–4) or "For many are the trees of God that grow/ In Paradise, and various" (9.618–19). In place of adjective + noun + and + adjective, he tried noun + verb

+ and + noun, as in "he seemed / For dignity composed and high exploit" (2.110–11). The poet did not invent a "Babylonish Dialect." He wrote English with a high degree of originality, and his original poetry sublime unleashes a number of effects that had never been tried before in English verse.

Three Controversies

Attacks on Milton's verse early in the twentieth century by Ezra Pound, Herbert Read, F. R. Leavis, T. S. Eliot, and A. J. A. Waldock sparked a debate that eventually came to be known as the Milton Controversy (Murray 1–12). Although the notion of Milton's artistic greatness had never before been questioned so systematically, this was hardly an isolated incident. Historically Milton is by some measure the most controversial of the great English poets. He has given rise to an inordinate number of critical debates, altogether too many, in fact, for us to suppose that his poetry is itself innocent of contentiousness. Certainly in his prose Milton liked to mix it up. He was among the greatest controversialists of the day. The decades he spent fighting the wars of truth, Coleridge suggested, added a "controversial spirit" to his youthful character (Thorpe 91). But the early poems are also imbued with the love of argument (see introduction to *Paradise Regained*). When Milton in the first invocation to *Paradise Lost* refers to "this great argument," the word *argument* primarily means "plot," as in the prose "Argument" or plot summary attached to each book of the epic. Yet the great argument of the plot is wed to an "argument" of another kind, a rational contention, since Milton vows that "to the highth of this great argument" he will, if inspired, "assert eternal providence,/And justify the ways of God to men" (1.24–26).

Emerson wrote that no man in literary history, perhaps in all history, excelled Milton in the power to inspire: "Virtue goes out of him to others" (*Early Lectures* 1:148). No doubt some of the controversies about Milton have not demonstrated much of the poet's own idealism, but the generally high quality of Milton debates over the centuries is arguably the finest of the poet's gifts to our culture, as Christopher Ricks has pointed out. It is for good reason that Milton is "the most argued-about poet in English." He brings out the serious and passionate advocate in us:

> Of the needs to which he ministers, one of the greatest is our need to commit ourselves in passionate argument about literature. Not as part of the academic industry, but because literature is a supreme controversy concerning "the best that has been thought and said in the world" (to adopt the words which Matthew Arnold applied to culture). By the energy and sincerity of his poetry, Milton stands—as no other poet quite does—in heartening and necessary opposition to all aestheticisms, old and new. (xi)

Milton's argumentative art refuses to stay within aesthetic boundaries, however they may be drawn. Virtue goes out of him to his readers. His arguments come to life, and participating in them both pleases and elevates us.

One of the oldest of the Milton debates swirls about the character of Satan. Is he the hero of the epic? Is he so attractive as to upset the standard moral balance of Christianity? The first of these questions is the more easily answered. Early in the poem, Milton deliberately places Satan in the roles occupied by classical epic heroes. He founds a civilization in Hell. He undertakes a long and arduous journey. Compared to Odysseus, Addison observed, Satan "put in practice many more wiles and stratagems, and hides himself under a greater variety of shapes and appearances" (Shawcross 1:152). To some extent, Milton uses his Satan as a diagnostic test of the moral health of classical epic.

In the beginning of the poem especially, Satan exudes glamour. His appearance—huge, ruined, thunder-scarred, darkened, but still able to evoke the memory of his former luminescence in Heaven—makes a tremendous impression. The Satan glimpsed in Tasso's *Jerusalem Liberated* has, like the cheap special-effects devils of modern supernatural thrillers, massive horns, red eyes, a huge beard, an open mouth filthy with red blood and spewing rancid fumes (4.6–7). As William Hazlitt put it, the Satan of *Paradise Lost* "has no bodily deformity to excite our loathing or disgust. The horns and tail are not there. . . . Milton was too magnanimous and open an antagonist to support his argument by the bye-tricks of a hump and cloven foot" (Thorpe 109; see also Newton in Shawcross 2:154). Satan is proud, obstinate, the rebel of rebels. He speaks thrillingly of his "unconquerable will." For Milton, part of giving the devil his due is having the devil give God his due. Satan several times concedes the omnipotence of his foe. When he finds himself cursing the "free love" God gave to all the angels because it did not prevent him from falling, Satan fiercely, and in the name of truth, recoils on himself: "Nay cursed be thou; since against his thy will / Chose freely what it now so justly rues" (4.71–72).

William Blake took the romantic exaltation of Satan to an extreme in *The Marriage of Heaven and Hell*: "The reason Milton wrote in fetters when he wrote of Angels & God, and at liberty when of Devils & Hell, is, because he was a true poet and of the Devil's party without knowing it." Blake was something of a Gnostic, for whom Milton's God the Father was an evil and inferior God, and his satanic opposition the force of true deity (Nuttall 224). But readers whose imaginations remain responsive to the ordinary polarities of Christianity will probably not leave the poem with the favorable impression of Satan with which they began. As the work continues, they realize that Satan's cannonlike recoils inevitably issue in a fatalistic resolve to go on being himself and fulfill his initial plan of corrupting mankind. His speeches remake the same decision over and over again. Readers come to understand that conceding the omnipotence of God, far from being magnanimous, is the only way Satan can reconcile his pride with his defeat. Heroic resistance begins to look like habitual stubbornness. Satan would desperately like to believe that he is self-created. But his image of his own greatness is also his enemy, the uncreated Father. Satan sits in "God-like imitated state" (2.511). Declaring that evil is his good, he dreams of sharing "divided Empire with Heav'n's King" (4.111)—in other words, of being the equal of God in a Manichaean universe.

But Satan's true God is his own will. Milton always maintained that tyrants were self-enslaved. An unconquerable will sacrifices the willer and everyone under his sway. Most readers, their infatuation with Satan having run its course, savor his final comeuppance in the poem, as his triumphant return to Hell becomes the first of countless annual reenactments of the wicked self-harming travesty he is doomed to think a victory. The attractions of Satan are real, and beguiling, but in the end not so profound as his degradation.

Satan's heroism, though felt in its highest form by the Romantics, did not die with them and remains a main source of argument in modern Milton criticism. It is crucial, for example, to the middle period of Harold Bloom's work, which begins with *The Anxiety of Influence* (1973). Hazlitt noted that Milton showed no signs of alarm over a vast literary indebtedness that would have stymied many a lesser poet: "Milton has borrowed more than any other writer, and exhausted every source of imitation, sacred or profane; yet he is perfectly distinct from every other writer.... The quantity of art in him shows the strength of his genius: the weight of his intellectual obligations would have oppressed any other writer. Milton's learning has the effect of intuition" (Thorpe 101).

Bloom points to a great subtext in *Paradise Lost* concerning the apparent ease with which Milton masters the anxiety of being belated, preceded, and preempted. Satan is the modern poet (20). God is "cultural history, the dead poets, the embarrassments of a tradition grown too wealthy to need anything more" (21). Everything has been done. The world created, the Bible written, the classical epics finished, the romance versions of them already penned by Ariosto and Spenser. What is there to do? To rally what remains, to salvage all creative impulses that are not infected by devotion, while trying to fend off the knowledge that nothing remains, that one will wind up in one God-like imitated state or another. Wallace Stevens's famous aphorism "The death of Satan was a tragedy / For the imagination" ("Esthétique du Mal") seems pertinent here. Assuming that his death has occurred, or may soon occur, this reading of *Paradise Lost* shows the dimensions of the tragedy. For Satan *is* imagination. Bloom transformed the Satan controversy into a neo-Romantic fable for modern poets.

The arguments set forth in Stanley Fish's influential *Surprised by Sin: The Reader in Paradise Lost* (1967) are also to a large extent responses to the traditional Satan controversies. The author, a born Miltonist, loves to argue. Fish maintains that it is alright for the most serious readers, for readers in search of the author's intentional meaning, to allow heroic images of Satan to form in their minds, provided they are willing to sacrifice those images when the intentional meaning of the poem requires it (as it always will). Satan's attractiveness is not an unconscious or unintended effect of some sort. Milton wanted his readers to entertain false ideas of Satan's virtue. He deliberately and repeatedly trapped them into doing so, only to correct them in the next phrase or line or passage. Blake responded to attractive cues but refused to obey the corrective cues, and wound up losing touch with the poem. Milton himself is the creator of, and ultimate manager of, the Satan controversy. Fish's most impressive examples are of course drawn from the glamorous treatments of Satan in the first two books of the epic. The spasmodic self-corrections of his model reader uncannily resemble the recoils of Satan.

While impressed with the neatness of this argument, and the energy with which Fish has defended it, other critics have wondered at the infinite gullibility of Fish's model reader, who goes through the same experience again and again without learning his lesson, as if reading were less a process of illumination than an obsessive-compulsive ritual. They doubt Fish's implicit view of Milton as a dogmatist unable to admit to mixed feelings about the devil. They question whether great poetry could be as Pavlovian in its didacticism as Fish implies (Kerrigan 1974, 180n, 1983, 98–99; Rumrich 1996, 2–4, 7–11, 60–64; Pritchard; Leonard 2002).

A related and comparably venerable controversy concerns Milton's portrait of God. Pope observed that "God the Father turns a School-Divine" ("The First Epistle of the Second Book of Horace Imitated"). The word *school-divine* appears in many subsequent discussions of this issue. It means "a medieval scholastic theologian, of the sort that was taught in European universities," and was not usually a derogatory word, though it does appear to have pejorative charge for Pope. He seems to be referring primarily to God's speeches during the Heavenly Council at the opening of Book 3, where the Father explains the relationship between freedom and foreknowledge, and the doctrine of the Atonement, in a language compounded of standard theological terminology and statements from Scripture. Some have answered with Addison that in Book 3 the central mysteries of Christianity and the "whole dispensation of Providence with respect to man" are defined with admirable clarity and concision (Shawcross 1:178). Some have maintained that Milton went wrong in the very decision to assign speech to deity, since this procedure will inevitably bring God down to a human level (Wilkie in Shawcross 2:240–43).

But the deeper issue here is not whether God should speak at all and if he must in what vocabulary. Milton's God, foreseeing the development of human philosophy and theology, anticipates being held responsible for the sins of Adam and Eve. This forethought irritates him:

> so will fall
> He and his faithless progeny: whose fault?
> Whose but his own? Ingrate, he had of me
> All he could have; I made him just and right,
> Sufficient to have stood, though free to fall. (3.95–99)

The speech implies that man's theodical attacks continue the faithlessness of the Fall itself. If someone maintains that God did not make him in such a way that he could be responsible for the Fall, he manifests ingratitude. He wants to have been given more from God than mere freedom. He deems his divine endowment not "sufficient." With regard to the poem's readers, God is provocative and ill-tempered. "Go on," he seems to be saying, "blame me. Doing so can only show your fallenness, your faithlessness, your ingratitude, and your utter lack of responsibility."

The same sort of provocation, daring his audience to disagree or disobey, marks the Father's words when he is exalting the Son in Heaven. He demands that the angels kneel and "confess him [the Son] Lord":

> Him who disobeys
> Me disobeys, breaks union, and that day
> Cast out from God and blessed union, falls
> Into utter darkness, deep engulfed, his place
> Ordained without redemption, without end. (5.611–15)

It is difficult not to be reminded, as we contemplate such a passage, that Milton hated the bullying ways of earthly monarchs. Why did he make the Father, at times, into a threatening king?

Milton would probably have replied that because God is a king, almighty and eternal, no one else can be. For all others sit in God-like imitated state, aspiring to godhead like Satan himself. God's legitimacy through merit, not birthright, renders all other monarchies illegitimate, all other monarchs pretenders. This helps to explain why a republican like Milton can have a king for a God, but not why his God should be angry and threatening. God is not always that, to be sure, and at one point amuses the Son by acting the role of some chronicle-history Henry IV worried about usurping northern lords (5.721–32). His aims are merciful, and he praises the Son for seizing upon those aims and guaranteeing their future realization (3.274–343). When pretending that Adam does not need a mate, God seems playful, and appreciative of a creature whose freedom and rational self-confidence permit him to disagree with his creator (8.357–448). But as we have seen, Milton's God has a tough side.

This much can be said. Today we are somewhat embarrassed to think about God in terms of human emotions, unless the emotion in question is love. But the idea of God having in any sense a character—with exasperation, anger, jealousy, and wrath to go along with his love, mercy, and playfulness—probably seems childish or simplistic or even (though we have grown suspicious of this word) primitive. As Milton saw things, however, the portrait of God in the Bible was full of anthropomorphism. No form of divine symbolism can represent God as he is. But in the Bible, God delivered the metaphors through which he wished us to know him. There can be no shame in taking him at his word. "Why does our imagination shy away from a notion of God which he himself does not hesitate to promulgate in unambiguous terms?" (*CD* 1.2, p. 1148). Milton had little interest in the sort of God we sometimes associate with philosophers and mystics, known to us through some esoteric and reason-humbling symbolism. By the same token, he was relatively unexcited by the thought of contemplating the *visio dei.* His angels seem happiest, like Milton himself, when performing a divinely assigned task.

Both the God and the Satan Controversies animate William Empson's striking *Milton's God* (1960). In the process of indicting Christianity, this book invents a new way to praise Milton, albeit one that he himself would surely have deplored. Christianity, for Empson, is intractably evil. In any telling of the story of the Fall of man, God will in some manner be revealed as the responsible party. Milton was a Christian of uncommon moral sensitivity, and he did virtually all that one could do to improve the faith. There is, as we have noted, no torture. The Crucifixion, though recounted briefly (12.411–19), is hardly the centerpiece of Milton's religion. Temptation, the act of free moral decision, takes its place. Satan is more sympathetic than ever before. But God the Father is still provocative, still threatening. This portrait, far from being the failure it was conventionally assumed to be on one side of the God Controversy, shows Milton's honesty. His God manifests the dark impulse to rule, to wield power purely and simply, that the many attractive aspects of *Paradise Lost* conceal from our view. Dennis Danielson's aptly titled *Milton's Good God* (1982) defends Milton and Christianity against some of the main arguments in *Milton's God.*

The third of our controversies, about the character of Eve, first appeared in the feminist criticism of the twentieth century. "For the Romantics," Mary Nyquist and Margaret Ferguson wrote in 1987, "it was Satan who was oppressed by the author's consciously held beliefs. In our time it tends to be Eve" (xiv). Satan was the controversy of another day. Feminism has arrived, and it wants to argue about Eve.

Traditionally Milton had received mostly high marks for his characterizations of Adam and Eve. Coleridge thought the love of Adam and Eve was "removed from everything degrading," the creation of two people who give each other what is most permanent in them and achieve "a completion of each in the other" (Thorpe 96). Their love unfolds without flattery or falsehood. Hazlitt told of some men's club wit who maintained that Adam and Eve enjoyed only the least interesting of the pursuits of human life, the relations between man and wife. Hazlitt replied with a long catalog of the furniture of fallen life (wars, riches, contracts, et cetera) missing from the supreme pleasures of Eden: "Thank Heaven, all these were yet to come" (Thorpe 111). Extending Hazlitt's idea that Milton had the power to think "of nobler forms and nobler things than those he found about him" (Thorpe 98), Emerson praised the poet for giving us a new human ideal: "Better than any other he has discharged the office of every great man, namely, to raise the idea of Man in the minds of his contemporaries and of posterity. . . . Human nature in these ages is indebted to him for its best portrait" (*Early Lectures* 149).

But there was information of diverse sorts suggesting that Milton might have had a grudge against womankind. During the time that he was deserted by his first wife, Mary Powell, Milton wrote four pamphlets arguing in favor of divorce on the grounds of spiritual incompatibility. Mary's daughters did not get along with his subsequent wives. Now and then the daughters were asked to read to their blind father in languages they could not understand (Darbishire 177, 277). And there were also a few passages in the poetry cataloging domestic unhappinesses with a somewhat unbalanced fervor. Samuel Johnson brought all of these factors together in a memorably pithy sentence: "There appears in his books something like a Turkish contempt of females, as subordinate and inferior beings" (*Lives* 1:193).

But through the eighteenth, the nineteenth, and much of the twentieth centuries, Milton's misogynistic streak was usually considered an eccentricity, not a malign preoccupation at the center of his being. At the dawn of the feminist period, Sandra Gilbert and Susan Gubar, in their groundbreaking *The Madwoman in the Attic,* maintained that Milton's patriarchal version of Genesis had from the beginning intimidated and oppressed female writers. He taught that a divine Father and Son had created everything, that Sin was a cursed mother, that Eve was supposed to be obedient to Adam ("He for God only, she for God in him") but instead was corrupted by the devil (Gilbert 368–82; later in Gilbert and Gubar 187–212). Philip Gallagher objected immediately (Gallagher and Gilbert 319–22) and later expanded his views in the fervently argued *Milton, the Bible, and Misogyny* (1990).

Joseph Wittreich's *Feminist Milton* (1987) showed that, Gilbert and Gubar to the contrary, many women down through the years had been empowered by Milton's portrait of Eve. Early commentators on *Paradise Lost* were well aware that a passage such as Adam's enumeration of marital woes to come at 10.896–908 was forced and gratuitous, since Adam "could not very naturally be supposed at that time to foresee so very circumstantially the inconvenience attending our *straight conjunction with this sex,* as he expresses it" (Thyer, cited in Todd 3.321). A few passages on a pet peeve were not too high a price to pay for great literature. Most poets had bees in their bonnets. Shakespeare himself never had a good word for dogs and cats. But feminists feared that Milton, whether consciously or not, was the agent of patriarchy or logocentrism or bourgeois individualism—whatever its name, a large conspiracy of overlapping ideological commitments hostile to women and progressive civilization alike.

The main positions in feminist Milton studies are essentially the same as those adopted in Shakespeare studies, and no doubt in other literary disciplines. Some interpreters found that Milton's poetry, if read sympathetically, yields meanings surprisingly favorable to women (McColley 1983; Woods). Others of this persuasion explored the possibility that Milton was not primarily threatened by women but in fact identified with them in profound ways (Kerrigan 1983, 184–86, 188–89, and 1991; S. Davies; Turner 65–71, 142–48; Lieb 83–113). Some, by contrast, agreed with Gilbert and Gubar that Milton is irredeemably an obstruction and will have to be cleared away (Froula). There were also those evenhanded souls contending that Milton is pretty much all right so far as he goes, but does not go far enough. James Turner in *One Flesh* found Milton's Eden erotically liberating; yet the poem has "two quite different models of the politics of love: one is drawn from the experience of being in love with an equal, . . . the other from the hierarchical arrangement of the universe, and the craving for male supremacy" (285). Mary Nyquist conceded that Milton seemed progressive in championing companionate marriage based on conversational partnership but warned that a woman content with such by-products of individualism would be settling for too little. The "blear illusion" (*Masque* 155) of these bourgeois goods prevents women from appreciating the higher truths to their left (99–100, 115–24).

This is still a young tradition. Up to now it has no doubt been too caught up in the barren chore of ideological grading. But the arguments have begun.

Paradiſe Loſt.

A
POEM
IN
TWELVE BOOKS.

The Author
JOHN MILTON.

The Second Edition
Reviſed and Augmented by the
ſame Author.

LONDON,
Printed by *S. Simmons* next door to the
Golden Lion in *Alderſgate-ſtreet*, 1674.

Title page to the second edition of *Paradise Lost* (1674).

Introduction to Prefatory Poems

These laudatory poems first prefaced *Paradise Lost* in 1674. The Latin verses by Samuel Barrow concentrate on the expulsion of Satan and his followers from Heaven and its classical precedents, the defeat and punishment of the Titans and Giants. Given the literary triumph of this section of *Paradise Lost,* Barrow confidently welcomes Milton onto the stage of world poetry (where he has been ever since). The English verses by Andrew Marvell assert the religious propriety and superior artistry of Milton's achievement, stressing its capaciousness and aesthetic excellence by invoking the cramped neoclassical canons that prevailed after the Restoration. Aware of Dryden's desire to rewrite *Paradise Lost* as a drama in heroic couplets, Marvell detects traces of divine inspiration even in Milton's blank verse prosody, created like the world itself "in number, weight, and measure."

Barrow was noted for his affection for Charles I, had been much involved with the political maneuvering of the late 1650s leading to the Restoration, and yet had also been linked with Cromwell. Appointed a physician to Charles II in 1660, he was a discreet, well-connected man of science and a great admirer of Milton. Marvell had a similar history of shifting political allegiance and a well-deserved reputation for discretion. Like Barrow a Royalist sympathizer at the beginning of the English Revolution, he must have adopted the Republican cause by 1653, when Milton recommended him for a position in Cromwell's government. (He was not appointed until 1657.) After the Restoration, he served ably as member of Parliament for Hull and was widely respected. The participation of Barrow and Marvell in the second edition seems to have been orchestrated as a broad-based appeal to judicious men of learning and affairs on behalf of a poet much maligned for his political crimes. Marvell had earlier come to the aid of the embattled Milton. Immediately after the Restoration, he helped protect the defender of regicide against his enemies and was instrumental in clearing Milton of a supposed debt to the sergeant at arms after his imprisonment in 1660. A decade later, in *The Rehearsal Transpos'd,* he championed Milton against the scurrilous attack of Samuel Parker.

IN PARADISUM AMISSAM SUMMI POETAE IOHANNIS MILTONI

[*On the Supreme Poet John Milton's* Paradise Lost]

Qui legis Amissam Paradisum, grandia magni
Carmina Miltoni, quid nisi cuncta legis?
Res cunctas et cunctarum primordia rerum
Et fata et fines continet iste liber.
Intima panduntur magni penetralia mundi,
Scribitur et toto quicquid in orbe latet:
Terraeque tractusque maris coelumque profundum
Sulphureumque Erebi flammivomumque specus;
Quaeque colunt terras pontumque et Tartara caeca,
Quaeque colunt summi lucida regna poli;
Et quodcunque ullis conclusum est finibus usquam,
Et sine fine chaos et sine fine Deus,
Et sine fine magis, si quid magis est sine fine,
In Christo erga homines conciliatus amor.
Haec qui speraret quis crederet esse futurum?
Et tamen haec hodie terra Britanna legit.
O quantos in bella duces, quae protulit arma!
Quae canit et quanta praelia dira tuba!
Coelestes acies, atque in certamine coelum,
Et quae coelestes pugna deceret agros!
Quantus in aetheriis tollit se Lucifer armis,
Atque ipso graditur vix Michaele minor!
Quantis et quam funestis concurritur iris
Dum ferus hic stellas protegit, ille rapit!
Dum vulsos montes ceu tela reciproca torquent
Et non mortali desuper igne pluunt,
Stat dubius cui se parti concedat Olympus
Et metuit pugnae non superesse suae.
At simul in coelis Messiae insignia fulgent,
Et currus animes armaque digna Deo,
Horrendumque rotae strident, et saeva rotarum
Erumpunt torvis fulgura luminibus,
Et flammae vibrant, et vera tonitrua rauco
Admistis flammis insonuere polo,
Excidit attonitis mens omnis et impetus omnis,

You who read *Paradise Lost,* great Milton's grand poem, what do you read but everything? This book contains all things, and the origins of all things, and their fates and their ends. The innermost secrets of the great universe are displayed, and whatever in the whole world is hidden is written out: the lands and the expanses of the sea and deep heaven and the sulfurous and flame-vomiting cave of Erebus; and those things that inhabit the lands and the sea[9] and blind Tartarus, and those that inhabit the bright realms of highest heaven; and whatever anywhere is enclosed within any boundaries, and boundless Chaos, and boundless God; and more boundless—if anything is more boundless—Christ's love directed toward men. Who would have believed there would come someone who would aspire to such things?—and yet today the land of Britain reads them. How many chieftains he brought to war, and what weaponry! What battles he sings, and with what a trumpet!—battlelines in Heaven, and Heaven in conflict, and fighting that befits the fields of Heaven! What a Lucifer lifts himself to ethereal warfare, and strides scarcely lower than Michael himself! With what great and fatal rage the fight is joined while one in his fierceness protects the stars, the other assaults them! While they hurl uprooted mountains as retaliatory weapons and they rain down from above with no mortal fire, Olympus stands unsure to which side to yield, and fears it will not survive its own battle. But as soon as the Messiah's standards shine out in

9. **pontumque**: "portumque" (harbor) in the 1674 *Paradise Lost.*

Et cassis dextris irrita tela cadunt.
Ad poenas fugiunt, et ceu foret Orcus asylum
Infernis certant condere se tenebris.
Cedite romani scriptores, cedite Graii
Et quos fama recens vel celebravit anus.
Haec quicunque leget tantum cecinisse putabit
Maeonidem ranas, Virgilium culices.

S.B. M.D.

Heaven and you rouse his chariot and the arms worthy of God, and the wheels shriek horrifyingly and savage lightning breaks from the wheels with grim flashes, and flames shake and true thunderclaps resound with a mixture of flames in the clangorous sky, all consciousness falls from those who have been struck, and all strength, and their useless weapons drop from their empty hands. They flee to punishment, and as if the underworld were asylum they strive to settle themselves in the infernal shades. Yield, Roman writers, yield, Greeks, and those whom recent or ancient fame has celebrated; whoever reads this will think Homer just sang of frogs, Vergil of gnats.

S[amuel] B[arrow]

ON MR. MILTON'S *PARADISE LOST*

When I beheld the poet blind, yet bold,
In slender book his vast design unfold,
Messiah crowned, God's reconciled decree,
Rebelling angels, the Forbidden Tree,
Heav'n, Hell, Earth, Chaos, all; the argument
Held me a while misdoubting his intent,
That he would ruin (for I saw him strong)
The sacred truths to fable and old song,
(So Samson groped the temple's posts in spite)
The world o'erwhelming to revenge his sight.
    Yet as I read, soon growing less severe,
I liked his project, the success did fear;
Through that wide field how he his way should find
O'er which lame Faith leads Understanding blind,
Lest he perplexed the things he would explain,

5. **argument:** the plot or subject matter.

9. Marvel appears to have read *Samson Agonistes*, first published in 1671. But the primary allusion is to Judges 16.28, a passage that Milton does *not* represent in *SA*.

15. **perplexed:** complicated unnecessarily.

And what was easy he should render vain.
Or if a work so infinite be spanned,
Jealous I was that some less skilful hand
(Such as disquiet always what is well,
And by ill imitating would excel)
Might hence presume the whole Creation's day
To change in scenes and show it in a play.
Pardon me, mighty poet, nor despise
My causeless, yet not impious, surmise.
But I am now convinced that none will dare
Within thy labors to pretend a share.
Thou hast not missed one thought that could be fit,
And all that was improper dost omit:
So that no room is here for writers left,
But to detect their ignorance or theft.
That majesty which through thy work doth reign
Draws the devout, deterring the profane.
And things divine thou treat'st of in such state
As them preserves, and thee, inviolate.
At once delight and horror on us seize,
Thou sing'st with so much gravity and ease;
And above human flight dost soar aloft,
With plume so strong, so equal, and so soft.
The bird named from that paradise you sing
So never flags, but always keeps on wing.
Where couldst thou words of such a compass find?
Whence furnish such a vast expense of mind?
Just heaven thee, like Tiresias, to requite,
Rewards with prophecy thy loss of sight.
Well might'st thou scorn thy readers to allure
With tinkling rhyme, of thine own sense secure;
While the *Town-Bays* writes all the while and spells,
And like a pack horse tires without his bells.

18. **some less skilful hand:** Dryden, who asked Milton if he could make a rhymed drama of *Paradise Lost.* "Mr. Milton received him civilly, and told him he would give him leave to tag his verses" (Aubrey, p. xxx).

30. **detect:** expose.

39. **bird named from that paradise:** Birds of Paradise were thought to live entirely in the air, never touching ground.

43. **Tiresias:** The legendary seer, mentioned in *PL* 3.36, was given prophetic vision in recompense for his blindness.

46. **tinkling rhyme:** Cp. Milton's "jingling sound of like endings" in his remarks on "The Verse" of *PL.*

47. **Town-Bays:** In Buckingham's play *The Rehearsal,* Dryden is lampooned in the character of Bayes. The name alludes to the laurel used to crown poets, which by synecdoche refers to all fame-seeking versifiers.

Their fancies like our bushy points appear:
The poets tag them; we for fashion wear.
I too transported by the mode offend,
And while I meant to *praise* thee must *commend.*
Thy verse created like thy theme sublime,
In number, weight, and measure, needs not rhyme.

49. **bushy points:** Points attached the hose to the doublet. They were either tasseled (*bushy*) or gathered together, like modern shoe laces, in a metal *tag.* Tagging bushy laces is here a metaphor for introducing regular end-rhyme in Milton's flowing blank verse.

54. **In number, weight, and measure:** See Wisdom 11:20: "thou hast ordered all things in measure, and number, and weight."

PARADISE LOST

THE PRINTER TO THE READER[1]

Courteous Reader, there was no argument at first intended to the book, but for the satisfaction of many that have desired it, I have procured it, and withal a reason of that which stumbled many others, why the poem rhymes not. S. Simmons

The Verse

The measure is English heroic verse without rhyme, as that of Homer in Greek, and of Vergil in Latin; rhyme being no necessary adjunct or true ornament of poem or good verse, in longer works especially, but the invention of a barbarous age, to set off wretched matter and lame meter; graced indeed since by the use of some famous modern poets, carried away by custom, but much to their own vexation, hindrance, and constraint to express many things otherwise, and for the most part worse than else they would have expressed them. Not without cause therefore some both Italian and Spanish poets of prime note have rejected rhyme both in longer and shorter works, as have also long since our best English tragedies, as a thing of itself, to all judicious ears, trivial and of no true musical delight; which consists only in apt numbers, fit quantity of syllables, and the sense variously drawn out from one verse into another, not in the jingling sound of like endings, a fault avoided by the learned ancients both in poetry and all good oratory. This neglect then of rhyme so little is to be taken for a defect, though it may seem so perhaps to vulgar readers, that it rather is to be esteemed an example set, the first in English, of ancient liberty recovered to heroic poem from the troublesome and modern bondage of rhyming.

1. The defense of blank verse and the prose arguments summarizing each book "procured" by Milton's printer, Samuel Simmons, were inserted in bound copies of the first edition beginning in 1668, with this brief note.

Book I

The Argument

This first book proposes, first in brief, the whole subject, man's disobedience, and the loss thereupon of Paradise wherein he was placed: then touches the prime cause of his fall, the serpent, or rather Satan in the serpent, who revolting from God, and drawing to his side many legions of angels, was by the command of God driven out of Heaven with all his crew into the great deep. Which action passed over, the poem hastes into the midst of things, presenting Satan with his angels now fallen into Hell, described here, not in the center (for heaven and earth may be supposed as yet not made, certainly not yet accursed) but in a place of utter darkness, fitliest called Chaos. Here Satan with his angels lying on the burning lake, thunder-struck and astonished, after a certain space recovers, as from confusion, calls up him who next in order and dignity lay by him. They confer of their miserable fall. Satan awakens all his legions, who lay till then in the same manner confounded; they rise, their numbers, array of battle, their chief leaders named, according to the idols known afterwards in Canaan and the countries adjoining. To these Satan directs his speech, comforts them with hope yet of regaining Heaven, but tells them lastly of a new world and new kind of creature to be created, according to an ancient prophecy or report in Heaven; for that angels were long before this visible creation was the opinion of many ancient Fathers. To find out the truth of this prophecy, and what to determine thereon, he refers to a full council. What his associates thence attempt. Pandaemonium the palace of Satan rises, suddenly built out of the deep. The infernal peers there sit in council.

Of man's first disobedience, and the fruit
Of that forbidden tree, whose mortal taste

1. The first line's introduction of an exemplary man recalls the epics of Homer and Vergil. Milton's theme, however, is neither martial nor imperial but spiritual: humanity's disastrous failure to obey God counterpoised by the promise of redemption. **Of man's:** The proper name *Adam* is also the Hebrew word for generic man or humankind. He is both an individual male and, with Eve, the entire species: "so God created man . . . ; male and female he created them" (Gen. 1.27). *Of man* translates the Hebrew for "woman" (Gen. 2.23). **fruit:** Its dual meanings (outcome, food) are put in play by enjambment, a primary formal device by which Milton draws out sense "from one verse into another" (*The Verse*).

Brought death into the world, and all our woe,
With loss of Eden, till one greater man
Restore us, and regain the blissful seat,
Sing heav'nly Muse, that on the secret top
Of Oreb, or of Sinai, didst inspire
That shepherd, who first taught the chosen seed,
In the beginning how the heavens and earth
Rose out of Chaos: or if Sion hill
Delight thee more, and Siloa's brook that flowed
Fast by the oracle of God, I thence
Invoke thy aid to my advent'rous song,
That with no middle flight intends to soar
Above th' Aonian mount, while it pursues
Things unattempted yet in prose or rhyme.

4. **one greater man:** Jesus, second Adam (1 Cor. 15.21–22; Rom. 5.19). Cp. *PR* 1.1–4.

5. **blissful seat:** translates Vergil's epithet for Elysium, *Aen.* 6.639.

6. **Sing heav'nly Muse:** the verb and subject of the magnificently inverted sixteen-line opening sentence. By invoking a Muse, Milton follows a convention that dates from Homer. Yet Milton's Muse is not the muse of classical epic (Calliope) but the inspiration of Moses, David, and the prophets (cp. 17–18n). **secret:** set apart, not common. When the Lord descends to give Moses the law, thick clouds and smoke obscure the mountaintop, and the people are forbidden on pain of death to cross boundaries around the mountain (Exod. 19.16, 23).

8. **shepherd:** The vocation of shepherd is a key vehicle for Milton's integration of classical and scriptural traditions. Moses encounters God while tending sheep on Mount Horeb (*Oreb*) and later receives the law on *Sinai,* a spur of Horeb (Exod. 3; 19). (Or the doubling of names may simply acknowledge the inconsistency of Exod. 19.20 and Deut. 4.10.)

9. **In the beginning:** opening phrase of Genesis and the Gospel of John.

10. **Chaos:** classical term for the primeval state of being out of which God creates, also referred to as "the deep" (as in Gen. 1.2) and "the abyss" (as in l. 21). **Sion hill:** Mount Zion, site of Solomon's Temple, "the house of the Lord" (1 Kings 6.1, 13). Adding to the persistent doubleness of the invocation, Milton requests inspiration from two scriptural sites associated with God's presence and prophetic inspiration. Both sites receive dual designations: Mount Horeb/Sinai and Mount Zion/Siloa's brook.

11–12. **Siloa's brook . . . God:** spring whose waters flowed through an underground aqueduct, supplied a pool near (*Fast by*) Solomon's Temple, and irrigated the king's lush garden (cp. 4.225–30). Jerome says it ran directly beneath Mount Zion (A. Gilbert 1919, 269). Scripturally, it symbolizes David's monarchical line (Isa. 7–8, esp. 8.6). In opening the eyes of the man born blind, Jesus sends him to wash his eyes with its waters (John 9). Cp. 3.30–31. **oracle of God:** the holiest place in the Temple, the tabernacle of the Ark of the Covenant (1 Kings 6.19). The classical Muses haunt a spring (Aganippe) on Helicon (cp. 15n), "the sacred well, / That from beneath the seat of Jove doth spring" (*Lyc* 15–16). In identifying the spring near the "Holy of Holies" as similarly a site of inspiration, Milton again links scriptural and classical prophetic and poetic traditions.

14. **no middle flight:** Milton will go beyond middle air, whose upper boundary is as high as the peaks of tall mountains, and soar to the highest Empyrean, the abode of God. His soaring ambition recalls the myth of Icarus, whose failure to follow a *middle flight* caused him to tumble into the sea (cp. 7.12–20).

15. **Aonian mount:** Helicon, Greek mountain favored by the Muses (cp. 11–12n). Hesiod says that while he tended sheep on Helicon (like Moses on Horeb), the Muses called him to sing of the gods (*Theog.* 22).

16. Translates the opening of *Orlando Furioso* (1.2) and is reminiscent of *Masque* 43–45; cp. similar claims by Lucretius (*De Rerum Nat.* 1.925–30) and Horace (*Odes* 3.1.2–4).

And chiefly thou, O Spirit, that dost prefer
Before all temples th' upright heart and pure,
Instruct me, for thou know'st; thou from the first
Wast present, and with mighty wings outspread
Dove-like sat'st brooding on the vast abyss
And mad'st it pregnant: what in me is dark
Illumine, what is low raise and support,
That to the highth of this great argument
I may assert eternal providence,
And justify the ways of God to men.
　Say first, for Heav'n hides nothing from thy view
Nor the deep tract of Hell, say first what cause
Moved our grand parents in that happy state,
Favored of Heav'n so highly, to fall off
From their Creator, and transgress his will
For one restraint, lords of the world besides?
Who first seduced them to that foul revolt?
Th' infernal serpent; he it was, whose guile
Stirred up with envy and revenge, deceived
The mother of mankind, what time his pride
Had cast him out from Heav'n, with all his host
Of rebel angels, by whose aid aspiring
To set himself in glory above his peers,
He trusted to have equaled the Most High,
If he opposed; and with ambitious aim
Against the throne and monarchy of God
Raised impious war in Heav'n and battle proud

17–18. 1 Cor. 3.16–17, 6.19. The *Spirit* is the Holy Spirit (l. 21). In Milton's theology, the diverse functions of the Holy Spirit derive from "the virtue and power of God the Father," in this case "the force or voice of God, in whatever way it was breathed into the prophets" (*CD* 1.6, p. 1194). The site of revelation progresses from Horeb/Sinai to Sion hill/Siloa's brook to, finally, the individual human heart.

21. **brooding:** Milton thus renders the Hebrew word translated as "moved" in the *AV* (Gen. 1.2) but as *incubabat* (brooded) in St. Basil and other Latin patristic authors (see also 7.235). Cp. Sir Thomas Browne, *Religio Medici:* "This is that gentle heat that brooded on the waters, and in six days hatched the world" (73).

24. **argument:** subject matter; cp. 9.28.

25. **assert:** take the part of, champion.

26. **justify:** vindicate; cp. Pope, *Essay on Man:* "Laugh where we must, be candid where we can,/But vindicate the ways of God to man" (1.15–16). Milton's word order permits dual readings: either "justify (the ways of God to men)" or "justify (the ways of God) to men." Cp. *SA:* "Just are the ways of God,/And justifiable to men" (293–94).

27–28. Milton introduces the narrative with a query, an epic convention; cp. "Tell me, O Muse, the cause" (Vergil, *Aen.* 1.8). Homer also depicts the Muses as all-knowing: "Tell me now, ye Muses that have dwellings on Olympus—for ye are goddesses and are at hand and know all things" (*Il.* 2.484–85).

29. **grand:** great, original, all-inclusive; cp. line 122.

30. **fall off:** deviate, revolt (as in l. 33).

33. Cp. *Il.* 1.8.

36. **what time:** when; cp. *Masque* 291, *Lyc* 28.

With vain attempt. Him the Almighty Power
Hurled headlong flaming from th' ethereal sky
With hideous ruin and combustion down
To bottomless perdition, there to dwell
In adamantine chains and penal fire,
Who durst defy th' Omnipotent to arms.
Nine times the space that measures day and night
To mortal men, he with his horrid crew
Lay vanquished, rolling in the fiery gulf
Confounded though immortal: but his doom
Reserved him to more wrath; for now the thought
Both of lost happiness and lasting pain
Torments him; round he throws his baleful eyes
That witnessed huge affliction and dismay
Mixed with obdurate pride and steadfast hate:
At once as far as angels ken he views
The dismal situation waste and wild,
A dungeon horrible, on all sides round

44–49. **Him . . . arms:** "God spared not the angels that sinned, but cast them down to hell and delivered them into chains of darkness" (2 Pet. 2.4; cp. Jude 6).

45. "I beheld Satan as lightning fall from heaven" (Luke 10.18); cp. Homer's Hephaestus "hurled . . . from the heavenly threshold . . . headlong" (*Il.* 1.591–92).

46. **ruin:** a fall from a great height, from the Latin *ruina;* cp 6.867–68.

48. **adamantine:** unbreakable (Gk.); cp. Aeschylus's Prometheus, clamped "in shackles of binding adamant that cannot be broken" (*Prom.* 6). The myth of adamant persists today; the indestructible claws of the Marvel Comics hero Wolverine are made of "adamantium."

49. **durst:** dared.

50–52. The rebel angels regain consciousness after nine days falling from Heaven (6.871) and nine days *rolling in the fiery gulf.* Hesiod's Titans fall nine days from heaven to earth and another nine from earth to Tartarus (*Theog.* 720–25). Milton, like many Christian mythographers, deemed the Titans' rebellion a pagan analogue for Satan's fall.

53. **Confounded:** destroyed. Combined with *though immortal,* it neatly defines the Christian concept of damnation.

54. **Reserved:** "And the angels which kept not their first estate, but left their own habitation, he hath reserved in everlasting chains under darkness unto the judgment of the great day" (Jude 6; cp. 2 Pet. 2.4). In *CD,* Milton cites these verses and others to show that "bad angels are kept for punishment" (1.9, p. 1218).

56. **baleful:** Of Old English origin, *baleful* signifies evil in both its active and its passive aspects. Satan's eyes thus brim with his own suffering and with malice toward others.

57. **witnessed:** Like *baleful,* active and passive. Satan's eyes express spite and woe and also observe it in the surrounding scene.

59. **ken:** "are able to see." Possessive apostrophes do not appear in early modern texts, so that *ken* here could also mean "visual range" of angels. The word is used both as a verb and as a noun elsewhere in *PL* (5.265, 11.379).

63. **darkness visible:** Judged "difficult to imagine" by T. S. Eliot, the paradox has scriptural and classical precedents. See the description in Job of the realm of the dead, "where the light is as darkness" (10.22) or, in Euripides' *Bacchae,* Pentheus's command to imprison Dionysus "so that he may see only darkness" (510). Milton previously flirted with the paradox in *Il Pens* (79–80). Cp. Keats's marginalia: "It can scarcely be conceived how Milton's blindness might here aid the magnitude of his conceptions, as a bat in a large gothic vault" (Lau 74).

66–67. **And rest . . . all:** The inscription above the gate to Dante's Hell reads, "Abandon every hope, who enter here" (*Inf.* 3.9). Cp. Euripides, *Trojan Women* (681–82).

As one great furnace flamed, yet from those flames
No light, but rather darkness visible
Served only to discover sights of woe,
Regions of sorrow, doleful shades, where peace
And rest can never dwell, hope never comes
That comes to all; but torture without end
Still urges, and a fiery deluge, fed
With ever-burning sulfur unconsumed:
Such place eternal justice had prepared
For those rebellious, here their prison ordained
In utter darkness, and their portion set
As far removed from God and light of Heav'n
As from the center thrice to th' utmost pole.
O how unlike the place from whence they fell!
There the companions of his fall, o'erwhelmed
With floods and whirlwinds of tempestuous fire,
He soon discerns, and welt'ring by his side
One next himself in power, and next in crime,
Long after known in Palestine, and named
Beëlzebub. To whom th' Arch-Enemy,
And thence in Heav'n called Satan, with bold words
Breaking the horrid silence thus began.
"If thou beest he; but O how fall'n! How changed
From him, who in the happy realms of light
Clothed with transcendent brightness didst outshine
Myriads though bright: if he whom mutual league,
United thoughts and counsels, equal hope
And hazard in the glorious enterprise,
Joined with me once, now misery hath joined

67–68. **but . . . urges:** "The devil that deceived them was cast into the lake of fire and brimstone . . . and shall be tormented day and night for ever and ever" (Rev. 20.10). **Still:** constantly.

70. Cp. "the everlasting fire, prepared for the devil and his angels" (Matt. 25.41). Dante similarly depicts the inferno as an artifice of divine justice (*Inf.* 3.4).

72. **utter darkness:** destination of those excluded from the kingdom of Heaven (Matt. 8.12, 22.13, 25.30). The *AV* has "outer" instead of "utter"; cp. 3.16. The Geneva gloss on Matt. 8.12 explains, "there is nothing but mere darkness out of the kingdom of heaven."

73–74. Homer, Hesiod, and Vergil precede Milton in expressing as a ratio distances between heaven, earth, and the pit of hell (*Il.* 8.16; *Theog.* 722–25; *Aen.* 6.577–79).

74. **center:** the earth, at the center of the Ptolemaic cosmos; **pole:** the point on the outside of the cosmic sphere closest to heaven.

78. **welt'ring:** rolling on waves; cp. *Lyc* 13.

81. **Beëlzebub:** Phoenician god at Ekron consulted by King Ahaziah (2 Kings 1.2). The name in Hebrew means "Lord of Flies." In the Gospels, he is called "prince of the devils"; he was often identified with Satan (Matt. 12.24; cp. *CD* 1.9, p. 1219).

82. **Satan:** Hebrew word for adversary or enemy, first applied to Satan after his rebellion (5.658). He ultimately glories in the title (10.386–87).

84. **If . . . fall'n:** "How art thou fallen from heaven, O Lucifer, son of the morning!" (Isa. 14.12; cp. Vergil, *Aen.* 2.274). The appearance of the rebel angels is altered for the worse. They are also bereft of names (ll. 361–65). Hence Satan persists in the conditional salutation (l. 87).

In equal ruin: into what pit thou seest
From what highth fall'n, so much the stronger proved
He with his thunder: and till then who knew
The force of those dire arms? Yet not for those,
Nor what the potent victor in his rage
Can else inflict, do I repent or change,
Though changed in outward luster; that fixed mind
And high disdain, from sense of injured merit,
That with the mightiest raised me to contend,
And to the fierce contention brought along
Innumerable force of spirits armed
That durst dislike his reign, and me preferring,
His utmost power with adverse power opposed
In dubious battle on the plains of Heav'n,
And shook his throne. What though the field be lost?
All is not lost; the unconquerable will,
And study of revenge, immortal hate,
And courage never to submit or yield:
And what is else not to be overcome?
That glory never shall his wrath or might
Extort from me. To bow and sue for grace
With suppliant knee, and deify his power,
Who from the terror of this arm so late
Doubted his empire, that were low indeed,
That were an ignominy and shame beneath
This downfall; since by fate the strength of gods
And this empyreal substance cannot fail,
Since through experience of this great event
In arms not worse, in foresight much advanced,

98. **high disdain:** noble scorn. A relatively common reaction in an aristocratic era (Kerrigan 2000), it is characteristic of Satan (cp. 4.50, 82, 180).

103–5. Satan's account differs from Raphael's; cp. 6.832–34, 853–55.

107. **study:** pursuit.

109. "And what else does it mean 'not to be overcome'?"

114. **Doubted:** feared for.

115. **ignominy:** can be pronounced "ig-no-min-y" or "ig-no-my" (as it was often spelled). In the former case, the terminal *y* would coalesce with *and*. Cp. 2.207, 6.383.

116. **fate:** Satan makes fate the ultimate authority, distinct from the deity, as in Homer. God later defines fate as what he wills, 7.173; cp. *CD* 1.2, pp. 1145–46. The portrayal of fate as an independent governing principle is a feature of Stoic philosophy specifically criticized by Jesus in *PR* (4.313–18). **gods:** "Anyone can observe throughout the whole of the Old Testament . . . that angels often take upon them as their own the name . . . of God" (*CD* 1.5, p. 1185). God himself refers to the angels as gods (3.341). Cp. Herrick, *Of Angels:* "Angels are called gods; yet of them, none / Are gods, but by participation" (1–2).

117. **empyreal substance:** fiery essence, like the substance of Heaven; cp. 2.771. Heaven (the empyrean) and Hell both are based on the element of fire: in Hell it possesses only its destructive properties, in Heaven only its salutary ones. See 63n.

We may with more successful hope resolve
To wage by force or guile eternal war
Irreconcilable, to our grand foe,
Who now triumphs, and in th' excess of joy
Sole reigning holds the tyranny of Heav'n."
So spake th' apostate angel, though in pain,
Vaunting aloud, but racked with deep despair:
And him thus answered soon his bold compeer.
"O Prince, O chief of many thronèd powers,
That led th' embattled Seraphim to war
Under thy conduct, and in dreadful deeds
Fearless, endangered Heav'n's perpetual King,
And put to proof his high supremacy,
Whether upheld by strength, or chance, or fate,
Too well I see and rue the dire event,
That with sad overthrow and foul defeat
Hath lost us Heav'n, and all this mighty host
In horrible destruction laid thus low,
As far as gods and Heav'nly essences
Can perish: for the mind and spirit remains
Invincible, and vigor soon returns,
Though all our glory extinct, and happy state
Here swallowed up in endless misery.
But what if he our conqueror (whom I now
Of force believe almighty, since no less
Than such could have o'erpow'red such force as ours)
Have left us this our spirit and strength entire
Strongly to suffer and support our pains,
That we may so suffice his vengeful ire,
Or do him mightier service as his thralls

123. **triumphs:** Emphasis on the second syllable stresses a plosive-frictive fusion, as in *harumph.* It was common to accent the word thus.

125–27. Cp. Vergil's depiction of the seemingly optimistic Aeneas after he has rallied his distressed comrades: "So spake his tongue; while sick with weighty cares he feigns hope on his face, and deep in his heart stifles the anguish" (*Aen.* 1.208–9).

128–29. **powers . . . Seraphim:** Thrones and Powers, like *Seraphim,* are angelic orders. The phrase *thronèd powers* invokes no specific order of angel, however. It instead indicates the dignity and spiritual nature of those led by Satan, including the *Seraphim.*

134. **event:** outcome.

141. **glory:** effulgence or brilliant, radiant light (see 63n, 117n). *Glory* is a word with a broad range of meaning in the poem (cp. in Book 1, ll. 39, 110, 239, 370, 594, 612; see Rumrich 1987, 3–52). **extinct:** (be) put out, extinguished.

144. **Of force:** perforce; cp. 4.813.

147. **support:** endure.

148. **suffice:** satisfy.

149–50. **thralls/By right of war:** slaves by conquest. "The effects and consequences of this right are infinite so that there is nothing so unlawful but the lord may do it to his slaves . . . there are no torments but what may with impunity be imposed on them, nothing to be done but what they may be forced to do by all manner of rigor and severity." (Grotius, *Rights* 481; cp. *CD* 1.11).

By right of war, whate'er his business be
Here in the heart of Hell to work in fire,
Or do his errands in the gloomy deep;
What can it then avail though yet we feel
Strength undiminished, or eternal being
To undergo eternal punishment?"
Whereto with speedy words th' Arch-Fiend replied.
"Fall'n cherub, to be weak is miserable
Doing or suffering: but of this be sure,
To do aught good never will be our task,
But ever to do ill our sole delight,
As being the contrary to his high will
Whom we resist. If then his providence
Out of our evil seek to bring forth good,
Our labor must be to pervert that end,
And out of good still to find means of evil;
Which ofttimes may succeed, so as perhaps
Shall grieve him, if I fail not, and disturb
His inmost counsels from their destined aim.
But see the angry victor hath recalled
His ministers of vengeance and pursuit
Back to the gates of Heav'n: the sulfurous hail
Shot after us in storm, o'erblown hath laid
The fiery surge, that from the precipice
Of Heav'n received us falling, and the thunder,
Winged with red lightning and impetuous rage,
Perhaps hath spent his shafts, and ceases now
To bellow through the vast and boundless deep.
Let us not slip th' occasion, whether scorn,
Or satiate fury yield it from our foe.
Seest thou yon dreary plain, forlorn and wild,
The seat of desolation, void of light,
Save what the glimmering of these livid flames
Casts pale and dreadful? Thither let us tend

152. **deep:** chaos; see 10n.

153–55. The question crystallizes Satan and Beëlzebub's developing awareness of their plight: what possible advantage is there in being a mighty entity eternally sustained only to absorb eternal punishment?

158. **Doing or suffering:** The Stoic counterpoise of suffering and doing was a literary commonplace, with suicide sometimes seeming the active option. So Hamlet ponders whether it is nobler "to suffer/The slings and arrows of outrageous fortune / Or to take arms against a sea of troubles" (3.1.56–58). The antithesis is regularly and variously invoked in the first two books (see, e.g., 2.199) and later approaches personification in the characters of the aggressively suicidal Moloch and the craven Belial.

167. **fail:** err.

172. **o'erblown hath laid:** having blown over (or, having blown down from above) has calmed.

178. **slip:** neglect, miss.

182. **livid:** black and blue, like a bruise; furious.

From off the tossing of these fiery waves,
There rest, if any rest can harbor there,
And reassembling our afflicted powers,
Consult how we may henceforth most offend
Our enemy, our own loss how repair,
How overcome this dire calamity,
What reinforcement we may gain from hope,
If not what resolution from despair."
  Thus Satan talking to his nearest mate
With head uplift above the wave, and eyes
That sparkling blazed, his other parts besides
Prone on the flood, extended long and large
Lay floating many a rood, in bulk as huge
As whom the fables name of monstrous size,
Titanian, or Earth-born, that warred on Jove,
Briareos or Typhon, whom the den
By ancient Tarsus held, or that sea beast
Leviathan, which God of all his works
Created hugest that swim th' ocean stream:
Him haply slumb'ring on the Norway foam
The pilot of some small night-foundered skiff,
Deeming some island, oft, as seamen tell,
With fixèd anchor in his scaly rind
Moors by his side under the lee, while night
Invests the sea, and wishèd morn delays:
So stretched out huge in length the Arch-Fiend lay
Chained on the burning lake, nor ever thence
Had ris'n or heaved his head, but that the will
And high permission of all-ruling Heaven

186. **afflicted:** struck down, routed.

196. **rood:** a measure of length that varies from 5.5 to 8.0 yards (5.0 to 7.3 meters); a measure of land equal to a quarter acre, or 40 square rods (0.1 hectare).

198–99. **Titanian . . . Typhon:** In Greek myth the Titans, children of Heaven (Uranus) and Earth (Gaia), were of the generation before the Olympian gods. The Giants, monstrous and huge, were also *Earth-born.* The Titans and Giants *warred* against the Olympian gods on separate occasions, but the two battles were often confused. See 50–52n. *Briareos* was a Titan with a hundred hands; *Typhon,* a hundred-headed Giant, "the Earth-born dweller of the Cilician caves," in Aeschylus's phrase (*Prom.* 353–54; cp. Homer, *Il.* 2.783, Pindar, *Pyth.* 1.15).

200. **Tarsus:** the capital of ancient Cilicia.

201. **Leviathan:** gigantic sea beast, symbolic of God's creative power (Job 41), but in Isa. 27.1 a target of divine judgment, identified as Satan by commentators. Cp. 7.412–16.

203–8. Tales of enormous sea creatures and of mariners who mistook them for islands were common, as were moral applications of such stories.

204. **night-foundered:** sunk in night.

207. **lee:** the side away from the wind and thus sheltered from it.

208. **Invests:** cloaks.

210–15. **Chained . . . damnation:** Cp. lines 239–41. Some readers regard this providential logic with disapproval. See Tennyson's response, as recorded by his son Hallam: "I hope most of us have a higher idea in these modern times of the Almighty than this" (881).

Left him at large to his own dark designs,
That with reiterated crimes he might
Heap on himself damnation, while he sought
Evil to others, and enraged might see
How all his malice served but to bring forth
Infinite goodness, grace and mercy shown
On man by him seduced, but on himself
Treble confusion, wrath and vengeance poured.
Forthwith upright he rears from off the pool
His mighty stature; on each hand the flames
Driv'n backward slope their pointing spires, and rolled
In billows, leave i' th' midst a horrid vale.
Then with expanded wings he steers his flight
Aloft, incumbent on the dusky air
That felt unusual weight, till on dry land
He lights, if it were land that ever burned
With solid, as the lake with liquid fire,
And such appeared in hue, as when the force
Of subterranean wind transports a hill
Torn from Pelorus, or the shattered side
Of thund'ring Etna, whose combustible
And fueled entrails thence conceiving fire,
Sublimed with mineral fury, aid the winds,
And leave a singèd bottom all involved
With stench and smoke: such resting found the sole
Of unblest feet. Him followed his next mate,
Both glorying to have scaped the Stygian flood
As gods, and by their own recovered strength,
Not by the sufferance of supernal power.

224. **horrid:** bristling, spiky (as *pointing spires* suggests).

226. **incumbent:** pressing with his weight (cp. *recumbent*); cp. Spenser's description of the dragon's flight, *FQ* 1.11.18.

230. **hue:** not simply color but also form or aspect. Cp. Shakespeare, *Sonnets* (20.7).

230–35. **as . . . winds:** Milton's account of Etna erupting echoes Vergil in diction (*thund'ring, entrails*), but unlike Vergil, he describes a geological process rather than trace the eruption to a pent-up giant (*Aen.* 3.571–77). The seismic violence attributed to wind trapped underground is similarly described by Ovid (*Met.* 15.296–306) and Lucretius (*On the Nature of Things* 6.535–607). Cp. 6.195–98; *SA* 1647–48.

232. **Pelorus:** Cape Faro, promontory of northeastern Sicily, near Etna.

234. **fueled . . . fire:** combustible interior (*entrails*) igniting from the force of the wind and spreading.

235. Vaporized (*sublimed*) by the intense heat of burning rock, the fuel-laden interior becomes hot mineral gas that augments the wind expelled from the *shattered side* of the mountain.

239. **Stygian flood:** body of water like the river Styx; the *fiery gulf* (52).

240–41. Satan and Beëlzebub contradict the narrator's explanation (ll. 210–15). Cp. Homer's Aias, who, having been saved from the sea by Poseidon, "declared that it was in spite of the gods that he had escaped the great gulf" (*Od.* 4.504). Poseidon immediately kills him.

"Is this the region, this the soil, the clime,"
Said then the lost Archangel, "this the seat
That we must change for Heav'n, this mournful gloom
For that celestial light? Be it so, since he
Who now is sov'reign can dispose and bid
What shall be right: farthest from him is best
Whom reason hath equaled, force hath made supreme
Above his equals. Farewell happy fields
Where joy for ever dwells: hail horrors, hail
Infernal world, and thou profoundest Hell
Receive thy new possessor: one who brings
A mind not to be changed by place or time.
The mind is its own place, and in itself
Can make a Heav'n of Hell, a Hell of Heav'n.
What matter where, if I be still the same,
And what I should be, all but less than he
Whom thunder hath made greater? Here at least
We shall be free; th' Almighty hath not built
Here for his envy, will not drive us hence:
Here we may reign secure, and in my choice
To reign is worth ambition though in Hell:
Better to reign in Hell, than serve in Heav'n.
But wherefore let we then our faithful friends,
Th' associates and copartners of our loss
Lie thus astonished on th' oblivious pool,
And call them not to share with us their part

244. **change:** exchange.

252. **possessor:** one who occupies without ownership (a legal term).

253. Cp. Horace, "the sky not the mind changes in one who crosses the sea" (*Epist.* 1.11.27). Young Milton adopted this as his motto (Hanford 98).

254–56. The chiasmus concluding line 255 epitomizes Satan's claim for the mind's constitutive power. Cp. *Hamlet:* "There is nothing either good or bad, but thinking makes it so" (2.2.249–50). That Satan's condition is a function of his own unchanging psyche is later borne out, ironically and to his dismay; see 4.75, 9.118–23.

257. **all but less than:** This puzzling phrase is usually glossed as a combination of "only less than" and "all but equal to." Satan is not conceding inequality, however, but asserting parity. He is anything but less than God, who triumphed because of superior armament—"his only dreaded bolt" (6.491).

263. Cp. Plutarch's account of Caesar riding past a sorry barbarian village, "I would rather be first here than second at Rome" (*Lives* 469) or the sentiments of Euripides' Eteocles, "When I can rule, shall I be this man's slave?" (*Phoe.* 520). Satan's specific preference has plentiful precedent, typically to the contrary: "I should choose . . . to serve as the hireling . . . of some portionless man . . . rather than to be lord over all the dead" (*Od.* 11.489–91); "I had rather be a doorkeeper in the house of my God, than to dwell in the tents of wickedness" (Ps. 84.10). See Abdiel's similar declaration, 6.183–84.

265. **copartners:** equal participants (coheirs) in an inheritance.

266. **astonished:** shocked, thunderstruck; **oblivious:** producing oblivion; cp. 2.74.

In this unhappy mansion, or once more
With rallied arms to try what may be yet
Regained in Heav'n, or what more lost in Hell?"
So Satan spake, and him Beëlzebub
Thus answered. "Leader of those armies bright,
Which but th' Omnipotent none could have foiled,
If once they hear that voice, their liveliest pledge
Of hope in fears and dangers, heard so oft
In worst extremes, and on the perilous edge
Of battle when it raged, in all assaults
Their surest signal, they will soon resume
New courage and revive, though now they lie
Groveling and prostrate on yon lake of fire,
As we erewhile, astounded and amazed,
No wonder, fallen such a pernicious highth."
He scarce had ceased when the superior fiend
Was moving toward the shore; his ponderous shield
Ethereal temper, massy, large and round,
Behind him cast; the broad circumference
Hung on his shoulders like the moon, whose orb
Through optic glass the Tuscan artist views
At evening from the top of Fesole,
Or in Valdarno, to descry new lands,
Rivers or mountains in her spotty globe.
His spear, to equal which the tallest pine
Hewn on Norwegian hills, to be the mast
Of some great ammiral, were but a wand,
He walked with to support uneasy steps

268. **mansion:** abode; cp. John 14.2: "In my father's house are many mansions."

276. **edge:** critical moment; battle line (as at *PL* 6.108). Shakespeare's Henry IV calls it "the edge of war" (*1H4* 1.1.17).

281. **erewhile:** some time ago; **amazed:** stunned; a stronger term in Milton's era than in ours.

284. **Was moving:** began to move; a classical use of the imperfect tense.

288–91. **Tuscan . . . globe:** Galileo is *the Tuscan artist,* the only contemporary to whom Milton in *PL* overtly alludes or names (5.262). *Artist* here signifies one skilled in a science. In *Areopagitica,* Milton claims that he visited Galileo while touring Tuscany (p. 950). Galileo was by 1638 already blind or nearly so, making it unlikely that Milton witnessed him using his telescope (*optic glass*) to view the moon. Yet the poet was obviously fascinated by the new technology and the vistas it opened to imagination (Nicolson). *Fesole* overlooks the Arno river valley (*Valdarno*) and the city of Florence—a landscape and a society that Milton idolized. Galileo describes the moon's surface as mountainous in *Sidereal Messenger.*

292–94. Homer's Polyphemos, the Cyclops, wields "a staff . . . as large as is the mast of a black ship of twenty oars" (*Od.* 9.322). After he is blinded, "a lopped pine guides and steadies his steps" (Vergil, *Aen.* 3.659). Milton extends Homer's comparison into a ratio that renders a great ship's mast inadequate to indicate the size of Satan's spear.

294. **ammiral:** obsolete spelling of *admiral;* a vessel carrying an admiral, flagship.

Over the burning marl, not like those steps
On Heaven's azure, and the torrid clime
Smote on him sore besides, vaulted with fire;
Nathless he so endured, till on the beach
Of that inflamèd sea, he stood and called
His legions, angel forms, who lay entranced
Thick as autumnal leaves that strow the brooks
In Vallombrosa, where th' Etrurian shades
High overarched embow'r; or scattered sedge
Afloat, when with fierce winds Orion armed
Hath vexed the Red Sea coast, whose waves o'erthrew
Busiris and his Memphian chivalry,
While with perfidious hatred they pursued
The sojourners of Goshen, who beheld
From the safe shore their floating carcasses
And broken chariot wheels. So thick bestrown
Abject and lost lay these, covering the flood,
Under amazement of their hideous change.
He called so loud, that all the hollow deep
Of Hell resounded. "Princes, potentates,
Warriors, the flow'r of Heav'n, once yours, now lost,
If such astonishment as this can seize
Eternal spirits; or have ye chos'n this place
After the toil of battle to repose
Your wearied virtue, for the ease you find
To slumber here, as in the vales of Heav'n?
Or in this abject posture have ye sworn
To adore the conqueror, who now beholds

296. **marl:** rich, crumbly soil.

298. **vaulted:** The heavens are commonly described as an arched structure, or vault, like the ceiling of a cathedral. In Hell, even the sky is on fire.

299. **Nathless:** nonetheless.

302. **autumnal leaves:** Comparison of the dead to fallen leaves is commonplace; cp. Homer, *Il.* 6.146; Vergil, *Aen.* 6.309–10; Dante, *Inf.* 3.112–15. Milton's description is distinctly echoed in Dryden's 1697 translation of Vergil: "thick as the leaves in autumn strow the woods" (*Aen.* 6.428).

303. Milton likely visited the heavily wooded valley of *Vallombrosa* in the fall of 1638. The Italian place name literally means "shady valley." Note its somber aural combination with *autumnal, strow, brooks,* and *embow'r.* **Etruria:** classical name for the Tuscan region. *Shades* is a metonymy for trees as well as a name for spirits of the dead.

304. **sedge:** botanical transition from the autumnal leaves of Vallombrosa to the Red Sea of Exodus. The Hebrew name for the Red Sea means "Sea of Sedge."

305. **Orion armed:** constellation of a hunter with sword and club. Orion rising was associated with stormy weather.

307. **Busiris:** mythical Egyptian king often identified as an oppressor of the Hebrews but here as the scriptural Pharaoh whose army is engulfed after it pursues the Hebrews into the parted Red Sea (Exod. 14). **Memphian chivalry:** Memphis was the ancient capital of Egypt; *chivalry* refers to armed forces (cp. *PR* 3.344).

309. **sojourners of Goshen:** Hebrews fleeing Egypt, the land of Goshen (Gen. 47.27).

320. **virtue:** strength, valor.

Cherub and Seraph rolling in the flood
With scattered arms and ensigns, till anon
His swift pursuers from Heav'n gates discern
Th' advantage, and descending tread us down
Thus drooping, or with linkèd thunderbolts
Transfix us to the bottom of this gulf?
Awake, arise, or be for ever fall'n."
They heard, and were abashed, and up they sprung
Upon the wing, as when men wont to watch
On duty, sleeping found by whom they dread,
Rouse and bestir themselves ere well awake.
Nor did they not perceive the evil plight
In which they were, or the fierce pains not feel;
Yet to their general's voice they soon obeyed
Innumerable. As when the potent rod
Of Amram's son in Egypt's evil day
Waved round the coast, up called a pitchy cloud
Of locusts, warping on the eastern wind,
That o'er the realm of impious Pharaoh hung
Like night, and darkened all the land of Nile:
So numberless were those bad angels seen
Hovering on wing under the cope of Hell
'Twixt upper, nether, and surrounding fires;
Till, as a signal giv'n, th' uplifted spear
Of their great sultan waving to direct
Their course, in even balance down they light
On the firm brimstone, and fill all the plain;
A multitude, like which the populous north
Poured never from her frozen loins, to pass
Rhene or the Danaw, when her barbarous sons
Came like a deluge on the south, and spread
Beneath Gibraltar to the Libyan sands.
Forthwith from every squadron and each band

324. **Seraph:** singular of *seraphim* (on the model of *cherub/cherubim*).

325. **anon:** straightaway, instantly (not "in a little while").

327. **tread us down:** trample us in triumph; cp. 2.79.

337. The construction *obey to* is unusual but not unprecedented; see Shakespeare's *Phoenix:* "to whose sound chaste wings obey" (4); cp. Rom. 6.16.

339. **Amram's son:** Moses, who with his rod calls a black (*pitchy*) cloud of locusts to afflict Egypt (Exod. 10.12–15; cp. 12.185–86).

341. **warping:** floating and swarming.

345. **cope:** covering, vault, like that of the sky; cp. l. 298, 4.992.

348. **sultan:** ruler, despot, or tyrant.

351–55. Alludes to barbarian hoards (Goths, Huns, Vandals) who from the third to fifth centuries poured into the southern Roman Empire. The Vandals crossed from Spain (*Beneath Gibraltar*) into Northern Africa (*Libyan sands*).

353. **Rhene . . . Danaw:** Rhine, Danube.

The heads and leaders thither haste where stood
Their great commander; godlike shapes and forms
Excelling human, princely dignities,
And Powers that erst in Heaven sat on thrones;
Though of their names in Heav'nly records now
Be no memorial, blotted out and razed
By their rebellion, from the Books of Life.
Nor had they yet among the sons of Eve
Got them new names, till wand'ring o'er the Earth,
Through God's high sufferance for the trial of man,
By falsities and lies the greatest part
Of mankind they corrupted to forsake
God their Creator, and th' invisible
Glory of him that made them to transform
Oft to the image of a brute, adorned
With gay religions full of pomp and gold,
And devils to adore for deities:
Then were they known to men by various names,
And various idols through the heathen world.
Say, Muse, their names then known, who first, who last,
Roused from the slumber on that fiery couch,
At their great emperor's call, as next in worth
Came singly where he stood on the bare strand,
While the promiscuous crowd stood yet aloof?
The chief were those who from the pit of Hell
Roaming to seek their prey on earth, durst fix
Their seats long after next the seat of God,
Their altars by his altar, gods adored
Among the nations round, and durst abide
Jehovah thund'ring out of Sion, throned
Between the Cherubim; yea, often placed
Within his sanctuary itself their shrines,
Abominations; and with cursèd things

363. **Books:** On God's condemnation as erasure (*razed*) from the roll of eternal life, see Exod. 32.32–33 and Rev. 22.5. The fallen angels' previous identities no longer exist; cp. 84n.

372. **gay:** gaudy, wanton; cp. 4.942.

373. That pagan gods were fallen angels was a Christian commonplace rooted in classical and scriptural thought, as Verity details (672–74). Cp. *Nat Ode* 173–228, *PR* 2.121–26.

376. The catalog is conventional, as is the request of the Muse to supply it; cp. Homer, *Il.* 5.703; Vergil, *Aen.* 9.664. Invocation of the Muse, a pagan deity, may seem jarring here, though in the invocations to Books 1 and 7 Milton identifies his Muse with inspiration from God.

380. **promiscuous:** random, diverse.

386–87. **Sion . . . Cherubim:** Zion is the site of Solomon's Temple, which houses the Ark of the Covenant. The throne of God's invisible presence stands on top of the Ark between images of cherubim; see 10n.

389. **Abominations:** scripturally, causes of pollution, especially idols of false gods; objects that excite disgust and hatred in true believers.

His holy rites, and solemn feasts profaned,
And with their darkness durst affront his light.
First Moloch, horrid king besmeared with blood
Of human sacrifice, and parents' tears,
Though for the noise of drums and timbrels loud
Their children's cries unheard, that passed through fire
To his grim idol. Him the Ammonite
Worshipped in Rabba and her wat'ry plain,
In Argob and in Basan, to the stream
Of utmost Arnon. Nor content with such
Audacious neighborhood, the wisest heart
Of Solomon he led by fraud to build
His temple right against the temple of God
On that opprobrious hill, and made his grove
The pleasant valley of Hinnom, Tophet thence
And black Gehenna called, the type of Hell.
Next Chemos, th' obscene dread of Moab's sons,
From Aroar to Nebo, and the wild
Of southmost Abarim; in Hesebon
And Horonaim, Seon's realm, beyond
The flow'ry dale of Sibma clad with vines,
And Eleale to th' Asphaltic Pool.
Peor his other name, when he enticed
Israel in Sittim on their march from Nile

392–96. **Moloch . . . idol:** *Moloch,* whose name is Hebrew for "king," was an Ammonite god represented by an idol "of brass, having the head of a calf . . . with arms extended to receive the miserable sacrifice [an infant], seared to death with his burning embracements. For the idol was hollow within, filled with fire. And lest their lamentable shrieks should sad the hearts of their parents, the priests of Moloch did deaf their ears with the continual clang of trumpets and timbrels" (Sandys 1637, 186). Victims were said to be *passed through fire* to Moloch (2 Kings 23.10).

397–99. **Rabba:** Ammonite capital, the "city of waters" (2 Sam. 12.27); *Argob* was Ammonite territory in *Basan* (on the Eastern side of the Jordan). *Arnon* is the name of a river erroneously supposed to flow near Rabba.

400–405. Moloch dares induce worship among the Ammonites, whose realm bordered on Israel. Even more impudently, he leads Solomon to build him a temple opposite God's temple.

404. **Hinnom, Tophet thence:** valley sacred to Moloch, south of Jerusalem. The Greek for *Gehenna* ("valley of Hinnom") is in the *AV* translated as Hell (e.g., Matt. 23.33). *Hinnom* was thought to derive from the Hebrew for "outcry," referring to the screams of sacrificial babies; *Tophet* from the Hebrew for "timbrel," the instrument used to drown the screams (Selden 314). Post-exile Jews made the valley a dump where corpses of animals and criminals were burned. It thence symbolized the place of eternal punishment.

406–17. **Chemos:** god of the Moabites (*Moab's sons*); a Priapus-like idol also called Baal-Peör (412). See Selden 46–65. The scriptural place names in lines 407–11 demarcate Moabite territory on the east shore of the Dead Sea (*Asphaltic Pool*). During the Exodus, wandering Hebrews participated in his *wanton rites* and were punished with a plague (*woe*); see Num. 25, which Milton in *CMS* cites as the basis for a future work. Later, Solomon built a temple to Chemos on the mount (*hill of scandal*) where Moloch's temple also stood (1 Kings 11.7; see 400–405n). The fertility cult of Chemos practiced ritual sex; Moloch's worshipers burned babies: hence, *lust hard by hate.*

To do him wanton rites, which cost them woe.
Yet thence his lustful orgies he enlarged
Even to that hill of scandal, by the grove
Of Moloch homicide, lust hard by hate;
Till good Josiah drove them thence to Hell.
With these came they, who from the bord'ring flood
Of old Euphrates to the brook that parts
Egypt from Syrian ground, had general names
Of Baälim and Ashtaroth, those male,
These feminine. For spirits when they please
Can either sex assume, or both; so soft
And uncompounded is their essence pure,
Nor tied or manacled with joint or limb,
Nor founded on the brittle strength of bones,
Like cumbrous flesh; but in what shape they choose
Dilated or condensed, bright or obscure,
Can execute their airy purposes,
And works of love or enmity fulfill.
For those the race of Israel oft forsook
Their Living Strength, and unfrequented left
His righteous altar, bowing lowly down
To bestial gods; for which their heads as low
Bowed down in battle, sunk before the spear
Of despicable foes. With these in troop
Came Astoreth, whom the Phoenicians called
Astarte, queen of heav'n, with crescent horns;
To whose bright image nightly by the moon
Sidonian virgins paid their vows and songs,
In Sion also not unsung, where stood
Her temple on th' offensive mountain, built
By that uxorious king, whose heart though large,

418. **Josiah:** King of Judah admired by Reformers because he destroyed idols and defiled their sites of worship; see 2 Kings 23.10–14.

419–21. **from . . . ground:** I.e., the land of Israel or Canaan, distinguished by rivers that mark its northeastern and southwestern boundaries (Gen. 2.14).

422. **Baälim and Ashtaroth:** collective titles for Canaanite fertility gods and goddesses (sing. Baal, Ashtoreth—as at l. 438), often worshiped by ancient Israelites.

425. **uncompounded:** not differentiated into anatomical parts or systems.

433. **Living Strength:** epithet for God (cp. 1 Sam. 15.29).

438–41. Phoenician version of the Assyrian Istar and the Greek Aphrodite, called *Astartè.* Her image had the body of a woman and the head of a horned bull, representing the crescent moon; cp. *Nat Ode* 200 and *Masque* 1002. Jeremiah (7.18) titles her the Queen of Heaven. *Sidon* was a chief Phoenician seaport. See Selden 141–71.

444–46. **uxorious . . . foul:** The king is Solomon, who to please foreign wives (*fair idolatresses*) erects temples on the Mount of Olives (*th' offensive mountain*) to Moloch, Chemos, and Ashtoreth (2 Kings 11.1–8). Cp. lines 403, 416. Solomon's *large heart* refers to his intellectual capacity (1 Kings 3.9–12). His *uxorious* idolatry appears in *CMS* among subjects for future works.

Beguiled by fair idolatresses, fell
To idols foul. Thammuz came next behind,
Whose annual wound in Lebanon allured
The Syrian damsels to lament his fate
In amorous ditties all a summer's day,
While smooth Adonis from his native rock
Ran purple to the sea, supposed with blood
Of Thammuz yearly wounded: the love-tale
Infected Sion's daughters with like heat,
Whose wanton passions in the sacred porch
Ezekiel saw, when by the vision led
His eye surveyed the dark idolatries
Of alienated Judah. Next came one
Who mourned in earnest, when the captive ark
Maimed his brute image, head and hands lopped off
In his own temple, on the grunsel edge,
Where he fell flat, and shamed his worshippers:
Dagon his name, sea monster, upward man
And downward fish: yet had his temple high
Reared in Azotus, dreaded through the coast
Of Palestine, in Gath and Ascalon
And Accaron and Gaza's frontier bounds.
Him followed Rimmon, whose delightful seat
Was fair Damascus, on the fertile banks
Of Abbana and Pharphar, lucid streams.
He also against the house of God was bold:
A leper once he lost and gained a king,

446–52. **Thammuz . . . wounded:** Thammuz is beloved of Astartè, who precedes him in the catalog. He is the Phoenician (Syrian) original of Adonis, which is also the name of a river in Lebanon that runs red after the summer solstice, purportedly with blood from Thammuz's mortal wound. The river's source lies in a rocky coastal mountain range; hence its *native rock.* Adonis is a sun god whose annual death and revival signifies the changing of the seasons. See Sandys 1637, 20; Selden 239–49. Milton alludes to the familiar myth often, e.g., *Nat Ode* 204, *Manso* 11, and *Eikon,* where he scorns hypocritical mourning for the beheaded Charles (Yale 3:365).

455. **Ezekiel:** Like other prophets, he condemned idolatrous observances in Israel, among them "women weeping for Thammuz" (Ezek. 8.14).

457–66. **Next . . . bounds:** During the era of Judges, the Philistines captured the Ark of the Covenant (see 386–87n) and set it in the temple of their god, *Dagon.* His idol then fell before the Ark onto the temple threshold (*grunsel*) and broke (1 Sam. 5). Lines 464–66 name the chief cities of the Philistines. *Dag* is Hebrew for "fish." See Selden 173–89.

467–69. **Rimmon:** Syrian deity worshiped in Damascus, which lies between the rivers *Abbana* and *Pharphar.*

471. **A leper once he lost:** Elisha told the Syrian leper Naaman to cleanse himself in the Jordan. Naaman proclaimed the superiority of the rivers of Damascus but ultimately humbled himself, washed in the Jordan, and was cured (2 Kings 5.8–19).

471–76. **gained . . . vanquished:** King Ahaz of Judah defeated the Syrians but, returning to Jerusalem, erected an altar to Rimmon and worshiped him (2 Kings 16.10–16).

Ahaz his sottish conqueror, whom he drew
God's altar to disparage and displace
For one of Syrian mode, whereon to burn
His odious off'rings, and adore the gods
Whom he had vanquished. After these appeared
A crew who under names of old renown,
Osiris, Isis, Orus and their train
With monstrous shapes and sorceries abused
Fanatic Egypt and her priests, to seek
Their wand'ring gods disguised in brutish forms
Rather than human. Nor did Israel scape
Th' infection when their borrowed gold composed
The calf in Oreb: and the rebel king
Doubled that sin in Bethel and in Dan,
Lik'ning his Maker to the grazèd ox,
Jehovah, who in one night when he passed
From Egypt marching, equaled with one stroke
Both her first born and all her bleating gods.
Belial came last, than whom a spirit more lewd
Fell not from Heaven, or more gross to love
Vice for itself: to him no temple stood
Or altar smoked; yet who more oft than he
In temples and at altars, when the priest
Turns atheist, as did Eli's sons, who filled
With lust and violence the house of God.
In courts and palaces he also reigns

472. **sottish:** stupid.

478–82. **Osiris . . . human:** Ovid reports that when Typhon attacked Olympus (cp. 198–200n), some gods fled and wandered Egypt disguised as beasts (*Met.* 5.319–31). *Isis* and *Osiris* are Egyptian gods represented as having the heads of a cow and a bull. Plutarch wrote influentially about them, and their myth had a hold on Milton's imagination; see *Areop*, p. 955. Falcon-headed *Orus* was their son.

484–89. While Moses received the law on Mount Horeb (see 8n), the Hebrews pressured Aaron to forge a calf to worship (Exod. 12.35–36). It was made of Egyptian gold, *borrowed* by the Hebrews just before the Exodus (Deut. 9.8–21; Exod. 31.18, 32).

484–86. **rebel . . . ox:** Jeroboam, who rebelled against Solomon's son Rehoboam, *doubled* the sin at Horeb (see previous note) by repeating the former idolatry and by making two golden calves instead of one (2 Kings 12.12–23). "Thus they changed their glory into the similitude of an ox that eateth grass" (Ps. 106.20).

487–89. Refers to the Hebrews' departure from Egypt, when Jehovah smites "all the first born in the land of Egypt, both man and beast" and executes judgment "against all the gods of Egypt" (Exod. 12.12).

488. **equaled:** Jehovah with *one stroke* ends (and so proves equal to) many lives.

490. **Belial:** The Hebrew for *Belial* is not a proper noun, much less the name of a god, but refers to anyone opposing established authority, civil or religious. In English translations it became "worthless fellow" or "vile scoundrel." A Rabbinical etymology derives it from a verb meaning "throws off the yoke"; the Septuagint accordingly translates *Belial* with terms that signify lawlessness (*anomia* or *paranomos*). Milton with characteristic bite links Belial to organized religion and the court (cp. *PR* 2.182–83).

495. **Eli's sons:** For the lechery and sacrilege of Eli's sons, see 1 Sam. 2.12–24.

And in luxurious cities, where the noise
Of riot ascends above their loftiest tow'rs,
And injury and outrage: and when night
Darkens the streets, then wander forth the sons
Of Belial, flown with insolence and wine.
Witness the streets of Sodom, and that night
In Gibeah, when the hospitable door
Exposed a matron to avoid worse rape.
These were the prime in order and in might;
The rest were long to tell, though far renowned,
Th' Ionian gods, of Javan's issue held
Gods, yet confessed later than Heav'n and Earth
Their boasted parents; Titan Heav'n's first born
With his enormous brood, and birthright seized
By younger Saturn, he from mightier Jove
His own and Rhea's son like measure found;
So Jove usurping reigned: these first in Crete
And Ida known, thence on the snowy top
Of cold Olympus ruled the middle air
Their highest heav'n; or on the Delphian cliff,
Or in Dodona, and through all the bounds
Of Doric land; or who with Saturn old
Fled over Adria to th' Hesperian fields,
And o'er the Celtic roamed the utmost isles.

502. **flown:** filled to excess (obsolete past participle of *flow*).

503–4. **Sodom . . . Gibeah:** biblical cities in which gangs of men clamor at hosts' doors to rape male guests and are offered women instead—Lot's daughters in *Sodom* and the visiting Levite's concubine in *Gibeah* (Gen. 19, Judg. 19). 1667 reads "when hospitable doors / Yielded their matrons to prevent worse rape." 1674 concentrates on Gibeah, where the concubine, unlike Lot's daughters, actually is assaulted and in the morning deposited lifeless at the door where she had been *exposed.*

505. **matron:** Her Hebrew title is translated by "concubine," but Milton's diction is not prudish. In polygamous Hebrew culture, concubines were secondary wives, owed the same respect from other men as the primary wife.

508. **Javan's issue:** Noah's grandson Javan was deemed (*held*) the ancestor of the Ionian Greeks; his name in the Septuagint is a version of Ionia (Gen. 10.2). Cp. *SA* 715–16.

509–14. **Gods . . . reigned:** Uranus and Gaea (*Heav'n* and *Earth*) beget the Greek gods. According to the Roman republican poet Ennius Quintus (239–170 B.C.E.), Titan's younger brother, Saturn, took Titan's *birthright* (cited by Lactantius, *Divine Institutes* 1.14). *Jove,* Saturn's son by *Rhea,* usurped his father's throne.

515. **Ida:** mountain in *Crete* where Jove was born (cp. *Il Pens* 29).

516. **Olympus:** snow-capped peak where the Greeks supposed the gods resided; **middle air:** cooler region of the atmosphere, extending to the mountaintops. Milton makes it the postlapsarian possession of Satan and his followers (*PR* 1.44–46).

517. **Delphian cliff:** on the southern slope of Mount Parnassus, the seat of the oracle of Apollo.

518. **Dodona:** town in Epirus, where Zeus had an oracle.

519. **Doric land:** Greece.

520–21. Saturn and his followers flee west from Greece, over the Adriatic Sea to Italy (*Hesperian fields*), to France (*the Celtic*), and finally to northwestern islands, including Britain (*the utmost isles*); cp. *Masque* 59–61.

All these and more came flocking; but with looks
Downcast and damp, yet such wherein appeared
Obscure some glimpse of joy, to have found their chief
Not in despair, to have found themselves not lost
In loss itself; which on his count'nance cast
Like doubtful hue: but he his wonted pride
Soon recollecting, with high words, that bore
Semblance of worth, not substance, gently raised
Their fainting courage, and dispelled their fears.
Then straight commands that at the warlike sound
Of trumpets loud and clarions be upreared
His mighty standard; that proud honor claimed
Azazel as his right, a cherub tall:
Who forthwith from the glittering staff unfurled
Th' imperial ensign, which full high advanced
Shone like a meteor streaming to the wind
With gems and golden luster rich emblazed,
Seraphic arms and trophies: all the while
Sonorous metal blowing martial sounds:
At which the universal host upsent
A shout that tore Hell's concave, and beyond
Frighted the reign of Chaos and old Night.
All in a moment through the gloom were seen
Ten thousand banners rise into the air
With orient colors waving: with them rose
A forest huge of spears: and thronging helms
Appeared, and serried shields in thick array
Of depth immeasurable: anon they move
In perfect phalanx to the Dorian mood
Of flutes and soft recorders; such as raised

523. **damp:** dejected; cp. 11.293.

528. **recollecting:** remembering, reassembling; cp. 9.471.

532. **clarions:** "small shrill treble trumpet" (Hume).

534. **Azazel:** variously construed, but the Hebrew name suggests rugged strength. Cabbalistic lore made him one of Satan's standard-bearers, as Milton could have known from various sources (West 155ff).

537. **meteor:** comet.

538–39. **emblazed . . . trophies:** lit up or decorated with heraldic devices (*arms*) and memorials (*trophies*). Cp. 5.592–93.

540. **Sonorous metal:** synecdoche referring to the trumpets and clarions of line 532.

542. **tore Hell's concave:** carried through Hell's vaulted roof; see 8.242–44.

543. **reign:** realm; for *Chaos* and *Night* see 2.894–909, 959–1009. Their reaction is prophetic; Satan's activity will encroach on their realm; cp. 10.415–18.

546. **orient:** lustrous like a pearl; rising like the sun in the east.

548. **serried:** in close order.

550. **Dorian:** Plato would allow "manly" Dorian music in his ideal state because it inspires, in Aristotle's words, "a moderate and settled temper" (*Rep.* 3.398–99; *Pol.* 8.5). Cp. *Areop,* p. 943; *Of Ed,* p. 979. Thucydides' account (5.70) of the Spartans in unbroken *phalanx,* calmly marching into battle to the sound of flutes, lies behind lines 549–62.

To highth of noblest temper heroes old
Arming to battle, and instead of rage
Deliberate valor breathed, firm and unmoved
With dread of death to flight or foul retreat,
Nor wanting power to mitigate and swage
With solemn touches, troubled thoughts, and chase
Anguish and doubt and fear and sorrow and pain
From mortal or immortal minds. Thus they
Breathing united force with fixèd thought
Moved on in silence to soft pipes that charmed
Their painful steps o'er the burnt soil; and now
Advanced in view they stand, a horrid front
Of dreadful length and dazzling arms, in guise
Of warriors old with ordered spear and shield,
Awaiting what command their mighty chief
Had to impose: he through the armèd files
Darts his experienced eye, and soon traverse
The whole battalion views, their order due,
Their visages and stature as of gods,
Their number last he sums. And now his heart
Distends with pride, and hard'ning in his strength
Glories: for never since created man,
Met such embodied force, as named with these
Could merit more than that small infantry
Warred on by cranes: though all the giant brood
Of Phlegra with th' heroic race were joined
That fought at Thebes and Ilium, on each side
Mixed with auxiliar gods; and what resounds
In fable or romance of Uther's son
Begirt with British and Armoric knights;

556. **swage:** assuage.

563. **horrid:** bristling (with spears).

565. **warriors old:** from the reader's perspective only; humanity has not yet been created.

567–68. **files . . . traverse:** He looks down and across the lines of warriors.

571. **Their number last he sums:** David orders a census to count the warriors he might deploy, as Satan does here; God punishes Israel for David's presumption and implicit lack of faith (2 Sam. 24).

573. **since created man:** since man was created.

575. **small infantry:** pygmies, mentioned by Homer (*Il.* 3.3–6). Addison was "afraid" that Milton intended the pun on *infant* (*Spectator* 297, Feb. 9, 1712).

577. **Phlegra:** In Greek myth, the Olympian gods defeated the giants on their breeding ground at Phlegra (Pallene), the westernmost prong of the Chalcidicean peninsula in the Aegean. The place name derives from the Greek for fire (cp. *Phlegethon* 2.581–82), so called because of the volcanic soil. Some later writers claimed that the battle culminated in Italy, where Jupiter blasts the giants on similar turf—the Phlegraean plains near Vesuvius—and then imprisons them beneath regional volcanoes (*Diodorus* 4.21.5).

578. Thebes and Troy (*Ilium*) are main sites of Greek epic and tragedy.

579. **auxiliar:** In classical epic, the gods aid their mortal kin and other favorites.

580–81. King Arthur (*Uther's son*) and his knights, some from Brittany (*Armoric*). For Milton's fascination with Arthur, see *Damon* 166–68.

And all who since, baptized or infidel,
Jousted in Aspramont or Montalban,
Damasco, or Marocco, or Trebisond,
Or whom Biserta sent from Afric shore
When Charlemagne with all his peerage fell
By Fontarabia. Thus far these beyond
Compare of mortal prowess, yet observed
Their dread commander: he above the rest
In shape and gesture proudly eminent
Stood like a tow'r; his form had yet not lost
All her original brightness, nor appeared
Less than Archangel ruined, and th' excess
Of glory obscured: as when the sun new ris'n
Looks through the horizontal misty air
Shorn of his beams, or from behind the moon
In dim eclipse disastrous twilight sheds
On half the nations, and with fear of change
Perplexes monarchs. Darkened so, yet shone
Above them all th' Archangel: but his face
Deep scars of thunder had intrenched, and care
Sat on his faded cheek, but under brows
Of dauntless courage, and considerate pride
Waiting revenge: cruel his eye, but cast
Signs of remorse and passion to behold
The fellows of his crime, the followers rather
(Far other once beheld in bliss) condemned

583–84. **Aspramont . . . Trebisond:** Fighting against the Saracens, Roland wins honor at the castle of *Aspramont,* an episode often mentioned in Italian epic (see Ariosto, *OF* 17.14). *Montalban* is the site of the castle of Rinaldo, the hero to whom Tasso assigns victory in the battle for Jerusalem (*GL*). *Damasco, Marocco,* and *Trebisond* are also sites associated with great warriors and battles between Christian and Saracen.

585. **Biserta:** Tunisian seaport from which Saracens embarked to invade Spain.

586–87. **Charlemagne . . . Fontarabia:** According to the Spanish Jesuit historian and noted advocate of tyrannicide Juan de Mariana (1536–1624), Charlemagne fell—that is, suffered ruinous defeat—at Fontarabia (1699). The historical incident is the basis for the epic tale of the death of Roland and his twelve paladins at nearby Roncesvalles.

588. **observed:** heeded, reverenced. Though it exceeds the greatest historical and legendary human armies combined, Satan's army acknowledges the still greater excellence of its leader.

594. **glory:** a coronalike brilliance; see 141n.

596. **Shorn:** an allusion to Samson, whose name derives from the Hebrew word for "sun."

596–99. **from . . . monarchs:** Charles II's censor objected to these lines, presumably because the king himself had been born on the day of an eclipse in 1630, a coincidence later construed "as a portent of the interregnum" (Leonard).

599. **Perplexes:** torments, a stronger term in seventeenth-century usage than now; see, e.g., *OTH* 5.2.346.

601. **intrenched:** cut into.

603. **considerate:** thoughtful, deliberate.

605. **passion:** suffering or affliction, in contrast with *cruel,* disposed to inflict suffering.

For ever now to have their lot in pain,
Millions of spirits for his fault amerced
Of Heav'n, and from eternal splendors flung
For his revolt, yet faithful how they stood,
Their glory withered. As when heaven's fire
Hath scathed the forest oaks or mountain pines,
With singèd top their stately growth though bare
Stands on the blasted heath. He now prepared
To speak; whereat their doubled ranks they bend
From wing to wing, and half enclose him round
With all his peers: attention held them mute.
Thrice he assayed, and thrice in spite of scorn,
Tears such as angels weep burst forth: at last
Words interwove with sighs found out their way.
"O myriads of immortal spirits, O powers
Matchless, but with th' Almighty, and that strife
Was not inglorious, though th' event was dire,
As this place testifies, and this dire change
Hateful to utter: but what power of mind
Foreseeing or presaging, from the depth
Of knowledge past or present, could have feared,
How such united force of gods, how such
As stood like these, could ever know repulse?
For who can yet believe, though after loss,
That all these puissant legions, whose exile
Hath emptied Heav'n, shall fail to reascend
Self-raised, and repossess their native seat?
For me be witness all the host of Heav'n,
If counsels different, or danger shunned
By me, have lost our hopes. But he who reigns
Monarch in Heav'n, till then as one secure
Sat on his throne, upheld by old repute,

609. **amerced:** from the French for "at the mercy of"; a law term meaning "fined at the court's discretion." Milton's unidiomatic construction suggests that he had in mind a similar Greek verb used by Homer to explain the blindness of the bard Demodokos: "Of his sight [the Muse] deprived [*ámerse*] him" (*Od.* 8.64).

615. **blasted heath:** Cp. *MAC* 1.3.77.

620. **Tears . . . forth:** According to Raphael, angels digest food and make love. Here it seems that they also have the capacity to shed tears after their fashion (cp. 5.407–39, 8.622–29, 10.23–25). It was commonly supposed that males weep because they are born of women. Milton rejects this theory (see 10.1101–2, 11.494–97) and had precedent for presenting angels capable of weeping; see, e.g., Shakespeare, *MM* 2.2.879, *OTH* 3.3.371. In context, Satan's tears suggest those of the Persian tyrant Xerxes before his invasion of Greece. Reviewing his vast army, he was overcome by consciousness of his soldiers' mortality "at the time when he was hastening them to their fate, and to the intended destruction of the greatest people in the world, to gratify his own vain glory" (Newton). Cp. 10.307–11.

624. **event:** outcome.

632. **puissant:** powerful.

Consent or custom, and his regal state
Put forth at full, but still his strength concealed,
Which tempted our attempt, and wrought our fall.
Henceforth his might we know, and know our own
So as not either to provoke, or dread
New war, provoked; our better part remains
To work in close design, by fraud or guile
What force effected not: that he no less
At length from us may find, who overcomes
By force, hath overcome but half his foe.
Space may produce new worlds; whereof so rife
There went a fame in Heav'n that he ere long
Intended to create, and therein plant
A generation, whom his choice regard
Should favor equal to the sons of Heav'n:
Thither, if but to pry, shall be perhaps
Our first eruption, thither or elsewhere:
For this infernal pit shall never hold
Celestial spirits in bondage, nor th' abyss
Long under darkness cover. But these thoughts
Full counsel must mature: peace is despaired,
For who can think submission? War then, war
Open or understood must be resolved."
He spake: and to confirm his words, out flew
Millions of flaming swords, drawn from the thighs
Of mighty Cherubim; the sudden blaze
Far round illumined Hell: highly they raged
Against the Highest, and fierce with graspèd arms
Clashed on their sounding shields the din of war,
Hurling defiance toward the vault of Heav'n.
There stood a hill not far whose grisly top

641. **still:** invariably.

642. **tempted our attempt:** Milton's propensity for paronomasia—close repetition of similar-sounding words distinct in meaning—has long been derided as "jingling": "like marriages between persons too near of kin, to be avoided" (Hume). It is a figure distinctive of Hebrew Scripture, however, and one found in late Latin writers and Renaissance Italian poets. Milton often uses it in expressions of derision; see lines 666–67, 4.286, 5.869, 9.11, 9.648, 11.627, 12.78.

646. **close:** covert.

650. **Space may produce:** a notably active construction for a state commonly regarded as a passive locale or empty setting. By *worlds* Milton means what we would call "universes." The one that Satan proceeds to mention is our own, which "may be supposed as yet not made" (Argument; cp. 8.229–36).

651. **fame:** rumor; cp. 2.345–53, 830–35, 10.481–82.

653. **generation:** race; **choice regard:** selective estimation or judgment. *Regard* may also mean "purpose" or "intention," as in the description of Shakespeare's Henry V: "The King is full of grace, and fair regard" (1.2.22).

656. **eruption:** outbreak; the diction seems suggestive of "hell's volcanoes" (Leonard), but according to the *OED* the association of *eruption* with volcanic activity is not current in England until well into the eighteenth century.

Belched fire and rolling smoke; the rest entire
Shone with a glossy scurf, undoubted sign
That in his womb was hid metallic ore,
The work of sulfur. Thither winged with speed
A numerous brigade hastened. As when bands
Of pioneers with spade and pickax armed
Forerun the royal camp, to trench a field,
Or cast a rampart. Mammon led them on,
Mammon, the least erected spirit that fell
From Heav'n, for ev'n in Heav'n his looks and thoughts
Were always downward bent, admiring more
The riches of Heav'n's pavement, trodden gold,
Than aught divine or holy else enjoyed
In vision beatific: by him first
Men also, and by his suggestion taught,
Ransacked the center, and with impious hands
Rifled the bowels of their mother Earth
For treasures better hid. Soon had his crew
Opened into the hill a spacious wound
And digged out ribs of gold. Let none admire
That riches grow in Hell; that soil may best
Deserve the precious bane. And here let those
Who boast in mortal things, and wond'ring tell
Of Babel, and the works of Memphian kings,
Learn how their greatest monuments of fame,
And strength and art are easily outdone
By spirits reprobate, and in an hour
What in an age they with incessant toil
And hands innumerable scarce perform.

672. **scurf:** any incrustation upon the surface of a body (especially diseased or scabbed skin); here a sulfurous deposit.

673. **womb:** belly or cavity.

674. **work of sulfur:** "the offspring and production of sulfur, . . . the subterranean fire [that] concocts and boils up the crude and undigested earth into a more profitable consistence, and by its innate heat, hardens and bakes it into metals" (Hume).

676. **pioneers:** soldiers who do demolition or construction for siege or defense.

678. **Mammon:** like *Belial,* a common noun. Derived from the Arabic for "riches," it means "wealth"; cp. Matt. 6.24. By medieval times, Mammon had been personified as a Christian version of Pluto. See Spenser, *FQ* 2.7.

679. **erected:** upright in posture, lofty in character.

682. **Heav'n's pavement:** see Rev. 21.21.

684. **vision beatific:** literally, the "happy-making sight" (*On Time* 18); viewing God.

686. **center:** the earth's interior.

686–88. **impious . . . hid:** a commonplace that originates in Ovid's account of a maternally abusive degeneration from the original "golden" age of justice and temperance (*Met.* 1.137–40). See Spenser, *FQ* 2.7.16, for a similar association of Mammon with such impiety. Cp. Comus's reversal of the theme, 718–36.

688–90. **Soon . . . gold:** The diction anticipates the production of Eve at 8.463ff.

690. **ribs:** veins of ore; **admire:** wonder.

694. The Tower of Babel (see 12.43–62) and the Egyptian pyramids.

Nigh on the plain in many cells prepared,
That underneath had veins of liquid fire
Sluiced from the lake, a second multitude
With wondrous art founded the massy ore,
Severing each kind, and scummed the bullion dross:
A third as soon had formed within the ground
A various mold, and from the boiling cells
By strange conveyance filled each hollow nook,
As in an organ from one blast of wind
To many a row of pipes the soundboard breathes.
Anon out of the earth a fabric huge
Rose like an exhalation, with the sound
Of dulcet symphonies and voices sweet,
Built like a temple, where pilasters round
Were set, and Doric pillars overlaid
With golden architrave; nor did there want
Cornice or frieze, with bossy sculptures grav'n;
The roof was fretted gold. Not Babylon,
Nor great Alcairo such magnificence
Equaled in all their glories, to enshrine
Belus or Serapis their gods, or seat
Their kings, when Egypt with Assyria strove

700–704. The *massy ore* (gold is dense) extracted by the pioneers is melted (*founded*) in prepared *cells* heated from below by a second group of fallen angels, who use *liquid fire* conveyed from the burning lake in sluices (*Sluiced*). Smelting the metals separates (*severing*) the heavy gold from the less dense matter (*dross*), which rises to the top and is skimmed off (*scummed*), leaving pure gold in the cells. In line 703, 1674 prints *found out* instead of *founded* (1667).

705–9. *A various mold* (hollow form or matrix) has been shaped by yet another crew, which fills it with molten gold transported from the cells *by strange conveyance.* This process is compared to an intricate musical composition taking audible form from *one blast of wind* into an organ.

710. **fabric:** fabrication.

711–12. Structural principles of music (e.g., Pythagoras' golden section) were deemed basic to architecture and other plastic arts, including, as Milton later presents it, cuisine (see 5.333–49). Athenians played music at the dedication of temples like the Parthenon.

711. **exhalation:** vapor emitted by the earth.

713–17. **Built . . . gold:** The edifice looks like a pagan temple, with features that recall the Roman Pantheon (e.g., golden roof), though the satirical Milton presumably also has St. Peter's Basilica in mind.

713. **pilasters round:** square columns built into the wall; *round* modifies *set.*

714. **Doric:** the least ornamented style of Greek column; like the laconic music of line 550.

715. **architrave:** the "master beam" or basis of the upper section of a classical temple; it sits on top of the columns (hence *overlaid*).

716. **Cornice or frieze:** The *frieze* is a band that sits on the architrave and is often, as in the case of the Parthenon, decorated with sculptures that stand out in relief, as if embossed (*bossy*). The *cornice* caps the frieze and is also often ornamented.

717. **fretted gold:** gold wrought with ornamental designs, as in the Pantheon.

718. **Alcairo:** Memphis, ancient capital of Egypt, near modern Cairo.

720. **Belus:** name for Baal in Babylon, where he had a celebrated temple, described by Ralegh (1621, 183); **Serapis:** Ptolemaic amalgamation of Hades and Osiris, with splendid temples in Memphis and Alexandria.

In wealth and luxury. Th' ascending pile
Stood fixed her stately highth, and straight the doors
Op'ning their brazen folds discover wide
Within, her ample spaces, o'er the smooth
And level pavement: from the archèd roof
Pendant by subtle magic many a row
Of starry lamps and blazing cressets fed
With naphtha and asphaltus yielded light
As from a sky. The hasty multitude
Admiring entered, and the work some praise
And some the architect: his hand was known
In Heav'n by many a towered structure high,
Where sceptered angels held their residence,
And sat as princes, whom the supreme King
Exalted to such power, and gave to rule,
Each in his hierarchy, the orders bright.
Nor was his name unheard or unadored
In ancient Greece; and in Ausonian land
Men called him Mulciber; and how he fell
From Heav'n, they fabled, thrown by angry Jove
Sheer o'er the crystal battlements; from morn
To noon he fell, from noon to dewy eve,
A summer's day; and with the setting sun
Dropped from the zenith like a falling star,
On Lemnos th' Aegean isle: thus they relate,
Erring; for he with this rebellious rout
Fell long before; nor aught availed him now
To have built in Heav'n high tow'rs; nor did he scape
By all his engines, but was headlong sent
With his industrious crew to build in Hell.
Meanwhile the wingèd heralds by command
Of sov'reign power, with awful ceremony
And trumpets' sound throughout the host proclaim

722–23. **ascending pile / Stood fixed:** After rising like a vapor out of the ground, the magnificent building achieved its finished state.

728. **cressets:** iron baskets suspended from the ceiling, containing flaming pitch (*asphaltus*).

729. **naphtha:** liquid pitch, supplies the lamps.

739. **Ausonian land:** Greek name for a district of Italy.

740. **Mulciber:** smelter; another name for Vulcan, Roman counterpart to the Greek Hephaestus, god of fire and crafts. Homer mentions palaces he erects on Olympus (*Il.* 1.605–8), and Hesiod says he forged Pandora (cp. 688–90n; 4.714–19n).

740–48. **Men . . . before:** Homer's Hephaestus tells how Zeus threw him from Olympus to punish him for siding with Hera (*Il.* 1.591–95). Milton closely imitates that account but then corrects it.

745. **zenith:** (1) upper region of the sky, where vaporous meteorological phenomena such as *falling stars* were thought to ignite; (2) the highest point above the observer's horizon attained by a celestial body (the sun in this case).

750. **engines:** contrivances (it shares a common Latin root with *invention*); cp. 4.17.

A solemn council forthwith to be held
At Pandaemonium, the high capital
Of Satan and his peers: their summons called
From every band and squarèd regiment
By place or choice the worthiest; they anon
With hundreds and with thousands trooping came
Attended: all access was thronged, the gates
And porches wide, but chief the spacious hall
(Though like a covered field, where champions bold
Wont ride in armed, and at the soldan's chair
Defied the best of paynim chivalry
To mortal combat or career with lance)
Thick swarmed, both on the ground and in the air,
Brushed with the hiss of rustling wings. As bees
In springtime, when the sun with Taurus rides,
Pour forth their populous youth about the hive
In clusters; they among fresh dews and flowers
Fly to and fro, or on the smoothèd plank,
The suburb of their straw-built citadel,
New rubbed with balm, expatiate and confer
Their state affairs. So thick the airy crowd
Swarmed and were straitened; till the signal giv'n,
Behold a wonder! They but now who seemed
In bigness to surpass Earth's giant sons
Now less than smallest dwarfs, in narrow room
Throng numberless, like that pygmean race

756. **Pandaemonium:** Greek for "place of all the demons."

759. **By place or choice:** by virtue of rank or election.

764. **Wont:** were wont (accustomed) to; **soldan's:** sultan's (see 348n).

765. **paynim:** pagan.

766. **career:** short gallop at full speed, as in jousting.

767–75. **swarmed . . . affairs:** Bee similes occur frequently in classical literature, and the phrasing here variously echoes precursors (cp. Homer, *Il.* 2.87–90; Vergil, *Aen.* 1.430–36; 6.707–9, and especially *Georg.* 4.149–227). Bees are usually presented as exemplary creatures, beneficial to humanity. Milton bends the tradition so that the inaugural scene of *state affairs* in Satan's palace anticipates the final one, when the fallen angels are straitened into swarms of hissing serpents (cp. 10.508ff). Note the predominance of sibilants in both passages. When Milton was in Rome, the seemingly ubiquitous insignia of Pope Urban VIII was a bee, and his followers were called bees.

769. **Taurus:** The sun stays in the astrological sign of Taurus from April 20 till May 20, the period immediately after Aries, the sign under which the world was created and would have persisted had the Fall not occurred.

774. **expatiate:** (1) walk about; (2) speak at length. Bees communicate by moving their legs in view of other bees, relaying directions to the best sites for pollen. Although such entomological discoveries are relatively recent, beekeepers have long recognized that allowing bees to "walk about" each other augments the harvest of honey; hence the "suburban" plank laid outside the hive for that purpose.

778. **Earth's giant sons:** See 198–200n.

780–81. **Throng . . . mount:** The legendary Pygmies were commonly thought to live beyond the Ganges in secluded mountainous regions where the Cranes that they battle lay their eggs (cp. 575n).

Beyond the Indian mount, or faerie elves
Whose midnight revels, by a forest side
Or fountain some belated peasant sees,
Or dreams he sees, while overhead the moon
Sits arbitress, and nearer to the earth
Wheels her pale course, they on their mirth and dance
Intent, with jocund music charm his ear;
At once with joy and fear his heart rebounds.
Thus incorporeal spirits to smallest forms
Reduced their shapes immense, and were at large,
Though without number still amidst the hall
Of that infernal court. But far within
And in their own dimensions like themselves
The great Seraphic lords and Cherubim
In close recess and secret conclave sat
A thousand demigods on golden seats,
Frequent and full. After short silence then
And summons read, the great consult began.

783–84. **belated . . . he sees:** The phrasing is generally taken as a borrowing from Vergil, when Aeneas thinks he glimpses Dido's shade. But vacillation between seeing and dreaming and mention of a *belated peasant* make reminiscence of *MND* equally likely (4.1.204–14).

785. **arbitress:** observer and judge.

795. **close recess:** enclosed, secluded place; **conclave:** literally, "lockable room"; in the Catholic Church, it denotes the meeting held to select a new pope, so called from the secure room in which the meeting occurs.

797. **Frequent:** numerous.

798. **consult:** In seventeenth-century usage, the term is associated with secret meetings for plotting insurgency.

"Him the Almighty Power / Hurled headlong flaming from th' ethereal sky" (1.44–45).

Book II

The Argument

The consultation begun, Satan debates whether another battle be to be hazarded for the recovery of Heaven: some advise it; others dissuade. A third proposal is preferred, mentioned before by Satan: to search the truth of that prophecy or tradition in Heaven concerning another world and another kind of creature, equal or not much inferior to themselves, about this time to be created; their doubt who shall be sent on this difficult search. Satan their chief undertakes alone the voyage, is honored and applauded. The council thus ended, the rest betake them several ways and to several employments, as their inclinations lead them, to entertain the time till Satan return. He passes on his journey to Hell gates, finds them shut, and who sat there to guard them: by whom at length they are opened and discover to him the great gulf between Hell and Heaven; with what difficulty he passes through, directed by Chaos, the power of that place, to the sight of this new world which he sought.

High on a throne of royal state, which far
Outshone the wealth of Ormus and of Ind,
Or where the gorgeous East with richest hand
Show'rs on her kings barbaric pearl and gold,
Satan exalted sat, by merit raised
To that bad eminence; and from despair
Thus high uplifted beyond hope, aspires
Beyond thus high, insatiate to pursue
Vain war with Heav'n, and by success untaught
His proud imaginations thus displayed.

2. **Ormus:** Hormuz, famously wealthy island town ideally situated in the Persian Gulf for trade in spices and jewels. Ships of the British East India Company helped the Dutch take it from the Portuguese in 1622. For acquiescing in the unauthorized aggression, King James and the Duke of Buckingham pocketed large bribes. **Ind:** India, celebrated for precious stones; cp. *Masque* 606.

4. **barbaric:** Greek for "foreign," primarily used of Asia or *the gorgeous East.* Classical authors depict Asian rulers as profligate despots; hence Vergil describes the doors of Priam's palace as "proud with the spoils of barbaric gold" (*Aen.* 2.504).

5. **merit:** desert, good or bad.

9. **success:** outcome; like *merit,* ironically complicated by its more usual positive sense.

"Powers and Dominions, deities of Heav'n,
For since no deep within her gulf can hold
Immortal vigor, though oppressed and fall'n,
I give not Heav'n for lost. From this descent
Celestial Virtues rising, will appear
More glorious and more dread than from no fall,
And trust themselves to fear no second fate.
Me though just right, and the fixed laws of Heav'n
Did first create your leader, next, free choice,
With what besides, in counsel or in fight,
Hath been achieved of merit, yet this loss
Thus far at least recovered, hath much more
Established in a safe unenvied throne
Yielded with full consent. The happier state
In Heav'n, which follows dignity, might draw
Envy from each inferior; but who here
Will envy whom the highest place exposes
Foremost to stand against the Thunderer's aim
Your bulwark, and condemns to greatest share
Of endless pain? Where there is then no good
For which to strive, no strife can grow up there
From faction; for none sure will claim in Hell
Precedence, none, whose portion is so small
Of present pain, that with ambitious mind
Will covet more. With this advantage then
To union, and firm faith, and firm accord,
More than can be in Heav'n, we now return
To claim our just inheritance of old,
Surer to prosper than prosperity
Could have assured us; and by what best way,
Whether of open war or covert guile,
We now debate; who can advise, may speak."
He ceased, and next him Moloch, sceptered king,
Stood up, the strongest and the fiercest spirit

11. **Powers and Dominions:** two kinds of angels (Col. 1.16).

14. **I . . . lost:** "I refuse to concede the loss of Heaven."

15. **Virtues:** efficacious qualities (not moral virtues); also, members of a rank of angels.

18–21. **Me . . . merit:** The tortuous syntax makes Stoic principles—*just right* and *fixed laws*—agents of Satan's creation as leader. The direct object (*Me*) begins the clause. His created status, Satan says, has been confirmed by the *free choice* of his followers and by his own deeds.

24–25. **happier . . . dignity:** Satan claims that in Heaven, the higher one's rank, the happier one's existence, and that in Hell the reverse holds true, which should deter envy and promote unity.

28. **Thunderer:** classical epithet for Jove.

43. **Moloch:** Hebrew for "king"; see 1.392n; **sceptered king:** translates Homer's formulaic epithet for kings (e.g., *Il.* 1.279).

That fought in Heav'n, now fiercer by despair.
His trust was with th' Eternal to be deemed
Equal in strength, and rather than be less
Cared not to be at all; with that care lost
Went all his fear: of God, or Hell, or worse
He reck'd not, and these words thereafter spake.
"My sentence is for open war. Of wiles,
More unexpert, I boast not: them let those
Contrive who need, or when they need, not now.
For while they sit contriving, shall the rest,
Millions that stand in arms and longing wait
The signal to ascend, sit ling'ring here
Heav'n's fugitives, and for their dwelling place
Accept this dark opprobrious den of shame,
The prison of his tyranny who reigns
By our delay? No, let us rather choose
Armed with Hell flames and fury all at once
O'er Heav'n's high tow'rs to force resistless way,
Turning our tortures into horrid arms
Against the Torturer; when to meet the noise
Of his almighty engine he shall hear
Infernal thunder, and for lightning see
Black fire and horror shot with equal rage
Among his angels; and his throne itself
Mixed with Tartarean sulfur, and strange fire,
His own invented torments. But perhaps
The way seems difficult and steep to scale
With upright wing against a higher foe.
Let such bethink them, if the sleepy drench
Of that forgetful lake benumb not still,
That in our proper motion we ascend
Up to our native seat: descent and fall
To us is adverse. Who but felt of late
When the fierce foe hung on our broken rear
Insulting, and pursu'd us through the deep,

50. **reck'd:** heeded; cared.

51. **sentence:** judgment. Cp. line 291.

52. **More unexpert:** less knowledgeable or experienced.

63. **horrid:** bristling (*with Hell flames*).

65. **engine:** instrument of war (cp. 4.17); here, God's lightning and thunder.

69. **Tartarean:** infernal; horrible. Tartarus confines the rebellious Titans, according to Homer and Hesiod (*Il.* 14.278; 8.478–91; *Theog.* 713–45). **strange fire:** "Nadab and Abihu died because they offered strange fire before the Lord" (Num. 26.61; cp. Lev. 10.1). The Geneva Bible glosses *strange fire* as fire "not taken of the altar"—that is, unholy or illicit fire.

73. **drench:** dose; douse. Cp. *Animad* (Yale 1:685).

74. **forgetful:** causing a state of oblivion; cp. "oblivious pool" (1.266).

79. **Insulting:** springing upon scornfully; trampling in triumph. Cp. 1.327.

With what compulsion and laborious flight
We sunk thus low? Th' ascent is easy then;
Th' event is feared. Should we again provoke
Our stronger, some worse way his wrath may find
To our destruction, if there be in Hell
Fear to be worse destroyed. What can be worse
Than to dwell here, driv'n out from bliss, condemned
In this abhorrèd deep to utter woe;
Where pain of unextinguishable fire
Must exercise us without hope of end
The vassals of his anger, when the scourge
Inexorably, and the torturing hour
Calls us to penance? More destroyed than thus
We should be quite abolished and expire.
What fear we then? What doubt we to incense
His utmost ire? Which to the highth enraged,
Will either quite consume us and reduce
To nothing this essential, happier far
Than miserable to have eternal being:
Or if our substance be indeed divine,
And cannot cease to be, we are at worst
On this side nothing; and by proof we feel
Our power sufficient to disturb his Heav'n,
And with perpetual inroads to alarm,
Though inaccessible, his fatal throne:
Which if not victory is yet revenge."
He ended frowning, and his look denounced
Desperate revenge, and battle dangerous
To less than gods. On th' other side up rose

81. For Fowler, Moloch's claim is "belied by the allusion to *Aen.* 6.126–29": "easy is the descent to Avernus . . . but to recall thy steps and pass out to the upper air, this is the task, this the toil!" Cp. *PL* 2.432–33, 3.20–21. Unlike Aeneas, however, the rebels are spiritual beings: "bodies compounded and elemented of Earth do naturally descend; but to spirits, those divine, airy, agile beings, as our poet well observes, . . . all motion downward seems forced and contrary" (Hume).

82. **event:** outcome.

89. **exercise:** a range of meanings applies, from "agitate" or "vex" to the more common "train" or "cause to undergo a physical regimen or ascetic discipline."

90. **vassals:** slaves (see *PR* 4.133).

91. **torturing hour:** Shakespeare's Theseus seeks entertainment "to ease the anguish of a torturing hour"—the time between the marriage rite and its consummation (*MND* 5.1.37). The fallen angels will also pursue diversions from pain (ll. 458–62, 523–27), not least that of endlessly frustrated desire (4.508–11).

94. **doubt we:** makes us hesitate.

97. **essential:** essence or being (adj. for noun). On the active disposition to suicide represented by Moloch, see 1.158n.

100–101. **we . . . nothing:** "we could not be in a worse state than we are now." Cp. *PR* 3.204–11.

101. **proof:** experience, trial; also, testing artillery by firing a heavy charge (see 6.584–99).

104. **fatal:** allotted by fate; cp. 1.133.

106. **denounced:** threatened.

Belial, in act more graceful and humane;
A fairer person lost not Heav'n; he seemed
For dignity composed and high exploit:
But all was false and hollow; though his tongue
Dropped manna, and could make the worse appear
The better reason, to perplex and dash
Maturest counsels: for his thoughts were low;
To vice industrious, but to nobler deeds
Timorous and slothful: yet he pleased the ear,
And with persuasive accent thus began.
    "I should be much for open war, O peers,
As not behind in hate, if what was urged
Main reason to persuade immediate war,
Did not dissuade me most, and seem to cast
Ominous conjecture on the whole success:
When he who most excels in fact of arms,
In what he counsels and in what excels
Mistrustful, grounds his courage on despair
And utter dissolution, as the scope
Of all his aim, after some dire revenge.
First, what revenge? The tow'rs of Heav'n are filled
With armèd watch, that render all access
Impregnable; oft on the bordering deep
Encamp their legions, or with obscure wing
Scout far and wide into the realm of Night,
Scorning surprise. Or could we break our way
By force, and at our heels all Hell should rise
With blackest insurrection, to confound
Heav'n's purest light, yet our great enemy
All incorruptible would on his throne
Sit unpolluted, and th' ethereal mold
Incapable of stain would soon expel
Her mischief, and purge off the baser fire

109. **Belial:** "Belial . . . taketh the form of a beautiful angel; he speaketh fair" (Scot 15.2). See 1.158n and 1.490n.

113. **manna:** divinely provided food, sweet like honey (Exod. 16.31). So Homer describes the oratory of Nestor: "from whose tongue flowed speech sweeter than honey" (1.249). The ability to *make the worse appear / The better reason* defines sophistry and is a charge brought against Socrates (*Apology* 19b), as Milton observes: "that he ever made the worse cause seem the better" (*Tetrachordon,* p. 989).

123. **conjecture:** doubt; **success**: outcome.

124. **fact:** deed, feat. *Fact of arms* translates an idiom common in French and Italian.

127. **scope:** object, end.

139. **mold:** material substance; for celestial beings, light or pure fire (see Ps. 104.4). Cp. Comus's claim that he and his band are of "purer fire" than agents of morality (111).

141. **Her mischief:** the harm intended her (i.e., the *ethereal mold* of l. 139).

Victorious. Thus repulsed, our final hope
Is flat despair: we must exasperate
Th' almighty Victor to spend all his rage,
And that must end us, that must be our cure,
To be no more. Sad cure; for who would lose,
Though full of pain, this intellectual being,
Those thoughts that wander through eternity,
To perish rather, swallowed up and lost
In the wide womb of uncreated Night,
Devoid of sense and motion? And who knows,
Let this be good, whether our angry foe
Can give it, or will ever? How he can
Is doubtful; that he never will is sure.
Will he, so wise, let loose at once his ire,
Belike through impotence, or unaware,
To give his enemies their wish, and end
Them in his anger, whom his anger saves
To punish endless? 'Wherefore cease we then?'
Say they who counsel war, 'we are decreed,
Reserved and destined to eternal woe;
Whatever doing, what can we suffer more,
What can we suffer worse?' Is this then worst,
Thus sitting, thus consulting, thus in arms?
What when we fled amain, pursued and strook
With Heav'n's afflicting thunder, and besought
The deep to shelter us? This Hell then seemed
A refuge from those wounds. Or when we lay
Chained on the burning lake? That sure was worse.
What if the breath that kindled those grim fires
Awaked should blow them into sevenfold rage
And plunge us in the flames? Or from above
Should intermitted vengeance arm again
His red right hand to plague us? What if all

149–50. **swallowed . . . Night:** Satan will reiterate this fear (ll. 438–41, 10.476–77).

152. **Let this be good:** "were we to concede that nonexistence is desirable."

156. As if through lack of self-control, or unwittingly. The astute Belial ironically registers God's omnipotence and omniscience.

160. **they who:** "Belial avoids naming Moloch, who is in any case nameless" (Leonard). Naming a previous speaker is prohibited by Parliamentary rules of debate.

165. **amain:** at full speed.

170. "The breath of the Lord, like a stream of brimstone, doth kindle [hellfire]" (Isa. 30.33). Cp. the story of King Nebuchadnezzar, who fires his furnace "seven times more than it was wont" to incinerate his prisoners (Dan. 3.19). According to the *Geneva* gloss, angry tyrants exercise their wits by "inventing strange and cruel punishments."

173. **intermitted:** discontinued temporarily.

174. **red right hand:** translates Horace's account of Jove's *rubente dextera* (*Odes* 1.2.3–4.). Horace evokes Rome's panic at a catastrophic flood threatened by Jove's thunder. Belial conjures up a vision of Hell similarly inundated, but with fire.

Her stores were opened, and this firmament
Of Hell should spout her cataracts of fire
Impendent horrors, threat'ning hideous fall
One day upon our heads; while we perhaps
Designing or exhorting glorious war,
Caught in a fiery tempest shall be hurled
Each on his rock transfixed, the sport and prey
Of racking whirlwinds, or for ever sunk
Under yon boiling ocean, wrapped in chains;
There to converse with everlasting groans,
Unrespited, unpitied, unreprieved,
Ages of hopeless end. This would be worse.
War therefore, open or concealed, alike
My voice dissuades; for what can force or guile
With him, or who deceive his mind, whose eye
Views all things at one view? He from Heav'n's highth
All these our motions vain, sees and derides;
Not more almighty to resist our might
Than wise to frustrate all our plots and wiles.
Shall we then live thus vile, the race of Heav'n
Thus trampled, thus expelled to suffer here
Chains and these torments? Better these than worse
By my advice; since fate inevitable
Subdues us, and omnipotent decree,
The victor's will. To suffer, as to do,
Our strength is equal, nor the law unjust
That so ordains: this was at first resolved,
If we were wise, against so great a foe
Contending, and so doubtful what might fall.
I laugh, when those who at the spear are bold

175. **Her:** Hell's.

176. **cataracts:** heavy downpours.

180–82. **Caught . . . whirlwinds:** Cp. Pallas' vengeance on Ajax: "him, as with pierced breast he breathed forth flame, she caught in a whirlwind and impaled on a spiky crag" (Vergil, *Aen.* 1.44–45).

187–93. Belial offers impeccable theological rationale against either alternative on Satan's agenda (l. 41; cp. 1.661–62).

188. **what can force or guile:** "what can force or guile accomplish."

197–99. **since . . . will:** Belial's theological clarity persists as he accurately links *fate, omnipotent decree,* and *the victor's will* (cp. 5.602, 7.173).

199. **To suffer, as to do:** Editors since Newton cite Livy's quotation of the legendary Mutius Scaevola ("left-handed"), who earned his name by burning off his own right hand in response to captors' threats: "The strength of Rome is to do and also to suffer" (2.12). Cp. 1.158n and *PR* 3.195. Belial, by contrast—nameless on account of his crimes and already engulfed in flames—recommends passivity to reduce suffering (ll. 208–14). In the narrator's terms, he seeks *ignoble ease* through *peaceful sloth* (l. 227).

200–208. **Our strength . . . conqueror:** The *law* to which Belial refers is the law of conquest or right of war, which Milton in *CD* cites to justify the death sentence imposed on all of Adam and Eve's descendants (1.11). Cp. 1.149–50n.

And vent'rous, if that fail them, shrink and fear
What yet they know must follow, to endure
Exile, or ignominy, or bonds, or pain,
The sentence of their conqueror. This is now
Our doom; which if we can sustain and bear,
Our supreme foe in time may much remit
His anger, and perhaps thus far removed
Not mind us not offending, satisfied
With what is punished; whence these raging fires
Will slacken, if his breath stir not their flames.
Our purer essence then will overcome
Their noxious vapor, or inured not feel,
Or changed at length, and to the place conformed
In temper and in nature, will receive
Familiar the fierce heat, and void of pain;
This horror will grow mild, this darkness light,
Besides what hope the never-ending flight
Of future days may bring, what chance, what change
Worth waiting, since our present lot appears
For happy though but ill, for ill not worst,
If we procure not to ourselves more woe."
    Thus Belial with words clothed in reason's garb
Counseled ignoble ease, and peaceful sloth,
Not peace: and after him thus Mammon spake.
    "Either to disenthrone the King of Heav'n
We war, if war be best, or to regain
Our own right lost: him to unthrone we then
May hope when everlasting Fate shall yield
To fickle Chance, and Chaos judge the strife:
The former vain to hope argues as vain
The latter: for what place can be for us
Within Heav'n's bound, unless Heav'n's Lord supreme

213. **what is punished:** the punishment already inflicted.

213–19. **Whence . . . pain:** "If God were to stop stoking the fire, the purity of our native substance might overcome it. Or, we might grow accustomed to a less intense fire and not notice it. Or perhaps our physiology and substance will adapt, so that hellfire will feel natural to us." Belial's first alternative fits with his rejection of Moloch's plan; cp. lines 139–42. The last alternative anticipates Mammon's proposal—that they adapt themselves to Hell (ll. 274–78). On God as the bellows infuriating hellfire, see 170n.

220. **light:** Possible meanings include the overtly paradoxical "illumination," as well as less obviously contradictory adjectival senses, such as "luminous" and "less harsh." "The rhyme at 220–21 offers a suitably jingling accompaniment to the cheerful fantasy" (Fowler).

223–24. **since . . . worst:** "Insofar as happiness is concerned, our current situation is certainly a bad one, but for a bad situation, it is not the worst."

228. **Mammon:** See 1.678n.

We overpower? Suppose he should relent
And publish grace to all, on promise made
Of new subjection; with what eyes could we
Stand in his presence humble, and receive
Strict laws imposed, to celebrate his throne
With warbled hymns, and to his Godhead sing
Forced hallelujahs; while he lordly sits
Our envied Sov'reign, and his altar breathes
Ambrosial odors and ambrosial flowers,
Our servile offerings. This must be our task
In Heav'n, this our delight; how wearisome
Eternity so spent in worship paid
To whom we hate. Let us not then pursue
By force impossible, by leave obtained
Unacceptable, though in Heav'n, our state
Of splendid vassalage, but rather seek
Our own good from our selves, and from our own
Live to our selves, though in this vast recess,
Free, and to none accountable, preferring
Hard liberty before the easy yoke
Of servile pomp. Our greatness will appear
Then most conspicuous, when great things of small,
Useful of hurtful, prosperous of adverse
We can create, and in what place soe'er
Thrive under evil, and work ease out of pain
Through labor and endurance. This deep world
Of darkness do we dread? How oft amidst
Thick clouds and dark doth Heav'n's all-ruling Sire
Choose to reside, his glory unobscured,
And with the majesty of darkness round
Covers his throne; from whence deep thunders roar
Must'ring their rage, and Heav'n resembles Hell?
As he our darkness, cannot we his light
Imitate when we please? This desert soil
Wants not her hidden luster, gems and gold;
Nor want we skill or art, from whence to raise
Magnificence; and what can Heav'n show more?
Our torments also may in length of time

243. **hallelujahs:** songs of praise; in Hebrew, *hallelujah* means "praise God."

244. **breathes:** exhales or emanates, as a fragrance; cp. 5.482.

245. **Ambrosial:** divinely fragrant; classically, ambrosia is divine nourishment.

256. **easy yoke:** "who best / Bear his mild yoke, they serve him best" (*Sonnet 19* 10–11).

263–68. **How oft . . . Hell?:** "The Lord hath said that he would dwell in the thick darkness" (2 Chron. 6.1; see also Ps. 18.11–13).

271. **Wants not:** does not lack.

Become our elements, these piercing fires
As soft as now severe, our temper changed
Into their temper; which must needs remove
The sensible of pain. All things invite
To peaceful counsels, and the settled state
Of order, how in safety best we may
Compose our present evils, with regard
Of what we are and where, dismissing quite
All thoughts of war: ye have what I advise."
    He scarce had finished, when such murmur filled
Th' assembly, as when hollow rocks retain
The sound of blust'ring winds, which all night long
Had roused the sea, now with hoarse cadence lull
Seafaring men o'erwatched, whose bark by chance
Or pinnace anchors in a craggy bay
After the tempest: such applause was heard
As Mammon ended, and his sentence pleased,
Advising peace: for such another field
They dreaded worse than Hell: so much the fear
Of thunder and the sword of Michael
Wrought still within them; and no less desire
To found this nether empire, which might rise
By policy, and long process of time,
In emulation opposite to Heav'n.
Which when Beëlzebub perceived, than whom,
Satan except, none higher sat, with grave
Aspect he rose, and in his rising seemed
A pillar of state; deep on his front engraven
Deliberation sat and public care;
And princely counsel in his face yet shone,
Majestic though in ruin: sage he stood
With Atlantean shoulders fit to bear
The weight of mightiest monarchies; his look

275. **elements:** components, habitats (cp. *Il Pens* 93–94); Belial makes a similar conjecture at lines 217–18.

278. **sensible:** what is felt; sensation (adj. for noun).

281. **Compose:** adjust to (by becoming part of); calm.

282. **where:** 1667; "were" in 1674 edition.

288. **o'erwatched:** sleep deprived.

288–89. **bark, pinnace:** small sailing ships.

292. **such another field:** another battle such as they fought in Heaven.

297. **policy:** statecraft; in Milton's era, *policy* often implies Machiavellian cunning. **process of time:** Cp. Adam and Eve's prospects for improvement, "by tract of time" (5.498).

302. **front:** brow, face.

306. **Atlantean:** Atlas-like; Zeus doomed Atlas, a rebel Titan, to uphold the sky (cp. 4.987n). Statesmen were often compared to Atlas or to Hercules relieving Atlas of his burden. See Cowley's praise of King Charles: "On whom (like Atlas shoulders) the propped state/(As he were the *Primum Mobile* of fate)/Solely, relies" (*On his Majesty's Return out of Scotland*).

Drew audience and attention still as night
Or summer's noontide air, while thus he spake.
"Thrones and imperial Powers, offspring of Heav'n,
Ethereal Virtues; or these titles now
Must we renounce, and changing style be called
Princes of Hell? For so the popular vote
Inclines, here to continue, and build up here
A growing empire; doubtless; while we dream,
And know not that the King of Heav'n hath doomed
This place our dungeon, not our safe retreat
Beyond his potent arm, to live exempt
From Heav'n's high jurisdiction, in new league
Banded against his throne, but to remain
In strictest bondage, though thus far removed,
Under th' inevitable curb, reserved
His captive multitude: for he, be sure
In highth or depth, still first and last will reign
Sole king, and of his kingdom lose no part
By our revolt, but over Hell extend
His empire, and with iron scepter rule
Us here, as with his golden those in Heav'n.
What sit we then projecting peace and war?
War hath determined us, and foiled with loss
Irreparable; terms of peace yet none
Vouchsafed or sought; for what peace will be giv'n
To us enslaved, but custody severe,
And stripes, and arbitrary punishment
Inflicted? And what peace can we return,
But to our power hostility and hate,
Untamed reluctance, and revenge though slow,
Yet ever plotting how the Conqueror least

312. **style:** official name or title. The fallen angels' original titles indicated their authority, the defense of which Satan cited as cause for their initial rebellion (see, e.g., 5.772–802). Beëlzebub invokes these titles to ask if they are indeed willing to forsake their Heavenly identities, as Mammon has suggested. Cp. 10.460–62, *PR* 2.121–25.

315. We retain from 1674 the semicolons bracing *doubtless,* which seem intended to indicate deliberate pauses for rhetorical effect.

321. In reply to Belial's conjecture at lines 209–13.

324. **first and last:** Cp. the persistent account of God in Isaiah (41.4, 27; 43.10; 44.6; 48.12) and of the Son in Revelation (1.11, 17; 2.8; 21.6; 22.13).

327–28. **iron, golden:** The association of iron with severity and gold with mercy distinguishes between the regime of God in Hell and in Heaven. Cp. Ps. 2.9 and Esther 4.11. See also the iron and golden keys of St. Peter in *Lyc* 110–11.

329. **What:** why; **projecting:** scheming; devising.

330. **determined us:** settled our course. Cp. 11.227.

334. **stripes:** marks left by a whip.

337. **reluctance:** resistance, opposition.

338–40. **how . . . feel?:** "how to mitigate God's victory and pleasure in tormenting us?" These challenging lines initiate the figure of God as a reaper seeking to maximize his yield (cp. 4.983) and cap the debate's running concern with the balance of *suffering* and *doing* (see 199n).

May reap his conquest, and may least rejoice
In doing what we most in suffering feel?
Nor will occasion want, nor shall we need
With dangerous expedition to invade
Heav'n, whose high walls fear no assault or siege,
Or ambush from the deep. What if we find
Some easier enterprise? There is a place
(If ancient and prophetic fame in Heav'n
Err not) another world, the happy seat
Of some new race called Man, about this time
To be created like to us, though less
In power and excellence, but favored more
Of him who rules above; so was his will
Pronounced among the gods, and by an oath,
That shook Heav'n's whole circumference, confirmed.
Thither let us bend all our thoughts, to learn
What creatures there inhabit, of what mold,
Or substance, how endued, and what their power,
And where their weakness, how attempted best,
By force or subtlety: though Heav'n be shut,
And Heav'n's high arbitrator sit secure
In his own strength, this place may lie exposed
The utmost border of his kingdom, left
To their defense who hold it: here perhaps
Some advantageous act may be achieved
By sudden onset, either with Hell fire
To waste his whole creation, or possess
All as our own, and drive as we were driven,
The puny habitants, or if not drive,
Seduce them to our party, that their God
May prove their foe, and with repenting hand

349. **like to us:** a comparison indicative of the fallen angels' egocentrism, or antitheocentrism. Resemblance between humans and angels derives from their reflection of the same creator (cp. 3.100–128, 4.567).

349–51. **To be . . . above:** "Thou hast made him a little lower than the angels, and hast crowned him with glory and honor" (Ps. 8.5).

352–53. Fowler observes that the precedent for God's Heaven-shaking oath is both biblical and classical. See Isa. 13.12–13 and especially Heb. 6.17 (a crucial verse for *Lycidas* also); Homer, *Il.* 1.528–30, and Vergil, *Aen.* 9.104–6.

355. **mold:** form. Cp. line 139. The sense "constitutive substance" (in humanity's case, earth) is secondary here because *substance* follows. See Rumrich 1987, 53–69.

357. **attempted:** attacked or tempted. The options are elaborated through line 376.

367. **puny:** from the French *puis né,* later born.

368. **God:** "The first time in *PL* that any devil has spoken the name" (Leonard).

369–70. **May . . . works:** "And the Lord said, I will destroy man . . . for it repenteth me that I have made them" (Gen. 6.7). Following the Calvinist interpretive practice known as "accommodation," the Geneva Bible explains that "God doeth never repent, but he speaketh after our capacity." Milton refuses to go along: "God would not have said anything . . . about himself

Abolish his own works. This would surpass
Common revenge, and interrupt his joy
In our confusion, and our joy upraise
In his disturbance, when his darling sons
Hurled headlong to partake with us, shall curse
Their frail original, and faded bliss,
Faded so soon. Advise if this be worth
Attempting, or to sit in darkness here
Hatching vain empires." Thus Beëlzebub
Pleaded his devilish counsel, first devised
By Satan, and in part proposed: for whence,
But from the author of all ill could spring
So deep a malice, to confound the race
Of mankind in one root, and Earth with Hell
To mingle and involve, done all to spite
The great Creator? But their spite still serves
His glory to augment. The bold design
Pleased highly those infernal States, and joy
Sparkled in all their eyes; with full assent
They vote: whereat his speech he thus renews.
"Well have ye judged, well ended long debate,
Synod of gods, and like to what ye are,
Great things resolved, which from the lowest deep
Will once more lift us up, in spite of fate,
Nearer our ancient seat; perhaps in view
Of those bright confines, whence with neighboring arms
And opportune excursion we may chance
Re-enter Heav'n; or else in some mild zone
Dwell not unvisited of Heav'n's fair light
Secure, and at the bright'ning orient beam
Purge off this gloom; the soft delicious air,
To heal the scar of these corrosive fires
Shall breathe her balm. But first whom shall we send
In search of this new world, whom shall we find

---

unless he intended that it should be a part of our conception of him. . . . Let us believe that he did repent" (*CD* 1.2).

374. **Hurled headlong:** repeats 1.45, the account of the rebel angels' expulsion. Beëlzebub assumes that God will be consistent in punishing rebellion; hence *partake* (share) *with us.*

375. **original:** 1667 reads "originals." The meaning includes "parentage" but also the prelapsarian state of bliss (see 10.731–42). Cp. *RCG:* "run questing up as high as Adam to fetch their original" (Yale 1:762).

377. **to sit in darkness here:** "Such as sit in darkness and in the shadow of death, being bound in affliction and iron; Because they rebelled against the words of God and condemned the counsel of the most High" (Ps. 107.10–11).

379–80. **first devised/By Satan:** See 1.650–56.

383. **one root:** Adam and Eve, the genealogical root of humanity.

387. **States:** representatives, dignitaries.

391. **Synod:** meeting, assembly (usually of clergy or church elders); cp. 6.156, 11.67.

Sufficient? Who shall tempt with wand'ring feet
The dark unbottomed infinite abyss
And through the palpable obscure find out
His uncouth way, or spread his airy flight
Upborne with indefatigable wings
Over the vast abrupt, ere he arrive
The happy isle; what strength, what art can then
Suffice, or what evasion bear him safe
Through the strict senteries and stations thick
Of angels watching round? Here he had need
All circumspection, and we now no less
Choice in our suffrage; for on whom we send,
The weight of all and our last hope relies."
This said, he sat; and expectation held
His look suspense, awaiting who appeared
To second, or oppose, or undertake
The perilous attempt: but all sat mute,
Pondering the danger with deep thoughts; and each
In other's count'nance read his own dismay
Astonished: none among the choice and prime
Of those Heav'n-warring champions could be found
So hardy as to proffer or accept
Alone the dreadful voyage; till at last
Satan, whom now transcendent glory raised
Above his fellows, with monarchal pride
Conscious of highest worth, unmoved thus spake.
"O progeny of Heav'n, empyreal Thrones,
With reason hath deep silence and demur
Seized us, though undismayed: long is the way
And hard, that out of Hell leads up to light;
Our prison strong, this huge convex of fire,

404. **tempt:** make trial of, test.

405. **abyss:** Greek for "bottomless"; translates "the deep" in the Septuagint.

406. **palpable obscure:** tangible dark. Cp. the "darkness which may be felt" inflicted by God on Egypt (Exod. 10.21) and the threat of "thick and palpable clouds of darkness" invoked in the prefatory epistle to the *AV*.

407. **uncouth:** unknown, strange, unpleasant.

409. **abrupt:** chasm.

410. **happy isle:** the universe of this world, hung in the sea of chaos (ll. 1011, 1051). The phrasing recalls the Islands of the Blessed in Greek mythology.

412. **senteries:** sentries. The meter requires the three-syllable form, a variation common in the seventeenth century.

413. **had:** would have.

415. **Choice in our suffrage:** judgment in arriving at a consensus.

418. **suspense:** attentive, in suspense, as is appropriate for personified *expectation*.

430–66. Cp. Satan's corresponding speech at *PR* 1.44–105.

432–33. **long . . . light:** Satan echoes the warning of Vergil's Sibyl to Aeneas before his trip to the underworld (*Aen.* 6.126–29; cp. 81n, 3.20–21).

434. **convex:** hemisphere or domelike vault, seen from the outside.

Outrageous to devour, immures us round
Ninefold, and gates of burning adamant
Barred over us prohibit all egress.
These past, if any pass, the void profound
Of unessential night receives him next
Wide gaping, and with utter loss of being
Threatens him, plunged in that abortive gulf.
If thence he scape into whatever world,
Or unknown region, what remains him less
Than unknown dangers and as hard escape.
But I should ill become this throne, O Peers,
And this imperial sov'reignty, adorned
With splendor, armed with power, if aught proposed
And judged of public moment, in the shape
Of difficulty or danger could deter
Me from attempting. Wherefore do I assume
These royalties, and not refuse to reign,
Refusing to accept as great a share
Of hazard as of honor, due alike
To him who reigns, and so much to him due
Of hazard more, as he above the rest
High honored sits? Go therefore mighty Powers,
Terror of Heav'n, though fall'n; intend at home,
While here shall be our home, what best may ease
The present misery, and render Hell
More tolerable; if there be cure or charm
To respite or deceive, or slack the pain
Of this ill mansion: intermit no watch
Against a wakeful foe, while I abroad
Through all the coasts of dark destruction seek
Deliverance for us all: this enterprise
None shall partake with me." Thus saying rose

435. **Outrageous to devour:** fierce enough to destroy rapidly and completely.

436. **adamant:** from the Greek for "unbreakable."

438. **void profound:** translates Lucretius' *inane profundum* (*On the Nature of Things* 1.1108).

439. **unessential:** lacking essence; without entity. Cp. "unoriginal" (10.477), "unsubstantial" (*PR* 4.399). Satan proceeds to revisit Belial's fear (ll. 149–51), as he will again when he returns to Hell (10.476–77).

441. **abortive:** threatening *utter loss of being* (as at l. 440), as if one had never been born. The sense "preventive" may also apply because, by swallowing Satan, the preexistent womb of chaos would end his mission before it begins; see lines 932–38.

443. **remains:** awaits.

444. Beginning with Edition 4 (1688), editors often supply a question mark after *escape*. The sentence may be construed as interrogative in form, but Satan is not asking a question.

448. **moment:** consequence.

452. **Refusing:** "if I refuse."

457. **intend at:** attend to.

461. **respite or deceive:** relieve or beguile, parallel to *cure or charm* (460).

The monarch, and prevented all reply,
Prudent, lest from his resolution raised
Others among the chief might offer now
(Certain to be refused) what erst they feared;
And so refused might in opinion stand
His rivals, winning cheap the high repute
Which he through hazard huge must earn. But they
Dreaded not more th' adventure than his voice
Forbidding; and at once with him they rose;
Their rising all at once was as the sound
Of thunder heard remote. Towards him they bend
With awful reverence prone; and as a god
Extol him equal to the highest in Heav'n:
Nor failed they to express how much they praised,
That for the general safety he despised
His own: for neither do the spirits damned
Lose all their virtue; lest bad men should boast
Their specious deeds on earth, which glory excites,
Or close ambition varnished o'er with zeal.
Thus they their doubtful consultations dark
Ended rejoicing in their matchless chief:
As when from mountain tops the dusky clouds
Ascending, while the north wind sleeps, o'erspread
Heav'n's cheerful face, the louring element
Scowls o'er the darkened lantskip snow, or show'r;
If chance the radiant sun with farewell sweet
Extend his ev'ning beam, the fields revive,
The birds their notes renew, and bleating herds
Attest their joy, that hill and valley rings.
O shame to men! Devil with devil damned
Firm concord holds, men only disagree
Of creatures rational, though under hope

467. **prevented:** forestalled.

468. **raised:** buoyed, uplifted (by Satan's resolve); modifies *Others* (469).

478. **With awful reverence prone:** For Leonard, the phrase implies respect; for Fowler, groveling submission. The former reading suits the republican strain of Hell's polity, the latter its affinity with Asian tyranny. Cp. *CD* 2.13: "We nowhere read of obeisance being made to kings in any other way than by a low bow. Yet this same mark of respect was frequently used by one private individual to another"; also *PL* 4.958–60, 5.357–60.

483–85. **lest . . . zeal:** "to prevent bad men from boasting about actions that appear virtuous but are really motivated by fame or hidden ambition cloaked with enthusiasm."

489. **while the north wind sleeps:** "what time the might of the north wind sleepeth" (Homer, *Il.* 5.524).

490. **louring element:** threatening (thus "lowering") sky; the *element* is air.

491. **lantskip:** landscape (old spelling).

496–502. "There is more amity among serpents than among men" (Juvenal, *Satire* 15.159). According to Rusca, devils maintain harmony to tempt humanity more effectively (Hughes).

Of heavenly grace: and God proclaiming peace,
Yet live in hatred, enmity, and strife
Among themselves, and levy cruel wars,
Wasting the earth, each other to destroy:
As if (which might induce us to accord)
Man had not hellish foes enow besides,
That day and night for his destruction wait.
    The Stygian Counsel thus dissolved; and forth
In order came the grand infernal Peers:
Midst came their mighty Paramount, and seemed
Alone th' antagonist of Heav'n, nor less
Than Hell's dread Emperor with pomp supreme,
And God-like imitated state; him round
A globe of fiery Seraphim enclosed
With bright emblazonry, and horrent arms.
Then of their session ended they bid cry
With trumpets' regal sound the great result:
Toward the four winds four speedy Cherubim
Put to their mouths the sounding alchemy
By herald's voice explained: the hollow abyss
Heard far and wide, and all the host of Hell
With deaf'ning shout, returned them loud acclaim.
Thence more at ease their minds and somewhat raised
By false presumptuous hope, the rangèd powers
Disband, and wand'ring, each his several way
Pursues, as inclination or sad choice
Leads him perplexed, where he may likeliest find
Truce to his restless thoughts, and entertain
The irksome hours, till this great chief return.
Part on the plain, or in the air sublime
Upon the wing, or in swift race contend,
As at th' Olympian Games or Pythian fields;

504. **enow:** archaic plural of "enough."

511–13. The imitation of God's *state* (ceremonial pomp) is slavish in detail. As in the scriptural account of God on his throne (Isa. 6.1–7), Satan is surrounded by a host of *Seraphim* in a compact band (*globe;* cp. *PR* 4.581). Recent editors (Fowler, Leonard) cite the Hebrew verb "to burn" as the source of *Seraphim* (hence *fiery Seraphim*). But the *Jewish Encyclopedia* cites the Hebrew noun for "fiery flying serpents" (Num. 21.6–9; Deut. 8:15).

513. **emblazonry:** heraldic devices decorating shields; **horrent**: bristling, dreadful.

517. **alchemy:** goldlike alloy, "alchemy gold"; here, a synecdoche for trumpets.

526. **entertain:** occupy. See 91n.

528–69. Classical precedents abound for the diversions of the fallen angels. Cp. the Myrmidons' exercises during Achilles' absence from battle (*Il.* 2.774–79) or Horace's list of pursuits favored by various men (*Odes* 1.1). Milton's specific choice of model is ironic; see Vergil's inventory of the activities of the blessed dead in Elysium (*Aen.* 6.642–78).

528. **sublime:** aloft, uplifted; cp. *PR* 4.542.

530. **Pythian fields:** Delphi; site of games instituted by Apollo after he slew the Python.

Part curb their fiery steeds, or shun the goal
With rapid wheels, or fronted brigades form.
As when to warn proud cities war appears
Waged in the troubled sky, and armies rush
To battle in the clouds, before each van
Prick forth the airy knights, and couch their spears
Till thickest legions close; with feats of arms
From either end of heav'n the welkin burns.
Others with vast Typhoean rage more fell
Rend up both rocks and hills, and ride the air
In whirlwind; Hell scarce holds the wild uproar.
As when Alcides from Oechalia crowned
With conquest, felt th' envenomed robe, and tore
Through pain up by the roots Thessalian pines,
And Lichas from the top of Oeta threw
Into th' Euboic Sea. Others more mild,
Retreated in a silent valley, sing
With notes angelical to many a harp
Their own heroic deeds and hapless fall
By doom of battle; and complain that fate
Free virtue should enthrall to force or chance.
Their song was partial, but the harmony
(What could it less when spirits immortal sing?)
Suspended Hell, and took with ravishment

531. **shun the goal:** go tightly around the turning post, without touching it. Cp. "the turning post cleared with glowing wheel" (Horace, *Odes* 1.1.4–5).

532. **fronted:** directly opposed, front to front.

533–34. **As when . . . sky:** Cloudy apparitions preceded the fall of Jerusalem, writes Josephus (*The Wars of the Jews* 6.5.3), and atmospheric conditions at the time of Caesar's assassination also warned of strife, according to many authors. Portentous weather was similarly observed "about the time of [the] Civil Wars" in England (Hume). Milton persistently likens fallen angels to ominous or deceptive meteorological phenomena, in line with his account of airy angelic substance and the rebels' authority as "powers of air" (*PR* 1.44).

535. **van:** front line of a battle formation.

536. **Prick forth:** spur forward; **couch:** lower into position for attack.

538. **welkin:** sky.

539. **Typhoean:** Identified with Etna's volcanic power, Typhon was deemed father of the winds and is also an English word meaning *whirlwind* (l. 541). See 1.197–99. **fell:** of cruel or vicious character.

542–46. **As when . . . Euboic Sea:** Homeward bound after sacking *Oechalia,* Hercules asks *Lichas* to fetch a ceremonial robe. Hercules' unwitting wife supplies an *envenomed* garment, which fastens to his flesh and burns unrelentingly. Uprooting trees in blind fury (*pines* is Milton's detail), Hercules hurls Lichas into the *Euboic Sea* from atop Mount *Oeta* in southern Thessaly. Sophocles dramatizes the story in *Trachiniae,* and Seneca in *Hercules Oetaeus.* But Milton mainly follows Ovid (*Met.* 9.134–272, *Her.* 9).

552. **partial:** biased; "silent as to the corrupt motive of their conduct, and dwelt only on the sad consequences of it" (Cowper). The ensuing contrast with *harmony* suggests that "in parts" or "polyphonic" is not the intended sense.

554. **Suspended:** The *OED* cites this line to exemplify the sense "riveted the attention of," and recent editors agree. The more likely meaning, however, is "to bring about the temporary cessation" (of a condition). The parenthesis im-

The thronging audience. In discourse more sweet
(For eloquence the soul, song charms the sense)
Others apart sat on a hill retired,
In thoughts more elevate, and reasoned high
Of providence, foreknowledge, will, and fate,
Fixed fate, free will, foreknowledge absolute,
And found no end, in wand'ring mazes lost.
Of good and evil much they argued then,
Of happiness and final misery,
Passion and apathy, and glory and shame,
Vain wisdom all, and false philosophy:
Yet with a pleasing sorcery could charm
Pain for a while or anguish, and excite
Fallacious hope, or arm th' obdurèd breast
With stubborn patience as with triple steel.
Another part in squadrons and gross bands,
On bold adventure to discover wide
That dismal world, if any clime perhaps
Might yield them easier habitation, bend
Four ways their flying march, along the banks
Of four infernal rivers that disgorge
Into the burning lake their baleful streams;
Abhorrèd Styx the flood of deadly hate,
Sad Acheron of sorrow, black and deep;
Cocytus, named of lamentation loud
Heard on the rueful stream; fierce Phlegeton
Whose waves of torrent fire inflame with rage.

---

plies this sense by interrupting the syntax and deferring the verb, as Newton observed. Cp. the effect on Satan of the Garden's beauty (4.356, 9.462–66). Classical antecedents include Orpheus' suspension of Hell (Vergil, *Georg.* 4.481–84) and the effect of Alcaeus's music on the tormented Titans, "beguiled of their sufferings by the soothing sound" (Horace, *Odes* 2.13.38). **took:** charmed, enchanted (cp. l. 556).

558–69. Though well versed in classical philosophy and scholastic argument, Milton in later works includes passages critical of them (cp. *PR* 4.286–321, *SA* 300–306). God later makes his way through the mazy discourse of free will versus predestination (3.96–119); so does Milton in his theological treatise (*CD* 1.3, 4).

564. **apathy:** impassivity; signature virtue of Stoicism, one that Milton did not endorse. Cp. *CD* 2.10: "Sensibility to pain, and complaints or lamentations, are not inconsistent with true patience"; also, *PR* 4.300–18. Orthodox theology makes God the paragon of this virtue, denoted by the term *impassibility.* But Milton insists that we should deem God to be as passionate as Scripture says (see 369–70n).

568. **obdurèd:** hardened, especially in sinfulness; stubborn and unyielding, sometimes by divine intercession. See 6.785. Elledge cites *obdurèd* as an example of prolepsis, a figure in which the adjective describes a state yet to be produced by the action of the verb. If it is God who renders the rebels obdurate, however, the figure instead expresses a coincidence common in seventeenth-century theologies: the damned creature's philosophical appropriation of God's sentence; cp. 1.211–12, 240–41.

570. **gross:** dense, closely packed.

575–81. The account of each river is a translation of its Greek name; e.g., *Cocytus* derives from *kokutos,* Greek for "wailing" or *lamentation loud.*

Far off from these a slow and silent stream,
Lethe the river of oblivion rolls
Her wat'ry labyrinth, whereof who drinks,
Forthwith his former state and being forgets,
Forgets both joy and grief, pleasure and pain.
Beyond this flood a frozen continent
Lies dark and wild, beat with perpetual storms
Of whirlwind and dire hail, which on firm land
Thaws not, but gathers heap, and ruin seems
Of ancient pile; all else deep snow and ice,
A gulf profound as that Serbonian Bog
Betwixt Damiata and Mount Casius old,
Where armies whole have sunk: the parching air
Burns frore, and cold performs th' effect of fire.
Thither by harpy-footed Furies haled,
At certain revolutions all the damned
Are brought: and feel by turns the bitter change
Of fierce extremes, extremes by change more fierce,
From beds of raging fire to starve in ice
Their soft ethereal warmth, and there to pine
Immovable, infixed, and frozen round,
Periods of time, thence hurried back to fire.
They ferry over this Lethean sound
Both to and fro, their sorrow to augment,
And wish and struggle, as they pass, to reach
The tempting stream, with one small drop to lose
In sweet forgetfulness all pain and woe,
All in one moment, and so near the brink;
But fate withstands, and to oppose th' attempt

591. **pile:** vast building.

592–94. **A gulf . . . sunk:** Surrounded by hills of sand, Lake Serbonis lay between *Mount Casius* and *Damiata,* at the center of a notorious morass on the lower Egyptian coast. Diodorus Siculus (1.30) and Sandys (1637, 137) describe the fatally deceptive locale and report it swallowing *whole armies.* Apollonius makes it, not Etna, Zeus's prison for Typhon (2.1210–15). Related similes appear at 939–40 and 9.634–42.

595. **frore:** frosty. "When the cold north wind bloweth, and the water is congealed into ice, it . . . clotheth the water as with a breastplate. It . . . burneth the wilderness and consumeth the grass as fire" (*Ec.* 43.20–21). That Hell's torments include ice as well as fire was a commonplace; see Dante, *Inf.* 3.86–87, and Shakespeare, *MM* 3.1.121–22.

596. **harpy-footed:** with hooked claws, like a raptor. In Greek culture, Harpies were wind spirits thought to snatch people from this world and deliver them to the Furies (with whom they were sometimes confounded). They are particularly identified with sweeping storm winds (hence the power to carry away). 1667 and 1674 have "hailed," not "haled." The spellings were interchangeable in Milton's time, and the superimposed senses of wind-driven precipitation, of being summoned, and of being dragged are likely intended.

600. **starve:** die a lingering death from the cold.

604. **Lethean sound:** the river of forgetfulness, Lethe (see l. 583).

Medusa with Gorgonian terror guards
The ford, and of itself the water flies
All taste of living wight, as once it fled
The lip of Tantalus. Thus roving on
In confused march forlorn, th' advent'rous bands
With shudd'ring horror pale, and eyes aghast
Viewed first their lamentable lot, and found
No rest: through many a dark and dreary vale
They passed, and many a region dolorous,
O'er many a frozen, many a fiery alp,
Rocks, caves, lakes, fens, bogs, dens, and shades of death,
A universe of death, which God by curse
Created evil, for evil only good,
Where all life dies, death lives, and nature breeds,
Perverse, all monstrous, all prodigious things,
Abominable, inutterable, and worse
Than fables yet have feigned, or fear conceived,
Gorgons and Hydras, and Chimeras dire.
　Meanwhile the Adversary of God and man,
Satan with thoughts inflamed of highest design,
Puts on swift wings, and towards the gates of Hell
Explores his solitary flight; sometimes
He scours the right hand coast, sometimes the left,
Now shaves with level wing the deep, then soars
Up to the fiery concave tow'ring high.
As when far off at sea a fleet descried

611. **Medusa:** "snaky-headed Gorgon" (*Masque* 447), the most notorious of three terrifying sisters. All who beheld Medusa were literally petrified.

613. **wight:** creature.

614. **Tantalus:** Homer depicts him in Tartarus, where he suffers perpetual thirst and appetite while standing chin deep in a lake that flees his lips, under boughs of fugitive fruit (*Od.* 11.582–92; see also Horace, *Satires* 1.68). Cp. 4.325–36, 10.556–70.

621. The variation of iambic rhythm in the first six monosyllables is shocking, maybe unique. It describes the unrelenting variety of uniformly deathly landscape.

628. **Hydra:** a venomous serpent with multiple, regenerative heads; **Chimera:** a fire-breathing mix of lion, goat, and serpent (*Il.* 6.180–82). *Prolusion 1* presents these monsters as the horrors of a guilty conscience (p. 792). On *Gorgons,* see 611n. Cp. 10.524: "Scorpion and asp, and amphisbaena dire."

629. **Adversary:** See 1.82n.

632. **Explores:** makes trial of, reconnoiters.

633–34. **scours . . . shaves:** "moves quickly over . . . skims the surface of." As suggested by *explores,* Satan both makes a test flight and inspects the bounds of his new realm. The contact and coverage implied by *scours* and *shaves* is characteristic of the way Satan marks territory; cp. 9.63–66.

636–37. **As . . . clouds:** Sailing ships seen from afar (*descried*) appear suspended in air; Greek authors termed them *meteorous,* "hanging" or "aloft" (see Thucydides 1.48.3).

Hangs in the clouds, by equinoctial winds
Close sailing from Bengala, or the isles
Of Ternate and Tidore, whence merchants bring
Their spicy drugs: they on the trading flood
Through the wide Ethiopian to the Cape
Ply stemming nightly toward the pole. So seemed
Far off the flying Fiend: at last appear
Hell bounds high reaching to the horrid roof,
And thrice threefold the gates; three folds were brass,
Three iron, three of adamantine rock,
Impenetrable, impaled with circling fire,
Yet unconsumed. Before the gates there sat
On either side a formidable shape;
The one seemed woman to the waist, and fair,
But ended foul in many a scaly fold
Voluminous and vast, a serpent armed
With mortal sting: about her middle round
A cry of Hell-hounds never ceasing barked
With wide Cerberean mouths full loud, and rung
A hideous peal: yet, when they list, would creep,
If aught disturbed their noise, into her womb,
And kennel there, yet there still barked and howled,

637–42. **by . . . pole:** The comparison is to merchant ships, sailing either from Bengal (*Bengala*) in northeastern India or from *Ternate* and *Tidore,* "spice islands" in the East Indies. For the association of Satan's regime with the region, see 2n, 4n.

637. **equinoctial:** usually and incorrectly glossed as "at the equator" on the authority of the *OED.* The rest of the simile indicates that the *winds* in question are not the light and shifting breezes at the equator but monsoons. They dominate the climate of the Indian Ocean (*the wide Ethiopian*), reversing direction at the equinoxes (hence *equinoctial*), thus determining the schedule for shipping spices to Europe along the established commercial course (*trading flood*). During the southern winter (April to October), the monsoon blows to the northeast, out of Southern Africa. A fleet bent on sailing toward the *Cape* (of Good Hope) against that prevailing wind would set a course southwest, as *close* to the eye of the wind as possible, and tack repeatedly (*ply*).

642. **stemming . . . pole:** Ships bound for the Cape would alter course *nightly,* making headway (*stemming*) directly to the south (*toward the pole*), to avoid shallow coastal waters. In the southern winter, the higher the latitude, the longer the night.

647. **impaled:** surrounded, enclosed.

650–59. **The one . . . unseen:** Milton's allegory of Sin comes out of the Spenserian tradition: cp. Spenser's Error (*FQ* 1.1.14–15), Phineas Fletcher's Hamartia (*Purple Island* 12.27–31) and Sin (*Apollyonists* 1.10–12). Classical sources include Hesiod's Echidna (half woman, half snake) (*Theog.* 300–25). See also Vergil's Scylla (*Aen.* 3.426–32) and Ovid's story of her origin (*Met.* 14.50–67), to which Milton alludes at 659–61 (see note); cp. *Masque* 257–58.

652. **Voluminous:** winding or coiling, like a serpent.

653. **mortal sting:** "The sting of death is sin" (1 Cor. 15.56).

654. **cry:** pack; group noun for hounds.

655. **Cerberean:** In Greek myth, Cerberus is a many-headed guard dog at the entrance to Hades.

658. Cp. the complaint of Shakespeare's Margaret to the Duchess of York: "From forth the kennel of thy womb hath crept / A hell-hound that doth hunt us all to death" (*R3* 4.4.47–48).

Within unseen. Far less abhorred than these
Vexed Scylla bathing in the sea that parts
Calabria from the hoarse Trinacrian shore:
Nor uglier follow the night-hag, when called
In secret, riding through the air she comes
Lured with the smell of infant blood, to dance
With Lapland witches, while the laboring moon
Eclipses at their charms. The other shape,
If shape it might be called that shape had none
Distinguishable in member, joint, or limb,
Or substance might be called that shadow seemed,
For each seemed either; black it stood as night,
Fierce as ten Furies, terrible as Hell,
And shook a dreadful dart; what seemed his head
The likeness of a kingly crown had on.
Satan was now at hand, and from his seat
The monster moving onward came as fast
With horrid strides; Hell trembled as he strode.
Th' undaunted Fiend what this might be admired,
Admired, not feared; God and his Son except,
Created thing naught valued he nor shunned;
And with disdainful look thus first began.
"Whence and what art thou, execrable shape,

659–61. Circe poisons the sheltered coastal pool in which Scylla bathes. According to Ovid, she wades in up to her waist and "sees her loins disfigured with barking monster shapes . . . gaping dogs' heads, such as a Cerberus might have" (*Met.* 14.60–65). She then preys on sailors from a cave on the Sicilian (*Trinacrian*) coast near Messina, opposite the southern tip of the Italian mainland (*Calabria*). Milton may deem the shore along the Strait of Messina *hoarse* because of nearby Etna's frequent roaring.

662. **night-hag:** probably Hecate, the only Titan left at large by Zeus. The Greeks associated her with, among other things, infernal powers, the moon, and witchcraft. Howling dogs signaled her approach. See *Masque* 535, *MAC* 3.5.

664–66. **Lured . . . charms:** Witches were thought to use infant blood in their rites. Hence seventeenth-century authorities suspected midwives of practicing witchcraft and serving Satan by infanticide (Baillie 63, Ehrenreich and English). *Laboring* evokes the process of childbirth.

665. **Lapland:** northernmost portion of the Scandinavian peninsula. Hume records the common reputation of the inhabitants: "their diabolical superstitions, and vindictive natures, added to their gross stupidity, and the malicious imaginations of melancholy, have made them infamous for witchcraft and conjuration." **laboring:** That magic could afflict the moon, causing it to labor in its movement, was an old and widespread belief. One meaning of the Latin *laborare* is "to undergo eclipse."

673. Milton's representation of Death with a *kingly crown* may reflect his antimonarchical views. Cp. Shakespeare's R_2: "Within the hollow crown/That rounds the mortal temples of a king/Keeps Death his court" (3.2.160–62).

677. **admired:** wondered.

678–79. **God . . . shunned:** "When God was *except* (past participle, *OED* 3b: 'excluded'), no basis for value remained" (Fowler). Although this gloss may seem strained, the more common reading—"of all creation Satan values or shuns only God and the Son"—has a nodding Milton imply that God is created.

681. In asking his opponent's origin, Satan speaks in the manner of Achilles, though to ironically comic effect (cp. *Il.* 21.150).

That dar'st, though grim and terrible, advance
Thy miscreated front athwart my way
To yonder gates? Through them I mean to pass,
That be assured, without leave asked of thee:
Retire, or taste thy folly, and learn by proof,
Hell-born, not to contend with spirits of Heav'n."
To whom the Goblin full of wrath replied,
"Art thou that traitor angel, art thou he,
Who first broke peace in Heav'n and faith, till then
Unbroken, and in proud rebellious arms
Drew after him the third part of Heav'n's sons
Conjured against the highest, for which both thou
And they outcast from God, are here condemned
To waste eternal days in woe and pain?
And reckon'st thou thyself with spirits of Heav'n,
Hell-doomed, and breath'st defiance here and scorn,
Where I reign king, and to enrage thee more,
Thy king and lord? Back to thy punishment,
False fugitive, and to thy speed add wings,
Lest with a whip of scorpions I pursue
Thy ling'ring, or with one stroke of this dart
Strange horror seize thee, and pangs unfelt before."
So spake the grisly terror, and in shape,
So speaking and so threat'ning, grew tenfold
More dreadful and deform: on th' other side
Incensed with indignation Satan stood
Unterrified, and like a comet burned,
That fires the length of Ophiucus huge
In th' Arctic sky, and from his horrid hair

683. **miscreated front:** ugly face.

686. **taste:** learn by experience or *proof;* a figurative usage crucial to the epic action.

692. "[The dragon's] tail drew the third part of the stars of heaven, and did cast them to the earth" (Rev. 12.4). Satan tends to overstate his faction as "well nigh half" (9.141). The precise ratio had long been a point of scholastic controversy.

693. **Conjured:** sworn together (stress on the second syllable).

697. **Hell-doomed:** retort to Satan's scornful *Hell-born* (l. 687). Raphael's narrative of the rebellion (5.563ff) confirms Death's summary, which is oddly well informed and free from the infernal bias prevalent for most of the first two books.

701. Cp. Solomon's son Rehoboam to the Israelites: "My father hath chastised you with whips, but I will chastise you with scorpions" (1 Kings 12.11). The allusion suggests that God (Satan's punisher) is also Death's father, though we are about to learn otherwise.

705–11. **So speaking . . . war:** Cp. Satan's confrontation with Gabriel (4.985ff).

708–11. **Unterrified . . . war:** Vergil and Tasso, among others, precede Milton in comparing warriors to comets (*Aen.* 10.272–73; *GL* 7.52). They were since ancient times believed to presage pestilence, war, and change of kingdoms.

709. **Ophiucus:** serpent bearer; a large constellation that Milton associates with Satan, located in the Northern (hence *Arctic*) Hemisphere.

710. **horrid hair:** Another example of Milton's etymologically instructive wordplay. *Comet* derives from the Greek *kometes,* "long-haired." *Horrid* means "bristling" and derives from the same root as *hirsute* ("hairy").

Shakes pestilence and war. Each at the head
Leveled his deadly aim; their fatal hands
No second stroke intend, and such a frown
Each cast at th' other, as when two black clouds
With heav'n's artillery fraught, come rattling on
Over the Caspian, then stand front to front
Hov'ring a space, till winds the signal blow
To join their dark encounter in mid air:
So frowned the mighty combatants, that Hell
Grew darker at their frown, so matched they stood;
For never but once more was either like
To meet so great a foe: and now great deeds
Had been achieved, whereof all Hell had rung,
Had not the snaky sorceress that sat
Fast by Hell gate, and kept the fatal key,
Ris'n, and with hideous outcry rushed between.
    "O father, what intends thy hand," she cried,
"Against thy only son? What fury O son,
Possesses thee to bend that mortal dart
Against thy father's head? And know'st for whom;
For him who sits above and laughs the while
At thee ordained his drudge, to execute
Whate'er his wrath, which he calls justice, bids,
His wrath which one day will destroy ye both."
    She spake, and at her words the hellish pest
Forbore, then these to her Satan returned:
    "So strange thy outcry, and thy words so strange
Thou interposest, that my sudden hand
Prevented spares to tell thee yet by deeds
What it intends; till first I know of thee,
What thing thou art, thus double-formed, and why
In this infernal vale first met thou call'st
Me father, and that phantasm call'st my son?
I know thee not, nor ever saw till now
Sight more detestable than him and thee."
    T' whom thus the portress of Hell gate replied:
"Hast thou forgot me then, and do I seem

714–18. Boiardo's Orlando and Agricane are similarly opposed like *two black clouds* (*Orlando Innamorato* 1.16.10). Satan, whose realm will be "mid air" (*PR* 1.44–46), is persistently linked to meteorological phenomena.

716. **Caspian:** region commonly associated with storms (see, e.g., Horace, *Odes* 2.9.2–3).

722. **foe:** the Son of God. See 1 Cor. 15.25–26 and Heb. 2.14.

746. **portress:** "The *Porter* to th' infernal gate is *Sin*" (P. Fletcher, *Apollyonists* 1.10.1).

Now in thine eye so foul, once deemed so fair
In Heav'n, when at th' assembly, and in sight
Of all the Seraphim with thee combined
In bold conspiracy against Heav'n's King,
All on a sudden miserable pain
Surprised thee, dim thine eyes, and dizzy swum
In darkness, while thy head flames thick and fast
Threw forth, till on the left side op'ning wide,
Likest to thee in shape and count'nance bright,
Then shining heav'nly fair, a goddess armed
Out of thy head I sprung: amazement seized
All th' host of Heav'n; back they recoiled afraid
At first, and called me Sin, and for a sign
Portentous held me; but familiar grown,
I pleased, and with attractive graces won
The most averse, thee chiefly, who full oft
Thyself in me thy perfect image viewing
Becam'st enamored, and such joy thou took'st
With me in secret, that my womb conceived
A growing burden. Meanwhile war arose,
And fields were fought in Heav'n; wherein remained
(For what could else) to our almighty foe
Clear victory, to our part loss and rout
Through all the empyrean: down they fell
Driv'n headlong from the pitch of Heaven, down
Into this deep, and in the general fall
I also; at which time this powerful key
Into my hand was giv'n, with charge to keep
These gates for ever shut, which none can pass
Without my op'ning. Pensive here I sat
Alone, but long I sat not, till my womb

748. "This is a very just and instructive part of the allegory. . . . Sin, pleasant in contemplation and enjoyment, is foul in retrospect" (Cowper).

752–53. **All . . . thee:** Sin's narrative and Raphael's later narrative offer distinct explanations of Satan's first experience of pain; cp. 6.327ff, 432ff.

754–58. **while . . . sprung:** The general *amazement* at the cephalic delivery of Sin full-blown, as *a goddess armed,* recalls the account of Athena's birth in *Homeric Hymn* 28.

760. Critics preoccupied with postmodern semiotics belabor the proximity of *Sin* and *sign,* near homophones.

768. **fields:** battles; cp. 1.105.

771. **empyrean:** highest part of Heaven, where pure fire or light subsists.

772. **pitch:** pinnacle, height.

774–77. **at which time . . . op'ning:** Citing these lines, Fowler (746n) dismisses Empson's concern over God's choice of Sin and Death as guards. An allegory in which a personification of sin is expected to obey God's command is nonetheless perplexing.

778–87. **till . . . destroy:** "Then when lust hath conceived, it bringeth forth sin: and sin, when it is finished, bringeth forth death" (James 1.15). Cp. Shakespeare, *Sonnet 129.* As with the birth of Sin (754–58n), the delivery of Death echoes the discharge of Satan's artillery (6.586–90).

Pregnant by thee, and now excessive grown
Prodigious motion felt and rueful throes.
At last this odious offspring whom thou seest
Thine own begotten, breaking violent way
Tore through my entrails, that with fear and pain
Distorted, all my nether shape thus grew
Transformed: but he my inbred enemy
Forth issued, brandishing his fatal dart
Made to destroy: I fled, and cried out 'Death';
Hell trembled at the hideous name, and sighed
From all her caves, and back resounded 'Death.'
I fled, but he pursued (though more, it seems,
Inflamed with lust than rage) and swifter far,
Me overtook his mother all dismayed,
And in embraces forcible and foul
Engend'ring with me, of that rape begot
These yelling monsters that with ceaseless cry
Surround me, as thou saw'st, hourly conceived
And hourly born, with sorrow infinite
To me, for when they list into the womb
That bred them they return, and howl and gnaw
My bowels, their repast; then bursting forth
Afresh with conscious terrors vex me round,
That rest or intermission none I find.
Before mine eyes in opposition sits
Grim Death my son and foe, who sets them on,
And me his parent would full soon devour
For want of other prey, but that he knows
His end with mine involved; and knows that I
Should prove a bitter morsel, and his bane,
Whenever that shall be; so fate pronounced.
But thou O father, I forewarn thee, shun
His deadly arrow; neither vainly hope
To be invulnerable in those bright arms,
Though tempered heav'nly, for that mortal dint,
Save he who reigns above, none can resist."
    She finished, and the subtle Fiend his lore

789. Vergil similarly describes the sound produced by a spear thrown into the side of the Trojan horse: "With the womb's reverberation the vaults rang hollow, sending forth a moan" (*Aen.* 2.52–53).

795–802. The description of this hourly cycle suggests a nightmarish clock mechanism. Postlapsarian time consciousness is also consciousness of death; cp. 4.266–68; *On Time.*

809. **so fate pronounced:** Leonard cites Milton's theological treatise: "fate or *fatum* is only what is *fatum,* spoken, by some almighty power" (*CD* 1.2).

813. **dint:** blow, stroke.

Soon learned, now milder, and thus answered smooth.
"Dear daughter, since thou claim'st me for thy sire,
And my fair son here show'st me, the dear pledge
Of dalliance had with thee in Heav'n, and joys
Then sweet, now sad to mention, through dire change
Befall'n us unforeseen, unthought of, know
I come no enemy, but to set free
From out this dark and dismal house of pain,
Both him and thee, and all the heav'nly host
Of spirits that in our just pretenses armed
Fell with us from on high: from them I go
This uncouth errand sole, and one for all
Myself expose, with lonely steps to tread
Th' unfounded deep, and through the void immense
To search with wand'ring quest a place foretold
Should be, and, by concurring signs, ere now
Created vast and round, a place of bliss
In the purlieus of Heav'n, and therein placed
A race of upstart creatures, to supply
Perhaps our vacant room, though more removed,
Lest Heav'n surcharged with potent multitude
Might hap to move new broils: be this or aught
Than this more secret now designed, I haste
To know, and this once known, shall soon return,
And bring ye to the place where thou and Death
Shall dwell at ease, and up and down unseen
Wing silently the buxom air, embalmed
With odors; there ye shall be fed and filled
Immeasurably, all things shall be your prey."
He ceased, for both seemed highly pleased, and Death
Grinned horrible a ghastly smile, to hear
His famine should be filled, and blessed his maw
Destined to that good hour: no less rejoiced

825. **pretenses:** claims; the meaning "false claims" was equally current in Milton's time.

827. **uncouth errand sole:** unknown mission alone; cp. line 407.

829. **unfounded:** bottomless, unestablished.

833. **purlieus:** outskirts. "A French word (as most of our law terms are) of *pur* pure and *lieu* a place, and denotes the ground adjoining to, and being accounted part of any forest, by Henry II and other Kings, was . . . separated again from the same and adjudged *Purlieu,* that is pure and free from the Laws of the Forest" (Hume).

836. **surcharged:** overburdened.

837. **broils:** tumults, riots. Without once mentioning God, Satan insinuates that humanity's location outside Heaven is a security measure aimed at crowd control.

842. **buxom:** pliant, yielding (cp. 5.270); **embalmed:** balmy, aromatic; also, "preserved with balm and precious spices, as princes and great persons are at their death, a word well applied to caress the ugly phantom" (Hume).

His mother bad, and thus bespake her sire.
"The key of this infernal pit by due,
And by command of Heav'n's all-powerful King
I keep, by him forbidden to unlock
These adamantine gates; against all force
Death ready stands to interpose his dart,
Fearless to be o'ermatched by living might.
But what owe I to his commands above
Who hates me, and hath hither thrust me down
Into this gloom of Tartarus profound,
To sit in hateful office here confined,
Inhabitant of Heav'n, and heav'nly-born,
Here in perpetual agony and pain,
With terrors and with clamors compassed round
Of mine own brood, that on my bowels feed:
Thou art my father, thou my author, thou
My being gav'st me; whom should I obey
But thee, whom follow? Thou wilt bring me soon
To that new world of light and bliss, among
The gods who live at ease, where I shall reign
At thy right hand voluptuous, as beseems
Thy daughter and thy darling, without end."
Thus saying, from her side the fatal key,
Sad instrument of all our woe, she took;
And towards the gate rolling her bestial train,
Forthwith the huge portcullis high up drew,
Which but herself not all the Stygian powers
Could once have moved; then in the key-hole turns
Th' intricate wards, and every bolt and bar
Of massy iron or solid rock with ease
Unfastens: on a sudden open fly

861–62. Sin's plight is echoed in Milton's account of his situation at the Restoration (7.25–28).

868. **gods who live at ease:** translates Homer's epithet for the Olympian gods (*Il.* 6.138).

869–70. Milton has Sin prophesy in phrases burlesquing the Nicene Creed ("Christ . . . sits on the right hand of the father . . . [his] kingdom shall have no end"). Milton scorned prescribed statements of faith and thought the doctrine of the Trinity articulated in the Nicene Creed especially contemptible. In his epic, the closest thing to the orthodox Trinity is the incestuous unity and variety of Satan, Sin, and Death.

872. **all our woe:** repeats 1.3. Sin provides the instrument that permits Satan to seduce humanity to the *first disobedience* (1.1).

876–79. **then . . . Unfastens:** Cp. Homer's description of Penelope opening the door to the storeroom where Odysseus's bow is kept: "Straightaway she quickly loosed the thong from the handle and thrust in the key, and with sure aim shot back the bolts . . . quickly they flew open before her" (*Od.* 21.46–50).

877. **wards:** corresponding ridges or grooves in a lock and key.

With impetuous recoil and jarring sound
Th' infernal doors, and on their hinges grate
Harsh thunder, that the lowest bottom shook
Of Erebus. She opened, but to shut
Excelled her power; the gates wide open stood,
That with extended wings a bannered host
Under spread ensigns marching might pass through
With horse and chariots ranked in loose array;
So wide they stood, and like a furnace mouth
Cast forth redounding smoke and ruddy flame.
Before their eyes in sudden view appear
The secrets of the hoary deep, a dark
Illimitable ocean without bound,
Without dimension, where length, breadth, and highth,
And time and place are lost; where eldest Night
And Chaos, ancestors of Nature, hold
Eternal anarchy, amidst the noise
Of endless wars, and by confusion stand.
For Hot, Cold, Moist, and Dry, four champions fierce
Strive here for mast'ry, and to battle bring
Their embryon atoms; they around the flag
Of each his faction, in their several clans,
Light-armed or heavy, sharp, smooth, swift or slow,
Swarm populous, unnumbered as the sands

880–82. **With . . . thunder:** "Grating on harsh, jarring hinges, the infernal gates open" (*Aen.* 6.873–74).

883. **Erebus:** darkness, the underworld.

889. **redounding:** surging, rolling upward in superabundance.

891. **secrets:** places, parts, or causes unknown, perhaps intentionally concealed; cp. 3.707. The realm of Chaos and Night is described as a womb (see l. 911, 10.476–77), impregnated by the Spirit during creation (1.21–22). Satan's trespass could thus be construed as sexual prying or a violation of the maternal (cp. 1.684–88, 2.785ff). **hoary:** white-haired and thus old or ancient.

894–910. **where . . . all:** Milton describes *eldest Night* as *eternal,* like the *anarchy* over which she and *Chaos* preside (e.g., l. 150, 3.18, 10.477). His presentation of Chaos is indebted to Ovid and Lucretius (*Met.* 1.5–20; *On the Nature of Things* 2). Commenting on Ovid, Sandys objects that "by not expressing the original, he seems to intimate the eternity of his *Chaos*" (1632, 49). Only God is eternal. The attribution of eternal being to Chaos and Night thus renders Milton's account of primordial matter heretical in one of two ways: either Chaos represents a realm distinct from God and, like him, eternal and existentially independent, or Chaos represents an aspect of eternal God himself. The discussion of matter in *Christian Doctrine* indicates that Milton endorsed the latter heresy (1.7). Cp. 915–16n.

898. **Hot, Cold, Moist, and Dry:** These had long been considered the four fundamental qualities that combine to constitute all created phenomena: humors, elements, planets, or bodies in general. Thus, earth was dry and cold, water moist and cold, air moist and hot, fire dry and hot, et cetera.

900–903. **embryon atoms . . . unnumbered:** indivisible units of primal matter, undeveloped and unformed; cp. line 913. The relative weights, shapes, motions, and textures of these countless (*unnumbered*) "seeds of things," the *semina rerum* of Lucretian atomist philosophy, account for the phenomenal variety of the world (*On the Nature of Things* 2.62–833).

Of Barca or Cyrene's torrid soil,
Levied to side with warring winds, and poise
Their lighter wings. To whom these most adhere,
He rules a moment; Chaos umpire sits,
And by decision more embroils the fray
By which he reigns: next him high arbiter
Chance governs all. Into this wild abyss,
The womb of Nature and perhaps her grave,
Of neither sea, nor shore, nor air, nor fire,
But all these in their pregnant causes mixed
Confus'dly, and which thus must ever fight,
Unless th' Almighty Maker them ordain
His dark materials to create more worlds,
Into this wild abyss the wary Fiend
Stood on the brink of Hell and looked a while,
Pondering his Voyage; for no narrow frith
He had to cross. Nor was his ear less pealed
With noises loud and ruinous (to compare
Great things with small) than when Bellona storms,
With all her battering engines bent to raze
Some capital city; or less than if this frame
Of heav'n were falling, and these elements
In mutiny had from her axle torn
The steadfast Earth. At last his sail-broad vans
He spreads for flight, and in the surging smoke
Uplifted spurns the ground, thence many a league
As in a cloudy chair ascending rides
Audacious, but that seat soon failing, meets

904. **Barca or Cyrene's:** desert region of Northern Africa notorious for sandstorms.

906. **To whom these:** The referents of *whom* are the *four champions fierce* of line 898; *these* refers to the atoms.

907–10. **Chaos . . . all:** On the rule of *Chaos* and *Chance* in relation to fate and God's will, cp. lines 232–33, 915–16, and 7.172–73.

911. Except for the insertion of *perhaps,* the line loosely translates Lucretius's portrayal of the Earth (*On the Nature of Things* 5.259).

915–16. Milton allows that God could use the *dark materials* of chaos to create more worlds (universes, not simply planets), provoking the complaint that Milton heretically "supposes the Deity to have needed means with which to work . . . [though] the very word *creation* implies existence given to something which never before existed" (Cowper). As Milton recognized, however, the Hebrew verb *create* implies the opposite of what Cowper claimed it does (*CD* 1.7; see 894–910n).

919. **frith:** firth, channel.

920. **pealed:** assailed, rung.

921–22. **to compare . . . small:** Cp. 6.310–11, 10.306; *PR* 4.563–64, where Milton uses the same formula, borrowed from Vergil (*Ec.* 1.24, *Georg.* 4.176).

922. **Bellona:** Roman goddess of war, sister to Mars.

924. **frame:** that which supports the sky. Cp. Horace's admiration of "the man tenacious of his purpose in a righteous cause": "Were the vault of heaven to break and fall upon him, its ruins would smite him undismayed" (*Odes* 3.3.1, 7–8).

927. **vans:** wings. Milton persists in linking Satan to a sailing ship.

930. **cloudy chair:** car formed of clouds.

A vast vacuity: all unawares
Flutt'ring his pennons vain plumb down he drops
Ten thousand fathom deep, and to this hour
Down had been falling, had not by ill chance
The strong rebuff of some tumultuous cloud
Instinct with fire and niter hurried him
As many miles aloft: that fury stayed,
Quenched in a boggy Syrtis, neither sea,
Nor good dry land: nigh foundered on he fares,
Treading the crude consistence, half on foot,
Half flying; behooves him now both oar and sail.
As when a gryphon through the wilderness
With wingèd course o'er hill or moory dale,
Pursues the Arimaspian, who by stealth
Had from his wakeful custody purloined
The guarded gold: so eagerly the Fiend
O'er bog or steep, through strait, rough, dense, or rare,
With head, hands, wings or feet pursues his way,
And swims or sinks, or wades, or creeps, or flies:
At length a universal hubbub wild
Of stunning sounds and voices all confused
Born through the hollow dark assaults his ear
With loudest vehemence: thither he plies,
Undaunted to meet there whatever power
Or spirit of the nethermost abyss
Might in that noise reside, of whom to ask
Which way the nearest coast of darkness lies
Bordering on light; when straight behold the throne

933. **pennons:** pinions, wings.

935–38. **Down . . . aloft:** Satan's escape from oblivion owes to the *rebuff* (counterblast) of a cloud *instinct with* (moved or impelled by) *fire and niter,* ingredients of gunpowder, Satan's signature invention from chaotic materials (see 6.478–83, 511–15). Phenomena like shooting stars, comets, and lightning were attributed to the atmospheric ignition of such vapors. Cp. other instances of Satan's luck (4.530; 9.85, 421–23).

939. **Syrtis:** The Syrtes are two shallow gulfs (Sidra and Cabes) off the north coast of Libya, a region dreaded for its quicksands (e.g., Acts 27.17). Milton echoes Lucan's *Pharsalia* (9.364ff) in describing it as neither sea nor land.

942. **both oar and sail:** all possible force, might and main. Galley ships when pressed used both oars and sails; cp. *Aen.* 3.563.

943–45. **gryphon . . . Arimaspian:** The *gryphon* (or griffin) is a mythical guardian of gold, with the upper half of an eagle and lower of a lion. It can thus speed over varied terrain *with wingèd course* (with wings and feet) in pursuit of the *Arimaspian,* legendary one-eyed people who steal the guarded gold. See Herodotus 3.116; 4.13, 27.

948–49. The extended series of disjointed monosyllables and breakdowns in iambic meter express the difficulty of negotiating the helter-skelter of chaos.

951–54. **universal hubbub . . . vehemence:** Cp. the curse of Babel, 12.53–62.

954. **vehemence:** mindlessness; **plies**: alters course, tacks (see 637–42n).

Of Chaos, and his dark pavilion spread
Wide on the wasteful deep; with him enthroned
Sat sable-vested Night, eldest of things,
The consort of his reign; and by them stood
Orcus and Ades, and the dreaded name
Of Demogorgon; Rumor next and Chance,
And Tumult and Confusion all embroiled,
And Discord with a thousand various mouths.
T' whom Satan turning boldly, thus. "Ye Powers
And Spirits of this nethermost abyss,
Chaos and ancient Night, I come no spy,
With purpose to explore or to disturb
The secrets of your realm, but by constraint
Wand'ring this darksome desert, as my way
Lies through your spacious empire up to light,
Alone, and without guide, half lost, I seek
What readiest path leads where your gloomy bounds
Confine with Heav'n; or if some other place
From your dominion won, th' Ethereal King
Possesses lately, thither to arrive
I travel this profound, direct my course;
Directed, no mean recompense it brings
To your behoof, if I that region lost,
All usurpation thence expelled, reduce
To her original darkness and your sway
(Which is my present journey) and once more
Erect the standard there of ancient Night;

960–61. **Of Chaos . . . deep:** "He made darkness pavilions round about him, dark waters, and thick clouds of the skies" (2 Sam. 22.12; cp. Ps. 18.11).

961. **wasteful:** vast, desolate. Milton is prone to repetition of initial *w* sounds, and especially to alliterative compounds with *wide.* See 1.3, 2.1007, 6.253, 8.467, 11.121, 487; *Nat Ode* 51, 64; *Il Pens* 75, *Lyc* 13; *Sonnet 19* 2.

962. **sable-vested Night:** translates Euripides' epithet for Night, *Ion* 1150 (literally, "black-robed Night"). She and Chaos preside over a court of accessory personifications.

964. **Orcus and Ades:** Latin and Greek for the underworld and its ruler (the Greek word is usually spelled *Hades*).

965. **Demogorgon:** Boccaccio copied the *dreaded name* from a medieval manuscript's gloss of an allusion in Statius (*Thebiad* 4.516). The reference is to a deity whose name alone terrifies infernal powers. Boccaccio applied it to the primeval deity in his *Genealogy of the Gods.* Subsequent authors followed suit and often made Demogorgon master of the Fates. See, e.g., Spenser, *FQ* 1.1.37, 4.2.47. Cp. Milton's *Prolusion 1,* p. 787.

967. Milton transfers to *Discord* a trait ordinarily found in personifications of fame or rumor, as when Shakespeare has *Rumor* "painted full of tongues" speak the prologue to *2H4.* In *PL,* rumor seems to originate in God and is aligned with prophecy, though it does inspire conflict (see, *e.g.,* ll. 345–53, 831, 1.651, 10.481–82).

977. **Confine with:** border on.

980. **this profound:** the deep (adj. for noun). The punctuation and dodgy syntax of lines 980–86 suggest that Satan is improvising as he speaks.

982. **behoof:** advantage.

982–87. **if I . . . revenge:** Satan is setting up a double cross. Cp. 10.399–418.

Yours be th' advantage all, mine the revenge."
Thus Satan; and him thus the Anarch old
With falt'ring speech and visage incomposed
Answered. "I know thee, stranger, who thou art,
That mighty leading angel, who of late
Made head against Heav'n's King, though overthrown.
I saw and heard, for such a numerous host
Fled not in silence through the frighted deep
With ruin upon ruin, rout on rout,
Confusion worse confounded; and Heav'n gates
Poured out by millions her victorious bands
Pursuing. I upon my frontiers here
Keep residence; if all I can will serve,
That little which is left so to defend,
Encroached on still through our intestine broils
Weak'ning the scepter of old Night: first Hell
Your dungeon stretching far and wide beneath;
Now lately heaven and Earth, another world
Hung o'er my realm, linked in a golden chain
To that side Heav'n from whence your legions fell:
If that way be your walk, you have not far;
So much the nearer danger; go and speed;
Havoc and spoil and ruin are my gain."
He ceased; and Satan stayed not to reply,
But glad that now his sea should find a shore,
With fresh alacrity and force renewed
Springs upward like a pyramid of fire
Into the wild expanse, and through the shock
Of fighting elements, on all sides round

988. **Anarch:** anarchy's head of state.

989. **incomposed:** without composure or orderly arrangement; cp. "increate" (3.6).

993–98. **I saw . . . Pursuing:** Cp. 6.871–74.

1001. **our:** In light of lines 908–9, some editors substitute "your," construing *our intestine broils* as a reference to the War in Heaven rather than to the constitutional strife of chaos. Cp. Henry IV's account of the "intestine shock / And furious close of civil butchery" involving opponents "all of one nature, of one substance bred" (*1H4* 1.1.11–13).

1004. **heaven:** not the abode of God and the angels, as in line 1006, but the sky. The *world* of which Chaos speaks is in modern usage called the "universe."

1005. **golden chain:** Homer's Zeus boasts that the combined strength of the other gods could not prevent him from pulling them and the world up to heaven by a golden chain (*Il.* 8.18–27). Milton endorsed the traditional interpretation of this chain as a symbol of cosmic design and order (*Prolusion 2*, Yale 1:236).

1007. **walk:** distance to be covered; course of conduct or action.

1008. **danger:** As with much of what Chaos says, the meaning is difficult to pin down. Is Satan approaching danger, or is danger, in the person of Satan, approaching the world?

1013. "The pyramid is the solid which is the original element and seed of fire" (Plato, *Timaeus* 56b). In sharp contrast to the anarchy of *embryon atoms* (l. 900), Satan through sheer force of will launches himself toward creation in the atomic form of his own element (Kerrigan 1983, 138–39).

Environed wins his way; harder beset
And more endangered, than when Argo passed
Through Bosporus betwixt the jostling rocks:
Or when Ulysses on the larboard shunned
Charybdis, and by th' other whirlpool steered.
So he with difficulty and labor hard
Moved on, with difficulty and labor he;
But he once passed, soon after when man fell,
Strange alteration! Sin and Death amain
Following his track, such was the will of Heav'n,
Paved after him a broad and beaten way
Over the dark abyss, whose boiling gulf
Tamely endured a bridge of wondrous length
From Hell continued reaching th' utmost orb
Of this frail world; by which the spirits perverse
With easy intercourse pass to and fro
To tempt or punish mortals, except whom
God and good angels guard by special grace.
But now at last the sacred influence
Of light appears, and from the walls of Heav'n
Shoots far into the bosom of dim Night
A glimmering dawn; here Nature first begins
Her farthest verge, and Chaos to retire
As from her outmost works a broken foe
With tumult less and with less hostile din,
That Satan with less toil, and now with ease
Wafts on the calmer wave by dubious light
And like a weather-beaten vessel holds
Gladly the port, though shrouds and tackle torn;
Or in the emptier waste, resembling air,
Weighs his spread wings, at leisure to behold
Far off th' empyreal Heav'n, extended wide

1017. **Argo:** the ship of Jason and his crew (Argonauts). They encounter the clashing (*jostling*) rocks of the *Bosporos* (the Strait of Constantinople) (Apollonius 2.552–611).

1019. **larboard:** left side of a vessel, port.

1020. **Charybdis:** dreaded whirlpool in the Strait of Messina, just opposite man-eating Scylla (see 659–61n). Ulysses avoided the total destruction that *Charybdis* threatened by sailing nearer to Scylla (Homer, *Od.* 12.234–59).

1024–30. **Sin . . . world:** For construction of this *broad and beaten way* (cp. Matt. 7.13), see 10.293–305.

1024. **amain:** in full force, numbers.

1033. **special grace:** Cp. 3.183–84. See *Masque* 36–42, 216–20, 453–63.

1034. **sacred influence:** Light is inseparable from God himself (3.1–6). Its influence, whether sunlight or starlight, is the chief agent of creative growth; see 4.661–73, 6.476–81, 9.107, 192.

1039. **her outmost works:** Nature's *works* are fortifications against the tumult of chaos.

1043. **holds:** maintains heading for.

1044. **shrouds and tackle:** rigging on sailing ship; cp. *SA* 198–200, 717.

1046. **Weighs:** holds steady.

In circuit, undetermined square or round,
With opal tow'rs and battlements adorned
Of living sapphire, once his native seat;
And fast by hanging in a golden chain
This pendant world, in bigness as a star
Of smallest magnitude close by the moon.
Thither full fraught with mischievous revenge,
Accursed, and in a cursèd hour he hies.

1048. **undetermined:** The expanse of Heaven is so vast that one cannot tell whether it is circular or square.

1050. **living:** in its native condition and site, unlike Satan, whose connection with his *native seat* and the source of his being lies irretrievably in the past. The walls are also, like everything in Heaven, living in the literal sense (6.860–61, 878–79).

1052. **pendant world:** the entire universe, hanging like a jewel on a chain.

1055. **hies:** hastens. "Milton begins Book 3 with the same alliteration" (Leonard).

"High on a throne of royal state . . ." (2.1).

Book III

The Argument

God sitting on his throne sees Satan flying towards this world, then newly created; shows him to the Son who sat at his right hand; foretells the success of Satan in perverting mankind; clears his own justice and wisdom from all imputation, having created man free and able enough to have withstood his tempter; yet declares his purpose of grace towards him, in regard he fell not of his own malice, as did Satan, but by him seduced. The Son of God renders praises to his Father for the manifestation of his gracious purpose towards man; but God again declares that grace cannot be extended towards man without the satisfaction of divine justice; man hath offended the majesty of God by aspiring to Godhead, and therefore with all his progeny devoted to death must die, unless someone can be found sufficient to answer for his offense, and undergo his punishment. The Son of God freely offers himself a ransom for man: the Father accepts him, ordains his incarnation, pronounces his exaltation above all names in Heaven and Earth, commands all the angels to adore him. They obey, and hymning to their harps in full choir, celebrate the Father and the Son. Meanwhile Satan alights upon the bare convex of this world's outermost orb; where wandering he first finds a place since called the Limbo of Vanity; what persons and things fly up thither; thence comes to the gate of Heaven, described ascending by stairs, and the waters above the firmament that flow about it: his passage thence to the orb of the sun; he finds there Uriel the regent of that orb, but first changes himself into the shape of a meaner angel; and pretending a zealous desire to behold the new creation and man whom God had placed here, inquires of him the place of his habitation, and is directed; alights first on Mount Niphates.

Hail holy light, offspring of Heav'n first-born,
Or of th' Eternal coeternal beam
May I express thee unblamed? Since God is light,
And never but in unapproachèd light
Dwelt from eternity, dwelt then in thee,
Bright effluence of bright essence increate.
Or hear'st thou rather pure ethereal stream,
Whose fountain who shall tell? Before the sun,
Before the heavens thou wert, and at the voice
Of God, as with a mantle didst invest
The rising world of waters dark and deep,
Won from the void and formless infinite.
Thee I revisit now with bolder wing,
Escaped the Stygian pool, though long detained
In that obscure sojourn, while in my flight
Through utter and through middle darkness borne
With other notes than to th' Orphean lyre
I sung of Chaos and eternal Night,
Taught by the Heav'nly Muse to venture down
The dark descent, and up to reascend,
Though hard and rare: thee I revisit safe,

1–55. This passage of transition from Hell and Chaos to Heaven, known as "the invocation to light," is at once the most speculative and intimate of the poem's four invocations (at the openings of Books 1, 3, 7, and 9). The meaning of the light addressed has often been debated. Some identify *holy light* with physical light, the first of created things (Kelley 91–94), while others think that light here symbolizes some aspect of the Godhead, usually the Son (Hunter et al., 149–56). In the second case, however, Milton in lines 1–8 would be uncertain whether the Son was created in time, whereas elsewhere in the poem (3.384, 5.603), as in his prose (*CD* 1.5), he is definite on the Son's createdness. See 6n.

2. Or the beam coeternal with the Father (and therefore not *first-born*).

3–6. **Since . . . increate:** These lines expand on the likelihood that light, being the dwelling of God, is eternal.

3. **express:** describe, invoke; **unblamed:** without being judged blasphemous or improper; **God is light:** quoted from 1 John 1.5.

4. **unapproachèd light:** See 1 Tim. 6.16. Even angels shade their eyes with their wings when approaching the *dazzling* Father (ll. 375–82).

6. **effluence:** flowing out; **essence:** deity, the divine essence of the Father; **increate:** uncreated, without origin.

7. **hear'st thou rather:** do you prefer to be called; **ethereal:** composed of ether, the lightest and most subtle element, ubiquitous in the heavens; see 7.244n.

8. **Whose fountain who shall tell:** whose beginning is unknown and unknowable; see Job 38.19.

10. **invest:** clothe, wrap; see Ps. 104.2.

12. **void and formless infinite:** Chaos is void of form, not matter; on its infinity, see 7.168–71n.

14. **Stygian pool:** classical synecdoche for Hell; **long detained:** for Book 1 and nearly all of Book 2.

15. **sojourn:** place of temporary stay.

16. **utter . . . middle darkness:** *Utter darkness* is Hell; *middle darkness* is Chaos.

17. **other notes:** Orpheus sang before Pluto in order to secure his wife's release from death. Milton's song is not Orphean because he has not sought to charm or bargain with the ruler of Hell. Milton might also be deflating the obscure, pseudomystical night worship found in a poem ("Hymn to Night") often ascribed to Orpheus.

19. **Heav'nly Muse:** See 1.6, 7.1, 9.21.

20–21. **up . . . rare:** another echo of the Sybil's advice to Aeneas in *Aen.* 6.126–29; see 2.432–33n.

And feel thy sov'reign vital lamp; but thou
Revisit'st not these eyes, that roll in vain
To find thy piercing ray, and find no dawn;
So thick a drop serene hath quenched their orbs,
Or dim suffusion veiled. Yet not the more
Cease I to wander where the Muses haunt
Clear spring, or shady grove, or sunny hill,
Smit with the love of sacred song; but chief
Thee Sion and the flow'ry brooks beneath
That wash thy hallowed feet, and warbling flow,
Nightly I visit: nor sometimes forget
Those other two equaled with me in fate,
So were I equaled with them in renown,
Blind Thamyris and blind Maeonides,
And Tiresias and Phineus prophets old.
Then feed on thoughts, that voluntary move
Harmonious numbers; as the wakeful bird
Sings darkling, and in shadiest covert hid
Tunes her nocturnal note. Thus with the year
Seasons return, but not to me returns
Day, or the sweet approach of ev'n or morn,

23–24. **roll . . . ray:** Milton told his Athenian correspondent Leonard Philaras that "upon the eyes turning" he saw in the mist of his blindness "a minute quantity of light as if through a crack" (p. 780).

25. **drop serene:** an English translation of the Latin *gutta serena,* a medical term for complete blindness whose cause is not visible to the physician's eye. It was thought to result from normally airy spirits and humors congealing into obstructing tumors in the optical nerves. A main cause of the congealing was the body's inability to rid itself of vapors produced by digestion. See Banister, sec. 9, chap. 1. **quenched:** put out the sight of; in Milton's case, the spirits necessary for sight could not, because of the tumors, pass through his eyes. **orbs:** eyeballs.

26. **dim suffusion:** translates the Latin *suffusio nigra* or *obscura,* another medical term for blindness.

27. **where the Muses haunt:** Mount Helicon, here a symbol of classical literature itself.

30. **Sion:** the biblical equivalent of Helicon, and a symbol of Hebrew poetry. See *PR* 4.346–47 on the preference for Hebrew poetry.

34. "Would that I were their equal in fame."

35. **Thamyris:** A Thracian poet mentioned in Homer, *Il.* 2.594–600. After he boasted that he could outsing the Muses, they blinded him and deprived him of the ability to sing. **Maeonides:** Homer; his father's name was Maeon.

36. **Tiresias:** the blind Theban sage, best known from *Oedipus Rex.* Among the explanations for his blindness is the anger of Athena, whom he spied bathing. **Phineus:** Thracian king blinded for revealing the gods' will in accurate prophecies.

37. **voluntary move:** of themselves utter (without a further act of volition). The idea is that these thoughts need not be turned into poetry because they *are* poetry and naturally arrange themselves in harmonious verse.

38. **numbers:** verse; **wakeful bird:** the nightingale, who appears often in Milton's early poetry and also in *PL* (4.602–3, 7.435–36).

39. **darkling:** in the dark. The word, become poetic diction, appears in Keats's "Ode on a Nightingale," Arnold's "Dover Beach," and Hardy's "The Darkling Thrush."

Or sight of vernal bloom, or summer's rose,
Or flocks, or herds, or human face divine;
But cloud instead, and ever-during dark
Surrounds me, from the cheerful ways of men
Cut off, and for the book of knowledge fair
Presented with a universal blank
Of Nature's works to me expunged and razed,
And wisdom at one entrance quite shut out.
So much the rather thou celestial light
Shine inward, and the mind through all her powers
Irradiate, there plant eyes, all mist from thence
Purge and disperse, that I may see and tell
Of things invisible to mortal sight.
  Now had th' Almighty Father from above,
From the pure empyrean where he sits
High throned above all highth, bent down his eye,
His own works and their works at once to view:
About him all the sanctities of Heaven
Stood thick as stars, and from his sight received
Beatitude past utterance; on his right
The radiant image of his glory sat,
His only Son; on Earth he first beheld
Our two first parents, yet the only two
Of mankind, in the happy Garden placed,
Reaping immortal fruits of joy and love,
Uninterrupted joy, unrivaled love
In blissful solitude; he then surveyed
Hell and the gulf between, and Satan there
Coasting the wall of Heav'n on this side Night
In the dun air sublime, and ready now

47. **book of knowledge:** the book of Nature. "There are two books from whence I collect my divinity; besides that written one of God [the Bible], another of his servant Nature, that universal and public manuscript that lies expansed unto the eyes of all" (Browne, 1.16)—but not to the blind eyes of Milton.

48. **blank:** a white or blank page.

49. **expunged and razed:** "The Romans *expunged* writing on wax tablets by covering it with little pricks, or *razed* it by shaving the tables clean" (Leonard).

56–417. The dialogue between Father and Son is comparable to the "Parliament in Heaven" scene found in medieval mystery and morality plays (Lewalski 1985, 118–21). The four "daughters of God" (Mercy, Truth, Righteousness, and Peace) debated the fate of sinful man, with Truth and Righteousness opposing Mercy and Peace. After a thorough search to find a substitute for man, the Son's offer to redeem mankind resolved the debate in favor of Mercy and Peace.

60. **sanctities:** angels.

62. **on his right:** as in Heb. 1.2–3.

71. **this side Night:** the side of Chaos (the realm of Night) closest to Heaven.

72. **dun air sublime:** The light of the empyrean penetrates Chaos, making the *sublime* (lofty) air a *dun* (dusky) color.

To stoop with wearied wings and willing feet
On the bare outside of this world, that seemed
Firm land embosomed without firmament,
Uncertain which, in ocean or in air.
Him God beholding from his prospect high,
Wherein past, present, future he beholds,
Thus to his only Son foreseeing spake.
"Only begotten Son, seest thou what rage
Transports our Adversary, whom no bounds
Prescribed, no bars of Hell, nor all the chains
Heaped on him there, nor yet the main abyss
Wide interrupt can hold; so bent he seems
On desperate revenge, that shall redound
Upon his own rebellious head. And now
Through all restraint broke loose he wings his way
Not far off Heav'n, in the precincts of light,
Directly towards the new-created world,
And man there placed, with purpose to assay
If him by force he can destroy, or worse,
By some false guile pervert; and shall pervert;
For man will hearken to his glozing lies,
And easily transgress the sole command,
Sole pledge of his obedience: so will fall
He and his faithless progeny: whose fault?
Whose but his own? Ingrate, he had of me
All he could have; I made him just and right,
Sufficient to have stood, though free to fall.
Such I created all th' ethereal Powers
And spirits, both them who stood and them who failed;
Freely they stood who stood, and fell who fell.
Not free, what proof could they have giv'n sincere
Of true allegiance, constant faith or love,
Where only what they needs must do, appeared,
Not what they would? What praise could they receive?
What pleasure I from such obedience paid,

74. **this world:** not Earth but all creation.

74–76. **seemed . . . air:** Viewed from the outside, the universe appeared to be a solid sphere with no sky, surrounded by either air or water.

81. **Transports:** both "drives" and "bears."

83. **main abyss:** Chaos.

84. **Wide interrupt:** widely breached. Editors usually construe *interrupt* as a past participle rather than as a noun made from a verb; it indicates the interval between Hell and the realms of light.

90. **assay:** test.

93. **glozing:** falsely flattering.

99. As Satan admits at 4.63–68. See also 5.525–43; *CD* 1.3.

When will and reason (reason also is choice)
Useless and vain, of freedom both despoiled,
Made passive both, had served necessity,
Not me. They therefore as to right belonged,
So were created, nor can justly accuse
Their Maker, or their making, or their fate,
As if predestination overruled
Their will, disposed by absolute decree
Or high foreknowledge; they themselves decreed
Their own revolt, not I: if I foreknew,
Foreknowledge had no influence on their fault,
Which had no less proved certain unforeknown.
So without least impulse or shadow of fate,
Or aught by me immutably foreseen,
They trespass, authors to themselves in all
Both what they judge and what they choose; for so
I formed them free, and free they must remain,
Till they enthrall themselves: I else must change
Their nature, and revoke the high decree
Unchangeable, eternal, which ordained
Their freedom; they themselves ordained their fall.
The first sort by their own suggestion fell,
Self-tempted, self-depraved: man falls deceived
By the other first: man therefore shall find grace,
The other none: in mercy and justice both,
Through Heav'n and Earth, so shall my glory excel,
But mercy first and last shall brightest shine."
    Thus while God spake, ambrosial fragrance filled
All Heav'n, and in the blessèd spirits elect
Sense of new joy ineffable diffused:
Beyond compare the Son of God was seen
Most glorious, in him all his Father shone
Substantially expressed, and in his face
Divine compassion visibly appeared,
Love without end, and without measure grace,

108. **reason also is choice:** "For reason is but choosing" (*Areop*, p. 944). Cp. Aristotle, *Ethics* 3.2.

119. **had . . . unforeknown:** because foreknowledge, "since it exists only in the mind of the foreknower, has no effect on its object" (*CD* 1.3, p. 1158). Leonard's description of the passage as inconsistent with *Christian Doctrine* and symptomatic of a breakdown in Milton's theodicy is confused.

120. **impulse:** instigation.

129. **The first sort:** the rebel angels; **suggestion:** temptation; see 5.702.

135. **fragrance:** synesthesia; God's words smell rather than resound.

140. **Substantially:** In *CD* 1.5, Milton argues that the Father transferred "divine substance," but not "the whole essence," to the Son.

141. **visibly:** See 6.681–82.

Which uttering thus he to his Father spake.
"O Father, gracious was that word which closed
Thy sov'reign sentence, that man should find grace;
For which both Heav'n and Earth shall high extol
Thy praises, with th' innumerable sound
Of hymns and sacred songs, wherewith thy throne
Encompassed shall resound thee ever blest.
For should man finally be lost, should man
Thy creature late so loved, thy youngest son
Fall circumvented thus by fraud, though joined
With his own folly? That be from thee far,
That far be from thee, Father, who art judge
Of all things made, and judgest only right.
Or shall the Adversary thus obtain
His end, and frustrate thine, shall he fulfill
His malice, and thy goodness bring to naught,
Or proud return though to his heavier doom,
Yet with revenge accomplished and to Hell
Draw after him the whole race of mankind,
By him corrupted? Or wilt thou thyself
Abolish thy creation, and unmake,
For him, what for thy glory thou hast made?
So should thy goodness and thy greatness both
Be questioned and blasphemed without defense."
To whom the great Creator thus replied.
"O Son, in whom my soul hath chief delight,
Son of my bosom, Son who art alone
My Word, my wisdom, and effectual might,
All hast thou spoken as my thoughts are, all
As my eternal purpose hath decreed:
Man shall not quite be lost, but saved who will,
Yet not of will in him, but grace in me
Freely vouchsafed; once more I will renew
His lapsèd powers, though forfeit and enthralled
By sin to foul exorbitant desires;

143. **uttering:** making exterior, bringing out (as in the *utter*—exterior—darkness of line 16).

152. **circumvented:** entrapped.

153–54. See Abraham's plea for the Sodomites (Gen. 18.25).

166. **blasphemed:** defamed.

168. Cp. Matt. 3.17.

170. **My Word:** In the New Testament "word" (Gk. *logos,* Lat. *verbum*) is a title of the Son (Rev. 19.13); **effectual might:** the means by which the Father exercises power, as at the Creation; see John 1.1–3.

174. This line might seem to state the Calvinist position that people cannot contribute to their salvation, but see lines 187–90, 302.

Upheld by me, yet once more he shall stand
On even ground against his mortal foe,
By me upheld, that he may know how frail
His fall'n condition is, and to me owe
All his deliv'rance, and to none but me.
Some I have chosen of peculiar grace
Elect above the rest; so is my will:
The rest shall hear me call, and oft be warned
Their sinful state, and to appease betimes
Th' incensèd Deity, while offered grace
Invites; for I will clear their senses dark,
What may suffice, and soften stony hearts
To pray, repent, and bring obedience due.
To prayer, repentance, and obedience due,
Though but endeavored with sincere intent,
Mine ear shall not be slow, mine eye not shut.
And I will place within them as a guide
My umpire conscience, whom if they will hear,
Light after light well used they shall attain,
And to the end persisting, safe arrive.
This my long sufferance and my day of grace
They who neglect and scorn, shall never taste;
But hard be hardened, blind be blinded more,
That they may stumble on, and deeper fall;
And none but such from mercy I exclude.
But yet all is not done; man disobeying,
Disloyal breaks his fealty, and sins
Against the high supremacy of Heav'n,
Affecting Godhead, and so losing all,
To expiate his treason hath naught left,
But to destruction sacred and devote,
He with his whole posterity must die,
Die he or Justice must; unless for him
Some other able, and as willing, pay

183. **peculiar grace:** grace given uniquely to some extraordinary souls. See S. Fallon 1998, 95–97.

186. **betimes:** in time.

187–90. The language carefully indicates that God's *offered grace* is not irresistible. It only *invites,* and *may suffice* rather than "will suffice." The Protestant belief in conditional election and resistable grace is called Arminianism, after the Dutchman Jacobus Arminius (1560–1609), who tried to introduce free will into Calvin's deterministic theology.

189. **stony hearts:** See Ezek. 11.19.

197. **persisting:** remaining steadfast; **safe arrive:** attain salvation in the end.

200–202. In *CD* 1.8, Milton argues that when God blinds or hardens a sinner, "he is not the cause of sin."

204. **fealty:** allegiance.

208. **sacred and devote:** absolutely doomed; the words are near synonyms, with *sacred* meaning "dedicated to a deity for destruction" and *devote* meaning "given to destruction as by a vow."

The rigid satisfaction, death for death.
Say Heav'nly powers, where shall we find such love,
Which of ye will be mortal to redeem
Man's mortal crime, and just th' unjust to save,
Dwells in all Heaven charity so dear?"
He asked, but all the Heav'nly choir stood mute,
And silence was in Heav'n: on man's behalf
Patron or intercessor none appeared,
Much less that durst upon his own head draw
The deadly forfeiture, and ransom set.
And now without redemption all mankind
Must have been lost, adjudged to death and Hell
By doom severe, had not the Son of God,
In whom the fullness dwells of love divine,
His dearest mediation thus renewed.
"Father, thy word is past, man shall find grace;
And shall grace not find means, that finds her way,
The speediest of thy wingèd messengers,
To visit all thy creatures, and to all
Comes unprevented, unimplored, unsought,
Happy for man, so coming; he her aid
Can never seek, once dead in sins and lost;
Atonement for himself or offering meet,
Indebted and undone, hath none to bring:
Behold me then, me for him, life for life
I offer, on me let thine anger fall;
Account me man; I for his sake will leave
Thy bosom, and this glory next to thee
Freely put off, and for him lastly die
Well pleased, on me let Death wreck all his rage;
Under his gloomy power I shall not long
Lie vanquished; thou hast giv'n me to possess

212. The idea that the Atonement satisfied justice originated with Anselm's *Cur Deus Homo* 1.11–16, 19–21.

215. **just:** in that he is "able" and "willing" to "pay / The rigid satisfaction, death for death" (ll. 211–12).

219. **Patron:** advocate.

221. **ransom set:** put down the ransom price, which is a life.

224. **doom:** judgment.

226. **mediation:** One of the Son's traditional titles is mediator between God and man (and in Milton's poem, between God and angel as well).

231. **unprevented:** unanticipated (that is to say, not prayed for).

233. **dead in sins:** See Col. 2.13.

234. **meet:** adequate.

236–38. **me . . . me . . . me . . . me:** The self-emphasis of the repetition is perhaps balanced by the humility of *me* being in all four cases an unstressed syllable. *Me* is both repeated and stressed in the battlefield oration of 6.812–18.

241. **on me:** Here at last *me* occurs in the stressed position (see previous note); **wreck:** give vent to.

Life in myself forever, by thee I live,
Though now to Death I yield, and am his due
All that of me can die, yet that debt paid,
Thou wilt not leave me in the loathsome grave
His prey, nor suffer my unspotted soul
Forever with corruption there to dwell;
But I shall rise victorious, and subdue
My vanquisher, spoiled of his vaunted spoil;
Death his death's wound shall then receive, and stoop
Inglorious, of his mortal sting disarmed.
I through the ample air in triumph high
Shall lead Hell captive maugre Hell, and show
The powers of darkness bound. Thou at the sight
Pleased, out of Heaven shalt look down and smile,
While by thee raised I ruin all my foes,
Death last, and with his carcass glut the grave:
Then with the multitude of my redeemed
Shall enter Heaven long absent, and return,
Father, to see thy face, wherein no cloud
Of anger shall remain, but peace assured,
And reconcilement; wrath shall be no more
Thenceforth, but in thy presence joy entire."
His words here ended, but his meek aspect
Silent yet spake, and breathed immortal love
To mortal men, above which only shone
Filial obedience: as a sacrifice
Glad to be offered, he attends the will
Of his great Father. Admiration seized
All Heav'n, what this might mean, and whither tend
Wond'ring; but soon th' Almighty thus replied:
"O thou in Heav'n and Earth the only peace
Found out for mankind under wrath, O thou
My sole complacence! Well thou know'st how dear
To me are all my works, nor man the least
Though last created, that for him I spare
Thee from my bosom and right hand, to save,

244. Cp. John 5.26.

247–49. "Thou will not leave my soul in hell; neither wilt thou suffer thine Holy One to see corruption" (Ps. 16.10).

253. **his mortal sting disarmed:** 1 Cor. 15.55: "O death, where is thy sting?" See 12.432.

255. **maugre:** in spite of; **show:** to the Father.

258. **ruin:** hurl down.

259. **Death last:** 1 Cor. 15.26: "The last enemy that shall be destroyed is death." **glut the grave:** gratify to the full the appetite of the grave. For the commonplace metaphor of the hungry grave, see Shakespeare's *ROM* 5.3.45–48.

270. **attends:** awaits.

271. **Admiration:** wonder.

276. **complacence:** pleasure.

By losing thee a while, the whole race lost.
Thou therefore whom thou only canst redeem,
Their nature also to thy nature join;
And be thyself man among men on earth,
Made flesh, when time shall be, of virgin seed,
By wondrous birth: be thou in Adam's room
The head of all mankind, though Adam's son.
As in him perish all men, so in thee
As from a second root shall be restored,
As many as are restored, without thee none.
His crime makes guilty all his sons, thy merit
Imputed shall absolve them who renounce
Their own both righteous and unrighteous deeds,
And live in thee transplanted, and from thee
Receive new life. So man, as is most just,
Shall satisfy for man, be judged and die,
And dying rise, and rising with him raise
His brethren, ransomed with his own dear life.
So Heav'nly love shall outdo Hellish hate,
Giving to death, and dying to redeem,
So dearly to redeem what Hellish hate
So easily destroyed, and still destroys
In those who, when they may, accept not grace.
Nor shalt thou by descending to assume
Man's nature, lessen or degrade thine own.
Because thou hast, though throned in highest bliss
Equal to God, and equally enjoying
God-like fruition, quitted all to save
A world from utter loss, and hast been found
By merit more than birthright Son of God,
Found worthiest to be so by being good,
Far more than great or high; because in thee
Love hath abounded more than glory abounds,
Therefore thy humiliation shall exalt
With thee thy manhood also to this throne;
Here shalt thou sit incarnate, here shalt reign

281–82. "Therefore join your nature to the nature of those whom only you can redeem."

285. **room:** place, stead.

287–88. "As in Adam all die, even so in Christ shall all be made alive" (1 Cor. 15.22).

290–91. **thy merit/Imputed:** Christ's merit is imputed, "attributed vicariously," to saved human beings. Cp. 12.407–10; *CD* 1.22.

299. **Giving:** submitting.

300. **dearly:** both "lovingly" and "expensively."

301. **still:** always.

306. **Equal to God:** applies to *throned in highest bliss,* not to the Son's divine nature.

307. **fruition:** enjoyment; **quitted:** both "left" (in becoming incarnate) and "paid, redeemed" (man's debt of sin).

Both God and man, Son both of God and man,
Anointed universal King; all power
I give thee, reign forever, and assume
Thy merits; under thee as Head Supreme
Thrones, Princedoms, Powers, Dominions I reduce:
All knees to thee shall bow, of them that bide
In Heaven, or Earth, or under Earth in Hell;
When thou attended gloriously from Heav'n
Shalt in the sky appear, and from thee send
The summoning Archangels to proclaim
Thy dread tribunal: forthwith from all winds
The living, and forthwith the cited dead
Of all past ages to the general doom
Shall hasten, such a peal shall rouse their sleep.
Then all thy saints assembled, thou shalt judge
Bad men and angels, they arraigned shall sink
Beneath thy sentence; Hell, her numbers full,
Thenceforth shall be for ever shut. Meanwhile
The world shall burn, and from her ashes spring
New Heav'n and Earth, wherein the just shall dwell,
And after all their tribulations long
See golden days, fruitful of golden deeds,
With joy and love triumphing, and fair truth.
Then thou thy regal scepter shalt lay by,
For regal scepter then no more shall need,
God shall be all in all. But all ye gods,
Adore him, who to compass all this dies,
Adore the Son, and honor him as me."
 No sooner had th' Almighty ceased, but all
The multitude of angels with a shout
Loud as from numbers without number, sweet

317–18. **all power/I give thee:** "All power is given to me" (Matt. 28.18).

318–19. **assume/Thy merits:** echoes Horace's *Odes* 3.30.14–15.

320. The line lists the four orders of angels found in Col. 1.16; see also 5.840.

321–22. "At the name of Jesus every knee should bow, of things in heaven, and things in earth, and things under the earth" (Phil. 2.10). See Satan's resentment of this "knee-tribute" at 5.782.

326. **all winds:** all quarters of the compass.

327. **cited:** summoned.

328. **doom:** judgment.

329. Cp. *Nat Ode* 155–56.

330. **saints:** righteous worshipers.

331. **arraigned:** accused.

334. **The world shall burn:** See 2 Pet. 3.10–13.

340. **need:** be necessary. The regal conception of deity will in the end be abandoned.

341. **God shall be all in all:** See 1 Cor. 15.28.

342. **compass:** accomplish, but perhaps anticipating the compasses of 7.225.

343. **as me:** If this phrase means "as you do me," God is simply prescribing rites of adoration, but if it means "as if me" he is sharing or even handing over his kingship. Cp. John 5.23.

As from blest voices, uttering joy, Heav'n rung
With jubilee, and loud hosannas filled
Th' eternal regions: lowly reverent
Towards either throne they bow, and to the ground
With solemn adoration down they cast
Their crowns inwove with amarant and gold,
Immortal amarant, a flow'r which once
In Paradise, fast by the Tree of Life
Began to bloom, but soon for man's offense
To Heav'n removed where first it grew, there grows,
And flow'rs aloft shading the fount of life,
And where the river of bliss through midst of Heav'n
Rolls o'er Elysian flow'rs her amber stream;
With these that never fade the spirits elect
Bind their resplendent locks inwreathed with beams,
Now in loose garlands thick thrown off, the bright
Pavement that like a sea of jasper shone
Impurpled with celestial roses smiled.
Then crowned again their golden harps they took,
Harps ever tuned, that glittering by their side
Like quivers hung, and with preamble sweet
Of charming symphony they introduce
Their sacred song, and waken raptures high;
No voice exempt, no voice but well could join
Melodious part, such concord is in Heav'n.
    Thee Father first they sung omnipotent,
Immutable, immortal, infinite,
Eternal King; thee Author of all being,
Fountain of light, thyself invisible
Amidst the glorious brightness where thou sitt'st
Throned inaccessible, but when thou shad'st
The full blaze of thy beams, and through a cloud
Drawn round about thee like a radiant shrine,
Dark with excessive bright thy skirts appear,
Yet dazzle Heav'n, that brightest Seraphim
Approach not, but with both wings veil their eyes.

348. **jubilee:** jubilation; **hosannas:** from the Hebrew "Save, we pray."

353. **amarant:** a legendary immortal flower; see 11.78n, *Lyc* 149.

357. **fount of life:** See Rev. 7.17, 22.1–2.

359. **amber:** clear.

363. **sea of jasper:** See Rev. 21.11.

367. **preamble:** musical prelude.

370. **exempt:** excluded.

377. **but:** except.

381. **that:** so that.

382. **veil their eyes:** See Isa. 6.2.

Thee next they sang of all creation first,
Begotten Son, divine similitude,
In whose conspicuous count'nance, without cloud
Made visible, th' Almighty Father shines,
Whom else no creature can behold; on thee
Impressed the effulgence of his glory abides,
Transfused on thee his ample spirit rests.
He Heav'n of Heav'ns and all the Powers therein
By thee created, and by thee threw down
Th' aspiring Dominations: thou that day
Thy Father's dreadful thunder didst not spare,
Nor stop thy flaming chariot wheels, that shook
Heav'n's everlasting frame, while o'er the necks
Thou drov'st of warring angels disarrayed.
Back from pursuit thy powers with loud acclaim
Thee only extolled, Son of thy Father's might,
To execute fierce vengeance on his foes,
Not so on man; him through their malice fall'n,
Father of mercy and grace, thou didst not doom
So strictly, but much more to pity incline:
No sooner did thy dear and only Son
Perceive thee purposed not to doom frail man
So strictly, but much more to pity inclined,
He to appease thy wrath, and end the strife
Of mercy and justice in thy face discerned,
Regardless of the bliss wherein he sat
Second to thee, offered himself to die
For man's offense. O unexampled love,
Love nowhere to be found less than divine!
Hail Son of God, Savior of men, thy name
Shall be the copious matter of my song
Henceforth, and never shall my harp thy praise
Forget, nor from thy Father's praise disjoin.
    Thus they in Heav'n, above the starry sphere,
Their happy hours in joy and hymning spent.

383. **of all creation first:** The phrase has biblical precedent (Rev. 3.14, Col. 1.15–17), but for Milton such verses were not, as they were for believers in the orthodox Trinity, metaphorical. On Christ as the first creation, see *CD* 1.5, and, on Milton's Arianism, Bauman 1987.

387. **Whom . . . behold:** See Exod. 33.18–20; John 1.18, 14.9.

388. **effulgence:** radiance.

392. **Dominations:** usually one of the nine angelic orders, but here apparently, by synecdoche, a name for all of the nine orders.

397. **powers:** angels.

412–15. The promise to devote future songs to the praise of a god was conventional in classical hymns. See Callimachus, *Hymns* 3.137.

Meanwhile upon the firm opacous globe
Of this round world, whose first convex divides
The luminous inferior orbs, enclosed
From Chaos and th' inroad of darkness old,
Satan alighted walks: a globe far off
It seemed, now seems a boundless continent
Dark, waste, and wild, under the frown of Night
Starless exposed, and ever-threat'ning storms
Of Chaos blust'ring round, inclement sky;
Save on that side which from the wall of Heav'n
Though distant far some small reflection gains
Of glimmering air less vexed with tempest loud:
Here walked the fiend at large in spacious field.
As when a vulture on Imaüs bred,
Whose snowy ridge the roving Tartar bounds,
Dislodging from a region scarce of prey
To gorge the flesh of lambs or yeanling kids
On hills where flocks are fed, flies toward the springs
Of Ganges or Hydaspes, Indian streams;
But in his way lights on the barren plains
Of Sericana, where Chineses drive
With sails and wind their cany wagons light:
So on this windy sea of land, the Fiend
Walked up and down alone bent on his prey,
Alone, for other creature in this place
Living or lifeless to be found was none,
None yet, but store hereafter from the earth
Up hither like aërial vapors flew
Of all things transitory and vain, when Sin
With vanity had filled the works of men:
Both all things vain, and all who in vain things

418. **opacous:** opaque.

419. **first convex:** the outer sphere or *primum mobile* of our universe.

429. **vexed:** tossed about.

430. **at large:** freely.

431. **Imaüs:** mountains that were believed to stretch from Afghanistan to the Arctic.

432. **roving Tartar:** nomadic inhabitants of central Asia, "a people the most barbarous, bloody, and fierce of all mankind . . . the scourges of God on the civilized world" (Hume). *Tartar* is also a shortened form of *Tartarus,* or hell.

434. **yeanling:** newborn.

435. **the springs:** Both the *Ganges* and the *Hydaspes* (the modern Jhelum) have their *springs,* or sources, in the Himalayas.

438. **Sericana:** China; *Chineses* was the standard seventeenth-century plural form.

439. **With sails and wind:** Peter Heylyn, *Cosmography* (1620), notes that the Chinese "have carts and coaches driven with sails" (867); **cany:** made of cane or bamboo.

444. **store:** plenty.

444–97. Milton's Paradise of Fools has its seed in Ariosto's *OF* 34, where the English knight Astolfo goes to the Limbo of Vanity on the moon in search of his lost wits. Milton may also have been influenced by Ovid's House of Fame (*Met.* 12.52–61).

Built their fond hopes of glory or lasting fame,
Or happiness in this or th' other life;
All who have their reward on Earth, the fruits
Of painful superstition and blind zeal,
Naught seeking but the praise of men, here find
Fit retribution, empty as their deeds;
All th' unaccomplished works of Nature's hand,
Abortive, monstrous, or unkindly mixed,
Dissolved on Earth, fleet hither, and in vain,
Till final dissolution, wander here,
Not in the neighboring moon, as some have dreamed;
Those argent fields more likely habitants,
Translated saints or middle spirits hold
Betwixt th' angelical and human kind:
Hither of ill-joined sons and daughters born
First from the ancient world those giants came
With many a vain exploit, though then renowned:
The builders next of Babel on the plain
Of Sennaär, and still with vain design
New Babels, had they wherewithal, would build:
Others came single; he who to be deemed
A god, leaped fondly into Etna flames,
Empedocles, and he who to enjoy
Plato's Elysium, leaped into the sea,
Cleombrotus, and many more too long,
Embryos and idiots, eremites and friars
White, black and gray, with all their trumpery.

449. **fond:** foolish.

452. **painful:** painstaking.

454. **empty:** The Latin for *empty* is *vanus,* the etymological root of *vanity* (447).

455. **unaccomplished:** unfinished, lacking.

456. **Abortive:** fruitless, useless; **unkindly:** unnaturally.

457. **fleet:** glide away.

459. **some:** Ariosto for one (*OF* 34.73ff).

461. **Translated saints:** righteous men such as Enoch and Elijah, who were taken from Earth without having to die (cp. 11.670–71).

464. **giants:** sired by the Sons of God (fallen angels in one tradition) on human women (Gen. 6.4). See 11.573–627; *PR* 2.178–81.

467. **Sennaär:** Vulgate form of Shinar (Gen. 11.2).

470. **fondly:** foolishly.

471. **Empedocles:** a philosopher who threw himself into Etna to hide his mortality. The volcano threw back one of his sandals. See Horace, *De Arte Poetica* 464–66.

473. **Cleombrotus:** A philosopher who drowned himself after reading of Elysium in Plato's *Phaedo.* See Callimachus, *Epigrams* 25.

474. **Embryos:** beings in an unrealized state; **eremites:** hermits; **friars:** Franciscan friars taught that idiots and unbaptized infants went not to Heaven but to a limbo above the earth; Milton in a satirical gesture puts the friars in his Paradise of Fools along with *embryos and idiots.*

475. The Carmelites wore a white mantle, the Dominicans a black, and the Franciscans a gray. **trumpery:** religious ornaments.

Here pilgrims roam, that strayed so far to seek
In Golgotha him dead, who lives in Heav'n;
And they who to be sure of Paradise
Dying put on the weeds of Dominic,
Or in Franciscan think to pass disguised;
They pass the planets seven, and pass the fixed,
And that crystalline sphere whose balance weighs
The trepidation talked, and that first moved;
And now Saint Peter at Heav'n's wicket seems
To wait them with his keys, and now at foot
Of Heav'n's ascent they lift their feet, when lo
A violent crosswind from either coast
Blows them transverse ten thousand leagues awry
Into the devious air; then might ye see
Cowls, hoods and habits with their wearers tossed
And fluttered into rags, then relics, beads,
Indulgences, dispenses, pardons, bulls,
The sport of winds: all these upwhirled aloft
Fly o'er the backside of the world far off
Into a limbo large and broad, since called
The Paradise of Fools, to few unknown
Long after, now unpeopled, and untrod;
All this dark globe the fiend found as he passed,
And long he wandered, till at last a gleam
Of dawning light turned thitherward in haste

476–77. The pilgrims to Golgotha repeat the error of the Apostles before learning of the Resurrection: "Why seek ye the living among the dead? He is not here, but is risen" (Luke 24.5).

478–80. It was not uncommon for dying Roman Catholics to disguise themselves as members of religious orders to ease their passage to Heaven.

481–83. This depiction of the Ptolemaic cosmos includes *seven* planetary spheres, the sphere of the *fixed* stars (the eighth), the *crystálline sphere* (ninth), and the *primum mobile* or *that first moved* (tenth). The crystalline sphere was a late and controversial insertion, invented to account for precession of the equinoxes and a perceived oscillation of the starry sphere, i.e., *the trepidation talked.* The poles of this hypothetical crystalline orb were thought to correspond to the equinoctial opposites of Aries and Libra in the eighth. The *balance* that measures (*weighs*) the trepidation may thus refer to Libra ("the balance") (Fowler). Or it may refer to the librating axis of the crystalline sphere, which imparts (*weighs*) irregular motions as it moves back and forth like a beam holding scales. Cp. "trepidation of the spheres" in Donne's "A Valediction Forbidding Mourning."

484. **wicket:** a small door made in, or placed beside, a large one.

485. **keys:** the keys of the kingdom of Heaven given to Peter (Matt. 16.19). Cp. *Lyc* 108–11.

489. **devious:** off their main course.

491. **beads:** rosaries.

492. For Protestants, sale of *indulgences* granting released time from Purgatory was a main Catholic abuse. *Dispenses* or dispensations voided obligations. *Pardons* absolved from offenses. *Bulls* were papal edicts.

494. **backside of the world:** the dark side of the *primum mobile,* farthest from Heaven.

495. **limbo:** fringe region.

496. **Paradise of Fools:** a proverbial phrase; see Shakespeare, *ROM* 2.4.163.

His traveled steps; far distant he descries
Ascending by degrees magnificent
Up to the wall of Heaven a structure high,
At top whereof, but far more rich appeared
The work as of a kingly palace gate
With frontispiece of diamond and gold
Embellished; thick with sparkling orient gems
The portal shone, inimitable on Earth
By model, or by shading pencil drawn.
The stairs were such as whereon Jacob saw
Angels ascending and descending, bands
Of guardians bright, when he from Esau fled
To Padan-Aram, in the field of Luz
Dreaming by night under the open sky,
And waking cried, "This is the gate of Heav'n."
Each stair mysteriously was meant, nor stood
There always, but drawn up to Heav'n sometimes
Viewless, and underneath a bright sea flowed
Of jasper, or of liquid pearl, whereon
Who after came from Earth, sailing arrived,
Wafted by angels, or flew o'er the lake
Rapt in a chariot drawn by fiery steeds.
The stairs were then let down, whether to dare
The fiend by easy ascent, or aggravate
His sad exclusion from the doors of bliss.
Direct against which opened from beneath,
Just o'er the blissful seat of Paradise,
A passage down to th' Earth, a passage wide,
Wider by far than that of aftertimes

501. **traveled:** punning on "travailed, wearied."

502. **degrees:** steps, stairs.

506. **frontispiece:** ornamental pediment above an entranceway.

507. **orient:** lustrous as pearl.

510–15. See Gen. 28.10–17.

513. The 1667 and 1674 editions have no comma after *Padan-Aram* but include one after *Luz*. We insert the first and omit the second to avoid geographical confusion. Jacob's vision occurs in the vicinity of *Luz*, or Bethel, just north of Jerusalem. He sleeps there en route to *Padan-Aram* in northwest Mesopotamia.

516. **mysteriously:** symbolically, as an allegorical figure.

518. **Viewless:** unseen.

518–19. **bright sea . . . pearl:** The Argument identifies this *bright sea* as "waters above the firmament that flow about [the gate of Heaven]." Cp. 7.619.

521. **Wafted:** gently floated, as Lazarus was (Luke 16.22).

522. **Rapt:** carried away or caught up, as Elijah was (2 Kings 2.11; cp. *PR* 2.16–17).

526–28. **Direct . . . Earth:** At the bottom of the stairway, precisely above Paradise, a wide passage opened down to Earth.

Over Mount Sion, and, though that were large,
Over the Promised Land to God so dear,
By which, to visit oft those happy tribes,
On high behests his angels to and fro
Passed frequent, and his eye with choice regard
From Paneas the fount of Jordan's flood
To Beërsaba, where the Holy Land
Borders on Egypt and the Arabian shore;
So wide the op'ning seemed, where bounds were set
To darkness, such as bound the ocean wave.
Satan from hence now on the lower stair
That scaled by steps of gold to Heaven gate
Looks down with wonder at the sudden view
Of all this world at once. As when a scout
Through dark and desert ways with peril gone
All night; at last by break of cheerful dawn
Obtains the brow of some high-climbing hill,
Which to his eye discovers unaware
The goodly prospect of some foreign land
First seen, or some renowned metropolis
With glistering spires and pinnacles adorned,
Which now the rising sun gilds with his beams.
Such wonder seized, though after Heaven seen,
The spirit malign, but much more envy seized
At sight of all this world beheld so fair.
Round he surveys, and well might, where he stood
So high above the circling canopy

530. *That* refers to the passage over the *Promised Land,* described in lines 531–37. It is distinct from the passage traveled by Satan and from the one *over Mount Sion.* These occasional thoroughfares are presented as avenues of divine purpose, like the stairway.

534. **eye with choice regard:** "His eye also passed, with preferential attention." Angels are later identified as God's eyes (ll. 650–53).

535. **Paneas:** mountain spring at the northern border of Israel, a chief source of the Jordan River (*flood*); also, Greek name for Dan, the city associated with this *fount.* Cp. the scriptural idiom "from Dan even to Beersheba" (e.g., 1 Sam 3.20).

536. **Beërsaba:** Vulgate form of Beersheba, city on Israel's southern border.

538–39. The opening to the passageway occurs at the boundary separating light from the darkness of chaos.

543. **world:** cosmos, universe.

547. **discovers:** reveals.

552. **though after Heaven seen:** "Though previously he had witnessed the splendors of Heaven."

556–61. **circling . . . breadth:** Satan views the interior of the cosmos from an opening in the *primum mobile* at its most eastern point (corresponding to *Libra,* the scales). Peering down (westward), Satan sees the dark side of the Earth and its rotating, *canopy*like shadow (the shadow's rotation would be annual in a Copernican cosmos; diurnal in a Ptolemaic). At the western extreme from Satan, behind the Earth and sun, lies Aries, *the fleecy star* (astrologically, the ram). Its position in the sky is below that of *Andromeda* (mythological princess threatened by a sea monster). From Satan's perspective, the ram thus appears to bear the princess past the horizon of the western ocean (*Atlantic seas*). Finally, to observe the breadth of the cosmos before him, Satan looks north and south, *from pole to pole.*

Of night's extended shade; from eastern point
Of Libra to the fleecy star that bears
Andromeda far off Atlantic seas
Beyond th' horizon; then from pole to pole
He views in breadth, and without longer pause
Down right into the world's first region throws
His flight precipitant, and winds with ease
Through the pure marble air his oblique way
Amongst innumerable stars, that shone
Stars distant, but nigh hand seemed other worlds,
Or other worlds they seemed, or happy isles,
Like those Hesperian gardens famed of old,
Fortunate fields, and groves and flow'ry vales,
Thrice happy isles, but who dwelt happy there
He stayed not to inquire: above them all
The golden sun in splendor likest Heaven
Allured his eye: thither his course he bends
Through the calm firmament; but up or down
By center, or eccentric, hard to tell,
Or longitude, where the great luminary
Aloof the vulgar constellations thick,
That from his lordly eye keep distance due,
Dispenses light from far; they as they move
Their starry dance in numbers that compute
Days, months, and years, towards his all-cheering lamp
Turn swift their various motions, or are turned
By his magnetic beam, that gently warms
The universe, and to each inward part

562. **world's first region:** uppermost portion of the universe, above the sphere of the moon.

563–64. Satan dives straight down (*flight precipitant*) through the sparkling (*marble*) air. Once among the stars, however, he follows a characteristically indirect and slanted course (*winds . . . his oblique way*).

565–66. **shone/Stars distant:** "From a distance appeared to be stars" (Greek idiom).

567. **Or . . . or:** "either . . . or." Various seventeenth-century authors, and some ancients, speculated about other inhabited worlds. Milton is notably persistent about this possibility. Cp. line 670; 7.621–22; 8.140–58, 175–76. **happy isles:** Islands of the Blessed in Greek mythology, where a favored few abide in bliss rather than face death.

568. **Hesperian gardens:** where grew golden apples guarded by a dragon. Associated with Hesperus, the evening star, these gardens were thought to lie beyond the western ocean (where Aries bears Andromeda; see 556–61n). Cp. *Masque* 393–97, 981–83; *PR* 2.357.

571. **above:** more than.

573–76. **thither . . . longitude:** Milton's noncommittal description of Satan's route sunward accommodates competing seventeenth-century astronomical models.

577. **Aloof:** apart from (preposition).

580. **numbers:** music of the spheres regarded as the measure of a dance (cp. 8.125; *Masque* 112–14). The choric role of the stars in pacing the drama of creation was a classical commonplace.

583. **magnetic beam:** attractive power of the sun; a pre-Newtonian principle of celestial dynamics, proposed by Kepler.

With gentle penetration, though unseen,
Shoots invisible virtue even to the deep:
So wondrously was set his station bright.
There lands the fiend, a spot like which perhaps
Astronomer in the sun's lucent orb
Through his glazed optic tube yet never saw.
The place he found beyond expression bright,
Compared with aught on Earth, metal or stone;
Not all parts like, but all alike informed
With radiant light, as glowing iron with fire;
If metal, part seemed gold, part silver clear;
If stone, carbuncle most or chrysolite,
Ruby or topaz, to the twelve that shone
In Aaron's breastplate, and a stone besides
Imagined rather oft than elsewhere seen,
That stone, or like to that which here below
Philosophers in vain so long have sought,
In vain, though by their powerful art they bind
Volatile Hermes, and call up unbound
In various shapes old Proteus from the sea,
Drained through a limbec to his native form.
What wonder then if fields and regions here
Breathe forth elixir pure, and rivers run
Potable gold, when with one virtuous touch

586. **virtue:** efficacy; **the deep:** here means the farthest reaches and most inward parts of the created universe, including underground parts. Sunlight does not penetrate the realm of Chaos, which is also known as "the deep."

587. **station:** Although it suggests a sedentary sun, as in the Copernican system, *station* could also refer to the fixed sphere or course of the sun in the Ptolemaic cosmos.

588–90. Galileo built the first telescope (*glazed optic tube*) and published his discoveries, sunspots among them, in *Siderius Nuncius* (1610). Cp. 1.288. *Tube* was a common seventeenth-century term for telescope. Cp. Marvell, "To the King": "So his bold tube man to the sun applied/And spots unknown in the bright star descried" (1–2).

592. **metal:** Editions 1 and 2 have "medal." See the repetition of *metal* and *stone* at lines 595–96.

596. **carbuncle:** precious stone, fiery red, like little glowing coals (the word's etymological origin) or like serpents' eyes (9.500). The gems referred to were all thought to be luminous, i.e., *informed/With radiant light* (593–94). **chrysolite:** yellow-green gemstone.

597–98. **to . . . breastplate:** "the forementioned radiant stones plus the others on Aaron's breastplate, to the total of twelve." See Exod. 28.17–20 for a description of the breastplate.

598. **stone:** the philosopher's stone; the grand goal of alchemical aspiration, able to confer immortality and transmute base metal into gold.

601. **Philosophers:** alchemists.

602–5. **bind . . . form:** Alchemists considered mercury (*Hermes*) a primary basis of material being and subjected it to much experimentation. Liquid at room temperature, it was deemed *volatile*—difficult to *bind* or fix. *Proteus* is the shape-shifting sea god, symbolic of primary matter, who had to be restrained in his native form before he would speak true. *Limbec* is a corrupted form of *alembic,* a retort used by alchemists to distill and fix matter in its original condition. Note the repetitions of *stone* and *vain* in lines 598–602.

607–8. **Breathe . . . gold:** Like the fields and

Th' arch-chemic sun so far from us remote
Produces with terrestrial humor mixed
Here in the dark so many precious things
Of color glorious and effect so rare?
Here matter new to gaze the Devil met
Undazzled, far and wide his eye commands,
For sight no obstacle found here, nor shade,
But all sunshine, as when his beams at noon
Culminate from th' equator, as they now
Shot upward still direct, whence no way round
Shadow from body opaque can fall, and the air,
Nowhere so clear, sharpened his visual ray
To objects distant far, whereby he soon
Saw within ken a glorious angel stand,
The same whom John saw also in the sun:
His back was turned, but not his brightness hid;
Of beaming sunny rays, a golden tiar
Circled his head, nor less his locks behind
Illustrious on his shoulders fledge with wings
Lay waving round; on some great charge employed
He seemed, or fixed in cogitation deep.
Glad was the spirit impure as now in hope
To find who might direct his wand'ring flight
To Paradise the happy seat of man,
His journey's end and our beginning woe.
But first he casts to change his proper shape,
Which else might work him danger or delay:
And now a stripling Cherub he appears,

---

streams in Paradise (5.185–86), those on the sun *breathe forth* mists, but on the sun the exhaled mist is *elixir*—a vaporous manifestation of the philosopher's stone with life-extending properties, also identified as *potable gold*.

608. **virtuous:** efficacious.

609. **arch-chemic:** of supreme chemical power.

610. **terrestrial humor:** earthly fluid or moisture. Sunlight was thought to penetrate the earth's surface and produce precious gems from subterranean moisture (cp. l. 586). Cp. *Masque* 732–36. Similar processes occur in Heaven (6.475–81).

612. **effect:** appearance, efficacy.

617. **Culminate from th' equator:** reach their zenith relative to the equator, i.e., at equatorial noon.

618–19. **whence . . . fall:** In the prelapsarian cosmos, the sun's rays are perpendicular to the surface at equatorial noon so that *no way round* shadows fall. On the always shadowless solar surface, the sun's beams always (*still*) shoot directly *upward*.

620–21. **Nowhere . . . far:** According to some classical theories widely accepted in the seventeenth century, vision depends on extromission, "a beam issuing out of the eye to the object" (Hume; cp. *SA* 163). The eye was thus deemed a sunlike organ. Satan's eyebeam is *sharpened* in a literal sense, like one knife sharpened against another, and so made able to pierce *to objects distant far*.

622. **ken:** visual range.

623. "And I saw an angel standing in the sun" (Rev. 19.17).

625. **tiar:** crown.

627. **Illustrious:** brightly shining.

634. **casts:** contrives.

Not of the prime, yet such as in his face
Youth smiled celestial, and to every limb
Suitable grace diffused, so well he feigned;
Under a coronet his flowing hair
In curls on either cheek played, wings he wore
Of many a colored plume sprinkled with gold,
His habit fit for speed succinct, and held
Before his decent steps a silver wand.
He drew not nigh unheard, the angel bright,
Ere he drew nigh, his radiant visage turned,
Admonished by his ear, and straight was known
Th' Archangel Uriel, one of the sev'n
Who in God's presence, nearest to his throne
Stand ready at command, and are his eyes
That run through all the heav'ns, or down to th' Earth
Bear his swift errands over moist and dry,
O'er sea and land: him Satan thus accosts.
"Uriel, for thou of those sev'n spirits that stand
In sight of God's high throne, gloriously bright,
The first art wont his great authentic will
Interpreter through highest Heav'n to bring,
Where all his sons thy embassy attend;
And here art likeliest by supreme decree
Like honor to obtain, and as his eye
To visit oft this new creation round;
Unspeakable desire to see, and know
All these his wondrous works, but chiefly man,
His chief delight and favor, him for whom
All these his works so wondrous he ordained,
Hath brought me from the choirs of Cherubim
Alone thus wand'ring. Brightest Seraph tell
In which of all these shining orbs hath man
His fixèd seat, or fixèd seat hath none,
But all these shining orbs his choice to dwell;
That I may find him, and with secret gaze,

637. **prime:** first in order of existence or rank; primary.

643. **habit . . . succinct:** refers to the *wings he wore* (l. 641); literally, tucked up.

644. **decent:** becoming, proper.

648. **Uriel:** Hebrew for "light of God." The name is apocryphal (2 Esd. 4.1, 36). **the sev'n:** For the seven angels nearest God's throne, see Rev. 1.5, 8.2.

650–53. **his . . . land:** "Those seven, they are the eyes of the Lord, which run to and fro through the whole earth" (Zech. 4.10). Cp. lines 533–34.

656. **authentic:** authoritative.

658. **attend:** wait upon; cp. line 270.

664. **favor:** object of favor.

670. "But instead can choose to dwell in any of these shining orbs."

Or open admiration him behold
On whom the great Creator hath bestowed
Worlds, and on whom hath all these graces poured;
That both in him and all things, as is meet,
The Universal Maker we may praise;
Who justly hath driv'n out his rebel foes
To deepest Hell, and to repair that loss
Created this new happy race of men
To serve him better: wise are all his ways."
 So spake the false dissembler unperceived;
For neither man nor angel can discern
Hypocrisy, the only evil that walks
Invisible, except to God alone,
By his permissive will, through Heav'n and Earth:
And oft though wisdom wake, suspicion sleeps
At wisdom's gate, and to simplicity
Resigns her charge, while goodness thinks no ill
Where no ill seems: which now for once beguiled
Uriel, though Regent of the Sun, and held
The sharpest sighted spirit of all in Heav'n;
Who to the fraudulent impostor foul
In his uprightness answer thus returned.
"Fair angel, thy desire which tends to know
The works of God, thereby to glorify
The great Work-Master, leads to no excess
That reaches blame, but rather merits praise
The more it seems excess, that led thee hither
From thy empyreal mansion thus alone,
To witness with thine eyes what some perhaps
Contented with report hear only in Heav'n:
For wonderful indeed are all his works,
Pleasant to know, and worthiest to be all
Had in remembrance always with delight;
But what created mind can comprehend
Their number, or the wisdom infinite
That brought them forth, but hid their causes deep.
I saw when at his word the formless mass,
This world's material mold, came to a heap:
Confusion heard his voice, and wild uproar
Stood ruled, stood vast infinitude confined;
Till at his second bidding darkness fled,

709. **mold:** substance.

Light shone, and order from disorder sprung:
Swift to their several quarters hasted then
The cumbrous elements, earth, flood, air, fire,
And this ethereal quintessence of heav'n
Flew upward, spirited with various forms,
That rolled orbicular, and turned to stars
Numberless, as thou seest, and how they move;
Each had his place appointed, each his course,
The rest in circuit walls this universe.
Look downward on that globe whose hither side
With light from hence, though but reflected, shines;
That place is Earth the seat of man, that light
His day, which else as th' other hemisphere
Night would invade, but there the neighboring moon
(So call that opposite fair star) her aid
Timely interposes, and her monthly round
Still ending, still renewing, through mid-heav'n;
With borrowed light her countenance triform
Hence fills and empties to enlighten th' Earth,
And in her pale dominion checks the night.
That spot to which I point is Paradise,
Adam's abode, those lofty shades his bow'r.
Thy way thou canst not miss, me mine requires."
    Thus said, he turned, and Satan bowing low,
As to superior spirits is wont in Heav'n,
Where honor due and reverence none neglects,
Took leave, and toward the coast of Earth beneath,
Down from th' ecliptic, sped with hoped success,
Throws his steep flight in many an airy wheel,
Nor stayed, till on Niphates' top he lights.

715–16. The four elements are unwieldy compared with celestial ether, the agile fifth element or *quintessence,* which Milton in the invocation identifies with light itself (l. 7).

717. **spirited with:** animated by. The endowment of form triggers the animation of matter; cp. 7.464–66.

718. **orbicular:** in circles. The natural motion of ether was thought to be circular; see Aristotle, *On the Heavens* 270b.

721. "The ether left after the stars were formed enspheres the universe."

730. **triform:** waning, waxing, full. Cp. Horace, *Odes* 3.22.

731. **Hence:** from here.

740. **ecliptic:** the path of the sun.

742. **Niphates:** mountain bordering ancient Assyria (4.126).

Book IV

The Argument

Satan now in prospect of Eden, and nigh the place where he must now attempt the bold enterprise which he undertook alone against God and man, falls into many doubts with himself, and many passions: fear, envy, and despair; but at length confirms himself in evil; journeys on to Paradise, whose outward prospect and situation is described; overleaps the bounds, sits in the shape of a cormorant on the Tree of Life, as highest in the Garden, to look about him. The Garden described; Satan's first sight of Adam and Eve; his wonder at their excellent form and happy state, but with resolution to work their fall; overhears their discourse, thence gathers that the Tree of Knowledge was forbidden them to eat of, under penalty of death; and thereon intends to found his temptation, by seducing them to transgress: then leaves them a while, to know further of their state by some other means. Meanwhile Uriel descending on a sunbeam warns Gabriel, who had in charge the gate of Paradise, that some evil spirit had escaped the deep, and passed at noon by his sphere in the shape of a good angel down to Paradise, discovered after by his furious gestures in the mount. Gabriel promises to find him ere morning. Night coming on, Adam and Eve discourse of going to their rest: their bower described; their evening worship. Gabriel drawing forth his bands of night-watch to walk the round of Paradise, appoints two strong angels to Adam's bower, lest the evil spirit should be there doing some harm to Adam or Eve sleeping; there they find him at the ear of Eve, tempting her in a dream, and bring him, though unwilling, to Gabriel; by whom questioned, he scornfully answers, prepares resistance, but hindered by a sign from Heaven, flies out of Paradise.

O for that warning voice, which he who saw
Th' Apocalypse, heard cry in Heav'n aloud,

1–12. The most dramatic book of the epic opens like Shakespeare's *Henry V*, with a wistful exclamation. Milton echoes Rev. 12.3–12, which prophesies an apocalyptic war in Heaven, defeat of Satan's forces, and a retaliatory attack on Earth. The juxtaposition of the Apocalypse (future), the War in Heaven (past), Satan's arrival in Paradise (the narrative present), and Milton's own present as creator of the poem generates a dizzying temporal displacement, registered in shifting verb tenses around the repeated *now* of lines 5–9.

Then when the Dragon, put to second rout,
Came furious down to be revenged on men,
"Woe to the inhabitants on Earth!" That now,
While time was, our first parents had been warned
The coming of their secret foe, and scaped
Haply so scaped his mortal snare; for now
Satan, now first inflamed with rage, came down,
The Tempter ere th' Accuser of mankind,
To wreck on innocent frail man his loss
Of that first battle, and his flight to Hell:
Yet not rejoicing in his speed, though bold,
Far off and fearless, nor with cause to boast,
Begins his dire attempt, which nigh the birth
Now rolling, boils in his tumultuous breast,
And like a devilish engine back recoils
Upon himself; horror and doubt distract
His troubled thoughts, and from the bottom stir
The Hell within him, for within him Hell
He brings, and round about him, nor from Hell
One step no more than from himself can fly
By change of place: now conscience wakes despair
That slumbered, wakes the bitter memory
Of what he was, what is, and what must be
Worse; of worse deeds worse sufferings must ensue.
Sometimes towards Eden which now in his view
Lay pleasant, his grieved look he fixes sad,
Sometimes towards heav'n and the full-blazing sun,
Which now sat high in his meridian tow'r:
Then much revolving, thus in sighs began.
"O thou that with surpassing glory crowned,

3. **Then when:** Cp. line 970.

10. **Accuser:** St. John identifies Satan not as the devil (*diabolos*) but as the tempter of Adam and Eve and accuser (*kategoros*) of Christians seeking salvation (Rev. 12.10).

11. **wreck:** avenge (wreak); cp. 3.241.

16. **rolling:** heaving, surging.

17. **engine:** cannon (see 6.470–91). Satan is repeatedly associated with gunpowder and artillery (cp. ll. 814–18), which he invents in Book 6. Both *engine* and *invention* (or even *plot*) can translate the Latin *ingenium.*

20–23. **The Hell . . . place:** Cp. 1.253–55. The narrator's comment recalls *Doctor Faustus* 1.3.76; 2.1.121–22.

25. Cp. *SA* 22.

27–28. **Eden . . . pleasant:** Milton appears to have thought that *Eden* (now deemed Sumerian in origin) derived from the Hebrew for "delight."

30. **meridian:** noon or zenith. Richardson traces to Vergil the image of the midday sun as in a tower (*Culex* 41).

31. **revolving:** deliberating. Milton's word choice continues the characterization of Satan's mental processes as circular, often viciously so (*rolling, recoil*).

32–41. Edward Phillips, Milton's nephew and biographer, claims that he was shown these lines "several years before the poem was begun" and that they were "designed for the very beginning" of a tragedy on the same subject (Darbishire 72). In the Trinity College manuscript, Milton

Look'st from thy sole dominion like the God
Of this new world; at whose sight all the stars
Hide their diminished heads; to thee I call,
But with no friendly voice, and add thy name
O Sun, to tell thee how I hate thy beams
That bring to my remembrance from what state
I fell, how glorious once above thy sphere;
Till pride and worse ambition threw me down
Warring in Heav'n against Heav'n's matchless King:
Ah wherefore! He deserved no such return
From me, whom he created what I was
In that bright eminence, and with his good
Upbraided none; nor was his service hard.
What could be less than to afford him praise,
The easiest recompense, and pay him thanks,
How due! Yet all his good proved ill in me,
And wrought but malice; lifted up so high
I 'sdained subjection, and thought one step higher
Would set me highest, and in a moment quit
The debt immense of endless gratitude,
So burdensome still paying, still to owe;
Forgetful what from him I still received,
And understood not that a grateful mind
By owing owes not, but still pays, at once
Indebted and discharged; what burden then?
O had his powerful destiny ordained
Me some inferior angel, I had stood
Then happy; no unbounded hope had raised
Ambition. Yet why not? Some other power
As great might have aspired, and me though mean
Drawn to his part; but other powers as great
Fell not, but stand unshaken, from within
Or from without, to all temptations armed.
Hadst thou the same free will and power to stand?
Thou hadst: whom hast thou then or what to accuse,

---

outlines such a tragedy under the title "Adam Unparadised." Satan's soliloquy draws on Prometheus' first speech in Aeschylus' *Prometheus Bound.*

45. **Upbraided:** reproached; cp. James 1.5.

50. **'sdained:** disdained, in a form reminiscent of the Italian *sdegnare* (to disdain). An attitude of romantic as well as religious import, "disdain" in Satan's usage at line 82 is given allegorical agency antagonistic to "submission"; cp. line 770.

51. **quit:** usually glossed as "repay," but the sense here more nearly approximates "to cease to be engaged in or occupied with" (*OED* I.5.a).

53–56. **still:** always.

56. **By owing owes not:** Acknowledgment of an obligation ("owning up") satisfies it. Cp. Cicero, *De Officiis* 2.20; *Pro Plancio* 28.68.

61. **power:** a rank in the angelic hierarchy, here and in line 63 used loosely to mean any angel.

66–72. Satan interrogates himself (*thou*), and his

But Heav'n's free love dealt equally to all?
Be then his love accursed, since love or hate,
To me alike, it deals eternal woe.
Nay cursed be thou; since against his thy will
Chose freely what it now so justly rues.
Me miserable! Which way shall I fly
Infinite wrath, and infinite despair?
Which way I fly is Hell; myself am Hell;
And in the lowest deep a lower deep
Still threat'ning to devour me opens wide,
To which the Hell I suffer seems a Heav'n.
O then at last relent: is there no place
Left for repentance, none for pardon left?
None left but by submission; and that word
Disdain forbids me, and my dread of shame
Among the spirits beneath, whom I seduced
With other promises and other vaunts
Than to submit, boasting I could subdue
Th' Omnipotent. Ay me, they little know
How dearly I abide that boast so vain,
Under what torments inwardly I groan;
While they adore me on the throne of Hell,
With diadem and scepter high advanced
The lower still I fall, only supreme
In misery; such joy ambition finds.
But say I could repent and could obtain
By act of grace my former state; how soon
Would highth recall high thoughts, how soon unsay
What feigned submission swore: ease would recant
Vows made in pain, as violent and void.
For never can true reconcilement grow

---

replies corroborate God's earlier self-justification (3.100–101).

75. **myself am Hell:** In the early 1660s, Louis XIV of France reportedly identified himself with the state—*"L'Etat c'est moi"*—a sentence long regarded as the epitome of royal absolutism. Satan dwells on the ramifications of his identification with Hell. See 20–23n.

79–80. **no place/Left for repentance:** Hebrews 12.17 is widely cited as the source for Satan's phrasing. The quasi-allegorical expression of a psychological condition as a physical locality is general in this poem, however. Satan is irreversibly consigned to Hell, and his former place of bliss has been irreversibly estranged from him (5.615, 7.144).

87. **abide:** endure or persevere in; but the sense "remain in a place" is also present. See the preceding note.

90. **advanced:** exalted (referring to Satan on his throne).

94. **act of grace:** suspension of a legal penalty. While the reference to divine mercy is clear, Satan's legalese recalls Charles's phrasing in *Eikon Basilike:* "Is this the reward and thanks I am to receive for those many Acts of Grace I have lately passed?" (9.53).

97. **violent and void:** forced and therefore invalid.

Where wounds of deadly hate have pierced so deep:
Which would but lead me to a worse relapse
And heavier fall: so should I purchase dear
Short intermission bought with double smart.
This knows my punisher; therefore as far
From granting he, as I from begging peace:
All hope excluded thus, behold instead
Of us outcast, exiled, his new delight,
Mankind created, and for him this world.
So farewell hope, and with hope farewell fear,
Farewell remorse: all good to me is lost;
Evil be thou my good; by thee at least
Divided Empire with Heav'n's King I hold
By thee, and more than half perhaps will reign;
As man ere long, and this new world shall know."
   Thus while he spake, each passion dimmed his face
Thrice changed with pale, ire, envy and despair,
Which marred his borrowed visage, and betrayed
Him counterfeit, if any eye beheld.
For Heav'nly minds from such distempers foul
Are ever clear. Whereof he soon aware,
Each perturbation smoothed with outward calm,
Artificer of fraud; and was the first
That practiced falsehood under saintly show,
Deep malice to conceal, couched with revenge:
Yet not enough had practiced to deceive
Uriel once warned; whose eye pursued him down
The way he went, and on th' Assyrian mount
Saw him disfigured, more than could befall
Spirit of happy sort: his gestures fierce
He marked and mad demeanor, then alone,
As he supposed, all unobserved, unseen.
So on he fares, and to the border comes,
Of Eden, where delicious Paradise,
Now nearer, crowns with her enclosure green,

110. **Evil be thou my good:** Satan later recognizes that the reverse also holds true (9.122–23).

115. **pale:** darkness, gloom (cp. 10.1009). The light drains from Satan's disguised face three times (cp. 1.594–98). (Note that the Argument identifies *fear,* not ire, as the first of the three passions affecting him.) His *disfiguration* (l. 127) reverses scriptural accounts of Christ's transfiguration, in which the mountaintop illumination of Jesus—his "face shone like the sun"—manifests his heavenly nature (Matt. 17.2).

123. **couched:** lying in ambush, lurking; cp. 405–6.

126. **Assyrian mount:** Niphates (3.742).

132–45. **Eden . . . round:** Milton describes Paradise as a walled garden situated on the level summit (*champaign head*) of a hill (*steep wilderness*) on the eastern border of Eden. The trees on the densely wooded hillside resemble ascending rows of seats in a theater.

As with a rural mound the champaign head
Of a steep wilderness, whose hairy sides
With thicket overgrown, grotesque and wild,
Access denied; and overhead up grew
Insuperable highth of loftiest shade,
Cedar, and pine, and fir, and branching palm,
A sylvan scene, and as the ranks ascend
Shade above shade, a woody theater
Of stateliest view. Yet higher than their tops
The verdurous wall of Paradise up sprung:
Which to our general sire gave prospect large
Into his nether empire neighboring round.
And higher than that wall a circling row
Of goodliest trees loaden with fairest fruit,
Blossoms and fruits at once of golden hue
Appeared, with gay enameled colors mixed:
On which the sun more glad impressed his beams
Than in fair evening cloud, or humid bow,
When God hath show'red the earth; so lovely seemed
That lantskip: and of pure now purer air
Meets his approach, and to the heart inspires
Vernal delight and joy, able to drive
All sadness but despair: now gentle gales
Fanning their odoriferous wings dispense
Native perfumes, and whisper whence they stole
Those balmy spoils. As when to them who sail
Beyond the Cape of Hope, and now are past

136. **grotesque:** according to the *OED,* which cites this as the first such usage in English, "of a landscape: Romantic, picturesquely irregular" (B 2.b). The implied Miltonic innovation is dubious. The word had only recently entered English from the Italian *grotesca.* It referred to the style of painting and sculpture found in excavated Roman grottoes, which featured partial human and animal forms and interwoven foliage. It was an aesthetic term applied to antic, rugged, extravagant, or fanciful productions. The suggestiveness of Milton's description of the "hairy" hillside wildly overgrown with tangled thicket, its imaginative amalgamations of human and vegetable, qualify this usage as an instance of the original meaning (cp. 5.294–97).

140. **sylvan scene:** forest backdrop; translates Vergil's *sylvis scaena* (*Aen.* 1.164).

149. **enameled:** glossy, brilliant, as in coloring fixed by fire (cp. 9.525).

151. **humid bow:** rainbow (cp. *Masque* 992).

153. **lantskip:** landscape.

156. **gales:** breezes.

160–65. **Cape of Hope . . . smiles:** After rounding the southern tip of Africa (*Cape of Hope*), European trade ships bore *northeast* from *Mozambique.* Diodorus Siculus (3.46), on whom Milton appears to draw here and at lines 275–79, notes that the prevailing winds of spring carry fragrance from Saba (Sheba), a region in Arabia Felix (*Araby the Blest;* modern Yemen) renowned for the *grateful* (pleasing) smell of myrrh and frankincense. The phenomenon of the aromatic Arabian breeze scenting the ocean was by Milton's time a commonplace expressive of remote knowledge: "So we the Arabian coast do know, / At distance, when the spices blow" (Waller, *Night-piece* 39–40; cp. Herbert, *Prayer* 13–14). A related olfactory phenomenon occurs in Heaven (3.135–37).

Mozambique, off at sea northeast winds blow
Sabean odors from the spicy shore
Of Araby the Blest, with such delay
Well pleased they slack their course, and many a league
Cheered with the grateful smell old Ocean smiles.
So entertained those odorous sweets the fiend
Who came their bane, though with them better pleased
Than Asmodeus with the fishy fume,
That drove him, though enamored, from the spouse
Of Tobit's son, and with a vengeance sent
From Media post to Egypt, there fast bound.
  Now to th' ascent of that steep savage hill
Satan had journeyed on, pensive and slow;
But further way found none, so thick entwined,
As one continued brake, the undergrowth
Of shrubs and tangling bushes had perplexed
All path of man or beast that passed that way:
One gate there only was, and that looked east
On th' other side: which when th' arch-felon saw
Due entrance he disdained, and in contempt,
At one slight bound high over leaped all bound
Of hill or highest wall, and sheer within
Lights on his feet. As when a prowling wolf,
Whom hunger drives to seek new haunt for prey,
Watching where shepherds pen their flocks at eve
In hurdled cotes amid the field secure,
Leaps o'er the fence with ease into the fold:
Or as a thief bent to unhoard the cash
Of some rich burgher, whose substantial doors,
Cross-barred and bolted fast, fear no assault,
In at the window climbs, or o'er the tiles;
So clomb this first grand thief into God's fold:

168–71. **Asmodeus . . . bound:** In *Media* (now northwestern Iran), according to the apocryphal Book of Tobit, the demon *Asmodeus* (cp. Asmadai, 6.365 and *PR* 2.151) kills seven husbands of Sarah. Tobias, son of the blind *Tobit,* becomes her eighth husband. On the advice of the angel Raphael, Tobias repels the jealous demon by burning the heart and liver of a fish (whence the *fishy fume*). Fleeing hastily (*post*) to Egypt to escape the smell, Asmodeus is captured by the angel and bound (cp. 5.221–23).

172. **savage:** wooded, wild.

176. **had perplexed:** would have perplexed.

181. **bound . . . bound:** another instance of paronomasia, jingling wordplay common in late Latin and Italian writers and characteristic of Hebrew Scripture. Cp. 1.642n.

183–87. **wolf . . . fold:** Cp. John 10.1–10, where Christ identifies himself as the proper entrance to the flock and calls those who circumvent him thieves and robbers. See 193n.

186. **hurdled cotes:** fenced shelters made of poles and intertwined branches.

188. **unhoard the cash:** undo a hidden reserve of money by removing its contents, in this case *cash* with a play on *cache.*

192. **clomb:** archaic past tense of *climb.*

So since into his Church lewd hirelings climb.
Thence up he flew, and on the Tree of Life,
The middle tree and highest there that grew,
Sat like a cormorant; yet not true life
Thereby regained, but sat devising death
To them who lived; nor on the virtue thought
Of that life-giving plant, but only used
For prospect, what well used had been the pledge
Of immortality. So little knows
Any, but God alone, to value right
The good before him, but perverts best things
To worst abuse, or to their meanest use.
Beneath him with new wonder now he views
To all delight of human sense exposed
In narrow room Nature's whole wealth, yea more,
A Heav'n on Earth, for blissful Paradise
Of God the Garden was, by him in the east
Of Eden planted; Eden stretched her line
From Auran Eastward to the royal tow'rs
Of great Seleucia, built by Grecian kings,
Or where the sons of Eden long before
Dwelt in Telassar: in this pleasant soil
His far more pleasant Garden God ordained;
Out of the fertile ground he caused to grow
All trees of noblest kind for sight, smell, taste;
And all amid them stood the Tree of Life,
High eminent, blooming ambrosial fruit
Of vegetable gold; and next to life

193. **lewd:** base (with an ironic glance at the original meaning, "not of the clergy, lay"). In the Geneva Bible and *AV, lewd* can translate *poneron,* Greek for evil in general (e.g., Acts 17.5; cp. 1.490, 6.182). Christ scorns the "hireling," who when a wolf attacks, "fleeth, because he is an hireling, and careth not for the sheep" (John 10.13). Milton's frequent criticisms of corrupt clergy allude to this parable and tend to merge the hireling and the wolf. Cp. 12.507–11, *Lyc* 114–29, *Sonnet 16* 14.

194. **Tree of Life:** Gen. 2.9; Rev. 2.7.

196. **cormorant:** large, voracious seabird; figuratively, someone insatiably greedy, rapacious.

200. **pledge:** "anything . . . put in the possession of another . . . as a guarantee of good faith" (*OED* 2.a). The tree of prohibition is a corresponding pledge—of humanity's obedience and faith (8.325; cp. *CD* in Yale 6:352). Satan though immortal has lost "true life" (l. 196) and now subsists in Hell, where death lives (2.624).

207. **In . . . wealth:** Cp. Barabas's delight at "infinite riches in a little room" in Marlowe's *Jew of Malta* (1.1.37).

211. **Auran:** or Hauran; region south of Damascus, on Israel's eastern border (Ezek. 47.16, 18).

212. **Seleucia:** city on the Tigris River near Baghdad, built by Seleucus, c. 300 B.C.E., one of Alexander's successors and founder of a dynasty.

214. **Telassar:** ancient city within the boundaries set forth in lines 211–12, inhabited by "the children of Eden" but conquered by the Assyrians in the eighth century B.C.E. (2 Kings 19.12; Isa. 37.12). See line 285.

Our death the Tree of Knowledge grew fast by,
Knowledge of good bought dear by knowing ill.
Southward through Eden went a river large,
Nor changed his course, but through the shaggy hill
Passed underneath engulfed, for God had thrown
That mountain as his Garden mold high raised
Upon the rapid current, which through veins
Of porous earth with kindly thirst up drawn,
Rose a fresh fountain, and with many a rill
Watered the Garden; thence united fell
Down the steep glade, and met the nether flood,
Which from his darksome passage now appears,
And now divided into four main streams,
Runs diverse, wand'ring many a famous realm
And country whereof here needs no account,
But rather to tell how, if art could tell,
How from that sapphire fount the crispèd brooks,
Rolling on orient pearl and sands of gold,
With mazy error under pendant shades
Ran nectar, visiting each plant, and fed
Flow'rs worthy of Paradise which not nice art
In beds and curious knots, but Nature boon
Poured forth profuse on hill and dale and plain,
Both where the morning sun first warmly smote
The open field, and where the unpierced shade
Embrowned the noontide bow'rs: thus was this place,
A happy rural seat of various view;
Groves whose rich trees wept odorous gums and balm,
Others whose fruit burnished with golden rind
Hung amiable, Hesperian fables true,
If true, here only, and of delicious taste:
Betwixt them lawns, or level downs, and flocks
Grazing the tender herb, were interposed,
Or palmy hillock, or the flow'ry lap

222. "That doom which Adam fell into of knowing good and evil—that is to say, of knowing good by evil" (*Areop*, p. 939); "since it was tasted, not only do we know evil, but also we do not even know good except through evil" (*CD* 1.10, p. 1220).

223. **a river large:** the Tigris, named at 9.71.

228. **kindly:** natural.

237. **crispèd:** wavy.

239. **error:** used in the primary sense of the Latin noun *error*, "a wandering."

241. **nice:** fastidious, precise.

242. **curious knots:** flower beds of painstakingly intricate design; **boon:** bounteous.

246. **Embrowned:** darkened, per French and Italian usage (*embrunir; imbrunire*).

247. **seat:** local habitation, residence.

250. **amiable:** lovely (cp. Ps. 84.1 in the *AV* versus Milton's translation, p. 117); **Hesperian fables:** See 3.568n.

254. **lap:** a hollow among hills (*OED* 5.b; Milton antedates by nearly a century the *OED*'s earliest quotation of this usage).

Of some irriguous valley spread her store,
Flow'rs of all hue, and without thorn the rose:
Another side, umbrageous grots and caves
Of cool recess, o'er which the mantling vine
Lays forth her purple grape, and gently creeps
Luxuriant; meanwhile murmuring waters fall
Down the slope hills, dispersed, or in a lake,
That to the fringèd bank with myrtle crowned,
Her crystal mirror holds, unite their streams.
The birds their choir apply; airs, vernal airs,
Breathing the smell of field and grove, attune
The trembling leaves, while universal Pan
Knit with the Graces and the Hours in dance
Led on th' eternal spring. Not that fair field
Of Enna, where Proserpine gathering flow'rs
Herself a fairer flow'r by gloomy Dis
Was gathered, which cost Ceres all that pain
To seek her through the world; nor that sweet grove
Of Daphne by Orontes, and th' inspired
Castalian spring, might with this Paradise
Of Eden strive; nor that Nyseian isle
Girt with the river Triton, where old Cham,
Whom Gentiles Ammon call and Lybian Jove,

255. **irriguous:** well watered (cp. Horace, *Satires* 2.4.16).

256. **without thorn the rose:** Thorns were commonly deemed a postlapsarian phenomenon (Gen. 3.18). "Before man's fall the Rose was born/ St. Ambrose says, without the thorn" (Herrick, *The Rose*).

257. **umbrageous:** shady.

258. **mantling:** covering, like a cloak; cp. 5.279; **mantling vine:** cp. *Masque* 294.

262–63. **myrtle . . . mirror:** Fowler notes that myrtle and mirror are iconographical attributes of Venus, goddess of love and gardens, often associated with Eve. See lines 454–65.

264. **airs:** melodies; breezes.

266. **Pan:** nature god. In Greek, *pan* means "all."

267. **Graces and the Hours:** Sister goddesses (Euphrosyne, Aglaia, Thalia), the *Graces* dance in attending Aphrodite (cp. *FQ* 6.10.5–17). The *Hours* represent the seasons and in Hesiod crown Pandora with spring flowers (*Works and Days* 74–75).

268–72. **eternal . . . world:** Milton presents the seasons as a postlapsarian phenomenon (10.651–91). In classical myth, seasonal change owes to the rape of Proserpine. Ovid describes the Sicilian grove from which *Dis* abducts her (*Enna*) as a place of perpetual spring (*Met.* 5.385–91). While sorrowful *Ceres,* goddess of grain, seeks her daughter, the earth turns barren. Because Proserpine eats of a pomegranate while in Hades, she must return to Dis for part of each year, during which time Ceres mourns, and nothing grows. Cp. 9.395–96 and Milton's 1637 letter to Diodati.

273–74. **Daphne . . . spring:** The laurel grove of *Daphne* by the river *Orontes* near Antioch had a spring inspired by Apollo and named for the *Castalian spring* of Parnassus. See Purchas 83. For the myth of Apollo and Daphne, see Ovid, *Met.* 1.450–565.

275–79. **Nyseian . . . eye:** The third stage of this four-layer simile follows Diodorus's account of *Ammon,* King of Libya, his affair with *Amalthea,* and their son (*Bacchus*). Mother and son take refuge from *Rhea,* Ammon's wife, on the island Nysa (3:67–70). Ammon was identified with the Libyan Jupiter and with Ham (*Cham*), Noah's son.

Hid Amalthea and her florid son
Young Bacchus from his stepdame Rhea's eye;
Nor where Abassin kings their issue guard,
Mount Amara, though this by some supposed
True Paradise under the Ethiop line
By Nilus' head, enclosed with shining rock,
A whole day's journey high, but wide remote
From this Assyrian garden, where the fiend
Saw undelighted all delight, all kind
Of living creatures new to sight and strange:
Two of far nobler shape erect and tall,
Godlike erect, with native honor clad
In naked majesty seemed lords of all,
And worthy seemed, for in their looks divine
The image of their glorious Maker shone,
Truth, wisdom, sanctitude severe and pure,
Severe but in true filial freedom placed;
Whence true authority in men; though both
Not equal, as their sex not equal seemed;
For contemplation he and valor formed,
For softness she and sweet attractive grace,
He for God only, she for God in him:
His fair large front and eye sublime declared
Absolute rule; and hyacinthine locks
Round from his parted forelock manly hung
Clust'ring, but not beneath his shoulders broad:
She as a veil down to the slender waist
Her unadornèd golden tresses wore
Disheveled, but in wanton ringlets waved
As the vine curls her tendrils, which implied
Subjection, but required with gentle sway,
And by her yielded, by him best received,
Yielded with coy submission, modest pride,
And sweet reluctant amorous delay.

280–85. **Abassin . . . garden:** Heylyn describes *Amara* as being "a day's journey high" and the site of palaces where, to prevent sedition, younger sons of the Abyssinian emperor were secluded and educated (4:64). Like Heylyn, Purchas comments on the identification of this [illegible] as the "place of our fore-father's [illegible]).

[illegible]ead; **sublime:** lofty.

[illegible]**e:** like hyacinth petals, from [illegible].231).

304–8. Women's long hair was on St. Paul's authority understood to imply subjection (1 Cor. 11.7, 14–15). Like Homer's Aphrodite and Vergil's Venus, Milton's Eve is golden.

306. **wanton:** abundant, luxuriant; like the "mantling vine" of line 258.

310. **coy:** not demonstrative, shy.

311. **reluctant:** "struggling" (Hume). Cp. the fire of divine wrath struggling through "dusky wreaths" of smoke at 6.58. As uncomfortable as some readers may be with the suggestion of

Nor those mysterious parts were then concealed,
Then was not guilty shame, dishonest shame
Of nature's works, honor dishonorable,
Sin-bred, how have ye troubled all mankind
With shows instead, mere shows of seeming pure,
And banished from man's life his happiest life,
Simplicity and spotless innocence.
So passed they naked on, nor shunned the sight
Of God or angel, for they thought no ill:
So hand in hand they passed, the loveliest pair
That ever since in love's embraces met,
Adam the goodliest man of men since borne
His sons, the fairest of her daughters Eve.
Under a tuft of shade that on a green
Stood whispering soft, by a fresh fountain side
They sat them down, and after no more toil
Of their sweet gard'ning labor than sufficed
To recommend cool Zephyr, and made ease
More easy, wholesome thirst and appetite
More grateful, to their supper fruits they fell,
Nectarine fruits which the compliant boughs
Yielded them, sidelong as they sat recline
On the soft downy bank damasked with flow'rs:
The savory pulp they chew, and in the rind
Still as they thirsted scoop the brimming stream;
Nor gentle purpose, nor endearing smiles
Wanted, nor youthful dalliance as beseems
Fair couple, linked in happy nuptial league,
Alone as they. About them frisking played
All beasts of th' earth, since wild, and of all chase
In wood or wilderness, forest or den;
Sporting the lion ramped, and in his paw
Dandled the kid; bears, tigers, ounces, pards,
Gamboled before them, th' unwieldy elephant
To make them mirth used all his might, and wreathed

---

erotic struggle, the modern sense of *reluctant* as "unwilling" was not current in the seventeenth century, according to the *OED.*

312. **mysterious:** See 741–43n.

329. **Zephyr:** west wind; "the frolic wind that breathes the spring" (*L'All* 18).

331–36. Adam and Eve's contented meal reverses the punishment of Tantalus.

332. **Nectarine:** sweet as nectar; **compliant:** yielding.

334. **damasked:** many colored.

337. **gentle purpose:** well-bred conversation.

338. **Wanted:** were lacking.

341. **chase:** unenclosed land, game preserve; also, animals to be hunted.

343. **ramped:** reared, as if climbing.

344. **Dandled:** played with; cp. Isa. 11.6; **ounces, pards:** lynxes, leopards.

His lithe proboscis; close the serpent sly
Insinuating, wove with Gordian twine
His braided train, and of his fatal guile
Gave proof unheeded; others on the grass
Couched, and now filled with pasture gazing sat,
Or bedward ruminating: for the sun
Declined was hasting now with prone career
To th' ocean isles, and in th' ascending scale
Of heav'n the stars that usher evening rose:
When Satan still in gaze, as first he stood,
Scarce thus at length failed speech recovered sad.
"O Hell! What do mine eyes with grief behold,
Into our room of bliss thus high advanced
Creatures of other mold, earth-born perhaps,
Not spirits, yet to Heav'nly spirits bright
Little inferior; whom my thoughts pursue
With wonder, and could love, so lively shines
In them divine resemblance, and such grace
The hand that formed them on their shape hath poured.
Ah gentle pair, ye little think how nigh
Your change approaches, when all these delights
Will vanish and deliver ye to woe,
More woe, the more your taste is now of joy;
Happy, but for so happy ill secured
Long to continue, and this high seat your Heav'n
Ill fenced for Heav'n to keep out such a foe
As now is entered; yet no purposed foe
To you whom I could pity thus forlorn
Though I unpitied: league with you I seek,
And mutual amity so strait, so close,
That I with you must dwell, or you with me

348. **Insinuating:** artfully working into company, winding; **Gordian:** like the famously complicated knot.

352. **ruminating:** chewing the cud.

353. **prone career:** downward course, as of a galloping horse.

354. **ocean isles:** identified at line 592 as the Azores; **ascending scale:** ladder, stairway (*OED* n3, I.1.b), or more likely, the rising scale of a figurative cosmic balance "weighing night and day, the one ascending as the other sinks" (Newton). In the equinoctial Garden, day and night are counterpoised. At the vernal equinox, the sun is in Aries, opposite Libra (the Scales), the constellation in which the evening stars would rise (cp. Vergil, *Georg.* 1.208).

356. **as first he stood:** since he initially saw Adam and Eve (l. 288).

360. **mold:** shape, pattern; also, Earth as humanity's native element.

361–62. **to Heav'nly spirits bright/Little inferior:** "Scarce to be less than gods thou mad'st his lot" (Ps. 8.5, Milton's translation; cp. Heb. 2.7).

370. **for so happy:** for being as fortunate as you are; cp. "for Heav'n" (l. 372).

376. **strait:** intimate; also constricted.

Henceforth; my dwelling haply may not please
Like this fair Paradise, your sense, yet such
Accept your Maker's work; he gave it me,
Which I as freely give; Hell shall unfold,
To entertain you two, her widest gates,
And send forth all her kings; there will be room,
Not like these narrow limits, to receive
Your numerous offspring; if no better place,
Thank him who puts me loath to this revenge
On you who wrong me not for him who wronged.
And should I at your harmless innocence
Melt, as I do, yet public reason just,
Honor and empire with revenge enlarged,
By conquering this new world, compels me now
To do what else though damned I should abhor."
So spake the fiend, and with necessity,
The tyrant's plea, excused his devilish deeds.
Then from his lofty stand on that high tree
Down he alights among the sportful herd
Of those four-footed kinds, himself now one,
Now other, as their shape served best his end
Nearer to view his prey, and unespied
To mark what of their state he more might learn
By word or action marked: about them round
A lion now he stalks with fiery glare,
Then as a tiger, who by chance hath spied
In some purlieu two gentle fawns at play,
Straight couches close, then rising changes oft
His couchant watch, as one who chose his ground
Whence rushing he might surest seize them both
Gripped in each paw: when Adam first of men
To first of women Eve thus moving speech,
Turned him all ear to hear new utterance flow.
"Sole partner and sole part of all these joys,
Dearer thyself than all; needs must the power
That made us, and for us this ample world

380–83. **he . . . kings:** Cp. Matt. 10.8, Isa. 14.9.

382. **her widest gates:** her gates as wide as possible.

387. **for:** instead of.

389. **public reason just:** legitimate concerns of state, such as honor and empire. Cp. *SA* 865–70.

402. **lion:** Cp. 1 Pet. 5.8; Euripides, *Bacchae* 1015.

410. **Turned him all ear:** Satan turns eagerly to hear human speech. The phrasing also suggests Raphael's account of spiritual bodily function, 6.350. Cp. *Masque* 560. "All ear" is a common expression in Italian (*tutt' orecchi*).

411. **Sole . . . sole:** only . . . peerless. The repetition of *sole* and *part* invites wordplay touching the origin of Eve and paradisial marriage.

Be infinitely good, and of his good
As liberal and free as infinite,
That raised us from the dust and placed us here
In all this happiness, who at his hand
Have nothing merited, nor can perform
Aught whereof he hath need, he who requires
From us no other service than to keep
This one, this easy charge, of all the trees
In Paradise that bear delicious fruit
So various, not to taste that only Tree
Of Knowledge, planted by the Tree of Life,
So near grows death to life, whate'er death is,
Some dreadful thing no doubt; for well thou know'st
God hath pronounced it death to taste that Tree,
The only sign of our obedience left
Among so many signs of power and rule
Conferred upon us, and dominion giv'n
Over all other creatures that possess
Earth, air, and sea. Then let us not think hard
One easy prohibition, who enjoy
Free leave so large to all things else, and choice
Unlimited of manifold delights:
But let us ever praise him, and extol
His bounty, following our delightful task
To prune these growing plants, and tend these flow'rs,
Which were it toilsome, yet with thee were sweet."
    To whom thus Eve replied. "O thou for whom
And from whom I was formed flesh of thy flesh,
And without whom am to no end, my guide
And head, what thou hast said is just and right.
For we to him indeed all praises owe,
And daily thanks, I chiefly who enjoy
So far the happier lot, enjoying thee
Preeminent by so much odds, while thou
Like consort to thyself canst nowhere find.
That day I oft remember, when from sleep
I first awaked, and found myself reposed
Under a shade on flow'rs, much wond'ring where

425. **whate'er death is:** For unfallen Adam, death has no meaning beyond *pronounced* penalty (l. 427). After the Fall, the concept of death will be gradually fleshed out, culminating in Michael's gruesome visions of mortality (11.444–47, 462–65).

447. **odds:** amount or ratio by which one thing exceeds or falls short of another; common diction in Shakespeare, where it often concerns characters in competition.

451. **on:** per the first edition; the second reads "of."

And what I was, whence thither brought, and how.
Not distant far from thence a murmuring sound
Of waters issued from a cave and spread
Into a liquid plain, then stood unmoved
Pure as th' expanse of heav'n; I thither went
With unexperienced thought, and laid me down
On the green bank, to look into the clear
Smooth lake, that to me seemed another sky.
As I bent down to look, just opposite,
A shape within the wat'ry gleam appeared
Bending to look on me, I started back,
It started back, but pleased I soon returned,
Pleased it returned as soon with answering looks
Of sympathy and love; there I had fixed
Mine eyes till now, and pined with vain desire,
Had not a voice thus warned me, 'What thou seest,
What there thou seest fair creature is thyself,
With thee it came and goes: but follow me,
And I will bring thee where no shadow stays
Thy coming, and thy soft embraces, he
Whose image thou art, him thou shall enjoy
Inseparably thine, to him shalt bear
Multitudes like thyself, and thence be called
Mother of human race.' What could I do,
But follow straight, invisibly thus led?
Till I espied thee, fair indeed and tall,
Under a platan, yet methought less fair,
Less winning soft, less amiably mild,
Than that smooth wat'ry image; back I turned,
Thou following cried'st aloud, 'Return fair Eve,
Whom fli'st thou? Whom thou fli'st, of him thou art,

460–69. Eve's narration formally echoes and significantly varies Ovid's tale of Narcissus (*Met.* 3.415ff).

466. **pined:** from the Latin noun *poena,* meaning "penalty in satisfaction for an offense or in consequence of failure to fulfill an obligation." As an intransitive verb, *pine* means "to languish with intense desire." As a transitive verb, it means "to cause pain or anguish" or "to grieve." Cp. Satan at lines 511 and 848.

470. **stays:** awaits. This line is echoed by Satan at *PR* 3.244.

478. **platan:** plane; a favorite shade tree of the Greeks and Romans, commonly described as barren (Vergil, *Georg.* 2.70, 4.146). Plato presents Socrates as reclining beneath a spreading plane tree (*Phaedrus* 230a). Horace calls it *caelebs,* which used of men means "unmarried" and of trees "without vines" (*Odes* 2.15.4). Despite the conjugal arc of Eve's narrative, Fowler maintains that Adam's association with the plane tree owes not to its classical association with "erotic love" but to a "well-known allegory" that made it a symbol of Christ, Adam's "head."

480–89. **Than . . . yielded:** Eve flees Adam as Daphne flees Apollo (*Met.* 1.502ff). As with preceding situational references to Tantalus (ll. 331–36) and Narcissus (ll. 460–69), another classical myth of frustration is undone.

His flesh, his bone; to give thee being I lent
Out of my side to thee, nearest my heart
Substantial life, to have thee by my side
Henceforth an individual solace dear;
Part of my soul I seek thee, and thee claim
My other half.' With that thy gentle hand
Seized mine, I yielded, and from that time see
How beauty is excelled by manly grace
And wisdom, which alone is truly fair."
So spake our general Mother, and with eyes
Of conjugal attraction unreproved,
And meek surrender, half embracing leaned
On our first father, half her swelling breast
Naked met his under the flowing gold
Of her loose tresses hid: he in delight
Both of her beauty and submissive charms
Smiled with superior love, as Jupiter
On Juno smiles, when he impregns the clouds
That shed May flowers; and pressed her matron lip
With kisses pure: aside the Devil turned
For envy, yet with jealous leer malign
Eyed them askance, and to himself thus plained.
"Sight hateful, sight tormenting! Thus these two
Imparadised in one another's arms
The happier Eden, shall enjoy their fill
Of bliss on bliss, while I to Hell am thrust,
Where neither joy nor love, but fierce desire,
Among our other torments not the least,
Still unfulfilled with pain of longing pines;
Yet let me not forget what I have gained
From their own mouths; all is not theirs it seems:
One fatal Tree there stands of Knowledge called,
Forbidden them to taste: knowledge forbidden?
Suspicious, reasonless. Why should their Lord

486. **individual:** inseparable, distinctive.

487–88. **Part . . . half:** Cp. Horace, *Odes* 1.3.8, 2.17.5.

493. **unreproved:** not subject to rebuke. Eve's eyes work differently at 9.1036.

499–501. **Smiled . . . flowers:** The simile recalls Vergil's account of Aether embracing his wife and of showers quickening seed in the earth (*Georg.* 2.325–28).

500. **impregns:** impregnates.

505–35. Satan's third soliloquy of the book. Like Shakespeare in *Othello,* Milton insists that his audience share the development of his villain's strategy.

508–11. **thrust . . . pines:** Satan's account of torment by *unfulfilled . . . longing* continues the epic's extensive correlation of the spiritual with the erotic (cp. 10.992–98).

511. **Still:** always; cp. 53–56; **pines:** torments (transitive, with Satan as the understood object); cp. 466n.

515–22. **knowledge . . . ruin:** Critics debate the sincerity of Satan's sentiments: whether his indig-

Envy them that? Can it be sin to know,
Can it be death? And do they only stand
By ignorance, is that their happy state,
The proof of their obedience and their faith?
O fair foundation laid whereon to build
Their ruin! Hence I will excite their minds
With more desire to know, and to reject
Envious commands, invented with design
To keep them low whom knowledge might exalt
Equal with gods; aspiring to be such,
They taste and die: what likelier can ensue?
But first with narrow search I must walk round
This garden, and no corner leave unspied;
A chance but chance may lead where I may meet
Some wand'ring spirit of Heav'n, by fountain side,
Or in thick shade retired, from him to draw
What further would be learned. Live while ye may,
Yet happy pair; enjoy, till I return,
Short pleasures, for long woes are to succeed."
    So saying, his proud step he scornful turned,
But with sly circumspection, and began
Through wood, through waste, o'er hill, o'er dale his roam.
Meanwhile in utmost longitude, where heav'n
With earth and ocean meets, the setting sun
Slowly descended, and with right aspect
Against the eastern gate of Paradise
Leveled his evening rays: it was a rock
Of alabaster, piled up to the clouds,
Conspicuous far, winding with one ascent
Accessible from earth, one entrance high;
The rest was craggy cliff, that overhung
Still as it rose, impossible to climb.
Betwixt these rocky pillars Gabriel sat
Chief of th' angelic guards, awaiting night;

---

nation is genuine (Empson 1965, 69) or a rehearsal of his rhetorical strategy (Broadbent 151). But Satan is capable neither of sincerity nor of being merely strategic.

530. **A chance but chance:** "Perhaps luck . . ."

539. **utmost longitude:** farthest west.

541. **right aspect:** square attitude; the setting sun is perpendicular to the vertical gate.

548. **Still:** continually.

549. **Gabriel:** "God is my strength" (Hebr.); see lines 1006–10. Widely deemed one of the four archangels (with Uriel, Raphael, and Michael), Gabriel appears in Scripture to aid Daniel and foretell the birth of John the Baptist and Jesus (Dan. 8.16, 9.21; Luke 1.19, 26). Jewish traditions identify him as one of the three angels (with Michael and Raphael) who share a peaceful meal with Abraham (Gen. 18). He is also accounted the guardian of Paradise and the angel responsible for ripening fruit.

About him exercised heroic games
Th' unarmèd youth of Heav'n, but nigh at hand
Celestial armory, shields, helms, and spears,
Hung high with diamond flaming, and with gold.
Thither came Uriel, gliding through the even
On a sunbeam, swift as a shooting star
In autumn thwarts the night, when vapors fired
Impress the air, and shows the mariner
From what point of his compass to beware
Impetuous winds: he thus began in haste.
"Gabriel, to thee thy course by lot hath giv'n
Charge and strict watch that to this happy place
No evil thing approach or enter in;
This day at highth of noon came to my sphere
A Spirit, zealous, as he seemed, to know
More of th' Almighty's works, and chiefly man
Gods latest Image: I described his way
Bent all on speed, and marked his airy gait;
But in the mount that lies from Eden north,
Where he first lighted, soon discerned his looks
Alien from Heav'n, with passions foul obscured:
Mine eye pursued him still, but under shade
Lost sight of him; one of the banished crew
I fear, hath ventured from the deep, to raise
New troubles; him thy care must be to find."
To whom the wingèd warrior thus returned:
"Uriel, no wonder if thy perfect sight,
Amid the sun's bright circle where thou sitst,
See far and wide: in at this gate none pass
The vigilance here placed, but such as come

555. **even:** Newton was the first to explain the play on *even:* "His coming upon a sun-beam was the most direct and level course that he could take; for the sun's rays were now pointed right against the eastern gate . . . where Gabriel was sitting." Homer similarly compares Athena's descent to a shooting star, a sign portentous to mariners (*Il.* 4.74–79).

557. **thwarts:** crosses. Aristotle explains shooting stars as combustible exhalations drawn from the earth and ignited aloft either through compression and condensation or by their own quickening motion. The natural motion of fire is upward, but strong winds, thought to originate at high altitude, propel the ignited vapors downward. Their oblique (*thwart*) path results from the combination of their natural motion and the wind's downward compulsion (*Meteorology* 1.4). Cp. Vergil, *Georg.* 1.365–67.

558. **Impress:** mark by exerting pressure.

561. The practice of establishing orders or divisions (*courses*) by lot is common in Scripture, especially in accounts of temple duties (1 Chron. 23.6–26; Luke 1.8).

567. **described:** observed, spied (per a seventeenth-century confusion of *describe* and *descry*).

568. **airy gait:** flight path as well as comportment in flight (cp. 3.741).

580. **vigilance:** guard or watch; metonymy is an apt figure for designating angels, whose entire subjectivity is perfectly aligned with function (cp. l. 410, 6.350–51).

Well known from Heav'n; and since meridian hour
No creature thence: if spirit of other sort,
So minded, have o'erleaped these earthy bounds
On purpose, hard thou knowst it to exclude
Spiritual substance with corporeal bar.
But if within the circuit of these walks,
In whatsoever shape he lurk, of whom
Thou tell'st, by morrow dawning I shall know."
 So promised he, and Uriel to his charge
Returned on that bright beam, whose point now raised
Bore him slope downward to the sun now fall'n
Beneath th' Azores; whether the prime orb,
Incredible how swift, had thither rolled
Diurnal, or this less voluble Earth
By shorter flight to th' east, had left him there
Arraying with reflected purple and gold
The clouds that on his western throne attend:
Now came still evening on, and twilight gray
Had in her sober livery all things clad;
Silence accompanied, for beast and bird,
They to their grassy couch, these to their nests
Were slunk, all but the wakeful nightingale;
She all night long her amorous descant sung;
Silence was pleased: now glowed the firmament
With living sapphires: Hesperus that led
The starry host, rode brightest, till the moon
Rising in clouded majesty, at length
Apparent queen unveiled her peerless light,
And o'er the dark her silver mantle threw.
 When Adam thus to Eve: "Fair consort, th' hour
Of night, and all things now retired to rest
Mind us of like repose, since God hath set
Labor and rest, as day and night to men
Successive, and the timely dew of sleep

591. **slope downward:** Because the sun has continued to sink, Uriel no longer follows a flat trajectory. The moment thus occurs just after the balance point of equinoctial day and night.

592–97. **whether . . . attend:** Milton will not choose between the Copernican cosmos and the Ptolemaic, which requires the sun to revolve around the earth at unbelievable velocity.

592. **whether:** First and second editions have "whither."

594. **Diurnal:** daily; **voluble:** rolling (Lat. *volúbilis*).

603. **descant:** counterpointed song.

605. **Hesperus:** the evening star, Venus.

606–9. Milton plays on clothing as a vehicle for light, here culminating in the moon's paradoxical disrobing (cp. *L'All* 60–62, *Il Pens* 122–25, *Masque* 188–89).

608. **Apparent:** "readily seen," but also "heir" (to Hesperus, the brightest light in the night sky until the moon's appearance).

Now falling with soft slumbrous weight inclines
Our eyelids; other creatures all day long
Rove idle unemployed, and less need rest;
Man hath his daily work of body or mind
Appointed, which declares his dignity,
And the regard of Heav'n on all his ways;
While other animals unactive range,
And of their doings God takes no account.
To morrow ere fresh morning streak the east
With first approach of light, we must be ris'n,
And at our pleasant labor, to reform
Yon flow'ry arbors, yonder allies green,
Our walk at noon, with branches overgrown,
That mock our scant manuring, and require
More hands than ours to lop their wanton growth:
Those blossoms also, and those dropping gums,
That lie bestrown unsightly and unsmooth,
Ask riddance, if we mean to tread with ease;
Meanwhile, as nature wills, night bids us rest."
    To whom thus Eve with perfect beauty adorned.
"My author and disposer, what thou bidd'st
Unargued I obey; so God ordains,
God is thy Law, thou mine: to know no more
Is woman's happiest knowledge and her praise.
With thee conversing I forget all time,
All seasons and their change, all please alike.
Sweet is the breath of morn, her rising sweet,
With charm of earliest birds; pleasant the sun
When first on this delightful land he spreads
His orient beams, on herb, tree, fruit, and flow'r,
Glist'ring with dew; fragrant the fertile earth
After soft showers; and sweet the coming on
Of grateful evening mild, then silent night
With this her solemn bird and this fair moon,
And these the gems of heav'n, her starry train:
But neither breath of morn when she ascends
With charm of earliest birds, nor rising sun
On this delightful land, nor herb, fruit, flow'r,
Glist'ring with dew, nor fragrance after showers,
Nor grateful evening mild, nor silent night

628. **manuring:** cultivation by hand (Lat. *manus:* hand).

635. **author and disposer:** source and ruler.

640. **seasons:** periods of time, occasions.

642. **charm:** delightful harmony.

648. **solemn bird:** nightingale; cp. 7.435.

With this her solemn bird, nor walk by moon,
Or glittering starlight without thee is sweet.
But wherefore all night long shine these, for whom
This glorious sight, when sleep hath shut all eyes?"
To whom our general ancestor replied.
"Daughter of God and man, accomplished Eve,
These have their course to finish, round the Earth,
By morrow evening, and from land to land
In order, though to nations yet unborn,
Minist'ring light prepared, they set and rise;
Lest total darkness should by night regain
Her old possession, and extinguish life
In nature and all things, which these soft fires
Not only enlighten, but with kindly heat
Of various influence foment and warm,
Temper or nourish, or in part shed down
Their stellar virtue on all kinds that grow
On earth, made hereby apter to receive
Perfection from the sun's more potent ray.
These then, though unbeheld in deep of night,
Shine not in vain, nor think, though men were none,
That heav'n would want spectators, God want praise;
Millions of spiritual creatures walk the earth
Unseen, both when we wake, and when we sleep:
All these with ceaseless praise his works behold
Both day and night: how often from the steep
Of echoing hill or thicket have we heard
Celestial voices to the midnight air,
Sole, or responsive each to other's note
Singing their great Creator: oft in bands
While they keep watch, or nightly rounding walk
With Heav'nly touch of instrumental sounds
In full harmonic number joined, their songs
Divide the night, and lift our thoughts to Heaven."

661. **These:** Early editions have "Those." Citing lines 657 and 674, Newton substituted "These."

665–67. **Lest . . . things:** Previously, Satan persuaded Chaos and Night of his intention to return the newly created world "to her original darkness" and the *possession* of Night (2.982–86; cp. 10.415–18). It is axiomatic in this epic that, without light, chaos would come again.

667–75. Neoplatonic astrology classified animals, vegetables, and minerals according to the predominant *stellar virtue,* or astral power, that *tempers* (strengthens, attunes) them. Such *influence* was supposedly mediated by streaming ether. After the Fall, the cosmos is adjusted so that the stars' influence is not always *kindly,* or naturally favorable (cp. 10.651ff). Their postlapsarian fire can be *soft* (gentle) as here, or severe (cp. 2.276).

685. **rounding:** making the rounds (literally, since the Garden is circular).

688. **Divide the night:** into watches. Roman armies sounded a trumpet when changing the

Thus talking hand in hand alone they passed
On to their blissful bower; it was a place
Chos'n by the sov'reign planter, when he framed
All things to man's delightful use; the roof
Of thickest covert was inwoven shade
Laurel and myrtle, and what higher grew
Of firm and fragrant leaf; on either side
Acanthus, and each odorous bushy shrub
Fenced up the verdant wall; each beauteous flow'r,
Iris all hues, roses, and jessamine
Reared high their flourished heads between, and wrought
Mosaic; underfoot the violet,
Crocus, and hyacinth with rich inlay
Broidered the ground, more colored than with stone
Of costliest emblem: other creature here
Beast, bird, insect, or worm durst enter none;
Such was their awe of man. In shady bower
More sacred and sequestered, though but feigned,
Pan or Silvanus never slept, nor nymph,
Nor Faunus haunted. Here in close recess
With flowers, garlands, and sweet-smelling herbs
Espousèd Eve decked first her nuptial bed,
And heav'nly choirs the hymenaean sung,
What day the genial angel to our sire
Brought her in naked beauty more adorned,
More lovely than Pandora, whom the Gods
Endowed with all their gifts, and O too like

---

watch; angelic guards do it to multipart music (*full harmonic number*).

690. **blissfull bower:** Cp. Spenser's account of the bower within the Garden of Adonis where Venus sequesters the mortally wounded Adonis from "stygian gods" (*FQ* 3.6.43–49).

694. **Laurel and myrtle:** plants sacred to Apollo and Venus, respectively. Cp. Vergil, *Ec.* 2.54–55.

701. **Crocus, and hyacinth:** Atop Mount Ida, the hoodwinked Zeus beds the scheming Hera on these freshly risen flowers (*Il.* 14.348).

703. **emblem:** in the classical sense of a surface with inlaid ornamentation, a mosaic.

705. **shady:** The first edition has "shadier," preferred by some editors.

707–8. **Pan or Silvanus . . . Faunus:** pastoral hybrids, half man and half goat, associated with secret retreats and fecundity. For Pan as a nature god, see 266n.

708. **close:** secluded, exclusive.

709. **flowers:** a rare instance where the two-syllable pronunciation is intended.

711. **hymenaean:** wedding song (after the classical marriage god, Hymen). Cp. *L'All* 125–28; *Elegy 5* 105–8.

712. **genial:** of or relating to marriage; nuptial. In Adam's version, the voice of Eve's "Heav'nly Maker" guides her to Adam (8.484–86).

714–19. **Pandora:** "all gifts" (Gk.); her story was frequently deemed an analogue of the Fall. After Prometheus ("Forethinker") steals heaven's fire for humanity's sake, Pandora is divinely contrived to bring misery upon the world. Bearing a sealed jar containing the world's ills, she is conducted by Hermes to Prometheus' brother, Epimetheus ("Afterthought")—"the unwiser son." After Epimetheus marries her, the evils are released from her jar (*Theog.* 570–612; *Works and Days* 54–105).

In sad event, when to the unwiser son
Of Japhet brought by Hermes, she ensnared
Mankind with her fair looks, to be avenged
On him who had stole Jove's authentic fire.
  Thus at their shady lodge arrived, both stood
Both turned, and under open sky adored
The God that made both sky, air, Earth and heav'n
Which they beheld, the moon's resplendent globe
And starry pole: "Thou also mad'st the night,
Maker omnipotent, and thou the day,
Which we in our appointed work employed
Have finished happy in our mutual help
And mutual love, the crown of all our bliss
Ordained by thee, and this delicious place
For us too large, where thy abundance wants
Partakers, and uncropped falls to the ground.
But thou hast promised from us two a race
To fill the Earth, who shall with us extol
Thy goodness infinite, both when we wake,
And when we seek, as now, thy gift of sleep."
  This said unanimous, and other rites
Observing none, but adoration pure
Which God likes best, into their inmost bow'r
Handed they went; and eased the putting off
These troublesome disguises which we wear,
Straight side by side were laid, nor turned I ween

717. **Japhet:** Christian mythographers identified Iapetus, the Titan father of Prometheus and Epimetheus, as Noah's son Iaphet (Gen. 9.18–10.2).

719. **authentic:** possessing in itself the basis of its existence; genuine, original. Cp. 3.656.

724–35. **Thou . . . sleep:** Cp. Ps. 74.16–17. Milton shifts seamlessly from describing the prayer to quoting it.

724. **pole:** sky.

733. **fill the Earth:** Cp. Gen. 1.28.

735. **gift of sleep:** Cp. Homer, *Il.* 9.713; Vergil, *Aen.* 2.269; Ps. 127.2.

736–38. **This . . . best:** For early readers, the Puritan edge of this prescription for piety would have been keen; cp. 12.534–35.

736. **unanimous:** literally, one-souled.

739. **Handed:** hand in hand, as at line 689.

741–43. **nor . . . refused:** The use of *rites* to mean marital sex was a commonplace warranted by St. Paul's account (Eph. 5.32) of the bodily union of husband and wife as a "mystery" symbolizing Christ's union with the Church (cp. 8.487; Shakespeare, *ADO* 2.1.373, *OTH* 1.3.258; Jonson, *Hymenaei* 137). The reverence expressed here for conjugal coition is ordinarily reserved for sacraments. In related passages, it extends to human genitalia ("mysterious parts") and the "genial bed" (l. 312, 8.598). Insistence that Adam and Eve participate mutually, neither turning away nor refusing, suggests another scriptural source for this passage. *Rite* was often spelled *right* (cp. *CMS, Masque* 125) and included a strong sense of moral obligation. St. Paul deemed refusal of spousal "due benevolence" fraudulent (1 Cor. 7.3–5). Cp. "the starved lover . . . best quitted with disdain" (ll. 769–70).

741. **I ween:** I believe; "used parenthetically rather than as governing the sentence; in verse often a mere tag" (*OED* 1.h). Seventeenth-century retellings of Book 4 suggest that Milton's conviction found a sympathetic audience. Dryden's

Adam from his fair spouse, nor Eve the rites
Mysterious of connubial love refused:
Whatever hypocrites austerely talk
Of purity and place and innocence,
Defaming as impure what God declares
Pure, and commands to some, leaves free to all.
Our Maker bids increase, who bids abstain
But our destroyer, foe to God and man?
Hail wedded love, mysterious law, true source
Of human offspring, sole propriety,
In Paradise of all things common else.
By thee adulterous lust was driv'n from men
Among the bestial herds to range, by thee
Founded in reason, loyal, just, and pure,
Relations dear, and all the charities
Of father, son, and brother first were known.
Far be it, that I should write thee sin or blame,
Or think thee unbefitting holiest place,
Perpetual fountain of domestic sweets,
Whose bed is undefiled and chaste pronounced,
Present, or past, as saints and patriarchs used.
Here love his golden shafts employs, here lights
His constant lamp, and waves his purple wings,
Reigns here and revels; not in the bought smile
Of harlots, loveless, joyless, unendeared,
Casual fruition, nor in court amours
Mixed dance, or wanton masque, or midnight ball,
Or serenade, which the starved lover sings

Satan thus imagines Eve as Semele to his Jove: "Have not I, like these, a body too, / Form'd for the same delights which they pursue? / I could (so variously my passions move) / Enjoy, and blast her in the act of Love" (*State of Innocence* 3.1; cp. Hopkins, *Primitive Loves* 135–235).

744–49. **hypocrites . . . man:** These lines concentrate allusions to various scriptural passages on marriage: 1 Tim. 4.1–3 (*hypocrites*), 1 Cor. 7.1 (*commands to some*), Gen. 1.28 (*Our Maker bids increase*).

751. **propriety:** exclusive possession or right of use; ownership. Wedlock is a prelapsarian institution, unlike private property (with the exception of the nuptial bower).

756. **all the charities:** affections; "comprehends all the relations, all the endearments of consanguinity and affinity" (Newton).

760–65. **Perpetual fountain . . . revels:** The references and diction—*fountain, golden shafts, lamp, purple wings*—are erotically charged and culturally diffuse; cp. 8.511–20. *Reigns here and revels* translates a description of love by Marino (*L'Adone* 2.114), a sensuous Italian poet noteworthy to Milton on account of his patron, Manso, whose acquaintance Milton prized. See *Manso, Damon* 181–97.

761. **bed is undefiled:** Cp. Heb. 13.4.

763. **love:** Cupid, whose golden arrows (*shafts*) infuse love.

768. **Mixed dance:** men and women dancing together, a practice frowned upon by Puritans, including Milton; cp. *Of Ref* (Yale 1:589). **masque:** masquerade ball.

769. **serenade:** serenade (Italian form); **starved:** deprived of love, but also of warmth; cp. 2.600.

To his proud fair, best quitted with disdain.
These lulled by nightingales embracing slept,
And on their naked limbs the flow'ry roof
Show'red roses, which the morn repaired. Sleep on
Blest pair; and O yet happiest if ye seek
No happier state, and know to know no more.
Now had night measured with her shadowy cone
Half way up hill this vast sublunar vault,
And from their ivory port the Cherubim
Forth issuing at th' accustomed hour stood armed
To their night watches in warlike parade,
When Gabriel to his next in power thus spake.
"Uzziel, half these draw off, and coast the south
With strictest watch; these other wheel the north,
Our circuit meets full west." As flame they part
Half wheeling to the shield, half to the spear.
From these, two strong and subtle spirits he called
That near him stood, and gave them thus in charge.
"Ithuriel and Zephon, with winged speed
Search through this garden, leave unsearched no nook,
But chiefly where those two fair creatures lodge,
Now laid perhaps asleep secure of harm.
This evening from the sun's decline arrived
Who tells of some infernal spirit seen
Hitherward bent (who could have thought?) escaped

770. **quitted:** repaid; cp. line 51.

773. **repaired:** restored.

774. **Blest pair:** translates Vergil's celebration of Nisus and Euryalus (*Fortunati ambo!*), intimate friends slain by the enemy at rest in each other's arms (*Aen.* 9.446).

775. Note the repetition of *no* and *know.*

776–77. **shadowy . . . vault:** The earth's globe casts a conical shadow into the night sky, which, reaching from horizon to horizon, is portrayed as an arch (*vault*). At this moment, the *shadowy cone,* moving in diametrical opposition to the sun, has ascended halfway from the eastern horizon toward its midnight zenith. It is therefore nine o'clock, equinoctial time, the start of the second watch (ll. 779–80). Line 777 occurs halfway between line 539, where "the sun *in utmost longitude* begins its descent beneath the horizon, and 1015, the last line of Book 4," which occurs at midnight (Fowler).

778. **ivory port:** Recent editors identify this phrase as an allusion to the ivory gate of the realm of sleep, from which false dreams proceed according to Homer and Vergil (*Od.* 19.562–67; *Aen.* 6.893–96). A significant connection with the guards' imminent interruption of Eve's dream is then proposed. Such a connection is strained. Guards, not personified dreams, issue from this ivory port, which is the gate not of sleep but of Paradise (made of the white stone *alabaster* [l. 544] and thus like ivory in color).

782–85. **Uzziel:** "power of God" (Hebr.). Standing at the eastern gate, Gabriel splits the guard to check the northern and southern perimeters of the Garden until they meet again *full west. Shield* and *spear* translate a Greek idiom designating left and right.

788. **Ithuriel and Zephon:** "Discovery of God" and "Lookout" (Hebr.). Their names denote their roles as they search the interior of the Garden.

791. **secure:** unsuspecting.

793. **Who:** one who; that is, Uriel (see l. 555).

The bars of Hell, on errand bad no doubt:
Such where ye find, seize fast, and hither bring."
So saying, on he led his radiant files,
Dazzling the Moon; these to the bower direct
In search of whom they sought: him there they found
Squat like a toad, close at the ear of Eve;
Assaying by his devilish art to reach
The organs of her fancy, and with them forge
Illusions as he list, phantasms and dreams,
Or if, inspiring venom, he might taint
Th' animal spirits that from pure blood arise
Like gentle breaths from rivers pure, thence raise
At least distempered, discontented thoughts,
Vain hopes, vain aims, inordinate desires
Blown up with high conceits engend'ring pride.
Him thus intent Ithuriel with his spear
Touched lightly; for no falsehood can endure
Touch of celestial temper, but returns
Of force to its own likeness: up he starts
Discovered and surprised. As when a spark
Lights on a heap of nitrous powder, laid
Fit for the tun some magazine to store
Against a rumored war, the smutty grain
With sudden blaze diffused, inflames the air:
So started up in his own shape the fiend.
Back stepped those two faire angels half amazed
So sudden to behold the grisly king;
Yet thus, unmoved with fear, accost him soon.
"Which of those rebel spirits adjudged to Hell
Com'st thou, escaped thy prison, and transformed,

798. **these:** Ithuriel and Zephon.

802. **organs of her fancy:** Satan delves into Eve's psyche to manipulate her *fancy* or imagination, the faculty that produces mental images (*phantasms*). Cp. "raise up the organs of her fantasy" in *WIV* 5.5.55. *Organs* retains its Greek sense of "instruments"; it may also include the specific sense of "musical instrument." In Milton's time, the plural *organs* could mean "pipe organ." In effect, Satan plays upon Eve's mental apparatus as if it were a set of pipes, attempting to forge illusions in a manner reminiscent of the erection of Pandaemonium (1.708ff). Cp. *PR* 4.407–9.

804–9. **inspiring . . . pride:** If unable to play directly on Eve's imagination, Satan hopes to unsettle the perfect humoral balance (*temper*) of her *animal spirits*. These spirits were thought to originate from the blood and carry sensory data to the brain. Breathing venom into (*inspiring*) her ear, he aims to provoke *distempered* impulses and grandiose designs (*high conceits*).

812. **celestial temper:** The spear, like incisive Ithuriel, was produced (*tempered*) in Heaven.

815. **Lights:** lands on and ignites; **nitrous powder:** gunpowder.

816–17. ready for a barrel (*tun*) and storage in an arsenal (*magazine*) as preparation for (*against*) war; **smutty grain:** cereal grain blackened by a parasitic fungus.

821. **grisly:** gruesomely horrible; applied to Death (2.704) and Moloch (*Nat Ode* 209), both of whom are also described as kingly.

Why sat'st thou like an enemy in wait
Here watching at the head of these that sleep?"
"Know ye not then," said Satan, filled with scorn,
"Know ye not me? Ye knew me once no mate
For you, there sitting where ye durst not soar;
Not to know me argues yourselves unknown,
The lowest of your throng; or if ye know,
Why ask ye, and superfluous begin
Your message, like to end as much in vain?"
To whom thus Zephon, answering scorn with scorn.
"Think not, revolted Spirit, thy shape the same,
Or undiminished brightness, to be known
As when thou stood'st in Heav'n upright and pure;
That glory then, when thou no more wast good,
Departed from thee, and thou resemblest now
Thy sin and place of doom obscure and foul.
But come, for thou, be sure, shalt give account
To him who sent us, whose charge is to keep
This place inviolable, and these from harm."
So spake the Cherub, and his grave rebuke
Severe in youthful beauty, added grace
Invincible: abashed the Devil stood,
And felt how awful goodness is, and saw
Virtue in her shape how lovely, saw, and pined
His loss; but chiefly to find here observed
His luster visibly impaired; yet seemed
Undaunted. "If I must contend," said he,
"Best with the best, the sender not the sent,
Or all at once; more glory will be won,
Or less be lost." "Thy fear," said Zephon bold,
"Will save us trial what the least can do
Single against thee wicked, and thence weak."
The fiend replied not, overcome with rage;
But like a proud steed reined, went haughty on,
Champing his iron curb: to strive or fly

830. **argues:** is reason to think.

835–43. Zephon's retorted scorn makes pointed and repeated use of the second person singular (form of address used with inferiors).

836. Bentley would transpose *undiminished brightness*, for reasons grammatical.

845–47. **Severe . . . is:** Satan reacts similarly to the sight of Eve (9.459–62). Cp. Vergil's description of the grave rebuke delivered by the youthful and beautiful Euryalus (*Aen.* 5.344) and Dryden's distillation in *Hind and Panther:* "For vice, though frontless and of hardened face / Is daunted at the sight of awful grace" (3.1040–41).

848. **Virtue . . . lovely:** It is a commonplace of Platonically inspired philosophy and poetry that beauty is the aesthetic expression of virtue or goodness. **pined:** grieved; see 466n.

858–59. **like . . . curb:** The simile echoes Hermes' account of Prometheus (Aeschylus, *Prom.* 1008).

He held it vain; awe from above had quelled
His heart, not else dismayed. Now drew they nigh
The western point, where those half-rounding guards
Just met, and closing stood in squadron joined
Awaiting next command. To whom their chief
Gabriel from the front thus called aloud.
"O friends, I hear the tread of nimble feet
Hasting this way, and now by glimpse discern
Ithuriel and Zephon through the shade,
And with them comes a third of regal port,
But faded splendor wan; who by his gait
And fierce demeanor seems the Prince of Hell,
Not likely to part hence without contest;
Stand firm, for in his look defiance lours."
He scarce had ended, when those two approached
And brief related whom they brought, where found,
How busied, in what form and posture couched.
To whom with stern regard thus Gabriel spake.
"Why hast thou, Satan, broke the bounds prescribed
To thy transgressions, and disturbed the charge
Of others, who approve not to transgress
By thy example, but have power and right
To question thy bold entrance on this place;
Employed it seems to violate sleep, and those
Whose dwelling God hath planted here in bliss?
To whom thus Satan, with contemptuous brow.
"Gabriel, thou hadst in Heav'n th' esteem of wise,
And such I held thee; but this question asked
Puts me in doubt. Lives there who loves his pain?
Who would not, finding way, break loose from Hell,
Though thither doomed? Thou wouldst thyself, no doubt,
And boldly venture to whatever place
Farthest from pain, where thou mightst hope to change
Torment with ease, and soonest recompense
Dole with delight, which in this place I sought;

862. **half-rounding:** See 782–85n.

868. **shade:** trees.

870–71. Verity and Fowler take Gabriel's easy recognition of Satan as validation of his aristocratic slap at Zephon (l. 830), but Gabriel goes by gait, bearing (*port*), and demeanor, which Zephon had little chance to observe before Satan identified himself.

879. **transgressions:** both "sins" (as in l. 880) and "boundary crossings"; though sentenced to Hell for his crimes, Satan now trespasses in Paradise (see l. 909). **charge:** responsibility; child or member of a minister's congregation under protection.

880. **approve:** agree; try or test (see Satan's rejoinder, l. 896).

886. **esteem of wise:** reputation for good sense.

893–94. **recompense . . .delight:** exchange pain for pleasure.

To thee no reason; who know'st only good,
But evil hast not tried: and wilt object
His will who bound us? Let him surer bar
His iron gates, if he intends our stay
In that dark durance: thus much what was asked.
The rest is true, they found me where they say;
But that implies not violence or harm."
Thus he in scorn. The warlike angel moved,
Disdainfully half smiling thus replied.
"O loss of one in Heav'n to judge of wise,
Since Satan fell, whom folly overthrew,
And now returns him from his prison scaped,
Gravely in doubt whether to hold them wise
Or not, who ask what boldness brought him hither
Unlicensed from his bounds in Hell prescribed;
So wise he judges it to fly from pain
However, and to scape his punishment.
So judge thou still, presumptuous, till the wrath,
Which thou incurr'st by flying, meet thy flight
Sevenfold, and scourge that wisdom back to Hell,
Which taught thee yet no better, that no pain
Can equal anger infinite provoked.
But wherefore thou alone? Wherefore with thee
Came not all Hell broke loose? Is pain to them
Less pain, less to be fled, or thou than they
Less hardy to endure? Courageous chief,
The first in flight from pain, hadst thou alleged
To thy deserted host this cause of flight,
Thou surely hadst not come sole fugitive."
To which the fiend thus answered frowning stern.
"Not that I less endure, or shrink from pain,
Insulting angel, well thou know'st I stood
Thy fiercest, when in battle to thy aid
The blasting volleyed thunder made all speed
And seconded thy else not dreaded spear.
But still thy words at random, as before,

896. **object:** raise as an objection.

899. **durance:** forced confinement; **thus much what:** so much (in reply to) what.

904. Gabriel ironically laments the loss of Satan as an arbiter of wisdom; see line 886.

906. **returns:** can take either *Satan* (archaic usage, reflexive) or *folly* as its subject.

911. **However:** by any means.

926. **stood:** withstood.

928. **The:** per first edition; second edition has "Thy."

930–33. **But . . . Leader:** Gabriel's remarks, says Satan, reveal his ignorance about how a dedicated leader ought to proceed after arduous undertakings and failures.

930. **at random:** without discrimination.

Argue thy inexperience what behooves
From hard assays and ill successes past
A faithful Leader, not to hazard all
Through ways of danger by himself untried.
I therefore, I alone first undertook
To wing the desolate abyss, and spy
This new created world, whereof in Hell
Fame is not silent, here in hope to find
Better abode, and my afflicted powers
To settle here on Earth, or in mid-air;
Though for possession put to try once more
What thou and thy gay legions dare against;
Whose easier business were to serve their Lord
High up in Heav'n, with songs to hymn his throne,
And practiced distances to cringe, not fight."
To whom the warrior angel, soon replied.
"To say and straight unsay, pretending first
Wise to fly pain, professing next the spy,
Argues no leader but a liar traced,
Satan, and couldst thou faithful add? O name,
O sacred name of faithfulness profaned!
Faithful to whom? To thy rebellious crew?
Army of fiends, fit body to fit head;
Was this your discipline and faith engaged,
Your military obedience, to dissolve
Allegiance to th' acknowledged power supreme?
And thou sly hypocrite, who now wouldst seem
Patron of liberty, who more than thou
Once fawned, and cringed, and servilely adored
Heav'n's awful Monarch? Wherefore but in hope
To dispossess him, and thyself to reign?
But mark what I aread thee now, avaunt;
Fly thither whence thou fledd'st: if from this hour
Within these hallowed limits thou appear,

939. **afflicted:** struck down (cp. 1.186).

940. **mid-air:** After the Fall, Satan rules the middle region of the air, which extends as high as the mountaintops (1.516–17). See *PR* 1.39–47, 2.117; Eph. 2.2, 6.12.

942. **gay:** ebullient, showy, self-indulgent; a pointed retort to Zephon (ll. 838–40).

945. **practiced distances:** applies both to courtly protocol (*cringe*) and martial training, especially swordplay (*fight*).

949. Replying to Satan at lines 930–34.

958–60. Gabriel's reply allows that Heaven is a realm of groveling toadies (Empson 1965, 111). Fowler counters that the response simply conforms to Satan's insulting tenor (ll. 942–45). Cp. Prometheus' scornful words to Zeus's followers: "Worship, adore, and fawn upon . . . thy lord" (Aeschylus, *Prom.* 937).

962. **aread:** advise, order; **avaunt:** begone; diction used especially for expulsion of evil spirits.

Back to th' infernal pit I drag thee chained,
And seal thee so, as henceforth not to scorn
The facile gates of Hell too slightly barred."
So threat'ned he, but Satan to no threats
Gave heed, but waxing more in rage replied.
"Then when I am thy captive talk of chains,
Proud limitary Cherub, but ere then
Far heavier load thy self expect to feel
From my prevailing arm, though Heaven's King
Ride on thy wings, and thou with thy compeers,
Used to the yoke, draw'st his triumphant wheels
In progress through the road of Heav'n star-paved."
While thus he spake, th' angelic squadron bright
Turned fiery red, sharp'ning in moonèd horns
Their phalanx, and began to hem him round
With ported spears, as thick as when a field
Of Ceres ripe for harvest waving bends
Her bearded grove of ears, which way the wind
Sways them; the careful plowman doubting stands
Lest on the threshing floor his hopeful sheaves
Prove chaff. On th' other side Satan alarmed

965–67. With Gabriel's threat to *drag* a *chained* Satan to the pit and *seal* him there (note the emphatic present tense), Milton returns to the apocalyptic context evoked at lines 1–12 (Rev. 20.1–3).

967. **facile:** easily negotiated; the diction implies negligence, as does *too slightly barred,* though again Gabriel may only be responding in Satan's scornful terms (ll. 898–99).

971. **limitary:** stationed at a border or boundary; of limited authority (in reply to l. 964).

974. **Ride on thy wings:** "He rode upon a Cherub and did fly" (Ps. 18.10).

975–76. Satan refers to God's chariot (6.750ff); cp. Ezek. 1, 10, 11.22.

976. **progress:** royal tour.

978–80. **sharp'ning . . . spears:** Taken in their most specific military senses, *phalanx* and *ported* are inconsistent. Troops in a classical Greek *phalanx* interlock shields in a square formation and carry their spears projecting forward. *Ported spears* are held diagonally, across the body, spearhead at the left shoulder. The movement into a crescent shape (*sharp'ning in moonèd horns*) suggests that *phalanx* here is used in its more general sense of a group moving closely together.

980–83. **With . . . them:** The comparison of a group of warriors to a windswept field of grain is common in epic, beginning with Homer (*Il.* 2.147–50). Leonard argues that the simile, commonly used of demoralized troops (like a field of grain flattened by wind), implies the good angels' weakness. Milton's simile departs from its precedents, however. Gabriel's troops, spears ported, form a thick semicircle around Satan. Viewed together, the shafts of their spears would appear to slant in several directions, like stalks in a field of grain *waving* in the uncertain wind that precedes a storm.

981. **Ceres:** goddess of grain, mother of Proserpine (cp. 268–72n).

983–85. **the careful plowman . . . chaff:** The subject conveyed by *the careful plowman* is not clear. Satan seems an unlikely candidate in light of line 985. The identification of God as the plowman is more likely in light of literary precedent, the designation of God in this book as the planter of the Garden, and the scriptural imagery of sheaves and chaff, which fits the apocalyptic role of God. The choice attributed to the plowman is also consistent with subsequent imagery of God's scales.

Collecting all his might dilated stood,
Like Teneriffe or Atlas unremoved:
His stature reached the sky, and on his crest
Sat Horror plumed; nor wanted in his grasp
What seemed both spear and shield: now dreadful deeds
Might have ensued, nor only Paradise
In this commotion, but the starry cope
Of Heav'n perhaps, or all the elements
At least had gone to wrack, disturbed and torn
With violence of this conflict, had not soon
Th' Eternal to prevent such horrid fray
Hung forth in Heav'n his golden scales, yet seen
Betwixt Astrea and the Scorpion sign,
Wherein all things created first he weighed,
The pendulous round Earth with balanced air
In counterpoise, now ponders all events,
Battles and realms: in these he put two weights
The sequel each of parting and of fight;
The latter quick up flew, and kicked the beam;
Which Gabriel spying, thus bespake the fiend.
"Satan, I know thy strength, and thou know'st mine,
Neither our own but giv'n; what folly then
To boast what arms can do, since thine no more
Than Heav'n permits, nor mine, though doubled now

986. **dilated:** enlarged, owing to spirits' ability to shrink or swell at will (cp. 1.428–29).

987. **Teneriffe or Atlas unremoved:** The summit of Mount *Teneriffe* (two miles high, in the Canary Islands) was in Milton's century estimated at "fifteen miles" (Hume). **Atlas:** cloud-capped mountain in Libya on which the sky was imagined to rest, per the myth of Atlas. **unremoved:** Latinate past participle meaning immovable (cp. l. 493). The usage is likely ironic. Faith can move mountains (1 Cor. 13.2), as angels provoked by Satan amply demonstrate (6.645–49).

988. **His stature reached the sky:** Homer's description of Discord and Vergil's of Rumor are usually adduced (*Il.* 4.443; *Aen.* 4.177), but the rendition of Passover night in the apocryphal Wisdom of Solomon is a more apt precedent for the configuration of the scene: "Night in her swift course was half spent, when thy almighty Word leapt from thy royal throne in heaven into the midst of that doomed land like a relentless warrior . . . and stood and filled it all with death, his head touching the heavens, his feet on earth" (14–16).

992. **cope:** vault; see 776–77n. The threat seems overstated given God's authority over creatures: he curbs angelic muscle to preserve the landscape during the War in Heaven (6.225–29), and Gabriel will soon claim that his strength has been doubled (ll. 1006–10).

997. **golden scales:** translates Homer's phrase for the balance in which Zeus weighs destinies of opposed armies or warriors (*Il.* 8.69, 22.209). Here it refers to the constellation Libra (the *scales*) between *Astrea and the Scorpion sign.*

998. **Astrea:** the constellation of Virgo (the Virgin). *Astrea,* goddess of justice, resided on earth during the Golden Age, but human iniquity drove her up to heaven, where she became this constellation (Ovid, *Met.* 1.149ff).

999–1001. **Wherein . . . counterpoise:** Weight is a crucial quality in Scripture, where God as creator and judge is repeatedly depicted as using a scale (Job 28.24ff, Isa. 40.12, 1 Sam. 2.3).

1001. **ponders:** weighs, deliberates.

To trample thee as mire: for proof look up,
And read thy lot in yon celestial sign
Where thou art weigh'd, and shown how light, how weak,
If thou resist. The fiend looked up and knew
His mounted scale aloft: nor more; but fled
Murmuring, and with him fled the shades of night.

1012. In Homer and Vergil, the loser's balance sinks; the victor's ascends. But Milton follows scriptural precedent: "Thou art weighed in the balances and art found wanting" (Dan. 5.27). Gabriel's reading seems inconsistent with the claim that God weighs *the sequel each of parting and of fight* (l. 1003). The outcome is nevertheless consistent with Gabriel's threat to apprehend Satan only if he refused to depart (ll. 965–67).

1014. **nor more:** nor (said) more.

1015. Cp. the final lines of Vergil's *Aen.*

"Eastward among those trees, what glorious shape / Comes this way moving" (5.309–10).

Book V

The Argument

Morning approached, Eve relates to Adam her troublesome dream; he likes it not, yet comforts her. They come forth to their day labors. Their morning hymn at the door of their bower. God to render man inexcusable sends Raphael to admonish him of his obedience, of his free estate, of his enemy near at hand; who he is, and why his enemy, and whatever else may avail Adam to know. Raphael comes down to Paradise, his appearance described, his coming discerned by Adam afar off sitting at the door of his bower. He goes out to meet him, brings him to his lodge, entertains him with the choicest fruits of Paradise got together by Eve; their discourse at table. Raphael performs his message, minds Adam of his state and of his enemy; relates at Adam's request who that enemy is, and how he came to be so, beginning from his first revolt in Heaven, and the occasion thereof; how he drew his legions after him to the parts of the north, and there incited them to rebel with him, persuading all but only Abdiel, a Seraph, who in argument dissuades and opposes him, then forsakes him.

Now Morn her rosy steps in th' eastern clime
Advancing, sowed the earth with orient pearl,
When Adam waked, so customed, for his sleep
Was airy light, from pure digestion bred,
And temperate vapors bland, which th' only sound
Of leaves and fuming rills, Aurora's fan,
Lightly dispersed, and the shrill matin song
Of birds on every bough; so much the more
His wonder was to find unwakened Eve
With tresses discomposed, and glowing cheek,

5. **temperate vapors bland:** soothing and perfectly proportioned vapors. Sleep, it was believed, was caused by vapors arising in the stomach. Adam's benign internal system is here perfectly blended with the external breezes and streams of Eden. **th' only sound:** the sound only.

6. **fuming rills:** foaming brooks; some editors gloss fuming as "misting," but the exhalations of lines 185–6 are not said to rise from streams. **Aurora:** goddess of the dawn.

As through unquiet rest: he on his side
Leaning half-raised, with looks of cordial love
Hung over her enamored, and beheld
Beauty, which whether waking or asleep,
Shot forth peculiar graces; then with voice
Mild, as when Zephyrus on Flora breathes,
Her hand soft touching, whispered thus. "Awake
My fairest, my espoused, my latest found,
Heav'n's last best gift, my ever new delight,
Awake, the morning shines, and the fresh field
Calls us; we lose the prime, to mark how spring
Our tended plants, how blows the citron grove,
What drops the myrrh, and what the balmy reed,
How nature paints her colors, how the bee
Sits on the bloom extracting liquid sweet."
Such whispering waked her, but with startled eye
On Adam, whom embracing, thus she spoke.
"O sole in whom my thoughts find all repose,
My glory, my perfection, glad I see
Thy face, and morn returned, for I this night,
Such night till this I never passed, have dreamed,
If dreamed, not as I oft am wont, of thee,
Works of day past, or morrow's next design,
But of offense and trouble, which my mind
Knew never till this irksome night; methought
Close at mine ear one called me forth to walk
With gentle voice, I thought it thine; it said,
'Why sleep'st thou Eve? Now is the pleasant time,
The cool, the silent, save where silence yields
To the night-warbling bird, that now awake
Tunes sweetest his love-labored song; now reigns
Full orbed the moon, and with more pleasing light
Shadowy sets off the face of things; in vain,
If none regard; heav'n wakes with all his eyes,
Whom to behold but thee, nature's desire,
In whose sight all things joy, with ravishment

15. **peculiar:** its [beauty's] own, from the Latin *peculium,* "private property."

16. **Zephyrus on Flora breathes:** The west wind (*Zephyrus*) blows gently (*breathes*) on the flowers (*Flora,* goddess of flowers).

17–25. **Awake . . . liquid sweet:** The language of Adam's aubade is drawn from Song of Solomon 2.10–13, 7.12.

21. **prime:** sunrise, or the first hour of the day, which in Paradise is always six o'clock.

22. **blows:** blooms.

23. **balmy reed:** balsam.

38. **Why sleep'st thou Eve?:** Satan used much the same formula, as we will soon learn (l. 673), to awaken Beëlzebub, his first co-conspirator.

44. **his eyes:** the stars.

Attracted by thy beauty still to gaze.'
I rose as at thy call, but found thee not;
To find thee I directed then my walk;
And on, methought, alone I passed through ways
That brought me on a sudden to the tree
Of interdicted knowledge: fair it seemed,
Much fairer to my fancy than by day:
And as I wond'ring looked, beside it stood
One shaped and winged like one of those from Heav'n
By us oft seen; his dewy locks distilled
Ambrosia; on that tree he also gazed;
And 'O fair plant,' said he, 'with fruit surcharged,
Deigns none to ease thy load and taste thy sweet,
Nor god, nor man; is knowledge so despised?
Or envy, or what reserve forbids to taste?
Forbid who will, none shall from me withhold
Longer thy offered good, why else set here?'
This said he paused not, but with vent'rous arm
He plucked, he tasted; me damp horror chilled
At such bold words vouched with a deed so bold:
But he thus overjoyed, 'O fruit divine,
Sweet of thyself, but much more sweet thus cropped,
Forbidden here, it seems, as only fit
For gods, yet able to make gods of men:
And why not gods of men, since good, the more
Communicated, more abundant grows,
The author not impaired, but honored more?
Here, happy creature, fair angelic Eve,
Partake thou also; happy though thou art,
Happier thou may'st be, worthier canst not be:
Taste this, and be henceforth among the gods
Thyself a goddess, not to Earth confined,
But sometimes in the air, as we, sometimes
Ascend to Heav'n, by merit thine, and see
What life the gods live there, and such live thou.'
So saying, he drew nigh, and to me held,
Even to my mouth of that same fruit held part
Which he had plucked; the pleasant savory smell

47. **still:** always.

60. **god:** angel. See *CD* 1.5.

61. **reserve:** referring to both God's restriction on the fruit and man's self-restraint.

65. **horror chilled:** Cp. 9.890.

66. **vouched with:** affirmed by.

79. "The words *as we* are so placed between the two sentences, as equally to relate to both" (Todd).

So quickened appetite, that I, methought,
Could not but taste. Forthwith up to the clouds
With him I flew, and underneath beheld
The Earth outstretched immense, a prospect wide
And various: wond'ring at my flight and change
To this high exaltation; suddenly
My guide was gone, and I, methought, sunk down,
And fell asleep; but O how glad I waked
To find this but a dream!" Thus Eve her night
Related, and thus Adam answered sad.
　　"Best image of myself and dearer half,
The trouble of thy thoughts this night in sleep
Affects me equally; nor can I like
This uncouth dream, of evil sprung I fear;
Yet evil whence? In thee can harbor none,
Created pure. But know that in the soul
Are many lesser faculties that serve
Reason as chief; among these Fancy next
Her office holds; of all external things,
Which the five watchful senses represent,
She forms imaginations, airy shapes,
Which reason joining or disjoining, frames
All what we affirm or what deny, and call
Our knowledge or opinion; then retires
Into her private cell when nature rests,
Oft in her absence mimic Fancy wakes
To imitate her; but misjoining shapes,
Wild work produces oft, and most in dreams,
Ill matching words and deeds long past or late.
Some such resemblances methinks I find
Of our last evening's talk, in this thy dream,
But with addition strange; yet be not sad.
Evil into the mind of god or man
May come or go, so unapproved, and leave
No spot or blame behind: Which gives me hope

94. **sad:** grave, serious.

98. **uncouth:** strange, unpleasant.

100–13. **But . . . late:** The main outlines of this conventional account of the role of "Fancy" (sometimes called "Phantasy") in dreaming can be found in Renaissance encyclopedias (Svendsen 1969, 36–38); Sir John Davies, *Nosce Teipsum,* 46–47; and Robert Burton, *The Anatomy of Melancholy,* 139–40.

109. **cell:** ventricle of the brain.

115. **our last evening's talk:** Yesterday they spoke in general of the prohibition on the Tree of Knowledge (4.419–28) and, prompted by Eve's question, about why the stars shine at night (4.657–88). Both concerns reappear in Eve's dream. Yet only the second conversation took place at evening.

118. **so:** provided that it remains; **unapproved:** unchosen.

That what in sleep thou didst abhor to dream,
Waking thou never wilt consent to do.
Be not disheartened then, nor cloud those looks
That wont to be more cheerful and serene
Than when fair morning first smiles on the world,
And let us to our fresh employments rise
Among the groves, the fountains, and the flow'rs
That open now their choicest bosomed smells
Reserved from night, and kept for thee in store."
So cheered he his fair spouse, and she was cheered,
But silently a gentle tear let fall
From either eye, and wiped them with her hair;
Two other precious drops that ready stood,
Each in their crystal sluice, he ere they fell
Kissed as the gracious signs of sweet remorse
And pious awe, that feared to have offended.
So all was cleared, and to the field they haste.
But first from under shady arborous roof,
Soon as they forth were come to open sight
Of day-spring, and the sun, who scarce up risen
With wheels yet hov'ring o'er the ocean brim,
Shot parallel to the Earth his dewy ray,
Discovering in wide landscape all the east
Of Paradise and Eden's happy plains,
Lowly they bowed adoring, and began
Their orisons, each morning duly paid
In various style, for neither various style
Nor holy rapture wanted they to praise
Their Maker, in fit strains pronounced or sung
Unmeditated, such prompt eloquence
Flowed from their lips, in prose or numerous verse,
More tuneable than needed lute or harp
To add more sweetness, and they thus began.
"These are thy glorious works, parent of good,
Almighty, thine this universal frame,

123. **wont to be:** are accustomed to being.

133–34. **he ere they fell/Kissed:** Adam's tender gesture enacts the words *be not sad* (l. 116) and *Be not disheartened then, nor cloud those looks* (l. 122) from his just-concluded speech.

146–50. Their morning prayers unite the fallen alternatives of deliberate artistic elaboration (*various style*), favored by Anglicans in Milton's day, and spontaneous inspiration (*holy rapture, Unmeditated*), favored by Puritans.

147. **wanted:** lacked.

150. **numerous:** subject to numbers, therefore measured, rhythmic, musical.

153–208. Giving voice to Creation, the orisons evoke Psalm 148 primarily, with touches drawn from the "Song of the Three Children," prescribed for morning prayers as the canticle "Benedicite omnia opera Domini" in the Book of Common Prayer.

Thus wondrous fair; thyself how wondrous then!
Unspeakable, who sit'st above these heavens
To us invisible or dimly seen
In these thy lowest works, yet these declare
Thy goodness beyond thought, and power divine:
Speak ye who best can tell, ye sons of light,
Angels, for ye behold him, and with songs
And choral symphonies, day without night,
Circle his throne rejoicing, ye in Heav'n,
On Earth join all ye creatures to extol
Him first, him last, him midst, and without end.
Fairest of stars, last in the train of night,
If better thou belong not to the dawn,
Sure pledge of day, that crown'st the smiling morn
With thy bright circlet, praise him in thy sphere
While day arises, that sweet hour of prime.
Thou sun, of this great world both eye and soul,
Acknowledge him thy greater, sound his praise
In thy eternal course, both when thou climb'st,
And when high noon hast gained, and when thou fall'st.
Moon, that now meet'st the orient sun, now fli'st
With the fixed stars, fixed in their orb that flies,
And ye five other wand'ring fires that move
In mystic dance not without song, resound
His praise, who out of darkness called up light.
Air, and ye elements the eldest birth
Of nature's womb, that in quaternion run
Perpetual circle, multiform, and mix
And nourish all things, let your ceaseless change
Vary to our great Maker still new praise.
Ye mists and exhalations that now rise
From hill or steaming lake, dusky or gray,
Till the sun paint your fleecy skirts with gold,
In honor to the world's great author rise;
Whether to deck with clouds the uncolored sky,
Or wet the thirsty earth with falling showers,
Rising or falling still advance his praise.
His praise ye winds, that from four quarters blow,

165. Cp. Rev. 22.13 ("I am the Alpha and the Omega, the first and the last"), and Ben Jonson, "To Heaven," l. 10.

166–67. **Fairest of stars:** Venus or Lucifer; **last . . . dawn:** Venus, the last star of morning, is also, as Hesperus, the first star of evening.

178. **not without song:** the music of the spheres, inaudible on Earth after the Fall; see *Nat Ode* 125–29, *Arcades* 63–73.

181. **in quaternion:** in a group of four (earth, air, fire, and water).

Breathe soft or loud; and wave your tops, ye pines,
With every plant, in sign of worship wave.
Fountains and ye that warble as ye flow
Melodious murmurs, warbling tune his praise.
Join voices all ye living souls, ye birds,
That singing up to heaven gate ascend,
Bear on your wings and in your notes his praise;
Ye that in waters glide, and ye that walk
The earth, and stately tread, or lowly creep;
Witness if I be silent, morn or even,
To hill, or valley, fountain, or fresh shade
Made vocal by my song, and taught his praise.
Hail universal Lord, be bounteous still
To give us only good; and if the night
Have gathered aught of evil or concealed,
Disperse it, as now light dispels the dark."
  So prayed they innocent, and to their thoughts
Firm peace recovered soon and wonted calm.
On to their morning's rural work they haste
Among sweet dews and flow'rs; where any row
Of fruit trees over-woody reached too far
Their pampered boughs, and needed hands to check
Fruitless embraces: or they led the vine
To wed her elm; she spoused about him twines
Her marriageable arms, and with her brings
Her dow'r th' adopted clusters, to adorn
His barren leaves. Them thus employed beheld
With pity Heav'n's high King, and to him called
Raphael, the sociable spirit, that deigned
To travel with Tobias, and secured
His marriage with the seven-times-wedded maid.
  "Raphael," said he, "thou hear'st what stir on Earth
Satan from Hell scaped through the darksome gulf
Hath raised in Paradise, and how disturbed
This night the human pair, how he designs
In them at once to ruin all mankind.
Go therefore, half this day as friend with friend
Converse with Adam, in what bow'r or shade

205. **still:** always.

214. **pampered:** overgrown.

215–19. **Fruitless embraces . . . leaves:** The feminine vine curled about the masculine elm was a traditional emblem of marriage; cp. Eve's vine-like hair at 4.307.

221–23. *Raphael,* Hebrew for "Health of God," helps Tobias claim his bride in the apocryphal Book of Tobit. Raphael is often associated with Christian medicine; see Cotton Mather, 48–54.

Thou find'st him from the heat of noon retired,
To respite his day-labor with repast,
Or with repose; and such discourse bring on,
As may advise him of his happy state,
Happiness in his power left free to will,
Left to his own free will, his will though free,
Yet mutable; whence warn him to beware
He swerve not too secure: tell him withal
His danger, and from whom, what enemy
Late fall'n himself from Heav'n is plotting now
The fall of others from like state of bliss;
By violence, no, for that shall be withstood,
But by deceit and lies; this let him know,
Lest willfully transgressing he pretend
Surprisal, unadmonished, unforewarned."
So spake th' eternal Father, and fulfilled
All justice: nor delayed the wingèd saint
After his charge received, but from among
Thousand celestial ardors, where he stood
Veiled with his gorgeous wings, up springing light
Flew through the midst of Heav'n; th' angelic choirs
On each hand parting, to his speed gave way
Through all th' empyreal road; till at the gate
Of Heav'n arrived, the gate self-opened wide
On golden hinges turning, as by work
Divine the sov'reign architect had framed.
From hence, no cloud, or, to obstruct his sight,
Star interposed, however small he sees,
Not unconform to other shining globes,
Earth and the gard'n of God, with cedars crowned
Above all hills. As when by night the glass
Of Galileo, less assured, observes
Imagined lands and regions in the moon:
Or pilot from amidst the Cyclades

238. **swerve:** err; **secure:** overconfident.

244–45. **pretend/Surprisal:** claim to have been the victim of a surprise attack.

249. **ardors:** angels, ardent (burning) with the love of God.

250. **Veiled:** Cp. 3.382.

253. **empyreal:** belonging to the empyrean realm beyond the outermost sphere of Creation.

254. **self-opened:** Cp. the grating gates of Hell at 2.881–82.

257–59. No cloud or star interposed itself between Raphael and the sight of Earth, which appeared as small as the other stars.

259. **Not unconform to:** like to.

263. **Imagined:** conjectured. Galileo's conjectures about lunar topography are not rejected at 1.288–91; Raphael seems to sanction their rejection at 5.419–20, but leaves the question open at 8.144–45.

264–65. **Cyclades . . . Samos:** islands in the

Delos or Samos first appearing kens
A cloudy spot. Down thither prone in flight
He speeds, and through the vast ethereal sky
Sails between worlds and worlds, with steady wing
Now on the polar winds, then with quick fan
Winnows the buxom air; till within soar
Of tow'ring eagles, to all the fowls he seems
A phoenix, gazed by all, as that sole bird
When to enshrine his relics in the sun's
Bright temple, to Egyptian Thebes he flies.
At once on th' eastern cliff of Paradise
He lights, and to his proper shape returns
A Seraph winged; six wings he wore, to shade
His lineaments divine; the pair that clad
Each shoulder broad, came mantling o'er his breast
With regal ornament; the middle pair
Girt like a starry zone his waist, and round
Skirted his loins and thighs with downy gold
And colors dipped in Heav'n; the third his feet
Shadowed from either heel with feathered mail
Sky-tinctured grain. Like Maia's son he stood,
And shook his plumes, that Heav'nly fragrance filled
The circuit wide. Straight knew him all the bands
Of Angels under watch; and to his state,
And to his message high in honor rise;
For on some message high they guessed him bound.
Their glittering tents he passed, and now is come
Into the blissful field, through groves of myrrh,
And flow'ring odors, cassia, nard, and balm;
A wilderness of sweets; for nature here
Wantoned as in her prime, and played at will

Aegean, including the supposedly floating island of *Delos; Samos,* an island off the coast of Asia Minor, did not belong to the Cyclades.

265. **kens:** discerns.

266. **prone:** bent forward and downward.

270. **Winnows the buxom air:** parts the yielding air. On *buxom* see 2.842n and *L'All* 24n.

271. **tow'ring eagles:** Descending Raphael has just reached the apex of ascending eagles.

271–74. **to all . . . flies:** To earthly birds, the bright and unique Raphael seems a phoenix. This mythical bird, of which there was only one, regenerated every five hundred or one thousand years by immolating itself, then depositing its own ashes (*relics*) at the temple of the sun in the Egyptian city of Heliopolis.

277. **six wings:** like the angels in Isa. 6.2.

279. **mantling:** covering him, as with a mantle.

281. **starry zone:** belt of stars (cp. 11.247).

284. **feathered mail:** The feathers lie in overlapping rows suggestive of the metal plates in mail armor.

285. **Sky-tinctured:** blue, a sacred color among the Israelites, as Fowler notes, citing Cowley's *Davideis,* bk. 1, n. 60; **grain:** dye; **Maia's son:** Mercury, messenger of the gods.

288. **state:** status.

293. **cassia, nard, and balm:** aromatic spices.

Her virgin fancies, pouring forth more sweet,
Wild above rule or art; enormous bliss.
Him through the spicy forest onward come
Adam discerned, as in the door he sat
Of his cool bow'r, while now the mounted sun
Shot down direct his fervid rays to warm
Earth's inmost womb, more warmth than Adam needs;
And Eve within, due at her hour prepared
For dinner savory fruits, of taste to please
True appetite, and not disrelish thirst
Of nectarous draughts between, from milky stream,
Berry or grape: to whom thus Adam called.
"Haste hither Eve, and worth thy sight behold
Eastward among those trees, what glorious shape
Comes this way moving; seems another morn
Ris'n on mid-noon; some great behest from Heav'n
To us perhaps he brings, and will vouchsafe
This day to be our guest. But go with speed,
And what thy stores contain, bring forth and pour
Abundance, fit to honor and receive
Our Heav'nly stranger; well we may afford
Our givers their own gifts, and large bestow
From large bestowed, where nature multiplies
Her fertile growth, and by disburd'ning grows
More fruitful, which instructs us not to spare."
To whom thus Eve. "Adam, earth's hallowed mold
Of God inspired, small store will serve, where store,
All seasons, ripe for use hangs on the stalk;
Save what by frugal storing firmness gains
To nourish, and superfluous moist consumes:
But I will haste and from each bough and brake,
Each plant and juiciest gourd will pluck such choice
To entertain our angel guest, as he
Beholding shall confess that here on Earth
God hath dispensed his bounties as in Heav'n."

296. **more sweet:** Nature's splurging sweetness recalls Eve at 4.439, 641–56. She translates this aspect of Eden into the spiritual Paradise of their marriage.

297. **Wild above rule or art:** The organic at its height is superior to artifice at its height, as we have just seen in the "clothing" of Raphael; **enormous:** beyond the norm, immense.

300. **while now:** Raphael arrives precisely at noon.

305. **disrelish:** destroy the relish for.

306. **nectarous:** as sweet as nectar; **milky:** sweet (not salty).

319. **disburd'ning:** harvesting.

321. **earth's hallowed mold:** *Adam* is sometimes said to derive from the Hebrew for "red," alluding to the red earth from which he was formed.

324. **frugal:** careful in the use of food (from Lat. *frux*, "fruit"). Thriftiness is not implied.

So saying, with dispatchful looks in haste
She turns, on hospitable thoughts intent
What choice to choose for delicacy best,
What order, so contrived as not to mix
Tastes, not well joined, inelegant, but bring
Taste after taste upheld with kindliest change,
Bestirs her then, and from each tender stalk
Whatever Earth all-bearing mother yields
In India east or west, or middle shore
In Pontus or the Punic Coast, or where
Alcinous reigned, fruit of all kinds, in coat,
Rough, or smooth rined, or bearded husk, or shell
She gathers, tribute large, and on the board
Heaps with unsparing hand; for drink the grape
She crushes, inoffensive must, and meathes
From many a berry, and from sweet kernels pressed
She tempers dulcet creams, nor these to hold
Wants her fit vessels pure, then strews the ground
With rose and odors from the shrub unfumed.
Meanwhile our primitive great sire, to meet
His godlike guest, walks forth, without more train
Accompanied than with his own complete
Perfections, in himself was all his state,
More solemn than the tedious pomp that waits
On princes, when their rich retinue long
Of horses led, and grooms besmeared with gold
Dazzles the crowd, and sets them all agape.
Nearer his presence Adam though not awed,
Yet with submiss approach and reverence meek,
As to a superior nature, bowing low,
Thus said. "Native of Heav'n, for other place
None can than Heav'n such glorious shape contain;
Since by descending from the thrones above,

333–36. "Eve's composing of food" is "a trope for poetry" (D. McColley 1993, 133), the culinary equivalent of Milton's "the sense variously drawn out from one verse into another" (see his note on *The Verse,* p. 291).

339. **India:** Indies; **middle shore:** lands to the north (*Pontus,* the shore of the Black Sea) and the south (*Punic,* the shore of North Africa) of the Mediterranean Sea.

341. **Alcinous:** Homer's King of the Phaeacians, whose garden bore fruit in every season (*Od.* 7.112–32).

345. **meathes:** sweet drinks; obsolete spelling of *meads.*

346. Metrically, the double anapests make for an unusual line.

349. **unfumed:** unburned (unlike incense in the fallen world).

350. **primitive:** primary, original.

353. **state:** ceremonial display.

356. **besmeared with gold:** See Horace, *Odes* 4.9.14f.

Those happy places thou hast deigned a while
To want, and honor these, vouchsafe with us
Two only, who yet by sov'reign gift possess
This spacious ground, in yonder shady bow'r
To rest, and what the garden choicest bears
To sit and taste, till this meridian heat
Be over, and the sun more cool decline."
 Whom thus the angelic Virtue answered mild.
"Adam, I therefore came, nor art thou such
Created, or such place hast here to dwell,
As may not oft invite, though spirits of Heav'n
To visit thee; lead on then where thy bow'r
O'ershades; for these mid-hours, till evening rise
I have at will." So to the sylvan lodge
They came, that like Pomona's arbor smiled
With flow'rets decked and fragrant smells; but Eve
Undecked, save with herself more lovely fair
Than wood-nymph, or the fairest goddess feigned
Of three that in Mount Ida naked strove,
Stood to entertain her guest from Heav'n; no veil
She needed, virtue-proof, no thought infirm
Altered her cheek. On whom the angel "Hail"
Bestowed, the holy salutation used
Long after to blest Mary, second Eve.
 "Hail mother of mankind, whose fruitful womb
Shall fill the world more numerous with thy sons
Than with these various fruits the trees of God
Have heaped this table." Raised of grassy turf
Their table was, and mossy seats had round,
And on her ample square from side to side
All autumn piled, though spring and autumn here
Danced hand in hand. A while discourse they hold;
No fear lest dinner cool; when thus began
Our author. "Heav'nly stranger, please to taste

371. **Virtue:** one of the lower angelic orders. Milton uses these hierarchical titles interchangeably, since Raphael is also termed a Seraph (5.277) and an Archangel (7.41).

378. **Pomona's arbor:** the lodging of the goddess of fruit trees, to whom Eve is compared at 9.393.

381. **fairest goddess:** Aphrodite, whom Paris chose over Athena and Juno. Since his reward was Helen, his choice was the mythical origin of the Trojan War. The episode was popular in Renaissance painting and literature.

384. **virtue-proof:** armored by, and therefore protected by, virtue.

385–87. **"Hail" . . . second Eve:** The passage alludes to Luke 1.28, where the angel Gabriel greets Mary: "Hail, thou that art highly favored, the Lord is with thee: blessed art thou among women." On Mary as second Eve, see 10.183n.

397. **author:** progenitor.

These bounties which our Nourisher, from whom
All perfect good unmeasured out descends,
To us for food and for delight hath caused
The earth to yield; unsavory food perhaps
To spiritual natures; only this I know,
That one celestial father gives to all."
To whom the angel. "Therefore what he gives
(Whose praise be ever sung) to man in part
Spiritual, may of purest spirits be found
No ingrateful food; and food alike those pure
Intelligential substances require
As doth your rational; and both contain
Within them every lower faculty
Of sense, whereby they hear, see, smell, touch, taste,
Tasting concoct, digest, assimilate,
And corporeal to incorporeal turn.
For know, whatever was created, needs
To be sustained and fed; of elements
The grosser feeds the purer, earth the sea,
Earth and the sea feed air, the air those fires
Ethereal, and as lowest first the moon;
Whence in her visage round those spots, unpurged
Vapors not yet into her substance turned.
Nor doth the moon no nourishment exhale
From her moist continent to higher orbs.
The Sun that light imparts to all, receives
From all his alimental recompense
In humid exhalations, and at even
Sups with the ocean: though in Heav'n the trees
Of life ambrosial fruitage bear, and vines
Yield nectar, though from off the boughs each morn
We brush mellifluous dews, and find the ground
Covered with pearly grain: yet God hath here
Varied his bounty so with new delights,
As may compare with Heaven; and to taste

408. **Intelligential substances:** angels. The word *substance,* used variously in metaphysics, here declares that the angels inhabit a *degree* of matter (see ll. 473–74) in which intelligence is pervasive: smart stuff, as it were.

412. **concoct, digest, assimilate:** Three stages in the physiology of nourishment: in concoction, food is broken down into a milky fluid called "chyle"; it is then digested, or dispersed by means of blood to the various parts of the body; finally it is assimilated, transformed into the nourished being.

419–20. See 263n.

429. **mellifluous:** fluid, sweet.

430. **pearly grain:** dew, but also evoking the manna or angel's food of Exod. 16.14 and Ps. 78.

Think not I shall be nice." So down they sat,
And to their viands fell, nor seemingly
The angel, nor in mist, the common gloss
Of theologians, but with keen dispatch
Of real hunger, and concoctive heat
To transubstantiate; what redounds, transpires
Through spirits with ease; nor wonder; if by fire
Of sooty coal the empiric alchemist
Can turn, or holds it possible to turn
Metals of drossiest ore to perfect gold
As from the mine. Meanwhile at table Eve
Ministered naked, and their flowing cups
With pleasant liquors crowned: O innocence
Deserving Paradise! if ever, then,
Then had the sons of God excuse to have been
Enamored at that sight; but in those hearts
Love unlibidinous reigned, nor jealousy
Was understood, the injured lover's hell.
  Thus when with meats and drinks they had sufficed,
Not burdened nature, sudden mind arose
In Adam, not to let th' occasion pass
Given him by this great conference to know

433. **nice:** fastidious, hard to please.

434. **nor seemingly:** not just apparently (as opposed to really).

435. **nor in mist:** nor in vapor, as when a visiting angel takes on an airy body; **common gloss:** This part of the poem, we are given to know, is *not* conventional. That angels are corporeal, and therefore eat, is entailed by the spiritual materialism set forth in Milton's *CD* 1.7: all Creation is material, even the human soul (1.8).

437. **real hunger, and concoctive heat:** Raphael's body has the same heat that was thought to fuel the digestive process in the human body.

438. **transubstantiate:** to transform one substance (earthly fruit) into another (the angelic body).

438–39. **what . . . ease:** Unassimilated food (*what redounds*) escapes vaporously through the pores of angels, reminding fallen readers of the more trying evacuations they know so well. "This artfully avoids the indecent idea, which would else have been apt to have arisen on the Angel's feeding, and withal gives a delicacy to these spirits, which finely distinguishes them from us in one of the most humbling circumstances relating to our bodies" (Richardson).

439–43. **nor wonder . . . mine:** The upward transformations claimed in alchemy are intended to make the idea of an angel assimilating earthly food seem plausible rather than an inexplicable *wonder.* At least one physician in the Paracelsan tradition, Jean-Baptiste van Helmont, developed the idea of digestion as an "inner alchemist" (see Multhauf; Pagel 1955 and 1956).

440. **empiric:** experimental. The word is sometimes pejorative, and means "quack." Milton may be contrasting the *empiric alchemist,* concentrating on the refinement of metals, with adepts of a more philosophical and spiritual outlook.

445. **crowned:** filled to the top.

446–48. **if ever . . . sight:** Milton alludes to Gen. 6.2: "The sons of God saw the daughters of men that they were fair; and they took them wives." Most exegetes took "sons of God" to refer to men, but some thought them to be fallen angels. Milton is saying that if angels ever were attracted to earthly women, the desire would in this instance have been excusable, since it would have arisen in response to Eve's innocence, not her sexual wiles.

449–50. All three, in other words, loved without sexual desire, and Adam did not feel jealous.

Of things above his world, and of their being
Who dwell in Heav'n, whose excellence he saw
Transcend his own so far, whose radiant forms
Divine effulgence, whose high power so far
Exceeded human, and his wary speech
Thus to th' empyreal minister he framed.
"Inhabitant with God, now know I well
Thy favor, in this honor done to man,
Under whose lowly roof thou hast vouchsafed
To enter, and these earthly fruits to taste,
Food not of angels, yet accepted so,
As that more willingly thou couldst not seem
As Heav'n's high feasts to have fed: yet what compare?"
To whom the wingèd hierarch replied.
"O Adam, one Almighty is, from whom
All things proceed, and up to him return,
If not depraved from good, created all
Such to perfection, one first matter all,
Endued with various forms, various degrees
Of substance, and in things that live, of life;
But more refined, more spiritous, and pure,
As nearer to him placed or nearer tending
Each in their several active spheres assigned,
Till body up to spirit work, in bounds
Proportioned to each kind. So from the root
Springs lighter the green stalk, from thence the leaves
More airy, last the bright consummate flow'r
Spirits odorous breathes: flow'rs and their fruit
Man's nourishment, by gradual scale sublimed
To vital spirits aspire, to animal,
To intellectual, give both life and sense,
Fancy and understanding, whence the soul

467. **yet what compare?:** "Yet what comparison can there possibly be between heavenly and earthly feasts?" Adam asks for a comparison, a metaphor, joining Earth and Heaven, and in reply will be given the literal basis for all such metaphors: matter.

469. **O:** A speech about the circular journey of matter begins appropriately with a typographical circle.

472. **one first matter all:** A remarkable conjunction of major philosophical words. In *CD* 1.7, Milton argues that the world was created not out of nothing but rather out of preexistent matter, the realm of Chaos visited by Satan in 2.951–1022.

478. **bounds:** both "limits" and "leaps" (Leonard).

483–85. Raphael adopts the language of Galenic physiology, in which food is elevated or *sublimed* into *vital spirits,* which reside in the heart and are the vehicles of passion, and *animal* spirits, which reside in the brain and are the vehicles of rational thought. No source has ever been adduced for *intellectual* spirits, which Milton postulates, it would seem, in order to supply a material basis for the intuitive capacities of men and angels.

Reason receives, and reason is her being,
Discursive, or intuitive; discourse
Is oftest yours, the latter most is ours,
Differing but in degree, of kind the same.
Wonder not then, what God for you saw good
If I refuse not, but convert, as you,
To proper substance; time may come when men
With angels may participate, and find
No inconvenient diet, nor too light fare:
And from these corporal nutriments perhaps
Your bodies may at last turn all to spirit,
Improved by tract of time, and winged ascend
Ethereal, as we, or may at choice
Here or in Heav'nly paradises dwell;
If ye be found obedient, and retain
Unalterably firm his love entire
Whose progeny you are. Meanwhile enjoy
Your fill what happiness this happy state
Can comprehend, incapable of more."
To whom the patriarch of mankind replied.
"O favorable spirit, propitious guest,
Well hast thou taught the way that might direct
Our knowledge, and the scale of nature set
From center to circumference, whereon
In contemplation of created things
By steps we may ascend to God. But say,
What meant that caution joined, 'If ye be found
Obedient'? Can we want obedience then
To him, or possibly his love desert
Who formed us from the dust, and placed us here
Full to the utmost measure of what bliss
Human desires can seek or apprehend?"
To whom the Angel. "Son of Heav'n and Earth,

490. The epic's definitive statement on the ontological relationship of man to angel, Earth to Heaven, matter to spirit; that the phrase was in common use can be inferred from its appearance in the verse of Katherine Philips: "The same in kind, though diff'ring in degree" ("On Controversies in Religion"). She died in 1664, three years before the publication of Milton's epic, and was not likely to have seen it in manuscript.

497. Cp. *Masque,* 558–61.

498. **tract:** a stretch or lapse.

499–500. Utopias are often criticized for their stasis. Here Raphael introduces the possibility of dynamic improvement into Edenic life.

505. **incapable:** unable to contain.

509. **scale of nature:** The *scale* or ladder of Nature, by which the mind may ascend from particularity to unity or Earth to Heaven, is a commonplace image in philosophy and theology. It was often linked with Jacob's vision in Gen. 28.12 and with the golden chain connecting heaven and earth in Homer's *Il.* 8.19 (Macrobius, *Commentary on the Dream of Scipio,* 1.14.15).

Attend: that thou are happy, owe to God;
That thou continu'st such, owe to thyself,
That is, to thy obedience; therein stand.
This was that caution giv'n thee; be advised.
God made thee perfect, not immutable;
And good he made thee, but to persevere
He left it in thy power, ordained thy will
By nature free, not overruled by fate
Inextricable, or strict necessity;
Our voluntary service he requires,
Not our necessitated, such with him
Finds no acceptance, nor can find, for how
Can hearts, not free, be tried whether they serve
Willing or no, who will but what they must
By destiny, and can no other choose?
Myself and all th' angelic host that stand
In sight of God enthroned, our happy state
Hold, as you yours, while our obedience holds;
On other surety none; freely we serve,
Because we freely love, as in our will
To love or not; in this we stand or fall:
And some are fall'n, to disobedience fall'n,
And so from Heav'n to deepest Hell; O fall
From what high state of bliss into what woe!"
    To whom our great progenitor. "Thy words
Attentive, and with more delighted ear,
Divine instructor, I have heard, than when
Cherubic songs by night from neighboring hills
Aerial music send: nor knew I not
To be both will and deed created free;
Yet that we never shall forget to love
Our Maker, and obey him whose command
Single, is yet so just, my constant thoughts
Assured me, and still assure: though what thou tell'st
Hath passed in Heav'n, some doubt within me move,
But more desire to hear, if thou consent,
The full relation, which must needs be strange,
Worthy of sacred silence to be heard;
And we have yet large day, for scarce the sun
Hath finished half his journey, and scarce begins

538. **surety:** ground of certainty, guarantee of secure possession.

547. **Cherubic songs:** See 4.680–88.

552. **yet:** also.

557. **sacred silence:** echoing Horace, *Odes* 2.13.29–32.

His other half in the great zone of heav'n."
Thus Adam made request, and Raphael
After short pause assenting, thus began.
"High matter thou enjoin'st me, O prime of men,
Sad task and hard, for how shall I relate
To human sense th' invisible exploits
Of warring spirits; how without remorse
The ruin of so many glorious once
And perfect while they stood; how last unfold
The secrets of another world, perhaps
Not lawful to reveal? Yet for thy good
This is dispensed, and what surmounts the reach
Of human sense, I shall delineate so,
By lik'ning spiritual to corporal forms,
As may express them best, though what if Earth
Be but the shadow of Heav'n, and things therein
Each to other like, more than on Earth is thought?
"As yet this world was not, and Chaos wild
Reigned where these heav'ns now roll, where earth now rests
Upon her center poised, when on a day
(For time, though in eternity, applied
To motion, measures all things durable
By present, past, and future) on such day
As Heav'n's great year brings forth, th' empyreal host
Of angels by imperial summons called,
Innumerable before th' Almighty's throne
Forthwith from all the ends of Heav'n appeared
Under their hierarchs in orders bright;
Ten thousand thousand ensigns high advanced,
Standards, and gonfalons twixt van and rear

566. **remorse:** pity.

571. **dispensed:** made lawful.

573. **lik'ning spiritual to corporal forms:** But as we know from the discussion that arose over Raphael's eating, spiritual and corporal forms differ only in degree; metaphor has ontological sanction.

575–76. The idea of Earth being the shadow of Heaven is sometimes meant to stress the difference, but Milton clearly thinks of them as being alike, analogical.

576. **more than on Earth is thought:** The only time that an earthling thought heavenly things too little like earthly things was when Adam assumed that Raphael could not eat earthly food. The error will be multiplied in the future: not everyone is a spiritual materialist, and even Adam took some convincing.

580–82. **For time . . . future:** On the unconventional idea that time precedes the Creation, see Milton's *CD* 1.7. On the idea that time is the measure of motion, see Aristotle, *Physics* 4.2.219, and lines 7–8 of Milton's second epitaph on Hobson.

583. **Heav'n's great year:** On earth a *great year* is the time required for the fixed stars to complete a full revolution, computed by Plato at 36,000 years (*Timaeus* 39D); we are left to imagine what Heaven's analogue of this cycle would be.

589. **gonfalons:** banners hung from crosspieces affixed to standards, as to this day in religious ceremonies.

Stream in the air, and for distinction serve
Of hierarchies, of orders, and degrees;
Or in their glittering tissues bear emblazed
Holy memorials, acts of zeal and love
Recorded eminent. Thus when in orbs
Of circuit inexpressible they stood,
Orb within orb, the Father infinite,
By whom in bliss embosomed sat the Son,
Amidst as from a flaming mount, whose top
Brightness had made invisible, thus spake.
"'Hear all ye angels, progeny of light,
Thrones, Dominations, Princedoms, Virtues, Powers,
Hear my decree, which unrevoked shall stand.
This day I have begot whom I declare
My only Son, and on this holy hill
Him have anointed, whom ye now behold
At my right hand; your head I him appoint;
And by myself have sworn to him shall bow
All knees in Heav'n, and shall confess him Lord:
Under his great vicegerent reign abide
United as one individual soul
Forever happy: him who disobeys
Me disobeys, breaks union, and that day
Cast out from God and blessed vision, falls
Into utter darkness, deep engulfed, his place
Ordained without redemption, without end.'
"So spake th' Omnipotent, and with his words
All seemed well pleased, all seemed, but were not all.
That day, as other solemn days, they spent
In song and dance about the sacred hill,
Mystical dance, which yonder starry sphere
Of planets and of fixed in all her wheels
Resembles nearest, mazes intricate,

601. The line names five of the traditional nine orders of angels. Satan, obviously impressed by this aspect of divine rhetoric, repeats the sonorous roll call of titles throughout his career (1.315–16, 2.11, 2.430; 5.772; *PR* 2.121). He thinks they signify the inalienable right to rule Heaven (ll. 800–802).

603. **This day I have begot:** Considering Gen. 22.16, Ps. 2.6–7, and Heb. 1.5, Milton argued in *CD* 1.5 that the begetting of the Son was a metaphor for his exaltation above the angels. The passage dramatizes that interpretation.

607. **by myself have sworn:** the formula of God's vowing found in Gen. 22.16, Isa. 45.23, Heb. 6.13–19; see Donne, "A Hymn to God the Father," l. 15.

609. **vicegerent:** the representative of a ruler.

610. **individual:** indivisible.

611. **him who disobeys:** whoever disobeys him.

618. **solemn days:** days set aside for religious ceremonies.

621. **fixed:** fixed stars.

Eccentric, intervolved, yet regular
Then most, when most irregular they seem,
And in their motions harmony divine
So smooths her charming tones, that God's own ear
Listens delighted. Evening now approached
(For we have also our evening and our morn,
We ours for change delectable, not need)
Forthwith from dance to sweet repast they turn
Desirous; all in circles as they stood,
Tables are set, and on a sudden piled
With angel's food, and rubied nectar flows
In pearl, in diamond, and massy gold
Fruit of delicious vines, the growth of Heav'n.
On flow'rs reposed, and with fresh flow'rets crowned,
They eat, they drink, and in communion sweet
Quaff immortality and joy, secure
Of surfeit where full measure only bounds
Excess, before th' all bounteous King, who show'red
With copious hand, rejoicing in their joy.
Now when ambrosial night with clouds exhaled
From that high mount of God, whence light and shade
Spring both, the face of brightest Heav'n had changed
To grateful twilight (for night comes not there
In darker veil) and roseate dews disposed
All but the unsleeping eyes of God to rest,
Wide over all the plain, and wider far
Than all this globous earth in plain outspread,
(Such are the courts of God) th' angelic throng
Dispersed in bands and files their camp extend
By living streams among the trees of life,
Pavilions numberless, and sudden reared,
Celestial tabernacles, where they slept
Fanned with cool winds, save those who in their course
Melodious hymns about the sov'reign throne
Alternate all night long: but not so waked
Satan, so call him now, his former name
Is heard no more in Heav'n; he of the first,

623. **Eccentric:** In the Ptolemaic system, an eccentric is a planetary orbit of which the earth is not the center; these eccentric centers revolve about the earth. **intervolved:** interlocked, like the two centers of an eccentric orbit.

627. **now:** added in 1674.

636–40. These lines revise and expand Editon 1, which reads, "They eat, they drink, and with refection sweet/Are filled, before th' all bounteous King, who show'red."

637. **communion:** fellowship.

652. **streams among the trees of life:** See Rev. 22.2.

658. **former name:** his original, prerebellion name, now blotted out from the heavenly records

If not the first Archangel, great in power,
In favor and in pre-eminence, yet fraught
With envy against the Son of God, that day
Honored by his great Father, and proclaimed
Messiah King anointed, could not bear
Through pride that sight, and thought himself impaired.
Deep malice thence conceiving and disdain,
Soon as midnight brought on the dusky hour
Friendliest to sleep and silence, he resolved
With all his legions to dislodge, and leave
Unworshipped, unobeyed the throne supreme
Contemptuous, and his next subordinate
Awak'ning, thus to him in secret spake.
"'Sleep'st thou companion dear, what sleep can close
Thy eyelids? And remember'st what decree
Of yesterday, so late hath passed the lips
Of Heav'n's Almighty. Thou to me thy thoughts
Wast wont, I mine to thee was wont to impart;
Both waking we were one; how then can now
Thy sleep dissent? New laws thou seest imposed;
New laws from him who reigns, new minds may raise
In us who serve, new counsels, to debate
What doubtful may ensue, more in this place
To utter is not safe. Assemble thou
Of all those myriads which we lead the chief;
Tell them that by command, ere yet dim night
Her shadowy cloud withdraws, I am to haste,
And all who under me their banners wave,
Homeward with flying march where we possess
The quarters of the north, there to prepare
Fit entertainment to receive our King
The great Messiah, and his new commands,
Who speedily through all the hierarchies
Intends to pass triumphant, and give laws.'
"So spake the false Archangel, and infused

(1.362–63). One tradition, derived from Isa. 14.12, took the former name to be Lucifer, but Raphael does not confirm this directly until 5.760.

664. **Messiah:** Hebrew, meaning "anointed."

669. **dislodge:** break camp.

671. **subordinate:** His fallen name is Beëlzebub (1.81).

673. **Sleep'st thou:** An epic formula for awakening someone found in Homer (*Il.* 2.560), Vergil (*Aen.* 4.560, 7.421), and Milton's *On the Fifth of November,* 92.

680. **minds:** purposes.

685. **by command:** a lie, since God has not commanded their departure.

689. **north:** where Satan's throne was traditionally located (Isa. 14.13).

Bad influence into th' unwary breast
Of his associate; he together calls,
Or several one by one, the regent powers,
Under him regent, tells, as he was taught,
That the most high commanding, now ere night,
Now ere dim night had disencumbered Heav'n,
The great hierarchal standard was to move;
Tells the suggested cause, and cast between
Ambiguous words and jealousies, to sound
Or taint integrity; but all obeyed
The wonted signal, and superior voice
Of their great potentate; for great indeed
His name, and high was his degree in Heav'n;
His count'nance, as the morning star that guides
The starry flock, allured them, and with lies
Drew after him the third part of Heav'n's host:
Meanwhile th' eternal eye, whose sight discerns
Abstrusest thoughts, from forth his holy mount
And from within the golden lamps that burn
Nightly before him, saw without their light
Rebellion rising, saw in whom, how spread
Among the sons of morn, what multitudes
Were banded to oppose his high decree;
And smiling to his only Son thus said.
"'Son, thou in whom my glory I behold
In full resplendence, heir of all my might,
Nearly it now concerns us to be sure
Of our omnipotence, and with what arms
We mean to hold what anciently we claim
Of deity or empire, such a foe
Is rising, who intends to erect his throne
Equal to ours, throughout the spacious north;
Nor so content, hath in his thought to try
In battle, what our power is, or our right.
Let us advise, and to this hazard draw
With speed what force is left, and all employ

695. **Bad influence:** perhaps with an astrological undertone.

700. Night's removal of darkness and the stars is made to seem an echo of Satan moving his troops.

710. **the third part:** See Rev. 12.4.

712. **Abstrusest:** most secret.

718. **smiling:** alerting us to the mocking tone of the forthcoming speech, where the omnipotent Father speaks as a Shakespearean monarch alarmed by the threat of rebellion.

721. **Nearly:** "closely," "intimately," as in Shakespeare's "something nearly that concerns yourselves" (*MND* 1.1.126).

725–26. Cp. Isa. 14.12–13.

In our defense, lest unawares we lose
This our high place, our sanctuary, our hill.'
"To whom the Son with calm aspect and clear
Lightning divine, ineffable, serene,
Made answer. 'Mighty Father, thou thy foes
Justly hast in derision, and secure
Laugh'st at their vain designs and tumults vain,
Matter to me of glory, whom their hate
Illustrates, when they see all regal power
Giv'n me to quell their pride, and in event
Know whether I be dextrous to subdue
Thy rebels, or be found the worst in Heav'n.'
"So spake the Son, but Satan with his powers
Far was advanced on wingèd speed, an host
Innumerable as the stars of night,
Or stars of morning, dewdrops, which the sun
Impearls on every leaf and every flower.
Regions they passed, the mighty regencies
Of Seraphim and Potentates and Thrones
In their triple degrees, regions to which
All thy dominion, Adam, is no more
Than what this garden is to all the earth,
And all the sea, from one entire globose
Stretched into longitude; which having passed
At length into the limits of the north
They came, and Satan to his royal seat
High on a hill, far blazing, as a mount
Raised on a mount, with pyramids and tow'rs
From diamond quarries hewn, and rocks of gold,
The palace of great Lucifer, (so call
That structure in the dialect of men
Interpreted) which not long after, he

736. **Justly hast in derision:** Ps. 2.4: "He that sitteth in the heavens shall laugh: The Lord shall have them in derision."

739. **Illustrates:** makes illustrious (by defeating them in battle).

740. **in event:** by the outcome.

741. **dextrous:** both "skillful" and "right-handed" (the Son sits on God's right hand [l. 606], and is, so to speak, his right-hand man).

746. **Or stars of morning, dewdrops:** The sudden shift of magnitude from stars to dewdrops recalls the similes of Book 1.

748. **regencies:** dominions.

750. **triple degrees:** The nine orders of angels were often arranged in three groups of three; see Spenser's "trinal triplicities" in *FQ* 1.39.

750–54. **regions . . . longitude:** Again the issue is magnitude: the planet Earth, spread on a flat plane, is to the regions traversed by the rebel angels as Eden is to the entire earth.

758. **pyramids:** Milton's association of pyramids with pomp and immortal longings can be discerned as early as *On Shakespeare*. See also *RCG* (Yale 1:790).

Affecting all equality with God,
In imitation of that mount whereon
Messiah was declared in sight of Heav'n,
The Mountain of the Congregation called;
For thither he assembled all his train,
Pretending so commanded to consult
About the great reception of their King,
Thither to come, and with calumnious art
Of counterfeited truth thus held their ears.
"'Thrones, Dominations, Princedoms, Virtues, Powers,
If these magnific titles yet remain
Not merely titular, since by decree
Another now hath to himself engrossed
All power, and us eclipsed under the name
Of King anointed, for whom all this haste
Of midnight march, and hurried meeting here,
This only to consult how we may best
With what may be devised of honors new
Receive him coming to receive from us
Knee-tribute yet unpaid, prostration vile,
Too much to one, but double how endured,
To one and to his image now proclaimed?
But what if better counsels might erect
Our minds and teach us to cast off this yoke?
Will ye submit your necks, and choose to bend
The supple knee? Ye will not, if I trust
To know ye right, or if ye know yourselves
Natives and sons of Heav'n possessed before
By none, and if not equal all, yet free,
Equally free; for orders and degrees
Jar not with liberty, but well consist.
Who can in reason then or right assume
Monarchy over such as live by right
His equals, if in power and splendor less,
In freedom equal? Or can introduce
Law and edict on us, who without law
Err not, much less for this to be our Lord,
And look for adoration to th' abuse

763. **Affecting:** aspiring to, making an ostentatious display of.

764. **that mount:** referring to the mount of line 598.

766. **Mountain of the Congregation:** See Isa. 14.13.

775. **engrossed:** monopolized.

786. **this yoke:** Christ maintains that his yoke is "easy" in Matt. 11.29–30.

799. **this:** this entity placed over us only by improper law and edict.

Of those imperial titles which assert
Our being ordained to govern, not to serve?'
"Thus far his bold discourse without control
Had audience, when among the Seraphim
Abdiel, than whom none with more zeal adored
The deity, and divine commands obeyed,
Stood up, and in a flame of zeal severe
The current of his fury thus opposed.
" 'O argument blasphemous, false and proud!
Words which no ear ever to hear in Heav'n
Expected, least of all from thee, ingrate,
In place thyself so high above thy peers.
Canst thou with impious obloquy condemn
The just decree of God, pronounced and sworn,
That to his only Son by right endued
With regal scepter, every soul in Heav'n
Shall bend the knee, and in that honor due
Confess him rightful King? Unjust thou say'st,
Flatly unjust, to bind with laws the free,
And equal over equals to let reign,
One over all with unsucceeded power.
Shalt thou give law to God, shalt thou dispute
With him the points of liberty, who made
Thee what thou art, and formed the pow'rs of Heav'n
Such as he pleased, and circumscribed their being?
Yet by experience taught we know how good,
And of our good, and of our dignity
How provident he is, how far from thought
To make us less, bent rather to exalt
Our happy state under one head more near
United. But to grant it thee unjust,
That equal over equals monarch reign:
Thyself though great and glorious dost thou count,
Or all angelic nature joined in one,
Equal to him begotten Son, by whom
As by his Word the mighty Father made

805. **Abdiel:** Hebrew meaning "Servant of God." Milton's most important addition to the traditional cast of Judeo-Christian angels; see West 154 on the origins of the name. **zeal:** a trait admired by Protestants and by Milton, who defined it as "an eager desire to sanctify the divine name, together with a feeling of indignation against things which tend to the violation or contempt of religion" (*CD* 2.6; see also *Apology* in Yale 1:900–901).

821. **unsucceeded:** without successor, unending.

835–40. Based on Col. 1.16–17: "By him were all things created, . . . whether they be thrones, or dominions, or principalities, or powers: all things were created by him, and for him."

All things, ev'n thee, and all the spirits of Heav'n
By him created in their bright degrees,
Crowned them with glory, and to their glory named
Thrones, Dominations, Princedoms, Virtues, Powers,
Essential powers, nor by his reign obscured,
But more illustrious made, since he the head
One of our number thus reduced becomes,
His laws our laws, all honor to him done
Returns our own. Cease then this impious rage,
And tempt not these; but hasten to appease
Th' incensèd Father, and th' incensèd Son,
While pardon may be found in time besought.'
"So spake the fervent Angel, but his zeal
None seconded, as out of season judged,
Or singular and rash, whereat rejoiced
Th' Apostate, and more haughty thus replied.
'That we were formed then say'st thou? And the work
Of secondary hands, by task transferred
From Father to his Son? Strange point and new!
Doctrine which we would know whence learnt: who saw
When this creation was? Remember'st thou
Thy making, while the Maker gave thee being?
We know no time when we were not as now;
Know none before us, self-begot, self-raised
By our own quick'ning power, when fatal course
Had circled his full orb, the birth mature
Of this our native Heav'n, ethereal sons.
Our puissance is our own, our own right hand
Shall teach us highest deeds, by proof to try
Who is our equal: then thou shalt behold
Whether by supplication we intend
Address, and to begirt th' Almighty throne
Beseeching or besieging. This report,

842–45. **But . . . own:** "The argument seems to be that Christ, by becoming the head of the angels, became in a measure one of them, and so ennobled their nature" (Verity). Such, of course, is precisely the effect of his Incarnation on humankind.

856–58. See Augustine's *Confessions* 1.6 on how we do not remember our beginnings but cannot suppose that we fabricated ourselves, and therefore honor our Maker. Adam at his awakening follows this line of thought (8.270–82). Milton might have derived the idea of the rebel angels denying their creation from Dante, *Par.* 29.58–60.

860. **self-begot, self-raised:** The sudden eruption of the word *self* recalls Shakespeare's *R3*, 5.3.183–204, and glances at the despairing hell of selfhood at 4.73–113.

864. **own right hand:** as opposed to God's (see 741n). Cp. Ps. 45.4.

868. **Address:** dutiful approach, with also a military sense of skillful engagement.

869. **Beseeching or besieging:** Out of supplication comes, treacherously, a new way of approaching the throne of God; *besieging* only sounds like *beseeching*. Cp. 1.642n.

These tidings carry to th' anointed King;
And fly, ere evil intercept thy flight.'
"He said, and as the sound of waters deep
Hoarse murmur echoed to his words applause
Through the infinite host, nor less for that
The flaming seraph fearless, though alone
Encompassed round with foes, thus answered bold.
" 'O alienate from God, O spirit accursed,
Forsaken of all good; I see thy fall
Determined, and thy hapless crew involved
In this perfidious fraud, contagion spread
Both of thy crime and punishment: henceforth
Not more be troubled how to quit the yoke
Of God's Messiah; those indulgent laws
Will not be now vouchsafed, other decrees
Against thee are gone forth without recall;
That golden scepter which thou didst reject
Is now an iron rod to bruise and break
Thy disobedience. Well thou didst advise,
Yet not for thy advise or threats I fly
These wicked tents devoted, lest the wrath
Impendent, raging into sudden flame,
Distinguish not: for soon expect to feel
His thunder on thy head, devouring fire.
Then who created thee lamenting learn,
When who can uncreate thee thou shalt know.'
"So spake the Seraph Abdiel faithful found,
Among the faithless, faithful only he;
Among innumerable false, unmoved,
Unshaken, unseduced, unterrified,
His loyalty he kept, his love, his zeal;
Nor number, nor example with him wrought
To swerve from truth, or change his constant mind
Though single. From amidst them forth he passed,
Long way through hostile scorn, which he sustained
Superior, nor of violence feared aught;
And with retorted scorn his back he turned
On those proud tow'rs to swift destruction doomed."

883. **those indulgent laws:** alluding to the laws of line 693.

890. **devoted:** doomed.

899. Similar effects with the prefix *un-* occur at 2.185, 3.231. In describing Abdiel's solitary steadfastness, Milton may also have had in mind his own position at the Restoration.

906. **retorted scorn:** Abdiel's physical gesture of scornfully turning his back on the scornful rebel angels enacts the etymology of *retorted,* from the Latin *retortus,* "turned back."

Book VI

The Argument

Raphael continues to relate how Michael and Gabriel were sent forth to battle against Satan and his angels. The first fight described: Satan and his powers retire under night: he calls a council, invents devilish engines, which in the second day's fight put Michael and his angels to some disorder; but they at length pulling up mountains overwhelmed both the forces and machines of Satan. Yet the tumult not so ending, God on the third day sends Messiah his Son, for whom he had reserved the glory of that victory. He in the power of his Father coming to the place, and causing all his legions to stand still on either side, with his chariot and thunder driving into the midst of his enemies, pursues them unable to resist towards the wall of Heaven, which opening, they leap down with horror and confusion into the place of punishment prepared for them in the deep. Messiah returns with triumph to his Father.

"All night the dreadless angel unpursued
Through Heav'n's wide champaign held his way, till Morn,
Waked by the circling Hours, with rosy hand
Unbarr'd the gates of light. There is a cave
Within the Mount of God, fast by his throne,
Where light and darkness in perpetual round
Lodge and dislodge by turns, which makes through Heav'n
Grateful vicissitude, like day and night;
Light issues forth, and at the other door

1. **dreadless angel:** Abdiel, fearless and without a doubt (see 5.899–905).

2. **champaign:** (1) wide expanse of open countryside; (2) common land ("The least turf of hallowed glebe is with God himself of more value than all the champaign of common possession," Jeremy Taylor, 2.34); (3) a plain as a battlefield (see l. 15).

2–11. **Morn . . . Heav'n:** Like Book 5, Book 6 begins with an allusion to the best-known Homeric personification, rosy-fingered Dawn. Milton's Dawn is distinctively awakened by the *Hours* in the *circling* configuration of a clock (cp. 4.267). Unlike Hesiod, who puts the abode of alternating day and night in the abyss (*Theog.* 744–54), Milton elevates their *perpetual round* to Heaven's most sacred site, *fast by* (near) God's *throne.* Milton grew up in a household with its own clock, at a time when it first became possible for wealthier citizens to own one (see *On Time* headnote).

Obsequious darkness enters, till her hour
To veil the Heav'n, though darkness there might well
Seem twilight here; and now went forth the Morn
Such as in highest Heav'n, arrayed in gold
Empyreal, from before her vanished night,
Shot through with orient beams: when all the plain
Covered with thick embattled squadrons bright,
Chariots and flaming arms, and fiery steeds
Reflecting blaze on blaze, first met his view:
War he perceived, war in procinct, and found
Already known what he for news had thought
To have reported: gladly then he mixed
Among those friendly powers who him received
With joy and acclamations loud, that one
That of so many myriads fall'n, yet one
Returned not lost: on to the sacred hill
They led him high applauded, and present
Before the seat supreme; from whence a voice
From midst a golden cloud thus mild was heard.
"'Servant of God, well done, well hast thou fought
The better fight, who single hast maintained
Against revolted multitudes the cause
Of truth, in word mightier than they in arms;
And for the testimony of truth hast borne
Universal reproach, far worse to bear
Than violence: for this was all thy care
To stand approved in sight of God, though worlds
Judged thee perverse: the easier conquest now
Remains thee, aided by this host of friends,
Back on thy foes more glorious to return
Than scorned thou didst depart, and to subdue
By force, who reason for their law refuse,
Right reason for their law, and for their King
Messiah, who by right of merit reigns.

10. **Obsequious:** obedient, sequent; like one observing rites of mourning (cp. *Lyc* headnote; *SA* 1732).

19. **in procinct:** from the Latin *in procinctu*, "girded up, prepared for battle."

29–30. "Well done, thou good and faithful servant"(Matt. 25.21); "fight the good fight" (1 Tim. 6.12).

33–35. **for the testimony . . . violence:** "For thy sake I have borne reproach" (Ps. 69.7). Cp. Spenser: "Evil deeds may better than bad words be bore" (*FQ* 4.4.4).

42. **Right reason:** Scholastic theologians adapted the concept of an *a priori* faculty of moral judgment from the *recta ratio* of Stoic philosophy. Milton cites Cicero (*Philippics* 11.12.28): "Right reason [is] derived from divine will which commands what is right and forbids what is wrong" (*1Def*, Yale 4:1.383; cp. *Brief Notes*, Yale 7:479). See Hoopes.

Go Michael of celestial armies prince,
And thou in military prowess next
Gabriel, lead forth to battle these my sons
Invincible, lead forth my armèd Saints
By thousands and by millions ranged for fight;
Equal in number to that godless crew
Rebellious, them with fire and hostile arms
Fearless assault, and to the brow of Heav'n
Pursuing drive them out from God and bliss,
Into their place of punishment, the gulf
Of Tartarus, which ready opens wide
His fiery chaos to receive their fall.'
"So spake the sov'reign voice, and clouds began
To darken all the hill, and smoke to roll
In dusky wreaths, reluctant flames, the sign
Of wrath awaked: nor with less dread the loud
Ethereal trumpet from on high gan blow:
At which command the powers militant,
That stood for Heav'n, in mighty quadrate joined
Of union irresistible, moved on
In silence their bright legions, to the sound
Of instrumental harmony that breathed
Heroic ardor to advent'rous deeds
Under their godlike leaders, in the cause

44. **Michael:** "Who is like God?" (Hebr.). He is named as Satan's opponent in Revelation, Milton's main source for the War in Heaven (12.7). Milton transfers to Christ many of the distinctions traditionally accorded Michael, including credit for vanquishing Satan.

46. **Gabriel:** "man of God" (Hebr.). See 4.549n.

49. **Equal:** Equality is a slippery concept in the epic. As Satan later acknowledges, "most" (two-thirds) of the angels remain loyal to God (l. 166; cp. l. 156, 2.692, 5.710).

54. **Tartarus:** Hell; see 2.69n.

55. **chaos:** Fowler glosses this usage as indicating the uncreated realm of primordial matter, but God uses the term in its primitive sense of "yawning gulf, chasm" (*OED* 1; cp. ll. 871–75).

56–60. Editors note that smoke, fire, and trumpet signal God's presence when he gives Moses the Ten Commandments (Exod. 19.18–19). The typological structure of the narrative suggests that Milton alludes primarily to Hebrews 12, however, in which St. Paul localizes the Exodus account to insist on the apocalyptic transcendence and universality of Christ's kingdom: "For ye are not come unto the mount that might be touched, and that burned with fire, nor unto blackness, and darkness, and tempest, and the sound of a trumpet. . . . But ye are come unto mount Sion, and unto the city of the living God, the heavenly Jerusalem, and to an innumerable company of angels" (18–22). Cp. 833–34n.

58. **reluctant:** struggling (of the fire working through smoke); cp. 4.311. The *OED* does not cite an example of the modern sense before the eighteenth century.

60. **gan:** began to.

62. **stood for Heav'n:** maintained loyalty to God; (in contrast to the *Apostate;* cp. l. 100).

63–65. **Of union irresistible . . . harmony:** Cp. the quiet calm of the fallen angels, marching in squared formation to the sound of flutes playing Dorian music (1.549–61). "Homer thus marches his Grecians silent and sedate" (Todd; *Il.* 3.8).

Of God and his Messiah. On they move
Indissolubly firm; nor obvious hill,
Nor strait'ning vale, nor wood, nor stream divides
Their perfect ranks; for high above the ground
Their march was, and the passive air upbore
Their nimble tread, as when the total kind
Of birds in orderly array on wing
Came summoned over Eden to receive
Their names of thee; so over many a tract
Of Heav'n they marched, and many a province wide
Tenfold the length of this terrene: at last
Far in th' horizon to the north appeared
From skirt to skirt a fiery region, stretched
In battailous aspect, and nearer view
Bristled with upright beams innumerable
Of rigid spears, and helmets thronged, and shields
Various, with boastful argument portrayed,
The banded powers of Satan hasting on
With furious expedition; for they weened
That selfsame day by fight, or by surprise
To win the Mount of God, and on his throne
To set the envier of his state, the proud
Aspirer, but their thoughts proved fond and vain
In the mid way: though strange to us it seemed
At first, that angel should with angel war,
And in fierce hosting meet, who wont to meet
So oft in festivals of joy and love
Unanimous, as sons of one great Sire
Hymning th' Eternal Father: but the shout
Of battle now began, and rushing sound
Of onset ended soon each milder thought.
High in the midst exalted as a god
Th' Apostate in his sun-bright chariot sat

69. **obvious:** standing in the way.

73–76. **Their nimble tread . . . thee:** Cp. Gen. 2.20.

78. **terrene:** earthly (referring back to *province*).

79–83. **horizon . . . shields:** The full extent of the northern horizon is filled with Satan's troops, whose armor shines with fiery light. For Satan's association with the north, see 5.689.

84. **argument:** design, subject (cp. 1.24, 9.13, *Damon* 189).

86. **expedition:** speed, aggressiveness; **weened:** thought, expected.

90. **fond:** foolish, conceited.

91. **In the mid way:** little-used idiom, meaning "halfway through," e.g., one's life (11.631; cp. Mary Herbert's translation of Ps. 102.24). In other words, Satan and his army fall well short of their intended goal. Fowler suspects numerological resonance because the Son ascends the chariot to defeat the rebels halfway through the epic (l. 762). Cp. 129n.

93. **hosting:** battle, from the noun *host,* "army" (see l. 104), but with a play on "entertain hospitably"; **wont:** were used.

100. **Apostate:** Greek *apo* (from, off), *stat* (stand).

Idol of majesty divine, enclosed
With flaming Cherubim, and golden shields;
Then lighted from his gorgeous throne, for now
'Twixt host and host but narrow space was left,
A dreadful interval, and front to front
Presented stood in terrible array
Of hideous length: before the cloudy van,
On the rough edge of battle ere it joined,
Satan with vast and haughty strides advanced,
Came tow'ring, armed in adamant and gold;
Abdiel that sight endured not, where he stood
Among the mightiest, bent on highest deeds,
And thus his own undaunted heart explores.
"'O Heav'n! That such resemblance of the Highest
Should yet remain, where faith and realty
Remain not; wherefore should not strength and might
There fail where virtue fails, or weakest prove
Where boldest; though to sight unconquerable?
His puissance, trusting in th' Almighty's aid,
I mean to try, whose reason I have tried
Unsound and false; nor is it aught but just,
That he who in debate of truth hath won,
Should win in arms, in both disputes alike
Victor; though brutish that contest and foul,
When reason hath to deal with force, yet so
Most reason is that reason overcome.'
"So pondering, and from his armèd peers
Forth stepping opposite, half way he met
His daring foe, at this prevention more
Incensed, and thus securely him defied.
"'Proud, art thou met? Thy hope was to have reached
The highth of thy aspiring unopposed,
The throne of God unguarded, and his side
Abandoned at the terror of thy power

107. **cloudy van:** the front line (*van*) of an army massed for battle and thus resembling a threatening cloud, as Milton's simile at 2.533–38 indicates. On Satan's proclivity for the front line or *edge* of battle, see 1.276–77.

115. **realty:** reality, sincerity.

118. **boldest:** most insolent, presumptuous.

120. **tried:** proved, judged after trial.

125–26. **reason . . . reason:** playing on the distinction between the principle or faculty of *reason* (capitalized in early editions) and *reason* as the rationale or explanation for an outcome (lowercase).

129. **prevention:** obstruction, in the literal sense of "coming before." Abdiel stops Satan "in the mid way" (cp. l. 91).

130. **securely:** confidently.

131. **Proud:** continuing the evasion of Satan's previous name, Abdiel names him according to his dominant trait.

Or potent tongue; fool, not to think how vain
Against th' Omnipotent to rise in arms;
Who out of smallest things could without end
Have raised incessant armies to defeat
Thy folly; or with solitary hand
Reaching beyond all limit at one blow
Unaided could have finished thee, and whelmed
Thy legions under darkness; but thou seest
All are not of thy train; there be who faith
Prefer, and piety to God, though then
To thee not visible, when I alone
Seemed in thy world erroneous to dissent
From all: my sect thou seest, now learn too late
How few sometimes may know, when thousands err.'
"Whom the grand foe with scornful eye askance
Thus answered. 'Ill for thee, but in wished hour
Of my revenge, first sought for thou return'st
From flight, seditious angel, to receive
Thy merited reward, the first assay
Of this right hand provoked, since first that tongue
Inspired with contradiction durst oppose
A third part of the gods, in synod met
Their deities to assert, who while they feel
Vigor divine within them, can allow
Omnipotence to none. But well thou com'st
Before thy fellows, ambitious to win
From me some plume, that thy success may show
Destruction to the rest: this pause between
(Unanswered lest thou boast) to let thee know;
At first I thought that liberty and Heav'n
To Heav'nly souls had been all one; but now

137–39. **Who . . . folly:** "God hath chosen the weak things of the world to confound the things which are mighty; and base things of the world, and things which are despised, hath God chosen, yea, and things which are not, to bring to nought things which are: that no flesh should glory in his presence" (1 Cor. 1.27–29).

147. **sect:** body of followers or adherents; a term applied by contemptuous episcopal loyalists to all dissenters ("sectaries"), Milton among them. Cp. *Eikon:* "I never knew that time in England when men of truest religion were not counted sectaries" (p. 1066).

149. **askance:** a facial tic that becomes characteristic of Satan (cp. 4.504).

153. **assay:** endeavor, trial.

156. **synod:** assembly; during the seventeenth century, often used of ecclesiastical assemblies (especially Presbyterian) and astrological conjunctions (see 10.661). Shakespeare in his later plays also applies *synod* to meetings of gods, presumably because of the mythological identification of gods and heavenly bodies (see, e.g., *ANT* 3.10.4, *COR* 5.2.68–69). Cp. 2.391.

161. **success:** what follows; as elsewhere, in ironic play with its more usual positive sense (see 2.9).

163. **Unanswered . . . boast:** i.e., lest Abdiel boast that Satan had no reply. How Abdiel will boast after the destruction threatened him is not addressed.

I see that most through sloth had rather serve,
Minist'ring spirits, trained up in feast and song;
Such hast thou armed, the minstrelsy of Heav'n,
Servility with freedom to contend,
As both their deeds compared this day shall prove.'
"To whom in brief thus Abdiel stern replied.
'Apostate, still thou err'st, nor end wilt find
Of erring, from the path of truth remote:
Unjustly thou deprav'st it with the name
Of servitude to serve whom God ordains,
Or Nature; God and Nature bid the same,
When he who rules is worthiest, and excels
Them whom he governs. This is servitude,
To serve th' unwise, or him who hath rebelled
Against his worthier, as thine now serve thee,
Thyself not free, but to thyself enthralled;
Yet lewdly dar'st our minist'ring upbraid.
Reign thou in Hell thy kingdom, let me serve
In Heav'n God ever blest, and his divine
Behests obey, worthiest to be obeyed,
Yet chains in Hell, not realms expect: meanwhile
From me returned, as erst thou saidst, from flight,
This greeting on thy impious crest receive.'
"So saying, a noble stroke he lifted high,
Which hung not, but so swift with tempest fell
On the proud crest of Satan, that no sight,
Nor motion of swift thought, less could his shield
Such ruin intercept: ten paces huge
He back recoiled; the tenth on bended knee
His massy spear upstayed; as if on Earth
Winds under ground or waters forcing way

166–68. Scripturally, angels are deemed "ministers" and carry out executive duties as God's agents or representatives (Matt. 4.11, Heb. 1.14). Raphael on his mission to Paradise is thus called "empyreal minister" (5.640). Satan exploits the shared Latin root with *minstrel* to deride the obedient angels as servile entertainers, a theme he revisits at 4.941–45. Cp. Lear's condemnation of the thundering elements as "servile ministers" (*LR* 3.2.21), and Nashe's anticipation of the wordplay: "What a stir he keeps against dumb ministers, and never writes nor talks of them, but he calleth them minstrels" (8).

169. **Servility with freedom:** slaves with free angels (abstract for concrete).

174. **deprav'st:** disparage.

176–78. **God . . . governs:** "God being the author of nature, her voice is but his instrument" (Hooker 1.3). The same assumption of agreement between divine and natural law underlies Milton's concession in *Tetrachordon* that a wife would properly govern her husband if superior to him in reason (see p. 993).

182. **lewdly:** wickedly, basely; cp. 4.193.

183–84. **Reign . . . blest:** Satan voices his contrary preference at 1.263 (see n).

194. **bended knee:** Cp. the knee-tribute previously disdained (5.782, 787–88).

195–98. **as if . . . pines:** Raphael's simile recalls the narrator's resort to seismic pressures to convey

Sidelong, had pushed a mountain from his seat
Half sunk with all his pines. Amazement seized
The rebel Thrones, but greater rage to see
Thus foiled their mightiest, ours joy filled, and shout,
Presage of victory and fierce desire
Of battle: whereat Michael bid sound
Th' archangel trumpet; through the vast of Heaven
It sounded, and the faithful armies rung
Hosanna to the Highest: nor stood at gaze
The adverse legions, nor less hideous joined
The horrid shock: now storming fury rose,
And clamor such as heard in Heav'n till now
Was never, arms on armor clashing brayed
Horrible discord, and the madding wheels
Of brazen chariots raged; dire was the noise
Of conflict; overhead the dismal hiss
Of fiery darts in flaming volleys flew,
And flying vaulted either host with fire.
So under fiery cope together rushed
Both battles main, with ruinous assault
And inextinguishable rage; all Heav'n
Resounded, and had Earth been then, all Earth
Had to her center shook. What wonder? When
Millions of fierce encount'ring angels fought
On either side, the least of whom could wield
These elements, and arm him with the force
Of all their regions: how much more of power
Army against army numberless to raise
Dreadful combustion warring, and disturb,
Though not destroy, their happy native seat;
Had not th' Eternal King omnipotent
From his stronghold of Heav'n high overruled

---

the phenomena of Hell (see, e.g., 1.230–37). Mountains appear immovable, but Milton deems faith sufficient to move them, as 1 Cor. 13.2 implies (see ll. 649–50; cp. 4.987, *SA* 1647–48).

199. **rebel Thrones:** A single angelic order stands for all (synecdoche). Leonard remarks that the choice of *Thrones* is "politically suggestive" (see 12.36).

210. **madding:** manic. The diction is odd, but the general point is clear; the jarring sounds and sights of war produce insane frenzy.

213–14. The local conditions anticipate the environment of Hell, complete with a dome of fire produced by thick volleys of flaming arrows and the prophetic sound of their *dismal hiss* (cp. 1.298, 10.508).

216. **battles main:** central bodies of the armies.

222–23. **These elements . . . regions:** Raphael refers to the four *elements* that constitute Adam's world—earth, air, fire, and water—each predominating in its *region.*

225. **combustion:** tumult, wild commotion.

And limited their might; though numbered such
As each divided legion might have seemed
A numerous host, in strength each armèd hand
A legion; led in fight, yet leader seemed
Each warrior single as in chief, expert
When to advance, or stand, or turn the sway
Of battle, open when, and when to close
The ridges of grim war; no thought of flight,
None of retreat, no unbecoming deed
That argued fear; each on himself relied,
As only in his arm the moment lay
Of victory; deeds of eternal fame
Were done, but infinite: for wide was spread
That war and various; sometimes on firm ground
A standing fight, then soaring on main wing
Tormented all the air; all air seemed then
Conflicting fire: long time in even scale
The battle hung; till Satan, who that day
Prodigious power had shown, and met in arms
No equal, ranging through the dire attack
Of fighting Seraphim confused, at length
Saw where the sword of Michael smote, and felled
Squadrons at once; with huge two-handed sway
Brandished aloft the horrid edge came down
Wide-wasting; such destruction to withstand

229–36. **though numbered . . . war:** "Each legion was in number like an army, each single warrior was in strength like a legion, and, though led in fight, was as expert as a commander-in-chief. So that the angels are celebrated first for their *number,* then for their *strength,* and lastly for their *expertness* in war" (Newton).

236. **ridges:** ranks (per *close* in l. 235); the reference is probably agricultural (furrows), despite Lewis's objection (135).

239. **moment:** determining influence, that which tips the balance.

243. **main:** powerful.

244. **Tormented:** disturbed, stirred.

248. **No equal:** The phrase has long stirred critical controversy because it seems to contradict the scene in which Satan is *foiled* by Abdiel (l. 200). Newton explains that Abdiel's moment of triumph was accidental and that if the combat had continued, Satan would have "prov'd an overmatch for Abdiel." A. H. Gilbert cites the inconsistency as evidence that the combat with Abdiel is a late insertion to a battle narrative that originally adhered more closely to a Homeric model, "in which the leaders of the hosts fight" (1947, 5). For Fish, the apparent inconsistency is a didactic trap set by the narrator to undermine Abdiel's "sense of justice" and "military pretensions" (1967, 187). Those "pretensions" seem justified at lines 369–71, however, and the present editors take *no equal* to imply only that Abdiel is inferior to Satan in rank or hierarchical position. The primary sense of the noun *equal* signifies "one that is very similar to another in rank or position." The significance and dramatic impact of Abdiel's *noble stroke* is, if anything, underscored by his social inferiority.

250. **sword of Michael:** The Archangel's grand weapon is a telling point of reference in Milton's depiction of Satan (2.294–95, 11.247–48), though it has no basis in Scripture. Some regard it as the "two-handed engine" of *Lycidas.*

He hasted, and opposed the rocky orb
Of tenfold adamant, his ample shield
A vast circumference: at his approach
The great archangel from his warlike toil
Surceased, and glad as hoping here to end
Intestine war in Heav'n, the arch-foe subdued
Or captive dragged in chains, with hostile frown
And visage all enflamed first thus began.
"'Author of evil, unknown till thy revolt,
Unnamed in Heav'n, now plenteous, as thou seest
These acts of hateful strife, hateful to all,
Though heaviest by just measure on thyself
And thy adherents: how hast thou disturbed
Heav'n's blessèd peace, and into nature brought
Misery, uncreated till the crime
Of thy rebellion? How hast thou instilled
Thy malice into thousands, once upright
And faithful, now proved false? But think not here
To trouble holy rest; Heav'n casts thee out
From all her confines. Heav'n the seat of bliss
Brooks not the works of violence and war.
Hence then, and evil go with thee along
Thy offspring, to the place of evil, Hell,
Thou and thy wicked crew; there mingle broils,
Ere this avenging sword begin thy doom,
Or some more sudden vengeance winged from God
Precipitate thee with augmented pain.'
"So spake the prince of angels; to whom thus
The Adversary. 'Nor think thou with wind
Of airy threats to awe whom yet with deeds
Thou canst not. Hast thou turned the least of these
To flight, or if to fall, but that they rise
Unvanquished, easier to transact with me
That thou shouldst hope, imperious, and with threats

254–56. **rocky orb . . . circumference:** Satan's shield, vast as the moon's orb (1.287), is made of a mythical, impenetrable stone (*adamant*) ten layers thick.

259. **Intestine war:** civil war, but *intestine* also applies literally (e.g., ll. 587–88).

262–71. **Author . . . false:** Michael's rage and wonder seem genuine, not merely rhetorical. In light of his princely status and angel's characteristic imperturbability, this reaction is a striking measure of what Satan has wrought by his rebellion.

276. **Thy offspring:** perhaps an allusion to Sin (see 2.743–60).

282. **Adversary:** translates "Satan."

284–88. **Hast thou . . . hence?:** i.e., "Have you turned the weakest in my army to flight, or have any fallen failed to rise again undefeated, that you should hope to deal (*transact*) so easily with me as to chase me away with imperious threats?" Satan's speeches here and before his clash with Abdiel are incoherent.

To chase me hence? Err not that so shall end
The strife which thou call'st evil, but we style
The strife of glory: which we mean to win,
Or turn this Heav'n itself into the Hell
Thou fablest, here however to dwell free,
If not to reign: meanwhile thy utmost force,
And join him named Almighty to thy aid,
I fly not, but have sought thee far and nigh.'
"They ended parle, and both addressed for fight
Unspeakable; for who, though with the tongue
Of angels, can relate, or to what things
Liken on Earth conspicuous, that may lift
Human imagination to such highth
Of godlike power: for likest gods they seemed,
Stood they or moved, in stature, motion, arms
Fit to decide the empire of great Heav'n.
Now waved their fiery swords, and in the air
Made horrid circles; two broad suns their shields
Blazed opposite, while expectation stood
In horror; from each hand with speed retired
Where erst was thickest fight, th' angelic throng,
And left large field, unsafe within the wind
Of such commotion, such as to set forth
Great things by small, if nature's concord broke,
Among the constellations war were sprung,
Two planets rushing from aspect malign
Of fiercest opposition in mid sky,
Should combat, and their jarring spheres confound.
Together both with next to almighty arm,

288. **Err not that:** "don't erroneously suppose."

290. **The strife of glory:** Cp. the Son's interpretation of the conflict (5.738–39).

296. **parle:** parley; **addressed:** prepared, but in play with *parle* and *unspeakable.*

297–98. **tongue/Of angels:** recalls St. Paul's insistence on the emptiness of oratory without charity (1 Cor. 13.1), a fitting transition from talking to fighting.

299. **conspicuous:** "perceivable," modifies *things.* In asking what could *lift / Human imagination to such highth / Of godlike power,* Raphael seeks an aesthetic of the sublime.

303. **empire:** command, control.

306–7. **while expectation stood/In horror:** The personification of *expectation* conveys the angels' alarm; cp. Shakespeare, *ANT* 3.6.47, where expectation is "faint" from lack of satisfaction, and *H5* 2.Prol.8: "Now sits Expectation in the air."

310–15. Fowler notes the passage's ironic anticipation of the fallen world, when celestial order is deliberately altered so that malignant opposition between planets becomes a regular astrological occurrence (10.657–61). Here, however, cosmic *concord* is imagined not simply as altered for the worse but as broken, and the planets not merely in *aspect malign* but rushing toward each other "in mere oppugnancy," as Shakespeare's Ulysses says in a precedent passage (*TRO* 2.111). The sublimely horrifying prospect of Michael and Satan's imminent combat dwarfs (*great things by small*) that of planets hurtling toward each other on a collision course.

Uplifted imminent one stroke they aimed
That might determine, and not need repeat,
As not of power, at once; nor odds appeared
In might or swift prevention; but the sword
Of Michael from the armory of God
Was giv'n him tempered so, that neither keen
Nor solid might resist that edge: it met
The sword of Satan with steep force to smite
Descending, and in half cut sheer, nor stayed,
But with swift wheel reverse, deep ent'ring shared
All his right side; then Satan first knew pain,
And writhed him to and fro convolved; so sore
The griding sword with discontinuous wound
Passed through him, but th' ethereal substance closed
Not long divisible, and from the gash
A stream of nectarous humor issuing flowed
Sanguine, such as celestial spirits may bleed,
And all his armor stained erewhile so bright.
Forthwith on all sides to his aid was run
By angels many and strong, who interposed
Defense, while others bore him on their shields
Back to his chariot, where it stood retired
From off the files of war; there they him laid
Gnashing for anguish and despite and shame
To find himself not matchless, and his pride
Humbled by such rebuke, so far beneath
His confidence to equal God in power.
Yet soon he healed; for spirits that live throughout

318–19. **determine . . . once:** decide the outcome and not need to be repeated because it lacked the necessary power to finish the fight in itself (*at once*). The common gloss of *as not of power*—"because so powerful a blow could not be repeated"—is unconvincing.

320. **prevention:** anticipation.

321. **armory of God:** mentioned in Jer. 50.25. Cp. the irresistible sword given Arthegall by Astraea, goddess of justice: "Wheresoever it did light, it thoroughly sheared" (*FQ* 5.1.10).

323–27. **Nor solid might . . . side:** Though hardly Homeric in his dissection of battle, Raphael is careful to relate how Satan's wound occurs. Michael's sword *descending* cuts Satan's sword sheer in two; then Michael executes a *swift wheel reverse* (a backhand upstroke) that cuts off (*shared*) Satan's entire *right side.* Satan's left (Lat. *sinister*) side remains.

328. **convolved:** rolled together; coiled up. Satan's reaction to the pain prefigures his metamorphosis into a serpent (10.511ff).

329. **griding:** slashing, piercing; **discontinuous:** gaping; "in allusion to the old definition of a wound that it separates the continuity of the parts" (Newton).

332–33. **nectarous . . . bleed:** *Celestial spirits* bleed a bodily fluid, or *humor,* whose *sanguine* color owes to the "rubied nectar" they drink (5.633); cp. Homer's similar treatment of divine bleeding, *Il.* 5.339–42.

335–36. **was run/By angels:** Latinate syntax (*cursum est*) indicating that his troops ran to aid him. Such scenes occur frequently in Homer (e.g., *Il.* 14.428–32).

Vital in every part, not as frail man
In entrails, heart or head, liver or reins,
Cannot but by annihilating die;
Nor in their liquid texture mortal wound
Receive, no more than can the fluid air:
All heart they live, all head, all eye, all ear,
All intellect, all sense, and as they please,
They limb themselves, and color, shape or size
Assume, as likes them best, condense or rare.
"Meanwhile in other parts like deeds deserved
Memorial, where the might of Gabriel fought,
And with fierce Ensigns pierced the deep array
Of Moloch furious king, who him defied,
And at his chariot wheels to drag him bound
Threatened, nor from the Holy One of Heav'n
Refrained his tongue blasphemous; but anon
Down clov'n to the waste, with shattered arms
And uncouth pain fled bellowing. On each wing
Uriel and Raphael his vaunting foe,
Though huge, and in a rock of diamond armed,
Vanquished Adramelec, and Asmadai,
Two potent Thrones, that to be less than gods
Disdained, but meaner thoughts learned in their flight,
Mangled with ghastly wounds through plate and mail.

345–53. On the versatile homogeneity of angels, see 1.425n. Kerrigan notes how enviable such a physiology would be for a man with defective eyes (1983, 215–16, 227–28, 257–62; cp. *SA* 93–97).

346. **reins:** kidneys.

347. **annihilating:** Whether or not existence is escapable for angels is an open question; see 2.92–93, 151–54. In Milton's monist theory of creation *ex deo,* certainly no created being can, in the literal sense of annihilation, become "nothing." The closest to annihiliation a creature can come is dissolution into constituent atoms, or as Belial puts it, "swallowed up and lost/In the wide womb of uncreated Night" (2.149–50).

353. **likes:** pleases; an instance of the ethical dative; **condense or rare:** thick or thin in density.

356. **Ensigns:** standards or banners of military units, here also the units themselves.

357. **Moloch:** "The name is not supposed to exist until after man's Fall (see 1.364–65). Raphael might foreknow the names of future devils (cp. 12.140), but to name them here implies the failure of his mission. He had withheld 'Beëlzebub' from Bk. 5 . . . but now allows many devils' names to infiltrate Bk. 6" (Leonard). Like the narrator in Books 1 and 2, however, Raphael does not have many options. The original names of the fallen angels have been erased, and fallen humanity has not yet supplied them with new ones.

359–60. **nor . . . blasphemous:** "Whom hast thou reproached and blasphemed? . . . the Holy One of Israel" (2 Kings 19.22).

362. **uncouth:** unfamiliar.

363. *Raphael* refers to himself in the third person, which may owe to the historian's objectivity or indicate that Adam and Eve do not know the name of their guest.

364. **in a rock of diamond:** Cp. *Sonnet 6*, 7–8.

365. **Adramelec and Asmadai:** *Adramelec* was idolized by the Sepharvites in Samaria under Assyrian dominion (2 Kings 17.31). Worshiped as a sun god, he is defeated by Uriel, "regent of that orb" (3, Argument). *Asmadai* (Asmodeus) is vanquished by Raphael, his captor in the apocryphal Book of Tobit (see 4.168–71n).

Nor stood unmindful Abdiel to annoy
The atheist crew, but with redoubled blow
Ariel and Arioch, and the violence
Of Ramiel scorched and blasted overthrew.
I might relate of thousands, and their names
Eternize here on Earth; but those elect
Angels contented with their fame in Heav'n
Seek not the praise of men: the other sort
In might though wondrous and in acts of war,
Nor of renown less eager, yet by doom
Cancelled from Heav'n and sacred memory,
Nameless in dark oblivion let them dwell.
For strength from truth divided and from just,
Illaudable, naught merits but dispraise
And ignominy, yet to glory aspires
Vainglorious, and through infamy seeks fame:
Therefore eternal silence be their doom.
"And now their mightiest quelled, the battle swerved,
With many an inroad gored; deformèd rout
Entered, and foul disorder; all the ground
With shivered armor strown, and on a heap
Chariot and charioteer lay overturned
And fiery foaming steeds; what stood, recoiled
O'erwearied, through the faint Satanic host
Defensive scarce, or with pale fear surprised,
Then first with fear surprised and sense of pain
Fled ignominious, to such evil brought
By sin of disobedience, till that hour

371–72. **Ariel and Arioch . . . Ramiel:** The meaning of *Ariel* is uncertain, though it is often glossed as "lion of God." It is the proper name of a man as well as a poetic name for Jerusalem (e.g., Isa. 29.1–2). Milton would also have remembered Shakespeare's character (*TMP*). *Arioch* (lion-like) is the scriptural name of two kings and a captain (Gen. 14.1, 9; Judg. 1.6; Dan. 2.14). More pertinently, Rabbinical sources identify the king from Genesis with Antiochus Epiphanes (176–64 B.C.E.), King of Syria and perpetrator of "the Abomination of Desolation," in which a statue of Zeus was erected in the temple and Jews forced to worship it (1 Macc. 1.11–6.16). *Ramiel,* the most obscure reference, means "thunder of God"; Milton may have known the name from an extant fragment of the apocryphal Book of Baruch, which centers on the destruction of Jerusalem. If so, the three angels defeated by Abdiel are associated with apostasy and destruction in the holy city.

373–85. Content with God's praise, good angels *seek not the praise of men* (cp. *Lyc* 78–84). The rebels, their names *cancelled* from God's book, cannot win praise in Heaven, though they as creatures desire it instinctively. That they will seek the consolation of humanity's praise is left implicit. That they will succeed in their quest is presumed by the appearance of their earthly names in Raphael's narrative (see 357n).

382. **Illaudable:** unworthy of praise.

386. **the battle:** the [rebel] army.

391. **what:** those who.

393. **Defensive scarce:** scarcely defending themselves.

Not liable to fear or flight or pain.
Far otherwise th' inviolable saints
In cubic phalanx firm advanced entire,
Invulnerable, impenetrably armed:
Such high advantages their innocence
Gave them above their foes, not to have sinned,
Not to have disobeyed; in fight they stood
Unwearied, unobnoxious to be pained
By wound, though from their place by violence moved.
"Now night her course began, and over Heav'n
Inducing darkness, grateful truce imposed,
And silence on the odious din of war:
Under her cloudy covert both retired,
Victor and Vanquished: on the foughten field
Michael and his angels prevalent
Encamping, placed in guard their watches round,
Cherubic waving fires: on th' other part
Satan with his rebellious disappeared,
Far in the dark dislodged, and void of rest,
His potentates to council called by night;
And in the midst thus undismayed began.
" 'O now in danger tried, now known in arms
Not to be overpowered, companions dear,
Found worthy not of liberty alone,
Too mean pretense, but what we more affect,
Honor, dominion, glory, and renown,
Who have sustained one day in doubtful fight,
(And if one day, why not eternal days?)
What Heaven's Lord had powerfullest to send
Against us from about his throne, and judged
Sufficient to subdue us to his will,
But proves not so: then fallible, it seems,

399. **cubic phalanx:** Angels aloft, unlike human armies, can assume a cubic formation, both geometrically foursquare and, in the figurative sense, firm and unwavering. Cp. the hollow cube deployed by the rebels (l. 552).

404. **unobnoxious:** not liable (cp. l. 397).

410. **foughten field:** battlefield (cp. Shakespeare, *H5* 4.6.18).

411. **prevalent:** prevailing.

413. **Cherubic waving fires:** "flaming Cherubim" (l. 102), regularly assigned guard duty (e.g., 4.778–85).

415. **dislodged:** shifted position (5.669), or was forced to shift position. The active-passive ambiguity seems especially apt because the site of Satan's relocation is *far in the dark* (5.614).

416. Tactical councils on the night of a battlefield setback occur in Homer (*Il.* 9) and Vergil (*Aen.* 9.224–313).

421. **mean pretense:** "low aim," ironically accompanied by "base deception"; **affect:** "strive after," ironically accompanied by "pretend."

423. **doubtful fight:** indecisive conflict; cp. "dubious battle" (1.104).

Of future we may deem him, though till now
Omniscient thought. True is, less firmly armed,
Some disadvantage we endured and pain,
Till now not known, but known as soon contemned,
Since now we find this our empyreal form
Incapable of mortal injury
Imperishable, and though pierced with wound,
Soon closing, and by native vigor healed.
Of evil then so small as easy think
The remedy; perhaps more valid arms,
Weapons more violent, when next we meet,
May serve to better us, and worse our foes,
Or equal what between us made the odds,
In nature none: if other hidden cause
Left them superior, while we can preserve
Unhurt our minds, and understanding sound,
Due search and consultation will disclose.'
"He sat; and in th' assembly next upstood
Nisroch, of Principalities the prime;
As one he stood escaped from cruel fight,
Sore toiled, his riven arms to havoc hewn,
And cloudy in aspect thus answering spake.
'Deliverer from new lords, leader to free
Enjoyment of our right as gods; yet hard
For gods, and too unequal work we find
Against unequal arms to fight in pain,
Against unpained, impassive; from which evil
Ruin must needs ensue; for what avails
Valor or strength, though matchless, quelled with pain
Which all subdues, and makes remiss the hands
Of mightiest. Sense of pleasure we may well
Spare out of life perhaps, and not repine,
But live content, which is the calmest life:
But pain is perfect misery, the worst
Of evils, and excessive, overturns

429. **Of future:** Editors generally gloss "in future," after the idiom "of old." But Hume's reading of the phrase as a supposed limit on divine knowledge ("of future events") is also possible.

430. **Omniscient thought:** Yet Satan called a secret meeting (5.683ff).

432. **known as soon contemned:** no sooner felt than scorned.

440. **worse:** harm.

447. **Nisroch:** Assyrian deity; while worshiping at Nisroch's temple after a disastrous campaign against Israel, the Assyrian ruler Sennacherib was slain by his own sons (2 Kings 19.37, Isa. 37.38).

449. **to havoc hewn:** cut to pieces.

455. **impassive:** invulnerable to pain.

458. **remiss:** slack.

All patience. He who therefore can invent
With what more forcible we may offend
Our yet unwounded enemies, or arm
Ourselves with like defense, to me deserves
No less than for deliverance what we owe.'
"Whereto with look composed Satan replied.
'Not uninvented that, which thou aright
Believ'st so main to our success, I bring;
Which of us who beholds the bright surface
Of this ethereous mold whereon we stand,
This continent of spacious Heav'n, adorned
With plant, fruit, flow'r ambrosial, gems and gold,
Whose eye so superficially surveys
These things, as not to mind from whence they grow
Deep under ground, materials dark and crude,
Of spiritous and fiery spume, till touched
With Heav'n's ray, and tempered they shoot forth
So beauteous, op'ning to the ambient light.
These in their dark nativity the deep
Shall yield us pregnant with infernal flame,
Which into hollow engines long and round
Thick-rammed, at th' other bore with touch of fire
Dilated and infuriate shall send forth
From far with thund'ring noise among our foes
Such implements of mischief as shall dash
To pieces, and o'erwhelm whatever stands
Adverse, that they shall fear we have disarmed

464. **He who:** What follows is an implicit, conditional threat to Satan's sole leadership.

465. **offend:** hit, hurt.

467–68. **to me . . . owe:** "in my view deserves no less than what we owe [Satan] for our deliverance."

471. **main:** key.

472–81. For related accounts of light's productive interaction with potent subterranean matter, see 3.608–12, 8.91–97; cp. *Masque* 732–36.

473. **ethereous:** Milton substitutes the Greco-Latin form of the adjective rather than make the tongue-twisting combination *ethereal mold.*

478. **materials dark and crude:** Chaos substantiates Heaven too (MacCaffrey 162–64); cp. ll. 482–83, 510–12, 2.941.

479–80. The action of light touching potent sulfurous material and causing it to *shoot forth* appears to have suggested Satan's invention. It is the archetypal instance of Satan's bent for violating generative processes to accomplish his ends.

479. **spirituous:** highly refined, pure; **spume:** "of the Lat. *spuma,* froth, foam, a word expressing well the crude consistence of sulfur and other subterranean materials, the efficients of fertility" (Hume).

483. **infernal:** Satan uses the word in its classical sense of "underground," though the ironic association with Hell is unavoidable for Milton's readers.

484. **engines:** war machines; cp. 4.17–18. Milton was widely anticipated in laying the invention of artillery at the Devil's door; see, e.g., Spenser, *FQ* 1.7.13.

485. **bore:** hole bored into the cannon's barrel and filled with powder (called *touch*) that fired the cannon when lit.

The thunderer of his only dreaded bolt.
Nor long shall be our labor, yet ere dawn,
Effect shall end our wish. Meanwhile revive;
Abandon fear; to strength and counsel joined
Think nothing hard, much less to be despaired.'
He ended, and his words their drooping cheer
Enlightened, and their languished hope revived.
Th' invention all admired, and each, how he
To be th' inventor missed, so easy it seemed
Once found, which yet unfound most would have thought
Impossible: yet haply of thy race
In future days, if malice should abound,
Some one intent on mischief, or inspired
With dev'lish machination might devise
Like instrument to plague the sons of men
For sin, on war and mutual slaughter bent.
Forthwith from council to the work they flew,
None arguing stood, innumerable hands
Were ready, in a moment up they turned
Wide the celestial soil, and saw beneath
Th' originals of nature in their crude
Conception; sulfurous and nitrous foam
They found, they mingled, and with subtle art,
Concocted and adusted they reduced
To blackest grain, and into store conveyed:
Part hidden veins digged up (nor hath this Earth
Entrails unlike) of mineral and stone,
Whereof to found their engines and their balls
Of missive ruin; part incentive reed
Provide, pernicious with one touch to fire.
So all ere day-spring, under conscious night

494. **counsel:** judgment, wisdom. Physical prowess and strategic intelligence are classically the two main martial virtues, exemplified by Achilles and Odysseus.

496. **cheer:** mood, spirits.

498. **admired:** wondered at.

507–9. The abrupt style conveys haste.

510–20. The rebels' procedure here bears comparison with the construction of Pandaemonium (1.686ff).

512. **nitrous foam:** potassium nitrate or saltpeter; material of *spiritous and fiery spume* mentioned at line 479 and a basic ingredient of gunpowder.

514. **concocted and adusted:** combined and dried.

515. **blackest grain:** Satan in Book 4 is identified with the *smutty grain* of his invention (816–17 and n).

518. **found:** cast as in a foundry; cp. 1.703; **engines:** cannons.

519. **missive:** sent, delivered from a distance; **incentive reed:** match.

520. **pernicious:** deadly; sudden (meanings with distinct Latin roots).

521. **conscious:** privy to; translates Ovid's ***nox conscia*** and to a similar end (*Met.* 13.15). The common observation that Raphael here personifies night as a guiltily aware accomplice is unjustified.

Secret they finished, and in order set,
With silent circumspection unespied.
Now when fair morn orient in Heav'n appeared
Up rose the victor angels, and to arms
The matin trumpet sung: in arms they stood
Of golden panoply, refulgent host,
Soon banded; others from the dawning hills
Looked round, and scouts each coast light-armèd scour,
Each quarter, to descry the distant foe,
Where lodged, or whither fled, or if for fight,
In motion or in halt: him soon they met
Under spread ensigns moving nigh, in slow
But firm battalion; back with speediest sail
Zophiel, of Cherubim the swiftest wing,
Came flying, and in mid-air aloud thus cried.
"'Arm, warriors, arm for fight, the foe at hand,
Whom fled we thought, will save us long pursuit
This day, fear not his flight; so thick a cloud
He comes, and settled in his face I see
Sad resolution and secure: let each
His adamantine coat gird well, and each
Fit well his helm, grip fast his orbèd shield,
Borne ev'n or high, for this day will pour down,
If I conjecture aught, no drizzling shower,
But rattling storm of arrows barbed with fire.'
So warned he them aware themselves, and soon
In order, quit of all impediment;
Instant without disturb they took alarm,
And onward move embattled; when behold
Not distant far with heavy pace the foe
Approaching gross and huge; in hollow cube
Training his devilish enginery, impaled
On every side with shadowing squadrons deep,
To hide the fraud. At interview both stood

535. **Zophiel:** "spy of God"; one of Michael's chieftains, according to the Zohar (Soncino Zohar, Bemidbar, sec. 3, p. 154a).

541. **Sad:** serious, grim; **secure:** confident.

544. **ev'n or high:** in front of the body or overhead (to ward off flaming arrows).

547. **aware themselves:** already wary.

548. **impediment:** carriage and baggage of an army.

549. "Instantaneous, without disorder, they sprang to arms." Here as elsewhere, Milton indicates angels in action with substantive adjectives, rather than by using an adverb to describe how they act; see, e.g., "union of pure, with pure/Desiring" (8.627–28). The angels are *instant* in this case, with the result that they respond instantly.

550. **embattled:** in battle formation.

553. **Training:** dragging; **enginery:** artillery; **impaled:** hedged, enclosed.

555. **At interview:** in mutual view.

A while, but suddenly at head appeared
Satan: and thus was heard commanding loud.
“ ‘Vanguard, to right and left the front unfold;
That all may see who hate us, how we seek
Peace and composure, and with open breast
Stand ready to receive them, if they like
Our overture, and turn not back perverse;
But that I doubt, however witness Heaven,
Heav’n witness thou anon, while we discharge
Freely our part; ye who appointed stand
Do as you have in charge, and briefly touch
What we propound, and loud that all may hear.’
“So scoffing in ambiguous words, he scarce
Had ended when to right and left the front
Divided, and to either flank retired.
Which to our eyes discovered new and strange,
A triple-mounted row of pillars laid
On wheels (for like to pillars most they seemed
Or hollowed bodies made of oak or fir
With branches lopped, in wood or mountain felled)
Brass, iron, stony mold, had not their mouths
With hideous orifice gaped on us wide,
Portending hollow truce; at each behind
A Seraph stood, and in his hand a reed
Stood waving tipped with fire; while we suspense,
Collected stood within our thoughts amused,
Not long, for sudden all at once their reeds
Put forth, and to a narrow vent applied
With nicest touch. Immediate in a flame,
But soon obscured with smoke, all Heav’n appeared,
From those deep-throated engines belched, whose roar

560. **composure:** agreement, settlement; **breast:** heart, front lines; initiates the series of puns that infects the following lines.

562–67. **overture:** opening of negotiations; opening of a cannon’s muzzle (from Lat. *apertura,* hole). The more obvious puns in the following lines include *discharge, charge, touch,* and *loud* as Satan orders his troops to fire under the linguistic cover of a peace initiative. Editors and critics have long groaned over these puns, but Satan and the rebels are at last enjoying themselves.

572. **triple-mounted:** mounted threefold in a row (see ll. 604–5, 650), perhaps in anticipation of the Son’s *three-bolted thunder* (l. 764).

576. **mold:** substance. Raphael says that the cannons look like pillars or hollowed-out tree trunks on wheels, except that they are made of metal or stone.

580. **suspense:** undecided, with a play on “dangling in air.” The angels are literally and figuratively “hanging fire.”

581. **amused:** preoccupied; deceived.

585. As the cannons fire, the angels see *all Heav’n* first in a flame and then obscured in smoke.

586–89. **From those . . . glut:** Note the alimental imagery, predominantly of inversion and spasm: *deep-throated, belched, emboweled* (filled to bursting), *entrails tore, disgorging, glut.* Shared imagery ties Satan’s perverse engines of destruction to

Emboweled with outrageous noise the air,
And all her entrails tore, disgorging foul
Their devilish glut, chained thunderbolts and hail
Of iron globes, which on the victor host
Leveled, with such impetuous fury smote,
That whom they hit, none on their feet might stand,
Though standing else as rocks, but down they fell
By thousands, angel on archangel rolled;
The sooner for their arms, unarmed they might
Have easily as spirits evaded swift
By quick contraction or remove; but now
Foul dissipation followed and forced rout;
Nor served it to relax their serried files.
What should they do? If on they rushed, repulse
Repeated, and indecent overthrow
Doubled, would render them yet more despised,
And to their foes a laughter; for in view
Stood ranked of Seraphim another row
In posture to displode their second tire
Of thunder: back defeated to return
They worse abhorred. Satan beheld their plight,
And to his mates thus in derision called.
"'O friends, why come not on these victors proud?
Erewhile they fierce were coming, and when we,
To entertain them fair with open front
And breast, (what could we more?) propounded terms
Of composition, straight they changed their minds,
Flew off, and into strange vagaries fell,

---

his generative history with Sin and Death (cp. 2.755–802). See also God's description of the impact of Sin and Death on the world, 10.630–37.

589–94. **chained thunderbolts . . . rolled:** S. Fallon argues that Milton associates the Devil with Hobbes, who believed that everything that exists is matter in motion. With the moving of the angels, Milton gives the Devil (and Hobbes) his due (1991, 228–29).

595–97. **The sooner . . . remove:** On spirits' ability to reduce or expand their bodies, see, e.g., ll. 351–53, 1.789–90.

595. **The sooner for their arms:** Fish sees this as a mock-heroic moment because the armor of the good angels confers vulnerability (1967, 179). As many have suggested, however, their armor signifies the armor of faith, complete with shields "able to quench all the fiery darts of the wicked" (Eph. 6.16). Though their faith protects them from direct assault by evil, their vulnerability to deceit is considerable (see the deception of Uriel, 3.686–89).

598. **dissipation:** dispersion.

599. "Nor did it help any to open up their close ranks."

601. **indecent:** unseemly.

603. **laughter:** "a sudden glory arising from some sudden conception of some eminency in ourselves, by comparison with the infirmity of others, or with our own formerly" (Hobbes 55).

605. **displode:** fire; **tire:** volley.

611–12. **open front:** both "honest face" and "divided front line"; for *breast,* see 560n.

614–27. Satan continues scoffing at his opponents, describing their violent dispersal by artillery as if it were a response to a peace negotiation. Hence his plays on *result* (outcome, jump back), *stumble* (perplex, trip), *understand* (comprehend,

As they would dance, yet for a dance they seemed
Somewhat extravagant and wild, perhaps
For joy of offered peace: but I suppose
If our proposals once again were heard
We should compel them to a quick result.'
    "To whom thus Belial in like gamesome mood.
'Leader, the terms we sent were terms of weight,
Of hard contents, and full of force urged home,
Such as we might perceive amused them all,
And stumbled many: who receives them right,
Had need from head to foot well understand;
Not understood, this gift they have besides,
They show us when our foes walk not upright.'
    "So they among themselves in pleasant vein
Stood scoffing, heightened in their thoughts beyond
All doubt of victory, eternal might
To match with their inventions they presumed
So easy, and of his thunder made a scorn,
And all his host derided, while they stood
A while in trouble; but they stood not long,
Rage prompted them at length, and found them arms
Against such hellish mischief fit to oppose.
Forthwith (behold the excellence, the power
Which God hath in his mighty angels placed)
Their arms away they threw, and to the hills
(For Earth hath this variety from Heav'n
Of pleasure situate in hill and dale)
Light as the lightning glimpse they ran, they flew,
From their foundations loos'ning to and fro
They plucked the seated hills with all their load,
Rocks, waters, woods, and by the shaggy tops
Uplifting bore them in their hands: amaze,

---

prop up). In wondering whether they are dancing, he again taunts them with behaving like minstrels (166–68n); cp. Aeneas's similar scorn (Homer, *Il.* 16.617). It is ritual taunting revived in Westerns; tough guys don't dance.

623. **amused:** held their attention, diverted them.

635. Expanding Vergil's *furor arma ministrat* (*Aen.* 1.150). Instead of peasants throwing rocks, we witness angels heaving mountains.

639–46. Removal of hills and mountains features prominently in the epic's geological and geographical similes as well as its mythological and scriptural allusions, almost always with apocalyptic resonance (see 195–98n, 1.230–35n, 4.987n). In this instance, which has the distinction of being an actual narrative event, Milton alludes to the tribulation before the Second Coming. Here, however, furious angels "flee into the mountains" to tear them up by the roots and fling them, nearly destroying Heaven (Matt. 24.16–22). The final instance of mountain moving in the poem occurs as part of a divine judgment, when the Flood pushes the mount of Paradise from its place (11.829–38).

646. **amaze:** amazement, dread, with ironic allusion to Ps. 121.1: "I will lift up mine eyes unto the hills, whence cometh my help."

Be sure, and terror seized the rebel host,
When coming towards them so dread they saw
The bottom of the mountains upward turned,
Till on those cursèd engines' triple-row
They saw them whelmed, and all their confidence
Under the weight of mountains buried deep,
Themselves invaded next, and on their heads
Main promontories flung, which in the air
Came shadowing, and oppressed whole legions armed,
Their armor helped their harm, crushed in and bruised
Into their substance pent, which wrought them pain
Implacable, and many a dolorous groan,
Long struggling underneath, ere they could wind
Out of such prison, though spirits of purest light,
Purest at first, now gross by sinning grown.
The rest in imitation to like arms
Betook them, and the neighboring hills uptore;
So hills amid the air encountered hills
Hurled to and fro with jaculation dire
That underground they fought in dismal shade;
Infernal noise; war seemed a civil game
To this uproar; horrid confusion heaped
Upon confusion rose: and now all Heav'n
Had gone to wrack, with ruin overspread,
Had not th' almighty Father where he sits
Shrined in his sanctuary of Heav'n secure,
Consulting on the sum of things, foreseen
This tumult, and permitted all, advised:
That his great purpose he might so fulfill,
To honor his anointed Son avenged
Upon his enemies, and to declare
All power on him transferred: whence to his Son

650. **triple-row:** Cp. 572n.

653. **invaded:** attacked.

654. **Main:** massive, entire.

655. **oppressed:** crushed.

657. **pent:** closely confined; cp. Shakespeare: "a liquid prisoner pent in walls of glass" (*Sonnet 5*, l. 10).

665–66. **jaculation . . . dismal shade:** Cp. the *dismal hiss* of the *fiery darts* on the first day of the war and the hellish canopy of flame they form above the battlefield (ll. 212–13). *Jaculum* is Latin for "dart"; *jaculation* means "throw." The verb for throwing darts seems overtly out of scale when applied to hills or mountains. The war has escalated dramatically from the first day.

673. **sum of things:** Milton's literal translation of *summa rerum,* or the established order of existence (Lucretius 1.333, 756, 1008). Ovid uses a similar phrase to mean "the highest public interest" as he relates the myth of Phaeton, ironically pertinent here inasmuch as Apollo's inept son is blasted from his father's chariot to preserve universal order (*Met.* 5.379–391).

Th' assessor of his throne he thus began.
" 'Effulgence of my glory, Son beloved,
Son in whose face invisible is beheld
Visibly, what by deity I am,
And in whose hand what by decree I do,
Second omnipotence, two days are passed,
Two days, as we compute the days of Heav'n,
Since Michael and his powers went forth to tame
These disobedient; sore hath been their fight,
As likeliest was, when two such foes met armed;
For to themselves I left them, and thou know'st,
Equal in their creation they were formed,
Save what sin hath impaired, which yet hath wrought
Insensibly, for I suspend their doom;
Whence in perpetual fight they needs must last
Endless, and no solution will be found:
War wearied hath performed what war can do,
And to disordered rage let loose the reins,
With mountains as with weapons armed, which makes
Wild work in Heav'n, and dangerous to the main.
Two days are therefore passed, the third is thine;
For thee I have ordained it, and thus far
Have suffered, that the glory may be thine
Of ending this great war, since none but thou
Can end it. Into thee such virtue and grace
Immense I have transfused, that all may know
In Heav'n and Hell thy power above compare,
And this perverse commotion governed thus,
To manifest thee worthiest to be heir
Of all things, to be heir and to be King
By sacred unction, thy deservèd right.
Go then thou mightiest in thy Father's might,
Ascend my chariot, guide the rapid wheels
That shake Heav'n's basis, bring forth all my war,
My bow and thunder, my almighty arms

679. **assessor:** sharer; literally, "one who sits by."

681–82. **invisible is beheld/Visibly:** "the image of the invisible God" (Col. 1.15). The oxymoronic effect owes to the use of *invisible* as a noun, i.e., "one who is invisible."

684. **Second omnipotence:** indicates the derivative or secondary nature of the Son's power (ll. 703–5; cp. John 5.19).

698. **main:** continent of Heaven.

699. **the third is thine:** "Milton, by continuing the war for three days, and reserving the victory upon the third for the Messiah alone, plainly alludes to the circumstances of his death and resurrection" (Newton).

701. **suffered:** permitted.

707–8. **heir/Of all things:** quotation of Heb. 1.2.

712. **war:** synecdoche for instruments of war.

Gird on, and sword upon thy puissant thigh;
Pursue these sons of darkness, drive them out
From all Heav'n's bounds into the utter deep:
There let them learn, as likes them, to despise
God and Messiah his anointed King.'
"He said, and on his Son with rays direct
Shone full, he all his Father full expressed
Ineffably into his face received,
And thus the filial Godhead answering spake:
" 'O Father, O supreme of Heav'nly thrones,
First, highest, holiest, best, thou always seek'st
To glorify thy Son, I always thee,
As is most just; this I my glory account,
My exaltation, and my whole delight,
That thou in me well pleased, declar'st thy will
Fulfilled, which to fulfill is all my bliss.
Scepter and power, thy giving, I assume,
And gladlier shall resign, when in the end
Thou shalt be all in all, and I in thee
Forever, and in me all whom thou lov'st:
But whom thou hat'st, I hate, and can put on
Thy terrors, as I put thy mildness on,
Image of thee in all things; and shall soon,
Armed with thy might, rid Heav'n of these rebelled,
To their prepared ill mansion driven down
To chains of darkness, and th' undying worm,
That from thy just obedience could revolt,
Whom to obey is happiness entire.

716. **utter:** outer.

720–21. "For God, who commanded the light to shine out of darkness, hath shined in our hearts, to give the light of the knowledge of the glory of God in the face of Jesus Christ" (2 Cor. 4.6). Cp. 10.63–67. **expressed/Ineffably:** another seeming oxymoron (see ll. 681–82, 684), here describing the *full* expression of the Father into his Son's face. It is after this silent communication that the Son is called *the filial Godhead* (l. 722). His subsequent reply (ll. 723–41) is woven from scriptures detailing relations between Father and Son.

725. "Glorify thy Son, that thy Son also may glorify thee" (John 17.1).

728. **That thou in me well pleased:** "This is my beloved Son, in whom I am well pleased" (Matt. 3.17).

731–32. **gladlier . . . all:** "When all things shall be subdued unto him, then shall the Son also himself be subject unto him that put all things under him, that God may be all in all" (1 Cor. 15.28).

734. **But whom thou hat'st, I hate:** "Do I not hate them, O Lord, that hate thee? And am I not grieved with those that rise up against thee?" (Ps. 139.21).

738. **prepared ill mansion:** Hell. The grim counterpoint to John 14.2: "In my father's house are many mansions. . . . I go to prepare a place for you."

739. "God delivered them into chains of darkness" (2 Pet. 2.4); "where their worm dieth not" (Mark 9.44). Cp. Isa. 66.24, Jude 6.

Then shall thy saints unmixed, and from th' impure
Far separate, circling thy holy mount
Unfeignèd hallelujahs to thee sing,
Hymns of high praise, and I among them chief.'
So said, he o'er his scepter bowing, rose
From the right hand of glory where he sat,
And the third sacred morn began to shine
Dawning through Heav'n: forth rushed with whirlwind sound
The chariot of paternal deity,
Flashing thick flames, wheel within wheel undrawn,
Itself instinct with spirit, but convoyed
By four cherubic shapes, four faces each
Had wondrous, as with stars their bodies all
And wings were set with eyes, with eyes the wheels
Of beryl, and careering fires between;
Over their heads a crystal firmament,
Whereon a sapphire throne, inlaid with pure
Amber, and colors of the show'ry arch.
He in celestial panoply all armed
Of radiant urim, work divinely wrought,
Ascended, at his right hand Victory
Sat eagle-winged, beside him hung his bow
And quiver with three-bolted thunder stored,
And from about him fierce effusion rolled
Of smoke and bickering flame, and sparkles dire;
Attended with ten thousand thousand saints,
He onward came, far off his coming shone,

744. **Unfeignèd hallelujahs:** Contrast Mammon's disdain for *forc'd hallelujahs* (2.243).

749–59. **forth rushed . . . arch:** Milton's description of the throne-chariot of the deity and its four-faced cherubic transmission is built from details in Ezekiel 1 and 10. Noting the contrast between this animate chariot and the merely material weapons of the devils, S. Fallon argues that the War in Heaven pits Milton's animist materialism against Satan's (and Hobbes's) mechanist materialism (1991, 226–31, 237–41).

752. **instinct with:** impelled by.

756. **beryl:** transparent mineral; **careering:** darting, flashing.

759. **show'ry arch:** rainbow.

761. **radiant urim:** Milton thought *urim* among twelve gemstones mounted on the "breastplate of judgment," worn by the high priest and used as a divine oracle (Exod. 28.30): "Urim and Thummim, those oraculous gems/On Aaron's breast" (*PR* 3.14–15). Fowler cites hermetic writers' identification of urim with the philosopher's stone, but Milton more likely had Josephus's account in mind: "God declared beforehand, by those twelve stones . . . when they should be victorious in battle; for so great a splendor shone forth from them before the army began to march, that all the people were sensible of God's being present for their assistance" (*Antiq.* 3.8.9).

762–64. *Victory* is a winged goddess who aids Zeus in his thundering defeat of the Titans and the Giants. The eagle is his bird. Milton may have in mind Pausanias' description of the statue of Zeus at Olympia: "in his right hand a figure of Victory" (5.11.1).

766. **bickering:** quivering, flashing.

767–70. The numbers are scripturally based; see Rev. 5.11, Jude 14, Ps. 68.17.

And twenty thousand (I their number heard)
Chariots of God, half on each hand were seen:
He on the wings of Cherub rode sublime
On the crystalline sky, in sapphire throned.
Illustrious far and wide, but by his own
First seen, them unexpected joy surprised,
When the great ensign of Messiah blazed
Aloft by angels borne, his sign in Heav'n:
Under whose conduct Michael soon reduced
His army, circumfused on either wing,
Under their head embodied all in one.
Before him power divine his way prepared;
At his command the uprooted hills retired
Each to his place, they heard his voice and went
Obsequious, Heav'n his wonted face renewed,
And with fresh flow'rets hill and valley smiled.
This saw his hapless foes but stood obdured,
And to rebellious fight rallied their powers
Insensate, hope conceiving from despair.
In heav'nly spirits could such perverseness dwell?
But to convince the proud what signs avail,
Or wonders move th' obdurate to relent?
They hardened more by what might most reclaim,
Grieving to see his glory, at the sight
Took envy, and aspiring to his highth,
Stood re-embattled fierce, by force or fraud
Weening to prosper, and at length prevail
Against God and Messiah, or to fall
In universal ruin last, and now
To final battle drew, disdaining flight,
Or faint retreat; when the great Son of God
To all his host on either hand thus spake.
"'Stand still in bright array ye saints, here stand
Ye angels armed, this day from battle rest;

771. "And he rode upon a cherub, and did fly" (2 Sam. 22.11, Ps. 18.10). **sublime:** lifted up, on the chariot's *crystal firmament* and *sapphire throne* (ll. 757–58).

773. **Illustrious:** shining brightly; see 5.738–39.

776. **his sign:** "And then shall appear the sign of the Son of man in heaven" (Matt. 24.30).

777. **reduced:** "led back," with a secondary sense of "diminished." See next note.

779. **their head:** See 5.606 and cp. Abdiel's interpretation of the Son's exaltation: "he the head/ One of our number thus reduced becomes" (5.842–43).

785. **obdured:** hardened; cp. 3.200.

791. **hardened more:** like Pharaoh (see *CD* 1.4).

797. **last:** Bentley would change to "lost," not unreasonably.

801. **Stand still . . . saints:** Moses similarly orders the Hebrews to stand and witness the destruction of Pharaoh's army (Exod. 14.13).

Faithful hath been your warfare, and of God
Accepted, fearless in his righteous cause,
And as ye have received, so have ye done
Invincibly; but of this cursèd crew
The punishment to other hand belongs,
Vengeance is his, or whose he sole appoints;
Number to this day's work is not ordained
Nor multitude, stand only and behold
God's indignation on these godless poured
By me, not you but me they have despised,
Yet envied; against me is all their rage,
Because the Father, t' whom in Heav'n supreme
Kingdom and power and glory appertains,
Hath honored me according to his will.
Therefore to me their doom he hath assigned;
That they may have their wish, to try with me
In battle which the stronger proves, they all,
Or I alone against them, since by strength
They measure all, of other excellence
Not emulous, nor care who them excels;
Nor other strife with them do I vouchsafe.'
"So spake the Son, and into terror changed
His count'nance too severe to be beheld
And full of wrath bent on his enemies.
At once the Four spread out their starry wings
With dreadful shade contiguous, and the orbs
Of his fierce chariot rolled, as with the sound
Of torrent floods, or of a numerous host.
He on his impious foes right onward drove,
Gloomy as night; under his burning wheels
The steadfast empyrean shook throughout,

808. "Vengeance is mine; I will repay, saith the Lord" (Rom. 12.19; cp. Deut. 32.35).

815. "For thine is the kingdom, and the power, and the glory" (Matt. 6.13).

827. **the Four:** the chariot's *four cherubic shapes* (l. 753); **starry wings:** The wings were previously described as *set with eyes* (l. 755; cp. Ezek. 10.12); the poetic equation of eyes and stars is, however, commonplace.

828. **contiguous:** "Their wings were joined one to another" (Ezek. 1.9).

831. **right onward:** Milton thought of himself as proceeding in the same way; cp. *Sonnet 22* 8–9.

833–34. **The steadfast empyrean . . . God:** In the first speech of the epic, Satan claims that the battle did shake God's throne (1.105). Editors cite as Heaven-shaking precedents Hesiod's account of Zeus's battle with Typhoeus (*Theog.* 842–43) and various scriptures, including Isa. 13.12–13, and 2 Sam. 22.8. Overlooked is Heb. 12.26, the key verse for *Lycidas* (Tayler 1979, 234–36) and one fundamental to the typological structure and range of the War in Heaven, from Moses receiving the Law to Christ's Second Coming (cp. 56–60n): "[His] voice then shook the earth: but now he hath promised, saying, 'Yet once more I shake not the earth only, but also heaven.' "

All but the throne itself of God. Full soon
Among them he arrived; in his right hand
Grasping ten thousand thunders, which he sent
Before him, such as in their souls infixed
Plagues; they astonished all resistance lost,
All courage; down their idle weapons dropped;
O'er shields and helms, and helmèd heads he rode
Of Thrones and mighty Seraphim prostrate,
That wished the mountains now might be again
Thrown on them as a shelter from his ire.
Nor less on either side tempestuous fell
His arrows, from the fourfold-visaged Four,
Distinct with eyes, and from the living wheels
Distinct alike with multitude of eyes;
One spirit in them ruled, and every eye
Glared lightning, and shot forth pernicious fire
Among th' accursed, that withered all their strength,
And of their wonted vigor left them drained,
Exhausted, spiritless, afflicted, fall'n.
Yet half his strength he put not forth, but checked
His thunder in mid-volley, for he meant
Not to destroy, but root them out of Heav'n:
The overthrown he raised, and as a herd
Of goats or timorous flock together thronged
Drove them before him thunderstruck, pursued
With terrors and with furies to the bounds
And crystal wall of Heav'n, which op'ning wide,
Rolled inward, and a spacious gap disclosed
Into the wasteful deep; the monstrous sight
Strook them with horror backward, but far worse
Urged them behind; headlong themselves they threw

838. **Plagues:** afflictions, strokes of divine retribution. Editors cite the plagues of Egypt under Pharaoh, who is contextually present. In prophecy of the apocalypse, plagues, thunder, lightning, and earthquake are grouped together (see, e.g., Rev. 17).

840–41. In *Apology*, Milton personifies "the invincible warrior Zeal," riding a chariot like the one described in Ezekiel and driving "over the heads of scarlet prelates, and such as are insolent to maintain traditions, bruising their stiff necks under his flaming wheels" (Yale 1:900).

842–43. "And [they] said to the mountains and rocks, 'fall on us, and hide us from the . . . wrath of the Lamb'" (Rev. 6.16; cp. Luke 23.30, Hosea 10.8).

846. **Distinct:** adorned.

849. **pernicious:** deadly, sudden; cp. l. 520.

857. **goats:** In Scripture the damned are compared to goats, whom at the Last Judgment Christ will gather in his left hand before passing sentence: "Depart from me, ye cursed, into everlasting fire, prepared for the devil and his angels" (Matt. 25.41).

861. **Rolled inward:** rolled up or together; cp. Rev. 6.14: "And the heaven departed [was removed] as a scroll when it is rolled together." **disclosed:** bared, opened.

862. **wasteful:** full of emptiness (Elledge).

Down from the verge of Heav'n; eternal wrath
Burnt after them to the bottomless pit.
"Hell heard th' unsufferable noise, Hell saw
Heav'n ruining from Heav'n and would have fled
Affrighted; but strict fate had cast too deep
Her dark foundations, and too fast had bound.
Nine days they fell; confounded Chaos roared,
And felt tenfold confusion in their fall
Through his wild anarchy, so huge a rout
Encumbered him with ruin: Hell at last
Yawning received them whole, and on them closed,
Hell their fit habitation fraught with fire
Unquenchable, the house of woe and pain.
Disburdened Heav'n rejoiced, and soon repaired
Her mural breach, returning whence it rolled.
Sole victor from th' expulsion of his foes
Messiah his triumphal chariot turned:
To meet him all his saints, who silent stood
Eye-witnesses of his almighty acts,
With jubilee advanced; and as they went,
Shaded with branching palm, each order bright
Sung triumph, and him sung victorious King,
Son, Heir, and Lord, to him dominion giv'n,
Worthiest to reign: he celebrated rode
Triumphant through mid-Heav'n, into the courts
And temple of his mighty Father throned
On high: who into glory him received,
Where now he sits at the right hand of bliss.
"Thus measuring things in Heav'n by things on Earth
At thy request, and that thou may'st beware
By what is past, to thee I have revealed
What might have else to human race been hid;
The discord which befell, and war in Heav'n

868. **ruining:** falling.

869. **fate:** God's curse (2.622–23). "Fate or *fatum* is only what is *fatum,* spoken, by some almighty power" (*CD* 1.2).

871. **Nine days they fell:** After falling for nine days, they lie stunned for another nine on the lake in Hell (1.50–53). In Hesiod, the rebellious Titans fall for nine days from Heaven to Earth and nine more from earth to Tartarus (*Theog.* 720–25).

873. **rout:** mob, those defeated.

874–75. **Hell . . . closed:** "Therefore hell hath enlarged herself, and opened her mouth without measure" (Isa. 5.14).

884. **jubilee:** joyful shouting.

885. **palm:** symbolic of triumph, as at *SA* 1735. "[The people] took branches of palm trees, and went forth to meet him, and cried, Hosanna: Blessed is the King of Israel that cometh in the name of the Lord" (John 22.12–13; cp. Rev. 7.9).

892. **right hand:** St. Paul describes Christ after his ascension into Heaven as sitting "on the right hand of the Majesty on high" (Heb. 1.3).

Among th' angelic powers, and the deep fall
Of those too high aspiring, who rebelled
With Satan, he who envies now thy state,
Who now is plotting how he may seduce
Thee also from obedience, that with him
Bereaved of happiness thou may'st partake
His punishment, eternal misery;
Which would be all his solace and revenge,
As a despite done against the Most High,
Thee once to gain companion of his woe.
But listen not to his temptations, warn
Thy weaker; let it profit thee to have heard
By terrible example the reward
Of disobedience; firm they might have stood,
Yet fell; remember, and fear to transgress."

900–907. Raphael's most explicit and specific warning of Satan's plot against humanity and its motive. He does not mention the apprehension of Satan at Eve's ear during the previous night.

909. **Thy weaker:** Eve, the "weaker vessel" (1 Pet. 3.7). She is present for Raphael's narration and at this moment.

"headlong themselves they threw / Down from the verge of Heav'n" (6.864–65).

Book VII

The Argument

Raphael at the request of Adam relates how and wherefore this world was first created: that God, after the expelling of Satan and his angels out of Heaven, declared his pleasure to create another world and other creatures to dwell therein; sends his Son with glory and attendance of angels to perform the work of Creation in six days; the angels celebrate with hymns the performance thereof, and his reascension into Heaven.

Descend from Heav'n Urania, by that name
If rightly thou art called, whose voice divine
Following, above th' Olympian hill I soar,
Above the flight of Pegasean wing.
The meaning, not the name I call: for thou
Nor of the Muses nine, nor on the top
Of old Olympus dwell'st, but Heav'nly born,
Before the hills appeared, or fountain flowed,
Thou with eternal Wisdom didst converse,
Wisdom thy sister, and with her didst play
In presence of th' Almighty Father, pleased
With thy celestial song. Up led by thee
Into the Heav'n of Heav'ns I have presumed,
An earthly guest, and drawn empyreal air,
Thy temp'ring; with like safety guided down

1. **Descend from Heav'n:** evoking Horace's *descende caelo . . . Calliope* (*Odes* 4.1.2); **Urania:** the Muse of astronomy in Roman times, but transformed into the Muse of Christian poetry by du Bartas in *La Muse Chrestiene* (1574).
3. **above th' Olympian hill:** Cp. 1.15.
4. **Pegasean wing:** The winged horse Pegasus ascended to the heavens of Greek mythology, but Milton has risen incomparably higher, to the Heaven of the Christian God.
5. **The meaning, not the name:** *Urania* means "heavenly one" in Latin, but Milton calls upon a power found in the Christian Heaven.
9. **Wisdom:** Wisdom was born "before the hills," before all Creation, in Prov. 8.24–31. Milton identified her as a personification of the Father's wisdom (*CD* 1.7 in Yale 6:303–4). **converse:** live in company with (Lat. *conversari*).
13. **Heav'n of Heav'ns:** the supreme Heaven (an English version of the Hebrew superlative).
15. **Thy temp'ring:** "made suitable by thee for an earthly guest."

Return me to my native element:
Lest from this flying steed unreined, (as once
Bellerophon, though from a lower clime)
Dismounted, on th' Aleian field I fall
Erroneous there to wander and forlorn.
Half yet remains unsung, but narrower bound
Within the visible diurnal sphere;
Standing on earth, not rapt above the pole,
More safe I sing with mortal voice, unchanged
To hoarse or mute, though fall'n on evil days,
On evil days though fall'n, and evil tongues;
In darkness, and with dangers compassed round,
And solitude; yet not alone, while thou
Visit'st my slumbers nightly, or when morn
Purples the east: still govern thou my song,
Urania, and fit audience find, though few.
But drive far off the barbarous dissonance
Of Bacchus and his revellers, the race
Of that wild rout that tore the Thracian bard
In Rhodope, where woods and rocks had ears
To rapture, till the savage clamor drowned
Both harp and voice; nor could the Muse defend

17–20. Milton defines his hapless condition without the Muse's aid by reference to the fate of *Bellerophon,* who tried unsuccessfully to ride Pegasus (see l. 4) to heaven and fell upon the *Aleian field* (land of wandering), where he died *erroneous* (i.e., in a state of distraction). According to some, his fall blinded him (Conti, *Mythologiae* 9.4).

18. **clime:** region.

21–22. Save for episodes in Books 10 and 11, the remaining action of the poem takes place on Earth.

22. **visible diurnal sphere:** the visible universe, which appears to rotate around the Earth on a daily basis.

23. **rapt:** transported; **pole:** the highest spot in the universe, at which it is chained to Heaven (2.1051–52). Milton went *above the pole* when representing the divine council at the opening of Book 3.

25. **hoarse:** In *RCG,* Milton ruefully noted that pamphlets were "a troubled sea of noises and hoarse disputes" (p. 843). **mute:** probably alludes to the silencing of many Puritan authors during the Restoration. Milton's point is that his poem has suffered neither of the common fates (becoming *hoarse or mute*) of Puritan pamphleteers. **evil days:** After the restoration of the English monarchy in May 1660, an order was issued for Milton's arrest. He was in fact arrested after hiding out for some weeks, and released in December. During this time some of his books were burned.

26. **evil tongues:** Among the many authors who reviled Milton during the Restoration were Roger L'Estrange, George Starkey, David Lloyd, Thomas Ford, Robert South, and Samuel Parker.

27. **darkness:** blindness, from which Milton had suffered since 1652.

28–30. **while thou . . . east:** Biographers report that Milton composed either at night or early in the morning (Darbishire 33, 291). Cp. 3.29–32; 9.21–24.

32. **barbarous dissonance:** The phrase also appears in *Masque* (l. 550).

33–37. **the race . . . voice:** The poet Orpheus was torn to pieces by the Maenads, female followers of Bacchus, after he rejected the love of women. His mother, the epic Muse Calliope, could not save him, as Milton also stresses in *Lyc* 58–63. But Urania, a higher Muse, can protect her inspired poet.

Her son. So fail not thou, who thee implores:
For thou art Heav'nly, she an empty dream.
    Say Goddess, what ensued when Raphael,
The affable archangel, had forewarned
Adam by dire example to beware
Apostasy, by what befell in Heaven
To those apostates, lest the like befall
In Paradise to Adam or his race,
Charged not to touch the interdicted tree,
If they transgress, and slight that sole command,
So easily obeyed amid the choice
Of all tastes else to please their appetite,
Though wand'ring. He with his consorted Eve
The story heard attentive, and was filled
With admiration, and deep muse to hear
Of things so high and strange, things to their thought
So unimaginable as hate in Heav'n,
And war so near the peace of God in bliss
With such confusion: but the evil soon
Driv'n back redounded as a flood on those
From whom it sprung, impossible to mix
With blessedness. Whence Adam soon repealed
The doubts that in his heart arose: and now
Led on, yet sinless, with desire to know
What nearer might concern him, how this world
Of heav'n and earth conspicuous first began,
When, and whereof created, for what cause,
What within Eden or without was done
Before his memory, as one whose drouth
Yet scarce allayed still eyes the current stream,
Whose liquid murmur heard new thirst excites,
Proceeded thus to ask his Heav'nly guest.
    "Great things, and full of wonder in our ears,
Far differing from this world, thou hast revealed
Divine interpreter, by favor sent

46. **touch:** "Ye shall not eat of it, neither shall ye touch it, lest ye die" (Gen. 3.3); cp. 9.651.

47. **sole command:** The singularity of the commandment has already been stressed (1.32; 4.421, 423–24, 428).

50. **wand'ring:** innocently curious wandering at this point, but the word does have the fallen sense of "going astray, losing one's moral bearings," as perhaps in line 20. **consorted:** espoused.

52. **admiration:** wonder; **muse:** meditation.

57. **redounded:** recoiled.

59. **repealed:** recalled.

63. **conspicuous:** visible.

72. **Divine interpreter:** "Mercury, who is the president of language, is called *deorum hominumque interpres*" (Jonson, *Discoveries*, in Herford et al. 8:621). Raphael is the Christian Mercury. See also 3.656–57.

Down from the Empyrean to forewarn
Us timely of what might else have been our loss,
Unknown, which human knowledge could not reach:
For which to the infinitely Good we owe
Immortal thanks, and his admonishment
Receive with solemn purpose to observe
Immutably his sov'reign will, the end
Of what we are. But since thou hast vouchsafed
Gently for our instruction to impart
Things above earthly thought, which yet concerned
Our knowing, as to highest wisdom seemed,
Deign to descend now lower, and relate
What may no less perhaps avail us known,
How first began this heav'n which we behold
Distant so high, with moving fires adorned
Innumerable, and this which yields or fills
All space, the ambient air wide interfused
Embracing round this florid Earth; what cause
Moved the Creator in his holy rest
Through all eternity so late to build
In Chaos, and the work begun, how soon
Absolved, if unforbid thou may'st unfold
What we, not to explore the secrets ask
Of his eternal empire, but the more
To magnify his works, the more we know.
And the great light of day yet wants to run
Much of his race though steep, suspense in heav'n
Held by thy voice, thy potent voice he hears,
And longer will delay to hear thee tell
His generation, and the rising birth
Of nature from the unapparent deep:
Or if the star of ev'ning and the moon
Haste to thy audience, Night with her will bring
Silence, and Sleep list'ning to thee will watch,
Or we can bid his absence, till thy song

79. **end:** purpose.

83. **seemed:** seemed good.

85. **avail us known:** prove valuable to us when known.

88. **yields or fills:** Air "yields space to all bodies, and . . . fills up the deserted space [when the bodies move]" (Richardson).

94. **Absolved:** finished; **unforbid:** unforbidden.

97. **magnify:** glorify. "Remember that thou magnify his work, which men behold" (Job 36.24).

98. **yet wants:** still has to.

99. **suspense:** attentive, hanging.

100. **he hears:** The sun or *great light of day* in line 98 is here personified.

103. **unapparent deep:** no longer perceptible Chaos.

106. **will watch:** will stay awake. Sleep (personified) is the subject of this verb.

107. **his:** Sleep's.

End, and dismiss thee ere the morning shine."
  Thus Adam his illustrious guest besought:
And thus the godlike angel answered mild.
"This also thy request with caution asked
Obtain: though to recount almighty works
What words or tongue of Seraph can suffice,
Or heart of man suffice to comprehend?
Yet what thou canst attain, which best may serve
To glorify the Maker, and infer
Thee also happier, shall not be withheld
Thy hearing, such commission from above
I have received, to answer thy desire
Of knowledge within bounds; beyond abstain
To ask, nor let thine own inventions hope
Things not revealed, which th' invisible King,
Only omniscient, hath suppressed in night,
To none communicable in Earth or Heaven:
Enough is left besides to search and know.
But knowledge is as food, and needs no less
Her temperance over appetite, to know
In measure what the mind may well contain,
Oppresses else with surfeit, and soon turns
Wisdom to folly, as nourishment to wind.
  "Know then, that after Lucifer from Heav'n
(So call him, brighter once amidst the host
Of angels, than that star the stars among)
Fell with his flaming legions through the deep
Into his place, and the great Son returned
Victorious with his saints, th' omnipotent
Eternal Father from his throne beheld
Their multitude, and to his Son thus spake.
  " 'At least our envious foe hath failed, who thought
All like himself rebellious, by whose aid
This inaccessible high strength, the seat
Of Deity supreme, us dispossessed,

116. **infer:** render.
120. **Of knowledge within bounds:** On this theme, cp. 8.173–97.
121. **inventions:** speculations; **hope:** hope for.
124. **in earth or Heaven:** The passage has apparently been calling attention to the bounds on human knowledge, but now we learn that the bounds in question limit angelic knowledge as well.
132. **So call him:** In classical Latin, Lucifer (from Gk. for "light-bringer") refers to Venus, the morning star. The Christian Fathers called Satan by the name of Lucifer, perhaps in reference to his original brightness. In Milton's four drafts for a tragedy on the fall of man in the *CMS*, the character is referred to as Lucifer, not Satan. Cp. 5.760, 10.425.
136. **saints:** angels.

He trusted to have seized, and into fraud
Drew many, whom their place knows here no more;
Yet far the greater part have kept, I see,
Their station, Heav'n yet populous retains
Number sufficient to possess her realms
Though wide, and this high temple to frequent
With ministeries due and solemn rites:
But lest his heart exalt him in the harm
Already done, to have dispeopled Heav'n,
My damage fondly deemed, I can repair
That detriment, if such it be to lose
Self-lost, and in a moment will create
Another world, out of one man a race
Of men innumerable, there to dwell,
Not here, till by degrees of merit raised
They open to themselves at length the way
Up hither, under long obedience tried,
And Earth be chang'd to Heav'n, and Heav'n to Earth,
One kingdom, joy and union without end.
Meanwhile inhabit lax, ye powers of Heav'n,
And thou my Word, begotten Son, by thee
This I perform, speak thou, and be it done:
My overshadowing Spirit and might with thee
I send along, ride forth, and bid the deep
Within appointed bounds be heav'n and earth;
Boundless the deep, because I am who fill
Infinitude, nor vacuous the space.
Though I uncircumscribed myself retire,
And put not forth my goodness, which is free

143. **fraud:** The word has its usual meaning of dishonesty and deception, but also the sense of Latin *fraus* (crime, injury). Satan not only drew his followers into deceit; he ruined them.

144. **their place knows here no more:** a scriptural idiom (Ps. 101.16, Job 7.10); cp. 11.50–57.

145. **the greater part:** Cp. 2.692n.

146. **station:** post, duty.

150–55. Empson concludes that God creates us "to spite the devils" (1965, 56). The passage says as much; but God also stresses that the Creation was not necessitated by the defection of the rebel angels.

152. **fondly:** foolishly.

156. **men innumerable:** A finite number of angels were created; they do not reproduce. The breeding race of men, by contrast, is *innumerable* (unnumbered). See Augustine, *City of God* 22.1. Thomas Browne wrote of "the fertility of Adam, and the magic of that sperm that hath dilated into so many millions" (*Religio Medici* 1.48).

162. **inhabit lax:** "dwell at ease" (having vanquished the rebels) and "dwell at large" (having more of Heaven to yourselves).

165. The Son creates the world, but using the *Spirit* and *might* of the Father. This combination of agency and service is typical of Milton's Arian Christology (see 3.169–72, 384–96; 6.680–83).

168–71. **Boundless . . . goodness:** The passage is highly compressed. The *deep* (uncreated Chaos) will not be any less *boundless* because of Creation. It is infinite because filled by an infinite God, who can nonetheless, and also with no loss of infinity, *retire* from it.

171. **free:** "In God a certain immutable internal necessity to do good, independent of all outside

To act or not, necessity and chance
Approach not me, and what I will is fate.'
"So spake th' Almighty, and to what he spake
His Word, the filial Godhead, gave effect.
Immediate are the acts of God, more swift
Than time or motion, but to human ears
Cannot without process of speech be told,
So told as earthly notion can receive.
Great triumph and rejoicing was in Heav'n
When such was heard declared th' Almighty's will;
Glory they sung to the most high, good will
To future men, and in their dwellings peace:
Glory to him whose just avenging ire
Had driven out th' ungodly from his sight
And th' habitations of the just; to him
Glory and praise, whose wisdom had ordained
Good out of evil to create, instead
Of spirits malign a better race to bring
Into their vacant room, and thence diffuse
His good to worlds and ages infinite.
So sang the hierarchies: meanwhile the Son
On his great expedition now appeared,
Girt with omnipotence, with radiance crowned
Of majesty divine, sapience and love
Immense, and all his Father in him shone.
About his chariot numberless were poured
Cherub and Seraph, Potentates and Thrones,
And Virtues, wingèd spirits, and chariots winged,

---

influence, can be consistent with absolute freedom of action" (*CD* 1.3, p. 1155). It is crucial to Milton that God be free to put forth his goodness in Creation, or *not.*

172. **necessity and chance:** a philosophical binary that the Christian God was often said to transcend (Augustine, *City of God* 5.1.8–10, on necessity; Boethius, *The Consolation of Philosophy* 4.1–2, on chance). In Milton, Chance rules only embryonic atoms (2.907), and necessity is "the tyrant's plea" (4.394).

173. **what I will is fate:** "Fate or *fatum* is only what is *fatum,* spoken, by some almighty power" (*CD* 1.2, p. 1146). Paradoxes would seem to be on the horizon: if God wills our will to be free, then freedom is fate. But Milton tried to keep divine and human freedom at a distance from such dialectical cleverness. Theologically, politically, and aesthetically, liberty was his most cherished concept.

175. **the filial Godhead:** the Son.

176. **Immediate are the acts of God:** Augustine maintained that the six days of Creation in Genesis symbolize one instantaneous act (*De Genesi* 1.1–3).

178. **process of speech:** the successive acts that constitute speech.

179. **earthly notion:** human understanding.

180–83. The passage is based on Job 38.7 and Luke 2.14.

188. **Good out of evil:** remembering 1.162–63 and anticipating 7.613–16 and 12.469–78.

194. **Girt:** armed.

197. **poured:** crowded together; not arranged in an orderly fashion.

From the armory of God, where stand of old
Myriads between two brazen mountains lodged
Against a solemn day, harnessed at hand,
Celestial equipage; and now came forth
Spontaneous, for within them spirit lived,
Attendant on their Lord: Heav'n opened wide
Her ever-during gates, harmonious sound
On golden hinges moving, to let forth
The King of Glory in his powerful Word
And Spirit coming to create new worlds.
On Heav'nly ground they stood, and from the shore
They viewed the vast immeasurable abyss
Outrageous as a sea, dark, wasteful, wild,
Up from the bottom turned by furious winds
And surging waves, as mountains to assault
Heav'n's highth, and with the center mix the pole.
"'Silence, ye troubled waves, and thou deep, peace,'
Said then th' omnific Word, 'your discord end.'
"Nor stayed, but on the wings of Cherubim
Uplifted, in paternal glory rode
Far into Chaos, and the world unborn;
For Chaos heard his voice: him all his train
Followed in bright procession to behold
Creation, and the wonders of his might.
Then stayed the fervid wheels, and in his hand
He took the golden compasses, prepared
In God's eternal store, to circumscribe
This universe, and all created things:
One foot he centered, and the other turned
Round through the vast profundity obscure,
And said, 'Thus far extend, thus far thy bounds,
This be thy just circumference, O world.'
Thus God the heav'n created, thus the earth,

200. **armory of God:** "The Lord hath opened his armory" (Jer. 50.25). See 6.321.

201. Four chariots are seen between two mountains in Zech. 6.1.

202. **Against:** in readiness for.

203–5. **now . . . Lord:** See the animated chariot of 6.845–50.

205. **opened wide:** Cp. the self-opening gate of 5.254–55, derived from Ps. 24.7.

206. **ever-during:** everlasting.

212. **Outrageous:** immense, unrestrained; **wasteful:** desolate.

217. **omnific:** all-creating. We have replaced the colon at the end of this line in 1667 with a period and sacrificed an effect: as the colon would have suggested, *omnific Word* is the subject of the next syntactical unit's verbs (*stayed, uplifted, rode*).

224. **fervid:** glowing (from motion).

225. **compasses:** Wisdom declares in Prov. 8:27, "I was there: then he set a compass upon the face of the depth." Cp. Dante, *Par.* 19.40–42.

226. **circumscribe:** mark out the limits of.

231. **just:** exact.

Matter unformed and void: darkness profound
Covered th' abyss: but on the wat'ry calm
His brooding wings the Spirit of God outspread,
And vital virtue infused, and vital warmth
Throughout the fluid mass, but downward purged
The black tartareous cold infernal dregs
Adverse to life: then founded, then conglobed
Like things to like, the rest to several place
Disparted, and between spun out the air,
And Earth self-balanced on her center hung.
"'Let there be light,' said God, and forthwith light
Ethereal, first of things, quintessence pure
Sprung from the deep, and from her native east
To journey through the airy gloom began,
Sphered in a radiant cloud, for yet the sun
Was not; she in a cloudy tabernacle
Sojourned the while. God saw the light was good;
And light from darkness by the hemisphere
Divided: light the day, and darkness night
He named. Thus was the first day ev'n and morn:
Nor passed uncelebrated, nor unsung
By the celestial choirs, when orient light
Exhaling first from darkness they beheld;
Birthday of heav'n and Earth; with joy and shout
The hollow universal orb they filled,
And touched their golden harps, and hymning praised
God and his works; Creator him they sung,
Both when first ev'ning was, and when first morn.

233. **Matter unformed and void:** "The earth was without form, and void" (Gen. 1.2).

235. **brooding wings:** See 1.20–22.

236. **vital virtue:** the stuff of life.

238. **tartareous:** hellish.

239. **founded:** usually glossed as "laid the foundation," but Leonard's "attached" fits the context perfectly. The word has biblical precedent (Ps. 89.11; Prov. 3.19). **conglobed:** gathered into separate spheres.

241. **Disparted:** separated in different directions.

242. **self-balanced:** Cp. *Nat Ode* 117–24; **her center:** See 4.1000–1001; 5.578–79.

243–52. Milton's version of Gen. 1.3–5.

244. Since the sun and other heavenly bodies are not created until the fourth day, commentators had somehow to distinguish ordinary celestial light from the light of Gen. 1.3. Milton identifies the primal light with ether, a fifth element (*quintessence*) thought to be ubiquitous above the sphere of the moon.

248. **tabernacle:** dwelling. "He set a tabernacle for the sun" (Ps. 19.4).

252. **ev'n and morn:** The Hebrew day was measured from evening to evening, though the meaning of *evening* was disputed. According to Fowler, "Milton clearly followed Jerome in reckoning from sunset" (Introduction, 30). *Ev'n* here must therefore mean "sunset."

254. **orient:** bright, eastern.

255. **Exhaling:** rising as a vapor. The earth was thought to emit vaporous clouds (exhalations) that rose toward the heavens and often combusted. Milton implicitly compares the separation of light from darkness to this phenomenon.

"Again, God said, 'Let there be firmament
Amid the waters, and let it divide
The waters from the waters': and God made
The firmament, expanse of liquid, pure,
Transparent, elemental air, diffused
In circuit to the uttermost convex
Of this great round: partition firm and sure,
The waters underneath from those above
Dividing: for as Earth, so he the world
Built on circumfluous waters calm, in wide
Crystalline ocean, and the loud misrule
Of Chaos far removed, lest fierce extremes
Contiguous might distemper the whole frame:
And heav'n he named the firmament: so ev'n
And morning chorus sung the second day.
"The Earth was formed, but in the womb as yet
Of waters, embryon immature involved,
Appeared not: over all the face of Earth
Main ocean flowed, not idle, but with warm
Prolific humor soft'ning all her globe,
Fermented the great mother to conceive,
Satiate with genial moisture, when God said,
'Be gathered now ye waters under heav'n
Into one place, and let dry land appear.'
Immediately the mountains huge appear
Emergent, and their broad bare backs upheave
Into the clouds, their tops ascend the sky:
So high as heaved the tumid hills, so low
Down sunk a hollow bottom broad and deep,
Capacious bed of waters: thither they
Hasted with glad precipitance, uprolled
As drops on dust conglobing from the dry;
Part rise in crystal wall, or ridge direct,

261–74. Milton's version of Gen. 1.6–8. The waters above the firmament are identified with the space between the earth and the crystalline sphere at the rim of the universe; the lower waters are the earth's oceans.

264. **expanse:** a correct translation of the Hebrew word rendered "firmament" in the *AV*.

267. **this great round:** the universe.

269. **the world:** the universe.

273. **distemper the whole frame:** disturb the order of the elements, making the universe too hot or too cold.

277. **embryon immature involved:** wrapped (by waters) in an immature embryonic state.

281. **great mother:** Earth, who is both the mother and her child.

282. **genial:** fertilizing.

288. **tumid:** swollen.

291. **precipitance:** flowing, falling.

292. **conglobing:** assembling into spheres.

293. **crystal wall:** See the description of the parting of the Red Sea at 12.196–97. **ridge direct:** move forward like waves.

For haste; such flight the great command impressed
On the swift floods: as armies at the call
Of trumpet (for of armies thou hast heard)
Troop to their standard, so the wat'ry throng,
Wave rolling after wave, where way they found,
If steep, with torrent rapture, if through plain,
Soft-ebbing; nor withstood them rock or hill,
But they, or under ground, or circuit wide
With serpent error wand'ring, found their way,
And on the washy ooze deep channels wore;
Easy, ere God had bid the ground be dry,
All but within those banks, where rivers now
Stream, and perpetual draw their humid train.
The dry land, earth, and the great receptacle
Of congregated waters he called seas:
And saw that it was good, and said, 'Let th' earth
Put forth the verdant grass, herb yielding seed,
And fruit tree yielding fruit after her kind;
Whose seed is in herself upon the earth.'
He scarce had said, when the bare earth, till then
Desert and bare, unsightly, unadorned,
Brought forth the tender grass, whose verdure clad
Her universal face with pleasant green,
Then herbs of every leaf, that sudden flow'red
Op'ning their various colors, and made gay
Her bosom smelling sweet: and these scarce blown,
Forth flourished thick the clust'ring vine, forth crept
The swelling gourd, up stood the corny reed
Embattled in her field: add the humble shrub,
And bush with frizzled hair implicit: last
Rose as in dance the stately trees, and spread

299. **with torrent rapture:** with torrential force, with rapturous obedience.

302. **serpent error wand'ring:** a crucial text for critics who argue for the presence of unfallen and fallen languages in the poem, since all three words have a sinful signification, but also an "innocent" one: *serpent* could mean "serpentine"; *error* mean "winding course"; and *wand'ring* mean "moving now this way, now that way." See Ricks 1963, 110; Fish 1967, 130–41.

308. **congregated waters:** For Gen. 1.10 the Vulgate reads *congregationesque aquarum.*

309–33. Milton's version of Gen. 1.11–13.

313–19. **the bare earth . . . sweet:** Here, as throughout the account of Creation, Milton describes the shaping activity of *logoi spermatikoi* (seminal seeds) embedded in matter. Augustine had adapted from Stoic cosmology the notion of these seeds or *rationes seminales* informed with the Creator's ideas of all things (*De Trinitate* 3.8.3). The Son speaks, the *logoi spermatikoi* obediently unfold. For more on this tradition, see Curry 1937, 29–49.

321. **swelling:** Both 1667 and 1674 read "smelling."

322. **Embattled:** See the cornlike spears of 4.980–82; **add:** moreover.

323. **hair:** leaves and branches; **implicit:** entangled.

Their branches hung with copious fruit; or gemmed
Their blossoms: with high woods the hills were crowned,
With tufts the valleys and each fountain side,
With borders long the rivers. That Earth now
Seemed like to Heav'n, a seat where gods might dwell,
Or wander with delight, and love to haunt
Her sacred shades: though God had yet not rained
Upon the earth, and man to till the ground
None was, but from the earth a dewy mist
Went up and watered all the ground, and each
Plant of the field, which ere it was in the earth
God made, and every herb, before it grew
On the green stem; God saw that it was good:
So ev'n and morn recorded the third day.
    "Again th' Almighty spake: 'Let there be lights
High in th' expanse of heaven to divide
The day from night; and let them be for signs,
For seasons, and for days, and circling years,
And let them be for lights as I ordain
Their office in the firmament of heav'n
To give light on the Earth'; and it was so.
And God made two great lights, great for their use
To man, the greater to have rule by day,
The less by night altern: and made the stars,
And set them in the firmament of heav'n
To illuminate the Earth, and rule the day
In their vicissitude, and rule the night,
And light from darkness to divide. God saw,
Surveying his great work, that it was good:
For of celestial bodies first the sun
A mighty sphere he framed, unlightsome first,
Though of ethereal mold: then formed the moon
Globose, and every magnitude of stars,
And sowed with stars the heav'n thick as a field:
Of light by far the greater part he took,
Transplanted from her cloudy shrine, and placed
In the sun's orb, made porous to receive
And drink the liquid light, firm to retain

325. **gemmed:** budded (from Lat. *gemmare*).
332. **man to till the ground:** See Gen. 2.5.
338. **recorded:** bore witness to.
339–86. Milton's version of Gen. 1.14–19.
348. **altern:** by turns.
351. **vicissitude:** alternation.
356. **of ethereal mold:** made from quintessential matter (see 244n).
357. **every magnitude of stars:** stars of every degree of brightness.

Her gathered beams, great palace now of light.
Hither as to their fountain other stars
Repairing, in their golden urns draw light,
And hence the morning planet gilds her horns;
By tincture or reflection they augment
Their small peculiar, though from human sight
So far remote, with diminution seen.
First in his east the glorious lamp was seen,
Regent of day, and all th' horizon round
Invested with bright rays, jocund to run
His longitude through heav'n's high road: the gray
Dawn, and the Pleiades before him danced
Shedding sweet influence: less bright the moon,
But opposite in leveled west was set
His mirror, with full face borrowing her light
From him, for other light she needed none
In that aspect, and still that distance keeps
Till night, then in the east her turn she shines,
Revolved on heav'n's great axle, and her reign
With thousand lesser lights dividual holds,
With thousand thousand stars, that then appeared
Spangling the hemisphere: then first adorned
With their bright luminaries that set and rose,
Glad ev'ning and glad morn crowned the fourth day.
"And God said, 'Let the waters generate
Reptile with spawn abundant, living soul:
And let fowl fly above the earth, with wings
Displayed on the op'n firmament of heav'n.'
And God created the great whales, and each
Soul living, each that crept, which plenteously
The waters generated by their kinds,
And every bird of wing after his kind;

366. **morning planet:** Venus or Lucifer; **her:** So 1667; 1674 has "his." Venus would fit *her,* Lucifer *his,* but *morning planet* could be either, and there is no strong reason for preferring one reading to the other.

367. **tincture or reflection:** absorbing or reflecting the sun's light.

368. **Their small peculiar:** their own small light.

372. **Invested:** clothed, arrayed; **jocund to run:** See Ps. 19.4–5.

373. **longitude:** course from east to west.

374–75. **Pleiades . . . influence:** Job 38.31: "Canst thou bind the sweet influences to the Pleiades?"

376. **leveled west:** due west (directly opposite).

377. **His mirror:** in the sense that the moon reflects the sun's light.

379. **In that aspect:** in that position (when the moon is full).

381. **axle:** axis.

382. **dividual:** divided.

387–448. Milton's version of Gen. 1.20–23.

388. **Reptile:** creeping things, including fish.

390. **Displayed:** spread out.

393. **by their kinds:** according to their species.

And saw that it was good, and blessed them, saying,
'Be fruitful, multiply, and in the seas
And lakes and running streams the waters fill;
And let the fowl be multiplied on the earth.'
Forthwith the sounds and seas, each creek and bay
With fry innumerable swarm, and shoals
Of fish that with their fins and shining scales
Glide under the green wave, in schools that oft
Bank the mid sea: part single or with mate
Graze the seaweed their pasture, and through groves
Of coral stray, or sporting with quick glance
Show to the sun their waved coats dropped with gold,
Or in their pearly shells at ease, attend
Moist nutriment, or under rocks their food
In jointed armor watch: on smooth the seal,
And bended dolphins play: part huge of bulk
Wallowing unwieldy, enormous in their gait
Tempest the ocean: there leviathan
Hugest of living creatures, on the deep
Stretched like a promontory sleeps or swims,
And seems a moving land, and at his gills
Draws in, and at his trunk spouts out a sea.
Meanwhile the tepid caves, and fens and shores
Their brood as numerous hatch, from the egg that soon
Bursting with kindly rupture forth disclosed
Their callow young, but feathered soon and fledge
They summed their pens, and soaring th' air sublime
With clang despised the ground, under a cloud
In prospect; there the eagle and the stork
On cliffs and cedar tops their eyries build:
Part loosely wing the region, part more wise
In common, ranged in figure wedge their way,
Intelligent of seasons, and set forth

403. **Bank the mid sea:** form living banks or shelves.

409. **smooth:** smooth or calm water.

410. **bended:** arching themselves.

412. **leviathan:** the whale; an animal as opposed to the satanic emblem of 1.200–208.

415–16. **gills . . . trunk:** perhaps a residue of the medieval correspondence between whales and elephants, though words like *gills* and *trunk* had a considerable range of reference (see Edwards 110–13).

419. **kindly:** natural.

420. **callow:** unfeathered; **fledge:** fledged.

421. **summed their pens:** gained their full complement of feathers.

422. **clang:** harsh cry; **despised:** looked down upon.

422–23. **under a cloud/In prospect:** There was such a mass of birds that the ground seemed to be under a cloud.

425. **loosely:** singly.

427. **Intelligent:** cognizant. There are no seasons until the celestial adjustments of 10.651–707. No adjustments will have to be made in the birds themselves. They are hardwired from day one with the inclination to migrate.

Their airy caravan high over seas
Flying, and over lands with mutual wing
Easing their flight; so steers the prudent crane
Her annual voyage, born on winds; the air
Floats, as they pass, fanned with unnumbered plumes:
From branch to branch the smaller birds with song
Solaced the woods, and spread their painted wings
Till ev'n, nor then the solemn nightingale
Ceased warbling, but all night tuned her soft lays:
Others on silver lakes and rivers bathed
Their downy breast; the swan with archèd neck
Between her white wings mantling proudly, rows
Her state with oary feet: yet oft they quit
The dank, and rising on stiff pennons, tower
The mid-aerial sky: others on ground
Walked firm; the crested cock whose clarion sounds
The silent hours, and th' other whose gay train
Adorns him, colored with the florid hue
Of rainbows and starry eyes. The waters thus
With fish replenished, and the air with fowl,
Ev'ning and morn solemnized the fifth day.

"The sixth and of creation last arose
With ev'ning harps and matin, when God said,
'Let th' earth bring forth soul living in her kind,
Cattle and creeping things, and beast of the earth,
Each in their kind.' The earth obeyed, and straight
Op'ning her fertile womb teemed at a birth
Innumerous living creatures, perfect forms,
Limbed and full-grown: out of the ground uprose
As from his lair the wild beast where he wons
In forest wild, in thicket, brake, or den;
Among the trees in pairs they rose, they walked:
The cattle in the fields and meadows green:
Those rare and solitary, these in flocks

429–30. **Flying . . . flight:** Some migrating birds were supposed to take turns resting on one another (Svendsen 1969, 158).

432. **Floats:** undulates.

434. **Solaced:** cheered; **painted:** imitated from Vergil, *Aen.* 4.525.

439. **mantling:** forming a mantle (by raising their wings).

440. **Her state:** her stature or rank.

441. **dank:** pool; **pennons:** pinions; **tower:** rise into.

442. **mid-aerial sky:** the midair, a cold region where clouds are found.

444. **th' other:** the other cock (i.e., the peacock).

446. **eyes:** the eye-shaped configurations on the plumage of peacocks.

450–98. Milton's version of Gen. 1.24–25.

451. **soul:** Both early editions read "foul" (fowl), which have already been created.

454. **teemed:** brought forth.

457. **wons:** dwells.

461. **rare:** here and there.

Pasturing at once, and in broad herds upsprung.
The grassy clods now calved, now half appeared
The tawny lion, pawing to get free
His hinder parts, then springs as broke from bonds,
And rampant shakes his brinded main; the ounce,
The libbard, and the tiger, as the mole
Rising, the crumbled earth above them threw
In hillocks; the swift stag from under ground
Bore up his branching head: scarce from his mold
Behemoth biggest born of earth upheaved
His vastness: fleeced the flocks and bleating rose,
As plants: ambiguous between sea and land
The river horse and scaly crocodile.
At once came forth whatever creeps the ground,
Insect or worm; those waved their limber fans
For wings, and smallest lineaments exact
In all the liveries decked of summer's pride
With spots of gold and purple, azure and green:
These as a line their long dimension drew,
Streaking the ground with sinuous trace; not all
Minims of nature; some of serpent kind
Wondrous in length and corpulence involved
Their snaky folds, and added wings. First crept
The parsimonious emmet, provident
Of future, in small room large heart enclosed,
Pattern of just equality perhaps
Hereafter, joined in her popular tribes
Of commonalty: swarming next appeared
The female bee that feeds her husband drone

464. **lion:** the first land animal to be named, which seems to defer to the old bestiaries that accounted him "king of beasts." Milton's lion is *rampant* (rearing up), as in heraldry, but *calved* and *brinded* associate the lion with humbler beasts (Edwards 126).

471. **Behemoth:** the elephant.

474. **river horse:** translates "hippopotamus"; **scaly crocodile:** In the tradition of European natural history, the crocodile was the epitome of strangeness; see Shakespeare, *ANT* 2.7.41–51. It was famous for its false tears, its cruelty, its odd relationship to a bird that supposedly gnawed its entrails. In this respect, Milton's *scaly crocodile,* "stripped of lore and lessons," provides another example of his interest in "freeing animals from their symbolic places" (Edwards 120, 127).

476. **worm:** a designation for serpents as well as insects (which creep the ground).

482. **Minims:** smallest creatures.

483. **involved:** coiled.

485. **parsimonious emmet:** thrifty ant.

486. **large heart:** capacious intellect.

487–89. **Pattern . . . commonalty:** Ants were often praised for their prudence and democratic commonality; Aristotle had remarked that they knew no king (Svendsen 1969, 150–52).

490. **The female bee:** In Milton's day it was believed that worker bees were sterile females and drones male. Bees were traditionally monarchical (Shakespeare, *H5* 1.2.183–204), but Milton disputed that belief in *1Def.* (Yale 4:348–50).

Deliciously, and builds her waxen cells
With honey stored: the rest are numberless,
And thou their natures know'st, and gav'st them names,
Needless to thee repeated; nor unknown
The serpent subtlest beast of all the field,
Of huge extent sometimes, with brazen eyes
And hairy main terrific, though to thee
Not noxious, but obedient at thy call.
Now heav'n in all her glory shone, and rolled
Her motions, as the great First Mover's hand
First wheeled their course; Earth in her rich attire
Consummate lovely smiled; air, water, earth,
By fowl, fish, beast, was flown, was swum, was walked
Frequent; and of the sixth day yet remained;
There wanted yet the master work, the end
Of all yet done; a creature who not prone
And brute as other creatures, but endued
With sanctity of reason, might erect
His stature, and upright with front serene
Govern the rest, self-knowing, and from thence
Magnanimous to correspond with Heav'n,
But grateful to acknowledge whence his good
Descends, thither with heart and voice and eyes
Directed in devotion, to adore
And worship God supreme, who made him chief
Of all his works: therefore th' omnipotent
Eternal Father (for where is not he
Present) thus to his Son audibly spake.
"'Let us make now man in our image, man
In our similitude, and let them rule
Over the fish and fowl of sea and air,
Beast of the field, and over all the earth,
And every creeping thing that creeps the ground.'

493. **gav'st them names:** See 8.342–54.

497. **hairy main:** Vergil described the serpents that strangled Laocoön as having bloodred manes (*Aen.* 2.203–7); **terrific:** terrifying.

498. **Not noxious:** not evil or harmful.

504. **Frequent:** in throngs.

505. **the end:** the completion of Creation and the being for whom all the rest had been done.

508–10. **might . . . self-knowing:** Man's uprightness was noted by Ovid, *Met.* 1.76–86, and was commonly treated by Christian writers as a sign of moral and spiritual dignity.

509. **front:** forehead.

510. **self-knowing:** knowing himself as created in the image and likeness of God; Shakespeare's Isabella memorably declares that this knowledge is sadly curtailed among fallen men (*MM* 2.2.120–24). **from thence:** as a result of these qualities.

511. **Magnanimous:** great-souled, high-minded; **to correspond with:** to be an image of, to be in contact with.

519–34. Milton's version of Gen. 1.26–31.

This said, he formed thee, Adam, thee O man
Dust of the ground, and in thy nostrils breathed
The breath of life; in his own image he
Created thee, in the image of God
Express, and thou becam'st a living soul.
Male he created thee, but thy consort
Female for race; then blessed mankind, and said,
'Be fruitful, multiply, and fill the Earth,
Subdue it, and throughout dominion hold
Over fish of the sea, and fowl of the air,
And every living thing that moves on the Earth.'
Wherever thus created, for no place
Is yet distinct by name, thence, as thou know'st
He brought thee into this delicious grove,
This garden, planted with the trees of God,
Delectable both to behold and taste;
And freely all their pleasant fruit for food
Gave thee, all sorts are here that all th' Earth yields,
Variety without end; but of the tree
Which tasted works knowledge of good and evil,
Thou may'st not; in the day thou eat'st, thou di'st;
Death is the penalty imposed, beware,
And govern well thy appetite, lest Sin
Surprise thee, and her black attendant Death.
Here finished he, and all that he had made
Viewed, and behold all was entirely good;
So ev'n and morn accomplished the sixth day:
Yet not till the Creator from his work
Desisting, though unwearied, up returned
Up to the Heav'n of Heav'ns his high abode,
Thence to behold this new created world
Th' addition of his empire, how it showed
In prospect from his throne, how good, how fair,
Answering his great idea. Up he rode
Followed with acclamation and the sound
Symphonious of ten thousand harps that tuned
Angelic harmonies: the Earth, the air

528. **Express:** exactly depicted.
530–34. **blessed . . . Earth:** See Gen. 1.28.
537. **delicious:** delightful.
552. **unwearied:** The Son did not "rest" on the seventh day because his strength was in any sense depleted.
557. **idea:** the only occurrence of the word *idea* in Milton's English poetry. It bears the Platonic-Augustinian sense of "ideal form, pattern." Thus Simon Goulart: "The idea, the form and pattern of them [all things] was in the science and intelligence of God . . . as Saint Augustine and others have expounded" (1621, 8–9).
559. **Symphonius:** harmonious; **tuned:** played.

Resounded, (thou remember'st, for thou heard'st)
The heav'ns and all the constellations rung,
The planets in their stations list'ning stood,
While the bright pomp ascended jubilant.
'Open, ye everlasting gates,' they sung,
'Open, ye Heav'ns, your living doors; let in
The great Creator from his work returned
Magnificent, his six days' work, a world;
Open, and henceforth oft; for God will deign
To visit oft the dwellings of just men
Delighted, and with frequent intercourse
Thither will send his wingèd messengers
On errands of supernal grace.' So sung
The glorious train ascending: he through Heav'n,
That opened wide her blazing portals, led
To God's eternal house direct the way,
A broad and ample road, whose dust is gold
And pavement stars, as stars to thee appear,
Seen in the galaxy, that Milky Way
Which nightly as a circling zone thou seest
Powdered with stars. And now on Earth the seventh
Ev'ning arose in Eden, for the sun
Was set, and twilight from the east came on,
Forerunning night; when at the holy mount
Of Heav'n's high-seated top, th' imperial throne
Of Godhead, fixed forever firm and sure,
The Filial Power arrived, and sat him down
With his great Father, for he also went
Invisible, yet stayed (such privilege
Hath omnipresence) and the work ordained,
Author and end of all things, and from work
Now resting, blessed and hallowed the sev'nth day,
As resting on that day from all his work,
But not in silence holy kept; the harp
Had work and rested not, the solemn pipe,

564. **pomp:** procession; **jubilant:** shouting with joy.

565–67. Based on Ps. 23.7.

569–73. **for . . . grace:** *CD* 1.9 discusses the earthly missions of angels.

579. **Milky Way:** The road to Heaven is like the Milky Way but not the Milky Way itself, as it is in Ovid, *Met.* 1.168–71.

588–90. The editions of 1667 and 1674 punctuate confusingly: "With his great Father (for he also went/Invisible, yet stayed (such privilege/Hath omnipresence)."

594. **not in silence holy kept:** The prominence of music at the first Sabbath indicates Milton's disagreement with the stricter versions of Puritan Sabbatarianism (Berry 61–101).

And dulcimer, all organs of sweet stop,
All sounds on fret by string or golden wire
Tempered soft tunings, intermixed with voice
Choral or unison: of incense clouds
Fuming from golden censers hid the mount.
Creation and the six days' acts they sung,
'Great are thy works, Jehovah, infinite
Thy power; what thought can measure thee or tongue
Relate thee; greater now in thy return
Than from the giant angels; thee that day
Thy thunders magnified; but to create
Is greater than created to destroy.
Who can impair thee, mighty king, or bound
Thy empire? Easily the proud attempt
Of spirits apostate and their counsels vain
Thou hast repelled, while impiously they thought
Thee to diminish, and from thee withdraw
The number of thy worshippers. Who seeks
To lessen thee, against his purpose serves
To manifest the more thy might: his evil
Thou usest, and from thence creat'st more good.
Witness this new-made world, another Heav'n
From Heaven gate not far, founded in view
On the clear hyaline, the glassy sea;
Of amplitude almost immense, with stars
Numerous, and every star perhaps a world
Of destined habitation; but thou know'st
Their seasons: among these the seat of men,
Earth with her nether ocean circumfused,
Their pleasant dwelling place. Thrice happy men,
And sons of men, whom God hath thus advanced,
Created in his image, there to dwell
And worship him, and in reward to rule

596. **dulcimer:** a stringed instrument played with small hammers; **stop:** the register of an organ.

597. **fret:** a ridge on the fingerboard of a stringed instrument.

599. **Choral or unison:** in parts or in unison.

605. **giant angels:** referring to the defeat of the rebel angels but alluding to Jove's defeat of the giants. Cp. 1.50–52, 199–200, 230–37; 6.643–66.

606–7. **but . . . destroy:** Satan seeks glory from the lesser course of destroying the work of Creation (9.129–38).

619. **hyaline:** the transliterated Greek word for the "sea of glass" before God's throne in Rev. 4.6.

621–22. **every . . . habitation:** On the possibility of other worlds being inhabited, see 3.566–71, 8.152–58. On the possibility that man might colonize other worlds, see 3.667–70 and 5.500.

622–23. **thou know'st/Their seasons:** "It is not for you to know the times or the seasons, which the Father hath put in his own power" (Acts 1.7).

624. **nether ocean:** the earth's seas, the waters below the firmament.

628–29. **to rule/Over his works:** "Thou madest

Over his works, on earth, in sea, or air,
And multiply a race of worshippers
Holy and just: thrice happy if they know
Their happiness, and persevere upright.'
"So sung they, and the empyrean rung,
With hallelujahs: thus was Sabbath kept.
And thy request think now fulfilled, that asked
How first this world and face of things began,
And what before thy memory was done

From the beginning, that posterity
Informed by thee might know; if else thou seek'st
Aught, not surpassing human measure, say."
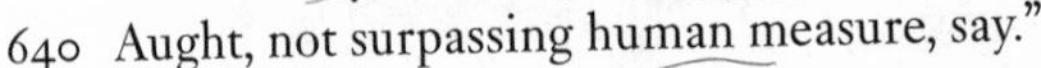

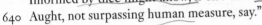

him to have dominion over the works of thy hands" (Ps. 8.6).

631–32. **thrice . . . happiness:** an adaptation of Vergil's *Georg.* 2.458, and one of a number of statements in the poem about the close relationship between Adam and Eve's happiness and their knowledge of that happiness. See 4.774–75 especially.

632. **persevere:** continue in a state of grace.

636. **face of things:** the visible world surrounding us.

Book VIII

THE ARGUMENT

Adam inquires concerning celestial motions, is doubtfully answered, and exhorted to search rather things more worthy of knowledge. Adam assents, and still desirous to detain Raphael, relates to him what he remembered since his own creation, his placing in Paradise, his talk with God concerning solitude and fit society, his first meeting and nuptials with Eve. His discourse with the angel thereupon, who after admonitions repeated departs.

The angel ended, and in Adam's ear
So charming left his voice, that he a while
Thought him still speaking, still stood fixed to hear;
Then as new waked thus gratefully replied.
"What thanks sufficient, or what recompense
Equal have I to render thee, divine
Historian, who thus largely hast allayed
The thirst I had of knowledge, and vouchsafed
This friendly condescension to relate
Things else by me unsearchable, now heard
With wonder, but delight, and, as is due,
With glory attributed to the high
Creator; something yet of doubt remains,
Which only thy solution can resolve.
When I behold this goodly frame, this world

1–4. The first three and half lines were added to the second edition of 1674. In the long Book 7 of 1667, the pause after Raphael's narration was marked by a single line: "To whom thus Adam gratefully replied."

9. **condescension:** courteous disregard of rank.

15–38. Eve was the first to wonder about the curious abundance of the nighttime sky (4.657–58). Adam tried to answer her query (4.660–88), as did Satan in the dream he created for Eve (5.41–47). Adam now broadens her question to include other celestial instances of apparent wastefulness and favoritism toward earth. Cp. *Prolusion 7* (pp. 795–96).

15. **this goodly frame:** a phrase used by Hamlet (2.2.316).

Of heav'n and Earth consisting, and compute
Their magnitudes, this Earth a spot, a grain,
An atom, with the firmament compared
And all her numbered stars, that seem to roll
Spaces incomprehensible (for such
Their distance argues and their swift return
Diurnal) merely to officiate light
Round this opacous Earth, this punctual spot,
One day and night; in all their vast survey
Useless besides, reasoning I oft admire,
How nature wise and frugal could commit
Such disproportions, with superfluous hand
So many nobler bodies to create,
Greater so manifold to this one use,
For aught appears, and on their orbs impose
Such restless revolution day by day
Repeated, while the sedentary Earth,
That better might with far less compass move,
Served by more noble than herself, attains
Her end without least motion, and receives,
As tribute such a sumless journey brought
Of incorporeal speed, her warmth and light;
Speed, to describe whose swiftness number fails."
    So spake our sire, and by his count'nance seemed
Ent'ring on studious thoughts abstruse, which Eve
Perceiving where she sat retired in sight,
With lowliness majestic from her seat,
And grace that won who saw to wish her stay,
Rose, and went forth among her fruits and flow'rs,
To visit how they prospered, bud and bloom,
Her nursery; they at her coming sprung
And touched by her fair tendance gladlier grew.
Yet went she not, as not with such discourse
Delighted, or not capable her ear
Of what was high: such pleasure she reserved,
Adam relating, she sole auditress;
Her husband the relater she preferred

17–18. **a spot, a grain,/An atom:** The tininess of the earth was apparent to ancient astronomers.

19. **numbered:** numerous, as in 7.621.

22. **officiate:** supply, minister.

23. **opacous:** dark; **punctual spot:** spot the size of a point (Lat. *punctum*) in relation to the spaces of the firmament, but also in the sense of "subject to exact timing."

25. **admire:** wonder, but with a sense of perplexity (the *something yet of doubt* in l. 13).

30. **For aught appears:** for all that can be seen.

32. **sedentary:** motionless.

36. **sumless:** immeasurable (see l. 38).

Before the angel, and of him to ask
Chose rather; he, she knew, would intermix
Grateful digressions, and solve high dispute
With conjugal caresses; from his lip
Not words alone pleased her. O when meet now
Such pairs, in love and mutual honor joined?
With goddesslike demeanor forth she went;
Not unattended, for on her as queen
A pomp of winning Graces waited still,
And from about her shot darts of desire
Into all eyes to wish her still in sight.
And Raphael now to Adam's doubt proposed
Benevolent and facile thus replied.
"To ask or search I blame thee not, for heav'n
Is as the book of God before thee set,
Wherein to read his wondrous works, and learn
His seasons, hours, or days, or months, or years:
This to attain, whether heav'n move or Earth,
Imports not, if thou reckon right; the rest
From man or angel the great Architect
Did wisely to conceal, and not divulge
His secrets to be scanned by them who ought
Rather admire; or if they list to try
Conjecture, he his fabric of the heav'ns
Hath left to their disputes, perhaps to move
His laughter at their quaint opinions wide
Hereafter, when they come to model heav'n
And calculate the stars, how they will wield
The mighty frame, how build, unbuild, contrive
To save appearances, how gird the sphere
With centric and eccentric scribbled o'er,

62. **darts of desire:** not sexual desire, as in love poetry, but desire that she remain *still in sight* (l. 63).

65. **facile:** affable. Raphael does not deem Adam's doubt about the wisdom of the celestial design malignant or accusatory.

67. **Is as the book of God:** Cp. 3.47.

70. **whether heav'n move or Earth:** a difference between the Ptolemaic and Copernican systems; but there were many compromise positions between the two (see G. McColley 217–44; Babb 78–94).

75. **admire:** behold with wonder.

78. **His laughter:** Psalm 2.4: "He that sitteth in the heavens shall laugh." A. O. Lovejoy considered Milton's God a "singularly detestable being" for devising cosmic riddles so that he could laugh at the false solutions (1962, 140). However, God will laugh not primarily at the falseness of astronomical theories but at the way astronomers play God in modeling the heavens. **quaint:** ingenious; **wide:** wide of the truth.

80. **calculate:** predict the motions of; **wield:** direct, guide.

82. **save appearances:** a scholastic term for fitting hypothesis to observation, a process particularly evident in the history of astronomy, where theories were modified repeatedly to account for local observations inconsistent with general assumptions.

83. **centric and eccentric:** spheres centered on,

Cycle and epicycle, orb in orb:
Already by thy reasoning this I guess,
Who art to lead thy offspring, and supposest
That bodies bright and greater should not serve
The less not bright, nor heav'n such journeys run,
Earth sitting still, when she alone receives
The benefit: consider first, that great
Or bright infers not excellence: the Earth
Though, in comparison of heav'n, so small,
Nor glistering, may of solid good contain
More plenty than the sun that barren shines
Whose virtue on itself works no effect,
But in the fruitful Earth; there first received
His beams, unactive else, their vigor find.
Yet not to Earth are those bright luminaries
Officious, but to thee Earth's habitant.
And for the heav'n's wide circuit, let it speak
The Maker's high magnificence, who built
So spacious, and his line stretched out so far;
That man may know he dwells not in his own;
An edifice too large for him to fill,
Lodged in a small partition, and the rest
Ordained for uses to his Lord best known.
The swiftness of those circles attribute,
Though numberless, to his omnipotence,
That to corporeal substances could add
Speed almost spiritual; me thou think'st not slow,
Who since the morning hour set out from Heav'n
Where God resides, and ere mid-day arrived
In Eden, distance inexpressible
By numbers that have name. But this I urge,

---

and not centered on, the earth. Kepler's teacher, Tycho Brahe, proposed that the sun was the center of the planetary orbits, while the fixed stars were centered on the earth. **scribbled o'er:** Raphael is making fun of complex astrological diagrams; cp. Donne, "An Anatomy of the World": "Man hath weaved out a net, and this net thrown / Upon the heavens, and now they are his own" (279–80).

84. In the Ptolemaic system planets traverse a circular *orb,* or orbit, but turn smaller circles (epicycles) within this larger cycle. Meant to account for observed differences of orbital velocity among the planets, the theory of epicycles is a notable example of "saving the appearances" (see 82n).

85–90. **Already . . . benefit:** Raphael maintains that he has been able to guess from Adam's thinking some of the forthcoming perplexity in the astronomy to be developed by his offspring. In particular, Adam mistakes brightness for excellence and on that ground supposes that the *opacous* earth (l. 23) should not be served by more resplendent heavenly bodies, such as the sun.

99. **Officious:** attentive, dutiful.

109–10. **That . . . spiritual:** The corporeal planets are almost as swift as spiritual angels, which is a sign of God's omnipotence in molding matter.

Admitting motion in the heav'ns, to show
Invalid that which thee to doubt it moved;
Not that I so affirm, though so it seem
To thee who hast thy dwelling here on Earth.
God to remove his ways from human sense,
Placed heav'n from Earth so far, that earthly sight,
If it presume, might err in things too high,
And no advantage gain. What if the sun
Be center to the world, and other stars
By his attractive virtue and their own
Incited, dance about him various rounds?
Their wand'ring course now high, now low, then hid,
Progressive, retrograde, or standing still,
In six thou seest, and what if sev'nth to these
The planet Earth, so steadfast though she seem,
Insensibly three different motions move?
Which else to several spheres thou must ascribe,
Moved contrary with thwart obliquities,
Or save the sun his labor, and that swift
Nocturnal and diurnal rhomb supposed,
Invisible else above all stars, the wheel
Of day and night; which needs not thy belief,
If Earth industrious of herself fetch day
Traveling east, and with her part averse
From the sun's beam meet night, her other part
Still luminous by his ray. What if that light
Sent from her through the wide transpicuous air,
To the terrestrial moon be as a star
Enlight'ning her by day, as she by night

117. **Not that I so affirm:** Raphael makes it clear that he is not delivering true, once-and-for-all knowledge of the heavens but confounding Adam's assumption that he had, or could in principle attain, such knowledge.

124. **attractive virtue:** Kepler supposed that the planets were held in their orbits by the sun's magnetism.

128. The *six* are the moon, Mercury, Venus, Mars, Jupiter, and Saturn.

129. **The planet Earth:** The most striking result of the Copernican theory was the idea that the earth was simply another planet (the seventh).

130. **three different motions:** "The three different motions, which the Copernicans attribute to the earth, are the *diural* round her own axis, the *annual* round the sun, and the *motion of libration* as it is called, whereby the earth so proceeds in her orbit, as that her axis is constantly parallel to the axis of the world [universe]" (Newton).

131–32. "Even if you do not posit a moving earth, you will have to posit spheres moving in contrary and awkward directions."

133–40. **Or save . . . ray:** Copernicus was able to make the sun responsible for astronomical effects earlier attributed to the *swift . . . rhomb,* or *primum mobile,* the great wheel turning rapidly beyond the fixed stars and imparting orbital motions to the planets. But this earlier picture of things *needs not thy belief,* need not be believed by Adam, if he assumes that the earth of its own power revolves on a daily basis, thus creating the alternation of day and night.

This Earth? Reciprocal, if land be there,
Fields and inhabitants: her spots thou seest
As clouds, and clouds may rain, and rain produce
Fruits in her softened soil, for some to eat
Allotted there; and other suns perhaps
With their attendant moons thou wilt descry
Communicating male and female light,
Which two great sexes animate the world,
Stored in each orb perhaps with some that live.
For such vast room in nature unpossessed
By living soul, desert and desolate,
Only to shine, yet scarce to contribute
Each orb a glimpse of light, conveyed so far
Down to this habitable, which returns
Light back to them, is obvious to dispute.
But whether thus these things, or whether not,
Whether the sun predominant in heav'n
Rise on the Earth, or Earth rise on the sun,
He from the east his flaming road begin,
Or she from west her silent course advance
With inoffensive pace that spinning sleeps
On her soft axle, while she paces ev'n,
And bears thee soft with the smooth air along,
Solicit not thy thoughts with matters hid,
Leave them to God above, him serve and fear;
Of other creatures, as him pleases best,
Wherever placed, let him dispose: joy thou
In what he gives to thee, this Paradise
And thy fair Eve; heav'n is for thee too high
To know what passes there; be lowly wise:
Think only what concerns thee and thy being;
Dream not of other worlds, what creatures there
Live, in what state, condition or degree,

145. **inhabitants:** Cp. 3.460–62.

148–49. **other suns . . . moons:** Advocates of an infinite universe, such as Giordano Bruno and Henry More, believed that the so-called fixed stars were suns with their own planetary systems; Galileo observed the *attendant moons* of Jupiter and Saturn. Cp. 1.650, 3.566–71, 7.621–22; also Spenser, *FQ* 2.1.3.

150. **male and female light:** original and reflected light.

151. No one has found a convincing source for this striking line, with its absolute confidence in the universality of gender and the conjunction of gender and life.

162. **He:** the sun.

163–66. These fine lines are sufficient to dispel the old idea that Milton found the Ptolemaic system inherently more poetic than the Copernican one.

163. **she:** the earth.

167. **Solicit not:** trouble not.

175. **what creatures:** That other planets might harbor life was a common speculation in Milton's day.

Contented that thus far hath been revealed
Not of Earth only but of highest Heav'n."
To whom thus Adam cleared of doubt, replied.
"How fully hast thou satisfied me, pure
Intelligence of Heav'n, angel serene,
And freed from intricacies, taught to live,
The easiest way, nor with perplexing thoughts
To interrupt the sweet of life, from which
God hath bid dwell far off all anxious cares,
And not molest us, unless we ourselves
Seek them with wand'ring thoughts, and notions vain.
But apt the mind or fancy is to rove
Unchecked, and of her roving is no end;
Till warned, or by experience taught, she learn,
That not to know at large of things remote
From use, obscure and subtle, but to know
That which before us lies in daily life,
Is the prime wisdom; what is more, is fume,
Or emptiness, or fond impertinence,
And renders us in things that most concern
Unpracticed, unprepared, and still to seek.
Therefore from this high pitch let us descend
A lower flight, and speak of things at hand
Useful, whence haply mention may arise
Of something not unseasonable to ask
By sufferance, and thy wonted favor deigned.
Thee I have heard relating what was done
Ere my remembrance: now hear me relate
My story, which perhaps thou hast not heard;
And day is yet not spent; till then thou seest
How subtly to detain thee I devise,
Inviting thee to hear while I relate,
Fond, were it not in hope of thy reply:
For while I sit with thee, I seem in Heav'n,
And sweeter thy discourse is to my ear
Than fruits of palm-tree pleasantest to thirst

183. **easiest way:** Milton entitled a prose work *The Ready and Easy Way* (1660). *Way,* which here means "course of action" (*OED* 12), is a key word in the poem. *Paradise Lost* intends to "justify the ways of God" (1.26) and ends with "way" (12.649). It should be borne in mind that in Acts 9.2, 19.9, 24.14, 24.22, et cetera, *way* signifies Christianity.

194. **fume:** literally "vapor" or "smoke," figuratively "something unsubstantial, transient, imaginary"; see *Apology* (Yale 1:193): "the pride of a metaphysical fume."

195. **fond:** foolish.

197. **still to seek:** without a clue.

202. **sufferance:** permission; **wonted:** customary.

209. **Fond:** foolish.

And hunger both, from labor, at the hour
Of sweet repast; they satiate, and soon fill,
Though pleasant, but thy words with grace divine
Imbued, bring to their sweetness no satiety."
 To whom thus Raphael answered Heav'nly meek.
"Nor are thy lips ungraceful, sire of men,
Nor tongue ineloquent; for God on thee
Abundantly his gifts hath also poured
Inward and outward both, his image fair:
Speaking or mute all comeliness and grace
Attends thee, and each word, each motion forms.
Nor less think we in Heav'n of thee on Earth
Than of our fellow servant, and inquire
Gladly into the ways of God with man:
For God we see hath honored thee, and set
On man his equal love: say therefore on;
For I that day was absent, as befell,
Bound on a voyage uncouth and obscure,
Far on excursion toward the gates of Hell;
Squared in full legion (such command we had)
To see that none thence issued forth a spy,
Or enemy, while God was in his work,
Lest he incensed at such eruption bold,
Destruction with creation might have mixed.
Not that they durst without his leave attempt,
But us he sends upon his high behests
For state, as sov'reign King, and to inure
Our prompt obedience. Fast we found, fast shut
The dismal gates, and barricadoed strong;
But long ere our approaching heard within
Noise, other than the sound of dance or song,
Torment, and loud lament, and furious rage.
Glad we returned up to the coasts of light
Ere Sabbath evening: so we had in charge.
But thy relation now; for I attend,

225. **fellow servant:** As the angel told a worshipful St. John, "I am thy fellow servant" (Rev. 22.9).
226. **ways of God with man:** See 183n, 1.26n.
229. **that day:** the sixth day of Creation? Presumably Raphael witnessed the other days, whose events he has just narrated.
230. **uncouth:** strange, desolate.
239. **state:** ceremony.
243–44. Cp. Aeneas hearing the groans and cries behind the gate to Tartarus (Vergil, *Aen.* 6.557–59), Astolfo listening at the gates of Hell (Ariosto, *OF* 34.4), and Dante greeted by wailings and lamentations upon entering Hell (*Inf.* 3.22–29).
246. **Sabbath evening:** the beginning of the seventh day of Creation. Milton here adopts the Hebrew custom of measuring the day from sunset to sunset.

Pleased with thy words no less than thou with mine."
So spake the godlike power, and thus our sire.
"For man to tell how human life began
Is hard; for who himself beginning knew?
Desire with thee still longer to converse
Induced me. As new waked from soundest sleep
Soft on the flow'ry herb I found me laid
In balmy sweat, which with his beams the sun
Soon dried, and on the reeking moisture fed.
Straight toward heav'n my wond'ring eyes I turned,
And gazed a while the ample sky, till raised
By quick instinctive motion up I sprung,
As thitherward endeavoring, and upright
Stood on my feet; about me round I saw
Hill, dale, and shady woods, and sunny plains,
And liquid lapse of murmuring streams; by these,
Creatures that lived, and moved, and walked, or flew,
Birds on the branches warbling; all things smiled,
With fragrance and with joy my heart o'erflowed.
Myself I then perused, and limb by limb
Surveyed, and sometimes went, and sometimes ran
With supple joints, as lively vigor led:
But who I was, or where, or from what cause,
Knew not; to speak I tried, and forthwith spake,
My tongue obeyed and readily could name
Whate'er I saw. 'Thou sun,' said I, 'fair light,
And thou enlightened earth, so fresh and gay,
Ye hills and dales, ye rivers, woods, and plains,
And ye that live and move, fair creatures, tell,
Tell, if ye saw, how came I thus, how here?
Not of myself; by some great Maker then,
In goodness and in power pre-eminent;
Tell me, how may I know him, how adore,
From whom I have that thus I move and live,
And feel that I am happier than I know.'

255. **balmy sweat:** In one of the first postmodern essays on *Paradise Lost,* Hartman declares that balmy sweat mingles "the balm of fruitfulness and the sweat of the curse, the labor to come and the regeneration to come from that" (147). But Edwards suggests that this reading spoils Paradise with the consequences of the Fall: "Adam's balmy sweat is, simply, sweet-scented sweat" (197).

256. **reeking:** steaming.

263. **lapse:** flow.

273–74. **Thou sun . . . earth:** In his very first words, Adam articulates in nascent form the ideas that lead to his puzzlement about the heavens (see 85–90n).

281. Acts 17.28: "For in him we live, and move, and have our being."

282. **happier than I know:** Cp. 4.774–75.

While thus I called, and strayed I knew not whither,
From where I first drew air, and first beheld
This happy light, when answer none returned,
On a green shady bank profuse of flow'rs
Pensive I sat me down; there gentle sleep
First found me, and with soft oppression seized
My drowsèd sense, untroubled, though I thought
I then was passing to my former state
Insensible, and forthwith to dissolve:
When suddenly stood at my head a dream,
Whose inward apparition gently moved
My fancy to believe I yet had being,
And lived: one came, methought, of shape divine,
And said, 'Thy mansion wants thee, Adam, rise,
First man, of men innumerable ordained
First father, called by thee I come thy guide
To the garden of bliss, thy seat prepared.'
So saying, by the hand he took me raised,
And over fields and waters, as in air
Smooth sliding without step, last led me up
A woody mountain, whose high top was plain,
A circuit wide, enclosed, with goodliest trees
Planted, with walks, and bowers, that what I saw
Of Earth before scarce pleasant seemed. Each tree
Loaden with fairest fruit, that hung to the eye
Tempting, stirred in me sudden appetite
To pluck and eat; whereat I waked, and found
Before mine eyes all real, as the dream
Had lively shadowed: here had new begun
My wand'ring, had not he who was my guide
Up hither, from among the trees appeared
Presence divine. Rejoicing, but with awe
In adoration at his feet I fell
Submiss: he reared me, and 'Whom thou sought'st I am,'
Said mildly, 'Author of all this thou seest
Above, or round about thee or beneath.
This Paradise I give thee, count it thine
To till and keep, and of the fruit to eat:

287. **Pensive:** The combination of happiness and pensiveness in this passage suggests that Milton, returning imaginatively to the themes of his youthful poetry, is blending elements of *L'Allegro* and *Il Penseroso.* The pensive man also goes to sleep during the daytime, and dreams (142–50), and the happy man speaks of "Such sights as youthful poets dream/On summer eves by haunted stream" (129–30).

288. **oppression:** weighing down.

302. **Smooth . . . led:** The *l-* sounds slide smoothly through the *s-* sounds.

Of every tree that in the garden grows
Eat freely with glad heart; fear here no dearth:
But of the tree whose operation brings
Knowledge of good and ill, which I have set
The pledge of thy obedience and thy faith,
Amid the garden by the Tree of Life,
Remember what I warn thee, shun to taste,
And shun the bitter consequence: for know,
The day thou eat'st thereof, my sole command
Transgressed, inevitably thou shalt die;
From that day mortal, and this happy state
Shalt lose, expelled from hence into a world
Of woe and sorrow.' Sternly he pronounced
The rigid interdiction, which resounds
Yet dreadful in mine ear, though in my choice
Not to incur; but soon his clear aspect
Returned and gracious purpose thus renewed.
'Not only these fair bounds, but all the Earth
To thee and to thy race I give; as lords
Possess it, and all things that therein live,
Or live in sea, or air, beast, fish, and fowl.
In sign whereof each bird and beast behold
After their kinds; I bring them to receive
From thee their names, and pay thee fealty
With low subjection; understand the same
Of fish within their wat'ry residence,
Not hither summoned, since they cannot change
Their element to draw the thinner air.'
As thus he spake, each bird and beast behold
Approaching two and two, these cow'ring low
With blandishment, each bird stooped on his wing.
I named them, as they passed, and understood
Their nature, with such knowledge God endued
My sudden apprehension: but in these
I found not what methought I wanted still;
And to the Heav'nly vision thus presumed.
" 'O by what name, for thou above all these,
Above mankind, or aught than mankind higher,

331. **From that day mortal:** the usual interpretation of Gen. 2.17: "For in the day you eat of it you shall die."

350. **two and two:** There is no indication in Gen. 2.19–20 that the animals parade by Adam in pairs, as they will again when entering Noah's ark "two and two" (Gen. 7.9). Milton's Adam seems intended to think about companionship, which he does (Gallagher 1990, 36).

Surpassest far my naming, how may I
Adore thee, Author of this universe,
And all this good to man, for whose well-being
So amply, and with hands so liberal
Thou hast provided all things: but with me
I see not who partakes. In solitude
What happiness, who can enjoy alone,
Or all enjoying, what contentment find?'
Thus I presumptuous; and the vision bright,
As with a smile more brightened, thus replied.
"'What call'st thou solitude, is not the Earth
With various living creatures, and the air
Replenished, and all these at thy command
To come and play before thee? Know'st thou not
Their language and their ways? They also know,
And reason not contemptibly; with these
Find pastime, and bear rule; thy realm is large.'
So spake the Universal Lord, and seemed
So ordering. I with leave of speech implored,
And humble deprecation thus replied.
"'Let not my words offend thee, Heav'nly power,
My Maker, be propitious while I speak.
Hast thou not made me here thy substitute,
And these inferior far beneath me set?
Among unequals what society
Can sort, what harmony or true delight?
Which must be mutual, in proportion due
Giv'n and received; but in disparity
The one intense, the other still remiss
Cannot well suit with either, but soon prove
Tedious alike: of fellowship I speak
Such as I seek, fit to participate
All rational delight, wherein the brute
Cannot be human consort; they rejoice
Each with their kind, lion with lioness;
So fitly them in pairs thou hast combined;
Much less can bird with beast, or fish with fowl
So well converse, nor with the ox the ape;

373. **Their language:** Since animals do not speak (9.557), Leonard must be right in asserting that *language* here means "inarticulate sounds used by the lower animals" (*OED* 1c).

379. See Abraham's similar preface when negotiating with God (Gen. 18.30).

383. **unequals:** Adam is here referring to the gap between himself and animals.

384. **sort:** fit.

387. **intense:** taut; **remiss:** slack.

Worse then can man with beast, and least of all.'
"Whereto th' Almighty answered, not displeased.
'A nice and subtle happiness I see
Thou to thyself proposest, in the choice
Of thy associates, Adam, and wilt taste
No pleasure, though in pleasure, solitary.
What think'st thou then of me, and this my state,
Seem I to thee sufficiently possessed
Of happiness, or not? Who am alone
From all eternity, for none I know
Second to me or like, equal much less.
How have I then with whom to hold converse
Save with the creatures which I made, and those
To me inferior, infinite descents
Beneath what other creatures are to thee?'
"He ceased, I lowly answered. 'To attain
The highth and depth of thy eternal ways
All human thoughts come short, supreme of things;
Thou in thyself art perfect, and in thee
Is no deficience found; not so is man,
But in degree, the cause of his desire
By conversation with his like to help,
Or solace his defects. No need that thou
Shouldst propagate, already infinite,
And through all numbers absolute, though one;
But man by number is to manifest
His single imperfection, and beget
Like of his like, his image multiplied,
In unity defective, which requires
Collateral love, and dearest amity.
Thou in thy secrecy although alone,
Best with thyself accompanied, seek'st not
Social communication, yet so pleased,

399. **nice:** refined, difficult to please (*OED* 7, the "good sense").

405–7. **who . . . less:** These lines are central to a debate over the identity of the divine presence speaking to Adam. Since Milton's Son is not co-eternal with the Father, the claim to be *alone/ From all eternity* suggests that the Father speaks.

417. **But in degree:** Man is perfect only in his station (which is of a kind to require a partner).

419. **solace:** alleviate.

419–21. **No need . . . one:** Adam, who began his religious life with the intuition of a Maker (ll. 278–79), here takes a leap forward in sophistication. *Through all numbers absolute* Englishes the Latin *omnibus numeris absolutus,* meaning "complete in every part," as in a well-written book (Pliny the Younger, *Letters* 9.38). Yet God is *infinite*—hence the completeness of his parts must be an innate idea, not an empirical observation. And God, despite his complete and infinite parts, is paradoxically *one.*

422–26. Man has a *single imperfection,* his *unity* is *defective,* because unlike God he requires another being to multiply his image.

426. **Collateral:** etymologically "side by side," accompanying.

Canst raise thy creature to what highth thou wilt
Of union or communion, deified;
I by conversing cannot these erect
From prone, nor in their ways complacence find.'
Thus I emboldened spake, and freedom used
Permissive, and acceptance found, which gained
This answer from the gracious voice divine.
"'Thus far to try thee, Adam, I was pleased,
And find thee knowing not of beasts alone,
Which thou hast rightly named, but of thyself,
Expressing well the spirit within thee free,
My image, not imparted to the brute,
Whose fellowship therefore unmeet for thee
Good reason was thou freely shouldst dislike,
And be so minded still; I, ere thou spak'st,
Knew it not good for man to be alone,
And no such company as then thou saw'st
Intended thee, for trial only brought,
To see how thou could'st judge of fit and meet:
What next I bring shall please thee, be assured,
Thy likeness, thy fit help, thy other self,
Thy wish exactly to thy heart's desire.'
"He ended, or I heard no more, for now
My earthly by his Heav'nly overpowered,
Which it had long stood under, strained to the highth
In that celestial colloquy sublime,
As with an object that excels the sense,
Dazzled and spent, sunk down, and sought repair
Of sleep, which instantly fell on me, called
By nature as in aid, and closed mine eyes.
Mine eyes he closed, but open left the cell
Of fancy my internal sight, by which
Abstract as in a trance methought I saw,
Though sleeping, where I lay, and saw the shape
Still glorious before whom awake I stood,
Who stooping opened my left side, and took

435. **Permissive:** allowed.

445. From Gen. 2.18: "God said, 'It is not good that man should be alone.'"

450. **thy other self:** an addition to Gen. 2.18 that Milton thought intended in the Hebrew (pp. 1000–1001). The Latin *alter ego* means "friend," which suggests that Milton is giving biblical sanction to the seventeenth-century ideal of "companionate marriage" (see Stone 361–74).

453. **earthly:** earthly nature.

454. **stood under:** been exposed to.

462–82. Cp. *Sonnet 23*.

465–67. **left side . . . fresh:** The Bible does not specify from which side the rib came, but tradition overwhelmingly chose the left, in part because of nearness to the heart (see l. 484; A. Williams 90–91).

From thence a rib, with cordial spirits warm,
And life-blood streaming fresh; wide was the wound,
But suddenly with flesh filled up and healed:
The rib he formed and fashioned with his hands;
Under his forming hands a creature grew,
Manlike, but different sex, so lovely fair,
That what seemed fair in all the world, seemed now
Mean, or in her summed up, in her contained
And in her looks, which from that time infused
Sweetness into my heart, unfelt before,
And into all things from her air inspired
The spirit of love and amorous delight.
She disappeared, and left me dark. I waked
To find her, or forever to deplore
Her loss, and other pleasures all abjure:
When out of hope, behold her, not far off,
Such as I saw her in my dream, adorned
With what all Earth or Heaven could bestow
To make her amiable: on she came,
Led by her Heav'nly Maker, though unseen,
And guided by his voice, nor uninformed
Of nuptial sanctity and marriage rites:
Grace was in all her steps, heav'n in her eye,
In every gesture dignity and love.
I overjoyed could not forbear aloud.
" 'This turn hath made amends; thou hast fulfilled
Thy words, Creator bounteous and benign,
Giver of all things fair, but fairest this
Of all thy gifts, nor enviest. I now see
Bone of my bone, flesh of my flesh, my self
Before me; woman is her name, of man
Extracted; for this cause he shall forgo
Father and mother, and to his wife adhere;
And they shall be one flesh, one heart, one soul.'
"She heard me thus, and though divinely brought,
Yet innocence and virgin modesty,
Her virtue and the conscience of her worth,

466. **cordial spirits:** vital spirits residing in the heart's blood.

481. **When out of hope:** when I had ceased to hope.

494. **nor enviest:** nor given reluctantly, begrudgingly.

499. **one heart, one soul:** an addition to Gen. 2.23–24, again suggesting companionate marriage (see 450n).

502. **conscience:** internal awareness. Cp. Eve's account of her initial turning away at 4.477–80.

That would be wooed, and not unsought be won,
Not obvious, not obtrusive, but retired,
The more desirable, or to say all,
Nature herself, though pure of sinful thought,
Wrought in her so, that seeing me, she turned;
I followed her, she what was honor knew,
And with obsequious majesty approved
My pleaded reason. To the nuptial bow'r
I led her blushing like the morn: all heav'n,
And happy constellations on that hour
Shed their selectest influence; the earth
Gave sign of gratulation, and each hill;
Joyous the birds; fresh gales and gentle airs
Whispered it to the woods, and from their wings
Flung rose, flung odors from the spicy shrub,
Disporting, till the amorous bird of night
Sung spousal, and bid haste the ev'ning star
On his hill top, to light the bridal lamp.
Thus I have told thee all my state, and brought
My story to the sum of earthly bliss
Which I enjoy, and must confess to find
In all things else delight indeed, but such
As used or not, works in the mind no change,
Nor vehement desire, these delicacies
I mean of taste, sight, smell, herbs, fruits, and flow'rs,
Walks, and the melody of birds; but here
Far otherwise, transported I behold,
Transported touch; here passion first I felt,
Commotion strange, in all enjoyments else
Superior and unmoved, here only weak
Against the charm of beauty's powerful glance.
Or nature failed in me, and left some part
Not proof enough such object to sustain,
Or from my side subducting, took perhaps
More than enough; at least on her bestowed

509. **obsequious:** acquiescent (not servile).

511. **blushing:** Most blushes in the fallen world indicate shame. But there are innocent blushes, too, compounded of shyness and a sense of awe at participating in a great thing. The syntax leaves open the possibility that Adam is also blushing.

513. **influence:** emanation from the heavens, here entirely favorable; cp. 10.661–64.

519. **ev'ning star:** Hesperus or Venus, whose appearance in the sky is a signal in the epithalamium tradition to light the bridal lamps and torches and bring the bride to the bridegroom. See Spenser, *Epithalamion* 286–95; *DDD*, pp. 873–74.

532–33. Cp. *SA* 1003–1007.

536. **subducting:** subtracting.

537–39. Cp. *SA* 1025–30.

Too much of ornament, in outward show
Elaborate, of inward less exact.
For well I understand in the prime end
Of nature her th' inferior, in the mind
And inward faculties, which most excel,
In outward also her resembling less
His image who made both, and less expressing
The character of that dominion giv'n
O'er other creatures; yet when I approach
Her loveliness, so absolute she seems
And in herself complete, so well to know
Her own, that what she wills to do or say,
Seems wisest, virtuousest, discreetest, best;
All higher knowledge in her presence falls
Degraded, wisdom in discourse with her
Looses discount'nanced, and like folly shows;
Authority and reason on her wait,
As one intended first, not after made
Occasionally; and to consummate all,
Greatness of mind and nobleness their seat
Build in her loveliest, and create an awe
About her, as a guard angelic placed."
To whom the Angel with contracted brow.
"Accuse not nature, she hath done her part;
Do thou but thine, and be not diffident
Of Wisdom; she deserts thee not, if thou
Dismiss not her when most thou need'st her nigh,
By attributing overmuch to things
Less excellent, as thou thyself perceiv'st.
For what admir'st thou, what transports thee so,
An outside? Fair no doubt, and worthy well
Thy cherishing, thy honoring, and thy love,
Not thy subjection: weigh with her thyself;
Then value: ofttimes nothing profits more
Than self-esteem, grounded on just and right
Well managed; of that skill the more thou know'st,

547. **absolute:** complete, perfect; Adam earlier used the word of God (ll. 419–21n).

553. **Looses:** goes to pieces.

555. **As one intended first:** Adam sees Eve as himself.

559. **guard angelic placed:** "Adam has just used, by ironic anticipation, the image of Paradise after he has been excluded from it," Frye wrote (1965, 64), thinking of 12.641–44.

556. **Occasionally:** on the occasion of Adam's request.

562. **diffident:** mistrustful.

572. **self-esteem:** Milton may well have coined the term in *Apology;* see p. 850 (Leonard).

The more she will acknowledge thee her head,
And to realities yield all her shows:
Made so adorn for thy delight the more,
So awful, that with honor thou may'st love
Thy mate, who sees when thou art seen least wise.
But if the sense of touch whereby mankind
Is propagated seem such dear delight
Beyond all other, think the same vouchsafed
To cattle and each beast; which would not be
To them made common and divulged, if aught
Therein enjoyed were worthy to subdue
The soul of man, or passion in him move.
What higher in her society thou find'st
Attractive, human, rational, love still;
In loving thou dost well, in passion not,
Wherein true love consists not; love refines
The thoughts, and heart enlarges, hath his seat
In reason, and is judicious, is the scale
By which to Heav'nly love thou may'st ascend,
Not sunk in carnal pleasure, for which cause
Among the beasts no mate for thee was found."
    To whom thus half abashed Adam replied.
"Neither her outside formed so fair, nor aught
In procreation common to all kinds
(Though higher of the genial bed by far,
And with mysterious reverence I deem)
So much delights me as those graceful acts,
Those thousand decencies that daily flow
From all her words and actions mixed with love
And sweet compliance, which declare unfeigned
Union of mind, or in us both one soul;
Harmony to behold in wedded pair
More grateful than harmonious sound to the ear.

574. **head:** "The head of the woman is the man" (1 Cor. 11.3).

575. **shows:** appearances. Turner finds the passage "particularly appalling" (280) because he takes *shows* to mean "pretenses, wiles," as if Eve were deliberately nurturing her husband's uxoriousness.

576. **adorn:** adorned.

577. **awful:** awe-inspiring.

583. **divulged:** done openly.

591–92. **the scale . . . ascend:** Earthly love as the *scale* or ladder by which we may ascend to *Heav'nly love* is a central feature of Neoplatonic works such as Marsilio Ficino's *Commentary on Plato's Symposium* and Spenser's *Four Hymns.*

598. **genial:** nuptial. As before he demonstrated his freedom in disputing with God (ll. 379–97, 412–33), so here Adam rejects Raphael's insistence that marital sexuality is no more than what animals do. He rather values it with the *reverence* appropriate to religious mysteries. Cp. *Tetrachordon* (p. 1004).

Yet these subject not; I to thee disclose
What inward thence I feel, not therefore foiled,
Who meet with various objects, from the sense
Variously representing; yet still free
Approve the best, and follow what I approve.
To love thou blam'st me not, for love thou say'st
Leads up to Heav'n, is both the way and guide;
Bear with me then, if lawful what I ask;
Love not the Heav'nly spirits, and how their love
Express they, by looks only, or do they mix
Irradiance, virtual or immediate touch?"
  To whom the angel with a smile that glowed
Celestial rosy red, love's proper hue,
Answered. "Let it suffice thee that thou know'st
Us happy, and without love no happiness.
Whatever pure thou in the body enjoy'st
(And pure thou wert created) we enjoy
In eminence, and obstacle find none
Of membrane, joint, or limb, exclusive bars:
Easier than air with air, if spirits embrace,
Total they mix, union of pure with pure
Desiring; nor restrained conveyance need
As flesh to mix with flesh, or soul with soul.
But I can now no more; the parting sun
Beyond the Earth's green cape and verdant isles
Hesperean sets, my signal to depart.
Be strong, live happy, and love, but first of all
Him whom to love is to obey, and keep
His great command; take heed lest passion sway
Thy judgment to do aught, which else free will

608. **foiled:** overcome.

617. **virtual:** in effect, not actually (modifies *touch*). Adam imagines three ways in which angels might express love (if they do): by looks, by mingling their radiance, or by actual (*immediate*) touch. Cp. his earlier interest in whether angels eat what humans eat (5.401–403, 466–67).

618–19. Todd: "Does not Milton here mean that the Angel both smiled and blushed at Adam's curiosity?" He does, and goes on to say that a red blush is love's *proper,* correct or natural, *hue.* Cp. 511n.

624–25. The passage has in mind the criticism of sexual intercourse voiced at the opening of Book 4 of Lucretius' *On the Nature of Things.* Human lovers desire full union, such as that enjoyed by Milton's angels, but are repeatedly frustrated in having to make do with the friction of surfaces: "Again they in each other would be lost,/But still by adamantine bars are crossed" (trans. John Dryden).

624. **In eminence:** in an elevated manner.

625. **exclusive:** excluding.

628. **restrained conveyance:** restraining transportation (such as the human body). Angels can apparently mix at a distance, uniting what Adam considered a disjunctive choice between *virtual* and *immediate touch* (l. 617).

631. **green cape:** Cape Verde; **verdant isles:** the Cape Verde Islands off the west (*Hesperean*) coast of Africa.

Would not admit; thine and of all thy sons
The weal or woe in thee is placed; beware.
I in thy persevering shall rejoice,
And all the blest: stand fast; to stand or fall
Free in thine own arbitrament it lies.
Perfect within, no outward aid require;
And all temptation to transgress repel."
    So saying, he arose; whom Adam thus
Followed with benediction. "Since to part,
Go Heav'nly guest, ethereal messenger,
Sent from whose sov'reign goodness I adore.
Gentle to me and affable hath been
Thy condescension, and shall be honored ever
With grateful memory: thou to mankind
Be good and friendly still, and oft return."
    So parted they, the angel up to Heav'n
From the thick shade, and Adam to his bow'r.

645. **Since to part:** since we must part.

Book IX

THE ARGUMENT

Satan having compassed the Earth, with meditated guile returns as a mist by night into Paradise, enters into the serpent sleeping. Adam and Eve in the morning go forth to their labors, which Eve proposes to divide in several places, each laboring apart. Adam consents not, alleging the danger, lest that enemy, of whom they were forewarned, should attempt her found alone. Eve, loath to be thought not circumspect or firm enough, urges her going apart, the rather desirous to make trial of her strength. Adam at last yields: the serpent finds her alone; his subtle approach, first gazing, then speaking, with much flattery extolling Eve above all other creatures. Eve, wondering to hear the serpent speak, asks how he attained to human speech and such understanding not till now. The serpent answers, that by tasting of a certain tree in the garden he attained both to speech and reason, till then void of both. Eve requires him to bring her to that tree, and finds it to be the Tree of Knowledge forbidden. The serpent now grown bolder, with many wiles and arguments induces her at length to eat. She, pleased with the taste, deliberates a while whether to impart thereof to Adam or not, at last brings him of the fruit, relates what persuaded her to eat thereof. Adam at first amazed, but perceiving her lost, resolves through vehemence of love to perish with her, and extenuating the trespass eats also of the fruit. The effects thereof in them both: they seek to cover their nakedness; then fall to variance and accusation of one another.

No more of talk where God or angel guest
With man, as with his friend, familiar used
To sit indulgent, and with him partake
Rural repast, permitting him the while
Venial discourse unblamed: I now must change

1. **No more:** *No/know* and *more* have earlier appeared in memorable formulations about the limits of knowledge that Adam and Eve must observe (4.637, 775; 8.194); now, at the beginning of the book in which those limits will be violated, Milton reconfigures these words to announce a fundamental break with unfallen existence. **God or angel:** Adam spoke with God (8.295–451), and Books 5–8 have chronicled the friendly visit of Raphael to Paradise.

2. **familiar:** in a familial manner, intimate.

5. **Venial:** innocent; **unblamed:** unblamable.

Those notes to tragic; foul distrust, and breach
Disloyal on the part of man, revolt,
And disobedience; on the part of Heav'n,
Now alienated, distance and distaste,
Anger and just rebuke, and judgment giv'n,
That brought into this world a world of woe,
Sin and her shadow Death, and Misery,
Death's harbinger: sad task, yet argument
Not less but more heroic than the wrath
Of stern Achilles on his foe pursued
Thrice fugitive about Troy wall; or rage
Of Turnus for Lavinia disespoused,
Or Neptune's ire or Juno's, that so long
Perplexed the Greek and Cytherea's son;
If answerable style I can obtain
Of my celestial patroness, who deigns
Her nightly visitation unimplored,
And dictates to me slumb'ring, or inspires
Easy my unpremeditated verse:
Since first this subject for heroic song
Pleased me long choosing, and beginning late;
Not sedulous by nature to indite
Wars, hitherto the only argument
Heroic deemed, chief mast'ry to dissect
With long and tedious havoc fabled knights
In battles feigned; the better fortitude
Of patience and heroic martyrdom
Unsung; or to describe races and games,
Or tilting furniture, emblazoned shields,
Impresses quaint, caparisons and steeds;
Bases and tinsel trappings, gorgeous knights

13. **sad task:** Raphael used the same phrase (5.564) in introducing his narrative of the fall of the rebel angels.

13–19. **yet . . . son:** Milton compares his *argument* or subject matter to earlier accounts of wrath in the epic tradition, Homer on Achilles' defeat of Hector (*Il.* 22), Vergil on the bellicose rage of Turnus (*Aen.* 7), Homer on Neptune's grudge against Odysseus, and Vergil on Juno's grudge against Aeneas, *Cytherea's* (Venus') *son.* The point is that the wrath in Milton's story, the wrath of the Christian God against human sin, is just, not capricious.

19. **Perplexed:** tormented.

20. **answerable:** commensurate (with his *more heroic* subject).

22. **unimplored:** Oddly, Milton in fact "implores" his muse at 7.38.

24. **unpremeditated:** Cp. the morning prayers of 5.149; in *Eikonoklastes,* Milton argues that prayers should not be imprisoned "in a pinfold of set words" (Yale 3:505).

27. **indite:** compose.

34. **tilting furniture:** jousting equipment, which Milton proceeds to list: shields emblazoned with *impresses quaint* (clever emblems), *caparisons* and *bases* (equestrian trappings).

At joust and tournament; then marshalled feast
Served up in hall with sewers and seneschals;
The skill of artifice or office mean,
Not that which justly gives heroic name
To person or to poem. Me of these
Nor skilled nor studious, higher argument
Remains, sufficient of itself to raise
That name, unless an age too late, or cold
Climate, or years damp my intended wing
Depressed, and much they may, if all be mine,
Not hers who brings it nightly to my ear.

The sun was sunk, and after him the star
Of Hesperus, whose office is to bring
Twilight upon the Earth, short arbiter
'Twixt day and night, and now from end to end
Night's hemisphere had veiled the horizon round:
When Satan who late fled before the threats
Of Gabriel out of Eden, now improved
In meditated fraud and malice, bent
On man's destruction, maugre what might hap
Of heavier on himself, fearless returned.
By night he fled, and at midnight returned
From compassing the Earth, cautious of day,
Since Uriel, Regent of the Sun, descried
His entrance, and forewarned the Cherubim

37–38. **then marshalled feast . . . seneschals:** The feast is *marshalled,* full of elaborate arrangements and displays. *Sewers,* supervised by their chief, the *seneschal,* seated the guests and served the meal. Milton's disdain for the ritual civility of the feast may in part be motivated by the primal bad feast he is soon to narrate.

39. **office:** position, duty. Romance is rejected as a poetry devoted to the superficial artifice of noble manners and amusements.

44. **That name:** the *heroic name* of line 40; **an age too late:** sometimes explained as universal decay, a theory Milton opposed in *Naturam non pati senium.* He might have felt that England, after the Restoration, had proved itself unworthy of a divinely inspired epic. He stated in *RCG* that the creation of ambitious Christian art might depend on the "fate of this age" (p. 841).

44–45. **unless . . . wing:** Milton feared that Aristotle was right in declaring that a cold climate such as England's (at least in comparison with the Mediterranean climates that spawned Homer and Vergil) might leave the mind unripe. See Fink.

45. **or years:** Milton was almost sixty when his epic was published; George Herbert's "The Forerunners," written in his thirties, anticipates senility. **damp:** discourage (*OED* 3).

46. **Depressed:** brought down. Psychological failure is here expressed in the metaphor of failed flight, lower than what Milton intends. Cp. the metaphor of winged flight at 3.13 and 7.4.

49. **Hesperus:** Venus, the evening star.

56. **maugre:** despite.

58–69. **By night . . . way:** Satan keeps to the darkness for an entire week to evade detection by Uriel. For three days he remains on the equator, flying ahead of the advance of sunlight. He spends the other four days compassing the earth from north to south, *traversing* each *colure*—a reference to two great circles that intersect at right angles on the earth's poles. "He crosses the world, but not in benediction" (Evans in Broadbent edition).

That kept their watch; thence full of anguish driv'n,
The space of seven continued nights he rode
With darkness, thrice the equinoctial line
He circled, four times crossed the car of night
From pole to pole, traversing each colure;
On the eighth returned, and on the coast averse
From entrance or Cherubic watch, by stealth
Found unsuspected way. There was a place,
Now not, though sin, not time, first wrought the change,
Where Tigris at the foot of Paradise
Into a gulf shot underground, till part
Rose up a fountain by the Tree of Life;
In with the river sunk, and with it rose
Satan involved in rising mist, then sought
Where to lie hid; sea he had searched and land
From Eden over Pontus, and the pool
Maeotis, up beyond the river Ob;
Downward as far Antarctic; and in length
West from Orontes to the ocean barred
At Darien, thence to the land where flows
Ganges and Indus: thus the orb he roamed
With narrow search; and with inspection deep
Considered every creature, which of all
Most opportune might serve his wiles, and found
The serpent subtlest beast of all the field.
Him after long debate, irresolute
Of thoughts revolved, his final sentence chose
Fit vessel, fittest imp of fraud, in whom
To enter, and his dark suggestions hide
From sharpest sight: for in the wily snake,
Whatever sleights none would suspicious mark,
As from his wit and native subtlety
Proceeding, which in other beasts observed
Doubt might beget of diabolic pow'r
Active within beyond the sense of brute.
Thus he resolved, but first from inward grief

67. **coast averse:** the north side of Eden, which is *averse* (turned away from) the eastern entrance, where cherubim keep watch.

77–82. **From Eden . . . Indus:** Satan spans the globe in search of his *fit vessel* (l. 89) in the animal kingdom. He journeys north from Paradise, to the *Pontus* (Black Sea), the *pool Maeotis* (Sea of Azov), and the *Ob* (a river in Siberia), then down the other side of the earth to Antarctica, and west to the *Orontes* (a river in Syria), to *Darien* (Panama), to the *Ganges* in India, and finally to the *Indus,* a river near Eden.

89. **fittest imp:** An *imp* is a graft or shoot; Satan's graft of fraud will be *fittest,* most likely to thrive, on the snake.

93. **native subtlety:** See Gen. 3.1.

His bursting passion into plaints thus poured:
"O Earth, how like to Heav'n, if not preferred
More justly, seat worthier of gods, as built
With second thoughts, reforming what was old!
For what god after better worse would build?
Terrestrial Heav'n, danced round by other heav'ns
That shine, yet bear their bright officious lamps,
Light above light, for thee alone, as seems,
In thee concent'ring all their precious beams
Of sacred influence: as God in Heav'n
Is center, yet extends to all, so thou
Cent'ring receiv'st from all those orbs; in thee,
Not in themselves, all their known virtue appears
Productive in herb, plant, and nobler birth
Of creatures animate with gradual life
Of growth, sense, reason, all summed up in man.
With what delight could I have walked thee round,
If I could joy in aught, sweet interchange
Of hill and valley, rivers, woods and plains,
Now land, now sea, and shores with forest crowned,
Rocks, dens, and caves; but I in none of these
Find place or refuge; and the more I see
Pleasures about me, so much more I feel
Torment within me, as from the hateful siege
Of contraries; all good to me becomes
Bane, and in Heav'n much worse would be my state.
But neither here seek I, no nor in Heav'n
To dwell, unless by mast'ring Heav'n's Supreme;
Nor hope to be myself less miserable
By what I seek, but others to make such
As I, though thereby worse to me redound:
For only in destroying I find ease
To my relentless thoughts; and him destroyed,
Or won to what may work his utter loss,
For whom all this was made, all this will soon
Follow, as to him linked in weal or woe;
In woe then, that destruction wide may range:

103–105. Adam suffered from the same misapprehension about the heavens (8.273–74n) and was corrected by Raphael (8.85–90n).

113. **growth, sense, reason:** progressing from vegetable (*growth*) to animal (*sense*) to rational (*reason*).

121–22. **hateful siege/Of contraries:** Here as elsewhere, Satan recoils from the beautiful, the pleasing, and the good. Cp. the "grateful vicissitude" of 6.8.

To me shall be the glory sole among
The infernal Powers, in one day to have marred
What he Almighty styled, six nights and days
Continued making, and who knows how long
Before had been contriving, though perhaps
Not longer than since I in one night freed
From servitude inglorious well nigh half
Th' angelic name, and thinner left the throng
Of his adorers: he to be avenged,
And to repair his numbers thus impaired,
Whether such virtue spent of old now failed
More angels to create, if they at least
Are his created, or to spite us more,
Determined to advance into our room
A creature formed of earth, and him endow,
Exalted from so base original,
With Heav'nly spoils, our spoils: what he decreed
He effected; man he made, and for him built
Magnificent this world, and Earth his seat,
Him lord pronounced, and, O indignity!
Subjected to his service angel wings,
And flaming ministers to watch and tend
Their earthy charge: of these the vigilance
I dread, and to elude, thus wrapped in mist
Of midnight vapor glide obscure, and pry
In every bush and brake, where hap may find
The serpent sleeping, in whose mazy folds
To hide me, and the dark intent I bring.
O foul descent! That I who erst contended
With gods to sit the highest, am now constrained
Into a beast, and mixed with bestial slime,
This essence to incarnate and imbrute,
That to the highth of deity aspired;
But what will not ambition and revenge
Descend to? Who aspires must down as low
As high he soared, obnoxious first or last
To basest things. Revenge, at first though sweet,

142. **name:** race, stock.

144. **to repair his numbers:** not, according to 3.289, God's original motive for the Creation, but a motive (7.152–53).

166. **This essence:** Satan's angelic matter, earlier said to be uncompounded or undifferentiated with regard to human fixities such as body parts (1.423–31). **incarnate:** Satan's parody of the Incarnation is undertaken with high-minded disdain, not love.

170. **obnoxious:** exposed.

171. **Revenge, at first though sweet:** repudiating the proverb "Revenge is sweet" (Tilley R90).

Bitter ere long back on itself recoils;
Let it; I reck not, so it light well aimed,
Since higher I fall short, on him who next
Provokes my envy, this new favorite
Of Heav'n, this man of clay, son of despite,
Whom us the more to spite his Maker raised
From dust: spite then with spite is best repaid."
So saying, through each thicket dank or dry,
Like a black mist low creeping, he held on
His midnight search, where soonest he might find
The serpent: him fast sleeping soon he found
In labyrinth of many a round self-rolled,
His head the midst, well stored with subtle wiles:
Not yet in horrid shade or dismal den,
Nor nocent yet, but on the grassy herb
Fearless unfeared he slept: in at his mouth
The Devil entered, and his brutal sense,
In heart or head, possessing soon inspired
With act intelligential, but his sleep
Disturbed not, waiting close th' approach of morn.
Now whenas sacred light began to dawn
In Eden on the humid flow'rs, that breathed
Their morning incense, when all things that breathe,
From th' Earth's great altar send up silent praise
To the Creator, and his nostrils fill
With grateful smell, forth came the human pair
And joined their vocal worship to the choir
Of creatures wanting voice; that done, partake
The season, prime for sweetest scents and airs;
Then commune how that day they best may ply
Their growing work: for much their work outgrew
The hands' dispatch of two gard'ning so wide.
And Eve first to her husband thus began.
"Adam, well may we labor still to dress
This garden, still to tend plant, herb and flow'r,
Our pleasant task enjoined, but till more hands
Aid us, the work under our labor grows,

172. **on itself recoils:** The metaphor of cannon, Satan's self-defining invention (cp. 4.17), continues in the gunnery language of lines 173–74.

174. **higher:** when aiming higher.

176. **son of despite:** son of scorn, with the added suggestion that man was created to spite Satan; on Satan's spite, see 2.384–85.

186. **Nor nocent:** not harmful. Milton's unusual phrase signifies "innocence" but suggests its opposite.

191. **close:** in hiding.

205. **still:** continually. For the first time, Eve initiates a conversation.

Luxurious by restraint; what we by day
Lop overgrown, or prune, or prop, or bind,
One night or two with wanton growth derides
Tending to wild. Thou therefore now advise
Or hear what to my mind first thoughts present;
Let us divide our labors, thou where choice
Leads thee, or where most needs, whether to wind
The woodbine round this arbor, or direct
The clasping ivy where to climb, while I
In yonder spring of roses intermixed
With myrtle, find what to redress till noon;
For while so near each other thus all day
Our task we choose, what wonder if so near
Looks intervene and smiles, or object new
Casual discourse draw on, which intermits
Our day's work brought to little, though begun
Early, and th' hour of supper comes unearned."
    To whom mild answer Adam thus returned.
"Sole Eve, associate sole, to me beyond
Compare above all living creatures dear,
Well hast thou motioned, well thy thoughts employed
How we might best fulfill the work which here
God hath assigned us, nor of me shalt pass
Unpraised: for nothing lovelier can be found
In woman than to study household good,
And good works in her husband to promote.
Yet not so strictly hath our Lord imposed
Labor, as to debar us when we need
Refreshment, whether food, or talk between,
Food of the mind, or this sweet intercourse
Of looks and smiles, for smiles from reason flow,
To brute denied, and are of love the food,
Love not the lowest end of human life.
For not to irksome toil, but to delight
He made us, and delight to reason joined.
These paths and bowers doubt not but our joint hands
Will keep from wilderness with ease, as wide

213. **hear:** 1667; 1674 reads "bear."

215–17. **to wind . . . to climb:** Both ivy and woodbine are in need of a prop, as Eve soon will be (ll. 431–33).

218. **spring:** thicket.

219. **redress:** put upright.

240. **of love the food:** For Ovid hope is the food of love (*Met.* 9.749); for Shakespeare's Orsino music is the food of love (*TN* 1.1.1); for Adam smiles are the food of love—and smiles, we know, lead to kisses (4.499–502).

As we need walk, till younger hands ere long
Assist us: but if much converse perhaps
Thee satiate, to short absence I could yield.
For solitude sometimes is best society,
And short retirement urges sweet return.
But other doubt possesses me, lest harm
Befall thee severed from me; for thou know'st
What hath been warned us, what malicious foe
Envying our happiness, and of his own
Despairing, seeks to work us woe and shame
By sly assault; and somewhere nigh at hand
Watches, no doubt, with greedy hope to find
His wish and best advantage, us asunder,
Hopeless to circumvent us joined, where each
To other speedy aid might lend at need;
Whether his first design be to withdraw
Our fealty from God, or to disturb
Conjugal love, than which perhaps no bliss
Enjoyed by us excites his envy more;
Or this, or worse, leave not the faithful side
That gave thee being, still shades thee and protects.
The wife, where danger or dishonor lurks,
Safest and seemliest by her husband stays,
Who guards her, or with her the worst endures."
    To whom the virgin majesty of Eve,
As one who loves, and some unkindness meets,
With sweet austere composure thus replied.
    "Offspring of Heav'n and Earth, and all Earth's lord,
That such an enemy we have, who seeks
Our ruin, both by thee informed I learn,
And from the parting angel overheard
As in a shady nook I stood behind,
Just then returned at shut of evening flow'rs.
But that thou shouldst my firmness therefore doubt

247–48. **but . . . yield:** Having dismissed the idea that Eden cannot be sufficiently tamed through their current work habits, Adam speculates that Eve has had enough *converse* (conversation).

249. Cp. *Masque* 375–80.

265. **Or:** whether.

270. **virgin majesty:** Technically, Eve is not a virgin. But *virgo* in Latin and *virginale* in Italian can sometimes denote "beauty," "freshness," "sweetness," "modesty" (Todd), or simply "woman" (Hume). In English, *virgin* can mean "chaste" (*OED* 1) and hence be applied to married women, as Puritans especially stressed.

272. **sweet austere composure:** The adjectives verge on oxymoron.

276. **parting angel overheard:** It is likely that Eve overheard 8.630–43, which begins with Raphael taking the "parting sun" to be his signal to "depart."

To God or thee, because we have a foe
May tempt it, I expected not to hear.
His violence thou fear'st not, being such,
As we, not capable of death or pain,
Can either not receive, or can repel.
His fraud is then thy fear, which plain infers
Thy equal fear that my firm faith and love
Can by his fraud be shaken or seduced;
Thoughts, which how found they harbor in thy breast
Adam, misthought of her to thee so dear?"
To whom with healing words Adam replied.
"Daughter of God and man, immortal Eve,
For such thou art, from sin and blame entire:
Not diffident of thee do I dissuade
Thy absence from my sight, but to avoid
Th' attempt itself, intended by our foe.
For he who tempts, though in vain, at least asperses
The tempted with dishonor foul, supposed
Not incorruptible of faith, not proof
Against temptation: thou thyself with scorn
And anger wouldst resent the offered wrong,
Though ineffectual found: misdeem not then,
If such affront I labor to avert
From thee alone, which on us both at once
The enemy, though bold, will hardly dare,
Or daring, first on me th' assault shall light.
Nor thou his malice and false guile contemn;
Subtle he needs must be, who could seduce
Angels, nor think superfluous others' aid.
I from the influence of thy looks receive
Access in every virtue, in thy sight
More wise, more watchful, stronger, if need were
Of outward strength; while shame, thou looking on,
Shame to be overcome or overreached
Would utmost vigor raise, and raised unite.
Why shouldst not thou like sense within thee feel
When I am present, and thy trial choose
With me, best witness of thy virtue tried."

292. **entire:** unblemished.

293. **diffident:** mistrustful.

296–301. **For he . . . found:** Adam seems to be falsely denying that he had entertained the thought (at ll. 265–69) that Eve, if apart from him, might fall. He temporarily projects that thought onto Satan, who does indeed have it.

310. **Access:** increase.

314. **raised unite:** unite all his strengths in a state of generally heightened vigor.

So spake domestic Adam in his care
And matrimonial love; but Eve, who thought
Less attributed to her faith sincere,
Thus her reply with accent sweet renewed.
"If this be our condition, thus to dwell
In narrow circuit straitened by a foe,
Subtle or violent, we not endued
Single with like defense, wherever met,
How are we happy, still in fear of harm?
But harm precedes not sin: only our Foe
Tempting affronts us with his foul esteem
Of our integrity: his foul esteem
Sticks no dishonor on our front, but turns
Foul on himself; then wherefore shunned or feared
By us? Who rather double honor gain
From his surmise proved false, find peace within,
Favor from Heav'n, our witness from th' event.
And what is faith, love, virtue unassayed
Alone, without exterior help sustained?
Let us not then suspect our happy state
Left so imperfect by the Maker wise,
As not secure to single or combined.
Frail is our happiness, if this be so,
And Eden were no Eden thus exposed."
To whom thus Adam fervently replied.
"O woman, best are all things as the will
Of God ordained them, his creating hand
Nothing imperfect or deficient left
Of all that he created, much less man,
Or aught that might his happy state secure,
Secure from outward force; within himself
The danger lies, yet lies within his power:
Against his will he can receive no harm.
But God left free the will, for what obeys
Reason, is free, and reason he made right,
But bid her well beware, and still erect,
Least by some fair appearing good surprised
She dictate false, and misinform the will
To do what God expressly hath forbid.
Not then mistrust, but tender love enjoins,

320. **Less:** too little.
326. **still:** always.
335–36. Cp. *Areop* (pp. 939, 944).
341. **Eden were no Eden:** See 4.27–28n.
353. **still:** always.

That I should mind thee oft, and mind thou me.
Firm we subsist, yet possible to swerve,
Since reason not impossibly may meet
Some specious object by the foe suborned,
And fall into deception unaware,
Not keeping strictest watch, as she was warned.
Seek not temptation then, which to avoid
Were better, and most likely if from me
Thou sever not: trial will come unsought.
Wouldst thou approve thy constancy, approve
First thy obedience; th' other who can know,
Not seeing thee attempted, who attest?
But if thou think, trial unsought may find
Us both securer than thus warned thou seem'st,
Go; for thy stay, not free, absents thee more;
Go in thy native innocence, rely
On what thou hast of virtue, summon all,
For God towards thee hath done his part, do thine."
So spake the patriarch of mankind, but Eve
Persisted, yet submiss, though last, replied.
"With thy permission then, and thus forewarned
Chiefly by what thy own last reasoning words
Touched only, that our trial, when least sought,
May find us both perhaps far less prepared,
The willinger I go, nor much expect
A foe so proud will first the weaker seek;
So bent, the more shall shame him his repulse."
Thus saying, from her husband's hand her hand
Soft she withdrew, and like a wood-nymph light
Oread or Dryad, or of Delia's train,
Betook her to the groves, but Delia's self
In gait surpassed and goddesslike deport,
Though not as she with bow and quiver armed,
But with such gard'ning tools as art yet rude,
Guiltless of fire had formed, or angels brought.
To Pales, or Pomona thus adorned,
Likeliest she seemed, Pomona when she fled

363. **she:** reason.

367. **approve:** prove.

371. **securer:** more careless.

372. **Go; for thy stay:** The conjunction of *go* and *stay* prepares, well over 3,000 lines in advance, for a major poetic effect at the end of the poem (12.615–20n, 648–49n).

386. **light:** light-footed.

387. **Oread:** mountain nymph; **Dryad:** wood nymph; **Delia's train:** the attendants of Diana, goddess of the moon, the hunt, and chastity.

393. **Pales:** the Roman goddess of flocks; **Pomona:** the goddess of fruit trees.

Vertumnus, or to Ceres in her prime,
Yet virgin of Proserpina from Jove.
Her long with ardent look his eye pursued
Delighted, but desiring more her stay.
Oft he to her his charge of quick return
Repeated, she to him as oft engaged
To be returned by noon amid the bow'r,
And all things in best order to invite
Noontide repast, or afternoon's repose.
O much deceived, much failing, hapless Eve,
Of thy presumed return! Event perverse!
Thou never from that hour in Paradise
Found'st either sweet repast, or sound repose;
Such ambush hid among sweet flow'rs and shades
Waited with hellish rancor imminent
To intercept thy way, or send thee back
Despoiled of innocence, of faith, of bliss.
For now, and since first break of dawn the fiend,
Mere serpent in appearance, forth was come,
And on his quest, where likeliest he might find
The only two of mankind, but in them
The whole included race, his purposed prey.
In bow'r and field he sought, where any tuft
Of grove or garden-plot more pleasant lay,
Their tendance or plantation for delight,
By fountain or by shady rivulet
He sought them both, but wished his hap might find
Eve separate; he wished, but not with hope
Of what so seldom chanced, when to his wish,
Beyond his hope, Eve separate he spies,
Veiled in a cloud of fragrance, where she stood,
Half spied, so thick the roses bushing round
About her glowed, oft stooping to support
Each flow'r of slender stalk, whose head though gay
Carnation, purple, azure, or specked with gold,

395. **Vertumnus:** a garden god who pursued Pomona.

396. **Yet virgin of Proserpina:** before she bore Proserpina, whose rape by Pluto anticipates Eve's fall. See 4.268–72n.

404–11. A rich apostrophe. The "Eve" in *deceived* and *event,* puns hitherto muted, erupts into full clarity. We first take *deceived* and *failing* in a general sense, announcing the whole process of her fall, but in the next lines must localize their reference to her failing, deceived presumption about her return. In this one mistake, however, lie all mistakes (Ricks 97). The loss of sound sleep and sweet repast recalls Shakespeare's conscience-stricken Macbeth.

405. **Event perverse:** unforeseen outcome.

413. **Mere:** pure, unmixed.

Hung drooping unsustained; them she upstays
Gently with myrtle band, mindless the while,
Herself, though fairest unsupported flow'r,
From her best prop so far, and storm so nigh.
Nearer he drew, and many a walk traversed
Of stateliest covert, cedar, pine, or palm,
Then voluble and bold, now hid, now seen
Among thick-woven arborets and flow'rs
Imbordered on each bank, the hand of Eve:
Spot more delicious than those gardens feigned
Or of revived Adonis, or renowned
Alcinous, host of old Laertes' son,
Or that, not mystic, where the sapient king
Held dalliance with his fair Egyptian spouse.
Much he the place admired, the person more.
As one who long in populous city pent,
Where houses thick and sewers annoy the air,
Forth issuing on a summer's morn to breathe
Among the pleasant villages and farms
Adjoined, from each thing met conceives delight,
The smell of grain, or tedded grass, or kine,
Or dairy, each rural sight, each rural sound;
If chance with nymphlike step fair virgin pass,
What pleasing seemed, for her now pleases more,
She most, and in her look sums all delight.
Such pleasure took the serpent to behold
This flow'ry plat, the sweet recess of Eve
Thus early, thus alone; her heav'nly form
Angelic, but more soft, and feminine,
Her graceful innocence, her every air
Of gesture or least action overawed
His malice, and with rapine sweet bereaved

431. **mindless:** heedless.

432. See 4.269–71.

436. **voluble:** from the Latin *volubilis,* rolling.

438. **Imbordered:** planted as borders; **hand:** handiwork.

439–44. The catalog of gardens less delicious than Eden begins with those of Adonis, which Spenser represented as a paradise (*FQ* 3.6.39–42), and Alcinous, whose garden is visited by Odysseus (Homer, *Od.* 7.112–35). The last, *not mystic* (allegorical), is the garden where *sapient* Solomon entertained his wife, Pharaoh's daughter (Song of Solomon 6.2).

446. **sewers annoy the air:** as they certainly annoyed the air of London; see John Evelyn, *Fumifugium: or, the Inconveniencie of the Aer and Smoak of London Dissipated* (1661), who argued that smoke and odors had made the city into "the suburbs of Hell" (6).

450. **tedded:** mown and spread out to dry; **kine:** archaic plural of *cow.*

453. **for:** because of.

456. **plat:** plot of ground.

458. **more soft:** Cp. 4.479.

His fierceness of the fierce intent it brought:
That space the evil one abstracted stood
From his own evil, and for the time remained
Stupidly good, of enmity disarmed,
Of guile, of hate, of envy, of revenge;
But the hot Hell that always in him burns,
Though in mid-Heav'n, soon ended his delight,
And tortures him now more, the more he sees
Of pleasure not for him ordained: then soon
Fierce hate he recollects, and all his thoughts
Of mischief, gratulating, thus excites.
"Thoughts, whither have ye led me, with what sweet
Compulsion thus transported to forget
What hither brought us, hate, not love, nor hope
Of Paradise for Hell, hope here to taste
Of pleasure, but all pleasure to destroy,
Save what is in destroying; other joy
To me is lost. Then let me not let pass
Occasion which now smiles; behold alone
The woman, opportune to all attempts,
Her husband, for I view far round, not nigh,
Whose higher intellectual more I shun,
And strength, of courage haughty, and of limb
Heroic built, though of terrestrial mold,
Foe not informidable, exempt from wound,
I not; so much hath Hell debased, and pain
Enfeebled me, to what I was in Heav'n.
She fair, divinely fair, fit love for gods,
Not terrible, though terror be in love
And beauty, not approached by stronger hate,
Hate stronger, under show of love well feigned,
The way which to her ruin now I tend."
So spake the enemy of mankind, enclosed
In serpent, inmate bad, and toward Eve
Addressed his way, not with indented wave,
Prone on the ground, as since, but on his rear,
Circular base of rising folds, that tow'red

463. **That space:** for that space of time.

467. Confirming lines 254–55, but ironically (the mind cannot make a Heaven of Hell).

472. **gratulating:** greeting; **excites:** stirs up (his thoughts, by addressing or greeting them).

480. **Occasion:** opportunity or falling together, from the Latin root *cadere,* "to fall."

485. **mold:** material.

490–92. "Beauty and love inspire awe, unless counteracted by a stronger hatred." The spondee in the chiasmic *Hate strong* makes the point metrically.

496. **indented:** sliding back and forth, zigzagging.

Fold above fold a surging maze, his head
Crested aloft, and carbuncle his eyes;
With burnished neck of verdant gold, erect
Amidst his circling spires, that on the grass
Floated redundant: pleasing was his shape,
And lovely, never since of serpent kind
Lovelier, not those that in Illyria changed
Hermione and Cadmus, or the god
In Epidaurus; nor to which transformed
Ammonian Jove, or Capitoline was seen,
He with Olympias, this with her who bore
Scipio the highth of Rome. With tract oblique
At first, as one who sought access, but feared
To interrupt, sidelong he works his way.
As when a ship by skillful steersman wrought
Nigh river's mouth or foreland, where the wind
Veers oft, as oft so steers, and shifts her sail;
So varied he, and of his tortuous train
Curled many a wanton wreath in sight of Eve,
To lure her eye; she busied heard the sound
Of rustling leaves, but minded not, as used
To such disport before her through the field,
From every beast, more duteous at her call,
Than at Circean call the herd disguised.
He bolder now, uncalled before her stood;
But as in gaze admiring: oft he bowed
His turret crest, and sleek enamelled neck,
Fawning, and licked the ground whereon she trod.
His gentle dumb expression turned at length
The eye of Eve to mark his play; he glad
Of her attention gained, with serpent tongue

500. **carbuncle:** red gem.

505–10. **Lovelier . . . Rome:** Satan is compared to serpents in classical literature into which men and gods were transformed. *Cadmus,* founder of Thebes, was changed into a snake, as was his wife, *Hermione,* when she embraced his serpentine form. The god of healing, Asclepius, journeyed as a serpent from his shrine in *Epidaurus* to Rome in order to stop a plague. In Plutarch's *Life of Alexander,* we learn that Philip of Macedonia saw his wife in bed with a snake. The oracle identified the serpent as Jupiter-Ammon. He was thus the divine father of Alexander the Great, foreshadowing Jupiter Capitolinus, who would assume a serpent body in siring *Scipio* Africanus.

510–14. Klemp (1977) noticed that the first letters of these lines spell *Satan.*

522. The sorceress Circe transformed men into obedient animals (*Od.* 10.212–19).

525. **turret:** towering; **enamelled:** smooth and variegated in color like enamel.

526. Here Satan, who balked at "prostration vile" in Heaven (5.782), invents *proskynesis,* the prostrate devotion paid to tyrants; Alexander the Great tried unsuccessfully to introduce this Persian custom into his court (Kerrigan 1998, 130).

529–30. **with . . . air:** Satan caused the serpent to

Organic, or impulse of vocal air,
His fraudulent temptation thus began.
    "Wonder not, sovereign mistress, if perhaps
Thou canst, who art sole wonder, much less arm
Thy looks, the heav'n of mildness, with disdain,
Displeased that I approach thee thus, and gaze
Insatiate, I thus single, nor have feared
Thy awful brow, more awful thus retired.
Fairest resemblance of thy Maker fair,
Thee all things living gaze on, all things thine
By gift, and thy celestial beauty adore
With ravishment beheld, there best beheld
Where universally admired; but here
In this enclosure wild, these beasts among,
Beholders rude, and shallow to discern
Half what in thee is fair, one man except,
Who sees thee? (and what is one?) who shouldst be seen
A goddess among gods, adored and served
By angels numberless, thy daily train."
    So glozed the tempter, and his proem tuned;
Into the heart of Eve his words made way,
Though at the voice much marveling; at length
Not unamazed she thus in answer spake.
"What may this mean? Language of man pronounced
By tongue of brute, and human sense expressed?
The first at least of these I thought denied
To beasts, whom God on their creation-day
Created mute to all articulate sound;
The latter I demur, for in their looks
Much reason, and in their actions oft appears.
Thee, serpent, subtlest beast of all the field
I knew, but not with human voice endued;
Redouble then this miracle, and say,
How cam'st thou speakable of mute, and how
To me so friendly grown above the rest
Of brutal kind, that daily are in sight?
Say, for such wonder claims attention due."

---

speak either by using its tongue as an instrument or by impressing his words on the nearby air (A. Williams 116–117).

532. **Wonder not:** punningly announcing the theme of one, oneness, and singularity that winds through the speech.

544. **shallow to discern:** without the intelligence to discern.

549. **glozed:** spoke flatteringly; **proem:** prelude.

558. **demur:** hesitate over.

563. **speakable:** able to speak.

To whom the guileful Tempter thus replied.
"Empress of this fair world, resplendent Eve,
Easy to me it is to tell thee all
What thou command'st, and right thou shouldst be obeyed:
I was at first as other beasts that graze
The trodden herb, of abject thoughts and low,
As was my food, nor aught but food discerned
Or sex, and apprehended nothing high:
Till on a day roving the field, I chanced
A goodly tree far distant to behold
Loaden with fruit of fairest colors mixed,
Ruddy and gold: I nearer drew to gaze;
When from the boughs a savory odor blown,
Grateful to appetite, more pleased my sense
Than smell of sweetest fennel or the teats
Of ewe or goat dropping with milk at ev'n,
Unsucked of lamb or kid, that tend their play.
To satisfy the sharp desire I had
Of tasting those fair apples, I resolved
Not to defer; hunger and thirst at once,
Powerful persuaders, quickened at the scent
Of that alluring fruit, urged me so keen.
About the mossy trunk I wound me soon,
For high from ground the branches would require
Thy utmost reach or Adam's: round the Tree
All other beasts that saw, with like desire
Longing and envying stood, but could not reach.
Amid the Tree now got, where plenty hung
Tempting so nigh, to pluck and eat my fill
I spared not, for such pleasure till that hour
At feed or fountain never had I found.
Sated at length, ere long I might perceive
Strange alteration in me, to degree
Of reason in my inward powers, and speech

571–612. The fourth and final of the major autobiographies in the poem: Sin's (2.747–809), Eve's (4.449–91), Adam's (8.250–520), and now the serpent's fraudulent story.

581. **fennel:** Serpents were supposed to be fond of this herb (Pliny, *Natural History* 19.9); they were also thought to suck the teats of sheep and goats. Serpent lore aside, it is brilliant strategy to present the Tree of Knowledge as, metaphorically, an unappreciated mother.

585. **apples:** The double sense of the Latin *malum* (apple, evil) sponsored a tradition identifying the forbidden fruit as an apple.

586. **defer:** delay.

596–97. Adam and Eve will entertain the same high estimate of the forbidden fruit's taste (ll. 786–87, 1022–24).

598–612. Having the serpent represent his powers of speech and reasoning as the effects of eating the forbidden fruit is a masterstroke. Evans (276–77) maintains that Milton's only precedent was Joseph Beaumont's *Psyche* (1648), a long and

Wanted not long, though to this shape retained.
Thenceforth to speculations high or deep
I turned my thoughts, and with capacious mind
Considered all things visible in heav'n,
Or Earth, or middle, all things fair and good;
But all that fair and good in thy divine
Semblance, and in thy beauty's heav'nly ray
United I beheld; no fair to thine
Equivalent or second, which compelled
Me thus, though importune perhaps, to come
And gaze, and worship thee of right declared
Sov'reign of creatures, universal dame."
So talked the spirited sly snake; and Eve
Yet more amazed unwary thus replied.
"Serpent, thy overpraising leaves in doubt
The virtue of that fruit, in thee first proved:
But say, where grows the tree, from hence how far?
For many are the trees of God that grow
In Paradise, and various, yet unknown
To us, in such abundance lies our choice,
As leaves a greater store of fruit untouched,
Still hanging incorruptible, till men
Grow up to their provision, and more hands
Help to disburden nature of her birth."
To whom the wily adder, blithe and glad.
"Empress, the way is ready, and not long,
Beyond a row of myrtles, on a flat,
Fast by a fountain, one small thicket past
Of blowing myrrh and balm; if thou accept
My conduct, I can bring thee thither soon."
"Lead then," said Eve. He leading swiftly rolled
In tangles, and made intricate seem straight,
To mischief swift. Hope elevates, and joy
Brightens his crest, as when a wand'ring fire,
Compact of unctuous vapor, which the night

---

uninspired poem whose serpent does indeed claim to have gained language and wisdom from the fruit (canto 6, ll. 1699–1710), and tempts Eve with the idea that she may gain even loftier wisdom from such a meal, since she is starting at a higher level than the brute (1711–22). But Beaumont only vaguely anticipates the crisp argument to be advanced by Milton's Satan (see 710–12n).

605. **middle:** the air.

606–608. **But . . . beheld:** Cp. 8.472–74.

613. **spirited sly snake:** a sibilant phrase, anticipating the prolonged hissing of 10.508–77.

616. **virtue:** power.

623. **their provision:** the fruits provided for them.

629. **blowing:** blooming.

634. **wand'ring fire:** the *ignis fatuus* or "will-o'-the-wisp," as in *Masque* 433. See Winny 168–70 and Burton, *The Anatomy of Melancholy* 166.

635. **Compact of:** composed of.

Condenses, and the cold environs round,
Kindled through agitation to a flame,
Which oft, they say, some evil spirit attends
Hovering and blazing with delusive light,
Misleads th' amazed night-wanderer from his way
To bogs and mires, and oft through pond or pool,
There swallowed up and lost, from succor far.
So glistered the dire snake, and into fraud
Led Eve our credulous mother, to the Tree
Of prohibition, root of all our woe;
Which when she saw, thus to her guide she spake.
"Serpent, we might have spared our coming hither,
Fruitless to me, though fruit be here to excess,
The credit of whose virtue rest with thee,
Wondrous indeed, if cause of such effects.
But of this Tree we may not taste nor touch;
God so commanded, and left that command
Sole daughter of his voice; the rest, we live
Law to ourselves, our reason is our law."
To whom the Tempter guilefully replied.
"Indeed? Hath God then said that of the fruit
Of all these garden trees ye shall not eat,
Yet lords declared of all in earth or air?"
To whom thus Eve yet sinless. "Of the fruit
Of each tree in the garden we may eat,
But of the fruit of this fair Tree amidst
The garden, God hath said, 'Ye shall not eat
Thereof, nor shall ye touch it, lest ye die.' "
She scarce had said, though brief, when now more bold
The tempter, but with show of zeal and love
To man, and indignation at his wrong,
New part puts on, and as to passion moved,
Fluctuates disturbed, yet comely and in act
Raised, as of some great matter to begin.
As when of old some orator renowned
In Athens or free Rome, where eloquence

640. **amazed:** both perplexed and lost, as in a labyrinth.

641. **pond or pool:** an indication that Eve is being led not just to the Tree of Knowledge but back to her initial infatuation with her own image (4.456–65).

644–45. " 'Into fraud led Eve . . .' overlaps magnificently with '. . . led Eve to the Tree,' so that what begins as a moving and ancient moral metaphor (lead us not into temptation) crystallizes with terrifying literalness" (Ricks 1963, 76).

648. **Fruitless:** pointless, but also literally fruitless, since she cannot eat this fruit; Milton anticipates the fully fallen sense of the word at line 1188.

668. **Fluctuates:** undulates.

Flourished, since mute, to some great cause addressed,
Stood in himself collected, while each part,
Motion, each act won audience ere the tongue,
Sometimes in highth began, as no delay
Of preface brooking through his zeal of right.
So standing, moving, or to highth upgrown
The tempter all impassioned thus began.
"O sacred, wise, and wisdom-giving plant,
Mother of science, now I feel thy power
Within me clear, not only to discern
Things in their causes, but to trace the ways
Of highest agents, deemed however wise.
Queen of this universe, do not believe
Those rigid threats of death; ye shall not die:
How should ye? By the fruit? It gives you life
To knowledge. By the threat'ner? Look on me,
Me who have touched and tasted, yet both live,
And life more perfect have attained than fate
Meant me, by vent'ring higher than my lot.
Shall that be shut to man, which to the beast
Is open? Or will God incense his ire
For such a petty trespass, and not praise
Rather your dauntless virtue, whom the pain
Of death denounced, whatever thing death be,
Deterred not from achieving what might lead
To happier life, knowledge of good and evil;
Of good, how just? Of evil, if what is evil
Be real, why not known, since easier shunned?
God therefore cannot hurt ye, and be just;
Not just, not God; not feared then, nor obeyed:
Your fear itself of death removes the fear.
Why then was this forbid? Why but to awe,
Why but to keep ye low and ignorant,

672. **since mute:** Eloquence itself is said to be extinct, not just in Greece and Rome; judging from *PR* 4.356–60, Milton may not have regarded the loss to be altogether negative.

674. **Motion:** gesture; **audience:** attention.

679–83. This speech, a brief travesty of *Paradise Lost* intending to prove the ways of God to man unjust, begins appropriately with an invocation to the *power* of the forbidden fruit inside the serpent and (so he claims) manifest in his very words. Cp. the four invocations at the beginnings of Books 1, 3, 7, and 9.

680. **science:** in the wide original sense of the Latin *scientia,* "knowledge."

698–99. **Of evil . . . shunned?:** A potent bit of sophistry stemming from the double meaning of *known:* (1) known by rational apprehension; (2) known by experience. Eve knows in sense 1 that eating the fruit is evil. But if eating the fruit becomes known in sense 2, she can hardly use that knowledge to shun evil. For in that case, she will have done evil. It is the difference between innocence and experience.

His worshipers; he knows that in the day
Ye eat thereof, your eyes that seem so clear,
Yet are but dim, shall perfectly be then
Opened and cleared, and ye shall be as gods,
Knowing both good and evil as they know.
That ye should be as gods, since I as man,
Internal man, is but proportion meet,
I of brute human, ye of human gods.
So ye shall die perhaps, by putting off
Human, to put on gods, death to be wished,
Though threatened, which no worse than this can bring.
And what are gods that man may not become
As they, participating godlike food?
The gods are first, and that advantage use
On our belief, that all from them proceeds;
I question it, for this fair Earth I see,
Warmed by the sun, producing every kind,
Them nothing: if they all things, who enclosed
Knowledge of good and evil in this Tree,
That whoso eats thereof, forthwith attains
Wisdom without their leave? And wherein lies
Th' offense, that man should thus attain to know?
What can your knowledge hurt him, or this Tree
Impart against his will if all be his?
Or is it envy, and can envy dwell
In heav'nly breasts? These, these and many more
Causes import your need of this fair fruit.
Goddess humane, reach then, and freely taste."
He ended, and his words replete with guile
Into her heart too easy entrance won:
Fixed on the fruit she gazed, which to behold
Might tempt alone, and in her ears the sound
Yet rung of his persuasive words, impregned

710–12. The power of speech becomes Satan's most tangible argument: as eating the fruit allowed him to change from brute to human, rising a notch in the chain of being, so eating the fruit will allow Eve to change from human to angel, a *proportion meet.* See 598–612n. The irony is pointed. The snake has not ascended the scale of being; Satan has in fact descended into the snake (ll. 163–71).

717. **participating:** partaking of.

720. **question:** Cp. 5.853–63, where Satan doubts whether the Son or anyone else created angels. The introduction of questioning is crucial; note the high proportion of questions in lines 686–732, 747–79.

722. **if they all things:** if they author all things.

732. **humane:** gracious, as in 2.109 and *PR* 1.221.

735–43. A passage built on the structure of the five senses, moving from sight to sound to smell, then to the desire *to touch or taste,* given imperative force in Satan's last words (*reach then, and freely taste,* l. 732), and in the end circling back to *her longing eye.*

With reason, to her seeming, and with truth;
Meanwhile the hour of noon drew on, and waked
An eager appetite, raised by the smell
So savory of that fruit, which with desire,
Inclinable now grown to touch or taste,
Solicited her longing eye; yet first
Pausing a while, thus to herself she mused.
"Great are thy virtues, doubtless, best of fruits,
Though kept from man, and worthy to be admired,
Whose taste, too long forborne, at first assay
Gave elocution to the mute, and taught
The tongue not made for speech to speak thy praise:
Thy praise he also who forbids thy use,
Conceals not from us, naming thee the Tree
Of Knowledge, knowledge both of good and evil;
Forbids us then to taste, but his forbidding
Commends thee more, while it infers the good
By thee communicated, and our want:
For good unknown, sure is not had, or had
And yet unknown, is as not had at all.
In plain then, what forbids he but to know,
Forbids us good, forbids us to be wise?
Such prohibitions bind not. But if death
Bind us with after-bands, what profits then
Our inward freedom? In the day we eat
Of this fair fruit, our doom is, we shall die.
How dies the serpent? He hath eat'n and lives,
And knows, and speaks, and reasons, and discerns,
Irrational till then. For us alone
Was death invented? Or to us denied
This intellectual food, for beasts reserved?
For beasts it seems: yet that one beast which first
Hath tasted, envies not, but brings with joy
The good befall'n him, author unsuspect,
Friendly to man, far from deceit or guile.
What fear I then, rather what know to fear
Under this ignorance of good and evil,
Of God or death, of law or penalty?

744. **to herself she mused:** the first time in the poem that Milton represents the silent inward speech of Adam or Eve.

756–57. **good unknown:** good unexperienced; **yet unknown:** good not apprehended rationally. The word-tree derived from "knowledge" has become a treacherous labyrinth. See 698–99n.

771. **author unsuspect:** authority above suspicion.

Here grows the cure of all, this fruit divine,
Fair to the eye, inviting to the taste,
Of virtue to make wise: what hinders then
To reach, and feed at once both body and mind?"
    So saying, her rash hand in evil hour
Forth reaching to the fruit, she plucked, she ate:
Earth felt the wound, and Nature from her seat
Sighing through all her works gave signs of woe,
That all was lost. Back to the thicket slunk
The guilty serpent, and well might, for Eve
Intent now wholly on her taste, naught else
Regarded, such delight till then, as seemed,
In fruit she never tasted, whether true
Or fancied so, through expectation high
Of knowledge, nor was Godhead from her thought.
Greedily she engorged without restraint,
And knew not eating death: satiate at length,
And heightened as with wine, jocund and boon,
Thus to herself she pleasingly began.
    "O sov'reign, virtuous, precious of all trees
In Paradise, of operation blessed
To sapience, hitherto obscured, infamed,
And thy fair fruit let hang, as to no end
Created; but henceforth my early care,
Not without song, each morning, and due praise
Shall tend thee, and the fertile burden ease
Of thy full branches offered free to all;
Till dieted by thee I grow mature
In knowledge, as the gods who all things know;
Though others envy what they cannot give;
For had the gift been theirs, it had not here
Thus grown. Experience, next to thee I owe,
Best guide; not following thee, I had remained
In ignorance, thou open'st wisdom's way,
And giv'st access, though secret she retire.
And I perhaps am secret; Heav'n is high,

776. **cure:** Eve means "remedy," but editors hear an unintended pun on the Latin *cura,* "care."

780. **hand:** Is hand the subject or object of *reaching* in line 781? (Evans in Broadbent); **evil hour:** noon.

784. **all was lost:** The poem has arrived at the meaning of its title.

792. **knew not eating death:** At least four meanings are copresent: "She did not experience death while eating"; "She did not know death, which devours"; "She did not know she was eating death"; "She did not gain knowledge when eating death."

797. **sapience:** knowledge, from the Latin *sapere,* "to taste."

High and remote to see from thence distinct
Each thing on Earth; and other care perhaps
May have diverted from continual watch
Our great forbidder, safe with all his spies
About him. But to Adam in what sort
Shall I appear? Shall I to him make known
As yet my change, and give him to partake
Full happiness with me, or rather not,
But keep the odds of knowledge in my power
Without copartner? So to add what wants
In female sex, the more to draw his love,
And render me more equal, and perhaps,
A thing not undesirable, sometime
Superior; for inferior who is free?
This may be well: but what if God have seen,
And death ensue? Then I shall be no more,
And Adam wedded to another Eve,
Shall live with her enjoying, I extinct;
A death to think. Confirmed then I resolve;
Adam shall share with me in bliss or woe:
So dear I love him, that with him all deaths
I could endure, without him live no life."
    So saying, from the Tree her step she turned,
But first low reverence done, as to the power
That dwelt within, whose presence had infused
Into the plant sciential sap, derived
From nectar, drink of gods. Adam the while
Waiting desirous her return, had wove
Of choicest flow'rs a garland to adorn
Her tresses, and her rural labors crown,
As reapers oft are wont their harvest queen.
Great joy he promised to his thoughts, and new
Solace in her return, so long delayed;
Yet oft his heart, divine of something ill,
Misgave him; he the falt'ring measure felt;

820. **odds:** advantage; see 4.447n.

823. **more equal:** The first words that Milton uses to define gender differences are "Not equal, as their sex not equal seemed" (4.296).

825. **for inferior who is free?:** as Satan has maintained (6.164–70).

827. **I shall be no more:** Heard at the opening of this book, *no more* is here applied to death and oblivion (see 1n).

835. **low reverence:** "She . . . now worships a vegetable" (Lewis 122).

837. **sciential:** conferring knowledge on those who partake of it.

845. **divine of something ill:** A stricken heart often signals a bad omen or premonition, as in *HAM* 5.2.208: "How ill all's here about my heart."

846. **falt'ring measure:** The elision of the middle syllable in *faltering* keeps Adam's *measure* or

And forth to meet her went, the way she took
That morn when first they parted; by the Tree
Of Knowledge he must pass, there he her met,
Scarce from the tree returning; in her hand
A bough of fairest fruit that downy smiled,
New gathered, and ambrosial smell diffused.
To him she hasted, in her face Excuse
Came prologue, and Apology to prompt,
Which with bland words at will she thus addressed.
"Hast thou not wondered, Adam, at my stay?
Thee I have missed, and thought it long, deprived
Thy presence, agony of love till now
Not felt, nor shall be twice, for never more
Mean I to try, what rash untried I sought,
The pain of absence from thy sight. But strange
Hath been the cause, and wonderful to hear:
This Tree is not as we are told, a tree
Of danger tasted, nor to evil unknown
Op'ning the way, but of divine effect
To open eyes, and make them gods who taste;
And hath been tasted such: the serpent wise,
Or not restrained as we, or not obeying,
Hath eaten of the fruit, and is become,
Not dead, as we are threatened, but thenceforth
Endued with human voice and human sense,
Reasoning to admiration, and with me
Persuasively hath so prevailed, that I
Have also tasted, and have also found
Th' effects to correspond, opener mine eyes,
Dim erst, dilated spirits, ampler heart,
And growing up to Godhead; which for thee
Chiefly I sought, without thee can despise.
For bliss, as thou hast part, to me is bliss,
Tedious, unshared with thee, and odious soon.
Thou therefore also taste, that equal lot
May join us, equal joy, as equal love;
Lest thou not tasting, different degree

---

heartbeat in an iambic mold; the pun on *falt/fault* (*fault'ring* was the original spelling) suggests cardiac problems to come.

851. **downy smiled:** seemed attractive covered with down.

853–54. **in her face . . . prompt:** "Excuse, the pleading expression on her face, was the prologue to Apology [Justification], and continued to serve as this actor's prompter."

855. **bland:** smooth, containing blandishments.

868. **Or . . . or:** either . . . or.

Disjoin us, and I then too late renounce
Deity for thee, when fate will not permit."
  Thus Eve with count'nance blithe her story told;
But in her cheek distemper flushing glowed.
On th' other side, Adam, soon as he heard
The fatal trespass done by Eve, amazed,
Astonied stood and blank, while horror chill
Ran through his veins, and all his joints relaxed;
From his slack hand the garland wreathed for Eve
Down dropped, and all the faded roses shed:
Speechless he stood and pale, till thus at length
First to himself he inward silence broke.
  "O fairest of creation, last and best
Of all God's works, creature in whom excelled
Whatever can to sight or thought be formed,
Holy, divine, good, amiable, or sweet!
How art thou lost, how on a sudden lost,
Defaced, deflow'red, and now to death devote?
Rather how hast thou yielded to transgress
The strict forbiddance, how to violate
The sacred fruit forbidd'n! Some cursèd fraud
Of enemy hath beguiled thee, yet unknown,
And me with thee hath ruined, for with thee
Certain my resolution is to die;
How can I live without thee, how forgo
Thy sweet converse and love so dearly joined,
To live again in these wild woods forlorn?
Should God create another Eve, and I
Another rib afford, yet loss of thee
Would never from my heart; no no, I feel
The link of nature draw me: flesh of flesh,
Bone of my bone thou art, and from thy state
Mine never shall be parted, bliss or woe."

890. **Astonied:** astonished, with pun on "as stone"; **horror chill:** cp. Vergil's *frigidus horror* (*Aen.* 3.29).

893. **faded roses:** A first instance of decay in Eden (Fowler). Evans thinks the faded roses symbolize Eve's mortality. But since fallen roses will acquire thorns (4.256), and since these woven flowers were intended to crown (l. 841), the decayed garland may also be meant to evoke Christ's crown of thorns.

895. **he inward silence broke:** as Eve also did before her fall (744n).

896. **last and best:** last but not best, Raphael warned (8.565–66).

901. **deflow'red:** Accounts of the Fall sometimes made use of sexual metaphors such as ravishment, seduction, and infidelity (A. Williams 120, 125), and sometimes included speculations about the actual deterioration of human sexuality (Turner 124–73). **devote:** consecrated.

911. **another Eve:** Eve also rejected this idea (ll. 828–30).

916. **bliss or woe:** echoing Eve at line 831.

So having said, as one from sad dismay
Recomforted, and after thoughts disturbed
Submitting to what seemed remediless,
Thus in calm mood his words to Eve he turned.
"Bold deed thou hast presumed, advent'rous Eve,
And peril great provoked, who thus hath dared
Had it been only coveting to eye
That sacred fruit, sacred to abstinence,
Much more to taste it under ban to touch.
But past who can recall, or done undo?
Not God omnipotent, nor Fate, yet so
Perhaps thou shalt not die, perhaps the fact
Is not so heinous now, foretasted fruit,
Profaned first by the serpent, by him first
Made common and unhallowed ere our taste;
Nor yet on him found deadly; he yet lives,
Lives, as thou saidst, and gains to live as man
Higher degree of life, inducement strong
To us, as likely tasting to attain
Proportional ascent, which cannot be
But to be gods, or angels, demi-gods.
Nor can I think that God, creator wise,
Though threat'ning, will in earnest so destroy
Us his prime creatures, dignified so high,
Set over all his works, which in our fall,
For us created, needs with us must fail,
Dependent made; so God shall uncreate,
Be frustrate, do, undo, and labor lose,
Not well conceived of God, who though his power
Creation could repeat, yet would be loath
Us to abolish, lest the Adversary
Triumph and say, 'Fickle their state whom God
Most favors; who can please him long? Me first
He ruined, now mankind; whom will he next?'
Matter of scorn, not to be given the foe.
However I with thee have fixed my lot,
Certain to undergo like doom; if death

924. **sacred:** set apart, unlike all other fruits (in being subject to abstinence).

926. The line contains two nearly synonymous proverbs: "Things past cannot be recalled" (Tilley T203) and "Things done cannot be undone" (Tilley T200).

928. **fact:** deed and crime.

936. **Proportional ascent:** echoing Satan at lines 710–12.

947–51. **lest . . . foe:** And indeed, Satan will not be allowed to gloat—a first intuition of the protevangelium (10.175–81n) and its enactment in Hell (10.504–77).

Consort with thee, death is to me as life;
So forcible within my heart I feel
The bond of nature draw me to my own,
My own in thee, for what thou art is mine;
Our state cannot be severed, we are one,
One flesh; to lose thee were to lose myself."
So Adam, and thus Eve to him replied.
"O glorious trial of exceeding love,
Illustrious evidence, example high!
Engaging me to emulate, but short
Of thy perfection, how shall I attain,
Adam, from whose dear side I boast me sprung,
And gladly of our union hear thee speak,
One heart, one soul in both; whereof good proof
This day affords, declaring thee resolved,
Rather than death or aught than death more dread
Shall separate us, linked in love so dear,
To undergo with me one guilt, one crime,
If any be, of tasting this fair fruit,
Whose virtue, for of good still good proceeds,
Direct, or by occasion hath presented
This happy trial of thy love, which else
So eminently never had been known.
Were it I thought death menaced would ensue
This my attempt, I would sustain alone
The worst, and not persuade thee, rather die
Deserted, than oblige thee with a fact
Pernicious to thy peace, chiefly assured
Remarkably so late of thy so true,
So faithful love unequaled; but I feel
Far otherwise th' event, not death, but life
Augmented, opened eyes, new hopes, new joys,
Taste so divine, that what of sweet before
Hath touched my sense, flat seems to this, and harsh.
On my experience, Adam, freely taste,
And fear of death deliver to the winds."
So saying, she embraced him, and for joy
Tenderly wept, much won that he his love
Had so ennobled, as of choice to incur

954. **death is to me as life:** Editors hear an echo of Satan's "Evil be thou my good" (4.110), but the resemblance is more verbal than moral or psychological.

980. **oblige:** make liable to a penalty (Lat. *obligare*).

988. **freely taste:** echoing Satan at line 732.

Divine displeasure for her sake, or death.
In recompense (for such compliance bad
Such recompense best merits) from the bough
She gave him of that fair enticing fruit
With liberal hand: he scrupled not to eat
Against his better knowledge, not deceived,
But fondly overcome with female charm.
Earth trembled from her entrails, as again
In pangs, and Nature gave a second groan;
Sky loured, and muttering Thunder, some sad drops
Wept at completing of the mortal sin
Original; while Adam took no thought,
Eating his fill, nor Eve to iterate
Her former trespass feared, the more to soothe
Him with her loved society, that now
As with new wine intoxicated both
They swim in mirth, and fancy that they feel
Divinity within them breeding wings
Wherewith to scorn the earth: but that false fruit
Far other operation first displayed,
Carnal desire inflaming; he on Eve
Began to cast lascivious eyes, she him
As wantonly repaid; in lust they burn:
Till Adam thus gan Eve to dalliance move.
"Eve, now I see thou art exact of taste,
And elegant, of sapience no small part,
Since to each meaning savor we apply,
And palate call judicious; I the praise
Yield thee, so well this day thou hast purveyed.
Much pleasure we have lost, while we abstained
From this delightful fruit, nor known till now
True relish, tasting; if such pleasure be
In things to us forbidden, it might be wished,
For this one tree had been forbidden ten.

998. **not deceived:** Cp. 1 Tim. 2.14: "Adam was not deceived, but the woman being deceived was in the transgression."

999. **fondly:** foolishly.

1003–1004. **sin/Original:** The only appearance of the famous theological phrase in the poem; for Milton's understanding of it, see *CD* 1.11.

1016. **dalliance:** amorous play.

1017–20. **Eve . . . judicious:** The idea, somewhat tortuously expressed, is that we apply words like *savor* and *judicious* to both questions of taste and questions of wisdom—hence the word *sapience,* epitomizing such usages, brilliantly denotes both taste and wisdom.

1018. **elegant:** in the sense of the Latin *elegans,* "refined in taste."

1025–26. **it . . . ten:** His fond wish will be granted when God delivers the Ten Commandments to Moses.

But come, so well refreshed, now let us play,
As meet is, after such delicious fare;
For never did thy beauty since the day
I saw thee first and wedded thee, adorned
With all perfections, so inflame my sense
With ardor to enjoy thee, fairer now
Than ever, bounty of this virtuous Tree."
    So said he, and forbore not glance or toy
Of amorous intent, well understood
Of Eve, whose eye darted contagious fire.
Her hand he seized, and to a shady bank,
Thick overhead with verdant roof embow'red
He led her nothing loath; flow'rs were the couch,
Pansies, and violets, and asphodel,
And hyacinth, earth's freshest softest lap.
There they their fill of love and love's disport
Took largely, of their mutual guilt the seal,
The solace of their sin, till dewy sleep
Oppressed them, wearied with their amorous play.
Soon as the force of that fallacious fruit,
That with exhilarating vapor bland
About their spirits had played, and inmost powers
Made err, was now exhaled, and grosser sleep
Bred of unkindly fumes, with conscious dreams
Encumbered, now had left them, up they rose
As from unrest, and each the other viewing,
Soon found their eyes how opened, and their minds
How darkened; innocence, that as a veil
Had shadowed them from knowing ill, was gone,
Just confidence, and native righteousness
And honor from about them, naked left
To guilty shame: he covered, but his robe
Uncovered more. So rose the Danite strong,

1028. **meet:** "appropriate," the deliciousness of the meal having awakened an appetite for its delicious purveyor; also glancing at *help meet,* one of Eve's titles, and by a pun on *meat* (meaning food in general), anticipating their new carnivorous diet.

1029–32. See Homer, *Od.* 14.314–16.

1037. **Her hand he seized:** not gently, as at 4.488–89.

1043. **of their mutual guilt the seal**: A *seal* makes a document official. So the mutual act of intercourse, as it were, brazenly authenticates their mutual crime: "We have done this, we who were given sexuality with the commandment to be fruitful and multiply."

1048. **spirits:** a technical term in medical physiology, denoting vaporous substances in the blood that carry out communications between the soul and body. See Thomas Wright, *The Passions of the Minde in Generall* (1604), 59–68 and passim; Donne, "The Extasie," 61–64.

1050. **unkindly:** unnatural; **conscious:** full of guilty knowledge.

1058. **he:** shame.

1059. **Danite:** Samson's father belonged to the tribe of Dan.

Herculean Samson, from the harlot-lap
Of Philistean Dalila, and waked
Shorn of his strength, they destitute and bare
Of all their virtue: silent, and in face
Confounded long they sat, as stricken mute,
Till Adam, though not less than Eve abashed,
At length gave utterance to these words constrained.
"O Eve, in evil hour thou didst give ear
To that false worm, of whomsoever taught
To counterfeit man's voice, true in our fall,
False in our promised rising; since our eyes
Opened we find indeed, and find we know
Both good and evil, good lost, and evil got,
Bad fruit of knowledge, if this be to know,
Which leaves us naked thus, of honor void,
Of innocence, of faith, of purity,
Our wonted ornaments now soiled and stained,
And in our faces evident the signs
Of foul concupiscence; whence evil store;
Even shame, the last of evils; of the first
Be sure then. How shall I behold the face
Henceforth of God or angel, erst with joy
And rapture so oft beheld? Those heav'nly shapes
Will dazzle now this earthly, with their blaze
Insufferably bright. O might I here
In solitude live savage, in some glade
Obscured, where highest woods impenetrable
To star or sunlight, spread their umbrage broad
And brown as evening: cover me ye pines,
Ye cedars, with innumerable boughs
Hide me, where I may never see them more.
But let us now, as in bad plight, devise
What best may for the present serve to hide
The parts of each from other, that seem most
To shame obnoxious, and unseemliest seen,
Some tree whose broad smooth leaves together sewed,
And girded on our loins, may cover round

1060. **Herculean:** strong like Hercules; **harlot-lap:** The word *harlot* does not appear in Milton's *Samson Agonistes,* where Dalila is the hero's wife.

1067. **Eve, in evil:** The pun is prelude to a host of accusations.

1078. **evil store:** evil aplenty.

1079. **Even shame, the last of evils:** Shame, because it initiates repentance, is the last manifestation of the evil that caused it (*the first*).

1083. **earthly:** earthly nature.

1087. **umbrage:** shadow, foliage.

1094. **obnoxious:** exposed.

Those middle parts, that this newcomer, Shame,
There sit not, and reproach us as unclean."
So counseled he, and both together went
Into the thickest wood; there soon they chose
The fig tree, not that kind for fruit renowned,
But such as at this day to Indians known
In Malabar or Deccan spreds her arms
Branching so broad and long, that in the ground
The bended twigs take root, and daughters grow
About the mother tree, a pillared shade
High overarched, and echoing walks between;
There oft the Indian herdsman shunning heat
Shelters in cool, and tends his pasturing herds
At loopholes cut through thickest shade: those leaves
They gathered, broad as Amazonian targe,
And with what skill they had, together sewed,
To gird their waist, vain covering if to hide
Their guilt and dreaded shame; O how unlike
To that first naked glory. Such of late
Columbus found th' American so girt
With feathered cincture, naked else and wild
Among the trees on isles and woody shores.
Thus fenced, and as they thought, their shame in part
Covered, but not at rest or ease of mind,
They sat them down to weep, nor only tears
Rained at their eyes, but high winds worse within
Began to rise, high passions, anger, hate,
Mistrust, suspicion, discord, and shook sore
Their inward state of mind, calm region once
And full of peace, now tossed and turbulent:
For understanding ruled not, and the will
Heard not her lore, both in subjection now
To sensual appetite, who from beneath
Usurping over sov'reign reason claimed
Superior sway: from thus distempered breast,
Adam, estranged in look and altered style,

1101. **fig tree:** the banyan, not the common variety. For details and sources, see Svendsen 1969, 31–32, 134–36.

1103. **Malabar:** southwest coast of India; **Deccan:** the peninsula of India (including Malabar).

1111. **as Amazonian targe:** as an Amazon's shield (notable for its size).

1115. **naked glory:** The paradoxical force of the phrase stems from the idea of *glory* (Heb. ***kabod***) as an adornment, a radiance of being (Rumrich 1987, 20–21, 131–32).

1116. **Columbus:** one of the two near contemporaries mentioned in the poem (see 1.288–91n).

1117. **cincture:** belt.

Speech intermitted thus to Eve renewed.
    "Would thou hadst hearkened to my words, and stayed
With me, as I besought thee, when that strange
Desire of wand'ring this unhappy morn.
I know not whence possessed thee; we had then
Remained still happy, not as now, despoiled
Of all our good, shamed, naked, miserable.
Let none henceforth seek needless cause to approve
The faith they owe; when earnestly they seek
Such proof, conclude, they then begin to fail."
    To whom soon moved with touch of blame thus Eve.
"What words have passed thy lips, Adam severe,
Imput'st thou that to my default, or will
Of wand'ring, as thou call'st it, which who knows
But might as ill have happened thou being by,
Or to thyself perhaps: hadst thou been there,
Or here th' attempt, thou couldst not have discerned
Fraud in the serpent, speaking as he spake;
No ground of enmity between us known,
Why he should mean me ill, or seek to harm.
Was I to have never parted from thy side?
As good have grown there still a lifeless rib.
Being as I am, why didst not thou the head
Command me absolutely not to go,
Going into such danger as thou saidst?
Too facile then thou didst not much gainsay,
Nay, didst permit, approve, and fair dismiss.
Hadst thou been firm and fixed in thy dissent,
Neither had I transgressed, nor thou with me."
    To whom then first incensed Adam replied.
"Is this the love, is this the recompense
Of mine to thee, ingrateful Eve, expressed
Immutable when thou wert lost, not I,
Who might have lived and joyed immortal bliss,
Yet willingly chose rather death with thee:
And am I now upbraided, as the cause
Of thy transgressing? Not enough severe,
It seems, in thy restraint: what could I more?
I warned thee, I admonished thee, foretold
The danger, and the lurking enemy
That lay in wait; beyond this had been force,

1133. **intermitted:** interrupted (by the quest for covering).

And force upon free will hath here no place.
But confidence then bore thee on, secure
Either to meet no danger, or to find
Matter of glorious trial; and perhaps
I also erred in overmuch admiring
What seemed in thee so perfect, that I thought
No evil durst attempt thee, but I rue
That error now, which is become my crime,
And thou th' accuser. Thus it shall befall
Him who to worth in women overtrusting
Lets her will rule; restraint she will not brook,
And left to herself, if evil thence ensue,
She first his weak indulgence will accuse."

Thus they in mutual accusation spent
The fruitless hours, but neither self-condemning,
And of their vain contest appeared no end.

1187. **mutual accusation:** *Mutual guilt* (l. 1043) has now deteriorated into a quarreling *mutual accusation.*

1188. **fruitless hours:** See 648n.

1189. **no end:** *No more* at the beginning of the book, declaring unfallen favors at an end, is balanced against the concluding *no end,* declaring fallen ills (so it appears) interminable.

"He bolder now, uncalled before her stood" (9.523).

Book X

The Argument

Man's transgression known, the guardian angels forsake Paradise, and return up to Heaven to approve their vigilance, and are approved, God declaring that the entrance of Satan could not be by them prevented. He sends his Son to judge the transgressors, who descends and gives sentence accordingly; then in pity clothes them both, and reascends. Sin and Death, sitting till then at the gates of Hell, by wondrous sympathy feeling the success of Satan in this new world, and the sin by man there committed, resolve to sit no longer confined in Hell, but to follow Satan their sire up to the place of man. To make the way easier from Hell to this world to and fro, they pave a broad highway or bridge over Chaos, according to the track that Satan first made; then preparing for Earth, they meet him proud of his success returning to Hell; their mutual gratulation. Satan arrives at Pandaemonium; in full assembly relates with boasting his success against man; instead of applause is entertained with a general hiss by all his audience, transformed with himself also suddenly into serpents, according to his doom given in paradise; then deluded with a show of the forbidden tree springing up before them, they greedily reaching to take of the fruit, chew dust and bitter ashes. The proceedings of Sin and Death; God foretells the final victory of his Son over them, and the renewing of all things, but for the present commands his angels to make several alterations in the heavens and elements. Adam more and more perceiving his fallen condition, heavily bewails, rejects the condolement of Eve. She persists and at length appeases him; then to evade the curse likely to fall on their offspring, proposes to Adam violent ways which he approves not, but conceiving better hope, puts her in mind of the late promise made them, that her seed should be revenged on the Serpent, and exhorts her with him to seek peace of the offended Deity, by repentance and supplication.

Meanwhile the heinous and despiteful act
Of Satan done in Paradise, and how
He in the serpent, had perverted Eve,
Her husband she, to taste the fatal fruit,
Was known in Heav'n; for what can scape the eye
Of God all-seeing, or deceive his heart

Omniscient, who in all things wise and just,
Hindered not Satan to attempt the mind
Of man, with strength entire, and free will armed,
Complete to have discovered and repulsed
Whatever wiles of foe or seeming friend.
For still they knew, and ought to have still remembered
The high injunction not to taste that fruit,
Whoever tempted; which they not obeying,
Incurred, what could they less, the penalty,
And manifold in sin, deserved to fall.
Up into Heav'n from Paradise in haste
Th' angelic guards ascended, mute and sad
For man, for of his state by this they knew,
Much wond'ring how the subtle fiend had stol'n
Entrance unseen. Soon as th' unwelcome news
From Earth arriv'd at Heaven Gate, displeased
All were who heard, dim sadness did not spare
That time celestial visages, yet mixed
With pity, violated not their bliss.
About the new-arrived, in multitudes
Th' ethereal people ran, to hear and know
How all befell: they towards the throne supreme
Accountable made haste to make appear
With righteous plea, their utmost vigilance,
And easily approved; when the Most High
Eternal Father from his secret cloud,
Amidst in thunder uttered thus his voice.
"Assembled angels, and ye Powers returned
From unsuccessful charge, be not dismayed,
Nor troubled at these tidings from the Earth,
Which your sincerest care could not prevent,
Foretold so lately what would come to pass,
When first this tempter crossed the gulf from Hell.
I told ye then he should prevail and speed
On his bad errand, man should be seduced
And flattered out of all, believing lies
Against his Maker; no decree of mine
Concurring to necessitate his fall,

10. **Complete:** fully equipped.

12. **still:** always.

16. **manifold in sin:** various in sin. On the multiplicity of the sin of the Fall, see *CD* 1.11; A. Williams 121–22.

29–31. **Accountable . . . approved:** "The guardian angels, accountable for their actions, hastily approached the throne to plead their vigilance, which God readily confirmed: the guards were not to blame."

40. **speed:** be successful.

Or touch with lightest moment of impulse
His free will, to her own inclining left
In even scale. But fall'n he is, and now
What rests but that the mortal sentence pass
On his transgression, death denounced that day,
Which he presumes already vain and void,
Because not yet inflicted, as he feared,
By some immediate stroke; but soon shall find
Forbearance no acquittance ere day end.
Justice shall not return as bounty scorned.
But whom send I to judge them? Whom but thee
Vicegerent Son, to thee I have transferred
All judgment, whether in Heav'n, or Earth, or Hell.
Easy it might be seen that I intend
Mercy colleague with justice, sending thee
Man's friend, his Mediator, his designed
Both ransom and Redeemer voluntary,
And destined man himself to judge man fall'n."
So spake the Father, and unfolding bright
Toward the right hand his glory, on the Son
Blazed forth unclouded deity; he full
Resplendent all his Father manifest
Expressed, and thus divinely answered mild.
"Father Eternal, thine is to decree,
Mine both in Heav'n and Earth to do thy will
Supreme, that thou in me thy Son beloved
May'st ever rest well pleased. I go to judge
On Earth these thy transgressors, but thou know'st,
Whoever judged, the worst on me must light,
When time shall be, for so I undertook
Before thee; and not repenting, this obtain
Of right, that I may mitigate their doom
On me derived, yet I shall temper so
Justice with mercy, as may illustrate most
Them fully satisfied, and thee appease.
Attendance none shall need, nor train, where none

45. **moment:** the minimum weight necessary to disturb the equilibrium of a balance (the *even scale* of l. 47). Cp. 6.239, 245–46.

48. **rests:** remains.

53. **Forbearance no acquittance:** A debt is not settled just because payment has not yet been demanded; see Tilley F584.

54. "Man will not scorn my justice [for not being duly delivered] as he scorned my gift of Paradise."

56–57. **to thee . . . judgment:** John 5.22.

78. **illustrate most:** show above all.

79. **Them:** justice and mercy. Cp. *Nat Ode,* stanza 15.

80. **Attendance none shall need:** "I will not need a retinue."

Are to behold the judgment but the judged,
Those two; the third best absent is condemned,
Convict by flight, and rebel to all law;
Conviction to the serpent none belongs."
    Thus saying, from his radiant seat he rose
Of high collateral glory: him Thrones and Powers,
Princedoms, and Dominations ministrant
Accompanied to Heaven gate, from whence
Eden and all the coast in prospect lay.
Down he descended straight; the speed of gods
Time counts not, though with swiftest minutes winged.
Now was the sun in western cadence low
From noon, and gentle airs due at their hour
To fan the earth now waked, and usher in
The evening cool, when he from wrath more cool
Came the mild Judge and Intercessor both
To sentence man: the voice of God they heard
Now walking in the garden, by soft winds
Brought to their ears, while day declined; they heard,
And from his presence hid themselves among
The thickest trees, both man and wife, till God
Approaching, thus to Adam called aloud.
    "Where art thou Adam, wont with joy to meet
My coming seen far off? I miss thee here,
Not pleased, thus entertained with solitude,
Where obvious duty erewhile appeared unsought:
Or come I less conspicuous, or what change
Absents thee, or what chance detain? Come forth."
He came, and with him Eve, more loath, though first
To offend, discount'nanced both, and discomposed;
Love was not in their looks, either to God
Or to each other, but apparent guilt,
And shame, and perturbation, and despair,
Anger, and obstinacy, and hate, and guile.
Whence Adam falt'ring long, thus answered brief.
    "I heard thee in the garden, and of thy voice
Afraid, being naked, hid myself." To whom

82. **the third:** Satan.
83. **Convict:** convicted.
84. **Conviction:** both "proof of guilt" and "condition of being convinced of sin" (*OED* 8).
86. **collateral:** side by side.
90–91. **the speed . . . winged:** The implication is that time, however finely measured, contains no unit short enough to express the instantaneous speed of the Son.
92. **cadence:** falling.
106. **obvious:** The word, meaning (1) "plain" and (2) "coming in the way," defines both the obviousness of the duty and the duty to be obvious before a visiting deity.

The gracious judge without revile replied.
  "My voice thou oft hast heard, and hast not feared,
But still rejoiced, how is it now become
So dreadful to thee? That thou art naked, who
Hath told thee? Hast thou eaten of the tree
Whereof I gave thee charge thou shouldst not eat?"
  To whom thus Adam sore beset replied.
"O Heav'n! In evil strait this day I stand
Before my Judge, either to undergo
Myself the total crime, or to accuse
My other self, the partner of my life;
Whose failing, while her faith to me remains,
I should conceal, and not expose to blame
By my complaint; but strict necessity
Subdues me, and calamitous constraint
Lest on my head both sin and punishment,
However insupportable, be all
Devolved; though should I hold my peace, yet thou
Wouldst easily detect what I conceal.
This woman whom thou mad'st to be my help,
And gav'st me as thy perfect gift, so good,
So fit, so acceptable, so divine,
That from her hand I could suspect no ill,
And what she did, whatever in itself,
Her doing seemed to justify the deed;
She gave me of the tree, and I did eat."
  To whom the sov'reign Presence thus replied.
"Was she thy God, that her thou didst obey
Before his voice, or was she made thy guide,
Superior, or but equal, that to her
Thou didst resign thy manhood, and the place
Wherein God set thee above her made of thee,
And for thee, whose perfection far excelled
Hers in all real dignity: adorned
She was indeed, and lovely to attract
Thy love, not thy subjection, and her gifts
Were such as under government well seemed,
Unseemly to bear rule, which was thy part

118. **revile:** reviling.
120. **still:** always, ever.
128. **other self:** See 8.450n.
135. **Devolved:** caused to fall upon (*OED* 3c).
137–43. Here Milton elaborates Gen. 3.12. Contrast Eve's simple confession in lines 159–62, where he closely follows Gen. 3.13.
155–56. **part/And person:** role and character (in a play).

And person, hadst thou known thyself aright."
So having said, he thus to Eve in few:
"Say woman, what is this which thou hast done?"
To whom sad Eve with shame nigh overwhelmed,
Confessing soon, yet not before her judge
Bold or loquacious, thus abashed replied.
"The Serpent me beguiled and I did eat."
Which when the Lord God heard, without delay
To judgment he proceeded on th' accused
Serpent though brute, unable to transfer
The guilt on him who made him instrument
Of mischief, and polluted from the end
Of his creation; justly then accursed,
As vitiated in nature: more to know
Concerned not man (since he no further knew)
Nor altered his offense; yet God at last
To Satan first in sin his doom applied,
Though in mysterious terms, judged as then best:
And on the serpent thus his curse let fall.
"Because thou hast done this, thou art accursed
Above all cattle, each beast of the field;
Upon thy belly groveling thou shalt go,
And dust shalt eat all the days of thy life.
Between thee and the woman I will put
Enmity, and between thine and her seed;
Her seed shall bruise thy head, thou bruise his heel."
So spake this oracle, then verified
When Jesus son of Mary, second Eve,
Saw Satan fall like lightning down from heav'n,
Prince of the Air; then rising from his grave
Spoiled Principalities and Powers, triumphed

165–66. **unable . . . instrument:** The serpent is unable to transfer the guilt to Satan, who made the serpent his instrument.

173. **mysterious:** mystical, prefiguring.

175–81. A major passage in the design of the poem, in that these *mysterious terms* are progressively opened or dilated in the remaining books until they convey the entirety of the Christian revelation. At lines 504–17 the curse on the serpent is literally transferred to Satan and the devils. The mysterious terms are then gradually explicated in lines 1030–40; 11.115–16, 154–55; 12.327–30, 376–85, 429–35, 451–55, 620–23. Genesis 3.15, on which this passage is based, is sometimes termed a "protevangelium" or "first gospel." Luther thought the first gospel was intended to console Eve, since *second Eve* (l. 183) will contribute humanity to Jesus, while Calvin insisted that "seed of the woman" meant all mankind. Milton presents both views. See Hunter et al., *A Milton Encyclopedia*, "Protevangelium."

183. **second Eve:** an idea familiar in Christian "figural" interpretation of the Bible (see Auerbach 11–78), as is the corresponding notion of Jesus as second or "last" Adam (1 Cor. 15.45).

184. **Satan fall like lightning:** Luke 10.18–19.

185. **Prince of the Air:** a commonplace epithet for Satan (Eph. 2.2). Cp. *PR* 1.39–47.

In open show, and with ascension bright
Captivity led captive through the air,
The realm itself of Satan long usurped,
Whom he shall tread at last under our feet;
Even he who now foretold his fatal bruise,
And to the woman thus his sentence turned.
"Thy sorrow I will greatly multiply
By thy conception; children thou shalt bring
In sorrow forth, and to thy husband's will
Thine shall submit, he over thee shall rule."
On Adam last thus judgment he pronounced.
"Because thou hast hearkened to the voice of thy wife,
And eaten of the tree concerning which
I charged thee, saying, 'Thou shalt not eat thereof,'
Cursed is the ground for thy sake, thou in sorrow
Shalt eat thereof all the days of thy life;
Thorns also and thistles it shall bring thee forth
Unbid, and thou shalt eat th' herb of th' field,
In the sweat of thy face shalt thou eat bread,
Till thou return unto the ground, for thou
Out of the ground wast taken, know thy birth,
For dust thou art, and shalt to dust return."
So judged he man, both Judge and Savior sent,
And th' instant stroke of death denounced that day
Removed far off; then pitying how they stood
Before him naked to the air, that now
Must suffer change, disdained not to begin
Thenceforth the form of servant to assume,
As when he washed his servants' feet, so now
As father of his family he clad
Their nakedness with skins of beasts, or slain,
Or as the snake with youthful coat repaid;
And thought not much to clothe his enemies:
Nor he their outward only with the skins

195–96. **thy husband's . . . rule:** Milton in *CD* 1.10 maintains that Adam's authority over Eve is strengthened after the Fall, but there are intimations in the poem that postlapsarian Adam and Eve enjoy new equalities—equal in guilt, equal in their Christian enmity toward the serpent, equal in "one faith unanimous" (12.603).

210. **denounced:** announced as a calamity soon to occur.

215. See John 13.5.

217–18. **or . . . Or:** either . . . or. The skins of Gen. 3.21 had long been a provocation to exegetes, as Hume noted: "Interpreters torment the text . . . with their curious inquiries, 'Who slew the beasts? Who flay'd 'em?' "

219. **thought not much:** thought it nothing to object to or hesitate to perform (*OED* 10d).

Of beasts, but inward nakedness, much more
Opprobrious, with his robe of righteousness,
Arraying covered from his Father's sight.
To him with swift ascent he up returned,
Into his blissful bosom reassumed
In glory as of old, to him appeased
All, though all-knowing, what had passed with man
Recounted, mixing intercession sweet.
Meanwhile ere thus was sinned and judged on Earth,
Within the gates of Hell sat Sin and Death,
In counterview within the gates, that now
Stood open wide, belching outrageous flame
Far into Chaos, since the fiend passed through,
Sin opening, who thus now to Death began.
"O Son, why sit we here each other viewing
Idly, while Satan our great author thrives
In other worlds, and happier seat provides
For us his offspring dear? It cannot be
But that success attends him; if mishap,
Ere this he had returned, with fury driv'n
By his avengers, since no place like this
Can fit his punishment, or their revenge.
Methinks I feel new strength within me rise,
Wings growing, and dominion giv'n me large
Beyond this deep; whatever draws me on,
Or sympathy, or some connatural force
Powerful at greatest distance to unite
With secret amity things of like kind
By secretest conveyance. Thou my shade
Inseparable must with me along:
For Death from Sin no power can separate.
But lest the difficulty of passing back
Stay his return perhaps over this gulf
Impassable, impervious, let us try

222. **robe of righteousness:** Isa. 61.10.

230. **Sin and Death:** Book 10 "has a greater variety of persons in it than any other in the whole poem. The author, upon the winding up of his action, introduces all those who had any concern in it, and shows with great beauty the influence which it had upon each of them. It is like the last act of a well-written tragedy" (Addison 157).

236. **author:** father.

241. **like this:** so well as this.

243–45. **Methinks . . . deep:** Since Adam and Eve feel wings growing on them soon after the Fall (9.1009–10), Sin's similar illusion may appear at the same moment (Fowler). Sin lays claim to the "dominion" originally given to Adam and Eve (4.430–32), and extends that rule to include Adam, Eve, and their offspring.

249. **conveyance:** communication.

254–323. Leonard notes that prodigious feats of building are conventional in epic; Milton has

Advent'rous work, yet to thy power and mine
Not unagreeable, to found a path
Over this main from Hell to that new world
Where Satan now prevails, a monument
Of merit high to all th' infernal host,
Easing their passage hence, for intercourse,
Or transmigration, as their lot shall lead.
Nor can I miss the way, so strongly drawn
By this new felt attraction and instinct."
 Whom thus the meager shadow answered soon.
"Go whither fate and inclination strong
Leads thee, I shall not lag behind, nor err
The way, thou leading, such a scent I draw
Of carnage, prey innumerable, and taste
The savor of death from all things there that live:
Nor shall I to the work thou enterprisest
Be wanting, but afford thee equal aid."
 So saying, with delight he snuffed the smell
Of mortal change on Earth. As when a flock
Of ravenous fowl, though many a league remote,
Against the day of battle, to a field
Where armies lie encamped, come flying, lured
With scent of living carcasses designed
For death, the following day, in bloody fight.
So scented the grim feature, and upturned
His nostril wide into the murky air,
Sagacious of his quarry from so far.
Then both from out Hell gates into the waste
Wide anarchy of Chaos damp and dark
Flew diverse, and with power (their power was great)
Hovering upon the waters; what they met
Solid or slimy, as in raging sea
Tossed up and down, together crowded drove
From each side shoaling towards the mouth of Hell.
As when two polar winds blowing adverse
Upon the Cronian Sea, together drive

---

already represented the raising of Pandaemonium (1.678–730), the invention of cannon (6.507–23), and the Creation.

257. **main:** Chaos's ocean.

261. **transmigration:** permanent migration to Earth.

264. **meager:** emaciated.

272. **snuffed:** detected by means of its odor.

275. **Against:** in anticipation of.

277. **designed:** marked out for.

279. **feature:** shape, form.

280. **murky:** dark.

281. **Sagacious:** (1) quick of scent and (2) wise. "A fit comparison for the *chief hell-hound*" (Hume).

284. **diverse:** in different directions.

288. **shoaling:** crowding together.

290. **Cronian Sea:** Arctic Ocean (icebound).

Mountains of ice, that stop th' imagined way
Beyond Petsora eastward, to the rich
Cathayan Coast. The aggregated soil
Death with his mace petrific, cold and dry,
As with a trident smote, and fixed as firm
As Delos floating once; the rest his look
Bound with Gorgonian rigor not to move,
And with asphaltic slime; broad as the gate,
Deep to the roots of Hell the gathered beach
They fastened, and the mole immense wrought on
Over the foaming deep high-arched, a bridge
Of length prodigious joining to the wall
Immovable of this now fenceless world
Forfeit to Death; from hence a passage broad,
Smooth, easy, inoffensive down to Hell.
So, if great things to small may be compared,
Xerxes, the liberty of Greece to yoke,
From Susa his Memnonian palace high
Came to the sea, and over Hellespont
Bridging his way, Europe with Asia joined,
And scourged with many a stroke th' indignant waves.
Now had they brought the work by wondrous art
Pontifical, a ridge of pendant rock
Over the vexed abyss, following the track
Of Satan, to the selfsame place where he
First lighted from his wing, and landed safe
From out of Chaos to the outside bare
Of this round world: with pins of adamant
And chains they made all fast, too fast they made

291–93. **th' imagined way . . . Coast:** the fabled northeast passage between Siberia—where the *Pechora* (Petsora) River is found; see Milton's *Muscovia* in Yale 8:479—and China (*Cathay*) that explorers such as Henry Hudson only *imagined,* since the waters were blocked with ice.

293–98. **The aggregated soil . . . slime:** With his petrifying mace (scepter), Death fixes the cold and dry qualities, and isolates the hot and moist, which he turns into a mortar, using both asphalt and his Gorgon-like ability to turn the objects of his gaze to stone.

296. **Delos:** Neptune secured the floating island of Delos by chains to the bottom of the Aegean Sea so that Latona could safely give birth to Apollo and Diana.

300. **mole:** great causeway or bridge.

305. **inoffensive:** free from obstacles, with a punning glance back at *fenceless* in line 303.

307–11. *Xerxes* of Persia built a bridge of ships across the *Hellespont* in order to invade Greece and ordered the sea whipped when the bridge was destroyed.

308. **Susa:** the winter palace of Persian kings, called *Memnonian* after Memnos, legendary son of Tithonus and Aurora.

311. **indignant:** both "resentful" from the Latin *indignans* and "unworthy of punishment" from the Latin *indignis* (Fowler).

312–13. **art/Pontifical:** both "bridge-building art" and "popish art." Eighteenth-century editors thought the pun in dubious taste (Todd).

314. **vexed:** storm torn.

And durable; and now in little space
The confines met of empyrean Heav'n
And of this world, and on the left hand Hell
With long reach interposed; three sev'ral ways
In sight, to each of these three places led.
And now their way to Earth they had descried,
To Paradise first tending, when behold
Satan in likeness of an angel bright
Betwixt the Centaur and the Scorpion steering
His zenith, while the sun in Aries rose:
Disguised he came, but those his children dear
Their parent soon discerned, though in disguise.
He after Eve seduced, unminded slunk
Into the wood fast by, and changing shape
To observe the sequel, saw his guileful act
By Eve, though all unweeting, seconded
Upon her husband, saw their shame that sought
Vain covertures; but when he saw descend
The Son of God to judge them, terrified
He fled, not hoping to escape, but shun
The present, fearing guilty what his wrath
Might suddenly inflict; that past, returned
By night, and list'ning where the hapless pair
Sat in their sad discourse, and various plaint,
Thence gathered his own doom, which understood
Not instant, but of future time. With joy
And tidings fraught, to Hell he now returned,
And at the brink of Chaos, near the foot
Of this new wondrous pontifice, unhoped
Met who to meet him came, his offspring dear.
Great joy was at their meeting, and at sight
Of that stupendous bridge his joy increased.
Long he admiring stood, till Sin, his fair
Enchanting daughter, thus the silence broke.
"O Parent, these are thy magnific deeds,

321. **confines:** borders.

328–29. **Betwixt . . . zenith:** Satan flies between the *Centaur* (Sagittarius) and the *Scorpion* (Scorpio), where the constellation Anguis, the serpent held by Ophiucus, is located. Satan entered the universe at the head of the serpent, in Libra (3.556–61n), and now leaves it at the tail of the serpent, enacting in astrological terms his possession of the snake. See Fowler for details. His entrance and exit also participate in the root image systems of eating and digestion.

334. **sequel:** consequence.

342–45. **list'ning . . . time:** This can only refer to lines 1030–40, which imply that the entire turbulent night of lines 720–1104 takes place earlier in chronological time than the present encounter between Satan, Sin, and Death (Leonard).

344. **which understood:** which he understood.

Thy trophies, which thou view'st as not thine own;
Thou art their author and prime architect:
For I no sooner in my heart divined,
My heart, which by a secret harmony
Still moves with thine, joined in connection sweet,
That thou on Earth hadst prospered, which thy looks
Now also evidence, but straight I felt
Though distant from thee worlds between, yet felt
That I must after thee with this thy son;
Such fatal consequence unites us three:
Hell could no longer hold us in her bounds,
Nor this unvoyageable gulf obscure
Detain from following thy illustrious track.
Thou hast achieved our liberty, confined
Within Hell gates till now, thou us empow'red
To fortify thus far, and overlay
With this portentous bridge the dark abyss.
Thine now is all this world, thy virtue hath won
What thy hands builded not, thy wisdom gained
With odds what war hath lost, and fully avenged
Our foil in Heav'n; here thou shalt monarch reign,
There didst not; there let him still victor sway,
As battle hath adjudged, from this new world
Retiring, by his own doom alienated,
And henceforth monarchy with thee divide
Of all things parted by th' empyreal bounds,
His quadrature, from thy orbicular world,
Or try thee now more dang'rous to his throne."
    Whom thus the Prince of Darkness answered glad.
"Fair daughter, and thou son and grandchild both,
High proof ye now have giv'n to be the race
Of Satan (for I glory in the name,
Antagonist of Heav'n's Almighty King)
Amply have merited of me, of all

364. **consequence:** of which Satan is the cause or author; evil's consequence is established in the opening lines of the epic, in the "fruit" whose taste brings Death into the world, and again when Satan as "cause" is first named at 1.34.

371. **portentous:** marvelous and ominous.

378. **doom:** judgment; **alienated:** See 9.9 for the apparent truth of Sin's claim; she does not yet understand the Incarnation, the countermovement to God's alienation.

379. Sin implies the Manichaean idea of a universe divided between God's and Satan's empires; see 4.110–12.

381. **His quadrature:** "And the city [of God] lieth four-square, and the length is as large as the breadth" (Rev. 21.16). The bounds of Heaven are left undetermined at 2.1048.

386–87. The name Satan is Hebrew for "adversary."

Th' infernal empire, that so near Heav'n's door
Triumphal with triumphal act have met,
Mine with this glorious work, and made one realm
Hell and this world, one realm, one continent
Of easy thoroughfare. Therefore while I
Descend through darkness, on your road with ease
To my associate powers, them to acquaint
With these successes, and with them rejoice,
You two this way, among these numerous orbs
All yours, right down to Paradise descend;
There dwell and reign in bliss, thence on the Earth
Dominion exercise and in the air,
Chiefly on man, sole lord of all declared,
Him first make sure your thrall, and lastly kill.
My substitutes I send ye, and create
Plenipotent on Earth, of matchless might
Issuing from me: on your joint vigor now
My hold of this new kingdom all depends,
Through Sin to Death exposed by my exploit.
If your joint power prevails, th' affairs of Hell
No detriment need fear. Go and be strong."
    So saying he dismissed them, they with speed
Their course through thickest constellations held
Spreading their bane; the blasted stars looked wan,
And planets, planet-struck, real eclipse
Then suffered. Th' other way Satan went down
The causey to Hell gate; on either side
Disparted Chaos overbuilt exclaimed,
And with rebounding surge the bars assailed,
That scorned his indignation: through the gate,
Wide open and unguarded, Satan passed,
And all about found desolate; for those
Appointed to sit there, had left their charge,

390. The triumphal arch of the bridge memorializes Satan's triumph on Earth.

400. Here Satan parodies God, who gave "dominion" over Creation to Adam and Eve. See lines 243–45n.

404. **Plenipotent:** fully powerful.

408. **prevails:** 1674; the 1667 edition reads "prevail."

409. **No detriment need fear:** alluding to the formula (*Providere nequid respublica detrimenti accipiat*) by which the Roman Senate conferred special powers on consuls (Newton); **detriment:** injury.

412. **blasted:** withered; an effect usually ascribed to ill wind or malignant astral influence.

413. **planet-struck:** struck by a malignant planet; **real eclipse:** not just apparently darkened, as in an eclipse beheld on earth, but really darkened.

415. **causey:** causeway, a raised and paved highway (*OED* 3).

416. Chaos, *disparted* (divided into parts) by the creation of the bridge, is enraged by Satan's betrayal (see 2.981–87).

Flown to the upper world; the rest were all
Far to the inland retired, about the walls
Of Pandaemonium, city and proud seat
Of Lucifer, so by allusion called,
Of that bright star to Satan paragoned.
There kept their watch the legions, while the grand
In council sat, solicitous what chance
Might intercept their Emperor sent, so he
Departing gave command, and they observed.
As when the Tartar from his Russian foe
By Astracan over the snowy plains
Retires, or Bactrian Sophy from the horns
Of Turkish crescent, leaves all waste beyond
The realm of Aladule, in his retreat
To Tauris or Casbeen. So these the late
Heav'n-banished host, left desert utmost Hell
Many a dark league, reduced in careful watch
Round their metropolis, and now expecting
Each hour their great adventurer from the search
Of foreign worlds: he through the midst unmarked,
In show plebeian angel militant
Of lowest order, passed; and from the door
Of that Plutonian hall, invisible
Ascended his high throne, which under state
Of richest texture spread, at th' upper end
Was placed in regal luster. Down awhile
He sat, and round about him saw unseen:
At last as from a cloud his fulgent head
And shape star-bright appeared, or brighter, clad
With what permissive glory since his fall
Was left him, or false glitter: all amazed
At that so sudden blaze the Stygian throng

426. **bright star:** Lucifer, the morning star; see 5.760, 7.131; **paragoned:** compared.

427. **the grand:** the "grand infernal Peers" of 2.507.

428. **solicitous:** concerned.

431–36. **As when . . . Casbeen:** The Tartars retreat from their Russian conquerors near *Astracan,* the ancient Tartar capital. The *Bactrian Sophy,* or Shah of Persia, retreats from the crescent battle formations of the Turks (*horns/Of Turkish crescent*) to Tabriz (*Tauris*) and Kazvin (*Casbeen*), Iranian cities, laying waste to lands once under the rule of King *Aladule.* Leonard notes that both of these defeated enemies were still dangerous.

438. **reduced:** led back, drawn together, diminished.

441–55. Analogues in the epic tradition include Homer, *Od.* 7.35–145; Vergil, *Aen.* 1.579–94; and Tasso, *GL,* 10.32–50. See S. Fallon 1984.

445. **state:** canopy. See *Arcades* 14n.

451. **permissive:** permitted (by God); cp. the "high permission" of 1.212.

453. **sudden blaze:** Cp. *Lyc* 74, where the context is also a nurtured ambition ready to publicize its achievements and about to be thwarted; *PR* 3.47.

Bent their aspect, and whom they wished beheld,
Their mighty chief returned: loud was th' acclaim:
Forth rushed in haste the great consulting peers,
Raised from their dark divan, and with like joy
Congratulant approached him, who with hand
Silence, and with these words attention won.
"Thrones, Dominations, Princedoms, Virtues, Powers,
For in possession such, not only of right,
I call ye and declare ye now, returned
Successful beyond hope, to lead ye forth
Triumphant out of this infernal pit
Abominable, accursed, the house of woe,
And dungeon of our tyrant: now possess,
As lords, a spacious world, to our native Heaven
Little inferior, by my adventure hard
With peril great achieved. Long were to tell
What I have done, what suffered, with what pain
Voyaged th' unreal, vast, unbounded deep
Of horrible confusion, over which
By Sin and Death a broad way now is paved
To expedite your glorious march; but I
Toiled out my uncouth passage, forced to ride
Th' untractable abyss, plunged in the womb
Of unoriginal Night and Chaos wild,
That jealous of their secrets fiercely opposed
My journey strange, with clamorous uproar
Protesting fate supreme; thence how I found
The new created world, which fame in Heav'n
Long had foretold, a fabric wonderful
Of absolute perfection, therein man
Placed in a Paradise, by our exile

457. **divan:** council (*OED* 1b). The Turkish origins of the term fit with Satan as "sultan" (1.348). The military successes of King Suleiman I (1520–1566) in Hungary, Armenia, Persia, and Africa caused widespread alarm in Europe, and led to commonplace associations between Turks and devils.

458. **Congratulant:** expressing congratulation.

460. The Father, when exalting his Son, was the first to use these titles (5.601), the meaning of which Satan (5.772) and Abdiel (5.840) dispute. Satan now declares the titles to be theirs not only by right but by possession (of estates formerly controlled by God).

471. **unreal:** formless, the equivalent of unreality in Aristotelian metaphysics.

475. **uncouth:** strange, unusual.

477. **unoriginal:** without origin, uncreated.

477–78. **Chaos . . . opposed:** Though the journey through Chaos was difficult, Chaos and Night hardly opposed Satan (2.910–1009); but see Chaos's indignation at lines 415–18.

480. **Protesting fate supreme:** Satan here identifies himself with supreme Fate, as usual parodying God (7.173).

481–82. **fame . . . foretold:** See 1.651–56, 2.345–76.

Made happy; him by fraud I have seduced
From his Creator, and the more to increase
Your wonder, with an apple; he thereat
Offended, worth your laughter, hath giv'n up
Both his beloved man and all his world,
To Sin and Death a prey, and so to us,
Without our hazard, labor, or alarm,
To range in, and to dwell, and over man
To rule, as over all he should have ruled.
True is, me also he hath judged, or rather
Me not, but the brute serpent in whose shape
Man I deceived: that which to me belongs,
Is enmity, which he will put between
Me and mankind; I am to bruise his heel;
His seed, when is not set, shall bruise my head:
A world who would not purchase with a bruise,
Or much more grievous pain? Ye have th' account
Of my performance: what remains, ye gods,
But up and enter now into full bliss."
  So having said, a while he stood, expecting
Their universal shout and high applause
To fill his ear, when contrary he hears
On all sides, from innumerable tongues
A dismal universal hiss, the sound
Of public scorn; he wondered, but not long
Had leisure, wond'ring at himself now more;
His visage drawn he felt to sharp and spare,
His arms clung to his ribs, his legs entwining
Each other, till supplanted down he fell
A monstrous serpent on his belly prone,
Reluctant, but in vain; a greater power

494–99. Like most of the biblical commentators (A. Williams 128), Satan supposes that the first part of the protevangelium (see 175–81n), condemning the serpent to grovel in the dust, applies only to the snake, whereas the second part, in which the seed of the woman will bruise the serpent in the head and be itself bruised in the heel, applies to him (Satan). He is about to be proven wrong. On the transformation of the devils into serpents, see Kerrigan 2004.

508–9. **universal hiss . . . scorn:** There is only one sound intelligible within the sign system of human language that both men and snakes can produce, and that is the hiss that greets a bad show. See Shakespeare's "serpent's tongue" (*MND* 5.1.433). On scorn, see Kerrigan 2000, 150–52.

509. **wondered:** ironically remembering Eve, who found the human speech of the serpent a "wonder" (9.566), as Satan now wonders at the serpentine hiss of his audience.

511–15. The passage imitates the serpent metamorphoses in Ovid, *Met.* 4.572–603, and Dante, *Inf.* 24, 25.

513. **supplanted:** tripped up, overthrown.

515. **Reluctant:** primarily in the sense of "writhing or struggling against" (Lat. *reluctari*).

Now ruled him, punished in the shape he sinned,
According to his doom: he would have spoke,
But hiss for hiss returned with forkèd tongue
To forkèd tongue, for now were all transformed
Alike, to serpents all as accessories
To his bold riot: dreadful was the din
Of hissing through the hall, thick swarming now
With complicated monsters head and tail,
Scorpion and asp, and amphisbaena dire,
Cerastes horned, hydrus, and ellops drear,
And dipsas (not so thick swarm'd once the soil
Bedropped with blood of Gorgon, or the Isle
Ophiusa); but still greatest he the midst,
Now dragon grown, larger than whom the sun
Engendered in the Pythian vale on slime,
Huge Python, and his power no less he seemed
Above the rest still to retain; they all
Him followed issuing forth to th' open field,
Where all yet left of that revolted rout
Heav'n-fall'n, in station stood or just array,
Sublime with expectation when to see
In triumph issuing forth their glorious chief;
They saw, but other sight instead, a crowd
Of ugly serpents; horror on them fell,
And horrid sympathy; for what they saw,
They felt themselves now changing; down their arms,
Down fell both spear and shield, down they as fast,
And the dire hiss renewed, and the dire form
Catched by contagion, like in punishment,
As in their crime. Thus was th' applause they meant,
Turned to exploding hiss, triumph to shame
Cast on themselves from their own mouths. There stood

517. **doom:** the judgment at lines 175–81.

524. **amphisbaena:** mythical snake with a head at both ends.

525. **Cerastes horned:** a snake with four horns; **hydrus . . . ellops:** water snakes.

526. **dipsas:** The bite of *dipsas* (from the Gk. word for "thirst") caused *scalding thirst* (l. 556).

526–27. **soil . . . Gorgon:** As Perseus flew over Libya with the head of Medusa, drops of her blood fell to the earth and became snakes—which explains why, according to Ovid, *Met.* 3.616, and Lucan, *Pharsalia* 9.696, serpents are so common there.

528. **Ophiusa:** a Mediterranean island, from the Gk. "full of snakes."

529. **dragon:** Satan had long been identified with the "great dragon" of Rev. 12.9. Cp. Fletcher, *The Purple Island* 7.11.

530. **Pythian vale:** Delphi.

531. **Python:** the great serpent born of the "slime" left behind by Deucalion's flood (Ovid, *Met.* 1.438) and eventually slain by Apollo.

536. **Sublime:** exalted, elated.

A grove hard by, sprung up with this their change,
His will who reigns above, to aggravate
Their penance, laden with fair fruit like that
Which grew in Paradise, the bait of Eve
Used by the Tempter: on that prospect strange
Their earnest eyes they fixed, imagining
For one forbidden tree a multitude
Now ris'n, to work them further woe or shame;
Yet parched with scalding thirst and hunger fierce,
Though to delude them sent, could not abstain,
But on they rolled in heaps, and up the trees
Climbing, sat thicker than the snaky locks
That curled Megaera: greedily they plucked
The fruitage fair to sight, like that which grew
Near that bituminous lake where Sodom flamed;
This more delusive, not the touch, but taste
Deceived; they fondly thinking to allay
Their appetite with gust, instead of fruit
Chewed bitter ashes, which th' offended taste
With spattering noise rejected: oft they assayed,
Hunger and thirst constraining, drugged as oft,
With hatefulest disrelish writhed their jaws
With soot and cinders filled; so oft they fell
Into the same illusion, not as man
Whom they triumphed once lapsed. Thus were they plagued
And worn with famine, long and ceaseless hiss,
Till their lost shape, permitted, they resumed,
Yearly enjoined, some say, to undergo
This annual humbling certain numbered days,
To dash their pride, and joy for man seduced.
However some tradition they dispersed
Among the heathen of their purchase got,
And fabled how the serpent, whom they called
Ophion with Eurynome, the wide-
Encroaching Eve perhaps, had first the rule

559–60. **snaky locks . . . Megaera:** Her hair, like Medusa's, was serpents (Ovid, *Met.* 4.771).

560–68. the *bituminous lake* is the Dead Sea, beside which Sodom and Gomorrah were situated. According to Josephus, *Wars* 4.8.4, the ashes of Sodom grow in the fruit of the area, which when plucked dissolve into smoke and ashes.

565. **gust:** gusto.

568. **drugged:** nauseated.

575. **some say:** A source has not been found for Milton's account of the annual metamorphosis of the devils.

578–84. Fowler notes that *purchase* can mean "annual return or rent from land," and thus alludes to the annual metamorphosis. According to some authorities, Milton says, the devils spread stories of primordial serpents in the ancient world, among them that of Ophion (from

Of high Olympus, thence by Saturn driv'n
And Ops, ere yet Dictaean Jove was born.
Meanwhile in Paradise the hellish pair
Too soon arrived, Sin there in power before,
Once actual, now in body, and to dwell
Habitual habitant; behind her Death
Close following pace for pace, not mounted yet
On his pale horse: to whom Sin thus began.
"Second of Satan sprung, all conquering Death,
What think'st thou of our empire now, though earned
With travail difficult, not better far
Than still at Hell's dark threshold to have sat watch,
Unnamed, undreaded, and thyself half starved?"
Whom thus the Sin-born monster answered soon.
"To me, who with eternal famine pine,
Alike is Hell, or Paradise, or Heaven,
There best, where most with ravin I may meet;
Which here, though plenteous, all too little seems
To stuff this maw, this vast unhidebound corpse."
To whom th' incestuous mother thus replied.
"Thou therefore on these herbs, and fruits, and flow'rs
Feed first, on each beast next, and fish, and fowl,
No homely morsels, and whatever thing
The scythe of Time mows down, devour unspared,
Till I in man residing through the race,
His thoughts, his looks, words, actions all infect,
And season him thy last and sweetest prey."
This said, they both betook them several ways,
Both to destroy, or unimmortal make
All kinds, and for destruction to mature
Sooner or later; which th' Almighty seeing,
From his transcendent seat the saints among,
To those bright orders uttered thus his voice.
"See with what heat these dogs of Hell advance
To waste and havoc yonder world, which I

Gk. for "serpent") and *Eurynome,* the first rulers of Olympus.

584. **Dictaean:** Jove was raised in Crete, in the vicinity of Mount Dicte.

586–87. **there . . . body:** a brief history of sin in Paradise: there by *power* or potential before the Fall, then *actual* at the Fall, *now in body,* as the character Sin arrives.

590. **pale horse:** See Rev. 6.8.

601. **unhidebound:** skin so loose that it can hold a great deal.

611. **unimmortal:** mortal; the negative of *immortal* neatly conveys the effect of the Fall.

617. **havoc:** Kings victorious on the battlefield had the privilege of shouting "havoc," a signal that no quarter should be given in slaughter and pillage. See Shakespeare, *JC* 3.1.273.

So fair and good created, and had still
Kept in that state, had not the folly of man
Let in these wasteful Furies, who impute
Folly to me, so doth the Prince of Hell
And his adherents, that with so much ease
I suffer them to enter and possess
A place so heav'nly, and conniving seem
To gratify my scornful enemies,
That laugh, as if transported with some fit
Of passion, I to them had quitted all,
At random yielded up to their misrule;
And know not that I called and drew them thither
My Hell-hounds, to lick up the draff and filth
Which man's polluting sin with taint hath shed
On what was pure, till crammed and gorged, nigh burst
With sucked and glutted offal, at one sling
Of thy victorious arm, well-pleasing Son,
Both Sin, and Death, and yawning grave at last
Through Chaos hurled, obstruct the mouth of Hell
Forever, and seal up his ravenous jaws.
Then heav'n and earth renewed shall be made pure
To sanctity that shall receive no stain:
Till then the curse pronounced on both precedes."
He ended, and the heav'nly audience loud
Sung hallelujah, as the sound of seas,
Through multitude that sung: "Just are thy ways,
Righteous are thy decrees on all thy works;
Who can extenuate thee? Next, to the Son,
Destined restorer of mankind, by whom
New heav'n and earth shall to the ages rise,
Or down from Heav'n descend." Such was their song,
While the Creator calling forth by name
His mighty angels gave them several charge,
As sorted best with present things. The sun
Had first his precept so to move, so shine,
As might affect the Earth with cold and heat
Scarce tolerable, and from the north to call
Decrepit winter, from the south to bring

627. **quitted:** handed over.
630. **draff:** refuse, swill.
633–34. **at one sling . . . arm:** "The souls of thine enemies, them shall he sling out, as out of the middle of a sling" (1 Sam. 25.29).
640. **precedes:** has precedence.
645. **extenuate:** disparage.

Solstitial summer's heat. To the blank moon
Her office they prescribed, to th' other five
Their planetary motions and aspects
In sextile, square, and trine, and opposite,
Of noxious efficacy, and when to join
In synod unbenign, and taught the fixed
Their influence malignant when to show'r,
Which of them rising with the sun, or falling,
Should prove tempestuous: to the winds they set
Their corners, when with bluster to confound
Sea, air, and shore, the thunder when to roll
With terror through the dark aerial hall.
Some say he bid his angels turn askance
The poles of Earth twice ten degrees and more
From the sun's axle; they with labor pushed
Oblique the centric globe: some say the sun
Was bid turn reins from th' equinoctial road
Like distant breadth to Taurus with the sev'n
Atlantic Sisters, and the Spartan Twins
Up to the Tropic Crab; thence down amain
By Leo and the Virgin and the Scales,
As deep as Capricorn, to bring in change
Of seasons to each clime; else had the spring
Perpetual smiled on Earth with vernant flow'rs,
Equal in days and nights, except to those
Beyond the polar circles; to them day
Had unbenighted shone, while the low sun
To recompense his distance, in their sight
Had rounded still th' horizon, and not known
Or east or west, which had forbid the snow
From cold Estotiland, and south as far
Beneath Magellan. At that tasted fruit

656. **blank:** pale.
658. **aspects:** astrological positions.
659. A list of aspects: *sextile* (60°), *square* (90°), *trine* (120°), and *opposite* (180°).
661. **synod:** conjunction; cp. 6.156n; **fixed:** fixed stars.
668–87. Before the Fall, the ecliptic follows the *equinoctial road* (l. 672) or equator, which produces *spring/Perpetual* (ll. 678–79), and a sun always in Aries. There are two ways to modify these conditions in order to produce a result consistent with astrological observations in the fallen world. In a heliocentric (Copernican) system, the axis of the earth must be tilted around 23°. In a terracentric (Ptolemaic) system, the plane of the sun's orbit must be tilted *like distant breadth* (that is, around 23°). Milton presents both explanations and does not choose between them. *Some say* (l. 668) the one, *some say* (l. 671) the other.
673–77. **Was bid . . . Capricorn:** Once resident in Aries, the sun now travels through the zodiac.
686. **Estotiland:** northern Labrador.
687. **Magellan:** Strait of Magellan.

The sun, as from Thyestean banquet, turned
His course intended; else how had the world
Inhabited, though sinless, more than now,
Avoided pinching cold and scorching heat?
These changes in the heav'ns, though slow, produced
Like change on sea and land, sideral blast,
Vapor, and mist, and exhalation hot,
Corrupt and pestilent: now from the north
Of Norumbega, and the Samoed shore
Bursting their brazen dungeon, armed with ice
And snow and hail and stormy gust and flaw,
Boreas and Caecias and Argestes loud
And Thrascias rend the woods and seas upturn;
With adverse blast upturns them from the south
Notus and Afer black with thund'rous clouds
From Serraliona; thwart of these as fierce
Forth rush the Levant and the ponent winds
Eurus and Zephyr with their lateral noise,
Sirocco, and Libecchio. Thus began
Outrage from lifeless things; but Discord first
Daughter of Sin, among th' irrational,
Death introduced through fierce antipathy:
Beast now with beast gan war, and fowl with fowl,
And fish with fish; to graze the herb all leaving,
Devoured each other; nor stood much in awe
Of man, but fled him, or with count'nance grim
Glared on him passing: these were from without
The growing miseries, which Adam saw
Already in part, though hid in gloomiest shade,
To sorrow abandoned, but worse felt within,
And in a troubled sea of passion tossed,

688. **Thyestean banquet:** In Seneca's tragedy *Thyestes,* the sun turns aside in horror from the sight of Thyestes eating his sons. A chorus (789–881) wonders if the sun's departure might not signal a return to "formless chaos" (832).

693. **sideral blast:** probably not malign astral influences, as Fowler and Leonard suggest, because Milton has shifted from celestial to terrestial change; perhaps exhalations or vapors released from the earth, drawn toward the stars (*sideral*) by the sun's heat, and thought to produce various *blasts* or explosions, such as shooting stars and comets.

696. **Norumbega:** a province of North America; **Samoed:** northeastern Siberia.

697. **brazen dungeon:** where Aeolus imprisoned the winds (*Aen.* 1.141).

699–706. The northern winds of *Boreas, Caecias, Argestes,* and *Thrascias* are opposed by the southern winds of *Notus* and *Afer.* This system is attacked at various side angles to the east and west (*thwart*) by winds named *Levant* et cetera.

714–17. **these . . . within:** a beautiful effect: the chain of bad external causes in lines 651–714 has led to the *part* (l. 716) Adam already sees, whereupon Milton shifts to his inner turbulence, which Adam then seeks to *disburden* through externalizing speech. We have moved back in time before the arrival of Sin and Death on Earth (342–45n).

Thus to disburden sought with sad complaint.
"O miserable of happy! Is this the end
Of this new glorious world, and me so late
The glory of that glory? Who now become
Accursed of blessed; hide me from the face
Of God, whom to behold was then my highth
Of happiness: yet well, if here would end
The misery, I deserved it, and would bear
My own deservings; but this will not serve;
All that I eat or drink, or shall beget,
Is propagated curse. O voice once heard
Delightfully, 'Increase and multiply,'
Now death to hear! For what can I increase
Or multiply, but curses on my head?
Who of all ages to succeed, but feeling
The evil on him brought by me, will curse
My head, 'Ill fare our ancestor impure,
For this we may thank Adam'? But his thanks
Shall be the execration; so besides
Mine own that bide upon me, all from me
Shall with a fierce reflux on me redound,
On me as on their natural center light
Heavy, though in their place. O fleeting joys
Of Paradise, dear bought with lasting woes!
Did I request thee, Maker, from my clay
To mold me man, did I solicit thee
From darkness to promote me, or here place
In this delicious garden? As my will
Concurred not to my being, it were but right
And equal to reduce me to my dust,
Desirous to resign, and render back
All I received, unable to perform
Thy terms too hard, by which I was to hold
The good I sought not. To the loss of that,
Sufficient penalty, why hast thou added
The sense of endless woes? Inexplicable

729. **propagated curse:** the curses of Adam's children upon their original forefather, increased and multiplied by the act of propagation. The commandment to "increase and multiply" is now literally transformed into ramifying curses, as Milton, an author much concerned with fame, has Adam confront the terror of infamy.

740–41. **On me . . . place:** When a body occupies its *natural center* in Aristotle's physics, it is weightless, but the curses of Adam's children are mysteriously *heavy.*

743–46. Isa. 45.9: "Woe unto him that striveth with his Maker! . . . Shall the clay say to him that fashioneth it, What makest thou?"

748. **equal:** equitable.

Thy justice seems; yet to say truth, too late,
I thus contest; then should have been refused
Those terms whatever, when they were proposed:
Thou didst accept them; wilt thou enjoy the good,
Then cavil the conditions? And though God
Made thee without thy leave, what if thy son
Prove disobedient, and reproved, retort,
'Wherefore didst thou beget me? I sought it not,'
Wouldst thou admit for his contempt of thee
That proud excuse? Yet him not thy election,
But natural necessity begot.
God made thee of choice his own, and of his own
To serve him, thy reward was of his grace,
Thy punishment then justly is at his will.
Be it so, for I submit, his doom is fair,
That dust I am, and shall to dust return:
O welcome hour whenever! Why delays
His hand to execute what his decree
Fixed on this day? Why do I overlive,
Why am I mocked with death, and lengthened out
To deathless pain? How gladly would I meet
Mortality my sentence, and be earth
Insensible, how glad would lay me down
As in my mother's lap! There I should rest
And sleep secure; his dreadful voice no more
Would thunder in my ears, no fear of worse
To me and to my offspring would torment me
With cruel expectation. Yet one doubt
Pursues me still, lest all I cannot die,
Lest that pure breath of life, the spirit of man
Which God inspired, cannot together perish
With this corporeal clod; then in the grave,
Or in some other dismal place who knows
But I shall die a living death? O thought
Horrid, if true! Yet why? It was but breath
Of Life that sinned; what dies but what had life
And sin? The body properly hath neither.

758. **Thou:** "I myself." Adam here addresses himself, not his Maker, as in lines 743–55.

762. Isa. 45.10: "Woe unto him that saith unto his father, 'What begettest thou?' "

782. **one doubt:** The same doubt reroutes the thoughts of Hamlet in his "To be, or not to be" soliloquy (3.1.56–88).

783. **all:** altogether, entirely.

786–92. **then . . . die:** Adam's reasoning here closely follows Milton's formulation of the mortalist heresy—the idea that body and soul die together (*CD* 1.13).

791. **The body properly hath neither:** Augustine, *City of God* 14.3.

All of me then shall die: let this appease
The doubt, since human reach no further knows.
For though the Lord of all be infinite,
Is his wrath also? Be it, man is not so,
But mortal doomed. How can he exercise
Wrath without end on man whom death must end?
Can he make deathless death? That were to make
Strange contradiction, which to God himself
Impossible is held, as argument
Of weakness, not of power. Will he draw out,
For anger's sake, finite to infinite
In punished man, to satisfy his rigor
Satisfied never? That were to extend
His sentence beyond dust and nature's law,
By which all causes else according still
To the reception of their matter act,
Not to th' extent of their own sphere. But say
That death be not one stroke, as I supposed,
Bereaving sense, but endless misery
From this day onward, which I feel begun
Both in me, and without me, and so last
To perpetuity; ay me, that fear
Comes thund'ring back with dreadful revolution
On my defenseless head; both Death and I
Am found eternal, and incorporate both,
Nor I on my part single, in me all
Posterity stands cursed: fair patrimony
That I must leave ye, sons; O were I able
To waste it all myself, and leave ye none!
So disinherited how would ye bless
Me now your curse! Ah, why should all mankind
For one man's fault thus guiltless be condemned,
If guiltless? But from me what can proceed,
But all corrupt, both mind and will depraved,
Not to do only, but to will the same
With me? How can they then acquitted stand
In sight of God? Him after all disputes
Forced I absolve: all my evasions vain,
And reasonings, though through mazes, lead me still

798–801. "The power of God is not exerted in those kinds of things which . . . imply a contradiction" (*CD* 1.2, p. 1150).

815–16. *Death and I* take the singular verb *am* because they are *incorporate,* united in one body.

But to my own conviction: first and last
On me, me only, as the source and spring
Of all corruption, all the blame lights due;
So might the wrath. Fond wish! Couldst thou support
That burden heavier than the Earth to bear,
Than all the world much heavier, though divided
With that bad woman? Thus what thou desir'st
And what thou fear'st, alike destroys all hope
Of refuge, and concludes thee miserable
Beyond all past example and future,
To Satan only like both crime and doom.
O conscience, into what abyss of fears
And horrors hast thou driv'n me; out of which
I find no way, from deep to deeper plunged!"
Thus Adam to himself lamented loud
Through the still night, not now, as ere man fell,
Wholesome and cool, and mild, but with black air
Accompanied, with damps and dreadful gloom,
Which to his evil conscience represented
All things with double terror: on the ground
Outstretched he lay, on the cold ground, and oft
Cursed his creation, Death as oft accused
Of tardy execution, since denounced
The day of his offense. "Why comes not Death,"
Said he, "with one thrice acceptable stroke
To end me? Shall Truth fail to keep her word,
Justice Divine not hasten to be just?
But Death comes not at call, Justice Divine
Mends not her slowest pace for prayers or cries.
O woods, O fountains, hillocks, dales and bow'rs,
With other echo late I taught your shades
To answer, and resound far other song."
Whom thus afflicted when sad Eve beheld,

831. **conviction:** See 84n.

831–34. **first and last . . . wish!:** Eve later gives voice to the same fond wish (ll. 933–36). The only being with the power to realize this desire is the Son (3.236–37).

837–38. **what thou desir'st:** Death; **what thou fear'st:** Death.

842–44. **O conscience . . . plunged:** evoking 4.75–78, and thus indeed *To Satan only like* (l. 841).

849–50. **Which . . . terror:** Greville observes that frightening hallucinations provoked by darkness "proper reflections of the error [original sin] be,/And images of self-confusednesses/Which hurt imaginations only see;/And from this nothing seen, tells news of devils,/Which but expressions be of inward evils" (*Caelica* C).

853–54. **since . . . offense:** "since it was announced that death would fall on the day man ate the fruit." Adam forgets that the sentence was delayed (see ll. 209–11).

Desolate where she sat, approaching nigh,
Soft words to his fierce passion she assayed:
But her with stern regard he thus repell'd.
"Out of my sight, thou serpent, that name best
Befits thee with him leagued, thyself as false
And hateful; nothing wants, but that thy shape,
Like his, and color serpentine may show
Thy inward fraud, to warn all creatures from thee
Henceforth; lest that too heav'nly form, pretended
To hellish falsehood, snare them. But for thee
I had persisted happy, had not thy pride
And wand'ring vanity, when least was safe,
Rejected my forewarning, and disdained
Not to be trusted, longing to be seen
Though by the Devil himself, him overweening
To overreach, but with the serpent meeting
Fooled and beguiled, by him thou, I by thee,
To trust thee from my side, imagined wise,
Constant, mature, proof against all assaults,
And understood not all was but a show
Rather than solid virtue, all but a rib
Crooked by nature, bent, as now appears,
More to the part sinister from me drawn,
Well if thrown out, as supernumerary
To my just number found. O why did God,
Creator wise, that peopled highest Heav'n
With spirits masculine, create at last
This novelty on Earth, this fair defect
Of nature, and not fill the world at once
With men as angels without feminine,

867–908. The speech bristles with misogyny, some of it standard, such as the opening allusion to a false etymology deriving *Eve* from *hevia* (Heb. for "snake"), the insult terming Eve *but a rib/Crooked by nature* (ll. 884–85), or the disparagement of the act of propagation, and some of it Miltonic, such as the closing catalog of the ways in which marriage will fail in the fallen world, which echoes complaints in the poet's divorce tracts. But it would be a mistake to confuse Adam's sour diatribe with Milton's own attitudes. His representation of Adam and Eve's subsequent behavior shows that the author did not subscribe to the articles of Adam's vituperation.

872–73. **pretended/To:** masking.

886. **sinister:** literally "left," figuratively "unlucky."

887. The line itself contains, in its feminine ending, a *supernumerary* syllable.

888–95. **O why . . . Mankind:** Adam's lament that God created woman at all follows Euripides, *Hippolytus* 616–19.

890. **spirits masculine:** Although, as we have earlier been told (1.424), angels (or at least fallen angels) can assume either sex, the ability to take on female form is evidently not the same thing as being female in sex. The angels of the poem are unwaveringly masculine in look and attitude.

891–92. **defect/Of nature:** as Aristotle had maintained in *On Generation* 737a28, 766a31–32, 766b8–15, 767b8–9.

Or find some other way to generate
Mankind? This mischief had not then befall'n,
And more that shall befall, innumerable
Disturbances on Earth through female snares,
And strait conjunction with this sex: for either
He never shall find out fit mate, but such
As some misfortune brings him, or mistake,
Or whom he wishes most shall seldom gain
Through her perverseness, but shall see her gained
By a far worse, or if she love, withheld
By parents, or his happiest choice too late
Shall meet, already linked and wedlock-bound
To a fell adversary, his hate or shame:
Which infinite calamity shall cause
To human life, and household peace confound."
He added not, and from her turned, but Eve
Not so repulsed, with tears that ceased not flowing,
And tresses all disordered, at his feet
Fell humble, and embracing them, besought
His peace, and thus proceeded in her plaint.
"Forsake me not thus, Adam, witness Heav'n
What love sincere, and reverence in my heart
I bear thee, and unweeting have offended,
Unhappily deceived; thy suppliant
I beg, and clasp thy knees; bereave me not,
Whereon I live, thy gentle looks, thy aid,
Thy counsel in this uttermost distress,
My only strength and stay: forlorn of thee,
Whither shall I betake me, where subsist?
While yet we live, scarce one short hour perhaps,
Between us two let there be peace, both joining,
As joined in injuries, one enmity
Against a foe by doom express assigned us,
That cruel serpent: on me exercise not
Thy hatred for this misery befall'n,
On me already lost, me than thyself
More miserable; both have sinned, but thou
Against God only, I against God and thee,
And to the place of judgment will return,
There with my cries importune Heaven, that all

925. Eve calls attention to the joint *enmity* against the serpent foretold in the protevangelium (175–81n).

The sentence from thy head removed may light
On me, sole cause to thee of all this woe,
Me me only just object of his ire."
She ended weeping, and her lowly plight,
Immovable till peace obtained from fault
Acknowledged and deplored, in Adam wrought
Commiseration; soon his heart relented
Towards her, his life so late and sole delight,
Now at his feet submissive in distress,
Creature so fair his reconcilement seeking,
His counsel whom she had displeased, his aid;
As one disarmed, his anger all he lost,
And thus with peaceful words upraised her soon.
"Unwary, and too desirous, as before,
So now of what thou know'st not, who desir'st
The punishment all on thyself; alas,
Bear thine own first, ill able to sustain
His full wrath whose thou feel'st as yet least part,
And my displeasure bear'st so ill. If prayers
Could alter high decrees, I to that place
Would speed before thee, and be louder heard,
That on my head all might be visited,
Thy frailty and infirmer sex forgiv'n,
To me committed and by me exposed.
But rise, let us no more contend, nor blame
Each other, blamed enough elsewhere, but strive
In offices of love, how we may light'n
Each other's burden in our share of woe;
Since this day's death denounced, if aught I see,
Will prove no sudden, but a slow-paced evil,
A long day's dying to augment our pain,
And to our seed (O hapless seed!) derived."
To whom thus Eve, recovering heart, replied.
"Adam, by sad experiment I know
How little weight my words with thee can find,
Found so erroneous, thence by just event
Found so unfortunate; nevertheless,
Restored by thee, vile as I am, to place
Of new acceptance, hopeful to regain

940. **Commiseration:** compassion for another's misery, precisely what was missing in his misogynistic diatribe (ll. 867–908).

965. **derived:** passed down by descent. Adam's return to the question of seed prompts Eve's next speech.

969. **event:** outcome, with a rueful pun on her name.

Thy love, the sole contentment of my heart,
Living or dying, from thee I will not hide
What thoughts in my unquiet breast are ris'n,
Tending to some relief of our extremes,
Or end, though sharp and sad, yet tolerable,
As in our evils, and of easier choice.
If care of our descent perplex us most,
Which must be born to certain woe, devoured
By Death at last, and miserable it is
To be to others cause of misery,
Our own begotten, and of our loins to bring
Into this cursèd world a woful race,
That after wretched life must be at last
Food for so foul a monster, in thy power
It lies, yet ere conception to prevent
The race unblest, to being yet unbegot.
Childless thou art, childless remain: so Death
Shall be deceived his glut, and with us two
Be forced to satisfy his rav'nous maw.
But if thou judge it hard and difficult,
Conversing, looking, loving, to abstain
From love's due rites, nuptial embraces sweet,
And with desire to languish without hope,
Before the present object languishing
With like desire, which would be misery
And torment less than none of what we dread,
Then both ourselves and seed at once to free
From what we fear for both, let us make short,
Let us seek Death, or he not found, supply
With our own hands his office on ourselves;
Why stand we longer shivering under fears,
That show no end but death, and have the power,

978. **As in:** considering.

979–1006. Adam has been lamenting at length his forthcoming infamy, but Eve cuts to the chase. Dread of our seed comes down to this: we can either abstain from the sexual act and have no seed, or, if such frustration seems unendurable, we can kill ourselves and again leave no seed. The speech seems to lift a veil from Adam's mind, reminding us that, as Milton emphasized at 9.1187–89, fallen men discern mistakes in others that they do not mark in themselves.

989. In early editions the words "so Death" were placed at the beginning of line 990. This is most likely an error, since otherwise 989 would be the only tetrameter line, and 990 the only hexameter line, in the poem.

990. **deceived:** cheated of.

994. **sweet:** The reintroduction of this key word in unfallen eroticism (4.298, 311, 641–56; 5.296; 8.603; 9.238, 407) suggests how severe the pangs of frustration would be and deftly reminds Adam of their mutual pleasures.

997–98. Satan has already verified that sexual frustration is "not the least" of Hell's torments (4.509–11).

Of many ways to die the shortest choosing,
Destruction with destruction to destroy."
She ended here, or vehement despair
Broke off the rest; so much of death her thoughts
Had entertained, as dyed her cheeks with pale.
But Adam with such counsel nothing swayed,
To better hopes his more attentive mind
Laboring had raised, and thus to Eve replied.
"Eve, thy contempt of life and pleasure seems
To argue in thee something more sublime
And excellent than what thy mind contemns;
But self-destruction therefore sought, refutes
That excellence thought in thee, and implies,
Not thy contempt, but anguish and regret
For loss of life and pleasure overloved.
Or if thou covet death, as utmost end
Of misery, so thinking to evade
The penalty pronounced, doubt not but God
Hath wiselier armed his vengeful ire than so
To be forestalled; much more I fear lest death
So snatched will not exempt us from the pain
We are by doom to pay; rather such acts
Of contumacy will provoke the Highest
To make death in us live: then let us seek
Some safer resolution, which methinks
I have in view, calling to mind with heed
Part of our sentence, that thy seed shall bruise
The serpent's head; piteous amends, unless
Be meant, whom I conjecture, our grand foe
Satan, who in the serpent hath contrived
Against us this deceit: to crush his head
Would be revenge indeed, which will be lost
By death brought on ourselves, or childless days
Resolved, as thou proposest; so our foe
Shall scape his punishment ordained, and we
Instead shall double ours upon our heads.
No more be mentioned then of violence
Against ourselves, and willful barrenness,
That cuts us off from hope, and savors only
Rancor and pride, impatience and despite,
Reluctance against God and his just yoke

1030–40. Again the protevangelium revives and guides.

Laid on our necks. Remember with what mild
And gracious temper he both heard and judged
Without wrath or reviling; we expected
Immediate dissolution, which we thought
Was meant by death that day, when lo, to thee
Pains only in child-bearing were foretold,
And bringing forth, soon recompensed with joy,
Fruit of thy womb: on me the curse aslope
Glanced on the ground, with labor I must earn
My bread; what harm? Idleness had been worse;
My labor will sustain me; and lest cold
Or heat should injure us, his timely care
Hath unbesought provided, and his hands
Clothed us unworthy, pitying while he judged;
How much more, if we pray him, will his ear
Be open, and his heart to pity incline,
And teach us further by what means to shun
Th' inclement seasons, rain, ice, hail and snow,
Which now the sky with various face begins
To show us in this mountain, while the winds
Blow moist and keen, shattering the graceful locks
Of these fair spreading trees; which bids us seek
Some better shroud, some better warmth to cherish
Our limbs benumbed, ere this diurnal star
Leave cold the night, how we his gathered beams
Reflected, may with matter sere foment,
Or by collision of two bodies grind
The air attrite to fire, as late the clouds
Justling or pushed with winds rude in their shock
Tine the slant lightning, whose thwart flame driv'n down
Kindles the gummy bark of fir or pine,
And sends a comfortable heat from far,
Which might supply the sun: such fire to use,
And what may else be remedy or cure

1053. **Fruit of thy womb:** anticipating Luke 1.41–42.

1053. **aslope:** Adam's curse (to earn his bread with labor) glanced off him and hit the ground (l. 201: *Cursed is the ground*) more directly than it hit him. Earlier, when he was in despair (ll. 720–42), his blessings seemed curses. Now that he is reinvigorated, his curse seems a blessing.

1062. **by what means:** The entire future of peaceful technology is anticipated here.

1066. **shattering:** shaking, breaking into pieces, as in *Lyc 5*, where leaves are also the verb's object.

1068. **shroud:** shelter.

1071. **foment:** heat.

1073. **attrite:** rubbed at.

1075. **Tine:** ignite. On the theological and philosophical implication of Adam's invention of fire, see Hoerner 1995.

To evils which our own misdeeds have wrought,
He will instruct us praying, and of grace
Beseeching him, so as we need not fear
To pass commodiously this life, sustained
By him with many comforts, till we end
In dust, our final rest and native home.
What better can we do, than to the place
Repairing where he judged us, prostrate fall
Before him reverent, and there confess
Humbly our faults, and pardon beg, with tears
Watering the ground, and with our sighs the air
Frequenting, sent from hearts contrite, in sign
Of sorrow unfeigned, and humiliation meek.
Undoubtedly he will relent and turn
From his displeasure; in whose look serene,
When angry most he seemed and most severe,
What else but favor, grace, and mercy shone?"
  So spake our father penitent, nor Eve
Felt less remorse: they forthwith to the place
Repairing where he judged them prostrate fell
Before him reverent, and both confessed
Humbly their faults, and pardon begged, with tears
Watering the ground, and with their sighs the air
Frequenting, sent from hearts contrite, in sign
Of sorrow unfeigned, and humiliation meek.

1086–1104. Another of the poem's many mirroring effects, this one being the only imitation in Milton's work of the extensive formulaic repetition found in Homer (e.g., *Il.* 9.122–57, 264–99). (Lines 1093–96 are not repeated because Adam and Eve's punishment will eventually include expulsion from Paradise.) Tayler 1979, 84 remarks that "not only do the narrator's words place a doctrinal seal upon this stage in the process of repentance" but they also create "a moment of stasis in which we all [Adam and Eve, the narrator, the reader] see things the same way": this is indeed the best thing to say, the best thing to do.

Book XI

The Argument

The Son of God presents to his Father the prayers of our first parents now repenting, and intercedes for them. God accepts them, but declares that they must no longer abide in Paradise; sends Michael with a band of Cherubim to dispossess them; but first to reveal to Adam future things; Michael's coming down. Adam shows to Eve certain ominous signs; he discerns Michael's approach, goes out to meet him: the angel denounces their departure. Eve's lamentation. Adam pleads, but submits. The angel leads him up to a high hill, sets before him in vision what shall happen till the Flood.

Thus they in lowliest plight repentant stood
Praying, for from the mercy-seat above
Prevenient grace descending had removed
The stony from their hearts, and made new flesh
Regenerate grow instead, that sighs now breathed
Unutterable, which the spirit of prayer
Inspired, and winged for Heav'n with speedier flight
Then loudest oratory: yet their port
Not of mean suiters, nor important less
Seemed their petition, than when th' ancient pair
In fables old, less ancient yet than these,
Deucalion and chaste Pyrrha to restore
The race of mankind drowned, before the shrine

1. **stood:** remained; the word, which may imply spiritual regeneration, is not intended to contradict "prostrate" in 10.1099.

2. **mercy-seat:** the cover of the Ark of the Covenant, whose cherubim represented intercession in Heaven; see Exod. 25.17–23.

3. **Prevenient grace:** grace that literally "comes before" human choice.

4. **stony . . . flesh:** From Ezek. 11.19: "I will take the stony heart out of their flesh, and will give them a heart of flesh."

5–6. **sighs now breathed/Unutterable:** Cp. Rom. 8.26, where "groanings which cannot be uttered" intercede for humankind. Cp. *Eikon* 16 (Yale 3:507).

8. **port:** bearing.

10–14. **th' ancient pair . . . devout:** *Deucalion* and his wife, *Pyrrha,* figures in Greek mythology, survived the flood in an ark. *Themis,* goddess of justice, told them to throw stones behind them, and the stones turned into people (echoing the transformation from stony to fleshly hearts in l. 4).

Of Themis stood devout. To Heav'n their prayers
Flew up, nor miss'd the way, by envious winds
Blown vagabond or frustrate: in they passed
Dimensionless through Heav'nly doors; then clad
With incense, where the golden altar fumed,
By their great Intercessor, came in sight
Before the Father's throne: them the glad Son
Presenting, thus to intercede began.
"See Father, what first fruits on Earth are sprung
From thy implanted grace in man, these sighs
And prayers, which in this golden censer, mixed
With incense, I thy priest before thee bring,
Fruits of more pleasing savor from thy seed
Sown with contrition in his heart, than those
Which his own hand manuring all the trees
Of Paradise could have produced, ere fall'n
From innocence. Now therefore bend thine ear
To supplication, hear his sighs though mute;
Unskillful with what words to pray, let me
Interpret for him, me his advocate
And propitiation, all his works on me
Good or not good ingraft; my merit those
Shall perfect, and for these my death shall pay.
Accept me, and in me from these receive
The smell of peace toward mankind, let him live
Before thee reconciled, at least his days
Numbered, though sad, till death, his doom (which I
To mitigate thus plead, not to reverse)
To better life shall yield him, where with me
All my redeemed may dwell in joy and bliss,
Made one with me as I with thee am one."
To whom the Father, without cloud, serene.
"All thy request for man, accepted Son,
Obtain, all thy request was my decree:
But longer in that Paradise to dwell,
The law I gave to nature him forbids:

14–16. **To Heav'n . . . frustrate:** Cp. the Paradise of Fools at 3.485–89.

17. **Dimensionless:** without spatial extension.

18. **incense:** See Rev. 8.3.

28. **manuring:** tending (by hand).

33–34. **me . . . propitiation:** "And if any man sin, we have an advocate with the Father, Jesus Christ the righteous: and he is the propitiation for our sins" (1 John 2.1–2). The repeated *me* in these lines echoes 3.178–82, 236–38. Cp. 10.830–32.

35. **ingraft:** See Rom. 11.16–24, for Protestants a key text on the superiority of faith to good works.

44. John 17.22–23: "that they may be one, even as we are one: I in them, and thou in me." Note how the symmetry of Milton's line takes shape about the central *as I*.

Those pure immortal elements that know
No gross, no unharmonious mixture foul,
Eject him tainted now, and purge him off
As a distemper, gross to air as gross,
And mortal food, as may dispose him best
For dissolution wrought by sin, that first
Distempered all things, and of incorrupt
Corrupted. I at first with two fair gifts
Created him endowed, with happiness
And immortality: that fondly lost,
This other served but to eternize woe;
Till I provided death; so death becomes
His final remedy, and after life
Tried in sharp tribulation, and refined
By faith and faithful works, to second life,
Waked in the renovation of the just,
Resigns him up with heav'n and Earth renewed.
But let us call to synod all the blest
Through Heav'n's wide bounds; from them I will not hide
My judgments, how with mankind I proceed,
As how with peccant angels late they saw;
And in their state, though firm, stood more confirmed."
He ended, and the Son gave signal high
To the bright minister that watched; he blew
His trumpet, heard in Oreb since perhaps
When God descended, and perhaps once more
To sound at general doom. Th' angelic blast
Filled all the regions: from their blissful bow'rs
Of amarantine shade, fountain or spring,
By the waters of life, where'er they sat
In fellowships of joy: the sons of light
Hasted, resorting to the summons high,
And took their seats; till from his throne supreme
Th' Almighty thus pronounced his sov'reign will.
"O Sons, like one of us man is become

53. **distemper:** medical term, denoting an imbalance of the four humors. The expulsion of Adam and Eve is here presented as an automatic purgation in which immortal elements rid themselves of tainted elements.

55. **dissolution:** death, disintegration.

59. **fondly:** foolishly.

60. **This other:** immortality (l. 59).

64. Cp. 12.427; *CD* 1.22.

66. **Resigns:** The subject of the verb is *death* (l. 61).

74. **heard in Oreb:** A trumpet sounded when God delivered the Ten Commandments (Exod. 19.19); see *Nat Ode* 156–59.

75. **perhaps once more:** reminiscent of the opening of *Lycidas,* which alludes to the "yet once more" of Heb. 12.26–27.

78. **amarantine:** blood red and unfading, like the legendary flower amaranthus (see 3.353).

To know both good and evil, since his taste
Of that defended fruit; but let him boast
His knowledge of good lost, and evil got,
Happier, had it sufficed him to have known
Good by itself, and evil not at all.
He sorrows now, repents, and prays contrite,
My motions in him; longer than they move,
His heart I know, how variable and vain
Self-left. Lest therefore his now bolder hand
Reach also of the Tree of Life, and eat,
And live forever, dream at least to live
Forever, to remove him I decree,
And send him from the garden forth to till
The ground whence he was taken, fitter soil.
"Michael, this my behest have thou in charge,
Take to thee from among the Cherubim
Thy choice of flaming warriors, lest the fiend
Or in behalf of man, or to invade
Vacant possession, some new trouble raise:
Haste thee, and from the Paradise of God
Without remorse drive out the sinful pair,
From hallowed ground th' unholy, and denounce
To them and to their progeny from thence
Perpetual banishment. Yet lest they faint
At the sad sentence rigorously urged,
For I behold them softened and with tears
Bewailing their excess, all terror hide.
If patiently thy bidding they obey,
Dismiss them not disconsolate; reveal
To Adam what shall come in future days,
As I shall thee enlighten, intermix
My cov'nant in the woman's seed renewed;
So send them forth, though sorrowing, yet in peace:
And on the east side of the garden place,
Where entrance up from Eden easiest climbs,
Cherubic watch, and of a sword the flame
Wide-waving, all approach far off to fright,
And guard all passage to the Tree of Life:

86. **defended:** forbidden.

91. **motions:** inward promptings of the soul; cp. *PR* 1.290, *SA* 1382.

93. **Self-left:** when left to itself.

93–98. **Lest . . . soil:** The passage is based on Gen. 3.22–23.

102. **Or . . . or:** either . . . or.

106. **denounce:** announce.

108. **faint:** lose heart.

111. **excess:** transgression. Cp. 3.696.

Lest Paradise a receptacle prove
To spirits foul, and all my trees their prey,
With whose stol'n fruit man once more to delude."
He ceased; and th' archangelic power prepared
For swift descent, with him the cohort bright
Of watchful Cherubim; four faces each
Had, like a double Janus, all their shape
Spangled with eyes more numerous than those
Of Argus, and more wakeful than to drowse,
Charmed with Arcadian pipe, the pastoral reed
Of Hermes, or his opiate rod. Meanwhile
To resalute the world with sacred light
Leucothea waked, and with fresh dews imbalmed
The Earth, when Adam and first matron Eve
Had ended now their orisons, and found
Strength added from above, new hope to spring
Out of despair, joy, but with fear yet linked;
Which thus to Eve his welcome words renewed.
"Eve, easily may faith admit, that all
The good which we enjoy, from Heav'n descends;
But that from us aught should ascend to Heav'n
So prevalent as to concern the mind
Of God high-blest, or to incline his will,
Hard to belief may seem; yet this will prayer,
Or one short sigh of human breath, upborne
Ev'n to the seat of God. For since I sought
By prayer th' offended Deity to appease,
Kneeled and before him humbled all my heart,
Methought I saw him placable and mild,
Bending his ear; persuasion in me grew
That I was heard with favor; peace returned
Home to my breast, and to my memory
His promise, that thy seed shall bruise our foe;
Which then not minded in dismay, yet now
Assures me that the bitterness of death
Is past, and we shall live. Whence hail to thee,

129. **Janus:** two-faced Roman god of gates, beginnings, transitions.

131. **Argus:** The hundred-eyed giant set to guard Io, whom *Hermes* (Mercury) put to sleep with his *pipe* and his *opiate rod,* then killed. See Ovid, *Met.* 1.568–779.

135. **Leucothea:** goddess of the dawn.

144. **prevalent:** potent.

157–58. **Assures . . . past:** Echoing the words of Agag ("surely the bitterness of death is past") just before he is killed by Samuel (1 Sam. 15.32).

158. **hail to thee:** Adam prefigures the Annunciation (Ave Maria).

Eve rightly called, Mother of all Mankind,
Mother of all things living, since by thee
Man is to live, and all things live for man."
    To whom thus Eve with sad demeanor meek.
"Ill-worthy I such title should belong
To me transgressor, who for thee ordained
A help, became thy snare; to me reproach
Rather belongs, distrust and all dispraise:
But infinite in pardon was my judge,
That I who first brought death on all, am graced
The source of life; next favorable thou,
Who highly thus to entitle me vouchsaf'st,
Far other name deserving. But the field
To labor calls us now with sweat imposed,
Though after sleepless night; for see the morn,
All unconcerned with our unrest, begins
Her rosy progress smiling; let us forth,
I never from thy side henceforth to stray,
Where'er our day's work lies, though now enjoined
Laborious, till day droop; while here we dwell,
What can be toilsome in these pleasant walks?
Here let us live, though in fall'n state, content."
    So spake, so wished much-humbled Eve, but fate
Subscribed not; nature first gave signs, impressed
On bird, beast, air, air suddenly eclipsed
After short blush of morn; nigh in her sight
The bird of Jove, stooped from his airy tour,
Two birds of gayest plume before him drove:
Down from a hill the beast that reigns in woods,
First hunter then, pursued a gentle brace,
Goodliest of all the forest, hart and hind;
Direct to th' eastern gate was bent their flight.
Adam observed, and with his eye the chase
Pursuing, not unmoved to Eve thus spake.
    "O Eve, some further change awaits us nigh,
Which Heav'n by these mute signs in nature shows
Forerunners of his purpose, or to warn

159. **Eve rightly called:** Here Adam confirms the epithet *mother* first given to Eve by the voice of God (4.475); *Eve* is cognate with Heb. *chai* or "life." See Gen. 3.20.

185. **The bird of Jove:** the eagle; **stooped:** having swooped down to strike his prey (technical term in falconry).

186. **Two birds of gayest plume:** The eagle chasing these birds is an augury of Michael's expulsion of Adam and Eve from the garden.

187. **the beast that reigns:** the lion, who is to land animals what the eagle is to birds. Another augury of Adam and Eve's expulsion from Eden.

188. **brace:** pair.

Us haply too secure of our discharge
From penalty, because from death released
Some days; how long, and what till then our life,
Who knows, or more than this, that we are dust,
And thither must return and be no more.
Why else this double object in our sight
Of flight pursued in th' air and o'er the ground
One way the selfsame hour? Why in the east
Darkness ere day's mid-course, and morning light
More orient in yon western cloud that draws
O're the blew firmament a radiant white,
And slow descends, with somthing Heav'nly fraught."
He erred not, for by this the Heav'nly bands
Down from a sky of jasper lighted now
In Paradise, and on a hill made halt,
A glorious apparition, had not doubt
And carnal fear that day dimmed Adam's eye.
Not that more glorious, when the angels met
Jacob in Mahanaim, where he saw
The field pavilioned with his guardians bright;
Nor that which on the flaming mount appeared
In Dothan, covered with a camp of fire,
Against the Syrian king, who to surprise
One man, assassin-like had levied war,
War unproclaimed. The princely hierarch
In their bright stand, there left his powers to seize
Possession of the garden; he alone,
To find where Adam sheltered, took his way,
Not unperceived of Adam, who to Eve,
While the great visitant approached, thus spake.
"Eve, now expect great tidings, which perhaps
Of us will soon determine, or impose
New laws to be observed; for I descry
From yonder blazing cloud that veils the hill
One of the Heav'nly host, and by his gait

196. **secure:** overconfident.
205. **orient:** bright.
208. **by this:** by this time.
209. **lighted:** landed.
210. **made halt:** came to a halt (military term).
214. **Mahanaim:** Jacob named the place (Heb. for "armies") when he saw an army of angels there (Gen. 32.1–2).
215. **pavilioned:** encamped. See Milton's version of Psalm 3, lines 17–18.
216–20. **Nor that . . . unproclaimed:** Elisha and his fearful servant also had a vision of an angelic army with "horses and chariots of fire" when the *Syrian king* laid siege to the city of *Dothan* (2 Kings 6.7).
221. **stand:** station (military term).
227. **determine:** bring to an end.

None of the meanest, some great potentate
Or of the Thrones above, such majesty
Invests him coming; yet not terrible,
That I should fear, nor sociably mild,
As Raphael, that I should much confide,
But solemn and sublime, whom not to offend,
With reverence I must meet, and thou retire."
He ended; and th' archangel soon drew nigh,
Not in his shape celestial, but as man
Clad to meet man; over his lucid arms
A military vest of purple flowed
Livelier than Meliboean, or the grain
Of Sarra, worn by kings and heroes old
In time of truce; Iris had dipped the woof;
His starry helm unbuckled showed him prime
In manhood where youth ended; by his side
As in a glistering zodiac hung the sword,
Satan's dire dread, and in his hand the spear.
Adam bowed low, he kingly from his state
Inclined not, but his coming thus declared.
"Adam, Heav'n's high behest no preface needs:
Sufficient that thy prayers are heard, and death,
Then due by sentence when thou didst transgress,
Defeated of his seizure many days
Giv'n thee of grace, wherein thou may'st repent,
And one bad act with many deeds well done
May'st cover: well may then thy Lord appeased
Redeem thee quite from death's rapacious claim;
But longer in this Paradise to dwell
Permits not; to remove thee I am come,
And send thee from the garden forth to till
The ground whence thou wast tak'n, fitter soil."
He added not, for Adam at the news
Heart-strook with chilling grip of sorrow stood,
That all his senses bound; Eve, who unseen
Yet all had heard, with audible lament

240. **lucid:** bright.

242–43. **Meliboean . . . Sarra:** The cities of Meliboea and Tyre (*Sarra*) were famous for dyes (*grain* = dye) made from local fish.

244. **Iris . . . woof:** Iris is goddess of the rainbow. Cp. *Masque* 83, where the Attendant Spirit doffs "sky robes spun out of Iris' woof," and *PL* 11.895–98.

254. **Defeated:** cheated.

256–57. **one . . . cover:** 1 Pet. 4.8: "For charity covers a multitude of sins."

259–62. Varied only slightly from lines 48–49, 96–98, in the manner of Homer's repetitive treatment of messages.

264. **grip:** spasm.

Discovered soon the place of her retire.
"O unexpected stroke, worse than of death!
Must I thus leave thee Paradise? Thus leave
Thee native soil, these happy walks and shades,
Fit haunt of gods? Where I had hope to spend,
Quiet though sad, the respite of that day
That must be mortal to us both. O flow'rs,
That never will in other climate grow,
My early visitation, and my last
At ev'n, which I bred up with tender hand
From the first op'ning bud, and gave ye names,
Who now shall rear ye to the sun, or rank
Your tribes, and water from th' ambrosial fount?
Thee lastly nuptial bower, by me adorned
With what to sight or smell was sweet; from thee
How shall I part, and whither wander down
Into a lower world, to this obscure
And wild, how shall we breathe in other air
Less pure, accustomed to immortal fruits?"
Whom thus the angel interrupted mild.
"Lament not Eve, but patiently resign
What justly thou hast lost; nor set thy heart,
Thus over-fond, on that which is not thine;
Thy going is not lonely, with thee goes
Thy husband, him to follow thou art bound;
Where he abides, think there thy native soil."
Adam by this from the cold sudden damp
Recovering, and his scattered spirits returned,
To Michael thus his humble words addressed.
"Celestial, whether among the Thrones, or named
Of them the highest, for such of shape may seem
Prince above princes, gently hast thou told
Thy message, which might else in telling wound,
And in performing end us; what besides
Of sorrow and dejection and despair

267. **Discovered:** revealed; **retire:** withdrawal.

270. **native soil:** "Paradise was the *native place* of Eve; but Adam was formed out of the dust of the ground, and was afterwards brought into Paradise" (Newton).

272. **respite:** temporary suspension of a death sentence (legal term).

277. **gave ye names:** Presumably this naming of the flowers, which has no biblical precedent, entailed, like Adam's naming of the creatures, an intuitive understanding of "their nature" (8.353).

283. **to this:** compared to this.

290–92. Eve will make this view her own in the last speech in the poem (12.615–18).

293. **by this:** by this time; **damp:** stupor, depression.

Our frailty can sustain, thy tidings bring,
Departure from this happy place, our sweet
Recess, and only consolation left
Familiar to our eyes, all places else
Inhospitable appear and desolate,
Nor knowing us nor known: and if by prayer
Incessant I could hope to change the will
Of him who all things can, I would not cease
To weary him with my assiduous cries:
But prayer against his absolute decree
No more avails than breath against the wind,
Blown stifling back on him that breathes it forth:
Therefore to his great bidding I submit.
This most afflicts me, that departing hence,
As from his face I shall be hid, deprived
His blessed count'nance; here I could frequent,
With worship, place by place where he vouchsafed
Presence divine, and to my sons relate,
"On this Mount he appeared, under this tree
Stood visible, among these pines his voice
I heard, here with him at this fountain talked."
So many grateful altars I would rear
Of grassy turf, and pile up every stone
Of luster from the brook, in memory,
Or monument to ages, and thereon
Offer sweet smelling gums and fruits and flow'rs:
In yonder nether world where shall I seek
His bright appearances, or footstep trace?
For though I fled him angry, yet recalled
To life prolonged and promised race, I now
Gladly behold though but his utmost skirts
Of glory, and far off his steps adore."
    To whom thus Michael with regard benign.
"Adam, thou know'st Heav'n his, and all the Earth,
Not this rock only; his omnipresence fills
Land, sea, and air, and every kind that lives,
Fomented by his virtual power and warmed:
All th' Earth he gave thee to possess and rule,
No despicable gift; surmise not then
His presence to these narrow bounds confined

309. **can:** is able to do, has knowledge of.

316. **from . . . hid:** a biblical idiom (Gen. 4.14, Ps. 104.27). Cp. 12.106–9 and *SA* 1749.

331. **promised race:** the human race.

338. **Fomented:** nurtured; **virtual:** potent.

Of Paradise or Eden: this had been
Perhaps thy capital seat, from whence had spread
All generations, and had hither come
From all the ends of th' Earth, to celebrate
And reverence thee their great progenitor.
But this preeminence thou hast lost, brought down
To dwell on even ground now with thy sons:
Yet doubt not but in valley and in plain
God is as here, and will be found alike
Present, and of his presence many a sign
Still following thee, still compassing thee round
With goodness and paternal love, his face
Express, and of his steps the track divine.
Which that thou may'st believe, and be confirmed
Ere thou from hence depart, know I am sent
To show thee what shall come in future days
To thee and to thy offspring; good with bad
Expect to hear, supernal grace contending
With sinfulness of men; thereby to learn
True patience, and to temper joy with fear
And pious sorrow, equally inured
By moderation either state to bear,
Prosperous or adverse: so shalt thou lead
Safest thy life, and best prepared endure
Thy mortal passage when it comes. Ascend
This hill; let Eve (for I have drenched her eyes)
Here sleep below while thou to foresight wak'st,
As once thou slept'st, while she to life was formed."
    To whom thus Adam gratefully replied.
"Ascend, I follow thee, safe guide, the path
Thou lead'st me, and to the hand of Heav'n submit,
However chast'ning, to the evil turn
My obvious breast, arming to overcome
By suffering, and earn rest from labor won,
If so I may attain." So both ascend
In the visions of God: it was a hill

356–58. **Ere . . . offspring:** As Addison was among the first to note, the idea of Adam's vision was probably suggested to Milton by the vision of his descendants given to Aeneas in the last book of the *Aeneid.* Addison also noted that the vision was necessary to console Adam, who "sees his offspring triumphing over his great enemy, and himself restored to a happier Paradise" (49).

361. **True patience:** Christian patience, which includes hope, as opposed to the apathy recommended by stoicism.

367. **drenched:** administered medicine (a sleeping potion) to. Cp. 2.73n.

374. **obvious:** vulnerable.

377. **visions of God:** visions sent by God.

Of Paradise the highest, from whose top
The hemisphere of earth in clearest ken
Stretched out to the amplest reach of prospect lay.
Not higher that hill nor wider looking round,
Whereon for different cause the Tempter set
Our second Adam in the wilderness,
To show him all Earth's kingdoms and their glory.
His eye might there command wherever stood
City of old or modern fame, the seat
Of mightiest empire, from the destined walls
Of Cambalu, seat of Cathayan Khan
And Samarkand by Oxus, Temir's throne,
To Paquin of Sinaean kings, and thence
To Agra and Lahore of Great Mogul
Down to the golden Chersonese, or where
The Persian in Ecbatan sat, or since
In Hispahan, or where the Russian Czar
In Moscow, or the Sultan in Bizance,
Turkestan-born; nor could his eye not ken
Th' Empire of Negus to his utmost port
Ercoco and the less maritime kings
Mombaza, and Quiloa, and Melind,
And Sofala thought Ophir, to the realm
Of Congo, and Angola farthest south;
Or thence from Niger flood to Atlas mount
The kingdoms of Almansor, Fez and Sus,
Morocco and Algiers, and Tremisen;

383. **second Adam:** See 10.183n.

388. **Cambalu:** capital of Cathay (China), modern Beijing, seat of the khans. Milton's geography of imperialism to come moves from east to west, like the sun, and like history as traditionally conceived in the West (see Chambers 1961).

389. **Samarkand by Oxus:** an Uzbekistan city on the river Oxus, the birthplace and royal residence of Tamburlaine (*Temir*).

390. **Paquin:** also a name for modern Beijing, where Chinese (*Sinaean*) kings ruled.

391. **Agra:** Mogul capital, where Akbar built the Taj Mahal; **Lahore:** Pakistani city where Mogul emperors sometimes resided.

392. **golden Chersonese:** area to the east of India, fabled for its wealth.

393. **Ecbatan:** Ecbatana, modern Hamadan in Iran, once the summer residence of Persian kings; **Hispahan:** Isfahan in Iran, made the Persian capital in the sixteenth century.

395. **Bizance:** Byzantium (modern Istanbul), conquered by the Ottoman Empire in the fifteenth century.

396. **Turkestan-born:** The Ottoman Turks originated in Turkistan.

397. **Negus:** title of Abyssinian emperors.

398. **Ercoco:** Arkiko, in modern Ethiopia.

399–400. **Mombaza** (modern Mombasa, in Kenya), **Quiloa** (Kilwa, in Tanzania), **Melind** (Malindi, in Kenya), and **Sofala** (in Mozambique) are port cities in eastern Africa visited by Vasco da Gama. Sofala was one of a number of candidates for the biblical *Ophir,* where Solomon found gold.

402. **Niger:** a West African river; **Atlas mount:** the Atlas Mountains of westernmost Africa.

403. **Almansor:** Muslim kings claimed the surname Al-Mansur (made victorious by God), and ruled over *Fez,* a Moroccan city, and *Sus* (Tunis).

404. **Tremisen:** an area of Algeria.

On Europe thence, and where Rome was to sway
The world: in spirit perhaps he also saw
Rich Mexico the seat of Motezume,
And Cusco in Peru, the richer seat
Of Atabalipa, and yet unspoiled
Guiana, whose great city Geryon's sons
Call El Dorado: but to nobler sights
Michael from Adam's eyes the film removed
Which that false fruit that promised clearer sight
Had bred; then purged with euphrasy and rue
The visual nerve, for he had much to see;
And from the Well of Life three drops instilled.
So deep the power of these ingredients pierced,
Even to the inmost seat of mental sight,
That Adam now enforced to close his eyes,
Sunk down and all his spirits became entranced:
But him the gentle angel by the hand
Soon raised, and his attention thus recalled.
"Adam, now ope thine eyes, and first behold
Th' effects which thy original crime hath wrought
In some to spring from thee, who never touched
Th' excepted tree, nor with the snake conspired,
Nor sinned thy sin, yet from that sin derive
Corruption to bring forth more violent deeds."
His eyes he opened, and beheld a field,
Part arable and tilth, whereon were sheaves
New reapt, the other part sheep-walks and folds;
I' th' midst an altar as the landmark stood
Rustic, of grassy sward; thither anon

406. **in spirit:** in a visionary extension of eyesight; the New World would have been hidden by the curvature of the earth.

407. **Motezume:** the Aztec emperor Montezuma, who surrendered to Hernán Cortés in 1520.

409. **Atabalipa:** Atahualpa, the Incan emperor slain by Francisco Pizarro in 1533; his Peruvian capital of *Cusco* fell to the Spaniards.

410. **Geryon's sons:** an epithet for Spaniards, based on a mythical monster named Geryon, who lived on a Spanish island and was slain by Hercules.

411. **El Dorado:** a mythical city in the New World that Sir Walter Ralegh among others sought in vain. See Ralegh's *The Discoverie of Guiana* (1595), 10.

412. **the film removed:** A god clearing mortal eyes is an epic convention (*Il.* 5.126; *Aen.* 2.604; *GL* 18.92f), but given the real physiological effects of the forbidden fruit (9.1011–12, 1044–51), it seems likely that this film is actual rather than metaphorical: Adam had incipient *gutta serena,* the "dim suffusion" (3.26) from which Milton suffered.

414. **euphrasy and rue:** medicinal herbs used in the treatment of eyesight. Milton might have taken salves made of these herbs in the course of going blind.

416. **the Well of Life:** perhaps the "fountain of life" of Ps. 36.9; **three drops:** a conspicuous dose in a poem that is not conventionally trinitarian.

426. **excepted:** forbidden.

427. **that sin:** 1667; 1674 drops "sin," spoiling the meter.

430. **tilth:** cultivated land.

433. **sward:** turf.

A sweaty reaper from his tillage brought
First fruits, the green ear, and the yellow sheaf,
Unculled, as came to hand; a shepherd next
More meek came with the firstlings of his flock
Choicest and best; then sacrificing, laid
The inwards and their fat, with incense strewed,
On the cleft wood, and all due rites performed.
His off'ring soon propitious fire from heav'n
Consumed with nimble glance, and grateful steam;
The other's not, for his was not sincere;
Whereat he inly raged, and as they talked,
Smote him into the midriff with a stone
That beat out life; he fell, and deadly pale
Groaned out his soul with gushing blood effused.
Much at that sight was Adam in his heart
Dismayed, and thus in haste to th' angel cried.
"O teacher, some great mischief hath befall'n
To that meek man, who well had sacrificed;
Is piety thus and pure devotion paid?"
T' whom Michael thus, he also moved, replied.
"These two are brethren, Adam, and to come
Out of thy loins; th' unjust the just hath slain,
For envy that his brother's offering found
From Heav'n acceptance; but the bloody fact
Will be avenged, and th' other's faith approved
Lose no reward, though here thou see him die,
Rolling in dust and gore." To which our sire.
"Alas, both for the deed and for the cause!
But have I now seen death? Is this the way
I must return to native dust? O sight
Of terror, foul and ugly to behold,
Horrid to think, how horrible to feel!"
To whom thus Michael. "Death thou hast seen
In his first shape on man; but many shapes
Of Death, and many are the ways that lead
To his grim cave, all dismal; yet to sense
More terrible at th' entrance than within.
Some, as thou saw'st, by violent stroke shall die,

436. **Unculled:** not picked by design.

441. **propitious fire from heav'n:** After Abel follows the rules for sacrificing in Lev. 1–8, Heaven consumes his offering (Gen. 4.4).

442. **glance:** flash.

447. **effused:** poured out.

457. **fact:** crime.

469. **his grim cave:** Cp. the cave to the underworld in *Aen.* 6.237, 273–94.

By fire, flood, famine; by intemperance more
In meats and drinks, which on the Earth shall bring
Diseases dire, of which a monstrous crew
Before thee shall appear; that thou may'st know
What misery th' inabstinence of Eve
Shall bring on men." Immediately a place
Before his eyes appeared, sad, noisome, dark,
A lazar-house it seemed, wherein were laid
Numbers of all diseased, all maladies
Of ghastly spasm, or racking torture, qualms
Of heart-sick agony, all feaverous kinds,
Convulsions, epilepsies, fierce catarrhs,
Intestine stone and ulcer, colic pangs,
Demoniac frenzy, moping melancholy
And moon-struck madness, pining atrophy,
Marasmus, and wide-wasting pestilence,
Dropsies, and asthmas, and joint-racking rheums.
Dire was the tossing, deep the groans; Despair
Tended the sick busiest from couch to couch;
And over them triumphant Death his dart
Shook, but delayed to strike, though oft invoked
With vows, as their chief good, and final hope.
Sight so deform what heart of rock could long
Dry-eyed behold? Adam could not, but wept,
Though not of woman born; compassion quelled
His best of man, and gave him up to tears
A space, till firmer thoughts restrained excess,
And scarce recovering words his plaint renewed.
"O miserable mankind, to what fall
Degraded, to what wretched state reserved!
Better end here unborn. Why is life giv'n
To be thus wrested from us? Rather why

479. **lazar-house:** hospital for those with infectious diseases, especially the dreaded leprosy; *lazar* comes from the name of the beggar in Luke 16.20. There were a number of lazar houses in England (Wilson 1963, 81).

481. **qualms:** faintings.

485–87. These lines were added in 1674.

487. **Marasmus:** consumption.

488. **Dropsies:** morbid retentions of fluid; **rheums:** mucous discharges.

496. **Though not of woman born:** Although the phrasing evokes *MAC* 4.1.80 and 5.3.13, Milton draws on Shakespeare's association between a man's tears and his internalized mother in *H5* 4.6.30–32 and *TN* 2.1.35–38.

497. **best of man:** manliness, normally impervious to tears. But Milton's Adam, apparently no exponent of tearless masculinity, weeps on his own here, and at lines 675, 754–58, and 12.372–73; Eve weeps on her own at 5.130–35, 9.990–91, and 10.910; they cry together at 9.1121, 10.1101–2, and 12.645.

502–507. **Better . . . peace:** A commonplace of both classical literature (Sophocles, *Oedipus at Colonus* 1224–26; Theognis of Megara, *Maxims,* 425–28; Seneca, *Ad Marciam: De Consolatione* 22.3)

Obtruded on us thus? Who if we knew
What we receive, would either not accept
Life offered, or soon beg to lay it down,
Glad to be so dismissed in peace. Can thus
Th' image of God in man created once
So goodly and erect, though faulty since,
To such unsightly sufferings be debased
Under inhuman pains? Why should not man,
Retaining still divine similitude
In part, from such deformities be free,
And for his Maker's image sake exempt?"
"Their Maker's image," answered Michael, "then
Forsook them, when themselves they vilified
To serve ungoverned appetite, and took
His image whom they served, a brutish vice,
Inductive mainly to the sin of Eve.
Therefore so abject is their punishment,
Disfiguring not God's likeness, but their own,
Or if his likeness, by themselves defaced
While they pervert pure nature's healthful rules
To loathsome sickness, worthily, since they
God's image did not reverence in themselves."
"I yield it just," said Adam, "and submit.
But is there yet no other way, besides
These painful passages, how we may come
To death, and mix with our connatural dust?"
"There is," said Michael, "if thou well observe
The rule of *not too much,* by temperance taught
In what thou eat'st and drink'st, seeking from thence
Due nourishment, not gluttonous delight,
Till many years over thy head return:
So may'st thou live, till like ripe fruit thou drop
Into thy mother's lap, or be with ease
Gathered, not harshly plucked, for death mature:
This is old age; but then thou must outlive
Thy youth, thy strength, thy beauty, which will change
To withered weak and gray; thy senses then

---

and Renaissance literature (*2H4* 3.1.45–56; Jonson, "To the Immortal Memory . . . Sir. Lucius Cary and Sir H. Morison," 1–20).

519. **Inductive:** traceable.

531. **The rule of *not too much:*** "Nothing too much" was inscribed on the temple of Apollo at Delphi (Plato, *Protagoras* 343B; see also Aristotle, *Nichomachean Ethics* 2.2.16).

535–37. The comparison stems from Cicero, *De Senectute* 19; cp. Donne, "A Valediction Forbidding Mourning": "As virtuous men pass mildly away. . . ."

Obtuse, all taste of pleasure must forgo,
To what thou hast, and for the air of youth
Hopeful and cheerful, in thy blood will reign
A melancholy damp of cold and dry
To weigh thy spirits down, and last consume
The balm of life." To whom our ancestor.
"Henceforth I fly not death, nor would prolong
Life much, bent rather how I may be quit
Fairest and easiest of this cumbrous charge,
Which I must keep till my appointed day
Of rend'ring up, and patiently attend
My dissolution." Michael replied,
"Nor love thy life, nor hate; but what thou liv'st
Live well, how long or short permit to Heav'n:
And now prepare thee for another sight."
He looked and saw a spacious plain, whereon
Were tents of various hue; by some were herds
Of cattle grazing: others, whence the sound
Of instruments that made melodious chime
Was heard, of harp and organ; and who moved
Their stops and chords was seen: his volant touch
Instinct through all proportions low and high
Fled and pursued transverse the resonant fugue.
In other part stood one who at the forge
Laboring, two massy clods of iron and brass
Had melted (whether found where casual fire
Had wasted woods on mountain or in vale,
Down to the veins of Earth, thence gliding hot
To some cave's mouth, or whether washed by stream
From underground) the liquid ore he drained
Into fit molds prepared; from which he formed
First his own tools; then, what might else be wrought
Fusile or grav'n in metal. After these,
But on the hither side a different sort
From the high neighboring hills, which was their seat,
Down to the plain descended: by their guise
Just men they seemed, and all their study bent

544. **damp:** Cp. 293; 9.45.

551–52. The first edition had only one line here: "Of rend'ring up. Michael to him replied."

553. **Nor love thy life, nor hate:** from Martial, *Epigrams,* 10.47.

556–97. Adam's third vision, concerning the descendants of Cain, derives from Gen. 4.19–22, 6.2–4.

561. **volant:** rapid, flying.

562. **Instinct:** instinctively.

563. **fugue:** from the Latin *fuga* (flight). A "skilful organist" plays fugues in *Of Ed* (p. 979).

573. **Fusile:** shaped by means of melting.

To worship God aright, and know his works
Not hid, nor those things last which might preserve
Freedom and peace to men: they on the plain
Long had not walked, when from the tents behold
A bevy of fair women, richly gay
In gems and wanton dress; to the harp they sung
Soft amorous ditties, and in dance came on:
The men though grave, eyed them, and let their eyes
Rove without rein, till in the amorous net
Fast caught, they liked, and each his liking chose;
And now of love they treat till th' ev'ning star
Love's harbinger appeared; then all in heat
They light the nuptial torch, and bid invoke
Hymen, then first to marriage rites invoked;
With feast and music all the tents resound.
Such happy interview and fair event
Of love and youth not lost, songs, garlands, flow'rs,
And charming symphonies attached the heart
Of Adam, soon inclined to admit delight,
The bent of nature; which he thus expressed.
"True opener of mine eyes, prime angel blest,
Much better seems this vision, and more hope
Of peaceful days portends, than those two past;
Those were of hate and death, or pain much worse,
Here nature seems fulfilled in all her ends."
To whom thus Michael. "Judge not what is best
By pleasure, though to nature seeming meet,
Created, as thou art, to nobler end
Holy and pure, conformity divine.
Those tents thou saw'st so pleasant, were the tents
Of wickedness, wherein shall dwell his race
Who slew his brother; studious they appear
Of arts that polish life, inventors rare,
Unmindful of their Maker, though his spirit
Taught them, but they his gifts acknowledged none.
Yet they a beauteous offspring shall beget;
For that fair female troop thou saw'st, that seemed
Of goddesses, so blithe, so smooth, so gay,
Yet empty of all good wherein consists

586. **amorous net:** Cp. *PR* 2.161–62; nets were conventional in erotic contexts.

593. **interview:** a mutual viewing as well as a verbal exchange; **event:** outcome.

595. **attached:** seized. Adam too readily warms to the sight of youthful pleasure *not lost.*

607. **tents:** Jabal was the father of tent dwellers (Gen. 4.20).

Woman's domestic honor and chief praise;
Bred only and completed to the taste
Of lustful appetence, to sing, to dance,
To dress, and troll the tongue, and roll the eye.
To these that sober race of men, whose lives
Religious titled them the Sons of God,
Shall yield up all their virtue, all their fame
Ignobly, to the trains and to the smiles
Of these fair atheists, and now swim in joy,
(Erelong to swim at large) and laugh; for which
The world erelong a world of tears must weep."
  To whom thus Adam of short joy bereft.
"O pity and shame, that they who to live well
Entered so fair, should turn aside to tread
Paths indirect, or in the mid way faint!
But still I see the tenor of man's woe
Holds on the same, from woman to begin."
  "From man's effeminate slackness it begins,"
Said th' angel, "who should better hold his place
By wisdom, and superior gifts received.
But now prepare thee for another scene."
  He looked and saw wide territory spread
Before him, towns, and rural works between,
Cities of men with lofty gates and tow'rs,
Concourse in arms, fierce faces threat'ning war,
Giants of mighty bone, and bold emprise;
Part wield their arms, part curb the foaming steed,
Single or in array of battle ranged
Both horse and foot, nor idly must'ring stood;
One way a band select from forage drives
A herd of beeves, fair oxen and fair kine
From a fat meadow ground; or fleecy flock,
Ewes and their bleating lambs over the plain,
Their booty; scarce with life the shepherds fly,

619. **appetence:** desire.

620. **troll:** wag; note the flashy rhyme with *roll.*

622. **Sons of God:** See 5.446–48n.

624. **trains:** tricks, stratagems.

626. **Erelong to swim at large:** Michael anticipates the Flood, the forthcoming punishment for this swimming in lewd joy.

631. **mid way:** Cp. 6.91n.

632–33. **man's woe . . . woman:** Adam turns *man's woe* into "woe-man," an old misogynistic joke.

638–73. The fourth vision is based on Gen. 6.4, with touches drawn from Homer's description of the shield of Achilles (*Il.* 18.478–540) and Vergil's imitation of it in *Aen.* 8.626–728.

642. **bold emprise:** martial enterprise; also found in *Masque* 610.

643. **curb the foaming steed:** Cp. 2.531n.

644. **ranged:** arranged.

But call in aid, which makes a bloody fray;
With cruel tournament the squadrons join;
Where cattle pastured late, now scattered lies
With carcasses and arms th' ensanguined field
Deserted: others to a city strong
Lay siege, encamped; by battery, scale, and mine,
Assaulting; others from the wall defend
With dart and jav'lin, stones and sulfurous fire;
On each hand slaughter and gigantic deeds.
In other part the sceptered heralds call
To council in the city gates: anon
Grey-headed men and grave, with warriors mixed,
Assemble, and harangues are heard, but soon
In factious opposition, till at last
Of middle age one rising, eminent
In wise deport, spake much of right and wrong,
Of justice, of religion, truth and peace,
And judgment from above: him old and young
Exploded and had seized with violent hands,
Had not a cloud descending snatched him thence
Unseen amid the throng: so violence
Proceeded, and oppression, and sword-law
Through all the plain, and refuge none was found.
Adam was all in tears, and to his guide
Lamenting turned full sad: "O what are these,
Death's ministers, not men, who thus deal death
Inhumanly to men, and multiply
Ten-thousandfold the sin of him who slew
His brother; for of whom such massacre
Make they but of their brethren, men of men?
But who was that just man, whom had not Heav'n
Rescued, had in his righteousness been lost?"
    To whom thus Michael. "These are the product
Of those ill-mated marriages thou saw'st:
Where good with bad were matched, who of themselves
Abhor to join; and by imprudence mixed,
Produce prodigious births of body or mind.
Such were these giants, men of high renown;

654. **ensanguined:** blood-soaked.

656. **battery, scale, and mine:** The sieging army can break through the walls of the city (*battery*), climb over them (*scale* = ladder), and dig underneath them (*mine*).

665. **one rising:** Enoch, the first of several forthcoming examples of solitary, Abdiel-like heroism (see 5.897–903).

669. **Exploded:** silenced with mockery, hissed.

687–88. "There were giants in the earth in those days" (Gen. 6.4).

For in those days might only shall be admired,
And valor and heroic virtue called;
To overcome in battle, and subdue
Nations, and bring home spoils with infinite
Manslaughter, shall be held the highest pitch
Of human glory, and for glory done
Of triumph, to be styled great conquerors,
Patrons of mankind, gods, and sons of gods,
Destroyers rightlier called and plagues of men.
Thus fame shall be achieved, renown on earth,
And what most merits fame in silence hid.
But he the sev'nth from thee, whom thou beheld'st
The only righteous in a world perverse,
And therefore hated, therefore so beset
With foes for daring single to be just,
And utter odious truth, that God would come
To judge them with his saints: him the Most High
Rapt in a balmy cloud with wingèd steeds
Did, as thou saw'st, receive, to walk with God
High in salvation and the climes of bliss,
Exempt from death, to show thee what reward
Awaits the good, the rest what punishment;
Which now direct thine eyes and soon behold."
He looked, and saw the face of things quite changed;
The brazen throat of war had ceased to roar,
All now was turned to jollity and game,
To luxury and riot, feast and dance,
Marrying or prostituting, as befell,
Rape or adultery, where passing fair
Allured them; thence from cups to civil broils.
At length a reverend sire among them came,
And of their doings great dislike declared,
And testified against their ways; he oft
Frequented their assemblies, whereso met,
Triumphs or festivals, and to them preached
Conversion and repentance, as to souls
In prison under judgments imminent:

700. **the sev'nth from thee:** See Jude 14.

707. **receive:** Enoch is one of only two men in the Bible to be received into Heaven without dying. The other is Elijah (see 2 Kings 2). For Milton's interest in this phenomenon, and its relation to the mortalist heresy, see Kerrigan 1975, 127–44.

712–53. The fifth vision concerns the Flood and the corruption that preceded it (Gen. 6–9).

715. **luxury:** lust.

717. **passing fair:** both "women passing by" and "surpassing beauty."

719. **reverend sire:** Noah. Cp. *Lyc* 103.

But all in vain: which when he saw, he ceased
Contending, and removed his tents far off;
Then from the mountain hewing timber tall,
Began to build a vessel of huge bulk,
Measured by cubit, length, and breadth, and highth,
Smeared round with pitch, and in the side a door
Contrived, and of provisions laid in large
For man and beast: when lo a wonder strange!
Of every beast, and bird, and insect small
Came sevens and pairs, and entered in, as taught
Their order: last the sire, and his three sons
With their four wives; and God made fast the door.
Meanwhile the south wind rose, and with black wings
Wide hovering, all the clouds together drove
From under Heav'n; the hills to their supply
Vapor, and exhalation dusk and moist,
Sent up amain; and now the thickened sky
Like a dark ceiling stood; down rushed the rain
Impetuous, and continued till the earth
No more was seen; the floating vessel swum
Uplifted, and secure with beakèd prow
Rode tilting o'er the waves, all dwellings else
Flood overwhelmed, and them with all their pomp
Deep under water rolled; sea covered sea,
Sea without shore; and in their palaces
Where luxury late reigned, sea-monsters whelped
And stabled; of mankind, so numerous late,
All left, in one small bottom swum embarked.
How didst thou grieve then, Adam, to behold
The end of all thy offspring, end so sad,
Depopulation; thee another flood,
Of tears and sorrow a flood thee also drowned,
And sunk thee as thy sons; till gently reared
By th' angel, on thy feet thou stood'st at last,
Though comfortless, as when a father mourns
His children, all in view destroyed at once;

730. **cubit:** a unit of length (the distance from the elbow to the fingertips); for the dimensions of the ark in cubits, see Gen. 6.15.

734. **insect:** Commentators often excluded insects from Noah's ark because they were thought to reproduce without coupling.

735. **sevens and pairs:** The ark contained seven pairs each of all clean animals and only one pair each of unclean animals (Gen. 7.2).

738–53. This passage draws from the description of Deucalion's flood in Ovid, *Met.* 1.262–347.

740. **supply:** assistance.

741. **exhalation dusk:** dark mist.

753. **bottom:** boat.

755–56. **The end . . . Depopulation:** See Matt. 6.34.

And scarce to th' angel utter'dst thus thy plaint.
"O visions ill foreseen! Better had I
Lived ignorant of future, so had borne
My part of evil only, each day's lot
Enough to bear; those now, that were dispensed
The burd'n of many ages, on me light
At once, by my foreknowledge gaining birth
Abortive, to torment me ere their being,
With thought that they must be. Let no man seek
Henceforth to be foretold what shall befall
Him or his childern, evil he may be sure,
Which neither his foreknowing can prevent,
And he the future evil shall no less
In apprehension than in substance feel
Grievous to bear: but that care now is past,
Man is not whom to warn: those few escaped
Famine and anguish will at last consume
Wand'ring that wat'ry desert: I had hope
When violence was ceased, and war on Earth,
All would have then gone well, peace would have crowned
With length of happy days the race of man;
But I was far deceived; for now I see
Peace to corrupt no less than war to waste.
How comes it thus? Unfold, celestial guide,
And whether here the race of man will end."
To whom thus Michael. "Those whom last thou saw'st
In triumph and luxurious wealth, are they
First seen in acts of prowess eminent
And great exploits, but of true virtue void;
Who having spilt much blood, and done much waste
Subduing nations, and achieved thereby
Fame in the world, high titles, and rich prey,
Shall change their course to pleasure, ease, and sloth,
Surfeit, and lust, till wantonness and pride
Raise out of friendship hostile deeds in peace.
The conquered also, and enslaved by war
Shall with their freedom lost all virtue lose
And fear of God, from whom their piety feigned
In sharp contest of battle found no aid

766. **dispensed:** portioned out (so much evil for this age, so much for that age, et cetera).
777. **Man is not whom:** No one remains.
797–807. In both his poetry and his prose, Milton often states his belief that moral corruption and the loss of political liberty go hand in hand. See *SA* 268–71.

Against invaders; therefore cooled in zeal
Thenceforth shall practice how to live secure,
Worldly or dissolute, on what their lords
Shall leave them to enjoy; for th' earth shall bear
More than enough, that temperance may be tried:
So all shall turn degenerate, all depraved,
Justice and temperance, truth and faith forgot;
One man except, the only son of light
In a dark age, against example good,
Against allurement, custom, and a world
Offended; fearless of reproach and scorn,
Or violence, he of their wicked ways
Shall them admonish, and before them set
The paths of righteousness, how much more safe,
And full of peace, denouncing wrath to come
On their impenitence; and shall return
Of them derided, but of God observed
The one just man alive; by his command
Shall build a wondrous ark, as thou beheld'st,
To save himself and household from amidst
A world devote to universal wrack.
No sooner he with them of man and beast
Select for life shall in the ark be lodged,
And sheltered round, but all the cataracts
Of heav'n set open on the earth shall pour
Rain day and night, all fountains of the deep
Broke up, shall heave the ocean to usurp
Beyond all bounds, till inundation rise
Above the highest hills: then shall this mount
Of Paradise by might of waves be moved
Out of his place, pushed by the hornèd flood,
With all his verdure spoiled, and trees adrift
Down the great river to the op'ning gulf,
And there take root an island salt and bare,
The haunt of seals and orcs, and sea-mews' clang.
To teach thee that God attributes to place
No sanctity, if none be thither brought

808. **One man:** Noah.

815. **denouncing:** proclaiming.

821. **devote:** consecrated to utter destruction, doomed.

835. **orcs:** whales; **sea-mews:** gulls; **clang:** shrill cry.

836–37. **to place/No sanctity:** One sign of the lack of sanctity for locality is the virtual absence of place names in Book 11. Indeed, even proper names are withheld, as if cults of personality were as false and distracting as cults of location.

By men who there frequent, or therein dwell.
And now what further shall ensue, behold."
He looked, and saw the ark hull on the flood,
Which now abated, for the clouds were fled,
Driv'n by a keen north wind, that blowing dry
Wrinkled the face of deluge, as decayed;
And the clear sun on his wide wat'ry glass
Gazed hot, and of the fresh wave largely drew,
As after thirst, which made their flowing shrink
From standing lake to tripping ebb, that stole
With soft foot towards the deep, who now had stopped
His sluices, as the heav'n his windows shut.
The ark no more now floats, but seems on ground
Fast on the top of some high mountain fixed.
And now the tops of hills as rocks appear;
With clamor thence the rapid currents drive
Towards the retreating sea their furious tide.
Forthwith from out the ark a raven flies,
And after him, the surer messenger,
A dove sent forth once and again to spy
Green tree or ground whereon his foot may light;
The second time returning, in his bill
An olive leaf he brings, pacific sign:
Anon dry ground appears, and from his ark
The ancient sire descends with all his train;
Then with uplifted hands, and eyes devout,
Grateful to Heav'n, over his head beholds
A dewy cloud, and in the cloud a bow
Conspicuous with three listed colors gay,
Betok'ning peace from God, and cov'nant new.
Whereat the heart of Adam erst so sad
Greatly rejoiced, and thus his joy broke forth.
"O thou who future things canst represent
As present, Heav'nly instructor, I revive
At this last sight, assured that man shall live

840–69. Adam's sixth and final vision focuses on God's turn to peace and reconciliation after the judgmental wrath of the Flood.

840. **hull:** drift.

845. **of the fresh wave largely drew:** Cp. the thirsty sun of 5.422–26.

847. **tripping:** softly flowing.

851. **some high mountain:** "The Ark rested . . . upon the mountains of Ararat" (Gen. 8.4).

856. **the surer messenger:** surer, because the dove represents peace.

866. **three listed colors:** stripes formed from the primary colors, red, yellow, and blue.

867. **cov'nant new:** The covenant, as explained in lines 892–901, that God will never again flood the earth, which will instead be renewed by a purging fire.

With all the creatures, and their seed preserve.
Far less I now lament for one whole world
Of wicked sons destroyed, than I rejoice
For one man found so perfect and so just,
That God vouchsafes to raise another world
From him, and all his anger to forget.
But say, what mean those colored streaks in heav'n,
Distended as the brow of God appeased,
Or serve they as a flow'ry verge to bind
The fluid skirts of that same wat'ry cloud,
Lest it again dissolve and show'r the Earth?"
  To whom th' Archangel. "Dextrously thou aim'st;
So willingly doth God remit his ire,
Though late repenting him of man depraved,
Grieved at his heart, when looking down he saw
The whole Earth filled with violence, and all flesh
Corrupting each their way; yet those removed,
Such grace shall one just man find in his sight,
That he relents, not to blot out mankind,
And makes a cov'nant never to destroy
The Earth again by flood, nor let the sea
Surpass his bounds, nor rain to drown the world
With man therein or beast; but when he brings
Over the Earth a cloud, will therein set
His triple-colored bow, whereon to look
And call to mind his cov'nant: day and night,
Seed time and harvest, heat and hoary frost
Shall hold their course, till fire purge all things new,
Both heav'n and earth, wherein the just shall dwell."

880. **Distended:** expanded or loosened, as opposed to a brow contracted in anger.

881. **verge:** border, hem.

885–87. **So willingly . . . heart:** based on Gen. 6.6–7, a passage central to Milton's discussion of metaphor in the biblical representation of God (*CD* 1.2).

886–901. Here Milton weaves together Gen. 6.6, 9, 11–12; 8.22; 9.11–17; 2 Pet. 3.12–13.

Book XII

The Argument

The angel Michael continues from the Flood to relate what shall succeed; then, in the mention of Abraham, comes by degrees to explain who that seed of the woman shall be which was promised Adam and Eve in the Fall; his incarnation, death, resurrection, and ascension; the state of the church till his second coming. Adam greatly satisfied and recomforted by these relations and promises descends the hill with Michael; wakens Eve, who all this while had slept, but with gentle dreams composed to quietness of mind and submission. Michael in either hand leads them out of Paradise, the fiery sword waving behind them, and the Cherubim taking their stations to guard the place.

As one who in his journey bates at noon,
Though bent on speed, so here the Archangel paused
Betwixt the world destroyed and world restored,
If Adam aught perhaps might interpose;
Then with transition sweet new speech resumes.
"Thus thou hast seen one world begin and end;
And man as from a second stock proceed.
Much thou hast yet to see, but I perceive
Thy mortal sight to fail; objects divine
Must needs impair and weary human sense:
Henceforth what is to come I will relate,
Thou therefore give due audience, and attend.
This second source of men, while yet but few,
And while the dread of judgment past remains

1–5. This passage first appeared in 1674, where the long Book 10 of 1667 was divided into the current Books 11 and 12.

1. **bates:** pauses at an inn for refreshment.

7. **second stock:** Noah now takes the place of Adam, but the passage also glances at Christ, the stock onto which we are grafted in Rom. 11.17–27.

11. **I will relate:** Adam's instruction switches from visions to narrations, and the pace doubles, since the visions of Book 11 were first described and then explained. The six visions in Book 11 are structurally balanced by Michael's six main speeches in Book 12.

Fresh in their minds, fearing the Deity,
With some regard to what is just and right
Shall lead their lives, and multiply apace,
Laboring the soil, and reaping plenteous crop,
Corn, wine and oil; and from the herd or flock,
Oft sacrificing bullock, lamb, or kid,
With large wine-offerings poured, and sacred feast,
Shall spend their days in joy unblamed, and dwell
Long time in peace by families and tribes
Under paternal rule; till one shall rise
Of proud ambitious heart, who not content
With fair equality, fraternal state,
Will arrogate dominion undeserved
Over his brethren, and quite dispossess
Concord and law of nature from the Earth;
Hunting (and men not beasts shall be his game)
With war and hostile snare such as refuse
Subjection to his empire tyrannous:
A mighty hunter thence he shall be styled
Before the Lord, as in despite of Heav'n,
Or from Heav'n claiming second sov'reignty;
And from rebellion shall derive his name,
Though of rebellion others he accuse.
He with a crew, whom like ambition joins
With him or under him to tyrannize,
Marching from Eden towards the west, shall find
The plain, wherein a black bituminous gurge
Boils out from under ground, the mouth of Hell;
Of brick, and of that stuff they cast to build
A city and tow'r, whose top may reach to Heav'n;
And get themselves a name, lest far dispersed
In foreign lands their memory be lost,
Regardless whether good or evil fame.
But God who oft descends to visit men

24. **one shall rise:** Nimrod; as in Book II, proper names and place names are for the time being withheld.

27. **arrogate dominion:** In biblical history, Nimrod is the first tyrant; see Ralegh, *History of the World,* I.10.1.

30. **Hunting:** In Gen. 10.9, Nimrod is "a mighty hunter before the Lord."

34–35. **as in despite . . . sov'reignty:** Michael says that Nimrod's epithet (see previous note) means that he either brazenly defies God or invents the blasphemous doctrine of the divine right of kings.

36. *Nimrod* was sometimes said to derive from the Hebrew *marad,* "to rebel." The sense is that he is rebelling against God.

38–62. In presenting Nimrod as the builder of Babel, Milton follows the view of Josephus (*Antiq.* 1.4.2).

41. **The plain:** the site of Babylon; **gurge:** whirlpool.

Unseen, and through their habitations walks
To mark their doings, them beholding soon,
Comes down to see their city, ere the tower
Obstruct Heav'n tow'rs, and in derision sets
Upon their tongues a various spirit to raze
Quite out their native language, and instead
To sow a jangling noise of words unknown:
Forthwith a hideous gabble rises loud
Among the builders; each to other calls
Not understood, till hoarse, and all in rage,
As mocked they storm; great laughter was in Heav'n
And looking down, to see the hubbub strange
And hear the din; thus was the building left
Ridiculous, and the work Confusion named."
Whereto thus Adam fatherly displeased.
"O execrable son so to aspire
Above his brethren, to himself assuming
Authority usurped, from God not giv'n:
He gave us only over beast, fish, fowl
Dominion absolute; that right we hold
By his donation; but man over men
He made not lord; such title to himself
Reserving, human left from human free.
But this usurper his encroachment proud
Stays not on man; to God his tow'r intends
Siege and defiance. Wretched man! What food
Will he convey up thither to sustain
Himself and his rash army, where thin air
Above the clouds will pine his entrails gross,
And famish him of breath, if not of bread?"
To whom thus Michael. "Justly thou abhorr'st
That son, who on the quiet state of men
Such trouble brought, affecting to subdue
Rational liberty; yet know withal,
Since thy original lapse, true liberty
Is lost, which always with right reason dwells

52. **in derision:** "The Lord shall have them in derision" (Ps. 2.4).

53–54. **to raze . . . language:** In the context of *Paradise Lost,* this well-known biblical episode suggests both the original names of the rebel angels razed from the Books of Life (1.362–63) and the senseless hissing and spitting of the metamorphosed devils (10.504–77).

60. **hubbub:** reminiscent of Chaos, "a universal hubbub wild/Of stunning sounds and voices all confused" (2.951–52).

62. **Confusion named:** *Babel* was sometimes said to derive from the Hebrew *balal,* "to confound."

82. **Rational liberty:** the freedom proper to rational animals (but not to the subjected beasts).

84. **right reason:** conscience, innate knowledge of

Twinned, and from her hath no dividual being:
Reason in man obscured, or not obeyed,
Immediately inordinate desires
And upstart passions catch the government
From reason, and to servitude reduce
Man till then free. Therefore since he permits
Within himself unworthy powers to reign
Over free reason, God in judgment just
Subjects him from without to violent lords;
Who oft as undeservedly enthrall
His outward freedom: tyranny must be,
Though to the tyrant thereby no excuse.
Yet sometimes nations will decline so low
From virtue, which is reason, that no wrong,
But justice, and some fatal curse annexed
Deprives them of their outward liberty,
Their inward lost: witness th' irreverent son
Of him who built the ark, who for the shame
Done to his father, heard this heavy curse,
'Servant of servants,' on his vicious race.
Thus will this latter, as the former world,
Still tend from bad to worse, till God at last
Wearied with their iniquities, withdraw
His presence from among them, and avert
His holy eyes, resolving from thenceforth
To leave them to their own polluted ways;
And one peculiar nation to select
From all the rest, of whom to be invoked,
A nation from one faithful man to spring:
Him on this side Euphrates yet residing,
Bred up in idol-worship; O that men
(Canst thou believe?) should be so stupid grown,
While yet the patriarch lived, who scaped the Flood,
As to forsake the living God, and fall

---

what is just and right. See Hoopes. Michael observes that this faculty was impaired by the Fall, so that true liberty, which is obedience to right reason, was lost in the microcosm of the human soul before it was lost in the macrocosm of human government. Cp. 6.42n.

85. **dividual:** separate.

103. **this heavy curse:** See Noah's curse on Ham's sons in Gen. 9.25.

104. **race:** descendants.

111. **one peculiar nation:** *Peculiar,* meaning "uniquely favored" and used of the Jews or of Christian believers in phrases such as "peculiar nation" or "peculiar people," was once a common idiom sanctioned by Bible translation (*OED* B.1.1a).

113. **one faithful man:** Abraham; Milton's account of him derives from Gen. 11–25.

115. **Bred up in idol-worship:** See Josh. 24.2.

117. **the patriarch:** Noah lived 350 years after the Flood (Gen. 9.28).

To worship their own work in wood and stone
For gods! Yet him God the Most High vouchsafes
To call by vision from his father's house,
His kindred and false gods, into a land
Which he will show him, and from him will raise
A mighty nation, and upon him shower
His benediction so, that in his seed
All nations shall be blest; he straight obeys,
Not knowing to what land, yet firm believes:
I see him, but thou canst not, with what faith
He leaves his gods, his friends, and native soil
Ur of Chaldea, passing now the ford
To Haran, after him a cumbrous train
Of herds and flocks, and numerous servitude;
Not wand'ring poor, but trusting all his wealth
With God, who called him, in a land unknown.
Canaan he now attains, I see his tents
Pitched about Sechem, and the neighboring plain
Of Moreh; there by promise he receives
Gift to his progeny of all that land;
From Hamath northward to the desert south
(Things by their names I call, though yet unnamed)
From Hermon east to the great western sea,
Mount Hermon, yonder sea, each place behold
In prospect, as I point them; on the shore
Mount Carmel; here the double-founted stream
Jordan, true limit eastward; but his sons
Shall dwell to Senir, that long ridge of hills.
This ponder, that all nations of the Earth
Shall in his seed be blessed; by that seed
Is meant thy great Deliverer, who shall bruise
The serpent's head; whereof to thee anon
Plainlier shall be revealed. This patriarch blest,
Whom 'faithful Abraham' due time shall call,
A son, and of his son a grandchild leaves,

130. **Ur:** a city in ancient Babylonia.

131. **Haran:** a city on the Belikh, a tributary of the Euphrates, on the border of Canaan.

132. **servitude:** slaves and servants.

136. **Sechem:** commercial center in Canaan, present-day Nablus.

139–45. A precise description of the Promised Land, drawn mostly from Num. 34. Its northern border is the district of *Hamath,* its southern the *desert* of Zin, its western the Mediterranean (*great western sea*), and its eastern the river *Jordan, double-founted* because of the supposed confluence of the Jor and the Dan.

140. **Things by their names I call:** Michael calls attention to the sudden reintroduction of place names and (with Abraham in line 152) proper names, hitherto missing from Adam's second education (see 11.836–37n; 12.24n).

153. **son:** Isaac; **grandchild:** Jacob.

Like him in faith, in wisdom, and renown;
The grandchild with twelve sons increased, departs
From Canaan, to a land hereafter called
Egypt, divided by the river Nile;
See where it flows, disgorging at seven mouths
Into the sea: to sojourn in that land
He comes invited by a younger son
In time of dearth, a son whose worthy deeds
Raise him to be the second in that realm
Of Pharaoh: there he dies, and leaves his race
Growing into a nation, and now grown
Suspected to a sequent king, who seeks
To stop their overgrowth, as inmate guests
Too numerous; whence of guests he makes them slaves
Inhospitably, and kills their infant males:
Till by two brethren (those two brethren call
Moses and Aaron) sent from God to claim
His people from enthralment, they return
With glory and spoil back to their promised land.
But first the lawless tyrant, who denies
To know their God, or message to regard,
Must be compelled by signs and judgments dire;
To blood unshed the rivers must be turned,
Frogs, lice and flies must all his palace fill
With loathed intrusion, and fill all the land;
His cattle must of rot and murrain die,
Botches and blains must all his flesh emboss,
And all his people; thunder mixed with hail,
Hail mixed with fire must rend th' Egyptian sky
And wheel on th' earth, devouring where it rolls;
What it devours not, herb, or fruit, or grain,
A darksome cloud of locusts swarming down
Must eat, and on the ground leave nothing green:
Darkness must overshadow all his bounds,
Palpable darkness, and blot out three days;
Last with one midnight stroke all the first-born
Of Egypt must lie dead. Thus with ten wounds

160. **younger son:** Joseph.
165. **Suspected to:** an object of suspicion to.
166. **overgrowth:** excessive growth.
173. **denies:** refuses.
175. **signs and judgments dire:** the ten plagues of Exod. 7–12.
179. **murrain:** a cattle plague.
180. **Botches:** boils; **blains:** pustules; **emboss:** swell.
188. **Palpable darkness:** See 2.406n.

The river-dragon tamed at length submits
To let his sojourners depart, and oft
Humbles his stubborn heart, but still as ice
More hardened after thaw, till in his rage
Pursuing whom he late dismissed, the sea
Swallows him with his host, but them lets pass
As on dry land between two crystal walls,
Awed by the rod of Moses so to stand
Divided, till his rescued gain their shore:
Such wondrous power God to his saint will lend,
Though present in his angel, who shall go
Before them in a cloud, and pillar of fire,
By day a cloud, by night a pillar of fire,
To guide them in their journey, and remove
Behind them, while th' obdurate king pursues:
All night he will pursue, but his approach
Darkness defends between till morning watch;
Then through the fiery pillar and the cloud
God looking forth will trouble all his host
And craze their chariot wheels: when by command
Moses once more his potent rod extends
Over the sea; the sea his rod obeys;
On their embattled ranks the waves return,
And overwhelm their war: the race elect
Safe towards Canaan from the shore advance
Through the wild desert, not the readiest way,
Lest ent'ring on the Canaanite alarmed
War terrify them inexpert, and fear
Return them back to Egypt, choosing rather
Inglorious life with servitude; for life
To noble and ignoble is more sweet
Untrained in arms, where rashness leads not on.
This also shall they gain by their delay
In the wide wilderness, there they shall found
Their government, and their great senate choose
Through the twelve tribes, to rule by laws ordained:
God from the mount of Sinai, whose gray top

207. **defends:** prevents.

210. **craze:** shatter.

214. **war:** soldiers.

216. **not the readiest way:** The detour was intended to circumvent the warlike Philistines (Exod. 13).

217. **alarmed:** called to arms.

225. **great senate:** the Seventy Elders of Exod. 24.19 and Num. 11.16–30. Milton cites the Sanhedrin as a model senate in *REW* (p. 1124).

Shall tremble, he descending, will himself
In thunder, lightning, and loud trumpet's sound
Ordain them laws; part such as appertain
To civil justice, part religious rites
Of sacrifice, informing them, by types
And shadows, of that destined seed to bruise
The serpent, by what means he shall achieve
Mankind's deliverance. But the voice of God
To mortal ear is dreadful; they beseech
That Moses might report to them his will,
And terror cease; he grants what they besought
Instructed that to God is no access
Without mediator, whose high office now
Moses in figure bears, to introduce
One greater, of whose day he shall foretell,
And all the prophets in their age the times
Of great Messiah shall sing. Thus laws and rites
Established, such delight hath God in men
Obedient to his will, that he vouchsafes
Among them to set up his tabernacle,
The Holy One with mortal men to dwell:
By his prescript a sanctuary is framed
Of cedar, overlaid with gold, therein
An ark, and in the ark his testimony,
The records of his cov'nant, over these
A mercy-seat of gold between the wings
Of two bright Cherubim; before him burn
Seven lamps as in a zodiac representing
The heav'nly fires; over the tent a cloud
Shall rest by day, a fiery gleam by night,
Save when they journey, and at length they come,
Conducted by his angel to the land
Promised to Abraham and his seed: the rest
Were long to tell, how many battles fought,
How many kings destroyed, and kingdoms won,
Or how the sun shall in mid-heav'n stand still
A day entire, and night's due course adjourn,

232–33. **types/And shadows:** prefigurations of Christianity; cp. *shadowy types* (l. 303).

241. **Moses in figure bears:** Moses prefigures Christ as mediator between man and God.

247. **his tabernacle:** the Ark of the Covenant, which contained manna, the tables of the law, and Aaron's rod.

255. **Seven lamps as in a zodiac:** Josephus, *Antiq.*, 3.6–7, maintained that the seven lamps of the candlestick (Exod. 25.37) represented the seven planets.

Man's voice commanding, 'Sun in Gibeon stand,
And thou moon in the vale of Aialon,
Till Israel overcome'; so call the third
From Abraham, son of Isaac, and from him
His whole descent, who thus shall Canaan win."
Here Adam interposed. "O sent from Heav'n,
Enlight'ner of my darkness, gracious things
Thou hast revealed, those chiefly which concern
Just Abraham and his seed: now first I find
Mine eyes true op'ning, and my heart much eased,
Erewhile perplexed with thoughts what would become
Of me and all mankind; but now I see
His day, in whom all nations shall be blest,
Favor unmerited by me, who sought
Forbidden knowledge by forbidden means.
This yet I apprehend not, why to those
Among whom God will deign to dwell on Earth
So many and so various laws are giv'n;
So many laws argue so many sins
Among them; how can God with such reside?"
To whom thus Michael. "Doubt not but that sin
Will reign among them, as of thee begot;
And therefore was law given them to evince
Their natural pravity, by stirring up
Sin against law to fight; that when they see
Law can discover sin, but not remove,
Save by those shadowy expiations weak,
The blood of bulls and goats, they may conclude
Some blood more precious must be paid for man,
Just for unjust, that in such righteousness
To them by faith imputed, they may find
Justification towards God, and peace

265–67. **Sun . . . overcome:** Paraphrasing the words of Joshua when routing the five Amorite kings at Gibeon (Josh. 10.12–13). The episode appears among the subjects for a tragic poem listed in the *CMS*.

267. **so call the third:** Jacob, who is named *Israel* ("he that strives with God") by a mysterious wrestling opponent in Gen. 32.24–28.

274. **eyes true op'ning:** Adam alludes to the opening of the eyes Satan falsely promised Eve upon her eating the forbidden fruit (9.706–8, 985, 1053).

277. **His:** Abraham's.

287. **therefore was law given them:** It is a dictum of Christian (especially Protestant) theology, stemming from Paul, that law can discover sin but not purge it (Rom. 3.19–28, 4.15–16, 5.12–15).

288. **natural pravity:** original sin. See *CD* 1.11.

292. **blood of bulls and goats:** "It is not possible that the blood of bulls and of goats should take away sins" (Heb. 10.4).

293. **blood more precious:** "the precious blood of Christ" (1 Pet. 1.19).

295. **imputed:** attributed vicariously.

296. **Justification:** a theological term: "The judg-

Of conscience, which the law by ceremonies
Cannot appease, nor man the moral part
Perform, and not performing cannot live.
So law appears imperfect, and but giv'n
With purpose to resign them in full time
Up to a better cov'nant, disciplined
From shadowy types to truth, from flesh to spirit,
From imposition of strict laws to free
Acceptance of large grace, from servile fear
To filial, works of law to works of faith.
And therefore shall not Moses, though of God
Highly beloved, being but the minister
Of law, his people into Canaan lead;
But Joshua whom the Gentiles Jesus call,
His name and office bearing, who shall quell
The adversary serpent, and bring back
Through the world's wilderness long wandered man
Safe to eternal Paradise of rest.
Meanwhile they in their earthly Canaan placed
Long time shall dwell and prosper, but when sins
National interrupt their public peace,
Provoking God to raise them enemies:
From whom as oft he saves them penitent
By judges first, then under kings; of whom
The second, both for piety renowned
And puissant deeds, a promise shall receive
Irrevocable, that his regal throne
Forever shall endure; the like shall sing
All prophecy, that of the royal stock
Of David (so I name this king) shall rise
A son, the woman's seed to thee foretold,
Foretold to Abraham, as in whom shall trust
All nations, and to kings foretold, of kings
The last, for of his reign shall be no end.
But first a long succession must ensue,
And his next son for wealth and wisdom famed,
The clouded ark of God till then in tents

ment of God . . . by virtue of which those who are regenerate . . . are absolved from sins and from death through Christ's absolutely full satisfaction, . . . not by the works of the law but through faith" (*CD* 1.22, Yale 6:485).

310. **Joshua . . . Jesus call:** *Joshua* in Hebrew and *Jesus* in Greek both mean "savior."

316. **but:** except.

322. **a promise:** "Thy throne shall be established forever," Nathan promises King David (2 Sam. 7.16).

332. **his next son:** Solomon.

Wand'ring, shall in a glorious temple enshrine.
Such follow him, as shall be registered
Part good, part bad, of bad the longer scroll,
Whose foul idolatries and other faults
Heaped to the popular sum, will so incense
God, as to leave them, and expose their land,
Their city, his temple, and his holy ark
With all his sacred things, a scorn and prey
To that proud city, whose high walls thou saw'st
Left in confusion, Babylon thence called.
There in captivity he lets them dwell
The space of seventy years, then brings them back,
Rememb'ring mercy, and his cov'nant sworn
To David, 'stablished as the days of Heav'n.
Returned from Babylon by leave of kings
Their Lords, whom God disposed, the house of God
They first re-edify, and for a while
In mean estate live moderate, till grown
In wealth and multitude, factious they grow;
But first among the priests dissension springs,
Men who attend the altar, and should most
Endeavor peace: their strife pollution brings
Upon the temple itself: at last they seize
The scepter, and regard not David's sons,
Then lose it to a stranger, that the true
Anointed King Messiah might be born
Barred of his right; yet at his birth a star
Unseen before in Heav'n proclaims him come,
And guides the eastern sages, who inquire
His place, to offer incense, myrrh, and gold;
His place of birth a solemn angel tells
To simple shepherds, keeping watch by night;
They gladly thither haste, and by a choir
Of squadroned angels hear his carol sung.
A virgin is his mother, but his sire
The power of the Most High; he shall ascend

338. **Heaped to the popular sum:** added to the sins of the people.

343–47. The seventy years of the Babylonian Captivity were foretold in Jer. 25.12 and are described in 2 Kings 25, 2 Chron. 36.

348. **kings:** Cyrus, Darius, and Artaxerxes, the Persian kings under whom Jerusalem was rebuilt.

349. **disposed:** put in a favorable mood.

350. **re-edify:** rebuild, with spiritual overtones (see Coolidge 23–54).

358. **a stranger:** Antipater, whom Julius Caesar appointed ruler of Judea (now a Roman colony).

360. **Barred of:** barred from; **a star:** the star of Bethlehem, proclaiming Christ the true king.

The throne hereditary, and bound his reign
With Earth's wide bounds, his glory with the Heav'ns."
He ceased, discerning Adam with such joy
Surcharged, as had like grief been dewed in tears,
Without the vent of words, which these he breathed.
"O prophet of glad tidings, finisher
Of utmost hope! Now clear I understand
What oft my steadiest thoughts have searched in vain,
Why our great expectation should be called
The seed of woman: Virgin Mother, hail,
High in the love of Heav'n, yet from my loins
Thou shalt proceed, and from thy womb the Son
Of God Most High; so God with man unites.
Needs must the serpent now his capital bruise
Expect with mortal pain: say where and when
Their fight, what stroke shall bruise the victor's heel."
To whom thus Michael. "Dream not of their fight,
As of a duel, or the local wounds
Of head or heel: not therefore joins the Son
Manhood to Godhead, with more strength to foil
Thy enemy; nor so is overcome
Satan, whose fall from Heav'n, a deadlier bruise,
Disabled not to give thee thy death's wound:
Which he who comes thy Savior shall recure,
Not by destroying Satan, but his works
In thee and in thy seed: nor can this be,
But by fulfilling that which thou didst want,
Obedience to the law of God, imposed
On penalty of death, and suffering death,
The penalty to thy transgression due,
And due to theirs which out of thine will grow:
So only can high justice rest apaid.
The law of God exact he shall fulfill
Both by obedience and by love, though love
Alone fulfill the law; thy punishment
He shall endure by coming in the flesh
To a reproachful life and cursèd death,

379. **hail:** See 11.158n.
383. **capital:** both "on the head" and "fatal."
393. **recure:** heal.
396. **want:** lack.
401. **apaid:** satisfied, the debt paid; see 3.246.
403. **by love:** "Love is the fulfilling of the law" (Rom. 13.10).
406. Crucifixion for the Jews was an ultimate punishment, virtually damnation (Gal. 3.13). The Romans also regarded it as the "extreme and ultimate punishment of slaves" (Cicero, *Against Verres,* 2.5.169).

Proclaiming life to all who shall believe
In his redemption, and that his obedience
Imputed becomes theirs by faith, his merits
To save them, not their own, though legal works.
For this he shall live hated, be blasphemed,
Seized on by force, judged, and to death condemned
A shameful and accursed, nailed to the cross
By his own nation, slain for bringing life;
But to the cross he nails thy enemies,
The law that is against thee, and the sins
Of all mankind, with him there crucified,
Never to hurt them more who rightly trust
In this his satisfaction; so he dies,
But soon revives, Death over him no power
Shall long usurp; ere the third dawning light
Return, the stars of morn shall see him rise
Out of his grave, fresh as the dawning light,
Thy ransom paid, which man from death redeems,
His death for man, as many as offered life
Neglect not, and the benefit embrace
By faith not void of works: this Godlike act
Annuls thy doom, the death thou shouldst have died,
In sin forever lost from life; this act
Shall bruise the head of Satan, crush his strength
Defeating Sin and Death, his two main arms,
And fix far deeper in his head their stings
Than temporal death shall bruise the victor's heel,
Or theirs whom he redeems, a death like sleep,
A gentle wafting to immortal life.
Nor after resurrection shall he stay
Longer on Earth than certain times to appear
To his disciples, men who in his life
Still followed him; to them shall leave in charge
To teach all nations what of him they learned
And his salvation, them who shall believe
Baptizing in the profluent stream, the sign

409. **Imputed:** See 295n. In the Protestant doctrine of justification, Christ's obedience is *imputed* or "attributed vicariously" to the faithful Christian, who cannot by means of his own works merit salvation.

415–16. **to the cross . . . sins:** See Col. 2.14.

423. **fresh as the dawning light:** Although dawn as a symbol of resurrection was commonplace, Milton found great poetry in it; recall the various dawns in *Nativity Ode* and *Lycidas.*

432. **fix far deeper in his head:** The stings of Sin and Death are returned to their source in Satan's head (Flannagan); see 2.758.

442. **profluent:** flowing; Milton favored baptism in *profluentum aquam* (running water) (*CD* 1.28).

from guilt of sin to life
nd prepared, if so befall,
that which the Redeemer died.
ey shall teach; for from that day
the sons of Abraham's loins
shall be preached, but to the sons
Of ... am's faith wherever through the world;
So in his seed all nations shall be blest.
Then to the Heav'n of Heav'ns he shall ascend
With victory, triumphing through the air
Over his foes and thine; there shall surprise
The serpent, Prince of Air, and drag in chains
Through all his realm, and there confounded leave;
Then enter into glory, and resume
His seat at God's right hand, exalted high
Above all names in Heav'n; and thence shall come,
When this world's disolution shall be ripe,
With glory and power to judge both quick and dead,
To judge th' unfaithful dead, but to reward
His faithful, and receive them into bliss,
Whether in Heav'n or Earth, for then the Earth
Shall all be Paradise, far happier place
Than this of Eden, and far happier days."
So spake th' Archangel Michael, then paused,
As at the world's great period; and our sire
Replete with joy and wonder thus replied.
"O goodness infinite, goodness immense!
That all this good of evil shall produce,
And evil turn to good; more wonderful
Than that which by creation first brought forth
Light out of darkness! Full of doubt I stand,
Whether I should repent me now of sin
By me done and occasioned, or rejoice

447–50. The universal teaching of the Apostles fulfills the promise to Abraham that all nations (men of faith throughout the world) shall be blessed in his seed.

454. **Prince of Air:** as in Eph. 2.2; **drag in chains:** as in Rev. 20.1.

460. **quick:** living.

467. **period:** end.

470. **shall produce:** The subject of this verb is *goodness* in line 469.

475. **or rejoice:** See Lovejoy 1937 on the tradition of the *felix culpa* or "fortunate fall," and Danielson (202–27) for a vigorous denial of its relevance to *Paradise Lost.* Milton's version of the *felix culpa* is the central paradox of the epic. The Fall is not fortunate; the Fall is fortunate. Though Danielson may go too far in excluding the fortunate fall from the poem, he demonstrates that Milton's is importantly more subdued than some versions of *felix culpa.* Adam wonders whether his sin is the precondition of Christian salvation. But he does not rejoice in his disobedience, emphasizing instead the glorious power of God to create, even from his sin, *goodness immense* (l. 469).

Much more, that much more good thereof shall spring,
To God more glory, more good will to men
From God, and over wrath grace shall abound.
But say, if our Deliverer up to Heav'n
Must reascend, what will betide the few
His faithful, left among th' unfaithful herd,
The enemies of truth; who then shall guide
His people, who defend? Will they not deal
Worse with his followers than with him they dealt?"
"Be sure they will," said th' angel. "But from Heav'n
He to his own a comforter will send,
The promise of the Father, who shall dwell
His Spirit within them, and the law of faith
Working through love, upon their hearts shall write,
To guide them in all truth, and also arm
With spiritual armor, able to resist
Satan's assaults, and quench his fiery darts,
What man can do against them, not afraid,
Though to the death, against such cruelties
With inward consolations recompensed,
And oft supported so as shall amaze
Their proudest persecutors: for the Spirit
Poured first on his apostles, whom he sends
To evangelize the nations, then on all
Baptized, shall them with wondrous gifts endue
To speak all tongues, and do all miracles,
As did their Lord before them. Thus they win
Great numbers of each nation to receive
With joy the tidings brought from Heav'n: at length
Their ministry performed, and race well run,
Their doctrine and their story written left,
They die; but in their room, as they forewarn,
Wolves shall succeed for teachers, grievous wolves,
Who all the sacred mysteries of Heav'n
To their own vile advantages shall turn

478. **over wrath grace shall abound:** "Where sin abounded, grace did much more abound" (Rom. 5.20).

486. **a comforter:** the Holy Spirit.

488. **the law of faith:** Rom. 3.27.

489. **upon their hearts shall write:** See Paul's contrast between the Old Testament Law, written "on tables of stone," and the Gospel, written by "the Spirit of the living God" on "fleshly tables of the heart" (2 Cor. 3.3).

491. **spiritual armor:** See Eph. 6.11–17.

501. **speak all tongues:** See Mark 16–17, Acts 2.4–7; this miracle is precisely opposite to Babel's confusion of tongues (ll. 52–59).

508. **grievous wolves:** See Paul's warning about corrupt priests in Acts 20.29; and see 4.193n.

Of lucre and ambition, and the truth
With superstitions and traditions taint,
Left only in those written records pure,
Though not but by the Spirit understood.
Then shall they seek to avail themselves of names,
Places and titles, and with these to join
Secular power, though feigning still to act
By spiritual, to themselves appropriating
The Spirit of God, promised alike and giv'n
To all believers; and from that pretense,
Spiritual laws by carnal power shall force
On every conscience; laws which none shall find
Left them enrolled, or what the Spirit within
Shall on the heart engrave. What will they then
But force the Spirit of Grace itself, and bind
His consort Liberty; what, but unbuild
His living temples, built by faith to stand,
Their own faith not another's: for on Earth
Who against faith and conscience can be heard
Infallible? Yet many will presume:
Whence heavy persecution shall arise
On all who in the worship persevere
Of Spirit and Truth; the rest, far greater part,
Will deem in outward rites and specious forms
Religion satisfied; Truth shall retire
Bestuck with sland'rous darts, and works of faith
Rarely be found: so shall the world go on,
To good malignant, to bad men benign,
Under her own weight groaning till the day
Appear of respiration to the just,
And vengeance to the wicked, at return
Of him so lately promised to thy aid
The woman's seed, obscurely then foretold,

511–14. **the truth . . . understood:** Protestants believe that God's truth in the Scriptures must be apprehended not through church tradition or the teachings of the priesthood but by the individual believer, whose interpretation will ideally be guided by the Holy Spirit.

523–24. **enrolled . . . engrave:** The oppressive laws binding the Christian conscience will be found neither in biblical writing (*enrolled*) nor in the Spirit's writing on the heart (see 489n).

527. **living temples:** 1 Cor. 3.16: "Know ye not that ye are the temple of God?" Cp. 1.17.

528–30. **for on Earth . . . Infallible?:** a dismissal of the idea of papal infallibility. See *A Treatise of Civil Power* (Yale 7:244).

534. Here we print "Will" (1667) rather than "Well" (1674).

539. **Under her own weight groaning:** a groaning that began with *sighing* at the moment of Eve's fall (9.783) and continued with a *second groan* at the moment of Adam's fall (9.1001).

540. **respiration:** breathing space.

Now amplier known thy Savior and thy Lord,
Last in the clouds from Heav'n to be revealed
In glory of the Father, to dissolve
Satan with his perverted world, then raise
From the conflagrant mass, purged and refined,
New heav'ns, new earth, ages of endless date
Founded in righteousness and peace and love
To bring forth fruits, joy and eternal bliss."
He ended; and thus Adam last replied.
"How soon hath thy prediction, seer blest,
Measured this transient world, the race of time,
Till time stand fixed: beyond is all abyss,
Eternity, whose end no eye can reach.
Greatly instructed I shall hence depart,
Greatly in peace of thought, and have my fill
Of knowledge, what this vessel can contain;
Beyond which was my folly to aspire.
Henceforth I learn, that to obey is best,
And love with fear the only God, to walk
As in his presence, ever to observe
His providence, and on him sole depend,
Merciful over all his works, with good
Still overcoming evil, and by small
Accomplishing great things, by things deemed weak
Subverting worldly strong, and worldly wise
By simply meek; that suffering for truth's sake
Is fortitude to highest victory,
And, to the faithful, death the gate of life;
Taught this by his example whom I now
Acknowledge my Redeemer ever blest."
To whom thus also th' angel last replied:
"This having learnt, thou hast attained the sum
Of wisdom; hope no higher, though all the stars
Thou knew'st by name, and all th' ethereal powers,
All secrets of the deep, all nature's works,
Or works of God in heav'n, air, earth, or sea,
And all the riches of this world enjoyedst,

546. **dissolve:** terminate. It is impossible to decide on the basis of this one verb whether Milton has here altered his opinion on the endless sufferings of the devils in Hell (*CD* 1.33).

549. **New heav'ns, new earth:** See 2 Pet. 3.13.

555. **stand fixed:** stands out clearly.

559. **vessel:** human being.

565. **Merciful . . . works:** "His tender mercies are over all his works" (Ps. 145.9).

565–66. **with good . . . evil:** "Overcome evil with good" (Rom. 12.21).

567–68. **things . . . strong:** "God hath chosen the weak things of the world to confound the things which are mighty" (1 Cor. 1.27).

ıd all the rule, one empire; only add
Deeds to thy knowledge answerable, add faith,
Add virtue, patience, temperance, add love,
By name to come called charity, the soul
Of all the rest: then wilt thou not be loath
To leave this Paradise, but shalt possess
A paradise within thee, happier far.
Let us descend now therefore from this top
Of speculation; for the hour precise
Exacts our parting hence; and see the guards,
By me encamped on yonder hill, expect
Their motion, at whose front a flaming sword,
In signal of remove, waves fiercely round;
We may no longer stay: go, waken Eve;
Her also I with gentle dreams have calmed
Portending good, and all her spirits composed
To meek submission: thou at season fit
Let her with thee partake what thou hast heard,
Chiefly what may concern her faith to know,
The great deliverance by her seed to come
(For by the woman's seed) on all mankind.
That ye may live, which will be many days,
Both in one faith unanimous though sad,
With cause for evils past, yet much more cheered
With meditation on the happy end."
He ended, and they both descend the hill;
Descended, Adam to the bower where Eve
Lay sleeping ran before, but found her waked;
And thus with words not sad she him received.
"Whence thou return'st, and whither went'st, I know;
For God is also in sleep, and dreams advise,
Which he hath sent propitious, some great good
Presaging, since with sorrow and heart's distress
Wearied I fell asleep: but now lead on;

581–85. **only add . . . rest:** A similar list of virtues, also emphasizing charity, appears in 2 Pet. 1.

582. **answerable:** corresponding with.

587. The *paradise within* is not biblical. It is Milton's addition to the largely traditional, biblical, Pauline spiritual vocabulary of Book 12, and has behind it the entire weight of his poem; cp. Satan's Hell within (4.20). See Duncan (257–68) for analogues. **happier far:** happier than continuing, having fallen, to live in Eden (for which Adam and Eve yearned at 11.263–333).

594. **stay: go:** Note the conjunction of these words, for they will appear in Eve's forthcoming speech; see 9.372 for the first conjoining of *go* and *stay*.

604. **With cause for evils past:** "With good reason (referring back to *sad* in l. 603), in view of past misdeeds."

608. **ran before:** who had run before (to the bower); **found her waked:** In the prose Argument, Adam *wakens Eve*.

In me is no delay; with thee to go,
Is to stay here; without thee here to stay,
Is to go hence unwilling; thou to me
Art all things under Heav'n, all places thou,
Who for my willful crime art banished hence.
This further consolation yet secure
I carry hence; though all by me is lost,
Such favor I unworthy am vouchsafed,
By me the promised seed shall all restore."
    So spake our mother Eve, and Adam heard
Well pleased, but answered not; for now too nigh
Th' Archangel stood, and from the other hill
To their fixed station, all in bright array
The Cherubim descended; on the ground
Gliding meteorous, as ev'ning mist
Ris'n from a river o're the marish glides,
And gathers ground fast at the laborer's heel
Homeward returning. High in front advanced,
The brandished sword of God before them blazed
Fierce as a comet; which with torrid heat,
And vapor as the Libyan air adust,
Began to parch that temperate clime; whereat
In either hand the hast'ning Angel caught
Our ling'ring parents, and to th' eastern gate
Led them direct, and down the cliff as fast
To the subjected plain; then disappeared.
They looking back, all th' eastern side beheld
Of Paradise, so late their happy seat,
Waved over by that flaming brand, the gate
With dreadful faces thronged and fiery arms:
Some natural tears they dropped, but wiped them soon;
The world was all before them, where to choose
Their place of rest, and providence their guide:

615–20. Now the words linked at 9.372 (see note) and 12.594 (see note) are woven into a beautiful love lyric, full of internal rhymes and repetitions, in which the *paradise within* widens to include their love and marriage: *with thee to go,/Is to stay here,* in Paradise. Cp. Shakespeare, *ANT* 1.3.101–5.

629. **meteorous:** above the ground; see Hill (in Hill and Kerrigan 117–28) on the word's associations with Aristophanes, Plato, and Luke 12.29.

630. **marish:** marsh.

631. **laborer's heel:** Milton's myth spills out into everyday reality: Adam, and all after him, bear the curse of laboring, and their *heel,* in the terms of the protevangelium (see 10.175–81n), will one day feel the serpent sting of death.

635. **adust:** burnt up, scorched.

640. **subjected:** lying beneath.

643. **brand:** sword.

They hand in hand with wand'ring steps and slow,
Through Eden took their solitary way.

648. **hand in hand:** See 4.448, 689, 739.

648–49. The end-words of the last two lines quietly, satisfyingly rhyme with *go* and *stay* (see ll. 615–20n).

Introduction to *Paradise Regained*

An interesting anecdote about the composition of *Paradise Regained* comes from the memoirs of a Quaker named Thomas Ellwood. As a young man in 1662, he had arranged to meet the blind Milton in the hope of bettering his education and found the retired statesman willing. In exchange for reading to Milton, Ellwood was tutored in Latin. One day (perhaps in 1665) Milton loaned him a manuscript of *Paradise Lost.* Upon returning it, Ellwood remarked in a pleasant tone, "Thou hast said much here of Paradise lost, but what hast thou to say of Paradise found?" Milton, not answering, "sat some time in a muse" before changing the subject. Some while thereafter, date uncertain, Milton showed Ellwood a second manuscript, that of *Paradise Regained,* and told him, "This is owing to you; for you put it into my head by the question you put to me" (233–34).

One strongly suspects that Ellwood never achieved an understanding of his teacher on these occasions. It seems likely that Milton sat in a muse not because Ellwood had suddenly alerted him to a spiritual defect in *Paradise Lost* but because he was momentarily stunned that a reader of *Paradise Lost* (and Ellwood must have been one of the first) could be so simpleminded as to charge it with having little or nothing to say of "Paradise found": the poem names the "one greater man" who shall "restore us" in its first invocation, presents the invention of Christian salvation in the heavenly council of Book 3, emphasizes the Christian promise of the woman's seed bruising the serpent's head in the judgment scene of Book 10, and points biblical history in Books 11 and 12 toward the two comings of Christ. In handing Ellwood the manuscript of *Paradise Regained,* and thanking him for having inspired it, Milton passed on a friendly if impish fabrication, giving Ellwood the gift of a distinction that in his continuing simplemindedness he would accept and probably never forget, as in fact he did not. In a draft elegy for Milton, Ellwood celebrated him as the author of two complementary poems: "Th' one shows how man of Eden was bereft; / In t'other man doth Paradise regain" (Shawcross 2:86).

Further anecdotal information about *Paradise Regained* comes from Edward Phillips, the poet's nephew and former pupil. Having served at least for a while as Milton's amanuensis, he was as likely as anyone to know what the author was writing when, and therefore, despite numerous attempts by modern scholars to suggest an earlier composition, we are strongly inclined to accept his clear assertion that *Paradise Regained* was written after the publication of *Paradise Lost* in 1667, and in a very short period of time. That Milton made, relatively speaking, quick work of *Paradise Regained* is important for dating *Samson Agonistes*, since on that basis it is reasonable to assume that he had time to compose both the new epic and the drama between August 1667 and September 10, 1670, when the two works were entered in the Stationer's Register (see introduction to *Samson Agonistes*). They were published in one volume in 1671. The title of the epic appeared first on the title page, and in larger type, no doubt in part because the publisher hoped to sell the volume to owners of *Paradise Lost.*

Phillips also reported that, despite the "sublimeness" of the work, "it is generally censured to be much inferior to the other [*Paradise Lost*]." Milton, however, "could not hear with patience any such thing when related to him." Phillips wondered if the subject of the poem allowed for the "variety of invention" found in *Paradise Lost.* But even this difference was not in his view decisive: "It is thought by the judicious to be little or nothing inferior to the other for style and decorum" (Darbishire 75–76). The two works are connected by their titles, their blank verse, their progression through Christian history, their focus on temptation (the disobedient first Adam saved by the obedient second Adam), and the shared characters of Satan and the Son. It may be this element of connection that drove Milton to impatience when he heard that *Lost* was preferred to *Regained:* in his mind they were in some ways one work, not two. The only invocation establishes that Milton's inspiration in the present poem continues the inspiration of *Paradise Lost.*

But as the author must have realized, there are differences as well. Far from being inherent in the material or the result of declining artistic powers, they appear to be entirely deliberate. The style throughout aspires to a magnificent plainness that is expressly justified in the work when Jesus prefers the Hebrew Psalms to Greek poetry. As early as 1642, Milton gave expression to this aesthetic conviction when explaining in *The Reason of Church Government* that he had switched his literary ambitions from Latin to "the adorning of my native tongue." Something he suspected or did not like in the word *adorning* led to an immediate qualification: "not to make verbal curiosities the end, that were a toilsome vanity, but to be an interpreter and relater of the best and sagest things" (p. 840). The biblical "toilsome vanity" rebukes an infatuation with "verbal curiosities" lurking in the treacherous "adorning." There are quite a large number of verbal curiosities in *Paradise Lost.* One could (and should!) argue that they are not "the end" but rather the means by which meanings are generated in the large epic. One could (and should!) argue that they are successes rather than failures. An appreciation for the opulence of *Paradise Lost* dooms most of the world to prefer it to *Paradise Regained.*

But the brief epic's "studied reserve of ornament," in the phrase of its first annotator, Charles Dunster (Shawcross 2:377), also doomed Milton to shake his head over our stubborn frivolity. For he believed in a higher style, a style suitable for "an interpreter and related of the best and sagest things." The curtailing of simile and the simpler syntax in *Paradise Regained* are examples of what Phillips's judicious readers called "decorum," the adjustment of style to subject. Milton thought that Jesus exemplified a sublime plainness in both his life and his preaching. However audacious such a notion may seem to us, the opening lines of the work make it clear that, in the author's Christian mind, *Paradise Regained* is the epic *Aeneid* to *Paradise Lost*'s *Eclogues* and *Georgics*. The flashy literariness of *Paradise Lost* yields in maturity to a studied reserve of ornament.

Elizabeth M. Pope's *Paradise Regained: The Tradition and the Poem* (1947) remains indispensable for acquiring a knowledge of how the temptations were understood in the traditions of biblical exegesis, theological commentary, and Christian art. Barbara K. Lewalski's *Milton's Brief Epic: The Genre, Meaning, and Art of Paradise Regained* (1966), the first of her notable studies of genre, argues that the poem is what Milton called a "brief" epic, citing the Book of Job as its model (Yale 1:813). But neither the Book of Job, nor the poems based on it, nor the other brief epics surveyed by Lewalski have quite the atmosphere of high-minded debate found in *Paradise Regained*. Milton had certainly experimented in *Paradise Lost* with poetic debates—the council of fallen angels in Book 2, the exchanges between Satan and the angelic guard in Book 4, the debate between Satan and Abdiel at the end of Book 6, the argument between Adam and Eve over working separately in Book 9, and the mutual accusations of the fallen pair at the end of Book 9. Indeed, his interest in the poetry of argument could be traced back to the temptation scene in *A Masque* or to *L'Allegro* and *Il Penseroso*. But in *Paradise Regained*, the whole poem is built on the conversing of absolute contraries. The main problem with Lewalski's study is that she makes the poem sound more traditional than it actually is. "Among numerous Italian and French Biblical poems of the sixteenth and seventeenth centuries, I have found none which even remotely resembles *Paradise Regained*," MacKellar reported. "Milton, in short, displays a singular independence of traditional literary forms" (Hughes et al. 4:10).

Others have sought the genre of the poem not in the Book of Job but in Vergil's *Georgics* (Martz; Fowler 1984; Low 1985, 296–352). But this sort of classifying admits into one's sense of genre a rather alarming elasticity. The *Georgics* is didactic but not meditative, contains no action, and unlike *Paradise Regained* relies stylistically on profuse pictorial imagery and mythological allusion (Hughes et al. 4:15). Critics in search of English analogues have usually adduced Giles Fletcher's *Christ's Victory and Triumph* and Joseph Beaumont's *Psyche*. But Fletcher does not represent Mary, a significant presence in Milton. Neither work has the immense historical precision of Milton's temptation of the kingdoms, or the profoundly ironic recognition scene that he fashioned in the third temptation. As Northrop Frye observed, the work is "practically *sui generis*. None of the ordinary literary categories apply to it; its poetic predecessors are nothing like it, and it has left no descendants" (1965, 235). *Paradise Regained* has nothing essential in common with the stiffly allegorical Fletcher or the diffuse

Beaumont. However one may rank it vis-à-vis *Paradise Lost,* the fierce originality of the work ought to be appreciated.

A good deal of crucial material in *Paradise Regained* is left tacit and implicit. Milton does not expressly inform his readers, for example, exactly how much his protagonists know of each other. From Satan's "His first-begot we know, and sore have felt, / When his fierce thunder drove us to the deep; / Who this is we must learn" (1.89–91), we deduce that while Satan knows that Jesus is the woman's seed destined to bruise his head (1.64–65), he does not recognize in Jesus the Son of Book 6 of *Paradise Lost,* whose elevation prompted his envious rebellion and whose decisive appearance on the third day of the war drove him and his troops from Heaven. Jesus also indicates no knowledge of those cosmic events. He understands by searching the Scriptures that he is the prophesied Messiah, destined to redeem mankind and deliver a weakening blow to Satan (1.259–67), but he does not realize that defeating Satan belongs to his divinity as much as to his humanity. John Carey insists that Jesus in this poem never acts as more than a man, albeit a perfect one (1970, 124–30). But this reading blocks out the cosmic dimension in the climactic irony. Satan and Jesus move toward a showdown on the pinnacle. The Son manifests his divinity; Satan reels in amazement. The moment recapitulates the climax of *Paradise Lost*'s War in Heaven, as again Satan falls (or rather hurls himself, as before in *PL* 6.864–65), and again the victorious Son is hymned by angels.

Phillips was surely wrong in supposing that Milton cut back on invention. The first temptation is rendered pretty much as in Luke 4.2–4, then expanded by the lavish demonic banquet. This enlargement by invention creates a pattern of expectation confirmed in the second temptation. The Bible's unspecified "kingdoms of the world" full of political and religious "power and glory" (Luke 4.5–6) first become incarnate in the kingdoms of Parthia and Rome. Thus far Milton's version is full of novelties but not exactly inventions, since he is filling in the Bible's unspecified kingdoms with plausible particulars. But the Athenian temptation, with its shift from political and religious power and glory to literary and intellectual power and glory, is a real addition.

Plots based on counting and repetition normally place their climax on the third time, third wish, third temptation. An alert reader of *Paradise Regained* comes to the third temptation eager to apprehend its novelty. And it awaits him there, the life of the work, the most extraordinary of Milton's inventions.

PARADISE REGAINED

Book I

I who erewhile the happy garden sung,
By one man's disobedience lost, now sing
Recovered Paradise to all mankind,
By one man's firm obedience fully tried
Through all temptation, and the tempter foiled
In all his wiles, defeated and repulsed,
And Eden raised in the waste wilderness.
    Thou Spirit who led'st this glorious eremite
Into the desert, his victorious field
Against the spiritual foe, and brought'st him thence
By proof the undoubted Son of God, inspire,
As thou art wont, my prompted song else mute,
And bear through highth or depth of nature's bounds
With prosperous wing full summed to tell of deeds
Above heroic, though in secret done,
And unrecorded left through many an age,
Worthy t' have not remained so long unsung.

1–2. The opening lines allude to *Paradise Lost* via a four-line passage that appears at the beginning of the *Aeneid* in many Renaissance editions, where Vergil contrasts his rural pastoral songs with the martial subject of his epic; see Spenser, proem to *FQ*. Milton audaciously suggests that *PL*'s *happy garden* (not altogether so!) is a youthful pastoral in relation to the superlative epic heroism of *PR*.

2–4. "For as by one man's disobedience many were made sinners, so by the obedience of one shall many be made righteous" (Rom. 5.19).

8. **Spirit:** "Then was Jesus led up of the spirit into the wilderness" (Matt. 4.1). Conventionally, "spirit" in this verse was identified with the Holy Spirit, but Milton in *CD* 1.6, arguing against the idea of the Holy Spirit as a distinct person in the Godhead, concludes that the Holy Spirit "cannot be a God nor an object of invocation" (Yale 6:295); **eremite:** hermit, desert dweller.

12. **As thou art wont:** referring to the inspiration-aided creation of *PL*, and possibly other works.

14. **full summed:** in full plumage (falconry term).

16. **unrecorded:** But the Gospel accounts were recorded. Leonard would clear the problem away by supposing that *unrecorded* means "not rendered in song," yet what of poems such as Vida's *Christiad* (see *Passion* 26n)? According to Carey, the line implies that "Milton believed the events he adds to the gospel narrative really happened, and are revealed to him by the heavenly Muse." A similar difficulty arises with regard to *PL* 1.16.

Now had the great proclaimer with a voice
More awful than the sound of trumpet, cried
Repentance, and Heaven's Kingdom nigh at hand
To all baptized: to his great baptism flocked
With awe the regions round, and with them came
From Nazareth the son of Joseph deemed
To the flood Jordan, came as then obscure,
Unmarked, unknown; but him the Baptist soon
Descried, divinely warned, and witness bore
As to his worthier, and would have resigned
To him his heav'nly office, nor was long
His witness unconfirmed: on him baptized
Heaven opened, and in likeness of a dove
The Spirit descended, while the Father's voice
From Heav'n pronounced him his beloved Son.
That heard the Adversary, who roving still
About the world, at that assembly famed
Would not be last, and with the voice divine
Nigh thunderstruck, th' exalted man, to whom
Such high attest was giv'n, a while surveyed
With wonder, then with envy fraught and rage
Flies to his place, nor rests, but in mid-air
To council summons all his mighty peers,
Within thick clouds and dark tenfold involved,
A gloomy consistory; and them amidst
With looks aghast and sad he thus bespake.
"O ancient powers of air and this wide world,
For much more willingly I mention air,
This our old conquest, than remember Hell
Our hated habitation; well ye know
How many ages, as the years of men,
This universe we have possessed, and ruled
In manner at our will th' affairs of earth,
Since Adam and his facile consort Eve
Lost Paradise deceived by me, though since

18. **great proclaimer:** John the Baptist.
20. Cp. Matt. 3.2.
23. **son of Joseph deemed:** Luke 3.23.
26. **divinely warned:** See John 1.33.
29–32. Milton mainly follows Matt. 3.16–17: "He saw the spirit of God descending like a dove: and lo a voice from heaven, saying, This is my beloved Son, in whom I am well pleased."
33. **the Adversary:** Satan; **still:** continually.
39. **place:** home; for the notion that devils rule the air, see Eph. 2.2.
42. **consistory:** council; the term was applied to the Catholic senate of the Pope and cardinals, and to the ecclesiastical court of the Anglican Church.
48. **as the years of men:** as men measure time.
51. **facile:** easily led.

With dread attending when that fatal wound
Shall be inflicted by the seed of Eve
Upon my head, long the decrees of Heav'n
Delay, for longest time to him is short;
And now too soon for us the circling hours
This dreaded time have compassed, wherein we
Must bide the stroke of that long threaten'd wound,
At least if so we can, and by the head
Broken be not intended all our power
To be infringed, our freedom and our being
In this fair empire won of earth and air;
For this ill news I bring, the woman's seed
Destined to this, is late of woman born;
His birth to our just fear gave no small cause,
But his growth now to youth's full flow'r, displaying
All virtue, grace and wisdom to achieve
Things highest, greatest, multiplies my fear.
Before him a great prophet, to proclaim
His coming, is sent harbinger, who all
Invites, and in the consecrated stream
Pretends to wash off sin, and fit them so
Purified to receive him pure, or rather
To do him honor as their king; all come,
And he himself among them was baptized,
Not thence to be more pure, but to receive
The testimony of Heav'n, that who he is
Thenceforth the nations may not doubt; I saw
The prophet do him reverence, on him rising
Out of the water, Heav'n above the clouds
Unfold her crystal doors, thence on his head
A perfect dove descend, whate'er it meant,
And out of Heav'n the sov'reign voice I heard,
'This is my Son beloved, in him am pleased.'

53. **attending:** awaiting.

53–55. **that fatal wound . . . head:** The protevangelium or "first gospel" of Gen. 3.15 is crucial to the design of both *PL* (see 10.175–81n) and *PR.*

56. **longest time to him is short:** "A thousand years in thy sight art but as yesterday" (Ps. 90.4).

57. **too soon for us:** God has delayed the realization of his sentence with the grand nonchalance of an eternal being—but not long enough for the guilty devils. **circling hours:** See *PL* 6.3.

59. **bide:** endure.

60. **if so we can:** Whether devils may be mortal is a point of speculation in *PL* 2.94–101, 145–59.

62. **infringed:** broken (from Lat. *infrangere*).

66. Satan did not learn of Jesus at his baptism but has followed his life from infancy.

73. **Pretends:** claims.

83. **whate'er it meant:** Amazement in the face of divine action often characterizes the opponents of God in Milton's work; see *Areop,* p. 960, *PL* 12.496–97, *SA* 1645, and the supreme instance of this motif, *PR* 4.562.

His mother then is mortal, but his sire,
He who obtains the monarchy of Heav'n,
And what will he not do to advance his Son?
His first-begot we know, and sore have felt,
When his fierce thunder drove us to the deep;
Who this is we must learn, for man he seems
In all his lineaments, though in his face
The glimpses of his Father's glory shine.
Ye see our danger on the utmost edge
Of hazard, which admits no long debate,
But must with something sudden be opposed,
Not force, but well-couched fraud, well-woven snares,
Ere in the head of nations he appear
Their king, their leader, and supreme on earth.
I, when no other durst, sole undertook
The dismal expedition to find out
And ruin Adam, and the exploit performed
Successfully; a calmer voyage now
Will waft me; and the way found prosperous once
Induces best to hope of like success."
He ended, and his words impression left
Of much amazement to th' infernal crew,
Distracted and surprised with deep dismay
At these sad tidings; but no time was then
For long indulgence to their fears or grief:
Unanimous they all commit the care
And management of this main enterprise
To him their great dictator, whose attempt
At first against mankind so well had thrived
In Adam's overthrow, and led their march
From Hell's deep-vaulted den to dwell in light,
Regents and potentates, and kings, yea gods
Of many a pleasant realm and province wide.
So to the coast of Jordan he directs

87. **obtains:** holds.

89. **first-begot:** the Son; Satan then remembers *PL* 6.749–866.

91. **Who this is we must learn:** The high theological comedy of *PR* stems from this benighted quest. Satan already knows a great deal about Jesus: that he is the prophesied "woman's seed," that his fulfillment of the prophecy has been announced by John the Baptist, and that God himself has acknowledged Jesus as his Son. But Satan does not recognize in Jesus the thunder-wielding conqueror of *PL* 6, in part because *His mother . . . is mortal,* whereas the Son in Heaven did not have a mother. See *PR* 4.500–540n.

94–95. **the utmost edge/Of hazard:** Cp. Shakespeare, *AWW* 3.3.6.

97. **well-couched:** well concealed.

100–102. **I . . . Adam:** See *PL* 2.430–66.

107. **amazement:** alarm.

113. **dictator:** Roman term for a person given extraordinary powers during a time of emergency.

His easy steps; girded with snaky wiles,
Where he might likeliest find this new-declared,
This man of men, attested Son of God,
Temptation and all guile on him to try;
So to subvert whom he suspected raised
To end his reign on earth so long enjoyed:
But contrary unweeting he fulfilled
The purposed council preordained and fixed
Of the Most High, who in full frequence bright
Of angels, thus to Gabriel smiling spake.
"Gabriel, this day by proof thou shalt behold,
Thou and all angels conversant on earth
With man or men's affairs, how I begin
To verify that solemn message late,
On which I sent thee to the virgin pure
In Galilee, that she should bear a son
Great in renown, and called the Son of God;
Then told'st her doubting how these things could be
To her a virgin, that on her should come
The Holy Ghost, and the power of the Highest
O'ershadow her: this man born and now upgrown,
To show him worthy of his birth divine
And high prediction, henceforth I expose
To Satan; let him tempt and now assay
His utmost subtlety, because he boasts
And vaunts of his great cunning to the throng
Of his apostasy; he might have learnt
Less overweening, since he failed in Job,
Whose constant perseverance overcame
Whate'er his cruel malice could invent.
He now shall know I can produce a man
Of female seed, far abler to resist
All his solicitations, and at length
All his vast force, and drive him back to Hell,
Winning by conquest what the first man lost
By fallacy surprised. But first I mean

126. A similar irony is found in *PL* 1.210–20.

128. **frequence:** assembly.

129. **Gabriel:** the angel of the Annunciation (Luke 1.26–38) and commander of the angels standing watch over Paradise in *PL* (4.549–50).

143. **assay:** practice by way of trial.

144. **His utmost subtlety:** probably Satan's utmost subtlety, though the phrase might refer to Jesus.

147. **overweening:** arrogance; **Job:** Milton believed that the Book of Job was the model for a "brief epic" (p. 840). On the relationship between *PR* and Job, see Lewalski 1966, 10–36 and *passim.*

To exercise him in the wilderness,
There he shall first lay down the rudiments
Of his great warfare, ere I send him forth
To conquer Sin and Death the two grand foes,
By humiliation and strong sufferance:
His weakness shall o'ercome Satanic strength
And all the world, and mass of sinful flesh;
That all the angels and ethereal powers,
They now, and men hereafter may discern,
From what consummate virtue I have chose
This perfect man, by merit called my Son,
To earn salvation for the sons of men."
 So spake the Eternal Father, and all Heav'n
Admiring stood a space, then into hymns
Burst forth, and in celestial measures moved,
Circling the throne and singing, while the hand
Sung with the voice, and this the argument.
 "Victory and triumph to the Son of God
Now ent'ring his great duel, not of arms,
But to vanquish by wisdom hellish wiles.
The Father knows the Son; therefore secure
Ventures his filial virtue, though untried,
Against whate'er may tempt, whate'er seduce,
Allure, or terrify, or undermine.
Be frustrate all ye stratagems of Hell,
And devilish machinations come to naught."
 So they in Heav'n their odes and vigils tuned:
Meanwhile the Son of God, who yet some days
Lodged in Bethabara where John baptized,
Musing and much revolving in his breast,
How best the mighty work he might begin
Of savior to mankind, and which way first
Publish his Godlike office now mature,
One day forth walked alone, the Spirit leading;
And his deep thoughts, the better to converse

156. **exercise:** train by practice; prepare for a task by performing a similar but less difficult one.
159. **Sin and Death:** In *PL*, the offspring of Satan (2.648–73).
161. "God hath chosen the weak things of the world to confound the things which are mighty" (1 Cor. 1.27).
161–62. **Satanic . . . world . . . flesh:** See the renunciation of the world, the flesh, and the devil that precedes baptism in the Book of Common Prayer.
171. **the hand:** musical instruments played by hand.
172. **argument:** subject matter.
182. **vigils:** night hymns.
188. **his Godlike office:** On the tripartite "office" or role of the Son—as Prophet, King, and Priest—see Lewalski 1966, 182–92.

With solitude, till far from track of men,
Thought following thought, and step by step led on,
He entered now the bordering desert wild,
And with dark shades and rocks environed round,
His holy meditations thus pursued.
"O what a multitude of thoughts at once
Awakened in me swarm, while I consider
What from within I feel myself, and hear
What from without comes often to my ears,
Ill sorting with my present state compared.
When I was yet a child, no childish play
To me was pleasing, all my mind was set
Serious to learn and know, and thence to do
What might be public good; myself I thought
Born to that end, born to promote all truth,
All righteous things: therefore above my years,
The law of God I read, and found it sweet,
Made it my whole delight, and in it grew
To such perfection, that ere yet my age
Had measured twice six years, at our great feast
I went into the temple, there to hear
The teachers of our Law, and to propose
What might improve my knowledge or their own;
And was admired by all, yet this not all
To which my Spirit aspired; victorious deeds
Flamed in my heart, heroic acts, one while
To rescue Israel from the Roman yoke,
Then to subdue and quell o'er all the earth
Brute violence and proud tyrannic power,
Till truth were freed, and equity restored:
Yet held it more humane, more heav'nly, first
By winning words to conquer willing hearts,
And make persuasion do the work of fear;
At least to try, and teach the erring soul
Not wilfully misdoing, but unware

200. **sorting:** corresponding.

209–14. **To such perfection . . . by all:** Luke 2.46–50, to which Milton adds the idea that Jesus came to the Temple to teach the doctors.

218. **subdue and quell:** The young Jesus already considered, and rejected, a military conquest of the kingdoms of the world, such as Satan will offer him in 3.152–805.

220. **equity:** fairness; in law, an appeal to general precepts of justice in order to correct or supplement the normal provisions of the law (*OED* 2.3); see Hooker, *Of the Laws of Ecclesiastical Polity*, 5.9.3.

223. **persuasion:** "Persuasion certainly is a more winning, and more manlike way to keep men in obedience than fear" (*RCG* in Yale 1:746).

Misled; the stubborn only to subdue.
These growing thoughts my mother soon perceiving
By words at times cast forth inly rejoiced,
And said to me apart, 'High are thy thoughts
O son, but nourish them and let them soar
To what highth sacred virtue and true worth
Can raise them, though above example high;
By matchless deeds express thy matchless sire.
For know, thou art no son of mortal man,
Though men esteem thee low of parentage,
Thy father is the Eternal King, who rules
All Heav'n and Earth, angels and sons of men.
A messenger from God foretold thy birth
Conceived in me a virgin, he foretold
Thou shouldst be great and sit on David's throne,
And of thy kingdom there should be no end.
At thy nativity a glorious choir
Of angels in the fields of Bethlehem sung
To shepherds watching at their folds by night,
And told them the Messiah now was born,
Where they might see him, and to thee they came;
Directed to the manger where thou lay'st,
For in the inn was left no better room:
A star, not seen before in heav'n appearing
Guided the wise men thither from the east,
To honor thee with incense, myrrh, and gold,
By whose bright course led on they found the place,
Affirming it thy star new-grav'n in heav'n,
By which they knew thee King of Israel born.
Just Simeon and prophetic Anna, warned
By vision, found thee in the temple, and spake
Before the altar and the vested priest,
Like things of thee to all that present stood.'
This having heard, straight I again revolved
The law and prophets, searching what was writ
Concerning the Messiah, to our scribes
Known partly, and soon found of whom they spake
I am; this chiefly, that my way must lie

226. **subdue:** 1671 reads "destroy," corrected in the errata to "subdue"; cp. *PL* 6.40–41.

233. **express:** manifest.

238. **messenger:** Gabriel; see Luke 1.26–33 and Matt. 1.20–23.

253. **grav'n:** fixed.

255. **Simeon:** See Luke 2.25–35; **Anna:** See Luke 2.36–38.

259. **revolved:** studied.

Through many a hard assay even to the death,
Ere I the promised kingdom can attain,
Or work redemption for mankind, whose sins'
Full weight must be transferred upon my head.
Yet neither thus disheartened or dismayed,
The time prefixed I waited, when behold
The Baptist (of whose birth I oft had heard,
Not knew by sight) now come, who was to come
Before Messiah and his way prepare.
I as all others to his baptism came,
Which I believed was from above; but he
Straight knew me, and with loudest voice proclaimed
Me him (for it was shown him so from Heav'n)
Me him whose harbinger he was; and first
Refused on me his baptism to confer,
As much his greater, and was hardly won;
But as I rose out of the laving stream,
Heaven opened her eternal doors, from whence
The Spirit descended on me like a dove,
And last the sum of all, my Father's voice,
Audibly heard from Heav'n, pronounced me his,
Me his beloved Son, in whom alone
He was well pleased; by which I knew the time
Now full, that I no more should live obscure,
But openly begin, as best becomes
The authority which I derived from Heav'n.
And now by some strong motion I am led
Into this wilderness, to what intent
I learn not yet, perhaps I need not know;
For what concerns my knowledge God reveals."
    So spake our morning star then in his rise,
And looking round on every side beheld
A pathless desert, dusk with horrid shades;
The way he came not having marked, return
Was difficult, by human steps untrod;
And he still on was led, but with such thoughts
Accompanied of things past and to come

279. **hardly won:** persuaded with difficulty.

286–87. **the time/Now full:** "When the fullness of time was come, God sent forth his Son" (Gal. 4.4).

290. **motion:** divine prompting in the soul.

292. **I learn not yet:** But he will; his doing of all things in a timely fashion, obedient to the providential scheme of the Father, lies at the center of his perfection. "Even the Son . . . does not know absolutely everything, for there are some secrets which the Father has kept to himself alone" (*CD* 1.5, Yale 6:265).

294. **morning star:** Rev. 22.16.

296. **horrid:** bristling, shaggy.

Lodged in his breast, as well might recommend
Such solitude before choicest society.
Full forty days he passed, whether on hill
Sometimes, anon in shady vale, each night
Under the covert of some ancient oak,
Or cedar, to defend him from the dew,
Or harbored in one cave, is not revealed;
Nor tasted human food, nor hunger felt
Till those days ended, hungered then at last
Among wild beasts: they at his sight grew mild,
Nor sleeping him nor waking harmed, his walk
The fiery serpent fled, and noxious worm,
The lion and fierce tiger glared aloof.
But now an aged man in rural weeds,
Following, as seemed, the quest of some stray ewe,
Or withered sticks to gather; which might serve
Against a winter's day when winds blow keen,
To warm him wet returned from field at eve,
He saw approach, who first with curious eye
Perused him, then with words thus uttered spake.
"Sir, what ill chance hath brought thee to this place
So far from path or road of men, who pass
In troop or caravan? For single none
Durst ever, who returned, and dropped not here
His carcass, pined with hunger and with drought.
I ask thee rather, and the more admire,
For that to me thou seem'st the man, whom late
Our new baptizing prophet at the ford
Of Jordan honored so, and called thee Son
Of God; I saw and heard, for we sometimes
Who dwell this wild, constrained by want, come forth
To town or village nigh (nighest is far)
Where aught we hear, and curious are to hear,
What happens new; fame also finds us out."
To whom the Son of God. "Who brought me hither
Will bring me hence, no other guide I seek."
"By miracle he may," replied the swain.
"What other way I see not, for we here

302. **solitude before choicest society:** See *Masque* 375–80, *PL* 9.249, and Abraham Cowley's essay "Of Solitude."

303. **Full forty days:** Milton, like Matt. 4.2, puts the temptation at the end of forty days of fasting; Mark 1.13 and Luke 4.3 maintain that the temptation took forty days.

312. **noxious worm:** poisonous snake.

334. **fame:** rumor.

Live on tough roots and stubs, to thirst inured
More than the camel, and to drink go far,
Men to much misery and hardship born;
But if thou be the Son of God, command
That out of these hard stones be made thee bread;
So shalt thou save thyself and us relieve
With food, whereof we wretched seldom taste."
He ended, and the Son of God replied.
"Think'st thou such force in bread? Is it not written
(For I discern thee other than thou seem'st)
Man lives not by bread only, but each word
Proceeding from the mouth of God; who fed
Our fathers here with manna; in the mount
Moses was forty days, nor eat nor drank,
And forty days Eliah without food
Wandered this barren waste, the same I now.
Why dost thou then suggest to me distrust,
Knowing who I am, as I know who thou art?"
Whom thus answered th' Arch-Fiend now undisguised.
" 'Tis true, I am that spirit unfortunate,
Who leagued with millions more in rash revolt
Kept not my happy station, but was driv'n
With them from bliss to the bottomless deep,
Yet to that hideous place not so confined
By rigor unconniving, but that oft
Leaving my dolorous prison I enjoy
Large liberty to round this globe of earth,
Or range in th' air, nor from the Heav'n of Heav'ns
Hath he excluded my resort sometimes.
I came among the sons of God, when he

349–50. **Man . . . God:** It is written in Matt. 4.14 and Deut. 8.3.

352. **Moses:** See Exod. 24.18.

353. **Eliah:** Milton's idiosyncratic spelling of *Elijah;* for his forty-day fast, see 1 Kings 19.8.

354. **the same I now:** Commentators often identified the desert wilderness in which Jesus was tempted with the desert in which the Jews wandered for forty years and Moses and Elijah fasted (Pope 110–12). Milton earlier (1.193) places Jesus, more probably, in the desert between Jerusalem and Jericho. As Carey and Leonard suggest, Milton apparently chose typological elegance over realism.

355. **distrust:** The first temptation, especially for Protestants, was an occasion to distrust God as provider.

356. **Knowing who I am:** Some read the line as proof that Satan, despite his earlier doubt (see 1.91), really knows who the Son is. But there is no evidence to suggest that either of them, at this point in the poem, recognizes each other from their previous encounter in the War in Heaven (*PL* 6). They have instead proportionate knowledge of each other: Satan knows that Jesus is the prophesied redeemer, entitled Son of God; Jesus knows that Satan is the tempter of Eve and head of the fallen angels.

363. **unconniving:** unwinking.

368. **I came among the sons of God:** "The sons

Gave up into my hands Uzzean Job
To prove him, and illustrate his high worth;
And when to all his angels he proposed
To draw the proud King Ahab into fraud
That he might fall in Ramoth, they demurring,
I undertook that office, and the tongues
Of all his flatt'ring prophets glibbed with lies
To his destruction, as I had in charge.
For what he bids I do; though I have lost
Much luster of my native brightness, lost
To be beloved of God, I have not lost
To love, at least contemplate and admire
What I see excellent in good, or fair,
Or virtuous; I should so have lost all sense.
What can be then less in me than desire
To see thee and approach thee, whom I know
Declared the Son of God, to hear attent
Thy wisdom, and behold thy Godlike deeds?
Men generally think me much a foe
To all mankind: why should I? They to me
Never did wrong or violence, by them
I lost not what I lost, rather by them
I gained what I have gained, and with them dwell
Copartner in these regions of the world,
If not disposer; lend them oft my aid,
Oft my advice by presages and signs,
And answers, oracles, portents and dreams,
Whereby they may direct their future life.
Envy they say excites me, thus to gain
Companions of my misery and woe.
At first it may be; but long since with woe
Nearer acquainted, now I feel by proof,
That fellowship in pain divides not smart,

---

of God came to present themselves before the Lord, and Satan came also among them" (Job 1.6).

369. **Uzzean Job:** Job was from "the land of Uz" (Job 1.1).

372. **Ahab:** See 1 Kings 22.19–35. The "lying spirit" sent to destroy Ahab was identified with Satan. **fraud:** the state of being deceived.

373. **they demurring:** while they hesitated.

375. **glibbed:** made smooth.

383. The snarled locution seems to mean that Satan can feel no less than a desire to see and approach Jesus, but it flirts with the opposite sense: "This is the last thing I want to do."

385. **attent:** attentive.

393. **disposer:** both "giver" and "ruler."

394. **my advice:** Here Milton alludes to the idea that the devils spoke through the pagan gods and oracles; see *PL* 1.364–75.

397. **Envy:** malice.

400. **proof:** experience.

401. Satan repudiates an old maxim found especially in the friendship tradition. See Cicero, *Laelius: On Friendship* 7.23; Seneca, *De Consola-*

Nor lightens aught each man's peculiar load.
Small consolation then, were man adjoined:
This wounds me most (what can it less) that man,
Man fall'n shall be restored, I never more."
   To whom our Savior sternly thus replied.
"Deservedly thou griev'st, composed of lies
From the beginning, and in lies wilt end;
Who boast'st release from Hell, and leave to come
Into the Heav'n of Heav'ns; thou com'st indeed,
As a poor miserable captive thrall
Comes to the place where he before had sat
Among the prime in splendor, now deposed,
Ejected, emptied, gazed, unpitied, shunned,
A spectacle of ruin or of scorn
To all the host of Heav'n; the happy place
Imparts to thee no happiness, no joy,
Rather inflames thy torment, representing
Lost bliss, to thee no more communicable,
So never more in Hell than when in Heav'n.
But thou art serviceable to Heaven's King.
Wilt thou impute to obedience what thy fear
Extorts, or pleasure to do ill excites?
What but thy malice moved thee to misdeem
Of righteous Job, then cruelly to afflict him
With all inflictions, but his patience won?
The other service was thy chosen task,
To be a liar in four hundred mouths;
For lying is thy sustenance, thy food.
Yet thou pretend'st to truth; all oracles
By thee are giv'n, and what confessed more true
Among the nations? That hath been thy craft,
By mixing somewhat true to vent more lies.
But what have been thy answers, what but dark
Ambiguous and with double sense deluding,
Which they who asked have seldom understood,
And not well understood as good not known?
Whoever by consulting at thy shrine

---

tione ad Polybium 12.2; Thomas Browne, *Christian Morals* 1.18.

414. **emptied:** devoid of merit.

420. A worthy addition to the line of new Heaven-and-Hell aphorisms strewn across *PL*. It is anticipated at *PL* 9.118–23 and might be viewed as a dire reconfiguration of Satan's "To which the Hell I suffer seems a Heav'n" (*PL* 4.78).

435. **Ambiguous:** Their ambiguity was a familiar complaint against the pagan oracles, and not only among the church fathers; witness Cicero, *Of Divination* 2.56.

Returned the wiser, or the more instruct
To fly or follow what concerned him most,
And run not sooner to his fatal snare?
For God hath justly giv'n the nations up
To thy delusions; justly, since they fell
Idolatrous, but when his purpose is
Among them to declare his Providence
To thee not known, whence hast thou then thy truth,
But from him or his angels president
In every province, who themselves disdaining
To approach thy temples, give thee in command
What to the smallest tittle thou shalt say
To thy adorers; thou with trembling fear,
Or like a fawning parasite obey'st;
Then to thyself ascrib'st the truth foretold.
But this thy glory shall be soon retrenched;
No more shalt thou by oracling abuse
The Gentiles; henceforth oracles are ceased,
And thou no more with pomp and sacrifice
Shalt be inquired at Delphos or elsewhere,
At least in vain, for they shall find thee mute.
God hath now sent his living oracle
Into the world, to teach his final will,
And sends his Spirit of Truth henceforth to dwell
In pious hearts, an inward oracle
To all truth requisite for men to know."
So spake our Savior; but the subtle fiend,
Though inly stung with anger and disdain,
Dissembled, and this answer smooth returned.
"Sharply thou hast insisted on rebuke,
And urged me hard with doings, which not will
But misery hath wrested from me; where
Easily canst thou find one miserable,
And not enforced ofttimes to part from truth,
If it may stand him more in stead to lie,
Say and unsay, feign, flatter, or abjure?
But thou art placed above me, thou art Lord;

447. **president:** presiding. Milton speculates in *CD* 1.9 that "angels are put in charge of nations, kingdoms and particular districts."

456. **oracles are ceased:** Christians believed that the prophecy of Micah 5.12 was confirmed by Plutarch's *The Obsolescence of Oracles.* The oracles became dumb at the birth of Jesus (as in *Nat Ode* 173–80).

462. **Spirit of Truth:** See John 16.13.

466. **disdain:** loathing.

474. **Say and unsay:** See Milton's contemptuous dismissal of such behavior in *PL* 4.947–49.

From thee I can and must submiss endure
Check or reproof, and glad to scape so quit.
Hard are the ways of truth, and rough to walk,
Smooth on the tongue discoursed, pleasing to th' ear,
And tunable as sylvan pipe or song;
What wonder then if I delight to hear
Her dictates from thy mouth? Most men admire
Virtue, who follow not her lore: permit me
To hear thee when I come (since no man comes)
And talk at least, though I despair to attain.
Thy Father, who is holy, wise and pure,
Suffers the hypocrite or atheous priest
To tread his sacred courts, and minister
About his altar, handling holy things,
Praying or vowing, and vouchsafed his voice
To Balaam reprobate, a prophet yet
Inspired; disdain not such access to me."
   To whom our Savior with unaltered brow.
"Thy coming hither, though I know thy scope,
I bid not or forbid; do as thou find'st
Permission from above; thou canst not more."
   He added not; and Satan bowing low
His gray dissimulation, disappeared
Into thin air diffused: for now began
Night with her sullen wing to double-shade
The desert, fowls in their clay nests were couched;
And now wild beasts came forth the woods to roam.

476. **submiss:** submissive (lit. "placed beneath").

477. **to scape so quit:** to escape with such a relatively mild reprisal.

487. **atheous:** impious.

491–92. **To Balaam . . ./Inspired:** When Balaam was ordered by his king to curse the Jews, he obeyed God and blessed them instead (Num. 23.20).

494. **scope:** purpose.

498. **gray dissimulation:** The phrase appears in Ford's *The Broken Heart* 4.2.101.

500. **double-shade:** Cp. *Masque* 335.

Book II

Meanwhile the new-baptized, who yet remained
At Jordan with the Baptist, and had seen
Him whom they heard so late expressly called
Jesus Messiah, Son of God declared,
And on that high authority had believed,
And with him talked, and with him lodged, I mean
Andrew and Simon, famous after known
With others though in Holy Writ not named,
Now missing him their joy so lately found,
So lately found, and so abruptly gone,
Began to doubt, and doubted many days,
And as the days increased, increased their doubt:
Sometimes they thought he might be only shown,
And for a time caught up to God, as once
Moses was in the mount, and missing long;
And the great Thisbite who on fiery wheels
Rode up to Heav'n, yet once again to come.
Therefore as those young prophets then with care
Sought lost Eliah, so in each place these
Nigh to Bethabara; in Jericho
The city of palms, Aenon, and Salem old,
Machaerus and each town or city walled
On this side the broad lake Genezaret,
Or in Perea, but returned in vain.
Then on the bank of Jordan, by a creek

14–15. **as once/Moses:** See Exod. 32.1.

16. **great Thisbite:** Elijah, born in the city of Thisbe; the story of his ascension appears in 2 Kings 2.11.

17. **yet once again to come:** as foretold in Mal. 4.5.

19. **Eliah:** Milton's way of spelling *Elijah,* though he uses the more familiar spelling in line 268.

21. **Aenon and Salem old:** cities where, as in Bethabara, John baptized (John 3.23).

22. **Machaerus:** a desert fortress, where John was believed to have been executed.

23. **lake Genezaret:** Sea of Galilee.

24. **Perea:** a land to the east of Jordan.

Where winds with reeds, and osiers whisp'ring play,
Plain fishermen, no greater men them call,
Close in a cottage low together got
Their unexpected loss and plaints outbreathed.
"Alas, from what high hope to what relapse
Unlooked for are we fall'n, our eyes beheld
Messiah certainly now come, so long
Expected of our fathers; we have heard
His words, his wisdom full of grace and truth,
Now, now, for sure, deliverance is at hand,
The kingdom shall to Israel be restored:
Thus we rejoiced, but soon our joy is turned
Into perplexity and new amaze:
For whither is he gone, what accident
Hath rapt him from us? Will he now retire
After appearance, and again prolong
Our expectation? God of Israel,
Send thy Messiah forth, the time is come;
Behold the kings of the earth, how they oppress
Thy chosen, to what highth their power unjust
They have exalted, and behind them cast
All fear of thee; arise and vindicate
Thy glory, free thy people from their yoke,
But let us wait; thus far he hath performed,
Sent his anointed, and to us revealed him,
By his great prophet, pointed at and shown,
In public, and with him we have conversed;
Let us be glad of this, and all our fears
Lay on his Providence; he will not fail
Nor will withdraw him now, nor will recall,
Mock us with his blest sight, then snatch him hence;
Soon we shall see our hope, our joy return."
Thus they out of their plaints new hope resume
To find whom at the first they found unsought:
But to his mother Mary, when she saw
Others returned from baptism, not her son,
Nor left at Jordan, tidings of him none;
Within her breast, though calm, her breast though pure,
Motherly cares and fears got head, and raised
Some troubled thoughts, which she in sighs thus clad.

27. Imitating the opening line of Spenser's *SC*: "A shepherd's boy (no better do him call)."

40. **rapt:** carried off.

50. **his anointed:** *Messiah* means "the anointed one."

"O what avails me now that honor high
To have conceived of God, or that salute
Hail highly favored, among women blest;
While I to sorrows am no less advanced,
And fears as eminent, above the lot
Of other women, by the birth I bore,
In such a season born when scarce a shed
Could be obtained to shelter him or me
From the bleak air; a stable was our warmth,
A manger his, yet soon enforced to fly
Thence into Egypt, till the murd'rous king
Were dead, who sought his life, and missing filled
With infant blood the streets of Bethlehem;
From Egypt home returned, in Nazareth
Hath been our dwelling many years, his life
Private, unactive, calm, contemplative,
Little suspicious to any king; but now
Full grown to man, acknowledged, as I hear,
By John the Baptist, and in public shown,
Son owned from Heaven by his Father's voice;
I looked for some great change; to honor? No,
But trouble, as old Simeon plain foretold,
That to the fall and rising he should be
Of many in Israel, and to a sign
Spoken against, that through my very soul
A sword shall pierce; this is my favored lot,
My exaltation to afflictions high;
Afflicted I may be, it seems, and blest;
I will not argue that, nor will repine.
But where delays he now? Some great intent
Conceals him: when twelve years he scarce had seen,
I lost him, but so found, as well I saw
He could not lose himself; but went about
His Father's business; what he meant I mused,
Since understand; much more his absence now
Thus long to some great purpose he obscures.
But I to wait with patience am inured;
My heart hath been a storehouse long of things

67. **that salute:** Gabriel's salutation at Luke 1.28.
76. **the murd'rous king:** Herod; see Matt. 2.16.
87. **Simeon plain foretold:** Luke 2.34–35.
96–99. **when . . . business:** Mary recalls the disputation in the Temple (see 1.209–14).
101. **obscures:** keeps secret.
103–4. Milton combines Luke 2.19 ("Mary kept all these things, and pondered them in her heart") and Luke 2.51 ("His mother kept all these sayings in her heart").

And sayings laid up, portending strange events."
Thus Mary pondering oft, and oft to mind
Recalling what remarkably had passed
Since first her salutation heard, with thoughts
Meekly composed awaited the fulfilling:
The while her son tracing the desert wild,
Sole but with holiest meditations fed,
Into himself descended, and at once
All his great work to come before him set;
How to begin, how to accomplish best
His end of being on Earth, and mission high:
For Satan with sly preface to return
Had left him vacant, and with speed was gone
Up to the middle region of thick air,
Where all his potentates in council sat;
There without sign of boast, or sign of joy,
Solicitous and blank he thus began.
"Princes, Heaven's ancient sons, ethereal Thrones,
Demonian spirits now, from the element
Each of his reign allotted, rightlier called,
Powers of fire, air, water, and earth beneath,
So may we hold our place and these mild seats
Without new trouble; such an enemy
Is risen to invade us, who no less
Threatens than our expulsion down to Hell;
I, as I undertook, and with the vote
Consenting in full frequence was empowered,
Have found him, viewed him, tasted him, but find
Far other labor to be undergone
Than when I dealt with Adam first of men,
Though Adam by his wife's allurement fell,
However to this man inferior far,
If he be man by mother's side at least,
With more than human gifts from Heav'n adorned,
Perfections absolute, graces divine,
And amplitude of mind to greatest deeds.
Therefore I am returned, lest confidence
Of my success with Eve in Paradise

115. **preface:** earlier saying (Lat. *praefatio*); Satan said he would return (1.483–85).

116. **vacant:** at leisure.

120. **Solicitous:** anxious; **blank:** nonplussed.

122–24. Cp. *Il Pens* 93–96.

130. **frequence:** assembly.

131. **tasted:** examined, tested.

139. **amplitude of mind:** Cp. Cicero's "largeness of soul" (*amplitudinem animi*) in *Tusculan Disputations* 2.26.

Deceive ye to persuasion oversure
Of like succeeding here; I summon all
Rather to be in readiness, with hand
Or counsel to assist; lest I who erst
Thought none my equal, now be overmatched."
So spake the old serpent doubting, and from all
With clamor was assured their utmost aid
At his command; when from amidst them rose
Belial, the dissolutest spirit that fell,
The sensualest, and after Asmodai
The fleshliest incubus, and thus advised.
"Set women in his eye and in his walk,
Among daughters of men the fairest found;
Many are in each region passing fair
As the noon sky; more like to goddesses
Than mortal creatures, graceful and discreet,
Expert in amorous arts, enchanting tongues
Persuasive, virgin majesty with mild
And sweet allayed, yet terrible to approach,
Skilled to retire, and in retiring draw
Hearts after them tangled in amorous nets.
Such object hath the power to soften and tame
Severest temper, smooth the rugged'st brow,
Enerve, and with voluptuous hope dissolve,
Draw out with credulous desire, and lead
At will the manliest, resolutest breast,
As the magnetic hardest iron draws.
Women, when nothing else, beguiled the heart
Of wisest Solomon, and made him build,
And made him bow to the gods of his wives."
To whom quick answer Satan thus returned.
"Belial, in much uneven scale thou weigh'st
All others by thyself; because of old
Thou thyself dot'st on womankind, admiring
Their shape, their color, and attractive grace,
None are, thou think'st, but taken with such toys.

150. **the dissolutest spirit:** Belial is the lewdest of the devils, according to *PL* 1.490–91.

151. **Asmodai:** His lust for Sarah led him to destroy seven husbands (Tob. 3.8).

152. **incubus:** a demon that has intercourse with sleeping women (Augustine, *City of God* 15.23).

160. **terrible to approach:** Cp. *PL* 9.489–91.

164. **temper:** temperament.

165. **Enerve:** enervate, weaken.

166. **Draw out:** attract (continuing the idea of *amorous nets* in l. 162 and looking forward to the magnetic *draws* of l. 168).

169–71. On the amorous and religious faults of Solomon see, 1 Kings 11.4–8.

177. **toys:** unworthy trifles.

Before the Flood thou with thy lusty crew,
False titled Sons of God, roaming the earth
Cast wanton eyes on the daughters of men,
And coupled with them, and begot a race.
Have we not seen, or by relation heard,
In courts and regal chambers how thou lurk'st,
In wood or grove by mossy fountain-side,
In valley or green meadow to waylay
Some beauty rare, Calisto, Clymene,
Daphne, or Semele, Antiopa,
Or Amymone, Syrinx, many more
Too long, then lay'st thy scapes on names adored,
Apollo, Neptune, Jupiter, or Pan,
Satyr, or Faun, or Sylvan? But these haunts
Delight not all; among the sons of men,
How many have with a smile made small account
Of beauty and her lures, easily scorned
All her assaults, on worthier things intent?
Remember that Pellean conqueror,
A youth, how all the beauties of the east
He slightly viewed, and slightly overpassed;
How he surnamed of Africa dismissed
In his prime youth the fair Iberian maid.
For Solomon he lived at ease, and full
Of honor, wealth, high fare, aimed not beyond
Higher design than to enjoy his state;
Thence to the bait of women lay exposed;
But he whom we attempt is wiser far
Than Solomon, of more exalted mind,
Made and set wholly on the accomplishment
Of greatest things; what woman will you find,
Though of this age the wonder and the fame,
On whom his leisure will vouchsafe an eye
Of fond desire? Or should she confident,
As sitting queen adored on Beauty's throne,
Descend with all her winning charms begirt

178–81. Here Milton adopts a patristic tradition that the "sons of God" in Gen. 6.2–4 were fallen angels; but see *PL* 11.573–87, where he adopts the counterview that they were the sons of Seth.

186–88. A list of mortal women pursued by Greek and Roman gods, but actually pursued (as Satan here reveals) by lewd Belial.

189. **lay'st thy scapes:** blamed your escapades.

196. **Pellean conqueror:** Alexander the Great, born at Pella, treated female captives honorably (Plutarch, *Alexander* 21).

199. **he surnamed of Africa:** Scipio Africanus, who was presented with a comely Spanish captive after conquering Carthage and returned her to her betrothed (Livy 26.50).

To enamor, as the zone of Venus once
Wrought that effect on Jove, so fables tell;
How would one look from his majestic brow
Seated as on the top of Virtue's hill,
Discount'nance her despised, and put to rout
All her array; her female pride deject,
Or turn to reverent awe? For beauty stands
In the admiration only of weak minds
Led captive; cease to admire, and all her plumes
Fall flat and shrink into a trivial toy,
At every sudden slighting quite abashed:
Therefore with manlier objects we must try
His constancy, with such as have more show
Of worth, of honor, glory, and popular praise;
Rocks whereon greatest men have oftest wrecked;
Or that which only seems to satisfy
Lawful desires of nature, not beyond;
And now I know he hungers where no food
Is to be found, in the wide wilderness;
The rest commit to me, I shall let pass
No advantage, and his strength as oft assay."
He ceased, and heard their grant in loud acclaim;
Then forthwith to him takes a chosen band
Of spirits likest to himself in guile
To be at hand, and at his beck appear,
If cause were to unfold some active scene
Of various persons each to know his part;
Then to the desert takes with these his flight;
Where still from shade to shade the Son of God
After forty days fasting had remained,
Now hung'ring first, and to himself thus said.
"Where will this end? Four times ten days I have passed
Wand'ring this woody maze, and human food
Nor tasted, nor had appetite; that fast
To virtue I impute not, or count part
Of what I suffer here; if nature need not,

214. **zone of Venus:** Hera wore the girdle (*zone*) of Aphrodite when seducing Zeus (*Il.* 14.214–351).

220. **turn to:** turn into.

222–23. **plumes . . . shrink:** Ovid, discoursing on female love of praise in *The Art of Love* 1.627–28, adduces the example of "Juno's peacock," who spreads her plumes when complimented but hides them when confronted with male silence.

235. **grant:** assent.

242. **shade to shade:** shelter to shelter.

244. **Now hung'ring first:** Leonard, following Lewalski, thinks the passage contradicts 1.309. But this is overly scrupulous. Jesus, after forty days of fasting, observes in a general assessment of his situation that he is now hungry, precisely as the narrator has observed in 1.309.

Or God support nature without repast
Though needing, what praise is it to endure?
But now I feel I hunger, which declares,
Nature hath need of what she asks; yet God
Can satisfy that need some other way,
Though hunger still remain: so it remain
Without this body's wasting, I content me,
And from the sting of famine fear no harm,
Nor mind it, fed with better thoughts that feed
Me hung'ring more to do my Father's will."
    It was the hour of night, when thus the Son
Communed in silent walk, then laid him down
Under the hospitable covert nigh
Of trees thick interwoven; there he slept,
And dreamed, as appetite is wont to dream,
Of meats and drinks, nature's refreshment sweet;
Him thought he by the brook of Cherith stood
And saw the ravens with their horny beaks
Food to Elijah bringing even and morn,
Though ravenous, taught to abstain from what they brought;
He saw the prophet also how he fled
Into the desert, and how there he slept
Under a juniper; then how awaked,
He found his supper on the coals prepared,
And by the angel was bid rise and eat,
And eat the second time after repose,
The strength whereof sufficed him forty days;
Sometimes that with Elijah he partook,
Or as a guest with Daniel at his pulse.
Thus wore out night, and now the herald lark
Left his ground-nest, high tow'ring to descry
The morn's approach, and greet her with his song:
As lightly from his grassy couch uprose
Our Savior, and found all was but a dream;
Fasting he went to sleep, and fasting waked.
Up to a hill anon his steps he reared,
From whose high top to ken the prospect round,

259. Cp. John 4.34: "My meat is to do the will of him who sent me."

266. **brook of Cherith:** where ravens brought food to Elijah (1 Kings 17.5–6).

270. **the prophet:** Elijah, twice fed by an angel before his forty-day fast (1 Kings 19.4–8).

278. **Daniel at his pulse:** Daniel preferred *pulse* (lentils, beans, peas, et cetera) to the rich table of Nebuchadnezzar (Dan. 1.13–21); cp. *Masque* 721.

If cottage were in view, sheep-cote or herd;
But cottage, herd or sheep-cote none he saw,
Only in a bottom saw a pleasant grove,
With chant of tuneful birds resounding loud;
Thither he bent his way, determined there
To rest at noon, and entered soon the shade
High-roofed and walks beneath, and alleys brown
That opened in the midst a woody scene,
Nature's own work it seemed (nature taught art)
And to a superstitious eye the haunt
Of wood-gods and wood-nymphs; he viewed it round,
When suddenly a man before him stood,
Not rustic as before, but seemlier clad,
As one in city, or court, or palace bred,
And with fair speech these words to him addressed.
"With granted leave officious I return,
But much more wonder that the Son of God
In this wild solitude so long should bide
Of all things destitute, and well I know,
Not without hunger. Others of some note,
As story tells, have trod this wilderness;
The fugitive bond-woman with her son,
Outcast Nebaioth, yet found he relief
By a providing angel; all the race
Of Israel here had famished, had not God
Rained from Heav'n manna, and that prophet bold
Native of Thebez wand'ring here was fed
Twice by a voice inviting him to eat.
Of thee these forty days none hath regard,
Forty and more deserted here indeed."
To whom thus Jesus, "What conclud'st thou hence?
They all had need, I as thou seest have none."
"How hast thou hunger then?" Satan replied,
"Tell me if food were now before thee set,
Wouldst thou not eat?" "Thereafter as I like
The giver," answered Jesus. "Why should that

289. **bottom:** valley.

295. **(nature taught art):** In parenthetical shorthand, Milton addresses the old question of the relation of art to nature; for a similar perspective, see Shakespeare, *WT* 4.4.89–97.

302. **officious:** eager to please, obliging.

308. **fugitive bond-woman:** When Hagar and her son Ishmael were banished by Sarah, an angel saved Ishmael's life by leading Hagar to a well (Gen. 21.9–21). Satan calls Ishmael *Nebaioth,* the name of his first son.

312. **manna:** See Exod. 16.35; **prophet bold:** Elijah; Milton has confused *Thebez,* a city mentioned in Judges 9.50, with Thisbe, where Elijah was born.

321–22. **Thereafter . . . giver:** Cp. *Masque* 702.

Cause thy refusal," said the subtle fiend,
"Hast thou not right to all created things,
Owe not all creatures by just right to thee
Duty and service, nor to stay till bid,
But tender all their power? Nor mention I
Meats by the law unclean, or offered first
To idols, those young Daniel could refuse;
Nor proffered by an enemy, though who
Would scruple that, with want oppressed? Behold
Nature ashamed, or better to express,
Troubled that thou shouldst hunger, hath purveyed
From all the elements her choicest store
To treat thee as beseems, and as her Lord
With honor; only deign to sit and eat."
He spake no dream, for as his words had end,
Our Savior lifting up his eyes beheld
In ample space under the broadest shade
A table richly spread, in regal mode,
With dishes piled, and meats of noblest sort
And savor, beasts of chase, or fowl of game,
In pastry built, or from the spit, or boiled,
Grisamber-steamed; all fish from sea or shore,
Freshet, or purling brook, of shell or fin,
And exquisitest name, for which was drained
Pontus and Lucrine bay, and Afric coast.
Alas how simple, to these cates compared,
Was that crude apple that diverted Eve!
And at a stately sideboard by the wine
That fragrant smell diffused, in order stood
Tall stripling youths rich-clad, of fairer hue
Than Ganymede or Hylas; distant more
Under the trees now tripped, now solemn stood
Nymphs of Diana's train, and Naiades

324. **right to all created things:** See Heb. 1.2.
329. **young Daniel could refuse:** See Dan. 1.8.
340. **A table richly spread:** The banquet temptation, with no precedent either in the Bible or in tradition, is Milton's invention. Pope (70–79) argues that Milton wanted to strengthen the parallel between the temptations of Eve and Jesus, but the scene is in any case a great poetic setpiece with precedents in history (Lucan 10.115–16), romance (*Sir Gawain and the Green Knight* 884–94), and epic (Tasso, *GL* 10.64).
344. **Grisamber:** ambergris.
345. **shell:** Mosaic law forbids the consumption of shellfish, yet Satan has insisted that his banquet will not contain *Meats by the law unclean* (l. 328).
347. **Pontus:** the Black Sea; **Lucrine bay:** lagoon near Naples, famed for its oysters; **Afric coast:** the Nile, famed for its fish.
353. **Ganymede:** the handsome boy who served Zeus as his cupbearer; he was associated with homoerotic love. **Hylas:** the attractive boy who served Hercules.
354. **tripped:** stepped lightly.
355. **Naiades:** water nymphs.

With fruits and flowers from Amalthea's horn,
And ladies of th' Hesperides, that seemed
Fairer than feigned of old, or fabled since
Of fairy damsels met in forest wide
By knights of Logres, or of Lyonesse,
Lancelot or Pelleas, or Pellenore,
And all the while harmonious airs were heard
Of chiming strings, or charming pipes, and winds
Of gentlest gale Arabian odors fanned
From their soft wings, and Flora's earliest smells.
Such was the splendor, and the tempter now
His invitation earnestly renewed.
  "What doubts the Son of God to sit and eat?
These are not fruits forbidden; no interdict
Defends the touching of these viands pure;
Their taste no knowledge works, at least of evil,
But life preserves, destroys life's enemy,
Hunger, with sweet restorative delight.
All these are spirits of air, and woods, and springs,
Thy gentle ministers, who come to pay
Thee homage, and acknowledge thee their Lord:
What doubt'st thou Son of God? Sit down and eat."
  To whom thus Jesus temperately replied:
"Said'st thou not that to all things I had right?
And who withholds my power that right to use?
Shall I receive by gift what of my own,
When and where likes me best, I can command?
I can at will, doubt not, as soon as thou,
Command a table in this wilderness,
And call swift flights of angels ministrant
Arrayed in glory on my cup to attend:

356. **Amalthea's horn:** the cornucopia or horn of plenty with which Amalthea fed the infant Jupiter (Ovid, *Fasti* 5.115–28).

357. **Hesperides:** The Hesperides, the daughters of Hesperus, tended a garden containing golden apples; Milton calls the garden by their name.

360. **Logres:** the central area of Arthurian England; **Lyonesse:** the legendary land of Arthur's birth, now submerged.

361. A list of three Arthurian characters, all of whom appear in Malory's *Morte d'Arthur.* The adulterous and sometimes inebriated *Lancelot* is a major figure, but the ferociously combative *Pelleas* is a somewhat puzzling choice (though he pursues the Blatant Beast in Spenser's *FQ* 6.12); *Pellenore* was King of the Isles.

365. **Flora:** goddess of flowers.

368. **What doubts:** why hesitates.

369. **not fruits forbidden:** Satan ignores the shellfish (see 345n).

370. **Defends:** forbids.

378. **temperately:** The adverb has almost an allegorical force, in that Jesus, as he speaks, *is* the ideal pattern of temperance.

382. **likes:** pleases.

384. See Ps. 78.19.

Why shouldst thou then obtrude this diligence,
In vain, where no acceptance it can find,
And with my hunger what has thou to do?
Thy pompous delicacies I contemn,
And count thy specious gifts no gifts but guiles."
    To whom thus answered Satan malcontent:
"That I have also power to give thou seest,
If of that power I bring thee voluntary
What I might have bestowed on whom I pleased,
And rather opportunely in this place
Chose to impart to thy apparent need,
Why shouldst thou not accept it? But I see
What I can do or offer is suspect;
Of these things others quickly will dispose
Whose pains have earned the far-fet spoil." With that
Both table and provision vanished quite
With sound of harpies' wings, and talons heard;
Only th' importune tempter still remained,
And with these words his temptation pursued.
    "By hunger, that each other creature tames,
Thou art not to be harmed, therefore not moved;
Thy temperance invincible besides,
For no allurement yields to appetite,
And all thy heart is set on high designs,
High actions; but wherewith to be achieved?
Great acts require great means of enterprise;
Thou art unknown, unfriended, low of birth,
A carpenter thy father known, thyself
Bred up in poverty and straits at home;
Lost in a desert here and hunger-bit:
Which way or from what hope dost thou aspire
To greatness? Whence authority deriv'st,
What followers, what retinue canst thou gain,
Or at thy heels the dizzy multitude,
Longer than thou canst feed them on thy cost?
Money brings honor, friends, conquest, and realms;
What raised Antipater the Edomite,

387. **diligence:** persistent effort to please.
401. **far-fet:** far-fetched.
403. **harpies' wings:** Harpies are large birds with female faces who snatch food and defile tables (Vergil, *Aen.* 3.225–28).
404. **importune:** persistent.
406. **that each other creature tames:** that tames every other creature.
420. "Or gain the dizzy multitude at your heels."
423. **Antipater:** Proconsul of Judea; Josephus, *Antiq.* 14.1, stresses his combination of wealth and seditiousness.

And his son Herod placed on Judah's throne
(Thy throne) but gold that got him puissant friends?
Therefore, if at great things thou wouldst arrive,
Get riches first, get wealth, and treasure heap,
Not difficult, if thou hearken to me,
Riches are mine, fortune is in my hand;
They whom I favor thrive in wealth amain,
While virtue, valor, wisdom sit in want."
To whom thus Jesus patiently replied;
"Yet wealth without these three is impotent,
To gain dominion or to keep it gained.
Witness those ancient empires of the earth,
In highth of all their flowing wealth dissolved:
But men endued with these have oft attained
In lowest poverty to highest deeds;
Gideon and Jephtha, and the shepherd lad,
Whose offspring on the throne of Judah sat
So many ages, and shall yet regain
That seat, and reign in Israel without end.
Among the heathen, (for throughout the world
To me is not unknown what hath been done
Worthy of memorial) canst thou not remember
Quintius, Fabricius, Curius, Regulus?
For I esteem those names of men so poor
Who could do mighty things, and could contemn
Riches though offered from the hand of kings.
And what in me seems wanting, but that I
May also in this poverty as soon
Accomplish what they did, perhaps and more?
Extol not riches then, the toil of fools,
The wise man's cumbrance if not snare, more apt
To slacken virtue, and abate her edge,
Than prompt her to do aught may merit praise.

432. **patiently:** again with virtually allegorical force (see 378n); the effect, at once simple and sublime, is repeated throughout the remainder of the poem.

439. **Gideon:** He stressed his impoverished background when commanded by God to lead Israel (Judg. 6.15); **Jephtha:** another champion of Israel with an impoverished youth (Judg. 11.2–3); **shepherd lad:** David, Jesus' ancestor who rose from shepherd to king and was promised that his seed would reign forever (Isa. 9.6–7).

446. A list, this time drawn from the Gentile world, of men who rose from poverty to power. **Quintius:** Lucius Quinctius Cincinnatus, b. c. 519 B.C.E., a Roman farmer who was briefly dictator; **Fabricius:** Gaius Fabricius Luscinus, d. after 275 B.C.E., a Roman war hero who resisted bribes; **Curius:** Manius Curius Dentatus, d. 270 B.C.E., another Roman war hero who refused to be bribed; **Regulus:** Marcus Atilius Regulus, d. c. 250 B.C.E., a captured Roman general who chose death rather than ransom.

What if with like aversion I reject
Riches and realms; yet not for that a crown,
Golden in show, is but a wreath of thorns,
Brings dangers, troubles, cares, and sleepless nights
To him who wears the regal diadem,
When on his shoulders each man's burden lies;
For therein stands the office of a king,
His honor, virtue, merit and chief praise,
That for the public all this weight he bears.
Yet he who reigns within himself, and rules
Passions, desires, and fears, is more a king;
Which every wise and virtuous man attains:
And who attains not, ill aspires to rule
Cities of men or head-strong multitudes,
Subject himself to anarchy within,
Or lawless passions in him which he serves.
But to guide nations in the way of truth
By saving doctrine, and from error lead
To know, and knowing worship God aright,
Is yet more kingly; this attracts the soul,
Governs the inner man, the nobler part,
That other o'er the body only reigns,
And oft by force, which to a generous mind
So reigning can be no sincere delight.
Besides to give a kingdom hath been thought
Greater and nobler done, and to lay down
Far more magnanimous, than to assume.
Riches are needless then, both for themselves,
And for thy reason why they should be sought,
To gain a scepter, oftest better missed.

458. **for that:** because. It is not the burdens of kingship that Jesus rejects.

459. **wreath of thorns:** anticipating the crown of thorns and the mocking "Hail, King of the Jews!" (Matt. 27.29).

476. **this:** ruling over oneself.

478. **That other:** political kingship; **o'er the body only reigns:** "Thoughts are no subjects" (Shakespeare, *MM* 5.1.451); see Tilley T244.

482–83. **to lay down . . . magnanimous:** Milton praised Cromwell for refusing kingship (*2Def,* p. 1102).

Book III

So spake the Son of God, and Satan stood
A while as mute confounded what to say,
What to reply, confuted and convinced
Of his weak arguing, and fallacious drift;
At length collecting all his serpent wiles,
With soothing words renewed, him thus accosts.
"I see thou know'st what is of use to know,
What best to say canst say, to do canst do;
Thy actions to thy words accord, thy words
To thy large heart give utterance due, thy heart
Contains of good, wise, just, the perfect shape.
Should kings and nations from thy mouth consult,
Thy counsel would be as the oracle
Urim and Thummim, those oraculous gems
On Aaron's breast: or tongue of seers old
Infallible; or wert thou sought to deeds
That might require th' array of war, thy skill
Of conduct would be such, that all the world
Could not sustain thy prowess, or subsist
In battle, though against thy few in arms.
These godlike virtues wherefore dost thou hide?
Affecting private life, or more obscure
In savage wilderness, wherefore deprive
All earth her wonder at thy acts, thyself
The fame and glory, glory the reward

2. **confounded:** a perplexity in defeat that will reappear, worsened, at the opening of Book 4, then become absolute in the *amazement* of 4.562.

14. **Urim and Thummim:** the gems in Aaron's breastplate, associated with divination (Num. 27.21).

16. **sought to:** called upon for.

25. **Fame and glory:** often assumed in classical culture to be the main motives for high achievement, as in Cicero, *On Duties* 1.8.26; the movement from the temptation of riches to the temptation of vainglory is mirrored in Spenser's *FQ* 2.

That sole excites to high attempts the flame
Of most erected spirits, most tempered pure
Ethereal, who all pleasures else despise,
All treasures and all gain esteem as dross,
And dignities and powers, all but the highest?
Thy years are ripe, and over-ripe; the son
Of Macedonian Philip had ere these
Won Asia and the throne of Cyrus held
At his dispose, young Scipio had brought down
The Carthaginian pride, young Pompey quelled
The Pontic king and in triumph had rode.
Yet years, and to ripe years judgment mature,
Quench not the thirst of glory, but augment.
Great Julius, whom now all the world admires,
The more he grew in years, the more inflamed
With glory, wept that he had lived so long
Inglorious: but thou yet art not too late."
  To whom our Savior calmly thus replied.
"Thou neither dost persuade me to seek wealth
For empire's sake, nor empire to affect
For glory's sake by all thy argument.
For what is glory but the blaze of fame,
The people's praise, if always praise unmixed?
And what the people but a herd confused,
A miscellaneous rabble, who extol
Things vulgar, and well weighed, scarce worth the praise?
They praise and they admire they know not what;
And know not whom, but as one leads the other;
And what delight to be by such extolled,
To live upon their tongues and be their talk,
Of whom to be dispraised were no small praise?
His lot who dares be singularly good.
Th' intelligent among them and the wise

27. **erected:** high-minded, exalted.

31. **Thy years:** According to Luke 3.23, Jesus at the time of his baptism was "about thirty years of age."

31–34. **the Son . . . dispose:** Alexander the Great had conquered the Persian Empire at twenty-five.

34–35. **young Scipio . . . pride:** Scipio at twenty-seven enjoyed victory over the Carthaginians in Spain.

35–36. **young Pompey . . . rode:** Actually, Pompey was in his forties when he defeated Mithridates, the *Pontic king*, and celebrated his triumph in Rome.

39–42. Plutarch, *Life of Caesar* 11.3, tells how Caesar began to weep when reading a life of Alexander; asked why, he replied that he had just cause to weep, since Alexander at his age had conquered so many nations, whereas he (Caesar) had done nothing.

47–56. Contempt for popular acclaim in classical culture often went along with contempt for the *miscellaneous rabble* (l. 50): see Cicero, *Tusculan Disputations* 5.36.

Are few, and glory scarce of few is raised.
This is true glory and renown, when God
Looking on the earth, with approbation marks
The just man, and divulges him through Heav'n
To all his angels, who with true applause
Recount his praises; thus he did to Job,
When to extend his fame through Heav'n and Earth,
As thou to thy reproach may'st well remember,
He asked thee, 'Hast thou seen my servant Job?'
Famous he was in Heav'n, on Earth less known,
Where glory is false glory, attributed
To things not glorious, men not worthy of fame.
They err who count it glorious to subdue
By conquest far and wide, to overrun
Large countries, and in field great battles win,
Great cities by assault: what do these worthies,
But rob and spoil, burn, slaughter, and enslave
Peaceable nations, neighboring, or remote,
Made captive, yet deserving freedom more
Than those their conquerors, who leave behind
Nothing but ruin wheresoe'er they rove,
And all the flourishing works of peace destroy,
Then swell with pride, and must be titled gods,
Great benefactors of mankind, deliverers,
Worshipped with temple, priest and sacrifice;
One is the son of Jove, of Mars the other,
Till conqueror Death discover them scarce men,
Rolling in brutish vices, and deformed,
Violent or shameful death their due reward.
But if there be in glory aught of good,
It may by means far different be attained
Without ambition, war, or violence;
By deeds of peace, by wisdom eminent,
By patience, temperance; I mention still
Him whom thy wrongs with saintly patience borne,
Made famous in a land and times obscure;
Who names not now with honor patient Job?

59. **few:** It is precisely to "fit audience . . . though few" that *PL* is addressed (7.31).

60. **true glory and renown:** Cp. the distinction between earthly and heavenly fame in *Lyc* 70–84.

64. **thus he did to Job:** See Job 1.8.

81. **titled gods:** Kings and conquerors throughout the ancient world styled themselves gods; the Roman Senate bestowed divine titles on emperors.

82. **benefactors:** "The kings of the Gentiles . . . are called benefactors" (Luke 22.25).

86. **brutish vices:** Alexander drank heavily.

Poor Socrates (who next more memorable?)
By what he taught and suffered for so doing,
For truth's sake suffering death unjust, lives now
Equal in fame to proudest conquerors.
Yet if for fame and glory aught be done,
Aught suffered; if young African for fame
His wasted country freed from Punic rage,
The deed becomes unpraised, the man at least,
And loses, though but verbal, his reward.
Shall I seek glory then, as vain men seek
Oft not deserved? I seek not mine, but his
Who sent me, and thereby witness whence I am."
To whom the tempter murmuring thus replied.
"Think not so slight of glory; therein least
Resembling thy great Father: he seeks glory,
And for his glory all things made, all things
Orders and governs, nor content in Heav'n
By all his angels glorified, requires
Glory from men, from all men good or bad,
Wise or unwise, no difference, no exemption;
Above all sacrifice, or hallowed gift
Glory he requires, and glory he receives
Promiscuous from all nations, Jew, or Greek,
Or barbarous, nor exception hath declared;
From us his foes pronounced glory he exacts."
To whom our Savior fervently replied.
"And reason; since his word all things produced,
Though chiefly not for glory as prime end,
But to show forth his goodness, and impart
His good communicable to every soul
Freely; of whom what could he less expect
Than glory and benediction, that is thanks,
The slightest, easiest, readiest recompense
From them who could return him nothing else,
And not returning that would likeliest render
Contempt instead, dishonor, obloquy?
Hard recompense, unsuitable return

105. **seek glory:** "I seek not mine own glory" (John 8.50).

108. **murmuring:** complaining, accusing.

111. **for his glory:** See Rev. 4.11 and Milton, *CD* 1.7, where a number of biblical verses are cited.

119. **barbarous:** from the Greek, "foreign, non-Hellenic."

122. **And reason:** "And with good reason."

123–24. **chiefly . . . goodness:** That God's chief end in creation was to communicate his goodness, not just to achieve glory, was the opinion of Boethius, *Consolation of Philosophy* 3.9.4–9; Aquinas, *Summa Theologica* 1.44.4; and numerous other authorities.

For so much good, so much beneficence.
But why should man seek glory? Who of his own
Hath nothing, and to whom nothing belongs
But condemnation, ignominy, and shame?
Who for so many benefits received
Turned recreant to God, ingrate and false,
And so of all true good himself despoiled,
Yet, sacrilegious, to himself would take
That which to God alone of right belongs;
Yet so much bounty is in God, such grace,
That who advance his glory, not their own,
Them he himself to glory will advance."
    So spake the Son of God; and here again
Satan had not to answer, but stood struck
With guilt of his own sin, for he himself
Insatiable of glory had lost all,
Yet of another plea bethought him soon.
    "Of glory as thou wilt," said he, "so deem,
Worth or not worth the seeking, let it pass:
But to a kingdom thou art born, ordained
To sit upon thy father David's throne;
By mother's side thy father, though thy right
Be now in powerful hands, that will not part
Easily from possession won with arms;
Judaea now and all the promised land
Reduced a province under Roman yoke,
Obeys Tiberius; nor is always ruled
With temperate sway; oft have they violated
The temple, oft the law with foul affronts,
Abominations rather, as did once
Antiochus: and think'st thou to regain
Thy right by sitting still or thus retiring?
So did not Maccabeus: he indeed
Retired unto the desert, but with arms;

138. **recreant:** faithless, false.

140. **sacrilegious:** In *CD* 2.4, Milton defines *sacrilege* as "the appropriation of things vowed and dedicated to God."

154. **By mother's side thy father:** Matt. 1.1–16 and Luke 3.23–38 trace Jesus' genealogy back to David through Joseph; subsequent commentators assumed that Mary was also a descendant of David.

155. **in powerful hands:** in fact, in the hands of the Roman Empire.

160–61. **oft . . . temple:** Josephus, *Antiq.* 14, records outrages against the Temple and the law.

163. **Antiochus:** This Syrian emperor looted the Temple and forced the Jews to perform abominations (1 Macc. 1.20–2.61).

165. **Maccabeus:** Judas Maccabeus retired to Modin and rallied the Jews to defeat Antiochus (1 Macc. 3–5).

And o'er a mighty king so oft prevailed,
That by strong hand his family obtained,
Though priests, the crown, and David's throne usurped,
With Modin and her suburbs once content.
If kingdom move thee not, let move thee zeal,
And duty; zeal and duty are not slow;
But on Occasion's forelock watchful wait.
They themselves rather are occasion best,
Zeal of thy Father's house, duty to free
Thy country from her heathen servitude;
So shalt thou best fulfill, best verify
The prophets old, who sung thy endless reign,
The happier reign the sooner it begins;
Reign then; what canst thou better do the while?"
    To whom our Savior answer thus returned.
"All things are best fulfilled in their due time,
And time there is for all things, Truth hath said:
If of my reign prophetic writ hath told,
That it shall never end, so when begin
The Father in his purpose hath decreed,
He in whose hand all times and seasons roll.
What if he hath decreed that I shall first
Be tried in humble state, and things adverse,
By tribulations, injuries, insults,
Contempts, and scorns, and snares, and violence,
Suffering, abstaining, quietly expecting
Without distrust or doubt, that he may know
What I can suffer, how obey? Who best
Can suffer, best can do; best reign, who first
Well hath obeyed; just trial ere I merit
My exaltation without change or end.
But what concerns it thee when I begin
My everlasting kingdom, why art thou
Solicitous, what moves thy inquisition?
Know'st thou not that my rising is thy fall,
And my promotion will be thy destruction?"
    To whom the tempter inly racked replied.

171. **kingdom:** kingship.
173. **Occasion's forelock:** an allegorical commonplace, in which Occasion (opportunity) has a forelock that must be grasped, since she is bald behind: an occasion must either be grasped quickly or lost forever.
174. **They:** zeal and duty.
183. **time there is for all things:** "To every thing there is a season, and a time to every purpose under the heaven" (Eccles. 3.1).
187. "It is not for you to know the times or the seasons, which the Father hath put in his own power" (Acts 1.7).
203. **inly racked:** as Satan was in *PL* 1.126.

"Let that come when it comes; all hope is lost
Of my reception into grace; what worse?
For where no hope is left, is left no fear;
If there be worse, the expectation more
Of worse torments me than the feeling can.
I would be at the worst; worst is my port,
My harbor and my ultimate repose,
The end I would attain, my final good.
My error was my error and my crime
My crime; whatever for itself condemned,
And will alike be punished; whether thou
Reign or reign not; though to that gentle brow
Willingly I could fly, and hope thy reign,
From that placid aspect and meek regard,
Rather than aggravate my evil state,
Would stand between me and thy Father's ire,
(Whose ire I dread more than the fire of Hell)
A shelter and a kind of shading cool
Interposition, as a summer's cloud.
If I then to the worst that can be haste,
Why move thy feet so slow to what is best,
Happiest both to thyself and all the world,
That thou who worthiest art shouldst be their king?
Perhaps thou linger'st in deep thoughts detained
Of the enterprise so hazardous and high;
No wonder, for though in thee be united
What of perfection can in man be found,
Or human nature can receive, consider
Thy life hath yet been private, most part spent
At home, scarce viewed the Galilean towns,
And once a year Jerusalem, few days'
Short sojourn; and what thence couldst thou observe?
The world thou hast not seen, much less her glory,
Empires, and monarchs, and their radiant courts,
Best school of best experience, quickest in sight
In all things that to greatest actions lead.
The wisest, unexperienced, will be ever

204. **Let that come when it comes:** proverbial courage; see Tilley C529.

206. **no hope . . . no fear:** See *PL* 4.108, spoken by Satan on Mount Niphates, where he is about to carry Jesus in *PR*. The following lines contain other reminiscences of Satan's soliloquy.

207–8. **the expectation . . . me:** "the expectation of worse torments me more."

222. **summer's cloud:** perhaps drawn from Isa. 25.5.

234. **once a year:** "His parents went to Jerusalem every year at the feast of the passover" (Luke 2.41).

Timorous and loth, with novice modesty,
(As he who seeking asses found a kingdom)
Irresolute, unhardy, unadvent'rous:
But I will bring thee where thou soon shalt quit
Those rudiments, and see before thine eyes
The monarchies of the earth, their pomp and state,
Sufficient introduction to inform
Thee, of thyself so apt, in regal arts,
And regal mysteries; that thou may'st know
How best their opposition to withstand."
With that (such power was giv'n him then) he took
The Son of God up to a mountain high.
It was a mountain at whose verdant feet
A spacious plain outstretched in circuit wide
Lay pleasant; from his side two rivers flowed,
Th' one winding, the other straight, and left between
Fair champaign with less rivers interveined,
Then meeting joined their tribute to the sea:
Fertile of corn the glebe, of oil and wine,
With herds the pastures thronged, with flocks the hills;
Huge cities and high towered, that well might seem
The seats of mightiest monarchs, and so large
The prospect was, that here and there was room
For barren desert fountainless and dry.
To this high mountain top the tempter brought
Our Savior, and new train of words began.
"Well have we speeded, and o'er hill and dale,
Forest and field, and flood, temples and towers
Cut shorter many a league; here thou behold'st
Assyria and her empire's ancient bounds,
Araxes and the Caspian lake, thence on
As far as Indus east, Euphrates west,

242. Saul, looking for his father's lost asses, found Samuel, who anointed him king (1 Sam. 9.3–10).

244. **But I will bring thee where:** Exactly the same locution appears in *PL* 4.470, where the context also involves a change from frustration to fulfillment.

249. **regal mysteries:** both "political skills" and "secrets of state."

252. **mountain high:** probably Niphates, as A. Gilbert (1919, 210) maintains.

255. **two rivers:** the Tigris (*straight*) and the Euphrates (*winding*), which after their confluence empty into the Persian Gulf.

259. **glebe:** cultivated land.

266. **new train of words:** The words that follow are in the ornate manner of the geographical and historical panoramas in *PL* 1.386–521 and 11.387–411, but here the poetic ornamentation expressly reflects a corrupt view of human aspiration.

270. **ancient bounds:** Satan describes the boundaries of the Assyrian Empire at its height between 722 and 626 B.C.E.

271. **Araxes:** a river (now the Aras) emptying into the Caspian Sea.

And oft beyond; to south the Persian Bay,
And inaccessible the Arabian drought:
Here Nineveh, of length within her wall
Several days' journey, built by Ninus old,
Of that first golden monarchy the seat,
And seat of Salmanassar, whose success
Israel in long captivity still mourns;
There Babylon the wonder of all tongues,
As ancient, but rebuilt by him who twice
Judah and all thy father David's house
Led captive, and Jerusalem laid waste,
Till Cyrus set them free; Persepolis
His city there thou seest, and Bactra there;
Ecbatana her structure vast there shows,
And Hecatompylos her hundred gates,
There Susa by Choaspes, amber stream,
The drink of none but kings; of later fame
Built by Emathian, or by Parthian hands,
The great Seleucia, Nisibis, and there
Artaxata, Teredon, Ctesiphon,
Turning with easy eye thou may'st behold.
All these the Parthian, now some ages past,
By great Arsaces led, who founded first
That empire, under his dominion holds,
From the luxurious kings of Antioch won.

274. **drought:** desert.

275. **Nineveh:** The sizable capital of Assyria, founded by Ninus.

278. **Salmanassar:** He captured the ten northern tribes of Israel (2 Kings 18.9–11).

280. **wonder of all tongues:** Editors, remembering the identification of Babel with Babylon in *PL* 12.342–43, hear a punning reference to the confusion of tongues here, but it is doubtful that Satan would find the joke amusing.

281. **rebuilt by him:** Nebuchadnezzer, who restored Babylon, captured Jerusalem and brought most of the Jews to his capital (2 Kings 25.1–22).

284. **Cyrus:** founder of the Persian Empire, who conquered Babylon and freed the Jews (Dan. 5); *Persepolis, Bactra, Ecbatana, Hecatompylos,* and *Susa* were key cities in his empire.

288. **Choaspes:** Herodotus 1.188 mentions that the kings of Persia drink only from the river Choaspes, but subsequent commentators, confused, maintained that only Persian kings drink the waters of the Choaspes—hence Milton's *The drink of none but kings.*

290. **Emathian:** Macedonian (successors of Alexander).

291. **great Seleucia:** Seleucus Nicator, one of Alexander's generals, founded the Syrian monarchy of the Seleucidae in 301 B.C.E. and built a number of cities named after himself, including one on the river Tigris called *great. Nisibus,* modern Nisibin, is a city in northwestern Mesopotamia.

292. **Artaxata:** Armenian city on the river Araxes (now the Aras); **Teredon:** city at the junction of the Tigris and the Euphrates; **Ctesiphon**: city on the Tigris, near great Seleucus.

294–301. *Arsaces,* c. 250 B.C.E., invaded the Seleucid province of Parthia, which eventually won independence. Its ruler in the time of Christ was Artabanus III, who resisted Roman expansion as well as the barbarian Scythians.

And just in time thou com'st to have a view
Of his great power; for now the Parthian king
In Ctesiphon hath gathered all his host
Against the Scythian, whose incursions wild
Have wasted Sogdiana; to her aid
He marches now in haste; see, though from far,
His thousands, in what martial equipage
They issue forth, steel bows, and shafts their arms
Of equal dread in flight, or in pursuit;
All horsemen, in which fight they most excel;
See how in warlike muster they appear,
In rhombs and wedges, and half moons, and wings."
He looked and saw what numbers numberless
The city gates outpoured, light-armèd troops
In coats of mail and military pride;
In mail their horses clad, yet fleet and strong,
Prancing their riders bore, the flower and choice
Of many provinces from bound to bound;
From Arachosia, from Candaor east,
And Margiana to the Hyrcanian cliffs
Of Caucasus, and dark Iberian dales,
From Atropatia and the neighboring plains
Of Adiabene, Media, and the south
Of Susiana to Balsara's hav'n.
He saw them in their forms of battle ranged,
How quick they wheeled, and flying behind them shot
Sharp sleet of arrowy showers against the face
Of their pursuers, and overcame by flight;
The field all iron cast a gleaming brown,
Nor wanted clouds of foot, nor on each horn,
Cuirassiers all in steel for standing fight;
Chariots or elephants endorsed with towers

302. **Sogdiana:** the northernmost province of Alexander's empire.

309. **rhombs:** diamond-shaped formations; **wedges:** half rhombs; **half moons:** formations with the wings curved back, presenting an opponent with the army's main force; **wings:** divisions to the extreme right and left.

316. **Arachosia:** easternmost section of Parthia; **Candaor:** a province now part of Afghanistan.

317. **Margiana:** a region east of the Caspian Sea; **Hyrcanian:** Fertile Hyrcania lay to the south of Margiana.

318. **dark Iberian dales:** Iberia, modern Georgia, noted for its dense forests.

319. **Atropatia:** the northern portion of Media.

320. **Adiabene:** a plain near Nineveh.

321. **Susiana:** the southernmost province of Parthia; **Balsara's hav'n:** modern Basra, at the confluence of the Tigris and the Euphrates.

327. **clouds of foot:** translating the ***nimbus peditum*** of *Aen.* 7.793; **horn**: the wing of a formation (see 309n).

328. **Cuirassiers:** cavalry outfitted in cuirasses (plated body armor).

329. **endorsed:** fitted on their backs.

Of archers, nor of laboring pioneers
A multitude with spades and axes armed
To lay hills plain, fell woods, or valleys fill,
Or where plain was raise hill, or overlay
With bridges rivers proud, as with a yoke;
Mules after these, camels and dromedaries,
And wagons fraught with utensils of war.
Such forces met not, nor so wide a camp,
When Agrican with all his northern powers
Besieged Albracca, as romances tell;
The city of Gallaphrone, from thence to win
The fairest of her sex Angelica
His daughter, sought by many prowest knights,
Both paynim, and the peers of Charlemagne.
Such and so numerous was their chivalry;
At sight whereof the fiend yet more presumed,
And to our Savior thus his words renewed.
"That thou may'st know I seek not to engage
Thy virtue, and not every way secure
On no slight grounds thy safety; hear, and mark
To what end I have brought thee hither and shown
All this fair sight; thy kingdom though foretold
By prophet or by angel, unless thou
Endeavor, as thy father David did,
Thou never shalt obtain; prediction still
In all things, and all men, supposes means;
Without means used, what it predicts revokes.
But say thou wert possessed of David's throne
By free consent of all, none opposite,
Samaritan or Jew; how couldst thou hope
Long to enjoy it quiet and secure,
Between two such enclosing enemies
Roman and Parthian? Therefore one of these
Thou must make sure thy own; the Parthian first
By my advice, as nearer and of late

337–44. Milton compares the *numbers numberless* (l. 310) of the Parthian army to the army of 2.2 million with which the Tartar king Agrican besieges Albracca in Boiardo's *Orlando Innamorato* 1.5–14.

347–49. **That . . . safety:** "So you may know that I do not intend to rouse your valor without making sure of your safety."

358. **opposite:** opposing.

359. **Samaritan or Jew:** By Christ's time, the Samaritans (whom the Jews despised as mongrels) occupied the northern territory where the ten tribes had lived. So Samaritans and Jews would have had to agree to accept Jesus as the king of David's old kingdom.

364–67. These events *of late* took place around 40 B.C.E. The Parthians invaded Syria and captured and eventually killed *Hyrcanus* II. But *Antigonus,*

Found able by invasion to annoy
Thy country, and captive lead away her kings
Antigonus, and old Hyrcanus bound,
Maugre the Roman: it shall be my task
To render thee the Parthian at dispose;
Choose which thou wilt by conquest or by league.
By him thou shalt regain, without him not,
That which alone can truly reinstall thee
In David's royal seat, his true successor,
Deliverance of thy brethren, those ten tribes
Whose offspring in his territory yet serve
In Habor, and among the Medes dispersed;
Ten sons of Jacob, two of Joseph lost
Thus long from Israel; serving as of old
Their fathers in the land of Egypt served,
This offer sets before thee to deliver.
These if from servitude thou shalt restore
To their inheritance, then, nor till then,
Thou on the throne of David in full glory,
From Egypt to Euphrates and beyond
Shalt reign, and Rome or Caesar not need fear."
  To whom our Savior answered thus unmoved.
"Much ostentation vain of fleshly arm,
And fragile arms, much instrument of war
Long in preparing, soon to nothing brought,
Before mine eyes thou hast set; and in my ear
Vented much policy, and projects deep
Of enemies, of aids, battles and leagues,
Plausible to the world, to me worth naught.
Means I must use thou say'st, prediction else
Will unpredict and fail me of the throne:
My time I told thee (and that time for thee
Were better farthest off) is not yet come;
When that comes think not thou to find me slack
On my part aught endeavoring, or to need

far from being captured, was installed as king of Judea. It is difficult to believe that Milton intended the inaccuracy.

368. **Maugre:** in spite of.

374. **ten tribes:** the tribes captured by Salmanassar (l. 278).

376. **Habor:** a tributary of the Euphrates.

377. **Jacob:** the patriarch of the ten lost tribes, two of which are also descended from his son *Joseph.*

384. **Egypt to Euphrates:** God told Abraham that the promised land stretched from "the river of Egypt unto . . . the river Euphrates" (Gen. 15.18).

387. **fleshly arm:** Cp. the "arm of flesh" that can do little without divine aid in 2 Chron. 32.8 and Jer. 17.5.

396–97. "My time is not yet come," Jesus tells his brothers in John 7.6.

Thy politic maxims, or that cumbersome
Luggage of war there shown me, argument
Of human weakness rather than of strength.
My brethren, as thou call'st them, those ten tribes
I must deliver, if I mean to reign
David's true heir, and his full scepter sway
To just extent over all Israel's sons;
But whence to thee this zeal, where was it then
For Israel, or for David, or his throne,
When thou stood'st up his tempter to the pride
Of numb'ring Israel, which cost the lives
Of threescore and ten thousand Israelites
By three days' pestilence? Such was thy zeal
To Israel then, the same that now to me.
As for those captive tribes, themselves were they
Who wrought their own captivity, fell off
From God to worship calves, the deities
Of Egypt, Baal next and Ashtaroth,
And all the idolatries of Heathen round,
Besides their other worse than heathenish crimes;
Nor in the land of their captivity
Humbled themselves, or penitent besought
The God of their forefathers; but so died
Impenitent, and left a race behind
Like to themselves, distinguishable scarce
From Gentiles, but by circumcision vain,
And God with idols in their worship joined.
Should I of these the liberty regard,
Who freed, as to their ancient patrimony,
Unhumbled, unrepentant, unreformed,
Headlong would follow, and to their gods perhaps
Of Bethel and of Dan? No, let them serve
Their enemies, who serve idols with God.
Yet he at length, time to himself best known,
Rememb'ring Abraham by some wond'rous call
May bring them back repentant and sincere,
And at their passing cleave the Assyrian flood,

401. **Luggage:** encumbrance.

410. **num'bring Israel:** Displeased by this census, God sent a plague that killed 70,000 (1 Chron. 21.1–14).

415–16. **fell off/From God:** Jesus remembers the heathenish practices of the ten tribes in 1 Kings 12.25–33, 16.31–32, 17.7–18.

425. **circumcision vain:** See Rom. 2.25.

428. **patrimony:** heritage (of worshiping idols).

436. **Assyrian flood:** the Euphrates, which figures in Isaiah's prophecy about the return of the lost tribes (Isa. 11.15–16).

While to their native land with joy they haste,
As the Red Sea and Jordan once he cleft,
When to the promised land their fathers passed;
To his due time and providence I leave them."
    So spake Israel's true King, and to the fiend
Made answer meet, that made void all his wiles.
So fares it when with truth falsehood contends.

438. God divided the Red Sea (Exod. 14.21–22) and the Jordan (Josh. 3.14–17).

Book IV

Perplexed and troubled at his bad success
The tempter stood, nor had what to reply,
Discovered in his fraud, thrown from his hope,
So oft, and the persuasive rhetoric
That sleeked his tongue, and won so much on Eve,
So little here, nay lost; but Eve was Eve,
This far his overmatch, who self-deceived
And rash, beforehand had no better weighed
The strength he was to cope with, or his own:
But as a man who had been matchless held
In cunning, over-reached where least he thought,
To salve his credit, and for very spite
Still will be tempting him who foils him still,
And never cease, though to his shame the more;
Or as a swarm of flies in vintage time,
About the wine-press where sweet must is poured,
Beat off, returns as oft with humming sound;
Or surging waves against a solid rock,
Though all to shivers dashed, the assault renew,
Vain battery, and in froth or bubbles end;
So Satan, whom repulse upon repulse
Met ever; and to shameful silence brought,
Yet gives not o'er though desperate of success,
And his vain importunity pursues.
He brought our Savior to the western side
Of that high mountain, whence he might behold
Another plain, long but in breadth not wide;
Washed by the southern sea, and on the north

5. **sleeked:** smoothed.
7. **This:** Jesus; **who:** Satan.
16. **must:** new wine.
19. **shivers:** fragments.

To equal length backed with a ridge of hills
That screened the fruits of the earth and seats of men
From cold Septentrion blasts, thence in the midst
Divided by a river, of whose banks
On each side an imperial city stood,
With towers and temples proudly elevate
On seven small hills, with palaces adorned,
Porches and theaters, baths, aqueducts,
Statues and trophies, and triumphal arcs,
Gardens and groves presented to his eyes,
Above the highth of mountains interposed.
By what strange parallax or optic skill
Of vision multiplied through air, or glass
Of telescope, were curious to inquire:
And now the tempter thus his silence broke.
"The city which thou seest no other deem
Than great and glorious Rome, queen of the earth
So far renowned, and with the spoils enriched
Of nations; there the Capitol thou seest
Above the rest lifting his stately head
On the Tarpeian rock, her citadel
Impregnable, and there Mount Palatine
The imperial palace, compass huge, and high
The structure, skill of noblest architects,
With gilded battlements, conspicuous far,
Turrets and terraces, and glittering spires.
Many a fair edifice besides, more like
Houses of gods (so well I have disposed
My airy microscope) thou mayst behold
Outside and inside both, pillars and roofs
Carved work, the hand of famed artificers
In cedar, marble, ivory or gold.

29. **ridge of hills:** the Apennines.

31. **Septentrion blasts:** north winds; the Latin *septentrionalis,* "north," derives from the *septentriones* or "seven plow oxen" in the northern consellation Ursa Major.

32. **a river:** the Tiber.

36. **Porches:** covered colonnades.

37. **trophies:** spoils of war; **arcs:** arches.

40. **parallax:** apparent change in the location of an object.

40–41. **optic skill . . . air:** perhaps, as Svendsen (1949) suggests, linking this passage to the *airy microscope* of line 57, a fanciful device such as the one described in Thomas Digges's *A Geometrical Practical Treatise Named Pantometria* (1591).

42. **curious:** excessively inquisitive.

49. **Tarpeian rock:** the cliffs of the Capitoline Hill.

51. **imperial palace:** probably, albeit anachronistically, the *Domus Aurea* or Golden House built by Nero after the fire of 64 C.E.

57. **airy microscope:** See 4.40–41n; by whatever trick of magnification he manages it, a desperate Satan hopes that views of the sumptuous exteriors and interiors of Roman buildings will weaken Jesus.

Thence to the gates cast round thine eye, and see
What conflux issuing forth, or ent'ring in,
Praetors, proconsuls to their provinces
Hasting or on return, in robes of state;
Lictors and rods the ensigns of their power,
Legions and cohorts, turms of horse and wings:
Or embassies from regions far remote
In various habits on the Appian road,
Or on the Aemilian, some from farthest south,
Syene, and where the shadow both way falls,
Meroe Nilotic isle, and more to west,
The realm of Bocchus to the Blackmoor sea;
From the Asian kings and Parthian among these,
From India and the golden Chersoness,
And utmost Indian isle Taprobane,
Dusk faces with white silken turbans wreathed:
From Gallia, Gades, and the British west,
Germans and Scythians, and Sarmatians north
Beyond Danubius to the Tauric pool.
All nations now to Rome obedience pay,
To Rome's great emperor, whose wide domain
In ample territory, wealth and power,
Civility of manners, arts, and arms,
And long renown thou justly mayst prefer
Before the Parthian; these two thrones except,
The rest are barbarous, and scarce worth the sight,
Shared among petty kings too far removed;
These having shown thee, I have shown thee all
The kingdoms of the world, and all their glory.
This Emperor hath no son, and now is old,

63. **Praetors:** judicial officers; **proconsuls:** governors of the Roman provinces.

65. **Lictors:** officials who executed the orders of Roman magistrates; **rods:** symbols of judicial power carried by lictors.

66. **Legion:** the largest unit of the Roman army; **cohorts:** a tenth part of a legion; **turms:** a tenth part of a wing; **wings:** cavalry deployed on either side of the infantry.

68–69. **Appian road . . . Aemilian:** The Via Appia and Via Aemilia were the chief roads to the south and north of Rome.

70. **Syene:** modern Aswan in Egypt; **the shadow both way falls:** On the equator, shadows fall southward in the summer and northward in the winter.

71. **Meroe:** Ethiopian capital on the Nile, thought to be on an island.

72. **realm of Bocchus:** Mauretania, in Northern Africa; **Blackmoor sea:** the Mediterranean bordering Mauretania, home of moors or "blackamoors."

74. **golden Chersoness:** region to the east of India.

75. **Taprobane:** probably Sumatra.

77. **Gallia:** France; **Gades:** Cádiz; **the British west:** probably Brittany.

78. **Scythians:** See 3.294–301n; **Sarmatians:** barbarians to the north of the Scythians.

79. **Danubius:** the Danube, the northeastern boundary of the Roman Empire; **Tauric pool:** the Sea of Azov.

90. **This Emperor:** Tiberius, who left Rome in 26

Old, and lascivious, and from Rome retired
To Capreae, an island small but strong
On the Campanian shore, with purpose there
His horrid lusts in private to enjoy,
Committing to a wicked favorite
All public cares, and yet of him suspicious,
Hated of all, and hating; with what ease,
Endued with regal virtues as thou art,
Appearing, and beginning noble deeds,
Might'st thou expel this monster from his throne
Now made a sty, and in his place ascending,
A victor people free from servile yoke!
And with my help thou mayst; to me the power
Is giv'n, and by that right I give it thee.
Aim therefore at no less than all the world,
Aim at the highest, without the highest attained
Will be for thee no sitting, or not long
On David's throne, be prophesied what will."
To whom the Son of God unmoved replied.
"Nor doth this grandeur and majestic show
Of luxury, though called magnificence,
More than of arms before, allure mine eye,
Much less my mind; though thou shouldst add to tell
Their sumptuous gluttonies, and gorgeous feasts
On citron tables or Atlantic stone;
(For I have also heard, perhaps have read)
Their wines of Setia, Cales, and Falerne,
Chios and Crete, and how they quaff in gold,
Crystal and myrrhine cups embossed with gems
And studs of pearl, to me should'st tell who thirst
And hunger still: then embassies thou show'st
From nations far and nigh; what honor that,
But tedious waste of time to sit and hear

C.E. and settled on Capri, where he indulged his lusts (Tacitus, *Annales* 4).

95. **wicked favorite:** Sejanus, executed in 31 C.E. after being denounced by Tiberius.

102. **servile yoke:** The oxen's yoke is a biblical symbol of slavery (Deut. 28.48, Gal. 5.1).

103–4. **to me the power / Is giv'n:** See Luke 4.6.

113. **thou should'st add to tell:** Jesus ironically intensifies Satan's tempting vision and shows that he too is a master of ornate description.

115. **citron:** made of citrus wood; **Atlantic stone:** perhaps marble, perhaps another way of saying *citron tables.*

117–18. **Their wines . . . Crete:** Roman poets praised the Italian wines of *Setia, Cales,* and *Falerne,* and also prized Greek wines from the islands of *Chios* and *Crete.*

119. **myrrhine:** The meaning of the Latin *murra* is uncertain; it might refer to glass, onyx, or Chinese porcelain.

123–25. **But . . . flatteries?:** As Cromwell's Latin Secretary, Milton received embassies, and knew whereof Jesus speaks.

So many hollow compliments and lies,
Outlandish flatteries? Then proceed'st to talk
Of the emperor, how easily subdued,
How gloriously; I shall, thou say'st, expel
A brutish monster: what if I withal
Expel a devil who first made him such?
Let his tormenter conscience find him out;
For him I was not sent, nor yet to free
That people victor once, now vile and base,
Deservedly made vassal, who once just,
Frugal, and mild, and temperate, conquered well,
But govern ill the nations under yoke,
Peeling their provinces, exhausted all
By lust and rapine; first ambitious grown
Of triumph, that insulting vanity;
Then cruel, by their sports to blood inured
Of fighting beasts, and men to beasts exposed,
Luxurious by their wealth, and greedier still,
And from the daily scene effeminate.
What wise and valiant man would seek to free
These thus degenerate, by themselves enslaved,
Or could of inward slaves make outward free?
Know therefore when my season comes to sit
On David's throne, it shall be like a tree
Spreading and overshadowing all the earth,
Or as a stone that shall to pieces dash
All monarchies besides throughout the world,
And of my kingdom there shall be no end:
Means there shall be to this, but what the means,
Is not for thee to know, nor me to tell."
    To whom the Tempter impudent replied.
"I see all offers made by me how slight
Thou valu'st, because offered, and reject'st:
Nothing will please the difficult and nice,
Or nothing more than still to contradict:
On the other side know also thou, that I
On what I offer set as high esteem,
Nor what I part with mean to give for naught;

132. **That people:** the Romans.

138. **insulting:** Cp. *PL* 2.79.

139. **their sports:** Here Jesus echoes the condemnation of Tertullian, *De Spectaculis.*

147–51. Like Christian commentators to come, Jesus sees his reign as the fulfillment of the visions of the tree in Dan. 4.10–12 and the stone in Dan. 2.31–35.

151. "And of his kingdom there shall be no end" (Luke 1.33).

157. **nice:** choosy.

158. **still:** always.

All these which in a moment thou behold'st,
The kingdoms of the world to thee I give;
For giv'n to me, I give to whom I please,
No trifle; yet with this reserve, not else,
On this condition, if thou wilt fall down,
And worship me as thy superior lord,
Easily done, and hold them all of me;
For what can less so great a gift deserve?"
 Whom thus our Savior answered with disdain.
"I never liked thy talk, thy offers less,
Now both abhor, since thou hast dared to utter
The abominable terms, impious condition;
But I endure the time, till which expired,
Thou hast permission on me. It is written
The first of all commandments, 'Thou shalt worship
The Lord thy God, and only him shalt serve;'
And dar'st thou to the Son of God propound
To worship thee accursed, now more accursed
For this attempt bolder than that on Eve,
And more blasphemous? Which expect to rue.
The kingdoms of the world to thee were giv'n,
Permitted rather, and by thee usurped,
Other donation none thou canst produce:
If giv'n, by whom but by the King of Kings,
God over all supreme? If giv'n to thee,
By thee how fairly is the giver now
Repaid? But gratitude in thee is lost
Long since. Wert thou so void of fear or shame,
As offer them to me the Son of God,
To me my own, on such abhorrèd pact,
That I fall down and worship thee as God?
Get thee behind me; plain thou now appear'st
That evil one, Satan forever damned."
 To whom the fiend with fear abashed replied.
"Be not so sore offended, Son of God;

166–67. See Matt. 4.9.

174–76. **It . . . serve:** "Jesus . . . said unto him, Get thee behind me, Satan: for it is written, Thou shalt worship the Lord thy God, and him only shalt thou serve" (Luke 4.8); it is written in Deut. 6.13. Milton reverses the biblical order of these statements; *get thee behind me* does not appear until line 193.

184. **donation:** the bestowal of property or benefit on an inferior by a superior (Lat. *donatio*).

188. **gratitude in thee is lost:** See *PL* 4.51–53.

191. **To me my own:** ambiguous: "You offer to me kingdoms for my own" and "You offer to me my own kingdoms."

Though sons of God both angels are and men,
If I to try whether in higher sort
Than these thou bear'st that title, have proposed
What both from men and angels I receive,
Tetrarchs of fire, air, flood, and on the earth
Nations besides from all the quartered winds,
God of this world invoked and world beneath;
Who then thou art, whose coming is foretold
To me so fatal, me it most concerns.
The trial hath endamaged thee no way,
Rather more honor left and more esteem;
Me naught advantaged, missing what I aimed.
Therefore let pass, as they are transitory,
The kingdoms of this world; I shall no more
Advise thee, gain them as thou canst, or not.
And thou thyself seem'st otherwise inclined
Than to a worldly crown, addicted more
To contemplation and profound dispute,
As by that early action may be judged,
When slipping from thy mother's eye thou went'st
Alone into the temple; there was found
Among the gravest Rabbis disputant
On points and questions fitting Moses' chair,
Teaching not taught; the childhood shows the man,
As morning shows the day. Be famous then
By wisdom; as thy empire must extend,
So let extend thy mind o'er all the world,
In knowledge, all things in it comprehend;
All knowledge is not couched in Moses' law,
The Pentateuch or what the prophets wrote;
The Gentiles also know, and write, and teach
To admiration, led by nature's light;

197. "For as many as are led by the Spirit of God, they are the sons of God" (Rom. 8.4); see also Hosea 1.10.

201. **Tetrarchs:** rulers of a fourth part, here referring to the rulers of the four elements.

215. **that early action:** See 1.209–14n.

219. **fitting Moses' chair:** befitting one sitting in Moses' chair (a scribe or Pharisee).

220–21. **childhood . . . day:** Mentioned alongside Wordsworth's "The child is father of the man" in *The Oxford Dictionary of English Proverbs,* ed. F. P. Wilson, and listed as a separate proverb in *A Dictionary of American Proverbs,* ed. Wolfgang Mieder.

221–22. **Be famous then/By wisdom:** Satan regards wisdom as another route to fame and glory (see 3.25n).

223. The idea of the mind as a kingdom was commonplace; see Dyer's "My mind to me a kingdom is," *HAM* 2.2.254–56, and *PL* 1.254–55.

226. **Pentateuch:** the first five books of the Old Testament.

228. **To admiration:** admirably; **nature's light:** a popular term in the theology of Milton's day, associated in particular with the Cambridge Platonists; see Nathanael Culverwel, *A Elegant and Learned Discourse of the Light of Nature* (1652).

And with the Gentiles much thou must converse,
Ruling them by persuasion as thou mean'st;
Without their learning how wilt thou with them,
Or they with thee hold conversation meet?
How wilt thou reason with them, how refute
Their idolisms, traditions, paradoxes?
Error by his own arms is best evinced.
Look once more ere we leave this specular mount
Westward, much nearer by southwest, behold
Where on the Aegean shore a city stands
Built nobly, pure the air, and light the soil,
Athens the eye of Greece, mother of arts
And eloquence, native to famous wits
Or hospitable, in her sweet recess,
City or suburban, studious walks and shades;
See there the olive grove of Academe,
Plato's retirement, where the Attic bird
Trills her thick-warbled notes the summer long;
There flowery hill Hymettus with the sound
Of bees' industrious murmur oft invites
To studious musing; there Ilissus rolls
His whispering stream; within the walls then view
The schools of ancient sages; his who bred
Great Alexander to subdue the world,
Lyceum there, and painted Stoa next:
There thou shalt hear and learn the secret power
Of harmony in tones and numbers hit
By voice or hand, and various-measured verse,
Aeolian charms and Dorian lyric odes,
And his who gave them breath, but higher sung,
Blind Melesigenes thence Homer called,

234. **idolisms:** idolatries; **paradoxes:** probably an allusion to moral maxims of the Stoic school, such as the ones Cicero discusses in *Paradoxa Stoicorum.*

235. **evinced:** conquered.

236. **specular:** affording an extensive view.

240. **eye of:** a classical idiom meaning "the seat of light or intelligence in."

244. **Academe:** the gymnasium west of Athens, planted with olive trees, where Plato taught.

245. **Attic bird:** the nightingale.

247. **Hymettus:** hills to the southeast of Athens, famous for their honey.

248. **industrious:** Vergil stressed the industry of bees in *Georg.* 4.149–250; cp. "th' industrious bee" of Marvell's "The Garden."

249. **Ilissus:** small river to the south of Athens.

251. **his:** Aristotle, tutor to Alexander the Great.

253. **Lyceum:** the gymnasium where Aristotle taught; **painted Stoa:** a colonnade decorated with frescoes where philosophers congregated and argued; but particularly associated with Zeno, whose followers were therefore known as "Stoics."

257. **Aeolian charms:** Alcaeus and Sappho wrote songs (*charms*) in the Aeolian dialect; **Dorian lyric odes:** Pindar wrote odes in the Dorian dialect.

259. **Melesigenes:** a name sometimes given to

Whose poem Phoebus challenged for his own.
Thence what the lofty grave tragedians taught
In chorus or iambic, teachers best
Of moral prudence, with delight received
In brief sententious precepts, while they treat
Of fate, and chance, and change in human life;
High actions, and high passions best describing:
Thence to the famous orators repair,
Those ancient, whose resistless eloquence
Wielded at will that fierce democraty,
Shook the Arsenal and fulmined over Greece,
To Macedon, and Artaxerxes' throne;
To sage philosophy next lend thine ear,
From Heav'n descended to the low-roofed house
Of Socrates, see there his tenement,
Whom well inspired the oracle pronounced
Wisest of men; from whose mouth issued forth
Mellifluous streams that watered all the schools
Of Academics old and new, with those
Surnamed Peripatetics, and the sect
Epicurean, and the Stoic severe;
These here revolve, or, as thou lik'st, at home,
Till time mature thee to a kingdom's weight;
These rules will render thee a king complete
Within thy self, much more with empire joined."
    To whom our Savior sagely thus replied.
"Think not but that I know these things, or think
I know them not; not therefore am I short

Homer, who was said to have been born on the banks of the river Meles; **thence Homer called:** so called because, by an ancient etymology, *Homer* derives from a Cumaean word meaning "blind."

260. Alluding to the *Greek Anthology* 9.455, where Apollo accuses Homer of plagiarizing him.

262. **In chorus or iambic:** Dialogue in Greek tragedy is written in the iambic meter, whereas the chorus has disparate meters.

269. **democraty:** democracy.

270. **Shook the Arsenal:** MacKellar cites E. C. Baldwin for the information that Demosthenes "shook" the *Arsenal* (dockyard) at Piraeus in that, on his advice, the building of it was suspended. **fulmined**: stormed in thunder and lightning.

271. **Artaxerxes' throne:** the Persian throne, hostile to Greece and occupied by several kings named Artaxerxes.

273. **From Heav'n descended:** "Socrates was the first to call philosophy down from heaven" (Cicero, *Tusculan Disputations* 5.4.10).

275. **the oracle pronounced:** The Delphic oracle did indeed say that no man was wiser than Socrates (Plato, *Apology* 21), but Socrates himself interpreted this to mean that like all men he knew nothing, but unlike all men knew that he knew nothing. Jesus will allude to this point in lines 293–94.

279. **Peripatetics:** Aristotelians.

286. **Think not but:** "Think nothing but."

287–88. **not therefore . . . ought:** "I am not short of knowing what I ought in either case [knowing these Greek things, or not knowing them]."

Of knowing what I ought: he who receives
Light from above, from the fountain of light,
No other doctrine needs, though granted true;
But these are false, or little else but dreams,
Conjectures, fancies, built on nothing firm.
The first and wisest of them all professed
To know this only, that he nothing knew;
The next to fabling fell and smooth conceits,
A third sort doubted all things, though plain sense;
Others in virtue placed felicity,
But virtue joined with riches and long life,
In corporal pleasure he, and careless ease;
The Stoic last in philosophic pride,
By him called virtue; and his virtuous man,
Wise, perfect in himself, and all possessing
Equal to God, oft shames not to prefer,
As fearing God nor man, contemning all
Wealth, pleasure, pain or torment, death and life,
Which when he lists, he leaves, or boasts he can,
For all his tedious talk is but vain boast,
Or subtle shifts conviction to evade.
Alas what can they teach, and not mislead;
Ignorant of themselves, of God much more,
And how the world began, and how man fell
Degraded by himself, on grace depending?
Much of the soul they talk, but all awry,
And in themselves seek virtue, and to themselves
All glory arrogate, to God give none;
Rather accuse him under usual names,
Fortune and Fate, as one regardless quite
Of mortal things. Who therefore seeks in these
True wisdom, finds her not, or by delusion
Far worse, her false resemblance only meets,

295. **The next:** Plato.

296. **third sort:** the Skeptics.

297. **Others:** the Peripatetics, who argued that happiness demanded both virtue and material goods (Aristotle, *Nicomachean Ethics* 1.11).

299. **he:** Epicurus; his teaching is more complex than Jesus allows.

302. **perfect in himself:** The Stoic ideal of autarchy (self-sufficiency) required the cultivation of *apatheia,* an utter indifference to all things outside the self.

306. **Which when he lists, he leaves:** Stoic self-sufficiency presupposed the possibility, should circumstances become intolerable, of committing suicide.

308. **subtle shifts:** the dialectical twists of Stoic argument.

317. **regardless quite:** The extremes in *regardless* deities in classical philosophy are the utterly indifferent gods of Lucretius, *On the Nature of Things,* 2.646–51.

An empty cloud. However, many books,
Wise men have said, are wearisome; who reads
Incessantly, and to his reading brings not
A spirit and judgment equal or superior,
(And what he brings, what needs he elsewhere seek)
Uncertain and unsettled still remains,
Deep-versed in books and shallow in himself,
Crude or intoxicate, collecting toys,
And trifles for choice matters, worth a sponge;
As children gathering pebbles on the shore.
Or if I would delight my private hours
With music or with poem, where so soon
As in our native language can I find
That solace? All our law and story strewed
With hymns, our psalms with artful terms inscribed,
Our Hebrew songs and harps in Babylon,
That pleased so well our victors' ear, declare
That rather Greece from us these arts derived;
Ill imitated, while they loudest sing
The vices of their deities, and their own
In fable, hymn, or song, so personating
Their gods ridiculous, and themselves past shame.
Remove their swelling epithets thick-laid
As varnish on a harlot's cheek, the rest,
Thin-sown with aught of profit or delight,
Will far be found unworthy to compare
With Sion's songs, to all true tastes excelling,
Where God is praised aright, and godlike men,
The Holiest of Holies, and his saints;

321. **empty cloud:** A likely allusion to the myth of Ixion, who embraced a cloud thinking it was Juno; the story often appears in indictments of erroneous intellectual pursuits.

321–22. **many books . . . wearisome:** "Of making many books there is no end; and much study is a weariness of the flesh" (Eccles. 12.12).

328. **Crude:** unable to digest.

329. **worth a sponge:** both "worth very little" and "worthy of being expunged" (sponges were used to wipe manuscripts clean so that the leaves could be overwritten).

336–37. Assyrian conquerors demand of captive Jews "songs of Zion" in Ps. 137.1–3.

338. **Greece from us these arts derived:** The Renaissance followed patristic sources in believing that the Jews invented the arts eventually adopted by the Egyptians and Greeks. Poetry "had her original from heaven, received thence from the Hebrews, and had in prime estimation with the Greeks, transmitted to the Latins, and all nations that professed civility" (Jonson, *Timber,* in *Works,* ed. Herford and Simpson, 8:636).

341. **personating**: representing.

343. **swelling:** bombastic, pompous.

347. **to all true tastes excelling:** "All profane authors seem of the seed of the serpent that creeps; thou [God, inspirer of the Scriptures] art the dove that flies" (Donne, *Devotions* 19); **tastes:** according to the *OED* the first instance of the word meaning "the faculty of perceiving what is excellent in art or literature."

Such are from God inspired, not such from thee;
Unless where moral virtue is expressed
By light of nature not in all quite lost.
Their orators thou then extoll'st, as those
The top of eloquence, statists indeed,
And lovers of their country, as may seem;
But herein to our prophets far beneath,
As men divinely taught, and better teaching
The solid rules of civil government
In their majestic unaffected style
Than all the oratory of Greece and Rome.
In them is plainest taught, and easiest learnt,
What makes a nation happy, and keeps it so,
What ruins kingdoms, and lays cities flat;
These only with our law best form a king."
    So spake the Son of God; but Satan now
Quite at a loss, for all his darts were spent,
Thus to our Savior with stern brow replied.
    "Since neither wealth, nor honor, arms nor arts,
Kingdom nor empire pleases thee, nor aught
By me proposed in life contemplative,
Or active, tended on by glory, or fame,
What dost thou in this world? The wilderness
For thee is fittest place, I found thee there,
And thither will return thee, yet remember
What I foretell thee, soon thou shalt have cause
To wish thou never hadst rejected thus
Nicely or cautiously my offered aid,
Which would have set thee in short time with ease
On David's throne; or throne of all the world,
Now at full age, fullness of time, thy season,
When prophecies of thee are best fulfilled.
Now contrary, if I read aught in heav'n,
Or heav'n write aught of fate, by what the stars
Voluminous, or single characters,

351. **Unless:** refers back to *unworthy to compare* in line 346.

352. **light of nature:** See 228n.

354. **statists:** statesmen.

377. **Nicely:** fastidiously.

380. **fullness of time:** "When the fullness of time was come, God sent forth his Son" (Gal. 4.4).

382. **Now contrary:** Satan sees an extraordinary difference between the *Now* of line 380 and this *Now*: Jesus' moment is past, or so his forthcoming horoscope will suggest. Horoscopes of Christ had in fact been cast, and during Milton's lifetime a notorious one was published by Jerome Cardan (Shumaker 53–90).

384. **Voluminous:** the heavens regarded as a large volume or book; **or single characters:** "or considering the stars as individual letters in the text of the book."

In their conjunction met, give me to spell,
Sorrows, and labors, opposition, hate,
Attends thee, scorns, reproaches, injuries,
Violence and stripes, and lastly cruel death;
A kingdom they portend thee, but what kingdom,
Real or allegoric I discern not,
Nor when, eternal sure, as without end,
Without beginning; for no date prefixed
Directs me in the starry rubric set."
So saying he took (for still he knew his power
Not yet expired) and to the wilderness
Brought back the Son of God, and left him there,
Feigning to disappear. Darkness now rose,
As daylight sunk, and brought in louring Night,
Her shadowy offspring, unsubstantial both,
Privation mere of light and absent day.
Our Savior meek and with untroubled mind
After his airy jaunt, though hurried sore,
Hungry and cold betook him to his rest,
Wherever, under some concourse of shades
Whose branching arms thick intertwined might shield
From dews and damps of night his sheltered head,
But sheltered slept in vain, for at his head
The tempter watched, and soon with ugly dreams
Disturbed his sleep; and either tropic now
'Gan thunder, and both ends of heav'n, the clouds
From many a horrid rift abortive poured
Fierce rain with lightning mixed, water with fire
In ruin reconciled: nor slept the winds
Within their stony caves, but rush'd abroad
From the four hinges of the world, and fell
On the vexed wilderness, whose tallest pines,
Though rooted deep as high, and sturdiest oaks

385. **conjunction:** when two stars or planets occupy the same sign of the zodiac; **spell:** read; cp. *Il Pens* 170–71.

390. It is, of course, both *real* and *allegoric.*

391–92. **as without end/Without beginning:** Satan speaks mockingly here. Christ's kingdom, being eternal, has the attribute of being endless, but it also has that other eternal attribute of being without beginning, and is therefore never to be established.

393. **starry rubric:** the heavens metaphorically considered as a *rubric,* or handbook of rules.

402. **jaunt:** tiring journey.

409. **either tropic:** north and south (Cancer and Capricorn).

410. **ends of heav'n:** east and west.

411. **horrid rift abortive:** "The clouds are imagined to be wombs that miscarry the elements of fire and water" (Leonard).

413. **ruin:** both "destruction" and "falling."

414. **caves:** where Aeolus imprisons the winds (*Aen.* 1.52–54).

415. **four hinges:** the four cardinal (Lat. *cardo,* "hinge") points of the compass.

Bowed their stiff necks, loaden with stormy blasts,
Or torn up sheer: ill wast thou shrouded then,
O patient Son of God, yet only stood'st
Unshaken; nor yet stayed the terror there;
Infernal ghosts, and hellish furies, round
Environed thee, some howled, some yelled, some shrieked,
Some bent at thee their fiery darts, while thou
Sat'st unappalled in calm and sinless peace.
Thus passed the night so foul till Morning fair
Came forth with pilgrim steps in amice gray;
Who with her radiant finger stilled the roar
Of thunder, chased the clouds, and laid the winds,
And grisly specters, which the fiend had raised
To tempt the Son of God with terrors dire.
And now the sun with more effectual beams
Had cheered the face of earth, and dried the wet
From drooping plant, or dropping tree; the birds
Who all things now behold more fresh and green,
After a night of storm so ruinous,
Cleared up their choicest notes in bush and spray
To gratulate the sweet return of morn;
Nor yet amidst this joy and brightest morn
Was absent, after all his mischief done,
The Prince of Darkness, glad would also seem
Of this fair change, and to our Savior came,
Yet with no new device, they all were spent,
Rather by this his last affront resolved,
Desperate of better course, to vent his rage
And mad despite to be so oft repelled.
Him walking on a sunny hill he found,
Backed on the north and west by a thick wood;
Out of the wood he starts in wonted shape;
And in a careless mood thus to him said.
"Fair morning yet betides thee Son of God,
After a dismal night; I heard the rack
As earth and sky would mingle; but myself
Was distant; and these flaws, though mortals fear them

419. **shrouded:** sheltered.
420. **only:** uniquely.
421. **nor yet stayed the terror there:** "nor yet did the terror [the *ugly dreams* of l. 408] cease."
422–23. Cp. Shakespeare *R3* 1.4.58–59.
427. **amice:** hood.
437. **Cleared up:** brightened, polished.
438. **gratulate:** welcome, give thanks for.
446. **despite:** hatred, resentment.
449. **wonted shape:** It is unclear whether this means "in his customary disguise (an old man)" or "as Satan, the fallen angel."
454. **flaws:** squalls.

As dang'rous to the pillared frame of heav'n,
Or to the Earth's dark basis underneath,
Are to the main as inconsiderable,
And harmless, if not wholesome, as a sneeze
To man's less universe, and soon are gone;
Yet as being ofttimes noxious where they light
On man, beast, plant, wasteful and turbulent,
Like turbulencies in th' affairs of men,
Over whose heads they roar, and seem to point,
They oft fore-signify and threaten ill:
This tempest at this desert most was bent;
Of men at thee, for only thou here dwell'st.
Did I not tell thee, if thou didst reject
The perfect season offered with my aid
To win thy destined seat, but wilt prolong
All to the push of fate, pursue thy way
Of gaining David's throne no man knows when,
For both the when and how is nowhere told,
Thou shalt be what thou art ordained, no doubt;
For angels have proclaimed it, but concealing
The time and means: each act is rightliest done,
Not when it must, but when it may be best.
If thou observe not this, be sure to find,
What I foretold thee, many a hard assay
Of dangers, and adversities and pains,
Ere thou of Israel's scepter get fast hold;
Whereof this ominous night that closed thee round,
So many terrors, voices, prodigies
May warn thee, as a sure foregoing sign."
So talked he, while the Son of God went on
And stayed not, but in brief him answered thus.
"Me worse than wet thou find'st not; other harm
Those terrors which thou speak'st of, did me none;
I never feared they could, though noising loud
And threat'ning nigh; what they can do as signs
Betok'ning, or ill-boding, I contemn
As false portents, not sent from God, but thee;
Who knowing I shall reign past thy preventing,
Obtrud'st thy offered aid, that I accepting

455. **pillared frame of heav'n:** See Job 26.11, and the "pillared firmament" of *Masque* 598.
457. **the main:** the world at large, the macrocosm.
470. **push:** critical juncture.
475–76. **each act . . . best:** See Jonson, "To the Immortal Memory and Friendship of . . . Sir. Lucius Cary and Sir. H. Morison," 59–62.

At least might seem to hold all power of thee,
Ambitious spirit, and wouldst be thought my God,
And storm'st refused, thinking to terrify
Me to thy will; desist, thou art discerned
And toil'st in vain, nor me in vain molest."
To whom the fiend now swoll'n with rage replied:
"Then hear, O son of David, virgin-born,
For Son of God to me is yet in doubt,
Of the Messiah I have heard foretold
By all the prophets; of thy birth at length
Announced by Gabriel with the first I knew,
And of th' angelic song in Bethlehem field,
On thy birth-night, that sung thee Savior born.
From that time seldom have I ceased to eye
Thy infancy, thy childhood, and thy youth,
Thy manhood last, though yet in private bred;
Till at the ford of Jordan whither all
Flocked to the Baptist, I among the rest,
Though not to be baptized, by voice from Heav'n
Heard thee pronounced the Son of God beloved.
Thenceforth I thought thee worth my nearer view
And narrower scrutiny, that I might learn
In what degree or meaning thou art called
The Son of God, which bears no single sense;
The son of God I also am, or was,
And if I was, I am; relation stands;
All men are sons of God; yet thee I thought
In some respect far higher so declared.
Therefore I watched thy footsteps from that hour,
And followed thee still on to this waste wild;
Where by all best conjectures I collect
Thou art to be my fatal enemy.
Good reason then, if I beforehand seek

496. **storm'st:** both "gets angry" and "raises a storm"; **refused:** when refused.

500–40. This angry (hence not primarily cunning) speech bears directly on the much-debated question of what Satan knows of Jesus. Personal observation, though it prompted the temptation to vainglorious learning (ll. 214–22), has supplied no proofs of divinity. Satan's knowledge of "Son of God" is largely scriptural; the baptismal theophany, though impressive, was just more words. Moreover, since Satan became Satan in resisting the divine elevation of the Son of God in Heaven (*PL* 5.600–907), he is prone to regard the whole subject of "Son of God" with doubt, faith's opposite.

515. **that I might learn:** Cp. 1.91 and note. Milton transforms the third temptation into a test of Christ's identity, the meaning of "Son of God." See 552n.

520. **All men are Sons of God:** "All of you are children of the most High" (Ps. 82.6–7).

524. **collect:** infer.

To understand my adversary, who
And what he is; his wisdom, power, intent,
By parle, or composition, truce, or league
To win him, or win from him what I can.
And opportunity I here have had
To try thee, sift thee, and confess have found thee
Proof against all temptation as a rock
Of adamant, and as a center, firm
To the utmost of mere man both wise and good,
Not more; for honors, riches, kingdoms, glory
Have been before contemned, and may again:
Therefore to know what more thou art than man,
Worth naming Son of God by voice from Heav'n,
Another method I must now begin."
So saying he caught him up, and without wing
Of hippogrif bore through the air sublime
Over the wilderness and o'er the plain;
Till underneath them fair Jerusalem,
The holy city, lifted high her towers,
And higher yet the glorious temple reared
Her pile, far off appearing like a mount
Of alabaster, topped with golden spires:
There on the highest pinnacle he set
The Son of God; and added thus in scorn:
"There stand, if thou wilt stand; to stand upright
Will ask thee skill; I to thy Father's house
Have brought thee, and highest placed; highest is best;
Now show thy progeny; if not to stand,
Cast thyself down; safely if Son of God:

529. **parle:** parley; **composition:** treaty.

532. **sift:** make trial of, scrutinize narrowly.

534. **adamant:** a mythical rock of impregnable hardness, with perhaps a play on *Adam.*

542. **hippogrif:** a fabulous creature, half griffin, half horse, that carries the heroes of Ariosto's *Orlando Furioso* on various wonderful journeys; **sublime:** raised aloft.

547–48. **far off . . . spires:** Josephus says that the front of the Temple, white marble covered with plates of gold, appeared at a distance "like a mountain covered with snow" (*Wars of the Jews,* 5.5.6)—thus Milton's *like a mount/Of alabaster.* This is not the Temple of Solomon but the one built on its site by Herod.

549. **highest pinnacle:** Both Matt. 4.6 and Luke 4.10 have Satan placing Christ on a "pinnacle," but the Greek word translated *pinnaculum* in the Vulgate is uncertain of meaning, particularly in view of the fact that the roof of the Temple was apparently flat. Milton seems to identify his pinnacle with one of the *golden spires* in line 548.

552. **Will ask thee skill:** Satan, speaking scornfully, does not believe that a man can stand on this pinnacle. A miracle is required, and in this regard Milton deviates from most commentators, who interpreted the third temptation (following the order in Luke) as one of presumption—that God would provide for someone who deliberately puts himself in danger.

555. **Cast thyself down:** In the Bible (Matt. 4.6, Luke 4.10) this injunction implies a choice: Jesus can either stand or presumptively cast himself down. Milton's Satan supposes that Jesus will either fall and die, proving himself no

For it is written, 'He will give command
Concerning thee to his angels, in their hands
They shall uplift thee, lest at any time
Thou chance to dash thy foot against a stone.' "
To whom thus Jesus: "Also it is written,
'Tempt not the Lord thy God,' " he said and stood.
But Satan smitten with amazement fell
As when Earth's son Antaeus (to compare
Small things with greatest) in Irassa strove
With Jove's Alcides, and oft foiled still rose,
Receiving from his mother Earth new strength,
Fresh from his fall, and fiercer grapple joined,
Throttled at length in the air, expired and fell;
So after many a foil the tempter proud,
Renewing fresh assaults, amidst his pride
Fell whence he stood to see his victor fall.
And as that Theban monster that proposed
Her riddle, and him who solved it not devoured;
That once found out and solved, for grief and spite
Cast herself headlong from th' Ismenian steep,
So struck with dread and anguish fell the fiend,
And to his crew, that sat consulting, brought
Joyless triumphals of his hoped success,
Ruin, and desperation, and dismay,

---

more than a perfect man, or fall and be saved by angels, proving himself something beyond that.

556. **For it is written:** Like the Satan of Luke 4.10–11, Milton's Satan quotes Ps. 91.11–12. But the Son is the stone—the *adamant* of line 534, the *solid rock* of line 18—against which Satan is dashed.

560–61. **Also . . . thy God:** quoting, as in Luke 4.12, Deut. 6.16: "Ye shall not tempt [make trial of] the Lord your God." Christ announces that he is God, then enacts, by standing, his words.

560. **smitten with amazement:** All of Satan's bafflements come to a head. Eve during the course of her temptation is progressively amazed (*PL* 9.552, 614, 640): the fate of the tempted in *Paradise Lost* now becomes the fate of the tempter. Satan, receiving the head bruise promised him by the protevangelium (see 1.53–55n), realizes that Jesus is both a man and the divine Son of God who drove him from Heaven in *PL* 6.856–66.

563–71. The giant *Antaeus* was the son of Ge (*Earth*). Wrestling Hercules (*Jove's Alcides*), he arose strengthened from each contact with mother Earth, until Hercules strangled him in the air (Lucan, *Pharsalia* 4.593–660). But Christ defeats Satan, "Prince of the power of the air" (Eph. 2.2), in his native element.

563–64. **to compare . . . greatest:** Milton adds the superlative *greatest* to Vergil's formula for comparing great (epic or urban) things with small (pastoral or rustic) things (*Ec.* 1.23; *Georg.* 4.176); Vergil's great things are Milton's small ones. Cp. *PL* 2.921–22, 6.310, 10.306.

571. Another confirmation that Satan expected Jesus to fall. Satan's fall, though known in visual representations, is not mentioned in the Bible or the commentary tradition.

572–75. The Sphinx leapt to her death from the acropolis at Thebes (*Ismenian steep*) when Oedipus answered her riddle: What creature goes first on four, then on two, and finally on three legs? "Man" was the answer. Satan, as it were, posed the riddle "Who is the Son of God?"—and "man" was only half the answer.

578. **triumphals:** tokens of success.

Who durst so proudly tempt the Son of God.
So Satan fell and straight a fiery globe
Of angels on full sail of wing flew nigh,
Who on their plumy vans received him soft
From his uneasy station, and upbore
As on a floating couch through the blithe air,
Then in a flow'ry valley set him down
On a green bank, and set before him spread
A table of celestial food, divine,
Ambrosial, fruits fetched from the Tree of Life,
And from the Fount of Life ambrosial drink,
That soon refreshed him wearied, and repaired
What hunger, if aught hunger had impaired,
Or thirst; and as he fed, angelic choirs
Sung Heav'nly anthems of his victory
Over temptation, and the tempter proud.
"True image of the Father whether throned
In the bosom of bliss, and light of light
Conceiving, or remote from Heav'n, enshrined
In fleshly tabernacle, and human form,
Wand'ring the wilderness, whatever place,
Habit, or state, or motion, still expressing
The Son of God, with Godlike force endued
Against th' attempter of thy Father's throne,
And thief of Paradise; him long of old
Thou didst debel, and down from Heaven cast
With all his army; now thou hast avenged
Supplanted Adam, and by vanquishing
Temptation, hast regained lost Paradise,
And frustrated the conquest fraudulent:
He never more henceforth will dare set foot

582. **angels:** "Angels came and ministered to him" (Matt. 4.11).

583. **vans:** wings; **him:** meaning Christ, but seemingly momentarily to refer to *Satan* in line 581; see Kerrigan 1983, 90–92.

584. **his uneasy station:** This phrase, Carey (1970) argued, proves his feat was human: an uneasy Jesus stands. MacCallum replied that the station, not the standing, is uneasy. Carey (1997) countered that *station* meant "manner of standing" (*OED* 1) as well as "place to stand" (*OED* 7a), but angels would not receive Jesus from a "manner of standing." MacCallum was right, and Carey recklessly mocked the consequences: "It would be curious if this meant 'uneasy for anyone else except the person here being discussed.' " Curious? That person is the *greatest* (563–64n).

587. **and set before him:** Christ also has a banquet laid before him in Giles Fletcher's poem on the temptation, *Christ's Victory and Triumph*, 2.61.

589. **the Tree of Life:** a human food, native to Eden, which balances the celestial food of line 588 and signifies that the Son has regained our lost Paradise.

590. **Fount of Life:** See Rev. 21.6.

598. **Conceiving:** receiving (perhaps an indication of Milton's heterodox views on the Son of God; see MacKellar).

605. **debel:** vanquish.

In Paradise to tempt; his snares are broke:
For though that seat of earthly bliss be failed,
A fairer Paradise is founded now
For Adam and his chosen sons, whom thou
A savior art come down to reinstall.
Where they shall dwell secure, when time shall be
Of tempter and temptation without fear.
But thou, infernal serpent, shalt not long
Rule in the clouds; like an autumnal star
Or lightning thou shalt fall from heav'n trod down
Under his feet: for proof, ere this thou feel'st
Thy wound, yet not thy last and deadliest wound
By this repulse received, and hold'st in Hell
No triumph; in all her gates Abaddon rues
Thy bold attempt; hereafter learn with awe
To dread the Son of God: he all unarmed
Shall chase thee with the terror of his voice
From thy demoniac holds, possession foul,
Thee and thy legions; yelling they shall fly,
And beg to hide them in a herd of swine,
Lest he command them down into the deep
Bound, and to torment sent before their time.
Hail Son of the Most High, heir of both worlds,
Queller of Satan, on thy glorious work
Now enter, and begin to save mankind."
  Thus they the Son of God our Savior meek
Sung victor, and from Heav'nly feast refreshed
Brought on his way with joy; he unobserved
Home to his mother's house private returned.

612. **be failed:** be extinguished; see *PL* 11.829–34.

613. **A fairer Paradise:** reminiscent of the "paradise within thee, happier far" in *PL* 12.587.

619. **autumnal star:** a comet or meteor; cp. the "ev'ning dragon" in *SA* 1692.

620. **Or lightning:** "I beheld Satan as lightning fall from heaven" (Luke 10.18); cp. *PL* 10.183–85.

621. **ere this:** before the fuller defeats to come.

622. **Thy wound:** the wound promised him by the protevangelium or "first gospel" woven into the first judgment of Gen. 3.15 (see 1.53–55n). This passage (ll. 618–32) concerns its typological unfolding. For the *last and deadliest wound,* see Rev. 20.10.

624. **Abaddon:** Hell (see Job 26.6).

628. **holds:** strongholds; **possession:** Satan's military positions (*holds*), and therefore "demonic possessions" as well.

630. See Matt. 8.28–34, Mark 5.1–13, Luke 8.26–33.

636. **Son of God our Savior meek:** "I am meek and lowly in heart" (Matt. 11.29).

Introduction to *Samson Agonistes*[1]

Samson Agonistes was first published in 1671, in the same volume as *Paradise Regained* but with its own supplementary title page and separate pagination. Through the first half of the twentieth century, it was almost always thought to have been composed soon after *Paradise Regained* in 1667–70, but in 1949 W. R. Parker's suggestion of an earlier date opened the way to decades of speculation about the beginning and finishing of *Samson Agonistes*. As is the case with *Paradise Lost*, the germ of *Samson* first appeared in a list of possible subjects for a tragic drama found in the Trinity College manuscript and usually dated 1640–41. Some authorities have pushed the composition back to the 1640s, before the advent of the author's full blindness in 1652, to a time when, so far as we know, Milton had no real hint of the affliction awaiting him. The early dating removes any personal element in the work's representation of blindness. Similarly, by placing the drama before the Restoration of 1660, the early dating removes any personal element from its political denunciation of the backsliding, self-enslaved Israelites. A work long savored for its autobiographical power becomes, if written in the 1640s, merely prescient.

But in the absence of compelling evidence, the traditional dating should be retained. With the exception of Samson's anger with Dalila, which may in some fashion tap Milton's resentment of his Royalist first wife, the emotions of the drama do not favor the 1640s. It is highly unlikely that Milton wrote an ambitious poem in the 1650s, a decade consumed by his secretaryship for the Cromwell government, his political pamphleteering, his adjustment to blindness, his efforts to forestall the Restoration, and in the end by his narrow survival of that turnaround. He might have begun the epic in 1658, as his nephew Edward Phillips seems to have reported to John Aubrey (p. xxviii), but one must agree with Jonathan Richardson that, given the tumultuous events of

1. The title, like the work, embodies the meeting of Hebrew (*Samson*) and Greek (*Agonistes*). The Greek epithet means "struggling" or "contending" or "agonizing" (see Sellin 1964). It was familiarly applied to athletes and champions, or to spiritual heroes who were metaphorically athletes and champions. Hale reminds us that *agonistes* also means "actor," and that it can be transferred to the character acted, as in our "antagonist" and "protagonist" (181); with this added meaning, the title glances at Samson playing a part in the Hebrew-Greek-Christian tragic drama Milton discerned in Judges.

those two years, "it seems probable he set not about the work in good earnest till after the Restoration" (Darbishire 288). In the first half of the 1660s, Milton wrote *Paradise Lost.* Let us assume that Ellwood was handed the manuscript of the large epic in 1665 and of its sequel in 1667 (see introduction to *Paradise Regained*). In this case, Milton would have had ample time to write *Samson* before the two works were licensed in June 1670 and entered in the Stationer's Register on September 10 of the same year. If he averaged twelve lines a day, which is about the pace at which *Paradise Lost* was composed, he would have needed around 143 working days for the drama. It is true, as William Parker emphasized (1949), that our best guide to matters of dating, Edward Phillips, declared that *Samson*'s time of composition "cannot certainly be concluded" (Darbishire 75), but Parker may have been wrong to weigh this uncertainty so heavily. During 1667–70, Phillips was tutor to the Earl of Pembroke's son and was no doubt often separated from his uncle.

When all the arguments about its dating have been examined, *Samson* still feels more like the end of something than a midcareer experiment. "And calm of mind, all passion spent." Could there be a better line on which to end a poetic career? A great ode, a great masque, two great pastoral elegies, a great epic, and a brief epic had been written. One last major genre remained to be conquered. Milton completed a career in heroic Christian poetry with *Paradise Lost.* He then published in one volume *Paradise Regained,* which recounts the beginning of a career that is the very pattern of Christian heroism, and *Samson Agonistes,* which deals with the end of a heroic career—an imperfectly human, not altogether exemplary or Christian one, into which a blind, politically disappointed Milton could pour a lifetime of "true experience" (l. 1756).

It was reading *Samson Agonistes,* in 1830, not *Paradise Lost,* that convinced Johann Wolfgang Goethe of Milton's greatness: "I have lately read his Samson," he told Eckermann, "which has more of the antique spirit than any other production of any other modern poet. He is very great, and his own blindness enabled him to describe with so much truth the situation of Samson. Milton was really a poet, to whom we owe all possible respect" (346–47). This high estimate rests on two accomplishments. The first may be termed romantic: his Samson is at once an objective character and an act of self-expression. The second is neoclassical: though many European dramatists tried to write a modern Greek tragedy, Milton alone succeeded. Samuel Taylor Coleridge also felt that *Samson* was "the finest imitation of the ancient Greek drama that ever had been, or ever would be written" (*Lectures* 14). Aside from Judges, the work has no sources other than Greek drama. Scholars have made claims for the Dutchman Joost van den Vondel's 1660 *Samson, of Heilige Wraeck, Treurspel* (translated in Kirkconnell), but they have been convincingly dismissed by Verity (1897, 158–68). From Judges itself, Milton takes only the catastrophe. The Danite companions, the visit of Dalila, the notion that she was Samson's wife, the entire character of

Harapha, Manoa's attempt to ransom Samson, the idea that the building toppled was a partially roofed theater—these and many other details are the poet's inventions.

Even the unpatterned rhymes, lawlessly shifting line lengths, and other prosodic peculiarities of the work, though critics have related them to Italian (Prince 145–69, 178–83), Greek, and Hebrew (Kermode) models, are essentially without precedent. In key letters to Robert Bridges (August 21, 1877) and R.W. Dixon (October 5, 1878), Gerard Manley Hopkins described the choruses of *Samson Agonistes* as unique instances of "counterpointed" rhythm, able simultaneously to support two mutually inconsistent scansions. One was conventional. The other was a revolutionary "sprung rhythm," free from the arithmetical regularities of standard accentual-syllabic verse.

Milton's finest poems are to a certain extent about their genres. Here the tragic form is clearly Greek. After an introductory soliloquy and an exchange between Samson and the Chorus, the drama proceeds through a series of episodes, each of them a dialogue between two people and all of them divided by choric interludes. The catastrophe takes place offstage and, as was conventional in Greek tragedy, is reported by a messenger. There is a great deal of Sophoclean irony, in which what is said takes on a second and ironic meaning in relation to the full plot. For a time in the early twentieth century, critics such as Richard Jebb wondered whether the work might be Greek in form but Hebraic or Christian in spirit. W. R. Parker laid this tradition to rest, at least for a couple of decades, by asserting that Greek drama is in spirit grave, elevated, thoughtful, didactic, and religious, all of which are characteristics of *Samson* (1937, 189–210). Like Coleridge and Goethe before him, A. W. Verity was right to suppose that "*Samson Agonistes* is unique because here the genius of Greek tragedy does live—really live. So oft invoked in vain, it wakes at last from the long sleep of centuries" (1897).

Samuel Johnson presented a fecund issue to the formal study of Milton's tragedy by observing that the play is defective in Aristotelian terms. For its middle scenes do not bring about the catastrophe: "The poem, therefore, has a beginning and end which Aristotle himself could not have disapproved; but it must be allowed to want a middle, since nothing passes between the first act and the last that either hastens or delays the death of Samson" (*Works* 4:376). Samson discusses with the Chorus and Manoa his wretched condition in relation to divine justice and his own responsibility. He denounces Dalila's claim to have acted out of high-minded religious and patriotic motives, or out of love, and threatens to tear her apart if she as much as touches him. He punctures the boastfulness of Harapha and dares the giant to close with him. The catastrophe approaches. But how has it been brought on by these events? Moreover, when the Philistine Officer relays the lords' command that Samson perform feats of strength at the festival of Dagon, Samson refuses (1319–21, 1332, 1342, 1345). He does not change his mind until "I begin to feel/Some rousing motions in me which dispose/To something extraordinary my thoughts" (1381–83). It is, apparently, the entrance of the will of God into dramatic time that points the play's inconsequential middle toward its catastrophe.

Johnson no doubt overstated the case. There is a causal middle of a sort in *Samson.* A frustrated Harapha stomps offstage, vowing that Samson will regret his insults "in irons loaden on thee" (1243). The Chorus remarks that "He will directly to the lords, I fear,/And with malicious counsel stir them up/Some way or other yet further to afflict thee" (1250–52). When, a few lines later, the Officer appears with the summons from "our lords" (l. 1310), it seems reasonable to infer that Harapha has indeed convinced them further to break and humiliate Samson. But this thin thread of causality does not constitute a solid Aristotelian middle, and nothing is here for tears. Johnson's criticism has actually had the effect of making the form of the drama seem mysterious and challenging rather than defective. Richard Cumberland addressed Johnson's strictures in 1785 (Shawcross 2:333–38). His answer animates many later discussions. Milton was not a determinist. The motions of divine guidance must be accepted by a freely willed act. In the course of the play we behold, alongside his terrible self-condemnation, the revival of Samson's fighting spirit. Accepting the blame and defending divine justice, denouncing Dalila, deflating Harapha, the disgraced and remorseful giant has again become able to see himself as God's champion. So he gropes his way toward an act that can be at once his revenge and his death, open as ever to the guidance of God. The revelation of his character, therefore, which is the main burden of the middle of the play, does in fact motivate or at least render comprehensible the tragic climax.

The question of the work's Christian spirit temporarily closed by Parker reemerged when a new generation of Miltonists, aware of the long and pervasive history of Christian typology, wanted to discuss how Milton modified Greek tragic structure to accommodate biblical figuralism. F. Michael Krouse demonstrated that commentaries on Judges identified Samson as a type of Christ. William Madsen cautioned that *type* did not mean "equivalent," and suggested that Milton was measuring the moral difference between Samson and Christ even as he connected them. Albert Cirillo found the Christological elements of the poem concentrated in the climactic appearance of the Phoenix (1971, 227–29).

Perhaps the structural soundness appropriate to a Christian Greek tragedy was not a middle, a causal paving making step after step into a linear road from the beginning to the end, but a pervasive irony that moves us back and forth from particular temporal moments to the full revelation at the conclusion. Anthony Low carefully categorized the kinds of irony in the work, ranging from simple reversals, in which characters do not in the end receive what they currently expect, to a unique "irony of alternatives" in which either-or disjunctions become both-and propositions from the perspective of the end (1974, 62–89). When Samson says, "This day will be remarkable in my life/By some great act, or of my days the last" (1388–89), the play ultimately collapses the pillars of his alternatives, revealing this day to be *both* remarkable by a great act *and* his last. Versions of this ironic effect appear throughout the work. Just a few lines later, Samson, leaving with the Officer, confesses that he does not know whether his life draws to an end: "The last of me or no I cannot warrant" (1426). Is it the last of him? He dies, but "though her body die, her fame survives" (1706), as the Chorus declares of the Samson-Phoenix. And does this ongoing fame contain the typological promise of the greater man to come, the beginning of whose career was in 1671 bound into the same volume containing Samson's ironically open end? Maintaining that the entire tragedy was adumbrated in the "guiding hand" of its opening passage, and repeatedly thereafter, even in the details of the imagery, Edward Tayler spoke of the work's "proleptic form": "We . . . find ourselves in the presence of a very considerable work of art, perhaps the unique example of specifically Christian tragedy; for Samson guided solely by God is not 'tragic,' as Samson guided solely by himself is not 'Christian.'" Downing the pillars of disjunctive logic, Milton invested Sophoclean irony with providential force (1979, 105–22).

A new chapter in Samson criticism was opened in 1986 with the publication of Joseph Wittreich's *Interpreting Samson Agonistes.* The catastrophe does not foreshadow Christ. The point of the 1671 volume is to manifest the ethical chasm between a sublime Christ and a barbarian Samson. His destruction of the temple is no better than vengeful mass murder. When Samson informs the Philistine assembly that he means to show them a feat of strength "of my own accord" (1643), he is telling them that he now acts on his own, without the sanction of God, despite the fact that in context he is distinguishing between his earlier commanded feats and his next uncommanded feat, and despite the fact that it is hard to fathom what his motive would be for so indirectly broaching this bit of theological news to uncomprehending Philistines. Wittreich claimed to find precedents for his view in the commentary tradition. His handling of historical evidence was called into question by Philip Gallagher (1987, 108–17) and Anthony Low (1987, 415–18); the books cited in *Interpreting Samson Agonistes* often fail to bear out the author's representation of them. But Wittreich's sense of the drama gained adherents. Galbraith Crump, Jacqueline DiSalvo, and others have accepted at least its general drift: Samson is a bad man. Aristotle thought the tragic hero should be somewhat better than ourselves (*Poetics* 13), since only in that case could real catharsis occur. The old idea of the work's Attic purity was quietly routed to oblivion along with recent discussions of the play's Christian form.

In 1994 a participant at the International Milton Seminar termed Samson a "terrorist." The practice has since become commonplace. "Could Milton have been celebrating the glory of an isolated terrorist?" Roy Flannagan asks, steering students toward the Wittreich interpretation. John Carey, in a piece written to commemorate the first anniversary of the 9/11 Al Qaeda attacks on the United

States, refers to the (in his mind) similar terrorist act at the climax of Milton's poem and announces that we are now once and for all beyond the old view of Samson acting with divine accord: "September 11 has changed *Samson Agonistes,* because it has changed the readings we can derive from it while still celebrating it as an achievement of the human imagination" (2002, 16; see also, mostly contra Carey, Fish 2006). This alarming statement would not allow us to discuss whether it should be taken at face value, as an odd but genuine expression of shock at the existence of violence in the world, or might instead be an instance of crass moral opportunism, allowing a critic to entertain the monstrously grandiose idea that his opponents have been smitten by history as profoundly as the Holocaust smote anti-Semites.

If Milton condemned Samson, might he have harbored goodwill toward Samson's opponents? William Empson, pre-Wittreich, wrote in defense of Dalila's worldliness, which he found attractive in contrast to the self-righteous fanaticism of her husband (1960). Empson declared himself to be alone in this endeavor, but admiring accounts of Dalila are now legion. John Ulreich observes of Dalila asking to touch Samson's hand, "Beneath all her elegant finery, Dalila is a woman desperately seeking love, struggling to find means by which to communicate her feelings to the man who hates her" (189). Any hint that Dalila might want to use sex to dominate and imprison Samson has been rigorously excluded from this airbrushed recitation of the episode. Roy Flannagan confesses that "Milton's Dalila is perhaps a more fascinating character than her male counterpart" (788). One cannot be quite sure what *counterpart* means here, since Dalila is not a giant, not a Philistine military hero, not a slayer of Israelites, not separate to Dagon, et cetera. Irene Samuel might have been in another world when she wrote, in an essay otherwise foreshadowing Wittreich's reading of the drama, "Dalila is surely the most bird-brained woman ever to have gotten herself involved in major tragedy" (248).

The Wittreich interpretation runs together a moral revulsion at the idea of God sanctioning the Philistine deaths with a corrective reading purporting to show that this revulsion is the play's intended sense. We should be clearer than we sometimes are about exactly what is at issue in assessing such claims. First of all, the judgment of this reading must not itself be driven by moral urgency. Wittreich's *Samson* should stand or fall as all readings do, by its support from the meanings of words and the formal designs of the work, by how plausibly it sorts with the author's other works and the works of his contemporaries. Were it to fail these tests, and the partnership of Samson and God celebrated in the choral victory ode (1660–1707) be deemed the work's probable intended meaning, any moral revulsion that readers feel at this sense would, of course, remain in place. This revulsion cannot be expected to disappear or conceal itself because the work could not legitimately be remade in its image. Like *Paradise Lost, Samson* is saturated with theodicy (Rumrich 2002). Disapproving readers should argue with Milton's God, or Milton, or the Western tradition's misuse of biblical folk-tales. Although one hears otherwise in the tense climate of current academic controversies, the defeat of an interpretation does not at all mean that a particular moral point of view will be "silenced." Times change. Interpretations come and go. The vast preponderance of them turn out to be wrong. But moral debates continue so long as there are proponents to be heard.

SAMSON AGONISTES

Of that Sort of Dramatic Poem which is Called Tragedy

Tragedy, as it was anciently composed, hath been ever held the gravest, moralest, and most profitable of all other poems: therefore said by Aristotle[1] to be of power by raising pity and fear, or terror, to purge the mind of those and such-like passions, that is to temper and reduce them to just measure with a kind of delight, stirred up by reading or seeing those passions well imitated. Nor is nature wanting in her own effects to make good his assertion: for so in physic things of melancholic hue and quality are used against melancholy, sour against sour, salt to remove salt humors.[2] Hence philosophers and other gravest writers, as Cicero, Plutarch, and others, frequently cite out of tragic poets, both to adorn and illustrate their discourse. The Apostle Paul himself thought it not unworthy to insert a verse of Euripides into the text of Holy Scripture, I Cor. 15.33, and Paraeus[3] commenting on the Revelation, divides the whole book as a tragedy, into acts distinguished each by a chorus of heavenly harpings and song between. Heretofore men in highest dignity have labored not a little to be thought able to compose a tragedy. Of that honor Dionysius the elder[4] was no less ambitious than before of his attaining to the tyranny. Augustus Caesar also had begun his *Ajax*,[5] but unable to please his own judgment with what he had begun, left it unfinished. Seneca the philosopher[6] is by some thought the author of those tragedies (at least the best of them) that go under that name. Gregory Nazianzen,[7] a Father of the Church, thought it not unbeseeming the sanctity of

1. **said by Aristotle:** Aristotle thought that "pity" was caused by the spectacle of a great man in distress, while "fear" resulted from our realization that a power higher than any human power determines events.
2. The analogy between tragic catharsis and homeopathic cures can be found in Minturno's *De Poeta* (1563) and Guarini's *Il Compendio della Poesia Tragicomica* (1601). See Sellin 1961.
3. **Paraeus:** David Paraeus, a German Calvinist, whose work on Revelation was translated into English as *On the Divine Apocalypse* (1644) by Elias Arnold.
4. **Dionysius the elder:** The Tyrant of Syracuse (431–367 B.C.E), who devoted much time to his poetry. He died while celebrating the news that one of his plays had at last won first prize at Athens.
5. **Augustus Caesar . . . Ajax:** Suetonius 2.85 says that Emperor Augustus, dissatisfied with his play *Ajax*, erased it.
6. **Seneca the philosopher:** Lucius Annaeus Seneca (55 B.C.E.–39 C.E.) wrote both philosophy and tragic drama, though there was some doubt over this fact in Milton's day.
7. **Gregory Nazianzen:** Fourth-century Bishop of Constantinople, and possible author of the play *Christus Patiens*, which contains passages from Euripides.

his person to write a tragedy, which he entitled *Christ Suffering*. This is mentioned to vindicate tragedy from the small esteem, or rather infamy, which in the account of many it undergoes at this day with other common interludes;[8] happening through the poet's error of intermixing comic stuff[9] with tragic sadness and gravity; or introducing trivial and vulgar persons, which by all judicious hath been counted absurd; and brought in without discretion, corruptly to gratify the people. And though ancient tragedy use no prologue,[10] yet using sometimes, in case of self-defense, or explanation, that which Martial[11] calls an epistle, in behalf of this tragedy coming forth after the ancient manner, much different from what among us passes for best, thus much beforehand may be epistled: that chorus is here introduced after the Greek manner, not ancient only, but modern, and still in use among the Italians.[12] In the modeling therefore of this poem, with good reason, the ancients and Italians are rather followed, as of much more authority and fame. The measure of verse used in the chorus is of all sorts, called by the Greeks monostrophic, or rather apolelymenon,[13] without regard had to strophe, antistrophe, or epode, which were a kind of stanzas framed only for the music, then used with the chorus that sung; not essential to the poem, and therefore not material; or being divided into stanzas or pauses, they may be called allaeostropha. Division into act and scene referring chiefly to the stage (to which this work never was intended) is here omitted.

It suffices if the whole drama be found not produced beyond the fifth act.[14] Of the style and uniformity, and that commonly called the plot, whether intricate or explicit,[15] which is nothing indeed but such economy, or disposition of the fable as may stand best with verisimilitude and decorum, they only will best judge who are not unacquainted with Aeschylus,[16] Sophocles, and Euripides, the three tragic poets unequaled yet by any, and the best rule to all who endeavor to write tragedy. The circumscription of time wherein the whole drama begins

8. **interludes:** comic plays.
9. **intermixing comic stuff:** Milton condemns the practice of mingling comic and tragic elements on the Elizabethan stage.
10. **prologue:** an initial speech in which a figure representing the author addresses the audience. In Greek drama, the "prologue" was the part of the play before the appearance of the Chorus. Samson's first speech (1–114) is, in the Greek sense, a prologue.
11. **Martial:** In the epistle to Book 2 of his *Epigrams,* Martial noted that plays, since they cannot speak for themselves, might need epistles. Dedicatory epistles were common features of Restoration plays in particular.
12. **among the Italians:** In part because of the influence of Seneca, the Chorus was a familiar feature of Italian Renaissance drama.
13. **monostrophic:** of only one stanza; **apolelymenon:** "freed" (from the restriction of a stanza pattern). In Greek drama the *strophe* was a stanza sung as the Chorus moved from right to left, while the *antistrophe* was a stanza sung during the opposite movement. The final *epode* was sung standing still. Milton suggests that if his choruses have stanzas, they are *allaeostropha,* or "irregular in strophes."
14. **not produced beyond the fifth act:** Horace maintained that a play should have five acts (*A.P.* 189). Dryden considered the matter in *An Essay of Dramatic Poesy* (*Essays* 1.45).
15. **intricate or explicit:** See Aristotle's *Poetics* 6, where plots are divided into complex and simple.
16. **Aeschylus:** At this time he was not commonly ranked with *Sophocles* and *Euripides,* but see Jonson, "To the Memory of . . . Shakespeare," 33–34.

and ends is according to ancient rule,[17] and best example, within the space of twenty-four hours.

The Argument

Samson made captive, blind, and now in the prison at Gaza, there to labor as in a common work-house, on a festival day, in the general cessation from labor, comes forth into the open air, to a place nigh, somewhat retired there to sit a while and bemoan his condition. Where he happens at length to be visited by certain friends and equals of his tribe, which make the Chorus, who seek to comfort him what they can; then by his old father Manoa, who endeavors the like, and withal tells him his purpose to procure his liberty by ransom; lastly, that this feast was proclaimed by the Philistines as a day of thanksgiving for their deliverance from the hands of Samson, which yet more troubles him. Manoa then departs to prosecute his endeavor with the Philistian lords for Samson's redemption; who in the meanwhile is visited by other persons; and lastly by a public officer to require his coming to the feast before the lords and people, to play or show his strength in their presence; he at first refuses, dismissing the public officer with absolute denial to come; at length persuaded inwardly that this was from God, he yields to go along with him, who came now the second time with great threatenings to fetch him; the Chorus yet remaining on the place, Manoa returns full of joyful hope, to procure ere long his son's deliverance: in the midst of which discourse an Hebrew comes in haste confusedly at first; and afterward more distinctly relating the catastrophe, what Samson had done to the Philistines, and by accident to himself; wherewith the tragedy ends.

The Persons

Samson
Manoa, the father of Samson
Dalila his wife
Harapha of Gath
Public Officer
Messenger
Chorus of Danites

The scene before the prison in Gaza

17. **ancient rule:** There was no ancient rule about circumscription of time except in the minds of Renaissance neoclassicists.

Samson. A little onward lend thy guiding hand
To these dark steps, a little further on;
For yonder bank hath choice of sun or shade,
There I am wont to sit, when any chance
Relieves me from my task of servile toil,
Daily in the common prison else enjoined me,
Where I a prisoner chained, scarce freely draw
The air imprisoned also, close and damp,
Unwholesome draft: but here I feel amends,
The breath of heav'n fresh-blowing, pure and sweet,
With day-spring born; here leave me to respire.
This day a solemn feast the people hold
To Dagon their sea-idol, and forbid
Laborious works; unwillingly this rest
Their superstition yields me; hence with leave
Retiring from the popular noise, I seek
This unfrequented place to find some ease,
Ease to the body some, none to the mind
From restless thoughts, that like a deadly swarm
Of hornets armed, no sooner found alone,
But rush upon me thronging, and present
Times past, what once I was, and what am now.
O wherefore was my birth from Heaven foretold
Twice by an angel, who at last in sight
Of both my parents all in flames ascended
From off the altar, where an off'ring burned,
As in a fiery column charioting
His godlike presence, and from some great act
Or benefit revealed to Abraham's race?
Why was my breeding ordered and prescribed

1–2. Milton imitates Greek models. Sophocles' *Oedipus at Colonus* opens with the blind Oedipus led by his daughter Antigone, and the blind Tiresias is likewise led by his daughter in Euripides' *Phoenician Women* 834–35.

3. **choice of sun or shade:** Cp. 1605–11, where the choice becomes a matter of life and death for Philistines attending the festival of Dagon.

5. **servile:** Grinding was a task given to slaves of the lowest class (Exod. 11.5, 12.29).

6. **else:** at other times.

11. **day-spring:** daybreak.

13. **Dagon their sea-idol:** Dagon, a Phoenician god particularly associated with Gaza and Ashdod, appears in *Paradise Lost* as a "sea monster, upward man/And downward fish" (1.462–63).

15–22. Cp. *PR* 1.196–200. In the first of many parallels with the companion poem, Samson like the Son of God retires to a place of solitude and is subject to swarming thoughts. The parallels also throw into relief fundamental differences between the heroes of the two poems.

22. **what once . . . am now:** Cp. *PL* 4.24–25.

23–24. **foretold / Twice by an angel:** Judg. 13.3–5 and 10–13. This double foretelling is recounted three times; see lines 361 and 635.

27. **charioting:** Samson is probably thinking of Elijah's translation to Heaven (2 Kings 3.11; also Ezek. 1 and 10).

28. **from some great act:** as from some great act.

As of a person separate to God,
Designed for great exploits, if I must die
Betrayed, captived, and both my eyes put out,
Made of my enemies the scorn and gaze,
To grind in brazen fetters under task
With this Heav'n-gifted strength? O glorious strength
Put to the labor of a beast, debased
Lower than bondslave! Promise was that I
Should Israel from Philistian yoke deliver;
Ask for this great deliverer now, and find him
Eyeless in Gaza at the mill with slaves,
Himself in bonds under Philistian yoke;
Yet stay, let me not rashly call in doubt
Divine prediction; what if all foretold
Had been fulfilled but through mine own default,
Whom have I to complain of but myself?
Who this high gift of strength committed to me,
In what part lodged, how easily bereft me,
Under the seal of silence could not keep,
But weakly to a woman must reveal it,
O'ercome with importunity and tears.
O impotence of mind, in body strong!
But what is strength without a double share
Of wisdom? Vast, unwieldly, burdensome,
Proudly secure, yet liable to fall
By weakest subtleties; not made to rule,
But to subserve where wisdom bears command.
God, when he gave me strength, to show withal
How slight the gift was, hung it in my hair.
But peace, I must not quarrel with the will
Of highest dispensation, which herein
Haply had ends above my reach to know:
Suffices that to me strength is my bane,
And proves the source of all my miseries;
So many, and so huge, that each apart

31. **separate:** Samson is a Nazarite, one set apart to serve God. The term derives from the Hebrew *nazar,* "to separate." See Num. 6.2–8.

34. **gaze:** display, spectacle.

37. **labor of a beast:** Asses were employed in mills; see line 1162.

38. **Promise was:** it was promised; see Judg. 13.5.

43–44. **Yet stay . . . prediction:** Like *A Masque* and *Paradise Lost, Samson Agonistes* is concerned with theodicy. See 60–62, 210, 1745–58.

50. **woman:** The implication is that it would have been bad enough to tell his secret to a man but worse to tell it to a woman.

55. **secure:** heedless, overconfident (from Lat. *securus*).

63. **suffices:** I.e., "it is enough that I realize."

Would ask a life to wail, but chief of all,
O loss of sight, of thee I most complain!
Blind among enemies, O worse than chains,
Dungeon, or beggary, or decrepit age!
Light, the prime work of God, to me is extinct,
And all her various objects of delight
Annulled, which might in part my grief have eased,
Inferior to the vilest now become
Of man or worm; the vilest here excel me,
They creep, yet see; I dark in light exposed
To daily fraud, contempt, abuse and wrong,
Within doors, or without, still as a fool,
In power of others, never in my own;
Scarce half I seem to live, dead more than half.
O dark, dark, dark, amid the blaze of noon,
Irrecoverably dark, total eclipse
Without all hope of day!
O first-created beam, and thou great word,
"Let there be light, and light was over all,"
Why am I thus bereaved thy prime decree?
The sun to me is dark
And silent as the moon,
When she deserts the night
Hid in her vacant interlunar cave.
Since light so necessary is to life,
And almost life itself, if it be true
That light is in the soul,
She all in every part, why was the sight
To such a tender ball as th' eye confined?
So obvious and so easy to be quenched,
And not as feeling through all parts diffused,
That she might look at will through every pore?
Then had I not been thus exiled from light;

66. **ask:** require, need.

68–79. This catalog of mutually aggravating evils is anticipated in the letter to Henry Oldenburg, July 6, 1654, where the blind Milton promises continued labors for liberty "if illness allow and this blindness, which is more oppressive than the whole of old age, and finally the cries of such brawlers" (Yale 4, pt. 2:866).

70. **prime work:** first creation (after Heaven and Earth); see Gen. 1.3.

77. **still:** always.

83. **Without all:** without any.

85. **bereaved:** robbed of.

87. **silent:** "of the moon: not shining" (*OED* 5a); see Pliny, *Natural History* 16.74.

89. **vacant:** "empty" and "at leisure"; **interlunar cave:** Following an ancient conception, Samson thinks of the moon as resting in a cave between the old and new moons.

93. **She all in every part:** Milton thought, with Augustine and others, that the soul is entire in every part of the body; see *CD* 1.7.

95. **obvious:** exposed, vulnerable.

96. **as feeling:** as feeling is.

As in the land of darkness yet in light,
To live a life half dead, a living death,
And buried; but O yet more miserable!
Myself my sepulcher, a moving grave,
Buried, yet not exempt
By privilege of death and burial
From worst of other evils, pains and wrongs,
But made hereby obnoxious more
To all the miseries of life,
Life in captivity
Among inhuman foes.
But who are these? For with joint pace I hear
The tread of many feet steering this way;
Perhaps my enemies who come to stare
At my affliction, and perhaps to insult,
Their daily practice to afflict me more.
Chorus. This, this is he; softly a while,
Let us not break in upon him;
O change beyond report, thought, or belief!
See how he lies at random, carelessly diffused,
With languished head unpropped,
As one past hope, abandoned,
And by himself given over;
In slavish habit, ill-fitted weeds
O'er-worn and soiled;
Or do my eyes misrepresent? Can this be he,
That heroic, that renowned,
Irresistible Samson? Whom unarmed
No strength of man, or fiercest wild beast could withstand;
Who tore the lion, as the lion tears the kid,
Ran on embattled armies clad in iron,
And weaponless himself,
Made arms ridiculous, useless the forgery
Of brazen shield and spear, the hammered cuirass,
Chalybean tempered steel, and frock of mail

100. **a living death:** a fate feared by Adam (*PL* 10.788).
106. **obnoxious:** exposed (to injury).
118. **at random:** without care; **diffused:** spread out.
119. **languished:** drooping.
128. **tore the lion:** Samson tears a lion in Judg. 14.5–6.
129. **embattled:** armed for battle and arranged in battle formations.
131. **forgery:** forging.
132. **cuirass:** breastplate.
133. **Chalybean:** The Chalybes, of Pontus on the Black Sea, were known for their work in iron and steel. **frock of mail:** coat of mail.

Adamantean proof;
But safest he who stood aloof,
When insupportably his foot advanced,
In scorn of their proud arms and warlike tools,
Spurned them to death by troops. The bold Ascalonite
Fled from his lion ramp, old warriors turned
Their plated backs under his heel;
Or grov'ling soiled their crested helmets in the dust.
Then with what trivial weapon came to hand,
The jaw of a dead ass, his sword of bone,
A thousand foreskins fell, the flower of Palestine
In Ramath-lechi famous to this day:
Then by main force pulled up, and on his shoulders bore
The gates of Azza, post, and massy bar
Up to the hill by Hebron, seat of giants old,
No journey of a Sabbath day, and loaded so;
Like whom the Gentiles feign to bear up heav'n.
Which shall I first bewail,
Thy bondage or lost sight,
Prison within prison
Inseparably dark?
Thou art become (O worst imprisonment!)
The dungeon of thyself; thy soul
(Which men enjoying sight oft without cause complain)
Imprisoned now indeed,
In real darkness of the body dwells,
Shut up from outward light

134. **Adamantean proof:** capable of withstanding adamant, the hardest substance.

136. **insupportably:** irresistibly.

137. **tools:** weapons.

138. **Spurned:** trampled; **Ascalonite:** Ascalon was a Philistine city near Gaza.

139. **lion ramp:** a lion reared on its hind legs, familiar in heraldry.

142–43. See Judg. 15.15–16 for Samson's feats with the jawbone of an ass.

144. **foreskins:** uncircumcised Philistines.

145. **Ramath-lechi:** Samson in Judg. 15.17 discards the jawbone in Ramath-lechi, which took its name from the Hebrew for "lifting up or casting away of a jawbone."

147. **Azza:** variant form of Gaza. Samson's exploit with the gate is taken from Judg. 16.3.

148. **Hebron:** Hebron was the home of giants, the sons of Anak (Num. 13.22–33).

149. **No journey of a Sabbath day:** Jewish law restricted travel on the Sabbath, depending on one's computation, to between a half mile and a mile and a half. Hebron is roughly forty miles from Gaza.

150. **whom . . . heav'n:** Atlas, one of the Titans, who was supposed to support the heavens on his head and shoulders.

156–63. **thy soul . . . visual beam:** The Neoplatonist commonplace that the soul is imprisoned in the body is mistaken (and therefore *without cause*) because, in Milton's materialist perspective, the soul and body are continuous. But because of Samson's blindness, with its blocking of the *visual beam* usually thought in Milton's time to travel from the perceiver to the perceived object, he is in a different and true sense trapped inside the dark walls of his body. His soul now *incorporates* (161), or becomes one body with, night and darkness.

To incorporate with gloomy night;
For inward light alas
Puts forth no visual beam.
O mirror of our fickle state,
Since man on earth unparalleled!
The rarer thy example stands,
By how much from the top of wondrous glory,
Strongest of mortal men,
To lowest pitch of abject fortune thou art fall'n.
For him I reckon not in high estate
Whom long descent of birth
Or the sphere of fortune raises;
But thee whose strength, while virtue was her mate,
Might have subdued the earth,
Universally crowned with highest praises.
Samson. I hear the sound of words, their sense the air
Dissolves unjointed ere it reach my ear.
Chorus. He speaks, let us draw nigh. Matchless in might,
The glory late of Israel, now the grief,
We come thy friends and neighbors not unknown
From Eshtaol and Zora's fruitful vale
To visit or bewail thee, or if better,
Counsel or consolation we may bring,
Salve to thy sores; apt words have power to 'suage
The tumors of a troubled mind,
And are as balm to festered wounds.
Samson. Your coming, friends, revives me, for I learn
Now of my own experience, not by talk,
How counterfeit a coin they are who friends
Bear in their superscription (of the most
I would be understood); in prosperous days
They swarm, but in adverse withdraw their head
Not to be found, though sought. Ye see, O friends,
How many evils have enclosed me round;
Yet that which was the worst now least afflicts me,
Blindness, for had I sight, confused with shame,

164. **mirror:** reflector; pattern, exemplar.

165. "Unparalleled since the creation of man."

169. **pitch:** Though *pitch* usually refers to height, here it clearly means depth.

172. **sphere of fortune:** the familiar metaphor of the "wheel of fortune" figured as a spinning globe.

181. **Eshtaol and Zora:** Manoa and his wife lived in Zora; Samson was first moved by the Spirit between Zora and nearby Eshtaol, and he was buried between the two cities (Judg. 13.2, 13.25, and 16.31).

185. **tumors:** the swelling of passion in the mind.

190. **superscription:** inscription on a coin.

190–91. **of the most/I would be understood:** "I am speaking of most people."

How could I once look up, or heave the head,
Who like a foolish pilot have shipwrecked
My vessel trusted to me from above,
Gloriously rigged; and for a word, a tear,
Fool, have divulged the secret gift of God
To a deceitful woman: tell me, friends,
Am I not sung and proverbed for a fool
In every street, do they not say, "How well
Are come upon him his deserts?" Yet why?
Immeasurable strength they might behold
In me, of wisdom nothing more than mean;
This with the other should, at least, have paired,
These two proportioned ill drove me transverse.
    Chorus. Tax not divine disposal; wisest men
Have erred, and by bad women been deceived;
And shall again, pretend they ne'er so wise.
Deject not then so overmuch thyself,
Who hast of sorrow thy full load besides;
Yet truth to say, I oft have heard men wonder
Why thou shouldst wed Philistian women rather
Than of thine own tribe fairer, or as fair,
At least of thy own nation, and as noble.
    Samson. The first I saw at Timna, and she pleased
Me, not my parents, that I sought to wed,
The daughter of an infidel: they knew not
That what I motioned was of God; I knew
From intimate impulse, and therefore urged
The marriage on; that by occasion hence

197. **heave:** lift, as in *Masque* 885; *L'All* 145.

198–200. **Who . . . rigged:** The first of several nautical metaphors in the poem; see also lines 710–19, 1044–45, 1061–63, and 1070.

200. **for:** because of.

207. **mean:** middling, average.

208. "His wisdom should have been equal to (*paired with*) his strength." Samson returns to an argument made in his first speech (52–57).

209. **transverse:** off course (continuing the ship metaphor).

210. **Tax not divine disposal:** "Do not blame God's direction of events."

210–11. **wisest men . . . been deceived:** Here as elsewhere Samson gives voice to Milton's preoccupations. He wrote in the *Doctrine and Discipline of Divorce* of the susceptibility of the best and wisest men to poor marriage choices: "It may yet befall a discreet man to be mistaken in his [marriage] choice, and we have plenty of examples. The soberest and best governed men are least practiced in these affairs" (p. 873). See also *Tetrachordon* (p. 999).

212. **pretend they ne'er so wise:** "however wise they claim to be" or "however wise their intentions may be" (*pretend* = intend).

216–18. In Judges, Samson marries only the woman of Timna; Dalila may or may not have been Philistian. Milton supposes her to be a Philistine and to be Samson's wife.

219–27. For Samson's marriage to the woman of Timna, see Judg. 14.1–20. Timna, modern Tibneh, is a town south of Gath.

222. **motioned:** proposed.

223. **intimate:** inward.

224. **by occasion hence:** by the chance or opportunity the marriage afforded.

I might begin Israel's deliverance,
The work to which I was divinely called;
She proving false, the next I took to wife
(O that I never had! Fond wish too late)
Was in the vale of Sorec, Dalila,
That specious monster, my accomplished snare.
I thought it lawful from my former act,
And the same end; still watching to oppress
Israel's oppressors: of what now I suffer
She was not the prime cause, but I myself,
Who, vanquished with a peal of words (O weakness!),
Gave up my fort of silence to a woman.
Chorus. In seeking just occasion to provoke
The Philistine, thy country's enemy,
Thou never wast remiss, I bear thee witness:
Yet Israel still serves with all his sons.
Samson. That fault I take not on me, but transfer
On Israel's governors and heads of tribes,
Who, seeing those great acts which God had done
Singly by me against their conquerors,
Acknowledged not, or not at all considered
Deliverance offered: I on th' other side
Used no ambition to commend my deeds;
The deeds themselves, though mute, spoke loud the doer;
But they persisted deaf, and would not seem
To count them things worth notice, till at length
Their lords, the Philistines, with gathered powers
Entered Judea seeking me, who then
Safe to the rock of Etham was retired,

228. **Fond:** foolish.

229. **in the vale of Sorec, Dalila:** See Judg. 16.4; the meter here and elsewhere tells us that Milton pronounced the name with stresses on the first and last syllables, "Dá li lá."

230. **specious:** fair-seeming but deceptive; **accomplished**: "complete," in that Samson has indeed been snared, and also a rueful reference to Dalila's many accomplishments (such as cunning, persuasiveness, ability to wound and humiliate).

231–32. **from my former act/And the same end:** Samson had done the same thing before (marry a Philistine), and for the same reason (to oppress the Philistines).

235. **peal:** The word was used of any loud noise. Given *fort* in the next line, Milton probably has in mind an artillery barrage.

241–76. While recounting events recorded in Judges 15, Milton almost certainly alludes to the Restoration and rebukes the English for rejecting their deliverers (among whom Milton claimed for himself a prominent place) and embracing servitude under a corrupt monarch.

247. **ambition:** active canvassing for public support and recognition.

251. **powers:** armed forces.

253. **rock of Etham:** Judg. 15.8. Note that Milton elides in his account what immediately precedes Samson's retirement to the rock of Etham, his firing of the grain fields of Timna by releasing foxes with burning tails, an episode that Milton once listed as a potential subject for a tragedy (Yale 8.556); in Milton's account, overtones of private grudge and vandalism are replaced by an emphasis on principled political action.

Not flying, but forecasting in what place
To set upon them, what advantaged best;
Meanwhile the men of Judah to prevent
The harrass of their land, beset me round;
I willingly on some conditions came
Into their hands, and they as gladly yield me
To the uncircumcised a welcome prey,
Bound with two cords; but cords to me were threads
Touched with the flame: on their whole host I flew
Unarmed, and with a trivial weapon felled
Their choicest youth; they only lived who fled.
Had Judah that day joined, or one whole tribe,
They had by this possessed the towers of Gath,
And lorded over them whom now they serve;
But what more oft in nations grown corrupt,
And by their vices brought to servitude,
Than to love bondage more than liberty,
Bondage with ease than strenuous liberty;
And to despise, or envy, or suspect
Whom God hath of his special favor raised
As their deliverer; if he aught begin,
How frequent to desert him, and at last
To heap ingratitude on worthiest deeds?
Chorus. Thy words to my remembrance bring
How Succoth and the fort of Penuel
Their great deliverer contemned,
The matchless Gideon in pursuit
Of Madian and her vanquished kings:
And how ingrateful Ephraim

254. **forecasting:** planning.

258. **on some conditions:** i.e., that the Israelites would not themselves attack Samson (Judg. 15.12).

261–62. **cords . . . flame:** Judg. 15.13–14.

263. See lines 142–45.

266. **by this:** by this time; **Gath:** Philistine city, home of Harapha (1068), here standing in for all of Philistia.

270–71. **to love bondage . . . strenuous liberty:** Samson here speaks in the accents of Milton's polemical prose. The same sentiment is placed, ironically, in the mouth of Mammon in *PL*: "preferring / Hard liberty before the easy yoke / Of servile pomp" (2.255–57).

272–76. As Masson suggested, Milton in these lines may well have had himself in mind. In his prose he often referred to himself as God's spokesperson and agent of liberty. After the Restoration, he found himself "fall'n on evil days, / . . . and evil tongues; / In darkness, and with dangers compassed round, / And solitude" (*PL* 7.25–28).

278–81. In Judg. 8.4–9, the Israelites in *Succoth* and *Penuel* refuse to help Gideon's army as it pursues Zebah and Zalmunna, the vanquished Midian kings.

282–89. Another example from Judges (11.12–33, 12.1–6). The Ephraimite Israelites, having refused to help *Jephtha* and the Gileadites against the *Ammonites,* threatened Jephtha after his victory. At the fords of the Jordan, Jephtha slaughtered the defeated Ephraimites, who were betrayed by their inability to pronounce "Shibboleth."

Had dealt with Jephtha, who by argument,
Not worse than by his shield and spear
Defended Israel from the Ammonite,
Had not his prowess quelled their pride
In that sore battle when so many died
Without reprieve adjudged to death,
For want of well pronouncing "Shibboleth."
Samson. Of such examples add me to the roll;
Me easily indeed mine may neglect,
But God's proposed deliverance not so.
Chorus. Just are the ways of God,
And justifiable to men,
Unless there be who think not God at all;
If any be, they walk obscure,
For of such doctrine never was there school
But the heart of the fool,
And no man therein doctor but himself.
Yet more there be who doubt his ways not just,
As to his own edicts, found contradicting,
Then give the reins to wand'ring thought,
Regardless of his glory's diminution;
Till by their own perplexities involved
They ravel more, still less resolved,
But never find self-satisfying solution.
As if they would confine th' interminable,
And tie him to his own prescript,
Who made our laws to bind us, not himself,
And hath full right to exempt
Whom so it pleases him by choice
From national obstriction, without taint
Of sin, or legal debt;

283. **Had dealt:** would have dealt.

291. **mine:** my compatriot Hebrews.

294. "Just and true are thy ways" (Ps. 145.17, Rev. 15.3). Theodicy is never far from Milton's mind; his main intention in *PL* is to "justify the ways of God to men" (1.26). See 43–44n.

295. **think not God:** do not think that God exists.

297. **such doctrine . . . school:** Atheism never became a sect professing a systematic philosophy.

298. **the heart of the fool:** "The fool hath said in his heart, There is no God" (Ps. 14.1). Milton quotes this verse at the beginning of *CD* 1.2, and goes on to remark: "But he [God] has left so many signs of himself in the human mind, so many traces of his presence through the whole of nature, that no sane person can fail to realize that he exists" (p. 1145).

299. **doctor:** learned man, teacher.

302. **wand'ring thought:** compare the devils' aimless and godless thinking, "in wand'ring mazes lost," and Belial's "thoughts that wander through eternity" in *PL* 2.561 and 2.148. Wandering thought in Milton is opposed to thought directed by apprehension of the divine plan.

305. **ravel:** become entangled; **still less resolved:** ever in greater doubt and perplexity.

312. **national obstriction:** legal obligation not to marry a Gentile (Deut. 7.3); the Chorus suggests that God can *dispense* with (abrogate, cancel) this law and move an Israelite to marry a

For with his own laws he can best dispense.
He would not else who never wanted means,
Nor, in respect of the enemy just cause
To set his people free,
Have prompted this heroic Nazarite,
Against his vow of strictest purity,
To seek in marriage that fallacious bride,
Unclean, unchaste.
Down Reason then, at least vain reasonings down,
Though Reason here aver
That moral verdict quits her of unclean:
Unchaste was subsequent, her stain not his.
But see here comes thy reverend sire
With careful step, locks white as down,
Old Manoa: advise
Forthwith how thou ought'st to receive him.
Samson. Ay me, another inward grief awaked,
With mention of that name renews th' assault.
Manoa. Brethren and men of Dan, for such ye seem,
Though in this uncouth place; if old respect,
As I suppose, towards your once gloried friend,
My son now captive, hither hath informed
Your younger feet, while mine cast back with age
Came lagging after; say if he be here.
Chorus. As signal now in low dejected state,
As erst in highest, behold him where he lies.
Manoa. O miserable change! Is this the man,
That invincible Samson, far renowned,
The dread of Israel's foes, who with a strength
Equivalent to angels walked their streets,
None offering fight; who single combatant
Dueled their armies ranked in proud array,
Himself an army, now unequal match
To save himself against a coward armed
At one spear's length? O ever-failing trust
In mortal strength! And O what not in man

Gentile; *strictest purity* (319) refers to avoidance of mixed marriages, not to celibacy, which was not required of Nazarites.

321. **Unclean:** according to Mosaic Law.

324. **quits:** acquits.

325. **Unchaste was subsequent:** The woman of Timna, having been rejected by Samson, was given to Samson's companion (Judg. 14.20), and thus the unchastity was subsequent to their wedding.

327. **careful:** full of care.

328. **advise:** consider.

332. **Dan:** the territory of Samson's tribe.

333. **uncouth:** unfamiliar.

335. **informed:** directed, guided.

338. **signal:** conspicuous.

Deceivable and vain! Nay what thing good
Prayed for, but often proves our woe, our bane?
I prayed for children, and thought barrenness
In wedlock a reproach; I gained a son,
And such a son as all men hailed me happy;
Who would be now a father in my stead?
O wherefore did God grant me my request,
And as a blessing with such pomp adorned?
Why are his gifts desirable, to tempt
Our earnest prayers, then, giv'n with solemn hand
As graces, draw a scorpion's tail behind?
For this did the angel twice descend? For this
Ordained thy nurture holy, as of a plant;
Select, and sacred, glorious for a while,
The miracle of men: then in an hour
Ensnared, assaulted, overcome, led bound,
Thy foes' derision, captive, poor, and blind,
Into a dungeon thrust, to work with slaves?
Alas methinks whom God hath chosen once
To worthiest deeds, if he through frailty err,
He should not so o'erwhelm, and as a thrall
Subject him to so foul indignities,
Be it but for honor's sake of former deeds.
    Samson. Appoint not Heavenly disposition, father,
Nothing of all these evils hath befall'n me
But justly; I myself have brought them on,
Sole author I, sole cause: if aught seem vile,
As vile hath been my folly, who have profaned
The mystery of God giv'n me under pledge
Of vow, and have betrayed it to a woman
A Canaanite, my faithless enemy.
This well I knew, nor was at all surprised
But warned by oft experience: did not she
Of Timna first betray me, and reveal
The secret wrested from me in her highth
Of nuptial love professed, carrying it straight

354. **as:** that.
363. **Select:** set aside.
373. **Appoint:** both "assign blame to" and "fix, or place a limit on."
377. **profaned:** disclosed a sacred secret (Lat. *profanum,* "outside the temple").
380. **Canaanite:** the Philistines had occupied Canaan.
384. **secret:** the solution to Samson's riddle (Judg. 14). Samson had posed a riddle to the thirty Philistine groomsmen at his first wedding; they prevailed upon the woman of Timna to draw the answer from Samson, who slew the thirty in a rage. The treachery of the woman of Timna foreshadows Dalila's, and thus adds to the *experience* (382) that makes Samson more culpable.

To them who had corrupted her, my spies,
And rivals? In this other was there found
More faith? Who also in her prime of love,
Spousal embraces, vitiated with gold,
Though offered only, by the scent conceived
Her spurious first-born, Treason against me?
Thrice she assayed with flattering prayers and sighs,
And amorous reproaches to win from me
My capital secret, in what part my strength
Lay stored, in what part summed, that she might know:
Thrice I deluded her, and turned to sport
Her importunity, each time perceiving
How openly, and with what impudence
She purposed to betray me, and (which was worse
Than undissembled hate) with what contempt
She sought to make me traitor to myself;
Yet the fourth time, when must'ring all her wiles,
With blandished parleys, feminine assaults,
Tongue-batteries, she surceased not day nor night
To storm me over-watched, and wearied out.
At times when men seek most repose and rest,
I yielded, and unlocked her all my heart,
Who with a grain of manhood well resolved
Might easily have shook off all her snares:
But foul effeminacy held me yoked
Her bond-slave. O indignity, O blot
To honor and religion! Servile mind
Rewarded well with servile punishment!
The base degree to which I now am fall'n,
These rags, this grinding, is not yet so base
As was my former servitude, ignoble,
Unmanly, ignominious, infamous,
True slavery, and that blindness worse than this,
That saw not how degenerately I served.
Manoa. I cannot praise thy marriage choices, son,

389–91. The mere offer, or *scent,* of gold is enough to impregnate Dalila with treason, her illegitimate, or *spurious,* child. **vitiated:** corrupted.

392–409. Judg. 16.6–22.

394. **capital:** both "lethal" and "pertaining to the head."

403. **blandished parleys:** flattering conversations.

405. **over-watched:** tired from being on alert.

414. **degree:** rank.

420. The line is sometimes said to be an example of bathetic understatement. But our desire for a humorous moment should not blind us to the disciplined plain speaking here, given that Manoa is but a man and cannot understand if or why God would lead his son to such women. Cp. the plainness of Jesus in *PR* 4.171: "I never liked thy talk, thy offers less."

Rather approved them not; but thou didst plead
Divine impulsion prompting how thou might'st
Find some occasion to infest our foes.
I state not that; this I am sure, our foes
Found soon occasion thereby to make thee
Their captive, and their triumph; thou the sooner
Temptation found'st, or over-potent charms
To violate the sacred trust of silence
Deposited within thee; which to have kept
Tacit was in thy power; true; and thou bear'st
Enough, and more the burden of that fault;
Bitterly hast thou paid, and still art paying
That rigid score. A worse thing yet remains:
This day the Philistines a popular feast
Here celebrate in Gaza, and proclaim
Great pomp, and sacrifice, and praises loud
To Dagon, as their god who hath delivered
Thee Samson bound and blind into their hands,
Them out of thine, who slew'st them many a slain.
So Dagon shall be magnified, and God,
Besides whom is no God, compared with idols,
Disglorified, blasphemed, and had in scorn
By th' idolatrous rout amidst their wine;
Which to have come to pass by means of thee,
Samson, of all thy sufferings think the heaviest,
Of all reproach the most with shame that ever
Could have befall'n thee and thy father's house.
Samson. Father, I do acknowledge and confess
That I this honor, I this pomp have brought
To Dagon, and advanced his praises high
Among the heathen round; to God have brought
Dishonor, obloquy, and oped the mouths
Of idolists and atheists; have brought scandal
To Israel, diffidence of God, and doubt

422. **prompting:** suggesting.

423. **infest:** annoy, plague.

424. **state not:** do not comment upon. Manoa will not discuss whether Samson's marriages were both divinely prompted but will instead pass on to the subject about which he is certain.

433. **rigid score:** stiff debt.

434–38. With Samson blinded and captive, the Philistine lords resolved "to offer a great sacrifice unto Dagon their god, and to rejoice: for they said, Our god hath delivered Samson our enemy into our hand" (Judg. 16.23).

439. **Them out of thine:** the Philistines out of Samson's hands; **slew'st them many a slain:** slew many of them, to their loss; an imitation of the Latin dative of disadvantage.

442. **Disglorified:** deprived of glory.

443. **rout:** multitude; the word is frequent in Milton, and always derogatory.

450. **advanced:** raised aloft.

454. **diffidence:** distrust.

In feeble hearts, propense enough before
To waver, or fall off and join with idols;
Which is my chief affliction, shame and sorrow,
The anguish of my soul, that suffers not
Mine eye to harbor sleep, or thoughts to rest.
This only hope relieves me, that the strife
With me hath end; all the contest is now
'Twixt God and Dagon; Dagon hath presumed,
Me overthrown, to enter lists with God,
His deity comparing and preferring
Before the God of Abraham. He, be sure,
Will not connive, or linger, thus provoked,
But will arise and his great name assert:
Dagon must stoop, and shall ere long receive
Such a discomfit, as shall quite despoil him
Of all these boasted trophies won on me,
And with confusion blank his worshippers.
    Manoa. With cause this hope relieves thee, and these words
I as a prophecy receive: for God,
Nothing more certain, will not long defer
To vindicate the glory of his name
Against all competition, nor will long
Endure it, doubtful whether God be Lord,
Or Dagon. But for thee what shall be done?
Thou must not in the meanwhile here forgot
Lie in this miserable loathsome plight
Neglected. I already have made way
To some Philistian lords, with whom to treat
About thy ransom: well they may by this
Have satisfied their utmost of revenge
By pains and slaveries, worse than death inflicted
On thee, who now no more canst do them harm.
    Samson. Spare that proposal, father, spare the trouble
Of that solicitation; let me here,
As I deserve, pay on my punishment;
And expiate, if possible, my crime,
Shameful garrulity. To have revealed

455. **propense:** ready, inclined.
456. **fall off:** break away from allegiance.
460. **only:** one, sole.
466. **connive:** tolerate; carries the Latin sense of "shut the eyes."
467. **assert:** champion.
469. **discomfit:** defeat.
470. **won on:** won over.
471. **confusion:** ruin, overthrow; **blank:** confound.
481–83. **I . . . ransom:** Milton adds Manoa's attempt to ransom Samson to the biblical account.
481–82. **made way/To:** approached.
483. **by this:** by this time.

Secrets of men, the secrets of a friend,
How heinous had the fact been, how deserving
Contempt, and scorn of all, to be excluded
All friendship, and avoided as a blab,
The mark of fool set on his front?
But I God's counsel have not kept, his holy secret
Presumptuously have published, impiously,
Weakly at least, and shamefully: a sin
That Gentiles in their parables condemn
To their abyss and horrid pains confined.
Manoa. Be penitent and for thy fault contrite,
But act not in thy own affliction, son,
Repent the sin, but if the punishment
Thou canst avoid, self-preservation bids;
Or th' execution leave to high disposal,
And let another hand, not thine, exact
Thy penal forfeit from thyself; perhaps
God will relent, and quit thee all his debt;
Who evermore approves and more accepts
(Best pleased with humble and filial submission)
Him who imploring mercy sues for life,
Than who self-rigorous chooses death as due;
Which argues over-just, and self-displeased
For self-offense, more than for God offended.
Reject not then what offered means, who knows
But God hath set before us, to return thee
Home to thy country and his sacred house,
Where thou may'st bring thy off'rings, to avert
His further ire, with prayers and vows renewed.
Samson. His pardon I implore; but as for life,
To what end should I seek it? When in strength
All mortals I excelled, and great in hopes
With youthful courage and magnanimous thoughts
Of birth from Heav'n foretold and high exploits,
Full of divine instinct, after some proof

493. **fact:** deed.

496. **front:** forehead.

499–501. **a sin . . . confined:** Tantalus was punished for revealing the gods' secrets (Euripides, *Orestes* 10). Ovid emphasizes his garrulity (*Ars Amatoria* 2.603–7).

503–15. In *CD* 2.8, Milton relates suicide to "a perverse hatred of oneself" (Yale 6:719). Manoa cautions Samson against suicide, advising his son to leave judgment and punishment to God. Samson often sounds suicidal (595–98, 647–52, 1262–67), and readers argue over whether his final act is a divinely authorized attack on the enemies of Israel or a blamable act of suicide or both (see 1584–86).

509. **quit thee all his debt:** cancel all your debt to him.

514. **argues over-just:** shows one to be overly scrupulous.

526. **instinct:** impulse; cp. lines 223 and 1382.

Of acts indeed heroic, far beyond
The sons of Anak, famous now and blazed,
Fearless of danger, like a petty god
I walked about admired of all and dreaded
On hostile ground, none daring my affront.
Then swoll'n with pride into the snare I fell
Of fair fallacious looks, venereal trains,
Softened with pleasure and voluptuous life;
At length to lay my head and hallowed pledge
Of all my strength in the lascivious lap
Of a deceitful concubine who shore me
Like a tame wether, all my precious fleece,
Then turned me out ridiculous, despoiled,
Shav'n, and disarmed among my enemies.
Chorus. Desire of wine and all delicious drinks,
Which many a famous warrior overturns,
Thou couldst repress, nor did the dancing ruby
Sparkling, out-poured, the flavor, or the smell,
Or taste that cheers the heart of gods and men,
Allure thee from the cool crystalline stream.
Samson. Wherever fountain or fresh current flowed
Against the eastern ray, translucent, pure,
With touch ethereal of Heav'n's fiery rod
I drank, from the clear milky juice allaying
Thirst, and refreshed; nor envied them the grape
Whose heads that turbulent liquor fills with fumes.
Chorus. O madness, to think use of strongest wines
And strongest drinks our chief support of health,
When God with these forbidd'n made choice to rear
His mighty champion, strong above compare,
Whose drink was only from the liquid brook.
Samson. But what availed this temperance, not complete
Against another object more enticing?
What boots it at one gate to make defense,

528. **sons of Anak:** giants; **blazed:** much spoken of.

531. **my affront:** to meet me.

533. **fallacious:** deceptive, perhaps with a pun on *phallic;* **venereal trains:** sexual traps.

535. **At length to lay:** at length so softened as to lay (see Judg. 26.19); **pledge:** his hair, the source of his strength and mark of divine favor.

537. **concubine:** Here Samson for once does not own Dalila as his wife.

538. **wether:** castrated ram.

541–46. As a Nazarite, Samson took a vow to abstain from alcohol (Judg. 13.4).

543. **dancing ruby:** flashing red wine.

549. **fiery rod:** sunbeam.

550. **milky juice:** pure, clear water; cp. *PL* 5.306.

552. **fumes:** undigested effluvia of wine, which cloud and befuddle the mind. Milton traced his own blindness to incompletely digested food.

557. **liquid:** clear, transparent.

560. **What boots it:** what good does it do.

And at another to let in the foe,
Effeminately vanquished? By which means,
Now blind, disheartened, shamed, dishonored, quelled,
To what can I be useful, wherein serve
My nation, and the work from Heav'n imposed,
But to sit idle on the household hearth,
A burdenous drone; to visitants a gaze,
Or pitied object, these redundant locks
Robustious to no purpose clust'ring down,
Vain monument of strength; till length of years
And sedentary numbness craze my limbs
To a contemptible old age obscure.
Here rather let me drudge and earn my bread,
Till vermin or the draff of servile food
Consume me, and oft-invocated death
Hasten the welcome end of all my pains.
Manoa. Wilt thou then serve the Philistines with that gift
Which was expressly given thee to annoy them?
Better at home lie bed-rid, not only idle,
Inglorious, unemployed, with age outworn.
But God who caused a fountain at thy prayer
From the dry ground to spring, thy thirst to allay
After the brunt of battle, can as easy
Cause light again within thy eyes to spring,
Wherewith to serve him better than thou hast;
And I persuade me so; why else this strength
Miraculous yet remaining in those locks?
His might continues in thee not for naught,
Nor shall his wondrous gifts be frustrate thus.
Samson. All otherwise to me my thoughts portend,
That these dark orbs no more shall treat with light,
Nor th' other light of life continue long,
But yield to double darkness nigh at hand:
So much I feel my genial spirits droop,
My hopes all flat, nature within me seems
In all her functions weary of herself;

568. **redundant:** abundant to fullness or even excess (*OED* 2.a).

569. **Robustious:** robust.

571. **craze:** impair.

574. **draff:** refuse, dregs; wash or swill given to pigs.

581–83. **But God . . . battle:** Judges 15.18–19. In the *AV,* the water comes from the jawbone itself. Milton follows another possibility in the ambiguous Hebrew version, and has water flowing at a rock named after the jawbone.

594. **genial:** arising from one's "genius" or natural character.

595. **flat:** overthrown.

My race of glory run, and race of shame,
And I shall shortly be with them that rest.
Manoa. Believe not these suggestions which proceed
From anguish of the mind and humors black,
That mingle with thy fancy. I however
Must not omit a father's timely care
To prosecute the means of thy deliverance
By ransom or how else: meanwhile be calm,
And healing words from these thy friends admit.
Samson. O that Torment should not be confined
To the body's wounds and sores
With maladies innumerable
In heart, head, breast, and reins;
But must secret passage find
To th' inmost mind,
There exercise all his fierce accidents,
And on her purest spirits prey,
As on entrails, joints, and limbs,
With answerable pains, but more intense,
Though void of corporal sense.
My griefs not only pain me
As a ling'ring disease,
But finding no redress, ferment and rage,
Nor less than wounds immedicable
Rankle, and fester, and gangrene,
To black mortification.
Thoughts my tormentors armed with deadly stings
Mangle my apprehensive tenderest parts,
Exasperate, exulcerate, and raise
Dire inflammation which no cooling herb
Or med'cinal liquor can assuage,
Nor breath of vernal air from snowy alp.
Sleep hath forsook and giv'n me o'er
To death's benumbing opium as my only cure.
Thence faintings, swoonings of despair,
And sense of Heav'ns desertion.
I was his nursling once and choice delight,

600. **humors black:** black bile, which when predominant causes melancholy. See the induction to Ben Jonson's *Every Man out of his Humour.*

603. **prosecute:** pursue, persist in.

609. **reins:** kidneys, thought to be the seat of feelings or affections.

612. **accidents:** unfavorable symptoms.

613. **purest spirits:** most refined corporal substance; cp. the "intellectual" spirits of *PL* 5.485.

615. **answerable:** corresponding.

622. **mortification:** gangrene.

624. **apprehensive:** receptive, sensitive.

625. **exulcerate:** cause ulcers.

628. **alp:** any high, snowcapped mountain.

His destined from the womb,
Promised by Heavenly message twice descending.
Under his special eye
Abstemious I grew up and thrived amain;
He led me on to mightiest deeds
Above the nerve of mortal arm
Against the uncircumcised, our enemies.
But now hath cast me off as never known,
And to those cruel enemies,
Whom I by his appointment had provoked,
Left me all helpless with th' irreparable loss
Of sight, reserved alive to be repeated
The subject of their cruelty, or scorn.
Nor am I in the list of them that hope;
Hopeless are all my evils, all remediless;
This one prayer yet remains, might I be heard,
No long petition, speedy death,
The close of all my miseries, and the balm.

Chorus. Many are the sayings of the wise
In ancient and in modern books enrolled,
Extolling patience as the truest fortitude,
And to the bearing well of all calamities,
All chances incident to man's frail life;
Consolatories writ
With studied argument, and much persuasion sought
Lenient of grief and anxious thought;
But with th' afflicted in his pangs their sound
Little prevails, or rather seems a tune,
Harsh, and of dissonant mood from his complaint,
Unless he feel within
Some source of consolation from above;
Secret refreshings, that repair his strength,
And fainting spirits uphold.

God of our fathers, what is man!
That thou towards him with hand so various,
Or might I say contrarious,

635. **message:** messenger.

637. **Abstemious:** abstaining from wine; **amain:** greatly, exceedingly.

639. **nerve:** muscle.

643. **appointment:** command.

645. **repeated:** repeatedly.

656. **incident:** likely to befall.

657. **Consolatories:** writings on the topic of consolation.

659. **Lenient:** soothing, softening.

662. **mood:** not only an emotional state but also a musical mode, picking up on *tune* in the previous line.

667. **what is man:** The question recalls, but reverses the emphasis of, the question in Job 7.17, "What is man, that thou shouldest magnify him?" (See also Ps. 8.4 and Heb. 2.6).

669. **contrarious:** both contradictory and hostile.

Temper'st thy providence through his short course,
Not evenly, as thou rul'st
The angelic orders and inferior creatures mute,
Irrational and brute.
Nor do I name of men the common rout,
That wand'ring loose about
Grow up and perish, as the summer fly,
Heads without name no more remembered;
But such as thou hast solemnly elected,
With gifts and graces eminently adorned
To some great work, thy glory,
And people's safety, which in part they effect:
Yet toward these thus dignified, thou oft,
Amidst their highth of noon,
Changest thy countenance, and thy hand with no regard
Of highest favors past
From thee on them, or them to thee of service.
    Nor only dost degrade them, or remit
To life obscured, which were a fair dismission,
But throw'st them lower than thou didst exalt them high,
Unseemly falls in human eye,
Too grievous for the trespass or omission,
Oft leav'st them to the hostile sword
Of heathen and profane, their carcasses
To dogs and fowls a prey, or else captívéd:
Or to th' unjust tribunals, under change of times,
And condemnation of the ingrateful multitude.
If these they scape, perhaps in poverty
With sickness and disease thou bow'st them down,

676. **the summer fly:** Summer flies typified short life; see Shakespeare, *LLL* 5.2.408, and George Herbert, "Complaining."

677. **Heads without name:** persons unknown to fame. Thomas Browne thought that most human beings were in fact destined to be *heads without name:* "The greater part must be content to be as though they had not been, to be found in the Register of God, not in the record of man" (*Urn Burial* 5).

678. **solemnly elected:** The sense of being specially elect by God for great service links Samson with Milton himself. Here the Chorus testifies to Samson's status.

687. **remit:** send back.

694. **To dogs and fowls a prey:** Literarily the image recalls the degrading exposure of Greek bodies in the first lines of the *Iliad.* But historically the allusion points to the Restoration.

695. **unjust tribunals, under change of times:** As Thomas Newton noted in 1749, this passage evokes prosecution of Milton's party at the Restoration. Buried Parliamentary leaders and regicides were exhumed and their *carcasses* (693) displayed (Leonard notes that Cromwell's skull was not reinterred until 1960); living ones were imprisoned, and Sir Henry Vane was hanged, drawn, and quartered, a grisly punishment that Milton came close to suffering. The reference to the *ingrateful multitude* (696) echoes Milton's frequent condemnation of the backsliding English. See the image of the "misguided and abused multitude" that closes *REW* (p. 1136).

Painful diseases and deformed,
In crude old age;
Though not disordinate, yet causeless suff'ring
The punishment of dissolute days: in fine,
Just or unjust, alike seem miserable,
For oft alike, both come to evil end.
So deal not with this once thy glorious champion,
The image of thy strength, and mighty minister.
What do I beg? How hast thou dealt already?
Behold him in this state calamitous, and turn
His labors, for thou canst, to peaceful end.
But who is this, what thing of sea or land?
Female of sex it seems,
That so bedecked, ornate, and gay,
Comes this way sailing
Like a stately ship
Of Tarsus, bound for th' isles
Of Javan or Gadier
With all her bravery on, and tackle trim,
Sails filled, and streamers waving,
Courted by all the winds that hold them play,
And amber scent of odorous perfume
Her harbinger, a damsel train behind;
Some rich Philistian matron she may seem,
And now at nearer view, no other certain
Than Dalila thy wife.
Samson. My wife, my traitress, let her not come near me.
Chorus. Yet on she moves, now stands and eyes thee fixed,
About t' have spoke, but now, with head declined
Like a fair flower surcharged with dew, she weeps
And words addressed seem into tears dissolved,

699. **deformed:** disfiguring.

700. **crude:** premature.

701–2. **Though not disordinate . . . days:** Although they have not led dissolute lives, they receive the punishment appropriate to the dissolute.

702. **in fine:** in conclusion.

706. **minister:** servant.

711–13. Reflecting literary practice, Milton has the Chorus compare Dalila to a ship.

714–15. **ship/Of Tarsus:** In the Old Testament, the ships of Tarshish are symbols of pride and objects of divine anger (Ps. 48.7, 2 Chron. 9.21). Milton identified *Tarsus* in Cilicia with Tarshish in Spain.

716. **Javan:** the Greek islands; Javan, Noah's grandson, was thought to be the ancestor of the Greeks. **Gadier:** modern Cádiz on the coast of Spain.

717. **bravery:** finery; **tackle trim:** rigging in good order.

719. **hold them play:** hold them in play, keep them occupied.

720. **amber scent:** fragrance, as of ambergris.

729. **addressed:** prepared.

Wetting the borders of her silken veil:
But now again she makes address to speak.
Dalila. With doubtful feet and wavering resolution
I came, still dreading thy displeasure, Samson,
Which to have merited, without excuse,
I cannot but acknowledge; yet if tears
May expiate (though the fact more evil drew
In the perverse event than I foresaw)
My penance hath not slack'ned, though my pardon
No way assured. But conjugal affection,
Prevailing over fear and timorous doubt,
Hath led me on desirous to behold
Once more thy face, and know of thy estate.
If aught in my ability may serve
To lighten what thou suffer'st, and appease
Thy mind with what amends is in my power,
Though late, yet in some part to recompense
My rash but more unfortunate misdeed.
Samson. Out, out hyena; these are thy wonted arts,
And arts of every woman false like thee,
To break all faith, all vows, deceive, betray,
Then as repentant to submit, beseech,
And reconcilement move with feigned remorse,
Confess, and promise wonders in her change,
Not truly penitent, but chief to try
Her husband, how far urged his patience bears,
His virtue or weakness which way to assail:
Then with more cautious and instructed skill
Again transgresses, and again submits;
That wisest and best men full oft beguiled,
With goodness principled not to reject
The penitent, but ever to forgive,
Are drawn to wear out miserable days,
Entangled with a pois'nous bosom snake,
If not by quick destruction soon cut off
As I by thee, to ages an example.

731. **makes address:** prepares.
736. **fact:** deed.
737. **event:** outcome.
739. **No way assured:** a Latinate construction, meaning "be no way assured."
748. **hyena:** The hyena was associated with deception and treachery. See Gosson's *School of Abuse:* "*Hyena* speaks like a friend, and devours like a foe" (1587, 3).
752. **move:** propose.
755. **bears:** endures.
759. **That:** so that.
760. **principled:** instructed.

Dalila. Yet hear me Samson; not that I endeavor
To lessen or extenuate my offence,
But that on th' other side, if it be weighed
By itself, with aggravations not surcharged,
Or else with just allowance counterpoised,
I may, if possible, thy pardon find
The easier towards me, or thy hatred less.
First granting, as I do, it was a weakness
In me, but incident to all our sex,
Curiosity, inquisitive, importune
Of secrets, then with like infirmity
To publish them, both common female faults:
Was it not weakness also to make known
For importunity, that is for naught,
Wherein consisted all thy strength and safety?
To what I did thou show'dst me first the way.
But I to enemies revealed, and should not.
Nor shouldst thou have trusted that to woman's frailty:
Ere I to thee, thou to thyself wast cruel.
Let weakness then with weakness come to parle,
So near related, or the same of kind;
Thine forgive mine, that men may censure thine
The gentler, if severely thou exact not
More strength from me, than in thyself was found.
And what if love, which thou interpret'st hate,
The jealousy of love, powerful of sway
In human hearts, nor less in mine towards thee,
Caused what I did? I saw thee mutable
Of fancy, feared lest one day thou wouldst leave me
As her at Timna, sought by all means therefore
How to endear, and hold thee to me firmest:
No better way I saw than by importuning
To learn thy secrets, get into my power
Thy key of strength and safety: thou wilt say,
Why then revealed? I was assured by those
Who tempted me, that nothing was designed
Against thee but safe custody, and hold:

769. **with aggravations not surcharged:** not weighted or made heavier with extrinsic circumstances.

775–76. **importune/Of:** persistent in uncovering.

782. **But:** but you will say.

785. **come to parle:** confer in order to settle disputed points.

786. **kind:** nature, quality.

794. **fancy:** love.

795. **her at Timna:** ironic, since the woman at Timna lost Samson's love, as did Dalila, by revealing her husband's secret.

800–802. In the *AV,* the Philistines want Samson's secret so that they may "afflict" him (Judges

That made for me; I knew that liberty
Would draw thee forth to perilous enterprises,
While I at home sat full of cares and fears
Wailing thy absence in my widowed bed;
Here I should still enjoy thee day and night
Mine and love's prisoner, not the Philistines',
Whole to myself, unhazarded abroad,
Fearless at home of partners in my love.
These reasons in love's law have passed for good,
Though fond and reasonless to some perhaps;
And love hath oft, well meaning, wrought much woe,
Yet always pity or pardon hath obtained.
Be not unlike all others, not austere
As thou art strong, inflexible as steel.
If thou in strength all mortals dost exceed,
In uncompassionate anger do not so.
Samson. How cunningly the sorceress displays
Her own transgressions, to upbraid me mine!
That malice not repentance brought thee hither,
By this appears: I gave, thou say'st, th' example,
I led the way; bitter reproach, but true,
I to myself was false ere thou to me;
Such pardon therefore as I give my folly,
Take to thy wicked deed: which when thou seest
Impartial, self-severe, inexorable,
Thou wilt renounce thy seeking, and much rather
Confess it feigned. Weakness is thy excuse,
And I believe it, weakness to resist
Philistian gold: if weakness may excuse,
What murderer, what traitor, parricide,
Incestuous, sacrilegious, but may plead it?
All wickedness is weakness: that plea therefore
With God or man will gain thee no remission.
But love constrained thee; call it furious rage
To satisfy thy lust: love seeks to have love;
My love how couldst thou hope, who took'st the way
To raise in me inexpiable hate,
Knowing, as needs I must, by thee betrayed?

16.5); Leonard notes that in the Greek of the Septuagint, the word is "humiliate," which may not give the lie to Dalila's claim here; in either reading, however, the hostile intent of the Philistines is clear.

803. **That made for me:** that influenced me, or that worked to my advantage.

812. **fond:** foolish.

826. **which:** referring to *pardon* in the previous line.

838. **hope:** hope for.

In vain thou striv'st to cover shame with shame,
Or by evasions thy crime uncover'st more.
Dalila. Since thou determin'st weakness for no plea
In man or woman, though to thy own condemning,
Hear what assaults I had, what snares besides,
What sieges girt me round, ere I consented;
Which might have awed the best resolved of men,
The constantest to have yielded without blame.
It was not gold, as to my charge thou lay'st,
That wrought with me: thou know'st the magistrates
And princes of my country came in person,
Solicited, commanded, threatened, urged,
Adjured by all the bonds of civil duty
And of religion, pressed how just it was,
How honorable, how glorious to entrap
A common enemy, who had destroyed
Such numbers of our nation: and the priest
Was not behind, but ever at my ear,
Preaching how meritorious with the gods
It would be to ensnare an irreligious
Dishonorer of Dagon: what had I
To oppose against such powerful arguments?
Only my love of thee held long debate,
And combated in silence all these reasons
With hard contest: at length that grounded maxim
So rife and celebrated in the mouths
Of wisest men, that to the public good
Private respects must yield, with grave authority
Took full possession of me and prevailed;
Virtue, as I thought, truth, duty so enjoining.
Samson. I thought where all thy circling wiles would end;
In feigned religion, smooth hypocrisy.
But had thy love, still odiously pretended,
Been, as it ought, sincere, it would have taught thee
Far other reasonings, brought forth other deeds.
I before all the daughters of my tribe
And of my nation chose thee from among
My enemies, loved thee, as too well thou knew'st,

841–42. **to cover . . . uncover'st more:** Leonard notes the likeness to *PL* 9.1057–61, when Adam and Eve are "naked left/To guilty Shame: he covered, but his robe/Uncovered more. So rose the Danite strong/Herculean Samson, from the harlot-lap/Of Philistean Dalila."

866. **rife:** widespread, often heard.

868. **respects:** considerations.

876–78. Samson's claims here and at lines 1192–93 ignore his earlier admission (227–33) that he married Dalila in order to find occasion to "oppress/Israel's oppressors."

Too well, unbosomed all my secrets to thee,
Not out of levity, but overpow'red
By thy request, who could deny thee nothing;
Yet now am judged an enemy. Why then
Didst thou at first receive me for thy husband?
Then, as since then, thy country's foe professed:
Being once a wife, for me thou wast to leave
Parents and country; nor was I their subject,
Nor under their protection but my own,
Thou mine, not theirs: if aught against my life
Thy country sought of thee, it sought unjustly,
Against the law of nature, law of nations,
No more thy country, but an impious crew
Of men conspiring to uphold their state
By worse than hostile deeds, violating the ends
For which our country is a name so dear;
Not therefore to be obeyed. But zeal moved thee;
To please thy gods thou didst it; gods unable
To acquit themselves and prosecute their foes
But by ungodly deeds, the contradiction
Of their own deity, gods cannot be:
Less therefore to be pleased, obeyed, or feared.
These false pretexts and varnished colors failing,
Bare in thy guilt how foul must thou appear?
Dalila. In argument with men a woman ever
Goes by the worse, whatever be her cause.
Samson. For want of words no doubt, or lack of breath,
Witness when I was worried with thy peals.
Dalila. I was a fool, too rash, and quite mistaken
In what I thought would have succeeded best.
Let me obtain forgiveness of thee, Samson,
Afford me place to show what recompense
Towards thee I intend for what I have misdone,
Misguided; only what remains past cure
Bear not too sensibly, nor still insist
To afflict thyself in vain: though sight be lost,
Life yet hath many solaces, enjoyed
Where other senses want not their delights

880. **levity:** "Gravity entails careful moderation of words and actions. . . . Opposed to this is levity" (*CD* 2.13).

897. **acquit themselves:** perform their offices.

901. **varnished colors:** false displays; in *Animad.*, Milton attacks the hypocrite for "painting his lewd and deceitfull principles with a smooth, and glossy varnish . . . to bring about his wickedest purposes" (Yale 1:720).

904. **Goes by:** gets.

913. **sensibly:** sensitively.

916. **want:** lack.

At home in leisure and domestic ease,
Exempt from many a care and chance to which
Eyesight exposes daily men abroad.
I to the lords will intercede, not doubting
Their favorable ear, that I may fetch thee
From forth this loathsome prison-house to abide
With me, where my redoubled love and care
With nursing diligence, to me glad office,
May ever tend about thee to old age
With all things grateful cheered, and so supplied,
That what by me thou hast lost thou least shalt miss.
Samson. No, no, of my condition take no care;
It fits not; thou and I long since are twain;
Nor think me so unwary or accursed
To bring my feet again into the snare
Where once I have been caught; I know thy trains
Though dearly to my cost, thy gins, and toils;
Thy fair enchanted cup, and warbling charms
No more on me have power, their force is nulled,
So much of adder's wisdom I have learned
To fence my ear against thy sorceries.
If in my flower of youth and strength, when all men
Loved, honored, feared me, thou alone could hate me
Thy husband, slight me, sell me, and forgo me;
How wouldst thou use me now, blind, and thereby
Deceiveable, in most things as a child
Helpless, thence easily contemned, and scorned,
And last neglected? How wouldst thou insult
When I must live uxorious to thy will
In perfect thraldom, how again betray me,
Bearing my words and doings to the lords
To gloss upon, and censuring, frown or smile?
This jail I count the house of liberty
To thine whose doors my feet shall never enter.
Dalila. Let me approach at least, and touch thy hand.

919. **abroad:** outdoors.

926. **grateful:** pleasing

929. **thou and I long since are twain:** Samson here exercises the Hebrew right of divorce that Milton argued for in the 1640s.

932–33. **trains . . . gins . . . toils:** various traps.

934. The *cup* and *charms* relate Dalila to Homer's Circe and to Milton's own Comus (*Masque* 51, 150).

935. **nulled:** annulled, canceled.

936–37. referring to the belief that adders are deaf (Ps. 58.4–5).

942. **Deceivable:** likely to be deceived.

948. **gloss upon:** comment upon; **censuring:** judging.

950. **To:** compared to.

Samson. Not for thy life, lest fierce remembrance wake
My sudden rage to tear thee joint by joint.
At distance I forgive thee, go with that;
Bewail thy falsehood, and the pious works
It hath brought forth to make thee memorable
Among illustrious women, faithful wives:
Cherish thy hastened widowhood with the gold
Of matrimonial treason: so farewell.

Dalila. I see thou art implacable, more deaf
To prayers, than winds and seas, yet winds to seas
Are reconciled at length, and sea to shore:
Thy anger, unappeasable, still rages,
Eternal tempest never to be calmed.
Why do I humble thus myself, and suing
For peace, reap nothing but repulse and hate?
Bid go with evil omen and the brand
Of infamy upon my name denounced?
To mix with thy concernments I desist
Henceforth, nor too much disapprove my own.
Fame if not double-faced is double-mouthed,
And with contrary blast proclaims most deeds;
On both his wings, one black, th' other white,
Bears greatest names in his wild airy flight.
My name perhaps among the circumcised
In Dan, in Judah, and the bordering tribes,
To all posterity may stand defamed,
With malediction mentioned, and the blot
Of falsehood most unconjugal traduced.
But in my country where I most desire,
In Ecron, Gaza, Asdod, and in Gath
I shall be named among the famousest
Of women, sung at solemn festivals,
Living and dead recorded, who to save
Her country from a fierce destroyer, chose

953. **tear thee joint by joint:** Samson has torn apart a lion (128). In Euripides' *Hecuba,* Polymestor threatens to tear apart Hecuba, who has blinded him. See Lieb 252–53.

954. **go with that:** leave content with that (my forgiveness at a distance).

958–59. **gold/Of:** gold gained by.

968. **denounced:** pronounced.

969. **concernments:** affairs.

971–73. For Milton's Fame, see *Aen.* 4.173ff. Milton is unusual in the tradition for making Fame male. By contrast, see *On the Fifth of November* 172–216.

971. **double-mouthed:** Chaucer describes Fame as attended by the trumpeter Aeolus, who bears two trumpets—a black one to announce infamous deeds and a golden one for good deeds (*House of Fame* 3.485–92, 582–98).

975. **the circumcised:** the Jews.

981. **Ecron . . . Gath:** major Philistine cities.

Above the faith of wedlock-bands, my tomb
With odors visited and annual flowers.
Not less renowned than in Mount Ephraim
Jael, who with inhospitable guile
Smote Sisera sleeping through the temples nailed.
Nor shall I count it heinous to enjoy
The public marks of honor and reward
Conferred upon me for the piety
Which to my country I was judged to have shown.
At this whoever envies or repines
I leave him to his lot, and like my own.
Chorus. She's gone, a manifest serpent by her sting
Discovered in the end, till now concealed.
Samson. So let her go; God sent her to debase me,
And aggravate my folly who committed
To such a viper his most sacred trust
Of secrecy, my safety, and my life.
Chorus. Yet beauty, though injurious, hath strange power,
After offense returning, to regain
Love once possessed, nor can be easily
Repulsed, without much inward passion felt
And secret sting of amorous remorse.
Samson. Love-quarrels oft in pleasing concord end,
Not wedlock-treachery endangering life.
Chorus. It is not virtue, wisdom, valor, wit,
Strength, comeliness of shape, or amplest merit
That woman's love can win or long inherit;
But what it is, hard is to say,
Harder to hit,
(Which way soever men refer it)
Much like thy riddle, Samson, in one day
Or seven, though one should musing sit;
If any of these or all, the Timnian bride
Had not so soon preferred
Thy paranymph, worthless to thee compared,
Successor in thy bed,
Nor both so loosely disallied

987. **odors:** incense.

988–90. The Israelite *Jael,* wife of Heber, lured the Canaanite leader Sisera to take refuge with her after his defeat by the Hebrews, and slew him (Judg. 4.17–24; 5.24–31).

1000. **aggravate**: The Latin sense, from *gravitas,* is "add to the weight of."

1008. See Terence, *Andria* 3.23.

1010–17. An elaborately rhymed passage in the middle of a mostly unrhymed poem. The rhyming continues, though less insistently, in lines 1018–33.

1020. **paranymph:** groomsman (see 384n).

1022. **both:** both wives.

Their nuptials, nor this last so treacherously
Had shorn the fatal harvest of thy head.
Is it for that such outward ornament
Was lavished on their sex, that inward gifts
Were left for haste unfinished, judgment scant,
Capacity not raised to apprehend
Or value what is best
In choice, but oftest to affect the wrong?
Or was too much of self-love mixed,
Of constancy no root infixed,
That either they love nothing, or not long?
Whate'er it be, to wisest men and best
Seeming at first all heavenly under virgin veil,
Soft, modest, meek, demure,
Once joined, the contrary she proves, a thorn
Intestine, far within defensive arms
A cleaving mischief, in his way to virtue
Adverse and turbulent, or by her charms
Draws him awry enslaved
With dotage, and his sense depraved
To folly and shameful deeds which ruin ends.
What pilot so expert but needs must wreck
Embarked with such a steers-mate at the helm?
Favored of Heav'n who finds
One virtuous, rarely found,
That in domestic good combines:
Happy that house! His way to peace is smooth:
But virtue which breaks through all opposition,
And all temptation can remove,
Most shines and most is acceptable above.
Therefore God's universal law
Gave to the man despotic power
Over his female in due awe,
Nor from that right to part an hour,

1025. **for that:** because.
1030. **affect:** prefer.
1034. **wisest men and best:** See 759n.
1035–36. Cf. Milton's *DDD*: "who knows not that the bashful muteness of a virgin may ofttimes hide all the unliveliness and natural sloth which is really unfit for conversation" (p. 873).
1037. **joined:** married.
1038. **Intestine:** domestic, internal.
1039. **cleaving:** both "clinging" and "dividing."
1039–40. **in his way . . . turbulent:** "Women were born to mar the lives of men / Ever, unto their surer overthrow" (Euripides, *Orestes* 605–6).
1048. "Who joins with her spouse in domestic happiness"; see Prov. 31.10ff for the praises of a virtuous wife.
1053–60. On the doctrine of male superiority, see *DDD* 15 and *PL* 4.295–99, 635–38; 9.1182–86; 10.145–56, 888–95.

Smile she or lour:
So shall he least confusion draw
On his whole life, not swayed
By female usurpation, or dismayed.
But had we best retire? I see a storm.
Samson. Fair days have oft contracted wind and rain.
Chorus. But this another kind of tempest brings.
Samson. Be less abstruse, my riddling days are past.
Chorus. Look now for no enchanting voice, nor fear
The bait of honeyed words; a rougher tongue
Draws hitherward, I know him by his stride,
The giant Harapha of Gath, his look
Haughty as is his pile high-built and proud.
Comes he in peace? What wind hath blown him hither
I less conjecture than when first I saw
The sumptuous Dalila floating this way:
His habit carries peace, his brow defiance.
Samson. Or peace or not, alike to me he comes.
Chorus. His fraught we soon shall know, he now arrives.
Harapha. I come not Samson, to condole thy chance,
As these perhaps, yet wish it had not been,
Though for no friendly intent. I am of Gath,
Men call me Harapha, of stock renowned
As Og or Anak and the Emims old
That Kiriathaim held, thou know'st me now
If thou at all art known. Much I have heard
Of thy prodigious might and feats performed
Incredible to me; in this displeased,
That I was never present on the place
Of those encounters, where we might have tried
Each other's force in camp or listed field:
And now am come to see of whom such noise
Hath walked about, and each limb to survey,
If thy appearance answer loud report.

1068. **Harapha:** Milton adds him to the biblical account; his name derives from the Hebrew *haraphah,* or "the giant." Like Dalila, the name is stressed on first and third syllables.

1069. **pile:** a lofty mass of buildings, here figurative of Harapha's huge body.

1073. **habit:** clothing.

1075. **fraught:** freight (his news or commands).

1076. **condole thy chance:** lament your fate.

1080. **Og . . . Anak . . . Emims:** biblical giants (see Num. 13.33, 21.33–35; Deut. 2.10–11, 3.11).

1081. **Kiriathaim:** home of the Emims (Gen. 14.5).

1081–82. **thou know'st . . . known:** Harapha echoes Milton's Satan, who tells Ithuriel and Zephon, "Not to know me argues yourselves unknown" (*PL* 4.830).

1087. **camp:** battlefield; **listed field:** field prepared for jousting.

1088. **noise:** fame, report.

Samson. The way to know were not to see but taste.
Harapha. Dost thou already single me; I thought
Gyves and the mill had tamed thee? O that fortune
Had brought me to the field where thou art famed
To have wrought such wonders with an ass's jaw;
I should have forced thee soon wish other arms,
Or left thy carcass where the ass lay thrown:
So had the glory of prowess been recovered
To Palestine, won by a Philistine
From the unforeskinned race, of whom thou bear'st
The highest name for valiant acts; that honor
Certain to have won by mortal duel from thee,
I lose, prevented by thy eyes put out.
Samson. Boast not of what thou wouldst have done, but do
What then thou wouldst; thou seest it in thy hand.
Harapha. To combat with a blind man I disdain,
And thou hast need much washing to be touched.
Samson. Such usage as your honorable lords
Afford me assassinated and betrayed,
Who durst not with their whole united powers
In fight withstand me single and unarmed,
Nor in the house with chamber ambushes
Close-banded durst attack me, no not sleeping,
Till they had hired a woman with their gold,
Breaking her marriage faith to circumvent me.
Therefore without feigned shifts let be assigned
Some narrow place enclosed, where sight may give thee,
Or rather flight, no great advantage on me;
Then put on all thy gorgeous arms, thy helmet
And brigandine of brass, thy broad habergeon,
Vantbrace and greaves, and gauntlet, add thy spear
A weaver's beam, and seven-times-folded shield,
I only with an oaken staff will meet thee,
And raise such outcries on thy clattered iron,
Which long shall not withhold me from thy head,

1091. **taste:** try, examine by touch.
1092. **single:** challenge to single combat.
1093. **Gyves:** chains, shackles.
1102. **mortal duel:** fight to the death.
1109. **Afford:** allow; **assassinated:** treacherously attacked.
1113. **Close-banded:** secretly combining.
1116. **feigned shifts:** deluding tricks.
1120–21. **brigandine:** body armor; **habergeon:** sleeveless coat of mail. **Vantbrace and greaves:** arm and leg armor; **gauntlet:** mailed glove.
1121–22. **spear / A weaver's beam:** a spear as large as a loom's heavy roller, like Goliath's spear (1 Sam. 17.7).
1122. **seven-times-folded shield:** made from a bull's hide folded seven times like the shields of Ajax (*Il.* 7.200) and Turnus (*Aen.* 12.925).

That in a little time while breath remains thee,
Thou oft shalt wish thyself at Gath to boast
Again in safety what thou wouldst have done
To Samson, but shalt never see Gath more.
Harapha. Thou durst not thus disparage glorious arms
Which greatest heroes have in battle worn,
Their ornament and safety, had not spells
And black enchantments, some magician's art,
Armed thee or charmed the strong, which thou from Heaven
Feign'dst at thy birth was giv'n thee in thy hair,
Where strength can least abide, though all thy hairs
Were bristles ranged like those that ridge the back
Of chafed wild boars, or ruffled porcupines.
Samson. I know no spells, use no forbidden arts;
My trust is in the living God who gave me
At my nativity this strength, diffused
No less through all my sinews, joints and bones,
Than thine, while I preserved these locks unshorn,
The pledge of my unviolated vow.
For proof hereof, if Dagon be thy god,
Go to his temple, invocate his aid
With solemnest devotion, spread before him
How highly it concerns his glory now
To frustrate and dissolve these magic spells,
Which I to be the power of Israel's God
Avow, and challenge Dagon to the test,
Offering to combat thee, his champion bold,
With th' utmost of his godhead seconded:
Then thou shalt see, or rather to thy sorrow
Soon feel, whose god is strongest, thine or mine.
Harapha. Presume not on thy god, whate'er he be,
Thee he regards not, owns not, hath cut off
Quite from his people, and delivered up
Into thy enemies' hand, permitted them
To put out both thine eyes, and fettered send thee
Into the common prison, there to grind
Among the slaves and asses thy comrades,
As good for nothing else, no better service

1132–40. Todd notes that Harapha's challenge and Samson's response echo the oath taken by knights engaged in trial by combat: "I do swear, that I have not upon me, nor on any of the *arms* I shall use, words, *charms,* or *enchantments,* to which I trust for help to conquer my enemy, but that *I do only trust in God,* in my right, and in the strength of my body and arms."

1138. **chafed:** enraged.

1146. **invocate:** pray for.

1147. **spread:** lay out.

With those thy boist'rous locks, no worthy match
For valor to assail, nor by the sword
Of noble warrior, so to stain his honor,
But by the barber's razor best subdued.
Samson. All these indignities, for such they are
From thine, these evils I deserve and more,
Acknowledge them from God inflicted on me
Justly, yet despair not of his final pardon
Whose ear is ever open; and his eye
Gracious to readmit the suppliant;
In confidence whereof I once again
Defy thee to the trial of mortal fight,
By combat to decide whose god is God,
Thine or whom I with Israel's sons adore.
Harapha. Fair honor that thou dost thy god, in trusting
He will accept thee to defend his cause,
A murderer, a revolter, and a robber.
Samson. Tongue-doughty giant, how dost thou prove me these?
Harapha. Is not thy nation subject to our lords?
Their magistrates confessed it, when they took thee
As a league-breaker and delivered bound
Into our hands: for hadst thou not committed
Notorious murder on those thirty men
At Ascalon, who never did thee harm,
Then like a robber stripp'dst them of their robes?
The Philistines, when thou hadst broke the league,
Went up with armèd powers thee only seeking,
To others did no violence nor spoil.
Samson. Among the daughters of the Philistines
I chose a wife, which argued me no foe;
And in your city held my nuptial feast:
But your ill-meaning politician lords,
Under pretense of bridal friends and guests,
Appointed to await me thirty spies,
Who, threat'ning cruel death, constrained the bride

1164. **boist'rous:** coarse, violent.

1169. **thine:** your people (the Philistines).

1181. **Tongue-doughty:** brave of tongue; **prove me these:** prove me to be these (murderer, revolter, robber).

1183–91. **Their magistrates . . . spoil:** The Israelites handed Samson over to the Philistines (Judg. 15.11–13) after he had killed thirty Askalonites, taking their robes to pay his debt to the thirty Philistines who had suborned the woman of Timna to discover and reveal the secret of Samson's riddle (Judg. 14.12 and 19). These events are recorded in lines 250–61 and 382–87.

1195. **politician:** scheming.

1197. **await:** wait upon; Milton from Josephus (*Antiq.* 5.8) borrows the idea that the thirty Philistines were guards posing as companions.

To wring from me and tell to them my secret,
That solved the riddle which I had proposed.
When I perceived all set on enmity,
As on my enemies, wherever chanced,
I used hostility, and took their spoil
To pay my underminers in their coin.
My nation was subjected to your lords.
It was the force of conquest; force with force
Is well ejected when the conquered can.
But I a private person, whom my country
As a league-breaker gave up bound, presumed
Single rebellion and did hostile acts.
I was no private but a person raised
With strength sufficient and command from Heav'n
To free my country; if their servile minds
Me their Deliverer sent would not receive,
But to their masters gave me up for naught,
Th' unworthier they; whence to this day they serve.
I was to do my part from Heav'n assigned,
And had performed it if my known offense
Had not disabled me, not all your force:
These shifts refuted, answer thy appellant
Though by his blindness maimed for high attempts,
Who now defies thee thrice to single fight,
As a petty enterprise of small enforce.
Harapha. With thee a man condemned, a slave enrolled,
Due by the law to capital punishment?
To fight with thee no man of arms will deign.
Samson. Cam'st thou for this, vain boaster, to survey me,
To descant on my strength, and give thy verdict?
Come nearer, part not hence so slight informed;
But take good heed my hand survey not thee.
Harapha. O Baäl-zebub! Can my ears unused
Hear these dishonors, and not render death?
Samson. No man withholds thee, nothing from thy hand
Fear I incurable; bring up thy van,
My heels are fettered, but my fist is free.

1201–3. **When I perceived . . . enemies:** When I saw all Philistines set on hatred, I treated all of them as enemies.

1208. **I a private person:** Samson, as line 1211 makes clear, is not conceding this point but simply characterizing Harapha's description of him.

1220. **appellant:** challenger.

1221. **maimed for:** made incapable of.

1223. **of small enforce:** of small difficulty, easy to do.

1228. **descant:** comment at length.

1231. **Baäl-zebub:** literally "god of the flies," a form of Baal, the Philistine sun god; **unused:** i.e., unused to hearing dishonors.

1234. **van:** first line of battle; i.e., begin to fight.

Harapha. This insolence other kind of answer fits.
Samson. Go baffled coward, lest I run upon thee,
Though in these chains, bulk without spirit vast
And with one buffet lay thy structure low,
Or swing thee in the air, then dash thee down
To the hazard of thy brains and shattered sides.
Harapha. By Astaroth, ere long thou shalt lament
These braveries in irons loaden on thee.
Chorus. His giantship is gone somewhat crestfall'n,
Stalking with less unconscionable strides,
And lower looks, but in a sultry chafe.
Samson. I dread him not, nor all his giant-brood,
Though fame divulge him father of five sons
All of gigantic size, Goliah chief.
Chorus. He will directly to the lords, I fear,
And with malicious counsel stir them up
Some way or other yet further to afflict thee.
Samson. He must allege some cause, and offered fight
Will not dare mention, lest a question rise
Whether he durst accept the offer or not,
And that he durst not plain enough appeared.
Much more affliction than already felt
They cannot well impose, nor I sustain,
If they intend advantage of my labors,
The work of many hands, which earns my keeping
With no small profit daily to my owners.
But come what will, my deadliest foe will prove
My speediest friend, by death to rid me hence,
The worst that he can give, to me the best.
Yet so it may fall out, because their end
Is hate, not help to me, it may with mine
Draw their own ruin who attempt the deed.
Chorus. Oh how comely it is, and how reviving
To the spirits of just men long oppressed!
When God into the hands of their deliverer
Puts invincible might

1237. **baffled:** publicly disgraced.

1242. **Astaroth:** a collective noun for manifestations of the Canaanite fertility goddess, Baal's counterpart. See *PL* 1.422–38.

1243. **braveries:** boasts.

1244. **His giantship:** mocking title.

1245. **unconscionable:** excessive.

1246. **sultry chafe:** angry rage.

1249. **Goliah:** Goliath; for the sons of the giant (*haraphah*) of Gath, see 2 Sam. 21.22.

1250–52. It is implied that the summons soon to be brought Samson by the officer (1310–18) was due to Harapha. In this sense, the visit of Harapha advances the drama toward its catastrophe.

To quell the mighty of the Earth, th' oppressor,
The brute and boist'rous force of violent men
Hardy and industrious to support
Tyrannic power, but raging to pursue
The righteous and all such as honor truth;
He all their ammunition
And feats of war defeats
With plain heroic magnitude of mind
And celestial vigor armed,
Their armories and magazines contemns,
Renders them useless, while
With wingèd expedition
Swift as the lightning glance he executes
His errand on the wicked, who surprised
Lose their defense, distracted and amazed.
But patience is more oft the exercise
Of saints, the trial of their fortitude,
Making them each his own deliverer,
And victor over all
That tyranny or fortune can inflict.
Either of these is in thy lot,
Samson, with might endued
Above the sons of men; but sight bereaved
May chance to number thee with those
Whom patience finally must crown.
This idol's day hath been to thee no day of rest,
Laboring thy mind
More than the working day thy hands.
And yet perhaps more trouble is behind,
For I descry this way
Some other tending, in his hand
A scepter or quaint staff he bears,
Comes on amain, speed in his look.
By his habit I discern him now
A public officer, and now at hand.
His message will be short and voluble.

1283. **expedition:** speed.

1286. **amazed:** confounded; stronger than the modern *astonished.*

1287. **patience:** The primary meaning is "suffering"; in *Paradise Lost,* Milton redefines heroism in terms of "patience and heroic martyrdom" (9.32).

1288. **saints:** the faithful and therefore blessed; the term from Protestant discourse is applied anachronistically here; Dunster, cited by Todd, faults Milton for using the "fanatical language of the republican party."

1300. **behind:** yet to come.

1303. **quaint:** curiously wrought.

1305. **habit:** clothing.

1307. **voluble:** quickly delivered.

Officer. Hebrews, the pris'ner Samson here I seek.
Chorus. His manacles remark him, there he sits.
Officer. Samson, to thee our lords thus bid me say;
This day to Dagon is a solemn feast,
With sacrifices, triumph, pomp, and games;
Thy strength they know surpassing human rate,
And now some public proof thereof require
To honor this great feast, and great assembly;
Rise therefore with all speed and come along,
Where I will see thee heartened and fresh clad
To appear as fits before th' illustrious lords.
Samson. Thou know'st I am an Hebrew, therefore tell them,
Our law forbids at their religious rites
My presence; for that cause I cannot come.
Officer. This answer, be assured, will not content them.
Samson. Have they not sword-players, and ev'ry sort
Of gymnic artists, wrestlers, riders, runners,
Jugglers and dancers, antics, mummers, mimics,
But they must pick me out with shackles tired,
And over-labored at their public mill,
To make them sport with blind activity?
Do they not seek occasion of new quarrels
On my refusal to distress me more,
Or make a game of my calamities?
Return the way thou cam'st, I will not come.
Officer. Regard thyself, this will offend them highly.
Samson. Myself? My conscience and internal peace.
Can they think me so broken, so debased
With corporal servitude, that my mind ever
Will condescend to such absurd commands?
Although their drudge, to be their fool or jester,
And in my midst of sorrow and heart-grief
To show them feats, and play before their god,
The worst of all indignities, yet on me
Joined with extreme contempt? I will not come.

1309. **remark:** distinguish, mark out.

1312. **triumph:** a procession celebrating a victory.

1313. **rate:** The 1671 edition's "race" was corrected by the Errata to "rate." The word means "degree."

1317. **heartened:** refreshed.

1320. **Our law forbids:** The Second Commandment forbids idol worship or service to other gods.

1325. **antics:** clowns; **mummers:** mimes.

1333. **Regard thyself:** look to your own interest.

1342. **Joined:** enjoined, imposed; **I will not come:** Samson repeats his refusal, by an ancient narrative and ritual formula, for the third time (see 1321 and 1332); for the significance of the repetition and the reversal at line 1384, see Kerrigan 1986.

Officer. My message was imposed on me with speed,
Brooks no delay: is this thy resolution?
Samson. So take it with what speed thy message needs.
Officer. I am sorry what this stoutness will produce.
Samson. Perhaps thou shalt have cause to sorrow indeed.
Chorus. Consider, Samson; matters now are strained
Up to the highth, whether to hold or break;
He's gone, and who knows how he may report
Thy words by adding fuel to the flame?
Expect another message more imperious,
More lordly thund'ring than thou well wilt bear.
Samson. Shall I abuse this consecrated gift
Of strength, again returning with my hair
After my great transgression, so requite
Favor renewed, and add a greater sin
By prostituting holy things to idols;
A Nazarite in place abominable
Vaunting my strength in honor to their Dagon?
Besides, how vile, contemptible, ridiculous,
What act more execrably unclean, profane?
Chorus. Yet with this strength thou serv'st the Philistines,
Idolatrous, uncircumcised, unclean.
Samson. Not in their idol-worship, but by labor
Honest and lawful to deserve my food
Of those who have me in their civil power.
Chorus. Where the heart joins not, outward acts defile not.
Samson. Where outward force constrains, the sentence holds,
But who constrains me to the temple of Dagon,
Not dragging? The Philistian Lords command.
Commands are no constraints. If I obey them,
I do it freely; venturing to displease
God for the fear of man, and man prefer,
Set God behind: which in his jealousy
Shall never, unrepented, find forgiveness.
Yet that he may dispense with me or thee

1344. **Brooks:** suffers.

1346. **I am sorry:** I am sorry to think; **stoutness:** defiance, courage.

1355. **again returning:** echoing Manoa at lines 586–87, and anticipating Manoa at 1496–99. Samson for the first time expresses an awareness of renewed strength.

1369. **sentence holds:** maxim holds true.

1375. **jealousy:** In promulgating the Second Commandment, God says, "I the Lord thy God am a jealous God" (Exod. 20:5).

1377. **Yet:** This word locates the *peripeteia* or "turning point," which Frye terms "the most precisely marked in the whole range of drama" (1973, 156).

1377–78. **may dispense . . . Present:** can grant a dispensation for you or me to be present.

Present in temples at idolatrous rites
For some important cause, thou need'st not doubt.
Chorus. How thou wilt here come off surmounts my reach.
Samson. Be of good courage, I begin to feel
Some rousing motions in me which dispose
To something extraordinary my thoughts.
I with this messenger will go along,
Nothing to do, be sure, that may dishonor
Our law, or stain my vow of Nazarite.
If there be aught of presage in the mind,
This day will be remarkable in my life
By some great act, or of my days the last.
Chorus. In time thou hast resolved, the man returns.
Officer. Samson, this second message from our lords
To thee I am bid say. Art thou our slave,
Our captive, at the public mill our drudge,
And dar'st thou at our sending and command
Dispute thy coming? Come without delay;
Or we shall find such engines to assail
And hamper thee, as thou shalt come of force,
Though thou wert firmlier fastened than a rock.
Samson. I could be well content to try their art,
Which to no few of them would prove pernicious.
Yet knowing their advantages too many,
Because they shall not trail me through their streets
Like a wild beast, I am content to go.
Masters' commands come with a power resistless
To such as owe them absolute subjection;
And for a life who will not change his purpose?
(So mutable are all the ways of men.)
Yet this be sure, in nothing to comply
Scandalous or forbidden in our Law.
Officer. I praise thy resolution, doff these links:
By this compliance thou wilt win the lords
To favor, and perhaps to set thee free.

1380. **come off:** escape.

1382. **motions:** workings of God in the soul. Recent readers vary on whether the motions are divine in origin or generated/imagined by Samson. The Argument declares that Samson was "persuaded inwardly that this was from God." See line 1426.

1389. **or:** By the end of the drama, we realize that the alternatives are simultaneously true, as Samson performs a great act on the last day of his life. This ironical play with the word *or* occurs often in the work. It was first noticed by Summers (158–59), termed "the irony of alternatives" by Low (1974, 79–83), and related to the effect of eternity on dramatic plot by Tayler (1979, 118–22).

1400. **pernicious:** deadly.

1402. **Because:** so that.

Samson. Brethren farewell, your company along
I will not wish, lest it perhaps offend them
To see me girt with friends; and how the sight
Of me as of a common enemy,
So dreaded once, may now exasperate them
I know not. Lords are lordliest in their wine;
And the well-feasted priest then soonest fired
With zeal, if aught religion seem concerned:
No less the people on their holy-days
Impetuous, insolent, unquenchable;
Happen what may, of me expect to hear
Nothing dishonorable, impure, unworthy
Our God, our law, my nation, or myself,
The last of me or no I cannot warrant.
Chorus. Go, and the Holy One
Of Israel be thy guide
To what may serve his glory best, and spread his name
Great among the heathen round:
Send thee the angel of thy birth, to stand
Fast by thy side, who from thy father's field
Rode up in flames after his message told
Of thy conception, and be now a shield
Of fire; that spirit that first rushed on thee
In the camp of Dan
Be efficacious in thee now at need.
For never was from Heaven imparted
Measure of strength so great to mortal seed,
As in thy wond'rous actions hath been seen.
But wherefore comes old Manoa in such haste
With youthful steps? Much livelier than erewhile
He seems: supposing here to find his son,
Or of him bringing to us some glad news?
Manoa. Peace with you brethren; my inducement hither
Was not at present here to find my son,
By order of the lords new parted hence
To come and play before them at their feast.
I heard all as I came, the city rings,

1420. **if aught:** if in any way.

1426. "I cannot be confident whether or not this is my last day."

1431–35. See lines 23–29.

1435–36. Samson first learned of his power when "the Spirit of the Lord began to move him at times in the camp of Dan" (Judg. 13.25).

1442. **Much livelier than erewhile:** See lines 336–37.

1445. **Peace with you:** a common salutation in the Bible (Judg. 6.23, 19.20).

And numbers thither flock; I had no will,
Lest I should see him forced to things unseemly.
But that which moved my coming now, was chiefly
To give ye part with me what hope I have
With good success to work his liberty.
Chorus. That hope would much rejoice us to partake
With thee; say reverend sire, we thirst to hear.
Manoa. I have attempted one by one the lords
Either at home, or through the high street passing,
With supplication prone and father's tears
To accept of ransom for my son their pris'ner.
Some much averse I found and wondrous harsh,
Contemptuous, proud, set on revenge and spite;
That part most reverenced Dagon and his priests:
Others more moderate seeming, but their aim
Private reward, for which both god and state
They easily would set to sale; a third
More generous far and civil, who confessed
They had enough revenged, having reduced
Their foe to misery beneath their fears,
The rest was magnanimity to remit,
If some convenient ransom were proposed.
What noise or shout was that? It tore the sky.
Chorus. Doubtless the people shouting to behold
Their once great dread, captive, and blind before them,
Or at some proof of strength before them shown.
Manoa. His ransom, if my whole inheritance
May compass it, shall willingly be paid
And numbered down: much rather I shall choose
To live the poorest in my tribe, than richest,
And he in that calamitous prison left.
No, I am fixed not to part hence without him.
For his redemption all my patrimony,
If need be, I am ready to forego

1450. **I had no will:** I had no desire to go to the feast.

1453. **give ye part:** let you share.

1454. **success:** outcome.

1457. **attempted:** entreated.

1459. **prone:** either prostrate or bending forward.

1461–66. **Some . . . to sale:** Early readers quoted by Todd recognized topical allusions here. According to Thyer, in describing the first group, that *reverenced Dagon and his priests,* Milton "indulges that inveterate spleen, which he always had against public and established religion." Dunster saw in the second, *more moderate seeming* group, the "Presbyterian party."

1470. They thought it magnanimous to give up the rest of their revenge.

1478. **numbered down:** counted out.

1481. **not to part hence without him:** Nor does he, albeit with Samson's dead body. This speech brims with ironies.

And quit: not wanting him, I shall want nothing.
Chorus. Fathers are wont to lay up for their sons,
Thou for thy son are bent to lay out all;
Sons wont to nurse their parents in old age,
Thou in old age car'st how to nurse thy son,
Made older than thy age through eyesight lost.
Manoa. It shall be my delight to tend his eyes,
And view him sitting in the house, ennobled
With all those high exploíts by him achieved,
And on his shoulders waving down those locks,
That of a nation armed the strength contained:
And I persuade me God had not permitted
His strength again to grow up with his hair
Garrisoned round about him like a camp
Of faithful soldiery, were not his purpose
To use him further yet in some great service,
Not to sit idle with so great a gift
Useless, and thence ridiculous about him.
And since his strength with eyesight was not lost,
God will restore him eyesight to his strength.
Chorus. Thy hopes are not ill founded, nor seem vain,
Of his delivery, and thy joy thereon
Conceived, agreeable to a father's love,
In both which we, as next, participate.
Manoa. I know your friendly minds—O what noise!
Mercy of Heav'n what hideous noise was that?
Horribly loud unlike the former shout.
Chorus. Noise call you it or universal groan
As if the whole inhabitation perished,
Blood, death, and deathful deeds are in that noise,
Ruin, destruction at the utmost point.
Manoa. Of ruin indeed methought I heard the noise,
O it continues, they have slain my son.
Chorus. Thy son is rather slaying them, that outcry
From slaughter of one foe could not ascend.
Manoa. Some dismal accident it needs must be;

1484. **wanting:** lacking.
1485. **wont:** accustomed to.
1495. **had not:** would not have.
1503. **to:** in addition to.
1504–5. **Thy hopes . . . delivery:** I.e., "Your hope of freeing Samson, as opposed to your hope for his recovered eyesight, is neither baseless nor foolish"; the Chorus, however, will in a moment join in that hope (1527–28).
1506. **agreeable to:** suitable to.
1507. **next:** next of kin (the Chorus are Danites).
1515. **ruin:** with its literal Latin meaning of "fall" or "collapse"; a favorite word of Milton's, e.g., Satan's fall from Heaven in "hideous ruin" (*PL* 1.46).

What shall we do, stay here or run and see?
Chorus. Best keep together here, lest running thither
We unawares run into danger's mouth.
This evil on the Philistines is fall'n,
From whom could else a general cry be heard?
The sufferers then will scarce molest us here,
From other hands we need not much to fear.
What if his eyesight (for to Israel's God
Nothing is hard) by miracle restored,
He now be dealing dole among his foes,
And over heaps of slaughtered walk his way?
Manoa. That were a joy presumptuous to be thought.
Chorus. Yet God hath wrought things as incredible
For his people of old; what hinders now?
Manoa. He can, I know, but doubt to think he will;
Yet hope would fain subscribe, and tempts belief.
A little stay will bring some notice hither.
Chorus. Of good or bad so great, of bad the sooner;
For evil news rides post, while good news baits.
And to our wish I see one hither speeding,
An Hebrew, as I guess, and of our tribe.
Messenger. O whither shall I run, or which way fly
The sight of this so horrid spectacle
Which erst my eyes beheld and yet behold;
For dire imagination still pursues me.
But providence or instinct of nature seems,
Or reason though disturbed, and scarce consulted,
To have guided me aright, I know not how,
To thee first reverend Manoa, and to these
My countrymen, whom here I knew remaining,
As at some distance from the place of horror,
So in the sad event too much concerned.
Manoa. The accident was loud, and here before thee
With rueful cry, yet what it was we hear not:
No preface needs, thou seest we long to know.

1527–37. In the 1671 edition, lines 1527–35 and 1537 were missing, but printed in the Omissa, and line 1536 was given to the Chorus, not Manoa. We print the passage as it appeared in the second edition of 1680.

1529. **dole:** dealing of blows, death, and the grief those deaths will cause.

1535. **fain subscribe:** assent willingly.

1538. **rides post:** travels quickly; **baits:** rests (and therefore travels slowly).

1539. **to:** according to.

1543. **erst:** just now.

1552. **accident:** as yet unexplained occurrence; the word has its root in the Latin *cadere,* "to fall," as does *Occasions* at line 1596.

Messenger. It would burst forth, but I recover breath
And sense distract, to know well what I utter.
Manoa. Tell us the sum, the circumstance defer.
Messenger. Gaza yet stands, but all her sons are fall'n,
All in a moment overwhelmed and fall'n.
Manoa. Sad, but thou know'st to Israelites not saddest
The desolation of a hostile city.
Messenger. Feed on that first, there may in grief be surfeit.
Manoa. Relate by whom.
Messenger. By Samson.
Manoa. That still less'ns
The sorrow, and converts it nigh to joy.
Messenger. Ah Mánoa I refrain, too suddenly
To utter what will come at last too soon;
Lest evil tidings with too rude irruption
Hitting thy agèd ear should pierce too deep.
Manoa. Suspense in news is torture, speak them out.
Messenger. Then take the worst in brief, Samson is dead.
Manoa. The worst indeed, O all my hope's defeated
To free him hence! But death who sets all free
Hath paid his ransom now and full discharge.
What windy joy this day had I conceived
Hopeful of his delivery, which now proves
Abortive as the first-born bloom of spring
Nipped with the lagging rear of winter's frost.
Yet ere I give the reins to grief, say first,
How died he? Death to life is crown or shame.
All by him fell thou say'st, by whom fell he,
What glorious hand gave Samson his death's wound?
Messenger. Unwounded of his enemies he fell.
Manoa. Wearied with slaughter then or how? Explain.
Messenger. By his own hands.
Manoa. Self-violence? What cause
Brought him so soon at variance with himself
Among his foes?
Messenger. Inevitable cause
At once both to destroy and be destroyed;
The edifice where all were met to see him
Upon their heads and on his own he pulled.
Manoa. O lastly over-strong against thyself!

1567. **irruption:** breaking in.
1574. **windy:** vain, empty.
1574–75. **conceived . . . delivery:** imagined . . . emancipation, with an implied metaphor of conception and birth.

A dreadful way thou took'st to thy revenge.
More than enough we know; but while things yet
Are in confusion, give us if thou canst,
Eye-witness of what first or last was done,
Relation more particular and distinct.
Messenger. Occasions drew me early to this city,
And as the gates I entered with sunrise,
The morning trumpets festival proclaimed
Through each high street: little I had dispatched
When all abroad was rumored that this day
Samson should be brought forth to show the people
Proof of his mighty strength in feats and games;
I sorrowed at his captive state, but minded
Not to be absent at that spectacle.
The building was a spacious theater
Half round on two main pillars vaulted high,
With seats where all the lords and each degree
Of sort, might sit in order to behold;
The other side was open, where the throng
On banks and scaffolds under sky might stand;
I among these aloof obscurely stood.
The feast and noon grew high, and sacrifice
Had filled their hearts with mirth, high cheer, and wine,
When to their sports they turned. Immediately
Was Samson as a public servant brought,
In their state livery clad; before him pipes
And timbrels, on each side went armèd guards,
Both horse and foot before him and behind
Archers, and slingers, cataphracts and spears.
At sight of him the people with a shout
Rifted the air, clamoring their god with praise,
Who had made their dreadful enemy their thrall.
He patient but undaunted where they led him,
Came to the place, and what was set before him
Which without help of eye might be assayed,
To heave, pull, draw, or break, he still performed

1595. **relation:** report.

1596. **Occasions:** business affairs.

1599. **little I had dispatched:** I had not completed much business.

1603. **minded:** decided.

1605–10. For the temple of Dagon, see Judg. 16.25–29; for the significance of Milton's modifications, see 1659n. The choice of sun or shade from the opening of the poem becomes, at the temple of Dagon, life or death.

1610. **banks:** benches; **scaffolds:** stands.

1616. **livery:** uniform. Cf. the officer's words at lines 1317–18.

1617. **timbrels:** tambourines.

1619. **cataphracts:** mounted and armored soldiers; **spears:** spearsmen.

All with incredible, stupendious force,
None daring to appear antagonist.
At length for intermission sake they led him
Between the pillars; he his guide requested
(For so from such as nearer stood we heard)
As overtired to let him lean a while
With both his arms on those two massy pillars
That to the archèd roof gave main support.
He unsuspicious led him; which when Samson
Felt in his arms, with head a while inclined,
And eyes fast fixed he stood, as one who prayed,
Or some great matter in his mind revolved.
At last with head erect thus cried aloud,
"Hitherto, lords, what your commands imposed
I have performed, as reason was, obeying,
Not without wonder or delight beheld.
Now of my own accord such other trial
I mean to show you of my strength, yet greater;
As with amaze shall strike all who behold."
This uttered, straining all his nerves he bowed,
As with the force of winds and waters pent,
When mountains tremble, those two massy pillars
With horrible convulsion to and fro
He tugged, he shook, till down they came and drew
The whole roof after them, with burst of thunder
Upon the heads of all who sat beneath,
Lords, ladies, captains, counsellors, or priests,
Their choice nobility and flower, not only
Of this but each Philistian city round
Met from all parts to solemnize this feast.
Samson with these immixed, inevitably
Pulled down the same destruction on himself;
The vulgar only scaped who stood without.

1630. **his guide:** the "lad" of Judg. 16.26; for the episode of the destruction of the Temple, see Judg. 16.23–30.

1637. **as one who prayed:** Milton is more ambiguous than his source. In Judg. 16.28–30, Samson clearly prays, and in doing so asks to die with the Philistines; see Allen 83f. In the poem, Samson appears to pray, and although he has wished to die throughout the work, we don't know definitely whether he does so at the end. See 1664–66n.

1645. **amaze:** confusion; see 1286n.

1647–48. Volcanoes and earthquakes were traced to subterranean motions of wind and water, as in *PL* 1.230–37 and 6.195–98. The winds of the earth were also thought to play a part in various meterological phenomena, such as comets and meteors.

1659. **vulgar:** common people; Milton changes Judges, in which three thousand watching from the roof perish in addition to the Philistine nobility, in order to save the common people. See 3n. Those who abhor the climactic violence often speak of it as an indiscriminate ethnic

Chorus. O dearly-bought revenge, yet glorious!
Living or dying thou hast fulfilled
The work for which thou wast foretold
To Israel, and now li'st victorious
Among thy slain self-killed
Not willingly, but tangled in the fold
Of dire necessity, whose law in death conjoined
Thee with thy slaughtered foes in number more
Than all thy life had slain before.

Semichorus. While their hearts were jocund and sublime,
Drunk with idolatry, drunk with wine,
And fat regorged of bulls and goats,
Chanting their idol, and preferring
Before our Living Dread who dwells
In Silo his bright sanctuary:
Among them he a spirit of frenzy sent,
Who hurt their minds,
And urged them on with mad desire
To call in haste for their destroyer;
They only set on sport and play
Unwittingly importuned
Their own destruction to come speedy upon them.
So fond are mortal men
Fall'n into wrath divine,
As their own ruin on themselves to invite,
Insensate left, or to sense reprobate,
And with blindness internal struck.

Semichorus. But he though blind of sight,
Despised and thought extinguished quite,
With inward eyes illuminated
His fiery virtue roused
From under ashes into sudden flame,

---

cleansing. But it is more precisely a slaughter of the Philistine aristocracy.

1660–1707. Hale discusses the way Pindaric elements appear in this passage and ultimately dominate the choral victory hymn, lifting the work into an epic realm (189–92).

1661. **Living or dying:** in your life and death alike.

1664–66. The Chorus agrees with St. Augustine and most annotators of Judges that Samson, because he acts on divine prompting, is not guilty of suicide; Hughes (1957) illustrates the contrary position from Donne's *Biathanatos* (3.5.4). The Argument speaks of "what Samson had done to the Philistines, and by accident to himself." It seems likely that the Chorus speaks for Milton, though the point cannot be proven.

1669. **sublime:** uplifted, elated.

1671. **fat:** Leonard notes that the eating of fat is prohibited in Lev. 3.17.

1674. **Silo:** Shiloh, then the location of the Ark of the Covenant.

1682. **fond:** foolish.

1685. "Left senseless or with godless (and therefore disordered) sense."

And as an ev'ning dragon came,
Assailant on the perchèd roosts,
And nests in order ranged
Of tame villatic fowl; but as an eagle
His cloudless thunder bolted on their heads.
So virtue giv'n for lost,
Depressed, and overthrown, as seemed,
Like that self-begott'n bird
In the Arabian woods embossed,
That no second knows nor third,
And lay erewhile a holocaust,
From out her ashy womb now teemed,
Revives, reflourishes, then vigorous most
When most unactive deemed,
And though her body die, her fame survives,
A secular bird ages of lives.
Manoa. Come, come, no time for lamentation now,
Nor much more cause; Samson hath quit himself
Like Samson, and heroic'ly hath finished
A life heroic, on his enemies
Fully revenged, hath left them years of mourning,
And lamentation to the sons of Caphtor
Through all Philistian bounds. To Israel
Honor hath left, and freedom, let but them
Find courage to lay hold on this occasion;
To himself and father's house eternal fame;

1692. **dragon:** serpent. Readers have traditionally pictured a large snake and been perplexed by the adjective *evening.* Tayler (1972) suggested the *draco volans,* or firedrake, a comet Londoners occasionally saw at evening over the Thames (Winny, 167–68). This identification makes better sense of *fiery virtue* and *sudden flame,* and also links with the *winds* of line 1647. Comets were thought to begin as windy exhalations from the earth.

1695. **villatic:** barnyard (Italian *villa* means "farmhouse"). **but as an eagle:** The second metaphorical bird, the eagle, traditionally delivered the thunderbolts of Jove and was immune to their power. Carey (1997) accuses Tayler of missing the "contrastive force" of *but* in identifying the evening dragon with a comet (see previous note). The word indicates that the eagle attacks suddenly from above while the evening dragon comes slowly and attacks from below, and cannot therefore be a comet. But it may be that the conjunction simply contrasts two ominous "birds" seen in the sky.

1696. **cloudless thunder:** Horace, *Odes* 1.34.5, attests to the extraordinary effect of hearing thunder on a clear day. See also Browne, *Pseudodoxia Epidemica* 2.5.

1697. **giv'n for:** considered.

1699. **self-begott'n bird:** The third and climactic bird, the mythical phoenix, was reborn from its ashes every five hundred or one thousand years.

1700. **embossed:** imbosked, sheltered by the woods.

1701. Only one phoenix exists at a time.

1702. **holocaust:** sacrifice consumed by fire.

1703. **teemed:** brought forth, born.

1707. **secular:** living for ages.

1709. **quit:** acquitted.

1713. **sons of Caphtor:** Philistines.

1715. **hath:** he has.

And which is best and happiest yet, all this
With God not parted from him, as was feared,
But favoring and assisting to the end.
Nothing is here for tears, nothing to wail
Or knock the breast, no weakness, no contempt,
Dispraise, or blame, nothing but well and fair,
And what may quiet us in a death so noble.
Let us go find the body where it lies
Soaked in his enemies' blood, and from the stream
With lavers pure and cleansing herbs wash off
The clotted gore. I with what speed the while
(Gaza is not in plight to say us nay)
Will send for all my kindred, all my friends
To fetch him hence and solemnly attend
With silent obsequy and funeral train
Home to his father's house: there will I build him
A monument, and plant it round with shade
Of laurel ever green, and branching palm,
With all his trophies hung, and acts enrolled
In copious legend, or sweet lyric song.
Thither shall all the valiant youth resort,
And from his memory inflame their breasts
To matchless valor, and adventures high:
The virgins also shall on feastful days
Visit his tomb with flowers, only bewailing
His lot unfortunate in nuptial choice,
From whence captivity and loss of eyes.
Chorus. All is best, though we oft doubt,
What th' unsearchable dispose
Of highest wisdom brings about,
And ever best found in the close.
Oft he seems to hide his face,
But unexpectedly returns
And to his faithful champion hath in place

1723. **nothing but well:** nothing but what is well.

1727. **lavers:** washbasins.

1728. **with what speed:** as quickly as I can.

1729. **not in plight:** not in a condition to.

1732. **obsequy:** funeral ceremony.

1736–37. **enrolled . . . legend:** written out in a detailed inscription.

1741–42. **The virgins . . . flowers:** This is the honor Dalila promised herself (986–87).

1745–48. These lines resemble the typical closing choruses of Euripides, which emphasize the unpredictable nature of divine intervention in human affairs.

1745–58. The Chorus's final speech, although mixing tetrameter and pentameter lines and including two trochaic lines, is modeled on the English or Shakespearean sonnet.

1746. **dispose:** disposition, dispensation.

1749. **hide his face:** God is figured as hiding his face in anger in Ps. 27.9 and 30.7.

Bore witness gloriously; whence Gaza mourns
And all that band them to resist
His uncontrollable intent;
His servants he with new acquist
Of true experience from this great event
With peace and consolation hath dismissed,
And calm of mind, all passion spent.

1755. **His servants:** Manoa, the Chorus, and Milton's sympathetic readers; **acquist:** acquisition.
1758. A perfect definition of regained faith and cathartic cure, and a perfect line on which to end a poetic career.

Prose Works

Familiar Letters

This section contains ten letters. With the exception of the so-called "Letter to a Friend," which was composed in English and for which there is a separate headnote, the letters by Milton are in Latin and cannot be regarded as mere mail, documents that have somehow survived from a private correspondence. "You ask what I am thinking of?" Milton writes to Diodati. "So help me God, an immortality of fame." However personal the thought may have been, it belongs as well to the genre in which Milton is writing. For the Latin familiar letter fused private and public, friendship and literary ambition. In Milton's day, such letters were written with an eye toward publication. As authors did the usual business of letter writing (thanking, requesting, praising, criticizing, excusing, seducing, opining, joking), they simultaneously demonstrated their mastery of Latin style, imitating the precedents of Cicero, Ovid, and Seneca. Milton published his *Epistolae Familiarum* in 1674, the last year of his life (see introduction to *Prolusions*). This book has been translated and annotated by Phyllis B. and E. M. W. Tillyard (1932).

The earliest of these ten pieces, probably, are the undated Greek letters sent to Milton by Charles Diodati, the great friend of his childhood. Together with the two Latin letters dated in September 1637 from Milton to Diodati, they convey the jocular yet somewhat tense idealism of this friendship. Diodati, who eventually studied medicine, chides Milton for his rigorous and possibly debilitating programs of self-study. Milton, for his part, readily confesses that his temperament "allows no delay, no rest, no anxiety . . . about scarcely anything to distract me, until I attain my object and complete some great period, as it were, of my studies." He pursues the idea of the beautiful as diligently as Ceres "sought her daughter Prosperina." The analogy is itself a pursuit of the beautiful.

In the 1628 letter to Alexander Gill, one of his teachers at St. Paul's grammar school, and son of its headmaster, Milton speaks diffidently of verses that he has sent, "light-minded nonsense" composed for a commencement ceremony at his college. Yet he is clearly eager for his former teacher, himself a poet, to evaluate them and to respond by sending verses of his own for Milton to read. Evidently, the scholasticism of Cambridge and the lack of preparation of his fellow students, clergy in training for the most part, had aroused Milton's skepticism and a corresponding nostalgia for the humanist training he received at St. Paul's.

The poet and statesman Sir Henry Wotton writes in 1638 to thank Milton for his gift of the anonymous 1638 edition of *A Masque*. After complimenting the work ("I must plainly confess to have seen yet nothing parallel in our language"), he proceeds to offer aid and advice with regard to the young poet's forthcoming trip to the Continent. Perhaps at the urging of the publisher, this letter was printed before *A Masque* in the 1645 *Poems*. It was omitted in the second edition of 1673.

Milton's letter to the Vatican librarian, Lukas Holste, was written during his second stay in Florence. Having just returned from Rome, Milton thanks Holste for his courtesies, praises his patron, Cardinal Barberini, and in his eager approval of Holste's various scholarly projects savors the humanist ideal of a republic of learning unspoiled by religious and political differences.

The Athens-born Leonard Philaras was a scholar, diplomat, and champion of Greek liberty. Visting London in 1654, he asked the blind Milton to supply him with an account of his symptoms in the hope that a French physician, François Thévenin, might be able to treat him. Milton's reply is our main authority for any attempt to diagnose his condition. Though he hopes for the best, Milton is clearly resigned to his blindness, and the letter closes with evocations of *Sonnet 22*.

This representative selection of Milton's private correspondence concludes with one of his two 1657 letters to Henry De Brass, a young man who wrote to ask Milton, then nearing fifty and totally blind, for his evaluation of Latin historians. Students who read Milton's *History of Britain* will find that he attempts to achieve the same brevity of style for which he praises Sallust. Milton no doubt felt that his experience as Latin Secretary for the Commonwealth had also made him equal to the task of "writing worthily of worthy deeds." The self-consciousness and worry that seem to break through his youthful letters have faded, and Milton's benign attitude toward his correspondent calls to mind the generosity the young Milton was shown by Sir Henry Wotton nearly twenty years before.

Our texts of the Greek and Latin letters follow the translations in the Yale edition of Milton's prose. We print the text of *Letter to a Friend* from a facsimile of the *CMS* (Wright 1972, 6–7).

Diodati Greets Milton Cheerfully[1]

The present state of the weather seems to be quite jealous of the arrangements we made when lately we parted, for it has been stormy and unsettled for two whole days now. But nevertheless, so much do I desire your company that in my longing I dream of and all but prophesy fair weather and calm, and everything golden for tomorrow, so that we may enjoy our fill of philosophical and learned conversation. Therefore I wished to write you to invite and encourage you, in fear lest you turn your mind to other plans, despairing of sunshine and enjoyment, for the time at least. But be of good cheer, my friend, and stand by the plans we made together, and adopt a festive spirit, gayer than that of today. For tomorrow all will be fair; the air and the sun and the river, and trees and little birds and earth and men will laugh and dance with us as we make holiday—but let this be said with humility. Only do you be ready to set out when called, or even uncalled, to come to me, who long to see you. "For Menelaus, good at the war-cry, came to him unbidden."[2] Farewell.

1. Two undated letters to Milton by his boyhood friend Charles Diodati (d. 1638) survive. Both are in Greek. On their friendship and correspondence, see Parker (1968, 1:59–61), Kerrigan (1983, 48–50), and Rumrich (1999). In this volume, see *Elegies 1* and *6*, *Damon*, and *Sonnet 4*. His name does not appear in Milton's English verse or in his prose.
2. Homer, *Il.* 2.408. Other Greek heroes must be called to Agamemnon's tent for a midnight council, but *Menelaus*, because of his heartfelt sympathy with his brother, comes without being bidden.

Diodati Greets Milton

I have no complaint with my present way of life with this one exception, that I lack some noble soul skilled in conversation. Such a person I do miss; but there is abundance of everything else here in the country. For what is lacking when the days are long, the countryside most lovely with flowers, and waving and teeming with leaves, on every branch a nightingale or goldfinch, or some other little bird singing and warbling in rivalry? Where are walks of utmost variety, a table neither scant nor overburdened, and quiet sleep. Could I but add to these a good companion, learned and initiate, I would be happier than the King of Persia. Still there is always something lacking in human affairs, wherefore one must be moderate. But you, extraordinary man, why do you despise the gifts of nature? Why such inexcusable perseverance, bending over books and studies day and night? Live, laugh, enjoy your youth and the hours, and stop reading the serious, the light, and the indolent works of ancient wise men, wearing yourself out the while. I, who in all other things am your inferior, in this one thing, in knowing the proper limit of labor, both seem to myself, and am, your better. Farewell, and be merry, but not in the manner of Sardanapalus in Soli.[3]

3. **Sardanapalus:** Greek name of a seventh-century Assyrian king, probably an amalgamation of several Assyrian kings. Classical authors present him as a sybaritic transvestite. *Soli* was a town in Cyprus under Assyrian control. Parker confuses it with a coastal town in Asia Minor by the same name (1968, 1:60).

To Alexander Gill[1]

In my former letter I did not so much answer you, as avoid the duty of answering;[2] and so I silently promised that another letter would soon follow, in which I should reply at somewhat greater length to your most friendly challenge. But even if I had not promised, it must be confessed that this letter is your most rightful due; for I think that each one of your letters cannot be repaid except by two of mine, or if it be reckoned more accurately, not even by a hundred of mine. Included with this letter, behold that project about which I wrote you somewhat more obscurely, a problem on which, when your letter reached me, I was laboring with great effort, harried by the shortness of time. For by chance a certain Fellow of our House,[3] who was going to act as respondent in the philosophical disputation at this academic assembly, entrusted to my puerility the verses which annual custom requires to be written on the questions, he himself being long past light-minded nonsense of that kind and more intent on serious things.[4] It is these, printed, that I have sent you, since I knew you to be the keenest judge of poetry in general and the most honest judge of mine. Now if you will deign to send me yours in turn, there will certainly be no one who will enjoy them more, though there will be, I confess, one who will better appraise their merit. Indeed whenever I remember your almost constant conversations with me (which even in Athens itself, nay in the very Academy, I long for and

1. Alexander Gill the younger (c. 1597–1644) was the son of the headmaster of St. Paul's school and taught there. He was already a published poet and, shortly after Milton wrote this letter, found himself in prison for unguarded expression of his political opinions (Parker 1968, 1:50–51).
2. Although two other letters to Gill survive, neither appears to be the letter to which Milton here refers.
3. **Fellow of our House:** that is, a graduate of Milton's college now in its employ.
4. Various short works have been proposed as candidates for the verses entrusted to Milton, among them *That Nature Does Not Suffer from Old Age* and *Of the Platonic Idea as Understood by Aristotle.* Both were composed around this time. The annual assembly to which Milton refers was Commencement, held on July 1, 1628, the day before the date of this letter.

need), I think immediately, not without sorrow, of how much benefit my absence has cheated me—me who never left you without a visible increase and growth of knowledge, quite as if I had been to some market of learning. There is really hardly anyone among us, as far as I know, who, almost completely unskilled and unlearned in philology and philosophy alike, does not flutter off to theology unfledged, quite content to touch that also most lightly, learning barely enough for sticking together a short harangue by any method whatever and patching it with worn-out pieces from various sources—a practice carried far enough to make one fear that the priestly ignorance of a former age may gradually attack our clergy.[5] And so, finding almost no intellectual companions here, I should longingly look straight to London, did I not consider retiring into a deeply literary leisure during this summer vacation and hiding as it were in the cloisters of the Muses. But since you already do so every day, I think it almost a crime to interrupt you longer with my noise at present. Farewell.

Cambridge, July 2, 1628.

5. See *Of Education* for a more developed version of Milton's critique of the universities' scholastic curriculum.

Letter to a Friend

The so-called "Letter to a Friend" survives in two drafts in the Trinity College manuscript (*CMS*) of Milton's minor poems, which also contains seven pages of notes for projected tragedies. Like those notes and the manuscript poems, which show evidence of considerable revision, the "Letter" opens a window on the mind of the young Milton. The intended recipient (we have no evidence that the letter was ever sent) is not specified. An emerging consensus pointed to Thomas Young, Presbyterian minister and Milton's tutor from 1618 to 1620 (from Milton's tenth through twelfth years), but recently Barbara Lewalski (2000) has taken the letter's composition in English as evidence that the recipient was neither a minister nor a university acquaintance. In any event, we know from the drafts themselves that the "friend" had questioned why Milton had not yet entered the ministry. William Riley Parker's persuasive dating of the letter in 1633 relies on this fact, as Milton would have become eligible for the ministry on his twenty-fourth birthday, in December 1632.

While we print what in the manuscript appears to be the final state of the draft letter, to look at the two drafts with their forests of strikeouts and interlinear and marginal additions is to see Milton in the process of composing himself. Although the tone is defensive in places, the revision process tends toward the effacement or qualification of hints of possible blameworthiness. The letter contains in small compass several themes that will become familiar in Milton's later writing: a concern with belatedness, a sense of special vocation, and an insistence on personal rectitude. One can also witness here one of Milton's favorite strategies, turning defense against criticism into assertion of unusual virtue and propriety. Note, for example, how he uses the parable of the laborers in the vineyard, in which those workers who come late receive the same reward as those who have worked all day. This apparent injustice calls for parabolic interpretation, the burden of which seems to be a rebuke to the self-righteous, who think they deserve more from God than others, and a demonstration of the mercy of God, who saves even those who come late. Milton reads the parable in a strained and self-referential manner, however, implying that the workers hired in the eleventh hour are less the objects of divine indulgence than they are particularly meritorious for having spent the earlier hours diligently preparing to serve well.

Sir,

Besides that in sundry other respects I must acknowledge me to profit by you whenever we meet, you are often to me, and were yesterday especially, as a good watchman to admonish that the hours of the night pass on (for so I call my life, as yet obscure and unserviceable to mankind) and that the day with me is at hand wherein Christ commands all to labor while there is light.[1] Which because I am persuaded you do to no other purpose than out of a true desire that God should be honored in everyone, I therefore think myself bound, though unasked, to give you account, as oft as occasion is, of this my tardy moving, according to the precept of my conscience, which I firmly trust is not without God. Yet now I will not strain for any set apology, but only refer myself to what my mind shall have at any time to declare herself at her best ease.

But if you think, as you said, that too much love of learning is in fault, and that I have given up myself to dream away my years in the arms of studious retirement like Endymion with the moon,[2] as the tale of Latmos goes,[3] yet consider that if it were no more but the mere love of learning, whether it proceed from a principle bad, good, or natural, it could not have held out thus long against so strong opposition on the other side of every kind. For if it be bad,[4]

1. Milton alludes to several biblical passages simultaneously here. The imperative to work while it is light is taken from John 9.3–4 and 12.35–36, but the watchman comes from Isa. 21.11–12, a passage often applied to ministers, as Lewalski notes (2000), and also from Matth. 24.42–44 and 25.13–14, passages that bracket the parable of the wise and foolish virgins and precede the parable of the talents, to which Milton alludes later.
2. **moon:** The moon goddess Selene, enchanted by the sight of the shepherd *Endymion* sleeping on Mount *Latmos*, visited him nightly and bore him fifty daughters. Various traditions explain Endymion's sleep: according to one, Selene placed him in an unbroken sleep so that she could enjoy him undisturbed; in another, particularly suited to this context, Endymion, offered anything he might desire by Zeus, chose eternal sleep with eternal youth.
3. **goes:** The manuscript reads, in error, "of goes."
4. **bad:** Here *bad* replaces the scratched-out "evil in me," one example among many in which Milton, as he revises, softens or excises suggestions of his own deficiency or delinquency.

why should not all the fond hopes that forward youth and vanity are fledge with, together with gain, pride, and ambition, call me forward more powerfully than a poor, regardless, and unprofitable sin of curiosity should be able to withhold me, whereby a man cuts himself off from all action, and becomes the most helpless, pusillanimous, and unweaponed creature in the world,[5] the most unfit and unable to do that which all mortals most aspire to, either to defend and be useful to his friends or to offend his enemies? Or if it be to be thought an natural proneness, there is against it a much more potent inclination inbred which about this time of a man's life solicits most, the desire of house and family of his own, to which nothing is esteemed more helpful than the early entering into credible employment, and nothing more hindering than this affected solitariness. And though this were enough, yet there is to this another act, if not of pure yet of refined nature, no less available to dissuade prolonged obscurity, a desire of honor and repute and immortal fame[6] seated in the breast of every true scholar, which all make haste to by the readiest ways of publishing and divulging conceived merits, as well those that shall as those that never shall obtain it. Nature therefore would presently work the more prevalent way if there were nothing but the inferior bent of herself to restrain her.

Lastly, this love of learning, as it is the pursuit of something good, it would sooner follow the more excellent and supreme good known and presented, and so be quickly diverted from the empty and fantastic chase of shadows and notions to the solid good flowing from due and timely obedience to that command in the gospel set out by the terrible seizing of him that hid the talent.[7] It is more probable therefore that not the endless delight of speculation but this very consideration of that great commandment does not press forward as soon as may be to undergo, but keeps off with a sacred reverence and religious advisement how best to undergo, not taking thought of being late so it give advantage to be more fit; for those that were latest lost nothing when the master of the vineyard came to give each one his hire.[8] And here I am come to a stream-head copious enough to disburden itself like Nilus at seven mouths into an ocean, but then I should also run into a reciprocal contradiction of ebbing and flowing at once, and do that which I excuse myself for not doing, preach and not preach. Yet that you may see that I am something suspicious of myself, and do take notice of a certain belatedness in me, I am the bolder to send you some of my nightward thoughts some while since (because they come in not altogether unfitly) made up in a Petrarchan stanza, which I told you of.[9]

5. **world:** The ms. reads "word," not "world." While we adopt the standard reading here, to be *unweaponed . . . in the word* is an explicable meaning in the context of a defense of delaying entry into the clergy.

6. **fame:** The description of the desire for fame as an *act, if not of pure yet of refined nature* foreshadows the description of fame in *Lyc* 71, as "that last infirmity of noble mind."

7. Matt. 25.14–30.

8. Matt. 20.1–16.

9. *Sonnet 7.* Milton copies the sonnet into the first draft of the letter; the second draft contains not the sonnet itself but a placeholder ("after the stanza").

How soon hath Time the subtle thief of youth
Stol'n on his wing my three and twentieth year!
My hasting days fly on with full career,
But my late spring no bud or blossom shew'th.
Perhaps my semblance might deceive the truth,
That I to manhood am arrived so near,
And inward ripeness doth much less appear,
That some more timely-happy spirits endu'th.
Yet be it less or more, or soon or slow,
It shall be still in strictest measure even
To that same lot, however mean or high,
Toward which Time leads me, and the will of Heav'n;
All is, if I have grace to use it so,
As ever in my great Taskmaster's eye.

after the stanza [*Sonnet 7*]

By this I believe you may well repent of having made mention at all of this matter, for if I have not all this while won you to this, I have certainly wearied you to it. This therefore alone may be a sufficient reason for me to keep me as I am, lest having thus tired you singly, I should deal worse with a whole congregation, and spoil all the patience of a parish. For I myself do not only see my own tediousness, but now grow offended with it that has hindered me thus long from coming to the last and best period of my letter, and that which must now chiefly work my pardon, that I am

Your true and unfeigned friend.

To Charles Diodati

Now at last I plainly see that you are trying to outdo me once in obstinate silence. If so, congratulations; have your little glory; see, I write first. Yet certainly, if ever we should debate the reasons why neither has written to the other for so long, do not doubt that I shall be much more excused than you. Obviously so, since I am naturally slow and lazy to write, as you well know; whereas you on the other hand, whether by nature or by habit, can usually be drawn into this sort of correspondence with ease. At the same time it is in my favor that your habit of studying permits you to pause frequently, visit friends, write much, and sometimes make a journey. But my temperament allows no delay, no rest, no anxiety—or at least thought—about scarcely anything to distract me, until I attain my object and complete some great period, as it were, of my studies. And wholly for this reason, not another please, has it happened that I undertake even courtesies more tardily than you. In returning them, however, my Diodati, I am not such a laggard; for I have never committed the crime of letting any letter of yours go unanswered by another of mine. How is it that you, as I hear, have written letters to the bookseller, even oftener to your brother, either of whom could conveniently enough, because of nearness, have been responsible for passing letters on to me—had there been any? But what I really complain of is that you, although you promised that you would visit us whenever you left the city, did not keep your promises. If you had once actually thought of these neglected promises, you would not have lacked immediate reason for writing. And so I had all these things to declaim against you, with reason I think; you will see to the answers yourself. But meanwhile, pray, how is everything? Are you quite well? Are there in those parts any fairly learned people with whom you can associate pleasantly and with whom you can talk, as we have been used to talking? When do you return? How long do you plan to linger among those Hyperboreans[1]? I should like you to answer these questions one by one. But you must not suppose that it is only now that I have your affairs at heart; for know that at the beginning of autumn I turned aside from a journey to see your brother, with the intention of finding out what you were doing. Again recently, when the news had been brought to me accidentally at London (by I know not whom) that you were in the city, immediately and as if by storm I hurried to your lodging, but " 'twas the vision of a shadow,"[2] for nowhere would you appear. Wherefore, if you conveniently can, fly hither with all speed and settle in some place which may offer brighter hope that somehow we may visit each other at least sometimes. Would that you could be as much my rustic neighbor as you are my urban one, but this as it pleases God. I wish I could say more, both about myself and about my studies, but I should prefer to do it in person. Furthermore, tomorrow we return to that country place of ours, and the journey presses so close that I have scarcely been able to throw these words hastily on paper. Farewell.

London, Septemb. [November?] 2. 1637.

1. **Hyperboreans:** those who dwell in the far north, literally "above the north wind." Diodati's actual whereabouts at the time are unknown.
2. Pindar, *Pyth.* 8.95. "In Milton's copy of Pindar at Harvard, the passage containing these words . . . is underlined" (Yale 1:324n4). In context it is an observation on the transience of human life.

To the Same

I see now why you wish me so many healths, when my other friends in their letters usually manage to wish me only one: you evidently want me to know that to those mere wishes which were all that you yourself could formerly and others can still offer, there are just now added to your art as well, and the whole mass as it were of medical power. For you bid me be well six hundred times, as well as I wish to be, and so on. Certainly you must have recently been made Health's wry steward, you so squander the whole store of salubrity; or rather

Health herself must doubtless now be your parasite,[1] you so act the king and order her to obey. And so I congratulate you and must thank you on two scores, both for your friendship and for your excellent skill. Indeed, since we had agreed upon it, I long expected letters from you; but though I had not yet received any, I did not, believe me, allow my old affection towards you to cool because of such a trifle. On the contrary, I had already suspected that you would use that very same excuse for tardiness which you have used at the beginning of your letter, and rightly so, considering the intimacy of our friendship. For I do not wish true friendship to be weighed by letters and salutations, which may all be false, but on either hand to rest and sustain itself upon the deep roots of the soul, and, begun with sincere and blameless motives, even though mutual courtesies cease, to be free for life from suspicion and blame. For fostering such a friendship there is need not so much for writing as for a living remembrance of virtues on both sides. Even if you had not written, that obligation would not necessarily remain unfulfilled. Your worth writes to me instead and inscribes real letters on my inmost consciousness; your candor of character writes, and your love of right; your genius writes too (by no means an ordinary one) and further recommends you to me. Therefore do not try to terrorize me, now that you hold that tyrannical citadel of medicine, as if you would take back your six hundred healths, withdrawing them little by little, to the last one, should I by chance desert friendship, which God forbid. And so remove that terrible battery which you seem to have trained on me, forbidding me to be sick without your permission. For lest you threaten too much, know that I cannot help loving people like you. For though I do not know what else God may have decreed for me, this certainly is true: he has instilled into me, if into anyone, a vehement love[2] of the beautiful. Not so diligently is Ceres, according to the Fables, said to have sought her daughter Proserpina, as I seek for this idea of the beautiful, as if for some glorious image, throughout all the shapes and forms of things ("for many are the shapes of things divine"); day and night I search and follow its lead eagerly as if by certain clear traces.[3] Whence it happens that if I find anywhere one who, despising the warped judgment of the public, dares to feel and speak and be that which the greatest wisdom throughout all ages has taught to be best, I shall cling to him immediately from a kind of necessity. But if I, whether by nature or by my fate, am so equipped that I can by no effort and labor of mine rise to such glory and height of fame, still, I think that neither men nor Gods forbid me to reverence and honor those who have attained that glory or who are successfully aspiring to it. But now I know you wish your curiosity satisfied. You make many anxious inquiries, even about what I am thinking. Listen, Diodati, but in secret, lest I blush;

1. **parasite:** one who obtains the hospitality or patronage of the powerful by being obsequious.
2. **vehement love:** Milton breaks from Latin to put this phrase in Greek. Cp. Adam's "vehemence of love" in the Argument to *PL* 9.
3. Milton refers to the search of Ceres for Proserpina after she had been taken to the underworld by Hades. The quoted passage is in Greek and appears in several of Euripides' tragedies, e.g., the concluding chorus of *Bacchae*.

and let me talk to you grandiloquently for a while. You ask what I am thinking of? So help me God, an immortality of fame.[4] What am I doing? Growing my wings and practicing flight.[5] But my Pegasus still raises himself on very tender wings. Let me be wise on my humble level. I shall now tell you seriously what I am planning: to move into some one of the Inns of Court,[6] wherever there is a pleasant and shady walk; for that dwelling will be more satisfactory, both for companionship, if I wish to remain at home, and as a more suitable headquarters, if I choose to venture forth. Where I am now, as you know, I live in obscurity and cramped quarters. You shall also hear about my studies. By continued reading I have brought the affairs of the Greeks to the time when they ceased to be Greeks. I have been occupied for a long time by the obscure history of the Italians under the Longobards, Franks, and Germans, to the time when liberty was granted them by Rudolph, King of Germany. From there it will be better to read separately about what each state did by its own effort.[7] But what about you? How long will you act the son of the family and devote yourself to domestic matters, forgetting urban companionships? For unless this step-motherly warfare be more hazardous than either the Dacian or Sarmatian, you must certainly hurry, and at least make your winter quarters with us.[8] Meanwhile, if you conveniently can, please send me Giustiniani, Historian of the Veneti.[9] On my word I shall see either that he is well cared for until your arrival, or, if you prefer, that he is returned to you shortly. Farewell.

London, Septemb. [November?] 23. 1637.

4. **immortality of fame:** Milton's Latin text simply reads "immortality" [*immortalitatem*], without mention of fame.
5. **Growing my wings:** Milton interjects the Greek verb for sprouting wings (πτεροφυῶ), which in this context suggests the winged soul's quest for immortality in Plato's *Phaedrus* (246e–252c). The Latin verb translated as "practicing" (*meditor*) is better rendered as "contemplating."
6. **Inns of Court:** public houses in the legal district of London.
7. At the time he wrote this letter, Milton's course of private study (1632–38) was drawing to an end. For what he read when, see Hanford 1921.
8. ***Dacian, Sarmatian:*** references to intermittent, fierce second-century conflicts between Rome and tribal forces in central Europe. The reference to *winter quarters* (Lat. *hiberna*) continues the allusion to Roman military history.
9. Milton refers either to Justianus Bernardus, *De Origine Urbis Venetiarum Rebusque ab Ipsa Gestis Historia* (Venice, 1492) or to later translations into Italian.

Sir Henry Wotton to Milton[1]

From the College, this 13. of April, 1638.

SIR,

It was a special favor, when you lately bestowed upon me here, the first taste of your acquaintance, though no longer then to make me know that I wanted

1. By the time he befriended Milton, Wotton (1568–1639) was nearing the end of a remarkable life, during which he was the admired friend of John Donne, George Herbert, and Izaak Walton among others. After his employment by the Earl of Essex in gathering foreign intelligence, he spent long periods abroad as King James's ambassador. He returned to England in 1624 and was made Provost of Eton.

more time to value it, and to enjoy it rightly; and in truth, if I could then have imagined your farther stay in these parts, which I understood afterwards by Mr. *H.*,[2] I would have been bold in our vulgar phrase to mend my draft (for you left me with an extreme thirst) and to have begged your conversation again, jointly with your said learned Friend, at a poor meal or two, that we might have banded together[3] some good Authors of the ancient time: among which, I observed you to have been familiar.

Since your going, you have charged me with new obligations, both for a very kind letter from you dated the sixth of this month, and for a dainty piece of entertainment which came therewith. Wherein I should much commend the tragical part, if the lyrical did not ravish me with a certain Doric delicacy in your songs and odes, whereunto I must plainly confess to have seen yet nothing parallel in our language: *Ipsa mollities.*[4] But I must not omit to tell you, that I now only owe you thanks for intimating unto me (how modestly so ever) the true artificer. For the work itself, I had viewed some good while before, with singular delight, having received it from our common friend Mr. *R.* in the very close of the late *R*'s Poems, printed at *Oxford,* whereunto it was added (as I now suppose) that the accessory might help out the principal, according to the art of stationers, and to leave the reader *con la bocca dolce.*[5]

Now sir, concerning your travels, wherein I may challenge a little more privilege of discourse with you; I suppose you will not blanch[6] Paris in your way; therefore I have been bold to trouble you with a few lines to Mr. M.B., whom you shall easily find attending the young Lord S. as his governor, and you may surely receive from him good directions for the shaping of your farther journey into Italy, where he did reside by my choice some time for the King, after mine own recess from Venice.[7]

I should think that your best line will be through the whole length of France to Marseilles, and thence by Sea to Genoa, whence the passage into Tuscany is as diurnal as a Gravesend barge:[8] I hasten as you do to Florence, or Siena, the rather to tell you a short story from the interest you have given me in your safety.

2. **Mr. *H.*:** "Probably John Hales, former fellow of Merton and now retired to a private fellowship at Eton" (Yale 1:340).
3. **banded together:** discussed in a group, bandied about.
4. **tragical:** dramatic, that part which imitates an action; **lyrical:** musically expressive; ***Doric:*** simple, rustic; ***Ipsa mollities:*** softness itself.
5. **Mr. *R.*:** Perhaps John Rouse, Oxford librarian (see the ode addressed to him, pp. 243–47) or Humphrey Robinson, a major London book trader. No volume of poetry published at Oxford about the time of this letter is known to have been bound with Milton's *Masque,* though Thomas Randolph's *Poems* (Oxford, 1638) has been proposed (Yale 1:341). Wotton suggests that the stationer's art of putting a profitable book together is like that of planning a successful meal, which ought to end *con la bocca dolce* (with a sweet taste).
6. **blanch:** omit, fail to see.
7. Michael Branthwaite, who had assisted Wotton in Venice, was serving as tutor to James Scudamore, son of the English ambassador in Paris, John Scudamore. In *2Def,* Milton says the elder Scudamore introduced him to Hugo Grotius and otherwise helped him on his way (see p. 1091).
8. **Diurnal . . . barge:** regularly recurring each day, like the *Gravesend barge* (a ferry).

At Siena I was tabled in the House of one Alberto Scipioni an old Roman Courtier in dangerous times, having been steward to the Duca di Pagliano, who with all his family were strangled, save this only man that escaped by foresight of the tempest. With him I had often much chat of those affairs; into which he took pleasure to look back from his native harbor; and at my departure toward Rome (which had been the center of his experience) I had won confidence enough to beg his advice, how I might carry myself securely there, without offense of others, or of mine own conscience. *Signor Arrigo mio* (says he) *I pensieri stretti, & il viso sciolto* will go safely over the whole world: Of which *Delphian* Oracle (for so I have found it) your judgment doth need no commentary;[9] and therefore (sir) I will commit you with it to the best of all securities, God's dear love, remaining

Your friend as much at command
as any of longer date
Henry Wootton.

Postscript.

SIR, I have expressly sent this my foot-boy to prevent[10] *your departure without some acknowledgement from me of the receipt of your obliging letter, having myself through some business, I know not how, neglected the ordinary conveyance. In any part where I shall understand you fixed, I shall be glad, and diligent to entertain you with home-novelties;*[11] *even for some fomentation*[12] *of our friendship, too soon interrupted in the cradle.*

9. Wotton took the passage in Italian to mean: "My Signor Harry, your thoughts close, and your countenance loose"; he had given the same advice to others (Yale 1:342). The entire paragraph suggests that Wotton wanted to impress upon Milton the need of a Protestant for discretion while traveling in Roman Catholic countries, especially Italy.

10. **prevent:** arrive before.

11. **home-novelties:** news of home.

12. **fomentation:** stimulation.

To Lukas Holste in the Vatican at Rome[1]

Although I can remember (and often do) many courteous and cordial favors which I have received in my hasty journey through Italy, still, I do not know whether I can rightly say that I have had greater tokens of kindness from anyone on such short acquaintance than from you. For when I went up to the Vatican to meet you, you received me with greatest kindness, though I was utterly unknown to you, unless perhaps I had been previously mentioned by Alessandro Cherubini.[2] At once courteously admitted to the Library, I was permitted to browse through the invaluable collection of books, and also the numerous

1. Born in Germany, *Lukas Holste* (Lat. Holstenius, 1596–1661) became a protégé of Cardinal Francesco Barberini, converted to Roman Catholicism, and by the time of Milton's visit worked in the Vatican Library. It was there in 1952 that the original manuscript of this letter was discovered.

2. Milton made his acquaintance in Rome. He died at twenty-eight, and little is known of him.

Greek authors in manuscript annotated by your nightly toil. Some of these, as yet unseen by our generation, seemed as if in readiness for action, like Vergil's

> —souls shut deep within a green valley, and about to cross the threshold
> of the upper world;

they seemed to demand only the ready hands of the printer and a delivery into the world.[3] Some, already edited by your labor, are being eagerly received everywhere by the learned; and I am sent forth enriched by your gift of two copies of one of these. Next, I could not help believing it the result of your mentioning me to Cardinal Francesco Barberini, that when, a few days later, he gave that public musical entertainment with truly Roman magnificence, he himself, waiting at the door, singled me out in so great a throng and, almost seizing me by the hand, welcomed me in an exceedingly honorable manner. When on this account I paid my respects to him the following day, it was again you yourself who gained both access for me and an opportunity to converse—an opportunity which, considering how important the man (though certainly no one of highest rank could be more kindly nor more courteous) and considering the time and place, was really rather ample than scant.[4] I am sure I do not know, most learned Holstenius, whether I alone have found you such a friend and host, or whether, remembering that you gave three years' work to scholarship at Oxford, you want to honor all Englishmen with attentions of that sort.[5] If the latter, you are indeed handsomely paying our—nay partly even your—England for what you learned there; and you deserve equal thanks in the name of each of us privately and of the country publicly. But if the former, if you have distinguished me from the rest and esteemed me enough to want my friendship, I both congratulate myself on your opinion and at the same time consider it due more to your generosity than to my merit. That commission which I understood you to have given me concerning the inspection of a Medicean codex,[6] I have faithfully referred to my friends, who, however, display scant hope of accomplishing the matter at present. In that library nothing can be copied except by previous permission, nor may one even bring a pen to the tables. They say, however, that Giovanni Battista Doni[7] is at Rome; he is expected daily, having

3. Milton quotes the *Aeneid* (6.679–80). His writings often represent books as bearing the lively potency of their authors; see *On Shakespeare* (p. 34) and *Areop* (p. 930).
4. Although in his writings Milton repeatedly registers a characteristically Puritan disdain for Roman Catholic presumption of religious and political authority, he was capable of maintaining amicable and dutiful relations with individual members of that church, including, as this letter indicates, one so powerful as Cardinal Barberini. While in Rome, he ate dinner with other Englishmen at the English Jesuit College and, at the cardinal's musical evening, may have heard Leonora Baroni sing. Her singing inspired three poems (see pp. 200–202).
5. Beginning in 1622, Holste performed research in Oxford and London.
6. **codex:** an unbound manuscript of some ancient classic. Since Milton sends the letter from Florence, home of the Medicis, he evidently refers to a manuscript in a library there. No more specific identification has been made of the library or manuscript in question.
7. **Doni:** another favorite of the Barberinis, admired for his learning in the arts and sciences both. He was a native of Florence but frequently stayed in Rome.

been called to Florence to give the public lectureship in Greek literature; and they say that through him you can easily obtain what you wish. Yet it would have given me very great pleasure if so eminently desirable a project could have been at least slightly furthered by my poor efforts, for it is a shame that in so worthy and splendid an undertaking you should not have the help of all men everywhere and their learning and fortunes. Finally, you will have bound me by a new obligation if you extend my most respectful greetings to his Eminence the Cardinal, whose great virtues and zeal for what is right, so ready to further all the liberal arts, are always before my eyes—also that gentle and, may I say, humble loftiness of spirit, which alone has taught him to distinguish himself by effacing himself, and about which it can be truly said, as of Ceres in Callimachus, though in a different sense: "Feet to the earth still cling, while the head is touching Olympus."[8] Such humility can prove to most other princes how alien to and how far different from true magnanimity are their surly arrogance and courtly haughtiness. Nor do I think that while he lives anyone will any longer miss the Estensi, Farnesi, or Medici, formerly the patrons of learned men. Farewell, most learned Holstenius, and if there is anyone who highly appreciates yourself and your works, please count me another of his kind, if you think it worthwhile, in whatever part of the world I may be.

Florence, March 30. 1639.

8. Callimachus, *Hymn 6, To Demeter,* 58.

To Leonard Philaras[1]

To Leonard Philaras, Athenian,

Since I have been from boyhood a worshipper of all things Greek and of your Athens first and foremost, I have always been most firmly convinced that this city would someday nobly recompense my goodwill towards her. Nor has the ancient spirit of your noble country belied my prophecy, but has given me you, both an Attic brother and a very loving one: it was you who addressed me most kindly by letter, though far distant and knowing me only by my writings;[2] and afterwards, arriving unexpectedly in London, you continued that kindness by going to see one who could not see, even in that misfortune which has made me more respectable to none, more despicable perhaps to many. And so, since you tell me that I should not give up all hope of regaining my sight, that you have a friend and intimate in the Paris physician Thévenot[3] (especially outstanding as an occulist), whom you will consult about my eyes if only I send you the means by which he can diagnose the causes and symptoms of the disease, I

1. For the circumstances that occasioned this letter, see the introduction.
2. He wrote to congratulate Milton on his *Defense of the English People.*
3. **Thévenot:** François Thévenin (Lat: *Tevenotus*). He died in 1656.

shall do what you urge, that I may not seem to refuse aid whencesoever offered, perhaps divinely.

It is ten years, I think, more or less, since I noticed my sight becoming weak and growing dim, and at the same time my spleen and all my viscera burdened and shaken with flatulence. And even in the morning, if I began as usual to read, I noticed that my eyes felt immediate pain deep within and turned from reading, though later refreshed after moderate bodily exercise; as often as I looked at a lamp, a sort of rainbow seemed to obscure it. Soon a mist appearing in the left part of the left eye (for that eye became clouded some years before the other) removed from my sight everything on that side. Objects further forward too seemed smaller, if I chanced to close my right eye. The other eye also failing slowly and gradually over a period of almost three years, some months before my sight was completely destroyed, everything which I distinguished when I myself was still seemed to swim, now to the right, now to the left. Certain permanent vapors seem to have settled upon my entire forehead and temples, which press and oppress my eyes with a sort of sleepy heaviness, especially from mealtime to evening, so that I often think of the Salmydessian seer Phineus in the *Argonauts*,

> All round him then there grew
> A purple thickness; and he thought the earth
> Whirling beneath his feet, and so he sank,
> Speechless at length, into a feeble sleep.[4]

But I must not omit that, while considerable sight still remained, when I would first go to bed and lie on one side or the other, abundant light would dart from my closed eyes; then, as sight daily diminished, colors proportionately darker would burst forth with violence and a sort of crash from within; but now, pure black, marked as if with extinguished or ashy light, and as if interwoven with it, pours forth. Yet the mist which always hovers before my eyes both night and day seems always to be approaching white rather than black; and upon the eyes turning, it admits a minute quantity of light as if through a crack.

Although some glimmer of hope too may radiate from that physician, I prepare and resign myself as if the case were quite incurable; and I often reflect that since many days of darkness are destined to everyone, as the wise man warns, mine thus far, by the signal kindness of Providence, between leisure and study, and the voices and visits of friends, are much more mild than those lethal ones.[5] But if, as it is written, man shall not live by bread alone, but by every word that proceedeth out of the mouth of God,[6] why should one not likewise find comfort in believing that he cannot see by the eyes alone, but by the guid-

4. Apollonius of Rhodes, *Argonautica* 2.205–8.

5. Milton alludes to Eccles. 11.8: "But if a man live many years, and rejoice in them all; yet let him remember the days of darkness; for they shall be many. All that cometh is vanity."

6. Deut. 8.3, quoted by Jesus to Satan, Matt. 4.4.

ance and wisdom of God. Indeed while he himself looks out for me and provides for me, which he does, and takes me as if by the hand and leads me throughout life, surely, since it has pleased him, I shall be pleased to grant my eyes a holiday. And you, my Philaras, whatever happens, I bid you farewell with a spirit no less stout and bold than if I were Lynceus.[7]

Westminster, September 28, 1654.

7. **Lynceus:** one of the Argonauts. His eyes were so sharp that he could see even through the earth.

To the Most Distinguished Mr. Henry de Brass[1]

I see, sir, that you, like very few of today's youth who wander through foreign lands, travel rightly and wisely, not for childish aims, but in the manner of ancient philosophers, to gather richer learning from every source. Yet whenever I regard what you write, you seem to have come abroad not so much to acquire foreign knowledge as to impart knowledge to others, to barter good merchandise rather than to buy it. And I wish that it were as easy for me to assist and promote those admirable studies of yours in every way as it is truly agreeable and pleasant that one of your distinguished talents should ask it of me. Yet as to your writing that you have decided to write to me and ask me to resolve those problems about which for many ages historians seem to have been in the dark, I have certainly never assumed nor would I dare assume anything of the sort. Concerning what you write of Sallust, I will say frankly, since you wish me to say freely what I think, that I prefer Sallust to any other Latin historian whatever, which was also the nearly unanimous opinion of the ancients. Your Tacitus has his merits, but certainly the greatest of these in my judgment is that he imitated Sallust with all his might. As far as I can tell from what you write, my discussing these matters personally with you seems to have made you feel almost the same way yourself about that most sagacious writer; and you even ask me, since he said at the beginning of the *Bellum Catilinae* that history is extremely difficult to write "because the style must be equal to the deeds," just how I think a historian could acquire such a style.[2] I think thus: he who would write worthily of worthy deeds ought to write with no less largeness of spirit and experience of the world than he who did them, so that he can comprehend and judge as an equal even the greatest, and, having comprehended, can narrate

1. As he grew older and achieved public prominence, Milton's private letters become more assured and, when he addresses younger men, particularly former pupils, magnanimous and avuncular. Although little is known about Henry De Brass beyond what Milton's letters to him tell us, Milton's tone toward him is characteristic of this period, and what he says provides valuable insight into his opinions on writing history.
2. "Milton does not use quotation marks, but his '*quod facta dictis exaequanda sunt*' are the exact words of Sallust, *Bellum Catilinae,* 3.2" (Yale 7:501).

them gravely and clearly in plain and temperate language.[3] For I do not insist on ornate language; I ask for a historian, not an orator. Nor would I favor injecting frequent maxims or judgments on historical exploits, lest by breaking the chain of events, the historian invade the province of the political writer; if, in explaining plans and narrating deeds, he follows to the best of his ability not his own invention or conjecture but the truth, he truly fulfills his function. I would also add of Sallust, what he himself praised most highly in Cato, that he can accomplish much in few words, which I believe no one can do without sharp judgment and a certain restraint. There are many in whose writing you will miss neither grace of style nor abundance of fact, but in my opinion the chief among the Latins who can join brevity with abundance, that is, who can say much in few words, is Sallust. I think these should be the excellences of the historian who expects to do justice to great deeds in words. But why should I say all this to you, who, with your ability, could reach these conclusions yourself, and who have entered a course on which if you proceed you will soon be able to consult no one more learned than yourself? And though you need no one's urging, still, lest I seem wholly unresponsive to your great need for my authority, I strongly urge and advise you to persevere. Farewell, and congratulations on your own excellence and on your zeal for gaining wisdom.

From Westminster, July 15, 1657.

3. Cp. *Apology*, p. 850.

Introduction to Prolusions

Toward the end of Milton's life, the bookseller Brabazon Aylmer planned a volume of his correspondence. Originally it was to have contained a group of familiar letters written over the years to various correspondents and a larger batch of letters of state composed by Milton during his tenure as Latin Secretary for the Cromwell government. But Aylmer was denied permission to reprint the state papers, and through an intermediary sought a replacement from the author. So it was that seven orations or "prolusions" composed during Milton's years at Cambridge University came to be published with his familiar letters in a 1674 volume entitled *Epistolarum Familiarum Liber Unus: Quibus Accesserunt, Ejusdem, jam olim in Collegio Adolescentis, Prolusiones Quaedam Oratoriae.* "I had no hesitation in publishing them," Aylmer said in his preface, "youthful work though they are, in the hope that I should find them as saleable (which is my chief personal concern) as those who originally heard them delivered found them enjoyable."

The prolusions show the young Milton already adept in the techniques of rhetoric and disputation later to be displayed in such argumentative masterpieces as *Paradise Lost, Paradise Regained,* and *Samson Agonistes.* For a modern student, they also offer a small window onto a lost tradition of pedagogy. The positions to be defended (that day is superior to night, that knowledge makes men happier than ignorance) were assigned. The student was expected to produce an oration defending the position in well-turned Latin, with appropriate allusions to classical literature and mythology, then to deliver the oration in persuasive fashion, and afterward, perhaps, to defend its position against objections from the audience. Such exercises were intended to produce men who, rarely at a loss for words, relished debate and associated winning an argument with superior learning. Milton, whether as poet or as prose controversialist, clearly drew much of his power from the seedbed of this training. The two prolusions we have chosen for this edition (1 and 7) anticipate memorable moments in a variety of his later works, including *Lycidas, Of Education, Areopagitica, Paradise Lost,* and *Paradise Regained.*

Our texts follow the translations in volume one of the Yale edition of Milton's prose works.

PROLUSION 1

DELIVERED IN COLLEGE

WHETHER DAY OR NIGHT IS THE MORE EXCELLENT

It is a frequent maxim of the most eminent masters of rhetoric, as you know well, Members of the University, that in every style of oration, whether demonstrative, deliberative, or judicial,[1] the speaker must begin by winning the good will of his audience; without it he cannot make any impression upon them, nor succeed as he would wish in his cause. If this be so (and, to tell the truth, I know that the learned are all agreed in regarding it as an established axiom), how unfortunate I am and to what a pass am I brought this day. At the very outset of my oration I fear I shall have to say something contrary to all the rules of oratory and be forced to depart from the first and chief duty of an orator. For how can I hope for your good-will, when in all this great assembly I encounter none but hostile glances, so that my task seems to be to placate the implacable? So provocative of animosity, even in the home of learning, is the rivalry of those who pursue different studies or whose opinions differ concerning studies they pursue in common. However, I care not if "Polydamas and the women of Troy prefer Labeo to me;—a trifle this."[2]

Yet to prevent complete despair, I see here and there, if I do not mistake, some who without a word show clearly by their looks how well they wish me. The approval of these, few though they be, is more precious to me than that of the countless hosts of the ignorant, who lack all intelligence, reasoning power, and sound judgment, and who pride themselves on the ridiculous effervescing froth of their verbiage. Stripped of their covering of patches borrowed from newfangled authors, they will prove to have no more in them than a serpent's slough, and once they have come to the end of their stock of phrases and platitudes you will find them unable to utter so much as a syllable, as dumb as the

1. **demonstrative:** describing in a laudatory or disparaging manner, such as panegyric or invective; **deliberative:** characterized by careful consideration in order to arrive at a decision; **judicial:** appropriate for legal controversy, critical or judicious.

2. Attius Labeo, author of a Latin translation of the *Iliad,* symbolized for Persius (34–62 C.E.) the Hellenization of Roman culture (*Satires* 1.4, 50). Polydamas and the Trojan ladies represent an unworthy audience.

frogs of Seriphus.[3] How difficult even Heraclitus would find it, were he still alive, to keep a straight face at the sight of these speechifiers (if I may call them so without offence), first grandly spouting their lines in the tragic part of Euripides' Orestes, or as the mad Hercules in his dying agony, and then, their slender stock of phrases exhausted and their glory all gone, drawing in their horns and crawling off like snails.[4]

But to return to the point, from which I have wandered a little. If there is anyone who has refused peace on any terms and declared war *à mort*[5] against me, I will for once stoop to beg and entreat him to lay aside his animosity for a moment and show himself an unbiased judge in this debate, and not to allow the speaker's fault (if such there be) to prejudice the best and most deserving of causes. If you consider that I have spoken with too much sharpness and bitterness, I confess, that I have done so intentionally, for I wish the beginning of my speech to resemble the first gleam of dawn, which presages the fairest day when overcast.

The question whether Day or Night is preferable is no common theme of discussion, and it is now my duty, the task meted out to me this morning, to probe the subject thoroughly and radically,[6] though it might seem better suited to a poetical exercise than to a contest of rhetoric.

Did I say that Night had declared war on Day? What should this portend? What means this daring enterprise? Are the Titans waging anew their ancient war, and renewing the battle of Phlegra's plain?[7] Has Earth brought forth new offspring of portentous stature to flout the gods of heaven? Or has Typhoeus forced his way from beneath the bulk of Etna piled upon him? Or last, has Briareus eluded Cerberus and escaped from his fetters of adamant?[8] What can it possibly be that has now thrice roused the hopes of the gods of hell to rule the empire of the heavens? Does Night so scorn the thunderbolt of Jove? Cares she nothing for the matchless might of Pallas,[9] which wrought such havoc in days of old among the Earth-born brothers? Has she forgotten Bacchus's[10] triumph over the shattered band of Giants, renowned through all the space of heaven?

3. **Seriphus:** an Aegean island turned to stone by Perseus; proverbially even its frogs were dumb as rocks.
4. **Heraclitus:** (c. 500 B.C.E.) Greek philosopher noted for his mournful attitude; **Orestes:** matricidal hero of Greek myth, driven insane by avenging furies; **Hercules:** An unbearably painful poison caused his madness and death.
5. **à mort:** to the death (French).
6. **radically:** to the root.
7. **Phlegra's plain:** In Greek myth, the Olympian gods defeated the giants on the ground out of which their mother (Earth) delivered them, Phlegra, the westernmost prong of the Chalcidicean peninsula in the Aegean. See *PL* 1.198–99n and 577n.
8. **Typhoeus:** Earth-born monster buried beneath Mount *Etna* by Zeus and deemed responsible for its volcanic unrest; **Briareus:** hundred-armed giant imprisoned in Tartarus, classical hell guarded by *Cerberus*, the three-headed dog.
9. **Pallas:** title of Athena, Greek goddess of wisdom.
10. **Bacchus:** aided Zeus in defending Olympus from the Giants' assault.

No, none of these. Full well she remembers, to her grief, how of those brothers most were slain by Jove, and the survivors driven in headlong flight even to the furthest corners of the underworld. Not for war, but for something far other, does she now anxiously prepare. Her thoughts now turn to complaints and accusations, and, womanlike, after a brave fight with tooth and nail, she proceeds to argument or rather abuse, to try, I suppose, whether her hands or her tongue are the better weapon. But I will soon show how unadvised, how arrogant, and how ill-founded is her claim to supremacy, compared with Day's. And indeed I see Day herself, awakened by the crowing of the cock, hastening hither more swiftly than is her wont, to hear her own praise.

Now since it is generally agreed that to be of noble lineage and to trace one's descent back to kings or gods of old is an essential qualification for honors and dignity, it behooves us to inquire, first, which of the two is of nobler birth, secondly, which can trace back her descent the furthest, and thirdly, which is of the greater service to mankind?

I find it stated by the most ancient authorities on mythology that Demogorgon,[11] the ancestor of all the gods (whom I suppose to be identical with the Chaos of the ancients), was the father of Earth, among his many children. Night was the child of Earth, by an unknown father (though Hesiod gives a slightly different pedigree and calls Night the child of Chaos, in the line "From Chaos sprang Erebus and black Night").[12] Whatever her parentage, when she had reached marriageable age, the shepherd Phanes asked her to wife. Her mother consented, but she herself opposed the match, refusing to contract an alliance with a man she did not know and had never seen, and one moreover whose style of life was so different from her own. Annoyed at the rebuff, and with his love turned to hatred, Phanes in his indignation pursued this dusky daughter of Earth through all the length and breadth of the world to slay her. She now feared his enmity as much as she had previously scorned his love. Therefore she did not feel secure enough even among the most distant peoples or in the most remote places, nor even in the very bosom of her mother, but fled for refuge, secretly and by stealth, to the incestuous embrace of her brother Erebus. Thus she found at once a release from her pressing fears and a husband who was certainly very like herself. From this pretty pair Ether and Day are said to have sprung, according to Hesiod, whom I have already quoted:

> From Night again sprang Ether and the Day
> Whom she conceived and bore by Erebus' embrace.[13]

11. **Demogorgon:** In *PL*, Milton does not make him identical to Chaos but does place him in his court; see 2.965 and note.
12. Milton is quoting Hesiod (*Theog.* 123).
13. In Hesiod, both *Night* and *Erebus* are accounted primeval offspring of Chaos; their union produces *Ether* (upper air or sky) and *Day*. Milton here quotes *Theog.* 124–25.

But the more cultured Muses and Philosophy herself, the neighbor of the gods, forbid us to place entire confidence in the poets who have given the gods their forms, especially the Greek poets; and no one should regard it as a reproach to them that in a question of such importance they hardly seem sufficiently reliable authorities. For if any of them has departed from the truth to some slight extent, the blame should not be laid upon their genius, which is most divine, but upon the perverse and blind ignorance of the age, which at that time was all-pervading. They have attained an ample meed of honor and of glory by gathering together in one place and forming into organized communities men who previously roamed like beasts at random through the forests and mountains, and by being the first to teach, by their divine inspiration, all the sciences which are known to-day, arraying them in the charming cloak of fable; and their best title to everlasting fame (and that no mean one) is that they have left to their successors the full development of that knowledge of the arts which they so happily began.

Do not then, whoever you are, hastily accuse me of arrogance, in shattering or altering the statements of all the ancient poets, without any authority to support me. For I am not taking upon myself to do that, but am only attempting to bring them to the test of reason, and thereby to examine whether they can bear the scrutiny of strict truth.

First, then, the story that makes Night the child of Earth is a learned and elegant allegory of antiquity; for what is it that makes night envelop the world but the dense and solid earth, coming between the sun's light and our horizon? Then, as to the statements of the mythologists, calling Night sometimes fatherless, sometimes motherless, these too are pleasing fictions, if we understand them to signify that she was a bastard or a changeling, or else that her parents refused for very shame to acknowledge so infamous and ignoble a child. But why they should believe that Phanes, endowed as he was with a wondrous and superhuman beauty, was so much in love with Night, a mere mulatto or silhouette, as even to wish to marry her, seems a problem hopelessly difficult to solve, unless the phenomenal scarcity of females at that time left him no choice.

But now let us come to close quarters with our subject. The ancients interpret Phanes as the sun or the day, and in relating that he at first sought Night in marriage and then pursued her to avenge his rejection, they mean only to signify the alternation of day and night. But why should they have thought it necessary, in order to show this, to represent Phanes as a suitor for the hand of Night, when their perpetual alternation and mutual repulsion, as it were, could be indicated far better by the figure of an innate and unremitting hatred? For it is well known that light and darkness have been divided from one another by an implacable hatred from the very beginning of time. It is in fact my opinion that Night got her Greek name of *euphrone*[14] for the very reason that she showed

14. **euphrone:** the kindly time, euphemism for *night.* The related Greek adjective, *euphroneon,* means "with kind or prudent mind."

caution and good sense in refusing to bind herself in wedlock to Phanes; for if she had once submitted to his embrace she would doubtless have been destroyed by his beams and by his unendurable radiance, and either annihilated altogether or utterly consumed by fire; like Semele, who, legend says, perished by fire, against the will of her lover Jove. For this reason, with a proper regard for her security, she preferred Erebus to Phanes. With reference to this, Martial aptly and wittily says, "Worst of husbands, worst of wives, I wonder not that you agree so well."[15]

It is, I think, proper to mention with what a handsome family, how like their mother, she presented her husband—namely Misery, Envy, Fear, Deceit, Fraud, Obstinacy, Poverty, Want, Hunger, Fretfulness, Sickness, Old Age, Pallor, Darkness, Sleep, Death and Charon,[16] her last child; so that the proverb *from a bad crow a bad egg* is exactly applicable to this case.

There are, however, some who maintain that Night also bore Aether and Day to her husband Erebus. But who in his senses would not howl down and turn out the advocate of such a theory, as he would anyone who seriously propounded Democritus' notions or the fairytales of childhood?[17] Is it indeed probable on the face of it that black and gloomy Night should be the mother of a child so comely, so sweet, so universally beloved and desired? Such a child; as soon as conceived, would have caused her mother's death by her birth before due time, would have driven her father Erebus into headlong flight, and forced old Charon to hide his dazzled eyes beneath the waters of the Styx and flee to seek what refuge he might in the realms below, as fast as his oars and sails could carry him. No, so far from being born in Hades, Day has never even shown her face there, nor can she find entrance even through a chink or cranny, except in defiance of Fate's decree. Nay, I dare rather declare that Day is older than Night, and that when the world had but newly emerged from Chaos, Day shed her wide-spreading rays over it, before ever the turn of Night had come—unless indeed we are so perverse as to call by the name of Night that foul and murky darkness, or regard it as identical with Demogorgon.[18]

Therefore I hold that Day is the eldest daughter of Heaven,[19] or rather of his son, begotten by him, it is said, to be the comfort of the race of men and the terror of the infernal gods, for fear lest Night should rule unopposed, lest Ghosts and Furies and all that loathsome brood of monsters, unchecked by any barrier between Earth and Hades, should leave the pit of Hell and make their way even

15. Milton refers to one of Martial's *Epigrams* (8.35), which actually concludes to opposite effect: "I wonder you don't agree" [*Mirror non bene convenire vobis*].

16. **Charon:** In Greek myth, the ferryman Charon conveys the dead across the river Styx.

17. The reference is to the Greek atomic theory of matter, founded by *Democritus* (c. 460–357 B.C.E.), and its ethical and religious ramifications.

18. In Book 2 of *PL*, Milton presents Night in just this way, describing her as "eldest" (894) and identifying Chaos as her realm (133).

19. In Greek myth *Heaven* (Gk. *Ouranos*) and Earth (*Gaia*) produce numerous children, among them Hyperion, the original sun god and presumably the *son* of Heaven to whom Milton refers.

to the upper world, and lest wretched Man, enveloped and surrounded by murky darkness, should suffer even in this life the tortures of the damned.

So far, Members of the University, I have endeavored to drag from their deep and dark hiding-places the obscure children of Night; you will immediately perceive how worthy they are of their parentage—especially if I should first devote the best of my small powers to the praise of Day, though Day herself must far transcend the eloquence of all who sing her praise.

In the first place, there is assuredly no need to describe to you how welcome and how desirable Day is to every living thing. Even the birds cannot hide their delight, but leave their nests at peep of dawn and noise it abroad from the treetops in sweetest song, or darting upwards as near as they may to the sun, take their flight to welcome the returning day. First of all these the wakeful cock acclaims the sun's coming, and like a herald bids mankind shake off the bonds of sleep, and rise and run with joy to greet the new-born day. The kids skip in the meadows, and beasts of every kind leap and gambol in delight. The sad heliotrope, who all night long has gazed toward the east, awaiting her beloved Sun, now smiles and beams at her lover's approach. The marigold too and rose, to add their share to the joy of all, open their petals and shed abroad their perfume, which they have kept for the Sun alone, and would not give to Night, shutting themselves up within their little leaves at fall of evening. And all the other flowers raise their heads, drooping and weighed down with dew, and offer themselves to the Sun, mutely begging him to kiss away the tear-drops which his absence brought. The Earth too decks herself in lovelier robes to honor the Sun's coming, and the clouds, arrayed in garb of every hue, attend the rising god in festive train and long procession. And last, that nothing may be lacking to proclaim his praise, the Persians and the Libyans give him divine honors; the Rhodians too have dedicated to his glory that far-famed Colossus of astounding size, created by the miraculous art of Chares of Lindus;[20] to the Sun too, we are told, the American Indians even to this day make sacrifice with incense and with every kind of ritual. You yourselves, Members of the University, must bear witness how delightful, how welcome, how long-awaited is the light of morning, since it recalls you to the cultured Muses from whom cruel Night parted you still unsatisfied and athirst. Saturn, hurled down to Hades from highest heaven, bears witness how gladly he would return to the light of day from that dread gloom, would Jove but grant the boon. Lastly, it is manifest that Pluto himself far preferred light to his own kingdom of darkness, since he so often strove to gain the realm of heaven. Thus Orpheus says with truth and with poetic skill in his hymn to Dawn—"Then of a truth do mortal men rejoice, nor is there one who flees thy face which shines above, when thou dost shake sweet sleep from their eyes. Every man is glad, and every creeping thing, all the tribes of beast and bird, and all the many creatures of the deep."[21]

20. **Chares:** Greek sculptor from *Lindus* (Rhodes). The Colossus of Rhodes, completed in 280 B.C.E., was a gigantic bronze statue of the sun god, deemed one of the seven wonders of the ancient world.

21. The Orphic *Hymn to Dawn* (28.7–11).

Nor is this to be wondered at, when we reflect that Day serves for use as well as pleasure, and is alone fitted to further the business of life; for who would have the hardihood to sail the wide and boundless seas, without a hope that Day would dawn? He would cross the ocean even as the ghosts cross Lethe and Acheron,[22] beset on every hand by fearsome darkness. Every man would then pass his life in his own mean hovel, hardly daring even to creep outside, so that the dissolution of human society must needs follow. To no purpose would Apelles have pictured Venus rising from the waves, in vain would Zeuxis have painted Helen, if dark, dense night hid from our eyes these wondrous sights.[23] In vain too would the earth bring forth in abundance vines twining in many a winding trail, in vain nobly towering trees; in vain would she deck herself anew with buds and blossoms, as with stars, striving to imitate the heaven above. Then indeed that noblest of the senses, sight, would lose its use to every creature; yes, and the light of the world's eye being quenched, all things would fade and perish utterly; nor would the men who dwelt upon the darkened earth long survive this tragedy, since nothing would be left to support their life, nor any means of staying the lapse of all things into the primeval Chaos.[24]

One might continue on this strain with unabating flow, but Day herself in modesty would not permit the full recital, but would hasten her downward course toward the sunset to check her advocate's extravagances. My day is now indeed already drawing to its close, and will soon give place to night, to prevent your saying in jest that this is the longest day though the season is midwinter. This alone I ask, that by your leave I may add a few words which I cannot well omit.

With good reason, then, have the poets declared that Night springs from Hell, since by no means whatever could so many grievous ills descend upon mankind from any other quarter. For when night falls all things grow foul and vile, no difference can then be seen between a Helen and a Canidia,[25] a precious jewel and a common stone (but that some gems have power to outshine the darkness). Then too the loveliest spots strike horror to the heart, a horror gathering force from a silence deep and sad. All creatures lingering in the fields, be they man or beast, hasten to house or lair for refuge; then, hiding their heads beneath their coverings, they shut their eyes against the dread aspect of Night. None may be seen abroad save thieves and rogues who fear the light, who, breathing murder and rapine, lie in wait to rob honest folk of their goods and

22. **Lethe and Acheron:** Rivers of hell. Cp. *PL* 2.575–86.

23. **Apelles:** Court painter in Macedon, fourth century B.C.E., he was considered the greatest of Greek painters. Though none of his paintings survived, description of his work did and inspired Renaissance painters, Botticelli among them. **Zeuxis:** famous Greek painter of the fifth century B.C.E. His celebrated painting of *Helen* (of Troy) was for the temple of Hera at Croton.

24. Cp. *PL* 4.664–66: "Minist'ring light prepared, they set and rise; / Lest total darkness should by night regain / Her old possession, and extinguish life."

25. **Helen:** the most beautiful woman; **Canidia:** a frightful witch (Horace, *Satires* 1.8.23–50).

wander forth by night alone, lest day betray them. For Day lays bare all crimes, nor ever suffers wrongdoing to pollute her light. None will you meet save ghosts and specters, and fearsome goblins who follow in Night's train from the realms below; it is their boast that all night long they rule the earth and share it with mankind. To this end, I think, night sharpens our hearing, that our ears may catch the sooner and our hearts perceive with greater dread the groans of specters, the screeching of owls and nightbirds, and the roaring of lions that prowl in search of prey. Hence clearly is revealed that man's deceit who says that night brings respite from their fears to men and lulls every care to rest. How false and vain is this opinion they know well from their own bitter experience who have ever felt the pangs of guilty consciences; they are beset by Sphinxes and Harpies, Gorgons and Chimaeras,[26] who hunt their victims down with flaming torches in their hands; those poor wretches too know it full well who have no friend to help or succor them, none to assuage their grief with words of comfort, but must pour out their useless plaints to senseless stones, longing and praying for the dawn of day. For this reason did that choicest poet Ovid rightly call Night the mighty foster-mother of cares.[27]

Some indeed say that it is above all by night that our bodies, broken and worn out by the labors of the day, are revived and restored. But this is the merciful ordinance of God, for which we owe no gratitude to Night. But even were it so, sleep is not a thing so precious that Night deserves honor for the bestowal of it. For when we betake ourselves to sleep, we do in truth but confess ourselves poor and feeble creatures, whose puny frames cannot endure even a little while without repose. And, to be sure, what is sleep but the image and semblance of death? Hence in Homer Sleep and Death are twins, conceived together and born at a single birth.[28]

Lastly, it is thanks to the sun that the moon, and the other stars display their fires by night, for they have no light to radiate but such as they borrow from the sun. Who then but a son of darkness, a robber; a gamester, or one whose wont it is to spend his nights in the company of harlots and snore away his days—who, I ask, but such a fellow would have undertaken to defend a cause so odious and discreditable? I wonder that he dare so much as look upon this sun, or share with other men, without a qualm, that light which he is slandering so ungratefully. He deserves to share the fate of Python,[29] slain by the stroke of the sun's hostile rays. He deserves to pass a long and loathsome life imprisoned in Cimmerian darkness.[30] He deserves, above all, to see sleep overcoming his hearers even as he speaks, so that his best eloquence affects them no more than an idle

26. **Sphinxes and Harpies, Gorgons and Chimaeras:** a gallery of fearsome classical monsters; *PL* 2.628.
27. *Letters from the Black Sea* 1.2.41–42.
28. *Il.* 14.230. See also 11.280, where death is described as "the sleep of bronze."
29. **Python:** monstrous serpent slain by Apollo.
30. In Homer, the Cimmerians dwell on the far shore of the western ocean, where the sun doesn't shine (*Od.* 11.13-22). Cp. *L'All* 10.

dream, till, drowsy himself, he is cheated into taking his hearers' nods and snores for nods of approval and murmurs of praise as he ends his speech.

But I see the black brows of Night, and note the advance of darkness; I must withdraw, lest Night overtake me unawares. I beg you then, my hearers, since Night is but the passing and the death of Day, not to give death the preference over life, but graciously to honor my cause with your votes; so may the Muses prosper your studies, and Dawn, the friend of the Muses, hear your prayers; and may the Sun, who sees and hears all things, hearken to all in this assembly who honor and support his cause. I have done.

PROLUSION 7

DELIVERED IN THE COLLEGE CHAPEL IN DEFENSE OF LEARNING AN ORATION

LEARNING BRINGS MORE BLESSINGS TO MEN THAN IGNORANCE

Although, gentlemen, nothing could give me greater pleasure and satisfaction than your presence here, than this eager crowd in cap and gown, or than the honorable office of speaker, which I have already once or twice discharged before you gladly enough, I must, to be candid, confess that I scarcely ever undertake these speeches of my own free will; even though my own disposition and the trend of my studies make no impediment. In fact, if the choice had been offered me, I could well have dispensed with this evening's task. For I have learnt from the writings and sayings of wise men that nothing common or mediocre can be tolerated in an orator any more than in a poet, and that he who would be an orator in reality as well as by repute must first acquire a thorough knowledge of all the arts and sciences to form a complete background to his own calling. Since however this is impossible at my age, I would rather endeavor truly to deserve that reputation by long and concentrated study and by the preliminary acquisition of that background, than snatch at a false repute by a premature and hastily acquired eloquence.[1]

Afire and aglow with these plans and notions, I found that there was no more serious hindrance or obstacle than the loss of time caused by these constant interruptions, while nothing better promoted the development and well-being of the mind, contrary to what is the case with the body, than a cultured and liberal leisure. This I believe to be the meaning of Hesiod's holy sleep and Endymion's

1. Cp. Milton's sense of his own belatedness in *Sonnet 7* and *Letter to a Friend.*

nightly meetings with the moon;[2] this was the significance of Prometheus' withdrawal, under the guidance of Mercury, to the lofty solitude of the Caucasus, where at last he became the wisest of gods and men, so that his advice was sought by Jupiter himself concerning the marriage of Thetis.[3] I can myself call to witness the woods and rivers and the beloved village elms, under whose shade I enjoyed in the summer just passed (if I may tell the secrets of goddesses) such sweet intercourse with the Muses, as I still remember with delight. There I too, amid rural scenes and woodland solitudes, felt that I had enjoyed a season of growth in a life of seclusion.

I might indeed have hoped to find here also the same opportunity for retirement, had not the distressing task of speaking been unseasonably imposed upon me. This so cruelly deprived me of my holy slumbers, so tormented my mind, intent upon other things, and so hindered and hampered me in the hard and arduous pursuit of learning, that I gave up all hope of finding any peace and began sadly to think how far removed I was from that tranquility which learning had at first promised me, how hard my life was like to be amid this turmoil and agitation, and that all attempts to pursue learning had best be abandoned. And so, almost beside myself, I rashly determined on singing the praise of ignorance, since that was not subject to these disturbances, and I proposed as the theme of dispute the question whether art or ignorance bestowed greater blessings on its devotees. I know not how it is, but somehow either my destiny or my disposition forbade me to give up my old devotion to the Muses; indeed, blind chance itself seemed of a sudden to be endowed with prudence and foresight and to join in the prohibition. Sooner than I could have expected, Ignorance had found her champion, and the defense of learning devolved on me. I am delighted thus to have been played with, and am not ashamed to confess that I owe the restoration of my sight to Fortune, who is herself blind. For this she deserves my gratitude. Now I may at any rate be permitted to sing the praises of learning, from whose embrace I have been torn, and as it were assuage my longing for the absent beloved by speaking of her. This can now hardly be called an interruption, for who would regard it as an interruption when he is called upon to praise or defend the object of his affection, his admiration, and his deepest desire?

But, gentlemen, it is my opinion that the power of eloquence is most manifest when it deals with subjects which rouse no particular enthusiasm. Those which most stir our admiration can hardly be compassed within the bounds of

2. **Hesiod's holy sleep:** presumably refers to the contemplative pastoral life in which the Muses called to Hesiod as he pastured his sheep under Mount Helicon. **Endymion:** The goddess of the moon came down to him as he was sleeping in a cave in Latmos. Cp. *Letter to a Friend* (p. 770).

3. The more usual version of the story is that Jupiter sent Mercury to bind *Prometheus* to Mount Caucasus as punishment for bringing fire to humanity. Jupiter's need to learn the bridal secret of the nymph *Thetis* (that her son would be greater than his father) brings him to request the guidance of Prometheus.

a speech: the very abundance of material is a drawback, and the multiplicity of subjects narrows and confines the swelling stream of eloquence. I am now suffering from this excess of material: that which should be my strength makes me weak, and that which should be my defense makes me defenseless. So I must make my choice, or at least mention only in passing rather than discuss at length the numerous arguments on whose powerful support our cause relies for its defense and security. On this occasion it seems to me that my efforts must be directed entirely to showing how and to what extent learning and ignorance respectively promote that happiness which is the aim of every one of us. With this question I shall easily deal in my speech, nor need I be over-anxious about what objections Folly may bring against knowledge, or ignorance against learning. Yet the very ability of ignorance to raise any objection, to make a speech, or even to open her lips in this great and learned assembly, she has received as a favor, or rather an alms, from learning.

It is, I think, a belief familiar and generally accepted that the great Creator of the world, while constituting all else fleeting and perishable, infused into man, besides what was mortal, a certain divine spirit, a part of himself, as it were, which is immortal, imperishable, and exempt from death and extinction. After wandering about upon the Earth for some time, like some heavenly visitant, in holiness and righteousness, this spirit was to take its flight upward to the heaven whence it had come and to return once more to the abode and home which was its birthright. It follows that nothing can be reckoned as a cause of our happiness which does not somehow take into account both that everlasting life and our ordinary life here on earth. This eternal life, as almost everyone admits, is to be found in contemplation alone, by which the mind is uplifted, without the aid of the body, and gathered within itself so that it attains, to its inexpressible joy, a life akin to that of the immortal gods. But without art the mind is fruitless, joyless, and altogether null and void. For who can worthily gaze upon and contemplate the ideas of things human or divine, unless he possesses a mind trained and ennobled by learning and study, without which he can know practically nothing of them: for indeed every approach to the happy life seems barred to the man who has no part in learning. God would indeed seem to have endowed us to no purpose, or even to our distress, with this soul which is capable and indeed insatiably desirous of the highest wisdom, if he had not intended us to strive with all our might toward the lofty understanding of those things, for which he had at our creation instilled so great a longing into the human mind. Survey from every angle the entire aspect of these things and you will perceive that the great Artificer of this mighty fabric established it for His own glory. The more deeply we delve into the wondrous wisdom, the marvelous skill, and the astounding variety of its creation (which we cannot do without the aid of learning), the greater grows the wonder and awe we feel for its Creator and the louder the praises we offer Him, which we believe and are fully persuaded that He delights to accept. Can we indeed believe, my hearers, that the vast spaces of boundless air are illuminated and adorned with everlasting lights, that these are endowed with such rapidity of motion and pass through such intricate revolutions, merely to serve as a lantern for base and slothful men, and to light the path of the idle and the sluggard here below? Do we perceive no purpose in the luxuriance of fruit and herb beyond the short-lived beauty of verdure? Of a truth, if we are so little able to appraise their value that we make no effort to go beyond the crass perceptions of the senses, we shall show ourselves not merely servile and abject, but ungracious and wicked before the goodness of God; for by our unresponsiveness and grudging spirit He is deprived of much of the glory which is His due, and of the reverence which His mighty power exacts.[4] If then Learning is our guide and leader in the search after happiness, if it is ordained and approved by almighty God, and most conformable to His glory, surely it cannot but bring the greatest blessings upon those who follow after it.

I am well aware, gentlemen, that this contemplation, by which we strive to reach the highest goal, cannot partake of true happiness unless it is conjoined with integrity of life and uprightness of character. I know, too, that many men eminent for learning have been of bad character, and slaves to anger, hatred, and evil passions, while on the other hand many utterly ignorant men have shown themselves righteous and just. What of it? Does it follow that ignorance is more blessed? By no means. For the truth is, gentlemen, that though the corrupt morals of their country and the evil communications of the illiterate have in some instances lured into wicked courses a few men distinguished for their learning, yet the influence of a single wise and prudent man has often kept loyal to their duty a large number of men who lacked the advantages of Learning. And indeed a single household, even a single individual, endowed with the gifts of Art and Wisdom, may often prove to be a great gift of God, and sufficient to lead a whole state to righteousness. But where no Arts flourish, where all scholarship is banished, there you will find no single trace of a good man, but savagery and barbarity stalk abroad. As instances of this I adduce no one country, province, or race alone, but Europe itself, forming as it does one fourth of the entire globe. Throughout this continent a few hundred years ago all the noble arts had perished and the Muses had deserted all the universities of the day, over which they had long presided; blind illiteracy had penetrated and entrenched itself everywhere, nothing was heard in the schools but the absurd doctrines of driveling monks, and that profane and hideous monster, Ignorance, assumed the gown and lorded it on our empty platforms and pulpits and in our deserted professorial chairs. Then Piety went in mourning, and Religion sickened and flagged, so that only after prolonged suffering, and hardly even to this very day, has she recovered from her grievous wound.

But, gentlemen, it is, I believe, an established maxim of philosophy that the

4. In *PL*, the themes sounded in the paragraph recur in various forms; cp. 3.694–704, 4.657–76, 8.10–38.

cognizance of every art and science appertains to the intellect only and that the home and sanctuary of virtue and uprightness is the will. But all agree that while the human intellect shines forth as the lord and governor of all the other faculties, it guides and illuminates with its radiance the will also, which would else be blind, and the will shines with a borrowed light, even as the moon does. So, even though we grant and willingly concede that virtue without learning is more conducive to happiness than learning without virtue, yet when these two are once wedded in happy union as they surely ought to be, and often are, then indeed Knowledge raises her head aloft and shows herself far superior, and shining forth takes her seat on high beside the king and governor, Intellect, and gazes upon the doings of the Will below as upon some object lying far beneath her feet; and thereafter for evermore she claims as her right all excellence and splendor and a majesty next to that of God himself.[5]

Let us now leave these heights to consider our ordinary life, and see what advantages learning and ignorance respectively can offer in private and in public life. I will say nothing of the argument that learning is the fairest ornament of youth, the strong defense of manhood, and the glory and solace of age. Nor will I mention that many men highly honored in their day, and even some of the greatest men of ancient Rome, after performing many noble deeds and winning great glory by their exploits, turned from the strife and turmoil of ambition to the study of literature as into a port and welcome refuge. Clearly these honored sages realized that the best part of the life which yet remained to them must be spent to the best advantage. They were first among men; they wished by virtue of these arts to be not the last among the gods. They had once striven for glory, and now strove for immortality. Their warfare against the foes of their country had been far other, but now that they were facing death, the greatest enemy of mankind, these were the weapons they took up, these the legions they enrolled, and these the resources from which they derived their strength.

But the chief part of human happiness is derived from the society of one's fellows and the formation of friendships, and it is often asserted that the learned are as a rule hard to please, lacking in courtesy, odd in manner, and seldom gifted with the gracious address that wins men's hearts. I admit that a man who is almost entirely absorbed and immersed in study finds it much easier to converse with gods than with men, either because he habitually associates with the gods but is unaccustomed to human affairs and a stranger among them, or because the mind, expanding through constant meditation on things divine and therefore feeling cramped within the narrow limits of the body, is less expert in the nicer formalities of social life. But if such a man once forms a worthy and congenial friendship, there is none who cultivates it more assiduously. For what can we imagine more delightful and happy than those conversations of learned

5. The relation between will and intellect that Milton here expresses hierarchically becomes an equation in later works: "reason is but choosing" (*Areop*, p. 944); "reason also is choice" (*PL* 3.108).

and wise men, such as those which the divine Plato is said often to have held in the shade of that famous plane-tree, conversations which all mankind might well have flocked to hear in spell-bound silence?[6] But gross talk and mutual incitement to indulge in luxury and lust is the friendship of ignorance, or rather the ignorance of friendship.

Moreover if this human happiness consists in the honorable and liberal joys of the mind, such a pleasure is to be found in study and learning as far surpasses every other. What a thing it is to grasp the nature of the whole firmament and of its stars, all the movements and changes of the atmosphere, whether it strikes terror into ignorant minds by the majestic roll of thunder or by fiery comets, or whether it freezes into snow or hail, or whether again it falls softly and gently in showers of dew; then perfectly to understand the shifting winds and all the exhalations and vapors which earth and sea give forth; next to know the hidden virtues of plants and metals and understand the nature and the feelings, if that may be, of every living creature; next the delicate structure of the human body and the art of keeping it in health; and, to crown all, the divine might and power of the soul, and any knowledge we may have gained concerning those beings which we call spirits and genii and daemons.[7] There is an infinite number of subjects besides these, a great part of which might be learnt in less time than it would take to enumerate them all. So at length, my hearers, when universal learning has once completed its cycle, the spirit of man, no longer confined within this dark prison-house, will reach out far and wide, till it fills the whole world and the space far beyond with the expansion of its divine greatness. Then at last most of the chances and changes of the world will be so quickly perceived that to him who holds this stronghold of wisdom hardly anything can happen in his life which is unforeseen or fortuitous. He will indeed seem to be one whose rule and dominion the stars obey, to whose command earth and sea hearken, and whom winds and tempests serve; to whom, lastly, Mother Nature herself has surrendered, as if indeed some god had abdicated the throne of the world and entrusted its rights, laws, and administration to him as governor.

Besides this, what delight it affords to the mind to take its flight through the history and geography of every nation and to observe the changes in the conditions of kingdoms, races, cities, and peoples, to the increase of wisdom and righteousness. This, my hearers, is to live in every period of the world's history, and to be as it were coeval with time itself. And indeed, while we look to the future for the glory of our name, this will be to extend and stretch our lives backward before our birth, and to wrest from grudging Fate a kind of retrospective immortality. I pass over a pleasure with which none can compare—to be the

6. In the *Phaedrus,* Socrates converses with his friend under the shade of a plane tree. For friendship and learning in the Platonic tradition, cp. the letters between Milton and Diodati.

7. The word translated as *spirits* is *lares,* Latin for guardian deities of households; *genii* perform a similar function for individuals. Although *daemons* are in one sense the Greek equivalents of *genii,* Milton uses the term to indicate a broader category of supernatural being, intermediate between gods and men as occasion demands, such as the Attendant Spirit in *A Mask.*

oracle of many nations, to find one's home regarded as a kind of temple, to be a man whom kings and states invite to come to them, whom men from near and far flock to visit, while to others it is a matter for pride if they have but set eyes on him once. These are the rewards of study, these are the prizes which learning can and often does bestow upon her votaries in private life.

What, then, of public life? It is true that few have been raised to the height of majesty through a reputation for learning, and not many more through a reputation for uprightness. Such men certainly enjoy a kingdom in themselves far more glorious than any earthly dominion; and who can lay claim to a twofold sovereignty without incurring the charge of ambition? I will, however, add this one thing more: that there have hitherto been but two men who have ruled the whole world, as by divine right, and shared an empire over all kings and princes equal to that of the gods themselves; namely Alexander the Great and Augustus, both of whom were students of philosophy.[8] It is as though Providence had specially singled them out as examples to humanity, to show to what sort of man the helm or reins of government should be entrusted.

But, it may be objected, many nations have won fame by their deeds or their wealth, without owing anything to learning. We know of but few Spartans, for example, who took any interest in liberal education, and the Romans only admitted philosophy within the walls of their city after a long time. But the Spartans found a lawgiver in Lycurgus, who was both a philosopher and so ardent a student of poetry that he was the first to gather together with extreme care the writings of Homer, which were scattered throughout Ionia.[9] The Romans, hardly able to support themselves after the various risings and disturbances which had taken place in the city, sent ambassadors to beg for the Decemviral Laws, also called the Twelve Tables, from Athens, which was at that time foremost in the study of the liberal Arts.[10]

How are we to answer the objection that the Turks of today have acquired an extensive dominion over the wealthy kingdoms of Asia in spite of being entirely devoid of culture? For my part, I have certainly never heard of anything in that state which deserves to be regarded as an example to us—if indeed one should dignify with the name of "state" the power which a horde of utter barbarians united by complicity in crime has seized by violence and murder. The provision of the necessaries of life, and their maintenance when acquired, we owe not to art but to nature; greedy attacks on the property of others, mutual assistance for purposes of plunder, and criminal conspiracy are the outcome of

8. Aristotle instructed *Alexander the Great* (356–23 B.C.E.); *Augustus* (63 B.C.E.–14 C.E.), the first Roman emperor, was interested in philosophy and literature as a means of encouraging social morality.

9. **Lycurgus:** legendary lawgiver of seventh-century B.C.E. (?) Sparta who, according to Plutarch (*Lives* 1.215), was introduced to Homer's works while in *Ionia* and made them widely known. *Ionia* is a storied region on the west coast of Asia Minor (Turkey).

10. **Decemviral:** refers to the ten men appointed in 451 B.C.E. to compile the laws brought back from Athens. They inscribed them on *twelve tables.* This paragraph rehearses examples that Milton later uses in his survey of the history of learning in *Areop.*

the perversion of nature. Some kind of justice indeed is exercised in such states, as might be expected; for while the other virtues are easily put to flight, Justice from her throne compels homage, for without her even the most unjust states would soon fall into decay. I must not, however, omit to mention that the Saracens,[11] to whom the Turks are indebted almost for their existence, enlarged their empire as much by the study of liberal culture as by force of arms.

If we go back to antiquity, we shall find that some states owed not merely their laws but their very foundation to culture: the oldest progenitors of every race are said to have wandered through the woods and mountains, seeking their livelihood after the fashion of wild beasts, with head erect but stooping posture. One might well think that they shared everything with the animals, except the dignity of their form; the same caves, the same dens, afforded them shelter from rain and frost. There were then no cities, no marble palaces, no shining altars or temples of the gods; they had no religion to guide them, no laws or law-courts, no bridal torches, no festal dance, no song at the joyful board, no funeral rites, no mourning, hardly even a grave paid honor to the dead. There were no feasts, no games; no sound of music was ever heard: all these refinements were then lacking which idleness now misuses to foster luxury. Then of a sudden the Arts and Sciences breathed their divine breath into the savage breasts of men, and instilling into them the knowledge of themselves, gently drew them to dwell together within the walls of cities. Therefore of a surety cities may well expect to have a long and happy history under the direction of those guides by whom they were first of all founded, then firmly based on laws, and finally fortified by wise counsels.

What now of ignorance? I perceive, gentlemen, that Ignorance is struck blind and senseless, skulks at a distance, casts about for a way of escape, and complains that life is short and art long. But if we do but remove two great obstacles to our studies, namely first our bad methods of teaching the arts, and secondly our lack of enthusiasm, we shall find that, with all deference to Galen or whoever may have been the author of the saying, quite the contrary is the truth, and that life is long and art short.[12] There is nothing so excellent and at the same time so exacting as art, nothing more sluggish and languid than ourselves. We allow ourselves to be outdone by laborers and husbandmen in working after dark and before dawn; they show greater energy in a mean occupation, to gain a miserable livelihood, than we do in the noblest of occupations, to win a life of true happiness. Though we aspire to the highest and best of human conditions we can endure neither hard work nor yet the reproach of idleness; in fact we are ashamed of owning the very character which we hate not to have imputed to us.

But, we object, our health forbids late hours and hard study. It is a shameful

11. **Saracens:** Used broadly, as here, it means Arabs in general.

12. The saying actually originates with the Greek physician Hippocrates (c. 460–c. 370 B.C.E.). Milton may be drawing on Seneca, who attributes the saying to "the greatest of healers" (*On the Brevity of Life* 1).

admission that we neglect to cultivate our minds out of consideration for our bodies, whose health all should be ready to impair if thereby their minds might gain the more. Yet those who make this excuse are certainly for the most part worthless fellows; for though they disregard every consideration of their time, their talents, and their health, and give themselves up to gluttony, to drinking like whales, and to spending their nights in gaming and debauchery, they never complain that they are any the worse for it. Since, then, it is their constant habit and practice to show eagerness and energy in the pursuit of vice, but listlessness and lethargy where any activity of virtue or intelligence is concerned, they cannot lay the blame on nature or the shortness of life with any show of truth or justice. But if we were to set ourselves to live modestly and temperately, and to tame the first impulses of headstrong youth by reason and steady devotion to study, keeping the divine vigor of our minds unstained and uncontaminated by any impurity or pollution, we should be astonished to find, gentlemen, looking back over a period of years, how great a distance we had covered and across how wide a sea of learning we had sailed, without a check on our voyage.

This voyage, too, will be much shortened if we know how to select branches of learning that are useful, and what is useful within them. In the first place, how many despicable quibbles there are in grammar and rhetoric! One may hear the teachers of them talking sometimes like savages and sometimes like babies. What about logic? That is indeed the queen of the Arts, if taught as it should be, but unfortunately how much foolishness there is in reason! Its teachers are not like men at all, but like finches which live on thorns and thistles. "O iron stomachs of the harvesters!"[13] What am I to say of that branch of learning which the Peripatetics call metaphysics?[14] It is not, as the authority of great men would have me believe, an exceedingly rich art; it is, I say, not an art at all, but a sinister rock, a Lernian bog[15] of fallacies, devised to cause shipwreck and pestilence. These are the wounds, to which I have already referred, which the ignorance of gownsmen inflicts; and this monkish disease has already infected natural philosophy to a considerable extent; the mathematicians too are afflicted with a longing for the petty triumph of demonstrative rhetoric. If we disregard and curtail all these subjects, which can be of no use to us, as we should, we shall be surprised to find how many whole years we shall save. Jurisprudence in particular suffers much from our confused methods of teaching, and from what is even worse, a jargon which one might well take for some Red Indian dialect,[16] or even no human speech at all. Often, when I have heard our lawyers shouting at each other in this lingo, it has occurred to me to wonder whether men who had neither a human tongue nor human speech could have any human feelings either. I do indeed fear that sacred justice will pay no atten-

13. Horace, *Epodes* 3.4: "O dura Messorum ilia!" *Stomachs* is a euphemism for bowels.
14. **Peripatetics:** philosophers in the Aristotelian tradition, such as the scholastics.
15. **Lernian bog:** noisome marshes of Lerna, near Argos, where Hercules confronted the Hydra.
16. **Red Indian dialect:** The Latin text reads *Americanus,* "American."

tion to us and that she will never understand our complaints and wrongs, as she cannot speak our language.

Therefore, gentlemen, if from our childhood onward we never allow a day to pass by without its lesson and diligent study, if we are wise enough to rule out of every art what is irrelevant, superfluous, or unprofitable, we shall assuredly, before we have attained the age of Alexander the Great, have made ourselves masters of something greater and more glorious than that world of his. And so far from complaining of the shortness of life and the slowness of Art, I think we shall be more likely to weep and wail, as Alexander did, because there are no more worlds for us to conquer.[17]

Ignorance is breathing her last, and you are now watching her final efforts and her dying struggle. She declares that glory is mankind's most powerful incentive, and that whereas a long succession and course of years has bestowed glory on the illustrious men of old, we live under the shadow of the world's old age and decrepitude, and of the impending dissolution of all things, so that even if we leave behind us anything deserving of everlasting fame, the scope of our glory is narrowed, since there will be few succeeding generations to remember us. It is therefore to no purpose that we produce so many books and noble monuments of learning, seeing that the approaching conflagration of the world will destroy them all.[18] I do not deny that this may indeed be so; but yet to have no thought of glory when we do well is above all glory. The ancients could indeed derive no satisfaction from the empty praise of men, seeing that no joy or knowledge of it could reach them when they were dead and gone. But we may hope for an eternal life, which will never allow the memory of the good deeds we performed on earth to perish; in which, if we have done well here, we shall ourselves be present to hear our praise; and in which, according to a wise philosophy held by many, those who have lived temperately and devoted all their time to noble arts, and have thus been of service to mankind, will be rewarded by the bestowal of a wisdom matchless and supreme over all others.[19]

Let the idle now cease to upbraid us with the uncertainties and perplexities of learning, which are indeed the fault not so much of learning as of the frailty of man. It is this consideration, gentlemen, which disproves or mitigates or compensates for Socrates' famous ignorance and the Skeptics' timid suspension of judgment.[20]

And finally, we may well ask, what is the happiness which Ignorance

17. *Of Education* develops some of the pedagogical reforms suggested in these paragraphs, with a particular eye toward efficient use of students' time.

18. The idea that time had almost run its course and the world had long been in decline was prevalent in the Renaissance. The *conflagration* to which Milton refers is apocalyptic.

19. Cp. *Lyc* 70–84.

20. *Socrates* was celebrated by the Oracle at Delphi as the wisest man alive because, he explained, he recognized his own ignorance (Plato, *Apology* 21a–b). The *Skeptics* of classical Greece argued that there were no adequate grounds for certainty as to the truth of any proposition. Hence they suspended judgment.

promises? To enjoy what one possesses, to have no enemies, to be beyond the reach of all care and trouble, to pass one's life in peace and quiet so far as may be—this is but the life of a beast, or of some bird which builds its little nest in the farthest depths of the forest as near to the sky as it can, in security, rears its offspring, flits about in search of sustenance without fear of the fowler, and pours forth its sweet melodies at dawn and dusk. Why should one ask for that divine activity of the mind in addition? Well, if such is the argument, we will offer Ignorance Circe's cup, and bid her throw off her human shape, walk no longer erect, and betake her to the beasts.[21] To the beasts, did I say? They will surely refuse to receive so infamous a guest, at any rate if they are either endowed with some kind of inferior reasoning power, as many maintain, or guided by some powerful instinct, enabling them to practice the arts, or something resembling the arts, among themselves. For Plutarch tells us that in the pursuit of game, dogs show some knowledge of dialectic, and if they chance to come to cross-roads, they obviously make use of a disjunctive syllogism. Aristotle points out that the nightingale in some sort instructs her offspring in the principles of music. Almost every animal is its own physician, and many of them have given valuable lessons in medicine to man; the Egyptian ibis teaches us the value of purgatives, the hippopotamus that of blood-letting. Who can maintain that creatures which so often give us warning of coming wind, rain, floods, or fair weather, know nothing of astronomy? What prudent and strict ethics are shown by those geese which check their dangerous loquacity by holding pebbles in their beaks as they fly over Mount Taurus! Our domestic economy owes much to the ants, our commonwealth to the bees, while military science admits its indebtedness to the cranes for the practice of posting sentinels and for the triangular formation in battle.[22] The beasts are too wise to admit Ignorance to their fellowship and society; they will force her to a lower station. What then? To stocks and stones? Why even trees, bushes, and whole woods once tore up their roots and hurried to hear the skilful strains of Orpheus. Often, too, they were endowed with mysterious powers and uttered divine oracles, as for instance did the oaks of Dodona. Rocks, too, show a certain aptitude for learning in that they reply to the sacred words of poets; will not these also reject Ignorance? Therefore, driven lower than any kind of beast, lower than stocks and stones, lower than any natural species, will Ignorance be permitted to find repose in the famous "non-existent" of the Epicureans?[23] No,

21. In Homer, the enchantress Circe uses her charmed cup and wand to transform Odysseus's men into swine (*Od.* 10.230–50).

22. In his *Apology for Raymond Sebond* (2.12), Montaigne had argued similarly but at greater length that beasts "reason not contemptibly" (*PL* 8.374) and included many of the same examples as Milton, including the syllogizing dog (known as "Chrysippus's dog"), a classical commonplace of considerable vogue in seventeenth-century philosophy.

23. A fundamental premise of Epicurean philosophy, one that contradicts the Christian doctrine of creation *ex nihilo*, is that nothing can come into being from that which is nonexistent. In his *Christian Doctrine*, the heretical Milton sides with the Epicureans on this point (1.7).

not even there; for Ignorance must be something yet worse, yet more vile, yet more wretched, in a word the very depth of degradation.

I come now to you, my clever hearers, for even without any words of mine I see in you not so much arguments on my side as darts which I shall hurl at Ignorance till she is slain. I have sounded the attack, do you rush into battle; put this enemy to flight, drive her from your porticos and walks. If you allow her to exist, you yourselves will be that which you know to be the most wretched thing in the world. This cause is the personal concern of you all. So, if I have perchance spoken at much greater length than is customary in this place, not forgetting that this was demanded by the importance of the subject, you will, I hope, pardon me, my judges, since it is one more proof of the interest I feel in you, of my zeal on your behalf, and of the nights of toil and wakefulness I consented to endure for your sakes. I have done.

Controversial Prose

Introduction to Selections from *Of Reformation*

In May 1641 appeared the first prose work that Milton wrote for publication, *Of Reformation, Touching Church-Discipline in England and the Causes that hitherto have hindered it. Two Books, Written to a Friend.* Over the next eleven months, there followed four additional antiprelatical tracts, or works attacking the legitimacy of episcopacy. By his own account in the 1654 *Second Defense,* Milton entered the lists late: "As Parliament acted with vigor, the haughtiness of the bishops began to deflate. As soon as freedom of speech . . . became possible, all mouths were opened against them. . . . I decided . . . to devote to this conflict all my talents and all my active powers" (see pp. 1093–94). In the 1630s, well before freedom of speech was possible, others—notably William Prynne, Henry Burton, and John Bastwick—had opened their mouths against bishops and been punished with imprisonment, branding, and the loss of their ears. The bishops were in retreat by the time Milton published *Of Reformation*: the House of Commons had charged Archbishop Laud with high treason, imprisoned him in the Tower, and pressed for exclusion of the bishops from the House of Lords. The increasingly powerful "Root and Branch" faction in Parliament, headed by Sir Henry Vane and Oliver Cromwell, sought not only to strip the bishops of secular power but also to remove them from the church altogether. Nearly twenty years later, it would require real physical courage for Milton to publish his antimonarchic prose works on the eve of a nearly universally popular Restoration, but with his antiprelatical tracts he could expect to meet an approving audience. He nevertheless published the work anonymously.

Milton had been trained to compose arguments in Latin (see the *Prolusions*), and *Of Reformation* betrays his lack of experience with vernacular prose. Long, convoluted, and sometimes broken sentences make this the most difficult of Milton's prose works to read in unmodernized form (even here, with sentences repunctuated and often divided, some difficulty remains). Don M. Wolfe has compared the tract's prose with "a hard pine log full of knots and unexpected twirls, rarely straight and smooth and easy to follow" (Yale 1:108). *Of Reformation* continues to be read, despite its difficult prose, for the brilliance of its imagery.

Milton would claim months later that, in the medium of prose, he had the use only of his "left hand" (*RCG,* p. 839), but the poet's right hand is manifest in *Of Reformation.* He unleashes a torrent of graphic images suggesting the bestial nature of the bishops and the disease and deformity they have inflicted upon a once pure church. Typical is his charge that under episcopal government "the obscene and surfeited priest scruples not to paw and mammock the sacramental bread as familiarly as his tavern biscuit" (p. 812). In the most famous set piece in the work, Milton compares episcopacy to a head-size "wen" growing from the neck of the body commonwealth, "a swollen tumor," "a bottle of vicious and hardened excrements," "a heap of hard and loathsome uncleanness, [which is] to the head a foul disfigurement and burden" (p. 822).

The vivid and often grotesque imagery overlays and sometimes overwhelms the structure of the tract's argument. Milton outlines the corruption of the church; laments that reformation, while beginning in England under Wycliffe, has stalled because of popish bishops; and traces the thwarting of reformation to three groups: "antiquitarians," as Milton calls them, "libertines," and "politicians." The bulk of Book 1 is occupied with an attack on antiquitarians, or those who defend episcopacy by way of the church fathers; here Milton contends that early bishops lived modestly and were elected by their flocks, that the texts of the fathers are at times contradictory and at times corrupt, and that the fathers themselves pointed to Scripture as the only authority. At the end of Book 1, Milton quickly dispatches the libertines, who fear that change in church government will restrain their licentiousness. In Book 2, Milton argues against the politicians that bishops undermine rather than support kings.

Milton would prove to be a quick study, and later works show a marked improvement in argumentation and readability as the author adjusts to what he calls "the cool element of prose" (see p. 839). Thomas N. Corns (1982) has demonstrated that, already by the mid-1640s, Milton moved toward a more functional, readable style, more sparing of imagery and neologisms.

The text of our selection is based on the copy of the first edition in the British Library's Thomason Collection.

Selections from

OF REFORMATION TOUCHING CHURCH-DISCIPLINE IN ENGLAND, AND THE CAUSES THAT HITHERTO HAVE HINDERED IT. IN TWO BOOKS. WRITTEN TO A FRIEND. 1641.

Sir,

Amidst those deep and retired thoughts which, with every man Christianly instructed, ought to be most frequent of God and of his miraculous ways and works amongst men, and of our religion and worship to be performed to him; after the story of our Savior Christ, suffering to the lowest bent of weakness in the flesh and presently triumphing to the highest pitch of glory in the spirit, which drew up his body also, till we in both be united to him in the revelation of his kingdom; I do not know of anything more worthy to take up the whole passion of pity on the one side and joy on the other, than to consider first the foul and sudden corruption, and then after many a tedious age the long-deferred, but much more wonderful and happy reformation of the church in these latter days. Sad it is to think how that doctrine of the gospel, planted by teachers divinely inspired and by them winnowed and sifted from the chaff of over-dated ceremonies, and refined to such a spiritual height and temper of purity and knowledge of the creator, that the body, with all the circumstances of time and place, were purified by the affections of the regenerate soul and nothing left impure, but sin; faith needing not the weak and fallible office of the senses, to be either the ushers or interpreters of heavenly mysteries, save where our Lord himself in his sacraments ordained; that such a doctrine should, through the grossness and blindness of her professors and the fraud of deceivable traditions, drag so downwards as to backslide one way into the Jewish beggary of old cast rudiments and stumble forward another way into the new-vomited paganism of sensual idolatry:[1] attributing purity or impurity to

1. The perspective of this complex temporal figure is primitive (and by extension reformed) Christianity; Milton castigates the Anglican Church for *backsliding* to a liturgy as highly articulated as the Jewish ceremonial law abrogated by Christ and for *stumbling forward* to the idolatrous *paganism* of the Roman Catholic Church, to which the Anglican Church, after the Reformation, has returned like a dog to its vomit (Prov. 26.11, 2 Pet. 2.22).

things indifferent, that they might bring the inward acts of the spirit to the outward and customary eye-service of the body, as if they could make God earthly and fleshly because they could not make themselves heavenly and spiritual.

They began to draw down all the divine intercourse betwixt God and the soul, yea, the very shape of God himself, into an exterior and bodily form; urgently pretending a necessity and obligement of joining the body in a formal reverence and worship circumscribed, they hallowed it, they fumed it, they sprinkled it, they bedecked it, not in robes of pure innocency, but of pure linen with other deformed and fantastic dresses in palls and miters, gold and gewgaws fetched from Aaron's old wardrobe, or the flamin's vestry.[2] Then was the priest set to con his motions and his postures, his liturgies and his lurries,[3] till the soul by this means of over-bodying herself, given up justly to fleshly delights, bated her wing apace downward; and finding the ease she had from her visible and sensuous colleague, the body, in performance of religious duties, her pinions now broken and flagging, shifted off from herself the labor of high soaring anymore, forgot her heavenly flight, and left the dull and droiling carcass to plod on in the old road and drudging trade of outward conformity.

And here, out of question from her perverse conceiting of God and holy things, she had fallen to believe no God at all, had not custom and the worm of conscience nipped her incredulity. Hence to all the duties of evangelical grace, instead of the adoptive and cheerful boldness which our new alliance with God requires, came servile and thrall-like fear; for in very deed, the superstitious man by his good will is an atheist, but being scared from thence by the pangs and gripes of a boiling conscience, all in a pudder[4] shuffles up to himself such a God and such a worship as is most agreeable to remedy his fear, which fear of his, as also is his hope, fixed only upon the flesh, renders likewise the whole faculty of his apprehension, carnal. And all the inward acts of worship, issuing from the native strength of soul, run out lavishly to the upper skin and there harden into a crust of formality. Hence men came to scan the scriptures by the letter, and in the covenant of our redemption magnified the external signs more than the quickening power of the spirit; and yet looking on them through their own guiltiness with a servile fear (and finding as little comfort, or rather terror from them again), they knew not how to hide their slavish approach to God's behests, by them not understood nor worthily received, but by cloaking their servile crouching to all religious presentments, sometimes lawful, sometimes

2. **palls, miters:** ecclesiastical vestments used by both the Roman and English churches; **Aaron's old wardrobe:** a reference to elaborate Jewish ritual clothing (Exod. 28), the *flamin's vestry* to the robes of ancient Roman priests.

3. **con his motions:** learn how to position and move his body during the liturgy; **lurries:** memorized or set lessons. Milton ridicules the prescribed and formulaic nature of Anglican (and Roman Catholic) liturgy.

4. **in a pudder:** in a tizzy.

idolatrous, under the name of humility, and terming the piebald frippery and ostentation of ceremonies, decency.[5]

Then was baptism changed into a kind of exorcism, and water sanctified by Christ's institute thought little enough to wash off the original spot without the scratch or cross impression of a priest's forefinger. And that feast of free grace[6] and adoption to which Christ invited his disciples to sit as brethren and coheirs of the happy covenant which at that table was to be sealed to them, even that feast of love and heavenly-admitted fellowship, the seal of filial grace, became the subject of horror and glouting[7] adoration, pageanted about like a dreadful idol, which sometimes deceives well-meaning men and beguiles them of their reward by their voluntary humility, which, indeed, is fleshly pride, preferring a foolish sacrifice and the rudiments of the world (as Saint Paul to Colossians [2.8] explaineth) before a savory obedience to Christ's example. Such was Peter's unseasonable humility, as then his knowledge was small, when Christ came to wash his feet; who, at an impertinent time, would needs strain courtesy with his master, and falling troublesomely upon the lowly, all-wise, and unexaminable intention of Christ in what he went with resolution to do, so provoked by his interruption the meek Lord, that he threatened to exclude him from his heavenly portion unless he could be content to be less arrogant and stiff-necked in his humility.[8]

But to dwell no longer in characterizing the depravities of the church and how they sprung and how they took increase, when I recall to mind at last, after so many dark ages wherein the huge overshadowing train of error had almost swept all the stars out of the firmament[9] of the church, how the bright and blissful reformation (by divine power) struck through the black and settled night of ignorance and antichristian tyranny, methinks a sovereign and reviving joy must needs rush into the bosom of him that reads or hears, and the sweet odor of the returning gospel imbathe his soul with the fragrancy of heaven. Then was the sacred Bible sought out of the dusty corners where profane falsehood and neglect had thrown it; the schools opened; divine and human learning raked out of the embers of forgotten tongues, the princes and cities trooping apace to the new erected banner of salvation; the martyrs, with the unresistible might of weakness, shaking the powers of darkness and scorning the fiery rage of the old red dragon.

The pleasing pursuit of these thoughts hath ofttimes led me into a serious question and debatement with myself, how it should come to pass that England (having had this grace and honor from God to be the first that should set up a

5. **decency:** a shorthand term for the uniform liturgy promoted by Laud, who decried the lack "of uniform and decent order in too many Churches" (*A Relation of the Conference* [1639], 3).

6. **feast of free grace:** i.e., the Lord's Supper.

7. **glouting:** looking sullen, frowning.

8. See John 13.5–11.

9. See Rev. 12.4. Throughout the tract, as here and at the end of the paragraph, Milton draws on the imagery of the apocalyptic final book of the Bible.

standard for the recovery of lost truth and blow the first evangelic trumpet to the nations, holding up, as from a hill,[10] the new lamp of saving light to all Christendom) should now be last and most unsettled in the enjoyment of that peace whereof she taught the way to others. Although indeed our Wycliffe's preaching,[11] at which all the succeeding reformers more effectually lighted their tapers, was to his countrymen but a short blaze soon damped and stifled by the pope and prelates for six or seven kings' reigns, yet methinks the precedency which God gave this island, to be the first restorer of buried truth, should have been followed with more happy success and sooner attained perfection in which as yet we are amongst the last. For, albeit in purity of doctrine we agree with our brethren, yet in discipline, which is the execution and applying of doctrine home, and laying the salve to the very orifice of the wound, yea, tenting[12] and searching to the core, without which pulpit preaching is but shooting at rovers,[13] in this we are no better than a schism from all the reformation and a sore scandal to them. For while we hold ordination to belong only to bishops, as our prelates do, we must of necessity hold also their ministers to be no ministers, and shortly after their church to be no church. Not to speak of those senseless ceremonies which we only retain as a dangerous earnest of sliding back to Rome, and serving merely either as a mist to cover nakedness where true grace is extinguished or as an interlude to set out the pomp of prelatism. Certainly it would be worth the while, therefore, and the pains, to inquire more particularly, what and how many the chief causes have been that have still hindered our uniform consent to the rest of the churches abroad, at this time especially when the kingdom is in a good propensity thereto, and all men in prayers, in hopes, or in disputes, either for or against it.

Yet will I not insist on that which may seem to be the cause on God's part (as his judgment on our sins, the trial of his own, the unmasking of hypocrites), nor shall I stay to speak of the continual eagerness and extreme diligence of the pope and papists to stop the furtherance of reformation, which know they have no hold or hope of England their lost darling, longer than the government of bishops bolsters them out; and therefore plot all they can to uphold them, as may be seen by the book of Santa Clara,[14] the popish priest in defense of bishops, which came out piping hot much about the time that one of our own prelates, out of an ominous fear, had writ on the same argument, as if they had joined their forces like good confederates to support one falling Babel.

10. See Matt. 5.14.

11. **Wycliffe:** John Wycliffe, well over a century before Martin Luther, articulated several central Reformation tenets, including the right of each believer to interpret Scripture and opposition to transubstantiation and papal infallibility. In 1380 he published the first English Bible. English Protestants pointed proudly to Wycliffe as the first reformer; Milton laments the irony that Wycliffe's nation is now less reformed than its continental neighbors.

12. **tenting:** probing a wound.

13. **shooting at rovers:** long-distance archery, in which arrows rarely hit the target.

14. **Santa Clara:** Franciscus Sancta Clara, a Franciscan priest, was born Christopher Davenport; he converted to Catholicism in 1617. Milton refers to his *Apologia Episcoporum seu Sacri Magistatus* (1640).

But I shall chiefly endeavor to declare those causes that hinder the forwarding of true discipline which are among ourselves. . . .

[*The omitted section offers a survey of missed opportunities for full reformation in England in the sixteenth century; Milton insists that the martyrdom of Cranmer, Latimer, and Ridley does not prove the lawfulness of prelacy, even as the martyrdom of various Christian heretics does not prove the truth of their doctrines.*]

And here withal I invoke the immortal deity, revealer and judge of secrets, that wherever I have in this book plainly and roundly (though worthily and truly) laid open the faults and blemishes of fathers,[15] martyrs, or Christian emperors, or have otherwise inveighed against error and superstition with vehement expressions, I have done it neither out of malice, nor list to speak evil, nor any vainglory, but of mere necessity to vindicate the spotless truth from an ignominious bondage, whose native worth is now become of such a low esteem that she is like to find small credit with us for what she can say, unless she can bring a ticket from Cranmer, Latimer, and Ridley,[16] or prove herself a retainer to Constantine[17] and wear his badge. More tolerable it were for the church of God that all these names were utterly abolished, like the brazen serpent,[18] than that men's fond opinion should thus idolize them, and the heavenly truth be thus captivated.

Now to proceed, whatsoever the bishops were, it seems they themselves were unsatisfied in matters of religion, as they then stood, by that commission granted to eight bishops, eight other divines, eight civilians, eight common lawyers, to frame ecclesiastical constitutions;[19] which no wonder if it came to nothing, for (as Hayward[20] relates) both their professions and their ends were different. Lastly, we all know by examples that exact reformation is not perfected at the first push, and those unwieldy times of Edward VI may hold some plea by this excuse: Now let any reasonable man judge whether that king's reign be a fit time from whence to pattern out the constitution of a church discipline, much less that it should yield occasion from whence to foster and establish the continuance of imperfection with the commendatory subscriptions of confessors and martyrs, to entitle and engage a glorious name to a gross corruption. It was not episcopacy that wrought in them the heavenly fortitude of martyrdom,

15. **fathers:** church fathers.
16. **Cranmer, Latimer, and Ridley:** Thomas Cranmer, Hugh Latimer, and Nicholas Ridley were Anglican bishops executed by the Catholic Queen Mary in 1555 and 1556; they are celebrated as martyrs of the Reformation in John Foxe's influential *Acts and Monuments* (1563). Milton is markedly idiosyncratic in taking a critical view of the three in this work.
17. **retainer to Constantine:** i.e., a Roman Catholic.
18. See Num. 21.9.
19. Cranmer proposed unsuccessfully a thirty-two-member commission to reform canon law in 1544.
20. **Hayward:** John Hayward, author of *The Life and Reign of King Edward the Sixth* (1630).

as little is it that martyrdom can make good episcopacy. But it was episcopacy that led the good and holy men, through the temptation of the enemy and the snare of this present world, to many blameworthy and opprobrious actions. And it is still episcopacy that before all our eyes worsens and slugs the most learned and seeming religious of our ministers, who no sooner advanced to it but, like a seething pot set to cool, sensibly exhale and reek out the greatest part of that zeal, and those gifts which were formerly in them, settling in a skinny congealment of ease and sloth at the top. And if they keep their learning by some potent sway of nature, 'tis a rare chance, but their devotion most commonly comes to that queasy temper of lukewarmness that gives a vomit to God[21] himself. . . .

[*Milton concludes his survey of missed opportunities in the previous century. He answers those who point to the great antiquity of Christian bishops first by arguing that early Christian bishops, unlike their modern successors, were elected by their flocks.*]

Thus then[22] did the spirit of unity and meekness inspire and animate every joint and sinew of the mystical body, but now the gravest and worthiest minister, a true bishop of his fold, shall be reviled and ruffled by an insulting and only canon-wise prelate, as if he were some slight, paltry companion. And the people of God, redeemed and washed with Christ's blood and dignified with so many glorious titles of saints and sons in the gospel, are now no better reputed than impure ethnics and lay dogs; stones and pillars and crucifixes have now the honor and the alms due to Christ's living members. The table of communion, now become a table of separation,[23] stands like an exalted platform upon the brow of the quire, fortified with bulwark and barricado to keep off the profane touch of the laics, whilst the obscene and surfeited priest scruples not to paw and mammock[24] the sacramental bread as familiarly as his tavern biscuit. And thus the people, vilified and rejected by them, give over the earnest study of virtue and godliness as a thing of greater purity than they need, and the search of divine knowledge as a mystery too high for their capacities and only for churchmen to meddle with, which is that the prelates desire—that when they have brought us back to popish blindness we might commit to their dispose the whole managing of our salvation, for they think it was never fair world with them since that time. But he that will mold a modern bishop into a primitive must yield him to be elected by the popular voice, undiocesed, unrevenued, unlorded, and leave him nothing but brotherly equality, matchless temperance, frequent fasting, incessant prayer, and preaching, continual watchings and

21. See Rev. 3.16.
22. **then:** in the early church, when bishops relied on the consent of their flocks.
23. Milton, like other Puritans, objected to Laud's returning the communion table to the old position of the altar, against the chancel wall at the east end of the church, most distant from the congregation.
24. **mammock:** to tear into shreds.

labors in his ministry, which what a rich booty it would be, what a plump endowment to the many-benefice-gaping mouth of a prelate, what a relish it would give to his canary-sucking and swan-eating palate, let old Bishop Mountain[25] judge for me.

How little therefore those ancient times make for modern bishops hath been plainly discoursed. But let them make for them as much as they will, yet why we ought not stand to their arbitrament shall now appear by a threefold corruption which will be found upon them. 1. The best times were spreadingly infected. 2. The best men of those times foully tainted. 3. The best writings of those men dangerously adulterated. These positions are to be made good out of those times witnessing of themselves.

[*In a lengthy section omitted here, Milton argues that corruption already touched the early church, that the writings of the church fathers have not always been reliably transmitted, and that the fathers themselves pointed to Scripture rather than to their own writings as authoritative.*]

But not to be endless in quotations, it may chance to be objected that there be many opinions in the fathers which have no ground in scripture. So much the less, may I say, should we follow them, for their own words shall condemn them and acquit us that lean not on them; otherwise these their words shall acquit them and condemn us. But it will be replied, the scriptures are difficult to be understood and therefore require the explanation of the fathers. 'Tis true there be some books, and especially some places in those books, that remain clouded; yet ever that which is most necessary to be known is most easy, and that which is most difficult so far expounds itself ever as to tell us how little it imports our saving knowledge. Hence, to infer a general obscurity over all the text is a mere suggestion of the devil to dissuade men from reading it, and casts an aspersion of dishonor both upon the mercy, truth, and wisdom of God. We count it no gentleness or fair dealing in a man of power amongst us to require strict and punctual obedience, and yet give out all his commands ambiguous and obscure; we should think he had a plot upon us; certainly such commands were no commands but snares.

The very essence of truth is plainness and brightness; the darkness and crookedness is our own. The wisdom of God created understanding fit and proportionable to truth, the object and end of it, as the eye to the thing visible. If our understanding have a film of ignorance over it or be blear with gazing on other false glisterings, what is that to truth? If we will but purge with sovereign eyesalve that intellectual ray which God hath planted in us, then we would believe the scriptures protesting their own plainness and perspicuity, calling to them to be instructed not only the wise and learned, but the simple, the poor,

25. **Bishop Mountain:** George Montaigne (1569–1628) rose from modest beginnings to become Archbishop of York.

the babes, foretelling an extraordinary effusion of God's spirit upon every age and sex, attributing to all men—and requiring from them—the ability of searching, trying, examining all things, and by the spirit discerning that which is good. And as the scriptures themselves pronounce their own plainness, so do the Fathers testify of them. . . .

[*Milton contrasts the clarity of Scripture with the "knotty Africanisms, the pampered metaphors, the intricate and involved sentences of the fathers."*]

I trust they for whom God hath reserved the honor of reforming this church will easily perceive their adversaries' drift in thus calling for antiquity. They fear the plain field of the scriptures; the chase is too hot; they seek the dark, the bushy, the tangled forest; they would imbosk.[26] They feel themselves struck in the transparent streams of divine truth; they would plunge and tumble and think to lie hid in the foul weeds and muddy waters, where no plummet can reach the bottom. But let them beat themselves like whales, and spend their oil till they be dredged ashore, though wherefore should the ministers give them so much line for shifts and delays? Wherefore should they not urge only the gospel, and hold it ever in their faces like a mirror of diamond, till it dazzle and pierce their misty eyeballs, maintaining it the honor of its absolute sufficiency and supremacy inviolable? For if the scripture be for reformation, and antiquity to boot, 'tis but an advantage to the dozen, 'tis no winning cast. And though antiquity be against it, while the scriptures be for it, the cause is as good as ought to be wished, antiquity itself sitting judge.

But to draw to an end: the second sort[27] of those that may be justly numbered among the hinderers of reformation are libertines. These suggest that the discipline sought would be intolerable: for one bishop now in a diocese we should then have a pope in every parish.[28] It will not be requisite to answer these men, but only to discover them; for reason they have none, but lust and licentiousness, and therefore answer can have none. It is not any discipline that they could live under, it is the corruption and remissness of discipline that they seek. Episcopacy duly executed, yea the Turkish and Jewish rigor against whoring and drinking, the dear and tender discipline of a father, the sociable and loving reproof of a brother, the bosom admonition of a friend is a presbytery and a consistory to them. 'Tis only the merry friar in Chaucer can disple[29] them.

26. **imbosk:** conceal themselves.
27. **second sort:** The three sorts are the "antiquitarians," whose arguments Milton has addressed in the body of the first book, the "libertines," whom he dispatches in a single paragraph here, and the "politicians," whom he answers in the second book.
28. A common charge against Presbyterian church government.
29. **disple:** to subject to religious discipline or penance.

Full sweetly heard he confession,
And pleasant was his absolution,
He was an easy man to give penance.[30]

And so I leave them, and refer the political discourse of episcopacy to a second book.

The Second Book

Sir,

It is a work good and prudent to be able to guide one man, of larger extended virtue to order well one house; but to govern a nation piously and justly, which only is to say happily, is for a spirit of the greatest size and divinest metal. And certainly of no less a mind, nor of less excellence in another way, were they who by writing laid the solid and true foundations of this science, which being of greatest importance to the life of man, yet there is no art that hath been more cankered in her principles, more soiled and slubbered with aphorisming pedantry than the art of policy, and that most, where a man would think should least be, in Christian commonwealths. They teach not that to govern well is to train up a nation in true wisdom and virtue and that which springs from thence, magnanimity (take heed of that), and that which is our beginning, regeneration, and happiest end, likeness to God, which in one word we call godliness; and that this is the true flourishing of a land, other things follow as the shadow does the substance. To teach thus were mere pulpitry to them. This is the masterpiece of a modern politician, how to qualify and mold the sufferance and subjection of the people to the length of that foot that is to tread on their necks, how rapine may serve itself with the fair and honorable pretences of public good, how the puny law may be brought under the wardship and control of lust and will. In which attempt, if they fall short, then must a superficial color of reputation by all means direct or indirect be gotten to wash over the unsightly bruise of honor.

To make men governable in this manner, their precepts mainly tend to break a national spirit and courage by countenancing open riot, luxury, and ignorance, till having thus disfigured and made men beneath men, as Juno in the fable of Io,[31] they deliver up the poor transformed heifer of the commonwealth to be stung and vexed with the breeze[32] and goad of oppression under the cus-

30. *Canterbury Tales,* "General Prologue," 221–23.

31. Zeus changed *Io* into a cow to protect her from the jealousy of *Juno,* who first set hundred-eyed *Argus* to watch Io and then sent a gadfly to drive Io through the world (Ovid, *Met.* 568–750).

32. **breeze:** stinging insect, gadfly.

tody of some Argus with a hundred eyes of jealousy. To be plainer, sir, how to solder, how to stop a leak, how to keep up the floating carcass of a crazy and diseased monarchy or state betwixt wind and water, swimming still upon her own dead lees, that now is the deep design of a politician.

Alas, sir! a commonwealth ought to be but as one huge Christian personage, one mighty growth and stature of an honest man, as big and compact in virtue as in body. For look what the grounds and causes are of single happiness to one man, the same ye shall find them to a whole state, as Aristotle, both in his *Ethics* and *Politics,* from the principles of reason lays down.[33] By consequence, therefore, that which is good and agreeable to monarchy will appear soonest to be so by being good and agreeable to the true welfare of every Christian, and that which can be justly proved hurtful and offensive to every true Christian will be evinced to be alike hurtful to monarchy; for God forbid that we should separate and distinguish the end and good of a monarch from the end and good of the monarchy, or of that from Christianity.

How then this third and last sort that hinder reformation[34] will justify that it stands not with reason of state, I much muse. For certain I am, the Bible is shut against them, as certain that neither Plato nor Aristotle is for their turns.[35] What they can bring us now from the schools of Loyola with his Jesuits or their Malvezzi that can cut Tacitus into slivers and steaks,[36] we shall presently hear. They allege, 1. that the church government must be conformable to the civil polity; next, that no form of church government is agreeable to monarchy but that of bishops. Must church government that is appointed in the Gospel, and has chief respect to the soul, be conformable and pliant to civil, that is arbitrary, and chiefly conversant about the visible and external part of man? This is the very maxim that molded the calves of Bethel and of Dan; this was the quintessence of Jeroboam's policy:[37] he made religion conform to his politic interests, and this was the sin that watched over the Israelites till their final captivity. If this state principle come from the prelates, as they affect to be counted statists, let them look back to Eleutherius,[38] bishop of Rome, and see what he thought of the policy of England. Being required by Lucius, the first Christian king of this island, to give his counsel for the founding of religious laws, little thought he of this sage caution, but bids him betake himself to the old and new testa-

33. See Aristotle, *Nichomachean Ethics* 1.9 (1099b30) and *Politics* 7.2 (1324a5).

34. Politicians; see note 27.

35. I.e., neither the Bible, Plato, nor Aristotle endorses what Milton calls in the first paragraph of this book the "masterpiece of a modern politician."

36. St. Ignatius of *Loyola* (1491–1556) founded the *Jesuits;* Virgilio *Malvezzi* (1595–1654) is the author of *Discourses upon Cornelius Tacitus,* an English translation of which appeared in 1642.

37. See 1 Kings 12.26-33. Because Rehoboam held Jerusalem with the Temple, his rival *Jeroboam* set up golden calves in *Bethel* and *Dan,* places he controlled, in order to shore up his authority with religious observance and sentiment.

38. According to tradition, *Lucius,* King of the Britons in the second century, sent to Rome to request from *Eleutherius* that he be made a Christian. See Bede's *Church History* 1.4 and Geoffrey of Monmouth's *History of Britain* 4.19.

ment and receive direction from them how to administer both church and commonwealth; that he was God's vicar and, therefore, to rule by God's laws; that the edicts of Caesar we may at all times disallow, but the statutes of God for no reason we may reject.

Now, certain if church-government be taught in the gospel, as the bishops dare not deny, we may well conclude of what late standing this position is, newly calculated for the altitude of bishop elevation and lettuce for their lips. But by what example can they show that the form of church discipline must be minted and modeled out to secular pretences? The ancient republic of the Jews is evident to have run through all the changes of civil estate, if we survey the story from the giving of the law to the Herods, yet did one manner of priestly government serve without inconvenience to all these temporal mutations: it served the mild aristocracy of elective dukes and heads of tribes joined with them, the dictatorship of the judges, the easy or hard-handed monarchies, the domestic or foreign tyrannies, lastly the Roman senate from without, the Jewish senate at home with the Galilean Tetrarch (yet the Levites had some right to deal in civil affairs).[39] But seeing the evangelical precept forbids churchmen to intermeddle with worldly employments,[40] what interweavings or interworkings can knit the minister and the magistrate in their several functions to the regard of any precise correspondency?

Seeing that the churchman's office is only to teach men the Christian faith, to exhort all, to encourage the good, to admonish the bad (privately, the less offender, publicly, the scandalous and stubborn), to censure and separate from the communion of Christ's flock the contagious and incorrigible, to receive with joy and fatherly compassion the penitent, all this must be done, and more than this is beyond any church authority. What is all this either here or there to the temporal regiment of weal public, whether it be popular, princely, or monarchical? Where doth it entrench upon the temporal governor, where does it come in his walk? Where does it make inroad upon his jurisdiction? Indeed if the minister's part be rightly discharged, it renders him the people more conscionable, quiet, and easy to be governed, if otherwise his life and doctrine will declare him. If, therefore, the constitution of the church be already set down by divine prescript, as all sides confess, then can she not be a handmaid to wait on civil commodities and respects; and if the nature and limits of church discipline be such as are either helpful to all political estates indifferently, or have no particular relation to any, then is there no necessity, nor indeed possibility, of linking the one with the other in special conformation.

Now for their second conclusion, "That no form of church government is agreeable to monarchy, but that of bishops,"[41] although it fall to pieces of itself

39. See 2 Chron. 19.8–11.

40. See Matt. 20.25–26.

41. James I in 1603 stated this principle both prophetically and pithily: "No bishop, no king" (see Yale 1:15–16).

by that which hath been said: yet to give them play front and rear, it shall be my task to prove that episcopacy, with that authority which it challenges in England, is not only not agreeable, but tending to the destruction of monarchy. While the primitive pastors of the church of God labored faithfully in their ministry, tending only their sheep, and not seeking but avoiding all worldly matters as clogs[42] (and indeed derogations and debasements to their high calling), little needed the princes and potentates of the earth, which way so ever the gospel was spread, to study ways how to make a coherence between the church's polity and theirs. Therefore, when Pilate heard once our Savior Christ professing that "his kingdom was not of this world" [John 18.36], he thought the man could not stand much in Caesar's light, nor much endamage the Roman empire: for if the life of Christ be hid to this world, much more is his scepter unoperative but in spiritual things.

And thus lived, for two or three ages, the successors of the apostles. But when through Constantine's lavish superstition they forsook their first love and set themselves up two gods instead, Mammon and their belly,[43] then taking advantage of the spiritual power which they had on men's consciences, they began to cast a longing eye to get the body also and bodily things into their command; upon which their carnal desires, the spirit daily quenching and dying in them, they knew no way to keep themselves up from falling to nothing, but by bolstering and supporting their inward rottenness by a carnal and outward strength. For a while they rather privily sought opportunity than hastily disclosed their project, but when Constantine was dead, and three or four emperors more, their drift became notorious and offensive to the whole world. For while Theodosius the younger reigned, thus writes Socrates the historian in his 7th book, 11th chapter: "Now began an ill name to stick upon the bishops of Rome and Alexandria, who beyond their priestly bounds now long ago had stepped into principality."[44] And this was scarce eighty years since their raising from the meanest worldly condition. Of courtesy now let any man tell me, if they draw to themselves a temporal strength and power out of Caesar's dominion, is not Caesar's empire thereby diminished? But this was a stolen bit, hitherto he was but a caterpillar secretly gnawing at monarchy, the next time you shall see him a wolf, a lion, lifting his paw against his raiser, as Petrarch expressed it, and finally an open enemy and subverter of the Greek empire. Philippicus and Leo,[45] with diverse other emperors after them, not without the advice of their patriarchs and at length of a whole eastern council of three hundred thirty-eight bishops, threw the images out of the churches as being decreed idolatrous.

42. **clogs:** originally denoted wooden blocks tied to legs in order to impede motion.

43. See Matt. 6.24: "Ye cannot serve God and mammon."

44. **Socrates:** Scholasticus lived in the fifth century. Milton translates from his *Church History* 8.11.

45. *Philippicus,* Emperor of Constantinople (711–713), abolished the canons of the Sixth Council of Constantinople, which had called for images of Christ as a human being; his successor *Leo* III, who reigned from 717 to 741, issued a series of edicts against image worship in the 720s.

Upon this goodly occasion the bishop of Rome[46] not only seizes the city and all the territory about into his own hands, and makes himself lord thereof, which till then was governed by a Greek magistrate, but absolves all Italy of their tribute and obedience due to the emperor, because he obeyed God's commandment in abolishing idolatry.

Mark, sir, here how the pope came by St. Peter's patrimony, as he feigns it; not the donation of Constantine, but idolatry and rebellion got it him. Ye need but read Sigonius,[47] one of his own sect, to know the story at large. And now to shroud himself against a storm from the Greek continent and provide a champion to bear him out in these practices, he takes upon him by papal sentence to unthrone Chilpericus, the rightful King of France, and gives the kingdom to Pepin for no other cause but that he seemed to him the more active man.[48] If he were a friend herein to monarchy I know not, but to the monarch I need not ask what he was.

Having thus made Pepin his fast friend, he calls him into Italy against Aistulphus the Lombard, that warred upon him for his late usurpation of Rome as belonging to Ravenna, which he had newly won.[49] Pepin, not unobedient to the pope's call, passing into Italy, frees him out of danger and wins for him the whole exarchate[50] of Ravenna, which, though it had been almost immediately before the hereditary possession of that monarchy which was his chief patron and benefactor, yet he takes and keeps it to himself as lawful prize and given to Saint Peter. What a dangerous fallacy is this, when a spiritual man may snatch to himself any temporal dignity or dominion under pretence of receiving it for the church's use? Thus he claims Naples, Sicily, England, and what not? To be short, under show of his zeal against the errors of the Greek church, he never ceased baiting and goring the successors of his best lord Constantine, what by his barking curses and excommunications, what by his hindering the western princes from aiding them against the Saracens and Turks, unless when they humored him. So that it may be truly affirmed, he was the subversion and fall of that monarchy which was the hoisting of him. This, besides Petrarch whom I have cited, our Chaucer also hath observed,[51] and gives from hence a caution to England to beware of her bishops in time, for that their ends and aims are no more friendly to monarchy than the pope's.

46. **bishop of Rome:** Pope Gregory III.

47. **Sigonius:** Carlo Sigonius (1523–1584), a historian, was the author of *De Regno Italiae*, the *sect* is Roman Catholicism.

48. Pope Zacharias, Gregory III's successor, took the crown of France from Chilperic and bestowed it on Pepin in 751. Milton notes this case and that of Leo in the preceding paragraph in his *Commonplace Book* (Yale 1:444).

49. Milton continues here to follow Sigonius.

50. **exarchate:** the territory of an exarch, or governor of an outlying province under the Byzantine emperors.

51. *The Plowman's Tale*, from which Milton quotes in the next paragraph, does not appear to have been written by Chaucer. Nevertheless, sixteenth-century editors accepted it as Chaucer's, as did Spenser and Milton.

Thus he brings in the Plowman speaking, 2nd Part, stanza 28.

The Emperor yafe the pope sometime
So high lordship him about
That at last the silly kime,
The proud pope put him out;
So of this realm is no doubt,
But lords beware and them defend,
For now these folks be wonders stout,
The king and lords now this amend.

And in the next stanza, which begins the third part of the tale, he argues that they ought not to be lords.

Moses Law forbode it tho
That priests should no Lordship welde[52]
Christ's gospel biddeth also,
That they should not lordships held
Ne Christ's apostles were never so bold
No such Lordships to hem embrace
But smeren[53] her Sheep, and keep her Fold.

And so forward. Whether the bishops of England have deserved thus to be feared by men so wise as our Chaucer is esteemed, and how agreeable to our monarchy and monarchs their demeanor has been, he that is but meanly read in our chronicles needs not be instructed. Have they not been as the Canaanites and Philistims[54] to this kingdom? What treasons, what revolts to the pope, what rebellions, and those the basest and most pretenseless, have they not been chief in? What could monarchy think when Becket durst challenge the custody of Rochester Castle and the Tower of London, as appertaining to his signory (to omit his other insolencies and affronts to regal majesty, till the lashes inflicted on the anointed body of the king washed off the holy unction with his blood drawn by the polluted hands of bishops, abbots, and monks)?[55]

What good upholders of royalty were the bishops when, by their rebellious opposition against King John, Normandy was lost, he himself deposed, and this kingdom made over to the pope?[56] When the Bishop of Winchester durst tell

52. **welde:** wield.
53. **smeren:** smear, to rub (sheep) with a mixture to keep wet out of the fleece and prevent disease or vermin.
54. **Philistims:** Philistines.
55. In this account of Thomas à Becket, Archbishop of Canterbury, Milton follows Raphael Holinshed's *Chronicles of England, Scotland and Ireland* (1587), 3.70, and John Speed's *History of Great Britain* (1627), p. 467.
56. In this paragraph, Milton continues to follow Speed and Holinshed (see Yale 1.581).

the nobles, the pillars of the realm, that there were no peers in England, as in France, but that the king might do what he pleased, what could tyranny say more? It would be petty now if I should insist upon the rendering up of Tournay by Wolsey's treason,[57] the excommunications, cursings, and interdicts upon the whole land. For haply I shall be cut off short by a reply, that these were the faults of the men and their popish errors, not of episcopacy, that hath now renounced the pope and is a Protestant. Yes, sure, as wise and famous men have suspected and feared the Protestant episcopacy in England, as those that have feared the papal.

You know, sir, what was the judgment of Padre Paolo,[58] the great Venetian antagonist of the pope, for it is extant in the hands of many men, whereby he declares his fear that when the hierarchy of England shall light into the hands of busy and audacious men, or shall meet with Princes tractable to the prelacy, then much mischief is like to ensue. And can it be nearer hand,[59] than when bishops shall openly affirm that "no bishop, no king"?[60] A trim paradox, and that ye may know where they have been a begging for it, I will fetch you the twin brother to it out of the Jesuit's cell; they, feeling the axe of God's reformation hewing at the old and hollow trunk of papacy and finding the Spaniard their surest friend and safest refuge, to sooth him up in his dream of a fifth monarchy, and withal to uphold the decrepit papalty, have invented this super-politic aphorism, as one terms it, "one pope and one king."[61]

Surely there is not any prince in Christendom who, hearing this rare sophistry, can choose but smile, and if we be not blind at home, we may as well perceive that this worthy motto, "no bishop, no king," is of the same batch and infanted out of the same fears, a mere ague-cake coagulated of a certain fever they have, presaging their time to be but short. And now, like those that are sinking, they catch round at that which is likeliest to hold them up, and would persuade regal power that if they dive he must after. But what greater debasement can there be to royal dignity, whose towering and steadfast heighth rests upon the unmovable foundations of justice and heroic virtue, than to chain it in a dependence of subsisting (or ruining) to the painted battlements and gaudy rottenness of prelatry, which want but one puff of the king's to blow them down like a pasteboard house built of court-cards.[62] Sir, the little ado which methinks

57. Cardinal Thomas *Wolsey,* Archbishop of York, was the power behind Henry VIII's throne from 1515 until shortly before his death in disgrace in 1530.

58. **Padre Paolo:** Paolo Sarpi (1552–1623), author of a history of the Counter-Reformation Council of Trent, was a religious reformer. His opposition to the papacy arises in part from tension between his native Venice and Rome.

59. **nearer hand:** i.e., nearer at hand.

60. See note 41.

61. Milton may have in mind the Dominican Tommaso Campanella's *De Monarchia Hispanica* (1640); *the Spaniard* is the King of Spain.

62. **court-cards:** face cards in a deck of playing cards.

I find in untacking these pleasant sophisms, puts me into the mood to tell you a tale ere I proceed further; and Menenius Agrippa[63] to speed us.

Upon a time the body summoned all the members to meet in the guild for the common good (as Aesop's chronicles aver many stranger accidents). The head by right takes the first seat, and next to it a huge and monstrous wen, little less than the head itself, growing to it by a narrower excrescency. The members amazed began to ask one another what he was that took place next their chief. None could resolve. Whereat the wen, though unwieldy, with much ado gets up and bespeaks the assembly to this purpose: that as in place he was second to the head, so by due of merit; that he was to it an ornament and strength, and of special near relation; and that if the head should fail, none were fitter than himself to step into his place; therefore he thought it for the honor of the body that such dignities and rich endowments should be decreed him, as did adorn and set out the noblest members. To this was answered, that it should be consulted. Then was a wise and learned philosopher sent for, that knew all the charters, laws, and tenures of the body. On him it is imposed by all, as chief committee,[64] to examine and discuss the claim and petition of right put in by the wen; who soon perceiving the matter and wondering at the boldness of such a swollen tumor, "wilt thou," quoth he "that art but a bottle of vicious and hardened excrements, contend with the lawful and freeborn members, whose certain number is set by ancient and unrepealable statute? Head thou art none, though thou receive this huge substance from it. What office bearest thou? What good canst thou show by thee done to the commonweal? The wen, not easily dashed, replies that his office was his glory, for so oft as the soul would retire out of the head from over the steaming vapors of the lower parts to divine contemplation, with him she found the purest and quietest retreat, as being most remote from soil and disturbance. "Lourdan,"[65] quoth the philosopher, "thy folly is as great as thy filth. Know that all the faculties of the soul are confined of old to their several vessels and ventricles, from which they cannot part without dissolution of the whole body, and that thou containest no good thing in thee, but a heap of hard and loathsome uncleanness, and art to the head a foul disfigurement and burden; when I have cut thee off and opened thee, as by the help of these implements I will do, all men shall see."

But to return whence was digressed, seeing that the throne of a king, as the wise King Solomon often remembers us,[66] is established in justice, which is the

63. In the next paragraph, Milton adapts a story from Livy's *Roman History* 2.32. In Livy, *Menenius Agrippa* pacifies an army protesting the actions of the consuls with an allegory of the debilitating effect of the revolt of the body's members against the belly, which seems to take but not to give. Milton's version is more graphic, and the emphasis changes; now a truly useless part attempts to aggrandize itself; thus Milton expresses what he sees as the grasping emptiness of episcopacy. Shakespeare dramatizes the episode of Menenius Agrippa in the first scene of *Coriolanus.*

64. **committee:** a person to whom some task or trust is committed.

65. **Lourdan:** sluggard, loafer.

66. Prov. 16.12.

universal justice that Aristotle so much praises,[67] containing in it all other virtues, it may assure us that the fall of prelacy, whose actions are so far distant from justice, cannot shake the least fringe that borders the royal canopy, but that their standing doth continually oppose and lay battery to regal safety, shall by that which follows easily appear. Amongst many secondary and accessory causes that support monarchy, these are not of least reckoning, though common to all other states: the love of the subjects, the multitude and valor of the people, and store of treasure. In all these things hath the kingdom been of late sore weakened, and chiefly by the prelates. First, let any man consider, that if any prince shall suffer under him a commission of authority to be exercised till all the land groan and cry out as against a whip of scorpions, whether this be not likely to lessen and keel[68] the affections of the subject? Next, what numbers of faithful and freeborn Englishmen and good Christians have been constrained to forsake their dearest home, their friends, and kindred, whom nothing but the wide ocean and the savage deserts of America could hide and shelter from the fury of the bishops?

O sir, if we could but see the shape of our dear mother England, as poets are wont to give a personal form to what they please, how would she appear, think ye, but in a mourning weed with ashes upon her head and tears abundantly flowing from her eyes, to behold so many of her children exposed at once and thrust from things of dearest necessity, because their conscience could not assent to things which the bishops thought indifferent? What more binding than conscience? What more free than indifferency? Cruel then must that indifferency needs be that shall violate the strict necessity of the conscience, merciless and inhumane that free choice and liberty that shall break asunder the bonds of religion. Let the astrologer be dismayed at the portentous blaze of comets, and impressions in the air, as foretelling troubles and changes to states; I shall believe there cannot be a more ill-boding sign to a nation (God turn the omen from us) than when the inhabitants, to avoid insufferable grievances at home, are enforced by heaps to forsake their native country.

Now whereas the only remedy and amends against the depopulation and thinness of a land within is the borrowed strength of firm alliance from without, these priestly policies of theirs, having thus exhausted our domestic forces, have gone the way also to leave us as naked of our firmest and faithfulest neighbors abroad, by disparaging and alienating from us all Protestant princes and commonwealths, who are not ignorant that our prelates, and as many as they can infect, account them no better than a sort of sacrilegious and puritanical rebels, preferring the Spaniard, our deadly enemy, before them, and set all orthodox writers at naught in comparison of the Jesuits, who are indeed the only corrupters of youth and good learning; and I have heard many wise and learned

67. Aristotle, *Nichomachean Ethics* 5.1 (1130a10).
68. **keel:** make less eager or ardent.

men in Italy say as much. It cannot be that the strongest knot of confederacy should not daily slacken when religion, which is the chief engagement of our league, shall be turned to their reproach. Hence it is that the prosperous and prudent states of the United Provinces, whom we ought to love, if not for themselves yet for our own good work in them, they having been in a manner planted and erected by us, and having been since to us the faithful watchmen and discoverers of many a popish and Austrian complotted treason,[69] and with us the partners of many a bloody and victorious battle,[70] whom the similitude of manners and language, the commodity of traffic, which founded the old Burgundian league betwixt us,[71] but chiefly religion should bind to us immortally, even such friends as these, out of some principles instilled into us by the prelates, have been often dismissed with distasteful answers and sometimes unfriendly actions. Nor is it to be considered to the breach of confederate nations whose mutual interest is of such high consequence, though their merchants bicker in the East Indies;[72] neither is it safe or wary, or indeed Christianly, that the French king, of a different faith, should afford our nearest allies as good protection as we.[73] Sir, I persuade myself, if our zeal to true religion and the brotherly usage of our truest friends were as notorious to the world as our prelatical schism and captivity to rochet[74] apothegms, we had ere this seen our old conquerors and afterward liege-men, the Normans, together with the Britains, our proper colony, and all the Gascoins that are the rightful dowry of our ancient kings,[75] come with cap and knee, desiring the shadow of the English scepter to defend them from the hot persecutions and taxes of the French. But when they come hither and see a tympany[76] of Spaniolized bishops swaggering in the foretop of the state and meddling to turn and dandle the royal ball with unskillful and pedantic palms, no marvel though they think it as unsafe to commit religion and liberty to their arbitrating as to a synagogue of Jesuits.

But what do I stand reckoning upon advantages and gains lost by the misrule and turbulency of the prelates? What do I pick up so thriftily their scatterings and diminishings of the meaner subject, whilst they by their seditious practices have endangered to lose the king one third of his main stock? What have they

69. Early in Elizabeth's reign, there were several plots to depose her and restore Catholic worship. One plot involved marrying the Catholic Duke of Norfolk, who had Spanish ties, to the Catholic Mary, Queen of Scots; another would have had Mary marry Don John of Austria.

70. English soldiers had fought against Spain as allies of the Dutch in the late sixteenth and early seventeenth centuries.

71. The *Burgundian league* of 1339 called for the settling of Flemish weavers in England, a leading wool producer; Milton apparently follows Speed's *History*.

72. Dutch and English traders competed forcefully for dominance in Asia, leading to intermittent armed conflict.

73. While the Catholic Louis XIII of France supported the Protestant Dutch against Catholic Spain, Charles I temporized and at times wished to ally himself with Spain.

74. **rochet:** a linen garment worn by bishops.

75. Milton laments England's relinquishing, owing to military defeats, its claims to French provinces.

76. **tympany:** a swelling, in this case, of pride and arrogance; the bishops are *Spaniolized* because won over to the cause of Catholic Spain.

not done to banish him from his own native country? But to speak of this as it ought would ask a volume by itself.

Thus as they have unpeopled the kingdom by expulsion of so many thousands, as they have endeavored to lay the skirts of it bare by disheartening and dishonoring our loyalest confederates abroad, so have they hamstrung the valor of the subject by seeking to effeminate us all at home. Well knows every wise nation that their liberty consists in manly and honest labors, in sobriety and rigorous honor to the marriage bed, which in both sexes should be bred up from chaste hopes to loyal enjoyments; and when the people slacken and fall to looseness and riot, then do they as much as if they had laid down their necks for some wily tyrant to get up and ride. Thus learnt Cyrus to tame the Lydians,[77] whom by arms he could not, whilst they kept themselves from luxury; with one easy proclamation to set up stews,[78] dancing, feasting, and dicing, he made them soon his slaves. I know not what drift the prelates had, whose brokers they were to prepare and supple us either for a foreign invasion or domestic oppression. But this I am sure, they took the ready way to despoil us both of manhood and grace at once, and that in the shamefullest and ungodliest manner upon that day which God's law and even our own reason hath consecrated, that we might have one day at least of seven set apart wherein to examine and increase our knowledge of God, to meditate and commune of our faith, our hope, our eternal city in heaven, and to quicken, withal, the study and exercise of charity. At such a time that men should be plucked from their soberest and saddest thoughts, and by the bishops, the pretended fathers of the church, instigated by public edict, and with earnest endeavor pushed forward to gaming, jigging, wassailing, and mixed dancing is a horror to think.[79] Thus did the reprobate hireling priest Balaam seek to subdue the Israelites to Moab, if not by force then by this devilish policy, to draw them from the sanctuary of God to the luxurious and ribald feasts of Baal-peor.[80] Thus have they trespassed not only against the monarchy of England, but of heaven also, as others, I doubt not, can prosecute against them.

I proceed within my own bounds to show you next what good agents they are about the revenues and riches of the kingdom, which declares of what moment they are to monarchy, or what avail. Two leeches they have that still suck and suck the kingdom: their ceremonies and their courts. If any man will contend that ceremonies be lawful under the gospel, he may be answered otherwhere. This doubtless that they ought to be many and overcostly, no true Protestant will affirm. Now I appeal to all wise men, what an excessive waste of treasury hath been within these few years in this land, not in the expedient but

77. *Cyrus* was taught to subdue the *Lydians* by encouraging them to wear luxurious clothing and to pursue music and dance (see Herodotus, *Histories* 1.155).

78. **stews:** brothels.

79. Like other Puritans, Milton decried Charles's 1633 *Book of Sports,* which encouraged the activities listed here; see Marcus 1986.

80. See Num. 22.5–41; 24; 25.1–3.

in the idolatrous erection of temples beautified exquisitely to outvie the papists, the costly and dear-bought scandals and snares of images, pictures, rich copes,[81] gorgeous altar-cloths. And by the courses they took and the opinions they held, it was not likely any stay would be, or any end of their madness, where a pious pretext is so ready at hand to cover their insatiate desires. What can we suppose this will come to? What other materials than these have built up the spiritual Babel to the height of her abominations? Believe it, sir, right truly it may be said, that Antichrist is Mammon's son. The sour leaven[82] of human traditions mixed in one putrefied mass with the poisonous dregs of hypocrisy in the hearts of prelates, that lie basking in the sunny warmth of wealth and promotion, is the serpent's egg that will hatch an Antichrist wheresoever and engender the same monster as big or little as the lump is which breeds him. If the splendor of gold and silver begin to lord it once again in the church of England, we shall see Antichrist[83] shortly wallow here, though his chief kennel be at Rome. If they had one thought upon God's glory and the advancement of Christian faith, they would be a means that with these expenses, thus profusely thrown away in trash, rather churches and schools might be built where they cry out for want and more added where too few are; a moderate maintenance distributed to every painful[84] minister that now scarce sustains his family with bread, while the prelates revel like Belshazzar with their full carouses in goblets and vessels of gold snatched from God's temple.[85] Which (I hope) the worthy men of our land will consider.

Now then for their courts. What a mass of money is drawn from the veins into the ulcers of the kingdom this way, their extortions, their open corruptions, the multitude of hungry and ravenous harpies that swarm about their offices declare sufficiently. And what though all this go not oversea? 'Twere better it did: better a penurious kingdom, than where excessive wealth flows into the graceless and injurious hands of common sponges to the impoverishing of good and loyal men, and that by such execrable, such irreligious courses.

If the sacred and dreadful works of holy discipline, censure, penance, excommunication, and absolution (where no profane thing ought to have access, nothing to be assistant but sage and Christianly admonition, brotherly love, flaming charity, and zeal; and then according to the effects, paternal sorrow, or paternal joy, mild severity melting compassion), if such divine ministries as these, wherein the angel of the church represents the person of Christ Jesus, must lie prostitute to sordid fees and not pass to and fro between our Savior

81. **copes:** ceremonial capes worn by priests.

82. Matt. 16.6.

83. **Antichrist:** i.e., the pope.

84. **painful:** painstaking, diligent.

85. Dan. 5.1–30. Belshazzar's revelry with the temple goblets prompted the miraculous writing, interpreted by Daniel, convicting the king of pride and blasphemy and predicting his downfall (he was slain that night). Milton, assuming Daniel's role, warns the bishops of their imminent fall.

(that of free grace redeemed us) and the submissive penitent, without the truckage[86] of perishing coin and the butcherly execution of tormentors, rooks, and rakeshames[87] sold to lucre, then have the Babylonish merchants of souls just excuse. Hitherto, sir, you have heard how the prelates have weakened and withdrawn the external accomplishments of kingly prosperity—the love of the people, their multitude, their valor, their wealth—mining and sapping the outworks and redoubts of monarchy, now hear how they strike at the very heart and vitals.

We know that monarchy is made up of two parts, the liberty of the subject and the supremacy of the king. I begin at the root. See what gentle and benign fathers they have been to our liberty. Their trade being, by the same alchemy that the pope uses to extract heaps of gold and silver out of the drossy bullion of the people's sins, and justly fearing that the quick-sighted Protestant's eye cleared in great part from the mist of superstition may at one time or other look with a good judgment into these their deceitful pedlaries,[88] to gain as many associates of guiltiness as they can, and to infect the temporal magistrate with the like lawless though not sacrilegious extortion, see a while what they do: they engage themselves to preach and persuade an assertion for truth the most false, and to this monarchy the most pernicious and destructive that could be chosen. What more baneful to monarchy than a popular commotion, for the dissolution of monarchy slides aptest into democraty;[89] and what stirs the Englishmen, as our wisest writers have observed, sooner to rebellion than violent and heavy hands upon their goods and purses? Yet these devout prelates, spite of our great charter and the souls of our progenitors that wrested their liberties out of the Norman grip with their dearest blood and highest prowess, for these many years have not ceased in their pulpits wrenching and spraining the text, to set at naught and trample under foot all the most sacred and lifeblood laws, statutes, and acts of Parliament that are the holy covenant of union and marriage between the king and his realm, by proscribing and confiscating from us all the right we have to our own bodies, goods, and liberties. What is this, but to blow a trumpet and proclaim a fire-cross[90] to a hereditary and perpetual civil war? Thus much against the subject's liberty hath been assaulted by them. . . .

[*In an omitted section, Milton offers examples of bishops and the pope challenging the secular authority of kings and emperors, praises God for frustrating the designs of prelates, and exhorts the English and Scottish to remain united in their pursuit of pure worship and civil justice.*]

86. **truckage:** barter.
87. **rakeshames:** ill-behaved, dissolute persons.
88. **pedlaries:** the base practices of a pedlar.
89. **democraty:** democracy.
90. **fire-cross:** a signal used in the Scottish Highlands to summon men to gather at the sudden outbreak of war.

Sir, you have now at length this question for the time, and as my memory would best serve me in such a copious and vast theme, fully handled, and you yourself may judge whether prelacy be the only church government agreeable to monarchy. Seeing, therefore, the perilous and confused estate into which we are fallen, and that,[91] to the certain knowledge of all men, through the irreligious pride and hateful tyranny of prelates (as the innumerable and grievous complaints of every shire cry out), if we will now resolve to settle affairs either according to pure religion or sound policy, we must first of all begin roundly to cashier and cut away from the public body the noisome and diseased tumor of prelacy and come from schism to unity with our neighbor reformed sister churches, which with the blessing of peace and pure doctrine have now long time flourished and, doubtless with all hearty joy and gratulation, will meet[92] and welcome our Christian union with them, as they have been all this while grieved at our strangeness and little better than separation from them. And for the discipline propounded,[93] seeing that it hath been inevitably proved that the natural and fundamental causes of political happiness in all governments are the same and that this church discipline is taught in the word of God, and, as we see, agrees according to wish with all such states as have received it, we may infallibly assure ourselves that it will as well agree with monarchy, though all the tribe of aphorismers and politicasters would persuade us there be secret and mysterious reasons against it. For upon the settling hereof mark what nourishing and cordial restorements to the state will follow: the ministers of the gospel attending only to the work of salvation, everyone within his limited charge; besides the diffusive blessing of God upon all our actions, the king shall sit without an old disturber,[94] a daily encroacher and intruder; shall rid his kingdom of a strong sequestered and collateral power; a confronting miter, whose potent wealth and wakeful ambition he had just cause to hold in jealousy: not to repeat the other present evils which only their removal will remove. And because things simply pure are inconsistent in the mass of nature, nor are the elements or humors in man's body exactly homogeneal, and hence the best founded commonwealths and least barbarous have aimed at a certain mixture and temperament, partaking the several virtues of each other state, that each part drawing to itself may keep up a steady and even uprightness in common.

There is no civil government that hath been known, no not the Spartan, not

91. **that:** i.e., the falling into the *perilous and confused state* just mentioned.

92. The spine of this complicated clause is as follows: *sister churches, which . . . have . . . flourished and . . . will meet.*

93. **the discipline propounded:** Presbyterian church government. By the mid-1640s, moved in part by the violent reaction of former Presbyterian allies to his argument for divorce, Milton would repudiate Presbyterianism and advocate Independency, or the self-governance of individual congregations; see his poem on the subject, *On the New Forcers of Conscience,* which ends "New *Presbyter* is but old *Priest* writ large" (p. 165).

94. **old disturber:** episcopacy in general, and perhaps Archbishop William Laud in particular.

the Roman, though both for this respect so much praised by the wise Polybius,[95] more divinely and harmoniously tuned, more equally balanced as it were by the hand and scale of justice, than is the commonwealth of England: where, under a free and untutored monarch, the noblest, worthiest, and most prudent men, with full approbation and suffrage of the people, have in their power the supreme and final determination of highest affairs. Now if conformity of church discipline to the civil be so desired, there can be nothing more parallel, more uniform, than when under the sovereign prince, Christ's vicegerent, using the scepter of David, according to God's law, the godliest, the wisest, and learnedest ministers in their several charges have the instructing and disciplining of God's people, by whose full and free election they are consecrated to that holy and equal aristocracy. And why should not the piety and conscience of Englishmen as members of the church be trusted in the election of pastors to functions that nothing concern a monarch, as well as their worldly wisdoms are privileged as members of the state in suffraging their knights and burgesses to matters that concern him nearly? And if in weighing these several offices, their difference in time and quality be cast in, I know they will not turn the beam of equal judgment the moiety of a scruple. . . .

[*In a brief omitted section, Milton, while elaborating on the parallels between the English secular government and Presbyterian church government, insists that ministers should not share in the elaborate honors and large stipends given to legislators and judges.*]

Here I might have ended, but that some objections, which I have heard commonly flying about, press me to the endeavor of an answer. We must not run, they say, into sudden extremes. This is a fallacious rule unless understood only of the actions of virtue about things indifferent, for if it be found that those two extremes be vice and virtue, falsehood and truth, the greater extremity of virtue and superlative truth we run into, the more virtuous and the more wise we become; and he that, flying from degenerate and traditional corruption, fears to shoot himself too far into the meeting embraces of a divinely-warranted reformation, had better not have run at all. And for the suddenness, it cannot be feared. Who should oppose it? The papists? They dare not. The Protestants otherwise affected? They were mad. There is nothing will be removed but what to them is professedly indifferent. The long affection which the people have born to it, what for itself, what for the odiousness of prelates, is evident. From the first year of Queen Elizabeth, it hath still been more and more propounded, desired, and beseeched, yea sometimes favorably forwarded by the Parliaments themselves. Yet if it were sudden and swift, provided still it be from worse to better, certainly we ought to hie us from evil like

95. See Polybius, *Histories* 6.48 and 6.12.

a torrent, and rid ourselves of corrupt discipline as we would shake fire out of our bosoms.

Speedy and vehement were the reformations of all the good kings of Judah,[96] though the people had been nuzzled in idolatry never so long before. They feared not the bugbear of danger, nor the lion in the way that the sluggish and timorous politician thinks he sees. No more did our brethren of the reformed churches abroad; they ventured (God being their guide) out of rigid popery into that which we in mockery call precise Puritanism, and yet we see no inconvenience befell them.

Let us not dally with God when he offers us a full blessing, to take as much of it as we think will serve our ends and turn him back the rest upon his hands, lest in his anger he snatch all from us again. Next, they allege the antiquity of episcopacy through all ages. What it was in the apostles' time, that questionless it must be still, and therein I trust the ministers will be able to satisfy the parliament. But if episcopacy be taken for prelacy,[97] all the ages they can deduce it through will make it no more venerable than papacy.

Most certain it is (as all our stories bear witness) that ever since their coming to the see[98] of Canterbury for near twelve hundred years, to speak of them in general, they have been in England to our souls a sad and doleful succession of illiterate and blind guides; to our purses and goods a wasteful band of robbers, a perpetual havoc and rapine; to our state a continual hydra of mischief and molestation, the forge of discord and rebellion. This is the trophy of their antiquity and boasted succession through so many ages. And for those prelate-martyrs[99] they glory of, they are to be judged what they were by the gospel and not the gospel to be tried by them. . . .

[*In a substantial omitted section, Milton answers a series of objections against Presbyterian church government: if episcopacy is woven into the common law, it can be woven out; not only is government by assembly true to the practice of the early church but it does not carry with it the danger of the meddling in politics by lordly and overweening bishops; on the continent, churches governed by assemblies do not intrude in secular affairs as bishops had done before the Reformation.*]

But let us not for fear of a scarecrow, or else through hatred to be reformed, stand hankering and politizing, when God with spread hands testifies to us and points us out the way to our peace.

Let us not be so overcredulous, unless God hath blinded us, as to trust our dear souls into the hands of men that beg so devoutly for the pride and gluttony

96. **good kings of Judah:** Asa (1 Kings 15.9–15), Hezekiah (2 Kings 18.4), and Josiah (2 Kings 23.1–25) have been proposed as instances.

97. Milton here distinguishes between episcopacy and prelacy; the bishops of the early church, according to Milton, did not claim lordship over their flocks.

98. **see:** diocese.

99. **prelate-martyrs:** a reference to Cranmer, Latimer, and Ridley (see note 16).

of their own backs and bellies, that sue and solicit so eagerly, not for the saving of souls, the consideration of which can have here no place at all, but for their bishoprics, deaneries, prebends, and chanonies.[100] How can these men not be corrupt, whose very cause is the bribe of their own pleading, whose mouths cannot open without the strong breath and loud stench of avarice, simony,[101] and sacrilege, embezzling the treasury of the church on painted and gilded walls of temples wherein God hath testified to have no delight, warming their palace kitchens, and from thence their unctuous and epicurean paunches, with the alms of the blind, the lame, the impotent, the aged, the orphan, the widow? For with these the treasury of Christ ought to be, here must be his jewels bestowed, his rich cabinet must be emptied here, as the constant martyr Saint Lawrence taught the Roman praetor.[102]

Sir, would you know what the remonstrance of these men[103] would have, what their petition[104] implies? They entreat us that we would not be weary of those insupportable grievances that our shoulders have hitherto cracked under. They beseech us that we would think 'em fit to be our justices of peace, our lords, our highest officers of state, though they come furnished with no more experience than they learnt between the cook and the manciple,[105] or more profoundly at the college audit, or the regent house, or (to come to their deepest insight) at their patron's table. They would request us to endure still the rustling of their silken cassocks, and that we would burst our midriffs rather than laugh to see them under sail in all their lawn and sarsenet,[106] their shrouds and tackle,[107] with geometrical rhomboids[108] upon their heads. They would bear us in hand that we must of duty still appear before them once a year in Jerusalem[109] like good circumcised males and females to be taxed by the poll,[110] to be sconsed our head money, our tuppences in their chaunlerly[111] shop-book of Easter. They pray us that it would please us to let them still hale us and worry us with their bandogs[112] and pursuivants;[113] and that it would please the

100. **chanonies:** canonries; a *canonry* is the benefice of a canon, a priest attached to a cathedral.
101. **simony:** the exchanging of rites and blessings for money.
102. Demanded under torture to hand over the riches of the church, St. Lawrence collected the poor and brought them to his persecutor. See Augustine, *Sermon* 302.9.
103. **these men:** the bishops.
104. **their petition:** A dismissive reference to *The Humble Petition of the University of Oxford, in Behalf of Episcopacy and Cathedrals*, published a month before *Of Reformation.*
105. **manciple:** a purchasing agent for a monastery.
106. **lawn:** fine linen, used in bishops' wide sleeves; **sarsenet:** a very fine and soft silk.
107. **shrouds and tackle:** parts of a ship's rigging; *shrouds* are ropes deployed in pairs to help brace the masthead; the ropes and pulleys with which the sails are deployed are the *tackle.* Milton often compares Satan to a sailing ship in *PL* (2.636–43, 4.159–65, 9.513–15).
108. **geometrical rhomboids:** miters.
109. It was the duty of Jewish men to appear once a year at the Temple in Jerusalem.
110. In Milton's time, a *tuppence* was required at Easter as a *poll* tax from parishioners old enough to take communion.
111. **chaunlerly:** relating to a chandler, or petty shopkeeper.
112. **bandogs:** mastiffs or bloodhounds.
113. **pursuivants:** warrant officers.

Parliament that they may yet have the whipping, fleecing, and flaying of us in their diabolical courts,[114] to tear the flesh from our bones, and into our wide wounds, instead of balm, to power in the oil of tartar, vitriol, and mercury. Surely a right reasonable innocent and soft-hearted petition! O the relenting bowels of the fathers! Can this be granted them unless God have smitten us with frenzy from above and with a dazzling giddiness at noonday?

Should not those men[115] rather be heard that come to plead against their own preferments, their worldly advantages, their own abundance; for honor and obedience to God's word, the conversion of souls, the Christian peace of the land, and union of the reformed catholic church,[116] the unappropriating and unmonopolizing the rewards of learning and industry from the greasy clutch of ignorance and high feeding? We have tried already, and miserably felt, what ambition, worldly glory, and immoderate wealth can do: what the boisterous and contradictional hand of a temporal, earthly, and corporeal spirituality can avail to the edifying of Christ's holy church. Were it such a desperate hazard to put to the venture the universal votes of Christ's congregation, the fellowly and friendly yoke of a teaching and laborious ministry, the pastor-like and apostolic imitation of meek and unlordly discipline, the gentle and benevolent mediocrity of church-maintenance,[117] without the ignoble hucksterage of piddling tithes?[118] Were it such an incurable mischief to make a little trial what all this would do to the flourishing and growing up of Christ's mystical body? As rather to use every poor shift and, if that serve not, to threaten uproar and combustion and shake the brand of civil discord?[119]

O sir, I do now feel myself enwrapped on the sudden into those mazes and labyrinths of dreadful and hideous thoughts, that which way to get out or which way to end I know not, unless I turn mine eyes and with your help lift up my hands to that eternal and propitious throne, where nothing is readier than grace and refuge to the distresses of mortal suppliants. And it were a shame to leave these serious thoughts less piously than the heathen were wont to conclude their graver discourses.

Thou therefore that sits in light and glory unapproachable, parent of angels and men! next thee I implore omnipotent king, redeemer of that lost remnant whose nature thou didst assume, ineffable and everlasting love! and thou the third subsistence of divine infinitude, illumining Spirit, the joy and solace of created things! One tri-personal godhead![120] look upon this thy poor and almost

114. **diabolical courts:** The bishops were particularly hated for their ecclesiastical courts.

115. **those men:** i.e., moderate Puritans.

116. **reformed catholic church:** the universal Protestant church, not the Roman Catholic Church.

117. **mediocrity of church-maintenance:** supporting ministers sufficiently but not luxuriously.

118. Milton's unwavering position that ministers should be supported by voluntary offerings rather than enforced tithes is the central subject of his 1659 work *Considerations Touching the Likeliest Means to Remove Hirelings out of the Church.*

119. Milton refers to the first and second Bishops' Wars of 1639 and 1640.

120. Milton would later reject Trinitarian beliefs, as is evident in *CD* 1.5 and in *Paradise Lost,* where, e.g., the Son lacks the Father's omnipresence (7.584–92).

spent and expiring church, leave her not thus a prey to these importunate wolves that wait and think long till they devour thy tender flock, these wild boars that have broke into thy vineyard, and left the print of their polluting hoofs on the souls of thy servants. O let them not bring about their damned designs, that stand now at the entrance of the bottomless pit, expecting the watchword to open and let out those dreadful locusts and scorpions to re-involve us in that pitchy cloud of infernal darkness, where we shall never more see the sun of thy truth again, never hope for the cheerful dawn, never more hear the bird of morning sing. Be moved with pity at the afflicted state of this our shaken monarchy, that now lies laboring under her throes and struggling against the grudges of more dreaded calamities.

O thou that, after the impetuous rage of five bloody inundations[121] and the succeeding sword of intestine war, soaking the land in her own gore, didst pity the sad and ceaseless revolution of our swift and thick-coming sorrows when we were quite breathless, of thy free grace didst motion peace and terms of covenant with us, and having first well-nigh freed us from antichristian thraldom, didst build up this Britannic empire to a glorious and enviable height with all her daughter islands about her, stay us in this felicity, let not the obstinacy of our half-obedience and will-worship bring forth that viper of sedition that for these fourscore years hath been breeding to eat through the entrails of our peace, but let her cast her abortive spawn without the danger of this travailing and throbbing kingdom. That we may still remember in our solemn thanksgivings, how for us the northern ocean even to the frozen Thule[122] was scattered with the proud shipwrecks of the Spanish armado, and the very maw of hell ransacked and made to give up her concealed destruction ere she could vent it in that horrible and damned blast.[123]

O how much more glorious will those former deliverances appear, when we shall know them not only to have saved us from the greatest miseries past but to have reserved us for greatest happiness to come. Hitherto thou has but freed us, and that not fully, from the unjust and tyrannous claim of thy foes, now unite us entirely and appropriate us to thyself, tie us everlastingly in willing homage to the prerogative of thy eternal throne.

And now we know, oh thou our most certain hope and defense, that thine enemies have been consulting all the sorceries of the great whore,[124] and have

121. **five bloody inundations:** most likely the five invasions of England by Romans, Picts and Scots, Anglo-Saxons, Danes, and Normans, described by Milton in his *History of Britain.*

122. **Thule:** Early geographers assigned this name to a land north of Britain, supposed to be the world's most northerly region. Milton gives dramatic emphasis to the 1588 English victory over the Spanish Armada.

123. A reference to the discovery of the Gunpowder Plot of 1605, which Milton celebrated in several juvenile poems (see the three poems titled "In proditionem bombaricam" and especially the mini-epic *On the Fifth of November*, pp. 205–13).

124. **great whore:** the Roman Catholic Church, associated by Protestants generally and Puritans in particular with the Whore of Babylon of Rev. 17.1.

joined their plots with that sad intelligencing tyrant[125] that mischiefs the world with his mines of Ophir, and lies thirsting to revenge his naval ruins that have larded our seas. But let them all take counsel together, and let it come to naught; let them decree, and do thou cancel it; let them gather themselves, and be scattered; let them embattle themselves, and be broken; let them embattle and be broken; for thou art with us.

Then, amidst the hymns and hallelujahs of saints, some one may perhaps be heard offering at high strains in new and lofty measures to sing and celebrate thy divine mercies and marvelous judgments in this land throughout all ages; whereby this great and warlike nation instructed and inured to the fervent and continual practice of truth and righteousness, and casting far from her the rags of her old vices, may press on hard to that high and happy emulation to be found the soberest, wisest, and most Christian people at that day when thou, the eternal and shortly expected king, shalt open the clouds to judge the several kingdoms of the world and, distributing national honors and rewards to religious and just commonwealths, shall put an end to all earthly tyrannies, proclaiming thy universal and mild monarchy through heaven and earth.[126] Where they undoubtedly that by their labors, counsels, and prayers have been earnest for the common good of religion and their country shall receive, above the inferior orders of the blessed, the regal addition of principalities, legions, and thrones into their glorious titles,[127] and in supereminence of beatific vision progressing the dateless and irrevoluble circle of eternity shall clasp inseparable hands with joy and bliss in overmeasure forever.

But they contrary that by the impairing and diminution of true faith, the distresses and servitude of their country, aspire to high dignity, rule, and promotion here, after a shameful end in this life (which God grant them) shall be thrown down eternally into the darkest and deepest gulf of hell, where, under the despiteful control, the trample and spurn of all the other damned that in the anguish of their torture shall have no other ease than to exercise a raving and bestial tyranny over them as their slaves and negroes, they shall remain in that plight forever, the basest, the lowermost, the most dejected, most underfoot, and downtrodden vassals of perdition.

The End

125. **sad intelligencing tyrant:** i.e., the Roman Catholic throne of Spain, which employed the gold of South America (described here with the biblical term *mines of Ophir* [1 Kings 10.11]) to further its goal of extirpating Protestantism.

126. A reference to the Second Coming of Christ (Matt. 24.29–25.46).

127. I.e., the heroes of reformation will join the angels in Heaven; *principalities* and *thrones* are two of the nine orders of angels (like other Protestants, Milton sometimes used the order names employed in the Roman Church without committing himself to the hierarchical arrangement of the orders).

A Selection from

THE REASON OF CHURCH GOVERNMENT URGED AGAINST PRELATY, THE SECOND BOOK

The Reason of Church Government Urged against Prelaty is the fourth of five works, published in the span of a year, attacking the episcopal hierarchy of the Church of England. Published in January or February 1642, *The Reason of Church Government* is the longest of these so-called antiprelatical tracts, and the first to which Milton affixed his name. The immediate occasion was the appearance in 1641 of *Certain Briefe Treatises, Written by Diverse Learned Men, Concerning the Ancient and Moderne Government of the Church,* which contained arguments in favor of episcopacy by Anglican champions such as Archbishop James Ussher, Lancelot Andrewes, and Richard Hooker. *The Reason of Church Government* is more moderate in its rhetoric than some of Milton's other tracts, notably the *Animadversions* and *An Apology for Smectymnuus,* which engage in harsh personal attacks.

While Milton's arguments against episcopacy hold interest for specialists, the tract is most often read for the remarkable autobiographical passage that takes up most of the Preface to Book 2. A relative unknown taking on illustrious elders, Milton probably believed it necessary to authorize his arguments by presenting himself as learned and virtuous, a rhetorical tactic known as the "ethical proof." But he goes well beyond the conventions of ethical proof. With characteristic egotism, Milton numbers himself among God's "selected heralds" and compares himself with the prophet Isaiah. He acknowledges an unbounded poetic ambition, promising to do for England what Homer did for Greece and Vergil for Rome, and, as a Christian, to trump them by writing a true epic to challenge their fictitious ones.

The text of our selection is based on the copy of the first edition in the British Library's Thomason Collection.

The Second Book

How happy were it for this frail and, as it may be truly called, mortal life of man, since all earthly things which have the name of good and convenient in our daily use are withal[1] so cumbersome and full of trouble, if knowledge yet which is the best and lightsomest possession of the mind were, as the common saying is, no burden, and that what it wanted of being a load to any part of the body, it did not with a heavy advantage overlay upon the spirit. For not to speak of that knowledge that rests in the contemplation of natural causes and dimensions,[2] which must needs be a lower wisdom as the object is low, certain it is that he who hath obtained in more than the scantest measure to know anything distinctly of God and of his true worship, and what is infallibly good and happy in the state of man's life, what in itself evil and miserable, though vulgarly not so esteemed, he that hath obtained to know this, the only high valuable wisdom indeed, remembering also that God even to a strictness requires the improvement of these his entrusted gifts,[3] cannot but sustain a sorer burden of mind, and more pressing, than any supportable toil or weight which the body can labor under; how and in what manner he shall dispose and employ those sums of knowledge and illumination which God hath sent him into this world to trade with.

And that which aggravates the burden more is that, having received amongst his allotted parcels certain precious truths of such an orient luster as no diamond can equal, which nevertheless he has in charge to put off[4] at any cheap rate, yea for nothing to them that will, the great merchants[5] of this world, fearing that this course would soon discover and disgrace the false glitter of their deceitful wares wherewith they abuse the people, like poor Indians with beads and glasses, practice by all means how they may suppress the venting of such rarities and such a cheapness as would undo them and turn their trash upon their hands. Therefore by gratifying the corrupt desires of men in fleshly doctrines, they stir them up to persecute with hatred and contempt all those that seek to bear themselves uprightly in this their spiritual factory[6]: which they foreseeing, though they cannot but testify of truth and the excellence of that heavenly traffic which they bring against what opposition or danger soever, yet needs must it sit heavily upon their spirits, that being, in God's prime intention and their own, selected heralds of peace and dispensers of treasure inestimable without price to them that have no pence, they find in the discharge of their commission that they are made the greatest variance and offense, a very sword

1. **withal:** at the same time.
2. Milton follows the tradition dividing knowledge available through the "contemplation of created things" (*PL* 5.511) from the higher knowledge available through revelation and right reason. Compare Bacon's *Advancement of Learning* 1.1.3.
3. Milton alludes to the parable of the talents (Matt. 25.14–31), as he does in *Sonnet 7* and *19*. For the importance of this parable in Milton, see Haskin 29–53.
4. **put off:** sell.
5. **great merchants:** Milton refers figuratively to the bishops.
6. **factory:** trading post. Milton distinguishes between upright traders in God's Word and the bishops who cheat the English as merchant traders cheated Native Americans or East Indians with cheap baubles.

and fire both in house and city over the whole earth.[7] This is that which the sad prophet Jeremiah laments, "Woe is me my mother, that thou hast born me a man of strife and contention" [Jer. 15:10].

And although divine inspiration must certainly have been sweet to those ancient prophets, yet the irksomeness of that truth which they brought was so unpleasant to them, that everywhere they call it a burden. Yea that mysterious book of Revelation which the great evangelist was bid to eat, as it had been some eye-brightening electuary[8] of knowledge and foresight, though it were sweet in his mouth and in the learning, it was bitter in his belly, bitter in the denouncing.[9] Nor was this hid from the wise poet Sophocles, who in that place of his tragedy where Tiresias is called to resolve King Oedipus in a matter which he knew would be grievous, brings him in bemoaning his lot, that he knew more than other men.[10] For surely to every good and peaceable man it must in nature needs be a hateful thing to be the displeaser and molester[11] of thousands; much better would it like him doubtless to be the messenger of gladness and contentment, which is his chief intended business to all mankind, but that they resist and oppose their own true happiness.

But when God commands to take the trumpet and blow a dolorous or a jarring blast, it lies not in man's will what he shall say or what he shall conceal. If he shall think to be silent, as Jeremiah did because of the reproach and derision he met with daily, and "all his familiar friends watched for his halting," to be revenged on him for speaking the truth, he would be forced to confess as he confessed, "his word was in my heart as a burning fire shut up in my bones; I was weary with forbearing, and could not stay" [Jer. 20:8-10]. Which might teach these times not suddenly to condemn all things that are sharply spoken or vehemently written as proceeding out of stomach,[12] virulence, and ill nature, but to consider rather that if the prelates have leave to say the worst that can be said and do the worst that can be done, while they strive to keep to themselves to their great pleasure and commodity those things which they ought to render up, no man can be justly offended with him that shall endeavor to impart and bestow, without any gain to himself, those sharp but saving words which would be a terror and a torment in him to keep back. For me, I have determined to lay up as the best treasure and solace of a good old age, if God vouchsafe it me, the honest liberty of free speech from my youth, where I shall think it available in so dear a concernment as the church's good. For if I be either by disposition, or what other cause too inquisitive or suspicious of myself and mine own doings, who can help it?

7. Matt. 10.34: "I come not to bring peace, but a sword."
8. **electuary:** medicine mixed with syrup or honey.
9. **denouncing:** proclaiming; in Rev. 10.9, John is told by an angel to eat a scroll that "shall make thy belly bitter, but it shall be in thy mouth sweet as honey."
10. In *Oedipus the King, Tiresias* must tell *Oedipus* that he has killed his father and married his mother.
11. **molester:** disturber.
12. **stomach:** angry pride.

But this I foresee, that should the church be brought under heavy oppression, and God have given me ability the while to reason against that man that should be the author of so foul a deed, or should she by blessing from above on the industry and courage of faithful men change this her distracted estate into better days without the least furtherance or contribution of those few talents[13] which God at that present had lent me, I foresee what stories I should hear within myself, all my life after, of discourage and reproach: "Timorous and ingrateful, the church of God is now again at the foot of her insulting enemies, and thou bewailest; what matters it for thee or thy bewailing? When time was, thou couldst not find a syllable of all that thou hadst read or studied, to utter in her behalf. Yet ease and leisure was given thee for thy retired thoughts out of the sweat of other men. Thou hadst the diligence, the parts, the language of a man if a vain subject were to be adorned or beautified, but when the cause of God and his church was to be pleaded, for which purpose that tongue was given thee which thou hast, God listened if he could hear thy voice among his zealous servants, but thou wert dumb as a beast; from henceforward be that which thine own brutish silence hath made thee." Or else I should have heard on the other ear: "Slothful, and ever to be set light by, the church hath now overcome her late distresses after the unwearied labors of many her true servants that stood up in her defense; thou also wouldst take upon thee to share amongst them of their joy. But wherefore thou? Where canst thou show any word or deed of thine which might have hastened her peace? Whatever thou dost now talk, or write, or look is the alms of other men's active prudence and zeal. Dare not now to say or do anything better than thy former sloth and infancy,[14] or if thou darest, thou dost impudently to make a thrifty purchase of boldness to thyself out of the painful merits of other men. What before was thy sin, is now thy duty, to be abject and worthless." These, and such like lessons as these, I know would have been my matins duly and my evensong. But now by this little diligence, mark what a privilege I have gained with good men and saints, to claim my right of lamenting the tribulations of the church, if she should suffer, when others that have ventured nothing for her sake have not the honor to be admitted mourners. But if she lift up her drooping head and prosper among those that have something more than wished her welfare I have my charter and freehold[15] of rejoicing to me and my heirs.

Concerning therefore this wayward[16] subject against prelaty, the touching whereof is so distasteful and disquietous to a number of men, as by what hath been said I may deserve of charitable readers to be credited that neither envy nor gall hath entered me upon this controversy, but the enforcement of conscience only and a preventive fear lest the omitting of this duty should be

13. See note 3.
14. **infancy:** speechlessness.
15. **charter and freehold:** i.e., unchallengeable right.
16. **wayward:** troublesome, likely to be offensive.

against me when I would store up to myself the good provision of peaceful hours; so lest it should be still imputed to me, as I have found it hath been, that some self-pleasing humor of vainglory hath incited me to contest with men of high estimation, now while green years are upon my head, from this needless surmisal I shall hope to dissuade the intelligent and equal[17] auditor, if I can but say successfully that which in this exigent[18] behooves me, although I would be heard only, if it might be, by the elegant and learned reader, to whom principally for a while I shall beg leave I may address myself. To him it will be no new thing though I tell him that if I hunted after praise by the ostentation of wit and learning, I should not write thus out of mine own season, when I have neither yet completed to my mind the full circle of my private studies, although I complain not of any insufficiency to the matter in hand; or were I ready to my wishes, it were a folly to commit anything elaborately composed to the careless and interrupted listening of these tumultuous times. Next, if I were wise only to mine own ends, I would certainly take such a subject as of itself might catch applause, whereas this hath all the disadvantages on the contrary, and such a subject as the publishing whereof might be delayed at pleasure, and time enough to pencil it over with all the curious[19] touches of art, even to the perfection of a faultless picture, whenas in this argument the not deferring is of great moment to the good speeding, that if solidity have leisure to do her office, art cannot have much. Lastly, I should not choose this manner of writing, wherein knowing myself inferior to myself, led by the genial power of nature to another task, I have the use, as I may account it, but of my left hand. And though I shall be foolish in saying more to this purpose, yet since it will be such a folly as wisest men going about to commit have only confessed and so committed, I may trust with more reason, because with more folly, to have courteous pardon. For although a poet soaring in the high region of his fancies[20] with his garland and singing robes about him might without apology speak more of himself than I mean to do, yet for me sitting here below in the cool element of prose, a mortal thing among many readers of no empyreal conceit,[21] to venture and divulge unusual things of myself, I shall petition to the gentler sort it may not be envy to me.

I must say, therefore, that after I had from my first years by the ceaseless diligence and care of my father, whom God recompense, been exercised to the tongues and some sciences[22] as my age would suffer,[23] by sundry masters and teachers both at home and at the schools, it was found that whether aught was

17. **equal:** impartial.
18. **exigent:** pressing circumstance.
19. **curious:** elegant.
20. **fancies:** imagination.
21. **of no empyreal conceit:** lacking sublime ideas; see *PL* 7.14.
22. **some sciences:** As a child Milton learned Latin, Greek, French, Italian, and Hebrew (see *To His Father* 79–85); by *sciences,* he means useful bodies of knowledge other than languages.
23. **suffer:** allow.

imposed me by them that had the overlooking, or betaken to of mine own choice in English or other tongue, prosing or versing, but chiefly this latter, the style, by certain vital signs it had, was likely to live. But much latelier in the private academies of Italy, whither I was favored to resort, perceiving that some trifles which I had in memory, composed at under twenty or thereabout (for the manner is that everyone must give some proof of his wit and reading there), met with acceptance above what was looked for, and other things, which I had shifted in scarcity of books and conveniences to patch up amongst them, were received with written encomiums, which the Italian is not forward to bestow on men of this side the Alps; I began thus far to assent both to them and divers of my friends here at home, and not less to an inward prompting which now grew daily upon me, that by labor and intent study (which I take to be my portion in this life) joined with the strong propensity of nature, I might perhaps leave something so written to aftertimes, as they should not willingly let it die. These thoughts at once possessed me and these other: that if I were certain to write as men buy leases, for three lives and downward, there ought no regard be sooner had than to God's glory, by the honor and instruction of my country.

For which cause, and not only for that I knew it would be hard to arrive at the second rank among the Latins, I applied myself to that resolution which Ariosto followed against the persuasions of Bembo,[24] to fix all the industry and art I could unite to the adorning of my native tongue; not to make verbal curiosities the end, that were a toilsome vanity, but to be an interpreter and relater of the best and sagest things among mine own citizens throughout this island in the mother dialect. That what the greatest and choicest wits of Athens, Rome, or modern Italy, and those Hebrews of old did for their country, I, in my proportion, with this over and above of being a Christian, might do for mine: not caring to be once named abroad, though perhaps I could attain to that, but content with these British islands as my world, whose fortune hath hitherto been, that if the Athenians, as some say, made their small deeds great and renowned by their eloquent writers, England hath had her noble achievements made small by the unskillful handling of monks and mechanics.[25]

Time serves not now,[26] and perhaps I might seem too profuse to give any certain account of what the mind at home in the spacious circuits of her musing hath liberty to propose to herself, though of highest hope and hardest attempting, whether that epic form whereof the two poems of Homer and those other two of Virgil and Tasso are a diffuse, and the book of Job a brief model;[27] or whether the rules of Aristotle herein are strictly to be kept, or nature to be

24. Ludovico *Ariosto,* sixteenth-century author of the *Orlando Furioso,* resisted the classicist Pietro *Bembo's* urging that he write in Latin rather than Italian.

25. **mechanics:** illiterate laborers, used figuratively for the medieval monks who chronicled British history.

26. **Time serves not now:** "There is not time now," or "Now is not the time."

27. Torquato Tasso's sixteenth-century *Geruselemme Liberata* echoed Vergil's and Homer's epics in form, and in devotion to a single action. The Book of Job was read in Milton's time as a brief epic.

followed, which in them that know art and use judgment is no transgression, but an enriching of art.[28] And lastly what king or knight before the conquest might be chosen in whom to lay the pattern of a Christian hero.[29] And as Tasso gave to a prince of Italy[30] his choice whether he would command him to write of Godfrey's expedition against the infidels, or Belisarius against the Goths, or Charlemagne against the Lombards, if to the instinct of nature and the emboldening of art aught may be trusted, and that there be nothing adverse in our climate[31] or the fate of this age, it haply would be no rashness from an equal diligence and inclination to present the like offer in our own ancient stories. Or whether those dramatic constitutions, wherein Sophocles and Euripides reign, shall be found more doctrinal and exemplary to a nation, the scripture also affords us a divine pastoral drama in the Song of Solomon consisting of two persons and a double chorus, as Origen rightly judges.[32] And the apocalypse of Saint John is the majestic image of a high and stately tragedy, shutting up and intermingling her solemn scenes and acts with a sevenfold chorus of hallelujahs and harping symphonies: and this my opinion the grave authority of Pareus commenting that book is sufficient to confirm. Or if occasion shall lead to imitate those magnificent odes and hymns wherein Pindarus and Callimachus[33] are in most things worthy, some others in their frame judicious, in their matter most an end[34] faulty. But those frequent songs throughout the law and prophets beyond all these, not in their divine argument alone, but in the very critical art of composition, may be easily made appear over all the kinds of lyric poesy to be incomparable.

These abilities, wheresoever they be found, are the inspired gift of God rarely bestowed, but yet to some (though most abuse) in every nation; and are of power beside the office of a pulpit to inbreed and cherish in a great people the seeds of virtue and public civility, to allay the perturbations of the mind and set the affections in right tune, to celebrate in glorious and lofty hymns the throne and equipage of God's almightiness and what he works and what he suffers to be wrought with high providence in his church, to sing the victorious agonies of martyrs and saints, the deeds and triumphs of just and pious nations doing valiantly through faith against the enemies of Christ, to deplore the general relapses of kingdoms and states from justice and God's true worship. Lastly, whatsoever in religion is holy and sublime, in virtue amiable or grave, whatsoever hath passion or admiration in all the changes of that which is called

28. Milton alludes to a vigorous Italian critical debate concerning the rule of epic form, with some favoring Tasso's Vergilian epic following Aristotle's rules (*Poetics* 26) and others defending the multiple plot and interlaced form favored by Ariosto, a model to which Spenser's *Faerie Queene* is indebted.
29. Milton years earlier had anticipated writing an epic of King Arthur (See *Manso* 80–84).
30. **prince of Italy:** Alfonso II, Duke of Ferrara.
31. Milton wonders in *PL* 9.44–46 if an epic can be written in England's damp, cold climate.
32. In his *Prologue to the Song of Songs,* cited by David Paraeus.
33. **Pindarus and Callimachus:** Pindar is famous for his odes, and Callimachus for his hymns.
34. **an end:** in the end.

fortune from without, or the wily subtleties and refluxes of man's thoughts from within, all these things with a solid and treatable smoothness to paint out and describe. Teaching over the whole book of sanctity and virtue through all the instances of example with such delight, to those especially of soft and delicious[35] temper, who will not so much as look upon Truth herself unless they see her elegantly dressed, that whereas the paths of honesty and good life appear now rugged and difficult, though they be indeed easy and pleasant, they would then appear to all men both easy and pleasant though they were rugged and difficult indeed.[36] And what a benefit this would be to our youth and gentry may be soon guessed by what we know of the corruption and bane which they suck in daily from the writings and interludes of libidinous and ignorant poetasters, who having scarce ever heard of that which is the main consistence of a true poem, the choice of such persons as they ought to introduce, and what is moral and decent to each one, do for the most part lap up vicious principles in sweet pills to be swallowed down, and make the taste of virtuous documents harsh and sour.

But because the spirit of man cannot demean itself lively in this body without some recreating intermission of labor and serious things, it were happy for the commonwealth if our magistrates, as in those famous governments of old, would take into their care, not only the deciding of our contentious law cases and brawls, but the managing of our public sports and festival pastimes, that they might be, not such as were authorized a while since, the provocations of drunkenness and lust,[37] but such as may inure and harden our bodies by martial exercises to all warlike skill and performance, and may civilize, adorn, and make discreet our minds by the learned and affable meeting of frequent academies, and the procurement of wise and artful recitations sweetened with eloquent and graceful enticements to the love and practice of justice, temperance, and fortitude, instructing and bettering the nation at all opportunities, that the call of wisdom and virtue may be heard everywhere, as Solomon saith, "she crieth without, she uttereth her voice in the streets, in the top of high places, in the chief concourse, and in the openings of the gates" [Prov. 1:20-21, 8:2-3]. Whether this may not be not only in pulpits but after another persuasive method, at set and solemn panegyries,[38] in theaters, porches,[39] or what other place or way may win most upon the people to receive at once both recreation and instruction, let them in authority consult.

35. **delicious:** sensuous.

36. Following Sidney's *Defense of Poetry* and his Italian predecessors, Milton voices a Renaissance critical commonplace, that poets can teach virtue by means of attractive examples.

37. Milton glances disapprovingly at the 1633 *Book of Sports,* by which Charles I promoted games, sports, and dancing on Sundays. As in *Of Education,* he proposes instead martial exercises and attendance at the kinds of literary and scientific academies he visited in Italy.

38. **panegyries:** religious festivals.

39. **porches:** church entranceways; medieval English drama originated in liturgical plays on church porches.

The thing which I had to say, and those intentions which have lived within me ever since I could conceive myself anything worth to my country, I return to crave excuse that urgent reason hath plucked from me by an abortive and foredated discovery.[40] And the accomplishment of them lies not but in a power above man's to promise; but that none hath by more studious ways endeavored, and with more unwearied spirit that none shall, that I dare almost aver of myself as far as life and free leisure will extend; and that the land had once enfranchised herself from this impertinent yoke of prelaty, under whose inquisitorious and tyrannical duncery no free and splendid wit can flourish. Neither do I think it shame to covenant with any knowing reader, that for some few years yet I may go on trust with him toward the payment of what I am now indebted, as being a work not to be raised from the heat of youth or the vapors of wine, like that which flows at waste from the pen[41] of some vulgar amorist or the trencher fury of a rhyming parasite, nor to be obtained by the invocation of Dame Memory and her siren daughters, but by devout prayer to that eternal Spirit who can enrich with all utterance and knowledge, and sends out his seraphim with the hallowed fire of his altar to touch and purify the lips of whom he pleases.[42] To this must be added industrious and select reading, steady observation, insight into all seemly and generous arts and affairs, till which in some measure be compassed, at mine own peril and cost I refuse not to sustain this expectation from as many as are not loath to hazard so much credulity upon the best pledges that I can give them.

Although it nothing content me to have disclosed thus much beforehand, but that I trust hereby to make it manifest with what small willingness I endure to interrupt the pursuit of no less hopes than these, and leave a calm and pleasing solitariness fed with cheerful and confident thoughts, to embark in a troubled sea of noises and hoarse disputes, put from beholding the bright countenance of truth in the quiet and still air of delightful studies to come into the dim reflection of hollow antiquities sold by the seeming bulk, and there be fain to club[43] quotations with men whose learning and belief lies in marginal stuffings, who when they have like good sumpters[44] laid ye down their horseload of citations and fathers at your door, with a rhapsody of who and who were bishops here or there, ye may take off their packsaddles, their day's work is done, and episcopacy, as they think, stoutly vindicated. Let any gentle apprehension that can distinguish learned pains from unlearned drudgery imagine what pleasure or profoundness can be in this, or what honor to deal against such adversaries. But were it the meanest under-service, if God by his secretary con-

40. **abortive and foredated discovery:** premature disclosure; Milton indicated earlier that he did not intend to discuss himself (see note 26).

41. For this double entendre Milton may be indebted to Shakespeare's *Sonnet 129* ("The expense of spirit in a waste of shame").

42. Isa. 6.6–7.

43. **club:** collect and trade.

44. **sumpters:** packhorse drivers.

science enjoin it, it were sad for me if I should draw back, for me especially, now when all men offer their aid to help ease and lighten the difficult labors of the church, to whose service by the intentions of my parents and friends I was destined of a child, and in mine own resolutions; till coming to some maturity of years and perceiving what tyranny had invaded the church, that he who would take orders must subscribe slave, and take an oath withal, which unless he took with a conscience that would retch, he must either straight perjure or split his faith, I thought it better to prefer a blameless silence before the sacred office of speaking bought and begun with servitude and forswearing. Howsoever, thus church-outed by the prelates,[45] hence may appear the right I have to meddle in these matters, as before the necessity and constraint appeared.

45. Because of his opposition to Archbishop William Laud and to the institution of episcopacy, Milton found himself unable in conscience to become a minister of the Church of England, the expected end of his Cambridge education.

A Selection from

AN APOLOGY FOR SMECTYMNUUS

The full title of Milton's final antiprelatical pamphlet, *An Apology against a Pamphlet Called A Modest Confutation of the Animadversions upon the Remonstrant against Smectymnuus,* tells us something about how the pamphlet wars unfolded, in a tangled skein of argument, reply, and ad hominem attack. The odd name "Smectymnuus" is composed of the initials of five Puritans—Stephen Marshall, Edmund Calamy, Thomas Young (Milton's childhood tutor), Matthew Newcomen, and William Spurstow—who a year earlier (March 1641) had attacked Bishop Joseph Hall's *Humble Remonstrance,* a moderate defense of episcopacy. Hall replied with *A Defence of the Humble Remonstrance, against . . . Smectymnuus* (April 1641), a work that Milton savaged in his anonymous *Animadversions* (July 1641). Late that year or early in the next appeared an anonymous reply, *A Modest Confutation of a Slanderous and Scurrilous Libell, Entituled, Animadversions,* which returned Milton's personal attacks, though with considerably less savagery. Milton, stung nevertheless, responded in *An Apology for Smectymnuus* (April 1642) with a bitter attack on Hall and his son Robert, whom he assumed, perhaps correctly, to be the authors of the *Confutation.* Like *The Reason of Church Government, An Apology* is now read most often for Milton's autobiographical portrait. Its greater emphasis on his ethical development and the virtuous tenor of his daily life derives from a perceived need to counter the confuter's personal attack. Milton emphasizes the chastity that he regarded as an essential and enabling virtue of the true Christian poet and asserts memorably that one wishing, like himself, to be a great poet "ought himself to be a true poem" (p. 850).

Our selection is based on the copy of the first edition in the Huntington Library (105698).

Thus having spent his first onset not in confuting but in a reasonless defaming of the book, the method of his malice hurries him[1] to attempt the like against the author;[2] not by proofs and testimonies, but "having no certain notice of me," as he professes, "further than what he gathers from the *Animadversions,*" blunders

1. **him:** the author of *A Modest Confutation,* whom Milton assumed to be Bishop Joseph Hall or his son.
2. **the author:** Milton.

at me for the rest and flings out stray crimes at a venture, which he could never, though he be a serpent, suck from anything that I have written, but from his own stuffed magazine[3] and hoard of slanderous inventions, over and above that which he converted to venom in the drawing. To me, readers, it happens as a singular contentment, and let it be to good men no slight satisfaction, that the slanderer here confesses he has "no further notice of me than his own conjecture." Although it had been honest to have inquired before he uttered such infamous words, and I am credibly informed he did inquire, but finding small comfort from the intelligence which he received, whereon to ground the falsities which he had provided, thought it is his likeliest course under a pretended ignorance to let drive at random, lest he should lose his odd ends which from some penurious Book of Characters[4] he had been culling out and would fain apply. Not caring to burden me with those vices whereof, among whom my conversation hath been, I have been ever least suspected; perhaps not without some subtlety to cast me into envy by bringing on me a necessity to enter into mine own praises. In which argument I know every wise man is more unwillingly drawn to speak than the most repining ear can be averse to hear.

Nevertheless, since I dare not wish to pass this life unpersecuted of slanderous tongues, for God hath told us that to be generally praised is woeful,[5] I shall rely on his promise to free the innocent from causeless aspersions.[6] Whereof nothing sooner can assure me than if I shall feel him now assisting me in the just vindication of myself, which yet I could defer, it being more meet that to those other matters of public debatement in this book I should give attendance first, but that I fear it would but harm the truth for me to reason in her behalf, so long as I should suffer my honest estimation to lie unpurged from these insolent suspicions. And if I shall be large or unwonted in justifying myself to those who know me not, for else it would be needless, let them consider that a short slander will ofttimes reach farther than a long apology; and that he who will do justly to all men, must begin from knowing how, if it so happen, to be not unjust to himself.

I must be thought, if this libeler (for now he shows himself to be so) can find belief, after an inordinate and riotous youth spent at the university, to have been at length "vomited out thence."[7] For which commodious lie, that he may be encouraged in the trade another time, I thank him; for it hath given me an apt occasion to acknowledge publicly with all grateful mind that more than ordinary favor and respect which I found above any of my equals[8] at the hands of those courteous and learned men, the fellows of that college wherein I spent

3. **magazine:** storehouse.
4. **Book of Characters:** Joseph Hall's 1608 *Characters of Virtues and Vices,* an example of the popular genre of witty character sketches, established his literary reputation.
5. Luke 6.26.
6. Matt. 5.11–12.
7. The confuter apparently refers to Milton's rustication (or suspension) from Cambridge in 1626. See *Elegy 1* for Milton's contemporary version of the episode.
8. **equals:** fellow students.

some years: who at my parting, after I had taken two degrees, as the manner is, signified many ways how much better it would content them that I would stay; as by many letters full of kindness and loving respect, both before that time and long after, I was assured of their singular good affection towards me. Which being likewise propense[9] to all such as were for their studious and civil life worthy of esteem, I could not wrong their judgments and upright intentions so much as to think I had that regard from them for other cause than that I might be still encouraged to proceed in the honest and laudable courses of which they apprehended I had given good proof. And to those ingenuous and friendly men who were ever the countenancers of virtuous and hopeful wits, I wish the best and happiest things that friends in absence wish one to another. As for the common approbation or dislike of that place as now it is, that I should esteem or disesteem myself or any other the more for that, too simple and too credulous is the confuter, if he think to obtain with me or any right discerner. Of small practice were that physician who could not judge by what both she or her sister[10] hath of long time vomited, that the worser stuff she strongly keeps in her stomach, but the better she is ever kecking[11] at, and is queasy. She vomits now out of sickness, but ere it be well with her she must vomit by strong physic.

In the meanwhile that "suburb sink,"[12] as this rude scavenger calls it (and more than scurrilously taunts it with the "plague," having a worse plague in his middle entrail), that suburb wherein I dwell shall be in my account a more honorable place than his university; which, as in the time of her better health and mine own younger judgment, I never greatly admired, so now much less. But he follows me to the city, still usurping[13] and forging beyond his book notice, which only he affirms to have had, "and where my morning haunts are he wisses[14] not." 'Tis wonder that, being so rare an alchemist of slander, he could not extract that as well as the university vomit and the suburb sink which his art could distill so cunningly, but because his limbec[15] fails him, to give him and envy the more vexation, I'll tell him. Those morning haunts are where they should be, at home, not sleeping or concocting[16] the surfeits of an irregular feast, but up and stirring—in winter often ere the sound of any bell awake men to labor or to devotion, in summer as oft with the bird that first rouses or not too much tardier—to read good authors, or cause them to be read, till the attention be weary or memory have his full fraught: then, with useful and generous labors preserving the body's health and hardiness, to render lightsome, clear, and not lumpish obedience to the mind, to the cause of religion, and our country's liberty, when it shall

9. **propense:** inclined.
10. **her sister:** Oxford.
11. **kecking:** retching.
12. **sink:** cesspool; the confuter accused Milton of visiting brothels in London suburbs.
13. **usurping:** going beyond his evidence.
14. **wisses:** knows.
15. **limbec:** an alembic, an alchemist's distilling device.
16. **concocting:** digesting.

require firm hearts in sound bodies to stand and cover their stations, rather than to see the ruin of our protestation[17] and the enforcement of a slavish life.

These are the morning practices. Proceed now to the afternoon: "in playhouses," he says, "and the bordellos." Your intelligence, unfaithful spy of Canaan?[18] He gives in his evidence, that "there he hath traced me." Take him at his word, readers, but let him bring good sureties ere ye dismiss him, that while he pretended to dog others, he did not turn in for his own pleasure. For so much in effect he concludes against himself, not contented to be caught in every other gin,[19] but he must be such a novice as to be still hampered in his own hemp. In the *Animadversions,*[20] saith he, I find the mention of old cloaks, false beards, nightwalkers, and salt lotion, therefore, the animadverter haunts playhouses and bordellos, for if he did not, how could he speak of such gear? Now that he may know what it is to be a child, and yet to meddle with edged tools, I turn his antistrophon[21] upon his own head; the confuter knows that these things are the furniture of playhouses and bordellos, therefore by the same reason the *confuter himself hath been traced in those places.* Was it such a dissolute speech, telling of some politicians who were wont to eavesdrop in disguises, to say they were often liable to a night-walking cudgeller, or the emptying of a urinal? What if I had writ as your friend the author of the aforesaid mime, *Mundus alter et idem,*[22] to have been ravished like some young Cephalus or Hylas by a troop of camping housewives in Viraginea, and that he was there forced to swear himself an uxorious varlet, then after a long servitude to have come into Aphrodisia, that pleasant country that gave such a sweet smell to his nostrils among the shameless courtesans of Desvergonia?[23] Surely he would have then concluded me as constant at the bordello as the galley-slave at his oar.

But since there is such necessity to the hearsay of a tire,[24] a periwig, or a vizard,[25] that plays must have been seen, what difficulty was there in that, when in the colleges so many of the young divines, and those in next aptitude to divinity, have been seen so oft upon the stage writhing and unboning their clergy limbs to all the antic and dishonest gestures of Trinculos,[26] buffoons, and bawds, prostituting the shame of that ministry which either they had, or were nigh

17. **protestation:** In the Protestation of May 3, 1641, the House of Commons affirmed English opposition to Roman Catholicism and reasserted English rights and liberties.
18. Returning from *Canaan,* Moses' spies "made all the congregation to murmur against him, by bringing up a slander upon the land" (Num. 14.36).
19. **gin:** trap.
20. ***Animadversions:*** Milton's earlier antiprelatical tract, attacked in *A Modest Confutation.*
21. **antistrophon:** a rhetorical figure turning an opponent's argument against him.
22. Earlier in *An Apology,* Milton ridiculed Joseph Hall's *Mundus alter et idem* as inept and frivolous.
23. *Cephalus* was taken from his wife by Aurora (Ovid, *Met.* 7.700–713); *Hylas* was seized by Hercules (Theocritus, *Idyll 13*). *Viraginea, Aphrodisia,* and *Desvergonia* are countries in Hall's imagined world, the homes respectively of viragos, erotic love, and licentiousness.
24. **tire:** costume.
25. **vizard:** mask.
26. **Trinculos:** either the character from *The Tempest* or a clown in *Albumazar,* a 1615 Cambridge University play by Thomas Tomkys.

having, to the eyes of courtiers and court ladies with their grooms and mademoiselles? There, while they acted and overacted, among other young scholars I was a spectator. They thought themselves gallant men, and I thought them fools; they made sport, and I laughed; they mispronounced, and I misliked; and, to make up the *atticism*,[27] they were out, and I hissed. Judge now whether so many good textmen were not sufficient to instruct me of false beards and vizards without more expositors. And how can this confuter take the face to object to me the seeing of that which his reverent prelates allow, and incite their young disciples to act? For if it be unlawful[28] to sit and behold a mercenary comedian personating that which is least unseemly for a hireling to do, how much more blameful is it to endure the sight of as vile things acted by persons either entered, or presently to enter into the ministry, and how much more foul and ignominious for them to be the actors?

But because, as well by this upbraiding to me the bordellos as by other suspicious glancings in his book, he would seem privily to point me out to his readers as one whose custom of life were not honest but licentious, I shall entreat to be borne with though I digress, and in a way not often trod acquaint ye with the sum of my thoughts in this matter through the course of my years and studies, although I am not ignorant how hazardous it will be to do this under the nose of the envious, as it were in skirmish to change the compact order and instead of outward actions to bring inmost thoughts into front. And I must tell ye, readers, that by this sort of men I have been already bitten at. Yet shall they not for me know how slightly they are esteemed, unless they have so much learning as to read what in Greek Ἀπειροκαλία[29] is, which, together with envy, is the common disease of those who censure books that are not for their reading. With me it fares now as with him whose outward garment hath been injured and ill bedighted; for having no other shift, what help but to turn the inside outwards, especially if the lining be of the same or, as it is sometimes, much better? So if my name and outward demeanor be not evident enough to defend me, I must make trial if the discovery of my inmost thoughts can. Wherein of two purposes both honest and both sincere, the one perhaps I shall not miss; although I fail to gain belief with others of being such as my perpetual thoughts shall here disclose me, I may yet not fail of success in persuading some to be such really themselves, as they cannot believe me to be more than what I fain.

I had my time, readers, as other have who have good learning bestowed upon them, to be sent to those places where, the opinion was, it might be soonest attained: and as the manner is, was not unstudied in those authors which are most commended. Whereof some were grave orators and historians, whose matter methought I loved indeed, but as my age then was, so I understood them;

27. ***atticism:*** a well-turned phrase.
28. Several months later, in September 1642, Parliament closed the theaters.
29. Ἀπειροκαλία: bad taste that leads to immoral conduct (the term is used in Plato's *Republic* 403c and 405b).

others were the smooth elegiac poets, whereof the schools are not scarce, whom both for the pleasing sound of their numerous[30] writing, which in imitation I found most easy and most agreeable to nature's part in me, and for their matter, which what it is there be few who know not, I was so allured to read that no recreation came to me better welcome. For that it was then those years with me which are excused though they be least severe, I may be saved the labor to remember ye. Whence having observed them to account it the chief glory of their wit, in that they were ablest to judge, to praise, and by that could esteem themselves worthiest to love those high perfections which under one or other name they took to celebrate, I thought with myself by every instinct and presage of nature, which is not wont to be false, that what emboldened them to this task might with such diligence as they used embolden me, and that what judgment, wit, or elegance was my share, would herein best appear, and best value itself, by how much more wisely and with more love of virtue I should choose (let rude ears be absent) the object of not unlike praises. For albeit these thoughts to some will seem virtuous and commendable, to others only pardonable, to a third sort perhaps idle, yet the mentioning of them now will end in serious.[31]

Nor blame it, readers, in those years to propose to themselves such a reward as the noblest dispositions above other things in this life have sometimes preferred—whereof not to be sensible when good and fair in one person meet, argues both a gross and shallow judgment, and withal[32] an ungentle and swainish[33] breast. For by the firm settling of these persuasions I became, to my best memory, so much a proficient that, if I found those authors anywhere speaking unworthy things of themselves or unchaste of those names which before they had extolled, this effect it wrought with me, from that time forward their art I still applauded, but the men I deplored; and above them all preferred the two famous renowners of Beatrice and Laura,[34] who never write but honor of them to whom they devote their verse, displaying sublime and pure thoughts without transgression. And long it was not after when I was confirmed in this opinion, that he who would not be frustrate of his hope to write well hereafter in laudable things ought himself to be a true poem, that is, a composition and pattern of the best and honorablest things—not presuming to sing high praises of heroic men or famous cities, unless he have in himself the experience and the practice of all that which is praiseworthy. These reasonings, together with a certain niceness of nature, an honest haughtiness, and self-esteem either of what I was or what I might be (which let envy call pride), and lastly that modesty whereof, though not in the title page, yet here I may be excused to make some beseeming profession, all these uniting the supply of their natural aid together,

30. **numerous:** metrical.
31. **will end in serious:** The meaning is unclear; the text may be corrupt.
32. **withal:** in addition.
33. **swainish:** low-bred.
34. Dante and Petrarch.

kept me still above those low descents of mind beneath which he must deject and plunge himself that can agree to saleable and unlawful prostitutions.

Next (for hear me out now readers), that I may tell ye whither[35] my younger feet wandered, I betook me among those lofty fables and romances, which recount in solemn cantos the deeds of knighthood founded by our victorious kings, and from hence had in renown over all Christendom.[36] There I read it in the oath of every knight that he should defend to the expense of his best blood, or of his life if it so befell him, the honor and chastity of virgin or matron. From whence even then I learnt what a noble virtue chastity sure must be, to the defense of which so many worthies by such a dear[37] adventure of themselves had sworn. And if I found in the story afterward any of them by word or deed breaking that oath, I judged it the same fault of the poet as that which is attributed to Homer, to have written indecent things of the gods.[38] Only this my mind gave me, that every free and gentle spirit, without that oath, ought to be born a knight, nor needed to expect the gilt spur or the laying of a sword upon his shoulder to stir him up both by his counsel and his arm to secure and protect the weakness of any attempted chastity. So that even those books which to many others have been the fuel of wantonness and loose living (I cannot think how, unless by divine indulgence) proved to me so many incitements, as you have heard, to the love and steadfast observation of that virtue which abhors the society of bordellos.

Thus, from the laureate fraternity of poets, riper years and the ceaseless round of study and reading led me to the shady spaces of philosophy, but chiefly to the divine volumes of Plato and his equal Xenophon.[39] Where, if I should tell ye what I learnt of chastity and love (I mean that which is truly so, whose charming cup is only virtue which she bears in her hand to those who are worthy—the rest are cheated with a thick intoxicating potion which a certain sorceress,[40] the abuser of love's name, carries about) and how the first and chiefest office of love begins and ends in the soul, producing those happy twins of her divine generation, knowledge and virtue, with such abstracted sublimities as these, it might be worth your listening, readers, as I may one day hope to have ye in a still time, when there shall be no chiding; not in these noises, the adversary, as ye know, barking at the door or searching for me at the bordellos, where it may be he has lost himself, and raps up without pity the sage and rheumatic old prelatess with all her young Corinthian laity,[41] to inquire for such a one.

35. **whither:** the text reads "whether," which, aside from its usual meaning, was a variant spelling of "whither"; either meaning fits, but "whither" seems to be the primary sense.

36. Milton may refer to medieval romances such as Malory's *Morte d'Arthur* or to Spenser's *Faerie Queene*.

37. **dear:** costly, arduous.

38. The criticism is Plato's (*Rep.* 377e).

39. **equal:** contemporary; *Xenophon's Memorabilia* records Socrates' moral teachings.

40. **sorceress:** Circe, the mother of Milton's Comus, who also tempts with a *charming cup* (*Masque* 51, 525, 811–13).

41. **Corinthian laity:** prostitutes; the association of Corinth and prostitution is ancient.

Last of all, not in time, but as perfection is last, that care was ever had of me, with my earliest capacity, not to be negligently trained in the precepts of Christian religion. This that I have hitherto related hath been to show that though Christianity had been but slightly taught me, yet a certain reservedness of natural disposition and moral discipline learnt out of the noblest philosophy, was enough to keep me in disdain of far less incontinences than this of the bordello. But having had the doctrine of holy Scripture unfolding those chaste and high mysteries with timeliest care infused, that "the body is for the Lord and the Lord for the body" [1 Cor. 6.13], thus also I argued to myself: that if unchastity in a woman, whom Saint Paul terms the glory of man, be such a scandal and dishonor, then certainly in a man, who is both the image and glory of God, it must, though commonly not so thought, be much more deflowering and dishonorable—in that he sins both against his own body, which is the perfecter sex, and his own glory, which is in the woman, and that which is worst, against the image and glory of God, which is in himself.[42] Nor did I slumber over that place expressing such high rewards of ever accompanying the Lamb, with those celestial songs to others inapprehensible, but not to those who were not defiled with women,[43] which doubtless means fornication: for marriage must not be called a defilement.

Thus large I have purposely been, that if I have been justly taxed with this crime, it may come upon me after all this my confession with a tenfold shame.

42. "Man . . . is the image and glory of God: but the woman is the glory of the man" (1 Cor. 11.7); cp. *PL* 4.299 ("He for God only, she for God in him").

43. Rev. 14.1–5; cp. the end of *Epitaph for Damon.*

Introduction to Selections from *The Doctrine and Discipline of Divorce*

In August 1643, Milton published anonymously *The Doctrine and Discipline of Divorce: Restored to the Good of Both Sexes, from the bondage of Canon Law and other mistakes, to Christian freedom, guided by the Rule of Charity. Wherein also many places of Scripture have recovered their long-lost meaning. Seasonable to be now thought on in the Reformation intended.* Early in 1644, a greatly expanded second edition appeared with a new subtitle: *Restored to the good of both Sexes, From the bondage of Canon Law and other mistakes, to the true meaning of Scripture in the Law and Gospel compared. Wherein also are set down the bad consequences of abolishing or condemning of Sin, that which the Law of God allows, and Christ abolished not. Now the second time revised and much augmented. In Two Books: To the Parliament of* England *with the Assembly.* The second edition, from which our selections are taken, includes Milton's initials on the title page and his full name affixed to a new prefatory letter to Parliament and the Westminster Assembly.

The topic was timely for both political and personal reasons. Parliament, in its efforts to settle the English church after the toppling of episcopacy and its system of canon law, had requested advice from the overwhelmingly Presbyterian Westminster Assembly. Among the topics addressed by the Assembly were marriage and divorce. Milton at this time found himself unhappily married (or deserted rather). He had met and married Mary Powell, a woman half his age, in June or July 1642. After two mutually disappointing months, she had returned to her family in Oxfordshire, and Milton was not to see her again until 1645. While it is true, as his *Commonplace Book* reveals, that Milton had been revolving ideas about marriage and divorce before he married Mary, the shock and unhappiness of his marriage is palpable in the pages of the *Doctrine and Discipline* (see Turner 188–229; Patterson 1990; and Fallon 2000). Milton himself observes in the prefatory letter that, when approaching questions like marriage and divorce, "it is incredible how cold, how dull, and far from all fellow feeling we are, without the spur of self-concernment" (p. 860).

As in his antiprelatical tracts, Milton faults the English for lagging in reformation, in this case by retaining the restrictive canon law teaching according to which divorce was allowable only for adultery and nonconsummation. He argues for divorce on wider grounds of incompatibility, mental as well as corporeal, citing Deuteronomy 24.1–2, where Moses says a man may divorce a woman when "she find[s] no favor in his eyes, because he hath found some uncleanness in her," and Genesis 2.18, where God announces that "it is not good that man should be alone; I will make him an help meet for him."

Milton insists that he is not talking about divorce for trivial causes. As true marriage is an endlessly unfolding spiritual exchange, a bonding of souls and bodies, so divorce is permitted to set free individuals who cannot achieve this union. Some couples, because of the "faultless proprieties of nature" (p. 867) resulting from the Fall, cannot love, and therefore cannot remedy each other's loneliness. Indeed, intercourse with an unloved spouse intensifies rather than remedies that loneliness. Fornication, or Moses' "uncleanness," moreover, means for Milton not only or even especially sexual sin but "continual headstrong behavior as tends to plain contempt of the husband" (p. 909).

Milton reinterprets Christ's apparently clear prohibition of divorce except for adultery in Matthew 19:3–9 as a coded teaching aimed at hard-hearted and hypocritical Pharisees. Because the Mosaic authorization of divorce is not merely positive judicial law but part of the moral law, Christ could not have prohibited divorce without involving God in the contradiction of allowing and even encouraging the Jews to sin. The emphasis on the continuing relevance of the Mosaic moral law and its value as a guide to reading the Gospel marks a departure from the antiprelatical tracts, in which Milton bridled at his opponents' efforts to invoke Jewish ritual law as precedent and justification for episcopacy.

Milton naïvely anticipated that his argument would be welcomed by his audience, and that he would "be reckoned among the public benefactors of civil and human life; above the inventors of wine and oil" (p. 868). Instead, he found himself, as he added in the second edition, subject to "evil report" as "the sole advocate of a discountenanced truth" (p. 858). Herbert Palmer, who chaired the Assembly's committee on marriage and divorce, vilified the *Doctrine and Discipline* in an August 13, 1644, sermon to Parliament as "a wicked book . . . deserving to be burnt, whose author hath been so impudent as to set his name to it and dedicate it to yourselves." A new epigraph in the second edition bears witness to the storm of criticism that greeted Milton's defense: "He that answereth a matter before he heareth it, it is folly and shame unto him" (Prov. 18.13).

The *Doctrine and Discipline,* like his other major divorce tract, *Tetrachordon,* is a divided work. Milton on the one hand mounts an argument for divorce for mutually blameless incompatibility; on the other hand he lashes out at women for disappointing the spiritual hopes of men. He articulates an ideal of nearly egalitarian, companionate marriage, and at the same time he insists, following 1 Corinthians 11.3, that man is "the head of the other sex which was made for him." He holds out a vision of chaste, redeemed sexuality, and he describes copulation in the most degrading terms ("instead of being one flesh, they will be rather two carcasses chained unnaturally together or . . . a living soul bound to a dead corpse" [p. 903]). This last division, however, is only apparent, for it is precisely Milton's idealism about the marriage bond and married sexuality that makes the loveless copulation of an unfit couple so abhorrent.

The divisions in the tract, both real and apparent, arise from and illustrate the "spur of self-concernment." The *Doctrine and Discipline* is punctuated by third-person descriptions of the virtuous young man who, like Milton, has delayed sexual gratification only to be mistaken in his choice of a mate and robbed of divinely sanctioned corporeal and spiritual intimacy. In the antiprelatical tracts and in his early poems, Milton had constructed a self-image in which prophetic gifts and prospective literary greatness are tied to his unspotted virtue and specifically his chastity. Now he contemplates the possibility of alienation from God under the weight of an unhappy marriage, and in the nation's response to his arguments on divorce finds himself vilified as a libertine. Hoping for a helpmeet and an idealized marriage as offered by God in Genesis 2.18, Milton finds himself trapped in wedlock with a woman whom apparently he does not love and with whom as a result copulation is a grinding slavery rather than a "fountain" of "the pure influence of peace and love" arising from "the soul's lawful contentment" (p. 873). The *Doctrine and Discipline* embodies both an idealized hope and the bitterness of failed expectations.

One can read the traces of the *Doctrine and Discipline*'s wrestling with gender relations through *Paradise Lost* and beyond. The assertion of male superiority found in the epic and the first divorce tract, however, is the common coin of Milton's time (and of the Bible). Milton's signature contribution, a vision of marriage built around the spiritual conversation between man and woman, informs his portrayal of Adam and Eve at its deepest levels. The vision is lyrically expressed, significantly by Eve, in one of the loveliest speeches in the poem ("With thee conversing I forget all time" [4.639–56]).

Ultimately, Milton's hope that he would be counted, by virtue of his argument on divorce, among "public benefactors of civil and human life" was not entirely misplaced. His conception of marriage as a union of "fit conversing soul[s]" (p. 875) and (in his best and happiest moments) as a yoking of equals or near equals was ahead of its time (Halkett 1970). If we think that unhappily married couples should be able to divorce without demonstrating adultery or their inability to consummate marriage, then we have followed Milton where virtually none of his contemporaries was willing to go. As a theorist of marriage and divorce, Milton has drawn the sustained and admiring attention of one of America's leading contemporary philosophers, Stanley Cavell, who with the poet as his powerful if improbable guide traces through Hollywood comedies the linked fates of marriage and freedom.

Our text is based on the copy of the second edition in the British Library's Thomason Collection (E.31[5]).

Selections from

THE DOCTRINE AND DISCIPLINE OF DIVORCE

Matt. 13.52. Every scribe instructed to the kingdom of heaven is like the master of a house which bringeth out of his treasury things new and old.

Prov. 18.13. He that answereth a matter before he heareth it, it is folly and shame unto him.

TO THE PARLIAMENT OF ENGLAND, WITH THE ASSEMBLY.

If it were seriously asked (and it would be no untimely question, renowned Parliament, select Assembly) who of all teachers and masters that have ever taught hath drawn the most disciples after him, both in religion and in manners, it might be not untruly answered, custom.[1] Though virtue be commended for the most persuasive in her theory, and conscience in the plain demonstration of the spirit finds most evincing,[2] yet whether it be the secret of divine will or the original blindness[3] we are born in, so it happens for the most part that custom still is silently received for the best instructor. Except it be because her method is so glib and easy, in some manner like to that vision of Ezekiel,[4] rolling up her sudden book of implicit knowledge for him that will to take and swallow down at pleasure, which proving but of bad nourishment in the concoction,[5] as it was heedless in the devouring, puffs up unhealthily a certain big face of pretended learning mistaken among credulous men for the wholesome habit of soundness and good constitution, but is indeed no other than that sworn visage of counterfeit knowledge and literature, which not only in private mars our education, but

1. As in the *Tenure of Kings and Magistrates,* five years later, Milton begins with an attack on custom.
2. **evincing:** convincing.
3. **original blindness:** spiritual blindness resulting from Original Sin.
4. In Ezek. 3.1–3, the prophet consumes God's words in the form of a scroll; Milton, oddly, compares Ezekiel's roll to the false teaching of Custom. In *The Reason of Church Government,* Milton compares himself with St. John, who alludes to Ezekiel when describing in Revelation his own consumption of God's word in the form of a scroll: "though it were sweet in his mouth and in the learning, it was bitter in his belly, bitter in the denouncing" (p. 837).
5. **concoction:** digestion.

also in public is the common climber into every chair where either religion is preached or law reported; filling each estate of life and profession with abject and servile principles, depressing the high and heaven-born spirit of man far beneath the condition wherein either God created him or sin hath sunk him.[6]

To pursue the allegory, custom being but a mere face, as echo is a mere voice, rests not in her unaccomplishment until by secret inclination she accorporate[7] herself with error, who being a blind and serpentine body[8] without a head willingly accepts what he wants and supplies what her incompleteness went seeking. Hence it is that error supports custom, custom countenances error. And these two between them would persecute and chase away all truth and solid wisdom out of humane life, were it not that God, rather than man, once in many ages calls together the prudent and religious counsels of men deputed to repress the encroachments and to work off the inveterate blots and obscurities wrought upon our minds by the subtle insinuating of error and custom: who, with the numerous and vulgar train of their followers, make it their chief design to envy and cry down the industry of free reasoning under the terms of humor[9] and innovation,[10] as if the womb of teeming truth were to be closed up if she presume to bring forth aught that sorts not with their unchewed notions and suppositions. Against which notorious injury and abuse of man's free soul to testify and oppose the utmost that study and true labor can attain, heretofore the incitement of men reputed grave hath led me among others. And now the duty and the right of an instructed Christian calls me through the chance of good or evil report, to be the sole advocate of a discountenanced truth:[11] a high enterprise, Lords and Commons, a high enterprise and a hard, and such as every seventh son of a seventh son[12] does not venture on.

Nor have I amidst the clamor of so much envy and impertinence whither to appeal, but to the concourse of so much piety and wisdom here assembled. Bringing in my hands an ancient and most necessary, most charitable, and yet most injured statute of Moses[13]: not repealed ever by him who only had the authority,[14] but thrown aside with much inconsiderate neglect under the rubbish of canonical ignorance, as once the whole law was by some such like con-

6. Milton suggests that, by blindly following custom, we bring ourselves lower than we have been brought by Original Sin, thus implying, as he argues in *Christian Doctrine* (1.7), that the human race is not wholly depraved after the Fall.

7. **accorporate:** incorporate.

8. **serpentine body:** Milton borrows from Spenser's allegorical embodiment of Error (*FQ* 1.1.13-24).

9. **humor:** fancy (literally, an idea resulting not from reason but from the predominance of one of the four bodily humors or fluids—blood, phlegm, black bile, and yellow bile).

10. **innovation:** Milton is anxious to deflect the charge that his argument is unprecedented (thus the title, *Doctrine and Discipline of Divorce: Restored . . .*).

11. While Milton was relatively late in his attack on episcopacy, he was far ahead of his time in his argument for divorce on the grounds of mutual incompatibility.

12. **seventh son of a seventh son:** one marked out for greatness.

13. **statute of Moses:** The Mosaic Law allowing divorce in Deut. 24.1–2.

14. I.e., Jesus.

veyance[15] in Josiah's time.[16] And he who shall endeavor the amendment of any old neglected grievance in church or state, or in the daily course of life, if he be gifted with abilities of mind that may raise him to so high an undertaking, I grant he hath already much whereof not to repent him. Yet let me aread[17] him, not to be the foreman of any misjudged opinion, unless his resolutions be firmly seated in a square and constant mind, not conscious to itself of any deserved blame, and regardless of ungrounded suspicions. For this let him be sure, he shall be boarded[18] presently by the ruder sort, but not by discreet and well-nurtured men, with a thousand idle descants[19] and surmises. Who when they cannot confute the least joint or sinew of any passage in the book, yet God forbid that truth should be truth, because they have a boisterous conceit of some pretences in the writer. But were they not more busy and inquisitive than the apostle[20] commends, they would hear him at least, "rejoicing, so the truth be preached, whether of envy or other pretence whatsoever." For truth is as impossible to be soiled by any outward touch as the sunbeam. Though this ill hap wait on her nativity, that she never comes into the world but like a bastard to the ignominy of him that brought her forth: till time, the midwife rather than the mother of truth, have washed and salted the infant, declared her legitimate, and churched the father of his young Minerva, from the needless causes of his purgation.[21] Yourselves can best witness this, worthy patriots, and better will, no doubt, hereafter. For who among ye of the foremost that have travailed in her behalf to the good of church or state, hath not been often traduced to be the agent of his own by-ends, under pretext of reformation. So much the more I shall not be unjust to hope that however infamy or envy may work in other men to do her fretful will against this discourse, yet that the experience of your own uprightness misinterpreted will put ye in mind to give it free audience and generous construction.

What though the brood of Belial,[22] the draff of men, to whom no liberty is pleasing, but unbridled and vagabond lust without pale or partition, will laugh broad perhaps to see so great a strength of scripture mustering up in favor, as they suppose, of their debaucheries? They will know better when they shall hence learn that honest liberty is the greatest foe to dishonest license. And what

15. **conveyance:** underhanded dealing.
16. See 2 Kings 22 and 23.
17. **aread:** advise, counsel.
18. **boarded:** attacked.
19. **descants:** remarks or criticisms.
20. **apostle:** Paul (Milton paraphrases Phil. 1.18).
21. Having given birth to his controversial argument as Jupiter gave birth to Minerva (or Wisdom), Milton expects to be misjudged as unclean, like the Hebrew and Anglican women subject to purification (Anglican "churching") after childbirth.
22. **brood of Belial:** The "children of Belial" is a label for enemies of God in Deut. 13.13 and Judg. 19.22. Milton, who would come to associate the term with the dissoluteness of the Cavaliers, condemns "the sons/Of Belial, flown with insolence and wine" (*PL* 1.501–2).

though others out of a waterish and queasy conscience, because ever crazy and never yet sound, will rail and fancy to themselves that injury and license is the best of this book? Did not the distemper of their own stomachs affect them with a dizzy megrim,[23] they would soon tie up their tongues, and discern themselves like that Assyrian blasphemer,[24] all this while reproaching not man but the Almighty, "the holy one of Israel," whom they do not deny to have belawgiven his own sacred people with this very allowance which they now call injury and license and dare cry shame on, and will do yet a while, till they get a little cordial sobriety to settle their qualming zeal.

But this question concerns not us perhaps. Indeed man's disposition though prone to search after vain curiosities, yet when points of difficulty are to be discussed, appertaining to the removal of unreasonable wrong and burden from the perplexed life of our brother, it is incredible how cold, how dull, and far from all fellow feeling we are, without the spur of self-concernment. Yet if the wisdom, the justice, the purity of God be to be cleared from foulest imputations which are not yet avoided, if charity be not to be degraded and trodden down under a civil ordinance, if matrimony be not to be advanced like that exalted perdition, written of to the Thessalonians, "above all that is called God,"[25] or goodness, nay, against them both, then I dare affirm there will be found in the contents of this book that which may concern us all. You it concerns chiefly, worthies in Parliament, on whom, as on our deliverers, all our grievances and cares by the merit of your eminence and fortitude are devolved. Me it concerns next, having with much labor and faithful diligence first found out, or at least with a fearless and communicative candor first published to the manifest good of Christendom, that which, calling to witness every thing mortal and immortal, I believe unfeignedly to be true. Let not other men think their conscience bound to search continually after truth, to pray for enlightening from above to publish what they think they have so obtained, and debar me from conceiving myself tied by the same duties.

Ye have now, doubtless by the savor and appointment of God, ye have now in your hands a great and populous nation to reform; from what corruption, what blindness in religion, ye know well; in what a degenerate and fallen spirit from the apprehension of native liberty and true manliness, I'm sure ye find: with what unbounded license rushing to whoredoms and adulteries, needs not long enquiry: insomuch that the fears which men have of too strict a discipline perhaps exceed the hopes that can be in others of ever introducing it with any great success. What if I should tell ye now of dispensations and indulgences,[26]

23. **megrim:** headache, migraine.

24. **Assyrian blasphemer:** Milton paraphrases and quotes Isaiah's rebuke of Sennacherib, king of Assyria (2 Kings 19.22).

25. To set (mistaken) marriage law above Christian charity is to repeat the error of "the son of *perdition*" who "*exalteth* himself above all that is called God" (2 Thess. 2.3–4).

26. **indulgences:** Milton suggests that if divorce is sinful, the Mosaic Law allowing it resembles the corrupt Roman Catholic doctrine of indulgences, which allowed the wealthy to buy their way out of sins.

to give a little the reins, to let them play and nibble with the bait a while; a people as hard of heart as that Egyptian colony[27] that went to Canaan. This is the common doctrine that adulterous and injurious divorces were not connived only, but with eye open allowed of old for hardness of heart. But that opinion, I trust, by then this following argument hath been well read, will be left for one of the mysteries of an indulgent antichrist to farm out incest by and those his other tributary pollutions. What middle way can be taken then, may some interrupt, if we must neither turn to the right nor to the left,[28] and that the people hate to be reformed? Mark then, judges and lawgivers, and ye whose office is to be our teachers, for I will utter now a doctrine, if ever any other, though neglected or not understood, yet of great and powerful importance to the governing of mankind. He who wisely would restrain the reasonable soul of man within due bounds, must first himself know perfectly how far the territory and dominion extends of just and honest liberty. As little must he offer to bind that which God hath loosened, as to loosen that which he hath bound. The ignorance and mistake of this high point hath heaped up one huge half of all the misery that hath been since Adam. In the Gospel we shall read a supercilious crew of masters, whose holiness, or rather whose evil eye, grieving that God should be so facile to man, was to set straiter limits to obedience than God had set, to enslave the dignity of man, to put a garrison upon his neck of empty and over-dignified precepts. And we shall read our Savior never more grieved and troubled than to meet with such a peevish madness among men against their own freedom.[29] How can we expect him to be less offended with us, when much of the same folly shall be found yet remaining where it least ought, to the perishing of thousands.

The greatest burden in the world is superstition, not only of ceremonies in the church but of imaginary and scarecrow sins at home. What greater weakening, what more subtle stratagem against our Christian warfare,[30] when, besides the gross body of real transgressions to encounter, we shall be terrified by a vain and shadowy menacing of faults that are not? When things indifferent[31] shall be set to overfront us under the banners of sin, what wonder if we be routed, and by this art of our adversary fall into the subjection of worst and deadliest offences. The superstition of the papist is, "touch not, taste not" [Col. 2.21],[32] when God bids both, and ours is, "part not, separate not," when God and charity both permits and commands. "Let all your things be done with charity," saith St. Paul

27. **Egyptian colony:** the Israelites, whose "hardness of heart," according to Jesus in Matt. 19.8 and Mark 10.5, was the reason Mosaic Law allowed divorce; Milton will reinterpret these passages.

28. See 2 Chron. 34.2.

29. Christ (Matt. 23) reprimanded the Pharisees for enforcing religious laws stricter than those in the Bible.

30. For *Christian warfare,* see 2 Cor. 10.4 and 1 Tim. 1.18; see also *Areop* (p. 939).

31. **things indifferent:** actions neither commanded nor forbidden in Scripture.

32. Milton quotes Paul's rebuke to those who, despite living in Christ, still consider themselves "subject to ordinances."

[1 Cor. 16.14], and his master saith, "She is the fulfilling of the Law" [Rom. 13.10].[33] Yet now a civil, an indifferent, a sometime dissuaded law of marriage, must be forced upon us to fulfill, not only without charity but against her. No place in heaven or earth, except hell, where charity may not enter: yet marriage, the ordinance of our solace and contentment, the remedy of our loneliness, will not admit now either of charity or mercy to come in and mediate or pacify the fierceness of this gentle ordinance, the unremedied loneliness of this remedy.

Advise ye well, supreme senate, if charity be thus excluded and expulsed, how ye will defend the untainted honor of your own actions and proceedings. He who marries, intends as little to conspire his own ruin, as he that swears allegiance: and as a whole people is in proportion to an ill government, so is one man to an ill marriage.[34] If they, against any authority, covenant, or statute, may by the sovereign edict of charity save not only their lives but honest liberties from unworthy bondage, as well may he against any private covenant, which he never entered to his mischief, redeem himself from unsupportable disturbances to honest peace and just contentment. And much the rather, for that to resist the highest magistrate though tyrannizing God never gave us express allowance, only he gave us reason, charity, nature, and good example to bear us out; but in this economical[35] misfortune thus to demean ourselves, besides the warrant of those four great directors,[36] which doth as justly belong hither, we have an express law of God, and such a law as whereof our Savior with a solemn threat forbid the abrogating.[37] For no effect of tyranny can sit more heavy on the commonwealth than this household unhappiness on the family. And farewell all hope of true reformation in the state, while such an evil as this lies undiscerned or unregarded in the house: on the redress whereof depends not only the spiritful and orderly life of our grown men, but the willing and careful education of our children.

Let this, therefore, be new examined: this tenure and freehold of mankind, this native and domestic charter given us by a greater Lord than that Saxon king the Confessor.[38] Let the statutes of God be turned over, be scanned anew, and considered, not altogether by the narrow intellectuals of quotationists and commonplacers, but (as was the ancient right of councils)[39] by men of what liberal profession soever, of eminent spirit and breeding joined with a diffuse and various knowledge of divine and human things; able to balance and define good

33. Milton in fact quotes Paul, not *his master,* Jesus, but Paul echoes here Jesus' teaching in Matt. 22.37–40. For the conception of Christian liberty, centrally important to Milton, see Barker (1942) and Bennett.
34. Ingeniously, Milton relates the spouse asserting a right to freedom from a bad marriage to his audience in Parliament, who had asserted their right to freedom from the misgovernment of Charles I and his advisers.
35. **economical:** household, domestic (the Greek root *oikos* means "household").
36. **four great directors:** i.e., the gifts enumerated earlier in the sentence.
37. Christ insists that "one jot or one tittle shall in no wise pass from the law" (Matt. 5.18).
38. Edward the Confessor (d. 1066), last of the Saxon kings, was widely and deeply revered.
39. Milton consistently championed the role of laypersons in theological and ecclesiastical deliberation.

and evil, right and wrong, throughout every state of life; able to show us the ways of the Lord, straight and faithful as they are, not full of cranks and contradictions and pit-falling dispenses, but with divine insight and benignity measured out to the proportion of each mind and spirit, each temper and disposition, created so different each from other, and yet by the skill of wise conducting all to become uniform in virtue.

To expedite these knots were worthy a learned and memorable Synod; while our enemies expect to see the expectation of the church tired out with dependencies and independencies[40] how they will compound, and in what calends.[41] Doubt not, worthy senators, to vindicate the sacred honor and judgment of Moses, your predecessor, from the shallow commenting of scholastics and canonists. Doubt not after him to reach out your steady hands to the misinformed and wearied life of man, to restore this his lost heritage into the household state. Wherewith be sure that peace and love, the best subsistence of a Christian family, will return home from whence they are now banished; places of prostitution will be less haunted, the neighbor's bed less attempted, the yoke of prudent and manly discipline will be generally submitted to; sober and well ordered living will soon spring up in the commonwealth.

Ye have an author great beyond exception, Moses; and one yet greater, he who hedged in from abolishing every smallest jot and tittle[42] of precious equity contained in that Law, with a more accurate and lasting Masoreth[43] than either the synagogue of Ezra,[44] or the Galilean school at Tiberias[45] hath left us. Whatever else ye can enact, will scarce concern a third part of the British name, but the benefit and good of this your magnanimous example will easily spread far beyond the banks of Tweed and the Norman isles.[46] It would not be the first or second time since our ancient druids (by whom this island was the cathedral of philosophy to France) left off their pagan rites, that England hath had this honor vouchsafed from heaven, to give out reformation to the world. Who was it but our English Constantine[47] that baptized the Roman Empire? Who but the Northumbrian Willibrode and Winifride of Devon[48] with their followers were the first apostles of Germany? Who but Alcuin[49] and Wyckliffe[50] our country-

40. **dependencies and independencies:** Presbyterians and Independents.

41. **calends:** date.

42. See note 37.

43. **Masoreth:** rabbinical scholars' textual commentary on the Hebrew Scriptures in the form of marginal notes.

44. **synagogue of Ezra:** established in the time of Ezra (fifth century B.C.E.), the "Great Synagogue" assumed the responsibility of maintaining the text of the Torah.

45. **Tiberias:** famous center of rabbinical scholarship on the Sea of Galilee.

46. **Norman isles:** the Channel Islands.

47. Milton shared the erroneous belief that the Emperor Constantine, who Christianized the Roman Empire, was English by birth.

48. *Willibrode* and *Winifride,* also known as St. Boniface, evangelized parts of Germany. They were successively bishops of Utrecht in the eighth century.

49. **Alcuin:** Alcuin, one of the leading intellectual figures of his age, was instrumental in the revival of learning at the court of Charlemagne in the eighth century.

50. **Wycliffe:** John Wycliffe was a fourteenth-century harbinger of the Reformation.

men opened the eyes of Europe, the one in arts, the other in religion. Let not England forget her precedence of teaching nations how to live.

Know, worthies, know and exercise the privilege of your honored country. A greater title I here bring ye than is either in the power or in the policy of Rome to give her monarchs. This glorious act will style ye the defenders of charity.[51] Nor is this yet the highest inscription that will adorn so religious and so holy a defense as this. Behold here the pure and sacred law of God and his yet purer and more sacred name, offering themselves to you first, of all Christian reformers, to be acquitted from the long suffered ungodly attribute of patronizing adultery. Defer not to wipe off instantly these imputative blurs and stains cast by rude fancies upon the throne and beauty itself of inviolable holiness, lest some other people more devout and wise than we bereave us this offered immortal glory, our wonted prerogative, of being the first asserters in every great vindication.

For me, as far as my part leads me, I have already my greatest gain, assurance and inward satisfaction to have done in this nothing unworthy of an honest life and studies well employed. With what event among the wise and right understanding handful of men I am secure. But how among the drove of custom and prejudice this will be relished by such whose capacity, since their youth run ahead into the easy creek of a system or a medulla,[52] sails there at will under the blown physiognomy of their unlabored rudiments; for them what their taste will be, I have also surety sufficient, from the entire league that hath been ever between formal ignorance and grave obstinacy. Yet, when I remember the little that our savior could prevail about this doctrine of charity against the crabbed textuists of his time, I make no wonder, but rest confident that who so prefers either matrimony or other ordinance before the good of man and the plain exigence of charity, let him profess papist, or Protestant, or what he will, he is no better than a pharisee and understands not the Gospel: whom as a misinterpreter of Christ I openly protest against, and provoke him to the trial of this truth before all the world. And let him bethink him withal how he will solder up the shifting flaws of his ungirt permissions, his venial and unvenial dispenses,[53] wherewith the law of God pardoning and unpardoning hath been shamefully branded for want of heed in glossing, to have eluded and baffled out all faith and chastity from the marriage bed of that holy seed with politic and judicial adulteries.

I seek not to seduce the simple and illiterate. My errand is to find out the choicest and the learnedest, who have this high gift of wisdom to answer solidly or to be convinced. I crave it from the piety, the learning, and the prudence which is housed in this place. It might perhaps more fitly have been written in

51. Milton echoes the title held by British monarchs since 1521, "Defender of the Faith."

52. **medulla:** marrow; used in titles of various digests of knowledge, notably William Ames's 1623 *Medulla Theologica,* which influenced Milton's *Christian Doctrine.*

53. **venial and unvenial dispenses:** dispensations for minor and mortal sins.

another tongue, and I had done so, but that the esteem I have of my country's judgment and the love I bear to my native language to serve it first with what I endeavor, made me speak it thus, ere I assay the verdict of outlandish readers.[54] And perhaps also here I might have ended nameless, but that the address of these lines chiefly to the Parliament of England might have seemed ungrateful not to acknowledge by whose religious care, unwearied watchfulness, courageous and heroic resolutions, I enjoy the peace and studious leisure to remain,

The honorer and attendant of their noble worth and virtues,

John Milton

THE DOCTRINE AND DISCIPLINE OF DIVORCE;

Restored to the good of both sexes

BOOK I

THE PREFACE.

That man is the occasion of his own miseries in most of those evils which he imputes to God's inflicting. The absurdity of our canonists in their decrees about divorce. The Christian imperial laws framed with more equity. The opinion of Hugo Grotius, *and* Paulus Fagius: *And the purpose, in general, of this discourse.*

Many men, whether it be their fate or fond[55] opinion, easily persuade themselves, if God would but be pleased a while to withdraw his just punishments from us and to restrain what power either the devil or any earthly enemy hath to work us woe, that then man's nature would find immediate rest and releasement from all evils. But verily they who think so, if they be such as have a mind large enough to take into their thoughts a general survey of human things, would soon prove themselves in that opinion far deceived. For though it were granted us by divine indulgence to be exempt from all that can be harmful to us from without, yet the perverseness of our folly is so bent that we should never lin[56] hammering out of our own hearts, as it were out of a flint, the seeds and sparkles of new misery to ourselves, till all were in a blaze again. And no marvel if out of our own hearts, for they are evil; but even out of those things which God meant us either for a principal good or a pure contentment, we are still hatching and contriving upon ourselves matter of continual sorrow and perplexity. What greater good to man than that revealed rule whereby God vouch-

54. Stung by the outcry against his writings on divorce, Milton would come to regret having published them in English. See *2Def.* "One thing only could I wish, that I had not written it in the vernacular, for then I would not have met with vernacular readers, who are usually ignorant of their own good, and laugh at the misfortunes of others" (p. 1089).

55. **fond:** foolish.

56. **lin:** cease.

safes to show us how he would be worshipped? And yet that not rightly understood became the cause that once a famous man in Israel could not but oblige his conscience to be the sacrificer, or, if not, the jailor of his innocent and only daughter;[57] and was the cause ofttimes that armies of valiant men have given up their throats to a heathenish enemy on the Sabbath day, fondly thinking their defensive resistance to be as then a work unlawful.[58]

What thing more instituted to the solace and delight of man than marriage? And yet the misinterpreting of some scripture directed mainly against the abusers of the law for divorce given by Moses[59] hath changed the blessing of matrimony not seldom into a familiar and coinhabiting mischief, at least into a drooping and disconsolate household captivity without refuge or redemption. So ungoverned and so wild a race doth superstition run us from one extreme of abused liberty into the other of unmerciful restraint. For although God in the first ordaining of marriage taught us to what end he did it, in words expressly implying the apt and cheerful conversation[60] of man with woman, to comfort and refresh him against the evil of solitary life, not mentioning the purpose of generation till afterwards, as being but a secondary end in dignity, though not in necessity; yet now, if any two be but once handed in the church and have tasted in any sort the nuptial bed, let them find themselves never so mistaken in their dispositions through any error, concealment, or misadventure, that through their different tempers, thoughts, and constitutions, they can neither be to one another a remedy against loneliness, nor live in any union or contentment all their days, yet they shall, so they be but found suitably weaponed to the least possibility of sensual enjoyment, be made, spite of antipathy,[61] to fadge together and combine as they may to their unspeakable wearisomeness and despair of all sociable delight in the ordinance which God established to that very end.

What a calamity is this, and as the wise man, if he were alive, would sigh out in his own phrase, what a "sore evil is this under the sun!"[62] All which we can refer justly to no other author than the canon law[63] and her adherents, not consulting with charity, the interpreter and guide of our faith, but resting in the mere element of the text; doubtless by the policy of the devil to make that gracious ordinance become unsupportable, that what with men not daring to venture upon wedlock, and what with men wearied out of it, all inordinate license might abound.

57. For the story of Jephthah, which recalls the story of Agamemnon and Iphigenia, see Judg. 11.29–40.

58. Mattathias's followers, for example, attacked by Antiochus on the Sabbath, allowed themselves to be massacred (1 Macc. 2.31–38).

59. See the discussion of Matt. 5.31–32 in 2.8.

60. **conversation:** companionship, intimacy.

61. **antipathy:** an incompatibility grounded in nature and therefore involuntary; this conception will play a major role in Milton's argument for divorce. See, e.g., his reference two paragraphs hence to the "faultless proprieties of nature" and the "secret power of nature's impression."

62. Eccles. 5.13; the *wise man* is Solomon.

63. **canon law:** ecclesiastical or church law.

It was for many ages that marriage lay in disgrace with most of the ancient doctors as a work of the flesh, almost a defilement, wholly denied to priests and the second time dissuaded to all, as he that reads Tertullian or Jerome[64] may see at large. Afterwards it was thought so sacramental that no adultery or desertion could dissolve it, and this is the sense of our canon courts in England to this day, but in no other reformed church else.[65] Yet there remains in them also a burden on it as heavy as the other two were disgraceful or superstitious, and of as much iniquity, crossing a law not only written by Moses, but charactered in us by nature, of more antiquity and deeper ground than marriage itself; which law is to force nothing against the faultless proprieties of nature. Yet that this may be colorably done, our Savior's words touching divorce are as it were congealed into a stony rigor, inconsistent both with his doctrine and his office, and that which he preached only to the conscience is by canonical tyranny snatched into the compulsive censure of a judicial court, where laws are imposed even against the venerable and secret power of nature's impression, to love whatever cause be found to loathe—which is a heinous barbarism both against the honor of marriage, the dignity of man and his soul, the goodness of Christianity, and all the humane respects of civility. Notwithstanding that some the wisest and gravest among the Christian Emperors who had about them to consult with, those of the Fathers then living, who for their learning and holiness of life are still with us in great renown, have made their statutes and edicts concerning this debate far more easy and relenting in many necessary cases, wherein the canon is inflexible. And Hugo Grotius,[66] a man of these times, one of the best learned, seems not obscurely to adhere in his persuasion to the equity of those imperial decrees in his notes upon the Evangelists, much allaying the outward roughness of the text, which hath for the most part been too immoderately expounded, and excites the diligence of others to enquire further into this question, as containing many points that have not yet been explained. Which ever likely to remain intricate and hopeless upon the suppositions commonly stuck to, the authority of Paulus Fagius,[67] one so learned and so eminent in England once, if it might persuade, would straight acquaint us with a solution of these differences, no less prudent than compendious. He, in his comment on the Pentateuch, doubted not to maintain that divorces might be as lawfully permitted by the magistrate to Christians as they were to the Jews.

64. *Tertullian* (c. 160–c. 230) and *St. Jerome* (c. 340–420) emphasized the superiority of the celibate life to the married life. Chaucer's Wife of Bath in her Prologue (674–76) also yokes the two church fathers in her criticism of the church's hostility to sexuality.

65. The Anglican Church, to Milton's dismay, is aligned with the Roman Catholic Church against the continental Protestant churches in its assertion of the sacramental nature and indissolubility of marriage.

66. **Hugo Grotius:** In arguing for divorce, Milton was influenced by the *Annotationes in Libros Evangeliorum* (1641) of the eminent Dutch scholar Hugo Grotius (1583–1645) who like Milton treated the fall of man in verse, in his 1601 *Adamus Exul.* Milton met Grotius in Paris in 1638.

67. **Paulus Fagius:** The eminent German reformer Paulus Fagius (1504–49) spent the last months of his life in England as Cambridge's Professor of Hebrew. He became a hero of the Protestant cause after his body was disinterred and desecrated during Mary's reign.

But because he is but brief, and these things of great consequence not to be kept obscure, I shall conceive it nothing above my duty, either for the difficulty or the censure that may pass thereon, to communicate such thoughts as I also have had, and do offer them now in this general labor of reformation to the candid view both of church and magistrate; especially because I see it the hope of good men, that those irregular and unspiritual courts have spun their utmost date in this land; and some better course must now be constituted.[68] This, therefore, shall be the task and period[69] of this discourse to prove, first, that other reasons of divorce besides adultery were by the Law of Moses, and are yet to be allowed by the Christian magistrate as a piece of justice, and that the words of Christ are not hereby contraried. Next, that to prohibit absolutely any divorce whatsoever, except those which Moses excepted, is against the reason of law, as in due place I shall show out of Fagius, with many additions. He, therefore, who by adventuring shall be so happy as with success to light the way of such an expedient liberty and truth as this, shall restore the much wronged and over-sorrowed state of matrimony, not only to those merciful and life-giving remedies of Moses, but, as much as may be, to that serene and blissful condition it was in at the beginning;[70] and shall deserve of all apprehensive men (considering the troubles and distempers which for want of this insight have been so oft in kingdoms, in states and families) shall deserve to be reckoned among the public benefactors of civil and human life; above the inventors of wine and oil. For this is a far dearer, far nobler, and more desirable cherishing to man's life, unworthily exposed to sadness and mistake, which he shall vindicate.

Not that license and levity and unconsented breach of faith should herein be countenanced, but that some conscionable and tender pity might be had of those who have unwarily, in a thing they never practiced before, made themselves the bondmen of a luckless and helpless matrimony. In which argument, he whose courage can serve him to give the first onset, must look for two several oppositions: the one from those who having sworn themselves to long custom and the letter of the text, will not out of the road; the other from those whose gross and vulgar apprehensions conceit but low of matrimonial purposes, and in the work of male and female think they have all. Nevertheless, it shall be here sought by due ways to be made appear that those words of God in the institution, promising a meet help against loneliness,[71] and those words of Christ, "That his yoke is easy, and his burden light" [Matt. 11.30], were not spoken in vain; for if the knot of marriage may in no case be dissolved but for adultery, all the burdens and services of the Law are not so intolerable.

68. Milton sees Parliament's recent abolition of ecclesiastical courts as an opportunity to reform marriage and divorce law in England.

69. **period:** aim.

70. I.e., in Eden before the Fall.

71. "And God said, It is not good that man should be alone" (Gen. 2.18).

This only is desired of them who are minded to judge hardly of thus maintaining, that they would be still and hear all out, nor think it equal to answer deliberate reason with sudden heat and noise; remembering this, that many truths now of reverend esteem and credit had their birth and beginning once from singular and private thoughts, while the most of men were otherwise possessed, and had the fate at first to be generally exploded and exclaimed on by many violent opposers. Yet I may err perhaps in soothing myself that this present truth revived will deserve on all hands to be not sinisterly received,[72] in that it undertakes the cure of an inveterate disease crept into the best part of human society; and to do this with no smarting corrosive, but with a smooth and pleasing lesson, which received hath the virtue to soften and dispel rooted and knotty sorrows; and, without enchantment (if that be feared) or spell used, hath regard at once both to serious pity and upright honesty that tends to the redeeming and restoring of none but such as are the object of compassion, having in an ill hour hampered themselves to the utter dispatch of all their most beloved comforts and repose for this life's term.

But if we shall obstinately dislike this new overture of unexpected ease and recovery, what remains but to deplore the frowardness of our hopeless condition, which neither can endure the estate we are in, nor admit of remedy either sharp or sweet. Sharp we ourselves distaste, and sweet, under whose hands we are, is scrupled and suspected as too luscious. In such a posture Christ found the Jews, who were neither won with the austerity of John the Baptist, and thought it too much license to follow freely the charming pipe of him who sounded and proclaimed liberty and relief to all distresses. Yet truth, in some age or other, will find her witness and shall be justified at last by her own children.[73]

CHAP. I

The position, proved by the Law of Moses. That Law expounded and asserted to a moral and charitable use, first by Paulus Fagius, *next with other additions.*

To remove, therefore, if it be possible, this great and sad oppression which through the strictness of a literal interpreting hath invaded and disturbed the dearest and most peaceable estate of household society, to the over-burdening if not the over-whelming of many Christians better worth than to be so deserted of the church's considerate care, this position shall be laid down, first proving, then answering what may be objected either from scripture or light of reason:

72. As is often the case, Milton's syntax becomes knotted when he writes about how his motives and actions will be judged.

73. See Luke 7.31–35 and Matt. 11.16–19 for Jesus' comment on those who found John the Baptist's model too severe and his own too permissive. The passage in Luke ends, "Wisdom is justified of all her children."

That indisposition, unfitness, or contrariety of mind, arising from a cause in nature unchangeable, hindering and ever likely to hinder the main benefits of conjugal society, which are solace and peace, is a greater reason of divorce than natural frigidity, especially if there be no children, and that there be mutual consent.

This I gather from the Law in Deut. 24.1: "When a man hath taken a wife and married her, and it come to pass that she find no favor in his eyes, because he hath found some uncleanness in her, let him write her a bill of divorcement, and give it in her hand, and send her out of his house," etc. This law, if the words of Christ may be admitted into our belief, shall never, while the world stands, for him be abrogated. First, therefore, I here set down what learned Fagius hath observed on this law: "the law of God," saith he, "permitted divorce for the help of human weakness. For every one that of necessity separates, cannot live single. That Christ denied divorce to his own hinders not, for what is that to the unregenerate, who hath not attained such perfection? Let not the remedy be despised which was given to weakness. And when Christ saith, who marries the divorced commits adultery, it is to be understood if he had any plot in the divorce." The rest I reserve until it be disputed how the magistrate is to do herein. From hence we may plainly discern a twofold consideration in this law: first, the end of the lawgiver and the proper act of the law, to command or to allow something just and honest or indifferent; secondly, his sufferance from some accidental result of evil by this allowance, which the law cannot remedy. For if this law have no other end or act but only the allowance of a sin, though never to so good intention, that law is no law but sin muffled in the robe of law, or law disguised in the loose garment of sin. Both which are too foul hypotheses to save the phenomenon of our Savior's answer to the Pharisees about this matter.[74] And I trust anon by the help of an infallible guide to perfect such Prutenic tables[75] as shall mend the astronomy of our wide expositors.

The cause of divorce mentioned in the law is translated "some uncleanness," but in the Hebrew it sounds "nakedness of aught, or any real nakedness," which by all the learned interpreters is referred to the mind as well as to the body. And what greater nakedness or unfitness of mind than that which hinders ever the solace and peaceful society of the married couple, and what hinders that more than the unfitness and defectiveness of an unconjugal mind? The cause, therefore, of divorce expressed in the position cannot but agree with that described in the best and equalest sense of Moses' Law. Which, being a matter of pure charity, is plainly moral, and more now in force than ever, therefore surely lawful. For if under the Law such was God's gracious indulgence as not to suffer the ordinance of his goodness and favor through any error to be seared and

74. See Matt. 19.3–9; see 2.1.

75. **Prutenic tables:** Copernicus's planetary tables, published under a title honoring the Duke of Prussia in 1551; they were superseded by Kepler's Rudolphine tables in 1627. Milton's appropriate reference to outmoded tables demonstrates scientific knowledge and rhetorical adroitness.

stigmatized upon his servants to their misery and thraldom, much less will he suffer it now under the covenant of grace, by abrogating his former grant of remedy and relief. But the first institution will be objected to have ordained marriage inseparable. To that a little patience until this first part have amply discoursed the grave and pious reasons of this divorcive law, and then I doubt not but with one gentle stroking to wipe away ten thousand tears out of the life of man. Yet thus much I shall now insist on, that whatever the institution were, it could not be so enormous,[76] nor so rebellious against both nature and reason, as to exalt itself above the end and person for whom it was instituted.

CHAP. 2

The first reason of this law grounded on the prime reason of matrimony. That no covenant whatsoever obliges against the main end both of itself and of the parties covenanting.

For all sense and equity reclaims[77] that any law or covenant, how solemn or strait soever, either between God and man, or man and man, though of God's joining, should bind against a prime and principal scope of its own institution, and of both or either party covenanting: neither can it be of force to engage a blameless creature to his own perpetual sorrow, mistaken for his expected solace, without suffering charity to step in and do a confessed good work of parting those whom nothing holds together but this of God's joining, falsely supposed against the express end of his own ordinance. And what his chief end was of creating woman to be joined with man, his own instituting words declare, and are infallible to inform us what is marriage and what is no marriage, unless we can think them set there to no purpose: "It is not good," saith he, "that man should be alone; I will make him a helpmeet for him" [Gen. 2.18]. From which words so plain, less cannot be concluded, nor is by any learned interpreter, than that in God's intention a meet and happy conversation is the chiefest and the noblest end of marriage, for we find here no expression so necessarily implying carnal knowledge as this prevention of loneliness to the mind and spirit of man. To this, Fagius, Calvin, Paræus, Rivetus,[78] as willingly and largely assent as can be wished.

And indeed it is a greater blessing from God, more worthy so excellent a creature as man is, and a higher end to honor and sanctify the league of marriage, whenas the solace and satisfaction of the mind is regarded and provided for before the sensitive pleasing of the body. And with all generous persons married thus it is that where the mind and person pleases aptly, there some unaccomplishment of the body's delight may be better born with than when the

76. **enormous:** outside the rule (or "norm").
77. **reclaims:** vigorously denies.
78. David *Paræus* (1548–1622) and André *Rivet* (1572–1651) were prominent Calvinist theologians.

mind hangs off in an unclosing disproportion, though the body be as it ought; for there all corporal delight will soon become unsavory and contemptible. And the solitariness of man, which God had namely and principally ordered to prevent by marriage, hath no remedy, but lies under a worse condition than the loneliest single life. For in single life the absence and remoteness of a helper might inure him to expect his own comforts out of himself, or to seek with hope, but here the continual sight of his deluded thoughts, without cure, must needs be to him, if especially his complexion[79] incline him to melancholy, a daily trouble and pain of loss in some degree like that which reprobates feel.

Lest therefore so noble a creature as man should be shut up incurably under a worse evil by an easy mistake in that ordinance which God gave him to remedy a less evil, reaping to himself sorrow while he went to rid away solitariness, it cannot avoid to be concluded that if the woman be naturally so of disposition[80] as will not help to remove but help to increase that same God-forbidden loneliness (which will in time draw on with it a general discomfort and dejection of mind not beseeming either Christian profession or moral conversation, unprofitable and dangerous to the commonwealth, when the household estate, out of which must flourish forth the vigor and spirit of all public enterprises, is so ill-contented and procured at home and cannot be supported), such a marriage can be no marriage, whereto the most honest end is wanting. And the aggrieved person shall do more manly, to be extraordinary and singular in claiming the due right whereof he is frustrated, than to piece up his lost contentment by visiting the stews, or stepping to his neighbor's bed, which is the common shift in this misfortune, or else by suffering his useful life to waste away and be lost under a secret affliction of an unconscionable size to human strength. Against all which evils, the mercy of this Mosaic Law was graciously exhibited.

CHAP. 3

The ignorance and iniquity of canon law providing for the right of the body in marriage, but nothing for the wrongs and grievances of the mind. An objection, that the mind should be better looked to before contract, answered.

How vain therefore is it, and how preposterous in the canon law, to have made such careful provision against the impediment of carnal performance, and to have had no care about the unconversing inability of mind, so defective to the purest and most sacred end of matrimony; and that the vessel of voluptuous enjoyment must be made good to him that has taken it upon trust without any

79. **complexion:** the proportions of one's four bodily humors.
80. Milton once again ascribes marital failure to a kind of bodily determinism, related to *complexion* (see note 61).

caution, whenas the mind, from whence must flow the acts of peace and love (a far more precious mixture than the quintessence of an excrement), though it be found never so deficient and unable to perform the best duty of marriage in a cheerful and agreeable conversation, shall be thought good enough, how ever flat and melancholious it be, and must serve, though to the eternal disturbance and languishing of him that complains him. Yet wisdom and charity, weighing God's own institution, would think that the pining of a sad spirit wedded to loneliness should deserve to be freed, as well as the impatience of a sensual desire so providently relieved. 'Tis read to us in the liturgy that "we must not marry to satisfy the fleshly appetite, like brute beasts that have no understanding";[81] but the canon so runs as if it dreamt of no other matter than such an appetite to be satisfied; for if it happen that nature hath stopped or extinguished the veins of sensuality, that marriage is annulled. But though all the faculties of the understanding and conversing part after trial appear to be so ill and so aversely met through nature's unalterable working[82] as that neither peace nor any sociable contentment can follow, 'tis as nothing—the contract shall stand as firm as ever, betide what will. What is this but secretly to instruct us that however many grave reasons are pretended to the married life, yet that nothing indeed is thought worth regard therein, but the prescribed satisfaction of an irrational heat? Which cannot be but ignominious to the state of marriage, dishonorable to the undervalued soul of man and even to Christian doctrine itself; while it seems more moved at the disappointing of an impetuous nerve than at the ingenuous grievance of a mind unreasonably yoked, and to place more of marriage in the channel of concupiscence,[83] than in the pure influence of peace and love, whereof the soul's lawful contentment is the only fountain.

But some are ready to object that the disposition ought seriously to be considered before. But let them know again that for all the wariness can be used, it may yet befall a discreet man to be mistaken in his choice, and we have plenty of examples.[84] The soberest and best governed men are least practiced in these affairs; and who knows not that the bashful muteness of a virgin may oft-times hide all the unliveliness and natural sloth which is really unfit for conversation. Nor is there that freedom of access granted or presumed as may suffice to a perfect discerning till too late; and where any indisposition is suspected, what more usual than the persuasion of friends, that acquaintance, as it increases, will amend all. And lastly, it is not strange though many who have spent their youth chastely are in some things not so quick-sighted, while they haste too ea-

81. Milton closely paraphrases from the marriage service in the Anglican Book of Common Prayer.

82. For *nature's unalterable working*, see note 61.

83. *Impetuous nerve* and *channel of concupiscence* are graphic anatomical images, balanced against the indefinite but erotically charged image that follows of a *fountain* pouring forth *peace and love*.

84. Milton adds the last clause to the second edition; it may mark his attempt to deflect attention from himself in this otherwise patently self-regarding paragraph.

gerly to light the nuptial torch.[85] Nor is it, therefore, that for a modest error a man should forfeit so great a happiness and no charitable means to release him, since they who have lived most loosely by reason of their bold accustoming prove most successful in their matches, because their wild affections, unsettling at will, have been as so many divorces to teach them experience. Whenas the sober man honoring the appearance of modesty, and hoping well of every social virtue under that veil, may easily chance to meet, if not with a body impenetrable, yet often with a mind to all other due conversation inaccessible, and to all the more estimable and superior purposes of matrimony useless and almost lifeless. And what a solace, what a fit help such a consort would be through the whole life of a man, is less pain to conjecture than to have experience.

CHAP. 4

The second reason of this law, because without it, marriage, as it happens oft, is not a remedy of that which it promises, as any rational creature would expect. That marriage, if we pattern from the beginning as our Savior bids, was not properly the remedy of lust, but the fulfilling of conjugal love and helpfulness.

And that we may further see what a violent and cruel thing it is to force the continuing of those together whom God and nature in the gentlest end of marriage never joined, diverse evils and extremities that follow upon such a compulsion shall here be set in view. Of evils, the first and greatest is that hereby a most absurd and rash imputation is fixed upon God and his holy laws, of conniving and dispensing with open and common adultery among his chosen people, a thing which the rankest politician would think it shame and disworship that his laws should countenance. How and in what manner this comes to pass I shall reserve till the course of method brings on the unfolding of many scriptures. Next, the Law and Gospel are hereby made liable to more than one contradiction, which I refer also thither. Lastly, the supreme dictate of charity is hereby many ways neglected and violated, which I shall forthwith address to prove. First, we know Saint Paul saith, "It is better to marry than to burn" [1 Cor. 7.9]. Marriage, therefore, was given as a remedy of that trouble—but what might this burning mean? Certainly not the mere motion of carnal lust, not the mere goad of a sensitive desire; God does not principally take care for such cattle.[86] What is it then but that desire which God put into Adam in paradise before he knew the sin of incontinence—that desire which God saw it was not good that man should be left alone to burn in—the desire and longing to put off an unkindly solitariness by uniting another body, but not without a fit soul, to his in the cheerful society of wedlock. Which if it were so needful before the fall, when man was much more perfect in himself, how much more is it needful

85. See *PL* 11.589–90: "Then all in heat / They light the nuptial torch."
86. See *PL* 8.579–94.

now against all the sorrows and casualties of this life to have an intimate and speaking help, a ready and reviving associate in marriage? Whereof who misses by chancing on a mute and spiritless mate, remains more alone than before, and in a burning less to be contained than that which is fleshly, and more to be considered, as being more deeply rooted even in the faultless innocence of nature.

As for that other burning, which is but as it were the venom of a lusty and over-abounding concoction, strict life and labor with the abatement of a full diet may keep that low and obedient enough: but this pure and more inbred desire of joining to itself in conjugal fellowship a fit conversing soul (which desire is properly called love) "is stronger than death," as the spouse of Christ thought, "many waters cannot quench it, neither can the floods drown it" [Song of Solomon 8.6–7].[87] This is that rational burning that marriage is to remedy, not to be allayed with fasting, nor with any penance to be subdued, which how can he assuage who by mishap hath met the unmeetest and most unsuitable mind? Who hath the power to struggle with an intelligible flame, not in paradise to be resisted, become now more ardent by being failed of what in reason it looked for, and even then most unquenched when the importunity of a provender[88] burning is well enough appeased and yet the soul hath obtained nothing of what it justly desires? Certainly, such a one forbidden to divorce is in effect forbidden to marry, and compelled to greater difficulties than in a single life. For if there be not a more human burning which marriage must satisfy, or else may be dissolved, than that of copulation, marriage cannot be honorable for the mere[89] reducing and terminating of lust between two; seeing many beasts in voluntary and chosen couples live together as unadulterously and are as truly married in that respect.

But all ingenuous men will see that the dignity and blessing of marriage is placed rather in the mutual enjoyment of that which the wanting soul needfully seeks than of that which the plenteous body would jollily give away. Hence it is that Plato in his festival discourse brings in Socrates relating what he feigned to have learnt from the prophetess Diotima, how Love was the son of Penury, begot of Plenty in the garden of Jupiter.[90] Which divinely sorts with that which in effect Moses tells us, that love was the son of loneliness, begot in paradise by that sociable and helpful aptitude which God implanted between man and woman toward each other. The same also is that burning mentioned by Saint Paul, whereof marriage ought to be the remedy; the flesh hath other natural and easy curbs which are in the power of any temperate man. When, therefore, this original and sinless penury or loneliness of the soul cannot lay itself down by

87. Milton follows a typical reading of the Song of Solomon, according to which the lover is Christ and the woman is the church.

88. **provender:** livestock feed. By this term, here used as an adjective, Milton suggests that sexual appetite is lower than the appetite for rational companionship.

89. We choose the reading of 1643, "meer," over the second editon's "meet."

90. In Plato's *Symposium* 203, Diotima relates an allegory of the birth of Eros (or Love) from the union of Poverty and Plenty. Milton goes on to compare this allegory to Gen. 2.18.

the side of such a meet and acceptable union as God ordained in marriage, at least in some proportion, it cannot conceive and bring forth love, but remains utterly unmarried under a formal wedlock and still burns in the proper meaning of Saint Paul. Then enters hate, not that hate that sins, but that which only is natural dissatisfaction and the turning aside from a mistaken object; if that mistake have done injury, it fails not to dismiss with recompense, for to retain still, and not be able to love, is to heap up more injury. Thence this wise and pious law of dismission now defended took beginning.

He therefore who, lacking of his due in the most native and human end of marriage, thinks it better to part than to live sadly and injuriously to that cheerful covenant (for not to be beloved and yet retained, is the greatest injury to a gentle spirit) he, I say, who[91] therefore seeks to part, is one who highly honors the married life and would not stain it, and the reasons which now move him to divorce are equal to the best of those that could first warrant him to marry. For, as was plainly shown, both the hate which now diverts him and the loneliness which leads him still powerfully to seek a fit help, hath not the least grain of a sin in it, if he be worthy to understand himself.

CHAP. 5

The third reason of this law, because without it, he who hath happened where he finds nothing but remediless offences and discontents, is in more and greater temptations than ever before.

Thirdly, yet it is next to be feared, if he must be still bound without reason by a deaf rigor, that when he perceives the just expectance of his mind defeated, he will begin even against law to cast about where he may find his satisfaction more complete, unless he be a thing heroically virtuous,[92] and that are not the common lump of men for whom chiefly the laws ought to be made—though not to their sins, yet to their unsinning weaknesses, it being above their strength to endure the lonely estate, which while they shunned they are fallen into. And yet there follows upon this a worse temptation. For if he be such as hath spent his youth unblamably and laid up his chiefest earthly comforts in the enjoyment of a contented marriage, nor did neglect that furtherance which was to be obtained therein by constant prayers, when he shall find himself bound fast to an uncomplying discord of nature—or, as it oft happens, to an image of earth and phlegm[93]—with whom he looked to be the copartner of a sweet and glad-

91. For the oscillation between the third person and the occulted first person in the locution *he, I say, who* and in the tract more generally, see Patterson 1990.

92. Contrast the heroic virtue Milton ascribes to himself in the *Apology* and *The Reason of Church Government.* Here Milton, who may need a divorce, indirectly associates himself with the *common lump of men.*

93. An excess of *phlegm,* one of the four bodily humors, was thought to cause apathy and sluggishness.

some society, and sees withal that his bondage is now inevitable, though he be almost the strongest Christian, he will be ready to despair in virtue and mutine[94] against divine providence. And this doubtless is the reason of those lapses and that melancholy despair which we see in many wedded persons, though they understand it not, or pretend other causes because they know no remedy, and is of extreme danger. Therefore when human frailty surcharged is at such a loss, charity ought to venture much and use bold physic, lest an over-tossed faith endanger to shipwreck.

CHAP. 6

The fourth reason of this law, that God regards love and peace in the family more than a compulsive performance of marriage, which is more broke by a grievous continuance than by a needful divorce.

Fourthly, marriage is a covenant the very being whereof consists not in a forced cohabitation and counterfeit performance of duties, but in unfeigned love and peace. And of matrimonial love, no doubt but that was chiefly meant, which by the ancient sages was thus parabled: that Love, if he be not twin-born, yet hath a brother wondrous like him, called Anteros,[95] whom while he seeks all about, his chance is to meet with many false and feigning desires that wander singly up and down in his likeness. By them in their borrowed garb, Love, though not wholly blind, as poets wrong him,[96] yet having but one eye, as being born an archer aiming, and that eye not the quickest in this dark region here below, which is not Love's proper sphere, partly out of the simplicity and credulity which is native to him, often deceived, embraces and consorts him with these obvious and suborned striplings, as if they were his mother's own sons, for so he thinks them, while they subtly keep themselves most on his blind side. But after a while, as his manner is, when soaring up into the high tower of his apogæum,[97] above the shadow of the earth, he darts out the direct rays of his then most piercing eyesight upon the impostures and trim disguises that were used with him, and discerns that this is not his genuine brother, as he imagined, he has no longer the power to hold fellowship with such a personated mate. For straight his arrows lose their golden heads and shed their purple feathers, his silken

94. **mutine:** mutiny.

95. *Anteros* appears in Plato's *Phaedrus* (255d); later mythographers filled in the story of Aphrodite's giving birth to this younger brother of Eros after she had been told that Eros would waste away unless he could see his likeness in another. For the tradition, see R. V. Merrill, "Eros and Anteros," *Speculum* 19 (1944): 265–84.

96. Spenser has E.K. in *SC* comment on the familiar (but, in Milton's eyes, erroneous because postclassical) image of Eros or Cupid as blind: "he is described of the poets to be . . . blindfolded because he maketh no difference of personages" (gloss to "March," l. 81).

97. **apogæum:** point in a celestial body's orbit most distant from the earth.

braids[98] untwine and slip their knots, and that original and fiery virtue given him by fate all on a sudden goes out and leaves him undeified and despoiled of all his force: till finding Anteros at last, he kindles and repairs the almost faded ammunition of his deity by the reflection of a coequal and homogeneal fire.

Thus mine author[99] sung it to me, and by the leave of those who would be counted the only grave ones, this is no mere amatorious novel (though to be wise and skilful in these matters, men heretofore of greatest name in virtue have esteemed it one of the highest arcs that human contemplation circling upward can make from the glassy sea[100] whereon she stands), but this is a deep and serious verity, showing us that love in marriage cannot live nor subsist unless it be mutual; and where love cannot be, there can be left of wedlock nothing but the empty husk of an outside matrimony as undelightful and unpleasing to God as any other kind of hypocrisy. So far is his command from tying men to the observance of duties which there is no help for, but they must be dissembled. If Solomon's advice be not overfrolic, "Live joyfully," saith he, "with the wife whom thou lovest, all thy days, for that is thy portion" [Eccles. 9.9]. How then, where we find it impossible to rejoice or to love, can we obey this precept? How miserably do we defraud ourselves of that comfortable portion which God gives us, by striving vainly to glue an error together which God and nature will not join, adding but more vexation and violence to that blissful society by our importunate superstition that will not hearken to Saint Paul, I Cor. 7[.15], who, speaking of marriage and divorce, determines plain enough in general that God therein "hath called us to peace" and not "to bondage." Yea, God himself commands in his Law more than once, and by his prophet Malachi, as Calvin and the best translations read, that "he who hates let him divorce";[101] that is, he who cannot love. Hence is it that the rabbins, and Maimonides (famous among the rest) in a book of his set forth by Buxtorfius, tells us that "divorce was permitted by Moses to preserve peace in marriage and quiet in the family."[102] Surely the Jews had their saving peace about them as well as we, yet care was taken that this wholesome provision for household peace should also be allowed them; and must this be denied to Christians? O perverseness! That the Law should be made more provident of peacemaking than the Gospel! That the Gospel should be put to beg a most necessary help of mercy from the Law, but must not have it. And that to grind in the mill of an undelighted and servile

98. The *braids* of Eros's bowstrings unravel.
99. No source has been found; *mine author* may well be Milton's invention, like Socrates' Diotima in the dialogue in which Anteros is found (see note 94).
100. **glassy sea:** Cp. the "sea of glass" in Rev. 4.6.
101. The translation of Mal. 2.16 was hotly contested. Milton's here differs from the *AV:* "For the Lord . . . saith that he hateth putting away [i.e., divorcing]."
102. Milton cites *The Guide for the Perplexed* of Moses *Maimonides* (1135–1204), the great synthesizer of rabbinic Judaism and Aristotelianism; Johann *Buxtorf* (1599–1664) translated the *Guide* into Latin in 1629.

copulation,[103] must be the only forced work of a Christian marriage, ofttimes with such a yoke-fellow, from whom both love and peace, both nature and religion, mourns to be separated.

I cannot therefore be so diffident, as not securely to conclude that he who can receive nothing of the most important helps in marriage, being thereby disenabled to return that duty which is his with a clear and hearty countenance, and thus continues to grieve whom he would not, and is no less grieved, that man ought even for love's sake and peace to move divorce upon good and liberal conditions to the divorced. And it is a less breach of wedlock to part with wise and quiet consent betimes, than still to soil and profane that mystery of joy and union[104] with a polluting sadness and perpetual distemper. For it is not the outward continuing of marriage that keeps whole that covenant, but whosoever does most according to peace and love, whether in marriage or in divorce, he it is that breaks marriage least; it being so often written that "Love only is the fulfilling of every Commandment" [Rom. 13.10].

CHAP. 7

The fifth reason, that nothing more hinders and disturbs the whole life of a Christian than a matrimony found to be incurably unfit, and doth the same in effect that an Idolatrous match.

Fifthly, as those priests of old were not to be long in sorrow, or if they were, they could not rightly execute their function,[105] so every true Christian in a higher order of priesthood[106] is a person dedicate to joy and peace, offering himself a lively sacrifice of praise and thanksgiving. And there is no Christian duty that is not to be seasoned and set off with cheerfulness, which in a thousand outward and intermitting crosses may yet be done well, as in this vale of tears; but in such a bosom affliction as this, crushing the very foundation of his inmost nature, when he shall be forced to love against a possibility and to use dissimulation against his soul in the perpetual and ceaseless duties of a husband, doubtless his whole duty of serving God must needs be blurred and tainted with a sad unpreparedness and dejection of spirit, wherein God has no delight. Who sees not, therefore, how much more Christianly it would be to break by divorce that which is more broken by undue and forcible keeping, rather than "to cover the Altar of the Lord with continual tears, so that he regardeth not the offering any more" [Mal. 2.13]; rather than that the whole worship of a Christ-

103. Foreshadowing *Samson Agonistes*, in which Samson grinds in a mill (35–41) and recoils from the touch of Dalila (951–54).

104. See Eph. 5.31–32.

105. For Jewish law's restriction on the mourning of priests, see Lev. 21.1–6 and Ezek. 44.25–27.

106. Milton endorses the Reformation principle of the priesthood of all believers.

ian man's life should languish and fade away beneath the weight of an immeasurable grief and discouragement? And because some think the children of a second matrimony succeeding a divorce would not be a holy seed, it hindered not the Jews from being so. And why should we not think them more holy than the offspring of a former, ill-twisted wedlock, begotten only out of a bestial necessity, without any true love or contentment or joy to their parents, so that in some sense we may call them the "children of wrath" [Eph. 2.3] and anguish, which will as little conduce to their sanctifying, as if they had been bastards? For nothing more than disturbance of mind suspends us from approaching to God. Such a disturbance especially as both assaults our faith and trust in God's providence, and ends, if there be not a miracle of virtue on either side,[107] not only in bitterness and wrath, the canker of devotion, but in a desperate and vicious carelessness, when he sees himself (without fault of his) trained by a deceitful bait into a snare of misery, betrayed by an alluring ordinance and then made the thrall of heaviness and discomfort by an undivorcing law of God (as he erroneously thinks, but of man's iniquity, as the truth is). For that God prefers the free and cheerful worship of a Christian before the grievous and exacted observance of an unhappy marriage, besides that the general maxims of religion assure us, will be more manifest by drawing a parallel argument from the ground of divorcing an idolatress, which was lest he should alienate his heart from the true worship of God. And what difference is there whether she pervert him to superstition by her enticing sorcery or disenable him in the whole service of God through the disturbance of her unhelpful and unfit society, and so drive him at last through murmuring and despair to thoughts of atheism? Neither doth it lessen the cause of separating in that the one willingly allures him from the faith, the other perhaps unwillingly drives him, for in the account of God it comes all to one that the wife loses him a servant; and therefore by all the united force of the decalogue she ought to be disbanded, unless we must set marriage above God and charity, which is the doctrine of devils, no less than forbidding to marry.[108]

CHAP. 8

That an idolatrous heretic ought to be divorced after a convenient space given to hope of conversion. That place of Corinth. 7 restored from a twofold erroneous exposition; and that the common expositors flatly contradict the moral law....

107. Although the unhappily married Milton argues that we need divorce in part because we are not *miracles of virtue,* he had consistently described himself as extraordinarily virtuous (see note 91).
108. Milton condemns the prohibition of divorce by associating it with the Roman Catholic prescription of priestly celibacy.

CHAP. 9

That adultery is not the greatest breach of matrimony, that there may be other violations as great.

Now whether idolatry or adultery be the greatest violation of marriage if any demand, let him thus consider that among Christian writers touching matrimony there be three chief ends thereof agreed on: Godly society, next civil, and thirdly, that of the marriage-bed.[109] Of these, the first in name to be the highest and most excellent, no baptized man can deny; nor that idolatry smites directly against this prime end, nor that such as the violated end is, such is the violation: but he who affirms adultery to be the highest breach, affirms the bed to be the highest of marriage, which is in truth a gross and boorish opinion, how common soever; as far from the countenance of scripture, as from the light of all clean philosophy or civil nature. And out of question the cheerful help that may be in marriage toward sanctity of life is the purest and so the noblest end of that contract. But if the particular of each person be considered, then of those three ends which God appointed, that to him is greatest which is most necessary; and marriage is then most broken to him when he utterly wants the fruition of that which he most sought therein, whether it were religious, civil, or corporal society. Of which wants to do him right by divorce only for the last and meanest is a perverse injury, and the pretended reason of it as frigid as frigidity itself, which the Code[110] and canon are only sensible of.

Thus much of this controversy. I now return to the former argument.[111] And having shown that disproportion, contrariety, or numbness of mind may justly be divorced, by proving already that the prohibition thereof opposes the express end of God's institution, suffers not marriage to satisfy that intellectual and innocent desire (which God himself kindled in man to be the bond of wedlock) but only to remedy a sublunary and bestial burning, which frugal diet without marriage would easily chasten. Next, that it drives many to transgress the conjugal bed, while the soul wanders after that satisfaction which it had hope to find at home, but hath missed. Or else it sits repining even to atheism, finding itself hardly dealt with, but misdeeming the cause to be in God's Law, which is in man's unrighteous ignorance. I have shown also how it unties the inward knot of marriage, which is peace and love (if that can be untied which was never knit), while it aims to keep fast the outward formality; how it lets perish the Christian man to compel impossibly the married man.

109. Milton leaves out a principal end mentioned by most Christian writers, the procreation of children.
110. **Code:** an apparent reference to the Justinian Code, standing in here for all civil law.
111. **former argument:** the argument of the eighth chapter.

CHAP. 10

The sixth reason of this law, that to prohibit divorce sought for natural causes is against nature.

The sixth place declares this prohibition to be as respectless of human nature as it is of religion, and therefore is not of God. He teaches that an unlawful marriage may be lawfully divorced, and that those who having thoroughly discerned each other's disposition, which ofttimes cannot be till after matrimony, shall then find a powerful reluctance and recoil of nature on either side blasting all the content of their mutual society, that such persons are not lawfully married; to use the apostle's words, "say I these things as a man, or saith not the Law also the same? For it is written" [1 Cor. 9.8-9]; Deut. 22[.9-10], "Thou shalt not sow thy vineyard with divers seeds, lest thou defile both. Thou shalt not plow with an ox and an ass together," and the like. I follow the pattern of Saint Paul's reasoning: "Doth God care for asses and oxen, how ill they yoke together, or is it not said altogether for our sakes? For our sakes no doubt this is written" [1 Cor. 9.9-10].[112] Yea, the apostle himself in the fore-cited 2 *Cor.* 6.14. alludes from that place of Deut. to forbid misyoking marriage, as by the Greek word is evident, though he instance but in one example of mismatching with an infidel. Yet next to that what can be a fouler incongruity, a greater violence to the reverend secret of nature, than to force a mixture of minds that cannot unite, and to sow the furrow of man's nativity[113] with seed of two incoherent and uncombining dispositions? Which act being kindly and voluntary, as it ought, the Apostle in the language he wrote called *eunoia,* and the Latin "benevolence,"[114] intimating the original thereof to be in the understanding and the will. If not, surely there is nothing which might more properly be called a malevolence rather, and is the most injurious and unnatural tribute that can be extorted from a person endowed with reason, to be made pay out the best substance of his body, and of his soul too, as some think,[115] when either for just and powerful causes he cannot like or from unequal causes finds not recompense. And that there is a hidden efficacy of love and hatred in man as well as in other kinds, not moral but natural, which though not always in the choice, yet in the success of marriage will ever be most predominant, besides daily experience, the author of Ecclesiasticus,

112. The passage from 1 Corinthians interprets Deut. 25.4; Milton claims to interpret in Pauline fashion the passage from Deut. 22.9–10.

113. **furrow of man's nativity:** vagina; Milton's descriptions of sexuality in the tract are graphic (see note 83) even when metaphorical.

114. See 1 Cor. 7.3.

115. As Milton himself argues in *CD* 1.7, where he refers to "Aristotle's argument, which I think a very strong one indeed, that if the soul is wholly contained in all the body and wholly in any given part of that body, how can the human seed, that intimate and most noble part of the body, be imagined destitute and devoid of the soul of the parents, or at least of the father, when communicated to the son in the act of generation?" Milton's divorce tracts contain foreshadowings of his mature materialist monism.

whose wisdom hath set him next the Bible, acknowledges, 13.16: "A man," saith he, "will cleave to his like." But what might be the cause, whether each one's allotted genius or proper star, or whether the supernal influence of schemes and angular aspects or this elemental crasis[116] here below, whether all these jointly or singly meeting friendly, or unfriendly in either party, I dare not, with the men I am likest to clash, appear so much a philosopher as to conjecture. The ancient proverb in Homer less abstruse entitles[117] this work of leading each like person to his like peculiarly to God himself,[118] which is plain enough also by his naming of a meet or like help in the first espousal instituted. And that every woman is meet for every man, none so absurd as to affirm. Seeing then there is indeed a twofold seminary or stock in nature, from whence are derived the issues of love and hatred distinctly flowing through the whole mass of created things, and that God's doing ever is to bring the due likenesses and harmonies of his works together, except when out of two contraries met to their own destruction he molds a third existence, and that it is error or some evil angel which either blindly or maliciously hath drawn together in two persons ill embarked in wedlock the sleeping discords and enmities of nature lulled on purpose with some false bait, that they may wake to agony and strife later than prevention could have wished; if from the bent of just and honest intentions beginning what was begun and so continuing, all that is equal, all that is fair and possible hath been tried and no accommodation likely to succeed, what folly is it still to stand combating and battering against invincible causes and effects, with evil upon evil, till either the best of our days be lingered out, or ended with some speeding sorrow? The wise Ecclesiasticus advises rather, 37.27, "My son, prove thy soul in thy life, see what is evil for it, and give not that unto it." Reason he had to say so; for if the noisomeness or disfigurement of body can soon destroy the sympathy of mind to wedlock duties, much more will the annoyance and trouble of mind infuse itself into all the faculties and acts of the body, to render them invalid, unkindly, and even unholy against the fundamental law book of nature, which Moses never thwarts, but reverences. Therefore he commands us to force nothing against sympathy[119] or natural order, no not upon the most abject creatures, to show that such an indignity cannot be offered to man without an impious crime. And certainly those divine meditating words, of finding out a meet and like help to man, have in them a consideration of more than the indefinite likeness of womanhood, nor are they to be made waste paper on for the dullness of Canon divinity, no nor those other allegoric precepts of beneficence fetched out of the closet of nature to teach us goodness and compassion in not compelling together unmatchable societies (or if they meet through mischance, by all consequence to disjoin them), as God and

116. **crasis:** combining of elements.
117. **entitles:** assigns.
118. Milton paraphrases *Od.* 17.218.
119. See note 61.

nature signifies and lectures to us not only by those recited decrees, but even by the first and last of all his visible works, when by his divorcing command[120] the world first rose out of chaos, nor can be renewed again out of confusion but by the separating of unmeet consorts.

CHAP. 11

The seventh reason, that sometimes continuance in marriage may be evidently the shortening or endangering of life to either party, both law and divinity concluding that life is to be preferred before marriage, the intended solace of life. . . .

CHAP. 12

The eighth reason, it is probable, or rather certain, that every one who happens to marry hath not the calling, and therefore upon unfitness found and considered force ought not to be used. . . .

CHAP. 13

The ninth reason, because marriage is not a mere carnal coition but a human society; where that cannot reasonably be had, there can be no true matrimony. Marriage compared with all other covenants and vows warrantably broken for the good of man. Marriage, the papist's sacrament, and unfit marriage, the Protestant's idol.

Ninthly, I suppose it will be allowed us that marriage is a human society, and that all human society must proceed from the mind rather than the body, else it would be but a kind of animal or beastish meeting. If the mind, therefore, cannot have that due company by marriage that it may reasonably and humanly desire, that marriage can be no human society, but a certain formality or gilding over of little better than a brutish congress, and so in very wisdom and pureness to be dissolved.

But marriage is more than human, "the covenant of God" (Prov. 2. 17), therefore man cannot dissolve it. I answer, if it be more than human so much the more it argues the chief society thereof to be in the soul rather than in the body, and the greatest breach thereof to be unfitness of mind rather than defect of body; for the body can have least affinity in a covenant more than human, so that the reason of dissolving holds good the rather. Again I answer, that the Sabbath is a higher institution, a command of the first table,[121] for the breach whereof God hath far more and oftener testified his anger than for divorces, which from Moses to Malachi he never took displeasure at, nor then neither if

120. Gen. 1.4: "And God divided the light from the darkness."

121. I.e., among the first three of the Ten Commandments, those prescribing man's duty directly to God (Deut. 5.6–21).

we mark the text,[122] and yet as oft as the good of man is concerned, he not only permits but commands to break the Sabbath. What covenant more contracted with God and less in man's power than the vow which hath once past his lips? Yet if it be found rash, if offensive, if unfruitful either to God's glory or the good of man, our doctrine forces not error and unwillingness irksomely to keep it, but counsels wisdom and better thoughts boldly to break it. Therefore to enjoin the indissoluble keeping of a marriage found unfit against the good of man both soul and body, as hath been evidenced, is to make an idol of marriage, to advance it above the worship of God and the good of man, to make it a transcendent command, above both the second and first table, which is a most prodigious doctrine.

Next, whereas they cite out of the Proverbs that it is "the covenant of God," and therefore more than human, that consequence is manifestly false; for so the covenant which Zedechiah made with the infidel king of Babel, is called the Covenant of God" (Ezek. 17.19), which would be strange to hear counted more than a human covenant. So every covenant between man and man bound by oath may be called the covenant of God, because God therein is attested. So of marriage he is the author and the witness yet hence will not follow any divine astriction more than what is subordinate to the glory of God and the main good of either party. For as the glory of God and their esteemed fitness one for the other was the motive which led them both at first to think without other revelation that God had joined them together, so when it shall be found by their apparent unfitness that their continuing to be man and wife is against the glory of God and their mutual happiness, it may assure them that God never joined them; who hath revealed his gracious will not to set the ordinance above the man for whom it was ordained, not to canonize marriage either as a tyranness or a goddess over the enfranchised life and soul of man. For wherein can God delight, wherein be worshipped, wherein be glorified by the forcible continuing of an improper and ill-yoking couple? He that loved not to see the disparity of several cattle at the plow[123] cannot be pleased with vast unmeetness in marriage. Where can be the peace and love which must invite God to such a house? May it not be feared that the not divorcing of such a helpless disagreement will be the divorcing of God finally from such a place?

But it is a trial of our patience, they say. I grant it, but which of Job's afflictions were sent him with that law that he might not use means to remove any of them if he could? And what if it subvert our patience and our faith too? Who shall answer for the perishing of all those souls perishing by stubborn expositions of particular and inferior precepts against the general and supreme rule of charity? They dare not affirm that marriage is either a sacrament or a mystery,[124] though all those sacred things give place to man, and yet they invest it

122. See the discussion of Mal. 2.16 in Chapter 6.

123. Deut. 22.10; see note 112.

124. Milton brands his opponents by association with Roman Catholics, who, unlike Protestants, view marriage as a sacrament.

with such an awful sanctity, and give such adamantine chains to bind with, as if it were to be worshipped like some Indian deity, when it can confer no blessing upon us but works more and more to our misery. To such teachers the saying of Saint Peter at the council of Jerusalem will do well to be applied, "Why tempt ye God to put a yoke upon the necks" of Christian men, which neither the Jews, God's ancient people, "nor we are able to bear" [Acts 15.10], and nothing but unwary expounding hath brought upon us.

CHAP. 14

Considerations concerning Familism, Antinomianism, and why it may be thought that such opinions may proceed from the undue restraint of some just liberty, than which no greater cause to contemn discipline.

To these considerations this also may be added as no improbable conjecture: seeing that sort of men who follow Anabaptism, Familism, Antinomianism,[125] and other fanatic dreams (if we understand them not amiss)[126] be such most commonly as are by nature addicted to religion, of life also not debauched, and that their opinions having full swing do end in satisfaction of the flesh, it may come[127] with reason into the thoughts of a wise man, whether all this proceed not partly, if not chiefly, from the restraint of some lawful liberty, which ought to be given men and is denied them—as by physic we learn in menstruous bodies, where nature's current hath been stopped, that the suffocation and upward forcing of some lower part affects the head and inward sense with dotage and idle fancies. And, on the other hand, whether the rest of vulgar men not so religiously professing do not give themselves much the more to whoredom and adulteries, loving the corrupt and venial discipline of clergy courts, but hating to hear of perfect reformation; whenas they foresee that then fornication shall be austerely censured, adultery punished, and marriage the appointed refuge of nature, though it hap to be never so incongruous and displeasing, must yet of force be worn out, when it can be to no other purpose but of strife and hatred, a thing odious to God.[128] This may be worth the study of skillful men in theology and the reason of things; and lastly to examine whether some undue and ill-grounded strictness upon the blameless nature of man be not the cause, in

125. *Anabaptism,* named for its condemnation of infant baptism, originated in Germany in the early sixteenth century. The Family of Love was founded by Hendrik Niclaes in Friesland in 1540. *Antinomianism* is a generic term for the doctrine, held by the Familists, Ranters, and other radical sectarians, that Christians are freed from the moral law.

126. This parenthesis, a significant qualification of the criticism of sectarians, is new to the second edition; this may suggest that the experience of writing, and being criticized for, his argument for divorce contributed to Milton's move toward the radical sectarians.

127. Second edition reads "it may be come." Either the compositor erred or Milton meant "perhaps it is with reason concluded that . . ."

128. It is very difficult to construe this sentence, which may be corrupt.

those places where already reformation is, that the discipline of the church, so often and so unavoidably broken, is brought into contempt and derision. And if it be thus, let those who are still bent to hold this obstinate literality, so prepare themselves as to share in the account for all these transgressions, when it shall be demanded at the last day by one who will scan and sift things with more than a literal wisdom of equity. For if these reasons be duly pondered and that the Gospel is more jealous of laying on excessive burdens than ever the Law was, lest the soul of a Christian, which is inestimable, should be over-tempted and cast away, considering also that many properties of nature, which the power of regeneration itself never alters, may cause dislike of conversing even between the most sanctified, which continually grating in harsh tune together may breed some jar and discord, and that end in rancor and strife, a thing so opposite both to marriage and to Christianity, it would perhaps be less scandal to divorce a natural disparity than to link violently together an unchristian dissention, committing two ensnared souls inevitably to kindle one another, not with the fire of love, but with a hatred inconcilable, who, were they dissevered, would be straight friends in any other relation. But if an alphabetical servility[129] must be still urged, it may so fall out that the true church may unwittingly use as much cruelty in forbidding to divorce, as the church of antichrist doth willfully in forbidding to marry.

THE SECOND BOOK

CHAP. I

The ordinance of Sabbath and marriage compared. Hyperbole no infrequent figure in the Gospel. Excess cured by contrary excess. Christ neither did nor could abrogate the law of divorce, but only reprove the abuse thereof.

Hitherto the position undertaken hath been declared and proved by a law of God, that law proved to be moral and unabolishable for many reasons equal, honest, charitable, just, annexed thereto. It follows now that those places of scripture which have a seeming to revoke the prudence of Moses, or rather that merciful decree of God, be forthwith explained and reconciled. For what are all these reasonings worth, will some reply, whenas the words of Christ are plainly against all divorce, "except in case of fornication" [Matt. 5.32]? To whom he whose mind were to answer no more but this, "except also in case of charity," might safely appeal to the more plain words of Christ in defense of so excepting. "Thou shalt do no manner of work" saith the commandment of the Sabbath [Exod. 20.10]. Yes, saith Christ, works of charity.[130] And shall we be more severe

129. **alphabetical servility:** obedience to the letter (as opposed to the spirit) of the law.
130. See Luke 13.10–17, 14.1–6.

in paraphrasing the considerate and tender Gospel than he was in expounding the rigid and peremptory law? What was ever in all appearance less made for man, and more for God alone, than the Sabbath? Yet when the good of man comes into the scales, we hear that voice of infinite goodness and benignity that "Sabbath was made for man, not man for Sabbath" [Mark 2.27]. What thing ever was more made for man alone and less for God than marriage? And shall we load it with a cruel and senseless bondage utterly against both the good of man and the glory of God? Let who so will now listen. I want neither pall nor miter, I stay neither for ordination nor induction, but in the firm faith of a knowing Christian, which is the best and truest endowment of the keys,[131] I pronounce, the man who shall bind so cruelly a good and gracious ordinance of God hath not in that the spirit of Christ. Yet that every text of scripture seeming opposite may be attended with a due exposition, this other part ensues and makes account to find no slender arguments for this assertion out of those very scriptures which are commonly urged against it.

First therefore let us remember, as a thing not to be denied, that all places of scripture wherein just reason of doubt arises from the letter are to be expounded by considering upon what occasion everything is set down, and by comparing other texts. The occasion which induced our Savior to speak of divorce was either to convince the extravagance of the Pharisees in that point, or to give a sharp and vehement answer to a tempting question.[132] And in such cases that we are not to repose all upon the literal terms of so many words, many instances will teach us: wherein we may plainly discover how Christ meant not to be taken word for word, but like a wise physician, administering one excess against another to reduce us to a perfect mean. Where the Pharisees were strict, there Christ seems remiss; where they were too remiss, he saw it needful to seem most severe. In one place he censures an unchaste look to be adultery already committed, another time he passes over actual adultery with less reproof than for an unchaste look, not so heavily condemning secret weakness as open malice.[133] So here he may be justly thought to have given this rigid sentence against divorce not to cut off all remedy from a good man who finds himself consuming away in a disconsolate and unenjoyed matrimony, but to lay a bridle upon the bold abuses of those overweening rabbis; which he could not more effectually do than by a countersway of restraint curbing their wild exorbitance almost into the other extreme, as when we bow things the contrary way to make them come to their natural straightness. And that this was the only intention of Christ is most evident if we attend but to his own words and protestation made in the same sermon, not many verses before he treats of divorcing,

131. Cp. Milton's claim in *CD* 1.29 that the "keys of the kingdom of heaven are not entrusted to [Peter] alone" but "with everyone else who professes the same faith."

132. See Matt. 19.3–9.

133. See Matt. 5.28, "Whosoever looketh on a woman to lust after her hath committed adultery with her already in his heart," and John 8.11, where Christ tells the woman taken in adultery, "Neither do I condemn thee; go, and sin no more."

that he came not to abrogate from the Law "one jot or tittle" [Matt. 5.18] and denounces against them that shall so teach.

But Saint Luke, the verse immediately before-going that of divorce, inserts the same caveat,[134] as if the latter could not be understood without the former; and as a witness to produce against this our willful mistake of abrogating, which must needs confirm us that whatever else in the political law of more special relation to the Jews might cease to us, yet that of those precepts concerning divorce, not one of them was repealed by the doctrine of Christ, unless we have vowed not to believe his own cautious and immediate profession. For if these our Savior's words inveigh against all divorce and condemn it as adultery, except it be for adultery, and be not rather understood against the abuse of those divorces permitted in the Law, then is that law of Moses, Deut. 24.1. not only repealed and wholly annulled against the promise of Christ and his known profession not to meddle in matters judicial, but, that which is more strange, the very substance and purpose of that law is contradicted and convinced both of injustice and impurity, as having authorized and maintained legal adultery by statute. Moses also cannot scape to be guilty of unequal and unwise decrees, punishing one act of secret adultery by death and permitting a whole life of open adultery by law. And albeit lawyers write that some political edicts, though not approved, are yet allowed to the scum of the people and the necessity of the times, these excuses have but a weak pulse. For first, we read not that the scoundrel people, but the choicest, the wisest, the holiest of that nation have frequently used these laws, or such as these, in the best and holiest times. Secondly, be it yielded that in matters not very bad or impure, a human lawgiver may slacken something of that which is exactly good, to the disposition of the people and the times, but if the perfect, the pure, the righteous Law of God (for so are all his statutes and his judgments) be found to have allowed smoothly, without any certain reprehension, that which Christ afterward declares to be adultery, how can we free this Law from the horrible indictment of being both impure, unjust, and fallacious?

CHAP. 2

How divorce was permitted for hardness of heart, cannot be understood by the common exposition. That the Law cannot permit, much less enact, a permission of sin.

Neither will it serve to say this was permitted for the hardness of their hearts, in that sense as it is usually explained,[135] for the Law were then but a corrupt

134. Luke 16.17–18: "And it is easier for heaven and earth to pass, than one tittle of the law to fall. Whosoever putteth away his wife and marrieth another, committeth adultery."

135. The Yale editor cites the arguments of Paræus (see note 78) and the prominent English Calvinist William Perkins that Mosaic Law allowed divorce, despite its sinfulness, to prevent greater sin.

and erroneous schoolmaster,[136] teaching us to dash against a vital maxim of religion by doing foul evil in hope of some uncertain good.

This only text not to be matched again throughout the whole scripture, whereby God in his perfect Law should seem to have granted to the hard hearts of his holy people under his own hand a civil immunity and free charter to live and die in a long successive adultery under a covenant of works, till the Messiah, and then that indulgent permission to be strictly denied by a covenant of grace; besides the incoherence of such a doctrine, cannot, must not be thus interpreted, to the raising of a paradox never known till then, only hanging by the twined thread of one doubtful scripture, against so many other rules and leading principles of religion, of justice, and purity of life. For what could be granted more either to the fear or to the lust of any tyrant, or politician,[137] than this authority of Moses thus expounded, which opens him a way at will to dam up justice, and not only to admit of any Romish or Austrian[138] dispenses, but to enact a statute of that which he dares not seem to approve, even to legitimate vice, to make sin itself, the ever alien and vassal sin, a free citizen of the commonwealth, pretending only these or these plausible reasons. And well he might, all the while that Moses shall be alleged to have done as much without showing any reason at all. Yet this could not enter into the heart of David, Psal. 94.20, how any such authority as endeavors "to fashion wickedness by a law" should derive itself from God. And Isaiah lays "woe upon them that decree unrighteous decrees," 10.1. Now which of these two is the better lawgiver, and which deserves most a woe, he that gives out an edict singly unjust, or he that confirms to generations a fixed and unmolested impunity of that which is not only held to be unjust but also unclean, and both in a high degree, not only, as they themselves affirm, an injurious expulsion of one wife, but also an unclean freedom by more than a patent to wed another adulterously? How can we therefore with safety thus dangerously confine the free simplicity of our Savior's meaning to that which merely amounts from so many letters, whenas it can consist neither with his former and cautionary words, nor with other more pure and holy principles, nor finally with the scope of charity, commanding by his express commission in a higher strain. But all rather of necessity must be understood as only against the abuse of that wise and ingenuous liberty which Moses gave, and to terrify a roving conscience from sinning under that pretext.

136. Paul compares the law to a schoolmaster in Gal. 3.24.

137. **politician:** This word is usually derogatory in Milton.

138. For the Protestant Milton, Rome is the seat of hostile foreign intrigue, and in his *Commonplace Book* (Yale 1:503) he records from Camden's *Annales* John of Austria's plot to invade England and depose Elizabeth.

CHAP. 3

That to allow sin by law is against the nature of law, the end of the lawgiver, and the good of the people. Impossible therefore in the Law of God. That it makes God the author of sin, more than anything objected by the Jesuits or Arminians against predestination.

[*In an omitted section of several pages, Milton maintains by argument and authority that God could not have allowed sin (divorce) by law. "Sin," he writes, "can have no tenure by law at all, but is rather an eternal outlaw, and in hostility with law past all atonement: both diagonal contraries, as much allowing one another, as day and night together in one hemisphere."*]

If it be affirmed that God as being Lord may do what he will, yet we must know that God hath not two wills, but one will, much less two contrary.[139] If he once willed adultery should be sinful and to be punished by death, all his omnipotence will not allow him to will the allowance that his holiest people might, as it were by his own antinomy or counter-statute, live unreproved in the same fact, as he himself esteemed it according to our common explainers. The hidden ways of his providence we adore and search not, but the Law is his revealed will, his complete, his evident, and certain will. Herein he appears to us as it were in human shape, enters into covenant with us, swears to keep it, binds himself like a just lawgiver to his own prescriptions, gives himself to be understood by men, judges and is judged, measures and is commensurate to right reason; cannot require less of us in one cantle[140] of his Law than in another, his legal justice cannot be so fickle and so variable, sometimes like a devouring fire[141] and by and by connivent[142] in the embers, or, if I may so say, oscitant[143] and supine. The vigor of his law could no more remit than the hallowed fire on his altar could be let go out.[144] The lamps that burnt before him might need snuffing, but the light of his law never. Of this also more beneath, in discussing a solution of Rivetus.[145]

The Jesuits and that sect among us which is named of Arminius[146] are wont

139. Cp. *CD* 1.4, p. 1163, where Milton denies the Calvinist assertion of God's twofold will: the revealed will by which he calls all to believe and the secret will by which he withholds from some the grace necessary for belief.

140. **cantle:** nook or section.

141. Exod. 24.17.

142. **connivent:** dozing.

143. **oscitant:** drowsy.

144. Lev. 6.13.

145. In the next chapter, here omitted.

146. **Arminius:** Jacob Arminius (1560–1609), a theologian of the Reformed Church of the Netherlands, having been assigned to refute attacks on Calvinist predestination, became convinced by those attacks. His defense of universal, sufficient, and resistible grace against the Calvinist tenets of particular and irresistible grace, which for Arminius amounted to making God the author of sin, was condemned at the Synod of Dort. Milton's later understanding of grace and salvation, both in *CD* 1.3–4 and in *Paradise Lost,* is firmly Arminian. See Danielson and S. Fallon (1999).

to charge us of making God the author of sin in two degrees especially, not to speak of his permissions. 1. Because we hold that he hath decreed some to damnation and consequently to sin, say they. Next, because those means which are of saving knowledge to others, he makes to them an occasion of greater sin. Yet considering the perfection wherein man was created and might have stood, no decree necessitating his free will, but subsequent though not in time yet in order to causes which were in his own power, they might methinks be persuaded to absolve both God and us.[147] When as the doctrine of Plato and Chrysippus[148] with their followers the Academics and the Stoics, who knew not what a consummate and most adorned Pandora was bestowed upon Adam to be the nurse and guide of his arbitrary[149] happiness and perseverance, I mean his native innocence and perfection, which might have kept him from being our true Epimetheus,[150] and though they taught of virtue and vice to be both the gift of divine destiny, they could yet find reasons not invalid, to justify the counsels of God and fate from the insulsity[151] of mortal tongues: that man's own will self-corrupted is the adequate and sufficient cause of his disobedience besides fate, as Homer also wanted not to express both in his *Iliad* and *Odyssey*.[152] And Manilius, the poet, although in his fourth book he tells of some "created both to sin and punishment," yet without murmuring and with an industrious cheerfulness acquits the deity.[153] They were not ignorant in their heathen lore that it is most God-like to punish those who of his creatures became his enemies with the greatest punishment; and they could attain also to think that the greatest, when God himself throws a man furthest from him, which then they held he did, when he blinded, hardened, and stirred up his offenders to finish and pile up their disparate work since they had undertaken it. To banish forever into a local hell, whether in the air or in the center, or in that uttermost and bottomless gulf of chaos, deeper from holy bliss than the world's diameter multiplied, they thought not a punishing so proper and proportionate for God to inflict as to punish sin with sin. Thus were the common sort of Gentiles wont to think, without any wry thoughts cast upon divine governance. And therefore Cicero, not in his Tusculan or Campanian retirements among the learned wits of that age but even in the senate to a mixed auditory (though he were sparing otherwise to broach his philosophy among statists and lawyers) yet as to this point,

147. I.e., the bondage to sin, having resulted from Adam and Eve's sin, is the responsibility of the human race and not of God.

148. *Plato's Laws* contains the argument that evil derives from the wills of individuals (10.904); *Chrysippus* (280–7 B.C.E.) was reported to have taught that human beings, because their wills are free, are responsible for the outcomes of their choices.

149. **arbitrary:** up to one's choice.

150. *Epimetheus,* by opening *Pandora*'s box, released the evils that have since plagued human beings; cp. *PL* 4.714–19.

151. **insulsity:** stupidity, senselessness.

152. Milton seems to refer to the opening lines of the *Iliad,* concerning Achilles' wrath; for the *Odyssey,* see the passages (1.7 and 1.32ff) quoted at the end of *CD* 1.4.

153. See Marcus Manilius's *Astronomicon* (4.108–18).

both in his *Oration against Piso* and in that which is about the answers of the soothsayers against Clodius, he declares it publicly as no paradox to common ears that God cannot punish man more, nor make him more miserable, than still by making him more sinful.[154] Thus we see how in this controversy the justice of God stood upright even among heathen disputers. But if anyone be truly and not pretendedly zealous for God's honor, here I call him forth before men and angels, to use his best and most advised skill lest God more unavoidably than ever yet, and in the guiltiest manner, be made the author of sin—if he shall not only deliver over and incite his enemies by rebukes to sin as a punishment, but shall by patent under his own broad seal allow his friends whom he would sanctify and save, whom he would unite to himself and not disjoin, whom he would correct by wholesome chastening and not punish as he doth the damned by lewd sinning, if he shall allow these in his Law (the perfect rule of his own purest will and our most edified conscience) the perpetrating of an odious and manifold sin without the lest contesting. 'Tis wondered how there can be in God a secret and a revealed will; and yet what wonder if there be in man two answerable causes. But here there must be two revealed wills grappling in a fraternal war with one another without any reasonable cause apprehended. This cannot be less than to engraft sin into the substance of the Law, which Law is to provoke sin by crossing and forbidding, not by complying with it. Nay this is, which I tremble in uttering, to incarnate sin into the unpunishing and well-pleased will of God. To avoid these dreadful consequences that tread upon the heels of those allowances to sin will be a task of far more difficulty than to appease those minds which perhaps out of a vigilant and wary conscience except against predestination. Thus finally we may conclude, that a law wholly giving license cannot upon any good consideration be given to a holy people, for hardness of heart in the vulgar sense.

CHAP. 4

That if divorce be no command, no more is marriage. That divorce could be no dispensation if it were sinful. The Solution of Rivetus, *that God dispensed by some unknown way, ought not to satisfy a Christian mind. . . .*

CHAP. 5

What a dispensation is. . . .

154. Hughes notes that "in the oration to the Senate *On Behalf of Milo* (86) *Cicero* dramatically described the Latian gods as having been outraged by Clodius, and as having inspired him and his gang with the madness that drove them to their deaths in their lawless attack on Milo. . . . In the oration *Against Piso* (20) Cicero asserted that the extreme crimes of the wicked are 'the most inevitable of the penalties ordained for them by the immortal gods.'"

CHAP. 6

That the Jew had no more right to this supposed dispense than the Christian hath and rather not so much....

CHAP. 7

That the Gospel is apter to dispense than the Law. Paræus *answered....*

CHAP. 8

The true sense how Moses suffered divorce for hardness of heart.

What may we do then to salve this seeming inconsistence?[155] I must not dissemble that I am confident that it can be done no other way than this.

Moses (Deut. 24.1) established a grave and prudent law, full of moral equity, full of due consideration towards nature, that cannot be resisted, a law consenting with the laws of wisest men and civilest nations: that "when a man hath married a wife, if it come to pass he cannot love her by reason of some displeasing natural quality or unfitness in her, let him write her a bill of divorce."[156] The intent of which law undoubtedly was this, that if any good and peaceable man should discover some helpless disagreement or dislike either of mind or body, whereby he could not cheerfully perform the duty of a husband without the perpetual dissembling of offense and disturbance to his spirit, rather than to live uncomfortably and unhappily both to himself and to his wife, rather than to continue undertaking a duty which he could not possibly discharge, he might dismiss her whom he could not tolerably and so not conscionably retain. And this law the spirit of God by the mouth of Solomon (Prov. 30.21,23) testifies to be a good and a necessary law, by granting it that "a hated woman" (for so the Hebrew word signifies, rather than odious, though it come all to one), "that a hated woman when she is married is a thing that the earth cannot bear." What follows then but that the charitable law must remedy what nature cannot undergo.

Now that many licentious and hardhearted men took hold of this law to cloak their bad purposes is nothing strange to believe. And these were they, not for whom Moses made the law, God forbid, but whose hardness of heart taking ill advantage by this law he held it better to suffer as by accident, where it could not be detected, rather than good men should lose their just and lawful privilege of remedy. Christ therefore having to answer these tempting Pharisees, ac-

155. I.e., between Moses' permitting and the Gospel's apparent prohibiting of divorce.

156. Milton here quotes Deut. 24.1, though his "by reason of some displeasing natural quality or unfitness in her" replaces the *AV*'s "because he hath found some uncleanness in her."

cording as his custom was, not meaning to inform their proud ignorance what Moses did in the true intent of the law, which they had ill cited, suppressing the true cause for which Moses gave it and extending it to every slight matter, tells them their own, what Moses was forced to suffer by their abuse of his law; which is yet more plain if we mark that our Savior in the fifth of Matth[ew] cites not the Law of Moses but the Pharisaical tradition falsely grounded upon that Law.[157] And in those other places, chap. 19 and Mark 10, the Pharisees cite the law but conceal the wise and human reason there expressed, which our Savior corrects not in them whose pride deserved not his instruction, only returns them what is proper to them: "Moses for the hardness of your heart suffered you," that is, such as you, "to put away your wives" [Matt. 19.8]; and "to you he wrote this precept" [Mark 10.5] for that cause, which "to you" must be read with an impression[158] and understood limitedly of such as covered ill purposes under that law. For it was seasonable that they should hear their own unbounded license rebuked, but not seasonable for them to hear a good man's requisite liberty explained.

But us he hath taught better, if we have ears to hear. He himself acknowledged it to be a law (Mark 10), and being a law of God it must have an undoubted "end of charity, which may be used with a pure heart, a good conscience, and faith unfeigned" [1 Tim. 1.5], as was heard. It cannot allow sin, but is purposely to resist sin, as by the same chapter to Timothy appears. There we learn also "that the Law is good, if a man use it lawfully" [1 Tim. 1.8]. Out of doubt then there must be a certain good in this Law which Moses willingly allowed. And there might be an unlawful use made thereof by hypocrites, and that was it which Moses unwillingly suffered, foreseeing it in general but not able to discern it in particulars. Christ therefore mentions not here what Moses and the Law intended; for good men might know that by many other rules, and the scornful Pharisees were not fit to be told until they could employ that knowledge they had less abusively. Only he acquaints them with what Moses by them was put to suffer.

CHAP. 9

The words of the institution how to be understood, and of our Savior's answer to his disciples.

And to entertain a little their overweening arrogance as best befitted, and to amaze them yet further, because they thought it no hard matter to fulfill the Law, he draws them up to that unseparable institution which God ordained in

157. Matt. 5.31: "It hath been said, Whosoever shall put away his wife, let him give her a writing of divorcement."

158. **impression:** emphasis.

the beginning before the fall, when man and woman were both perfect and could have no cause to separate; just as in the same chapter he stands not to contend with the arrogant young man who boasted his observance of the whole Law, whether he had indeed kept it or not, but screws him up higher to a task of that perfection which no man is bound to imitate.[159] And in like manner that pattern of the first institution he set before the opinionative Pharisees to dazzle them and not to bind us. For this is a solid rule, that every command given with a reason binds our obedience no otherwise than that reason holds. Of this sort was that command in Eden: "therefore shall a man cleave to his wife and they shall be one flesh" [Gen. 2.24], which we see is no absolute command, but with an inference: "therefore." The reason then must be first considered, that[160] our obedience be not mis-obedience. The first is, for it is not single, because the wife is to the husband "flesh of his flesh," as in the verse going before. But this reason cannot be sufficient of itself; for why then should he for his wife leave his father and mother, with whom he is far more "flesh of flesh and bone of bone," as being made of their substance? And, besides, it can be but a sorry and ignoble society of life whose inseparable injunction depends merely upon flesh and bones.[161] Therefore we must look higher, since Christ himself recalls us to the beginning, and we shall find that the primitive reason of never divorcing was that sacred and not vain promise of God to remedy man's loneliness by "making him a meet help for him" [Gen 2.18], though not now in perfection as at first, yet still in proportion as things now are.[162] And this is repeated (verse 20) when all other creatures were fitly associated and brought to Adam, as if the divine power had been in some care and deep thought because "there was not yet found a help meet for man." And can we so slightly depress the all-wise purpose of a deliberating God, as if his consultation had produced no other good for man but to join him with an accidental companion of propagation, which his sudden word had already made for every beast? Nay, a far less good to man it will be found, if she must at all adventures be fastened upon him individually.[163] And therefore even plain sense and equity and, which is above them both, the all-interpreting voice of charity herself cries loud that this primitive reason, this consulted promise of God "to make a meet help," is the only cause that gives authority to this command of not divorcing, to be a command. And it might be further added that if the true definition of a wife were asked in good earnest, this clause of being "a meet help" would show itself so necessary and so essential in that demonstrative argument, that it might be logically concluded, therefore, she who naturally and perpetually is no meet help, can be no wife, which clearly takes away the difficulty of dismissing of such a one.

159. Matt. 19.16–22.

160. **that:** so that.

161. Cp. *PL* 8.499: "And they shall be one flesh, one heart, one soul."

162. Milton's argument for divorce will depend in part on the possibility of incompatibility that results from the Fall.

163. **individually:** indivisibly, inseparably.

If this be not thought enough, I answer yet further, that marriage, unless it mean a fit and tolerable marriage, is not inseparable neither by nature nor institution. Not by nature, for then those Mosaic divorces had been against nature, if separable and inseparable be contraries, as who doubts they be? And what is against nature is against law, if soundest philosophy abuse us not.[164] By this reckoning Moses should be most un-Mosaic, that is, most illegal, not to say most unnatural. Nor is it inseparable by the first institution: for then no second institution in the same law for so many causes could dissolve it; it being most unworthy a human (as Plato's judgment is in the fourth book of his *Laws*)[165] much more a divine lawgiver to write two several decrees upon the same thing. But what would Plato have deemed if the one of these were good, the other evil to be done? Lastly, suppose it be inseparable by institution, yet in competition with higher things, as religion and charity in mainest matters, and when the chief end is frustrate for which it was ordained (as hath been shown), if still it must remain inseparable, it holds a strange and lawless propriety from all other works of God under heaven.

From these many considerations we may safely gather that so much of the first institution as our Savior mentions, for he mentions not all, was but to quell and put to nonplus the tempting Pharisees and to lay open their ignorance and shallow understanding of the scriptures. For, saith he, "have ye not read that he which made them at the beginning, made them male and female, and said, 'for this cause shall a man cleave to his wife'?" [Matt. 19.4-5]; which these blind usurpers of Moses' chair could not gainsay: as if this single respect of male and female were sufficient against a thousand inconveniences and mischiefs to clog a rational creature to his endless sorrow unrelinquishably, under the guileful superscription of his intended solace and comfort. What if they had thus answered, master, if thou mean to make wedlock as inseparable as it was from the beginning, let it be made also a fit society as God meant it, which we shall soon understand it ought to be if thou recite the whole reason of the law? Doubtless our Savior had applauded their just answer. For then they had expounded this command of paradise, even as Moses himself expounds it by his laws of divorce, that is, with due and wise regard had to the premises and reasons of the first command, according to which, without unclean and temporizing permissions, he instructs us in this imperfect state what we may lawfully do about divorce.

But if it be thought that the disciples, offended at the rigor of Christ's answer, could yet obtain no mitigation of the former sentence pronounced to the Pharisees, it may be fully answered that our Savior continues the same reply to his disciples, as men leavened with the same customary license which the Pharisees maintained and displeased at the removing of a traditional abuse whereto they had so long not unwillingly been used. It was no time then to contend with

164. Cp. Aquinas, *Summa Theologica* 1–2. Q.95. art 2: "A human law has so much the nature of law, as it is consistent with the law of nature."

165. In *Laws* 4 (719d), Plato argues that the lawgiver must make only one law about the same thing.

their slow and prejudicial belief, in a thing wherein an ordinary measure of light in scripture (with some attention) might afterwards inform them well enough. And yet ere Christ had finished this argument, they might have picked out of his own concluding words an answer more to their minds, and in effect the same with that which hath been all this while entreating audience. "All men," said he, "cannot receive this saying, save they to whom it is given; he that is able to receive it let him receive it" [Matt. 19.11–12]. What saying is this which is left to a man's choice to receive or not receive? What but the married life? Was our Savior then so mild and favorable to the weakness of a single man, and is he turned on the sudden so rigorous and inexorable to the distresses and extremities of an ill-wedded man? Did he so graciously give leave to change the better single life for the worse married life? Did he open so to us this hazardous and accidental door of marriage to shut upon us like the gate of death without retracting or returning, without permitting to change the worst, most insupportable, most unchristian mischance of marriage for all the mischiefs and sorrows that can ensue, being an ordinance which was especially given as a cordial and exhilarating cup of solace the better to bear our other crosses and afflictions? Questionless, this were a hardheartedness of undivorcing worse than that in the Jews which they say extorted the allowance from Moses, and is utterly dissonant from all the doctrine of our Savior.

After these considerations, therefore, to take a law out of paradise given in time of original perfection, and to take it barely without those just and equal inferences and reasons which mainly establish it (nor so much as admitting those needful and safe allowances wherewith Moses himself interprets it to the fallen condition of man), argues nothing in us but rashness and contempt of those means that God left us in his pure and chaste law, without which it will not be possible for us to perform the strict imposition of this command; or, if we strive beyond our strength, we shall strive to obey it otherwise than God commands it. And lamented experience daily teaches the bitter and vain fruits of this our presumption, forcing men in a thing wherein we are not able to judge either of their strength or of their sufferance. Whom neither one vice nor other by natural addiction, but only marriage ruins; which doubtless is not the fault of that ordinance, for God gave it as a blessing, nor always of man's mis-choosing, it being an error above wisdom to prevent, as examples of wisest men so mistaken manifest. It is the fault therefore of a perverse opinion that will have it continued in despite of nature and reason, when indeed it was never truly joined. All those expositors upon the fifth of Matthew confess the Law of Moses to be the Law of the Lord wherein no addition or diminution hath place; yet coming to the point of divorce, as if they feared not to be called least in the kingdom of heaven,[166] any slight evasion will content them to reconcile those contradictions which they make between Christ and Moses, between Christ and Christ.[167]

166. Matt. 5.19.

167. Milton might be said here to displace the charges of evasion and contradiction that might be brought against his own reading of Matt. 19.

CHAP. 10

The vain shift of those who make the law of divorce to be only the premises of a succeeding law. . . .

CHAP. 11

The other shift of saying divorce was permitted by law, but not approved. More of the institution. . . .

CHAP. 12

The third shift of them who esteem it a mere judicial law. Proved again to be a law of moral equity. . . .

CHAP. 13

The ridiculous opinion, that divorce was permitted from the custom in Egypt. That Moses gave not this law unwillingly. Perkins *confesses this law was not abrogated. . . .*

CHAP. 14

That Beza's *opinion of regulating sin by a politic law cannot be sound.*

Yet Beza's opinion is that a politic law (but what politic law I know not, unless one of Machiavel's) may regulate sin,[168] may bear indeed, I grant, with imperfection for a time, as the Apostles did in ceremonial things. But as for sin, the essence of it cannot consist with rule, and if the Law fall to regulate sin, and not to take it utterly away, it necessarily confirms and establishes sin. To make a regularity of sin by law, either the Law must straighten sin into no sin, or sin must crook the Law into no law. The judicial law can serve to no other end than to be the protector and champion of religion and honest civility, as is set down plainly (Rom. 13),[169] and is but the arm of moral law, which can no more be separate from justice than justice from virtue. Their office also in a different manner steers the same course: the one teaches what is good by precept, the other unteaches what is bad by punishment. But if we give way to politic dispensations of lewd uncleanness, the first good consequence of such a relax will be the

168. Milton has in mind the *Annotationes Majores in Novum Testamentum* (1594) of Calvin's successor in Geneva, Theodore *Beza* (1519–1605); commenting on Matt. 19.8, Beza distinguishes between moral law, which always commands the good and prohibits evil, and civil law, which must at times regulate sins that it cannot abolish.

169. Rom. 13.1: "For there is no power but of God: the powers that be are ordained of God."

justifying of papal stews,[170] joined with a toleration of epidemic whoredom. Justice must revolt from the end of her authority, and become the patron of that whereof she was created the punisher. The example of usury, which is commonly alleged, makes against the allegation which it brings, as I touched before. Besides that usury, so much as is permitted by the magistrate and demanded with common equity, is neither against the word of God nor the rule of charity, as hath been often discussed by men of eminent learning and judgment.[171] There must be therefore some other example found out to show us wherein civil policy may with warrant from God settle wickedness by law, and make that lawful which is lawless. Although I doubt not but, upon deeper consideration, that which is true in physic will be found as true in policy, that as of bad pulses those that beat most in order are much worse than those that keep the most inordinate circuit, so of popular vices those that may be committed legally will be more pernicious than those that are left to their own course at peril, not under a stinted privilege to sin orderly and regularly, which is an implicit contradiction, but under due and fearless execution of punishment.

The political law, since it cannot regulate vice, is to restrain it, by using all means to root it out. But if it suffer the weed to grow up to any pleasurable or contented height upon what pretext soever, it fastens the root, it prunes and dresses vice, as if it were a good plant. Let no man doubt therefore to affirm that it is not so hurtful or dishonorable to a commonwealth, nor so much to the hardening of hearts, when those worse faults pretended to be feared, are committed by who so dares under strict and executed penalty, as when those less faults, tolerated for fear of greater, harden their faces, not their hearts only, under the protection of public authority. For what less indignity were this, than as if Justice herself, the queen of virtues, descending from her sceptered royalty, instead of conquering should compound and treat with sin, her eternal adversary and rebel, upon ignoble terms? Or as if the judicial law were like that untrusty steward in the Gospel, and, instead of calling in the debts of his moral master, should give out subtle and sly acquittances to keep himself from begging?[172] Or let us person him like some wretched itinerary judge, who, to gratify his delinquents before him, would let them basely break his head, lest they should pull him from the bench and throw him over the bar. Unless we had rather think both moral and judicial full of malice and deadly purpose conspired to let the debtor Israelite, the seed of Abraham, run on upon a bankrout[173] score, flattered with insufficient and ensnaring discharges, that so he might be haled to a more cruel forfeit for all the indulgent arrears which

170. Protestant polemicists often charged that the papacy allowed and, by taxation, profited from Roman brothels.

171. Milton's father was a usurer; Milton met and married Mary Powell while visiting her family to collect on a loan from his father to hers.

172. See Luke 16.1–8.

173. **bankrout:** bankrupt.

those judicial acquitments had engaged him in. No, no, this cannot be, that the Law whose integrity and faithfulness is next to God, should be either the shameless broker of our impurities or the intended instrument of our destruction. The method of holy correction, such as became the commonwealth of Israel, is not to bribe sin with sin, to capitulate and hire out one crime with another; but, with more noble and graceful severity than Popilius the Roman legate used with Antiochus,[174] to limit and level out the direct way from vice to virtue, with straightest and exactest lines on either side, not winding or indenting so much as to the right hand of fair pretences. Violence indeed and insurrection may force the law to suffer what it cannot mend, but to write a decree in allowance of sin, as soon can the hand of Justice rot off. Let this be ever concluded as a truth that will outlive the faith of those that seek to bear it down.

CHAP. 15

That divorce was not given for wives only, as Beza *and* Paræus *write. More of the institution.*

Lastly, if divorce were granted, as Beza and others say,[175] not for men but to release afflicted wives, certainly it is not only a dispensation, but a most merciful law; and why it should not yet be in force, being wholly as needful, I know not what can be in cause but senseless cruelty. But yet to say divorce was granted for relief of wives, rather than of husbands is but weakly conjectured, and is manifest the extreme shift of a huddled exposition. Whenas it could not be found how hardness of heart should be lessened by liberty of divorce, a fancy was devised to hide the flaw by commenting that divorce was permitted only for the help of wives. Palpably uxorious! Who can be ignorant that woman was created for man and not man for woman, and that a husband may be injured as insufferably in marriage as a wife. What an injury is it after wedlock not to be beloved, what to be slighted, what to be contended with in point of house-rule who shall be the head, not for any parity of wisdom (for that were something reasonable) but out of a female pride? "I suffer not," saith St. Paul, "the woman to usurp authority over the man."[176] If the apostle could not suffer it, into what mould is he mortified that can? Solomon saith, "that a bad wife is to her husband as rottenness to his bones, a continual dropping: better dwell in a corner of the housetop, or in the wilderness" than with such a one.[177] "Who so hideth her hideth the wind, and one of the four mischiefs that the earth cannot bear."[178] If the spirit of

174. Gaius *Popilius* stopped *Antiochus* IV's invasion of Egypt by commanding him not to step outside a circle drawn about him until he agreed to the terms of the Roman Senate (Polybius, *Histories* 29.27).

175. Milton refers to Beza's *Annotationes Majores in Novum Testamentum* (see note 165) and David Paræus's *Operum Theologicorum* (1605), 1.784.

176. 1 Tim. 2.12.

177. Milton stitches together Prov. 12.4, 19.13, 21.9, 21.19.

178. Milton quotes Prov. 27.16 and digests Prov. 30.21–23.

God wrote such aggravations as these and, as may be guessed by these similitudes, counsels the man rather to divorce than to live with such a colleague, and yet on the other side expresses nothing of the wife's suffering with a bad husband, is it not most likely that God in his Law had more pity towards man thus wedlocked than towards the woman that was created for another? The same spirit relates to us the course which the Medes and Persians took by occasion of Vashti, whose mere denial to come at her husband's sending lost her the being queen any longer and set up a wholesome law, "that every man should bear rule in his own house" [Esth. 1.22]. And the divine relater shows us not the least sign of disliking what was done. How should he, if Moses long before was nothing less mindful of the honor and preeminence due to man? So that to say divorce was granted for woman rather than man was but fondly invented.

Esteeming therefore to have asserted thus an injured law of Moses from the unwarranted and guilty name of a dispensation, to be again a most equal and requisite law, we have the word of Christ himself, that he came not to alter the least tittle of it, and signifies no small displeasure against him that shall teach to do so. On which relying, I shall not much waver to affirm that those words which are made to intimate as if they forbade all divorce but for adultery (though Moses have constituted otherwise), those words taken circumscriptly,[179] without regard to any precedent law of Moses or attestation of Christ himself or without care to preserve those his fundamental and superior laws of nature and charity to which all other ordinances give up their seals, are as much against plain equity and the mercy of religion, as those words of "take, eat, this is my body" [Matt. 26.26; Mark 14.22], elementally understood,[180] are against nature and sense.

And surely the restoring of this degraded law hath well recompensed the diligence was used, by enlightening us further to find out wherefore Christ took off the Pharisees from alleging the law and referred them to the first institution, not condemning, altering, or abolishing this precept of divorce, which is plainly moral, for that were against his truth, his promise, and his prophetic office. But knowing how fallaciously they had cited and concealed the particular and natural reason of the law, that they might justify any froward reason of their own, he lets go that sophistry unconvinced, for that had been to teach them else, which his purpose was not. And since they had taken a liberty which the law gave not, he amuses[181] and repels their tempting pride with a perfection of paradise, which the law required not. Not thereby to oblige our performance to that whereto the law never enjoined the fallen estate of man; for if the first in-

179. **circumscriptly:** out of context.

180. **elementally understood:** i.e., understood as referring literally to the transformation of *elements* (bread and wine to body and blood); Milton brands the common teaching on divorce by association with Roman Catholic notions of the Eucharist.

181. **amuses:** baffles, perplexes.

stitution must make wedlock, whatever happen, inseparable to us, it must make it also as perfect, as meetly helpful, and as comfortable, as God promised it should be, at least in some degree. Otherwise it is not equal or proportionable to the strength of man that he should be reduced into such indissoluble bonds to his assured misery, if all the other conditions of that covenant be manifestly altered.

CHAP. 16

How to be understood that they must be one flesh. And how that those whom God hath joined man should not sunder.

Next he saith, "they must be one flesh" [Gen. 2.24], which, when all conjecturing is done, will be found to import no more but to make legitimate and good the carnal act, which else might seem to have something of pollution in it. And infers thus much over, that the fit union of their souls be such as may even incorporate them to love and amity, but that can never be where no correspondence is of the mind. Nay, instead of being one flesh, they will be rather two carcasses chained unnaturally together or, as it may happen, a living soul bound to a dead corpse, a punishment too like that inflicted by the tyrant Mezentius,[182] so little worthy to be received as that remedy of loneliness which God meant us. Since we know it is not the joining of another body will remove loneliness but the uniting of another compliable mind, and that it is no blessing but a torment, nay a base and brutish condition, to be one flesh, unless where nature can in some measure fix a unity of disposition.

The meaning, therefore, of these words, "For this cause shall a man leave his father and his mother, and shall cleave to his wife" [Matt. 19.5], was first to show us the dear affection which naturally grows in every not unnatural marriage, even to the leaving of parents or other familiarity whatsoever. Next, it justifies a man in so doing, that nothing is done undutifully to father or mother. But that he should be[183] here sternly commanded to cleave to his error, a disposition which to his he finds will never cement, a quotidian of sorrow and discontent in his house, let us be excused to pause a little and bethink us every way round ere we lay such a flat solecism upon the gracious and certainly not inexorable, not ruthless and flinty ordinance of marriage. For if the meaning of these words must be thus blocked up within their own letters from all equity and fair deduction, they will serve then well indeed their turn who affirm divorce to have been granted only for wives—whenas we see no word of this text binds women, but men only, what it binds. No marvel then if Salomith, sister to Herod, sent a writ

182. Vergil describes the grisly torture enacted by the cruel Etruscan king *Mezentius* (*Aen.* 8.485–88).

183. The second edition here reads, apparently erroneously, "But he that should be . . ." We substitute the first edition's wording.

of ease to Costobarus her husband, which as Josephus there attests was lawful only to men.[184] No marvel though Placidia, the sister of Honorius, threatened the like to Earl Constantius for a trivial cause, as Photius relates from Olympiodorus.[185] No marvel any thing if letters must be turned into palisadoes[186] to stake out all requisite sense from entering to their due enlargement.

Lastly, Christ himself tells who should not be put asunder, namely those whom God hath joined. A plain solution of this great controversy, if men would but use their eyes—for when is it that God may be said to join? When the parties and their friends consent? No, surely, for that may concur to lewdest ends. Or is it when church rites are finished? Neither, for the efficacy of those depends upon the presupposed fitness of either party. Perhaps, after carnal knowledge? Least of all, for that may join persons whom neither law nor nature dares join. 'Tis left, that only then, when the minds are fitly disposed and enabled to maintain a cheerful conversation to the solace and love of each other, according as God intended and promised in the very first foundation of matrimony, "I will make him a help meet for him" [Gen. 2.18]. For surely what God intended and promised, that only can be thought to be his joining and not the contrary. So, likewise, the apostle witnesseth (1 Cor. 7.15) that in marriage "God hath called us to peace." And doubtless in what respect he hath called us to marriage, in that also he hath joined us.

The rest whom either disproportion or deadness of spirit, or something distasteful and averse in the immutable bent of nature renders unconjugal, error may have joined, but God never joined against the meaning of his own ordinance. And if he joined them not, then is there no power above their own consent to hinder them from unjoining when they cannot reap the soberest ends of being together in any tolerable sort. Neither can it be said properly that such twain were ever divorced, but only parted from each other, as two persons unconjunctive and unmarriable together. But if, whom God hath made a fit help, frowardness or private injuries hath made unfit, that being the secret of marriage God can better judge than man, neither is man indeed fit or able to decide this matter. However it be, undoubtedly a peaceful divorce is a less evil and less in scandal than a hateful, hardhearted, and destructive continuance of marriage, in the judgment of Moses and of Christ; that justifies him in choosing the less evil, which if it were an honest and civil prudence in the law, what is there in the Gospel forbidding such a kind of legal wisdom, though we should admit the common expositors[187]?

184. Josephus renders this judgment on Salome's divorce of her husband in *Antiq.* 15.7.

185. Photius relates from Olympiodorus's *Histories* the story of Photia's threatening divorce to her husband unless he removed a visiting magician (*Bibliotheca* 80).

186. **palisadoes:** a fence made of stakes.

187. **common expositors:** For this term, see Williams 1948; Milton mostly likely has in mind the standard Calvinist authorities previously cited.

CHAP. 17

The sentence of Christ concerning divorce how to be expounded. What Grotius *hath observed. Other additions.*

Having thus unfolded those ambiguous reasons wherewith Christ, as his wont was, gave to the Pharisees that came to sound him such an answer as they deserved, it will not be uneasy[188] to explain the sentence itself that now follows: "Whosoever shall put away his wife, except it be for fornication, and shall marry another, committeth adultery" [Matt. 19.9]. First, therefore, I will set down what is observed by Grotius upon this point, a man of general learning.[189] Next I produce what mine own thoughts gave me, before I had seen his annotations. Origen,[190] saith he, notes that Christ named adultery rather as one example of other like cases, than as one only exception. And that is frequent, not only in human but in divine laws, to express one kind of fact, whereby other causes of like nature may have the like plea: as Exod. 21.18,19,20,26, Deut. 19.5. And from the maxims of civil law he shows that even in sharpest penal laws, the same reason hath the same right: and in gentler laws that from like causes to like the law interprets rightly. But it may be objected, saith he, that nothing destroys the end of wedlock so much as adultery. To which he answers, that marriage was not ordained only for copulation, but for mutual help and comfort of life, and if we mark diligently the nature of our Savior's commands, we shall find that both their beginning and their end consists in charity, whose will is that we should so be good to others, as that we be not cruel to ourselves. And hence it appears why Mark, and Luke, and St. Paul to the Cor[inthians], mentioning this precept of Christ, add no exception, because exceptions that arise from natural equity are included silently under general terms. It would be considered, therefore, whether the same equity may not have place in other cases less frequent.

Thus far he.[191] From hence is what I add. First, that this saying of Christ, as it is usually expounded, can be no law at all, that a man for no cause should separate but for adultery, except it be a supernatural law, not binding us as we now are.[192] Had it been the law of nature, either the Jews or some other wise and civil nation would have pressed it. Or let it be so, yet that law (Deut. 24.1) whereby a man hath leave to part, whenas for just and natural cause discovered he cannot love, is a law ancienter and deeper engraven in blameless nature than the other. Therefore the inspired lawgiver, Moses, took care that this should be specified and allowed; the other he let vanish in silence, not once repeated in

188. **uneasy:** hard.
189. Milton is referring to Grotius's *Annotationes* (see note *66*).
190. **Origen:** (c. 185–c. 254), a leading church father.
191. **he:** i.e., Grotius, whose argument Milton has been paraphrasing.
192. **as we now are:** i.e., after the Fall.

the volume of his law, even as the reason of it vanished with paradise. Secondly, this can be no new command, for the Gospel enjoins no new morality, save only the infinite enlargement of charity, which in this respect is called the "new commandment" by St. John, as being the accomplishment of every command.[193] Thirdly, it is no command of perfection further than it partakes of charity, which is "the bond of perfection" [Col. 3.14]. Those commands therefore which compel us to self-cruelty, above our strength, so hardly will help forward to perfection, that they hinder and set backward in all the common rudiments of Christianity, as was proved.

It being thus clear that the words of Christ can be no kind of command, as they are vulgarly taken, we shall now see in what sense they may be a command, and that an excellent one, the same with that of Moses and no other. Moses had granted that only for a natural annoyance, defect, or dislike, whether in body or mind (for so the Hebrew words plainly note),[194] which a man could not force himself to live with, he might give a bill of divorce, thereby forbidding any other cause wherein amendment or reconciliation might have place. This law, the Pharisees depraving,[195] extended to any slight contentious cause whatsoever. Christ therefore, seeing where they halted,[196] urges the negative part of that law, which is necessarily understood (for the determinate permission of Moses binds them from further license), and checking their supercilious drift, declares that no accidental, temporary, or reconcilable offence, except fornication, can justify a divorce. He touches not here those natural and perpetual hindrances of society, whether in body or mind, which are not to be removed, for such, as they are aptest to cause an unchangeable offence, so are they not capable of reconcilement because not of amendment. They do not break, indeed, but they annihilate the bands of marriage more than adultery. For that fault committed argues not always a hatred either natural or incidental against whom it is committed; neither does it infer a disability of all future helpfulness, or loyalty, or loving agreement, being once past and pardoned where it can be pardoned. But that which naturally distastes, and "finds no favor in the eyes" of matrimony, can never be concealed, never appeased, never intermitted, but proves a perpetual nullity of love and contentment, a solitude, and dead vacation[197] of all acceptable conversing. Moses therefore permits divorce, but in cases only that have no hands to join and more need separating than adultery. Christ forbids it, but in matters only that may accord,[198] and those less than fornication. Thus is Moses' law here plainly confirmed, and those causes which he permitted not a jot gainsaid.

And that this is the true meaning of this place, I prove also by no less an

193. John 13.34.
194. See 1.1.
195. I.e., this law, having been depraved by the Pharisees.
196. **halted:** fell short.
197. **vacation:** cessation.
198. **accord:** be brought into concord.

author than St. Paul himself, 1 Cor. 7.10, 11, upon which text interpreters agree that the apostle only repeats the precept of Christ; where while he speaks of "the wife's reconcilement to her husband," he puts it out of controversy that our Savior meant chiefly matters of strife and reconcilement, of which sort he would not that any difference should be the occasion of divorce, except fornication. And that we may learn better how to value a grave and prudent law of Moses, and how unadvisedly we smatter with our lips when we talk of Christ's abolishing any judicial law of his great Father (except in some circumstances which are judaical[199] rather than judicial, and need no abolishing but cease of themselves), I say again, that this recited law of Moses contains a cause of divorce greater beyond compare than that for adultery; and whoso cannot so conceive it, errs and wrongs exceedingly a law of deep wisdom for want of well fathoming. For let him mark, no man urges the just divorcing of adultery as it is a sin but as it is an injury to marriage, and though it be but once committed and that without malice, whether through importunity or opportunity, the Gospel does not therefore dissuade him who would therefore divorce; but that natural hatred whenever it arises is a greater evil in marriage than the accident of adultery, a greater defrauding, a greater injustice, and yet not blamable, he who understands not after all this representing, I doubt his will like a hard spleen draws faster than his understanding can well sanguify.[200] Nor did that man ever know or feel what it is to love truly, nor ever yet comprehend in his thoughts what the true intent of marriage is.[201] And this also will be somewhat above his reach, but yet no less a truth for lack of his perspective, that as no man apprehends what vice is so well as he who is truly virtuous; no man knows hell like him who converses most in heaven, so there is none that can estimate the evil and the affliction of a natural hatred in matrimony, unless he have a soul gentle enough and spacious enough to contemplate what is true love.

And the reason why men so disesteem this wise judging law of God and count hate or "the not finding of favor," as it is there termed, a humorous,[202] a dishonest, and slight cause of divorce, is because themselves apprehend so little of what true concord is. For if they did, they would be juster in their balancing between natural hatred and casual adultery; this being but a transient injury, and soon amended, I mean as to the party against whom the trespass is, but the other being an unspeakable and unremitting sorrow and offense, whereof no amends can be made, no cure, no ceasing but by divorce, which like a divine touch in one moment heals all, and like the word of a God, in one in-

199. **judaical:** i.e., involving only the Jewish ceremonial law as opposed to moral law.

200. **sanguify:** generate blood. Milton's figure is based on a physiological model under which the liver generates blood, which in turn is purified by the spleen—in the absence of the product of the understanding, the will labors in vain, like the spleen in the absence of blood.

201. Here and in the next sentence, Milton links his innovative teaching on divorce to an all too rare understanding of marriage. His is the *soul gentle enough and spacious enough* to understand what love is.

202. **humorous:** slight and capricious.

stant hushes outrageous tempests into a sudden stillness and peaceful calm.[203] Yet all this so great a good of God's own enlarging to us is by the hard reins of them that sit us wholly diverted and embezzled from us. Maligners of mankind! But who hath taught ye to mangle thus and make more gashes in the miseries of a blameless creature with the leaden daggers of your literal decrees, to whose ease you cannot add the tithe of one small atom but by letting alone your unhelpful surgery? As for such as think wandering concupiscence to be here newly and more precisely forbidden than it was before, if the apostle can convince them, we know that we are to "know lust by the law" [Rom 7.7] and not by any new discovery of the gospel. The law of Moses knew what it permitted and the Gospel knew what it forbid. He that under a peevish conceit of debarring concupiscence shall go about to make a novice of Moses (not to say a worse thing for reverence sake) and such a one of God himself, as is a horror to think, to bind our Savior in the default of a downright promise breaking, and to bind the disunions of complaining nature in chains together and curb them with a canon bit,[204] 'tis he that commits all the whoredom and adultery which himself adjudges, besides the former guilt so manifold that lies upon him. And if none of these considerations with all their weight and gravity can avail to the dispossessing him of his precious literalism, let some one or other entreat him but to read on in the same 19 of Matth[ew], till he come to that place that says, "Some make themselves eunuchs for the kingdom of heaven's sake" [Matt. 19.12]. And if then he please to make use of Origen's knife, he may do well to be his own carver.[205]

CHAP. 18

Whether the words of our Savior be rightly expounded only of actual fornication to be the cause of divorce. The opinion of Grotius *with other reasons.*

But because we know that Christ never gave a judicial law and that the word fornication is variously significant in scripture, it will be much right done to our Savior's words to consider diligently whether it be meant here that nothing but actual fornication, proved by witness, can warrant a divorce, for so our canon law judges. Nevertheless, as I find that Grotius on this place hath observed, the Christian emperors, Theodosius the Second and Justinian, men of high wisdom and reputed piety, decreed it to be a divorsive fornication if the wife attempted either against the knowledge or obstinately against the will of her husband, such things as gave open suspicion of adulterizing: as the willful haunting of feasts and invitations with men not of her near kindred, the lying forth of her house without probable cause, the frequenting of theaters against her husband's

203. See Matt. 8.26, Mark 4.39.

204. A play on words, drawing together the *canon bit,* a kind of riding bit, with the Canon Law.

205. Origen is said to have castrated himself after reading the verse from Matthew just quoted.

mind, her endeavor to prevent or destroy conception.[206] Hence that of Jerome, "Where fornication is suspected, the wife may lawfully be divorced." Not that every motion of a jealous mind should be regarded, but that it should not be exacted to prove all things by the visibility of law witnessing, or else to hoodwink the mind: for the law is not able to judge of these things but by the rule of equity and by permitting a wise man to walk the middle way of prudent circumspection, neither wretchedly jealous nor stupidly and tamely patient: to this purpose hath Grotius in his notes. He shows also that fornication is taken in scripture for such a continual headstrong behavior as tends to plain contempt of the husband, and proves it out of Judges 19.2, where the Levite's wife is said to have played the whore against him, which Josephus and the Septuagint[207] with the Chaldaean interpret only of stubbornness and rebellion against her husband.[208] And to this I add that Kimchi[209] and the two other Rabbis who gloss the text, are in the same opinion. Ben Gersom reasons that had it been whoredom, a Jew and a Levite would have disdained to fetch her again. And this I shall contribute, that had it been whoredom, she would have chosen any other place to run to than to her father's house, it being so infamous for an Hebrew woman to play the harlot and so opprobrious to the parents. Fornication, then, in this place of the Judges is understood for stubborn disobedience against the husband, and not for adultery....

CHAP. 19

Christ's manner of teaching. St. Paul *adds to this matter of divorce without command, to show the matter to be of equity, not of rigor. That the bondage of a Christian may be as much, and his peace as little in some other marriages besides idolatrous. If those arguments, therefore, be good in that one case, why not in those other? Therefore the apostle himself adds* ἐν τοῖς τοιούτοις.[210]

Thus at length we see, both by this[211] and by other places, that there is scarce any one saying in the Gospel but must be read with limitations and distinctions to be rightly understood; for Christ gives no full comments or continued discourses, but, as Demetrius the rhetorician phrases it,[212] speaks oft in monosyllables, like a master scattering the heavenly grain of his doctrine like pearl here and there, which requires a skillful and laborious gatherer who must compare the words he finds with other precepts, with the end of every ordinance, and

206. This sentence and the next two translate and paraphrase a passage from Grotius' *Annotationes.*

207. **Septuagint:** third-century Greek version of the Hebrew Scriptures.

208. Once again Milton paraphrases Grotius; as the Yale editor notes, Milton fails to mention that Grotius relates this argument without endorsing it.

209. David *Kimchi,* like Levi *ben Gersom* in the next sentence, were learned rabbis of the Middle Ages.

210. "In such cases" (1 Cor. 7.15).

211. Matt. 5.32, which Milton has been addressing in the second book.

212. In *On Style* (fourth century B.C.E.).

with the general analogy of evangelic doctrine. Otherwise many particular sayings would be but strange repugnant riddles, and the church would offend in granting divorce for frigidity, which is not here excepted with adultery but by them added. And this was it undoubtedly which gave reason to St. Paul of his own authority, as he professes, and without command from the Lord, to enlarge the seeming construction of those places in the Gospel, by adding a case wherein a person deserted, which is something less than divorced, may lawfully marry again. And having declared his opinion in one case, he leaves a further liberty for Christian prudence to determine in cases of like importance, using words so plain as are not to be shifted off, "that a brother or a sister is not under bondage in such cases," adding also that "God hath called us to peace" in marriage [1 Cor. 7.15].

Now if it be plain that a Christian may be brought into unworthy bondage, and his religious peace not only interrupted now and then but perpetually and finally hindered in wedlock by mis-yoking with a diversity of nature as well as of religion, the reasons of St. Paul cannot be made special to that one case of infidelity, but are of equal moment to a divorce wherever Christian liberty and peace are without fault equally obstructed; that the ordinance which God gave to our comfort may not be pinned upon us to our undeserved thraldom, to be cooped up, as it were, in mockery of wedlock, to a perpetual betrothed loneliness and discontent, if nothing worse ensue. There being naught else of marriage left between such but a displeasing and forced remedy against the sting of a brute desire, which fleshly accustoming[213] without the soul's union and commixture of intellectual delight, as it is rather a soiling than a fulfilling of marriage rites, so it is enough to imbase the mettle of a generous spirit, and sinks him to a low and vulgar pitch of endeavor in all his actions, or, which is worse, leaves him in a despairing plight of abject and hardened thoughts. Which condition rather than a good man should fall into, a man useful in the service of God and mankind, Christ himself hath taught us to dispense with the most sacred ordinances of his worship, even for a bodily healing to dispense with that holy and speculative rest of Sabbath,[214] much more than with the erroneous observance of an ill-knotted marriage, for the sustaining of an overcharged faith and perseverance.

CHAP. 20

The meaning of St. Paul, *that* charity believeth all things. *What is to be said to the license which is vainly feared will grow hereby. What to those who never have done prescribing patience in this case. The papist most severe against divorce, yet most easy to all license.*

213. **accustoming:** sexual intimacy.

214. See 2.1.

Of all the miseries in marriage God is to be cleared and the fault to be laid on man's unjust laws.

And though bad causes would take license by this pretext, if that cannot be remedied, upon their conscience be it who shall so do. This was that hardness of heart and abuse of a good law which Moses was content to suffer rather than good men should not have it at all to use needfully. And he who to run after one lost sheep left ninety-nine of his own flock at random in the wilderness[215] would little perplex his thought for the obduring[216] of nine-hundred and ninety such as will daily take worse liberties, whether they have permission or not. To conclude, as without charity God hath given no commandment to men, so without it neither can men rightly believe any commandment given. For every act of true faith, as well that whereby we believe the law as that whereby we endeavor[217] the law, is wrought in us by charity, according to that in the divine hymn of St. Paul, 1 Cor. 13[.7], "charity believeth all things." Not as if she were so credulous, which is the exposition hitherto current, for that were a trivial praise, but to teach us that charity is the high governess of our belief, and that we cannot safely assent to any precept written in the Bible but as charity commends it to us. Which agrees with that of the same apostle to the Ephes[ians] (4.14–15), where he tells us that the way to get a sure undoubted knowledge of things is to hold that for truth which accords most with charity. Whose unerring guidance and conduct having followed as a lodestar with all diligence and fidelity in this question, I trust, through the help of that illuminating spirit which hath favored me, to have done no everyday's work in asserting,[218] after many ages, the words of Christ with other scriptures of great concernment from burdensome and remorseless obscurity, tangled with manifold repugnances to their native luster and consent between each other; hereby also dissolving tedious and Gordian[219] difficulties which have hitherto molested the church of God and are now decided, not with the sword of Alexander but with the immaculate hands of charity to the unspeakable good of Christendom.

And let the extreme literalist sit down now and revolve whether this in all necessity be not the due result of our Savior's words. Or if he persist to be otherwise opinioned, let him well advise lest, thinking to grip fast the Gospel, he be found instead with the canon law in his fist, whose boisterous edicts tyrannizing the blessed ordinance of marriage into the quality of a most unnatural and unchristianly yoke have given the flesh this advantage to hate it and turn aside, ofttimes unwillingly, to all dissolute uncleanness, even till punishment it-

215. See Matt. 18.12–13 and Luke 15.4–6.
216. **obduring:** the act of becoming or being obdurate, or hardened.
217. **endeavor:** attempt to fulfill.
218. **asserting:** here carries the meaning of "rescuing."
219. **Gordian:** an allusion to the Gordian knot, which could not be untied.

self is weary and overcome by the incredible frequency of trading lust and uncontrolled adulteries.

Yet men whose creed is custom I doubt not but will be still endeavoring to hide the sloth of their own timorous capacities with this pretext, that for all this 'tis better to endure with patience and silence this affliction which God hath sent. And I agree 'tis true, if this be exhorted and not enjoined, but withal it will be wisely done to be as sure as may be that what man's iniquity hath laid on be not imputed to God's sending, lest under the color of an affected patience we detain ourselves at the gulf's mouth of many hideous temptations, not to be withstood without proper gifts, which, as Perkins well notes, God gives not ordinarily, no not to most earnest prayers.[220] Therefore we pray, "Lead us not into temptation," a vain prayer, if, having led ourselves thither, we love to stay in that perilous condition. God sends remedies as well as evils, under which he who lies and groans, that may lawfully acquit himself, is accessory to his own ruin. Nor will it excuse him, though he suffer through a sluggish fearfulness to search thoroughly what is lawful, for fear of disquieting the secure falsity of an old opinion.

Who doubts not but that it may be piously said to him who would dismiss frigidity, "bear your trial, take it as if God would have you live this life of continence"? If he exhort this, I hear him as an angel, though he speak without warrant, but if he would compel me, I know him for Satan. To him who divorces an adulteress, piety might say, "pardon her, you may show much mercy, you may win a soul"; yet the law both of God and man leaves it freely to him, for God loves not to plow out the heart of our endeavors with over-hard and sad tasks. God delights not to make a drudge of virtue, whose actions must be all elective and unconstrained. Forced virtue is as a bolt overshot,[221] it goes neither forward nor backward and does no good as it stands.

Seeing therefore that neither scripture nor reason hath laid this unjust austerity upon divorce, we may resolve that nothing else hath wrought it but that letter-bound servility of the canon doctors, supposing marriage to be a sacrament, and out of the art they have to lay unnecessary burdens upon all men, to make a fair show in the fleshly observance of matrimony, though peace and love with all other conjugal respects fare never so ill. And indeed the papists, who are the strictest forbidders of divorce, are the easiest libertines to admit of grossest uncleanness, as if they had a design by making wedlock a supportless[222] yoke, to violate it most under color of preserving it most inviolable; and withal delighting, as their mystery[223] is, to make men the day-laborers of their own af-

220. Milton paraphrases from the *Christian Oeconomie* (1609) of the leading Calvinist theologian of Elizabethan England, William Perkins (1558–1602).
221. The comparison is to a jammed lock.
222. **supportless:** unbearable, insupportable.
223. **mystery:** hidden design.

flictions, as if there were such a scarcity of miseries from abroad that we should be made to melt our choicest home blessings and coin them into crosses, for want whereby to hold commerce with patience.

If any, therefore, who shall hap to read this discourse, hath been through misadventure ill engaged in this contracted evil here complained of and finds the fits and workings of a high impatience frequently upon him, of all those wild words which men in misery think to ease themselves by uttering, let him not open his lips against the providence of heaven or tax the ways of God and his divine truth—for they are equal, easy, and not burdensome. Nor do they ever cross the just and reasonable desires of men, nor involve this our portion of mortal life into a necessity of sadness and malcontent by laws commanding over the unreducible antipathies of nature sooner or later found, but allow us to remedy and shake off those evils into which human error hath led us through the midst of our best intentions and to support our incident extremities by that authentic precept of sovereign charity, whose grand commission is to do and to dispose over all the ordinances of God to man, that love and truth may advance each other to everlasting. While we, literally superstitious through customary faintness of heart, not venturing to pierce with our free thoughts into the full latitude of nature and religion, abandon ourselves to serve under the tyranny of usurped opinions, suffering those ordinances which were allotted to our solace and reviving to trample over us and hale us into a multitude of sorrows which God never meant us. And where he set us in a fair allowance of way, with honest liberty and prudence to our guard, we never leave subtilizing and casuisting[224] till we have straitened and pared that liberal path into a razor's edge to walk on between a precipice of unnecessary mischief on either side. And starting at every false alarm, we do not know which way to set a foot forward with manly confidence and Christian resolution through the confused ringing in our ears of panic scruples and amazements.

CHAP. 21

That the matter of divorce is not to be tried by law, but by conscience, as many other sins are. The magistrate can only see that the condition of divorce be just and equal. The opinion of Fagius *and the reasons of this assertion.*

Another act of papal encroachment it was to pluck the power and arbitrament of divorce from the master of family, into whose hands God and the law of all nations had put it and Christ so left it, preaching only to the conscience and not authorizing a judicial court to toss about and divulge the unaccountable and secret reasons of disaffection between man and wife, as a thing most improperly

224. **casuisting:** practicing casuistry, a sophisticated and, in Milton's view, sophistical Roman Catholic art of moral reasoning.

answerable to any such kind of trial. But the popes of Rome, perceiving the great revenue and high authority it would give them even over princes to have the judging and deciding of such a main consequence in the life of man as was divorce, wrought so upon the superstition of those ages as to divest them of that right which God from the beginning had entrusted to the husband. By which means they subjected that ancient and naturally domestic prerogative to an external and unbefitting judicature. For although differences in divorce about dowries, jointures, and the like, besides the punishing of adultery, ought not to pass without referring, if need be, to the magistrate, yet that the absolute and final hindering of divorce cannot belong to any civil or earthly power against the will and consent of both parties, or of the husband alone, some reasons will be here urged.... [*In an omitted passage, Milton cites the authority of Grotius and Fagius.*]

If there remain a furlong yet to end the question, these following reasons may serve to gain it with any apprehension not too unlearned or too wayward. First, because ofttimes the causes of seeking divorce reside so deeply in the radical and innocent affections of nature as is not within the diocese of law to tamper with. Other relations may aptly enough be held together by a civil and virtuous love, but the duties of man and wife are such as are chiefly conversant in that love which is most ancient and merely[225] natural, whose two prime statutes are to join itself to that which is good and acceptable and friendly and to turn aside and depart from what is disagreeable, displeasing and unlike. Of the two this latter is the strongest and most equal to be regarded, for although a man may often be unjust in seeking that which he loves, yet he can never be unjust or blamable in retiring from his endless trouble and distaste, whenas his tarrying can redound to no true content on either side. Hate is of all things the mightiest divider, nay, is division itself. To couple hatred therefore, though wedlock try all her golden links and borrow to her aid all the iron manacles and fetters of law, it does but seek to twist a rope of sand,[226] which was a task, they say, that posed the devil. And that sluggish fiend in hell, Ocnus, whom the poems tell of, brought his idle cordage to as good effect, which never served to bind with but to feed the ass that stood at his elbow.[227] And that the restrictive law against divorce attains as little to bind anything truly in a disjointed marriage or to keep it bound, but serves only to feed the ignorance and definitive impertinence of a doltish canon, were no absurd allusion.

To hinder therefore those deep and serious regresses of nature in a reasonable soul parting from that mistaken help which he justly seeks in a person created for him, recollecting[228] himself from an unmeet help which was never

225. **merely:** entirely.

226. A proverbial expression for an impossible feat and for a fetter that does not bind; cp. George Herbert, "The Collar."

227. *Ocnus* was condemned in hell to make from straw a rope, which his ass immediately ate (Pausanias, *Description of Greece* 10.29.1–2).

228. **recollecting:** withdrawing.

meant, and to detain him by compulsion in such an unpredestined misery as this, is in diameter against[229] both nature and institution; but to interpose a jurisdictive power upon the inward and irremediable disposition of man, to command love and sympathy, to forbid dislike against the guiltless instinct of nature, is not within the province of any law to reach, and were indeed an incommodious rudeness, not a just power. For that law may bandy with nature and traverse her sage motions was an error in Callicles, the rhetorician, whom Socrates from high principles confutes in Plato's *Gorgias*.[230] If therefore divorce may be so natural and that law and nature are not to go contrary, then to forbid divorce compulsively is not only against nature, but against law.

Next, it must be remembered that all law is for some good that may be frequently attained without the admixture of a worse inconvenience, and therefore many gross faults (as ingratitude and the like, which are too far within the soul to be cured by constraint of law) are left only to be wrought on by conscience and persuasion; which made Aristotle, in the 10th of his *Ethics* to Nicomachus, aim at a kind of division of law into private or persuasive and public or compulsive.[231] Hence it is that the law forbidding divorce never attains to any good end of such prohibition, but rather multiplies evil. For if nature's resistless sway in love or hate be once compelled, it grows careless of itself, vicious, useless to friend, unserviceable and spiritless to the commonwealth, which Moses rightly foresaw, and all wise lawgivers that ever knew man, what kind of creature he was. The Parliament also and clergy of England were not ignorant of this when they consented that Harry the Eighth might put away his queen Anne of Cleve, whom he could not like after he had been wedded half a year,[232] unless it were that contrary to the proverb, they made a necessity of that which might have been a virtue in them to do. For even the freedom and eminence of man's creation gives him to be a law in this matter to himself, being the head of the other sex which was made for him,[233] whom therefore, though he ought not to injure, yet neither should he be forced to retain in society to his own overthrow, nor to hear any judge therein above himself. It being also an unseemly affront to the sequestered and veiled modesty of that sex to have her unpleasingness and other concealments bandied up and down, and aggravated in open court by those hired masters of tongue-fence.[234] . . . [*In several omitted sentences, Milton offers an example from the divorce proceedings of Henry VIII and Catherine of Aragon.*] That woman whose honor is not appeached[235] is less injured by a silent dismission, being otherwise not illiberally dealt with, than to

229. **in diameter against:** diametrically opposed to.

230. Socrates argues against Callicles that justice is inherent in things and not merely a matter of convention (*Gorgias* 482–510).

231. *Nichomachean Ethics* 10.9.

232. Henry VIII was divorced from Anne of Cleves in 1540, after six months of marriage.

233. Cp. 1 Cor. 11.3: "The head of the woman is the man."

234. **hired masters of tongue-fence:** i.e., lawyers.

235. **appeached:** impeached.

endure a clamoring debate of utterless things in a business of that civil secrecy and difficult discerning, as not to be overmuch questioned by nearest friends. Which drew that answer from the greatest and worthiest Roman of his time, Paulus Emilius, being demanded why he would put away his wife for no visible reason: "This shoe," saith he, and held it out on his foot, "is a neat shoe, a new shoe, and yet none of you know where it wrings me."[236] Much less by the unfamiliar cognizance of a feed gamester can such a private difference be examined, neither ought it.

Again, if law aim at the firm establishment and preservation of matrimonial faith, we know that cannot thrive under violent means, but is the more violated. It is not when two unfortunately met are by the canon forced to draw in that yoke an unmerciful day's work of sorrow till death unharnesse 'em, that then the law keeps marriage most unviolated and unbroken; but when the law takes order that marriage be accountant and responsible to perform that society, whether it be religious, civil, or corporal, which may be conscionably required and claimed therein, or else to be dissolved if it cannot be undergone. This is to make marriage most indissoluble, by making it a just and equal dealer, a performer of those due helps which instituted the covenant, being otherwise a most unjust contract and no more to be maintained under tuition[237] of law than the vilest fraud, or cheat, or theft that may be committed. But because this is such a secret kind of fraud or theft, as cannot be discerned by law but only by the plaintiff himself, therefore to divorce was never counted a political or civil offense neither to Jew nor Gentile, nor any judicial intendment of Christ further than could be discerned to transgress the allowance of Moses, which was of necessity so large that it doth all one as if it sent back the matter undeterminable at law and intractable by rough dealing, to have instructions and admonitions bestowed about it by them whose spiritual office is to adjure and to denounce, and so left to the conscience.

The law can only appoint the just and equal conditions of divorce, and is to look how it is an injury to the divorced. Which in truth it can be none as a mere separation: for if she consent, wherein has the law to right her? Or consent not, then is it either just and so deserved, or if unjust, such in all likelihood was the divorcer, and to part from an unjust man is a happiness and no injury to be lamented. But suppose it be an injury, the law is not able to amend it, unless she think it other than a miserable redress to return back from whence she was expelled, or but entreated to be gone, or else to live apart still married without marriage, a married widow. Last, if it be to chasten the divorcer, what law punishes a deed which is not moral but natural, a deed which cannot certainly be found to be an injury? Or how can it be punished by prohibiting the divorce, but that the innocent must equally partake both in the shame and in the smart? So

236. Milton draws the story from Plutarch, *Aemilius Paulus* 5.1–2.
237. **tuition:** protection.

that which way soever we look the law can to no rational purpose forbid divorce, it can only take care that the conditions of divorce be not injurious. Thus then we see the trial of law how impertinent it is to this question of divorce, how helpless next, and then how hurtful.

CHAP. 22

The last reason why divorce is not to be restrained by law, it being against the law of nature and of nations. The larger proof whereof referred to Mr. Selden's *Book* De jure naturali & gentium. *An objection of* Paræus *answered. How it ought to be ordered by the church. That this will not breed any worse inconvenience nor so bad as is now suffered.*

Therefore the last reason why it should not be, is the example we have not only from the noblest and wisest commonwealths, guided by the clearest light of human knowledge, but also from the divine testimonies of God himself, lawgiving in person to a sanctified people. That all this is true, whoso desires to know at large with least pains and expects not here overlong rehearsals of that which is by others already so judiciously gathered, let him hasten to be acquainted with that noble volume written by our learned Selden, *Of the Law of Nature and of Nations*,[238] a work more useful and more worthy to be perused, whosoever studies to be a great man in wisdom, equity, and justice, than all those decretals, and sumless sums,[239] which the pontifical clerks have doted on ever since that unfortunate mother famously[240] sinned thrice[241] and died impenitent of her bringing into the world those two misbegotten infants, and forever infants, Lombard & Gratian, him the compiler of canon iniquity, t'other the Tubalcain[242] of scholastic sophistry, whose overspreading barbarism hath not only infused their own bastardy upon the fruitfullest part of human learning, not only dissipated and dejected the clear light of nature in us and of nations, but hath tainted also the fountains of divine doctrine and rendered the pure and solid law of God unbeneficial to us by their calumnious dunceries.

Yet this law, which their unskilfulness hath made liable to all ignominy, the purity and wisdom of this law shall be the buckler of our dispute. Liberty of divorce we claim not, we think not, but from this law; the dignity, the faith, the authority thereof is now grown among Christians, O astonishment! A labor of

238. John Selden (1584–1654), a leading scholar and Parliamentarian, published his *De Jure Naturali et Gentium* in 1640; he is thought to have influenced Milton's thinking on divorce and other matters. See *CD* 1.10, n. 28.

239. **sumless sums:** Milton plays on the title *summa,* used for compendia or digests (e.g., Aquinas's *Summa Theologica*).

240. **famously:** notoriously.

241. According to legend, the twelfth-century writers Peter *Lombard,* Johannes *Gratian,* and Peter Comestor, reputed to be the founders of Canon Law, theology, and biblical scholarship, were brothers.

242. See Gen. 4.22, where *Tubalcain* is "an instructor of every artificer in brass and iron."

no mean difficulty and envy[243] to defend. That it should not be counted a faltering dispense, a flattering permission of sin, the bill of adultery, a snare, is the expense of all this apology. And all that we solicit is that it may be suffered to stand in the place where God set it amidst the firmament of his holy laws, to shine, as it was wont, upon the weaknesses and errors of men perishing else in the sincerity of their honest purposes. For certain there is no memory of whoredoms and adulteries left among us now, when this warranted freedom of God's own giving is made dangerous and discarded for a scroll of license. It must be your suffrages and votes, O Englishmen, that this exploded decree of God and Moses may scape and come off fair without the censure of a shameful abrogating, which, if yonder sun[244] ride sure and mean not to break word with us tomorrow, was never yet abrogated by our Savior. Give sentence, if you please, that the frivolous canon may reverse the infallible judgment of Moses and his great director.

Or if it be the reformed writers whose doctrine persuades this rather, their reasons I dare affirm are all silenced, unless it be only this: Paræus, on the Corinthians, would prove that hardness of heart in divorce is no more now to be permitted, but to be amerced with fine and imprisonment.[245] I am not willing to discover the forgettings of reverend men, yet here I must. What article or clause of the whole new covenant can Paræus bring to exasperate the judicial law upon any infirmity under the Gospel? (I say infirmity, for if it were the high hand of sin, the law as little would have endured it as the Gospel.) It would not stretch to the dividing of an inheritance;[246] it refused to condemn adultery,[247] not that these things should not be done at law, but to show that the Gospel hath not the least influence upon judicial courts, much less to make them sharper and more heavy—least of all to arraign before a temporal judge that which the Law without summons acquitted. But, saith he, the Law was the time of youth under violent affections, the Gospel in us is mature age and ought to subdue affections.[248] True, and so ought the Law too, if they be found inordinate and not merely natural and blameless.

Next, I distinguish that the time of the Law is compared to youth and pupilage in respect of the ceremonial part, which led the Jews as children through corporal and garish rudiments, until the fullness of time should reveal to them the higher lessons of faith and redemption. This is not meant of the moral part; therein it soberly concerned them not to be babies, but to be men in good earnest. The sad and awful majesty of that Law was not to be jested with. To bring a bearded nonage with lascivious dispensations before that throne had been a lewd affront, as it is now a gross mistake. But what discipline is this

243. **envy:** unpopularity.
244. A pun on *Son.*
245. Milton summarizes Paraeus's comment on 1 Cor. 7.10–11.
246. See Luke 12.13–14.
247. See John 8.3–11.
248. This sentence translates and paraphrases Paraeus's commentary on 1 Corinthians.

Paræus to nourish violent affections in youth by cockering[249] and wanton indulgences, and to chastise them in mature age with a boyish rod of correction? How much more coherent is it to Scripture that the Law as a strict schoolmaster should have punished every trespass without indulgence so baneful to youth, and that the Gospel should now correct that by admonition and reproof only, in free and mature age, which was punished with stripes in the childhood and bondage of the Law.[250] What therefore it allowed then so fairly, much less is to be whipped now, especially in penal courts, and if it ought now to trouble the conscience, why did that angry accuser and condemner law reprieve it?

So then, neither from Moses nor from Christ hath the magistrate any authority to proceed against it. But what? Shall then the disposal of that power return again to the master of family? Wherefore not? Since God there put it and the presumptuous canon thence bereft it. This only must be provided, that the ancient manner be observed in the presence of the minister and other grave selected elders, who after they shall have admonished and pressed upon him the words of our Savior, and he shall have protested in the faith of the eternal Gospel and the hope he has of happy resurrection, that otherwise than thus he cannot do, and thinks himself and this his case not contained in that prohibition of divorce which Christ pronounced, the matter not being of malice, but of nature, and so not capable of reconciling. To constrain him further were to unchristen him, to unman him, to throw the mountain of Sinai upon him, with the weight of the whole Law to boot, flat against the liberty and essence of the Gospel, and yet nothing available either to the sanctity of marriage, the good of husband, wife, or children, nothing profitable either to church or commonwealth, but hurtful and pernicious to all these respects. But this will bring in confusion.[251]

Yet these cautious mistrusters might consider that what they thus object lights not upon this book but upon that which I engage against them, the book of God and of Moses,[252] with all the wisdom and providence which had forecast the worst of confusion that could succeed, and yet thought fit of such a permission. But let them be of good cheer, it wrought so little disorder among the Jews, that from Moses till after the captivity not one of the prophets thought it worth rebuking; for that of Malachi, well looked into, will appear to be not against divorcing, but rather against keeping strange concubines to the vexation of their Hebrew wives.[253] If therefore we Christians may be thought as good and tractable as the Jews were, and certainly the prohibiters of divorce presume us to be better, then less confusion is to be feared for this among us than was among them. If we be worse or but as bad, which lamentable examples confirm

249. **cockering:** indulgent, coddling.
250. See Gal. 3.24–25.
251. Milton characterizes his opponents' position.
252. Milton suggests that attacks on his position amount to attacks on the Bible.
253. See Mal. 2.16; see 1.6, and n. 101.

we are, then have we more—or at least as much—need of this permitted law as they to whom God therefore gave it (as they say) under a harsher covenant.

Let not therefore the frailty of man go on thus inventing needless troubles to itself, to groan under the false imagination of a strictness never imposed from above, enjoining that for duty which is an impossible and vain supererogating. "Be not righteous overmuch," is the counsel of Ecclesiastes, "why shouldst thou destroy thyself?" [Eccles. 7.16]. Let us not be thus over-curious to strain at atoms,[254] and yet to stop every vent and cranny of permissive liberty, lest nature, wanting those needful pores and breathing places which God hath not debarred our weakness, either suddenly break out into some wide rupture of open vice and frantic heresy or else inwardly fester with repining and blasphemous thoughts under an unreasonable and fruitless rigor of unwarranted law. Against which evils nothing can more beseem the religion of the church or the wisdom of the state than to consider timely and provide. And in so doing, let them not doubt but they shall vindicate the misreputed honor of God and his great lawgiver, by suffering him to give his own laws according to the condition of man's nature best known to him, without the insufferable imputation of dispensing legally with many ages of ratified adultery. They shall recover the misattended words of Christ to the sincerity of their true sense from manifold contradictions and shall open them with the key of charity. Many helpless Christians they shall raise from the depth of sadness and distress, utterly unfitted as they are to serve God or man. Many they shall reclaim from obscure and giddy sects, many regain from dissolute and brutish license, many from desperate hardness, if ever that were justly pleaded. They shall set free many daughters of Israel, not wanting much of her sad plight "whom Satan had bound eighteen years" [Luke 13.16]. Man they shall restore to his just dignity and prerogative in nature, preferring the soul's free peace before the promiscuous draining of a carnal rage. Marriage, from a perilous hazard and snare, they shall reduce to be a more certain haven and retirement of happy society, when they shall judge according to God and Moses (and how not then according to Christ?), when they shall judge it more wisdom and goodness to break that covenant seemingly and keep it really, than by compulsion of law to keep it seemingly, and by compulsion of blameless nature to break it really, at least if it were ever truly joined. The vigor of discipline they may then turn with better success upon the prostitute looseness of the times, when men, finding in themselves the infirmities of former ages, shall not be constrained above the gift of God in them to unprofitable and impossible observances never required from the civilest, the wisest, the holiest nations, whose other excellencies in moral virtue they never yet could equal. Last of all, to those whose mind still is to maintain textual restrictions whereof the bare sound cannot consist sometimes with humanity, much less with charity, I would ever answer by putting them in remembrance of a command above all commands, which they seem to have forgot, and who spake it, in comparison

254. **atoms:** particles of dust; cp. Matt. 23.24: "Ye blind guides, which strain at a gnat."

whereof this, which they so exalt, is but a petty and subordinate precept): "Let them go therefore" (with whom I am loathe to couple them, yet they will needs run into the same blindness with the Pharisees),[255] "let them go therefore" and consider well what this lesson means, "I will have mercy and not sacrifice" [Matt. 9.13]; for on that "saying all the law and prophets depend" [Matt. 22.40], much more the Gospel whose end and excellence is mercy and peace. Or if they cannot learn that, how will they hear this (which yet I shall not doubt to leave with them as a conclusion)? that God the son hath put all other things under his own feet, but his commandments he hath left all under the feet of charity.

The end.

255. Milton compares his opponents to the Pharisees rebuked by Christ in Matt. 9.

AREOPAGITICA;

A

SPEECH

OF

Mr. JOHN MILTON

For the Liberty of UNLICENC'D PRINTING,

To the PARLAMENT of ENGLAND.

Τοὐλεύθερον δ' ἐκεῖνο, εἴ τις θέλει πόλει
Χρηστόν τι βούλευμ' εἰς μέσον φέρειν, ἔχων.
Καὶ ταῦθ' ὁ χρῄζων, λαμπρὸς ἔσθ', ὁ μὴ θέλων,
Σιγᾷ, τί τούτων ἐστὶν ἰσαίτερον πόλει;

Euripid. Hicetid.

This is true Liberty when free born men
Having to advise the public may speak free,
Which he who can, and will, deserv's high praise,
Who neither can nor will, may hold his peace;
What can be juster in a State then this?

Euripid. Hicetid.

LONDON,
Printed in the Yeare, 1644.

Title page to *Areopagitica* (1644).

Introduction to *Areopagitica*

Despite a Parliamentary order of June 1643 prohibiting unlicensed publications, *Areopagitica* was in November 1644 printed without license. Milton composed it as if he were speaking before Parliament, observing that its members had restored the most perverse and repressive system of censorship ever devised, one first inflicted on the English by the feared and loathed Court of the Star Chamber. King Charles and Archbishop Laud had harnessed that court's wide-ranging powers to enforce "thorough" conformity. Yet two years after abolishing the Star Chamber, Parliament reimposed its system of censorship, forbidding publication of any book "unless the same be first approved and licensed by such . . . as shall be thereto appointed." The main difference under the new regime was that the licensers were Parliament's presbyters instead of Archbishop Laud's priests—a change that Milton later observed did not extend beyond the two syllables difference in their titles (*On the New Forcers of Conscience* 20).

The expanded liberty of expression enjoyed upon the demise of the Star Chamber in 1641 did not last long, but if statistics are any guide, it was energetically exploited. Excluding serials, 867 items were published in 1640, the last full year of Stuart censorship. During 1642, the one full year in which Parliament allowed the book trade to go unregulated, that total jumped to 2,968 items. The numbers bear out Milton's stirring account of embattled Londoners "disputing, reasoning, reading, inventing, discoursing, even to a rarity and admiration, things not before discoursed or written of." Milton himself in 1641–42 produced five tracts, all of them supporting the Presbyterian assault on episcopacy. His next barrage of pamphlets, however, published in 1643–44, scandalized his former allies by advocating a scriptural right of divorce. The uproar came to a head in the second half of 1644, when the dogged divorcer was denounced in broadsides and reprobated from pulpits. In a baleful sermon preached before Parliament in August of that year, Herbert Palmer declared Milton's most current divorce tract intolerable, "deserving to be burnt" (an evaluation of Milton's controversial writings regularly repeated and sometimes acted upon in years to come). That same August, the Stationers' Company, which controlled the

London book trade, delivered a petition to the House of Commons that evidently complained of the failure of Milton and others to submit to the licensing order. On Milton's part, the defiance was real and persistent. The first edition of the *Doctrine and Discipline of Divorce* was published a month after the Licensing Order of 1643, and the second edition more than six months after. Neither was registered with the Stationers' Company—as *Areopagitica* and subsequent works were not. Although it is not clear what the perceived risk was in 1643–44 for those who chose to publish unlicensed books, we do know that the still anonymous printer of *Areopagitica* took pains to use only nondescript materials in producing the pamphlet—one that bears John Milton's name on its title page.

Milton's address to Parliament, like other of his works advocating or defending political and religious liberties, takes the form of a classical oration. Its title and the topic of censorship recall Isocrates' seventh oration, the so-called *Areopagitic Discourse* (c. 355 B.C.E.), recommending moral reform to the Athenian Council of the Areopagus (Mars hill). Several centuries later, the apostle Paul would stand on that same hill, as Milton's audience well knew, quoting Greek poetry to evangelize the Athenians (Acts 17.22–34). St. Paul hoped to persuade them that his God was the unknown deity whom their cult acknowledged and poets intimated. It was their recognition that religious truth might lie beyond their ken that allowed the Athenians to learn of a faith that seemed strange, even foolish, but one that Milton's audience, sixteen centuries later, accepted as absolutely true and the sole means of salvation.

The first part of Milton's aptly titled oration is historical and traces the invention of licensing to the Roman Catholic Inquisition. The second affirms temperance as the sole means of fostering individual virtue: temperance understood not as unreasoning habit but as a rationally informed discipline fortified in the process of confronting, identifying, and rejecting the deceptive evils of the world. "Promiscuous" reading is well suited to this virtuous exercise, or so Milton insists in a passage that remains strikingly pertinent: "They are not skilful considerers of human things who imagine to remove sin by removing the matter of sin." Even if humanity did possess innate virtue to protect from exposure to corruption, mere regulation of printing, as the third part of the argument wittily elaborates, would not suffice: "Who shall silence all the airs and madrigals that whisper softness in chambers?" The fourth part develops the claim that licensing will fail to achieve the end it seeks and instead perversely undermine the virtue of English souls. Even if a belief to which one obediently but mindlessly conformed were true, one would be no more than a "heretic in the truth." Faith not rationally tried by the believer does not in Milton's view qualify as authentic.

As social policy, Milton's advocacy of limited freedom of the press and toleration of Protestant sects, though courageous enough in its historical moment, was hardly inspiring to future generations. His representation of truth as being, in this world, partial, fragmentary, and multiple, however, continues to encourage a commitment to pluralism and tolerance as conducive rather than corrosive to human virtue. Milton claims that truth once was readily accessible, indeed wholly present in the world, but, after the era of Christ and his apostles, "straight arose a wicked race of deceivers," who "took the virgin Truth, hewed her lovely form into a thousand pieces and scattered them to the four winds." The rest of history affords "the sad friends of truth" the opportunity to recover the pieces, just as in myth Isis recovered the mangled body of her beloved Osiris. This pious effort, Milton insists, will not be complete until Christ's Second Coming, and Parliament should not in the meantime obstruct "them that continue seeking."

Readers of *Areopagitica* have long found that such moments of myth and poetic symbol possess a sudden and unqualified force missing from the oration's discursive argument. Ernst Sirluck explained this inconsistency by identifying Parliamentary factions that any proposal would need to negotiate rhetorically if it were to succeed (Yale 2:169–78). More recently, Christopher Kendrick elaborated on Sirluck's thesis to argue that the discursive argument's recurring imagery of trade and commerce signals Milton's unconscious allegiance to the emergent bourgeoisie, in whose interest freedom of expression would still be regulated. For Stanley Fish, however, Milton quite consciously recognized freedom of speech as being always conditional, a privilege extended by those in power to those of like mind (1994).

We can of course never know precisely what rhetorical strategy Milton in 1644 thought he was pursuing or what political interest he may have served, consciously or unconsciously, by his appeal to Parliament. We do know that in its own time *Areopagitica* had little or no impact. Parliament actually stepped up its efforts to suppress heretical opinion. Only a half century later, Walter Blount would publish a condensed version of Milton's oration as if it were his own composition, under the title "A Just Vindication of Learning and the Liberty of the Press." Yet the book in which Milton's oration was printed did survive, and, according to its own definition of a "good book," Milton survived with it. The material process by which "the precious life-blood of a master spirit" is "embalmed and treasured up on purpose to a life beyond life" haunts the oration's imagery and diction (Dobranski). Evidently, the vitalist materialism central to Milton's epic poetry and heretical theology is the imaginative and doctrinal culmination of a persistent tendency in his thought. His definition of a good book is famously engraved over the doorway of the main reading room of the New York Public Library. But in Milton's view, his posthumous existence, like Shakespeare's, persists not in piled stones, however inscribed, but in the minds of his readers. By the eighteenth century, especially in revolutionary America and France, Milton's oration at last found an audience in whom his version of truth might live. Since then, *Areopagitica* has in the West been widely considered the most complete and inspirational argument for freedom of the press ever composed, "the foundational essay of the free speech tradition" (Blasi).

Our text is based on the copy of the first edition in the British Library's Thomason Collection, checked against the copy held in the Carl H. Pforzheimer Library in the Harry Ransom Humanities Research Center, Austin, Texas.

AREOPAGITICA:
A SPEECH OF MR. JOHN MILTON FOR THE LIBERTY OF UNLICENSED PRINTING TO THE PARLIAMENT OF ENGLAND.

Τοὐλεύθερον δ' ἐκεῖνο, εἴ τις θέλει πόλει
Χρηστόν τι βούλευμ' εἰς μέσον φέρειν ἔχων;
Καὶ ταῦθ' ὁ χρῄζων, λαμπρὸς ἔσθ', ὁ μὴ θέλων,
Σιγᾷ. τί τούτων ἔστιν ἰσαίτερον πόλει;
Euripid. Hicetid.

This is true liberty when freeborn men
Having to advise the public may speak free,
Which he who can, and will, deserves high praise,
Who neither can nor will, may hold his peace;
What can be juster in a state than this?
[Euripid. Hicetid.[1]]

For the Liberty of Unlicensed Printing:

They who to states and governors of the commonwealth direct their speech, high court of Parliament, or wanting such access in a private condition, write that which they foresee may advance the public good, I suppose them as at the beginning of no mean endeavor, not a little altered and moved inwardly in their minds: some with doubt of what will be the success, others with fear of what will be the censure; some with hope, others with confidence of what they have to speak. And me, perhaps, each of these dispositions, as the subject was whereon I entered, may have at other times variously affected; and likely might in these foremost expressions now also disclose which of them swayed most, but that the very attempt of this address thus made, and the thought of whom it hath recourse to, hath got the power within me to a passion far more welcome than incidental to a preface.

Which though I stay not to confess ere any ask, I shall be blameless, if it be no

1. Euripides, *The Suppliants* 438.41. The passage in Greek appears with Milton's translation on the title page of the first edition. Euripides is quoting the words with which the assembly at Athens opened.

other than the joy and gratulation which it brings to all who wish and promote their country's liberty, whereof this whole discourse proposed will be a certain testimony, if not a trophy. For this is not the liberty which we can hope, that no grievance ever should arise in the commonwealth—that let no man in this world expect. But when complaints are freely heard, deeply considered, and speedily reformed, then is the utmost bound of civil liberty attained that wise men look for. To which if I now manifest by the very sound of this which I shall utter, that we are already in good part arrived, and yet from such a steep disadvantage of tyranny and superstition grounded into our principles as was beyond the manhood of a Roman recovery,[2] it will be attributed first, as is most due, to the strong assistance of God our deliverer, next to your faithful guidance and undaunted wisdom, Lords and Commons of England. Neither is it in God's esteem the diminution of his glory when honorable things are spoken of good men and worthy magistrates; which if I now first should begin to do, after so fair a progress of your laudable deeds and such a long obligement[3] upon the whole realm to your indefatigable virtues, I might be justly reckoned among the tardiest, and the unwillingest of them that praise ye.

Nevertheless, there being three principal things without which all praising is but courtship and flattery. First, when that only is praised which is solidly worth praise; next, when greatest likelihoods are brought that such things are truly and really in those persons to whom they are ascribed; the other, when he who praises, by showing that such his actual persuasion is of whom he writes, can demonstrate that he flatters not. The former two of these I have heretofore endeavored, rescuing the employment from him who went about to impair your merits with a trivial and malignant encomium;[4] the latter as belonging chiefly to mine own acquittal, that whom I so extolled I did not flatter, hath been reserved opportunely to this occasion. For he who freely magnifies what hath been nobly done and fears not to declare as freely what might be done better gives ye the best covenant of his fidelity and that his loyalest affection and his hope waits on your proceedings. His highest praising is not flattery, and his plainest advice is a kind of praising. For though I should affirm and hold by argument that it would fare better with truth, with learning, and the commonwealth, if one of your published orders which I should name were called in, yet at the same time it could not but much redound to the luster of your mild and equal government whenas private persons are hereby animated to think ye better pleased with public advice than other statists have been delighted heretofore with public flattery. And men will then see what difference there is

2. **Roman recovery:** The English, having cast off the yoke of King Charles and the bishops, achieved what the Romans, subject to emperors and then popes, could not.

3. **obligement:** indebtedness for benefits received. The Long Parliament first convened in November 1640, four years before the publication of *Areopagitica.*

4. In *An Apology for Smectymnuus,* Milton objects to the covert Royalism of Bishop Hall's praise of Parliament and counters it with what he deems more fitting praise (Yale 1:919–20).

between the magnanimity of a triennial parliament[5] and that jealous haughtiness of prelates and cabin counselors that usurped of late, whenas they shall observe ye in the midst of your victories and successes[6] more gently brooking written exceptions against a voted order than other courts, which had produced nothing worth memory but the weak ostentation of wealth, would have endured the least signified dislike at any sudden proclamation.

If I should thus far presume upon the meek demeanor of your civil and gentle greatness, Lords and Commons, as what your published order hath directly said, that to gainsay, I might defend myself with ease, if any should accuse me of being new or insolent, did they but know how much better I find ye esteem it to imitate the old and elegant humanity of Greece than the barbaric pride of a Hunnish and Norwegian stateliness. And out of those ages, to whose polite wisdom and letters we owe that we are not yet Goths and Jutlanders, I could name him who from his private house wrote that discourse to the Parliament of Athens[7] that persuades them to change the form of democracy which was then established. Such honor was done in those days to men who professed the study of wisdom and eloquence, not only in their own country but in other lands, that cities and seignories heard them gladly and with great respect if they had aught in public to admonish the state. Thus did Dion Prusæus, a stranger and a private orator, counsel the Rhodians against a former edict,[8] and I abound with other like examples which to set here would be superfluous. But if from the industry of a life wholly dedicated to studious labors and those natural endowments haply not the worst for two and fifty degrees of northern latitude[9] so much must be derogated as to count me not equal to any of those who had this privilege, I would obtain to be thought not so inferior as yourselves are superior to the most of them who received their counsel. And how far you excel them, be assured, Lords and Commons, there can no greater testimony appear, than when your prudent spirit acknowledges and obeys the voice of reason from what quarter soever it be heard speaking, and renders ye as willing to repeal any act of your own setting forth as any set forth by your predecessors.[10]

If ye be thus resolved, as it were injury to think ye were not, I know not what should withhold me from presenting ye with a fit instance wherein to show both that love of truth which ye eminently profess, and that uprightness of your

5. According to the Triennial Parliaments Act (February 1641), a new parliament would automatically be summoned three years after the last was dismissed.

6. Parliamentary forces had won a string of victories in the spring and summer of 1644, culminating in the battle of Marston Moor (July 2), which gave Parliament control of the north.

7. A private citizen, Isocrates addressed his *Areopagitic Discourse* (c. 355 B.C.E.) to the popular assembly of Athens.

8. The *Rhodian Discourse* of Dion Prusaeus (d. 117 C.E.) urges repeal of a law permitting replacement of the original names on public monuments.

9. Milton often blames the cold and damp northern climate for English dullness (e.g., *PL* 9.44–45).

10. This sentence ends the introduction, or *exordium;* what follows is the statement of the case, or *narratio.*

judgment which is not wont to be partial to yourselves, by judging over again that order which ye have ordained "to regulate printing, that no book, pamphlet, or paper shall be henceforth printed, unless the same be first approved and licensed by such,"[11] or at least one of such as shall be thereto appointed. For that part which preserves justly every man's copy[12] to himself or provides for the poor I touch not, only wish they be not made pretenses to abuse and persecute honest and painful men who offend not in either of these particulars. But that other clause of licensing books, which we thought had died with his brother quadragesimal and matrimonial[13] when the prelates expired, I shall now attend with such a homily as shall lay before ye: first, the inventors of it to be those whom ye will be loath to own; next, what is to be thought in general of reading, whatever sort the books be; and, that this order avails nothing to the suppressing of scandalous, seditious, and libelous books, which were mainly intended to be suppressed. Last, that it will be primely to the discouragement of all learning and the stop of truth, not only by disexercising[14] and blunting our abilities in what we know already, but by hindering and cropping the discovery that might be yet further made both in religious and civil wisdom.

I deny not but that it is of greatest concernment in the church and commonwealth to have a vigilant eye how books demean themselves as well as men, and thereafter to confine, imprison, and do sharpest justice on them as malefactors. For books are not absolutely dead things, but do contain a potency of life in them to be as active as that soul was whose progeny they are; nay, they do preserve as in a vial the purest efficacy and extraction of that living intellect that bred them. I know they are as lively and as vigorously productive as those fabulous dragon's teeth, and, being sown up and down, may chance to spring up armed men.[15] And yet, on the other hand, unless wariness be used, as good almost kill a man as kill a good book. Who kills a man kills a reasonable creature, God's image, but he who destroys a good book kills reason itself, kills the image of God, as it were, in the eye. Many a man lives a burden to the earth, but a good book is the precious lifeblood of a master spirit, embalmed and treasured up on purpose to a life beyond life. 'Tis true, no age can restore a life, whereof perhaps there is no great loss, and revolutions of ages do not oft recover the loss of a rejected truth, for the want of which whole nations fare the worse. We should be wary therefore what persecution we raise against the living labors of public men, how we spill[16] that seasoned life of man preserved and stored up in books, since we see a kind of homicide may be thus committed, sometimes a martyr-

11. Milton recites (though he does not quote exactly) the text of the order.

12. **copy:** copyright.

13. Milton refers to ecclesiastical licenses to dispense with Lenten dietary rules (*quadragesimal*) and rules requiring publication of marriage banns (*matrimonial*).

14. **disexercising:** depriving of exercise.

15. Mythical dragon's teeth were sown by both Cadmus and Jason and quickly grew into armed warriors (Ovid, *Met.* 3.101–30, 7.121–42).

16. **spill:** destroy.

dom, and if it extend to the whole impression, a kind of massacre, whereof the execution ends not in the slaying of an elemental life, but strikes at that ethereal and fifth essence,[17] the breath of reason itself, slays an immortality rather than a life. But lest I should be condemned of introducing license while I oppose licensing, I refuse not the pains to be so much historical as will serve to show what hath been done by ancient and famous commonwealths against this disorder, till the very time that this project of licensing crept out of the Inquisition,[18] was catched up by our prelates, and hath caught some of our presbyters.

In Athens, where books and wits were ever busier than in any other part of Greece, I find but only two sorts of writings which the magistrate cared to take notice of: those either blasphemous and atheistical, or libelous. Thus the books of Protagoras were by the judges of Areopagus commanded to be burnt and himself banished the territory for a discourse begun with his confessing not to know "whether there were gods or whether not." And against defaming, it was decreed that none should be traduced by name, as was the manner of *Vetus Comœdia*,[19] whereby we may guess how they censured libeling. And this course was quick enough, as Cicero writes, to quell both the desperate wits of other atheists and the open way of defaming as the event showed. Of other sects and opinions, though tending to voluptuousness and the denying of divine providence, they took no heed. Therefore we do not read that either Epicurus, or that libertine school of Cyrene, or what the Cynic impudence uttered, was ever questioned by the laws.[20] Neither is it recorded that the writings of those old comedians were suppressed, though the acting of them were forbid; and that Plato commended the reading of Aristophanes, the loosest of them all, to his royal scholar Dionysius, is commonly known, and may be excused, if holy Chrysostom, as is reported, nightly studied so much the same author and had the art to cleanse a scurrilous vehemence into the style of a rousing sermon.

That other leading city of Greece, Lacedæmon, considering that Lycurgus their lawgiver was so addicted to elegant learning as to have been the first that brought out of Ionia the scattered works of Homer, and sent the poet Thales from Crete to prepare and mollify the Spartan surliness with his smooth songs and odes, the better to plant among them law and civility, it is to be wondered how museless and unbookish they were, minding naught but the feats of war. There needed no licensing of books among them, for they disliked all but their

17. The *fifth essence,* or quintessence, is not *elemental,* like earth, air, fire, and water, but *ethereal.* From it derives Heaven and the pure intellectual substance of angels (cp. *PL* 3.714–18).

18. **Inquisition:** tribunal of the Roman Catholic Church (1232–1820) created to discover and suppress heresy.

19. **Vetus Comœdia:** The old comedy of Greece regularly attacked public figures by name; Aristophanes is the best known of the old comedians.

20. Followers of *Epicurus* (c. 341–270 B.C.E.) were associated with devotion to pleasure. *Cyrene* was the home of Hedonism, a philosophy linked to sensual self-indulgence. *Cynics* were noted for insolence to authority.

own laconic apothegms and took a slight occasion to chase Archilochus out of their city, perhaps for composing in a higher strain than their own soldierly ballads and roundels could reach to; or if it were for his broad verses, they were not therein so cautious, but they were as dissolute in their promiscuous conversing,[21] whence Euripides affirms in *Andromache* that their women were all unchaste. Thus much may give us light after what sort books were prohibited among the Greeks.

The Romans also, for many ages trained up only to a military roughness, resembling most the Lacedæmonian guise, knew of learning little but what their twelve tables and the Pontific College with their augurs and flamens[22] taught them in religion and law, so unacquainted with other learning that when Carneades and Critolaus, with the Stoic Diogenes coming ambassadors to Rome, took thereby occasion to give the city a taste of their philosophy, they were suspected for seducers by no less a man than Cato the Censor, who moved it in the Senate to dismiss them speedily, and to banish all such Attic babblers out of Italy.[23] But Scipio and others of the noblest senators withstood him and his old Sabine austerity, honored and admired the men, and the Censor himself at last in his old age fell to the study of that whereof before he was so scrupulous. And yet at the same time, Nævius and Plautus, the first Latin comedians, had filled the city with all the borrowed scenes of Menander and Philemon.[24]

Then began to be considered there also what was to be done to libelous books and authors; for Nævius was quickly cast into prison for his unbridled pen and released by the tribunes upon his recantation. We read also that libels were burnt and the makers punished by Augustus. The like severity no doubt was used if aught were impiously written against their esteemed gods. Except in these two points, how the world went in books, the magistrate kept no reckoning. And therefore Lucretius without impeachment versifies his Epicurism to Memmius, and had the honor to be set forth the second time by Cicero, so great a father of the commonwealth, although himself disputes against that opinion in his own writings.[25] Nor was the satirical sharpness or naked plainness of Lucilius, or Catullus, or Flaccus, by any order prohibited. And for mat-

21. Spartan men and women exercised naked together, a practice presumed to spur sexual license.

22. **twelve tables:** earliest Roman law code. **Pontific College:** Rome's supreme religious authority. **augurs and flamens:** priests who consulted natural omens to guide public policy and priests devoted to the service of a particular deity, respectively.

23. This anecdote from the second century B.C.E. indicates the Roman republic's initial distrust of Greek intellectuals, especially as rhetorical performers (*Attic babblers*). The skeptic *Carneades* (213?–129 B.C.E.), the Aristotelian *Critolaus* (fl. second century B.C.E.), and the Stoic *Diogenes* (fl. second century B.C.E.) were opposed by the notoriously rigorous and conservative *Cato* (234–149 B.C.E.). *Scipio* the Younger (185–29 B.C.E.) was, by contrast, a leading Roman patron of Greek culture. *Censors* were elected public officials who took the census and supervised Rome's public works, finance, and morality.

24. *Menander* and *Philemon* were major authors of Athenian New Comedy; *Nævius* and *Plautus* were Roman playwrights deeply influenced by them. Though Rome came to embrace Greek learning, libel was still suppressed, as Nævius discovered when he was imprisoned for satirizing Scipio.

25. In *De Rerum Natura, Lucretius* gave epic expression to Epicurean materialism. *Memmius,* to whom the work was dedicated, was praetor in 58 B.C.E. *Cicero* was its putative editor.

ters of state, the story of Titus Livius, though it extolled that part which Pompey held, was not therefore suppressed by Octavius Cæsar of the other faction.[26] But that Naso was by him banished in his old age for the wanton poems of his youth was but a mere covert of state over some secret cause, and besides, the books were neither banished nor called in.[27] From hence we shall meet with little else but tyranny in the Roman Empire, that we may not marvel, if not so often bad as good books were silenced. I shall therefore deem to have been large enough in producing what among the ancients was punishable to write, save only which all other arguments were free to treat on.

By this time the emperors were become Christians, whose discipline in this point I do not find to have been more severe than what was formerly in practice. The books of those whom they took to be grand heretics were examined, refuted, and condemned in the general councils and not till then were prohibited or burnt by authority of the emperor. As for the writings of heathen authors, unless they were plain invectives against Christianity, as those of Porphyrius and Proclus,[28] they met with no interdict that can be cited, till about the year 400 in a Carthaginian council, wherein bishops themselves were forbid to read the books of gentiles, but heresies they might read; while others long before them, on the contrary, scrupled more the books of heretics than of gentiles. And that the primitive councils and bishops were wont only to declare what books were not commendable, passing no further, but leaving it to each one's conscience to read or to lay by, till after the year 800, is observed already by Padre Paolo, the great unmasker of the Trentine Council.[29]

After which time the popes of Rome, engrossing what they pleased of political rule into their own hands, extended their dominion over men's eyes as they had before over their judgments, burning and prohibiting to be read what they fancied not—yet sparing in their censures, and the books not many which they so dealt with; till Martin the Fifth by his bull not only prohibited, but was the first that excommunicated the reading of heretical books,[30] for about that time Wycliffe and Huss,[31] growing terrible, were they who first drove the papal court to a stricter policy of prohibiting. Which course Leo the Ninth and his successors followed, until the Council of Trent and the Spanish Inquisition, engendering together, brought forth or perfected those catalogues and expurging indexes[32]

26. The historian *Titus Livius* (Livy) praised *Pompey* highly and was alleged to have had the approval of *Octavius Cæsar* (Augustus), Pompey's victorious opponent, for doing so.

27. The licentious verse of Ovid (Publius Ovidius *Naso*) was the alleged reason for his exile by Augustus. Although Ovid was banished, his books were not.

28. Late classical Neoplatonic scholars, *Porphyrius* (or Porphyry, 233–304) and *Proclus* (or Proculus, 410–485) opposed Christianity and defended paganism.

29. *Padre Paolo* is the religious name of Pietro Sarpi (1552–1623), a leader of the Venetian opposition to the papacy's secular authority, which was affirmed by the Council of Trent (1545–63). Milton's account of censorship and church councils since 400 follows Sarpi's *History of the Council of Trent.*

30. Pope Martin the Fifth (1368–1431) in 1418 issued a bull condemning the reading of heretical works.

31. The English reformer John *Wycliffe* (c. 1329–84), and his follower, John *Huss* of Bohemia (1369–1415).

32. *Leo the Tenth* was pope from 1513 to 1521. The Church created the *index* of prohibited books in 1559.

that rake through the entrails of many an old good author with a violation worse than any could be offered to his tomb. Nor did they stay in matters heretical, but any subject that was not to their palate they either condemned in a prohibition or had it straight into the new purgatory of an index.

To fill up the measure of encroachment, their last invention was to ordain that no book, pamphlet, or paper should be printed (as if St. Peter had bequeathed them the keys of the press also out of paradise) unless it were approved and licensed under the hands of two or three glutton friars. For example:

> "Let the Chancellor Cini be pleased to see if in this present work be contained aught that may withstand the printing."
>
> Vincent Rabbatta, Vicar of Florence.

> "I have seen this present work, and find nothing athwart the Catholic faith and good manners: in witness whereof I have given, etc."
>
> Nicolò Cini, Chancellor of Florence.

> "Attending the precedent relation, it is allowed that this present work of Davanzati may be printed."
>
> Vincent Rabbatta, etc.

> "It may be printed, July 15."
>
> Friar Simon Mompei d'Amelia,
> Chancellor of the holy office in Florence.

Sure they have a conceit, if he of the bottomless pit had not long since broke prison, that this quadruple exorcism would bar him down. I fear their next design will be to get into their custody the licensing of that which they say Claudius intended, but went not through with.[33] Vouchsafe to see another of their forms the Roman stamp:

> "*Imprimatur,* If it seem good to the reverend Master of the holy Palace."
>
> Belcastro, Vicegerent.

> "Imprimatur"
>
> Friar Nicolò Rodolphi,
> Master of the holy Palace.

Sometimes five *imprimaturs* are seen together dialogue-wise in the piazza of one title page, complimenting and ducking each to other with their shaven rever-

33. The margin of the first edition quotes Suetonius's *Lives of the Caesars* (5.32) regarding the legislative officiousness of Claudius: *"Quo veniam daret statum crepitumque ventris in convivio emittendi. Sueton. in Claudio"* [He is even said to have thought of an edict allowing the privilege of breaking wind quietly or noisily at table].

ences,[34] whether the author, who stands by in perplexity at the foot of his epistle, shall to the press or to the sponge. These are the pretty responsories, these are the dear antiphonies,[35] that so bewitched of late our prelates and their chaplains with the goodly echo they made and besotted us to the gay imitation of a lordly *imprimatur,* one from Lambeth house, another from the west end of Paul's,[36] so apishly romanizing that the word of command still was set down in Latin, as if the learned grammatical pen that wrote it would cast no ink without Latin, or perhaps, as they thought, because no vulgar tongue was worthy to express the pure conceit of an *imprimatur,* but rather, as I hope, for that our English, the language of men ever famous and foremost in the achievements of liberty, will not easily find servile letters enow to spell such a dictatory presumption [in] English.[37]

And thus ye have the inventors and the original of book-licensing ripped up and drawn as lineally as any pedigree. We have it not, that can be heard of, from any ancient state, or polity, or church, nor by any statute left us by our ancestors elder or later, nor from the modern custom of any reformed city, or church abroad, but from the most antichristian council and the most tyrannous inquisition that ever inquired.

Till then books were ever as freely admitted into the world as any other birth; the issue of the brain was no more stifled than the issue of the womb; no envious Juno sat cross-legged over the nativity of any man's intellectual offspring;[38] but if it proved a monster, who denies but that it was justly burnt or sunk into the sea? But that a book, in worse condition than a peccant soul, should be to stand before a jury ere it be born to the world, and undergo yet in darkness the judgment of Rhadamanth and his colleagues ere it can pass the ferry backward into light,[39] was never heard before, till that mysterious iniquity, provoked and troubled at the first entrance of reformation, sought out new limbos and new hells wherein they might include our books also within the number of their damned.[40] And this was the rare morsel so officiously snatched up and so ill-favoredly imitated by our inquisiturient bishops and the attendant minorites, their chaplains.[41] That ye like not now these most certain authors of this licensing order, and that all sinister intention was far distant from your

34. A reference to clerics' shorn crowns (tonsures).

35. *Responsories* and *antiphonies* are verses and replies, spoken or sung by a priest and congregation.

36. *Lambeth house* is a residence of the Archbishop of Canterbury; the Bishop of London used to reside near St. *Paul's* Cathedral.

37. **enow:** the archaic plural of *enough.* The 1644 edition omits "in" before "English."

38. Juno instructed the goddess of childbirth to block the birth of Hercules by sitting cross-legged while his mother labored.

39. In classical literature, Rhadamanth, his brother Minos, and Aeacus judged the dead. Milton pictures them judging instead the unborn before they can be ferried backward across the Styx to the realm of the living.

40. *Mysterious iniquity* refers to the Church of Rome, incited by the Protestant Reformation to damn books to freshly invented infernal realms (*new limbos and new hells*).

41. Milton coins *inquisiturient* in scorn of clergy eager to play inquisitor. By referring to English chaplains as *attendant minorites,* he links them with Franciscan friars (Friars Minor).

thoughts when ye were importuned the passing it, all men who know the integrity of your actions and how ye honor truth will clear ye readily.

But some will say, what though the inventors were bad, the thing for all that may be good. It may be so; yet if that thing be no such deep invention, but obvious, and easy for any man to light on, and yet best and wisest commonwealths through all ages and occasions have forborne to use it, and falsest seducers and oppressors of men were the first who took it up, and to no other purpose but to obstruct and hinder the first approach of reformation, I am of those who believe it will be a harder alchemy than Lullius ever knew to sublimate any good use out of such an invention.[42] Yet this only is what I request to gain from this reason, that it may be held a dangerous and suspicious fruit, as certainly it deserves, for the tree that bore it, until I can dissect one by one the properties it has. But I have first to finish, as was propounded, what is to be thought in general of reading books, whatever sort they be, and whether be more the benefit or the harm that thence proceeds?

Not to insist upon the examples of Moses, Daniel, and Paul, who were skillful in all the learning of the Egyptians, Chaldeans, and Greeks, which could not probably be without reading their books of all sorts; in Paul especially, who thought it no defilement to insert into holy scripture the sentences of three Greek poets, and one of them a tragedian.[43] The question was notwithstanding sometimes controverted among the primitive doctors, but with great odds on that side which affirmed it both lawful and profitable, as was then evidently perceived, when Julian the Apostate and subtlest enemy to our faith made a decree forbidding Christians the study of heathen learning; for, said he, they wound us with our own weapons, and with our own arts and sciences they overcome us.[44] And indeed, the Christians were put so to their shifts by this crafty means, and so much in danger to decline into all ignorance, that the two Apollinarii were fain, as a man may say, to coin all the seven liberal sciences out of the Bible, reducing it into diverse forms of orations, poems, dialogues, even to the calculating of a new Christian grammar. But, sayeth the historian Socrates, the providence of God provided better than the industry of Apollinarius and his son, by taking away that illiterate law with the life of him who devised it.[45]

So great an injury they then held it to be deprived of Hellenic learning, and thought it a persecution more undermining and secretly decaying the church than the open cruelty of Decius or Diocletian.[46] And perhaps it was the same

42. **Lullius:** Raymond Lully (c. 1234–1315), renowned alchemist. *Sublimation* is the alchemical process by which base substances are refined and exalted.

43. For Moses' learning, see Acts 7.22; for Daniel's, Dan. 1.17; for Paul's, Acts 22.3. Paul quotes Greek poets at Acts 17.28, Titus 1.12, and 1 Cor. 15.33. The *tragedian* is Euripides.

44. Flavius Claudius Julianus (332–63) became Roman Emperor in 361. His policy in religion was to promote Rome's old religion and discourage Christianity.

45. In his *Ecclesiastical History,* the Greek historian Socrates Scholasticus (380–450) relates the story of the two Apollinarii and Julian's early death.

46. The Roman Emperor *Decius* (d. 251) in 249 initiated the first imperial persecution of Christians. *Diocletian,* emperor from 284 to 305, ordered the last.

politic drift that the devil whipped St. Jerome in a lenten dream for reading Cicero, or else it was a phantasm bred by the fever which had then seized him.[47] For had an angel been his discipliner, unless it were for dwelling too much upon Ciceronianisms, and had chastised the reading not the vanity, it had been plainly partial: first to correct him for grave Cicero, and not for scurril Plautus, whom he confesses to have been reading not long before; next to correct him only, and let so many more ancient fathers wax old in those pleasant and florid studies without the lash of such a tutoring apparition, insomuch that Basil teaches how some good use may be made of *Margites,* a sportful poem, not now extant, writ by Homer; and why not then of *Morgante,* an Italian romance much to the same purpose?[48]

But if it be agreed we shall be tried by visions, there is a vision recorded by Eusebius far ancienter than this tale of Jerome to the nun Eustochium, and besides, has nothing of a fever in it.[49] Dionysius Alexandrinus was, about the year 240, a person of great name in the church for piety and learning, who had wont to avail himself much against heretics by being conversant in their books; until a certain presbyter laid it scrupulously to his conscience, how he durst venture himself among those defiling volumes. The worthy man, loath to give offense, fell into a new debate with himself what was to be thought, when suddenly a vision sent from God (it is his own epistle that so avers it) confirmed him in these words: "Read any books whatever come to thy hands, for thou art sufficient both to judge aright and to examine each matter." To this revelation he assented the sooner, as he confesses, because it was answerable to that of the apostle to the Thessalonians: "Prove all things, hold fast that which is good." And he might have added another remarkable saying of the same author: "To the pure, all things are pure"; not only meats and drinks, but all kind of knowledge whether of good or evil; the knowledge cannot defile, nor consequently the books, if the will and conscience be not defiled.[50]

For books are as meats and viands are: some of good, some of evil substance, and yet God in that unapocryphal vision, said without exception, "Rise Peter, kill and eat," leaving the choice to each man's discretion.[51] Wholesome meats to a vitiated stomach differ little or nothing from unwholesome, and best books to a naughty mind are not unappliable to occasions of evil. Bad meats will scarce breed good nourishment in the healthiest concoction, but herein the difference

47. In an epistle (18) identified by Milton in the next paragraph, St. Jerome (c. 342–420) relates a dream in which an angel whips him for excessive devotion to Cicero.

48. *Basil* the Great (330–379) became Bishop of Caesarea in 370. He advised reading pagan literature from a Christian perspective. *Margites* and *Il Morgante Maggiore* (by Luigi Pulci, 1431–87) are mock heroic works.

49. *Eusebius* (264–340) was the Bishop of Caesarea and the Church's first historian. In his *Ecclesiastical History* (7.7), he tells of a letter in which *Dionysius,* Bishop of Alexandria (247–65), justifies having read heretical works by claiming that a vision commanded him to read whatever came into his hands. Milton substitutes *a certain presbyter* for the scrupulous priests of the original account.

50. The apostle Paul in 1 Thess. 5.21 and Titus 1.15.

51. Acts 10.13.

is of bad books, that they to a discreet and judicious reader serve in many respects to discover, to confute, to forewarn, and to illustrate. Whereof what better witness can ye expect I should produce than one of your own now sitting in Parliament, the chief of learned men reputed in this land, Mr. Selden, whose volume of natural and national laws proves, not only by great authorities brought together, but by exquisite reasons and theorems almost mathematically demonstrative, that all opinions, yea errors, known, read, and collated, are of main service and assistance toward the speedy attainment of what is truest.[52] I conceive, therefore, that when God did enlarge the universal diet of man's body, saving ever the rules of temperance, he then also, as before, left arbitrary the dieting and repasting of our minds, as wherein every mature man might have to exercise his own leading capacity.

How great a virtue is temperance, how much of moment through the whole life of man![53] Yet God commits the managing so great a trust, without particular law or prescription, wholly to the demeanor of every grown man. And therefore when he himself tabled the Jews from heaven, that omer which was every man's daily portion of manna is computed to have been more than might have well sufficed the heartiest feeder thrice as many meals.[54] For those actions which enter into a man, rather than issue out of him and therefore defile not,[55] God uses not to captivate under a perpetual childhood of prescription but trusts him with the gift of reason to be his own chooser. There were but little work left for preaching, if law and compulsion should grow so fast upon those things which heretofore were governed only by exhortation. Solomon informs us that much reading is a weariness to the flesh,[56] but neither he, nor other inspired author tells us that such or such reading is unlawful; yet certainly had God thought good to limit us herein, it had been much more expedient to have told us what was unlawful than what was wearisome. As for the burning of those Ephesian books by St. Paul's converts, 'tis replied the books were magic—the Syriac so renders them.[57] It was a private act, a voluntary act, and leaves us to a voluntary imitation: the men in remorse burnt those books which were their own; the magistrate by this example is not appointed; these men practiced the books; another might perhaps have read them in some sort usefully.

Good and evil we know in the field of this world grow up together almost inseparably; and the knowledge of good is so involved and interwoven with the knowledge of evil, and in so many cunning resemblances hardly to be discerned, that those confused seeds which were imposed on Psyche as an inces-

52. John *Selden* (1584–1654) served in Parliament and was one of England's most distinguished scholars, especially of legal history. He begins *De Jure Naturali et Gentium juxta Disciplinam Ebraeorum* (1640) with the claim that truth is best served when dissent is published.

53. On knowledge, nourishment, and temperance, cp. *PL* 7.126–30.

54. See Exod. 16.

55. One of Jesus' sayings (Mark 7.15).

56. Eccles. 12.12.

57. See Acts 19.19.

sant labor to cull out and sort asunder, were not more intermixed.[58] It was from out the rind of one apple tasted that the knowledge of good and evil as two twins cleaving together leapt forth into the world. And perhaps this is that doom which Adam fell into of knowing good and evil, that is to say, of knowing good by evil.

As therefore the state of man now is, what wisdom can there be to choose, what continence to forbear without the knowledge of evil? He that can apprehend and consider vice with all her baits and seeming pleasures, and yet abstain, and yet distinguish, and yet prefer that which is truly better, he is the true warfaring[59] Christian. I cannot praise a fugitive and cloistered virtue, unexercised and unbreathed, that never sallies out and sees her adversary, but slinks out of the race where that immortal garland is to be run for, not without dust and heat. Assuredly we bring not innocence into the world, we bring impurity much rather: that which purifies us is trial, and trial is by what is contrary. That virtue therefore which is but a youngling in the contemplation of evil and knows not the utmost that vice promises to her followers, and rejects it, is but a blank virtue, not a pure; her whiteness is but an excremental[60] whiteness; which was the reason why our sage and serious poet, Spenser, whom I dare be known to think a better teacher than Scotus or Aquinas,[61] describing true temperance under the person of Guyon, brings him in with his palmer through the cave of Mammon and the bower of earthly bliss that he might see and know and yet abstain.[62] Since therefore the knowledge and survey of vice is in this world so necessary to the constituting of human virtue, and the scanning of error to the confirmation of truth, how can we more safely and with less danger scout into the regions of sin and falsity than by reading all manner of tractates and hearing all manner of reason? And this is the benefit which may be had of books promiscuously read.

But of the harm that may result hence, three kinds are usually reckoned. First is feared the infection that may spread. But then all human learning and controversy in religious points must remove out of the world, yea the Bible itself; for that ofttimes relates blasphemy not nicely, it describes the carnal sense of wicked men not unelegantly, it brings in holiest men passionately murmuring against providence through all the arguments of Epicurus.[63] In other great disputes it answers dubiously and darkly to the common reader; and ask a Talmudist what ails the modesty of his marginal Keri, that Moses and all the

58. Apuleius tells of Psyche and the heap of mixed seeds (*Golden Ass* 4–6).

59. Cp. Eph. 6.11. The first edition has "wayfaring," but in all known presentation copies *y* is crossed out and *r* substituted. The change is thus probably authorial.

60. **excremental:** external, superficial.

61. John Duns *Scotus* (1265–1308) and St. Thomas *Aquinas* (c. 1225–74) were scholastic philosophers much studied in the universities.

62. Milton's account of Spenser is significantly erroneous. The palmer, representing reason, does not accompany Guyon, the Knight of Temperance, into Mammon's cave.

63. That is, the skepticism of holy men as recorded in Scripture sometimes corresponds to arguments of Epicurus (see, e.g., Eccles. 8.15). **nicely:** delicately.

Prophets cannot persuade him to pronounce the textual Chetiv.[64] For these causes we all know the Bible itself put by the papist into the first rank of prohibited books. The ancientest fathers must be next removed, as Clement of Alexandria, and that Eusebian book of evangelic preparation, transmitting our ears through a hoard of heathenish obscenities to receive the gospel.[65] Who finds not that Irenæus, Epiphanius, Jerome, and others discover more heresies than they well confute, and that oft for heresy which is the truer opinion?[66]

Nor boots it to say for these and all the heathen writers of greatest infection, if it must be thought so, with whom is bound up the life of human learning, that they writ in an unknown tongue, so long as we are sure those languages are known as well to the worst of men, who are both most able and most diligent to instill the poison they suck, first into the courts of princes, acquainting them with the choicest delights and criticisms of sin. As perhaps did that Petronius whom Nero called his arbiter, the master of his revels, and that notorious ribald of Arezzo, dreaded and yet dear to the Italian courtiers.[67] I name not him for posterity's sake, whom Harry the Eighth named in merriment his vicar of hell.[68] By which compendious way all the contagion that foreign books can infuse will find a passage to the people far easier and shorter than an Indian voyage, though it could be sailed either by the north of Cataio[69] eastward or of Canada westward, while our Spanish licensing gags the English press never so severely.

But on the other side that infection which is from books of controversy in religion is more doubtful and dangerous to the learned than to the ignorant; and yet those books must be permitted untouched by the licenser. It will be hard to instance where any ignorant man hath been ever seduced by papistical book in English, unless it were commended and expounded to him by some of that clergy; and indeed all such tractates whether false or true are, as the prophecy of Isaiah was to the eunuch, not to be "understood without a guide."[70] But of our priests and doctors how many have been corrupted by studying the comments of Jesuits and Sorbonists,[71] and how fast they could transfuse that corruption into the people, our experience is both late and sad. It is not forgot,

64. When reading Hebrew Scripture aloud, the Talmudic scholar (or *Talmudist*) substitutes a gloss in the margin (*Keri*) for an actual written text (*Chetiv*) deemed inappropriate or erroneous.

65. *Clement of Alexandria* (c. 150–c. 215) was among the first Christian theologians to incorporate Greek philosophy in his writings. Eusebius in *Preparatio Evangelica* argues that the Greek tradition is inferior to the Hebrew and, like Clement, details pagan indecencies.

66. *Irenæus* (c. 130–200), *Epiphanius* (c. 315–403), and *Jerome* (c. 342–420) wrote against various heresies, which consequently became more widely known.

67. *Petronius* Arbiter (d. 66), author of *Satyricon*, is usually identified with a like-named hedonist who reportedly guided Nero in his choice of pleasures (Tacitus 16.18). Born in Arezzo, Pietro Aretino (1492–1556) was a satirist whose lewd satirical wit was so feared that potential targets paid protection money to stay on his good side.

68. Sir Francis Bryan (d. 1550), called Henry's *vicar of hell*, was notorious for his loose ways.

69. **Cataio:** Cathay, or China.

70. See Acts 8.27-39.

71. The Sorbonne in Paris was a primary institution of Roman Catholic learning.

since the acute and distinct Arminius was perverted merely by the perusing of a nameless discourse written at Delft, which at first he took in hand to confute.[72]

Seeing therefore that those books, and those in great abundance which are likeliest to taint both life and doctrine, cannot be suppressed without the fall of learning and of all ability in disputation; and that these books of either sort are most and soonest catching to the learned, from whom to the common people whatever is heretical or dissolute may quickly be conveyed; and that evil manners are as perfectly learned without books a thousand other ways which cannot be stopped; and evil doctrine not with books can propagate except a teacher guide, which he might also do without writing, and so beyond prohibiting, I am not able to unfold, how this cautelous[73] enterprise of licensing can be exempted from the number of vain and impossible attempts. And he who were pleasantly disposed could not well avoid to liken it to the exploit of that gallant man who thought to pound up the crows by shutting his park gate.

Besides another inconvenience, if learned men be the first receivers out of books and dispreaders both of vice and error, how shall the licensers themselves be confided in, unless we can confer upon them, or they assume to themselves above all others in the land, the grace of infallibility and uncorruptedness? And, again, if it be true that a wise man like a good refiner can gather gold out of the drossiest volume, and that a fool will be a fool with the best book, yea or without book, there is no reason that we should deprive a wise man of any advantage to his wisdom, while we seek to restrain from a fool that which being restrained will be no hindrance to his folly. For if there should be so much exactness always used to keep that from him which is unfit for his reading, we should in the judgment of Aristotle not only, but of Solomon and of our Savior,[74] not vouchsafe him good precepts, and by consequence not willingly admit him to good books, as being certain that a wise man will make better use of an idle pamphlet than a fool will do of sacred scripture.

'Tis next alleged we must not expose ourselves to temptations without necessity, and, next to that, not employ our time in vain things. To both these objections one answer will serve out of the grounds already laid, that to all men such books are not temptations, nor vanities, but useful drugs and materials wherewith to temper and compose effective and strong medicines which man's life cannot want.[75] The rest, as children and childish men who have not the art to qualify and prepare these working minerals, well may be exhorted to forbear, but hindered forcibly they cannot be by all the licensing that sainted inquisition

72. Jacobus *Arminius* (1560–1609) was a Dutch Calvinist whose opposition to strict predestination led to an alternative system of salvation that came to be known as Arminianism. His dissent reportedly began in an attempt to rebut criticisms of orthodox Calvinism by ministers from Delft. Milton says that Arminius was *perverted,* but *Areopagitica* is implicitly Arminian, and Milton's mature theology explicitly so (cp. *CD* 1.4).

73. **cautelous:** cautious; deceitful.

74. Aristotle, *Nicomachean Ethics* 1.3 (1095a); Prov. 23.9 (for Solomon); Matt. 7.6 (Jesus).

75. I.e., which man's life requires.

could ever yet contrive. Which is what I promised to deliver next—that this order of licensing conduces nothing to the end for which it was framed—and hath almost prevented[76] me by being clear already while thus much hath been explaining. See the ingenuity[77] of Truth, who, when she gets a free and willing hand, opens herself faster than the pace of method and discourse can overtake her.

It was the task which I began with, to show that no nation or well instituted state, if they valued books at all, did ever use this way of licensing. And it might be answered that this is a piece of prudence lately discovered. To which I return, that as it was a thing slight and obvious to think on, so if it had been difficult to find out, there wanted not among them long since who suggested such a course, which they, not following, leave us a pattern of their judgment, that it was not the not knowing but the not approving which was the cause of their not using it.

Plato, a man of high authority indeed, but least of all for his commonwealth, in the book of his *Laws,* which no city ever yet received, fed his fancy with making many edicts to his airy burgomasters, which they who otherwise admire him wish had been rather buried and excused in the genial cups of an academic night-sitting.[78] By which laws he seems to tolerate no kind of learning but by unalterable decree, consisting most of practical traditions, to the attainment whereof a library of smaller bulk than his own dialogues would be abundant. And there also enacts that no poet should so much as read to any private man what he had written until the judges and law-keepers had seen it and allowed it. But that Plato meant this law peculiarly to that commonwealth which he had imagined and to no other is evident. Why was he not else a lawgiver to himself, but a transgressor, and to be expelled by his own magistrates, both for the wanton epigrams and dialogues which he made, and his perpetual reading of Sophron Mimus and Aristophanes, books of grossest infamy, and also for commending the latter of them, though he were the malicious libeler of his chief friends, to be read by the tyrant Dionysius, who had little need of such trash to spend his time on?[79] But that he knew this licensing of poems had reference and dependence to many other provisos there set down in his fancied republic which in this world could have no place. And so neither he himself nor any magistrate or city ever imitated that course, which taken apart from those other collateral injunctions must needs be vain and fruitless.

For if they fell upon one kind of strictness, unless their care were equal to

76. **prevented:** come before (its allotted place in the oration).
77. **ingenuity:** ingenuousness, candor.
78. Plato wrote both the *Republic,* on the principles of an ideal society, and the *Laws,* on the legal code for a deserted city soon to be reestablished.
79. Plato's *Symposium* and *Phaedrus* feature drinking, loose talk, and homoeroticism. Plato admired *Sophron Mimus* (fifth century B.C.E.), who gave literary form to the often ribald dramatic sketches known as mime (not pantomime). Although Aristophanes mocked Socrates and friends in *Clouds,* Plato reportedly recommended his works to Dionysius the First of Syracuse (430–367 B.C.E.).

regulate all other things of like aptness to corrupt the mind, that single endeavor they knew would be but a fond labor, to shut and fortify one gate against corruption and be necessitated to leave others round about wide open. If we think to regulate printing, thereby to rectify manners, we must regulate all recreations and pastimes, all that is delightful to man. No music must be heard, no song be set or sung, but what is grave and Doric.[80] There must be licensing dancers, that no gesture, motion, or deportment be taught our youth but what by their allowance shall be thought honest, for such Plato was provided of. It will ask more than the work of twenty licensers to examine all the lutes, the violins, and the guitars in every house; they must not be suffered to prattle as they do, but must be licensed what they may say. And who shall silence all the airs and madrigals that whisper softness in chambers? The windows also and the balconies must be thought on—there are shrewd books with dangerous frontispieces set to sale—who shall prohibit them, shall twenty licensers? The villages also must have their visitors to inquire what lectures the bagpipe and the rebeck reads even to the balladry and the gamut of every municipal fiddler, for these are the countryman's Arcadias and his Montemayors.[81]

Next, what more national corruption for which England hears ill abroad than household gluttony; who shall be the rectors of our daily rioting? And what shall be done to inhibit the multitudes that frequent those houses where drunkenness is sold and harbored? Our garments also should be referred to the licensing of some more sober workmasters to see them cut into a less wanton garb. Who shall regulate all the mixed conversation of our youth, male and female together, as is the fashion of this country? Who shall still appoint what shall be discoursed, what presumed, and no further? Lastly, who shall forbid and separate all idle resort, all evil company? These things will be and must be; but how they shall be least hurtful, how least enticing, herein consists the grave and governing wisdom of a state.

To sequester out of the world into Atlantic and Utopian[82] polities which never can be drawn into use will not mend our condition, but to ordain wisely as in this world of evil, in the midst whereof God hath placed us unavoidably. Nor is it Plato's licensing of books will do this, which necessarily pulls along with it so many other kinds of licensing as will make us all both ridiculous and weary, and yet frustrate, but those unwritten or at least unconstraining laws of virtuous education, religious and civil nurture, which Plato there men-

80. Plato preferred Dorian music because it inspires, in Aristotle's words, "a moderate and settled temper" (*Rep.* 3.398–99; *Pol.* 8.5). Cp. *PL* 1.550; *Of Ed* (see p. 979).

81. *Visitors* is a euphemism for censors, here depicted as absurdly concerned with the regulation of ballads. A *rebeck* is a two- or three-stringed fiddle (cp. *L'All.* 94). Romantic or sentimental country music is in Milton's view the illiterate counterpart of literary romances, such as Sidney's *Arcadia* or *Montemayor's Diana Enamorada,* deemed morally corrosive by Puritans.

82. *Sequester* is used intransitively to mean "withdraw." Plato describes the primeval excellence of the island of Atlantis in *Critias* and *Timaeus.* Thomas More tells of an ideal island society in *Utopia* (1516), as does Francis Bacon in *New Atlantis* (1627). Milton's point is that none of these places actually exist.

tions,[83] as the bonds and ligaments of the commonwealth, the pillars and the sustainers of every written statute. These they be which will bear chief sway in such matters as these, when all licensing will be easily eluded. Impunity and remissness for certain are the bane of a commonwealth, but here the great art lies to discern in what the law is to bid restraint and punishment, and in what things persuasion only is to work. If every action which is good or evil in man at ripe years were to be under pittance, and prescription, and compulsion, what were virtue but a name, what praise could be then due to well-doing, what gramercy[84] to be sober, just, or continent?

Many there be that complain of divine providence for suffering Adam to transgress. Foolish tongues! When God gave him reason, he gave him freedom to choose, for reason is but choosing; he had been else a mere artificial Adam, such an Adam as he is in the motions.[85] We ourselves esteem not of that obedience, or love, or gift, which is of force. God therefore left him free, set before him a provoking object, ever almost in his eyes; herein consisted his merit, herein the right of his reward, the praise of his abstinence. Wherefore did he create passions within us, pleasures round about us, but that these rightly tempered are the very ingredients of virtue? They are not skillful considerers of human things who imagine to remove sin by removing the matter of sin. For, besides that it is a huge heap increasing under the very act of diminishing, though some part of it may for a time be withdrawn from some persons, it cannot from all, in such a universal thing as books are; and when this is done, yet the sin remains entire. Though ye take from a covetous man all his treasure, he has yet one jewel left, ye cannot bereave him of his covetousness. Banish all objects of lust, shut up all youth into the severest discipline that can be exercised in any hermitage, ye cannot make them chaste that came not thither so: such great care and wisdom is required to the right managing of this point.

Suppose we could expel sin by this means; look how much we thus expel of sin, so much we expel of virtue. For the matter of them both is the same; remove that, and ye remove them both alike. This justifies the high providence of God, who though he command us temperance, justice, continence, yet pours out before us even to a profuseness all desirable things and gives us minds that can wander beyond all limit and satiety. Why should we then affect a rigor contrary to the manner of God and of nature, by abridging or scanting those means which books freely permitted are, both to the trial of virtue and the exercise of truth? It would be better done to learn that the law must needs be frivolous which goes to restrain things uncertainly and yet equally working to good and to evil. And were I the chooser, a dram of well-doing should be preferred before many times as much the forcible hindrance of evil-doing. For God sure es-

83. Plato, *Laws* 1 (643–45), a passage that may have suggested the ensuing puppetry metaphor.
84. **gramercy:** occasion for thanks.
85. For the identification of reason and choice, cp. *PL* 3.95–128. **motions:** puppet shows.

teems the growth and completing of one virtuous person more than the restraint of ten vicious.

And albeit whatever thing we hear or see, sitting, walking, traveling, or conversing may be fitly called our book, and is of the same effect that writings are, yet grant the thing to be prohibited were only books, it appears that this order hitherto is far insufficient to the end which it intends. Do we not see—not once or oftener, but weekly—that continued court-libel against the Parliament and City printed, as the wet sheets can witness, and dispersed among us, for all that licensing can do?[86] Yet this is the prime service a man would think wherein this order should give proof of itself. If it were executed, you'll say. But certain, if execution be remiss or blindfold now and in this particular what will it be hereafter and in other books? If then the order shall not be vain and frustrate, behold a new labor, Lords and Commons, ye must repeal and proscribe all scandalous and unlicensed books already printed and divulged—after ye have drawn them up into a list, that all may know which are condemned and which not—and ordain that no foreign books be delivered out of custody till they have been read over. This office will require the whole time of not a few overseers, and those no vulgar men. There be also books which are partly useful and excellent, partly culpable and pernicious; this work will ask as many more officials to make expurgations and expunctions, that the commonwealth of learning be not damnified.[87] In fine, when the multitude of books increase upon their hands, ye must be fain to catalogue all those printers who are found frequently offending and forbid the importation of their whole suspected typography. In a word, that this your order may be exact and not deficient, ye must reform it perfectly according to the model of Trent and Seville,[88] which I know ye abhor to do.

Yet though ye should condescend to this, which God forbid, the order still would be but fruitless and defective to that end whereto ye meant it. If to prevent sects and schisms, who is so unread or so uncatechized in story that hath not heard of many sects refusing books as a hindrance and preserving their doctrine unmixed for many ages only by unwritten traditions? The Christian faith, for that was once a schism, is not unknown to have spread all over Asia ere any gospel or epistle was seen in writing. If the amendment of manners be aimed at, look into Italy and Spain, whether those places be one scruple the better, the honester, the wiser, the chaster, since all the inquisitional rigor that hath been executed upon books.

Another reason, whereby to make it plain that this order will miss the end it seeks, consider by the quality which ought to be in every licenser. It cannot be denied but that he who is made judge to sit upon the birth or death of books

86. Milton refers to the weekly Royalist newspaper, *Mercurius Aulicus,* published from 1642 to 1645.
87. **damnified:** injured or impaired.
88. Milton has already identified the Council of *Trent* (1545–63) as the historical origin of prepublication licensing. The Spanish Inquisition, instituted in 1481, had its seat in *Seville.*

whether they may be wafted into this world or not, had need to be a man above the common measure, both studious, learned, and judicious. There may be else no mean mistakes in the censure of what is passable or not, which is also no mean injury. If he be of such worth as behooves him, there cannot be a more tedious and unpleasing journey-work,[89] a greater loss of time levied upon his head, than to be made the perpetual reader of unchosen books and pamphlets, ofttimes huge volumes. There is no book that is acceptable unless at certain seasons; but to be enjoined the reading of that at all times, and in a hand scarce legible, whereof three pages would not down[90] at any time in the fairest print, is an imposition I cannot believe how he that values time and his own studies, or is but of a sensible nostril, should be able to endure. In this one thing I crave leave of the present licensers to be pardoned for so thinking; who doubtless took this office up, looking on it through their obedience to the Parliament, whose command perhaps made all things seem easy and unlaborious to them; but that this short trial hath wearied them out already, their own expressions and excuses to them who make so many journeys to solicit their license are testimony enough. Seeing therefore those who now possess the employment by all evident signs wish themselves well rid of it, and that no man of worth, none that is not a plain unthrift of his own hours, is ever likely to succeed them, except he mean to put himself to the salary of a press corrector,[91] we may easily foresee what kind of licensers we are to expect hereafter, either ignorant, imperious, and remiss, or basely pecuniary. This is what I had to show wherein this order cannot conduce to that end whereof it bears the intention.

I lastly proceed, from the no good it can do, to the manifest hurt it causes in being first the greatest discouragement and affront that can be offered to learning and to learned men.

It was the complaint and lamentation of prelates, upon every least breath of a motion to remove pluralities[92] and distribute more equally church revenues, that then all learning would be forever dashed and discouraged. But as for that opinion, I never found cause to think that the tenth part of learning stood or fell with the clergy, nor could I ever but hold it for a sordid and unworthy speech of any churchman who had a competency left him.[93] If therefore ye be loath to dishearten utterly and discontent, not the mercenary crew of false pretenders to learning, but the free and ingenuous sort of such as evidently were born to study and love learning for itself, not for lucre or any other end but the service of God and of truth, and perhaps that lasting fame and perpetuity of praise which God and good men have consented shall be the reward of those whose published labors advance the good of mankind, then know, that so far to distrust

89. **journey-work:** day labor.
90. **down:** i.e., go down (like food or drink, as *be . . . of a sensible nostril* suggests).
91. **press corrector:** proofreader.
92. **pluralities:** the possession by clergymen of more than one benefice or living.
93. **tenth part of learning:** The phrasing suggests the system of tithing for support of the church. **competency:** income sufficient to meet living expenses.

the judgment and the honesty of one who hath but a common repute in learning, and never yet offended, as not to count him fit to print his mind without a tutor and examiner, lest he should drop a schism or something of corruption, is the greatest displeasure and indignity to a free and knowing spirit that can be put upon him.

What advantage is it to be a man over it is to be a boy at school, if we have only scaped the ferula to come under the fescue[94] of an *imprimatur;* if serious and elaborate writings, as if they were no more than the theme of a grammar lad under his pedagogue, must not be uttered without the cursory eyes of a temporizing and extemporizing licenser? He who is not trusted with his own actions, his drift not being known to be evil, and standing to the hazard of law and penalty, has no great argument to think himself reputed, in the commonwealth wherein he was born, for other than a fool or a foreigner. When a man writes to the world, he summons up all his reason and deliberation to assist him; he searches, meditates, is industrious, and likely consults and confers with his judicious friends; after all which done he takes himself to be informed in what he writes, as well as any that writ before him. If in this the most consummate act of his fidelity and ripeness, no years, no industry, no former proof of his abilities can bring him to that state of maturity, as not to be still mistrusted and suspected, unless he carry all his considerate diligence, all his midnight watchings, and expense of Palladian[95] oil, to the hasty view of an unleisured licenser, perhaps much his younger, perhaps far his inferior in judgment, perhaps one who never knew the labor of book-writing, and if he be not repulsed or slighted, must appear in print like a puny[96] with his guardian and his censor's hand on the back of his title to be his bail and surety that he is no idiot or seducer; it cannot be but a dishonor and derogation to the author, to the book, to the privilege and dignity of learning.

And what if the author shall be one so copious of fancy as to have many things well worth the adding come into his mind after licensing, while the book is yet under the press, which not seldom happens to the best and diligentest writers, and that perhaps a dozen times in one book. The printer dares not go beyond his licensed copy. So often then must the author trudge to his leave-giver, that those his new insertions may be viewed, and many a jaunt will be made, ere that licenser, for it must be the same man, can either be found, or found at leisure. Meanwhile, either the press must stand still, which is no small damage, or the author lose his accuratest thoughts and send the book forth worse than he had made it, which to a diligent writer is the greatest melancholy and vexation that can befall. And how can a man teach with authority, which is the life of teaching, how can he be a doctor in his book as he ought to be (or else had better be silent), whenas all he teaches, all he delivers, is but under the

94. **ferula:** teacher's rod; **fescue:** teacher's pointer.
95. **Palladian:** pertaining to Pallas Athena, Greek goddess of wisdom.
96. **puny:** minor, youth; someone young in learning (from French *puis-né:* later-born).

tuition, under the correction of his patriarchal licenser to blot or alter what precisely accords not with the hidebound humor which he calls his judgment?[97] When every acute reader upon the first sight of a pedantic license will be ready with these like words to ding the book a quoit's distance[98] from him: "I hate a pupil teacher; I endure not an instructor that comes to me under the wardship of an overseeing fist. I know nothing of the licenser, but that I have his own hand here for his arrogance. Who shall warrant me his judgment?"

"The state, sir," replies the stationer,[99] but has a quick return: "the state shall be my governors, but not my critics; they may be mistaken in the choice of a licenser, as easily as this licenser may be mistaken in an author; this is some common stuff"; and he might add from Sir Francis Bacon, that "such authorized books are but the language of the times."[100] For though a licenser should happen to be judicious more than ordinary, which will be a great jeopardy of the next succession, yet his very office and his commission enjoins him to let pass nothing but what is vulgarly received already.

Nay, which is more lamentable, if the work of any deceased author, though never so famous in his lifetime and even to this day, come to their hands for license to be printed or reprinted; if there be found in his book one sentence of a venturous edge, uttered in the height of zeal, and who knows whether it might not be the dictate of a divine spirit, yet not suiting with every low decrepit humor of their own, though it were Knox himself, the reformer of a kingdom that spake it, they will not pardon him their dash. The sense of that great man shall to all posterity be lost for the fearfulness or the presumptuous rashness of a perfunctory licenser. And to what an author this violence hath been lately done, and in what book of greatest consequence to be faithfully published, I could now instance, but shall forbear till a more convenient season.[101]

Yet if these things be not resented seriously and timely by them who have the remedy in their power, but that such iron molds[102] as these shall have authority to gnaw out the choicest periods of exquisitest books and to commit such a treacherous fraud against the orphan remainders of worthiest men after death, the more sorrow will belong to that hapless race of men whose misfortune it is to have understanding. Henceforth let no man care to learn or care to be more than worldly wise, for certainly in higher matters to be ignorant and

97. At his trial in March 1644, Archbishop Laud was charged with bargaining to restore England to the Catholic Church so that he might become Patriarch of Great Britain. The allusion is reinforced, according to Sirluck (*Yale* 2.533), by Milton's assertion that licensers did not just *blot* but altered what authors wrote, an offense with which Laud was also charged.

98. **ding:** throw violently. **quoit:** a ring-shaped piece of iron, the classical discus.

99. **stationer:** bookseller or publisher.

100. The quotation is rough but substantially accurate. See *A Wise and Moderate Discourse Concerning Church-Affaires,* 11 (1641), composed by Bacon in 1589 as *An Advertisement touching the Controversies of the Church of England.*

101. Works usually cited as examples include John Knox's *History of the Reformation* (1644) and Edward Coke's *Institutes of Laws of England* (1641). Both suffered cuts before publication.

102. **iron molds:** stains caused by rusty iron or ink, here used figuratively of the licensers' efforts.

slothful, to be a common, steadfast dunce, will be the only pleasant life, and only in request.

And as it is a particular disesteem of every knowing person alive, and most injurious to the written labors and monuments of the dead, so to me it seems an undervaluing and vilifying of the whole nation. I cannot set so light by all the invention, the art, the wit, the grave and solid judgment which is in England, as that it can be comprehended in any twenty capacities how good soever, much less that it should not pass except their superintendence be over it, except it be sifted and strained with their strainers, that it should be uncurrent without their manual stamp. Truth and understanding are not such wares as to be monopolized[103] and traded in by tickets and statutes and standards. We must not think to make a staple commodity of all the knowledge in the land, to mark and license it like our broadcloth and our woolpacks. What is it but a servitude like that imposed by the Philistines not to be allowed the sharpening of our own axes and coulters, but we must repair from all quarters to twenty licensing forges.[104] Had any one written and divulged erroneous things and scandalous to honest life, misusing and forfeiting the esteem had of his reason among men, if after conviction this only censure were adjudged him, that he should never henceforth write but what were first examined by an appointed officer, whose hand should be annexed to pass his credit for him that now he might be safely read, it could not be apprehended less than a disgraceful punishment. Whence to include the whole nation and those that never yet thus offended under such a diffident and suspectful prohibition may plainly be understood what a disparagement it is. So much the more whenas debtors and delinquents may walk abroad without a keeper,[105] but unoffensive books must not stir forth without a visible jailer in their title.

Nor is it to the common people less than a reproach. For if we be so jealous over them as that we dare not trust them with an English pamphlet, what do we but censure them for a giddy, vicious, and ungrounded people, in such a sick and weak estate of faith and discretion as to be able to take nothing down but through the pipe[106] of a licenser? That this is care or love of them we cannot pretend, whenas in those popish places where the laity are most hated and despised, the same strictness is used over them. Wisdom we cannot call it, because it stops but one breach of license, nor that neither whenas those corruptions which it seeks to prevent break in faster at other doors, which cannot be shut.

103. Commercial monopolies, on which Charles I had increasingly depended during the 1630s, caused great outrage and constituted a prominent Parliamentary grievance.

104. The Philistines did not permit the subject Israelites to have forges. To sharpen tools, they had to go to the Philistines (1 Sam. 13.19–21).

105. In Milton's era (and long after) debtors could be jailed, though in certain exempt districts they were able to walk without fear of apprehension. Parliament in 1643 ruled that those who had aided the king were *delinquents*, expropriated their property, and left them liable to imprisonment. By 1644, this action had been much mitigated, and relatively easy settlement was made available (Sirluck, Yale 2:536).

106. **pipe:** tube for giving medicine.

And in conclusion, it reflects to the disrepute of our ministers also, of whose labors we should hope better, and of the proficiency which their flock reaps by them, than that after all this light of the gospel which is and is to be, and all this continual preaching, they should be still frequented with such an unprincipled, unedified, and laic rabble, as that the whiff of every new pamphlet should stagger them out of their catechism and Christian walking.[107] This may have much reason to discourage the ministers, when such a low conceit is had of all their exhortations and the benefiting of their hearers, as that they are not thought fit to be turned loose to three sheets of paper without a licenser, that all the sermons, all the lectures preached, printed, vented in such numbers and such volumes as have now well nigh made all other books unsaleable, should not be armor enough against one single enchiridion, without the castle of St. Angelo of an *imprimatur*.[108]

And lest some should persuade ye, Lords and Commons, that these arguments of learned men's discouragement at this your order are mere flourishes and not real, I could recount what I have seen and heard in other countries where this kind of inquisition tyrannizes: when I have sat among their learned men, for that honor I had, and been counted happy to be born in such a place of philosophic freedom as they supposed England was, while themselves did nothing but bemoan the servile condition into which learning amongst them was brought; that this was it which had damped the glory of Italian wits; that nothing had been there written now these many years but flattery and fustian. There it was that I found and visited the famous Galileo grown old, a prisoner to the Inquisition, for thinking in astronomy otherwise than the Franciscan and Dominican licensers thought.[109] And though I knew that England then was groaning loudest under the prelatical yoke, nevertheless I took it as a pledge of future happiness that other nations were so persuaded of her liberty.

Yet was it beyond my hope that those worthies were then breathing in her air who should be her leaders to such a deliverance as shall never be forgotten by any revolution of time that this world hath to finish. When that was once begun, it was as little in my fear that what words of complaint I heard among learned men of other parts uttered against the Inquisition, the same I should hear by as learned men at home uttered in time of Parliament against an order of licensing. And that so generally, that when I had disclosed myself a companion of their discontent, I might say, if without envy, that he whom an honest quæstorship had endeared to the Sicilians was not more by them importuned against Verres,[110]

107. Christians are exhorted to walk wisely at Eph. 5.15–16 and Col. 4.5.

108. **conceit:** concept, imagination; **enchiridion:** handbook (with a pun on the Greek for "dagger"); **castle of St. Angelo:** papal prison in Rome.

109. Galileo (1564–1642) published *Dialogue on the Two Chief Systems,* which undermined church teaching on the stationary centrality of the earth, in 1632. He was made to recant and spent the rest of his life under house arrest. Milton claims to have met him in Tuscany in 1638.

110. In 75 B.C.E., Cicero served as *quaestor* (financial officer) for Sicily. Afterward, *Verres* became governor (73–71), and the Sicilians asked Cicero to prosecute him for corruption, which he did with brilliant success.

than the favorable opinion which I had among many who honor ye, and are known and respected by ye, loaded me with entreaties and persuasions that I would not despair to lay together that which just reason should bring into my mind toward the removal of an undeserved thraldom upon learning. That this is not therefore the disburdening of a particular fancy, but the common grievance of all those who had prepared their minds and studies above the vulgar pitch to advance truth in others, and from others to entertain it, thus much may satisfy.

And in their name I shall for neither friend nor foe conceal what the general murmur is: that if it come to inquisitioning again, and licensing, and that we are so timorous of ourselves and so suspicious of all men as to fear each book and the shaking of every leaf before we know what the contents are; if some who but of late were little better than silenced from preaching shall come now to silence us from reading except what they please, it cannot be guessed what is intended by some but a second tyranny over learning, and will soon put it out of controversy that bishops and presbyters are the same to us both name and thing.[111] That those evils of prelaty, which before from five or six and twenty sees[112] were distributively charged upon the whole people, will now light wholly upon learning is not obscure to us, whenas now the pastor of a small unlearned parish on the sudden shall be exalted archbishop over a large diocese of books and yet not remove but keep his other cure too, a mystical pluralist.[113] He who but of late cried down the sole ordination of every novice bachelor of art and denied sole jurisdiction over the simplest parishioner, shall now at home in his private chair assume both these over worthiest and excellentest books and ablest authors that write them.[114] This is not—ye covenants and protestations[115] that we have made!—this is not to put down prelaty; this is but to chop an episcopacy;[116] this is but to translate the palace metropolitan[117] from one kind of dominion into another; this is but an old canonical sleight of commuting our penance.

To startle thus betimes at a mere unlicensed pamphlet will after a while be afraid of every conventicle, and a while after will make a conventicle of every Christian meeting.[118] But I am certain that a state governed by the rules of jus-

111. In supporting Presbyterian opposition to episcopal hierarchy, Milton had argued that *bishop* and *presbyter* were in Scripture synonymous terms for "priest" (Yale 1:650). He suggests that presbyters now risk becoming the same as bishops in more than name. Cp. *On the New Forcers of Conscience.*

112. **sees:** seats of episcopal power.

113. **mystical pluralist:** By overseeing "a large diocese of books," while simultaneously remaining in his local parish, the pastor mysteriously manages to occupy two places at once.

114. Presbyterians had disputed the sole right of bishops to ordain new ministers and exercise spiritual authority, yet they now assume similar rights over authors and books.

115. **covenants and protestations:** Milton invokes various resolutions in Scotland and England from 1638 to 1643 that spelled out Presbyterian opposition to episcopal discipline and upheld the rights and liberties of the people.

116. **chop an episcopacy:** exchange one church hierarchy for another.

117. **palace metropolitan:** residence of the presiding bishop. The Archbishop of Canterbury resided in Lambeth Palace.

118. **To startle:** to take fright (corresponds with [*to*] *be afraid of*); **conventicle:** a meeting of religious nonconformists, held secretly to avoid persecution.

tice and fortitude, or a church built and founded upon the rock of faith and true knowledge, cannot be so pusillanimous. While things are yet not constituted in religion,[119] that freedom of writing should be restrained by a discipline imitated from the prelates, and learnt by them from the Inquisition to shut us up all again into the breast of a licenser, must needs give cause of doubt and discouragement to all learned and religious men. Who cannot but discern the fineness[120] of this politic drift and who are the contrivers, that while bishops were to be baited down, then all presses might be open; it was the people's birthright and privilege in time of Parliament; it was the breaking forth of light.

But now, the bishops abrogated and voided out of the church, as if our Reformation sought no more but to make room for others into their seats under another name, the episcopal arts begin to bud again, the cruse[121] of truth must run no more oil, liberty of printing must be enthralled again under a prelatical commission of twenty, the privilege of the people nullified, and, which is worse, the freedom of learning must groan again, and to her old fetters—all this the Parliament yet sitting. Although their own late arguments and defenses against the prelates might remember them that this obstructing violence meets for the most part with an event utterly opposite to the end which it drives at: instead of suppressing sects and schisms, it raises them and invests them with a reputation. "The punishing of wits enhances their authority," sayeth the Viscount St. Albans,[122] "and a forbidden writing is thought to be a certain spark of truth that flies up in the faces of them who seek to tread it out." This order, therefore, may prove a nursing mother to sects, but I shall easily show how it will be a stepdame to Truth, and first by disenabling us to the maintenance of what is known already.

Well knows he who uses to consider, that our faith and knowledge thrives by exercise as well as our limbs and complexion.[123] Truth is compared in scripture to a streaming fountain; if her waters flow not in a perpetual progression they sicken into a muddy pool of conformity and tradition. A man may be a heretic in the truth; and if he believe things only because his pastor says so or the Assembly[124] so determines, without knowing other reason, though his belief be true, yet the very truth he holds becomes his heresy. There is not any burden that some would gladlier post off to another than the charge and care of their religion. There be (who knows not that there be?) of Protestants and professors who live and die in as arrant an implicit faith as any lay papist of Loretto.[125] A

119. The episcopacy had been uprooted, and a new church discipline had not yet been settled.
120. **fineness:** cunning, subtle strategy (finesse).
121. In 1 Kings 17.12–16, a widow's small jar (*cruse*) of oil never fails, as Elijah promised.
122. Sir Francis Bacon, whose *Wise and Moderate Discourse Concerning Church-Affaires* is again quoted, from the same page as previously. See note 99.
123. **uses:** is accustomed to; **complexion:** bodily constitution; natural disposition.
124. The Westminster Assembly of divines was convened to advise Parliament on church affairs.
125. The *those* preceding *who* in this sentence is understood. **professors:** Puritans who publicly declare their faith; **implicit:** blindly trusting; **Loretto:** Italian shrine to which it was believed angels had transported Mary and Jesus' house from Nazareth.

wealthy man, addicted to his pleasure and to his profits, finds religion to be a traffic so entangled and of so many piddling accounts that of all mysteries[126] he cannot skill to keep a stock going upon that trade. What should he do? Fain he would have the name to be religious; fain he would bear up with his neighbors in that. What does he, therefore, but resolves to give over toiling and to find himself out some factor to whose care and credit he may commit the whole managing of his religious affairs; some divine of note and estimation that must be. To him he adheres, resigns the whole warehouse of his religion with all the locks and keys into his custody; and indeed makes the very person of that man his religion; esteems his associating with him a sufficient evidence and commendatory of his own piety. So that a man may say his religion is now no more within himself, but is become a dividual movable,[127] and goes and comes near him according as that good man frequents the house. He entertains him, gives him gifts, feasts him, lodges him; his religion comes home at night, prays, is liberally supped, and sumptuously laid to sleep, rises, is saluted, and after the malmsey or some well spiced brewage, and better breakfasted than he whose morning appetite would have gladly fed on green figs between Bethany and Jerusalem,[128] his religion walks abroad at eight and leaves his kind entertainer in the shop trading all day without his religion.

Another sort there be who, when they hear that all things shall be ordered, all things regulated and settled, nothing written but what passes through the customhouse of certain publicans that have the tunnaging and the poundaging of all freespoken truth,[129] will straight give themselves up into your hands, make 'em and cut 'em out what religion ye please. There be delights, there be recreations and jolly pastimes that will fetch the day about from sun to sun, and rock the tedious year as in a delightful dream. What need they torture their heads with that which others have taken so strictly and so unalterably into their own purveying? These are the fruits which a dull ease and cessation of our knowledge will bring forth among the people. How goodly, and how to be wished, were such an obedient unanimity as this; what a fine conformity would it starch us all into? Doubtless a staunch and solid piece of framework as any January could freeze together.

Nor much better will be the consequence even among the clergy themselves. It is no new thing never heard of before, for a parochial minister, who has his reward and is at his Hercules' pillars[130] in a warm benefice, to be easily in-

126. **mysteries:** professions, occupations, trades.

127. **dividual movable:** separable piece of property or commodity.

128. Hungry, Jesus sought figs to eat on the way from Bethany to Jerusalem (Matt. 11.12–14).

129. **publicans:** tax collectors; **tunnaging and poundaging:** excise taxes on wine (by the tun) and other commodities. Sirluck complains that the modernization of "tunnage to tonnage . . . betrays a misconception." But "*tonnage* is the more usual form," according to the *OED* (1.1), and has been since the fifteenth century.

130. **Hercules' pillars:** rocks on either side of the Strait of Gibraltar, anciently thought to mark the western limit of the world and to have been established by Hercules.

clinable, if he have nothing else that may rouse up his studies, to finish his circuit in an English concordance and a topic folio,[131] the gatherings and savings of a sober graduateship, a harmony and a catena,[132] treading the constant round of certain common doctrinal heads, attended with their uses, motives, marks, and means; out of which, as out of an alphabet or sol-fa, by forming and transforming, joining and disjoining variously, a little bookcraft, and two hours' meditation, might furnish him unspeakably to the performance of more than a weekly charge of sermoning—not to reckon up the infinite helps of interlinearies, breviaries, synopses, and other loitering gear.

But as for the multitude of sermons ready printed and piled up on every text that is not difficult, our London trading St. Thomas in his vestry and add to boot St. Martin and St. Hugh have not within their hallowed limits more vendible ware of all sorts ready made: so that penury he never need fear of pulpit provision, having where so plenteously to refresh his magazine.[133] But if his rear and flanks be not impaled,[134] if his back door be not secured by the rigid licenser, but that a bold book may now and then issue forth and give the assault to some of his old collections in their trenches, it will concern him then to keep waking, to stand in watch, to set good guards and sentinels about his received opinions, to walk the round and counter-round with his fellow inspectors, fearing lest any of his flock be seduced, who also then would be better instructed, better exercised and disciplined. And God send that the fear of this diligence which must then be used do not make us affect the laziness of a licensing church.

For if we be sure we are in the right and do not hold the truth guiltily, which becomes not, if we ourselves condemn not our own weak and frivolous teaching, and the people for an untaught and irreligious gadding rout, what can be more fair, than when a man judicious, learned, and of a conscience, for aught we know as good as theirs that taught us what we know, shall not privily from house to house, which is more dangerous, but openly by writing publish to the world what his opinion is, what his reasons, and wherefore that which is now thought cannot be sound. Christ urged it as wherewith to justify himself that he preached in public;[135] yet writing is more public than preaching and more easy to refutation, if need be, there being so many whose business and profession

131. **topic folio:** commonplace book, notebook.

132. **harmony:** handbook that arranges parallel scriptural passages respecting the same events to show their agreement or consistency; **catena:** chain of connected passages chosen from biblical commentaries, arranged so that each passage is related to the preceding and following ones. The rest of the sentence refers to commonly taught means of organizing a sermon.

133. The Church of St. Thomas, Apostle, had clothiers nearby (see Dekker and Middleton, *Roaring Girl* 3.1.199); St. Martin le Grand, shoemakers. St. Hugh was a patron saint of shoemakers (Dekker, *Shoemakers' Holiday* 5.5.157–60). Milton thus puns on *vestry* and *boot* (apparel and shoes) as he suggests that religion is being regulated and standardized like any commerce.

134. **impaled:** fenced in, protected.

135. John 18.19–20.

merely it is to be the champions of truth, which if they neglect, what can be imputed but their sloth or inability?

Thus much we are hindered and disinured[136] by this course of licensing toward the true knowledge of what we seem to know. For how much it hurts and hinders the licensers themselves in the calling of their ministry, more than any secular employment, if they will discharge that office as they ought, so that of necessity they must neglect either the one duty or the other, I insist not, because it is a particular, but leave it to their own conscience, how they will decide it there.

There is yet behind[137] of what I purposed to lay open the incredible loss and detriment that this plot of licensing puts us to; more than if some enemy at sea should stop up all our havens and ports, and creeks, it hinders and retards the importation of our richest merchandize, truth. Nay, it was first established and put in practice by antichristian malice and mystery on set purpose to extinguish, if it were possible, the light of reformation and to settle falsehood, little differing from that policy wherewith the Turk upholds his Alcoran,[138] by the prohibition of printing. 'Tis not denied, but gladly confessed, we are to send our thanks and vows to heaven louder than most of nations, for that great measure of truth which we enjoy, especially in those main points between us and the Pope, with his appurtenances the prelates. But he who thinks we are to pitch our tent here and have attained the utmost prospect of reformation that the mortal glass[139] wherein we contemplate can show us till we come to beatific vision, that man by this very opinion declares that he is yet far short of truth.

Truth indeed came once into the world with her divine Master and was a perfect shape most glorious to look on. But when he ascended and his apostles after him were laid asleep, then straight arose a wicked race of deceivers, who, as that story goes of the Egyptian Typhon with his conspirators, how they dealt with the good Osiris, took the virgin Truth, hewed her lovely form into a thousand pieces, and scattered them to the four winds.[140] From that time ever since, the sad friends of Truth, such as durst appear, imitating the careful search that Isis made for the mangled body of Osiris, went up and down gathering up limb by limb still as they could find them. We have not yet found them all, Lords and Commons, nor ever shall do, till her Master's second coming. He shall bring together every joint and member, and shall mold them into an immortal feature[141] of loveliness and perfection. Suffer not these licensing prohibitions to stand at every place of opportunity, forbidding and disturbing them that con-

136. **disinured:** rendered unaccustomed or unfamiliar.
137. **yet behind:** still to show.
138. **Alcoran:** sacred writings of Islam; the Koran.
139. **mortal glass:** the mirror of mortal existence (cp. 1 Cor. 13.12: "Now we see through a glass darkly; but then face to face"; see also 2 Cor. 3.17–19).
140. Milton's application of the myth of Osiris and Typhon recalls Plutarch's in "Isis and Osiris."
141. **feature:** shape.

tinue seeking, that continue to do our obsequies to the torn body of our martyred saint.

We boast our light, but if we look not wisely on the sun itself, it smites us into darkness. Who can discern those planets that are oft combust,[142] and those stars of brightest magnitude that rise and set with the sun, until the opposite motion of their orbs bring them to such a place in the firmament where they may be seen evening or morning? The light which we have gained, was given us, not to be ever staring on, but by it to discover onward things more remote from our knowledge. It is not the unfrocking of a priest, the unmitering of a bishop, and the removing him from off the Presbyterian shoulders that will make us a happy nation. No, if other things as great in the church and in the rule of life both economical and political be not looked into and reformed, we have looked so long upon the blaze that Zwinglius and Calvin[143] hath beaconed up to us that we are stark blind.

There be who perpetually complain of schisms and sects, and make it such a calamity that any man dissents from their maxims. 'Tis their own pride and ignorance which causes the disturbing, who neither will hear with meekness, nor can convince, yet all must be suppressed which is not found in their syntagma.[144] They are the troublers, they are the dividers of unity, who neglect and permit not others to unite those dissevered pieces which are yet wanting to the body of Truth. To be still searching what we know not by what we know, still closing up truth to truth as we find it (for all her body is homogeneal and proportional), this is the golden rule[145] in theology as well as in arithmetic and makes up the best harmony in a church, not the forced and outward union of cold and neutral and inwardly divided minds.

Lords and Commons of England, consider what nation it is whereof ye are, and whereof ye are the governors: a nation not slow and dull, but of a quick, ingenious, and piercing spirit, acute to invent, subtle and sinewy to discourse, not beneath the reach of any point the highest that human capacity can soar to. Therefore the studies of learning in her deepest sciences have been so ancient and so eminent among us that writers of good antiquity and ablest judgment have been persuaded that even the school of Pythagoras and the Persian wisdom took beginning from the old philosophy of this island.[146] And that wise and

142. A planet within eight and a half degrees of the sun is said to be *combust,* its light subsumed by the sun's and its astrological influence "burnt up." Mars and Venus are regularly eclipsed by the sun but at other times can be seen morning and evening.

143. Ulrich *Zwingli* (1484–1531) was the principal figure of the Swiss Reformation. John *Calvin* (1509–64), a Frenchman who established a theocracy in Geneva, became the principal theologian of the Reformation.

144. **syntagma:** a systematic collection of doctrines.

145. **golden rule:** also known as the rule of three, a method of finding an unknown number from three given numbers, where the first is in the same proportion to the second as the third is to the unknown fourth.

146. **Persian wisdom:** occult arts, magic; **old philosophy:** that of the Druids, who practiced magic and, like the Pythagoreans, believed in the transmigration of souls.

civil Roman, Julius Agricola, who governed once here for Caesar, preferred the natural wits of Britain before the labored studies of the French.[147] Nor is it for nothing that the grave and frugal Transylvanian sends out yearly from as far as the mountainous borders of Russia and beyond the Hercynian wilderness,[148] not their youth, but their staid men to learn our language and our theologic arts.

Yet that which is above all this, the favor and the love of Heaven, we have great argument to think in a peculiar manner propitious and propending[149] towards us. Why else was this nation chosen before any other, that out of her as out of Sion should be proclaimed and sounded forth the first tidings and trumpet of reformation to all Europe? And had it not been the obstinate perverseness of our prelates against the divine and admirable spirit of Wycliffe, to suppress him as a schismatic and innovator, perhaps neither the Bohemian Huss and Jerome, no, nor the name of Luther or of Calvin, had been ever known; the glory of reforming all our neighbors had been completely ours.[150] But now, as our obdurate clergy have with violence demeaned the matter, we are become hitherto the latest and backwardest scholars of whom God offered to have made us the teachers.

Now once again by all concurrence of signs and by the general instinct of holy and devout men as they daily and solemnly express their thoughts, God is decreeing to begin some new and great period in his church, even to the reforming of reformation itself. What does he then but reveal himself to his servants, and, as his manner is, first to his Englishmen? I say as his manner is, first to us, though we mark not the method of his counsels and are unworthy. Behold now this vast city, a city of refuge, the mansion house of liberty, encompassed and surrounded with his protection. The shop of war hath not there more anvils and hammers waking, to fashion out the plates and instruments of armed justice in defence of beleaguered truth, than there be pens and heads there, sitting by their studious lamps, musing, searching, revolving new notions and ideas wherewith to present, as with their homage and their fealty, the approaching reformation; others as fast reading, trying all things, assenting to the force of reason and convincement. What could a man require more from a nation so pliant and so prone to seek after knowledge? What wants there to such a towardly and pregnant soil but wise and faithful laborers to make a knowing people a nation of prophets, of sages, and of worthies?[151] We reckon more than five months

147. *Agricola* (40–93) was a Roman general and governor of Britain. Tacitus, his son-in-law, records his regard for British ingenuity (*Agricola* 21).

148. **Hercynian wilderness:** forested region in central and southern Germany. Transylvania ("beyond the forest") was an independent state in Milton's era and zealously Protestant.

149. **propending:** inclining.

150. The reformist doctrines of John *Wycliffe* (c. 1330–1384) found supporters in England but were ultimately condemned and proscribed by the Church. John *Huss,* influenced by Wycliffe, was a reformer in Prague burned alive for heresy in 1414. His friend *Jerome* (1370–1416), also of Prague, was likewise influenced by Wycliffe and burned at the stake.

151. I.e., "What does this intellectually and spiritually apt country lack to fulfill its potential but those seekers of religious truth whose reasoned efforts can make it a land of the wise and holy?"

yet to harvest. There need not be five weeks; had we but eyes to lift up, the fields are white already.[152] Where there is much desire to learn, there of necessity will be much arguing, much writing, many opinions: for opinion in good men is but knowledge in the making. Under these fantastic[153] terrors of sect and schism, we wrong the earnest and zealous thirst after knowledge and understanding which God hath stirred up in this city.

What some lament of, we rather should rejoice at, should rather praise this pious forwardness among men to reassume the ill-deputed care of their religion into their own hands again. A little generous prudence, a little forbearance of one another, and some grain of charity might win all these diligences to join and unite into one general and brotherly search after truth, could we but forgo this prelatical tradition of crowding free consciences and Christian liberties into canons and precepts of men. I doubt not, if some great and worthy stranger should come among us, wise to discern the mold and temper of a people and how to govern it, observing the high hopes and aims, the diligent alacrity of our extended thoughts and reasonings in the pursuance of truth and freedom, but that he would cry out as Pyrrhus did, admiring the Roman docility and courage: "if such were my Epirots, I would not despair the greatest design that could be attempted to make a church or kingdom happy."[154]

Yet these are the men cried out against for schismatics and sectaries; as if, while the temple of the Lord was building, some cutting, some squaring the marble, others hewing the cedars, there should be a sort of irrational men who could not consider there must be many schisms and many dissections made in the quarry and in the timber ere the house of God can be built.[155] And when every stone is laid artfully together, it cannot be united into a continuity, it can but be contiguous in this world. Neither can every piece of the building be of one form; nay, rather the perfection consists in this, that out of many moderate varieties and brotherly dissimilitudes that are not vastly disproportional arises the goodly and the graceful symmetry that commends the whole pile and structure.

Let us therefore be more considerate builders, more wise in spiritual architecture, when great reformation is expected. For now the time seems come, wherein Moses, the great prophet, may sit in Heaven rejoicing to see that memorable and glorious wish of his fulfilled, when, not only our seventy elders, but all the Lord's people are become prophets. No marvel then though some men—and some good men too, perhaps, but young in goodness, as Joshua then was—envy them.[156] They fret and out of their own weakness are in agony lest

152. See John 4.35: "Say not ye, There are yet four months, and then cometh harvest? Behold, I say unto you, Lift up your eyes, and look on the fields; for they are white already to harvest."

153. **fantastic:** imaginary.

154. After a costly victory, King *Pyrrhus* of Epirus (319–272 B.C.E.) said that with soldiers like those of Rome, he could conquer the world.

155. On the hewing and cutting for Solomon's Temple, see 1 Kings 5–7 and 2 Chron. 2–4.

156. The young *Joshua* bid Moses to forbid other Hebrews from prophesying, but Moses replied, "Enviest thou for my sake? Would God that all the Lord's people were prophets" (Num. 11.29).

these divisions and subdivisions will undo us. The adversary again applauds and waits the hour. "When they have branched themselves out," sayeth he, "small enough into parties and partitions, then will be our time." Fool! He sees not the firm root out of which we all grow, though into branches; nor will beware until he see our small-divided maniples cutting through at every angle of his ill-united and unwieldy brigade.[157] And that we are to hope better of all these supposed sects and schisms, and that we shall not need that solicitude—honest, perhaps, though over-timorous—of them that vex in this behalf, but shall laugh in the end at those malicious applauders of our differences, I have these reasons to persuade me.

First, when a city shall be as it were besieged and blocked about, her navigable river infested, inroads and incursions round, defiance and battle oft rumored to be marching up even to her walls and suburb trenches, that then the people, or the greater part, more than at other times, wholly taken up with the study of highest and most important matters to be reformed, should be disputing, reasoning, reading, inventing, discoursing, even to a rarity and admiration, things not before discoursed or written of, argues first a singular goodwill, contentedness, and confidence in your prudent foresight and safe government, Lords and Commons.[158] And from thence derives itself to a gallant bravery and well-grounded contempt of their enemies, as if there were no small number of as great spirits among us as his was, who, when Rome was nigh besieged by Hannibal, being in the city, bought that piece of ground at no cheap rate whereon Hannibal himself encamped his own regiment.[159]

Next, it is a lively and cheerful presage of our happy success and victory. For as in a body, when the blood is fresh, the spirits pure and vigorous, not only to vital but to rational faculties, and those in the acutest and the pertest operations of wit and subtlety, it argues in what good plight and constitution the body is, so when the cheerfulness of the people is so sprightly up as that it has not only wherewith to guard well its own freedom and safety, but to spare, and to bestow upon the solidest and sublimest points of controversy and new invention, it betokens us not degenerated nor drooping to a fatal decay, but casting off the old and wrinkled skin of corruption to outlive these pangs and wax young again, entering the glorious ways of truth and prosperous virtue destined to become great and honorable in these latter ages.

Methinks I see in my mind a noble and puissant nation rousing herself like a strong man after sleep and shaking her invincible locks. Methinks I see her as an eagle mewing[160] her mighty youth and kindling her undazzled eyes at the full midday beam, purging and unscaling her long-abused sight at the fountain

157. **maniples:** small units (literally "handfuls") of soldiers. A *brigade* is a much larger unit.

158. This sentence recalls the situation in October 1642, when the Royalist army was poised to attack London. Cp. *Sonnet 8.* The threat of attack continued intermittently.

159. The story of a Roman citizen who paid full price for land then occupied by Hannibal's besieging troops appears in Livy's *History* (26.11).

160. **mewing:** molting, though some editors amend to "newing" (renewing).

itself of heavenly radiance, while the whole noise of timorous and flocking birds, with those also that love the twilight, flutter about, amazed at what she means, and in their envious gabble would prognosticate a year of sects and schisms.

What would ye do then; should ye suppress all this flowery crop of knowledge and new light sprung up and yet springing daily in this city? Should ye set an oligarchy of twenty engrossers[161] over it to bring a famine upon our minds again, when we shall know nothing but what is measured to us by their bushel? Believe it, Lords and Commons, they who counsel ye to such a suppressing do as good as bid ye suppress yourselves, and I will soon show how.

If it be desired to know the immediate cause of all this free writing and free speaking, there cannot be assigned a truer than your own mild and free and human government. It is the liberty, Lords and Commons, which your own valorous and happy counsels have purchased us, liberty which is the nurse of all great wits. This is that which hath rarified and enlightened our spirits like the influence of heaven; this is that which hath enfranchised, enlarged, and lifted up our apprehensions degrees above themselves. Ye cannot make us now less capable, less knowing, less eagerly pursuing of the truth, unless ye first make yourselves, that made us so, less the lovers, less the founders of our true liberty. We can grow ignorant again, brutish, formal, and slavish, as ye found us; but you then must first become that which ye cannot be, oppressive, arbitrary, and tyrannous, as they were from whom ye have freed us. That our hearts are now more capacious, our thoughts more erected to the search and expectation of greatest and exactest things, is the issue of your own virtue propagated in us; ye cannot suppress that unless ye reinforce an abrogated and merciless law that fathers may dispatch at will their own children.[162] And who shall then stick closest to ye and excite others? Not he who takes up arms for coat and conduct, and his four nobles of Danegelt. Although I dispraise not the defense of just immunities, yet love my peace better, if that were all.[163] Give me the liberty to know, to utter, and to argue freely according to conscience, above all liberties.

What would be best advised then, if it be found so hurtful and so unequal[164] to suppress opinions for the newness or the unsuitableness to a customary acceptance, will not be my task to say. I only shall repeat what I have learned from one of your own honorable number, a right noble and pious lord, who, had he not sacrificed his life and fortunes to the church and commonwealth, we had

161. **engrossers:** those who obtain sole possession; monopolizers.

162. The Roman law giving fathers the power of life and death over children was abolished in 318.

163. **coat and conduct:** tax levied on counties to pay for the equipment and transport of troops; **danegelt:** a tax imposed originally to fend off the Danes from English shores, and subsequently for other ends, such as the defense of the coast. Charles's attempt to revive and extend it without consent of Parliament was challenged as a violation of *just immunities* from such impositions. The sense of this passage seems to be that those who stood by Parliament against the Royalists did so not for money but to establish freedom of inquiry and expression.

164. **unequal:** unjust.

not now missed and bewailed a worthy and undoubted patron of this argument. Ye know him I am sure; yet I for honor's sake (and may it be eternal to him) shall name him, the Lord Brooke.[165] He, writing of episcopacy and by the way treating of sects and schisms, left ye his vote, or rather now the last words of his dying charge (which I know will ever be of dear and honored regard with ye) so full of meekness and breathing charity, that, next to his last testament who bequeathed love and peace to his disciples,[166] I cannot call to mind where I have read or heard words more mild and peaceful. He there exhorts us to hear with patience and humility those, however they be miscalled, that desire to live purely, in such a use of God's ordinances as the best guidance of their conscience gives them, and to tolerate them, though in some disconformity to ourselves. The book itself will tell us more at large, being published to the world and dedicated to the Parliament by him who, both for his life and for his death, deserves that what advice he left be not laid by without perusal.

And now the time in special is by privilege[167] to write and speak what may help to the further discussing of matters in agitation. The temple of Janus with his two controversial faces might now not unsignificantly be set open.[168] And though all the winds of doctrine were let loose to play upon the earth, so Truth be in the field, we do injuriously by licensing and prohibiting to misdoubt her strength.[169] Let her and Falsehood grapple; who ever knew Truth put to the worse in a free and open encounter? Her confuting is the best and surest suppressing. He who hears what praying there is for light and clearer knowledge to be sent down among us would think of other matters to be constituted beyond the discipline of Geneva, framed and fabricked already to our hands.[170]

Yet when the new light which we beg for shines in upon us, there be who envy and oppose if it come not first in at their casements. What a collusion is this, whenas we are exhorted by the wise man to use diligence, "to seek for wisdom as for hidden treasures early and late,"[171] that another order shall enjoin us to know nothing but by statute? When a man hath been laboring the hardest labor in the deep mines of knowledge, hath furnished out his findings in all their equipage, drawn forth his reasons as it were a battle ranged, scattered and defeated all objections in his way, calls out his adversary into the plain, offers him the advantage of wind and sun, if he please, only that he may try the mat-

165. Robert Greville (1608–43), the second *Lord Brooke,* a general of the Parliamentary army, was killed at the attack on Lichfield. Milton refers to his *Discourse Opening the Nature of that Episcopacy, which is Exercised in England* (1641).

166. See John 14.27.

167. **in special:** especially; **by privilege:** an idiom used to signify the right to print or publish a book or the like.

168. **Janus:** Roman god of gates and doorways. His two faces looked *controversially,* that is, in opposed directions. His temple lay open in time of war, closed in time of peace.

169. In opposing the *winds of doctrine* to *Truth,* Milton alludes to Eph. 4.14–15.

170. **discipline of Geneva:** Presbyterianism, which followed Calvin; **fabricked:** fashioned.

171. Though printed as a quotation in the first edition, this imperative combines and paraphrases Prov. 2.4, 8.11, and Matt. 13.44.

ter by dint of argument; for his opponents then to skulk, to lay ambushments, to keep a narrow bridge of licensing where the challenger should pass, though it be valor enough in soldiership, is but weakness and cowardice in the wars of Truth.

For who knows not that Truth is strong next to the Almighty; she needs no policies, nor stratagems, nor licensings to make her victorious, those are the shifts and the defenses that error uses against her power. Give her but room and do not bind her when she sleeps, for then she speaks not true as the old Proteus did, who spake oracles only when he was caught and bound,[172] but then rather she turns herself into all shapes, except her own, and perhaps tunes her voice according to the time, as Micaiah did before Ahab, until she be adjured into her own likeness.[173]

Yet is it not impossible that she may have more shapes than one? What else is all that rank of things indifferent[174] wherein Truth may be on this side or on the other without being unlike herself? What but a vain shadow else is the abolition of "those ordinances, that handwriting nailed to the cross"?[175] What great purchase is this Christian liberty which Paul so often boasts of?[176] His doctrine is that he who eats or eats not, regards a day or regards it not, may do either to the Lord.[177] How many other things might be tolerated in peace and left to conscience, had we but charity, and were it not the chief stronghold of our hypocrisy to be ever judging one another? I fear yet this iron yoke of outward conformity hath left a slavish print upon our necks; the ghost of a linen decency[178] yet haunts us. We stumble and are impatient at the least dividing of one visible congregation from another, though it be not in fundamentals. And through our forwardness to suppress and our backwardness to recover any enthralled piece of truth out of the grip of custom,[179] we care not to keep truth separated from truth, which is the fiercest rent and disunion of all. We do not see that while we still affect by all means a rigid external formality, we may as soon fall again into a gross conforming stupidity, a stark and dead congealment of "wood and hay and stubble" [1 Cor. 3.12][180] forced and frozen together, which is more to the sudden degenerating of a church than many subdichotomies of petty schisms.

Not that I can think well of every light separation, or that all in a Church is

172. On oracular *Proteus,* the shape-changing sea god, see Homer, *Od.* 4.384–93.

173. For *Ahab* and *Micaiah,* see 1 Kings 22.1–38.

174. **things indifferent:** points of religion not explicitly set out in Scripture, a much debated category in Milton's era.

175. **those . . . cross:** the old law, superseded through the sacrifice of Christ, as expressed by St. Paul (Col. 2.14).

176. See, e.g., Gal. 5.1, Rom. 8.21.

177. See Rom. 14.1–13.

178. **linen decency:** The phrase evokes priestly vestments dictated by Archbishop Laud and condemned by the Puritans.

179. See the preface to *DDD* on the opposition of truth and custom.

180. Another part of the same verse is quoted in the next sentence.

to be expected "gold and silver and precious stones." It is not possible for man to sever the wheat from the tares, the good fish from the other fry; that must be the angels' ministry at the end of mortal things.[181] Yet if all cannot be of one mind (as who looks they should be?), this doubtless is more wholesome, more prudent, and more Christian that many be tolerated, rather than all compelled. I mean not tolerated popery and open superstition, which as it extirpates all religions and civil supremacies, so itself should be extirpate, provided first that all charitable and compassionate means be used to win and regain the weak and the misled; that also which is impious or evil absolutely either against faith or manners no law can possibly permit, that intends not to unlaw itself. But those neighboring differences, or rather indifferences, are what I speak of, whether in some point of doctrine or of discipline, which though they may be many, yet need not interrupt "the unity of spirit," if we could but find among us "the bond of peace."[182]

In the meanwhile, if any one would write and bring his helpful hand to the slow-moving reformation which we labor under, if Truth have spoken to him before others, or but seemed at least to speak, who hath so bejesuited[183] us that we should trouble that man with asking license to do so worthy a deed?—and not consider this, that if it come to prohibiting, there is not aught more likely to be prohibited than truth itself, whose first appearance to our eyes, bleared and dimmed with prejudice and custom, is more unsightly and unplausible than many errors, even as the person[184] is of many a great man slight and contemptible to see to. And what do they tell us vainly of new opinions, when this very opinion of theirs, that none must be heard but whom they like, is the worst and newest opinion of all others and is the chief cause why sects and schisms do so much abound, and true knowledge is kept at distance from us; besides yet a greater danger which is in it. For when God shakes a kingdom with strong and healthful commotions to a general reforming, 'tis not untrue that many sectaries and false teachers are then busiest in seducing. But yet more true it is that God then raises to his own work men of rare abilities and more than common industry, not only to look back and revise what hath been taught heretofore, but to gain further and go on some new enlightened steps in the discovery of truth.

For such is the order of God's enlightening his church, to dispense and deal out by degrees his beam so as our earthly eyes may best sustain it. Neither is God appointed[185] and confined where and out of what place these his chosen shall be first heard to speak. For he sees not as man sees,[186] chooses not as man

181. Milton alludes to the parable of the wheat and the tares (Matt. 13.24–30, 36–43).
182. See Eph. 4.3.
183. **bejesuited:** initiated to Jesuitism.
184. **person:** bodily form.
185. **appointed:** fixed by agreement; settled beforehand.
186. Before choosing the shepherd David as King of Israel, God informs the prophet Samuel that "the Lord seeth not as man seeth" (1 Sam. 16.7).

chooses, lest we should devote ourselves again to set places, and assemblies, and outward callings of men, planting our faith one while in the old convocation house and another while in the chapel at Westminster;[187] when all the faith and religion that shall be there canonized is not sufficient without plain convincement,[188] and the charity of patient instruction to supple[189] the least bruise of conscience, to edify the meanest Christian who desires to walk in the spirit and not in the letter of human trust, for all the number of voices that can be there made; no, though Harry the Seventh himself there, with all his liege tombs about him, should lend them voices from the dead to swell their number.

And if the men be erroneous who appear to be the leading schismatics, what withholds us but our sloth, our self-will, and distrust in the right cause, that we do not give them gentle meeting and gentle dismissions, that we debate not and examine the matter thoroughly with liberal and frequent audience, if not for their sakes yet for our own? Seeing no man who hath tasted learning but will confess the many ways of profiting by those who, not contented with stale receipts, are able to manage and set forth new positions to the world. And were they but as the dust and cinders of our feet, so long as in that notion they may yet serve to polish and brighten the armory of truth, even for that respect they were not utterly to be cast away. But if they be of those whom God hath fitted for the special use of these times with eminent and ample gifts—and those perhaps neither among the priests nor among the pharisees—and we in the haste of a precipitant zeal shall make no distinction but resolve to stop their mouths because we fear they come with new and dangerous opinions (as we commonly forejudge them ere we understand them), no less than woe to us while, thinking thus to defend the Gospel, we are found the persecutors.

There have been not a few since the beginning of this Parliament, both of the presbytery and others, who, by their unlicensed books to the contempt of an *imprimatur*, first broke that triple ice clung about our hearts and taught the people to see day. I hope that none of those were the persuaders to renew upon us this bondage which they themselves have wrought so much good by contemning. But if neither the check that Moses gave to young Joshua, nor the countermand which our Savior gave to young John,[190] who was so ready to prohibit those whom he thought unlicensed, be not enough to admonish our elders how unacceptable to God their testy mood of prohibiting is; if neither their own remembrance what evil hath abounded in the church by this let of licensing, and

187. The bishops who until the 1640s set church policy in England met in the Jerusalem Chamber at Westminster. Once the episcopacy was undone, the *Westminster* Assembly of Divines met in the chapel of Henry VII (named at the end of the paragraph) to establish a new church discipline.

188. **convincement:** conviction of conscience.

189. **supple:** soften or mollify.

190. When *Joshua* wanted to forbid others from prophesying, *Moses* checked him (Num. 11.29). See note 156. Jesus tells *John* not to forbid others from acting in Jesus' name: "He that is not against us is for us" (Luke 9.50).

what good they themselves have begun by transgressing it, be not enough but that they will persuade and execute the most Dominican part of the Inquisition over us,[191] and are already with one foot in the stirrup so active at suppressing, it would be no unequal distribution in the first place to suppress the suppressors themselves, whom the change of their condition hath puffed up more than their late experience of harder times hath made wise.

And as for regulating the press, let no man think to have the honor of advising ye better than yourselves have done in that order published next before this, that no book be printed unless the printer's and the author's name, or at least the printer's, be registered.[192] Those which otherwise come forth, if they be found mischievous and libelous, the fire and the executioner will be the timeliest and the most effectual remedy that man's prevention can use. For this authentic Spanish policy of licensing books, if I have said aught, will prove the most unlicensed book itself within a short while, and was the immediate image of a Star Chamber decree to that purpose made in those very times when that court did the rest of those her pious works, for which she is now fallen from the stars with Lucifer.[193] Whereby ye may guess what kind of state prudence, what love of the people, what care of religion or good manners there was at the contriving, although with singular hypocrisy it pretended to bind books to their good behavior. And how it got the upper hand of your precedent order so well constituted before, if we may believe those men whose profession gives them cause to inquire most, it may be doubted[194] there was in it the fraud of some old patentees and monopolizers in the trade of bookselling; who, under pretence of the poor in their company not to be defrauded, and the just retaining of each man his several copy[195] (which God forbid should be gainsaid), brought diverse glossing colors[196] to the House, which were indeed but colors and serving to no end except it be to exercise a superiority over their neighbors, men who do not therefore labor in an honest profession to which learning is indebted that they should be made other men's vassals. Another end is thought was aimed at by some of them in procuring by petition this order,[197] that having power in their hands, malignant books might the easier scape abroad, as the event shows.

But of these sophisms and elenchs of merchandise I skill not.[198] This I know, that errors in a good government and in a bad are equally almost incident,[199] for

191. *Dominican* friars often served as licensers and were strict enforcers of doctrine.

192. Milton cites the Order of Parliament regulating printing that was made in January 1642.

193. The Court of the Star Chamber on July 11, 1637, gave control of the press to the Church. In July 1641, the Court was abolished. Milton compares its demise to the fall of Lucifer, the "morning star" (see Isa. 14.12, Rev. 12.4).

194. **doubted:** suspected.

195. **copy:** copyright.

196. **glossing colors:** explanations intended to disguise the truth.

197. In April 1643, the Stationers' Company petitioned Parliament to reinstitute control of the press.

198. I.e., "But of such fallacious arguments born of commercial interest, I profess ignorance."

199. **incident:** likely to occur.

what magistrate may not be misinformed, and much the sooner if liberty of printing be reduced into the power of a few. But to redress willingly and speedily what hath been erred, and in highest authority to esteem a plain advertisement[200] more than others have done a sumptuous bribe, is a virtue, honored Lords and Commons, answerable to your highest actions, and whereof none can participate but greatest and wisest men.

The End.

200. **advertisement:** warning.

Introduction to *Of Education*

Today *humanism* has become a slippery term. But for scholars of the early modern period it refers to an educational program based on the extant writings of Greek and Latin antiquity. The program can be traced to the thirteenth century, in Italy, and its rise has often been thought to be the defining feature of the Renaissance itself as a period in Western culture. Milton's essay *Of Education,* though in crucial ways a defense of traditional humanism, nonetheless owes its genesis to a movement in seventeenth-century European education dedicated to ending once and for all the cultural reign of humanism, and thus to ending, in some views at least, the Renaissance.

A new pedagogy had come into being. Most of its adherents were Protestants, though its leading figure, the Czech educator Johann Amos Comenius (1592–1670), was not. Gradually, over several centuries, and after undergoing numerous historical transformations, the new pedagogy carried the field. Most of its proposed changes are now firmly instituted in educational systems around the world.

Here are some of its tenets. Scientific empiricism should dominate the curriculum. The work of Francis Bacon, especially the assault on traditional logic and rhetoric in his *Novum Organum* (1620), was much admired by these reformers, and presented as a shining alternative to the arid culture of Greek and Latin studies. Literature, the humanities in general, amounted to a tyranny of words, occasioning a pedantic, snobbish, elitist pseudo-learning confined to its own word-world, not the world God created and Bacon taught us to number, weigh, and measure. Comenius favored state-sponsored schools offering an empirical, vocational education to all children, male and female. In a humanistic curriculum students would read Herodotus to learn about the conflicts between Greece and Asia, Donatus to discover the laws of drama, Quintilian and Cicero to discern the techniques and ethics of public speaking, and so on, through a whole host of ever-relevant originators, the *fontes* (springs) of civilized culture. Education meant having read and understood them. But Comenius hoped to subvert this reliance on great and seminal writers by collecting "Pansophy" (all truth) in a single book, a précis of knowledge in its entirety, or as Samuel Hartlib put it, "a true anatomy of the universe" (Comenius 13). Latin would still be taught, but in a vastly streamlined fashion. The new emphasis would fall on the twin virtues of the shortcut and the simplification.

Hartlib was a main champion of the new pedagogy in the England of Milton's day. Adopting the role of unofficial adviser to the mid-century Protestant Parliaments, Hartlib championed a wide variety of causes, from better use of farmland in England to utopian social schemes in the Virginia colony. He brought Comenius himself to England in 1641. He promoted a stable of like-minded authors, and it was no doubt this lifelong urge to proselytize that led him, at some point in the early 1640s, to invite Milton, then earning his living as a schoolmaster, to write about education. Perhaps Hartlib already knew or strongly suspected what the nation would find out in the decades ahead: that John Milton, graduate of St. Paul's, a grammar school designed by the formidable sixteenth-century humanist John Colet, and of Trinity College, Cambridge, was the supreme living product of humanistic learning. What a victory that would be! A Milton endorsing a Comenius!

Milton did agree wholeheartedly with certain of the Comenian indictments of Renaissance pedagogy. He thought his education wasteful, inefficient, and dispiriting. He detested the barren brambles of logic. He deplored the absence of Baconian subjects in the traditional curriculum. Like proponents of vocational instruction, he considered it wise to learn from actual practitioners. But Milton was also humanist-trained and Renaissance-inspired. Hartlib and Comenius had little or nothing to say about the power of art and literature to enrich and elevate, whereas that power was the central truth of Milton's existence. He also detested the idea of handbooks and compendiums. When Milton assures Hartlib that he has not looked into "what many modern *Januas* and *Didactics,* more than ever I shall read, have projected," he is alluding to two of the best-known books by Comenius, the *Janua Linguarum Reserata* (The Door of Languages Unlocked) and the *Didactica Magna* (Great Instruction), joking with evident contempt that even in the work of Comenius himself the dream of one Pansophic book had turned plural, and there were already too many of these supposedly time-saving digests to waste his time reading.

In the ideal school Milton envisions, there is time for the venerable humanistic authors as well as Baconian practicality, for Christian education with its imperative "to repair the ruins of our first parents by regaining to know God aright," as well as classical education, with its goal of preparing men "to perform justly, skilfully, and magnanimously all the offices both private and public of peace and war." There is time for Scripture and epic, music and martial exercise—time, magically, for *everything.* As the historian Charles Webster put it, "Milton is perhaps the only leading writer to embody a compromise between the old and new pedagogies" (113).

A telling feature of Milton's pedagogical scheme is the postponement of original composition until the entire curriculum has been mastered. Then, as education's crowning act, "will be the season of forming them to be able writers and composers." He clearly resented having been forced to write prematurely of various subjects through the course of his studies. The belief that composition should be the supreme act of maturity, and the anxious fear that this maturity, this readiness, may not yet have been attained, became part of the drama of his poetic compositions. A concern with the spiritual discipline of "inward ripeness" marks *Sonnet 7*, the 1633 "Letter to a Friend" that contains a draft of *Sonnet 7*, and the opening lines of *Lycidas*, where the premature death of a shepherd forces an unready author to begin his eulogy "before the mellowing year." *Of Education* was published in 1644. It would not be long before the publication of the 1645 *Poems*, whose dated works announce that the author has finally reached a first stage in artistic maturity and can now, at long last, submit his labors to public scrutiny. That the author himself felt a deep affinity between the pedagogical ideals expressed in *Of Education* and the fulfillment of his poetic ambitions is suggested by the fact that the 1673 edition of his *Poems Upon Several Occasions*, which appeared a year before Milton's death, reprints the "small tractate Of Education to Mr. Hartlib" after the early verse. This is the sole instance of Milton publishing his poetry and one of his prose works between the same covers.

Our text is based on the copy of the first edition in the Carl H. Pforzheimer Library in the Harry Ransom Humanities Research Center, Austin, Texas.

OF EDUCATION. TO MASTER SAMUEL HARTLIB.

Master Hartlib,

I am long since persuaded that to say or do aught worth memory and imitation, no purpose or respect should sooner move us than simply the love of God and of mankind. Nevertheless, to write now the reforming of education, though it be one of the greatest and noblest designs that can be thought on, and for the want whereof this nation perishes, I had not yet at this time been induced but by your earnest entreaties and serious conjurements; as having my mind, for the present, half-diverted in the pursuance of some other assertions, the knowledge and the use of which cannot but be a great furtherance both to the enlargement of truth and honest living with much more peace.

Nor should the laws of any private friendship have prevailed with me to divide thus or transpose my former thoughts, but that I see those aims, those actions which have won you with me the esteem of a person sent hither by some good providence from a far country to be the occasion and the incitement of great good to this island.[1] And, as I hear, you have obtained the same repute with men of most approved wisdom, and some of highest authority among us. Not to mention the learned correspondence which you hold in foreign parts, and the extraordinary pains and diligence which you have used in this matter both here and beyond the seas, either by the definite will of God so ruling or the peculiar sway of nature,[2] which also is God's working. Neither can I think that, so reputed and so valued as you are, you would, to the forfeit of your own discerning ability, impose upon me an unfit and over-ponderous argument, but that the satisfaction which you profess to have received from those incidental discourses which we have wandered into hath pressed and almost constrained you into a persuasion that what you require from me in this point I neither ought nor can in conscience defer beyond this time both of so much need at once and so much opportunity to try what God hath determined.[3]

I will not resist, therefore, whatever it is either of divine or human obligement that you lay upon me, but will forthwith set down in writing, as you re-

1. A native of Prussia, Hartlib (1600–62) attended Cambridge briefly around 1625. By 1628 he returned to England, where he maintained a voluminous international correspondence and tirelessly advocated educational and other reforms.

2. **peculiar sway of nature:** i.e., Hartlib's own natural bent.

3. In 1641 Parliament dedicated land taken from prelates to the advancement of learning, providing the resources, in Milton's view, to attempt to fulfill God's will.

quest me, that voluntary[4] idea, which hath long in silence presented itself to me, of a better education—in extent and comprehension far more large, and yet of time far shorter and of attainment far more certain—than hath been yet in practice. Brief I shall endeavor to be: for that which I have to say, assuredly this nation hath extreme need should be done sooner than spoken. To tell you, therefore, what I have benefited herein among old renowned authors, I shall spare; and to search what many modern *Januas* and *Didactics*[5] (more than ever I shall read) have projected, my inclination leads me not. But if you can accept of these few observations which have flowered off and are, as it were, the burnishing of many studious and contemplative years altogether spent in the search of religious and civil knowledge, and such as pleased you so well in the relating, I here give you them to dispose of.

The end then of learning is to repair the ruins of our first parents[6] by regaining to know God aright, and out of that knowledge to love him, to imitate him, to be like him as we may the nearest by possessing our souls of true virtue, which, being united to the heavenly grace of faith, makes up the highest perfection. But, because our understanding cannot in this body found itself but on sensible things, nor arrive so clearly to the knowledge of God and things invisible as by orderly conning over the visible and inferior creature,[7] the same method is necessarily to be followed in all discreet teaching. And, seeing every nation affords not experience and tradition enough for all kind of learning, therefore we are chiefly taught the languages of those people who have at any time been most industrious after wisdom; so that language is but the instrument conveying to us things useful to be known. And though a linguist should pride himself to have all the tongues that Babel cleft the world into, yet if he have not studied the solid things in them, as well as the words and lexicons, he were nothing so much to be esteemed a learned man as any yeoman or tradesman competently wise in his mother dialect only.

Hence appear the many mistakes which have made learning generally so unpleasing and so unsuccessful. First, we do amiss to spend seven or eight years merely in scraping together so much miserable Latin and Greek as might be learnt otherwise easily and delightfully in one year.[8] And that which casts our proficiency therein so much behind is our time lost, partly in too oft idle vacancies[9] given both to schools and universities, partly in a preposterous[10] exaction forcing the empty wits of children to compose themes, verses, and orations,

4. **voluntary:** spontaneous, unbidden.

5. Works by Johann Amos Comenius (1592–1670), Moravian pedagogical theorist who inspired Hartlib's project in England. He held that the end of education is the development of Christian virtue and that learning begins in the sensible realm.

6. In Christian teaching, the fall of Adam and Eve devastated human understanding.

7. **visible and inferior creature:** visible creation; the world we perceive.

8. Aubrey records that Milton taught his nephews to sight-read Latin within a year (p. xxv).

9. **vacancies:** vacations; holidays.

10. **preposterous:** literally, putting the last thing first; backward.

which are the acts of ripest judgment and the final work of a head filled, by long reading and observing, with elegant maxims and copious invention.[11] These are not matters to be wrung from poor striplings like blood out of the nose or the plucking of untimely fruit—besides the ill habit which they get of wretched barbarizing against the Latin and Greek idiom with their untutored Anglicisms,[12] odious to be read, yet not to be avoided without a well-continued and judicious conversing among pure authors digested, which they scarce taste; whereas, if after some preparatory grounds of speech by their certain forms got into memory, they were led to the praxis[13] thereof in some chosen short book, lessoned thoroughly to them, they might then forthwith proceed to learn the substance of good things and arts in due order, which would bring the whole language quickly into their power. This I take to be the most rational and most profitable way of learning languages, and whereby we may best hope to give account to God of our youth spent herein.

And for the usual method of teaching arts, I deem it to be an old error of universities not yet well recovered from the scholastic grossness of barbarous ages that, instead of beginning with arts most easy (and those be such as are most obvious to the sense), they present their young, unmatriculated[14] novices at first coming with the most intellective abstractions of logic and metaphysics.[15] So that they, having but newly left those grammatic flats and shallows where they stuck unreasonably to learn a few words with lamentable construction, and now on the sudden transported under another climate to be tossed and turmoiled with their unballasted wits in fathomless and unquiet deeps of controversy,[16] do for the most part grow into hatred and contempt of learning, mocked and deluded all this while with ragged notions and babblements while they expected worthy and delightful knowledge; till poverty or youthful years call them importunately their several ways and hasten them with the sway of friends[17] either to an ambitious and mercenary or ignorantly zealous divinity;[18] some allured to the trade of law, grounding their purposes not on the prudent and heavenly contemplation of justice and equity, which was never taught them, but on the promising and pleasing thoughts of litigious terms,[19] fat contentions,[20] and flowing fees; others betake them to state affairs, with souls so un-

11. In classical rhetoric, *inventio* refers to research, finding out all materials relevant to a given topic. *Copia* refers to the full use of these materials to address the topic fruitfully.
12. **Anglicisms:** expressions in Latin or Greek that follow English usage.
13. **praxis:** practice.
14. **unmatriculated:** not yet enrolled in a college or university.
15. In *Prolusion 7,* Milton laments that logic, "the queen of the Arts," is mistaught and scorns metaphysics as a "bog of fallacies" (1827).
16. As may be seen from Milton's *Prolusions,* school exercises typically took the form of disputations, often on metaphysical topics.
17. **sway of friends:** influence of relatives.
18. **divinity:** career in the clergy.
19. **litigious terms:** periods when courts were in session and dockets full.
20. **fat contentions:** lucrative legal disputes.

principled in virtue and true generous breeding that flattery and court shifts[21] and tyrannous aphorisms[22] appear to them the highest points of wisdom, instilling their barren hearts with a conscientious slavery if, as I rather think, it be not feigned. Others, lastly, of a more delicious[23] and airy[24] spirit, retire themselves, knowing no better, to the enjoyments of ease and luxury, living out their days in feast and jollity—which indeed is the wisest and the safest course of all these, unless they were with more integrity undertaken. And these are the fruits of misspending our prime youth at the schools and universities as we do, either in learning mere words or such things chiefly as were better unlearnt.

I shall detain you no longer in the demonstration of what we should not do, but straight conduct ye to a hillside, where I will point ye out the right path of a virtuous and noble education—laborious indeed at the first ascent, but else so smooth, so green, so full of goodly prospect and melodious sounds on every side that the harp of Orpheus was not more charming.[25] I doubt not but ye shall have more ado to drive our dullest and laziest youth, our stocks and stubs,[26] from the infinite desire of such a happy nurture, than we have now to haul and drag our choicest and hopefullest wits to that asinine feast of sow-thistles and brambles which is commonly set before them as all the food and entertainment of their tenderest and most docible[27] age. I call therefore a complete and generous[28] education that which fits a man to perform justly, skillfully, and magnanimously all the offices both private and public of peace and war. And how all this may be done between twelve and one and twenty (less time than is now bestowed in pure trifling at grammar and sophistry) is to be thus ordered.

First, to find out a spacious house and ground about it fit for an academy, and big enough to lodge a hundred and fifty persons, whereof twenty or thereabout may be attendants, all under the government of one who shall be thought of desert sufficient and ability either to do all or wisely to direct and oversee it done. This place should be at once both school and university, not needing a remove to any other house of scholarship, except it be some peculiar college of law or physic[29] where they mean to be practitioners; but as for those general studies which take up all our time from Lily[30] to the commencing, as they term it, Master of Art, it should be absolute.[31] After this pattern, as many edifices may

21. **shifts:** subterfuges; sophistries.

22. **aphorisms:** customary maxims; *tyrannous* because untested by reason.

23. **delicious:** prone to sensuous indulgence.

24. **airy:** unsubstantial, vain. The sentence echoes parts of Comus's first speech (*Masque* 102–12).

25. In Greek myth, Orpheus was a poet-musician whose song enraptured and civilized listeners, even beasts, rocks, and trees—or in this case stocks and stubs.

26. **stocks and stubs:** tree stumps, here signifying "blockheads."

27. **docible:** teachable.

28. **generous:** appropriate for one of noble lineage.

29. **peculiar college of law or physic:** specialized school of law or medicine.

30. The standard Latin grammar used in English schools for over two centuries was written by the eponymous William Lily (c. 1468–1522). John Colet made him the first headmaster of St. Paul's School, Milton's alma mater.

31 **absolute:** complete, entire.

be converted to this use as shall be needful in every city throughout this land, which would tend much to the increase of learning and civility[32] everywhere. This number, less or more, thus collected to the convenience of a foot company,[33] or interchangeably two troops of cavalry, should divide their days' work into three parts as it lies orderly: their studies, their exercise, and their diet.

For their studies: first, they should begin with the chief and necessary rules of some good grammar, either that now used or any better; and while this is doing, their speech is to be fashioned to a distinct and clear pronunciation, as near as may be to the Italian, especially in the vowels. For we Englishmen, being far northerly, do not open our mouths in the cold air wide enough to grace a southern tongue, but are observed by all other nations to speak exceeding close and inward—so that to smatter[34] Latin with an English mouth is as ill a-hearing as law-French.[35]

Next, to make them expert in the usefullest points of grammar, and withal to season them and win them early to the love of virtue and true labor ere any flattering seducement or vain principle seize them wandering, some easy and delightful book of education would be read to them, whereof the Greeks have store, as Cebes, Plutarch, and other Socratic discourses.[36] But in Latin we have none of classic authority extant except the two or three first books of Quintilian[37] and some select pieces elsewhere. But here the main skill and groundwork will be to temper[38] them such lectures and explanations, upon every opportunity, as may lead and draw them in willing obedience, inflamed with the study of[39] learning and the admiration of virtue, stirred up with high hopes of living to be brave men and worthy patriots, dear to God and famous to all ages. That they may despise and scorn all their childish and ill-taught qualities to delight in manly and liberal[40] exercises; which he who hath the art and proper eloquence to catch them with—what with mild and effectual persuasions, and what with the intimation of some fear if need be, but chiefly by his own example—might in a short space gain them to an incredible diligence and courage, infusing into their young breasts such an ingenuous[41] and noble ardor as would not fail to make many of them renowned and matchless men.

At the same time, some other hour of the day might be taught them the rules of arithmetic and soon after the elements of geometry, even playing as the old

32. **civility:** good citizenship.
33. **convenience of a foot company:** number of soldiers in an infantry company (about one hundred).
34. **smatter:** both "to besmirch" and "to speak ignorantly."
35. **law-French:** corrupt variety of French used in English legal books.
36. Among the Greek works to which Milton refers are Cebes' *Table,* Plutarch's *On the Education of Children* and *Moralia,* and Plato's *Republic* and *Laws.* There were Latin translations of these texts that could pull the double duty Milton envisions, teaching grammar and inculcating high ideals at one stroke.
37. The first three books of Quintilian's *Institutes* concern pedagogy and rhetoric.
38. **temper:** adapt for.
39. **study of:** devotion to.
40. **liberal:** befitting a gentleman.
41. **ingenous:** high-minded.

manner was.[42] After evening repast till bedtime, their thoughts will be best taken up in the easy[43] grounds of religion and the story of scripture. The next step would be to the authors of agriculture—Cato, Varro, and Columella[44]—for the matter is most easy; and if the language be difficult, so much the better: it is not a difficulty above their years. And here will be an occasion of inciting and enabling them hereafter to improve the tillage of their country, to recover the bad soil, and to remedy the waste that is made of good, for this was one of Hercules' praises.[45] Ere half these authors be read, which will soon be with plying hard and daily, they cannot choose but be masters of any ordinary prose. So that it will be then seasonable for them to learn in any modern author the use of the globes and all the maps, first with the old names and then with the new;[46] or they might be then capable to read any compendious method of natural philosophy.

And at the same time might be entering into the Greek tongue, after the same manner as was before prescribed in the Latin, whereby the difficulties of grammar being soon overcome, all the historical physiology of Aristotle and Theophrastus are open before them, and, as I may say, under contribution.[47] The like access will be to Vitruvius, to Seneca's *Natural Questions,* to Mela, Celsus, Pliny, or Solinus.[48] And having thus passed the principles of arithmetic, geometry, astronomy, and geography, with a general compact of physics, they may descend in mathematics to the instrumental science of trigonometry and from thence to fortification, architecture, enginery,[49] or navigation. And in natural philosophy they may proceed leisurely from the history of meteors, minerals, plants, and living creatures as far as anatomy. Then also in course might be read to them out of some not tedious writer the institution of physic, that they may know the tempers, the humors, the seasons, and how to manage a crudity;[50]

42. The use of games to teach mathematics was recommended by Plato and Quintilian in *Laws* and *Institutes,* respectively. "The prominence given to mathematics in Milton's educational plan, here and later, is progressive if not indeed unique for his time" (Sirluck; Yale 2:386).

43. **easy:** advantageous, comforting.

44. All three Romans wrote standard agricultural tracts entitled *De Re Rustica* (On Rural Concerns).

45. The cleansing of the Augean stables, one of Hercules' twelve labors, was commonly allegorized as the first manuring of Italian soil.

46. Both classical and vernacular place names appeared on maps of Milton's era.

47. The zoological works of Aristotle and the botanical works of his pupil Theophrastus. **under contribution:** rendered tributary.

48. *Vitruvius,* first-century B.C.E. Roman authority on architecture, was highly regarded in the Renaissance. In *Natural Questions, Seneca* (4 B.C.E.–65 C.E.) summarizes classical knowledge about the natural world. Pomponius *Mela* wrote the earliest surviving Latin geography (c. 43 C.E.); Anlus Cornelius *Celsus* was a first-century Roman encyclopedist whose surviving volumes concern medicine; *Pliny* the Elder (c. 23–79 C.E.) produced a thirty-seven-volume *Natural History;* the geographer Julius *Solinus* (fl. c. 200 C.E.) compiled a digest of Mela and Pliny.

49. **enginery:** military engineering.

50. **institution of physic:** fundamentals of medicine. Ancient physiology identified four personality types or *tempers* (choleric, melancholic, sanguine, and phlegmatic) that varied according to the four *seasons* of the year as well as to the proportions of the four basic bodily fluids or *humors* (yellow bile, black bile, blood, and phlegm). **crudity:** an imperfect "concoction" of the humors, indigestion.

which he who can wisely and timely do is not only a great physician to himself and to his friends but also may at some time or other save an army by this frugal and expenseless means only and not let the healthy and stout bodies of young men rot away under him for want of this discipline, which is a great pity and no less a shame to the commander.

To set forward all these proceedings in nature and mathematics, what hinders but that they may procure, as oft as shall be needful, the helpful experiences of hunters, fowlers, fishermen, shepherds, gardeners, apothecaries, and, in the other sciences, architects, engineers, mariners, anatomists, who doubtless would be ready, some for reward and some to favor such a hopeful seminary. And this will give them such a real tincture of natural knowledge as they shall never forget but daily augment with delight. Then also those poets which are now counted most hard will be both facile and pleasant: Orpheus, Hesiod, Theocritus, Aratus, Nicander, Oppian, Dionysius, and in Latin Lucretius, Manilius, and the rural part of Vergil.[51]

By this time, years and good general precepts will have furnished them more distinctly with that act of reason which in ethics is called *proairesis*,[52] that they may with some judgment contemplate upon moral good and evil. Then will be required a special reinforcement of constant and sound indoctrinating to set them right and firm, instructing them more amply in the knowledge of virtue and the hatred of vice while their young and pliant affections are led through all the moral works of Plato, Xenophon, Cicero, Plutarch, Laertius, and those Locrian remnants[53]—but still to be reduced in their nightward studies, wherewith they close the day's work, under the determinate sentence of David or Solomon or the evangels and apostolic scriptures.[54]

Being perfect in the knowledge of personal duty, they may then begin the study of economics.[55] And either now, or before this, they may have easily learnt at any odd hour the Italian tongue. And soon after, but with wariness and good antidote, it would be wholesome enough to let them taste some choice comedies, Greek, Latin, or Italian; those tragedies also that treat of household matters, as *Trachinae, Alcestis,* and the like.[56]

The next remove must be to the study of politics—to know the beginning, end, and reasons of political societies—that they may not in a dangerous fit of the commonwealth be such poor, shaken, uncertain reeds of such a tottering

51. Milton lists Greek and Roman poets whose writings on the natural world would be easily understood by students versed in the "visible creature." (The didactic poem *Lithica,* on the magical properties of stones, had long been attributed to the legendary Orpheus.).

52. **proairesis:** Aristotle's widely adopted term for the power of individual moral choice.

53. Timaeus of Locri (fifth century B.C.E.), namesake of Plato's *Timaeus,* was long deemed the author of *On the Soul of the World and Nature.*

54. I.e., pagan ethical philosophy must always be subjected to the definitive judgment of David, Solomon, the Gospels, and apostolic writings.

55. **economics:** the science or art of household management.

56. Classical comedy is more likely than tragedy to treat household affairs, though there are exceptions, such as Sophocles' *Trachiniae* and Euripides' *Alcestis* (cp. *Sonnet 23*).

conscience as many of our great counselors have lately shown themselves, but steadfast pillars of the state. After this they are to dive into the grounds of law and legal justice, delivered first and with best warrant by Moses and, as far as human prudence can be trusted, in those extolled remains of Grecian lawgivers, Lycurgus, Solon, Zaleucus, Charondas,[57] and thence to all the Roman edicts and tables with their Justinian,[58] and so down to the Saxon and common laws of England and the statutes. Sundays also and every evening may be now understandingly spent in the highest matters of theology and church history ancient and modern; and ere this time the Hebrew tongue at a set hour might have been gained, that the Scriptures may be now read in their own original, whereto it would be no impossibility to add the Chaldee and the Syrian dialect.[59] When all these employments are well conquered, then will the choice histories, heroic poems, and Attic tragedies of stateliest and most regal argument, with all the famous political orations, offer themselves, which if they were not only read but some of them got by memory and solemnly pronounced with right accent and grace, as might be taught, would endue them even with the spirit and vigor of Demosthenes or Cicero, Euripides or Sophocles.

And now lastly will be the time to read with them those organic arts[60] which enable men to discourse and write perspicuously, elegantly, and according to the fitted style of lofty, mean, or lowly. Logic, therefore, so much as is useful, is to be referred to this due place with all her well-couched heads[61] and topics until it be time to open her contracted palm[62] into a graceful and ornate rhetoric taught out of the rule of Plato, Aristotle, Phalereus, Cicero, Hermogenes, Longinus.[63]

To which poetry would be made subsequent, or indeed, rather precedent, as being less subtle[64] and fine but more simple, sensuous and passionate. I mean not here the prosody of a verse, which they could not but have hit on before among the rudiments of grammar, but that sublime art which in Aristotle's *Poetics,* in Horace, and the Italian commentaries of Castelvetro, Tasso, Mazzoni,[65] and others, teaches what the laws are of a true epic poem, what of a dramatic,

57. Ancient lawgivers who helped form or reform early constitutions in Greece and its Italian colonies.

58. **Justinian:** sixth-century emperor who codified and rationalized the Roman legal system.

59. Aramaic dialects in which parts of the Bible had been preserved.

60. **organic arts:** instrumental disciplines, such as logic, rhetoric, and poetry.

61. **well-couched heads:** strategically arranged points.

62. **contracted palm:** The closed fist symbolizes logic; the open palm, rhetoric.

63. Classical authors, actual or reputed, of standard works on rhetoric. See, e.g., Plato's *Gorgias* and *Phaedrus,* and Aristotle's *Rhetoric.* Cicero was the most influential of those Milton lists; see especially *De Oratore.* The Athenian statesman Demetrius *Phalereus* was traditionally but mistakenly identified as the author of *On Style,* and the Greek rhetorician Cassius *Longinus* as the author of *On the Sublime. Hermogenes* of Tarsus, a Greek grammarian who wrote on style and rhetoric, is the least known of those Milton names.

64. **precedent:** could mean both "earlier" in time and "superior or prime in value"; **subtle:** analytical.

65. Ludovico *Castelvetro* (1505–71) translated Aristotle's *Poetics* into Italian; his rigorous conception of the dramatic unities fostered neoclassical theory. Torquato *Tasso* (1544–95) profoundly influenced Milton's understanding of heroic poetry. Giacomo *Mazzoni* (1548–98) championed Dante.

what of a lyric, what decorum[66] is, which is the grand masterpiece to observe. This would make them soon perceive what despicable creatures our common rhymers and playwrights be, and show them what religious, what glorious and magnificent use might be made of poetry both in divine and human things. From hence, and not till now, will be the right season of forming them to be able writers and composers in every excellent matter, when they shall be thus fraught[67] with an universal insight into things. Or whether they be to speak in parliament or counsel, honor and attention would be waiting on their lips. There would then also appear in pulpits other visages, other gestures, and stuff otherwise wrought than what we now sit under, oft-times to as great a trial of our patience as any other that they preach to us.

These are the studies wherein our noble and our gentle youth ought to bestow their time in a disciplinary way from twelve to one-and-twenty—unless they rely more upon their ancestors dead than upon themselves living. In which methodical course it is so supposed they must proceed, by the steady pace of learning, onward, as at convenient times for memory's sake to retire back into the middleward,[68] and sometimes into the rear of what they have been taught, until they have confirmed and solidly united the whole body of their perfected knowledge, like the last embattling[69] of a Roman legion. Now will be worth the seeing what exercises and recreations may best agree and become these studies.

THEIR EXERCISE

The course of study hitherto briefly described is, what I can guess by reading, likest to those ancient and famous schools of Pythagoras, Plato, Isocrates, Aristotle, and such others, out of which were bred up[70] such a number of renowned philosophers, orators, historians, poets, and princes all over Greece, Italy, and Asia, besides the flourishing studies of Cyrene and Alexandria.[71] But herein it shall exceed them and supply a defect as great as that which Plato noted in the commonwealth of Sparta: whereas that city trained up their youth most for war and these, in their academies and Lyceum, all for the gown,[72] this institution of breeding which I here delineate shall be equally good both for peace and war. Therefore about an hour and a half ere they eat at noon should be allowed them

66. **decorum:** that which is proper to the nature, unity, or harmony of a literary composition.
67. **fraught:** laden, supplied.
68. **middleward:** middle part of an army.
69. **embattling:** arrangement of troops in battle order.
70. Aristotle, for example, was *bred up* or educated in Plato's Academy and later founded his own school, the Lyceum.
71. **Cyrene and Alexandria:** third-century centers of medicine and physical sciences.
72. **gown:** peacetime careers (Roman usage).

for exercise and due rest afterwards—but the time for this may be enlarged at pleasure, according as their rising in the morning shall be early.

The exercise which I commend first is the exact use of their weapon,[73] to guard and to strike safely with edge or point. This will keep them healthy, nimble, strong, and well in breath; is also the likeliest means to make them grow large and tall and to inspire them with a gallant and fearless courage, which, being tempered with seasonable lectures and precepts to them of true fortitude and patience, will turn into a native and heroic valor and make them hate the cowardice of doing wrong. They must be also practiced in all the locks and grips of wrestling, wherein Englishmen were wont to excel, as need may often be in fight to tug or grapple, and to close. And this perhaps will be enough wherein to prove and heat their single strength.[74]

The interim of unsweating themselves regularly and convenient rest before meat may both with profit and delight be taken up in recreating and composing their travailed spirits with the solemn and divine harmonies of music heard or learnt; either while the skillful organist plies his grave and fancied descant in lofty fugues, or the whole symphony with artful and unimaginable touches adorn and grace the well-studied chords of some choice composer; sometimes the lute or soft organ-stop waiting on elegant voices either to religious, martial, or civil ditties; which, if wise men and prophets be not extremely out,[75] have a great power over dispositions and manners to smooth and make them gentle from rustic harshness and distempered passions. The like also would not be unexpedient after meat to assist and cherish nature in her first concoction[76] and send their minds back to study in good tune and satisfaction.

Where, having followed it close under vigilant eyes till about two hours before supper, they are by a sudden alarum or watchword to be called out to their military motions, under sky or covert according to the season, as was the Roman wont; first on foot, then, as their age permits, on horseback to all the art of cavalry. That having in sport, but with much exactness and daily muster, served out the rudiments of their soldiership in all the skill of embattling, marching, encamping, fortifying, besieging, and battering, with all the helps of ancient and modern stratagems, tactics, and warlike maxims, they may, as it were out of a long war, come forth renowned and perfect commanders in the service of their country. They would not then, if they were trusted with fair and hopeful armies, suffer them, for want of just and wise discipline, to shed away from about them like sick feathers, though they be never so oft supplied; they would not suffer their empty and unrecruitable[77] colonels of twenty men in a

73. **weapon:** sword (cp. *2Def*, p. 1079).
74. **prove . . . strength:** test and arouse their individual fortitude.
75. **out:** mistaken.
76. **cherish . . . concoction:** encourage vital functioning as the digestive process begins.
77. **unrecruitable:** incapable of getting recruits.

company to quaff out or convey into secret hoards the wages of a delusive list and a miserable remnant[78]—yet in the meanwhile to be overmastered with a score or two of drunkards, the only soldiery left about them, or else to comply with all rapines and violences. No, certainly, if they knew aught of that knowledge that belongs to good men or good governors, they would not suffer these things.

But to return to our own institute: besides these constant exercises at home, there is another opportunity of gaining experience to be won from pleasure itself abroad;[79] in those vernal seasons of the year when the air is calm and pleasant, it were an injury and sullenness against nature not to go out and see her riches and partake in her rejoicing with heaven and earth. I should not therefore be a persuader to them of studying much then, after two or three years that they have well laid their grounds, but to ride out in companies with prudent and staid guides to all the quarters of the land: learning and observing all places of strength, all commodities[80] of building and of soil for towns and tillage, harbors and ports for trade. Sometimes taking sea as far as to our navy, to learn there also what they can in the practical knowledge of sailing and of sea-fight.

These ways would try all their peculiar[81] gifts of nature, and if there were any secret excellence among them, would fetch it out and give it fair opportunities to advance itself by, which could not but mightily redound to the good of this nation, and bring into fashion again those old admired virtues and excellencies with far more advantage now in this purity of Christian knowledge. Nor shall we then need the monsieurs of Paris to take our hopeful youth into their slight and prodigal custodies and send them over back again transformed into mimics, apes, and kickshaws.[82] But if they desire to see other countries at three or four and twenty years of age, not to learn principles, but to enlarge experience and make wise observation, they will by that time be such as shall deserve the regard and honor of all men where they pass and the society and friendship of those in all places who are best and most eminent. And perhaps then other nations will be glad to visit us for their breeding, or else to imitate us in their own country.

Now lastly for their diet there cannot be much to say, save only that it would be best in the same house—for much time else would be lost abroad, and many ill habits got—and that it should be plain, healthful, and moderate, I suppose is out of controversy.

Thus, Mr. Hartlib, you have a general view in writing, as your desire was, of that which at several times I had discoursed with you concerning the best and

78. **colonels . . . remnant:** Unable to recruit soldiers, the colonel commands a small company depleted by desertion and illness but submits a deceptive list of his troops, padded with false names, then embezzles the wages of both his real and his imaginary soldiers.

79. **abroad:** outdoors.

80. **commodities:** material advantages.

81. **peculiar:** special, individual.

82. **kickshaws:** fantastical, frivolous persons (Fr. *quelques choses*).

noblest way of education; not beginning, as some have done, from the cradle, which yet might be worth many considerations; if brevity had not been my scope, many other circumstances also I could have mentioned, but this,[83] to such as have the worth in them to make trial, for light and direction may be enough. Only I believe that this is not a bow for every man to shoot in that counts himself a teacher, but will require sinews almost equal to those which Homer gave Ulysses;[84] yet I am withal persuaded that it may prove much more easy in the assay than it now seems at distance, and much more illustrious, howbeit not more difficult than I imagine, and that imagination presents me with nothing but very happy and very possible according to best wishes,[85] if God have so decreed, and this age have spirit and capacity enough to apprehend.

The End

83. **this:** what I have here proposed.

84. In Book 21 of Homer's *Odyssey,* Odysseus (*Ulysses*) alone can string his famed bow, much to the chagrin of his wife's suitors.

85. I.e., the actual attempt to establish such an academy may prove easier than it might now appear, and much more obviously beneficial (*illustrious*) although no more difficult than Milton imagines, and his imagination presents only happy and manageable prospects in line with the best intentions.

Introduction to Selections from *Tetrachordon*

In March 1645 appeared *Tetrachordon: Expositions upon the four chief Places in Scripture which treat of Marriage or nullities in Marriage. On Gen. 1:27, 28. compared and explained by Gen. 2:18, 23, 24; Deut. 24:1, 2; Matt. 5:31, 32 with Matt. 19, from verse 3 to 11; 1 Cor. 7, from verse 10 to 16. Wherein the Doctrine and Discipline of Divorce, as was late published, is confirmed by explanation of Scripture, by testimony of ancient Fathers, of civil laws in the Primitive Church, of famousest Reformed Divines, and lastly, by an intended Act of the Parliament and Church of England in the last year of Edward the sixth. By the former Author J. M.* The title, which means "four-stringed," points to the four main biblical texts that Milton hopes to harmonize in his argument for divorce. The main challenge, as in *The Doctrine and Discipline,* was reconciling Christ's apparent prohibition of divorce in the Gospel of Matthew with the Mosaic allowance of divorce in Deuteronomy.

Milton again argues that God would contradict himself were the Mosaic permission to be overturned by a Gospel prohibition. The most important new element in *Tetrachordon* is a reinterpretation of Matthew 19:8: "He saith unto them, Moses because of the hardness of your hearts suffered you to put away your wives: but from the beginning it was not so." Earlier Milton, taking hard-heartedness as characterizing a subset of the Jews, argued that God allowed divorce for the relief of the conscientious despite knowing that the hard-hearted would abuse the law by divorcing for trivial reasons. Now, by identifying another meaning of *hard-heartedness*—the imperfection or weakness among even the good after the Fall—Milton salvages for virtuous Christians (such as himself) the Mosaic allowance of divorce as glossed by Christ in Matthew 19:8, without having to evoke a complex and ironical interpretive setting (Yale 2:153–55). When Christ adds "from the beginning it was not so," he refers not to the time before Moses but to Paradise, before the Fall resulted in the kinds of temperamental differences that can make marital union impossible. Given that the Mosaic Law is adapted to our weakness after the Fall, it is inconceivable to Milton that the Gospel Law would be harsher and less merciful. Not only the lawfulness of divorce but the rest of "the secondary law of nature and of nations" is adapted to our fallen condition (p. 1015); the implication is that the Mosaic (and by extension Christian) authorization of divorce is a universal law.

The new reading of "hardness of heart" seems to promise a firmer foundation for the no-fault divorce advanced in the *Doctrine and Discipline.* The earlier argument, however, all but disappears from *Tetrachordon,* in which marriages fail almost invariably owing to the wife's willfulness and hostility.

As in the *Doctrine and Discipline,* Milton holds out an ideal of companionate marriage that should resonate today. The differences between the sexes can make for a happy meeting of "most resembling unlikeness, and most unlike resemblance" (p. 998), and Milton explicitly takes Augustine to task for his "crabbed opinion" that, were woman not required for procreation, Adam would have been better off with a man as his companion (p. 998).

Tetrachordon fared no better with its audience than did the *Doctrine and Discipline.* Milton turns the tables on his attackers among the Scottish Presbyterians with his sharply satirical *Sonnet 11,* "A book was writ of late called *Tetrachordon.*" In his related *Sonnet 12,* "I did but prompt the age to quit their clogs," Milton rebukes those who have pronounced his idealistic argument on marriage and divorce licentious: they "bawl for freedom in their senseless mood, / And still revolt when truth would set them free. / License they mean when they cry libertie; / For who loves that, must first be wise and good."

Our text follows the copy of the first edition in the British Library's Thomason Collection (E. 271[12]).

Selections from

TETRACHORDON

Σκαιοῖσι καινὰ προσφέρων σοφὰ
Δόξεις ἀρχεῖος, κοὐ σοφὸς πεφυκέναι.
Τῶν δ' αὖ δοκαύντων εἰδέναι τι ποικίλον,
Κρείσσων νομισθεὶς ἐν πόλει, λυπρὸς φανῇ.[1]
Euripid[es], *Medea*

TO THE PARLIAMENT

That which I knew to be the part of a good magistrate, aiming at true liberty through the right information of religious and civil life, and that which I saw, and was partaker of, your vows and solemn covenants,[2] Parliament of England, your actions also manifestly tending to exalt the truth and to depress the tyranny of error and ill custom with more constancy and prowess than ever yet any, since that Parliament which put the first scepter of this kingdom into his hand whom God and extraordinary virtue made their monarch,[3] were the causes that moved me, one else not placing much in the eminence of a dedication, to present your high notice with a discourse, conscious to itself of nothing more than of diligence and firm affection to the public good. And that ye took it so as wise and impartial men, obtaining so great power and dignity, are wont to accept, in matters both doubtful and important, what they think offered them well meant, and from a rational ability, I had no less than to persuade me.

And on that persuasion am returned as to a famous and free port, myself also bound by more than a maritime Law, to expose as freely what freightage I conceive to bring of no trifles. For although it be generally known, how and by whom ye have been instigated to a hard censure of that former book,[4] entitled

1. Euripides, *Medea* 298–301: "If you put new ideas before the eyes of fools/They'll think you foolish and worthless into the bargain;/And if you are thought to be superior to those who have/Some reputation for learning, you will become hated" (tr. Rex Warner).

2. **solemn covenants:** An allusion to the Solemn Covenant of 1643, by which Parliament and the Westminster Assembly agreed to bring the churches of England, Scotland, and Wales into uniformity of doctrine, worship, and church government, under the model of the Presbyterian national church of Scotland.

3. Most likely a reference to Parliament's 1534 Act of Supremacy, which placed Henry VIII at the head of the English Church.

4. A reference to the Presbyterian clergy, and particularly to Herbert Palmer, who denounced the author of the *Doctrine and Discipline* in a sermon preached to Parliament on August 13, 1644, a special Day of Humiliation.

The Doctrine and Discipline of Divorce, an opinion held by some of the best among reformed writers without scandal or confutement, though now thought new and dangerous by some of our severe Gnostics[5] (whose little reading and less meditating holds ever with hardest obstinacy that which it took up with easiest credulity), I do not find yet that aught, for the furious incitements which have been used, hath issued by your appointment that might give the least interruption or disrepute either to the author, or to the book. Which he who will be better advised than to call your neglect or connivance at a thing imagined so perilous, can attribute it to nothing more justly than to the deep and quiet stream of your direct and calm deliberations, that gave not way either to the fervent rashness or the immaterial gravity of those who ceased not to exasperate without cause. For which uprightness and incorrupt refusal of what ye were incensed to, Lords and Commons, (though it were done to justice, not to me, and was a peculiar demonstration how far your ways are different from the rash vulgar) besides those allegiances of oath and duty, which are my public debt to your public labors, I have yet a store of gratitude laid up which cannot be exhausted; and such thanks perhaps they may live to be, as shall more than whisper to the next ages.

Yet that the author may be known to ground himself upon his own innocence and the merit of his cause, not upon the favor of a diversion or a delay to any just censure, but wishes rather he might see those his detractors at any fair meeting, as learned debatements are privileged with a due freedom under equal moderators, I shall here briefly single one of them[6] (because he hath obliged me to it), who I persuade me having scarce read the book nor knowing him who writ it, or at least feigning the latter, hath not forborne to scandalize him, unconferred with, unadmonished, undealt with by any pastorly or brotherly convincement, in the most open and invective manner, and at the most bitter opportunity that drift or set design could have invented. And this, whenas the canon Law, though commonly most favoring the boldness of their priests, punishes the naming or traducing of any person in the Pulpit, was by him made no scruple. If I shall therefore take license by the right of nature, and that liberty wherein I was born, to defend my self publicly against a printed calumny, and do willingly appeal to those judges to whom I am accused, it can be no immoderate or unallowable course of seeking so just and needful reparations. Which I had done long since, had not these employments, which are now visible, deferred me.

It was preached before ye, Lords and Commons, in August last upon a special Day of Humiliation, that "there was a wicked book abroad," and ye were taxed of sin that it was yet "uncensured, the book deserving to be burnt"; and

5. By calling his opponents *Gnostics,* Milton implies that to oppose divorce for incompatibility is to condone hateful, loathsome sexuality (the sex of people who hate each other), and in that sense to show a gnostic contempt for physical life.

6. Herbert Palmer (see note 4).

"impudence" also was charged upon the author, who durst "set his name to it, and dedicate it to yourselves." First, Lords and Commons, I pray to that God, before whom ye then were prostrate, so to forgive ye those omissions and trespasses which ye desire most should find forgiveness, as I shall soon show to the world how easily ye absolve yourselves of that which this man calls your sin, and is indeed your wisdom and your nobleness, whereof to this day ye have done well not to repent. He terms it "a wicked book" and (why but "for allowing other causes of divorce, than Christ and his Apostles mention"?); and with the same censure condemns of wickedness not only Martin Bucer, that elect instrument of reformation, highly honored and had in reverence by Edward the Sixth, and his whole Parliament, whom also I had published in English by a good providence about a week before this calumnious digression was preached,[7] so that if he knew not Bucer then, as he ought to have known, he might at least have known him some months after, ere the sermon came in print; wherein notwithstanding he persists in his former sentence, and condemns again of wickedness, either ignorantly or willfully, not only Martin Bucer and all the choicest and holiest of our reformers, but the whole Parliament and church of England in those best and purest times of Edward the Sixth. All which I shall prove with good evidence at the end of these explanations. And then let it be judged and seriously considered with what hope the affairs of our religion are committed to one among others,[8] who hath now only left him which of the twain he will choose, whether this shall be his palpable ignorance, or the same wickedness of his own book, which he so lavishly imputes to the writings of other men: and whether this of his, that thus peremptorily defames and attaints of wickedness unspotted churches, unblemished Parliaments, and the most eminent restorers of Christian doctrine, deserve not to be burnt first.

And if his heat had burst out only against the opinion, his wonted passion had no doubt been silently borne with wonted patience. But since, against the charity of that solemn place and meeting, it served him further to inveigh opprobriously against the person, branding him with no less than impudence only for setting his name to what he had written, I must be excused not to be so wanting to the defense of an honest name, or to the reputation of those good men who afford me their society, but to be sensible of such a foul endeavored disgrace; not knowing aught either in mine own deserts or the laws of this land why I should be subject, in such a notorious and illegal manner, to the intemperancies of this man's preaching choler. And indeed to be so prompt and ready, in the midst of his humbleness, to toss reproaches of this bulk and size, argues as if they were the weapons of his exercise, I am sure not of his ministry, or of that day's work. Certainly to subscribe my name at what I was to own, was what the state had ordered and requires. And he who lists not to be malicious would

7. Milton published his translation of Bucer as *The Judgement of Martin Bucer concerning Divorce* in early August 1644.

8. Palmer chaired the committee charged with revising the doctrine of marriage.

call it ingenuity,[9] clear conscience, willingness to avouch what might be questioned, or to be better instructed. And if God were so displeased with those (Isa. 58[.4]) who "on the solemn fast were wont to smite with the fist of wickedness," it could be no sign of his own humiliation accepted, which disposed him to smite so keenly with a reviling tongue.

But if only to have writ my name must be counted "impudence," how doth this but justify another who might affirm, with as good warrant, that the late discourse of *Scripture and Reason,* which is certain to be chiefly his own draught, was published without a name, out of base fear and the sly avoidance of what might follow to his detriment if the party at court should hap to reach him?[10] And I, to have set my name where he accuses me to have set it, am so far from recanting that I offer my hand also, if need be, to make good the same opinion which I there maintain by inevitable consequences drawn parallel from his own principal arguments in that of *Scripture and Reason,* which I shall pardon him if he can deny without shaking his own composition to pieces. The "impudence" therefore, since he weighed so little what a gross revile that was to give his equal, I send him back again for a phylactery[11] to stitch upon his arrogance, that censures not only before conviction, so bitterly without so much as one reason given, but censures the congregation of his governors to their faces, for not being so hasty as himself to censure.

And wheras my other crime is that I addressed the dedication of what I had studied to the Parliament, how could I better declare the loyalty which I owe to that supreme and majestic tribunal, and the opinion which I have of the high-entrusted judgment, and personal worth assembled in that place? With the same affections therefore, and the same addicted fidelity, Parliament of England, I here again have brought to your perusal on the same argument these following expositions of scripture. The former book, as pleased some to think who were thought judicious, had of reason in it to a sufficiency; what they required was that the scriptures there alleged might be discussed more fully. To their desires thus much further hath been labored in the scriptures. Another sort also, who wanted more authorities and citations, have not been here unthought of. If all this attain not to satisfy them, as I am confident that none of those our great controversies at this day hath had a more demonstrative explaining, I must confess to admire what it is; for doubtless it is not reason nowadays that satisfies or suborns the common credence of men, to yield so easily and grow so vehement in matters much more disputable and far less conducing to the daily good and peace of life.

Some whose necessary shifts have long inured them to cloak the defects of

9. **ingenuity:** frankness, ingenuousness.

10. In *Scripture and Reason Pleaded for Defensive Arms* (1643), Palmer and his coauthors argued against the divine right of kings.

11. **phylactery:** Leather prayer box containing excerpts of Deuteronomy and Exodus, worn by Jews during morning prayer as a sign of obedience to the law. Milton uses the term figuratively to mean an ostentatious or hypocritical show of piety or rectitude.

their unstudied years and hatred now to learn, under the appearance of a grave solidity (which estimation they have gained among weak perceivers), find the ease of slighting what they cannot refute, and are determined, as I hear, to hold it not worth the answering. In which number I must be forced to reckon that doctor,[12] who in a late equivocating treatise plausibly set afloat against the Dippers, diving the while himself with a more deep prelatical malignance against the present state and church government, mentions with ignominy "the Tractate of Divorce"; yet answers nothing, but instead thereof (for which I do not commend his marshalling) sets Moses also among the crew of his Anabaptists, as one who to a holy nation, the commonwealth of Israel, gave laws "breaking the bonds of marriage to inordinate lust." These are no mean surges of blasphemy, not only dipping Moses the divine lawgiver, but dashing with a high hand against the justice and purity of God himself, as these ensuing scriptures plainly and freely handled shall verify to the lancing of that old apostemated[13] error. Him therefore I leave now to his repentance.

Others, which is their courtesy, confess that wit and parts may do much to make that seem true which is not (as was objected to Socrates by them who could not resist his efficacy, that he ever made the worse cause seem the better),[14] and thus, thinking themselves discharged of the difficulty, love not to wade further into the fear of a convincement. These will be their excuses to decline the full examining of this serious point. So much the more I press it and repeat it, Lords and Commons, that ye beware while time is, ere this grand secret and only art of ignorance affecting tyranny, grow powerful and rule among us. For if sound argument and reason shall be thus put off, either by an undervaluing silence, or the masterly censure of a railing word or two in the pulpit, or by rejecting the force of truth as the mere cunning of eloquence and sophistry, what can be the end of this, but that all good learning and knowledge will suddenly decay? Ignorance and illiterate presumption, which is yet but our disease, will turn at length into our very constitution, and prove the hectic evil of this age, worse to be feared, if it get once to reign over us, than any Fifth Monarchy.[15]

If this shall be the course, that what was wont to be a chief commendation and the ground of other men's confidence in an author, his diligence, his learning, his elocution, whether by right or by ill meaning granted him, shall be turned now to a disadvantage and suspicion against him, that what he writes,

12. Daniel Featley, who in *The Dippers Dipt* (1645) attacked the Anabaptists for, among other things, permitting divorce. In this sentence, which ends by quoting Featley's attack on his own *Doctrine and Discipline,* Milton, as elsewhere, both implicitly associates himself with fringe sectarians and adroitly positions his opponents as enemies to the mainstream.

13. **apostemated:** abscessed.

14. See Plato's *Apology* 18b.

15. The *Fifth Monarchy,* the last of the succession of kingdoms foretold in the apocalyptic Book of Daniel (2.44), was interpreted in Milton's time as the reign of Christ after the Second Coming. Fifth Monarchy Men hoped to usher in that reign by force.

though unconfuted, must therefore be mistrusted, therefore not received for the industry, the exactness, the labor in it, confessed to be more than ordinary; as if wisdom had now forsaken the thirsty and laborious inquirer, to dwell against her nature with the arrogant and shallow babbler. To what purpose all those pains and that continual searching required of us by Solomon to the attainment of understanding?[16] Why are men bred up with such care and expense to a life of perpetual studies? Why do yourselves with such endeavor seek to wipe off the imputation of intending to discourage the progress and advance of learning?

He, therefore, whose heart can bear him to the high pitch of your noble enterprises, may easily assure himself that the prudence and far-judging circumspectness of so grave a magistracy sitting in Parliament, who have before them the prepared and purposed act of their most religious predecessors to imitate in this question, cannot reject the clearness of these reasons and these allegations both here and formerly offered them; nor can overlook the necessity of ordaining more wholesomely and more humanely in the casualties of divorce than our laws have yet established, if the most urgent and excessive grievances happening in domestic life be worth the laying to heart, which, unless charity be far from us, cannot be neglected. And that these things, both in the right constitution and in the right reformation of a commonwealth, call for speediest redress and ought to be the first considered, enough was urged in what was prefaced to that monument of Bucer which I brought to your remembrance, and the other time before.

Henceforth, except new cause be given, I shall say less and less. For if the law make not timely provision, let the law, as reason is, bear the censure of those consequences which her own default now more evidently produces. And if men want manliness to expostulate the right of their due ransom, and to second their own occasions, they may sit hereafter and bemoan themselves to have neglected through faintness the only remedy of their sufferings, which a seasonable and well-grounded speaking might have purchased them. And perhaps in time to come, others will know how to esteem what is not every day put into their hands, when they have marked events, and better weighed how hurtful and unwise it is to hide a secret and pernicious rupture under the ill counsel of a bashful silence. But who would distrust aught, or not be ample in his hopes of your wise and Christian determinations? Who have the prudence to consider, and should have the goodness, like gods as ye are called,[17] to find out readily, and by just law to administer, those redresses which have of old, not without God ordaining, been granted to the adversities of mankind, ere they who needed were put to ask. Certainly, if any other have enlarged his thoughts to expect from this government, so justly undertaken and by frequent assistances

16. See, e.g., Prov. 2.4.
17. Milton plays on a Hebrew word for God, *elohim,* which literally means "powers" and was also used for rulers and judges.

from Heaven so apparently upheld, glorious changes and renovations both in church and state, he among the foremost might be named, who prays that the fate of England may tarry for no other deliverers.

John Milton

TETRACHORDON,

Expositions upon the four chief places in scripture which treat of marriage or nullities in marriage.

GEN. 1.27.

"So God created man in his own image, in the image of God created he him; male and female created he them.

28. "And God blessed them, and God said unto them, Be fruitful," etc.

GEN. 2.18.

"And the Lord God said, It is not good that man should be alone, I will make him a help meet for him.

23. "And Adam said, This is now bone of my bones, and flesh of my flesh; she shall be called woman, because she was taken out of man.
24. "Therefore shall a man leave his father and his mother, and shall cleave unto his wife, and they shall be one flesh."

GEN. 1.27.

["So God created Man in his own image."][18] To be informed aright in the whole history of marriage, that we may know for certain, not by a forced yoke but by an impartial definition, what marriage is and what is not marriage, it will undoubtedly be safest, fairest, and most with our obedience, to inquire, as our Savior's direction is, how it was in the beginning. And that we begin so high as man created after God's own image, there want not earnest causes. For nothing nowadays is more degenerately forgotten than the true dignity of man, almost in every respect, but especially in this prime institution of matrimony, wherein his native preeminence ought most to shine. Although if we consider that just and natural privileges men neither can rightly seek, nor dare fully claim, unless they be allied to inward goodness and steadfast knowledge, and that the want of

18. Here and throughout, the bracketed paragraph-heading quotations are Milton's.

this quells them to a servile sense of their own conscious unworthiness, it may save the wondering why in this age many are so opposite both to human and to Christian liberty,[19] either while they understand not or envy others that do; contenting or rather priding themselves in a specious humility and strictness bred out of low ignorance, that never yet conceived the freedom of the Gospel; and is therefore by the Apostle to the Colossians ranked with no better company than will-worship and the mere show of wisdom.[20] And how injurious herein they are, if not to themselves yet to their neighbors, and not to them only but to the all-wise and bounteous grace offered us in our redemption, will orderly appear.

["In the image of God created he him."] It is enough determined that this image of God wherein man was created, is meant wisdom, purity, justice, and rule over all creatures. All which, being lost in Adam, was recovered with gain by the merits of Christ. For albeit our first parent had lordship over sea, and land, and air, yet there was a law without him, as a guard set over him. But Christ having cancelled the handwriting of ordinances which was against us (Coloss. 2.14) and interpreted the fulfilling of all through charity, hath in that respect set us over law, in the free custody of his love, and left us victorious under the guidance of his living Spirit, not under the dead letter; to follow that which most edifies, most aids and furthers a religious life, makes us holiest and likest to his immortal image, not that which makes us most conformable and captive to civil and subordinate precepts; whereof the strictest observance may ofttimes prove the destruction not only of many innocent persons and families, but of whole nations. Although indeed no ordinance, human or from heaven, can bind against the good of man, so that to keep them strictly against that end is all one with to break them. Men of most renowned virtue have sometimes by transgressing most truly kept the law, and wisest magistrates have permitted and dispensed it, while they looked not peevishly at the letter, but with a greater spirit at the good of mankind, if always not written in the characters of law, yet engraven in the heart of man by a divine impression.

This heathens could see, as the well-read in story can recount of Solon and Epaminondas, whom Cicero in his first book of *Invention*[21] nobly defends. "All law," saith he, "we ought refer to the common good, and interpret by that, not by the scroll of letters. No man observes law for law's sake, but for the good of them for whom it was made." The rest might serve well to lecture these times, deluded through belly doctrines[22] into a devout slavery. The scripture also af-

19. *Human liberty* denotes external freedom from burdensome and inappropriate laws; *Christian liberty* denotes the internal freedom of the regenerate Christian to follow God's law willingly, made possible because Christ, as Milton phrases it later, "redeemed us to a state above prescriptions by dissolving the whole law into charity."

20. Col. 2.23: "Which things have indeed a show of wisdom in will worship, and humility."

21. Cicero, *On Invention* 1.38.

22. See Rom. 16.18.

fords us David in the shewbread, Hezekiah in the Passover,[23] sound and safe transgressors of the literal command, which also dispensed not seldom with itself; and taught us on what just occasions to do so: until our Savior, for whom that great and Godlike work was reserved, redeemed us to a state above prescriptions by dissolving the whole law into charity. And have we not the soul to understand this, and must we against this glory of God's transcendent love towards us be still the servants of literal indictment?

["Created he him."] It might be doubted why he saith, "In the image of God created he him," not them, as well as "male and female" them; especially since that image might be common to them both, but, male and female, could not, however the Jews fable and please themselves with the accidental concurrence of Plato's wit, as if man at first had been created hermaphrodite[24] (but then it must have been male and female created he him). So had the image of God been equally common to them both, it had no doubt been said, 'In the image of God created he them.' But St. Paul ends the controversy, by explaining that the woman is not primarily and immediately the image of God, but in reference to the man: "The head of the woman," saith he (1 Cor. 11[.3,7]), "is the man"; "he the image and glory of God, she the glory of the man"; he not for her, but she for him.[25] Therefore his precept is, "Wives be subject to your husbands as is fit in the Lord" (Coloss. 3.18). "In everything" (Eph. 5.24). Nevertheless man is not to hold her as a servant, but receives her into a part of that empire which God proclaims him to, though not equally, yet largely, as his own image and glory. For it is no small glory to him, that a creature so like him should be made subject to him. Not but that particular exceptions may have place, if she exceed her husband in prudence and dexterity, and he contentedly yield; for then a superior and more natural law comes in, that the wiser should govern the less wise, whether male or female.

But that which far more easily and obediently follows from this verse is that, seeing woman was purposely made for man, and he her head, it cannot stand before the breath of this divine utterance that man, the portraiture of God, joining to himself for his intended good and solace an inferior sex, should so become her thrall, whose willfulness or inability to be a wife frustrates the occasional end[26] of her creation, but that he may acquit himself to freedom by his natural birthright and that indelible character of priority which God crowned him with. If it be urged that sin hath lost him this, the answer is not far to seek, that from her the sin first proceeded, which keeps her justly in the same proportion still beneath. She is not to gain by being first in the transgression, that man

23. For David, see 1 Sam. 21.2–6; for Hezekiah, see 2 Chron. 30.18–19.

24. The notion that human beings were originally hermaphroditic appears both in Plato's *Symposium* and in Jewish sources.

25. Cp. *PL* 4.299: "He for God only, she for God in him."

26. Milton agrees with the tradition that woman was made for a purpose or *occasional end,* though he viewed that purpose as companionship for the man rather than, as commonly thought, procreation.

should further lose to her, because already he hath lost by her means. Oft it happens that in this matter he is without fault, so that his punishment herein is causeless; and God hath the praise in our speeches of him, to sort his punishment in the same kind with the offence. Suppose he erred; it is not the intent of God or man to hunt an error so to the death with a revenge beyond all measure and proportion.

But if we argue thus, this affliction is befallen him for his sin, therefore he must bear it without seeking the only remedy: first, it will be false that all affliction comes for sin, as in the case of Job and of the man born blind (John 9.3) was evident; next, by that reason, all miseries coming for sin, we must let them all lie upon us like the vermin of an Indian Catharist,[27] which his fond religion forbids him to molest. Were it a particular punishment inflicted through the anger of God upon a person or upon a land, no law hinders us in that regard, no law but bids us remove it if we can; much more if it be a dangerous temptation withal, much more yet, if it be certainly a temptation, and not certainly a punishment, though a pain. As for what they say we must bear with patience, to bear with patience and to seek effectual remedies implies no contradiction. It may no less be for our disobedience, our unfaithfulness, and other sins against God, that wives become adulterous to the bed, and questionless we ought to take the affliction as patiently as Christian prudence would wish; yet hereby is not lost the right of divorcing for adultery. No, you say, because our Savior excepted that only. But why, if he were so bent to punish our sins and try our patience in binding on us a disastrous marriage, why did he except adultery? Certainly to have been bound from divorce in that case also had been as plentiful a punishment to our sins, and not too little work for the patientest. Nay, perhaps they will say it was too great a sufferance. And with as slight a reason, for no wise man but would sooner pardon the act of adultery once and again committed by a person worth pity and forgiveness, than to lead a wearisome life of unloving and unquiet conversation with one who neither affects nor is affected, much less with one who exercises all bitterness, and would commit adultery too, but for envy lest the persecuted condition should thereby get the benefit of his freedom. 'Tis plain therefore that God enjoins not this supposed strictness of not divorcing either to punish us or to try our patience.

Moreover, if man be the image of God, which consists in holiness, and woman ought in the same respect to be the image and companion of man, in such wise to be loved as the Church is beloved of Christ; and if, as God is the head of Christ, and Christ the head of man, so man is the head of woman; I cannot see by this golden dependence of headship and subjection, but that piety and religion is the main tie of Christian matrimony. So as if there be found between the pair a notorious disparity either of wickedness or heresy, the husband by all manner of right is disengaged from a creature not made and inflicted on

27. The *Cathars* were an ascetic sect in medieval Europe.

him to the vexation of his righteousness. The wife also, as her subjection is terminated in the Lord, being herself the redeemed of Christ, is not still bound to be the vassal of him who is the bond-slave of Satan; she being now neither the image nor the glory of such a person, nor made for him, nor left in bondage to him, but hath recourse to the wing of charity and protection of the church, unless there be a hope on either side. Yet such a hope must be meant, as may be a rational hope and not an endless servitude. Of which hereafter.

But usually it is objected that, if it be thus, then there can be no true marriage between misbelievers and irreligious persons. I might answer, let them see to that who are such; the church hath no commission to judge those without (1 Cor. 5). But this they will say, perhaps, is but penuriously to resolve a doubt. I answer therefore, that where they are both irreligious, the marriage may be yet true enough to them in a civil relation. For there are left some remains of God's image in man, as he is merely man; which reason God gives against the shedding of man's blood (Gen. 9.[5–6]), as being made in God's image, without expression whether he were a good man or a bad, to exempt the slayer from punishment. So that in those marriages where the parties are alike void of religion, the wife owes a civil homage and subjection, the husband owes a civil loyalty. But where the yoke is misyoked, heretic with faithful, godly with ungodly, to the grievance and manifest endangering of a brother or sister, reasons of a higher strain than matrimonial bear sway; unless the Gospel, instead of freeing us, debase itself to make us bondmen, and suffer evil to control good.

["Male and female created he them."] This contains another end of matching man and woman, being the right and lawfulness of the marriage-bed, though much inferior to the former end of her being his image and help in religious society. And who of weakest insight may not see that this creating of them male and female cannot in any order of reason, or Christianity, be of such moment against the better and higher purposes of their creation, as to enthrall husband or wife to duties or to sufferings, unworthy and unbeseeming the image of God in them? Now whenas not only men, but good men, do stand upon their right, their estimation, their dignity, in all other actions and deportments with warrant enough and good conscience, as having the image of God in them, it will not be difficult to determine what is unworthy and unseemly for a man to do or suffer in wedlock (and the like proportionally may be found for woman), if we love not to stand disputing below the principles of humanity. He that said, "Male and female created he them," immediately before that said also in the same verse, "In the image of God created he him," and redoubled it, that our thoughts might not be so full of dregs as to urge this poor consideration of "male and female," without remembering the nobleness of that former repetition; lest when God sends a wise eye to examine our trivial glosses, they be found extremely to creep upon the ground. Especially since they confess that what here concerns marriage is but a brief touch, only preparative to the institution which follows more expressly in the next chapter. And that Christ so took it, as desiring to be briefest with them who came to tempt him, account shall be given in due place.

> Ver. 28. "And God blessed them, and God said unto them, be fruitful and multiply, and replenish the earth," etc.

This declares another end of matrimony, the propagation of mankind, and is again repeated to Noah and his sons.[28] Many things might be noted on this place not ordinary, nor unworth the noting, but I undertook not a general comment. Hence therefore we see the desire of children is honest and pious; if we be not less zealous in our Christianity than Plato was in his heathenism, who, in the sixth of his *Laws*,[29] counts offspring therefore desirable, that we may leave in our stead sons of our sons, continual servants of God; a religious and prudent desire, if people knew as well what were required to breeding as to begetting; which desire perhaps was a cause why the Jews hardly could endure a barren wedlock, and Philo in his book of special laws esteems him only worth pardon that sends not barrenness away.[30] Carvilius, the first recorded in Rome to have sought divorce, had it granted him for the barrenness of his wife, upon his oath that he married to the end he might have children, as Dionysius and Gellius are authors.[31] But to dismiss a wife only for barrenness is hard; and yet in some the desire of children is so great, and so just, yea sometime so necessary, that to condemn such a one to a childless age, the fault apparently not being in him, might seem perhaps more strict than needed. Sometimes inheritances, crowns, and dignities are so interested and annexed in their common peace and good to such or such lineal descent, that it may prove a great moment both in the affairs of men and of religion, to consider thoroughly what might be done herein, notwithstanding the waywardness of our school doctors.

GEN. 2.18.

> "And the Lord said, It is not good that man should be alone; I will make him a help meet for him."

> V 23. "And Adam said," etc. V 24. "Therefore shall a man leave," etc.

This second chapter is granted to be a commentary on the first; and these verses granted to be an exposition of that former verse, "Male and female created he them," and yet when this male and female is by the explicit words of

28. See Gen. 9.1.

29. *Laws* 6 (774a).

30. In his *Special Laws* (3.35), Philo, condemning men who marry barren women as moved only by lust, insists that barren wives be divorced; he recognizes the dilemma of men who, not aware at first of their wives' barrenness, develop affection for them.

31. Dionysius of Helicarnassus, *Roman Antiquities* 2.25; Aulus Gellius, *Noctes Aticae* 4.3.

God himself here declared to be not meant other than a fit help, and meet society, some, who would engross to themselves the whole trade of interpreting, will not suffer the clear text of God to do the office of explaining itself.

["And the Lord God said it is not good."] A man would think that the consideration of who spake should raise up the attention of our minds to inquire better, and obey the purpose of so great a Speaker. For as we order the business of marriage, that which he here speaks is all made vain, and in the decision of matrimony, or not matrimony, nothing at all regarded. Our presumption hath utterly changed the state and condition of this ordinance. God ordained it in love and helpfulness to be indissoluble, and we in outward act and formality to be a forced bondage; so that being subject to a thousand errors in the best men, if it prove a blessing to any, it is of mere accident, as man's law hath handled it, and not of institution.

["It is not good for man to be alone."] Hitherto all things that have been named were approved of God to be very good. Loneliness is the first thing which God's eye named not good (whether it be a thing, or the want of something, I labor not; let it be their tendance, who have the art to be industriously idle). And here "alone" is meant alone without woman; otherwise Adam had the company of God himself and angels to converse with, all creatures to delight him seriously, or to make him sport. God could have created him out of the same mold a thousand friends and brother Adams to have been his consorts, yet for all this, till Eve was given him, God reckoned him to be alone.

["It is not good."] God here presents himself like to a man deliberating; both to show us that the matter is of high consequence, and that he intended to found it according to natural reason, not impulsive command; but that the duty should arise from the reason of it, not the reason be swallowed up in a reasonless duty. "Not good" was as much to Adam before his fall as not pleasing, not expedient; but since the coming of sin into the world, to him who hath not received the continence, it is not only not expedient to be alone, but plainly sinful. And therefore he who willfully abstains from marriage, not being supernaturally gifted, and he who by making the yoke of marriage unjust and intolerable causes men to abhor it, are both in a diabolical sin, equal to that of Antichrist, who forbids to marry.[32] For what difference at all whether he abstain men from marrying, or restrain them in a marriage happening totally discommodious, distasteful, dishonest and pernicious to him, without the appearance of his fault? For God does not here precisely say, I make a female to this male, as he did before, but expounding himself here on purpose, he saith, because it is not good for man to be alone, I make him therefore a meet help. God supplies the privation of not good, with the perfect gift of a real and positive good; it is man's perverse cooking who hath turned this bounty of God into a scorpion, either by weak and shallow constructions or by proud arrogance and cruelty to them who neither in their purposes nor in their actions have offended against the due honor of wedlock.

32. A reference to the Roman Catholic prescription of priestly celibacy.

Now whereas the apostle speaking in the Spirit (1 Cor. 7[.1]) pronounces quite contrary to this word of God, "It is good for a man not to touch a woman," and God cannot contradict himself, it instructs us that his commands and words, especially such as bear the manifest title of some good to man, are not to be so strictly wrung as to command without regard to the most natural and miserable necessities of mankind. Therefore the apostle adds a limitation in the 26th verse of that chapter, for the present necessity it is good; which he gives us doubtless as a pattern how to reconcile other places by the general rule of charity.

["*For man to be alone.*"] Some would have the sense hereof to be in respect of procreation only; and Austin contests that manly friendship in all other regards had been a more becoming solace for Adam, than to spend so many secret years in an empty world with one woman.[33] But our writers deservedly reject this crabbed opinion, and defend that there is a peculiar comfort in the married state besides the genial bed,[34] which no other society affords. No mortal nature can endure, either in the actions of religion or study of wisdom, without sometime slackening the cords of intense thought and labor, which, lest we should think faulty, God himself conceals us not his own recreations before the world was built: "I was," saith the eternal Wisdom, "daily his delight, playing always before him" [Prov. 8.30]. And to him indeed wisdom is as a high tower of pleasure, but to us a steep hill, and we toiling ever about the bottom. He executes with ease the exploits of his omnipotence, as easy as with us it is to will, but no worthy enterprise can be done by us without continual plodding and wearisomeness to our faint and sensitive abilities. We cannot therefore always be contemplative, or pragmatical abroad, but have need of some delightful intermissions, wherein the enlarged soul may leave off a while her severe schooling, and, like a glad youth in wandering vacancy, may keep her holidays to joy and harmless pastime; which as she cannot well do without company, so in no company so well as where the different sex in most resembling unlikeness, and most unlike resemblance, cannot but please best and be pleased in the aptitude of that variety.

Whereof lest we should be too timorous, in the awe that our flat sages would form us and dress us, wisest Solomon among his gravest Proverbs[35] countenances a kind of ravishment and erring fondness in the entertainment of wedded leisures; and in the Song of Songs, which is generally believed, even in the jolliest expressions, to figure the spousals of the church with Christ, sings of a thousand raptures between those two lovely ones far on the hither side of carnal enjoyment. By these instances, and more which might be brought, we may imagine how indulgently God provided against man's loneliness; that he approved it not, as by himself declared not good; that he approved the remedy

33. Milton accurately paraphrases the sense of Augustine in *De Genesi ad Litteram* 9.5.
34. **genial:** related to procreation; cp. Adam's parallel discussion of the "genial bed" in *PL* 8.596–606.
35. See Prov. 5.18–19.

thereof, as of his own ordaining, consequently good; and as he ordained it, so doubtless proportionably to our fallen estate he gives it; else were his ordinance at least in vain, and we for all his gift still empty-handed. Nay, such an unbounteous giver we should make him, as in the fables Jupiter was to Ixion, giving him a cloud instead of Juno; giving him a monstrous issue by her, the breed of Centaurs, a neglected and unloved race, the fruits of a delusive marriage; and, lastly, giving him her with a damnation to that wheel in hell, from a life thrown into the midst of temptations and disorders. But God is no deceitful giver, to bestow that on us for a remedy of loneliness, which if it bring not a sociable mind as well as a conjunctive body, leaves us no less alone than before; and, if it bring a mind perpetually averse and disagreeable, betrays us to a worse condition than the most deserted loneliness. God cannot in the justice of his own promise and institution so unexpectedly mock us by forcing that upon us as the remedy of solitude, which wraps us in a misery worse than any wilderness, as the Spirit of God himself judges (Prov. 19);[36] especially knowing that the best and wisest men amidst the sincere and most cordial designs of their heart do daily err in choosing.

We may conclude therefore, seeing orthodoxal expositors confess to our hands, that by loneliness is not only meant the want of copulation, and that man is not less alone by turning in a body to him, unless there be within it a mind answerable; that it is a work more worthy the care and consultation of God to provide for the worthiest part of man, which is his mind, and not unnaturally to set it beneath the formalities and respects of the body, to make it a servant of its own vassal. I say we may conclude that such a marriage, wherein the mind is so disgraced and vilified below the body's interest, and can have no just or tolerable contentment, is not of God's institution, and therefore no marriage. Nay, in concluding this, I say we conclude no more than what the common expositors themselves give us, both in that which I have recited and much more hereafter. But the truth is, they give us in such a manner as they who leave their own mature positions like the eggs of an ostrich in the dust. I do but lay them in the sun; their own pregnancies hatch the truth. And I am taxed of novelties and strange producements, while they, like that inconsiderate bird, know not that these are their own natural breed.

["I will make him a help meet for him."] Here the heavenly institutor, as if he labored not to be mistaken by the supercilious hypocrisy of those that love to master their brethren, and to make us sure that he gave us not now a servile yoke, but an amiable knot, contents not himself to say, I will make him a wife; but resolving to give us first the meaning before the name of a wife, saith graciously, "I will make him a help meet for him." And here again, as before, I do not require more full and fair deductions than the whole consent of our divines usually raise from this text, that in matrimony there must be first a mutual help

36. Prov. 19.13: "The contentions of a wife are a continual dropping."

to piety, next to civil fellowship of love and amity, then to generation, so to household affairs, lastly the remedy of incontinence. And commonly they reckon them in such order as leaves generation and incontinence to be last considered. This I amaze me at, that though all the superior and nobler ends both of marriage and of the married persons be absolutely frustrate, the matrimony stirs not, loses no hold, remains as rooted as the center. But if the body bring but in a complaint of frigidity, by that cold application only this adamantine Alp of wedlock has leave to dissolve, which else all the machinations of religious or civil reason at the suit of a distressed mind, either for divine worship or human conversation violated, cannot unfasten. What courts of concupiscence are these, wherein fleshly appetite is heard before right reason, lust before love or devotion? They may be pious Christians together, they may be loving and friendly, they may be helpful to each other in the family, but they cannot couple—that shall divorce them, though either party would not. They can neither serve God together, nor one be at peace with the other, nor be good in the family one to other, but live as they were dead, or live as they were deadly enemies in a cage together—'tis all one, they can couple, they shall not divorce till death, no, though this sentence be their death.

What is this besides tyranny, but to turn nature upside down, to make both religion and the mind of man wait upon the slavish errands of the body, and not the body to follow either the sanctity or the sovereignty of the mind, unspeakably wronged and with all equity complaining? What is this but to abuse the sacred and mysterious bed of marriage to be the compulsive sty of an ingrateful and malignant lust, stirred up only from a carnal acrimony,[37] without either love or peace, or regard to any other thing holy or human. This I admire, how possibly it should inhabit thus long in the sense of so many disputing theologians, unless it be the lowest lees of a canonical infection liver-grown to their sides, which perhaps will never uncling without the strong abstersive[38] of some heroic magistrate, whose mind equal to his high office dares lead him both to know and to do without their frivolous case-putting. For certain he shall have God and this institution plainly on his side. And if it be true both in divinity and law, that consent alone, though copulation never follow, makes a marriage, how can they dissolve it for the want of that which made it not, and not dissolve it for that not continuing which made it, and should preserve it in love and reason, and difference it from a brute conjugality?

["*Meet for him.*"] The original here is more expressive than other languages word for word can render it, but all agree effectual conformity of disposition and affection to be hereby signified; which God, as it were, not satisfied with the naming of a help, goes on describing "another self," "a second self," "a very self itself." Yet now there is nothing in the life of man, through our misconstruction, made more uncertain, more hazardous and full of chance, than this divine

37. **acrimony:** sharpness. Milton refers to the sting of lust.
38. **abstersive:** having the quality of purging and washing away impurities.

blessing with such favorable significance here conferred upon us; which if we do but err in our choice, the most unblamable error that can be, err but one minute, one moment after those mighty syllables pronounced, which take upon them to join heaven and hell together unpardonably till death pardon, this divine blessing that looked but now with such a humane smile upon us, and spoke such gentle reason, straight vanishes like a fair sky, and brings on such a scene of cloud and tempest as turns all to shipwreck without haven or shore, but to a ransomless captivity. And then they tell us it is our sin; but let them be told again, that sin through the mercy of God hath not made such waste upon us as to make utterly void to our use any temporal benefit, much less any so much availing to a peaceful and sanctified life, merely for a most incident error which no wariness can certainly shun. And wherefore serves our happy redemption, and the liberty we have in Christ, but to deliver us from calamitous yokes not to be lived under without the endangerment of our souls, and to restore us in some competent measure to a right in every good thing both of this life and the other? Thus we see how treatably and distinctly God hath here taught us what the prime ends of marriage are: mutual solace and help. That we are now, upon the most irreprehensible mistake in choosing, defeated and defrauded of all this original benignity was begun first through the snare of anti-Christian canons long since obtruded upon the church of Rome, and not yet scoured off by reformation, out of a lingering vainglory that abides among us to make fair shows in formal ordinances, and to enjoin continence and bearing of crosses in such a garb as no scripture binds us, under the thickest arrows of temptation, where we need not stand. Now we shall see with what acknowledgment and assent Adam received this new associate which God brought him. . . .

[*In an omitted section on Genesis 2.23, Milton argues that, except in the case of Adam and Eve, who were literally "flesh of flesh," marriage is a civil rather than a natural relation.*]

V. 24. "Therefore shall a man leave his father and his mother, and shall cleave unto his wife; and they shall be one flesh."

This verse, as our common heed expounds it, is the great knot-tier, which hath undone by tying, and by tangling, millions of guiltless consciences. This is that grisly porter, who having drawn men—and wisest men—by subtle allurement within the train of an unhappy matrimony, claps the dungeon-gate upon them, as irrecoverable as the grave. But if we view him well, and hear him with not too hasty and prejudicant[39] ears, we shall find no such terror in him. For, first, it is not here said absolutely without all reason he shall cleave to his wife, be it to his weal or to his destruction as it happens, but he shall do this upon the premises and considerations of that meet help and society before mentioned: "Therefore he shall cleave to his wife," no otherwise a wife, than a fit help. He

39. **prejudicant:** prejudging.

is not bid to leave the dear cohabitation of his father, mother, brothers and sisters, to link himself inseparably with the mere carcass of a marriage, perhaps an enemy. This joining particle "therefore" is in all equity, nay in all necessity of construction, to comprehend first and most principally what God spake concerning the inward essence of marriage in his institution, that we may learn how far to attend what Adam spake of the outward materials thereof in his approbation. For if we shall bind these words of Adam only to a corporal meaning, and that the force of this injunction upon all us his sons to live individually with any woman which hath befallen us in the most mistaken wedlock, shall consist not in[40] those moral and relative causes of Eve's creation, but in the mere anatomy of a rib, and that Adam's insight concerning wedlock reached no further, we shall make him as very an idiot as the Socinians[41] make him (which would not be reverently done of us). Let us be content to allow our great forefather so much wisdom as to take the instituting words of God along with him into this sentence, which, if they be well-minded,[42] will assure us that flesh and ribs are but of a weak and dead efficacy to keep marriage united where there is no other fitness.

The rib of marriage, to all since Adam, is a relation much rather than a bone. The nerves and sinews thereof are love and meet help; they knit not every couple that marries, and where they knit they seldom break. But where they break, which for the most part is where they never truly joined, to such at the same instant both flesh and rib cease to be in common; so that here they argue nothing to the continuance of a false or violated marriage, but must be led back to receive their meaning from those institutive words of God which give them all the life and vigor they have.

["Therefore shall a man leave his father," etc.] What to a man's thinking more plain by this appointment, that the fatherly power should give place to conjugal prerogative? Yet it is generally held by reformed writers against the papist, that though in persons at discretion the marriage in itself be never so fit, though it be fully accomplished with benediction, board and bed, yet the father not consenting, his main will without dispute shall dissolve all. And this they affirm only from collective reason, not any direct law. For that in Exod. 22.17, which is most particular, speaks that a father may refuse to marry his daughter to one who hath deflowered her, not that he may take her away from one who hath soberly married her. Yet because the general honor due to parents is great, they hold he may, and perhaps hold not amiss. But again when the question is of harsh and rugged parents, who defer to bestow their children seasonably, they agree jointly that the church or magistrate may bestow them, though without the father's consent; and for this they have no express authority in scripture. So that they may see by their own handling of this very place, that it is not the

40. **shall not consist in:** will not be consistent with.

41. The *Socinians* were thought to hold that Adam was created ignorant.

42. **well-minded:** i.e., kept in mind by the reader.

stubborn letter must govern us, but the divine and softening breath of charity, which turns and winds the dictate of every positive command, and shapes it to the good of mankind.

Shall the outward accessory of a father's will wanting rend the fittest and most affectionate marriage in twain, after all nuptial consummations, and shall not the want of love and the privation of all civil and religious concord, which is the inward essence of wedlock, do as much to part those who were never truly wedded? Shall a father have this power to vindicate his own willful honor and authority to the utter breach of a most dearly united marriage, and shall not a man in his own power have the permission to free his soul, his life, and all his comfort of life from the disaster of a no-marriage? Shall fatherhood, which is but man, for his own pleasure dissolve matrimony, and shall not matrimony, which is God's ordinance, for its own honor and better conservation dissolve itself, when it is wrong, and not fitted to any of the chief ends which it owes us?

["And they shall be one flesh."] These words also infer that there ought to be an individuality[43] in marriage, but without all question presuppose the joining causes. Not a rule yet that we have met with, so universal in this whole institution, but hath admitted limitations and conditions according to human necessity. The very foundation of matrimony, though God laid it so deliberately, "that it is not good for man to be alone," holds not always, if the apostle can secure us. Soon after we are bid leave father and mother, and cleave to a wife, but must understand the father's consent withal, else not. "Cleave to a wife," but let her be a wife, let her be a meet help, a solace, not a nothing, not an adversary, not a desertrice. Can any law or command be so unreasonable as to make men cleave to calamity, to ruin, to perdition?

In like manner here, "They shall be one flesh"; but let the causes hold, and be made really good, which only have the possibility to make them one flesh. We know that flesh can neither join, nor keep together two bodies of itself. What is it then must make them one flesh, but likeness, but fitness of mind and disposition, which may breed the spirit of concord and union between them? If that be not in the nature of either, and that there has been a remediless mistake, as vain we go about to compel them into one flesh as if we undertook to weave a garment of dry sand. It were more easy to compel the vegetable and nutritive power of nature to assimilations and mixtures which are not alterable each by other, or force the concoctive stomach to turn that into flesh which is so totally unlike that substance as not to be wrought on.

For as the unity of mind is nearer and greater than the union of bodies, so doubtless is the dissimilitude greater and more dividual, as that which makes between bodies all difference and distinction. Especially whenas besides the singular and substantial differences of every soul, there is an intimate quality of good or evil, through the whole progeny of Adam, which like a radical heat or

43. **individuality:** indivisibility. Milton acknowledges the inseparability of a married couple, but a couple is truly married only if the ends of God's original institution are fulfilled.

mortal chillness joins them or disjoins them irresistibly. In whom therefore either the will, or the faculty is found to have never joined, or now not to continue so, 'tis not to say, they shall be one flesh, for they cannot be one flesh. God commands not impossibilities, and all the ecclesiastical glue that liturgy or laymen can compound is not able to solder up two such incongruous natures into the one flesh of a true beseeming marriage.

Why did Moses then set down their uniting into one flesh? And I again ask, why the Gospel so oft repeats the eating of our Savior's flesh, the drinking of his blood? "That we are one body with him, the members of his body, flesh of his flesh and bone of his bone" (Ephes. 5[.30]). Yet lest we should be Capernaitans,[44] as we are told there that the flesh profiteth nothing, so we are told here, if we be not as deaf as adders, that this union of the flesh proceeds from the union of a fit help and solace. We know that there was never a more spiritual mystery than this Gospel taught us under the terms of body and flesh, yet nothing less intended than that we should stick there. What a stupidness then is it, that in marriage, which is the nearest resemblance of our union with Christ, we should deject ourselves to such a sluggish and underfoot philosophy, as to esteem the validity of marriage merely by the flesh, though never so broken and disjointed from love and peace, which only can give a human qualification to that act of the flesh and distinguish it from bestial. The text therefore uses this phrase, that "they shall be one flesh," to justify and make legitimate the rites of marriage-bed; which was not unneedful, if for all this warrant they were suspected of pollution by some sects of philosophy and religions of old, and latelier among the papists, and other heretics elder than they.

Some think there is a high mystery in those words, from that which Paul saith of them (Ephes. 5[.32]), "This is a great mystery, but I speak of Christ and the Church," and thence they would conclude marriage to be inseparable. For me I dispute not now whether matrimony be a mystery or no; if it be of Christ and his church, certainly it is not meant of every ungodly and miswedded marriage, but then only mysterious, when it is a holy, happy, and peaceful match. But when a saint is joined with a reprobate, or both alike wicked with wicked, fool with fool, a he-drunkard with a she, when the bed hath been nothing else for twenty years or more but an old haunt of lust and malice mixed together, no love, no goodness, no loyalty, but counterplotting and secret wishing one another's dissolution, this is to me the greatest mystery in the world, if such a marriage as this can be the mystery of aught, unless it be the mystery of iniquity: according to that which Paræus cites out of Chrysostom, that a bad wife is a help for the devil,[45] and the like may be said of a bad husband. Since therefore none but a fit and pious Matrimony can signify the union of Christ and his church, there cannot hence be any hindrance of divorce to that wedlock wherein there can be no good mystery. Rather it might to a Christian con-

44. In Matt. 11.23 and Luke 10.15, Jesus denounces the residents of Capernaum for their lack of faith.
45. Paraeus, *In Genesin* (1614), col. 420.

science be matter of finding itself so much less satisfied than before, in the continuance of an unhappy yoke, wherein there can be no representation either of Christ, or of his Church. . . .

[*In the remainder of this section, Milton defines the Aristotelian causes of marriage (material: man and woman; efficient: God and the couple's consent; formal: conjugal love; and final: help and society) and defines marriage as "a divine institution joining man and woman in a love fitly disposed to the helps and comforts of domestic life."*]

DEUT. 24. 1, 2.

1. "When a man hath taken a wife, and married her, and it come to pass that she find no favor in his eyes, because he hath found some uncleanness in her, then let him write her a bill of divorcement, and give it in her hand, and send her out of his house.
2. "And when she is departed out of his house, she may go and be another man's wife."

[*In an omitted section, Milton argues that if divorce among the Jews had been merely an evil custom, Mosaic Law would have forbidden it and that the "uncleanness" of Deuteronomy 24.1, though usually read as adultery, refers instead to "any defect, annoyance, or ill quality in nature, which to be joined with, makes life tedious, and such company worse than solitude."*]

Now although Moses needed not to add other reason of this law than that one there expressed, yet to these ages wherein canons, and Scotisms, and Lombard laws[46] have dulled and almost obliterated the lively sculpture of ancient reason and humanity, it will be requisite to heap reason upon reason, and all little enough to vindicate the whiteness and the innocence of this divine law from the calumny it finds at this day of being a door to license and confusion. Whenas indeed there is not a judicial point in all Moses consisting of more true equity, high wisdom, and God-like pity than this law; not derogating, but preserving the honor and peace of marriage, and exactly agreeing with the sense and mind of that institution in Genesis.

For first, if marriage be but an ordained relation, as it seems not more, it cannot take place above the prime dictates of nature; and if it be of natural right, yet it must yield to that which is more natural, and before it by eldership and precedence in nature. Now it is not natural that Hugh marries Beatrice, or Thomas, Rebecca, being only a civil contract, and full of many chances; but that these men seek them meet helps, that only is natural; and that they espouse them such, that only is marriage. But if they find them neither fit helps nor tolerable society, what thing more natural, more original, and first in nature than

46. Milton alludes scornfully to Canon Law and the writings of the scholastic theologians John Duns Scotus (c. 1265–1308) and Peter Lombard (c. 1100–1160).

to depart from that which is irksome, grievous, actively hateful, and injurious even to hostility, especially in a conjugal respect, wherein antipathies are invincible, and where the forced abiding of the one can be no true good, no real comfort to the other? For if he find no contentment from the other, how can he return it from himself; or no acceptance, how can he mutually accept? What more equal, more pious, than to untie a civil knot for a natural enmity held by violence from parting, to dissolve an accidental conjunction of this or that man and woman, for the most natural and most necessary disagreement of meet from unmeet, guilty from guiltless, contrary from contrary? It being certain that the mystical and blessed unity of marriage can be no way more unhallowed and profaned than by the forcible uniting of such disunions and separations. Which if we see ofttimes they cannot join or piece up to a common friendship, or to a willing conversation in the same house, how should they possibly agree to the most familiar and united amity of wedlock?

Abraham and Lot, though dear friends and brethren in a strange country, chose rather to part asunder than to infect their friendship with the strife of their servants.[47] Paul and Barnabas, joined together by the Holy Ghost to a spiritual work, thought it better to separate when once they grew at variance.[48] If these great saints, joined by nature, friendship, religion, high providence, and revelation, could not so govern a casual difference, a sudden passion, but must in wisdom divide from the outward duties of a friendship, or a colleagueship in the same family, or in the same journey, lest it should grow to a worse division, can anything be more absurd and barbarous than that they, whom only error, casualty, art, or plot hath joined, should be compelled, not against a sudden passion but against the permanent and radical discords of nature, to the most intimate and incorporating duties of love and embracement, therein only rational and human as they are free and voluntary, being else an abject and servile yoke, scarce not brutish? And that there is in man such a peculiar sway of liking or disliking in the affairs of matrimony is evidently seen before marriage among those who can be friendly, can respect each other, yet to marry each other would not for any persuasion. If then this unfitness and disparity be not till after marriage discovered, through many causes and colors and concealments that may overshadow, undoubtedly it will produce the same effects, and perhaps with more vehemence, that such a mistaken pair would give the world to be unmarried again. And their condition Solomon to the plain justification of divorce expresses (Prov. 30.21, 23), where he tells us of his own accord that a "hated" or a "hateful woman when she is married is a thing for which the earth is disquieted and cannot bear it"; thus giving divine testimony to this divine law, which bids us nothing more than is the first and most innocent lesson of nature, to turn away peaceably from what afflicts and hazards our destruction; especially when our staying can do no good, and is exposed to all evil. . . .

47. Gen. 13.6–12.
48. Acts 15.37–40.

[*In an omitted section, Milton argues again that no law or covenant can bind against the welfare, properly understood, of those governed by the law or party to the covenant.*]

Fourthly, the law is not to neglect men under greatest sufferances, but to see covenants of greatest moment faithfullest performed. And what injury comparable to that sustained in a frustrate and false-dealing marriage, to lose, for another's fault against him, the best portion of his temporal comforts, and of his spiritual too, as it may fall out? It was the law that, for man's good and quiet, reduced things to propriety, which were at first in common.[49] How much more lawlike were it to assist nature in disappropriating that evil which by continuing proper becomes destructive? But he might have bewared. So he might in any other covenant, wherein the law does not constrain error to so dear a forfeit. And yet in these matters wherein the wisest are apt to err, all the wariness that can be ofttimes nothing avails. But the law can compel the offending party to be more duteous. Yes, if all these kind of offences were fit in public to be complained on, or being compelled were any satisfaction to a mate not sottish or malicious. And these injuries work so vehemently, that if the law remedy them not by separating the cause when no way else will pacify, the person not relieved betakes him either to such disorderly courses, or to such a dull dejection, as renders him either infamous or useless to the service of God and his country. Which the law ought to prevent as a thing pernicious to the commonwealth; and what better prevention than this which Moses used?

Fifthly, the law is to tender the liberty and the human dignity of them that live under the law, whether it be the man's right above the woman or the woman's just appeal against wrong and servitude. But the duties of marriage contain in them a duty of benevolence,[50] which to do by compulsion against the soul, where there can be neither peace, nor joy, nor love, but an enthrallment to one who either cannot or will not be mutual in the godliest and the civilest ends of that society, is the ignoblest and the lowest slavery that a human shape can be put to. This law therefore justly and piously provides against such an unmanly task of bondage as this. The civil law, though it favored the setting free of a slave, yet if he proved ungrateful to his patron, reduced him to a servile condition. If that law did well to reduce from liberty to bondage for an ingratitude not the greatest, much more became it the law of God to enact the restorement of a freeborn man from an unpurposed and unworthy bondage to a rightful liberty for the most unnatural fraud and ingratitude that can be committed against him. And if the civilian emperor, in his title of *Donations*, permit the giver to recall his gift from him who proves unthankful towards him (yea, though he had subscribed and signed in the deed of his gift not to recall it, though for this very cause of ingratitude),[51] with much more equity doth Moses permit here the

49. **reduced . . . in common:** i.e., assigned things held communally to private ownership.
50. **duty of benevolence:** obligation to participate in sexual relations with one's spouse.
51. The Yale editor points to the *Juris Civilis, Code*, book 8, title 56, ¶s 1, 10.

giver to recall no petty gift, but the gift of himself, from one who most injuriously and deceitfully uses him against the main ends and conditions of his giving himself, expressed in God's institution.

Sixthly, although there be nothing in the plain words of this law that seems to regard the afflictions of a wife, how great soever, yet expositors determine, and doubtless determine rightly, that God was not uncompassionate of them also in the framing of this law. For should the rescript of Antoninus in the civil law give release to servants flying for refuge to the emperor's statue, by giving leave to change their cruel masters,[52] and should God, who in his law also is good to injured servants by granting them their freedom in diverse cases, not consider the wrongs and miseries of a wife, which is no servant? Though herein the countersense of our divines, to me, I must confess, seems admirable; who teach that God gave this as a merciful law, not for man whom he here names, and to whom by name he gives this power, but for the wife whom he names not, and to whom by name he gives no power at all. For certainly if man be liable to injuries in marriage, as well as woman, and man be the worthier person, it were a preposterous law to respect only the less worthy, her whom God made for marriage, and not him at all for whom marriage was made. . . .

[*In the omitted section, Milton cites prescriptions in Jewish law that implicitly confirm the right of divorce.*]

Ninthly, suppose it might be imputed to a man that he was too rash in his choice, and why he took not better heed, let him now smart, and bear his folly as he may; although the law of God, that terrible law, do not thus upbraid the infirmities and unwilling mistakes of man in his integrity. But suppose these and the like proud aggravations of some stern hypocrite, more merciless in his mercies than any literal law in the vigor of severity, must be patiently heard; yet all law, and God's law especially, grants everywhere to error easy remitments, even where the utmost penalty exacted were no undoing. With great reason therefore and mercy doth it here not torment an error, if it be so, with the endurance of a whole life lost to all household comfort and society, a punishment of too vast and huge dimension for an error, and the more unreasonable for that the like objection may be opposed against the plea of divorcing for adultery: he might have looked better before to her breeding under religious parents. Why did he not then more diligently inquire into her manners, into what company she kept? Every glance of her eye, every step of her gait, would have prophesied adultery, if the quick scent of these discerners had been took along; they had the divination to have foretold you all this, as they have now the divinity to punish an error inhumanly. As good reason to be content, and forced to be con-

52. The Yale editor points here to the *Juris Civilis, Institutes,* book 1, title 8, ¶ 2.

tent with your adulteress, if these objectors might be the judges of human frailty.

But God, more mild and good to man than man to his brother, in all this liberty given to divorcement, mentions not a word of our past errors and mistakes, if any were, which these men objecting from their own inventions prosecute with all violence and iniquity. For if the one be to look so narrowly what he takes, at the peril of ever keeping, why should not the other be made as wary what is promised, by the peril of losing? For without those promises the treaty of marriage had not proceeded. Why should his own error bind him, rather than the other's fraud acquit him? Let the buyer beware, saith the old law-beaten termer. Belike then there is no more honesty nor ingenuity in the bargain of a wedlock than in the buying of a colt. We must, it seems, drive it on as craftily with those whose affinity we seek, as if they were a pack of sale-men and complotters. But the deceiver deceives himself in the unprosperous marriage, and therein is sufficiently punished. I answer that the most of those who deceive are such as either understand not or value not the true purposes of marriage; they have the prey they seek, not the punishment. Yet say it prove to them some cross, it is not equal that error and fraud should be linked in the same degree of forfeiture, but rather that error should be acquitted, and fraud bereaved his morsel, if the mistake were not on both sides; for then on both sides the acquitment will be reasonable, if the bondage be intolerable; which this law graciously determines, not unmindful of the wife, as was granted willingly to the common expositors, though beyond the letter of this law, yet not beyond the spirit of charity.

Tenthly, marriage is a solemn thing, some say a holy, the resemblance of Christ and his Church; and so indeed it is where the persons are truly religious. And we know all sacred things not performed sincerely as they ought are no way acceptable to God in their outward formality. And that wherein it differs from personal duties, if they be not truly done, the fault is in ourselves; but marriage, to be a true and pious marriage, is not in the single power of any person; the essence whereof, as of all other covenants, is in relation to another, the making and maintaining causes thereof are all mutual, and must be a communion of spiritual and temporal comforts. If then either of them cannot, or obstinately will not, be answerable in these duties, so as that the other can have no peaceful living, or enduring the want of what he justly seeks, and sees no hope, then straight from that dwelling love, which is the soul of wedlock, takes his flight, leaving only some cold performances of civil and common respects; but the true bond of marriage, if there were ever any there, is already burst like a rotten thread. Then follows dissimulation, suspicion, false colors, false pretences, and, worse than these, disturbance, annoyance, vexation, sorrow, temptation even in the faultless person, weary of himself and of all action, public or domestic; then comes disorder, neglect, hatred, and perpetual strife, all these the enemies of holiness and Christianity, and every one of these, persisted in, a remediless violation to matrimony. Therefore God, who hates all feigning and formality where there should be all faith and sincereness, and abhors to see the inevitable discord where there should be greatest concord, when through another's default faith and concord cannot be, counts it neither just to punish the innocent with the transgressor, nor holy, nor honorable for the sanctity of marriage, that should be the union of peace and love, to be made the commitment, and close fight of enmity and hate. And therefore doth in this law what best agrees with his goodness, loosening a sacred thing to peace and charity, rather than binding it to hatred and contention; loosening only the outward and formal tie of that which is already inwardly and really broken, or else was really never joined.

Eleventhly, one of the chief matrimonial ends is said to seek a holy seed, but where an unfit marriage administers continual cause of hatred and distemper, there, as was heard before, cannot choose but much unholiness abide. Nothing more unhallows a man, more unprepares him to the service of God in any duty, than a habit of wrath and perturbation, arising from the importunity of troublous causes never absent. And where the household stands in this plight, what love can there be to the unfortunate issue, what care of their breeding, which is of main conducement to their being holy? God therefore knowing how unhappy it would be for children to be born in such a family, gives this law either as a prevention, that, being an unhappy pair, they should not add to be unhappy parents, or else as a remedy that if there be children, while they are fewest, they may follow either parent, as shall be agreed or judged, from the house of hatred and discord to place of more holy and peaceable education.

Twelfthly, all law is available to some good end, but the final prohibition of divorce avails to no good end, causing only the endless aggravation of evil. And therefore this permission of divorce was given to the Jews by the wisdom and fatherly providence of God, who knew that law cannot command love, without which matrimony hath no true being, no good, no solace, nothing of God's instituting, nothing but so sordid and so low as to be disdained of any generous person. Law cannot enable natural inability either of body or mind, which gives the grievance; it cannot make equal those inequalities; it cannot make fit those unfitnesses; and where there is malice more than defect of nature, it cannot hinder ten thousand injuries and bitter actions of despite too subtle and too unapparent for law to deal with. And while it seeks to remedy more outward wrongs, it exposes the injured person to other more inward and more cutting. All these evils unavoidably will redound upon the children, if any be, and the whole family.

It degenerates and disorders the best spirits, leaves them to unsettled imaginations and degraded hopes, careless of themselves, their households, and their friends, unactive to all public service, dead to the commonwealth; wherein they are by one mishap, and no willing trespass of theirs, outlawed from all the benefits and comforts of married life and posterity. It confers as little to the honor and inviolable keeping of matrimony, but sooner stirs up temptations and occasions to secret adulteries and unchaste roving. But it maintains public honesty.[53] Public folly, rather; who shall judge of public honesty? The law of God and of ancientest Christians, and all civil nations, or the illegitimate law of monks and canonists, the most malevolent, most unexperienced, and incompetent judges of matrimony?

These reasons, and many more that might be alleged, afford us plainly to perceive both what good cause this law had to do for good men in mischances, and what necessity it had to suffer accidentally the hard-heartedness of bad men, which it could not certainly discover, or discovering could not subdue, no nor endeavor to restrain without multiplying sorrow to them, for whom all was endeavored. The guiltless therefore were not deprived their needful redresses, and the hard hearts of others, unchastisable in those judicial courts, were so remitted there, as bound over to the higher session of conscience.

Notwithstanding all this, there is a loud exception against this law of God, nor can the holy author save his law from this exception, that it opens a door to all license and confusion. But this is the rudest, I was almost saying the most graceless objection, and with the least reverence to God and Moses, that could be devised. This is to cite God before man's tribunal, to arrogate a wisdom and holiness above him. Did not God then foresee what event of license or confusion could follow? Did not he know how to ponder these abuses with more prevailing respects, in the most even balance of his justice and pureness, till these correctors came up to show him better? The law is, if it stir up sin any way, to stir it up by forbidding, as one contrary excites another (Rom. 7).[54] But if it once come to provoke sin by granting license to sin, according to laws that have no other honest end but only to permit the fulfilling of obstinate lust, how is God not made the contradicter of himself?

No man denies that best things may be abused, but it is a rule resulting from many pregnant experiences, that what doth most harm in the abusing, used rightly doth most good. And such a good to take away from honest men, for being abused by such as abuse all things, is the greatest abuse of all. That the whole law is no further useful than as a man uses it lawfully, St. Paul teaches (1 Tim. 1).[55] And that Christian liberty may be used for an occasion to the flesh, the same Apostle confesses (Galat. 5),[56] yet thinks not of removing it for that, but bids us rather "stand fast in the liberty wherewith Christ hath freed us, and not be held again in the yoke of bondage" [Gal. 5.1]. The very permission which Christ gave to divorce for adultery may be foully abused by any whose hardness of heart can either feign adultery or dares commit, that he may divorce. And for this cause the pope and hitherto the church of England forbid all divorce from

53. Milton voices, in order to answer, the argument of his opponents.

54. Rom. 7.7: "I had not known sin, but by the law; for I had not known lust, except the law had said, Thou shalt not covet."

55. 1 Tim. 1.8: "But we know that the law is good, if a man use it lawfully."

56. Gal. 5.13: "Ye have been called unto liberty; only use not liberty for an occasion to the flesh."

the bond of marriage, though for openest adultery. If then it be righteous to hinder, for the fear of abuse, that which God's law, notwithstanding that caution, hath warranted to be done, doth not our righteousness come short of Antichrist, or do we not rather herein conform ourselves to his unrighteousness in this undue and unwise fear? For God regards more to relieve by this law the just complaints of good men, than to curb the license of wicked men, to the crushing withal and the overwhelming of his afflicted servants. He loves more that his law should look with pity upon the difficulties of his own, than with rigor upon the boundless riots of them who serve another master, and, hindered here by strictness, will break another way to worse enormities.

If this law therefore have many good reasons for which God gave it, and no intention of giving scope to lewdness, but as abuse by accident comes in with every good law and every good thing, it cannot be wisdom in us, while we can content us with God's wisdom, nor can be purity, if his purity will suffice us, to except against this law as if it fostered license. But if they affirm this law had no other end but to permit obdurate lust because it would be obdurate, making the law of God intentionally to proclaim and enact sin lawful, as if the will of God were become sinful, or sin stronger than his direct and law-giving will, the men would be admonished to look well to it, that while they are so eager to shut the door against license, they do not open a worse door to blasphemy.

And yet they shall be here further shown their iniquity. What more foul and common sin among us than drunkenness? And who can be ignorant that, if the importation of wine and the use of all strong drink were forbid, it would both clean rid the possibility of committing that odious vice, and men might afterwards live happily and healthfully without the use of those intoxicating liquors. Yet who is there, the severest of them all, that ever propounded to lose his sack, his ale, toward the certain abolishing of so great a sin? Who is there of them, the holiest, that less loves his rich canary[57] at meals, though it be fetched from places that hazard the religion of them who fetch it, and though it make his neighbor drunk out of the same tune? While they forbid not therefore the use of that liquid merchandise, which forbidden would utterly remove a most loathsome sin, and not impair either the health or the refreshment of mankind, supplied many other ways, why do they forbid a law of God, the forbidding whereof brings into excessive bondage ofttimes the best of men, and betters not the worse? He, to remove a national vice, will not pardon his cups, nor think it concerns him to forbear the quaffing of that outlandish grape, in his unnecessary fullness, though other men abuse it never so much, nor is he so abstemious as to intercede with the magistrate that all matter of drunkenness be banished the commonwealth; and yet for the fear of a less inconvenience unpardonably requires of his brethren, in their extreme necessity, to debar themselves the use of God's permissive law, though it might be their saving, and no man's endan-

57. **canary:** sweet wine from the Canary Islands. Cp. Jonson, "Inviting a Friend to Supper," l. 29: "a pure cup of rich canary wine."

gering the more. Thus this peremptory strictness we may discern of what sort it is, how unequal, and how unjust.

But it will breed confusion.[58] What confusion it would breed, God himself took the care to prevent in the fourth verse of this chapter [Deut. 24.4], that the divorced, being married to another, might not return to her former husband. And Justinian's law counsels the same in his title of *Nuptials.* And what confusion else can there be in separation, to separate upon extreme urgency the religious from the irreligious, the fit from the unfit, the willing from the willful, the abused from the abuser? Such a separation is quite contrary to confusion. But to bind and mix together holy with atheist, heavenly with hellish, fitness with unfitness, light with darkness, antipathy with antipathy, the injured with the injurer, and force them into the most inward nearness of a detested union, this doubtless is the most horrid, the most unnatural mixture, the greatest confusion that can be confused![59]

Thus by this plain and Christian Talmud[60] vindicating the law of God from irreverent and unwary expositions, I trust, where it shall meet with intelligible perusers, some stay at least of men's thoughts will be obtained, to consider these many prudent and righteous ends of this divorcing permission. That it may have, for the great author's sake, hereafter some competent allowance to be counted a little purer than the prerogative of a legal and public ribaldry granted to that holy seed. So that from hence we shall hope to find the way still more open to the reconciling of those places which treat this matter in the Gospel. And thither now without interruption the course of method brings us.

MATT. 5.31, 32.

31. "It hath been said, Whosoever shall put away his wife, let him give her a writing of divorcement.
32. "But I say unto you that whosoever shall put away his wife," etc.

MATT. 19.3, 4 &C.

3. "And the Pharisees also came unto him tempting him," etc.

. . .

[*In a lengthy omitted section, Milton acknowledges that his argument will not seem to fit the letter of Matthew but argues that Christ would have us read the Gospel in the light of charity, not literal rigor. Because marriage and divorce fall under the moral law as opposed to the merely positive ceremonial and judical laws, to assume, as orthodox opinion did in his day, that Christ's teaching on divorce diverged from Mosaic Law on divorce amounts to a*

58. Once again Milton articulates an objection before countering it.
59. Despite the argument elsewhere in the tract for divorce for mutually blameless incompatibility, Milton's binaries in these sentences assign blame, with the single exception of *antipathy with antipathy.*
60. **Talmud:** ancient Jewish writings interpreting Scripture.

kind of Manichaeanism, with one God in the Old Testament and another in the New. Christ's apparent prohibition of divorce in Matthew 19, Milton argues, is in fact a response to the Pharisees' attempt to trap him; it is "not so much a teaching [for us], but an entangling [of the Pharisees]." Because they had abused the Mosaic permission of divorce, and because they had treated marriage as merely the carnal work of male and female, Christ answers them according to their degraded capacity. At the same time, Christ implies that marriage is only marriage when the purposes of the original institution are fulfilled.]

> Ver. 7. "They say unto him, Why did Moses then command to give a writing of divorcement, and to put her away?
> Ver. 8. "He saith unto them, Moses because of the hardness of your hearts suffered you to put away your wives, but from the beginning it was not so."

. . .

[*In another lengthy section, Milton argues, as he had in the* Doctrine and Discipline (*see Book 2, chapter 3*), *that to insist that Christ overturns the Mosaic permission of divorce is to imply that God lured the Jews into a sinful practice, and that God is thus the author of their sins. The argument that the Mosaic Law is designed to limit rather than to encourage sin is fallacious, for sin by its nature is chaotic and boundless, and it cannot be limited.*]

["Moses suffered you to put away," etc.] Not commanded you, says the common observer, and therefore cared not how soon it were abolished, being but suffered; herein declaring his annotation to be slight and nothing law-prudent. For in this place "commanded" and "suffered" are interchangeably used in the same sense both by our Savior and the Pharisees. Our Savior, who here saith, "Moses suffered you," in the 10th of Mark saith, "Moses wrote you this command." And the Pharisees who here say, "Moses commanded," and would mainly have it a command, in that place of Mark say, "Moses suffered," which had made against them in their own mouths if the word of "suffering" had weakened the command. So that "suffered" and "commanded" is here taken for the same thing on both sides of the controversy, as Cameron[61] also and others on this place acknowledge. And lawyers know that all the precepts of law are divided into obligatory and permissive, containing either what we must do, or what we may do; and of this latter sort are as many precepts as of the former, and all as lawful. Tutelage, an ordainment than which nothing more just, being for the defense of orphans, the *Institutes* of Justinian say, "is given and permitted by the civil law," and "to parents it is permitted to choose and appoint by will the guardians of their children."[62] What more equal? And yet the civil law calls this "permission." So likewise to "manumise," to adopt, to make a will, and to be

61. Johannes Cameron makes this point in his *Myrothecium Evangelicum* (1632, 98).
62. *Juris Civiles, Institutes,* book 1, title 13, ¶s 1, 3.

made an heir is called "permission" by law. Marriage itself, and this which is already granted, to divorce for adultery, obliges no man, is but a permission by law, is but suffered. By this we may see how weakly it hath been thought that all divorce is utterly unlawful, because the law is said to suffer it: whenas to "suffer" is but the legal phrase denoting what by law a man may do or not do.

["Because of the hardness of your hearts."] Hence they argue that therefore he allowed it not, and therefore it must be abolished. But the contrary to this will sooner follow, that because he suffered it for a cause, therefore in relation to that cause he allowed it. Next, if he in his wisdom and in the midst of his severity allowed it for hardness of heart, it can be nothing better than arrogance and presumption to take stricter courses against hardness of heart than God ever set an example, and that under the Gospel,[63] which warrants them to no judicial act of compulsion in this matter, much less to be more severe against hardness of extremity, than God thought good to be against hardness of heart. He suffered it rather than worse inconveniences; these men wiser, as they make themselves, will suffer the worst and heinousest inconveniences to follow rather than they will suffer what God suffered. Although they can know, when they please, that Christ spake only to the conscience, did not judge on the civil bench, but always disavowed it. What can be more contrary to the ways of God than these their doings?

If they be such enemies to hardness of heart, although this groundless rigor proclaims it to be in themselves, they may yet learn or consider that hardness of heart hath a twofold acceptation in the Gospel. One, when it is in a good man taken for infirmity and imperfection, which was in all the apostles, whose weakness only, not utter want of belief, is called hardness of heart (Mark 16).[64] Partly for this hardness of heart, the imperfection and decay of man from original righteousness, it was that God suffered not divorce only, but all that which by civilians[65] is termed the "secondary law of nature and of nations." He suffered his own people to waste and spoil and slay by war, to lead captives, to be some masters, some servants, some to be princes, others to be subjects; he suffered propriety to divide all things by several possession, trade, and commerce, not without usury; in his commonwealth some to be undeservedly rich, others to be undeservingly poor. All which, till hardness of heart came in, was most unjust; whenas prime nature made us all equal, made us equal coheirs by common right and dominion over all creatures. In the same manner and for the same cause, he suffered divorce as well as marriage, our imperfect and degenerate condition of necessity requiring this law among the rest, as a remedy against

63. **and that under the Gospel:** i.e., it would be particularly arrogant and presumptuous to act so under the new law.

64. Mark 16.14: "Afterward he appeared unto the eleven as they sat at meat, and upbraided them with their unbelief and hardness of heart, because they believed not them which had seen him after he was raised."

65. **civilians:** students of civil law.

intolerable wrong and servitude above the patience of man to bear. Nor was it given only because our infirmity or (if it must be so called) hardness of heart could not endure all things, but because the hardness of another's heart might not inflict all things upon an innocent person, whom far other ends brought into a league of love and not of bondage and indignity.

If therefore we abolish divorce as only suffered for hardness of heart, we may as well abolish the whole law of nations, as only suffered for the same cause; it being shown us by Saint Paul (1 Cor. 6[.7]) that the very seeking of a man's right by law, and at the hands of a worldly magistrate, is not without the hardness of our hearts: "For why do ye not rather take wrong," saith he, "why suffer ye not rather yourselves to be defrauded?" If nothing now must be suffered for hardness of heart, I say the very prosecution of our right by way of civil justice can no more be suffered among Christians, for the hardness of heart wherewith most men pursue it. And that would next remove all our judicial laws, and this restraint of divorce also in the number, which would more than half end the controversy. But if it be plain that the whole juridical law and civil power is only suffered under the Gospel for the hardness of our hearts, then wherefore should not that which Moses suffered be suffered still by the same reason?

In a second signification, hardness of heart is taken for a stubborn resolution to do evil. And that God ever makes any law purposely to such, I deny. For he vouchsafes not to enter covenant with them but as they fortune to be mixed with good men and pass undiscovered, much less that he should decree an unlawful thing only to serve their licentiousness. But that God "suffers" this reprobate hardness of heart I affirm, not only in this law of divorce but throughout all his best and purest commandments. He commands all to worship in singleness of heart according to all his ordinances; and yet suffers the wicked man to perform all the rites of religion hypocritically and in the hardness of his heart. He gives us general statutes and privileges in all civil matters, just and good of themselves, yet suffers unworthiest men to use them, and by them to prosecute their own right, or any color of right, though for the most part maliciously, covetously, rigorously, revengefully. He allowed by law the discreet father and husband to forbid, if he thought fit, the religious vows of his wife or daughter (Num. 30[.3-8]), and in the same law suffered the hard-heartedness of impious and covetous fathers or husbands abusing this law to forbid their wives or daughters in their offerings and devotions of greatest zeal. If then God suffer hardness of heart equally in the best laws, as in this of divorce, there can be no reason that for this cause this law should be abolished.

But other laws, they object, may be well used, this never. How often shall I answer, both from the institution of marriage and from other general rules in scripture, that this law of divorce hath many wise and charitable ends besides the being suffered for hardness of heart (which is indeed no end, but an accident happening through the whole law), which gives to good men right, and to bad men (who abuse right under false pretences) gives only sufferance. Now although Christ express no other reasons here, but only what was suffered, it nothing follows that this law had no other reason to be permitted but for hardness of heart. The scripture seldom or never in one place sets down all the reasons of what it grants or commands, especially when it talks to enemies and tempters. St. Paul permitting marriage (1 Cor. 7[.2]) seems to permit even that also for hardness of heart only, lest we should run into fornication; yet no intelligent man thence concludes marriage allowed in the Gospel only to avoid an evil, because no other end is there expressed. Thus Moses of necessity suffered many to put away their wives for hardness of heart, but enacted the law of divorce doubtless for other good causes, not for this only sufferance. He permitted not divorce by law as an evil, for that was impossible to divine law, but permitted by accident the evil of them who divorced against the law's intention undiscoverably.

This also may be thought not improbably, that Christ, stirred up in his spirit against these tempting Pharisees, answered them in a certain form of indignation usual among good authors; whereby the question or the truth is not directly answered, but something which is fitter for them who ask to hear. So in the ecclesiastical stories, one demanding how God employed himself before the world was made, had answer, that he was making hell for curious questioners.[66] Another (and Libanius the Sophist, as I remember) asking in derision some Christian what the carpenter, meaning our Savior, was doing, now that Julian so prevailed, had it returned him, that the carpenter was making a coffin for the apostate.[67] So Christ, being demanded maliciously why Moses made the law of divorce, answers them in a vehement scheme, not telling them the cause why he made it, but what was fittest to be told them, that "for the hardness of their hearts" he suffered them to abuse it. And albeit Mark say not "he suffered you," but "to you he wrote this precept," Mark may be warrantably expounded by Matthew the larger. And whether he suffered or gave precept (being all one, as was heard), it changes not the trope of indignation, fittest account for such askers. Next, "for the hardness of your hearts to you he wrote this precept" infers not therefore for this cause only he wrote it, as was paralleled by other scriptures.

Lastly, it may be worth the observing that Christ, speaking to the Pharisees, does not say in general that for hardness of heart he gave this precept, but "you he suffered, and to you he gave this precept for your hardness of heart." It cannot be easily thought that Christ here included all the children of Israel under the person of these tempting Pharisees, but that he conceals wherefore he gave the better sort of them this law, and expresses by saying emphatically "To you" how he gave it to the worser, such as the Pharisees best represented, that is to

66. See, e.g., Augustine's *Confessions* 11.12.
67. See Theodoret, *Ecclesiasticae Historiae* 3.18.

say, for the hardness of your hearts (as indeed to wicked men and hardened hearts he gives the whole law and the Gospel also, to harden them the more). Thus many ways it may orthodoxally be understood how God or Moses suffered such as the demanders were, to divorce for hardness of heart. Whereas the vulgar expositor beset with contradictions and absurdities round, and resolving at any peril to make an exposition of it (as there is nothing more violent and boisterous than a reverend ignorance in fear to be convicted), rushes brutely and impetuously against all the principles both of nature, piety, and moral goodness; and in the fury of his literal expounding overturns them all.

["But from the beginning it was not so."] Not how from the beginning? Do they suppose that men might not divorce at all, not necessarily, not deliberately, except for adultery, but that some law (like canon law presently) attached them both before and after the flood, till stricter Moses came and with law brought license into the world? That were a fancy indeed to smile at. Undoubtedly as to point of judicial law, divorce was more permissive from the beginning before Moses than under Moses. But from the beginning (that is to say, by the institution in Paradise) it was not intended that matrimony should dissolve for every trivial cause, as you Pharisees accustom. But that it was not thus suffered from the beginning ever since the race of men corrupted and laws were made, he who will affirm must have found out other antiquities than are yet known. Besides we must consider now, what can be so as from the beginning, not only what should be so. In the beginning, had men continued perfect, it had been just that all things should have remained as they began to Adam and Eve. But after that the sons of men grew violent and injurious, it altered the lore of justice and put the government of things into a new frame. While man and woman were both perfect each to other, there needed no divorce; but when they both degenerated to imperfection, and ofttimes grew to be an intolerable evil each to other, then law more justly did permit the alienating of that evil which mistake made proper, than it did the appropriating of that good which nature at first made common. For if the absence of outward good be not so bad as the presence of a close evil, and that propriety, whether by covenant or possession, be but the attainment of some outward good, it is more natural and righteous that the law should sever us from an intimate evil than appropriate any outward good to us from the community of nature. The Gospel indeed, tending ever to that which is perfectest, aimed at the restorement of all things as they were in the beginning. And therefore all things were in common to those primitive Christians in the Acts, which Ananias and Sapphira dearly felt.[68] That custom also continued more or less till the time of Justin Martyr, as may be read in his second *Apology*, which might be writ after that act of communion perhaps some forty years above a hundred.[69] But who will be the man shall introduce this kind

68. See Acts 5.1–10.

69. See *Apologia I, Pro Christianis* 15.

of commonwealth, as Christianity now goes? If then marriage must be as in the beginning, the persons that marry must be such as then were; the institution must make good, in some tolerable sort, what it promises to either party. If not, it is but madness to drag this one ordinance back to the beginning, and draw down all other to the present necessity and condition, far from the beginning, even to the tolerating of extortions and oppressions. Christ only told us that from the beginning it was not so; that is to say, not so as the Pharisees manured[70] the business; did not command us that it should be forcibly so again in all points as at the beginning; or so at least in our intentions and desires, but so in execution, as reason and present nature can bear. Although we are not to seek, that the institution itself from the first beginning was never but conditional, as all covenants are: because thus and thus, therefore so and so; if not thus, then not so. Then moreover was perfectest to fulfill each law in itself; now is perfectest in this estate of things to ask of charity how much law may be fulfilled, else the fulfilling ofttimes is the greatest breaking. If any therefore demand which is now most perfection, to ease an extremity by divorce or to enrage and fester it by the grievous observance of a miserable wedlock, I am not destitute to say which is most perfection (although some who believe they think favorably of divorce, esteem it only venial to infirmity). Him I hold more in the way to perfection who forgoes an unfit, ungodly, and discordant wedlock, to live according to peace and love and God's institution in a fitter choice, than he who debars himself the happy experience of all godly, which is peaceful conversation in his family, to live a contentious and unchristian life not to be avoided, in temptations not to be lived in, only for the false keeping of a most unreal nullity, a marriage that hath no affinity with God's intention, a daring phantasm, a mere toy of terror awing weak senses, to the lamentable superstition of ruining themselves, the remedy whereof God in his law vouchsafes us. Which not to dare use, he warranting, is not our perfection, is our infirmity, our little faith, our timorous and low conceit of charity; and in them who force us, it is their masking pride and vanity, to seem holier and more circumspect than God. So far is it that we need impute to him infirmity, who thus divorces: since the rule of perfection is not so much that which was done in the beginning, as that which now is nearest to the rule of charity. This is the greatest, the perfectest, the highest commandment. . . .

[*In the rest of this section, Milton distinguishes between those who wish to divorce for fleeting or contingent causes and those who find themselves deprived of the ends of the institution of marriage for immutable causes. As in the* Doctrine and Discipline, *he argues that "fornication" is not limited to sexual infidelity but that it signifies a "constant alienation and disaffection of mind" between husband and wife.*]

70. **manured:** handled.

I COR. 7.10, ETC.

10. "And unto the married I command," etc.
11. "And let not the husband put away his wife."

[*Milton examines Paul's teaching on a Christian's divorcing an unbelieving spouse, and he argues that life with one unable or unwilling to fulfill the ends of marriage is worse than marriage to an infidel. In a coda at the end of the work, Milton, while deprecating "the weaker sort" of readers and teachers who rely on authority, supplies for their benefit arguments supporting his own from church fathers and reformers.*]

Introduction to Selections from *The Tenure of Kings and Magistrates*

The path of Milton's life in relation to English public affairs from the 1630s to the 1660s might be compared to the orbit of a comet that comes out of nowhere and completes a turn of compelling brilliance and apparent sway before receding into the interstellar distance. *Tenure of Kings and Magistrates* was published at the pivotal moment of Milton's eccentric orbit of civic pertinence, and if comets are indeed malignant to monarchs, his first regicide tract would seem to justify the celestial analogy. Biographers have assumed that its argument brought Milton to the attention of Oliver Cromwell and the Council of State because shortly after its publication he was appointed Secretary for Foreign Tongues and asked to reply to Charles's posthumous *Eikon Basilike*. Thereafter, "John Milton Englishman" became the brand author of the English Commonwealth, his name and nationality appearing above the titles of his works defending it. The increasing prominence of this public persona profoundly influenced Milton's conception of himself until the Restoration and continued to do so afterward, if we judge by his later masterpieces.

Politically, *Tenure* is Milton's most radical work. David Masson singles it out as unequivocal evidence of his complicity in "compassing or imagining" the death of Charles I and insists that it would certainly have cost Milton his life upon the return of Charles II had the public eye not been averted, or intentionally distracted, at the proper moment (6:170–92). One scarcely need read the pamphlet's full title to see Masson's point: *The Tenure of Kings and Magistrates: proving that it is lawful, and hath been held so through all ages, for any, who have the power, to call to account a tyrant or wicked king, and after due conviction, to depose and put him to death if the ordinary magistrate have neglected or denied to do it*. . . . Not until the nineteenth century did British editors begin including *Tenure* with Milton's collected works, and then they introduced it with an apology or condemned the pamphlet outright: "Enunciation of this elaborate and wicked title is quite enough to deter any from wasting time in the perusal of the treatise itself," said the Reverend James Graham in his 1870 edition of Milton's prose (230). One hundred years earlier, on the other side of the Atlantic, it had made a much different impression on John Adams and Thomas Jefferson, and along with other of Milton's works figured in the revolutionary transformation of the American colonies into the United States of America. Indeed, the proposition on which Milton's entire argument depends—that "all men naturally were born free" (p. 1028)—is one embraced and developed in the Declaration of Independence.

Milton's radical insistence that governmental authority derives from the people recapitulates a major development in his thought, one that originated in the divorce tracts' conception of marriage as society's most fundamental institution. His advocacy of divorce in 1643 invoked concepts new to his writings, of individual rights, equity, natural law, and the contingency of social bonds. It was written, after all, in the midst of an intense political debate on the propriety of violating one's allegiance to a bad king: "He who marries, intends as little to conspire his own ruin, as he that swears allegiance: and as a whole people is in proportion to an ill government, so is one man to an ill marriage" (*DDD*, p. 862). By comparing marriage to the bond between subject and ruler, Milton aimed to win over influential Presbyterians who in 1643 were intent on justifying Parliament's militant defiance of Charles I. The choice of rhetorical strategy was questionable at best, and Milton was publicly and harshly condemned by his former allies. He evidently bore this embarrassing episode in mind. The same Herbert Palmer who in August 1644 lashed Milton the divorcer in a sermon before Parliament had a year earlier published *Scripture and Reason*. In it, he supported the right to bear "defensive" arms against the king. Milton singles out *Scripture and Reason* in *Tenure* to illustrate the inconsistency and hypocrisy of the Presbyterians' position in 1649 by comparing it with more bellicose arguments they had made earlier in the decade.

On one crucial point, however, Presbyterian criticism of the effort to put Charles on trial seemed to make good sense. In the early 1640s, the full and frequent Long Parliament opposed Charles. Now, however, it was the Rump, that is, the Long Parliament purged (as of December 1648) of those who advocated compromise with Charles. According to Presbyterian arguments, the soldiers who purged Parliament were a group of private citizens lacking governmental authority, and the Rump, being the consequence of that illegal action, similarly lacked authority. It therefore could not bring Charles to account. But Milton in the first edition of *Tenure* argues that to remove a tyrant is an imperative of natural law and an inalienable right of every man, as the title to which the Reverend Graham so vehemently objected insists: "It is lawful for any, who have the power, to call to account a tyrant or a wicked king." The position is subject to abuse, obviously, and the second edition, published probably eight months after the first, retreats from it by addition. By then the political situation had changed greatly. A new government of dubious legitimacy and with many opponents was in place. It needed to shore up its support or at least undermine its opposition. The radical argument of the first edition remains intact, but the additions to it, as Martin Dzelzainis argues (xi–xix), especially the concluding list of quotations culled from the writings of revered reformers, support the more conservative conclusion that resistance to the magistrate properly comes only from within a duly elected government: "to do justice on a lawless king is to a private man unlawful, to an inferior magistrate lawful" (p. 1054). Perhaps after due consideration Milton wanted to back away from a position that he himself had come to see as too extreme. More likely he wanted to remind the Presbyterians to restrain their own opposition by citing the opinion of the authorities they most honored. Although our text follows the second edition, we indicate its additions to the first with brackets.

Our text is based on the copy of the second edition held in the Wrenn Library of the Harry Ransom Humanities Research Center, University of Texas, Austin, with reference to the copy of the first edition held in the Carl H. Pforzheimer Library in the Harry Ransom Humanities Research Center, Austin, Texas.

Selections from

THE TENURE OF KINGS AND MAGISTRATES

If men within themselves would be governed by reason and not generally give up their understanding to a double tyranny of custom[1] from without and blind affections within, they would discern better what it is to favor and uphold the tyrant of a nation. But being slaves within doors, no wonder that they strive so much to have the public state conformably governed to the inward vicious rule by which they govern themselves. For indeed none can love freedom heartily but good men; the rest love not freedom but license, which never hath more scope or more indulgence than under tyrants. Hence is it that tyrants are not often offended, nor stand much in doubt of bad men, as being all naturally servile. But in whom[2] virtue and true worth most is eminent, them they fear in earnest, as by right their masters; against them lies all their hatred and suspicion. Consequently, neither do bad men hate tyrants, but have been always readiest with the falsified names of *loyalty* and *obedience* to color over their base compliances.[3]

And although sometimes for shame, and when it comes to their own grievances, of purse especially, they would seem good patriots and side with the better cause, yet when others for the deliverance of their country, endued with fortitude and heroic virtue to fear nothing but the curse written against those "that do the work of the Lord negligently,"[4] would go on to remove not only the calamities and thraldoms of a people but the roots and causes whence they spring, straight these men and sure helpers at need, as if they hated only the miseries but not the mischiefs, after they have juggled and paltered with the world, bandied and borne arms against their king, divested him, disanointed him, nay, cursed him all over in their pulpits and their pamphlets to the engaging of sincere and real men beyond what is possible or honest to retreat from,

1. For similar attacks on custom, see *DDD* (pp. 857–58) and *Eikon* (pp. 1059, 1060).

2. **in whom:** those in whom. Milton claims that tyrants do not doubt the allegiance of bad men, however vicious, because bad men are intrinsically servile. Tyrants fear good men, because the virtuous are intrinsically self-governing.

3. The distinction between liberty and license, and its political application, is common in Milton's poetry and prose (e.g., *Sonnet 12*; *DDD*, pp. 859–60). His views reflect arguments developed in Aristotle's *Politics* and *Nichomachean Ethics* on the servility of those who lack virtue; conversely, the self-rule of the virtuous fits them for political sovereignty (Hawkes). Cp. *PL* 12.82–96.

4. Jer. 48.10. The marginal gloss in the second edition erroneously cites Jer. 48.19.

not only turn revolters from those principles which only could at first move them, but lay the stain of disloyalty and worse on those proceedings which are the necessary consequences of their own former actions, nor disliked by themselves, were they managed to the entire advantages of their own faction; not considering the while that he toward whom they boasted their new fidelity counted them accessory and, by those statutes and laws which they so impotently brandish against others, would have doomed them to a traitor's death for what they have done already.[5] 'Tis true, that most men are apt enough to civil wars and commotions as a novelty, and for a flash[6] hot and active; but through sloth or inconstancy and weakness of spirit, either fainting ere their own pretenses,[7] though never so just, be half attained, or through an inbred falsehood and wickedness, betray ofttimes to destruction with themselves men of noblest temper joined with them for causes whereof they in their rash undertakings were not capable.

If God and a good cause give them victory, the prosecution whereof for the most part inevitably draws after it the alteration of laws, change of government, downfall of princes with their families, then comes the task to those worthies which are the soul of that enterprise, to be sweat and labored out amidst the throng and noises of vulgar and irrational men. Some contesting for privileges, customs, forms, and that old entanglement of iniquity, their gibberish laws, though the badge of their ancient slavery.[8] Others who have been fiercest against their prince under the notion of a tyrant, and no mean incendiaries of the war against him, when God out of his providence and high disposal hath delivered him into the hand of their brethren, on a sudden and in a new garb of allegiance, which their doings have long since canceled, they plead for him, pity him, extol him, protest against those that talk of bringing him to the trial of justice, which is the sword of God, superior to all mortal things, in whose hand soever by apparent signs his testified will is to put it. But certainly if we consider who and what they are, on a sudden grown so pitiful,[9] we may conclude their pity can be no true and Christian commiseration but either levity and shallowness of mind or else a carnal admiring of that worldly pomp and greatness from whence they see him fallen; or rather lastly a dissembled and seditious pity, feigned of industry[10] to beget new discord. As for mercy, if it be to a tyrant, under which name they themselves have cited him so oft in the hearing of God, of angels, and the holy church assembled, and there charged him with the

5. The former allies of Parliament described in this paragraph are the Presbyterians. Milton insists that Charles would have had them drawn and quartered for their early opposition, regardless of their late change of course.
6. **for a flash:** for brief moment.
7. **pretenses:** assertions or claims of rights.
8. Milton refers to the Levellers, who, though they objected to the Norman influence over English law and the class system since the Conquest, nevertheless deemed Charles's trial illegal.
9. **pitiful:** i.e., full of pity.
10. **of industry:** on purpose, intentionally.

spilling of more innocent blood by far than ever Nero[11] did, undoubtedly the mercy which they pretend is the mercy of wicked men. And "their mercies," we read, "are cruelties,"[12] hazarding the welfare of a whole nation to have saved one whom so oft they have termed Agag,[13] and vilifying the blood of many Jonathans that have saved Israel;[14] insisting with much niceness on the unnecessariest clause of their Covenant[15] [wrested], wherein the fear of change and the absurd contradiction of a flattering hostility had hampered them, but not scrupling to give away for compliments, to an implacable revenge, the heads of many thousand Christians more.

Another sort there is who (coming in the course of these affairs to have their share in great actions above the form of law or custom, at least to give their voice and approbation) begin to swerve and almost shiver at the majesty and grandeur of some noble deed, as if they were newly entered into a great sin; disputing precedents, forms, and circumstances, when the commonwealth nigh perishes for want of deeds in substance, done with just and faithful expedition. To these I wish better instruction, and virtue equal to their calling; the former of which, that is to say instruction, I shall endeavor, as my duty is, to bestow on them; and exhort them not to startle from the just and pious resolution of adhering with all their strength and assistance to the present Parliament and army, in the glorious way wherein justice and victory hath set them—the only warrants through all ages, next under immediate revelation, to exercise supreme power—in those proceedings which hitherto appear equal to what hath been done in any age or nation heretofore justly or magnanimously.

Nor let them be discouraged or deterred by any new apostate scarecrows, who, under show of giving counsel, send out their barking monitories and *mementoes,* empty of aught else but the spleen of a frustrated faction.[16] For how can that pretended counsel be either sound or faithful, when they that give it see not, for madness and vexation of their ends lost, that those statutes and scriptures which both falsely and scandalously they wrest against their friends and associates, would, by sentence of the common adversary, fall first and heaviest upon their own heads. Neither let mild and tender dispositions be foolishly

11. Protestant social theorists typically construed civil obedience as a religious duty. The limiting case was whether the Christian subject owed obedience even to a tyrant such as *Nero.*

12. Milton here refers to Prov. 12.10.

13. **Agag:** impious Amalekite king "hewn to pieces" by Samuel (1 Sam. 15.33–34). The biblical books of Samuel and Kings, particularly as they concern the origin and early course of kingship in Israel, were often cited in early modern debates over monarchy.

14. *Jonathan,* after battling heroically against the Philistine enemy, remained unscathed upon his return despite orders from his father, King Saul, to have him killed on account of a ceremonial infraction (1 Sam. 14.1–45).

15. The Solemn League and Covenant (1643) was an agreement meant to uphold Parliament's rights. Its third article demanded that the sovereign's personal safety and authority be defended while Parliament sought civil liberty and the establishment of true religion.

16. William Prynne wrote *A Brief Memento to the Present Unparliamentary Junto* (1649); John Gauden, the self-proclaimed "faithful monitor," wrote *The Religious and Loyal Protestation* (1649).

softened from their duty and perseverance with the unmasculine rhetoric of any puling priest or chaplain—sent as a friendly letter of advice, for fashion sake in private, and forthwith published by the sender himself (that we may know how much of friend there was in it) to cast an odious envy upon them to whom it was pretended to be sent in charity.[17] Nor let any man be deluded by either the ignorance or the notorious hypocrisy and self-repugnance of our dancing divines, who have the conscience and the boldness to come with scripture in their mouths, glossed and fitted for their turns with a double contradictory sense, transforming the sacred verity of God to an idol with two faces, looking at once two several ways, and with the same quotations to charge others, which in the same case they made serve to justify themselves. For while the hope to be made classic and provincial lords led them on, while pluralities greased them thick and deep to the shame and scandal of religion more than all the sects and heresies they exclaim against[18]—then to fight against the king's person and no less a party of his Lords and Commons or to put force upon both the Houses, was good, was lawful, was no resisting of superior powers; they only were powers not to be resisted who countenanced the good and punished the evil.

But now that their censorious domineering is not suffered to be universal, truth and conscience to be freed, tithes and pluralities to be no more, though competent allowance provided and the warm experience of large gifts, and they so good at taking them—yet now to exclude and seize upon impeached members,[19] to bring delinquents without exemption to a fair tribunal by the common national law against murder, is now to be no less than Corah, Dathan, and Abiram.[20] He who but erewhile in the pulpits was a cursed tyrant, an enemy to God and saints, laden with all the innocent blood spilt in three kingdoms, and so to be fought against, is now, though nothing penitent or altered from his first principles, a lawful magistrate, a sovereign lord, the Lord's anointed, not to be touched, though by themselves imprisoned. As if this only were obedience, to preserve the mere useless bulk of his person, and that only in prison, not in the field, and to disobey his commands, deny him his dignity and office, everywhere to resist his power but where they think it only surviving in their own faction.

But who in particular is a tyrant cannot be determined in a general discourse, otherwise than by supposition. His particular charge and the sufficient proof of it must determine that; which I leave to magistrates, at least to the

17. Gauden (see previous note) appealed to the army to demonstrate masculine and Christian heroism by taking pity on Charles.

18. In Presbyterian church organization, parishes were grouped in "classes," and representative divines met in provincial assemblies. **pluralities:** multiple church livings held by a single, privileged cleric.

19. The army in 1647 impeached eleven members of Parliament suspected of conspiring with the queen.

20. These men rebelled against Moses; two of them were swallowed up by the earth, making them traditional examples of justly punished rebels (Num. 16.1–33).

uprighter sort of them and of the people, though in number less by many, in whom faction least hath prevailed above the law of nature and right reason, to judge as they find cause. But this I dare own as part of my faith, that if such a one there be, by whose commission whole massacres have been committed on his faithful subjects,[21] his provinces offered to pawn or alienation as the hire of those whom he had solicited to come in and destroy whole cities and countries[22]—be he king, or tyrant, or emperor, the sword of justice is above him, in whose hand soever is found sufficient power to avenge the effusion and so great a deluge of innocent blood. For if all human power to execute not accidentally but intendedly the wrath of God upon evildoers without exception be of God, then that power whether ordinary or, if that fail, extraordinary so executing that intent of God is lawful and not to be resisted.[23]

But to unfold more at large this whole question, though with all expedient brevity, I shall here set down from first beginning the original of kings, how and wherefore exalted to that dignity above their brethren; and from thence shall prove that, turning to tyranny, they may be as lawfully deposed and punished, as they were at first elected. This I shall do by authorities and reasons not learnt in corners among schisms and heresies, as our doubling divines are ready to calumniate, but fetched out of the midst of choicest and most authentic learning, and no prohibited authors, nor many heathen, but Mosaical, Christian, orthodoxal, and, which must needs be more convincing to our adversaries, presbyterial.

No man who knows aught can be so stupid to deny that all men naturally were born free, being the image and resemblance of God himself, and were by privilege above all the creatures born to command and not to obey; and that they lived so till from the root of Adam's transgression falling among themselves to do wrong and violence, and foreseeing that such courses must needs tend to the destruction of them all, they agreed by common league to bind each other from mutual injury and jointly to defend themselves against any that gave disturbance or opposition to such agreement. Hence came cities, towns, and commonwealths. And because no faith in all was found sufficiently binding, they saw it needful to ordain some authority that might restrain by force and punishment what was violated against peace and common right. This authority and power of self-defense and preservation being originally and naturally in every one of them and unitedly in them all, for ease, for order, and, lest each man should be his own partial judge, they communicated and derived either to one, whom for the eminence of his wisdom and integrity they chose above the rest, or to more than one whom they thought of equal deserving. The first was

21. Milton alludes to the Irish rebellion against English rule under the Long Parliament and the subsequent massacre of Protestants in Ulster (1641).

22. In exchange for military aid, Charles had offered to cede counties to the Irish and Scots.

23. As his introductory remarks draw to an end, Milton alludes to Rom. 12.2, which had been interpreted to vindicate those who take it upon themselves to execute justice when magistrates fail to perform that divinely appointed duty.

called a king, the other, magistrates: not to be their lords and masters (though afterward those names in some places were given voluntarily to such as had been authors of inestimable good to the people) but to be their deputies and commissioners, to execute, by virtue of their entrusted power, that justice which else every man by the bond of nature and of covenant must have executed for himself and for one another. And to him that shall consider well why among free persons one man by civil right should bear authority and jurisdiction over another, no other end or reason can be imaginable.

These for a while governed well and with much equity decided all things at their own arbitrement,[24] till the temptation of such a power left absolute in their hands, perverted them at length to injustice and partiality. Then did they, who now by trial had found the danger and inconveniences of committing arbitrary power to any, invent laws either framed or consented to by all, that should confine and limit the authority of whom they chose to govern them: that so[25] man, of whose failing they had proof, might no more rule over them, but law and reason abstracted as much as might be from personal errors and frailties: [while, as the magistrate was set above the people, so the law was set above the magistrate].[26] When this would not serve, but that the law was either not executed, or misapplied, they were constrained from that time, the only remedy left them, to put conditions and take oaths from all kings and magistrates at their first installment to do impartial justice by law: who, upon those terms and no other, received allegiance from the people, that is to say, bond or covenant to obey them in execution of those laws which they the people had themselves made or assented to. And this ofttimes with express warning, that if the king or magistrate proved unfaithful to his trust, the people would be disengaged.

They added also counselors and parliaments, nor to be only at his beck, but with him or without him, at set times, or at all times when any danger threatened, to have care of the public safety. Therefore saith Claudius Sesell, a French statesman, "The parliament was set as a bridle to the king";[27] which I instance rather, not because our English lawyers have not said the same long before, but because that French monarchy is granted by all to be a far more absolute than ours. That this and the rest of what hath hitherto been spoken is most true, might be copiously made appear throughout all stories heathen and Christian, even of those nations where kings and emperors have sought means to abolish all ancient memory of the people's right by their encroachments and usurpations. But I spare long insertions, appealing to the known constitutions of both the latest Christian empires in Europe, the Greek and German, besides the French, Italian, Aragonian, English, and not least the Scottish histories: not forgetting this only by the way, that William the Norman, though a conqueror,

24. **arbitrement:** free choice, the right or capacity to decide for oneself.
25. **that so:** i.e., they legislated these limitations on arbitrary power so that . . .
26. Cp. Cicero, *On the Laws* 3.1.
27. Claude de Seissel, *La Grand Monarchie de France* (1519).

and not unsworn at his coronation, was compelled the second time to take oath at St. Albans, ere the people would be brought to yield obedience.

It being thus manifest that the power of kings and magistrates is nothing else but what is only derivative, transferred and committed to them in trust from the people to the common good of them all, in whom the power yet remains fundamentally and cannot be taken from them without a violation of their natural birthright, and seeing that from hence Aristotle and the best of political writers have defined a king, him[28] who governs to the good and profit of his people and not for his own ends, it follows from necessary causes that the titles of sovereign lord, natural lord, and the like, are either arrogancies, or flatteries, not admitted by emperors and kings of best note, and disliked by the church both of Jews (Isa. 26.13) and ancient Christians, as appears by Tertullian and others. Although generally the people of Asia, and with them the Jews also, especially since the time they chose a king against the advice and counsel of God, are noted by wise authors much inclinable to slavery.[29]

Secondly, that to say, as is usual, the king hath as good right to his crown and dignity as any man to his inheritance, is to make the subject no better than the king's slave, his chattel, or his possession that may be bought and sold. And doubtless if hereditary title were sufficiently inquired, the best foundation of it would be found either but in courtesy or convenience. But suppose it to be of right hereditary, what can be more just and legal, if a subject for certain crimes be to forfeit by law from himself and posterity all his inheritance to the king, than that a king for crimes proportional should forfeit all his title and inheritance to the people? Unless the people must be thought created all for him, he not for them, and they all in one body inferior to him single, which were a kind of treason against the dignity of mankind to affirm.

Thirdly, it follows that to say kings are accountable to none but God, is the overturning of all law and government. For if they may refuse to give account, then all covenants made with them at coronation, all oaths are in vain and mere mockeries, all laws which they swear to keep made to no purpose. For if the king fear not God (as how many of them do not?), we hold then our lives and estates by the tenure of his mere grace and mercy, as from a God, not a mortal magistrate, a position that none but court parasites or men besotted would maintain. [Aristotle, therefore, whom we commonly allow for one of the best interpreters of nature and morality, writes in the fourth of his *Politics*, chap. 10, that "monarchy unaccountable is the worst sort of tyranny, and least of all to be endured by freeborn men."]

And [surely] no Christian prince, not drunk with high mind and prouder than those pagan Caesars that deified themselves, would arrogate so unreasonably above human condition, or derogate so basely from a whole nation of men

28. I.e., defined a king *as* him who governs . . .

29. E.g., Aristotle, *Politics* (7.7), John Calvin, *Institutes* (4.20.8).

his brethren, as if for him only subsisting, and to serve his glory; valuing them in comparison of his own brute will and pleasure, no more than so many beasts or vermin under his feet, not to be reasoned with, but to be trod on; among whom there might be found so many thousand men for wisdom, virtue, nobleness of mind, and all other respects but the fortune of his dignity, far above him. Yet some would persuade us that this absurd opinion was King David's because in the 51 Psalm he cries out to God, "Against thee only have I sinned"; as if David had imagined that to murder Uriah and adulterate his wife had been no sin against his neighbor, when as that law of Moses was to the king expressly not to think so highly of himself above his brethren.[30] David therefore by those words could mean no other than either that the depth of his guiltiness was known to God only or to so few as had not the will or power to question him, or that the sin against God was greater beyond compare than against Uriah. Whatever his meaning were, any wise man will see that the pathetical words of a psalm can be no certain decision to a point that hath abundantly more certain rules to go by.

How much more rationally spake the heathen king Demophoön, in a tragedy of Euripides, than these interpreters would put upon King David: "I rule not my people by tyranny, as if they were barbarians, but am myself liable, if I do unjustly, to suffer justly."[31] Not unlike was the speech of Trajan, the worthy emperor, to one whom he made general of his praetorian forces: "Take this drawn sword," saith he, "to use for me, if I reign well; if not, to use against me."[32] Thus Dion[33] relates. And not Trajan only, but Theodosius the younger,[34] a Christian emperor and one of the best, caused it to be enacted as a rule undeniable and fit to be acknowledged by all kings and emperors, that a prince is bound to the laws, that on the authority of law the authority of a prince depends, and to the laws ought submit. Which edict of his remains yet in the Code of Justinian (Bk. 1, title 24) as a sacred constitution to all the succeeding emperors.[35] How then can any king in Europe maintain and write himself accountable to none but God, when emperors in their own imperial statutes have written and decreed themselves accountable to law. And indeed where such account is not feared, he that bids a man reign over him above law, may bid as well a savage beast.

It follows, lastly, that since the king or magistrate holds his authority of the

30. Ps. 51.4; 2 Sam. 11.22–27; Deut. 17.20.

31. Euripides, *Heraclidae* 423–24.

32. *Trajan* was a Roman emperor (98–117 C.E.) who, along with Theodosius, was lauded for respecting the rule of law. The *praetorian* guard were the emperor's bodyguards.

33. **Dion:** also known as Dio Cassius (150–235), Roman historian. Only fragments of his eighty-volume history of Rome survive, though subsequent historians relay some of what is missing. This account of Trajan was widely reported.

34. Theodosius II, Byzantine emperor whose edict at Ravenna (429) declared the ruler's authority to be dependent upon the law.

35. *Justinian* was Roman emperor at Constantinople (527–65); he issued his law code in 529.

people, both originally and naturally for their good in the first place, and not his own, then may the people, as oft as they shall judge it for the best, either choose him or reject him, retain him or depose him, though no tyrant, merely by the liberty and right of freeborn men to be governed as seems to them best. This, though it cannot but stand with plain reason, shall be made good also by scripture (Deut. 17.14): "When thou art come into the land which the Lord thy God giveth thee, and shalt say I will set a king over me, like as all the nations about me." These words confirm us that the right of choosing, yea of changing their own government, is by the grant of God himself in the people. And therefore when they desired a king, though then under another form of government, and though their changing displeased him, yet he that was himself their king and rejected by them would not be a hindrance to what they intended, further than by persuasion, but that they might do therein as they saw good (1 Sam. 8). Only he reserved to himself the nomination of who should reign over them. Neither did that exempt the king, as if he were to God only accountable, though by his especial command anointed. Therefore "David first made a covenant with the Elders of Israel, and so was by them anointed king" [2 Sam 5.3]; 1 Chron. 11. And Jehoiada the priest, making Jehoash king, made a covenant between him and the people (2 Kings 11.17). Therefore when Roboam at his coming to the crown rejected those conditions which the Israelites brought him, hear what they answer him, "What portion have we in David, or inheritance in the son of Jesse? See to thine own house, David."[36] And for the like conditions not performed, all Israel before that time deposed Samuel, not for his own default but for the misgovernment of his sons.

But some will say to both these examples, it was evilly done. I answer that not the latter, because it was expressly allowed them in the law to set up a king if they pleased; and God himself joined with them in the work, though in some sort it was at that time displeasing to him, in respect of old Samuel who had governed them uprightly. As Livy praises the Romans who took occasion from Tarquinius, a wicked prince, to gain their liberty, which to have extorted, saith he, from Numa, or any of the good kings before, had not been seasonable. Nor was it in the former example done unlawfully; for, when Roboam had prepared a huge army to reduce the Israelites, he was forbidden by the prophet, 1 Kings 12.24: "Thus saith the Lord: 'Ye shall not go up, nor fight against your brethren, for this thing is from me.'" He calls them their brethren, not rebels, and forbids to be proceeded against them, owning the thing himself, not by single providence but by approbation, and that not only of the act, as in the former example, but of the fit season also. He had not otherwise forbid to molest them. And those grave and wise counselors, whom Rehoboam[37] first advised with, spake no such thing as our old gray-headed flatterers now are wont: "Stand upon your

36. See 1 Kings 12.16. The northern kingdom rejected his government.

37. **Rehoboam:** the more common spelling of the name of the tyrannical king of Judah (previously spelled *Roboam*).

birthright, scorn to capitulate, you hold of God, not of them." For they knew no such matter, unless conditionally, but gave him politic counsel, as in a civil transaction.

Therefore kingdom and magistracy, whether supreme or subordinate, is [without difference] called a "human ordinance," 1 Pet. 2.13 etc., which we are there taught is the will of God we should [alike] submit to, so far as for the punishment of evildoers and the encouragement of them that do well. "Submit," saith he, "as free men." [But to any civil power unaccountable, unquestionable, and not to be resisted, no, not in wickedness and violent actions, how can we submit as free men?] "There is no power but of God," saith Paul, Rom. 13,[38] as much as to say, God put it into man's heart to find out that way at first for common peace and preservation, approving the exercise thereof; else it contradicts Peter, who calls the same authority an ordinance of man. It must be also understood of lawful and just power, else we read of great power in the affairs and kingdoms of the world permitted to the devil: for saith he to Christ, Luke 4.6, "All this power will I give thee and the glory of them, for it is delivered to me, and to whomsoever I will, I give it." Neither did he lie, or Christ gainsay what he affirmed, for in the thirteenth of the Revelation we read how the dragon gave to the beast "his power, his seat, and great authority," which beast so authorized most expound to be the tyrannical powers and kingdoms of the earth. Therefore Saint Paul in the fore-cited chapter tells us that such magistrates he means as are not a terror to the good but to the evil, such as bear not the sword in vain but to punish offenders and to encourage the good.[39]

If such only be mentioned here as powers to be obeyed, and our submission to them only required, then doubtless those powers that do the contrary are no powers ordained of God, and by consequence no obligation laid upon us to obey or not to resist them. And it may be well observed that both these apostles, whenever they give this precept, express it in terms not concrete but abstract, as logicians are wont to speak; that is, they mention the ordinance, the power, the authority before the persons that execute it; and what that power is, lest we should be deceived, they describe exactly. So that if the power be not such, or the person execute not such power, neither the one nor the other is of God, but of the devil, and by consequence to be resisted. From this exposition Chrysostom[40] also on the same place dissents not, explaining that these words were not written in behalf of a tyrant. And this is verified by David, himself a king, and likeliest to be author of the Psalm 94.20, which saith, "Shall the throne of iniquity have fellowship with thee?" And it were worth the knowing, since kings [in these days,] and that by scripture, boast the justness of their title by holding it immediately of God yet cannot show the time when God ever set on the throne

38. Along with 1 Pet. 2, Rom. 13.1–2 was often cited by Royalist apologists as scriptural authority for royal prerogative.

39. Rom. 13.4.

40. St. John Chrysostom, archbishop of Constantinople (c. 400) and prolific exegete.

them or their forefathers, but only when the people chose them; why by the same reason, since God ascribes as oft to himself the casting down of princes from the throne, it should not be thought as lawful and as much from God when none are seen to do it but the people, and that for just causes. For if it needs must be a sin in them to depose, it may as likely be a sin to have elected. And contrary, if the people's act in election be pleaded by a king as the act of God and the most just title to enthrone him, why may not the people's act of rejection be as well pleaded by the people as the act of God and the most just reason to depose him? So that we see the title and just right of reigning or deposing, in reference to God, is found in scripture to be all one, visible only in the people, and depending merely upon justice and demerit. Thus far hath been considered briefly the power of kings and magistrates, how it was and is originally the people's, and by them conferred in trust only to be employed to the common peace and benefit; with liberty therefore and right remaining in them to reassume it to themselves if by kings or magistrates it be abused, or to dispose of it by any alteration as they shall judge most conducing to the public good.[41]

We may from hence with more ease and force of argument determine what a tyrant is, and what the people may do against him. A tyrant, whether by wrong or by right coming to the crown, is he who, regarding neither law nor the common good, reigns only for himself and his faction. Thus St. Basil among others defines him.[42] And because his power is great, his will boundless and exorbitant, the fulfilling whereof is for the most part accompanied with innumerable wrongs and oppressions of the people—murders, massacres, rapes, adulteries, desolation, and subversion of cities and whole provinces, look how great a good and happiness a just king is, so great a mischief is a tyrant; as he the public father of his country, so this the common enemy. Against whom what the people lawfully may do, as against a common pest and destroyer of mankind, I suppose no man of clear judgment need go further to be guided than by the very principles of nature in him.

But because it is the vulgar folly of men to desert their own reason and shutting their eyes to think they see best with other men's, I shall show by such examples as ought to have most weight with us, what hath been done in this case heretofore. The Greeks and Romans, as their prime authors witness, held it not only lawful, but a glorious and heroic deed, rewarded publicly with statues and garlands, to kill an infamous tyrant at any time without trial. And but reason, that he who trod down all law, should not be vouchsafed the benefit of law. Insomuch that Seneca the tragedian brings in Hercules the grand suppressor of tyrants, thus speaking,

41. This concludes the general statement of Milton's case: that it belongs to the people to choose or depose their king for the common good. He now proceeds to elaborate on what makes a king a tyrant and thus subject to be deposed justly.

42. *St. Basil* the Great, bishop of Cappadocia (370–79). His definition of a tyrant also appears in Milton's *Commonplace Book* (Yale 1:453).

——— ——— *Victima haud ulla amplior*
Potest, magisque opima mactari Jovi
Quam Rex iniquus ——— ———
——— ——— There can be slain
No sacrifice to God more acceptable
Than an unjust and wicked king.[43] ——— ———

But of these I name no more, lest it be objected they were heathen, and come to produce another sort of men that had the knowledge of true religion. Among the Jews this custom of tyrant-killing was not unusual. First Ehud, a man whom God had raised to deliver Israel from Eglon, king of Moab, who had conquered and ruled over them eighteen years, being sent to him as an ambassador with a present, slew him in his own house.[44] But he was a foreign prince, an enemy, and Ehud besides had special warrant from God. To the first I answer, it imports not whether foreign or native. For no prince so native but professes to hold by law; which when he himself overturns, breaking all the covenants and oaths that gave him title to his dignity and were the bond and alliance between him and his people, what differs he from an outlandish king or from an enemy?[45]

For look how much right the king of Spain hath to govern us at all, so much right hath the king of England to govern us tyrannically. If he, though not bound to us by any league, coming from Spain in person to subdue us or to destroy us, might lawfully by the people of England either be slain in fight or put to death in captivity, what hath a native king to plead, bound by so many covenants, benefits, and honors to the welfare of his people; why he through the contempt of all laws and parliaments, the only tie of our obedience to him, for his own will's sake and a boasted prerogative unaccountable, after seven years warring and destroying of his best subjects, overcome, and yielded prisoner, should think to scape unquestionable as a thing divine, in respect of whom so many thousand Christians destroyed should lie unaccounted for, polluting with their slaughtered carcasses all the land over and crying for vengeance against the living that should have righted them? Who knows not that there is a mutual bond of amity and brotherhood between man and man over all the world?[46] Neither is it the English Sea that can sever us from that duty and relation: a

43. Seneca, *Hercules Furens* 2.922–24.

44. Judg. 3.12–23. Royalist authors knew that Ehud could be construed as a precedent and objected to it for reasons that Milton rehearses in the next sentence.

45. Milton questions the distinction drawn by constitutional theorists between two kinds of tyrants: tyrants by practice (duly appointed rulers who proceed to act tyrannically) and tyrants without title (usurpers or foreign conquerors). It was generally agreed that the first sort could be removed only by governmental authority, not by the common people or an inspired individual like Ehud. Theorists could not agree over which sort of tyrants the oppressors of Israel had been. Dzelzainis argues that Milton chose the story of Ehud as an example "precisely because of the pivotal place it occupied in the controversy over who may lawfully resist a tyrant" (xiii).

46. Cicero regularly argues for a general brotherhood among men on the basis of reason. See, e.g., *On the Nature of the Gods* 1.2.4, where he asserts that the only division in human society should be between rational men and tyrants.

straiter bond yet there is between fellow-subjects, neighbors, and friends. But when any of these do one to another so as hostility could do no worse, what doth the law decree less against them than open enemies and invaders? Or if the law be not present, or too weak, what doth it warrant us to less than single defense or civil war? And from that time forward the law of civil defensive war differs nothing from the law of foreign hostility. Nor is it distance of place that makes enmity, but enmity that makes distance. He therefore that keeps peace with me, near or remote, of whatsoever nation, is to me as far as all civil and human offices an Englishman and a neighbor. But if an Englishman, forgetting all laws, human, civil and religious, offend against life and liberty, to him offended and to the law in his behalf, though born in the same womb, he is no better than a Turk, a Saracen,[47] a heathen.

This is gospel, and this was ever law among equals; how much rather then in force against any king whatever, who in respect of the people is confessed inferior and not equal. To distinguish therefore of a tyrant by outlandish, or domestic, is a weak evasion. To the second that he was an enemy, I answer, "What tyrant is not?" Yet Eglon by the Jews had been acknowledged as their sovereign. They had served him eighteen years, as long almost as we our William the Conqueror, in all which time he could not be so unwise a statesman but to have taken of them oaths of fealty and allegiance, by which they made themselves his proper subjects, as their homage and present sent by Ehud testified. To the third, that he had special warrant to kill Eglon in that manner, it cannot be granted, because not expressed. 'Tis plain that he was raised by God to be a deliverer, and went on just principles such as were then and ever held allowable to deal so by a tyrant that could no[48] otherwise be dealt with.

Neither did Samuel, though a prophet, with his own hand abstain from Agag, a foreign enemy no doubt. But mark the reason: "As thy sword hath made women childless,"[49] a cause that by the sentence of law itself nullifies all relations. And as the law is between brother and brother, father and son, master and servant, wherefore not between king, or rather tyrant, and people? And whereas Jehu had special command to slay Jehoram, a successive and hereditary tyrant, it seems not the less imitable for that.[50] For where a thing grounded so much on natural reason hath the addition of a command from God, what does it but establish the lawfulness of such an act?[51] Nor is it likely that God, who had so many ways of punishing the house of Ahab, would have sent a subject against his prince, if the fact in itself, as done to a tyrant, had been of bad example. And

47. **Saracen:** archaic term for "Arab," often used simply to mean a nonbeliever.

48. The first edition reads "not."

49. 1 Sam. 15.33.

50. 2 Kings 9.1–2.

51. The position that reason alone can provide grounds enough for tyrannicide represents a sharp turn from Puritan voluntarism: "The individualistic, even anarchic nature of this claim should not be underestimated—nor should its secularism" (Dzelzainis xv).

if David refused to lift his hand against the Lord's anointed, the matter between them was not tyranny but private enmity, and David as a private person had been his own revenger, not so much the people's.[52] But when any tyrant at this day can show to be the Lord's anointed, the only mentioned reason why David withheld his hand, he may then but not till then presume on the same privilege.

We may pass therefore hence to Christian times. And first our Savior himself, how much he favored tyrants, and how much intended they should be found or honored among Christians, declares his mind not obscurely: accounting their absolute authority no better than Gentilism, yea, though they flourished it over with the splendid name of benefactors;[53] charging those that would be his disciples to usurp no such dominion, but that they who were to be of most authority among them should esteem themselves ministers and servants to the public. Matt. 20.25, "The princes of the Gentiles exercise lordship over them," and Mark 10.42, "They that seem to rule," saith he, either slighting or accounting them no lawful rulers, "but ye shall not be so, but the greatest among you shall be your servant." And although he himself were the meekest and came on earth to be so, yet to a tyrant we hear him not vouchsafe an humble word, but, "Tell that fox" (Luke 13).[54] [So far we ought to be from thinking that Christ and his gospel should be made a sanctuary for tyrants from justice, to whom his law before never gave such protection.] And wherefore did his mother, the Virgin Mary, give such praise to God in her prophetic song, that he had now by the coming of Christ cut down *dynastas*[55] or proud monarchs from the throne, if the church, when God manifests his power in them to do so, should rather choose all misery and vassalage to serve them, and let them still sit on their potent seats to be adored for doing mischief?

Surely it is not for nothing that tyrants by a kind of natural instinct both hate and fear none more than the true church and saints of God, as the most dangerous enemies and subverters of monarchy, though indeed of tyranny. Hath not this been the perpetual cry of courtiers and court prelates? Whereof no likelier cause can be alleged but that they well discerned the mind and principles of most devout and zealous men, and indeed the very discipline of church, tending to the dissolution of all tyranny. No marvel then if since the faith of Christ received, in purer or impurer times, to depose a king and put him to death for tyranny hath been accounted so just and requisite that neighbor kings have both upheld and taken part with subjects in the action. And Ludovicus Pius,[56] himself an emperor, and son of Charles the Great, being made judge (du Haillan

52. David's refusal to harm Saul (1 Sam. 24.5) was a mainstay of Royalist arguments that the people should be submissive to their rulers, however vicious.

53. Luke 22.25.

54. Luke 13.32. Jesus is referring to Herod.

55. **dynastas:** Milton is translating Luke 1.52, where Mary prophesies that her son will cast down great powers (Gk. *dynastas*) from their thrones.

56. **Ludovicus Pius:** Louis the Pious, Holy Roman emperor (814–40).

is my author) between Milegast, king of the Vultzes, and his subjects who had deposed him, gave his verdict for the subjects and for him whom they had chosen in his room. Note here that the right of electing whom they please is by the impartial testimony of an emperor in the people. For, said he, "A just prince ought to be preferred before an unjust, and the end of government before the prerogative."[57] And Constantinus Leo, another emperor, in the Byzantine Laws saith "that the end of a king is for the general good, which, he not performing, is but the counterfeit of a king."[58]

And to prove that some of our own monarchs have acknowledged that their high office exempted them not from punishment, they had the sword of St. Edward borne before them by an officer who was called Earl of the Palace, even at the times of their highest pomp and solemnities, to mind them, saith Matthew Paris, the best of our historians, that if they erred the sword had power to restrain them.[59] And what restraint the sword comes to at length, having both edge and point, if any skeptic will doubt, let him feel. It is also affirmed from diligent search made in our ancient books of law that the peers and barons of England had a legal right to judge the king, which was the cause most likely, for it could be no slight cause, that they were called his peers or equals. This however may stand immovable, so long as man hath to deal with no better than man, that if our law judge all men to the lowest by their peers, it should in all equity ascend also and judge the highest.

And so much I find both in our own and foreign story, that dukes, earls, and marquises were at first not hereditary, not empty and vain titles, but names of trust and office,[60] and with the office ceasing, as induces me to be of opinion, that every worthy man in Parliament (for the word baron imports no more) might for the public good be thought a fit peer and judge of the king, without regard had to petty caveats and circumstances, the chief impediment in high affairs and ever stood upon most by circumstantial men.[61] Whence doubtless our ancestors who were not ignorant with what rights either nature or ancient constitution had endowed them, when oaths both at coronation and renewed in Parliament would not serve, thought it no way illegal to depose and put to death their tyrannous kings. Insomuch that the Parliament drew up a charge against Richard the Second, and the Commons requested to have judgment decreed against him that the realm might not be endangered.[62] And Peter Martyr,

57. See Du Haillan, Bernard de Girard (1535–1610), *Histoire Générale des Rois de France* (Paris, 1576), 248.

58. Quoting from the *Eclogue* of Johann Leunclavius, *Juris Graceo-Romani,* issued in 740, toward the end of the reign of Leo III.

59. Matthew Paris (1200–1259), *Historia Maior* (London, 1644), 421, relates that the Earl of Chester carried the sword of King Edward the Confessor (1042–66) as a symbolic gesture of monarchical self-restraint.

60. Cp. Du Haillan, 163, 316.

61. **circumstantial men:** distinguished merely by the "pomp and circumstance" of their position (*OED*).

62. Cp. Holinshed, 3.512.

a divine of foremost rank, on the third of Judges approves their doings.[63] Sir Thomas Smith also a Protestant and a statesman, in his *Commonwealth of England,* putting the question whether it be lawful to rise against a tyrant, answers that the vulgar judge of it according to the event and the learned according to the purpose of them that do it.[64]

But far before these days, Gildas, the most ancient of all our historians, speaking of those times wherein the Roman Empire, decaying, quitted and relinquished what right they had by conquest to this island and resigned it all into the people's hands, testifies that the people thus re-invested with their own original right, about the year 446, both elected them kings whom they thought best (the first Christian British kings that ever reigned here since the Romans) and by the same right, when they apprehended cause, usually deposed and put them to death. This is the most fundamental and ancient tenure that any king of England can produce or pretend to, in comparison of which all other titles and pleas are but of yesterday. If any object that Gildas condemns the Britons for so doing, the answer is as ready, that he condemns them no more for so doing than he did before for choosing such; for saith he, "They anointed them kings, not of God, but such as were more bloody than the rest."[65] Next he condemns them not at all for deposing or putting them to death, but for doing it over hastily without trial or well examining the cause, and for electing others worse in their room.

Thus we have here both domestic and most ancient examples that the people of Britain have deposed and put to death their kings in those primitive Christian times. And to couple reason with example, if the Church in all ages, primitive, Romish, or Protestant, held it ever no less their duty than the power of their keys, though without express warrant of scripture, to bring indifferently both king and peasant under the utmost rigor of their canons and censures ecclesiastical, even to the smiting him with a final excommunion, if he persist impenitent; what hinders but that the temporal law both may and ought, though without a special text or precedent, extend with like indifference the civil sword, to the cutting off without exemption him that capitally offends, seeing that justice and religion are from the same God, and works of justice ofttimes more acceptable? Yet because that some lately with the tongues and arguments of malignant backsliders have written that the proceedings now in Parliament against the king are without precedent from any Protestant state or kingdom, the examples which follow shall be all Protestant and chiefly Presbyterian.[66]

63. *Peter Martyr,* or Pietro Martire Vermigli (1499–1562), Augustinian monk turned Reformation theologian. Milton refers to his commentary on Judges, chapter 3.

64. Smith, 1.5.

65. Cp. Habingdon's translation (1638) of the same passage: "Kings were anointed, not as God appointed, but such as in cruelty excelled others" (43).

66. Concluding the portion of his argument devoted to asserting the propriety of bringing tyrants to justice, Milton will now cite Presbyterian authorities to refute the claim that it is wrong to subject a king to lawful judgment.

In the year 1546, The Duke of Saxony, Landgrave of Hessen, and the whole Protestant league raised open war against Charles the Fifth, their emperor, sent him a defiance, renounced all faith and allegiance towards him, and debated long in council whether they should give him so much as the title of Caesar. Sleidan, Bk. 17.[67] Let all men judge what this wanted of deposing or of killing but the power to do it.

In the year 1559, the Scotch Protestants claiming promise of their Queen Regent for liberty of conscience, she answering that promises were not to be claimed of princes beyond what was commodious for them to grant, told her to her face in the Parliament then at Stirling that if it were so they renounced their obedience; and soon after betook them to arms (Buchanan, *Hist.*, Bk. 16).[68] Certainly, when allegiance is renounced, that very hour the king or queen is in effect deposed.

In the year 1564, John Knox, a most famous divine and the reformer of Scotland to the Presbyterian discipline, at a general assembly maintained openly in a dispute against Lethington,[69] the Secretary of State, that subjects might and ought execute God's judgments upon their king; that the fact of Jehu and others against their king, having the ground of God's ordinary command to put such and such offenders to death, was not extraordinary, but to be imitated of all that preferred the honor of God to the affection of flesh and wicked princes; that kings, if they offend, have no privilege to be exempted from the punishments of law more than any other subject: so that if the king be a murderer, adulterer, or idolater, he should suffer, not as a king, but as an offender; and this position he repeats again and again before them. Answerable was the opinion of John Craig, another learned divine, and that laws made by the tyranny of princes or the negligence of people, their posterity might abrogate, and reform all things according to the original institution of commonwealths. And Knox, being commanded by the nobility to write to Calvin and other learned men for their judgment in that question, refused, alleging that both himself was fully resolved in conscience and had heard their judgments and had the same opinion under handwriting of many the most godly and most learned that he knew in Europe, that if he should move the question to them again, what should he do but show his own forgetfulness or inconstancy? All this is far more largely in the *Ecclesiastic History Of Scotland*, Bk. 4,[70] with many other passages to this effect all

67. Milton cites Johann Philippson [Sleidan], *De Statu Religionis et Reipublicae Carolo V Caesare, Commentarii XXV Libris Comprehensi* (Strasburg, 1555).
68. Milton here and in subsequent citations refers to George Buchanan, *Rerum Scoticarum Historia* (Edinburgh, 1582). As sixteenth-century reformers venerated by the Presbyterians, Knox and Buchanan "could not be disowned," though their "radicalism was now likely to embarrass their seventeenth-century descendents" (Dzelzainis, xii).
69. William Maitland of Lethington (1528–73); what follows is an account of the debate between Maitland and Knox, in which Lethington defended Queen Mary's controversial decision to marry Henry Stuart Darnley.
70. John Knox, *History of the Reformation of the Church of Scotland* (London, 1644), which Milton paraphrases, more or less, throughout his account of the debate.

the book over, set out with diligence by Scotchmen of best repute among them at the beginning of these troubles, as if they labored to inform us what we were to do, and what they intended upon the like occasion.

And to let the world know that the whole church and Protestant state of Scotland in those purest times of reformation were of the same belief, three years after, they met in the field, Mary, their lawful and hereditary queen, took her prisoner yielding before fight, kept her in prison, and the same year deposed her. Buchan. *Hist.* Bk. 18.

And four years after that, the Scots, in justification of their deposing Queen Mary, sent ambassadors to Queen Elizabeth, and in a written declaration alleged that they had used toward her more lenity than she deserved; that their ancestors had heretofore punished their kings by death or banishment; that the Scots were a free nation, made king whom they freely chose, and with the same freedom unkinged him if they saw cause, by right of ancient laws and ceremonies yet remaining, and old customs yet among the Highlanders in choosing the head of their clans, or families; all which, with many other arguments, bore witness that regal power was nothing else but a mutual covenant or stipulation between king and people. Buch. *Hist.*, Bk. 20. These were Scotchmen and Presbyterians: but what measure then have they lately offered to think such liberty less beseeming us than themselves, presuming to put him upon us for a master whom their law scarce allows to be their own equal? If now then we hear them in another strain than heretofore in the purest times of their church, we may be confident it is the voice of faction speaking in them, not of truth and reformation. [Which no less in England than in Scotland, by the mouths of those faithful witnesses commonly called puritans and non-conformists, spake as clearly for the putting down, yea, the utmost punishing of kings, as in their several treatises may be read even from the first reign of Elizabeth to these times. Insomuch that one of them, whose name was Gibson,[71] foretold King James he should be rooted out and conclude his race if he persisted to uphold bishops. And that very inscription stamped upon the first coins at his coronation, a naked sword in a hand with these words, *Si mereor in me,* "Against me, if I deserve," not only manifested the judgment of that State, but seemed also to presage the sentence of divine justice in this event upon his son.[72]]

In the year 1581, the states of Holland in a general assembly at the Hague abjured all obedience and subjection to Philip, king of Spain, and in a declaration justify their so doing, for that by his tyrannous government, against faith so many times given and broken, he had lost his right to all the Belgic provinces; that therefore they deposed him and declared it lawful to choose another in his stead. Thuan. Bk. 74.[73] From that time to this, no state or kingdom in the world

71. James Gibson reportedly warned James in 1586 that he would share the fate of Jeroboam if he upheld bishops (Dzelzainis 25).

72. **his son:** Charles I.

73. Jacques-Auguste de Thou [Thuanus], *History of His Own Times* [*Historiarum sui Temporis*] (Geneva, 1620).

hath equally prospered. But let them remember not to look with an evil and prejudicial eye upon their neighbors walking by the same rule.[74]

But what need these examples to Presbyterians, I mean to those who now of late would seem so much to abhor deposing, whenas they to all Christendom have given the latest and the liveliest example of doing it themselves. I question not the lawfulness of raising war against a tyrant in defense of religion or civil liberty, for no Protestant church from the first Waldenses of Lyons and Languedoc[75] to this day but have done it round and maintained it lawful. But this I doubt not to affirm, that the Presbyterians, who now so much condemn deposing, were the men themselves that deposed the king, and cannot with all their shifting and relapsing wash off the guiltiness from their own hands. For they themselves by these their late doings have made it guiltiness and turned their own warrantable actions into rebellion. There is nothing that so actually makes a king of England as rightful possession and supremacy "in all causes both civil and ecclesiastical," and nothing that so actually makes a subject of England as those two oaths of allegiance and supremacy "observed without equivocating or any mental reservation."[76] Out of doubt then, when the king shall command things already constituted in church or state, obedience is the true essence of a subject, either to do, if it be lawful, or, if he hold the thing unlawful, to submit to that penalty which the law imposes, so long as he intends to remain a subject. Therefore when the people or any part of them shall rise against the king and his authority, executing the law in any thing established, civil or ecclesiastical, I do not say it is rebellion, if the thing commanded though established be unlawful, and that they sought first all due means of redress (and no man is further bound to law). But I say it is an absolute renouncing both of supremacy and allegiance, which in one word is an actual and total deposing of the king and the setting up of another supreme authority over them.

And whether the Presbyterians have not done all this and much more, they will not put me, I suppose, to reckon up a seven years' story fresh in the memory of all men. Have they not utterly broke the oath of allegiance, rejecting the king's command and authority sent them from any part of the kingdom whether in things lawful or unlawful? Have they not abjured the oath of supremacy by setting up the Parliament without the king, supreme to all their obedience, and though their vow and Covenant bound them in general to the Parliament, yet sometimes adhering to the lesser part of Lords and Commons

74. Having listed Presbyterian authorities who refuted the claim that monarchy was above the law, Milton moves to conclude his argument with persuasive force.

75. Milton's source of information about the Waldensians, a sect founded in the twelfth century by Peter Waldo of Lyons, was Pierre Gilles, *Histoire Ecclesiastique des Eglises Reformees* [*Ecclesiastical History of the Reformed Churches*] (Geneva, 1644). Cp. *Sonnet 18.* **Languedoc:** region of south-central France.

76. Milton quotes from "An act for the better discovering and repressing of popish recusants" (1606), drafted by James I. The Oaths of Supremacy and Allegiance acknowledging the supremacy of the king were originally instituted by Henry VIII for the detection and suppression of closet Catholicism.

that remained faithful, as they term it, and even of them, one while to the Commons without the Lords, another while to the Lords without the Commons? Have they not still declared their meaning, whatever their oath were, to hold them only for supreme whom they found at any time most yielding to what they petitioned? Both these oaths which were the straightest bond of an English subject in reference to the king, being thus broke and made void, it follows undeniably that the king from that time was by them in fact absolutely deposed, and they no longer in reality to be thought his subjects, notwithstanding their fine clause in the Covenant to preserve his person, crown, and dignity,[77] set there by some dodging casuist with more craft than sincerity to mitigate the matter in case of ill success and not taken, I suppose, by any honest man, but as a condition subordinate to every the least particle that might more concern religion, liberty, or the public peace.

To prove it yet more plainly that they are the men who have deposed the king, I thus argue. We know that king and subject are relatives, and relatives have no longer being than in the relation. The relation between king and subject can be no other than regal authority and subjection. Hence I infer, past their defending, that if the subject, who is one relative, take away the relation, of force he takes away also the other relative.[78] But the Presbyterians who were one relative, that is to say subjects, have for this seven years taken away the relation, that is to say the king's authority and their subjection to it. Therefore the Presbyterians for these seven years have removed and extinguished the other relative, that is to say the king, or to speak more in brief have deposed him; not only by depriving him the execution of his authority, but by conferring it upon others.

If then their oaths of subjection broken, new supremacy obeyed, new oaths and covenants taken, notwithstanding frivolous evasions, have in plain terms unkinged the king, much more than hath their seven years war not deposed him only, but outlawed him and defied him as an alien, a rebel to law, and enemy to the state—it must needs be clear to any man not averse from reason, that hostility and subjection are two direct and positive contraries, and can no more in one subject stand together in respect of the same king, than one person at the same time can be in two remote places. Against whom therefore the subject is in act of hostility, we may be confident that to him he is in no subjection; and in whom hostility takes place of subjection, for they can by no means consist together, to him the king can be not only no king, but an enemy.

So that from hence we shall not need dispute whether they have deposed him, or what they have defaulted towards him as no king, but show manifestly how much they have done toward the killing him. Have they not levied all these

77. See note 15.

78. Milton's position on relation differs from Satan's in *PR* (4.518–19): "The son of God I also am or was, / And if I was, I am; relation stands."

wars against him whether offensive or defensive (for defense in war equally offends, and most prudently beforehand)[79] and given commission to slay where they knew his person could not be exempt from danger? And if chance or flight had not saved him, how often had they killed him, directing their artillery without blame or prohibition to the very place where they saw him stand? Have they not [sequestered him, judged or unjudged, and] converted his revenue to other uses, detaining from him [as a grand delinquent] all means of livelihood, so that for them long since he might have perished or have starved? Have they not hunted and pursued him round about the kingdom with sword and fire? Have they not formerly denied to treat with him,[80] and their now recanting ministers preached against him as a reprobate incurable, an enemy to God and his church, marked for destruction, and therefore not to be treated with? Have they not besieged him and to their power forbidden him water and fire, save what they shot against him to the hazard of his life? Yet while they thus assaulted and endangered it with hostile deeds, they swore in words to defend it with his crown and dignity; not in order, as it seems now, to a firm and lasting peace or to his repentance after all this blood, but simply, without regard, without remorse, or any comparable value of all the miseries and calamities suffered by the poor people, or to suffer hereafter through his obstinacy or impenitence.

No understanding man can be ignorant that covenants are ever made according to the present state of persons and of things, and have ever the more general laws of nature and of reason included in them, though not expressed. If I make a voluntary covenant as with a man to do him good, and he prove afterward a monster to me, I should conceive a disobligement. If I covenant not to hurt an enemy, in favor of him and forbearance and hope of his amendment, and he after that shall do me tenfold injury and mischief to what he had done when I so covenanted and still be plotting what may tend to my destruction, I question not but that his after actions release me; nor know I covenant so sacred that withholds me from demanding justice on him.

Howbeit, had not their distrust in a good cause and the fast and loose of our prevaricating divines overswayed, it had been doubtless better not to have inserted in a covenant unnecessary obligations and words not works of a supererogating[81] allegiance to their enemy; no way advantageous to themselves had the king prevailed, as to their cost many would have felt, but full of snare and distraction to our friends; useful only, as we now find, to our adversaries, who under such a latitude and shelter of ambiguous interpretation have ever since been plotting and contriving new opportunities to trouble all again. How

79. The Presbyterians in Parliament had insisted that their campaign against Charles had been defensive. See note 90.

80. In January 1648, frustrated by the king's maneuvering, Parliament passed a resolution of "No More Addresses." By September, it reversed itself under political pressure and resumed negotiations. See note 86.

81. **supererogating:** beyond what is required or expected.

much better had it been and more becoming an undaunted virtue, to have declared openly and boldly whom and what power the people were to hold supreme; as on the like occasion Protestants have done before, and many conscientious men now in these times have more than once besought the Parliament to do, that they might go on upon a sure foundation and not with a riddling Covenant in their mouths, seeming to swear counter, almost in the same breath, allegiance and no allegiance; which doubtless had drawn off all the minds of sincere men from siding with them had they not discerned their actions far more deposing him than their words upholding him; which words made now the subject of cavillous[82] interpretations, stood ever in the Covenant, by judgment of the more discerning sort, an evidence of their fear, not of their fidelity.

What should I return to speak on, of those attempts for which the king himself hath often charged the Presbyterians of seeking his life, whenas in the due estimation of things they might without a fallacy be said to have done the deed outright? Who knows not that the king is a name of dignity and office, not of person? Who therefore kills a king, must kill him while he is a king. Then they certainly who by deposing him have long since taken from him the life of a king, his office, and his dignity, they in the truest sense may be said to have killed the king, nor only by their deposing and waging war against him (which besides the danger to his personal life, set him in the farthest opposite point from any vital function of a king) but by their holding him in prison, vanquished and yielded into their absolute and despotic power, which brought him to the lowest degradement and incapacity of the regal name.[83] I say not by whose matchless valor[84] next under God, lest the story of their ingratitude thereupon carry me from the purpose in hand, which is to convince them that they, which I repeat again, were the men who in the truest sense killed the king, not only as is proved before, but by depressing him their king far below the rank of a subject to the condition of a captive, without intention to restore him (as the Chancellor of Scotland[85] in a speech told him plainly at Newcastle) unless he granted fully all their demands, which they knew he never meant. Nor did they treat or think of treating with him, till their hatred to the army that delivered them, not their love or duty to the king, joined them secretly with men sentenced so oft for reprobates in their own mouths, by whose subtle inspiring they grew mad upon a most tardy and improper treaty.[86] Whereas if the whole bent of their actions had not been against the king himself, but [only] against

82. **cavillous:** hairsplitting.

83. In May 1646, Charles I surrendered to the Scots, who a year later released him to agents for Parliament, then controlled by Presbyterians.

84. Presumably Cromwell and the New Model Army.

85. In 1646, John Campbell, Earl of Loudon and Scottish Chancellor, negotiated with Charles, then confined at Newcastle-on-Tyne.

86. Negotiations for the Treaty of Newport took place between Parliamentary representatives and the king in 1648, from September to November, while Charles was held on the Isle of Wight. See note 80.

his evil counselors, as they feigned and published, wherefore did they not restore him all that while to the true life of a king, his office, crown, and dignity, when he was in their power and they themselves his nearest counselors. The truth, therefore, is both that they would not, and that indeed they could not without their own certain destruction, having reduced him to such a final pass as was the very death and burial of all in him that was regal, and from whence never king of England yet revived, but by the new reinforcement of his own party, which was a kind of resurrection to him.

Thus having quite extinguished all that could be in him of a king, and from a total privation clad him over, like another specifical thing,[87] with forms and habitudes destructive to the former, they left in his person, dead as to law and all the civil right either of king or subject, the life only of a prisoner, a captive, and a malefactor. Whom the equal and impartial hand of justice finding, was no more to spare than another ordinary man; not only made obnoxious[88] to the doom of law by a charge more than once drawn up against him and his own confession to the first article at Newport,[89] but summoned and arraigned in the sight of God and his people, cursed and devoted to perdition worse than any Ahab, or Antiochus,[90] with exhortation to curse all those in the name of God that made not war against him, as bitterly as Meroz was to be cursed that went not out against a Canaanitish king,[91] almost in all the sermons, prayers, and fulminations that have been uttered this seven years by those cloven tongues of falsehood and dissention, who now, to the stirring up of new discord, acquit him; and against their own discipline, which they boast to be the throne and scepter of Christ, absolve him, unconfound him—though unconverted, unrepentant, unsensible of all their precious saints and martyrs whose blood they have so oft laid upon his head. And now again with a new sovereign anointment can wash it all off, as if it were as vile and no more to be reckoned for than the blood of so many dogs in a time of pestilence, giving the most opprobrious lie to all the acted zeal that for these many years hath filled their bellies and fed

87. **specifical thing:** i.e., a different species or kind of thing. The terminology used in this sentence—*privation, specifical, forms, habitudes*—is scholastic. Milton claims that Charles has been deprived of the essence of kingship and all that remains of the former king is a prisoner devoid of his previous identity.

88. **obnoxious:** liable or subject.

89. "Whereas both Houses of the Parliament of England have been necessitated to undertake a war in their just and lawful defense." So read the preamble to the articles presented to Charles at Newport (see note 86). Charles agreed to it provisionally, on the condition that all other issues were completely settled.

90. **Ahab:** king of Israel (c. 869–850 B.C.E.) condemned by the prophet Elijah for permitting his wife's idolatry and the murder of Naboth for his vineyard (1 Kings 16–22). **Antiochus:** a Greek who ruled over the Jews (175–64 B.C.E.) and strove to wipe out their religion. A heroic resistance eventually defeated him and restored the Hebrew religion. Cp. the apocryphal book 1 Maccabees. Presbyterian preachers had once compared Charles to both Ahab and Antiochus.

91. The Song of Deborah says that Meroz's inhabitants are cursed "because they came not to the help of the Lord against the mighty" (Judg. 5.23), specifically Jabin the Canaanite king.

them fat upon the foolish people. Ministers of sedition, not of the gospel, who, while they saw it manifestly tend to civil war and bloodshed, never ceased exasperating the people against him; and now that they see it likely to breed new commotion, cease not to incite others against the people that have saved them from him, as if sedition were their only aim, whether against him or for him.

But God, as we have cause to trust, will put other thoughts into the people and turn them from giving ear or heed to these mercenary noisemakers of whose fury and false prophecies we have enough experience, and from the murmurs of new discord will incline them to hearken rather with erected minds to the voice of our supreme magistracy, calling us to liberty and the flourishing deeds of a reformed commonwealth; with this hope, that as God was heretofore angry with the Jews who rejected him and his form of government to choose a king,[92] so that he will bless us and be propitious to us who reject a king to make him only our leader and supreme governor, in the conformity, as near as may be, of his own ancient government; if we have at least but so much worth in us to entertain the sense of our future happiness, and the courage to receive what God vouchsafes us wherein we have the honor to precede other nations who are now laboring to be our followers.

For as to this question in hand what the people by their just right may do in change of government or of governor, we see it cleared sufficiently, besides other ample authority, even from the mouths of princes themselves. And surely they that shall boast, as we do, to be a free nation, and not have in themselves the power to remove or to abolish any governor supreme or subordinate, with the government itself upon urgent causes, may please their fancy with a ridiculous and painted freedom, fit to cozen babies; but are indeed under tyranny and servitude, as wanting that power which is the root and source of all liberty, to dispose and economize[93] in the land which God hath given them, as masters of family in their own house and free inheritance. Without which natural and essential power of a free nation, though bearing high their heads, they can in due esteem be thought no better than slaves and vassals born, in the tenure and occupation of another inheriting lord, whose government, though not illegal, or intolerable, hangs over them as a lordly scourge, not as a free government, and therefore to be abrogated.

How much more justly then may they fling off tyranny or tyrants, who being once deposed can be no more than private men, as subject to the reach of justice and arraignment as any other transgressors. And certainly if men, not to speak of heathen, both wise and religious, have done justice upon tyrants what way they could soonest, how much more mild and humane then is it, to give them fair and open trial? To teach lawless kings, and all who so much adore them, that not mortal man, or his imperious will, but justice is the only true

92. 1 Sam. 8.

93. **economize:** to act as the governor of a household (*OED*, citing this passage as the sole example).

sovereign and supreme majesty upon earth? Let men cease therefore out of faction and hypocrisy to make outcries and horrid things of things so just and honorable.

[Though perhaps till now no Protestant state or kingdom can be alleged to have openly put to death their king, which lately some have written and imputed to their great glory, much mistaking the matter: it is not, neither ought to be, the glory of a Protestant state never to have put their king to death; it is the glory of a Protestant king never to have deserved death.][94] And if the Parliament and Military Council do what they do without precedent, if it appear their duty, it argues the more wisdom, virtue, and magnanimity, that they know themselves able to be a precedent to others, who perhaps in future ages, if they prove not too degenerate, will look up with honor and aspire toward these exemplary and matchless deeds of their ancestors, as to the highest top of their civil glory and emulation. Which, heretofore, in the pursuance of fame and foreign dominion, spent itself vaingloriously abroad, but henceforth may learn a better fortitude—to dare execute highest justice on them that shall by force of arms endeavor the oppressing and bereaving of religion and their liberty at home, that no unbridled potentate or tyrant, but to his sorrow, for the future may presume such high and irresponsible license over mankind, to havoc and turn upside-down whole kingdoms of men as though they were no more in respect of his perverse will than a nation of pismires.[95]

As for the party called Presbyterian, of whom I believe very many to be good and faithful Christians though misled by some of turbulent spirit, I wish them earnestly and calmly not to fall off from their first principles nor to affect rigor and superiority over men not under them; not to compel unforcible things, in religion especially, which, if not voluntary, becomes a sin; nor to assist the clamor and malicious drifts of men whom they themselves have judged to be the worst of men, the obdurate enemies of God and his church: nor to dart against the actions of their brethren, for want of other argument, those wrested laws and scriptures thrown by prelates and malignants against their own sides, which though they hurt not otherwise, yet taken up by them to the condemnation of their own doings, give scandal to all men and discover[96] in themselves either extreme passion or apostasy. Let them not oppose their best friends and associates, who molest them not at all, infringe not the least of their liberties (unless they call it their liberty to bind other men's consciences), but are still seeking to live at peace with them and brotherly accord. Let them beware an old and perfect enemy, who, though he hope by sowing discord to make them his instruments, yet cannot forbear a minute the open threatening of his destined revenge upon them, when they have served his purposes. Let them fear therefore, if they be wise, rather what they have done already, than what re-

94. Dzelzainis sees in this passage a possible reference to Salmasius's *Defensio Regia*.
95. **pismires:** ants.
96. **discover:** reveal.

mains to do, and be warned in time they put no confidence in princes whom they have provoked, lest they be added to the examples of those that miserably have tasted the event.

Stories[97] can inform them how Christiern the Second, king of Denmark, not much above a hundred years past, driven out by his subjects and received again upon new oaths and conditions, broke through them all to his most bloody revenge, slaying his chief opposers when he saw his time, both them and their children invited to a feast for that purpose. How Maximilian dealt with those of Bruges,[98] though by mediation of the German princes reconciled to them by solemn and public writings drawn and sealed. How the massacre at Paris[99] was the effect of that credulous peace which the French Protestants made with Charles the Ninth, their king. And that the main visible cause which to this day hath saved the Netherlands from utter ruin was their final not believing the perfidious cruelty which, as a constant maxim of state, hath been used by the Spanish kings on their subjects that have taken arms and after trusted them, as no later age but can testify, heretofore in Belgia[100] itself and this very year in Naples.[101] And to conclude with one past exception though far more ancient, David[, whose sanctified prudence might be alone sufficient, not to warrant us only but to instruct us,] when once he had taken arms never after that trusted Saul, though with tears and much relenting he twice promised not to hurt him. These instances, few of many, might admonish them both English and Scotch not to let their own ends and the driving on of a faction betray them blindly into the snare of those enemies whose revenge looks on them as the men who first begun, fomented, and carried on, beyond the cure of any sound or safe accommodation, all the evil which hath since unavoidably befallen them and their king.

I have something also to the divines, though brief to what were needful; not to be disturbers of the civil affairs, being in hands better able and more belonging to manage them; but to study harder and to attend the office of good pastors, knowing that he whose flock is least among them hath a dreadful charge, not performed by mounting twice into the chair[102] with a formal preachment huddled up at the odd hours of a whole lazy week, but by incessant pains and watching, "in season and out of season," "from house to house" over the souls of whom they have to feed.[103] Which if they ever well considered, how little leisure would they find to be the most pragmatical sidesmen[104] of every popular

97. **Stories:** histories. Dzelzainis notes that most of the examples listed in this paragraph appear in de Thou, *History of His Own Times* 3.423–24. See note 73.

98. Maximilian I, Holy Roman emperor, cruelly put down an uprising by inhabitants of the city of Bruges in 1490.

99. The 1572 slaughter of Huguenots on St. Bartholomew's Eve.

100. **Belgia:** the Netherlands.

101. Despite a formal pledge not to, the Spaniards crushed a Neapolitan revolt in 1648.

102. **chair:** pulpit.

103. Milton quotes 2 Tim. 4.2 and Acts 20:20.

104. **sidesmen:** officious partisans.

tumult and sedition? And all this while are[105] to learn what the true end and reason is of the gospel which they teach, and what a world it differs from the censorious and supercilious lording over conscience. It would be good also they lived so as might persuade the people they hated covetousness, which, worse than heresy, is idolatry; hated pluralities and all kind of simony; left rambling from benefice to benefice like ravenous wolves seeking where they may devour the biggest. Of which if some well and warmly seated from the beginning be not guilty, 'twere good they held not conversation with such as are. Let them be sorry that being called to assemble about reforming the church, they fell to progging[106] and soliciting the Parliament, though they had renounced the name of priests, for a new settling of their tithes and oblations, and double lined[107] themselves with spiritual places of commodity beyond the possible discharge of their duty. Let them assemble in consistory with their elders and deacons, according to ancient ecclesiastical rule, to the preserving of church discipline, each in his several charge, and not a pack of clergymen by themselves to belly-cheer[108] in their presumptuous Sion, or to promote designs, abuse and gull the simple laity, and stir up tumult, as the prelates did, for the maintenance of their pride and avarice.

These things if they observe and wait with patience, no doubt but all things will go well without their importunities or exclamations; and the printed letters which they send subscribed with the ostentation of great characters and little moment[109] would be more considerable than now they are. But if they be the ministers of Mammon instead of Christ and scandalize his church with the filthy love of gain—aspiring also to sit the closest and the heaviest of all tyrants upon the conscience—and fall notoriously into the same sins whereof so lately and so loud they accused the prelates, as God rooted out those [wicked ones] immediately before, so will he root out them their imitators; and, to vindicate his own glory and religion, will uncover their hypocrisy to the open world and visit upon their own heads that "Curse ye Meroz," the very motto of their pulpits, wherewith so frequently, not as Meroz but more like atheists, they have blasphemed the vengeance of God and [traduced] the zeal of his people. [And that they be not what they go for, true ministers of the Protestant doctrine, taught by those abroad, famous and religious men who first reformed the church, or by those no less zealous who withstood corruption and the bishops here at home, branded with the name of Puritans and Nonconformists, we shall abound with testimonies to make appear: that men may yet more fully know the difference between Protestant divines and these pulpit-firebrands.

105. **are:** have yet.
106. **progging:** prodding.
107. **double lined:** crammed or stuffed.
108. **belly-cheer:** feast luxuriously, in this case at Sion College, the seat of the Presbyterian provincial assembly.
109. Milton contrasts the abundance of capital letters and poverty of substance in books published by Presbyterian divines.

[*In the section omitted Milton quotes from eminent Protestant reformers to support his claim that a monarch's authority derives from the people and that wicked rulers ought to be deposed by the people. The authorities he quotes include Martin Luther, John Calvin, Huldrich Zwingli, Martin Bucer, David Paraeus, John Knox, and Christopher Goodman.*]

These were the true Protestant divines of England, our fathers in the faith we hold. This was their sense, who for so many years laboring under prelacy, through all storms and persecutions kept religion from extinguishing and delivered it pure to us till there arose a covetous and ambitious generation of divines (for divines they call themselves) who, feigning on a sudden to be new converts and proselytes from episcopacy, under which they had long temporized, opened their mouths at length, in show against pluralities and prelacy, but with intent to swallow them down both; gorging themselves like harpies on those simonious places and preferments of their outed[110] predecessors, as the quarry for which they hunted, not to plurality only but to multiplicity; for possessing which they had accused them their brethren, and aspiring under another title to the same authority and usurpation over the consciences of all men.

Of this faction, diverse reverend and learned divines (as they are styled in the phylactery[111] of their own title page) pleading the lawfulness of defensive arms against this king in a treatise called *Scripture and Reason*, seem in words to disclaim utterly the deposing of a king.[112] But both the scripture and the reasons which they use draw consequences after them which, without their bidding, conclude it lawful. For if by scripture, and by that especially to the Romans,[113] which they most insist upon, kings, doing that which is contrary to St. Paul's definition of a magistrate, may be resisted, they may altogether with as much force of consequence be deposed or punished. And if by reason the unjust authority of kings "may be forfeited in part, and his power be reassumed in part, either by the parliament or people, for the case in hazard and the present necessity," as they affirm, p. 34, there can no scripture be alleged, no imaginable reason given that necessity continuing—as it may always, and they in all prudence and their duty may take upon them to foresee it—why in such a case they may not finally amerce him with the loss of his kingdom, of whose amendment they have no hope. And if one wicked action persisted in against religion, laws, and liberties may warrant us to thus much in part, why may not forty times as many tyrannies by him committed warrant us to proceed on restraining him till the restraint become total? For the ways of justice are exactest proportion. If for one trespass of a king it require so much remedy or satisfaction,

110. **harpies:** mythical monsters, rapacious plunderers; **simonious:** tainted by the practice of using religion for profit; **outed:** expelled.

111. **phylactery:** See *Tetrachordon,* note 11.

112. Herbert Palmer, *Scripture and Reason Pleaded for Defensive Arms* (London, 1643). Milton cites this text by page number later in the paragraph.

113. Rom. 13.1–2.

then for twenty more as heinous crimes, it requires of him twenty-fold, and so proportionably, till it come to what is utmost among men. If in these proceedings against their king they may not finish by the usual course of justice what they have begun, they could not lawfully begin at all. For this golden rule of justice and morality as well as of arithmetic, out of three terms which they admit, will as certainly and unavoidably bring out the fourth, as any problem that ever Euclid or Apollonius made good by demonstration.[114]

And if the Parliament, being undeposable but by themselves, as is affirmed, (pp. 37, 38), might for his whole life, if they saw cause, take all power, authority, and the sword out of his hand, which in effect is to unmagistrate him, why might they not, being then themselves the sole magistrates in force, proceed to punish him who being lawfully deprived of all things that define a magistrate, can be now no magistrate to be degraded lower but an offender to be punished? Lastly, whom they may defy and meet in battle, why may they not as well prosecute by justice? For lawful war is but the execution of justice against them who refuse law. Among whom if it be lawful, as they deny not (pp. 19, 20), to slay the king himself coming in front at his own peril, wherefore may not justice do that intendedly, which the chance of a defensive war might without blame have done casually, nay, purposely, if there it find him among the rest. They ask (p. 19), "By what rule of conscience or God a state is bound to sacrifice religion, laws, and liberties, rather than a prince, defending such as subvert them, should come in hazard of his life." And I ask by what conscience, or divinity, or law, or reason, a state is bound to leave all these sacred concernments under a perpetual hazard and extremity of danger, rather than cut off a wicked prince, who sits plotting day and night to subvert them.

They tell us that the law of nature justifies any man to defend himself, even against the king in person. Let them show us then why the same law may not justify much more a state or whole people to do justice upon him against whom each private man may lawfully defend himself; seeing all kind of justice done is a defense to good men, as well as a punishment to bad, and justice done upon a tyrant is no more but the necessary self-defense of a whole commonwealth. To war upon a king that his instruments may be brought to condign[115] punishment and thereafter to punish them the instruments, and not to spare only but to defend and honor him the author, is the strangest piece of justice to be called Christian, and the strangest piece of reason to be called human, that by men of reverence and learning, as their style imports them, ever yet was vented. They maintain in the third and fourth section[116] that a judge or inferior magistrate is

114. In arithmetic, *golden rule* refers to a method of finding an unknown number from three given numbers, where the first is in the same proportion to the second as the third is to the unknown fourth. Milton repeatedly presents the mathematical golden rule as an expression of proportion analogous to the golden rule of morality and justice. Cp. *Areop*, p. 956. *Euclid* (328–283 B.C.E.) and *Apollonius* of Perga (262?–190 B.C.E.) were pioneers in geometry.

115. **condign:** well deserved, completely appropriate.

116. Palmer, *Scripture and Reason*, 33–37.

anointed of God, is his minister, hath the sword in his hand, is to be obeyed by St. Peter's rule[117] as well as the supreme and without difference anywhere expressed: and yet will have us fight against the supreme till he remove and punish the inferior magistrate (for such were greatest delinquents) when as by scripture and by reason there can no more authority be shown to resist the one than the other; and altogether as much, to punish or depose the supreme himself, as to make war upon him till he punish or deliver up his inferior magistrates, whom in the same terms we are commanded to obey and not to resist.

Thus while they, in a cautious line or two here and there stuffed in, are only verbal against the pulling down or punishing of tyrants, all the scripture and the reason which they bring is in every leaf direct and rational to infer it altogether as lawful as to resist them. And yet in all their sermons, as hath by others been well noted, they went much further. For divines, if ye observe them, have their postures and their motions no less expertly and with no less variety than they that practice feats in the artillery-ground. Sometimes they seem furiously to march on, and presently march counter. By and by they stand, and then retreat, or if need be can face about, or wheel in a whole body with that cunning and dexterity as is almost unperceivable, to wind themselves by shifting ground into places of more advantage. And "Providence" only must be the drum, "Providence" the word of command that calls them from above, but always to some larger benefice, or acts[118] them into such or such figures and promotions. At their turns and doublings no men readier, to the right, or to the left; for it is their turns which they serve chiefly; herein only singular, that with them there is no certain hand right or left, but as their own commodity[119] thinks best to call it. But if there come a truth to be defended which to them and their interest of this world seems not so profitable, straight these nimble motionists can find no even legs to stand upon and are no more of use to reformation thoroughly performed and not superficially, or to the advancement of Truth (which among mortal men is always in her progress[120]), than if on a sudden they were struck maim and crippled. Which the better to conceal, or the more to countenance by a general conformity to their own limping, they would have scripture, they would have reason also, made to halt with them for company, and would put us off with impotent conclusions, lame and shorter than the premises.[121]

In this posture they seem to stand with great zeal and confidence on the wall of Sion, but like Jebusites, not like Israelites or Levites. Blind also as well as

117. 1 Pet. 2.13–14.

118. **acts:** impels, moves to action.

119. **commodity:** advantage, profit.

120. **progress:** onward march, journey.

121. Like Shakespeare before him (cp. *OTH* 2.1.161), Milton may have had in mind Quintilian, whose *Institutes of Oratory* were a staple of English schools: "The conclusions of clauses sometimes seem to halt or hang" (9.4.70).

lame, they discern not David from Adonibezek,[122] but cry him up for the Lord's anointed whose thumbs and great toes not long before they had cut off upon their pulpit cushions. Therefore he who is our only King, the Root of David, and whose Kingdom is eternal righteousness, with all those that war under him, whose happiness and final hopes are laid up in that only just and rightful Kingdom (which we pray incessantly may come soon, and in so praying wish hasty ruin and destruction to all tyrants), even he our immortal King and all that love him, must of necessity have in abomination these blind and lame defenders of Jerusalem, as the soul of David hated them, and forbid them entrance into God's house and his own.[123] But as to those before them which I cited first (and with an easy search, for many more might be added), as they there stand, without more in number, being the best and chief of Protestant divines, we may follow them for faithful guides and without doubting may receive them as witnesses abundant of what we here affirm concerning tyrants. And indeed I find it generally the clear and positive determination of them all (not prelatical, or of this late faction subprelatical) who have written on this argument, that to do justice on a lawless king is to a private man unlawful, to an inferior magistrate lawful.[124] Or if they were divided in opinion, yet greater than these here alleged, or of more authority in the church, there can be none produced.

If anyone shall go about by bringing other testimonies to disable these, or by bringing these against themselves in other cited passages of their books, he will not only fail to make good that false and impudent assertion of those mutinous ministers—that the deposing and punishing of a king or tyrant "is against the constant judgment of all Protestant divines" (it being quite the contrary),[125] but will prove rather what perhaps he intended not, that the judgment of divines, if it be so various and inconstant to itself, is not considerable or to be esteemed at all. Ere which be yielded, as I hope it never will, these ignorant asserters in their own art will have proved themselves more and more not to be Protestant divines (whose constant judgment in this point they have so audaciously belied) but rather to be a pack of hungry church-wolves, who in the steps of Simon Magus[126] their father, following the hot scent of double livings and pluralities, advowsons, donatives, inductions, and augmentations (though uncalled to the flock of Christ but by the mere suggestion of their bellies, like those priests of

122. **Adonibezek:** Lord of Bezek, a Canaanite king. He was defeated by the Israelites, who cut off his thumbs and big toes, the punishment he had inflicted on his prisoners. See Judg. 1.5–7.

123. See 2 Sam. 5.6–8.

124. Dzelzainis finds this conclusion, based on the second edition's citations from the greatest reformers, to be a departure from Milton's effort in the first edition to undermine the distinction between private citizen and public official. That is, Milton's original, more radical, and even anarchic position was that any individual citizen has the inalienable right to remove a tyrant from power.

125. Milton's quotation condenses a passage in Palmer, *Scripture and Reason,* 11.

126. Simon the magician (*Magus*) was rebuked by Peter for attempting to traffic in spiritual power (Acts 8). The offense of simony derives from his name.

Bel, whose pranks Daniel found out),[127] have got possession or rather seized upon the pulpit as the stronghold and fortress of their sedition and rebellion against the civil magistrate. Whose friendly and victorious hand having rescued them from the bishops, their insulting lords, fed them plenteously, both in public and in private, raised them to be high and rich of poor and base, only suffered not their covetousness and fierce ambition (which as the pit that sent out their fellow locusts hath been ever bottomless and boundless)[128] to interpose in all things, and over all persons, their impetuous ignorance and importunity.]

127. **advowsons:** rights to appoint clergy to an endowed position; **donatives:** endowed positions that patrons can present on their own authority; **inductions:** formal introductions of clergymen to church offices and incomes; **augmentations:** increases in clerical stipends obtained through legal action. In the apocryphal *Bel and the Dragon,* Daniel exposes corrupt priests who hoard sacrifices that worshipers intended for their gods.

128. Rev. 9.1–3 describes "smoke like the smoke of a great furnace" rising from the "bottomless pit." Out of the smoke come locusts to torment humanity.

Frontispiece to *Eikon Basilike* (1644),
engraving by William Marshall (cp. p. 243).

Introduction to Selections from *Eikonoklastes*

Eikonoklastes, published in October 1649, is the first of several works that Milton wrote in his role as Secretary for Foreign Tongues of the interregnum Council of State. The Greek title positions the author as an iconoclast, or "image or idol breaker." Barbara Lewalski observes that among the idols Milton attempts to smash are "rote prayers, liturgical forms, the Solemn League and Covenant, kings, bishops, and the church of Rome" (2000, 270). The main idol, and the immediate occasion of the Council's command, is Charles I's posthumous and wildly popular *Eikon Basilike* (or "image of the king"), which followed hard upon Charles's execution on January 30, 1649, and which boasted an astounding thirty-five editions in English printed in England by the end of the year, not to mention numerous editions in Latin, Dutch, French, and German. In the *Eikon,* Charles presents himself (or rather the ghostwriter John Gauden presents him) as a saint and martyr, roles captured in William Marshall's famous frontispiece (opposite). This strategy's resounding success, like the shocked response to the public execution, complicated matters for the nascent interregnum government. Turning to Milton, no doubt impressed by the persuasive power of *The Tenure of Kings and Magistrates,* the Council hoped to blunt the force of *Eikon Basilike* and mold public opinion in its favor.

Milton was in the unenviable position of not merely arguing against but impugning the character of a dead man (to say nothing of a martyr). His response, as he writes, is to treat Charles "as in his book alive" (p. 1061). Milton labors to replace *Eikon*'s image of the king with his own image of Charles (see Loewenstein 1990), who now appears as a selfish, prevaricating, treasonous tyrant and vassal of Rome. The book's method is point-by-point, chapter-by-chapter refutation of Charles's, or Gauden's, work. The selections included here, the Preface and the peroration (or rhetorically charged conclusion), betray Milton's frustration and sense of injured merit as he observes what he calls "an inconstant, irrational, and image-doting rabble" (p. 1068) enchanted and deluded by the display of the king's name and image, turning against the "truth and wisdom" of Milton's party, which is already in danger of becoming, even at the beginning of the interregnum experiment, the "sole remainder" (p. 1066) of the faithful. Whatever the later verdict of history, and particularly of literary scholars, *Eikonoklastes* proved no match for the *Eikon Basilike,* seeing only two editions in the author's lifetime.

The text of our selection is based on a copy of the enlarged second edition in the British Library (1507/1350).

Selections from

EIKONOKLASTES

IN ANSWER TO A BOOK ENTITLED *EIKON BASILIKE, THE PORTRAITURE OF HIS SACRED MAJESTY IN HIS SOLITUDES AND SUFFERINGS*

The Preface

To descant on the misfortunes of a person fallen from so high a dignity, who hath also paid his final debt both to nature and his faults, is neither of itself a thing commendable nor the intention of this discourse. Neither was it fond ambition or the vanity to get a name, present or with posterity, by writing against a king: I never was so thirsty after fame nor so destitute of other hopes and means better and more certain to attain it. For kings have gained glorious titles from their favorers by writing against private men, as Henry the Eighth did against Luther,[1] but no man ever gained much honor by writing against a king, as not usually meeting with that force of argument in such courtly antagonists which to convince might add to his reputation. Kings most commonly, though strong in legions, are but weak at arguments; as they who ever have accustomed from the cradle to use their will only as their right hand, their reason always as their left. Whence, unexpectedly constrained to that kind of combat, they prove but weak and puny adversaries. Nevertheless, for their sakes who through custom, simplicity, or want of better teaching have not more seriously considered kings than in the gaudy name of majesty, and admire them and their doings as if they breathed not the same breath with other mortal men, I shall make no scruple to take up (for it seems to be the challenge both of him and all his party) to take up this gauntlet, though a king's, in the behalf of liberty, and the commonwealth.

And further, since it appears manifestly the cunning drift of a factious and defeated party[2] to make the same advantage of his book which they did before

1. Milton refers to Henry's *Assertio Septem Sacramentorum adversus Martinum Lutherum* (1521).

2. Milton refers not only to the Royalists but also to the Presbyterian party, which had earlier opposed Charles but which had late in the 1640s attempted to enter a treaty separately with him to the disadvantage of the Independent party represented by Cromwell's New Model Army. Excluded from the

of his regal name and authority, and intend it not so much the defense of his former actions as the promoting of their own future designs (making thereby the book their own rather than the king's, as the benefit now must be their own more than his), now the third time to corrupt and disorder the minds of weaker men by new suggestions and narrations, either falsely or fallaciously representing the state of things to the dishonor of this present government and the retarding of a general peace (so needful to this afflicted nation and so nigh obtained), I suppose it no injury to the dead, but a good deed rather to the living, if by better information given them or, which is enough, by only remembering them the truth of what they themselves know to be here[3] misaffirmed, they may be kept from entering the third time unadvisedly into war and bloodshed. For as to any moment[4] of solidity in the book itself, save only that a king is said to be the author, a name than which there needs no more among the blockish vulgar to make it wise, and excellent, and admired, nay to set it next the Bible, though otherwise containing little else but the common grounds of tyranny and popery dressed up, the better to deceive, in a new Protestant guise, and trimly garnished over, or as to any need of answering, in respect of staid and well-principled men, I take it on me as a work assigned rather than by me chosen or affected,[5] which was the cause both of beginning it so late, and finishing it so leisurely in the midst of other employments and diversions.

And though well it might have seemed in vain to write at all, considering the envy and almost infinite prejudice likely to be stirred up among the common sort against whatever can be written or gainsaid to the king's book, so advantageous to a book it is only to be a king's, and though it be an irksome labor to write with industry and judicious pains that which, neither weighed nor well read, shall be judged without industry or the pains of well-judging by faction and the easy literature of custom and opinion, it shall be ventured yet, and the truth not smothered but sent abroad in the native confidence of her single self, to earn, how she can, her entertainment in the world, and to find out her own readers; few perhaps, but those few of such[6] value and substantial worth, as truth and wisdom, not respecting numbers and big names, have been ever wont in all ages to be contented with.

And if the late king had thought sufficient those answers and defenses made

Long Parliament in Pride's Purge of December 1648, the Presbyterian party denounced the execution of the king. In *The Tenure of Kings and Magistrates,* Milton warns the Presbyterians that their rediscovered allegiance to Charles will do them no good.

3. **here:** in Charles's *Eikon Basilike.*
4. **moment:** particle.
5. In the *Second Defense* (p. 1096), Milton will claim that he was assigned the task of writing *Eikonoklastes*: "Not long afterwards there appeared a book attributed to the king, and plainly written with great malice against Parliament. Bidden to reply to this, I opposed to the *Eikon* the *Eikonoklastes,* not, as I am falsely charged, 'insulting the departed spirit of the king,' but thinking that Queen Truth should be preferred to King Charles."
6. **of such:** Although the 1650 edition prints "such of," the phrase has in our copy text been transposed by hand to read "of such," an emendation we have adopted.

for him in his lifetime, they who on the other side accused his evil government, judging that on their behalf enough also hath been replied, the heat of this controversy was in likelihood drawing to an end; and the further mention of his deeds, not so much unfortunate as faulty, had in tenderness to his late sufferings been willingly forborne, and perhaps for the present age might have slept with him unrepeated, while his adversaries, calmed and assuaged with the success of their cause, had been the less unfavorable to his memory. But since he himself, making new appeal to truth and the world, hath left behind him this book as the best advocate and interpreter of his own actions, and that his friends by publishing, dispersing, commending, and almost adoring it, seem to place therein the chief strength and nerves of their cause, it would argue doubtless in the other party great deficience and distrust of themselves not to meet the force of his reason in any field whatsoever, the force and equipage of whose arms they have so often met victoriously. And he who at the bar stood excepting against the form and manner of his judicature and complained that he was not heard,[7] neither he nor his friends shall have that cause now to find fault, being met and debated with in this open and monumental court of his own erecting; and not only heard uttering his whole mind at large, but answered—which to do effectually, if it be necessary that to his book nothing the more respect be had for being his, they of his own party can have no just reason to exclaim.

For it were too unreasonable that he, because dead, should have the liberty in his book to speak all evil of the Parliament; and they, because living, should be expected to have less freedom, or any for them, to speak home the plain truth of a full and pertinent reply. As he, to acquit himself, hath not spared his adversaries to load them with all sorts of blame and accusation, so to him, as in his book alive, there will be used no more courtship than he uses; but what is properly his own guilt, not imputed any more to his evil counselors (a ceremony used longer by the Parliament than he himself desired)[8] shall be laid here without circumlocutions at his own door. That they who from the first beginning or but now of late, by what unhappiness I know not, are so much affatuated[9] not with his person only but with his palpable faults, and dote upon his deformities, may have none to blame but their own folly if they live and die in such a strucken blindness, as next to that of Sodom[10] hath not happened to any sort of men more gross or more misleading. Yet neither let his enemies expect to find recorded here all that hath been whispered in the court or alleged openly of the king's bad actions, it being the proper scope of this work in hand

7. During his trial, Charles repeatedly denied the authority of his Parliamentary judges and claimed that a king was not subject to any earthly court.

8. In Chapter 15, not included in this edition, Milton quotes Charles's rejection in *Eikon Basilike* of the conventional pretense that opposition to a king's policies is opposition not to the king but to evil counselors.

9. **affatuated:** infatuated.

10. Destroyed with fire after failing to reform in response to repeated warnings (Gen. 19.24), *Sodom* was a common figure for spiritual blindness.

not to rip up and relate the misdoings of his whole life, but to answer only and refute the missayings of his book.

First, then, that some men (whether this were by him intended, or by his friends) have by policy accomplished after death that revenge upon their enemies which in life they were not able, hath been oft related. And among other examples we find that the last will of Caesar being read to the people, and what bounteous legacies he had bequeathed them, wrought more in that vulgar audience to the avenging of his death than all the art he could ever use to win their favor in his lifetime.[11] And how much their intent who published these over-late apologies and meditations of the dead king, drives to the same end of stirring up the people to bring him that honor, that affection, and by consequence that revenge to his dead corpse which he himself living could never gain to his person, it appears both by the conceited portraiture before his book,[12] drawn out to the full measure of a masking scene[13] and set there to catch fools and silly gazers, and by those Latin words after the end, *"Vota dabunt quæ bella negarunt,"* intimating that "what he could not compass by war, he should achieve by his meditations." For in words which admit of various sense the liberty is ours to choose that interpretation which may best mind us of what our restless enemies endeavor and what we are timely to prevent.

And here may be well observed the loose and negligent curiosity of those who took upon them to adorn the setting out of this book. For though the picture set in front would martyr him and saint him to befool the people, yet the Latin motto in the end, which they understand not, leaves him as it were a politic contriver to bring about that interest by fair and plausible words which the force of arms denied him. But quaint emblems and devices, begged from the old pageantry of some Twelfth-night's entertainment at Whitehall,[14] will do but ill to make a saint or martyr. And if the people resolve to take him sainted at the rate of such a canonizing, I shall suspect their calendar more than the Gregorian.[15] In one thing I must commend his openness who gave the title to this book, Εικὼν Βασιλικὴ, that is to say, *The King's Image;* and by the shrine

11. See Suetonius's *Lives of the Caesars* 83, for Caesar's generosity even to those who would murder him, an episode dramatized in Shakespeare's *Julius Caesar,* in which Mark Antony states that Caesar's will would lead the Romans to "go kiss dead Caesar's wounds" (3.2.140).

12. Milton refers here, and at the beginning of the next paragraph, to *Eikon Basilike*'s elaborate frontispiece, which depicts Charles as a saint and martyr at prayer.

13. **masking scene:** a tableau in a mask, or masque, an elaborate courtly entertainment typically celebrating the royal family as guarantors of universal order. Milton's own masques, *Arcades* and especially *A Masque Presented at Ludlow Castle,* stayed at arm's length from the usual ideology of the genre. In the body of his work, Milton accuses Charles of being a mere poet, one who trades in fiction: "I begun to think that the whole Book might perhaps be intended a peece of Poetrie. The words are good, the fiction smooth and cleanly; there wanted only Rime" (Yale 3:406).

14. Entertainments customarily marked the end of the Christmas season at court; Shakespeare's *Twelfth Night* is an example.

15. The *Gregorian* calendar, proclaimed by Pope Gregory XIII in 1582 and the standard today, was suspect in part because of its Roman Catholic association; England would continue to use the Julian calendar until 1752.

he dresses out for him certainly would have the people come and worship him. For which reason this answer also is entitled *Eikonoklastes,* the famous surname of many Greek emperors who, in their zeal to the command of God, after long tradition of idolatry in the church, took courage and broke all superstitious images to pieces.[16]

But the people, exorbitant and excessive in all their motions, are prone ofttimes not to a religious only, but to a civil kind of idolatry in idolizing their kings, though never more mistaken in the object of their worship; heretofore being wont to repute for saints those faithful and courageous barons who lost their lives in the field making glorious war against tyrants for the common liberty: as Simon de Montfort, Earl of Leicester, against Henry the Third; Thomas Plantagenet, Earl of Lancaster, against Edward the Second.[17] But now, with a besotted and degenerate baseness of spirit, except some few who yet retain in them the old English fortitude and love of freedom and have testified it by their matchless deeds, the rest, imbastardized from the ancient nobleness of their ancestors, are ready to fall flat and give adoration to the image and memory of this man, who hath offered at more cunning fetches to undermine our liberties, and put tyranny into an art, than any British king before him. Which low dejection and debasement of mind in the people, I must confess, I cannot willingly ascribe to the natural disposition of an Englishman, but rather to two other causes. First, to the prelates and their fellow-teachers, though of another name and sect,[18] whose pulpit stuff, both first and last, hath been the doctrine and perpetual infusion of servility and wretchedness to all their hearers; whose lives the type of worldliness and hypocrisy, without the least true pattern of virtue, righteousness, or self-denial in their whole practice. I attribute it next to the factious inclination of most men divided from the public by several ends and humors of their own.

At first no man less beloved, no man more generally condemned, than was the king; from the time that it became his custom to break Parliaments at home and either willfully or weakly to betray Protestants abroad, to the beginning of these combustions. All men inveighed against him; all men except court-vassals opposed him and his tyrannical proceedings; the cry was universal; and this full Parliament was at first unanimous in their dislike and protestation against his evil government. But when they who sought themselves and not the public began to doubt that all of them could not by one and the same way attain to

16. The name had been given to Leo III, who in 726 outlawed the use of images and image worship, in opposition to Pope Gregory II.

17. Polemicists during the Civil War replayed the thirteenth-century struggle between Simon de Montfort, Earl of Leicester, and Henry the Third. Royalists, such as Edward Chamberlayne in his *The Present War Parallel'd. Or, a briefe Relation of the five yeares Civil Warres of Henry the Third* (1647), painted Montfort and the barons as traitors. Parliamentary polemicists, such as George Walker in his *Anglo-Tyrannus, Represented in the parallel Reignes of Henry the Third and Charles King of England* (1650), portrayed the same figures as defenders of liberty.

18. Another shot at the Presbyterians (see note 2), branded by association with the Laudian high church party.

their ambitious purposes, then was the king, or his name at least, as a fit property, first made use of, his doings made the best of, and by degrees justified. Which begot him such a party as, after many wiles and strugglings with his inward fears, emboldened him at length to set up his standard against the Parliament. Whenas before that time all his adherents, consisting most of dissolute swordmen and suburb roisterers, hardly amounted to the making up of one ragged regiment strong enough to assault the unarmed House of Commons. After which attempt, seconded by a tedious and bloody war on his subjects, wherein he hath so far exceeded those his arbitrary violences in time of peace, they who before hated him for his high misgovernment, nay, fought against him with displayed banners in the field, now applaud him and extol him for the wisest and most religious prince that lived. By so strange a method amongst the mad multitude is a sudden reputation won, of wisdom by willfulness and subtle shifts, of goodness by multiplying evil, of piety by endeavoring to root out true religion.

But it is evident that the chief of his adherents never loved him, never honored either him or his cause, but as they took him to set a face upon their own malignant designs; nor bemoan his loss at all, but the loss of their own aspiring hopes, like those captive women whom the poet notes in his *Iliad* to have bewailed the death of Patroclus in outward show, but indeed their own condition:

Πάτρόκλον πρόφασιν, σφῶν δ'αὔτων κήδε' ἑκάστη.
Hom[er] *Iliad* 19.[302][19]

And it needs must be ridiculous to any judgment unenthralled, that they who in other matters express so little fear either of God or man should in this one particular outstrip all precisianism[20] with their scruples and cases and fill men's ears continually with the noise of their conscientious loyalty and allegiance to the king, rebels in the meanwhile to God in all their actions beside; much less that they whose professed loyalty and allegiance led them to direct arms against the king's person and thought him nothing violated by the sword of hostility drawn by them against him, should now in earnest think him violated by the unsparing sword of justice,[21] which undoubtedly so much the less in vain she bears among men, by how much greater and in highest place the offender. Else justice, whether moral or political, were not justice, but a false counterfeit of that impartial and godlike virtue. The only grief is that the head was not struck off to the best advantage and commodity of them that held it by

19. Milton quotes the narrator's comment, following Briseis's grief-stricken speech in Book 19, that she and her companions bewailed "Patroclus' fortunes in pretext, but in sad truth their own" (George Chapman's translation).
20. **precisianism:** a derogatory term for Puritanism.
21. Here, as in the *Tenure,* Milton ridicules Presbyterians for protesting the trial of Charles after they had taken up arms against him.

the hair—an ingrateful and perverse generation,[22] who having first cried to God to be delivered from their king, now murmur against God that heard their prayers, and cry as loud for their king against those that delivered them.

But as to the author of these soliloquies, whether it were undoubtedly the late king, as is vulgarly believed, or any secret coadjutor (and some stick not to name him),[23] it can add nothing, nor shall take from the weight, if any be, of reason which he brings. But allegations, not reasons, are the main contents of this book, and need no more than other contrary allegations to lay the question before all men in an even balance; though it were supposed that the testimony of one man in his own cause affirming, could be of any moment to bring in doubt the authority of a Parliament denying. But if these his fair-spoken words shall be here fairly confronted and laid parallel to his own far differing deeds, manifest and visible to the whole nation, then surely we may look on them who notwithstanding shall persist to give to bare words more credit than to open deeds, as men whose judgment was not rationally evinced and persuaded, but fatally stupefied and bewitched into such a blind and obstinate belief. For whose cure it may be doubted, not whether any charm, though never so wisely murmured, but whether any prayer can be available.

This however would be remembered and well noted, that while the king, instead of that repentance which was in reason and in conscience to be expected from him, without which we could not lawfully readmit him, persists here to maintain and justify the most apparent of his evil doings, and washes over with a court-fucus[24] the worst and foulest of his actions, disables and uncreates the Parliament itself, with all our laws and native liberties that ask not his leave, dishonors and attaints all Protestant churches not prelatical,[25] and what they piously reformed, with the slander of rebellion, sacrilege, and hypocrisy. They who seemed of late to stand up hottest for the Covenant,[26] can now sit mute and much pleased to hear all these opprobrious things uttered against their faith, their freedom, and themselves in their own doings made traitors to boot. The divines also, their wizards, can be so brazen as to cry "hosanna" to this his book,

22. Cp. Matt. 17.17.

23. John Gauden was Charles's ghostwriter; he was to be rewarded with the bishoprics of Exeter and Worcester.

24. **fucus:** a liquid cosmetic.

25. In the *Tenure,* Milton praises the nonprelatical churches (i.e., churches without bishops) of the continent for resisting tyranny and labels his backsliding Presbyterian contemporaries "subprelatical."

26. In 1643 the Scots and the English Parliament entered into the Solemn League and Covenant, agreeing to reform religion in England and Ireland on the Presbyterian model. Though motivated by shared opposition to Charles's attempts to impose episcopal church government on Scotland, the covenanters pledged to preserve not only "the Rights and Priviledges of the Parliament" but also "the Kings Majesties Person and Authority." After the Presbyterians' political influence was eclipsed by the Independents under Oliver Cromwell, they attempted to negotiate with the defeated king to advance their agenda. Although they had once fought against him, now they emphasized the clause concerning the preservation of the king's person.

which cries louder against them for no disciples of Christ, but of Iscariot;[27] and to seem now convinced with these withered arguments and reasons here, the same which in some other writings of that party and in his own former declarations and expresses,[28] they have so often heretofore endeavored to confute and to explode—none appearing all this while to vindicate church or state from these calumnies and reproaches but a small handful of men whom they defame and spit at with all the odious names of schism and sectarism. I never knew that time in England when men of truest religion were not counted sectaries.[29] But wisdom now, valor, justice, constancy, prudence—united and embodied to defend religion and our liberties both by word and deed against tyranny—is counted schism and faction.

Thus in a graceless age things of highest praise and imitation under a right name, to make them infamous and hateful to the people, are miscalled. Certainly, if ignorance and perverseness will needs be national and universal, then they who adhere to wisdom and to truth are not therefore to be blamed for being so few as to seem a sect or faction. But in my opinion it goes not ill with that people where these virtues grow so numerous and well joined together as to resist and make head against the rage and torrent of that boisterous folly and superstition that possesses and hurries on the vulgar sort. This therefore we may conclude to be a high honor done us from God and a special mark of his favor, whom he hath selected as the sole remainder,[30] after all these changes and commotions, to stand upright and steadfast in his cause, dignified with the defense of truth and public liberty; while others, who aspired to be the top of zealots[31] and had almost brought religion to a kind of trading monopoly, have not only by their late silence and neutrality belied their profession, but foundered themselves and their consciences to comply with enemies in that wicked cause and interest which they have too often cursed in others, to prosper now in the same themselves.

[*In twenty-eight long chapters, Milton answers the* Eikon Basilike *point for point, ridiculing Charles's pretensions to piety and love for his subjects. The selection here is the peroration that concludes Chapter 28 and the book. Quotation marks indicate passages from the* Eikon Basilike.]

27. The followers of Judas *Iscariot* are traitors.
28. **expresses:** royal communications less formal than *declarations.*
29. From the mid-1640s, Milton was increasingly sympathetic to the sects. Cp. Abdiel's defiant vaunt to Satan at the beginning of the War in Heaven: "My sect thou seest, now learn too late / How few sometimes may know, when thousands err" (*PL* 6.147–48).
30. Milton compares those remaining faithful to Parliament with the faithful "remnant" of Israel (Isa. 11.16).
31. Milton's use of the term *zealots* alludes to the faction of Jews who betrayed the chief priest during the siege of Titus in 70 C.E. (Josephus, *Wars of the Jews*).

He[32] would fain bring us out of conceit with the good "success" which God hath vouchsafed us. We measure not our cause by our success, but our success by our cause. Yet certainly in a good cause success is a good confirmation, for God hath promised it to good men almost in every leaf of scripture.[33] If it argue not for us, we are sure it argues not against us; but as much or more for us than ill success argues for them, for to the wicked God hath denounced ill success in all that they take in hand.[34]

He hopes much of those "softer tempers," as he calls them, and "less advantaged by his ruin, that their consciences do already" gripe them. 'Tis true, there be a sort of moody, hot-brained, and always unedified consciences, apt to engage their leaders into great and dangerous affairs past retirement, and then, upon a sudden qualm and swimming of their conscience, to betray them basely in the midst of what was chiefly undertaken for their sakes. Let such men never meet with any faithful Parliament to hazard for them; never with any noble spirit to conduct and lead them out; but let them live and die in servile condition and their scrupulous queasiness, if no instruction will confirm them. Others there be in whose consciences the loss of gain and those advantages they hoped for hath sprung a sudden leak. These are they that cry out the Covenant broken,[35] and to keep it better slide back into neutrality or join actually with incendiaries and malignants.[36] But God hath eminently begun to punish those, first in Scotland,[37] then in Ulster,[38] who have provoked him with the most hateful kind of mockery to break his Covenant under pretense of strictest keeping it; and hath subjected them to those malignants with whom they scrupled not to be associates. In God therefore we shall not fear what their false fraternity can do against us.

He seeks again with cunning words to turn our success into our sin, but might call to mind that the scripture speaks of those also who, "when God slew them, then sought him," yet did but "flatter him with their mouth, and lied to him with their tongues; for their heart was not right with him."[39] And there was one, who in the time of his affliction trespassed more against God: "This was that King Ahaz."[40]

32. **He:** Charles.

33. See, e.g., Ps. 1.1–3.

34. Ps. 1.6: "The way of the ungodly shall perish."

35. The London Presbyterian clergy had appealed against Parliament on January 24, 1649, to the "Covenant-keeping Citizens," and on February 24 the Scottish Commissioners in London had declared that they "detested the execution of the late King" and had charged Parliament with "breach of the Solemn League and Covenant" (Hughes's note).

36. **malignants:** Royalists.

37. A reference to the defeat of the Marquis of Montrose, Charles II's supporter, in April 1650.

38. The *Ulster* Scots, from Milton's perspective, shared in the August 1649 defeat of the Duke of Ormond by Parliamentary forces. Ormond had attempted to establish Charles II's authority in Ireland.

39. Milton here paraphrases Ps. 78.34–37, in response to Charles's invoking of Ps. 5.9: "For there is no faithfulness in their mouth; . . . they flatter with their tongue").

40. 2 Chron. 28.22.

He glories much in the forgiveness of his enemies. So did his grandmother at her death.[41] Wise men would sooner have believed him had he not so often told us so. But he hopes to erect "the trophies of his charity over us." And trophies of charity no doubt will be as "glorious" as trumpets before the alms of hypocrites, and more especially the trophies of such an aspiring charity as offers in his prayer to share victory with God's "compassion," which is over all his works. Such prayers as these may haply catch the people, as was intended. But how they please God is to be much doubted, though prayed in secret, much less written to be divulged. Which perhaps may gain him after death a short, contemptible, and soon fading reward; not what he aims at, to stir the constancy and solid firmness of any wise man or to unsettle the conscience of any knowing Christian (if he could ever aim at a thing so hopeless and above the genius of his cleric elocution),[42] but to catch the worthless approbation of an inconstant, irrational, and image-doting rabble; that like a credulous and hapless herd, begotten to servility and enchanted with these popular institutes of tyranny (subscribed with a new device of the king's picture at his prayers),[43] hold out both their ears with such delight and ravishment to be stigmatized and bored through in witness of their own voluntary and beloved baseness. The rest, whom perhaps ignorance without malice, or some error less than fatal, hath for the time misled, on this side sorcery or obduration, may find the grace and good guidance to bethink themselves and recover.

41. Like her grandson, Mary Queen of Scots had denied the jurisdiction of the court that tried her. Before her execution in 1587, she prayed for Elizabeth and her other enemies.

42. Milton surmised correctly that the *Eikon Basilike* was ghostwritten by a cleric (see n. 23).

43. Another reference to the frontispiece of Charles as a martyr at prayer.

INTRODUCTION TO SELECTIONS FROM *SECOND DEFENSE OF THE ENGLISH PEOPLE*

Milton was ordered by the Council of State to compose two major works of controversy before the *Second Defense.* In September 1649 came *Eikonoklastes* ("The Image Breaker"), aimed at discrediting *Eikon Basilike* (The King's Image), which appeared about a week after the execution of King Charles, its putative author, on January 30, 1649. Charles's maudlin self-portrait as a saintly martyr succeeded better with the home audience than Milton's fierce if factually accurate exposure of the late king's ill doing. Not only did the royal image remain unbroken but, by telling hard truths about the dead king, Milton incurred centuries of Royalist abuse—for having "bespatter[ed] the white robes of [Charles's] spotless life . . . with the dirty filth of his satirical pen" (G.S., *Epistle Dedicatory*).

Milton's second major effort on behalf of the Commonwealth was better received. *A Defense of the English People* appeared in February 1651, little more than a year after *A Defense of Kingship,* a massive tome by the renowned French scholar Claude de Saumaise. Writing in Latin for an elite European audience, Saumaise (Salmasius, his Latin pen name) ponderously asserted the divine right of kings and the odious impiety of regicide. Milton, relatively unknown, efficiently rebutted his charges and, mixing invective with argument in a manner reminiscent of Cicero's *Philippics,* attacked his opponent's integrity and mocked his manhood. "All Europe took part in the paper-war of these two great men," Isaac D'Israeli observed, adding that Milton "perfectly massacred Salmasius" (237).

More than three years separated Milton's first two major secretarial efforts from the *Second Defense of the English People,* which came out in May 1654. The attack it answered, *The Cry of the Royal Blood to Heaven, against the English Parricides* (hereafter, *The Cry*), was published in the summer of 1652 by Adriaan Vlacq, who also signed the prefatory epistle dedicating the book to Charles II. Although Milton was made aware of the fresh attack and asked to rebut it, he could not have read it himself, since earlier that year his blindness had become total. Compounding that trauma, his wife and fifteen-month-old son died in quick succession over the next few months. Under these circumstances it would have been surprising had Milton managed to produce a third major polemical work more quickly than he did. Yet he offers no personal excuses for the delay, claiming instead that it was owing the promise of a renewed assault by the infuriated giant Salmasius: "I thought it better to wait, so that I might keep my strength intact for the more formidable adversary." A smarting Salmasius seemed a worthier opponent than the reputed author of *The Cry,* that "fornicating priest" Alexander More (Parker 1:423).

Published anonymously, as Salmasius's *Defense of Kingship* had been, *The Cry* was attributed to More soon after its publication. His authorship was confirmed in 1653 and early 1654 by usually reliable government spies and by Milton's own continental correspondents (Parker 2:1026, n. 54). Yet it was Peter Du Moulin, an Anglican divine residing in Oxford, who composed *The Cry* and sent it to Salmasius to use as he saw fit. Though not the author, More was Salmasius's protégé and an intimate of his household. The mistaken attribution occurred because it was More, at Salmasius's behest, who saw to its publication. After penning the dedication and lacing it with threats of Salmasius's imminent revenge, More delivered the manuscript to Vlacq, arranging for the printer to take responsibility for the dedication. Ironically, that last dodge was easily ferreted out (the merely mercenary Vlacq had no reason to keep silent) and led to the misidentification of More as author of the entire work. Only after Milton had completed the *Second Defense* was he informed of the error and entreated not to publish his work. He refused and has long been blamed for stubbornness and unjustified cruelty to More. Yet it is difficult to sympathize with More, or to wish Milton's chastisement undone, given More's sniping dedication and servile instrumentality in publishing *The Cry.*

We also find it difficult to blame Milton for wishing to publish the entire work, complete with its attacks on the man who arranged for its publication and wrote but would not sign its dedication. As it happens, More in Latin is *Morus,* which also means "mulberry tree" and "fool," and invites puns with other near homonyms. Milton took full advantage. The rumors that had More seducing and impregnating Salmasius's serving girl (also fortunately named) were true, as had been those concerning Salmasius's domineering wife, which Milton exploited in the *First Defense.* Although not known for his sense of humor, as a satirist Milton could be wickedly funny, never more brilliantly than in this tract. Some may deem the humor low and obscene, but it is nonetheless marvelously inventive.

Still, there is more to the *Second Defense* than More, and he could have been left out had Milton wished. Indeed, because most of the virtuoso wit is lost in translation, the excerpts printed here largely omit Milton's rapid-fire slaps at More. Balancing the invective and sexual innuendo are noble panegyrics on Cromwell, Fairfax, Overton, Fleetwood, and Bradshaw, among others, which we have included for their abiding historical interest. The people Milton chooses to praise and the reasons for which he praises them have often been understood as a submerged petition to Cromwell, now Lord Protector, to protect freedom of conscience and reconcile with those who opposed his recent assumption of kinglike power. Robert Fallon has skeptically and we think properly questioned the claim that these laudatory portraits amount to a Miltonic critique of Cromwell. Yet readers have long recognized that worries about the future direction of the commonwealth haunt the panegyrics of this nonetheless undoubted loyalist "ready to place high hopes in Cromwell's semi-royal government" (Norbrook 18).

Overall, as with other of his tracts advocating political liberty (e.g., *Areopagitica, Tenure of Kings and Magistrates*), the *Second Defense* takes the form of a classical oration, a genre that, as Milton well knew, originated and flourished in free states, precisely in the face of threats to their liberty. It is Demosthenes of Athens and Cicero of "free Rome" that he emulates (*PL* 9.671), but through the power of print he imagines himself addressing not the citizens of Athens or the Roman Senate but "virtually all of Europe," indeed, "the entire assembly and council of all the most influential men, cities, and nations everywhere." David Loewenstein has suggested that the *Second Defense* "succeeds brilliantly" in its effective merger of "personal drama with its epic vision of history" (1990, 171). Yet this merger, however successful, left Milton open to the criticism that he was following the precedent of Charles in establishing an exaggerated, self-serving image of his own virtue (S. Fallon 2002, 119). Isolated by blindness and deaths in his immediate family, Milton may well have compensated by exaggerating the significance of his accomplishment. His accounts of his triumph over Salmasius, in both *Second Defense* and *Sonnet 22*, clearly reveal that he took solace in the reputation he had won as a champion of liberty. Also, the extended autobiographical passages in *Second Defense* that are the kernel of all subsequent Milton biographies suggest a powerful retrospective effort to shape his past as if it had found its culmination in his present triumph.

Leaving aside the question of whether, or to what degree, Milton overstates the righteous coherence of his life and the heroic sacrifice of his eyesight in opposing Salmasius, we must at least recognize that he nursed false hopes about the subsequent willingness of his countrymen to heed their champion. By the end of the 1650s, Milton had become a prophet without honor in his own country. The once celebrated defender of the English people was rejected as a "blind guide" and ridiculed for having "scribbled [his] eyes out" for "little or no purpose" (*No Blind Guides; Censure of the Rota* 4). Some who wrote against him were explicit and eager in their desire to see him drawn and quartered when Charles II took his father's throne.

Yet Milton survived to write his greatest work in the crucible of a defeat so crushing that we find it difficult to imagine him strong enough to persevere. Although he did not suffer public execution, the image he had created of himself as a prophet of liberty came under an iconoclastic attack more severe and sustained than any he had mounted against Charles. Still, by 1688, events in England vindicated his opposition to divine right monarchy, and in the following century his political orations would inspire republican revolutionaries in North America and France. His image and reputation survived the desertion of his countrymen, as he anticipated it would: "It will seem to posterity that a mighty harvest of glory was at hand, together with the opportunity for doing the greatest deeds, but that to this opportunity men were wanting. Yet there was not one wanting who could rightly counsel, encourage, and inspire, who could honor both the noble deeds and those who had done them, and make both deeds and doers illustrious with praises that will never die" (p. 1110).

Our text follows the translation in volume four, part one of the Yale edition of Milton's prose works.

Selections from

John Milton *ENGLISHMAN* *Second Defense* of The English People Against the Base Anonymous Libel, Entitled *The Cry of the Royal Blood to Heaven, against the English Parricides.*[1]

BY JOHN MILTON, ENGLISHMAN[2]

In the whole life and estate of man the first duty is to be grateful to God and mindful of his blessings, and to offer particular and solemn thanks without delay when his benefits have exceeded hope and prayer. Now, on the very threshold of my speech, I see three most weighty reasons for my discharge of this duty.[3] First that I was born at a time in the history of my country when her citizens, with preeminent virtue and a nobility and steadfastness surpassing all the glory of their ancestors, invoked the Lord, followed his manifest guidance, and after accomplishing the most heroic and exemplary achievements since the foundation of the world, freed the state from grievous tyranny and the church from unworthy servitude. Secondly, that when a multitude had sprung up which in the wonted manner of a mob venomously attacked these noble achievements, and when one man above all, swollen and complacent with his empty grammarian's conceit and the esteem of his confederates, had in a book of unparalleled baseness attacked us and wickedly assumed the defense of all tyrants, it was I and no other who was deemed equal to a foe of such repute and

1. The original Latin title of the tract to which Milton replies is *Regii Sanguinis Clamor ad Coelum, Adversus Parricidas Anglicanos,* published by Adriaan Vlacq, at The Hague (1652).
2. Milton regularly adjoins his nationality to his name in works intended for a foreign readership.
3. The rhetorical structure of *Second Defense,* like those of *Areopagitica* and the *Tenure of Kings and Magistrates,* is that of a classical oration. The political orators he names as models in *Of Education* are Demosthenes and Cicero, both of whom spoke in opposition to tyranny.

to the task of speaking on so great a theme, and who received from the very liberators of my country this role, which was offered spontaneously with universal consent, the task of publicly defending (if anyone ever did) the cause of the English people and thus of Liberty herself.[4] Lastly, I thank God that in an affair so arduous and so charged with expectation, I did not disappoint the hope or the judgment of my countrymen about me, nor fail to satisfy a host of foreigners, men of learning and experience, for by God's grace I so routed my audacious foe that he fled, broken in spirit and reputation.[5] For the last three years of his life, he did in his rage utter frequent threats, but gave us no further trouble, save that he sought the secret help of certain rogues and persuaded some bungling and immoderate panegyrists to repair, if they could, his fresh and unlooked-for disgrace. All this will shortly be made clear.

In the belief that such great blessings come from on high and that they should properly be recognized both out of gratitude to God and in order to secure favorable auspices for the work in hand, I held that they should be reverently proclaimed, as they are, at the outset. For who does not consider the glorious achievements of his country as his own? But what can tend more to the honor and glory of any country than the restoration of liberty both to civil life and to divine worship? What nation, what state has displayed superior fortune or stouter courage in securing for itself such liberty in either sphere? In truth, it is not in warfare and arms alone that courage shines forth, but she pours out her dauntless strength against all terrors alike, and thus those illustrious Greeks and Romans whom we particularly admire expelled the tyrants from their cities without other virtues than the zeal for freedom, accompanied by ready weapons and eager hands. All else they easily accomplished amid universal praise, applause, and joyful omens. Nor did they hasten so much towards danger and doubtful issues as towards the fair and glorious trial of virtue, towards distinctions, in short, and garlands, and the sure hope of immortality. For not yet was tyranny a sacred institution. Not yet had tyrants, suddenly become viceroys, indeed, and vicars of Christ, sheltered themselves behind the blind superstition of the mob, when they could not fortify themselves with their good will.[6] Not yet had the common people, maddened by priestly machinations, sunk to a barbarism fouler than that which stains the Indians, themselves the most stupid of mortals. The Indians indeed worship as gods malevolent demons whom they cannot exorcize, but this mob of ours, to avoid driving out its

4. The renowned French scholar Claude de Saumaise (1588–1653) or, in Latin, Claudius Salmasius, authored *Defensio Regia pro Carolo I* (*Defense of Kingship on behalf of Charles I*), published in November 1649. Though he studied philosophy and law, Salmasius was best known in the field of literary studies. He published numerous editions of classical authors and was especially celebrated for his discovery in 1606 of the unique Palatine manuscript of *The Greek Anthology.* The Council of State in January 1650 ordered Milton to pen a reply to his defense of monarchy.

5. Ill health occasioned Salmasius's departure from Stockholm. He died before finishing a reply to Milton's *Defense.*

6. Milton thus characterizes divine right polity, in which monarchs such as Charles I claimed that their right to rule derived directly from God.

tyrants, even when it could, has set up as gods over it the most impotent of mortals and to its own destruction has consecrated the enemies of mankind.[7] And against all this close array of long-held opinions, superstitions, slanders, and fears, more dreadful to other men than the enemy[8] himself, the English people had to contend. Being better instructed and doubtless inspired by heaven, they overcame all these obstacles with such confidence in their cause and such strength of mind and courage that although they were indeed a multitude in numbers, yet the lofty exaltation of their minds kept them from being a mob. Britain herself, which was once called a land teeming with tyrants, shall hereafter deserve the everlasting praise of all the ages as a country where liberators flourish. The English people were not driven to unbridled license by scorn for the laws or desecration of them. They were not inflamed with the empty name of liberty by a false notion of virtue and glory, or senseless emulation of the ancients. It was their purity of life and their blameless character which showed them the one direct road to true liberty, and it was the most righteous defense of law and religion that of necessity gave them arms. And so, trusting completely in God, with honorable weapons, they put slavery to flight.

Although I claim for myself no share in this glory, yet it is easy to defend myself from the charge of timidity or cowardice, should such a charge be leveled. For I did not avoid the toils and dangers of military service without rendering to my fellow citizens another kind of service that was much more useful and no less perilous. In time of trial I was neither cast down in spirit nor unduly fearful of envy or death itself. Having from early youth been especially devoted to the liberal arts, with greater strength of mind than of body, I exchanged the toils of war, in which any stout trooper might outdo me, for those labors which I better understood, that with such wisdom as I owned I might add as much weight as possible to the counsels of my country and to this excellent cause, using not my lower but my higher and stronger powers. And so I concluded that if God wished those men to achieve such noble deeds, He also wished that there be other men by whom these deeds, once done, might be worthily praised and extolled, and that truth defended by arms be also defended by reason—the only defense truly appropriate to man.[9] Hence it is that while I admire the heroes victorious in battle, I nevertheless do not complain about my own role. Indeed I congratulate myself and once again offer most fervent thanks to the heavenly bestower of gifts that such a lot has befallen me—a lot that seems much more a source of envy to others than of regret to myself. And yet, to no

7. Milton scorned the religious practices of Indians as reported in travel literature of his time, particularly the worship of deities that inflict misery. Cp. *DDD* (Yale 2:277–78): "worshipped like some Indian deity, when it can confer no blessing"; *Tetrachordon* (Yale 2:590): "the vermin of an Indian Catharist, which his fond religion forbids him to molest."

8. **enemy:** The Latin original is *hostis,* which means an enemy met in open battle, as opposed to the "close array" of customary bias and social pressure tactics.

9. Cp. *PL* 6.121–23: "Nor is it aught but just,/That he who in debate of truth hath won,/Should win in arms."

one, even the humblest, do I willingly compare myself, nor do I say one word about myself in arrogance, but whenever I allow my mind to dwell upon this cause, the noblest and most renowned of all, and upon the glorious task of defending the very defenders, a task assigned me by their own vote and decision,[10] I confess that I can scarcely restrain myself from loftier and bolder flights than are permissible in this exordium,[11] and from the search for a more exalted manner of expression. Indeed, in the degree that the distinguished orators of ancient times undoubtedly surpass me, both in their eloquence and in their style (especially in a foreign tongue, which I must of necessity use, and often to my own dissatisfaction),[12] in that same degree shall I outstrip all the orators of every age in the grandeur of my subject and my theme. This circumstance has aroused so much anticipation and notoriety that I do not now feel that I am surrounded, in the Forum or on the Rostra, by one people alone, whether Roman or Athenian, but that, with virtually all of Europe attentive, in session, and passing judgment, I have in the *First Defense* spoken out and shall in the *Second* speak again to the entire assembly and council of all the most influential men, cities, and nations everywhere. I seem now to have embarked on a journey and to be surveying from on high far-flung regions and territories across the sea, faces numberless and unknown, sentiments in complete agreement with mine. Here the manly strength of the Germans, hostile to slavery, meets my eye; there the lively and generous ardor of the Franks, worthy of their name; here the well-considered courage of the Spaniards; there the serene and self-controlled magnanimity of the Italians. Wherever liberal sentiment, wherever freedom, or wherever magnanimity either prudently conceals or openly proclaims itself, there some in silence approve, others openly cast their votes, some make haste to applaud, others, conquered at last by the truth, acknowledge themselves my captives.

Now, surrounded by such great throngs, from the Pillars of Hercules all the way to the farthest boundaries of Father Liber,[13] I seem to be leading home again everywhere in the world, after a vast space of time, Liberty herself, so long expelled and exiled. And, like Triptolemus of old, I seem to introduce to the nations of the earth a product from my own country, but one far more excellent than that of Ceres.[14] In short, it is the renewed cultivation of freedom

10. Milton refers here to his 1649 appointment as Secretary for Foreign Tongues, a position whose duties included replying to foreign censure of the new republic.

11. **exordium:** the opening of the five-part classical oration.

12. Milton writes in Latin, because it was the international language of his intended audience. The claim of dissatisfaction may seem disingenuous, given Milton's polish as a Latinist, but it comes in a comparison with the greatest classical orators speaking in their native tongues.

13. The imagined crowd stretches from the conventional western limit of Europe, Gibraltar (*the Pillars of Hercules*) to India as its eastern limit, the realm of Dionysus, identified as *Father Liber* by the Romans. Milton may resort to this less familiar name so that he can pun on *liberty.*

14. In Greek myth, Ceres sent Triptolemus to introduce the arts of agriculture to the world once the golden age had ended, so that humanity might sustain itself. In his final paragraph, Milton will claim that he has spread the word successfully and that "a mighty harvest of glory" is at hand if only the English will rise to the occasion.

and civic life that I disseminate throughout cities, kingdoms, and nations. But not entirely unknown, nor perhaps unwelcome, shall I return if I am he who disposed of the contentious satellite of tyrants, hitherto deemed unconquerable, both in the view of most men and in his own opinion.[15] When he with insults was attacking us and our battle array, and our leaders looked first of all to me, I met him in single combat and plunged into his reviling throat this pen,[16] the weapon of his own choice. And (unless I wish to reject outright and disparage the views and opinions of so many intelligent readers everywhere, in no way bound or indebted to me) I bore off the spoils of honor. That this is actually the truth and no empty boast finds ready proof in the following event—which I believe did not occur without the will of God—namely, that when Salmasius (or Salmasia,[17] for which of the two he was, the open domination of his wife, both in public and in private, had made it quite difficult to determine), when Salmasius had been courteously summoned by Her Most Serene Majesty, the Queen of the Swedes (whose devotion to the liberal arts and to men of learning has never been surpassed) and had gone thither, there in the very place where he was living as a highly honored guest, he was overtaken by my *Defence,* while he was expecting nothing of the kind. Nearly everyone read it immediately, and the Queen herself, who had been among the first to do so, having regard only for what was worthy of her, omitted nothing of her earlier kindness and generosity towards her guest. But for the rest, if I may report what is frequently mentioned and is no secret, so great a reversal of opinion suddenly took place that he who the day before yesterday had flourished in the highest favor now all but withered away. When he departed, not much later, with good leave, there was but one doubt in many minds, namely, whether he came more honored or went more despised. Nor in other places, it is certain, did less harm befall his reputation.

Yet I have not referred to all these matters with the intention of ingratiating myself with anyone (for there is no need), but only to show more copiously that which I undertook at the outset, for what reasons—and what weighty ones—I began by offering my most fervent thanks to almighty God. I would show that this proem,[18] in which I offer so many convincing proofs that, although by no means exempt from the disasters common to humanity, I and my interests are nevertheless under the protection of God—this proem, I say, will be a source of honor and credit to me. I would show that with respect to matters of well-nigh primary importance, relating to the immediate needs of my country and destined to be of the greatest service to civil life and religion, when I speak, not on behalf of one people nor yet one defendant, but rather for the entire human

15. The reference is to Salmasius, whose accomplishments and reputation were indeed formidable.

16. **pen:** The Latin original is *stilo,* which literally refers to a long, sharply pointed piece of metal for inscribing letters on a wax tablet. Milton also knew it as an Italian word for "dagger."

17. The feminine form of the name. Rumor had it that Salmasius's wife lorded it over him; Milton in the *First Defense* repeatedly mocked him for his effeminate slackness.

18. **proem:** introduction, preamble.

race against the foes of human liberty, amid the common and well-frequented assembly (so to speak) of all nations, I have been aided and enriched by the favor and assistance of God. Anything greater or more glorious than this I neither can, nor wish to, claim. Accordingly, I beg the same immortal God that, just as, depending on his familiar help and grace alone, I lately defended deeds of supreme courage and justice, so with the same or greater honesty, industry, fidelity, and even good fortune, I may be able to defend from undeserved insults and slanders both the doers of those deeds and myself, who have been linked with these great men for the purpose of ignominy, rather than honor. And if there is anyone who thinks that these attacks might better have been ignored, I for my part agree, provided that they were circulated among men who had an accurate knowledge of us. But how in the world will everyone else be convinced that the lies our enemy has told are not the truth? Yet when I shall have seen to it (as is proper) that Truth the avenger shall follow wherever calumny has gone before, I believe that men will cease to think wrongly of us, and that that creature will perhaps be ashamed of his lies. If he feel no shame, then at last we may properly ignore him.

Meanwhile I should more quickly have sped him a reply in accord with his merits, had he not protected himself up until now with false reports, announcing again and again that Salmasius was sweating at the anvil, forging new charges against us, always on the very point of publishing them. By these tactics he achieved but one result—that of postponing for a little while the payment of the penalty for slander, for I thought it better to wait, so that I might keep my strength intact for the more formidable adversary.[19] But with Salmasius, since he is dead, I think my war is over. How he died, I shall not say, for I shall not impute his death as a crime to him, as he imputed my blindness to me.[20] Yet there are those who even place the responsibility for his death on me and on those barbs of mine, too keenly sharpened.[21] While he fixed them more deeply in himself by his resistance, while he saw that the work which he had in hand was proceeding too slowly, that the time for reply had passed and the welcome accorded his work had died, when he realized that his reputation was gone, along with his good name, and finally that the favor of princes was diminished, so far as he was concerned, because of his poor defense of the royal cause,[22] they say that at last, after a three-year illness, worn away by mental distress rather than by bodily disease, he died. However that may be, if I must wage a posthumous war as well, and with a familiar enemy whose attacks I easily sustained when

19. Nearly two years had passed since *The Cry* was published, in the summer of 1652; here Milton explains the delay.
20. Salmasius had not impugned his blindness, but the preface to *The Cry* claimed that, when Salmasius did reply, he would give Milton "the castigation he deserves, a monster horrible, deformed, huge, and sightless."
21. "Salmasius died at the Spa, September 3, 1653; and, as controvertists are commonly said to be killed by their last dispute, Milton was flattered with the credit of destroying him" (Johnson 1:115).
22. Actually, the *Defense of Kingship* was favorably received by European royalty.

they were fierce and vigorous, there is no reason for me to fear his efforts when feeble and dying.

[*Milton distinguishes between kingship and tyranny, derides the authors of* Defense of Kingship *and* The Cry *for their anonymity, and names Alexander More as the author of the latter. He mocks him as a philanderer with a penchant for servant girls, particularly Pontia, a maid in the employ of Salmasius's wife. He characterizes Vlacq, the tract's printer and ostensible author of the prefatory letter addressed to Charles, as a profligate opportunist and a shill of Salmasius and More. He ridicules the letter for being of uncertain authorship and for its empty threats of a forthcoming reply by Salmasius. In the excerpt that follows, Milton responds to the attacks that have been made on him.*]

Let us now come to the charges against me. Is there anything in my life or character which he could criticize? Nothing, certainly. What then? He does what no one but a brute and barbarian would have done—casts up to me my appearance and my blindness.

"A monster, dreadful, ugly, huge, deprived of sight." Never did I think that I should rival the Cyclops in appearance.[23] But at once he corrects himself. "Yet not huge, for there is nothing more feeble, bloodless, and pinched." Although it ill befits a man to speak of his own appearance, yet speak I shall, since here too there is reason for me to thank God and refute liars, lest anyone think me to be perhaps a dog-headed ape or a rhinoceros, as the rabble in Spain, too credulous of their priests, believe to be true of heretics, as they call them.[24] Ugly I have never been thought by anyone, to my knowledge, who has laid eyes on me. Whether I am handsome or not, I am less concerned. I admit that I am not tall, but my stature is closer to the medium than to the small. Yet what if it were small, as is the case with so many men of the greatest worth in both peace and war? (Although why is that stature called small which is great enough for virtue?) But neither am I especially feeble, having indeed such spirit and such strength that when my age and manner of life required it, I was not ignorant of how to handle or unsheathe a sword, nor unpracticed in using it each day. Girded with my sword, as I generally was, I thought myself equal to anyone, though he was far more sturdy, and I was fearless of any injury that one man could inflict on another.[25] Today I possess the same spirit, the same strength, but not the same eyes. And yet they have as much the appearance of being uninjured, and are as clear and bright, without a cloud, as the eyes of men who see most keenly. In this respect alone, against my will, do I deceive. In my face, than which he says there is "nothing more bloodless," still lingers a color exactly

23. The insulting description of Milton derives from Vergil's account of Polyphemus, the Cyclops blinded by Odysseus (*Aen.* 3.658).

24. Heretics in Spanish writing and theater were often portrayed as monsters. Such representations were not unknown in England. English Protestants credulously repeated accounts of monstrous births delivered to heretic mothers in New England (Rumrich 1996, 103–4).

25. Milton practiced fencing as exercise and in *Of Education* included it as part of the curriculum.

opposite to the bloodless and pale, so that although I am past forty, there is scarcely anyone to whom I do not seem younger by about ten years. Nor is it true that either my body or my skin is shriveled. If I am in any way deceitful in respect to these matters, I should deserve the mockery of many thousands of my fellow-citizens, who know me by sight, and of not a few foreigners as well. But if this fellow is proved such a bold and gratuitous liar in a matter by no means calling for deceit, you will be able to draw the same conclusion as to the rest.

So much have I been forced to say about my appearance. Concerning yours, although I have heard that it is utterly despicable and the living image of the falseness and malice that dwell within you, I do not care to speak nor does anyone care to hear.[26] Would that it were equally possible to refute this brutish adversary on the subject of my blindness, but it is not possible. Let me bear it then. Not blindness but the inability to endure blindness is a source of misery. Why should I not bear that which every man ought to prepare himself to bear with equanimity, if it befall him—that which I know may humanly befall any mortal and has indeed befallen certain men who are the most eminent and virtuous in all history? Or shall I recall those ancient bards and wise men of the most distant past, whose misfortune the gods, it is said, recompensed with far more potent gifts, and whom men treated with such respect that they preferred to blame the very gods than to impute their blindness to them as a crime? The tradition about the seer Tiresias is well known. Concerning Phineus,[27] Apollonius sang as follows in the *Argonautica:*

> Nor did he fear Jupiter himself,
> Revealing truly to men the divine purpose.
> Wherefore he gave him a prolonged old age,
> But deprived him of the sweet light of his eyes.[28]

But God himself is truth! The more veracious a man is in teaching truth to men, the more like must he be to God and the more acceptable to him. It is impious to believe that God is grudging of truth or does not wish it to be shared with men as freely as possible. Because of no offence, therefore, does it seem that this man who was godlike and eager to enlighten the human race was deprived of his eyesight, as were a great number of philosophers. Or should I

26. The underlying premise, that outward appearance reflects intrinsic value, is Platonic (see *Phaedo* 81; *Timaeus* 90). It informs Adam and Raphael's discussion in *PL* 8 concerning the problematic beauty of Eve as well as their discussion of celestial dynamics.

27. In one tradition, Hera struck Tiresias blind when he affirmed Zeus's claim that women take more pleasure in sex than men. Zeus then compensated him with prophetic vision. Explanations for the blindness of Phineus are also multiple. In one version, Zeus blinds the legendary King of Salmydessus because he revealed divine secrets, but Milton resists the inference that he was punished for teaching the truth, suggesting that prophetic insight richly compensates for loss of vision.

28. In the original text, Milton quotes Apollonius's Greek (*Argonautica* 2.181–84) and provides a Latin translation.

mention those men of old who were renowned for statecraft and military achievements? First, Timoleon of Corinth, who freed his own city and all Sicily, than whom no age has borne a man greater or more venerated in his state.[29] Next, Appius Claudius, whose vote, nobly expressed in the Senate, delivered Italy from Pyrrhus, her mortal enemy, but not himself from blindness.[30] Thirdly, Caecilius Metellus, the Pontifex, who, while he saved from fire not the city alone but also the Palladium, the symbol of its destiny, and its innermost mysteries, lost his own eyes, although on other occasions certainly God has given proof that he favors such remarkable piety, even among the heathen.[31] Therefore what has befallen such a man should scarcely, I think, be regarded as an evil.

Why should I add to the list other men of later times, such as the famous Doge of Venice, Dandolo,[32] by far the most eminent of all, or Zizka, the brave leader of the Bohemians and the bulwark of the orthodox faith[33]? Why should I add theologians of the highest repute, Hieronymus Zanchius[34] and some others, when it is established that even Isaac[35] the patriarch himself—and no mortal was ever dearer to God—lived in blindness for many years, as did also (for a few years perhaps) Jacob,[36] his son, who was no less beloved by God. When, finally, it is perfectly certain from the divine testimony of Christ our Savior that the man who was healed by Him had been blind from the very womb, through no sin of his own or of his parents.[37]

For my part, I call upon Thee, my God, who knowest my inmost mind and all my thoughts, to witness that (although I have repeatedly examined myself on this point as earnestly as I could, and have searched all the corners of my life) I am conscious of nothing, or of no deed, either recent or remote, whose wickedness could justly occasion or invite upon me this supreme misfortune.

29. The Corinthian statesman and soldier was sent with a small force to Syracuse to help the natives resist the tyrant Dionysius II. Triumphant, he retired into venerated private life in Syracuse, losing his vision as he grew old.

30. In his old age, when blind, the former censor (312–8 B.C.E.) in a celebrated speech successfully attacked the proposals of Pyrrhus for peace (279/8 B.C.E.).

31. Lucius *Caecilius Metellus*, consul 251 B.C.E., pontifex maximus 243, died in 221. Hero of the First Punic War, in 241 he rescued the Palladium when the temple of Vesta was on fire and lost his sight as a result. A sacred image of Athena that legend traced back to Troy, the Palladium was thought to protect Rome from danger so long as it remained safe.

32. Milton includes the famed Doge of Venice Enrico Dandolo (c. 1108–1205) in his list of blind statesmen. Dandolo, who personally directed the Fourth Crusade in the sack of Constantinople, had poor sight but was not blind. Milton apparently accepted the spurious rumor that he was blinded by the Emperor of Byzantium.

33. John Zizka (1376–1424), Bohemian military leader and head of the Hussite forces during Catholic crusades against them. He lost his eyes in battle. As elsewhere, by "orthodox faith" (*orthodoxae fidei*) Milton means "Protestant." The Hussites followed John Huss (1373–1415), Bohemian supporter of the early reformer John Wyclifffe (1329–84).

34. In *Christian Doctrine,* Milton repeatedly cites the monk turned Calvinist theologian Jerome Zanchius (1516–90), though usually in disagreement (see, e.g., 1.14). He lost the power of sight in his old age.

35. For the blindness of Isaac, see Gen. 27.1.

36. For the blindness of Jacob, see Gen. 48.10.

37. John 9.1–41.

As for what I have at any time written (since the royalists think that I am now undergoing this suffering as a penance, and they accordingly rejoice), I likewise call God to witness that I have written nothing of such kind that I was not then and am not now convinced that it was right and true and pleasing to God. And I swear that my conduct was not influenced by ambition, gain, or glory, but solely by considerations of duty, honor, and devotion to my country. I did my utmost not only to free my country, but also to free the church. Hence, when the business of replying to the royal defense had been officially assigned to me, and at that same time I was afflicted at once by ill health[38] and the virtual loss of my remaining eye, and the doctors were making learned predictions that if I should undertake this task, I would shortly lose both eyes, I was not in the least deterred by the warning. I seemed to hear, not the voice of the doctor (even that of Aesculapius, issuing from the shrine at Epidaurus), but the sound of a certain more divine monitor within.[39] And I thought that two lots had now been set before me by a certain command of fate: the one, blindness, the other, duty. Either I must necessarily endure the loss of my eyes, or I must abandon my most solemn duty. And there came into my mind those two fates which, the son of Thetis[40] relates, his mother brought back from Delphi, where she inquired concerning him:

> Two destinies lead me to the end, which is death:
> If staying here I fight around the city of Troy,
> Return is denied me, but immortal will be my fame.
> If homeward I return to my dear native land,
> Lost is fair fame, but long will be my life.

Then I reflected that many men have bought with greater evil smaller good; with death, glory. To me, on the contrary, was offered a greater good at the price of a smaller evil: that I could at the cost of blindness alone fulfill the most honorable requirement of my duty. As duty is of itself more substantial than glory, so it ought to be for every man more desirable and illustrious. I resolved therefore that I must employ this brief use of my eyes while yet I could for the greatest possible benefit to the state. You see what I chose, what I rejected, and why.

Then let those who slander the judgments of God cease to speak evil and invent empty tales about me. Let them be sure that I feel neither regret nor shame for my lot, that I stand unmoved and steady in my resolution, that I nei-

38. Milton reports in a letter to Leonard Philaras of Athens that the deterioration of his eyesight over several years was accompanied by intestinal distress and intense ocular pain.

39. **Aesculapius:** Latin for Asclepius, Apollo's son and the Greek god of healing. The ancient Greek city of *Epidaurus* was the center of his cult. By *more divine monitor,* Milton seems to mean the voice of conscience.

40. Achilles in the *Iliad,* from which Milton took the following excerpt (9.411–16). He quotes the original Greek and adds a Latin translation.

ther discern nor endure the anger of God, that in fact I know and recognize in the most momentous affairs his fatherly mercy and kindness towards me, and especially in this fact, that with his consolation strengthening my spirit I bow to his divine will, dwelling more often on what he has bestowed on me than on what he has denied. Finally, let them rest assured that I would not exchange the consciousness of my achievement for any deed of theirs, be it ever so righteous, nor would I be deprived of the recollection of my deeds, ever a source of gratitude and repose.

Finally, as to my blindness, I would rather have mine, if it be necessary, than either theirs, More, or yours. Your blindness, deeply implanted in the inmost faculties, obscures the mind, so that you may see nothing whole or real. Mine, which you make a reproach, merely deprives things of color and superficial appearance. What is true and essential in them is not lost to my intellectual vision. How many things there are, moreover, which I have no desire to see, how many things that I should be glad not to see, how few remain that I should like to see.[41] Nor do I feel pain at being classed with the blind, the afflicted, the suffering, and the weak (although you hold this to be wretched), since there is hope that in this way I may approach more closely the mercy and protection of the Father Almighty.[42] There is a certain road which leads through weakness, as the apostle teaches, to the greatest strength.[43] May I be entirely helpless, provided that in my weakness there may arise all the more powerfully this immortal and more perfect strength; provided that in my shadows the light of the divine countenance may shine forth all the more clearly. For then I shall be at once the weakest and the strongest, at the same time blind and most keen in vision. By this infirmity may I be perfected, by this completed. So in this darkness, may I be clothed in light.

To be sure, we blind men are not the least of God's concerns, for the less able we are to perceive anything other than himself, the more mercifully and graciously does he deign to look upon us. Woe to him who mocks us, woe to him who injures us. He deserves to be cursed with a public malediction. Divine law[44] and divine favor have rendered us not only safe from the injuries of men, but almost sacred, nor do these shadows around us seem to have been created so much by the dullness of our eyes as by the shade of angels' wings. And divine favor not infrequently is wont to lighten these shadows again, once made, by an inner and far more enduring light. To this circumstance I refer the fact that my friends now visit, esteem, and attend me more diligently even than before, and

41. Milton here distinguishes between the world of Platonic forms containing the essence of things, which he can still see with "intellectual vision," and the everyday world of objects, which contains little that he still wishes to see even if he were able. Cp. *Phaedrus* 247.

42. Cp. *PL* 1.157–58: "To be weak is miserable/Doing or suffering."

43. Here and in the rest of the paragraph, Milton alludes to 2 Cor. 12, especially verse 9: "My strength is made perfect in weakness." His inscription of verse 9 in several autograph albums during the 1650s indicates that it became his motto (Kerrigan 1983, 134).

44. See, e.g., Deut. 27.18.

that there are some with whom I might as with true friends exchange the conversation of Pylades [with Orestes] and Theseus [with Heracles]:

ORESTES: Go slowly as the rudder of my feet.
PYLADES: A precious care is this to me.

And elsewhere:

THESEUS: Give your hand to your friend and helper.
Put your arm around my neck, and I will be your guide.[45]

For my friends do not think that by this calamity I have been rendered altogether worthless, nor that whatever is characteristic of an honest and prudent man resides in his eyes. In fact, since the loss of my eyesight has not left me sluggish from inactivity but tireless and ready among the first to risk the greatest dangers for the sake of liberty, the chief men in the state do not desert me either, but, considering within themselves what human life is like, they gladly favor and indulge me, and grant to me rest and leisure, as to one who well deserves it. If I have any distinction, they do not remove it, if any public office, they do not take it away, if any advantage from that office, they do not diminish it, and although I am no longer as useful as I was, they think that they should reward me no less graciously.[46] They pay me the same honor as if, according to the custom of ancient Athens, they had decreed that I take my meals in the Prytaneum.[47]

So long as I find in God and man such consolation for my blindness, let no one mourn for my eyes, which were lost in the cause of honor. Far be it from me either to mourn. Far be it from me to have so little spirit that I cannot easily despise the revilers of my blindness, or so little charity that I cannot even more easily pardon them. To you, whoever you are, I return, who with but little consistency regard me now as a dwarf, now as Antaeus.[48] You have (finally) no more ardent desire "for the United Provinces of Holland than that they should dispose of this war as easily and successfully as Salmasius will dispose of Milton."[49] If I give glad assent to this prayer, I think that I express no bad omen or evil wish against our success and the cause of England.

But listen! Another Cry, something strange and hissing. I take it that geese are flying in from somewhere or other. Now I realize what it is. I remember that

45. The quotations are from plays by Euripides: the first, *Orestes* (795); the second, *Heracles* (1398, 1402). His devoted friend Pylades helps Orestes endure the madness that visits him after he kills his mother. After madness so deludes Hercules that he kills his family, his friend Theseus comforts him. Both quotations appear in the original Greek followed by Latin translations.
46. Although Milton stopped attending conferences with ambassadors after blindness set in, his appointment as Latin Secretary was not affected.
47. **Prytaneum:** state house where distinguished Athenians were rewarded with free meals.
48. **Antaeus:** a giant, the son of the sea god Poseidon and Gaia (Earth).
49. Holland and England had been engaged in a naval war since May 1652.

this is the Tragedy of a Cry.[50] The Chorus appears. Behold, two poetasters[51]—either two or a single one, twofold in appearance and of two colors. Should I call it a sphinx, or that monster which Horace describes in the *Ars Poetica,* with the head of a woman, the neck of an ass, clad in varied plumage, with limbs assembled from every source?[52] Yes, this is that very monster. It must be some rhapsode or other, strewn with centos and patches.[53] Whether it is one or two is uncertain, for it also is anonymous.

Now, poets who deserve the name, I love and cherish, and I delight in hearing them frequently. Most of them, I know, are bitterly hostile to tyrants, if I should list them from the first down to our own Buchanan.[54] But these peddlers of effeminate little verses—who would not despise them? Nothing could be more foolish, more idle, more corrupt, or more false than such as they. They praise, they censure, without choice, without discrimination, judgment, or measure, now princes, now commoners, the learned as well as the ignorant, whether honest or wicked, it makes no difference, according as they are puffed up and swept away by the bottle, by the hope of a halfpenny, or by that empty frenzy of theirs. From every source they accumulate their absurdities of diction and matter, so many, so inconsistent, so disgusting, that it is far better for the object of their praise to suffer their neglect and live, as the saying is, with a crooked nose,[55] than to receive such praise. But he whom they attack should consider it no small honor that he finds no favor with such absurd and paltry fools.[56]

It is doubtful whether the first[57] (if there really are two of them) should be called a poet or a plasterer, to such a degree does he whitewash the façade of Salmasius, or rather whiten and plaster him entirely, as if he were a wall. He brings on in a "triumphal" chariot, no less, the giant-fighting hero, brandishing his "javelins and boxing-gloves" and all manner of trifling weapons, with all the scholars following the chariot on foot, but a tremendous distance to the rear, since he is the one "whom divine providence has raised up in evil times for the salvation of the world. At last, therefore, the time was at hand for kings to be protected by such a shield—the parent [no less] of law and empire." Salmasius must have been mad and in his second childhood not only to have been so

50. With *Cry,* Milton mocks the title of the tract for which he holds both More and Vlacq responsible as if they were a hybrid author.

51. **poetasters:** writers of poor or trashy verse.

52. The description of the monster paraphrases the first three lines of *Epistula ad Pisones* [Letters to Piso], usually known as *Ars Poetica* [The Art of Poetry].

53. In ancient Greece, *rhapsodes* recited epic poetry, particularly Homer's, and often improvised, including pieces by other poets in their performances. In Milton's time, collectors of literary pieces were also known as rhapsodists. **centos:** pieces of patchwork; patched garments.

54. The Scottish author George Buchanan (1506–82) wrote prose tracts regarding monarchy that anticipated Milton's. Most of his efforts in poetry were translations.

55. **with a crooked nose:** i.e., with his nose out of joint (indignant at their neglect).

56. Cp. *PR* 3.56: "Of whom to be dispraised were no small praise."

57. Vlacq.

hugely gratified by such praises but also to have taken such pains to have them printed with all possible haste. Wretched too and ignorant of propriety was the poet if he thought a mere schoolmaster worthy of such immoderate eulogy, since that breed of men has always been at the service of poets and inferior to them.[58]

The other, however, does not write verses, but simply raves, himself the most insane of all the possessed whom he so rabidly assails. As if he were an executioner for Salmasius, a son of Syrian Dama,[59] he calls for the floggers and Cadmus;[60] then drunk with hellebore,[61] he vomits up out of the index to Plautus[62] all the filthy language of slaves and scoundrels that can be found anywhere. You would suppose that he was speaking Oscan,[63] not Latin, or was croaking like a frog from the hellish swamps in which he swims. Then, to show you how great is his mastery of iambics, he is guilty of two false quantities in a single word, one syllable incorrectly prolonged, the other shortened:

Hi trucidate rege per horrendum nefas.[64]

Take away, you ass, those saddlebags filled with your "emptinesses" and bring us at last just three words, if you can, like a sane and sober man, provided that that pumpkinhead of yours, that "blockhead," can be sensible even for a second. Meanwhile I hand you over, an Orbilius, to be executed by the "harvest of rods" of your pupils.[65]

Continue to curse me as being "worse than Cromwell" in your estimation—the highest praise you could bestow on me. But should I call you a friend, a fool, or a crafty foe? A friend you surely are not, for your words prove you a foe. Why then have you been so inept in your slander that it occurred to you to exalt me above so great a man? Is it possible that you do not understand, or think that I do not understand, that the greater the hatred you show towards me, the greater is your advertisement of my merits with respect to the Commonwealth, and that your insults amount to so many eulogies of me among my own people? For

58. Milton calls Salmasius a schoolmaster or grammarian [*grammaticum*], but Salmasius was a professor and eminent scholar. Milton himself instructed students but scoffs at the idea that teachers merit such praise as Vlacq lavishes on Salmasius. In the passage quoted, Salmasius is depicted in a manner that oddly anticipates Milton's epic account of Messiah's single-handed assault on the rebel angels (*PL* 6.760–843).

59. **Dama:** in Horace's *Satires* (1.6.38–39), a slave who threatens a freeborn man with death.

60. Mentioned in the same passage from Horace's *Satires, Cadmus* was an infamously cruel executioner.

61. **hellebore:** a plant used as poison but also as a treatment for mental disease.

62. Titus Maccius *Plautus* (c. 250–184 B.C.E.), Roman dramatist particularly known for his comic representations of slaves and other low characters.

63. **Oscan:** a primitive dialect of southern Italy.

64. The iambic meter used by the author of the ode in *The Cry* mangles the pronunciation of *trucidate* in two of its syllables, making the short *u* long and the long *i* short.

65. *Orbilius* was Horace's schoolmaster, notoriously liberal with the cane. Milton suggests that, for More's mistakes in prosody, the roles should be reversed, and More should take a beating from his students.

if you hate me most of all, surely I am the one who has injured you most of all, hurt you most of all, and damaged your cause. If such is the case, I am also the one who has deserved most highly of my fellow-citizens, for the testimony or judgment of an enemy, even if in other circumstances somewhat unreliable, is nevertheless by far the most weighty when it concerns his own suffering. Or do you not remember that when Ajax and Ulysses vied for the weapons of the dead Achilles, the poet chose as judges, on the advice of Nestor, not Greeks, their fellow-countrymen, but Trojans, their enemies?

Therefore let the prudent Trojans decide this quarrel.

And a little later:

Who will give just judgment concerning these men
Partial to neither party, since all the Achaeans with equal bitterness
They hate, mindful of their grievous loss.

These are the words of the poet of Smyrna or Calabria.[66]

Hence it follows that you are a crafty foe and take pains to cast infamy on me, when with malicious intent and the purpose of inflicting still deeper injury you pervert and debase that judgment which is wont in the case of an enemy to be impartial and honest. So perverted are you, not just as a man, but even as an enemy. Yet, my fine fellow, I shall without difficulty circumvent you. For although I should like to be Ulysses—should like, that is, to have deserved as well as possible of my country—yet I do not covet the arms of Achilles. I do not seek to bear before me heaven painted on a shield,[67] for others, not myself to see in battle, while I carry on my shoulders a burden, not painted, but real, for myself, and not for others to perceive.

Since I bear no grudge whatever nor harbor private quarrels against any man, nor does any man, so far as I know, bear any grudge against me, I endure with the greater equanimity all the curses that are uttered against me, all the insults that are hurled, so long as they are suffered for the sake of the state, not for myself. Nor do I complain that to me has fallen the tiniest share of the rewards and benefits which thus accrue, but the greatest share of ignominy. I am content to have sought for their own sake alone, and to accomplish without recompense, those deeds which honor bade me do. Let others look to that, and do you rest assured that I have not touched these "abundances" and "riches" of which you accuse me, nor have I become a penny richer by reason of that renown with which especially you charge me.

66. Quintus of Smyrna, whose epic *Posthomerica* was found in Calabria. Milton quotes the original Greek and provides a Latin translation.

67. The famous shield wrought for Achilles by Hephaestus depicts the entire cosmos. Ulysses, not Ajax, was awarded the arms of Achilles as the most deserving of the Greeks.

[*Milton continues his attacks on More, charging him with blasphemy for comparing Charles's execution to Christ's Crucifixion, then turns again to Salmasius, whom he brands a lowly pedant undeserving of his high reputation. He lavishly praises the Queen of Sweden, whom he claims admired his* Defense *and reviled the defeated Salmasius, and sets her up as an example of a just monarch to further distinguish between kings and tyrants.*]

Now I must return to the work from which I digressed, a very different matter. We "became frantic," you say, "at the news of the *Defensio Regia* and therefore" we "hunted out some starveling little schoolmaster,[68] who would consent to lend his corrupt pen to the defense of parricide." This tale you have maliciously invented out of your recollection that the royalists, when they were seeking a herald for their own lies and abuse, approached a grammarian, who was, if not hungry, at least more than a little thirsty for gold—Salmasius. He gladly sold them, not only his services at that time, but also his intellectual powers, if any were his before. The tale springs also from your recollection that Salmasius, his reputation now lost and ruined, when he was casting about for some one who might be able in some way to repair his good name, thus damaged and disgraced, found you, by the just judgment of God, not the minister of Geneva (whence you had been expelled) but the bishop of Lampsacus, that is, a Priapus from the garden, the defiler of his own home.[69] Thereafter, revolted by your insipid praises, which he had purchased with such dishonor, he was converted from a friend into the bitterest enemy and uttered many curses against you, his eulogist, as he died.

"Only one man was found, most assuredly a great hero, whom they could oppose to Salmasius, a certain John Milton." I did not realize that I was a hero, although you may, so far as I am concerned, be the son, perhaps, of some hero or other, since you are totally noxious.[70] And that I alone was found to defend the cause of the people of England, certainly I regret, if I consider the interests of the Commonwealth, but if I consider the glory involved, I am perfectly content that I have no one with whom to share it. Who I am and whence I come is uncertain, you say; so once it was uncertain who Homer was, and who Demosthenes.[71] But in fact, I had learned to hold my peace, I had mastered the art of not writing,[72] a lesson that Salmasius could never learn. And I carried silently in my breast that which, if I had then wished to publish it, would long since have made me as famous as I am today. But I was not greedy for fame, whose gait is slow, nor did I ever intend to publish even this, unless a fitting opportunity presented itself. It made no difference to me even if others did not realize

68. *Grammaticastum,* i.e., petty grammarian.

69. *Priapus,* a god of fertility represented in garden statues as a grotesque figure with an incongruously swollen phallus, had a cult in Lampascus, a city in Asia Minor.

70. A Latin proverb, *Heroum filii nexae,* holds that the sons of heroes are nothing.

71. Demosthenes was seven when his father died. His guardians mismanaged the estate, and the boy grew up in obscurity and neglect.

72. *Posse non scribere,* or, literally, the power not to write.

that I knew whatever I knew, for it was not fame, but the opportune moment for each thing that I awaited. Hence it happened that I was known to a good many, long before Salmasius was known to himself. Now he is better known than the nag Andraemon.[73]

"Is he a man or a worm?" Indeed I should prefer to be a worm, which even King David confesses that he is, rather than hide in my breast your worm that dieth not.[74] "They say," you continue, "that this fellow, expelled from the University of Cambridge, because of his offences, fled his disgrace and his country and traveled to Italy." Even from this statement one can infer how truthful were your sources of information, for on this point everyone who knows me knows that both you and your informants lie most shamelessly, and I shall at once make this fact clear. If I had actually been expelled from Cambridge, why should I travel to Italy, rather than to France or Holland, where you, enveloped in so many offenses, a minister of the Gospel, not only live in safety, but preach, and even defile with your unclean hands the sacred offices, to the extreme scandal of your church? But why to Italy, More? Another Saturn, I presume, I fled to Latium that I might find a place to lurk.[75] Yet I knew beforehand that Italy was not, as you think, a refuge or asylum for criminals, but rather the lodging-place of *humanitas*[76] and of all the arts of civilization, and so I found it.

"Returning, he wrote his book on divorce." I wrote nothing different from what Bucer had written before me—and copiously—about the kingdom of Christ, nothing different from what Fagius had written on Deuteronomy, Erasmus on the first Epistle to the Corinthians (a commentary intended for the benefit of the English people), nothing different from what many other illustrious men wrote for the common good. No one blamed them for so doing, and I fail to understand why it should be to me above all a source of reproach. One thing only could I wish, that I had not written it in the vernacular, for then I would not have met with vernacular readers, who are usually ignorant of their own good, and laugh at the misfortunes of others. But do you, vilest of men, protest about divorce, you who procured the most brutal of all divorces from Pontia, the maidservant engaged to you, after you seduced her under cover of that engagement? Moreover, she was a servant of Salmasius, an English woman it is said, warmly devoted to the royalist cause. It is beyond question that you wickedly courted her as royal property and left her as public property. Take care lest you yourself prove to have been the author of the very conversion which you profess to find so distasteful. Take care, I repeat, lest with the rule of Salmasius utterly overthrown you may yourself have converted Pontia into a "republic."[77]

73. *Andraemon,* a horse driven by the famous charioteer Scorpus, probably was, as Martial insisted, better known than the celebrated poet (*Epigrams* 10.9).

74. In Ps. 22.6, David confesses he is "a worm and no man, scorned by men and despised by the people"; in Mark 9.48, Jesus describes "hell, where their worm dieth not."

75. According to Vergil (*Aen.* 8.314–23), Saturn took refuge in Latium after being deposed by Jupiter.

76. ***humanitas:*** civility, culture.

77. Milton is punning on the Latin for "republic," *res publica,* literally, "public thing."

And take care lest in this way, you, though a royalist, may be said to have founded many "republics" in a single city, or as minister of state to have served them after their foundation by other men. These are your divorces, or, if you prefer, diversions, from which you emerge against me as a veritable Curius.[78]

Now you continue with your lies. "When the conspirators were agitating the decapitation of the king, Milton wrote to them, and when they were wavering urged them to the wicked course." But I did not write to them, nor did it rest with me to urge men who had already without me determined on precisely this course. Yet I shall describe hereafter what I did write on this subject, and I shall also speak of *Eikonoklastes.* Now since this fellow (I am uncertain whether to call him a man or the dregs of manhood), progressing from adultery with servant girls to the adulteration of all truth, has tried to render me infamous among foreigners, by piling up a whole series of lies against me, I ask that no one take it amiss or make it a source of reproach, or resent it, if I have said previously and shall say hereafter more about myself than I would wish, so that if I cannot rescue my eyes from blindness or my name from oblivion or slander, I can at least bring my life into the light out of that darkness which accompanies disgrace. And I must do this for more reasons than one. First, in order that the many good and learned men in all the neighboring countries who are now reading my works and thinking rather well of me, may not despise me on account of this man's abuse, but may persuade themselves that I am incapable of ever disgracing honorable speech by dishonorable conduct, or free utterances by slavish deeds, and that my life, by the grace of God, has ever been far removed from all vice and crime. Next, in order that those distinguished and praiseworthy men whom I undertake to extol may know that I should consider nothing more shameful than to approach the task of praising them while myself deserving blame and censure. Finally, in order that the English people whose defense their own virtue has impelled me to undertake (whether it be my fate or my duty) may know that if I have always led a pure and honorable life, my *Defense* (whether it will be to their honor or dignity I know not) will certainly never be for them a source of shame or disgrace.

Who I am, then, and whence I come, I shall now disclose.[79] I was born in London, of an honorable family. My father was a man of supreme integrity, my mother a woman of purest reputation, celebrated throughout the neighborhood for her acts of charity.[80] My father destined me in early childhood for the study of literature, for which I had so keen an appetite that from my twelfth year scarcely ever did I leave my studies for my bed before the hour of midnight. This was the first cause of injury to my eyes, whose natural weakness was augmented by frequent headaches. Since none of these defects slackened my

78. Manius *Curius* Dentatus (d. 270 B.C.E.), Roman general and exemplar of simple and severe republican virtues. The philanderer More, Milton says, postures as such a model of rectitude.
79. The narrative that follows underlies all subsequent accounts of Milton's life.
80. *Eleemosynis* ["for her acts of charity"] is more precisely translated as "for almsgiving."

assault upon knowledge, my father took care that I should be instructed daily both in school and under other masters at home.[81] When I had thus become proficient in various languages and had tasted by no means superficially the sweetness of philosophy, he sent me to Cambridge, one of our two universities. There, untouched by any reproach, in the good graces of all upright men, for seven years I devoted myself to the traditional disciplines and liberal arts, until I had attained the degree of Master, as it is called, *cum laude*. Then, far from fleeing to Italy, as that filthy rascal alleges, of my own free will I returned home, to the regret of most of the fellows of the college, who bestowed on me no little honor.[82] At my father's country place, whither he had retired to spend his declining years, I devoted myself entirely to the study of Greek and Latin writers, completely at leisure, not, however, without sometimes exchanging the country for the city, either to purchase books or to become acquainted with some new discovery in mathematics or music, in which I then took the keenest pleasure.[83]

When I had occupied five years in this fashion, I became desirous, my mother having died, of seeing foreign parts,[84] especially Italy, and with my father's consent I set forth, accompanied by a single attendant. On my departure Henry Wotton, a most distinguished gentleman, who had long served as King James' ambassador to the Venetians, gave signal proof of his esteem for me, writing a graceful letter which contained good wishes and precepts of no little value to one going abroad.[85] On the recommendation of others I was warmly received in Paris by the noble Thomas Scudamore, Viscount Sligo, legate of King Charles.[86] He on his own initiative introduced me, in company with several of his suite, to Hugo Grotius, a most learned man (then ambassador from the Queen of Sweden to the King of France) whom I ardently desired to meet.[87] When I set out for Italy some days thereafter, Scudamore gave me letters to English merchants along my projected route, that they might assist me as they could. Sailing from Nice, I reached Genoa, then Leghorn and Pisa, and after that Florence. In that city, which I have always admired above all others because of the elegance, not just of its tongue, but also of its wit, I lingered for about two months. There I at once became the friend of many gentlemen eminent in rank

81. Cp. *To His Father* (78–92), where Milton thanks his father for supporting his education.

82. Actually, Milton was passed over in 1630 for an available fellowship, which was awarded instead to Edward King, whose subsequent death occasioned *Lycidas*. Milton's repudiation of the priesthood and indeed all other traditional career paths rendered moot any possibility of formal retention by the university, however much its fellows may have esteemed him.

83. These years "at leisure" were also devoted to poetry; some of Milton's most celebrated early works date from this period, including *Arcades*, *A Masque*, and *Lycidas*.

84. What Sara Milton's death had to do with Milton's wanderlust remains a subject of critical conjecture. See, e.g., Kerrigan 1983, 56; Boesky.

85. Sir Henry Wotton (1568–1639) was a favorite of James I, who knighted him and made him ambassador to Venice. He was provost of Eton (near Milton's country retreat in Horton) from 1624 until his death. In *Poems* (1645) Milton prefaces his *Masque* with the letter from Wotton.

86. The legate of King Charles in Paris was John, not Thomas, Scudamore, Viscount Sligo.

87. Grotius, well-known for his works on international law, also wrote Latin poetry that was an early source of inspiration for Milton. He is cited as an authority in the divorce tracts.

and learning, whose private academies I frequented—a Florentine institution which deserves great praise not only for promoting humane studies but also for encouraging friendly intercourse. Time will never destroy my recollection—ever welcome and delightful—of you, Jacopo Gaddi, Carlo Dati, Frescobaldi, Coltellini, Buonmattei, Chimentelli, Francini, and many others.[88]

From Florence I traveled to Siena and thence to Rome. When the antiquity and venerable repute of that city had detained me for almost two months and I had been graciously entertained there by Lukas Holste[89] and other men endowed with both learning and wit, I proceeded to Naples. Here I was introduced by a certain Eremite Friar, with whom I had made the journey from Rome, to Giovanni Battista Manso, Marquis of Villa, a man of high rank and influence, to whom the famous Italian poet, Torquato Tasso, dedicated his work on friendship.[90] As long as I was there I found him a very true friend. He personally conducted me through the various quarters of the city and the Viceregal Court, and more than once came to my lodgings to call. When I was leaving he gravely apologized because even though he had especially wished to show me many more attentions, he could not do so in that city, since I was unwilling to be circumspect in regard to religion.[91] Although I desired also to cross to Sicily and Greece, the sad tidings of civil war from England summoned me back. For I thought it base that I should travel abroad at my ease for the cultivation of my mind, while my fellow-citizens at home were fighting for liberty. As I was on the point of returning to Rome, I was warned by merchants that they had learned through letters of plots laid against me by the English Jesuits, should I return to Rome, because of the freedom with which I had spoken about religion. For I had determined within myself that in those parts I would not indeed begin a conversation about religion, but if questioned about my faith would hide nothing, whatever the consequences. And so, I nonetheless returned to Rome. What I was, if any man inquired, I concealed from no one. For almost two more months, in the very stronghold of the Pope, if anyone attacked the orthodox religion, I openly, as before, defended it. Thus, by the will of God, I returned again in safety to Florence, revisiting friends who were as anxious to see me as if it were my native land to which I had returned. After gladly lingering there for as many months as before (except for an excursion of a few days to Lucca[92]) I crossed the Apennines and hastened to Venice by way of Bologna and

88. Among these Italian friends were lawyers, priests, poets, and aristocratic patrons of the arts. Dati, then only nineteen, seems to have been the closest friend Milton made while in Italy. Correspondence between them is extant; Milton mentions him in *Damon* (137–38); and a tribute from him appears in *Poems* (1645).

89. A German scholar and librarian to Cardinal Barberini, Holste (Holstenius) showed Milton books and manuscripts in the Vatican Library. See Milton's letter to him (1784–87).

90. Cp. *Manso.*

91. One of Henry Wotton's "precepts of no little value to one going abroad" had been to maintain a politic discretion, advice that Milton evidently ignored when it came to religious matters.

92. **Lucca:** the ancestral home of the family of Milton's dearest friend, Charles Diodati. News of Diodati's death may have reached Milton in Naples and spurred his return home (Rumrich 1999).

Ferrara. When I had spent one month exploring that city and had seen to the shipping of the books which I had acquired throughout Italy, I proceeded to Geneva by way of Verona, Milan, and the Pennine Alps, and then along Lake Leman. Geneva, since it reminds me of the slanderer More, impels me once again to call God to witness that in all these places, where so much license exists, I lived free and untouched by the slightest sin or reproach, reflecting constantly that although I might hide from the gaze of men, I could not elude the sight of God. In Geneva I conversed daily with John Diodati,[93] the learned professor of theology. Then by the same route as before, through France, I returned home after a year and three months, more or less, at almost the same time as Charles broke the peace and renewed the war with the Scots, which is known as the second Bishops' War.

The royalist troops were routed in the first engagement of this war, and Charles, when he perceived that all the English, as well as the Scots, were extremely—and justly—ill disposed towards him, soon convened Parliament, not of his own free will but compelled by disaster. I myself, seeking a place to become established, could I but find one anywhere in such upset and tumultuous times, rented a house in town,[94] sufficiently commodious for myself and my books, and there, blissfully enough, devoted myself to my interrupted studies, willingly leaving the outcome of these events, first of all to God, and then to those whom the people had entrusted with this office. Meanwhile, as Parliament acted with vigor, the haughtiness of the bishops began to deflate. As soon as freedom of speech (at the very least) became possible, all mouths were opened against them. Some complained of the personal defects of the bishops, others of the defectiveness of the episcopal rank itself. It was wrong, they said, that their church alone should differ from all other reformed churches. It was proper for the church to be governed by the example of the brethren, but first of all by the word of God.[95] Now, thoroughly aroused to these concerns, I perceived that men were following the true path to liberty and that from these beginnings, these first steps, they were making the most direct progress towards the liberation of all human life from slavery—provided that the discipline arising from religion should overflow into the morals and institutions of the state. Since, moreover, I had so practiced myself from youth that I was above all things unable to disregard the laws of God and man, and since I had asked myself whether I should be of any future use if I now failed my country (or rather the church and so many of my brothers who were exposing themselves to danger for the sake of the Gospel) I decided, although at that time occupied with

93. Charles Diodati's uncle, expatriated from Lucca for his conversion to Protestantism.

94. The house was in St. Bride's Churchyard. In it Milton began the private school in which he instructed John and Edward Phillips. "I cannot but remark a kind of respect, perhaps unconsciously paid to this great man by his biographers: every house in which he resided is historically mentioned, as if it were an injury to neglect naming any place that he honored by his presence" (Johnson 1:127).

95. In Milton's view, there was no scriptural justification for the clerical hierarchy found in Catholicism and retained by the Church of England.

certain other matters,[96] to devote to this conflict all my talents and all my active powers.

First, therefore, I addressed to a certain friend two books on the reformation of the English church.[97] Then, since two bishops of particularly high repute were asserting their prerogatives against certain eminent ministers,[98] and I concluded that on those subjects which I had mastered solely for love of truth and out of regard for Christian duty, I could express myself at least as well as those who were wrangling for their own profit and unjust authority, I replied to one of the bishops in two books, of which the first was entitled *Of Prelatical Episcopacy* and the second *The Reason of Church-Government*, while to the other bishop I made reply in certain *Animadversions* and later in an *Apology*. I brought succor to the ministers, who were, as it was said, scarcely able to withstand the eloquence of this bishop, and from that time onward, if the bishops made any response, I took a hand. When they, having become a target for the weapons of all men, had at last fallen and troubled us no more, I directed my attention elsewhere, asking myself whether I could in any way advance the cause of true and substantial liberty, which must be sought, not without, but within, and which is best achieved, not by the sword, but by a life rightly undertaken and rightly conducted. Since, then, I observed that there are, in all, three varieties of liberty without which civilized life is scarcely possible, namely ecclesiastical liberty, domestic or personal liberty, and civil liberty, and since I had already written about the first, while I saw that the magistrates were vigorously attending to the third, I took as my province the remaining one, the second or domestic kind. This too seemed to be concerned with three problems: the nature of marriage itself, the education of the children, and finally the existence of freedom to express oneself. Hence I set forth my views on marriage, not only its proper contraction, but also, if need be, its dissolution. My explanation was in accordance with divine law, which Christ did not revoke; much less did He give approval in civil life to any other law more weighty than the law of Moses. Concerning the view which should be held on the single exception, that of fornication, I also expressed both my own opinion and that of others. Our distinguished countryman Selden still more fully explained this point in his *Hebrew Wife*, published about two years later.[99] For in vain does he prattle about liberty in assembly and market-place who at home endures the slavery most unworthy of man, slavery to an inferior. Concerning this matter then I published several books,[100] at the

96. Presumably, these *other matters* include the schooling of his nephews and plans to pen an epic on British history.
97. *Of Reformation* comprises two books.
98. Milton attacked the two bishops, James Ussher and Joseph Hall, on behalf of the five antiprelatical clergymen whose initials formed the pen name Smectymnuus, including his former tutor, Thomas Young.
99. Milton also cites this work by the eminent jurist John Selden in *CD* (1.10).
100. *The Doctrine and Discipline of Divorce* (1643, 1st ed.; 1644, 2nd ed.), *The Judgment of Martin Bucer Concerning Divorce* (1644), *Tetrachordon* (1645), and *Colasterion* (1645).

very time when man and wife were often bitter foes, he dwelling at home with their children, she, the mother of the family, in the camp of the enemy, threatening her husband with death and disaster. Next, in one small volume, I discussed the education of children,[101] a brief treatment, to be sure, but sufficient, as I thought, for those who devote to the subject the attention it deserves. For nothing can be more efficacious than education in molding the minds of men to virtue (whence arises true and internal liberty), in governing the state effectively, and preserving it for the longest possible space of time.

Lastly I wrote, on the model of a genuine speech, the *Areopagitica,* concerning freedom of the press, that the judgment of truth and falsehood, what should be printed and what suppressed, ought not to be in the hands of a few men (and these mostly ignorant and of vulgar discernment) charged with the inspection of books, at whose will or whim virtually everyone is prevented from publishing aught that surpasses the understanding of the mob. Civil liberty, which was the last variety, I had not touched upon, for I saw that it was being adequately dealt with by the magistrates, nor did I write anything about the right of kings, until the king, having been declared an enemy by Parliament and vanquished in the field, was pleading his cause as a prisoner before the judges and was condemned to death. Then at last, when certain Presbyterian ministers, formerly bitter enemies of Charles, but now resentful that the Independent parties were preferred to theirs and carried more weight in Parliament, persisted in attacking the decree which Parliament had passed concerning the king (wroth, not because of the fact, but because their own faction had not performed it) and caused as much tumult as they could, even daring to assert that the doctrines of Protestants and all reformed churches shrank from such an outrageous sentence against kings, I concluded that I must openly oppose so open a lie. Not even then, however, did I write or advise anything concerning Charles, but demonstrated what was in general permissible against tyrants, adducing not a few testimonies from the foremost theologians. And I attacked, almost as if I were haranguing an assembly, the pre-eminent ignorance or insolence of these ministers, who had given promise of better things. This book did not appear until after the death of the king, having been written to reconcile men's minds, rather than to determine anything about Charles (which was not my affair, but that of the magistrates, and which had by then been effected).[102] This service of mine, between private walls, I freely gave, now to the church and now to the state. To me, in return, neither the one nor the other offered more than protection, but the deeds themselves undoubtedly bestowed on me a good conscience, good repute among good men, and this honorable freedom of speech. Other men gained for themselves advantages, other men secured offices at no cost to themselves. As for me, no man has ever seen me seeking office, no man has ever seen me soliciting aught through my friends, clinging with suppliant expression

101. *Of Education* (1644).
102. *The Tenure of Kings and Magistrates* (1649).

to the doors of Parliament, or loitering in the hallways of the lower assemblies. I kept myself at home for the most part, and from my own revenues, though often they were in large part withheld because of the civil disturbance, I endured the tax—by no means entirely just—that was laid on me and maintained my frugal way of life.

When these works had been completed and I thought that I could look forward to an abundance of leisure, I turned to the task of tracing in unbroken sequence, if I could, the history of my country, from the earliest origins even to the present day.[103] I had already finished four books when the kingdom of Charles was transformed into a republic, and the so-called Council of State, which was then for the first time established by the authority of Parliament, summoned me, though I was expecting no such event, and desired to employ my services, especially in connection with foreign affairs. Not long afterwards there appeared a book attributed to the king, and plainly written with great malice against Parliament. Bidden to reply to this, I opposed to the *Eikon* the *Eikonoklastes,* not, as I am falsely charged, "insulting the departed spirit of the king," but thinking that Queen Truth should be preferred to King Charles. Indeed, since I saw that this slander would be at hand for any calumniator, in the very introduction (and as often as I could elsewhere) I averted this reproach from myself. Then Salmasius appeared. So far were they from spending a long time (as More alleges) seeking one who would reply to him, that all, of their own accord, at once named me, then present in the Council. I have given an account of myself to this extent in order to stop your mouth, More, and refute your lies, chiefly for the sake of those good men who otherwise would know me not. Do you then, I bid you, unclean More, be silent. Hold your tongue, I say![104] For the more you abuse me, the more copiously will you compel me to account for my conduct. From such accounting you can gain nothing save the reproach, already most severe, of telling lies, while for me you open the door to still higher praise of my own integrity.

[*Returning to his favorite theme—More's lechery—Milton also derides his opponent for using anecdotal rather than theoretical arguments. He then answers the charges that the regicides lacked popular support, judicial legitimacy, and ecclesiastical backing by citing the incompetence and riotousness of the masses, extolling John Bradshaw* (*the judge who presided over Charles's trial*), *and alleging the hypocrisy of the Church of England. He ridicules the idealization of Charles as a martyr, praises the behavior of the British troops, and defends the seizure of church assets.*]

You now presume to deal with political considerations, you slave of the chair (or rather the easy-chair), namely our offences against all kings and peoples.

103. *The History of Britain* (1670).

104. In Mark 1.23–25, Jesus heals a supplicant possessed by an unclean spirit by ordering the spirit to be silent. Milton wrote the command in the Greek of the New Testament, [φιμώσητι], which literally means "be muzzled."

What offences? For we had no such design. We merely attended to our own affairs and dismissed the affairs of others. If any good has redounded to our neighbors from our example, we do not begrudge it; if any evil, we hold that it occurs through the fault, not of ourselves, but of those who abuse our principles. And pray, what kings or peoples established you, a mere buffoon, as the spokesman of their wrongs? Certainly other men in Parliament, and I myself in the Council, have often heard their ambassadors and legates, when they were given an audience, so far from complaining about their grievances, actually asking of their own free will for our friendship and alliance, even, in fact, congratulating us on our affairs in the names of their own kings and princes, wishing us well indeed and invoking eternal peace and security and the continuance of the same auspicious success. These are not the words of enemies nor of those who hate us, as you allege. Either you must be condemned for lying (in you a trifle) or the kings themselves for fraud and wicked designs (which to them would be a great disgrace). But you reproach us with our writings, in which we admit, "We have given an example beneficial to all people, dreadful to all tyrants." It is a monstrous crime that you describe, to be sure; almost the same as if someone had said, "Take warning, learn to practice justice and respect the gods."[105] Could any utterance be more baleful?

"Cromwell wrote this message to the Scots after the battle of Dunbar." And it was worthy of him and of that noble victory. "The unspeakable pages of Milton are sprinkled with this kind of sesame and poppy."[106] Illustrious indeed is the comrade whom you always associate with me, and in this crime you clearly make me his equal and sometimes his superior. With this title I should think myself most highly honored by you, if from you could proceed anything honorable. "Those pages have been burned," you assert, "by the public hangman in Paris, at the instance of the supreme Parliament."[107] In no wise, I have learned, was this done by Parliament, but by some city official, a *locum tenens,*[108] whether civil or uncivil I do not know, at the instigation of certain clergymen, lazy beasts, who foresaw from a distance and at a great remove what I pray may someday befall their own paunch. Do you not perceive that we too could in turn have burned Salmasius' *Royal Defense*? Even I myself could easily have obtained this request from our magistrates, if I had not thought the insult better avenged by contempt. You, hastening to put out one fire with another, built a Herculean pyre, whence I might rise to greater fame. We more sensibly decided that the frigidity of the *Royal Defense* should not be kindled into flame. I marvel that the people of Toulouse (for I have heard that I was burned also at Toulouse)

105. The quotation is a paraphrase of Vergil (*Aen.* 6.620).

106. *Sesame* was used to induce vomiting; the *poppy,* sleep.

107. Milton's *Defense* was condemned and ordered to be burned by the hangman at Paris, June 26, 1651. Contemporary correspondence from the Dutch scholar Isaac Vossius to Nicholas Heinsius observes that "men come under the executioner's hands for the most part for their crimes and depravity, but books for their worth and excellence" (quoted in Masson 4:342).

108. ***locum tenens:*** a place holder; one who holds office temporarily, as a substitute.

have become so unlike their ancestors that in the city where under the counts Raimond both liberty and religion were once so nobly defended, the Defense of liberty and religion has now been burned. "Would that the writer had been burned as well," you say. So, you slave? But you have taken extraordinary care that I should not return a similar greeting to you, More, for you have long since been consumed by far darker flames—the flames of your adulteries, the flames of your foul deeds, the flames of your prejudices, with the help of which you faithlessly discarded the woman who was betrothed to you by her own seduction. You are consumed by your fits of desperate madness, which drove you to lust after the holiest of rites, foul wretch that you are. They drove you as a priest to defile with incestuous[109] hands the unperceived body of the Lord, and, even as you feigned holiness, to threaten with this Cry of yours all dreadful consequences to those who feign holiness. The flames of madness drove you to untangle your own infamous head, condemned by your own pronouncement. With these crimes and infamies you are all afire, with these raging flames you are scorched night and day, and you pay us a penalty more severe than that which any foe could invoke against you. Meanwhile these burnings of yours do not injure, do not touch me, and I have a great many consolations that delight and gratify my mind, with which to counter those insults of yours. One court, one Parisian hangman, impelled by evil auspices, has perhaps burned me, but a very great many good and learned men throughout all France nonetheless read, approve, and embrace me, as do great numbers throughout the boundless reaches of all Germany, the very home of liberty, and throughout all other countries as well, wherever any of her footprints still remain. And even Greece herself, Athens herself in Attica, as if come to life again, has applauded me in the voice of Philaras,[110] her most illustrious nursling. Indeed, I can truthfully assert that from the time when my *Defense* was first published, and kindled the enthusiasm of its readers, no ambassador from any prince or state who was then in the city failed to congratulate me, if we chanced to meet, or omitted to seek an interview with me at his own house, or to visit me at mine. It would be a sacrilege to omit mention of your departed spirit, Adrian Pauw, glory and ornament of the Netherlands, you who were sent to us with the highest dignity as Ambassador and took care that, although we chanced never to meet, many messages should often assure me of your great and singular good will towards me.[111] Even more often is it a pleasure to recall what I think could never have happened without the favor of God—that on me, whose writings seemed to have attacked kings, the royal majesty itself benignly smiled and bore witness to my integrity and the superior truth of my judgment, with a testimony neighboring on the divine. For why should I shrink from such an epithet, when I contem-

109. **incestuous:** adulterous.

110. Leonard *Philaras,* ambassador to France who, when he visited England and learned of Milton's blindness, recommended a Paris specialist to him. Cp. letter *To Leonard Philaras.*

111. Adrian de Pauw visited London on a diplomatic mission in 1652.

plate that most august queen and the high praise with which she is celebrated on the lips of all men? Indeed, I should not regard the wisest of Athenians (to whom, however, I do not compare myself) as more honored even by the oracle of the Pythian himself, than I by the judgment of that queen.[112] But if it had been my fate to write these words in my youth, and if orators were allowed the same license as poets, I should not have hesitated to exalt my lot above that of certain gods, for they, being gods, contended before a human judge concerning beauty alone, or music, while I, a human being, with a goddess for judge, have come off victorious in by far the noblest contest of all. When I had been so honored, no one would dare to treat me with contempt, save only a public hangman, whether he who gave the orders or he who carried them out.

[*Milton defends the English Church and invokes the support of other European Protestants, specifically the French and Dutch. He cites precedents for aggression against tyrants in European and classical history, and celebrates England for being the first to execute a tyrant. More, he argues, is also destined for the gallows for his adulterous crimes. After defending Cromwell from charges made against him, Milton proceeds with the following laudatory history.*]

But I shall have accomplished nothing if I merely prove that this great man, who has deserved so well of the state, has done no wrong. For it is to the interest not only of the state, but of myself as well (since I have been so deeply involved in the same slanderous accusations) to show to all peoples and all ages, so far as I can, how supremely excellent he is, how worthy of all praise.

Oliver Cromwell is sprung of renowned and illustrious stock. The name was celebrated in former times for good administration under the monarchy and became more glorious as soon as the orthodox religion was reformed, or rather established among us for the first time. He had grown up in the seclusion of his own home, until he reached an age mature and settled, and this too he passed as a private citizen, known for nothing so much as his devotion to the Puritan religion and his upright life. For an occasion of supreme importance he had nourished in his silent heart a faith dependent on God and a mighty spirit. When Parliament was for the last time convened by the king, Cromwell was chosen by his town's electorate and won a seat.[113] There he at once became known for his upright sentiments and steadfast counsels. When war broke out, he offered his services and was put in command of a squadron of horse, but because of the concourse of good men who flocked to his standards from all sides, his force was greatly increased and he soon surpassed well-nigh the greatest generals both in the magnitude of his accomplishments and in the speed with

112. In Plato's *Apology* (21a), the oracle of Apollo (*the Pythian*) at Delphi declares Socrates the wisest of all men.

113. Cromwell first served in Parliament in 1628 for his hometown of Huntingdon; at the 1640 initiation of the last session convened by Charles, the Long Parliament, he was a member for Cambridge.

which he achieved them. Nor was this remarkable, for he was a soldier well-versed in self-knowledge, and whatever enemy lay within—vain hopes, fears, desires—he had either previously destroyed within himself or had long since reduced to subjection. Commander first over himself, victor over himself, he had learned to achieve over himself the most effective triumph, and so, on the very first day that he took service against an external foe, he entered camp a veteran and past-master in all that concerned the soldier's life.

It is impossible for me within the confines of this discourse to describe with fitting dignity the capture of the many cities, to list the many battles, and indeed such great ones, in which he was never conquered nor put to flight, but traversed the entire realm of Britain with uninterrupted victory. Such deeds require the grand scope of a true history, a second battlefield, so to speak, on which they may be recounted, and a space for narration equal to the deeds themselves. The following single proof of his rare and all-but-divine excellence suffices—that there flourished in him so great a power, whether of intellect and genius or of discipline (established not merely according to military standards, but rather according to the code of Christian virtue) that to his camp, as to the foremost school, not just of military science, but of religion and piety, he attracted from every side all men who were already good and brave, or else he made them such, chiefly by his own example. Throughout the entire war, and sometimes even in the intervening periods of peace, amid the many shifts of opinion and circumstance, in spite of opposition, he kept them at their duty, and does so still, not by bribes and the licentiousness typical of the military, but by his authority and their wages alone. No greater praise is wont to be attributed to Cyrus or Epaminondas[114] or any other pre-eminent general among the ancients. And so no one has ever raised a larger or better-disciplined army in a shorter space of time than did Cromwell, an army obedient to his command in all things, welcomed and cherished by their fellow-citizens, formidable indeed to the enemy in the field, but wonderfully merciful to them once they had surrendered. On the estates and under the roofs of the enemy this army proved so mild and innocent of all offence that when the royalists considered the violence of their own soldiery, their drunkenness, impiety, and lust, they rejoiced in their altered lot and believed that Cromwell's men had come, not as enemies, but as guests, a bulwark to all good men, a terror to the wicked, and in fact an inspiration to all virtue and piety.[115]

Nor should I pass you by, Fairfax, in whom nature and divine favor have joined with supreme courage supreme modesty and supreme holiness. By your own right and merit you deserve to be called upon to share these praises, al-

114. *Cyrus* the Great (d. 530 B.C.E.) founded the Persian Empire, vastly expanded its territories, and ruled it with unprecedented tolerance. *Epaminondas* (d. 362 B.C.E.), Theban general and statesman, made his city the most powerful in Greece.

115. Even the Royalists conceded that Cromwell's New Model Army surpassed their own in moral conduct. Troops were forbidden to plunder, abuse prisoners, or harm noncombatants.

though in your present retreat you conceal yourself as well as you can, like Scipio Africanus of old in Liternum.[116] You have defeated, not only the enemy, but ambition as well, and the thirst for glory which conquers all the most eminent men, and you are reaping the reward of your virtues and noble deeds amid that most delightful and glorious retirement which is the end of all labors and human action, even the greatest. When the heroes of old, after wars and honors no greater than yours, enjoyed such repose, the poets who sought to praise them despaired of being able fittingly to describe its nature in any other way than by creating a myth to the effect that they had been received into heaven and were sharing the banquets of the gods. But whether ill health, as I suspect, or some other reason has withdrawn you from public life, I am firmly convinced that nothing could have torn you from the needs of the State had you not seen how great a defender of liberty, how strong and faithful a pillar and support of English interests you were leaving in your successor.[117] For while you, Cromwell, are safe, he does not have sufficient faith even in God himself who would fear for the safety of England, when he sees God everywhere so favorable to you, so unmistakably at your side. But you were now left alone to fight upon another battleground.

Yet why go on at length? The greatest events I shall relate, if I can, with brevity comparable to the speed with which you are wont to achieve them. When all Ireland was lost, but for a single city, you transported the army and in one battle instantly broke the power of Hibernia. You were completing the task day by day, when suddenly you were recalled to the Scottish War. Then, tireless, you proceeded against the Scots who with their king were preparing an invasion of England, and in about one year you completely subdued and added to the wealth of England that realm which all our kings for eight hundred years had been unable to master. When the remnant of their forces, still powerful and marching swiftly with no encumbrances, set out in utter desperation for England, which was then almost stripped of defenses, and, making an unforeseen attack, got as far as Worcester, you pursued them with forced marches and in one battle destroyed them, capturing almost all their noblemen. Afterwards peace was maintained at home.

Then, but not for the first time, we perceived that you were as mighty in deliberation as in the arts of war. Daily you toiled in Parliament, that the treaty made with the enemy might be honored, or that decrees in the interest of the State might at once be passed. When you saw delays being contrived and every man more attentive to his private interest than to that of the state, when you saw the people complaining that they had been deluded of their hopes and circumvented by the power of the few, you put an end to the domination of these few

116. Publius Cornelius Scipio, or *Scipio Africanus* Major (c. 200 B.C.E.), was the greatest Roman general of the Second Punic War. He retired to his country home in Liternum following a political controversy in which he was charged with misconduct.

117. Milton neglects to mention that Fairfax withdrew because he disapproved of the regicide.

men, since they, although so often warned, had refused to do so. Another Parliament was convened anew, and the suffrage granted only to those who deserved it.[118] The elected members came together. They did nothing. When they in turn had at length exhausted themselves with disputes and quarrels, most of them considering themselves inadequate and unfit for executing such great tasks, they of their own accord dissolved the Parliament.

Cromwell, we are deserted! You alone remain.[119] On you has fallen the whole burden of our affairs. On you alone they depend. In unison we acknowledge your unexcelled virtue. No one protests save such as seek equal honors, though inferior themselves, or begrudge the honors assigned to one more worthy, or do not understand that there is nothing in human society more pleasing to God, or more agreeable to reason, nothing in the state more just, nothing more expedient, than the rule of the man most fit to rule. All know you to be that man, Cromwell! Such have been your achievements as the greatest and most illustrious citizen, the director of public counsels, the commander of the bravest armies, the father of your country. It is thus that you are greeted by the spontaneous and heartfelt cries of all upright men. Your deeds recognize no other name as worthy of you; no other do they allow, and the haughty titles which seem so great in the opinion of the mob, they properly reject. For what is a title, except a certain limited degree of dignity? Your deeds surpass all degrees, not only of admiration, but surely of titles too, and like the tops of pyramids, bury themselves in the sky, towering above the popular favor of titles. But since it is, not indeed worthy, but expedient for even the greatest capacities to be bounded and confined by some sort of human dignity, which is considered an honor, you assumed a certain title very like that of father of your country. You suffered and allowed yourself, not indeed to be borne aloft, but to come down so many degrees from the heights and be forced into a definite rank, so to speak, for the public good.[120] The name of king you spurned from your far greater eminence, and rightly so.[121] For if, when you became so great a figure, you were captivated by the title which as a private citizen you were able to send under the yoke and reduce to nothing, you would be doing almost the same thing as if, when you had subjugated some tribe of idolaters with the help of the true God, you were to worship the gods that you had conquered. May you then, O Cromwell, increase in your magnanimity, for it becomes you. You, the liberator of your country, the author of liberty, and likewise its guardian and savior,

118. After Cromwell dissolved the Rump Parliament in April 1653, he convened a new one, the Barebones Parliament, its members chosen by the officers of the army from among those nominated by the Independent churches of each county.

119. Cromwell accepted the abdication of the Barebones Parliament and assumed sovereign power under the title Lord Protector in December 1653.

120. Milton's interpretation of Cromwell's assumption of the title Lord Protector bears comparison with Abdiel's interpretation of the Son's installation as head of the angels (*PL* 5.831–45).

121. Led by General Lambert, a group of army officers had indeed urged Cromwell to accept the title of king in the last days of the Barebones Parliament.

can undertake no more distinguished role and none more august. By your deeds you have outstripped not only the achievements of our kings, but even the legends of our heroes.

Consider again and again how precious a thing is this liberty which you hold, committed to your care, entrusted and commended to you by how dear a mother, your native land. That which she once sought from the most distinguished men of the entire nation, she now seeks from you alone and through you alone hopes to achieve. Honor this great confidence reposed in you, honor your country's singular hope in you. Honor the faces and the wounds of the many brave men, all those who under your leadership have striven so vigorously for liberty. Honor the shades of those who have fallen in that very struggle. Honor too what foreign nations think and say of us, the high hopes which they have for themselves as a result of our liberty, so bravely won, and our republic, so gloriously born. If the republic should miscarry, so to speak, and as quickly vanish, surely no greater shame and disgrace could befall this country. Finally, honor yourself, so that, having achieved that liberty in pursuit of which you endured so many hardships and encountered so many perils, you may not permit it to be violated by yourself or in any degree diminished by others. Certainly you yourself cannot be free without us, for it has so been arranged by nature that he who attacks the liberty of others is himself the first of all to lose his own liberty and learns that he is the first of all to become a slave. And he deserves this fate. For if the very patron and tutelary god of liberty, as it were, if that man than whom no one has been considered more just, more holy, more excellent, shall afterwards attack that liberty which he himself has defended, such an act must necessarily be dangerous and well-nigh fatal not only to liberty itself but also to the cause of all virtue and piety. Honor itself, virtue itself will seem to have melted away, religious faith will be circumscribed, reputation will hereafter be a meager thing. A deeper wound than this, after that first wound,[122] can never be inflicted on the human race. You have taken upon yourself by far the heaviest burden, one that will put to the test your inmost capacities, that will search you out wholly and intimately, and reveal what spirit, what strength, what authority are in you, whether there truly live in you that piety, faith, justice, and moderation of soul which convince us that you have been raised by the power of God beyond all other men to this most exalted rank. To rule with wisdom three powerful nations, to desire to lead their peoples from base customs to a better standard of morality and discipline than before, to direct your solicitous mind and thoughts into the most distant regions, to be vigilant, to exercise foresight, to refuse no toil, to yield to no allurements of pleasure, to flee from the pomp of wealth and power, these are arduous tasks compared to which war is a mere game. These trials will buffet you and shake you; they require a man supported by divine help, advised and instructed by all-but-divine inspiration.

122. **first wound:** i.e., Original Sin.

Such matters and still others I have no doubt that you consider and reflect upon, times without number, and also the following concern—by what means you can best, can not only accomplish these momentous ends, but also restore to us our liberty, unharmed and even enhanced. In my judgment you can do this in no better way than by admitting those men whom you first cherished as comrades in your toils and dangers to the first share in your counsels—as indeed you do—men who are eminently modest, upright, and brave, men who from the sight of so much death and slaughter before their very eyes have learned, not cruelty or hardness of heart, but justice, the fear of God, and compassion for the lot of mankind, have learned finally that liberty is to be cherished the more dearly in proportion to the gravity of the dangers to which they have exposed themselves for her sake. These men come not from the off-scourings of the mob or of foreign countries. They are no random throng, but most of them citizens of the better stamp, of birth either noble or at least not dishonorable, of ample or moderate means. What if some are more highly valued because of their very poverty? It was not booty that attracted them, but the most troubled times, when our situation was beyond question dubious and often desperate, inspired them to free the state by killing the tyrant. And they were ready, not merely to bandy speeches and views with one another in a place of safety or in Parliament, but to join battle with the enemy. Therefore, unless we are for ever to pursue vague and empty hopes, I see not in what men faith can finally be reposed if not in them, or in their like. Of their loyalty we have the surest and most indubitable pledge in that they were willing to meet death itself for their country, if such had been their destiny. Of their piety in that, after humbly imploring God's assistance and so often receiving notable help from him, they were accustomed to assign the whole glory of their successful enterprises to him from whom they were wont to seek aid. Of their justice in that they brought even the king to trial, and, when he was condemned, refused to spare him. Of their moderation, in that we have now for a long time tasted it, and also in that if the peace which they themselves have secured should be broken through their own fault, they would themselves be the first to feel the evils that would then ensue. They would themselves receive in their own bodies the first wounds and must fight again for all those fortunes and distinctions which they had just now so gloriously secured. Of their courage, at last, in that other men have never recovered their liberty with better fortune or greater bravery. Let us not suppose that any others can preserve it with greater care.

My discourse is on fire to commemorate the names of these illustrious men: first you, Fleetwood, whom I know to have shown the same civility, gentleness, and courtesy from your earliest days in the army even to those military commands which you now hold, next to the very highest.[123] The enemy found you brave and fearless, but also merciful in victory. You, Lambert, who as a mere youth and the leader of a bare handful of men checked the advance of the Duke

123. Charles *Fleetwood* was then commander in chief of Ireland.

of Hamilton and kept him in check, though around him was the flower and strength of all Scotland's young manhood.[124] You, Desborough, and you, Whalley, whom, when I heard or read about the most violent battles of this war, I always sought and found where the enemy was thickest.[125] You, Overton, who for many years have been linked to me with a more than fraternal harmony, by reason of the likeness of our tastes and the sweetness of your disposition.[126] At the unforgettable Battle of Marston Moor, when our left wing had been routed, the leaders, looking behind them in flight, beheld you making a stand with your infantry and repelling the attacks of the enemy amid dense slaughter on both sides. Then, in the war in Scotland, once the shores of Fife had been seized by your efforts under the leadership of Cromwell and a way laid open beyond Stirling, the Scots of the West and the North admit that you were a most humane foe, and the farthest Orkneys confess you a merciful conqueror. I shall name others too, whom you summoned to share your counsels, men famous in private life and the arts of peace, and known to me either through friendship or by report. Whitelocke, Pickering, Strickland, Sydenham, and Sidney (which glorious name I rejoice has ever been loyal to our side), Montague, Lawrence,[127] both of them men of supreme genius, cultivated in the liberal arts, and a great many other citizens of pre-eminent merits, some already famed for service in Parliament, some for military distinction. To these most illustrious men and honored citizens it would beyond doubt be appropriate for you to entrust our liberty. Indeed, it would be hard to say to whom that liberty could more safely be committed.

Next, I would have you leave the church to the church and shrewdly relieve yourself and the government of half your burden (one that is at the same time completely alien to you), and not permit two powers, utterly diverse, the civil and the ecclesiastical, to make harlots of each other and while appearing to strengthen, by their mingled and spurious riches, actually to undermine and at length destroy each other. I would have you remove all power from the church (but power will never be absent so long as money, the poison of the church, the quinsy[128] of truth, extorted by force even from those who are unwilling, remains

124. John *Lambert* was only twenty-nine when he defeated the invading Scottish forces led by Hamilton, and had already achieved a rank second only to Fairfax and Cromwell.

125. John *Desborough* almost captured Charles II in the battle at Worcester, and Edmund *Whalley* commanded the regiment responsible for Charles I while he was at Hampton Court.

126. Robert *Overton,* the governor of Hull, played a prominent part in the battle of Marston Moor but openly criticized the new Protectorate.

127. Bulstrode Whitelocke and Gilbert *Pickering* served in Parliament from 1640 until its dissolution in 1653. Walter *Strickland* and William *Sydenham* both served in the Barebones Parliament, the latter after a distinguished career as a colonel. Algernon *Sidney,* a captain of horse who sustained serious injury at Marston Moor, was nevertheless twice suspected of Royalist sympathies but proved loyal to the Parliamentarians. Edward *Montague* and Henry *Lawrence* were both expelled from the Long Parliament in the 1648 purge, but the former later served in the Council of State, and the latter ascended to the position of Lord President of Cromwell's Supreme Council. Milton wrote *Sonnet 20* for Henry's son, Edward.

128. **quinsy:** tonsillitis.

the price of preaching the Gospel). I would have you drive from the temple the money-changers, who buy and sell, not doves, but the Dove, the Holy Spirit Himself. Then may you propose fewer new laws than you repeal old ones, for there are often men in the state who itch with a kind of lust to promulgate many laws, as versifiers itch to pour forth many poems. But the greater the number, the worse in general is the quality of the laws, which become, not precautions, but pitfalls. You should keep only those laws that are essential and pass others—not such as subject good men with bad to the same yoke, nor, while they take precautions against the wiles of the wicked, forbid also that which should be free for good men—but rather such laws as appertain only to crimes and do not forbid actions of themselves licit, merely because of the guilt of those who abuse them. For laws are made only to curb wickedness, but nothing can so effectively mould and create virtue as liberty.

Next, would that you might take more thought for the education and morality of the young than has yet been done, nor feel it right for the teachable and the unteachable, the diligent and the slothful to be instructed side by side at public expense. Rather should you keep the rewards of the learned for those who have already acquired learning, those who already deserve the reward. Next, may you permit those who wish to engage in free inquiry to publish their findings at their own peril without the private inspection of any petty magistrate, for so will truth especially flourish, nor will the censure, the envy, the narrow-mindedness, or the superstition of the half-educated always mete out the discoveries of other men, and indeed knowledge in general, according to their own measure and bestow it on us according to their whim.[129] Lastly, may you yourself never be afraid to listen to truth or falsehood, whichever it is, but may you least of all listen to those who do not believe themselves free unless they deny freedom to others, and who do nothing with greater enthusiasm or vigor than cast into chains, not just the bodies, but also the consciences of their brothers, and impose on the state and the church the worst of all tyrannies, that of their own base customs or opinions. May you always take the side of those who think that not just their own party or faction, but all citizens equally have an equal right to freedom in the state. If there be any man for whom such liberty, which can be maintained by the magistrates, does not suffice, he is, I judge, more in love with self-seeking and mob-rule than with genuine liberty, for a people torn by so many factions (as after a storm, when the waves have not yet subsided) does not itself permit that condition in public affairs which is ideal and perfect.

For, my fellow countrymen, your own character is a mighty factor in the acquisition or retention of liberty. Unless your liberty is such as can neither be won nor lost by arms, but is of that kind alone which, sprung from piety, justice, temperance, in short, true virtue, has put down the deepest and most far-reaching roots in your souls, there will not be lacking one who will shortly

129. Here Milton restates the gist of *Areopagitica*.

wrench from you, even without weapons, that liberty which you boast of having sought by force of arms. Many men has war made great whom peace makes small. If, having done with war, you neglect the arts of peace, if warfare is your peace and liberty, war your only virtue, your supreme glory, you will find, believe me, that peace itself is your greatest enemy. Peace itself will be by far your hardest war, and what you thought liberty will prove to be your servitude. Unless with true and sincere devotion to God and men—not empty and verbose, but effective and fruitful devotion—you drive from your minds the superstitions that are sprung from ignorance of real and genuine religion, you will have those who will perch upon your back and shoulders as if on beasts of burden, who will sell you at public auction, though you be victors in the war, as if you were their own booty, and will reap rich reward from your ignorance and superstition. Unless you expel avarice, ambition, and luxury from your minds, yes, and extravagance from your families as well, you will find at home and within that tyrant who, you believed, was to be sought abroad and in the field—now even more stubborn. In fact, many tyrants, impossible to endure, will from day to day hatch out from your very vitals. Conquer them first. This is the warfare of peace, these are its victories, hard indeed, but bloodless, and far more noble than the gory victories of war. Unless you be victors here as well, that enemy and tyrant whom you have just now defeated in the field has either not been conquered at all or has been conquered in vain. For if the ability to devise the cleverest means of putting vast sums of money into the treasury, the power readily to equip land and sea forces, to deal shrewdly with ambassadors from abroad, and to contract judicious alliances and treaties has seemed to any of you greater, wiser, and more useful to the state than to administer incorrupt justice to the people, to help those cruelly harassed and oppressed, and to render to every man promptly his own deserts, too late will you discover how mistaken you have been, when those great affairs have suddenly betrayed you and what now seems to you small and trifling shall then have turned against you and become a source of ruin. Nay, the loyalty of the armies and allies in whom you trust is fleeting, unless it be maintained by the power of justice alone. Wealth and honors, which most men pursue, easily change masters; they desert to the side which excels in virtue, industry, and endurance of toil, and they abandon the slothful. Thus nation presses upon nation, or the sounder part of a nation overthrows the more corrupt. Thus did you drive out the royalists. If you begin to slip into the same vices, to imitate those men, to seek the same goals, to clutch at the same vanities, you actually are royalists yourselves, at the mercy either of the same men who up to now have been your enemies, or of others in turn, who, depending on the same prayers to God, the same patience, integrity, and shrewdness which were at first your strength, will justly subdue you, who have now become so base and slipped into royalist excess and folly. Then in truth, as if God had become utterly disgusted with you—a horrid state—will you seem to have passed through the fire only to perish in the smoke. Then will you be as much despised by all men as you are now admired and will leave behind you only this salutary lesson (which could in the future perhaps be of assistance to others, though not to you), how great might have been the achievements of genuine virtue and piety, when the mere counterfeit and shadow of these qualities—cleverly feigned, no more—could embark upon such noble undertakings and through you progress so far towards execution.

For if through your want of experience, of constancy, or of honesty such glorious deeds have issued in failure, it will yet be possible for better men to do as much hereafter, and no less must be expected of them. But no one, not even Cromwell himself, nor a whole tribe of liberating Brutuses, if Brutus[130] were to come to life again, either could if they would, or would if they could, free you a second time, once you had been so easily corrupted. For why should anyone then claim for you freedom to vote or the power of sending to Parliament whomever you prefer? So that each of you could elect in the cities men of his own faction, or in the country towns choose that man, however unworthy, who has entertained you more lavishly at banquets and supplied farmers and peasants with more abundant drink? Under such circumstances, not wisdom or authority, but faction and gluttony would elect to Parliament in our name either inn-keepers and hucksters of the state from city taverns or from country districts ploughboys and veritable herdsmen. Who would commit the state to men whom no one would trust with his private affairs? the treasury and revenues to men who have shamefully wasted their own substance? Who would hand over to them the public income, to steal and convert from public to private? Or how could they suddenly become legislators for the whole nation who themselves have never known what law is, what reason, what right or justice, straight or crooked, licit or illicit; who think that all power resides in violence, all grandeur in pride and arrogance; who in Parliament give priority to showing illegitimate favor to their friends and persistent hostility to their foes; who establish their relatives and friends in every section of the country to levy taxes and confiscate property—men for the most part mean and corrupt, who by bidding at their own auctions collect therefrom great sums of money, embezzle what they have collected, defraud the state, ravage the provinces, enrich themselves, and suddenly emerge into opulence and pride from the beggary and rags of yesterday? Who could endure such thieving servants, the deputies of their masters? Who could believe the masters and patrons of such thieves to be fit guardians of liberty, or think his own liberty enlarged one iota by such caretakers of the state (though the customary number of five hundred be thus elected from all the towns), since there would then be so few among the guardians and watchdogs of liberty who either knew how to enjoy, or deserved to possess, it?

Lastly (a reflection not to be neglected), men who are unworthy of liberty most often prove ungrateful to their very liberators. Who would now be willing to fight, or even encounter the smallest danger for the liberty of such men? It is

130. Lucius Junius Brutus (c. 500 B.C.E.), legendary founder of the Roman republic, liberated Rome from the Tarquins.

not fitting, it is not meet, for such men to be free. However loudly they shout and boast about liberty, slaves they are at home and abroad, although they know it not. When at last they do perceive it and like wild horses fretting at the bit try to shake off the yoke, driven not by the love of true liberty (to which the good man alone can rightly aspire), but by pride and base desires, even though they take arms in repeated attempts, they will accomplish naught.[131] They can perhaps change their servitude; they cannot cast it off.[132] This often happened even to the ancient Romans, once they had been corrupted and dissipated by luxury; still more often to the modern Romans; when after a long interval they sought under the auspices of Crescentius Nomentanus and later under the leadership of Cola di Rienzi, self-styled Tribune of the People, to renew the ancient glory of Rome and restore the Republic.[133] For rest assured (that you may not be vexed, or seek to blame someone other than yourselves), rest assured, I say, that to be free is precisely the same as to be pious, wise, just, and temperate and just, careful of one's property, aloof from another's, and thus finally to be magnanimous and brave, so to be the opposite to these qualities is the same as to be a slave. And by the customary judgment and, so to speak, just retaliation of God, it happens that a nation which cannot rule and govern itself, but has delivered itself into slavery to its own lusts, is enslaved also to other master whom it does not choose, and serves not only voluntarily but also against its will. Such is the decree of law and of nature herself, that he who cannot control himself, who through poverty of intellect or madness cannot properly administer his own affairs, should not be his own master, but like a ward be given over to the power of another.[134] Much less should he be put in charge of the affairs of other men, or of the state. You, therefore, who wish to remain free, either be wise at the outset or recover your senses as soon as possible. If to be a slave is hard, and you do not wish it, learn to obey right reason, to master yourselves. Lastly refrain from factions, hatreds, superstitions, injustices, lusts, and rapine against one another. Unless you do this with all your strength you cannot seem either to God

131. According to Masson (4:547–52), the Protectorate was opposed both by those who wanted a republican form of government, not single-person rule, and by those loyal to the Stuarts. Both factions actively plotted against Cromwell.

132. Cp. *Sonnet 12* 8–12: "But this is got by casting pearl to hogs,/That bawl for freedom in their senseless mood,/And still revolt when truth would set them free./License they mean when they cry libertie;/ For who loves that, must first be wise and good"; also, *TKM:* "None can love freedom heartily but good men. The rest love not freedom, but license; which never hath more scope, or more indulgence, than under tyrants."

133. *Crescentius Nomentanus* (c. 950–98), who like the rest of his powerful clan (the Crescentii) affected the ways of classical Rome, actively opposed the dominion of Saxon rulers over Rome's affairs. Otto III besieged, captured, and had him beheaded. *Cola di Rienzi* (1313–54) took the title of tribune and sought fiscal, political, and judicial reform in Rome. Ultimately successful in enlisting papal support, he returned to Rome from exile and was killed by the mob.

134. The theological application of this classical principle of ethics and political theory pervades Milton's late masterpieces. See *PL* 12.90–95: "Therefore since he permits/Within himself unworthy powers to reign/Over free reason, God in judgment just/Subjects him from without to violent lords;/ Who oft as undeservedly enthrall/His outward freedom"; also, with specific application to the descent of Rome from republican virtue to imperial servility *PR* 4.132–45.

or to men, or even to your recent liberators, fit to be entrusted with the liberty and guidance of the state and the power of commanding others, which you arrogate to yourselves so greedily. Then indeed, like a nation in wardship, you would rather be in need of some tutor, some brave and faithful guardian of your affairs.

As for me, whatever the issue, I have bestowed my services by no means grudgingly nor, I hope, in vain, where I judged that they would be most useful to the state. I have not borne arms for liberty merely on my own doorstep, but have also wielded them so far afield that the reason and justification of these by no means commonplace events, having been explained and defended both at home and abroad, and having surely won the approval of all good men, are made splendidly manifest to the supreme glory of my countrymen and as an example to posterity. If the most recent deeds of my fellow countrymen should not correspond sufficiently to their earliest, let them look to it themselves. I have borne witness, I might almost say I have erected a monument that will not soon pass away, to those deeds that were illustrious, that were glorious, that were almost beyond any praise, and if I have done nothing else, I have surely redeemed my pledge. Moreover, just as the epic poet, if he is scrupulous and disinclined to break the rules, undertakes to extol, not the whole life of the hero whom he proposes to celebrate in his verse, but usually one event of his life (the exploits of Achilles at Troy, let us say, or the return of Ulysses, or the arrival of Aeneas in Italy) and passes over the rest, so let it suffice me too, as my duty or my excuse, to have celebrated at least one heroic achievement of my countrymen. The rest I omit. Who could extol all the achievements of an entire nation? If after such brave deeds you ignobly fail, if you do aught unworthy of yourselves, be sure that posterity will speak out and pass judgment: the foundations were soundly laid, the beginnings, in fact more than the beginnings, were splendid, but posterity will look in vain, not without a certain distress, for those who were to complete the work, who were to put the pediment in place. It will be a source of grief that to such great undertakings, such great virtues, perseverance was lacking. It will seem to posterity that a mighty harvest of glory was at hand, together with the opportunity for doing the greatest deeds, but that to this opportunity men were wanting. Yet there was not one wanting who could rightly counsel, encourage, and inspire, who could honor both the noble deeds and those who had done them, and make both deeds and doers illustrious with praises that will never die.[135]

135. In defining his historical role in the last two sentences, Milton returns to the agricultural myth invoked early in this work, when he compared himself to "Triptolemus of old" disseminating "the renewed cultivation of freedom and civic life." The *mighty harvest of glory* waiting to be reaped owes much to his oratorical efforts. See note 14.

Introduction to *The Ready and Easy Way to Establish a Free Commonwealth*

The Ready and Easy Way to Establish a Free Commonwealth; and the Excellence Thereof Compared with the Inconveniences and Dangers of Readmitting Kingship in this Nation appeared in two editions in late February and early April 1660, amid conditions that were from Milton's perspective rapidly deteriorating (Norbrook 1999; Lewalski 2000; Knoppers 2001). Although Milton wrote both versions in great haste in order to keep pace with events, *The Ready and Easy Way* is at once a grimly and gloriously eloquent work. The immediate political context was the unpopular rule of the Rump Parliament, agitation by Republication army leaders, and the arrival in London of General George Monck's army. In January and early February, Monck reiterated his support of the Commonwealth and his opposition to the restoration of monarchy, but his true intentions were as much a subject of debate and speculation among his contemporaries as they are among scholars today.

It is clear from the first edition of *The Ready and Easy Way* that Milton placed in Monck his hopes for the continuation of republican government. On February 21, however, before Milton could see the first edition through the press, Monck reinstated the Presbyterian MPs excluded in Pride's Purge of 1648, making the return of Charles II all but inevitable. In the greatly expanded second edition, reprinted here, Milton by turns adjusts to and pointedly ignores Monck's ominous about-face. While Milton refers in the opening lines to the "resolution of those who are in power tending to the establishment of a free commonwealth," the end had come for the Good Old Cause of antimonarchic republicanism. The Rump's "writs for new elections," in which eligibility depended on opposition to a rule by a "single person," had been recalled, and public sentiment was gathering for the restoration of Charles II. By the time of the second edition, the restored Long Parliament had called its own new elections, and it was clear that the new body, elected without the Rump's qualifications, would restore monarchy. Milton's thinly veiled plea that Monck thwart pro-monarchist sentiment by force underlines the bleakness of anti-monarchism prospects: "More just it is, doubtless, if it come to force, that a less number compel a greater to retain (which can be no wrong to them) their liberty, than that a greater number, for the pleasure of their baseness, compel a less most injuriously to be their fellow slaves" (pp. 1131–32).

If there was an element of bandwagon jumping in the publication of the antiprelatical tracts (see the introduction to *Of Reformation*), the circumstances surrounding *The Ready and Easy Way* could not have been more different. Milton was the last republican to put his name to a work opposing monarchy before the Restoration. His claim that "with all hazard I have ventured what I thought my duty to speak" (p. 1136) is no exaggeration. Publishing the work at a time of growing public opposition to the Rump and growing support for the restoration of monarchy took remarkable physical courage. Within months, the new House of Commons had successfully called for the burning of several of Milton's books, and Milton was imprisoned. It is not altogether clear how the author escaped the punishment for treason: hanging until half-dead, disembowelment while alive, and quartering.

The title refers to Milton's plan for a grand council (a national assembly perpetuating the Long Parliament, with members granted life tenure) and for regional assemblies. Members of the grand council are to be chosen by a series of nominations and elections that gradually sift and refine candidate lists, a process superior in Milton's eyes to "committing all to the noise and shouting of a rude multitude" (p. 1126). Milton may have seen his model as "ready and easy," but he must have also recognized by late February that popular sentiment made its implementation impossible. It may be significant in this connection that Milton in his later poetry was critical of ready ways and of ease (see, e.g., *PL* 2.81 and 12.214–26 and *SA* 268–71).

The Ready and Easy Way is simultaneously a groundbreaking work of political theory and the last gasp of the Good Old Cause. Blair Hoxby (2002) argues persuasively that Milton invents here the federalist republican balance between central and local authority. At the same time, Milton in his prophetic mode unleashes a jeremiad against the backsliding English, who like the Israelites are an elect nation but who have, again like the Israelites, chosen "a captain back for Egypt" (p. 1136; Knoppers 1990). After years in which the spokesperson of the party in power had moderated his style (Corns 1982), Milton returns in the rhetoric of *The Ready and Easy Way* to the fiery incandescence of his early prose works, as he articulates a principle close to his heart: external tyranny, though an apt punishment for those who are slaves within, is an insupportable outrage when imposed on those endowed with inward freedom. Milton's passionate conviction fuels the tract's language, culminating in a peroration justly celebrated as one of the high points of Milton's prose.

Our copy text for the second edition of April 1660 is a Harvard University Library copy (14496.17.2*).

THE READY AND EASY WAY TO ESTABLISH A FREE COMMONWEALTH

Et nos
Consilium dedimus Syllae, demus populo nunc.[1]

Although since the writing of this treatise the face of things hath had some change, writs for new elections have been recalled, and the members at first chosen readmitted from exclusion,[2] yet not a little rejoicing to hear declared the resolution of those who are in power tending to the establishment of a free commonwealth,[3] and to remove, if it be possible, this noxious humor of returning to bondage (instilled of late by some deceivers, and nourished from bad principles and false apprehensions among too many of the people), I thought best not to suppress what I had written, hoping that it may now be of much more use and concernment to be freely published in the midst of our elections to a free parliament, or their sitting to consider freely of the government, whom it behooves to have all things represented to them that may direct their judgment therein. And I never read of any state, scarce of any tyrant, grown so incurable as to refuse counsel from any in a time of public deliberation, much less to be offended. If their absolute determination be to enthrall us, before so long a Lent of servitude they may permit us a little shroving time[4] first, wherein to speak freely and take our leaves of liberty. And because in the former edition, through haste, many faults escaped, and many books were suddenly dispersed ere the note to mend them could be sent, I took the opportunity from this occasion to revise and somewhat to enlarge the whole discourse, especially that

1. Juvenal's *Satires* I ("And we have given advice to Sulla, now let us give it to the people"). Under the name of the Roman ruler Lucius Cornelius Sulla (138–78 B.C.E.), who paved the way for the monarchy of Julius Caesar, Milton points to General George Monck, to whom he had recently addressed proposals for preventing the restoration of monarchy; having in the meantime lost confidence in Monck, he turns now to the people.

2. In the days before the publication of the first edition, *new elections* for Parliament, in which Royalists would be ineligible, were called off after the Presbyterian and largely Royalist members purged in 1648 (see n. 13) had been *readmitted from exclusion* as a result of Monck's intervention. With this change, the restoration of monarchy became inevitable. By the time of the second edition, things looked even bleaker from Milton's perspective.

3. The Rump emphatically and Monck and the army officers at least nominally were opposed to the *returning to bondage,* i.e., the restoration of monarchy; Milton is grasping at straws.

4. **shroving time:** Shrovetide, which precedes Ash Wednesday and Lent, was set aside for confession and carnivals (Shrove Tuesday is the English *Mardi Gras*).

part which argues for a perpetual senate. The treatise thus revised and enlarged is as follows.

The parliament of England, assisted by a great number of the people who appeared and stuck to them faithfulest in defense of religion and their civil liberties, judging kingship by long experience a government unnecessary, burdensome, and dangerous, justly and magnanimously abolished it,[5] turning regal bondage into a free commonwealth, to the admiration and terror of our emulous neighbors. They took themselves not bound by the light of nature or religion to any former covenant,[6] from which the king himself, by many forfeitures of a latter date or discovery, and our own longer consideration thereon, had more and more unbound us, both to himself and his posterity, as hath been ever the justice and the prudence of all wise nations that have ejected tyranny. They covenanted "to preserve the king's person and authority in the preservation of the true religion and our liberties," not in his endeavoring to bring in upon our consciences a popish religion, upon our liberties thraldom, upon our lives destruction, by his occasioning (if not complotting, as was after discovered) the Irish massacre,[7] his fomenting and arming the rebellion, his covert leaguing with the rebels against us, his refusing, more than seven times, propositions[8] most just and necessary to the true religion and our liberties, tendered him by the parliament both of England and Scotland. They made not their covenant concerning him with no difference between a king and a god, or promised him, as Job did to the Almighty, "to trust in him, though he slay us."[9] They understood that the solemn engagement[10] wherein we all forswore kingship was no more a breach of the covenant than the covenant was of the protestation[11] before, but a faithful and prudent going on both in the words, well weighed, and in the true sense of the covenant, "without respect of persons,"[12] when we could not serve two contrary masters, God and the king, or the king and that more supreme law sworn in the first place to maintain our safety and our liberty.

They knew the people of England to be a free people, themselves the representers of that freedom. And although many were excluded,[13] and as many fled

5. In February 1649, shortly after the execution of Charles I, the Rump Parliament abolished monarchy.

6. **covenant:** the Solemn League and Covenant of 1643, quoted several lines later.

7. Although Charles was not behind the massacre of English Protestants by Irish Catholics in 1641, he did attempt to secure the military help of Irish Catholic armies during the Civil War.

8. **propositions:** In the seven years preceding his execution, Charles received seven or more sets of proposals from the English and Scottish Parliaments.

9. Milton paraphrases Job 13.15.

10. **engagement:** oath of loyalty to the Commonwealth mandatory for Members of Parliament following October 1649.

11. **protestation:** In a formal protest in May 1641, Parliament tied the duties of defending the king and defending the Church of England; Milton believed that the first duty lapsed when Charles sought alliance with Irish Catholics.

12. Milton again quotes from the Solemn League and Covenant.

13. **excluded:** Presbyterian M.P.'s with Royalist sympathies were expelled by Pride's Purge in 1648.

(so they pretended) from tumults to Oxford,[14] yet they were left a sufficient number to act in parliament: therefore not bound by any statute of preceding parliaments but by the law of nature only, which is the only law of laws truly and properly to all mankind fundamental, the beginning and the end of all government, to which no parliament or people that will thoroughly reform but may and must have recourse—as they had and must yet have in church reformation (if they thoroughly intend it) to evangelic rules, not to ecclesiastical canons, though never so ancient, so ratified and established in the land by statutes, which for the most part are mere positive laws,[15] neither natural nor moral—and so by any parliament, for just and serious considerations, without scruple to be at any time repealed.

If others of their number in these things were under force, they were not, but under free conscience; if others were excluded by a power which they could not resist, they were not therefore to leave the helm of government in no hands, to discontinue their care of the public peace and safety, to desert the people in anarchy and confusion, no more than when so many of their members left them as made up in outward formality a more legal parliament of three estates against them.[16] The best affected also and best principled of the people stood not numbering or computing on which side were most voices in parliament, but on which side appeared to them most reason, most safety, when the house divided upon main matters. What was well motioned and advised, they examined not whether fear or persuasion carried it in the vote. Neither did they measure votes and counsels by the intentions of them that voted, knowing that intentions either are but guessed at or not soon enough known, and, although good, can neither make the deed such nor prevent the consequence from being bad. Suppose bad intentions in things otherwise well done; what was well done was, by them who so thought, not the less obeyed or followed in the state, since in the church who had not rather follow Iscariot[17] or Simon the magician,[18] though to covetous ends preaching, than Saul, though in the uprightness of his heart persecuting the gospel?

Safer they therefore judged what they thought the better counsels, though carried on by some perhaps to bad ends, than the worse by others, though endeavored with best intentions. And yet they were not to learn[19] that a greater

14. In 1644, Royalist members of Parliament had answered Charles's call for an alternative Parliament in Oxford.

15. **positive laws:** laws not entailed by the law of nature, and therefore merely conventional.

16. **three estates:** king, lords, and commons; Milton's strained argument is that, just as the Long Parliament, without the king, was more legitimate than the Royalist Oxford Parliament, so the Rump Parliament gained rather than lost legitimacy with the exclusion by military force of elected members in Pride's Purge.

17. **Iscariot:** Judas, who before betraying Christ for silver preached the good news.

18. Simon Magus offered money to Peter and John for the power of the Holy Spirit (Acts 8.9–25).

19. **were not to learn:** did not need to be taught.

number might be corrupt within the walls of a parliament as well as of a city,[20] whereof in matters of nearest concernment all men will be judges; nor easily permit that the odds of voices in their greatest council shall more endanger them by corrupt or credulous votes than the odds of enemies by open assaults, judging that most voices ought not always to prevail where main matters are in question. If others hence will pretend to disturb all counsels, what is that to them who pretend not, but are in real danger?—not they only so judging, but a great, though not the greatest, number of their chosen patriots, who might be more in weight than the others in number, there being in number little virtue, but by weight and measure wisdom working all things. And the dangers on either side they seriously thus weighed: from the treaty, short fruits of long labors and seven years war—security for twenty years, if we can hold it; reformation in the church for three years[21]—then put to shift again with our vanquished master. His justice, his honor, his conscience declared quite contrary to ours, which would have furnished him with many such evasions, as in a book entitled *An Inquisition for Blood*[22] soon after were not concealed: bishops not totally removed but left, as it were, in ambush, a reserve, with ordination in their sole power; their lands already sold, not to be alienated but rented, and the sale of them called "sacrilege"; delinquents,[23] few of many brought to condign[24] punishment; accessories punished, the chief author[25] above pardon, though after utmost resistance vanquished, not to give but to receive laws; yet besought, treated with, and to be thanked for his gracious concessions, to be honored, worshiped, glorified.

If this we swore to do, with what righteousness in the sight of God, with what assurance that we bring not by such an oath the whole sea of blood-guiltiness upon our own heads?[26] If on the other side we prefer a free government, though for the present not obtained, yet all those suggested fears and difficulties, as the event will prove, easily overcome, we remain finally secure from the exasperated regal power and out of snares; shall retain the best part of our liberty, which is our religion; and the civil part will be from these who defer[27] us much more easily recovered, being neither so subtle nor so awful as a king reenthroned. Nor were their actions less both at home and abroad than might become the hopes of a glorious, rising commonwealth; nor were the expressions

20. Presbyterians now sympathetic to Charles formed the majority in Parliament (before their expulsion) and in London.
21. Milton refers dismissively to terms of the 1648 Treaty of Newport between Parliament and Charles, *our vanquished master,* at the end of *seven years* of civil war.
22. James Howell's Royalist pamphlet (July 1649) argued that Charles, having acted only in his public capacity, was not bound personally by his concessions in the Treaty of Newport.
23. **delinquents:** those who opposed Parliamentary forces in the Civil War.
24. **condign:** deserved.
25. **chief author:** Charles I.
26. I.e., if in the Solemn League and Covenant we swore to be loyal to the king even in his crimes against his people, then we share his guilt for those killed in the Civil War.
27. **defer:** delay.

both of army and people, whether in their public declarations or several writings, other than such as testified a spirit in this nation no less noble and well fitted to the liberty of a commonwealth than in the ancient Greeks or Romans. Nor was the heroic cause unsuccessfully defended to all Christendom against the tongue of a famous and thought invincible adversary,[28] nor the constancy and fortitude that so nobly vindicated our liberty, our victory at once against two the most prevailing usurpers over mankind, superstition and tyranny, unpraised or uncelebrated in a written monument likely to outlive detraction, as it hath hitherto convinced or silenced not a few of our detractors, especially in parts abroad.

After our liberty and religion thus prosperously fought for, gained, and many years possessed (except in those unhappy interruptions which God hath removed), now that nothing remains but in all reason the certain hopes of a speedy and immediate settlement forever in a firm and free commonwealth for this extolled and magnified nation, regardless both of honor won or deliverances vouchsafed from heaven, to fall back, or rather to creep back so poorly, as it seems the multitude would, to their once abjured and detested thraldom of kingship, to be ourselves the slanderers of our own just and religious deeds (though done by some to covetous and ambitious ends, yet not therefore to be stained with their infamy, or they to asperse the integrity of others); and yet these now by revolting from the conscience of deeds well done both in church and state, to throw away and forsake or rather to betray a just and noble cause for the mixture of bad men who have ill managed and abused it (which had our fathers done heretofore, and on the same pretence deserted true religion, what had long ere this become of our gospel and all Protestant reformation so much intermixed with the avarice and ambition of some reformers?), and by thus relapsing to verify all the bitter predictions of our triumphing enemies—who will now think they wisely discerned and justly censured both us and all our actions as rash, rebellious, hypocritical and impious—not only argues a strange, degenerate contagion suddenly spread among us, fitted and prepared for new slavery, but will render us a scorn and derision to all our neighbors.

And what will they at best say of us and of the whole English name but scoffingly, as of that foolish builder, mentioned by our savior, who began to build a tower and was not able to finish it?[29] Where is this goodly tower of a commonwealth, which the English boasted they would build to overshadow kings and be another Rome in the west? The foundation indeed they laid gallantly, but fell into a worse confusion, not of tongues but of factions, than those at the tower of Babel, and have left no memorial of their work behind them remaining but in the common laughter of Europe. Which must needs redound the more to our

28. **adversary:** Salmasius, the eminent French scholar whose defense of Charles I Milton answered in a *written monument,* his Latin *First Defense of the English People* (1651). Heroic self-portraits are frequent in Milton's polemical prose.

29. Luke 14.28–30.

shame if we but look on our neighbors the United Provinces,[30] to us inferior in all outward advantages, who notwithstanding, in the midst of greater difficulties, courageously, wisely, constantly went through with the same work and are settled in all the happy enjoyments of a potent and flourishing republic to this day.

Besides this, if we return to kingship and soon repent, as undoubtedly we shall when we begin to find the old encroachments coming on by little and little upon our consciences, which must necessarily proceed from king and bishop united inseparably in one interest, we may be forced perhaps to fight over again all that we have fought, and spend over again all that we have spent, but are never like to attain thus far as we are now advanced to the recovery of our freedom, never to have it in possession as we now have it, never to be vouchsafed hereafter the like mercies and signal assistances from heaven in our cause, if by our ingrateful backsliding we make these fruitless; flying now to regal concessions from his divine condescensions and gracious answers to our once importuning prayers against the tyranny which we then groaned under; making vain and viler than dirt the blood of so many thousand faithful and valiant Englishmen, who left us in this liberty bought with their lives; losing by a strange aftergame of folly all the battles we have won, together with all Scotland as to our conquest,[31] hereby lost, which never any of our kings could conquer, all the treasure we have spent, not that corruptible treasure only, but that far more precious of all our late miraculous deliverances treading back again with lost labor all our happy steps in the progress of reformation and most pitifully depriving ourselves the instant fruition of that free government which we have so dearly purchased, a free commonwealth, not only held by wisest men in all ages the noblest, the manliest, the equallest, the justest government, the most agreeable to all due liberty and proportioned equality, both human, civil, and Christian, most cherishing to virtue and true religion, but also (I may say it with greatest probability) plainly commended, or rather enjoined, by our Savior himself to all Christians, not without remarkable disallowance and the brand of gentilism upon kingship.[32]

God in much displeasure gave a king to the Israelites, and imputed it a sin to them that they sought one,[33] but Christ apparently forbids his disciples to admit of any such heathenish government. "The kings of the gentiles," saith he, "exercise lordship over them," and they that "exercise authority upon them are called benefactors: but ye shall not be so; but he that is greatest among you, let him be as the younger, and he that is chief, as he that serveth" [Luke 22.25–27]. The occasion of these his words was the ambitious desire of Zebedee's two

30. **United Provinces:** the Netherlands, a Protestant republic.

31. Cromwell had defeated the Scots at Dunbar and Worcester.

32. "Ye know that they which are accounted to rule over the Gentiles exercise lordship over them. . . . But so shall it not be among you" (Mark 10.42–43).

33. 1 Sam. 8.11–18.

sons[34] to be exalted above their brethren in his kingdom, which they thought was to be ere long upon earth. That he speaks of civil government is manifest by the former part of the comparison, which infers the other part to be always in the same kind. And what government comes nearer to this precept of Christ than a free commonwealth, wherein they who are greatest are perpetual servants and drudges to the public at their own cost and charges, neglect their own affairs, yet are not elevated above their brethren, live soberly in their families, walk the streets as other men, may be spoken to freely, familiarly, friendly, without adoration? Whereas a king must be adored like a demigod, with a dissolute and haughty court about him of vast expense and luxury, masks and revels, to the debauching of our prime gentry both male and female; not in their pastimes only, but in earnest, by the loose employments of court service, which will be then thought honorable. There will be a queen also of no less charge, in most likelihood outlandish and a papist, besides a queen mother such already, together with both their courts and numerous train;[35] then a royal issue, and ere long severally their sumptuous courts, to the multiplying of a servile crew not of servants only but of nobility and gentry, bred up then to the hopes not of public, but of court offices, to be stewards, chamberlains, ushers, grooms, even of the close-stool;[36] and the lower their minds debased with court opinions, contrary to all virtue and reformation, the haughtier will be their pride and profuseness. We may well remember this not long since at home, or need but look at present into the French court, where enticements and preferments daily draw away and pervert the Protestant nobility.

As to the burden of expense, to our cost we shall soon know it; for any good to us deserving to be termed no better than the vast and lavish price of our subjection and their debauchery, which we are now so greedily cheapening,[37] and would so fain by paying most inconsiderately to a single person, who, for anything wherein the public really needs him, will have little else to do but to bestow the eating and drinking of excessive dainties, to set a pompous face upon the superficial actings of state, to pageant himself up and down in progress among the perpetual bowings and cringings of an abject people, on either side deifying and adoring him for nothing done that can deserve it. For what can he more than another man, who, even in the expression of a late court poet, sits only like a great cipher[38] set to no purpose before a long row of other significant figures? Nay, it is well and happy for the people if their king be but a cipher, being ofttimes a mischief, a pest, a scourge of the nation, and, which is worse,

34. **Zebedee's two sons:** James and John, who asked to sit next to Christ in glory (Mark 10.37).

35. **outlandish:** foreign; the *queen mother,* Henrietta Maria, was a French Catholic; following the Restoration, Charles II would marry a Portuguese Catholic princess, Catherine of Braganza.

36. **close-stool:** chamber pot.

37. **cheapening:** bargaining over.

38. **cipher:** arithmetical o, which multiplies figures placed before it; Milton slyly places the o before the other numbers, thus rendering it worthless (his source is unknown, though Sir William Davenant and George Chapman have been suggested).

not to be removed, not to be controlled—much less accused or brought to punishment—without the danger of a common ruin, without the shaking and almost subversion of the whole land; whereas in a free commonwealth, any governor or chief counselor offending may be removed and punished without the least commotion.

Certainly then that people must needs be mad or strangely infatuated that build the chief hope of their common happiness or safety on a single person, who if he happen to be good can do no more than another man, if to be bad hath in his hands to do more evil without check than millions of other men. The happiness of a nation must needs be firmest and certainest in a full and free council of their own electing, where no single person, but reason only, sways. And what madness is it for them who might manage nobly their own affairs themselves, sluggishly and weakly to devolve all on a single person, and, more like boys under age than men, to commit all to his patronage and disposal who neither can perform what he undertakes, and yet for undertaking it, though royally paid, will not be their servant, but their lord? How unmanly must it needs be to count such a one the breath of our nostrils, to hang all our felicity on him, all our safety, our well-being, for which, if we were aught else but sluggards or babies, we need depend on none but God and our own counsels, our own active virtue and industry. "Go to the ant, thou sluggard," saith Solomon, "consider her ways, and be wise; which, having no prince, ruler, or lord, provides her meat in the summer and gathers her food in the harvest" [Prov. 6.6–8]:[39] which evidently shows us that they who think the nation undone without a king, though they look grave or haughty, have not so much true spirit and understanding in them as a pismire.[40] Neither are these diligent creatures hence concluded to live in lawless anarchy, or that commended, but are set the examples to imprudent and ungoverned men of a frugal and self-governing democraty or commonwealth, safer and more thriving in the joint providence and counsel of many industrious equals than under the single domination of one imperious Lord.

It may be well wondered that any nation styling themselves free can suffer any man to pretend hereditary right over them as their lord, whenas, by acknowledging that right, they conclude themselves his servants and his vassals, and so renounce their own freedom. Which how a people and their leaders especially can do, who have fought so gloriously for liberty, how they can change their noble words and actions, heretofore so becoming the majesty of a free people, into the base necessity of court flatteries and prostrations, is not only strange and admirable,[41] but lamentable to think on. That a nation should be so valorous and courageous to win their liberty in the field, and, when they have

39. The ant colony and beehive were often cited to support the natural legitimacy and strength of, respectively, republican and monarchic governments.

40. **pismire:** ant.

41. **admirable:** astonishing, to be wondered at.

won it, should be so heartless[42] and unwise in their counsels as not to know how to use it, value it, what to do with it or with themselves, but, after ten or twelve years' prosperous war and contestation with tyranny, basely and besottedly to run their necks again into the yoke which they have broken and prostrate all the fruits of their victory for naught at the feet of the vanquished, besides our loss of glory and such an example as kings or tyrants never yet had the like to boast of, will be an ignominy if it befall us that never yet befell any nation possessed of their liberty; worthy indeed themselves, whatsoever they be, to be forever slaves—but that part of the nation which consents not with them, as I persuade me of a great number, far worthier than by their means to be brought into the same bondage.

Considering these things so plain, so rational, I cannot but yet further admire on the other side how any man who hath the true principles of justice and religion in him can presume or take upon him to be a king and lord over his brethren, whom he cannot but know, whether as men or Christians, to be for the most part every way equal or superior to himself; how he can display with such vanity and ostentation his regal splendor so supereminently above other mortal men, or, being a Christian, can assume such extraordinary honor and worship to himself while the kingdom of Christ, our common King and Lord, is hid to this world, and such gentilish[43] imitation forbid in express words by himself to all his disciples. All Protestants hold that Christ in his church hath left no vicegerent[44] of his power, but himself without deputy is the only head thereof, governing it from heaven. How then can any Christian man derive his kingship from Christ, but with worse usurpation than the pope his headship over the church, since Christ not only hath not left the least shadow of a command for any such vicegerence from him in the state as the pope pretends for his in the Church, but hath expressly declared that such regal dominion is from the gentiles, not from him, and hath strictly charged us not to imitate them therein?

I doubt not but all ingenuous and knowing men will easily agree with me that a free commonwealth without single person or House of Lords is by far the best government, if it can be had.[45] "But we have all this while," say they, "been expecting[46] it, and cannot yet attain it." 'Tis true indeed, when monarchy was dissolved, the form of a commonwealth should have forthwith been framed, and the practice thereof immediately begun, that the people might have soon been satisfied and delighted with the decent order, ease, and benefit thereof. We had been then by this time firmly rooted, past fear of commotions or mutations, and now flourishing. This care of timely settling a new government instead of the old, too much neglected, hath been our mischief. Yet the cause thereof may

42. **heartless:** cowardly.
43. **gentilish:** see note 32.
44. **vicegerent:** one appointed to act in the place of a ruler.
45. The bland assertion of a highly contested opinion as self-evident is a Miltonic signature.
46. **expecting:** awaiting.

be ascribed with most reason to the frequent disturbances, interruptions, and dissolutions which the parliament hath had, partly from the impatient or disaffected people, partly from some ambitious leaders in the army;[47] much contrary, I believe, to the mind and approbation of the army itself and their other commanders, once undeceived or in their own power.

Now is the opportunity, now the very season, wherein we may obtain a free commonwealth and establish it forever in the land without difficulty or much delay. Writs are sent out for elections, and, which is worth observing, in the name not of any king but of the keepers of our liberty, to summon a free parliament,[48] which then only will indeed be free, and deserve the true honor of that supreme title, if they preserve us a free people; which never parliament was more free to do, being now called not as heretofore by the summons of a king, but by the voice of liberty. And if the people, laying aside prejudice and impatience, will seriously and calmly now consider their own good both religious and civil, their own liberty, and the only means thereof, as shall be here laid before them, and will elect their knights and burgesses[49] able men, and according to the just and necessary qualifications (which for aught I hear remain yet in force unrepealed, as they were formerly decreed in parliament),[50] men not addicted to a single person or house of lords, the work is done; at least the foundation firmly laid of a free commonwealth, and good part also erected of the main structure. For the ground and basis of every just and free government (since men have smarted so oft for committing all to one person) is a general council of ablest men, chosen by the people to consult of public affairs from time to time for the common good. In this grand council must the sovereignty (not transferred but delegated only, and as it were deposited) reside, with this caution: they must have the forces by sea and land committed to them for preservation of the common peace and liberty; must raise and manage the public revenue, at least with some inspectors deputed for satisfaction of the people, how it is employed; must make or propose, as more expressly shall be said anon, civil laws, treat of commerce, peace, or war with foreign nations; and, for the carrying on some particular affairs with more secrecy and expedition, must elect, as they have already out of their own number and others, a council of state.[51]

And, although it may seem strange at first hearing, by reason that men's

47. Milton certainly refers to two dissolutions of Parliament under pressure from army leaders in 1659; he may also refer to Oliver Cromwell's expulsion of the Rump and dissolution of the Barebones Parliament.

48. In March 1660, the Long Parliament, elected in 1640 and having gone through many permutations as a result of defections, expulsions, and reinstatements, issued writs for new election and dissolved itself.

49. **knights and burgesses:** Knights represented counties and shires; burgesses represented cities, towns, and the universities of Oxford and Cambridge.

50. The measures Milton describes, while passed by the Rump at the beginning of 1660, were repealed after excluded members were readmitted in late February.

51. Milton refers to both the executive councils attempted by the Rump in 1659–60 and the perpetual *grand or general council* that he is about to propose.

minds are prepossessed with the notion of successive parliaments, I affirm that the grand or general council, being well chosen, should be perpetual; for so their business is or may be, and ofttimes urgent, the opportunity of affairs gained or lost in a moment. The day of council cannot be set as the day of a festival, but must be ready always to prevent or answer all occasions.[52] By this continuance they will become every way skilfullest, best provided of intelligence from abroad, best acquainted with the people at home, and the people with them. The ship of the commonwealth is always under sail. They sit at the stern, and if they steer well, what need is there to change them, it being rather dangerous? Add to this that the grand council is both foundation and main pillar of the whole state, and to move pillars and foundations not faulty cannot be safe for the building.

I see not, therefore, how we can be advantaged by successive and transitory parliaments; but that they are much likelier continually to unsettle rather than to settle a free government, to breed commotions, changes, novelties, and uncertainties, to bring neglect upon present affairs and opportunities, while all minds are suspense[53] with expectation of a new assembly, and the assembly, for a good space, taken up with the new settling of itself. After which, if they find no great work to do, they will make it by altering or repealing former acts or making and multiplying new, that they may seem to see what their predecessors saw not and not to have assembled for nothing, till all law be lost in the multitude of clashing statutes.

But if the ambition of such as think themselves injured that they also partake not of the government, and are impatient till they be chosen, cannot brook the perpetuity of others chosen before them, or if it be feared that long continuance of power may corrupt sincerest men, the known expedient is, and by some lately propounded, that annually (or if the space be longer, so much perhaps the better) the third part of senators may go out according to the precedence of their election, and the like number be chosen in their places, to prevent the settling of too absolute a power, if it should be perpetual: and this they call "partial rotation."[54] But I could wish that this wheel or partial wheel in state, if it be possible, might be avoided as having too much affinity with the wheel of fortune. For it appears not how this can be done without danger and mischance of putting out a great number of the best and ablest, in whose stead new elections may bring in as many raw, unexperienced, and otherwise affected, to the weakening and much altering for the worse of public transactions. Neither do I think a perpetual senate, especially chosen and entrusted by the people, much in this land to be feared, where the well-affected[55] either in a standing army or in a

52. I.e., anticipate and address all emergencies.

53. **suspense:** in suspense.

54. The *lately propounded* proposal for a rotating senate is James Harrington's, in *Oceana* (1656); it is associated with the republican Rota Club. The *wheel* in the next sentence is a play on the proposal and the club's name (Lat. *rota* = wheel).

55. **well-affected:** loyal and right thinking.

settled militia have their arms in their own hands. Safest therefore to me it seems, and of least hazard or interruption to affairs, that none of the grand council be moved unless by death or just conviction of some crime: for what can be expected firm or steadfast from a floating foundation? However, I forejudge not any probable expedient, any temperament that can be found in things of this nature so disputable on either side.

Yet lest this which I affirm be thought my single opinion, I shall add sufficient testimony. Kingship itself is therefore counted the more safe and durable because the king, and for the most part his council, is not changed during life. But a commonwealth is held immortal, and therein firmest, safest, and most above fortune. For the death of a king causeth ofttimes many dangerous alterations, but the death now and then of a senator is not felt, the main body of them still continuing permanent in greatest and noblest commonwealths, and as it were eternal. Therefore among the Jews the supreme council of seventy, called the Sanhedrim, founded by Moses, in Athens that of Areopagus, in Sparta that of the ancients,[56] in Rome the senate, consisted of members chosen for term of life; and by that means remained as it were still the same to generations. In Venice they change indeed ofter than every year some particular councils of state, as that of six, or such other; but the true senate, which upholds and sustains the government, is the whole aristocracy immovable.[57] So in the United Provinces, the States-General, which are indeed but a council of state deputed by the whole union, are not usually the same persons for above three or six years; but the states of every city, in whom the sovereignty hath been placed time out of mind, are a standing senate, without succession, and accounted chiefly in that regard the main prop of their liberty. And why they should be so in every well-ordered commonwealth, they who write of policy[58] give these reasons: "That to make the senate successive not only impairs the dignity and luster of the senate but weakens the whole commonwealth and brings it into manifest danger, while by this means the secrets of state are frequently divulged, and matters of greatest consequence committed to inexpert and novice counselors, utterly to seek[59] in the full and intimate knowledge of affairs past."[60] I know not therefore what should be peculiar in England to make successive parliaments thought safest, or convenient here more than in other nations, unless it be the fickleness which is attributed to us as we are islanders. But good education and acquisite[61]

56. The *Sanhedrim,* or Sanhedrin, which Milton later calls "great senate" (*PL* 12.225), was Israel's legislative and judicial assembly, established by Moses (Num. 11.16–17); the *Areopagus* was the seat of the Athenian Council of State and, after Solon's reforms, its judicial tribunal; Lycurgus established the assembly of *ancients* in Sparta. Milton's reference to the legendary founders of these assemblies is calculated to flatter and persuade Parliament.

57. As Milton indicates, the Doge of Venice and his advisory Council of Six served brief terms, while members of the Grand Council served for life.

58. **policy:** politics, government.

59. **to seek:** lacking.

60. Milton adapts this passage from Jean Bodin's *De Republica* (1576).

61. **acquisite:** acquired.

wisdom ought to correct the fluxible[62] fault, if any such be, of our watery situation.

It will be objected that in those places where they had perpetual senates, they had also popular remedies against their growing too imperious: as in Athens, besides Areopagus, another senate of four or five hundred; in Sparta, the Ephori; in Rome, the tribunes of the people.[63] But the event tells us that these remedies either little availed the people, or brought them to such a licentious and unbridled democraty[64] as in fine[65] ruined themselves with their own excessive power. So that the main reason urged why popular assemblies are to be trusted with the people's liberty, rather than a senate of principal men—because great men will be still endeavoring to enlarge their power, but the common sort will be contented to maintain their own liberty—is by experience found false, none being more immoderate and ambitious to amplify their power than such popularities; which was seen in the people of Rome, who, at first contented to have their tribunes, at length contended with the senate that one consul, then both, soon after that the censors and praetors also, should be created plebeian, and the whole empire put into their hands; adoring lastly those who most were adverse to the senate, till Marius, by fulfilling their inordinate desires, quite lost them all the power for which they had so long been striving, and left them under the tyranny of Sylla.[66]

The balance therefore must be exactly so set as to preserve and keep up due authority on either side, as well in the senate as in the people. And this annual rotation of a senate to consist of three hundred, as is lately propounded, requires also another popular assembly upward of a thousand, with an answerable rotation. Which, besides that it will be liable to all those inconveniences found in the foresaid remedies, cannot but be troublesome and chargeable,[67] both in their motion[68] and their session, to the whole land, unwieldy with their own bulk, unable in so great a number to mature their consultations as they ought, if any be allotted them, and that they meet not from so many parts remote to sit a whole year lieger[69] in one place, only now and then to hold up a forest of fingers, or to convey each man his bean or ballot into the box, without reason shown or common deliberation; incontinent of secrets, if any be imparted to

62. **fluxible:** fluid, and therefore changeable.

63. The office of Spartan *Ephors,* like that of Roman *Tribunes,* was established as a check on the power of ancients and senators who served for life; in each case the office established as a curb on arbitrary power itself became subject to abuse.

64. In Milton's time, *democraty,* or democracy, was as often as not a pejorative term; two paragraphs later, Milton cautions against trusting elections to "the noise and shouting of a rude multitude."

65. **in fine:** in the end.

66. Gaius *Marius,* of plebeian or common birth, amassed power by military victories, alliance with demagogues, and the massacre of patricians; after his death in 86 B.C.E., he was succeeded by the patrician Lucius Cornelius *Sulla* (see epigraph and note 1).

67. **chargeable:** expensive.

68. **motion:** travel.

69. **lieger:** residing, particularly as an agent or ambassador.

them, emulous and always jarring with the other senate.[70] The much better way doubtless will be, in this wavering condition of our affairs, to defer the changing or circumscribing of our senate more than may be done with ease, till the commonwealth be thoroughly settled in peace and safety, and they themselves give us the occasion.

Military men hold it dangerous to change the form of battle in view of an enemy; neither did the people of Rome bandy with their senate while any of the Tarquins[71] lived, the enemies of their liberty, nor sought by creating tribunes to defend themselves against the fear of their patricians, till, sixteen years after the expulsion of their kings and in full security of their state, they had or thought they had just cause given them by the senate. Another way will be to well qualify and refine elections: not committing all to the noise and shouting of a rude multitude, but permitting only those of them who are rightly qualified to nominate as many as they will, and out of that number others of a better breeding to choose a less number more judiciously, till after a third or fourth sifting and refining of exactest choice, they only be left chosen who are the due number and seem by most voices the worthiest.

To make the people fittest to choose, and the chosen fittest to govern, will be to mend our corrupt and faulty education, to teach the people faith not without virtue, temperance, modesty, sobriety, parsimony, justice; not to admire wealth or honor; to hate turbulence and ambition; to place everyone his private welfare and happiness in the public peace, liberty, and safety. They shall not then need to be much mistrustful of their chosen patriots in the grand council, who will be then rightly called the true keepers of our liberty, though the most of their business will be in foreign affairs. But to prevent all mistrust, the people then will have their several ordinary assemblies (which will henceforth quite annihilate the odious power and name of committees[72]) in the chief towns of every county—without the trouble, charge, or time lost of summoning and assembling from far in so great a number, and so long residing from their own houses, or removing of their families—to do as much at home in their several shires, entire or subdivided, toward the securing of their liberty, as a numerous assembly of them all formed and convened on purpose with the wariest rotation. Whereof I shall speak more ere the end of this discourse, for it may be referred to time,[73] so we be still[74] going on by degrees to perfection. The people well weighing and performing these things, I suppose would have no cause to fear, though the parliament, abolishing that name as originally signifying but the "parley" of our lords and commons with their Norman king when he pleased to call them, should,

70. Milton criticizes Harrington's proposal for a bicameral parliament, with a 300-member senate to debate and propose laws, and a second chamber of 1,050 that would simply vote the senate's proposals up or down.

71. The Roman republic was founded after the expulsion of the final Tarquin king, in 510 B.C.E.

72. **committees:** local governing bodies that enforced loyalty to Cromwell.

73. **it may be referred to time:** discussed later.

74. **still:** always.

with certain limitations of their power, sit perpetual, if their ends be faithful and for a free commonwealth, under the name of a grand or general council.

Till this be done, I am in doubt whether our state will be ever certainly and thoroughly settled, never likely till then to see an end of our troubles and continual changes, or at least never the true settlement and assurance of our liberty. The grand council being thus firmly constituted to perpetuity, and still, upon the death or default of any member, supplied and kept in full number, there can be no cause alleged why peace, justice, plentiful trade, and all prosperity should not thereupon ensue throughout the whole land, with as much assurance as can be of human things that they shall so continue (if God favor us, and our willful sins provoke him not) even to the coming of our true and rightful and only to be expected king, only worthy as he is our only Savior, the Messiah, the Christ, the only heir of his eternal father, the only by him anointed and ordained since the work of our redemption finished, universal Lord of all mankind.[75]

The way propounded is plain, easy, and open before us, without intricacies, without the introducement of new or obsolete forms, or terms, or exotic models—ideas that would effect nothing but with a number of new injunctions to manacle the native liberty of mankind, turning all virtue into prescription, servitude, and necessity, to the great impairing and frustrating of Christian liberty. I say again, this way lies free and smooth before us, is not tangled with inconveniences, invents no new encumbrances, requires no perilous, no injurious alteration or circumscription of men's lands and proprieties;[76] secure that in this commonwealth, temporal and spiritual lords removed, no man or number of men can attain to such wealth or vast possession as will need the hedge of an agrarian law[77] (never successful, but the cause rather of sedition, save only where it began seasonably with first possession) to confine them from endangering our public liberty. To conclude, it can have no considerable objection made against it that it is not practicable, lest it be said hereafter that we gave up our liberty for want of a ready way or distinct form proposed of a free commonwealth. And this facility we shall have above our next neighboring commonwealth (if we can keep us from the fond conceit[78] of something like a duke of Venice, put lately into many men's heads by some one or other subtly driving on under that notion his own ambitious ends to lurch[79] a crown) that our liberty shall not be hampered or hovered over by any engagement to such a potent family as the house of Nassau,[80] of whom to stand in perpetual doubt and suspicion, but we shall live the clearest and absolutest free nation in the world.

75. Milton, believing that only the Son of God is worthy to be a king, voices a millenarian vision of the reign of Christ on Earth.

76. **proprieties:** properties.

77. In *Oceana,* Harrington proposed a law limiting the size of landed estates.

78. **fond conceit:** foolish idea; apparently a suggestion that Richard Cromwell, who had succeeded his father as Protector, be returned to power as something like the Doge of Venice (see note 57).

79. **lurch:** steal.

80. **house of Nassau:** The heirs of William of Orange inherited the powers he had gained as Stadtholder in the Dutch republic.

On the contrary, if there be a king, which the inconsiderate multitude are now so mad upon, mark how far short we are like to come of all those happinesses which in a free state we shall immediately be possessed of. First, the grand council, which, as I showed before, should sit perpetually (unless their leisure give them now and then some intermissions or vacations, easily manageable by the council of state left sitting), shall be called, by the king's good will and utmost endeavor, as seldom as may be. For it is only the king's right, he will say, to call a parliament, and this he will do most commonly about his own affairs rather than the kingdom's, as will appear plainly so soon as they are called. For what will their business then be, and the chief expense of their time, but an endless tugging between petition of right and royal prerogative,[81] especially about the negative voice,[82] militia, or subsidies, demanded and ofttimes extorted without reasonable cause appearing to the commons, who are the only true representatives of the people and their liberty, but will be then mingled with a court faction. Besides which, within their own walls, the sincere part of them who stand faithful to the people will again have to deal with two troublesome counterworking adversaries from without, mere creatures of the king, spiritual, and the greater part, as is likeliest, of temporal lords, nothing concerned with the people's liberty.[83]

If these prevail not in what they please, though never so much against the people's interest, the parliament shall be soon dissolved, or sit and do nothing, not suffered to remedy the least grievance or enact aught advantageous to the people. Next, the council of state shall not be chosen by the parliament, but by the king, still his own creatures, courtiers and favorites, who will be sure in all their counsels to set their master's grandeur and absolute power, in what they are able, far above the people's liberty. I deny not but that there may be such a king who may regard the common good before his own, may have no vicious favorite, may hearken only to the wisest and incorruptest of his parliament. But this rarely happens in a monarchy not elective, and it behooves not a wise nation to commit the sum of their well-being, the whole state of their safety, to fortune. What need they? And how absurd would it be, whenas they themselves, to whom his[84] chief virtue will be but to hearken, may with much better management and dispatch, with much more commendation of their own worth and magnanimity, govern without a master? Can the folly be paralleled, to adore and be the slaves of a single person for doing that which it is ten thousand to one whether he can or will do, and we without him might do more easily, more effectually, more laudably ourselves? Shall we never grow old enough to be wise to make seasonable use of gravest authorities, experiences, examples? Is it such an unspeakable joy to serve, such felicity to wear a yoke, to clink our shackles locked

81. In 1628, Parliament, resisting Charles I's assertion of *royal prerogative,* forced him to agree to the Petition of Right.

82. **negative voice:** royal veto.

83. I.e., a restored king would recall the House of Lords, abolished in 1649.

84. **his:** the king's.

on by pretended law of subjection, more intolerable and hopeless to be ever shaken off than those which are knocked on by illegal injury and violence?[85]

Aristotle, our chief instructor in the universities (lest this doctrine be thought sectarian, as the royalist would have it thought), tells us in the third of his *Politics* that certain men at first, for the matchless excellence of their virtue above others, or some great public benefit, were created kings by the people, in small cities and territories, and in the scarcity of others to be found like them; but when they abused their power and governments grew larger and the number of prudent men increased, that then the people, soon deposing their tyrants, betook them in all civilest places to the form of a free commonwealth.[86] And why should we thus disparage and prejudicate[87] our own nation as to fear a scarcity of able and worthy men united in counsel to govern us, if we will but use diligence and impartiality to find them out and choose them, rather yoking ourselves to a single person, the natural adversary and oppressor of liberty; though good, yet far easier corruptible by the excess of his singular power and exaltation, or at best not comparably sufficient to bear the weight of government, nor equally disposed to make us happy in the enjoyment of our liberty under him?

But admit that monarchy of itself may be convenient to some nations, yet to us who have thrown it out, received back again it cannot but prove pernicious. For kings to come, never forgetting their former ejection, will be sure to fortify and arm themselves sufficiently for the future against all such attempts hereafter from the people, who shall be then so narrowly watched and kept so low that, though they would never so fain (and at the same rate of their blood and treasure), they never shall be able to regain what they now have purchased and may enjoy, or to free themselves from any yoke imposed upon them. Nor will they dare to go about it, utterly disheartened for the future, if these their highest attempts prove unsuccessful; which will be the triumph of all tyrants hereafter over any people that shall resist oppression. And their[88] song will then be to others, "how sped the rebellious English?" to our posterity, "how sped the rebels your fathers?"

This is not my conjecture, but drawn from God's known denouncement against the gentilizing[89] Israelites, who, though they were governed in a commonwealth of God's own ordaining, he only their king,[90] they his peculiar[91] people, yet affecting rather to resemble heathen, but pretending the misgovernment of Samuel's sons (no more a reason to dislike their commonwealth, than the violence of Eli's sons was imputable to that priesthood or religion) clamored

85. I.e., is subservience so attractive that we will place manacles on ourselves worse than any placed upon us by force?

86. Milton paraphrases Aristotle's *Politics* III.15 (1286b).

87. **prejudicate:** prejudge unfairly.

88. **their:** the tyrants'.

89. **gentilizing:** imitating the Gentiles in their desire for a king (1 Sam. 8.4–22); see notes 32 and 33.

90. See note 75.

91. **peculiar:** chosen, particular.

for a king. They had their longing, but with this testimony of God's wrath: "Ye shall cry out in that day because of your king whom ye shall have chosen, and the Lord will not hear you in that day" [1 Sam. 8.18]. Us if he shall hear now, how much less will he hear when we cry hereafter, who once delivered by him from a king, and not without wondrous acts of his providence, insensible and unworthy of those high mercies, are returning precipitantly, if he withhold us not, back to the captivity from whence he freed us.

Yet neither shall we obtain or buy at an easy rate this new gilded yoke which thus transports us. A new royal revenue must be found, a new episcopal, for those are individual.[92] Both which being wholly dissipated, or bought by private persons, or assigned for service done (and especially to the army), cannot be recovered without a general detriment and confusion to men's estates or a heavy imposition on all men's purses[93]—benefit to none but to the worst and ignoblest sort of men, whose hope is to be either the ministers of court riot and excess or the gainers by it. But not to speak more of losses and extraordinary levies on our estates, what will then be the revenges and offenses remembered and returned, not only by the chief person but by all his adherents; accounts and reparations that will be required, suits, indictments, inquiries, discoveries, complaints, informations, who knows against whom or how many, though perhaps neuters,[94] if not to utmost infliction, yet to imprisonment, fines, banishment, or molestation? if not these, yet disfavor, discountenance, disregard, and contempt on all but the known royalist, or whom he favors, will be plenteous.

Nor let the new royalized Presbyterians[95] persuade themselves that their old doings, though now recanted, will be forgotten, whatever conditions be contrived or trusted on. Will they not believe this, nor remember the pacification, how it was kept to the Scots,[96] how other solemn promises many a time to us? Let them now but read the diabolical forerunning libels, the faces, the gestures that now appear foremost and briskest in all public places, as the harbingers of those that are in expectation to reign over us. Let them but hear the insolencies, the menaces, the insultings of our newly animated common enemies crept lately out of their holes, their hell I might say by the language of their infernal pamphlets, the spew of every drunkard, every ribald; nameless, yet not for want of license, but for very shame of their own vile persons, not daring to name themselves while they traduce others by name.[97] And give us to foresee that

92. **individual:** both inseparable and distinct.

93. In the event, those who purchased or who had been awarded lands confiscated from the bishops and from Charles I's supporters were not compensated when the lands were returned after the Restoration.

94. **neuters:** neutrals.

95. In *The Tenure of Kings and Magistrates,* Milton castigates the Presbyterians for supporting the imprisoned Charles after working to bring down the monarchy.

96. There are several broken agreements between Charles and the Scottish Presbyterians to which Milton could refer here.

97. Milton was among those attacked *by name* in the *forerunning libels,* e.g., in Sir Roger L'Estrange's *No Blinde Guides* (1660).

they intend to second their wicked words, if ever they have power, with more wicked deeds.

Let our zealous backsliders forethink now with themselves how their necks yoked with these tigers of Bacchus,[98] these new fanatics of not the preaching- but the sweating-tub, inspired with nothing holier than the venereal pox,[99] can draw one way under monarchy to the establishing of church discipline with these new-disgorged atheisms. Yet shall they not have the honor to yoke with these, but shall be yoked under them. These shall plow on their backs. And do they among them who are so forward to bring in the single person think to be by him trusted or long regarded? So trusted they shall be and so regarded as by kings are wont reconciled enemies: neglected and soon after discarded, if not prosecuted for old traitors; the first inciters, beginners, and more than to the third part actors of all that followed.

It will be found also that there must be then, as necessarily as now (for the contrary part will be still feared), a standing army, which for certain shall not be this, but of the fiercest cavaliers, of no less expense, and perhaps again under Rupert.[100] But let this army[101] be sure they shall be soon disbanded, and likeliest without arrear or pay, and, being disbanded, not be sure but they may as soon be questioned for being in arms against their king. The same let them fear who have contributed money, which will amount to no small number that must then take their turn to be made delinquents and compounders.[102]

They who past reason and recovery are devoted to kingship perhaps will answer that a greater part by far of the nation will have it so, the rest therefore must yield. Not so much to convince these, which I little hope, as to confirm them who yield not, I reply that this greatest part[103] have both in reason and the trial of just battle lost the right of their election what the government shall be. Of them who have not lost that right, whether they for kingship be the greater number, who can certainly determine? Suppose they be, yet of freedom they partake all alike, one main end of government; which if the greater part value not, but will degenerately forgo, is it just or reasonable that most voices against the main end of government should enslave the less number that would be free? More just it is, doubtless, if it come to force, that a less number compel a greater to retain (which can be no wrong to them) their liberty, than that a greater number, for the pleasure of their baseness, compel a less most injuriously to be

98. **tigers of Bacchus:** tigers pulled the chariot of the god of wine; Milton associated the monarchist Cavaliers with Bacchus, for their devotion to pleasure.

99. The *preaching-tub* was the improvised pulpit of street preachers; the *sweating-tub* was used to treat *venereal pox,* or syphilis.

100. Prince *Rupert,* nephew of Charles I, commanded the Royalist army, and afterward the navy, during the Civil War.

101. **this army:** the current, republican army.

102. **delinquents and compounders:** Royalist *delinquents,* who had their estates confiscated during the Civil War, were allowed to keep them if they *compounded,* or made a specified payment; Milton assumes that the Royalists would do the same to commonwealth supporters at the Restoration.

103. **this greatest part:** the Royalists, having lost the war, have lost the right to vote.

their fellow slaves. They who seek nothing but their own just liberty have always right to win it and to keep it whenever they have power, be the voices never so numerous that oppose it. And how much we above others are concerned to defend it from kingship, and from them who in pursuance thereof so perniciously would betray us and themselves to most certain misery and thraldom, will be needless to repeat.

Having thus far shown with what ease we may now obtain a free commonwealth, and by it, with as much ease, all the freedom, peace, justice, plenty that we can desire, on the other side the difficulties, troubles, uncertainties, nay, rather impossibilities, to enjoy these things constantly under a monarch, I will now proceed to show more particularly wherein our freedom and flourishing condition will be more ample and secure to us under a free commonwealth than under kingship.

The whole freedom of man consists either in spiritual or civil liberty. As for spiritual, who can be at rest, who can enjoy anything in this world with contentment, who hath not liberty to serve God and to save his own soul according to the best light which God hath planted in him to that purpose, by the reading of his revealed will and the guidance of his holy spirit? That this is best pleasing to God, and that the whole Protestant church allows no supreme judge or rule in matters of religion but the scriptures, and these to be interpreted by the scriptures themselves, which necessarily infers liberty of conscience, I have heretofore proved at large in another treatise,[104] and might yet further by the public declarations, confessions, and admonitions of whole churches and states, obvious in all history since the Reformation.

This liberty of conscience, which above all other things ought to be to all men dearest and most precious, no government more inclinable not to favor only, but to protect, than a free commonwealth, as being most magnanimous, most fearless, and confident of its own fair proceedings. Whereas kingship, though looking big, yet indeed most pusillanimous, full of fears, full of jealousies, startled at every umbrage,[105] as it hath been observed of old to have ever suspected most and mistrusted them who were in most esteem for virtue and generosity of mind, so it is now known to have most in doubt and suspicion them who are most reputed to be religious. Queen Elizabeth, though herself accounted so good a Protestant, so moderate, so confident of her subjects' love, would never give way so much as to Presbyterian reformation in this land, though once and again besought, as Camden[106] relates; but imprisoned and persecuted the very proposers thereof, alleging it as her mind and maxim unalterable that such reformation would diminish regal authority.

What liberty of conscience can we then expect of others, far worse principled from the cradle, trained up and governed by popish and Spanish coun-

104. *A Treatise of Civil Power in Ecclesiastical Causes* (1659).

105. **umbrage:** shadow.

106. Milton refers to William Camden's *History of the Most Renowned and Victorious Princess Elizabeth.*

sels,[107] and on such depending hitherto for subsistence? Especially what can this last parliament expect, who, having revived lately and published the covenant,[108] have re-engaged themselves never to readmit episcopacy? Which no son of Charles returning but will most certainly bring back with him, if he regard the last and strictest charge of his father, "to persevere in not the doctrine only but government of the church of England, not to neglect the speedy and effectual suppressing of errors and schisms,"[109] among which he accounted presbytery one of the chief. Or if, notwithstanding that charge of his father, he submit to the covenant, how will he keep faith to us with disobedience to him, or regard that faith given which must be founded on the breach of that last and solemnest paternal charge, and the reluctance, I may say the antipathy, which is in all kings against Presbyterian and Independent discipline?[110] For they hear the gospel speaking much of liberty, a word which monarchy and her bishops both fear and hate, but a free commonwealth both favors and promotes, and not the word only, but the thing itself. But let our governors beware in time lest their hard measure to liberty of conscience be found the rock whereon they shipwreck themselves, as others have now done before them in the course wherein God was directing their steerage to a free commonwealth; and the abandoning of all those whom they call "sectaries," for the detected falsehood and ambition of some, be a willful rejection of their own chief strength and interest in the freedom of all Protestant religion, under what abusive name soever calumniated.

The other part of our freedom consists in the civil rights and advancements of every person according to his merit: the enjoyment of those never more certain, and the access to these never more open, than in a free commonwealth. Both which, in my opinion, may be best and soonest obtained if every county in the land were made a kind of subordinate commonalty or commonwealth, and one chief town or more, according as the shire is in circuit,[111] made cities, if they be not so called already; where the nobility and chief gentry, from a proportionable compass of territory annexed to each city, may build houses or palaces befitting their quality, may bear part in the government, make their own judicial laws, or use these that are, and execute them by their own elected judicatures and judges without appeal, in all things of civil government between man and man. So they shall have justice in their own hands, law executed fully and finally in their own counties and precincts, long wished and spoken of, but

107. Charles II, the son of a French Catholic mother, allied himself with the Spanish against Cromwell in the Battle of Flanders (1658).

108. The 1643 Solemn League and Covenant pledging loyalty to the king had been reinstated in March 1660.

109. Milton conflates two passages from Charles I's *Eikon Basilike,* chap. 27; he paraphrases the same passages in his own *Eikonoklastes* (Yale 3:571, 573).

110. **Independent discipline:** Milton's preferred system, under which individual churches govern themselves, as opposed to subordination to a hierarchy of bishops or Presbyterian synods.

111. **in circuit:** in size.

never yet obtained. They shall have none then to blame but themselves if it be not well administered, and fewer laws to expect or fear from the supreme authority. Or to those that shall be made of any great concernment to public liberty, they may, without much trouble in these commonalties or in more general assemblies called to their cities from the whole territory on such occasion, declare and publish their assent or dissent by deputies within a time limited sent to the grand council; yet so as this their judgment declared shall submit to the greater number of other counties or commonalties, and not avail them to any exemption of themselves, or refusal of agreement with the rest, as it may in any of the United Provinces, being sovereign within itself, ofttimes to the great disadvantage of that union.

In these employments they may, much better than they do now, exercise and fit themselves till their lot fall to be chosen into the grand council, according as their worth and merit shall be taken notice of by the people. As for controversies that shall happen between men of several counties, they may repair, as they do now, to the capital city, or any other more commodious, indifferent[112] place, and equal[113] judges. And this I find to have been practiced in the old Athenian commonwealth, reputed the first and ancientest place of civility in all Greece: that they had in their several cities a peculiar,[114] in Athens a common, government;[115] and their right, as it befell them, to the administration of both.

They should have here also schools and academies at their own choice, wherein their children may be bred up in their own sight to all learning and noble education, not in grammar only, but in all liberal arts and exercises. This would soon spread much more knowledge and civility, yea religion, through all parts of the land, by communicating the natural heat of government and culture more distributively to all extreme parts which now lie numb and neglected; would soon make the whole nation more industrious, more ingenuous at home, more potent, more honorable abroad. To this a free commonwealth will easily assent (nay, the parliament hath had already some such thing in design), for of all governments a commonwealth aims most to make the people flourishing, virtuous, noble, and high spirited. Monarchs will never permit, whose aim is to make the people wealthy indeed perhaps and well fleeced for their own shearing and the supply of regal prodigality, but otherwise softest, basest, viciousest, servilest, easiest to be kept under. And not only in fleece, but in mind also sheepishest, and will have all the benches of judicature annexed to the throne, as a gift of royal grace that we have justice done us, whenas nothing can be more essential to the freedom of a people than to have the administration of justice and all public ornaments[116] in

112. **indifferent:** impartial.
113. **equal:** fair.
114. **peculiar:** separate.
115. Milton's proposal for a federal constitution follows Aristotle's description of Athenian reform (*Athenian Constitution* 21.3–22).
116. **ornaments:** a usage not recorded in the *OED;* Milton may refer to judgeships, which bring honor to those chosen.

their own election and within their own bounds, without long traveling or depending on remote places to obtain their right or any civil accomplishment; so it be not supreme, but subordinate to the general power and union of the whole republic.

In which happy firmness, as in the particular above mentioned, we shall also far exceed the United Provinces by having, not as they (to the retarding and distracting ofttimes of their counsels or urgentest occasions), many sovereignties united in one commonwealth, but many commonwealths under one united and entrusted sovereignty. And when we have our forces by sea and land, either of a faithful army or a settled militia, in our own hands to the firm establishing of a free commonwealth, public accounts under our own inspection, general laws and taxes, with their causes, in our own domestic suffrages, judicial laws, offices, and ornaments at home in our own ordering and administration, all distinction of lords and commoners that may any way divide or sever the public interest removed, what can a perpetual senate have then wherein to grow corrupt, wherein to encroach upon us or usurp? Or if they do, wherein to be formidable? Yet if all this avail not to remove the fear or envy of a perpetual sitting, it may be easily provided to change a third part of them yearly or every two or three years, as was above mentioned; or that it be at those times in the people's choice whether they will change them or renew their power, as they shall find cause.

I have no more to say at present. Few words will save us, well considered; few and easy things, now seasonably done. But if the people be so affected as to prostitute religion and liberty to the vain and groundless apprehension that nothing but kingship can restore trade, not remembering the frequent plagues[117] and pestilences that then wasted this city, such as through God's mercy we never have felt since, and that trade flourishes nowhere more than in the free commonwealths of Italy, Germany, and the Low Countries before their eyes at this day; yet if trade be grown so craving and importunate through the profuse living of tradesmen that nothing can support it but the luxurious expenses of a nation upon trifles or superfluities, so as if the people generally should betake themselves to frugality, it might prove a dangerous matter, lest tradesmen should mutiny for want of trading, and that therefore we must forgo and set to sale religion, liberty, honor, safety, all concernments divine or human to keep up trading; if, lastly, after all this light among us, the same reason shall pass for current to put our necks again under kingship, as was made use of by the Jews to return back to Egypt and to the worship of their idol queen,[118] because they falsely imagined that they then lived in more plenty and prosperity, our condition is not sound, but rotten,[119] both in religion and all civil prudence,

117. There had not been a plague in England since 1625, in James I's reign; there would not be another until 1665, during the reign of Charles II.

118. See Num. 11 for the story of Moses' displeasure with his followers' desire to return to Egypt; Milton may be alluding to God's instructions to Moses to call a council of elders to address the crisis (Num. 11.16–18) as a model for his own grand council.

119. Milton comes finally to the main clause, after three long dependent clauses.

and will bring us soon, the way we are marching, to those calamities which attend always and unavoidably on luxury, all national judgments under foreign or domestic slavery. So far we shall be from mending our condition by monarchizing our government, whatever new conceit now possesses us.

However, with all hazard I have ventured what I thought my duty to speak in season, and to forewarn my country in time, wherein I doubt not but there be many wise men in all places and degrees, but am sorry the effects of wisdom are so little seen among us. Many circumstances and particulars I could have added in those things whereof I have spoken, but a few main matters now put speedily in execution will suffice to recover us and set all right. And there will want at no time who are good at circumstances,[120] but men who set their minds on main matters and sufficiently urge them, in these most difficult times I find not many.

What I have spoken is the language of that which is not called amiss "the good old cause."[121] If it seem strange to any, it will not seem more strange, I hope, than convincing to backsliders. Thus much I should perhaps have said though I were sure I should have spoken only to trees and stones, and had none to cry to, but with the prophet, "O earth, earth, earth!" [Jer. 22.29] to tell the very soil itself what her perverse inhabitants are deaf to. Nay, though what I have spoke should happen (which Thou suffer not, who didst create mankind free, nor Thou next, who didst redeem us from being servants of men!) to be the last words of our expiring liberty. But I trust I shall have spoken persuasion to abundance of sensible and ingenuous men; to some perhaps whom God may raise of these stones to become children of reviving liberty,[122] and may reclaim, though they seem now choosing them a captain back for Egypt, to bethink themselves a little and consider whither they are rushing; to exhort this torrent also of the people not to be so impetuous, but to keep their due channel; and at length recovering and uniting their better resolutions, now that they see already how open and unbounded the insolence and rage is of our common enemies, to stay these ruinous proceedings, justly and timely fearing to what a precipice of destruction the deluge of this epidemic madness would hurry us, through the general defection of a misguided and abused multitude.

120. **who are good at circumstances:** people who can work out the details.

121. **"the good old cause":** Milton reclaims the republican rallying cry; Royalist adversaries were using it ironically against Milton's party as the Restoration approached.

122. Milton echoes another voice crying in the wilderness, John the Baptist: "I say unto you, That God is able of these stone to raise up children unto Abraham" (Matt. 3.9, Luke 3.8).

Introduction to Selections from *Christian Doctrine*

The heavily and repeatedly revised Latin manuscript of Milton's *Christian Doctrine* was found in 1823, in a storage compartment in London's Old State Paper Office. It had Milton's name on it, was bundled with copies of his State Papers, and appeared to be the final product of his lifelong study of Scripture, scriptural commentaries, and precedent theological systems. The prefatory epistle to the treatise describes its genesis and growth, and this account dovetails neatly with references in Milton's *Commonplace Book* to a "theological index" and Edward Phillips's mention of his uncle's theological "tractate" (Darbishire 1932, 61). Since discovery of the manuscript, scholars have gradually pieced together a documentary record that with the evidence of the manuscript itself establishes the following: (1) Though it was the evolving product of a lifetime of devotional searching, work on the treatise proceeded most intensively from 1658 to 1660, about the time *Paradise Lost* began to be composed. (2) After Milton's death a young man named Daniel Skinner had possession of the manuscripts of both the treatise and Milton's State Papers. (3) In 1675, Skinner tried to have both published in Amsterdam, but even there, where freedom of the press flourished by comparison with Restoration England, the prospective publisher decided to suppress the treatise because of its heresies. (4) By 1677, Skinner, ignorant of the publisher's decision, came under pressure from the British government, specifically its Secretary of State, Sir Joseph Williamson, to prevent publication. (5) Williamson successfully intimidated and manipulated Skinner, confiscated the manuscripts, and put them in storage, where they remained until 1823. The most thorough and up-to-date account of the documentary evidence establishing these circumstances appears in Campbell et al. (1997, 67–89).

Had Milton himself attempted to publish the treatise during the Restoration, its heretical contents would likely have caused him serious trouble, especially on account of his Arian rejection of the Trinity. That *Arian* is the correct theological category for Milton's views has been definitively demonstrated (Bauman 1987), and it is precisely the label that was applied to them in the seventeenth century. The Dutch professor of theology consulted by the Amsterdam publisher advised against publication of the treatise specifically "because the strongest Arianism was to be found throughout it" (Campbell et al. 1997, 69). Even without the treatise, various early readers of *Paradise Lost* suspected Milton of holding just such views (Bauman 1986).

In the seventeenth century, denial of Christ's full divinity was among the gravest heresies. Bartholomew Legate and Edward Wightman were burned to death during the reign of James I for maintaining such opinions. Even after the recovery of the treatise in the nineteenth century, its Arianism provoked strong reaction, both from disappointed Christian readers (except, of course, Unitarians) and, during the last half of the twentieth century, from scholars inclined to see Milton as being "closer to the great traditions of Christianity, no longer associated with a merely eccentric fringe" (Hunter 1992, 166). The result has been a long and varied history of erudite evasion, culminating in an effort to deny Milton's original authorship of the treatise through statistical analysis of its style (Corns et al. 1998). Although this long-running dispute has made scholars more attentive to the history of Milton's treatise and the exact nature of his theological opinions, the effort to uncouple Milton from authorship of a work its prefatory epistle calls his "dearest and best possession" has proven unconvincing. For rebuttal of that effort, see S. Fallon (1998, 1999), Hill (1994), Kelley (1994), Lewalski (1992, 1998), and Rumrich (1998, 2004).

Space does not permit characterization of all Milton's deviations from orthodox Protestant dogma of his time—Arminianism, antinomianism, vitalist materialism, and polygamy prominent among them. Some of these heterodoxies are at least as pertinent to Milton's poetry as his Arianism, and it is unfortunate that sensitivity to this particular heresy should have drawn critical attention away from the others. Interested readers should begin with Maurice Kelley's edition of the treatise, and particularly the relevant section of his introduction (Yale 6:43–99). Rather than list here the heresies detailed by Kelley, we would stress that the treatise took shape as Milton was composing *Paradise Lost* and that his epic narrative developed in dialogue with his ongoing attempt to make a systematic account of his faith (cp. introduction to *Paradise Lost*). Not surprisingly, the mutual pertinence of Milton's theological treatise and his epic is the implicit premise of some of the most useful recent scholarship.

Telling precedent informs Milton's effort as a systematic theologian of Protestantism. Among those closest to *Christian Doctrine* in structure, in many points of theology, and even in the expression of some of these points are *Compendium Theologiae Christianae* (1626) by Johannes Wollebius and *Medulla Theologica* (1623) by the Englishman Guilielmus Amesius (William Ames), whom Milton quotes in book 2, chapter 7. Ames's work was soon translated into English as *The Marrow of Sacred Divinity* (1650) and became highly influential in the North American colonies. The most distinctive characteristic of the treatise and of Milton as a theologian is his unremitting reliance on Scripture. According to Bauman (1989, 178), the treatise includes a staggering 9,346 citations of canonical Scripture and apocrypha, and many of these accompany generous quotation. As Milton himself puts it in the prefatory epistle, he strove "to cram [his] pages even to overflowing, with quotations drawn from all part of the Bible and to leave as little space as possible for my own words." The primary interest of the present volume nevertheless lies in Milton's own words. Although we have retained the scriptural citations, many quotations have been deleted for reasons of space. We have indicated our deletions with ellipses in brackets. All other ellipses are Milton's own.

Our text is based on John Carey's translation for the Yale edition of Milton's prose works. Some chapters and sections of chapters have been omitted, but where possible we have kept discussion of doctrine that seems to us relevant to Milton's other writings. Our notes point to some of these connections and where necessary summarize what has been omitted. But because this work is a systematic treatise in discrete chapters, bridging summaries of the sort provided for other selected prose works in this edition do not appear. The cross-references in our notes sometimes repeat without specific acknowledgment connections made by Maurice Kelley before us, as indeed Kelley himself sometimes repeated cross-references put forward by the treatise's first translator, Charles Sumner.

Selections from

CHRISTIAN DOCTRINE

John Milton

ENGLISHMAN

To All the Churches of Christ and to All in any part of the world who profess the Christian Faith, Peace, Knowledge of the Truth, and Eternal Salvation in God the Father and in our Lord Jesus Christ.[1]

The process of restoring religion to something of its pure original state, after it had been defiled with impurities for more than thirteen hundred years,[2] dates from the beginning of the last century. Since that time many theological systems have been propounded, aiming at further purification, and providing sometimes brief, sometimes more lengthy and methodical expositions of almost all the chief points of Christian doctrine. This being so, I think I should explain straight away why, if any work has yet been published on this subject which is as exhaustive as possible, I have been dissatisfied with it, and why, on the other hand, if all previous writers have failed in this attempt, I have not been discouraged from making the same attempt myself.

If I were to say that I had focused my studies principally upon Christian doctrine because nothing else can so effectually wipe away those two repulsive afflictions, tyranny and superstition,[3] from human life and the human mind, I should show that I had been concerned not for religion but for life's well-being.

But in fact I decided not to depend upon the belief or judgment of others in religious questions for this reason: God has revealed the way of eternal salva-

1. "Renaissance theologians tended to address their works to noblemen, patrons, friends, or to the reader; and I have not noted another Renaissance systematic theology directed, like Milton's, to the combined churches of Christ and all Christians" (Kelley).
2. That is, from the early fourth century, when Constantine (306–37) legalized Christianity and the Council of Nicaea (325) formulated the doctrine of the Trinity.
3. Cp. *1Def* (Yale 4:535): "the two greatest evils in human life, the most fatal to virtue, namely, tyranny and superstition"; *REW:* "the two most prevailing usurpers over mankind, superstition and tyranny" (p. 1117).

tion only to the individual faith of each man, and demands of us that any man who wishes to be saved should work out his beliefs for himself. So I made up my mind to puzzle out a religious creed for myself by my own exertions, and to acquaint myself with it thoroughly. In this the only authority I accepted was God's self-revelation, and accordingly I read and pondered the Holy Scriptures themselves with all possible diligence, never sparing myself in any way.

I shall mention those methods that proved profitable for me, in case desire for similar profit should, perhaps, lead someone else to start out upon the same path in the future. I began by devoting myself when I was a boy to an earnest study of the Old and New Testaments in their original languages, and then proceeded to go carefully through some of the shorter systems of theologians. I also started, following the example of these writers, to list under general headings[4] all passages from the scriptures which suggested themselves for quotation, so that I might have them ready at hand when necessary. At length, gaining confidence, I transferred my attention to more diffuse volumes of divinity, and to the conflicting arguments in controversies over certain heads of faith. But, to be frank, I was very sorry to find, in these works, that the authors frequently evaded an opponent's point in a thoroughly dishonest way, or countered it, in appearance rather than in reality, by an affected display of logical ingenuity or by constant linguistic quibbles. Such writers, moreover, often defended their prejudices tooth and nail, though with more fervor than force, by misinterpretations of biblical texts or by the false conclusions which they wrung from these. Hence, they sometimes violently attacked the truth as error and heresy, while calling error and heresy truth and upholding them not upon the authority of the Bible but as a result of habit and partisanship.

So I considered that I could not properly entrust either my creed or my hope of salvation to such guides. But I still thought that it was absolutely necessary to possess a systematic exposition of Christian teaching, or at any rate a written investigation of it, which could assist my faith or my memory or both. It seemed, then, safest and most advisable for me to make a fresh start and compile for myself, by my own exertion and long hours of study, some work of this kind which might be always at hand. I should derive this from the word of God and from that alone, and should be scrupulously faithful to the text, for to do otherwise would be merely to cheat myself. After I had painstakingly persevered in this work for several years, I saw that the citadel of reformed religion was adequately fortified against the Papists. Through neglect, however, it was open to attack in many other places where defenses and defenders were alike wanting to make it safe. In religion as in other things, I discerned, God offers all

4. The phrase *general headings* translates *loci communes,* more literally rendered "common places." "Authorship within a commonplace tradition implies readily observable stylistic consequences. The point is straightforward enough. Where *De Doctrina Christiana* does *not* disagree with the exegetical tradition . . . , it simply restates it, though—and the import of this authorial contribution should not be underestimated—it often supplements the tradition with scriptural citations and fresh or altered arguments" (Rumrich 2004, 223). Kelley's introduction to the treatise (Yale 6:16–22) discusses Milton's composition of the work and identifies precursors consulted by Milton.

his rewards not to those who are thoughtless and credulous, but to those who labor constantly and seek tirelessly after truth.[5] Thus I concluded that there was more than I realized which still needed to be measured with greater strictness against the yardstick of the Bible, and reformed with greater care. I pursued my studies, and so far satisfied myself that eventually I had no doubt about my ability to distinguish correctly in religion between matters of faith and matters of opinion. It was, furthermore, my greatest comfort that I had constructed, with God's help, a powerful support for my faith, or rather that I had laid up provision for the future in that I should not thenceforth be unprepared or hesitant when I needed to give an account of my beliefs.

God is my witness that it is with feelings of universal brotherhood and good will that I make this account public. By so doing I am sharing, and that most willingly, my dearest and best possession with as many people as possible. I hope, then, that all my readers will be sympathetic, and will avoid prejudice and malice, even though they see at once that many of the views I have published are at odds with certain conventional opinions. I implore all friends of truth not to start shouting that the church is being thrown into confusion by free discussion and inquiry. These are allowed in academic circles, and should certainly be denied to no believer. For we are ordered to find out the truth about all things, and the daily increase of the light of truth fills the church much rather with brightness and strength than with confusion. I do not see how anyone should be able or is able to throw the church into confusion by searching after truth, any more than the heathen were thrown into confusion when the gospel was first preached. For assuredly I do not urge or enforce anything upon my own authority. On the contrary, I advise every reader, and set him an example by doing the same myself, to withold his consent from those opinions about which he does not feel fully convinced, until the evidence of the Bible convinces him and induces his reason to assent and to believe. I do not seek to conceal any part of my meaning. Indeed I address myself with much more confidence to learned than to untutored readers or, if the very learned are not always the best judges and critics of such matters, at any rate to mature, strong-minded men who thoroughly understand the teaching of the gospel. Most authors who have dealt with this subject at the greatest length in the past have been in the habit of filling their pages almost entirely with expositions of their own ideas. They have relegated to the margin, with brief reference to chapter and verse, the scriptural texts upon which all that they teach is utterly dependent. I, on the other hand, have striven to cram my pages even to overflowing, with quotations drawn from all parts of the Bible and to leave as little space as possible for my own words, even when they arise from the putting together of actual scriptural texts.[6]

5. Cp. *Areop*, pp. 956–60.
6. "I have discovered no systematic theology, Protestant or other, that is even remotely as biblically grounded as Milton's. For page after page, the range and number of his biblical references easily outstrip those of every other comparable text" (Bauman 1989, 9).

I intend also to make people understand how much it is in the interests of the Christian religion that men should be free not only to sift and winnow any doctrine, but also openly to give their opinions of it and even to write about it, according to what each believes. This I aim to achieve not only by virtue of the intrinsic soundness and power of the arguments, new or old, which my readers will find me bringing forward, but much more by virtue of the authority of the Bible, upon very frequent citations of which these arguments are based. Without this freedom to which I refer, there is no religion and no gospel. Violence alone prevails; and it is disgraceful and disgusting that the Christian religion should be supported by violence. Without this freedom, we are still enslaved: not, as once, by the law of God but, what is vilest of all, by human law, or rather, to be more exact, by an inhuman tyranny. There are some irrational bigots who, by a perversion of justice, condemn anything they consider inconsistent with conventional beliefs and give it an invidious title—"heretic" or "heresy"—without consulting the evidence of the Bible upon the point. To their way of thinking, by branding anyone out of hand with this hateful name, they silence him with one word and need take no further trouble. They imagine that they have struck their opponent to the ground, as with a single blow, by the impact of the name heretic alone. I do not expect that my unprejudiced and intelligent readers will behave in this way: such conduct would be utterly unworthy of them. But to these bigots I retort that, in apostolic times, before the New Testament was written, the word heresy, whenever it was used as an accusation, was applied only to something which contradicted the teaching of the apostles as it passed from mouth to mouth. Heretics were then, according to Rom. 16.17, 18, only those people who *caused divisions of opinion and offences contrary to the teaching of the apostles: serving not our Lord Jesus Christ but their own belly.* On the same grounds I hold that, since the compilation of the New Testament, nothing can correctly be called heresy unless it contradicts that.[7] For my own part, I devote my attention to the Holy Scriptures alone. I follow no other heresy or sect. I had not even studied any of the so-called heretical writers, when the blunders of those who are styled orthodox, and their unthinking distortions of the sense of scripture, first taught me to agree with their opponents whenever these agreed with the Bible. If this is heresy, I confess, as does Paul in Acts 24.14, that *following the way which is called heresy I worship the God of my fathers, believing all things that are written in the law and the prophets* and, I add, whatever is written in the New Testament as well.[8] In common with the whole Protestant Church I refuse to recognize any other arbiters of or any other supreme authorities for Christian belief, or any faith not independently arrived at but "implicit," as it is termed. For the rest, brethren, cherish the truth with love for your fellow men. Assess this work as God's spirit shall direct you. Do not accept or reject what I

7. Hunter observes the close correspondence of this view of heresy with Milton's position in *Civil Power* and in *True Religion* (Yale 7:247, n. 23).

8. On Milton's understanding of the term *heresy,* see Mueller.

say unless you are absolutely convinced by the clear evidence of the Bible. Lastly, live in the spirit of our Lord and Savior Jesus Christ, and so I bid you farewell.

J.M.

BOOK 1

CHAPTER I

WHAT CHRISTIAN DOCTRINE IS, AND HOW MANY ITS PARTS

Christian doctrine is the doctrine which, in all ages, CHRIST (though he was not known by that name from the beginning) taught by divine communication, for the glory of God and the salvation of mankind, about God and about worshipping him.

[. . .][9]

I do not teach anything new in this work. I aim only to assist the reader's memory by collecting together, as it were, into a single book texts which are scattered here and there throughout the Bible, and by systematizing them under definite headings, in order to make reference easy. This procedure might well be defended on grounds of Christian prudence, but in fact a more powerful argument in its favor is that apparently it fulfils God's own command: Matt. 13.52: *every scribe who has been instructed in the kingdom of heaven, is like a householder who brings out of his treasure new and old possessions.* So also the apostle says to Timothy, 2 Tim. 1.13: ὑποτύπωσιν ἔχε, "Hold fast the pattern," which the author of the epistle to the Hebrews seems to have been determined to do, so as to teach the main points of Christian doctrine methodically: Heb. 6.1–3: *of repentance, faith, the doctrine of Baptisms, and of the laying on of hands, the resurrection of the dead and eternal judgment: and this we will do if God permit.* This was a very convenient way of instructing catechumens when they were making their first profession of faith in the Church. The same method is indicated in Rom. 6.17: *You have listened from the heart to that pattern of doctrine which you were taught.* In this quotation the Greek word τύπος, like ὑποτύπωσις in 2 Tim. 1.13, seems to mean either those parts of the gospels that were actually written at the time (as in Rom. 2.20 the word μόρφωσις, meaning "form" or "semblance", signifies the law itself in the phrase "the *form* of knowledge and of truth in the law"), or else some systematic course of instruction derived from those parts or from the whole doctrine of the gospel. It appears from Acts 20.27: *I have not avoided making known to you God's whole counsel,* that there is a complete corpus of doctrine, conceived in terms

9. The deleted passage cites Scripture to elaborate the definition of Christian doctrine.

of a definite course of instruction. This was of no great length, however, since the whole course was completed, and perhaps even repeated several times, in about three years, while Paul was at Ephesus.

The PARTS of CHRISTIAN DOCTRINE are two: FAITH, or KNOWLEDGE OF GOD, and LOVE, or THE WORSHIP OF GOD.[10] Gen. 17.1: *walk in sight of me and be perfect;* Ps. 37.3: *have faith in God, and do good;* Luke 11.28: *blessed are those who hear and obey;* Acts 24.14; *I, as one who believes,* and 24.16: *I train myself;* 2 Tim. 1.13: *hold fast the pattern of words with faith and love, which is in Christ Jesus;* 1 Tim. 1.19 [. . .]; Titus 3.8 [. . .]; 1 John 3.23 [. . .].

Although these two parts are distinguished in kind, and are divided for the purpose of instruction, in practice they are inseparable. Rom. 2.13: *not hearers but doers;* James 1.22 [. . .]. Besides, obedience and love are always the best guides to knowledge, and often cause it to increase and flourish, though very small at first. Ps. 25.14: *the secret of Jehovah is with those who reverence him;* John 7.17: *if any man wants what he wills, he shall know about the doctrine,* and 8.31, 32: *if you remain, you will know, and the truth will make you free;* 1 John 2.3: *if we keep his commandments we know, by this, that we know him.*

Faith, however, in this section, does not mean the habit of believing, but the things which must habitually be believed. Acts 6.7: *was obedient to the faith;* Gal. 1.23: *he preaches the faith.*

CHAPTER 2

OF GOD

That there is a God, many deny: *for the fool says in his heart, There is no God,* Ps. 14.1.[11] But he has left so many signs of himself in the human mind, so many traces of his presence through the whole of nature, that no sane person can fail to realize that he exists. Job 12.9: *who does not know from all these things?;* Ps. 19.2: *the heavens declare the glory of God;* Acts 14.17: *he did not allow himself to exist without evidence,* and 17.27, 28: *he is not far from every one of us;* Rom. 1.19, 20: *that which can be known about God is obvious,* and 2.14, 15 [. . .]; 1 Cor. 1.21 [. . .]. It is indisputable that all the things which exist in the world, created in perfection of beauty and order for some definite purpose, and that a good one, provide proof that a supreme creative being existed before the world, and had a definite purpose of his own in all created things.

There are some who prattle about nature or fate, as if they were to be identified with this supreme being. But nature or *natura* implies by its very name that it was *natam,* born. Strictly speaking it means nothing except the specific character of a thing, or that general law in accordance with which everything

10. Cp. *Of Civil Power* (Yale 7:255): "What evangelic religion is, is told in two words, faith and charity; or belief and practice." Hunter's note explains that these "traditional divisions" underlie "Milton's arrangement of the *Christian Doctrine* into two books." See also *PL* 3.103–4; 12.583–85.

11. Cp. *SA* 295–99.

comes into existence and behaves.[12] Surely, too, fate or *fatum* is only what is *fatum,* spoken, by some almighty power. [13]

Moreover, those who want to prove that all things are created by nature, have to introduce the concept of chance as well, to share godhead with nature. What, then, do they gain by their theory? In place of one God, whom they find intolerable, they are forced to set up as universal rulers two goddesses who are almost always at odds with each other. In fact, then, many visible proofs, the fulfillment of many prophecies and the narration of many marvels have driven every nation to the belief that either God or some supreme evil power of unknown name presides over the affairs of men. But it is intolerable and incredible that evil should be stronger than good and should prove the true supreme power. Therefore God exists.

Further evidence for the existence of God is provided by the phenomenon of conscience, or right reason. This cannot be altogether asleep, even in the most evil men. If there were no God, there would be no dividing line between right and wrong. What was to be called virtue, and what vice, would depend upon mere arbitrary opinion. No one would try to be virtuous, no one would refrain from sin because he felt ashamed of it or feared the law, if the voice of conscience or right reason did not speak from time to time in the heart of every man, reminding him, however unwilling he may be to remember it, that a God does exist, that he rules and governs all things, and that everyone must one day render to him an account of his actions, good and bad alike.

The whole of scripture proves the same point, and it is absolutely requisite that those who wish to learn Christian doctrine should be convinced of this fact from the outset. This is stated in Heb. 11.6: *he who comes to God must believe that he is God.* The fact that the Jews, an extremely ancient nation, are now dispersed all over the world, demonstrates the same thing. God often warned them that this would be the outcome of their sins. Amidst the constant flux of history they have been preserved in this state, scattered among the other nations, right up to the present day. This has been done not only to make them pay the penalty of their sins but much rather to give the whole world a perpetual, living proof of the existence of God and the truth of the scriptures.

No one, however, can form correct ideas about God guided by nature or reason alone, without the word or message of God: Rom. 10.14: *how shall they believe in him about whom they have not heard?*

We know God, in so far as we are permitted to know him, from either his nature or his efficiency.

When we talk about knowing God, it must be understood in terms of man's limited powers of comprehension. God, as he really is, is far beyond man's

12. Cp. *PL* 11.48–49: "But longer in that Paradise to dwell,/The law I gave to nature him forbids"; 10.804–7: "that were to extend/His sentence beyond dust and nature's law,/By which all causes else according still/To the reception of their matter act."

13. Cp. *PL* 7.173: "and what I will is Fate"; *Art of Logic* (Yale 8:229): "fate or divine decree."

imagination, let alone his understanding: 1 Tim. 6.16: *dwellin light.* God has revealed only so much of himself as our mind the weakness of our nature can bear: Ex. 33.20, 23: *no one can s will see my back parts;* Isa. 6.1: [...]; John 1.18: [...] and 6.46: [...] 13.12: [...].

It is safest for us to form an image of God in our minds which corresponds to his representation and description of himself in the sacred writings. Admittedly, God is always described or outlined not as he really is but in such a way as will make him conceivable to us. Nevertheless, we ought to form just such a mental image of him as he, in bringing himself within the limits of our understanding, wishes us to form. Indeed he has brought himself down to our level expressly to prevent our being carried beyond the reach of human comprehension, and outside the written authority of scripture, into vague subtleties of speculation.[14]

In my opinion, then, theologians do not need to employ anthropopathy, or the ascription of human feelings to God. This is a rhetorical device thought up by grammarians to explain the nonsense poets write about Jove. Sufficient care has been taken, without any doubt, to ensure that the holy scriptures contain nothing unfitting to God or unworthy of him. This applies equally to those passages in scripture where God speaks about his own nature. So it is better not to think about God or form an image of him in anthropopathetic terms, for to do so would be to follow the example of men, who are always inventing more and more subtle theories about him. Rather we should form our ideas with scripture as a model, for that is the way in which he has offered himself to our contemplation. We ought not to imagine that God would have said anything or caused anything to be written about himself unless he intended that it should be a part of our conception of him. On the question of what is or what is not suitable for God, let us ask for no more dependable authority than God himself. If *Jehovah repented that he had created man,* Gen. 6.6, *and repented because of their groanings,* Judges 2.18, let us believe that he did repent. But let us not imagine that God's repentance arises from lack of foresight, as man's does, for he has warned us not to think about him in this way: Num. 23.19: *God is not a man that he should lie, nor the son of man that he should repent.* The same point is made in 1 Sam. 15.29. If *he grieved in his heart* Gen. 6.6, and if, similarly, *his soul was grieved,* Judges 10.16, let us believe that he did feel grief. For those states of mind which are good in a good man, and count as virtues, are holy in God. If it is said that God, after working for six days, *rested and was refreshed,* Ex. 31.17, and if he *feared his enemy's displeasure,* Deut. 32.27, let us believe that it is not beneath God to feel what grief he does feel, to be refreshed by what refreshes him, and to fear what he does

14. Milton recommends acquiescence to scriptural metaphor in terms similar to those that Raphael uses in warning Adam against abstruse astronomical investigations (8.119–22): "God to remove his ways from human sense,/Placed heav'n from Earth so far, that earthly sight,/If it presume, might err in things too high,/And no advantage gain."

.ear. For however you may try to tone down these and similar texts about God by an elaborate show of interpretative glosses, it comes to the same thing in the end. After all, if *God is said to have created man in his own image, after his own likeness,* Gen. 1.26, and not only his mind but also his external appearance (unless the same words mean something different when they are used again in Gen. 5.3: *Adam begot his son after his own likeness, in his own image*), and if God attributes to himself again and again a human shape and form, why should we be afraid of assigning to him something he assigns to himself, provided we believe that what is imperfect and weak in us is, when ascribed to God, utterly perfect and utterly beautiful? We may be certain that God's majesty and glory were so dear to him that he could never say anything about himself which was lower or meaner than his real nature, nor would he ever ascribe to himself any property if he did not wish us to ascribe it to him. Let there be no question about it: they understand best what God is like who adjust their understanding to the word of God, for he has adjusted his word to our understanding, and has shown what kind of an idea of him he wishes us to have. In short, God either is or is not really like he says he is. If he really is like this, why should we think otherwise? If he is not really like this, on what authority do we contradict God? If, at any rate, he wants us to imagine him in this way, why does our imagination go off on some other tack? Why does our imagination shy away from a notion of God which he himself does not hesitate to promulgate in unambiguous terms? For God in his goodness has revealed to us in ample quantity those things which we need to understand about him for our salvation: Deut. 29.29: *hidden things are in the power of Jehovah, but the things which are revealed are revealed to us that we may do them.* We do not imply by this argument that God, in all his parts and members, is of human form, but that, so far as it concerns us to know, he has that form which he attributes to himself in Holy Writ. God, then, has disclosed just such an idea of himself to our understanding as he wishes us to possess. If we form some other idea of him, we are not acting according to his will, but are frustrating him of his purpose, as if, indeed, we wished to show that our concept of God was not too debased, but that his concept of us was.[15]

Since it has no causes, we cannot define the "divine nature." However, this is the name given to it in 2 Pet. 1.4: *that you might be made sharers of the divine nature* (though "nature" here does not mean the essence but the image of God) and in Gal. 4.8: *which by nature are not Gods,* while θεοτὴς in Col. 2.9, θειοτὴς in Rom. 1.20, and τό θεῖον in Acts 17.29 are all translated "godhead." But though God, by his very nature, transcends everything, including definition, some description of him may be gathered from his names and attributes, as in Isa. 28.29.

[. . . .][16]

15. Calvin proposed an interpretive theory of accommodation that attributes theologically embarrassing scriptural moments, e.g., when God "repents," to divine condescension (*Institutes* 1.13.1). Milton concedes that scriptural accounts of God's emotions may not be accurate but insists that readers of Scripture should think of the deity as he has chosen to depict himself rather than judge the accuracy of Scripture on the basis of doctrine.

16. The deleted passage discusses the implied meanings of three Hebrew names for God.

The ATTRIBUTES which show the essential nature of God are, first, that he is the TRUE GOD: Jer. 10.10: *Jehovah the true God;* John 17.3 [. . .]; 1 Thess. 1.9 [. . .]; 1 John 5.20 [. . .].

Secondly, that God in his most simple nature is a SPIRIT. Ex. 3.14, 15: *I am who I am;* Rom. 11.35, 36: *from him and through him are all things;* John 4.24: *God is a spirit.* Moreover, it is shown what a spirit is, or rather, what it is not: Isa. 31.3: *flesh, not spirit;* Luke 24.39: *a spirit does not have flesh and bones.* From this it may be understood that the essence of God, since it is utterly simple, allows nothing to be compounded with it, and that the word *hypostasis,* Heb. 1.3, which is variously translated *substance, subsistence,* or *person,* is nothing but that most perfect essence by which God exists from himself, in himself, and through himself. For neither *substance* nor *subsistence* can add anything to an utterly complete essence, and the word *person,* in its more recent use, means any individual thing gifted with intelligence, while *hypostasis* means not the thing itself but the essence of the thing in the abstract. *Hypostasis,* therefore, is clearly the same as essence, and in the passage cited above many translate it by the Latin word *essentia.*[17] Therefore, just as God is an utterly simple essence, so he is an utterly simple subsistence.

Thirdly, he is IMMENSE and INFINITE:[18] 1 Kings 8.27: *the heaven of heavens cannot contain you;* Job 11.8: *higher than the highest heavens, deeper than the lowest depth,* and 36.26: so *great that we do not know.*

Fourthly, that he is ETERNAL: everyone agrees that nothing can properly be called eternal unless it has no beginning and no end. It can be seen that both these are true of God from the following passages; not, indeed from each of them separately, but from a comparison of the several texts. [. . . .][19]

The fifth attribute, derived from the fourth, is that God is IMMUTABLE.[20] Ps. 102.28: *but you are the same;* Mal. 3.6: *I, Jehovah, am not changed;* James 1.17: *with whom there is no variation or shadow caused by change.*

The sixth, also derived from the fourth attribute, is that he is INCORRUPTIBLE:[21] Ps. 102.26, 27: you *remain;* Rom. 1.23: *of God, who is not corrupted;* 1 Tim. 1.17 [. . .].

The seventh attribute, which is a consequence of his infinity, is that God is PRESENT EVERYWHERE.[22] Ps. 139.8, 9: *if I climb up to the heavens you are there,* etc.; Prov. 15.3: *Jehovah's eyes are in every place;* Jer. 23.24 [. . .]; Eph. 4.6 [. . .]. Our ideas about the omnipresence of God, as it is called, should be only such as appear most reconcilable with the reverence we ought to have for him.

17. The terms addressed by Milton in this paragraph have a vexed history in Christian theology. See Prestige; also Rumrich 1982.

18. Cp. *PL* 7.168–69: "Boundless the deep, because I am who fill/Infinitude."

19. The rest of the paragraph cites verses that together imply the eternity of God and concludes with the observation that "the concept of what is, strictly speaking, eternity, is expressed in the Hebrew language by inference rather than by distinct words."

20. Cp. *PL* 3.372–73: "Thee Father first they sung omnipotent,/Immutable."

21. Cp. *PL* 2.137–38: "our great enemy/All incorruptible."

22. Cp. *PL* 11.336–37: "his omnipresence fills/Land, sea, and air, and every kind that lives."

The eighth attribute, that God is OMNIPOTENT: 2 Chron. 20.6: *might and power are in your hand;* Job 42.2: *I know that you can do everything;* Ps. 33.9 [. . .] and 115.3 [. . .], and similarly 135.6. Matt. 19.26 [. . .]. Luke 1.37 [. . .]. Because of this attribute the name El Shaddai is applied to God. Gen. 17.1: *I am the omnipotent God,* literally, *the sufficiently powerful God* [. . .]. Hence it appears that God cannot rightly be called Actus Purus, or pure actuality, as is customary in Aristotle, for thus he could do nothing except what he does do, and he would do that of necessity, although in fact he is omnipotent and utterly free in his actions.[23] It should be noted, however, that the power of God is not exerted in those kinds of things which, as the term goes, imply a contradiction: 2 Tim. 2.13: *he cannot deny himself;* Tit. 1.2 [. . .]; Heb. 6.18 [. . .].[24]

The ninth attribute, that God is ONE,[25] proceeds from the eight previous attributes and is, as it were, the logical conclusion of them all. Still further proof of it is to be found, however: Deut. 4.35: *that Jehovah is God and that there is no God except him,* 4.39 [. . .], 6.4: *Hear, Israel, Jehovah our God is one Jehovah,* and 32.39 [. . .]; 1 Kings 8.60: *that all the peoples of the earth may know that Jehovah is God and that there is no one else except him;* 2 Kings 19.15 [. . .]; Isa. 44.1 [. . .], and 44.8 [. . .]; and 45.5 [. . .]; and 45.21 [. . .]; 45.22: *I am God and there is none besides,* that is, no spirit, no person, no being besides him is God, for "none" is a negative of general application: Isa. 46.9: *that I am God and that there is no God besides me, and that no one is like me.* What could be more plain and straightforward? What could be better adapted to the average intelligence, what more in keeping with everyday speech, so that God's people should understand that there is numerically one God and one spirit, just as they understand that there is numerically one of anything else. It was indeed fitting, and thoroughly in accordance with reason, that God should communicate his first and therefore greatest commandment, which he wanted all people, even the lowest, scrupulously to obey, in terms like these which contain nothing ambiguous or obscure that might mislead his worshippers or leave them in doubt. Certainly the Israelites under the law and the prophets always understood that God was without question numerically one, and that there was no other besides him, let alone any equal to him.[26] The schoolmen, to be sure, had not yet appeared on the scene. When they did, by relying upon subtleties,

23. St. Thomas Aquinas used Aristotle's concept of pure actuality to characterize the divine nature and distinguish God from his creatures. Milton's heterodox claim that God's essence includes potentiality is motivated not only by his insistence on divine immunity from necessity but also on God's containing the matter (and thus the material potency) that he shaped in creating the world (see Chapter 7).

24. Cp. *PL* 10.798–801: "Can he make deathless Death? That were to make/Strange contradiction, which to God himself/Impossible is held; as argument/Of weakness, not of power."

25. "Milton is laying groundwork for his antitrinitarian doctrine. To the attribute of unity, he pauses to devote more than a manuscript page, citing proof texts first from the Old Testament and then from the New, and establishing in his exegesis of Mark 12.28–32 the concord of the two. This authority of the scripture he buttresses with appeals to reason: the simplicity of the Bible, the mathematical concept on oneness, and the axiom that God cannot be involved in anything that implies a contradiction—three points that Milton will again urge in chapter 5" (Kelley).

26. Cp. *PL* 8.406–7: "for none I know/Second to me or like, equal much less."

or rather upon utterly contradictory arguments, they threw doubt upon the unity of God, which they ostensibly asserted. But, as I pointed out earlier, everyone agrees that an exception must be made to God's omnipotence, namely that he cannot do things which, as it is put, imply a contradiction. Accordingly we must remember here that nothing can be said of the one God that is inconsistent with his unity, and which makes him both one and not one. Now let us look at the evidence of the New Testament. It is no less clear upon the points already dealt with, and in this respect even clearer: it asserts that this one God is the Father of Our Lord Jesus Christ. When Christ was asked, in Mark 12.28–29, what was the first commandment of all, he replied, quoting from Deut. 6.4, a passage already cited, and understood here in no other sense than the customary one: *Hear, Israel, the Lord our God is one Lord.* The lawyer agreed with this reply, Mark 12.42: *Master, he said, you have spoken well and truthfully, for there is one God and there is no other except him;* John 17.3: *this is eternal life, that they may know that you are the only true God;* Rom. 3.30: *there is one God;* 1 Cor. 8.4 [. . .], 8.6 [. . .]; Gal. 3.20: *an intermediary however is not needed for one person acting alone, but God is one;* Eph. 4.6 [. . .]; 1 Tim. 2.5 [. . .].[27]

So far I have dealt with those attributes which represent God's nature. Some of them are positive attributes: some are negative, in that they show God is not imperfect as created things are. For example, when God is called immense or infinite or immortal, these are negative attributes. The attributes which follow are those which show his divine power and virtue. They are grouped under the concepts of LIFE, INTELLECT, and WILL.

First, LIFE: Deut. 32.40: *I live for ever,* hence the expression *the living God,* Ps. 42.3, and elsewhere. John 5.26: *the Father has life in himself.*

Secondly, under the concept of INTELLECT, God is OMNISCIENT: Gen. 6.5: *he saw human thoughts,* and 18.14 [. . .]; 1 Chron. 28.9 [. . .]; 2 Chron. 6.30 [. . .]; Ps. 33.15 [. . .], and 139.2 [. . .]; 139.4 [. . .]; and 147.5 [. . .]; Job 11.7–9 [. . .] and 26.6 [. . .]; Prov. 15.11: *Hell and destruction are within Jehovah's sight; how much more are the hearts of men!,* and 16.2 [. . .] and 17.3 [. . .]; Isa. 40.28: *his powers of foresight are beyond discovery;* Jer. 17.10: *it is I who scrutinize the heart and test the affections,* whence he is called, Acts 1.24: καρδιογνώστης πάντων, "he who knows the hearts of all men." Jer. 23.23, 24: *Am I a God from near at hand, says Jehovah, and not from far away? Can anyone hide in secret places so that he is out of my sight?;* Heb. 4.13 [. . .]. Hence he is named *the only wise,* Dan. 2.10; Rom. 16.27; 1 Tim. 1.17. God has complete foreknowledge, so he knows what men, who are free in their actions, will think and do, even before they are born and even though these thoughts and deeds will not take place until many centuries have passed. Deut. 31.16: *behold, you will sleep,* etc. *but this people will rise up and go whoring,* etc., and 31.20, 21 [. . .]; 2 Kings 8.12: [. . .].

Thirdly, under the concept of WILL, God is in the first place SUPREMELY PURE and HOLY. Ex. 15.11: *magnificent in holiness;* Josh. 24.19: *he is most holy;*

27. Three deleted sentences at the end of this paragraph concern the singular application of plural Hebrew terms for God.

1 Sam. 2.2: *there is none as holy as Jehovah,* and 6.20 [. . .]; Job 15.15: *the heavens are not clean in his eyes;* Isa. 6.2 [. . .], 6.3 [. . .]; 40.25 [. . .], and 41.20 [. . .]; Hab. 1.13 [. . .].

Secondly, also under the concept of WILL, God is SUPREMELY KIND. Ex. 34.6: *merciful, gracious, patient, of great kindness and fidelity.* Similarly Ps. 86.15 and 103.8 and 5.4: *evil will not dwell with you,* and 25.6: *kindnesses from the beginning of the world,* 103.11 [. . .] and 103.17 [. . .] and 119.68 [. . .]; Lam. 3.22 [. . .]; Matt. 19.17 [. . .]; Luke 6.36 [. . .]; 2 Cor. 1.3 [. . .]; Eph. 2.4 [. . .]; 1 John 4.8 [. . .]. From God's supreme wisdom and goodness may be deduced a further proof of his immutability, for a being supremely wise and good neither would nor could, without contradicting his own nature, change his state of supreme goodness.

Thirdly, just as God is the true God by nature, so with respect to his WILL he is TRUE and FAITHFUL. Ps. 19.8: *the testimony of Jehovah is true;* and John 7.28: *he who sent me is true;* Rom 3.4: *let God be true, but every man a liar;* 2 Tim. 2.13 [. . .]; 1 Cor. 1.9 and 10.13 [. . .]; Rev. 6.10 [. . .].

Fourthly, he is JUST. Deut. 32.4: *all his ways are justice, he is without iniquity, just and right;* Ps. 36.6 [. . .] and 119.137 [. . .]; Isa. 5.16 [. . .]. But I am not concerned at this juncture to discuss God's justice, and what is consistent or inconsistent with it, more widely. For either it is self-evident, or it will be dealt with more conveniently when occasion arises later in the work. Severity, also, is attributed to God: Rom. 11.22: *abrupt severity to those who fell away.*

The flower of all these attributes is that supreme excellence of God, by virtue of which he is truly perfect and truly blessed in supreme glory, and through which he is most justly and deservedly the supreme Lord of all things, as he is often called. Ps. 16.11: *in your sight is an abundance of joys,* and 104.1: *you have clothed yourself in glory and majesty;* Dan. 7.10 [. . .]; Matt. 5.48: *as the Father is perfect;* 1 Tim. 1.11 [. . .]; 6.15 [. . .].

Some description is extant of this divine glory, in so far as mortals can comprehend it. Ex. 19.18, etc.: *Mount Sinai smoked . . . ,* and 24.10, etc.: *they saw the God of Israel, and beneath his feet something resembling a pavement of sapphire, and like the very body of heaven in brightness;* 33.9, 10: *as the cloudy pillar descending,* etc., and 33.18; 1 Kings 19.11 [. . .]; 8.10, 11 [. . .], 22.19 [. . .]; Ps. 18.8, etc., and 104; Micah 1.3, etc.; Nahum 1.3, etc.; Isa. 6.; Ezek. 1 and 8.1–3 and 10.1, etc., and 43.2, 3; Hab. 3.3, etc.; Dan. 7.9; Rev. 4.

It follows, finally, that we must call God WONDERFUL and INCOMPREHENSIBLE. Judges 13.18: *why do you make eager enquiries about my name, since it is an object for wonder?;* Ps. 145.3: *there is no finding out his greatness;* Isa. 40.28 [. . .].

CHAPTER 3

OF DIVINE DECREE

Up to now I have examined God from the point of view of his nature: now we must learn more about him by investigating his efficiency.

God's EFFICIENCY is either INTERNAL or EXTERNAL.

God's INTERNAL EFFICIENCY is that which begins and ends within God himself. His decrees come into this category: Eph. 1.9: *which he had determined beforehand in his own mind.*

A DECREE of God is either GENERAL or SPECIAL.

God's GENERAL DECREE is that by which HE DECREED FROM ETERNITY, WITH ABSOLUTE FREEDOM, WITH ABSOLUTE WISDOM AND WITH ABSOLUTE HOLINESS, ALL THOSE THINGS WHICH HE PROPOSED OR WHICH HE WAS GOING TO PERFORM.

ALL THOSE THINGS WHICH, etc.: Eph. 1.11: *who does all things according to the resolution of his own will.* This does not mean the things which others perform, or which God performs in co-operation with others, to whom he has granted, by nature, freedom of action, but rather the things he performs or purposes singly and by himself. For example, he decreed by himself to create the world, and he decreed by himself that he would not curse the earth any longer, Gen. 8.21.

FROM ETERNITY. Acts 15.18: *all God's works are known to him from the beginning* of *the world;* 1 Cor. 2.7 [. . .].

WITH ABSOLUTE FREEDOM: that is, not forced, not impelled by any necessity,[28] but just as he wished: Eph. 1.11, as above.

WITH ABSOLUTE WISDOM: that is, according to his perfect foreknowledge of all things that were to be created. Acts 2.23: *by the deliberate counsel and foreknowledge of God,* and 4.28: *to do whatever your power and counsel foreordained,* 15.18: *all God's works are known to him from the beginning of the world;* 1 Cor. 2.7 [. . .]; Eph. 3.10, 11 [. . .].

It is absurd, then, to separate God's decree or intention from his eternal resolution and foreknowledge and give the former chronological priority. For God's foreknowledge is simply his wisdom under another name, or that idea of all things which, to speak in human terms, he had in mind before he decreed anything.[29]

So we must conclude that God made no absolute decrees about anything which he left in the power of men, for men have freedom of action. The whole course of scripture shows this: [. . .]. In 2 Kings 20.1, though God said that Hezekiah would die straight away, this did not happen: therefore God had not decreed it without reservation. The death of Josiah was not positively decreed, but he did not listen to Necho's speech, which was derived from the word of God, warning him not to march out, 2 Chron. 35.22. Again, Jer. 18.9, 10: *at that moment when I speak about a nation or a kingdom, saying that I will build or plant it, if, through not paying attention to my voice, it do something that seems evil in my sight, I shall, in turn, repent of the good which I said I should do for it.* In other words, I shall reverse

28. The Latin of the manuscript reads *"nulla necessitate impulsus."* Cp. *PL* 3.120: "So without least impulse or shadow of fate."

29. Cp. *PL* 7.554–57: "Thence to behold this new created world/Th' addition of his empire, how it showed/In prospect from his throne, how good, how fair/Answering his great idea."

my decree because that nation did not keep the condition upon which the decree depended. Here we have a rule given by God himself! He wishes us always to understand his decrees in the light of this agreement, and always clearly to appreciate the condition upon which the decree depends. Jer. 26.3: *if it should happen that they are obedient and that each man turn from his evil path, so that I repent the harm I intend to do them because of the depravity of their behavior.* So, too, God had not decreed absolutely even upon the destruction of Jerusalem: Jer. 38.17, etc [. . .]; Jonah 3.4: *yet forty days and Nineveh will be overthrown,* but, at 3.10, when he saw they had reformed God repented, although Jonah was angry and thought it did not become God in the least.[30] Acts 27.24, 31: *I have given you all as a gift. But unless these men stay on board . . . ;* here Paul revokes the divinely inspired statement which he had made: God takes back the gift given to Paul unless they all take care of themselves to the utmost of their ability.

Judging from these passages of scripture then, and from many others of the same kind, which we are immediately bound to acknowledge as authoritative, it is beyond dispute that the supreme God has not absolutely decreed all things.

Each side of this controversy has hosts of adherents, all arguing at great length and with altogether more subtlety than weight. However, if it is allowable to apply the standards of mortal reason to divine decrees, this method of making decrees in a non-absolute way can be readily defended, even with regard to human considerations, as supremely wise and in no way unworthy of God. For if the decrees of God quoted above, and others of the same kind which frequently occur, were interpreted in an absolute sense without any implied conditions, God would seem to contradict himself and be changeable.

[. . .][31]

It is no good replying that this necessity is not the result of compulsion but that it springs from God's immutability, by virtue of which everything is decreed, or from his infallibility of foreknowledge, by virtue of which everything is foreknown. I shall give a full exposure of these two purely academic types of necessity later. Meanwhile I recognize no other type of necessity than the one which Logic, that is, reason teaches:[32] namely, when a given cause produces some single unalterable effect either as a result of its own inherent propensity, as when fire burns, which is called natural necessity, or as the result of the compulsion of some external force, which is called compulsory necessity. In the latter case, whatever effect the given cause produces is said to be produced *per*

30. On divine repentance and its implications, see previous chapter, note 15.

31. In the deleted paragraph, Milton considers and rejects the claim that God predestines not only the end but the means to the end of his decree. Milton revisits the point in chapter 4.

32. Cp. *Art of Logic* (Yale 8:211): "For the theologians produce rules about God, about divine substances, and about sacraments purportedly out of the middle of logic, as though these rules had been furnished simply for their own convenience, although nothing is more foreign to logic, or indeed to reason itself, than the grounds for these rules as formulated by them."

accidens.[33] Now any necessity operating externally upon a given cause either makes it produce a certain effect or limits it from producing other effects. In either case it is clear that the cause loses all freedom of action. In God a certain immutable internal necessity to do good, independent of all outside influence, can be consistent with absolute freedom of action. For in the same divine nature each tends to the same result. However, it does not follow from this that I must allow the same possibility where two different natures are concerned, namely the nature of God and the nature of man. For in this case the external immutability of the one and the internal liberty of the other may not have the same aim at all but point in opposite directions. Nor, incidentally, do I concede the point that there is in God any necessity to act. I grant only that he is necessarily God. For scripture itself bears witness to the fact that his decrees and still more his actions, whatever they may be, are absolutely free.[34]

But it is said that divine necessity, or the necessity of a first cause, does not bring any compulsion to bear upon the liberty of free agents. I reply that, if it does not compel, then either it restricts liberty within certain limits, or assists it, or does nothing. If it restricts or assists then it is either the only or the joint and principal cause of every action,[35] good and bad, of the free agent. If it does nothing, it is not a cause at all, still less should it be called necessity.

We imagine nothing unworthy of God if we maintain that those results, those conditions which God himself has chosen to place within man's free power, depend upon man's free will. In fact, God made his decrees conditional in this way for the very purpose of allowing free causes to put into effect that freedom which he himself gave them.[36] It would be much more unworthy of God to announce that man is free but really deprive him of freedom; and freedom is destroyed or at least obscured if we admit any such sophistical concept of necessity as that which, we are asked to believe, results not from compulsion but from immutability or infallibility. This concept has misled and continues to mislead a lot of people.

However, I affirm that, strictly speaking, the divine plan depends only upon God's own wisdom. By this wisdom he had perfect foreknowledge of all things

33. Cp. *Art of Logic* (Yale 8:226–27): "An efficient cause is such either *per se* or *per accidens*. . . . A *per se* efficient cause is one which causes efficiently through its own power, that is, one which produces an effect from an intrinsic principle. . . . A *per accidens* efficient cause is one which causes through an eternal power, that is, one not its own."

34. Cp. *Art of Logic* (Yale 8:227): "Only God does all things with absolute freedom, that is, He does whatever he wills; and He can act or not act. This is attested to throughout Sacred Scripture." See S. Fallon 1988.

35. Cp. *Art of Logic* (Yale 8:224): "An efficient cause works either by itself or along with other efficient causes, and of all these often one will be the principal cause, while another is less principal, or an assisting and helping cause."

36. Cp. *Art of Logic* (Yale 8:227): "Only those causes act freely *ex hypothesi* which do things through reason and deliberation, as angels and men—on the hypothesis, to be sure, of the divine will, which in the beginning gave them the power to act freely. For freedom is the power to do or not to do this or that, unless of course God wills otherwise or some other force violently interferes."

in his own mind, and knew what they would be like and what their consequence would be when it eventually occurred.

But, you ask, how can these consequences which, on account of man's free will, are uncertain, be reconciled with God's absolutely firm decree? For it is written, Ps. 33.11: *Jehovah's intention will be stable for ever,* similarly Prov. 19.21; Isa. 46.10; Heb. 6.17: *the immutability of his plan.* My reply is that, in the first place, these consequences are not uncertain from God's point of view, but known with absolute certainty. They are not, however, inevitable, as we shall see later. Secondly, in all the passages quoted the divine plan is said to stand in the face of all human power and intention. It is not said to stand in opposition to the freedom of the will in matters where God himself has made man his own master, and decreed to make him so from all eternity. If it were otherwise, one of God's decrees would contradict another. This would lead to the result you object to in the arguments of others, that is, God becomes mutable so long as you make those things which by his command are matters of free will, appear inevitabilities. But God is not mutable if he makes no positive decree about anything which, through the freedom he decided to give man, could turn out otherwise. He would be mutable, and his intention would not be stable, if, by a second decree, he thwarted the freedom he had once decided upon, or cast the least shadow of necessity over it.

From the concept of freedom, then, all idea of necessity must be removed. No place must be given even to that shadowy and peripheral idea of necessity based on God's immutability and foreknowledge. If any idea of necessity remains, as I have said before, it either restricts free agents to a single course, or compels them against their will, or assists them when they are willing, or does nothing at all. If it restricts free agents to a single course, this makes man the natural cause of all his actions and therefore of his sins, just as if he were created with an inherent propensity towards committing sins. If it compels free agents against their will, this means that man is subject to the force of another's decree, and is thus the cause of sins only *per accidens,* God being the cause of the sin *per se.* If it assists free agents when they are willing, this makes God either the principal or the joint cause of sins. Lastly, if it does nothing at all, no necessity exists. By doing nothing it reduces itself to nothingness. For it is quite impossible that God should have made an inflexible decree about something which we know man is still at liberty to do or not to do. It is also impossible that a thing should be immutable which afterwards might or might not take place.

Whatever was a matter of free will for the first created man, could not then have been immutably or absolutely decreed from all eternity. Obviously, either nothing ever was in the power of man, or if anything was, God cannot be said to have made a firm decree about it.[37]

37. This statement opposes Calvinist orthodoxy. Cp. Calvin, *Institutes* (3.23.7): "The decree is dreadful, I confess. Yet no one can deny that God foreknew what end man was to have before he created him, and consequently foreknew because he so ordained by his decree."

The absurdities which are said to ensue from this argument are either not absurdities or do not ensue from it. For it is neither absurd nor impious to say that the idea of certain things or events might come to God from some other source. Since God has decreed from eternity that man should have free will to enable him either to fall or not to fall, the idea of that evil event, the fall, was clearly present in God from some other source: everyone admits this.

It cannot be deduced from this that something temporal may cause or limit something eternal; for nothing temporal, but rather eternal wisdom supplied a cause for the divine plan.

The matter or object of the divine plan was that angels and men alike should be endowed with free will, so that they could either fall or not fall. Doubtless God's actual decree bore a close resemblance to this, so that all the evils which have since happened as a result of the fall could either happen or not: if you stand firm, you will stay; if you do not, you will be thrown out: if you do not eat it, you will live; if you do, you will die.

Those, then, who argue that man's freedom of action is subordinate to an absolute decree by God, wrongly conclude that God's decree is the cause of his foreknowledge and antecedent to it. But really, if we must discuss God in terms of our own habits and understandings, it seems more consonant with reason to foresee first and then decree, and indeed this is more in keeping with scripture, and with the nature of God himself, since, as I have just proved, he decreed everything with supreme wisdom in accordance with his foreknowledge.

I do not deny that God's will is the first cause of everything. But neither do I divorce his foreknowledge and wisdom from his will, much less pretend that the latter is antecedent. In short, God's will is no less the first cause of everything if he decrees that certain things shall depend upon the will of man, than if he had decreed to make all things inevitable.

To sum up these numerous arguments in a few words, this is briefly how the matter stands, looked at from a thoroughly reasonable angle. By virtue of his wisdom God decreed the creation of angels and men as beings gifted with reason and thus with free will.[38] At the same time he foresaw the direction in which they would tend when they used this absolutely unimpaired freedom. What then? Shall we say that God's providence or foreknowledge imposes any necessity upon them? Certainly not: no more than if some human being possessed the same foresight. For an occurrence foreseen with absolute certainty by a human being will no less certainly take place than one foretold by God. For example, Elisha foresaw what evils King Hazael would bring upon the Israelites in a few years' time: 2 Kings 8.12. But no one would claim that these happened inevitably as a result of Elisha's foreknowledge: for these events, no less than any others, clearly arose from man's will, which is always free.[39] Similarly, nothing happens

38. Cp. *PL* 3.108: "reason also is choice"; also 9.351–52: "But God left free the will, for what obeys/Reason, is free."

39. *"arbitrio semper libro."* In classical usage, *arbitrio libro* denotes discretionary power.

because God has foreseen it, but rather he has foreseen each event because each is the result of particular causes which, by his decree, work quite freely and with which he is thoroughly familiar. So the outcome does not rest with God who foresees it, but only with the man whose action God foresees. As I have demonstrated above, there can be no absolute divine decree about the action of free agents. Moreover, divine foreknowledge can no more affect the action of free agents than can human foreknowledge, that is, not at all, because in both cases the foreknowledge is within the mind of the foreknower and has no external effect.[40] Divine foreknowledge definitely cannot itself impose any necessity, nor can it be set up as a cause, in any sense, of free actions. If it is set up in this way, then liberty will be an empty word, and will have to be banished utterly not only from religion but also from morality and even from indifferent matters. Nothing will happen except by necessity, since there is nothing God does not foresee.

To conclude, we should feel certain that God has not decreed that everything must happen inevitably. Otherwise we should make him responsible for all the sins ever committed, and should make demons and wicked men blameless. But we should feel certain also that God really does foreknow everything that is going to happen. My opponent, of course, snatches up this last remark and thinks I have conceded enough for him to prove either that God does not foreknow everything, or that all future events must happen by necessity because God has foreknown them. But though future events will certainly happen, because divine foreknowledge cannot be mistaken, they will not happen by necessity, because foreknowledge, since it exists only in the mind of the foreknower, has no effect on its object.[41] A thing which is going to happen quite freely in the course of events is not then produced as a result of God's foreknowledge, but arises from the free action of its own causes, and God knows in what direction these will, of their own accord, tend. In this way he knew that Adam would, of his own accord, fall. Thus it was certain that he would fall, but it was not necessary, because he fell of his own accord and that is irreconcilable with necessity.[42] [...]. From all that has been said it is sufficiently clear that neither God's decree nor his foreknowledge can shackle free causes with any kind of necessity. There are some people, however, who, struggling to oppose this doctrine through thick and thin, do not hesitate to assert that God is, in himself, the cause and author of sin.[43] If I did not believe that they said such a thing from

40. Cp. *Art of Logic* (Yale 8:236): "While [an end] is still only in the mind . . . and has not been achieved, it does not yet truly exist; and since it does not yet exist, how can it be a cause?"

41. Cp. *Art of Logic* (Yale 8:229): "Theology will discuss providence better than logic will. But in passing let this much be said: fate or divine decree does not force anyone to do evil, and on the hypothesis of divine foreknowledge all things are certain, to be sure, but not necessary."

42. Cp. *PL* 3.111–23.

43. Arminius, whose theology of free will and predestination anticipates Milton's, writes that the doctrine that God by eternal decree determines our choice or inclines us in one direction or another "makes God to be the author of sin, and man to be exempt from blame. . . . It constitutes God as the real, proper, and only sinner" (*Apology or Defense,* art. 7, in *The Writings of James Arminius,* trans. James Nichols and W. R. Bagnall, 3 vols. [Baker Book House, 1956], 1.298). See Danielson.

error rather than wickedness, I should consider them of all blasphemers the most utterly damned. If I should attempt to refute them, it would be like inventing a long argument to prove that God is not the Devil. So much for God's GENERAL DECREE.

God's first and most excellent SPECIAL DECREE of all concerns HIS SON: primarily by virtue of this he is called FATHER:[44] Ps. 2.7: *I shall declare the decree: Jehovah said to me, You are my son I have begotten you today;* Heb. 1.5 [. . .]. And again *"I shall be a Father to him and he shall be a son to me";* 1 Pet. 1.19, 20 [. . .]; Isa. 42.1 [. . .]; 1 Pet. 2.14 [. . .]. From all these quotations it appears that the Son of God was begotten by a decree of the Father.

Distinct mention is nowhere made of a SPECIAL DECREE of God about THE ANGELS: but it is implied in 1 Tim. 5.21: *of the elect angels;* Eph. 1.9, 10: *the mystery of his will* etc. *that he might collect together under a single head in Christ, all things in heaven,* etc.

CHAPTER 4

OF PREDESTINATION

The principal SPECIAL DECREE of God which concerns men is called PREDESTINATION: by which GOD, BEFORE THE FOUNDATIONS OF THE WORLD WERE LAID, HAD MERCY ON THE HUMAN RACE, ALTHOUGH IT WAS GOING TO FALL OF ITS OWN ACCORD, AND, TO SHOW THE GLORY OF HIS MERCY, GRACE AND WISDOM, PREDESTINED TO ETERNAL SALVATION, ACCORDING TO HIS PURPOSE or plan IN CHRIST, THOSE WHO WOULD IN THE FUTURE BELIEVE AND CONTINUE IN THE FAITH.

In academic circles the word "predestination" is habitually used to refer to reprobation as well as to election. For the discussion of such an exacting problem, however, this usage is too slapdash. Whenever the subject is mentioned in scripture, specific reference is made only to election: Rom. 8.29, 30: *he predestined that they should be shaped to the likeness of his son: and those whom he has predestined he has also called, justified and made glorious;* 1 Cor. 2.7 [. . .]; Eph. 1.5 [. . .], and 1.11 [. . .]; Acts 2.23: *when he had been given to you by the deliberate counsel and foreknowledge of God,* compared with 4.28: *that they might do everything which your power and your counsel predestined would be done*—in order, that is, to procure the salvation of man.

When other terms are used to signify predestination, the reference is always to election alone: Rom. 8.28: *who are called according to his purpose,* or plan, and 9.23, 24: *vessels of mercy which he prepared for glory beforehand; even those whom he has called;*

44. "Milton is here laying the foundation for his argument against the eternal generation of the Son: the Son was begotten in consequence of a decree; the decree preceded the execution of the decree; therefore the Son was begotten within the limits of time" (Kelley). On the prominence of Psalm 2 in contexts concerning the generation of the Son, see chapter 5, note 74.

Eph. 3.11 [. . .]; 2 Tim. 1.9 [. . .]; 1 Thess. 5.9: *God has not appointed us to anger, but to obtain salvation through our Lord Jesus Christ.* It does not follow from the negative part of this last quotation that others are appointed to anger. Nor does the clause in 1 Pet. 2.8: *to which they had been appointed,* mean that they were predestined from eternity, but rather from some time after they rebelled, just as the apostles are said to be "elected" in time and "appointed" by Christ to their employment, John 15.16.

If, in such a controversial question, any importance can be attached to metaphor and allegory, it is worth noting that mention is often made of "enrollment among the living" and of "the book of life," but never of the "book of death": Isa. 4.3: *enrolled among the living;* Dan. 12.1: *at that time the people will be set free, each one that will be found written in that book;* Luke 10.20 [. . .]; Phillip. 4.3 [. . .]. However this metaphor from writing does not seem to signify predestination from eternity, which is general, but rather some particular decree made by God within the bounds of time, and referring to certain men, on account of their works. Ps. 69.28: *let them be blotted out from the book of life, and not enrolled with the righteous:* it follows they were not enrolled from eternity. Isa. 65.6 [. . .]; Rev. 20.12: *the dead were judged in accordance with the things which had been written in these books, in accordance with the things they had done*—clearly, then, this was not the book of eternal predestination, but of their deeds.[45] Similarly those people were not marked down from eternity who are described in Jude 4 as *marked down for this doom long ago.* Why should we extend the sense of *long ago* so much, and not interpret it rather as "from the time when they became inveterate and hardened sinners"? Why, I repeat, should we extend the meaning of *long ago* so far into the past, either in this quotation or in the passage from which it seems to be taken, 2 Pet. 2.3: *the judgment long ago decreed for them has not been idle; destruction waits for them with unsleeping eyes?* Here it clearly means "from the time of their apostasy," however long they concealed it.

Another text which is quoted against me is Prov. 16.4: *Jehovah has made all things for himself, even the wicked man for the day of evil.* But God did not make man wicked, much less did he make him so "for himself." What did he do? He threatened the wicked man with the punishment he deserved, as was just, but did not predestine to punishment the man who did not deserve it. The point is clearer in Eccles. 7.29: *that God has made man upright, but they have thought up numerous devices.* The day of evil follows as certainly from this as if the wicked man had been made for it.

PREDESTINATION, then, must always be taken to refer to election, and seems often to be used instead of that term. What Paul says, Rom. 8.29: *those whom he foreknew, he also predestined* has the same meaning as 1 Pet. 1.2: *elect according to foreknowledge;* Rom. 9.11 [. . .] and 11.5 [. . .]; Eph. 1.4 [. . .]; Col. 3.12 [. . .]; 2 Thess. 2.13 [. . .]. There could, then, be nothing of reprobation in predestination: 1 Tim. 2.4: *who wishes that all men should be saved and should come to a knowledge of the*

45. Cp. *PL* 1.362–63: "blotted out and razed/By their rebellion, from the Books of Life."

truth; 2 Pet. 3.9: *he is patiently disposed towards us, not wishing that any should perish but that all should come to repentance. Towards us,* that is, all men: not only the elect, as some propose, but particularly towards the wicked; thus Rom. 9.22: *tolerated the vessels of wrath.* If, as some object, Peter would hardly have numbered himself among the unbelievers, then surely neither would he have numbered himself, in the previous quotation, among the elect who had not yet repented. Besides, God does not delay on account of the elect, but hurries rather: Matt. 24.22: *those days shall be shortened.*

I do not understand by the term election that general or, so to speak, national election by which God chose the whole nation of Israel as his own people, Deut. 4.37: *because he loved your forefathers and elected their seed after them,* and 7.6–8: *Jehovah selected you to be a people peculiar to him,* and elsewhere, Isa. 45.4 [. . .].[46] Nor do I mean the election by which, after rejecting the Jews, God chose the Gentiles to whom he wished the gospel should be preached. This is spoken of particularly in Rom. 9 and 11. Nor do I mean the election by which he chooses an individual for some employment, 1 Sam. 10.24: *do you see whom Jehovah has chosen?;* John 6.70: *have I not chosen you twelve, and one of you is a devil;* whence they are sometimes called elect who are superior to the rest for any reason, as 2 John 1: *to the elect Lady,* which means, as it were, most excellent, and 2 John 13: *of your elect sister;* 1 Pet. 2.6: *the elect stone, precious;* 1 Tim. 5. 21: *of the elect angels.* I mean, rather, that special election which is almost the same as eternal predestination. Election, then, is not a part of predestination; much less is reprobation. Predestination, strictly speaking, includes a concept of aim, namely the salvation at least of believers, a thing in itself desirable. The aim of reprobation, on the other hand, is the destruction of unbelievers, a thing in itself repulsive and hateful. Clearly, then, God did not predestine reprobation at all, or make it his aim. Ezek. 18.32: *I have no pleasure in the death of a man who dies,* and 33.11: *may I not live,* etc. *if I have pleasure in the death of the wicked, but* etc. If God wished neither for sin nor for the death of the sinner, that is neither for the cause nor for the effect of reprobation, then certainly he did not wish for reprobation itself. Reprobation, therefore, is no part of divine predestination.

BY WHICH GOD: meaning, of course, the Father.[47] Luke 12.32: *it was your father's pleasure;* similarly whenever mention is made of the divine decree or plan: John 17.2: *as many as you have given him;* 17.6 [. . .]; similarly 11.24. Eph. 1.4 [. . .], 1.5 [. . .], 1.11: *predestined according to his purpose.*

BEFORE THE FOUNDATIONS OF THE WORLD WERE LAID: Eph. 1.4; 2 Tim. 1.9: *before the world began;* similarly Tit. 1.2.

HAD MERCY ON THE HUMAN RACE, ALTHOUGH IT WAS GOING TO FALL OF ITS OWN ACCORD. The matter or object of predestination was not simply man who was to be created, but man who was going to fall of his own free will. For the demonstration of divine mercy and grace which

46. Cp. *PL* 12.111–12: "And one peculiar nation to select/From all the rest"; also 12.214–15.

47. As the next chapter makes clear, in Milton's view, the Father alone is truly God.

God purposed as the final end of predestination necessarily presupposes man's sin and misery, originating in man alone. Everyone agrees that man could have avoided falling.[48] But if, because of God's decree, man could not help but fall (and the two contradictory opinions are sometimes voiced by the same people), then God's restoration of fallen man was a matter of justice not grace. For once it is granted that man fell, though not unwillingly, yet by necessity, it will always seem that that necessity either prevailed upon his will by some secret influence, or else guided his will in some way. But if God foresaw that man would fall of his own accord, then there was no need for him to make a decree about the fall, but only about what would become of man who was going to fall. Since, then, God's supreme wisdom foreknew the first man's falling away, but did not decree it, it follows that, before the fall of man, predestination was not absolutely decreed either. Predestination, even after the fall, should always be considered and defined not so much as the result of an actual decree but as arising from the immutable condition of a decree.[49]

PREDESTINED: that is designated, elected. He made the salvation of man the goal and end, as it were, of his purpose. Hence may be refuted those false theories about preterition from eternity and the abandonment of the non-elect. For in opposition to these God has clearly and frequently declared, as I have quoted above, that he desires the salvation of all and the death of none, that he hates nothing he has made, and has omitted nothing which might provide salvation for everyone.

TO SHOW THE GLORY OF HIS MERCY, GRACE AND WISDOM. This is the supreme end of predestination: Rom. 9.23: *that he might make known the riches of his glory towards the vessels of mercy;* Eph. 1.6 [. . .]; 1 Cor. 2.7 [. . .].

ACCORDING TO HIS PURPOSE or plan IN CHRIST: Eph. 3.10, 11: *the wisdom of God in all its forms; according to his eternal purpose, which he appointed in Jesus Christ our Lord;* 1.4 [. . .]; and 1.5 [. . .]; 1.11: *in him, in whom indeed we have been given our share, as we were predestined according to his purpose.* Hence that love of God shown to us in Christ: John 3.16: *God loved the world so much that he gave his only begotten Son;* Eph. 2.4, 5 [. . .]; 1 John 4.9, 10 [. . .], etc. Except for Christ, then, who was foreknown, no grace was decided upon, no reconciliation between God and man who was going to fall.[50] Since God has so openly declared that predestination is the effect of his mercy, love, grace, and wisdom in Christ, we ought not attribute it, as is usually done, to his absolute and inscrutable will, even in those

48. In fact, not everyone agreed that man could have avoided falling. For the argument that God not only foresaw but necessitated the Fall of Adam and Eve, see Calvin's *Institutes* 2.12.5 and 3.23.7–8. Blithe assertion of a contested opinion is characteristic of Milton; cp. *TKM* (p. 1028): "No man who knows aught can be so stupid to deny that all men naturally were born free."

49. Cp. *PL* 3.124–34.

50. Cp. *PL* 3.274–75: "O thou in Heav'n and Earth the only peace / Found out for mankind under wrath." Arminian soteriology tends to stress the Son's unique role in effecting God's decision to show mercy. This emphasis is even more pronounced in Milton's works because his Arianism also renders the Son's self-sacrifice voluntary; see chapter 14.

passages which mention will alone: Ex. 33.19: *I shall be gracious to him to whom I shall be gracious,* that is, not to elaborate further upon the causes of my graciousness at present. Rom. 9.18: *he has mercy on whom he will,* that is to say, by the method he determined upon in Christ: and in passages of this kind God is, in fact, usually speaking of his extraordinary grace and mercy, as will be evident when we examine particular texts. Thus Luke 12.32: *it was your father's pleasure;* Eph. 1.5: *by himself through Jesus Christ, according to the good pleasure of his will,* 1.11 [. . .]; James 1.18: *because he wished it he has begotten us by the word of truth,* that is, through Christ, who is the word and truth of God.

THOSE WHO WOULD IN THE FUTURE BELIEVE AND CONTINUE IN THE FAITH. This is the immutable condition of his decree. It does not attribute any mutability to God or his decrees. *This, God's solid foundation, stands sure and bears this inscription,* 2 Tim. 2.19: *the Lord knows his own, and these are all who leave wickedness and name the name of Christ,* that is, all who believe. The mutability is all on the side of those who renounce their faith: thus in 2 Tim. 2.13: *if we do not believe, nevertheless he remains faithful, he cannot deny himself.* It seems, then, that predestination and election are not particular but only general: that is, they belong to all who believe in their hearts and persist in their belief. Peter is not predestined or elected as Peter, or John as John, but each only insofar as he believes and persists in his belief. Thus the general decree of election is individually applicable to each believer, and is firmly established for those who persevere.[51]

The whole of scripture makes this very clear. It offers salvation and eternal life to all equally, on condition of obedience to the Old Testament and faith in the New. Without doubt the decree as it was made public was consistent with the decree itself. Otherwise we should have to pretend that God was insincere, and said one thing but kept another hidden in his heart. This is, indeed, the effect of that academic distinction which ascribes a twofold will to God: the revealed will, by which he instructs us what he wants us to do, and the will of his good pleasure, by which he decrees that we will never do it.[52] As good split the will in two and say: will in God is twofold—a will by which he wishes, and a will by which he contradicts that wish! But, my opponents reply, we find in scripture these two statements about the same matter: God wishes Pharaoh to let the people go, because he orders it: he does not wish it, because he hardens Pharaoh's heart. But, in fact, God wished it only. Pharaoh did not wish it, and to make him more unwilling God hardened his heart. He postponed the accomplishment of his will, which was the opposite of Pharaoh's, so that he might punish the latter all the more severely for his prolonged unwillingness. To order us to do right but decree that we shall do wrong!—this is not the way God dealt with our forefather, Adam, nor is it the way he deals with those he calls and invites to grace. Could anything be imagined more absurd than such a

51. Cp. *PL* 3.185–97.

52. Cp. *DDD* (p. 891), where Milton similarly rejects the Calvinist tenet of God's twofold will.

theory? To make it work, you have to invent a necessity which does not necessitate and a will which does not will.

The other point which must be proved is that the decree, as it was made public, is everywhere conditional: Gen. 2.17: *do not eat of this, for on the day you eat it you will die.* This is clearly as if God had said: I do not wish you to eat of this, and therefore I have certainly not decreed that you will eat it; for if you eat it you will die, if you do not you will live. Thus the decree itself was conditional before the fall, and it is evident from numerous other passages that it was conditional after the fall as well: Gen. 4.7: *surely, if you do well, lenity awaits you? but if you do not do well, sin is at the door,* or rather, sin's penalty, ever watchful. Ex. 32.32, 33: *blot me out now from your book which you have written. I shall blot out from my book the man who sins against me.* Here Moses, on account of his love for his people, forgot that the faithful cannot be blotted out so long as they remain faithful: or perhaps his speech should be modified by reference to Rom. 9.1, etc.: *indeed I should wish, if it were possible* . . . But God's reply, though metaphorical, shows quite clearly that the principle of predestination has a conditional basis: *I shall blot out the man who sins.* This is shown at greater length when the compact of the law is laid down, Deut. 7.6, 7, 8. [. . .][53]

Two difficult texts remain, which must be explained by reference to many clearer passages which resemble them; for clear things are not elucidated by obscure things, but obscure by clear.[54] The first passage is Acts 13.48, the second Rom. 8.28–30. I shall deal first with the latter as in my opinion it is less difficult. The words are as follows: *but we know that with those who love God all things work together for good; with those who are called according to his purpose. For those whom he foreknew he also predestined that they should be shaped to the likeness of his Son,* etc. *and those whom he has predestined he has also called; those he has called, he has also justified, and those he has justified he has also made glorious.*[55]

First it must be noticed that, in 8.28, *those who love God* and *those who are called according to his purpose* are the same, and that they are identical with *those whom he foreknew* and *those whom he has predestined* and *those he has called* in 8.30. Hence it is evident that the method and order of general election is being outlined here, not of the election of certain individuals in preference to others. It is just as if Paul had said: We know that with those who love God, that is, those who believe (for those who love, believe) all things work together for good: and the order of events is as follows. First, God foreknew those who would believe; that is, he

53. In the deleted passage, Milton cites various examples of divine decree conditional on the law in the Old and on faith in the New Testament.

54. Cp. *Areop* (p. 956): "To be still searching what we know not by what we know, still closing up truth to truth as we find it . . . , this is the golden rule in theology as well as in arithmetic"; also, *Art of Logic* (Yale 8:391).

55. Cp. *Art of Logic* (Yale 8:388), where Milton quotes these verses to exemplify *sorites:* "propositions proceeding in a continuous series in such a way that the predicate of the preceding proposition is invariably the subject of the following, until finally the consequent of the last proposition is concluded of the antecedent of the first." (The final clause of Rom. 8.30 reads, "Therefore, those whom he has foreknown, he has glorified.")

decided or approved that it should be those alone upon whom, through Christ, he would look kindly: in fact, then, that it should be all men, if they believed. He predestined these to salvation, and, in various ways, he called all men to believe, that is, truly to acknowledge God. He justified those who believed in this way, and finally glorified those who persevered in their belief. But to make it clearer who they are whom God has foreknown, it must be realized that there are three different ways in which God is said to know a person or thing. First, by universal knowledge, as in Acts 15.8: *all God's works are known to him from the beginning of time.* Secondly, by knowledge which implies approval or grace, which is a Hebraic idiom, and must therefore be explained more fully: Ex. 33.12: *I know you by name, and also you have found grace in my eyes;* Ps. 1.6 [. . .]; Matt. 7.23 [. . .]. Thirdly, by knowledge which implies displeasure: Deut. 31.21: *I know the product of their imagination* etc.; 2 Kings 19.27 [. . .]; Rev. 3.1: *I know all your works, that you have a name for being alive, but are dead.* It is clear that, in our passage, the knowledge which implies approval can alone be intended. [. . .].[56] God has predestined and elected each person who believes and persists in his belief. What is the point of knowing whether God had prescience about who in the future would believe or not believe? For no man believes because God had prescience about it, but rather God had prescience about it because the man was going to believe.[57] It is hard to see what purpose is served by introducing God's prescience or foreknowledge about particular individuals into the doctrine of predestination, except that of raising useless and utterly unanswerable questions. For why should God foreknow particular individuals? What could he foreknow in them which might induce him to predestine them in particular, rather than all in general, once the general condition of belief had been laid down? Suffice it to know, without investigating the matter any further, that God, out of his supreme mercy and grace in Christ, has predestined to salvation all who shall believe.

The other passage is Acts 13.48: *when the Gentiles heard this they were glad and glorified the word of the Lord; and as many as were ordained to eternal life, believed.* The difficulty lies in the author's sudden introduction of an idea which is at first sight quite inconsistent with the rest of scripture, including the part he wrote himself. For he had just recorded Peter's speech, Acts 10.34, 35: *truly I perceive that God is no respecter of the person* or, of the appearance, *but anyone in any nation who fears him and follows righteousness is acceptable to him.* "Acceptable" here certainly means elect. Moreover, in case it should be objected that Cornelius was already a proselyte, Paul says the same even of those who are ignorant of the law: Rom. 2.10, 11, 14: *with God there is no respect of persons. He who has not the law,* etc.; 1 Pet. 1.17: *who, without respect of persons, judges according to each man's work.* But those who teach that each man believes because he was ordained, not that he was ordained because he was going to believe, cannot avoid the conclusion that God is a

56. The deleted sentences discuss intricacies of divine foreknowledge, causes of a believer's faith, and predestination.

57. Cp. *PL* 3.102–22.

respecter of persons which, as he so often asserts, he does not wish to be thought. Again, if the Gentiles believed because they were ordained to do so, this same reason will account for the Jews' failure to believe, Acts 13.46, which excuses them to a large extent, for it would appear that eternal life was not offered them but merely shown them. If this were so, moreover, it would not be likely to encourage other nations, for they would immediately draw the conclusion that what was necessary for eternal life was not any will or exertion of their own, but some sort of fatal decree. But on the contrary, scripture is absolutely clear on this point throughout: all who have been ordained to eternal life believe, not simply because they have been ordained, but because they were ordained on condition that they believed. For this reason interpreters who are, in my opinion, more acute, think there is some ambiguity in the Greek word τεταγμένοι, normally translated *ordained.* They consider it equivalent to "well or moderately disposed or affected," that is, of a composed, attentive, upright and not disorderly mind, and, with reference to eternal life, unlike those Jews who had rejected God's word and shown themselves unworthy of it. A similar sense of this word "ordained" is not unknown among the Greek writers: it is found in Plutarch's *Pompey.* In 2 Thess. 3.6, 11 we find *those who behaved in a disorderly way,* meaning, undoubtedly, disorderly from the point of view of attaining eternal life. This meaning, and the very application which we wish to give it, is not uncommonly found in the scriptures, expressed in other words: Luke 9.62: *well disposed* or *fit for the kingdom of God;* Mark 12.34: *not far from the kingdom of God;* 2 Tim. 2.21: *a vessel fit to grace his Lord's use, and prepared for every good work.* For, as we shall show later, some traces of the divine image remain in man,[58] and when they combine in an individual he becomes more suitable, and as it were, more properly disposed for the kingdom of God than another. Since we are not mere puppets, some cause at least should be sought in human nature itself why some men embrace and others reject this divine grace. One thing may be established at the outset: although all men are dead in sin and children of wrath, nevertheless some are worse than others. This may be observed every day, in the nature, disposition, and habits of those who are most estranged from God's grace. It may also be inferred from that parable in Matt. 13 where, before any seed had been sown, there were four, or at any rate three kinds of soil, some stony, some covered with thorns, and some, compared at least with the rest, quite good. See also Matt, 10.11, etc.: *inquire who is worthy in it,* etc. *and if the house is worthy let your peace come upon it.* How could anyone be worthy before hearing the gospel preached, unless he were ordained, in the sense of being well inclined or disposed to eternal life? Christ teaches that others will be made to feel the truth of this by the punishment which they suffer after death: Matt. 11.22: *it will be more tolerable for Tyre and Sidon,* etc.; Luke 12.47, 48: *he shall be beaten with many stripes, he with few.* Lastly, everyone is provided with a sufficient degree of innate reason for him to be able to resist evil desires by his own effort; so no one can add

58. Cp. *PL* 11.512–13: "Retaining still divine similitude / In part."

strength to his excuse by complaining that his own nature is peculiarly depraved. But, you will object, God does not aim to pick out the less wicked from among the wicked, but prefers more often the inferior, Deut. 9.5: *it is not on account of your righteousness or your upright mind that you are going to march in and possess their land,* and Luke 10.13: *if the miracles that were performed in you had been performed in Tyre and Sidon, they would have repented long ago, sitting in sackcloth and ashes.* My answer is that we cannot be sure from these passages what it is God looks for in those he chooses. [. . .].[59] Finally, you will quote at me: *it does not depend on him that wills or on him that runs but on God who is merciful,* Rom. 9.16. But I reply, I am not talking about anyone willing or running, but about someone being less unwilling, less backward, less opposed, and I grant that God is still merciful, and is, at the same time, supremely wise and just. On the other hand, those that say *it does not depend on him that wills or on him that runs,* do presuppose a man willing and running, only they deny him any praise or merit. However, when God determined to restore mankind, he also decided unquestionably (and what could be more just?) to restore some part at least of man's lost freedom of will. So he gave a greater power of willing or running (that is, of believing) to those whom he saw willing or running already by virtue of the fact that their wills had been freed either before or at the actual time of their call. These, probably, represent here the "ordained." Thus we find: 1 Sam. 16.7: *Jehovah looks on the heart,* that is, either on the natural disposition as it is in itself, or as it is after receiving grace from God, who calls to it. The famous quotation, *to him that has shall be given,* illustrates the same point. [. . .].[60]

But the following objection may, perhaps be made: if you decide that God has predestined men only on condition that they believe and persist in their belief, then predestination will not be entirely a matter of grace but will depend upon human will and faith, so that the esteem in which divine grace is held will not, in fact, be consistent with its real importance. I insist, on the contrary, that it will be absolutely consistent, not less so in any way, but indeed much more so, and far more clearly so than if we were to accept the theory of those who raise this objection. For God's grace is acknowledged supreme, firstly, because when we were going to fall through our own fault, he had any pity for us at all; secondly, because he loved the world so much that he gave his only begotten Son for it; lastly, because he granted that we should once again be able to use our wills, that is, to act freely, when we had recovered liberty of the will through renewing of the Spirit. In this way he opened Lydia's heart, Acts 16.14. The condition upon which God's decision depends, then, entails the action of a will which he himself has freed and a belief which he himself demands from men. If this condition is left in the power of men who are free to act, it is absolutely in keeping with justice and does not detract at all from the importance of divine grace.

59. The deleted sentences reply to two minor objections to Milton's account of human responsibility.

60. The deleted sentences cite more scriptural examples of those more or less naturally suitable for eternal life.

For the power to will and believe is either the gift of God or, insofar as it is inherent in man at all, has no relation to good work or merit but only to the natural faculties. God does not then, by my argument, depend upon the will of man, but accomplishes his own will, and in doing so has willed that in the love and worship of God, and thus in their own salvation, men should always use their free will. If we do not, whatever worship or love we men offer to God is worthless and of no account. The will which is threatened or overshadowed by any external decree cannot be free, and once force is imposed, all esteem for services rendered grows faint and vanishes altogether.[61]

Many people decry this theory and violently attack it. They say that, since repentance and faith have been foreseen already, predestination is made subsequent to man's works. Thus, they say, this predestination depends upon human will. They say this deprives God of some of the glory of our salvation. They say that man is thus swollen with pride, that Christian consolation in life and death is shaken, and that gratuitous justification is denied. None of these objections can be allowed. On the contrary, this theory makes the method and consequently the glory not only of divine grace, but also of divine wisdom and justice considerably more apparent, and to show this was God's principal aim in predestination.

It is quite clear, then, that God has predestined from eternity all who would believe and persist in their belief. It follows, therefore, that there is no reprobation except for those who do not believe or do not persist, and that this is rather a matter of consequence than of an express decree by God. Thus there is no reprobation from eternity of particular men. For God has predestined to salvation all who use their free will, on one condition, which applies to all. None are predestined to destruction except through their own fault and, in a sense, *per accidens.* Thus, for example, even the gospel is said to be a stumbling-block and a bane to many. [. . .].

If God decreed unconditionally that some people must be condemned, and there is no scriptural authority for such a belief, it follows from this theory of unconditionally decreed reprobation that God also decided upon the means without which he could not fulfill his decree. But the means are sin, and that alone. It is no use evading the issue in the conventional way by saying that God did not decree sin but decreed that he would permit sin, for there is this objection: if he decreed that he would permit, then he does not merely permit, because he who permits a thing does not decree anything, but leaves it free.

[. . .].[62]

If, then, God rejects none except the disobedient and the unbeliever, he undoubtedly bestows grace on all, and if not equally upon each, at least sufficient

61. Cp. *PL* 3.103–6: "Not free, what proof could they have giv'n sincere/Of true allegiance, constant faith or love,/Where only what they needs must do, appeared,/Not what they would? What praise could they receive?"

62. The deleted paragraph insists that even if Scripture admitted the possibility of divine reprobation, repentance on the part of the reprobate would undo it.

to enable everyone to attain knowledge of the truth and salvation.[63] I say not equally upon each, because he has not distributed grace equally, even among the reprobate, as they are called: Matt. 11.21, 23: *woe to you* etc. *For if the miracles which were performed in you had been performed in Tyre and Sidon,* similarly Luke 10.13. For like anyone else, where his own possessions are concerned, God claims for himself the right of making decrees about them as he thinks fit, without being obliged to give a reason for his decree, though he could give a very good one if he wished: Rom. 9.20, 21: *indeed, who are you, man, to answer God back? Shall the statue say to the sculptor, Why have you made me like this? Has not the potter power over his clay?* So God does not consider everyone worthy of equal grace, and the cause of this is his supreme will.[64] But he considers all worthy of sufficient grace, and the cause is his justice. [. . .]. Clearly he wishes only that sinners should turn from their wickedness, Ezek. 33.11, as above, if he wishes that everyone should be saved, 1 Tim. 2.4, and that none should perish, 2 Pet. 3.9, he must also wish that no one should lack sufficient grace for salvation. Otherwise it is not clear how he can demonstrate his truthfulness to mankind. It is not enough that the grace in question should be sufficient only to deprive us of any excuse: we should perish without excuse even if we had no grace at all. But once grace has been revealed and offered, surely those who perish will always have some excuse, and will perish unjustly, unless it is quite clear that that grace is really adequate for salvation. So what Moses said, Deut. 29.4, in his address to the Israelites, *Jehovah has not given you a mind to understand, eyes to see and ears to hear until today,* must be explained by reference to Moses' kindness and tenderness. These made him avoid the accusations of severity or harshness which he would have incurred had he openly, before so large an assembly of the people, reproved the hardness of their hearts at that particular time, when they were about to enter into covenant with God. Their impenitence might be ascribed to two causes: either God, who was free to turn their minds to penitence whenever he wished, had not yet done so, or they had not yet obeyed him. Accordingly Moses mentioned only the first, God's free will, and left the second, their obstinacy, to be understood. For indeed no one can fail to understand that, in the first place, if God had not turned their minds to penitence until that day, their own obstinacy was the chief cause, and, secondly, that God who had performed so many miracles for their sake, had in fact given them mind, eyes and ears in ample measure, though they had refused to make use of his gifts.

Of one thing, then, we may be absolutely positive: God, to show the glory of his long-suffering and justice, excludes no man from the way of penitence and eternal salvation, unless that man has continued to reject and despise the offer

63. Cp. *PL* 3.185–90: "The rest shall hear me call, and oft be warned/Their sinful state, and to appease betimes/Th' incensèd Deity, while offered grace/Invites; for I will clear their senses dark,/What may suffice, and soften stony hearts/To pray, repent, and bring obedience due."

64. Cp. *PL* 3.183–84: "Some I have chosen of peculiar grace/Elect above the rest; so is my will."

of grace, and of grace sufficient for salvation, until it is too late.[65] For God has nowhere declared, unambiguously and directly, that his will is the cause of reprobation. On the contrary he has frequently explained the considerations which influence his will in the matter of reprobation: namely, the heinous sins of the reprobate, either already committed or foreseen by God; the absence of penitence; the contempt for grace; and the refusal to listen to God's repeated call. Unlike the election of grace, then, reprobation must not be attributed to the divine will alone: Deut. 9.5: *it is not on account of your righteousness or your upright mind that you are going to march in; but Jehovah is expelling those nations on account of their wickedness.* It is unnecessary to give any cause or reason for the exercise of mercy, other than God's own merciful will. On the other hand, the cause of reprobation, which is followed by punishment, must, if it is to be just, be man's sin alone, not God's will. I say sin, meaning sin either committed or foreseen, and when the sinner has either spurned grace right to the end, or has looked for it too late, and then only because he fears punishment, when the time-limit for grace has already passed. God does not reprobate for one reason, and condemn and assign to death for another, though this distinction is commonly made. Rather, those whom he has condemned for their sin, he has also reprobated for their sin, as in time, so from eternity. This reprobation lies not so much in God's will as in their own obstinate minds, and is not so much God's decree as theirs, resulting from their refusal to repent while they have an opportunity: Acts 13.46: *since you reject it and consider yourselves unworthy of eternal life;* Matt. 21.43: *the stone they rejected,* etc. *therefore the kingdom of God shall be taken away from you.* Similarly 1 Peter 2.7, 8. Matt. 23.37: *how often have I wished,* etc. *and you would not?* It would be no less unjust to decree reprobation for any cause other than sin than it would be to condemn for any cause other than sin. Condemnation does not occur except because of unbelief or sin, John 3.18, 19: *he who does not believe is already condemned because he has not believed,* etc. *this is the condemnation: light came into the world, but men loved darkness rather than light,* and 7.48 [. . .] 2 Thess. 2.12 [. . .]. Similarly all the texts which are produced to prove a decree of reprobation will be seen to point to the fact that no one is excluded by a decree of God from the way of penitence and eternal salvation unless he has rejected and despised the offer of grace until it is too late. [. . .][66]

[. . .] That is, it was appointed that they should be disobedient. Why? Because they had rejected the stone and stumbled over it: they rejected it themselves, before they were rejected. Attention to these points will quickly reveal the fact that, in discussion of this doctrine, difficulty mostly arises when no distinction

65. Cp. *PL* 3.198–202: "This my long sufferance and my day of grace/They who neglect and scorn, shall never taste;/But hard be hardened, blind be blinded more,/That they may stumble on, and deeper fall;/And none but such from mercy I exclude."

66. The deleted passage continues the discussion of election owing to God's good will and reprobation owing to the sinner's perverse will, particularly with respect to "the undeserved calling of the Gentiles after the Jews' merited rejection" (Yale 6:196). We resume the excerpt in the midst of the chapter's final paragraph.

is made between a decree of reprobation and that punishment which involves the hardening of a sinner's heart. Prov. 19.3 has an apt comment: *man's foolishness leads him astray, and his spirit is roused in indignation against Jehovah.* For those who believe in a decree of reprobation do, in fact, accuse God, however strongly they may deny it. Even a heathen like Homer emphatically reproves such people in *Odyssey* 1.7:[67]

They perished by their own impieties.

—and again, through the mouth of Jupiter, 1.32:

O how falsely men
Accuse us gods as authors of their ill,
Where by the bane their own bad lives instill
They suffer all the miseries of their states—
Past our inflictions and beyond their fates.

CHAPTER 5

PREFACE

I am now going to talk about the Son of God and the Holy Spirit, and I do not think I should broach such a difficult subject without some fresh preliminary remarks. The Roman Church demands implicit obedience on all points of faith. If I professed myself a member of it, I should be so indoctrinated, or at any rate so besotted by habit, that I should yield to its authority and to its mere decree even if it were to assert that the doctrine of the Trinity, as accepted at present, could not be proved from any passage of scripture. As it happens, however, I am one of those who recognize God's word alone as the rule of faith; so I shall state quite openly what seems to me much more clearly deducible from the text of scripture than the currently accepted doctrine. I do not see how anyone who calls himself a Protestant or a member of the Reformed Church, and who acknowledges the same rule of faith as myself, could be offended with me for this, especially as I am not trying to browbeat anyone, but am merely pointing out what I consider the more credible doctrine. This one thing I beg of my reader: that he will weigh each statement and evaluate it with a mind innocent of prejudice and eager only for the truth. For I take it upon myself to refute, whenever necessary, not scriptural authority, which is inviolable, but human interpretations. That is my right, and indeed my duty as a human being. Of course, if my opponents could show that the doctrine they defend was revealed to them by a voice from heaven, he would be an impious wretch who dared to raise so much

67. Cp. *DDD* (p. 892): "Man's own free will corrupted is the adequate and sufficient cause of his disobedience besides fate; as Homer also wanted not to express both in his *Iliad* and *Odyssey.*"

as a murmur against it, let alone a sustained protest.[68] But in fact they can lay claim to nothing more than human powers and that spiritual illumination which is common to all men.[69] What is more just, then, than that they should allow someone else to play his part in the business of research and discussion: someone else who is hunting the same truth, following the same track, and using the same methods as they, and who is equally anxious to benefit his fellow men? Now, relying on God's help, let us come to grips with the subject itself.

OF THE SON OF GOD

So far the efficiency of God has been treated as INTERNAL, residing in his decrees.

His EXTERNAL efficiency takes the form of the execution of these decrees. By this he effects outside himself something he has decreed within himself.

EXTERNAL efficiency subdivides into GENERATION, CREATION, and THE GOVERNMENT OF THE UNIVERSE.[70]

By GENERATION God begot his only Son, in accordance with his decree. That is the chief reason why he is called Father.

Generation must be an example of external efficiency, since the Son is a different person from the Father. Theologians themselves admit as much when they say that there is a certain emanation of the Son from the Father. This point will appear more clearly in the discussion of the Holy Spirit, for although they maintain that the Spirit is of the same essence as the Father, they admit that it emanates and issues and proceeds and is breathed from the Father, and all these expressions denote external efficiency. They also hold that the Son is of the same essence as the Father, and generated from all eternity. So this question, which is quite difficult enough in itself, becomes very complicated indeed if you follow the orthodox line. In scripture there are two senses in which the Father is said to have begotten the Son: one literal, with reference to production; the other metaphorical, with reference to exaltation. Many commentators have cited those passages which allude to the exaltation of the Son, and to his function as mediator, as evidence of his generation from eternity. As a matter of fact

68. Milton alludes to 2 Pet. 1.16–18, where "cleverly devised myths" about the Son are set against the revelation received by Peter when Jesus was transfigured: "We were eyewitnesses of his majesty. For when he received honor and glory from God the Father and the voice was borne to him by the Majestic Glory, 'This is my beloved Son, with whom I am well pleased,' we heard this voice borne from heaven, for we were with him on the holy mountain."

69. That all men receive spiritual illumination sufficient to effect salvation is an Arminian tenet. See 1.4, pp. 1168–69: "God . . . undoubtedly bestows grace on all, and if not equally upon each, at least sufficient to enable everyone to attain knowledge of the truth and salvation"; cp. *PL* 3.185–90.

70. Orthodox doctrine deemed generation an internal efficiency essential to the deity. Milton instead makes divine generation external, contingent, and, like any other of God's acts, voluntary, not necessary.

they have some excuse, if there is any room for excuse at all, because not a scrap of real evidence for the eternal generation of the Son can be found in the whole of scripture. Whatever certain modern scholars may say to the contrary, it is certain that the Son existed in the beginning, under the title of the Word or Logos, that he was the first of created things,[71] and that through him all other things, both in heaven and earth, were afterwards made.[72] John 1.1–3: *in the beginning was the Word, and the Word was with God and the Word was God,* etc., and 17.5: *now therefore glorify me, Father, with your own self, with the glory which I had with you before the world was;* Col. 1.15, 18 [. . .]; Rev. 3.14 [. . .]; 1 Cor. 8.6 [. . .]; Eph. 3.9 [. . .]; Col. 1.16 [. . .], etc.; Heb. 1.2: *through whom also he made the world*—hence 1.10: *you have created.* For more on this subject see below, chapter 7 (On the Creation). All these passages prove that the Son existed before the creation of the world, but not that his generation was from eternity. The other texts which are cited indicate only metaphorical generation, that is resurrection from the dead or appointment to the functions of mediator, according to St. Paul's own interpretation of the second Psalm: Ps. 2.7: *I will declare the decree: Jehovah has said to me, You are my Son, I have begotten you today,* which Paul interprets thus, Acts 13.32, 33: *having raised up Jesus, as indeed it is written in the second Psalm, You are my Son, I have begotten you today.* Rom. 1.4: *powerfully defined as the Son of God, according to the Spirit of holiness, by the resurrection from the dead;* hence Col. 1.18; Rev. 1.4: *the firstborn from the dead.* Then, again, we have Heb. 1.5, where it is written of the Son's exaltation above the angels: *for to which of the angels did he ever say, You are my Son, I have begotten you today? And again, I will be to him a Father, and he shall be to me a Son.* And 5.5, 6, with reference to the priesthood of Christ: so *also Christ did not confer upon himself the glory of becoming high priest, but he who said to him, You are my Son, I have begotten you today.* As also in another Psalm he says, *You are a priest for ever,* etc. From the second Psalm it will also be seen that God begot the Son in the sense of making him a king, Ps. 2.6, 7: *anointing my king, I have set him upon my holy hill of Sion.* Then, in the next verse, having anointed his king, from which process the name "Christ" is derived, he says: *I have begotten you today.*[73] Similarly Heb. 1.4, 5: *made as superior to the angels as the name he has obtained as his lot is more excellent than theirs.* What name, if not "Son"? The next verse drives the point home: *for to which of the angels did he ever say, You are my Son, I have begotten you today?* The Son declares the same of himself, John 10.35, 36: *do you say that I, whom the Father has sanctified and sent into the world, blaspheme, because I have said, I am the Son of God?* By the same figure of speech, though in a much less exalted sense, the saints also are said to have been begotten by God.

71. Cp. *PL* 3.383: "Thee next they sang of all creation first." In orthodox doctrine, the Son is not created but eternally and continuously generated by the Father.

72. Cp. *PL* 5.835–37: "begotten Son, by whom/As by his Word the mighty Father made/All things."

73. Cp. *PL* 5.602–6: "Hear my decree, which unrevoked shall stand./This day I have begot whom I declare/My only Son, and on this holy hill/Him have anointed, whom ye now behold/At my right hand"; 6.708–9: "to be heir and to be King/By sacred unction, thy deservèd right"; 5.776–77: "and us eclipsed under the name/Of King anointed."

When all the above passages, especially the second Psalm, have been compared and digested carefully, it will be apparent that, however the Son was begotten, it did not arise from natural necessity, as is usually maintained, but was just as much a result of the Father's decree and will as the Son's priesthood, kingship, and resurrection from the dead.[74] The fact that he is called "begotten," whatever that means, and God's *own Son,* Rom. 8.32, does not stand in the way of this at all. He is called God's own Son simply because he had no other Father but God, and this is why he himself said that God was his Father, John 5.18. For to Adam, formed out of the dust, God was creator rather than Father; but he was in a real sense Father of the Son, whom he made of his own substance. It does not follow, however, that the Son is of the same essence as the Father. Indeed, if he were, it would be quite incorrect to call him Son. For a real son is not of the same age as his father, still less of the same numerical essence: otherwise father and son would be one person. This particular Father begot his Son not from any natural necessity but of his own free will: a method more excellent and more in keeping with paternal dignity, especially as this Father is God.[75] For it has already been demonstrated from the text of scripture that God always acts with absolute freedom, working out his own purpose and volition. Therefore he must have begotten his Son with absolute freedom.

God could certainly have refrained from the act of generation and yet remained true to his own essence, for he stands in no need of propagation.[76] So generation has nothing to do with the essence of deity. And if a thing has nothing to do with his essence or nature, he does not do it from natural necessity like a natural agent.[77] Moreover, if natural necessity was the deciding factor, then God violated his own essence by begetting, through the force of nature, an equal. He could no more do this than deny himself. Therefore he could not have begotten the Son except of his own free will and as a result of his own decree.

So God begot the Son as a result of his own decree. Therefore it took place within the bounds of time, for the decree itself must have preceded its execution (the insertion of the word *today* makes this quite clear). As for those who maintain that the Son's generation was from eternity, I cannot discover on what passage in the scriptures they ground their belief. Micah 5.2 refers to his works, not his generation, and states only that these were from the beginning of the world—but more of this later. The Son is also called *only begotten,* John 1.14: *and we saw his glory, a glory indeed as of the only begotten having proceeded from the Father,*

74. The Father's exaltation of the Son in Book 5 of *PL* (600–615) echoes Psalm 2, which, according to the 1673 *Poems,* Milton translated on August 8, 1653. Orthodox theologians inferred the necessity of the Son's begetting from the premise of a triune Godhead.

75. Cp. *PL* 10.760–65: "what if thy son/Prove disobedient, and reproved, retort,/'Wherefore didst thou beget me? I sought it not':/Wouldst thou admit for his contempt of thee/That proud excuse? Yet him not thy election,/But natural necessity begot."

76. Cp. *PL* 8.419–20: "No need that thou/Shouldst propagate, already infinite."

77. Cp. *Art of Logic* (Yale 8:227): "Causes which act through nature do so out of necessity."

and 1.18 [. . .]; 3.16: *that he gave his only begotten Son,* similarly 3.18. 1 John 4.9: *he sent his only begotten Son.* Notice that it is not said that he is of the same essence as the Father but, on the contrary, that he is visible and given by, sent from, and proceeding from the Father. He is called *only begotten* to distinguish him from the numerous other people who are likewise said to be begotten by God, John 1.13: *begotten by God;* 1 John 3.9: *whoever is born of God,* etc.; James 1.18 [. . .]; 1 John 5.1 [. . .]; 1 Pet. 1.3 [. . .], etc. But since nowhere in the scriptures is the Son said to be begotten except, as above, in a metaphorical sense, it is probable that he is called *only begotten* chiefly because he is the only mediator between God and man.

Then, again, the Son is called *the first born,* Rom. 8.29: *that he might be the first born among many brothers;* Col. 1.15: *the first born of all created things;* 1.18: *the first born from the dead;* Heb. 1.6: *when he brings in the first born.* All these passages preclude the possibility of his being co-essential with the Father, and of his generation from eternity. Furthermore, the same thing is said of Israel, Ex. 4.22: *thus says Jehovah, Israel is my Son, my first born,* and of Ephraim, Jer. 31.9: *he is my first born,* and of all the blessed, Heb. 12.23: *to the assembly of the first born.*

Up to now all mention of generation has been entirely metaphorical. But if one in fact begets another being, who did not previously exist, one brings him into existence. And if God begets as a result of physical necessity, he can beget only a God equal to himself (though really a God cannot be begotten at all). It would follow from the first hypothesis that there are two infinite Gods, and from the second that a first cause can become an effect, which no sane man will allow. So it is necessary to inquire how and in what sense God the Father begot the Son. Once again, we can quickly find the answer in scripture. When the Son is said to be *the first born of every creature* and, Rev. 3.14, *the beginning of God's creation,* it is as plain as it could possibly be that God voluntarily created or generated or produced the Son before all things: the Son, who was endowed with divine nature and whom, similarly, when the time was ripe, God miraculously brought forth in his human nature from the Virgin Mary. The generation of the divine nature is by no one more sublimely or more fully explained than by the apostle to the Hebrews, 1.2, 3: *whom he has appointed heir of all things, through whom also he made the world. Who, since he is the brightness of his glory and the image of his substance,* etc. What can this imply but that God imparted to the Son as much as he wished of the divine nature, and indeed of the divine substance also? But do not take *substance* to mean total essence. If it did, it would mean that the Father gave his essence to his Son and at the same time retained it, numerically unaltered, himself. That is not a means of generation but a contradiction of terms. What I have quoted is all that is revealed from heaven about the generation of the Son of God. Anyone who wants to be wiser than this is really not wise at all. Lured on by empty philosophy or sophistry, he becomes hopelessly entangled and loses himself in the dark.

In spite of the fact that we all know there is only one God, Christ in scripture is called not merely *the only begotten Son of God* but also, frequently, *God.*

Many people, pretty intelligent people in their own estimation, felt sure that this was inconsistent. So they hit upon the bizarre and senseless idea that the Son, although personally and numerically distinct, was nevertheless essentially one with the Father, and so there was still only one God.

The numerical significance of "one" and of "two" must be unalterable and the same for God as for man. It would have been a waste of time for God to thunder forth so repeatedly that first commandment which said that he was the one and only God, if it could nevertheless be maintained that another God existed as well, who ought himself to be thought of as the only God. Two distinct things cannot be of the same essence. God is one being, not two. One being has one essence, and also one subsistence—by which is meant simply a substantial essence. If you were to ascribe two subsistences or two persons to one essence, it would be a contradiction in terms. You would be saying that the essence was at once one and not one. If one divine essence is common to two components, then that essence or divinity will be in the position of a whole in relation to its parts, or of a genus in relation to its several species, or lastly of a common subject, in relation to its non-essential qualities.[78] If you should grant none of these, there would be no escaping the absurdities which follow, as that one essence can be one third of two or more components of an essence.

If my opponents had paid attention to God's own words when he was addressing kings and magnates, Ps. 82.6: *I say, you are Gods, and all of you sons of the Most High,* and to the words of Christ, John 10.35: *if he called those to whom the word of God came, Gods; and the scripture cannot be blotted out,* and to the words of Paul, 1 Cor. 8.5, 6: *although there are those that are called Gods, both in heaven and earth,* (*for there are many Gods and many Lords*), *nevertheless for us there is one God, the Father, from whom all things,* etc., and lastly to the words of Peter 2. 1.4: *that through these things you might be made partakers or sharers of the divine nature* (which implies much more than the title *gods* in the sense in which kings are said to be gods, and yet no one would conclude from this text that the saints were of one essence with God)—if, I say, my opponents had paid attention to these words, they would not have found it necessary to fly in the face of reason or, indeed, of so much glaring scriptural evidence.

But let us disregard reason when discussing sacred matters and follow exclusively what the Bible teaches. Accordingly let no one expect me to preface what I have to say with a long metaphysical introduction, or bring into my argument all that play-acting of the persons of the godhead. For a start, it is absolutely clear from innumerable passages of scripture that there is in reality one true and independent supreme God. Since he is called "one"; since human reason and the conventions of language and God's people, the Jews, have always interpreted the term "only one person" to mean one in number, let us examine the sacred books to discover who this one, true, supreme God is. Let us look first at the gospel. This should provide the clearest evidence, for here we find the plain

78. These categories of distributive relation are discussed in *Art of Logic* (Yale 8:299–308).

and exhaustive doctrine of the one God which Christ expounded to his apostles and they to their followers. It is very unlikely that the gospel should be ambiguous or obscure on this point. For it was given not for the purpose of spreading new or incredible ideas about God's nature, ideas that his people had never heard of before, but to announce the salvation of the Gentiles through Messiah, the Son of God, which God had promised to Abraham: *no one has ever seen God: the only begotten Son who is in the bosom of the Father, he has revealed him to us,* John 1.18. So first of all let us consult the Son on the subject of God.

According to the Son's clearest possible testimony, the Father is that one true God from whom are all things. Mark 12.28, 29, 32, Christ, asked by the lawyer which was the first commandment of all, replied by quoting Deut. 6.4: *the first commandment of all is: hear, Israel, the Lord our God is one Lord* or, as it is in the Hebrew, *Jehovah our God is one Jehovah.* The lawyer agreed: *there is one God and there is no other except him.* Christ approved of him for agreeing, Mark 12.34. Now it is absolutely clear that this lawyer and all the Jews understood that there was one God in the sense that he was one person, as that phrase is commonly understood. That this God was none other than the Father is proved by John 8.41–54: *we have one Father, God. It is my Father who glorifies me, whom you say is your God,* and 4.21: *neither on this mountain nor in Jerusalem shall you worship the Father.* Christ therefore agrees with all God's people that the Father is that one and only God. Who can believe that the very first of the commandments was so obscure that it was utterly misunderstood by the Church for so many centuries? Who can believe that these two other persons could have gone without their divine honors and remained wholly unknown to God's people right down to the time of the gospel? Indeed God, teaching his people about their worship under the gospel, warns them that they will have for their God the one Jehovah that they have always had, and David, that is, Christ, for their king and their Lord. Jer. 30.9: *they shall serve Jehovah their God and David their king, whom I will raise up for them.*[79] In this passage Christ, as God wished him to be known and worshipped by his people under the gospel, is firmly distinguished, both by nature and title, from the one God Jehovah. Christ himself, then, the Son of God, teaches us nothing in the gospel about the one God other than what the law had taught us already. He asserts everywhere, quite clearly, that it is the Father. John 17.3: *this is eternal life, that they may know you, the only true God, and Jesus Christ whom you have sent,* 20.17: *I ascend to my Father and your Father, and to my God and your God.* If the Father is Christ's God and our God, and if there is only one God, who can be God except the Father?

Paul, the apostle and interpreter of Christ, makes this same point very clearly and distinctly, almost as if it were the sum of his teaching. So much so, that no instructor in the church could have taught a novice under his care more skillfully or more plainly about the one God—one, that is, in the numerical

79. Like other interpreters, Milton understands Jeremiah's promise of a Davidic king as a prophecy of Christ.

sense in which human reason always understands it. 1 Cor. 8.4–6: *we know that an idol is nothing in the world, and that there is no other God but one: for although there are those that are called Gods both in heaven and earth* (*for there are many Gods and many Lords*), *nevertheless for us there is one God, the Father, from whom all things are and in whom we are, and one Lord Jesus Christ, through whom all things are and through whom we are.* Here, *there is no other* or *second* God, *but one,* excludes not only a second essence but any second person whatsoever. For it is expressly stated, 8.6: *the Father is that one God;* therefore there is no *other* person, but one only. There is no other person, that is, in the sense in which Church divines usually argue that there is when they use John 14.16 as proof of the existence of the Holy Spirit as a person. Again, the single *God, the Father, from whom all things are* is numerically opposed to *those that are called Gods both in heaven and earth,* and *one* is numerically opposed to *many.* Though the Son be another God, here he is called only *Lord.* He *from whom all things are* is clearly distinguished from him *through whom all things are,* and since a difference in method of causation proves a difference in essence, the two are distinguished from the point of view of essence as well. Besides, since a numerical difference is the result of a difference in essence, if two things are two numerically, they must also be two essentially.[80] [. . .].

All this is so obvious in itself that it really needs no explanation. It is quite clear that the Father alone is a self-existent God: clear, too, that a being who is not self-existent cannot be a God. But it is amazing what nauseating subtlety, not to say trickery, some people have employed in their attempts to evade the plain meaning of these scriptural texts. They have left no stone unturned; they have followed every red herring they could find; they have tried everything. Indeed they have made it apparent that, instead of preaching the plain, straightforward truth of the gospel to poor and simple men, they are engaged in maintaining an extremely absurd paradox with the maximum of obstinacy and argumentativeness. To save this paradox from utter collapse they have availed themselves of the specious assistance of certain strange terms and sophistries borrowed from the stupidity of the schools.

Their excuse, however, is that though these opinions may seem inconsistent with reason they are, on account of some other scriptural passages, to be countenanced; otherwise there will appear to be inconsistencies in scripture. So let us, again, disregard reason and concentrate on the text of scripture.

Only two passages are relevant. The first is John 10.30: *I and the Father are one,* that is, as it is commonly interpreted, one in essence. But for God's sake let us not come to any rash conclusions about God! There is more than one way in which two things can be called one. Scripture says and the Son says *I and the*

80. Cp. *Art of Logic* (Yale 8:233): "Number, as Scaliger correctly says, is a property consequent upon essence, and never do things differ in number without also differing in essence. *Here let the Theologians take notice.*" Although Kelley notes that Milton took this passage from an antecedent work, he neglects to mention that the italicized sentence is Milton's own insertion. The rest of this paragraph and the next cite Scripture to elaborate the numerical and therefore essential distinction between God and the Son.

Father are one. I agree. Someone or other guesses that this means one in essence. I reject it as man's invention. For whoever it was in the Church who first took it upon himself to guess about it, the Son has not left the question of how he is one with the Father to our conjecture. On the contrary, he explains the doctrine very clearly himself, insofar as it concerns us to know it. The Father and the Son are certainly not one in essence, for the Son had himself asserted the contrary in the preceding verse, *my Father, who gave me them, is greater than all,* (indeed, he also says, 14.28: *he is greater than I*), and in the following verses he expressly denies that by saying *I and the Father are one* he was setting himself up as God. He claims that what he said was only what follows in the next quotation, which amounts to much less, 10.36: *do you say that I whom the Father has sanctified and sent into the world, blaspheme because I have said, I am the Son of God?* It must be that this is said of two persons, distinct in essence and, moreover, not equal to each other. If the Son is here teaching about the one divine essence of two persons of the Trinity, why does he not rather talk about the one essence of the three persons? Why does he divide the indivisible Trinity? That which is not a whole is not one. So it follows from the convictions of those very people who affirm the truth of the Trinity that the Son and the Father, without the Spirit, are not one in essence. How, then, are they one? The Son alone can tell us this, and he does. Firstly, they are one in that they speak and act as one. He explains himself to this effect in the same chapter, after the Jews have misunderstood his statement: 10.38: *believe in my works so that you may know and believe that the Father is in me and I in him.* Similarly 14.10: *do you not believe that I am in the Father and the Father in me? I myself am not the source of the words which I speak to you; but the Father who dwells in me, he performs the works.* Here it is evident that Christ distinguishes the Father from the whole of his own being. However, he does say that the Father dwells in him, though this does not mean that their essence is one, only that their communion is extremely close. Secondly, he declares that he and the Father are one in the same way as we are one with him: that is, not in essence but in love, in communion, in agreement, in charity, in spirit, and finally in glory.[81] John 15.20, 21: *on that day you will know that I am in my Father, and you in me, and I in you. He who has my commandments and keeps them, he it is that loves me; and he that loves me shall be loved by my Father,* and 17.21 [...] and 17.23 [...] and 17.22 [...]. Since the Son plainly teaches that there are so many ways in which the Father and he are one, shall I pay no attention to all these ways of being one? Shall I put my mind to it and think up some other way of being one, namely that of being one in essence? Shall I give preference to this idea when some other mere man has thought it up beforehand? Who will stand surety for me if I do? The Church? The orthodox Church herself teaches me otherwise, and rightly. She tells me that I should listen to Christ before her.

The second passage, and that which is generally thought the clearest of all, upon which the orthodox view of the essential unity of the three persons of the

81. *PL* 11.43–44: "All my redeemed may dwell in joy and bliss,/Made one with me as I with thee am one."

Trinity is based, is 1 John 5.7: *there are three witnesses in heaven, the Father, the Word and the Holy Spirit, and these three are one.* This verse, however, is not found in the Syriac or the other two Oriental versions, the Arabic and the Ethiopic, nor in the majority of the ancient Greek codices. Moreover, in those manuscripts where it does appear a remarkable variety of readings occurs.[82] Anyway, quite apart from this, the verse does not prove that those who are said to be one in heaven are necessarily one in essence, any more than it proves that about those who, in the next verse, are said to be one on earth. The fact that John is speaking here (if John really wrote the verse) only about unity of consent and testimony, as in the last-quoted passage, was not only realized by Erasmus but even admitted by Beza, though reluctantly.[83] (You can go and look at their works to prove it.) Besides, who are these three witnesses? You will admit that there are not three Gods; therefore the *one* in the passage is not a God but the one testimony of the three witnesses; one witnessing. But he who is not essentially one with God the Father cannot be the Father's equal. This text will be discussed more fully, however, in the next chapter.

But it is maintained that, although scripture does not say in so many words that the Father and the Son are essentially one, the fact can be reasonably deduced from these texts and from others. To begin with, granting this to be the case (and I do not, in fact, grant it at all) when the point at issue is so sublime and so far above the reach of our understanding, and involves the very elements and, as it were, the first postulates of our faith, we can really base our belief only on God's word, and God's word at its clearest and most distinct, not on mere reason at all. Anyway, reason is loud in its denunciation of the doctrine in question. I ask you, what can reason do here? Can reason maintain an unreasonable opinion? The product of reason must be reason, not absurd notions which are utterly alien to all human ways of thinking. The conclusion must be, then, that this opinion is consonant neither with reason nor scripture. Of the two alternatives only one can remain: namely, that if God is one God, and the Father, and yet the Son is also called God, then he must have received the divine name and nature from God the Father, in accordance with the Father's decree and will, as I said before. This is in no way opposed to reason, and is supported by innumerable texts from scripture.

But not all those who insist that the Son is one with God the Father rely for proof on the two texts I have quoted above. So although deprived of that evi-

82. Milton's account of 1 John 5.7 as a late variant of suspect textual authority is accurate. The so-called Johannine comma is now generally deemed spurious and omitted in modern critical editions. Isaac Newton in 1690 would likewise critique it in a manuscript he shared with John Locke but withheld from publication, entitled *A Historical Account of Two Notable Corruptions of Scripture.* It was first published in 1841.

83. Desiderius *Erasmus* (1466–1536), Dutch scholar, was the greatest of the Renaissance humanists. His translation of the Greek New Testament into Latin exposed errors in the Vulgate. He influenced Luther and other reformers, though he remained in the Catholic Church and disagreed with the course of the Reformation. Theodore *Beza* (1519–1605), Swiss reformed theologian, followed Calvin as leader in Geneva. In 1565 he published the first critical edition of the Greek New Testament.

dence, they are still confident that they can prove their point quite clearly if they can show, by frequent scriptural quotation, that the name, attributes and works of God, and the divine office itself, are habitually attributed to the Son. To proceed, therefore, in the same line of argument: I do not ask them to believe that the Father alone, and no one else, is God, unless I demonstrate and prove beyond question the following points. First, that all the above particulars are everywhere expressly attributed, both by the Son himself and by his apostles, only to one God, the Father. Second, that if these particulars are anywhere attributed to the Son, it is in such a way that they are easily understood to be attributable, in their primary and proper sense, to the Father alone, and that the Son admits that he possesses whatever measure of Deity is attributed to him, by virtue of the peculiar gift and kindness of the Father, as the apostles also testify. Third, that the Son himself and his apostles acknowledge in everything they say and write that the Father is greater than the Son in all things.

[. . .].[84]

However, some will still argue vehemently that the Son is at times called God and even Jehovah, and that all the divine attributes are ascribed to him as well, in many passages in both the Old and the New Testaments.

This, then, is the second of the points that I undertook to prove at the beginning. I have already demonstrated satisfactorily, from the agreement of scriptural texts, that when both Father and Son are mentioned, the name, attributes, and works of God, and also the divine honor, are always ascribed to the one and only God the Father. I will now demonstrate that when these things are ascribed to the Son, it is done in such a way as to make it easily intelligible that they should all be attributed primarily and properly to the Father alone.

We should notice first of all that the name "God" is, by the will and permission of God the Father, not infrequently bestowed even upon angels and men (how much more, then, upon the only begotten Son, the image of the Father!).

Upon angels: Ps. 8.6: *less than gods,* and 97.7, 9, compared with Heb. 1.6. Upon judges: Ex. 21.6: *his Master shall make him stand in the presence of the gods,* that is, of the magistrates; and similarly 22.8, 9, 28; Ps. 82.1, 6: *I have said you are gods and all of you sons of the Highest.* Upon the whole house of David, or upon all the saints: Zech. 12.8: *the house of David shall be as gods as an angel before them.*

[. . .][85]

Even the principal texts which are quoted as proof of the Son's divinity show quite plainly, when they are closely and carefully studied, that he is God in the

84. The deleted passage develops the first of the three points just introduced, asserting that "those who have not numerically the same understanding and the same will cannot have the same essence. There is no way of evading this conclusion, since the Son himself has revealed this in discussing his own divine nature" (Yale 6:229).

85. In the deleted passage, Milton surveys Hebrew and Greek terms for God and characterizes the application of the plurals of such terms to singular subjects as a mark of "respect or reverence" and not as evidence of multiple persons in God. He then notes that in Scripture angels are often called "God," as are men who speak for or otherwise represent him.

way I have suggested. John 1.1: *in the beginning was the Word, and the Word was with,* that is, *in company with God, and the Word was God. In the beginning,* it says, not from eternity. *The Word* must be audible, but God is inaudible just as he is invisible, John 5.37; therefore the Word is not of the same essence as God. *In company with God, and was God*—was God, in fact, because he was in company with God, that is, in the Father's bosom, as it is later said in verse 18. Does it follow that the Son is essentially one with someone in whose company, or with whom he is? Surely no more than it follows that the disciple who was reclining against Jesus' breast, John 13.23, was essentially one with Christ. Reason rejects the idea, and scripture nowhere supports it; so let us leave the lies of men behind and follow the evangelist himself, who is his own interpreter. Rev. 19.13: *his name is called the Word of God:* that is, of the one God, he himself being a distinct person. Distinct from whom? From God, of course, who is one. How, then, is he himself God? The answer must be, through the will of the one God, which is how he is the Word and the only begotten Son as well. For this reason, apparently, John repeats the words in the second verse, *he was in the beginning with,* that is, in company with *God.* Thus he drives home what he wants us to see as his chief point: that Christ was not, in the beginning, God, but that he was with, or in company with God. John does this to show that Christ was God not in essence but only by nearness and love: a fact which he subsequently explains in innumerable passages of his gospel.

A second passage is the speech of Thomas in John 20.28: *my Lord and my God.* Anyone who tries to elicit from this abrupt exclamation a new confession of faith, a confession not recognized as such by the other disciples, must be really exceedingly credulous. In his surprise Thomas calls not only upon Christ, his own Lord, but upon the God of his ancestors as well, that is, God the Father. It is as if he had said, "Lord! What do I see: what do I hear: what do I touch?" Christ, whom Thomas is here supposed to call God, has said of himself just before, 20.17: *I ascend to my God and your God.* Now the God of a God cannot be essentially one with him whose God he is. If Thomas really called Christ his God, whose word will provide a safer model for our faith? Christ's, when Christ is giving quite clear information, or Thomas', when Thomas is a novice who was at first incredulous, and who now cries out suddenly in wonder and amazement? For when he had thrust in his fingers, he called the man whom he had touched God, as if unconscious of what he was saying. It is incredible that he should so quickly have perceived the hypostatic union of a person whose resurrection he had just doubted. Besides, Peter's faith is praised, though he had said only, *you are the Son of the living God. Blessed are you, Simon,* said Christ, Matt. 16.16, 17. Thomas' faith, although far more spectacular, as commonly interpreted, in that it asserts Christ's deity, is not praised but, in fact, belittled and almost reproved in the next verse: *Thomas, because you have seen me you have believed; blessed are those who have not seen and yet have believed.* The slowness of his belief may have deserved blame. But surely the clarity of his attestation of Christ's godhead would have been praised, for, if the usual interpretations of it are correct, it is the clearest attestation to be found anywhere. But it was not praised at all. So nothing stands in the way of the interpretation suggested above, namely, that in the disputed passage *my Lord* is to be taken as referring to Christ, and *my God* as referring to God the Father, who had just proved that Christ was his Son by raising him from the dead in such a miraculous way.

Similarly Heb. 1.8: *to the Son,* or, *of the Son: Your throne, O God, is for all ages:* but 1.9: *you have loved righteousness,* etc. *therefore God, your God, has anointed you with the oil of exultation above your fellows.* Almost every word here shows in what sense Christ is God. In fact these were the words spoken by Jehovah through the mouths of the bridesmaids, Ps. 45. They might have been cited by this writer for any other purpose rather than that of demonstrating the Son's equality with the Father. Why? Because in the Psalm they are applied to Solomon who, in accordance with scriptural usage, could also be called God because he was a king.

These three passages are just about the most convincing of those my opponents adduce. That text in Matt. 1.23: *they shall call* (for that is the reading in most of the Greek codices) *his name Immanuel, which means, if you interpret it, God with us,* does not prove that the person they are going to call Immanuel is necessarily God, but only that he is sent by God, as Zacharias sang, Luke 1.68, 69: *blessed is the Lord God of Israel, for he has visited and redeemed his people, and has raised up,* etc. Nor can anything be proved from the text in Acts 16.31, 34: *believe in the Lord Jesus Christ. He rejoiced with his whole house, because he had believed in God.* It does not follow from this that Christ is God. The apostles have never taught explicitly that Christ is the ultimate object of belief. These are the words of the historian, who is making a brief paraphrase of what the apostles doubtless expounded at greater length, that is, faith in God the Father through Christ. Nothing can be proved from the passage in Acts 20.28, either: *the Church of God, which he has bought with his own blood.* This means, with his own Son, as it is expressed elsewhere; for God, properly speaking, has no blood, and the word *blood* is very frequently used to mean offspring.

[. . .][86]

It is surprising, however, that those who maintain that the Father and Son are one in essence, should turn back from the gospel to the times of the law, and thus try to illuminate light with darkness. Granted the Son is called not only God but also Jehovah, as appears from a comparison of several passages in both testaments. But although they insist that, as Jehovah is the one and supreme

86. The deleted passage continues the scrutiny of scriptural verses construed by the orthodox to support the Trinity. Milton's analysis delves into linguistic detail, variant readings, and the possibility of textual corruption. He concludes that "where the very fundamentals of our faith are at stake, we should not place our confidence in something which has to be forced or wrenched, so to speak, from passages dealing with a quite unrelated topic, in which there are sometimes variant readings, and where the meaning is questionable. Nor should we believe in something which has to be lured out from among articles and particles by some sort of verbal bird-catcher, or which has to be dug out from a mass of ambiguities and obscurities like the answers of an oracle. Rather, we should drink our fill from the clearest fountains of truth. For this open simplicity, this true light, this promised clarity of doctrine is what makes the gospel superior to the law" (Yale 6:245–46).

God, therefore Father and Son are one in essence, in fact it will quickly appear how weak an argument the attribution of the name Jehovah to the Son really is. For the name Jehovah is granted even to the angels, and in no other sense than the one in which I have shown the name of God is granted to them, that is, as representatives of the divine presence and person and as spokesmen for Jehovah's own words. [. . .].[87]

It is certain then, from the declaration of the sacred writer himself, that the name Jehovah was attributed to an angel. The fact that those very persons to whom angels appeared believed this, is further proof. The name was attributed, moreover, not only to an angel, but to the universal church, Jer. 33.16, see below. But since it seems incredible to Placæus of Saumur[88] that an angel should bear the name of Jehovah, and thus be a sort of counterfeit Jehovah, a playacting Jehovah, as it were, I will show you where God himself declares that his name is in an angel. Ex. 23.20, 21: *behold, I send an angel before you, to keep you in this way* etc. *beware of him and obey his voice, in case you provoke him: for he will not bear your defection, because my name is in him.* The angel who spoke to the Israelites from that time on, and whose voice they were commanded to obey, was always called Jehovah although he was not really Jehovah. My opponents say he was Jehovah because he was Christ, 1 Cor. 10.9: *nor let us tempt Christ,* etc. I reply, it is irrelevant now whether or not he was Christ. The question is whether the children of Israel believed that the angel really was Jehovah or not. If they did, they must have believed either that there were two Jehovahs, or that Jehovah and the angel were essentially one. No one in his right mind would claim that they believed this, and if anyone did claim it, Ex. 33.2, 3, 5 would give him the lie: *I will send an angel: I will not go up, lest I consume you. And when the people heard this evil news, they mourned.* If the people believed that Jehovah and the angel were one in essence, equal in divinity and glory, why did they mourn? Why did they prefer that Jehovah should go up before them, even though angry, than that the angel should? If indeed the angel had been Christ, he would have been a mediator and a peacemaker. If they did not believe that the angel was Jehovah, they must have believed, as I do, that he bore the name of Jehovah. There is nothing absurd or play-like about this either. When he is eventually persuaded to go up with them in person, he grants only this, 33.14: *my appearance shall go before you.* What can this mean but the representation of his name and glory in some angel?[89] But whoever is referred to, whether Christ or some other angel, Jehovah's own words show that he was not one with nor equal to Jehovah. The Israelites were commanded to obey his voice not on account of his own name, but because the name of Jehovah was in him. If, however, my opponents assert that this angel

87. The deleted passage exhaustively details the usage of *Jehovah* in Scripture, especially as that most sacrosanct title was applied to angels.

88. **Placæus:** French Protestant divine (1606?–65). In 1625 he became pastor of the Reformed Church at Nantes and in 1632 was appointed professor of theology at *Saumur.*

89. Cp. *PL* 12.200–202: "Such wondrous power God to his saint will lend,/Though present in his angel, who shall go/Before them in a cloud, and pillar of fire."

was Christ, what do they prove except that Christ was an angel, according to their interpretation of Gen. 48.16: *that angel who redeemed me.* Isa. 43.9: *the angel of his appearance,* that is, the angel who bears his appearance or glory and plays his part. [. . .]

The style of the prophetical Book of Revelation must be considered from the same point of view: compare 1.1 with 1.8, 11: *he signified it, sending it through his angel;* then that angel (who is described in almost the same words as the angel in Dan. 10.5, etc.) says: *I am Alpha and Omega says the Lord, who is, who was and who will be,* and 13 [. . .], and 17 [. . .], and 2.17 and elsewhere, [. . .]; and 22.6 [. . .], and 8 [. . .] and 9 [. . .]. Then the same angel says, 22.12 [. . .] and 13 [. . .], again 14 [. . .] and 16 [. . .]. These passages led Beza to suppose that certain verses in the last chapter had been disordered and transposed by some Arian. As the book had been recognized by the Church as the work of the apostle at a rather late date, he thought it might have been preserved somewhat carelessly. So he considered it necessary to restore the verses to what seemed to him their right place. This would have been unnecessary had he noticed what anyone can observe throughout the whole of the Old Testament, that is, that angels often take upon them as their own the name, the person and the very words of God and Jehovah. Also an angel sometimes assumes the person and the very words of God, even without taking the name of Jehovah or God, but with the name of an angel only, or even of a man, as Junius[90] himself admits, Judges 2.1, etc. But theologians say that the name Jehovah signifies one of two things: either the nature of God or the fulfillment of his words or promises. If it signifies the nature and therefore the person of God, why, when he lays his person and presence upon someone, does he not also lay upon him the name which signifies them? If it means the fulfillment of his words or promises, why should not he to whom words which befit God alone are so frequently attributed, have also the attribution of the name Jehovah, by which the fulfillment of those words and promises is signified? Moreover, if this name pleased God so much that he wished it to be always sacrosanct and proper to himself alone, why did he utterly abandon it in the New Testament, where his promises are most markedly fulfilled? There he retained only the name Lord, which he had always shared with angels and men. Finally, if the idea of a name is so near to God's heart, why has he revealed himself to us in the gospel without any proper name at all?

My opponents insist, however, that there are places where Christ himself, in his own name and person, is called Jehovah: for example, Isa. 8.13, 14: *sanctify the Jehovah of armies himself, and let him be your fear,* etc. *and he will be a sanctuary for you: but he will be a stumbling block for both the houses of Israel and a rock for them to trip over,* etc.; compare 1 Pet. 2.7: *he is made the head corner stone and a stumbling block,* etc. I reply that it is apparent from a comparison of Isa. 8.13 with 8.11: *for Jehovah spoke thus to me,* that these are not the words of Christ exhorting the Israelites to sanc-

90. Franciscus *Junius* (1545–1602) was a French Huguenot theologian; with John Immanuel Tremellius (1510–80), he published a Latin translation of the Bible from Hebrew and Syriac (Frankfurt, 1579).

tify and fear him (for they did not yet know him), but the words of the Father who, as in other places, is threatening to be *as a stone,* etc. *to both the houses of Israel,* that is, to all the Israelites, especially those of that age. Even if these words do refer to Christ, it is not unusual in the prophetic books for God the Father to declare that he is going to do something which he afterwards does through his Son under the gospel. Thus Peter says *he is made the head corner stone and a stumbling block*—but who did the making, if not the Father? And 1 Pet. 3.15, where this very passage of Isaiah is quoted, clearly proves that the Father spoke these words with reference to himself: *but sanctify the Lord God.* No one would claim that this means Christ. My opponents also adduce Zech. 11.13: *Jehovah said to me, Throw them away for the potter to gather up. It is a fine price they price me at!* I reply that, granted this refers to Christ, we should remember that this is not his own name but the name of Jehovah who is in him (see Ex. 23.21); this point will be clarified below. Moreover there is in fact nothing to prevent us from taking these as words spoken by the Father in his own name. He regards the things which the Jews are going to do to his Son as if they were offences against himself.[91] In the same way the Son says that what is done to those who believe in him, is done to him: Matt. 25.35, 40: *I was hungry and you gave me* etc. *inasmuch as you have done it to one of the least of these my brothers, you have done it to me.* [. . .].[92]

Now, using the evidence of the gospel itself, which should be our principal foundation, and particularly that of the evangelist John, whose chief purpose was to declare explicitly the nature of the Son's deity, I shall proceed to demonstrate the other point which I promised to deal with in my division of the subject above. That is, that the Son himself reports that he received from the Father not only the name of God and Jehovah, but also whatever else he has. The apostles, later, bear witness to the same fact: that he received from the Father his individuality, his life itself, his attributes, his works, and, lastly, his divine honor: John 3.35: *the Father loves the Son and has given all things into his hand,* and 13.3: *Jesus, knowing that the Father had given all things into his hand, and that he had come from God;* Matt. 11.27: *all things are given over to me by my Father.* But here, perhaps, my opponents will break in again with the same objection as before; for they use the two natures of Christ, and their conjunction in the office of mediator, as a convenient little device for evading any arguments brought against them, with the result that they are more difficult to pin down than Vertumnus.[93] They apply what scripture says about the Son to either the Son of God or the Son of man separately, as it suits them—now to the mediator as God, now as man, and sometimes as both together. But the Son himself says distinctly *the Father loves the Son and has given all things into his hand,* John 3.35—has given them, that is, be-

91. Cp. *PL* 5.611–12, "him who disobeys/Me disobeys."

92. In the deleted passage, Milton discusses other instances where the Son stands in for the Father. He then moves to the third point in his argument.

93. Cp. *Tetrachordon* (Yale 2:675): "Let him try which way he can wind in his Vertumnian distinctions and evasions." *Vertumnus,* Roman god of orchards and fruit, presided over the changing seasons and was himself a shape-shifter.

cause he loves him, not because he begot him, and has given them to the Son, not to the mediator only. If Christ had meant what my opponents claim he meant, how much more satisfactory it would have been, and how much easier for us to understand, if he had said *the Father loves Christ* or *loves the mediator* or *loves the Son of man.* He does not, however. He says simply *loves the Son—the Son* or, in other words, "whatever meaning the name Son can cover." I ask again, as I did above, is Christ still, after being made a mediator, the same God as, in my opponents' opinion, he was before, or not? If he is the same, why does he ask and receive all things from the Father and not from himself? If all things are from the Father, why is it necessary for the mediatorial office that, as my opponents maintain, the Son should be the true and supreme God? For he receives everything from the Father: everything—not only what belongs to him as mediator, but also what belongs to him as Son. If he is not still the same God after being made mediator, then he was never the supreme God. This clarifies the text in John 16.15: *all things which the Father has are mine*—that is, by the gift of the Father. Also 17.9, 10: *which you have given me because they are yours; and all mine are yours, and yours are mine.*

First of all, then, it is quite clear that the Son receives his name from the Father, Isa. 9.6: *Jehovah calls his name Wonderful,* etc. *the everlasting Father*—if that is the correct interpretation of the elliptical syntax of this passage: for, strictly speaking, the Son is not the Father, and cannot be called the Father. Moreover, even if we grant that he is in some sense or other called *Father* here, he is not called so elsewhere. Furthermore, *the everlasting Father* is usually translated *the Father of a future age*—in other words, the teacher of a future age, for a teacher is often called a father. Phil. 2.7, 9: *on account of this also God has exalted him, and of his grace has given him* (καὶ ἐχαρίσατο) *a name which is above every name;* Heb. 1.4: *as the name he has inherited,* or, *obtained as his lot, is more excellent than theirs;* Eph. 1.20, 21 [. . .]. Why should not that name be Jehovah, or any more excellent name for God, if there is one? It does not alter the fact that the giving of a name is always acknowledged to be the function of a superior, whether father or lord.

But why should we worry about the name, when the Son, in the same way, receives his very being from the Father? John 7.29: *I am from him.* The same is implied in John 1.1: *in the beginning,* for the idea of eternity is excluded here by the decree, as I showed above, and also by the name *Son* and by sentences like *I have begotten you today,* and *I will be a Father to him. Beginning* here can only mean "before the creation of the world," as in John 17.5. Col. 1.15–17 shows this: *the firstborn of all created things: for through him all things in the heavens and on the earth were created* etc. *As he is before all things and all things exist through him.* Here the Son is himself called the firstborn of all created things, and not as man, nor as mediator, but as creator. Similarly Heb. 2.11: [. . .] and 3.2 [. . .]. Indisputably the Father can never have begotten a being who was begotten from eternity. What was made from eternity, was never in the process of being made. Any being whom the Father begot from eternity, he must still be begetting, for an action which has no beginning can have no end. If the Father is still begetting him, he is not yet begotten, and is therefore not a Son. It seems, then, utterly impossible that the Son either should be or was begotten from eternity. If he is a son, then either he was once in the Father and proceeded from him, or else he must always have existed, as now, separate from the Father, with a separate and independent identity. If he was once in the Father but now exists separately, then he must once have undergone a change, and is therefore mutable.[94] If he has always been separate from the Father, how is he *from* the Father, how *begotten,* how a *Son* and how, lastly, is he separate in subsistence unless he is separate in essence too? For, leaving aside the nonsense of quibbling metaphysicians, a substantial essence and a subsistence are the same thing. Anyway, no one will deny that the Son is numerically different from the Father. And the fact that things numerically different are also different in their proper essences, as logicians call it, is so obvious that no reasonable being could contradict it.[95] Therefore the Father and Son differ from each other in essence. This is certainly the reasonable conclusion. My opponents still claim that it is not the conclusion reached by scripture: let them prove it! Although they put so much confidence in that property which is prefigured in Melchisedec, it does not really go against my case, Heb. 7.3: *without father, without mother, without descent; having neither beginning of days nor end of life, but made like the Son of God.* Insofar as the Son lacked an earthly father, it is true that he did not have a *beginning of days.* But this does not prove that he had no *beginning of days* from all eternity any more than it proves that he did not have a Father and was therefore not a Son. If he did derive his essence from the Father, let my opponents prove how that essence can be supremely divine or, in other words, one with and the same as the Father's essence. For the divine essence, which is always one, cannot possibly generate or be generated by an essence the same as itself. Nor can any subsistence or person possibly act or be acted upon in this way, without its whole essence also acting or being acted upon in a similar way. Now generation produces something that is and exists apart from its generator. Therefore God cannot generate a God equal to himself, because he is by definition one and infinite. Since therefore the Son derives his essence from the Father, the Son undoubtedly comes after the Father not only in rank but also in essence (a distinction, incidentally, which has no scriptural authority, though a good many people are taken in by it). The name "Son," upon which my opponents chiefly build their theory of his supreme divinity, is in fact itself the best refutation of their theory. For a supreme God is self-existent, but a God who is not self-existent, who did not beget but was begotten, is not a first cause but an effect, and is therefore not a supreme God. Moreover it is obvious that anyone who was begotten from all eternity, has existed from all

94. "Possibly a reference to and rejection of early speculation of stoic origin on a two-stage theory of the Logos: the Logos existed first only internally in God's thought and later was generated as a person when God externalized his thought into an intelligible universe" (Kelley). Hunter's claim that Milton endorsed an orthodox variation of this "two-stage Logos theory" (1959) has been rejected by Kelley (1961) and Bauman (1987).

95. Milton repeats his earlier point that number follows essence. Cp. note 80.

eternity. But if a being who has existed from all eternity has also been begotten, why should not the Father have been begotten, and have had a father? Anyway "father" and "son" are relative terms and differ both in theory and practice. According to the laws of opposites, the father is not the son, nor the son the father.[96] If Father and Son were of one essence, which, because of their relationship, is impossible, it would follow that the Father was the Son's son and the Son the Father's father. Anyone who is not a lunatic can see what kind of a conclusion this is. For I have said enough already to show that more than one hypostasis cannot be fitted into one essence. Lastly, if the Son is of the same essence as the Father, and if the same Son, after a hypostatical union, coalesces in one person with man, I do not see how to avoid the conclusion that man, also, is the same person as the Father—a conclusion which might produce quite a few paradoxes! But perhaps I shall have more to say about this when I deal with the incarnation of Christ.[97]

On the subject of his life, John 5.26: *as the Father has life in himself, so has he given it to the Son to have life in himself,* and 6.57 [. . .]. His life is for ever:[98] Heb. 1.8: *but to the Son, your throne, God, is for ever and ever;* hence 1.11, 12 [. . .].

On the subject of attributes, first, omnipresence: for if the Father has given the Son everything, even his very existence and life, he has also given it to him to be wherever he is. John 1.49 is to be understood in this light: *before Philip called you, I saw you.* For Nathaniel deduced nothing from this except what he declared in 1.50: *you are the Son of God,* and 3.13: *the Son of man who is in heaven.* These words can never prove that the Son, whether of man or of God, is of the same essence as the Father. They can prove only that the Son of man came down from heaven when he was conceived in the virgin's womb, and that, although his body was living on the earth, he was in heaven—that is, his whole mind and spirit were, as befitted a supreme prophet. Alternatively they can prove that he who is now, with the very highest degree of virtue, made man, is, even now, by that virtue or because of a superior nature given to him in the beginning, in heaven (or rather "was" in heaven, for ὢν can mean either). Again, Matt. 18.20: *there I am in their midst,* and 28.20: *I shall be with you until;* etc. But these texts do not amount to a proof of infinite omnipresence, as the next chapter will show.

[. . .].[99]

Lastly, divine glory:[100] John 1.1: *the Word was with God, and the Word was God,* and 1.14: *we saw his glory as of the only begotten having proceeded from the Father,*

96. Cp. *Art of Logic* (Yale 8:254–55): "Opposites cannot be attributed to one and the same thing by reason of the same thing, with reference to the same thing and at the same time. . . . Thus Socrates cannot be . . . father and son of the same."

97. In chapter 14.

98. Cp. *PL* 3.243–44: "thou hast giv'n me to possess/Life in myself forever, by thee I live."

99. The deleted paragraphs consider a series of divine traits and activities in which the Son participates according to the Father's wishes: omniscience, authority, omnipotence, works, creation, remission of sins, preservation, renovation, the power of conferring gifts, mediatorial work, bringing back to life, judgment, divine honor, and baptism.

100. The deleted sentences elaborate the Son's inferiority to the father and cite Greek idioms implying the essential distinction between God and the Son.

παρὰ πατρός; and 1.18 [. . .]; and 6.46: *not that anyone has seen the Father, except him who is from God,* ὁ ὢν παρὰ τοῦ θεοῦ compared with 17.5: *glorify me, Father, with your own self, with the glory which I had with you before the world was.* No one doubts that, when the Son ascended to him, the Father restored him to that place of glory which he had previously occupied and which he is praying for here. Moreover the place in question is, no one will deny, the right hand of God. Therefore that was his place of glory from the beginning, and it was from that place that he descended. But the right hand of God implies a glory not primarily or supremely divine, but only approaching that of God. [. . .] The fact that he derived his glory, even in his divine nature, before the foundations of the world were laid, not from himself but from the Father, who gave it because he loved him, makes it obvious that he is inferior to the Father. So Matt. 16.27: *with his Father's glory;* Acts 3.13: *the God of Abraham and of Isaac and of Jacob, the God of our fathers, has glorified his Son Jesus;* Col. 1.19: *since it pleased the Father that all fullness should dwell in him,* compared with 2.9: *the whole fullness of the Godhead dwells in him bodily,* and Eph. 3.19: *that you may be filled with all God's fullness.* These passages make it clear that Christ has received his fullness from God in the same sense as that in which we shall receive ours from Christ. For the word *bodily,* which is added, may mean *solidly,* as opposed to the *vain deceit* mentioned in the preceding verse, and anyway it certainly does nothing to prove that his essence is the same as God's.[101] 1 Pet. 1.21: *he has given him glory, that your faith and hope may be in God,* and 2.4 [. . .]; and 2 Pet. 1.16, 17 [. . .]; also 1 Pet. 4.11 compared with 2 Pet. 3.18: *that in all things God may be glorified through Jesus Christ; to whom is glory and strength for ever and ever. Grow in grace and knowledge of our Lord and of our Savior Jesus Christ: to whom is glory both now and for ever.* By reference to the previous passage we can see that, as often, the name *Lord* must be understood here as applying to the Father. But if it refers to the Son, it makes no difference: the doctrine of the previous passage is not affected. Thus John 12.41, quoting from Isa. 43.5: *Esaias said these things when he saw his glory,* that is, the glory of the only begotten, which the Father gave to the Son. My point is not invalidated by Isa. 42.8: *I am Jehovah, that is my name, and I will not give my glory to another nor my praise to statues.* It is true that the Son is *another,* but what God is saying here is that he will not give his glory to statues or to alien gods, not that he will not give it to his Son, who is the brightness of his glory and the image of his substance, and upon whom he had promised to place his spirit, 42.1. For the glory which the Father gives the Son is not lost to him, since the Son everywhere glorifies the Father:[102] John 13.31: *now the Son of man is glorified, and God is glorified in him,* and 8.50 [. . .].

Thus it is quite clear in what sense those things which belong to the Father are said to belong to the Son. John 16.15: *all things which the Father has are mine,* and 17.6, 7 [. . .]. Hence 17.10: *all mine are yours and yours are mine,* that is, in the same

101. Col. 2.9 is cited four times in the treatise. In chapter 6, Milton will use it to claim that God *must* possess a body to allow him to contribute "bodily" to his Son's body.

102. Cp. *PL* 6.724–26: "thou always seek'st/To glorify thy Son, I always thee,/As is most just."

sense in which the Son called the kingdom his, Luke 22.30: for he had said in the preceding verse *I give you a kingdom as my Father gave it to me.* Then again, his coming to judge the world, 1 Tim. 6.14: *until the bright coming of our Lord Jesus Christ, which at the fore-ordained,* or, in his own *time, he, the blessed one, will show; he, the King of kings and Lord of lords; he who alone has immortality, dwelling in unapproachable light; he whom no man has seen or can see.*

Since he received all these things from the Father, and was in the form of God, *he did not reckon it robbery to be equal with God,* Phil. 2.6, that is, because he had received it as a gift, not by robbery. But if the sense of the passage is that he is an equal, it rather refutes than proves the theory that he is of one essence with God. For equality cannot exist except between two or more essences. Furthermore the words *he did not reckon,* meaning "he did not consider," and the words *he emptied himself,* etc., do not seem compatible with the supreme God. For "to consider" means, surely, to have an opinion, but there is no place for "opinion" in God. Similarly a God who is infinite can no more empty himself than contradict himself, for infinity and emptiness are mutually exclusive terms. But since he emptied himself of that form of God in which he had previously existed, if the form of God were to be taken to mean the essence of God, it would prove that he had emptied himself of the very essence of God, which is impossible.

The Son himself—and this is the last point I undertook to prove—openly acknowledges and declares that the Father is greater than he: John 10.29: *the Father is greater than all,* and 14.28: *the Father is greater than I.* You will say that he is speaking as a man, but did his disciples believe that he spoke only as a man? Did Christ wish to be believed in, only as a man? I do not imagine you will say so. He spoke, then, not only as a man (for no one ever doubted that the Father was greater than he was as a man), but as he wished himself to be believed, that is, as man and God. If that is so, he should undoubtedly be understood as if he had said openly, My Father is greater than I, however great I am, both as man and God. Otherwise the speaker was not the person in whom they believed; nor did he teach them, but tricked them with a *double entendre.* His comparison, then, was between God's nature and his own person, not between the nature of God the Father and the human nature of the Son. So 14.31: *I do just as my Father commanded me;* also John 5.18, 19, when accused by the Jews of making himself equal with God, he expressly denies it: *the Son,* he says, *cannot perform anything by himself . . . ,* and 5.30: *as I hear, I judge; and my judgment is just, because I do not seek my will but the will of him who sent me,* that is, *the Father;* and 6.38 [. . .]. Now, the Father sent his only begotten Son: therefore the Father's will is distinct from and greater than the will of the only begotten Son. So 7.28 [. . .]; also 8.29: *for he who sent me is with me: my Father has not left me alone; because I always do the things which please him.* If he is saying this as God, how, if the Father were essentially one with him, could the Father leave him? If he is speaking as a man, then what would it matter to him to be left alone, if he were anyway supported by a power of deity equal to the Father's? Moreover, why does the Father not leave him alone? Not because he is essentially one with him, but because the Son *always does the things which please him,* that is, as an inferior does the things which please a superior. And 8.42: *for I have not come from myself*—not, therefore, by virtue of his own deity, *but he sent me: he,* therefore, is someone different from and greater than *myself:* 8.49: *I honor my Father,* 50: *I do not seek my own glory,* and 54: *if I glorify myself my glory is nothing*—therefore it is less than the Father's glory. Also John 10.24, 25 [. . .], and 15.10 [. . .], and 16.25 [. . .], and 20.17 [. . .]. Compare Rev. 1.11 [. . .], and 1.17: *I am the first and the last,* and 2.8, as also 3.12: *I shall make him a pillar in the temple of my God*—this is repeated three times. Thus the person who had just called himself *the first and the last* now admits that the Father is his God: Matt. 11.25, 26: *I confess* or *I give thanks to you, Father, Lord of heaven and earth, because this . . . because, Father, it pleased you to do so.*

So far we have heard the Son's evidence about the Father. Now let us hear what the Father has to say about the Son: for it is written, Matt. 11.27: *no one knows the Son except the Father, nor does anyone know the Father except the* Son *and anyone to whom the Son wishes to reveal him;* 1 John 5.9: *this is God's testimony about his Son . . . ;* here the Father, who is going to testify about his Son, is called simply *God,* and his testimony is, moreover, absolutely clear: Matt. 3.17: *this is my beloved Son, with whom I have been pleased;* Isa. 42.1, compared with Matt. 12.18: *behold my servant, whom I uphold, my chosen one whom my soul cherishes: I shall place my spirit upon him;* and again, Matt. 17.5, which is to the same effect. 2 Pet. 1.17 [. . .]: Mal. 3.1 [. . .], and most plainly of all in Ps. 2,[103] where God the Father is introduced in his own person openly declaring the nature and offices of his Son, 2.7, 8, 11, 12 [. . .]; add to this Heb. 1.8, 9 [. . .]. Finally, we may add the evidence of the angel Gabriel: Luke 1.32: *he will be great, and will be called the Son of the Highest, and the Lord God will give him the throne of his father, David.* The Son of the Highest, not, therefore, the highest himself. The apostles everywhere corroborate this fact, and so, first of all, does John the Baptist: John 1.29: *behold the Lamb of God;* and 1.33, 34 [. . .]. Also 3.32, etc.: *what he has seen and heard, that he testifies . . . : he* meaning not only *he that is of the earth* or he who speaks only *of earthly things,* 3.31, but he who *is above all* and comes *from heaven:* I point this out in case anyone should go on insisting that this passage, and others of the same kind, refer to Christ as a man. 2 Cor. 4.4, 6: *lest the light of the glory of the gospel of Christ, who is the image of God, should shine upon them;* Col. 1.15: *who is the image of the invisible God, and the first born of all created things;* Phil. 2.6 [. . .]; Heb. 1.2 [. . .], and 1.3 [. . .]. All these passages imply a comparison and all refer numerically to two people, thus proving that the two people are not of one essence, and that one of them is inferior to the other. Similarly 1.4: *made as superior to the angels as the name he has inherited is more excellent than theirs;* 1 Cor. 3.23: *but you are Christ's and Christ is God's.* Where would it be more likely to find Christ called God than here? But he is called *God's,* not God. The point is clarified even further by the following passages: 1 Cor. 11.3: *I would have you know that the head of Christ is God;* Eph. 1.17 [. . .]; 1 Cor. 15.27: *when it says "all things" are subjected to him, obviously this means all things except him who subjected all things to him.*

103. Psalm 2 weighs heavily in Milton's conception of the Father's relation to the Son. Cp. note 74.

And after everything has been made subject to him, then the Son himself will be made subject to him who subjected all things to him, so that God may be all in all.[104] Here my opponents cannot wriggle out of it, as they usually do, by claiming that Christ's mediatorial function is being discussed. The passage states that, when Christ has completed his mediatorial office, and when there is nothing left to stop him from resuming his original glory as the only begotten Son, even then he will be subject to the Father.

This was the faith of the saints concerning the Son of God; this also the celebrated confession of that faith: this alone is taught, is acceptable to God, and holds promise of eternal salvation: Matt. 16.15–19: *who do you say that I am? Peter replied, You are Christ, the Son of the living God: then Jesus said, Blessed are you Simon, for flesh and blood did not reveal this to you, but my Father, who is in heaven. On this rock I will build my church . . . ;* Luke 9.20 [. . .]; John 1.50, 51 [. . .], and 6.69 [. . .] and 9.35–38 [. . .]; and 11.22, 26, 27 [. . .]; and 16.27, 30, 31 [. . .]; and 17.3, 7, 8, 21 [. . .]; Acts 8.37 [. . .]; Rom. 10.9 [. . .]; Col. 2.2 [. . .]; Phil. 4.6, 7 [. . .]; 1 Pet. 1.21 [. . .]; 1 John 4.15: *if anyone confesses that Jesus is the Son of God, God dwells in him and he in God;* and 5.1: *whoever believes that Jesus is the Christ, is begotten by God,* and 5.5 [. . .]. Finally, the Apostles' Creed itself, the most ancient and the most widely accepted creed which the Church possesses, offers us this belief and no other.

CHAPTER 6

OF THE HOLY SPIRIT

So much for the Father and the Son: the next thing to be discussed is the Holy Spirit, for this is called the spirit both of the Father and of the Son. The Bible, however, says nothing about what the Holy Spirit is like, how it exists, or where it comes from—a warning to us not to be too hasty in our conclusions. Granted it is a spirit, in the sense in which that term is correctly applied to the Father and the Son, and granted that Christ, in John 20.22, is said to have given the Holy Spirit to his disciples (or, rather, some symbol or pledge of the spirit) by breathing upon them: who, on this evidence, would dare to maintain, in a discussion of the nature of the Holy Spirit, that it was breathed from the Father and the Son? The terms "emanation" and "procession" are irrelevant to the question of the Holy Spirit's nature. Theologians use them on the authority of John 15.26, where the reference is to the *spirit of truth,* ὁ παρὰ τοῦ πατρὸς ἐκπορεύεται, *which proceeds* or goes out from *the Father.* This one word is a pretty slender basis for our belief in so great a mystery. Anyway it refers to the mission, not the nature of the spirit. In the same sense the Son is often said ἐξελθεῖν, as well, that is either *to go out from* or *to proceed from* the Father, whichever translation you prefer: there is nothing to choose between them as far as I can see. Indeed, we are said

104. Cp. *PL* 3.339–41: "Then thou thy regal scepter shalt lay by,/For regal scepter then no more shall need,/God shall be all in all."

to *live by every word,* ἐκπορευομένῳ *that proceeds* or *goes out, through the mouth of God,* Matt 4.4.[105] The spirit, then, is not said to be generated or created, and it cannot be decided, from biblical evidence, how else it exists. So we must leave the point open, since the sacred writers are so noncommittal about it.

The name "spirit" is habitually applied to God, to the angels, and even to the minds of men. When the term "spirit of God" or "holy spirit" occurs in the Old Testament, it sometimes means God the Father, as in Gen. 6.3: *my spirit will not always strive.*

Sometimes it means the power and virtue of the Father, especially that divine breath which creates and nourishes everything. In the latter sense many interpreters, both ancient and modern, understand that passage in Gen. 1.2: *the spirit of God brooded.* It seems more likely, however, that we should here interpret the word as a reference to the Son, through whom, as we are constantly told, the Father created all things. Job 26.13: *by his spirit he decked the heavens,* and 27.3: *the spirit of God is in my nostrils,* and 33.4 [. . .]; Ps. 104.30: *when you send your spirit out, they are recreated;* and 139.7 [. . .]; Ezek. 37.14 [. . .]. There are many other passages of the same sort.

Sometimes "spirit" means an angel, Isa. 48.16: *the Lord Jehovah and his spirit has sent me;* Ezek. 3.12: *then the spirit took me up . . . ;* similarly 3.14 and 24 and elsewhere.

Sometimes it means Christ, whom, most people think, the Father sent to lead the Israelites into the land of Canaan. Isa. 43.10, 11: *afflicting with grief the spirit of his holiness. Who placed in their midst the spirit of his holiness*—that is, the angel upon which he bestowed his own name: that is, Christ, whom they tempted, Num. 21.5 etc., compared with 1 Cor. 10.9.

Sometimes it means the force or voice of God, in whatever way it was breathed into the prophets: Neh. 9.30: *since you testified against them by your spirit through your prophets.*

[. . . .][106]

Let us assume that, appropriately enough, when God wants us to understand and thus believe in a particular doctrine as a primary point of faith, he teaches it to us not obscurely or confusedly, but simply and clearly, in plain words. Let us also take it for granted that, in religion, we should beware above all of exposing ourselves to the charge which Christ brought against the Samaritans in John 4.22: *you worship something you do not know.* Assume, too, that in matters of faith, that saying of Christ, *we worship something which we know,* should be regarded as axiomatic. If these assumptions are correct, then, as the above passages comprise just about all we are told in express terms about the Holy Spirit, they also represent all we can or ought to know on the subject. What they amount to is

105. In this passage, the Greek phrase or word precedes the italicized translation. Milton's point is that the distinct Greek words meaning "proceed from" and "go out from" could well mean the same thing in the contexts in which he quotes them. Believers have no good textual reason to attach special theological significance to "proceed from."

106. In the deleted paragraphs, Milton continues his demonstration that scriptural accounts are variable and obscure in what they imply about the nature of the Holy Spirit.

this: the Holy Spirit, unlike the Son, is nowhere said to have submitted himself to any mediatorial function. He is nowhere said to be under an obligation, as a son is, to pay obedience to the Father. Nevertheless he is obviously inferior to both the Father and the Son, inasmuch as he is represented as being and is said to be subservient and obedient in all things; to have been promised, sent and given; to speak nothing of his own accord; and even to have been given as a pledge. You cannot avoid the issue here by talking about his human nature. [. . .] It remains to be seen, then, on what grounds we are to believe that the Holy Spirit is God, and what arguments there are for it. When the point at issue is as difficult to grasp as the present one, and when, like the present one, it is reckoned to be of primary importance and absolutely indispensable, it is inconsiderate and dangerous to burden believers with the necessity of accepting a doctrine which cannot be deduced from the clear testimony of God's word: a doctrine, moreover, which, although itself contrary to human reason, can only be ascertained by human reason, or rather by dubious logic-chopping.

Thus it is usual to defend the theory that the Holy Spirit is God by saying, first, that the name of God seems to be attributed to the Holy Spirit: Acts 5.3 compared with 5.4: *as you have lied to the Holy Spirit, you have not lied to men but to God.* But if we pay proper attention to what is previously said about the Holy Spirit by the Son, this passage will appear a pretty poor reason for asserting such a mysterious doctrine. For since it is explicitly stated that the Spirit is sent by the Father and in the name of the Son, clearly the man who lies to the Spirit lies to God, just as the man who receives an apostle receives God who sent him, Matt. 10.40; John 13.20. Paul himself puts an end to any argument about this passage, and explains it in the most apposite way, when he expounds what is obviously the same idea in a more developed form; 1 Thess. 4.8: *the man who despises these things despises not man but God, who has placed his Holy Spirit in us.* Besides, it is questionable whether, in the passage from Acts, *Holy Spirit* does not really mean God the Father, for Peter says, 5.9: *why . . . that you might tempt the spirit of the Lord,* that is, God the Father himself and his divine intelligence, which no mortal can deceive or be concealed from. And in Acts 5.32 it is evident that the Holy Spirit is called not God but, like the apostles, a witness to Christ—a witness *whom God has given to those who obey him.* Similarly Acts 2.38: *you will receive the gift of the Holy Spirit*—receive it, that is, from God. But how can the gift of God be God himself—especially the supreme God?

The second passage adduced is Acts 28.25, compared with Isa. 6.8, 9: *the Lord said. The Holy Spirit has said,* and similarly Jer. 31.31, compared with Heb. 10.15. But I demonstrated above[107] that in the Old Testament the names "Lord" and "Jehovah" are frequently attributed to whatever angels God sends on his errands. Moreover, in the New Testament, the Son himself openly gives evidence about the Holy Spirit to this effect, John 16.13: *that he does not speak of his own accord, but*

107. In chapter 5, p. 1181.

speaks the things he hears. So the Holy Spirit cannot be proved God from this passage either.

The third passage is 1 Cor. 3.16, compared with 6.19 and with 2 Cor. 6.16: *the temple of God. The temple of the Spirit.* But it is not stated here, nor does it in any way follow from this that the Holy Spirit is God. For it is because the Father and the Son, not only the Holy Spirit *live in us,* John 14.23, that we are called *the temple of God.* So in 1 Cor. 6.19, where we are called *the temple of the Spirit,* Paul has added *which you have from God,* as if he were anxious to prevent us from drawing any false conclusions about the Holy Spirit from the expression he uses. How could anyone deduce from this passage, then, that what we have from God, is God? Paul explains more fully in what sense we are called *the temple of the Spirit* in Eph. 2.22: *you, too, are built together in him to be the home of God through the Spirit.*

[. . .][108]

Although the scriptures do not tell us explicitly who or what the Holy Spirit is, we need not be completely ignorant about it, as this much may be understood from the texts quoted above. The Holy Spirit, since he is a minister of God, and therefore a creature, was created, that is, produced, from the substance of God, not by natural necessity, but by the free will of the agent, maybe before the foundations of the world were laid, but after the Son, to whom he is far inferior, was made. You will say that this does not really distinguish the Holy Spirit from the Son. I reply that, in the same way, the expressions *to go forth from* and *to go out from* and *to proceed from the Father,* which are all the same in the Greek, do not distinguish the Son from the Holy Spirit, since they are used about both and signify the mission not the nature of each. There is sufficient reason for placing the name and also the nature of the Son above that of the Holy Spirit, when discussing matters relative to the Deity, in that the brightness of God's glory and the image of his divine subsistence are said to have been impressed on the Son but not on the Holy Spirit.

CHAPTER 7

OF THE CREATION

The second[109] kind of external efficiency is commonly called CREATION. Anyone who asks what God did before the creation of the world is a fool; and

108. The deleted passage argues that the attributes of true deity cannot be properly assigned to the Holy Spirit any more than they could be to the Son. It culminates with further discussion of 1 John 5.7, which asserts that "the Father, the Word and the Holy Spirit . . . are one," a verse whose spuriousness was detailed in note 82.

109. "Milton's antitrinitarianism dictates this numbering. According to orthodox theologians the external efficiency of God manifests itself in creation, by which he governs that which he produces. To these Milton adds an earlier species, the generation of the Son, so that creation and providence become the second and third rather than the standard first and second species of the Father's external efficiency" (Kelley).

anyone who answers him is not much wiser.[110] Most people think they have given an account of the matter when they have quoted 1 Cor. 2.7: *that he preordained, before the creation of the world, his wisdom, hidden in a mystery,* which they take to mean that he was occupied with election and reprobation, and with deciding other related matters. But it would clearly be disproportionate for God to have been totally occupied from eternity in decreeing things which it was to take him only six days to create: things which were to be governed in various ways for a few thousand years, and then finally either received into an unchanging state with God for ever, or else for ever thrown away.

That the world was created, must be considered an article of faith: Heb. 11.3: *through faith we understand that the world was made by God's word.*

CREATION is the act by which GOD THE FATHER PRODUCED EVERYTHING THAT EXISTS BY HIS WORD AND SPIRIT, that is, BY HIS WILL, IN ORDER TO SHOW THE GLORY OF HIS POWER AND GOODNESS.

BY WHICH GOD THE FATHER: Job 9.8: *who alone spreads out the heavens;* Isa. 44.24: *I, Jehovah, make all things, I alone spread out the heavens, and I stretch forth the earth by myself,* and 45.6, 7 [. . .]. If such things as common sense and accepted idiom exist at all, then these words preclude the possibility not only of there being any other God, but also of there being any person, of any kind whatever, equal to him.[111] Neh. 9.6 [. . .]; Mal. 2.10: *have we not all one father? Has not one mighty and unparalleled God created us?* Thus Christ himself says, Matt. 11.25: *Father, Lord of heaven and earth;* and so do all the apostles: Acts 4.24, compared with 4.27: *Lord, you are that God who created the heaven and the earth, the sea and all that is in* them . . . against *your Son;* Rom. 11.36: *from him and through him and in him are all things;* 1 Cor. 8.6 [. . .] and 2 Cor. 4.6 [. . .]; Heb. 2.10 [. . .] and 3.4 [. . .].

BY HIS WORD: Gen. 1. *passim, he said . . . ;* Ps. 33.6: *by Jehovah's word,* and 33.9: *he speaks;* Ps. 148.5: *he commanded;* 2 Pet. 3.5: *through the word of God,* that is, as we learn from other passages, through the Son, who apparently derives from this his title of the Word.[112] John 1.3, 10: *all things were made through him: through him the world was made;* 1 Cor. 8.6: *one God, the Father, from whom all things are. And one Lord Jesus Christ, through whom all things are;* Eph. 3.9 [. . .]; Col. 1.16 [. . .]; Heb. 1.2: *through whom also he made the world,* hence 1.10: *you have created.* The preposition *through* sometimes denotes the principal cause, as in Matt. 12.28: *through the Spirit of God I cast out devils,* 1 Cor. 1.9: *through whom you are called,* and sometimes the instrumental or less important cause, as in the passages quoted above.[113] It does not

110. Cp. *Tetrachordon,* p. 1017: "One demanding how God employed himself before the world was made, had answer: that he was making hell for curious questioners."

111. Cp. *PL* 8.406–7: "for none I know/Second to me or like, equal much less."

112. On the significance of the distinction between the roles of the Word and the Son, see Rumrich 1987, 162–64. Cp. *PL* 5.814–18.

113. Cp. *Art of Logic* (Yale 8:224–25): "Properly speaking, instruments do not act, but are rather acted upon or help. And anyone who has only instruments as helping cause can correctly be called a solitary cause."

denote the principal cause in these passages, because if it did the Father himself, by whom all things are, would not be the principal. Nor does it denote a joint cause, because then it would be said not that the Father created *by* the Word and Spirit but *with* the Word and Spirit, or alternatively that the Father, the Word, and the Spirit created. These formulae are nowhere to be found in scripture. Again, "to be *by* the Father" and "to be *through* the Son" are phrases which do not signify the same kind of efficient cause. If they are not of the same kind, then there can be no question of a joint cause, and if there is no joint cause then "the Father *by* whom all things are" will unquestionably be a more important cause than "the Son *through* whom all things are." For the Father is not only he *by* whom, but also he *from* whom, in whom, *through* whom, and *on account of* whom all things are, as I have shown above, inasmuch as he comprehends within himself all lesser causes. But the Son is only he *through* whom all things are, and is therefore the less principal cause. So we often find it said that the Father created the world through the Son, but nowhere that the Son, in the same sense, created the world through the Father. But some try to prove from Rev. 3.14 that the Son was the joint cause of the creation with the Father, or even the principal cause. The reference there is to *the beginning of God's creation,* and they interpret the word *beginning* as meaning *beginner,* on the authority of Aristotle. But in the first place, the Hebrew language, from which this expression is taken, never allows this use of the word *beginning,* but rather requires a quite contrary sense, as in Gen. 49.3: *Reuben, the beginning of my strength.* Secondly, there are two passages in Paul, referring to Christ himself, which make it absolutely clear that the word *beginning* is here used to mean not an agent but something acted upon: Col. 1.15, 18: *the first born of all created things. The beginning, the first born from the dead.* Here both the Greek accent and the verbal passive πϱοτότοϰος, show that the Son of God was *the first born of all created things* in the same sense as the Son of man was the πϱοτότοϰος or *first born* of Mary, Matt. 1.25. The second passage is Rom. 8.29: *the first born among many brothers,* where *first born* has, of course, a passive sense. Finally it should be noted that Christ is not called merely the *beginning of creation,* but *the beginning of God's creation,* and that can only mean that he was the first of the things which God created. How, then, can he be God himself? Some of the Fathers have suggested that the reason why he is called *the first born of all created things* in Col. 1.15 is that *through him all things were created,* as it says in the next verse. But this argument cannot be admitted, because if St. Paul had meant this, he would have said "who was before every creature" (which is what these Fathers insist that the words mean, although it is a forced reading), not, *who was the first born of all created things.* The words *first born* here are certainly superlative in sense, but they also, in a way, imply that only part of a collective whole is being spoken of. This last remark is true only because the production of Christ was apparently a kind of "birth" or creation: it is not true where Christ is also called the first born *man.* For he is called *first born* in that phrase not just as a title of dignity, but to distinguish him from other men for the chronological reason that *through him all things which are in the heavens were created,* Col. 1.16.

Prov. 8.22, 23 is no better as a basis for argument, even if we admit that the chapter as a whole should be interpreted as a reference to Christ: *Jehovah possessed me, the beginning of his way; I was anointed before the world.* A thing which was *possessed* and *anointed* could not itself be the primary cause. Besides, even a creature is called the beginning of the ways of God in Job 40.19: *he is the beginning of God's ways.* As for the eighth chapter of Proverbs, I should say that the figure introduced as a speaker there is not the Son of God but a poetical personification of Wisdom, as in Job 28.20–27: *From where, then, is that wisdom . . . ? then he saw her. . . .*

Another argument is based on Isa. 45.12, 23: *I have made the earth . . . ; shall bow to me.* My opponents say that these words are spoken by Christ, and they quote St. Paul in their support: Rom. 14.10, 11: *we shall all stand before the judgment seat of Christ: for it is written, As I live, says the Lord, every knee shall bow to me. . . .* But it is obvious from the parallel passage, Phil. 2.9–11, that this is said by God the Father, who gave that judgment seat, and all judgment, to the Son, *that at the name of Jesus every knee shall bow . . . ; to the glory of God the Father,* or in other words, *every tongue shall confess to God.*

AND SPIRIT. Gen. 1.2: *the Spirit of God brooded,* that is to say, God's divine power, not any particular person, as I showed in Chapter 6, Of the Holy Spirit.[114] For if it was a person, why is the Spirit named and nothing said about the Son, by whose labor, as we so often read, the world was made? (Unless, of course, the Spirit referred to was Christ, who, as I have shown, is sometimes called *the Spirit* in the Old Testament.) Anyway, even if we grant that it was a person, it seems only to have been a subordinate, since, after God had created heaven and earth, the Spirit merely brooded upon the face of the waters which had already been created. Similarly Job 26.13: *by his spirit he decked the heavens;* Ps. 33.6: *the heavens were made by Jehovah's word, and all the host of them by the spirit of his mouth.* The person of the Spirit certainly does not seem to have proceeded more from God's mouth than from Christ's, who *shall consume the antichrist with the spirit of his mouth,* 2 Thess. 2.8, compared with Isa. 11.4: *the rod of his mouth.*

BY HIS WILL. Ps. 135.6: *whatever pleases you;* Rev. 4.11: *as a result of your will.*

IN ORDER TO SHOW. Gen. 1.31: *whatever he had done, it was very good,* similarly 1 Tim. 4.4; Ps. 19.2, 3: *the heavens declare the glory of God;* Prov. 16.4 [. . .]; Acts 14.15 [. . .] and 17.24 [. . .] etc.; Rom. 1.20: *for both his eternal power and his eternal godhead are discerned.*[115] So far I have established that God the Father is the first efficient cause of all things.

114. Milton never states decisively whether or not the force brooding was contained in a specific person. He admits no doubt, however, that ultimately it is the power of the Father, regardless of whether it was channeled through a person or not.

115. Cp. *PR* 3.110–14: "he seeks glory,/And for his glory all things made, all things / Orders and governs, nor content in Heaven/By all his Angels glorified, requires/Glory from men, from all men, good or bad."

There is a good deal of controversy, however, about what the original matter was. On the whole the moderns are of the opinion that everything was formed out of nothing (which is, I fancy, what their own theory is based on!). In the first place it is certain that neither the Hebrew verb בָּרָא nor the Greek κτίζειν, nor the Latin *creare* means "to make out of nothing." On the contrary, each of them always means "to make out of something." Gen. 1.21, 27: *God created . . . which the waters brought forth abundantly, he created them male and female;* Isa. 54.16: *I have created the maker, I have created the destroyer.* Anyone who says, then, that "to create" means "to produce out of nothing," is, as logicians say, arguing from an unproved premise. The passages of scripture usually quoted in this context do not at all confirm the received opinion, but tend to imply the contrary, namely that all things were not made out of nothing, 2 Cor. 4.6: *God who commanded light to shine out of darkness.* It is clear from Isa. 45.7 that this darkness was far from being a mere nothing: *I am Jehovah,* etc. *I form the light and create the darkness.* If the darkness is nothing, then when God created the darkness he created nothing, that is he both created and did not create, which is a contradiction in terms. Again, Heb. 11.3, all we are required *to understand through faith* about *earthly times,* that is, about the world, is that *the things which are seen were not put together from the things which appear.* Now because things do not appear, they must not be considered synonymous with nothing. For one thing, you cannot have a plural of nothing, and for another, a thing cannot be *put together* from nothing as it can from a number of components. The meaning is, rather, that these things are not as they now appear. I might also mention the apocryphal writers, as closest to the scriptures in authority: Wisdom 11.17: *who created the world out of formless matter;* 2 Macc. 7.28: *out of things that were not.* But it is said of Rachel's children in Matt. 2.18, *they are not,* and this does not mean *they are nothing* but, as frequently in the Hebrew language, they are not among the living.

It is clear, then, that the world was made out of some sort of matter. For since "action" and "passivity" are relative terms, and since no agent can act externally unless there is something, and something material, which can be acted upon, it is apparent that God could not have created this world out of nothing. *Could* not, that is, not because of any defect of power or omnipotence on his part, but because it was necessary that something should have existed previously, so that it could be acted upon by his supremely powerful active efficacy. Since, then, both the Holy Scriptures and reason itself suggest that all these things were made not out of nothing but out of matter, matter must either have always existed, independently of God, or else originated from God at some point in time. That matter should have always existed independently of God is inconceivable. In the first place, it is only a passive principle, dependent upon God and subservient to him; and, in the second place, there is no inherent force or efficacy in time or eternity, any more than there is in the concept of number. But if matter did not exist from eternity, it is not very easy to see where it originally came from. There remains only this solution, especially if we allow ourselves to be guided by scripture, namely, that all things came from God. Rom. 11.36: *from him and through him and in him are all things;* 1 Cor. 8.6: *one God, the Father, from whom all things are,—from,* as the Greek reads in both cases. Heb. 2.11: *for both he who sanctifies and he who is sanctified, are all from one.*

There are, to begin with, as everyone knows, four kinds of causes, efficient, material, formal and final.[116] Since God is the first, absolute and sole cause of all things, he unquestionably contains and comprehends within himself all these causes. So the material cause must be either God or nothing. But nothing is no cause at all; (though my opponents want to prove that forms and, what is more, human forms were created from nothing). Now matter and form are, as it were, internal causes. These are the things which go to make up the object itself. So either all objects must have had only two causes, external causes that is, or else God was not the perfect and absolute cause of all things. Secondly, it is a demonstration of supreme power and supreme goodness that such heterogeneous, multiform and inexhaustible virtue should exist in God, and exist substantially (for that virtue cannot be accidental which admits various degrees and is, as it were, susceptible to augmentation and remission, according his will). It is, I say, a demonstration of God's supreme power and goodness that he should not shut up this heterogeneous and substantial virtue within himself, but should disperse, propagate and extend it as far as, and in whatever way, he wills. For this original matter was not an evil thing, nor to be thought of as worthless: it was good, and it contained the seeds of all subsequent good. It was a substance, and could only have been derived from the source of all substance. It was in a confused and disordered state at first, but afterwards God made it ordered and beautiful.[117]

Those who object to this theory, on the grounds that matter was apparently imperfect, should also object to the theory that God originally produced it out of nothing in an imperfect and formless state. What does it matter whether God produced this imperfect matter out of nothing or out of himself? To argue that there could have been no imperfection in a substance which God produced out of himself, is only to transfer the imperfection to God's efficiency. For why did he not, starting from nothing, make everything absolutely perfect straight away? But in fact, matter was not, by nature, imperfect. The addition of forms (which, incidentally, are themselves material) did not make it more perfect but only more beautiful. But, you will say, how can something corruptible result from something incorruptible? I might well reply, how can God's virtue and efficiency result from nothing? But in fact matter, like the form and nature of the

116. Cp. *Art of Logic* (Yale 8:223).

117. Here we find the theological justification for Milton's vitalist materialism: that a *multiform and inexhaustible virtue* is intrinsic to God's absolute excellence; it is the substantial power that permits him to produce a materially and formally diverse creation. The claim seems inconsistent with the allegorical representation in *Paradise Lost* of a hostile Chaos. For divergent critical views of this apparent inconsistency, see Schwartz; Rumrich 1995.

angels, came from God in an incorruptible state, and even since the fall it is still incorruptible, so far as its essence is concerned.

But the same problem, or an even greater one, still remains. How can anything sinful have come, if I may so speak, from God? My usual reply to this is to ask, how can anything sinful have come from that virtue and efficiency which themselves proceed from God? But really it is not the matter nor the form which sins. When matter or form has gone out from God and become the property of another, what is there to prevent its being infected and polluted, since it is now in a mutable state, by the calculations of the devil or of man, calculations which proceed from these creatures themselves? But, you will say, body cannot emanate from spirit. My reply is, much less can it emanate from nothing. Moreover spirit, being the more excellent substance, virtually, as they say, and eminently contains within itself what is clearly the inferior substance; in the same way as the spiritual and rational faculty contains the corporeal, that is, the sentient and vegetative faculty. For not even God's virtue and efficiency could have produced bodies out of nothing (as it is vulgarly believed he did) unless there had been some bodily force in his own substance, for no one can give something he has not got.

And indeed, St. Paul himself did not hesitate to attribute something bodily to God, Col. 2.9: *the whole fullness of the Godhead dwells in him bodily*. And it is not any more incredible that a bodily force should be able to issue from a spiritual substance, than that something spiritual should be able to arise from a body; and that is what we trust will happen to our own bodies at the resurrection. Lastly, I do not see how God can truthfully be called infinite if there is anything which might be added to him. And if something did exist, in the nature of things, which had not first been from God and in God, then that might be added to him.

It seems to me that, with the guidance of scripture, I have proved that God produced all things not out of nothing but out of himself. Now I think I ought to go on to consider the necessary consequence of this, which is that, since all things come not only from God but out of God, no created thing can be utterly annihilated. To begin with, there is not a word in the Bible about any such annihilation. That is the very best reason for rejecting the concept of annihilation altogether, but I will also suggest some other reasons. First, because it seems to me that God neither wishes to nor, properly speaking, can altogether annihilate anything.[118] He does not wish to, because he makes everything to some definite end, and nothing cannot be the end either of God or of any created thing. It cannot be the end of God, because he is himself his own end; and it cannot be the end of any created thing, because the end of all created things is some kind of good, whereas nothing is neither good nor any kind of thing at all. All entity is good: nonentity, not good. It is not consistent, then, with the goodness and

118. Cp. *PL* 2.151–54; 6.347.

wisdom of God, to make out of entity, which is good, something which is not good, or nothing. Moreover God cannot annihilate anything, because by making nothing he would both make and not make at the same time, which involves a contradiction. But, you will say, God does make something when he annihilates: he makes something which exists, cease to exist. My reply is that any complete action involves two things, motion, and something brought about by the motion. Here the motion is the act of annihilation, but there is not anything brought about by the motion, that is, nothing is brought about, no effect: and if there is no effect there is no efficient.

CREATION is of THINGS INVISIBLE or of THINGS VISIBLE.

THINGS INVISIBLE, at least to us, are the highest heaven, the throne and dwelling place of God, and the heavenly beings, or angels.

This is the distinction which the apostle makes in Col. 1.16. Things invisible deserve priority by virtue of dignity if not of origin. For the highest heaven is, as it were, God's supreme citadel and dwelling-place (see Deut. 26.15; 1 Kings 8.27, 30: *of the heaven of heavens;* Neh. 9.6; similarly Isa. 63.15): *it is far above all heavens,* Eph. 4.10; where God *dwells in unapproachable light, whom no man can see,* 1 Tim. 6.16. Bliss and glory and a kind of perpetual heaven have, apparently, emanated from this light and exist as a result of it; see Ps. 16.11: *eternal pleasures at your right hand;* Isa. 57.15: *whose name dwells in eternity and is holy; I who live in a high and holy place.*

It is not likely that God built a dwelling-place of this kind for his majesty only the day before yesterday, only, that is, from the beginning of the world. If God really has a dwelling-place where he pours forth his glory and the brightness of his majesty in a particular and extraordinary way, why should I believe that it was made at the same time as the fabric of this world, and not ages before? But it does not follow that heaven is eternal, nor, if it is eternal, that it is God. For God could always produce any effect he pleased both when and how he chose. We cannot imagine light without some source of light, but we do not therefore think that a source of light is the same thing as light, or equal in excellence. Similarly we do not consider that what are called *the back parts* of God in Ex. 33, are, strictly speaking, God, yet we do not deny that they are eternal. I prefer to think in the same way about the heavens of heavens, the throne and dwelling-place of God, rather than believe that God was without a heaven until the first of the six days of creation. I say this not because I dare be at all dogmatic on such a subject, but in order to show that other people have been too rashly dogmatic in affirming that that invisible and supreme heaven was, like the heaven we see above us, made on the first day of creation. Since Moses had set himself the task of writing only about the visible heaven, and this visible universe, why should it have concerned him to say what was above the world?

The heaven of the blessed seems to be a part of this highest heaven. It is sometimes called Paradise, Luke 23.43; 2 Cor. 12.2, 4; and sometimes Abraham's bosom, Luke 16.22 compared with Matt. 8.11. Here God reveals himself to the sight of the angels and saints (insofar as they are capable of seeing him); and after the end of the world he will reveal himself more fully, 1 Cor. 13.12. John 14.2, 3: *in my Father's house there are many mansions;* Heb. 11.10, 16 [. . .].

Most people argue that the angels should be understood as included in and created along with "the heavens" at the creation of the world. We may well believe that the angels were, in fact, created at a particular time, see Num. 16.22: *God of spirits,* and similarly 27.16; Heb. 1.7; Col. 1.16: *through him were invisible things made, whether they be thrones* . . . But that they were created on the first or on any one of the six days is asserted by the general mob of theologians with, as usual, quite unjustifiable confidence, chiefly on the authority of the repetition in Gen. 2.1: *thus the heavens and the earth were finished, and all the army of them:* quite unjustifiable, that is, unless we are supposed to pay more attention to this conclusion than to the preceding narrative, and to interpret this *army* which inhabits the visible heavens as a reference to the angels. The fact that they *shouted for joy* before God at the creation, as we read in Job 38.7, proves that they were then already created, not that they were first created at that time. Certainly many of the Greek Fathers, and some of the Latin, were of the opinion that angels, inasmuch as they were spirits, existed long before this material world. Indeed it seems likely that that apostasy, as a result of which so many myriads of them fled, beaten, to the lowest part of heaven, took place before even the first beginnings of this world.[119] There is certainly no reason why we should conform to the popular belief that motion and time, which is the measure of motion, could not, according to our concepts of "before" and "after," have existed before this world was made. For Aristotle, who taught that motion and time are inherent only in this world, asserted, nevertheless, that this world was eternal.[120]

Angels are spirits, Matt. 8.16 and 12.45. Indeed a whole legion of evil angels was able to get inside one man, Luke 8.30; Heb. 1.14 [. . .]. They are ethereal by nature: 1 Kings 22.21; Ps. 104.4 compared with Matt. 8.31; Heb. 1.7: *like lightning;* Luke 10.18; for which reason they are also called Seraphim.[121] They are immortal, Luke 20.36: *they cannot die.* Remarkable for their wisdom, 2 Sam. 14.20. Extremely strong, Ps. 103.20; 2 Pet. 2.11; 2 Kings 19.35; 2 Thess. 1.7. Extremely swift, as if they had wings, Ezek. 1.6; so numerous that they are almost innumerable, Deut. 33.2; Job 25.3; Dan. 7.10; Matt. 26.53; Heb. 12.22; Rev. 5.11, 12. They were created perfect in holiness and righteousness, Luke 9. 26; John 8.44; 2 Cor. 11.14, 15: *angels of light, ministers of righteousness;* Matt. 6.10 [. . .], and 25.31 [. . .]. So they are also called sons of God,[122] Job 1.6 and 38.7; Dan. 3.25, compared with 3.28; and they are even called Gods, Ps. 8.6 and 97.7. But they are not to be compared with God; Job 4.18: *he will give light to his angels,* and 15.15 [. . .]*s,* and 25.5 [. . .]; Isa. 6.2 [. . .]. They are distinguished one from another by their duties and their

119. Cp. *PL* 1, Argument: "for that angels were long before this visible creation, was the opinion of many ancient Fathers"; also 5.577ff.

120. Cp. *PL* 5.580–82: "(For time, though in eternity, applied/To motion, measures all things durable/By present, past, and future)."

121. The name of this angelic order is related to the Hebrew word for "fire."

122. Cp. *PL* 5.447; 11.84; and *PR* 1.368; 4.197.

ranks, Matt. 25.41; Rom. 8.38; Col. 1.16; Eph. 1.21 and 3.10; 1 Pet. 3.22; Rev. 12.7. Cherubim, Gen. 3.24. Seraphim, Isa. 6.22. They are also distinguished by their personal names, Dan. 8.16 and 9.21 and 10.13; Luke 1.19. Michael, Jude 9. Rev. 12.7; 1 Thess. 4.16: *with the voice of an archangel.* Josh. 6.2. See more on the subject of angels in chapter 9, below. Those who tried to say more about the nature of angels earned the apostle's rebuke, Col. 2.18: *intruding into those things which he has not seen, rashly puffed up by his fleshly intelligence.*

THINGS VISIBLE are this visible world and whatever it contains, and above all the human race.

The creation of the world and of its individual parts is narrated in Gen. 1. It is described in Job 26.7 etc. and 38, and in various passages of the Psalms and Prophets: Ps. 33.6, 9 and 104 and 148.5; Prov. 8.26, etc.; Amos 4.13; 2 Pet. 3.5. But when God is about to make man he speaks like a person giving careful consideration to something, as if to imply that this is a still greater work; Gen. 1.26: *after this God said, let us make man in our image, after our own likeness.* So it was not only the body but also the soul which he made at that time, for it is in our souls that we are most like God. I say this in case anyone should think that souls, which God created at that time, really existed beforehand. Some people have imagined this, but they are refuted by Gen. 2.7: *God formed man out of the dust of the earth, and breathed the breath of life into his nostrils. Thus man became a living soul;* Job 32.8: *truly this spirit is in man, and the breath of the Almighty makes them intelligent beings.* He did not merely breathe that spirit into man, but shaped it in each individual as a fundamental attribute, and separated its various faculties, making it beautiful and orderly, Zech. 12.1: *forming the spirit of man within him.*

We may, however, be absolutely sure, from other scriptural passages, that when God breathed that breath of life into man, he did not make him a sharer in anything divine, any part of the divine essence, as it were. He imparted to him only something human which was proportionate to divine virtue. For he breathed the breath of life into other living things besides man, as we can see from Ps. 104.29, 30: *you take back their spirit, they die: when you send your spirit out, they are re-created.* We learn, then, that all living creatures receive their life from the same source of life and spirit; and that when God takes back that spirit or breath of life, they die. Eccl. 3.19: *they all have the same spirit.* In Holy Scripture that word *spirit* means nothing but the breath of life, which we breathe; or the vital or sensitive or rational faculty, or some action or affection belonging to them.

When man had been created in this way, it is said, finally: *thus man became a living soul.* Unless we prefer to be instructed about the nature of the soul by heathen authors, we must interpret this as meaning that man is a living being, intrinsically and properly one and individual. He is not double or separable: not, as is commonly thought, produced from and composed of two different and distinct elements, soul and body. On the contrary, the whole man is the soul, and the soul the man: a body, in other words, or individual substance, animated, sensitive, and rational. The breath of life mentioned in Genesis was not a part of the divine essence, nor was it the soul, but a kind of air or breath of divine virtue, fit for the maintenance of life and reason and infused into the organic body. For man himself, the whole man, I say, when finally created, is specifically referred to as *a living soul.* Hence the word soul is interpreted by the apostle, 1 Cor. 15.45, as meaning *animal.* And all properties of the body are attributed to the soul as well: touch, Lev. 5.2: *when the soul has touched any unclean thing,* and elsewhere: the ability to eat, 7.18: *the soul which eats of it,* 7.20: *the soul which eats the flesh,* and frequently elsewhere: hunger, Prov. 13.25 and 27.7: thirst, Prov. 25.25: *as cool waters to a weary soul;* Isa. 29.8: apprehensibility, 1 Sam. 24.11: *although you harass my soul in order to capture it;* Ps. 7.6: *let him pursue my soul and capture it.*

But in a context where "body" means merely physical trunk, "soul" may mean either the spirit or its secondary faculties, such as the vital or sensitive faculty. So, to avoid confusion, "soul" is as frequently distinguished from "spirit" as it is from "body": for example Luke 1.46, 47; 1 Thess. 5.23: *the whole spirit, soul and body;* Heb. 4.12: *to the division of soul and spirit.* The idea that the spirit of man is separate from his body, so that it may exist somewhere in isolation, complete and intelligent, is nowhere to be found in scripture, and is plainly at odds with nature and reason, as I will demonstrate more fully below. For it is said of every kind of animal in Gen. 1.30: *in them is a living soul,* and 7.22: *of all that was on the dry land, everything which had in its nostrils the breath of the spirit of life, died.* But no one believes that beasts have therefore souls which enjoy some kind of separate existence.

On the seventh day God ceased to create, and completed the entire work of creation, Gen. 2.2, 3.

So it would seem that the human soul is generated by the parents in the course of nature, and not created daily by the immediate act of God.[123] Tertullian and Apollinarius saw this as the more probable theory, and it seemed so, too, to Augustine and the whole western church in the time of Jerome, as he himself testifies, Tom. 2, Epist. 82, and Gregory of Nyssa in his treatise on the soul. If God still created every day as many souls as man's frequently unlawful passion creates bodies in every part of the world, then he would have left himself a huge and, in a way, a servile task, even after that sixth day of creation—a task which would still remain to be performed, and from which he would not be able to rest even one day in seven. But in fact the force of the divine blessing, that each creature should reproduce in its own likeness, is as fully applicable to man as it is to all other animals; Gen. 1.21, 28. So God made the mother of all things living out of a simple rib, without having to breathe the breath of life a second time, Gen. 2.22; and Adam himself begot his son in his own image and likeness, Gen. 5.3. 1 Cor. 15.49: *as we have borne the image of the earthly,* and this means not only in the body but in the soul, just as it was chiefly with reference

123. The belief that the individual soul is generated by the parents along with the body is called "traducianism." The more standard view (creationism) was that God himself creates each individual soul and infuses it into the body during gestation.

to his soul that Adam was made in God's image. So Gen. 46.26: *all the souls which came out of Jacob's loins;* Heb. 7.10: *Levi was in Abraham's loins.* Hence in scripture an offspring is called "seed," and Christ is said to be *the seed of the woman. I will be your God and the God of your seed,* Gen. 17.7. 1 Cor. 15.44: *it is sown an animal body* and 15.46: *the spiritual is not first but the animal.*

Rational arguments can also be adduced. A man who is born, or formed and conceived in sin (and we all are, not only David, Ps. 51.5), must, if he is able to receive his soul immediately from God, receive it from God in a sinful state. For what do "to be born" and "to be conceived" mean, except to receive soul with body? But if we receive the soul straight from God, it must be a pure soul: for who would dare to call it impure? And if it is pure, in what way are we "conceived in sin" when we receive a pure soul which might well sanctify our impure bodies? How can a pure soul deserve to be charged with bodily sins? But, my opponents insist, God does not create impure souls but only souls which, from the viewpoint of original righteousness, are weakened and impaired. My answer is that to create pure souls which lack original righteousness, and then to put them into contaminated and vicious bodies, to surrender them to the body as to an enemy, imprisoned, innocent and unarmed, with blinded intellect and with will enchained, quite deprived, in other words, of the strength which is needed to resist the body's vicious tendencies—to do all this would argue injustice just as much as to have created them impure would argue impurity. It would be equally unjust to have created the first man, Adam, with his original righteousness weakened and impaired.

Again, if sin is transmitted from the parents to the child in the act of generation, then the πρῶτον δεκτικόν or original subject of sin, namely the rational soul, must also be propagated by the parents.[124] For no one will deny that all sin proceeds in the first instance from the soul. Lastly, by what sort of law could we make a soul answerable for a crime which Adam committed, when that soul was never in Adam and never came from him? Add to this Aristotle's argument, which I think a very strong one indeed, that if the soul is wholly contained in all the body and wholly in any given part of that body, how can the human seed, that intimate and most noble part of the body, be imagined destitute and devoid of the soul of the parents, or at least of the father, when communicated to the son in the act of generation? Nearly everyone agrees that all form—and the human soul is a kind of form—is produced by the power of matter.[125]

124. Cp. *Art of Logic* (Yale 8:242): "A subject has its various modes.... [It] can be divided into *receiving* subject, which the Greeks call δεκτικόν, and *appropriating* subject, which is commonly called *object* because in it the adjuncts are appropriated ...; the subject receiving its attributes into itself either sustains and as it were supports them, so that they are called *implanted* or *inhering*, or it contains them."

125. The Latin phrase is *"ex potentia materiae."* Cp. *Art of Logic* (Yale 8:230): "*Matter is the cause out of which a thing is.* ... We think of matter as common to all beings and non-beings.... Of whatever sort the things themselves may be, such, too, should be their matter." Also, *PL* 5.472–74: "one first matter all,/Endued with various forms, various degrees/Of substance, and in things that live, of life." On Milton's understanding of the power of matter, see Hunter 1952.

I suppose that it was arguments of this kind which brought Augustine to the point where he admitted he had not been able to discover by reading, praying or reasoning how the doctrine of original sin could be reconciled with that of the creation of souls: Epist. 28 *ad Hieron.* and 157 *ad Optat.* The passages which are usually cited, Eccl. 12.7, Isa. 57.20, Zech. 12.1, certainly indicate the nobility of the soul's origin, in that it was breathed from the mouth of God. However they no more prove an immediate and separate creation for each soul, than the following texts prove that each body is directly molded by God in the womb: Job 10.8–10: *your hands have made me; you have poured me like milk;* Ps. 33.15 [. . .]; Job 31.15 [. . .]; Isa. 44.24 [. . .]; Acts 17.26 [. . .]. But it does not follow from these passages that natural causes have not in each case made their usual contribution towards the propagation of the body. Nor does the fact that the soul, on account of its origin, returns again at death to elements different from those of the body, prove that it is not handed on from father to son.

As for that passage in Heb. 12.9 where *fathers of the flesh* are contrasted with *the father of spirits,* my answer to that is that it should be taken in a theological sense, not in a physical sense as if the father of the body were opposed to the father of the soul. For *flesh* does not signify here or anywhere else, as far as I know, the body without the soul; and *the father of spirits* does not refer to the father of the soul, who is concerned in the act of generation. On the contrary, *father of flesh* means here nothing more nor less than the earthly, natural father who begets in sin; and *the father of spirits* means either the heavenly Father, who once created all spirits, angels and men alike, or the spiritual father who, according to John 3.6, regenerates the faithful: *that which is born from flesh is flesh: that born from spirit, spirit.* The argument of the passage in Hebrews runs more smoothly, moreover, if it is understood from the viewpoint of castigation, not generation. For the passage does not tell who generated us or what part of us he generated, but who may more usefully chastise and educate us. The apostle might well have used the same argument to persuade his readers to put up with his censure, since he was their spiritual father. As a matter of fact God is as truly Father of the flesh as he is of the spirits of the flesh, Num. 16.22: but that is not the point at issue here, and conclusions squeezed out from a passage of scripture which really deals with a quite different subject are extremely untrustworthy.

As for the soul of Christ, it is enough to say that its generation was supernatural, so it cannot be used as an argument in this controversy. But even he is called *the seed of the woman, the seed of David from the fleshly point of view,* which means, unquestionably, from the point of view of his human nature.

Since man was formed in the image of God, he must have been endowed with natural wisdom, holiness and righteousness: Gen. 1.27, 31 and 2.25; Eccl. 7.29; Eph. 4.24; Col. 3.10; 2 Cor. 3.18. Moreover he could not have given names to the animals in that extempore way, without very great intelligence: Gen. 2.20. I do not see why anyone should make the human soul into an anomaly. For, as I have shown above, God breathed the breath of life into other living things besides man, and when he had breathed it, he mixed it with matter in a very fundamental way, so that the human form, like all other forms, should be propagated and produced as a result of that power which God had implanted in matter.

CHAPTER 8

OF GOD'S PROVIDENCE OR HIS UNIVERSAL GOVERNMENT OF THINGS

The last kind of external divine efficiency is the GOVERNMENT OF THE UNIVERSE.

This is either GENERAL or SPECIAL.

GENERAL GOVERNMENT is that by which GOD THE FATHER VIEWS AND PRESERVES ALL CREATED THINGS AND GOVERNS THEM WITH SUPREME WISDOM AND HOLINESS, ACCORDING TO THE CONDITIONS OF HIS DECREE.

[. . .][126]

ACCORDING TO THE CONDITIONS OF HIS DECREE. We must add this qualification because God has not preserved angels or men or anything else absolutely, but only so far as the condition of his decree extends. For ever since man fell of his own free will God has preserved him and all other things with him only in the sense that he has continued their existence, not their original perfection.

[. . .][127]

ALL THINGS. Gen. 8.1: *God remembered Noah, and all beasts and all cattle,* and 9.9, 10, 12, 15 [. . .]; Prov. 15.3: *Jehovah's eyes are in every place watching the evil and the good.*

Even the smallest things: Job 34.21: *for his eyes are turned towards each man's ways, and he counts all his steps;* Ps. 104.21 [. . .], and 147.9 [. . .]; Matt. 6.26 and 10.29, 30: *a sparrow does not fall to the ground without your Father. The hairs of your head are numbered.*

But God does not consider all things worthy of equal care and providence: 1 Cor. 9.9: *is God concerned about oxen?*—as much, that is, as he is about men? Zech. 2.8: *he who touches you touches the pupil of his own eye;* 1 Tim. 4.10: *savior of all, especially of believers.*

Natural things. Ex. 3.21: *I will make this people pleasing in the sight of the Egyptians*—that is, by altering their natural affections. Jer. 51.16 [. . .]; Amos 5.8:

126. In the deleted passage Milton cites Scripture to elaborate term by term GOD THE FATHER VIEWS AND PRESERVES from his definition of GENERAL GOVERNMENT.

127. In the deleted passage Milton cites Scripture to elaborate GOVERNS THEM WITH SUPREME WISDOM AND HOLINESS.

calling together the waters of the sea and pouring them out on the face of the earth; Jehovah by name.

And supernatural as well. Lev. 25.20, 21 [. . .]; Deut. 8.3, 4: *he fed you with manna. . .your clothing has not worn out and ceased to be a covering for you, and your foot has not swollen these forty years,* similarly 29.5. 1 Kings 17.4 [. . .], and 17.14 [. . .].

Contingencies or chance happenings. Ex. 21.13: *if God delivers him to his hand;* Prov. 16.33: *the arrangement of the lot comes from Jehovah.* Those passages of scripture which do not scruple to use the words "fortune" or "chance," imply nothing derogatory to divine providence by such expressions, but merely rule out the possibility of any human causation.[128] Eccl. 9.11: *but time and chance happen to them all;* Luke 10.31 [. . .].

And voluntary actions. 2 Chron. 10.15: *so when the king did not listen to the people, for the cause came from God;* Prov. 16.9: *man's mind thinks out his own way, but Jehovah lays down his path,* and 20.24 [. . .]; and 21.1 [. . .]; Jer. 10.23 [. . .]. But the freedom of the will always remains uninfringed, otherwise we shall have to deprive man of freedom not only in any good but also in any indifferent or evil act.

Lastly, evil occurrences just as much as good ones. Ex. 21.13: *if God delivers him to his hand;* Isa. 45.7: *making peace and creating evil*—that is, what afterwards became and is now evil, for whatever God created was originally good, as he himself testifies, Gen. 1; Matt. 18.7: *woe to the world and its offences; for it must be that offences shall come: nevertheless, woe to that man;* 1 Cor. 11.19 [. . .].

But God either merely allows evil to happen, by not impeding natural causes and free agents, as in Acts 2.23 [. . .] and 14.16: *he allowed all nations to go their own ways;* and 1 Pet. 3.17: *if he wishes it, that though you act righteously you are afflicted with evils,* and 4.19: *who suffer according to the will of God*—or else he causes evil by administering chastisement, and this is called the evil of punishment. 2 Sam. 12.11: *I shall in justice bring evil upon you, that is, punishment, out of your own house.* Prov. 16.4: *Jehovah has created all things for himself, yes, even the wicked for the day of evil,* that is, the man who later became wicked, by his own fault; as I have already said in connection with Isa. 45.7. Isa. 54.16: *I have created the murderer to destroy;* Lam. 3.38, 39 [. . .]; Amos 3.6 [. . .].

For God, who is supremely good, cannot be the source of wickedness or of the evil of crime: on the contrary, he created good out of man's wickedness; Gen. 45.5: *God sent me before you to provide sustenance,* and 50.20: *you had thought evil, but God thought to turn it to good.*

I am writing not for those who are wholly ignorant of Christian doctrine, but for those who are already fairly well informed. So I may be permitted, while I am on the subject of God's general providence, to anticipate a later stage in my argument and say something about sin, though I have not yet reached the place where I deal with that subject. Even in sin, then, we see God's providence at

128. *Art of Logic* (Yale 8:229): "For fortune surely is to be placed in heaven, but its name should be changed and it should be called 'divine providence.' "

work, not only in permitting it or withdrawing his grace, but often in inciting sinners to commit sin, hardening their hearts and blinding them.

In inciting: Ex. 9.16: *I have made you oppose me;* Judges 9.23: *God sent an evil spirit between Abimelech and the men of Shechem;* 2 Sam. 12.11, 12: *I shall raise up evil against you; and I will hand over your wives to your neighbor; I shall do this thing,* and 16.10 [. . .], and 24.1 [. . .]. Compare 1 Chron. 21.1. 1 Kings 22.20 [. . .]; Ps. 105.25 [. . .]; Ezek. 14.9 [. . .].

Hardening their hearts. Ex. 4.21: *I will make his heart stubborn,* similarly 7.6. Deut. 2.30 [. . .]; Josh. 11.20 [. . .]; John 12.39, 40: *they were unable to believe, because Esaias said again, he has hardened their hearts;* Rom. 9.18: *he hardens whom he wishes.*

Blinding them. Deut. 28.28: *Jehovah will strike you with madness and blindness and numbness of heart;* 1 Sam. 16.14 [. . .]; 1 Kings 22.22 [. . .]; Isa. 8.14: *he will be a stumbling block and a rock for them to trip over; a snare and a noose,* and 19.14 [. . .], and 29.10 [. . .]; Matt. 13.13: *I speak to them in parables, because seeing they do not see;* John 12.40: *he has blinded their eyes,* compared with Isa. 6.9. Rom. 1.28: *God gave them up to a mind devoid of all judgment;* 2 Thess. 2.11: *God will send them a powerful delusion, so that they believe a lie.*

Although in these quotations and in many others from both Testaments God openly confesses that it is he who incites the sinner, hardens his heart, blinds him and drives him into error, it must not be concluded that he is the originator even of the very smallest sin, for he is supremely holy. Hos. 14.9: *the ways of Jehovah are straight, and the just shall walk in them; but transgressors shall kick against them;* Ps. 5.5, 6, 7 [. . .]; Rom. 7.8 [. . .]; James 1.13, 14: *let no man say when he is tempted, I am tempted by God: for God cannot be tempted with evil, nor does he tempt anyone; but every man is tempted when he is drawn on and enticed by his own lust,* and 4.1: *where do the wars and fighting among you come from? Do they not come from here, here from your lusts which make war in your members?;* 1 John 2.16 [. . .]. For God does not drive the human heart to sinfulness and deceit when it is innocent and pure and shrinks from sin. But when it has conceived sin, when it is heavy with it, and already giving birth to it, then God as the supreme arbiter of all things turns and points it in this or that direction or towards this or that object. Ps. 94.23: *he turns their own wickedness against them, and destroys them with their own viciousness; Jehovah destroys them*—that is, by his punishment. Neither does God make an evil will out of a good one, but he directs a will which is already evil so that it may produce out of its own wickedness either good for others or punishment for itself, though it does so unknowingly, intending something quite different: Prov. 16.9: *man's mind thinks out his own way, but Jehovah lays down his path.* So when, in Ezek. 21.26, 27, the King of Babylon was in doubt whether to attack the Ammonites or the Jews, God controlled the omens, so that the King chose to set out for Jerusalem. Or, to use the common simile, as a rider who spurs on a lame horse in a chosen direction is the cause of the horse's increased speed but not of its lameness, so God, who is the supreme governor of the whole universe, may urge on a criminal although he is in no sense the cause of his crime. I shall say more about this simile later. Let me give an example: God saw that as a result of his power King David's spirit was so haughty and puffed up that even without anyone inciting him he was on the point of doing something that would unmistakably reveal his pride. This being so, God incited him to number the people. He did not incite him to become vainglorious and swollen with pride, but only to show in this particular way rather than any other that haughtiness of spirit which, though hidden, was on the point of breaking out. So God was the instigator of the deed itself, but David alone was responsible for all the wickedness and pride which it involved. The sinner, then, is nearly always evil or unjust in his aims, but God always produces something good and just out of these and creates, as it were, light out of darkness.[129] To this end he explores a man's innermost thoughts. In other words, he makes a man see clearly the evil which lies hidden in his own heart, so that he may reform or become thoroughly inexcusable in the eyes of the world; or alternatively, so that both the malefactor and his victim may pay the penalty for some previous offence. We should, however, be wary of the common saying, that God punishes sins with sins. He does not do this by forcing or helping anyone to sin, but by taking away his usual light-giving grace and the power to resist sin. There is, to be sure, a proverb which says, he who prevents not when he can, commands.[130] Men are bound by this principle as a moral duty, but not God. God says, speaking like a man, that he incites, when really he only omits to prevent, and this does not mean that he commands, for he is not bound by any moral duty to prevent. Ps. 81.12, 13: *they did not hear me or obey me, so I sent them off to follow their own devices,* and so we find in Rom. 1.24: *because of this he has given them up to filthy lusts,* in other words he left them to be driven by and to follow their own desires. For strictly speaking God does not either incite or hand over someone if he leaves him entirely to himself, that is, to his own desires and devices and to the ceaseless promptings of Satan. It is in the same sense that the Church is said to hand over to Satan a recalcitrant member when really it only excludes him from its communion. As for the business of the numbering of the people by David, it can be explained in a single word, for it is not God but Satan who is said to have incited him, 2 Sam. 24.1, 1 Chron. 21.1. A similar explanation is applicable to that passage in 2 Sam. 12.11, 12: *behold I shall raise up evil against you out of your own house,* the evil, that is, of punishment, and *I will take your wives and hand them over to your neighbor,* that is, I will leave them to your son, for him to debauch, on the advice of Achitophel—for this is what *to hand over* means, as I have just shown. That popular simile of the lame horse is itself a bit lame, because the sinner, unlike the horse, is not simply incited to act, if in fact he is incited at all, but to act badly: in other words, because he is lame he is incited to limp. In both passages

129. Cp. *PL* 1.211–18: "the will/And high permission of all-ruling Heaven/Left him at large to his own dark designs,/That with reiterated crimes he might/Heap on himself damnation, while he sought/Evil to others, and enraged might see/How all his malice served but to bring forth/Infinite goodness, grace and mercy."

130. Cp. *Tetrachordon* (Yale 2:655): "Where else are all our grave and faithful sayings, that he whose office is to forbid and forbids not, bids, exhorts, encourages."

cited above God had determined to punish publicly David's secret adultery. He saw Absalom, ready to dash into any kind of wickedness: he saw Achitophel's evil counsels. All he did was to direct their minds, which were already ripe for any atrocity, so that when the opportunity presented itself they should commit one crime rather than another. This is in keeping with the text quoted above, Prov. 16.9: *man's mind thinks out his own way, but Jehovah lays down his path.* For by offering an opportunity for sin you do not make a sinner, but only reveal one. The fact that God gives a good outcome to every evil deed, contrary to the intentions of the sinner, and overcomes evil with good, is well enough illustrated by the example of the selling of Joseph by his brothers: Gen. 45.8, quoted above.[131] It is the same with Christ's crucifixion. Pilate was anxious not to lose Caesar's favor: the Jews wanted to satisfy their hatred and their thirst for vengeance. But God *whose power and counsel had determined everything that was to be done,* Acts 4.28, redeemed mankind through their cruelty and violence, Rom. 11.11: *through their offence salvation has come to the Gentiles;* 1 Cor. 11.19 [. . .]; Phil. 1.12,14 [. . .].

In the same way, just as when God incites to sin he is nevertheless not the cause of anyone's sinning, so when he hardens the heart of a sinner or blinds him, he is not the cause of sin. For he does not do this by infusing wickedness into the man. The means he uses are just and kindly, and ought rather to soften the hearts of sinners than harden them.[132] They are: first, his long-suffering; Rom. 2.4, 5: *do you despise the wealth of his tolerance, and in your hardness lay up anger for yourself?;* second, his insistence upon his own good and just commandments in opposition to the stubbornness of the wicked. This hardens them in the same way as an anvil or steel is said to be hardened by hammering. Thus Pharaoh became more obstinate and more furious when God's commands ran counter to his will; Ex. 5.2 [. . .] and 7.2, 3 [. . .]; Isa. 6.10: *make the heart of that people grow fat,* that is, by drumming commandments into them, as in 28.13: *but the word of Jehovah gave them command after command, . . . so that they should go on and fall headlong. . . .* Third, correction or punishment, Ezek. 3.20: *but if a righteous man turns away from his righteousness and commits a crime, and I place a stumbling block before him,* etc.; Jer. 5.3: *you strike them but they are not hurt, they have made their faces harder than rock.* Hardening of the heart, then, is usually the last punishment inflicted on inveterate wickedness and unbelief in this life; Sam. 2.25: *they did not listen, because Jehovah wished to kill them.* God often hardens the hearts of powerful and arrogant world-leaders to a remarkable degree so that through their pride and arrogance his glory may be more clearly seen by the nations: Ex. 9.16: *to show my power in you,* and 10.2, also, compared with Rom. 9.17: *I have raised you up for this very purpose, to show my power in you.* Ex. 14.4 [. . .], similarly 14.17. But the hardening of the wicked is not solely God's doing. They themselves do a great deal to

131. This verse is *not* quoted previously in the treatise; Milton's claim to the contrary may indicate revision.

132. Cp. *PL* 6.789–91: "But to convince the proud what signs avail,/Or wonders move th' obdurate to relent?/They hardened more by what might most reclaim."

bring about God's purpose, though not in the least intending to please him. Thus Pharaoh is said to harden his own heart; Ex. 9.34: *when he saw that the rain had ceased* [. . .] *he continued to sin: for he hardened his heart, he and his servants;* 2 Chron. 36.13 [. . .]; Ps. 95.8 [. . .]; Zech. 7.12 [. . .].

The same applies to blinding: Deut. 28.15 compared with 28: *but it will happen if you do not listen to the voice of Jehovah your God, Jehovah will afflict you with madness and blindness and numbness of heart,* that is, by taking away the light of his grace, and by confusing the faculties of the mind or making them dull, or simply by allowing Satan to do this: Rom. 1.28: *just as it did not seem fit to them to acknowledge God, so God gave them up to emptiness of mind;* 2 Cor. 4.4 [. . .]; Eph. 2.2 [. . .]; 2 Thess. 2.10, 11 [. . .]. Lastly, God is said to entice men, but not to sin. He entices them either as punishment, or for the accomplishment of some good end. Ezek. 14.9–11: *but when the prophet himself is enticed into saying something, it will be I, Jehovah, who enticed that prophet: and I will stretch out my hand against* etc. *so they will bear the punishment of their wrongdoing* etc. *so that the house of Israel may not go astray from following me any more.* But God enticed a prophet who was already corrupt and avaricious, and easily misled him into giving the answers which the people wanted. Then he justly destroyed both the questioner, because he had asked his question with an evil intention, and the prophet who had been questioned, because he had answered falsely, without command from God. God did this so that in future others would be afraid to commit the same sin.

To this system of providence must be referred what is called Temptation, by which God either tempts a man or allows him to be tempted by the devil or his agents.

Temptation is either good or evil.

It is evil when God, by the methods outlined above, either withdraws his grace from a man or throws opportunities for sin in his path or hardens his heart or blinds him. This is generally an evil temptation from the point of view of the man tempted, but on God's part it is absolutely just, for the reasons I have given above, as for example when it is used to unmask hypocrisy. For God tempts no one in the sense of enticing or persuading him to sin (see James 1.13 above), although he quite justly allows some men to be tempted by the devil in this way. We are taught to pray against temptations of this kind in the Lord's prayer: Matt. 6.13: *do not lead us into temptation, but deliver us from that evil.*

Good temptations are those which God uses to tempt even righteous men, in order to prove them. He does this not for his own sake—as if he did not know what sort of men they would turn out to be—but either to exercise or demonstrate their faith or patience, as in the case of Abraham and Job, or to lessen their self-confidence and prove them guilty of weakness, so that they may become wiser, and others may be instructed. Thus in 2 Chron. 32.31: *God left* Hezekiah, temporarily or partially, *so that by tempting him he might find out whatever was in his mind.* In the same way he tempted the Israelites in the desert, Deut. 8.2, etc.: *to afflict you, by tempting you to find out what was in your mind, whether you would keep his commandments or not . . . ;* Ps. 66.10, etc. [. . .]; 1 Pet. 1.7 [. . .], and 4.12 [. . .]; Rev. 2.10: *behold, it will happen that the devil will throw some of you into prison, so that you may be tried.*

Good temptation, then, is rather to be desired. Ps. 26.2: *prove me Jehovah and try me, make trial of my reins and my heart;* James 1.2, 3: *esteem it a great joy, my brothers, whenever you fall into various temptations, knowing that the trial of your faith produces patience.*

And God promises a happy outcome. 1 Cor. 10.13: *no temptation has entrapped you, except what is common to man: but God is faithful and will not allow you to be tempted beyond your powers. Along with the temptation he will supply an escape, so that you will be able to bear it;* James 1.12: *blessed is the man who endures temptation; for when he is found righteous, he will receive the crown of life.*

But even the faithful are sometimes insufficiently aware of all these methods of divine providence, until they examine the subject more deeply and become better informed about the word of God. Ps. 73.2, 17: *my feet had almost gone astray, until I went into the sanctuary of God: then I understood their end;* Dan. 12.10 [. . .]. Since I said in my prefatory definition that the providence of God cares for and governs all created things, it may usefully be asked here whether God has laid down any definite limit to human life, beyond which no one can go. Holy Scripture shows very clearly that this is the case; Job 14.5: *since his days are cut short, the number of his months is in your sight: you have set him limits, which he may not overstep;* Ps. 90.10: *in the days of our years there are seventy years, or (if we are very strong) eighty years, yet the best of them is labor and sorrow; it is quickly cut off and away we fly.* From these and similar passages, and especially from the early history of the world, it is clear that God, at any rate after the fall of man, laid down a certain limit for human life. It is also clear that in the course of the years down to the time of David this limit gradually became smaller. Whether the limit is one and the same for all mortals, or whether it is fixed at a different point for each individual, it is certain that no man can prolong it or exceed it. That is in the power of God alone, as is proved by his promise of long life to his people, and by the fifteen years he added to the life of the dying Hezekiah.[133] As for cutting short or anticipating this term of life, not only does God do it as a reward or punishment, but also any mortal may do it by his guiltiness or vice, and this often happens. Prov. 10.27: *reverence for Jehovah adds to one's days, but the years of the wicked will be cut short;* Ex. 20.12: *honor your father,* etc. *that your days may be prolonged,* etc., and there are many other passages in the Old Testament to the same effect. Ps. 55.24: *bloody and deceitful men shall not live out half their days,* that is, the sum total of days which, by virtue of their strong constitutions, they might otherwise have attained.[134] Suicides, and those who hasten their deaths by a depraved way of life, must also be included in this category.

God's providence is either ordinary or extraordinary.

133. Cp. *PL* 11.554: "Live well, how long or short permit to Heav'n."
134. Cp. *PL* 11.527–34.

God's ordinary providence is that by which he maintains and preserves that constant and ordered system of causes which was established by him in the beginning.

This is commonly and indeed too frequently called Nature; for nature cannot mean anything except the wonderful power and efficacy of the divine voice which went forth in the beginning, and which all things have obeyed ever since as a perpetual command. Job 38.12: *have you ever given rules to the morning?,* and 38.33: *or do you know about the laws of the sky?;* Ps. 148.8 [. . .]; Isa. 45.12 [. . .]; Jer. 31.36 [. . .], and 33.20 [. . .].

The extraordinary providence of God is that by which he produces some effect outside the normal order of nature or gives to some chosen person the power of producing this effect. This is what we call a miracle.

Thus God alone is the primary author of miracles, as he alone is able to invert the order of nature which he has appointed: Ps. 72.18: *who alone works miracles;* John 10.21 [. . .]; 2 Thess. 2.9 [. . .].

The purpose of miracles is to demonstrate divine power and strengthen our faith: Ex. 6.6, 7: *with great judgments . . . , thus you will find out,* and 8.22: *I will make an exception of the land of Goshen . . . so that you shall know that I am Jehovah;* 1 Kings 17.24 [. . .]; Mark 16.20 [. . .]; Heb. 2.4: *it was confirmed for us, since God bore witness to them with signs and with omens and with various manifestations of power and with gifts of the Holy Ghost, according to his own will.*[135]

Another purpose of miracles is to ensure a weightier condemnation for those who do not believe. Matt. 11.21 [. . .]; John 15.24: *if I had not performed among them works such as no one else performed, they would not be sinful. But now . . . .*

CHAPTER 9

OF THE SPECIAL GOVERNMENT OF ANGELS

We have been discussing GENERAL PROVIDENCE. SPECIAL PROVIDENCE is concerned particularly with angels and men, as they are far superior to all other creatures.

There are, however, both good and evil angels. Luke 9.26 and 8.2, for it is well known that a great many of them revolted from God of their own free will before the fall of man: John 8.44: *he did not stand firm in the truth, for there is no truth in him, he speaks like what he is, the father of lies;* 2 Pet. 2.4: *he did not spare the angels who sinned;* Jude 6: *the angels who did not maintain their original position;* 1 John 3.8 [. . .]; Ps. 106.37 [. . .].

It seems to some people that the good angels now maintain their position not so much by their own strength as by the grace of God. 1 Tim. 5.21: *of the elect angels,* that is, of those who did not revolt; Eph. 1.10: *that he might collect together all*

135. Cp. *PL* 12.497–504.

things under a single head in Christ, the things in heaven as well; Col. 1 20 [. . .]; Job 4.18 [. . .], similarly 15.

Hence the angels take great pleasure in examining the mystery of man's salvation: 1 Pet. 1.12: *things which the angels desire to look into;* Eph.3.10 [. . .]; Luke 2.13, 14: *a multitude of the armies praising God,* that is, on account of the birth of Christ; and 15.10: *there is joy in the presence of the angels over one man who repents.*

As a result, also, they adore Christ: Heb. 1.6: *let all the angels of God adore him;* Matt. 4.11 [. . .]; Phil. 2.10: *that every knee shall bow, among the heavenly creatures . . . ;* 2 Thess. 1.7 [. . .]; 1 Pet. 3.22 [. . .]; Rev. 5.11, 12 [. . .]. It seems more reasonable, however, to suppose that the good angels stand by their own strength, no less than man did before his fall, and that they are called "elect" only in the sense that they are beloved or choice:[136] also that they desire to contemplate the mystery of our salvation simply out of love,[137] and not from any interest of their own, that they are not included in any question of reconciliation, and that they are reckoned as being under Christ because he is their head, not their Redeemer.[138] [. . .].

They are absolutely obedient[139] to God in all things: Gen. 28.12: *behold the angels of God ascending and descending on it;* Ps. 103.20: *doing his word;* Zech. 1.10 [. . .].

Their chief ministry concerns believers: Heb. 1.14: *they are all ministering spirits who are sent out to minister for the sake of the heirs of salvation;* Ps. 34.8 [. . .], and 91.11 [. . .]; Isa. 63.9 [. . .]; Matt. 18.10 [. . .], and 13.41 [. . .], and 24.31 [. . .]; Acts 12.15 [. . .]; 1 Cor. 11.10: *on account of the angels,* that is, as some suppose, the angels who guard over the meetings of the faithful. There are innumerable examples available besides these.

And seven of them particularly patrol the earth:[140] Zech. 4.10: *these seven are the eyes of Jehovah which go to and fro over the earth,* compared with Rev. 5.6: *who are those seven spirits of God sent forth into the whole earth,* see also 1.4 and 4.5.

It is probable, too, that angels are put in charge of nations, kingdoms and particular districts:[141] Dan. 4.13, 17: *this word is from the decree of the watchers,* and 12.1: *that prince who stands for your fellow-countrymen,* and 10.13 [. . .]; 2 Pet. 2.11 [. . .]; Gen. 3.24: *to guard the way to the tree of life.*

Sometimes they are ministers of divine vengeance,[142] sent from heaven to punish mortal sins. They destroy cities and peoples: Gen. 19.13; 2 Sam. 24.16;

136. Cp. *PL* 4.66–67: "Hadst thou the same free will and power to stand?/Thou hadst."

137. Cp. *PL* 8.224–26: "Nor less think we in Heav'n of thee on Earth/Than of our fellow servant, and inquire/Gladly into the ways of God with man"; 8:639–40: "I in thy persevering shall rejoice,/And all the blest."

138. Cp. *PL* 5.606: "your head I him appoint"; also 5.830–31: "under one head more near/United."

139. **absolutely obedient:** The Latin original reads *"obsequentissimi."*

140. Cp. *PL* 3.648–61.

141. Cp. *PR* 1.447–48: "his angels president/In every province"; also *PL* 4.561–63: "Gabriel, to thee thy course by lot hath giv'n/Charge and strict watch that to this happy place/No evil thing approach or enter in."

142. Cp. *PL* 1.170: "His ministers of vengeance."

1 Chron. 21.16: *David saw the angel of Jehovah threatening Jerusalem with a drawn sword.* They strike down whole armies with unexpected calamity: 2 Kings 19.35, and similar passages.

As a result they often appeared looking like soldiers: Gen. 32.1, 2: *God's battle-array;* Josh. 6.2: *leader of Jehovah's soldiery;* 2 Kings 6.17: *with horses and chariots of fire;* Ps. 68.18 [. . .]; Luke 2.13 [. . .].

They are also described in Isa. 6; Hos. 1.7; Matt. 28.2, 3; Rev. 10.1.

There seems to be a leader among the good angels, and he is often called Michael: Josh. 6.2: *I am the leader of Jehovah's soldiery;* Dan. 10.13: *Michael is the first of the chief princes,*[143] and 12.1: *the greatest prince;* Rev. 12.7, 8 [. . .].

A lot of people are of the opinion that Michael is Christ. But whereas Christ alone vanquished Satan and trod him underfoot, Michael is introduced as leader of the angels and Ἀντίπαλος (antagonist) of the prince of the devils: their respective forces were drawn up in battle array and separated after a fairly even fight,[144] Rev. 12.7, 8. And Jude says of Michael *when disputing about Moses' body he did not dare* [. . .], whereas it would be quite improper to say this about Christ, especially if he is God. See also 1 Thess. 4.16: *the Lord himself will descend with the voice of an archangel.* Finally, it would be very strange for an apostle of the Gospel to talk in such an obscure way, and to call Christ by another name, when reporting these odd and unheard-of things about him.

The good angels do not see into all God's thoughts, as the Papists pretend. They know by revelation only those things which God sees fit to show them, and they know other things by virtue of their very high intelligence, but there are many things of which they are ignorant.[145] For we find an angel full of curiosity and asking questions: Dan. 8.13: *how long is this vision?,* and 12.6: *how far off is its end?;* Matt. 24.36: *no one knows of that day, not even the angels;* Eph. 3.10 [. . .]; Rev. 5.3 [. . .].

Bad angels are kept for punishment: Matt. 8.29: *have you come here to torment us before the appointed time?;* 2 Pet. 2.4: *he thrust them down to hell and chained them in dark chains, to be kept for damnation;* Jude 6: [. . .]; 1 Cor. 6.3 [. . .]; Matt. 25.41 [. . .]; Rev. 20.10 [. . .].

But sometimes they are able to wander all over the earth, the air, and even heaven, to carry out God's judgments:[146] Job 1.7: *from going to and fro on the earth;* 1 Sam. 16.15: *the spirit of Jehovah had left Saul, and an evil spirit from Jehovah troubled him;* 1 Pet. 5.8: [. . .]; John 12.31: [. . .]; 2 Cor. 4.4 [. . .]; Matt. 12.43 [. . .]; Eph. 2.2 [. . .], and 6.12 [. . .]. They even come into the presence of God:[147] Job 1.6 and 2.1; 1

143. Cp. *PL* 6.44: "Go Michael of celestial armies prince."

144. Michael was traditionally represented as Satan's vanquisher. But the action of *PL* 6 is consistent with the idiosyncratic version of the War in Heaven presented here.

145. Cp. *PL* 3.681–85; 7.112–13; 11.67–69.

146. Cp. *PL* 1.209–13: "the Arch-Fiend lay/Chained on the burning lake, nor ever thence/Had ris'n or heaved his head, but that the will/And high permission of all-ruling Heav'n/Left him at large to his own dark designs." Also 2.1025; 7.233–37; and *PR* 1.362–77.

147. Cp. *PR* 1.366–67: "nor from the Heav'n of Heav'ns/Hath he excluded my resort sometimes."

Kings 22.21 [. . .]; Zech. 3.1: *he showed me Joshua standing in the presence of the angel of Jehovah, and Satan standing at his right hand to oppose him;* Luke 10.18 [. . .]; Rev. 12.12 [. . .].

But their proper place is hell, which they cannot leave without permission:[148] Luke 8.31: *they asked him not to command them to go away to hell;* Matt. 12.43: *seeking rest through dry places;* Mark 5.10 [. . .]; Rev. 20.3 [. . .]. They cannot do anything unless God commands them:[149] Job 1.12: *look, let them be in your power;* Matt. 8.31: *allow us to go away into this herd of swine;* Rev. 20.2: *he seized the dragon and bound him.*

Their knowledge is great, but it is a torment to them rather than a consolation; so that they utterly despair of their salvation:[150] Matt. 8.29: *what have we to do with you, Jesus? Have you come here to torment us before the appointed time?,* similarly Luke 4.34; James 2.19: *the devils believe and are horrified*—because they are kept for punishment, as I said before.

The devils have their prince too: Matt. 12.24: *Beelzebub prince of devils,* similarly Luke 11.15; Matt. 25.41: *for the devil and his angels;* Rev. 12.9: *that great dragon and his angels.*

They also keep their ranks: Col. 2.15: *having plundered principalities and powers;* Eph. 6.12: *against powers and principalities.*

Their chief is the author of all wickedness and hinders all good:[151] Job 1 and 2; Zech. 3.1: *Satan;* John 8.44: *the father of lies;* 1 Thess. 2.18 [. . .]; Acts 5.3 [. . .]; Rev. 20.3, 8 [. . .]; Eph. 2.2 [. . .].

As a result he has been given a number of titles, which suit his actions. He is frequently called *Satan,* that is, enemy or adversary, Job 1.6, 1 Chron. 21.1: also *the great dragon, the old serpent, the devil,* that is, the calumniator, Rev. 12.9 [. . .].

CHAPTER 10

OF THE SPECIAL GOVERNMENT OF MAN BEFORE THE FALL: DEALING ALSO WITH THE SABBATH AND MARRIAGE

The providence of God which governs man relates either to man's prelapsarian or to his fallen state.

The providence which relates to his prelapsarian state is that by which God placed man in the garden of Eden and supplied him with every good thing necessary for a happy life. And, so that there might be some way for man to show

148. Cp. *PR* 1:494–96: "Thy coming hither, though I know thy scope,/I bid not or forbid; do as thou find'st/Permission from above; thou canst not more."

149. Cp. *PR* 1.451–52: "thou with trembling fear,/Or like a fawning parasite obey'st."

150. Cp. *PR* 3.204–15.

151. Cp. *PL* 6.262: "Author of evil"; 2.380–82: "for whence,/But from the author of all ill could spring/So deep a malice"; 1.159–60: "To do aught good never will be our task,/But ever to do ill our sole delight."

his obedience, God ordered him to abstain only from the tree of the knowledge of good and evil, and threatened him with death if he disobeyed: Gen. 1.28: *subdue the earth and have dominion,* and 2.15, 16, 17: *he placed him in the garden. You may eat freely the fruit of every tree. On the day you eat the fruit of the tree of the knowledge of good and evil, you will die.*

Some people call this "the covenant of works," though it does not appear from any passage of scripture to have been either a covenant or of works.[152] Adam was not required to perform any works; he was merely forbidden to do one thing. It was necessary that one thing at least should be either forbidden or commanded, and above all something which was in itself neither good nor evil, so that man's obedience might in this way be made evident. For man was by nature good and holy, and was naturally disposed to do right, so it was certainly not necessary to bind him by the requirements of any covenant to something which he would do of his own accord. And he would not have shown obedience at all by performing good works, since he was in fact drawn to these by his own natural impulses, without being commanded. Besides a command, whether it comes from God or from a magistrate, should not be called a covenant just because rewards and punishments are attached: it is rather a declaration of power.

The tree of the knowledge of good and evil was not a sacrament, as is commonly thought, for sacraments are meant to be used, not abstained from; but it was a kind of pledge or memorial of obedience.[153]

It was called the tree of knowledge of good and evil because of what happened afterwards: for since it was tasted, not only do we know evil, but also we do not even know good except through evil.[154] For where does virtue shine, where is it usually exercised, if not in evil?

I do not know whether the tree of life ought to be called a sacrament, rather than a symbol of eternal life or even perhaps the food of eternal life: Gen. 3.22: *lest he eat and live for ever;* [155] Rev. 2.7: *to the victor I will give food from the tree of life.*

Man was made in the image of God, and the whole law of nature was so implanted and innate in him that he was in need of no command. It follows, then, that if he received any additional commands, whether about the tree of knowledge or about marriage, these had nothing to do with the law of nature, which is itself sufficient to teach whatever is in accord with right reason (i.e., whatever is intrinsically good). These commands, then, were simply a matter of what is called positive right. Positive right comes into play when God, or anyone else

152. According to Calvin (*Institutes* 2.9–11), salvation history may be understood as a series of covenants between God and humanity. In *"the covenant of works,"* God promises life in return for humanity's obedience and establishes death as the penalty for disobedience. In Milton's England, the Independent divine John Owen (1616–83) was a proponent of "Covenant Theology."

153. Cp. *PL* 3.94–95: "the sole command,/Sole pledge of his obedience"; 8.323–25: "the tree whose operation brings/Knowledge of good and ill, which I have set/The pledge of thy obedience and thy faith."

154. Cp. *Areop* (p. 939).

155. Cp. *PL* 11.93–96: "Lest therefore his now bolder hand/Reach also of the Tree of Life, and eat,/And live forever, dream at least to live/Forever"; see also 4.194–201.

invested with lawful power, commands or forbids things which, if he had not commanded or forbidden them, would in themselves have been neither good nor bad, and would therefore have put no one under any obligation.[156] As for the Sabbath, it is clear that God sanctified it as his own, in memory of the completion of his task, and dedicated it to rest;[157] Gen. 2.2, 3, compared with Ex. 31.17. But it is not known, because there is nothing about it in scripture, whether this was ever disclosed to Adam or whether any commandment about the observance of the Sabbath existed before the giving of the law on Mount Sinai, let alone before the fall of man. Probably Moses, who seems to have written the book of Genesis long after the giving of the law, inserted this sentence from the fourth commandment in what was, as it were, an opportune place. Thus he seized an opportunity of reminding the people about the reason, which was, so to speak, topical at this point in his narrative, but which God had really given many years later to show why he wanted the Sabbath to be observed by his people, with whom he had at long last made a solemn covenant. For an example of a similar insertion see Ex. 16.34, 35: *Moses said to Aaron, take a pot . . . So Aaron set it up . . .*—which, however, happened long afterwards. We read in Ex. 16 that, shortly before the giving of the law, it was commanded that the Sabbath should be observed in the wilderness; for God had said that he would rain manna on every day except the seventh, so that no one should go out to look for it on that day. Judging from a comparison of 16.5 with 16.22–30, it seems that this command was first given to the Israelites at that time, as a kind of groundwork for the law which was going to be promulgated more clearly a little later on, and that they were previously ignorant about the observation of the Sabbath. For the elders, who ought to have known the commandment about the Sabbath better than anyone else, wondered why the people had gathered twice as much manna on the sixth day, and asked Moses, who told them only then, as if it were something new, that tomorrow would be the Sabbath. So he writes, as if he had just narrated how the Sabbath first came to be observed, *thus the people rested on the seventh day,* 16.30.

More than one passage in the prophets seems to confirm that the Israelites had not even heard anything about the Sabbath before that time: Ezek. 20.10–12: *I led them away into the wilderness; where I gave them my statutes and made my laws known to them. Also I gave them my sabbaths, to be a sign between me and them, that they might know that I, Jehovah, sanctify them;* Neh. 9.13, 14 [. . .]. But see Book 2 Chapter 7 for more on the subject of the Sabbath.

Marriage also, if it was not commanded, was at any rate instituted, and consisted in the mutual love, delight, help and society of husband and wife, though

156. Cp. *PL* 9.651–54: "But of this tree we may not taste nor touch;/God so commanded, and left that command/Sole daughter of his voice; the rest, we live/Law to ourselves, our reason is our law."

157. Cp. *PL* 7.591–93: "and from work/Now resting, blessed and hallowed the sev'nth day,/As resting on that day from all his work."

with the husband having greater authority:[158] Gen. 2.18: *it is not good for the man to be alone; I will make him a help before his eyes, as it were;* 1 Cor. 11.7–9: *since the man is the image and glory of God, but the woman is the glory of her husband. For the man did not come from the woman, but the woman from the man: so the man was not given for the woman's sake but the woman for the man's.* The husband's authority became still greater after the fall:[159] Gen. 3.16: *your desire or your obedience will be towards your husband.* So in Hebrew the same word, בַּעַל, means both *husband* and *lord.* Thus Sarah is said, 1 Pet. 3.6, to have called her husband Abraham *lord.* 1 Tim. 2.12–14: *I do not allow a woman to teach or to usurp authority over a man; she should be silent. For Adam was made first, then Eve; and Adam was not deceived, but the woman was deceived and was the cause of the transgression.*

Marriage, then, is a very intimate relationship between man and woman instituted by God for the procreation of children or the help and solace of life. As a result it is written, Gen. 2.24: *so a man will leave his father and mother and cling to his wife, and they will be one flesh.* This is neither a law nor a commandment, but an effect or natural consequence of that very intimate relationship which would have existed between Adam and Eve in man's unfallen state. Nothing is being discussed in the passage except the origin of families. In my definition I have not said, as most people do, *between one man and one woman.* I have not done so, in order to avoid accusing the most holy patriarchs and pillars of our faith, Abraham, and others who had more than one wife, of constant fornication and adultery. Otherwise I should be forced to exclude from God's sanctuary as bastards all their most holy offspring, all the children of Israel, in fact, for whom the sanctuary itself was made. For it is written, Deut. 23.2: *a bastard shall not come into the congregation of Jehovah, even to his tenth generation.*

So either polygamy is a true form of marriage, or else all children born in it are bastards: and that means the whole race of Jacob, the twelve holy tribes chosen by God. But it would be absolutely absurd and even downright blasphemous to suggest this. Also it is very unjust, and a very dangerous precedent in religion to consider something a sin when it is not a sin. So I am of the opinion that it is not irrelevant but on the contrary absolutely vital to find out whether polygamy is lawful or not.

Those who deny its lawfulness try to prove their case from Gen. 2.24: *he will cling to his wife and they will be one flesh,* compared with Matt. 19.5: *those two will be one flesh. He will cling* they say *to his wife* not *to his wives;* and *those two* not *those several people.* Brilliant! Let me add also Ex. 20.17: *you shall not covet your neighbor's house nor his manservant nor his maidservant nor his ox nor his ass:* therefore no one has more than one house, manservant, maidservant, ox or ass! How ridiculous it would be to argue like this—it says *house* not *houses, servant* not *servants* and even

158. Cp. *PL* 4.635–37: "My author and disposer, what thou bidd'st/Unargued I obey; so God ordains,/God is thy Law, thou mine." See also 4.295–309, 440–43; 10.146–51; 11.632–34.

159. Cp. *PL* 10.195–96: "and to thy husband's will/Thine shall submit, he over thee shall rule"; also 11.290–91.

neighbor's not *neighbors'*—and not to realize that in nearly all the commandments the singular of the noun signifies not the number but the species of each thing mentioned. As for the fact that Matt. 19.5 says *those two* and not *those several people,* it must be understood that this passage deals only with one man and with the wife whom he wanted to divorce, and that it is in no way concerned with whether he had one wife or several. Then again, it must be understood that marriage is a kind of relationship and that there are only two sides to any one relationship. So that in the same way, if anyone has a number of sons, his paternal relationship towards them all will be various, but towards each one it will be single and complete in itself. Similarly, if anyone has several wives, his relationship towards each one will be no less complete, and the husband will be no less *one flesh* with each one of them, than if he had only one wife.[160] So it is correctly said of Abraham, with Sarah and with Hagar respectively, that *these two were one flesh.* And with good reason, for anyone who associates with prostitutes, however many they may be, is still said to be *one flesh* with each of them. 1 Cor. 6.16: *do you not know that he who couples with a prostitute is one body with her? For those two,* he says, *will be one flesh.* So this expression may be used about a husband, even though he has several wives, just as correctly as if he had only one; and may be understood in the same sense as if he had only one. It follows, then, that polygamy is neither forbidden nor opposed by this so-called commandment which, as I have shown above, is not really a commandment at all. Otherwise we must assume either that the Mosaic law contradicts this instruction, or else that though the relevant passage had been frequently studied by innumerable priests, Levites and prophets and by very holy men of all ranks who were most acceptable to God, nevertheless they were so wanting in reason that they were swept by a blind impulse to this passion for constant fornication. This is what we must assume if the effect of the instruction we are considering is to make polygamy an unlawful form of marriage.

The second text quoted to prove polygamy unlawful is Lev. 18.18: *you shall not take a woman to her sister, to make enemies of them and to uncover her nakedness, besides the other in her lifetime.* Here Junius translates *a woman to another woman,* instead of *a woman to her sister,* so that with this interpretation, which is plainly forced and inadmissible, he should have some grounds for proving polygamy unlawful. But in drawing up laws, as in writing definitions, it is necessary to use precise words and to interpret them properly, not in any metaphorical way. He claims, however, that these words are found elsewhere in the sense he gives them. I confess that they are, but in a context where there can be no ambiguity, as in Gen. 26.31: *they swore, each man to his brother,* that is, to the other man. For who would think of

160. *Art of Logic* (Yale 8:259): "Nor do I any more see why in one singular relative there cannot be a multiple relation to many things, provided that there be numerically only one relation between two things and that it be considered as many times as there are relatives; the relation of father certainly as many times as there are children; of child as there are parents, namely father and mother; of brother as there are brothers and sisters."

arguing from this that Isaac was Abimelich's brother? And who could fail to conclude that the Leviticus passage was clearly about not taking one sister in marriage after another, especially in a chapter where the verses which immediately precede this deal with the degrees of kinship to which marriage is forbidden? Moreover by taking one sister in marriage after another, *nakedness is uncovered,* which is what this passage warns against.[161] If it is another woman who is taken, not the sister of nor related to the first, then there is no need for this caution, because in this case no nakedness would be uncovered. Lastly, why is *in her lifetime* added? Because, though there could not be any doubt that it was permissible, after the death of one wife, to marry another who was not her sister nor related to her, there could be some doubt whether it was permissible to marry the first wife's sister. But, my opponent objects, marriage with a wife's sister is already forbidden by analogy in 18.16, so this prohibition is superfluous. I reply, first, that there is no analogy, for by marrying a brother's wife, the brother's nakedness is uncovered, but by marrying a wife's sister it is not a sister's nakedness but only that of a relation by marriage which is uncovered. Secondly, if nothing may be prohibited which has already been prohibited by analogy, why, after marriage with one's father has been forbidden, is marriage with one's mother forbidden as well? Why forbid marriage with one's mother's sister after forbidding it with one's father's sister? If such prohibitions are unnecessary it must be concluded that more than half the laws relating to incest are unnecessary. Moreover if polygamy were really forbidden by this passage, much stronger reasons ought to have been given—reasons affecting the institution itself, as was done in the establishment of the Sabbath—whereas the chief reason suggested here is the prevention of enmity.

The third passage which is adduced, Deut. 17.17, does not condemn polygamy either in a king or in anyone else, indeed it expressly allows it, while merely imposing a limit to it in the same way as it imposes a limit to the keeping of horses or the accumulation of wealth. This is clear from the verse cited and the previous one.

Except for the three passages, which are actually irrelevant, no trace of the censure of polygamy can be seen throughout the whole law. Nor, for that matter, can any be found even in all the writings of the prophets, although they interpreted the law very severely, and were constantly censuring the vices of the people. The one exception is a passage in Malachi, the last of the prophets, which some people think utterly destroys the case for polygamy. It would be a real *volte-face* and a long-delayed one at that if a thing which ought to have been prohibited many centuries before was prohibited at long last only after the

161. The critique of Junius's translation (see chapter 5, n. 90) is apt, but Milton's reading of the phrase "nakedness is uncovered" seems oddly figurative after his warning about metaphor. In modern translation (*Revised English Bible*), Lev. 18.18 states: "You must not take a woman who is your wife's sister to make her a rival wife, and to have intercourse with her during her sister's lifetime." The point of the prohibition, it seems, is not to warn against uncovering nakedness but, as Milton recognizes at the end of the paragraph, to prevent enmity between sisters.

Babylonian captivity. If it really had been a sin, how could it have escaped the censure of all the prophets who preceded Malachi? What we can be sure of is that if polygamy is not forbidden in the law then it is not forbidden here either, because Malachi did not write a new law. But let us take a look at the words themselves, as Junius translates them, 2.15: *nonne unum effecit? Quamvis reliqui spiritus ipsi essent: quid autem unum?*—[*did he not make one? although the remains of the spirit were his: but why one?*]. It would certainly be far too rash and dangerous to make up one's mind on such an important point, and to impose an article of faith upon one's fellow men, on the evidence of such an obscure passage as this: a passage which various interpreters twist and turn in so many different ways. But whatever the words *nonne unum effecit* mean, what do they prove? Does *unum* mean "one woman"; and does the passage therefore establish the fact that a man should marry only one woman? No, because the word is the wrong gender; and as a matter of fact it is the wrong case as well, because nearly all the other translators render the passage: *annon unus fecit? et residuum spiritus ipsi? et quid ille unus?*—[*did not one make? and is not the rest of the spirit his? and why that one?*] We cannot, then, force a condemnation of polygamy from this very obscure passage, and no such doctrine is mentioned anywhere else, or only in doubtful terms. What we should derive from the passage, rather, is something which we can find all through the scriptures, and which is the chief subject of this very chapter from verse eleven onwards, namely a condemnation of marriage with the daughter of an alien god. As Ezra and Nehemia show it was very common at that time for the Jews to defile themselves by such marriages.

As for the words of Christ, Matt. 5.32 and 19.5, he repeats the passage from Gen. 2.24 in order to condemn not polygamy but unlicensed divorce, which is a very different matter; and you have to wrench his words if you want to make them fit polygamy. Some people argue from Matt. 5.32 that if a man who marries another wife after rejecting his first commits adultery, then he does so much more certainly if he marries another and keeps his first wife. But this argument is adulterate itself, and ought itself to be rejected. For in the first place, it is the actual precepts that bind us, not the consequences deduced from them by human reasoning: for what seems to be a reasonable deduction to one person may not seem so to another, though equally intelligent. Secondly, a man who rejects his first wife and marries another, is not said to commit adultery because he marries another, but because when he married the second wife he did not keep the first though he ought to have behaved like a dutiful husband to her as well. So Mark 10.11 says quite plainly: *he commits adultery against her.* Moreover God himself teaches that it is possible to behave like a dutiful husband towards the first wife, even after marrying a second, Ex. 21.10: *if he takes another wife he shall not diminish her food, her clothing or her portion of time*—and God did not make his provisions for adulterers.

It is not correct to argue from 1 Cor. 7.2: *let every man have his own wife,* that he should therefore not have more than one. The text says that he should have *his own* wife, meaning that he should keep her for himself, not that she should be the only one. Bishops and priests are explicitly required to have only one wife, 1 Tim. 3.2 and Tit. 1.6: *let them be husbands of one wife;* I suppose this was so that they could carry out the ecclesiastical duties which they had undertaken more diligently. And the requirement itself shows plainly enough that polygamy was not forbidden to other people, and that it was common in the church at that time.

Lastly, as for the argument which is based on 1 Cor. 7.4: *but in the same way the husband does not have power over his own body, but the wife does,* this is quickly answered by pointing out, as before, that the word *wife* here refers to species not number. Furthermore, the wife's power over her husband's body cannot be different now from what it was under the law, and in Hebrew this power is called עוֹנָה, Ex. 21.10, which means *her appointed time.* In the present chapter the same idea is expressed by the phrase *due benevolence,* but the Hebrew word makes it quite clear what *due* means.[162]

On the other hand, the following texts clearly admit polygamy: Ex. 21.10: *if he takes another wife he shall not diminish her food, her clothing, or her portion of time;* Deut. 17.17: *let him not increase his wives, lest his heart turn from me.* Who would have worded this law so loosely, if it were not meant to grant more than one wife? And who would be so bold as to add to this: therefore let him have only one? The previous verse says *let him not increase his horses,* so shall we add to that: therefore he must have only one horse? We know well enough that the first institution of marriage applied to the king as well as his people: if it allows only one wife, then it does not allow more even to the king. Moreover the reason given for the law is *lest his heart turn from me*—a danger which might arise if he were to marry a great many wives, especially foreign ones, as Solomon afterwards did. But if this law was meant as a renewal of the first institution of marriage, what could have been more appropriate than to have cited that institution here, instead of giving only this other reason?

Let us listen to God himself, the author of the law, and his own best interpreter: 2 Sam. 12.8: *I have handed over your master's wives into your breast: and if they were not enough I would have added such and such things.* There is no escape here: God gave wives: he gave them to the man he loved among a number of other great benefits: he would have given more if these had not been enough. Besides, the very argument which God uses against David is more forceful when applied to the gift of wives than to any other: you should at least have abstained from another man's wife, not so much because I had given you your master's house or his kingdom, as because I had given you the royal wives. But, says Beza, therefore David committed incest, with the wives of his father-in-law. Beza forgets, however, a point which is made clear by Esther 2.12, 13, that the kings had two harems, one for virgins and the other for concubines, and it is understood that David was given the former, not the latter. This is evident from

162. Cp. *PL* 10.994: "love's due rites, nuptial embraces sweet." *Due* in the phrase *due benevolence* includes the sense "belonging to by right."

1 Kings 1.4 as well: *the king did not know her;* Song of Solomon 6.8: *eighty concubines and countless virgins.* Although as a matter of fact God could be said to have given him his master's wives if he had given him not necessarily the same wives, but as many wives as his master had, and similar ones. In the same way he did not give him the actual house and retinue of his master, but a house and retinue equally royal and magnificent.

The law itself, then, and even the authority of God's own voice, wholly approve of this practice. So it is not surprising that the holy prophets should speak of it in their divine hymns as something absolutely honorable: Ps. 45.10, (which is called "A Song of Sweethearts"): *kings' daughters among your dear ones,* and 15, 16: *after her the virgins, her friends, shall be brought to you.* Indeed the words of these sweethearts are quoted by the apostle, Heb. 1.7, etc.: *to the Son, Your throne, O God,* as the words of God himself to his Son; and no words anywhere in scripture attribute godhead to the Son more clearly than these words of theirs. Would it have been proper for God the Father to speak through the mouths of prostitutes and reveal the godhead of his holy Son to men through the love-songs of whores? So, too, in the Song of Solomon, 6.8, 9, 10, both queens and concubines are clearly given honorable mention, and are all considered worthy to sing the praises of the bride: *sixty queens and eighty concubines and countless virgins: the queens will bless that only one and the concubines will praise her, saying* . . . Nor should we forget that passage in 2 Chron. 24.2, 3: *and during the whole lifetime of Jehoiada the priest, Joash did what was right in the sight of the Jehovah, and Jehoiada took two wives for him.* For here the two facts, that he did what was right on the instructions of Jehoiada, and that on Jehoiada's authority he married two wives, are not stated in isolation or in opposition to each other, but in conjunction. In eulogies of kings, if anything which was less admirable than the rest was added on at the end, it was usually explicitly excepted from what went before, contrary to what is done here: thus 1 Kings 15.5: *except in the matter of Uriah,* and 11, 14: *and Asa did what was right . . . though the high places were not removed; nevertheless Asa's heart was perfect.* The fact that Joash's bigamy is mentioned straight after his right conduct, without any exception being made, indicates, then, that it was not considered wrong. For the sacred writer would not have missed such a convenient opportunity for making an exception in the customary way if there had been anything less deserving of commendation than the rest.

Moreover God himself in Ezek. 23.4 says that he has taken two wives, Aholah and Aholibah. He would certainly not have spoken about himself like this at such great length, not even in a parable, nor adopted this character or likeness at all, if the thing itself had been intrinsically dishonorable or base.

But how can anything be dishonorable or base when it is forbidden to no one, even under the gospel (for that dispensation does not annul any of the merely civil regulations which existed previous to its introduction)? The only stipulation made is that priests and deacons should be chosen from among men who had only one wife; see 1 Tim. 3 and Tit. 1.6, cited above. And this is stipulated not because it would be a sin to marry more than one wife, for then it would have been forbidden to everyone else as well, but so that priests and deacons should be less involved in household affairs and therefore more at leisure to attend to the business of the church. Since then polygamy is forbidden here only to ecclesiastics, and even then not because it is a sin, and since neither here nor anywhere else is it forbidden to any other members of the church, it follows that it was permitted to all other members of the church, as I said before, and that it was adopted by many without offence.

Lastly, I argue as follows from Heb. 13.4: polygamy is either marriage or fornication or adultery—for the apostle admits no halfway state between these. Let no one dare to say that it is fornication or adultery: the shame this would bring upon so many patriarchs who were polygamists will, I hope, prevent anyone from doing so. For *God will judge fornicators and adulterers,* whereas he loved the patriarchs above all, and declared that they were very dear to him. If, then, polygamy is nothing but marriage, it must, in the opinion of the same apostle, be lawful and honorable as well: *marriage is honorable for all, and the bed unstained.*

[. . .][163]

The form of marriage consists in the mutual goodwill, love, help and solace of husband and wife, as the institution itself, or its definition, shows.

The end of marriage is almost the same as the form. Its proper fruit is the procreation of children. Since the fall of Adam, the relief of sexual desire has become a kind of secondary end: 1 Cor. 7.2.

So not everyone is bound by the command to marry, but only those who cannot live chastely and continently outside marriage: Matt. 19.11: *not all are able.*

Marriage is intrinsically honorable, and it is not forbidden to any order of men. So, the Papists are wrong to prohibit their priests from marrying: it is allowable for anyone to marry:[164] Heb. 13.4: *marriage is honorable in all;* Gen. 2.24; 1 Cor. 9.5 [. . .]; 1 Tim. 3.2 [. . .], and 3.4 [. . .].

Marriage is, by definition, a union of the most intimate kind, but it is not indissoluble or indivisible. Some people argue that it is, on the grounds that in Matt. 19.5 the words *those two will be one flesh* are added. But these words, rightly considered, do not mean that marriage is absolutely indissoluble, only that it should not be easily dissolved. For this mention of the indissolubility of marriage, whether it is given as a command, or to describe a natural consequence, depends upon what has gone before (i.e., the institution of marriage itself and the due observation of each of its parts). So we find it written: *for this reason he will leave . . . and they will be one flesh*—if, in other words, the wife, according to the institution described in the preceding verses, Gen. 2.18, 20, is a *fit help* for the husband: that is, if goodwill, love, help, solace and fidelity are firm on both sides,

163. The deleted passage presents a long list of holy men in Scripture with more than one wife and then, in a series of short paragraphs, considers various impediments to marriage, from incest to difference in religion.

164. Cp. *PL* 4.744–49: "Whatever hypocrites austerely talk/Of purity and place and innocence,/ Defaming as impure what God declares/Pure, and commands to some, leaves free to all./Our Maker bids increase; who bids abstain/But our destroyer, foe to God and man?"

which, as all admit, is the essential form of marriage. But when the form is dissolved it follows that the marriage must really be dissolved as well.

My opponents emphasize above all those words in Matt. 19.6: *what God has joined together, let no man separate.* The institution of marriage itself shows clearly what it is that God has joined together. He has joined together things compatible, fit, good and honorable: he has not joined chalk and cheese: he has not joined things base, wretched, ill-omened and disastrous. It is violence or rashness or error or some evil genius which joins things like this, not God.

What is there, then, to prevent us from getting rid of an evil so distressing and so deep-seated?

This will not be to separate those whom God has joined together, by his most holy institution, but those whom he has himself separated by his no less holy law: a law which should carry the same weight now as it did with his people of old. As for my opponents' argument about Christian perfection, perfection is not to be forced upon men by penal laws but only encouraged by Christian admonition. It is certainly only a man who does the separating, when he adds to God's law things which the law does not command, and then under cover of the law separates whom he thinks fit. For it should be remembered that God in his most holy, just and pure law has not only allowed divorce on various grounds, but has even, on some occasions, sanctioned it and on others very firmly insisted upon it: Ex. 21.4, 10, 11; Deut. 21.14 and 24.1; Ezra 10.3; Neh. 13.23, 30.

But, say my opponents, he did this *because of the hardness of their hearts,* Matt. 19.8. My answer is that Christ is here making a reply appropriate to the occasion. The Pharisees were tempting him, and his intention, as usual, was to deflate their arrogance and avoid their snares.[165] But he had no intention of giving an explanation of the question of divorce in general. He is replying only to those who, on the grounds of Deut. 24.1, taught that it was lawful to divorce a wife for any reason at all, so long as a bill of divorce was given. This is clear from the same chapter, Matt. 19.3:[166] *is it lawful for every cause?*—because a lot of people were giving bills of divorce not for the single reason allowed by Moses (i.e., the discovery of some uncleanness in the woman that might turn love into hatred), but merely on the pretext of uncleanness, without any just cause. Since, however, the law was not able to convict these people, Christ considered that they ought to be tolerated, although they were hard-hearted, rather than

165. Cp. *DDD* (p. 888): "The occasion which induced our Savior to speak of divorce, was either to convince the extravagance of the Pharisees in that point, or to give a sharp and vehement answer to a tempting question."

166. Cp. *Tetrachordon* (Yale 2:642): "The manner of these men coming to our Savior, not to learn, but to tempt him, may give us to expect that their answer will be such as is fittest for them, not so much a teaching, as an entangling. No man though never so willing or so well enabled to instruct, but if he discern his willingness and candor made use of to entrap him, will suddenly draw in himself, and laying aside the facile vein of perspicuity, will know his time to utter clouds and riddles. . . . This the Pharisees held, that for every cause they might divorce, for every accidental cause, any quarrel or difference that might happen."

that earthly marriages should be indissoluble. For in his opinion marriage was of so much importance in life as a source either of happiness or of misery.

The fact is that if we examine the causes of divorce one by one, we shall find that divorce was always sanctioned for an absolutely just and sufficient reason, and not as a concession to hard-heartedness at all. The first passage is Ex. 21.1–4: *these are the judgments which you shall set before them. When you buy a Hebrew slave . . . in the seventh year he shall go free, without paying anything. If he is married, then his wife shall go with him. If his master has given him a wife, and she has borne him sons or daughters, the wife and her children shall be the master's, and the man shall go by himself.* What could be more just? This law certainly did not make allowances for hardness of heart but, on the contrary, opposed it. For it prevented a Hebrew slave, however much he had cost, from being a slave for more than seven years: at the same time it preferred the right of the master to that of the husband.[167] Again, 21.10, 11: *if he takes another wife, he shall not diminish her food, her clothing or her portion of time. If he does not maintain these three things, then she shall go free without payment.* Who can fail to appreciate the supreme humanity and justice of this law? The husband is not allowed to divorce his wife merely because of his hard heart; but on the other hand the wife is allowed to leave her husband if he is harsh and inhuman, which is a very just reason indeed. Again (Deut. 21.13, 14), it is permissible by the right of war and of property both to marry and to divorce a female captive; but it is not permissible either to sell her after divorcing her, or to keep her for profit, both of which would have been a concession to hard-heartedness.[168] The third passage is Deut. 24.1: *if anyone marries a wife and becomes her husband, and it happens that she does not find favor in his eyes, because he has found some nakedness or shameful thing in her, he shall write her a bill of divorce and give it to her, and send her out of his house.* Here, if the cause is a real one, not a mere fiction, what hardness of heart can there be? For it is clear from the institution of marriage itself that when God originally gave man a wife he intended her to be his help, solace and delight.[169] So if, as often happens, she is found to be a source of grief, shame, deception, ruin and calamity instead, why should we think it displeasing to God if we divorce her?[170] In fact I should be inclined to attribute a thick skin to the man who could keep such a wife, rather than a hard heart to the man who sent her packing. And I am not the only one: Solomon is of the same opinion, or rather the Spirit of God itself is, speaking through the mouth of Solomon, Prov. 30.21, 23: *three things shake the earth; or rather there are four things which it cannot bear:*

167. Cp. *Tetrachordon* (Yale 2:627–28): "[Marriage] gives place to masterly power, for the master might take away from an Hebrew servant the wife which he gave him, *Ex.* 21."

168. Cp. *Tetrachordon* (Yale 2:628): "Lastly, it gives place to the right of war, for a captive woman lawfully married, and afterward not beloved, might be dismissed, only without ransom, *Deut.* 21."

169. Cp. *PL* 8.449–50: "What next I bring shall please thee, be assured,/Thy likeness, thy fit help, thy other self"; 4.486: "Henceforth an individual solace dear"; 8.576: "Made so adorn for thy delight the more." See also 10.137, 940–41; 11.163–65.

170. Cp. *Tetrachordon* (Yale 2:620): "God permitted divorce for whatever was unalterably distasteful, whether in body or mind."

an odious woman when she is married....[171] And on the other hand, Eccles. 9.12: *enjoy your life under the sun, all the days of your fragile life, with the wife whom you love; indeed God has given this to you:* the wife whom you love, notice, not the wife you hate. Thus Mal. 2.16: *whoever hates* or *because he hates, let him send her away;* as everyone before Junius[172] interpreted the passage. So it seems that God enacted this law through Moses, and repeated it through the mouths of the prophets, not in order to make any concessions to the hard-heartedness of husbands, but to rescue the wretched wives from any hard-heartedness which might occur. For where is the hard-heartedness in sending away honorably and freely a woman who, through her own fault, you cannot love? But that a woman who is not loved but justly neglected, a woman who is loathed and hated, should, in obedience to the harshest of laws, be kept beneath the yoke of a crushing slavery (for that is what marriage is without love), by a man who has no love or liking for her: that is a hardship harder than any divorce. So God gave laws of divorce which, if not abused, are absolutely just, equitable and humane. He even extended these laws to those whom he knew would abuse them, because of their hard-heartedness. For he considered it preferable to put up with the hard-heartedness of the wicked, rather than fail to help the righteous in their affliction or save the institution of marriage itself from imminent danger. And this danger was that instead of being a God-given benefit, marriage should become the bitterest misery of all. The fourth and fifth passages, Ezra 10.3 and Neh. 13.23, 30 do not allow divorce, as a concession to hard-heartedness, but rigorously command it for the most sacred religious reasons. But on what authority? These prophets were certainly not bearers of a new law, so what authority could they have except the law of Moses? But the law of Moses nowhere commands the dissolution of this kind of marriage. It does, however, forbid its contraction, Ex. 34.15, 16; Deut. 7.3, 4.[173] From this they argued that a marriage which should not have been contracted, ought to be dissolved. Hence you can see the falsity of the common saying that "What's done can't be undone."

So marriage gives way to religion, and it gives way, as I showed above, to the right of .a master; though it is generally agreed, on the grounds of the scriptural passages cited above, and of numerous provisions in the civil law and the law of nations, that the right of a husband is much the same as the right of a master. Finally, marriage must give way to that natural aversion which anyone may feel for a disgusting object, and also to any really irresistible antipathy. But as for

171. Cp. *Tetrachordon* (p. 1006): "*Solomon* to the plain justification of divorce.... Prov. 30.21, 23 ... tells us of his own accord that a *hated* or a *hateful* woman *when she is married is a thing for which the earth is disquieted and cannot bear it;* thus giving divine testimony to this divine law."

172. Cp. *Tetrachordon* (Yale 2:615): "as if it were to be thus rendered, *The Lord God sayeth that he hateth putting away.* But this new interpretation rests only in the authority of *Junius;* for neither *Calvin* nor *Vatablus* himself, nor any other known divine so interpreted before. And they of best note who have translated the scripture since, and *Diodati* for one, follow not his reading."

173. Cp. *Tetrachordon* (Yale 2:681): "the law of *Moses, Ex.* 34.16. *Deut.* 7.3–6, interpreted by *Ezra* and *Nehemiah* two infallible authors, commands to divorce an infidel not for the fear only of a ceremonious defilement but of an irreligious seducement.... *Nehem.* 13.24–26."

hard-heartedness—if that is really set up as the sole or primary reason for the law's enactment—marriage nowhere gives way to that. Deut. 22.19 makes this even clearer: *because he has defamed a virgin of Israel, she shall be his wife: he may not send her away as long as he lives,* and 22.29: *she shall be his wife; because he has ravished her, he may not send her away as long as he lives.* Now in this case the Mosaic law does not yield to the hard-heartedness of the ravisher or the defamer if he wishes to send away the ravished virgin or the defamed wife. Why then should it be imagined that it yields only to the hard-heartedness of that man who has formed an aversion because of some uncleanness?[174] In fact, then, Christ was reproving the hard-heartedness of those who abuse this law, that is the Pharisees and those like them, when he said *on account of your hard-heartedness he allowed you to send away your wives.* He did not abrogate the law itself or its legitimate use, for he says that Moses permitted it on account of their hard-heartedness, not that he permitted it wrongly or unjustly. And in this sense almost all the civil law was given on account of their hard-heartedness. This is why Paul rebukes the brethren, 1 Cor. 6.6, for using it at all; but no one argues from that that the civil law is or ought to be abrogated. How much less can anyone who understands what the gospel is, believe that it denies to man something which the law allowed, whether it allowed it rightly or through an indulgent attitude towards human weakness?

Christ's words in Matt. 19.8: *it was not so from the beginning* are only a repetition of what he had said more plainly in 19.4: *the maker made them from the beginning . . . ;* that is, marriage was first made by God in such a way that it could not be destroyed, even by death. For there was no such thing as death yet, nor was there any sin. But once marriage had been violated by the sin of one of the parties, necessity taught them that death must put an end to it, and reason told them that it must often come to an end, even before death.[175] No age or memorial since the fall of man records any other *beginning* from which *it was not so.* Certainly in the very beginning of our faith Abraham himself, the father of the faithful, sent away his argumentative and quarrelsome wife, Hagar, and had God's authority for it; Gen. 21.10, 12, 14.[176]

Moreover Christ himself, Matt. 19.9, permitted divorce on grounds of fornication. He could not have done this if those whom God had once joined in the bond of matrimony were never afterwards to be separated. Furthermore, as Selden demonstrated particularly well in his *Uxor Hebraea,* with the help of nu-

174. Cp. *Tetrachordon* (Yale 2:629) "The absolute forbidding of divorce was in part the punishment of a deflowerer and a defamer. Yet not so but that the wife questionless might depart when she pleased. Otherwise this course had not so much righted her, as delivered her up to more spite and cruel usage. This law therefore doth justly distinguish the privilege of an honest and blameless man in the matter of divorce from the punishment of a notorious offender."

175. Cp. *Tetrachordon* (p. 1018): "While man and woman were both perfect each to other, there needed no divorce; but when they both degenerated to imperfection & oft times grew to be an intolerable evil each to other, then law more justly did permit the alienating of that evil which mistake made proper."

176. Cp. *DDD* (Yale 2:263): "while we remember that God commanded *Abraham* to send away his irreligious wife and her son for the offences which they gave in a pious family."

merous rabbinical texts, the word *fornication,* if it is considered in the light of the idiom of oriental languages, does not mean only adultery.[177] It can mean also either what is called *some shameful thing* (i.e., the lack of some quality which might reasonably be required in a wife), Deut. 24.1, or it can signify anything which is found to be persistently at variance with love, fidelity, help and society (i.e., with the original institution of marriage).[178] I have proved this elsewhere, basing my argument on several scriptural texts,[179] and Selden has demonstrated the same thing. It would be almost laughable to tell the Pharisees, when they asked whether it was lawful to send away one's wife for every cause, that it was not lawful except in the case of adultery. Because everyone already knew that it was not merely lawful but one's duty to send away an adulteress, and not simply to divorce her but to send her to her death. So the word *fornication* must be interpreted here in a much broader sense than that of adultery. The best text to demonstrate this, and there are many, is Judg. 19.2: *she fornicated against him.* This was not by committing adultery, because then she would not have dared to run home to her father, but by behaving in an obstinate way towards her husband.[180] To take another example, Paul would not have been able to grant divorce on grounds of desertion by an unbeliever, unless this was a kind of fornication as well. And it is, in fact, irrelevant that an unbeliever was concerned in this case, because anyone who deserts his family *is worse than an unbeliever,* 1 Tim. 5.8. For what could be more natural or more in keeping with the original institution of marriage than that a couple whom love, honor and mutual assistance in life have joined together, should be separated if hatred or implacable dislike comes between them, or some dishonorable act for which one of them is responsible? So when human nature was perfect, before the fall, God, in paradise, established marriage as an indissoluble bond. But when man had fallen, he granted by the law of nature and by the Mosaic law, which Christ did not contradict, that it should of necessity be subject to dissolution. In this he intended to prevent the innocent from being exposed to perpetual injury at the hands of the wicked. In the same way practically every treaty and contract is meant to be permanent and indissoluble when it is made, but it is immediately nullified if either party breaks his word. No one has so far been able to produce any good

177. The noted jurist John Selden (1584–1654) won fame as an Orientalist with the treatise *De Diis Syriis* (1617). Milton here refers to a work published in 1646, after his divorce tracts had been published. Selden's study concerns marriage and divorce among the Jews and, like most of his writing, exhibits extensive knowledge of Rabbinical commentaries. Regarding "fornication," Milton in *Second Defense* (p. 1094) had previously noted his anticipation of Selden: "Concerning the view which should be held on the single exception, that of fornication, I also expressed both my own opinion and that of others. Our distinguished countryman Selden still more fully explained this point in his *Hebrew Wife* [*Uxor Hebraica*], published about two years later." See *DDD,* p. 917 n. 235.

178. Cp. *Tetrachordon* (Yale 2:673): "The word fornication is to be understood . . . for a constant alienation and disaffection of the mind, or for the continual practice of disobedience and crossness from the duties of love and peace, that, in sum, when to be a tolerable wife is either naturally not in their power, or obstinately not in their will."

179. I.e., *Tetrachordon.* This is the treatise's only explicit reference to another of Milton's works.

180. Cp. *Tetrachordon* (Yale 2:672) and *DDD* (p. 909), both of which cite Judg. 19.2 in making the same point.

reason why marriage should be an exception to this rule. What is more, the apostle has freed even brothers and sisters from their obligations, not only in cases of desertion, but *in things of that kind,* that is, in any circumstances which result in a shameful subjection: 1 Cor. 7.15: *a brother or sister is not bound to subjection in cases of this kind, for God has called us in peace,* or *to peace.* He has not called us, then, so that we should be tormented by continual wrangling and annoyance. We are called to peace and liberty, not to marriage, and certainly not to the perpetual squabbles and the slavish pounding-mill of unhappy marriage which, if the apostle is right, is particularly shameful for a free Christian man.[181] It is quite unthinkable that Christ should have expunged from the Mosaic law any provision which could sanction the extension of charity towards the wretched and the afflicted. It is unthinkable, too, that he should have sanctioned a measure which was far more severe than the civil law. We must conclude that, having reprimanded the abuse of this law, he proceeded to teach what the perfect line of action would be, not by compulsion but, as elsewhere, simply by admonition: for he always utterly renounced the role of a judge. So it is the most flagrant error to twist these injunctions of Christ in the gospels into civil statutes, enforcible by magistrates.

It may be asked why, if Christ was apparently not laying down anything new about divorce, or anything more severe than the existing law, it gave such little satisfaction to the disciples that they said, Matt. 19.10: *if this is the position of a man with his wife, is it a bad thing to marry?* My reply is that it is not surprising if the disciples, imbued as they were with the doctrines of their time, should have had the same opinions about divorce as the Pharisees. That is why it seemed strange and burdensome to them that it should be unlawful to send away a wife, once she had been given a bill of divorce, for every cause.[182]

Finally, to put the whole thing in a nutshell: everyone admits that marriage may be dissolved if the prime end and form of marriage is violated; and most people say that this is the reason why Christ permitted divorce only on grounds of adultery. But the prime end and form of marriage is not the bed, but conjugal love and mutual assistance in life: nearly everyone admits that this is so. For the prime end and form of marriage can only be what is mentioned in the original institution, and mention is there made of pleasant companionship (a thing which ceases to exist if someone is left by himself), and of the mutual assistance of a married couple (a thing which only thrives where there is love). No mention is made of the bed or of procreation, which can take place even where there is hatred. It follows that wedded love is older and more important than the mere marriage bed, and far more worthy to be considered as the prime end and form of marriage. Who is so base and swinish[183] as to deny that this is so?

181. Cp. *Tetrachordon* (Yale 2:688–89), where Milton also construes 1 Cor. 7.15 as a principle that implies the right of divorce.

182. Cp. *Tetrachordon* (Yale 2:678), which interprets Matt. 19.10 in the same way.

183. *"tam prono tamque porcino animo."* Cp. *Colasterion,* where Milton describes a critic of his divorce tracts as one of "ignoble and swinish mind" (Yale 2:740).

Violation of the marriage bed is only serious because it violates peace and love. Divorce, then, should rather be granted because love and peace are perpetually being violated by quarrels and arguments, than because of adultery. Christ himself admitted this for, as I have proved above, it is absolutely certain that the word *fornication* means not so much adultery as the wife's constant contrariness, faithlessness and disobedience, which all show that her mind is not her husband's even if her body is. Moreover the common, though mistaken interpretation, which makes an exception only in the case of adultery, although it is meant to protect the law, does, in fact, break it. For the Mosaic law did not sanction the divorce of an adulteress, but her trial and execution.

CHAPTER II

OF THE FALL OF OUR FIRST PARENTS, AND OF SIN

The PROVIDENCE of God with regard to the fall of man may be discerned both in man's sin and the misery which followed it, and also in his restoration.

SIN, as defined by the apostle, is ἀνομία or the breaking of the law, 1 John 3.4.

Here the word *law* means primarily that law which is innate and implanted in man's mind; and secondly it means the law which proceeded from the mouth of God; Gen. 2.17: *do not eat of this:* for the law written down by Moses is of a much later date. So it is written, Rom. 2.12: *those who have sinned without law will perish without law.*

SIN is either THE SIN COMMON TO ALL MEN or THE SIN OF EACH INDIVIDUAL.

THE SIN COMMON TO ALL MEN IS THAT WHICH OUR FIRST PARENTS, AND IN THEM ALL THEIR POSTERITY[184] COMMITTED WHEN THEY ABANDONED THEIR OBEDIENCE AND TASTED THE FRUIT OF THE FORBIDDEN TREE.

OUR FIRST PARENTS: Gen. 3.6: *the woman took some of the fruit and ate it, and gave some to her husband, and he ate it.* Hence 1 Tim. 2.14: *Adam was not deceived, but the woman was deceived and was the cause of the transgression.* This sin was instigated first by the devil,[185] as is clear from the course of events, Gen. 3 and 1 John 3.8: *the man who commits sin is of the devil; for the devil sins from the beginning.* Secondly it was instigated by man's own inconstant nature, which meant that he, like the devil before him *did not stand firm in the truth,* John 8.44. He did not keep his original state, but left his home, Jude 6. Anyone who examines this sin carefully will admit, and rightly, that it was a most atrocious offence, and that it broke every part of the law.[186] For what fault is there which man did not commit in commit-

184. Cp. *PL* 10.817–18: "in me all/Posterity stands cursed."
185. Cp. *PL* 1.33–34: "Who first seduced them to that foul revolt?/Th' infernal serpent."
186. Cp. *PL* 10.16: "And manifold in sin, deserved to fall."

ting this sin? He was to be condemned both for trusting Satan and for not trusting God; he was faithless, ungrateful, disobedient, greedy, uxorious; she, negligent of her husband's welfare; both of them committed theft, robbery with violence, murder against their children (i.e., the whole human race); each was sacrilegious and deceitful, cunningly aspiring to divinity although thoroughly unworthy of it, proud and arrogant. And so we find in Eccles. 7.29: *God has made man upright, but they have thought up numerous devices,* and in James 2.10: *whoever keeps the whole law, and yet offends in one point, is guilty of all.*

AND IN THEM ALL THEIR POSTERITY: for they are judged and condemned in them, although not yet born, Gen. 3.16, etc., so they must obviously have sinned in them as well. Rom. 5.12: *sin came into the world through one man,* 5.15: *through the offence of that one man many are dead,* and 5.16 [. . .], and 5.17 [. . .], and 5.18 [. . .], and 5.19 [. . .]; 1 Cor. 15.22: *in Adam all die:* so it is certain that all sinned in Adam.

For Adam, the parent and head of all men, either stood or fell as a representative of the whole human race: this was true both when the covenant was made, that is, when he received God's commands, and also when he sinned. In the same way *Levi also paid tithes in Abraham . . . while he was still in his father's loins,* Heb. 7.9, 10; *for God has made the whole human race from the blood of one man, Adam,* Acts 17.26. If all men did not sin in Adam, why was the condition of all made worse by his fall? Some modern thinkers would say that this deterioration was not moral but physical. But I say that it would be quite as unjust to impair the physical perfection of innocent men, especially as this has so much effect on their morals.

Moreover, it is not only a constant principle of divine justice but also a very ancient law among all races and all religions, that when a man has committed sacrilege (and this tree we are discussing was sacred),[187] not only he but also the whole of his posterity becomes an anathema and a sin-offering.[188]

This was so in the flood, in the burning of Sodom and in the destruction of Korah, Num. 16.27, 32, and in the punishment of Achan, Josh. 7.24, 25. When Jericho was demolished, the children paid for the sins of their fathers, and even the cattle were given up to slaughter along with their masters, Josh. 6.21. So, too, with the posterity of Eli, the priest, 1 Sam. 2.31, 33, 36; and Saul's sons paid the penalty for his slaughter of the Gibeonites, 2 Sam. 21.1, etc.

God declares that this is his justice, Ex. 20.5: *punishing the sin of the fathers in the persons of the children, grandchildren and great-grandchildren of those who pursue me with hatred;* Num. 14.33: *your sons, feeding their flocks in the wilderness for forty years, will pay the penalty for your fornication:* they were not guiltless themselves, however.[189] God himself explains what the method behind this justice is: Lev. 26.39: *pining away because of their iniquity and also because of the iniquity of their fathers;*

187. Cp. *PL* 9.904: "The sacred fruit forbidd'n."
188. Cp. *PL* 3.208: "But to destruction sacred and devote."
189. Cp. *PL* 12.398–400: "and suffering death,/The penalty to thy transgression due,/And due to theirs which out of thine will grow."

2 Kings 17.14: *they had stiffened their necks as their ancestors stiffened theirs;* and Ezek. 18.4 [. . .]. As for infants, the problem is solved by the consideration that all souls are God's, and that though innocent they were the children of sinful parents, and God saw that they would turn out to be like their parents. With everybody else, the explanation is that no one perishes unless he has himself sinned. Thus Agag and his people paid the penalty for the crime of their ancestors four hundred years after the latter had attacked the Israelite fugitives while they were on the march from Egypt, 1 Sam. 15.2, 3; true, they were themselves far from guiltless, 15.33. Then again, Hosea, king of Israel, was better than his ancestors; but when he was guilty of the idolatry of the Gentiles, he paid the penalty for his own sins and the sins of his ancestors as well by the loss of his kingdom, 2 Kings 17.2–4. Similarly Manasseh's sins overflowed onto his children (though they were hardly innocent themselves), 23.26: *because of all the provocations with which Manasseh had provoked him,* compared with Jer. 25.3, 4, etc.: *from the thirteenth year of Josiah king of Judah, right up to this day, the word of Jehovah has come to me: and I have spoken it to you incessantly from daybreak onwards, but you have not listened;* and 2 Kings 24.5: *on account of sins just like those which Manasseh had committed.* So the good king Josiah, and those who were like him, were exempt from the greater part of the punishment. The Pharisees, however, were not exempt, Matt. 23.34, 35: *you shall kill some of them* etc. *that all righteous blood may come upon you, from the blood of righteous Abel,* etc.

Accordingly penitents are ordered to confess both their own sins and the sins of their fathers: Lev. 26.40: *if they will confess their iniquity and the iniquity of their fathers,* and Neh. 9.2: *they confessed their sins and the iniquities of their ancestors:* and frequently elsewhere.

So even a whole family may become guilty because of the crime committed by its head: Gen. 12.14: *Jehovah afflicted Pharaoh and his family with great plagues,* and 20.7 [. . .].

Subjects have to pay the penalty, too, for the sins of their king, as all Egypt did for Pharaoh's sins. Even King David, who thought it unjust that subjects should suffer in this way, also thought it quite equitable that sons should be punished for and with their fathers: 2 Sam. 24.17: *look, I have sinned and done wrong: but these, these sheep, what have they done? I beg that your hand may be against me and against my father's house.*

Indeed, sometimes a whole nation is punished for the sin of one citizen, Josh. 7, and the offence of a single person is imputed to all, 7.1, 11.

Furthermore, even the most just men have thought it right that a crime committed against them should be atoned for by the punishment not only of the criminal but also of his children. Thus Noah considered that Ham's offence should be avenged upon Ham's son, Canaan,[190] Gen. 9.25.

This feature of divine justice, the insistence upon propitiatory sacrifices for

190. Cp. *PL* 12.101–4: "witness th' irreverent son/Of him who built the ark, who for the shame/Done to his father, heard this heavy curse,/'Servant of servants,' on his vicious race."

sin, was well known among other nations, and never thought to be unfair. So we find in Thucydides 1:[191] *For this they and their family are held to be accursed and offenders against the goddess.* And Virgil, *Aeneid,* 1:[192]

Could angry Pallas, with revengeful spleen,
The Grecian navy burn, and drown the men?
She for the fault of one offending foe . . .

The same fact could easily be demonstrated by a host of other examples and proofs from the pagan writers.

Again, a man convicted of high treason, which is only an offence against another man, forfeits not only his own estate and civil rights but also those of all his family, and lawyers have decided upon the same sentence in other cases of a similar kind. Everyone knows, too, what the right of war is, and that it extends not only to those who are responsible, but to everyone who is in the enemy's power, women, for example, and even children, and people who have done nothing towards the war nor intended to.[193]

THE SIN OF EACH INDIVIDUAL is THE SIN WHICH EACH MAN COMMITS ON HIS OWN ACCOUNT, QUITE APART FROM THAT SIN WHICH IS COMMON TO ALL. All men commit sin of this kind: Job 9.20: *if I were to call myself righteous, my own mouth would condemn me . . . ,* and 10.15 [. . .]; Ps. 143.2: *no living man is righteous in your sight;* Prov. 20.9 [. . .]; Eccles. 7.20 [. . .]; Rom. 3.23 [. . .].

Each type of sin, common and personal, has two subdivisions, whether we call them degrees or parts or modes of sin, or whether they are related to each other as cause and effect. These subdivisions are evil desire, or the will to do evil, and the evil deed itself. James 1.14, 15: *every man is tempted when he is drawn on and enticed by his own lust: then, when lust has conceived, it brings forth sin.* This same point is neatly expressed by the poet:[194]

Mars sees her; seeing desires her; desiring enjoys her

It was evil desire that our first parents were originally guilty of. Then they implanted it in all their posterity, since their posterity too was guilty of that original sin, in the shape of a certain predisposition towards, or, to use a metaphor, a sort of tinder to kindle sin.

This is called in scripture *the old man* and *the body of sin,* Rom. 6.6, Eph. 4.22, Col. 3.9: or simply *sin,* Rom. 7.8: *sin seized its opportunity by means of that commandment; sin dwelling in me,* Rom. 7.17, 20; *evil which is present,* 7.21; [. . .] 7.23; [. . .] 7.24; [. . .] 8.2.

191. *History of the Peloponnesian War* 1.126.11.
192. Lines 39–41.
193. The right of war gives absolute power over a vanquished enemy. Cp. *PL* 1.149–50n; 2.200–208n.
194. Ovid, *Fast.* 3.21.

Apparently Augustine, in his writings against Pelagius, was the first to call this ORIGINAL SIN. He used the word *original,* I suppose, because in the *origin* or generation of man this sin was transmitted to posterity by our first parents. But if that is what he meant, the term is too narrow, because this evil desire, this law of sin, was not only inbred in us, but also took possession of Adam after his fall,[195] and from his point of view it could not be called *original.*[196]

The depravity which all human minds have in common, and their propensity to sin, are described in Gen. 6.5: *that all the thoughts of his heart were always evil and evil alone;* 8.21: *the devices of a man's heart are evil from childhood;* Jer. 17.9 [. . .]; Matt. 15.19 [. . .]; Rom. 7.14 [. . .]; and 8.7 [. . .]; Gal. 5.17 [. . .]; Eph. 4.22: *the old man who is corrupted by deceitful lusts.*

Our first parents implanted it in us: Job 14.4: *who produces purity from impurity?,* and 15.14 [. . .]; Ps. 51.7: *I was formed in iniquity and my mother nursed me in sin;* and 58.4 [. . .]; Isa. 48.8 [. . .]; John 3.6 [. . .]. Eph. 2.3: *we were by nature children of anger, like the others*—even those who were born of regenerate parents, for although faith removes each man's personal guilt, it does not altogether root out the vice which dwells within us. So it is not man as a regenerate creature, but man as an animal, that begets man: Just as the seed, though cleansed from straw and chaff, produces not only the ear or the grain but also the stalk and the husk. Christ alone was free from this contagion, since he was produced by supernatural generation, although descended from Adam: Heb. 7.26: *holy, spotless.*

Some interpret this term original sin primarily as guiltiness. But guiltiness is not a sin, it is the imputation of sin, called elsewhere *the judgment of God:* Rom. 1.32: *knowing the judgment of God.* As a result of this sinners are held *worthy of death,* and ὑπόδικοι, that is, *liable to condemnation and punishment,* Rom. 3.19, and *are under sin,* 3.9. Thus as soon as the fall occurred, our first parents became guilty, though there could have been no original sin in them. Moreover all Adam's descendants were included in the guilt, though original sin had not yet been implanted in them. Finally, guilt is taken away from the regenerate, but they still have original sin.

Others define original sin as the loss of original righteousness and the corruption of the whole mind. But this loss must be attributed to our first parents before it is attributed to us, and they could not have been subject to original sin, as I said before. Their sin was what is called "actual" sin, which these same theologians, as part of their theory, distinguish from original sin. Anyway their loss was a consequence of sin, rather than a sin itself; or if it was a sin, it was only a sin of ignorance, because they did not expect for a moment that they would lose anything good by eating the fruit, or that they would be worse off in any way at all.[197] So I shall not consider this loss under the heading of sin, but under that of punishment in the next chapter.

195. Cp. *PL* 9.1077–78: "And in our faces evident the signs/Of foul concupiscence."

196. Yet Milton at *PL* 9.1003–4 calls the first disobedience "the mortal sin/Original."

197. Cp. *PL* 10.334–36: "his guileful act/By Eve, though all unwilling, seconded/Upon her husband." Milton represents Adam, however, as fully aware of the fatal impact of eating the fruit (*PL* 9.896–907).

The second subdivision of sin, after evil desire, is the evil action or crime itself, which is commonly called "actual" sin.[198] It can be committed not only through actions, as such, but also through words and thoughts and even through the omission of a good action.

It is called "actual" not because sin is really an action, on the contrary it is a deficiency, but because it usually exists in some action. For every action is intrinsically good; it is only its misdirection or deviation from the set course of law which can properly be called evil. So action is not the material out of which sin is made, but only the ὑποκείμενον, the essence or element in which it exists.

Through words: Matt. 12.36: *for every idle word they will be called to account,* and 15.11: *whatever comes out, defiles a man.*

Through thoughts: Ex. 20.17: *you shall not covet your neighbor's house;* Ps. 7.14: *see, he will bring forth vanity; as he conceived trouble so he will bring forth lies;* Prov. 24.8 [...]; Jer. 17.9 [...], etc.; Matt. 5.28 [...], and 15.19 [...]; 1 John 3.15 [...].

Through omission: Matt. 12.30: *he who is not with me is against me; and he who does not gather with me, scatters,* similarly Luke 11.23 and 6.9, where not to save a man is considered the same as destroying him. Matt. 25.42: *I was hungry and you did not give;* James 4.17: *a man who knows how to do right and does not do it, is in the power of sin.*

But all sins are not, as the Stoics maintained, equally great: Ezek. 5.6: *into wickedness more than the nations,* and 8.15 [...]; John 19.11: *he has the greater sin.*

This inequality arises from many and various circumstances of person, place, time, and the like: Isa. 26.10: *in the land of righteousness he will deal unjustly.*

A discussion of the difference between mortal and venial sin will fit in better elsewhere. Meanwhile it is indisputable that even the least sin renders a man liable to condemnation: Luke 16.10: *he who is unjust in little is also unjust in much.*

CHAPTER 12

OF THE PUNISHMENT OF SIN

So far I have spoken of sin. After sin came death, as its affliction or punishment: Gen. 2.17: *on the day you eat it, you will die;* Rom. 5.12: *through sin is death,* and 6.23: *the wages of sin is death,* and 7.5: *the effects of sin, to bring forth fruit to death.*

But in scripture every evil, and everything which seems to lead to destruction, is indeed under the name of *death.* For physical death, as it is called, did not follow *on the same day as* Adam's sin, as God had threatened.[199]

198. Cp. *PL* 10.586–88: "Sin there in power before,/Once actual, now in body, and to dwell/Habitual habitant."

199. Cp. *PL* 8.329–33: "my sole command/Transgressed, inevitably thou shalt die;/From that day mortal, and this happy state/Shalt lose, expelled from hence into a world/Of woe and sorrow"; 10.49–53: "death denounced that day,/Which he presumes already vain and void,/Because not yet inflicted, as he feared,/By some immediate stroke; but soon shall find/Forbearance no acquittance ere day end."

So four degrees of death may conveniently be distinguished. First, as I said above, come ALL EVILS WHICH TEND TO DEATH AND WHICH, IT IS AGREED, CAME INTO THE WORLD AS SOON AS MAN FELL. I will here set out the most important of these. First: guiltiness, which, although it is a thing imputed to us by God, is nevertheless a sort of partial death or prelude to death in us, by which we are fettered to condemnation and punishment as by some actual bond: Gen. 3.7: *then both their eyes opened, and they knew that they were naked;* Lev. 5.2, etc. [. . .]; Rom. 3.19 [. . .]. As a result guiltiness is either accompanied or followed by terrors of conscience:[200] Gen. 3.8: *they heard the voice of God, and Adam hid himself: he said, I was afraid;* Rom. 8.15 [. . .]; Heb. 2.15: *all those who through fear of death were condemned to slavery all their lives,* and 10.27: *a terrifying expectation of judgment:* also by the loss of divine protection and favor, which results in the lessening of the majesty of the human countenance, and the degradation of the mind:[201] Gen. 3.7: *they knew that they were naked.* Thus the whole man is defiled: Tit. 1.15: *both their mind and their conscience is defiled.* Hence comes shame: Gen. 3.7: *they sewed leaves together and made themselves aprons;* Rom. 6.21: *for which you are now ashamed, for the end of those things is death.*

The second degree of death is called SPIRITUAL DEATH. This is the loss of that divine grace and innate righteousness by which, in the beginning, man lived with God: Eph. 2.1: *since you were dead in trespasses and sins,* and 4.18: *alienated from the life of God;* Col. 2.13 [. . .]; Rev. 3.1 [. . .]. And this death took place at the same moment as the fall of man, not merely on the same day. Those who are delivered from it are said to be regenerated and born again and created anew. As I will show in my chapter on Regeneration,[202] this is not the work of God alone.

This death consists, first, in the loss or at least the extensive darkening of that right reason, whose function it was to discern the chief good, and which was, as it were, the life of the understanding: Eph. 4.18: *having a mind obscured by darkness, and alienated from the life of God on account of the ignorance which is in them,* and 5.8 [. . .]; John 1.5 [. . .]; Jer. 6.10 [. . .]; John 8.43 [. . .]; 1 Cor. 2.14 [. . .]; 2 Cor. 3.5: *not that we are fit to think anything out by ourselves,* and 4.4: *the god of this world has blinded their minds;* Col. 1.13 [. . .]: secondly, in that extinction of righteousness and of the liberty to do good, and in that slavish subjection to sin and the devil which is, as it were, the death of the will.[203] John 8.34: *whoever commits sin is the slave of sin.* We have all committed sin in Adam, therefore we are born slaves; Rom. 7.14: *sold to be subject to sin,* and 8.3 [. . .], and 8.7 [. . .]; Rom. 6.16, 17 [. . .]; Phil. 3.19 [. . .]; Acts 26.18 [. . .]; 2 Tim. 2.26: *out of the snare of the devil, who are made captive by him at his*

200. Cp. *PL* 10.842–43: "O conscience, into what abyss of fears/And horrors hast thou driv'n me."
201. Cp. *PL* 9.1077–78: "And in our faces evident the signs/Of foul concupiscence."
202. Chapter 18 of Book 1, not included in our selection.
203. Cp. *PL* 12.83–90: "Since thy original lapse, true liberty/Is lost, which always with right reason dwells/Twinned, and from her hath no dividual being:/Reason in man obscured, or not obeyed,/Immediately inordinate desires/And upstart passions catch the government/From reason, and to servitude reduce/Man till then free."

will; Eph. 2.2 [. . .]. Lastly sin is its own punishment, and the death of the spiritual life; especially when sins are heaped upon sins: Rom. 1.26: *for this reason he has given them up to filthy desires.* The reason for this is not hard to see. As sins increase so they bind the sinners to death more surely, make them more miserable and constantly more vile, and deprive them more and more of divine help and grace, and of their own former glory. No one should have the least doubt that sin is in itself alone the gravest evil of all, for it is opposed to the chief good, that is, to God. Punishment, on the other hand, seems to be opposed only to the good of the creature, and not always to that.

However, it cannot be denied that some traces of the divine image still remain in us, which are not wholly extinguished by this spiritual death.[204] This is quite clear, not only from the holiness and wisdom in both word and deed of many of the heathens, but also from Gen. 9.2: *every beast shall have fear of you,* and 9.6: *who sheds man's blood . . . because God made man in his image.* These traces remain in our intellect, Ps. 19.2: *the heavens declare . . .*—obviously they do not *declare* it to beings who cannot hear. Rom. 1.19, 20: *that which can be known about God . . . the invisible things are evident from the creation of the world,* and 1.32 [. . .], and 2.15 [. . .]; 7.23, 24: *I see another law in my members battling against the law of my mind . . . I am a wretched man. Who will rescue me from this body of death?* The freedom of the will is not entirely extinct: first of all, in indifferent matters, whether natural or civil: 1 Cor. 7.36, 37, 39: *let him do what he will. He has power over his will. She is free to marry whom she likes.* Secondly, this freedom has clearly not quite disappeared even where good works are concerned, or at least good attempts, at any rate after God has called us and given us grace. But it is so weak and of such little moment, that it only takes away any excuse we might have for doing nothing, and does not give us the slightest reason for being proud of ourselves: Deut. 30.19: *choose life, that you and your seed may live;* Ps. 78.8 [. . .]; Jer. 8.13–16: *because when I speak to you from the dawn onwards, you do not hear, and when I shout at you, you do not answer, therefore . . .*—but why, if he had only been speaking to incapable blockheads? And 31.18: *turn to me and I will be turned;* Zech. 1.3 [. . .]; Mark 9.23, 24 [. . .]; Rom. 2.14: *when the Gentiles who have not the law do by nature the things contained in the law,* and 6.16: *do you not know that when you present yourselves as slaves to obey someone, you are the slaves of him whom you obey, whether slaves of sin, to death, or slaves of obedience, to righteousness,* and 7.18 [. . .], and 7.21 [. . .]. Paul seems to speak these words in the person of a man not yet fully regenerate who, although called by God and given grace, had not yet been subject to his regenerating influence. This is clear from 7.14: *I am carnal, sold to be subject to sin.* As for his words in 7.25: *I thank God through Jesus Christ . . . ,* these and similar things could be said and done by a man who had only been called. Rom. 9.31: *by following the law of righteousness they did not attain the law of righteousness,* and 10.2: *they have zeal for God, but not from knowledge;* 1 Cor. 9.17 [. . .]; Philipp. 3.6 [. . .]; 1 Pet. 5.2 [. . .]. As a result nearly all human

204. Cp. *PL* 11.511–13: "man,/Retaining still divine similitude/In part." This claim also distinguishes Milton's views from Calvinist orthodoxy, which insisted on humanity's total depravity.

beings profess some concern for virtue, and have an abhorrence of some of the more atrocious crimes: 1 Cor. 5.1: *fornication of a kind which is not mentioned even among the Gentiles.*

As a vindication of God's justice, especially when he calls man, it is obviously fitting that some measure of free will should be allowed to man, whether this is something left over from his primitive state, or something restored to him as a result of the call of grace. It is also fitting that this will should operate in good works or at least good attempts, rather than in things indifferent. For if God rules all human actions, both natural and civil, by his absolute command, then he is not doing anything more than he is entitled to do, and no one need complain. But if he turns man's will to moral good or evil just as he likes, and then rewards the good and punishes the wicked, it will cause an outcry against divine justice from all sides. It would seem then that God's general government of all things, which is so often referred to, should be understood as operating in natural and civil matters and in things indifferent and in chance happenings—in fact in anything rather than in moral or religious concerns. There are several scriptural texts which corroborate this. 2 Chron. 15.12, 14: *they entered into a covenant to seek Jehovah the God of their ancestors with all their heart and with all their soul: and they swore to Jehovah;* Ps. 119.106: *I have sworn (and I will perform it), to keep your righteous judgments.* Obviously if religious matters were not under our control, or to some extent within our power and choice, God could not enter into a covenant with us, and we could not keep it, let alone swear to keep it.

CHAPTER 13

OF THE DEATH WHICH IS CALLED THE DEATH OF THE BODY

The third degree of death is what is usually called the DEATH OF THE BODY. The body's sufferings and hardships and diseases are nothing but the prelude to this bodily death. Gen. 3.16: *I greatly multiply your grief* and 3.17 [. . .] and 3.19 [. . .]; Job 5.7 [. . .]; Deut. 28.22 [. . .]; Hos. 2.18 [. . .]; Rom. 2.9: *affliction and distress upon every man who instigates evil.* The curse of death extends to the whole of nature,[205] because of man—Gen. 3.17: *because of you, the ground shall be cursed;* Rom. 8.20, 21: *the world is made subject to vanity, but not on its own account*—and even to the beasts, Gen. 3.14 and 6.7; the firstborn in Egypt, Ex. 11.5.

Although some people disagree, this bodily death should really be thought of as a punishment for sin, just as much as the other degrees of death: Rom. 5.13, 14: *sin was in the world until the* law . . . *but death reigned from Adam to Moses;* 1 Cor. 15.21: *since death came through man*—death in this world, that is, as well as eternal death, as the second half of the sentence indicates—*through man came also the resurrection of the dead.* Therefore that bodily death which precedes resurrection

205. Cp. *PL* 10.846–48, 678–80, 687–91.

came about not naturally but through man's sin. This refutes those who attribute death in this world to nature, and eternal death alone to sin.

The death of the body, as it is called, is the loss or extinction of life. For the separation of body and soul, which is the usual definition of death, cannot possibly be death at all. What part of man dies when this separation takes place? The soul? Even those who adhere to the usual definition deny that. The body? But how can that be said to die which never had any life of its own?[206] This separation, then, cannot be called the death of man.

This gives rise to a very important question which, because of the prejudice of theologians, has usually been dismissed out of hand, instead of receiving proper and careful examination. Does the whole man die, or only the body? It is a question which can be debated without detriment to faith or devotion, whichever side we may be on. So I shall put forward quite unreservedly the doctrine which seems to me to be instilled by virtually innumerable passages of scripture. I assume that no one thinks you should look for truth among philosophers and schoolmen rather than in the Bible!

Man is always said to be made up of body, spirit and soul, whatever we may think about where one starts and the other leaves off. So I will first prove that the whole man dies, and then that each separate part dies. First of all, we should consider that God pronounced the sentence of death upon the whole sinful man, without making an exception of any part. For what could be more just than that the whole man should die since the whole man had sinned; and that the part, whether soul or spirit, which was found to have the chief hand in the sin should die above all? Or, to put it another way, what could be more absurd than that the part which sinned most (i.e., the soul) should escape the sentence of death; or that the body, which was just as immortal as the soul before sin brought death into the world, should alone pay the penalty for sin by dying although it had no actual part in the sin?

It is quite obvious that all the saints and believers, patriarchs, prophets and apostles alike, were of this same opinion: Jacob, Gen. 37.35: *I will go down mourning to my son in the grave,* and 42.36 [. . .]; Job 3.12–18 [. . .], similarly Job 10.21. Also Job 14.11: *when man has died, where is he?* and 14.13: *when man has lain down, he does not rise again until the heavens are no more,* and 17.12 [. . .], and 17.14, 15 [. . .], and there are many other passages; David, too, as is evident from the reason he so often gave when praying to be delivered from death, Ps. 6.5: *there is no remembrance of you in death, who shall praise you in the tomb,* and similarly 88.11–13, 115.17 [. . .], and 39.14: *before I go away and am no more,* and 146.2: *I will praise my God while I still exist.* Clearly if he had believed that his soul would survive and would be received into heaven without delay he would not have used this kind of argument, be-

206. Cp. *PL* 10.789–92: "It was but breath/Of Life that sinned; what dies but what had life/And sin? The body properly hath neither./All of me then shall die."

cause he would know that he would soon take his flight to a place where he could praise God unceasingly. What David believed of himself, Peter believed about David, Acts 2.29, 34: *let me speak freely among you about the patriarch David: that he is both dead and buried, and his monument is with us to this very day: for David did not ascend into heaven.* Hezekiah shows clearly how convinced he was that all of him would die, when he complains that he will not be able to praise God in the tomb: Isa. 38.18, 19: *the grave cannot praise you. They that go down to the grave have no hope in your faith: the living, the living shall praise you as I do today.* The voice of God himself bears witness to the same truth: Isa. 57.5, 6: *the just man perishes, and no one takes it to heart: merciful men are taken, and no one considers that the just man is taken away before the arrival of that evil. He shall enter into peace, they shall rest in their beds;* Jer. 31.15 compared with Matt. 2.18 [. . .]; so does Daniel, Dan. 12.2 [. . .]. Christ himself proves that God is the God of the living, Luke 20.37, etc., by arguing that they will be resurrected. If they were alive already, it would not necessarily follow from his argument that there was going to be a resurrection of the body. Thus he says, John 11.25: *I am the resurrection and the life.* So, too, he quite openly declares that, before the resurrection, there is no dwelling place in heaven even for the saints, John 14.2, 3: *I am going to prepare a place for you, and if I go away and prepare a place for you, I shall come again and take you to myself, that where I am, you may be also.* No satisfactory reason can be produced for taking this to refer only to physical bodies. So presumably it was spoken about, and should be understood to refer to the soul and the spirit, as well as the body, and to their reception into heaven, after the second coming of the Lord. So, too, Luke 20.35 and Acts 7.60: *when he had said this, he fell asleep* and 23.6: *of the hope and resurrection*—that is, the hope of resurrection, which was the only hope he said he had. Similarly Luke 24.21 and 26.6–8, and 1 Cor. 15.17–19: *if Christ has not risen* (which was done so that the dead might rise again) *then those who sleep in Christ shall perish.* So we see that there are here two, and only two alternatives: either to rise again or to perish. For *if we have hope in Christ in this life only, we are of all men the most miserable:* again there are two alternatives, either to believe in resurrection or to place all one's hopes in this life alone. Also, 1 Cor. 15.29, 30: *if the dead are not raised, why do we put ourselves in danger* and 15.32: *let us eat and drink, for tomorrow we die,* die altogether, that is, otherwise the argument would be worthless. From 15.42 to 50 the reasoning proceeds from the simply mortal to the simply immortal, from death to resurrection. There is not so much as a word about any intermediate state. Even Paul affirmed that he would not gain his own crown of righteousness before that last day came: 2 Tim. 4.8: *as for the rest, a crown of righteousness is laid up for me, which the Lord, the righteous judge, will give me on that day: but not only to me, but also to all those who have longed for his glorious coming.* A crown is laid up for Paul: therefore it is not to be obtained immediately after death. When is it to be obtained, then? At that time when crowns are to be given to all the others: in other words, not before Christ's *glorious coming.* Philipp. 2.16 [. . .], and 3.11 [. . .], and 3.20, 21: *our city is in heaven, from which place, also, we look for a savior, the Lord Jesus Christ: who shall transform our vile body, so that it may become like his glorious body.* Our citizenship, then, is in the heavens: not in that place where we now live, but in the place from which we expect a savior who will lead us back with him. Luke 20.35, 36: *but those who shall be held worthy to obtain that existence, and the resurrection from the dead,* etc. *for they are equal to the angels,* etc. *being sons of the resurrection:* that is, they will eventually be. It follows that they will not attain that heavenly existence before their resurrection.

So far I have proved that the whole man dies. But in case anyone should start quibbling, and should claim that because the whole man dies it does not mean that the whole *of* man dies, I will now prove the same thing about the three components, body, spirit and soul, which I enumerated above. As for the body, no one has any doubt that it dies.

The same thing will be equally apparent in the case of the spirit, once it is agreed that the spirit is not divine but merely human, as I showed in Chapter 7. It must also be conceded that no cause can be found why, when God sentenced the whole sinful man to death, the spirit alone should have been exempted from the punishment of death. After all, the spirit was the chief offender. So, then, before sin came into the world, all man's component parts were equally immortal, but since the advent of sin they have all become equally subject to death, as a result of God's sentence. But now for the proofs. The Preacher himself, the wisest of all mortals, distinctly says that the spirit is not exempt from death: Eccles. 3.18–20: *that as the beast dies, so the man dies, they all have the same spirit. Each of them goes to the same place;* and 3.21 condemns the ignorance of those who are so bold as to affirm that the spirit of a man and the spirit of a beast go different ways after death: *who knows whether the spirit of man goes upwards?;* Ps. 146.4: *his spirit goes out, the man returns to his earth: in that day his thoughts perish*—but his *thoughts* are in his soul and spirit, not in his body. If they *perish,* then the conclusion must be that the soul and spirit themselves also suffer the same fate as the body. 1 Cor. 5.5: *that the spirit may be saved on the day of the Lord Jesus.* Paul does not say *on the day of death,* but *on the day of the Lord.* Lastly there are plenty of texts which prove that the soul also suffers both natural and violent death, whether we take the term *soul* to mean the whole human make-up, or whether we take it as synonymous with *spirit.* Num. 23.14: *may my soul die the death of the righteous.* True, these words are said by Balaam, not one of the most upright of prophets, but they are words which God put into his mouth, 23.9; Job 33.18: *he may keep back his soul from the pit* and 36.14: *their soul dies in youth;* Ps. 22.21 [. . .], and 78.50 [. . .] and 89.49 [. . .] and 94.17 [. . .]. So, too, man, when dead, is referred to as a *soul:* Lev. 19.28 and 21.1, 11: *nor go to any dead souls,* and elsewhere. Isa. 38.17: *you have delivered my soul from the pit.* But the most convincing explanation I can adduce for the death of the soul is God's own, Ezek. 18.20: *the soul which sins shall itself die.* Thus even Christ's soul succumbed to death for a short time when he died for our sins. The prophet, the apostle and Christ himself corroborate this: Ps. 16.10, compared with Acts 2.27, 28, 31: *that his soul was not left in the sepulcher, nor his flesh;*

Matt. 26.38: *my soul is sad, sad to death.*[207] The souls are never spoken of as being summoned to or assembling for judgment from heaven or hell; they are always said to be called out of the grave, or at least to have been in the state of the dead. John 5.28, 29: *the time will come when all who are in their graves will hear his voice, and they will come forth,* etc. Here those who rise again, those who hear and come forth, whether just or unjust, are in their tombs and nowhere else. 1 Cor. 15.52 [...]; 1 Thess. 4.13–17: *but I do not want you to be ignorant, brothers, about those who have gone to sleep, in case you should grieve, like those other people who have no hope. For if we believe that Jesus was dead and rose again, so too God, through Jesus, will bring with him those who have been asleep. For we say this to you by the words of the Lord, that we who shall be left alive when the Lord comes, shall not go before those who have been asleep: for the Lord himself,* etc. *and those who died in Christ shall rise first; then we who are left alive will be snatched up into the clouds along with them, to meet the Lord in the air, and so we shall always be with the Lord.* They *have gone to sleep:* the lifeless body, however, does not sleep, unless, that is, you could say that a piece of stone, for example, sleeps. *In case you should grieve, like those other people who have no hope:* but why should they grieve, why should they have no hope, if they believed that, whatever might happen to the body, the soul would be in a state of salvation and blessedness even before the resurrection? Of course *those other people* who had no hope despaired of the soul as well as of the body, because they did not believe in any resurrection. That is why Paul directs the hope of all believers to the resurrection: *God, through Jesus, will bring with him those who have been asleep,* bring them, that is, into heaven from the grave. *That we who shall be left alive when the Lord comes, shall not go before those who have been asleep:* but there would be no question of *us* going before them if those who had gone to sleep had flown off to heaven long ago. And if they had, they would not now go *to meet the Lord,* but would come back with him. In fact, though, *we who are alive shall be snatched up together with them,* not after them, *and so we shall always be with the Lord:* after the resurrection, that is, not before. And then eventually *the just shall be separated from the wicked,* Matt. 13.49. Dan. 12.2: *many of those sleeping in the dust of the earth shall awake: some to eternal life, some to shame and eternal contempt.* I should say that it was in this same sleep that Lazarus lay, if anyone were to ask where his soul went during those four days of death. Indeed, I should not hesitate to answer that in my opinion his soul was not called down from heaven, to undergo a second time the inconveniences of the body, but was called up from the grave and awakened from the sleep of death. Christ's own words lead me to this conclusion: John 11.11, 13: *our friend Lazarus sleeps, but I am going to awake him from sleep: but Jesus said this of his death:* and if it was really a miracle, then it must really have been death. Christ's behavior when he raised Lazarus points to the same thing, 11.43: *he called*

207. Cp. *PL* 3.245–49: "Though now to Death I yield, and am his due/All that of me can die, yet that debt paid,/Thou wilt not leave me in the loathsome grave/His prey, nor suffer my unspotted soul/Forever with corruption there to dwell."

with a loud voice, Lazarus, come out of there. If Lazarus' soul, that is Lazarus' real self, was not in *there,* why did Christ call to the dead body, for that would not be able to hear. And if he called to the soul, why did he call it from a place where it was not? If he had wanted it to be believed that the soul was separated from the body, then clearly he would have directed his eyes to the place from which the soul of Lazarus ought to return, in other words, to heaven. To call something from the grave which is not in the grave is like seeking the living among the dead, which the angel censured as ignorance in the disciples, Luke 24.5. The same thing is apparent in the raising of the widow's son, Luke 7.14.

On the other hand there are some who insist that the soul is exempt from death. They say that once it has thrown off the body it goes directly to or is led by angels to the place appointed for reward or punishment, and that there it remains in isolation until the end of the world. Their case rests fundamentally on the following texts: Ps. 49.16: *God is going to redeem my soul from the grave.* But this, like the various texts I quoted above, proves rather that the soul goes down into the grave with the body, and therefore stands in need of redemption (i.e., at the resurrection, *when God is going to receive it with power,* as it is said in the same verse). As for the others, *whose redemption is forever wanting,* 49.9, *they are like beasts,* 49.13, 15.

The second text is Eccles. 12.9: *the spirit returning to God, who gave it.* But my opponents cannot prove their point from this either, because *returning to God* must be understood in a very broad sense: after all the wicked do not go to God at death, but far away from him. Moreover, it has already been said in 3.20, that *each of them goes to the same place.* In fact God is referred to as having given spirits to all animals, and as taking them to himself again when the body returns to dust, Job 34.14, 15: if . . . he *takes its spirit and its soul to himself: all flesh will die together, and man will turn back to dust.* Ps. 104.29, 30 says the same. Euripides, in the *Suppliants,* has given a far better interpretation of this passage than my opponents, without knowing it:[208]

Each various part
That constitutes the frame of man, returns
Whence it was taken; to th' ethereal sky
The soul, the body to its earth

that is, when soul and body part, each component returns to the place it came from, to its own element. This is confirmed by Ezek. 37.9: *come from the four winds, o spirit:* obviously the spirit of man must have first gone to *the four winds* if it is now to return from them. I suppose this is what Matt. 24.31 refers to: *they will collect together his elect from the four winds.* Why should they not collect spirits

208. Milton quotes lines 532–34. He praises Euripides to similar effect in *TKM* (p. 1031): "How much more rationally spake the heathen king Demophoön in a tragedy of Euripides than these interpreters would put upon King David."

together just as they do the tiniest particles of bodies, which are often scattered far and wide over the face of the earth? The same goes for 1 Kings 17.21: *I pray that the boy's soul may return.* This, however, is an idiom applied to recovery from any kind of unconsciousness: Judges 15.19: *his spirit returned and he lived,* similarly 1 Sam. 30.12. I have quoted only a few of the very large number of texts which prove that the dead do not have any kind of life. Obviously, however, the passages I have cited above about the death of the spirit are enough to deal with this particular part of my opponents' case.

The third passage they refer to is Matt. 10.28: *they kill the body, they cannot kill the soul.* I reply that strictly speaking the body cannot be killed either, since it is in itself lifeless.[209] So the word *body* here, as usual in scripture, must be taken to stand for the whole human make-up, as it is called, or for the animal and temporal life. The word *soul* must mean that spiritual life which we are to put on after the end of the world. This is clear from the remainder of the verse and from 1 Cor. 15.44.

The fourth passage which they quote is Phil. 1.23: *wishing to be dissolved and to be with Christ.* I will not bother to say anything about the disputed and uncertain translation of the word ἀναλῦσαι which means nothing less than *to be dissolved.*[210] What I will say, however, is that it is true Paul wanted to obtain the highest perfection and glory at once. It was, as it were, his ultimate aim: a thing which all men wish to achieve. But that does not prove that when someone's soul leaves his body it is received into heaven or hell without delay. Paul desired to *be with Christ* at Christ's second coming, an event which all believers confidently hoped would take place in the very near future. In the same way, someone who is going on a voyage wants to set sail and to reach port safely, and hardly mentions the intervening journey. And what about the theory that there is no time without motion? Aristotle illustrates this (*Phys.* 4.11) by the story of those men who were said to have gone to sleep in the temple of the heroes and who, on waking, thought that they had gone to sleep one moment and woken up the next, and were not aware of any interim. It is even more likely that, for those who have died, all intervening time will be as nothing, so that to them it will seem that they die and are with Christ at the same moment. But Christ himself indicates very clearly the time at which we shall eventually be with him, John 14.3: *for after I have gone and prepared a place for you, I shall come again and take you to myself, that where I am, you may be also.*

The fifth passage which my opponents quote obviously favors my argument: 1 Pet. 3.19: *to the spirits which are in prison,* literally *under guard,* or, as the Syriac version has it, *in the grave,* which comes to the same thing, for the grave is the common guardian of everyone until the day of judgment.[211] The apostle repeats the

209. See note 206.

210. The usual translation is "to depart" or, more literally, "to unloose," as in a boat unloosed from its moorings, as the subsequent comparison with a voyage suggests.

211. Milton refers to the Tremellius translation of the Syriac, in the Junius-Tremellius Bible; see 1.5, n. 90.

idea more plainly in 4.5, 6: *he is ready to judge the living and the dead; for this reason the gospel was preached to those who are dead as well,* whereas in the first passage he was speaking metaphorically. It follows that *the spirits which are under guard* are dead spirits.

The sixth passage quoted is Rev. 6.9: *I saw the souls beneath the altar.* My answer is that in biblical idiom the word *soul* is regularly used to mean the whole animate body, and that here the reference is to souls not yet born, unless, that is, the fifth seal had already been opened in John's day. Similarly, Christ makes no distinction whatsoever, in the parable about Dives and Lazarus in Luke 16, between the soul and the body. He does, however, for purposes of instruction, speak of things which will not happen until after the day of judgment as if they had already happened, and represents the dead as existing in two different states.

The seventh passage quoted is Luke 23.43: *then Jesus said to him, I tell you truly today you will be with me in paradise.* This text has, for various reasons, worried a lot of people, so much so that they have not hesitated to alter the punctuation, as if it had been written with a comma after *today.* In other words, *although today I seem to everyone to be utterly wretched and contemptible, I give you my word that you will be with me in paradise. In paradise* means *in some pleasant place* (for strictly speaking paradise is not heaven), or *in some delightful spiritual state which both soul and body enjoy.* This is how other commentators read Matt. 27.52, 53. During the earthquake (which was on the same day, not three days after, as is commonly believed) the graves were opened and the dead arose and came out. Then, 27.52 καὶ ἐξελθόντες, *when they had come out,* they eventually entered the holy city, after the resurrection of Christ. According to Erasmus, that is how the ancient Greeks punctuated the passage, and the Syriac quite clearly supports it: *and they came out, and after his resurrection they entered,* etc. The spiritual state of the souls and bodies of those saints, when they rose from their graves, might well be called paradise, and presumably it was in that state that the penitent thief was united with the other saints, without doing them any harm. Moreover, there is no need to take the word *today* in its strict sense. It can mean merely *in a short time,* as it does in 2 Sam. 16.3 and Heb. 3.7. Anyway, such a large amount of quite unequivocal evidence should not be discounted because of one very obscure text, the meaning of which has never been properly understood.

The eighth text cited is from the same chapter, Luke 23, 46: *I give up my spirit into your hands.* But this does not mean that the spirit is necessarily separable from the body, nor that it is not subject to death. David speaks in the same way, though he was not at the time near to death, Ps. 31.6: *into your hand,* he says, *I resign my spirit,* though it is still in and with his body. Stephen, too, says, Acts 7.59: *Lord Jesus, receive my spirit,* but then, *when he had said this, he fell asleep.* What does this mean? It means that it was not the bare spirit, separated from the body, that he commended to Christ but, as 1 Thess. 5.23 puts it, the whole spirit with the body and the soul. And whereas Christ's spirit, body and soul were to be raised again after three days, Stephen's were to be kept until the Lord's coming. Similarly 1 Pet. 4.19: *let them resign their souls to him, as to a faithful creator, with well doing.*

The ninth passage quoted is 2 Cor. 5.1–20. However it is quite obvious that this does not assert the separation of the soul and body, but merely contrasts the earthly and animal life of the whole man with his spiritual and heavenly life. Thus, in the first verse, *the house of this tabernacle* is not contrasted with the soul, but with *a building* and *a home,* that is, with the final renewal of the whole man, as Beza also explains it, which will take place when we are clothed in the heavens (*clothed, not naked,* 5.3). The fourth verse clearly bears this out: *we do not desire to put off that in which we are created, but to put something on over it, so that mortality may be swallowed up by life:* so does the fifth verse: *God has created us for the same thing.* It is quite plain that this does not mean, for separation of the soul from the body, but rather for us to attain perfection of both. So the eighth verse, *to be absent from the body and to be present with the Lord,* must, in fact, be understood as a reference to our final and perfect beatitude. The word *body* must here be taken to mean this frail worldly life, as is common in the sacred writers, and the word ἐκδήμησιν in the ninth verse should be interpreted as an indication of our eternal removal to a heavenly existence. Similarly, *to be present in the body and to live away from the Lord,* in the sixth verse, seems to mean the same as to be entangled in worldly matters, and so have less time for heavenly things. The reason for this state of affairs is given in the seventh verse: *for we walk by faith, not by sight.* This explains the eighth verse: *we are confident and think it right rather to be absent from the body and to be at home with the Lord:* that is, to renounce worldly things as much as possible and concentrate upon heavenly things. The ninth verse shows still more plainly that the terms *to be absent* and *to be at home* both refer to this life. It says that we strive, whether living at home with God or away from him, to be accepted by him. Obviously, we do not strive in any future life to be acceptable to God in heaven at our resurrection. That is the work of this life alone, and its reward is not to be looked for until the second coming of Christ. For Paul says, 5.10: *we must appear at the judgment-seat of Christ, so that everyone may be paid back for the things which he has done in the body, according to what he has done, whether good or evil.* It follows that there is no rewarding of good or evil after death until that day of judgment. Compare 1 Cor. 15, the whole of which throws a good deal of light on this text. 2 Pet. 1.13–15 should also be compared with the same passage: *as long as I am in this tabernacle,* etc., that is, in this life. What more is there to say? There is virtually no scriptural text left which cannot be countered by one or other of the arguments which I have already produced.

The last degree of death is ETERNAL DEATH, THE PUNISHMENT OF THE DAMNED. Chapter 27 deals with this.[212]

212. Actually, this topic is dealt with in chapter 33.

CHAPTER 14

OF MAN'S RESTORATION AND OF CHRIST THE REDEEMER

We have seen how God's providence operated in man's fall: now let us see how it operates in his restoration.

MAN'S RESTORATION is the act by which man, freed from sin and death by God the Father through Jesus Christ, is raised to a far more excellent state of grace and glory than that from which he fell. Rom. 5.15: *but the free gift does not correspond to the offense: for if through the offense of that one man many are dead, much more has God's grace, and the gift through grace, which is of one man Jesus Christ, overflowed to many,* also 5.17 [. . .], and 5.21 says the same. Eph. 1.9, 10 [. . .]; 1 John 3.8: *the man who commits sin is of the* devil . . . *for this purpose the Son of God was made manifest: that he might destroy the works of the devil.*

ITS COMPONENTS ARE REDEMPTION AND RENOVATION.

REDEMPTION IS THAT ACT BY WHICH CHRIST, SENT IN THE FULNESS OF TIME, REDEEMED ALL BELIEVERS AT THE PRICE OF HIS OWN BLOOD, WHICH HE PAID VOLUNTARILY, IN ACCORDANCE WITH THE ETERNAL PLAN AND GRACE OF GOD THE FATHER.[213]

ACCORDING TO THE ETERNAL PLAN OF GOD THE FATHER. 1 Pet. 1.20: *of the lamb foreknown before the foundations of the world were laid.* See the other relevant passages in Chapter 4, Of Predestination.

AND GRACE. For in pronouncing punishment upon the serpent, at a time when man had only grudgingly confessed his guilt, God promised that he would raise up from the seed of the woman a man who would bruise the serpent's head, Gen. 3.15. This was before he got as far as passing sentence on the man. Thus he prefaced man's condemnation with a free redemption:[214] John 3.16 [. . .]; Rom. 3.25: *whom God has set forth as a means of appeasement through faith,* and 5.8 [. . .]; Heb. 2.9 [. . .]; 1 John 4.9, 10 [. . .]. For this reason the Father is frequently called *our Savior,* as it is by his eternal counsel and grace alone that we are saved.[215] Luke 1.47: *my spirit rejoices in God my Savior,* and 1.68, 69 [. . .]; 1 Tim. 1.1 [. . .], and 2.3 [. . .], and 4.10 [. . .]; Tit. 1.3 [. . .], and 2.10 [. . .] and 3.4–6 [. . .]; Jude 25 [. . .].

CHRIST, SENT IN THE FULLNESS OF TIME: Gal. 4.4 [. . .]; Eph. 1.10: *in the dispensation of the fullness of times.*

AT THE PRICE OF HIS OWN BLOOD: Isa. 53.1, etc., Acts 20.28: *the Church of God, which he has bought with his own blood;* Rom. 3.25 [. . .]; 1 Cor. 6.20 [. . .], simi-

213. Cp. *PL* 3.171–72: "All hast thou spoken as my thoughts are, all/As my eternal purpose hath decreed."
214. Cp. *PL* 11.113–17 and 12.232–35.
215. Cp. *PL* 3.173–75: "Man shall not quite be lost, but saved who will,/Yet not of will in him, but grace in me/Freely vouchsafed"; and 3.181–82: "and to me owe/All his deliv'rance, and to none but me."

larly 7.23. Gal. 3.13 [. . .]; Eph. 5.2 [. . .]; Heb. 2.9 [. . .], and 13.20 [. . .]; 1 Pet. 1.19 [. . .], and 3.18 [. . .]; Rev. 1.5 [. . .], and 5.9: *you have redeemed us to God through your blood,* and 3.8 [. . .].

WHICH HE PAID VOLUNTARILY:[216] Isa. 53.10: *he has laid himself bare;* Matt. 20.28 [. . .]; John 10.15, 18: *no one has taken life from me, but I lay it down: I have power to lay it down and to take it up again;* Eph. 5.2 [. . .]; Phil. 2.8 [. . .]; 1 Tim. 2.6 [. . .].

ALL BELIEVERS:[217] Rom. 3.25: *a means of appeasement through faith in his blood.*

Christ is the only redeemer or mediator: Acts 4.12: *nor is there salvation in any other, for there is no other name under the sky which may be given to men, through which we must be saved;*[218] 1 Tim. 2.5: *one mediator, the man Jesus Christ;* John 14.6 [. . .].

Moreover this promise was made to all mankind, more or less distinctly, and the fulfillment of it expected, right from the time of man's fall.[219] Gen. 3.15 [. . .], and 22. 8: *in your seed all the nations of the earth will be blessed,* similarly 26.4 and 28.14, also 49.10 [. . .]; Deut. 18.15 [. . .]; Job 19.25, 26 [. . .]. The point is made even more clearly throughout the Psalms and the prophetic books. Ps. 89.36, 37: *I have sworn once by my holiness that I will not lie to David: his seed shall endure for ever . . . ;* Isa. 11.1, etc. [. . .]; Jer. 30.9 [. . .], and 33.15 [. . .].

He was sent into the world at a pre-ordained time, see Gal. 4.4, above.

Two things must be considered when we think of Christ as a redeemer: his NATURE and his OFFICE.

His NATURE is double, divine and human. Matt. 16.16: *Christ, the Son of the living God;* Gen. 3.15: *the seed of woman;* John 1.1, 14 [. . .] and 3.13 [. . .], and 3.31 [. . .]; Acts 2.30 [. . .], similarly Rom. 1.3. Rom. 8.3 [. . .], and 9.5 [. . .], *God;* 1 Cor. 15.47 [. . .]; Gal. 4.4 [. . .]; Phil. 2.7, 8 [. . .]; Heb. 2.14, 16: *he himself was made a sharer in flesh and blood; he did not choose the angels, but the seed of Abraham,* and 10.5, etc. [. . .]; 1 John 1.7 [. . .], and 4.2 [. . .]; Col. 2.9: *the whole fullness of the godhead dwells in him bodily.* I should deduce from this passage not Christ's divine nature but the absolute and complete virtue of the Father. I prefer to read *fullness* as *fulfillment,* and take it to mean that the entire fulfillment of the Father's promises resides in, but is not hypostatically united with Christ as a man.[220] And I should say that the word *bodily* ought to be interpreted as meaning *in reality*—not, that is to say, merely in the rudimentary ceremonies of this world.[221] This interpretation is in accordance with Isa. 11.1, 2, etc.: *the spirit of Jehovah shall rest upon him, the spirit of wisdom;* and John 3.34: *God does not measure out the spirit to him,* and 1.17: *grace and truth through Jesus Christ.* Similarly 1 Tim. 3.16: *God made manifest in flesh,* that is, in

216. Cp. Argument, *PL* 3: "The Son of God freely offers himself a ransom for man."

217. Cp. *PL* 12.407–8: "Proclaiming life to all who shall believe/In his redemption."

218. Cp. *PL* 3.274–75: "O thou in Heav'n and Earth the only peace/Found out for mankind under wrath."

219. Cp. *PL* 10.1031–35: "Part of our sentence, that thy seed shall bruise/The serpent's head; piteous amends, unless/Be meant, whom I conjecture, our grand foe/Satan, who in the serpent hath contrived/Against us this deceit"; also 10.182–90.

220. Milton also quotes this verse in chapters 2 and 7, construing it differently each time.

221. The phrase *rudimentary ceremonies of the world* alludes to Gal. 4.3; cp. *PR* 1.157.

his incarnate Son, his image. As for Christ's divine nature, the reader should recollect the arguments I presented in my chapter on the Son of God. Through Christ all things were made, both in heaven and earth, even the angels. In the beginning he was the Word. He was God with God, and although he was not supreme, he was the firstborn of all creation. It follows that he must have existed before his incarnation, whatever subtleties may have been invented to provide an escape from this conclusion, by those who argue that Christ was a mere man.[222]

Christ, then, although he was God, put on human nature, and was made flesh, but did not cease to be numerically one Christ. Theologians are of the opinion that this incarnation is by far the greatest mystery of our religion, next to that of the three persons existing in one divine essence. There is, however, not a single word in the Bible about the mystery of the Trinity, whereas the incarnation is frequently spoken of as a mystery: 1 Tim. 3.16: *the mystery of godliness is unquestionably great, God was made manifest in flesh . . . ;* Col. 2.2, 3 [. . .]; Eph. 1.9, 10 [. . .] and 3.4 [. . .]; similarly Col. 4.3. Eph. 3.9 [. . .]; Col. 1.26, 27 [. . .].

As this is such a great mystery, let its very magnitude put us on our guard from the outset, to prevent us from making any rash or hasty assertions or depending upon the trivialities of mere philosophy. Let it prevent us from adding anything of our own, or even from placing weight upon any scriptural text which can be easily invalidated. Instead, let us make do with the most unambiguous of texts, even though these may be few. If we pay attention only to texts of this kind, and are willing to be satisfied with the simple truth, ignoring the glosses of metaphysicians, how many prolix and monstrous controversies we shall put an end to! How many opportunities for heresy we shall remove: how much of the raw material for heresy we shall cut away! How many huge volumes, the works of dabblers in theology, we shall fling out of God's temple as filth and rubbish! If teachers, teachers even of the reformed church, had learned by now to rely on divine authorities alone where divine matters are concerned, and to concentrate upon the contents of the Bible, then nothing would be more straightforward than what the Christian faith propounds as essential for our salvation. Nothing would be more reasonable, or more adapted to the understanding even of the least intelligent. We should easily see the essentials, once they were disentangled froth the windings of controversy, and we should let mysteries alone and not tamper with them. We should be afraid to pry into things further than we were meant.

I will now outline the orthodox position, as it stands today and as, indeed, it has stood for a great many years.[223] The assumption which we came across earlier was that there were three persons in one natural entity, the Trinity. This time, however, it is assumed that there are two natures in the one person of

222. Socinians denied the divinity and thus the preexistence of Christ.

223. For Milton's view of the Incarnation in relation to orthodox doctrine, see Lewalski 1966 and Rumrich 2003.

Christ. Furthermore it is assumed that Christ has a real and perfect subsistence in one of these natures, without that nature having a subsistence of its own. Thus two natures make one person. This is what is called, by scholastic philosophers, the hypostatic union. Zanchius explains it as follows, Vol. 1, Pt. 2, Bk. 2, Chap. 7. He took upon him not, strictly speaking, man, he writes, but the human nature. *For when the Logos was in the virgin's womb, it took human nature upon itself by forming a body for itself out of the substance of Mary, and at the same time creating a soul for that body. And he assumed this nature in and for himself in such a way that the nature never subsisted by itself, independent of the Logos, but has always subsisted, both at first and ever since, in the Logos alone.*

I will not bother to point out that there is no mention of these curious secrets anywhere in the Bible. Zanchius is rash enough to expound them on his own authority, and does so as confidently as if he had been present in Mary's womb and witnessed the mystery himself. But what an absurd idea, that someone should take human nature upon himself without taking manhood as well! For human nature, that is, the form of man contained in flesh, must, at the very moment when it comes into existence, bring a man into existence too, and a whole man, with no part of his essence or his subsistence (if that word signifies anything) or his personality missing.[224] As a matter of fact subsistence does not really mean anything except substantial existence, and personality is merely a word which has been wrenched from its proper meaning to help patch up the holes in the arguments of theologians. Obviously the Logos became what it assumed, and if it assumed human nature, but not manhood, then it became an example of human nature, not a man. But, of course, the two things are really inseparable.

I will now go on to demonstrate the sheer vacuity of the orthodox view. But first I will explain and differentiate between the meanings of three words which commonly recur in this discussion: *nature, person* and *hypostasis* or, as it is translated in Latin, *substantia* (substance) or *subsistentia* (subsistence). *Nature,* in this context, can only mean either the essence itself or the properties of that essence. But as these properties are inseparable from the essence itself, and as the unity of natures is *hypostatical* not *accidental,* we must conclude that *nature* can mean nothing in this context except the essence itself. *Person* is a theatrical term which has been adopted by scholastic theologians to mean any one individual being, as the logicians put it: any intelligent ens, numerically one whether it be one God or one angel or one man. The Greek word *hypostasis* can, in this context, mean only what is expressed by the Latin words *substantia* or

224. Milton rejects the orthodox doctrine that Christ took on generic human nature. Logicians typically make form generic and matter specific. But for Milton, form is the principle of individuation and numerical difference; matter the principle of commonality (cp. *Art of Logic,* Yale 8:233–34; *PL* 5.472–75). The Son by taking human matter becomes generically human; by assuming the specific form of Jesus he becomes an individual man.

subsistentia (i.e., substance or subsistence). It denotes, then, merely a perfect essence existing *per se*, and is therefore usually used in opposition to *accidents*.

It follows that the union of two natures in Christ was the mutual hypostatic union of two essences. Because where a perfect substantial essence exists, there must also be a hypostasis or subsistence, since they are quite evidently the same thing. So one Christ, one ens, and one person is formed from this mutual hypostatic union of two natures. There is no need to be afraid that two persons will result from the union of two hypostases, any more than from the union of two natures, that is, of two essences. But supposing Christ's human nature never had its own separate subsistence, or supposing the Son did not take that subsistence upon himself: it would follow that he could not have been a real man, and that he could not have taken upon himself the true and perfect substance or essence of man. He could not have done so, that is, any more than he could cause his body to be present in the sacrament without mass or local extension, which is what the Papists maintain.[225] They explain this phenomenon, if you please, by reference to divine power, their usual shift in such cases. But it is no good pleading divine power if you cannot prove it on divine authority. There is, then, in Christ a mutual hypostatic union of two natures or, in other words, of two essences, of two substances and consequently of two persons. And there is nothing to stop the properties of each from remaining individually distinct. It is quite certain that this is so. We do not know how it is so, and it is best for us to be ignorant of things which God wishes to remain secret.[226] After all, if it were legitimate to be definite and dogmatic about mysteries of this kind, why should we not play the philosopher and start asking questions about the external form common to these two natures? Because if the divine nature and the human nature coalesced in one person, that is to say, as my opponents themselves admit, in a rational being numerically one, then they must have coalesced in one external form as well. As a result the divine form, if it were not previously identical with the human, must have been either destroyed or blended with the human, both of which seem absurd. Or else the human form, if it did not precisely resemble the divine, must have been either destroyed or blended with the divine. Or else Christ must have had two forms. How much better for us, then, to know only that the Son of God, our Mediator, was made flesh and that he is called and is in fact both God and man.[227] The Greeks express this concept very neatly by the single word θεάνθρωπος. As God has not revealed to us how this comes about it is much better for us to hold our tongues and be wisely ignorant.[228]

However, the opinion I have advanced here about the hypostatic union cor-

225. Cp. *DDD* (p. 902): "those words . . . are as much against plain equity, and the mercy of religion, as those words of 'Take, eat, this is my body,' elementally understood, are against nature and sense."

226. Cp. *PL* 8.71–78 and 172–74.

227. *PL* 3.238: "Account me man"; and 3.315–16: "Here shalt thou sit incarnate, here shalt reign / Both God and man, Son both of God and man." Also 3.283–85, 303–4; 10.60–62; 12.380–82.

228. *PL* 8.173: "be lowly wise."

roborates further the conclusion of my more lengthy discussion of the Son of God in the fifth chapter (i.e. that the essence of the Son is not the same as the essence of the Father). For if it were the same the Son could not have coalesced in one person with man, unless the Father had also been included in the same union—unless, in fact, man had become one person with the Father as well as with the Son, which is impossible.

So let us get rid of those arguments which are produced to prove that the person who was made flesh must necessarily be the supreme God. First of all there is that text from Heb. 7.26, 27: *such a high priest was fitting for us, holy, removed from all evil, spotless, separate from sinners, and made higher than the heavens.* But these words do not prove even that he is God, let alone that he must have been God. To begin with he was *holy* not only as God but as man, since he was conceived through the Holy Spirit and by the power of the Most High. Furthermore, he is not said to have been higher than the heavens, but to have been *made higher* than them. Again *to last for ever,* 7.24, is common both to angels and to men, and the fact that he *can save those who come to God through him,* 7.25, does not prove that he is God either. Finally, it is said that *the word of the oath, taken since the law, makes the Son perfect for ever,* 7.28, and it certainly does not follow from this that he is God. Besides, the Bible nowhere states that only God can approach God, or take away sin, or fulfil the law, or endure and overcome the anger of God, the power of Satan and temporal and eternal death, or recover the blessings lost by us. What it does state is that he whom God has empowered to do all this can do it: in other words, God's beloved Son with whom God has declared himself pleased.

So since we must believe that Christ, after his incarnation, remained one Christ it is not for us to ask whether he retained a two-fold intellect or a two-fold will, for the Bible says nothing of these things. For he could, with the same intellect, both *increase in wisdom,* Luke 2.52, after he had emptied himself, and *know everything,* John 21.17, that is, after the Father had instructed him, as he himself acknowledges.[229] That single text, Matt. 26.39: *not as I will but as you will,* does not imply a two-fold will, unless he and the Father are the same, and as I have already shown this cannot be so.

The fact that Christ had a body shows that he was a real man, Luke 24.39: *a spirit does not have flesh and bones, as you see I have;* so does the fact that he had a soul,[230] Mark 10.45: *that he might give his soul for many,* and 14.34: *my soul is sad, sad to death;* and a spirit, Luke 23.46: *I give up my spirit into your hands.* True, God also claims that he himself has a soul and a spirit. But the Bible gives some absolutely unambiguous reasons why Christ must have been a man: 1 Cor. 15.21: *for since death came through man, through man came also the resurrection of the dead;* Heb. 2.14: *since children are sharers in flesh and blood, he too, likewise . . . that through death he*

229. Cp. *PR* 1.293: "For what concerns my knowledge God reveals."

230. *PL* 3.247–49: "Thou wilt not leave me in the loathsome grave/His prey, nor suffer my unspotted soul/Forever with corruption there to dwell."

might smash him in whose power the strength of death lies, that is, the devil, and 2.17 [. . .], and 2.18 [. . .]; and 4.15 [. . .], and 5.2 [. . .]. Moreover, God would not accept any other sacrifice, since any other would have been less worthy. Heb. 10.5: *you did not want a sacrifice, but you have prepared a body for me,* and 8.3 [. . .], and 9.22 [. . .].

Since Christ's two natures add up to a single person, there are certain things which seem to be said about him in an unrestricted way which actually have to be applied to one or other of the two natures. This way of speaking is known as *communicatio idiomatum* or *proprietatum.* It means that something which is proper to one of the two natures is, by idiomatic license, transferred to the other. John 3.13: *the Son of man, who is in heaven, came down from heaven,* and 8.58: *before Abraham existed, I am.* So these and similar passages, whenever they occur, are to be understood κατ' ἄλλο καὶ ἄλλο, as theologians put it: ἄλλο καὶ ἄλλο not ἄλλος καὶ ἄλλος because it refers not to Christ's self, but to his *person* (i.e. his office of mediator).[231] As for his natures themselves, they constitute in my opinion too deep a mystery for anyone to say anything definite about them.

But sometimes attributes which belong to Christ as a whole are applied to one or other of his natures. 1 Tim. 2.5: *the mediator between God and men, the man Christ Jesus.* It is not as man, however, that Christ is mediator, but as θεάνθρωπος.

It is more usual for the Bible to distinguish the things which are peculiar to his human nature. Acts 2.30: *from David's loins* τὸ κατὰ σάρκα *insofar as the flesh is concerned;* also Rom. 9.5. 1 Pet. 3.18: *having been put to death in the flesh,* that is principally and more obviously in the flesh than in any other way. This point will be raised again in Chapter 16.

There are two parts to Christ's incarnation: the conception and the nativity. The efficient cause of the former was the Holy Spirit, Matt. 1.20: *that which is conceived in her is of the Holy Spirit;* Luke 1.35: *the Holy Spirit shall come upon you, and the power of the Highest shall overshadow you.* I should say that these words refer to the power and spirit of the Father himself, as I have shown before: compare Ps. 40.7 with Heb. 10.5, 6: *you have prepared a body for me.*

The aim of this miraculous conception was to evade the pollution of Adam's sin. Heb. 7.26: *such a high priest was fitting for us, holy, spotless, separate from sinners.*

Christ's birth is foretold by all the prophets, and more particularly in Mic. 5.2: *but you Bethlehem Ephratah;* Isa. 7.14 [. . .], and 11.1 [. . .]. It is narrated in Matt. 1.18 onwards; Luke 1.42: *blessed is the fruit of your womb,* and 2.6, 7 [. . .], and 2.22 [. . .].

The following arguments can be used to prove that, in spite of what the Jews believe, the Messiah has already come. First, the cities of Bethlehem and Nazareth are now destroyed. It was in these that the Christ was to be born and educated: Mic. 5.2; Zech. 6.12: *behold a man whose name is Nazer or the offshoot.* Secondly, it was foretold that he would come while the second temple and the

231. Milton distinguishes between the neuter ἄλλο and masculine ἄλλος forms of the Greek word for "other, another." Christ's *self,* Milton insists, is masculine, though the communicable *office* he fulfills is neuter.

Jewish republic were still in existence. Hag. 2.7, 9 [. . .]; Dan. 9.24 [. . .], and 9.26 [. . .], and 9.27 [. . .]; Zech. 9.9 [. . .]; Gen. 49.10: *the people shall not depart from Judah, nor a lawgiver from between his feet, until Shiloh comes.* The three most ancient Jewish commentators, Onkelos, Jonathan and Hierosolymitanus took this name to mean the Messiah. Dan. 2.44: *in the days of those kings the God of heaven will set up a kingdom.* Thirdly, the Gentiles have long since left off worshipping other gods and have embraced the faith of Christ, and it was foretold that this would not happen before Christ's coming: Gen. 49.10: *and the obedience of the peoples will be to him;* Isa. 2.2: *it will happen in the last days that all the Gentiles will come flocking to him,* similarly Mic. 4.1; Hag. 2.7 [. . .]; Mal. 3.1 [. . .], etc.

CHAPTER 16

OF THE ADMINISTRATION OF REDEMPTION

[. . .][232]

ON BEHALF OF ALL MEN. Rom. 5.18: *a benefit upon all men;* 2 Cor. 5.15: *that if one died for all, then surely all were dead.* If this follows, then the converse is also true, that if all were dead because Christ died for all, then he died for all who were dead, that is, for everyone. Eph. 1.10: *to collect together all things in Christ, both the things in heaven and the things on earth* (i.e., everything on earth, without exception, as well as everything in heaven). Col. 1.20: *that through him he might reconcile all things;* 1 Tim. 2.4 [. . .] also 2.6; Heb. 2.9: *for all men,* also 2 Pet. 3.9. Moreover there are numerous texts which say that Christ was given for the whole world: John 3.16, 17: *God loved the world so much that he gave his only begotten Son, so that everyone who believes in him may not perish but have eternal life,* etc., and 6.51 [. . .]. Also 1 John 4.14. But those who maintain that Christ made satisfaction for the elect alone, argue that *the world* should be interpreted as meaning only the elect in the world. They take as proof of this the fact that in other passages Christ is said to have made satisfaction *for us* which they, of course, take to mean *for the elect:* Rom. 8.34; 2 Cor. 5.21 and Tit. 2.14: *for us.* But to begin with, anyone who examines these texts at all carefully will soon see that it cannot be only the elect in *the world* who are meant. For if anyone were to explain the first passage from St. John according to their theory (*God loved the world,* that is, *the elect, so much that everyone of the elect who believes in him shall not perish*), it would be ridiculous. For who is elect and does not believe? So it must be that God has here divided the world into believers and unbelievers; and when on the one hand he declared *that everyone who believes in him shall not perish,* he must have meant that, conversely, *everyone shall perish who does not believe.* What is more, when *the world*

232. The deleted section concerns the mediatorial functions of the incarnate Son's righteous life, sacrificial death, and subsequent exaltation. According to Calvinist orthodoxy as defined at the Synod of Dort (1618–19), the Son suffered on behalf of the elect only. In the ensuing excerpt, the Arminian Milton asserts instead that Christ died for all humanity.

does not mean *everyone* it quite frequently means *the worst people in the world:* John 14.17: *the spirit of truth, which the world cannot receive,* and 15.19: *the world hates you,* and often elsewhere. Besides, where Christ is said to have made satisfaction *for us,* it is quite explicitly stated that other people are not excluded: 1 John 2.2: *not for ours alone, but for the sins of the whole world.* What could be more comprehensive? The same applies in those passages where Christ is said to act *for his sheep,* John 10.16, or *for the church,* Acts 20.28; Eph. 5.23, 25. Furthermore, as I have demonstrated above,[233] sufficient grace is imparted to all men. So it must follow that Christ has made satisfaction for all men to a sufficient extent and efficaciously enough to meet the requirements of God's plan and will. For without that absolutely full satisfaction even the smallest measure of grace could not possibly have been imparted at all. It is true that a large number of passages may be cited where Christ is said to have paid the price *for many,* as for example Matt. 20.28: *a ransom for many;* Heb. 9.28: *of many,* and others of the same sort. These passages, however, in no way deny that he paid it *for all;* for *all* are certainly *many.* Should anyone choose to argue that if a thing is *for many* it is not *for all,* there are other quite unambiguous texts which plainly contradict this assertion. The principal one is Rom. 5.19: *as through one man's disobedience many were made sinners.* Who would deny that here *many* means *all*? But suppose these opponents of mine should interpret *for all* as if it means *for anyone you please to name.* Suppose they should take it to mean, as they themselves put it, for kinds of individuals, not for individuals of all kinds. Even then they would not prove their point, quite apart from the fact that they are ignoring the accepted sense of a general term merely for the sake of their own theories. For the Bible testifies that Christ made satisfaction for individuals of every class, saying as it does so frequently that he died *for all* and *for the whole world* and *for none who are not to be saved,* 2 Pet. 3.9. It bears witness to this just as firmly as that lone text, Rev. 5.9, does to the fact that Christ made satisfaction for kinds of individuals *from every tribe and tongue and people and nation.* It may be proved, moreover, that Christ made satisfaction not only for the elect but also for the so-called reprobate: Matt. 18.11: *the Son of man has come to save that which had perished.* But all men had perished. It follows that he came to save all men, the reprobate and the so-called elect alike. John 3.17: *God did not send his Son into the world to condemn the world* (though that is what he was sent for, according to those people who say that he was sent for the elect alone, and in order to make the condemnation of the reprobate more heavy), *but that the world might be saved through him.* This must refer to the so-called reprobate, because it would be superfluous to foretell salvation for the elect. Similarly John 12.4 and John 6.32: *my Father gives you that true heavenly bread: you,* that is, *unbelievers,* 6.36; and *gives,* that is, offers in a sincere way. *For that bread of God gives life to the world,* that is, to everyone, because it gives life *even to you unbelievers* provided that you do not yourselves reject it: Acts 17.30, 31: *now he commands all men everywhere to repent, because he has fixed a day upon which he will judge the world justly.* Obviously he will

233. See chapter 4.

call to repentance those whom he is going to judge, and as he is going to judge every individual it follows that he calls every individual to repentance. However, no one would have been thought worthy of this gracious call had not Christ interposed and made a satisfaction, and a satisfaction which was not only sufficient in itself but also effectual, insofar as God's will was concerned, for all men. This must be so, unless the call was not meant seriously. But though the call and the gift are God's concern, the acceptance of them depends upon the faith of man. If there is not enough faith to make the satisfaction effectual, then it does not mean that the satisfaction was not given effectually, but simply that it was not accepted.

[. . .][234]

There is no need to be afraid that by this reasoning we shall help to establish the doctrine of human merit. The fact that we shape ourselves to Christ's image does not add anything at all to Christ's full and perfect satisfaction, any more than our good works add anything to our faith. It is faith that justifies, but a faith not without works. If we deserve anything, if we are worthy in any sense, then it is God who has made us worthy in Christ: Col. 1.12: *giving thanks to the Father, who has made us fit . . .* ; 2 Thess. 1.11: *that he may count you worthy.* See more on this point in the chapter on justification.[235] But insofar as Christ's election and our election by God the Father are concerned, the restitution of man is simply a matter of grace. So it is often said in the gospel that the Father has given those who are the Son's to the Son, and also that he has given the Son to those that are the Son's.

The Papists' tale about a purgatory in which sins are melted down and cleansed or purged by fire is obviously untrue for a whole host of reasons, but above all because of the full satisfaction which Christ has made. Quite apart from the fact that there is not a word about any kind of purgatory in the Bible, if Christ's blood has made full satisfaction for us and thoroughly cleansed us from every stain then nothing at all can be left for the fire to purge. There are some who take *that fire* mentioned in 1 Cor. 3.13, 15 to be a real fire. But they must realize that this is not purgatory; it is merely the fire prepared to test false teachers. *The day,* that is, the light of truth, will make it plain whether their teaching was flashy and decked out with a lot of trumpery or whether it was crude and boorish. Like *the fire of afflictions* in 1 Pet. 4.12, this fire does not purge us in the life to come but tests us in this. Besides, all retribution after this life, all sense of pleasure or pain, is deferred until Christ's judgment day, 2 Cor. 5.10: *that everyone may be paid back for the things which he has done in the body, according to what he has done, whether good or evil.* Moreover if, as I have shown above, the soul as well as the body goes to sleep until the day of resurrection, then obviously there can be no stronger argument against the idea of a purgatory. To those who

234. In the deleted passage, Milton argues that Christ made satisfaction for sinners, and for the elect only as they were formerly sinners. He explains that the redeemed share in Christ's humiliation and exaltation.

235. That is, chapter 22.

are going to be saved no middle state, except death, is assigned between the *earthly house* of this life and *that eternal home in the heavens,* 2 Cor. 5.1. 2 Tim. 4.8: *a crown of righteousness is laid up for me which the Lord, the righteous judge, will give me on that day.*

CHAPTER 17

OF RENOVATION AND ALSO OF VOCATION

I have now dealt with man's REDEMPTION and will go on to discuss his RENOVATION.

It is by MAN'S RENOVATION that he is BROUGHT TO A STATE OF GRACE AFTER BEING CURSED AND SUBJECT TO GOD'S ANGER. Eph. 2.3, 5, etc.: *we were by nature children of anger: you are saved by grace,* and 1.3, 5 [. . .]; Col. 3.10 [. . .]; Eph. 4.23, 24: *renewed in the true spirit of your mind, and to put on that new man, who is created according to God, to righteousness and true holiness;* 2 Cor. 4.16 [. . .]; Tit. 3.5 [. . .]; Rom. 12.2 [. . .]; Heb. 6.4, 6 [. . .].

When dealing with renovation we must consider both how it takes place, and how this shows itself.

Renovation takes place either naturally or supernaturally. When I say that it takes place naturally I mean that it affects only the natural man. This includes vocation, and the alteration in the natural man which follows it.

VOCATION is that natural method of renovation by which GOD THE FATHER, ACCORDING TO HIS PRECONCEIVED PURPOSE IN CHRIST, INVITES FALLEN MEN TO A KNOWLEDGE OF THE WAY TO PLACATE AND WORSHIP HIS GODHEAD AND, OUT OF GRATUITOUS KINDNESS, INVITES BELIEVERS TO SALVATION SO THAT THOSE WHO DO NOT BELIEVE ARE DEPRIVED OF ALL EXCUSE.

[. . .] [236]

Vocation, then, is either general or special. It is by general vocation that God invites all men to a knowledge of his true godhead. He does this in various ways, but all of them are sufficient to his purpose: John 1.9: *that was the true light, which gives light to every man who comes into the world;* Acts 14.17: *he did not allow himself to exist without evidence;* Rom. 1.19 [. . .] and 2.15 [. . .].

But, you may object, it is not true that everyone has known Christ. I reply that this does not alter the fact that everyone is called and called in Christ alone. Because if Christ had not been given to the world God would not have called anyone at all. Since, moreover, the price of redemption which he has paid is sufficient for all mankind, it follows that everyone is called to share in that grace although everyone may not know how the grace is given. After all, Job believed that his sacrifice would be valid for his children, even though they were

236. Cp. *PL* 3.185–202. In the deleted passage, Milton substantiates each phrase of this definition with multiple citations of Scripture, without commentary.

not present when it was offered and had, perhaps, nothing of the sort in mind, Job 1.5. And the Jews who returned believed that it was not in vain for them to make sacrifices on behalf of the remainder of the ten tribes, although they were then a long way away and quite ignorant of what was going on at Jerusalem. How much more, then, ought we to believe that Christ's perfect sacrifice is in every way sufficient even for those who have never heard of his name, but who only believe in God. I shall say more about this when I discuss faith.

Special vocation means that God, whenever he chooses, invites certain selected individuals, either from the so-called elect or from the reprobate, more clearly and more insistently than is normal.

Certain selected individuals: he called Abraham, for example, out of his house, when he probably had not the slightest idea that such a thing would happen, Gen. 12.1, etc. and when, in fact, he was an idolater:[237] Josh. 24.2, 3: *they worshipped strange gods. But I took your father Abraham . . .* He also called the Israelites, for the sake of his name and of the promises he had made to their forbears. Ps. 147.19, 20: *he shows his words to Jacob . . . : he has not treated any nation like this, with the result that they have ignored his judgments.* Another reason is given in Matt. 9.13: *I have not come to call the righteous but sinners,* and 15.26 [. . .]; Acts 16.6, 7 [. . .], and 16.9 [. . .].

Either elect. Rom. 8.28–30: *with those who love God, with those, that is, who are called according to his purpose;* 1 Cor. 1.26: *you see your vocation, brothers . . . God has chosen the foolish things of the world;* 2 Tim. 1.9 [. . .]; Rev. 19.9 [. . .].

Or reprobate: Isa. 28.13: *but the word of Jehovah gave them command after command;* Ezek. 2.4, 5: *as they are obdurate children;* see also 2.7, 17, 21 and 3.12; Matt. 10.18 [. . .], and 11.21 [. . .], and 22.8, 9 [. . .], and 22.10 [. . .], and 23.37 [. . .]; Luke 7.30: *they have scorned God's counsel;* Acts 7.51: *you always strive against the Holy Spirit,* and 13.46 [. . .].

Whenever he chooses . . . Matt. 20.1–3, etc.: *he went out about the third hour;* Acts 14.16 [. . .] and 17.27, 30: *he turned a blind eye upon those times of ignorance, but now he commands all men . . . ;* Eph. 3.5 [. . .]; Rom. 16.25 [. . .]. Then at last the gospel was proclaimed, Matt. 28.19: *go out and teach all nations . . . ;* Mark 16.15: *to every creature;* Rom. 10.18 [. . .]; Col. 1.26 [. . .].

The change in man which follows his vocation is that whereby the mind and will of the natural man are partially renewed and are divinely moved towards knowledge of God, and undergo a change for the better, at any rate for the time being.

Since this change comes from God it is called *light* and *the gift of will.* Sometimes the Father is named as its source: Eph. 1.17, 18: *the God of our Lord Jesus Christ . . . , having given light to the eyes of your mind;* 2 Cor. 4.6 [. . .]; James 1.17 [. . .]; Luke 11.13 [. . .]: sometimes the Son, John 1.9: *that was the true light, which gives light to every man who comes into the world:* and sometimes the Holy Spirit, Heb. 6.4, etc.: *enlightened, and sharers of the Holy Spirit.*

237. Cp. *PL* 12.113–15: "A nation from one faithful man to spring: / . . . / Bred up in idol-worship."

As this change is by way of being an effect produced in man, and as it happens in answer to the call, it is sometimes called a *hearing* or a *listening,* though it is usually understood that the ability to hear or listen is itself a gift from God. It is also sometimes called *a taste.*[238] Hearing, Matt. 11.15: *he who has ears to hear, let him hear:* Thus Herod is said to have *willingly heard* John the Baptist, Mark 6.20, and Agrippa, Paul, Acts 26.28 and 16.14: *the Lord opened her heart so that she should attend to . . . ;* Rom. 6.17 [. . .]; Heb. 3.7 [. . .]. Taste, Heb. 6.4: *enlightened and have tasted that heavenly gift, sharers of the Holy* Spirit . . . if *they fall away* . . . Even man's weakest effort is ascribed to this source. Luke 11.13: *how much more shall your heavenly Father give the Holy Spirit to those who ask him?;* Phil. 2.12, 13: *work out your own salvation with fear and trembling. For it is God who works in you to will and act for his pleasure.* What can this mean but that God gives us the power to act freely, which we have not been able to do since the fall unless called and restored? We cannot be given the gift of will unless we are also given freedom of action, because that is what free will means.

[. . .][239]

CHAPTER 22

OF JUSTIFICATION

[. . .][240]

Now here is a question over which there is very fierce controversy: does faith alone justify? Our theologians say yes; and hold, moreover, that works are the effects of faith, not the causes of justification, Rom. 3.24, 27, 28; Gal. 2.16, as above. Others contend that we are not justified by faith alone, and they base their argument on James 2.24: *that man is justified by works, and not by faith only.* As the two points of view seem incompatible, our theologians argue that James must be talking about justification in the sight of men, not in the sight of God. But anyone who reads carefully from verse fourteen to the end of the chapter will see that the main topic is justification in God's sight. The faith which is being discussed is the faith of which James asks the usefulness, it is the faith which lives and saves. It cannot, therefore, be the faith which justifies only in the sight of men, since this faith might be hypocritical. What the apostle is saying is that we are not justified only by a useful, true and living faith, a faith which saves, but by works as well. As it is, then, the apostles pay very particular attention to this part of our religion. Their conclusion is never *that man is justified by faith alone,*

238. Cp. *PL* 3.198–99: "This my long sufferance and my day of grace/They who neglect and scorn, shall never taste."

239. The deleted passage identifies penitence and faith as two aspects of the change in man brought about by his vocation.

240. The deleted passage defines justification as a function of God's mercy, effected by "Christ's absolutely full satisfaction." The parts of the definition are substantiated almost entirely through scriptural quotations without additional comment.

but generally *that man is justified by faith without the works of the law,* Rom. 3.28. I cannot imagine what came into our theologians' heads to make them abridge the words of the apostles' conclusion. Had they not done so they would have seen that the two points of view, *that man is justified by faith without the works of the law,* and *that man is justified by works, not by faith alone,* are quite compatible. For Paul does not say that man is justified simply through faith, without works, but *without the works of the law.* Nor does he say that he is justified by faith alone, but *by faith working through charity,* Gal. 5.6. Faith has its own works, which may be different from the works of the law. We are justified, then, by faith, but a living faith, not a dead one, and the only living faith is a faith which acts, James 2.17, 20, 26. So we are justified by faith without the works of the law, but not without the works of faith; for a true and living faith cannot exist without works, though these may be different from the works of the written law. Take for example the works of Abraham and of Rahab. The one offered his son as a sacrifice, the other harbored spies. They are both cited by James as examples of the works of faith. To these two instances I should add that of Phinehas. His action was *imputed to him as righteousness,* Ps. 106.31, and these are the very words which are used when Abraham's faith is *imputed to* him, Gen. 15.6; Rom. 4.9. It will be difficult for anyone to deny that Phinehas was justified in the sight of God rather than in the sight of man, or that his act, which is recorded in Num. 25.11, 12, was a work of faith and not of the law. It follows that Phinehas was not justified by faith alone but by the works of faith as well. I will explain the principle of this doctrine more fully later, when I discuss the gospel and Christian liberty.

The above argument does not establish the doctrine of human merit, since both faith itself and the works of faith are works of the Spirit, not our own. Eph. 2.8–10: *by grace you are saved through faith: and this is not something which comes from you, it is the gift of God. Not by works, in case anyone should boast; for we are his work, created in Christ Jesus for good works, which God has prepared that we may perform them.* Here the works about which a man might boast are distinguished from those works which do not give rise to boasting, that is to say, from the works of faith. Similarly Rom. 3.27, 28: *where is boasting then? It is excluded. By what law? The law of works? No: but by the law of faith.* But what is the law of faith except the works of faith? So whenever the words *of the law* are omitted after the word *works,* as in Rom. 4.2, they must be supplied. Alternatively the words *of the flesh* may be supplied, as they are in 4.1 (*of the law* would not do here since the subject is Abraham, who lived before the law). If these words are not supplied Paul will be contradicting himself as well as James. He will be contradicting himself by saying that Abraham had reason to boast of his works, when he had said in the previous chapter, 3.27, 28, that *by the law of faith,* that is *by the works of faith, boasting* was *excluded.* And he will be flatly contradicting James who asserts, as I quoted above, *that man is justified by works and not by faith alone.* He will be contradicting him, that is, unless we understand that James is referring to the works of faith, and not to the works of the law. Similarly Rom. 4.13: *not through the law, . . . but through the righteousness of faith.* We are meant to interpret Matt. 5.20 in the same way: *unless your righteousness is more abundant than that of the lawyers and the Pharisees, you will not...* The righteousness of the doctors of the law and of the Pharisees was absolutely scrupulous, insofar as the law was concerned. James 1.25: *because he is not a forgetful hearer but a doer of the work;* Heb. 12.14: *seek for peace with all men, and holiness, without which no man shall see the Lord.* Hence, perhaps, Rev. 2.26: *if anyone gives attention to my works;* 1 John 3.7: *little children, let no one deceive you, the man that behaves righteously is righteous.*

This line of argument does not in any way belittle Christ's satisfaction. Our faith is imperfect, so it follows that the works of faith cannot be pleasing to God except insofar as they depend upon his mercy and Christ's righteousness. It is this mercy and this righteousness alone that makes them valid. Phil. 3.9: *that I may be found in him, not having my righteousness from to the law, but through the faith of Christ, righteousness from God through faith;* Tit. 3.5–7 [...] ; 1 John 2.29 [...].

In the opinion of the Papists it is as absurd to say that we are made righteous by the righteousness of another, as to say that a man is learned by the learning of another. But this is not really an analogy. For the relationship between one man and another is not at all the same as that between a believer and Christ, his head. At the same time the Papists do not realize the palpable absurdity of their own doctrine that the righteousness of the dead, or of monks, can be imputed to other people.

They argue too, on the authority of several biblical texts, that man is justified by his own works: Ps. 18.21, 25: *Jehovah has rewarded me according to my righteousness ...;* Rom. 2.6: *he shall repay each man according to his works.* But it is one thing to repay a man *according to* his works, and another to repay him *because of* them. It does not follow from the texts quoted that works have any inherent justifying power, or that they deserve anything on their own account. For if we do anything right, and if God rewards righteous actions at all, it is entirely thanks to his grace. That is why we find, in the previous verse of the same psalm: *he delivers me because he delights in me,* and in Ps. 62.12: *that kindness is yours, O Lord, you will repay each man according to his work.* Moreover the psalmist who attributes righteousness to himself attributes iniquity also, in the same sentence, Ps. 18.24: *when I am perfect before him, and beware of my iniquity.*

As for Matt. 25.34, 35: *possess the* kingdom ... for *I was hungry and you gave me...;* this should be explained as follows. Christ will give sentence on the judgment day with reference not to faith, which is the internal cause of justification, but to the effects and signs of faith or, in other words, the works of faith. He will do this in order to demonstrate the justice of his sentence more clearly to all mankind.

It is true that sometimes a man is said to be perfect or righteous in the sight of God. This happens in Luke 1.6, for example, when Zacharias and his wife are under discussion: *they were both righteous in the sight of God, walking in all the commandments and ordinances of the Lord, blameless.* But this is always to be understood with reference to human standards of perfection. It is a comparative estimate, made with other mortals in mind. Or it may simply mean that they were sincere and blameless, without any dissimulation, as in Deut. 18.13: *be blameless with Jehovah your God.* The words *in the sight of God* seem to favor this interpretation; compare Gen. 17.1: *walk always in my sight;* Ps. 19.13 [. . .]; Eph. 1.4: *he has chosen us that we may be holy and blameless in his sight, with charity.* Or, finally, it may mean that he is called righteous by God through grace and faith, as Noah was, Gen. 6.8: *he found grace in the eyes of Jehovah,* and so, 6.9: *Noah, a just man, was perfect in his days, and he always followed God.* Compare Heb. 11.7: *he was made the heir of righteousness which is by faith.*

As for Luke 7.47: *her many sins are forgiven, for she has loved much,* it should be noticed that love was here not the cause but the sign or even the effect of forgiveness. This is evident from the parable, which begins at 7.40, and in which the debtors are not forgiven because they loved a great deal, but on the contrary they loved because they were forgiven a great deal. The same thing is apparent from the words which follow: *he to whom little is forgiven, loves little,* and the point is made even more clearly by 7.50: *your faith has saved you.* Obviously the quality which saved her was the quality which justified her, and that was not love, but faith, and faith which was itself the cause of her love. See 2.1, below, on the subject of merit.

It is only from an awareness of justification that peace and true tranquility of mind arise. Rom. 5.1, etc.: *justified, we have peace with God;* 1 Cor. 7.15: *God has called us to peace;* Phil. 4.7 [. . .]; Col. 3.15 [. . .]. This is that peace which the apostles repeatedly wish upon the church when they send it greeting.

CHAPTER 25

OF INCOMPLETE GLORIFICATION ALSO OF THE ASSURANCE OF SALVATION AND THE PERSEVERANCE OF THE SAINTS

[. . .][241]

These three, regeneration, growth and preservation, considered as proximate causes for which God is responsible; and their effects, such as *faith, charity* and so on for which man is responsible, or which take place in man, combine to produce the ASSURANCE OF SALVATION and the PERSEVERANCE OF THE SAINTS.

Insofar as God's responsibility is concerned, the primary and more remote cause is his predestination or election of believers: Rom. 8.30 [. . .], 11.29 [. . .]; Heb. 6.17, 18: *in this thing God, wishing abundantly to show the immutability of his plan to the heirs of promise, gave surety on oath that through two immutable things, in which it was impossible for God to lie, we may have strong consolation,* etc.; 2 Pet. 1.4 [. . .].

ASSURANCE OF SALVATION, then, is A CERTAIN DEGREE OF

241. The deleted passage introduces the topic of this chapter—progressive intimations of divine favor toward the regenerate—and illustrates it with a string of quotations from Pauline epistles.

FAITH. IT MEANS THAT A MAN IS PERSUADED BY THE TESTIMONY OF THE SPIRIT, AND FIRMLY BELIEVES THAT IF HE BELIEVES AND PERSISTS IN FAITH AND CHARITY, HE WILL WITHOUT ANY DOUBT ATTAIN ETERNAL LIFE AND PERFECT GLORY, SINCE HE IS ALREADY JUSTIFIED, ADOPTED AND PARTIALLY GLORIFIED BY UNION AND COMMUNION WITH CHRIST AND THE FATHER.

[. . .][242]

The PERSEVERANCE OF THE SAINTS is a GIFT OF GOD THE PRESERVER. IT MEANS THAT THOSE WHO ARE FOREKNOWN, ELECT, REGENERATE AND SEALED THROUGH THE HOLY SPIRIT, PERSEVERE TO THE END IN THE FAITH AND GRACE OF GOD. NO POWER OR GUILE OF WORLD OR DEVIL MAKES THEM ENTIRELY FALL AWAY, SO LONG AS THEY DO NOT PROVE WANTING IN THEMSELVES, AND SO LONG AS THEY CLING TO FAITH AND CHARITY WITH ALL THEIR MIGHT.[243]

A GIFT OF GOD THE PRESERVER. Ps. 26.1: *I trust in Jehovah, I shall not waver;* Luke 22.32 [. . .]; John 6.37 [. . .]; Rom. 5.5 [. . .]; Jude 1 [. . .].

FOREKNOWN. 2 Tim. 2.19: *the foundation of God stands firm, having this seal, The Lord knows his own,* and *Let all who name the name of Christ leave wickedness.*

REGENERATE. John 8.35: *the slave does not stay in the house for ever, but the Son stays for ever.*

NO POWER OR GUILE OF WORLD OR DEVIL. Matt. 24.24 [. . .]; John 10.28, 29 [. . .], and 17.15 [. . .]; Rom. 8.35, 38, 39: *who shall separate us from the love of Christ? Shall affliction, or hardship, or persecution, or hunger, or nakedness, or danger, or the sword? For I am persuaded that neither death, nor life, nor angels, nor principalities, nor powers, nor things present, nor things to come, nor height, nor depth, nor any other created thing can separate us from the love of God, which is in Christ Jesus our Lord.*

SO LONG AS THEY DO NOT PROVE WANTING IN THEMSELVES . . . What made me add this exception was the overall tendency of scripture: Ps. 125.1, 2 [. . .]; 2 Chron. 15.2 [. . .]; Jer. 32.40 *I will make an everlasting covenant with them, that I shall not turn from them when they follow me, in order to do them good, and I will put my reverence in their minds, that they shall not depart from me.* God here promises to put reverence for him into their minds, so that they may not depart from him. In other words he promises to fulfill his own responsibility and give them enough grace to prevent their departure. He also makes a covenant, however, and the conditions of a covenant have to be fulfilled not by

242. The deleted passage cites Scripture to substantiate the definition of ASSURANCE OF SALVATION.

243. The closing conditional clauses in this definition mark the distance between Milton's Arminian position on soteriology (i.e., doctrine pertaining to salvation) and the orthodox Calvinist position. Calvin and his followers argued that the elect could *not* prove wanting in themselves or fail to cling to faith and charity. God had determined their perseverance in advance.

one party alone but by both. One of the conditions here is *that they shall not depart from me.* This means, *from my external worship,* as is clear from the whole chapter, from verse thirty-seven to the end, and from verses twenty and twenty-one of the next chapter: *if you can break my covenant of the* day . . . then *my covenant with my servant David may be broken . . . and with the Levites.* Lastly, it is certain that the people into whose minds God promised to put his reverence on this occasion, to prevent them departing from him, did in fact depart. Thus the same promise is made to their children in 32.39. So the event proved that although God fulfilled the covenant and put reverence into their minds to keep them from departing, nevertheless they did depart through their own viciousness, and it was their fault. What is more, these words are spoken to and about all the Jews, and since all the Jews were not elect, the argument that this speech applies only to the elect just will not work.

Thus Ezek. 11.19–21[. . .]; Matt. 7.24, 25 [. . .]; John 4.14 [. . .], and 6.51 [. . .]; 1 Cor. 10.12: *let him who seems to himself to stand firm take care lest he fall;* Phil. 2.12 [. . .]; 1 John 2.17: [. . .], and 2.28: [. . .].

For this same reason I have added these words to my definition: SO LONG AS THEY CLING TO FAITH AND CHARITY WITH ALL THEIR MIGHT. John 15.2: *every branch in me which does not bear fruit, he removes,* and 15.6: *if a man does not abide in me, he is cast away at once like a branch from the vine, and withers; then those branches are gathered together and thrown into the fire, and they burn,* and 15.10 [. . .]; Rom. 11.20 [. . .], and 11.22 [. . .]. Thus God's gifts are said to be ἀμεταμέλητα, 11.29, that is, *not liable to repentance,* because he did not repent that he had made a promise to Abraham and his seed, although the majority of them revolted. It does not follow that he did not change his mind about them when they had changed theirs about him. 2 Cor. 1.24 [. . .]; Eph. 3.18 [. . .]; 1 Pet. 1.5: *you are guarded by God's power through faith;* 2 Pet. 1.5, etc.: *and moreover, applying yourselves with all diligence, add virtue to your faith . . . for if you have these things, and to an abundant degree, they will ensure that you are not sluggish* or *barren, and fruitless, for if you do these things you will never stumble . . .* The same author points out, however, that even a genuine believer may sometimes fall irrecoverably, 2.18: *they entice through the lusts of the flesh and lasciviousness some who had really escaped from those who live in error.* If, that is, we are right to read *really* or *in actual fact* here, rather than *to a small extent,* which some maintain is the correct reading. Perhaps, too, the expression *knowledge of the Lord,* which occurs two verses later, does not imply a saving faith but merely an historical one; and perhaps *having left the pollutions of the world* implies only an outward and formal morality, not a really regenerate and Christian purity of life. The passage, then, seems distinctly ambiguous. Ezek. 18.26 is clearer: *when a righteous man turns away from his* righteousness . . . he *shall die.* This must mean true righteousness, because anyone turning from it dies. It might be argued that the sentence is conditional, *if he turns away,* but that really he will never turn away. In fact, however, there is no condition in the Hebrew, and even if there were, it is out of keeping with God's nature to lay down impossible or absurd conditions. The passage puts forward two equally probable suppositions: *if a wicked man turns,* 18.21 and *if a righteous man turns,* 18.26: *this is the justice of God's ways,* 18.25. The same argument is repeated in 33.12, 13, etc. Paul was a true believer, but he says, 1 Cor. 9.27: *I beat my body and reduce it to subjection, for fear that somehow, after preaching to others, I should find myself rejected.* The apostle to the Hebrews seems also to touch upon the possible final falling away of a true believer in 6.4–6, or so it appears from a careful consideration of the last words in the extract: *and having fallen away, should be renewed again to repentance.* The people concerned seem to be those who have shown signs of regeneration. For the same reason Christ prayed to the Father that Peter's faith should not fail, Luke 22.32. Peter's faith could have failed through his own fault, even though God's gift of grace was maintained as usual. So Christ prayed that Peter's faith, not God's grace, should not fail. There was, at the time, some risk of its failing without the help of an abnormal supply of grace from God, and that is what Christ prayed for. 1 Tim. 1.19: *keeping faith and a good conscience, by abandoning which some have made a shipwreck of their faith.* Unquestionably the faith and good conscience which some have abandoned here, and the faith of which they have made a shipwreck, were both genuine.

For this reason those who persevere, not those who are elect, are said to attain salvation. Matt. 24.12, 13: *the charity of many shall grow cold: but he who perseveres to the end will be saved,* and 10.22, similarly; Heb. 3.6 [. . .], and 3.14 [. . .]; 1 John 2.24 [. . .]; Rev. 2.10 [. . .], and 3.11 [. . .]; John 8.31: *if you remain in my word, then you will really be my disciples.*

[. . .][244]

In the same epistle, however, we find 3.9: *whoever is born of God, does not sin, because God's seed remains in him; nor can he sin, because he is born of God.* Some people argue from this, if he cannot sin, then much less can he leave the faith. But we should not tear a particular verse from its context in this way. We ought carefully to compare it with the other verses in the same chapter and epistle, and indeed with other passages throughout the Bible as a whole, in case it should appear that John is contradicting himself or any of the other sacred authors. He is explaining, in the verse quoted above, what a strong defense against sin God has placed in us. In 3.3 he had explained what we are required to do for ourselves: *everyone who has this hope in him purifies himself, just as he is pure.* This point is made again in 3.10: *this is how the sons of God and the sons of the devil are made known: everyone who does not do righteousness, is not of God; also the man who does not love his brother,* and 4.16: *God is charity, and he who lives in charity lives in God, and God in him,* and 5.18: *whoever is born of God, does not sin, and he that is begotten of God keeps himself safe.* It is true, then, that anyone who is born of God cannot sin, and therefore cannot leave the faith. But this is only true provided that he purifies himself as much as he possibly can, does righteousness, loves his brother, remains in charity himself so that God and God's seed may remain in him, and

244. In the deleted passage, Milton addresses 1 John 2.19, taken by some to support the impossibility of a saint's falling away.

keeps himself safe. Then again, why does John say *he cannot sin,* when he has already asserted that 1.8: *if we say that we have no sin we deceive ourselves?* It is obvious that *he cannot sin* must here mean that he does not sin easily or willingly or intentionally. It must mean that he does not devote his mind and energies to sin, but sins with reluctance and remorse, and that he does not persist in sin, as a habit. For these reasons his sin is not imputed to him, thanks chiefly to Christ. A great deal of caution is essential, then, in interpreting even the one word *sin.* This being so, we ought to be equally careful in interpreting the words in the rest of the verse. We should not take advantage of the simple style which this apostle always employs, and so father upon him an otherwise absurd doctrine. The word *cannot,* as the Remonstrants[245] have rightly observed, does not always imply impossibility either in common speech or in the Bible. We often say *I cannot do this* when we mean *I cannot do it conveniently, or honorably, or easily, or with a clear conscience, or without being ashamed, or disgraced, or undignified, or forsworn.* Thus in Luke 11.7 we find *I cannot rise and give you,* etc., although the speaker presently gets up; and in Acts 4.20: *we cannot help but speak of the things we have seen and heard.* Also Matt. 12.34: *how can you speak good things, when you are evil?* In fact, of course, it is easy, even for hypocrites, to speak good things. So here *he cannot sin* means he cannot easily sin, and therefore cannot easily leave the faith. The reason offered by the apostle, *because God's seed remains in him,* is explained by the Remonstrants with equal insight and equal scrupulousness. They point out that *remains in him* is identical in meaning with *is in him.* Thus in John 14.17 we have: *he remains with you and will be in you;* and in verse fourteen of this very chapter: *he who does not love his brother remains in death.* In other words, *so long as* he does not love his brother he is in death: if it did not mean this, it would mean that no one who had ever, at any time, failed to love his brother, could escape death. *Everyone,* then, *who is born of God, cannot sin because God's seed remains* or is *in him.* But it is in him only so long as he does not himself extinguish it, for even the spirit can be extinguished. It remains in him, too, so long as he remains in charity.

[...].[246]

245. Those who belonged to the Arminian party in the Dutch Reformed Church were called Remonstrants, from the Remonstrance of 1610, which the Synod of Dort (1618–19) rejected point for point.

246. The chapter concludes by distinguishing between the believer who may stumble several times but who ultimately is faithful and the unregenerate person who falls and does not rise again.

CHAPTER 27

OF THE GOSPEL AND CHRISTIAN LIBERTY

[. . .][247]

Once the gospel, the new covenant through faith in Christ, is introduced, then all the old covenant, in other words the entire Mosaic law, is abolished.[248] Jer. 31.31–33, as above; Luke 16.16: *the law and the prophets existed until John*; Acts 15.10 [. . .]; Rom. 3.21, 22: *but now God's righteousness is revealed without the law,* and 6.14: *you are not under the law but under grace,* and 7.4 [. . .], and 7.6 [. . .]. At the beginning of the same chapter Paul shows that we are released from the law in the same way as a wife is released from her dead husband. Also 7.7: *I did not know sin except through the law*: that is, the whole law, *for I should not have known lust if the law had not said, Do not lust*. . . The law referred to here is the decalogue, so it follows that we are released from the decalogue too. See also 8.15: *you have not received the spirit of slavery again in fear,* and 14.20: *indeed all things are pure* . . . , compared with Tit. 1.15: *to the pure, all things are pure: but to the polluted and the unbelieving nothing is pure, but both their mind and their conscience is defiled*; 1 Cor. 6.12 [. . .] and 10.23 [. . .]; 2 Cor. 3.3 [. . .], and 3.6–8 [. . .], and 11 [. . .], and 13 [. . .], and 5.17 [. . .]; Gal. 3.19: *why, then, the law? It was added because of transgressions, until that seed should come to whom the promise was made,* and 3.25: *but after the faith comes we are no longer under a schoolmaster,* and 4.1, etc. [. . .], also 4.21, spoken to those who desired to be under the law, and 4.24, on the subject of Hagar and Sarah: *these are the two covenants; Agar bringing forth offspring to slavery: the other,* 4.26: *is free.* Hence 4.30: *throw out the bondwoman and her son; for the bondwoman's son shall not be heir with the freewoman's son,* and 5.18: *if you are led by the Spirit, you are not under the law*; Eph. 2.14, 15: *the barrier of the dividing wall,* that is *enmity, he has abolished in his flesh; and has annulled that law of commandments, contained in decrees.* Now not only the ceremonial code, but the whole positive law of Moses was a law of commandments and contained in decrees. Moreover, the Jews were distinguished from the Gentiles not only by the ceremonial code, as Zanchius, commenting on this passage, claims, but by the whole Mosaic law. They were *alienated from the state of Israel and excluded from the promise of the covenants,* 2.12, and this *promise* was made with reference to the works of the whole law, not only to ceremonies. [. . .].[249]

The usual retort is that all these passages should be taken to refer to the abo-

247. The previous chapter makes the transition from Milton's discussion of the process of renovation to its "manifestation or exhibition in the covenant of grace," indistinctly under Hebrew law, discussed in chapter 26, and more clearly under the Gospel, the topic of this chapter. The excerpt printed here concerns Christian liberty in relation to Mosaic Law.

248. After making the same assertion briefly in *Of Civil Power,* Milton promises "of these things perhaps more some other time," a statement that Hunter notes for its apparent reference to the extensive treatment in this chapter (Yale 7:271–72).

249. The deleted passages from Scripture elaborate Milton's claim that the whole law has been superceded.

lition of the ceremonial code only.[250] This argument can be quickly refuted, firstly, by the definition of the law itself, as given in the previous chapter, which contains all the reasons for the law's enactment. When all the causes of the law, considered as a whole, have been removed or have become obsolete, then the whole law must be annulled too. The principal reasons given for the enactment of the law as a whole, are as follows: to stimulate our depravity, and thus cause anger; to inspire us with slavish fear, as a result of the enmity and the written accusation directed against us; to be a schoolmaster to bring us to the righteousness of Christ, and so on.[251] Now the texts quoted above prove not only that every one of these reasons has now been removed, but also that they have nothing at all to do with ceremonies.

First, then, the law is abolished above all because it is a law of works, and in order that it may give place to a law of grace. Rom. 3.27: *By what law? The law of works? No: but by the law of faith,* and 11.6: *if through grace, then no longer from works; otherwise grace is not grace.* Now the law of works was not only the ceremonial law but the whole law.

2. *the law brings anger: for where there is no law there is no transgression,* 4.15. It is no single part of the law, but the whole law, which causes anger, for a transgression is a transgression of the whole, not only of a part. Moreover the law causes anger but the gospel produces grace, and as anger and grace are incompatible, it follows that the law and the gospel are incompatible too.

3. It was the whole law which promised life and salvation to those who obeyed and carried out the things written in it, Lev. 18.5, Gal. 3.12, and which cursed those who did otherwise, Deut. 27.26, Gal. 3.10. Christ has redeemed us from the curse of that law, Gal. 3.13—the law, that is, whose demands we were unable to fulfill. Now we could have fulfilled the demands of the ceremonial code without any difficulty, so it must have been the entire Mosaic law from which Christ redeemed us. Again, the curse was directed against those who did not fulfill the demands of the whole law, so Christ cannot redeem us from that curse unless he has annulled the whole law for us. If he has annulled the whole law, then obviously we cannot be bound by any part of it.

4. We are told that the law *which was written on tablets of stone* was *the ministry of death,* and therefore *transitory,* 2 Cor. 3. But this law was the decalogue itself.

5. It is unquestionably not only the ceremonial code, then, but the whole law that is a law of sin and of death. It is a law of sin because it stimulates sin, and of death because it produces death and is opposed to the law of the spirit of life. But it is this same complete law which is abolished: Rom. 8.2: *the law of the spirit of life, which is in Christ Jesus, has freed me from the law of sin and of death.*

6. It was certainly not merely the ceremonial law through which the desires

250. Protestant theologians typically distinguished between Jewish ceremonial law, from which Christians were exempt, and moral law, which they were obliged to obey.

251. Cp. *PL* 12.287–90: "And therefore was law given them to evince/Their natural pravity, by stirring up/Sin against law to fight; that when they see/Law can discover sin, but not remove."

of sins flourished in our members to bring forth fruit to death, Rom. 7.5. But it is that law to which we are dead, 7.4, and which is dead to us, 7.6, and from which we are therefore freed as a wife from her dead husband, 7.3. It follows that we are freed not only from the ceremonial law but from the whole Mosaic law, 7.7, as above.

7. All believers should undoubtedly be considered righteous, since they are justified by God through faith. But Paul distinctly says that there is no law for the righteous, Gal. 5.22, 23, 1 Tim. 1.9. If there were to be any law for the righteous, it would only be a law which justifies. Now justification is beyond the scope not of the ceremonial law alone, but of the whole Mosaic law: I have already established this fact in my discussion of justification; Gal. 3.11, and so on. Therefore it is the whole law and not only the ceremonial code which is repealed because of its inability to justify.

In addition, this law not only cannot justify, it disturbs believers and makes them waver. It even tempts God, if we try to fulfill it. It contains no promise, in fact it breaks and puts an end to all promises—of inheritance, of adoption, of grace itself and even of the spirit. What is more, it makes us accursed. The law which does all this is surely repealed. Now it was not only the ceremonial law but the whole law, the law of works, which did these things. Therefore the whole law is repealed. There is the clearest scriptural proof that the law really did every one of the things I have specified: Acts 15.24: *we have heard that certain people who went out from us have disturbed you by their words, and made your souls waver, saying that you ought to be circumcised and keep the law* . . . and 15.10: *why do you tempt God to put a yoke* . . . ? The Pharisees who had believed wanted believers to be subject to the whole law, 15.5, therefore it was the whole law which, Peter argued, should be removed from the necks of the disciples. Secondly, the law which contains no promise is not merely the ceremonial law but the whole law. This is evident, because if any part of the law were to contain a promise, that would be enough, but the law about which Paul says so much contains no promise in any part of it. Rom. 4.13, 16: *it was not through the law that the promise was granted to Abraham or to his seed that he would be the heir of the world; but through the righteousness of faith;* Gal. 3.18: *if inheritance is from the law, it is no longer from the promise. But God gave it to Abraham through the promise*—not, therefore, through the law or any part of it. Thus Paul proves that either the whole law or the promise itself must be abolished, Rom. 4.14: *for if those who are of the law are heirs, faith is made vain and the promise an empty one.* Also Gal. 3.18, as above. If the promise is abolished, then inheritance and adoption are abolished too, and fear and slavery, which are incompatible with adoption, are brought back, Rom. 8.15, Gal. 4.1, etc. and 4.21, 24, 26, 30, as above. In that case union and communion with Christ are destroyed as well, Gal. 5.4: *cut off from Christ, you have disappeared, all of you who are justified through the law.* Thus glorification is lost and grace itself is destroyed, unless the whole law is destroyed, Gal. 5.4: *all of you who are justified through the law have fallen from grace.* There are various factors which make it obvious that the whole law is being spoken of here, one of which is the previous verse, where obeying the whole law is mentioned. Finally, the Spirit itself is excluded, unless the whole law is destroyed, Gal. 5.18: *if you are led by the Spirit you are not under the law,* therefore, conversely, if you are under the law, you are not led by the Spirit. What is left, is the curse, Gal. 3.10: *all who are of the works of the law are under a curse, for it is written, cursed is everyone who does not continue to observe all the injunctions which are written in the book of the law.* It follows that all the things which are written in the law, and not only the ceremonial law, make us liable to the curse. Thus Christ, when he redeemed us from the curse, 3.13, redeemed us also from the causes of the curse, that is to say, from the works of the law, or from the whole law of works, which is the same thing, and this, as I showed above, does not mean merely the ceremonial law. Even if these results did not follow, there is obviously no point in obeying a law which contains no promise. If you do no good unless you obey the law in every detail, and if it is absolutely impossible to obey it in every detail, then it is ridiculous to obey it at all, especially if it has been superseded by a better law of faith, which God, in Christ, has given us both the will and the ability to obey.[252]

All these arguments and authorities serve to prove that the whole Mosaic law is abolished by the gospel. But in reality the law, that is the substance of the law, is not broken by this abolition. On the contrary its purpose is attained in that love of God and of our neighbor which is born of faith, through the spirit. Thus Christ quite truthfully asserted the law, Matt. 5.17, etc.: *do not think that I have come to repeal the law and the prophets: I have not come to repeal but to fulfill* etc.; Rom. 3.31: *do we then make the law vain, through faith? God forbid: why, we establish the law!,* and 8.4: *that the righteousness of the law might be fulfilled in us who walk not according to the flesh but according to the spirit.*

The common objection to this doctrine is countered by Paul himself. He firmly maintains that sin is not strengthened, on the contrary, either dispersed altogether or at least diminished by this abrogation of the law: Rom. 6.14, 15: *sin will not govern you: for you are not under the law but under grace. What then? shall we sin because we are not under the law but under grace? God forbid . . .* The substance of the law, love of God and of our neighbor, should not, I repeat, be thought of as destroyed. We must realize that only the written surface has been changed, and that the law is now inscribed on believers' hearts by the spirit. At the same time, however, it sometimes appears that, where particular commandments are concerned, the spirit is at variance with the letter. This happens when by breaking the letter of the law we behave in a way which conforms better with our love of God and of our neighbor. Thus Christ himself broke the letter of the law, Mark 2.27: look at the fourth commandment, and then compare his words, *the sabbath was made for man, not man for the sabbath.* Paul did the same when he said that marriage with an unbeliever was not to be dissolved, contrary, to the express

252. Cp. *PL* 12.295–99: "they may find/Justification towards God, and peace/Of conscience, which the law by ceremonies/Cannot appease, nor man the moral part/Perform, and not performing cannot live."

injunction of the law. 1 Cor. 7.12: *I, not the Lord.* In interpreting both these commandments, the commandment about the Sabbath and that about marriage, attention to the requirements of charity is given precedence over any written law. The other commandments should all be treated in the same way. Matt. 22.37, 39, 40: *on these two commandments,* that is, those which concern love for God and for our neighbor, *all the law and the prophets depend.* Neither of these, however, is found, in so many words, among the ten commandments. The first occurs in Deut. 6.5 and the second in Lev. 19.18, and not before. Nevertheless we are told that they are preeminent and include not only the ten commandments but, what is more, all the law and the prophets. Also Matt. 7.12: *whatever you wish men to do to you, do it to them; for that is the law and the prophets;* Rom. 13.8, 10: *he who loves another has fulfilled the demands of the law: charity is the fulfilling of the demands of the law;* Gal. 5.14: *the whole law can be summed up in one sentence: love your neighbor as yourself;* 1 Tim. 1.5 [. . .]. This is the end of the Mosaic commandment, and the same thing is even more true of the commandment of the gospel. James 2.8: *if you obey the royal law according to the scripture, you will love your neighbor as yourself.* Thus anyone with any sense interprets the precepts of Christ in the Sermon on the Mount not in a literal way but in a way that is in keeping with the spirit of charity. The same applies to Paul's remark in 1 Cor. 11.4: *every man praying or prophesying with his head covered . . . ,* a text which will be dealt with later, in book 2 chapter 4, when I discuss the matter of how those who pray should dress. Hence we find, in Rom. 4.15: *where there is no law there is no transgression,* that is, no transgression of the letter, so long as the substance of the law, love for God and for one's neighbor, is, by the Spirit's guidance, preserved. [. . .].[253]

But all the rest stick to the doctrine propounded by the converted Pharisees, and believe that the law should still be observed even in gospel times. This is a doctrine which did a good deal of harm in the early days of the church. It is maintained that the law has many uses even for us Christians. For example, it forces us to be more aware of sin, and thus to receive grace more eagerly, and to understand God's will better. I should reply that, to begin with, my argument does not apply to people who need to be forced to come to Christ, but to those who are already believers and thus already firmly attached to Christ. Secondly, the will of God is best understood from the teaching of the gospel itself, under the promised guidance of the Spirit of truth, and from God's law, written in the hearts of believers. Besides, we are made aware of sin and are forced towards an acceptance of Christ's grace merely by knowing the law, not by obeying it; for as scripture constantly reminds us, we do not draw nearer to Christ by the works of the law but wander further away from him.

Then again, those theologians with whom I disagree, particularly Polanus,[254]

253. The deleted paragraph is devoted to noting that two other theologians agree with Milton, most prominently the Italian Protestant Jerome Zanchius (1516–90).

254. Of Czech origin, Amandus Polanus von Polansdorf (1561–1610) was the leader of the conservative Calvinists in Basel. His *Syntagma Theologiae Christianae* was published in Hanover in 1609. He also composed commentaries on the Old Testament and translated the New Testament into German.

make the following distinction: *the fact that one is not under the law does not mean that one does not owe obedience to the law, but that one is free from the curse and constraint of the law and from its provocation to sin.* But if this is so, what do believers gain from the gospel? For believers, even under the law, were exempt from its curse and its provocation to sin. Moreover what, I ask you, can it mean to be free from the constraint of the law, if not to be entirely exempt from the law, as I maintain we are? For so long as the law exists, it constrains, because it is a law of slavery. Constraint and slavery are as inseparable from the law as liberty is from the gospel. I will make this clear presently.

Polanus contends, in his comment on Gal. 4.4, 5: *to redeem those who were subject to the law,* that "to say Christians are redeemed from the subjection of the law, and are not under the law, does not mean simply that they owe no more obedience to the law. The words have, instead, a less absolute meaning, which is that Christians are no longer required to fulfil the law of God perfectly in this life, because Christ has fulfilled it for them." Anyone can see, however, that this is not so at all. It is not a less perfect life that is required from Christians but, in fact, a more perfect life than was required of those who were under the law. The whole tenor of Christ's teaching shows this. There is, however, one difference. Moses imposed the literal or external law even on those who were unwilling to receive it;[255] whereas Christ writes the internal law of God on the hearts of believers through his Spirit, and leads them as willing followers.[256] Under the law men who trusted in God were justified through their faith, but not without the works of the law, Rom. 4.12: *the Father of the circumcised,* etc. But the gospel justifies through faith without the works of the law. So we, freed from the works of the law, follow not the letter but the spirit, not the works of the law but the works of faith. Thus it is not said to us, *whatever is not of the law, is sin,* but *whatever is not of faith.* Faith, not law, is our rule. It follows from this that, as faith cannot be compelled, the works of faith cannot be either. See more on this subject in chapter 15, above, on Christ's kingly office and the internal law of the spirit by which he governs the church. Also Book 2, chapter 1 on the form of good works.

The law of slavery having been abrogated through the gospel, the result is Christian Liberty. It is true that liberty is primarily the fruit of adoption, and was consequently not unknown in the time of the law, as I said in Chapter 23. However, our liberty could not be perfect or manifest before the advent of Christ, our liberator. Therefore liberty is a matter relevant chiefly to the gospel, and is associated with it. This is so, first, because truth exists chiefly under the gospel, John 1.17: *grace and truth are present through Jesus Christ,* and truth liberates, 8.31, 32: *if you remain in my word, then you will really be my disciples, and you will know the truth, and the truth will make you free,* and 8.36 [...]. Secondly, because the pecu-

255. Cp. *PL* 12.304–5: "From imposition of strict laws, to free/Acceptance of large grace."
256. Cp. *PL* 12.523–24: "what the Spirit within/Shall on the heart engrave."

liar gift of the gospel is the Spirit and: *where the Spirit of the Lord is, there is liberty,* 2 Cor. 3.17.

CHRISTIAN LIBERTY means that CHRIST OUR LIBERATOR FREES US FROM THE SLAVERY OF SIN AND THUS FROM THE RULE OF THE LAW AND OF MEN, AS IF WE WERE EMANCIPATED SLAVES. HE DOES THIS SO THAT, BEING MADE SONS INSTEAD OF SERVANTS[257] AND GROWN MEN INSTEAD OF BOYS, WE MAY SERVE GOD IN CHARITY THROUGH THE GUIDANCE OF THE SPIRIT OF TRUTH. Gal. 5.1: *stand fast, then, in the liberty by which Christ has freed us, and do not be entangled again in the yoke of slavery*; Rom. 8.2 [. . .], and 8.15 [. . .]; Gal. 4.7 [. . .]; Heb. 2.15 [. . .]; 1 Cor. 7.23: *you are bought with a price, do not be slaves of men*; James 1.25: *who looks into that perfect law of liberty,* and 2.12: *speak and act like those who are to be judged by the law of liberty.*

THAT WE MAY SERVE GOD. Matt. 11.29, 30: *take my yoke upon you: for my yoke is good,* or *easy, and my burden is light,* compared with 1 John 5.3–5: *to love God, is to keep his commandments, and his commandments are not burdensome*. . .; Rom. 6.18: *freed from sin, you became servants of righteousness,* and 6.22 [. . .], and 7.6 [. . .]; Rom. 12.1, 2 [. . .]; James 1.25: [. . .]; 1 Pet. 2.16: *as free, and not using your liberty as a veil for malice, but as servants of God.* Thus we are freed from the judgments of men, and especially from coercion and legislation in religious matters, Rom. 14.4 [. . .], and 14.8 [. . .]; Matt. 7.1: *do not judge, so that you may not be judged*; Rom. 14.10: *but why do you condemn your brother, why do you think him worth nothing? For we shall all stand before the judgment seat of Christ.* We are forbidden, then, where matters of conscience and religion are concerned, to *judge* or *condemn* our brothers even in everyday speech. So we are certainly forbidden to judge them in a court of law, which has very plainly nothing to do with such matters. St. Paul refers all cases of conscience or religion to the judgment-seat not of man but of Christ. James 2.12: *speak and act like those who are to be judged by the law of liberty*—judged, that is, in questions of religion by God, not by men.[258] If God is going to judge us in these questions according to the law of liberty, why should man prejudge us according to the law of slavery?

IN CHARITY THROUGH THE GUIDANCE OF THE SPIRIT OF TRUTH. Rom. 14, and 15.1–15. In these chapters, however, Paul first warns us to beware of two things. First, that however we employ this liberty of ours, we should act in firm faith, convinced that we are allowed to do so: 14.5: *let every man be fully certain in his own mind,* and 23: *whatever is not of faith, is sin.* Secondly, that we should give no just cause of offence to a weak brother: 14.20, 21: *do not destroy the work of God for the sake of food: all things indeed are pure, but it is evil for a man to give offence when he eats* . . . ; 1 Cor. 8.13 [. . .]. This, however, was the effect of Paul's extraordinary love for his brothers. It does not constitute a duty incumbent upon every believer to abstain from meat for ever in case a weaker brother

257. Cp. *PL* 12.305–6: "from servile fear/To filial, works of law to works of faith."
258. Cp. *PL* 12.528–30: "for on Earth/Who against faith and conscience can be heard/Infallible?"

should think vegetable food alone lawful. See also 9.19–22 [. . .], and 10.23: *all things are lawful for me but not all things are good for me . . .* , as above. Gal. 5.13 [. . .]; 2 Pet. 2.19 [. . .]; 1 Cor. 8.9 [. . .].

This seems to have been the only reason for the command given to the churches, Acts 15.28, 29: *to abstain from blood and from things strangled.* It was, that is to say, in case the Jews who were not yet sufficiently firm in their faith should take offense. It is clear that the prohibition of blood was purely ceremonial, from the reason given in Lev. 17.11: *for the life of all flesh is in the blood, and I . . .* Thus the eating of fat was also forbidden in the law, 7.23, etc., but no one thinks that it is therefore unlawful to eat fat. The prohibition applies only to sacrificial times, Acts 10.13, etc.

No consideration is to be shown, however, to the malicious or the obstinate: Gal. 2.4, 5: *but because of false brothers who had crept in. They had entered secretly to find out about the liberty which we enjoy in Christ Jesus, intending to bring us into slavery. We did not yield to them by subjection even for a moment, so that the truth of the gospel might persist among you.* Christ did not worry about giving offence to the Pharisees; instead he defended his disciples when they did not wash their hands before eating, Matt. 15.2, 3, and also when they plucked ears of corn, which was then considered unlawful on the Sabbath day, Luke 6.1, etc. If it were always necessary to satisfy the malicious and the envious, Christ would not have allowed a woman to anoint his feet with such precious ointment. He would not have allowed the same wealthy woman to wipe them with her soft hair: he would not have defended and praised her action, as, indeed, he did, John 12.3, etc. Nor would he have taken advantage of the services and liberality of the women who accompanied him wherever he went, Luke 8.2–3.

No regard is to be paid even to one's fellow-Christians, if they behave in a disingenuous way. Gal. 2.11, etc.: *but when Peter had come to Antioch I opposed him to his face, because he was culpable . . .*

Moreover the weak should not be over-hasty in judging the freedom of the strong. Rather, they should present themselves for instruction. Rom. 14.13: *so let us not judge one another any more.*

So neither this reason, nor even the reason I mentioned before, that is, consideration for the weak, is enough to necessitate magisterial ordinances which compel believers to uniformity or deprive them of any part of their freedom. Paul argues along these lines in 1 Cor. 9.19: *although I am free from all men I have made myself a slave to all*—I was not made a slave by anyone else: *free from all men*—and therefore, of course, from the magistrate, at any rate in matters of this kind.[259] If a magistrate takes this freedom away he takes the gospel away too: at least, he deprives the good as well as the bad, contrary to the well-known

259. Cp. *Of Civil Power* (Yale 7.267): "None more cautious of giving scandal than St. Paul. Yet while he made himself *servant to all,* that he *might gain the more,* he made himself so of his own accord, was not made so by outward force, testifying at the same time that he *was free from all men,* 1 Cor. 9.19."

precept in Matt. 13.29: *in case when gathering the tares you root up the wheat at the same time: let both grow together until harvest.*[260]

CHAPTER 28

OF THE EXTERNAL SEALING OF THE COVENANT OF GRACE

[. . .][261]

Under the gospel the first of the sacraments commonly so called is BAPTISM. AT BAPTISM THE BODIES OF BELIEVERS WHO PLEDGE THEMSELVES TO PURITY OF LIFE ARE IMMERSED IN RUNNING WATER.[262] THIS IS TO SIGNIFY OUR REGENERATION THROUGH THE HOLY SPIRIT AND ALSO OUR UNION WITH CHRIST THROUGH HIS DEATH, BURIAL AND RESURRECTION.

OF BELIEVERS. Matt. 28.19: *teach all nations, baptizing them* . . . ; Mark 16.15, 16: *preach the gospel . . . he who believes and has been baptized will be saved*; Acts 8.36, 37 [. . .]; Eph. 5.26: *purifying with a bath of water through the word*; 1 Pet. 3.21: *the symbol of baptism, which now corresponds to this, saves us* (*not because the filth of the flesh is washed away, but by the obligation of a good conscience before God*) *through the resurrection of Jesus Christ.*

It follows that infants are not fit for baptism. They cannot be taught, they cannot believe or undertake an obligation, they cannot pledge themselves or answer for themselves, or even hear the word. How can infants, who do not understand a word, be purified by the word? It means as much to them, as it does to an adult to hear an unknown language. For we are not saved by that outward baptism which washes away merely the filth of the flesh, but, as Peter says, *by the obligation of a good conscience*, and conscience is not a property of infants. Besides, baptism is a covenant, containing an obligation which is not only imposed but must also be undertaken, and this an infant cannot do. What is more, baptism is a vow, and infants cannot make or be forced to make vows. I shall have more to say about this in Book 2, Chapter 4, where I discuss vows.

It is amazing what futile arguments those theologians employ who oppose this doctrine. Matt. 19.14: *allow little children to come to me and do not forbid them, for the kingdom of heaven belongs to such as these.* But no one was bringing them to be baptized, 19.13: *they were brought for him to put his hands upon them and pray*—and

260. Cp. *Of Civil Power* (Yale 7.245): "Seeing that in matters of religion . . . none can judge or determine here on earth, no not church governors themselves, against the consciences of other believers, my inference is, or rather not mine but our Savior's own, that in those matters they neither can command or use constraint; lest they run rashly on a pernicious consequence forewarned in that parable Matt. 13. from the 26 to the 31 verse: *lest while ye gather up the tares, ye root up also the wheat with them. Let both grow together until the harvest* . . ."

261. The deleted passage describes sacraments as ceremonies that visibly represent the sealing of a covenant between God and his people. For the Jews, according to Milton, the sacraments are circumcision and Passover, for Christians, baptism and the Lord's Supper.

262. Cp. *PL* 12.442: "Baptizing in the profluent stream."

Christ did not baptize them, he merely laid his hands upon them, 19.15; *and when he had taken them in his arms he laid his hands upon them and blessed them,* Mark 10.16. But if the children were not taken to Christ for baptism, and if he took them in his arms but did not baptize them, who could possibly deduce from this that they ought to have been baptized? What kind of an argument is this for saying not merely that children but that infants are fit for baptism? For if they are proved fit for baptism by this text, then they are, on the same grounds, fit to be sharers in the Lord's Supper. The church, then, should receive infants who come to her as Christ received them: she should lay hands on them and bless them, not baptize them. But, my opponents insist, *the kingdom of heaven belongs to such as these.* Does this refer to all children, or only to those who will later believe? However well God may know those that are his, the church does not know them: what they are in the sight of God is one thing; what they are by church privilege, another. So *to such as these* must mean such as have the simplicity and innocence of children. But neither simplicity nor innocence can properly be attributed to infants, who are not yet rational beings. Moreover it does not follow that because the kingdom of heaven is theirs, any religious sacrament is theirs as well. Nor does it follow that because the covenant is theirs, they are also in possession of each seal of the covenant, for this calls for the intelligence and faith of a grown-up man. The thing signified in the Lord's Supper applies to infants just as much as the thing signified in baptism. But infants are not admitted to the Lord's Supper, though they did take part in the Passover which it replaced. So you can see how weak it is to argue that, as baptism has replaced circumcision, and as infants were circumcised, infants may be baptized. Because it is just as certain that the Passover has been replaced by the Lord's Supper, and yet infants were admitted to the one and are excluded from the other.

But, my opponents insist, *we were all baptized in the cloud and in the sea,* 1 Cor. 10.2, and *all* must include infants. Very well, but *all ate the same spiritual food and all drank the same spiritual drink,* 10.3, 4, yet infants are not therefore allowed to take part in the Lord's Supper.

My opponents also place emphasis upon Gen. 17.7: *I establish my covenant between me and you and your seed after you throughout their generations.* But no one in his senses would say that this referred to infants, or deny that *throughout their generations* applied to the adult descendants of Abraham. It is not to infants, in the next verse, that the land is to be given: it is not infants who, in the verse after that, are commanded to keep the covenant. There is a similar text in Acts 2.39: *the promise is made to you and to your children and to all those far off in the future, to whoever the Lord our God will call.* My opponents take *to your children* to mean, to infants: in other words, God calls those who cannot understand and addresses those who cannot hear. Such infantile reasoning is enough to make anyone blush. If these commentators had only read two verses further, they would have found it clearly stated, 2.41: *those who willingly received his word were baptized.* Here both understanding and will are requisite for baptism, and infants have neither.

Similarly Acts 8.37: *if you believe with all your heart, you may be baptized*—but infants cannot believe even with the least little bit of their hearts. As for that text which my opponents make so much fuss about, *the promise is made to you and to your seed,* I wish they would pay some attention to the way in which Paul explains this passage, Rom. 9.7, 8. If they did so they would understand that the evangelical promises were not made to anyone's seed, that is, not to the *sons* of anyone's *flesh,* not even *Abraham*'s, but only to *the sons of God,* that is, to believers. Under the gospel only believers *are sons of the promise* and *are counted among the seed.* But no one can be considered a believer by the church before he has professed his faith. The church, then, should not place its seal upon the promises by baptism when the persons concerned are quite obviously not those to whom the promises were made.

Then again, my opponents allege an analogy between baptism and circumcision, which was performed during infancy: Col. 2.11: *in whom you are circumcised with a circumcision which is not made by any hand. You put off the body of the sins of the flesh through the circumcision of Christ: buried with him through baptism.* But to begin with there is after all no analogy between being *circumcised* and being *buried with him*—no analogy, that is, except that which exists between all sacraments, in spite of their different modes of signification. Secondly, who would claim that things which are analogous must correspond to each other in every respect? Women were able to go without circumcision quite safely, but they cannot go without baptism, either because it is a more perfect sign or because it represents a more perfect thing. It is true that circumcision was *a seal of the righteousness of faith,* Rom. 4.11, 12. But it was a seal of this kind only for Abraham, who had already believed before he was circumcised, and for those like him who would believe in the same way. It was not a seal of the righteousness of faith for those who were, in later times, circumcised during infancy, and who were therefore unable to believe before circumcision. For them it was a sign in the flesh, and a very obscure one at that, of the grace which was to be made known long afterwards. Baptism, on the other hand, is a seal of grace already revealed, of the remission of sins, of sanctification and a sign of our death and resurrection with Christ. Circumcision was given under the law and the sacrifices, and the man circumcised was bound to obey the whole law, Gal. 5.3. This was a slavish kind of service, a mere menial, as it were, employed to bring children to school.[263] Through baptism, on the other hand, we are initiated into the gospel, which is a rational, manly and utterly free service. Under the law men were not only born infants, they grew old as infants; but under the gospel and baptism we are born men. So in baptism knowledge and faith are first required from us, as con-

263. **A mere menial:** translates *paedagogicus,* the title of a slave in a well-to-do Greek or Roman family whose task was to attend children on the way to school and watch their behavior. St. Paul twice compares the law to such a servant (Gal. 3.24, 1 Cor. 4.15). The more usual translation is "guide" or "custodian." Carey's resort to a definition in translating the term may be a reaction to Sumner's misleading if traditional choice of "schoolmaster."

ditions which grown men can fulfill, but in circumcision, as with slaves under the law and infants, no conditions are imposed. Lastly, circumcision was not performed by the priests or Levites, but either by the father of the family, Gen. 17, or by the mother, Ex. 4.26, or by any other person as, for example, a surgeon. Baptism, on the other hand, cannot be performed, or so my opponents maintain, except by a minister of the gospel, and certainly everyone would agree that it can be performed only by a believer, and by one who is neither a new convert nor uneducated. Why should this be so, except to ensure that the person who is going to be baptized is thoroughly saturated with Christian doctrine before he is dipped in the water? Therefore he cannot be an infant. It follows that circumcision and baptism are not analogous. We should pay attention, in the sacraments, not to evidently shaky analogies but to the Lord's own institution, and follow that always and above all. Even the theologians who oppose me agree in this.

But, they say, circumcision was *the seal of the righteousness of faith,* Rom. 4.11, 12, yet infants, who could not believe, were nevertheless circumcised. I reply, as above, that it was a seal of the righteousness of faith, but only to Abraham and to those who followed his example and believed before circumcision. With infants it was quite another thing: nothing more, in fact, than the outward consecration of a whole nation to the external worship of God, and particularly to the Mosaic form of worship, as it was eventually to be ordained.

Lastly, my opponents say that the apostles baptized whole families, therefore they baptized infants. The weakness of this argument is very clearly shown by Acts 8.12: *when they* believed . . . they *were baptized, both men and women,* not, therefore, infants; 16.31–34: *believe in the Lord Jesus Christ and you shall be saved, you and your house. And they spoke the word of the Lord to him and to all that were of his house, and he was baptized, he and all his household, there and then. And he rejoiced that he and all his house had believed in God.* Here *all his house* obviously means those who had believed, and cannot, therefore, include infants. Only those people to whom the word of the Lord was spoken, and who believed, were baptized. This is evident from 11.17 as well: *if, then, God has given them a gift equal to ours, who believe . . .*, and 18.8: *he believed in the Lord with all his house. And many of the Corinthians who heard believed and were baptized.* Finally, even John's baptism, which was a kind of prelude to Christ's, is called *the baptism of repentance,* Mark 1.4, and those he baptized *confessed their sins,* Matt. iii. 6. But infants can obviously not repent or confess. So if infants were not fit to receive John's baptism, how can they be fit to receive Christ's, the prerequisites of which are instruction, repentance and faith?

IMMERSION. Some people have substituted sprinkling for immersion in baptism. They argue, from Mark 7.4 and Luke 11.38, that baptism means sprinkling. There is, however, nothing in this argument: when you wash your hands you do not just sprinkle them, you put them right in the water.

TO REGENERATION. John 3.5: *unless a man is born from water and the spirit he cannot enter the kingdom of God*—cannot, that is, if it is found that his omission proceeds from neglect, Acts 22.16: *why do you delay? Rise, be baptized and washed clean from your sins, calling on the name of the Lord*; 1 Cor. 6.11 [. . .]; Eph. 5.26 [. . .]; Tit. 3.5 [. . .].

UNION THROUGH DEATH. 1 Cor. 12.13: *through one spirit we are all baptized into one body*; Gal. 3.27 [. . .]; Rom. 6.3: *do you not know that as many of us as were baptized into Jesus Christ, were baptized into his death? Thus we were buried with him through baptism into death*; Col. 2.12 [. . .]. So baptism is a symbol for Christ's painful life, his death and his burial, in which he was, so to speak, immersed for a time: Mark 10.38: *and be baptized with the baptism with which I am baptized*, similarly Luke 12.50. As for the administration of baptism, see below, Chapters 29 and 31, on the visible church and on particular churches.

The baptism of John was essentially the same as the baptism of Christ. It differed, however, in the form of words used in its administration and in the immediacy of its efficacy. If it had not been essentially the same it would follow that we had not received the same baptism as Christ did, that our baptism had not been sanctified by the person of Christ, that Christ had not fulfilled all righteousness, Matt. 3.15, and that the apostles were baptized twice, though no second baptism is mentioned. It was not, however, the same in every respect. Although both baptisms were from God, Luke 3.2, 3 and 7.29, 30, and although both required repentance and faith, Acts 19.4, 5, the one baptized, somewhat obscurely, into a Christ who had not yet been properly revealed, the other, more clearly, into a Christ who was now fully known. The baptism of Christ was accompanied by a more solemn form of words—*in the name of the Father, and of the Son, and of the Holy Ghost*—though, as a matter of fact, it is nowhere recorded that the apostles ever used this formula. It also had a more immediate efficacy, as I said above. For John's baptism only baptized with water, Matt. 3.11, John 1.23, Acts 1.5 and 19.2, except, that is, on the one occasion when Christ received it. This exception was made, moreover, in order to bear witness to Christ, rather than to show the power of John's baptism. Thus we see why the apostles did not receive the Holy Spirit until long after their baptism, Acts 1.5, and why the Ephesians, who had been baptized with the baptism of John, *had not even heard whether there was any Holy Spirit*, 19.1, 2. Christ's baptism, on the other hand, baptized with water and with the Spirit, and conferred the gifts of the Spirit straight away.

The usual answer is that these passages are not making a distinction between baptism with water and baptism with the Spirit but are contrasting the part played by the minister in baptism with the part played by Christ. If this were so, however, the same thing would be said about the other apostles when they administer baptism; but that never happens. On the contrary, it is quite certain that the other apostles baptized both with water and with the Holy Spirit.

The baptism of John, then, either did not confer the Spirit at all, or not immediately. It seems to have been a kind of initiation or purification, rather than an absolute sealing of the covenant: for only the Spirit seals, 1 Cor. 12.13. Thus it would conform to the old Hebrew custom, by which all proselytes were baptized.

It appears that, as a result, it was possible, though not necessary, to add the baptism of Christ to that of John: Acts 19.5: *having heard these things they were baptized in the name of the Lord Jesus.* This refers to people who had previously been baptized by John, 19.3. I say not necessary because it seems that the apostles and many others remained satisfied with John's baptism. Taking them as my model I should be inclined to conclude that those who have been baptized in infancy, and in every respect irregularly, do not need to be baptized again when they grow up. Indeed I should consider baptism itself necessary only for proselytes, not for those brought up in the church, if the apostle had not taught us that baptism is not merely an initiation but a kind of symbol of our death, burial and resurrection with Christ.

The type of baptism, before the Mosaic law, was Noah's ark; 1 Pet. 3.20, 21: *while the ark was being built,* etc. *to which the type of baptism now corresponds.* Under the law, the type was the cloud: 1 Cor. 10.2: *that all were baptized in Moses in the cloud and in the sea.*

THE LORD'S SUPPER commemorates the death of Christ by the breaking of bread and the pouring out of wine: both are tasted by all present, and the benefits of his death are thus sealed to believers: Matt. 26.26–29: *as they were eating Jesus took the bread and blessed it and then he broke it and gave it to his disciples and said, Take, eat, this is my body; and he took the cup and when he had given thanks he gave it to them, saying, All drink from this, for this is my blood of the new covenant, which is shed for many for the remission of sins. From this time on I will not drink from the fruit of the vine until . . . ,* similarly Mark 14.22–5; Luke 22.19, 20 [. . .]; John 6.33 [. . .], and 6.35 [. . .], and 50, 51 [. . .], similarly 6.53, and 54–57: *he who eats my flesh and drinks my blood dwells in me and I in him. As the living Father has sent me, and I live through the Father, so too he who eats me shall also live through me,* similarly 58, and 63: *the spirit is that which gives life; flesh is no use; the words which I speak to you are the spirit and are life.* It is true that this chapter of John does not refer exclusively to the Lord's Supper, but to any kind of acceptance, through faith, of the benefits of Christ's incarnation. That is why the action which is so often referred to in terms of eating and drinking from 6.50 onwards, is previously spoken of, 6.35, as *coming* and *believing.* Similarly 4.10, 14: *the living water, anyone who drinks of it shall never thirst,* cannot be related either to baptism or to the Lord's Supper. Nevertheless these words of Christ explain the Lord's Supper, which was instituted very soon afterwards (for *the passover was near,* 6.4), in a most effective way. They show us quite clearly that the mere flesh is of no use here any more than it was in feeding the five thousand: also that not teeth but faith is needed to eat his flesh: also that what he gave was the heavenly and spiritual bread which had come down from heaven. It was not the earthly bread, which had been born from the virgin and which, had he merely given his flesh, he would have given, but a bread which was, so to speak, more heavenly than the manna itself, and which *he who eats shall live for ever,* 6.58. The Papists hold that it is Christ's actual flesh which is eaten by all in the Mass. But if this were so, even the most wicked of the communicants, not to mention the mice and worms which often eat the eucharist, would attain eternal life by virtue of that heavenly bread. That living bread which, Christ says, is his flesh, and the true drink which, he says, is his blood, can only be the doctrine which teaches us that Christ was made man in order to pour out his blood for us. The man who accepts this doctrine with true faith will live for ever. This is as certain as that actual eating and drinking sustain this mortal life of ours for a little while—indeed, much more certain. For it means that Christ will dwell in us and we in him, as the above quotation says. Whereas if we eat his flesh it will not remain in us, but, to speak candidly, after being digested in the stomach, it will be at length exuded.

It is called *the Lord's Supper* by Paul, I Cor. 11.20, and its institution by our Lord is recorded and explained, 11.23–30: *for I have received from the Lord that which I have handed on to you; that the Lord Jesus, that night on which he was betrayed, took bread; and when he had given thanks he broke it and said, Take, eat; this is my body which is broken for you; do this in remembrance of me: similarly, after he had dined, he took the cup, saying, This cup is the new covenant made through my blood; do this, as often as you drink it, in remembrance of me. For as often as you eat this bread and drink this cup you proclaim the Lord's death, until his coming.* It is also incidentally explained, 10.16, 17, 21: *the cup of blessing which we bless: is it not the communion of the blood of Christ? The bread which we break, is it not the communion of the body of Christ? Since the bread is one, we many are one body, for we all partake of that one bread.*

Under the law the type of the Lord's Supper was the manna, and the water which flowed from the rock: I Cor. 10.3, 4: *and that they all ate the same spiritual food and all drank the same spiritual drink, for they drank from the spiritual rock which followed them: and that rock was Christ.* If under a fleshly covenant they ate a spiritual Christ, then certainly we, under a spiritual covenant, do not eat a fleshly Christ.

I have quoted these passages at length because they include the whole doctrine of the Lord's Supper. If anyone will interpret them with that simplicity of heart which characterized the early Christians, and according to the evident meaning of the words themselves, he will wonder why so many monstrous doctrines concerning this subject should have disturbed the church of God in the past, practically turning the Lord's Supper into a cannibal feast.

Consubstantiation and particularly transubstantiation and papal ἀνθρωποφάγια or cannibalism are utterly alien to reason, common sense and human behavior. What is more, they are irreconcilable with sacred doctrine, with the nature and the fruit of a sacrament, with the analogy of baptism, with the normal use of words, with the human nature of Christ and with the heavenly state of glory in which he is to remain until the day of judgment.

In the so-called sacrament, as in most matters where the question of analogy arises, it is to be noted that a certain trope or figure of speech was frequently employed. By this I mean that a thing which in any way illustrates or signifies another thing is mentioned not so much for what it really is as for what it illustrates or signifies. Failure to recognize this figure of speech in the sacraments, where the relationship between the symbol and the thing symbolized is very close, has been a widespread source of error, and still is today.[264] Thus in Gen. 17.10 circumcision is called a *covenant,* and in 11, *a sign of the covenant.* In Ex. 12.11 a lamb is called *the passover,* and there are parallel passages which support this text against the objections which my opponents may take to it: Luke 22.7: *the passover be killed,* and 8: *prepare us the passover,* and 11 [. . .], and 12 [. . .]. 2 Sam. 23.17 is figurative in the same way: *whether I should drink the blood of those men who went in danger of their lives?.* The same figure is used of baptism: Eph. 5.26: *purified with a bath of water through the word;* Col. 2.12: *buried with him through baptism;* and of the Lord's Supper: Matt. 26.26, 27: *as they were eating . . . ; take, eat, this is my body . . . ;* and in Mark, and Luke 22.20: *this cup is the new testament,* and 1 Cor. 11.25. Similarly 1 Cor. 10.4: *that rock was Christ.* The biblical writers seem to have employed this figure of speech to denote the close relationship between the symbol and the thing symbolized, and also to show that these spiritual matters were sealed with absolute certainty. Thus the same form of speech is used in other instances where the absolute certainty of a thing is to be expressed: Gen. 41.27: *the seven cows are seven years . . . ;* Rev. 1.20 and 17.9: *the seven heads are seven mountains,* and 17.12: *the ten horns are ten kings.*

Finally, every sacrament is a seal of the covenant of grace. Thus it is clear that the Papists are wrong when they attribute to the outward sign the power of conferring salvation or grace. They think that this power is released whenever the rite itself is performed. But the sacraments cannot impart salvation or grace of themselves. They are merely seals or symbols of salvation and grace for believers: 1 Pet. 3.21: *not because the filth of the flesh is washed away, but by the obligation of good conscience . . .*

It follows that sacraments are not absolutely necessary: 1. because many have achieved salvation without them; women without circumcision for example, and the crucified thief without baptism, and no doubt many infants and many converts who were still receiving instruction and had not been baptized. Thus also many received the gifts of the spirit through the word and faith alone, Acts 10.44, etc.: *the Holy Spirit fell on all those who heard this word . . .* Even John, the first minister of baptism, was not himself baptized, although we have his word for it that he, too, needed baptism, Matt. 3.14. Perhaps even Apollos was unbaptized. He was born in Alexandria and first went to Ephesus long after John the Bap-

264. Protestants could not agree on how to understand Christ's words about the sacramental bread and wine: "This is my body"; "This is my blood." Lutherans, and Anglicans after them, came closest to Catholic doctrine, insisting that Christ's *is* means that the body and blood of Christ are locally present and partaken by believer and unbeliever alike. Milton scorns this notion as cannibalism. Calvin agreed that Christ's words were not figurative but rejected local presence, insisting that the body and blood of Christ are present only by virtue of the power of the Holy Spirit uniting believers with Christ, and thus are partaken of only by believers—which left unbelievers partaking of the outward sign only. Milton's position is closest to that of Zwingli, who claimed that when Christ said *is,* he spoke figuratively and meant "signifies" or "represents." Cp. *Art of Logic* (Yale 8:339): "So that we are not perhaps deceived by this conversion—for it is not the most trustworthy—certain precautions are customarily taken. The first is that the terms should not be figurative, as in *Bread is the Body of Christ.*"

tist's time. It is said that he knew only the baptism of John, but this does not necessarily prove that he had ever undergone the ceremony. However, Aquila and Priscilla simply instructed him more fully—there is no mention of their first having had him baptized, Acts 18.24–26. 2. because seals do not constitute the covenant but only make it public. Thus Abraham was circumcised as a seal of righteousness when he had already believed and been justified. True, John 3.5 lays down that *unless a man has been born again from water and the spirit, he cannot enter the kingdom of God.* But we must understand that this assumes that the man had a reasonable chance of being baptized, and that there was no question of his having been negligent. The same applies to Eph. 5.26: *purified with a bath of water through the word,* and Tit. 3.5: *through the bath of regeneration.* For the gospel is said to be *the power of God making for salvation,* Rom. 1.16, and in 1 Pet. 1.23 we are said to be *born again through the word,* but nevertheless those who die in infancy or without any outward instruction in the gospel and the word, must either be regenerated by the Spirit alone or perish altogether. Similarly, the man who simply believes drinks that living water, the blood of Christ, and eats that heavenly bread, the flesh of Christ, and has eternal life, John 4 and 6, as above. As regards the necessity of sacraments, then, it can safely be said that it is the Spirit which gives life and it is faith which feeds, and that actual feeding, in the physical sense, cannot always conveniently take place and is not absolutely necessary. Clearly, if the sacrament is nothing but a seal, or rather a sort of symbol, it is not wrong for a man to have just as much trust in God, even without the seal, when it is not convenient for him to receive it properly. After all, he can give thanks to God and commemorate the death of Christ in many other ways every day of his life, even if he does not do so in the ceremonial way which God has instituted.

There is nothing in the Bible about the Lord's Supper being administered. The early Christians are said to have taken part in it regularly and in their own homes: Acts 2.42: *they persisted in the apostles' doctrines and fellowship and in the breaking of bread and in prayers,* and 2.46 [. . .], and 20.7 [. . .]. So I do not know why ministers should forbid anyone except themselves to celebrate the Lord's Supper. It might be said that Christ handed the bread and wine to his disciples, but he certainly did not give them to each individually, and besides he was acting as the founder of a new institution, not as a minister. True, 1 Cor. 4.1 says, *let a man look upon us as ministers of Christ and stewards of God's mysteries.* However, Paul is here speaking of himself and the other ministers of his order, and they were the only stewards of God's mysteries, in that they were stewards of the doctrine of the gospel which was at that time first revealed by God. Paul is not speaking of them as ministers of bread and wine, for they did not minister or serve at tables, as Acts 6.2 points out, not even at those at which, in all probability, they frequently met together. Similarly Paul was sent, according to 1 Cor. 1.17, not to baptize but to preach the gospel. Moreover, the next verse shows that the *mysteries* mentioned refer only to doctrine: *it is required of stewards that a man should be found faithful.* It would obviously be too mean a thing to require of so great a steward that he should be found faithful in dispensing bread and wine, which are mere elements, not mysteries. See also 10.16, 17: here the blessing of the cup and the breaking of the bread are allowed to all those who are not prohibited from the communion of the body and blood of Christ. For Christ is the only priest of the new testament, Heb. 7.23, 24, so there is no order of men that can rightly claim for itself alone the function of giving or distributing the sacred elements. We are all equally priests in Christ, 1 Pet. 2.9; Rev. 1.6. And even if we were not, is there so very much difference between the Passover and the Lord's Supper? The distribution of the Passover was not limited or assigned to the priests or Levites; and that was under the law, when no one but a priest or a Levite was even allowed to touch the sacred objects. Now we are under the gospel, which has done away with all those regulations about touching things: now the rights and liberties of believers have been made more comprehensive. Does it seem probable, then, that, since the distribution of the Lord's Supper is assigned to no one in particular, we are right to restrict it only to ministers of the church? Does it seem right that the head of a family, or anyone appointed by him, should not now be at liberty to distribute the Lord's Supper to his dependents, as he once distributed the Passover? Does it seem right, that is, even if we assume that some distribution of the elements by a particular individual ever was, or is now, requisite?

We ought not to approach the sacraments until we have thoroughly searched our consciences and renounced our sins: 2 Chron. 30.13–15: *they arose and took away the altars that were in Jerusalem, and they took away all the altars for incense, and threw them into the brook Kidron: then they killed the passover;* Ezra 6.21 [. . .]; 1 Cor. 11.28 [. . .].

To neglect the sacraments and to receive them in an unworthy way are both equally displeasing to the Deity: Ex. 4.24–26 [. . .]; 1 Cor. 11.29, etc.: *for he who eats and drinks unworthily, eats and drinks judgment upon himself, if he does not discern the Lord's body: for this reason many are ill among you . . .*

So the sacraments can and should be put off until one has a proper time and place, a pure mind, holiness of life and a regular communion of believers. Ex. 13.5: *it shall be, when Jehovah shall bring you into the land of the* Canaanites . . . that *you shall engage in that worship this month;* Num. 9.10, 11 [. . .]; similarly 2 Chron. 30.2, 3; Josh. 5.4 [. . .]. The papist Mass is not at all the same as the Lord's Supper. 1. The one was instituted by the Lord, the other by the Pope. 2. The Lord's Supper commemorates the fact that Christ, as the only priest, offered himself, Heb. 7.24, 25, 27 and 9.15, 25, 26 and 10.10, 12, 14. The Mass, on the other hand, is a daily offering, made by innumerable priests. 3. Christ offered himself, not at the holy supper, but on the cross; but in the Mass Christ is sacrificed each day by the priest. 4. At the Lord's Supper the actual body of the living Lord, made from the Virgin Mary, was present. Whereas in the Mass it is supposed to be made out of bread at the moment when the priest murmurs the four words, *this is my body,* and to be broken as soon as it is made. 5. In the holy supper the bread and wine remain unchanged after consecration in substance as in name. But in the Mass, so we are told, only the outward appearance remains, and each is metamorphosed into the body of our Lord. 6. In the holy supper, by Christ's command, all drank from the cup, but in the Mass the cup is denied to the laity. Finally the Mass brings down Christ's holy body from its supreme exaltation at the right hand of God. It drags it back to the earth, though it has suffered every pain and hardship already, to a state of humiliation even more wretched and degrading than before: to be broken once more and crushed and ground, even by the fangs of brutes. Then, when it has been driven through all the stomach's filthy channels, it shoots it out—one shudders even to mention it—into the latrine.

It is quite clear to us, from the very definition of the word *sacrament,* that the other things which the Papists call sacraments—CONFIRMATION, PENANCE, EXTREME UNCTION, ORDINATION and MATRIMONY—are not really sacraments at all. They are not divinely instituted, and they contain no sign appointed by God to seal the covenant of grace.

CONFIRMATION or THE LAYING ON OF HANDS was, it is true, employed by Christ, not as a sacrament, however, but as a symbol of blessing. This was in accordance with the custom of his people, probably derived from the patriarchs, who laid their hands on their children when they blessed them, as did magistrates on those who succeeded them in the magistracy, see Num. 27.18 where Moses lays his hands on Joshua. Thus the apostles usually laid their hands on those who were elected to any ecclesiastical office, or were baptized. I say usually, not always, because although we read that hands were laid upon the seven deacons, Acts 6.6, there is no mention of this happening in Acts 1.26 when Matthias was added to the number of the apostles. It is true that, in the case of the baptized this laying on of hands conferred miraculous gifts of the Holy Spirit and wonderful, though not saving, grace; Acts 8.17 etc. and 19.6, and 1 Tim. 4.14, and 2 Tim. 1.6. So although it is clearly improper that it should remain in the church as a sacrament, it is just and profitable that it should be retained as a symbol of blessing: Heb. 6.2: *the doctrine of baptisms and of the laying on of hands.*

As for PENANCE for sins committed after baptism (which is the only kind of penance the Papists consider a sacrament), and HOLY ORDERS, I have no objection to their being called sacraments if the word is used loosely, implying only that they represent sacred things, as did the old custom of washing the feet, and other customs of the same kind. I do not see why much trouble should be taken to establish the precise meaning of the word when it does not even occur in the Bible. Certainly penance does not contain any real sign, nor does it seal anything, any more than faith does.

But MATRIMONY, since it is something which belongs to all men indiscriminately, by the common law of nations, should clearly not, unless the term is limited to mean the matrimony of believers, be called a sacred thing at all, let alone a sacrament. On the contrary, it is obviously a civil matter and therefore its celebration is definitely not part of the function of ministers of religion.[265]

As for the UNCTION OF THE SICK, it is true that the apostles *anointed the sick with oil and healed them,* Mark 6.13, and James gives the practice his support, 5.14, 15. But these rites were not sacraments, they were merely the natural accompaniment of miracles, and ceased along with the gift of miracles. So the extreme unction of the modern Papist does not in any way resemble that ancient practice. The apostles did not only anoint those who were at the point of death, as is now the custom, but anyone who was seriously ill and, furthermore, they cured them. Mark 6.13. What more can I say? Sacraments were chiefly instituted to set the seal upon grace and to confirm our faith. Therefore all sacraments should be distributed equally to all believers. But of these five papist sacraments, four are not available to all but only to particular men: penance to the lapsed, unction to the sick, orders to the clergy, and marriage only to the laity.

CHAPTER 29

OF THE VISIBLE CHURCH

[. . .][266]

Just as Christ is the head of the mystical church, so no one is rightly or can possibly be at the head of the visible church, except Christ. Matt. 18.20: *there I am in their midst,* and 28.20 [. . .]; 1 Cor. 5.4 [. . .]; Heb. 3.6 [. . .]; Rev. 2.1 [. . .].

Those people are in error, therefore, who set up anyone as an earthly head over the church, particularly Peter and his so-called successors, the Popes of Rome. There is no divine authority for doing this.

Peter certainly does not seem to have been preferred to the other apostles, either by virtue of his mission, Matt. 10.1, or of his instructions, John 20.21, 22, or because of any authority in deciding controversies, Acts 15.2, 6, 7, 19, 23, 25. He does not seem to have excelled them in knowledge, and certainly not in constancy, since, to begin with, he fell in a particularly marked way when he denied Christ, and since he fell again, though less seriously, on that occasion when he was reproved by Paul, Gal. 2.11. He was *a presbyter,* as they were, 1 Pet. 5.1, and did not enjoy a higher degree of honor than they, Matt. 19.28. In fact nothing special is attributed to him any more than it is to James, or John, or Paul, or Barnabas; Gal. 2.9. He was merely the apostle of the circumcised, as Paul was of the Gen-

265. Cp. *Likeliest Means* (Yale 7:299): "As for marriages that ministers should meddle with them, as not sanctified or legitimate without their celebration, I find no ground in scripture either of precept or example . . . being of itself a civil ordinance, a household contract, a thing indifferent and free to the whole race of mankind, not as religious, but as men."

266. In the omitted portion, Milton defines the *Visible Church* and its manifestations, including signs and miracles, neither of which are essential to the church, unlike charity, which is.

tiles, 2.8, 9, and Paul was *in no way inferior to the chief apostles,* 2 Cor. 11.5. Moreover Peter was sent into Samaria as John's colleague, Acts 8.14, and gave an account of his apostleship to those who argued against him, 11.2. The church is said to be *built on the foundation,* not of Peter alone, but *of the apostles,* Eph. 2.20; Rev. 21.14. And anyway, how could a *foundation* have any successors? As for that famous text, Matt. 16.18, 19, which the Pope perverts in order to make it the letters patent of his papacy, it confers nothing on Peter which be does not share with everyone else who professes the same faith. For, as the evangelists make clear, many other people had confessed no less explicitly that Christ was the Son of God. So Christ's answer is not *on you, Peter,* but *on this rock,* or in other words, on this faith which you have in common with other believers. For Christ is the true rock, 1 Cor. 10.4, and the sole foundation, 3.11, and thus faith in Christ is called a foundation, Jude 20: *building up yourselves on your most holy faith,* and so are Christ's apostles, rather than anyone else, see Eph. 2.20, above. Moreover the keys of the kingdom of heaven are not entrusted to Peter alone. The power of the keys, that is the power of binding and loosing, is not committed to him exclusively, Matt. 18.18, 19: *whatever you bind . . . ;* John 20.23: *if you remit their sins . . .* Again, that passage in John 21.15, etc. does not mean that the feeding of Christ's flock was entrusted to Peter rather than to anyone else. It was because Peter had fallen by denying Christ three times that he is, in this passage, restored to the place from which he had fallen by a confession which is three times repeated. He had been too self-confident, and had declared that he loved Christ more than anyone else, Matt. 26.33; now he has been tried and found wanting, and is blamed for that self-confidence. He is reminded that, if he really loves Christ more than the other disciples, he should show this love by feeding Christ's sheep, and particularly the lambs. As a matter of fact he had been reminded of the same thing before, Luke 22.32: *when you are converted, confirm your brothers.* It was, of course, the common task of all the apostles to feed Christ's flock, that is, to teach all nations, Matt. 28.19.[267]

Even if we were to grant all that is claimed for Peter, what is there to prove that the same things are granted to his successors, or that these successors are the Popes of Rome?

THE VISIBLE CHURCH is either UNIVERSAL or PARTICULAR.

THE UNIVERSAL VISIBLE CHURCH is THE WHOLE MULTITUDE OF THOSE WHO ARE CALLED FROM ANY PART OF THE WHOLE WORLD, AND WHO OPENLY WORSHIP GOD THE FATHER IN CHRIST EITHER INDIVIDUALLY OR IN CONJUNCTION WITH OTHERS.

[. . .][268]

267. Milton's views concerning Peter and the papacy are commonplaces of Protestantism. He extends these arguments to the institution of monarchy in *REW* (p. 1121): "All Protestants hold that Christ in his church hath left no vicegerent of his power, but himself without deputy is the only head thereof, governing it from heaven: how then can any Christian man derive his kingship from Christ but with worse usurpation than the Pope his headship over the church?"

268. The deleted passage substantiates the parts of the preceding definition with scriptural citations. In the same way, it then defines and elaborates the meaning of *MINISTERS of the universal church.*

The MINISTERS of the universal church are either ORDINARY or EXTRAORDINARY: 1 Cor. 12.28, as above; Eph. 4.11–13: *so he gave some apostles, and some prophets, and some evangelists, and some pastors and teachers, for making the saints perfect, for the work of the ministry, for the building of the body of Christ, until we all come into the unity of the faith, into the knowledge of the Son of God.* Here, notice, *pastors* are synonymous with *teachers.* The apostle does not say, *he gave some pastors, some teachers,* but merely adds the second word as an explanation of the first, which is a figurative term. This proves the futility of the modern academic title *doctor.* Both the doctor (or teacher) and the pastor teach and exhort: the function is twofold, but the office and the agent are one. Of course, one individual may be better than another at performing either task, and may sometimes be distinguished for this reason: Rom. 12.7, 8.

EXTRAORDINARY MINISTERS are sent and inspired by God to set up or to reform the church both by preaching and by writing.

To this class the prophets, apostles, evangelists and others of that kind belonged: 1 Cor. 4.1: *let a man look upon us as ministers of Christ, and stewards of God's mysteries*; Gal. 1.1: *Paul, made an apostle not by men nor through man, but through Jesus Christ and God the Father who raised him from the dead,* and 1.17 [. . .], and 2.6 [. . .]; Acts 13.2 [. . .]; 2 Tim. 4.5 [. . .].

Any believer can be an ORDINARY MINISTER, whenever necessary, so long as he is provided with certain gifts (which constitute his mission).

Before the law the fathers or eldest sons of families came into this category,[269] as, for example, Abel, Noah, Abraham, etc., and Jethro, Ex. 18.12 and 19.22: *let the ministers of the holy things, who come near to Jehovah, sanctify themselves . . . ,* and 24.5: *he sent young men of the children of Israel who offered burnt-offerings and sacrificed thank-offerings to Jehovah.*

Also in this category, under the law, came Aaron and his posterity, the whole tribe of Levi, and lastly the prophets. Furthermore, anyone who seemed suitable, although neither priest nor Levite, was able to teach publicly in the synagogue: Christ was given permission to do this; so was Paul, Acts 13.15: *after the reading of the law and the prophets they sent, . . . saying, Men and brothers, if you have any word of exhortation for the people, speak.* So it is even more allowable, under the gospel, for any believer endowed with similar gifts to do the same. Mark 9.38, 39 clearly permits it: *we saw a man who does not follow us casting out devils in your name, and we forbade him . . . Do not forbid*; Acts 8.4: *those who were scattered went through the land preaching the word of God,* and 11.19, etc. [. . .]. But our modern clergy, if that is the right name for them, who claim the right of preaching as theirs alone, would not have been glad had they seen this grace extended to the laity, as they call them, but would have been more likely to condemn it. See also 18.24, 25 [. . .]; 2 Tim. 2.2 [. . .]; Ex. 19.6, compared with Isa. 41.6: *you shall be called the priests of Jehovah, you will be styled the ministers of our God,* and with 1 Pet. 2.9: *you are*

269. Cp. *Likeliest Means* (Yale 7:286): "In those days there was no priest, but the father or the first born of each family."

a chosen generation, a royal priesthood, a holy nation, a people whom the Lord claims as his own, to proclaim the powers of him who has called us from darkness into his marvelous light; Rev. 1.6 [. . .]. Again, 1 Pet. 5.3: *not as domineering over the clergy.* If the term *clergy*, which ecclesiastics have since appropriated to themselves, means anything here, then it must signify the whole church.[270] Moreover the term *prophet* is applied not only to a man able to foretell the future but also to anyone endowed with exceptional piety and wisdom for the purpose of teaching: Gen. 20.7, of Abraham, *he is a prophet, and when he prays for you you shall live.* Similarly Miriam is called a prophetess, Ex. 15.20, and so is Deborah, Judges 4.4, and all believers, Ps. 105.15: *do not touch my anointed, and do no harm to my prophets.* Thus under the gospel the simple gift of teaching, especially of public teaching, is called *prophecy*: 1 Cor. 14.1 [. . .], and 14.3 [. . .], and so on, until the end of the chapter. 1 Cor. 3.8, etc. [. . .]. It is not the universities, then, but God who has given us pastors and teachers:[271] that same God who gave us apostles and prophets, 1 Pet. 4.10, 11: *whatever gift each man has received, let him use it to serve his fellows, like a good steward of God's various grace. If any man can speak, let him speak as if he spoke the declarations of God . . . .*

If, then, any believer can preach the gospel, so long as he is endowed with certain gifts, it follows that any believer can administer baptism, because baptism is less important than the preaching of the gospel: John 4.12: *Jesus did not baptise, but his disciples did*; 1 Cor. 1.17 [. . .]. Thus Ananias, though he was only a disciple, baptised Paul, Acts 9.10, 18, also 10.48: *he told them to be baptised in the name of the Lord.* Those he told to do the baptising were those who had come with him, and they are called merely *brothers* and *believers*, 10.23, 45. It is commonly supposed, moreover, that baptism has taken the place of circumcision, and resembles it closely. If this is so, why should not any Christian be able to administer baptism, so long as he is a suitable person, that is to say, not uninstructed? After all, any Jew was able to administer circumcision.

I showed in the last chapter that the communion of the Lord's Supper is something which belongs to all believers, and that its administration is not the particular right of any man or order of men.

The celebration of marriages or funerals has even less to do with ministers of the church. However, these hirelings customarily claim it as their exclusive right, without a shadow of scriptural justification and without even the excuse that the custom is derived from the priests and Levites.

THE PEOPLE of the universal church are *all nations;* Matt. 28.19, 20: *go out and teach all nations.* It is the duty of every man to do his best to procure and promote their conversion: Rom. 1.14: *I am a debtor both to the Greeks and to the barbarians; both to the wise and to the unwise.*

270. Cp. *RCG* (Yale 1:838): "the title of clergy St. Peter gave to all God's people."

271. Cp. *Likeliest Means* (Yale 7:315, 316): "It is a fond error . . . to think that the university make a minister of the gospel"; "by whom sent? By the university? . . . No, surely: but sent from God only."

CHAPTER 30

OF THE HOLY SCRIPTURE

The writings of the prophets, the apostles and the evangelists, since they were divinely inspired, are called THE HOLY SCRIPTURE; 2 Sam. 23.2: *the Spirit of Jehovah spoke in me, and his word was on my tongue;* Matt. 22.43: *David, through the Spirit, calls him Lord, saying . . . ;* 2 Cor. 13.3 [. . .]; 2 Tim: 3.16 [. . .].

As can be seen from standard editions of the Bible, there is general agreement among the orthodox[272] about which books of the Old and New Testaments may be called CANONICAL, that is to say, accepted as the genuine writings of the prophets, apostles and evangelists.

The books usually added to these, and known as the APOCRYPHAL books, have nothing like the same authority as the canonical, and are not admitted as evidence in deciding points of faith.

The reasons for this are: 1. Because although they were written in Old Testament times, they are not in the Hebrew language. They certainly ought to have been, if genuine, because at that time, before the Gentiles had been called, the church existed only among the Hebrews, Rom. 3.2 and 9.4. It would obviously have been ridiculous to write in the language of a people who had nothing as yet to do with the things written about. 2. Their authority is deservedly called in question because they are never cited in the New Testament. 3. Because they contain many things which contradict the canonical scriptures, and some which are fantastic, low, trifling and quite foreign to real sagacity and religion.

The Holy Scriptures were not written merely for particular occasions, as the Papists teach. They were written for the use of the church throughout all succeeding ages, not only under the law but also under the gospel. Exod. 34.27: *write for yourself these words, because according to the intent of these words I make a covenant with you and with Israel;* Deut. 31.19 [. . .]; Isa. 8.20: [. . .], and 30.8 [. . .]; Hab. 2.2 [. . .]; Luke 16.29 [. . .]; John 5.39 [. . .]; Rom. 15.4: *the things which were written beforehand were written for our instruction, that through patience and the consolation of the scriptures we might still have hope;* 1 Cor. 10.11: [. . .].

Almost everything in the New Testament is proved by reference to the Old. The function of the books of the New Testament is made clear in John 20.31: *these things are written that you may believe . . . ;* Eph. 2.20 [. . .]; Phil. 3.1 [. . .]; 1 Thess. 5.27 [. . .]; 1 Tim. 3.15 [. . .]; 2 Tim. 3.15–17: *that you have known the Holy Scriptures from childhood, and they are able to make you wise and lead you to salvation through the faith which is in Christ Jesus. All scripture is divinely inspired, and useful for teaching, for reproof, for correction, for discipline in right living, so that the man of God may be fully prepared and equipped for every good work.* It is true that the scriptures which Timothy

272. " '*Orthodoxos*,' i.e., Protestant. This usage appears also in *Second Defense* . . . where Milton speaks of his defense in Italy of '*orthodoxam religionem*' " (Kelley; see p. 1099).

is said to have *known from childhood,* and which *are able to make* one *wise through faith in Christ,* seem to have been only the books of the Old Testament. It is not apparent that any book of the New Testament had been written when Timothy was a child. However, in the next verse the same claim is made for the whole divinely inspired scripture. This claim is that it is *useful for teaching*... even those who are already learned and wise, 1 Cor. 10.15: *as I say this to intelligent men, consider what I say,* and even those who have arrived at full maturity, Phil. 3.15: *let as many of us as are adults think this*—such as Timothy himself and Titus, to whom Paul wrote. Also, that it is useful to the strong, 1 John 2.14: *I have written to you, young men, because you are strong, and the word of God dwells in you;* 2 Pet. 1.12, 15 [...], and 3.15, 16 [...]; Paul addressed his epistle to the Romans, 1.7, 15, but Peter here says that he wrote not only to them but to all believers; 2 Pet. 3.1, 2 [...]; 1 John 2.21: *I have not written to you because you are ignorant of the truth, but because you know it;* Rev. 1.19 [...].

It is clear from all these texts that no one should be forbidden to read the scriptures. On the contrary, it is very proper that all sorts and conditions of men should read them or hear them read regularly. This includes the king, Deut. 17.19; magistrates, Josh. 1.8; and every kind of person, Deut. 31.9–11, etc. [. . .], 11.18–20: *you shall store up these my words in your heart and in your soul, and shall bind them as a sign to your hand . . . and you shall write them on the doorposts of your house and on your gates;* and 29.29 [...], and 30.11 [...]; 2 Chron. 34.30 [...]; Isa. 8.20 [...]; Nehem. 9.3: *and they got up in their places and read in the book of the law,* etc., that is, all the people, as the second verse shows. Or again, take a writer whom my opponents consider canonical: 1 Macc. 1.59, 60: *wherever anyone was found with the book of the covenant.*

The evidence is clearer in the New Testament: Luke 10.26: *what is written in the law? How do you read it?* The man whom Christ asked this question was an interpreter of the law. It is generally agreed that there were, at that time, many interpreters, Pharisees and others, who were neither priests nor Levites. Moreover Christ himself, whom they did not consider at all learned, was not forbidden to interpret the law even in the synagogue, so obviously there would have been no objection to his reading the scriptures in his own home. Also 16.29: *they have Moses and the prophets, let them hear them;* John 5.39: *examine the scriptures;* Acts 8.28 [...], and 17.11 [...], and 18.24 [...]; 2 Tim. 3.15 [...]; Rev. 1.3: *blessed is he who reads.*

Thus the scriptures are, both in themselves and through God's illumination absolutely clear. If studied carefully and regularly, they are an ideal instrument for educating even unlearned readers in those matters which have most to do with salvation. Ps. 19.8: *the doctrine of Jehovah is perfect, restoring the soul; the testimony of Jehovah is true, making the unlearned wise* ..., and 119.105 [...], 119.130: *the entrance of your words gives light, it gives the simple prudence*—another proof that the scriptures ought to be read by everyone; 119.18 [...]; Luke 24.45 [...]; Acts 18.28 [...]; 2 Pet. 1.20, 21: *that no prophecy of the scriptures is susceptible of particular interpretation: for, at the time when it came, the prophecy was not brought by the will of man* . . . The prophecy, then, must not be interpreted by the intellect of a particular individual, that is to say, not by his merely human intellect, but with the help of the Holy Spirit, promised to each individual believer.[273] Hence the gift of prophecy, 1 Cor. 14.

The scriptures, then, are plain and sufficient in themselves. Thus they *can make a man wise and fit for salvation through faith,* and *through them the man of God may be fully prepared and fully provided for every good work.* Through what madness is it, then, that even members of the reformed church persist in explaining and illustrating and interpreting the most holy truths of religion, as if they were conveyed obscurely in the Holy Scriptures? Why do they shroud them in the thick darkness of metaphysics? Why do they employ all their useless technicalities and meaningless distinctions and barbarous jargon in their attempt to make the scriptures plainer and easier to understand, when they themselves are continually claiming how supremely clear they are already? As if scripture did not contain the clearest of all lights in itself: as if it were not in itself sufficient, especially in matters of faith and holiness: as if the sense of the divine truth, itself absolutely plain, needed to be brought out more clearly or more fully, or otherwise explained, by means of terms imported from the most abstruse of human sciences—which does not, in fact, deserve the name of a science at all!

The scriptures are difficult or obscure, at any rate in matters where salvation is concerned, only to those who perish: Luke 8.10: *to you it is given to know the mysteries of the kingdom of God, but to others I speak through parables; so that they may look but not see, and hear but not understand;* 1 Cor. 1.18 [. . .], also 2.14 [. . .], also 2 Cor. 4.2, 3 [. . .]; 2 Pet. 3.16, speaking of the epistles of St. Paul: *in which some things are difficult to understand, which those who are untaught and unstable distort, as they do the other scriptures, to their own destruction.*

Each passage of scripture has only a single sense, though in the Old Testament this sense is often a combination of the historical and the typological, take Hosea 11.1, for example, compared with Matt. 2.15: *I have called my son out of Egypt.* This can be read correctly in two senses, as a reference both to the people of Israel and to Christ in his infancy.

The custom of interpreting scripture in the church is mentioned in Neh. 8.9, 10: *they read the book of God distinctly, and by explaining the sense gave them understanding through the scripture: then said Nehemiah (he is the king's legate), and Ezra, the priest, well-read in the law, and the Levites who taught the people . . . ;* 2 Chron. 17.9, 10 [. . .]; Luke 4.17 [. . .]; 1 Cor. 14.1, etc. [. . .]

The right method of interpreting the scriptures has been laid down by theologians. This is certainly useful, but no very careful attention is paid to it. The requisites are linguistic ability, knowledge of the original sources, consideration of the overall intent, distinction between literal and figurative language, examination of the causes and circumstances, and of what comes before and

273. Cp. *PL* 12.511–14: "the truth, .../Left only in those written records pure,/Though not but by the Spirit understood."

after the passage in question, and comparison of one text with another.[274] It must always be asked, too, how far the interpretation is in agreement with faith. Finally, one often has to take into account the anomalies of syntax, as, for example, when a relative does not refer to its immediate antecedent but to the principal word in the sentence, although it is not so near to it. Compare 2 Kings 16.2 with 16.1: *Ahaz was twenty years old when he began to reign.* Here *he* refers to Jotham, Ahaz's father, as is apparent if you consider the age at which Hezekiah began his reign, 18.2. Similarly 2 Chron. 36.9: *when he began to reign,* compared with 2 Kings 24.10. Ps. 99.6 [. . .]; John 8.44 [. . .]. Lastly, no inferences should be made from the text, unless they follow necessarily from what is written. This precaution is necessary, otherwise we may be forced to believe something which is not written instead of something which is, and to accept human reasoning, generally fallacious, instead of divine doctrine, thus mistaking the shadow for the substance. What we are obliged to believe are the things written in the sacred books, not the things debated in academic gatherings.

Every believer is entitled to interpret the scriptures; and by that I mean interpret them for himself. He has the spirit, who guides truth, and he has the mind of Christ.[275] Indeed, no one else can usefully interpret them for him, unless that person's interpretation coincides with the one he makes for himself and his own conscience. There is more on this subject in the next chapter, where I deal with the people of particular churches. Whoever God has appointed as apostle or prophet or evangelist or pastor or teacher, is entitled to interpret the scriptures for others in public, 1 Cor. 12.8, 9; Eph. 4.11–13: in other words, anyone endowed with the gift of teaching, *every teacher of the law who has been instructed in readiness for the kingdom of heaven,* Matt. 13.52. This does not mean those who are appointed to professional chairs by mere men or by universities: of these it can often be said, as in Luke 11.52: *woe to you, interpreters of the law, for you have taken away the key of knowledge. You did not enter yourselves, and you stopped those who were entering.*

No visible church, then, let alone any magistrate, has the right to impose its own interpretations upon the consciences of men as matters of legal obligation, thus demanding implicit faith.

If there is disagreement about the sense of scripture among apparent believers, they should tolerate each other until God reveals the truth to all: Phil. 3.15, 16: *let as many of us as are adults think this: if you think differently about anything, God will reveal the truth to you also. However, in things which we have already mastered, let us walk by the same rule and share the same opinion.* Similarly Rom. 14.4 [. . .].

274. Cp. *DDD* (p. 888): "All places of scripture wherein just reason of doubt arises from the letter are to be expounded by considering upon what occasion everything is set down and by comparing other texts." For Miltonic hermeneutics, see Haskin.

275. Cp. *Of Civil Power* (Yale 7:244): "Every true Christian able to give a reason of his faith hath the word of God before him, the promised Holy Spirit, and the mind of Christ within him, 1 Cor. 2.16."

The rule and canon of faith, therefore, is scripture alone: Ps. 19.10: *the judgments of Jehovah are truth itself.* In controversies there is no arbitrator except scripture, or rather, each man is his own arbitrator, so long as he follows scripture and the Spirit of God. It is true that Paul says, 1 Tim. 3.15: *the church of the living God is the pillar and ground of the truth.* Some people turn these words into a claim that the visible church, however defined, has the supreme authority of interpretation and of arbitration in controversy. However, once we examine this and the previous verse, it becomes evident that such people are very far from the truth. Paul wrote these words to Timothy, and for him they were meant to have the force of Holy Scripture. The intention was *that he might know,* through these words, *how he ought to behave in the house of God, which is the church*—that is, in any assembly of believers. Therefore it was not the house of God, or the church, which was to be a rule to him *that he might know,* but the Holy Scripture which he had received from Paul. The church is, or at least ought to be, for it is sometimes not, *the pillar and ground,* that is to say the guardian, repository and confirmer *of the truth.* But though it is all these things, it does not follow that it is the rule or arbiter of truth and scripture. For the house of God is not a rule to itself: it receives its rule from the word of God, and it ought, at any rate, to keep very closely to this. Besides, the writings of the prophets and of the apostles, which constitute the scriptures, are the foundations of the church. Eph. 2.20: *built on,* etc. Now if the church is built on a foundation, it cannot itself be the rule or arbiter of that foundation.

Apparently not all the instructions which the apostles gave the churches were written down, or if they were written down they have not survived: see 2 John 12: *although I had many things to write to you, I did not want to put them down in black and white;* similarly 3 John 13. Col. 4.16 [. . .].

We should conclude that these instructions, though useful, were not necessary for salvation. They ought, then, to be supplied either from other passages of scripture or, if it is doubtful whether this is possible, not from the decrees of popes or councils, much less from the edicts of magistrates, but from that same Spirit operating in us through faith and charity: John 16.12, 13: *I still have many things to say to you; but you cannot bear them now. However when he, the Spirit of truth, comes, he will lead you into all truth.* Peter also warns us, in the same way, *that attention must be paid to the prophetic word, until the day dawns, and the day-star arises in our hearts,* 2 Pet. 1.19. The reference here is to the light of the gospel, which is to be sought in our hearts just as much as in written records: 2 Cor. 3.3: *that you are the epistle of Christ, ministered by us, written not with ink but with the Spirit of the living God; not on tablets of stone, but on the fleshly tablets of the heart;* Eph. 6.17 [. . .]; 1 John 2.20 [. . .], and 2.27 [. . .]. So when the Corinthians asked Paul about certain matters on which scripture had not laid down anything definite, he answered them in accordance with the spirit of Christianity, and by means of that spiritual anointing which he had received: 1 Cor. 7.12: *I say this, not the Lord,* 25, 26: *I have no command from the Lord about virgins, but I give my own opinion, as one to whom the Lord through his mercy has granted faith. I think, then . . . ,* 40 [. . .]. Thus he reminds them that they are able to supply answers for themselves in questions of this kind, 7.15: *a brother or sister is not bound to subjection in cases of this kind,* and 36 [. . .].

We have, particularly under the gospel, a double scripture. There is the external scripture of the written word and the internal scripture of the Holy Spirit which he, according to God's promise, has engraved upon the hearts of believers, and which is certainly not to be neglected. See above, Chapter 27, on the gospel. Isa. 59.21: *as for me, this will be my covenant with them, says Jehovah; my spirit which is in you, and my words which I have placed in your mouth, shall not leave your mouth or the mouth of your seed or the mouth of your seed's seed, says Jehovah, from this time forward, for ever;* Jer. 31.33, 34; Acts 5.32 [. . .]; 1 Cor. 2.12 [. . .].

Nowadays the external authority for our faith, in other words, the scriptures, is of very considerable importance and, generally speaking, it is the authority of which we first have experience. The pre-eminent and supreme authority, however, is the authority of the Spirit, which is internal, and the individual possession of each man.

I will say nothing about those books which are not a genuine part of scripture. Paul himself has warned us to beware of these, 2 Thess. 2.2 [. . .], and 3.17 [. . .]. But quite apart from these, the external scripture, particularly the New Testament, has often been liable to corruption and is, in fact, corrupt. This has come about because it has been committed to the care of various untrustworthy authorities, has been collected together from an assortment of divergent manuscripts, and has survived in a medley of transcripts and editions. But no one can corrupt the Spirit which guides man to truth, and a spiritual man is not easily deceived; 1 Cor. 2.15, 16: *the spiritual man judges all things discriminatingly but is himself judged by no one. For who knows the mind of the Lord? Who will be his instructor? But we have the mind of Christ,* and 12.10 [. . .]. An example of a corrupt text found in nearly all the manuscripts is Matt. 27.9, where a quotation attributed to Jeremiah actually occurs only in Zechariah. Innumerable other instances occur on almost every page of Erasmus, Beza and other New-Testament editors.

In early times the ark of the covenant, which was sacrosanct, held the law of Moses. After the Babylonish captivity the law passed into the care of its pledged protectors, the priests and prophets and other divinely instructed men, as, for example, Ezra, Zechariah and Malachi. Unquestionably these men handed down God's holy books in an uncorrupted state, to be preserved in the sanctuary by the priests who succeeded them. In every period the priests considered it a matter of supreme importance that no word should be changed, and they had no theories which might have made them alter anything. It is true that the other books, particularly the historical ones, cannot be certainly ascribed to a particular date or author, and also that the chronological accuracy of their narrative often seems suspect. Few or none, however, have called in doubt their doctrinal part. The New Testament, on the other hand, has been entrusted throughout the ages, as I said before, to a variety of hands, some more corrupt than others. We possess no autograph copy: no exemplar which we can rely on as more trustworthy than the others. Thus Erasmus, Beza, and other learned men have edited from the various manuscripts what seems to them to be the most authentic text. I do not know why God's providence should have committed the contents of the New Testament to such wayward and uncertain guardians, unless it was so that this very fact might convince us that the Spirit which is given to us is a more certain guide than scripture, and that we ought to follow it.

It is certain, too, that it is not the visible church but the hearts of believers which, since Christ's ascension, have continually constituted the *pillar* and *ground of truth.* They are the real *house and church of the living God,* 1 Tim. 3.15.

Clearly the editors and interpreters of the Greek Testament, which is of prime authority, rest all their decisions upon the weight and reliability of the manuscript evidence, not upon the visible church. If the reliability of the manuscripts varies or is uncertain, these editors must be at a loss. They have nothing which they can then follow or establish as the genuine, uncorrupted text, the indisputable word of God. This happens in the story of the woman taken in adultery, and in some other passages.

However, we believe in the scriptures in a general and overall way first of all, and we do so because of the authority either of the visible church or of the manuscripts. Later we believe in the church, in those very manuscripts, and in particular sections of them, because of the authority and internal consistency of the whole scripture. Finally we believe in the whole scripture because of that Spirit which inwardly persuades every believer. Thus the Samaritans believed in Christ first of all because of the words of the woman. Later they believed not so much because of her words as because of Christ's words as he spoke before them, John 4.42. Thus, too, on the evidence of scripture itself, all things are eventually to be referred to the Spirit and the unwritten word.

Each believer is ruled by the Spirit of God. So if anyone imposes any kind of sanction or dogma upon believers against their will, whether he acts in the name of the church or of a Christian magistrate, he is placing a yoke not only upon man but upon the Holy Spirit itself.[276] The apostles themselves, in a council over which the Holy Spirit presided, refused to impose even the divine law upon believers. They considered it an intolerable yoke, Acts 15.10, 19, 28: *why do you tempt God*... Much less can any modern church, which is unable to claim for itself with any real certainty the presence of the Spirit, and least of all can a magistrate impose rigid beliefs upon the faithful, beliefs which are either not found in scripture at all, or only deduced from scripture by a process of human reasoning which does not carry any conviction with it.

Human traditions, written or unwritten, are expressly forbidden, Deut. 4.2: *do not add to the word which I command you, nor subtract from it,* etc.; Prov. 30.6 [. . .];

276. Cp. *PL* 12.520–25: "from that pretense,/Spiritual laws by carnal power shall force/On every conscience; laws which none shall find/Left them enrolled, or what the Spirit within/Shall on the heart engrave. What will they then/But force the Spirit of Grace itself."

Rev. 22.18, 19 [. . .], etc. [. . .], etc.; Isa. 29.13, 14 [. . .]; Matt. 15.3, 9; Gal. 1.8 [. . .]; 1 Tim. 6.3 [. . .]; Tit. 1.14 [. . .]; 1 Tim. 1.4 [. . .]; Col. 2.8: *look out, lest anyone rob you by means of philosophy and delusive vanities, based on human traditions and worldly principles, and not on Christ.*

In a matter of this sort we should not rely upon our predecessors or upon antiquity, 2 Chron. 29.6, etc.: *for our fathers did not act uprightly . . . ;* Ps. 78.8, etc. [. . .]; Ezek. 20.18 [. . .]; Amos 2.1 [. . .]; Mal. 3.7 [. . .]; Eccles. 7.10 [. . .]. It is true that Jeremiah advises the people to *seek out the old ways,* but only to find *what the good way is,* and to choose that, 6.16—otherwise this would be an argument in favor of idol-worship, and of the Pharisees and Samaritans; Jer. 44.17, etc. [. . .]; Matt. 15.2, etc.: *why do your disciples act in a way contrary to the tradition of their elders?* Christ opposes to this God's commandment, 15.3: *and why do you act in a way contrary to the commandment of God by your tradition . . . ?* Similarly Mark 7.8, 9., John 4.20 [. . .].

We should not attribute too much even to the venerable name of our mother the church[277] (Hos. 2.2: *dispute with your mother, dispute with her; tell her that she is not my wife nor I her husband, so that she may get rid of her fornications*) unless by the church we mean exclusively the mystical church in heaven, Gal. 4.26: *Jerusalem, which is above, is free, and is the mother of us all.*

CHAPTER 31

OF PARTICULAR CHURCHES

[. . .][278]

As for the remuneration of ministers, both those of the universal church and those of each particular church, it is true that some remuneration is allowable, since it is both just in itself and also has the sanction of God's law and of the authority of Christ and his apostle: Matt. 10.10 [. . .]; 1 Cor. 9.7–13 [. . .]; Gal. 6.6: *let the catechumen* or *him who is instructed in the word share all good things with him who has instructed him;* 1 Tim. 5.7, 18 [. . .]: thus it is right and proper, and in accordance with God's own provision, 1 Cor. 9.14: *that those who preach the gospel should get their living from the gospel.* But it is better to serve God's church for nothing and, following our Lord's example, to minister and to serve without pay. This is not only more exemplary, but also it is a more likely way to avoid all offence or suspicion, and a more bright and beautiful way of exulting in God: Matt. 20.28 [. . .] and 10.8 [. . .]; Acts 20.35: *remember the words of the Lord Jesus: he said, It is more blessed to give than to receive.* By his own example Paul proposed and recommended the same course of action for the imitation of all ministers of the church: 20.34, 35:

277. *Cp. Of Civil Power* (Yale 7:248): "Then ought we to believe what in our conscience we apprehend the scripture to say, though the visible church with all her doctors gainsay."

278. The deleted passage concerns "ordinary ministers" of a particular church, their titles, functions, qualifications, and succession. What follows is Milton's account of their proper remuneration.

you yourselves know that these hands have ministered to my needs and to those of my companions. I have shown you everything: that you ought to support the weak by laboring in this way . . . ; 2 Thess. 3.7–9 [. . .]; 1 Cor. 9.15, 18 [. . .]; and 2 Cor. 11.8 [. . .], and 11.9 [. . .], and 11.10 [. . .], and 11.12 [. . .], and 12.14 [. . .], and 12.17 [. . .] and 12.18: *did Titus make a profit in any transaction with you? Have we not been guided by the same Spirit?,* and 12.19: *but all these things, beloved, are for your edification.* And if at any time, he was compelled by dire necessity to accept any aid from the churches, even though it was freely and spontaneously given, it worried and annoyed him so much that he seems to consider himself guilty of robbery, 2 Cor. 11.8: *I robbed other churches, taking wages from them, so that to you . . .*

If ministers nowadays cannot attain to this high degree of virtue, the next best thing is that they should rely on the providence of God who calls them, and should look to the church, the willing flock of willing shepherds, for the necessaries of life, rather than to any edicts of the civil power. Matt. 10.11 [. . .]; Luke 10.7, 8 [. . .], and 22.35 [. . .]; 2 Cor. 11.9: *the brothers supplied my wants when they came from Macedonia;* Philipp. 4.15, etc. [. . .].

But because a thing is right in itself, and because there are the best of reasons why it should be done, and because it is sanctioned by the word of God, it does not follow that the civil law and the magistracy ought to demand or enforce it. Paul uses the same argument and almost the same words to prove that the ministers of the church should be fed and maintained as he does to prove that alms should be given to the Jews by the Gentiles, 1 Cor. 9.11, compared with Rom. 15.27: *they have decided to do so, as I say, and indeed they are their debtors: for if they have shared their spiritual goods with the Gentiles, it is the Gentiles' duty to supply their material needs:* yet no one concludes that alms should be demanded or extracted by force. If, then, mere moral and civil gratitude is not to be enforced, how much more ought gratitude for the gospel be freed from every trace of force or constraint? Similarly, monetary considerations should weigh least of all with anyone who preaches the gospel; Acts 8.20: *may your money perish with you, because you thought that you could buy God's gift with money.* If it is wicked to buy the gospel, it must be much more wicked to sell it. O you of little faith, whose incredulous voices I have often heard exclaiming "If you take away ecclesiastical revenues, you destroy the gospel"[279]—what I say is that if the Christian religion is based upon and supported by violence and money, why should it be thought any more worthy of respect than Mohammedanism?[280]

To bargain for or exact tithes or gospel-taxes, to extort a subsidy from the flock by force or by the intervention of the magistrates, to invoke the civil law in order to secure church revenue, and to take such matters into the courts—

279. Cp. *Likeliest Means* (Yale 7:318): "They are to be reviled and shamed, who cry out with the distinct voice of notorious hirelings, that if ye settle not our maintenance by law, farewell the gospel."

280. Cp. *Likeliest Means* (Yale 7:318): "How can any Christian object it to a Turk that his religion stands by force only and not justly fear from him this reply, 'yours both by force and money in the judgment of your own preachers.' "

these are the actions of wolves, not ministers of the gospel; Acts 20.29 [. . .], and 20.33 [. . .].[281] Paul, then, did not exact such things himself, and did not think that any minister of the gospel should do so: 1 Tim. 3.3: *not desiring shameful profit or money*—certainly not exacting it, then. Similarly 3.8 and Tit. 1.7 and 11 and 1 Pet. 5.2, 3: *feed the flock of God, which is in your keeping . . . not for shameful profit but with an eager heart.* It is hardly allowable for a Christian man to go to law with anyone, even about his own property, Matt. 5.39, 40; 1 Cor. 6.7. How disgraceful is it, then, for a man of the church to enter into litigation with his flock, or rather with a flock which is not strictly speaking his at all, for the sake of tithes, which are the property of others. This sort of thing does not go on in any reformed church except ours.[282] Tithes originated either in the spoils of war, or in the voluntary vow of some individual, or in that agrarian law which was not only abrogated long ago but which never had anything to do with us anyway. These were the things which once made it obligatory to pay tithes, though to ministers of another sect than ours, but now they should not be paid to anyone. If the flock does belong to the minister, how avaricious it is for him to be so eager to make a profit out of his holy office; and if it does not, how unjust his behavior is! How officious, to force his instruction upon those who do not want to be taught by him at all! How extortionate, to exact payment for teaching from a man who rejects you as a teacher and whom you would reject as a pupil if it were not for the money! For *the hireling, to whom the sheep do not belong, runs away because he is a hireling and because he does not care for the sheep,* John 10.12, 13. Nowadays there are a great many who answer to this description. They run away and jump about from flock to flock on the slightest pretext, not so much because they are afraid of wolves as because they themselves become wolves whenever the prey of a more lucrative living in some other parish appears. Unlike real shepherds, they are continually chasing after richer pastures not for their flock but for themselves.[283]

[. . .].[284]

This is the difference between a particular church and a Jewish synagogue. The synagogue was a particular assembly, and a religious one, but it was not a particular church, because the total and entire worship of God could not properly be performed in the synagogue. Sacrifices and ceremonies were to be carried out only in the temple. But now everything that has to do with the worship of God and the salvation of believers, everything, in fact, that is necessary to constitute a church may be performed in a correct and properly ordered way

281. The comparison of hirelings to wolves is a favorite of Milton's. See *PL* 4.183–93; 12.507–11; *History of Britain* (Yale 5:175); *2Def* (Yale 4:650); *Likeliest Means* (Yale 7:280).

282. Cp. *Likeliest Means* (Yale 7:281): "Under the gospel as under the law, say our English divines, and they only of all Protestants, . . . tithes."

283. Cp. *Lyc* (114–15): "such as for their bellies' sake/Creep and intrude, and climb into the fold."

284. In the deleted paragraphs, Milton argues that ministers can and should support themselves by practicing trades, as did Christ and the apostles. He proposes that a church's members should be sufficiently knowledgeable in their faith to be able to test their ministers.

in a particular church, within the walls of a private house where no great number of believers are assembled. Indeed a church of this kind which, through the greed of its pastors, has become numerically larger than it should be, deprives itself to a large extent of the advantages to be derived from meeting together.

It was at first necessary for Jews and proselytes to travel to Jerusalem from all over the world for the sake of their religion, Acts 2.5 etc. and 8.27. This was because there was at that time only one national or universal Jewish church, and no particular churches. But now there is no national church and a great number of particular churches, each absolute in itself and equal to the others in divine right and power.[285] These, like similar and homogenous components, joined together by a bond of mutual equality, form a single, Catholic Church. No one of them has any need to go to another for anything which it does not itself possess.

However, particular churches can consult together in fraternal harmony and cooperate to achieve what they trust will be to the benefit of the universal church, 2 Cor. 8.19: *he was chosen by the votes of the churches as the companion of our travels,* and 1.24 [. . .]; 1 Pet. 5.3 [. . .].

Of councils, I find no trace in scripture. The decision recorded in Acts 15.2 etc. should rather be called an oracular utterance elicited from the inspired apostles. When a controversy arose they were consulted as the supreme arbitrators of disputed points, since at that time no written gospel existed. Our modern councils of bishops and presbyters are a different matter altogether. Their members are no more inspired than anyone else, their authority is less than that of the written word, and they are just as liable to error as other men, for they certainly cannot say, as the apostles did, *it has seemed to the Holy Spirit and to us,* Acts 15.28. Nevertheless they dare to arrogate to themselves the right of imposing laws on the churches, and to demand that everyone else should obey their decrees. At the synod which met in Jerusalem, on the other hand, the whole crowd of believers took part and recorded their votes, Acts 15.12, 22, 23. If, however, these councils satisfy themselves with performing the brotherly task of admonition, no one should contemn them.

The opponents of the church are heretics and wicked people inspired with enmity.

Heretics are heretics either because of their own evil disposition, Philipp. 1.16: *others preach Christ through quarrelsomeness, not religiously . . . ,* or because some unnecessary restriction has been placed upon the church, Matt. 9.16: *the patch tears away from the garment, and makes a worse hole.*

285. Cp. *Likeliest Means* (Yale 7:292): "a national church of many incomplete synagogues, uniting the accomplishment of divine worship in one temple . . . but the Christian church is universal; not tied to nation, diocese or parish, but consisting of many particular churches complete in themselves." Milton's idiom for distributive perfection ("*in se numeris omnes absolutae*") is classical and characteristic of both his Latin and his English writings. See *1Def* (Yale 4:509); *Defense of Himself* (Yale 4:759); *PL* 8.421; and the passage from *Likeliest Means* just quoted.

Even heretics are not useless, 1 Cor. 11.19: *for there must also be heresies among you, that those who are righteous among you may be clearly shown.*

[. . .].[286]

CHAPTER 33

OF COMPLETE GLORIFICATION, ALSO OF CHRIST'S SECOND COMING, THE RESURRECTION OF THE DEAD, AND THE CONFLAGRATON OF THIS WORLD

I have already spoken, in Chapter 25, about OUR INCOMPLETE GLORIFICATION, that is, our glorification in this life. I must now turn, finally, to that COMPLETE GLORIFICATION which must eventually be achieved in eternity.

Before the law the type of this glorification was Enoch, who was taken up into heaven, Gen. 5.24, and Elijah, 2 Kings 2.11.

Its fulfillment and consummation will begin with Christ's second coming to judge the world, and with the resurrection of the dead, Luke 21.28: *when these things begin to happen, look up and lift your heads high, for your redemption is approaching;* 2 Thess. 1.7 [. . .].

THE COMING OF THE LORD TO JUDGMENT, WHEN HE, WITH HIS HOLY ANGELS, SHALL JUDGE THE WORLD, was predicted first by Enoch and the prophets and then by Christ himself and his apostles, Jude 14, 13: *Enoch too, the seventh from Adam, prophesied about these things, and said, see the Lord is coming with thousands of his saints, to bring judgment upon all, and to convict all those who are ungodly among them of all the ungodly acts which they have performed and of all the hard things which have been spoken against him by ungodly sinners;* Dan. 7.22 [. . .]; Matt. 25.31 [. . .]; Acts 1.11 [. . .], and 10.42 [. . .], and 17.31 [. . .]; 2 Thess. 1.7, 8 [. . .].

Only the Father knows the day and the hour of Christ's coming; Matt. 24.36; Mark 13.32 [. . .]; Acts 1.7 [. . .]; Dan. 12.8, 9: *I said, My Lord, what will be the end of these things? And he said, Go, Daniel, for these things are shut up and sealed until the time prescribed.* The seventh volume of Zanchius' book on the end of the world may also be usefully consulted on this point.

The end, then, will be sudden. Matt. 25.6 [. . .]; Luke 17.26, etc. [. . .], and 21.34, 35 [. . .]; 1 Thess. 5.2, 3: *you know that the day of the Lord will come like a thief in the night: for when they say, Peace and safety, then sudden destruction will come upon them . . .*

286. At the end of the chapter, Milton describes the enemies of the church and their leader Antichrist, and offers counsel on dealing with persecution. Chapter 32 concerns church discipline, i.e., "the common consent of the church to order its life correctly, according to Christian doctrine, and to perform everything in a decent and orderly way at its meetings" (Yale 6:607). The phrase *common consent* indicates that such discipline is voluntarily agreed upon by each worshiper in the congregation.

Certain signs have, however, been described by Christ and his apostles which will warn us of its approach: Matt. 24.3–27, compared with Mark 13 and Luke 21.

These signs are either common or special.

The common signs are those which are common to the destruction of Jerusalem, the type of Christ's second coming, and his second coming itself. To this category belong false prophets, false Christs, wars, earthquakes, persecutions, plague, famine, and the dwindling of faith and charity right down to the last day itself, Matt. 24.3–27, 2 Tim. 3.1, etc.

The special signs are extreme carelessness and impiety, and almost universal rebellion. Luke 18.8: *when the Son of man comes, shall he find faith on the earth?;* 2 Thess. 2.3: *the day of Christ will not come, unless rebellion comes first . . . ;* 1 Tim. 4.1.

Secondly, the revelation of antichrist, and his destruction through the spirit of Christ's mouth. 2 Thess. 2.3 [. . .], and 2.8: *and then he will be revealed, that outlaw, whom the Lord shall consume with the spirit of his mouth, and cause to vanish by the brightness of his coming.* Some authorities think that a further portent will herald this event, namely, the calling of the entire nation not only of the Jews but also of the Israelites.[287] Isa. 11.11, 12: *for it will happen in that time that the Lord will turn his hand a second time . . . ,* and 14.1, etc. [. . .], and 27.14, 15 [. . .]; Jer. 3.7 [. . .], and 3.13 [. . .], and 30.3 [. . .], and 31.5 [. . .], and 31.36, etc. [. . .], and 33.7: *I will lead back the captive multitude of Judah and the captive multitude of Israel . . . ;* Ezek. 20.41, 42 [. . .], and 37.21, 22 [. . .] ; Hos. 3.5 [. . .]; Amos 9.14, 15 [. . .]; Zech. 8.23 [. . .], and 12.4, etc. [. . .]. Thus the Jews, when they had returned, Ezra 6.17: *offered twelve sucking goats for the sins of the whole of Israel, one for each of the tribes of Israel,* since God still reckoned all these tribes as his own, although they have not, even today, returned from their captivity. Luke 21.24: *Jerusalem will be trodden down by the Gentiles, until the times of the Gentiles have run their course;* Rom. 11.12, 13 [. . .], and 11.15 [. . .], and 11.25 [. . .].

Christ will be slow to come. 2 Thess. 2.1–3: *but, brothers, about the coming of our Lord Jesus Christ and our gathering together to him: we beg you, do not suddenly lose your heads, whether at some spirit or utterance or at some letter purporting to come from us, as if the day of Christ were at hand. Let no one deceive you in any way whatever. For the day of Christ will not come unless there comes . . . ;* 2 Pet. 3.3, 4, etc. [. . .], to the end of the chapter, where the reason is given why the Lord will put off the day of his coming.

His coming will be full of light. Matt. 24.27: *as lightning from the east flashing as far as the west, will be the coming of the Son of man,* and 24.30: *they will see the Son of man coming on the clouds of heaven with power and great glory;* similarly Luke 21.27; Matt 25.31 [. . .]; 1 Thess. 4.16 [. . .]; and 2 Thess. 1.10 [. . .]; Tit. 2.13 [. . .]; Jude 14 [. . .].

It will be terrible. Isa. 66.15, 16: *for see, Jehovah will come with fire, and with his chariots like a whirlwind, to display his anger with fury and his rebuke with burning*

287. Cp. *PR* 3.433–39.

flames, and 13.9, 10 compared with Matt. 24.29, 30: *but immediately after the affliction of those days the sun will be darkened, and the moon will not give her light, and the stars will fall from the sky, and the powers of the heavens will be shaken;* similarly Mark 13.24, 25; Luke 21.25, 26 [. . .]; 2 Thess. 1.7, 8 [. . .]; Rev. 6.12 to the end of the chapter [. . .].

The resurrection of the dead and the last judgment will follow Christ's second coming.

It was not under the gospel that the RESURRECTION OF THE DEAD was first believed in. Job 19.25, 26, etc.: *I know indeed that my redeemer lives and that he will rise above the last dust. And that after worms pierce through this body, I shall awake, and then in my flesh I shall see God;* Ps. 16.10, etc. [. . .], and 17.14, 15 [. . .], and 49.15, 16 [. . .]; Isa. 51.6, etc. [. . .], and 26.19: *your dead men will live again, and my corpses will rise again: awake, I say, and sing, you who inhabit the dust . . .*; Zech. 3.7 [. . .]; Dan. 12.2 [. . .]; Hos. 13.14, compared with 1 Cor. 15.54 [. . .]; Acts 24.15 [. . .], and 26.6–8 [. . .]; Heb. 11.10 [. . .].

Then, under the gospel, it was corroborated by Christ. Matt. 12.41 [. . .]; John 5.28, 29: *the time will come when all who are in their graves will hear his voice. And they will come forth, those who have done good things to the resurrection of life, but those who have done evil to the resurrection of condemnation;* similarly 6.39, 40 and 1 Cor. 6.14, also 15.52: *the trumpet will sound and the dead will be raised uncorrupted;* and 2 Cor. 4.14 [. . .], similarly 1 Thess. 4.14.

In addition to this evidence for resurrection, certain arguments in favor of it are also given: 1. because the covenant with God is not dissolved by death, Matt. 22.32: *God is not God of the dead but of the living;* 2. *if there is no future resurrection, then not even Christ has yet been resurrected,* 1 Cor. 15.13–20, and 15.23 [. . .]; John 11.25 [. . .]; 3. otherwise the righteous would be of all men the most wretched, and the wicked the most fortunate, because in this life their share is the more sumptuous by far. This state of affairs would be quite irreconcilable with God's providence and justice. 1 Cor. 15.19: *if we have hope in Christ in this life only . . . ;* and 15.30–32 [. . .].

The resurrection will consist partly of the raising of the dead to life, partly of the sudden transformation of the living.

It appears that each man will rise with the same identity as he had before; Job 19.26, 27: *after worms pierce through this body, I shall awake, and then in my flesh I shall see God. He will be seen by me as I am, not by another, by my very own eyes;* 1 Cor. 15.53 [. . .]; 2 Cor. 5.4: *enclosed in this, we do not desire to put off that in which we are created, but to put something on over it, so that our mortality may be swallowed up by life,* and 5.10 [. . .]. If this were not so we should not be like Christ. He entered into glory with that very same body, that very same flesh and blood, with which he had died and risen again.

We learn of the transformation of the living in 1 Cor. 15.51, 52: *behold, a mystery . . . ; we shall all be changed . . . ;* 1 Thess. 4.15, 17, 18: *for we say these things to you by the words of the Lord, that we who shall be left alive when the Lord comes shall not go before those who have been asleep. Those who died in Christ shall rise first, and then we who are left alive will be snatched up into the clouds along with them to meet the Lord in the air. And so we shall always be with the Lord.*

THE LAST JUDGMENT is that at which CHRIST WITH THE SAINTS, ARRAYED IN THE GLORY AND THE POWER OF THE FATHER, WILL JUDGE THE FALLEN ANGELS AND THE WHOLE HUMAN RACE.

[. . .][288]

The standard of judgment will be the individual conscience itself, and so each man will be judged according to the light which he has received. John 12.48: *he who disdains me and does not accept my words has one to condemn him: the word which I have spoken will condemn him on the last day;* Rom. 2.12 [. . .], and 2.14 [. . .]; James 2.2 [. . .]; Rev. 20.12 [. . .].

At the time of this last judgment it seems that the often-promised and glorious reign of Christ and his saints on this earth will begin. I say *at the time of,* rather than *on the day of,* because the word *day* is often used to mean some indefinite period of time, and because it does not seem likely that so many millions of angels and men could be assembled and judged within the space of a single day. Christ's reign, then, will extend from the beginning to the end of this time of judgment, and will continue for some time after the judgment has finished, until all his enemies are subdued. It is true, of course, that his reign of grace, also called *the kingdom of heaven,* began with his first advent, when it was proclaimed by John the Baptist. But his reign of glory will not begin until his second coming, Dan. 7.13, 14: *look, he came with the clouds of heaven, like the Son of man, . . . : and dominion, glory and rule were given to him . . . ;* given to him, that is, from the time when he came with the clouds to the time when he was to put an end to his reign, 1 Cor. 15.24: *then will come the end . . .*—but more of this later. Christ's second coming is always described as coming *with the clouds,* so it is certainly his second coming which is referred to in the Daniel passage: not his birth, as Junius claims, but his coming to judge the world. Otherwise the passage would be saying that he was like the Son of man before he was man at all, which obviously cannot be so. There are any number of texts which show that Christ's reign will take place on the earth; Ps. 2.8, 9, compared with Rev. 2.25–27 [. . .], and 110.5, 6 [. . .]; Isa. 9.7 [. . .]; Dan. 7.22 [. . .], and 7.27 [. . .]; Luke 1.32, 33: *the Lord God will give him the throne of his father David: and he will reign in the house of Jacob for ever, and there will be no end to his kingdom;* Matt. 19.28 [. . .]; Luke 22.29, 30: *I give you a kingdom, as my Father gave it to me, so that you may eat and drink at my table in my kingdom; and so that you may sit upon thrones giving judgment to the twelve tribes of Israel.* This *judgment,* it seems, will not last for one day only but for a considerable length of time, and will really be a reign, rather than a judicial session. The same sense of the word *judgment* is applicable in the case of Gideon, Jephthah and the other *judges* who are said to have *judged* Israel for many years. 1 Cor. 15.23–26: *every man*

288. The deleted passage cites Scripture for each part of the preceding definition.

in his turn; Christ the first-fruits, then those who are Christ's at his coming; then will come the end . . .; Rev. 5.10 [. . .], and 11.15 [. . .], and 20.1–7 [. . .].

After a thousand years Satan will come again, raging, and will besiege the church with huge forces, with all the enemies of the church collected together. But he will be thrown down by fire from heaven and condemned to everlasting punishment. Rev. 20.7–9 [. . .]; 2 Thess. 2.8: *and then he will be revealed, that outlaw, whom the Lord shall consume with the spirit of his mouth, and cause to vanish by the brightness of his coming.*

The judgment of the evil angels and of the chief enemies of God will be followed by that of the whole human race. Rev. 20.11, to the end of the chapter [. . .].

Then it appears that sentence will be pronounced. Matt. 25.34: *Come here, my Father's blessed ones, possess the kingdom that has been ready for you from the time when the world's foundations were laid,* and 25.41: *you cursed ones, go from me into the eternal fire which is prepared for the devil and his angels.*

The sentence will be followed by its execution: that is, by the punishment of the wicked and the complete glorification of the righteous. Matt. 25.46: *and these will go away to eternal punishment; but the righteous to eternal life;* Rev. 20.14, 15 [. . .].

Then at last the end will come; the end spoken of in 1 Cor. 15.24–28: *then will come the end, when he shall hand over the kingdom to God the Father, after annihilating all domination, authority and power. For he is to rule until he has put down all enemies under his feet. The last enemy to be annihilated will be death: for "he has subjected all things beneath his feet." But when it says "all things" are subjected to him, obviously this means all things except him who subjected all things to him. And after everything has been made subject to him, then the Son himself will be made subject to him who subjected all things to him, so that God may be all in all.*

But, you may say, if Christ is to hand over the kingdom to God the Father, how can there be any truth in texts like Heb. 1.8: *but to the Son, Your throne, O God, is for all ages,* or Dan. 7.14: *his dominion is an everlasting dominion which does not pass away, and his kingdom a kingdom which is not destroyed;* or Luke 1.33 [. . .]? My reply is that there will be no end to his kingdom *for all ages,* that is, while the ages of the world endure, until *time will be no more,* Rev. 10.6, and until all the aims for which he took up the kingdom in the first place have been accomplished.[289] Thus his kingdom will not *pass away,* like something ineffectual, nor will it be *destroyed.* Its end will not be one of dissolution but of perfection and consummation, like the end of the law, Matt. 5.18. There are a lot of other things which, it is said, will never *pass away* in this sense, but will be *everlasting* and eternal—circumcision, for example, Gen. 17.13, and the ceremonial law, Lev. 3.17 and 24.8, and the Land of Canaan, Gen. 13.15, Jer. 7.7 and 25.5, and the Sabbath, Exod. 31.16, and the priesthood of Aaron, Num. 18.8, and the memorial stone at the river

289. Cp. *PL* 3.339–41: "Then thou thy regal scepter shalt lay by,/For regal scepter then no more shall need,/God shall be all in all."

Jordan, Josh. 4.7, and the signs of heaven, Ps. 148.6, and the earth, Eccles. 1.4. But all these things have either come to an end already or will eventually do so.

The *second death* is called *second* to distinguish it from the first or so-called physical death. In addition to the three degrees of death dealt with in Chapter 13 under the subject of the punishment of sin, there is a fourth and last degree of death, namely, eternal death, or the punishment of the damned.

Under this heading can be included the death of this foul and polluted world itself, that is, its end and conflagration. Whether this end means the actual abolition of the world's substance, or only a change in its qualities, is uncertain, and does not really concern us. But we are told as much as it is useful for us to know about the end of the world and the conflagration, Job 14.13 [. . .]; Ps. 102.27 [. . .]; Isa. 34.4 [. . .], and 51.6 [. . .]; Matt. 24.35: *heaven and earth will pass away . . . ;* 1 Cor. 7.31 [. . .]; 2 Pet. 3.7 [. . .], and 10 [. . .] and 12 [. . .]; Rev. 10.6 [. . .], and 21.1 [. . .].

The second death, the punishment of the damned, seems to consist of the loss of the supreme good, that is, divine grace and protection and the beatific vision, which is commonly called the punishment of loss. It consists also of eternal torment, and the usual name for this is the punishment of sense. Matt. 25.41: *you cursed ones, go from me into the eternal fire which is prepared for the devil and his angels;* Luke 13.27, 28 [. . .], and 16.23 [. . .]; 2 Thess. 1.9 [. . .].

There are various descriptions of the severity and duration of these punishments. Isa. 30.33: *the place of destruction is already prepared; it is made ready for the king himself. Jehovah has made it very wide and deep, his pyre has fire and logs in great plenty; the breath of Jehovah kindles it like a stream of sulfur,* and 66.24, compared with Mark 9.44: *where their worm does not die and the fire is not quenched;* Dan. 12.2 [. . .]; Matt. 8.12 [. . .], and 13.42, and elsewhere; Mark 9.43 [. . .]; Rom. 2.8, 9 [. . .]; 2 Thess. 1.9 [. . .]; Rev. 14.11 [. . .], similarly 19.3, also 21.8 [. . .].

These punishments are, however, graduated according to the sins of the sufferers: Matt. 11.22 [. . .]; Luke 12.47, 48: *he shall be beaten with many stripes; he with few.*

The place of punishment is called HELL: *Tophet,* Isa. 30.33; *the fire Gehenna,* Matt. 5.22, and, more clearly, 10.28; *outer darkness,* 8.12 and 22.13 and 25.30; *a furnace of fire,* 13.42; ᾅδης Luke 16.23 and elsewhere [. . .], 16.28 [. . .], Rev. 9.1 [. . .], 20.15 [. . .], 21.8.

Hell seems to be situated outside this world. Luke 16.26: *there is a huge chasm fixed between us and you, so that those who wish . . . ; outer darkness,* as above; Rev. 22.14, 15 [. . .].

It is not hard to see why. The hell of the damned is the same as the place which was prepared for the devil and his angels, Matt. 25.41, as above. The devil's fall preceded that of man. Therefore it is highly improbable that hell should have been prepared within this world, that is, in the bowels of the earth, when the earth had not yet been cursed.[290] This is said to have been the opin-

290. Cp. the Argument of *PL* 1: "Hell, described here, not in the center (for heaven and earth may be supposed as yet not made, certainly not yet accursed) but in a place of utter darkness, fitliest called Chaos."

ion of Chrysostom and also of Luther and other more recent scholars. Besides, if the whole world must eventually be destroyed by fire, as I have already demonstrated from various passages in the New Testament, what will become of hell if it is situated in the centre of the earth? Obviously it will have to be destroyed as well, along with the earth. If this were to happen it would be very nice for the damned, no doubt!

So much for the punishment of the wicked: now we must turn to the complete glorification of the righteous.

Complete glorification consists in eternal and utterly happy life, arising chiefly from the sight of God.[291] It is described in Ps. 16.11: *you show me the path of life; that in your sight is an abundance of the most delightful joys; at your right hand eternally,* and 17.15: *in righteousness I will see your face; I will be satisfied with your likeness when I awake;* Dan. 12.3 [. . .]; Matt. 13.43 [. . .], and 22.30 [. . .], and 5.8 [. . .]; 1 Cor. 2.9 [. . .], and 13.12 [. . .], and 15.42, 43 [. . .]; 2 Cor. 4.16, 17 [. . .], and 5.1 [. . .]; Eph. 2.6 [. . .]; Philipp. 3.21 [. . .]; 1 Thess. 4.17 [. . .]; 2 Tim. 4.8 [. . .]; 1 Pet. 1.4 [. . .], and 5.4 [. . .], and 5.10 [. . .]; 1 John 3.2 [. . .]; Rev. 7.14–17: *these are those who . . . therefore they are before the throne of God, and worship him day and night in his temple; and he who sits upon the throne will cover them with a shade. They will not be hungry any more, nor . . .*, and 21.4: *God will wipe away every tear from their eyes: and death will be no more, nor will grief or crying or pain,* and 22.1–5 [. . .].

It appears that the saints will not all be equally glorified in heaven. Dan. 12.3: *teachers shall shine like the brightness of the heavens, and those who justify many, like the stars, for ever and ever;* Matt. 20.23 [. . .]; 1 Cor. 15.41, 42 [. . .].

IN HEAVEN. Matt. 5.12: *your reward is great in heaven;* Luke 12.33: *provide for yourselves . . . a never-failing treasure in heaven;* Phil. 3.20 [. . .]; Heb. 10.34 [. . .].

Our glorification will be accompanied by the renovation of, and our possession of, heaven and earth and all those creatures in both which may be useful or delightful to us.[292] Isa. 65.17: *for see, I will create new heavens and a new earth, and the former will not be remembered, nor come to mind,* and 66.22 [. . .]; Acts 3.21 [. . .]; Matt. 19.29 [. . .], and 26.29 [. . .]; Luke 14.15: *one of those who sat down to eat at the same time said to him, Blessed is he who eats bread in the kingdom of God*—and the speaker here is not reproved by Christ; also 22.30: *that you may eat and drink at my table in my kingdom;* Rom. 8.19–24 [. . .]; 2 Pet. 3.13 [. . .]; Rev. 5.10: *you have made us kings and priests to our God, and we shall reign on the earth,* and 21.1, etc.: *then I saw a new heaven and a new earth: for the first heaven and the first earth had gone, and there was no more sea. And I, John, saw the holy city, new Jerusalem, coming down from God out of heaven, prepared as a bride adorned for her husband.*

291. Cp. *PL* 3.60–62: "About him all the sanctities of Heaven/Stood thick as stars, and from his sight received/Beatitude past utterance"; also 1.680–84.

292. Cp. *PL* 12.547–51: "then raise/From the conflagrant mass, purged and refined,/New heav'ns, new earth, ages of endless date/Founded in righteousness and peace and love/To bring forth fruits, joy and eternal bliss"; and 10.638–40.

BOOK 2

CHAPTER I

OF GOOD WORKS

The first book dealt with FAITH and THE KNOWLEDGE OF GOD. This second book is about THE WORSHIP OF GOD and CHARITY.

What chiefly constitutes the true worship of God is eagerness to do good works: Matt. 16.27: *then he will repay every man according to his work;* Rom. 2.13: *it is not those who hear the law that are just in God's sight; but it is those who do the law that shall be justified;* Phil. 1.11 [. . .], and 4.8 [. . .]; 2 Tim. 3.17 [. . .]; Tit. 2.11, 12 [. . .]; and 3.8 [. . .]; James 1.22 [. . .]; 2 Pet. 1.5, etc. [. . .].

GOOD WORKS are those which WE DO WHEN THE SPIRIT OF GOD WORKS WITHIN US, THROUGH TRUE FAITH, TO GOD'S GLORY, THE CERTAIN HOPE OF OUR OWN SALVATION, AND THE INSTRUCTION OF OUR NEIGHBOR.

WHEN THE SPIRIT OF GOD WORKS WITHIN US. John 3.21: *that his works may be made manifest, that they have been done in God;* 1 Cor. 15.10: *by the grace of God I am what I am, and his grace, which was bestowed upon me, was not in vain; on the contrary, I have worked more effectively than all of them—not I, though, but the grace of God which is with me;* and 2 Cor. 3.5 [. . .]; Gal. 5.22 [. . .]; Eph. 2.10 [. . .]; and 5.9 [. . .]; Phil. 2.13 [. . .].

THROUGH FAITH: John 15.5: *the man who abides in me, and in whom I abide bears much fruit; for without me you can do nothing;* Heb. 11.6 [. . .]; James 2.22: *you see that faith took a hand in his works, and by his works his faith was made perfect*—that is, faith, as form, gives form to the works, so that they can be good, and is itself brought to perfection by these same works, as by an end or fruit.

Some theologians insist that the form of good works is their conformity with the Ten Commandments, insofar as they are covered by the terms of the commandments. But I do not see how this can possibly be true under the gospel. Throughout the whole of his letter to the Romans, and elsewhere, Paul quite distinctly teaches that, Rom. 14.23: *whatever is not in accordance with faith, is sin.* Notice that he does not say *whatever is not in accordance with the Ten Commandments is sin,* but *whatever is not in accordance with faith.* So it is conformity with faith, not with the Ten Commandments, which must be considered as the form of good works. Thus if I keep the Sabbath, in accordance with the Ten Commandments, when my faith prompts me to do otherwise, my precise compliance with the commandments will be counted as sin and as ἀνομία or unlawful behavior. It is faith that justifies, not compliance with the commandments; and only that which justifies can make any work good. It follows that no work of ours can be good except through faith. Faith, then, is the form of good works, because the definition of *form* is *that through which a thing is what it is.*[293] As for passages like 1 John 2.4 and 3.24 and various others, where the keeping of God's commandments is mentioned, these should be understood as referring to the commandments of God in the gospel which always give faith precedence over the works of the law. If in the gospel faith is given precedence over the works of the law, it certainly ought to be given precedence over the commandments of the law, for the works are the end and fulfillment of these commandments. If anyone should, then, under the gospel, keep the commandments of the whole Mosaic Law with absolute scrupulousness, but have no faith, it would do him no good. So good works must obviously be defined with reference to faith, not to the commandments. Thus we ought to consider the form of good works to be conformity not with the written but with the unwritten law, that is, with the law of the Spirit which the Father has given us to lead us into truth. For the works of the faithful are the works of the Holy Spirit itself. These never run contrary to the love of God and of our neighbor, which is the sum of the law. They may, however, sometimes deviate from the letter even of the gospel precepts (particularly those which are special rather than general), in pursuance of their overriding motive, which is charity.[294] Christ himself showed this by his abolition of the observance of the Sabbath, and on several other occasions. See above, Book 1, Chapter 27, on the gospel.

[. . .][295]

The Papists talk about works of supererogation, meaning that more is done than is prescribed in the law. They believe that as a result of these some of the saints stored up so much merit that they can purchase eternal life both for themselves and for others. But this is impossible. We are commanded both in the gospel and in the law to love and worship God with all our strength and with all our mind, and to love our neighbor as ourselves. So an excess of godliness or charity is simply impossible. What service could we possibly do God that would be so dutiful as to be considered more than or, indeed, as much as our duty required? Luke 17.10: *when you have done all those things which you were commanded to do, say, We are unprofitable servants, for we have done what it was our duty to do.* The Papists claim that the gospel contains counsels, of a higher nature than its precepts, and that if a man follows them although he need not, he may be said to perform a work of supererogation. But really these are not counsels, nor are they of a higher nature than precepts. They ought rather to be thought of as particular precepts, given not to all mankind but to certain individuals for special reasons and under special circumstances. Thus in Matt. 19.11 celibacy is required from those who are gifted with continence and can therefore under-

293. Cp. *Art of Logic* (Yale 8:232): "*The form is the cause through which a thing is what it is.*" Also *Tetrachordon* (Yale 2:608): "the *form* by which the thing is what it is."

294. Cp. *Tetrachordon* (p. 992): "Christ having cancelled the handwriting of ordinances which was against us (Col. 2.14) and interpreted the fulfilling of all through charity, hath in that respect set us over law."

295. The deleted passage scripturally elaborates the rest of Milton's definition of good works.

take to remain celibate: it is required, that is, whenever it may appear to conduce to the glory of God and the good of the church. Similarly, whether you call the advice given to the young man in Matt. 19.21 a precept or a counsel, the young man would certainly not have done anything more than his duty had he obeyed Christ in every particular, any more than Abraham did when he went to sacrifice his son. For God's command, whether it be general or special or addressed to a single individual, is absolutely binding from the point of view of those to whom it is addressed—mankind, a collection of men, or an individual man, as the case may be. In the example just cited obedience to the general precept about loving God above all things was demanded from the arrogant young man as a single and particular specimen of duty. This was done in order to shake his complacency and his vain confidence in his works, and in order to let him see how far he was from the perfection to which he pretended. There was no perfection in selling all he had: men have done that without charity. The perfection lay in leaving his possessions and following Christ. As for celibacy, 1 Cor. 7, this is clearly not decreed either as a precept or as a counsel, but is left absolutely free as a matter of personal discretion, to be decided with reference to the particular state of affairs. Besides, if any works were works of supererogation, then it would be apparent that all precepts were imperfect since counsels (a superior order of things) have to be added to them as a supplement. Or again, if counsels really were of a higher order than the law, who would be able to obey them, seeing that no mortal is able to comply even with the law? What is more, absolutely vital precepts of general applicability are sometimes called counsels, as in Rev. 3.18: *I give you counsel to buy from me gold tried in the fire.* Finally, praying for forgiveness—and we all pray for forgiveness each day in the prayer which Christ taught us—is irreconcilable with this kind of vain commendation of human works.

Of course, one work may be more perfect than another in matters where Christian liberty is exercised; 1 Cor. 7.38: *he does well, he does better,* and 2 Cor. 11.23: *are they ministers of Christ? I am better.* But nevertheless there is nothing by which God's glory or our neighbor's instruction may most effectually be promoted which is not a matter of duty. Paul did not have to preach the gospel without payment, 1 Cor. 9.7, etc. It seemed to him, however, that giving his service to the gospel for nothing was the easiest way of avoiding calumny and the best way of instructing God's church, 1 Cor. 9.18 and 2 Cor. 11.12. As a result, he did no more than his duty in preaching for nothing: nor did Zaccheus when, without being ordered to do so, he gave half his possessions to the poor, Luke 19.8: nor did that widow when she threw into the sacred treasury all the money she had at that time, Mark 12.42: nor did the disciples when they sold their lands and divided the proceeds among their fellows, Acts 4.34. None of these performed works of supererogation. They merely loved their neighbors (particularly those who were believers) as themselves. True, such singular proofs of love as these arise from free choice rather than obligation, Acts 5.4; for true perfection is set before all men as a goal, but not all are required to reach it.

The worthlessness of our merits becomes quickly apparent when we consider that even our good deeds are not really ours but God's, who works in us,[296] and that even if they were certainly ours they would still be no more than our duty. Moreover, however well we perform our duty it cannot possibly bear comparison with the richness of the promised reward, Rom. 6.23: *the gift of God is eternal life,* and 8.18: *I reckon that the sufferings of the present time are not in the least worthy of the glory to be revealed to us.*

It is true that King Hezekiah mentions his own integrity before God, Isa. 38.3: *I beseech you, Jehovah, remember at this time that I have always walked before you, faithfully and with integrity, and have done what seemed good in your eyes.* But he does not claim that he has deserved any reward: on the contrary, he confesses that God's kindness has pardoned his sins, 38.17: *kindly through love you have delivered my soul from the fatal pitfall, for you have thrust away my sins behind your back.* It is the same with Nehemiah, 13.22: *my God, remember this of me also, and spare me through your abundant kindness.* God's own declaration provides further evidence, Ex. 20.6.

Anyway, what merit could there be in our doing works of which God has no need at all?[297] Job 22.2, etc.: *can a man be profitable to the mighty God?*—and 35.7 [. . .] Luke 17.10 [. . .]. Rom. 11.35 [. . .]. See above, Book 1, Chapter 22, Of Justification.

The opposite of good works are evil works. Isaiah shows very clearly the vanity and bitterness of these, 59.4, etc.: *they conceive pain and bring forth falsehood: they hatch adders' eggs . . . ;* Prov. 11.3: *the perversity of evil-doers ruins them,* and 11.5: *the wicked man falls through his own wickedness,* and 13.15 [. . .], and 22.5 [. . .].

A good man is known by his good works. Matt. 12.35: *the good man brings forth good things out of the good treasury of his heart;* 1 John 3.7: *the man that behaves righteously is righteous, as he is righteous.* He is described in Job 29.11, onwards: *for the ear heard me and blessed me . . . ,* and elsewhere.

Sometimes, however, certain temporary virtues (or at any rate, what look like virtues) are found in the wicked: in Saul, for example, 1 Sam. 19, and in the Jews, Jer. 34. Some appearance of liberality, gratitude and justice was discernible in the king of Sodom, along with a regard for the interest of his subjects; Gen. 14.21. Eglon, Judges 3.20 and Belshazzar, Dan. 5.29, are examples of the same thing.

The evil man is described in Ps. 10.3, onwards: *the wicked man praises his own soul . . . ;* and 14.1, onwards: *the fool says in his heart . . . ;* Prov. 1.11, onwards: *if they say, Come with us, let us lie in wait for blood . . . ,* and 4.14, onwards: *do not set your foot on the path of the wicked . . . ,* and 28.5, etc.: *men given over to wickedness do not understand what is right . . . .*

296. Cp. *PL* 11.90–91: "He sorrows now, repents, and prays contrite,/My motions in him."
297. Cp. *Sonnet 19.*

CHAPTER 6[298]

OF ZEAL

I have called the first part of true religion, dealt with so far, INVOCATION. There remains the second part, THE SANCTIFICATION OF THE DIVINE NAME IN EVERY CIRCUMSTANCE OF OUR LIFE.

An eager desire to sanctify the divine name, together with a feeling of indignation against things which tend to the violation or contempt of religion, is called ZEAL.

[. . .].[299]

It is a fact, however, that all Greek writers, sacred as well as profane, use the word *blasphemy* in a general sense to mean any kind of evil-speaking, directed against any person. Jewish writers use the corresponding Hebrew words, which I mentioned, in the same general sense. Thus in Isa. 43.28: *I shall expose Israel to curses,* and in 51.7: *do not grow alarmed because of their abuse,* and in Ezek. 5.15: *a reproach and a taunt,* that is, to the Jews; and in Zeph. 2.8: *the taunts of the Ammonites, with which they insulted my people*—in all these passages the same word is employed, and it means blasphemy. Similarly in Matt. 15.19: *false witnesses, curses* (in the Greek: *blasphemies*), and in Mark 7.22 and 1 Tim. 6.1: *that God's name and doctrine be not blasphemed;* and again in Tit. 2.5 and 2 Pet. 2.10: *they are not afraid to insult dignitaries* (Greek: *blaspheme*), and 2.11: *whereas the angels themselves bring no evil-speaking* (Greek: *blasphemous judgment*) *against them before the Lord.* I repeat, even writers of religious works applied the Greek word *blasphemy* to any kind of evil-speaking. I think, therefore, that it was misleading and ill-advised of certain authors to introduce this foreign word into the Latin language, and to limit what had been a general term to mean only evil-speaking against God, while at the same time extending its meaning in one particular direction so that, since people generally no longer understood the term, these authors should be able to denounce out of hand as blasphemy pretty well any opinion about God or religious matters which did not tally with their own.[300] In this they resemble the lawyers in Matt. 9.3 who, when Christ had simply said, 9.2: *your sins are forgiven,* immediately *said to themselves, This man blasphemes.* In fact, though, to blaspheme God is, as the above examples make clear, nothing more nor less than to curse or abuse God openly and *high-handedly,* Num. 15.30. There is also Matt. 15.19:

298. Book 2, chapters 2–5, concerns the immediate causes of good works (e.g., good habits), virtues related to worship of God (e.g., love of God), external worship or religion (e.g., religious rituals), and finally, oath taking and casting of lots. Milton considers the last three topics as they pertain to the proper invocation or religious adoration of God. The present chapter discusses how to infuse the rest of one's life with the same worshipful attitude.

299. The deleted passage lists relevant scriptural examples of ZEAL and of its opposite, blasphemy. In *Paradise Lost,* when Satan argues that the angels should not adore or submit to the Son, zealous Abdiel characterizes his position as "blasphemous, false and proud!" (5.809).

300. Milton similarly objects to the narrow definition of blasphemy in *Of Civil Power* (Yale 7:246). On the politics of blasphemy in Milton's era, see Loewenstein 1998, 176–98.

blasphemies come from the heart—meaning blasphemies against God or against men. Those who, in all sincerity, and with no desire to stir up controversy, teach or discuss some doctrine concerning the deity which they have quite apparently, as they see it, learned from the Holy Scriptures, are in no sense guilty of the sin of blasphemy. But if the meaning of *blasphemy* is to be derived from the Hebrew, it will be very extensive indeed: every obstinate sinner, in fact, will be guilty of blasphemy and thus, as some insist, of a capital offence: Num. 15.30: *the soul which behaves high-handedly, abuses* or *blasphemes Jehovah and that soul will, without fail, be extirpated from among his people;* Ezek. 20.27, 28: *yet in this your fathers have abused* (Vulgate: *blasphemed*) *me, trespassing against me, for they saw each hill* . . . .

[. . .].[301]

CHAPTER 7

OF THE TIME FOR DIVINE WORSHIP, WITH A CONSIDERATION OF THE SABBATH, THE LORD'S DAY, AND RELIGIOUS FESTIVALS

So far I have dealt with the various components of divine worship. Now it is time to discuss the circumstances in which it takes place.

The CIRCUMSTANCES OF DIVINE WORSHIP, as of all sensible phenomena, are two: TIME AND PLACE.[302]

Before the law of Moses there was no fixed and regular place for public worship. Under the law it was held partly in the synagogues and partly in the temple. Finally, under the gospel it may be held in any convenient place, John 4.21, 23: *neither on this mountain, nor in Jerusalem. But the time is coming, and is indeed here already, when true worshippers shall worship the Father in spirit and in truth:* as the Father had predicted in Mal. 1.11: *incense in every place* . . .

It is not certain what the regular TIME for public worship was before the law of Moses.

Under the law it was the SABBATH, that is, the seventh day, which was consecrated to God from the beginning of the world, Gen. 2.2, 3. But the Sabbath was not observed, nor was its observation commanded, so far as we can ascertain, before the second month of the departure of the Israelites from Egypt (see Book 1, Chapter 10, above, and Ex. 16.1, 23, 25, 29). After that it was enforced with severe prohibitions, 16.23: *tomorrow is Jehovah's sabbath rest: cook what you are going to cook, today, and boil what you are going to boil, and put whatever is left over on one side, to be kept for the morrow,* and 20.8, etc.: *remember the sabbath day, so that you may keep it holy* . . . : *remember* it, that is, as it is laid down in 16: or perhaps *remember* is used

301. The rest of the chapter, deleted here, includes standard discussions of martyrdom and of consecration to the glory of God.

302. For Milton's understanding of time and place as circumstantial modes "common to absolutely all things," see Book 1, chapters 10 and 11, *Art of Logic* (Yale 8:242–49).

here as a word to give emphasis to the admonition. And 31.14: *you shall keep the sabbath, because it is a holy thing for you: every one of those who profane it shall be put to death without fail*..., and 34.21 [...]; and 35.2, 3 [...]; Lev. 23.3 [...]; Num. 15.32, etc. [...]; 2 Chron. 36.20, 21 [...]; Jer. 17.21, 22 [...]; Neh. 10.32 [...], and 13.15, etc. [...].

Now the Israelites were commanded to keep the Sabbath holy and inviolable for a number of reasons, most of which are applicable to themselves alone, and which are recorded in different parts of the Mosaic law.

Firstly, as a memorial of God's completion of creation on the seventh day; Ex. 20.11 and 31.15, 17: *so the children of Israel shall keep the sabbath, observing the sabbath throughout their generations, as a perpetual covenant. Because in six days Jehovah made the heaven and the earth, but on the seventh day he rested and refreshed himself.* Although the reason given here for observing the Sabbath day may seem to apply equally well to all nations, the Israelites alone are in fact commanded to observe it. The same is true of the command about not eating reptiles, Lev. 11.44: *that you may sanctify yourselves and be holy, for I am holy: so do not pollute yourselves with any reptile;* and of the command about not disfiguring the body, and other similar commands, Deut. 14.1: *you are the sons of God*... These reasons are equally applicable to all believers at the present day, but the commands themselves do not apply to them. Our countryman, Ames, has noted this in his *Marrow of Divinity* 2.13.[303] "That principle," he says, "of interpreting the scriptures commonly given out by certain men, 'that all duties which are bound up with moral and immutable reasons are themselves moral and immutable,' is not universally true unless it is understood to apply to duties which follow inevitably from the stated reasons, without the interposition of a special command from God."[304] Duties like those mentioned above cannot be said to come into this category, and the duty of Sabbath-observance cannot either.

[...][305]

It is certain, then, that under the law the Sabbath was imposed only upon the Israelites, and that the intention was to distinguish them from other nations by this very sign. It follows that we who live under the gospel and are, as I proved in my first book, quite freed from the law, must be emancipated above all from this law about Sabbath-observance, because the distinction upon which it was founded has been removed. Both Christ's teaching and his example quite apparently corroborated this, and that is why he was so severely censured by the Pharisees: John 10.16: *this man is not from God, for he does not keep the Sabbath*....

[...].[306]

303. William *Ames* [Guilielmi Amesii] (1576–1633), English Calvinist theologian particularly influential in Colonial America, was educated at Cambridge, where his strongly Puritan and anti-Arminian views developed. He left England for Holland in 1610. Milton quotes from *Medulla Theologica,* a work translated into English as *The Marrow of Sacred Divinity.*

304. *Medulla* 2.13.9. Kelley notes that Milton alters the quotation slightly.

305. The deleted passage lists more reasons for Sabbath observance under the Mosaic Law.

306. In the deleted passage, Milton repeats that for Christians the Sabbath no longer applies and cites Paul to claim that God has not instituted another particular day for his worship in its place.

It remains to be seen what there is to be said for those who maintain that the Lord's day ought to be celebrated as a day ordained by God for public worship—a kind of new Sabbath. God, they say, rested on the seventh day. True, and with reason, for he had created heaven and earth—no small task. If they insist that we are to imitate him in his rest, without being commanded to do so (and no command has yet been produced), let them also insist that, like Prometheus in the legend, we imitate his work, which only a God can in fact perform. But, they reply, God sanctified that day. Granted: he sanctified it, that is made it holy, for himself (*for on that day he rested and refreshed himself,* Ex. 31.17), but not for us as well: that would have meant adding a command, to make us keep it holy. For it is commands that bind us, not examples—not even the example of God himself. But, they insist, the Sabbath was observed even before the time of the Mosaic law. They make this claim with more eagerness than probability, but even if we grant that it is true (and there can be no certainty either way), it is also true that sacrificial rites, and distinction between things clean and things unclean, and other practices of the same sort were current in pre-Mosaic times, but we do not therefore have to include them among our moral duties.

But, they reply, the Sabbath has been ratified since that time by the fourth commandment. Unquestionably so: and the Sabbath referred to is the seventh day. What has this to do with the first day of the week? Are you going to force me to observe a particular day on the grounds that God commanded it, and then swop one day for another without any command from him at all? You make so bold as to say that not merely the seventh day—which was specified only for the Israelites—but any day of the seven you like to choose ought, at all events, to be kept sacred because of this commandment, and that this should be considered a moral duty, as it is termed, incumbent upon all nations.

I do not see, to begin with, what authority there is for such an assertion. Certainly no such sense can possibly be extracted from the words of the commandment in question. The actual motive for the commandment, God's relaxation after the creation of the world, applies to the seventh day and obviously cannot be shifted to the first, and no alternative motive can be supplied—whether the resurrection of the Lord, or some other—without divine sanction. There is, then, more than one scriptural text to prove to us that the Sabbath has been abolished, and nowhere in scripture is there any mention of its being changed from one day to another, or any justification for such a change. Thus, though it became the practice of the church to make this change, she did not obey any divine command, for there was none any longer, but merely gave evidence of her own freedom of action (either freedom of action or madness—one of these it was). For whether my opponents hold that this commandment of God's has been abrogated or not, it is equally dangerous and equally reprehensible for them to alter it in any way. If it has not been abrogated, then by changing it they, in effect, abrogate it, and if it has they, in effect, revive it. It is up to them to show us what moral excellence there can possibly be in the number seven. It is up to them to show us why, released from Sabbath-observation, we should still be bound by a seven—by a mere number, without force or efficacy. The fact is that, if any Sabbath-rest still remains for us under the gospel, then it is a spiritual and eternal one, and the observance of it belongs not to this life, but to the next, Heb. 4.9–11: *so there remains a sabbath-rest for the people of God: for anyone who enters his rest rests from his own work as God did from his. So let us endeavor to enter that rest, so that no one may fall through following this example of stubbornness.* If this commandment was given only to those whom God *brought out of the land of Egypt and the house of slavery,* then it will obviously not apply to us as Christians. If, however, as my opponents maintain, it does apply to us in that we have been rescued from the slavery of a spiritual Egypt, then the Sabbath, like the rescue, must be spiritual and evangelical, not physical and Mosaic. It must, in short, be spontaneous, not enforced; otherwise we shall be brought out of one Egypt and into another. The spirit cannot be subjected to force. To maintain that what we ought, as Christians, to do every day, is in fact enjoined by divine decree only on one day in seven, is to disparage the Christian religion and not enforce but frustrate God's commandments.

Some claim that it is by this fourth commandment that the practice of public worship has been established in perpetuity in the church. I grant that public worship is commended and even recommended under the gospel, but I deny that it is imposed upon believers as a duty either by this commandment or by any Sinaitical precept. I am not one of those who consider the decalogue a faultless moral code. Indeed I am amazed that such an opinion should have become so widespread. For it is clear that the decalogue is nothing but a summary of the Mosaic law as a whole, and its fourth commandment in particular summarizes the whole ceremonial law. It can therefore contain nothing relevant to gospel worship.

The Lord's Day is mentioned only once in scripture, Rev. 1.10. What it was called and, indeed, whether it was weekly or annual, are matters upon which no one may venture to pronounce with any certainty. Nowhere in scripture may any word be found of its institution, nor any instructions as to its celebration, as, for example, in the case of the Lord's Supper. If it is the day of the Lord's resurrection why, may I ask, is that day to be considered the Lord's Day any more than the day of his birth or the day of his death or the day of his ascension? Why should we consider it more important or more solemn than the day on which the Holy Spirit was sent to us? And why should it be celebrated once a week while the others are not even necessarily celebrated once a year, but only at the discretion of each believer?

But Christ, it is argued, appeared twice to his disciples on this day. Even if the words *after eight days* in John 20.26 really mean "on the eighth day after," however, this is still a very shaky argument for the divine institution of a new Sabbath. For one thing, there can be no doubt that he appeared on other days as well, Luke 24.36 and John 21.3–4: *Peter said, I am going fishing.* It was not lawful to fish on the Sabbath, so the following day, on the morning of which Christ appeared, cannot possibly have been the Lord's Day. But let us say, for sake of argument, that it was. What reason is this for assuming that a new Sabbath has been imposed upon us? It is the merest conjecture: there is no commandment and no reason for such an institution anywhere in scripture.

Now let us pass from commandments (of which, as we have seen, there are none in this case) to examples. In fact no mere example can weaken the force of a contrary commandment; however, I shall demonstrate that what are produced as examples are really not examples at all. Take first Acts 20.7, where the disciples dwelling at Troas *came together*, we are told, *to break bread on the first day of the week.* Who can say with absolute certainty whether this was a regular weekly meeting, or one which the disciples happened to arrange on that day, of their own free choice? Who can say whether it was a religious meeting or merely a brotherly meal; whether it was a special assembly, taking place on that particular day, or a mere daily event, like those recorded in 2.42, compared with 46; whether it was held by order of the apostles, or whether, as often, they were merely acting in compliance with the popular custom?

The deduction which my opponents make from 1 Cor. 16.2 is, again, a thoroughly unsatisfactory piece of evidence. Paul does not lay down any rules there about the observance of the Lord's Day. What he does is to advise that *on the first day of each week* (if this is what *per unam sabbathorum* means) *each person should put aside and keep by him* (that is, at home) something for the relief of the poor. Nothing is said about a public assembly on that day or about any sort of collection taking place at it. Possibly he wished this sum to be set aside on the first day of the week either because our alms ought to be set aside as a sort of first-fruits to God, or because the first day seemed the most convenient for the arrangement of the family accounts. And what if we were to grant that the Corinthians did hold a religious assembly on that day? It does not follow that we, without any divine command to that effect, are bound to follow their example, any more than that we are bound to observe the Jewish Sabbath because the Philippians, and Paul himself, were in the habit of doing so. Acts 16.13: *on the sabbath day we went out of the city to the river, where it was the custom to offer prayer,* and 17.2: *Paul, as was his custom, went in to them, and for three sabbath days he had discussions with them about the scriptures,* and 18.3, 4: *he lived with them and worked. And every sabbath day he went and debated in the synagogue . . .*—on the other six days, as it seems, he attended to his own affairs at home.

The expression "the Lord's Day" is found, then, only once in the whole of scripture. Let those who venture to make this the grounds for the introduction of a divinely instituted sacred day—a sort of new Sabbath—beware. It may turn out that they are setting a very bad and dangerous example in scriptural interpretation.

This being so, let us draw our conclusions. First, where divine worship is concerned, no special day is appointed under the gospel in preference to another. The church may, of course, of its own authority, set aside a day of voluntary observance upon which we may freely and of our own choice gather together in our congregations. On this day, too, we may be at leisure to neglect our worldly affairs and devote ourselves wholly to religious services, so far as is consistent with the duties of charity. Secondly, that this may conveniently recur once every seven days, and particularly on the first day of each week. But it must be the authority of the church which encourages this: there must be no question of its being enforced by the civil authority. And our consciences must not be ensnared by the allegation of a divine command, borrowed from the decalogue. St. Paul expressly warns us to beware of this; Col. 2.16: *so let no man condemn you.* If we are to use the decalogue as a guide in fixing the time of our public worship under the gospel, it will certainly be much safer to select the seventh day, according to the express commandment of God, rather than the first day, which has nothing to recommend it beyond mere human conjecture. I may add that all the most learned theologians—BUCER, CALVIN, PETER MARTYR, MUSCULUS, URSINUS, GOMARUS and others—seem to have been more or less of this opinion.

CHAPTER II

OF MAN'S DUTY TOWARDS HIS NEIGHBOR, AND THE VIRTUES CONNECTED WITH THIS

[. . .][307]

There is some hatred, however, which is a religious duty, as when we hate the enemies of God or of the church. 2 Chron. 19.2: *should you love those that hate Jehovah?;* Ps. 31.7 [. . .] and 139.21, 22 [. . .], etc.; Prov. 28.4 [. . .], and 29.27 [. . .]; Jer. 48.10: *cursed is the man who does the work of Jehovah deceitfully, and cursed is the man who keeps his sword from blood:* or as when we hate even those who are in other respects our nearest and dearest, if they hinder or deter us from the love of God and from our reverence for the true religion: Ex. 32.27: *every man kill his brother, and every man his friend, and every man his neighbor . . . ;* Deut. 13.6–8 [. . .]; Luke 14.26 [. . .]. Thus Christ says to Peter, who was otherwise very dear to him, Mark 8.33: *get away from me, Satan . . .*

[. . .].

FRIENDSHIP is the intimate conjunction of two or more people who perform every virtuous or at least every courteous service for one another. Eccles. 4.5, etc: *two are better than one because. . . .*

It takes precedence over all blood-relationships. Deut. 13.6: *your friend, who is as dear to you as yourself;* Prov. 17.17 [. . .], and 18.24 [. . .], and 27.10 [. . .].

307. Milton's account of Christian social virtues is standard for the time. It begins with charity as defined in Lev. 19.18: "You shall love your neighbor as yourself." *Neighbor* is a term that applies chiefly "to fellow-Christians," however. The passage excerpted here notes the usual exceptions to the duty of charity toward others. We include the discussion of friendship from the other social virtues detailed in this chapter.

And friendship with good men, or even mere association with them, is safe and beneficial. Gen. 12.3: *I will bless those who bless you* . . . , and 18.26, etc. [. . .], and 19.21 [. . .], and 20.7 [. . .]; Num. 11.2 [. . .], and 14.19, 20 [. . .]; 1 Sam. 15.6 [. . .]; Ps. 119.63 [. . .]; Prov. 13.20 [. . .]; Isa. 65.8 [. . .]; Ezek. 12.30 [. . .]. It is also useful as a source of good advice. Ex. 18.14 [. . .], and 18.24 [. . .]; Prov. 12.15 [. . .], and 27.9: *as ointment and sweet smoke make the heart joyful, so does the sweetness of a man's friend, more than his own counsel.* But it does not lead to eternal salvation, not even for those who were Christ's companions on earth; Matt. 12.46 etc.; Mark 3.35; Luke 11.27 and 13.26; John 7.5.

Opposed to this is counterfeit friendship. Job 19.13, etc.: *he has driven my brothers far from me and my companions estrange themselves from me* . . . ; Ps. 55.13, etc. [. . .]; Prov. 19.4, 6, 7 [. . .]. The traitor Judas is an example of this.

[. . .].

CHAPTER 13[308]

OF THE SECOND CLASS OF SPECIAL DUTIES TOWARDS ONE'S NEIGHBOR

[. . .].

Falsehood is usually defined as the EXPRESSION OF AN UNTRUTH, EITHER BY WORDS OR ACTIONS, WITH DECEITFUL INTENT. In practice, however, it frequently happens that not only to disguise or conceal the truth, but actually to tell lies with deceitful intent makes for the safety or advantage of one's neighbor. We must therefore turn our attention to producing a better definition of falsehood. Homicide and various other activities which I shall discuss later have to be considered with reference not so much to the act itself as to the end and object. I do not see why the same cannot be said of falsehood. Who but a madman would deny that we are absolutely justified in concluding that some people ought to be deceived? What about children, or lunatics, or people who are ill, or drunk, or hostile, or themselves deceitful? What about thieves? In the words of the old adage, *You cannot wrong a wrongdoer.* Is it really a religious duty to tell the truth even to these people? According to the above definition we must not deceive them either by word or deed. But I should certainly not give back to a madman a sword or other weapon which he had left with me while he was sane. So why should I reveal the truth to someone who never left it with me, and is quite unfit to receive it, and will turn it to evil ends? What is more, if giving an answer which is intended to deceive to

308. In chapter 12 of Book 2, Milton addressed the first class of "special virtues or duties towards one's neighbor," defined as those that affect his "internal well-being." These include "harmlessness," "gentleness," and "placability" (Yale 6:753–54). The second class of such virtues Milton defines as those that affect the neighbor's "reputation" or "fortune." In the excerpt included here, Milton works out a practical definition of falsehood as a wicked counterpart to veracity.

someone who asks you a question must always be accounted falsehood, then nothing was more common for the saints and prophets than to tell falsehoods.

So what about defining falsehood like this: FALSEHOOD must arise from EVIL INTENT and entails EITHER THE DELIBERATE MISREPRESENTATION OF THE TRUTH OR THE TELLING OF AN ACTUAL LIE TO SOMEONE, WHOEVER HE MAY BE, TO WHOM IT IS THE SPEAKER'S DUTY TO BE TRUTHFUL? Thus the devil, when he took the form of the serpent, was the first liar, Gen. 3.4. Cain, too, was a liar, 4.9; and Sarah, 18.15, who did not apologize and frankly confess her fault to the angels, who were rightly put out; also Abraham 12.13 and 20, whose story about Sarah being his sister, though it was intended only to save his own life, was, as he might have learned from his previous experience in Egypt, likely to lead men who did not know the truth into sin and unlawful desire; also David, 1 Sam. 21.3, who, when he was running away from Saul, ought not to have exposed his host, Abimelech, to such great danger by concealing from him how matters stood between himself and the king; also Ananias and Sapphira, Acts 5.

It is evident from this definition, as indeed from the previous one I quoted, that parables, hyperboles, fables and the various uses of irony are not falsehoods since they are calculated not to deceive but to instruct: 1 Kings 18.27: *that Elijah mocked them and said, Shout loudly, for he is a God . . .*, and 22.15: *he said to him, Go on and prosper, for Jehovah will deliver it into the hand of the king.* It is evident, secondly, that, in the proper sense of the word "deceit," no one can be deceived unless he is, at the same time, injured in some way. If, then, we do not injure him in any way but, on the contrary, either assist him, or prevent him from inflicting or suffering injury, we do not really deceive him, not even if we tell him a thousand lies, but rather do him a service of which he is unaware. Thirdly, everyone agrees that the strategems and tactics of warfare, provided they do not involve treachery or perjury, do not constitute falsehood. Once this is granted it is obviously fatal to the first definition I quoted. For hardly any of the ambushes or surprise-tactics common in warfare can be carried out without the telling of a great many flagrant untruths which are quite specifically designed to deceive. If the first definition is correct, they cannot be cleared of the charge of falsehood. We ought rather to conclude, then, that strategems are allowable, even when they entail falsehood, because if it is not our duty to tell someone the truth, it does not matter if we lie to him whenever it is convenient. Moreover I do not see why this should apply to peace any less than to war, especially when we may, by a salutary and commendable falsehood, save ourselves or our neighbor from harm or danger.

The scriptural texts which are cited condemning falsehood must be understood, then, to refer to that kind of falsehood which evidently injures our neighbor or detracts from the glory of God. Texts of this sort, besides those quoted above, are Lev. 19.11: *do not tell lies or deal falsely with your neighbor;* Ps. 101.7: *a man who practices deception shall not dwell in my house, and he that speaks falsehoods shall not stand in my sight;* Prov. 6.16, 17 [. . .]; Jer. 9.5 [. . .]. These and similar texts command us to speak the truth: but to whom? Not to enemies, or madmen, or thugs, or murderers, but to our neighbor—one with whom we are at peace, and whose lawful society we enjoy. If, then, we are commanded to speak the truth only to our neighbor, it is clear that we are not forbidden to tell lies, as often as need be, to those who have not earned the name of neighbor. If anyone disagrees I should like to ask him which of the Ten Commandments forbids falsehood. No doubt he will reply, the ninth. Right then, let him repeat the words of that commandment, and he will no longer disagree with me. For what that commandment forbids is presented as an injury to one's neighbor, so if a falsehood does not injure one's neighbor it is certainly not forbidden by that commandment.

Thus we may absolve all those holy men who, according to the common judgment of theologians, are guilty of falsehood: Abraham, for example, Gen. 22.5. When he told his servants that he would come back with his son he intended to deceive them so that they would not suspect anything. He himself was quite sure that his son would be sacrificed and left behind. Had he not been sure of this, what sort of trial of his faith would there have been? But he was an intelligent man and he realized that it was not his servants' concern to know what was going on, and that it was convenient that they should not know for the time being. Rebecca and Jacob, Gen. 27, come in the same category. Their prudence, adroitness and circumspection made accessible to Jacob that birthright which his brother had sold for so poor a price—a birthright which was, indeed, already Jacob's both by prophetic prediction and by right of purchase. But, you will say, he deceived his father. Say rather that he corrected, and not before time, the error of his father who was swayed by his absurd passion for Esau. Joseph too, if the usual definition holds good, was obviously guilty of a great many falsehoods, Gen. 42.7, etc. How many lies he told to deceive his brothers! His intentions, however, were not evil but very much to his brothers' advantage. The Hebrew midwives may also be mentioned, Ex. 1.19, etc., whose conduct earned the approval of God himself, in that though they deceived Pharaoh they did him not an injury but a service because they deprived him of an opportunity for committing a crime. Moses may be added to the list, Ex. 3, for he was commanded by God himself to ask Pharaoh for permission to make a three days' journey into the desert, ostensibly for religious purposes but really with the intention of pulling the wool over Pharaoh's eyes. Thus he alleged a quite false reason for their departure, or at least substituted what was only an invented reason for the true one. Indeed the Israelites as a whole may be included, Ex. 11 and 12. It was, once more, at God's command that they borrowed gold and utensils and costly clothes from the Egyptians, no doubt promising to pay them back, though intending to deceive them—and why not, when they were enemies of God and violators of hospitality who had for years been robbing the Israelites? Rahab is another example, Josh. 2.45: she lied nobly and not dishonestly because she deceived those whom God wished to be deceived, though they were her fellow-countrymen and magistrates, and saved those he wished to be saved, rightly preferring religious to civil duty. Then, too, there was Ehud who deceived Eglon with a double lie, Judges 3.19, 20 (and justifiably, since Eglon was an enemy and Ehud acted upon divine prompting): and there was Jael who enticed Sisera to his death when he sought refuge with her, Judges 4.18, 19, though he was God's enemy rather than hers. (Junius claims that she achieved this by a pious fraud rather than by falsehood—as if there were any difference!).[309] Then there was Jonathan who at his friend David's request gave his father an invented reason for David's absence, 1 Sam. 20.6, 28. He had more regard for the safety of an innocent man than for his father's cruelty. It was more in keeping with charity that he should protect the life of his innocent friend, though at the cost of a lie, than that he should assist in the commission of a crime and gratify his father by a confession of the truth which could only do harm. So we see that my more accurate inquiry into this question of falsehood rescues the above-mentioned, plus a great many other very saintly men, from that limbo to which the old definition had condemned them.

[. . .][310]

URBANITY entails not only elegance and wit (of a decent kind) in conversation, but also the ability to discourse and to reply in an acute and apposite way. Prov. 24.26: *he will kiss the lips of the man who answers aptly,* and 25.11: *like golden apples placed on silverwork is an apposite word;* 1 Kings 18.27 [. . .]; Col. 4.6 [. . .].

Opposed to this are scurrility and banter. Eph. 4.29: *let no bad language come from your mouth,* and 5.4: [. . .]; Col. 3.8: *have done with all these things: anger . . . obscene talk.* Strictly speaking no word or thing is obscene. The obscenity is in the dirty mind of the man who perverts words or things out of prurience or to get a laugh. Thus those words in the Hebrew Bible for which the Jewish commentators offer marginal equivalents, which they consider more decent, are not to be thought of as obscene.[311] Their presence is to be attributed, rather, to the vehemence or indignation of the speaker.[312] Nor is there anything obscene about those words in Deut. 22.17: *they shall spread out the sheet before the elders.*

[. . .][313]

309. Cp. *SA* (989–90), where Dalila, to excuse her betrayal of Samson, cites Jael as precedent: "who with inhospitable guile/Smote Sisera sleeping through the temples nailed." In the Junius-Tremellius translation, the explanation of Jael's action as a "pious fraud" occurs in a note to Judg. 4.20.

310. In the deleted passage, Milton lists and cites biblical examples of behavior opposed to candor, such as "evil suspicion," "prying," "calumny," "abuse and disparagement," "litigiousness," and "at the other extreme," "flattery" and "unjustified praise or blame." He goes on to discuss "candor" in the now obsolete sense of "sweetness of temper" or "freedom from malice." Of various traits that Milton goes on to name as allied or opposed to candor in this now obsolete sense, we include two particularly characteristic of him.

311. See *Areop,* n. 62.

312. Milton defends himself similarly from criticism of his rough language in controversy. Cp. *Defense of Himself* (Yale 4:744–45).

313. In the deleted passage, Milton cites biblical examples of "frankness" (the virtue that "makes us speak the truth fearlessly") and its opposite, "timidity." He continues in the same way to define "admonitoriness" (the virtue that "makes us warn all sinners of their danger frankly and fearlessly"), a virtue not to be exercised on "stubborn sinners" or those who will "only scoff at such a warning."

CHAPTER 14

MORE ABOUT THE SECOND CLASS OF SPECIAL DUTIES TOWARDS ONE'S NEIGHBOR

[. . .][314]

It is a violation of justice to charge excessive interest on loans, and if the loan is made to a poor man, any interest at all is excessive. Ex. 22.25: *do not lend money at interest to a poor man;* Lev. 25.35–37: *when your brother is in straitened circumstances and his hand shakes before you, then you shall encourage him to live with you, even if he is a foreigner or a stranger; and you shall not take any interest from him, but you shall fear your God . . . so that your brother may live with you.* This is the meaning of Deut. 23.19: *do not lend to your brother at interest, interest of money or of food or of anything which is lent at interest.*

There are many conflicting opinions about usury, however, and as the controversy is of some relevance to this section let us now take a quick look at the rights and wrongs of the matter.

Most people agree that usury is not always illicit, and that in judging it we should take into account the usurer's motives, the rate of interest, and the borrower.

As for the borrower, they agree that it is legitimate to take interest from anyone who is well enough off to pay it.

They agree too, that the rate should square with justice, if not with charity.

They agree that, where motive is concerned, the usurer should have some consideration for his neighbor as well as for himself.

Given these conditions, they maintain, no fault can be found with usury—and they are certainly right about the conditions, for unless they are observed pretty well all business transactions are illicit. Usury, then, is no more reprehensible in itself than any other kind of lawful commerce. The proof of this is, in the first place, that if it were blameworthy in itself God would not have let the Israelites take interest from foreigners, Deut. 23.20, especially as he elsewhere instructs them to do no injury to foreigners but rather to assist them in all kindness, particularly those in need. Secondly, if we may make a profit out of cattle, land, houses and the like, why should we not out of money? When money is borrowed, as it often is, not to relieve hardship but simply for the purpose of gain, it tends to be more profitable to the borrower than to the lender. It is true that God did not wish the Israelites to devote the produce of their land

314. In the deleted passage, Milton discusses virtues by which one shows "regard for our neighbor' fortune," that is, "honesty and generosity." The excerpt printed here concerns usury, which comes under the heading of "commutative justice," which concerns "buying and selling, hiring, lending and borrowing, and the retention and restoration of deposits." Milton's father lent money for interest, and Milton occasionally aided him in this part of his business. Roman Catholic orthodoxy forbade usury.

to usury, but this was for purely ceremonial reasons, as was his desire that they should not sell their land permanently, Lev. 25.23. We see, then, that usury is only to be condemned if it is practiced at the expense of the poor, or solely out of avarice, or to an uncharitable and unjust extent; and these conditions apply to every kind of profit-making transaction just as much as they do to usury. Any transaction which disregards these conditions deserves, just as much as does usury, to be called נֶשֶׁךְ, "a bite." It is this kind of usury which is forbidden in Ex. 22.25: *if you lend money to one of my people, to one of the poor among you, do not be like a usurer to him . . .*, and Lev. 25.35–7, as above. Since these two passages are the very first to deal with the subject, they certainly ought to throw light upon later passages, and that exception which they contain must be inferred elsewhere; for example, in Deut. 23.19, as above; Ps. 15.5: *who does not put out his money to usury;* Prov. 28: *he who increases his capital by usury, will amass a fortune for one who will give generously to the poor;* Ezek. 18.8 [. . .].

[. . .][315]

CHAPTER 17[316]

OF PUBLIC DUTIES TOWARDS OUR NEIGHBOR

[. . .].

Above all it is the duty of magistrates to foster religion and the worship—particularly the public worship—of God, and to respect the church. Isa. 49.23: *kings will be your foster-fathers, and their queens your nurses; they will bow down their faces to the earth in your honor, and lick up the dust at your feet.* But churches do not need the supervision of magistrates. Provided that there is peace, they are perfectly well able to rule themselves according to their own laws and discipline, and also to enlarge themselves. There is evidence for this assertion in Acts 9.31: *the churches throughout the whole of Judea and Galilee and Samaria enjoyed peace and built up their strength; and progressing in the fear of the Lord and with the comfort of the Holy Ghost, they grew more numerous.*

Thus magistrates should protect religion, not enforce it, Josh. 24.15: *if it seems evil in your eyes . . . choose today whom you will serve . . . but I and my family will serve Jehovah;* Ps. 105. 14: *he did not allow anyone to oppress them; he even reproved kings for*

315. After a brief discussion of deposits, Milton defines and cites scriptural examples of "moderation" and "generosity," the latter including "liberality" and "munificence" and opposed by "niggardliness" and "prodigality." He concludes with a brief mention of the corresponding virtue of "gratitude" and its opposite, "ingratitude."

316. In chapters 15 and 16 of Book 2, Milton addresses "reciprocal duties toward his neighbor, particularly private duties" (Yale 6:781). Chapter 15 primarily concerns duties toward family and quasi-family members; chapter 16, "duties toward those not of your own household" (Yale 6:789) The section of the final chapter included here addresses church-state relations, freedom of conscience, ethical limits on the subject's obedience to a ruler, and international affairs.

their sake, saying, Do not touch my anointed, or do my prophets harm. If kings are here forbidden to subject religious persons to any kind of compulsion, then a king must certainly not force the consciences of such people in the matter of religion itself (particularly over controversial issues where a king or magistrate can be—and often is—just as mistaken as the Pope), unless he wants to be called antichrist as the Pope, chiefly for this reason, is. It is true that, in ancient times, the kings and magistrates of the Jews gave judgments in matters of religion, and even enforced their execution. This happened, however, only when the law of God was absolutely explicit, so that the magistrate's decision could be unquestionably correct. Nowadays, on the other hand, Christians are often persecuted or punished over things which are controversial, or permitted by Christian liberty, or about which the gospel says nothing explicit.[317] Magistrates who do this sort of thing are Christians in name alone, and there are plenty of Jewish and heathen magistrates who can be cited as evidence against them: Pontius Pilate himself, to begin with. He had enough respect for the Jews to go outside and talk to them, though he was a proconsul, when they would not enter the praetorium because of their religion, John 18.28, 29: also Gamaliel, Acts 5.39: *but if it is from God, your hands have not the power . . . ;* and Gallio, Acts 18.15: *I will not be a judge of these things.*

Even an ecclesiastical minister does not have the right to domineer over the church, let alone a magistrate. 2 Cor. 1.24: *not that we may domineer over your faith, but that we may contribute to your happiness; for you stand by faith;* Col. 2.18 [. . .]; 1 Pet. 5.3 [. . .]; Rom. 14.4 [. . .]; similarly James 4.12. Further proof may be found in my first book, in the discussions of Christ's kingdom, faith, the gospel, Christian liberty and church-government and its object. We may be sure that, since Christ's kingdom is not of this world, it does not stand by force and constraint, the constituents of worldly authority. So the gospel should not be made a matter of compulsion, and faith, liberty and conscience cannot be. These are the concern of ecclesiastical discipline, and are quite outside the province of civil jurisdiction. To compel religious people to profess a religion of which they do not approve, and to compel the profane, whom God keeps from holy things, to take part in public worship, are equally senseless and impious acts. Ps. 1.16, 17; *God says to the wicked man, What business have you to tell of my decrees or take my covenant in your mouth . . . ?;* Prov. 15.8 and 21.27: *the sacrifice of the wicked is an abomination, and much more so when he offers it impiously.*

THE DUTIES OF THE PEOPLE TOWARDS THE MAGISTRATE are prescribed in Ex. 22.28: *you shall not revile the magistrates, or curse the ruler of your*

317. Cp. *Of Civil Power* (Yale 7:259): "Now is the state of grace, manhood, freedom and faith; to which belongs willingness and reason, not force; the law was then written on tables of stone, and to be performed according to the letter, willingly or unwillingly; the gospel, our new covenant, upon the heart of every believer, to be interpreted only by the sense of charity and inward persuasion."

people; 2 Sam. 21.17 [. . .]; Prov. 24.21, 22 [. . .], and 29.26 [. . .]; Eccles. 7.1, etc. [. . .]; Matt. 22.21 [. . .]; Rom. 13.1, etc. [. . .]; 1 Tim. 2.1, 2 [. . .]; Tit. 3.1: *prompt them to be submissive to the government and the authorities, to be obedient, to be ready for any good work;* 1 Pet. 2.13, etc.: *submit to every human ordinance, for the sake of the Lord.*

Even towards unjust magistrates: Matt. 17.26, 27: *their own citizens are free: but so that we shall not cause difficulty, go . . . ;* Acts 23.3, etc. [. . .].

Except in things which are unlawful. Ex. 1.17: *but the midwives feared God, and did not do as the king of Egypt had told them;* Ex. 2.2 [. . .]; 1 Sam. 14.45, etc. [. . .], and 20.2, etc. [. . .], and 22.17 [. . .]; Josh. 1.17 [. . .]; 2 Chron. 21.10 [. . .], and 26.18 [. . .]; Esther 3.2–4 [. . .]; Dan. 3.16 [. . .], and 3.18 [. . .], and 6.11 [. . .]; Acts 4.19: *decide for yourselves whether it is right in the sight of God to obey you rather than God;* Heb. 11.23: *through faith Moses was hidden for three months by his parents, and they were not afraid of the king's edict.*

Opposed to this is rebellion: Num. 16.1, etc.: *but Korah took men . . . ;* 2 Sam. 20.1, etc. [. . .].

And obedience in unlawful things. 1 Sam. 22.18: *so Doeg turned . . . .*

Some maintain that magistrates must be obeyed not only when they are god-fearing but also when they are tyrannical and when their commands are wicked. There is, however, no divine authority for such an opinion. When 1 Pet. 2.13 talks about obeying *every human ordinance,* it means every kind of human ordinance which can legitimately be obeyed, as the next verse makes perfectly clear. As for 2.18, it is addressed to slaves, and has nothing to do with the duties of free peoples, who must be judged by standards quite different from those which apply to slaves, serfs and mercenaries. Again, the Israelites obeyed Pharaoh. True: but was their obedience willing or unwilling, right or wrong? Who knows? We read nowhere that they were commanded to obey him or praised for doing so. And as for Daniel's behavior in captivity, it, too, is irrelevant to the argument. What else could he do? He was a prisoner. Look at Ps. 60.4: *you have given a banner to those who fear you, to be used mightily in the service of truth.*

I do not deny that in lawful matters it may be prudent to obey even a tyrant, or at any rate to be a time-server, in the interest of public peace and personal safety.

The duties of magistrate and people TOWARDS NEIGHBORING STATES concern either peace or war.

The duties of PEACE include the making of treaties. In order to know whether it is right or wrong to make treaties with the wicked, we must first understand the reasons for which treaties are concluded, namely: to strengthen the existing peace, or to ensure mutual defense and reinforce the friendship between neighboring states.

Of the first class are the treaties made by Abraham with the natives and with Abimelech, Gen. 14.13 and 21.27; that of Isaac with Abimelech, 26.29–31; and that of Solomon with Hiram, 1 Kings 5.12. These examples place the lawfulness of such treaties beyond question.

Of the second class are the treaties made by Asa with Benhadad, 1 Kings 15.19, and with Baasha, 2 Chron. 16.7; by Jehoshaphat with the house of Ahab, 18.1 compared with 19.2, etc.; by Amaziah with the Israelites, 25.7, 8; by Ahaz with the Assyrians, 2 Kings 16.7; and the treaty which the Jews attempted to make with the Egyptians, Isa. 30.2, etc. Each of these was forbidden and had an unhappy outcome: Ex. 23.32, 33: *you shall not make a treaty with them* . . . , and 34.12 [. . .], similarly 34.15; Deut. 7.4 [. . .]; Ezek. 16.26, etc. [. . .]; 2 Cor. 6.14: *do not couple with unbelievers, it is an unequal match; for what has righteousness to do with wickedness, and what have light and darkness in common?.*

Examples of treaty-breakers are Asa, 2 Chron. 16.3, and Zedekiah, 36.13. See also Ezek. 17.

Num. 34 and 35.15, and Deut. 23.15 deal with the subject of asylum.

As for WAR, we are instructed, in the first place, that it is to be undertaken only after extremely careful consideration, Prov. 20.18 and 24.6; Luke 14.31 [. . .] ; secondly, that it is to be waged knowledgeably and skillfully, 1 Sam. 14.29 [. . .], and 23.22 [. . .]; Prov. 21.22 [. . .]; and thirdly, with moderation, Deut. 20.19: *you shall not destroy its trees* . . . ; and fourthly, in holiness, Deut. 23. 9, etc.: *when the army goes out against your enemies, then beware of anything evil* . . . , and 32.29, 30 [. . .]; 1 Sam. 7.9 [. . .]; Isa. 31.6, etc. [. . .]; Amos 1.13 [. . .]; fifthly, that a cruel enemy should not be spared, 1 Sam. 15.33 [. . .]; Ps. 18.42, 43 [. . .], and 60.10 [. . .]; Jer. 48.10: *cursed is the man who keeps his sword from blood;* sixthly, that we should not trust in the strength of our forces, but in God alone, Ex. 14.17, 18 [. . .]; Deut. 20.1, etc. [. . .]; 1 Sam. 14.6 [. . .], and 17.47 [. . .]; Ps. 33.16, 17 [. . .], and 44.3, etc. [. . .], and 60.1, 2, etc. [. . .], and 127.1 [. . .], and 144.1, 2: *blessed be Jehovah, my rock, who teaches my hands battle* . . . , and 147.10 [. . .], and 147.13 [. . .]; Prov. 21.31: *the horse is prepared for the day of battle, but safety is Jehovah's;* 2 Chron. 14.11 [. . .], and 20.21 [. . .], and 24.24 [. . .]; Isa. 5.26, etc. [. . .]; Jer. 21.4 [. . .], and 37.10 [. . .]; Ezek. 13.5 [. . .]; Zech. 10.4–6 [. . .]; Amos 2.11 [. . .]; seventhly, that the spoil should be divided equally and fairly, Num. 31.27, etc.: *that you divide the booty between those who fought this battle, and marched out to war, and the whole assembly* . . . ; Deut. 20.14 [. . .]; Josh. 22.8, etc. [. . .]; 1 Sam. 30.24 [. . .].

There is no reason why war should be any less lawful now than it was in the time of the Jews. It is not forbidden in the New Testament. Ps. 149.6: *with a two-edged sword in their hand* . . . Two centurions, Cornelius and the man from Capernaum, are included among the faithful, Matt. 8, Acts 10; and it was not against war but against unjust plunder and rapine that John warned the soldiers, Luke 3.14: *he said to the soldiers, Do not bully anyone to extort money* . . . ; 1 Cor. 9.7 [. . .]; Paul availed himself of a military bodyguard, Acts 23.17 [. . .].

Obedience to God's commandments makes nations prosperous in every respect; see Lev. 26. It makes them fortunate, wealthy and victorious, Deut. 15.4–6, and lords over other nations; see Deut. 15.6 and 26.17–19, and particularly 28.1, etc.—a passage which politicians should read over and over again. See also Deut. 29 and 4; Judges 2 and 3; Ps. 33.12: *blessed is the nation whose God is Jehovah;*

Prov. 11.11 [. . .], and 14.34 [. . .], and 28.2 [. . .]; Isa. 3 and 24 and 48.18: *if only you had listened . . . ;* Jer. 5; Ezek. 7.

The converse is also true, Isa. 3.8: *in my house there is neither bread nor clothing, do not make me a ruler of the people . . . ,* and 57.13, 14, 17 [. . .]; Hos. 5.13 [. . .], and 7.11, 12 [. . .], and 12.2 [. . .]; Habak. 2.12 [. . .].

[. . .][318]

318. The rest of the chapter addresses duties of ministers toward the church as a whole and toward individual believers as well as the duties of the church and believers toward ministers.

Works Cited

I. Editions of Milton

Bentley, Richard. *Milton's "Paradise Lost."* Jacob Tonson, 1732.

Broadbent, J. B. (gen. ed.). *The Cambridge Milton.* Cambridge Univ. Press, 1972.

Browne, R. C. *English Poems by John Milton.* 2 vols. Clarendon Press, 1870.

Bush, Douglas. *The Complete Poetical Works of John Milton.* Houghton Mifflin, 1965.

Carey, John. *Complete Shorter Poems.* 2nd ed. Longman, 1997.

Cowper, William. *Latin and Italian Poems of John Milton: Translated into English Verse, and a Fragment of a Commentary on Paradise Lost.* J. Johnson, 1808.

Darbishire, Helen. *The Manuscript of Milton's Paradise Lost Book I.* Clarendon Press, 1931.

Dzelzainis, Martin. *John Milton: Political Writings.* Cambridge Univ. Press, 1991.

Elledge, Scott. *John Milton: "Paradise Lost."* 2nd ed. Norton, 1993.

Flannagan, Roy. *The Riverside Milton.* Houghton Mifflin, 1998.

Fletcher, Harris F. *John Milton's Complete Poetical Works, Reproduced in Photographic Facsimile.* 4 vols. Univ. of Illinois Press, 1943–48.

Fowler, Alastair. *Paradise Lost.* 2nd ed. Longman, 1998.

Graham, James. *Selections from the Prose Works of John Milton.* Hurst & Blackett, 1870.

Hanford, James Holly. *Poems of John Milton.* Ronald Press, 1953.

Honigmann, E. A. J. *Milton's Sonnets.* St. Martin's Press, 1966.

Hughes, Merritt Y. *Complete Poems and Major Prose.* Odyssey Press, 1957.

Leonard, John. *John Milton: The Complete Poems.* Penguin, 1998.

———. *Paradise Lost.* Penguin, 2000.

Masson, David. *The Poetical Works of John Milton.* 3 vols. Macmillan, 1882.

Newton, Thomas. *"Paradise Lost": A Poem in Twelve Books.* 2 vols. J. and R. Tonson, 1749.

Ricks, Christopher. *John Milton: "Paradise Lost" and "Paradise Regained."* Signet Classics, 1968.

Smart, John S. *The Sonnets of Milton.* Maclehose, 1921.

Tillyard, Phyllis B., and E. M. W. Tillyard. *Milton: Private Correspondence and Academic Exercises.* Cambridge Univ. Press, 1932.

Todd, H. J. *The Poetical Works of John Milton.* 6 vols. R. Gilpert, 1826.

Verity, A. W. *Milton's Ode on the Morning of Christ's Nativity, L'Allegro, Il Penseroso and Lycidas.* Cambridge Univ. Press, 1891.

———. *Milton's Samson Agonistes.* Cambridge Univ. Press, 1897.

———. *Comus.* Cambridge Univ. Press, 1909.

———. *Paradise Lost.* 2 vols. Cambridge Univ. Press, 1921.

Warton, Thomas. *Poems upon Several Occasions . . . by John Milton.* James Dodsley, 1785.

Wolfe, Don M., et al. *The Complete Prose Works of John Milton.* 8 vols. Yale Univ. Press, 1953–82.
Wright, B. A. *Shorter Poems of John Milton.* Macmillan, 1938.
Wright, William A. *Poems Reproduced in Facsimile from the Manuscript in Trinity College, Cambridge, with a Transcript.* Scolar Press, 1972.

II. Critical and Historical Works

________. *The Censure of the Rota Upon Mr. Milton's Book.* Paul Giddy, 1660.
Addison, Joseph. *Criticisms on Milton.* Cassell and Co., 1898.
Adler, Cyrus, and Isidore Singer, eds. *The Jewish Encyclopedia.* 12 vols. Funk & Wagnalls, Co., 1901–7.
Allen, D.C. *The Harmonious Vision: Studies in Milton's Poetry.* Johns Hopkins Univ. Press, 1954.
Amesii, Guilielmi [Ames, William]. *Medulla Theologica* [*Marrow of Sacred Divinity*]. Ioannem Ianssonium, 1623.
Aquinas, Thomas. *Summa Theologica.* Trans. Fathers of the English Dominican Province. 5 vols. Christian Classics, 1981.
Aristotle. *The Art of Poetry.* Ed. W. Hamilton Fyfe. Clarendon Press, 1940.
Aubrey, John. *Aubrey's Brief Lives.* Ed. Oliver Lawson Dick. Secker and Warburg, 1950.
Auerbach, Erich. *Scenes from the Drama of European Literature.* Meridian Books, 1959.
Babb, Lawrence. *The Moral Cosmos of Paradise Lost.* Michigan State Univ. Press, 1970.
Bacon, Francis. *Of the Proficiencie and Advancement of Learning.* Henrie Tomes, 1605.
Baillie, Robert. *A Dissuasive from the Errours of the Time.* Samuel Gillibrand, 1646.
Baldwin, Edward C. "Shook the Arsenal: A Note on *Paradise Regained*," *Philological Quarterly* 18 (1939): 218–22.
Banister, Richard. *A Treatise of One Hundred and Thirteen Diseases of the Eyes.* 1622.
Barker, Arthur. "The Pattern of Milton's *Nativity Ode*," *University of Toronto Quarterly* 10 (1940–41): 167-81.
———. *Milton and the Puritan Dilemma.* Univ. of Toronto Press, 1942.
Bauman, Michael. "Heresy in Paradise and the Ghost of Readers Past," *College Language Association Journal* 30 (1986): 59-68.
———. *Milton's Arianism.* Peter Lang, 1987.
———. *A Scripture Index to John Milton's De Doctrina Christiana.* Medieval and Renaissance Texts Society, 1989.
Bennett, Joan S. *Reviving Liberty: Radical Christian Humanism in Milton's Great Poems.* Cambridge Univ. Press, 1989.
Berry, Boyd M. *Process of Speech: Puritan Religious Writing and Paradise Lost.* Johns Hopkins Univ. Press, 1976.
Berryman, John. *The Freedom of the Poet.* Farrar, Straus & Giroux, 1976.
Binyon, Lawrence. "A Note on Milton's Imagery and Rhythm." In John Dover Wilson, ed., *Seventeenth-Century Studies Presented to Sir Herbert Grierson*, pp. 184–92. Clarendon Press, 1938.
Blasi, Vincent. "Milton's *Areopagitica* and the First Amendment," *Ideas* 4 (1996) <http://www.nhc.rtp.nc.us./Ideasv42/Ideas.htm>.
Bloom, Harold. *The Anxiety of Influence: A Theory of Poetry.* Oxford Univ. Press, 1973.

Boddy, Margaret. "Milton's Translation of Psalms 80–88," *Modern Philology* 64 (1966): 1–9.
Boesky, Amy. "The Maternal Shape of Mourning: A Reconsideration of *Lycidas*," *Modern Philology* 95 (1998): 463–83.
Boone, Lalia P. "The Language of Book VI, *Paradise Lost*." In J. Max Patrick, ed., *SAMLA Studies in Milton.* Univ. of Florida Press, 1953.
Breasted, Barbara. "*Comus* and the Castlehaven Scandal," *Milton Studies* 3 (1971): 201–24.
Brooks, Cleanth, and John Hardy. *Poems of Mr. John Milton.* Harcourt, Brace, 1951.
Brown, Cedric C. *John Milton's Aristocratic Entertainments.* Cambridge Univ. Press, 1985.
Browne, Sir Thomas. *Religio Medici.* Andrew Crooke, 1642.
Burges, Cornelius, et al. *Sermons Before Parliament* [Nov. 17, 1640–June 30, 1647]. London, 1641–47.
Burton, Robert. *The Anatomy of Melancholy.* Ed. Floyd Dell and Paul Jordon-Smith. Tudor, 1927.
Calvin, John. *Institutes of the Christian Religion.* 2 vols. Trans. Ford Lewis Battles. Eerdmans, 1986.
Campbell, Gordon. *A Milton Chronology.* Macmillan, 1997.
Campbell, Gordon, Thomas N. Corns, John K. Hale, David I. Holmes, and Fiona Tweedie. "The Provenance of *De Doctrina Christiana*," *Milton Quarterly* 31 (1997): 67–117.
Carey, John. "Milton's *Ad Patrem*, 35–37," *Review of English Studies* 15 (1964): 180–84.
———. *Milton.* Arco, 1970.
———. "A Work in Praise of Terrorism?" *TLS*, 6 Sept. 2002: 15–16.
Cavell, Stanley. *Pursuits of Happiness: The Hollywood Comedy of Remarriage.* Harvard Univ. Press, 1981.
Chambers, A. B. "'Goodfriday, 1913. Riding Westward': The Poem and the Tradition," *English Literary History* 28 (1961): 31–53.
———. "Chaos in *Paradise Lost*," *Journal of the History of Ideas* 24 (1963): 55–84.
Channing, William Ellery. *Remarks on the Character and Writings of John Milton.* Issac Butts, 1826.
Charles I. *Eikon Basilike: Pourtraicture of his Sacred Majestie in his Solitudes and Sufferings.* Roger Daniel, 1646.
Cirillo, Albert R. "Noon-Midnight and the Temporal Structure of *Paradise Lost*," *English Literary Renaissance* 29 (1962): 372–95.
———. "Time, Light, and the Phoenix: The Design of *Samson Agonistes*." In Joseph A. Wittreich, ed., *Calm of Mind: Tercentenary Essays on Paradise Regained and Samson Agonistes*, pp. 209–33. Press of Case Western Reserve Univ., 1971.
Clark, Andrew, ed. *Aubrey's Brief Lives.* 2 vols. Clarendon Press, 1898.
Coleridge, S. T. *Table Talk.* Ed. Henry Morley. Routledge and Sons, 1886.
———. *Lectures and Notes on Shakespeare and Other English Poets.* Ed. T. Ashe. G. Bell & Sons, 1902.
Colgrave, Bertram, and R. A. B. Mynors, eds. *Bede's Ecclesiastical History of the English People.* Clarendon Press, 1969.
Comenius, Johann Amos. *A Reformation of Schools.* Trans. Samuel Hartlib. Michael Sparks, 1642.
Conti, Natale. *Mythologiae.* Ed. Stephen Orgel. Garland Pub., 1979.
Coolidge, John S. *The Pauline Renaissance in England: Puritanism and the Bible.* Clarendon Press, 1970.

Corns, Thomas. *The Development of Milton's Prose Style.* Oxford Univ. Press, 1982.

———. *Milton's Language.* London: Basil Blackwell, 1990.

Crick, Julia C., et al. *Historia Regum Britannie of Geoffrey of Monmouth.* Woodbridge, 1989.

Crump, Galbraith. "Milton: Generic Dualist," *Sewanee Review* 95 (1987): 648–56.

Cudworth, Ralph. *True Intellectual System of the Universe.* Ed. J. L. Mosheim. 3 vols. Thomas Tegg, 1845.

Curry, Walter Clyde. *Shakespeare's Philosophical Patterns.* Louisiana State Univ. Press, 1937.

Danielson, Dennis. *Milton's Good God: A Study in Literary Theodicy.* Cambridge Univ. Press, 1982.

Dante. *Inferno.* Trans. Allen Mandelbaum. Berkeley: Univ. of California Press, 1980.

Darbishire, Helen. *Early Lives of Milton.* Oxford Univ. Press, 1932.

Davies, Sir John. *Poems.* Columbia Univ. Press, 1941.

Davies, Stevie. *The Feminine Reclaimed: The Idea of the Women in Spenser, Shakespeare, and Milton.* Univ. Press of Kentucky, 1986.

Defoe, Daniel. *Political History of the Devil.* T. Warner, 1726.

Demaray, John G. *Milton and the Masque Tradition.* Harvard Univ. Press, 1968.

Dennis, John. *The Grounds of Criticism in Poetry.* George Strahan, 1704.

Diodorus. *Biblioteca Historica.* Trans. C. H. Oldfather. London: Harvard Univ. Press, 1935.

DiSalvo, Jacqueline. "Intestine Thorn: Samson's Struggle with the Woman Within." In Julia M. Walker, ed., *Milton and the Idea of Woman,* pp. 211–29. Univ. of Illinois Press, 1988.

———. "Make Love Not War: On *Samson Agonistes* and *The Caucasian Chalk Circle,*" *Milton Studies* 24 (1988): 203–32.

D'Israeli, Isaac. *Curiosities of Literature.* Routledge, 1859.

Dobranski, Stephen B. *Milton, Authorship, and the Book Trade.* Cambridge Univ. Press, 1998.

Dorian, Donald C. *The English Diodatis: A History of Charles Diodati's Family and of His Friendship with Milton.* Rutgers Univ. Press, 1950.

Dryden, John. *Critical and Miscellaneous Prose Works.* Ed. Edmond Malone. 3 vols. H. Baldwin and Son, 1800.

———. *Essays of John Dryden.* Ed. W. P. Ker. 2 vols. Clarendon Press, 1926.

Duncan, Joseph E. *Milton's Earthly Paradise: A Historical Study of Eden.* Univ. of Minnesota Press, 1972.

Edwards, Karen L. *Milton and the Natural World: Science and Poetry in Paradise Lost.* Cambridge Univ. Press, 1999.

Eliot, T. S. *On Poetry and Poets.* Faber, 1957.

———. *Selected Essays.* Harcourt, Brace & World, 1964.

———. *The Varieties of Metaphysical Poetry.* Ed. Ronald Schuchard. Faber & Faber, 1993.

Elledge, Scott, ed. *Milton's "Lycidas": Edited to Serve as an Introduction to Criticism.* Harper & Row, 1966.

Ellwood, Thomas. *The History of the Life of Thomas Ellwood.* J. Sowle, 1714.

Emerson, Ralph Waldo. *The Early Lectures of Ralph Waldo Emerson.* Ed. Stephen E. Whicher and Robert E. Spiller. 3 vols. Harvard Univ. Press, 1959.

Empson, William. "A Defense of Delilah," *Sewanee Review* 68 (1960): 240–55.

———. *Milton's God.* 2nd ed. Chatto & Windus, 1965.

Evans, J. Martin. *Paradise Lost and the Genesis Tradition.* Oxford Univ. Press, 1968.

Evelyn, John. *Fumifugium: or, The Inconveniencie of the Aer and Smoak of London Dissipated.* W. Godbid, 1661.

Fallon, Robert. "*A Second Defence:* Milton's Critique of Cromwell?" *Milton Studies* 40 (2000): 167–82.

Fallon, Stephen M. "Satan's Return to Hell: Milton's Concealed Dialogue with Homer and Virgil," *Milton Quarterly* 18 (1984): 78–81.

———. " 'To Act or Not': Milton's Conception of Divine Freedom," *Journal of the History of Ideas* 49 (1988): 425–49.

———. *Milton Among the Philosophers: Poetry and Materialism in Seventeenth-Century England.* Cornell Univ. Press, 1991.

———. " 'Elect Above the Rest': Theology as Self-Representation in Milton." In *Milton and Heresy,* ed. Stephen B. Dobranski and John Rumrich, pp. 93–116. Cambridge Univ. Press, 1998.

———. "Milton's Arminianism and the Authorship of *De Doctrina Christiana,*" *Texas Studies in Literature and Language* 41 (1999): 103–27.

——. " 'The Spur of Self-Concernment': Milton in His Divorce Tracts." In *John Milton: The Writer in His Works, Milton Studies* 38, ed. Albert C. Labiola and Michael Lieb, pp. 220–42. Univ. of Pittsburgh Press, 2000.

———. "Alexander More Reads Milton." In *Milton and the Terms of Liberty,* ed. Graham Parry and Joad Raymond, pp. 111–24. D. S. Brewer, 2002.

Felltham, Owen. *Resolves.* George Purslowe, 1628.

Ficino, Marsilio. *Commentary on Plato's Symposium on Love.* Trans. Sears Jayne. Spring Publications, 1985.

Fink, Zera S. "Milton and the Theory of Climatic Influence," *Modern Language Quarterly* 2 (1941): 67–80.

Fish, Stanley. *Surprised by Sin: The Reader in Paradise Lost.* St. Martin's Press, 1967.

———. *There's No Such Thing as Free Speech.* Oxford Univ. Press, 1994.

———. " 'There Is Nothing He Cannot Ask': Milton, Liberalism, and Terrorism," in Michael Lieb and Albert C. Labriola, eds., *Milton in the Age of Fish: Essays on Authorship, Text, and Terrorism,* pp. 243–64. Duquesne Univ. Press, 2006.

Fixler, Michael. *Milton and the Kingdoms of God.* Faber, 1964.

Fletcher, Harris F. *The Intellectual Development of John Milton.* 2 vols. Univ. of Illinois Press, 1961.

Flosdorf, J. W. " 'Gums of Glutinous Heat': A Query," *Milton Quarterly* 7 (1973): 4–5.

Fowler, Alastair. "Paradise Regained: Some Problems of Style." In Piero Boitano, and Anna Torli, eds., *Medieval and Pseudo-Medieval Literature,* pp. 181–89. Cambridge Univ. Press, 1984.

Freccero, John. *Dante: The Poetics of Conversion.* Ed. Rachel Jacoff. Harvard Univ. Press, 1986.

Froula, Christine. "When Eve Reads Milton: Undoing the Canonical Economy," *Critical Inquiry* 10 (1983): 321–47.

Frye, Northrop. "The Typology of Paradise Regained," *Modern Philology* 53 (1956): 227–38.

———. *The Return to Eden: Five Essays on Milton's Epics.* Univ. of Toronto Press, 1965.

———. "Agon and Logos: Revolution and Revelation." In Balachandra Rajan, ed., *The Prison and the Pinnacle,* pp. 135–36. Univ. of Toronto Press, 1973.

G. S. *Monarchy Triumphing over Traitorous Republicans.* T. R. for William Palmer, 1661.

Galilei, Galileo. *Sidereus Nuncius.* Th. Baglionum, 1610.

Gallagher, Philip J. "On Reading Joseph Wittreich: A Review Essay," *Milton Quarterly* 21 (1987): 108–13.

———. *Milton, the Bible, and Misogyny.* Univ. of Missouri Press, 1990.

Gallagher, Philip J., and Sandra Gilbert. "Milton's Bogey," *Publications of the Modern Language Association* 94 (1979): 319–22.

Gaskell, Phillip. *From Writer to Reader: Studies in Editorial Method.* Clarendon Press, 1978.

Gilbert, Allan H. *A Geographical Dictionary of Milton.* Yale Univ. Press, 1919.

———. *On the Composition of Paradise Lost: A Study of the Ordering and Insertion of Material.* Univ. of North Carolina Press, 1947.

Gilbert, Sandra. "Patriarchal Poetry and Women Readers: Reflections on Milton's Bogey," *Publications of the Modern Language Association* 93 (1978): 368–82.

Gilbert, Sandra, and Susan Gubar, *The Madwoman in the Attic: The Woman Writer and the Nineteenth-Century Literary Imagination.* Yale Univ. Press, 1979.

Gildas (516?–570), *The Epistle of Gildas.* Trans. Thomas Habingdon. T. Cotes for W. Cooke, 1638.

Goethe, Johann Wolfgang. *Conversations with Eckermann.* J. M. Dent, 1930.

Goldberg, Jonathan. *James I and the Politics of Literature.* Johns Hopkins Univ. Press, 1983.

Gollancz, Israel. *The Caedmon Manuscript of Anglo-Saxon Biblical Poetry.* Oxford Univ. Press, 1927.

Goulart, Simon. *A Learned Summary upon the Poems of William of Saluste, Lord of Bartas. . . .* Trans. Thomas Lodge. John Grismand, 1621.

Grossman, Marshall. "The Fruit of One's Labor in Miltonic Practice and Marxian Theory," *English Literary History* 59 (1992): 77–105.

Grotius, Hugo. *Of the Rights of Peace and War.* Trans. William Evats. M.W., 1682.

Hale, John. *Milton's Languages: The Impact of Multilingualism on Style.* Cambridge Univ. Press, 1997.

Halkett, John. *Milton and the Idea of Matrimony: A Study of the Divorce Tracts and Paradise Lost.* Yale Univ. Press, 1970.

Hammond, Gerald. *Fleeting Things: English Poets and Poems, 1616–1660.* Harvard Univ. Press, 1990.

Hanford, James Holly. "The Chronology of Milton's Private Studies," *Publications of the Modern Language Association* 36 (1921): 251–314.

Harding, Davis P. *The Club of Hercules: Studies in the Classical Background of Paradise Lost.* Illinois Studies in Language and Literature, vol. 50. Univ. of Illinois Press, 1962.

Hartman, Geoffrey. *Beyond Formalism: Literary Essays 1958–1970.* Yale Univ. Press, 1970.

Haskin, Dayton. *Milton's Burden of Interpretation.* Univ. of Pennsylvania Press, 1994.

Havens, Raymond Dexter. *The Influence of Milton on English Poetry.* Russell & Russell, 1961.

Hawkes, David. "The Politics of Character in John Milton's Divorce Tracts," *Journal of the History of Ideas* 62 (2001): 141–60.

Heninger, S. K. *Touches of Sweet Harmony: Pythagorean Cosmology and Renaissance Poetics.* Huntington Library, 1974.

Herford, C. H.; Simpson, Percy; Simpson, Evelyn, eds. *Ben Jonson.* 11 vols. Clarendon Press, 1935–47.

Heylyn, Peter. *Cosmography in Four Books.* P. C. T. Passenger, B. Tooke, and T. Sawbridge, 1682.

Hill, Christopher. *The English Bible and the Seventeenth-Century Revolution.* Penguin, 1993.

———. "Professor William B. Hunter, Bishop Burgess, and John Milton," *Studies in English Literature* 34 (1994): 165–93.

Hobbes, Thomas. *Hobbs's Tripos, in Three Discourses.* Matt. Gilliflower and Henry Rogers, 1684.

Hoerner, Fred. "'Fire to Use': A Practice Theory Approach to *Paradise Lost,*" *Representations* 51 (1995): 94–117.

Holinshed, Raphael. *Chronicles of England.* London, 1587.

Hooker, Richard. *Of the Laws of Ecclesiastical Polity.* John Windet, 1593.

Hoopes, Robert. *Right Reason in the English Renaissance.* Harvard Univ. Press, 1962.

Hoxby, Blair. *Mammon's Music: Literature and Economics in the Age of Milton.* Yale Univ. Press, 2002.

Hughes, Merritt Y. "'Lydian Airs,'" *MLN* 40 (1925): 129–37.

———. "The Arthurs of The Faerie Queene," *Études Anglaises* 6 (1953): 193–213.

Hughes, Merritt Y., et al. *A Variorum Commentary on the Poems of John Milton.* 4 vols. Columbia Univ. Press, 1970–75.

Hume, Patrick. *Annotations on Milton's 'Paradise Lost.'* J. Tonson, 1695.

Hunter, William B. "Milton's Power of Matter," *Journal of the History of Ideas* 13 (1952): 551–62.

———. "Milton's Arianism Reconsidered," *Harvard Theological Review* 52 (1959): 9–35.

———. "Milton Translates the Psalms," *Philological Quarterly* 40 (1961): 485–97.

Hunter, William B., gen. ed. *A Milton Encyclopedia.* 9 vols. Bucknell Univ. Press, 1978–83.

Hunter, William B., C. A. Patrides, and J. H. Adamson. *Bright Essence.* Univ. of Utah Press, 1971.

Huntley, Frank Livingstone. *Bishop Joseph Hall and Protestant Meditation in Seventeenth-Century England.* Medieval and Renaissance Texts and Studies, 1981.

Huttar, Charles A. "The Passion of Christ in *PR,*" *English Literary Notes* 19 (1982): 236–60.

Ingram, James. *An Inaugural Lecture on the Utility of Anglo-Saxon Literature.* Oxford Univ. Press, 1807.

Jebb, Richard. "*Samson Agonistes* and the Hellenic Drama," *Proceedings of the British Academy* 3 (1907–8): 341–48.

Jefferson, Thomas. *Papers of Thomas Jefferson.* Ed. Julian Boyd. 27 vols. Princeton Univ. Press, 1950–95.

Johnson, Samuel. *Lives of the English Poets.* Ed. George Birkbeck Hill. 3 vols. Clarendon Press, 1905.

———. *The Yale Edition of the Works of Samuel Johnson.* Ed. W. J. Bate and Albrecht B. Strauss. Yale Univ. Press, 1958.

Jones, Richard Foster. *Ancients and Moderns: A Study of the Rise of the Scientific Movement in Seventeenth-Century England.* Univ. of California Press, 1961.

Josephus, Flavius. *Works.* Trans. William Whiston. Armstrong and Plaskitt, 1832.

Kates, Judith A. *Tasso and Milton: The Problem of Christian Epic.* Associated Univ. Presses, 1983.

Kelley, Maurice. "Milton's Arianism Again Considered," *Harvard Theological Review* 54 (1961): 195–205.

Kendrick, Chistopher. *Milton: A Study in Ideology and Form.* Methuen, 1986.

Kermode, Frank. "*Samson Agonistes* and Hebrew Prosody," *Durham Univer. Journal* 14 (1953): 59–63.

Kerrigan, William. *The Prophetic Milton.* Univ. Press of Virginia, 1974.

———. "The Heretical Milton: From Assumption to Mortalism," *English Literary Renaissance* 5 (1975): 127–44.

———. *The Sacred Complex: On the Psychogenesis of Paradise Lost.* Harvard Univ. Press, 1983.

———. "The Irrational Coherence of *Samson Agonistes*," *Milton Studies* 22 (1986): 217–32.

———. "Gender and Confusion in Milton and Everyone Else," *Hellas* 2 (1991): 195–220.

———. "The Politically Correct *Comus*: A Reply to John Leonard," *Milton Quarterly* 27 (1993): 150–54.

———. "Of Scorn." In *The Wit to Know: Essays on English Renaissance Literature for Edward Tayler*, Eugene Hill and William Kerrigan, eds., pp. 143–63. George Herbert Journal Special Studies and Monographs, 2000.

———. "Complicated Monsters: Essence and Metamorphosis in Milton," *Texas Studies in Literature and Language* 46 (2004): 324–39.

Kerrigan, William, and Gordon Braden. *The Idea of the Renaissance.* Johns Hopkins Univ. Press, 1989.

Kirkconnell, Watson. *That Invincible Samson: The Theme of Samson Agonistes in World Literature with Translations of the Major Analogues.* Univ. of Toronto Press, 1964.

Klein, Robert. *Form and Meaning: Writings on the Renaissance and Modern Art.* Viking, 1979.

Klemp, Paul J. " 'Now Hid, Now Seen': An Acrostic in *Paradise Lost*," *Milton Quarterly* 11 (1977): 91–92.

Klibansky, Raymond, Erwin Panofsky, and Fritz Saxl. *Saturn and Melancholy.* Nelson, 1964.

Knoppers, Laura Lunger. "*The Readie and Easie Way* and the English Jeremiad." In *Politics, Poetics, and Hermeneutics in Milton's Prose*, David Loewenstein and James Grantham Turner, eds., pp. 213–25. Cambridge Univ. Press, 1990.

———. "Late Political Prose." Thomas N. Corns, ed., *A Companion to Milton*, pp. 309–25. Blackwell, 2002.

Krouse, F. Michael. *Milton's Samson and the Christian Tradition.* Princeton Univ. Press, 1949.

La Primaudaye, Pierre. *The Third Volume of the French Academie.* Trans. R. Doman. 1601.

Lactantius. *Divine Institutes*, Books 1–7. Trans. Sister Mary Francis McDonald. Catholic Univ. of America Press, 1964.

Lau, Beth. *Keats's Paradise Lost.* Univ. Press of Florida, 1998.

Laud, William. *A Relation of the Conference between William Laud . . . and Mr. Fisher the Jesuit, By Command of King James.* Richard Badger, 1639.

Leavis, F. R. *Revaluation: Tradition and Development in English Poetry.* George W. Stewart, 1947.

LeComte, Edward. *Milton's Unchanging Mind: Three Essays.* Kennikat Press, 1973.

Lee, Sidney, and C. T. Onions, eds. *Shakespeare's England: An Account of the Life and Manners of His Age.* 2 vols. Clarendon Press, 1916.

Leishman, J. B. *Translating Horace.* B. Cassirer, 1956.

Leonard, John. *Naming in Paradise: Milton and the Language of Adam and Eve.* Oxford Univ. Press, 1990.

———. "Saying 'No' to Freud: Milton's *A Mask* and Sexual Assault," *Milton Quarterly* 25 (1991): 129–40.

———. "Did Milton Go to the Devil's Party?" *New York Review of Books* 18 (July 2002): 28–31.

Lewalski, Barbara Kiefer. *Milton's Brief Epic: The Genre, Meaning, and Art of Paradise Regained.* Brown Univ. Press, 1966.

———. *Paradise Lost and the Rhetoric of Literary Forms.* Princeton Univ. Press, 1985.

———. "Milton and *De Doctrina Christiana*: Evidences of Authorship," *Milton Studies* 36 (1998): 203–28.

———. *The Life of John Milton: A Critical Biography.* Blackwell, 2000.

Lewis, C. S. *A Preface to Paradise Lost.* Oxford Univ. Press, 1942.

Lieb, Michael. *Milton and the Culture of Violence.* Cornell Univ. Press, 1994.

Loewenstein, David. *Milton and the Drama of History.* Cambridge Univ. Press, 1990.

———. "Treason Against God and State." In Stephen B. Dobranski and John Rumrich, eds., *Milton and Heresy,* pp. 176–98. Cambridge Univ. Press, 1998.

Lovejoy, Arthur O. "Milton and the Paradox of the Fortunate Fall," *English Literary History* 4 (1937): 161–79.

———. "Milton's Dialogue on Astronomy." In Joseph A. Mazzeo, ed., *Reason and Imagination: Studies in the History of Ideas, 1600–1800,* pp. 129–42. Columbia Univ. Press, 1962.

Low, Anthony. *The Blaze of Noon: A Reading of Samson Agonistes.* Columbia Univ. Press, 1974.

———. *The Georgic Revolution.* Princeton Univ. Press, 1985.

———. Review of Joseph Wittreich, *Interpreting Samson Agonistes, Journal of English and Germanic Philology* 86 (1987): 415-18.

Lynch, Kathleen M. *Jacob Tonson: Kit-Cat Publisher.* Univ. of Tennessee Press, 1971.

Macaulay, Thomas Babington. *Macaulay's Essay on Milton.* Ed. Herbert Augustine Smith. Ginn, 1998.

MacCaffrey, Isabel. *Paradise Lost as Myth.* Harvard Univ. Press, 1959.

MacCallum, Hugh. *Milton and the Sons of God: The Divine Image in Milton's Epic Poetry.* Univ. of Toronto Press, 1986.

MacKellar, Walter. *A Variorum Commentary on the Poems of John Milton,* vol. 4: *Paradise Regained.* Columbia Univ. Press, 1975.

McColley, Diane Kelsey. *Milton's Eve.* Univ. of Illinois Press, 1983.

———. *A Gust for Paradise: Milton's Eden and the Visual Arts.* Univ. of Illinois Press, 1993.

McColley, Grant. *Paradise Lost: An Account of Its Growth and Major Origins.* Packard and Co., 1940.

McIlwain, Charles Howard, ed. *The Political Works of James I.* Harvard Univ. Press, 1918.

Madsen, William. "From Shadowy Types to Truth." In Joseph H. Summers, ed., *The Lyric and Dramatic Milton,* pp. 94–114. Columbia Univ. Press, 1965.

Maimonides, Moses. *The Guide for the Perplexed.* Trans. M. Friedlander. Routledge, 1904.

Marcus, Leah. "The Milieu of Milton's *Comus*: Judicial Reform at Ludlow and the Problem of Sexual Assault," *Criticism* 25 (1983): 293–327.

———. *The Politics of Mirth: Jonson, Herrick, Milton, Marvell, and the Defense of Old Holiday Pastimes.* Univ. of Chicago Press, 1986.

Mariana, Juan de. *De rege et regis institutione.* 2nd ed. Mainz (?), 1611.

———. *General History of Spain.* Trans. John Stevens. London, 1699.

Martz, Louis. "*Paradise Regained:* The Meditative Combat," *English Literary History* 27 (1960): 223–47.

Masson, David. *The Life of John Milton.* 6 vols. Peter Smith, 1965.

Merrill, R. V. "Eros and Anteros," *Speculum* 19 (1944): 265–84.

Mieder, Wolfgang, ed. *A Dictionary of American Proverbs.* Oxford Univ. Press, 1992.

Milgate, W., ed. *The Satires, Epigrams and Verse Letters of John Donne.* Clarendon Press, 1967.

Miller, Leo. "John Milton's 'Lost' Sonnet to Mary Powell," *Milton Quarterly* 25 (1991): 102–7.

More, Sir Thomas. *Utopia.* In Burton Milligan, ed., *Three Renaissance Classics.* Charles Scribner's Sons, 1953.

Morse, C. J. "The Dating of Milton's Sonnet XIX," *TLS,* 15 Sept. 1961:620.

Moseley, C. W. R. D. *The Poetic Birth: Milton's Poems of 1645.* Scolar Press, 1991.

Moyles, R. G. *The Text of Paradise Lost: A Study in Editorial Procedure.* Univ. of Toronto Press, 1985.

Mueller, Janel. "Milton on Heresy," in *Milton and Heresy,* ed. Stephen B. Dobranski and John Rumrich, pp. 21–38. Cambridge Univ. Press, 1998.

Multhauf, Robert P. "Van Helmont's Reformation of the Galenic Doctrine of Digestion," *Bulletin of the History of Medicine* 29 (1955): 154–63.

Mundhenk, Rosemary K. "Dark Scandal and the Sun-Clad Power of Chastity: The Historical Milieu of Milton's *Comus,*" *Studies in English Literature* 15 (1975): 141–52.

Murray, Patrick. *Milton: The Modern Phase.* Barnes & Noble, 1967.

Nashe, Thomas. *An Almond for a Parrat.* Eliot's Court Press (?), 1589.

Nelson, Jr., Lowry. *Baroque Lyric Poetry.* Yale Univ. Press, 1961.

Newton, Isaac. *An Historical Account of Two Notable Corruptions of Scripture.* J. Green, 1841.

Nicolson, Marjorie Hope. "Milton and the Telescope," *English Literary History* 2 (1935): 1–32.

———. *The Breaking of the Circle: Studies in the Effect of the "New Science" on Seventeenth-Century Poetry.* Columbia Univ. Press, 1960.

Norbrook, David. *Writing the English Republic.* Cambridge Univ. Press, 1999.

Nuttall, A. D. *The Alternative Trinity: Gnostic Heresy in Marlowe, Milton, and Blake.* Clarendon Press, 1998.

Nyquist, Mary. "The Genesis of Gendered Subjectivity in the Divorce Tracts and *Paradise Lost,*" in Nyquist and Ferguson, eds., *Re-membering Milton,* pp. 99–127.

Nyquist, Mary, and Margaret Ferguson, eds. *Re-membering Milton: Essays on the Texts and Traditions.* Methuen, 1987.

O'Reilly, Mary Oates. "A New Song: Singing Space in Milton's Nativity Ode." In Eugene Hill and William Kerrigan, eds., *The Wit to Know: Essays on English Renaissance Literature for Edward Tayler,* pp. 95–116. George Herbert Journal Monographs, 2000.

Orgel, Stephen. *The Illusion of Power: Political Theater in the English Renaissance.* Univ. of California Press, 1975.

Pagel, Walter. "J. B. Van Helmont's Reformation of the Galenic Doctrine of Digestion—and Paracelsus," *Bulletin of the History of Medicine* 29 (1955): 564–66.

———. "Van Helmont's Idea on Gastric Digestion and the Gastric Acid," *Bulletin of the History of Medicine* 30 (1956): 524–36.

Panofsky, Irwin. *Studies in Iconology.* Harper & Row, 1967.

Parker, William R. *Milton's Debt to Greek Tragedy in Samson Agonistes.* Johns Hopkins Univ. Press, 1937.

———. "Milton's Last Sonnet," *RES* 21 (1945): 235–38.

———. "The Date of *Samson Agonistes,*" *PQ* 18 (1949): 145–66.

———. *Milton: A Biography.* 2 vols. Clarendon Press, 1968.

———. *Milton's Contemporary Reputation.* Haskell House, 1971.

Parry, Graham. *The Golden Age Restor'd: The Culture of the Stuart Court, 1603–42.* St. Martin's Press, 1981.

Paterson, James. *A Complete Commentary with Etymological, Explanatory, Critical and Classical Notes on Milton's "Paradise Lost."* R. Walker, 1744.

Patrides, C. A. "Milton and the Arian Controversy," *Proceedings of the American Philosophical Society* 120 (1976): 245–52.

Patrides, C. A., ed. *Milton's Lycidas: The Tradition and the Poem.* Univ. of Missouri Press, 1983.

Patterson, Annabel. " 'Forc'd fingers': Milton's Early Poems and Ideological Constraint." In C. J. Summers and T.-L. Pebworth, eds., *'The Muses Common-Weale': Poetry and Politics in the Seventeenth Century,* pp. 9–22. Univ. of Missouri Press, 1988.

———. "No Meer Amatorious Novel." In David Loewenstein and James Grantham Turner, eds., *Politics, Poetics, and Hermeneutics in Milton's Prose,* pp. 88–95. Cambridge Univ. Press, 1990.

Peck, Francis. *New Memoirs of the Life and Poetical Works of Mr. John Milton.* T. Evans, 1740.

Photius. *Bibliotheca.* Augustae Vindelicorum, 1606.

Pope, Elizabeth M. *Paradise Regained: The Tradition and the Poem.* Johns Hopkins Univ. Press, 1947.

Pordage, Samuel. *Mundorum Explicatium or the Explanation of an Hieroglyphical Figure.* T.R., 1661.

Prestige, G. L. *God in Patristic Thought.* SPCK, 1952.

Prince, F. T. *The Italian Element in Milton's Verse.* Clarendon Press, 1954.

Pritchard, William H. "Fish Contemplating a Bust of Milton," *New England Review* 22 (Fall 2001): 177–85.

Purchas, Samuel. *Purchas His Pilgrimage, or Relations of the World and the Religions Observed,* 3rd ed. William Stansby, 1617.

Quint, David. "Expectation and Prematurity in Milton's Nativity Ode," *Modern Philology* 97 (1999): 195–219.

Rajan, Balachandra. *Milton and the Seventeenth-Century Reader.* Barnes & Noble, 1966.

Ralegh, Sir Walter. *The Discoverie of Guiana.* Robert Robinson, 1595.

———. *History of the World.* William Iaggard, 1621.

Raleigh, Sir Walter. *Milton.* Edward Arnold, 1900.

Redfield, James. *Nature and Culture in the Iliad: The Tragedy of Hector.* Univ. of Chicago Press, 1975.

Richardson(s), Jonathan. *Explanatory Notes and Remarks on Milton's 'Paradise Lost.'* John James and Paul Knapton, 1734.

Richardson, Robert D. *Emerson: The Mind on Fire.* Univ. of California Press, 1995.

Ricks, Christopher. *Milton's Grand Style.* Oxford Univ. Press, 1963.

Ricoeur, Paul. *The Symbolism of Evil.* Trans. Emerson Buchanan. Harper & Row, 1967.

Ripa, Cesare. *Iconologia.* Donato Pasquardi, 1611.

Rohr-Sauer, Philipp von. *English Metrical Psalms from 1600 to 1660.* Poppen & Ortmann, 1938.

Rumrich, John Peter. "Milton's Concept of Substance," *ELN* 19 (1982): 218–33.

———. *Matter of Glory: A New Preface to Paradise Lost.* Univ. of Pittsburgh Press, 1987.

———. "Milton's God and the Matter of Chaos," *PMLA* 110 (1995): 1035–46.

———. *Milton Unbound: Controversy and Reinterpretation.* Cambridge Univ. Press, 1996.

———. "The Erotic Milton," *Texas Studies in Literature and Language* 41 (1999): 128–41.

———. "Samson and the Excluded Middle." In *Altering Eyes: New Perspectives on Samson Agonistes,* Mark R. Kelley and Joseph A. Wittreich, eds., pp. 307–32. Univ. of Delaware Press, 2002.

———. "Milton's *Theanthropos:* The Body of Christ in *Paradise Regained,*" *Milton Studies* 42 (2003): 50–67.

———. "The Provenance of *De Doctrina Christiana*: A View of the Present State of the Controversy." In Michael Lieb and John Shawcross, eds., *Milton and the Grounds of Contention,* pp. 214–33. Duquesne Univ. Press, 2004.

Rusca, Antonio. *De Inferno et Statu Daemonum.* Milan, 1621.

Rust, George. *A Letter of Resolution Concerning Origen and the Chief of His Opinions.* Columbia Univ. Press, 1933.

Rymer, Thomas. *The Tragedies of the Last Age.* Richard Tonson, 1678.

———. *Monsieur Rapin's Reflections on Aristotle's Treatise of Poesie.* T. Warren, 1694.

S., G. "Epistle Dedicatory," *The Dignity of Kingship Asserted.* H. Seile and W. Palmer, 1660.

Salmasius, Claudius. *Defensio Regia, pro Carolo I* [*Defense of Kingship, on behalf of Charles I*]. Sumptibus Regiis, 1650.

Samuel, Irene. "*Samson Agonistes* as Tragedy." In Joseph A. Wittreich, ed., *Calm of Mind,* pp. 335–58. Press of Case Western Reserve Univ., 1971.

Sandys, George. *Ovid's Metamorphosis Englished.* John Lichfield, 1632.

———. *Relation of a Journey.* Thomas Cotes, 1637.

Schwartz, Regina M. *Remembering and Repeating: Biblical Creation in Paradise Lost.* Cambridge Univ. Press, 1988.

Scot, Reginald. *The Discovery of Witchcraft.* Henry Denham, 1584.

Selden, John. *De Dis Syris.* Guilielmus Stansbeins, 1617.

———. *Uxor Hebraica.* Richardi Bishopii, 1646.

Sellin, Paul R. "Sources of Milton's Catharsis: A Reconsideration," *Journal of English and Germanic Philology* 60 (1961): 712–20.

———. "Milton's Epithet Agonistes," *Studies in English Literature* 4 (1964): 137–62.

Shawcross, John T. *Milton: The Critical Heritage.* 2 vols. Routledge, 1970–72.

Shumaker, Wayne. *Renaissance Curiosa.* Center for Medieval and Early Renaissance Studies, 1982.

Smith, G. C. Moore. "Milton and Randolph," *TLS,* 19 Jan. 1922:44.

Smith, Sir Thomas. *The Commonwealth of England.* John Smethwicke, 1609.

Speed, John. *History of Great Britian.* George Humble, 1632.

Sperling, Harry and Maurice Simon, trans. *The Zohar.* 5 vols. Soncino Press, 1949.

Spitzer, Leo. *Classical and Christian Ideas of World Harmony,* ed. A. G. Hatcher. Johns Hopkins Univ. Press, 1963.

Sprott, S. E. *John Milton: "A Maske," the Earlier Versions.* Univ. of Toronto Press, 1973.

Stone, Lawrence. *The Family, Sex and Marriage in England 1500–1800.* Harper & Row, 1977.

Studley, Marian H. "Milton and the Paraphrases of the Psalms," *Philological Quarterly* 4 (1925): 364–72.

Summers, Joseph, ed. *The Lyric and Dramatic Milton.* Columbia Univ. Press, 1965.

Svendsen, Kester. "Milton's Aery Microscope," *Modern Language Notes* 64 (1949): 525–27.

———. *Milton and Science.* Greenwood Press, 1969.

Tayler, Edward W. "Milton's Firedrake," *Milton Quarterly* 6 (1972): 7–10.

———. *Milton's Poetry: Its Development in Time.* Duquesne Univ. Press, 1979.

———. "Milton's Grim Laughter and Second Choices." In Roland Hegenbüchle and Laura Skandera, eds., *Poetry and Epistemology: Turning Points in the History of Knowledge,* pp. 72–93. Friedrich Pustet, 1986.

Taylor, Jeremy. *The Great Exemplar.* Francis Ash, 1649.

Tennyson, Hallam. *Alfred Lord Tennyson: A Memoir.* London: Macmillan, 1899.

Theodoret, et al. *Historia Ecclesiastica.* Petri le Petit, 1673.

Thorpe, James, ed. *Milton Criticism: Selections from Four Centuries.* Octagon Books, 1966.

Tilley, Morris Palmer. *A Dictionary of the Proverbs in England in the Sixteenth and Seventeenth Centuries.* Univ. of Michigan Press, 1966.

Toland, John. *The Life of John Milton.* John Darby, 1699.

Turner, James Grantham. *One Flesh: Paradisal Marriage and Sexual Relations in the Age of Milton.* Oxford Univ. Press, 1987.

Tuve, Rosemond. *Images and Themes in Five Poems by Milton.* Harvard Univ. Press, 1957.

Tweedie, Fiona, et al. "The Provenance of *De Doctrina Christiana,* attributed to John Milton: A Statistical Investigation," *Literary and Linguistic Computing* 13 (1998): 77–87.

Ulreich, John C. " 'Incident of All Our Sex': The Tragedy of Dalila." In Julia M. Walker, ed., *Milton and the Idea of Woman,* pp. 185–210. Univ. of Illinois Press, 1988.

Voltaire. *La Henriade.* Chez Veuve Duchesne, 1787.

Walker, D. P. *The Decline of Hell: Seventeenth-Century Discussions of Eternal Torment.* Univ. of Chicago Press, 1964.

Webster, Charles. *The Great Instauration: Science, Medicine and Reform 1626–1660.* Gerald Duckworth, 1975.

Welsford, Enid. *The Court Masque.* Cambridge Univ. Press, 1927.

West, Robert. *Milton and the Angels.* Univ. of Georgia Press, 1955.

Williams, Arnold. *The Common Expositor: An Account of the Commentaries on Genesis 1527–1633.* Univ. of North Carolina Press, 1948.

Williams, R. F., ed. *The Court and Times of Charles the First.* 2 vols. H. Colburn, 1848.

Wilson, F. P. *The Plague in Shakespeare's London.* 2nd ed. Oxford Univ. Press, 1963.

Wilson, F. P., ed. *The Oxford Dictionary of English Proverbs.* Clarendon Press, 1970.

Winny, James, ed. *The Frame of Order: An Outline of Elizabethan Belief Taken from Treatises of the Late Sixteenth Century.* Allen & Unwin, 1957.

Wittkower, Rudolf, and Margot Wittkower. *Born Under Saturn.* Norton, 1963.

Wittreich, Joseph A. *Interpreting Samson Agonistes.* Princeton Univ. Press, 1986.

———. *Feminist Milton.* Cornell Univ. Press, 1987.

Woodhouse, A. S. P. "Notes on Milton's Early Development," *University of Toronto Quarterly* 13 (1943–44): 66–101.

Woods, Suzanne. "How Free Are Milton's Women?" In Julia M. Walker, ed., *Milton and the Idea of Woman,* pp. 15–31. Univ. of Illinois Press, 1988.

Wright, George. "Hendiadys and *Hamlet,*" *Publications of the Modern Language Association* 96 (1981): 168–93.

Wright, Thomas. *The Passions of the Minde in Generall.* Valentine Simmes, 1604.

Yates, Frances A. *Giordano Bruno and the Hermetic Tradition.* Vintage, 1969.

Zagorin, Perez. *John Milton: Aristocrat and Rebel.* D. S. Brewster, 1992.

Index

This index includes names of historical persons and authors to whom Milton refers, or who are mentioned in the accompanying text and footnotes. Names of biblical and mythological characters are omitted. Milton's name and the titles of his works are not indexed; however, his Milton and Phillips relatives are included.

Abrams, M. H., 99
Adams, John, 1022
Adamson, J. H., 262
Addison, Joseph, 271, 276, 278, 314n.575, 559n.230, 595n.356–58
Aeschylus, 49n.99, 296n.48, 301n.198–99, 385–86n.32–41, 411n.858–59, 414n.958–60, 708
Aesop, 170, 822
Agricola, Julius, 957
Agrippa, Menenius, 822, 1264
Aistulphus, 819
Alcaeus, 226n.22, 340–41n.554, 685n.257
Alcibiades, 181n.23
Alcuin, 863–64
Alexander the Great, 145, 145n.10, 181, 181n.25, 391n.212, 532n.505–10, 532n.526, 655, 655n.196, 665, 665n.31–34, 665n.39–42, 666n.86, 673n.302, 685, 799, 802, 911
Allen, D. C., 8n.23–27, 29n.227–28, 757n.1637
Amesii, Guilielmi (William Ames), 864n.52, 1138, 1319
Andrewes, Lancelot, 177–79, 213, 835
Anne of Cleves, 915
Anselm, 367n.212
Antiochus Epiphanes, 458n.371–72, 668, 866n.58, 1046
Antipater, 621n.358, 661
Antoninus (Roman emperor), 1008
Apelles, 791
Apollinarius (father and son), 936, 1206
Apollonius of Perga, 1052
Apollonius of Rhodes, xxv, 245n.33, 342n.592–94, 357n.1017, 780, 781, 1080
Appius Claudius, 1081
Apuleius, 98n.1004–8, 98n.1011
Aquinas, Thomas, 158n.12–14, 667n.123–24, 897n.164, 917n.239, 939, 1150n.23
Aratus, xxv, 976
Archilochus, 214, 214n.20, 932
Archimedes, 160
Aretino, Pietro, 940, 940n.67
Ariosto, Ludovico, 75n.322–26, 81n.515, 132, 277, 294n.16, 315n.583–84, 373n.444–97, 374n.459, 504n.243–44, 694n.541, 840, 841n.28
Aristophanes, 629n.629, 931, 942
Aristotle, 13n.53–58, 14n.90, 41n.1, 181, 181n.25, 218, 519n.44–45, 685, 685n.251, 701, 707, 803, 816, 882n.115, 941, 943n.80, 975, 976n.52, 977, 978, 1005, 1150, 1198, 1204, 1207
Athenian Constitution, 1134n.115
Categories, 13n.53–58, 14n.87–88
Ethics, 364n.108
History of the Animals, 21n.68, 491n.487–89
Metaphysics, 218
Meteorology, 402n.557
Nichomachean Ethics, 600n.531, 687n.297, 816, 823, 915, 941n.74, 1024n.3

Aristotle (*cont'd*)
On Generation, 578n.891–92
On The Heavens, 36n.5, 383n.718
Physics, 36n.7, 435n.580–82, 574n.740–41, 1249
Poetics, 268, 269, 703, 708n.15, 841n.28, 977
Politics, 816, 1024n.3, 1030, 1129
Rhetoric, 977n.63
Arius, 262
Arminius, Jacobus, 263, 264, 366n.187–90, 891, 941, 1158n.43, 1172n.69, 1259n.232, 1268n.243, 1271n.245
Arnold, Elias, 707n.3
Arnold, Matthew, 16, 270, 274, 275, 361n.39
Atahualpa (Atahalipa), 597
Aubrey, John, xxiii–xxx, 173n.15, 251, 288n.18, 699, 971n.8
Auerbach, Erich, 557n.183
Augustine (saint), 493n.557, 712n.93, 758n.1664–66, 984, 1206, 1208, 1239
City of God, 481n.156, 482n.172, 575n.791, 654n.152
Confessions, 443n.856–58, 1017n.66
De Genesi ad Litteram, 482n.176, 998, 998n.33
De Trinitate, 486n.302
Sermon, 831n.102
Augustus (Octavius Caesar), 707, 799, 932
Aylmer, Brabazon, 253, 783

Babb, Lawrence, 258, 260, 499n.70499n.70
Bacon, Francis (viscount St. Albans), 943, 948, 952, 952n.122
Advancement of Learning, 836n.2
New Atlantis, 943n.82
Novum Organum, 967
Of Truth, 161
Wisdom of the Ancients, 221n.20
Baillie, Robert, 164n.12, 345n.664–66
Baldwin, E. C., 686n.270
Banister, Richard, 361n.25
Barberini, Francesco (cardinal), 766, 777n.1, 778, 779, 1092n.89
Barker, Arthur, 18, 862n.33
Baroni, Leonora, 200–2
Barrow, Samuel, 252, 285, 286–87
Basil the Great (saint), 295n.21, 937, 1034
Bastwick, John, 805
Bauman, Michael, 263, 372n.383, 1137, 1138, 1142n.6, 1188n.94
Beaumont, Joseph, 534–35n.598–612, 633–34
Becket, Thomas à, 820n.55
Bede (saint), 816n.38
Behn, Aphra, 93n.864
Bembo, Pietro, 149, 840
Ben Gersom, Levi, 909
Bennett, Joan S., 862n.33
Benson, William, 16
Bentley, Richard, 253–54, 411n.836, 471n.797
Berry, Boyd M., 494n.594
Berryman, John, 100
Betjeman, John, 271
Beza, Theodore, 899, 901, 1180, 1185, 1226, 1251, 1300, 1301
Binyon, Lawrence, 124
Bion, 100n.8, 109n.189, 233
Blake, William, 276, 278
Blasi, Vincent, 926
Bloom, Harold, 277
Blount, Walter, 925
Boccaccio, Giovanni, 219n.4, 355n.965
Boddy, Margaret, 110
Bodin, Jean, 1124n.60
Boesky, Amy, 1091n.84
Boethius, 60n.22, 482n.172, 667n.113–24
Boiardo, Matteo Maria, 347n.714–18, 674n.337–44
Boone, Laila P., 273
Botticelli, Sandro, 791n.23
Braden, Gordon, 137, 140
Bradshaw, John, 1070, 1096
Brahe, Tycho, 499–500n.83
Branthwaite, Michael, 776n.7
Breasted, Barbara, 63
Bridges, Robert, 701
Bridgewater, 1st earl of (John Egerton), 52, 61–62, 63, 65, 65n.31
Broadbent, J. B., 400–1n.515–22, 540n.780
Brooks, Cleanth, 108n.153
Brown, Cedric C., 62, 63
Browne, R. C., 46n.141
Browne, Thomas
Christian Morals, 646–47n.401
Pseudodoxia Epidemica, 27n.173, 101n.28, 759n.1696
Religio Medici, 295n.21, 362n.47, 481n.156
Urn Burial, 730n.677

Browne, William, 30n.239, 63, 73n.253, 110n.192
Browning, Robert, 270
Bruno, Giordano, 502n.148–49
Bryan, Francis, 940, 940n.68
Bucer, Martin, 987, 990, 1051, 1089, 1323
Buchanan, George, 1040, 1041, 1085
Buckingham, 1st duke of (George Villiers), 288n.47, 323n.1
Buonmattei, Benedetto, 1092
Burton, Henry, 805
Burton, Robert, 421n.100–13, 535n.634
Bush, Douglas, 159n.13, 254
Butler, Samuel, 273
Buxtorf, Johann, 878

Caedmon, 269, 270
Calamy, Edmund, 845
Callicles, 915
Callimachus, 103n.77, 374n.473, 841, 230n.38, 372n.412–15, 779
Calvin, John, 263, 265, 366n.187–90, 557n.175–81, 871, 878, 899n.168, 956, 957, 1040, 1051, 1180n.82, 1231n.172, 1248n.104, 1259n.232, 1268n.243, 1287n.264, 1323
Institutes, 90n.787, 1030n.29, 1148n.15, 1156n.37, 1162n.48, 1220n.152
Camden, William, 102n.52, 108n.161, 108n.162, 236, 240, 890n.138, 1132
Cameron, Johannes, 1014
Campanella, Tommaso, 821n.57
Campbell, Gordon, 57, 262, 1137, 1138
Cardan, Jerome, 689n.382
Carew, Thomas, 88n.737–54, 93n.864
Carey, John, 6, 32n.34–35, 69n.139, 72n.243, 172, 193n.89, 218, 222n.35, 634, 635n.16, 645n.354, 696n.584, 703–4, 759n.1695, 1139, 1282
Carneades, 932
Carvilius, 996
Casella, 150
Castelvetro, Ludovico, 977
Castlehaven, 2nd earl of, 63
Catherine of Aragon, 915
Catherine of Braganza, 1119, 1119n.35
Cato, xxv, 782, 932, 975
Catullus, 188n.105, 247, 248n.1, 932
Cavell, Stanley, 855–56
Cebes, 974
Celsus, Anlus Cornelius, 975
Cerdogni family, 98n.1023
Chamberlayne, Edward, 1063n.17
Chambers, A. B., 255, 596n.388
Channing, William Ellery, 261–62
Chapman, George, 1064n.19, 1119n.38
Chappell, William, xxv, 102n.36, 172, 173n.15
Chares, 790
Charlemagne, 315, 674, 841, 863n.49, 1037
Charles I (king of England), 145, 146n.1, 146n.5–6, 152, 154, 180, 248n.3, 264, 285, 310n.446–52, 332n.306, 387n.94, 824n.73, 825n.79, 842n.37, 862n.34, 923, 928, 949n.103, 960n.163, 1021, 1022, 1025n.5, 1025n.8, 1027, 1027n.17, 1028, 1028n.22, 1041, 1041n.72, 1042–46, 1057, 1059–60n.2, 1060–69, 1071, 1074n.6, 1079, 1088, 1090, 1093, 1095, 1096, 1099, 1104, 1105n.124, 1113n.109, 1114, 1115n.14, 1116, 1128n.81, 1130n.93, 1130nn.95–96, 1131n.100
Charles II (king of England), 153n.9, 154, 251, 285, 315n.596–99, 1021, 1067n.37, 1069, 1071, 1105n.125, 1111, 1119n.35, 1133n.107 1135n.117
Charles IX (king of France), 1049
Charles V (Holy Roman emperor), 1040
Charles X (king of Sweden), 160, 160n.8
Charondas, 977
Chaucer, Geoffrey, 41, 229n.34, 237n.117, 738n.971, 819, 820
Canterbury Tales, 50, 50n.109, 814–15, 867n.64
Cheke, John, 148
Cherubini, Alessandro, 777
Chester, earl of, 1038n.59
Chilperic (king of France), 819
Chimentelli, Valerio, 1092
Christian II (king of Denmark), 1049
Christina (queen of Sweden), 1077, 1088, 1091, 1098–99
Chrysippus, 892
Chrysostom, John (saint), 931, 1004, 1033, 1312
Cicero, 707, 765, 892–93, 931, 932, 937, 967, 976, 977, 1071, 1073n.3
Against Verres, 622n.406, 950, 950n.110
De Officiis (On Duties), 386n.56, 664n.23
De Oratore, 977n.63
De Senectute, 600n.535–37
Of Divination, 647n.435

Cicero (*cont'd*)
On Invention, 992
Laelius: On Friendship, 646–47n.401
On Behalf of Milo, 893n.154
On the Chief Good and Evil, 86n.663
On the Laws, 1029n.26
On the Nature of the Gods, 1035n.46
Oration against Piso, 893
Paradoxa Stoicorum, 685n.234
Philippics, 446n.42, 1069
Pro Plancio, 386n.56
Somnium Scipionis, 222n.35
Tusculan Disputations, 47–56, 653n.139, 665n, 686n.273
Cincinnatus, Lucius Quinctius, 662, 662n.446
Cirillo, Albert R., 259, 702
Clark, Andrew, xxiii
Clarke, Deborah Milton (daughter of poet), xxv, xxviii, 161
Claudian, 213n.221, 219n.4
Claudius (Roman emperor), 934
Clement of Alexandria, 940
Cleombrotus, 374
Clodius, 893
Coke, Edward, 159, 159n.1, 948n.101
Coleridge, Samuel Taylor, 269, 275, 280, 700, 701
Colet, John, 968, 973n.30
Collins, William, 16
Coltellini, Agostino, 1092
Columbus, Christopher, 549
Columella, xxv, 975
Comenius, Johan Amos, 967, 968, 971n.5
Comestor, Peter, 917, 917n.241
Condell, Henry, 34n.10
Constantine (emperor), 239, 863, 1140n.2
Constantius, 904
Conti, Natale, 477n.17–20
Coolidge, John S., 621n.350
Copernicus, 258, 377n.556–61, 379n.587, 403n.592–97, 499n.70, 501n.133–40, 501nn.129–30, 502n.163–66, 572n.668–87, 870n.75
Corns, Thomas N., 806, 1138
Cortés, Hern·n, 597n.407
Costobarus, 904
Cowley, Abraham, 158, 266, 332n.306, 426n.285, 644
Cowper, William, 340n.552, 348n.748, 353n.915–16
Craig, John, 1040
Crane, Hart, 270
Cranmer, Thomas, 811, 830, 830n.99
Crashaw, Richard, 31
Crescentius Nomentanus, 1109
Critolaus, 932
Cromwell, Oliver, xxix, 138, 152, 153, 154, 155, 158, 285, 681n.123–25, 699, 730n.695, 805, 1021, 1045n.84, 1065n.26, 1070, 1071, 1086, 1097, 1099–1100, 1101–4, 1105, 1108, 1109n.131, 1118n.31, 1122n.47, 1126n.72
Cromwell, Richard, 1127n.78
Crump, Galbraith, 703
Cudworth, Ralph, 262
Culverwell, Nathanael, 684n.228
Cumberland, Richard, 702
Curius Dentatus, Manius, 662, 1090
Curry, Walter Clyde, 486n.313–19
Cyrus the Great, 621n.348, 672, 825, 1100

Dandolo, Enrico, 1081
Daniel, John, 88n.737–54
Danielson, Dennis, 256, 264, 280, 624n.475, 891n.146, 1158n.43
Dante, 124, 138, 258, 274, 850, 977
Inferno, 65n.37, 132, 257, 296n.66–67, 297n.70, 305n.302, 342n.595, 504n.243–44, 567n.511–15
Paradiso, 105n.113–29, 106n.126, 443n.856–58, 483n.225
Purgatorio, 150, 150n.12–14
Darbishire, Helen, xxiii, 6, 146, 158, 159, 159n.12, 160n.1–2, 251, 252, 259, 281, 385n.32–41, 477n.28–30, 632, 700, 1137
Dati, Carlo, 238, 1092
Davenant, William, 266, 1119n.38
Davies, John, 421n.100–13
Davies, Stevie, 281
De Brass, Henry, 766, 781–82
De Thou, Jacques-Auguste, 1041n.73, 1049n.97
Decius (Roman emperor), 936
Defoe, Daniel, 262
Dekker, Thomas, 954n.133
Demaray, John, 63, 96n.964
Demetrius the rhetorician, 909

Democritus, 789
Demosthenes, 686n.270, 977, 1071, 1073n.3, 1088
Dennis, John, 267
Derby, dowager countess of (Alice Spenser Egerton), 52–57, 62
Desborough, John, 1105
Digges, Thomas, 679n.40–41
Diocletian (Roman emperor), 936
Diodati, Charles, xxiv, 18n.1, 142, 172, 190–93, 232–42, 393n.268–71, 765, 767–68, 772–75, 798n.6, 1092n.92
Diodati, John, 1093, 1231n.172
Diodati, Theodore, 215
Diodorus Siculus, 229n.26, 342n.592–94, 389n.160–65, 393n.275–79
Diogenes the Cynic, 87n.708, 932
Dion (Dio Cassius), 132, 1031
Dion Prusaeus, 929
Dionysius Afer, xxv
Dionysius (bishop of Alexandria), 937
Dionysius I of Syracuse, 942
Dionysius II of Syracuse, 931, 1081n.29
Dionysius of Helicarnassus, 147n.7, 976, 996
Dionysus the elder, 707
DiSalvo, Jacqueline, 703
D'Israeli, Isaac, 1069
Dixon, R. W., 701
Dobranski, Stephen B., 925
Donatus, 967
Doni, Giovanni Battista, 778
Donne, John, 36, 93n.864, 138, 177, 775n.1
"An Anatomy of the World," 100n., 499–500n.83
Biathanatos, 758n.1664–66
Devotions, 688n.338
"The Extasie," 547n.1048
Holy Sonnets, 137
A Hymn to Christ, 51n.160
"A Hymn to God the Father," 436n.607
La Corona, 137
Satires, 146n.4
"A Valediction Forbidding Mourning," 375n.481–83, 600n.535–37
Dorian, Donald C., 238n.127
Drayton, Michael
England's Heroical Epistles, 88n.737–54
Polyolbion, 15n.91, 91n.824–41, 102n.54
Dryden, John, xxviii, xxx, 252, 253, 285, 288n.18, 288n.47, 305n.302
Critical and Miscellaneous Prose Works, 268
Essays, 271, 708n.14
Hind and Panther, 411n.845–47
The State of Innocence, 252, 407–8n.741, 515n.624–25
Du Bartas, Guillaume de Salluste, 19n.15, 476n.1
Du Haillan, Bernard de Girard, 1037–38
Du Moulin, Peter, xxix, 1070
Duncan, Joseph E., 628n.587
Duns Scotus, John, 939, 1005
Dunster, Charles, 632, 747n.1288, 752n.1461–66
Dyer, Edward, 684n.223
Dzelzainis, Martin, 1022, 1035n.45, 1036n.51, 1040n.68, 1048n.94, 1049n.97, 1054n.124

Eckermann, Johann Peter von, 700
Edward II (king of England), 1063
Edward the Confessor, 862, 862n.38, 1038n.59
Edward VI (king of England), 811, 983, 987
Edwards, Jonathan, 257
Edwards, Karen L., 489n.415–16, 491n.464, 491n.474, 505n.255
Edwards, Thomas, 164
Egerton, Alice, 62, 64, 150
Egerton, Alice Spenser (dowager countess of Derby), 52–57, 62
Egerton, John (1st earl of Bridgewater), 52, 61–62, 63, 65, 65n.31
Egerton, John (viscount Brackley), 62, 64, 150
Egerton, Thomas (Lord Keeper), 52
Egerton, Thomas, 62, 64, 150
Ehrenreich, Barbara, 345n.664–66
Eleutherius, 816
Eliot, T. S., 108, 177, 266, 273, 275, 296n.63
Elizabeth I (queen of England), 209, 209n.104, 824n.69, 829, 890n.138, 1041, 1132
Elledge, Scott, 99, 254, 341n.568, 473n.862
Ellwood, Thomas, 631, 700
Emerson, Ralph Waldo, 99–100, 271, 275, 280
Emilius, Paulus, 916
Empedocles, 374
Empson, William, 254, 257, 280, 348n.774–77, 400–1n.515–22, 414n.958–60, 491n.150–55, 704

Ennius Quintus, 312n.509–14
Epicurus, 687, 687n.299, 931, 937
Epiphanius, 940
Erasmus, Desiderius (Gerhard Gerhards), 1089, 1180, 1250, 1300, 1301
Essex, 2nd earl of (Robert Devereaux), 775n.1
Essex, 3rd earl of (Robert Devereaux), 145
Este, Leonora d', 201n.1
Euclid, 160, 1052
Euripides, 49nn.99–100, 145, 145n.12–14, 707, 708, 760n.1745–48, 841, 936n.43, 977
  Alcestis, 163n.2, 976n.56
  Andromache, 932
  Bacchae, 296n.63, 397n.402, 774n.3
  Electra, 145n.12–14
  Hecuba, 738n.953
  Heraclidae, 1031, 1084n.45
  Hippolytus, 578n.888–95
  Ion, 246, 355n.962
  Medea, 87n.703, 985n.1
  Orestes, 725n.499–501, 740n.1039–40, 786, 1084n.45
  Phoenissae (Phoenician Women), 303n.263, 710n.1–2
  Supplices (The Suppliants), 133, 927, 1248
  Trojan Women, 296n.66–67
Eusebius, 937, 940
Eustochium, 937
Evans, J. Martin, 519n.58–69, 534–35n.598–612, 540n.780
Evans, Margery, 63
Evelyn, John, 530n.446

Fabricius, Gaius Luscinus, 662
Fabricius, Germanus, xxix
Fagius, Paulus, 867–68, 869, 870, 871, 913, 914, 1089
Fairfax, Maria, 152
Fairfax of Cameron, 3rd lord (Thomas Fairfax), xxix, 138, 152, 1070, 1100–1, 1105n.124
Fallon, Robert, 1071
Fallon, Stephen M., 79n.463, 264, 366n.183, 465n.589–94, 470n.749–59, 565n.441–55, 853, 891n.146, 1071, 1138
Fawkes, Guy, 198–99, 205, 212n.194
Featley, Daniel, 989, 989n.12
Felltham, Owen, 103n.71
Felton, Nicholas, 213
Ferguson, Margaret, 280
Ferrara, duke of (Alfonso II), 841, 841n.30
Ficino, Marsilio, 49n.93, 241n.191, 514n.591–92
Fink, Zera S., 519n.44–45
Fish, Stanley, 277–78, 453, 453n.248, 465n.595, 486n.302, 704, 925
Fixler, Michael, 123–24
Flaccus, 932
Flannagan, Roy, 254, 623n.432, 703, 704
Fleetwood, Charles, 1070, 1104
Fletcher, Giles, 633, 696n.587
Fletcher, Harris F., 270
Fletcher, John, 63
Fletcher, Phineas
  Apollyonists, 344n.650–59, 347n.746
  Piscatory Eclogues, 104n.103
  The Purple Island, 344n.650–59, 568n.529
Flosdorf, J. W., 95n.917
Fogle, French, 270
Ford, John, 649n.498
Ford, Thomas, 477n.26
Fowler, Alastair, 254, 259, 270, 326n.81, 330n.220, 334n.352–53, 338n.478, 339n.511–13, 345n.678–79, 348n.774–77, 375n.481–83, 393n.262–63, 399n.478, 409n.776–77, 412n.870–71, 414n.958–60, 426n.285, 447n.55, 448n.91, 455n.310–15, 470n.761, 484n.252, 543n.893, 559n.243–45, 561n.311, 562n.328–29, 569–70n.578–84, 573n.693, 633
Foxe, John, xxviin.7, 811n.16
Francini, Antonio, 238, 1029
Francis (saint), 208
Frescobaldi, Piero, 1092
Frost, Robert, 271
Froula, Christine, 282
Frye, Northrop, 267, 514n.559, 633, 749n.1377

G.S., 1069
Gaddi, Jacopo, 1092
Galen, 800
Galilei, Galileo, 257–59, 260, 304n.288–91, 379n.588–90, 425, 502n.148–49, 950
Gallagher, Philip J., 281, 507n.350, 703
Gallus, Cornelius, 228
Gama, Vasco da, 596n.399–400

Gascoigne, George, 30n.239
Gaskell, Phillip, 62
Gauden, John, 1026n.16, 1027n.17, 1057, 1065n.23
Gellius, Aulus, 996
Geoffrey of Monmouth, 91n.824–41, 92n.831, 95n.923, 134, 175n.73, 230n.46, 239n.164, 240n.166, 816n.38
Gibson, James, 1041
Gilbert, Allan H., 294n.11–12, 453n.248, 671n.252
Gilbert, Sandra, 281
Gildas, 1039
Gill, Alexander, xxiv, 218, 225, 270, 765, 768
Gilles, Pierre, 1042n.75
Giustiniani, Bernardo, 775
Goethe, Johann Wolfgang von, 700, 701
Goldberg, Jonathan, 63
Gomarus, Franciscus, 1323
Goodman, Christopher, 1051
Goodman, Geoffrey, 215
Gosson, Stephen, 732n.748
Gostlin, John, 203
Goulart, Simon, 493n.557
Graham, James, 1021, 1022
Gratian, Johannes, 917
Gregory II (pope), 1063n.16
Gregory III (pope), 819
Gregory Nazianzen (saint), 707–708
Gregory of Nyssa (saint), 1206
Gregory XIII (pope), 1062n.15
Greville, Fulke, 577n.849–50
Greville, Robert (2nd lord Brooke), 960–61, 961n.165
Grossman, Marshall, 40
Grotius, Hugo, 299n.149–50, 776n.7, 867, 905, 908, 909, 914, 1091
Guarini, Gianbattista, 707n.1
Gubar, Susan, 281

Haak, Theodore, xxix
Habingdon, Thomas, 1039n.65
Hakewill, George, 215
Hale, John, 273, 699n.1, 758n.1660–1707, 776, 776n.2
Halkett, John, 855
Hall, Joseph (bishop), 163, 845, 846n.4, 848n.22, 928n.4, 1094n.98
Hall, Robert, 845
Hamilton, 1st duke of, 1104–5
Hammond, Gerald, 162, 163n.8
Hanford, James Holly, 85n.638, 303n.253, 775n.7
Hannibal, 154, 154n.4, 959
Harding, Davis P., 68n.131
Hardy, Thomas, 361n.39
Harrington, James, 1123n.54, 1126n.70, 1127n.77
Hartlib, Samuel, 967, 968, 969, 970, 980
Hartman, Geoffrey, 505n.255
Haskin, Dayton, 157, 836n.3, 1298n.274
Havens, Raymond, 16, 40
Hawkes, David, 1024n.3
Hayward, John, 811
Hazlitt, William, 271, 276, 277, 280
Heinsius, Nicholas, 1097n.107
Helmont, Jean-Baptiste van, 431n.439–43
Heming, John, 34n.10
Heninger, S. K., 57
Henrietta Maria (queen of England), 1119, 1119n.35
Henry III (king of England), 1063
Henry VII (king of England), 964
Henry VIII (king of England), 821n.57, 915, 940, 985n.3, 1042n.76, 1059
Heraclitus, 786
Herbert, George, 31, 775n.1
  "The Answer," 138
  "The Collar," 914n.226
  "Complaining," 730n.676
  "The Forerunners," 519n.44–45
  Prayer, 160–65
  "The Sacrifice," 61n.28
Herbert, Mary, 448
Herford, C. H., 478n.72, 688n.338
Hermes Trismegistus, 49, 49n.88, 220, 220n.33
Hermogenes of Tarsus, 977
Herodotus, 5n.46, 29n.220, 108n.164, 222n.60, 229, 229n.22, 354n.943–45, 672n.288, 825n.77, 967
Herrick, Robert, 36, 158
  "The Bell-man," 49n.83
  Hesperides, 100n.8
  Of Angels, 298n.116
  "The Rose," 256

Hesiod, xxv, 255, 320n.740, 793, 794n.2, 976
Theogony, 9n.47, 48n.48, 97n.982–83, 214n.32, 216n.9, 294n.15, 296n.50–52, 297n.73–74, 325n.69, 344n.650–59, 406n.714–19, 445n.2–11, 472n.833–34, 474n.871, 787
Works and Days, 393n.267, 406n.714–19
Hesse, landgrave of (Philip I), xxiv, 1040
Heylyn, Peter, 373, 394n.280–85
Hill, Abraham, xxix
Hill, Christopher, 110, 123, 1138
Hill, Eugene, 629n.629
Hippocrates, 800n.12
Hobbes, Thomas, xxx, 465n.589–94, 465n.603, 470n.749–59
Hobson, Thomas, 35–37, 435n.580–82
Hobson (captain), 146
Hoerner, Fred, 583n.1075
Holinshed, Raphael, 820nn.55–56, 1038n.62
Holste, Lukas, 766, 777–79, 1092
Homer, 81n.515, 85n.638, 93n.869, 173, 226, 229, 251, 253, 267, 268, 269, 287, 291, 293, 294, 298n.116, 327n.113, 361, 361n.35, 394, 417n.1012, 445n.2–11, 453n.248, 456n.323–27, 519n.44–45, 592n.259–62, 685–86, 799, 835, 851, 931, 937, 1085n.53, 1088
Iliad, 93n.877, 163n.13–14, 204n.13, 204n.15, 204n.23, 211n.178, 259, 295n.27–28, 295n.33, 296n.45, 297n.73–74, 301n.198–99, 305n.302, 307n.376, 314n.575, 320n.740, 321n.767–75, 324n.43, 325n.69, 334n.352–53, 338n.489, 339n.528–69, 343n.628, 345n.681, 351n.868, 356n.1005, 361n.35, 402n.555, 407n.735, 415n.980–83, 416n.988, 416n.997, 433n.509, 438n.673, 447n.63–65, 456n.332–33, 456n.335–36, 459n.416, 465–66n.614–27, 518n.13–19, 584n.1086–1104, 597n.412, 603n.638–73, 730n.694, 742n.1122, 767n.2, 785n.2, 792, 840, 840n.27, 892, 1064, 1082, 1082n.40, 1171n.67
Odyssey, 9n.40, 13n.48, 41n.10, 49n.100, 63, 66n.51, 66n.66–77, 73n.253, 73n.254, 86n.675–76, 92n.838, 142n.14, 175n.88, 193n.74–76, 207n.60, 302n.240–41, 303n.263, 304n.292–94, 316n.609, 343n.614, 351n.876–79, 357n.1020, 394n.301, 409n.778, 428n.341, 518n.13–19, 530n.439–44, 547n.1029–32, 565n.441–55, 737n.934, 792n.30, 803n.21, 840, 840n.27, 883, 892, 962n.172, 981, 1171n.67
Honigmann, E.A.J., 139, 145, 152n.12
Honorius, 904
Hooker, Richard, 451, 641n.220, 835
Hoopes, Robert, 446n.42, 613–14n.84
Hopkins, Gerard Manley, 701
Hopkins, J., 407–8n.741
Horace, 11, 138, 156, 977, 1086n.65
De Arte Poetica (Ars Poetica), 374n.471, 708n.14, 1085
Epistles, 133, 148n.3, 193n.71, 214n.20, 228n.4, 303n.253
Epodes, 68n.129, 100n.11, 801n.13
Odes, 13n.53, 16–17, 45n.135, 90n.797, 101n.31, 177n.5, 181n.19, 191, 191n.27, 192n.48, 227n.36, 235n.65, 245n.25, 294n.16, 328n.174, 339n.528–69, 340n.531, 340–41n.554, 347n.716, 353n.924, 370n.318–19, 383n.730, 399n.478, 400n.487–88, 428n.356, 434n.557, 476n.1, 759n.1696
Satires, 133, 343n.614, 393n.255, 791n.25, 1086nn.59–60
Horwood, A. I., 169
Howell, James, 1116n.22
Hoxby, Blair, 1112
Hudson, Henry, 561n.291–93
Hughes, Merritt Y., 7, 29n.227–28, 82n.534, 83n.187, 102n.52, 136, 151, 159n.13, 195n.89, 210n.150, 254, 338n.496–502, 633, 758n.1664–66, 893n.154, 1067n.35
Hume, Patrick, 253, 313n.532, 317n.642, 318n.674, 326n.81, 340n.533–34, 345n.665, 350n.833, 350n.842, 373n.432, 380n.620–21, 394n.311, 416n.987, 460n.429, 461n.479, 525n.270, 558n.217–18, 560n.281
Hunter, William B., 110, 262, 263, 360n.1–55, 557n.175–81, 1138, 1143n.7, 1145n.10, 1188n.94, 1207n.125, 1272n.248
Huntley, Frank Livingstone, 100n.
Huss, John, 933, 957, 1081n.33
Huttar, Charles A., 270

Ignatius of Loyola (saint), 816
Ingram, James, 270

Irenaeus, 940
Isocrates, 147, 147n.7, 924, 929, 929n.7, 978

James I (king of England), 146n.1, 199, 200, 205, 209, 210, 212, 323n.1, 775n.1, 817n.41, 1041, 1042n.76, 1091, 1135n.117, 1138
Jebb, Richard, 701
Jefferson, Thomas, 263, 264, 1022
Jerome of Prague, 957
Jerome (saint), 294n.11–12, 484n.252, 867, 909, 937, 940, 1206
John (king of England), 820
John of Austria, 824n.69, 890n.138
Johnson, Samuel, 251, 273, 281, 701, 702, 1093n.94
Jones, Richard Foster, 215
Jonson, Ben, 36, 37, 41, 45, 99, 138, 158, 229n.30
  Discoveries, 478n.72
  Epigram 76, 41n.11
  Every Man out of his Humor, 728n.600
  His Excuse for Loving, 96n.970–71
  Hymenaei, 407n.741–43
  "Inviting a Friend to Supper," 160n.6
  Love Restored, 44n.105
  Masque of Beauty, 52
  Masque of Blackness, 52, 92n.834
  "On My First Daughter," 11n.71
  "On My First Son," 11n.71
  Pleasure Reconciled with Virtue, 63, 66n.56, 76n.373–74
  The Satyr, 44n.103
  Timber, 688n.338
  "To Heaven," 423n.165
  "To the Immortal Memory . . . of . . . Cary and . . . Morison," 599–600n.502–507, 692n.475–76
  To the Memory of . . . Shakespeare, 34n 1–2, 708n.16
Josephus, Flavius, 909
  Jewish Antiquities, 470n.761, 612n.38–62, 618n.255, 661n.423, 668n.160–61, 744n.1197, 904
  Wars of the Jews, 340n.533–34, 569n.560–68, 694n.147–48, 1066n.31
Julian the Apostate (Flavius Claudius Julianus), 936, 1017
Julius Caesar, 621n.358, 665, 1062, 1113n.1
Junius, Franciscus, 269, 1185, 1223, 1224n.161, 1225, 1231, 1249n.211, 1309, 1327
Justin Martyr, 1018
Justinian (Roman emperor), 908, 977, 1013, 1014, 1031
Juvenal, 68, 248, 338n.496–502, 1113n.1

Kates, Judith A., 267
Keats, John, 270, 296n.63, 361n.39
Kelley, Maurice, 261, 360n.1–55, 1138, 1139, 1140n.1, 1141n.4, 1150n.25, 1159n.44, 1178n.80, 1188n.94, 1196n.109, 1295n.272, 1319n.304
Kemp, Will, 68n.116
Kendrick, Christopher, 925
Kepler, Johannes, 378n.583, 499–500n.83, 501n.124, 870n.75
Kermode, Frank, 701
Kerrigan, William, 95n.917, 273, 278, 281, 298n.98, 356n.1013, 457n.345–53, 532n.526, 567n.494–99, 567n.508–9, 605n.707, 695n.583, 748n.1342, 767n.1, 1083n.43, 1091n.84
Kimchi, David, 909
King, Edward, 99, 105n.109, 232, 1091n.82
Kirkconnell, Watson, 700
Klein, Robert, 142n.5
Klemp, Paul J., 532n.510–14
Klibansky, Raymond, 47n.24
Knoppers, Laura Lunger, 1111, 1112
Knox, John, 948, 1040, 1051
Krouse, F. Michael, 702

La Primaudaye, Pierre, 22n.71
Labeo, Attius, 785n.2
Lactantius, 241n.187, 312n.509–14
Laertius, 976
Lambert, John, 1102n.121, 1104–5
Lancaster, 2nd earl of (Thomas Plantagenet), 1063
Landor, Walter Savage, 273
Latimer, Hugh, 811, 830, 830n.99
Lau, Beth, 296n.63
Laud, William (archbishop), 805, 809n.5, 812n.23, 828n.94, 844n.45, 923, 948n.97, 962n.178, 1063n.18

Lawes, Henry, 53, 62, 67n.84–88, 80n.494, 84n.619, 131, 150
Lawrence, Edward, 158–69, 1105n.127
Lawrence, Henry, 158, 1105
Lawrence (saint), 831
Leavis, F. R., 63, 275
LeComte, Edward, 6
Lee, Margaret. *See* Ley, Margaret
Lee, Sidney, 68n.116
Legate, Bartholomew, 1138
Leishman, J. B., 17
Leo III (emperor), 818, 819n.48, 1038, 1063n.16
Leo X (pope), 933, 933n.32
Leonard, John, 69n.139, 90n.787, 92n.853, 149n.10, 156n.12–14, 242n.213, 254, 256, 278, 315n.596–99, 317n.656, 328n.160, 334n.368, 338n.478, 339n.511–13, 349n.809, 358n.1055, 362n.49, 364n.119, 415n.980–83, 432n.478, 452n.199, 457n.357, 484n.139, 508n.373, 513n.572, 559–60n.254–323, 562n.342–45, 565n.431–36, 573n.693, 635n.16, 645n.354, 656n.244, 690n.411, 730n.695, 733–34n.800–802, 735n.841–42, 758n.1671
L'Estrange, Roger, 477n.26, 1130n.97
Leunclavius, Johann, 1038
Lewalski, Barbara Kiefer, 267, 362n.56–417, 633, 639n.147, 640n.188, 656n.244, 769, 770n.1, 1057, 1111, 1138, 1254n.223
Lewis, C. S., 261, 262, 266, 453n.236, 541n.835
Ley, James (earl of Marlborough), 147, 147n.1, 147n.5–6
Ley, Margaret, 146–47
Libanius the Sophist, 1017
Lieb, Michael, 281, 738n.953
Lily, William, 973
Livy (Titus Livius), xxix, 329n.199, 655n.199, 822n.63, 933, 959n.159, 1032
Lloyd, David, 477n.26
Locke, John, 261–62, 1180n.82
Loewenstein, David, 1057, 1071, 1317n.300
Lombard, Peter, 917, 1005
Longinus, Cassius, 977
Loudon, 1st earl of, 1045, 1045n.85
Louis the Pious (emperor), 1037–38
Louis XIII (king of France), 824, 824n.73
Louis XIV (king of France), 387n.75
Lovejoy, A. O., 499n.78, 624n.475
Lovelace, Richard, 36, 158
Low, Anthony, 633, 702, 703, 750n.1389
Lucan, 27n.179, 354n.939, 568n.526–27, 659n.340, 695n.563–71
Lucilius, 932
Lucretius, xxv, 467n.673, 976
De Rerum Natura, 294n.16, 302n.230–35, 337n.438, 352n.894–910, 352n.900–903, 353n.911, 515n.624–25, 687n.317, 932
Lully, Raymond (Lullius), 936, 936n.42
Luther, Martin, 557n.175–81, 810n.11, 957, 1051, 1059, 1180n.83, 1312
Lycurgus, 799, 931, 977, 1124n.56
Lydgate, John, 47n.18
Lynch, Kathleen M., 253

Macaulay, Thomas B., 262
MacCaffrey, Isabel, 461n.478
MacCallum, Hugh, 696n.584
Machiavelli, Niccolò, 94n.906, 155n.8, 899
MacKellar, Walter, 633, 686n.270, 686n.598
Macrobius, 222n.35, 433n.509
Madsen, William, 702
Maecenas, 228
Maimonides, Moses, 878
Maitland of Lethington, William, 1040
Malory, Thomas, 851n.36
Malvezzi, Virgilio, 816
Manilius, Marcus, xxv, 253, 892, 976
Manso, Giovanni Battista, 227–32, 240, 408n.760–65, 1092
Mantuan, 170
Marcus, Leah, 63, 95n.917, 825
Mariana, Juan de, 315n.586–87
Marino, Giambattista, 227, 229, 230, 408n.760–65
Marius, Gaius, 1125
Marlborough, earl of (James Ley), 147, 147n.1, 147n.5–6
Marlowe, Christopher, 46n.151–52, 88–89n.738, 385n.20–23, 391n.207
Marshall, Stephen, 845
Marshall, William, 242, 1057
Marston, John, 52, 53
Martial, 213n.221, 248, 248n.6, 501n.553, 708, 789, 1089n.73
Martin V (pope), 933
Martz, Louis, 633

Marvell, Andrew, xxx, 152, 252, 285
Horatian Ode, 153
"On Mr. Milton's Paradise Lost," 285, 287–89
The Rehearsal Transpos'd, 285
"The Garden," 685n.248
"To the King," 379n.588–90
Mary of Guise, 1040
Mary (queen of England), 209, 209n.104, 811n.16, 867n.67
Mary (queen of Scots), 824n.69, 1041, 1068, 1068n.41
Masson, David, 103n.77, 1021, 1097n.107, 1109n.131
Mather, Cotton, 424n.221–23
Maximilian I (Holy Roman emperor), 1049
Mazzoni, Giacomo, 977
McColley, Diane Kelsey, 281, 428n.333–36
McColley, Grant, 499n.70
Mede, Joseph, 102n.36
Mela, Pomponius, 975
Melicertes, 93, 93n.876, 108n.164
Memmius, 932
Menander, 932
Merrill, R. V., 877
Metellus, Lucius Caecilius, 1081
Middleton, Thomas, 954n.133
Mieder, Wolfgang, 684n.220–21
Milgate, W., 146n.4
Miller, Leo, 145
Milo, 893n.154
Milton, Christopher (brother of poet), xxiv, 62
Milton, Deborah. *See* Clarke, Deborah Milton (daughter of poet)
Milton, Elizabeth Minshull (third wife of poet), xxvi
Milton, John, Sr. (father of poet), xxiii, xxiv, xxvii, 3, 99, 156, 220–24, 839, 900n.171, 1090–91
Milton, Katharine Woodcock (second wife of poet), xxvi, 161–62, 251
Milton, Mary (daughter of poet), xxviii
Milton, Mary Powell (first wife of poet), xxv–xxvi, 145, 146, 161–62, 251, 281, 853, 900n.171
Milton, Sara (mother of poet), xxiii, 99, 1090, 1091
Minturno, Antonio Sebastiano, 707n.1
Mithridates, 665, 665n.35–36
Monck, George, 1111, 1113nn.1–3
Montague, Edward, 1105
Montaigne, George ("Bishop Mountain"), 813n.25
Montaigne, Michel Eyquem de, 803n.22
Monteagle, 4th baron, 212n.194
Montemayor, Jorge de, 943
Montezuma (Motezume), 597
Montfort, Simon de (earl of Leicester), 1063
Montrose, 1st marquis of, 1067n.37
More, Alexander, xxix, 248, 1070, 1079, 1085n.50, 1086n.65, 1088, 1089–90, 1093, 1096–98, 1099
More, Henry, 59n.12, 502n.148–49
More, Thomas, 51n.160, 943
Morland, Michael, 155
Morse, C. J., 156
Moschus, 101n.15, 102n.39–44, 109n.189, 233
Moseley, C.W.R.D., 18
Moyles, R. G., 253
Mueller, Janel, 1143n.8
Multhauf, Robert P., 431n.439–43
Mundhenk, Rosemary K., 63
Murray, Patrick, 275
Musculus, Wolfgang, 1323

Naevius, 932
Nashe, Thomas, 15, 451n.166–68
Nelson, Lowry, Jr., 19n.19
Nero (Roman emperor), 679n.51, 940, 1026
Newcomen, Matthew, 845
Newton, Isaac, 261–62, 1180n.82
Newton, Thomas, 254, 276, 316n.620, 329n.199, 340–41n.554, 396n.354, 402n.55, 405n.661, 408n.756, 453n.229–36, 453n.248, 456n.329, 468n.699, 501n.130, 564n.409, 593n.270, 730n.695
Nicander, 976
Nichols, James, 1158n.43
Niclaes, Hendrik, 886n.125
Nicolson, Marjorie Hope, 59n.12, 258, 260, 304n.288–91
Norbrook, David, 1071, 1111
Norfolk, 4th duke of, 824n.69
Norwood, Alfred, 131

Nuttall, A. D., 276
Nyquist, Mary, 280, 282

Oldenburg, Henry, 712n.68–79
Olympiodorus, 904
Oppian, xxv, 976
Orbilius, 1086
O'Reilly, Mary Oates, 18
Orgel, Stephen, 63
Origen, 841, 905, 908
Ormond, duke of (James Butler), 1067n.38
Otto III (Holy Roman emperor), 1109n.133
Overton, Robert, 1070, 1105n.124
Ovid (Publius Ovidius Naso), 173n.21, 174n.69, 191, 191n.20, 765, 933
Amores, xxvii, 179n.68
Ars Amatoria, 174n.69, 192n.51, 656n.222–23, 725n.499–501
Fasti, 71n.221–25, 176n.9, 236n.88, 660n.356, 1238, 1238n.194
Heroides, 174n.63
Ibis, 214, 214n.18
Letters from the Black Sea, 792
Metamorphoses, 8n.8–9, 8n.25–27, 22n.84, 38n.20, 46n.147, 50n.124, 66n.48, 66n.51, 68n.131, 73n.256–59, 75n.341, 86n.661, 91n.816, 93nn.874–75, 93n.879, 102n.39–44, 102n.58–63, 108n.164, 149n.5–7, 150n.4, 174n.57, 176n.7, 181n.11, 183n.81, 186n.40, 187n.66, 188n.91, 195n.31, 195n.37, 211n.172, 217n.33, 218n.62, 222n.48, 236n.88, 302n.230–35, 311n.478–82, 318n.686–88, 340n.542–46, 344n.650–59, 345n.659–61, 352n.894–910, 373n.444–97, 393n.268–71, 393n.273–74, 399n.460–69, 399n.480–89, 416n.998, 462n.521, 467n.673, 492n.508–10, 494n.579, 524n.240, 567n.511–15, 568n.526–27, 568n.531, 569n.559–60, 589n.131, 606n.738–53, 815n.31, 848n.23, 930n.15
Tristia, 180n.1, 190n.8, 191n.20
Owen, John, 153, 1220n.152
Oxford, 17th earl of, 177n.11

Pagel, Walter, 431n.439–43
Pagett (doctor), xxx
Palgrave, Francis Turner, 15
Palmer, Herbert, 854, 923, 985n.4, 986, 986n.6, 987, 987n.8, 988, 988n.10, 1022, 1051, 1051n.112, 1052, 1052n.116, 1053, 1054n.125
Panofsky, Irwin, 216n.14
Paraeus, David, 707, 841, 871, 889n.135, 894, 901, 917, 918–19, 1004, 1051
Paris, Matthew, 1038
Parker, Samuel, 285, 477n.26
Parker, William Riley, 148, 161, 699, 700, 701, 702, 767n.1, 768n.1, 768n.3, 769, 1070
Parry, Graham, 63
Paterson, James, 254
Patrides, C. A., 99, 262
Patterson, Annabel, 40, 853, 876n.91
Pau, Adrian de, 1098
Paulet, Charles, 38n.24
Pausanias, 470n.762–64, 914n.227
Peele, George, 63
Pelagius, 1239
Pembroke, 6th earl of, 700
Pepin (king of France), 819
Perkins, William, 889n.135, 899, 912
Persius, 247, 785n.2
Peter Martyr (Pietro Martire Vermigli), 1038–39, 1323
Petrarch, 105n.113–29, 106n.126, 132, 138, 139, 140, 143, 144, 818, 819, 850
Petronius Arbiter, 940
Phalereus, Demetrius, 977
Philaras, Leonard, 361n.23–24, 766, 779–81, 1082n.38, 1098
Philip II (king of Spain), 1041
Philip of Macedonia, 147n.7, 532n.505–10, 655
Philippicus, 818
Philips, Katherine, 433n.490
Phillips, Anne (niece of poet), 6–11
Phillips, Anne (sister of poet), xxvii, 6, 7, 11, 62, 220
Phillips, Edward (nephew of poet), xxiii, xxv, xxvii, xxviii, xxix, 6, 146, 152, 153, 158, 159n.12, 251, 252, 385n.32–41, 631–32, 633, 634, 699, 700, 1093n.94, 1094n.96, 1137
Phillips, Elizabeth (niece of poet), 7
Phillips, John (nephew of poet), xxiii, xxv, 1093n.94, 1094n.96
Philo, 996

Photius, 904
Pickering, Gilbert, 1105
Pindarus (Pindar), 145, 145n.10, 191, 685n.257, 758n.1660–1707, 841
Pythian Odes, 33n.56, 301n.198–99301n.198–99, 773n.2
Pitt, Moses, xxvi
Pizarro, Francisco, 597n.409
Placaeus of Saumur, 1184
Placidia, 904
Plato, 49, 64n.3, 198n.5, 218, 220, 220n.35, 262, 374, 411n.848, 493n.557, 629n.629, 684n.228, 685, 687, 687n.295, 798, 816, 851, 892, 931, 943–44, 976, 977, 978, 993
Apology, 686n.275, 802n.20, 989n.14, 1099n.112
Critias, 943n.82
Gorgias, 915, 977n.63
Laws, 892n.148, 897, 942, 944n.83, 974n.36, 975n.42, 996
Phaedo, 9n.40, 64n.6, 79n.461–75, 80n.470–75, 97n.976, 219n.19, 374n.473, 1080n.26
Phaedrus, 21n.48, 399n.478, 775n.5, 798, 798n.6, 877n.95, 942n.79, 977n.63, 1083n.41
Politics, 313n.550, 943n.80
Protagoras, 600n.531
Republic, 45n.136, 55n.63, 55n.65, 57n.1, 220n.35, 313n.550, 849n.29, 851n.38, 942n.78, 943n.80, 974n.36
Symposium, 181n.23, 241n.191, 875, 942n.79, 993n.24
Timaeus, 356n.1013, 435n.583, 943n.82, 976n.53, 1080n.26
Plautus, Titus Maccius, 932, 937, 1086
Pliny the Elder, 189n.116, 534n.581, 712n.87, 975
Pliny the Younger, 509n.419–21
Plutarch, 22n.89, 311, 707, 803, 974, 976
Aemilius Paulus, 916n.236
"Isis and Osiris," 955n.140
Life of Alexander, 145n.10, 181n.25, 532n.505–10, 655n.196
Life of Caesar, 665n.39–42
Lives, 303n.263, 799n.9
Lysander, 145n.12–14
The Obsolescence of Oracles, 22n.89, 27n.173, 648n.456
Pompey, 1166
Polanus, Amandus, 1276–77
Polybius, 829, 901n.174
Pompey, 665, 933
Pope, Alexander, 104n.79, 295n.26, 278
Pope, Elizabeth M., 633, 645n.354, 659n.340
Popilius, Gaius, 901
Porphyrius, 933
Pound, Ezra, 275
Prestige, G. L., 1149n.17
Prince, F. T., 141n.10, 274, 701
Pritchard, William H., 278
Proclus, 933
Protagoras, 931
Prynne, William, 165n.47, 805, 1026n.16
Pseudo-Dionysius, 158n.12–14
Ptolemy, 236n.90, 258, 260, 375n.481–83, 377n.556–61, 379n.587, 403n.592–97, 437n.623, 499n.70, 500n.84, 502n.163–66, 572n.668–87
Pulci, Luigi, 937n.48
Purchas, Samuel, 393n.273–74, 394n.280–85
Pyrrhus, 154, 154n.4, 958, 1081
Pythagoras, 192, 192n.59, 319n.711–12, 956, 978

Quint, David, 18
Quintilian, 148, 148n.11, 967, 974, 975n.42, 1053n.121
Quintus of Smyrna (Quintus Calaber), xxv, 1087, 1087n.66
Quirinus, 207

Raimond (count of Toulouse), 1098
Rajan, Balachandra, 262
Ralegh, Walter, 163n.1, 319n.720, 597n.411, 612n.27
Raleigh, Walter Alexander, 274
Randolph, Thomas, 42n.24, 87–88n.710–36, 776n.5
Ravenscroft, Thomas, 3
Read, Herbert, 275
Regulus, Marcus Attilius, 662
Richard II (king of England), 1038
Richardson, Jonathan, 254, 259, 262, 267–68, 385n.30, 431n.438–39, 479n.88, 699
Richardson, Robert D., 100, 271
Richelieu, cardinal-duc de, 267

Ricks, Christopher, 254, 274, 275, 486n.302, 529n.404–11, 536n.644–45
Ricoeur, Paul, 256
Ridding, Richard, 175–76
Ridley, Nicholas, 811, 830, 830n.99
Rienzi, Cola di, 1109
Ripa, Cesare, 10n.54
Rivers, George, 15n.91
Rivers, Nizel, 15n.91
Rivetus (André Rivet), 871, 891, 893
Robinson, Edwin Arlington, 270
Robinson, Humphrey, 776n.5
Rochester, 2nd earl of, 93n.864
Rohr-Sauer, Philipp von, 123–24
Rouse, John, 243, 246–47, 776n.5
Rudolph I (king of Germany), 775
Rumrich, John Peter, 256, 278, 299n.141, 334n.355, 549n.1115, 704, 767n.1, 1079n.24, 1092n.92, 1138, 1141n.4, 1149n.17, 1197n.112, 1201n.117, 1254n.223
Rupert (prince), 1131
Rusca, Antonio, 338n.496–502
Ruskin, John, 105n.119
Russell (tailor), xxv, xxvi
Rust, George, 79n.459–63
Rutherford, Samuel, 164
Rymer, Thomas, 266–67

Sallust, 766, 781, 782
Salmasius, Claudius (Claude de Saumaise), xxvi, 186n.30, 210n.143, 247–48, 1071, 1074nn.4–5, 1077, 1078–79, 1080, 1083, 1084, 1085–86, 1088, 1089
  Defensio Regia, 161n.11, 247, 248n.1, 1048n.94, 1069, 1070, 1073, 1074, 1074n.4, 1088, 1097, 1117n.28
Salzilli, Giovanni, 226–27
Samuel, Irene, 704
Sandys, George, 91n.816, 308n.392–96, 310n.446–52, 342n.592–94, 352n.894–910
Sannazaro, Jacopo, 53n
Santa Clara, Franciscus, 810
Sappho, 226n.22, 685n.257
Sardanapalus, 768
Sarpi, Pietro (Padre Paolo), 821, 933, 933n.29
Savoy, duke of (Charles Emmanuel II), 155
Saxony, duke of (Mauritz I), 1040
Scaevola, Mutius, 329n.199
Scholasticus, 818, 818n.44, 936
Schwartz, Regina, 256, 1201n.117
Scipio, Publius Cornelius (Scipio Africanus Major), 532, 655, 655n.199, 665, 667, 1101
Scipio the Younger, 932
Scipione, Alberto, 777
Scot, Reginald, 327n.109
Scudamore, James, 776n.7
Scudamore, John (viscount Sligo), 776n.7, 1091
Secundus, Johannes (Jan Everaerts), 103n.69
Seissel, Claude de, 1029
Sejanus, 681, 681n.95
Selden, John, 308n.404, 309n.438–41, 310n.446–52, 917, 938, 1094, 1232–33
Seleucus, 391n.212
Seleucus Nicator (Nisibis Seleucia), 672
Sellin, Paul R., 699n.1, 707n.1
Seneca, Lucius Annaeus, 707, 708n.12, 765
  Ad Marciam, 599n.502–507
  De Consolatione, 599n.502–507, 646–47n.401
  Hercules Furens, 134, 1034–35
  Hercules Oetaeus, 340n.542–46
  Hippolytus, 87n.710–36
  Natural Questions, 975
  On the Brevity of Life, 800n.12
  Thyestes, 573n.688
Servius, 8n.23–27
Shakespeare, William, 7n.1–2, 7n.6–7, 34, 41, 45, 64n.5, 229n.30, 253, 254, 270, 281, 306n.337, 398n.447, 925
  All's Well That Ends Well, 638n.94–95
  Antony and Cleopatra, 450n.156, 455n.306–7, 491n.474, 629n.615–20
  As You Like It, 15
  Coriolanus, 109n.171, 450n.156, 822n.63
  Cymbeline, 239n.164
  Hamlet, 30n.232–34, 78n.432, 300n.158, 303n.254–56, 497n.15, 541n.845, 575n.782, 684n.223
  Julius Caesar, 570n.617, 1062n.11
  King Henry the Fifth, 317n.653, 384n.1–12, 455n.306–7, 459n.410, 491n.490, 599n.496
  King Henry the Fourth, Part I, 304n.176, 356n.1001
  King Henry the Fourth, Part II, 355n.967, 599–600n.502–507

King Lear, 89n.768–74, 451n.166–68
King Richard the Second, 345n.673
King Richard the Third, 344n.658, 443n.860, 691n.422–23
Love's Labor's Lost, 80n.478, 730n.676
Macbeth, 316n.615, 345n.662, 529n.404–11, 599n.496
Measure for Measure, 316n.620, 342n.595, 492n.510, 663n.478
The Merchant of Venice, 96n.964
A Midsummer Night's Dream, 30n.232–34, 322n.783–84, 326n.91, 439n.721, 567n.508–9
Much Ado About Nothing, 407n.741–43
Othello, 316n.620, 400n.505–35, 407n.741–43, 1053n.121
Romeo and Juliet, 44n.102, 50n.122, 76n.373–74, 368n.259, 375n.496
Sonnets, 138, 139, 157n.1, 302n.230, 348n.778–87, 467n.657, 843n.41
The Tempest, 94n.897, 458n.371–72, 848n.26
Troilus and Cressida, 455n.310–15
Twelfth Night, 524n.240, 599n.496, 1062n.14
The Winter's Tale, 106n.142–50, 658n.295
Shawcross, John T., 271, 276, 278, 631, 632, 702
Shumaker, Wayne, 689n.382
Sidney, Algernon, 1105
Sidney, Philip, 53n, 88n.737–54, 266, 842n.36, 943
Sigonius, Carlo, 819
Sikes, George, 154
Simmons, Samuel, 252, 253, 291
Simon Magus, 1054, 1115
Sirluck, Ernest, 925, 948n.97, 949n.105, 953n.129, 975n.42
Skinner, Cyriack, xxiii, xxx, 159–61
Skinner, Daniel, 1137
Sleidan (Johann Philippson), 1040
Smart, John S., 140n.1–2
SMECTYMNUUS, 163, 180, 845, 1094n.98
Smith, G. C. Moore, 87–88n.710–36
Smith, Thomas, 1039
Socrates, 64n.6, 181, 181n.23, 327n.113, 399n.478, 667, 686, 687, 798n.6, 802, 851, 875, 878n.99, 915, 942n.79, 974, 989, 1099n.122, 1189n.96
Socrates Scholasticus. *See* Scholasticus
Solinus, Julius, 975
Solon, 977, 992, 1124n.56
Sophocles, 49nn.99–100, 701, 703, 708, 841, 977
Electra, 133
Oedipus at Colonus, 599n.502–507, 710n.1–2
Oedipus the King, 837, 837n.10
Trachiniae, 340n.542–46, 976n.56
Sophron Mimus, 942
South, Robert, 477n.26
Southampton, 3rd earl of, 177n.11
Speed, John, xxvii, 820nn.55–56, 824n.71
Spenser, Edmund, 25n.155, 34n.4, 50n.112, 50n.120, 81n.515, 90n.786–87, 91n.822, 138, 252, 253, 270, 277, 819n.51, 939
Astrophel, 100n.8–9
Colin Clouts Come Home Again, 52, 53
Epithalamion, 512n.519
The Faerie Queene, 15n.91, 16n.3, 50n.112, 65n.37, 76n.373–74, 91n.817, 91n.822, 98n.999, 98n.1002, 98n.1011, 302n.226, 318n.678, 318n.686–88, 344n.650–59, 355n.965, 393n.267, 406n.690, 440n.750, 446n.33–35, 456n.321, 461n.484, 502n.148–49, 530n.439–44, 635n.1–2, 660n.361, 664n.25, 841n.28, 851n.36, 858n.8
Four Hymns, 514n.591–92
The Shepheardes Calender, 22n.74, 22n.89, 105n.113–29, 229n.34, 651n.27, 877n.96
Tears of the Muses, 52, 53
Spitzer, Leo, 57
Sprott, S. E., 62
Spurstow, William, 845
Starkey, George, 477n.26
Statius, 197n.84, 355n.965
Stevens, Wallace, 270–71, 277
Stewart, Adam ("A.S."), 164, 164n.8
Stone, Lawrence, 510n.450
Strickland, Walter, 1105
Studley, Marian H., 123–24
Suetonius, 707n.1, 934n.33, 1062n.11
Suleiman I (Turkish sultan), 566n.457
Sulla, Lucius Cornelius, 1113n.1, 1125
Summers, Joseph, 750n.1389
Sumner, Charles Richard, 261, 1139, 1282
Surrey, 1st earl of, 270
Svendsen, Kester, 26n.164, 421n.100–13, 490n.429–30, 491n.487–89, 549n.1101, 679n.40–41
Sydenham, William, 1105

Tacitus, Cornelius, 102n.54, 103n.71, 680–81n.90, 781, 816, 940n.67, 957n.147
Tamburlaine (Temir), 596, 596n.389
Tarquinius, 1032
Tasso, Torquato, 81n.515, 201, 201n.1, 226, 227, 228, 229, 230, 267, 268, 977, 1092
Gerusalemme Liberata, 276, 315n.583–84, 346n.708–11, 565n.441–55, 597n.412, 659n.340, 840, 840n.27, 841
Heroic Sonnets, 138, 140
Le Fenice, 243n.187
Tayler, Edward W., 19n.19, 100n.1, 106n.130, 472n.833–34, 584n.1086–1104, 703, 750n.1389, 759n.1692, 759n.1695
Taylor, Jeremy, 445
Tennyson, Alfred, 16, 270, 301n.210–15
Tennyson, Hallam, 301n.210–15
Terence, 739n.1008
Tertullian, 682n.139, 867, 1030, 1206
Thales, 931
Thamyris, 361
Theocritus, 80n.494, 100n.8, 101n.15, 102n.50, 104n.85–87, 109n.189, 233n.1, 848n.23, 976
Theodoret (bishop of Cyrus), 1017n.67
Theodosius II (emperor), 908, 1031
Theognis of Megara, 599n.502–507
Theophrastus, 975
Thévenin, François, 766, 779
Thomason, Catharine, 151
Thomason, George, 151
Thomson, James, 270
Thorpe, James, 251, 271, 273, 275, 276, 277, 280
Thucydides, 313n.550, 343n.636–37, 1238
Thyer, Robert, 281, 752n.1461–66
Tiberius, 668, 680–81, 680–81n.90, 681n.95
Tilley, Morris Palmer, 75n.322–26, 76n.362, 139n.5–7, 522n.171, 544n.926, 554n.53, 663n.478, 670n.294
Tillyard, E.M.W., 765
Tillyard, Phyllis B., 765
Timaeus of Locri, 976, 976n.53
Timoleon of Corinth, 1081
Todd, Henry J., 254, 281, 420n.79, 447n.63–65, 515n.618–19, 525n.270, 561n.312–13, 743n.1132–40, 747n.1288, 752n.1461–66
Toland, John, xxiii, 262
Tomkys, Thomas, 848n.26
Tonson, Jacob, 253
Tovey, Nathaniel, xxv, xxvn.3
Townshend, Aurelian, 63
Trajan, 1031
Tremellius, John Immanuel, 1185n.90, 1249n.211, 1327
Turner, James Grantham, 281, 282, 514n.575, 543n.901, 853
Tuve, Rosemond, 18, 27n.173–236

Ulreich, John, 704
Urban VIII (pope), 321n.767–75
Ursinus, Zacharius, 1323
Ussher, James (archbishop), 831, 1094n.98

Vane, Henry (elder), 154
Vane, Henry (younger), 154–55, 730n.695, 805
Varro, xxv, 975
Vatablus, Franciscus, 1231
Vere, Horace, 177n.11
Vergil, 81n.515, 104n.85–87, 173, 181n.19, 226, 228n.4, 251, 253, 267, 287, 291, 293, 394n.304–8, 417n.1012, 519n.44–45, 835
Aeneid, 21n.48, 41n.3, 54n.21, 73n.255, 79n.463, 82n.534, 93n.865, 104n.96, 163n.13–14, 170n.3, 176n.17, 184n.119, 211n.172, 219n.19, 221n.25, 234n.23, 264, 270, 294n.5, 295n.27–28, 297n.73–74, 297n.84, 299n.125–27, 302n.230–35, 304n.292–94, 305n.302, 307n.376, 321n.767–75, 322n.783–84, 323n.4, 324n.43, 325n.69, 326n.81, 329n.180–82, 334n.352–53, 336n.432–33, 339n.528–69, 344n.650–59, 346n.708–11, 349n.789, 352n.880–82, 354n.942, 360n.20–21, 366n.183, 389n.140, 407n.735, 409n.774, 409n.778, 411n.845–47, 416n.988, 417n.1015, 438n.673, 459n.416, 465n.589–94, 466n.635, 470n.749–59, 490n.434, 492n.497, 504n.243–44, 518n.13–19, 543n.890, 565n.441–55, 595n.356–58, 597n.412, 603n.638–73, 633, 635n.1–2, 661n.403, 673n.327, 690n.414, 738n.971–73, 742n.1122, 778, 840, 840n.27, 903n.182, 1079n.23, 1089n.75, 1097, 1097n.105, 1238
Culex, 385n.30

Eclogues, 25n.135, 62, 80n.494, 91n.822, 100n.8, 100n.10, 101n.15, 102n.50, 103n.66, 103n.68, 103n.77, 232, 234n.18, 237n.117, 240n.180, 241n.203, 342n.595, 353n.921–22, 406n.694, 633, 695n.563–64
Georgics, 94n.880, 102n.58–63, 321n.767–75, 340–41n.554, 353n.921–22, 396n.354, 399n.478, 400n.499–500, 402n.557, 496n.631–32, 633, 685n.248, 695n.563–64, 976
Verity, A.W., 254, 307n.373, 412n.870–71, 443n.842–45, 700, 701
Vida, Marco Girolamo, 32, 32n.26, 635n.16
Vitruvius, 975
Vlacq, Adriaan, 1069, 1070, 1073n.1, 1079, 1085n.50, 1086n.58
Voltaire (François Marie Arouet), 268
Vondel, Joost van den, 700
Vossius, Isaac, 1097n.107

Waldo, Peter, 1042n.75
Waldock, A.J.A., 275
Walker, D. P., 257
Walker, George, 1063n.17
Waller, Edmund, xxix, 389n.160–65
Walton, Izaak, 775n.1
Warner, Rex, 985n.1
Warton, Thomas, 16, 45n.137, 109n.173
Webster, Charles, 968
Welsford, Enid, 63
West, Robert, 313n.534, 442n.805
Whalley, Edmund, 1105
Whitelocke, Bulstrode, 1105
Wightman, Edward, 1138
Wilkie, William, 278
William the Conqueror, 1029–30, 1036
Williams, Arnold, 510n.465–67, 532–33n.529–30, 543n.901, 553n.16, 567n.494–99, 904n.187
Williams, Raymond F., 40
Williamson, Joseph, 1137
Willibrode, 863
Wilson, F. P., 177n.3, 599n.479, 684n.220–21
Winchester, marchioness of (Jane Savage Paulet), 37–40
Winchester, marquis of (John Paulet), 37, 38n.16
Winifride (St. Boniface), 863
Winny, James, 535n.634, 759n.1692
Wittkower, Margot, 41n.1
Wittkower, Rudolf, 41n.1
Wittreich, Joseph, 281, 703, 704
Wolfe, Don M., 805
Wollebius, Johannes, 1138
Wolsey, Thomas (cardinal), 821
Wood, Anthony ·, xxiii
Woodhouse, A.S.P., 185
Woods, Suzanne, 281
Wordworth, William, 138, 270, 648n.220–21
Wotton, Henry, xxiv, 62, 765, 775–77, 1091, 1092n.91
Wright, B. A., 85n.638, 106n.137, 108n.162
Wright, George, 64n.5, 84n.620
Wright, Thomas, 547n.1048
Wright, William A., 766
Wycliffe, John, 806, 810, 863–64, 933, 957, 1081n.33

Xenophon, 851, 976
Xerxes, 316n.620, 561

Yates, Frances A., 220n.33
Young, Thomas, 141, 180–84, 769, 845, 1094n.98

Zagorin, Perez, 265
Zaleucus, 977
Zanchius, Jerome, 1081, 1255, 1272, 1276, 1306
Zeuxis, 791
Zizka, John, 1081
Zwingli, Huldrich, 956, 1051, 1287n.264

About the Editors

William Kerrigan is the author of many books, including *The Sacred Complex: On the Psychogenesis of Paradise Lost,* for which he won the James Holly Hanford Award of the Milton Society of America. A former president of the Milton Society, he has also earned numerous honors and distinctions from that group, including its award for lifetime achievement. He is professor emeritus at the University of Massachusetts.

John Rumrich is the author of *Matter of Glory: A New Preface to Paradise Lost* and *Milton Unbound: Controversy and Reinterpretation.* An award-winning editor and writer, he is A. J. and W. D. Thaman Professor of English at the University of Texas at Austin, where he teaches early modern British literature.

Stephen M. Fallon is the author of *Milton's Peculiar Grace: Self-Representation and Authority* and *Milton among the Philosophers: Poetry and Materialism in Seventeenth-Century England,* winner of the Milton Society's Hanford Award. He is professor of liberal studies and English at the University of Notre Dame.

A Note on the Type

The principal text of this Modern Library edition was set in a digitized version of Janson, a typeface that dates from about 1690 and was cut by Nicholas Kis, a Hungarian working in Amsterdam. The original matrices have survived and are held by the Stempel foundry in Germany. Hermann Zapf redesigned some of the weights and sizes for Stempel, basing his revisions on the original design.